INDIANA RULES OF COURT: KEYRULES

VOLUME IIA - FEDERAL

2017

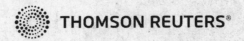

Mat #41778237

ISBN: 978-0-314-68062-4

PREFACE

Indiana Rules of Court: KeyRules provides the practitioner with a comprehensive "single source" procedural guide for civil practice in the United States District Courts for the Northern and Southern Districts of Indiana, combining applicable provisions of the Federal Rules of Civil Procedure, United States Code, local rules of practice, and analytical materials.

This book consists of outlines of the applicable rules of practice, timing requirements, filing and service requirements, hearing requirements, checklists, and other pertinent documents related to pleadings, motions, and discovery requests in United States District Courts.

THE PUBLISHER

December 2016

CONTACT US

For additional information or research assistance call our reference attorneys at 1-800-REF-ATTY (1-800-733-2889). Contact our U.S. legal editorial department directly with your questions and suggestions by email at editors.us-legal@tr.com.

Courts Covered

Table of Contents

NORTHERN DISTRICT OF INDIANA

SOUTHERN DISTRICT OF INDIANA

TABLE OF CONTENTS

APPENDIX - RELATED COURT DOCUMENTS

UNITED STATES DISTRICT COURT

NORTHERN DISTRICT OF INDIANA

Pleadings
Complaint

Document Last Updated December 2016

A. Checklist

(I) ❑ Matters to be considered by plaintiff

    (a) ❑ Required documents

        (1) ❑ Civil cover sheet

        (2) ❑ Complaint

        (3) ❑ Summons

        (4) ❑ Filing fee

        (5) ❑ Affidavit proving service

    (b) ❑ Supplemental documents

        (1) ❑ Notice and request for waiver of service

        (2) ❑ Notice of constitutional question

        (3) ❑ Notice of issue concerning foreign law

        (4) ❑ Nongovernmental corporate disclosure statement

        (5) ❑ Request for three-judge court

        (6) ❑ Report on the filing or determination of an action regarding a patent or trademark

        (7) ❑ Report on the filing or determination of an action or appeal regarding a copyright

        (8) ❑ Index of exhibits

        (9) ❑ Copy of document with self-addressed envelope

        (10) ❑ Notice of manual filing

        (11) ❑ Courtesy copies

        (12) ❑ Declaration that party was unable to file in a timely manner

    (c) ❑ Timing

        (1) ❑ A civil action is commenced by filing a complaint with the court

        (2) ❑ If a defendant is not served within ninety (90) days after the complaint is filed, the court—on motion or on its own after notice to the plaintiff—must dismiss the action without prejudice against that defendant or order that service be made within a specified time

(II) ❑ Matters to be considered by defendant

    (a) ❑ Required documents

        (1) ❑ Answer

        (2) ❑ Certificate of service

    (b) ❑ Supplemental documents

        (1) ❑ Waiver of the service of summons

    (2) ❏ Notice of constitutional question

    (3) ❏ Notice of issue concerning foreign law

    (4) ❏ Nongovernmental corporate disclosure statement

    (5) ❏ Request for three-judge court

    (6) ❏ Index of exhibits

    (7) ❏ Copy of document with self-addressed envelope

    (8) ❏ Notice of manual filing

    (9) ❏ Courtesy copies

    (10) ❏ Declaration that party was unable to file in a timely manner

(c) ❏ Timing

    (1) ❏ A defendant must serve an answer:

        (i) ❏ Within twenty-one (21) days after being served with the summons and complaint; or

        (ii) ❏ If it has timely waived service under FRCP 4(d), within sixty (60) days after the request for a waiver was sent, or within ninety (90) days after it was sent to the defendant outside any judicial district of the United States

    (2) ❏ The United States, a United States agency, or a United States officer or employee sued only in an official capacity must serve an answer to a complaint, counterclaim, or crossclaim within sixty (60) days after service on the United States attorney

    (3) ❏ A United States officer or employee sued in an individual capacity for an act or omission occurring in connection with duties performed on the United States' behalf must serve an answer to a complaint, counterclaim, or crossclaim within sixty (60) days after service on the officer or employee or service on the United States attorney, whichever is later

    (4) ❏ Unless the court sets a different time, serving a motion under FRCP 12 alters these periods as follows:

        (i) ❏ If the court denies the motion or postpones its disposition until trial, the responsive pleading must be served within fourteen (14) days after notice of the court's action; or

        (ii) ❏ If the court grants a motion for a more definite statement, the responsive pleading must be served within fourteen (14) days after the more definite statement is served

    (5) ❏ Defendant is given a reasonable time of at least thirty (30) days after a waiver of service request is sent—or at least sixty (60) days if sent to defendant outside any judicial district of the United States—to return the waiver

B. Timing

1. *Commencing an action.* A civil action is commenced by filing a complaint with the court. FRCP 3.

    a. *Statute of limitations.* An action will be barred if it is not commenced within the period set forth in the applicable statute of limitations. Under the Federal Rules of Civil Procedure (FRCP), an action is commenced by filing a complaint with the court. Thus, in a suit on a right created by federal law, filing a complaint suffices to satisfy the statute of limitations. FEDPROF § 61:2.

        i. *Federal question cases.* Absent a specific statutory provision for tolling the statute of limitations, in federal question cases, the filing of the complaint will toll the statute, even if not all filing fees have been paid, although some courts have added the requirement of reasonable diligence in effecting service. FEDPROF § 61:2.

        ii. *Diversity cases.* In diversity actions the matter is less clear. In the landmark Ragan case, the Supreme Court held in construing FRCP 3 that if, under local law, an action is not commenced until the defendant has been served, the statute is not tolled until service has been accomplished. FEDPROF § 61:2; Ragan v. Merchants Transfer & Warehouse Co., 337 U.S. 530, 69 S.Ct. 1233, 93 L.Ed. 1520 (1949). However, in a subsequent case, the Supreme Court distinguished Ragan in holding that the provision of FRCP 4 governing methods of service prevails over a conflicting state rule requiring personal service. FEDPROF § 61:2; Hanna v. Plumer, 380 U.S. 460, 85 S.Ct. 1136, 14 L.Ed.2d 8 (1965). The court reaffirmed Ragan and held that (1) a state law mandating actual service of a summons to toll the statute of limitations must be followed in a diversity case, and (2) FRCP 3 only governs other timing requirements in the federal rules. FEDPROF § 61:2; Walker v. Armco Steel Corp., 446 U.S. 740, 100 S.Ct. 1978, 64 L.Ed.2d 659 (1980).

2. *Service of summons and complaint.* If a defendant is not served within ninety (90) days after the complaint is filed, the court—on motion or on its own after notice to the plaintiff—must dismiss the action without prejudice against that defendant or order that service be made within a specified time. But if the plaintiff shows good cause for the failure, the court must extend the time for service for an appropriate period. FRCP 4(m) does not apply to service in a foreign country under FRCP 4(f), FRCP 4(h)(2), or FRCP 4(j)(1). FRCP 4(m).

3. *Computation of time*

   a. *Computing time.* FRCP 6 applies in computing any time period specified in the Federal Rules of Civil Procedure, in any local rule or court order, or in any statute that does not specify a method of computing time. FRCP 6(a).

      i. *Period stated in days or a longer unit.* When the period is stated in days or a longer unit of time:
         - Exclude the day of the event that triggers the period;
         - Count every day, including intermediate Saturdays, Sundays, and legal holidays; and
         - Include the last day of the period, but if the last day is a Saturday, Sunday, or legal holiday, the period continues to run until the end of the next day that is not a Saturday, Sunday, or legal holiday. FRCP 6(a)(1).

      ii. *Period stated in hours.* When the period is stated in hours:
         - Begin counting immediately on the occurrence of the event that triggers the period;
         - Count every hour, including hours during intermediate Saturdays, Sundays, and legal holidays; and
         - If the period would end on a Saturday, Sunday, or legal holiday, the period continues to run until the same time on the next day that is not a Saturday, Sunday, or legal holiday. FRCP 6(a)(2).

      iii. *Inaccessibility of the clerk's office.* Unless the court orders otherwise, if the clerk's office is inaccessible:
         - On the last day for filing under FRCP 6(a)(1), then the time for filing is extended to the first accessible day that is not a Saturday, Sunday, or legal holiday; or
         - During the last hour for filing under FRCP 6(a)(2), then the time for filing is extended to the same time on the first accessible day that is not a Saturday, Sunday, or legal holiday. FRCP 6(a)(3).

      iv. *"Last day" defined.* Unless a different time is set by a statute, local rule, or court order, the last day ends:
         - For electronic filing, at midnight in the court's time zone; and
         - For filing by other means, when the clerk's office is scheduled to close. FRCP 6(a)(4).

      v. *"Next day" defined.* The "next day" is determined by continuing to count forward when the period is measured after an event and backward when measured before an event. FRCP 6(a)(5).

      vi. *"Legal holiday" defined.* "Legal holiday" means:
         - The day set aside by statute for observing New Year's Day, Martin Luther King Jr.'s Birthday, Washington's Birthday, Memorial Day, Independence Day, Labor Day, Columbus Day, Veterans' Day, Thanksgiving Day, or Christmas Day;
         - Any day declared a holiday by the President or Congress; and

- For periods that are measured after an event, any other day declared a holiday by the state where the district court is located. FRCP 6(a)(6).

b. *Computation of electronic filing deadlines.* Filing documents electronically does not alter any filing deadlines or any time computation pursuant to FRCP 6. The counties of Lake, Porter, LaPorte, Pulaski and Starke are located in the Central time zone and the remaining counties in the Northern District of Indiana are located in the Eastern time zone. Nevertheless, all electronic transmissions of documents must be completed (i.e., received completely by the clerk's office) prior to midnight Eastern Time, (South Bend/Fort Wayne/Lafayette time) in order to be considered timely filed that day, regardless of the local time in the division where the case is pending. Although documents can be filed electronically twenty-four (24) hours a day, filers are strongly encouraged to file all documents during hours when the CM/ECF Help Line is available, from 9:00 a.m. to 4:00 p.m. local time. IN R USDCTND CM/ECF(II)(I).

   i. *Technical failures.* If the attorney is unable to file a document in a timely manner due to technical difficulties in the user's system, the attorney must file a document with the court as soon as possible notifying the court of the inability to file the document. A sample document entitled Declaration that Party was Unable to File in a Timely Manner Due to Technical Difficulties is attached hereto as Form 5. IN R USDCTND CM/ECF(VI)(B). [Editor's note: the reference to Form 5 is likely meant to be a reference to Form 3 (IN R USDCTND CM/ECF(Form 3)].

c. *Extending time*

   i. *In general.* When an act may or must be done within a specified time, the court may, for good cause, extend the time:

      - With or without motion or notice if the court acts, or if a request is made, before the original time or its extension expires; or

      - On motion made after the time has expired if the party failed to act because of excusable neglect. FRCP 6(b)(1).

   ii. *Exceptions.* A court must not extend the time to act under FRCP 50(b), FRCP 50(d), FRCP 52(b), FRCP 59(b), FRCP 59(d), FRCP 59(e), and FRCP 60(b). FRCP 6(b)(2).

   iii. Refer to the United States District Court for the Northern District of Indiana KeyRules Motion for Continuance/Extension of Time document for more information on extending time.

C. General Requirements

1. *Pleading, generally*

   a. *Pleadings allowed.* Only these pleadings are allowed: (1) a complaint; (2) an answer to a complaint; (3) an answer to a counterclaim designated as a counterclaim; (4) an answer to a crossclaim; (5) a third-party complaint; (6) an answer to a third-party complaint; and (7) if the court orders one, a reply to an answer. FRCP 7(a).

   b. *Pleading to be concise and direct.* Each allegation must be simple, concise, and direct. No technical form is required. FRCP 8(d)(1).

   c. *Alternative statements of a claim or defense.* A party may set out two or more statements of a claim or defense alternatively or hypothetically, either in a single count or defense or in separate ones. If a party makes alternative statements, the pleading is sufficient if any one of them is sufficient. FRCP 8(d)(2).

   d. *Inconsistent claims or defenses.* A party may state as many separate claims or defenses as it has, regardless of consistency. FRCP 8(d)(3).

   e. *Construing pleadings.* Pleadings must be construed so as to do justice. FRCP 8(e).

2. *Pleading special matters*

   a. *Capacity or authority to sue; Legal existence*

      i. *In general.* Except when required to show that the court has jurisdiction, a pleading need not allege:

         - A party's capacity to sue or be sued;

- A party's authority to sue or be sued in a representative capacity; or
- The legal existence of an organized association of persons that is made a party. FRCP 9(a)(1).

    ii. *Raising those issues.* To raise any of those issues, a party must do so by a specific denial, which must state any supporting facts that are peculiarly within the party's knowledge. FRCP 9(a)(2).

b. *Fraud or mistake; Conditions of mind.* In alleging fraud or mistake, a party must state with particularity the circumstances constituting fraud or mistake. Malice, intent, knowledge, and other conditions of a person's mind may be alleged generally. FRCP 9(b).

c. *Conditions precedent.* In pleading conditions precedent, it suffices to allege generally that all conditions precedent have occurred or been performed. But when denying that a condition precedent has occurred or been performed, a party must do so with particularity. FRCP 9(c).

d. *Official document or act.* In pleading an official document or official act, it suffices to allege that the document was legally issued or the act legally done. FRCP 9(d).

e. *Judgment.* In pleading a judgment or decision of a domestic or foreign court, a judicial or quasi-judicial tribunal, or a board or officer, it suffices to plead the judgment or decision without showing jurisdiction to render it. FRCP 9(e).

f. *Time and place.* An allegation of time or place is material when testing the sufficiency of a pleading. FRCP 9(f).

g. *Special damages.* If an item of special damage is claimed, it must be specifically stated. FRCP 9(g).

h. *Admiralty or maritime claim*

    i. *How designated.* If a claim for relief is within the admiralty or maritime jurisdiction and also within the court's subject-matter jurisdiction on some other ground, the pleading may designate the claim as an admiralty or maritime claim for purposes of FRCP 14(c), FRCP 38(e), and FRCP 82 and the Supplemental Rules for Admiralty or Maritime Claims and Asset Forfeiture Actions. A claim cognizable only in the admiralty or maritime jurisdiction is an admiralty or maritime claim for those purposes, whether or not so designated. FRCP 9(h)(1).

    ii. *Designation for appeal.* A case that includes an admiralty or maritime claim within FRCP 9(h) is an admiralty case within 28 U.S.C.A. § 1292(a)(3). FRCP 9(h)(2).

3. *Complaint.* A pleading that states a claim for relief must contain: (1) a short and plain statement of the grounds for the court's jurisdiction, unless the court already has jurisdiction and the claim needs no new jurisdictional support; (2) a short and plain statement of the claim showing that the pleader is entitled to relief; and (3) a demand for the relief sought, which may include relief in the alternative or different types of relief. FRCP 8(a).

a. *Statement of jurisdiction.* Federal courts are courts of limited jurisdiction, and it is presumed that they are without jurisdiction unless the contrary affirmatively appears. FEDPROC § 62:38; Kirkland Masonry, Inc. v. C.I.R., 614 F.2d 532 (5th Cir. 1980). Therefore, in order for a complaint to comply with the requirement that it contain a short and plain statement of the grounds upon which the court's jurisdiction depends, the jurisdictional basis must be alleged affirmatively and distinctly on the face of the complaint. FEDPROC § 62:38; Spain v. U.S. Through Atomic Nuclear Regulatory Commission Through U.S. Atomic Safety and Licensing Bd., 397 F.Supp. 15 (M.D.La. 1975).

    i. Although it has been said that the jurisdictional statement requirement contemplates reference to a federal statute, a sufficient jurisdictional statement is not made by simply citing a federal statute without alleging facts which bring the plaintiff within the purview of the statute. FEDPROC § 62:38; Atkins v. School Bd. of Halifax County, 379 F.Supp. 1060 (W.D.Va. 1974); Sims v. Mercy Hospital of Monroe, 451 F.2d 171 (6th Cir. 1971).

    ii. Improper venue is an affirmative defense, and a complaint need not include allegations showing venue to be proper. FEDPROC § 62:38; Ripperger v. A.C. Allyn & Co., 113 F.2d 332 (2d Cir. 1940).

b. *Statement of claim*

    i. *Notice pleading.* Because the only function left exclusively to the pleadings by the Federal

Rules of Civil Procedure is that of giving notice, federal courts frequently have said that the Federal Rules of Civil Procedure have adopted a system of "notice pleading." FPP § 1202; Swierkiewicz v. Sorema N.A., 534 U.S. 506, 122 S.Ct. 992, 152 L.Ed.2d 1 (2002). To comply with the requirement that a complaint contain a short and plain statement of the claim, a pleading must give the opposing party fair notice of the nature of a claim and of the basis or grounds for it, so that the defendant will at least be notified as to which of its actions gave rise to the claim upon which the complaint is based. FEDPROC § 62:45.

- *Plausibility standard.* Bell Atlantic Corporation v. Twombly and Ashcroft v. Iqbal have paved the way for a heightened "plausibility" pleading standard that requires plaintiffs to provide greater factual development in their complaints in order to survive a FRCP 12(b)(6) motion to dismiss. FPP § 1202; Bell Atlantic Corp. v. Twombly, 550 U.S. 544, 127 S.Ct. 1955, 167 L.Ed.2d 929, 68 Fed.R.Serv.3d 661 (2007); Ashcroft v. Iqbal, 556 U.S. 662, 129 S.Ct. 1937, 173 L.Ed.2d 868 (2009). In discussing what appears to be the new plausibility standard, the Court [in Bell Atlantic Corp. v. Twombly] stated: "While a complaint attacked by a Rule 12(b)(6) motion to dismiss does not need detailed factual allegations. . .a plaintiff's obligation to provide the 'grounds' of his 'entitle[ment] to relief' requires more than labels and conclusions, and a formulaic recitation of the elements of a cause of action will not do. . .Factual allegations must be enough to raise a right to relief above the speculative level." FPP § 1216; Bell Atlantic Corp. v. Twombly, 550 U.S. 544, 127 S.Ct. 1955, 167 L.Ed.2d 929, 68 Fed.R.Serv.3d 661 (2007).

ii. *Facts and evidence.* The complaint need only state enough facts to raise a reasonable expectation that discovery will reveal evidence of the necessary elements. FEDPROC § 62:52; Phillips v. County of Allegheny, 515 F.3d 224 (3d Cir. 2008). A complaint is not intended to formulate issues or fully summarize the facts involved. FEDPROC § 62:52; Hill v. MCI WorldCom Communications, Inc., 141 F.Supp.2d 1205 (S.D.Iowa 2001). Under notice pleading, the full development of the facts and the narrowing of contested issues are accomplished through discovery and other pretrial procedures. FEDPROC § 62:52.

iii. *Particularity.* The claim should be particularized sufficiently for the defendant to prepare an adequate defense, file a responsive pleading, determine whether the defense of res judicata is appropriate, and commence discovery, and should insure that the court is sufficiently informed to determine the issue presented and to decide whether the complaint states a claim upon which relief can be had. FEDPROC § 62:45; Kelly v. Schmidberger, 806 F.2d 44, 6 Fed.R.Serv.3d 798 (2d Cir. 1986); Frank v. Mracek, 58 F.R.D. 365 (M.D.Ala. 1973); Barlow v. Pep Boys, Inc., 625 F.Supp. 130 (E.D.Pa. 1985); Philadelphia Dressed Beef Co. v. Wilson & Co., 19 F.R.D. 198 (E.D.Pa. 1956); Luckett v. Cohen, 145 F.Supp. 155 (S.D.N.Y. 1956).

c. *Pro se complaints.* Parties representing themselves must prepare the following types of complaints on clerk-supplied forms:

i. Complaints alleging claims arising under The Civil Rights Act, 42 U.S.C.A. § 1983. IN R USDCTND L.R. 8-1.

ii. Complaints alleging claims arising under The Social Security Act, 42 U.S.C.A. § 405(g). IN R USDCTND L.R. 8-1.

iii. Complaints alleging employment discrimination under a federal statute. IN R USDCTND L.R. 8-1.

d. *Demand for relief sought.* FRCP 8(a)(3) does not require a party to frame the demand for judgment according to a prescribed form or set of particular words; any concise statement identifying the remedies and the parties against whom relief is sought will be sufficient. FPP § 1255; Chandler v. McKee Foods Corp., 2009 WL 210858 (W.D.Va. 2009). Moreover, the pleader need only make one demand for relief regardless of the number of claims that are asserted. FPP § 1255; Liberty Mut. Ins. Co. v. Wetzel, 424 U.S. 737, 96 S.Ct. 1202, 47 L.Ed.2d 435 (1976).

i. Relief must be requested as to each defendant. FEDPROC § 62:58; RKO-Stanley Warner Theatres, Inc. v. Mellon Nat. Bank & Trust Co., 436 F.2d 1297 (3d Cir. 1970).

4. *Joinder*

    a. *Joinder of claims.* A party asserting a claim, counterclaim, crossclaim, or third-party claim may join, as independent or alternative claims, as many claims as it has against an opposing party. FRCP 18(a).

        i. *Joinder of contingent claims.* A party may join two claims even though one of them is contingent on the disposition of the other; but the court may grant relief only in accordance with the parties' relative substantive rights. In particular, a plaintiff may state a claim for money and a claim to set aside a conveyance that is fraudulent as to that plaintiff, without first obtaining a judgment for the money. FRCP 18(b).

    b. *Joinder of parties; Required*

        i. *Persons required to be joined if feasible; Required party.* A person who is subject to service of process and whose joinder will not deprive the court of subject-matter jurisdiction must be joined as a party if:

- In that person's absence, the court cannot accord complete relief among existing parties; or
- That person claims an interest relating to the subject of the action and is so situated that disposing of the action in the person's absence may: (1) as a practical matter impair or impede the person's ability to protect the interest; or (2) leave an existing party subject to a substantial risk of incurring double, multiple, or otherwise inconsistent obligations because of the interest. FRCP 19(a)(1).

        ii. *Joinder of parties by court order.* If a person has not been joined as required, the court must order that the person be made a party. A person who refuses to join as a plaintiff may be made either a defendant or, in a proper case, an involuntary plaintiff. FRCP 19(a)(2).

        iii. *Venue.* If a joined party objects to venue and the joinder would make venue improper, the court must dismiss that party. FRCP 19(a)(3).

        iv. *When joinder of parties is not feasible.* If a person who is required to be joined if feasible cannot be joined, the court must determine whether, in equity and good conscience, the action should proceed among the existing parties or should be dismissed. FRCP 19(b). For a list of the factors for the court to consider in determining whether joinder of parties is feasible, refer to FRCP 19(b)(1) through FRCP 19(b)(4).

        v. *Pleading the reasons for nonjoinder.* When asserting a claim for relief, a party must state:

- The name, if known, of any person who is required to be joined if feasible but is not joined; and
- The reasons for not joining that person. FRCP 19(c).

        vi. *Exception for class actions.* FRCP 19 is subject to FRCP 23. FRCP 19(d). For information on class actions, refer to FRCP 23.

    c. *Joinder of parties; Permissible*

        i. *Persons who may join or be joined*

- *Plaintiffs.* Persons may join in one action as plaintiffs if: (1) they assert any right to relief jointly, severally, or in the alternative with respect to or arising out of the same transaction, occurrence, or series of transactions or occurrences; and (2) any question of law or fact common to all plaintiffs will arise in the action. FRCP 20(a)(1).
- *Defendants.* Persons—as well as a vessel, cargo, or other property subject to admiralty process in rem—may be joined in one action as defendants if: (1) any right to relief is asserted against them jointly, severally, or in the alternative with respect to or arising out of the same transaction, occurrence, or series of transactions or occurrences; and (2) any question of law or fact common to all defendants will arise in the action. FRCP 20(a)(2).
- *Extent of relief.* Neither a plaintiff nor a defendant need be interested in obtaining or defending against all the relief demanded. The court may grant judgment to one or more plaintiffs according to their rights, and against one or more defendants according to their liabilities. FRCP 20(a)(3).

      ii.   *Protective measures.* The court may issue orders—including an order for separate trials—to protect a party against embarrassment, delay, expense, or other prejudice that arises from including a person against whom the party asserts no claim and who asserts no claim against the party. FRCP 20(b).

    d.   *Misjoinder and nonjoinder of parties.* Misjoinder of parties is not a ground for dismissing an action. On motion or on its own, the court may at any time, on just terms, add or drop a party. The court may also sever any claim against a party. FRCP 21.

5.   *Right to a jury trial; Demand*

    a.   *Right preserved.* The right of trial by jury as declared by U.S.C.A. Const. Amend. VII, or as provided by a federal statute, is preserved to the parties inviolate. FRCP 38(a).

    b.   *Demand.* On any issue triable of right by a jury, a party may demand a jury trial by:

        i.   Serving the other parties with a written demand—which may be included in a pleading—no later than fourteen (14) days after the last pleading directed to the issue is served; and

        ii.   Filing the demand in accordance with FRCP 5(d). FRCP 38(b).

    c.   *Specifying issues.* In its demand, a party may specify the issues that it wishes to have tried by a jury; otherwise, it is considered to have demanded a jury trial on all the issues so triable. If the party has demanded a jury trial on only some issues, any other party may—within fourteen (14) days after being served with the demand or within a shorter time ordered by the court—serve a demand for a jury trial on any other or all factual issues triable by jury. FRCP 38(c).

    d.   *Waiver; Withdrawal.* A party waives a jury trial unless its demand is properly served and filed. A proper demand may be withdrawn only if the parties consent. FRCP 38(d).

    e.   *Admiralty and maritime claims.* The rules in FRCP 38 do not create a right to a jury trial on issues in a claim that is an admiralty or maritime claim under FRCP 9(h). FRCP 38(e).

6.   *Appearances.* Attorneys not representing the United States or its agencies must file an appearance when they represent (either in person or by filing a paper) a party. IN R USDCTND L.R. 83-8(a). For more information, refer to IN R USDCTND L.R. 83-8.

7.   *Notice of related action.* A party must file a notice of related action as soon as it appears that the party's case and another pending case: (1) arise out of the same transaction or occurrence; (2) involve the same property; or (3) involve the validity or infringement of the same patent, trademark, or copyright. IN R USDCTND L.R. 40-1(d). For more information, refer to IN R USDCTND L.R. 40-1.

8.   *Alternative dispute resolution (ADR).* After they confer as required by FRCP 26(f), the parties must advise the court which, if any, alternative-dispute-resolution processes they expect to pursue and when they expect to undertake the process. IN R USDCTND L.R. 16-6(a). For more information on alternative dispute resolution (ADR), refer to IN R USDCTND L.R. 16-6 and IN R USDCTND Order 2003-21.

9.   *Settlement or resolution.* The parties must immediately notify the court if they reasonably expect to settle the case or resolve a pending motion. IN R USDCTND L.R. 16-1(g).

10.   *Modification or suspension of rules.* The court may, on its own motion or at the request of a party, suspend or modify any rule in a particular case in the interest of justice. IN R USDCTND L.R. 1-1(c).

D. Documents

1.   *Required documents*

    a.   *Civil cover sheet.* All new civil complaints must be filed electronically in CM/ECF, and should be accompanied by a Civil Cover Sheet (JS-44). IN R USDCTND CM/ECF(II)(B). A civil cover sheet is submitted with each civil complaint filed in the district court. Copies of the cover sheet may be obtained from the Clerk of Court. 2 FEDFORMS § 3:29(Comment).

    b.   *Complaint.* Refer to the General Requirements section of this document for the form and contents of the complaint.

    c.   *Summons.* A summons must be served with a copy of the complaint. FRCP 4(c)(1). All new civil complaints must be filed electronically in CM/ECF, and should be accompanied by. . .summons forms with the top portion completed. IN R USDCTND CM/ECF(II)(B). A summons must:

 i. Name the court and the parties;

 ii. Be directed to the defendant;

 iii. State the name and address of the plaintiff's attorney or—if unrepresented—of the plaintiff;

 iv. State the time within which the defendant must appear and defend;

 v. Notify the defendant that a failure to appear and defend will result in a default judgment against the defendant for the relief demanded in the complaint;

 vi. Be signed by the clerk; and

 vii. Bear the court's seal. FRCP 4(a)(1).

d. *Filing fee.* The clerk of each district court shall require the parties instituting any civil action, suit or proceeding in such court, whether by original process, removal or otherwise, to pay a filing fee. 28 U.S.C.A. § 1914(a). Each district court by rule or standing order may require advance payment of fees. 28 U.S.C.A. § 1914(c). For information on filing fees and the District Court Miscellaneous Fee Schedule, refer to 28 U.S.C.A. § 1914.

e. *Affidavit proving service.* Unless service is waived, proof of service must be made to the court. Except for service by a United States marshal or deputy marshal, proof must be by the server's affidavit. FRCP 4(l)(1). Refer to the Filing and Service Requirements section of this document for more information.

2. *Supplemental documents*

a. *Notice and request for waiver of service.* An individual, corporation, or association that is subject to service under FRCP 4(e), FRCP 4(f), or FRCP 4(h) has a duty to avoid unnecessary expenses of serving the summons. The plaintiff may notify such a defendant that an action has been commenced and request that the defendant waive service of a summons. The notice and request must:

 i. Be in writing and be addressed:

  • To the individual defendant; or

  • For a defendant subject to service under FRCP 4(h), to an officer, a managing or general agent, or any other agent authorized by appointment or by law to receive service of process;

 ii. Name the court where the complaint was filed;

 iii. Be accompanied by a copy of the complaint, two (2) copies of a waiver form appended to FRCP 4, and a prepaid means for returning the form;

 iv. Inform the defendant, using the form appended to FRCP 4, of the consequences of waiving and not waiving service;

 v. State the date when the request is sent;

 vi. Give the defendant a reasonable time of at least thirty (30) days after the request was sent—or at least sixty (60) days if sent to the defendant outside any judicial district of the United States—to return the waiver; and

 vii. Be sent by first-class mail or other reliable means. FRCP 4(d)(1).

b. *Notice of constitutional question.* A party that files a pleading, written motion, or other paper drawing into question the constitutionality of a federal or state statute must promptly:

 i. *File notice.* File a notice of constitutional question stating the question and identifying the paper that raises it, if:

  • A federal statute is questioned and the parties do not include the United States, one of its agencies, or one of its officers or employees in an official capacity; or

  • A state statute is questioned and the parties do not include the state, one of its agencies, or one of its officers or employees in an official capacity; and

ii. *Serve notice.* Serve the notice and paper on the Attorney General of the United States if a federal statute is questioned—or on the state attorney general if a state statute is questioned—either by certified or registered mail or by sending it to an electronic address designated by the attorney general for this purpose. FRCP 5.1(a).

iii. *When to file the notice.* A party required to file a notice of constitutional question under FRCP 5.1 must do so by the later of: (1) the day the parties tender their proposed case-management plan (if one is required); or (2) 21 days after filing the pleading, written motion, or other paper questioning the constitutionality of a federal or state statute. IN R USDCTND L.R. 5.1-1(a).

iv. *Service on government officials.* The party must also serve the notice and the pleading, written motion, or other paper questioning the constitutionality of a federal or state statute on: (1) the Attorney General of the United States and the United States Attorney for the Northern District of Indiana, if a federal statute is challenged; or (2) the Attorney General for the state if a state statute is challenged. IN R USDCTND L.R. 5.1-1(b). Service required under IN R USDCTND L.R. 5.1-1(b) may be made either by certified or registered mail or by emailing it to an address designated by those officials for this purpose. IN R USDCTND L.R. 5.1-1(c).

v. *No forfeiture.* A party's failure to file and serve the notice, or the court's failure to certify, does not forfeit a constitutional claim or defense that is otherwise timely asserted. FRCP 5.1(d).

c. *Notice of issue concerning foreign law.* A party who intends to raise an issue about a foreign country's law must give notice by a pleading or other writing. In determining foreign law, the court may consider any relevant material or source, including testimony, whether or not submitted by a party or admissible under the Federal Rules of Evidence. The court's determination must be treated as a ruling on a question of law. FRCP 44.1.

d. *Nongovernmental corporate disclosure statement*

i. *Contents.* A nongovernmental corporate party must file two (2) copies of a disclosure statement that:

- Identifies any parent corporation and any publicly held corporation owning ten percent (10%) or more of its stock; or

- States that there is no such corporation. FRCP 7.1(a).

ii. *Time to file; Supplemental filing.* A party must:

- File the disclosure statement with its first appearance, pleading, petition, motion, response, or other request addressed to the court; and

- Promptly file a supplemental statement if any required information changes. FRCP 7.1(b).

e. *Request for three-judge court.* If a party believes the law requires a three-judge court in a case or proceeding, the party must: (1) print "Three-Judge District Court Requested" or the equivalent immediately following the title on the first pleading asserting a claim requiring a three-judge court; and (2) set forth the basis for the request in the pleading or in a short statement attached to the pleading, unless the basis is apparent from the pleading. IN R USDCTND L.R. 9-2(a). The words "Three-Judge District Court Requested" or the equivalent on a pleading constitutes a "request" under 28 U.S.C.A. § 2284(b)(1). IN R USDCTND L.R. 9-2(b).

f. *Report on the filing or determination of an action regarding a patent or trademark.* If the complaint alleges a violation of a patent [or] trademark,. . .a completed AO 120 (Patent & Trademark). . .form should also be attached. IN R USDCTND CM/ECF(II)(B).

g. *Report on the filing or determination of an action or appeal regarding a copyright.* If the complaint alleges a violation of a. . .copyright, a completed. . .AO 121 (Copyright) form should also be attached. IN R USDCTND CM/ECF(II)(B).

h. *Index of exhibits.* Any pleading, motion, brief, affidavit, notice, or proposed order, whether filed electronically or by delivering it to the clerk, must: include a separate index identifying and briefly describing each exhibit if there are more than four (4) exhibits. IN R USDCTND L.R. 5-4(a)(8).

i. *Copy of document with self-addressed envelope.* A party who wants a file-stamped copy of a paper must include with the filing an additional copy of the paper and a self-addressed envelope with adequate postage. IN R USDCTND L.R. 5-4(b)(6).

j. *Notice of manual filing.* However, if that is not physically possible, counsel shall electronically file a .pdf document titled Notice of Manual Filing as a notation on the docket sheet that filings are being held in the clerk's office in paper. A sample Notice of Manual Filing is attached as Form 2 (IN R USDCTND CM/ECF(Form 2)). IN R USDCTND CM/ECF(III)(A)(1).

k. *Courtesy copies.* If documents are filed in paper format, counsel must provide an original for the clerk's office, a copy for the judge and a copy must be served on all parties in the case. IN R USDCTND CM/ECF(III)(A)(1).

l. *Declaration that party was unable to file in a timely manner.* If the attorney is unable to file a document in a timely manner due to technical difficulties in the user's system, the attorney must file a document with the court as soon as possible notifying the court of the inability to file the document. A sample document entitled Declaration that Party was Unable to File in a Timely Manner Due to Technical Difficulties is attached hereto as Form 5. IN R USDCTND CM/ECF(VI)(B). [Editor's note: the reference to Form 5 is likely meant to be a reference to Form 3 (IN R USDCTND CM/ECF(Form 3)].

E. Format

1. *Form of documents*

    a. *Paper.* Any pleading, motion, brief, affidavit, notice, or proposed order, whether filed electronically or by delivering it to the clerk, must: use eight and one-half by eleven (8-1/2 x 11) inch pages. IN R USDCTND L.R. 5-4(a)(2).

        i. *Manual filings.* Papers delivered to the clerk for filing must: be flat, unfolded, and on good-quality, white paper. IN R USDCTND L.R. 5-4(b)(1)(A).

            • *Covers or backing.* Papers delivered to the clerk for filing must: not have a cover or a back. IN R USDCTND L.R. 5-4(b)(1)(B).

            • *Recycled paper.* The court encourages using recycled paper. IN R USDCTND L.R. 5-4(b)(7).

    b. *Margins.* Any pleading, motion, brief, affidavit, notice, or proposed order, whether filed electronically or by delivering it to the clerk, must: have at least one (1) inch margins. IN R USDCTND L.R. 5-4(a)(3).

    c. *Spacing.* Any pleading, motion, brief, affidavit, notice, or proposed order, whether filed electronically or by delivering it to the clerk, must: be double spaced (except for headings, footnotes, and quoted material). IN R USDCTND L.R. 5-4(a)(5).

    d. *Text.* Any pleading, motion, brief, affidavit, notice, or proposed order, whether filed electronically or by delivering it to the clerk, must: be plainly typewritten, printed, or prepared by a clearly legible copying process. IN R USDCTND L.R. 5-4(a)(1).

        i. Any pleading, motion, brief, affidavit, notice, or proposed order, whether filed electronically or by delivering it to the clerk, must: use at least twelve (12) point type in the body and at least ten (10) point type in footnotes. IN R USDCTND L.R. 5-4(a)(4).

    e. *Page numbering.* Any pleading, motion, brief, affidavit, notice, or proposed order, whether filed electronically or by delivering it to the clerk, must: have consecutively numbered pages. IN R USDCTND L.R. 5-4(a)(6).

    f. *Caption; Names of parties.* Every pleading must have a caption with the court's name, a title, a file number, and a FRCP 7(a) designation. The title of the complaint must name all the parties; the title of other pleadings, after naming the first party on each side, may refer generally to other parties. FRCP 10(a). Any pleading, motion, brief, affidavit, notice, or proposed order, whether filed electronically or by delivering it to the clerk, must: include a title on the first page. IN R USDCTND L.R. 5-4(a)(7).

        i. *Request for three-judge court.* If a party believes the law requires a three-judge court in a case or proceeding, the party must: print "Three-Judge District Court Requested" or the equivalent immediately following the title on the first pleading asserting a claim requiring a three-judge court. IN R USDCTND L.R. 9-2(a)(1). Refer to the Documents section of this document for more information.

    ii. *Class actions.* A party seeking to maintain a case as a class action (whether for or against a class) must include in the complaint, crossclaim, or counterclaim: (1) the words "Class Action" in the document's title; and (2) a reference to each part of FRCP 23 that the party relies on in seeking to maintain the case as a class action. IN R USDCTND L.R. 23-1.

g. *Filer's information.* Any pleading, motion, brief, affidavit, notice, or proposed order, whether filed electronically or by delivering it to the clerk, must: except in proposed orders and affidavits, include the filer's name, address, telephone number, fax number (where available), and e-mail address (where available). IN R USDCTND L.R. 5-4(a)(9).

h. *Paragraphs; Separate statements.* A party must state its claims or defenses in numbered paragraphs, each limited as far as practicable to a single set of circumstances. A later pleading may refer by number to a paragraph in an earlier pleading. If doing so would promote clarity, each claim founded on a separate transaction or occurrence—and each defense other than a denial—must be stated in a separate count or defense. FRCP 10(b).

i. *Adoption by reference; Exhibits.* A statement in a pleading may be adopted by reference elsewhere in the same pleading or in any other pleading or motion. A copy of a written instrument that is an exhibit to a pleading is a part of the pleading for all purposes. FRCP 10(c).

j. *Citation of local rules.* The Local Civil Rules of the United States District Court for the Northern District of Indiana may be cited as "N.D. Ind. L.R." IN R USDCTND L.R. 1-1(a)(1).

k. *Acceptance by the clerk.* The clerk must not refuse to file a paper solely because it is not in the form prescribed by the Federal Rules of Civil Procedure or by a local rule or practice. FRCP 5(d)(4).

    i. *Sanctions for formatting errors; Non-compliance.* If a person files a paper that does not comply with the rules governing the format of papers filed with the court, the court may: (1) strike the paper from the record; or (2) fine the person up to one thousand dollars ($1,000). IN R USDCTND L.R. 1-3(a).

- *Notice.* Before sanctioning a person under IN R USDCTND L.R. 1-3(a)(2), the court must: (1) notify the person that the paper is noncompliant; and (2) give the person the opportunity either to be heard or to revise the paper. IN R USDCTND L.R. 1-3(b).

2. *Form of electronic documents.* Electronically filed documents must meet the same requirements of format and page limits as documents "conventionally filed" (as defined in IN R USDCTND CM/ECF(III)(A)) pursuant to the Federal Rules of Civil Procedure and the Local Civil Rules of the United States District Court for the Northern District of Indiana. IN R USDCTND CM/ECF(II)(A)(2).

a. *PDF format required.* Documents filed in the CM/ECF must be in .pdf format. A document created with almost any word-processing program can be converted to .pdf format. The .pdf program in effect takes a picture of the original document and allows anyone to open the converted document across a broad range of hardware and software, with layout, format, links, and images intact. IN R USDCTND CM/ECF(FN2).

b. *Title of documents.* The person electronically filing a pleading or other document will be responsible for designating a title for the pleading or other document by using one of the categories contained in the events listed in the CM/ECF Menu. IN R USDCTND CM/ECF(II)(G).

c. *Combining documents.* All documents which form part of a single pleading and which are being filed at the same time and by the same party may be electronically filed together under one document number, e.g., the motion and a supporting affidavit, with the exception of memoranda in support. Memoranda in support shall be electronically filed separately and shown as a related document to the motion. IN R USDCTND CM/ECF(II)(A)(4).

d. *Exhibits and attachments.* Filing users must submit in electronic form all documents referenced as exhibits or attachments, unless the court permits conventional filing. A filing user must submit as

exhibits or attachments only those excerpts of the referenced documents that are directly germane to the matter under consideration by the court. Excerpted material must be clearly and prominently identified as such. Filing users who file excerpts of documents as exhibits or attachments do so without prejudice to their right to timely file additional excerpts or the complete document. Responding parties may timely file additional excerpts or the complete document that they believe are directly germane. The court may require parties to file additional excerpts or the complete document. IN R USDCTND CM/ECF(II)(A)(6).

e. *Hyperlinks.* Electronically filed documents may contain hyperlink references to an external document as a convenient mechanism for accessing material cited in the document. A hyperlink reference is neither validated for content nor considered a part of the court's records. The court neither endorses the product or organization at the destination of a hyperlink reference, nor does the court exercise any responsibility over the content at the destination. In order to preserve the integrity of the court record, attorneys wishing to insert hyperlinks in court filings shall continue to use the traditional citation method for the cited authority, in addition to the hyperlink. A hyperlink contained in a filing is no more than a convenient mechanism for accessing material cited in the document and a hyperlink reference is extraneous to any filed document and is not part of the court's record. IN R USDCTND CM/ECF(II)(A)(3).

3. *Signing of pleadings, motions and other papers*

   a. *Signature.* Every pleading, written motion, and other paper must be signed by at least one attorney of record in the attorney's name—or by a party personally if the party is unrepresented. The paper must state the signer's address, e-mail address, and telephone number. FRCP 11(a).

      i. *Signatures on manual filings.* Papers delivered to the clerk for filing must: include the filer's original signature. IN R USDCTND L.R. 5-4(b)(1)(C).

         • *Rubber-stamped and faxed signatures.* An original paper with a rubber-stamped or faxed signature is unsigned for purposes of FRCP 11 and FRCP 26(g). IN R USDCTND L.R. 5-4(b)(2).

         • *Affidavits.* Only the affiant need sign an affidavit. IN R USDCTND L.R. 5-4(b)(3).

      ii. *Electronic signatures.* Pursuant to FRCP 11, every pleading, motion, and other paper (except lists, schedules, statements or amendments thereto) shall be signed by at least one attorney of record or, if the party is not represented by an attorney, all papers shall be signed by the party. An attorney's/participant's password issued by the court combined with the user's identification, serves as and constitutes the attorney/participant's signature for FRCP 11 and other purposes. IN R USDCTND CM/ECF(I)(C). Documents which must be filed and which must contain original signatures other than those of a participating attorney or which require either verification or an unsworn declaration under any rule or statute, shall be filed electronically, with originally executed copies maintained by the filer. The pleading or other document electronically filed shall contain "s/" signature(s), as noted in IN R USDCTND CM/ECF(II)(E)(3)(b). IN R USDCTND CM/ECF(II)(E)(1).

         • *Multiple signatures.* In the case of a stipulation or other document to be signed by two or more attorneys, the following procedure should be used: The filing attorney shall initially confirm that the content of the document is acceptable to all persons required to sign the document and shall obtain the physical signatures of all attorneys on the document. IN R USDCTND CM/ECF(II)(E)(3)(a). The filing attorney then shall file the document electronically, indicating the signatories, e.g., "s/Jane Doe," "s/John Doe," etc. IN R US-DCTND CM/ECF(II)(E)(3)(b). The filing attorney shall retain the hard copy of the document containing the original signatures. IN R USDCTND CM/ECF(II)(E)(3)(c).

      iii. *No verification or accompanying affidavit required for pleadings.* Unless a rule or statute specifically states otherwise, a pleading need not be verified or accompanied by an affidavit. FRCP 11(a).

      iv. *Unsigned papers.* The court must strike an unsigned paper unless the omission is promptly corrected after being called to the attorney's or party's attention. FRCP 11(a).

b. *Representations to the court.* By presenting to the court a pleading, written motion, or other paper—whether by signing, filing, submitting, or later advocating it—an attorney or unrepresented party certifies that to the best of the person's knowledge, information, and belief, formed after an inquiry reasonable under the circumstances:

    i. It is not being presented for any improper purpose, such as to harass, cause unnecessary delay, or needlessly increase the cost of litigation;

    ii. The claims, defenses, and other legal contentions are warranted by existing law or by a nonfrivolous argument for extending, modifying, or reversing existing law or for establishing new law;

    iii. The factual contentions have evidentiary support or, if specifically so identified, will likely have evidentiary support after a reasonable opportunity for further investigation or discovery; and

    iv. The denials of factual contentions are warranted on the evidence or, if specifically so identified, are reasonably based on belief or a lack of information. FRCP 11(b).

c. *Sanctions.* If, after notice and a reasonable opportunity to respond, the court determines that FRCP 11(b) has been violated, the court may impose an appropriate sanction on any attorney, law firm, or party that violated FRCP 11(b) or is responsible for the violation. FRCP 11(c)(1). Refer to the United States District Court for the Northern District of Indiana KeyRules Motion for Sanctions document for more information.

4. *Privacy protection for filings made with the court*

a. *Redacted filings.* Counsel should not include sensitive information in any document filed with the court unless such inclusion is necessary and relevant to the case. IN R USDCTND CM/ECF(VII). Unless the court orders otherwise, in an electronic or paper filing with the court that contains an individual's Social Security number, taxpayer-identification number, or birth date, the name of an individual known to be a minor, or a financial-account number, a party or nonparty making the filing may include only:

    i. The last four (4) digits of the Social Security number and taxpayer-identification number;

    ii. The year of the individual's birth;

    iii. The minor's initials; and

    iv. The last four (4) digits of the financial-account number. FRCP 5.2(a); IN R USDCTND Order 2005-3.

b. *Exemptions from the redaction requirement.* The redaction requirement does not apply to the following:

    i. A financial-account number that identifies the property allegedly subject to forfeiture in a forfeiture proceeding;

    ii. The record of an administrative or agency proceeding;

    iii. The official record of a state-court proceeding;

    iv. The record of a court or tribunal, if that record was not subject to the redaction requirement when originally filed;

    v. A filing covered by FRCP 5.2(c) or FRCP 5.2(d); and

    vi. A pro se filing in an action brought under 28 U.S.C.A. § 2241, 28 U.S.C.A. § 2254, or 28 U.S.C.A. § 2255. FRCP 5.2(b).

    vii. In cases filed under the Social Security Act, 42 U.S.C.A. § 405(g), there is no need for redaction of any information from the documents filed in the case. IN R USDCTND Order 2005-3.

c. *Limitations on remote access to electronic files; Social Security appeals and immigration cases.* Unless the court orders otherwise, in an action for benefits under the Social Security Act, and in an action or proceeding relating to an order of removal, to relief from removal, or to immigration benefits or detention, access to an electronic file is authorized as follows:

    i. The parties and their attorneys may have remote electronic access to any part of the case file, including the administrative record;

ii. Any other person may have electronic access to the full record at the courthouse, but may have remote electronic access only to:

- The docket maintained by the court; and

- An opinion, order, judgment, or other disposition of the court, but not any other part of the case file or the administrative record. FRCP 5.2(c).

d. *Filings made under seal.* The court may order that a filing be made under seal without redaction. The court may later unseal the filing or order the person who made the filing to file a redacted version for the public record. FRCP 5.2(d). For information on filing documents under seal, refer to IN R USDCTND L.R. 5-3, IN R USDCTND CM/ECF(IV)(A), and IN R USDCTND ECF Order 2004-19.

e. *Protective orders.* For good cause, the court may by order in a case:

i. Require redaction of additional information; or

ii. Limit or prohibit a nonparty's remote electronic access to a document filed with the court. FRCP 5.2(e).

f. *Option for additional unredacted filing under seal.* A person making a redacted filing may also file an unredacted copy under seal. The court must retain the unredacted copy as part of the record. FRCP 5.2(f); IN R USDCTND Order 2005-3.

i. The unredacted version of the document or the reference list shall be retained by the court under seal as part of the record. This paper shall be retained by the court as part of the record. The court may, however, still require the party to file a redacted copy for the public file. IN R USDCTND Order 2005-3.

g. *Option for filing a reference list.* A filing that contains redacted information may be filed together with a reference list that identifies each item of redacted information and specifies an appropriate identifier that uniquely corresponds to each item listed. The list must be filed under seal and may be amended as of right. Any reference in the case to a listed identifier will be construed to refer to the corresponding item of information. FRCP 5.2(g); IN R USDCTND Order 2005-3.

i. The unredacted version of the document or the reference list shall be retained by the court under seal as part of the record. This paper shall be retained by the court as part of the record. The court may, however, still require the party to file a redacted copy for the public file. IN R USDCTND Order 2005-3.

h. *Responsibility for redaction.* The responsibility for redacting these personal identifiers rests solely with counsel and the parties. The Clerk will not review each paper for compliance with IN R USDCTND Order 2005-3. IN R USDCTND Order 2005-3.

i. *Waiver of protection of identifiers.* A person waives the protection of FRCP 5.2(a) as to the person's own information by filing it without redaction and not under seal. FRCP 5.2(h).

F. Filing and Service Requirements

1. *Filing requirements.* A civil action is commenced by filing a complaint with the court. FRCP 3. The first step in a civil action in a United States district court is the filing of the complaint with the clerk or the judge. FPP § 1052. Filing a complaint requires nothing more than delivery of the document to a court officer authorized to receive it. FPP § 1052; Central States, Southeast & Southwest Areas Pension Fund v. Paramount Liquor Co., 34 F.Supp.2d 1092 (N.D.Ill. 1999). Papers not filed electronically must be filed with the clerk, not a judge. IN R USDCTND L.R. 5-4(b)(4). Parties manually filing a paper that requires the clerk to give others notice, must give the clerk: (1) sufficient copies of the notice; and (2) the name and address of each person entitled to receive the notice. IN R USDCTND L.R. 5-4(b)(8).

a. *Where to file.* Papers not filed electronically must be filed in the division where the case is pending, unless: (1) a person will be prejudiced if the paper is not filed the same day it is tendered; and (2) it includes an adequately sized envelope addressed to the clerk's office in the division where the case is pending and with adequate postage. IN R USDCTND L.R. 5-4(b)(5).

b. *Pro se incarcerated litigants.* Individuals who are incarcerated and are filing their legal documents pro se may benefit from a special "mailbox rule," which fixes the time of commencement of an action at the point when the complaint enters the prison mail system, rather than when it reaches the court clerk. FPP § 1052; Houston v. Lack, 487 U.S. 266, 276, 108 S.Ct. 2379, 2385, 101 L.Ed.2d 245 (1988).

c. *Electronic filing*

   i. *Authorization of electronic filing program.* A court may, by local rule, allow papers to be filed, signed, or verified by electronic means that are consistent with any technical standards established by the Judicial Conference of the United States. A local rule may require electronic filing only if reasonable exceptions are allowed. A paper filed electronically in compliance with a local rule is a written paper for purposes of the Federal Rules of Civil Procedure. FRCP 5(d)(3).

   - Papers must be filed, signed, and verified electronically unless excepted by the court's CM/ECF Civil and Criminal User Manual (IN R USDCTND CM/ECF). IN R USDCTND L.R. 5-1.

   ii. *Mandatory electronic filing.* Unless otherwise permitted by these procedures or otherwise authorized by the assigned judge, all documents submitted for filing in this district in civil and criminal cases, no matter when a case was originally filed, shall be filed electronically using the System. IN R USDCTND CM/ECF(II)(A)(1). The requirement that "all documents" be filed electronically includes briefs, and attachments and exhibits used in support of motions. IN R USDCTND CM/ECF(FN1).

   - Sending a document or pleading to the court via e-mail or facsimile does not constitute "electronic filing." IN R USDCTND CM/ECF(I)(A).

   iii. *Conventional filing.* As used in these procedures, a "conventionally" filed or submitted document or pleading is one presented to the Clerk or a party in paper or other non-electronic, tangible format. The following documents shall be filed conventionally and not electronically unless specifically authorized by the Court:

   - Exhibits and other documents which cannot be converted to a legible electronic form. Whenever possible, counsel is responsible for converting filings to an electronic form. However, if that is not physically possible, counsel shall electronically file a .pdf document titled Notice of Manual Filing as a notation on the docket sheet that filings are being held in the clerk's office in paper. A sample Notice of Manual Filing is attached as Form 2 (IN R USDCTND CM/ECF(Form 2)). If documents are filed in paper format, counsel must provide an original for the clerk's office, a copy for the judge and a copy must be served on all parties in the case. Large documents which do not exist in an electronic format shall be scanned into .pdf format by counsel, in small batches if necessary, and filed electronically as separate attachments in the System. IN R USDCTND CM/ECF(III)(A)(1).

   - Certain documents which are listed in IN R USDCTND CM/ECF(II)(E)(2). IN R USDCTND CM/ECF(III)(A)(2).

   - Documents filed by pro se litigants. IN R USDCTND CM/ECF(III)(A)(3).

   iv. For more information on electronic filing, refer to IN R USDCTND CM/ECF.

2. *Issuance of summons.* On or after filing the complaint, the plaintiff may present a summons to the clerk for signature and seal. If the summons is properly completed, the clerk must sign, seal, and issue it to the plaintiff for service on the defendant. A summons—or a copy of a summons that is addressed to multiple defendants—must be issued for each defendant to be served. FRCP 4(b).

   a. *Electronic issuance.* The court may sign, seal and issue a summons on paper or electronically. IN R USDCTND CM/ECF(II)(B).

   b. *Amendments.* The court may permit a summons to be amended. FRCP 4(a)(2).

3. *Service requirements.* A summons must be served with a copy of the complaint. The plaintiff is responsible for having the summons and complaint served within the time allowed by FRCP 4(m) and

must furnish the necessary copies to the person who makes service. FRCP 4(c)(1). A party may not electronically serve a summons and complaint, but instead must perfect service according to FRCP 4. IN R USDCTND CM/ECF(II)(D)(3); IN R USDCTND CM/ECF(II)(B).

a. *By whom served.* Any person who is at least 18 years old and not a party may serve a summons and complaint. FRCP 4(c)(2).

    i. *By a marshal or someone specially appointed.* At the plaintiff's request, the court may order that service be made by a United States marshal or deputy marshal or by a person specially appointed by the court. The court must so order if the plaintiff is authorized to proceed in forma pauperis under 28 U.S.C.A. § 1915 or as a seaman under 28 U.S.C.A. § 1916. FRCP 4(c)(3).

b. *Serving an individual within a judicial district of the United States.* Unless federal law provides otherwise, an individual—other than a minor, an incompetent person, or a person whose waiver has been filed—may be served in a judicial district of the United States by:

    i. Following state law for serving a summons in an action brought in courts of general jurisdiction in the state where the district court is located or where service is made; or

    ii. Doing any of the following:

- Delivering a copy of the summons and of the complaint to the individual personally;
- Leaving a copy of each at the individual's dwelling or usual place of abode with someone of suitable age and discretion who resides there; or
- Delivering a copy of each to an agent authorized by appointment or by law to receive service of process. FRCP 4(e).

c. *Serving an individual in a foreign country.* Unless federal law provides otherwise, an individual—other than a minor, an incompetent person, or a person whose waiver has been filed—may be served at a place not within any judicial district of the United States:

    i. By any internationally agreed means of service that is reasonably calculated to give notice, such as those authorized by the Hague Convention on the Service Abroad of Judicial and Extrajudicial Documents;

    ii. If there is no internationally agreed means, or if an international agreement allows but does not specify other means, by a method that is reasonably calculated to give notice:

- As prescribed by the foreign country's law for service in that country in an action in its courts of general jurisdiction;
- As the foreign authority directs in response to a letter rogatory or letter of request; or
- Unless prohibited by the foreign country's law, by: (1) delivering a copy of the summons and of the complaint to the individual personally; or (2) using any form of mail that the clerk addresses and sends to the individual and that requires a signed receipt; or
- By other means not prohibited by international agreement, as the court orders. FRCP 4(f).

d. *Serving a minor or an incompetent person.* A minor or an incompetent person in a judicial district of the United States must be served by following state law for serving a summons or like process on such a defendant in an action brought in the courts of general jurisdiction of the state where service is made. A minor or an incompetent person who is not within any judicial district of the United States must be served in the manner prescribed by FRCP 4(f)(2)(A), FRCP 4(f)(2)(B), or FRCP 4(f)(3). FRCP 4(g).

e. *Serving a corporation, partnership, or association.* Unless federal law provides otherwise or the defendant's waiver has been filed, a domestic or foreign corporation, or a partnership or other unincorporated association that is subject to suit under a common name, must be served:

    i. In a judicial district of the United States:

- In the manner prescribed by FRCP 4(e)(1) for serving an individual; or
- By delivering a copy of the summons and of the complaint to an officer, a managing or general agent, or any other agent authorized by appointment or by law to receive service

of process and—if the agent is one authorized by statute and the statute so requires—by also mailing a copy of each to the defendant; or

   ii. At a place not within any judicial district of the United States, in any manner prescribed by FRCP 4(f) for serving an individual, except personal delivery under FRCP 4(f)(2)(C)(i). FRCP 4(h).

f. *Serving the United States and its agencies, corporations, officers, or employees*

   i. *United States.* To serve the United States, a party must:

- Deliver a copy of the summons and of the complaint to the United States attorney for the district where the action is brought—or to an assistant United States attorney or clerical employee whom the United States attorney designates in a writing filed with the court clerk—or send a copy of each by registered or certified mail to the civil-process clerk at the United States attorney's office;

- Send a copy of each by registered or certified mail to the Attorney General of the United States at Washington, D.C.; and

- If the action challenges an order of a nonparty agency or officer of the United States, send a copy of each by registered or certified mail to the agency or officer. FRCP 4(i)(1).

   ii. *Agency; Corporation; Officer or employee sued in an official capacity.* To serve a United States agency or corporation, or a United States officer or employee sued only in an official capacity, a party must serve the United States and also send a copy of the summons and of the complaint by registered or certified mail to the agency, corporation, officer, or employee. FRCP 4(i)(2).

   iii. *Officer or employee sued individually.* To serve a United States officer or employee sued in an individual capacity for an act or omission occurring in connection with duties performed on the United States' behalf (whether or not the officer or employee is also sued in an official capacity), a party must serve the United States and also serve the officer or employee under FRCP 4(e), FRCP 4(f), or FRCP 4(g). FRCP 4(i)(3).

   iv. *Extending time.* The court must allow a party a reasonable time to cure its failure to:

- Serve a person required to be served under FRCP 4(i)(2), if the party has served either the United States attorney or the Attorney General of the United States; or

- Serve the United States under FRCP 4(i)(3), if the party has served the United States officer or employee. FRCP 4(i)(4).

g. *Serving a foreign, state, or local government*

   i. *Foreign state.* A foreign state or its political subdivision, agency, or instrumentality must be served in accordance with 28 U.S.C.A. § 1608. FRCP 4(j)(1).

   ii. *State or local government.* A state, a municipal corporation, or any other state-created governmental organization that is subject to suit must be served by:

- Delivering a copy of the summons and of the complaint to its chief executive officer; or

- Serving a copy of each in the manner prescribed by that state's law for serving a summons or like process on such a defendant. FRCP 4(j)(2).

h. *Notice by publication.* When published notice is required: (1) the clerk must send the notice to the party originating the notice; and (2) the party must deliver the notice to the appropriate newspapers for publication. IN R USDCTND L.R. 5-4(d).

i. *Territorial limits of effective service*

   i. *In general.* Serving a summons or filing a waiver of service establishes personal jurisdiction over a defendant:

- Who is subject to the jurisdiction of a court of general jurisdiction in the state where the district court is located;

- Who is a party joined under FRCP 14 or FRCP 19 and is served within a judicial district of the United States and not more than one hundred (100) miles from where the summons was issued; or

- When authorized by a federal statute. FRCP 4(k)(1).

ii. *Federal claim outside state-court jurisdiction.* For a claim that arises under federal law, serving a summons or filing a waiver of service establishes personal jurisdiction over a defendant if:

- The defendant is not subject to jurisdiction in any state's courts of general jurisdiction; and
- Exercising jurisdiction is consistent with the United States Constitution and laws. FRCP 4(k)(2).

j. *Asserting jurisdiction over property or assets*

i. *Federal law.* The court may assert jurisdiction over property if authorized by a federal statute. Notice to claimants of the property must be given as provided in the statute or by serving a summons under FRCP 4. FRCP 4(n)(1).

ii. *State law.* On a showing that personal jurisdiction over a defendant cannot be obtained in the district where the action is brought by reasonable efforts to serve a summons under FRCP 4, the court may assert jurisdiction over the defendant's assets found in the district. Jurisdiction is acquired by seizing the assets under the circumstances and in the manner provided by state law in that district. FRCP 4(n)(2).

k. *Proving service*

i. *Affidavit required.* Unless service is waived, proof of service must be made to the court. Except for service by a United States marshal or deputy marshal, proof must be by the server's affidavit. FRCP 4(l)(1).

ii. *Service outside the United States.* Service not within any judicial district of the United States must be proved as follows:

- If made under FRCP 4(f)(1), as provided in the applicable treaty or convention; or
- If made under FRCP 4(f)(2) or FRCP 4(f)(3), by a receipt signed by the addressee, or by other evidence satisfying the court that the summons and complaint were delivered to the addressee. FRCP 4(l)(2).

iii. *Validity of service; Amending proof.* Failure to prove service does not affect the validity of service. The court may permit proof of service to be amended. FRCP 4(l)(3).

iv. *Results of filing a waiver of service.* When the plaintiff files a waiver, proof of service is not required and FRCP 4 applies as if a summons and complaint had been served at the time of filing the waiver. FRCP 4(d)(4).

l. *Service of other process.* For information on service of other process, refer to FRCP 4.1.

G. Hearings

1. There is no hearing contemplated in the federal statutes or rules for the complaint and summons.

H. Forms

1. Official Federal Complaint and Summons Forms

a. Rule 4 notice of a lawsuit and request to waive service of summons. FRCP 4.

2. Federal Complaint and Summons Forms

a. Summons. 2 FEDFORMS § 3:23.

b. Summons; With proof of service. 2 FEDFORMS § 3:24.

c. Summons; Suit against officers of the United States. 2 FEDFORMS § 3:26.

d. Request for summons. 2 FEDFORMS § 3:27.

e. Civil cover sheet. 2 FEDFORMS § 3:29.

f. Motion for appointment of person to serve process. 2 FEDFORMS § 3:30.

g.   Motion for appointment of United States marshal to serve process. 2 FEDFORMS § 3:34.

h.   Notice of lawsuit and request for waiver of service of summons and waiver of summons. 2 FEDFORMS § 3:36.

i.   Motion for payment of costs of personal service. 2 FEDFORMS § 3:37.

j.   Affidavit of personal service; Delivery to individual. 2 FEDFORMS § 3:54.

k.   Declaration of service; Delivery to individual. 2 FEDFORMS § 3:55.

l.   Declaration of service; Delivery at usual place of abode or residence. 2 FEDFORMS § 3:56.

m.   Declaration of service; Service on corporation; Delivery to officer. 2 FEDFORMS § 3:57.

n.   Declaration of service; Service on United States. 2 FEDFORMS § 3:69.

o.   Declaration of service; Service on officer of United States. 2 FEDFORMS § 3:71.

p.   Complaint. 2 FEDFORMS § 7:14.

q.   Introductory clause; Single claim stated. 2 FEDFORMS § 7:16.

r.   Introductory clause; Several claims stated in separate counts. 2 FEDFORMS § 7:18.

s.   Allegations on information and belief. 2 FEDFORMS § 7:19.

t.   General prayer for relief. 2 FEDFORMS § 7:21.

u.   Disparate treatment; Sex discrimination; Sexual harassment and constructive discharge. 2A FEDFORMS § 7:143.

v.   Against manufacturer for negligent design and manufacture. 2B FEDFORMS § 7:426.

w.   Complaint; Single count. FEDPROF § 1:68.

x.   Complaint; Multiple counts; With same jurisdictional basis. FEDPROF § 1:69.

y.   Complaint; Multiple counts; With different jurisdictional basis for each. FEDPROF § 1:70.

z.   Civil cover sheet; General form (form JS-44). FEDPROF § 1:144.

3. Forms for the Northern District of Indiana

a.   Notice of manual filing. IN R USDCTND CM/ECF(Form 2).

b.   Declaration that party was unable to file in a timely manner. IN R USDCTND CM/ECF(Form 3).

I.   Applicable Rules

1.   *Federal rules*

a.   District court; Filing and miscellaneous fees; Rules of court. 28 U.S.C.A. § 1914.

b.   Commencing an action. FRCP 3.

c.   Summons. FRCP 4.

d.   Serving and filing pleadings and other papers. FRCP 5.

e.   Constitutional challenge to a statute; Notice, certification, and intervention. FRCP 5.1.

f.   Privacy protection for filings made with the court. FRCP 5.2.

g.   Computing and extending time; Time for motion papers. FRCP 6.

h.   Pleadings allowed; Form of motions and other papers. FRCP 7.

i.   Disclosure statement. FRCP 7.1.

j.   General rules of pleading. FRCP 8.

k.   Pleading special matters. FRCP 9.

l.   Form of pleadings. FRCP 10.

m.   Signing pleadings, motions, and other papers; Representations to the court; Sanctions. FRCP 11.

n.   Joinder of claims. FRCP 18.

o.   Required joinder of parties. FRCP 19.

p.   Permissive joinder of parties. FRCP 20.

q.   Misjoinder and nonjoinder of parties. FRCP 21.

r.   Right to a jury trial; Demand. FRCP 38.

s.   Determining foreign law. FRCP 44.1.

2. *Local rules*

a.   Citation and scope of the rules. IN R USDCTND L.R. 1-1.

b.   Sanctions for formatting errors. IN R USDCTND L.R. 1-3.

c.   Electronic filing required. IN R USDCTND L.R. 5-1.

d.   Constitutional questions. IN R USDCTND L.R. 5.1-1.

e.   Format of papers. IN R USDCTND L.R. 5-4.

f.   Pro se complaints. IN R USDCTND L.R. 8-1.

g.   Request for three-judge court. IN R USDCTND L.R. 9-2.

h.   Pretrial procedure. IN R USDCTND L.R. 16-1.

i.   Alternative dispute resolution. IN R USDCTND L.R. 16-6.

j.   Class actions. IN R USDCTND L.R. 23-1.

k.   Case assignment. IN R USDCTND L.R. 40-1.

l.   Appearance and withdrawal of appearance. IN R USDCTND L.R. 83-8.

m.   CM/ECF civil and criminal user manual. IN R USDCTND CM/ECF.

n.   In re: privacy and public access to civil electronic case files. IN R USDCTND Order 2005-3.

Pleadings
Answer

Document Last Updated December 2016

A. **Checklist**

(I)   ❏ Matters to be considered by plaintiff

(a)   ❏ Required documents

(1)   ❏ Civil cover sheet

(2)   ❏ Complaint

(3)   ❏ Summons

(4)   ❏ Filing fee

(5)   ❏ Affidavit proving service

(b)   ❏ Supplemental documents

(1)   ❏ Notice and request for waiver of service

(2)   ❏ Notice of constitutional question

(3)   ❏ Notice of issue concerning foreign law

(4)   ❏ Nongovernmental corporate disclosure statement

(5)   ❏ Request for three-judge court

(6)   ❏ Report on the filing or determination of an action regarding a patent or trademark

(7)   ❏ Report on the filing or determination of an action or appeal regarding a copyright

(8) ❏ Index of exhibits

(9) ❏ Copy of document with self-addressed envelope

(10) ❏ Notice of manual filing

(11) ❏ Courtesy copies

(12) ❏ Declaration that party was unable to file in a timely manner

(c) ❏ Timing

    (1) ❏ A civil action is commenced by filing a complaint with the court

    (2) ❏ If a defendant is not served within ninety (90) days after the complaint is filed, the court—on motion or on its own after notice to the plaintiff—must dismiss the action without prejudice against that defendant or order that service be made within a specified time

(II) ❏ Matters to be considered by defendant

  (a) ❏ Required documents

    (1) ❏ Answer

    (2) ❏ Certificate of service

  (b) ❏ Supplemental documents

    (1) ❏ Waiver of the service of summons

    (2) ❏ Notice of constitutional question

    (3) ❏ Notice of issue concerning foreign law

    (4) ❏ Nongovernmental corporate disclosure statement

    (5) ❏ Request for three-judge court

    (6) ❏ Index of exhibits

    (7) ❏ Copy of document with self-addressed envelope

    (8) ❏ Notice of manual filing

    (9) ❏ Courtesy copies

   (10) ❏ Declaration that party was unable to file in a timely manner

  (c) ❏ Timing

    (1) ❏ A defendant must serve an answer:

      (i) ❏ Within twenty-one (21) days after being served with the summons and complaint; or

      (ii) ❏ If it has timely waived service under FRCP 4(d), within sixty (60) days after the request for a waiver was sent, or within ninety (90) days after it was sent to the defendant outside any judicial district of the United States

    (2) ❏ The United States, a United States agency, or a United States officer or employee sued only in an official capacity must serve an answer to a complaint, counterclaim, or crossclaim within sixty (60) days after service on the United States attorney

    (3) ❏ A United States officer or employee sued in an individual capacity for an act or omission occurring in connection with duties performed on the United States' behalf must serve an answer to a complaint, counterclaim, or crossclaim within sixty (60) days after service on the officer or employee or service on the United States attorney, whichever is later

    (4) ❏ Unless the court sets a different time, serving a motion under FRCP 12 alters these periods as follows:

      (i) ❏ If the court denies the motion or postpones its disposition until trial, the responsive pleading must be served within fourteen (14) days after notice of the court's action; or

      (ii) ❏ If the court grants a motion for a more definite statement, the responsive pleading must be served within fourteen (14) days after the more definite statement is served

(5) ☐ Defendant is given a reasonable time of at least thirty (30) days after a waiver of service request is sent—or at least sixty (60) days if sent to defendant outside any judicial district of the United States—to return the waiver

B. Timing

1. *Answer.* Unless another time is specified by FRCP 12 or a federal statute. . .a defendant must serve an answer: (1) within twenty-one (21) days after being served with the summons and complaint; or (2) if it has timely waived service under FRCP 4(d), within sixty (60) days after the request for a waiver was sent, or within ninety (90) days after it was sent to the defendant outside any judicial district of the United States. FRCP 12(a)(1)(A).

   a. *Time to serve other responsive pleadings.* Unless another time is specified by FRCP 12 or a federal statute, the time for serving a responsive pleading is as follows:

      i. *Answer to counterclaim or crossclaim.* A party must serve an answer to a counterclaim or crossclaim within twenty-one (21) days after being served with the pleading that states the counterclaim or crossclaim. FRCP 12(a)(1)(B).

      ii. *Reply to an answer.* A party must serve a reply to an answer within twenty-one (21) days after being served with an order to reply, unless the order specifies a different time. FRCP 12(a)(1)(C).

   b. *United States and its agencies, officers, or employees sued in an official capacity.* The United States, a United States agency, or a United States officer or employee sued only in an official capacity must serve an answer to a complaint, counterclaim, or crossclaim within sixty (60) days after service on the United States attorney. FRCP 12(a)(2).

   c. *United States officers or employees sued in an individual capacity.* A United States officer or employee sued in an individual capacity for an act or omission occurring in connection with duties performed on the United States' behalf must serve an answer to a complaint, counterclaim, or crossclaim within sixty (60) days after service on the officer or employee or service on the United States attorney, whichever is later. FRCP 12(a)(3).

   d. *Effect of a FRCP 12 motion on the time to serve a responsive pleading.* Unless the court sets a different time, serving a motion under FRCP 12 alters the periods in FRCP 12(a) as follows:

      i. If the court denies the motion or postpones its disposition until trial, the responsive pleading must be served within fourteen (14) days after notice of the court's action; or

      ii. If the court grants a motion for a more definite statement, the responsive pleading must be served within fourteen (14) days after the more definite statement is served. FRCP 12(a)(4).

2. *Waiver of service.* The notice and request for waiver must give the defendant a reasonable time of at least thirty (30) days after the request was sent—or at least sixty (60) days if sent to defendant outside any judicial district of the United States—to return the waiver. FRCP 4(d)(1)(F).

   a. *Time to answer after a waiver.* A defendant who, before being served with process, timely returns a waiver need not serve an answer to the complaint until sixty (60) days after the request was sent—or until ninety (90) days after it was sent to the defendant outside any judicial district of the United States. FRCP 4(d)(3).

3. *Automatic initial extension.* The deadline to respond to a pleading or a discovery request—including requests for admission—is automatically extended when an extension notice is filed with the court and: (1) the deadline has not been extended before; (2) the extension is for twenty-eight (28) or fewer days; and (3) the notice states: (A) the original deadline; (B) the new deadline; and (C) that all opposing attorneys the attorney could reach agreed to the extension; or that the party could not reach any other opposing attorneys despite due diligence. IN R USDCTND L.R. 6-1(b).

   a. *Pro se parties.* The automatic initial extension does not apply to pro se parties. IN R USDCTND L.R. 6-1(c).

4. *Computation of time*

   a. *Computing time.* FRCP 6 applies in computing any time period specified in the Federal Rules of Civil

Procedure, in any local rule or court order, or in any statute that does not specify a method of computing time. FRCP 6(a).

i. *Period stated in days or a longer unit.* When the period is stated in days or a longer unit of time:

- Exclude the day of the event that triggers the period;

- Count every day, including intermediate Saturdays, Sundays, and legal holidays; and

- Include the last day of the period, but if the last day is a Saturday, Sunday, or legal holiday, the period continues to run until the end of the next day that is not a Saturday, Sunday, or legal holiday. FRCP 6(a)(1).

ii. *Period stated in hours.* When the period is stated in hours:

- Begin counting immediately on the occurrence of the event that triggers the period;

- Count every hour, including hours during intermediate Saturdays, Sundays, and legal holidays; and

- If the period would end on a Saturday, Sunday, or legal holiday, the period continues to run until the same time on the next day that is not a Saturday, Sunday, or legal holiday. FRCP 6(a)(2).

iii. *Inaccessibility of the clerk's office.* Unless the court orders otherwise, if the clerk's office is inaccessible:

- On the last day for filing under FRCP 6(a)(1), then the time for filing is extended to the first accessible day that is not a Saturday, Sunday, or legal holiday; or

- During the last hour for filing under FRCP 6(a)(2), then the time for filing is extended to the same time on the first accessible day that is not a Saturday, Sunday, or legal holiday. FRCP 6(a)(3).

iv. *"Last day" defined.* Unless a different time is set by a statute, local rule, or court order, the last day ends:

- For electronic filing, at midnight in the court's time zone; and

- For filing by other means, when the clerk's office is scheduled to close. FRCP 6(a)(4).

v. *"Next day" defined.* The "next day" is determined by continuing to count forward when the period is measured after an event and backward when measured before an event. FRCP 6(a)(5).

vi. *"Legal holiday" defined.* "Legal holiday" means:

- The day set aside by statute for observing New Year's Day, Martin Luther King Jr.'s Birthday, Washington's Birthday, Memorial Day, Independence Day, Labor Day, Columbus Day, Veterans' Day, Thanksgiving Day, or Christmas Day;

- Any day declared a holiday by the President or Congress; and

- For periods that are measured after an event, any other day declared a holiday by the state where the district court is located. FRCP 6(a)(6).

b. *Computation of electronic filing deadlines.* Filing documents electronically does not alter any filing deadlines or any time computation pursuant to FRCP 6. The counties of Lake, Porter, LaPorte, Pulaski and Starke are located in the Central time zone and the remaining counties in the Northern District of Indiana are located in the Eastern time zone. Nevertheless, all electronic transmissions of documents must be completed (i.e., received completely by the clerk's office) prior to midnight Eastern Time, (South Bend/Fort Wayne/Lafayette time) in order to be considered timely filed that day, regardless of the local time in the division where the case is pending. Although documents can be filed electronically twenty-four (24) hours a day, filers are strongly encouraged to file all documents during hours when the CM/ECF Help Line is available, from 9:00 a.m. to 4:00 p.m. local time. IN R USDCTND CM/ECF(II)(I).

i. *Technical failures.* If the attorney is unable to file a document in a timely manner due to technical difficulties in the user's system, the attorney must file a document with the court as

soon as possible notifying the court of the inability to file the document. A sample document entitled Declaration that Party was Unable to File in a Timely Manner Due to Technical Difficulties is attached hereto as Form 5. IN R USDCTND CM/ECF(VI)(B). [Editor's note: the reference to Form 5 is likely meant to be a reference to Form 3 (IN R USDCTND CM/ECF(Form 3)].

   c. *Extending time*

      i. *In general.* When an act may or must be done within a specified time, the court may, for good cause, extend the time:

- With or without motion or notice if the court acts, or if a request is made, before the original time or its extension expires; or

- On motion made after the time has expired if the party failed to act because of excusable neglect. FRCP 6(b)(1).

      ii. *Exceptions.* A court must not extend the time to act under FRCP 50(b), FRCP 50(d), FRCP 52(b), FRCP 59(b), FRCP 59(d), FRCP 59(e), and FRCP 60(b). FRCP 6(b)(2).

      iii. Refer to the United States District Court for the Northern District of Indiana KeyRules Motion for Continuance/Extension of Time document for more information on extending time.

   d. *Additional time after certain kinds of service.* When a party may or must act within a specified time after being served and service is made under FRCP 5(b)(2)(C) (mail), FRCP 5(b)(2)(D) (leaving with the clerk), or FRCP 5(b)(2)(F) (other means consented to), three (3) days are added after the period would otherwise expire under FRCP 6(a). FRCP 6(d).

C. General Requirements

1. *Pleading, generally*

   a. *Pleadings allowed.* Only these pleadings are allowed: (1) a complaint; (2) an answer to a complaint; (3) an answer to a counterclaim designated as a counterclaim; (4) an answer to a crossclaim; (5) a third-party complaint; (6) an answer to a third-party complaint; and (7) if the court orders one, a reply to an answer. FRCP 7(a).

   b. *Pleading to be concise and direct.* Each allegation must be simple, concise, and direct. No technical form is required. FRCP 8(d)(1).

   c. *Alternative statements of a claim or defense.* A party may set out two or more statements of a claim or defense alternatively or hypothetically, either in a single count or defense or in separate ones. If a party makes alternative statements, the pleading is sufficient if any one of them is sufficient. FRCP 8(d)(2).

   d. *Inconsistent claims or defenses.* A party may state as many separate claims or defenses as it has, regardless of consistency. FRCP 8(d)(3).

   e. *Construing pleadings.* Pleadings must be construed so as to do justice. FRCP 8(e).

2. *Pleading special matters*

   a. *Capacity or authority to sue; Legal existence*

      i. *In general.* Except when required to show that the court has jurisdiction, a pleading need not allege:

- A party's capacity to sue or be sued;

- A party's authority to sue or be sued in a representative capacity; or

- The legal existence of an organized association of persons that is made a party. FRCP 9(a)(1).

      ii. *Raising those issues.* To raise any of those issues, a party must do so by a specific denial, which must state any supporting facts that are peculiarly within the party's knowledge. FRCP 9(a)(2).

   b. *Fraud or mistake; Conditions of mind.* In alleging fraud or mistake, a party must state with particularity the circumstances constituting fraud or mistake. Malice, intent, knowledge, and other conditions of a person's mind may be alleged generally. FRCP 9(b).

c. *Conditions precedent.* In pleading conditions precedent, it suffices to allege generally that all conditions precedent have occurred or been performed. But when denying that a condition precedent has occurred or been performed, a party must do so with particularity. FRCP 9(c).

d. *Official document or act.* In pleading an official document or official act, it suffices to allege that the document was legally issued or the act legally done. FRCP 9(d).

e. *Judgment.* In pleading a judgment or decision of a domestic or foreign court, a judicial or quasi-judicial tribunal, or a board or officer, it suffices to plead the judgment or decision without showing jurisdiction to render it. FRCP 9(e).

f. *Time and place.* An allegation of time or place is material when testing the sufficiency of a pleading. FRCP 9(f).

g. *Special damages.* If an item of special damage is claimed, it must be specifically stated. FRCP 9(g).

h. *Admiralty or maritime claim*

   i. *How designated.* If a claim for relief is within the admiralty or maritime jurisdiction and also within the court's subject-matter jurisdiction on some other ground, the pleading may designate the claim as an admiralty or maritime claim for purposes of FRCP 14(c), FRCP 38(e), and FRCP 82 and the Supplemental Rules for Admiralty or Maritime Claims and Asset Forfeiture Actions. A claim cognizable only in the admiralty or maritime jurisdiction is an admiralty or maritime claim for those purposes, whether or not so designated. FRCP 9(h)(1).

   ii. *Designation for appeal.* A case that includes an admiralty or maritime claim within FRCP 9(h) is an admiralty case within 28 U.S.C.A. § 1292(a)(3). FRCP 9(h)(2).

3. *Answer*

   a. *Form.* Responsive pleadings under FRCP 7(a) must: (1) restate verbatim the paragraphs from the pleading they respond to; and (2) immediately following each restated paragraph, state the response to that paragraph. IN R USDCTND L.R. 10-1(a).

      i. *Exception.* IN R USDCTND L.R. 10-1 does not apply to pro se cases. IN R USDCTND L.R. 10-1(b).

   b. *Defenses; Admissions and denials*

      i. *In general.* In responding to a pleading, a party must: (1) state in short and plain terms its defenses to each claim asserted against it; and (2) admit or deny the allegations asserted against it by an opposing party. FRCP 8(b)(1).

         • The purpose of an answer is to formulate issues by means of defenses addressed to the allegations of the complaint, and to give the plaintiff notice of the defenses he or she will be called upon to meet. FEDPROC § 62:70; Lopez v. U.S. Fidelity & Guaranty Co., 15 Alaska 633, 18 F.R.D. 59 (1955); Moriarty v. Curran, 18 F.R.D. 461 (S.D.N.Y. 1956).

         • An answer is adequate where it accomplishes these purposes, even if it contains general and specific denials and at the same time asserts additional facts by way of justification or explanation, and even if it sets forth conclusions of law. FEDPROC § 62:70; Johnston v. Jones, 178 F.2d 481 (3d Cir. 1949); Burke v. Mesta Mach. Co., 5 F.R.D. 134 (W.D.Pa. 1946).

      ii. *Denials; Responding to the substance.* A denial must fairly respond to the substance of the allegation. FRCP 8(b)(2).

      iii. *General and specific denials.* A party that intends in good faith to deny all the allegations of a pleading—including the jurisdictional grounds—may do so by a general denial. A party that does not intend to deny all the allegations must either specifically deny designated allegations or generally deny all except those specifically admitted. FRCP 8(b)(3).

      iv. *Denying part of an allegation.* A party that intends in good faith to deny only part of an allegation must admit the part that is true and deny the rest. FRCP 8(b)(4).

      v. *Lacking knowledge or information.* A party that lacks knowledge or information sufficient to form a belief about the truth of an allegation must so state, and the statement has the effect of a denial. FRCP 8(b)(5).

- An answer merely stating that the defendant lacks knowledge to form a belief as to the plaintiff's allegations, and making no statement as to his or her lack of information, has been held to be insufficient, the court suggesting that the phrase might be used in an attempt to mask the defendant's inability to make a good-faith denial of the allegations. FEDPROC § 62:73; Gilbert v. Johnston, 127 F.R.D. 145 (N.D.Ill. 1989).

vi. *Effect of failing to deny.* An allegation—other than one relating to the amount of damages—is admitted if a responsive pleading is required and the allegation is not denied. If a responsive pleading is not required, an allegation is considered denied or avoided. FRCP 8(b)(6).

c. *Affirmative defenses.* In responding to a pleading, a party must affirmatively state any avoidance or affirmative defense, including: (1) accord and satisfaction; (2) arbitration and award; (3) assumption of risk; (4) contributory negligence; (5) duress; (6) estoppel; (7) failure of consideration; (8) fraud; (9) illegality; (10) injury by fellow servant; (11) laches; (12) license; (13) payment; (14) release; (15) res judicata; (16) statute of frauds; (17) statute of limitations; and (18) waiver. FRCP 8(c)(1).

i. *Mistaken designation.* If a party mistakenly designates a defense as a counterclaim, or a counterclaim as a defense, the court must, if justice requires, treat the pleading as though it were correctly designated, and may impose terms for doing so. FRCP 8(c)(2).

d. *How to present defenses.* Every defense to a claim for relief in any pleading must be asserted in the responsive pleading if one is required. But a party may assert the following defenses by motion: (1) lack of subject-matter jurisdiction; (2) lack of personal jurisdiction; (3) improper venue; (4) insufficient process; (5) insufficient service of process; (6) failure to state a claim upon which relief can be granted; and (7) failure to join a party under FRCP 19. FRCP 12(b).

i. A motion asserting any of these defenses must be made before pleading if a responsive pleading is allowed. If a pleading sets out a claim for relief that does not require a responsive pleading, an opposing party may assert at trial any defense to that claim. FRCP 12(b).

ii. Refer to the United States District Court for the Northern District of Indiana KeyRules Motion to Dismiss for Lack of Subject Matter Jurisdiction, Motion to Dismiss for Lack of Personal Jurisdiction, Motion to Dismiss for Improper Venue, and Motion to Dismiss for Failure to State a Claim documents for more information on motions under FRCP 12(b)(1), FRCP 12(b)(2), FRCP 12(b)(3), and FRCP 12(b)(6).

e. *Waiving and preserving certain defenses.* No defense or objection is waived by joining it with one or more other defenses or objections in a responsive pleading or in a motion. FRCP 12(b).

i. *When some are waived.* A party waives any defense listed in FRCP 12(b)(2) through FRCP 12(b)(5) by:

- Omitting it from a motion in the circumstances described in FRCP 12(g)(2); or

- Failing to either: (1) make it by motion under FRCP 12; or (2) include it in a responsive pleading or in an amendment allowed by FRCP 15(a)(1) as a matter of course. FRCP 12(h)(1).

ii. *When to raise others.* Failure to state a claim upon which relief can be granted, to join a person required by FRCP 19(b), or to state a legal defense to a claim may be raised:

- In any pleading allowed or ordered under FRCP 7(a);

- By a motion under FRCP 12(c); or

- At trial. FRCP 12(h)(2).

iii. *Lack of subject matter jurisdiction.* If the court determines at any time that it lacks subject-matter jurisdiction, the court must dismiss the action. FRCP 12(h)(3).

4. *Counterclaim and crossclaim*

    a. *Compulsory counterclaim*

        i. *In general.* A pleading must state as a counterclaim any claim that—at the time of its service—the pleader has against an opposing party if the claim:

- Arises out of the transaction or occurrence that is the subject matter of the opposing party's claim; and

- Does not require adding another party over whom the court cannot acquire jurisdiction. FRCP 13(a)(1).

        ii. *Exceptions.* The pleader need not state the claim if:

- When the action was commenced, the claim was the subject of another pending action; or

- The opposing party sued on its claim by attachment or other process that did not establish personal jurisdiction over the pleader on that claim, and the pleader does not assert any counterclaim under FRCP 13. FRCP 13(a)(2).

    b. *Permissive counterclaim.* A pleading may state as a counterclaim against an opposing party any claim that is not compulsory. FRCP 13(b).

    c. *Relief sought in a counterclaim.* A counterclaim need not diminish or defeat the recovery sought by the opposing party. It may request relief that exceeds in amount or differs in kind from the relief sought by the opposing party. FRCP 13(c).

    d. *Counterclaim against the United States.* The Federal Rules of Civil Procedure do not expand the right to assert a counterclaim—or to claim a credit—against the United States or a United States officer or agency. FRCP 13(d).

    e. *Counterclaim maturing or acquired after pleading.* The court may permit a party to file a supplemental pleading asserting a counterclaim that matured or was acquired by the party after serving an earlier pleading. FRCP 13(e).

    f. *Crossclaim against a coparty.* A pleading may state as a crossclaim any claim by one party against a coparty if the claim arises out of the transaction or occurrence that is the subject matter of the original action or of a counterclaim, or if the claim relates to any property that is the subject matter of the original action. The crossclaim may include a claim that the coparty is or may be liable to the cross-claimant for all or part of a claim asserted in the action against the cross-claimant. FRCP 13(g).

    g. *Joining additional parties.* FRCP 19 and FRCP 20 govern the addition of a person as a party to a counterclaim or crossclaim. FRCP 13(h).

    h. *Separate trials; Separate judgments.* If the court orders separate trials under FRCP 42(b), it may enter judgment on a counterclaim or crossclaim under FRCP 54(b) when it has jurisdiction to do so, even if the opposing party's claims have been dismissed or otherwise resolved. FRCP 13(i).

5. *Third-party practice*

    a. *Timing of the summons and complaint.* A defending party may, as third-party plaintiff, serve a summons and complaint on a nonparty who is or may be liable to it for all or part of the claim against it. But the third-party plaintiff must, by motion, obtain the court's leave if it files the third-party complaint more than fourteen (14) days after serving its original answer. FRCP 14(a)(1).

    b. *Third-party defendant's claims and defenses.* The person served with the summons and third-party complaint—the "third-party defendant":

        i. Must assert any defense against the third-party plaintiff's claim under FRCP 12;

        ii. Must assert any counterclaim against the third-party plaintiff under FRCP 13(a), and may assert any counterclaim against the third-party plaintiff under FRCP 13(b) or any crossclaim against another third-party defendant under FRCP 13(g);

        iii. May assert against the plaintiff any defense that the third-party plaintiff has to the plaintiff's claim; and

        iv. May also assert against the plaintiff any claim arising out of the transaction or occurrence that is the subject matter of the plaintiff's claim against the third-party plaintiff. FRCP 14(a)(2).

c. For more information on third-party practice, refer to FRCP 14.

6. *Right to a jury trial; Demand*

   a. *Right preserved.* The right of trial by jury as declared by U.S.C.A. Const. Amend. VII, or as provided by a federal statute, is preserved to the parties inviolate. FRCP 38(a).

   b. *Demand.* On any issue triable of right by a jury, a party may demand a jury trial by:

      i. Serving the other parties with a written demand—which may be included in a pleading—no later than fourteen (14) days after the last pleading directed to the issue is served; and

      ii. Filing the demand in accordance with FRCP 5(d). FRCP 38(b).

   c. *Specifying issues.* In its demand, a party may specify the issues that it wishes to have tried by a jury; otherwise, it is considered to have demanded a jury trial on all the issues so triable. If the party has demanded a jury trial on only some issues, any other party may—within fourteen (14) days after being served with the demand or within a shorter time ordered by the court—serve a demand for a jury trial on any other or all factual issues triable by jury. FRCP 38(c).

   d. *Waiver; Withdrawal.* A party waives a jury trial unless its demand is properly served and filed. A proper demand may be withdrawn only if the parties consent. FRCP 38(d).

   e. *Admiralty and maritime claims.* The rules in FRCP 38 do not create a right to a jury trial on issues in a claim that is an admiralty or maritime claim under FRCP 9(h). FRCP 38(e).

7. *Appearances.* Attorneys not representing the United States or its agencies must file an appearance when they represent (either in person or by filing a paper) a party. IN R USDCTND L.R. 83-8(a). For more information, refer to IN R USDCTND L.R. 83-8.

8. *Notice of related action.* A party must file a notice of related action as soon as it appears that the party's case and another pending case: (1) arise out of the same transaction or occurrence; (2) involve the same property; or (3) involve the validity or infringement of the same patent, trademark, or copyright. IN R USDCTND L.R. 40-1(d). For more information, refer to IN R USDCTND L.R. 40-1.

9. *Alternative dispute resolution (ADR).* After they confer as required by FRCP 26(f), the parties must advise the court which, if any, alternative-dispute-resolution processes they expect to pursue and when they expect to undertake the process. IN R USDCTND L.R. 16-6(a). For more information on alternative dispute resolution (ADR), refer to IN R USDCTND L.R. 16-6 and IN R USDCTND Order 2003-21.

10. *Settlement or resolution.* The parties must immediately notify the court if they reasonably expect to settle the case or resolve a pending motion. IN R USDCTND L.R. 16-1(g).

11. *Modification or suspension of rules.* The court may, on its own motion or at the request of a party, suspend or modify any rule in a particular case in the interest of justice. IN R USDCTND L.R. 1-1(c).

D. Documents

1. *Required documents*

   a. *Answer.* Refer to the General Requirements section of this document for information on the form and contents of the answer.

   b. *Certificate of service.* FRCP 5(d) requires that the person making service under FRCP 5 certify that service has been effected. FRCP 5(Advisory Committee Notes). Having such information on file may be useful for many purposes, including proof of service if an issue arises concerning the effectiveness of the service. FRCP 5(Advisory Committee Notes).

      i. *Certificate of service for electronically-filed documents.* A Certificate of Service is still a requirement when filing documents electronically. A sample Certificate of Service is attached as Form 1 (IN R USDCTND CM/ECF(Form 1)). IN R USDCTND CM/ECF(II)(H).

2. *Supplemental documents*

   a. *Waiver of the service of summons.* An individual, corporation, or association that is subject to service under FRCP 4(e), FRCP 4(f), or FRCP 4(h) has a duty to avoid unnecessary expenses of serving the summons. FRCP 4(d)(1). Waiving service of a summons does not waive any objection to personal jurisdiction or to venue. FRCP 4(d)(5). If a defendant located within the United States fails, without good cause, to sign and return a waiver requested by a plaintiff located within the United States, the court must impose on the defendant:

    i.   The expenses later incurred in making service; and

    ii.   The reasonable expenses, including attorney's fees, of any motion required to collect those service expenses. FRCP 4(d)(2).

b. *Notice of constitutional question.* A party that files a pleading, written motion, or other paper drawing into question the constitutionality of a federal or state statute must promptly:

    i.   *File notice.* File a notice of constitutional question stating the question and identifying the paper that raises it, if:

- A federal statute is questioned and the parties do not include the United States, one of its agencies, or one of its officers or employees in an official capacity; or

- A state statute is questioned and the parties do not include the state, one of its agencies, or one of its officers or employees in an official capacity; and

    ii.   *Serve notice.* Serve the notice and paper on the Attorney General of the United States if a federal statute is questioned—or on the state attorney general if a state statute is questioned—either by certified or registered mail or by sending it to an electronic address designated by the attorney general for this purpose. FRCP 5.1(a).

    iii.   *When to file the notice.* A party required to file a notice of constitutional question under FRCP 5.1 must do so by the later of: (1) the day the parties tender their proposed case-management plan (if one is required); or (2) 21 days after filing the pleading, written motion, or other paper questioning the constitutionality of a federal or state statute. IN R USDCTND L.R. 5.1-1(a).

    iv.   *Service on government officials.* The party must also serve the notice and the pleading, written motion, or other paper questioning the constitutionality of a federal or state statute on: (1) the Attorney General of the United States and the United States Attorney for the Northern District of Indiana, if a federal statute is challenged; or (2) the Attorney General for the state if a state statute is challenged. IN R USDCTND L.R. 5.1-1(b). Service required under IN R USDCTND L.R. 5.1-1(b) may be made either by certified or registered mail or by emailing it to an address designated by those officials for this purpose. IN R USDCTND L.R. 5.1-1(c).

    v.   *No forfeiture.* A party's failure to file and serve the notice, or the court's failure to certify, does not forfeit a constitutional claim or defense that is otherwise timely asserted. FRCP 5.1(d).

c. *Notice of issue concerning foreign law.* A party who intends to raise an issue about a foreign country's law must give notice by a pleading or other writing. In determining foreign law, the court may consider any relevant material or source, including testimony, whether or not submitted by a party or admissible under the Federal Rules of Evidence. The court's determination must be treated as a ruling on a question of law. FRCP 44.1.

d. *Nongovernmental corporate disclosure statement*

    i.   *Contents.* A nongovernmental corporate party must file two (2) copies of a disclosure statement that:

- Identifies any parent corporation and any publicly held corporation owning ten percent (10%) or more of its stock; or

- States that there is no such corporation. FRCP 7.1(a).

    ii.   *Time to file; Supplemental filing.* A party must:

- File the disclosure statement with its first appearance, pleading, petition, motion, response, or other request addressed to the court; and

- Promptly file a supplemental statement if any required information changes. FRCP 7.1(b).

e. *Request for three-judge court.* If a party believes the law requires a three-judge court in a case or proceeding, the party must: (1) print "Three-Judge District Court Requested" or the equivalent immediately following the title on the first pleading asserting a claim requiring a three-judge court;

and (2) set forth the basis for the request in the pleading or in a short statement attached to the pleading, unless the basis is apparent from the pleading. IN R USDCTND L.R. 9-2(a). The words "Three-Judge District Court Requested" or the equivalent on a pleading constitutes a "request" under 28 U.S.C.A. § 2284(b)(1). IN R USDCTND L.R. 9-2(b).

f. *Index of exhibits.* Any pleading, motion, brief, affidavit, notice, or proposed order, whether filed electronically or by delivering it to the clerk, must: include a separate index identifying and briefly describing each exhibit if there are more than four (4) exhibits. IN R USDCTND L.R. 5-4(a)(8).

g. *Copy of document with self-addressed envelope.* A party who wants a file-stamped copy of a paper must include with the filing an additional copy of the paper and a self-addressed envelope with adequate postage. IN R USDCTND L.R. 5-4(b)(6).

h. *Notice of manual filing.* However, if that is not physically possible, counsel shall electronically file a .pdf document titled Notice of Manual Filing as a notation on the docket sheet that filings are being held in the clerk's office in paper. A sample Notice of Manual Filing is attached as Form 2 (IN R USDCTND CM/ECF(Form 2)). IN R USDCTND CM/ECF(III)(A)(1).

i. *Courtesy copies.* If documents are filed in paper format, counsel must provide an original for the clerk's office, a copy for the judge and a copy must be served on all parties in the case. IN R USDCTND CM/ECF(III)(A)(1).

j. *Declaration that party was unable to file in a timely manner.* If the attorney is unable to file a document in a timely manner due to technical difficulties in the user's system, the attorney must file a document with the court as soon as possible notifying the court of the inability to file the document. A sample document entitled Declaration that Party was Unable to File in a Timely Manner Due to Technical Difficulties is attached hereto as Form 5. IN R USDCTND CM/ECF(VI)(B). [Editor's note: the reference to Form 5 is likely meant to be a reference to Form 3 (IN R USDCTND CM/ECF(Form 3)].

E. Format

1. *Form of documents*

   a. *Paper.* Any pleading, motion, brief, affidavit, notice, or proposed order, whether filed electronically or by delivering it to the clerk, must: use eight and one-half by eleven (8-1/2 x 11) inch pages. IN R USDCTND L.R. 5-4(a)(2).

      i. *Manual filings.* Papers delivered to the clerk for filing must: be flat, unfolded, and on good-quality, white paper. IN R USDCTND L.R. 5-4(b)(1)(A).

         • *Covers or backing.* Papers delivered to the clerk for filing must: not have a cover or a back. IN R USDCTND L.R. 5-4(b)(1)(B).

         • *Recycled paper.* The court encourages using recycled paper. IN R USDCTND L.R. 5-4(b)(7).

   b. *Margins.* Any pleading, motion, brief, affidavit, notice, or proposed order, whether filed electronically or by delivering it to the clerk, must: have at least one (1) inch margins. IN R USDCTND L.R. 5-4(a)(3).

   c. *Spacing.* Any pleading, motion, brief, affidavit, notice, or proposed order, whether filed electronically or by delivering it to the clerk, must: be double spaced (except for headings, footnotes, and quoted material). IN R USDCTND L.R. 5-4(a)(5).

   d. *Text.* Any pleading, motion, brief, affidavit, notice, or proposed order, whether filed electronically or by delivering it to the clerk, must: be plainly typewritten, printed, or prepared by a clearly legible copying process. IN R USDCTND L.R. 5-4(a)(1).

      i. Any pleading, motion, brief, affidavit, notice, or proposed order, whether filed electronically or by delivering it to the clerk, must: use at least twelve (12) point type in the body and at least ten (10) point type in footnotes. IN R USDCTND L.R. 5-4(a)(4).

   e. *Page numbering.* Any pleading, motion, brief, affidavit, notice, or proposed order, whether filed electronically or by delivering it to the clerk, must: have consecutively numbered pages. IN R USDCTND L.R. 5-4(a)(6).

f. *Caption; Names of parties.* Every pleading must have a caption with the court's name, a title, a file number, and a FRCP 7(a) designation. The title of the complaint must name all the parties; the title of other pleadings, after naming the first party on each side, may refer generally to other parties. FRCP 10(a). Any pleading, motion, brief, affidavit, notice, or proposed order, whether filed electronically or by delivering it to the clerk, must: include a title on the first page. IN R USDCTND L.R. 5-4(a)(7).

　i. *Request for three-judge court.* If a party believes the law requires a three-judge court in a case or proceeding, the party must: print "Three-Judge District Court Requested" or the equivalent immediately following the title on the first pleading asserting a claim requiring a three-judge court. IN R USDCTND L.R. 9-2(a)(1). Refer to the Documents section of this document for more information.

　ii. *Class actions.* A party seeking to maintain a case as a class action (whether for or against a class) must include in the complaint, crossclaim, or counterclaim: (1) the words "Class Action" in the document's title; and (2) a reference to each part of FRCP 23 that the party relies on in seeking to maintain the case as a class action. IN R USDCTND L.R. 23-1.

g. *Filer's information.* Any pleading, motion, brief, affidavit, notice, or proposed order, whether filed electronically or by delivering it to the clerk, must: except in proposed orders and affidavits, include the filer's name, address, telephone number, fax number (where available), and e-mail address (where available). IN R USDCTND L.R. 5-4(a)(9).

h. *Paragraphs; Separate statements.* A party must state its claims or defenses in numbered paragraphs, each limited as far as practicable to a single set of circumstances. A later pleading may refer by number to a paragraph in an earlier pleading. If doing so would promote clarity, each claim founded on a separate transaction or occurrence—and each defense other than a denial—must be stated in a separate count or defense. FRCP 10(b).

i. *Adoption by reference; Exhibits.* A statement in a pleading may be adopted by reference elsewhere in the same pleading or in any other pleading or motion. A copy of a written instrument that is an exhibit to a pleading is a part of the pleading for all purposes. FRCP 10(c).

j. *Citation of local rules.* The Local Civil Rules of the United States District Court for the Northern District of Indiana may be cited as "N.D. Ind. L.R." IN R USDCTND L.R. 1-1(a)(1).

k. *Acceptance by the clerk.* The clerk must not refuse to file a paper solely because it is not in the form prescribed by the Federal Rules of Civil Procedure or by a local rule or practice. FRCP 5(d)(4).

　i. *Sanctions for formatting errors; Non-compliance.* If a person files a paper that does not comply with the rules governing the format of papers filed with the court, the court may: (1) strike the paper from the record; or (2) fine the person up to one thousand dollars ($1,000). IN R USDCTND L.R. 1-3(a).

　　• *Notice.* Before sanctioning a person under IN R USDCTND L.R. 1-3(a)(2), the court must: (1) notify the person that the paper is noncompliant; and (2) give the person the opportunity either to be heard or to revise the paper. IN R USDCTND L.R. 1-3(b).

2. *Form of electronic documents.* Electronically filed documents must meet the same requirements of format and page limits as documents "conventionally filed" (as defined in IN R USDCTND CM/ECF(III)(A)) pursuant to the Federal Rules of Civil Procedure and the Local Civil Rules of the United States District Court for the Northern District of Indiana. IN R USDCTND CM/ECF(II)(A)(2).

a. *PDF format required.* Documents filed in the CM/ECF must be in .pdf format. A document created with almost any word-processing program can be converted to .pdf format. The .pdf program in effect takes a picture of the original document and allows anyone to open the converted document across a broad range of hardware and software, with layout, format, links, and images intact. IN R USDCTND CM/ECF(FN2).

b. *Title of documents.* The person electronically filing a pleading or other document will be responsible for designating a title for the pleading or other document by using one of the categories contained in the events listed in the CM/ECF Menu. IN R USDCTND CM/ECF(II)(G).

c. *Combining documents.* All documents which form part of a single pleading and which are being filed

at the same time and by the same party may be electronically filed together under one document number, e.g., the motion and a supporting affidavit, with the exception of memoranda in support. Memoranda in support shall be electronically filed separately and shown as a related document to the motion. IN R USDCTND CM/ECF(II)(A)(4).

d. *Exhibits and attachments.* Filing users must submit in electronic form all documents referenced as exhibits or attachments, unless the court permits conventional filing. A filing user must submit as exhibits or attachments only those excerpts of the referenced documents that are directly germane to the matter under consideration by the court. Excerpted material must be clearly and prominently identified as such. Filing users who file excerpts of documents as exhibits or attachments do so without prejudice to their right to timely file additional excerpts or the complete document. Responding parties may timely file additional excerpts or the complete document that they believe are directly germane. The court may require parties to file additional excerpts or the complete document. IN R USDCTND CM/ECF(II)(A)(6).

e. *Hyperlinks.* Electronically filed documents may contain hyperlink references to an external document as a convenient mechanism for accessing material cited in the document. A hyperlink reference is neither validated for content nor considered a part of the court's records. The court neither endorses the product or organization at the destination of a hyperlink reference, nor does the court exercise any responsibility over the content at the destination. In order to preserve the integrity of the court record, attorneys wishing to insert hyperlinks in court filings shall continue to use the traditional citation method for the cited authority, in addition to the hyperlink. A hyperlink contained in a filing is no more than a convenient mechanism for accessing material cited in the document and a hyperlink reference is extraneous to any filed document and is not part of the court's record. IN R USDCTND CM/ECF(II)(A)(3).

3. *Signing of pleadings, motions and other papers*

a. *Signature.* Every pleading, written motion, and other paper must be signed by at least one attorney of record in the attorney's name—or by a party personally if the party is unrepresented. The paper must state the signer's address, e-mail address, and telephone number. FRCP 11(a).

   i. *Signatures on manual filings.* Papers delivered to the clerk for filing must: include the filer's original signature. IN R USDCTND L.R. 5-4(b)(1)(C).

      • *Rubber-stamped and faxed signatures.* An original paper with a rubber-stamped or faxed signature is unsigned for purposes of FRCP 11 and FRCP 26(g). IN R USDCTND L.R. 5-4(b)(2).

      • *Affidavits.* Only the affiant need sign an affidavit. IN R USDCTND L.R. 5-4(b)(3).

   ii. *Electronic signatures.* Pursuant to FRCP 11, every pleading, motion, and other paper (except lists, schedules, statements or amendments thereto) shall be signed by at least one attorney of record or, if the party is not represented by an attorney, all papers shall be signed by the party. An attorney's/participant's password issued by the court combined with the user's identification, serves as and constitutes the attorney/participant's signature for FRCP 11 and other purposes. IN R USDCTND CM/ECF(I)(C). Documents which must be filed and which must contain original signatures other than those of a participating attorney or which require either verification or an unsworn declaration under any rule or statute, shall be filed electronically, with originally executed copies maintained by the filer. The pleading or other document electronically filed shall contain "s/" signature(s), as noted in IN R USDCTND CM/ECF(II)(E)(3)(b). IN R USDCTND CM/ECF(II)(E)(1).

      • *Multiple signatures.* In the case of a stipulation or other document to be signed by two or more attorneys, the following procedure should be used: The filing attorney shall initially confirm that the content of the document is acceptable to all persons required to sign the document and shall obtain the physical signatures of all attorneys on the document. IN R USDCTND CM/ECF(II)(E)(3)(a). The filing attorney then shall file the document electronically, indicating the signatories, e.g., "s/Jane Doe," "s/John Doe," etc. IN R USDCTND CM/ECF(II)(E)(3)(b). The filing attorney shall retain the hard copy of the document containing the original signatures. IN R USDCTND CM/ECF(II)(E)(3)(c).

    iii. *No verification or accompanying affidavit required for pleadings.* Unless a rule or statute specifically states otherwise, a pleading need not be verified or accompanied by an affidavit. FRCP 11(a).

    iv. *Unsigned papers.* The court must strike an unsigned paper unless the omission is promptly corrected after being called to the attorney's or party's attention. FRCP 11(a).

b. *Representations to the court.* By presenting to the court a pleading, written motion, or other paper—whether by signing, filing, submitting, or later advocating it—an attorney or unrepresented party certifies that to the best of the person's knowledge, information, and belief, formed after an inquiry reasonable under the circumstances:

    i. It is not being presented for any improper purpose, such as to harass, cause unnecessary delay, or needlessly increase the cost of litigation;

    ii. The claims, defenses, and other legal contentions are warranted by existing law or by a nonfrivolous argument for extending, modifying, or reversing existing law or for establishing new law;

    iii. The factual contentions have evidentiary support or, if specifically so identified, will likely have evidentiary support after a reasonable opportunity for further investigation or discovery; and

    iv. The denials of factual contentions are warranted on the evidence or, if specifically so identified, are reasonably based on belief or a lack of information. FRCP 11(b).

c. *Sanctions.* If, after notice and a reasonable opportunity to respond, the court determines that FRCP 11(b) has been violated, the court may impose an appropriate sanction on any attorney, law firm, or party that violated FRCP 11(b) or is responsible for the violation. FRCP 11(c)(1). Refer to the United States District Court for the Northern District of Indiana KeyRules Motion for Sanctions document for more information.

4. *Privacy protection for filings made with the court*

a. *Redacted filings.* Counsel should not include sensitive information in any document filed with the court unless such inclusion is necessary and relevant to the case. IN R USDCTND CM/ECF(VII). Unless the court orders otherwise, in an electronic or paper filing with the court that contains an individual's Social Security number, taxpayer-identification number, or birth date, the name of an individual known to be a minor, or a financial-account number, a party or nonparty making the filing may include only:

    i. The last four (4) digits of the Social Security number and taxpayer-identification number;

    ii. The year of the individual's birth;

    iii. The minor's initials; and

    iv. The last four (4) digits of the financial-account number. FRCP 5.2(a); IN R USDCTND Order 2005-3.

b. *Exemptions from the redaction requirement.* The redaction requirement does not apply to the following:

    i. A financial-account number that identifies the property allegedly subject to forfeiture in a forfeiture proceeding;

    ii. The record of an administrative or agency proceeding;

    iii. The official record of a state-court proceeding;

    iv. The record of a court or tribunal, if that record was not subject to the redaction requirement when originally filed;

    v. A filing covered by FRCP 5.2(c) or FRCP 5.2(d); and

    vi. A pro se filing in an action brought under 28 U.S.C.A. § 2241, 28 U.S.C.A. § 2254, or 28 U.S.C.A. § 2255. FRCP 5.2(b).

    vii. In cases filed under the Social Security Act, 42 U.S.C.A. § 405(g), there is no need for redaction of any information from the documents filed in the case. IN R USDCTND Order 2005-3.

c. *Limitations on remote access to electronic files; Social Security appeals and immigration cases.* Unless the court orders otherwise, in an action for benefits under the Social Security Act, and in an action or proceeding relating to an order of removal, to relief from removal, or to immigration benefits or detention, access to an electronic file is authorized as follows:

    i. The parties and their attorneys may have remote electronic access to any part of the case file, including the administrative record;

    ii. Any other person may have electronic access to the full record at the courthouse, but may have remote electronic access only to:

- The docket maintained by the court; and

- An opinion, order, judgment, or other disposition of the court, but not any other part of the case file or the administrative record. FRCP 5.2(c).

d. *Filings made under seal.* The court may order that a filing be made under seal without redaction. The court may later unseal the filing or order the person who made the filing to file a redacted version for the public record. FRCP 5.2(d). For information on filing documents under seal, refer to IN R USDCTND L.R. 5-3, IN R USDCTND CM/ECF(IV)(A), and IN R USDCTND ECF Order 2004-19.

e. *Protective orders.* For good cause, the court may by order in a case:

    i. Require redaction of additional information; or

    ii. Limit or prohibit a nonparty's remote electronic access to a document filed with the court. FRCP 5.2(e).

f. *Option for additional unredacted filing under seal.* A person making a redacted filing may also file an unredacted copy under seal. The court must retain the unredacted copy as part of the record. FRCP 5.2(f); IN R USDCTND Order 2005-3.

    i. The unredacted version of the document or the reference list shall be retained by the court under seal as part of the record. This paper shall be retained by the court as part of the record. The court may, however, still require the party to file a redacted copy for the public file. IN R USDCTND Order 2005-3.

g. *Option for filing a reference list.* A filing that contains redacted information may be filed together with a reference list that identifies each item of redacted information and specifies an appropriate identifier that uniquely corresponds to each item listed. The list must be filed under seal and may be amended as of right. Any reference in the case to a listed identifier will be construed to refer to the corresponding item of information. FRCP 5.2(g); IN R USDCTND Order 2005-3.

    i. The unredacted version of the document or the reference list shall be retained by the court under seal as part of the record. This paper shall be retained by the court as part of the record. The court may, however, still require the party to file a redacted copy for the public file. IN R USDCTND Order 2005-3.

h. *Responsibility for redaction.* The responsibility for redacting these personal identifiers rests solely with counsel and the parties. The Clerk will not review each paper for compliance with IN R USDCTND Order 2005-3. IN R USDCTND Order 2005-3.

i. *Waiver of protection of identifiers.* A person waives the protection of FRCP 5.2(a) as to the person's own information by filing it without redaction and not under seal. FRCP 5.2(h).

F. Filing and Service Requirements

1. *Filing requirements.* Any paper after the complaint that is required to be served—together with a certificate of service—must be filed within a reasonable time after service. FRCP 5(d)(1).

    a. *How filing is made; In general.* A paper is filed by delivering it:

        i. To the clerk; or

ii. To a judge who agrees to accept it for filing, and who must then note the filing date on the paper and promptly send it to the clerk. FRCP 5(d)(2).

- Papers not filed electronically must be filed with the clerk, not a judge. IN R USDCTND L.R. 5-4(b)(4).

iii. Parties manually filing a paper that requires the clerk to give others notice, must give the clerk: (1) sufficient copies of the notice; and (2) the name and address of each person entitled to receive the notice. IN R USDCTND L.R. 5-4(b)(8).

b. *Where to file.* Papers not filed electronically must be filed in the division where the case is pending, unless: (1) a person will be prejudiced if the paper is not filed the same day it is tendered; and (2) it includes an adequately sized envelope addressed to the clerk's office in the division where the case is pending and with adequate postage. IN R USDCTND L.R. 5-4(b)(5).

c. *Electronic filing*

i. *Authorization of electronic filing program.* A court may, by local rule, allow papers to be filed, signed, or verified by electronic means that are consistent with any technical standards established by the Judicial Conference of the United States. A local rule may require electronic filing only if reasonable exceptions are allowed. A paper filed electronically in compliance with a local rule is a written paper for purposes of the Federal Rules of Civil Procedure. FRCP 5(d)(3).

- Papers must be filed, signed, and verified electronically unless excepted by the court's CM/ECF Civil and Criminal User Manual (IN R USDCTND CM/ECF). IN R USDCTND L.R. 5-1.

ii. *Mandatory electronic filing.* Unless otherwise permitted by these procedures or otherwise authorized by the assigned judge, all documents submitted for filing in this district in civil and criminal cases, no matter when a case was originally filed, shall be filed electronically using the System. IN R USDCTND CM/ECF(II)(A)(1). The requirement that "all documents" be filed electronically includes briefs, and attachments and exhibits used in support of motions. IN R USDCTND CM/ECF(FN1).

- Sending a document or pleading to the court via e-mail or facsimile does not constitute "electronic filing." IN R USDCTND CM/ECF(I)(A).

iii. *Conventional filing.* As used in these procedures, a "conventionally" filed or submitted document or pleading is one presented to the Clerk or a party in paper or other non-electronic, tangible format. The following documents shall be filed conventionally and not electronically unless specifically authorized by the Court:

- Exhibits and other documents which cannot be converted to a legible electronic form. Whenever possible, counsel is responsible for converting filings to an electronic form. However, if that is not physically possible, counsel shall electronically file a .pdf document titled Notice of Manual Filing as a notation on the docket sheet that filings are being held in the clerk's office in paper. A sample Notice of Manual Filing is attached as Form 2 (IN R USDCTND CM/ECF(Form 2)). If documents are filed in paper format, counsel must provide an original for the clerk's office, a copy for the judge and a copy must be served on all parties in the case. Large documents which do not exist in an electronic format shall be scanned into .pdf format by counsel, in small batches if necessary, and filed electronically as separate attachments in the System. IN R USDCTND CM/ECF(III)(A)(1).

- Certain documents which are listed in IN R USDCTND CM/ECF(II)(E)(2). IN R USDCTND CM/ECF(III)(A)(2).

- Documents filed by pro se litigants. IN R USDCTND CM/ECF(III)(A)(3).

iv. For more information on electronic filing, refer to IN R USDCTND CM/ECF.

2. *Service requirements*

   a. *Service; When required*

      i. *In general.* Unless the Federal Rules of Civil Procedure provide otherwise, each of the following papers must be served on every party:

         - An order stating that service is required;

         - A pleading filed after the original complaint, unless the court orders otherwise under FRCP 5(c) because there are numerous defendants;

         - A discovery paper required to be served on a party, unless the court orders otherwise;

         - A written motion, except one that may be heard ex parte; and

         - A written notice, appearance, demand, or offer of judgment, or any similar paper. FRCP 5(a)(1).

      ii. *If a party fails to appear.* No service is required on a party who is in default for failing to appear. But a pleading that asserts a new claim for relief against such a party must be served on that party under FRCP 4. FRCP 5(a)(2).

      iii. *Seizing property.* If an action is begun by seizing property and no person is or need be named as a defendant, any service required before the filing of an appearance, answer, or claim must be made on the person who had custody or possession of the property when it was seized. FRCP 5(a)(3).

   b. *Service; How made*

      i. *Serving an attorney.* If a party is represented by an attorney, service under FRCP 5 must be made on the attorney unless the court orders service on the party. FRCP 5(b)(1).

      ii. *Service in general.* A paper is served under FRCP 5 by:

         - Handing it to the person;

         - Leaving it: (1) at the person's office with a clerk or other person in charge or, if no one is in charge, in a conspicuous place in the office; or (2) if the person has no office or the office is closed, at the person's dwelling or usual place of abode with someone of suitable age and discretion who resides there;

         - Mailing it to the person's last known address—in which event service is complete upon mailing;

         - Leaving it with the court clerk if the person has no known address;

         - Sending it by electronic means if the person consented in writing—in which event service is complete upon transmission, but is not effective if the serving party learns that it did not reach the person to be served; or

         - Delivering it by any other means that the person consented to in writing—in which event service is complete when the person making service delivers it to the agency designated to make delivery. FRCP 5(b)(2).

      iii. *Electronic service.* Electronically filed papers may be served electronically if service is consistent with the CM/ECF User Manual (IN R USDCTND CM/ECF). IN R USDCTND L.R. 5-2(a).

         - *Waiver of other service.* An attorney's registration will constitute a waiver of conventional service of documents and the attorney agrees to accept service of notice on behalf of the client of the electronic filing by hand, facsimile or authorized email. IN R USDCTND CM/ECF(I)(B)(3).

         - *Serving registered persons.* The System will generate a "Notice of Electronic Filing" when any document is filed. This notice represents service of the document on parties who are registered participants with the System. Except as provided in IN R USDCTND CM/ECF(III)(B), the filing party shall not be required to serve any pleading or other documents on any party receiving electronic notice. IN R USDCTND CM/ECF(II)(D)(1). The term "pleading" refers only to those documents listed in FRCP 7(a). IN R USDCTND CM/ECF(FN3).

- *When electronic service is deemed completed.* A person registered to use the court's electronic-filing system is served with an electronically filed paper when a "Notice of Electronic Filing" is transmitted to that person through the court's electronic filing-system. IN R USDCTND L.R. 5-2(b).

- *Serving non-registered persons.* A person who has not registered to use the court's electronic-filing system but who is entitled to service of a paper must be served according to the Local Civil Rules of the United States District Court for the Northern District of Indiana and the Federal Rules of Civil Procedure. IN R USDCTND L.R. 5-2(c); IN R USDCTND CM/ECF(II)(D)(2). If such service of a paper copy is to be made, it shall be done in the manner provided in the Federal Rules of Civil Procedure and the Local Civil Rules of the United States District Court for the Northern District of Indiana. IN R USDCTND CM/ECF(II)(D)(2).

iv. *Service of conventional filings.* Pleadings or other documents which are filed conventionally rather than electronically shall be served in the manner provided for in the Federal Rules of Civil Procedure and the Local Civil Rules of the United States District Court for the Northern District of Indiana, except as otherwise provided by order of the Court. IN R USDCTND CM/ECF(III)(B).

v. *Using court facilities.* If a local rule so authorizes, a party may use the court's transmission facilities to make service under FRCP 5(b)(2)(E). FRCP 5(b)(3).

c. *Serving numerous defendants*

i. *In general.* If an action involves an unusually large number of defendants, the court may, on motion or on its own, order that:

- Defendants' pleadings and replies to them need not be served on other defendants;

- Any crossclaim, counterclaim, avoidance, or affirmative defense in those pleadings and replies to them will be treated as denied or avoided by all other parties; and

- Filing any such pleading and serving it on the plaintiff constitutes notice of the pleading to all parties. FRCP 5(c)(1).

ii. *Notifying parties.* A copy of every such order must be served on the parties as the court directs. FRCP 5(c)(2).

G. Hearings

1. *Hearing on FRCP 12 defenses before trial.* If a party so moves, any defense listed in FRCP 12(b)(1) through FRCP 12(b)(7)—whether made in a pleading or by motion—and a motion under FRCP 12(c) must be heard and decided before trial unless the court orders a deferral until trial. FRCP 12(i).

H. Forms

1. Official Federal Answer Forms

a. Rule 4 waiver of the service of summons. FRCP 4.

2. Federal Answer Forms

a. Generally. 2B FEDFORMS § 8:10.

b. Introduction to separate defenses. 2B FEDFORMS § 8:11.

c. Presenting defenses. 2B FEDFORMS § 8:12.

d. With counterclaim for interpleader. 2B FEDFORMS § 8:13.

e. Denials and admissions. 2B FEDFORMS § 8:14.

f. Denials, admissions and affirmative defenses. 2B FEDFORMS § 8:15.

g. Separate answer of two defendants; Duty of fair representation. 2B FEDFORMS § 8:16.

h. Separate answer of third defendant. 2B FEDFORMS § 8:17.

i. Reciting paragraphs and subparagraphs of complaint; Account malpractice. 2B FEDFORMS § 8:18.

j. One of multiple defendants. 2B FEDFORMS § 8:21.

k. Answer to complaint for employment discrimination. 2B FEDFORMS § 8:22.

l. Denial of particular averment. 2B FEDFORMS § 8:24.

m. Admission of particular averment. 2B FEDFORMS § 8:25.

n. Denial of all averments of paragraph. 2B FEDFORMS § 8:26.

o. Admission of all averments of paragraph. 2B FEDFORMS § 8:27.

p. Denial in part and admission in part of paragraph. 2B FEDFORMS § 8:28.

q. General denial. 2B FEDFORMS § 8:29.

r. Qualified general denial. 2B FEDFORMS § 8:30.

s. Denial of knowledge or information sufficient to form a belief. 2B FEDFORMS § 8:31.

t. Denial of jurisdictional allegations; Jurisdictional amount. 2B FEDFORMS § 8:32.

u. Denial of jurisdictional allegations; Federal question. 2B FEDFORMS § 8:34.

v. Denial of jurisdictional allegations; Diversity of citizenship. 2B FEDFORMS § 8:37.

w. Contributory negligence. 2B FEDFORMS § 8:58.

x. Fraud. 2B FEDFORMS § 8:74.

y. Mistake. 2B FEDFORMS § 8:85.

z. Statute of limitations. 2B FEDFORMS § 8:103.

3. Forms for the Northern District of Indiana

a. Certificate of service. IN R USDCTND CM/ECF(Form 1).

b. Notice of manual filing. IN R USDCTND CM/ECF(Form 2).

c. Declaration that party was unable to file in a timely manner. IN R USDCTND CM/ECF(Form 3).

I. Applicable Rules

1. *Federal rules*

a. Summons. FRCP 4.

b. Serving and filing pleadings and other papers. FRCP 5.

c. Constitutional challenge to a statute; Notice, certification, and intervention. FRCP 5.1.

d. Privacy protection for filings made with the court. FRCP 5.2.

e. Computing and extending time; Time for motion papers. FRCP 6.

f. Pleadings allowed; Form of motions and other papers. FRCP 7.

g. Disclosure statement. FRCP 7.1.

h. General rules of pleading. FRCP 8.

i. Pleading special matters. FRCP 9.

j. Form of pleadings. FRCP 10.

k. Signing pleadings, motions, and other papers; Representations to the court; Sanctions. FRCP 11.

l. Defenses and objections; When and how presented; Motion for judgment on the pleadings; Consolidating motions; Waiving defenses; Pretrial hearing. FRCP 12.

m. Counterclaim and crossclaim. FRCP 13.

n. Third-party practice. FRCP 14.

o. Right to a jury trial; Demand. FRCP 38.

p. Determining foreign law. FRCP 44.1.

2. *Local rules*

   a. Citation and scope of the rules. IN R USDCTND L.R. 1-1.

   b. Sanctions for formatting errors. IN R USDCTND L.R. 1-3.

   c. Electronic filing required. IN R USDCTND L.R. 5-1.

   d. Constitutional questions. IN R USDCTND L.R. 5.1-1.

   e. Electronic service. IN R USDCTND L.R. 5-2.

   f. Format of papers. IN R USDCTND L.R. 5-4.

   g. Extensions of time. IN R USDCTND L.R. 6-1.

   h. Request for three-judge court. IN R USDCTND L.R. 9-2.

   i. Responsive pleadings. IN R USDCTND L.R. 10-1.

   j. Pretrial procedure. IN R USDCTND L.R. 16-1.

   k. Alternative dispute resolution. IN R USDCTND L.R. 16-6.

   l. Class actions. IN R USDCTND L.R. 23-1.

   m. Case assignment. IN R USDCTND L.R. 40-1.

   n. Appearance and withdrawal of appearance. IN R USDCTND L.R. 83-8.

   o. CM/ECF civil and criminal user manual. IN R USDCTND CM/ECF.

   p. In re: privacy and public access to civil electronic case files. IN R USDCTND Order 2005-3.

Pleadings
Amended Pleading

Document Last Updated December 2016

A. Checklist

(I) ❏ Matters to be considered by plaintiff or defendant

   (a) ❏ Required documents

      (1) ❏ Amended pleading

      (2) ❏ Certificate of service

   (b) ❏ Supplemental documents

      (1) ❏ Notice of constitutional question

      (2) ❏ Notice of issue concerning foreign law

      (3) ❏ Index of exhibits

      (4) ❏ Copy of document with self-addressed envelope

      (5) ❏ Notice of manual filing

      (6) ❏ Courtesy copies

      (7) ❏ Declaration that party was unable to file in a timely manner

   (c) ❏ Timing

      (1) ❏ A party may amend its pleading once as a matter of course within:

         (i) ❏ Twenty-one (21) days after serving it, or

         (ii) ❏ If the pleading is one to which a responsive pleading is required, twenty-one (21) days after service of a responsive pleading or twenty-one (21) days after service of a motion under FRCP 12(b), FRCP 12(e), or FRCP 12(f), whichever is earlier

B. Timing

1. *Amended pleading*

    a. *Amending as a matter of course.* A party may amend its pleading once as a matter of course within:

        i. Twenty-one (21) days after serving it, or

        ii. If the pleading is one to which a responsive pleading is required, twenty-one (21) days after service of a responsive pleading or twenty-one (21) days after service of a motion under FRCP 12(b), FRCP 12(e), or FRCP 12(f), whichever is earlier. FRCP 15(a)(1).

    b. *Extension of time.* If the time for serving the responsive pleading is extended by a motion for enlargement of time under FRCP 6(b), or by a stipulation, the period for amending as of right also may be enlarged. FPP § 1480.

    c. *Other amendments.* In all other cases, a party may amend its pleading only with the opposing party's written consent or the court's leave. The court should freely give leave when justice so requires. FRCP 15(a)(2). Refer to the United States District Court for the Northern District of Indiana KeyRules Motion for Leave to Amend document for more information.

2. *Time to respond to an amended pleading.* Unless the court orders otherwise, any required response to an amended pleading must be made within the time remaining to respond to the original pleading or within fourteen (14) days after service of the amended pleading, whichever is later. FRCP 15(a)(3).

3. *Automatic initial extension.* The deadline to respond to a pleading or a discovery request—including requests for admission—is automatically extended when an extension notice is filed with the court and: (1) the deadline has not been extended before; (2) the extension is for twenty-eight (28) or fewer days; and (3) the notice states: (A) the original deadline; (B) the new deadline; and (C) that all opposing attorneys the attorney could reach agreed to the extension; or that the party could not reach any other opposing attorneys despite due diligence. IN R USDCTND L.R. 6-1(b).

    a. *Pro se parties.* The automatic initial extension does not apply to pro se parties. IN R USDCTND L.R. 6-1(c).

4. *Computation of time*

    a. *Computing time.* FRCP 6 applies in computing any time period specified in the Federal Rules of Civil Procedure, in any local rule or court order, or in any statute that does not specify a method of computing time. FRCP 6(a).

        i. *Period stated in days or a longer unit.* When the period is stated in days or a longer unit of time:

        - Exclude the day of the event that triggers the period;

        - Count every day, including intermediate Saturdays, Sundays, and legal holidays; and

        - Include the last day of the period, but if the last day is a Saturday, Sunday, or legal holiday, the period continues to run until the end of the next day that is not a Saturday, Sunday, or legal holiday. FRCP 6(a)(1).

        ii. *Period stated in hours.* When the period is stated in hours:

        - Begin counting immediately on the occurrence of the event that triggers the period;

        - Count every hour, including hours during intermediate Saturdays, Sundays, and legal holidays; and

        - If the period would end on a Saturday, Sunday, or legal holiday, the period continues to run until the same time on the next day that is not a Saturday, Sunday, or legal holiday. FRCP 6(a)(2).

        iii. *Inaccessibility of the clerk's office.* Unless the court orders otherwise, if the clerk's office is inaccessible:

        - On the last day for filing under FRCP 6(a)(1), then the time for filing is extended to the first accessible day that is not a Saturday, Sunday, or legal holiday; or

        - During the last hour for filing under FRCP 6(a)(2), then the time for filing is extended to the same time on the first accessible day that is not a Saturday, Sunday, or legal holiday. FRCP 6(a)(3).

iv. *"Last day" defined.* Unless a different time is set by a statute, local rule, or court order, the last day ends:

- For electronic filing, at midnight in the court's time zone; and

- For filing by other means, when the clerk's office is scheduled to close. FRCP 6(a)(4).

v. *"Next day" defined.* The "next day" is determined by continuing to count forward when the period is measured after an event and backward when measured before an event. FRCP 6(a)(5).

vi. *"Legal holiday" defined.* "Legal holiday" means:

- The day set aside by statute for observing New Year's Day, Martin Luther King Jr.'s Birthday, Washington's Birthday, Memorial Day, Independence Day, Labor Day, Columbus Day, Veterans' Day, Thanksgiving Day, or Christmas Day;

- Any day declared a holiday by the President or Congress; and

- For periods that are measured after an event, any other day declared a holiday by the state where the district court is located. FRCP 6(a)(6).

b. *Computation of electronic filing deadlines.* Filing documents electronically does not alter any filing deadlines or any time computation pursuant to FRCP 6. The counties of Lake, Porter, LaPorte, Pulaski and Starke are located in the Central time zone and the remaining counties in the Northern District of Indiana are located in the Eastern time zone. Nevertheless, all electronic transmissions of documents must be completed (i.e., received completely by the clerk's office) prior to midnight Eastern Time, (South Bend/Fort Wayne/Lafayette time) in order to be considered timely filed that day, regardless of the local time in the division where the case is pending. Although documents can be filed electronically twenty-four (24) hours a day, filers are strongly encouraged to file all documents during hours when the CM/ECF Help Line is available, from 9:00 a.m. to 4:00 p.m. local time. IN R USDCTND CM/ECF(II)(I).

i. *Technical failures.* If the attorney is unable to file a document in a timely manner due to technical difficulties in the user's system, the attorney must file a document with the court as soon as possible notifying the court of the inability to file the document. A sample document entitled Declaration that Party was Unable to File in a Timely Manner Due to Technical Difficulties is attached hereto as Form 5. IN R USDCTND CM/ECF(VI)(B). [Editor's note: the reference to Form 5 is likely meant to be a reference to Form 3 (IN R USDCTND CM/ECF(Form 3)].

c. *Extending time*

i. *In general.* When an act may or must be done within a specified time, the court may, for good cause, extend the time:

- With or without motion or notice if the court acts, or if a request is made, before the original time or its extension expires; or

- On motion made after the time has expired if the party failed to act because of excusable neglect. FRCP 6(b)(1).

ii. *Exceptions.* A court must not extend the time to act under FRCP 50(b), FRCP 50(d), FRCP 52(b), FRCP 59(b), FRCP 59(d), FRCP 59(e), and FRCP 60(b). FRCP 6(b)(2).

iii. Refer to the United States District Court for the Northern District of Indiana KeyRules Motion for Continuance/Extension of Time document for more information on extending time.

d. *Additional time after certain kinds of service.* When a party may or must act within a specified time after being served and service is made under FRCP 5(b)(2)(C) (mail), FRCP 5(b)(2)(D) (leaving with the clerk), or FRCP 5(b)(2)(F) (other means consented to), three (3) days are added after the period would otherwise expire under FRCP 6(a). FRCP 6(d).

C. General Requirements

1. *Pleading, generally*

   a. *Pleadings allowed.* Only these pleadings are allowed: (1) a complaint; (2) an answer to a complaint; (3) an answer to a counterclaim designated as a counterclaim; (4) an answer to a crossclaim; (5) a third-party complaint; (6) an answer to a third-party complaint; and (7) if the court orders one, a reply to an answer. FRCP 7(a).

   b. *Pleading to be concise and direct.* Each allegation must be simple, concise, and direct. No technical form is required. FRCP 8(d)(1).

   c. *Alternative statements of a claim or defense.* A party may set out two or more statements of a claim or defense alternatively or hypothetically, either in a single count or defense or in separate ones. If a party makes alternative statements, the pleading is sufficient if any one of them is sufficient. FRCP 8(d)(2).

   d. *Inconsistent claims or defenses.* A party may state as many separate claims or defenses as it has, regardless of consistency. FRCP 8(d)(3).

   e. *Construing pleadings.* Pleadings must be construed so as to do justice. FRCP 8(e).

2. *Pleading special matters*

   a. *Capacity or authority to sue; Legal existence*

      i. *In general.* Except when required to show that the court has jurisdiction, a pleading need not allege:

         • A party's capacity to sue or be sued;

         • A party's authority to sue or be sued in a representative capacity; or

         • The legal existence of an organized association of persons that is made a party. FRCP 9(a)(1).

      ii. *Raising those issues.* To raise any of those issues, a party must do so by a specific denial, which must state any supporting facts that are peculiarly within the party's knowledge. FRCP 9(a)(2).

   b. *Fraud or mistake; Conditions of mind.* In alleging fraud or mistake, a party must state with particularity the circumstances constituting fraud or mistake. Malice, intent, knowledge, and other conditions of a person's mind may be alleged generally. FRCP 9(b).

   c. *Conditions precedent.* In pleading conditions precedent, it suffices to allege generally that all conditions precedent have occurred or been performed. But when denying that a condition precedent has occurred or been performed, a party must do so with particularity. FRCP 9(c).

   d. *Official document or act.* In pleading an official document or official act, it suffices to allege that the document was legally issued or the act legally done. FRCP 9(d).

   e. *Judgment.* In pleading a judgment or decision of a domestic or foreign court, a judicial or quasi-judicial tribunal, or a board or officer, it suffices to plead the judgment or decision without showing jurisdiction to render it. FRCP 9(e).

   f. *Time and place.* An allegation of time or place is material when testing the sufficiency of a pleading. FRCP 9(f).

   g. *Special damages.* If an item of special damage is claimed, it must be specifically stated. FRCP 9(g).

   h. *Admiralty or maritime claim*

      i. *How designated.* If a claim for relief is within the admiralty or maritime jurisdiction and also within the court's subject-matter jurisdiction on some other ground, the pleading may designate the claim as an admiralty or maritime claim for purposes of FRCP 14(c), FRCP 38(e), and FRCP 82 and the Supplemental Rules for Admiralty or Maritime Claims and Asset Forfeiture Actions. A claim cognizable only in the admiralty or maritime jurisdiction is an admiralty or maritime claim for those purposes, whether or not so designated. FRCP 9(h)(1).

      ii. *Designation for appeal.* A case that includes an admiralty or maritime claim within FRCP 9(h) is an admiralty case within 28 U.S.C.A. § 1292(a)(3). FRCP 9(h)(2).

3. *Amended pleading*

    a. *Amendments before trial.* The function of FRCP 15(a), which provides generally for the amendment of pleadings, is to enable a party to assert matters that were overlooked or were unknown at the time the party interposed the original complaint or answer. FPP § 1473; Smiga v. Dean Witter Reynolds, Inc., 766 F.2d 698, 703 (2d Cir. 1985).

        i.   *Matters contained in amended pleading under FRCP 15(a).* Although FRCP 15(a) does not expressly state that an amendment must contain only matters that occurred within a particular time period, FRCP 15(d) provides that any "transaction, occurrence, or event that happened after the date of the pleading" should be set forth in a supplemental pleading. FPP § 1473. Thus, impliedly, an amended pleading, whether prepared with or without leave of court, only should relate to matters that have taken place prior to the date of the earlier pleading. FPP § 1473; Ford Motor Co. v. U.S., 19 C.I.T. 946, 896 F.Supp. 1224, 1230 (1995).

        ii. *Amending as a matter of course.* The right to amend as of course is not restricted to any particular litigant or pleading. FPP § 1480. It is a right conferred on all of the parties to an action and thus extends to persons who were not original parties to the litigation, but are brought into the action by way of counterclaim, crossclaim, third-party claim, or defensive interpleader. FPP § 1480; Johnson v. Walsh, 65 F.Supp. 157 (W.D.Mo. 1946).

            •   *Amending a complaint with multiple defendants.* When a number of defendants are involved in an action, some of whom have answered and some of whom have filed no responsive pleading, the plaintiff can amend as a matter of course as to those defendants who have not answered. FEDPROC § 62:267; Pallant v. Sinatra, 7 F.R.D. 293 (S.D.N.Y. 1945). On the other hand, a plaintiff may not file an amended complaint as of right against those defendants who have not yet answered, if he or she has amended the complaint once already as a matter of course. FEDPROC § 62:267; Glaros v. Perse, 628 F.2d 679 (1st Cir. 1980).

        iii. *Amending with leave of court.* Refer to the United States District Court for the Northern District of Indiana KeyRules Motion for Leave to Amend document for information on amending the pleadings with leave of court.

        iv. *Types of amendments permitted under FRCP 15(a)*

            •   *Cure a defective pleading.* Perhaps the most common use of FRCP 15(a) is by a party seeking to amend in order to cure a defective pleading. FPP § 1474.

            •   *Correct insufficiently stated claims or defenses.* A more common use of FRCP 15(a) amendments is to correct insufficiently stated claims or defenses. Typically, amendments of this character involve either adding a necessary allegation in order to state a claim for relief or correcting a misnomer of a party to the action. FPP § 1474.

            •   *Change nature or theory of claim or capacity of party.* Courts also have allowed a party to amend in order to change the nature or theory of the party's claim or the capacity in which the party is bringing the action. FPP § 1474.

            •   *State additional claims or defenses or drop claims or defenses.* Plaintiffs and defendants also have been permitted to amend their pleadings to state additional claims, to assert additional defenses, or to drop claims or defenses. FPP § 1474; Weinberger v. Retail Credit Co., 498 F.2d 552, 554, n.4 (4th Cir. 1974).

            •   *Increase amount of damages or elect a different remedy.* A FRCP 15(a) amendment also is appropriate for increasing the amount of damages sought, or for electing a different remedy than the one originally requested. FPP § 1474; McFadden v. Sanchez, 710 F.2d 907 (2d Cir. 1983).

            •   *Add, substitute, or drop parties.* Finally, a party may make a FRCP 15(a) amendment to add, substitute, or drop parties to the action. FPP § 1474.

    b. *Amendments during and after trial*

        i.   *Based on an objection at trial.* If, at trial, a party objects that evidence is not within the issues raised in the pleadings, the court may permit the pleadings to be amended. The court should freely permit an amendment when doing so will aid in presenting the merits and the objecting party fails to satisfy the court that the evidence would prejudice that party's action or defense on the merits. The court may grant a continuance to enable the objecting party to meet the evidence. FRCP 15(b)(1).

    ii. *For issues tried by consent.* When an issue not raised by the pleadings is tried by the parties' express or implied consent, it must be treated in all respects as if raised in the pleadings. A party may move—at any time, even after judgment—to amend the pleadings to conform them to the evidence and to raise an unpleaded issue. But failure to amend does not affect the result of the trial of that issue. FRCP 15(b)(2).

    iii. Refer to the United States District Court for the Northern District of Indiana KeyRules Motion for Leave to Amend document for more information on moving to amend the pleadings.

  c. *Relation back of amendments*

    i. *When an amendment relates back.* An amendment to a pleading relates back to the date of the original pleading when:

- The law that provides the applicable statute of limitations allows relation back;
- The amendment asserts a claim or defense that arose out of the conduct, transaction, or occurrence set out—or attempted to be set out—in the original pleading; or
- The amendment changes the party or the naming of the party against whom a claim is asserted, if FRCP 15(c)(1)(B) is satisfied and if, within the period provided by FRCP 4(m) for serving the summons and complaint, the party to be brought in by amendment: (1) received such notice of the action that it will not be prejudiced in defending on the merits; and (2) knew or should have known that the action would have been brought against it, but for a mistake concerning the proper party's identity. FRCP 15(c)(1).

    ii. *Notice to the United States.* When the United States or a United States officer or agency is added as a defendant by amendment, the notice requirements of FRCP 15(c)(1)(C)(i) and FRCP 15(c)(1)(C)(ii) are satisfied if, during the stated period, process was delivered or mailed to the United States attorney or the United States attorney's designee, to the Attorney General of the United States, or to the officer or agency. FRCP 15(c)(2).

  d. *Effect of an amended pleading.* A pleading that has been amended under FRCP 15(a) supersedes the pleading it modifies and remains in effect throughout the action unless it subsequently is modified. FPP § 1476. Once an amended pleading is interposed, the original pleading no longer performs any function in the case and any subsequent motion made by an opposing party should be directed at the amended pleading. FPP § 1476; Ferdik v. Bonzelet, 963 F.2d 1258, 1262 (9th Cir. 1992); Davis v. TXO Production Corp., 929 F.2d 1515, 1517 (10th Cir. 1991).

4. *Amended complaint.* Refer to the United States District Court for the Northern District of Indiana KeyRules Complaint document for the requirements specific to the amended complaint.

5. *Amended answer.* Refer to the United States District Court for the Northern District of Indiana KeyRules Answer document for the requirements specific to the amended answer.

6. *Right to a jury trial; Demand*

  a. *Right preserved.* The right of trial by jury as declared by U.S.C.A. Const. Amend. VII, or as provided by a federal statute, is preserved to the parties inviolate. FRCP 38(a).

  b. *Demand.* On any issue triable of right by a jury, a party may demand a jury trial by:

    i. Serving the other parties with a written demand—which may be included in a pleading—no later than fourteen (14) days after the last pleading directed to the issue is served; and

    ii. Filing the demand in accordance with FRCP 5(d). FRCP 38(b).

  c. *Specifying issues.* In its demand, a party may specify the issues that it wishes to have tried by a jury; otherwise, it is considered to have demanded a jury trial on all the issues so triable. If the party has demanded a jury trial on only some issues, any other party may—within fourteen (14) days after being served with the demand or within a shorter time ordered by the court—serve a demand for a jury trial on any other or all factual issues triable by jury. FRCP 38(c).

d. *Waiver; Withdrawal.* A party waives a jury trial unless its demand is properly served and filed. A proper demand may be withdrawn only if the parties consent. FRCP 38(d).

e. *Admiralty and maritime claims.* The rules in FRCP 38 do not create a right to a jury trial on issues in a claim that is an admiralty or maritime claim under FRCP 9(h). FRCP 38(e).

7. *Appearances.* Attorneys not representing the United States or its agencies must file an appearance when they represent (either in person or by filing a paper) a party. IN R USDCTND L.R. 83-8(a). For more information, refer to IN R USDCTND L.R. 83-8.

8. *Notice of related action.* A party must file a notice of related action as soon as it appears that the party's case and another pending case: (1) arise out of the same transaction or occurrence; (2) involve the same property; or (3) involve the validity or infringement of the same patent, trademark, or copyright. IN R USDCTND L.R. 40-1(d). For more information, refer to IN R USDCTND L.R. 40-1.

9. *Alternative dispute resolution (ADR).* After they confer as required by FRCP 26(f), the parties must advise the court which, if any, alternative-dispute-resolution processes they expect to pursue and when they expect to undertake the process. IN R USDCTND L.R. 16-6(a). For more information on alternative dispute resolution (ADR), refer to IN R USDCTND L.R. 16-6 and IN R USDCTND Order 2003-21.

10. *Settlement or resolution.* The parties must immediately notify the court if they reasonably expect to settle the case or resolve a pending motion. IN R USDCTND L.R. 16-1(g).

11. *Modification or suspension of rules.* The court may, on its own motion or at the request of a party, suspend or modify any rule in a particular case in the interest of justice. IN R USDCTND L.R. 1-1(c).

D. Documents

1. *Required documents*

   a. *Amended pleading.* Amendments to a pleading: (1) must reproduce the entire pleading as amended, unless the court allows otherwise; and (2) must not incorporate another pleading by reference. IN R USDCTND L.R. 15-1(b). Refer to the General Requirements section of this document for the form and contents of the amended pleading.

   b. *Certificate of service.* FRCP 5(d) requires that the person making service under FRCP 5 certify that service has been effected. FRCP 5(Advisory Committee Notes). Having such information on file may be useful for many purposes, including proof of service if an issue arises concerning the effectiveness of the service. FRCP 5(Advisory Committee Notes).

      i. *Certificate of service for electronically-filed documents.* A Certificate of Service is still a requirement when filing documents electronically. A sample Certificate of Service is attached as Form 1 (IN R USDCTND CM/ECF(Form 1)). IN R USDCTND CM/ECF(II)(H).

2. *Supplemental documents*

   a. *Notice of constitutional question.* A party that files a pleading, written motion, or other paper drawing into question the constitutionality of a federal or state statute must promptly:

      i. *File notice.* File a notice of constitutional question stating the question and identifying the paper that raises it, if:

         • A federal statute is questioned and the parties do not include the United States, one of its agencies, or one of its officers or employees in an official capacity; or

         • A state statute is questioned and the parties do not include the state, one of its agencies, or one of its officers or employees in an official capacity; and

      ii. *Serve notice.* Serve the notice and paper on the Attorney General of the United States if a federal statute is questioned—or on the state attorney general if a state statute is questioned—either by certified or registered mail or by sending it to an electronic address designated by the attorney general for this purpose. FRCP 5.1(a).

      iii. *When to file the notice.* A party required to file a notice of constitutional question under FRCP

5.1 must do so by the later of: (1) the day the parties tender their proposed case-management plan (if one is required); or (2) 21 days after filing the pleading, written motion, or other paper questioning the constitutionality of a federal or state statute. IN R USDCTND L.R. 5.1-1(a).

    iv. *Service on government officials.* The party must also serve the notice and the pleading, written motion, or other paper questioning the constitutionality of a federal or state statute on: (1) the Attorney General of the United States and the United States Attorney for the Northern District of Indiana, if a federal statute is challenged; or (2) the Attorney General for the state if a state statute is challenged. IN R USDCTND L.R. 5.1-1(b). Service required under IN R USDCTND L.R. 5.1-1(b) may be made either by certified or registered mail or by emailing it to an address designated by those officials for this purpose. IN R USDCTND L.R. 5.1-1(c).

    v. *No forfeiture.* A party's failure to file and serve the notice, or the court's failure to certify, does not forfeit a constitutional claim or defense that is otherwise timely asserted. FRCP 5.1(d).

  b. *Notice of issue concerning foreign law.* A party who intends to raise an issue about a foreign country's law must give notice by a pleading or other writing. In determining foreign law, the court may consider any relevant material or source, including testimony, whether or not submitted by a party or admissible under the Federal Rules of Evidence. The court's determination must be treated as a ruling on a question of law. FRCP 44.1.

  c. *Index of exhibits.* Any pleading, motion, brief, affidavit, notice, or proposed order, whether filed electronically or by delivering it to the clerk, must: include a separate index identifying and briefly describing each exhibit if there are more than four (4) exhibits. IN R USDCTND L.R. 5-4(a)(8).

  d. *Copy of document with self-addressed envelope.* A party who wants a file-stamped copy of a paper must include with the filing an additional copy of the paper and a self-addressed envelope with adequate postage. IN R USDCTND L.R. 5-4(b)(6).

  e. *Notice of manual filing.* However, if that is not physically possible, counsel shall electronically file a .pdf document titled Notice of Manual Filing as a notation on the docket sheet that filings are being held in the clerk's office in paper. A sample Notice of Manual Filing is attached as Form 2 (IN R USDCTND CM/ECF(Form 2)). IN R USDCTND CM/ECF(III)(A)(1).

  f. *Courtesy copies.* If documents are filed in paper format, counsel must provide an original for the clerk's office, a copy for the judge and a copy must be served on all parties in the case. IN R USDCTND CM/ECF(III)(A)(1).

  g. *Declaration that party was unable to file in a timely manner.* If the attorney is unable to file a document in a timely manner due to technical difficulties in the user's system, the attorney must file a document with the court as soon as possible notifying the court of the inability to file the document. A sample document entitled Declaration that Party was Unable to File in a Timely Manner Due to Technical Difficulties is attached hereto as Form 5. IN R USDCTND CM/ECF(VI)(B). [Editor's note: the reference to Form 5 is likely meant to be a reference to Form 3 (IN R USDCTND CM/ECF(Form 3)].

3. *Documents required for an amended complaint adding a new claim for relief or new party.* Refer to the United States District Court for the Northern District of Indiana KeyRules Complaint document for the documents for an amended complaint adding a new claim for relief or being filed and served against a new party.

E. Format

1. *Form of documents*

  a. *Paper.* Any pleading, motion, brief, affidavit, notice, or proposed order, whether filed electronically or by delivering it to the clerk, must: use eight and one-half by eleven (8-1/2 x 11) inch pages. IN R USDCTND L.R. 5-4(a)(2).

    i. *Manual filings.* Papers delivered to the clerk for filing must: be flat, unfolded, and on good-quality, white paper. IN R USDCTND L.R. 5-4(b)(1)(A).

      • *Covers or backing.* Papers delivered to the clerk for filing must: not have a cover or a back. IN R USDCTND L.R. 5-4(b)(1)(B).

- *Recycled paper.* The court encourages using recycled paper. IN R USDCTND L.R. 5-4(b)(7).

b. *Margins.* Any pleading, motion, brief, affidavit, notice, or proposed order, whether filed electronically or by delivering it to the clerk, must: have at least one (1) inch margins. IN R USDCTND L.R. 5-4(a)(3).

c. *Spacing.* Any pleading, motion, brief, affidavit, notice, or proposed order, whether filed electronically or by delivering it to the clerk, must: be double spaced (except for headings, footnotes, and quoted material). IN R USDCTND L.R. 5-4(a)(5).

d. *Text.* Any pleading, motion, brief, affidavit, notice, or proposed order, whether filed electronically or by delivering it to the clerk, must: be plainly typewritten, printed, or prepared by a clearly legible copying process. IN R USDCTND L.R. 5-4(a)(1).

    i. Any pleading, motion, brief, affidavit, notice, or proposed order, whether filed electronically or by delivering it to the clerk, must: use at least twelve (12) point type in the body and at least ten (10) point type in footnotes. IN R USDCTND L.R. 5-4(a)(4).

e. *Page numbering.* Any pleading, motion, brief, affidavit, notice, or proposed order, whether filed electronically or by delivering it to the clerk, must: have consecutively numbered pages. IN R USDCTND L.R. 5-4(a)(6).

f. *Caption; Names of parties.* Every pleading must have a caption with the court's name, a title, a file number, and a FRCP 7(a) designation. The title of the complaint must name all the parties; the title of other pleadings, after naming the first party on each side, may refer generally to other parties. FRCP 10(a). Any pleading, motion, brief, affidavit, notice, or proposed order, whether filed electronically or by delivering it to the clerk, must: include a title on the first page. IN R USDCTND L.R. 5-4(a)(7).

g. *Filer's information.* Any pleading, motion, brief, affidavit, notice, or proposed order, whether filed electronically or by delivering it to the clerk, must: except in proposed orders and affidavits, include the filer's name, address, telephone number, fax number (where available), and e-mail address (where available). IN R USDCTND L.R. 5-4(a)(9).

h. *Paragraphs; Separate statements.* A party must state its claims or defenses in numbered paragraphs, each limited as far as practicable to a single set of circumstances. A later pleading may refer by number to a paragraph in an earlier pleading. If doing so would promote clarity, each claim founded on a separate transaction or occurrence—and each defense other than a denial—must be stated in a separate count or defense. FRCP 10(b).

i. *Adoption by reference; Exhibits.* A statement in a pleading may be adopted by reference elsewhere in the same pleading or in any other pleading or motion. A copy of a written instrument that is an exhibit to a pleading is a part of the pleading for all purposes. FRCP 10(c).

j. *Citation of local rules.* The Local Civil Rules of the United States District Court for the Northern District of Indiana may be cited as "N.D. Ind. L.R." IN R USDCTND L.R. 1-1(a)(1).

k. *Acceptance by the clerk.* The clerk must not refuse to file a paper solely because it is not in the form prescribed by the Federal Rules of Civil Procedure or by a local rule or practice. FRCP 5(d)(4).

    i. *Sanctions for formatting errors; Non-compliance.* If a person files a paper that does not comply with the rules governing the format of papers filed with the court, the court may: (1) strike the paper from the record; or (2) fine the person up to one thousand dollars ($1,000). IN R USDCTND L.R. 1-3(a).

        - *Notice.* Before sanctioning a person under IN R USDCTND L.R. 1-3(a)(2), the court must: (1) notify the person that the paper is noncompliant; and (2) give the person the opportunity either to be heard or to revise the paper. IN R USDCTND L.R. 1-3(b).

2. *Form of electronic documents.* Electronically filed documents must meet the same requirements of format and page limits as documents "conventionally filed" (as defined in IN R USDCTND CM/ECF(III)(A)) pursuant to the Federal Rules of Civil Procedure and the Local Civil Rules of the United States District Court for the Northern District of Indiana. IN R USDCTND CM/ECF(II)(A)(2).

a. *PDF format required.* Documents filed in the CM/ECF must be in .pdf format. A document created with almost any word-processing program can be converted to .pdf format. The .pdf program in effect takes a picture of the original document and allows anyone to open the converted document across a broad range of hardware and software, with layout, format, links, and images intact. IN R USDCTND CM/ECF(FN2).

b. *Title of documents.* The person electronically filing a pleading or other document will be responsible for designating a title for the pleading or other document by using one of the categories contained in the events listed in the CM/ECF Menu. IN R USDCTND CM/ECF(II)(G).

c. *Combining documents.* All documents which form part of a single pleading and which are being filed at the same time and by the same party may be electronically filed together under one document number, e.g., the motion and a supporting affidavit, with the exception of memoranda in support. Memoranda in support shall be electronically filed separately and shown as a related document to the motion. IN R USDCTND CM/ECF(II)(A)(4).

d. *Exhibits and attachments.* Filing users must submit in electronic form all documents referenced as exhibits or attachments, unless the court permits conventional filing. A filing user must submit as exhibits or attachments only those excerpts of the referenced documents that are directly germane to the matter under consideration by the court. Excerpted material must be clearly and prominently identified as such. Filing users who file excerpts of documents as exhibits or attachments do so without prejudice to their right to timely file additional excerpts or the complete document. Responding parties may timely file additional excerpts or the complete document that they believe are directly germane. The court may require parties to file additional excerpts or the complete document. IN R USDCTND CM/ECF(II)(A)(6).

e. *Hyperlinks.* Electronically filed documents may contain hyperlink references to an external document as a convenient mechanism for accessing material cited in the document. A hyperlink reference is neither validated for content nor considered a part of the court's records. The court neither endorses the product or organization at the destination of a hyperlink reference, nor does the court exercise any responsibility over the content at the destination. In order to preserve the integrity of the court record, attorneys wishing to insert hyperlinks in court filings shall continue to use the traditional citation method for the cited authority, in addition to the hyperlink. A hyperlink contained in a filing is no more than a convenient mechanism for accessing material cited in the document and a hyperlink reference is extraneous to any filed document and is not part of the court's record. IN R USDCTND CM/ECF(II)(A)(3).

3. *Signing of pleadings, motions and other papers*

a. *Signature.* Every pleading, written motion, and other paper must be signed by at least one attorney of record in the attorney's name—or by a party personally if the party is unrepresented. The paper must state the signer's address, e-mail address, and telephone number. FRCP 11(a).

i. *Signatures on manual filings.* Papers delivered to the clerk for filing must: include the filer's original signature. IN R USDCTND L.R. 5-4(b)(1)(C).

   • *Rubber-stamped and faxed signatures.* An original paper with a rubber-stamped or faxed signature is unsigned for purposes of FRCP 11 and FRCP 26(g). IN R USDCTND L.R. 5-4(b)(2).

   • *Affidavits.* Only the affiant need sign an affidavit. IN R USDCTND L.R. 5-4(b)(3).

ii. *Electronic signatures.* Pursuant to FRCP 11, every pleading, motion, and other paper (except lists, schedules, statements or amendments thereto) shall be signed by at least one attorney of record or, if the party is not represented by an attorney, all papers shall be signed by the party. An attorney's/participant's password issued by the court combined with the user's identification, serves as and constitutes the attorney/participant's signature for FRCP 11 and other purposes. IN R USDCTND CM/ECF(I)(C). Documents which must be filed and which must contain original signatures other than those of a participating attorney or which require either verification or an unsworn declaration under any rule or statute, shall be filed electronically, with originally executed copies maintained by the filer. The pleading or other document electronically filed shall contain "s/" signature(s), as noted in IN R USDCTND CM/ECF(II)(E)(3)(b). IN R USDCTND CM/ECF(II)(E)(1).

   • *Multiple signatures.* In the case of a stipulation or other document to be signed by two or

more attorneys, the following procedure should be used: The filing attorney shall initially confirm that the content of the document is acceptable to all persons required to sign the document and shall obtain the physical signatures of all attorneys on the document. IN R USDCTND CM/ECF(II)(E)(3)(a). The filing attorney then shall file the document electronically, indicating the signatories, e.g., "s/Jane Doe," "s/John Doe," etc. IN R US-DCTND CM/ECF(II)(E)(3)(b). The filing attorney shall retain the hard copy of the document containing the original signatures. IN R USDCTND CM/ECF(II)(E)(3)(c).

    iii. *No verification or accompanying affidavit required for pleadings.* Unless a rule or statute specifically states otherwise, a pleading need not be verified or accompanied by an affidavit. FRCP 11(a).

    iv. *Unsigned papers.* The court must strike an unsigned paper unless the omission is promptly corrected after being called to the attorney's or party's attention. FRCP 11(a).

b. *Representations to the court.* By presenting to the court a pleading, written motion, or other paper—whether by signing, filing, submitting, or later advocating it—an attorney or unrepresented party certifies that to the best of the person's knowledge, information, and belief, formed after an inquiry reasonable under the circumstances:

    i. It is not being presented for any improper purpose, such as to harass, cause unnecessary delay, or needlessly increase the cost of litigation;

    ii. The claims, defenses, and other legal contentions are warranted by existing law or by a nonfrivolous argument for extending, modifying, or reversing existing law or for establishing new law;

    iii. The factual contentions have evidentiary support or, if specifically so identified, will likely have evidentiary support after a reasonable opportunity for further investigation or discovery; and

    iv. The denials of factual contentions are warranted on the evidence or, if specifically so identified, are reasonably based on belief or a lack of information. FRCP 11(b).

c. *Sanctions.* If, after notice and a reasonable opportunity to respond, the court determines that FRCP 11(b) has been violated, the court may impose an appropriate sanction on any attorney, law firm, or party that violated FRCP 11(b) or is responsible for the violation. FRCP 11(c)(1). Refer to the United States District Court for the Northern District of Indiana KeyRules Motion for Sanctions document for more information.

4. *Privacy protection for filings made with the court*

a. *Redacted filings.* Counsel should not include sensitive information in any document filed with the court unless such inclusion is necessary and relevant to the case. IN R USDCTND CM/ECF(VII). Unless the court orders otherwise, in an electronic or paper filing with the court that contains an individual's Social Security number, taxpayer-identification number, or birth date, the name of an individual known to be a minor, or a financial-account number, a party or nonparty making the filing may include only:

    i. The last four (4) digits of the Social Security number and taxpayer-identification number;

    ii. The year of the individual's birth;

    iii. The minor's initials; and

    iv. The last four (4) digits of the financial-account number. FRCP 5.2(a); IN R USDCTND Order 2005-3.

b. *Exemptions from the redaction requirement.* The redaction requirement does not apply to the following:

    i. A financial-account number that identifies the property allegedly subject to forfeiture in a forfeiture proceeding;

    ii. The record of an administrative or agency proceeding;

    iii. The official record of a state-court proceeding;

    iv. The record of a court or tribunal, if that record was not subject to the redaction requirement when originally filed;

v. A filing covered by FRCP 5.2(c) or FRCP 5.2(d); and

vi. A pro se filing in an action brought under 28 U.S.C.A. § 2241, 28 U.S.C.A. § 2254, or 28 U.S.C.A. § 2255. FRCP 5.2(b).

vii. In cases filed under the Social Security Act, 42 U.S.C.A. § 405(g), there is no need for redaction of any information from the documents filed in the case. IN R USDCTND Order 2005-3.

c. *Limitations on remote access to electronic files; Social Security appeals and immigration cases.* Unless the court orders otherwise, in an action for benefits under the Social Security Act, and in an action or proceeding relating to an order of removal, to relief from removal, or to immigration benefits or detention, access to an electronic file is authorized as follows:

i. The parties and their attorneys may have remote electronic access to any part of the case file, including the administrative record;

ii. Any other person may have electronic access to the full record at the courthouse, but may have remote electronic access only to:

- The docket maintained by the court; and

- An opinion, order, judgment, or other disposition of the court, but not any other part of the case file or the administrative record. FRCP 5.2(c).

d. *Filings made under seal.* The court may order that a filing be made under seal without redaction. The court may later unseal the filing or order the person who made the filing to file a redacted version for the public record. FRCP 5.2(d). For information on filing documents under seal, refer to IN R USDCTND L.R. 5-3, IN R USDCTND CM/ECF(IV)(A), and IN R USDCTND ECF Order 2004-19.

e. *Protective orders.* For good cause, the court may by order in a case:

i. Require redaction of additional information; or

ii. Limit or prohibit a nonparty's remote electronic access to a document filed with the court. FRCP 5.2(e).

f. *Option for additional unredacted filing under seal.* A person making a redacted filing may also file an unredacted copy under seal. The court must retain the unredacted copy as part of the record. FRCP 5.2(f); IN R USDCTND Order 2005-3.

i. The unredacted version of the document or the reference list shall be retained by the court under seal as part of the record. This paper shall be retained by the court as part of the record. The court may, however, still require the party to file a redacted copy for the public file. IN R USDCTND Order 2005-3.

g. *Option for filing a reference list.* A filing that contains redacted information may be filed together with a reference list that identifies each item of redacted information and specifies an appropriate identifier that uniquely corresponds to each item listed. The list must be filed under seal and may be amended as of right. Any reference in the case to a listed identifier will be construed to refer to the corresponding item of information. FRCP 5.2(g); IN R USDCTND Order 2005-3.

i. The unredacted version of the document or the reference list shall be retained by the court under seal as part of the record. This paper shall be retained by the court as part of the record. The court may, however, still require the party to file a redacted copy for the public file. IN R USDCTND Order 2005-3.

h. *Responsibility for redaction.* The responsibility for redacting these personal identifiers rests solely with counsel and the parties. The Clerk will not review each paper for compliance with IN R USDCTND Order 2005-3. IN R USDCTND Order 2005-3.

i. *Waiver of protection of identifiers.* A person waives the protection of FRCP 5.2(a) as to the person's own information by filing it without redaction and not under seal. FRCP 5.2(h).

F. Filing and Service Requirements

1. *Filing requirements.* Any paper after the complaint that is required to be served—together with a certificate of service—must be filed within a reasonable time after service. FRCP 5(d)(1).

   a. *How filing is made; In general.* A paper is filed by delivering it:

      i. To the clerk; or

      ii. To a judge who agrees to accept it for filing, and who must then note the filing date on the paper and promptly send it to the clerk. FRCP 5(d)(2).

         • Papers not filed electronically must be filed with the clerk, not a judge. IN R USDCTND L.R. 5-4(b)(4).

      iii. Parties manually filing a paper that requires the clerk to give others notice, must give the clerk: (1) sufficient copies of the notice; and (2) the name and address of each person entitled to receive the notice. IN R USDCTND L.R. 5-4(b)(8).

   b. *Where to file.* Papers not filed electronically must be filed in the division where the case is pending, unless: (1) a person will be prejudiced if the paper is not filed the same day it is tendered; and (2) it includes an adequately sized envelope addressed to the clerk's office in the division where the case is pending and with adequate postage. IN R USDCTND L.R. 5-4(b)(5).

   c. *Electronic filing*

      i. *Authorization of electronic filing program.* A court may, by local rule, allow papers to be filed, signed, or verified by electronic means that are consistent with any technical standards established by the Judicial Conference of the United States. A local rule may require electronic filing only if reasonable exceptions are allowed. A paper filed electronically in compliance with a local rule is a written paper for purposes of the Federal Rules of Civil Procedure. FRCP 5(d)(3).

         • Papers must be filed, signed, and verified electronically unless excepted by the court's CM/ECF Civil and Criminal User Manual (IN R USDCTND CM/ECF). IN R USDCTND L.R. 5-1.

      ii. *Mandatory electronic filing.* Unless otherwise permitted by these procedures or otherwise authorized by the assigned judge, all documents submitted for filing in this district in civil and criminal cases, no matter when a case was originally filed, shall be filed electronically using the System. IN R USDCTND CM/ECF(II)(A)(1). The requirement that "all documents" be filed electronically includes briefs, and attachments and exhibits used in support of motions. IN R USDCTND CM/ECF(FN1).

         • Sending a document or pleading to the court via e-mail or facsimile does not constitute "electronic filing." IN R USDCTND CM/ECF(I)(A).

      iii. *Conventional filing.* As used in these procedures, a "conventionally" filed or submitted document or pleading is one presented to the Clerk or a party in paper or other non-electronic, tangible format. The following documents shall be filed conventionally and not electronically unless specifically authorized by the Court:

         • Exhibits and other documents which cannot be converted to a legible electronic form. Whenever possible, counsel is responsible for converting filings to an electronic form. However, if that is not physically possible, counsel shall electronically file a .pdf document titled Notice of Manual Filing as a notation on the docket sheet that filings are being held in the clerk's office in paper. A sample Notice of Manual Filing is attached as Form 2 (IN R USDCTND CM/ECF(Form 2)). If documents are filed in paper format, counsel must provide an original for the clerk's office, a copy for the judge and a copy must be served on all parties in the case. Large documents which do not exist in an electronic format shall be scanned into .pdf format by counsel, in small batches if necessary, and filed electronically as separate attachments in the System. IN R USDCTND CM/ECF(III)(A)(1).

         • Certain documents which are listed in IN R USDCTND CM/ECF(II)(E)(2). IN R USDCTND CM/ECF(III)(A)(2).

- Documents filed by pro se litigants. IN R USDCTND CM/ECF(III)(A)(3).

    iv. For more information on electronic filing, refer to IN R USDCTND CM/ECF.

2. *Service requirements*

  a. *Service; When required*

    i. *In general.* Unless the Federal Rules of Civil Procedure provide otherwise, each of the following papers must be served on every party:

- An order stating that service is required;
- A pleading filed after the original complaint, unless the court orders otherwise under FRCP 5(c) because there are numerous defendants;
- A discovery paper required to be served on a party, unless the court orders otherwise;
- A written motion, except one that may be heard ex parte; and
- A written notice, appearance, demand, or offer of judgment, or any similar paper. FRCP 5(a)(1).

    ii. *If a party fails to appear.* No service is required on a party who is in default for failing to appear. But a pleading that asserts a new claim for relief against such a party must be served on that party under FRCP 4. FRCP 5(a)(2).

    iii. *Seizing property.* If an action is begun by seizing property and no person is or need be named as a defendant, any service required before the filing of an appearance, answer, or claim must be made on the person who had custody or possession of the property when it was seized. FRCP 5(a)(3).

  b. *Service; How made*

    i. *Serving an attorney.* If a party is represented by an attorney, service under FRCP 5 must be made on the attorney unless the court orders service on the party. FRCP 5(b)(1).

    ii. *Service in general.* A paper is served under FRCP 5 by:

- Handing it to the person;
- Leaving it: (1) at the person's office with a clerk or other person in charge or, if no one is in charge, in a conspicuous place in the office; or (2) if the person has no office or the office is closed, at the person's dwelling or usual place of abode with someone of suitable age and discretion who resides there;
- Mailing it to the person's last known address—in which event service is complete upon mailing;
- Leaving it with the court clerk if the person has no known address;
- Sending it by electronic means if the person consented in writing—in which event service is complete upon transmission, but is not effective if the serving party learns that it did not reach the person to be served; or
- Delivering it by any other means that the person consented to in writing—in which event service is complete when the person making service delivers it to the agency designated to make delivery. FRCP 5(b)(2).

    iii. *Electronic service.* Electronically filed papers may be served electronically if service is consistent with the CM/ECF User Manual (IN R USDCTND CM/ECF). IN R USDCTND L.R. 5-2(a).

- *Waiver of other service.* An attorney's registration will constitute a waiver of conventional service of documents and the attorney agrees to accept service of notice on behalf of the client of the electronic filing by hand, facsimile or authorized email. IN R USDCTND CM/ECF(I)(B)(3).
- *Serving registered persons.* The System will generate a "Notice of Electronic Filing" when any document is filed. This notice represents service of the document on parties who are

registered participants with the System. Except as provided in IN R USDCTND CM/ECF(III)(B), the filing party shall not be required to serve any pleading or other documents on any party receiving electronic notice. IN R USDCTND CM/ECF(II)(D)(1). The term "pleading" refers only to those documents listed in FRCP 7(a). IN R USDCTND CM/ECF(FN3).

- *When electronic service is deemed completed.* A person registered to use the court's electronic-filing system is served with an electronically filed paper when a "Notice of Electronic Filing" is transmitted to that person through the court's electronic filing-system. IN R USDCTND L.R. 5-2(b).

- *Serving non-registered persons.* A person who has not registered to use the court's electronic-filing system but who is entitled to service of a paper must be served according to the Local Civil Rules of the United States District Court for the Northern District of Indiana and the Federal Rules of Civil Procedure. IN R USDCTND L.R. 5-2(c); IN R USDCTND CM/ECF(II)(D)(2). If such service of a paper copy is to be made, it shall be done in the manner provided in the Federal Rules of Civil Procedure and the Local Civil Rules of the United States District Court for the Northern District of Indiana. IN R USDCTND CM/ECF(II)(D)(2).

    iv. *Service of conventional filings.* Pleadings or other documents which are filed conventionally rather than electronically shall be served in the manner provided for in the Federal Rules of Civil Procedure and the Local Civil Rules of the United States District Court for the Northern District of Indiana, except as otherwise provided by order of the Court. IN R USDCTND CM/ECF(III)(B).

    v. *Using court facilities.* If a local rule so authorizes, a party may use the court's transmission facilities to make service under FRCP 5(b)(2)(E). FRCP 5(b)(3).

  c. *Serving numerous defendants*

    i. *In general.* If an action involves an unusually large number of defendants, the court may, on motion or on its own, order that:

- Defendants' pleadings and replies to them need not be served on other defendants;

- Any crossclaim, counterclaim, avoidance, or affirmative defense in those pleadings and replies to them will be treated as denied or avoided by all other parties; and

- Filing any such pleading and serving it on the plaintiff constitutes notice of the pleading to all parties. FRCP 5(c)(1).

    ii. *Notifying parties.* A copy of every such order must be served on the parties as the court directs. FRCP 5(c)(2).

3. *Service requirements of an amended complaint asserting new or additional claims for relief.* The service of amended pleadings is generally governed by FRCP 5. Thus, except for an amended pleading against a defaulting party that does not assert new or additional claims for relief, an amended pleading must be served in accordance with FRCP 5. FEDPROC § 62:263; International Controls Corp. v. Vesco, 556 F.2d 665, 23 Fed.R.Serv.2d 923 (2d Cir. 1977). However, while FRCP 5 permits service of an amended complaint on counsel, where the amended complaint contains an entirely different cause of action that could not have been properly served originally by the method used in serving the original complaint, the amended complaint must be served in accordance with the terms of FRCP 4. FEDPROC § 62:263; Lasch v. Antkies, 161 F.Supp. 851 (E.D.Pa. 1958). Refer to the United States District Court for the Northern District of Indiana KeyRules Complaint document for more information on serving the amended complaint in accordance with FRCP 4.

G. Hearings

1. *Hearings, generally.* Generally, there is no hearing contemplated in the federal statutes or rules for the amended pleading.

  a. *Amended answer; Hearing on FRCP 12 defenses before trial.* If a party so moves, any defense listed in FRCP 12(b)(1) through FRCP 12(b)(7)—whether made in a pleading or by motion—and a motion under FRCP 12(c) must be heard and decided before trial unless the court orders a deferral until trial. FRCP 12(i).

H. Forms

1. Federal Amended Pleading Forms

a. Notice; Of filing amended pleading as of course. AMJUR PP FEDPRAC § 153.

b. Amendment; Of pleading as of course. AMJUR PP FEDPRAC § 154.

c. Civil cover sheet. 2 FEDFORMS § 3:29.

d. Notice of lawsuit and request for waiver of service of summons and waiver of summons. 2 FEDFORMS § 3:36.

e. Complaint. 2 FEDFORMS § 7:14.

f. Generally. 2B FEDFORMS § 8:10.

g. Presenting defenses; Official form. 2B FEDFORMS § 8:12.

h. Denials, admissions and affirmative defenses. 2B FEDFORMS § 8:15.

i. Denial of particular averment. 2B FEDFORMS § 8:24.

j. Admission of particular averment. 2B FEDFORMS § 8:25.

k. Denial of all averments of paragraph. 2B FEDFORMS § 8:26.

l. Admission of all averments of paragraph. 2B FEDFORMS § 8:27.

m. Denial in part and admission in part of paragraph. 2B FEDFORMS § 8:28.

n. Notice of amended complaint. 2C FEDFORMS § 14:10.

o. Amendment to complaint. 2C FEDFORMS § 14:47.

p. Amendment to complaint; Short version. 2C FEDFORMS § 14:48.

q. Amendment to complaint; As of course. 2C FEDFORMS § 14:49.

r. Complaint; Single count. FEDPROF § 1:68.

s. Complaint; Multiple counts; With same jurisdictional basis. FEDPROF § 1:69.

t. Amendment of pleading; As matter of course. FEDPROF § 1:220.

u. Notice of filing amended pleading; Where amendment is matter of course. FEDPROF § 1:221.

v. Amendment of pleading; Particular clauses. FEDPROF § 1:224.

w. Amendment of pleading; Clause; Change in title of action. FEDPROF § 1:225.

x. Amendment of pleading; Clause; To show amount in controversy. FEDPROF § 1:227.

y. Amendment of pleading; Clause; To show diversity of citizenship. FEDPROF § 1:228.

z. Amendment of pleading; Clause; Prayer for relief. FEDPROF § 1:229.

2. Forms for the Northern District of Indiana

a. Certificate of service. IN R USDCTND CM/ECF(Form 1).

b. Notice of manual filing. IN R USDCTND CM/ECF(Form 2).

c. Declaration that party was unable to file in a timely manner. IN R USDCTND CM/ECF(Form 3).

I. Applicable Rules

1. *Federal rules*

a. Serving and filing pleadings and other papers. FRCP 5.

b. Constitutional challenge to a statute; Notice, certification, and intervention. FRCP 5.1.

c. Privacy protection for filings made with the court. FRCP 5.2.

d. Computing and extending time; Time for motion papers. FRCP 6.

    e.   Pleadings allowed; Form of motions and other papers. FRCP 7.

    f.   General rules of pleading. FRCP 8.

    g.   Pleading special matters. FRCP 9.

    h.   Form of pleadings. FRCP 10.

    i.   Signing pleadings, motions, and other papers; Representations to the court; Sanctions. FRCP 11.

    j.   Defenses and objections; When and how presented; Motion for judgment on the pleadings; Consolidating motions; Waiving defenses; Pretrial hearing. FRCP 12.

    k.   Amended and supplemental pleadings. FRCP 15.

    l.   Right to a jury trial; Demand. FRCP 38.

    m.   Determining foreign law. FRCP 44.1.

2. *Local rules*

    a.   Citation and scope of the rules. IN R USDCTND L.R. 1-1.

    b.   Sanctions for formatting errors. IN R USDCTND L.R. 1-3.

    c.   Electronic filing required. IN R USDCTND L.R. 5-1.

    d.   Constitutional questions. IN R USDCTND L.R. 5.1-1.

    e.   Electronic service. IN R USDCTND L.R. 5-2.

    f.   Format of papers. IN R USDCTND L.R. 5-4.

    g.   Extensions of time. IN R USDCTND L.R. 6-1.

    h.   Amending pleadings. IN R USDCTND L.R. 15-1.

    i.   Pretrial procedure. IN R USDCTND L.R. 16-1.

    j.   Alternative dispute resolution. IN R USDCTND L.R. 16-6.

    k.   Case assignment. IN R USDCTND L.R. 40-1.

    l.   Appearance and withdrawal of appearance. IN R USDCTND L.R. 83-8.

    m.   CM/ECF civil and criminal user manual. IN R USDCTND CM/ECF.

    n.   In re: privacy and public access to civil electronic case files. IN R USDCTND Order 2005-3.

Motions, Oppositions and Replies
Motion to Strike

Document Last Updated December 2016

A. **Checklist**

    (I) ❑ Matters to be considered by moving party

        (a) ❑ Required documents

            (1) ❑ Notice of motion and motion

            (2) ❑ Brief

            (3) ❑ Certificate of service

        (b) ❑ Supplemental documents

            (1) ❑ Deposition

            (2) ❑ Notice of constitutional question

            (3) ❑ Nongovernmental corporate disclosure statement

            (4) ❑ Index of exhibits

            (5) ❑ Request for oral argument

(6) ❑ Request for evidentiary hearing

(7) ❑ Copy of authority

(8) ❑ Proposed order

(9) ❑ Copy of document with self-addressed envelope

(10) ❑ Notice of manual filing

(11) ❑ Courtesy copies

(12) ❑ Declaration that party was unable to file in a timely manner

(c) ❑ Timing

(1) ❑ The court may act on motion made by a party either before responding to the pleading or, if a response is not allowed, within twenty-one (21) days after being served with the pleading

(2) ❑ A written motion and notice of the hearing must be served at least fourteen (14) days before the time specified for the hearing, with the following exceptions: (i) when the motion may be heard ex parte; (ii) when the Federal Rules of Civil Procedure set a different time; or (iii) when a court order—which a party may, for good cause, apply for ex parte—sets a different time

(3) ❑ Any affidavit supporting a motion must be served with the motion

(II) ❑ Matters to be considered by opposing party

(a) ❑ Required documents

(1) ❑ Response brief

(2) ❑ Certificate of service

(b) ❑ Supplemental documents

(1) ❑ Deposition

(2) ❑ Notice of constitutional question

(3) ❑ Index of exhibits

(4) ❑ Request for oral argument

(5) ❑ Request for evidentiary hearing

(6) ❑ Copy of authority

(7) ❑ Copy of document with self-addressed envelope

(8) ❑ Notice of manual filing

(9) ❑ Courtesy copies

(10) ❑ Declaration that party was unable to file in a timely manner

(c) ❑ Timing

(1) ❑ A party must file any response brief to a motion within fourteen (14) days after the motion is served

(2) ❑ Except as FRCP 59(c) provides otherwise, any opposing affidavit must be served at least seven (7) days before the hearing, unless the court permits service at another time

B. Timing

1. *Motion to strike.* The court may act on motion made by a party either before responding to the pleading or, if a response is not allowed, within twenty-one (21) days after being served with the pleading. FRCP 12(f)(2).

2. *Timing of motions, generally*

a. *Motion and notice of hearing.* A written motion and notice of the hearing must be served at least fourteen (14) days before the time specified for the hearing, with the following exceptions:

i. When the motion may be heard ex parte;

    ii.   When the Federal Rules of Civil Procedure set a different time; or

    iii.   When a court order—which a party may, for good cause, apply for ex parte—sets a different time. FRCP 6(c)(1).

  b. *Supporting affidavit.* Any affidavit supporting a motion must be served with the motion. FRCP 6(c)(2).

3. *Timing of opposing papers.* A party must file any response brief to a motion within fourteen (14) days after the motion is served. IN R USDCTND L.R. 7-1(d)(2)(A).

  a. *Opposing affidavit.* Except as FRCP 59(c) provides otherwise, any opposing affidavit must be served at least seven (7) days before the hearing, unless the court permits service at another time. FRCP 6(c)(2).

  b. *Extensions.* The court may extend response- and reply-brief deadlines, but only for good cause. IN R USDCTND L.R. 7-1(d)(3).

  c. *Summary rulings.* The court may rule on a motion summarily if an opposing party does not file a response before the deadline. IN R USDCTND L.R. 7-1(d)(4).

4. *Timing of reply papers.* Where the respondent files an answering affidavit setting up a new matter, the moving party ordinarily is allowed a reasonable time to file a reply affidavit since failure to deny the new matter by affidavit may operate as an admission of its truth. AMJUR MOTIONS § 25.

  a. *Reply brief.* The moving party must file any reply brief within seven (7) days after the response brief is served. IN R USDCTND L.R. 7-1(d)(2)(B).

  b. *Extensions.* The court may extend response- and reply-brief deadlines, but only for good cause. IN R USDCTND L.R. 7-1(d)(3).

5. *Effect of a FRCP 12 motion on the time to serve a responsive pleading.* Unless the court sets a different time, serving a motion under FRCP 12 alters the periods in FRCP 12(a) as follows:

  a. If the court denies the motion or postpones its disposition until trial, the responsive pleading must be served within fourteen (14) days after notice of the court's action; or

  b. If the court grants a motion for a more definite statement, the responsive pleading must be served within fourteen (14) days after the more definite statement is served. FRCP 12(a)(4).

6. *Computation of time*

  a. *Computing time.* FRCP 6 applies in computing any time period specified in the Federal Rules of Civil Procedure, in any local rule or court order, or in any statute that does not specify a method of computing time. FRCP 6(a).

    i. *Period stated in days or a longer unit.* When the period is stated in days or a longer unit of time:

      • Exclude the day of the event that triggers the period;

      • Count every day, including intermediate Saturdays, Sundays, and legal holidays; and

      • Include the last day of the period, but if the last day is a Saturday, Sunday, or legal holiday, the period continues to run until the end of the next day that is not a Saturday, Sunday, or legal holiday. FRCP 6(a)(1).

    ii. *Period stated in hours.* When the period is stated in hours:

      • Begin counting immediately on the occurrence of the event that triggers the period;

      • Count every hour, including hours during intermediate Saturdays, Sundays, and legal holidays; and

      • If the period would end on a Saturday, Sunday, or legal holiday, the period continues to run until the same time on the next day that is not a Saturday, Sunday, or legal holiday. FRCP 6(a)(2).

    iii. *Inaccessibility of the clerk's office.* Unless the court orders otherwise, if the clerk's office is inaccessible:

      • On the last day for filing under FRCP 6(a)(1), then the time for filing is extended to the first accessible day that is not a Saturday, Sunday, or legal holiday; or

- During the last hour for filing under FRCP 6(a)(2), then the time for filing is extended to the same time on the first accessible day that is not a Saturday, Sunday, or legal holiday. FRCP 6(a)(3).

iv. *"Last day" defined.* Unless a different time is set by a statute, local rule, or court order, the last day ends:

- For electronic filing, at midnight in the court's time zone; and

- For filing by other means, when the clerk's office is scheduled to close. FRCP 6(a)(4).

v. *"Next day" defined.* The "next day" is determined by continuing to count forward when the period is measured after an event and backward when measured before an event. FRCP 6(a)(5).

vi. *"Legal holiday" defined.* "Legal holiday" means:

- The day set aside by statute for observing New Year's Day, Martin Luther King Jr.'s Birthday, Washington's Birthday, Memorial Day, Independence Day, Labor Day, Columbus Day, Veterans' Day, Thanksgiving Day, or Christmas Day;

- Any day declared a holiday by the President or Congress; and

- For periods that are measured after an event, any other day declared a holiday by the state where the district court is located. FRCP 6(a)(6).

b. *Computation of electronic filing deadlines.* Filing documents electronically does not alter any filing deadlines or any time computation pursuant to FRCP 6. The counties of Lake, Porter, LaPorte, Pulaski and Starke are located in the Central time zone and the remaining counties in the Northern District of Indiana are located in the Eastern time zone. Nevertheless, all electronic transmissions of documents must be completed (i.e., received completely by the clerk's office) prior to midnight Eastern Time, (South Bend/Fort Wayne/Lafayette time) in order to be considered timely filed that day, regardless of the local time in the division where the case is pending. Although documents can be filed electronically twenty-four (24) hours a day, filers are strongly encouraged to file all documents during hours when the CM/ECF Help Line is available, from 9:00 a.m. to 4:00 p.m. local time. IN R USDCTND CM/ECF(II)(I).

i. *Technical failures.* If the attorney is unable to file a document in a timely manner due to technical difficulties in the user's system, the attorney must file a document with the court as soon as possible notifying the court of the inability to file the document. A sample document entitled Declaration that Party was Unable to File in a Timely Manner Due to Technical Difficulties is attached hereto as Form 5. IN R USDCTND CM/ECF(VI)(B). [Editor's note: the reference to Form 5 is likely meant to be a reference to Form 3 (IN R USDCTND CM/ECF(Form 3)].

c. *Extending time*

i. *In general.* When an act may or must be done within a specified time, the court may, for good cause, extend the time:

- With or without motion or notice if the court acts, or if a request is made, before the original time or its extension expires; or

- On motion made after the time has expired if the party failed to act because of excusable neglect. FRCP 6(b)(1).

ii. *Exceptions.* A court must not extend the time to act under FRCP 50(b), FRCP 50(d), FRCP 52(b), FRCP 59(b), FRCP 59(d), FRCP 59(e), and FRCP 60(b). FRCP 6(b)(2).

iii. Refer to the United States District Court for the Northern District of Indiana KeyRules Motion for Continuance/Extension of Time document for more information on extending time.

d. *Additional time after certain kinds of service.* When a party may or must act within a specified time after being served and service is made under FRCP 5(b)(2)(C) (mail), FRCP 5(b)(2)(D) (leaving with the clerk), or FRCP 5(b)(2)(F) (other means consented to), three (3) days are added after the period would otherwise expire under FRCP 6(a). FRCP 6(d).

C. General Requirements

1. *Motions, generally*

   a. *Requirements.* A request for a court order must be made by motion. The motion must:

      i. Be in writing unless made during a hearing or trial;

      ii. State with particularity the grounds for seeking the order; and

      iii. State the relief sought. FRCP 7(b)(1).

   b. *Notice of motion.* A party interested in resisting the relief sought by a motion has a right to notice thereof, and an opportunity to be heard. AMJUR MOTIONS § 12.

      i. In addition to statutory or court rule provisions requiring notice of a motion—the purpose of such a notice requirement having been said to be to prevent a party from being prejudicially surprised by a motion—principles of natural justice dictate that an adverse party generally must be given notice that a motion will be presented to the court. AMJUR MOTIONS § 12.

      ii. "Notice," in this regard, means reasonable notice, including a meaningful opportunity to prepare and to defend against allegations of a motion. AMJUR MOTIONS § 12.

   c. *Writing requirement.* The writing requirement is intended to insure that the adverse parties are informed and have a record of both the motion's pendency and the grounds on which the movant seeks an order. FPP § 1191; Feldberg v. Quechee Lakes Corp., 463 F.3d 195 (2d Cir. 2006).

      i. It is sufficient "if the motion is stated in a written notice of the hearing of the motion." FPP § 1191.

   d. *Particularity requirement.* The particularity requirement insures that the opposing parties will have notice of their opponent's contentions. FEDPROC § 62:364; Goodman v. 1973 26 Foot Trojan Vessel, Arkansas Registration No. AR1439SN, 859 F.2d 71, 12 Fed.R.Serv.3d 645 (8th Cir. 1988). That requirement ensures that notice of the basis for the motion is provided to the court and to the opposing party so as to avoid prejudice, provide the opponent with a meaningful opportunity to respond, and provide the court with enough information to process the motion correctly. FEDPROC § 62:364; Andreas v. Volkswagen of America, Inc., 336 F.3d 789, 56 Fed.R.Serv.3d 6 (8th Cir. 2003).

      i. Reasonable specification of the grounds for a motion is sufficient. However, where a movant fails to state even one ground for granting the motion in question, the movant has failed to meet the minimal standard of "reasonable specification." FEDPROC § 62:364; Martinez v. Trainor, 556 F.2d 818, 23 Fed.R.Serv.2d 403 (7th Cir. 1977).

      ii. The court may excuse the failure to comply with the particularity requirement if it is inadvertent, and where no prejudice is shown by the opposing party. FEDPROC § 62:364.

   e. *Motions must be filed separately.* Motions must be filed separately, but alternative motions may be filed in a single paper if each is named in the title following the caption. IN R USDCTND L.R. 7-1(a).

2. *Motion to strike.* The court may strike from a pleading an insufficient defense or any redundant, immaterial, impertinent, or scandalous matter. The court may act: (1) on its own; or (2) on motion made by a party either before responding to the pleading or, if a response is not allowed, within twenty-one (21) days after being served with the pleading. FRCP 12(f). FRCP 12(f) also is designed to reinforce the requirement in FRCP 8(e) that pleadings be simple, concise, and direct. However, as the cases make clear, it is neither an authorized nor a proper way to procure the dismissal of all or a part of a complaint, or a counterclaim, or to strike an opponent's affidavits. FPP § 1380.

   a. *Practice on a motion to strike.* All well-pleaded facts are taken as admitted on a motion to strike but conclusions of law or conclusions drawn from the facts do not have to be treated in that fashion by the district judge. FPP § 1380. Both because striking a portion of a pleading is a drastic remedy and because it often is sought by the movant simply as a dilatory or harassing tactic, numerous judicial decisions make it clear that motions under FRCP 12(f) are viewed with disfavor by the federal courts and are infrequently granted. FPP § 1380.

   b. *Striking an insufficient defense.* Only if a defense is insufficient as a matter of law will it be stricken. If a defense cannot succeed under any set of circumstances alleged, the defense may be deemed insufficient as a matter of law. In other words, a defense may be stricken if, on the face of the pleadings, it is patently frivolous, or if it is clearly invalid as a matter of law. FEDPROC § 62:412.

  i. A defense will be stricken if it could not possibly prevent recovery by the plaintiff on its claim. FEDPROC § 62:413. In addition, a defense may be stricken if:

  - The defense requires separate statements;
  - The defense has been previously advanced and rejected; or
  - The defense cannot be waived. FEDPROC § 62:413.

c. *Striking immaterial or impertinent matter.* Immaterial or impertinent matter will be stricken from a pleading if it is clear that it can have no possible bearing upon the subject matter of the litigation, and that its inclusion will prejudice the movant. If there is any doubt as to whether under any contingency the matter may raise an issue, the motion should be denied. FEDPROC § 62:415.

  i. "Immaterial matter," for purposes of FRCP 12(f), is matter which has no essential or important relationship to the claim for relief or the defenses being pleaded. FEDPROC § 62:414. A statement of unnecessary particulars in connection with and descriptive of that which is material may be stricken as immaterial matter. FEDPROC § 62:416.

  ii. "Impertinent matter," for purposes of FRCP 12(f), consists of statements that do not pertain, and are not necessary, to the issues in question. FEDPROC § 62:414.

d. *Striking redundant matter.* "Redundant matter," for purposes of FRCP 12(f), consists of allegations that constitute a needless repetition of other averments or which are wholly foreign to the issue to be decided. However, even if allegations are redundant, they need not be stricken if their presence in the pleading cannot prejudice the moving party. FEDPROC § 62:417.

  i. Merely duplicative remedies do not necessarily make claims "redundant," within the meaning of FRCP 12(f), if the claims otherwise require proof of different elements, but a claim that merely recasts the same elements under the guise of a different theory may be stricken as redundant. FEDPROC § 62:417.

e. *Striking scandalous matter.* A matter is deemed scandalous, for purposes of FRCP 12(f), when it improperly casts a derogatory light on someone, usually a party to the action. Scandalous matter also consists of any unnecessary allegation which reflects cruelly upon the moral character of an individual, or states anything in repulsive language which detracts from the dignity of the court. To be scandalous, degrading charges must be irrelevant, or, if relevant, must go into in unnecessary detail. FEDPROC § 62:418.

  i. Allegations may be stricken as scandalous if the matter bears no possible relation to the controversy or may cause the objecting party prejudice. FEDPROC § 62:418.

  ii. But there are several limitations on the court's willingness to strike scandalous allegations. For example, it is not enough that the matter offends the sensibilities of the objecting party or the person who is the subject of the statements in the pleading, if the challenged allegations describe acts or events that are relevant to the action. FPP § 1382.

f. *Striking sham or false matter.* FRCP 12(f) does not authorize a motion to strike part or all of a pleading on the ground that it is sham, and the grounds for a motion to strike similarly do not include falsity of the matter alleged. FEDPROC § 62:419; PAE Government Services, Inc. v. MPRI, Inc., 514 F.3d 856 (9th Cir. 2007). However, it has been said that a court will strike a pleading according to FRCP 12(f) when it appears beyond peradventure that it is a sham and false and that its allegations are devoid of factual basis. FEDPROC § 62:419.

g. *Striking conclusions of law.* Unwarranted conclusions of law may be stricken from a pleading pursuant to FRCP 12(f), but ordinarily an allegation is not subject to being stricken merely because it is a conclusion of law. To the contrary, the Federal Rules of Civil Procedure do not condemn conclusions of law, but rather encourage them as at times the clearest and simplest way of stating a claim for relief. Conclusions of law must be unwarranted enough to justify a motion to strike, such as when a plaintiff states causes of action under a federal statute which provides no explicit private right of action. FEDPROC § 62:420.

h. *Striking other particular matter.* Under FRCP 12(f), which permits a court to order stricken from any pleading any redundant, immaterial, impertinent, or scandalous matter, courts have the authority to strike a prayer for relief seeking damages that are not recoverable as a matter of law. A motion to strike may be used to remove an excessive or unauthorized claim for damages. Furthermore, a motion to strike a demand for punitive damages under FRCP 12(f) may be proper if such damages are clearly not collectible, such as in an ordinary breach of contract action. However, there are other ways to raise this issue, and in a particular case, one of these other methods may be more appropriate, such as a motion to dismiss for failure to state a claim pursuant to FRCP 12(b)(6). FEDPROC § 62:421.

i. *Form.* On a motion to strike portions of a pleading, the movant must indicate what paragraphs are being challenged in order to fulfill the particularity requirement; the movant cannot merely state the conclusion that the allegations are too indefinite and insufficient to state a claim or defense. FPP § 1192.

j. *Joining motions*

    i. *Right to join.* A motion under FRCP 12 may be joined with any other motion allowed by FRCP 12. FRCP 12(g)(1).

    ii. *Limitation on further motions.* Except as provided in FRCP 12(h)(2) or FRCP 12(h)(3), a party that makes a motion under FRCP 12 must not make another motion under FRCP 12 raising a defense or objection that was available to the party but omitted from its earlier motion. FRCP 12(g)(2).

3. *Opposing papers.* The Federal Rules of Civil Procedure do not require any formal answer, return, or reply to a motion, except where the Federal Rules of Civil Procedure or local rules may require affidavits, memoranda, or other papers to be filed in opposition to a motion. Such papers are simply to apprise the court of such opposition and the grounds of that opposition. FEDPROC § 62:359.

a. *Effect of failure to respond to motion.* Although in the absence of statutory provision or court rule, a motion ordinarily does not require a written answer, when a party files a motion and the opposing party fails to respond, the court may construe such failure to respond as nonopposition to the motion or an admission that the motion was meritorious, may take the facts alleged in the motion as true—the rule in some jurisdictions being that the failure to respond to a fact set forth in a motion is deemed an admission—and may grant the motion if the relief requested appears to be justified. AMJUR MOTIONS § 28.

b. *Assent or no opposition not determinative.* However, a motion will not be granted automatically simply because an "assent" or a notation of "no opposition" has been filed; federal judges frequently deny motions that have been assented to when it is thought that justice so dictates. FPP § 1190.

c. *Responsive pleading inappropriate as response to motion.* An attempt to answer or oppose a motion with a responsive pleading usually is not appropriate. FPP § 1190.

4. *Reply papers.* A moving party may be required or permitted to prepare papers in addition to his original motion papers. AMJUR MOTIONS § 25. Papers answering or replying to opposing papers may be appropriate, in the interests of justice, where it appears there is a substantial reason for allowing a reply. Thus, a court may accept reply papers where a party demonstrates that the papers to which it seeks to file a reply raise new issues that are material to the disposition of the question before the court, or where the court determines, sua sponte, that it wishes further briefing of an issue raised in those papers and orders the submission of additional papers. FEDPROC § 62:360.

a. *Function of reply papers.* The function of a reply affidavit is to answer the arguments made in opposition to the position taken by the movant and not to permit the movant to introduce new arguments in support of the motion. AMJUR MOTIONS § 25.

b. *Issues raised for the first time in a reply document.* However, the view has been followed in some jurisdictions, that as a matter of judicial economy, where there is no prejudice and where the issues could be raised simply by filing a motion to dismiss, the trial court has discretion to consider arguments raised for the first time in a reply memorandum, and that a trial court may grant a motion to strike issues raised for the first time in a reply memorandum. AMJUR MOTIONS § 26.

5.   *Appearances.* Attorneys not representing the United States or its agencies must file an appearance when they represent (either in person or by filing a paper) a party. IN R USDCTND L.R. 83-8(a). For more information, refer to IN R USDCTND L.R. 83-8.

6.   *Notice of related action.* A party must file a notice of related action as soon as it appears that the party's case and another pending case: (1) arise out of the same transaction or occurrence; (2) involve the same property; or (3) involve the validity or infringement of the same patent, trademark, or copyright. IN R USDCTND L.R. 40-1(d). For more information, refer to IN R USDCTND L.R. 40-1.

7.   *Alternative dispute resolution (ADR).* After they confer as required by FRCP 26(f), the parties must advise the court which, if any, alternative-dispute-resolution processes they expect to pursue and when they expect to undertake the process. IN R USDCTND L.R. 16-6(a). For more information on alternative dispute resolution (ADR), refer to IN R USDCTND L.R. 16-6 and IN R USDCTND Order 2003-21.

8.   *Settlement or resolution.* The parties must immediately notify the court if they reasonably expect to settle the case or resolve a pending motion. IN R USDCTND L.R. 16-1(g).

9.   *Modification or suspension of rules.* The court may, on its own motion or at the request of a party, suspend or modify any rule in a particular case in the interest of justice. IN R USDCTND L.R. 1-1(c).

D. Documents

1.   *Documents for moving party*

   a.   *Required documents*

   i.   *Notice of motion and motion.* The party must not specify a hearing date in the notice of a motion or petition unless the court or the clerk has authorized it. IN R USDCTND L.R. 7-5(b)(2). Refer to the General Requirements section of this document for information on the notice of motion and motion.

   ii.   *Brief.* Parties must file a supporting brief with any motion under: FRCP 12. IN R USDCTND L.R. 7-1(b)(1). Refer to the Format section of this document for the format of briefs.

   iii.   *Certificate of service.* FRCP 5(d) requires that the person making service under FRCP 5 certify that service has been effected. FRCP 5(Advisory Committee Notes). Having such information on file may be useful for many purposes, including proof of service if an issue arises concerning the effectiveness of the service. FRCP 5(Advisory Committee Notes).

   • *Certificate of service for electronically-filed documents.* A Certificate of Service is still a requirement when filing documents electronically. A sample Certificate of Service is attached as Form 1 (IN R USDCTND CM/ECF(Form 1)). IN R USDCTND CM/ECF(II)(H).

   b.   *Supplemental documents.* Matter outside the pleadings normally is not considered on a FRCP 12(f) motion; for example, affidavits in support of or in opposition to the motion typically may not be used. FPP § 1380.

   i.   *Deposition.* Notwithstanding the general rule that matters outside the pleadings should ordinarily not be considered in passing upon a motion to strike under FRCP 12(f), a court may consider a deposition in deciding a FRCP 12(f) motion if the attorneys for both the plaintiff and the defendant, in their respective briefs, refer to the deposition and to the testimony contained therein. FEDPROC § 62:407.

   • *Materials necessary for motion.* A party must file those portions of discovery requests or responses (including deposition transcripts) that the party relies on to support a motion that could result in a final order on an issue. IN R USDCTND L.R. 26-2(c).

   ii.   *Notice of constitutional question.* A party that files a pleading, written motion, or other paper drawing into question the constitutionality of a federal or state statute must promptly:

   • *File notice.* File a notice of constitutional question stating the question and identifying the paper that raises it, if: (1) a federal statute is questioned and the parties do not include the United States, one of its agencies, or one of its officers or employees in an official capacity; or (2) a state statute is questioned and the parties do not include the state, one of its agencies, or one of its officers or employees in an official capacity; and

- *Serve notice.* Serve the notice and paper on the Attorney General of the United States if a federal statute is questioned—or on the state attorney general if a state statute is questioned—either by certified or registered mail or by sending it to an electronic address designated by the attorney general for this purpose. FRCP 5.1(a).

- *When to file the notice.* A party required to file a notice of constitutional question under FRCP 5.1 must do so by the later of: (1) the day the parties tender their proposed case-management plan (if one is required); or (2) 21 days after filing the pleading, written motion, or other paper questioning the constitutionality of a federal or state statute. IN R USDCTND L.R. 5.1-1(a).

- *Service on government officials.* The party must also serve the notice and the pleading, written motion, or other paper questioning the constitutionality of a federal or state statute on: (1) the Attorney General of the United States and the United States Attorney for the Northern District of Indiana, if a federal statute is challenged; or (2) the Attorney General for the state if a state statute is challenged. IN R USDCTND L.R. 5.1-1(b). Service required under IN R USDCTND L.R. 5.1-1(b) may be made either by certified or registered mail or by emailing it to an address designated by those officials for this purpose. IN R USDCTND L.R. 5.1-1(c).

- *No forfeiture.* A party's failure to file and serve the notice, or the court's failure to certify, does not forfeit a constitutional claim or defense that is otherwise timely asserted. FRCP 5.1(d).

iii. *Nongovernmental corporate disclosure statement*

- *Contents.* A nongovernmental corporate party must file two (2) copies of a disclosure statement that: (1) identifies any parent corporation and any publicly held corporation owning ten percent (10%) or more of its stock; or (2) states that there is no such corporation. FRCP 7.1(a).

- *Time to file; Supplemental filing.* A party must: (1) file the disclosure statement with its first appearance, pleading, petition, motion, response, or other request addressed to the court; and (2) promptly file a supplemental statement if any required information changes. FRCP 7.1(b).

iv. *Index of exhibits.* Any pleading, motion, brief, affidavit, notice, or proposed order, whether filed electronically or by delivering it to the clerk, must: include a separate index identifying and briefly describing each exhibit if there are more than four (4) exhibits. IN R USDCTND L.R. 5-4(a)(8).

v. *Request for oral argument.* A party may request oral argument on a motion by filing and serving a separate document explaining why oral argument is necessary and estimating how long the court should allow for the argument. IN R USDCTND L.R. 7-5(a)(1). The request must be filed and served with the party's supporting brief, response brief, or reply brief. IN R USDCTND L.R. 7-5(a)(2).

vi. *Request for evidentiary hearing.* A party may request an evidentiary hearing by filing and serving a separate document explaining why the hearing is necessary and estimating how long the court should allow for it. IN R USDCTND L.R. 7-5(b)(1).

vii. *Copy of authority.* A copy of any decision, statute, or regulation cited in a motion or brief must be attached to the paper if—and only if—it is not available on Westlaw or Lexis. But if a copy of a decision, statute, or regulation is only available electronically, a party must provide it to the court or another party upon request. IN R USDCTND L.R. 7-1(f).

viii. *Proposed order.* Parties filing a paper that requires the judge or clerk to enter a routine or uncontested order must include a suitable form of order. IN R USDCTND L.R. 5-4(c).

- Proposed orders shall not be filed electronically either as a separate document or as an attachment to the main pleading or other document. Instead, all proposed orders must be e-mailed to the chambers of the appropriate judicial officer for the case. The proposed order must be in WordPerfect Format or Rich Text Format (RTF). Proposed orders should be attached to an e-mail and sent to the appropriate judicial officer at the address listed in IN R USDCTND CM/ECF(II)(F). The subject line of the email message should indicate the case title, cause number and document number of the motion, e.g., Smith v. Jones 1:02-cv-1234, motion# ___. IN R USDCTND CM/ECF(II)(F).

ix. *Copy of document with self-addressed envelope.* A party who wants a file-stamped copy of a paper must include with the filing an additional copy of the paper and a self-addressed envelope with adequate postage. IN R USDCTND L.R. 5-4(b)(6).

x. *Notice of manual filing.* However, if that is not physically possible, counsel shall electronically file a .pdf document titled Notice of Manual Filing as a notation on the docket sheet that filings are being held in the clerk's office in paper. A sample Notice of Manual Filing is attached as Form 2 (IN R USDCTND CM/ECF(Form 2)). IN R USDCTND CM/ECF(III)(A)(1).

xi. *Courtesy copies.* If documents are filed in paper format, counsel must provide an original for the clerk's office, a copy for the judge and a copy must be served on all parties in the case. IN R USDCTND CM/ECF(III)(A)(1).

xii. *Declaration that party was unable to file in a timely manner.* If the attorney is unable to file a document in a timely manner due to technical difficulties in the user's system, the attorney must file a document with the court as soon as possible notifying the court of the inability to file the document. A sample document entitled Declaration that Party was Unable to File in a Timely Manner Due to Technical Difficulties is attached hereto as Form 5. IN R USDCTND CM/ECF(VI)(B). [Editor's note: the reference to Form 5 is likely meant to be a reference to Form 3 (IN R USDCTND CM/ECF(Form 3)].

2. *Documents for opposing party*

   a. *Required documents*

      i. *Response brief.* Refer to the Format section of this document for the format of briefs. Refer to the General Requirements section of this document for information on the opposing papers.

      ii. *Certificate of service.* FRCP 5(d) requires that the person making service under FRCP 5 certify that service has been effected. FRCP 5(Advisory Committee Notes). Having such information on file may be useful for many purposes, including proof of service if an issue arises concerning the effectiveness of the service. FRCP 5(Advisory Committee Notes).

         • *Certificate of service for electronically-filed documents.* A Certificate of Service is still a requirement when filing documents electronically. A sample Certificate of Service is attached as Form 1 (IN R USDCTND CM/ECF(Form 1)). IN R USDCTND CM/ECF(II)(H).

   b. *Supplemental documents.* Matter outside the pleadings normally is not considered on a FRCP 12(f) motion; for example, affidavits in support of or in opposition to the motion typically may not be used. FPP § 1380.

      i. *Deposition.* Notwithstanding the general rule that matters outside the pleadings should ordinarily not be considered in passing upon a motion to strike under FRCP 12(f), a court may consider a deposition in deciding a FRCP 12(f) motion if the attorneys for both the plaintiff and the defendant, in their respective briefs, refer to the deposition and to the testimony contained therein. FEDPROC § 62:407.

         • *Materials necessary for motion.* A party must file those portions of discovery requests or responses (including deposition transcripts) that the party relies on to support a motion that could result in a final order on an issue. IN R USDCTND L.R. 26-2(c).

      ii. *Notice of constitutional question.* A party that files a pleading, written motion, or other paper drawing into question the constitutionality of a federal or state statute must promptly:

         • *File notice.* File a notice of constitutional question stating the question and identifying the paper that raises it, if: (1) a federal statute is questioned and the parties do not include the United States, one of its agencies, or one of its officers or employees in an official capacity; or (2) a state statute is questioned and the parties do not include the state, one of its agencies, or one of its officers or employees in an official capacity; and

- *Serve notice.* Serve the notice and paper on the Attorney General of the United States if a federal statute is questioned—or on the state attorney general if a state statute is questioned—either by certified or registered mail or by sending it to an electronic address designated by the attorney general for this purpose. FRCP 5.1(a).

- *When to file the notice.* A party required to file a notice of constitutional question under FRCP 5.1 must do so by the later of: (1) the day the parties tender their proposed case-management plan (if one is required); or (2) 21 days after filing the pleading, written motion, or other paper questioning the constitutionality of a federal or state statute. IN R USDCTND L.R. 5.1-1(a).

- *Service on government officials.* The party must also serve the notice and the pleading, written motion, or other paper questioning the constitutionality of a federal or state statute on: (1) the Attorney General of the United States and the United States Attorney for the Northern District of Indiana, if a federal statute is challenged; or (2) the Attorney General for the state if a state statute is challenged. IN R USDCTND L.R. 5.1-1(b). Service required under IN R USDCTND L.R. 5.1-1(b) may be made either by certified or registered mail or by emailing it to an address designated by those officials for this purpose. IN R USDCTND L.R. 5.1-1(c).

- *No forfeiture.* A party's failure to file and serve the notice, or the court's failure to certify, does not forfeit a constitutional claim or defense that is otherwise timely asserted. FRCP 5.1(d).

iii. *Index of exhibits.* Any pleading, motion, brief, affidavit, notice, or proposed order, whether filed electronically or by delivering it to the clerk, must: include a separate index identifying and briefly describing each exhibit if there are more than four (4) exhibits. IN R USDCTND L.R. 5-4(a)(8).

iv. *Request for oral argument.* A party may request oral argument on a motion by filing and serving a separate document explaining why oral argument is necessary and estimating how long the court should allow for the argument. IN R USDCTND L.R. 7-5(a)(1). The request must be filed and served with the party's supporting brief, response brief, or reply brief. IN R USDCTND L.R. 7-5(a)(2).

v. *Request for evidentiary hearing.* A party may request an evidentiary hearing by filing and serving a separate document explaining why the hearing is necessary and estimating how long the court should allow for it. IN R USDCTND L.R. 7-5(b)(1).

vi. *Copy of authority.* A copy of any decision, statute, or regulation cited in a motion or brief must be attached to the paper if—and only if—it is not available on Westlaw or Lexis. But if a copy of a decision, statute, or regulation is only available electronically, a party must provide it to the court or another party upon request. IN R USDCTND L.R. 7-1(f).

vii. *Copy of document with self-addressed envelope.* A party who wants a file-stamped copy of a paper must include with the filing an additional copy of the paper and a self-addressed envelope with adequate postage. IN R USDCTND L.R. 5-4(b)(6).

viii. *Notice of manual filing.* However, if that is not physically possible, counsel shall electronically file a .pdf document titled Notice of Manual Filing as a notation on the docket sheet that filings are being held in the clerk's office in paper. A sample Notice of Manual Filing is attached as Form 2 (IN R USDCTND CM/ECF(Form 2)). IN R USDCTND CM/ECF(III)(A)(1).

ix. *Courtesy copies.* If documents are filed in paper format, counsel must provide an original for the clerk's office, a copy for the judge and a copy must be served on all parties in the case. IN R USDCTND CM/ECF(III)(A)(1).

x. *Declaration that party was unable to file in a timely manner.* If the attorney is unable to file a document in a timely manner due to technical difficulties in the user's system, the attorney must file a document with the court as soon as possible notifying the court of the inability to file the document. A sample document entitled Declaration that Party was Unable to File in a Timely Manner Due to Technical Difficulties is attached hereto as Form 5. IN R USDCTND

CM/ECF(VI)(B). [Editor's note: the reference to Form 5 is likely meant to be a reference to Form 3 (IN R USDCTND CM/ECF(Form 3)].

E. Format

1. *Form of documents.* The rules governing captions and other matters of form in pleadings apply to motions and other papers. FRCP 7(b)(2).

    a. *Paper.* Any pleading, motion, brief, affidavit, notice, or proposed order, whether filed electronically or by delivering it to the clerk, must: use eight and one-half by eleven (8-1/2 x 11) inch pages. IN R USDCTND L.R. 5-4(a)(2).

        i. *Manual filings.* Papers delivered to the clerk for filing must: be flat, unfolded, and on good-quality, white paper. IN R USDCTND L.R. 5-4(b)(1)(A).

            - *Covers or backing.* Papers delivered to the clerk for filing must: not have a cover or a back. IN R USDCTND L.R. 5-4(b)(1)(B).

            - *Recycled paper.* The court encourages using recycled paper. IN R USDCTND L.R. 5-4(b)(7).

    b. *Margins.* Any pleading, motion, brief, affidavit, notice, or proposed order, whether filed electronically or by delivering it to the clerk, must: have at least one (1) inch margins. IN R USDCTND L.R. 5-4(a)(3).

    c. *Spacing.* Any pleading, motion, brief, affidavit, notice, or proposed order, whether filed electronically or by delivering it to the clerk, must: be double spaced (except for headings, footnotes, and quoted material). IN R USDCTND L.R. 5-4(a)(5).

    d. *Text.* Any pleading, motion, brief, affidavit, notice, or proposed order, whether filed electronically or by delivering it to the clerk, must: be plainly typewritten, printed, or prepared by a clearly legible copying process. IN R USDCTND L.R. 5-4(a)(1).

        i. Any pleading, motion, brief, affidavit, notice, or proposed order, whether filed electronically or by delivering it to the clerk, must: use at least twelve (12) point type in the body and at least ten (10) point type in footnotes. IN R USDCTND L.R. 5-4(a)(4).

    e. *Page numbering.* Any pleading, motion, brief, affidavit, notice, or proposed order, whether filed electronically or by delivering it to the clerk, must: have consecutively numbered pages. IN R USDCTND L.R. 5-4(a)(6).

    f. *Caption; Names of parties.* Every pleading must have a caption with the court's name, a title, a file number, and a FRCP 7(a) designation. The title of the complaint must name all the parties; the title of other pleadings, after naming the first party on each side, may refer generally to other parties. FRCP 10(a). Any pleading, motion, brief, affidavit, notice, or proposed order, whether filed electronically or by delivering it to the clerk, must: include a title on the first page. IN R USDCTND L.R. 5-4(a)(7).

        i. *Alternative motions.* Motions must be filed separately, but alternative motions may be filed in a single paper if each is named in the title following the caption. IN R USDCTND L.R. 7-1(a).

    g. *Filer's information.* Any pleading, motion, brief, affidavit, notice, or proposed order, whether filed electronically or by delivering it to the clerk, must: except in proposed orders and affidavits, include the filer's name, address, telephone number, fax number (where available), and e-mail address (where available). IN R USDCTND L.R. 5-4(a)(9).

    h. *Paragraphs; Separate statements.* A party must state its claims or defenses in numbered paragraphs, each limited as far as practicable to a single set of circumstances. A later pleading may refer by number to a paragraph in an earlier pleading. If doing so would promote clarity, each claim founded on a separate transaction or occurrence—and each defense other than a denial—must be stated in a separate count or defense. FRCP 10(b).

    i. *Adoption by reference; Exhibits.* A statement in a pleading may be adopted by reference elsewhere in the same pleading or in any other pleading or motion. A copy of a written instrument that is an exhibit to a pleading is a part of the pleading for all purposes. FRCP 10(c).

j. *Citation of local rules.* The Local Civil Rules of the United States District Court for the Northern District of Indiana may be cited as "N.D. Ind. L.R." IN R USDCTND L.R. 1-1(a)(1).

k. *Acceptance by the clerk.* The clerk must not refuse to file a paper solely because it is not in the form prescribed by the Federal Rules of Civil Procedure or by a local rule or practice. FRCP 5(d)(4).

   i. *Sanctions for formatting errors; Non-compliance.* If a person files a paper that does not comply with the rules governing the format of papers filed with the court, the court may: (1) strike the paper from the record; or (2) fine the person up to one thousand dollars ($1,000). IN R USDCTND L.R. 1-3(a).

   - *Notice.* Before sanctioning a person under IN R USDCTND L.R. 1-3(a)(2), the court must: (1) notify the person that the paper is noncompliant; and (2) give the person the opportunity either to be heard or to revise the paper. IN R USDCTND L.R. 1-3(b).

2. *Form of electronic documents.* Electronically filed documents must meet the same requirements of format and page limits as documents "conventionally filed" (as defined in IN R USDCTND CM/ECF(III)(A)) pursuant to the Federal Rules of Civil Procedure and the Local Civil Rules of the United States District Court for the Northern District of Indiana. IN R USDCTND CM/ECF(II)(A)(2).

a. *PDF format required.* Documents filed in the CM/ECF must be in .pdf format. A document created with almost any word-processing program can be converted to .pdf format. The .pdf program in effect takes a picture of the original document and allows anyone to open the converted document across a broad range of hardware and software, with layout, format, links, and images intact. IN R USDCTND CM/ECF(FN2).

b. *Title of documents.* The person electronically filing a pleading or other document will be responsible for designating a title for the pleading or other document by using one of the categories contained in the events listed in the CM/ECF Menu. IN R USDCTND CM/ECF(II)(G).

c. *Combining documents.* All documents which form part of a single pleading and which are being filed at the same time and by the same party may be electronically filed together under one document number, e.g., the motion and a supporting affidavit, with the exception of memoranda in support. Memoranda in support shall be electronically filed separately and shown as a related document to the motion. IN R USDCTND CM/ECF(II)(A)(4).

d. *Exhibits and attachments.* Filing users must submit in electronic form all documents referenced as exhibits or attachments, unless the court permits conventional filing. A filing user must submit as exhibits or attachments only those excerpts of the referenced documents that are directly germane to the matter under consideration by the court. Excerpted material must be clearly and prominently identified as such. Filing users who file excerpts of documents as exhibits or attachments do so without prejudice to their right to timely file additional excerpts or the complete document. Responding parties may timely file additional excerpts or the complete document that they believe are directly germane. The court may require parties to file additional excerpts or the complete document. IN R USDCTND CM/ECF(II)(A)(6).

e. *Hyperlinks.* Electronically filed documents may contain hyperlink references to an external document as a convenient mechanism for accessing material cited in the document. A hyperlink reference is neither validated for content nor considered a part of the court's records. The court neither endorses the product or organization at the destination of a hyperlink reference, nor does the court exercise any responsibility over the content at the destination. In order to preserve the integrity of the court record, attorneys wishing to insert hyperlinks in court filings shall continue to use the traditional citation method for the cited authority, in addition to the hyperlink. A hyperlink contained in a filing is no more than a convenient mechanism for accessing material cited in the document and a hyperlink reference is extraneous to any filed document and is not part of the court's record. IN R USDCTND CM/ECF(II)(A)(3).

3. *Form of briefs*

a. *Page limits.* Supporting and response briefs (excluding tables of contents, tables of authorities, and appendices) ordinarily must not exceed twenty-five (25) pages. Reply briefs must not exceed fifteen (15) pages. IN R USDCTND L.R. 7-1(e)(1).

   i. *Exception.* The court may allow a party to file a brief exceeding these page limits for extraordinary and compelling reasons. But if the court permits a brief to exceed twenty-five (25) pages, it must include:

- A table of contents with page references;
- An issue statement; and
- A table of authorities including: (1) all cases (alphabetically arranged), statutes, and other authorities cited in the brief; and (2) references to where the authorities appear in the brief. IN R USDCTND L.R. 7-1(e)(2).

4. *Signing of pleadings, motions and other papers*

   a. *Signature.* Every pleading, written motion, and other paper must be signed by at least one attorney of record in the attorney's name—or by a party personally if the party is unrepresented. The paper must state the signer's address, e-mail address, and telephone number. FRCP 11(a).

      i. *Signatures on manual filings.* Papers delivered to the clerk for filing must: include the filer's original signature. IN R USDCTND L.R. 5-4(b)(1)(C).

         - *Rubber-stamped and faxed signatures.* An original paper with a rubber-stamped or faxed signature is unsigned for purposes of FRCP 11 and FRCP 26(g). IN R USDCTND L.R. 5-4(b)(2).

         - *Affidavits.* Only the affiant need sign an affidavit. IN R USDCTND L.R. 5-4(b)(3).

      ii. *Electronic signatures.* Pursuant to FRCP 11, every pleading, motion, and other paper (except lists, schedules, statements or amendments thereto) shall be signed by at least one attorney of record or, if the party is not represented by an attorney, all papers shall be signed by the party. An attorney's/participant's password issued by the court combined with the user's identification, serves as and constitutes the attorney/participant's signature for FRCP 11 and other purposes. IN R USDCTND CM/ECF(I)(C). Documents which must be filed and which must contain original signatures other than those of a participating attorney or which require either verification or an unsworn declaration under any rule or statute, shall be filed electronically, with originally executed copies maintained by the filer. The pleading or other document electronically filed shall contain "s/" signature(s), as noted in IN R USDCTND CM/ECF(II)(E)(3)(b). IN R USDCTND CM/ECF(II)(E)(1).

         - *Multiple signatures.* In the case of a stipulation or other document to be signed by two or more attorneys, the following procedure should be used: The filing attorney shall initially confirm that the content of the document is acceptable to all persons required to sign the document and shall obtain the physical signatures of all attorneys on the document. IN R USDCTND CM/ECF(II)(E)(3)(a). The filing attorney then shall file the document electronically, indicating the signatories, e.g., "s/Jane Doe," "s/John Doe," etc. IN R US-DCTND CM/ECF(II)(E)(3)(b). The filing attorney shall retain the hard copy of the document containing the original signatures. IN R USDCTND CM/ECF(II)(E)(3)(c).

     iii. *No verification or accompanying affidavit required for pleadings.* Unless a rule or statute specifically states otherwise, a pleading need not be verified or accompanied by an affidavit. FRCP 11(a).

     iv. *Unsigned papers.* The court must strike an unsigned paper unless the omission is promptly corrected after being called to the attorney's or party's attention. FRCP 11(a).

   b. *Representations to the court.* By presenting to the court a pleading, written motion, or other paper—whether by signing, filing, submitting, or later advocating it—an attorney or unrepresented party certifies that to the best of the person's knowledge, information, and belief, formed after an inquiry reasonable under the circumstances:

      i. It is not being presented for any improper purpose, such as to harass, cause unnecessary delay, or needlessly increase the cost of litigation;

      ii. The claims, defenses, and other legal contentions are warranted by existing law or by a nonfrivolous argument for extending, modifying, or reversing existing law or for establishing new law;

  iii. The factual contentions have evidentiary support or, if specifically so identified, will likely have evidentiary support after a reasonable opportunity for further investigation or discovery; and

  iv. The denials of factual contentions are warranted on the evidence or, if specifically so identified, are reasonably based on belief or a lack of information. FRCP 11(b).

 c. *Sanctions.* If, after notice and a reasonable opportunity to respond, the court determines that FRCP 11(b) has been violated, the court may impose an appropriate sanction on any attorney, law firm, or party that violated FRCP 11(b) or is responsible for the violation. FRCP 11(c)(1). Refer to the United States District Court for the Northern District of Indiana KeyRules Motion for Sanctions document for more information.

5. *Privacy protection for filings made with the court*

 a. *Redacted filings.* Counsel should not include sensitive information in any document filed with the court unless such inclusion is necessary and relevant to the case. IN R USDCTND CM/ECF(VII). Unless the court orders otherwise, in an electronic or paper filing with the court that contains an individual's Social Security number, taxpayer-identification number, or birth date, the name of an individual known to be a minor, or a financial-account number, a party or nonparty making the filing may include only:

  i. The last four (4) digits of the Social Security number and taxpayer-identification number;

  ii. The year of the individual's birth;

  iii. The minor's initials; and

  iv. The last four (4) digits of the financial-account number. FRCP 5.2(a); IN R USDCTND Order 2005-3.

 b. *Exemptions from the redaction requirement.* The redaction requirement does not apply to the following:

  i. A financial-account number that identifies the property allegedly subject to forfeiture in a forfeiture proceeding;

  ii. The record of an administrative or agency proceeding;

  iii. The official record of a state-court proceeding;

  iv. The record of a court or tribunal, if that record was not subject to the redaction requirement when originally filed;

  v. A filing covered by FRCP 5.2(c) or FRCP 5.2(d); and

  vi. A pro se filing in an action brought under 28 U.S.C.A. § 2241, 28 U.S.C.A. § 2254, or 28 U.S.C.A. § 2255. FRCP 5.2(b).

  vii. In cases filed under the Social Security Act, 42 U.S.C.A. § 405(g), there is no need for redaction of any information from the documents filed in the case. IN R USDCTND Order 2005-3.

 c. *Limitations on remote access to electronic files; Social Security appeals and immigration cases.* Unless the court orders otherwise, in an action for benefits under the Social Security Act, and in an action or proceeding relating to an order of removal, to relief from removal, or to immigration benefits or detention, access to an electronic file is authorized as follows:

  i. The parties and their attorneys may have remote electronic access to any part of the case file, including the administrative record;

  ii. Any other person may have electronic access to the full record at the courthouse, but may have remote electronic access only to:

   • The docket maintained by the court; and

   • An opinion, order, judgment, or other disposition of the court, but not any other part of the case file or the administrative record. FRCP 5.2(c).

 d. *Filings made under seal.* The court may order that a filing be made under seal without redaction. The court may later unseal the filing or order the person who made the filing to file a redacted version for the public record. FRCP 5.2(d). For information on filing documents under seal, refer to IN R USDCTND L.R. 5-3, IN R USDCTND CM/ECF(IV)(A), and IN R USDCTND ECF Order 2004-19.

e. *Protective orders.* For good cause, the court may by order in a case:

    i. Require redaction of additional information; or

    ii. Limit or prohibit a nonparty's remote electronic access to a document filed with the court. FRCP 5.2(e).

f. *Option for additional unredacted filing under seal.* A person making a redacted filing may also file an unredacted copy under seal. The court must retain the unredacted copy as part of the record. FRCP 5.2(f); IN R USDCTND Order 2005-3.

    i. The unredacted version of the document or the reference list shall be retained by the court under seal as part of the record. This paper shall be retained by the court as part of the record. The court may, however, still require the party to file a redacted copy for the public file. IN R USDCTND Order 2005-3.

g. *Option for filing a reference list.* A filing that contains redacted information may be filed together with a reference list that identifies each item of redacted information and specifies an appropriate identifier that uniquely corresponds to each item listed. The list must be filed under seal and may be amended as of right. Any reference in the case to a listed identifier will be construed to refer to the corresponding item of information. FRCP 5.2(g); IN R USDCTND Order 2005-3.

    i. The unredacted version of the document or the reference list shall be retained by the court under seal as part of the record. This paper shall be retained by the court as part of the record. The court may, however, still require the party to file a redacted copy for the public file. IN R USDCTND Order 2005-3.

h. *Responsibility for redaction.* The responsibility for redacting these personal identifiers rests solely with counsel and the parties. The Clerk will not review each paper for compliance with IN R USDCTND Order 2005-3. IN R USDCTND Order 2005-3.

i. *Waiver of protection of identifiers.* A person waives the protection of FRCP 5.2(a) as to the person's own information by filing it without redaction and not under seal. FRCP 5.2(h).

F. Filing and Service Requirements

1. *Filing requirements.* Any paper after the complaint that is required to be served—together with a certificate of service—must be filed within a reasonable time after service. FRCP 5(d)(1). Motions must be filed separately, but alternative motions may be filed in a single paper if each is named in the title following the caption. IN R USDCTND L.R. 7-1(a).

a. *How filing is made; In general.* A paper is filed by delivering it:

    i. To the clerk; or

    ii. To a judge who agrees to accept it for filing, and who must then note the filing date on the paper and promptly send it to the clerk. FRCP 5(d)(2).

       • Papers not filed electronically must be filed with the clerk, not a judge. IN R USDCTND L.R. 5-4(b)(4).

    iii. Parties manually filing a paper that requires the clerk to give others notice, must give the clerk: (1) sufficient copies of the notice; and (2) the name and address of each person entitled to receive the notice. IN R USDCTND L.R. 5-4(b)(8).

b. *Where to file.* Papers not filed electronically must be filed in the division where the case is pending, unless: (1) a person will be prejudiced if the paper is not filed the same day it is tendered; and (2) it includes an adequately sized envelope addressed to the clerk's office in the division where the case is pending and with adequate postage. IN R USDCTND L.R. 5-4(b)(5).

c. *Electronic filing*

    i. *Authorization of electronic filing program.* A court may, by local rule, allow papers to be filed,

signed, or verified by electronic means that are consistent with any technical standards established by the Judicial Conference of the United States. A local rule may require electronic filing only if reasonable exceptions are allowed. A paper filed electronically in compliance with a local rule is a written paper for purposes of the Federal Rules of Civil Procedure. FRCP 5(d)(3).

- Papers must be filed, signed, and verified electronically unless excepted by the court's CM/ECF Civil and Criminal User Manual (IN R USDCTND CM/ECF). IN R USDCTND L.R. 5-1.

ii. *Mandatory electronic filing.* Unless otherwise permitted by these procedures or otherwise authorized by the assigned judge, all documents submitted for filing in this district in civil and criminal cases, no matter when a case was originally filed, shall be filed electronically using the System. IN R USDCTND CM/ECF(II)(A)(1). The requirement that "all documents" be filed electronically includes briefs, and attachments and exhibits used in support of motions. IN R USDCTND CM/ECF(FN1).

- Sending a document or pleading to the court via e-mail or facsimile does not constitute "electronic filing." IN R USDCTND CM/ECF(I)(A).

iii. *Conventional filing.* As used in these procedures, a "conventionally" filed or submitted document or pleading is one presented to the Clerk or a party in paper or other non-electronic, tangible format. The following documents shall be filed conventionally and not electronically unless specifically authorized by the Court:

- Exhibits and other documents which cannot be converted to a legible electronic form. Whenever possible, counsel is responsible for converting filings to an electronic form. However, if that is not physically possible, counsel shall electronically file a .pdf document titled Notice of Manual Filing as a notation on the docket sheet that filings are being held in the clerk's office in paper. A sample Notice of Manual Filing is attached as Form 2 (IN R USDCTND CM/ECF(Form 2)). If documents are filed in paper format, counsel must provide an original for the clerk's office, a copy for the judge and a copy must be served on all parties in the case. Large documents which do not exist in an electronic format shall be scanned into .pdf format by counsel, in small batches if necessary, and filed electronically as separate attachments in the System. IN R USDCTND CM/ECF(III)(A)(1).

- Certain documents which are listed in IN R USDCTND CM/ECF(II)(E)(2). IN R USDCTND CM/ECF(III)(A)(2).

- Documents filed by pro se litigants. IN R USDCTND CM/ECF(III)(A)(3).

iv. For more information on electronic filing, refer to IN R USDCTND CM/ECF.

2. *Service requirements*

a. *Service; When required*

i. *In general.* Unless the Federal Rules of Civil Procedure provide otherwise, each of the following papers must be served on every party:

- An order stating that service is required;

- A pleading filed after the original complaint, unless the court orders otherwise under FRCP 5(c) because there are numerous defendants;

- A discovery paper required to be served on a party, unless the court orders otherwise;

- A written motion, except one that may be heard ex parte; and

- A written notice, appearance, demand, or offer of judgment, or any similar paper. FRCP 5(a)(1).

ii. *If a party fails to appear.* No service is required on a party who is in default for failing to appear. But a pleading that asserts a new claim for relief against such a party must be served on that party under FRCP 4. FRCP 5(a)(2).

   iii. *Seizing property.* If an action is begun by seizing property and no person is or need be named as a defendant, any service required before the filing of an appearance, answer, or claim must be made on the person who had custody or possession of the property when it was seized. FRCP 5(a)(3).

b. *Service; How made*

   i. *Serving an attorney.* If a party is represented by an attorney, service under FRCP 5 must be made on the attorney unless the court orders service on the party. FRCP 5(b)(1).

   ii. *Service in general.* A paper is served under FRCP 5 by:

- Handing it to the person;

- Leaving it: (1) at the person's office with a clerk or other person in charge or, if no one is in charge, in a conspicuous place in the office; or (2) if the person has no office or the office is closed, at the person's dwelling or usual place of abode with someone of suitable age and discretion who resides there;

- Mailing it to the person's last known address—in which event service is complete upon mailing;

- Leaving it with the court clerk if the person has no known address;

- Sending it by electronic means if the person consented in writing—in which event service is complete upon transmission, but is not effective if the serving party learns that it did not reach the person to be served; or

- Delivering it by any other means that the person consented to in writing—in which event service is complete when the person making service delivers it to the agency designated to make delivery. FRCP 5(b)(2).

   iii. *Electronic service.* Electronically filed papers may be served electronically if service is consistent with the CM/ECF User Manual (IN R USDCTND CM/ECF). IN R USDCTND L.R. 5-2(a).

- *Waiver of other service.* An attorney's registration will constitute a waiver of conventional service of documents and the attorney agrees to accept service of notice on behalf of the client of the electronic filing by hand, facsimile or authorized email. IN R USDCTND CM/ECF(I)(B)(3).

- *Serving registered persons.* The System will generate a "Notice of Electronic Filing" when any document is filed. This notice represents service of the document on parties who are registered participants with the System. Except as provided in IN R USDCTND CM/ECF(III)(B), the filing party shall not be required to serve any pleading or other documents on any party receiving electronic notice. IN R USDCTND CM/ECF(II)(D)(1). The term "pleading" refers only to those documents listed in FRCP 7(a). IN R USDCTND CM/ECF(FN3).

- *When electronic service is deemed completed.* A person registered to use the court's electronic-filing system is served with an electronically filed paper when a "Notice of Electronic Filing" is transmitted to that person through the court's electronic filing-system. IN R USDCTND L.R. 5-2(b).

- *Serving non-registered persons.* A person who has not registered to use the court's electronic-filing system but who is entitled to service of a paper must be served according to the Local Civil Rules of the United States District Court for the Northern District of Indiana and the Federal Rules of Civil Procedure. IN R USDCTND L.R. 5-2(c); IN R USDCTND CM/ECF(II)(D)(2). If such service of a paper copy is to be made, it shall be done in the manner provided in the Federal Rules of Civil Procedure and the Local Civil Rules of the United States District Court for the Northern District of Indiana. IN R USDCTND CM/ECF(II)(D)(2).

   iv. *Service of conventional filings.* Pleadings or other documents which are filed conventionally rather than electronically shall be served in the manner provided for in the Federal Rules of

Civil Procedure and the Local Civil Rules of the United States District Court for the Northern District of Indiana, except as otherwise provided by order of the Court. IN R USDCTND CM/ECF(III)(B).

    v. *Using court facilities.* If a local rule so authorizes, a party may use the court's transmission facilities to make service under FRCP 5(b)(2)(E). FRCP 5(b)(3).

  c. *Serving numerous defendants*

    i. *In general.* If an action involves an unusually large number of defendants, the court may, on motion or on its own, order that:

- Defendants' pleadings and replies to them need not be served on other defendants;

- Any crossclaim, counterclaim, avoidance, or affirmative defense in those pleadings and replies to them will be treated as denied or avoided by all other parties; and

- Filing any such pleading and serving it on the plaintiff constitutes notice of the pleading to all parties. FRCP 5(c)(1).

    ii. *Notifying parties.* A copy of every such order must be served on the parties as the court directs. FRCP 5(c)(2).

G. Hearings

1. *Hearings, generally*

  a. *Oral argument.* Due process does not require that oral argument be permitted on a motion and, except as otherwise provided by local rule, the district court has discretion to determine whether it will decide the motion on the papers or hear argument by counsel (and perhaps receive evidence). FPP § 1190; F.D.I.C. v. Deglau, 207 F.3d 153 (3d Cir. 2000).

    i. *Request for oral argument.* A party may request oral argument on a motion by filing and serving a separate document explaining why oral argument is necessary and estimating how long the court should allow for the argument. IN R USDCTND L.R. 7-5(a)(1). Refer to the Documents section of this document for more information.

    ii. *Additional evidence forbidden.* Parties may not present additional evidence at oral argument. IN R USDCTND L.R. 7-5(a)(3).

  b. *Providing a regular schedule for oral hearings.* A court may establish regular times and places for oral hearings on motions. FRCP 78(a).

  c. *Providing for submission on briefs.* By rule or order, the court may provide for submitting and determining motions on briefs, without oral hearings. FRCP 78(b).

  d. *Evidentiary hearings.* A party may request an evidentiary hearing by filing and serving a separate document explaining why the hearing is necessary and estimating how long the court should allow for it. IN R USDCTND L.R. 7-5(b)(2). Refer to the Documents section of this document for more information.

  e. *Court's authority.* The court may: (1) grant or deny a request for oral argument or an evidentiary hearing in its discretion; (2) set oral argument or an evidentiary hearing without a request from a party; or (3) order any oral argument or evidentiary hearing to be held anywhere within the district regardless of where the case will be tried. IN R USDCTND L.R. 7-5(c).

2. *Courtroom and courthouse decorum.* For information on courtroom and courthouse decorum, refer to IN R USDCTND L.R. 83-3.

H. Forms

1. Federal Motion to Strike Forms

  a. Motion; By plaintiff; To strike insufficient defense from answer. AMJUR PP FEDPRAC § 441.

  b. Motion; To strike redundant, immaterial, impertinent, or scandalous matter from pleading. AMJUR PP FEDPRAC § 442.

  c. Motion; To strike portions of complaint. AMJUR PP FEDPRAC § 444.

d. Motion to strike insufficient affirmative defenses. 2C FEDFORMS § 11:151.

e. Motion to strike insufficient defense in answer; Stating particular reason. 2C FEDFORMS § 11:153.

f. Notice of motion and motion to strike insufficient affirmative defense. 2C FEDFORMS § 11:155.

g. Motion to strike impertinence and scandal. 2C FEDFORMS § 11:157.

h. Motion to strike impertinence and immateriality. 2C FEDFORMS § 11:158.

i. Motion to strike redundancy and scandal. 2C FEDFORMS § 11:159.

j. Motion to strike immaterial defense. 2C FEDFORMS § 11:160.

k. Motion to strike for immateriality. 2C FEDFORMS § 11:161.

l. Motion to strike counterclaim for lack of evidence. 2C FEDFORMS § 11:162.

m. Opposition; To motion; General form. FEDPROF § 1:750.

n. Affidavit; Supporting or opposing motion. FEDPROF § 1:751.

o. Brief; Supporting or opposing motion. FEDPROF § 1:752.

p. Statement of points and authorities; Opposing motion. FEDPROF § 1:753.

q. Motion; To strike material outside statute of limitations. FEDPROF § 1:773.

r. Opposition to motion; Material not contained in pleading. FEDPROF § 1:774.

s. General form. GOLDLTGFMS § 20:8.

t. General form; Federal form. GOLDLTGFMS § 20:10.

u. Notice and motion to strike immaterial, redundant or scandalous matter. GOLDLTGFMS § 20:13.

v. Motion to strike complaint and dismiss action as to one defendant. GOLDLTGFMS § 20:14.

w. Defendant's motion to strike. GOLDLTGFMS § 20:16.

x. Defendant's motion to strike; Plaintiff's response. GOLDLTGFMS § 20:17.

y. Motion to strike answer. GOLDLTGFMS § 20:19.

z. Objections to motion to strike. GOLDLTGFMS § 20:20.

2. Forms for the Northern District of Indiana

a. Certificate of service. IN R USDCTND CM/ECF(Form 1).

b. Notice of manual filing. IN R USDCTND CM/ECF(Form 2).

c. Declaration that party was unable to file in a timely manner. IN R USDCTND CM/ECF(Form 3).

I. Applicable Rules

1. *Federal rules*

a. Serving and filing pleadings and other papers. FRCP 5.

b. Constitutional challenge to a statute; Notice, certification, and intervention. FRCP 5.1.

c. Privacy protection for filings made with the court. FRCP 5.2.

d. Computing and extending time; Time for motion papers. FRCP 6.

e. Pleadings allowed; Form of motions and other papers. FRCP 7.

f. Disclosure statement. FRCP 7.1.

g. Form of pleadings. FRCP 10.

h. Signing pleadings, motions, and other papers; Representations to the court; Sanctions. FRCP 11.

i. Defenses and objections; When and how presented; Motion for judgment on the pleadings; Consolidating motions; Waiving defenses; Pretrial hearing. FRCP 12.

j. Hearing motions; Submission on briefs. FRCP 78.

2. *Local rules*

a. Citation and scope of the rules. IN R USDCTND L.R. 1-1.

b. Sanctions for formatting errors. IN R USDCTND L.R. 1-3.

c. Electronic filing required. IN R USDCTND L.R. 5-1.

d. Constitutional questions. IN R USDCTND L.R. 5.1-1.

e. Electronic service. IN R USDCTND L.R. 5-2.

f. Format of papers. IN R USDCTND L.R. 5-4.

g. Motion practice. IN R USDCTND L.R. 7-1.

h. Oral arguments and evidentiary hearings. IN R USDCTND L.R. 7-5.

i. Pretrial procedure. IN R USDCTND L.R. 16-1.

j. Alternative dispute resolution. IN R USDCTND L.R. 16-6.

k. Filing of discovery and other materials. IN R USDCTND L.R. 26-2.

l. Case assignment. IN R USDCTND L.R. 40-1.

m. Appearance and withdrawal of appearance. IN R USDCTND L.R. 83-8.

n. CM/ECF civil and criminal user manual. IN R USDCTND CM/ECF.

o. In re: privacy and public access to civil electronic case files. IN R USDCTND Order 2005-3.

Motions, Oppositions and Replies
Motion to Dismiss for Improper Venue

Document Last Updated December 2016

A. Checklist

(I) ❑ Matters to be considered by moving party

   (a) ❑ Required documents

      (1) ❑ Notice of motion and motion

      (2) ❑ Brief

      (3) ❑ Certificate of service

   (b) ❑ Supplemental documents

      (1) ❑ Supporting evidence

      (2) ❑ Notice of constitutional question

      (3) ❑ Nongovernmental corporate disclosure statement

      (4) ❑ Index of exhibits

      (5) ❑ Request for oral argument

      (6) ❑ Request for evidentiary hearing

      (7) ❑ Copy of authority

      (8) ❑ Proposed order

      (9) ❑ Copy of document with self-addressed envelope

     (10) ❑ Notice of manual filing

     (11) ❑ Courtesy copies

     (12) ❑ Declaration that party was unable to file in a timely manner

   (c) ❑ Timing

      (1) ❑ Every defense to a claim for relief in any pleading must be asserted in the responsive pleading if one is required

(2) ❑ A motion asserting any of the defenses in FRCP 12(b) must be made before pleading if a responsive pleading is allowed

(3) ❑ If a pleading sets out a claim for relief that does not require a responsive pleading, an opposing party may assert at trial any defense to that claim

(4) ❑ A written motion and notice of the hearing must be served at least fourteen (14) days before the time specified for the hearing, with the following exceptions: (i) when the motion may be heard ex parte; (ii) when the Federal Rules of Civil Procedure set a different time; or (iii) when a court order—which a party may, for good cause, apply for ex parte—sets a different time

(5) ❑ Any affidavit supporting a motion must be served with the motion

(II) ❑ Matters to be considered by opposing party

   (a) ❑ Required documents

      (1) ❑ Response brief

      (2) ❑ Certificate of service

   (b) ❑ Supplemental documents

      (1) ❑ Supporting evidence

      (2) ❑ Notice of constitutional question

      (3) ❑ Index of exhibits

      (4) ❑ Request for oral argument

      (5) ❑ Request for evidentiary hearing

      (6) ❑ Copy of authority

      (7) ❑ Copy of document with self-addressed envelope

      (8) ❑ Notice of manual filing

      (9) ❑ Courtesy copies

     (10) ❑ Declaration that party was unable to file in a timely manner

   (c) ❑ Timing

      (1) ❑ A party must file any response brief to a motion within fourteen (14) days after the motion is served

      (2) ❑ Except as FRCP 59(c) provides otherwise, any opposing affidavit must be served at least seven (7) days before the hearing, unless the court permits service at another time

B. Timing

1. *Motion to dismiss for improper venue*

   a. *In a responsive pleading.* Every defense to a claim for relief in any pleading must be asserted in the responsive pleading if one is required. FRCP 12(b).

   b. *By motion.* A motion asserting any of the defenses in FRCP 12(b) must be made before pleading if a responsive pleading is allowed. FRCP 12(b). Although FRCP 12(b) encourages the responsive pleader to file a motion to dismiss before filing the answer, nothing in FRCP 12 prohibits the filing of a motion to dismiss with the answer. An untimely motion to dismiss may be considered if the defense asserted in the motion was previously raised in the responsive pleading. FEDPROC § 62:427.

   c. *At trial.* If a pleading sets out a claim for relief that does not require a responsive pleading, an opposing party may assert at trial any defense to that claim. FRCP 12(b).

2. *Timing of motions, generally*

   a. *Motion and notice of hearing.* A written motion and notice of the hearing must be served at least fourteen (14) days before the time specified for the hearing, with the following exceptions:

     i. When the motion may be heard ex parte;

    ii.   When the Federal Rules of Civil Procedure set a different time; or

    iii.   When a court order—which a party may, for good cause, apply for ex parte—sets a different time. FRCP 6(c)(1).

  b.   *Supporting affidavit.* Any affidavit supporting a motion must be served with the motion. FRCP 6(c)(2).

3.   *Timing of opposing papers.* A party must file any response brief to a motion within fourteen (14) days after the motion is served. IN R USDCTND L.R. 7-1(d)(2)(A).

  a.   *Opposing affidavit.* Except as FRCP 59(c) provides otherwise, any opposing affidavit must be served at least seven (7) days before the hearing, unless the court permits service at another time. FRCP 6(c)(2).

  b.   *Extensions.* The court may extend response- and reply-brief deadlines, but only for good cause. IN R USDCTND L.R. 7-1(d)(3).

  c.   *Summary rulings.* The court may rule on a motion summarily if an opposing party does not file a response before the deadline. IN R USDCTND L.R. 7-1(d)(4).

4.   *Timing of reply papers.* Where the respondent files an answering affidavit setting up a new matter, the moving party ordinarily is allowed a reasonable time to file a reply affidavit since failure to deny the new matter by affidavit may operate as an admission of its truth. AMJUR MOTIONS § 25.

  a.   *Reply brief.* The moving party must file any reply brief within seven (7) days after the response brief is served. IN R USDCTND L.R. 7-1(d)(2)(B).

  b.   *Extensions.* The court may extend response- and reply-brief deadlines, but only for good cause. IN R USDCTND L.R. 7-1(d)(3).

5.   *Effect of a FRCP 12 motion on the time to serve a responsive pleading.* Unless the court sets a different time, serving a motion under FRCP 12 alters the periods in FRCP 12(a) as follows:

  a.   If the court denies the motion or postpones its disposition until trial, the responsive pleading must be served within fourteen (14) days after notice of the court's action; or

  b.   If the court grants a motion for a more definite statement, the responsive pleading must be served within fourteen (14) days after the more definite statement is served. FRCP 12(a)(4).

6.   *Computation of time*

  a.   *Computing time.* FRCP 6 applies in computing any time period specified in the Federal Rules of Civil Procedure, in any local rule or court order, or in any statute that does not specify a method of computing time. FRCP 6(a).

    i.   *Period stated in days or a longer unit.* When the period is stated in days or a longer unit of time:

- Exclude the day of the event that triggers the period;

- Count every day, including intermediate Saturdays, Sundays, and legal holidays; and

- Include the last day of the period, but if the last day is a Saturday, Sunday, or legal holiday, the period continues to run until the end of the next day that is not a Saturday, Sunday, or legal holiday. FRCP 6(a)(1).

    ii.   *Period stated in hours.* When the period is stated in hours:

- Begin counting immediately on the occurrence of the event that triggers the period;

- Count every hour, including hours during intermediate Saturdays, Sundays, and legal holidays; and

- If the period would end on a Saturday, Sunday, or legal holiday, the period continues to run until the same time on the next day that is not a Saturday, Sunday, or legal holiday. FRCP 6(a)(2).

    iii.   *Inaccessibility of the clerk's office.* Unless the court orders otherwise, if the clerk's office is inaccessible:

- On the last day for filing under FRCP 6(a)(1), then the time for filing is extended to the first accessible day that is not a Saturday, Sunday, or legal holiday; or

- During the last hour for filing under FRCP 6(a)(2), then the time for filing is extended to the same time on the first accessible day that is not a Saturday, Sunday, or legal holiday. FRCP 6(a)(3).

iv. *"Last day" defined.* Unless a different time is set by a statute, local rule, or court order, the last day ends:

- For electronic filing, at midnight in the court's time zone; and

- For filing by other means, when the clerk's office is scheduled to close. FRCP 6(a)(4).

v. *"Next day" defined.* The "next day" is determined by continuing to count forward when the period is measured after an event and backward when measured before an event. FRCP 6(a)(5).

vi. *"Legal holiday" defined.* "Legal holiday" means:

- The day set aside by statute for observing New Year's Day, Martin Luther King Jr.'s Birthday, Washington's Birthday, Memorial Day, Independence Day, Labor Day, Columbus Day, Veterans' Day, Thanksgiving Day, or Christmas Day;

- Any day declared a holiday by the President or Congress; and

- For periods that are measured after an event, any other day declared a holiday by the state where the district court is located. FRCP 6(a)(6).

b. *Computation of electronic filing deadlines.* Filing documents electronically does not alter any filing deadlines or any time computation pursuant to FRCP 6. The counties of Lake, Porter, LaPorte, Pulaski and Starke are located in the Central time zone and the remaining counties in the Northern District of Indiana are located in the Eastern time zone. Nevertheless, all electronic transmissions of documents must be completed (i.e., received completely by the clerk's office) prior to midnight Eastern Time, (South Bend/Fort Wayne/Lafayette time) in order to be considered timely filed that day, regardless of the local time in the division where the case is pending. Although documents can be filed electronically twenty-four (24) hours a day, filers are strongly encouraged to file all documents during hours when the CM/ECF Help Line is available, from 9:00 a.m. to 4:00 p.m. local time. IN R USDCTND CM/ECF(II)(I).

i. *Technical failures.* If the attorney is unable to file a document in a timely manner due to technical difficulties in the user's system, the attorney must file a document with the court as soon as possible notifying the court of the inability to file the document. A sample document entitled Declaration that Party was Unable to File in a Timely Manner Due to Technical Difficulties is attached hereto as Form 5. IN R USDCTND CM/ECF(VI)(B). [Editor's note: the reference to Form 5 is likely meant to be a reference to Form 3 (IN R USDCTND CM/ECF(Form 3)].

c. *Extending time*

i. *In general.* When an act may or must be done within a specified time, the court may, for good cause, extend the time:

- With or without motion or notice if the court acts, or if a request is made, before the original time or its extension expires; or

- On motion made after the time has expired if the party failed to act because of excusable neglect. FRCP 6(b)(1).

ii. *Exceptions.* A court must not extend the time to act under FRCP 50(b), FRCP 50(d), FRCP 52(b), FRCP 59(b), FRCP 59(d), FRCP 59(e), and FRCP 60(b). FRCP 6(b)(2).

iii. Refer to the United States District Court for the Northern District of Indiana KeyRules Motion for Continuance/Extension of Time document for more information on extending time.

d. *Additional time after certain kinds of service.* When a party may or must act within a specified time after being served and service is made under FRCP 5(b)(2)(C) (mail), FRCP 5(b)(2)(D) (leaving with the clerk), or FRCP 5(b)(2)(F) (other means consented to), three (3) days are added after the period would otherwise expire under FRCP 6(a). FRCP 6(d).

C. General Requirements

1. *Motions, generally*

    a. *Requirements.* A request for a court order must be made by motion. The motion must:

        i. Be in writing unless made during a hearing or trial;

        ii. State with particularity the grounds for seeking the order; and

        iii. State the relief sought. FRCP 7(b)(1).

    b. *Notice of motion.* A party interested in resisting the relief sought by a motion has a right to notice thereof, and an opportunity to be heard. AMJUR MOTIONS § 12.

        i. In addition to statutory or court rule provisions requiring notice of a motion—the purpose of such a notice requirement having been said to be to prevent a party from being prejudicially surprised by a motion—principles of natural justice dictate that an adverse party generally must be given notice that a motion will be presented to the court. AMJUR MOTIONS § 12.

        ii. "Notice," in this regard, means reasonable notice, including a meaningful opportunity to prepare and to defend against allegations of a motion. AMJUR MOTIONS § 12.

    c. *Writing requirement.* The writing requirement is intended to insure that the adverse parties are informed and have a record of both the motion's pendency and the grounds on which the movant seeks an order. FPP § 1191; Feldberg v. Quechee Lakes Corp., 463 F.3d 195 (2d Cir. 2006).

        i. It is sufficient "if the motion is stated in a written notice of the hearing of the motion." FPP § 1191.

    d. *Particularity requirement.* The particularity requirement insures that the opposing parties will have notice of their opponent's contentions. FEDPROC § 62:364; Goodman v. 1973 26 Foot Trojan Vessel, Arkansas Registration No. AR1439SN, 859 F.2d 71, 12 Fed.R.Serv.3d 645 (8th Cir. 1988). That requirement ensures that notice of the basis for the motion is provided to the court and to the opposing party so as to avoid prejudice, provide the opponent with a meaningful opportunity to respond, and provide the court with enough information to process the motion correctly. FEDPROC § 62:364; Andreas v. Volkswagen of America, Inc., 336 F.3d 789, 56 Fed.R.Serv.3d 6 (8th Cir. 2003).

        i. Reasonable specification of the grounds for a motion is sufficient. However, where a movant fails to state even one ground for granting the motion in question, the movant has failed to meet the minimal standard of "reasonable specification." FEDPROC § 62:364; Martinez v. Trainor, 556 F.2d 818, 23 Fed.R.Serv.2d 403 (7th Cir. 1977).

        ii. The court may excuse the failure to comply with the particularity requirement if it is inadvertent, and where no prejudice is shown by the opposing party. FEDPROC § 62:364.

    e. *Motions must be filed separately.* Motions must be filed separately, but alternative motions may be filed in a single paper if each is named in the title following the caption. IN R USDCTND L.R. 7-1(a).

2. *Motion to dismiss for improper venue.* A party may assert the defense of improper venue by motion. FRCP 12(b)(3). The court will not rule on a defense under FRCP 12 until the party who raised it files a motion and brief. IN R USDCTND L.R. 7-1(c). Objections to venue typically stem from a failure to adhere to the requirements specified in the general venue statute, 28 U.S.C.A. § 1391, or some other statutory venue provision. FPP § 1352.

    a. *Forum selection clauses.* In recent years, however, there have been what appears to be an increasing number of venue motions based on the enforcement of forum selection clauses in contracts. FPP § 1352; Tropp v. Corp. of Lloyd's, 385 Fed.Appx. 36, 37 (2d Cir. 2010). The courts of appeal are split as to whether dismissal of the action is proper pursuant to FRCP 12(b)(3) or FRCP 12(b)(6) when it is based on one of these forum selection clauses rather than on noncompliance with a federal venue statute; most of the decided cases use the former rule as the basis, however. FPP § 1352.

        i. The Supreme Court resolved this split in its 2013 decision Atlantic Marine Construction Co. Inc. v. United States District Court for the Western District of Texas by holding that the appropriate method for enforcing a valid forum-selection clause is the use of transfer to the contractually selected forum under 28 U.S.C.A. § 1404(a). FPP § 1352; Atlantic Marine

Construction Co. Inc. v. United States District Court for the Western District of Texas, 134 S.Ct. 568, 187 L.Ed.2d 487 (2013); Martinez v. Bloomberg LP, 740 F.3d 211, 216 (2d Cir. 2014).

    ii.   Forum-selection clauses cannot make venue "wrong" or "improper" within the meaning of 28 U.S.C.A. § 1406(a) or FRCP 12(b)(3), which is why FRCP 12(b)(3) is no longer an appropriate method for enforcing forum selection clauses. FPP § 1352; Atlantic Marine Construction Co. Inc. v. United States District Court for the Western District of Texas, 134 S.Ct. 568, 579, 187 L.Ed.2d 487 (2013).

b. *Burden.* On a motion under FRCP 12(b)(3), facts must be shown that will defeat the plaintiff's assertion of venue. FPP § 1352; Pierce v. Shorty Small's of Branson Inc., 137 F.3d 1190 (10th Cir. 1998). Courts have not agreed as to which party has the burden of proof on a motion for improper venue. FEDPROC § 62:450.

    i.   *On defendant.* A number of federal courts have concluded that the burden of doing so is on the defendant, since venue is a "personal privilege" that can be waived and a lack of venue should be established by the party asserting it. FPP § 1352; Myers v. American Dental Ass'n, 695 F.2d 716 (3d Cir. 1982).

    ii.   *On plaintiff.* On the other hand, an equal (perhaps a larger) number of federal courts have imposed the burden on the plaintiff in keeping with the rule applied in the context of subject matter and personal jurisdiction defenses. FPP § 1352. The latter view seems correct inasmuch as it is the plaintiff's obligation to institute his action in a permissible forum, both in terms of jurisdiction and venue. FPP § 1352; Pierce v. Shorty Small's of Branson Inc., 137 F.3d 1190 (10th Cir. 1998).

       • If the court chooses to rely on pleadings and affidavits, the plaintiff need only make a prima facie showing of venue, but if the court holds an evidentiary hearing, the plaintiff must demonstrate venue by a preponderance of the evidence. FEDPROF § 1:830; Gulf Ins. Co. v. Glasbrenner, 417 F.3d 353, 62 Fed.R.Serv.3d 592 (2d Cir. 2005).

c. *Form.* A motion to dismiss for lack of venue must be denied as insufficient where it is not apparent which venue provision the moving party wishes to invoke or, assuming that the general venue statute 28 U.S.C.A. § 1391 is contemplated, which paragraph is considered controlling. FEDPROC § 62:449.

d. *Practice on a FRCP 12(b)(3) motion.* All well-pleaded allegations in the complaint bearing on the venue question generally are taken as true, unless contradicted by the defendant's affidavits. A district court may examine facts outside the complaint to determine whether its venue is proper. FPP § 1352; Ambraco, Inc. v. Bossclip B.V., 570 F.3d 233 (5th Cir. 2009). And, as is consistent with practice in other contexts, such as construing the complaint, the court must draw all reasonable inferences and resolve all factual conflicts in favor of the plaintiff. FPP § 1352.

e. *Dismissal versus transfer.* The chances of a motion to dismiss for improper venue being successful have been diminished even further by the liberal attitude of the courts in permitting venue defects to be cured. FPP § 1352.

    i.   A motion to dismiss for improper venue under FRCP 12(b)(3) no longer is necessary in order to object to an inconvenient forum. FPP § 1352. With the enactment of 28 U.S.C.A. § 1404(a) as part of the 1948 revision of the Judicial Code, the district courts now have authority to transfer any case to a more convenient forum if the transfer is in the interest of justice. FPP § 1352; Norwood v. Kirkpatrick, 349 U.S. 29, 75 S.Ct. 544, 99 L.Ed. 789 (1955). Consideration of a dismissal for improper venue must take into account 28 U.S.C.A. § 1406(a) as well as FRCP 12(b)(3). FEDPROC § 62:452.

       • The district court of a district in which is filed a case laying venue in the wrong division or district shall dismiss, or if it be in the interest of justice, transfer such case to any district or division in which it could have been brought. 28 U.S.C.A. § 1406(a).

       • For the convenience of parties and witnesses, in the interest of justice, a district court may transfer any civil action to any other district or division where it might have been brought or to any district or division to which all parties have consented. 28 U.S.C.A. § 1404(a).

      ii. Technically speaking, motions to transfer are made pursuant to a motion under 28 U.S.C.A. § 1404(a) rather than under FRCP 12(b)(3), although little, other than the possible application of the consolidation requirement in FRCP 12(g), turns on this distinction. FPP § 1352.

  f. *Joining motions*

      i. *Right to join.* A motion under FRCP 12 may be joined with any other motion allowed by FRCP 12. FRCP 12(g)(1).

      ii. *Limitation on further motions.* Except as provided in FRCP 12(h)(2) or FRCP 12(h)(3), a party that makes a motion under FRCP 12 must not make another motion under FRCP 12 raising a defense or objection that was available to the party but omitted from its earlier motion. FRCP 12(g)(2).

  g. *Waiving and preserving certain defenses.* No defense or objection is waived by joining it with one or more other defenses or objections in a responsive pleading or in a motion. FRCP 12(b).

      i. *Waiver by consent.* The defendant may waive the right to obtain a dismissal prior to trial either by express consent to be sued in a certain district or by some conduct that will be construed as implying consent. FPP § 1352.

      ii. *When some are waived.* A party waives any defense listed in FRCP 12(b)(2) through FRCP 12(b)(5) by:

- Omitting it from a motion in the circumstances described in FRCP 12(g)(2); or
- Failing to either: (1) make it by motion under FRCP 12; or (2) include it in a responsive pleading or in an amendment allowed by FRCP 15(a)(1) as a matter of course. FRCP 12(h)(1).

      iii. *When to raise others.* Failure to state a claim upon which relief can be granted, to join a person required by FRCP 19(b), or to state a legal defense to a claim may be raised:

- In any pleading allowed or ordered under FRCP 7(a);
- By a motion under FRCP 12(c); or
- At trial. FRCP 12(h)(2).

      iv. *Lack of subject matter jurisdiction.* If the court determines at any time that it lacks subject-matter jurisdiction, the court must dismiss the action. FRCP 12(h)(3).

3. *Venue, generally*

  a. *Applicability of 28 U.S.C.A. § 1391.* Except as otherwise provided by law:

      i. 28 U.S.C.A. § 1391 shall govern the venue of all civil actions brought in district courts of the United States; and

      ii. The proper venue for a civil action shall be determined without regard to whether the action is local or transitory in nature. 28 U.S.C.A. § 1391(a).

  b. *Venue in general.* A civil action may be brought in:

      i. A judicial district in which any defendant resides, if all defendants are residents of the State in which the district is located;

      ii. A judicial district in which a substantial part of the events or omissions giving rise to the claim occurred, or a substantial part of property that is the subject of the action is situated; or

      iii. If there is no district in which an action may otherwise be brought as provided in 28 U.S.C.A. § 1391, any judicial district in which any defendant is subject to the court's personal jurisdiction with respect to such action. 28 U.S.C.A. § 1391(b).

  c. *Residency.* For all venue purposes:

      i. A natural person, including an alien lawfully admitted for permanent residence in the United States, shall be deemed to reside in the judicial district in which that person is domiciled;

      ii. An entity with the capacity to sue and be sued in its common name under applicable law, whether or not incorporated, shall be deemed to reside, if a defendant, in any judicial district in which such defendant is subject to the court's personal jurisdiction with respect to the civil action in question and, if a plaintiff, only in the judicial district in which it maintains its principal place of business; and

    iii. A defendant not resident in the United States may be sued in any judicial district, and the joinder of such a defendant shall be disregarded in determining where the action may be brought with respect to other defendants. 28 U.S.C.A. § 1391(c).

d. *Residency of corporations in states with multiple districts.* For purposes of venue Chapter 87 of the United States Code (28 U.S.C.A. § 1390, et seq.), in a State which has more than one judicial district and in which a defendant that is a corporation is subject to personal jurisdiction at the time an action is commenced, such corporation shall be deemed to reside in any district in that State within which its contacts would be sufficient to subject it to personal jurisdiction if that district were a separate State, and, if there is no such district, the corporation shall be deemed to reside in the district within which it has the most significant contacts. 28 U.S.C.A. § 1391(d).

e. *Actions where defendant is officer or employee of the United States*

    i. *In general.* A civil action in which a defendant is an officer or employee of the United States or any agency thereof acting in his official capacity or under color of legal authority, or an agency of the United States, or the United States, may, except as otherwise provided by law, be brought in any judicial district in which: (1) a defendant in the action resides, (2) a substantial part of the events or omissions giving rise to the claim occurred, or a substantial part of property that is the subject of the action is situated, or (3) the plaintiff resides if no real property is involved in the action. Additional persons may be joined as parties to any such action in accordance with the Federal Rules of Civil Procedure and with such other venue requirements as would be applicable if the United States or one of its officers, employees, or agencies were not a party. 28 U.S.C.A. § 1391(e)(1).

    ii. *Service.* The summons and complaint in such an action shall be served as provided by the Federal Rules of Civil Procedure except that the delivery of the summons and complaint to the officer or agency as required by the Federal Rules of Civil Procedure may be made by certified mail beyond the territorial limits of the district in which the action is brought. 28 U.S.C.A. § 1391(e)(2).

f. *Civil actions against a foreign state.* A civil action against a foreign state as defined in 28 U.S.C.A. § 1603(a) may be brought:

    i. In any judicial district in which a substantial part of the events or omissions giving rise to the claim occurred, or a substantial part of property that is the subject of the action is situated;

    ii. In any judicial district in which the vessel or cargo of a foreign state is situated, if the claim is asserted under 28 U.S.C.A. § 1605(b);

    iii. In any judicial district in which the agency or instrumentality is licensed to do business or is doing business, if the action is brought against an agency or instrumentality of a foreign state as defined in 28 U.S.C.A. § 1603(b); or

    iv. In the United States District Court for the District of Columbia if the action is brought against a foreign state or political subdivision thereof. 28 U.S.C.A. § 1391(f).

g. *Multiparty, multiforum litigation.* A civil action in which jurisdiction of the district court is based upon 28 U.S.C.A. § 1369 may be brought in any district in which any defendant resides or in which a substantial part of the accident giving rise to the action took place. 28 U.S.C.A. § 1391(g).

4. *Opposing papers.* The Federal Rules of Civil Procedure do not require any formal answer, return, or reply to a motion, except where the Federal Rules of Civil Procedure or local rules may require affidavits, memoranda, or other papers to be filed in opposition to a motion. Such papers are simply to apprise the court of such opposition and the grounds of that opposition. FEDPROC § 62:359.

a. *Effect of failure to respond to motion.* Although in the absence of statutory provision or court rule, a motion ordinarily does not require a written answer, when a party files a motion and the opposing party fails to respond, the court may construe such failure to respond as nonopposition to the motion or an admission that the motion was meritorious, may take the facts alleged in the motion as true—the rule in some jurisdictions being that the failure to respond to a fact set forth in a motion is deemed an admission—and may grant the motion if the relief requested appears to be justified. AMJUR MOTIONS § 28.

b. *Assent or no opposition not determinative.* However, a motion will not be granted automatically simply because an "assent" or a notation of "no opposition" has been filed; federal judges frequently deny motions that have been assented to when it is thought that justice so dictates. FPP § 1190.

c. *Responsive pleading inappropriate as response to motion.* An attempt to answer or oppose a motion with a responsive pleading usually is not appropriate. FPP § 1190.

5. *Reply papers.* A moving party may be required or permitted to prepare papers in addition to his original motion papers. AMJUR MOTIONS § 25. Papers answering or replying to opposing papers may be appropriate, in the interests of justice, where it appears there is a substantial reason for allowing a reply. Thus, a court may accept reply papers where a party demonstrates that the papers to which it seeks to file a reply raise new issues that are material to the disposition of the question before the court, or where the court determines, sua sponte, that it wishes further briefing of an issue raised in those papers and orders the submission of additional papers. FEDPROC § 62:360.

a. *Function of reply papers.* The function of a reply affidavit is to answer the arguments made in opposition to the position taken by the movant and not to permit the movant to introduce new arguments in support of the motion. AMJUR MOTIONS § 25.

b. *Issues raised for the first time in a reply document.* However, the view has been followed in some jurisdictions, that as a matter of judicial economy, where there is no prejudice and where the issues could be raised simply by filing a motion to dismiss, the trial court has discretion to consider arguments raised for the first time in a reply memorandum, and that a trial court may grant a motion to strike issues raised for the first time in a reply memorandum. AMJUR MOTIONS § 26.

6. *Appearances.* Attorneys not representing the United States or its agencies must file an appearance when they represent (either in person or by filing a paper) a party. IN R USDCTND L.R. 83-8(a). For more information, refer to IN R USDCTND L.R. 83-8.

7. *Notice of related action.* A party must file a notice of related action as soon as it appears that the party's case and another pending case: (1) arise out of the same transaction or occurrence; (2) involve the same property; or (3) involve the validity or infringement of the same patent, trademark, or copyright. IN R USDCTND L.R. 40-1(d). For more information, refer to IN R USDCTND L.R. 40-1.

8. *Alternative dispute resolution (ADR).* After they confer as required by FRCP 26(f), the parties must advise the court which, if any, alternative-dispute-resolution processes they expect to pursue and when they expect to undertake the process. IN R USDCTND L.R. 16-6(a). For more information on alternative dispute resolution (ADR), refer to IN R USDCTND L.R. 16-6 and IN R USDCTND Order 2003-21.

9. *Settlement or resolution.* The parties must immediately notify the court if they reasonably expect to settle the case or resolve a pending motion. IN R USDCTND L.R. 16-1(g).

10. *Modification or suspension of rules.* The court may, on its own motion or at the request of a party, suspend or modify any rule in a particular case in the interest of justice. IN R USDCTND L.R. 1-1(c).

D. Documents

1. *Documents for moving party*

a. *Required documents*

i. *Notice of motion and motion.* The party must not specify a hearing date in the notice of a motion or petition unless the court or the clerk has authorized it. IN R USDCTND L.R. 7-5(b)(2). Refer to the General Requirements section of this document for information on the notice of motion and motion.

ii. *Brief.* Parties must file a supporting brief with any motion under: FRCP 12. IN R USDCTND L.R. 7-1(b)(1). Refer to the Format section of this document for the format of briefs.

iii. *Certificate of service.* FRCP 5(d) requires that the person making service under FRCP 5 certify that service has been effected. FRCP 5(Advisory Committee Notes). Having such information on file may be useful for many purposes, including proof of service if an issue arises concerning the effectiveness of the service. FRCP 5(Advisory Committee Notes).

- *Certificate of service for electronically-filed documents.* A Certificate of Service is still a requirement when filing documents electronically. A sample Certificate of Service is attached as Form 1 (IN R USDCTND CM/ECF(Form 1)). IN R USDCTND CM/ECF(II)(H).

b. *Supplemental documents*

  i. *Supporting evidence.* When a motion relies on facts outside the record, the court may hear the matter on affidavits or may hear it wholly or partly on oral testimony or on depositions. FRCP 43(c).

- *Materials necessary for motion.* A party must file those portions of discovery requests or responses (including deposition transcripts) that the party relies on to support a motion that could result in a final order on an issue. IN R USDCTND L.R. 26-2(c).

  ii. *Notice of constitutional question.* A party that files a pleading, written motion, or other paper drawing into question the constitutionality of a federal or state statute must promptly:

- *File notice.* File a notice of constitutional question stating the question and identifying the paper that raises it, if: (1) a federal statute is questioned and the parties do not include the United States, one of its agencies, or one of its officers or employees in an official capacity; or (2) a state statute is questioned and the parties do not include the state, one of its agencies, or one of its officers or employees in an official capacity; and

- *Serve notice.* Serve the notice and paper on the Attorney General of the United States if a federal statute is questioned—or on the state attorney general if a state statute is questioned—either by certified or registered mail or by sending it to an electronic address designated by the attorney general for this purpose. FRCP 5.1(a).

- *When to file the notice.* A party required to file a notice of constitutional question under FRCP 5.1 must do so by the later of: (1) the day the parties tender their proposed case-management plan (if one is required); or (2) 21 days after filing the pleading, written motion, or other paper questioning the constitutionality of a federal or state statute. IN R USDCTND L.R. 5.1-1(a).

- *Service on government officials.* The party must also serve the notice and the pleading, written motion, or other paper questioning the constitutionality of a federal or state statute on: (1) the Attorney General of the United States and the United States Attorney for the Northern District of Indiana, if a federal statute is challenged; or (2) the Attorney General for the state if a state statute is challenged. IN R USDCTND L.R. 5.1-1(b). Service required under IN R USDCTND L.R. 5.1-1(b) may be made either by certified or registered mail or by emailing it to an address designated by those officials for this purpose. IN R USDCTND L.R. 5.1-1(c).

- *No forfeiture.* A party's failure to file and serve the notice, or the court's failure to certify, does not forfeit a constitutional claim or defense that is otherwise timely asserted. FRCP 5.1(d).

  iii. *Nongovernmental corporate disclosure statement*

- *Contents.* A nongovernmental corporate party must file two (2) copies of a disclosure statement that: (1) identifies any parent corporation and any publicly held corporation owning ten percent (10%) or more of its stock; or (2) states that there is no such corporation. FRCP 7.1(a).

- *Time to file; Supplemental filing.* A party must: (1) file the disclosure statement with its first appearance, pleading, petition, motion, response, or other request addressed to the court; and (2) promptly file a supplemental statement if any required information changes. FRCP 7.1(b).

iv. *Index of exhibits.* Any pleading, motion, brief, affidavit, notice, or proposed order, whether filed electronically or by delivering it to the clerk, must: include a separate index identifying and briefly describing each exhibit if there are more than four (4) exhibits. IN R USDCTND L.R. 5-4(a)(8).

v. *Request for oral argument.* A party may request oral argument on a motion by filing and serving a separate document explaining why oral argument is necessary and estimating how long the court should allow for the argument. IN R USDCTND L.R. 7-5(a)(1). The request must be filed and served with the party's supporting brief, response brief, or reply brief. IN R USDCTND L.R. 7-5(a)(2).

vi. *Request for evidentiary hearing.* A party may request an evidentiary hearing by filing and serving a separate document explaining why the hearing is necessary and estimating how long the court should allow for it. IN R USDCTND L.R. 7-5(b)(1).

vii. *Copy of authority.* A copy of any decision, statute, or regulation cited in a motion or brief must be attached to the paper if—and only if—it is not available on Westlaw or Lexis. But if a copy of a decision, statute, or regulation is only available electronically, a party must provide it to the court or another party upon request. IN R USDCTND L.R. 7-1(f).

viii. *Proposed order.* Parties filing a paper that requires the judge or clerk to enter a routine or uncontested order must include a suitable form of order. IN R USDCTND L.R. 5-4(c).

- Proposed orders shall not be filed electronically either as a separate document or as an attachment to the main pleading or other document. Instead, all proposed orders must be e-mailed to the chambers of the appropriate judicial officer for the case. The proposed order must be in WordPerfect Format or Rich Text Format (RTF). Proposed orders should be attached to an e-mail and sent to the appropriate judicial officer at the address listed in IN R USDCTND CM/ECF(II)(F). The subject line of the email message should indicate the case title, cause number and document number of the motion, e.g., Smith v. Jones 1:02-cv-1234, motion# ___. IN R USDCTND CM/ECF(II)(F).

ix. *Copy of document with self-addressed envelope.* A party who wants a file-stamped copy of a paper must include with the filing an additional copy of the paper and a self-addressed envelope with adequate postage. IN R USDCTND L.R. 5-4(b)(6).

x. *Notice of manual filing.* However, if that is not physically possible, counsel shall electronically file a .pdf document titled Notice of Manual Filing as a notation on the docket sheet that filings are being held in the clerk's office in paper. A sample Notice of Manual Filing is attached as Form 2 (IN R USDCTND CM/ECF(Form 2)). IN R USDCTND CM/ECF(III)(A)(1).

xi. *Courtesy copies.* If documents are filed in paper format, counsel must provide an original for the clerk's office, a copy for the judge and a copy must be served on all parties in the case. IN R USDCTND CM/ECF(III)(A)(1).

xii. *Declaration that party was unable to file in a timely manner.* If the attorney is unable to file a document in a timely manner due to technical difficulties in the user's system, the attorney must file a document with the court as soon as possible notifying the court of the inability to file the document. A sample document entitled Declaration that Party was Unable to File in a Timely Manner Due to Technical Difficulties is attached hereto as Form 5. IN R USDCTND CM/ECF(VI)(B). [Editor's note: the reference to Form 5 is likely meant to be a reference to Form 3 (IN R USDCTND CM/ECF(Form 3)].

2. *Documents for opposing party*

   a. *Required documents*

   i. *Response brief.* Refer to the Format section of this document for the format of briefs. Refer to the General Requirements section of this document for information on the opposing papers.

   ii. *Certificate of service.* FRCP 5(d) requires that the person making service under FRCP 5 certify that service has been effected. FRCP 5(Advisory Committee Notes). Having such information on file may be useful for many purposes, including proof of service if an issue arises concerning the effectiveness of the service. FRCP 5(Advisory Committee Notes).

- *Certificate of service for electronically-filed documents.* A Certificate of Service is still a requirement when filing documents electronically. A sample Certificate of Service is attached as Form 1 (IN R USDCTND CM/ECF(Form 1)). IN R USDCTND CM/ECF(II)(H).

b. *Supplemental documents*

   i. *Supporting evidence.* When a motion relies on facts outside the record, the court may hear the matter on affidavits or may hear it wholly or partly on oral testimony or on depositions. FRCP 43(c).

   - *Materials necessary for motion.* A party must file those portions of discovery requests or responses (including deposition transcripts) that the party relies on to support a motion that could result in a final order on an issue. IN R USDCTND L.R. 26-2(c).

   ii. *Notice of constitutional question.* A party that files a pleading, written motion, or other paper drawing into question the constitutionality of a federal or state statute must promptly:

   - *File notice.* File a notice of constitutional question stating the question and identifying the paper that raises it, if: (1) a federal statute is questioned and the parties do not include the United States, one of its agencies, or one of its officers or employees in an official capacity; or (2) a state statute is questioned and the parties do not include the state, one of its agencies, or one of its officers or employees in an official capacity; and

   - *Serve notice.* Serve the notice and paper on the Attorney General of the United States if a federal statute is questioned—or on the state attorney general if a state statute is questioned—either by certified or registered mail or by sending it to an electronic address designated by the attorney general for this purpose. FRCP 5.1(a).

   - *When to file the notice.* A party required to file a notice of constitutional question under FRCP 5.1 must do so by the later of: (1) the day the parties tender their proposed case-management plan (if one is required); or (2) 21 days after filing the pleading, written motion, or other paper questioning the constitutionality of a federal or state statute. IN R USDCTND L.R. 5.1-1(a).

   - *Service on government officials.* The party must also serve the notice and the pleading, written motion, or other paper questioning the constitutionality of a federal or state statute on: (1) the Attorney General of the United States and the United States Attorney for the Northern District of Indiana, if a federal statute is challenged; or (2) the Attorney General for the state if a state statute is challenged. IN R USDCTND L.R. 5.1-1(b). Service required under IN R USDCTND L.R. 5.1-1(b) may be made either by certified or registered mail or by emailing it to an address designated by those officials for this purpose. IN R USDCTND L.R. 5.1-1(c).

   - *No forfeiture.* A party's failure to file and serve the notice, or the court's failure to certify, does not forfeit a constitutional claim or defense that is otherwise timely asserted. FRCP 5.1(d).

   iii. *Index of exhibits.* Any pleading, motion, brief, affidavit, notice, or proposed order, whether filed electronically or by delivering it to the clerk, must: include a separate index identifying and briefly describing each exhibit if there are more than four (4) exhibits. IN R USDCTND L.R. 5-4(a)(8).

   iv. *Request for oral argument.* A party may request oral argument on a motion by filing and serving a separate document explaining why oral argument is necessary and estimating how long the court should allow for the argument. IN R USDCTND L.R. 7-5(a)(1). The request must be filed and served with the party's supporting brief, response brief, or reply brief. IN R USDCTND L.R. 7-5(a)(2).

   v. *Request for evidentiary hearing.* A party may request an evidentiary hearing by filing and

serving a separate document explaining why the hearing is necessary and estimating how long the court should allow for it. IN R USDCTND L.R. 7-5(b)(1).

vi. *Copy of authority.* A copy of any decision, statute, or regulation cited in a motion or brief must be attached to the paper if—and only if—it is not available on Westlaw or Lexis. But if a copy of a decision, statute, or regulation is only available electronically, a party must provide it to the court or another party upon request. IN R USDCTND L.R. 7-1(f).

vii. *Copy of document with self-addressed envelope.* A party who wants a file-stamped copy of a paper must include with the filing an additional copy of the paper and a self-addressed envelope with adequate postage. IN R USDCTND L.R. 5-4(b)(6).

viii. *Notice of manual filing.* However, if that is not physically possible, counsel shall electronically file a .pdf document titled Notice of Manual Filing as a notation on the docket sheet that filings are being held in the clerk's office in paper. A sample Notice of Manual Filing is attached as Form 2 (IN R USDCTND CM/ECF(Form 2)). IN R USDCTND CM/ECF(III)(A)(1).

ix. *Courtesy copies.* If documents are filed in paper format, counsel must provide an original for the clerk's office, a copy for the judge and a copy must be served on all parties in the case. IN R USDCTND CM/ECF(III)(A)(1).

x. *Declaration that party was unable to file in a timely manner.* If the attorney is unable to file a document in a timely manner due to technical difficulties in the user's system, the attorney must file a document with the court as soon as possible notifying the court of the inability to file the document. A sample document entitled Declaration that Party was Unable to File in a Timely Manner Due to Technical Difficulties is attached hereto as Form 5. IN R USDCTND CM/ECF(VI)(B). [Editor's note: the reference to Form 5 is likely meant to be a reference to Form 3 (IN R USDCTND CM/ECF(Form 3)].

E. Format

1. *Form of documents.* The rules governing captions and other matters of form in pleadings apply to motions and other papers. FRCP 7(b)(2).

   a. *Paper.* Any pleading, motion, brief, affidavit, notice, or proposed order, whether filed electronically or by delivering it to the clerk, must: use eight and one-half by eleven (8-1/2 x 11) inch pages. IN R USDCTND L.R. 5-4(a)(2).

      i. *Manual filings.* Papers delivered to the clerk for filing must: be flat, unfolded, and on good-quality, white paper. IN R USDCTND L.R. 5-4(b)(1)(A).

         • *Covers or backing.* Papers delivered to the clerk for filing must: not have a cover or a back. IN R USDCTND L.R. 5-4(b)(1)(B).

         • *Recycled paper.* The court encourages using recycled paper. IN R USDCTND L.R. 5-4(b)(7).

   b. *Margins.* Any pleading, motion, brief, affidavit, notice, or proposed order, whether filed electronically or by delivering it to the clerk, must: have at least one (1) inch margins. IN R USDCTND L.R. 5-4(a)(3).

   c. *Spacing.* Any pleading, motion, brief, affidavit, notice, or proposed order, whether filed electronically or by delivering it to the clerk, must: be double spaced (except for headings, footnotes, and quoted material). IN R USDCTND L.R. 5-4(a)(5).

   d. *Text.* Any pleading, motion, brief, affidavit, notice, or proposed order, whether filed electronically or by delivering it to the clerk, must: be plainly typewritten, printed, or prepared by a clearly legible copying process. IN R USDCTND L.R. 5-4(a)(1).

      i. Any pleading, motion, brief, affidavit, notice, or proposed order, whether filed electronically or by delivering it to the clerk, must: use at least twelve (12) point type in the body and at least ten (10) point type in footnotes. IN R USDCTND L.R. 5-4(a)(4).

   e. *Page numbering.* Any pleading, motion, brief, affidavit, notice, or proposed order, whether filed electronically or by delivering it to the clerk, must: have consecutively numbered pages. IN R USDCTND L.R. 5-4(a)(6).

f. *Caption; Names of parties.* Every pleading must have a caption with the court's name, a title, a file number, and a FRCP 7(a) designation. The title of the complaint must name all the parties; the title of other pleadings, after naming the first party on each side, may refer generally to other parties. FRCP 10(a). Any pleading, motion, brief, affidavit, notice, or proposed order, whether filed electronically or by delivering it to the clerk, must: include a title on the first page. IN R USDCTND L.R. 5-4(a)(7).

    i. *Alternative motions.* Motions must be filed separately, but alternative motions may be filed in a single paper if each is named in the title following the caption. IN R USDCTND L.R. 7-1(a).

g. *Filer's information.* Any pleading, motion, brief, affidavit, notice, or proposed order, whether filed electronically or by delivering it to the clerk, must: except in proposed orders and affidavits, include the filer's name, address, telephone number, fax number (where available), and e-mail address (where available). IN R USDCTND L.R. 5-4(a)(9).

h. *Paragraphs; Separate statements.* A party must state its claims or defenses in numbered paragraphs, each limited as far as practicable to a single set of circumstances. A later pleading may refer by number to a paragraph in an earlier pleading. If doing so would promote clarity, each claim founded on a separate transaction or occurrence—and each defense other than a denial—must be stated in a separate count or defense. FRCP 10(b).

i. *Adoption by reference; Exhibits.* A statement in a pleading may be adopted by reference elsewhere in the same pleading or in any other pleading or motion. A copy of a written instrument that is an exhibit to a pleading is a part of the pleading for all purposes. FRCP 10(c).

j. *Citation of local rules.* The Local Civil Rules of the United States District Court for the Northern District of Indiana may be cited as "N.D. Ind. L.R." IN R USDCTND L.R. 1-1(a)(1).

k. *Acceptance by the clerk.* The clerk must not refuse to file a paper solely because it is not in the form prescribed by the Federal Rules of Civil Procedure or by a local rule or practice. FRCP 5(d)(4).

    i. *Sanctions for formatting errors; Non-compliance.* If a person files a paper that does not comply with the rules governing the format of papers filed with the court, the court may: (1) strike the paper from the record; or (2) fine the person up to one thousand dollars ($1,000). IN R USDCTND L.R. 1-3(a).

        • *Notice.* Before sanctioning a person under IN R USDCTND L.R. 1-3(a)(2), the court must: (1) notify the person that the paper is noncompliant; and (2) give the person the opportunity either to be heard or to revise the paper. IN R USDCTND L.R. 1-3(b).

2. *Form of electronic documents.* Electronically filed documents must meet the same requirements of format and page limits as documents "conventionally filed" (as defined in IN R USDCTND CM/ECF(III)(A)) pursuant to the Federal Rules of Civil Procedure and the Local Civil Rules of the United States District Court for the Northern District of Indiana. IN R USDCTND CM/ECF(II)(A)(2).

a. *PDF format required.* Documents filed in the CM/ECF must be in .pdf format. A document created with almost any word-processing program can be converted to .pdf format. The .pdf program in effect takes a picture of the original document and allows anyone to open the converted document across a broad range of hardware and software, with layout, format, links, and images intact. IN R USDCTND CM/ECF(FN2).

b. *Title of documents.* The person electronically filing a pleading or other document will be responsible for designating a title for the pleading or other document by using one of the categories contained in the events listed in the CM/ECF Menu. IN R USDCTND CM/ECF(II)(G).

c. *Combining documents.* All documents which form part of a single pleading and which are being filed at the same time and by the same party may be electronically filed together under one document number, e.g., the motion and a supporting affidavit, with the exception of memoranda in support. Memoranda in support shall be electronically filed separately and shown as a related document to the motion. IN R USDCTND CM/ECF(II)(A)(4).

d. *Exhibits and attachments.* Filing users must submit in electronic form all documents referenced as exhibits or attachments, unless the court permits conventional filing. A filing user must submit as

exhibits or attachments only those excerpts of the referenced documents that are directly germane to the matter under consideration by the court. Excerpted material must be clearly and prominently identified as such. Filing users who file excerpts of documents as exhibits or attachments do so without prejudice to their right to timely file additional excerpts or the complete document. Responding parties may timely file additional excerpts or the complete document that they believe are directly germane. The court may require parties to file additional excerpts or the complete document. IN R USDCTND CM/ECF(II)(A)(6).

e. *Hyperlinks.* Electronically filed documents may contain hyperlink references to an external document as a convenient mechanism for accessing material cited in the document. A hyperlink reference is neither validated for content nor considered a part of the court's records. The court neither endorses the product or organization at the destination of a hyperlink reference, nor does the court exercise any responsibility over the content at the destination. In order to preserve the integrity of the court record, attorneys wishing to insert hyperlinks in court filings shall continue to use the traditional citation method for the cited authority, in addition to the hyperlink. A hyperlink contained in a filing is no more than a convenient mechanism for accessing material cited in the document and a hyperlink reference is extraneous to any filed document and is not part of the court's record. IN R USDCTND CM/ECF(II)(A)(3).

3. *Form of briefs*

a. *Page limits.* Supporting and response briefs (excluding tables of contents, tables of authorities, and appendices) ordinarily must not exceed twenty-five (25) pages. Reply briefs must not exceed fifteen (15) pages. IN R USDCTND L.R. 7-1(e)(1).

    i. *Exception.* The court may allow a party to file a brief exceeding these page limits for extraordinary and compelling reasons. But if the court permits a brief to exceed twenty-five (25) pages, it must include:

- A table of contents with page references;

- An issue statement; and

- A table of authorities including: (1) all cases (alphabetically arranged), statutes, and other authorities cited in the brief; and (2) references to where the authorities appear in the brief. IN R USDCTND L.R. 7-1(e)(2).

4. *Signing of pleadings, motions and other papers*

a. *Signature.* Every pleading, written motion, and other paper must be signed by at least one attorney of record in the attorney's name—or by a party personally if the party is unrepresented. The paper must state the signer's address, e-mail address, and telephone number. FRCP 11(a).

    i. *Signatures on manual filings.* Papers delivered to the clerk for filing must: include the filer's original signature. IN R USDCTND L.R. 5-4(b)(1)(C).

- *Rubber-stamped and faxed signatures.* An original paper with a rubber-stamped or faxed signature is unsigned for purposes of FRCP 11 and FRCP 26(g). IN R USDCTND L.R. 5-4(b)(2).

- *Affidavits.* Only the affiant need sign an affidavit. IN R USDCTND L.R. 5-4(b)(3).

    ii. *Electronic signatures.* Pursuant to FRCP 11, every pleading, motion, and other paper (except lists, schedules, statements or amendments thereto) shall be signed by at least one attorney of record or, if the party is not represented by an attorney, all papers shall be signed by the party. An attorney's/participant's password issued by the court combined with the user's identification, serves as and constitutes the attorney/participant's signature for FRCP 11 and other purposes. IN R USDCTND CM/ECF(I)(C). Documents which must be filed and which must contain original signatures other than those of a participating attorney or which require either verification or an unsworn declaration under any rule or statute, shall be filed electronically, with originally executed copies maintained by the filer. The pleading or other document electronically filed shall contain "s/" signature(s), as noted in IN R USDCTND CM/ECF(II)(E)(3)(b). IN R USDCTND CM/ECF(II)(E)(1).

- *Multiple signatures.* In the case of a stipulation or other document to be signed by two or

more attorneys, the following procedure should be used: The filing attorney shall initially confirm that the content of the document is acceptable to all persons required to sign the document and shall obtain the physical signatures of all attorneys on the document. IN R USDCTND CM/ECF(II)(E)(3)(a). The filing attorney then shall file the document electronically, indicating the signatories, e.g., "s/Jane Doe," "s/John Doe," etc. IN R US-DCTND CM/ECF(II)(E)(3)(b). The filing attorney shall retain the hard copy of the document containing the original signatures. IN R USDCTND CM/ECF(II)(E)(3)(c).

    iii. *No verification or accompanying affidavit required for pleadings.* Unless a rule or statute specifically states otherwise, a pleading need not be verified or accompanied by an affidavit. FRCP 11(a).

    iv. *Unsigned papers.* The court must strike an unsigned paper unless the omission is promptly corrected after being called to the attorney's or party's attention. FRCP 11(a).

b. *Representations to the court.* By presenting to the court a pleading, written motion, or other paper—whether by signing, filing, submitting, or later advocating it—an attorney or unrepresented party certifies that to the best of the person's knowledge, information, and belief, formed after an inquiry reasonable under the circumstances:

    i. It is not being presented for any improper purpose, such as to harass, cause unnecessary delay, or needlessly increase the cost of litigation;

    ii. The claims, defenses, and other legal contentions are warranted by existing law or by a nonfrivolous argument for extending, modifying, or reversing existing law or for establishing new law;

    iii. The factual contentions have evidentiary support or, if specifically so identified, will likely have evidentiary support after a reasonable opportunity for further investigation or discovery; and

    iv. The denials of factual contentions are warranted on the evidence or, if specifically so identified, are reasonably based on belief or a lack of information. FRCP 11(b).

c. *Sanctions.* If, after notice and a reasonable opportunity to respond, the court determines that FRCP 11(b) has been violated, the court may impose an appropriate sanction on any attorney, law firm, or party that violated FRCP 11(b) or is responsible for the violation. FRCP 11(c)(1). Refer to the United States District Court for the Northern District of Indiana KeyRules Motion for Sanctions document for more information.

5. *Privacy protection for filings made with the court*

a. *Redacted filings.* Counsel should not include sensitive information in any document filed with the court unless such inclusion is necessary and relevant to the case. IN R USDCTND CM/ECF(VII). Unless the court orders otherwise, in an electronic or paper filing with the court that contains an individual's Social Security number, taxpayer-identification number, or birth date, the name of an individual known to be a minor, or a financial-account number, a party or nonparty making the filing may include only:

    i. The last four (4) digits of the Social Security number and taxpayer-identification number;

    ii. The year of the individual's birth;

    iii. The minor's initials; and

    iv. The last four (4) digits of the financial-account number. FRCP 5.2(a); IN R USDCTND Order 2005-3.

b. *Exemptions from the redaction requirement.* The redaction requirement does not apply to the following:

    i. A financial-account number that identifies the property allegedly subject to forfeiture in a forfeiture proceeding;

    ii. The record of an administrative or agency proceeding;

    iii. The official record of a state-court proceeding;

    iv. The record of a court or tribunal, if that record was not subject to the redaction requirement when originally filed;

v. A filing covered by FRCP 5.2(c) or FRCP 5.2(d); and

vi. A pro se filing in an action brought under 28 U.S.C.A. § 2241, 28 U.S.C.A. § 2254, or 28 U.S.C.A. § 2255. FRCP 5.2(b).

vii. In cases filed under the Social Security Act, 42 U.S.C.A. § 405(g), there is no need for redaction of any information from the documents filed in the case. IN R USDCTND Order 2005-3.

c. *Limitations on remote access to electronic files; Social Security appeals and immigration cases.* Unless the court orders otherwise, in an action for benefits under the Social Security Act, and in an action or proceeding relating to an order of removal, to relief from removal, or to immigration benefits or detention, access to an electronic file is authorized as follows:

i. The parties and their attorneys may have remote electronic access to any part of the case file, including the administrative record;

ii. Any other person may have electronic access to the full record at the courthouse, but may have remote electronic access only to:

- The docket maintained by the court; and

- An opinion, order, judgment, or other disposition of the court, but not any other part of the case file or the administrative record. FRCP 5.2(c).

d. *Filings made under seal.* The court may order that a filing be made under seal without redaction. The court may later unseal the filing or order the person who made the filing to file a redacted version for the public record. FRCP 5.2(d). For information on filing documents under seal, refer to IN R USDCTND L.R. 5-3, IN R USDCTND CM/ECF(IV)(A), and IN R USDCTND ECF Order 2004-19.

e. *Protective orders.* For good cause, the court may by order in a case:

i. Require redaction of additional information; or

ii. Limit or prohibit a nonparty's remote electronic access to a document filed with the court. FRCP 5.2(e).

f. *Option for additional unredacted filing under seal.* A person making a redacted filing may also file an unredacted copy under seal. The court must retain the unredacted copy as part of the record. FRCP 5.2(f); IN R USDCTND Order 2005-3.

i. The unredacted version of the document or the reference list shall be retained by the court under seal as part of the record. This paper shall be retained by the court as part of the record. The court may, however, still require the party to file a redacted copy for the public file. IN R USDCTND Order 2005-3.

g. *Option for filing a reference list.* A filing that contains redacted information may be filed together with a reference list that identifies each item of redacted information and specifies an appropriate identifier that uniquely corresponds to each item listed. The list must be filed under seal and may be amended as of right. Any reference in the case to a listed identifier will be construed to refer to the corresponding item of information. FRCP 5.2(g); IN R USDCTND Order 2005-3.

i. The unredacted version of the document or the reference list shall be retained by the court under seal as part of the record. This paper shall be retained by the court as part of the record. The court may, however, still require the party to file a redacted copy for the public file. IN R USDCTND Order 2005-3.

h. *Responsibility for redaction.* The responsibility for redacting these personal identifiers rests solely with counsel and the parties. The Clerk will not review each paper for compliance with IN R USDCTND Order 2005-3. IN R USDCTND Order 2005-3.

i. *Waiver of protection of identifiers.* A person waives the protection of FRCP 5.2(a) as to the person's own information by filing it without redaction and not under seal. FRCP 5.2(h).

F. Filing and Service Requirements

1. *Filing requirements.* Any paper after the complaint that is required to be served—together with a

certificate of service—must be filed within a reasonable time after service. FRCP 5(d)(1). Motions must be filed separately, but alternative motions may be filed in a single paper if each is named in the title following the caption. IN R USDCTND L.R. 7-1(a).

a. *How filing is made; In general.* A paper is filed by delivering it:

    i. To the clerk; or

    ii. To a judge who agrees to accept it for filing, and who must then note the filing date on the paper and promptly send it to the clerk. FRCP 5(d)(2).

        • Papers not filed electronically must be filed with the clerk, not a judge. IN R USDCTND L.R. 5-4(b)(4).

    iii. Parties manually filing a paper that requires the clerk to give others notice, must give the clerk: (1) sufficient copies of the notice; and (2) the name and address of each person entitled to receive the notice. IN R USDCTND L.R. 5-4(b)(8).

b. *Where to file.* Papers not filed electronically must be filed in the division where the case is pending, unless: (1) a person will be prejudiced if the paper is not filed the same day it is tendered; and (2) it includes an adequately sized envelope addressed to the clerk's office in the division where the case is pending and with adequate postage. IN R USDCTND L.R. 5-4(b)(5).

c. *Electronic filing*

    i. *Authorization of electronic filing program.* A court may, by local rule, allow papers to be filed, signed, or verified by electronic means that are consistent with any technical standards established by the Judicial Conference of the United States. A local rule may require electronic filing only if reasonable exceptions are allowed. A paper filed electronically in compliance with a local rule is a written paper for purposes of the Federal Rules of Civil Procedure. FRCP 5(d)(3).

        • Papers must be filed, signed, and verified electronically unless excepted by the court's CM/ECF Civil and Criminal User Manual (IN R USDCTND CM/ECF). IN R USDCTND L.R. 5-1.

    ii. *Mandatory electronic filing.* Unless otherwise permitted by these procedures or otherwise authorized by the assigned judge, all documents submitted for filing in this district in civil and criminal cases, no matter when a case was originally filed, shall be filed electronically using the System. IN R USDCTND CM/ECF(II)(A)(1). The requirement that "all documents" be filed electronically includes briefs, and attachments and exhibits used in support of motions. IN R USDCTND CM/ECF(FN1).

        • Sending a document or pleading to the court via e-mail or facsimile does not constitute "electronic filing." IN R USDCTND CM/ECF(I)(A).

    iii. *Conventional filing.* As used in these procedures, a "conventionally" filed or submitted document or pleading is one presented to the Clerk or a party in paper or other non-electronic, tangible format. The following documents shall be filed conventionally and not electronically unless specifically authorized by the Court:

        • Exhibits and other documents which cannot be converted to a legible electronic form. Whenever possible, counsel is responsible for converting filings to an electronic form. However, if that is not physically possible, counsel shall electronically file a .pdf document titled Notice of Manual Filing as a notation on the docket sheet that filings are being held in the clerk's office in paper. A sample Notice of Manual Filing is attached as Form 2 (IN R USDCTND CM/ECF(Form 2)). If documents are filed in paper format, counsel must provide an original for the clerk's office, a copy for the judge and a copy must be served on all parties in the case. Large documents which do not exist in an electronic format shall be scanned into .pdf format by counsel, in small batches if necessary, and filed electronically as separate attachments in the System. IN R USDCTND CM/ECF(III)(A)(1).

        • Certain documents which are listed in IN R USDCTND CM/ECF(II)(E)(2). IN R USDCTND CM/ECF(III)(A)(2).

- Documents filed by pro se litigants. IN R USDCTND CM/ECF(III)(A)(3).

iv. For more information on electronic filing, refer to IN R USDCTND CM/ECF.

2. *Service requirements*

a. *Service; When required*

   i. *In general.* Unless the Federal Rules of Civil Procedure provide otherwise, each of the following papers must be served on every party:

- An order stating that service is required;
- A pleading filed after the original complaint, unless the court orders otherwise under FRCP 5(c) because there are numerous defendants;
- A discovery paper required to be served on a party, unless the court orders otherwise;
- A written motion, except one that may be heard ex parte; and
- A written notice, appearance, demand, or offer of judgment, or any similar paper. FRCP 5(a)(1).

   ii. *If a party fails to appear.* No service is required on a party who is in default for failing to appear. But a pleading that asserts a new claim for relief against such a party must be served on that party under FRCP 4. FRCP 5(a)(2).

   iii. *Seizing property.* If an action is begun by seizing property and no person is or need be named as a defendant, any service required before the filing of an appearance, answer, or claim must be made on the person who had custody or possession of the property when it was seized. FRCP 5(a)(3).

b. *Service; How made*

   i. *Serving an attorney.* If a party is represented by an attorney, service under FRCP 5 must be made on the attorney unless the court orders service on the party. FRCP 5(b)(1).

   ii. *Service in general.* A paper is served under FRCP 5 by:

- Handing it to the person;
- Leaving it: (1) at the person's office with a clerk or other person in charge or, if no one is in charge, in a conspicuous place in the office; or (2) if the person has no office or the office is closed, at the person's dwelling or usual place of abode with someone of suitable age and discretion who resides there;
- Mailing it to the person's last known address—in which event service is complete upon mailing;
- Leaving it with the court clerk if the person has no known address;
- Sending it by electronic means if the person consented in writing—in which event service is complete upon transmission, but is not effective if the serving party learns that it did not reach the person to be served; or
- Delivering it by any other means that the person consented to in writing—in which event service is complete when the person making service delivers it to the agency designated to make delivery. FRCP 5(b)(2).

   iii. *Electronic service.* Electronically filed papers may be served electronically if service is consistent with the CM/ECF User Manual (IN R USDCTND CM/ECF). IN R USDCTND L.R. 5-2(a).

- *Waiver of other service.* An attorney's registration will constitute a waiver of conventional service of documents and the attorney agrees to accept service of notice on behalf of the client of the electronic filing by hand, facsimile or authorized email. IN R USDCTND CM/ECF(I)(B)(3).
- *Serving registered persons.* The System will generate a "Notice of Electronic Filing" when any document is filed. This notice represents service of the document on parties who are

registered participants with the System. Except as provided in IN R USDCTND CM/ECF(III)(B), the filing party shall not be required to serve any pleading or other documents on any party receiving electronic notice. IN R USDCTND CM/ECF(II)(D)(1). The term "pleading" refers only to those documents listed in FRCP 7(a). IN R USDCTND CM/ECF(FN3).

- *When electronic service is deemed completed.* A person registered to use the court's electronic-filing system is served with an electronically filed paper when a "Notice of Electronic Filing" is transmitted to that person through the court's electronic filing-system. IN R USDCTND L.R. 5-2(b).

- *Serving non-registered persons.* A person who has not registered to use the court's electronic-filing system but who is entitled to service of a paper must be served according to the Local Civil Rules of the United States District Court for the Northern District of Indiana and the Federal Rules of Civil Procedure. IN R USDCTND L.R. 5-2(c); IN R USDCTND CM/ECF(II)(D)(2). If such service of a paper copy is to be made, it shall be done in the manner provided in the Federal Rules of Civil Procedure and the Local Civil Rules of the United States District Court for the Northern District of Indiana. IN R USDCTND CM/ECF(II)(D)(2).

iv. *Service of conventional filings.* Pleadings or other documents which are filed conventionally rather than electronically shall be served in the manner provided for in the Federal Rules of Civil Procedure and the Local Civil Rules of the United States District Court for the Northern District of Indiana, except as otherwise provided by order of the Court. IN R USDCTND CM/ECF(III)(B).

v. *Using court facilities.* If a local rule so authorizes, a party may use the court's transmission facilities to make service under FRCP 5(b)(2)(E). FRCP 5(b)(3).

c. *Serving numerous defendants*

i. *In general.* If an action involves an unusually large number of defendants, the court may, on motion or on its own, order that:

- Defendants' pleadings and replies to them need not be served on other defendants;

- Any crossclaim, counterclaim, avoidance, or affirmative defense in those pleadings and replies to them will be treated as denied or avoided by all other parties; and

- Filing any such pleading and serving it on the plaintiff constitutes notice of the pleading to all parties. FRCP 5(c)(1).

ii. *Notifying parties.* A copy of every such order must be served on the parties as the court directs. FRCP 5(c)(2).

G. Hearings

1. *Hearings, generally*

a. *Oral argument.* Due process does not require that oral argument be permitted on a motion and, except as otherwise provided by local rule, the district court has discretion to determine whether it will decide the motion on the papers or hear argument by counsel (and perhaps receive evidence). FPP § 1190; F.D.I.C. v. Deglau, 207 F.3d 153 (3d Cir. 2000).

i. *Request for oral argument.* A party may request oral argument on a motion by filing and serving a separate document explaining why oral argument is necessary and estimating how long the court should allow for the argument. IN R USDCTND L.R. 7-5(a)(1). Refer to the Documents section of this document for more information.

ii. *Additional evidence forbidden.* Parties may not present additional evidence at oral argument. IN R USDCTND L.R. 7-5(a)(3).

b. *Providing a regular schedule for oral hearings.* A court may establish regular times and places for oral hearings on motions. FRCP 78(a).

c. *Providing for submission on briefs.* By rule or order, the court may provide for submitting and determining motions on briefs, without oral hearings. FRCP 78(b).

d. *Evidentiary hearings.* A party may request an evidentiary hearing by filing and serving a separate document explaining why the hearing is necessary and estimating how long the court should allow for it. IN R USDCTND L.R. 7-5(b)(2). Refer to the Documents section of this document for more information.

e. *Court's authority.* The court may: (1) grant or deny a request for oral argument or an evidentiary hearing in its discretion; (2) set oral argument or an evidentiary hearing without a request from a party; or (3) order any oral argument or evidentiary hearing to be held anywhere within the district regardless of where the case will be tried. IN R USDCTND L.R. 7-5(c).

2. *Hearing on FRCP 12 defenses before trial.* If a party so moves, any defense listed in FRCP 12(b)(1) through FRCP 12(b)(7)—whether made in a pleading or by motion—and a motion under FRCP 12(c) must be heard and decided before trial unless the court orders a deferral until trial. FRCP 12(i).

3. *Courtroom and courthouse decorum.* For information on courtroom and courthouse decorum, refer to IN R USDCTND L.R. 83-3.

H. Forms

1. Federal Motion to Dismiss for Improper Venue Forms

a. Defense; Improper venue; Defendant resident of another district. FEDPROF § 1:184.

b. Motion; For dismissal or transfer of action on grounds of improper venue; Diversity case. FEDPROF § 1:371.

c. Motion; For dismissal; Improper venue; Lack of personal jurisdiction. FEDPROF § 1:371.50.

d. Motion; General form. FEDPROF § 1:746.

e. Notice; Of motion; General form. FEDPROF § 1:747.

f. Notice; Of motion; With costs of motion. FEDPROF § 1:748.

g. Notice; Of motion; Containing motion. FEDPROF § 1:749.

h. Opposition; To motion; General form. FEDPROF § 1:750.

i. Affidavit; Supporting or opposing motion. FEDPROF § 1:751.

j. Brief; Supporting or opposing motion. FEDPROF § 1:752.

k. Statement of points and authorities; Opposing motion. FEDPROF § 1:753.

l. Motion; To dismiss; Improper venue; Diversity action. FEDPROF § 1:916.

m. Motion to dismiss; Improper venue; Action not founded solely on diversity. FEDPROF § 1:917.

n. Motion to dismiss; Improper venue; Corporate defendant not subject to personal jurisdiction in district. FEDPROF § 1:918.

o. Motion to dismiss; Improper venue; Action of local nature. FEDPROF § 1:919.

p. Motion; To dismiss or, alternatively, to transfer action; Improper venue. FEDPROF § 1:920.

q. Affidavit; In support of motion to dismiss for improper venue; Corporate defendant not subject to personal jurisdiction in district. FEDPROF § 1:921.

r. Motion; To dismiss action for improper venue. FEDPROF § 22:56.

s. Motion to dismiss complaint; General form. GOLDLTGFMS § 20:24.

t. Affidavit in support of motion to dismiss complaint. GOLDLTGFMS § 20:32.

u. Motion; Federal form. GOLDLTGFMS § 45:4.

v. Affidavit in support of motion; Improper venue. GOLDLTGFMS § 45:15.

2. Forms for the Northern District of Indiana

a. Certificate of service. IN R USDCTND CM/ECF(Form 1).

b. Notice of manual filing. IN R USDCTND CM/ECF(Form 2).

c. Declaration that party was unable to file in a timely manner. IN R USDCTND CM/ECF(Form 3).

I. Applicable Rules

1. *Federal rules*

   a. Venue generally. 28 U.S.C.A. § 1391.

   b. Serving and filing pleadings and other papers. FRCP 5.

   c. Constitutional challenge to a statute; Notice, certification, and intervention. FRCP 5.1.

   d. Privacy protection for filings made with the court. FRCP 5.2.

   e. Computing and extending time; Time for motion papers. FRCP 6.

   f. Pleadings allowed; Form of motions and other papers. FRCP 7.

   g. Disclosure statement. FRCP 7.1.

   h. Form of pleadings. FRCP 10.

   i. Signing pleadings, motions, and other papers; Representations to the court; Sanctions. FRCP 11.

   j. Defenses and objections; When and how presented; Motion for judgment on the pleadings; Consolidating motions; Waiving defenses; Pretrial hearing. FRCP 12.

   k. Taking testimony. FRCP 43.

   l. Hearing motions; Submission on briefs. FRCP 78.

2. *Local rules*

   a. Citation and scope of the rules. IN R USDCTND L.R. 1-1.

   b. Sanctions for formatting errors. IN R USDCTND L.R. 1-3.

   c. Electronic filing required. IN R USDCTND L.R. 5-1.

   d. Constitutional questions. IN R USDCTND L.R. 5.1-1.

   e. Electronic service. IN R USDCTND L.R. 5-2.

   f. Format of papers. IN R USDCTND L.R. 5-4.

   g. Motion practice. IN R USDCTND L.R. 7-1.

   h. Oral arguments and evidentiary hearings. IN R USDCTND L.R. 7-5.

   i. Pretrial procedure. IN R USDCTND L.R. 16-1.

   j. Alternative dispute resolution. IN R USDCTND L.R. 16-6.

   k. Filing of discovery and other materials. IN R USDCTND L.R. 26-2.

   l. Case assignment. IN R USDCTND L.R. 40-1.

   m. Appearance and withdrawal of appearance. IN R USDCTND L.R. 83-8.

   n. CM/ECF civil and criminal user manual. IN R USDCTND CM/ECF.

   o. In re: privacy and public access to civil electronic case files. IN R USDCTND Order 2005-3.

Motions, Oppositions and Replies
Motion for Leave to Amend

Document Last Updated December 2016

A. Checklist

(I) ❑ Matters to be considered by moving party

   (a) ❑ Required documents

      (1) ❑ Notice of motion and motion

      (2) ❑ Proposed amendment

      (3) ❑ Certificate of service

(b) ❑ Supplemental documents

    (1) ❑ Brief

    (2) ❑ Supporting evidence

    (3) ❑ Notice of constitutional question

    (4) ❑ Index of exhibits

    (5) ❑ Request for oral argument

    (6) ❑ Request for evidentiary hearing

    (7) ❑ Copy of authority

    (8) ❑ Proposed order

    (9) ❑ Copy of document with self-addressed envelope

    (10) ❑ Notice of manual filing

    (11) ❑ Courtesy copies

    (12) ❑ Declaration that party was unable to file in a timely manner

(c) ❑ Timing

    (1) ❑ Unlike amendments as of course, amendments under FRCP 15(a)(2) may be made at any stage of the litigation

    (2) ❑ A party may move—at any time, even after judgment—to amend the pleadings to conform them to the evidence and to raise an unpleaded issue

    (3) ❑ A written motion and notice of the hearing must be served at least fourteen (14) days before the time specified for the hearing, with the following exceptions: (i) when the motion may be heard ex parte; (ii) when the Federal Rules of Civil Procedure set a different time; or (iii) when a court order—which a party may, for good cause, apply for ex parte—sets a different time

    (4) ❑ Any affidavit supporting a motion must be served with the motion

(II) ❑ Matters to be considered by opposing party

(a) ❑ Required documents

    (1) ❑ Response brief

    (2) ❑ Certificate of service

(b) ❑ Supplemental documents

    (1) ❑ Supporting evidence

    (2) ❑ Notice of constitutional question

    (3) ❑ Index of exhibits

    (4) ❑ Request for oral argument

    (5) ❑ Request for evidentiary hearing

    (6) ❑ Copy of authority

    (7) ❑ Copy of document with self-addressed envelope

    (8) ❑ Notice of manual filing

    (9) ❑ Courtesy copies

    (10) ❑ Declaration that party was unable to file in a timely manner

(c) ❑ Timing

    (1) ❑ A party must file any response brief to a motion within fourteen (14) days after the motion is served

    (2) ❑ Except as FRCP 59(c) provides otherwise, any opposing affidavit must be served at least seven (7) days before the hearing, unless the court permits service at another time

B. Timing

1. *Motion for leave to amend.* Unlike amendments as of course, amendments under FRCP 15(a)(2) may be made at any stage of the litigation. FPP § 1484.

   a. *Amendments to conform to the evidence.* A party may move—at any time, even after judgment—to amend the pleadings to conform them to the evidence and to raise an unpleaded issue. FRCP 15(b)(2).

   b. *Time to respond to an amended pleading.* Unless the court orders otherwise, any required response to an amended pleading must be made within the time remaining to respond to the original pleading or within fourteen (14) days after service of the amended pleading, whichever is later. FRCP 15(a)(3).

2. *Timing of motions, generally*

   a. *Motion and notice of hearing.* A written motion and notice of the hearing must be served at least fourteen (14) days before the time specified for the hearing, with the following exceptions:

      i. When the motion may be heard ex parte;

      ii. When the Federal Rules of Civil Procedure set a different time; or

      iii. When a court order—which a party may, for good cause, apply for ex parte—sets a different time. FRCP 6(c)(1).

   b. *Supporting affidavit.* Any affidavit supporting a motion must be served with the motion. FRCP 6(c)(2).

3. *Timing of opposing papers.* A party must file any response brief to a motion within fourteen (14) days after the motion is served. IN R USDCTND L.R. 7-1(d)(2)(A).

   a. *Opposing affidavit.* Except as FRCP 59(c) provides otherwise, any opposing affidavit must be served at least seven (7) days before the hearing, unless the court permits service at another time. FRCP 6(c)(2).

   b. *Extensions.* The court may extend response- and reply-brief deadlines, but only for good cause. IN R USDCTND L.R. 7-1(d)(3).

   c. *Summary rulings.* The court may rule on a motion summarily if an opposing party does not file a response before the deadline. IN R USDCTND L.R. 7-1(d)(4).

4. *Timing of reply papers.* Where the respondent files an answering affidavit setting up a new matter, the moving party ordinarily is allowed a reasonable time to file a reply affidavit since failure to deny the new matter by affidavit may operate as an admission of its truth. AMJUR MOTIONS § 25.

   a. *Reply brief.* The moving party must file any reply brief within seven (7) days after the response brief is served. IN R USDCTND L.R. 7-1(d)(2)(B).

   b. *Extensions.* The court may extend response- and reply-brief deadlines, but only for good cause. IN R USDCTND L.R. 7-1(d)(3).

5. *Computation of time*

   a. *Computing time.* FRCP 6 applies in computing any time period specified in the Federal Rules of Civil Procedure, in any local rule or court order, or in any statute that does not specify a method of computing time. FRCP 6(a).

      i. *Period stated in days or a longer unit.* When the period is stated in days or a longer unit of time:

      - Exclude the day of the event that triggers the period;

      - Count every day, including intermediate Saturdays, Sundays, and legal holidays; and

      - Include the last day of the period, but if the last day is a Saturday, Sunday, or legal holiday, the period continues to run until the end of the next day that is not a Saturday, Sunday, or legal holiday. FRCP 6(a)(1).

    ii.   *Period stated in hours.* When the period is stated in hours:

- Begin counting immediately on the occurrence of the event that triggers the period;

- Count every hour, including hours during intermediate Saturdays, Sundays, and legal holidays; and

- If the period would end on a Saturday, Sunday, or legal holiday, the period continues to run until the same time on the next day that is not a Saturday, Sunday, or legal holiday. FRCP 6(a)(2).

    iii.   *Inaccessibility of the clerk's office.* Unless the court orders otherwise, if the clerk's office is inaccessible:

- On the last day for filing under FRCP 6(a)(1), then the time for filing is extended to the first accessible day that is not a Saturday, Sunday, or legal holiday; or

- During the last hour for filing under FRCP 6(a)(2), then the time for filing is extended to the same time on the first accessible day that is not a Saturday, Sunday, or legal holiday. FRCP 6(a)(3).

    iv.   *"Last day" defined.* Unless a different time is set by a statute, local rule, or court order, the last day ends:

- For electronic filing, at midnight in the court's time zone; and

- For filing by other means, when the clerk's office is scheduled to close. FRCP 6(a)(4).

    v.   *"Next day" defined.* The "next day" is determined by continuing to count forward when the period is measured after an event and backward when measured before an event. FRCP 6(a)(5).

    vi.   *"Legal holiday" defined.* "Legal holiday" means:

- The day set aside by statute for observing New Year's Day, Martin Luther King Jr.'s Birthday, Washington's Birthday, Memorial Day, Independence Day, Labor Day, Columbus Day, Veterans' Day, Thanksgiving Day, or Christmas Day;

- Any day declared a holiday by the President or Congress; and

- For periods that are measured after an event, any other day declared a holiday by the state where the district court is located. FRCP 6(a)(6).

b. *Computation of electronic filing deadlines.* Filing documents electronically does not alter any filing deadlines or any time computation pursuant to FRCP 6. The counties of Lake, Porter, LaPorte, Pulaski and Starke are located in the Central time zone and the remaining counties in the Northern District of Indiana are located in the Eastern time zone. Nevertheless, all electronic transmissions of documents must be completed (i.e., received completely by the clerk's office) prior to midnight Eastern Time, (South Bend/Fort Wayne/Lafayette time) in order to be considered timely filed that day, regardless of the local time in the division where the case is pending. Although documents can be filed electronically twenty-four (24) hours a day, filers are strongly encouraged to file all documents during hours when the CM/ECF Help Line is available, from 9:00 a.m. to 4:00 p.m. local time. IN R USDCTND CM/ECF(II)(I).

    i.   *Technical failures.* If the attorney is unable to file a document in a timely manner due to technical difficulties in the user's system, the attorney must file a document with the court as soon as possible notifying the court of the inability to file the document. A sample document entitled Declaration that Party was Unable to File in a Timely Manner Due to Technical Difficulties is attached hereto as Form 5. IN R USDCTND CM/ECF(VI)(B). [Editor's note: the reference to Form 5 is likely meant to be a reference to Form 3 (IN R USDCTND CM/ECF(Form 3)].

c. *Extending time*

    i.   *In general.* When an act may or must be done within a specified time, the court may, for good cause, extend the time:

- With or without motion or notice if the court acts, or if a request is made, before the original time or its extension expires; or

- On motion made after the time has expired if the party failed to act because of excusable neglect. FRCP 6(b)(1).

   ii. *Exceptions*. A court must not extend the time to act under FRCP 50(b), FRCP 50(d), FRCP 52(b), FRCP 59(b), FRCP 59(d), FRCP 59(e), and FRCP 60(b). FRCP 6(b)(2).

   iii. Refer to the United States District Court for the Northern District of Indiana KeyRules Motion for Continuance/Extension of Time document for more information on extending time.

  d. *Additional time after certain kinds of service*. When a party may or must act within a specified time after being served and service is made under FRCP 5(b)(2)(C) (mail), FRCP 5(b)(2)(D) (leaving with the clerk), or FRCP 5(b)(2)(F) (other means consented to), three (3) days are added after the period would otherwise expire under FRCP 6(a). FRCP 6(d).

C. General Requirements

1. *Motions, generally*

  a. *Requirements*. A request for a court order must be made by motion. The motion must:

   i. Be in writing unless made during a hearing or trial;

   ii. State with particularity the grounds for seeking the order; and

   iii. State the relief sought. FRCP 7(b)(1).

  b. *Notice of motion*. A party interested in resisting the relief sought by a motion has a right to notice thereof, and an opportunity to be heard. AMJUR MOTIONS § 12.

   i. In addition to statutory or court rule provisions requiring notice of a motion—the purpose of such a notice requirement having been said to be to prevent a party from being prejudicially surprised by a motion—principles of natural justice dictate that an adverse party generally must be given notice that a motion will be presented to the court. AMJUR MOTIONS § 12.

   ii. "Notice," in this regard, means reasonable notice, including a meaningful opportunity to prepare and to defend against allegations of a motion. AMJUR MOTIONS § 12.

  c. *Writing requirement*. The writing requirement is intended to insure that the adverse parties are informed and have a record of both the motion's pendency and the grounds on which the movant seeks an order. FPP § 1191; Feldberg v. Quechee Lakes Corp., 463 F.3d 195 (2d Cir. 2006).

   i. It is sufficient "if the motion is stated in a written notice of the hearing of the motion." FPP § 1191.

  d. *Particularity requirement*. The particularity requirement insures that the opposing parties will have notice of their opponent's contentions. FEDPROC § 62:364; Goodman v. 1973 26 Foot Trojan Vessel, Arkansas Registration No. AR1439SN, 859 F.2d 71, 12 Fed.R.Serv.3d 645 (8th Cir. 1988). That requirement ensures that notice of the basis for the motion is provided to the court and to the opposing party so as to avoid prejudice, provide the opponent with a meaningful opportunity to respond, and provide the court with enough information to process the motion correctly. FEDPROC § 62:364; Andreas v. Volkswagen of America, Inc., 336 F.3d 789, 56 Fed.R.Serv.3d 6 (8th Cir. 2003).

   i. Reasonable specification of the grounds for a motion is sufficient. However, where a movant fails to state even one ground for granting the motion in question, the movant has failed to meet the minimal standard of "reasonable specification." FEDPROC § 62:364; Martinez v. Trainor, 556 F.2d 818, 23 Fed.R.Serv.2d 403 (7th Cir. 1977).

   ii. The court may excuse the failure to comply with the particularity requirement if it is inadvertent, and where no prejudice is shown by the opposing party. FEDPROC § 62:364.

  e. *Motions must be filed separately*. Motions must be filed separately, but alternative motions may be filed in a single paper if each is named in the title following the caption. IN R USDCTND L.R. 7-1(a).

2. *Motion for leave to amend*. FRCP 15(a)(2) provides that after a party has amended a pleading once as of course or the time for amendments of that type has expired, a party may amend only by obtaining leave of the court or if the adverse party consents to it. FPP § 1484; In re Cessna Distributorship Antitrust

Litigation, 532 F.2d 64 (8th Cir. 1976). FRCP 15(a) does not set forth any specific procedure for obtaining leave to amend. Typically, it is sought by a motion addressed to the court's discretion. FPP § 1485.

a. *Pleadings to be amended.* As in the case of amendments as of course under FRCP 15(a)(1), any of the pleadings enumerated in FRCP 7(a) may be amended with the court's leave and FRCP 15 does not restrict the purposes for which an amendment may be made or its character. FPP § 1484.

b. *Prerequisites for leave to amend.* The only prerequisites are that the district court have jurisdiction over the case and an appeal must not be pending. FPP § 1484. If these two conditions are met, the court will proceed to examine the effect and the timing of the proposed amendments to determine whether they would prejudice the rights of any of the other parties to the suit. FPP § 1484; Nilsen v. City of Moss Point, Miss., 674 F.2d 379, 388 (5th Cir. 1982).

c. *When leave or consent is not obtained.* In general, if an amendment that cannot be made as of right is served without obtaining the court's leave or the opposing party's consent, it is without legal effect and any new matter it contains will not be considered unless the amendment is resubmitted for the court's approval. Some courts have held, however, that an untimely amended pleading served without judicial permission may be considered as properly introduced when leave to amend would have been granted had it been sought and when it does not appear that any of the parties will be prejudiced by allowing the change. FPP § 1484.

d. *Form.* A motion to amend under FRCP 15(a), as is true of motions generally, is subject to the requirements of FRCP 7(b), and must set forth with particularity the relief or order requested and the grounds supporting the application. In order to satisfy these prerequisites a copy of the amendment should be submitted with the motion so that the court and the adverse party know the precise nature of the pleading changes being proposed. FPP § 1485.

e. *Oral motion for leave to amend.* Courts have held that an oral request to amend a pleading that is made before the court in the presence of opposing party's counsel may be sufficient if the adverse party is put on notice of the nature and purpose of the request and is given the same opportunity to present objections to the proposed amendment as would have occurred if a formal motion had been made. FPP § 1485.

f. *Conditions imposed on leave to amend.* While FRCP 15(a) does not specifically authorize the district court to impose conditions on its granting of leave to amend, it is well settled that the court may impose such conditions to avoid or minimize any prejudice to the opposing party. FEDPROC § 62:276. Conditions frequently are imposed because the amending party knew of the facts sought to be asserted in the amendment but failed to assert such facts until later, to the prejudice of the opposing party. Conversely, the court may decline to impose conditions where the amendment was asserted with relative promptness. FEDPROC § 62:276.

   i. The moving party's refusal to comply with the conditions imposed by the court normally will result in a denial of the right to amend. FPP § 1486.

g. *When leave to amend may be granted.* If the underlying facts or circumstances relied upon by a plaintiff may be a proper subject of relief, he ought to be afforded an opportunity to test his claim on the merits. In the absence of any apparent or declared reason—such as undue delay, bad faith or dilatory motive on the part of the movant, repeated failure to cure deficiencies by amendments previously allowed, undue prejudice to the opposing party by virtue of allowance of the amendment, futility of amendment, etc.—the leave sought should, as the rules require, be "freely given." FPP § 1487; Foman v. Davis, 371 U.S. 178, 182, 83 S.Ct. 227, 230, 9 L.Ed.2d 222 (1962).

3. *Amendments, generally*

a. *Amendments before trial.* The function of FRCP 15(a), which provides generally for the amendment of pleadings, is to enable a party to assert matters that were overlooked or were unknown at the time the party interposed the original complaint or answer. FPP § 1473; Smiga v. Dean Witter Reynolds, Inc., 766 F.2d 698, 703 (2d Cir. 1985).

   i. *Matters contained in amended pleading under FRCP 15(a).* Although FRCP 15(a) does not expressly state that an amendment must contain only matters that occurred within a particular time period, FRCP 15(d) provides that any "transaction, occurrence, or event that happened after the date of the pleading" should be set forth in a supplemental pleading. FPP § 1473. Thus, impliedly, an amended pleading, whether prepared with or without leave of court, only should relate to matters that have taken place prior to the date of the earlier pleading. FPP § 1473; Ford Motor Co. v. U.S., 19 C.I.T. 946, 896 F.Supp. 1224, 1230 (1995).

ii. *Amending as a matter of course.* A party may amend its pleading once as a matter of course within: (1) twenty-one (21) days after serving it, or if the pleading is one to which a responsive pleading is required, twenty-one (21) days after service of a responsive pleading or twenty-one (21) days after service of a motion under FRCP 12(b), FRCP 12(e), or FRCP 12(f), whichever is earlier. FRCP 15(a)(1). Refer to the United States District Court for the Northern District of Indiana KeyRules Amended Pleading document for more information on amending as a matter of course.

iii. *Other amendments.* In all other cases, a party may amend its pleading only with the opposing party's written consent or the court's leave. The court should freely give leave when justice so requires. FRCP 15(a)(2).

iv. *Types of amendments permitted under FRCP 15(a)*

- *Cure a defective pleading.* Perhaps the most common use of FRCP 15(a) is by a party seeking to amend in order to cure a defective pleading. FPP § 1474.

- *Correct insufficiently stated claims or defenses.* A more common use of FRCP 15(a) amendments is to correct insufficiently stated claims or defenses. Typically, amendments of this character involve either adding a necessary allegation in order to state a claim for relief or correcting a misnomer of a party to the action. FPP § 1474.

- *Change nature or theory of claim or capacity of party.* Courts also have allowed a party to amend in order to change the nature or theory of the party's claim or the capacity in which the party is bringing the action. FPP § 1474.

- *State additional claims or defenses or drop claims or defenses.* Plaintiffs and defendants also have been permitted to amend their pleadings to state additional claims, to assert additional defenses, or to drop claims or defenses. FPP § 1474; Weinberger v. Retail Credit Co., 498 F.2d 552, 554, n.4 (4th Cir. 1974).

- *Increase amount of damages or elect a different remedy.* A FRCP 15(a) amendment also is appropriate for increasing the amount of damages sought, or for electing a different remedy than the one originally requested. FPP § 1474; McFadden v. Sanchez, 710 F.2d 907 (2d Cir. 1983).

- *Add, substitute, or drop parties.* Finally, a party may make a FRCP 15(a) amendment to add, substitute, or drop parties to the action. FPP § 1474.

b. *Amendments during and after trial*

i. *Based on an objection at trial.* If, at trial, a party objects that evidence is not within the issues raised in the pleadings, the court may permit the pleadings to be amended. The court should freely permit an amendment when doing so will aid in presenting the merits and the objecting party fails to satisfy the court that the evidence would prejudice that party's action or defense on the merits. The court may grant a continuance to enable the objecting party to meet the evidence. FRCP 15(b)(1).

ii. *For issues tried by consent.* When an issue not raised by the pleadings is tried by the parties' express or implied consent, it must be treated in all respects as if raised in the pleadings. A party may move—at any time, even after judgment—to amend the pleadings to conform them to the evidence and to raise an unpleaded issue. But failure to amend does not affect the result of the trial of that issue. FRCP 15(b)(2).

c. *Relation back of amendments*

i. *When an amendment relates back.* An amendment to a pleading relates back to the date of the original pleading when:

- The law that provides the applicable statute of limitations allows relation back;

- The amendment asserts a claim or defense that arose out of the conduct, transaction, or occurrence set out—or attempted to be set out—in the original pleading; or

- The amendment changes the party or the naming of the party against whom a claim is asserted, if FRCP 15(c)(1)(B) is satisfied and if, within the period provided by FRCP 4(m) for serving the summons and complaint, the party to be brought in by amendment: (1) received such notice of the action that it will not be prejudiced in defending on the merits; and (2) knew or should have known that the action would have been brought against it, but for a mistake concerning the proper party's identity. FRCP 15(c)(1).

    ii. *Notice to the United States.* When the United States or a United States officer or agency is added as a defendant by amendment, the notice requirements of FRCP 15(c)(1)(C)(i) and FRCP 15(c)(1)(C)(ii) are satisfied if, during the stated period, process was delivered or mailed to the United States attorney or the United States attorney's designee, to the Attorney General of the United States, or to the officer or agency. FRCP 15(c)(2).

  d. *Effect of an amended pleading.* A pleading that has been amended under FRCP 15(a) supersedes the pleading it modifies and remains in effect throughout the action unless it subsequently is modified. FPP § 1476. Once an amended pleading is interposed, the original pleading no longer performs any function in the case and any subsequent motion made by an opposing party should be directed at the amended pleading. FPP § 1476; Ferdik v. Bonzelet, 963 F.2d 1258, 1262 (9th Cir. 1992); Davis v. TXO Production Corp., 929 F.2d 1515, 1517 (10th Cir. 1991).

4. *Opposing papers.* The Federal Rules of Civil Procedure do not require any formal answer, return, or reply to a motion, except where the Federal Rules of Civil Procedure or local rules may require affidavits, memoranda, or other papers to be filed in opposition to a motion. Such papers are simply to apprise the court of such opposition and the grounds of that opposition. FEDPROC § 62:359.

  a. *Effect of failure to respond to motion.* Although in the absence of statutory provision or court rule, a motion ordinarily does not require a written answer, when a party files a motion and the opposing party fails to respond, the court may construe such failure to respond as nonopposition to the motion or an admission that the motion was meritorious, may take the facts alleged in the motion as true—the rule in some jurisdictions being that the failure to respond to a fact set forth in a motion is deemed an admission—and may grant the motion if the relief requested appears to be justified. AMJUR MOTIONS § 28.

  b. *Assent or no opposition not determinative.* However, a motion will not be granted automatically simply because an "assent" or a notation of "no opposition" has been filed; federal judges frequently deny motions that have been assented to when it is thought that justice so dictates. FPP § 1190.

  c. *Responsive pleading inappropriate as response to motion.* An attempt to answer or oppose a motion with a responsive pleading usually is not appropriate. FPP § 1190.

5. *Reply papers.* A moving party may be required or permitted to prepare papers in addition to his original motion papers. AMJUR MOTIONS § 25. Papers answering or replying to opposing papers may be appropriate, in the interests of justice, where it appears there is a substantial reason for allowing a reply. Thus, a court may accept reply papers where a party demonstrates that the papers to which it seeks to file a reply raise new issues that are material to the disposition of the question before the court, or where the court determines, sua sponte, that it wishes further briefing of an issue raised in those papers and orders the submission of additional papers. FEDPROC § 62:360.

  a. *Function of reply papers.* The function of a reply affidavit is to answer the arguments made in opposition to the position taken by the movant and not to permit the movant to introduce new arguments in support of the motion. AMJUR MOTIONS § 25.

  b. *Issues raised for the first time in a reply document.* However, the view has been followed in some jurisdictions, that as a matter of judicial economy, where there is no prejudice and where the issues could be raised simply by filing a motion to dismiss, the trial court has discretion to consider arguments raised for the first time in a reply memorandum, and that a trial court may grant a motion to strike issues raised for the first time in a reply memorandum. AMJUR MOTIONS § 26.

6. *Appearances.* Attorneys not representing the United States or its agencies must file an appearance when

they represent (either in person or by filing a paper) a party. IN R USDCTND L.R. 83-8(a). For more information, refer to IN R USDCTND L.R. 83-8.

7. *Notice of related action.* A party must file a notice of related action as soon as it appears that the party's case and another pending case: (1) arise out of the same transaction or occurrence; (2) involve the same property; or (3) involve the validity or infringement of the same patent, trademark, or copyright. IN R USDCTND L.R. 40-1(d). For more information, refer to IN R USDCTND L.R. 40-1.

8. *Alternative dispute resolution (ADR).* After they confer as required by FRCP 26(f), the parties must advise the court which, if any, alternative-dispute-resolution processes they expect to pursue and when they expect to undertake the process. IN R USDCTND L.R. 16-6(a). For more information on alternative dispute resolution (ADR), refer to IN R USDCTND L.R. 16-6 and IN R USDCTND Order 2003-21.

9. *Settlement or resolution.* The parties must immediately notify the court if they reasonably expect to settle the case or resolve a pending motion. IN R USDCTND L.R. 16-1(g).

10. *Modification or suspension of rules.* The court may, on its own motion or at the request of a party, suspend or modify any rule in a particular case in the interest of justice. IN R USDCTND L.R. 1-1(c).

D. Documents

1. *Documents for moving party*

   a. *Required documents*

      i. *Notice of motion and motion.* The party must not specify a hearing date in the notice of a motion or petition unless the court or the clerk has authorized it. IN R USDCTND L.R. 7-5(b)(2). Refer to the General Requirements section of this document for information on the notice of motion and motion.

      ii. *Proposed amendment.* Motions to amend a pleading must include the original signed proposed amendment as an attachment. IN R USDCTND L.R. 15-1(a). In order to file a document which requires leave of court such as an amended complaint or a document to be filed out of time, the proposed document shall be attached as an exhibit to a motion. IN R USDCTND CM/ECF(II)(A)(5). In order to satisfy the prerequisites of FRCP 7(b), a copy of the amendment should be submitted with the motion so that the court and the adverse party know the precise nature of the pleading changes being proposed. FPP § 1485. The amending party should submit a copy of the proposed amendment at least by the date of the hearing on the motion for leave to amend. FEDPROC § 62:274; Grombach v. Oerlikon Tool & Arms Corp. of America, 276 F.2d 155 (4th Cir. 1960).

      - Amendments to a pleading: (1) must reproduce the entire pleading as amended, unless the court allows otherwise; and (2) must not incorporate another pleading by reference. IN R USDCTND L.R. 15-1(b).

      - The documents accompanying the motion for leave to amend may be an appropriate substitute for a formally proposed amendment, if the documents sufficiently indicate the gist of the amendment. FEDPROC § 62:274.

      - Failing to comply with IN R USDCTND L.R. 15-1 is not grounds to deny the motion. IN R USDCTND L.R. 15-1(c).

      iii. *Certificate of service.* FRCP 5(d) requires that the person making service under FRCP 5 certify that service has been effected. FRCP 5(Advisory Committee Notes). Having such information on file may be useful for many purposes, including proof of service if an issue arises concerning the effectiveness of the service. FRCP 5(Advisory Committee Notes).

      - *Certificate of service for electronically-filed documents.* A Certificate of Service is still a requirement when filing documents electronically. A sample Certificate of Service is attached as Form 1 (IN R USDCTND CM/ECF(Form 1)). IN R USDCTND CM/ECF(II)(H).

   b. *Supplemental documents*

      i. *Brief.* Refer to the Format section of this document for the format of briefs.

ii. *Supporting evidence.* When a motion relies on facts outside the record, the court may hear the matter on affidavits or may hear it wholly or partly on oral testimony or on depositions. FRCP 43(c).

- *Materials necessary for motion.* A party must file those portions of discovery requests or responses (including deposition transcripts) that the party relies on to support a motion that could result in a final order on an issue. IN R USDCTND L.R. 26-2(c).

iii. *Notice of constitutional question.* A party that files a pleading, written motion, or other paper drawing into question the constitutionality of a federal or state statute must promptly:

- *File notice.* File a notice of constitutional question stating the question and identifying the paper that raises it, if: (1) a federal statute is questioned and the parties do not include the United States, one of its agencies, or one of its officers or employees in an official capacity; or (2) a state statute is questioned and the parties do not include the state, one of its agencies, or one of its officers or employees in an official capacity; and

- *Serve notice.* Serve the notice and paper on the Attorney General of the United States if a federal statute is questioned—or on the state attorney general if a state statute is questioned—either by certified or registered mail or by sending it to an electronic address designated by the attorney general for this purpose. FRCP 5.1(a).

- *When to file the notice.* A party required to file a notice of constitutional question under FRCP 5.1 must do so by the later of: (1) the day the parties tender their proposed case-management plan (if one is required); or (2) 21 days after filing the pleading, written motion, or other paper questioning the constitutionality of a federal or state statute. IN R USDCTND L.R. 5.1-1(a).

- *Service on government officials.* The party must also serve the notice and the pleading, written motion, or other paper questioning the constitutionality of a federal or state statute on: (1) the Attorney General of the United States and the United States Attorney for the Northern District of Indiana, if a federal statute is challenged; or (2) the Attorney General for the state if a state statute is challenged. IN R USDCTND L.R. 5.1-1(b). Service required under IN R USDCTND L.R. 5.1-1(b) may be made either by certified or registered mail or by emailing it to an address designated by those officials for this purpose. IN R USDCTND L.R. 5.1-1(c).

- *No forfeiture.* A party's failure to file and serve the notice, or the court's failure to certify, does not forfeit a constitutional claim or defense that is otherwise timely asserted. FRCP 5.1(d).

iv. *Index of exhibits.* Any pleading, motion, brief, affidavit, notice, or proposed order, whether filed electronically or by delivering it to the clerk, must: include a separate index identifying and briefly describing each exhibit if there are more than four (4) exhibits. IN R USDCTND L.R. 5-4(a)(8).

v. *Request for oral argument.* A party may request oral argument on a motion by filing and serving a separate document explaining why oral argument is necessary and estimating how long the court should allow for the argument. IN R USDCTND L.R. 7-5(a)(1). The request must be filed and served with the party's supporting brief, response brief, or reply brief. IN R USDCTND L.R. 7-5(a)(2).

vi. *Request for evidentiary hearing.* A party may request an evidentiary hearing by filing and serving a separate document explaining why the hearing is necessary and estimating how long the court should allow for it. IN R USDCTND L.R. 7-5(b)(1).

vii. *Copy of authority.* A copy of any decision, statute, or regulation cited in a motion or brief must be attached to the paper if—and only if—it is not available on Westlaw or Lexis. But if a copy of a decision, statute, or regulation is only available electronically, a party must provide it to the court or another party upon request. IN R USDCTND L.R. 7-1(f).

viii. *Proposed order.* Parties filing a paper that requires the judge or clerk to enter a routine or uncontested order must include a suitable form of order. IN R USDCTND L.R. 5-4(c).

- Proposed orders shall not be filed electronically either as a separate document or as an

attachment to the main pleading or other document. Instead, all proposed orders must be e-mailed to the chambers of the appropriate judicial officer for the case. The proposed order must be in WordPerfect Format or Rich Text Format (RTF). Proposed orders should be attached to an e-mail and sent to the appropriate judicial officer at the address listed in IN R USDCTND CM/ECF(II)(F). The subject line of the email message should indicate the case title, cause number and document number of the motion, e.g., Smith v. Jones 1:02-cv-1234, motion# ___. IN R USDCTND CM/ECF(II)(F).

ix. *Copy of document with self-addressed envelope.* A party who wants a file-stamped copy of a paper must include with the filing an additional copy of the paper and a self-addressed envelope with adequate postage. IN R USDCTND L.R. 5-4(b)(6).

x. *Notice of manual filing.* However, if that is not physically possible, counsel shall electronically file a .pdf document titled Notice of Manual Filing as a notation on the docket sheet that filings are being held in the clerk's office in paper. A sample Notice of Manual Filing is attached as Form 2 (IN R USDCTND CM/ECF(Form 2)). IN R USDCTND CM/ECF(III)(A)(1).

xi. *Courtesy copies.* If documents are filed in paper format, counsel must provide an original for the clerk's office, a copy for the judge and a copy must be served on all parties in the case. IN R USDCTND CM/ECF(III)(A)(1).

xii. *Declaration that party was unable to file in a timely manner.* If the attorney is unable to file a document in a timely manner due to technical difficulties in the user's system, the attorney must file a document with the court as soon as possible notifying the court of the inability to file the document. A sample document entitled Declaration that Party was Unable to File in a Timely Manner Due to Technical Difficulties is attached hereto as Form 5. IN R USDCTND CM/ECF(VI)(B). [Editor's note: the reference to Form 5 is likely meant to be a reference to Form 3 (IN R USDCTND CM/ECF(Form 3)].

2. *Documents for opposing party*

  a. *Required documents*

    i. *Response brief.* Refer to the Format section of this document for the format of briefs. Refer to the General Requirements section of this document for information on the opposing papers.

    ii. *Certificate of service.* FRCP 5(d) requires that the person making service under FRCP 5 certify that service has been effected. FRCP 5(Advisory Committee Notes). Having such information on file may be useful for many purposes, including proof of service if an issue arises concerning the effectiveness of the service. FRCP 5(Advisory Committee Notes).

      • *Certificate of service for electronically-filed documents.* A Certificate of Service is still a requirement when filing documents electronically. A sample Certificate of Service is attached as Form 1 (IN R USDCTND CM/ECF(Form 1)). IN R USDCTND CM/ECF(II)(H).

  b. *Supplemental documents*

    i. *Supporting evidence.* When a motion relies on facts outside the record, the court may hear the matter on affidavits or may hear it wholly or partly on oral testimony or on depositions. FRCP 43(c).

      • *Materials necessary for motion.* A party must file those portions of discovery requests or responses (including deposition transcripts) that the party relies on to support a motion that could result in a final order on an issue. IN R USDCTND L.R. 26-2(c).

    ii. *Notice of constitutional question.* A party that files a pleading, written motion, or other paper drawing into question the constitutionality of a federal or state statute must promptly:

      • *File notice.* File a notice of constitutional question stating the question and identifying the paper that raises it, if: (1) a federal statute is questioned and the parties do not include the United States, one of its agencies, or one of its officers or employees in an official capacity; or (2) a state statute is questioned and the parties do not include the state, one of its agencies, or one of its officers or employees in an official capacity; and

- *Serve notice.* Serve the notice and paper on the Attorney General of the United States if a federal statute is questioned—or on the state attorney general if a state statute is questioned—either by certified or registered mail or by sending it to an electronic address designated by the attorney general for this purpose. FRCP 5.1(a).

- *When to file the notice.* A party required to file a notice of constitutional question under FRCP 5.1 must do so by the later of: (1) the day the parties tender their proposed case-management plan (if one is required); or (2) 21 days after filing the pleading, written motion, or other paper questioning the constitutionality of a federal or state statute. IN R USDCTND L.R. 5.1-1(a).

- *Service on government officials.* The party must also serve the notice and the pleading, written motion, or other paper questioning the constitutionality of a federal or state statute on: (1) the Attorney General of the United States and the United States Attorney for the Northern District of Indiana, if a federal statute is challenged; or (2) the Attorney General for the state if a state statute is challenged. IN R USDCTND L.R. 5.1-1(b). Service required under IN R USDCTND L.R. 5.1-1(b) may be made either by certified or registered mail or by emailing it to an address designated by those officials for this purpose. IN R USDCTND L.R. 5.1-1(c).

- *No forfeiture.* A party's failure to file and serve the notice, or the court's failure to certify, does not forfeit a constitutional claim or defense that is otherwise timely asserted. FRCP 5.1(d).

iii. *Index of exhibits.* Any pleading, motion, brief, affidavit, notice, or proposed order, whether filed electronically or by delivering it to the clerk, must: include a separate index identifying and briefly describing each exhibit if there are more than four (4) exhibits. IN R USDCTND L.R. 5-4(a)(8).

iv. *Request for oral argument.* A party may request oral argument on a motion by filing and serving a separate document explaining why oral argument is necessary and estimating how long the court should allow for the argument. IN R USDCTND L.R. 7-5(a)(1). The request must be filed and served with the party's supporting brief, response brief, or reply brief. IN R USDCTND L.R. 7-5(a)(2).

v. *Request for evidentiary hearing.* A party may request an evidentiary hearing by filing and serving a separate document explaining why the hearing is necessary and estimating how long the court should allow for it. IN R USDCTND L.R. 7-5(b)(1).

vi. *Copy of authority.* A copy of any decision, statute, or regulation cited in a motion or brief must be attached to the paper if—and only if—it is not available on Westlaw or Lexis. But if a copy of a decision, statute, or regulation is only available electronically, a party must provide it to the court or another party upon request. IN R USDCTND L.R. 7-1(f).

vii. *Copy of document with self-addressed envelope.* A party who wants a file-stamped copy of a paper must include with the filing an additional copy of the paper and a self-addressed envelope with adequate postage. IN R USDCTND L.R. 5-4(b)(6).

viii. *Notice of manual filing.* However, if that is not physically possible, counsel shall electronically file a .pdf document titled Notice of Manual Filing as a notation on the docket sheet that filings are being held in the clerk's office in paper. A sample Notice of Manual Filing is attached as Form 2 (IN R USDCTND CM/ECF(Form 2)). IN R USDCTND CM/ECF(III)(A)(1).

ix. *Courtesy copies.* If documents are filed in paper format, counsel must provide an original for the clerk's office, a copy for the judge and a copy must be served on all parties in the case. IN R USDCTND CM/ECF(III)(A)(1).

x. *Declaration that party was unable to file in a timely manner.* If the attorney is unable to file a document in a timely manner due to technical difficulties in the user's system, the attorney must file a document with the court as soon as possible notifying the court of the inability to file the document. A sample document entitled Declaration that Party was Unable to File in a Timely Manner Due to Technical Difficulties is attached hereto as Form 5. IN R USDCTND

CM/ECF(VI)(B). [Editor's note: the reference to Form 5 is likely meant to be a reference to Form 3 (IN R USDCTND CM/ECF(Form 3)].

E. Format

1. *Form of documents.* The rules governing captions and other matters of form in pleadings apply to motions and other papers. FRCP 7(b)(2).

    a. *Paper.* Any pleading, motion, brief, affidavit, notice, or proposed order, whether filed electronically or by delivering it to the clerk, must: use eight and one-half by eleven (8-1/2 x 11) inch pages. IN R USDCTND L.R. 5-4(a)(2).

        i. *Manual filings.* Papers delivered to the clerk for filing must: be flat, unfolded, and on good-quality, white paper. IN R USDCTND L.R. 5-4(b)(1)(A).

        - *Covers or backing.* Papers delivered to the clerk for filing must: not have a cover or a back. IN R USDCTND L.R. 5-4(b)(1)(B).

        - *Recycled paper.* The court encourages using recycled paper. IN R USDCTND L.R. 5-4(b)(7).

    b. *Margins.* Any pleading, motion, brief, affidavit, notice, or proposed order, whether filed electronically or by delivering it to the clerk, must: have at least one (1) inch margins. IN R USDCTND L.R. 5-4(a)(3).

    c. *Spacing.* Any pleading, motion, brief, affidavit, notice, or proposed order, whether filed electronically or by delivering it to the clerk, must: be double spaced (except for headings, footnotes, and quoted material). IN R USDCTND L.R. 5-4(a)(5).

    d. *Text.* Any pleading, motion, brief, affidavit, notice, or proposed order, whether filed electronically or by delivering it to the clerk, must: be plainly typewritten, printed, or prepared by a clearly legible copying process. IN R USDCTND L.R. 5-4(a)(1).

        i. Any pleading, motion, brief, affidavit, notice, or proposed order, whether filed electronically or by delivering it to the clerk, must: use at least twelve (12) point type in the body and at least ten (10) point type in footnotes. IN R USDCTND L.R. 5-4(a)(4).

    e. *Page numbering.* Any pleading, motion, brief, affidavit, notice, or proposed order, whether filed electronically or by delivering it to the clerk, must: have consecutively numbered pages. IN R USDCTND L.R. 5-4(a)(6).

    f. *Caption; Names of parties.* Every pleading must have a caption with the court's name, a title, a file number, and a FRCP 7(a) designation. The title of the complaint must name all the parties; the title of other pleadings, after naming the first party on each side, may refer generally to other parties. FRCP 10(a). Any pleading, motion, brief, affidavit, notice, or proposed order, whether filed electronically or by delivering it to the clerk, must: include a title on the first page. IN R USDCTND L.R. 5-4(a)(7).

        i. *Alternative motions.* Motions must be filed separately, but alternative motions may be filed in a single paper if each is named in the title following the caption. IN R USDCTND L.R. 7-1(a).

    g. *Filer's information.* Any pleading, motion, brief, affidavit, notice, or proposed order, whether filed electronically or by delivering it to the clerk, must: except in proposed orders and affidavits, include the filer's name, address, telephone number, fax number (where available), and e-mail address (where available). IN R USDCTND L.R. 5-4(a)(9).

    h. *Paragraphs; Separate statements.* A party must state its claims or defenses in numbered paragraphs, each limited as far as practicable to a single set of circumstances. A later pleading may refer by number to a paragraph in an earlier pleading. If doing so would promote clarity, each claim founded on a separate transaction or occurrence—and each defense other than a denial—must be stated in a separate count or defense. FRCP 10(b).

    i. *Adoption by reference; Exhibits.* A statement in a pleading may be adopted by reference elsewhere in the same pleading or in any other pleading or motion. A copy of a written instrument that is an exhibit to a pleading is a part of the pleading for all purposes. FRCP 10(c).

j. *Citation of local rules.* The Local Civil Rules of the United States District Court for the Northern District of Indiana may be cited as "N.D. Ind. L.R." IN R USDCTND L.R. 1-1(a)(1).

k. *Acceptance by the clerk.* The clerk must not refuse to file a paper solely because it is not in the form prescribed by the Federal Rules of Civil Procedure or by a local rule or practice. FRCP 5(d)(4).

   i. *Sanctions for formatting errors; Non-compliance.* If a person files a paper that does not comply with the rules governing the format of papers filed with the court, the court may: (1) strike the paper from the record; or (2) fine the person up to one thousand dollars ($1,000). IN R USDCTND L.R. 1-3(a).

   - *Notice.* Before sanctioning a person under IN R USDCTND L.R. 1-3(a)(2), the court must: (1) notify the person that the paper is noncompliant; and (2) give the person the opportunity either to be heard or to revise the paper. IN R USDCTND L.R. 1-3(b).

2. *Form of electronic documents.* Electronically filed documents must meet the same requirements of format and page limits as documents "conventionally filed" (as defined in IN R USDCTND CM/ECF(III)(A)) pursuant to the Federal Rules of Civil Procedure and the Local Civil Rules of the United States District Court for the Northern District of Indiana. IN R USDCTND CM/ECF(II)(A)(2).

   a. *PDF format required.* Documents filed in the CM/ECF must be in .pdf format. A document created with almost any word-processing program can be converted to .pdf format. The .pdf program in effect takes a picture of the original document and allows anyone to open the converted document across a broad range of hardware and software, with layout, format, links, and images intact. IN R USDCTND CM/ECF(FN2).

   b. *Title of documents.* The person electronically filing a pleading or other document will be responsible for designating a title for the pleading or other document by using one of the categories contained in the events listed in the CM/ECF Menu. IN R USDCTND CM/ECF(II)(G).

   c. *Combining documents.* All documents which form part of a single pleading and which are being filed at the same time and by the same party may be electronically filed together under one document number, e.g., the motion and a supporting affidavit, with the exception of memoranda in support. Memoranda in support shall be electronically filed separately and shown as a related document to the motion. IN R USDCTND CM/ECF(II)(A)(4).

   d. *Exhibits and attachments.* Filing users must submit in electronic form all documents referenced as exhibits or attachments, unless the court permits conventional filing. A filing user must submit as exhibits or attachments only those excerpts of the referenced documents that are directly germane to the matter under consideration by the court. Excerpted material must be clearly and prominently identified as such. Filing users who file excerpts of documents as exhibits or attachments do so without prejudice to their right to timely file additional excerpts or the complete document. Responding parties may timely file additional excerpts or the complete document that they believe are directly germane. The court may require parties to file additional excerpts or the complete document. IN R USDCTND CM/ECF(II)(A)(6).

   e. *Hyperlinks.* Electronically filed documents may contain hyperlink references to an external document as a convenient mechanism for accessing material cited in the document. A hyperlink reference is neither validated for content nor considered a part of the court's records. The court neither endorses the product or organization at the destination of a hyperlink reference, nor does the court exercise any responsibility over the content at the destination. In order to preserve the integrity of the court record, attorneys wishing to insert hyperlinks in court filings shall continue to use the traditional citation method for the cited authority, in addition to the hyperlink. A hyperlink contained in a filing is no more than a convenient mechanism for accessing material cited in the document and a hyperlink reference is extraneous to any filed document and is not part of the court's record. IN R USDCTND CM/ECF(II)(A)(3).

3. *Form of briefs*

   a. *Page limits.* Supporting and response briefs (excluding tables of contents, tables of authorities, and appendices) ordinarily must not exceed twenty-five (25) pages. Reply briefs must not exceed fifteen (15) pages. IN R USDCTND L.R. 7-1(e)(1).

      i. *Exception.* The court may allow a party to file a brief exceeding these page limits for extraordinary and compelling reasons. But if the court permits a brief to exceed twenty-five (25) pages, it must include:

- A table of contents with page references;
- An issue statement; and
- A table of authorities including: (1) all cases (alphabetically arranged), statutes, and other authorities cited in the brief; and (2) references to where the authorities appear in the brief. IN R USDCTND L.R. 7-1(e)(2).

4. *Signing of pleadings, motions and other papers*

    a. *Signature.* Every pleading, written motion, and other paper must be signed by at least one attorney of record in the attorney's name—or by a party personally if the party is unrepresented. The paper must state the signer's address, e-mail address, and telephone number. FRCP 11(a).

        i. *Signatures on manual filings.* Papers delivered to the clerk for filing must: include the filer's original signature. IN R USDCTND L.R. 5-4(b)(1)(C).

- *Rubber-stamped and faxed signatures.* An original paper with a rubber-stamped or faxed signature is unsigned for purposes of FRCP 11 and FRCP 26(g). IN R USDCTND L.R. 5-4(b)(2).
- *Affidavits.* Only the affiant need sign an affidavit. IN R USDCTND L.R. 5-4(b)(3).

        ii. *Electronic signatures.* Pursuant to FRCP 11, every pleading, motion, and other paper (except lists, schedules, statements or amendments thereto) shall be signed by at least one attorney of record or, if the party is not represented by an attorney, all papers shall be signed by the party. An attorney's/participant's password issued by the court combined with the user's identification, serves as and constitutes the attorney/participant's signature for FRCP 11 and other purposes. IN R USDCTND CM/ECF(I)(C). Documents which must be filed and which must contain original signatures other than those of a participating attorney or which require either verification or an unsworn declaration under any rule or statute, shall be filed electronically, with originally executed copies maintained by the filer. The pleading or other document electronically filed shall contain "s/" signature(s), as noted in IN R USDCTND CM/ECF(II)(E)(3)(b). IN R USDCTND CM/ECF(II)(E)(1).

- *Multiple signatures.* In the case of a stipulation or other document to be signed by two or more attorneys, the following procedure should be used: The filing attorney shall initially confirm that the content of the document is acceptable to all persons required to sign the document and shall obtain the physical signatures of all attorneys on the document. IN R USDCTND CM/ECF(II)(E)(3)(a). The filing attorney then shall file the document electronically, indicating the signatories, e.g., "s/Jane Doe," "s/John Doe," etc. IN R USDCTND CM/ECF(II)(E)(3)(b). The filing attorney shall retain the hard copy of the document containing the original signatures. IN R USDCTND CM/ECF(II)(E)(3)(c).

        iii. *No verification or accompanying affidavit required for pleadings.* Unless a rule or statute specifically states otherwise, a pleading need not be verified or accompanied by an affidavit. FRCP 11(a).

        iv. *Unsigned papers.* The court must strike an unsigned paper unless the omission is promptly corrected after being called to the attorney's or party's attention. FRCP 11(a).

    b. *Representations to the court.* By presenting to the court a pleading, written motion, or other paper—whether by signing, filing, submitting, or later advocating it—an attorney or unrepresented party certifies that to the best of the person's knowledge, information, and belief, formed after an inquiry reasonable under the circumstances:

        i. It is not being presented for any improper purpose, such as to harass, cause unnecessary delay, or needlessly increase the cost of litigation;

        ii. The claims, defenses, and other legal contentions are warranted by existing law or by a nonfrivolous argument for extending, modifying, or reversing existing law or for establishing new law;

iii. The factual contentions have evidentiary support or, if specifically so identified, will likely have evidentiary support after a reasonable opportunity for further investigation or discovery; and

iv. The denials of factual contentions are warranted on the evidence or, if specifically so identified, are reasonably based on belief or a lack of information. FRCP 11(b).

c. *Sanctions.* If, after notice and a reasonable opportunity to respond, the court determines that FRCP 11(b) has been violated, the court may impose an appropriate sanction on any attorney, law firm, or party that violated FRCP 11(b) or is responsible for the violation. FRCP 11(c)(1). Refer to the United States District Court for the Northern District of Indiana KeyRules Motion for Sanctions document for more information.

5. *Privacy protection for filings made with the court*

a. *Redacted filings.* Counsel should not include sensitive information in any document filed with the court unless such inclusion is necessary and relevant to the case. IN R USDCTND CM/ECF(VII). Unless the court orders otherwise, in an electronic or paper filing with the court that contains an individual's Social Security number, taxpayer-identification number, or birth date, the name of an individual known to be a minor, or a financial-account number, a party or nonparty making the filing may include only:

i. The last four (4) digits of the Social Security number and taxpayer-identification number;

ii. The year of the individual's birth;

iii. The minor's initials; and

iv. The last four (4) digits of the financial-account number. FRCP 5.2(a); IN R USDCTND Order 2005-3.

b. *Exemptions from the redaction requirement.* The redaction requirement does not apply to the following:

i. A financial-account number that identifies the property allegedly subject to forfeiture in a forfeiture proceeding;

ii. The record of an administrative or agency proceeding;

iii. The official record of a state-court proceeding;

iv. The record of a court or tribunal, if that record was not subject to the redaction requirement when originally filed;

v. A filing covered by FRCP 5.2(c) or FRCP 5.2(d); and

vi. A pro se filing in an action brought under 28 U.S.C.A. § 2241, 28 U.S.C.A. § 2254, or 28 U.S.C.A. § 2255. FRCP 5.2(b).

vii. In cases filed under the Social Security Act, 42 U.S.C.A. § 405(g), there is no need for redaction of any information from the documents filed in the case. IN R USDCTND Order 2005-3.

c. *Limitations on remote access to electronic files; Social Security appeals and immigration cases.* Unless the court orders otherwise, in an action for benefits under the Social Security Act, and in an action or proceeding relating to an order of removal, to relief from removal, or to immigration benefits or detention, access to an electronic file is authorized as follows:

i. The parties and their attorneys may have remote electronic access to any part of the case file, including the administrative record;

ii. Any other person may have electronic access to the full record at the courthouse, but may have remote electronic access only to:

- The docket maintained by the court; and

- An opinion, order, judgment, or other disposition of the court, but not any other part of the case file or the administrative record. FRCP 5.2(c).

d. *Filings made under seal.* The court may order that a filing be made under seal without redaction. The court may later unseal the filing or order the person who made the filing to file a redacted version for the public record. FRCP 5.2(d). For information on filing documents under seal, refer to IN R USDCTND L.R. 5-3, IN R USDCTND CM/ECF(IV)(A), and IN R USDCTND ECF Order 2004-19.

e. *Protective orders.* For good cause, the court may by order in a case:

   i. Require redaction of additional information; or

   ii. Limit or prohibit a nonparty's remote electronic access to a document filed with the court. FRCP 5.2(e).

f. *Option for additional unredacted filing under seal.* A person making a redacted filing may also file an unredacted copy under seal. The court must retain the unredacted copy as part of the record. FRCP 5.2(f); IN R USDCTND Order 2005-3.

   i. The unredacted version of the document or the reference list shall be retained by the court under seal as part of the record. This paper shall be retained by the court as part of the record. The court may, however, still require the party to file a redacted copy for the public file. IN R USDCTND Order 2005-3.

g. *Option for filing a reference list.* A filing that contains redacted information may be filed together with a reference list that identifies each item of redacted information and specifies an appropriate identifier that uniquely corresponds to each item listed. The list must be filed under seal and may be amended as of right. Any reference in the case to a listed identifier will be construed to refer to the corresponding item of information. FRCP 5.2(g); IN R USDCTND Order 2005-3.

   i. The unredacted version of the document or the reference list shall be retained by the court under seal as part of the record. This paper shall be retained by the court as part of the record. The court may, however, still require the party to file a redacted copy for the public file. IN R USDCTND Order 2005-3.

h. *Responsibility for redaction.* The responsibility for redacting these personal identifiers rests solely with counsel and the parties. The Clerk will not review each paper for compliance with IN R USDCTND Order 2005-3. IN R USDCTND Order 2005-3.

i. *Waiver of protection of identifiers.* A person waives the protection of FRCP 5.2(a) as to the person's own information by filing it without redaction and not under seal. FRCP 5.2(h).

F. Filing and Service Requirements

1. *Filing requirements.* Any paper after the complaint that is required to be served—together with a certificate of service—must be filed within a reasonable time after service. FRCP 5(d)(1). Motions must be filed separately, but alternative motions may be filed in a single paper if each is named in the title following the caption. IN R USDCTND L.R. 7-1(a).

   a. *How filing is made; In general.* A paper is filed by delivering it:

      i. To the clerk; or

      ii. To a judge who agrees to accept it for filing, and who must then note the filing date on the paper and promptly send it to the clerk. FRCP 5(d)(2).

         • Papers not filed electronically must be filed with the clerk, not a judge. IN R USDCTND L.R. 5-4(b)(4).

      iii. Parties manually filing a paper that requires the clerk to give others notice, must give the clerk: (1) sufficient copies of the notice; and (2) the name and address of each person entitled to receive the notice. IN R USDCTND L.R. 5-4(b)(8).

   b. *Where to file.* Papers not filed electronically must be filed in the division where the case is pending, unless: (1) a person will be prejudiced if the paper is not filed the same day it is tendered; and (2) it includes an adequately sized envelope addressed to the clerk's office in the division where the case is pending and with adequate postage. IN R USDCTND L.R. 5-4(b)(5).

   c. *Electronic filing*

      i. *Authorization of electronic filing program.* A court may, by local rule, allow papers to be filed,

signed, or verified by electronic means that are consistent with any technical standards established by the Judicial Conference of the United States. A local rule may require electronic filing only if reasonable exceptions are allowed. A paper filed electronically in compliance with a local rule is a written paper for purposes of the Federal Rules of Civil Procedure. FRCP 5(d)(3).

- Papers must be filed, signed, and verified electronically unless excepted by the court's CM/ECF Civil and Criminal User Manual (IN R USDCTND CM/ECF). IN R USDCTND L.R. 5-1.

ii. *Mandatory electronic filing.* Unless otherwise permitted by these procedures or otherwise authorized by the assigned judge, all documents submitted for filing in this district in civil and criminal cases, no matter when a case was originally filed, shall be filed electronically using the System. IN R USDCTND CM/ECF(II)(A)(1). The requirement that "all documents" be filed electronically includes briefs, and attachments and exhibits used in support of motions. IN R USDCTND CM/ECF(FN1).

- Sending a document or pleading to the court via e-mail or facsimile does not constitute "electronic filing." IN R USDCTND CM/ECF(I)(A).

iii. *Conventional filing.* As used in these procedures, a "conventionally" filed or submitted document or pleading is one presented to the Clerk or a party in paper or other non-electronic, tangible format. The following documents shall be filed conventionally and not electronically unless specifically authorized by the Court:

- Exhibits and other documents which cannot be converted to a legible electronic form. Whenever possible, counsel is responsible for converting filings to an electronic form. However, if that is not physically possible, counsel shall electronically file a .pdf document titled Notice of Manual Filing as a notation on the docket sheet that filings are being held in the clerk's office in paper. A sample Notice of Manual Filing is attached as Form 2 (IN R USDCTND CM/ECF(Form 2)). If documents are filed in paper format, counsel must provide an original for the clerk's office, a copy for the judge and a copy must be served on all parties in the case. Large documents which do not exist in an electronic format shall be scanned into .pdf format by counsel, in small batches if necessary, and filed electronically as separate attachments in the System. IN R USDCTND CM/ECF(III)(A)(1).

- Certain documents which are listed in IN R USDCTND CM/ECF(II)(E)(2). IN R US-DCTND CM/ECF(III)(A)(2).

- Documents filed by pro se litigants. IN R USDCTND CM/ECF(III)(A)(3).

iv. For more information on electronic filing, refer to IN R USDCTND CM/ECF.

2. *Service requirements*

a. *Service; When required*

i. *In general.* Unless the Federal Rules of Civil Procedure provide otherwise, each of the following papers must be served on every party:

- An order stating that service is required;

- A pleading filed after the original complaint, unless the court orders otherwise under FRCP 5(c) because there are numerous defendants;

- A discovery paper required to be served on a party, unless the court orders otherwise;

- A written motion, except one that may be heard ex parte; and

- A written notice, appearance, demand, or offer of judgment, or any similar paper. FRCP 5(a)(1).

ii. *If a party fails to appear.* No service is required on a party who is in default for failing to appear. But a pleading that asserts a new claim for relief against such a party must be served on that party under FRCP 4. FRCP 5(a)(2).

    iii. *Seizing property.* If an action is begun by seizing property and no person is or need be named as a defendant, any service required before the filing of an appearance, answer, or claim must be made on the person who had custody or possession of the property when it was seized. FRCP 5(a)(3).

b. *Service; How made*

    i. *Serving an attorney.* If a party is represented by an attorney, service under FRCP 5 must be made on the attorney unless the court orders service on the party. FRCP 5(b)(1).

    ii. *Service in general.* A paper is served under FRCP 5 by:

- Handing it to the person;

- Leaving it: (1) at the person's office with a clerk or other person in charge or, if no one is in charge, in a conspicuous place in the office; or (2) if the person has no office or the office is closed, at the person's dwelling or usual place of abode with someone of suitable age and discretion who resides there;

- Mailing it to the person's last known address—in which event service is complete upon mailing;

- Leaving it with the court clerk if the person has no known address;

- Sending it by electronic means if the person consented in writing—in which event service is complete upon transmission, but is not effective if the serving party learns that it did not reach the person to be served; or

- Delivering it by any other means that the person consented to in writing—in which event service is complete when the person making service delivers it to the agency designated to make delivery. FRCP 5(b)(2).

    iii. *Electronic service.* Electronically filed papers may be served electronically if service is consistent with the CM/ECF User Manual (IN R USDCTND CM/ECF). IN R USDCTND L.R. 5-2(a).

- *Waiver of other service.* An attorney's registration will constitute a waiver of conventional service of documents and the attorney agrees to accept service of notice on behalf of the client of the electronic filing by hand, facsimile or authorized email. IN R USDCTND CM/ECF(I)(B)(3).

- *Serving registered persons.* The System will generate a "Notice of Electronic Filing" when any document is filed. This notice represents service of the document on parties who are registered participants with the System. Except as provided in IN R USDCTND CM/ECF(III)(B), the filing party shall not be required to serve any pleading or other documents on any party receiving electronic notice. IN R USDCTND CM/ECF(II)(D)(1). The term "pleading" refers only to those documents listed in FRCP 7(a). IN R USDCTND CM/ECF(FN3).

- *When electronic service is deemed completed.* A person registered to use the court's electronic-filing system is served with an electronically filed paper when a "Notice of Electronic Filing" is transmitted to that person through the court's electronic filing-system. IN R USDCTND L.R. 5-2(b).

- *Serving non-registered persons.* A person who has not registered to use the court's electronic-filing system but who is entitled to service of a paper must be served according to the Local Civil Rules of the United States District Court for the Northern District of Indiana and the Federal Rules of Civil Procedure. IN R USDCTND L.R. 5-2(c); IN R USDCTND CM/ECF(II)(D)(2). If such service of a paper copy is to be made, it shall be done in the manner provided in the Federal Rules of Civil Procedure and the Local Civil Rules of the United States District Court for the Northern District of Indiana. IN R USDCTND CM/ECF(II)(D)(2).

    iv. *Service of conventional filings.* Pleadings or other documents which are filed conventionally rather than electronically shall be served in the manner provided for in the Federal Rules of

Civil Procedure and the Local Civil Rules of the United States District Court for the Northern District of Indiana, except as otherwise provided by order of the Court. IN R USDCTND CM/ECF(III)(B).

    v.   *Using court facilities.* If a local rule so authorizes, a party may use the court's transmission facilities to make service under FRCP 5(b)(2)(E). FRCP 5(b)(3).

c.   *Serving numerous defendants*

    i.   *In general.* If an action involves an unusually large number of defendants, the court may, on motion or on its own, order that:

- Defendants' pleadings and replies to them need not be served on other defendants;
- Any crossclaim, counterclaim, avoidance, or affirmative defense in those pleadings and replies to them will be treated as denied or avoided by all other parties; and
- Filing any such pleading and serving it on the plaintiff constitutes notice of the pleading to all parties. FRCP 5(c)(1).

    ii. *Notifying parties.* A copy of every such order must be served on the parties as the court directs. FRCP 5(c)(2).

G. Hearings

1. *Hearings, generally*

    a. *Oral argument.* Due process does not require that oral argument be permitted on a motion and, except as otherwise provided by local rule, the district court has discretion to determine whether it will decide the motion on the papers or hear argument by counsel (and perhaps receive evidence). FPP § 1190; F.D.I.C. v. Deglau, 207 F.3d 153 (3d Cir. 2000).

       i.   *Request for oral argument.* A party may request oral argument on a motion by filing and serving a separate document explaining why oral argument is necessary and estimating how long the court should allow for the argument. IN R USDCTND L.R. 7-5(a)(1). Refer to the Documents section of this document for more information.

      ii. *Additional evidence forbidden.* Parties may not present additional evidence at oral argument. IN R USDCTND L.R. 7-5(a)(3).

    b. *Providing a regular schedule for oral hearings.* A court may establish regular times and places for oral hearings on motions. FRCP 78(a).

    c. *Providing for submission on briefs.* By rule or order, the court may provide for submitting and determining motions on briefs, without oral hearings. FRCP 78(b).

    d. *Evidentiary hearings.* A party may request an evidentiary hearing by filing and serving a separate document explaining why the hearing is necessary and estimating how long the court should allow for it. IN R USDCTND L.R. 7-5(b)(2). Refer to the Documents section of this document for more information.

    e. *Court's authority.* The court may: (1) grant or deny a request for oral argument or an evidentiary hearing in its discretion; (2) set oral argument or an evidentiary hearing without a request from a party; or (3) order any oral argument or evidentiary hearing to be held anywhere within the district regardless of where the case will be tried. IN R USDCTND L.R. 7-5(c).

2. *Courtroom and courthouse decorum.* For information on courtroom and courthouse decorum, refer to IN R USDCTND L.R. 83-3.

H. Forms

1. Federal Motion for Leave to Amend Forms

    a. Leave to amend complaint; Attaching copy of amendment. 2C FEDFORMS § 14:18.

    b. Leave to amend complaint; Inserting amendment. 2C FEDFORMS § 14:19.

    c. Leave to amend complaint; Interlineation. 2C FEDFORMS § 14:20.

    d. Leave to amend complaint; Responding to motion to dismiss complaint. 2C FEDFORMS § 14:21.

e. Leave to amend complaint; Close to trial. 2C FEDFORMS § 14:22.

f. Leave to amend complaint; Adding new count. 2C FEDFORMS § 14:24.

g. Leave to amend complaint; Asserting lack of knowledge of facts at time of original complaint. 2C FEDFORMS § 14:25.

h. Leave to amend complaint; Seeking fourth amendment. 2C FEDFORMS § 14:26.

i. Leave to amend complaint; Substituting plaintiff and dropping defendant. 2C FEDFORMS § 14:27.

j. Leave to amend answer. 2C FEDFORMS § 14:30.

k. Leave to amend answer; With leave endorsed. 2C FEDFORMS § 14:31.

l. Leave to amend answer; Correcting errors, deleting and interlining. 2C FEDFORMS § 14:32.

m. Leave to amend answer; Adding paragraph. 2C FEDFORMS § 14:33.

n. Leave to amend answer; Adding defense. 2C FEDFORMS § 14:34.

o. Leave to amend answer; During trial. 2C FEDFORMS § 14:35.

p. Defendant's response to motion for leave to amend complaint a fourth time. 2C FEDFORMS § 14:36.

q. Motion and notice; For leave to file amended pleading. FEDPROF § 1:222.

r. Motion; To amend pleading to conform to findings of master. FEDPROF § 1:223.

s. Affidavit; In support of motion for amendment of pleading. FEDPROF § 1:230.

t. Opposition; To motion; General form. FEDPROF § 1:750.

u. Affidavit; Supporting or opposing motion. FEDPROF § 1:751.

v. Brief; Supporting or opposing motion. FEDPROF § 1:752.

w. Statement of points and authorities; Opposing motion. FEDPROF § 1:753.

x. Motion for leave to amend pleading. GOLDLTGFMS § 14:3.

y. Motion to file second amended complaint on ground of newly discovered evidence. GOLDLTGFMS § 14:20.

z. Motion for leave to file amended answer. GOLDLTGFMS § 14:22.

2. **Forms for the Northern District of Indiana**

a. Certificate of service. IN R USDCTND CM/ECF(Form 1).

b. Notice of manual filing. IN R USDCTND CM/ECF(Form 2).

c. Declaration that party was unable to file in a timely manner. IN R USDCTND CM/ECF(Form 3).

I. Applicable Rules

1. *Federal rules*

a. Serving and filing pleadings and other papers. FRCP 5.

b. Constitutional challenge to a statute; Notice, certification, and intervention. FRCP 5.1.

c. Privacy protection for filings made with the court. FRCP 5.2.

d. Computing and extending time; Time for motion papers. FRCP 6.

e. Pleadings allowed; Form of motions and other papers. FRCP 7.

f. Form of pleadings. FRCP 10.

g. Signing pleadings, motions, and other papers; Representations to the court; Sanctions. FRCP 11.

h. Amended and supplemental pleadings. FRCP 15.

i. Taking testimony. FRCP 43.

j. Hearing motions; Submission on briefs. FRCP 78.

2. *Local rules*

    a.   Citation and scope of the rules. IN R USDCTND L.R. 1-1.

    b.   Sanctions for formatting errors. IN R USDCTND L.R. 1-3.

    c.   Electronic filing required. IN R USDCTND L.R. 5-1.

    d.   Constitutional questions. IN R USDCTND L.R. 5.1-1.

    e.   Electronic service. IN R USDCTND L.R. 5-2.

    f.   Format of papers. IN R USDCTND L.R. 5-4.

    g.   Motion practice. IN R USDCTND L.R. 7-1.

    h.   Oral arguments and evidentiary hearings. IN R USDCTND L.R. 7-5.

    i.   Amending pleadings. IN R USDCTND L.R. 15-1.

    j.   Pretrial procedure. IN R USDCTND L.R. 16-1.

    k.   Alternative dispute resolution. IN R USDCTND L.R. 16-6.

    l.   Filing of discovery and other materials. IN R USDCTND L.R. 26-2.

    m.   Case assignment. IN R USDCTND L.R. 40-1.

    n.   Appearance and withdrawal of appearance. IN R USDCTND L.R. 83-8.

    o.   CM/ECF civil and criminal user manual. IN R USDCTND CM/ECF.

    p.   In re: privacy and public access to civil electronic case files. IN R USDCTND Order 2005-3.

Motions, Oppositions and Replies
Motion for Continuance/Extension of Time

Document Last Updated December 2016

A. Checklist

  (I)   ❑ Matters to be considered by moving party

    (a) ❑ Required documents

        (1) ❑ Notice of motion and motion

        (2) ❑ Certificate of service

    (b) ❑ Supplemental documents

        (1) ❑ Brief

        (2) ❑ Supporting evidence

        (3) ❑ Notice of constitutional question

        (4) ❑ Nongovernmental corporate disclosure statement

        (5) ❑ Index of exhibits

        (6) ❑ Request for oral argument

        (7) ❑ Request for evidentiary hearing

        (8) ❑ Copy of authority

        (9) ❑ Proposed order

      (10) ❑ Copy of document with self-addressed envelope

      (11) ❑ Notice of manual filing

      (12) ❑ Courtesy copies

      (13) ❑ Declaration that party was unable to file in a timely manner

(c) ❑ Timing

    (1) ❑ Continuance: there are no specific timing requirements for moving for a continuance

    (2) ❑ Extension of time: when an act may or must be done within a specified time, the court may, for good cause, extend the time:

        (i) ❑ With or without motion or notice if the court acts, or if a request is made, before the original time or its extension expires; or

        (ii) ❑ On motion made after the time has expired if the party failed to act because of excusable neglect

    (3) ❑ A written motion and notice of the hearing must be served at least fourteen (14) days before the time specified for the hearing, with the following exceptions: (i) when the motion may be heard ex parte; (ii) when the Federal Rules of Civil Procedure set a different time; or (iii) when a court order—which a party may, for good cause, apply for ex parte—sets a different time

    (4) ❑ Any affidavit supporting a motion must be served with the motion

(II) ❑ Matters to be considered by opposing party

    (a) ❑ Required documents

        (1) ❑ Response brief

        (2) ❑ Certificate of service

    (b) ❑ Supplemental documents

        (1) ❑ Supporting evidence

        (2) ❑ Notice of constitutional question

        (3) ❑ Index of exhibits

        (4) ❑ Request for oral argument

        (5) ❑ Request for evidentiary hearing

        (6) ❑ Copy of authority

        (7) ❑ Copy of document with self-addressed envelope

        (8) ❑ Notice of manual filing

        (9) ❑ Courtesy copies

        (10) ❑ Declaration that party was unable to file in a timely manner

    (c) ❑ Timing

        (1) ❑ A party must file any response brief to a motion within fourteen (14) days after the motion is served

        (2) ❑ Except as FRCP 59(c) provides otherwise, any opposing affidavit must be served at least seven (7) days before the hearing, unless the court permits service at another time

B. Timing

1. *Motion for continuance/extension of time*

    a. *Continuance.* There are no specific timing requirements for moving for a continuance.

    b. *Extension of time.* When an act may or must be done within a specified time, the court may, for good cause, extend the time:

        i. With or without motion or notice if the court acts, or if a request is made, before the original time or its extension expires; or

        ii. On motion made after the time has expired if the party failed to act because of excusable neglect. FRCP 6(b)(1).

2. *Timing of motions, generally*

    a. *Motion and notice of hearing.* A written motion and notice of the hearing must be served at least fourteen (14) days before the time specified for the hearing, with the following exceptions:

        i. When the motion may be heard ex parte;

        ii. When the Federal Rules of Civil Procedure set a different time; or

        iii. When a court order—which a party may, for good cause, apply for ex parte—sets a different time. FRCP 6(c)(1).

    b. *Supporting affidavit.* Any affidavit supporting a motion must be served with the motion. FRCP 6(c)(2).

3. *Timing of opposing papers.* A party must file any response brief to a motion within fourteen (14) days after the motion is served. IN R USDCTND L.R. 7-1(d)(2)(A).

    a. *Opposing affidavit.* Except as FRCP 59(c) provides otherwise, any opposing affidavit must be served at least seven (7) days before the hearing, unless the court permits service at another time. FRCP 6(c)(2).

    b. *Extensions.* The court may extend response- and reply-brief deadlines, but only for good cause. IN R USDCTND L.R. 7-1(d)(3).

    c. *Summary rulings.* The court may rule on a motion summarily if an opposing party does not file a response before the deadline. IN R USDCTND L.R. 7-1(d)(4).

4. *Timing of reply papers.* Where the respondent files an answering affidavit setting up a new matter, the moving party ordinarily is allowed a reasonable time to file a reply affidavit since failure to deny the new matter by affidavit may operate as an admission of its truth. AMJUR MOTIONS § 25.

    a. *Reply brief.* The moving party must file any reply brief within seven (7) days after the response brief is served. IN R USDCTND L.R. 7-1(d)(2)(B).

    b. *Extensions.* The court may extend response- and reply-brief deadlines, but only for good cause. IN R USDCTND L.R. 7-1(d)(3).

5. *Computation of time*

    a. *Computing time.* FRCP 6 applies in computing any time period specified in the Federal Rules of Civil Procedure, in any local rule or court order, or in any statute that does not specify a method of computing time. FRCP 6(a).

        i. *Period stated in days or a longer unit.* When the period is stated in days or a longer unit of time:

- Exclude the day of the event that triggers the period;

- Count every day, including intermediate Saturdays, Sundays, and legal holidays; and

- Include the last day of the period, but if the last day is a Saturday, Sunday, or legal holiday, the period continues to run until the end of the next day that is not a Saturday, Sunday, or legal holiday. FRCP 6(a)(1).

        ii. *Period stated in hours.* When the period is stated in hours:

- Begin counting immediately on the occurrence of the event that triggers the period;

- Count every hour, including hours during intermediate Saturdays, Sundays, and legal holidays; and

- If the period would end on a Saturday, Sunday, or legal holiday, the period continues to run until the same time on the next day that is not a Saturday, Sunday, or legal holiday. FRCP 6(a)(2).

        iii. *Inaccessibility of the clerk's office.* Unless the court orders otherwise, if the clerk's office is inaccessible:

- On the last day for filing under FRCP 6(a)(1), then the time for filing is extended to the first accessible day that is not a Saturday, Sunday, or legal holiday; or

- During the last hour for filing under FRCP 6(a)(2), then the time for filing is extended to the same time on the first accessible day that is not a Saturday, Sunday, or legal holiday. FRCP 6(a)(3).

iv. *"Last day" defined.* Unless a different time is set by a statute, local rule, or court order, the last day ends:

- For electronic filing, at midnight in the court's time zone; and

- For filing by other means, when the clerk's office is scheduled to close. FRCP 6(a)(4).

v. *"Next day" defined.* The "next day" is determined by continuing to count forward when the period is measured after an event and backward when measured before an event. FRCP 6(a)(5).

vi. *"Legal holiday" defined.* "Legal holiday" means:

- The day set aside by statute for observing New Year's Day, Martin Luther King Jr.'s Birthday, Washington's Birthday, Memorial Day, Independence Day, Labor Day, Columbus Day, Veterans' Day, Thanksgiving Day, or Christmas Day;

- Any day declared a holiday by the President or Congress; and

- For periods that are measured after an event, any other day declared a holiday by the state where the district court is located. FRCP 6(a)(6).

b. *Computation of electronic filing deadlines.* Filing documents electronically does not alter any filing deadlines or any time computation pursuant to FRCP 6. The counties of Lake, Porter, LaPorte, Pulaski and Starke are located in the Central time zone and the remaining counties in the Northern District of Indiana are located in the Eastern time zone. Nevertheless, all electronic transmissions of documents must be completed (i.e., received completely by the clerk's office) prior to midnight Eastern Time, (South Bend/Fort Wayne/Lafayette time) in order to be considered timely filed that day, regardless of the local time in the division where the case is pending. Although documents can be filed electronically twenty-four (24) hours a day, filers are strongly encouraged to file all documents during hours when the CM/ECF Help Line is available, from 9:00 a.m. to 4:00 p.m. local time. IN R USDCTND CM/ECF(II)(I).

i. *Technical failures.* If the attorney is unable to file a document in a timely manner due to technical difficulties in the user's system, the attorney must file a document with the court as soon as possible notifying the court of the inability to file the document. A sample document entitled Declaration that Party was Unable to File in a Timely Manner Due to Technical Difficulties is attached hereto as Form 5. IN R USDCTND CM/ECF(VI)(B). [Editor's note: the reference to Form 5 is likely meant to be a reference to Form 3 (IN R USDCTND CM/ECF(Form 3)].

c. *Extending time.* Refer to the General Requirements section of this document for information on extending time.

d. *Additional time after certain kinds of service.* When a party may or must act within a specified time after being served and service is made under FRCP 5(b)(2)(C) (mail), FRCP 5(b)(2)(D) (leaving with the clerk), or FRCP 5(b)(2)(F) (other means consented to), three (3) days are added after the period would otherwise expire under FRCP 6(a). FRCP 6(d).

C. General Requirements

1. *Motions, generally*

a. *Requirements.* A request for a court order must be made by motion. The motion must:

i. Be in writing unless made during a hearing or trial;

ii. State with particularity the grounds for seeking the order; and

iii. State the relief sought. FRCP 7(b)(1).

b. *Notice of motion.* A party interested in resisting the relief sought by a motion has a right to notice thereof, and an opportunity to be heard. AMJUR MOTIONS § 12.

i. In addition to statutory or court rule provisions requiring notice of a motion—the purpose of such a notice requirement having been said to be to prevent a party from being prejudicially surprised by a motion—principles of natural justice dictate that an adverse party generally must be given notice that a motion will be presented to the court. AMJUR MOTIONS § 12.

    ii. "Notice," in this regard, means reasonable notice, including a meaningful opportunity to prepare and to defend against allegations of a motion. AMJUR MOTIONS § 12.

c. *Writing requirement.* The writing requirement is intended to insure that the adverse parties are informed and have a record of both the motion's pendency and the grounds on which the movant seeks an order. FPP § 1191; Feldberg v. Quechee Lakes Corp., 463 F.3d 195 (2d Cir. 2006).

    i. It is sufficient "if the motion is stated in a written notice of the hearing of the motion." FPP § 1191.

d. *Particularity requirement.* The particularity requirement insures that the opposing parties will have notice of their opponent's contentions. FEDPROC § 62:364; Goodman v. 1973 26 Foot Trojan Vessel, Arkansas Registration No. AR1439SN, 859 F.2d 71, 12 Fed.R.Serv.3d 645 (8th Cir. 1988). That requirement ensures that notice of the basis for the motion is provided to the court and to the opposing party so as to avoid prejudice, provide the opponent with a meaningful opportunity to respond, and provide the court with enough information to process the motion correctly. FEDPROC § 62:364; Andreas v. Volkswagen of America, Inc., 336 F.3d 789, 56 Fed.R.Serv.3d 6 (8th Cir. 2003).

    i. Reasonable specification of the grounds for a motion is sufficient. However, where a movant fails to state even one ground for granting the motion in question, the movant has failed to meet the minimal standard of "reasonable specification." FEDPROC § 62:364; Martinez v. Trainor, 556 F.2d 818, 23 Fed.R.Serv.2d 403 (7th Cir. 1977).

    ii. The court may excuse the failure to comply with the particularity requirement if it is inadvertent, and where no prejudice is shown by the opposing party. FEDPROC § 62:364.

e. *Motions must be filed separately.* Motions must be filed separately, but alternative motions may be filed in a single paper if each is named in the title following the caption. IN R USDCTND L.R. 7-1(a).

2. *Motion for continuance/extension of time*

a. *Continuance.* The court may continue proceedings in a civil case on its own or on the motion of one or more parties. IN R USDCTND L.R. 16-3(a). Attorneys must consult with their clients before asking the court to continue a trial. IN R USDCTND L.R. 16-3(b). Absent a controlling statute, the grant or denial of a continuance rests in the discretion of the trial judge to whom application is made, taking into consideration not only the facts of the particular case but also all of the demands on counsel's time and the court's. FEDPROC § 77:28; Star Financial Services, Inc. v. AASTAR Mortg. Corp., 89 F.3d 5 (1st Cir. 1996); Streber v. Hunter, 221 F.3d 701, 55 Fed.R.Evid.Serv. 376 (5th Cir. 2000). The court may order a party seeking a continuance to reimburse other parties for their actual expenses caused by the delay. IN R USDCTND L.R. 16-3(e). The grounds upon which a continuance is sought may include the following:

    i. Unpreparedness of a party. FEDPROC § 77:29; U.S. v. 110 Bars of Silver, 3 Crucibles of Silver, 11 Bags of Silver Coins, 508 F.2d 799 (5th Cir. 1975).

    ii. Absence of a party. FEDPROC § 77:29. Since it is generally recognized that a party to a civil action ordinarily has a right to attend the trial, an illness severe enough to prevent a party from appearing in court is always a legitimate ground for asking for a continuance. FEDPROC § 77:30; Davis v. Operation Amigo, Inc., 378 F.2d 101 (10th Cir. 1967). However, the failure of the moving party to produce any competent medical evidence of the reasons and necessities for the party's unavailability will result in the denial of the continuance. FEDPROC § 77:30; Weisman v. Alleco, Inc., 925 F.2d 77 (4th Cir. 1991). Some courts, moreover, require a showing that the party has some particular contribution to make to the trial as a material witness or otherwise before granting a continuance due to the party's illness. FEDPROC § 77:30; Johnston v. Harris County Flood Control Dist., 869 F.2d 1565 (5th Cir. 1989).

    iii. Absence of counsel. FEDPROC § 77:29. The courts have shown greater leniency when the illness of counsel is the ground for the continuance, especially where the case presents complex issues. FEDPROC § 77:31; Smith-Weik Machinery Corp. v. Murdock Mach. & Engineering

Co., 423 F.2d 842 (5th Cir. 1970). However, many courts do not favor the granting of a continuance where counsel is unavailable due to a claimed engagement elsewhere or where it is not clear that counsel's illness was genuine. FEDPROC § 77:31; Community Nat. Life Ins. Co. v. Parker Square Sav. & Loan Ass'n, 406 F.2d 603 (10th Cir. 1969); Williams v. Johanns, 518 F.Supp.2d 205 (D.D.C. 2007).

iv. Absence of a witness or evidence. FEDPROC § 77:29. The moving party must show. . .that the witness's testimony would be competent and material and that there are no other witnesses who can establish the same facts. FEDPROC § 77:32; Krodel v. Houghtaling, 468 F.2d 887 (4th Cir. 1972); Vitarelle v. Long Island R. Co., 415 F.2d 302 (2d Cir. 1969).

- *Stipulation to absent evidence.* The court may not continue a trial because evidence is unavailable if all parties stipulate to the content of the unavailable evidence. Despite the stipulation, the parties may contest the stipulated evidence as if it had been available at trial. IN R USDCTND L.R. 16-3(d).

v. Surprise and prejudice. FEDPROC § 77:29. The action complained of should not be one which could have been anticipated by due diligence or of which the movant had actual notice. FEDPROC § 77:33; Communications Maintenance, Inc. v. Motorola, Inc., 761 F.2d 1202, 2 Fed.R.Serv.3d 126 (7th Cir. 1985). Surprise and prejudice are often claimed as a result of the court allowing the other party to amend its pleadings under FRCP 15(b). FEDPROC § 77:29.

vi. In determining whether to grant a continuance, the court will consider a variety of factors, including:

- Good faith on the part of the moving party;
- Due diligence of the moving party;
- The likelihood that the need prompting the request for a continuance will be met if the continuance is granted;
- Inconvenience to the court and the nonmoving party, including the witnesses, if the continuance is granted;
- Possible harm to the moving party if the continuance is denied;
- Prior delays in the proceedings;
- The court's prior refusal to grant the opposing party a continuance;
- Judicial economy. FEDPROC § 77:29; Amarin Plastics, Inc. v. Maryland Cup Corp., 946 F.2d 147, 34 Fed.R.Evid.Serv. 528 (1st Cir. 1991); Lewis v. Rawson, 564 F.3d 569 (2d Cir. 2009); U.S. v. 2.61 Acres of Land, More or Less, Situated in Mariposa County, State of Cal., 791 F.2d 666 (9th Cir. 1985); In re Homestore.com, Inc. Securities Litigation, 347 F.Supp.2d 814 (C.D.Cal. 2004).

b. *Extension of time.* Ordinarily, requests for an extension of time not made in open court or at a conference must: (1) be made by written motion; (2) state the original deadline and the requested deadline; and (3) either: (A) state that there is no objection to the extension; or (B) describe the requesting party's efforts to get opposing attorneys to agree to the extension if there is an objection. IN R USDCTND L.R. 6-1(a). When an act may or must be done within a specified time, the court may, for good cause, extend the time:

i. *Before original time or its extension expires.* With or without motion or notice if the court acts, or if a request is made, before the original time or its extension expires. FRCP 6(b)(1)(A).

- An application for the enlargement of time under FRCP 6(b)(1)(A) normally will be granted in the absence of bad faith on the part of the party seeking relief or prejudice to the adverse party. FPP § 1165.
- Neither a formal motion for enlargement nor notice to the adverse party is expressly required by FRCP 6(b). FPP § 1165.

ii. *After the time has expired.* On motion made after the time has expired if the party failed to act because of excusable neglect. FRCP 6(b)(1)(B).

- *Excusable neglect.* Excusable neglect is intended and has proven to be quite elastic in its application. In essence it is an equitable concept that must take account of all relevant circumstances of the party's failure to act within the required time. FPP § 1165.

- *Burden.* The burden is on the movant to establish that the failure to act in a timely manner was the result of excusable neglect. FEDPROC § 77:5. Common sense indicates that among the most important factors are the possibility of prejudice to the other parties, the length of the applicant's delay and its impact on the proceeding, the reason for the delay and whether it was within the control of the movant, and whether the movant has acted in good faith. FPP § 1165; Kettle Range Conservation Group v. U.S. Forest Service, 8 Fed.Appx. 729 (9th Cir. 2001).

- *Motion required.* No relief may be granted under FRCP 6(b)(1)(B) after the expiration of the specified period, even though the failure to act may have been the result of excusable neglect, if no motion is made by the party who failed to act. FEDPROC § 77:3.

iii. *Exceptions.* A court must not extend the time to act under FRCP 50(b), FRCP 50(d), FRCP 52(b), FRCP 59(b), FRCP 59(d), FRCP 59(e), and FRCP 60(b). FRCP 6(b)(2). FRCP 6(b) does not require the district courts to extend a time period where the extension would contravene a local court rule and does not apply to periods of time that are definitely fixed by statute. FEDPROC § 77:4; Truncale v. Universal Pictures Co., 82 F.Supp. 576 (S.D.N.Y. 1949); Lusk v. Lyon Metal Products, 9 F.R.D. 250 (W.D.Mo. 1949).

iv. *Automatic initial extension.* The deadline to respond to a pleading or a discovery request—including requests for admission—is automatically extended when an extension notice is filed with the court and: (1) the deadline has not been extended before; (2) the extension is for twenty-eight (28) or fewer days; and (3) the notice states: (A) the original deadline; (B) the new deadline; and (C) that all opposing attorneys the attorney could reach agreed to the extension; or that the party could not reach any other opposing attorneys despite due diligence. IN R USDCTND L.R. 6-1(b).

- *Pro se parties.* The automatic initial extension does not apply to pro se parties. IN R USDCTND L.R. 6-1(c).

3. *Opposing papers.* The Federal Rules of Civil Procedure do not require any formal answer, return, or reply to a motion, except where the Federal Rules of Civil Procedure or local rules may require affidavits, memoranda, or other papers to be filed in opposition to a motion. Such papers are simply to apprise the court of such opposition and the grounds of that opposition. FEDPROC § 62:359.

a. *Effect of failure to respond to motion.* Although in the absence of statutory provision or court rule, a motion ordinarily does not require a written answer, when a party files a motion and the opposing party fails to respond, the court may construe such failure to respond as nonopposition to the motion or an admission that the motion was meritorious, may take the facts alleged in the motion as true—the rule in some jurisdictions being that the failure to respond to a fact set forth in a motion is deemed an admission—and may grant the motion if the relief requested appears to be justified. AMJUR MOTIONS § 28.

b. *Assent or no opposition not determinative.* However, a motion will not be granted automatically simply because an "assent" or a notation of "no opposition" has been filed; federal judges frequently deny motions that have been assented to when it is thought that justice so dictates. FPP § 1190.

c. *Responsive pleading inappropriate as response to motion.* An attempt to answer or oppose a motion with a responsive pleading usually is not appropriate. FPP § 1190.

4. *Reply papers.* A moving party may be required or permitted to prepare papers in addition to his original motion papers. AMJUR MOTIONS § 25. Papers answering or replying to opposing papers may be appropriate, in the interests of justice, where it appears there is a substantial reason for allowing a reply. Thus, a court may accept reply papers where a party demonstrates that the papers to which it seeks to file a reply raise new issues that are material to the disposition of the question before the court, or where the court determines, sua sponte, that it wishes further briefing of an issue raised in those papers and orders the submission of additional papers. FEDPROC § 62:360.

a. *Function of reply papers.* The function of a reply affidavit is to answer the arguments made in opposition to the position taken by the movant and not to permit the movant to introduce new arguments in support of the motion. AMJUR MOTIONS § 25.

 b. *Issues raised for the first time in a reply document.* However, the view has been followed in some jurisdictions, that as a matter of judicial economy, where there is no prejudice and where the issues could be raised simply by filing a motion to dismiss, the trial court has discretion to consider arguments raised for the first time in a reply memorandum, and that a trial court may grant a motion to strike issues raised for the first time in a reply memorandum. AMJUR MOTIONS § 26.

5. *Appearances.* Attorneys not representing the United States or its agencies must file an appearance when they represent (either in person or by filing a paper) a party. IN R USDCTND L.R. 83-8(a). For more information, refer to IN R USDCTND L.R. 83-8.

6. *Notice of related action.* A party must file a notice of related action as soon as it appears that the party's case and another pending case: (1) arise out of the same transaction or occurrence; (2) involve the same property; or (3) involve the validity or infringement of the same patent, trademark, or copyright. IN R USDCTND L.R. 40-1(d). For more information, refer to IN R USDCTND L.R. 40-1.

7. *Alternative dispute resolution (ADR).* After they confer as required by FRCP 26(f), the parties must advise the court which, if any, alternative-dispute-resolution processes they expect to pursue and when they expect to undertake the process. IN R USDCTND L.R. 16-6(a). For more information on alternative dispute resolution (ADR), refer to IN R USDCTND L.R. 16-6 and IN R USDCTND Order 2003-21.

8. *Settlement or resolution.* The parties must immediately notify the court if they reasonably expect to settle the case or resolve a pending motion. IN R USDCTND L.R. 16-1(g).

9. *Modification or suspension of rules.* The court may, on its own motion or at the request of a party, suspend or modify any rule in a particular case in the interest of justice. IN R USDCTND L.R. 1-1(c).

D. Documents

1. *Documents for moving party*

 a. *Required documents*

  i. *Notice of motion and motion.* The party must not specify a hearing date in the notice of a motion or petition unless the court or the clerk has authorized it. IN R USDCTND L.R. 7-5(b)(2). Refer to the General Requirements section of this document for information on the notice of motion and motion.

  ii. *Certificate of service.* FRCP 5(d) requires that the person making service under FRCP 5 certify that service has been effected. FRCP 5(Advisory Committee Notes). Having such information on file may be useful for many purposes, including proof of service if an issue arises concerning the effectiveness of the service. FRCP 5(Advisory Committee Notes).

   • *Certificate of service for electronically-filed documents.* A Certificate of Service is still a requirement when filing documents electronically. A sample Certificate of Service is attached as Form 1 (IN R USDCTND CM/ECF(Form 1)). IN R USDCTND CM/ECF(II)(H).

 b. *Supplemental documents*

  i. *Brief.* Refer to the Format section of this document for the format of briefs.

  ii. *Supporting evidence.* When a motion relies on facts outside the record, the court may hear the matter on affidavits or may hear it wholly or partly on oral testimony or on depositions. FRCP 43(c).

   • *Materials necessary for motion.* A party must file those portions of discovery requests or responses (including deposition transcripts) that the party relies on to support a motion that could result in a final order on an issue. IN R USDCTND L.R. 26-2(c).

   • *Unavailable evidence.* A party seeking to continue a trial because evidence is unavailable must include with the motion an affidavit showing: (1) that the evidence is material; (2) that the party has acted diligently to obtain it; (3) where the evidence might be; and (4) if the evidence is the testimony of an absent witness: (A) the name and residence of the witness, if known; (B) the likelihood of procuring the testimony within a reasonable time; (C) that neither the party nor anyone at the party's request or with the party's knowledge procured the witness's absence; (D) the facts the party believes the witness will truthfully testify to; and (E) that the party cannot prove the facts by another witness whose testimony can be readily procured. IN R USDCTND L.R. 16-3(c).

iii. *Notice of constitutional question.* A party that files a pleading, written motion, or other paper drawing into question the constitutionality of a federal or state statute must promptly:

- *File notice.* File a notice of constitutional question stating the question and identifying the paper that raises it, if: (1) a federal statute is questioned and the parties do not include the United States, one of its agencies, or one of its officers or employees in an official capacity; or (2) a state statute is questioned and the parties do not include the state, one of its agencies, or one of its officers or employees in an official capacity; and

- *Serve notice.* Serve the notice and paper on the Attorney General of the United States if a federal statute is questioned—or on the state attorney general if a state statute is questioned—either by certified or registered mail or by sending it to an electronic address designated by the attorney general for this purpose. FRCP 5.1(a).

- *When to file the notice.* A party required to file a notice of constitutional question under FRCP 5.1 must do so by the later of: (1) the day the parties tender their proposed case-management plan (if one is required); or (2) 21 days after filing the pleading, written motion, or other paper questioning the constitutionality of a federal or state statute. IN R USDCTND L.R. 5.1-1(a).

- *Service on government officials.* The party must also serve the notice and the pleading, written motion, or other paper questioning the constitutionality of a federal or state statute on: (1) the Attorney General of the United States and the United States Attorney for the Northern District of Indiana, if a federal statute is challenged; or (2) the Attorney General for the state if a state statute is challenged. IN R USDCTND L.R. 5.1-1(b). Service required under IN R USDCTND L.R. 5.1-1(b) may be made either by certified or registered mail or by emailing it to an address designated by those officials for this purpose. IN R USDCTND L.R. 5.1-1(c).

- *No forfeiture.* A party's failure to file and serve the notice, or the court's failure to certify, does not forfeit a constitutional claim or defense that is otherwise timely asserted. FRCP 5.1(d).

iv. *Nongovernmental corporate disclosure statement*

- *Contents.* A nongovernmental corporate party must file two (2) copies of a disclosure statement that: (1) identifies any parent corporation and any publicly held corporation owning ten percent (10%) or more of its stock; or (2) states that there is no such corporation. FRCP 7.1(a).

- *Time to file; Supplemental filing.* A party must: (1) file the disclosure statement with its first appearance, pleading, petition, motion, response, or other request addressed to the court; and (2) promptly file a supplemental statement if any required information changes. FRCP 7.1(b).

v. *Index of exhibits.* Any pleading, motion, brief, affidavit, notice, or proposed order, whether filed electronically or by delivering it to the clerk, must: include a separate index identifying and briefly describing each exhibit if there are more than four (4) exhibits. IN R USDCTND L.R. 5-4(a)(8).

vi. *Request for oral argument.* A party may request oral argument on a motion by filing and serving a separate document explaining why oral argument is necessary and estimating how long the court should allow for the argument. IN R USDCTND L.R. 7-5(a)(1). The request must be filed and served with the party's supporting brief, response brief, or reply brief. IN R USDCTND L.R. 7-5(a)(2).

vii. *Request for evidentiary hearing.* A party may request an evidentiary hearing by filing and

serving a separate document explaining why the hearing is necessary and estimating how long the court should allow for it. IN R USDCTND L.R. 7-5(b)(1).

viii. *Copy of authority.* A copy of any decision, statute, or regulation cited in a motion or brief must be attached to the paper if—and only if—it is not available on Westlaw or Lexis. But if a copy of a decision, statute, or regulation is only available electronically, a party must provide it to the court or another party upon request. IN R USDCTND L.R. 7-1(f).

ix. *Proposed order.* Parties filing a paper that requires the judge or clerk to enter a routine or uncontested order must include a suitable form of order. IN R USDCTND L.R. 5-4(c).

- Proposed orders shall not be filed electronically either as a separate document or as an attachment to the main pleading or other document. Instead, all proposed orders must be e-mailed to the chambers of the appropriate judicial officer for the case. The proposed order must be in WordPerfect Format or Rich Text Format (RTF). Proposed orders should be attached to an e-mail and sent to the appropriate judicial officer at the address listed in IN R USDCTND CM/ECF(II)(F). The subject line of the email message should indicate the case title, cause number and document number of the motion, e.g., Smith v. Jones 1:02-cv-1234, motion# ___. IN R USDCTND CM/ECF(II)(F).

x. *Copy of document with self-addressed envelope.* A party who wants a file-stamped copy of a paper must include with the filing an additional copy of the paper and a self-addressed envelope with adequate postage. IN R USDCTND L.R. 5-4(b)(6).

xi. *Notice of manual filing.* However, if that is not physically possible, counsel shall electronically file a .pdf document titled Notice of Manual Filing as a notation on the docket sheet that filings are being held in the clerk's office in paper. A sample Notice of Manual Filing is attached as Form 2 (IN R USDCTND CM/ECF(Form 2)). IN R USDCTND CM/ECF(III)(A)(1).

xii. *Courtesy copies.* If documents are filed in paper format, counsel must provide an original for the clerk's office, a copy for the judge and a copy must be served on all parties in the case. IN R USDCTND CM/ECF(III)(A)(1).

xiii. *Declaration that party was unable to file in a timely manner.* If the attorney is unable to file a document in a timely manner due to technical difficulties in the user's system, the attorney must file a document with the court as soon as possible notifying the court of the inability to file the document. A sample document entitled Declaration that Party was Unable to File in a Timely Manner Due to Technical Difficulties is attached hereto as Form 5. IN R USDCTND CM/ECF(VI)(B). [Editor's note: the reference to Form 5 is likely meant to be a reference to Form 3 (IN R USDCTND CM/ECF(Form 3)].

2. *Documents for opposing party*

   a. *Required documents*

      i. *Response brief.* Refer to the Format section of this document for the format of briefs. Refer to the General Requirements section of this document for information on the opposing papers.

      ii. *Certificate of service.* FRCP 5(d) requires that the person making service under FRCP 5 certify that service has been effected. FRCP 5(Advisory Committee Notes). Having such information on file may be useful for many purposes, including proof of service if an issue arises concerning the effectiveness of the service. FRCP 5(Advisory Committee Notes).

         - *Certificate of service for electronically-filed documents.* A Certificate of Service is still a requirement when filing documents electronically. A sample Certificate of Service is attached as Form 1 (IN R USDCTND CM/ECF(Form 1)). IN R USDCTND CM/ECF(II)(H).

   b. *Supplemental documents*

      i. *Supporting evidence.* When a motion relies on facts outside the record, the court may hear the matter on affidavits or may hear it wholly or partly on oral testimony or on depositions. FRCP 43(c).

         - *Materials necessary for motion.* A party must file those portions of discovery requests or

responses (including deposition transcripts) that the party relies on to support a motion that could result in a final order on an issue. IN R USDCTND L.R. 26-2(c).

ii. *Notice of constitutional question.* A party that files a pleading, written motion, or other paper drawing into question the constitutionality of a federal or state statute must promptly:

- *File notice.* File a notice of constitutional question stating the question and identifying the paper that raises it, if: (1) a federal statute is questioned and the parties do not include the United States, one of its agencies, or one of its officers or employees in an official capacity; or (2) a state statute is questioned and the parties do not include the state, one of its agencies, or one of its officers or employees in an official capacity; and

- *Serve notice.* Serve the notice and paper on the Attorney General of the United States if a federal statute is questioned—or on the state attorney general if a state statute is questioned—either by certified or registered mail or by sending it to an electronic address designated by the attorney general for this purpose. FRCP 5.1(a).

- *When to file the notice.* A party required to file a notice of constitutional question under FRCP 5.1 must do so by the later of: (1) the day the parties tender their proposed case-management plan (if one is required); or (2) 21 days after filing the pleading, written motion, or other paper questioning the constitutionality of a federal or state statute. IN R USDCTND L.R. 5.1-1(a).

- *Service on government officials.* The party must also serve the notice and the pleading, written motion, or other paper questioning the constitutionality of a federal or state statute on: (1) the Attorney General of the United States and the United States Attorney for the Northern District of Indiana, if a federal statute is challenged; or (2) the Attorney General for the state if a state statute is challenged. IN R USDCTND L.R. 5.1-1(b). Service required under IN R USDCTND L.R. 5.1-1(b) may be made either by certified or registered mail or by emailing it to an address designated by those officials for this purpose. IN R USDCTND L.R. 5.1-1(c).

- *No forfeiture.* A party's failure to file and serve the notice, or the court's failure to certify, does not forfeit a constitutional claim or defense that is otherwise timely asserted. FRCP 5.1(d).

iii. *Index of exhibits.* Any pleading, motion, brief, affidavit, notice, or proposed order, whether filed electronically or by delivering it to the clerk, must: include a separate index identifying and briefly describing each exhibit if there are more than four (4) exhibits. IN R USDCTND L.R. 5-4(a)(8).

iv. *Request for oral argument.* A party may request oral argument on a motion by filing and serving a separate document explaining why oral argument is necessary and estimating how long the court should allow for the argument. IN R USDCTND L.R. 7-5(a)(1). The request must be filed and served with the party's supporting brief, response brief, or reply brief. IN R USDCTND L.R. 7-5(a)(2).

v. *Request for evidentiary hearing.* A party may request an evidentiary hearing by filing and serving a separate document explaining why the hearing is necessary and estimating how long the court should allow for it. IN R USDCTND L.R. 7-5(b)(1).

vi. *Copy of authority.* A copy of any decision, statute, or regulation cited in a motion or brief must be attached to the paper if—and only if—it is not available on Westlaw or Lexis. But if a copy of a decision, statute, or regulation is only available electronically, a party must provide it to the court or another party upon request. IN R USDCTND L.R. 7-1(f).

vii. *Copy of document with self-addressed envelope.* A party who wants a file-stamped copy of a paper must include with the filing an additional copy of the paper and a self-addressed envelope with adequate postage. IN R USDCTND L.R. 5-4(b)(6).

viii. *Notice of manual filing.* However, if that is not physically possible, counsel shall electronically file a .pdf document titled Notice of Manual Filing as a notation on the docket sheet that filings are being held in the clerk's office in paper. A sample Notice of Manual Filing is attached as Form 2 (IN R USDCTND CM/ECF(Form 2)). IN R USDCTND CM/ECF(III)(A)(1).

ix. *Courtesy copies.* If documents are filed in paper format, counsel must provide an original for the clerk's office, a copy for the judge and a copy must be served on all parties in the case. IN R USDCTND CM/ECF(III)(A)(1).

x. *Declaration that party was unable to file in a timely manner.* If the attorney is unable to file a document in a timely manner due to technical difficulties in the user's system, the attorney must file a document with the court as soon as possible notifying the court of the inability to file the document. A sample document entitled Declaration that Party was Unable to File in a Timely Manner Due to Technical Difficulties is attached hereto as Form 5. IN R USDCTND CM/ECF(VI)(B). [Editor's note: the reference to Form 5 is likely meant to be a reference to Form 3 (IN R USDCTND CM/ECF(Form 3)].

E. Format

1. *Form of documents.* The rules governing captions and other matters of form in pleadings apply to motions and other papers. FRCP 7(b)(2).

   a. *Paper.* Any pleading, motion, brief, affidavit, notice, or proposed order, whether filed electronically or by delivering it to the clerk, must: use eight and one-half by eleven (8-1/2 x 11) inch pages. IN R USDCTND L.R. 5-4(a)(2).

      i. *Manual filings.* Papers delivered to the clerk for filing must: be flat, unfolded, and on good-quality, white paper. IN R USDCTND L.R. 5-4(b)(1)(A).

         • *Covers or backing.* Papers delivered to the clerk for filing must: not have a cover or a back. IN R USDCTND L.R. 5-4(b)(1)(B).

         • *Recycled paper.* The court encourages using recycled paper. IN R USDCTND L.R. 5-4(b)(7).

   b. *Margins.* Any pleading, motion, brief, affidavit, notice, or proposed order, whether filed electronically or by delivering it to the clerk, must: have at least one (1) inch margins. IN R USDCTND L.R. 5-4(a)(3).

   c. *Spacing.* Any pleading, motion, brief, affidavit, notice, or proposed order, whether filed electronically or by delivering it to the clerk, must: be double spaced (except for headings, footnotes, and quoted material). IN R USDCTND L.R. 5-4(a)(5).

   d. *Text.* Any pleading, motion, brief, affidavit, notice, or proposed order, whether filed electronically or by delivering it to the clerk, must: be plainly typewritten, printed, or prepared by a clearly legible copying process. IN R USDCTND L.R. 5-4(a)(1).

      i. Any pleading, motion, brief, affidavit, notice, or proposed order, whether filed electronically or by delivering it to the clerk, must: use at least twelve (12) point type in the body and at least ten (10) point type in footnotes. IN R USDCTND L.R. 5-4(a)(4).

   e. *Page numbering.* Any pleading, motion, brief, affidavit, notice, or proposed order, whether filed electronically or by delivering it to the clerk, must: have consecutively numbered pages. IN R USDCTND L.R. 5-4(a)(6).

   f. *Caption; Names of parties.* Every pleading must have a caption with the court's name, a title, a file number, and a FRCP 7(a) designation. The title of the complaint must name all the parties; the title of other pleadings, after naming the first party on each side, may refer generally to other parties. FRCP 10(a). Any pleading, motion, brief, affidavit, notice, or proposed order, whether filed electronically or by delivering it to the clerk, must: include a title on the first page. IN R USDCTND L.R. 5-4(a)(7).

      i. *Alternative motions.* Motions must be filed separately, but alternative motions may be filed in a single paper if each is named in the title following the caption. IN R USDCTND L.R. 7-1(a).

   g. *Filer's information.* Any pleading, motion, brief, affidavit, notice, or proposed order, whether filed electronically or by delivering it to the clerk, must: except in proposed orders and affidavits, include the filer's name, address, telephone number, fax number (where available), and e-mail address (where available). IN R USDCTND L.R. 5-4(a)(9).

   h. *Paragraphs; Separate statements.* A party must state its claims or defenses in numbered paragraphs,

each limited as far as practicable to a single set of circumstances. A later pleading may refer by number to a paragraph in an earlier pleading. If doing so would promote clarity, each claim founded on a separate transaction or occurrence—and each defense other than a denial—must be stated in a separate count or defense. FRCP 10(b).

i. *Adoption by reference; Exhibits.* A statement in a pleading may be adopted by reference elsewhere in the same pleading or in any other pleading or motion. A copy of a written instrument that is an exhibit to a pleading is a part of the pleading for all purposes. FRCP 10(c).

j. *Citation of local rules.* The Local Civil Rules of the United States District Court for the Northern District of Indiana may be cited as "N.D. Ind. L.R." IN R USDCTND L.R. 1-1(a)(1).

k. *Acceptance by the clerk.* The clerk must not refuse to file a paper solely because it is not in the form prescribed by the Federal Rules of Civil Procedure or by a local rule or practice. FRCP 5(d)(4).

  i. *Sanctions for formatting errors; Non-compliance.* If a person files a paper that does not comply with the rules governing the format of papers filed with the court, the court may: (1) strike the paper from the record; or (2) fine the person up to one thousand dollars ($1,000). IN R USDCTND L.R. 1-3(a).

   • *Notice.* Before sanctioning a person under IN R USDCTND L.R. 1-3(a)(2), the court must: (1) notify the person that the paper is noncompliant; and (2) give the person the opportunity either to be heard or to revise the paper. IN R USDCTND L.R. 1-3(b).

2. *Form of electronic documents.* Electronically filed documents must meet the same requirements of format and page limits as documents "conventionally filed" (as defined in IN R USDCTND CM/ECF(III)(A)) pursuant to the Federal Rules of Civil Procedure and the Local Civil Rules of the United States District Court for the Northern District of Indiana. IN R USDCTND CM/ECF(II)(A)(2).

a. *PDF format required.* Documents filed in the CM/ECF must be in .pdf format. A document created with almost any word-processing program can be converted to .pdf format. The .pdf program in effect takes a picture of the original document and allows anyone to open the converted document across a broad range of hardware and software, with layout, format, links, and images intact. IN R USDCTND CM/ECF(FN2).

b. *Title of documents.* The person electronically filing a pleading or other document will be responsible for designating a title for the pleading or other document by using one of the categories contained in the events listed in the CM/ECF Menu. IN R USDCTND CM/ECF(II)(G).

c. *Combining documents.* All documents which form part of a single pleading and which are being filed at the same time and by the same party may be electronically filed together under one document number, e.g., the motion and a supporting affidavit, with the exception of memoranda in support. Memoranda in support shall be electronically filed separately and shown as a related document to the motion. IN R USDCTND CM/ECF(II)(A)(4).

d. *Exhibits and attachments.* Filing users must submit in electronic form all documents referenced as exhibits or attachments, unless the court permits conventional filing. A filing user must submit as exhibits or attachments only those excerpts of the referenced documents that are directly germane to the matter under consideration by the court. Excerpted material must be clearly and prominently identified as such. Filing users who file excerpts of documents as exhibits or attachments do so without prejudice to their right to timely file additional excerpts or the complete document. Responding parties may timely file additional excerpts or the complete document that they believe are directly germane. The court may require parties to file additional excerpts or the complete document. IN R USDCTND CM/ECF(II)(A)(6).

e. *Hyperlinks.* Electronically filed documents may contain hyperlink references to an external document as a convenient mechanism for accessing material cited in the document. A hyperlink reference is neither validated for content nor considered a part of the court's records. The court neither endorses the product or organization at the destination of a hyperlink reference, nor does the court exercise any responsibility over the content at the destination. In order to preserve the integrity of the court record, attorneys wishing to insert hyperlinks in court filings shall continue to use the traditional citation method for the cited authority, in addition to the hyperlink. A hyperlink contained in a filing is no more than a convenient mechanism for accessing material cited in the document and a hyperlink reference is extraneous to any filed document and is not part of the court's record. IN R USDCTND CM/ECF(II)(A)(3).

3. *Form of briefs*

  a. *Page limits.* Supporting and response briefs (excluding tables of contents, tables of authorities, and appendices) ordinarily must not exceed twenty-five (25) pages. Reply briefs must not exceed fifteen (15) pages. IN R USDCTND L.R. 7-1(e)(1).

    i. *Exception.* The court may allow a party to file a brief exceeding these page limits for extraordinary and compelling reasons. But if the court permits a brief to exceed twenty-five (25) pages, it must include:

- A table of contents with page references;
- An issue statement; and
- A table of authorities including: (1) all cases (alphabetically arranged), statutes, and other authorities cited in the brief; and (2) references to where the authorities appear in the brief. IN R USDCTND L.R. 7-1(e)(2).

4. *Signing of pleadings, motions and other papers*

  a. *Signature.* Every pleading, written motion, and other paper must be signed by at least one attorney of record in the attorney's name—or by a party personally if the party is unrepresented. The paper must state the signer's address, e-mail address, and telephone number. FRCP 11(a).

    i. *Signatures on manual filings.* Papers delivered to the clerk for filing must: include the filer's original signature. IN R USDCTND L.R. 5-4(b)(1)(C).

- *Rubber-stamped and faxed signatures.* An original paper with a rubber-stamped or faxed signature is unsigned for purposes of FRCP 11 and FRCP 26(g). IN R USDCTND L.R. 5-4(b)(2).
- *Affidavits.* Only the affiant need sign an affidavit. IN R USDCTND L.R. 5-4(b)(3).

    ii. *Electronic signatures.* Pursuant to FRCP 11, every pleading, motion, and other paper (except lists, schedules, statements or amendments thereto) shall be signed by at least one attorney of record or, if the party is not represented by an attorney, all papers shall be signed by the party. An attorney's/participant's password issued by the court combined with the user's identification, serves as and constitutes the attorney/participant's signature for FRCP 11 and other purposes. IN R USDCTND CM/ECF(I)(C). Documents which must be filed and which must contain original signatures other than those of a participating attorney or which require either verification or an unsworn declaration under any rule or statute, shall be filed electronically, with originally executed copies maintained by the filer. The pleading or other document electronically filed shall contain "s/" signature(s), as noted in IN R USDCTND CM/ECF(II)(E)(3)(b). IN R USDCTND CM/ECF(II)(E)(1).

- *Multiple signatures.* In the case of a stipulation or other document to be signed by two or more attorneys, the following procedure should be used: The filing attorney shall initially confirm that the content of the document is acceptable to all persons required to sign the document and shall obtain the physical signatures of all attorneys on the document. IN R USDCTND CM/ECF(II)(E)(3)(a). The filing attorney then shall file the document electronically, indicating the signatories, e.g., "s/Jane Doe," "s/John Doe," etc. IN R US-DCTND CM/ECF(II)(E)(3)(b). The filing attorney shall retain the hard copy of the document containing the original signatures. IN R USDCTND CM/ECF(II)(E)(3)(c).

    iii. *No verification or accompanying affidavit required for pleadings.* Unless a rule or statute specifically states otherwise, a pleading need not be verified or accompanied by an affidavit. FRCP 11(a).

    iv. *Unsigned papers.* The court must strike an unsigned paper unless the omission is promptly corrected after being called to the attorney's or party's attention. FRCP 11(a).

  b. *Representations to the court.* By presenting to the court a pleading, written motion, or other paper—whether by signing, filing, submitting, or later advocating it—an attorney or unrepresented party certifies that to the best of the person's knowledge, information, and belief, formed after an inquiry reasonable under the circumstances:

    i.   It is not being presented for any improper purpose, such as to harass, cause unnecessary delay, or needlessly increase the cost of litigation;

    ii.   The claims, defenses, and other legal contentions are warranted by existing law or by a nonfrivolous argument for extending, modifying, or reversing existing law or for establishing new law;

    iii.   The factual contentions have evidentiary support or, if specifically so identified, will likely have evidentiary support after a reasonable opportunity for further investigation or discovery; and

    iv.   The denials of factual contentions are warranted on the evidence or, if specifically so identified, are reasonably based on belief or a lack of information. FRCP 11(b).

c.   *Sanctions.* If, after notice and a reasonable opportunity to respond, the court determines that FRCP 11(b) has been violated, the court may impose an appropriate sanction on any attorney, law firm, or party that violated FRCP 11(b) or is responsible for the violation. FRCP 11(c)(1). Refer to the United States District Court for the Northern District of Indiana KeyRules Motion for Sanctions document for more information.

5.   *Privacy protection for filings made with the court*

a.   *Redacted filings.* Counsel should not include sensitive information in any document filed with the court unless such inclusion is necessary and relevant to the case. IN R USDCTND CM/ECF(VII). Unless the court orders otherwise, in an electronic or paper filing with the court that contains an individual's Social Security number, taxpayer-identification number, or birth date, the name of an individual known to be a minor, or a financial-account number, a party or nonparty making the filing may include only:

    i.   The last four (4) digits of the Social Security number and taxpayer-identification number;

    ii.   The year of the individual's birth;

    iii.   The minor's initials; and

    iv.   The last four (4) digits of the financial-account number. FRCP 5.2(a); IN R USDCTND Order 2005-3.

b.   *Exemptions from the redaction requirement.* The redaction requirement does not apply to the following:

    i.   A financial-account number that identifies the property allegedly subject to forfeiture in a forfeiture proceeding;

    ii.   The record of an administrative or agency proceeding;

    iii.   The official record of a state-court proceeding;

    iv.   The record of a court or tribunal, if that record was not subject to the redaction requirement when originally filed;

    v.   A filing covered by FRCP 5.2(c) or FRCP 5.2(d); and

    vi.   A pro se filing in an action brought under 28 U.S.C.A. § 2241, 28 U.S.C.A. § 2254, or 28 U.S.C.A. § 2255. FRCP 5.2(b).

    vii.   In cases filed under the Social Security Act, 42 U.S.C.A. § 405(g), there is no need for redaction of any information from the documents filed in the case. IN R USDCTND Order 2005-3.

c.   *Limitations on remote access to electronic files; Social Security appeals and immigration cases.* Unless the court orders otherwise, in an action for benefits under the Social Security Act, and in an action or proceeding relating to an order of removal, to relief from removal, or to immigration benefits or detention, access to an electronic file is authorized as follows:

    i.   The parties and their attorneys may have remote electronic access to any part of the case file, including the administrative record;

    ii. Any other person may have electronic access to the full record at the courthouse, but may have remote electronic access only to:

- The docket maintained by the court; and
- An opinion, order, judgment, or other disposition of the court, but not any other part of the case file or the administrative record. FRCP 5.2(c).

d. *Filings made under seal.* The court may order that a filing be made under seal without redaction. The court may later unseal the filing or order the person who made the filing to file a redacted version for the public record. FRCP 5.2(d). For information on filing documents under seal, refer to IN R USDCTND L.R. 5-3, IN R USDCTND CM/ECF(IV)(A), and IN R USDCTND ECF Order 2004-19.

e. *Protective orders.* For good cause, the court may by order in a case:

    i. Require redaction of additional information; or

    ii. Limit or prohibit a nonparty's remote electronic access to a document filed with the court. FRCP 5.2(e).

f. *Option for additional unredacted filing under seal.* A person making a redacted filing may also file an unredacted copy under seal. The court must retain the unredacted copy as part of the record. FRCP 5.2(f); IN R USDCTND Order 2005-3.

    i. The unredacted version of the document or the reference list shall be retained by the court under seal as part of the record. This paper shall be retained by the court as part of the record. The court may, however, still require the party to file a redacted copy for the public file. IN R USDCTND Order 2005-3.

g. *Option for filing a reference list.* A filing that contains redacted information may be filed together with a reference list that identifies each item of redacted information and specifies an appropriate identifier that uniquely corresponds to each item listed. The list must be filed under seal and may be amended as of right. Any reference in the case to a listed identifier will be construed to refer to the corresponding item of information. FRCP 5.2(g); IN R USDCTND Order 2005-3.

    i. The unredacted version of the document or the reference list shall be retained by the court under seal as part of the record. This paper shall be retained by the court as part of the record. The court may, however, still require the party to file a redacted copy for the public file. IN R USDCTND Order 2005-3.

h. *Responsibility for redaction.* The responsibility for redacting these personal identifiers rests solely with counsel and the parties. The Clerk will not review each paper for compliance with IN R USDCTND Order 2005-3. IN R USDCTND Order 2005-3.

i. *Waiver of protection of identifiers.* A person waives the protection of FRCP 5.2(a) as to the person's own information by filing it without redaction and not under seal. FRCP 5.2(h).

F. Filing and Service Requirements

1. *Filing requirements.* Any paper after the complaint that is required to be served—together with a certificate of service—must be filed within a reasonable time after service. FRCP 5(d)(1). Motions must be filed separately, but alternative motions may be filed in a single paper if each is named in the title following the caption. IN R USDCTND L.R. 7-1(a).

a. *How filing is made; In general.* A paper is filed by delivering it:

    i. To the clerk; or

    ii. To a judge who agrees to accept it for filing, and who must then note the filing date on the paper and promptly send it to the clerk. FRCP 5(d)(2).

- Papers not filed electronically must be filed with the clerk, not a judge. IN R USDCTND L.R. 5-4(b)(4).

    iii. Parties manually filing a paper that requires the clerk to give others notice, must give the clerk: (1) sufficient copies of the notice; and (2) the name and address of each person entitled to receive the notice. IN R USDCTND L.R. 5-4(b)(8).

b. *Where to file.* Papers not filed electronically must be filed in the division where the case is pending, unless: (1) a person will be prejudiced if the paper is not filed the same day it is tendered; and (2) it includes an adequately sized envelope addressed to the clerk's office in the division where the case is pending and with adequate postage. IN R USDCTND L.R. 5-4(b)(5).

c. *Electronic filing*

    i. *Authorization of electronic filing program.* A court may, by local rule, allow papers to be filed, signed, or verified by electronic means that are consistent with any technical standards established by the Judicial Conference of the United States. A local rule may require electronic filing only if reasonable exceptions are allowed. A paper filed electronically in compliance with a local rule is a written paper for purposes of the Federal Rules of Civil Procedure. FRCP 5(d)(3).

        • Papers must be filed, signed, and verified electronically unless excepted by the court's CM/ECF Civil and Criminal User Manual (IN R USDCTND CM/ECF). IN R USDCTND L.R. 5-1.

    ii. *Mandatory electronic filing.* Unless otherwise permitted by these procedures or otherwise authorized by the assigned judge, all documents submitted for filing in this district in civil and criminal cases, no matter when a case was originally filed, shall be filed electronically using the System. IN R USDCTND CM/ECF(II)(A)(1). The requirement that "all documents" be filed electronically includes briefs, and attachments and exhibits used in support of motions. IN R USDCTND CM/ECF(FN1).

        • Sending a document or pleading to the court via e-mail or facsimile does not constitute "electronic filing." IN R USDCTND CM/ECF(I)(A).

    iii. *Conventional filing.* As used in these procedures, a "conventionally" filed or submitted document or pleading is one presented to the Clerk or a party in paper or other non-electronic, tangible format. The following documents shall be filed conventionally and not electronically unless specifically authorized by the Court:

        • Exhibits and other documents which cannot be converted to a legible electronic form. Whenever possible, counsel is responsible for converting filings to an electronic form. However, if that is not physically possible, counsel shall electronically file a .pdf document titled Notice of Manual Filing as a notation on the docket sheet that filings are being held in the clerk's office in paper. A sample Notice of Manual Filing is attached as Form 2 (IN R USDCTND CM/ECF(Form 2)). If documents are filed in paper format, counsel must provide an original for the clerk's office, a copy for the judge and a copy must be served on all parties in the case. Large documents which do not exist in an electronic format shall be scanned into .pdf format by counsel, in small batches if necessary, and filed electronically as separate attachments in the System. IN R USDCTND CM/ECF(III)(A)(1).

        • Certain documents which are listed in IN R USDCTND CM/ECF(II)(E)(2). IN R US-DCTND CM/ECF(III)(A)(2).

        • Documents filed by pro se litigants. IN R USDCTND CM/ECF(III)(A)(3).

    iv. For more information on electronic filing, refer to IN R USDCTND CM/ECF.

2. *Service requirements*

a. *Service; When required*

    i. *In general.* Unless the Federal Rules of Civil Procedure provide otherwise, each of the following papers must be served on every party:

        • An order stating that service is required;

        • A pleading filed after the original complaint, unless the court orders otherwise under FRCP 5(c) because there are numerous defendants;

        • A discovery paper required to be served on a party, unless the court orders otherwise;

- A written motion, except one that may be heard ex parte; and

- A written notice, appearance, demand, or offer of judgment, or any similar paper. FRCP 5(a)(1).

  ii. *If a party fails to appear.* No service is required on a party who is in default for failing to appear. But a pleading that asserts a new claim for relief against such a party must be served on that party under FRCP 4. FRCP 5(a)(2).

  iii. *Seizing property.* If an action is begun by seizing property and no person is or need be named as a defendant, any service required before the filing of an appearance, answer, or claim must be made on the person who had custody or possession of the property when it was seized. FRCP 5(a)(3).

b. *Service; How made*

  i. *Serving an attorney.* If a party is represented by an attorney, service under FRCP 5 must be made on the attorney unless the court orders service on the party. FRCP 5(b)(1).

  ii. *Service in general.* A paper is served under FRCP 5 by:

- Handing it to the person;

- Leaving it: (1) at the person's office with a clerk or other person in charge or, if no one is in charge, in a conspicuous place in the office; or (2) if the person has no office or the office is closed, at the person's dwelling or usual place of abode with someone of suitable age and discretion who resides there;

- Mailing it to the person's last known address—in which event service is complete upon mailing;

- Leaving it with the court clerk if the person has no known address;

- Sending it by electronic means if the person consented in writing—in which event service is complete upon transmission, but is not effective if the serving party learns that it did not reach the person to be served; or

- Delivering it by any other means that the person consented to in writing—in which event service is complete when the person making service delivers it to the agency designated to make delivery. FRCP 5(b)(2).

  iii. *Electronic service.* Electronically filed papers may be served electronically if service is consistent with the CM/ECF User Manual (IN R USDCTND CM/ECF). IN R USDCTND L.R. 5-2(a).

- *Waiver of other service.* An attorney's registration will constitute a waiver of conventional service of documents and the attorney agrees to accept service of notice on behalf of the client of the electronic filing by hand, facsimile or authorized email. IN R USDCTND CM/ECF(I)(B)(3).

- *Serving registered persons.* The System will generate a "Notice of Electronic Filing" when any document is filed. This notice represents service of the document on parties who are registered participants with the System. Except as provided in IN R USDCTND CM/ECF(III)(B), the filing party shall not be required to serve any pleading or other documents on any party receiving electronic notice. IN R USDCTND CM/ECF(II)(D)(1). The term "pleading" refers only to those documents listed in FRCP 7(a). IN R USDCTND CM/ECF(FN3).

- *When electronic service is deemed completed.* A person registered to use the court's electronic-filing system is served with an electronically filed paper when a "Notice of Electronic Filing" is transmitted to that person through the court's electronic filing-system. IN R USDCTND L.R. 5-2(b).

- *Serving non-registered persons.* A person who has not registered to use the court's electronic-filing system but who is entitled to service of a paper must be served according to the Local Civil Rules of the United States District Court for the Northern District of

Indiana and the Federal Rules of Civil Procedure. IN R USDCTND L.R. 5-2(c); IN R USDCTND CM/ECF(II)(D)(2). If such service of a paper copy is to be made, it shall be done in the manner provided in the Federal Rules of Civil Procedure and the Local Civil Rules of the United States District Court for the Northern District of Indiana. IN R USDCTND CM/ECF(II)(D)(2).

    iv. *Service of conventional filings.* Pleadings or other documents which are filed conventionally rather than electronically shall be served in the manner provided for in the Federal Rules of Civil Procedure and the Local Civil Rules of the United States District Court for the Northern District of Indiana, except as otherwise provided by order of the Court. IN R USDCTND CM/ECF(III)(B).

    v. *Using court facilities.* If a local rule so authorizes, a party may use the court's transmission facilities to make service under FRCP 5(b)(2)(E). FRCP 5(b)(3).

  c. *Serving numerous defendants*

    i. *In general.* If an action involves an unusually large number of defendants, the court may, on motion or on its own, order that:

- Defendants' pleadings and replies to them need not be served on other defendants;

- Any crossclaim, counterclaim, avoidance, or affirmative defense in those pleadings and replies to them will be treated as denied or avoided by all other parties; and

- Filing any such pleading and serving it on the plaintiff constitutes notice of the pleading to all parties. FRCP 5(c)(1).

    ii. *Notifying parties.* A copy of every such order must be served on the parties as the court directs. FRCP 5(c)(2).

G. Hearings

1. *Hearings, generally*

  a. *Oral argument.* Due process does not require that oral argument be permitted on a motion and, except as otherwise provided by local rule, the district court has discretion to determine whether it will decide the motion on the papers or hear argument by counsel (and perhaps receive evidence). FPP § 1190; F.D.I.C. v. Deglau, 207 F.3d 153 (3d Cir. 2000).

    i. *Request for oral argument.* A party may request oral argument on a motion by filing and serving a separate document explaining why oral argument is necessary and estimating how long the court should allow for the argument. IN R USDCTND L.R. 7-5(a)(1). Refer to the Documents section of this document for more information.

    ii. *Additional evidence forbidden.* Parties may not present additional evidence at oral argument. IN R USDCTND L.R. 7-5(a)(3).

  b. *Providing a regular schedule for oral hearings.* A court may establish regular times and places for oral hearings on motions. FRCP 78(a).

  c. *Providing for submission on briefs.* By rule or order, the court may provide for submitting and determining motions on briefs, without oral hearings. FRCP 78(b).

  d. *Evidentiary hearings.* A party may request an evidentiary hearing by filing and serving a separate document explaining why the hearing is necessary and estimating how long the court should allow for it. IN R USDCTND L.R. 7-5(b)(2). Refer to the Documents section of this document for more information.

  e. *Court's authority.* The court may: (1) grant or deny a request for oral argument or an evidentiary hearing in its discretion; (2) set oral argument or an evidentiary hearing without a request from a party; or (3) order any oral argument or evidentiary hearing to be held anywhere within the district regardless of where the case will be tried. IN R USDCTND L.R. 7-5(c).

2. *Courtroom and courthouse decorum.* For information on courtroom and courthouse decorum, refer to IN R USDCTND L.R. 83-3.

H. Forms

1. Federal Motion for Continuance/Extension of Time Forms

a. Opposition in federal district court; To motion for continuance; On ground of additional time required to prepare for trial; No excusable neglect shown. AMJUR PP CONTIN § 79.

b. Affidavit in opposition to motion for continuance; By plaintiff's attorney; Lack of due diligence in discovery of documents. AMJUR PP CONTIN § 80.

c. Affidavit in opposition to motion for continuance; By plaintiff's attorney; Defendant's absent witness previously absent; Lack of due diligence in compelling attendance of witness. AMJUR PP CONTIN § 81.

d. Affidavit in opposition to motion for continuance; By plaintiff; Admission that absent witness of defendant would testify according to affidavit. AMJUR PP CONTIN § 83.

e. Affidavit in opposition to defendant's motion for continuance; By plaintiff's counsel; Testimony of absent witness merely cumulative. AMJUR PP CONTIN § 85.

f. Motion for enlargement of time. 2 FEDFORMS § 5:11.

g. Motion for enlargement of time; By plaintiff. 2 FEDFORMS § 5:12.

h. Motion for enlargement of time; To answer motion. 2 FEDFORMS § 5:14.

i. Motion for continuance. 2 FEDFORMS § 5:36.

j. Motion for continuance; Reciting supporting facts; New allegations in amended answer. 2 FEDFORMS § 5:37.

k. Motion for continuance; Reciting supporting facts; Absence of witness. 2 FEDFORMS § 5:38.

l. Motion for continuance; Reciting supporting facts; Absence of witness; Witness outside the country. 2 FEDFORMS § 5:39.

m. Motion for continuance or in the alternative for change of venue; Hostility against defendant. 2 FEDFORMS § 5:40.

n. Notice; Of motion; Containing motion. FEDPROF § 1:749.

o. Brief; Supporting or opposing motion. FEDPROF § 1:752.

p. Opposition to motion; For continuance; No excusable neglect. FEDPROF § 1:808.

q. Affidavit; Opposing motion for continuance; Offer to stipulate to testimony of unavailable witness. FEDPROF § 1:813.

r. Reply to motion for extension of time. GOLDLTGFMS § 10:40.

s. Motions; Extension of time to file jury demand. GOLDLTGFMS § 12:6.

t. Motion for extension of time. GOLDLTGFMS § 25:37.

u. Motion for extension of time to answer. GOLDLTGFMS § 26:13.

v. Motion to extend time for serving answers. GOLDLTGFMS § 26:14.

w. Motion for continuance. GOLDLTGFMS § 43:2.

x. Motion for continuance; Lawyer unavailable. GOLDLTGFMS § 43:3.

y. Motion for continuance; Witness unavailable. GOLDLTGFMS § 43:4.

z. Motion for continuance; Party in military service. GOLDLTGFMS § 43:6.

2. Forms for the Northern District of Indiana

a. Certificate of service. IN R USDCTND CM/ECF(Form 1).

b. Notice of manual filing. IN R USDCTND CM/ECF(Form 2).

c. Declaration that party was unable to file in a timely manner. IN R USDCTND CM/ECF(Form 3).

I. Applicable Rules

1. *Federal rules*

   a. Serving and filing pleadings and other papers. FRCP 5.

   b. Constitutional challenge to a statute; Notice, certification, and intervention. FRCP 5.1.

   c. Privacy protection for filings made with the court. FRCP 5.2.

   d. Computing and extending time; Time for motion papers. FRCP 6.

   e. Pleadings allowed; Form of motions and other papers. FRCP 7.

   f. Disclosure statement. FRCP 7.1.

   g. Form of pleadings. FRCP 10.

   h. Signing pleadings, motions, and other papers; Representations to the court; Sanctions. FRCP 11.

   i. Taking testimony. FRCP 43.

   j. Hearing motions; Submission on briefs. FRCP 78.

2. *Local rules*

   a. Citation and scope of the rules. IN R USDCTND L.R. 1-1.

   b. Sanctions for formatting errors. IN R USDCTND L.R. 1-3.

   c. Electronic filing required. IN R USDCTND L.R. 5-1.

   d. Constitutional questions. IN R USDCTND L.R. 5.1-1.

   e. Electronic service. IN R USDCTND L.R. 5-2.

   f. Format of papers. IN R USDCTND L.R. 5-4.

   g. Extensions of time. IN R USDCTND L.R. 6-1.

   h. Motion practice. IN R USDCTND L.R. 7-1.

   i. Oral arguments and evidentiary hearings. IN R USDCTND L.R. 7-5.

   j. Pretrial procedure. IN R USDCTND L.R. 16-1.

   k. Continuances. IN R USDCTND L.R. 16-3.

   l. Alternative dispute resolution. IN R USDCTND L.R. 16-6.

   m. Filing of discovery and other materials. IN R USDCTND L.R. 26-2.

   n. Case assignment. IN R USDCTND L.R. 40-1.

   o. Appearance and withdrawal of appearance. IN R USDCTND L.R. 83-8.

   p. CM/ECF civil and criminal user manual. IN R USDCTND CM/ECF.

   q. In re: privacy and public access to civil electronic case files. IN R USDCTND Order 2005-3.

Motions, Oppositions and Replies
Motion for Summary Judgment

Document Last Updated December 2016

A. Checklist

(I) ❑ Matters to be considered by moving party

    (a) ❑ Required documents

        (1) ❑ Notice of motion and motion

        (2) ❑ Brief

        (3) ❑ Certificate of service

(b) ❏ Supplemental documents

    (1) ❏ Supporting evidence

    (2) ❏ Notice of constitutional question

    (3) ❏ Nongovernmental corporate disclosure statement

    (4) ❏ Index of exhibits

    (5) ❏ Notice to pro se litigant

    (6) ❏ Request for oral argument

    (7) ❏ Request for evidentiary hearing

    (8) ❏ Copy of authority

    (9) ❏ Proposed order

    (10) ❏ Copy of document with self-addressed envelope

    (11) ❏ Notice of manual filing

    (12) ❏ Courtesy copies

    (13) ❏ Declaration that party was unable to file in a timely manner

(c) ❏ Timing

    (1) ❏ Unless a different time is set by local rule or the court orders otherwise, a party may file a motion for summary judgment at any time until thirty (30) days after the close of all discovery

    (2) ❏ A written motion and notice of the hearing must be served at least fourteen (14) days before the time specified for the hearing, with the following exceptions: (i) when the motion may be heard ex parte; (ii) when the Federal Rules of Civil Procedure set a different time; or (iii) when a court order—which a party may, for good cause, apply for ex parte—sets a different time

    (3) ❏ Any affidavit supporting a motion must be served with the motion

(II) ❏ Matters to be considered by opposing party

  (a) ❏ Required documents

    (1) ❏ Response brief

    (2) ❏ Certificate of service

  (b) ❏ Supplemental documents

    (1) ❏ Supporting evidence

    (2) ❏ Notice of constitutional question

    (3) ❏ Index of exhibits

    (4) ❏ Motion disputing admissibility of evidence

    (5) ❏ Request for oral argument

    (6) ❏ Request for evidentiary hearing

    (7) ❏ Copy of authority

    (8) ❏ Copy of document with self-addressed envelope

    (9) ❏ Notice of manual filing

    (10) ❏ Courtesy copies

    (11) ❏ Declaration that party was unable to file in a timely manner

  (c) ❏ Timing

    (1) ❏ A party opposing the motion must, within twenty-eight (28) days after the movant serves the

motion, file and serve (1) a response brief and (2) any materials that the party contends raise a genuine dispute

(2) ❑ Except as FRCP 59(c) provides otherwise, any opposing affidavit must be served at least seven (7) days before the hearing, unless the court permits service at another time

B. Timing

1. *Motion for summary judgment.* Unless a different time is set by local rule or the court orders otherwise, a party may file a motion for summary judgment at any time until thirty (30) days after the close of all discovery. FRCP 56(b).

2. *Timing of motions, generally*

   a. *Motion and notice of hearing.* A written motion and notice of the hearing must be served at least fourteen (14) days before the time specified for the hearing, with the following exceptions:

      i. When the motion may be heard ex parte;

      ii. When the Federal Rules of Civil Procedure set a different time; or

      iii. When a court order—which a party may, for good cause, apply for ex parte—sets a different time. FRCP 6(c)(1).

   b. *Supporting affidavit.* Any affidavit supporting a motion must be served with the motion. FRCP 6(c)(2).

3. *Timing of opposing papers.* Summary-judgment motions are subject to the deadlines in IN R USDCTND L.R. 56-1(b) and IN R USDCTND L.R. 56-1(c). IN R USDCTND L.R. 7-1(d)(1). A party opposing the motion must, within twenty-eight (28) days after the movant serves the motion, file and serve: (1) a response brief; and (2) any materials that the party contends raise a genuine dispute. IN R USDCTND L.R. 56-1(b)(1).

   a. *Opposing affidavit.* Except as FRCP 59(c) provides otherwise, any opposing affidavit must be served at least seven (7) days before the hearing, unless the court permits service at another time. FRCP 6(c)(2).

   b. *Extensions.* The court may extend response- and reply-brief deadlines, but only for good cause. IN R USDCTND L.R. 7-1(d)(3).

   c. *Summary rulings.* The court may rule on a motion summarily if an opposing party does not file a response before the deadline. IN R USDCTND L.R. 7-1(d)(4).

4. *Timing of reply papers.* Where the respondent files an answering affidavit setting up a new matter, the moving party ordinarily is allowed a reasonable time to file a reply affidavit since failure to deny the new matter by affidavit may operate as an admission of its truth. AMJUR MOTIONS § 25.

   a. *Reply brief.* Summary-judgment motions are subject to the deadlines in IN R USDCTND L.R. 56-1(b) and IN R USDCTND L.R. 56-1(c). IN R USDCTND L.R. 7-1(d)(1). The movant may file a reply brief within fourteen (14) days after a response is served. IN R USDCTND L.R. 56-1(c).

   b. *Extensions.* The court may extend response- and reply-brief deadlines, but only for good cause. IN R USDCTND L.R. 7-1(d)(3).

5. *Computation of time*

   a. *Computing time.* FRCP 6 applies in computing any time period specified in the Federal Rules of Civil Procedure, in any local rule or court order, or in any statute that does not specify a method of computing time. FRCP 6(a).

      i. *Period stated in days or a longer unit.* When the period is stated in days or a longer unit of time:

         • Exclude the day of the event that triggers the period;

         • Count every day, including intermediate Saturdays, Sundays, and legal holidays; and

         • Include the last day of the period, but if the last day is a Saturday, Sunday, or legal holiday, the period continues to run until the end of the next day that is not a Saturday, Sunday, or legal holiday. FRCP 6(a)(1).

ii. *Period stated in hours.* When the period is stated in hours:

- Begin counting immediately on the occurrence of the event that triggers the period;
- Count every hour, including hours during intermediate Saturdays, Sundays, and legal holidays; and
- If the period would end on a Saturday, Sunday, or legal holiday, the period continues to run until the same time on the next day that is not a Saturday, Sunday, or legal holiday. FRCP 6(a)(2).

iii. *Inaccessibility of the clerk's office.* Unless the court orders otherwise, if the clerk's office is inaccessible:

- On the last day for filing under FRCP 6(a)(1), then the time for filing is extended to the first accessible day that is not a Saturday, Sunday, or legal holiday; or
- During the last hour for filing under FRCP 6(a)(2), then the time for filing is extended to the same time on the first accessible day that is not a Saturday, Sunday, or legal holiday. FRCP 6(a)(3).

iv. *"Last day" defined.* Unless a different time is set by a statute, local rule, or court order, the last day ends:

- For electronic filing, at midnight in the court's time zone; and
- For filing by other means, when the clerk's office is scheduled to close. FRCP 6(a)(4).

v. *"Next day" defined.* The "next day" is determined by continuing to count forward when the period is measured after an event and backward when measured before an event. FRCP 6(a)(5).

vi. *"Legal holiday" defined.* "Legal holiday" means:

- The day set aside by statute for observing New Year's Day, Martin Luther King Jr.'s Birthday, Washington's Birthday, Memorial Day, Independence Day, Labor Day, Columbus Day, Veterans' Day, Thanksgiving Day, or Christmas Day;
- Any day declared a holiday by the President or Congress; and
- For periods that are measured after an event, any other day declared a holiday by the state where the district court is located. FRCP 6(a)(6).

b. *Computation of electronic filing deadlines.* Filing documents electronically does not alter any filing deadlines or any time computation pursuant to FRCP 6. The counties of Lake, Porter, LaPorte, Pulaski and Starke are located in the Central time zone and the remaining counties in the Northern District of Indiana are located in the Eastern time zone. Nevertheless, all electronic transmissions of documents must be completed (i.e., received completely by the clerk's office) prior to midnight Eastern Time, (South Bend/Fort Wayne/Lafayette time) in order to be considered timely filed that day, regardless of the local time in the division where the case is pending. Although documents can be filed electronically twenty-four (24) hours a day, filers are strongly encouraged to file all documents during hours when the CM/ECF Help Line is available, from 9:00 a.m. to 4:00 p.m. local time. IN R USDCTND CM/ECF(II)(I).

i. *Technical failures.* If the attorney is unable to file a document in a timely manner due to technical difficulties in the user's system, the attorney must file a document with the court as soon as possible notifying the court of the inability to file the document. A sample document entitled Declaration that Party was Unable to File in a Timely Manner Due to Technical Difficulties is attached hereto as Form 5. IN R USDCTND CM/ECF(VI)(B). [Editor's note: the reference to Form 5 is likely meant to be a reference to Form 3 (IN R USDCTND CM/ECF(Form 3)].

c. *Extending time*

i. *In general.* When an act may or must be done within a specified time, the court may, for good cause, extend the time:

- With or without motion or notice if the court acts, or if a request is made, before the original time or its extension expires; or

- On motion made after the time has expired if the party failed to act because of excusable neglect. FRCP 6(b)(1).

   ii. *Exceptions.* A court must not extend the time to act under FRCP 50(b), FRCP 50(d), FRCP 52(b), FRCP 59(b), FRCP 59(d), FRCP 59(e), and FRCP 60(b). FRCP 6(b)(2).

   iii. Refer to the United States District Court for the Northern District of Indiana KeyRules Motion for Continuance/Extension of Time document for more information on extending time.

  d. *Additional time after certain kinds of service.* When a party may or must act within a specified time after being served and service is made under FRCP 5(b)(2)(C) (mail), FRCP 5(b)(2)(D) (leaving with the clerk), or FRCP 5(b)(2)(F) (other means consented to), three (3) days are added after the period would otherwise expire under FRCP 6(a). FRCP 6(d).

C. General Requirements

1. *Motions, generally*

  a. *Requirements.* A request for a court order must be made by motion. The motion must:

   i. Be in writing unless made during a hearing or trial;

   ii. State with particularity the grounds for seeking the order; and

   iii. State the relief sought. FRCP 7(b)(1).

  b. *Notice of motion.* A party interested in resisting the relief sought by a motion has a right to notice thereof, and an opportunity to be heard. AMJUR MOTIONS § 12.

   i. In addition to statutory or court rule provisions requiring notice of a motion—the purpose of such a notice requirement having been said to be to prevent a party from being prejudicially surprised by a motion—principles of natural justice dictate that an adverse party generally must be given notice that a motion will be presented to the court. AMJUR MOTIONS § 12.

   ii. "Notice," in this regard, means reasonable notice, including a meaningful opportunity to prepare and to defend against allegations of a motion. AMJUR MOTIONS § 12.

  c. *Writing requirement.* The writing requirement is intended to insure that the adverse parties are informed and have a record of both the motion's pendency and the grounds on which the movant seeks an order. FPP § 1191; Feldberg v. Quechee Lakes Corp., 463 F.3d 195 (2d Cir. 2006).

   i. It is sufficient "if the motion is stated in a written notice of the hearing of the motion." FPP § 1191.

  d. *Particularity requirement.* The particularity requirement insures that the opposing parties will have notice of their opponent's contentions. FEDPROC § 62:364; Goodman v. 1973 26 Foot Trojan Vessel, Arkansas Registration No. AR1439SN, 859 F.2d 71, 12 Fed.R.Serv.3d 645 (8th Cir. 1988). That requirement ensures that notice of the basis for the motion is provided to the court and to the opposing party so as to avoid prejudice, provide the opponent with a meaningful opportunity to respond, and provide the court with enough information to process the motion correctly. FEDPROC § 62:364; Andreas v. Volkswagen of America, Inc., 336 F.3d 789, 56 Fed.R.Serv.3d 6 (8th Cir. 2003).

   i. Reasonable specification of the grounds for a motion is sufficient. However, where a movant fails to state even one ground for granting the motion in question, the movant has failed to meet the minimal standard of "reasonable specification." FEDPROC § 62:364; Martinez v. Trainor, 556 F.2d 818, 23 Fed.R.Serv.2d 403 (7th Cir. 1977).

   ii. The court may excuse the failure to comply with the particularity requirement if it is inadvertent, and where no prejudice is shown by the opposing party. FEDPROC § 62:364.

  e. *Motions must be filed separately.* Motions must be filed separately, but alternative motions may be filed in a single paper if each is named in the title following the caption. IN R USDCTND L.R. 7-1(a).

2. *Motion for summary judgment.* A party may move for summary judgment, identifying each claim or defense—or the part of each claim or defense—on which summary judgment is sought. The court shall grant summary judgment if the movant shows that there is no genuine dispute as to any material fact and

the movant is entitled to judgment as a matter of law. The court should state on the record the reasons for granting or denying the motion. FRCP 56(a).

a. *Burden of proof and presumptions*

  i. *Movant's burden.* It is well-settled that the party moving for summary judgment has the burden of demonstrating that the FRCP 56(c) test—"no genuine issue as to any material fact"—is satisfied and that the movant is entitled to judgment as a matter of law. FPP § 2727; Adickes v. S. H. Kress & Co., 398 U.S. 144, 157, 90 S.Ct. 1598, 1608, 26 L.Ed.2d 142 (1970).

  - The movant is held to a stringent standard. FPP § 2727. Before summary judgment will be granted it must be clear what the truth is and any doubt as to the existence of a genuine dispute of material fact will be resolved against the movant. FPP § 2727; Poller v. Columbia Broadcasting Sys., Inc., 368 U.S. 464, 82 S.Ct. 486, 7 L.Ed.2d 458 (1962); Adickes v. S. H. Kress & Co., 398 U.S. 144, 90 S.Ct. 1598, 26 L.Ed.2d 142 (1970).

  - Because the burden is on the movant, the evidence presented to the court always is construed in favor of the party opposing the motion and the opponent is given the benefit of all favorable inferences that can be drawn from it. FPP § 2727; Scott v. Harris, 550 U.S. 372, 127 S.Ct. 1769, 167 L.Ed.2d 686 (2007).

  - Finally, facts asserted by the party opposing the motion, if supported by affidavits or other evidentiary material, are regarded as true. FPP § 2727; McLaughlin v. Liu, 849 F.2d 1205, 1208 (9th Cir. 1988).

  ii. *Opponent's burden.* If the summary-judgment movant makes out a prima facie case that would entitle him to a judgment as a matter of law if uncontroverted at trial, summary judgment will be granted unless the opposing party offers some competent evidence that could be presented at trial showing that there is a genuine dispute as to a material fact. FPP § 2727.2; Scott v. Harris, 550 U.S. 372, 127 S.Ct. 1769, 167 L.Ed.2d 686 (2007). In this way the burden of producing evidence is shifted to the party opposing the motion. FPP § 2727.2; Celotex Corp. v. Catrett, 477 U.S. 317, 331, 106 S.Ct. 2548, 2557, 91 L.Ed.2d 265 (1986).

  - The burden on the nonmoving party is not a heavy one; the nonmoving party simply is required to show specific facts, as opposed to general allegations, that present a genuine issue worthy of trial. FPP § 2727.2; Lujan v. Defenders of Wildlife, 504 U.S. 555, 112 S.Ct. 2130, 119 L.Ed.2d 351 (1992).

  - The nonmoving party has two options once the moving party has met its burden of production of evidence demonstrating the absence of a genuine issue of material fact: either come forward with countervailing evidence showing that a genuine issue does exist, or submit an affidavit under FRCP 56(f) demonstrating that more time or further discovery are necessary to enable it to oppose the summary judgment motion. FEDPROC § 62:589.

b. *Failing to properly support or address a fact.* If a party fails to properly support an assertion of fact or fails to properly address another party's assertion of fact as required by FRCP 56(c), the court may:

  i. Give an opportunity to properly support or address the fact;

  ii. Consider the fact undisputed for purposes of the motion;

  iii. Grant summary judgment if the motion and supporting materials—including the facts considered undisputed—show that the movant is entitled to it; or

  iv. Issue any other appropriate order. FRCP 56(e).

c. *Judgment independent of the motion.* After giving notice and a reasonable time to respond, the court may:

  i. Grant summary judgment for a nonmovant;

  ii. Grant the motion on grounds not raised by a party; or

  iii. Consider summary judgment on its own after identifying for the parties material facts that may not be genuinely in dispute. FRCP 56(f).

d. *Failing to grant all the requested relief.* If the court does not grant all the relief requested by the motion, it may enter an order stating any material fact—including an item of damages or other relief—that is not genuinely in dispute and treating the fact as established in the case. FRCP 56(g).

e. *Affidavit or declaration submitted in bad faith.* If satisfied that an affidavit or declaration under FRCP 56 is submitted in bad faith or solely for delay, the court—after notice and a reasonable time to respond—may order the submitting party to pay the other party the reasonable expenses, including attorney's fees, it incurred as a result. An offending party or attorney may also be held in contempt or subjected to other appropriate sanctions. FRCP 56(h).

f. *Conversion of motions under FRCP 12(b)(6) and FRCP 12(c).* If, on a motion under FRCP 12(b)(6) or FRCP 12(c), matters outside the pleadings are presented to and not excluded by the court, the motion must be treated as one for summary judgment under FRCP 56. FRCP 12(d).

3. *Opposing papers*

a. *Opposing papers, generally.* The Federal Rules of Civil Procedure do not require any formal answer, return, or reply to a motion, except where the Federal Rules of Civil Procedure or local rules may require affidavits, memoranda, or other papers to be filed in opposition to a motion. Such papers are simply to apprise the court of such opposition and the grounds of that opposition. FEDPROC § 62:359.

    i. *Effect of failure to respond to motion.* Although in the absence of statutory provision or court rule, a motion ordinarily does not require a written answer, when a party files a motion and the opposing party fails to respond, the court may construe such failure to respond as nonopposition to the motion or an admission that the motion was meritorious, may take the facts alleged in the motion as true—the rule in some jurisdictions being that the failure to respond to a fact set forth in a motion is deemed an admission—and may grant the motion if the relief requested appears to be justified. AMJUR MOTIONS § 28.

    ii. *Assent or no opposition not determinative.* However, a motion will not be granted automatically simply because an "assent" or a notation of "no opposition" has been filed; federal judges frequently deny motions that have been assented to when it is thought that justice so dictates. FPP § 1190.

    iii. *Responsive pleading inappropriate as response to motion.* An attempt to answer or oppose a motion with a responsive pleading usually is not appropriate. FPP § 1190.

b. *Opposition to motion for summary judgment.* The party opposing summary judgment does not have a duty to present evidence in opposition to a motion under FRCP 56 in all circumstances. FPP § 2727.2; Jaroma v. Massey, 873 F.2d 17 (1st Cir. 1989).

    i. *When facts are unavailable to the nonmovant.* If a nonmovant shows by affidavit or declaration that, for specified reasons, it cannot present facts essential to justify its opposition, the court may:

- Defer considering the motion or deny it;
- Allow time to obtain affidavits or declarations or to take discovery; or
- Issue any other appropriate order. FRCP 56(d).

4. *Reply papers.* A moving party may be required or permitted to prepare papers in addition to his original motion papers. AMJUR MOTIONS § 25. Papers answering or replying to opposing papers may be appropriate, in the interests of justice, where it appears there is a substantial reason for allowing a reply. Thus, a court may accept reply papers where a party demonstrates that the papers to which it seeks to file a reply raise new issues that are material to the disposition of the question before the court, or where the court determines, sua sponte, that it wishes further briefing of an issue raised in those papers and orders the submission of additional papers. FEDPROC § 62:360.

a. *Function of reply papers.* The function of a reply affidavit is to answer the arguments made in opposition to the position taken by the movant and not to permit the movant to introduce new arguments in support of the motion. AMJUR MOTIONS § 25.

b. *Issues raised for the first time in a reply document.* However, the view has been followed in some jurisdictions, that as a matter of judicial economy, where there is no prejudice and where the issues could be raised simply by filing a motion to dismiss, the trial court has discretion to consider arguments raised for the first time in a reply memorandum, and that a trial court may grant a motion to strike issues raised for the first time in a reply memorandum. AMJUR MOTIONS § 26.

5. *Appearances.* Attorneys not representing the United States or its agencies must file an appearance when they represent (either in person or by filing a paper) a party. IN R USDCTND L.R. 83-8(a). For more information, refer to IN R USDCTND L.R. 83-8.

6. *Notice of related action.* A party must file a notice of related action as soon as it appears that the party's case and another pending case: (1) arise out of the same transaction or occurrence; (2) involve the same property; or (3) involve the validity or infringement of the same patent, trademark, or copyright. IN R USDCTND L.R. 40-1(d). For more information, refer to IN R USDCTND L.R. 40-1.

7. *Alternative dispute resolution (ADR).* After they confer as required by FRCP 26(f), the parties must advise the court which, if any, alternative-dispute-resolution processes they expect to pursue and when they expect to undertake the process. IN R USDCTND L.R. 16-6(a). For more information on alternative dispute resolution (ADR), refer to IN R USDCTND L.R. 16-6 and IN R USDCTND Order 2003-21.

8. *Settlement or resolution.* The parties must immediately notify the court if they reasonably expect to settle the case or resolve a pending motion. IN R USDCTND L.R. 16-1(g).

9. *Modification or suspension of rules.* The court may, on its own motion or at the request of a party, suspend or modify any rule in a particular case in the interest of justice. IN R USDCTND L.R. 1-1(c).

D. Documents

1. *Documents for moving party*

   a. *Required documents*

   i. *Notice of motion and motion.* The party must not specify a hearing date in the notice of a motion or petition unless the court or the clerk has authorized it. IN R USDCTND L.R. 7-5(b)(2). Refer to the General Requirements section of this document for information on the notice of motion and motion.

   ii. *Brief.* Parties must file a supporting brief with any motion under: FRCP 56. IN R USDCTND L.R. 7-1(b)(3). Refer to the Format section of this document for the format of briefs.

   - *Statement of material facts.* The brief supporting a summary-judgment motion or the brief's appendix must include a section labeled "Statement of Material Facts" that identifies the facts that the moving party contends are not genuinely disputed. IN R USDCTND L.R. 56-1(a).

   iii. *Certificate of service.* FRCP 5(d) requires that the person making service under FRCP 5 certify that service has been effected. FRCP 5(Advisory Committee Notes). Having such information on file may be useful for many purposes, including proof of service if an issue arises concerning the effectiveness of the service. FRCP 5(Advisory Committee Notes).

   - *Certificate of service for electronically-filed documents.* A Certificate of Service is still a requirement when filing documents electronically. A sample Certificate of Service is attached as Form 1 (IN R USDCTND CM/ECF(Form 1)). IN R USDCTND CM/ECF(II)(H).

   b. *Supplemental documents*

   i. *Supporting evidence.* When a motion relies on facts outside the record, the court may hear the matter on affidavits or may hear it wholly or partly on oral testimony or on depositions. FRCP 43(c).

   - *Materials necessary for motion.* A party must file those portions of discovery requests or responses (including deposition transcripts) that the party relies on to support a motion that could result in a final order on an issue. IN R USDCTND L.R. 26-2(c).

   - *Supporting factual positions.* A party asserting that a fact cannot be or is genuinely disputed must support the assertion by: (1) citing to particular parts of materials in the record, including depositions, documents, electronically stored information, affidavits or declarations, stipulations (including those made for purposes of the motion only), admissions, interrogatory answers, or other materials; or (2) showing that the materials cited do not establish the absence or presence of a genuine dispute, or that an adverse party cannot produce admissible evidence to support the fact. FRCP 56(c)(1).

- *Objection that a fact is not supported by admissible evidence.* A party may object that the material cited to support or dispute a fact cannot be presented in a form that would be admissible in evidence. FRCP 56(c)(2).

- *Materials not cited.* The court need consider only the cited materials, but it may consider other materials in the record. FRCP 56(c)(3).

- *Affidavits or declarations.* An affidavit or declaration used to support or oppose a motion must be made on personal knowledge, set out facts that would be admissible in evidence, and show that the affiant or declarant is competent to testify on the matters stated. FRCP 56(c)(4).

ii.   *Notice of constitutional question.* A party that files a pleading, written motion, or other paper drawing into question the constitutionality of a federal or state statute must promptly:

- *File notice.* File a notice of constitutional question stating the question and identifying the paper that raises it, if: (1) a federal statute is questioned and the parties do not include the United States, one of its agencies, or one of its officers or employees in an official capacity; or (2) a state statute is questioned and the parties do not include the state, one of its agencies, or one of its officers or employees in an official capacity; and

- *Serve notice.* Serve the notice and paper on the Attorney General of the United States if a federal statute is questioned—or on the state attorney general if a state statute is questioned—either by certified or registered mail or by sending it to an electronic address designated by the attorney general for this purpose. FRCP 5.1(a).

- *When to file the notice.* A party required to file a notice of constitutional question under FRCP 5.1 must do so by the later of: (1) the day the parties tender their proposed case-management plan (if one is required); or (2) 21 days after filing the pleading, written motion, or other paper questioning the constitutionality of a federal or state statute. IN R USDCTND L.R. 5.1-1(a).

- *Service on government officials.* The party must also serve the notice and the pleading, written motion, or other paper questioning the constitutionality of a federal or state statute on: (1) the Attorney General of the United States and the United States Attorney for the Northern District of Indiana, if a federal statute is challenged; or (2) the Attorney General for the state if a state statute is challenged. IN R USDCTND L.R. 5.1-1(b). Service required under IN R USDCTND L.R. 5.1-1(b) may be made either by certified or registered mail or by emailing it to an address designated by those officials for this purpose. IN R USDCTND L.R. 5.1-1(c).

- *No forfeiture.* A party's failure to file and serve the notice, or the court's failure to certify, does not forfeit a constitutional claim or defense that is otherwise timely asserted. FRCP 5.1(d).

iii.   *Nongovernmental corporate disclosure statement*

- *Contents.* A nongovernmental corporate party must file two (2) copies of a disclosure statement that: (1) identifies any parent corporation and any publicly held corporation owning ten percent (10%) or more of its stock; or (2) states that there is no such corporation. FRCP 7.1(a).

- *Time to file; Supplemental filing.* A party must: (1) file the disclosure statement with its first appearance, pleading, petition, motion, response, or other request addressed to the court; and (2) promptly file a supplemental statement if any required information changes. FRCP 7.1(b).

iv.   *Index of exhibits.* Any pleading, motion, brief, affidavit, notice, or proposed order, whether filed electronically or by delivering it to the clerk, must: include a separate index identifying and briefly describing each exhibit if there are more than four (4) exhibits. IN R USDCTND L.R. 5-4(a)(8).

v.   *Notice to pro se litigant.* A party seeking summary judgment against an unrepresented party must serve that party with the notice contained in Appendix C (IN R USDCTND App. C). IN R USDCTND L.R. 56-1(f).

vi. *Request for oral argument.* A party may request oral argument on a motion by filing and serving a separate document explaining why oral argument is necessary and estimating how long the court should allow for the argument. IN R USDCTND L.R. 7-5(a)(1). The request must be filed and served with the party's supporting brief, response brief, or reply brief. IN R USDCTND L.R. 7-5(a)(2).

vii. *Request for evidentiary hearing.* A party may request an evidentiary hearing by filing and serving a separate document explaining why the hearing is necessary and estimating how long the court should allow for it. IN R USDCTND L.R. 7-5(b)(1).

viii. *Copy of authority.* A copy of any decision, statute, or regulation cited in a motion or brief must be attached to the paper if—and only if—it is not available on Westlaw or Lexis. But if a copy of a decision, statute, or regulation is only available electronically, a party must provide it to the court or another party upon request. IN R USDCTND L.R. 7-1(f).

ix. *Proposed order.* Parties filing a paper that requires the judge or clerk to enter a routine or uncontested order must include a suitable form of order. IN R USDCTND L.R. 5-4(c).

   • Proposed orders shall not be filed electronically either as a separate document or as an attachment to the main pleading or other document. Instead, all proposed orders must be e-mailed to the chambers of the appropriate judicial officer for the case. The proposed order must be in WordPerfect Format or Rich Text Format (RTF). Proposed orders should be attached to an e-mail and sent to the appropriate judicial officer at the address listed in IN R USDCTND CM/ECF(II)(F). The subject line of the email message should indicate the case title, cause number and document number of the motion, e.g., Smith v. Jones 1:02-cv-1234, motion# ___. IN R USDCTND CM/ECF(II)(F).

x.   *Copy of document with self-addressed envelope.* A party who wants a file-stamped copy of a paper must include with the filing an additional copy of the paper and a self-addressed envelope with adequate postage. IN R USDCTND L.R. 5-4(b)(6).

xi. *Notice of manual filing.* However, if that is not physically possible, counsel shall electronically file a .pdf document titled Notice of Manual Filing as a notation on the docket sheet that filings are being held in the clerk's office in paper. A sample Notice of Manual Filing is attached as Form 2 (IN R USDCTND CM/ECF(Form 2)). IN R USDCTND CM/ECF(III)(A)(1).

xii. *Courtesy copies.* If documents are filed in paper format, counsel must provide an original for the clerk's office, a copy for the judge and a copy must be served on all parties in the case. IN R USDCTND CM/ECF(III)(A)(1).

xiii. *Declaration that party was unable to file in a timely manner.* If the attorney is unable to file a document in a timely manner due to technical difficulties in the user's system, the attorney must file a document with the court as soon as possible notifying the court of the inability to file the document. A sample document entitled Declaration that Party was Unable to File in a Timely Manner Due to Technical Difficulties is attached hereto as Form 5. IN R USDCTND CM/ECF(VI)(B). [Editor's note: the reference to Form 5 is likely meant to be a reference to Form 3 (IN R USDCTND CM/ECF(Form 3)].

2. *Documents for opposing party*

   a. *Required documents*

      i. *Response brief.* Refer to the Format section of this document for the format of briefs. Refer to the General Requirements section of this document for information on the opposing papers.

         • *Statement of genuine disputes.* The response brief or its appendix must include a section labeled "Statement of Genuine Disputes" that identifies the material facts that the party contends are genuinely disputed so as to make a trial necessary. IN R USDCTND L.R. 56-1(b)(2).

ii. *Certificate of service.* FRCP 5(d) requires that the person making service under FRCP 5 certify that service has been effected. FRCP 5(Advisory Committee Notes). Having such information on file may be useful for many purposes, including proof of service if an issue arises concerning the effectiveness of the service. FRCP 5(Advisory Committee Notes).

- *Certificate of service for electronically-filed documents.* A Certificate of Service is still a requirement when filing documents electronically. A sample Certificate of Service is attached as Form 1 (IN R USDCTND CM/ECF(Form 1)). IN R USDCTND CM/ECF(II)(H).

b. *Supplemental documents*

i. *Supporting evidence.* When a motion relies on facts outside the record, the court may hear the matter on affidavits or may hear it wholly or partly on oral testimony or on depositions. FRCP 43(c).

- *Materials necessary for motion.* A party must file those portions of discovery requests or responses (including deposition transcripts) that the party relies on to support a motion that could result in a final order on an issue. IN R USDCTND L.R. 26-2(c).

- *Supporting factual positions.* A party asserting that a fact cannot be or is genuinely disputed must support the assertion by: (1) citing to particular parts of materials in the record, including depositions, documents, electronically stored information, affidavits or declarations, stipulations (including those made for purposes of the motion only), admissions, interrogatory answers, or other materials; or (2) showing that the materials cited do not establish the absence or presence of a genuine dispute, or that an adverse party cannot produce admissible evidence to support the fact. FRCP 56(c)(1).

- *Objection that a fact is not supported by admissible evidence.* A party may object that the material cited to support or dispute a fact cannot be presented in a form that would be admissible in evidence. FRCP 56(c)(2).

- *Materials not cited.* The court need consider only the cited materials, but it may consider other materials in the record. FRCP 56(c)(3).

- *Affidavits or declarations.* An affidavit or declaration used to support or oppose a motion must be made on personal knowledge, set out facts that would be admissible in evidence, and show that the affiant or declarant is competent to testify on the matters stated. FRCP 56(c)(4).

ii. *Notice of constitutional question.* A party that files a pleading, written motion, or other paper drawing into question the constitutionality of a federal or state statute must promptly:

- *File notice.* File a notice of constitutional question stating the question and identifying the paper that raises it, if: (1) a federal statute is questioned and the parties do not include the United States, one of its agencies, or one of its officers or employees in an official capacity; or (2) a state statute is questioned and the parties do not include the state, one of its agencies, or one of its officers or employees in an official capacity; and

- *Serve notice.* Serve the notice and paper on the Attorney General of the United States if a federal statute is questioned—or on the state attorney general if a state statute is questioned—either by certified or registered mail or by sending it to an electronic address designated by the attorney general for this purpose. FRCP 5.1(a).

- *When to file the notice.* A party required to file a notice of constitutional question under FRCP 5.1 must do so by the later of: (1) the day the parties tender their proposed case-management plan (if one is required); or (2) 21 days after filing the pleading, written motion, or other paper questioning the constitutionality of a federal or state statute. IN R USDCTND L.R. 5.1-1(a).

- *Service on government officials.* The party must also serve the notice and the pleading, written motion, or other paper questioning the constitutionality of a federal or state statute on: (1) the Attorney General of the United States and the United States Attorney for the Northern District of Indiana, if a federal statute is challenged; or (2) the Attorney General for the state if a state statute is challenged. IN R USDCTND L.R. 5.1-1(b). Service required under IN R USDCTND L.R. 5.1-1(b) may be made either by certified or registered mail or by emailing it to an address designated by those officials for this purpose. IN R USDCTND L.R. 5.1-1(c).

- *No forfeiture.* A party's failure to file and serve the notice, or the court's failure to certify, does not forfeit a constitutional claim or defense that is otherwise timely asserted. FRCP 5.1(d).

iii. *Index of exhibits.* Any pleading, motion, brief, affidavit, notice, or proposed order, whether filed electronically or by delivering it to the clerk, must: include a separate index identifying and briefly describing each exhibit if there are more than four (4) exhibits. IN R USDCTND L.R. 5-4(a)(8).

iv. *Motion disputing admissibility of evidence.* Any dispute regarding the admissibility of evidence should be addressed in a separate motion in accordance with IN R USDCTND L.R. 7-1. IN R USDCTND L.R. 56-1(e).

v. *Request for oral argument.* A party may request oral argument on a motion by filing and serving a separate document explaining why oral argument is necessary and estimating how long the court should allow for the argument. IN R USDCTND L.R. 7-5(a)(1). The request must be filed and served with the party's supporting brief, response brief, or reply brief. IN R USDCTND L.R. 7-5(a)(2).

vi. *Request for evidentiary hearing.* A party may request an evidentiary hearing by filing and serving a separate document explaining why the hearing is necessary and estimating how long the court should allow for it. IN R USDCTND L.R. 7-5(b)(1).

vii. *Copy of authority.* A copy of any decision, statute, or regulation cited in a motion or brief must be attached to the paper if—and only if—it is not available on Westlaw or Lexis. But if a copy of a decision, statute, or regulation is only available electronically, a party must provide it to the court or another party upon request. IN R USDCTND L.R. 7-1(f).

viii. *Copy of document with self-addressed envelope.* A party who wants a file-stamped copy of a paper must include with the filing an additional copy of the paper and a self-addressed envelope with adequate postage. IN R USDCTND L.R. 5-4(b)(6).

ix. *Notice of manual filing.* However, if that is not physically possible, counsel shall electronically file a .pdf document titled Notice of Manual Filing as a notation on the docket sheet that filings are being held in the clerk's office in paper. A sample Notice of Manual Filing is attached as Form 2 (IN R USDCTND CM/ECF(Form 2)). IN R USDCTND CM/ECF(III)(A)(1).

x. *Courtesy copies.* If documents are filed in paper format, counsel must provide an original for the clerk's office, a copy for the judge and a copy must be served on all parties in the case. IN R USDCTND CM/ECF(III)(A)(1).

xi. *Declaration that party was unable to file in a timely manner.* If the attorney is unable to file a document in a timely manner due to technical difficulties in the user's system, the attorney must file a document with the court as soon as possible notifying the court of the inability to file the document. A sample document entitled Declaration that Party was Unable to File in a Timely Manner Due to Technical Difficulties is attached hereto as Form 5. IN R USDCTND CM/ECF(VI)(B). [Editor's note: the reference to Form 5 is likely meant to be a reference to Form 3 (IN R USDCTND CM/ECF(Form 3)].

E. Format

1. *Form of documents.* The rules governing captions and other matters of form in pleadings apply to motions and other papers. FRCP 7(b)(2).

   a. *Paper.* Any pleading, motion, brief, affidavit, notice, or proposed order, whether filed electronically

or by delivering it to the clerk, must: use eight and one-half by eleven (8-1/2 x 11) inch pages. IN R USDCTND L.R. 5-4(a)(2).

    i. *Manual filings.* Papers delivered to the clerk for filing must: be flat, unfolded, and on good-quality, white paper. IN R USDCTND L.R. 5-4(b)(1)(A).

        • *Covers or backing.* Papers delivered to the clerk for filing must: not have a cover or a back. IN R USDCTND L.R. 5-4(b)(1)(B).

        • *Recycled paper.* The court encourages using recycled paper. IN R USDCTND L.R. 5-4(b)(7).

b. *Margins.* Any pleading, motion, brief, affidavit, notice, or proposed order, whether filed electronically or by delivering it to the clerk, must: have at least one (1) inch margins. IN R USDCTND L.R. 5-4(a)(3).

c. *Spacing.* Any pleading, motion, brief, affidavit, notice, or proposed order, whether filed electronically or by delivering it to the clerk, must: be double spaced (except for headings, footnotes, and quoted material). IN R USDCTND L.R. 5-4(a)(5).

d. *Text.* Any pleading, motion, brief, affidavit, notice, or proposed order, whether filed electronically or by delivering it to the clerk, must: be plainly typewritten, printed, or prepared by a clearly legible copying process. IN R USDCTND L.R. 5-4(a)(1).

    i. Any pleading, motion, brief, affidavit, notice, or proposed order, whether filed electronically or by delivering it to the clerk, must: use at least twelve (12) point type in the body and at least ten (10) point type in footnotes. IN R USDCTND L.R. 5-4(a)(4).

e. *Page numbering.* Any pleading, motion, brief, affidavit, notice, or proposed order, whether filed electronically or by delivering it to the clerk, must: have consecutively numbered pages. IN R USDCTND L.R. 5-4(a)(6).

f. *Caption; Names of parties.* Every pleading must have a caption with the court's name, a title, a file number, and a FRCP 7(a) designation. The title of the complaint must name all the parties; the title of other pleadings, after naming the first party on each side, may refer generally to other parties. FRCP 10(a). Any pleading, motion, brief, affidavit, notice, or proposed order, whether filed electronically or by delivering it to the clerk, must: include a title on the first page. IN R USDCTND L.R. 5-4(a)(7).

    i. *Alternative motions.* Motions must be filed separately, but alternative motions may be filed in a single paper if each is named in the title following the caption. IN R USDCTND L.R. 7-1(a).

g. *Filer's information.* Any pleading, motion, brief, affidavit, notice, or proposed order, whether filed electronically or by delivering it to the clerk, must: except in proposed orders and affidavits, include the filer's name, address, telephone number, fax number (where available), and e-mail address (where available). IN R USDCTND L.R. 5-4(a)(9).

h. *Paragraphs; Separate statements.* A party must state its claims or defenses in numbered paragraphs, each limited as far as practicable to a single set of circumstances. A later pleading may refer by number to a paragraph in an earlier pleading. If doing so would promote clarity, each claim founded on a separate transaction or occurrence—and each defense other than a denial—must be stated in a separate count or defense. FRCP 10(b).

i. *Adoption by reference; Exhibits.* A statement in a pleading may be adopted by reference elsewhere in the same pleading or in any other pleading or motion. A copy of a written instrument that is an exhibit to a pleading is a part of the pleading for all purposes. FRCP 10(c).

j. *Citation of local rules.* The Local Civil Rules of the United States District Court for the Northern District of Indiana may be cited as "N.D. Ind. L.R." IN R USDCTND L.R. 1-1(a)(1).

k. *Acceptance by the clerk.* The clerk must not refuse to file a paper solely because it is not in the form prescribed by the Federal Rules of Civil Procedure or by a local rule or practice. FRCP 5(d)(4).

    i. *Sanctions for formatting errors; Non-compliance.* If a person files a paper that does not comply with the rules governing the format of papers filed with the court, the court may: (1) strike the paper from the record; or (2) fine the person up to one thousand dollars ($1,000). IN R USDCTND L.R. 1-3(a).

- *Notice.* Before sanctioning a person under IN R USDCTND L.R. 1-3(a)(2), the court must: (1) notify the person that the paper is noncompliant; and (2) give the person the opportunity either to be heard or to revise the paper. IN R USDCTND L.R. 1-3(b).

2. *Form of electronic documents.* Electronically filed documents must meet the same requirements of format and page limits as documents "conventionally filed" (as defined in IN R USDCTND CM/ECF(III)(A)) pursuant to the Federal Rules of Civil Procedure and the Local Civil Rules of the United States District Court for the Northern District of Indiana. IN R USDCTND CM/ECF(II)(A)(2).

   a. *PDF format required.* Documents filed in the CM/ECF must be in .pdf format. A document created with almost any word-processing program can be converted to .pdf format. The .pdf program in effect takes a picture of the original document and allows anyone to open the converted document across a broad range of hardware and software, with layout, format, links, and images intact. IN R USDCTND CM/ECF(FN2).

   b. *Title of documents.* The person electronically filing a pleading or other document will be responsible for designating a title for the pleading or other document by using one of the categories contained in the events listed in the CM/ECF Menu. IN R USDCTND CM/ECF(II)(G).

   c. *Combining documents.* All documents which form part of a single pleading and which are being filed at the same time and by the same party may be electronically filed together under one document number, e.g., the motion and a supporting affidavit, with the exception of memoranda in support. Memoranda in support shall be electronically filed separately and shown as a related document to the motion. IN R USDCTND CM/ECF(II)(A)(4).

   d. *Exhibits and attachments.* Filing users must submit in electronic form all documents referenced as exhibits or attachments, unless the court permits conventional filing. A filing user must submit as exhibits or attachments only those excerpts of the referenced documents that are directly germane to the matter under consideration by the court. Excerpted material must be clearly and prominently identified as such. Filing users who file excerpts of documents as exhibits or attachments do so without prejudice to their right to timely file additional excerpts or the complete document. Responding parties may timely file additional excerpts or the complete document that they believe are directly germane. The court may require parties to file additional excerpts or the complete document. IN R USDCTND CM/ECF(II)(A)(6).

   e. *Hyperlinks.* Electronically filed documents may contain hyperlink references to an external document as a convenient mechanism for accessing material cited in the document. A hyperlink reference is neither validated for content nor considered a part of the court's records. The court neither endorses the product or organization at the destination of a hyperlink reference, nor does the court exercise any responsibility over the content at the destination. In order to preserve the integrity of the court record, attorneys wishing to insert hyperlinks in court filings shall continue to use the traditional citation method for the cited authority, in addition to the hyperlink. A hyperlink contained in a filing is no more than a convenient mechanism for accessing material cited in the document and a hyperlink reference is extraneous to any filed document and is not part of the court's record. IN R USDCTND CM/ECF(II)(A)(3).

3. *Form of briefs*

   a. *Page limits.* Supporting and response briefs (excluding tables of contents, tables of authorities, and appendices) ordinarily must not exceed twenty-five (25) pages. Reply briefs must not exceed fifteen (15) pages. IN R USDCTND L.R. 7-1(e)(1).

      i. *Exception.* The court may allow a party to file a brief exceeding these page limits for extraordinary and compelling reasons. But if the court permits a brief to exceed twenty-five (25) pages, it must include:

         - A table of contents with page references;
         - An issue statement; and
         - A table of authorities including: (1) all cases (alphabetically arranged), statutes, and other

authorities cited in the brief; and (2) references to where the authorities appear in the brief. IN R USDCTND L.R. 7-1(e)(2).

4. *Signing of pleadings, motions and other papers*

  a. *Signature.* Every pleading, written motion, and other paper must be signed by at least one attorney of record in the attorney's name—or by a party personally if the party is unrepresented. The paper must state the signer's address, e-mail address, and telephone number. FRCP 11(a).

   i. *Signatures on manual filings.* Papers delivered to the clerk for filing must: include the filer's original signature. IN R USDCTND L.R. 5-4(b)(1)(C).

   - *Rubber-stamped and faxed signatures.* An original paper with a rubber-stamped or faxed signature is unsigned for purposes of FRCP 11 and FRCP 26(g). IN R USDCTND L.R. 5-4(b)(2).

   - *Affidavits.* Only the affiant need sign an affidavit. IN R USDCTND L.R. 5-4(b)(3).

   ii. *Electronic signatures.* Pursuant to FRCP 11, every pleading, motion, and other paper (except lists, schedules, statements or amendments thereto) shall be signed by at least one attorney of record or, if the party is not represented by an attorney, all papers shall be signed by the party. An attorney's/participant's password issued by the court combined with the user's identification, serves as and constitutes the attorney/participant's signature for FRCP 11 and other purposes. IN R USDCTND CM/ECF(I)(C). Documents which must be filed and which must contain original signatures other than those of a participating attorney or which require either verification or an unsworn declaration under any rule or statute, shall be filed electronically, with originally executed copies maintained by the filer. The pleading or other document electronically filed shall contain "s/" signature(s), as noted in IN R USDCTND CM/ECF(II)(E)(3)(b). IN R USDCTND CM/ECF(II)(E)(1).

   - *Multiple signatures.* In the case of a stipulation or other document to be signed by two or more attorneys, the following procedure should be used: The filing attorney shall initially confirm that the content of the document is acceptable to all persons required to sign the document and shall obtain the physical signatures of all attorneys on the document. IN R USDCTND CM/ECF(II)(E)(3)(a). The filing attorney then shall file the document electronically, indicating the signatories, e.g., "s/Jane Doe," "s/John Doe," etc. IN R USDCTND CM/ECF(II)(E)(3)(b). The filing attorney shall retain the hard copy of the document containing the original signatures. IN R USDCTND CM/ECF(II)(E)(3)(c).

   iii. *No verification or accompanying affidavit required for pleadings.* Unless a rule or statute specifically states otherwise, a pleading need not be verified or accompanied by an affidavit. FRCP 11(a).

   iv. *Unsigned papers.* The court must strike an unsigned paper unless the omission is promptly corrected after being called to the attorney's or party's attention. FRCP 11(a).

  b. *Representations to the court.* By presenting to the court a pleading, written motion, or other paper—whether by signing, filing, submitting, or later advocating it—an attorney or unrepresented party certifies that to the best of the person's knowledge, information, and belief, formed after an inquiry reasonable under the circumstances:

   i. It is not being presented for any improper purpose, such as to harass, cause unnecessary delay, or needlessly increase the cost of litigation;

   ii. The claims, defenses, and other legal contentions are warranted by existing law or by a nonfrivolous argument for extending, modifying, or reversing existing law or for establishing new law;

   iii. The factual contentions have evidentiary support or, if specifically so identified, will likely have evidentiary support after a reasonable opportunity for further investigation or discovery; and

   iv. The denials of factual contentions are warranted on the evidence or, if specifically so identified, are reasonably based on belief or a lack of information. FRCP 11(b).

  c. *Sanctions.* If, after notice and a reasonable opportunity to respond, the court determines that FRCP

11(b) has been violated, the court may impose an appropriate sanction on any attorney, law firm, or party that violated FRCP 11(b) or is responsible for the violation. FRCP 11(c)(1). Refer to the United States District Court for the Northern District of Indiana KeyRules Motion for Sanctions document for more information.

5. *Privacy protection for filings made with the court*

    a. *Redacted filings.* Counsel should not include sensitive information in any document filed with the court unless such inclusion is necessary and relevant to the case. IN R USDCTND CM/ECF(VII). Unless the court orders otherwise, in an electronic or paper filing with the court that contains an individual's Social Security number, taxpayer-identification number, or birth date, the name of an individual known to be a minor, or a financial-account number, a party or nonparty making the filing may include only:

        i. The last four (4) digits of the Social Security number and taxpayer-identification number;

        ii. The year of the individual's birth;

        iii. The minor's initials; and

        iv. The last four (4) digits of the financial-account number. FRCP 5.2(a); IN R USDCTND Order 2005-3.

    b. *Exemptions from the redaction requirement.* The redaction requirement does not apply to the following:

        i. A financial-account number that identifies the property allegedly subject to forfeiture in a forfeiture proceeding;

        ii. The record of an administrative or agency proceeding;

        iii. The official record of a state-court proceeding;

        iv. The record of a court or tribunal, if that record was not subject to the redaction requirement when originally filed;

        v. A filing covered by FRCP 5.2(c) or FRCP 5.2(d); and

        vi. A pro se filing in an action brought under 28 U.S.C.A. § 2241, 28 U.S.C.A. § 2254, or 28 U.S.C.A. § 2255. FRCP 5.2(b).

        vii. In cases filed under the Social Security Act, 42 U.S.C.A. § 405(g), there is no need for redaction of any information from the documents filed in the case. IN R USDCTND Order 2005-3.

    c. *Limitations on remote access to electronic files; Social Security appeals and immigration cases.* Unless the court orders otherwise, in an action for benefits under the Social Security Act, and in an action or proceeding relating to an order of removal, to relief from removal, or to immigration benefits or detention, access to an electronic file is authorized as follows:

        i. The parties and their attorneys may have remote electronic access to any part of the case file, including the administrative record;

        ii. Any other person may have electronic access to the full record at the courthouse, but may have remote electronic access only to:

            • The docket maintained by the court; and

            • An opinion, order, judgment, or other disposition of the court, but not any other part of the case file or the administrative record. FRCP 5.2(c).

    d. *Filings made under seal.* The court may order that a filing be made under seal without redaction. The court may later unseal the filing or order the person who made the filing to file a redacted version for the public record. FRCP 5.2(d). For information on filing documents under seal, refer to IN R USDCTND L.R. 5-3, IN R USDCTND CM/ECF(IV)(A), and IN R USDCTND ECF Order 2004-19.

    e. *Protective orders.* For good cause, the court may by order in a case:

        i. Require redaction of additional information; or

    ii.   Limit or prohibit a nonparty's remote electronic access to a document filed with the court. FRCP 5.2(e).

  f. *Option for additional unredacted filing under seal.* A person making a redacted filing may also file an unredacted copy under seal. The court must retain the unredacted copy as part of the record. FRCP 5.2(f); IN R USDCTND Order 2005-3.

    i.   The unredacted version of the document or the reference list shall be retained by the court under seal as part of the record. This paper shall be retained by the court as part of the record. The court may, however, still require the party to file a redacted copy for the public file. IN R USDCTND Order 2005-3.

  g. *Option for filing a reference list.* A filing that contains redacted information may be filed together with a reference list that identifies each item of redacted information and specifies an appropriate identifier that uniquely corresponds to each item listed. The list must be filed under seal and may be amended as of right. Any reference in the case to a listed identifier will be construed to refer to the corresponding item of information. FRCP 5.2(g); IN R USDCTND Order 2005-3.

    i.   The unredacted version of the document or the reference list shall be retained by the court under seal as part of the record. This paper shall be retained by the court as part of the record. The court may, however, still require the party to file a redacted copy for the public file. IN R USDCTND Order 2005-3.

  h. *Responsibility for redaction.* The responsibility for redacting these personal identifiers rests solely with counsel and the parties. The Clerk will not review each paper for compliance with IN R USDCTND Order 2005-3. IN R USDCTND Order 2005-3.

  i. *Waiver of protection of identifiers.* A person waives the protection of FRCP 5.2(a) as to the person's own information by filing it without redaction and not under seal. FRCP 5.2(h).

F. Filing and Service Requirements

1. *Filing requirements.* Any paper after the complaint that is required to be served—together with a certificate of service—must be filed within a reasonable time after service. FRCP 5(d)(1). Motions must be filed separately, but alternative motions may be filed in a single paper if each is named in the title following the caption. IN R USDCTND L.R. 7-1(a).

  a. *How filing is made; In general.* A paper is filed by delivering it:

    i.   To the clerk; or

    ii.   To a judge who agrees to accept it for filing, and who must then note the filing date on the paper and promptly send it to the clerk. FRCP 5(d)(2).

       • Papers not filed electronically must be filed with the clerk, not a judge. IN R USDCTND L.R. 5-4(b)(4).

    iii. Parties manually filing a paper that requires the clerk to give others notice, must give the clerk: (1) sufficient copies of the notice; and (2) the name and address of each person entitled to receive the notice. IN R USDCTND L.R. 5-4(b)(8).

  b. *Where to file.* Papers not filed electronically must be filed in the division where the case is pending, unless: (1) a person will be prejudiced if the paper is not filed the same day it is tendered; and (2) it includes an adequately sized envelope addressed to the clerk's office in the division where the case is pending and with adequate postage. IN R USDCTND L.R. 5-4(b)(5).

  c. *Electronic filing*

    i.   *Authorization of electronic filing program.* A court may, by local rule, allow papers to be filed, signed, or verified by electronic means that are consistent with any technical standards established by the Judicial Conference of the United States. A local rule may require electronic filing only if reasonable exceptions are allowed. A paper filed electronically in compliance with a local rule is a written paper for purposes of the Federal Rules of Civil Procedure. FRCP 5(d)(3).

       • Papers must be filed, signed, and verified electronically unless excepted by the court's

CM/ECF Civil and Criminal User Manual (IN R USDCTND CM/ECF). IN R USDCTND L.R. 5-1.

ii. *Mandatory electronic filing.* Unless otherwise permitted by these procedures or otherwise authorized by the assigned judge, all documents submitted for filing in this district in civil and criminal cases, no matter when a case was originally filed, shall be filed electronically using the System. IN R USDCTND CM/ECF(II)(A)(1). The requirement that "all documents" be filed electronically includes briefs, and attachments and exhibits used in support of motions. IN R USDCTND CM/ECF(FN1).

- Sending a document or pleading to the court via e-mail or facsimile does not constitute "electronic filing." IN R USDCTND CM/ECF(I)(A).

iii. *Conventional filing.* As used in these procedures, a "conventionally" filed or submitted document or pleading is one presented to the Clerk or a party in paper or other non-electronic, tangible format. The following documents shall be filed conventionally and not electronically unless specifically authorized by the Court:

- Exhibits and other documents which cannot be converted to a legible electronic form. Whenever possible, counsel is responsible for converting filings to an electronic form. However, if that is not physically possible, counsel shall electronically file a .pdf document titled Notice of Manual Filing as a notation on the docket sheet that filings are being held in the clerk's office in paper. A sample Notice of Manual Filing is attached as Form 2 (IN R USDCTND CM/ECF(Form 2)). If documents are filed in paper format, counsel must provide an original for the clerk's office, a copy for the judge and a copy must be served on all parties in the case. Large documents which do not exist in an electronic format shall be scanned into .pdf format by counsel, in small batches if necessary, and filed electronically as separate attachments in the System. IN R USDCTND CM/ECF(III)(A)(1).
- Certain documents which are listed in IN R USDCTND CM/ECF(II)(E)(2). IN R US-DCTND CM/ECF(III)(A)(2).
- Documents filed by pro se litigants. IN R USDCTND CM/ECF(III)(A)(3).

iv. For more information on electronic filing, refer to IN R USDCTND CM/ECF.

2. *Service requirements*

a. *Service; When required*

i. *In general.* Unless the Federal Rules of Civil Procedure provide otherwise, each of the following papers must be served on every party:

- An order stating that service is required;
- A pleading filed after the original complaint, unless the court orders otherwise under FRCP 5(c) because there are numerous defendants;
- A discovery paper required to be served on a party, unless the court orders otherwise;
- A written motion, except one that may be heard ex parte; and
- A written notice, appearance, demand, or offer of judgment, or any similar paper. FRCP 5(a)(1).

ii. *If a party fails to appear.* No service is required on a party who is in default for failing to appear. But a pleading that asserts a new claim for relief against such a party must be served on that party under FRCP 4. FRCP 5(a)(2).

iii. *Seizing property.* If an action is begun by seizing property and no person is or need be named as a defendant, any service required before the filing of an appearance, answer, or claim must be made on the person who had custody or possession of the property when it was seized. FRCP 5(a)(3).

b. *Service; How made*

i. *Serving an attorney.* If a party is represented by an attorney, service under FRCP 5 must be made on the attorney unless the court orders service on the party. FRCP 5(b)(1).

ii. *Service in general.* A paper is served under FRCP 5 by:

- Handing it to the person;

- Leaving it: (1) at the person's office with a clerk or other person in charge or, if no one is in charge, in a conspicuous place in the office; or (2) if the person has no office or the office is closed, at the person's dwelling or usual place of abode with someone of suitable age and discretion who resides there;

- Mailing it to the person's last known address—in which event service is complete upon mailing;

- Leaving it with the court clerk if the person has no known address;

- Sending it by electronic means if the person consented in writing—in which event service is complete upon transmission, but is not effective if the serving party learns that it did not reach the person to be served; or

- Delivering it by any other means that the person consented to in writing—in which event service is complete when the person making service delivers it to the agency designated to make delivery. FRCP 5(b)(2).

iii. *Electronic service.* Electronically filed papers may be served electronically if service is consistent with the CM/ECF User Manual (IN R USDCTND CM/ECF). IN R USDCTND L.R. 5-2(a).

- *Waiver of other service.* An attorney's registration will constitute a waiver of conventional service of documents and the attorney agrees to accept service of notice on behalf of the client of the electronic filing by hand, facsimile or authorized email. IN R USDCTND CM/ECF(I)(B)(3).

- *Serving registered persons.* The System will generate a "Notice of Electronic Filing" when any document is filed. This notice represents service of the document on parties who are registered participants with the System. Except as provided in IN R USDCTND CM/ECF(III)(B), the filing party shall not be required to serve any pleading or other documents on any party receiving electronic notice. IN R USDCTND CM/ECF(II)(D)(1). The term "pleading" refers only to those documents listed in FRCP 7(a). IN R USDCTND CM/ECF(FN3).

- *When electronic service is deemed completed.* A person registered to use the court's electronic-filing system is served with an electronically filed paper when a "Notice of Electronic Filing" is transmitted to that person through the court's electronic filing-system. IN R USDCTND L.R. 5-2(b).

- *Serving non-registered persons.* A person who has not registered to use the court's electronic-filing system but who is entitled to service of a paper must be served according to the Local Civil Rules of the United States District Court for the Northern District of Indiana and the Federal Rules of Civil Procedure. IN R USDCTND L.R. 5-2(c); IN R USDCTND CM/ECF(II)(D)(2). If such service of a paper copy is to be made, it shall be done in the manner provided in the Federal Rules of Civil Procedure and the Local Civil Rules of the United States District Court for the Northern District of Indiana. IN R USDCTND CM/ECF(II)(D)(2).

iv. *Service of conventional filings.* Pleadings or other documents which are filed conventionally rather than electronically shall be served in the manner provided for in the Federal Rules of Civil Procedure and the Local Civil Rules of the United States District Court for the Northern District of Indiana, except as otherwise provided by order of the Court. IN R USDCTND CM/ECF(III)(B).

v. *Using court facilities.* If a local rule so authorizes, a party may use the court's transmission facilities to make service under FRCP 5(b)(2)(E). FRCP 5(b)(3).

   c. *Serving numerous defendants*

      i. *In general.* If an action involves an unusually large number of defendants, the court may, on motion or on its own, order that:

- Defendants' pleadings and replies to them need not be served on other defendants;

- Any crossclaim, counterclaim, avoidance, or affirmative defense in those pleadings and replies to them will be treated as denied or avoided by all other parties; and

- Filing any such pleading and serving it on the plaintiff constitutes notice of the pleading to all parties. FRCP 5(c)(1).

      ii. *Notifying parties.* A copy of every such order must be served on the parties as the court directs. FRCP 5(c)(2).

G. Hearings

1. *Hearings, generally*

   a. *Oral argument.* Due process does not require that oral argument be permitted on a motion and, except as otherwise provided by local rule, the district court has discretion to determine whether it will decide the motion on the papers or hear argument by counsel (and perhaps receive evidence). FPP § 1190; F.D.I.C. v. Deglau, 207 F.3d 153 (3d Cir. 2000).

      i. *Request for oral argument.* A party may request oral argument on a motion by filing and serving a separate document explaining why oral argument is necessary and estimating how long the court should allow for the argument. IN R USDCTND L.R. 7-5(a)(1). Refer to the Documents section of this document for more information.

      ii. *Additional evidence forbidden.* Parties may not present additional evidence at oral argument. IN R USDCTND L.R. 7-5(a)(3).

   b. *Providing a regular schedule for oral hearings.* A court may establish regular times and places for oral hearings on motions. FRCP 78(a).

   c. *Providing for submission on briefs.* By rule or order, the court may provide for submitting and determining motions on briefs, without oral hearings. FRCP 78(b).

   d. *Evidentiary hearings.* A party may request an evidentiary hearing by filing and serving a separate document explaining why the hearing is necessary and estimating how long the court should allow for it. IN R USDCTND L.R. 7-5(b)(2). Refer to the Documents section of this document for more information.

   e. *Court's authority.* The court may: (1) grant or deny a request for oral argument or an evidentiary hearing in its discretion; (2) set oral argument or an evidentiary hearing without a request from a party; or (3) order any oral argument or evidentiary hearing to be held anywhere within the district regardless of where the case will be tried. IN R USDCTND L.R. 7-5(c).

2. *Hearing on motion for summary judgment.* Even though FRCP 56(c) makes reference to a hearing on the motion for summary judgment, FRCP 56 confers no right to an oral hearing on the summary judgment motion, nor is a hearing required by due process considerations. FEDPROC § 62:673; Forjan v. Leprino Foods, Inc., 209 Fed.Appx. 8, 2006 WL 3623496 (2d Cir. 2006).

   a. *Oral argument.* The court will decide summary-judgment motions without oral argument unless a request under IN R USDCTND L.R. 7-5 is granted or the court directs otherwise. IN R USDCTND L.R. 56-1(d). Oral argument on a motion for summary judgment may be considered ordinarily appropriate, so that as a general rule, a district court should grant a request for oral argument on all but frivolous summary judgment motions, or a nonmovant's request for oral argument must be granted unless summary judgment is also denied, according to some courts. FEDPROC § 62:674; Season-All Industries, Inc. v. Turkiye Sise Ve Cam Fabrikalari, A. S., 425 F.2d 34 (3d Cir. 1970); Houston v. Bryan, 725 F.2d 516 (9th Cir. 1984); Fernhoff v. Tahoe Regional Planning Agency, 803 F.2d 979 (9th Cir. 1986).

      i. Oral argument on a summary judgment motion may be deemed waived where the opposing party does not request it. FEDPROC § 62:674; McCormack v. Citibank, N.A., 100 F.3d 532, 30 UCC Rep.Serv.2d 1175 (8th Cir. 1996).

3. *Courtroom and courthouse decorum.* For information on courtroom and courthouse decorum, refer to IN R USDCTND L.R. 83-3.

H. Forms

1. Federal Motion for Summary Judgment Forms

a. Answer; To plaintiff's motion for summary judgment. AMJUR PP SUMMARY § 56.

b. Affidavit opposing defendant's motion for summary judgment; By plaintiff. AMJUR PP SUMMARY § 64.

c. Affidavit opposing motion for summary judgment; By party; Dispute as to issues of fact. AMJUR PP SUMMARY § 73.

d. Affidavit opposing motion for summary judgment; By party; Inability to present facts. AMJUR PP SUMMARY § 74.

e. Affidavit opposing motion for summary judgment; By party; Good defense to part of claim. AMJUR PP SUMMARY § 77.

f. Statement of disputed and undisputed material facts; In opposition to motion for summary judgment. AMJUR PP SUMMARY § 89.

g. Motion and notice of motion for summary judgment. 4 FEDFORMS § 4708.

h. Motion for summary judgment by plaintiff. 4 FEDFORMS § 4709.

i. Motion for summary judgment by defendant. 4 FEDFORMS § 4713.

j. Motion for summary judgment by defendant; Claims of plaintiff and counterclaims of defendant. 4 FEDFORMS § 4717.

k. Motion for summary judgment by defendant; Interpleader against another claimant. 4 FEDFORMS § 4718.

l. Motion for summary judgment by defendant; Failure of plaintiff to produce evidence. 4 FEDFORMS § 4719.

m. Motion for summary judgment by defendant; Statute of limitations. 4 FEDFORMS § 4720.

n. Notice of motion for summary judgment. 4 FEDFORMS § 4744.

o. Affidavit in support of motion for summary judgment. 4 FEDFORMS § 4773.

p. Movant's contention there are no genuine issues of material facts. 4 FEDFORMS § 4776.

q. Opposition to statement of uncontested material facts. 4 FEDFORMS § 4777.

r. Response to movant's contention there are no genuine issues with respect to listed material facts. 4 FEDFORMS § 4778.

s. Motion; For summary judgment; By claimant. FEDPROF § 1:1298.

t. Motion; For summary judgment; By defending party. FEDPROF § 1:1302.

u. Motion; By plaintiff; For partial summary judgment. FEDPROF § 1:1305.

v. Notice of cross motion; For summary judgment; By defending party. FEDPROF § 1:1306.

w. Statement of material facts; In support of summary judgment motion. FEDPROF § 1:1311.

x. Statement in support of defendant's summary judgment motion; By codefendant. FEDPROF § 1:1312.

y. Affidavit; Opposing claimant's motion for summary judgment; Witnesses unavailable. FEDPROF § 1:1316.

z. Affidavit; Opposing part of claim. FEDPROF § 1:1317.

2. Forms for the Northern District of Indiana

a. Notice to pro se litigant. IN R USDCTND App. C.

b. Certificate of service. IN R USDCTND CM/ECF(Form 1).

    c.   Notice of manual filing. IN R USDCTND CM/ECF(Form 2).

    d.   Declaration that party was unable to file in a timely manner. IN R USDCTND CM/ECF(Form 3).

I. Applicable Rules

1. *Federal rules*

    a.   Serving and filing pleadings and other papers. FRCP 5.

    b.   Constitutional challenge to a statute; Notice, certification, and intervention. FRCP 5.1.

    c.   Privacy protection for filings made with the court. FRCP 5.2.

    d.   Computing and extending time; Time for motion papers. FRCP 6.

    e.   Pleadings allowed; Form of motions and other papers. FRCP 7.

    f.   Disclosure statement. FRCP 7.1.

    g.   Form of pleadings. FRCP 10.

    h.   Signing pleadings, motions, and other papers; Representations to the court; Sanctions. FRCP 11.

    i.   Defenses and objections; When and how presented; Motion for judgment on the pleadings; Consolidating motions; Waiving defenses; Pretrial hearing. FRCP 12.

    j.   Taking testimony. FRCP 43.

    k.   Summary judgment. FRCP 56.

    l.   Hearing motions; Submission on briefs. FRCP 78.

2. *Local rules*

    a.   Citation and scope of the rules. IN R USDCTND L.R. 1-1.

    b.   Sanctions for formatting errors. IN R USDCTND L.R. 1-3.

    c.   Electronic filing required. IN R USDCTND L.R. 5-1.

    d.   Constitutional questions. IN R USDCTND L.R. 5.1-1.

    e.   Electronic service. IN R USDCTND L.R. 5-2.

    f.   Format of papers. IN R USDCTND L.R. 5-4.

    g.   Motion practice. IN R USDCTND L.R. 7-1.

    h.   Oral arguments and evidentiary hearings. IN R USDCTND L.R. 7-5.

    i.   Pretrial procedure. IN R USDCTND L.R. 16-1.

    j.   Alternative dispute resolution. IN R USDCTND L.R. 16-6.

    k.   Filing of discovery and other materials. IN R USDCTND L.R. 26-2.

    l.   Case assignment. IN R USDCTND L.R. 40-1.

    m.   Summary judgment procedure. IN R USDCTND L.R. 56-1.

    n.   Appearance and withdrawal of appearance. IN R USDCTND L.R. 83-8.

    o.   CM/ECF civil and criminal user manual. IN R USDCTND CM/ECF.

    p.   In re: privacy and public access to civil electronic case files. IN R USDCTND Order 2005-3.

Motions, Oppositions and Replies
Motion for Sanctions

Document Last Updated December 2016

A. Checklist

(I) ❑ Matters to be considered by moving party

    (a) ❑ Required documents

        (1) ❑ Notice of motion and motion

        (2) ❑ Certificate of service

    (b) ❑ Supplemental documents

        (1) ❑ Brief

        (2) ❑ Supporting evidence

        (3) ❑ Notice of constitutional question

        (4) ❑ Nongovernmental corporate disclosure statement

        (5) ❑ Index of exhibits

        (6) ❑ Request for oral argument

        (7) ❑ Request for evidentiary hearing

        (8) ❑ Copy of authority

        (9) ❑ Proposed order

        (10) ❑ Copy of document with self-addressed envelope

        (11) ❑ Notice of manual filing

        (12) ❑ Courtesy copies

        (13) ❑ Declaration that party was unable to file in a timely manner

    (c) ❑ Timing

        (1) ❑ A party who is aware of a FRCP 11 violation should act promptly; however, motions for sanctions can be timely even when filed well after the original pleadings

            (i) ❑ It must not be filed or be presented to the court if the challenged paper, claim, defense, contention, or denial is withdrawn or appropriately corrected within twenty-one (21) days after service or within another time the court sets

        (2) ❑ A written motion and notice of the hearing must be served at least fourteen (14) days before the time specified for the hearing, with the following exceptions: (i) when the motion may be heard ex parte; (ii) when the Federal Rules of Civil Procedure set a different time; or (iii) when a court order—which a party may, for good cause, apply for ex parte—sets a different time

        (3) ❑ Any affidavit supporting a motion must be served with the motion

(II) ❑ Matters to be considered by opposing party

    (a) ❑ Required documents

        (1) ❑ Response brief

        (2) ❑ Certificate of service

    (b) ❑ Supplemental documents

        (1) ❑ Supporting evidence

        (2) ❑ Notice of constitutional question

        (3) ❑ Index of exhibits

  (4) ❑ Request for oral argument

  (5) ❑ Request for evidentiary hearing

  (6) ❑ Copy of authority

  (7) ❑ Copy of document with self-addressed envelope

  (8) ❑ Notice of manual filing

  (9) ❑ Courtesy copies

  (10) ❑ Declaration that party was unable to file in a timely manner

 (c) ❑ Timing

  (1) ❑ A party must file any response brief to a motion within fourteen (14) days after the motion is served

  (2) ❑ Except as FRCP 59(c) provides otherwise, any opposing affidavit must be served at least seven (7) days before the hearing, unless the court permits service at another time

B. Timing

1. *Motion for sanctions.* The deterrent purpose of FRCP 11 can best be served by imposing sanctions at or near the time of the violation. FEDPROC § 62:777. Accordingly, a party who is aware of a FRCP 11 violation should act promptly. FEDPROC § 62:777; Oliveri v. Thompson, 803 F.2d 1265, 5 Fed.R.Serv.3d 761 (2d Cir. 1986). However, whether a case is well-grounded in fact will often not be evident until a plaintiff has been given a chance to conduct discovery. Therefore, motions for sanctions can be timely even when filed well after the original pleadings. FEDPROC § 62:777; Runfola & Associates, Inc. v. Spectrum Reporting II, Inc., 88 F.3d 368, 35 Fed.R.Serv.3d 434, 1996 Fed.App. 0198P (6th Cir. 1996).

 a. *Safe harbor provision.* The motion must be served under FRCP 5, but it must not be filed or be presented to the court if the challenged paper, claim, defense, contention, or denial is withdrawn or appropriately corrected within twenty-one (21) days after service or within another time the court sets. FRCP 11(c)(2).

2. *Timing of motions, generally*

 a. *Motion and notice of hearing.* A written motion and notice of the hearing must be served at least fourteen (14) days before the time specified for the hearing, with the following exceptions:

  i. When the motion may be heard ex parte;

  ii. When the Federal Rules of Civil Procedure set a different time; or

  iii. When a court order—which a party may, for good cause, apply for ex parte—sets a different time. FRCP 6(c)(1).

 b. *Supporting affidavit.* Any affidavit supporting a motion must be served with the motion. FRCP 6(c)(2).

3. *Timing of opposing papers.* A party must file any response brief to a motion within fourteen (14) days after the motion is served. IN R USDCTND L.R. 7-1(d)(2)(A).

 a. *Opposing affidavit.* Except as FRCP 59(c) provides otherwise, any opposing affidavit must be served at least seven (7) days before the hearing, unless the court permits service at another time. FRCP 6(c)(2).

 b. *Extensions.* The court may extend response- and reply-brief deadlines, but only for good cause. IN R USDCTND L.R. 7-1(d)(3).

 c. *Summary rulings.* The court may rule on a motion summarily if an opposing party does not file a response before the deadline. IN R USDCTND L.R. 7-1(d)(4).

4. *Timing of reply papers.* Where the respondent files an answering affidavit setting up a new matter, the moving party ordinarily is allowed a reasonable time to file a reply affidavit since failure to deny the new matter by affidavit may operate as an admission of its truth. AMJUR MOTIONS § 25.

 a. *Reply brief.* The moving party must file any reply brief within seven (7) days after the response brief is served. IN R USDCTND L.R. 7-1(d)(2)(B).

b. *Extensions.* The court may extend response- and reply-brief deadlines, but only for good cause. IN R USDCTND L.R. 7-1(d)(3).

5. *Computation of time*

a. *Computing time.* FRCP 6 applies in computing any time period specified in the Federal Rules of Civil Procedure, in any local rule or court order, or in any statute that does not specify a method of computing time. FRCP 6(a).

    i. *Period stated in days or a longer unit.* When the period is stated in days or a longer unit of time:

- Exclude the day of the event that triggers the period;

- Count every day, including intermediate Saturdays, Sundays, and legal holidays; and

- Include the last day of the period, but if the last day is a Saturday, Sunday, or legal holiday, the period continues to run until the end of the next day that is not a Saturday, Sunday, or legal holiday. FRCP 6(a)(1).

    ii. *Period stated in hours.* When the period is stated in hours:

- Begin counting immediately on the occurrence of the event that triggers the period;

- Count every hour, including hours during intermediate Saturdays, Sundays, and legal holidays; and

- If the period would end on a Saturday, Sunday, or legal holiday, the period continues to run until the same time on the next day that is not a Saturday, Sunday, or legal holiday. FRCP 6(a)(2).

    iii. *Inaccessibility of the clerk's office.* Unless the court orders otherwise, if the clerk's office is inaccessible:

- On the last day for filing under FRCP 6(a)(1), then the time for filing is extended to the first accessible day that is not a Saturday, Sunday, or legal holiday; or

- During the last hour for filing under FRCP 6(a)(2), then the time for filing is extended to the same time on the first accessible day that is not a Saturday, Sunday, or legal holiday. FRCP 6(a)(3).

    iv. *"Last day" defined.* Unless a different time is set by a statute, local rule, or court order, the last day ends:

- For electronic filing, at midnight in the court's time zone; and

- For filing by other means, when the clerk's office is scheduled to close. FRCP 6(a)(4).

    v. *"Next day" defined.* The "next day" is determined by continuing to count forward when the period is measured after an event and backward when measured before an event. FRCP 6(a)(5).

    vi. *"Legal holiday" defined.* "Legal holiday" means:

- The day set aside by statute for observing New Year's Day, Martin Luther King Jr.'s Birthday, Washington's Birthday, Memorial Day, Independence Day, Labor Day, Columbus Day, Veterans' Day, Thanksgiving Day, or Christmas Day;

- Any day declared a holiday by the President or Congress; and

- For periods that are measured after an event, any other day declared a holiday by the state where the district court is located. FRCP 6(a)(6).

b. *Computation of electronic filing deadlines.* Filing documents electronically does not alter any filing deadlines or any time computation pursuant to FRCP 6. The counties of Lake, Porter, LaPorte, Pulaski and Starke are located in the Central time zone and the remaining counties in the Northern District of Indiana are located in the Eastern time zone. Nevertheless, all electronic transmissions of documents must be completed (i.e., received completely by the clerk's office) prior to midnight Eastern Time, (South Bend/Fort Wayne/Lafayette time) in order to be considered timely filed that day, regardless of the local time in the division where the case is pending. Although documents can be filed electronically twenty-four (24) hours a day, filers are strongly encouraged to file all

documents during hours when the CM/ECF Help Line is available, from 9:00 a.m. to 4:00 p.m. local time. IN R USDCTND CM/ECF(II)(I).

    i. *Technical failures.* If the attorney is unable to file a document in a timely manner due to technical difficulties in the user's system, the attorney must file a document with the court as soon as possible notifying the court of the inability to file the document. A sample document entitled Declaration that Party was Unable to File in a Timely Manner Due to Technical Difficulties is attached hereto as Form 5. IN R USDCTND CM/ECF(VI)(B). [Editor's note: the reference to Form 5 is likely meant to be a reference to Form 3 (IN R USDCTND CM/ECF(Form 3)].

c. *Extending time*

    i. *In general.* When an act may or must be done within a specified time, the court may, for good cause, extend the time:

- With or without motion or notice if the court acts, or if a request is made, before the original time or its extension expires; or

- On motion made after the time has expired if the party failed to act because of excusable neglect. FRCP 6(b)(1).

    ii. *Exceptions.* A court must not extend the time to act under FRCP 50(b), FRCP 50(d), FRCP 52(b), FRCP 59(b), FRCP 59(d), FRCP 59(e), and FRCP 60(b). FRCP 6(b)(2).

    iii. Refer to the United States District Court for the Northern District of Indiana KeyRules Motion for Continuance/Extension of Time document for more information on extending time.

d. *Additional time after certain kinds of service.* When a party may or must act within a specified time after being served and service is made under FRCP 5(b)(2)(C) (mail), FRCP 5(b)(2)(D) (leaving with the clerk), or FRCP 5(b)(2)(F) (other means consented to), three (3) days are added after the period would otherwise expire under FRCP 6(a). FRCP 6(d).

C. General Requirements

1. *Motions, generally*

a. *Requirements.* A request for a court order must be made by motion. The motion must:

    i. Be in writing unless made during a hearing or trial;

    ii. State with particularity the grounds for seeking the order; and

    iii. State the relief sought. FRCP 7(b)(1).

b. *Notice of motion.* A party interested in resisting the relief sought by a motion has a right to notice thereof, and an opportunity to be heard. AMJUR MOTIONS § 12.

    i. In addition to statutory or court rule provisions requiring notice of a motion—the purpose of such a notice requirement having been said to be to prevent a party from being prejudicially surprised by a motion—principles of natural justice dictate that an adverse party generally must be given notice that a motion will be presented to the court. AMJUR MOTIONS § 12.

    ii. "Notice," in this regard, means reasonable notice, including a meaningful opportunity to prepare and to defend against allegations of a motion. AMJUR MOTIONS § 12.

c. *Writing requirement.* The writing requirement is intended to insure that the adverse parties are informed and have a record of both the motion's pendency and the grounds on which the movant seeks an order. FPP § 1191; Feldberg v. Quechee Lakes Corp., 463 F.3d 195 (2d Cir. 2006).

    i. It is sufficient "if the motion is stated in a written notice of the hearing of the motion." FPP § 1191.

d. *Particularity requirement.* The particularity requirement insures that the opposing parties will have notice of their opponent's contentions. FEDPROC § 62:364; Goodman v. 1973 26 Foot Trojan Vessel, Arkansas Registration No. AR1439SN, 859 F.2d 71, 12 Fed.R.Serv.3d 645 (8th Cir. 1988). That requirement ensures that notice of the basis for the motion is provided to the court and to the opposing party so as to avoid prejudice, provide the opponent with a meaningful opportunity to

respond, and provide the court with enough information to process the motion correctly. FEDPROC § 62:364; Andreas v. Volkswagen of America, Inc., 336 F.3d 789, 56 Fed.R.Serv.3d 6 (8th Cir. 2003).

    i. Reasonable specification of the grounds for a motion is sufficient. However, where a movant fails to state even one ground for granting the motion in question, the movant has failed to meet the minimal standard of "reasonable specification." FEDPROC § 62:364; Martinez v. Trainor, 556 F.2d 818, 23 Fed.R.Serv.2d 403 (7th Cir. 1977).

    ii. The court may excuse the failure to comply with the particularity requirement if it is inadvertent, and where no prejudice is shown by the opposing party. FEDPROC § 62:364.

e. *Motions must be filed separately.* Motions must be filed separately, but alternative motions may be filed in a single paper if each is named in the title following the caption. IN R USDCTND L.R. 7-1(a).

2. *Motion for sanctions.* A motion for sanctions under FRCP 11 may be filed by either the plaintiff or the defendant. FEDPROC § 62:774. Only parties and other "participants" in an action have standing to seek sanctions, however. FEDPROC § 62:774; New York News, Inc. v. Kheel, 972 F.2d 482, 23 Fed.R.Serv.3d 317 (2d Cir. 1992).

a. *Basis for motion for sanctions.* FRCP 11(c) authorizes sanctions for misconduct relating to representations to the court. These representations are based on misconduct relating to the presentation (whether by signing, filing, submitting, or later advocating) of a pleading, written motion, or other paper to the court. Improper conduct includes, but is not limited to: (1) the filing of a frivolous suit or document; (2) the filing of a document or lawsuit for an improper purpose; and (3) the filing of actions that needlessly increase the cost or length of litigation. LITGTORT § 20:7. Refer to the Format section of this document for more information on representations to the court.

b. *Informal notice.* In most cases, counsel should be expected to give informal notice to the other party, whether in person or by a telephone call or letter, of a potential violation before proceeding to prepare and serve a FRCP 11 motion. FRCP 11(Advisory Committee Notes).

c. *Safe harbor provision.* A motion for sanctions must be made separately from any other motion and must describe the specific conduct that allegedly violates FRCP 11(b). The motion must be served under FRCP 5, but it must not be filed or be presented to the court if the challenged paper, claim, defense, contention, or denial is withdrawn or appropriately corrected within twenty-one (21) days after service or within another time the court sets. If warranted, the court may award to the prevailing party the reasonable expenses, including attorney's fees, incurred for the motion. FRCP 11(c)(2).

    i. These provisions are intended to provide a type of "safe harbor" against motions under FRCP 11 in that a party will not be subject to sanctions on the basis of another party's motion unless, after receiving the motion, it refuses to withdraw that position or to acknowledge candidly that it does not currently have evidence to support a specified allegation. FRCP 11(Advisory Committee Notes).

d. *Imposition of sanctions.* If, after notice and a reasonable opportunity to respond, the court determines that FRCP 11(b) has been violated, the court may impose an appropriate sanction on any attorney, law firm, or party that violated FRCP 11(b) or is responsible for the violation. Absent exceptional circumstances, a law firm must be held jointly responsible for a violation committed by its partner, associate, or employee. FRCP 11(c)(1).

    i. *Government agencies and their counsel.* FRCP 11 applies to government agencies and their counsel as well as private parties. Thus, the United States is bound by FRCP 11 just as are private parties, and must have reasonable grounds to make allegations within its complaint or answer. FEDPROC § 62:769.

    ii. *Pro se litigants.* In applying FRCP 11, the court may consider the special circumstances of pro se litigants. FEDPROC § 62:771; Maduakolam v. Columbia University, 866 F.2d 53, 51 Ed.Law.Rep. 441, 12 Fed.R.Serv.3d 1271 (2d Cir. 1989). Pro se litigants are held to a more lenient standard than professional counsel, with FRCP 11's application determined on a sliding scale according to the litigant's level of sophistication. FEDPROC § 62:771.

e. *Nature of a sanction.* A sanction imposed under FRCP 11 must be limited to what suffices to deter repetition of the conduct or comparable conduct by others similarly situated. The sanction may include nonmonetary directives; an order to pay a penalty into court; or, if imposed on motion and warranted for effective deterrence, an order directing payment to the movant of part or all of the reasonable attorney's fees and other expenses directly resulting from the violation. FRCP 11(c)(4).

    f.   *Counsel's liability for excessive costs.* Any attorney or other person admitted to conduct cases in any court of the United States or any Territory thereof who so multiplies the proceedings in any case unreasonably and vexatiously may be required by the court to satisfy personally the excess costs, expenses, and attorneys' fees reasonably incurred because of such conduct. 28 U.S.C.A. § 1927.

    g.   *Limitations on monetary sanctions.* The court must not impose a monetary sanction:

        i.   Against a represented party for violating FRCP 11(b)(2); or

        ii.   On its own, unless it issued the show-cause order under FRCP 11(c)(3) before voluntary dismissal or settlement of the claims made by or against the party that is, or whose attorneys are, to be sanctioned. FRCP 11(c)(5).

    h.   *Requirements for an order.* An order imposing a sanction must describe the sanctioned conduct and explain the basis for the sanction. FRCP 11(c)(6).

        i.   *On the court's initiative.* On its own, the court may order an attorney, law firm, or party to show cause why conduct specifically described in the order has not violated FRCP 11(b). FRCP 11(c)(3).

3. *Opposing papers.* The Federal Rules of Civil Procedure do not require any formal answer, return, or reply to a motion, except where the Federal Rules of Civil Procedure or local rules may require affidavits, memoranda, or other papers to be filed in opposition to a motion. Such papers are simply to apprise the court of such opposition and the grounds of that opposition. FEDPROC § 62:359.

    a.   *Effect of failure to respond to motion.* Although in the absence of statutory provision or court rule, a motion ordinarily does not require a written answer, when a party files a motion and the opposing party fails to respond, the court may construe such failure to respond as nonopposition to the motion or an admission that the motion was meritorious, may take the facts alleged in the motion as true—the rule in some jurisdictions being that the failure to respond to a fact set forth in a motion is deemed an admission—and may grant the motion if the relief requested appears to be justified. AMJUR MOTIONS § 28.

    b.   *Assent or no opposition not determinative.* However, a motion will not be granted automatically simply because an "assent" or a notation of "no opposition" has been filed; federal judges frequently deny motions that have been assented to when it is thought that justice so dictates. FPP § 1190.

    c.   *Responsive pleading inappropriate as response to motion.* An attempt to answer or oppose a motion with a responsive pleading usually is not appropriate. FPP § 1190.

4. *Reply papers.* A moving party may be required or permitted to prepare papers in addition to his original motion papers. AMJUR MOTIONS § 25. Papers answering or replying to opposing papers may be appropriate, in the interests of justice, where it appears there is a substantial reason for allowing a reply. Thus, a court may accept reply papers where a party demonstrates that the papers to which it seeks to file a reply raise new issues that are material to the disposition of the question before the court, or where the court determines, sua sponte, that it wishes further briefing of an issue raised in those papers and orders the submission of additional papers. FEDPROC § 62:360.

    a.   *Function of reply papers.* The function of a reply affidavit is to answer the arguments made in opposition to the position taken by the movant and not to permit the movant to introduce new arguments in support of the motion. AMJUR MOTIONS § 25.

    b.   *Issues raised for the first time in a reply document.* However, the view has been followed in some jurisdictions, that as a matter of judicial economy, where there is no prejudice and where the issues could be raised simply by filing a motion to dismiss, the trial court has discretion to consider arguments raised for the first time in a reply memorandum, and that a trial court may grant a motion to strike issues raised for the first time in a reply memorandum. AMJUR MOTIONS § 26.

5. *Appearances.* Attorneys not representing the United States or its agencies must file an appearance when they represent (either in person or by filing a paper) a party. IN R USDCTND L.R. 83-8(a). For more information, refer to IN R USDCTND L.R. 83-8.

6. *Notice of related action.* A party must file a notice of related action as soon as it appears that the party's case and another pending case: (1) arise out of the same transaction or occurrence; (2) involve the same property; or (3) involve the validity or infringement of the same patent, trademark, or copyright. IN R USDCTND L.R. 40-1(d). For more information, refer to IN R USDCTND L.R. 40-1.

7. *Alternative dispute resolution (ADR).* After they confer as required by FRCP 26(f), the parties must advise the court which, if any, alternative-dispute-resolution processes they expect to pursue and when they expect to undertake the process. IN R USDCTND L.R. 16-6(a). For more information on alternative dispute resolution (ADR), refer to IN R USDCTND L.R. 16-6 and IN R USDCTND Order 2003-21.

8. *Settlement or resolution.* The parties must immediately notify the court if they reasonably expect to settle the case or resolve a pending motion. IN R USDCTND L.R. 16-1(g).

9. *Modification or suspension of rules.* The court may, on its own motion or at the request of a party, suspend or modify any rule in a particular case in the interest of justice. IN R USDCTND L.R. 1-1(c).

D. Documents

1. *Documents for moving party*

   a. *Required documents*

      i. *Notice of motion and motion.* The party must not specify a hearing date in the notice of a motion or petition unless the court or the clerk has authorized it. IN R USDCTND L.R. 7-5(b)(2). Refer to the General Requirements section of this document for information on the notice of motion and motion.

      ii. *Certificate of service.* FRCP 5(d) requires that the person making service under FRCP 5 certify that service has been effected. FRCP 5(Advisory Committee Notes). Having such information on file may be useful for many purposes, including proof of service if an issue arises concerning the effectiveness of the service. FRCP 5(Advisory Committee Notes).

         • *Certificate of service for electronically-filed documents.* A Certificate of Service is still a requirement when filing documents electronically. A sample Certificate of Service is attached as Form 1 (IN R USDCTND CM/ECF(Form 1)). IN R USDCTND CM/ECF(II)(H).

   b. *Supplemental documents*

      i. *Brief.* Refer to the Format section of this document for the format of briefs.

      ii. *Supporting evidence.* When a motion relies on facts outside the record, the court may hear the matter on affidavits or may hear it wholly or partly on oral testimony or on depositions. FRCP 43(c).

         • *Materials necessary for motion.* A party must file those portions of discovery requests or responses (including deposition transcripts) that the party relies on to support a motion that could result in a final order on an issue. IN R USDCTND L.R. 26-2(c).

      iii. *Notice of constitutional question.* A party that files a pleading, written motion, or other paper drawing into question the constitutionality of a federal or state statute must promptly:

         • *File notice.* File a notice of constitutional question stating the question and identifying the paper that raises it, if: (1) a federal statute is questioned and the parties do not include the United States, one of its agencies, or one of its officers or employees in an official capacity; or (2) a state statute is questioned and the parties do not include the state, one of its agencies, or one of its officers or employees in an official capacity; and

         • *Serve notice.* Serve the notice and paper on the Attorney General of the United States if a federal statute is questioned—or on the state attorney general if a state statute is questioned—either by certified or registered mail or by sending it to an electronic address designated by the attorney general for this purpose. FRCP 5.1(a).

         • *When to file the notice.* A party required to file a notice of constitutional question under FRCP 5.1 must do so by the later of: (1) the day the parties tender their proposed case-management plan (if one is required); or (2) 21 days after filing the pleading, written

motion, or other paper questioning the constitutionality of a federal or state statute. IN R USDCTND L.R. 5.1-1(a).

- *Service on government officials.* The party must also serve the notice and the pleading, written motion, or other paper questioning the constitutionality of a federal or state statute on: (1) the Attorney General of the United States and the United States Attorney for the Northern District of Indiana, if a federal statute is challenged; or (2) the Attorney General for the state if a state statute is challenged. IN R USDCTND L.R. 5.1-1(b). Service required under IN R USDCTND L.R. 5.1-1(b) may be made either by certified or registered mail or by emailing it to an address designated by those officials for this purpose. IN R USDCTND L.R. 5.1-1(c).

- *No forfeiture.* A party's failure to file and serve the notice, or the court's failure to certify, does not forfeit a constitutional claim or defense that is otherwise timely asserted. FRCP 5.1(d).

iv. *Nongovernmental corporate disclosure statement*

- *Contents.* A nongovernmental corporate party must file two (2) copies of a disclosure statement that: (1) identifies any parent corporation and any publicly held corporation owning ten percent (10%) or more of its stock; or (2) states that there is no such corporation. FRCP 7.1(a).

- *Time to file; Supplemental filing.* A party must: (1) file the disclosure statement with its first appearance, pleading, petition, motion, response, or other request addressed to the court; and (2) promptly file a supplemental statement if any required information changes. FRCP 7.1(b).

v. *Index of exhibits.* Any pleading, motion, brief, affidavit, notice, or proposed order, whether filed electronically or by delivering it to the clerk, must: include a separate index identifying and briefly describing each exhibit if there are more than four (4) exhibits. IN R USDCTND L.R. 5-4(a)(8).

vi. *Request for oral argument.* A party may request oral argument on a motion by filing and serving a separate document explaining why oral argument is necessary and estimating how long the court should allow for the argument. IN R USDCTND L.R. 7-5(a)(1). The request must be filed and served with the party's supporting brief, response brief, or reply brief. IN R USDCTND L.R. 7-5(a)(2).

vii. *Request for evidentiary hearing.* A party may request an evidentiary hearing by filing and serving a separate document explaining why the hearing is necessary and estimating how long the court should allow for it. IN R USDCTND L.R. 7-5(b)(1).

viii. *Copy of authority.* A copy of any decision, statute, or regulation cited in a motion or brief must be attached to the paper if—and only if—it is not available on Westlaw or Lexis. But if a copy of a decision, statute, or regulation is only available electronically, a party must provide it to the court or another party upon request. IN R USDCTND L.R. 7-1(f).

ix. *Proposed order.* Parties filing a paper that requires the judge or clerk to enter a routine or uncontested order must include a suitable form of order. IN R USDCTND L.R. 5-4(c).

- Proposed orders shall not be filed electronically either as a separate document or as an attachment to the main pleading or other document. Instead, all proposed orders must be e-mailed to the chambers of the appropriate judicial officer for the case. The proposed order must be in WordPerfect Format or Rich Text Format (RTF). Proposed orders should be attached to an e-mail and sent to the appropriate judicial officer at the address listed in IN R USDCTND CM/ECF(II)(F). The subject line of the email message should indicate the case title, cause number and document number of the motion, e.g., Smith v. Jones 1:02-cv-1234, motion# ___. IN R USDCTND CM/ECF(II)(F).

x. *Copy of document with self-addressed envelope.* A party who wants a file-stamped copy of a paper must include with the filing an additional copy of the paper and a self-addressed envelope with adequate postage. IN R USDCTND L.R. 5-4(b)(6).

xi. *Notice of manual filing.* However, if that is not physically possible, counsel shall electronically file a .pdf document titled Notice of Manual Filing as a notation on the docket sheet that filings are being held in the clerk's office in paper. A sample Notice of Manual Filing is attached as Form 2 (IN R USDCTND CM/ECF(Form 2)). IN R USDCTND CM/ECF(III)(A)(1).

xii. *Courtesy copies.* If documents are filed in paper format, counsel must provide an original for the clerk's office, a copy for the judge and a copy must be served on all parties in the case. IN R USDCTND CM/ECF(III)(A)(1).

xiii. *Declaration that party was unable to file in a timely manner.* If the attorney is unable to file a document in a timely manner due to technical difficulties in the user's system, the attorney must file a document with the court as soon as possible notifying the court of the inability to file the document. A sample document entitled Declaration that Party was Unable to File in a Timely Manner Due to Technical Difficulties is attached hereto as Form 5. IN R USDCTND CM/ECF(VI)(B). [Editor's note: the reference to Form 5 is likely meant to be a reference to Form 3 (IN R USDCTND CM/ECF(Form 3)].

2. *Documents for opposing party*

   a. *Required documents*

   i. *Response brief.* Refer to the Format section of this document for the format of briefs. Refer to the General Requirements section of this document for information on the opposing papers.

   ii. *Certificate of service.* FRCP 5(d) requires that the person making service under FRCP 5 certify that service has been effected. FRCP 5(Advisory Committee Notes). Having such information on file may be useful for many purposes, including proof of service if an issue arises concerning the effectiveness of the service. FRCP 5(Advisory Committee Notes).

   - *Certificate of service for electronically-filed documents.* A Certificate of Service is still a requirement when filing documents electronically. A sample Certificate of Service is attached as Form 1 (IN R USDCTND CM/ECF(Form 1)). IN R USDCTND CM/ECF(II)(H).

   b. *Supplemental documents*

   i. *Supporting evidence.* When a motion relies on facts outside the record, the court may hear the matter on affidavits or may hear it wholly or partly on oral testimony or on depositions. FRCP 43(c).

   - *Materials necessary for motion.* A party must file those portions of discovery requests or responses (including deposition transcripts) that the party relies on to support a motion that could result in a final order on an issue. IN R USDCTND L.R. 26-2(c).

   ii. *Notice of constitutional question.* A party that files a pleading, written motion, or other paper drawing into question the constitutionality of a federal or state statute must promptly:

   - *File notice.* File a notice of constitutional question stating the question and identifying the paper that raises it, if: (1) a federal statute is questioned and the parties do not include the United States, one of its agencies, or one of its officers or employees in an official capacity; or (2) a state statute is questioned and the parties do not include the state, one of its agencies, or one of its officers or employees in an official capacity; and

   - *Serve notice.* Serve the notice and paper on the Attorney General of the United States if a federal statute is questioned—or on the state attorney general if a state statute is questioned—either by certified or registered mail or by sending it to an electronic address designated by the attorney general for this purpose. FRCP 5.1(a).

   - *When to file the notice.* A party required to file a notice of constitutional question under FRCP 5.1 must do so by the later of: (1) the day the parties tender their proposed case-management plan (if one is required); or (2) 21 days after filing the pleading, written motion, or other paper questioning the constitutionality of a federal or state statute. IN R USDCTND L.R. 5.1-1(a).

   - *Service on government officials.* The party must also serve the notice and the pleading, written motion, or other paper questioning the constitutionality of a federal or state statute on: (1) the Attorney General of the United States and the United States Attorney for the Northern District of Indiana, if a federal statute is challenged; or (2) the Attorney General for the state if a state statute is challenged. IN R USDCTND L.R. 5.1-1(b). Service required under IN R USDCTND L.R. 5.1-1(b) may be made either by certified or registered mail or by emailing it to an address designated by those officials for this purpose. IN R USDCTND L.R. 5.1-1(c).

- *No forfeiture.* A party's failure to file and serve the notice, or the court's failure to certify, does not forfeit a constitutional claim or defense that is otherwise timely asserted. FRCP 5.1(d).

iii. *Index of exhibits.* Any pleading, motion, brief, affidavit, notice, or proposed order, whether filed electronically or by delivering it to the clerk, must: include a separate index identifying and briefly describing each exhibit if there are more than four (4) exhibits. IN R USDCTND L.R. 5-4(a)(8).

iv. *Request for oral argument.* A party may request oral argument on a motion by filing and serving a separate document explaining why oral argument is necessary and estimating how long the court should allow for the argument. IN R USDCTND L.R. 7-5(a)(1). The request must be filed and served with the party's supporting brief, response brief, or reply brief. IN R USDCTND L.R. 7-5(a)(2).

v. *Request for evidentiary hearing.* A party may request an evidentiary hearing by filing and serving a separate document explaining why the hearing is necessary and estimating how long the court should allow for it. IN R USDCTND L.R. 7-5(b)(1).

vi. *Copy of authority.* A copy of any decision, statute, or regulation cited in a motion or brief must be attached to the paper if—and only if—it is not available on Westlaw or Lexis. But if a copy of a decision, statute, or regulation is only available electronically, a party must provide it to the court or another party upon request. IN R USDCTND L.R. 7-1(f).

vii. *Copy of document with self-addressed envelope.* A party who wants a file-stamped copy of a paper must include with the filing an additional copy of the paper and a self-addressed envelope with adequate postage. IN R USDCTND L.R. 5-4(b)(6).

viii. *Notice of manual filing.* However, if that is not physically possible, counsel shall electronically file a .pdf document titled Notice of Manual Filing as a notation on the docket sheet that filings are being held in the clerk's office in paper. A sample Notice of Manual Filing is attached as Form 2 (IN R USDCTND CM/ECF(Form 2)). IN R USDCTND CM/ECF(III)(A)(1).

ix. *Courtesy copies.* If documents are filed in paper format, counsel must provide an original for the clerk's office, a copy for the judge and a copy must be served on all parties in the case. IN R USDCTND CM/ECF(III)(A)(1).

x. *Declaration that party was unable to file in a timely manner.* If the attorney is unable to file a document in a timely manner due to technical difficulties in the user's system, the attorney must file a document with the court as soon as possible notifying the court of the inability to file the document. A sample document entitled Declaration that Party was Unable to File in a Timely Manner Due to Technical Difficulties is attached hereto as Form 5. IN R USDCTND CM/ECF(VI)(B). [Editor's note: the reference to Form 5 is likely meant to be a reference to Form 3 (IN R USDCTND CM/ECF(Form 3)].

E. Format

1. *Form of documents.* The rules governing captions and other matters of form in pleadings apply to motions and other papers. FRCP 7(b)(2).

   a. *Paper.* Any pleading, motion, brief, affidavit, notice, or proposed order, whether filed electronically

or by delivering it to the clerk, must: use eight and one-half by eleven (8-1/2 x 11) inch pages. IN R USDCTND L.R. 5-4(a)(2).

   i. *Manual filings.* Papers delivered to the clerk for filing must: be flat, unfolded, and on good-quality, white paper. IN R USDCTND L.R. 5-4(b)(1)(A).

- *Covers or backing.* Papers delivered to the clerk for filing must: not have a cover or a back. IN R USDCTND L.R. 5-4(b)(1)(B).

- *Recycled paper.* The court encourages using recycled paper. IN R USDCTND L.R. 5-4(b)(7).

b. *Margins.* Any pleading, motion, brief, affidavit, notice, or proposed order, whether filed electronically or by delivering it to the clerk, must: have at least one (1) inch margins. IN R USDCTND L.R. 5-4(a)(3).

c. *Spacing.* Any pleading, motion, brief, affidavit, notice, or proposed order, whether filed electronically or by delivering it to the clerk, must: be double spaced (except for headings, footnotes, and quoted material). IN R USDCTND L.R. 5-4(a)(5).

d. *Text.* Any pleading, motion, brief, affidavit, notice, or proposed order, whether filed electronically or by delivering it to the clerk, must: be plainly typewritten, printed, or prepared by a clearly legible copying process. IN R USDCTND L.R. 5-4(a)(1).

   i. Any pleading, motion, brief, affidavit, notice, or proposed order, whether filed electronically or by delivering it to the clerk, must: use at least twelve (12) point type in the body and at least ten (10) point type in footnotes. IN R USDCTND L.R. 5-4(a)(4).

e. *Page numbering.* Any pleading, motion, brief, affidavit, notice, or proposed order, whether filed electronically or by delivering it to the clerk, must: have consecutively numbered pages. IN R USDCTND L.R. 5-4(a)(6).

f. *Caption; Names of parties.* Every pleading must have a caption with the court's name, a title, a file number, and a FRCP 7(a) designation. The title of the complaint must name all the parties; the title of other pleadings, after naming the first party on each side, may refer generally to other parties. FRCP 10(a). Any pleading, motion, brief, affidavit, notice, or proposed order, whether filed electronically or by delivering it to the clerk, must: include a title on the first page. IN R USDCTND L.R. 5-4(a)(7).

   i. *Alternative motions.* Motions must be filed separately, but alternative motions may be filed in a single paper if each is named in the title following the caption. IN R USDCTND L.R. 7-1(a).

g. *Filer's information.* Any pleading, motion, brief, affidavit, notice, or proposed order, whether filed electronically or by delivering it to the clerk, must: except in proposed orders and affidavits, include the filer's name, address, telephone number, fax number (where available), and e-mail address (where available). IN R USDCTND L.R. 5-4(a)(9).

h. *Paragraphs; Separate statements.* A party must state its claims or defenses in numbered paragraphs, each limited as far as practicable to a single set of circumstances. A later pleading may refer by number to a paragraph in an earlier pleading. If doing so would promote clarity, each claim founded on a separate transaction or occurrence—and each defense other than a denial—must be stated in a separate count or defense. FRCP 10(b).

i. *Adoption by reference; Exhibits.* A statement in a pleading may be adopted by reference elsewhere in the same pleading or in any other pleading or motion. A copy of a written instrument that is an exhibit to a pleading is a part of the pleading for all purposes. FRCP 10(c).

j. *Citation of local rules.* The Local Civil Rules of the United States District Court for the Northern District of Indiana may be cited as "N.D. Ind. L.R." IN R USDCTND L.R. 1-1(a)(1).

k. *Acceptance by the clerk.* The clerk must not refuse to file a paper solely because it is not in the form prescribed by the Federal Rules of Civil Procedure or by a local rule or practice. FRCP 5(d)(4).

   i. *Sanctions for formatting errors; Non-compliance.* If a person files a paper that does not comply with the rules governing the format of papers filed with the court, the court may: (1) strike the paper from the record; or (2) fine the person up to one thousand dollars ($1,000). IN R USDCTND L.R. 1-3(a).

- *Notice.* Before sanctioning a person under IN R USDCTND L.R. 1-3(a)(2), the court must: (1) notify the person that the paper is noncompliant; and (2) give the person the opportunity either to be heard or to revise the paper. IN R USDCTND L.R. 1-3(b).

2. *Form of electronic documents.* Electronically filed documents must meet the same requirements of format and page limits as documents "conventionally filed" (as defined in IN R USDCTND CM/ECF(III)(A)) pursuant to the Federal Rules of Civil Procedure and the Local Civil Rules of the United States District Court for the Northern District of Indiana. IN R USDCTND CM/ECF(II)(A)(2).

   a. *PDF format required.* Documents filed in the CM/ECF must be in .pdf format. A document created with almost any word-processing program can be converted to .pdf format. The .pdf program in effect takes a picture of the original document and allows anyone to open the converted document across a broad range of hardware and software, with layout, format, links, and images intact. IN R USDCTND CM/ECF(FN2).

   b. *Title of documents.* The person electronically filing a pleading or other document will be responsible for designating a title for the pleading or other document by using one of the categories contained in the events listed in the CM/ECF Menu. IN R USDCTND CM/ECF(II)(G).

   c. *Combining documents.* All documents which form part of a single pleading and which are being filed at the same time and by the same party may be electronically filed together under one document number, e.g., the motion and a supporting affidavit, with the exception of memoranda in support. Memoranda in support shall be electronically filed separately and shown as a related document to the motion. IN R USDCTND CM/ECF(II)(A)(4).

   d. *Exhibits and attachments.* Filing users must submit in electronic form all documents referenced as exhibits or attachments, unless the court permits conventional filing. A filing user must submit as exhibits or attachments only those excerpts of the referenced documents that are directly germane to the matter under consideration by the court. Excerpted material must be clearly and prominently identified as such. Filing users who file excerpts of documents as exhibits or attachments do so without prejudice to their right to timely file additional excerpts or the complete document. Responding parties may timely file additional excerpts or the complete document that they believe are directly germane. The court may require parties to file additional excerpts or the complete document. IN R USDCTND CM/ECF(II)(A)(6).

   e. *Hyperlinks.* Electronically filed documents may contain hyperlink references to an external document as a convenient mechanism for accessing material cited in the document. A hyperlink reference is neither validated for content nor considered a part of the court's records. The court neither endorses the product or organization at the destination of a hyperlink reference, nor does the court exercise any responsibility over the content at the destination. In order to preserve the integrity of the court record, attorneys wishing to insert hyperlinks in court filings shall continue to use the traditional citation method for the cited authority, in addition to the hyperlink. A hyperlink contained in a filing is no more than a convenient mechanism for accessing material cited in the document and a hyperlink reference is extraneous to any filed document and is not part of the court's record. IN R USDCTND CM/ECF(II)(A)(3).

3. *Form of briefs*

   a. *Page limits.* Supporting and response briefs (excluding tables of contents, tables of authorities, and appendices) ordinarily must not exceed twenty-five (25) pages. Reply briefs must not exceed fifteen (15) pages. IN R USDCTND L.R. 7-1(e)(1).

      i. *Exception.* The court may allow a party to file a brief exceeding these page limits for extraordinary and compelling reasons. But if the court permits a brief to exceed twenty-five (25) pages, it must include:

         - A table of contents with page references;
         - An issue statement; and
         - A table of authorities including: (1) all cases (alphabetically arranged), statutes, and other

authorities cited in the brief; and (2) references to where the authorities appear in the brief. IN R USDCTND L.R. 7-1(e)(2).

4. *Signing of pleadings, motions and other papers*

   a. *Signature.* Every pleading, written motion, and other paper must be signed by at least one attorney of record in the attorney's name—or by a party personally if the party is unrepresented. The paper must state the signer's address, e-mail address, and telephone number. FRCP 11(a).

      i. *Signatures on manual filings.* Papers delivered to the clerk for filing must: include the filer's original signature. IN R USDCTND L.R. 5-4(b)(1)(C).

         • *Rubber-stamped and faxed signatures.* An original paper with a rubber-stamped or faxed signature is unsigned for purposes of FRCP 11 and FRCP 26(g). IN R USDCTND L.R. 5-4(b)(2).

         • *Affidavits.* Only the affiant need sign an affidavit. IN R USDCTND L.R. 5-4(b)(3).

      ii. *Electronic signatures.* Pursuant to FRCP 11, every pleading, motion, and other paper (except lists, schedules, statements or amendments thereto) shall be signed by at least one attorney of record or, if the party is not represented by an attorney, all papers shall be signed by the party. An attorney's/participant's password issued by the court combined with the user's identification, serves as and constitutes the attorney/participant's signature for FRCP 11 and other purposes. IN R USDCTND CM/ECF(I)(C). Documents which must be filed and which must contain original signatures other than those of a participating attorney or which require either verification or an unsworn declaration under any rule or statute, shall be filed electronically, with originally executed copies maintained by the filer. The pleading or other document electronically filed shall contain "s/" signature(s), as noted in IN R USDCTND CM/ECF(II)(E)(3)(b). IN R USDCTND CM/ECF(II)(E)(1).

         • *Multiple signatures.* In the case of a stipulation or other document to be signed by two or more attorneys, the following procedure should be used: The filing attorney shall initially confirm that the content of the document is acceptable to all persons required to sign the document and shall obtain the physical signatures of all attorneys on the document. IN R USDCTND CM/ECF(II)(E)(3)(a). The filing attorney then shall file the document electronically, indicating the signatories, e.g., "s/Jane Doe," "s/John Doe," etc. IN R USDCTND CM/ECF(II)(E)(3)(b). The filing attorney shall retain the hard copy of the document containing the original signatures. IN R USDCTND CM/ECF(II)(E)(3)(c).

      iii. *No verification or accompanying affidavit required for pleadings.* Unless a rule or statute specifically states otherwise, a pleading need not be verified or accompanied by an affidavit. FRCP 11(a).

      iv. *Unsigned papers.* The court must strike an unsigned paper unless the omission is promptly corrected after being called to the attorney's or party's attention. FRCP 11(a).

   b. *Representations to the court.* By presenting to the court a pleading, written motion, or other paper—whether by signing, filing, submitting, or later advocating it—an attorney or unrepresented party certifies that to the best of the person's knowledge, information, and belief, formed after an inquiry reasonable under the circumstances:

      i. It is not being presented for any improper purpose, such as to harass, cause unnecessary delay, or needlessly increase the cost of litigation;

      ii. The claims, defenses, and other legal contentions are warranted by existing law or by a nonfrivolous argument for extending, modifying, or reversing existing law or for establishing new law;

      iii. The factual contentions have evidentiary support or, if specifically so identified, will likely have evidentiary support after a reasonable opportunity for further investigation or discovery; and

      iv. The denials of factual contentions are warranted on the evidence or, if specifically so identified, are reasonably based on belief or a lack of information. FRCP 11(b).

   c. *Sanctions.* Refer to the General Requirements section of this document for information on sanctions.

5. *Privacy protection for filings made with the court*

    a. *Redacted filings.* Counsel should not include sensitive information in any document filed with the court unless such inclusion is necessary and relevant to the case. IN R USDCTND CM/ECF(VII). Unless the court orders otherwise, in an electronic or paper filing with the court that contains an individual's Social Security number, taxpayer-identification number, or birth date, the name of an individual known to be a minor, or a financial-account number, a party or nonparty making the filing may include only:

        i. The last four (4) digits of the Social Security number and taxpayer-identification number;

        ii. The year of the individual's birth;

        iii. The minor's initials; and

        iv. The last four (4) digits of the financial-account number. FRCP 5.2(a); IN R USDCTND Order 2005-3.

    b. *Exemptions from the redaction requirement.* The redaction requirement does not apply to the following:

        i. A financial-account number that identifies the property allegedly subject to forfeiture in a forfeiture proceeding;

        ii. The record of an administrative or agency proceeding;

        iii. The official record of a state-court proceeding;

        iv. The record of a court or tribunal, if that record was not subject to the redaction requirement when originally filed;

        v. A filing covered by FRCP 5.2(c) or FRCP 5.2(d); and

        vi. A pro se filing in an action brought under 28 U.S.C.A. § 2241, 28 U.S.C.A. § 2254, or 28 U.S.C.A. § 2255. FRCP 5.2(b).

        vii. In cases filed under the Social Security Act, 42 U.S.C.A. § 405(g), there is no need for redaction of any information from the documents filed in the case. IN R USDCTND Order 2005-3.

    c. *Limitations on remote access to electronic files; Social Security appeals and immigration cases.* Unless the court orders otherwise, in an action for benefits under the Social Security Act, and in an action or proceeding relating to an order of removal, to relief from removal, or to immigration benefits or detention, access to an electronic file is authorized as follows:

        i. The parties and their attorneys may have remote electronic access to any part of the case file, including the administrative record;

        ii. Any other person may have electronic access to the full record at the courthouse, but may have remote electronic access only to:

           • The docket maintained by the court; and

           • An opinion, order, judgment, or other disposition of the court, but not any other part of the case file or the administrative record. FRCP 5.2(c).

    d. *Filings made under seal.* The court may order that a filing be made under seal without redaction. The court may later unseal the filing or order the person who made the filing to file a redacted version for the public record. FRCP 5.2(d). For information on filing documents under seal, refer to IN R USDCTND L.R. 5-3, IN R USDCTND CM/ECF(IV)(A), and IN R USDCTND ECF Order 2004-19.

    e. *Protective orders.* For good cause, the court may by order in a case:

        i. Require redaction of additional information; or

        ii. Limit or prohibit a nonparty's remote electronic access to a document filed with the court. FRCP 5.2(e).

    f. *Option for additional unredacted filing under seal.* A person making a redacted filing may also file

an unredacted copy under seal. The court must retain the unredacted copy as part of the record. FRCP 5.2(f); IN R USDCTND Order 2005-3.

    i.   The unredacted version of the document or the reference list shall be retained by the court under seal as part of the record. This paper shall be retained by the court as part of the record. The court may, however, still require the party to file a redacted copy for the public file. IN R USDCTND Order 2005-3.

g.   *Option for filing a reference list.* A filing that contains redacted information may be filed together with a reference list that identifies each item of redacted information and specifies an appropriate identifier that uniquely corresponds to each item listed. The list must be filed under seal and may be amended as of right. Any reference in the case to a listed identifier will be construed to refer to the corresponding item of information. FRCP 5.2(g); IN R USDCTND Order 2005-3.

    i.   The unredacted version of the document or the reference list shall be retained by the court under seal as part of the record. This paper shall be retained by the court as part of the record. The court may, however, still require the party to file a redacted copy for the public file. IN R USDCTND Order 2005-3.

h.   *Responsibility for redaction.* The responsibility for redacting these personal identifiers rests solely with counsel and the parties. The Clerk will not review each paper for compliance with IN R USDCTND Order 2005-3. IN R USDCTND Order 2005-3.

i.   *Waiver of protection of identifiers.* A person waives the protection of FRCP 5.2(a) as to the person's own information by filing it without redaction and not under seal. FRCP 5.2(h).

F. Filing and Service Requirements

1.   *Filing requirements.* Any paper after the complaint that is required to be served—together with a certificate of service—must be filed within a reasonable time after service. FRCP 5(d)(1). Motions must be filed separately, but alternative motions may be filed in a single paper if each is named in the title following the caption. IN R USDCTND L.R. 7-1(a).

   a.   *How filing is made; In general.* A paper is filed by delivering it:

      i.   To the clerk; or

      ii.   To a judge who agrees to accept it for filing, and who must then note the filing date on the paper and promptly send it to the clerk. FRCP 5(d)(2).

        •   Papers not filed electronically must be filed with the clerk, not a judge. IN R USDCTND L.R. 5-4(b)(4).

     iii.   Parties manually filing a paper that requires the clerk to give others notice, must give the clerk: (1) sufficient copies of the notice; and (2) the name and address of each person entitled to receive the notice. IN R USDCTND L.R. 5-4(b)(8).

   b.   *Where to file.* Papers not filed electronically must be filed in the division where the case is pending, unless: (1) a person will be prejudiced if the paper is not filed the same day it is tendered; and (2) it includes an adequately sized envelope addressed to the clerk's office in the division where the case is pending and with adequate postage. IN R USDCTND L.R. 5-4(b)(5).

   c.   *Electronic filing*

      i.   *Authorization of electronic filing program.* A court may, by local rule, allow papers to be filed, signed, or verified by electronic means that are consistent with any technical standards established by the Judicial Conference of the United States. A local rule may require electronic filing only if reasonable exceptions are allowed. A paper filed electronically in compliance with a local rule is a written paper for purposes of the Federal Rules of Civil Procedure. FRCP 5(d)(3).

        •   Papers must be filed, signed, and verified electronically unless excepted by the court's CM/ECF Civil and Criminal User Manual (IN R USDCTND CM/ECF). IN R USDCTND L.R. 5-1.

     ii.   *Mandatory electronic filing.* Unless otherwise permitted by these procedures or otherwise authorized by the assigned judge, all documents submitted for filing in this district in civil and criminal cases, no matter when a case was originally filed, shall be filed electronically using the System. IN R USDCTND CM/ECF(II)(A)(1). The requirement that "all documents" be filed electronically includes briefs, and attachments and exhibits used in support of motions. IN R USDCTND CM/ECF(FN1).

- Sending a document or pleading to the court via e-mail or facsimile does not constitute "electronic filing." IN R USDCTND CM/ECF(I)(A).

iii. *Conventional filing.* As used in these procedures, a "conventionally" filed or submitted document or pleading is one presented to the Clerk or a party in paper or other non-electronic, tangible format. The following documents shall be filed conventionally and not electronically unless specifically authorized by the Court:

- Exhibits and other documents which cannot be converted to a legible electronic form. Whenever possible, counsel is responsible for converting filings to an electronic form. However, if that is not physically possible, counsel shall electronically file a .pdf document titled Notice of Manual Filing as a notation on the docket sheet that filings are being held in the clerk's office in paper. A sample Notice of Manual Filing is attached as Form 2 (IN R USDCTND CM/ECF(Form 2)). If documents are filed in paper format, counsel must provide an original for the clerk's office, a copy for the judge and a copy must be served on all parties in the case. Large documents which do not exist in an electronic format shall be scanned into .pdf format by counsel, in small batches if necessary, and filed electronically as separate attachments in the System. IN R USDCTND CM/ECF(III)(A)(1).

- Certain documents which are listed in IN R USDCTND CM/ECF(II)(E)(2). IN R US-DCTND CM/ECF(III)(A)(2).

- Documents filed by pro se litigants. IN R USDCTND CM/ECF(III)(A)(3).

iv. For more information on electronic filing, refer to IN R USDCTND CM/ECF.

2. *Service requirements*

   a. *Service; When required*

      i. *In general.* Unless the Federal Rules of Civil Procedure provide otherwise, each of the following papers must be served on every party:

         - An order stating that service is required;

         - A pleading filed after the original complaint, unless the court orders otherwise under FRCP 5(c) because there are numerous defendants;

         - A discovery paper required to be served on a party, unless the court orders otherwise;

         - A written motion, except one that may be heard ex parte; and

         - A written notice, appearance, demand, or offer of judgment, or any similar paper. FRCP 5(a)(1).

      ii. *If a party fails to appear.* No service is required on a party who is in default for failing to appear. But a pleading that asserts a new claim for relief against such a party must be served on that party under FRCP 4. FRCP 5(a)(2).

      iii. *Seizing property.* If an action is begun by seizing property and no person is or need be named as a defendant, any service required before the filing of an appearance, answer, or claim must be made on the person who had custody or possession of the property when it was seized. FRCP 5(a)(3).

   b. *Service; How made*

      i. *Serving an attorney.* If a party is represented by an attorney, service under FRCP 5 must be made on the attorney unless the court orders service on the party. FRCP 5(b)(1).

      ii. *Service in general.* A paper is served under FRCP 5 by:

         - Handing it to the person;

- Leaving it: (1) at the person's office with a clerk or other person in charge or, if no one is in charge, in a conspicuous place in the office; or (2) if the person has no office or the office is closed, at the person's dwelling or usual place of abode with someone of suitable age and discretion who resides there;

- Mailing it to the person's last known address—in which event service is complete upon mailing;

- Leaving it with the court clerk if the person has no known address;

- Sending it by electronic means if the person consented in writing—in which event service is complete upon transmission, but is not effective if the serving party learns that it did not reach the person to be served; or

- Delivering it by any other means that the person consented to in writing—in which event service is complete when the person making service delivers it to the agency designated to make delivery. FRCP 5(b)(2).

iii. *Electronic service.* Electronically filed papers may be served electronically if service is consistent with the CM/ECF User Manual (IN R USDCTND CM/ECF). IN R USDCTND L.R. 5-2(a).

- *Waiver of other service.* An attorney's registration will constitute a waiver of conventional service of documents and the attorney agrees to accept service of notice on behalf of the client of the electronic filing by hand, facsimile or authorized email. IN R USDCTND CM/ECF(I)(B)(3).

- *Serving registered persons.* The System will generate a "Notice of Electronic Filing" when any document is filed. This notice represents service of the document on parties who are registered participants with the System. Except as provided in IN R USDCTND CM/ECF(III)(B), the filing party shall not be required to serve any pleading or other documents on any party receiving electronic notice. IN R USDCTND CM/ECF(II)(D)(1). The term "pleading" refers only to those documents listed in FRCP 7(a). IN R USDCTND CM/ECF(FN3).

- *When electronic service is deemed completed.* A person registered to use the court's electronic-filing system is served with an electronically filed paper when a "Notice of Electronic Filing" is transmitted to that person through the court's electronic filing-system. IN R USDCTND L.R. 5-2(b).

- *Serving non-registered persons.* A person who has not registered to use the court's electronic-filing system but who is entitled to service of a paper must be served according to the Local Civil Rules of the United States District Court for the Northern District of Indiana and the Federal Rules of Civil Procedure. IN R USDCTND L.R. 5-2(c); IN R USDCTND CM/ECF(II)(D)(2). If such service of a paper copy is to be made, it shall be done in the manner provided in the Federal Rules of Civil Procedure and the Local Civil Rules of the United States District Court for the Northern District of Indiana. IN R USDCTND CM/ECF(II)(D)(2).

iv. *Service of conventional filings.* Pleadings or other documents which are filed conventionally rather than electronically shall be served in the manner provided for in the Federal Rules of Civil Procedure and the Local Civil Rules of the United States District Court for the Northern District of Indiana, except as otherwise provided by order of the Court. IN R USDCTND CM/ECF(III)(B).

v. *Using court facilities.* If a local rule so authorizes, a party may use the court's transmission facilities to make service under FRCP 5(b)(2)(E). FRCP 5(b)(3).

c. *Serving numerous defendants*

i. *In general.* If an action involves an unusually large number of defendants, the court may, on motion or on its own, order that:

- Defendants' pleadings and replies to them need not be served on other defendants;

- Any crossclaim, counterclaim, avoidance, or affirmative defense in those pleadings and replies to them will be treated as denied or avoided by all other parties; and
- Filing any such pleading and serving it on the plaintiff constitutes notice of the pleading to all parties. FRCP 5(c)(1).

ii. *Notifying parties.* A copy of every such order must be served on the parties as the court directs. FRCP 5(c)(2).

G. Hearings

1. *Hearings, generally*

   a. *Oral argument.* Due process does not require that oral argument be permitted on a motion and, except as otherwise provided by local rule, the district court has discretion to determine whether it will decide the motion on the papers or hear argument by counsel (and perhaps receive evidence). FPP § 1190; F.D.I.C. v. Deglau, 207 F.3d 153 (3d Cir. 2000).

      i. *Request for oral argument.* A party may request oral argument on a motion by filing and serving a separate document explaining why oral argument is necessary and estimating how long the court should allow for the argument. IN R USDCTND L.R. 7-5(a)(1). Refer to the Documents section of this document for more information.

      ii. *Additional evidence forbidden.* Parties may not present additional evidence at oral argument. IN R USDCTND L.R. 7-5(a)(3).

   b. *Providing a regular schedule for oral hearings.* A court may establish regular times and places for oral hearings on motions. FRCP 78(a).

   c. *Providing for submission on briefs.* By rule or order, the court may provide for submitting and determining motions on briefs, without oral hearings. FRCP 78(b).

   d. *Evidentiary hearings.* A party may request an evidentiary hearing by filing and serving a separate document explaining why the hearing is necessary and estimating how long the court should allow for it. IN R USDCTND L.R. 7-5(b)(2). Refer to the Documents section of this document for more information.

   e. *Court's authority.* The court may: (1) grant or deny a request for oral argument or an evidentiary hearing in its discretion; (2) set oral argument or an evidentiary hearing without a request from a party; or (3) order any oral argument or evidentiary hearing to be held anywhere within the district regardless of where the case will be tried. IN R USDCTND L.R. 7-5(c).

2. *Courtroom and courthouse decorum.* For information on courtroom and courthouse decorum, refer to IN R USDCTND L.R. 83-3.

H. Forms

1. Federal Motion for Sanctions Forms

   a. Motion; For order imposing sanctions pursuant to FRCP 11; Notice of removal frivolous, not well grounded in fact, or interposed for purpose of causing unnecessary delay and needlessly to increase cost of litigation. AMJUR PP FEDPRAC § 364.

   b. Notice of motion for sanctions. 2C FEDFORMS § 10:74.

   c. Notice of motion and motion for sanctions. 2C FEDFORMS § 10:75.

   d. Notice of motion and motion for sanctions; Including motion for sanctions under FRCP 37(c). 2C FEDFORMS § 10:76.

   e. Motion for sanctions; Including sanctions under FRCP 37(d). 2C FEDFORMS § 10:77.

   f. Defendant's summary of attorney fees. 2C FEDFORMS § 10:78.

   g. Motion; General form. FEDPROF § 1:746.

   h. Notice; Of motion; General form. FEDPROF § 1:747.

   i. Notice; Of motion; With costs of motion. FEDPROF § 1:748.

   j. Notice; Of motion; Containing motion. FEDPROF § 1:749.

k. Opposition; To motion; General form. FEDPROF § 1:750.

l. Affidavit; Supporting or opposing motion. FEDPROF § 1:751.

m. Brief; Supporting or opposing motion. FEDPROF § 1:752.

n. Statement of points and authorities; Opposing motion. FEDPROF § 1:753.

o. Illustrative forms; FRCP 11; Notice and motion for sanctions. LITGTORT § 20:36.

p. Illustrative forms; FRCP 11; Memorandum in support of motion. LITGTORT § 20:37.

q. Illustrative forms; FRCP 11; Declaration in support of motion. LITGTORT § 20:38.

r. Illustrative forms; FRCP 11 and 28 U.S.C.A. § 1927; Notice of motion and motion for sanctions. LITGTORT § 20:39.

s. Illustrative forms; FRCP 11 and 28 U.S.C.A. § 1927; Brief in support of motion. LITGTORT § 20:40.

2. **Forms for the Northern District of Indiana**

a. Certificate of service. IN R USDCTND CM/ECF(Form 1).

b. Notice of manual filing. IN R USDCTND CM/ECF(Form 2).

c. Declaration that party was unable to file in a timely manner. IN R USDCTND CM/ECF(Form 3).

I. Applicable Rules

1. *Federal rules*

a. Counsel's liability for excessive costs. 28 U.S.C.A. § 1927.

b. Serving and filing pleadings and other papers. FRCP 5.

c. Constitutional challenge to a statute; Notice, certification, and intervention. FRCP 5.1.

d. Privacy protection for filings made with the court. FRCP 5.2.

e. Computing and extending time; Time for motion papers. FRCP 6.

f. Pleadings allowed; Form of motions and other papers. FRCP 7.

g. Disclosure statement. FRCP 7.1.

h. Form of pleadings. FRCP 10.

i. Signing pleadings, motions, and other papers; Representations to the court; Sanctions. FRCP 11.

j. Taking testimony. FRCP 43.

k. Hearing motions; Submission on briefs. FRCP 78.

2. *Local rules*

a. Citation and scope of the rules. IN R USDCTND L.R. 1-1.

b. Sanctions for formatting errors. IN R USDCTND L.R. 1-3.

c. Electronic filing required. IN R USDCTND L.R. 5-1.

d. Constitutional questions. IN R USDCTND L.R. 5.1-1.

e. Electronic service. IN R USDCTND L.R. 5-2.

f. Format of papers. IN R USDCTND L.R. 5-4.

g. Motion practice. IN R USDCTND L.R. 7-1.

h. Oral arguments and evidentiary hearings. IN R USDCTND L.R. 7-5.

i. Pretrial procedure. IN R USDCTND L.R. 16-1.

j. Alternative dispute resolution. IN R USDCTND L.R. 16-6.

k. Filing of discovery and other materials. IN R USDCTND L.R. 26-2.

l. Case assignment. IN R USDCTND L.R. 40-1.

m. Appearance and withdrawal of appearance. IN R USDCTND L.R. 83-8.

n. CM/ECF civil and criminal user manual. IN R USDCTND CM/ECF.

o. In re: privacy and public access to civil electronic case files. IN R USDCTND Order 2005-3.

Motions, Oppositions and Replies
Motion to Compel Discovery

Document Last Updated December 2016

A. Checklist

(I) ❑ Matters to be considered by moving party

   (a) ❑ Required documents

      (1) ❑ Notice of motion and motion

      (2) ❑ Certificate of compliance

      (3) ❑ Brief

      (4) ❑ Discovery materials

      (5) ❑ Certificate of service

   (b) ❑ Supplemental documents

      (1) ❑ Supporting evidence

      (2) ❑ Notice of constitutional question

      (3) ❑ Index of exhibits

      (4) ❑ Request for oral argument

      (5) ❑ Request for evidentiary hearing

      (6) ❑ Copy of authority

      (7) ❑ Proposed order

      (8) ❑ Copy of document with self-addressed envelope

      (9) ❑ Notice of manual filing

      (10) ❑ Courtesy copies

      (11) ❑ Declaration that party was unable to file in a timely manner

   (c) ❑ Timing

      (1) ❑ A motion must simply be submitted within a reasonable time; however, a motion to compel discovery filed under FRCP 37(a) is premature if it is filed before any request for discovery is made

      (2) ❑ A written motion and notice of the hearing must be served at least fourteen (14) days before the time specified for the hearing, with the following exceptions: (i) when the motion may be heard ex parte; (ii) when the Federal Rules of Civil Procedure set a different time; or (iii) when a court order—which a party may, for good cause, apply for ex parte—sets a different time

      (3) ❑ Any affidavit supporting a motion must be served with the motion

(II) ❑ Matters to be considered by opposing party

   (a) ❑ Required documents

      (1) ❑ Response brief

      (2) ❑ Certificate of service

(b) ❑ Supplemental documents

    (1) ❑ Supporting evidence

    (2) ❑ Notice of constitutional question

    (3) ❑ Index of exhibits

    (4) ❑ Request for oral argument

    (5) ❑ Request for evidentiary hearing

    (6) ❑ Copy of authority

    (7) ❑ Copy of document with self-addressed envelope

    (8) ❑ Notice of manual filing

    (9) ❑ Courtesy copies

    (10) ❑ Declaration that party was unable to file in a timely manner

(c) ❑ Timing

    (1) ❑ A party must file any response brief to a motion within fourteen (14) days after the motion is served

    (2) ❑ Except as FRCP 59(c) provides otherwise, any opposing affidavit must be served at least seven (7) days before the hearing, unless the court permits service at another time

B. Timing

1. *Motion to compel discovery.* There is no specific time limit for a motion to compel discovery under FRCP 37(a); rather, a motion must simply be submitted within a reasonable time. FEDPROC § 26:779. However, a motion to compel discovery filed under FRCP 37(a) is premature if it is filed before any request for discovery is made. FEDPROC § 26:779; Bermudez v. Duenas, 936 F.2d 1064, 19 Fed.R.Serv.3d 1443 (9th Cir. 1991).

2. *Timing of motions, generally*

    a. *Motion and notice of hearing.* A written motion and notice of the hearing must be served at least fourteen (14) days before the time specified for the hearing, with the following exceptions:

        i. When the motion may be heard ex parte;

        ii. When the Federal Rules of Civil Procedure set a different time; or

        iii. When a court order—which a party may, for good cause, apply for ex parte—sets a different time. FRCP 6(c)(1).

    b. *Supporting affidavit.* Any affidavit supporting a motion must be served with the motion. FRCP 6(c)(2).

3. *Timing of opposing papers.* A party must file any response brief to a motion within fourteen (14) days after the motion is served. IN R USDCTND L.R. 7-1(d)(2)(A).

    a. *Opposing affidavit.* Except as FRCP 59(c) provides otherwise, any opposing affidavit must be served at least seven (7) days before the hearing, unless the court permits service at another time. FRCP 6(c)(2).

    b. *Extensions.* The court may extend response- and reply-brief deadlines, but only for good cause. IN R USDCTND L.R. 7-1(d)(3).

    c. *Summary rulings.* The court may rule on a motion summarily if an opposing party does not file a response before the deadline. IN R USDCTND L.R. 7-1(d)(4).

4. *Timing of reply papers.* Where the respondent files an answering affidavit setting up a new matter, the moving party ordinarily is allowed a reasonable time to file a reply affidavit since failure to deny the new matter by affidavit may operate as an admission of its truth. AMJUR MOTIONS § 25.

    a. *Reply brief.* The moving party must file any reply brief within seven (7) days after the response brief is served. IN R USDCTND L.R. 7-1(d)(2)(B).

b. *Extensions.* The court may extend response- and reply-brief deadlines, but only for good cause. IN R USDCTND L.R. 7-1(d)(3).

5. *Computation of time*

a. *Computing time.* FRCP 6 applies in computing any time period specified in the Federal Rules of Civil Procedure, in any local rule or court order, or in any statute that does not specify a method of computing time. FRCP 6(a).

    i. *Period stated in days or a longer unit.* When the period is stated in days or a longer unit of time:

- Exclude the day of the event that triggers the period;

- Count every day, including intermediate Saturdays, Sundays, and legal holidays; and

- Include the last day of the period, but if the last day is a Saturday, Sunday, or legal holiday, the period continues to run until the end of the next day that is not a Saturday, Sunday, or legal holiday. FRCP 6(a)(1).

    ii. *Period stated in hours.* When the period is stated in hours:

- Begin counting immediately on the occurrence of the event that triggers the period;

- Count every hour, including hours during intermediate Saturdays, Sundays, and legal holidays; and

- If the period would end on a Saturday, Sunday, or legal holiday, the period continues to run until the same time on the next day that is not a Saturday, Sunday, or legal holiday. FRCP 6(a)(2).

    iii. *Inaccessibility of the clerk's office.* Unless the court orders otherwise, if the clerk's office is inaccessible:

- On the last day for filing under FRCP 6(a)(1), then the time for filing is extended to the first accessible day that is not a Saturday, Sunday, or legal holiday; or

- During the last hour for filing under FRCP 6(a)(2), then the time for filing is extended to the same time on the first accessible day that is not a Saturday, Sunday, or legal holiday. FRCP 6(a)(3).

    iv. *"Last day" defined.* Unless a different time is set by a statute, local rule, or court order, the last day ends:

- For electronic filing, at midnight in the court's time zone; and

- For filing by other means, when the clerk's office is scheduled to close. FRCP 6(a)(4).

    v. *"Next day" defined.* The "next day" is determined by continuing to count forward when the period is measured after an event and backward when measured before an event. FRCP 6(a)(5).

    vi. *"Legal holiday" defined.* "Legal holiday" means:

- The day set aside by statute for observing New Year's Day, Martin Luther King Jr.'s Birthday, Washington's Birthday, Memorial Day, Independence Day, Labor Day, Columbus Day, Veterans' Day, Thanksgiving Day, or Christmas Day;

- Any day declared a holiday by the President or Congress; and

- For periods that are measured after an event, any other day declared a holiday by the state where the district court is located. FRCP 6(a)(6).

b. *Computation of electronic filing deadlines.* Filing documents electronically does not alter any filing deadlines or any time computation pursuant to FRCP 6. The counties of Lake, Porter, LaPorte, Pulaski and Starke are located in the Central time zone and the remaining counties in the Northern District of Indiana are located in the Eastern time zone. Nevertheless, all electronic transmissions of documents must be completed (i.e., received completely by the clerk's office) prior to midnight Eastern Time, (South Bend/Fort Wayne/Lafayette time) in order to be considered timely filed that day, regardless of the local time in the division where the case is pending. Although documents can be filed electronically twenty-four (24) hours a day, filers are strongly encouraged to file all

documents during hours when the CM/ECF Help Line is available, from 9:00 a.m. to 4:00 p.m. local time. IN R USDCTND CM/ECF(II)(I).

    i. *Technical failures.* If the attorney is unable to file a document in a timely manner due to technical difficulties in the user's system, the attorney must file a document with the court as soon as possible notifying the court of the inability to file the document. A sample document entitled Declaration that Party was Unable to File in a Timely Manner Due to Technical Difficulties is attached hereto as Form 5. IN R USDCTND CM/ECF(VI)(B). [Editor's note: the reference to Form 5 is likely meant to be a reference to Form 3 (IN R USDCTND CM/ECF(Form 3)].

  c. *Extending time*

    i. *In general.* When an act may or must be done within a specified time, the court may, for good cause, extend the time:

- With or without motion or notice if the court acts, or if a request is made, before the original time or its extension expires; or

- On motion made after the time has expired if the party failed to act because of excusable neglect. FRCP 6(b)(1).

    ii. *Exceptions.* A court must not extend the time to act under FRCP 50(b), FRCP 50(d), FRCP 52(b), FRCP 59(b), FRCP 59(d), FRCP 59(e), and FRCP 60(b). FRCP 6(b)(2).

    iii. Refer to the United States District Court for the Northern District of Indiana KeyRules Motion for Continuance/Extension of Time document for more information on extending time.

  d. *Additional time after certain kinds of service.* When a party may or must act within a specified time after being served and service is made under FRCP 5(b)(2)(C) (mail), FRCP 5(b)(2)(D) (leaving with the clerk), or FRCP 5(b)(2)(F) (other means consented to), three (3) days are added after the period would otherwise expire under FRCP 6(a). FRCP 6(d).

C. General Requirements

1. *Motions, generally*

  a. *Requirements.* A request for a court order must be made by motion. The motion must:

    i. Be in writing unless made during a hearing or trial;

    ii. State with particularity the grounds for seeking the order; and

    iii. State the relief sought. FRCP 7(b)(1).

  b. *Notice of motion.* A party interested in resisting the relief sought by a motion has a right to notice thereof, and an opportunity to be heard. AMJUR MOTIONS § 12.

    i. In addition to statutory or court rule provisions requiring notice of a motion—the purpose of such a notice requirement having been said to be to prevent a party from being prejudicially surprised by a motion—principles of natural justice dictate that an adverse party generally must be given notice that a motion will be presented to the court. AMJUR MOTIONS § 12.

    ii. "Notice," in this regard, means reasonable notice, including a meaningful opportunity to prepare and to defend against allegations of a motion. AMJUR MOTIONS § 12.

  c. *Writing requirement.* The writing requirement is intended to insure that the adverse parties are informed and have a record of both the motion's pendency and the grounds on which the movant seeks an order. FPP § 1191; Feldberg v. Quechee Lakes Corp., 463 F.3d 195 (2d Cir. 2006).

    i. It is sufficient "if the motion is stated in a written notice of the hearing of the motion." FPP § 1191.

  d. *Particularity requirement.* The particularity requirement insures that the opposing parties will have notice of their opponent's contentions. FEDPROC § 62:364; Goodman v. 1973 26 Foot Trojan Vessel, Arkansas Registration No. AR1439SN, 859 F.2d 71, 12 Fed.R.Serv.3d 645 (8th Cir. 1988). That requirement ensures that notice of the basis for the motion is provided to the court and to the opposing party so as to avoid prejudice, provide the opponent with a meaningful opportunity to

respond, and provide the court with enough information to process the motion correctly. FEDPROC § 62:364; Andreas v. Volkswagen of America, Inc., 336 F.3d 789, 56 Fed.R.Serv.3d 6 (8th Cir. 2003).

    i. Reasonable specification of the grounds for a motion is sufficient. However, where a movant fails to state even one ground for granting the motion in question, the movant has failed to meet the minimal standard of "reasonable specification." FEDPROC § 62:364; Martinez v. Trainor, 556 F.2d 818, 23 Fed.R.Serv.2d 403 (7th Cir. 1977).

    ii. The court may excuse the failure to comply with the particularity requirement if it is inadvertent, and where no prejudice is shown by the opposing party. FEDPROC § 62:364.

e. *Motions must be filed separately.* Motions must be filed separately, but alternative motions may be filed in a single paper if each is named in the title following the caption. IN R USDCTND L.R. 7-1(a).

2. *Motion to compel discovery.* On notice to other parties and all affected persons, a party may move for an order compelling disclosure or discovery. FRCP 37(a)(1). A party must request the specific documents in issue from the opposing party before filing a motion to compel the production of documents. FEDPROC § 26:778.

a. *Appropriate court.* A motion for an order to a party must be made in the court where the action is pending. A motion for an order to a nonparty must be made in the court where the discovery is or will be taken. FRCP 37(a)(2).

b. *Specific motions*

    i. *To compel disclosure.* If a party fails to make a disclosure required by FRCP 26(a), any other party may move to compel disclosure and for appropriate sanctions. FRCP 37(a)(3)(A). Refer to the United States District Court for the Northern District of Indiana KeyRules Motion for Discovery Sanctions document for more information on sanctions.

    ii. *To compel a discovery response.* A party seeking discovery may move for an order compelling an answer, designation, production, or inspection. This motion may be made if:

- A deponent fails to answer a question asked under FRCP 30 or FRCP 31;
- A corporation or other entity fails to make a designation under FRCP 30(b)(6) or FRCP 31(a)(4);
- A party fails to answer an interrogatory submitted under FRCP 33; or
- A party fails to produce documents or fails to respond that inspection will be permitted—or fails to permit inspection—as requested under FRCP 34. FRCP 37(a)(3)(B).

    iii. *Related to a deposition.* When taking an oral deposition, the party asking a question may complete or adjourn the examination before moving for an order. FRCP 37(a)(3)(C).

    iv. *Evasive or incomplete disclosure, answer, or response.* For purposes of FRCP 37(a), an evasive or incomplete disclosure, answer, or response must be treated as a failure to disclose, answer, or respond. FRCP 37(a)(4).

c. *Payment of expenses; Protective orders*

    i. *If the motion is granted (or disclosure or discovery is provided after filing).* If the motion is granted—or if the disclosure or requested discovery is provided after the motion was filed—the court must, after giving an opportunity to be heard, require the party or deponent whose conduct necessitated the motion, the party or attorney advising that conduct, or both to pay the movant's reasonable expenses incurred in making the motion, including attorney's fees. But the court must not order this payment if:

- The movant filed the motion before attempting in good faith to obtain the disclosure or discovery without court action;
- The opposing party's nondisclosure, response, or objection was substantially justified; or
- Other circumstances make an award of expenses unjust. FRCP 37(a)(5)(A).

    ii. *If the motion is denied.* If the motion is denied, the court may issue any protective order authorized under FRCP 26(c) and must, after giving an opportunity to be heard, require the movant, the attorney filing the motion, or both to pay the party or deponent who opposed the motion its reasonable expenses incurred in opposing the motion, including attorney's fees. But the court must not order this payment if the motion was substantially justified or other circumstances make an award of expenses unjust. FRCP 37(a)(5)(B).

   iii. *If the motion is granted in part and denied in part.* If the motion is granted in part and denied in part, the court may issue any protective order authorized under FRCP 26(c) and may, after giving an opportunity to be heard, apportion the reasonable expenses for the motion. FRCP 37(a)(5)(C).

3. *Opposing papers.* The Federal Rules of Civil Procedure do not require any formal answer, return, or reply to a motion, except where the Federal Rules of Civil Procedure or local rules may require affidavits, memoranda, or other papers to be filed in opposition to a motion. Such papers are simply to apprise the court of such opposition and the grounds of that opposition. FEDPROC § 62:359.

   a. *Effect of failure to respond to motion.* Although in the absence of statutory provision or court rule, a motion ordinarily does not require a written answer, when a party files a motion and the opposing party fails to respond, the court may construe such failure to respond as nonopposition to the motion or an admission that the motion was meritorious, may take the facts alleged in the motion as true—the rule in some jurisdictions being that the failure to respond to a fact set forth in a motion is deemed an admission—and may grant the motion if the relief requested appears to be justified. AMJUR MOTIONS § 28.

   b. *Assent or no opposition not determinative.* However, a motion will not be granted automatically simply because an "assent" or a notation of "no opposition" has been filed; federal judges frequently deny motions that have been assented to when it is thought that justice so dictates. FPP § 1190.

   c. *Responsive pleading inappropriate as response to motion.* An attempt to answer or oppose a motion with a responsive pleading usually is not appropriate. FPP § 1190.

4. *Reply papers.* A moving party may be required or permitted to prepare papers in addition to his original motion papers. AMJUR MOTIONS § 25. Papers answering or replying to opposing papers may be appropriate, in the interests of justice, where it appears there is a substantial reason for allowing a reply. Thus, a court may accept reply papers where a party demonstrates that the papers to which it seeks to file a reply raise new issues that are material to the disposition of the question before the court, or where the court determines, sua sponte, that it wishes further briefing of an issue raised in those papers and orders the submission of additional papers. FEDPROC § 62:360.

   a. *Function of reply papers.* The function of a reply affidavit is to answer the arguments made in opposition to the position taken by the movant and not to permit the movant to introduce new arguments in support of the motion. AMJUR MOTIONS § 25.

   b. *Issues raised for the first time in a reply document.* However, the view has been followed in some jurisdictions, that as a matter of judicial economy, where there is no prejudice and where the issues could be raised simply by filing a motion to dismiss, the trial court has discretion to consider arguments raised for the first time in a reply memorandum, and that a trial court may grant a motion to strike issues raised for the first time in a reply memorandum. AMJUR MOTIONS § 26.

5. *Appearances.* Attorneys not representing the United States or its agencies must file an appearance when they represent (either in person or by filing a paper) a party. IN R USDCTND L.R. 83-8(a). For more information, refer to IN R USDCTND L.R. 83-8.

6. *Notice of related action.* A party must file a notice of related action as soon as it appears that the party's case and another pending case: (1) arise out of the same transaction or occurrence; (2) involve the same property; or (3) involve the validity or infringement of the same patent, trademark, or copyright. IN R USDCTND L.R. 40-1(d). For more information, refer to IN R USDCTND L.R. 40-1.

7. *Alternative dispute resolution (ADR).* After they confer as required by FRCP 26(f), the parties must advise the court which, if any, alternative-dispute-resolution processes they expect to pursue and when they expect to undertake the process. IN R USDCTND L.R. 16-6(a). For more information on alternative dispute resolution (ADR), refer to IN R USDCTND L.R. 16-6 and IN R USDCTND Order 2003-21.

8. *Settlement or resolution.* The parties must immediately notify the court if they reasonably expect to settle the case or resolve a pending motion. IN R USDCTND L.R. 16-1(g).

9. *Modification or suspension of rules.* The court may, on its own motion or at the request of a party, suspend or modify any rule in a particular case in the interest of justice. IN R USDCTND L.R. 1-1(c).

D. Documents

1. *Documents for moving party*

   a. *Required documents*

      i. *Notice of motion and motion.* The party must not specify a hearing date in the notice of a motion or petition unless the court or the clerk has authorized it. IN R USDCTND L.R. 7-5(b)(2). Refer to the General Requirements section of this document for information on the notice of motion and motion.

      ii. *Certificate of compliance.* A party filing any discovery motion must file a separate certification that the party has conferred in good faith or attempted to confer with other affected parties in an effort to resolve the matter raised in the motion without court action. The certification must include: (1) the date, time, and place of any conference or attempted conference; and (2) the names of the parties participating in the conference. IN R USDCTND L.R. 37-1(a). The motion must include a certification that the movant has in good faith conferred or attempted to confer with the person or party failing to make disclosure or discovery in an effort to obtain it without court action. FRCP 37(a)(1).

      - *Failure to file certification.* The court may deny any motion described in IN R USDCTND L.R. 37-1(a)—except those motions brought by or against a person appearing pro se—if the required certification is not filed. IN R USDCTND L.R. 37-1(b).

      iii. *Brief.* Parties must file a supporting brief with any motion under: FRCP 37. IN R USDCTND L.R. 7-1(b)(2). Refer to the Format section of this document for the format of briefs.

      iv. *Discovery materials.* A party who files a motion for relief under FRCP 26(c) or FRCP 37 must file with the motion those parts of the discovery requests or responses that the motion pertains to. IN R USDCTND L.R. 26-2(b).

      v. *Certificate of service.* FRCP 5(d) requires that the person making service under FRCP 5 certify that service has been effected. FRCP 5(Advisory Committee Notes). Having such information on file may be useful for many purposes, including proof of service if an issue arises concerning the effectiveness of the service. FRCP 5(Advisory Committee Notes).

      - *Certificate of service for electronically-filed documents.* A Certificate of Service is still a requirement when filing documents electronically. A sample Certificate of Service is attached as Form 1 (IN R USDCTND CM/ECF(Form 1)). IN R USDCTND CM/ECF(II)(H).

   b. *Supplemental documents*

      i. *Supporting evidence.* When a motion relies on facts outside the record, the court may hear the matter on affidavits or may hear it wholly or partly on oral testimony or on depositions. FRCP 43(c).

      - *Materials necessary for motion.* A party must file those portions of discovery requests or responses (including deposition transcripts) that the party relies on to support a motion that could result in a final order on an issue. IN R USDCTND L.R. 26-2(c).

      ii. *Notice of constitutional question.* A party that files a pleading, written motion, or other paper drawing into question the constitutionality of a federal or state statute must promptly:

      - *File notice.* File a notice of constitutional question stating the question and identifying the paper that raises it, if: (1) a federal statute is questioned and the parties do not include the United States, one of its agencies, or one of its officers or employees in an official capacity; or (2) a state statute is questioned and the parties do not include the state, one of its agencies, or one of its officers or employees in an official capacity; and

- *Serve notice.* Serve the notice and paper on the Attorney General of the United States if a federal statute is questioned—or on the state attorney general if a state statute is questioned—either by certified or registered mail or by sending it to an electronic address designated by the attorney general for this purpose. FRCP 5.1(a).

- *When to file the notice.* A party required to file a notice of constitutional question under FRCP 5.1 must do so by the later of: (1) the day the parties tender their proposed case-management plan (if one is required); or (2) 21 days after filing the pleading, written motion, or other paper questioning the constitutionality of a federal or state statute. IN R USDCTND L.R. 5.1-1(a).

- *Service on government officials.* The party must also serve the notice and the pleading, written motion, or other paper questioning the constitutionality of a federal or state statute on: (1) the Attorney General of the United States and the United States Attorney for the Northern District of Indiana, if a federal statute is challenged; or (2) the Attorney General for the state if a state statute is challenged. IN R USDCTND L.R. 5.1-1(b). Service required under IN R USDCTND L.R. 5.1-1(b) may be made either by certified or registered mail or by emailing it to an address designated by those officials for this purpose. IN R USDCTND L.R. 5.1-1(c).

- *No forfeiture.* A party's failure to file and serve the notice, or the court's failure to certify, does not forfeit a constitutional claim or defense that is otherwise timely asserted. FRCP 5.1(d).

iii. *Index of exhibits.* Any pleading, motion, brief, affidavit, notice, or proposed order, whether filed electronically or by delivering it to the clerk, must: include a separate index identifying and briefly describing each exhibit if there are more than four (4) exhibits. IN R USDCTND L.R. 5-4(a)(8).

iv. *Request for oral argument.* A party may request oral argument on a motion by filing and serving a separate document explaining why oral argument is necessary and estimating how long the court should allow for the argument. IN R USDCTND L.R. 7-5(a)(1). The request must be filed and served with the party's supporting brief, response brief, or reply brief. IN R USDCTND L.R. 7-5(a)(2).

v. *Request for evidentiary hearing.* A party may request an evidentiary hearing by filing and serving a separate document explaining why the hearing is necessary and estimating how long the court should allow for it. IN R USDCTND L.R. 7-5(b)(1).

vi. *Copy of authority.* A copy of any decision, statute, or regulation cited in a motion or brief must be attached to the paper if—and only if—it is not available on Westlaw or Lexis. But if a copy of a decision, statute, or regulation is only available electronically, a party must provide it to the court or another party upon request. IN R USDCTND L.R. 7-1(f).

vii. *Proposed order.* Parties filing a paper that requires the judge or clerk to enter a routine or uncontested order must include a suitable form of order. IN R USDCTND L.R. 5-4(c).

- Proposed orders shall not be filed electronically either as a separate document or as an attachment to the main pleading or other document. Instead, all proposed orders must be e-mailed to the chambers of the appropriate judicial officer for the case. The proposed order must be in WordPerfect Format or Rich Text Format (RTF). Proposed orders should be attached to an e-mail and sent to the appropriate judicial officer at the address listed in IN R USDCTND CM/ECF(II)(F). The subject line of the email message should indicate the case title, cause number and document number of the motion, e.g., Smith v. Jones 1:02-cv-1234, motion# ___. IN R USDCTND CM/ECF(II)(F).

viii. *Copy of document with self-addressed envelope.* A party who wants a file-stamped copy of a paper must include with the filing an additional copy of the paper and a self-addressed envelope with adequate postage. IN R USDCTND L.R. 5-4(b)(6).

ix. *Notice of manual filing.* However, if that is not physically possible, counsel shall electronically file a .pdf document titled Notice of Manual Filing as a notation on the docket sheet that filings are being held in the clerk's office in paper. A sample Notice of Manual Filing is attached as Form 2 (IN R USDCTND CM/ECF(Form 2)). IN R USDCTND CM/ECF(III)(A)(1).

    x.   *Courtesy copies.* If documents are filed in paper format, counsel must provide an original for the clerk's office, a copy for the judge and a copy must be served on all parties in the case. IN R USDCTND CM/ECF(III)(A)(1).

   xi.   *Declaration that party was unable to file in a timely manner.* If the attorney is unable to file a document in a timely manner due to technical difficulties in the user's system, the attorney must file a document with the court as soon as possible notifying the court of the inability to file the document. A sample document entitled Declaration that Party was Unable to File in a Timely Manner Due to Technical Difficulties is attached hereto as Form 5. IN R USDCTND CM/ECF(VI)(B). [Editor's note: the reference to Form 5 is likely meant to be a reference to Form 3 (IN R USDCTND CM/ECF(Form 3)].

2.   *Documents for opposing party*

   a.   *Required documents*

      i.   *Response brief.* Refer to the Format section of this document for the format of briefs. Refer to the General Requirements section of this document for information on the opposing papers.

     ii.   *Certificate of service.* FRCP 5(d) requires that the person making service under FRCP 5 certify that service has been effected. FRCP 5(Advisory Committee Notes). Having such information on file may be useful for many purposes, including proof of service if an issue arises concerning the effectiveness of the service. FRCP 5(Advisory Committee Notes).

         •   *Certificate of service for electronically-filed documents.* A Certificate of Service is still a requirement when filing documents electronically. A sample Certificate of Service is attached as Form 1 (IN R USDCTND CM/ECF(Form 1)). IN R USDCTND CM/ECF(II)(H).

   b.   *Supplemental documents*

      i.   *Supporting evidence.* When a motion relies on facts outside the record, the court may hear the matter on affidavits or may hear it wholly or partly on oral testimony or on depositions. FRCP 43(c).

         •   *Materials necessary for motion.* A party must file those portions of discovery requests or responses (including deposition transcripts) that the party relies on to support a motion that could result in a final order on an issue. IN R USDCTND L.R. 26-2(c).

     ii.   *Notice of constitutional question.* A party that files a pleading, written motion, or other paper drawing into question the constitutionality of a federal or state statute must promptly:

         •   *File notice.* File a notice of constitutional question stating the question and identifying the paper that raises it, if: (1) a federal statute is questioned and the parties do not include the United States, one of its agencies, or one of its officers or employees in an official capacity; or (2) a state statute is questioned and the parties do not include the state, one of its agencies, or one of its officers or employees in an official capacity; and

         •   *Serve notice.* Serve the notice and paper on the Attorney General of the United States if a federal statute is questioned—or on the state attorney general if a state statute is questioned—either by certified or registered mail or by sending it to an electronic address designated by the attorney general for this purpose. FRCP 5.1(a).

         •   *When to file the notice.* A party required to file a notice of constitutional question under FRCP 5.1 must do so by the later of: (1) the day the parties tender their proposed case-management plan (if one is required); or (2) 21 days after filing the pleading, written motion, or other paper questioning the constitutionality of a federal or state statute. IN R USDCTND L.R. 5.1-1(a).

         •   *Service on government officials.* The party must also serve the notice and the pleading, written motion, or other paper questioning the constitutionality of a federal or state statute on: (1) the Attorney General of the United States and the United States Attorney for the

Northern District of Indiana, if a federal statute is challenged; or (2) the Attorney General for the state if a state statute is challenged. IN R USDCTND L.R. 5.1-1(b). Service required under IN R USDCTND L.R. 5.1-1(b) may be made either by certified or registered mail or by emailing it to an address designated by those officials for this purpose. IN R USDCTND L.R. 5.1-1(c).

- *No forfeiture.* A party's failure to file and serve the notice, or the court's failure to certify, does not forfeit a constitutional claim or defense that is otherwise timely asserted. FRCP 5.1(d).

iii. *Index of exhibits.* Any pleading, motion, brief, affidavit, notice, or proposed order, whether filed electronically or by delivering it to the clerk, must: include a separate index identifying and briefly describing each exhibit if there are more than four (4) exhibits. IN R USDCTND L.R. 5-4(a)(8).

iv. *Request for oral argument.* A party may request oral argument on a motion by filing and serving a separate document explaining why oral argument is necessary and estimating how long the court should allow for the argument. IN R USDCTND L.R. 7-5(a)(1). The request must be filed and served with the party's supporting brief, response brief, or reply brief. IN R USDCTND L.R. 7-5(a)(2).

v. *Request for evidentiary hearing.* A party may request an evidentiary hearing by filing and serving a separate document explaining why the hearing is necessary and estimating how long the court should allow for it. IN R USDCTND L.R. 7-5(b)(1).

vi. *Copy of authority.* A copy of any decision, statute, or regulation cited in a motion or brief must be attached to the paper if—and only if—it is not available on Westlaw or Lexis. But if a copy of a decision, statute, or regulation is only available electronically, a party must provide it to the court or another party upon request. IN R USDCTND L.R. 7-1(f).

vii. *Copy of document with self-addressed envelope.* A party who wants a file-stamped copy of a paper must include with the filing an additional copy of the paper and a self-addressed envelope with adequate postage. IN R USDCTND L.R. 5-4(b)(6).

viii. *Notice of manual filing.* However, if that is not physically possible, counsel shall electronically file a .pdf document titled Notice of Manual Filing as a notation on the docket sheet that filings are being held in the clerk's office in paper. A sample Notice of Manual Filing is attached as Form 2 (IN R USDCTND CM/ECF(Form 2)). IN R USDCTND CM/ECF(III)(A)(1).

ix. *Courtesy copies.* If documents are filed in paper format, counsel must provide an original for the clerk's office, a copy for the judge and a copy must be served on all parties in the case. IN R USDCTND CM/ECF(III)(A)(1).

x. *Declaration that party was unable to file in a timely manner.* If the attorney is unable to file a document in a timely manner due to technical difficulties in the user's system, the attorney must file a document with the court as soon as possible notifying the court of the inability to file the document. A sample document entitled Declaration that Party was Unable to File in a Timely Manner Due to Technical Difficulties is attached hereto as Form 5. IN R USDCTND CM/ECF(VI)(B). [Editor's note: the reference to Form 5 is likely meant to be a reference to Form 3 (IN R USDCTND CM/ECF(Form 3))].

E. Format

1. *Form of documents.* The rules governing captions and other matters of form in pleadings apply to motions and other papers. FRCP 7(b)(2).

   a. *Paper.* Any pleading, motion, brief, affidavit, notice, or proposed order, whether filed electronically or by delivering it to the clerk, must: use eight and one-half by eleven (8-1/2 x 11) inch pages. IN R USDCTND L.R. 5-4(a)(2).

      i. *Manual filings.* Papers delivered to the clerk for filing must: be flat, unfolded, and on good-quality, white paper. IN R USDCTND L.R. 5-4(b)(1)(A).

      - *Covers or backing.* Papers delivered to the clerk for filing must: not have a cover or a back. IN R USDCTND L.R. 5-4(b)(1)(B).

- *Recycled paper.* The court encourages using recycled paper. IN R USDCTND L.R. 5-4(b)(7).

b. *Margins.* Any pleading, motion, brief, affidavit, notice, or proposed order, whether filed electronically or by delivering it to the clerk, must: have at least one (1) inch margins. IN R USDCTND L.R. 5-4(a)(3).

c. *Spacing.* Any pleading, motion, brief, affidavit, notice, or proposed order, whether filed electronically or by delivering it to the clerk, must: be double spaced (except for headings, footnotes, and quoted material). IN R USDCTND L.R. 5-4(a)(5).

d. *Text.* Any pleading, motion, brief, affidavit, notice, or proposed order, whether filed electronically or by delivering it to the clerk, must: be plainly typewritten, printed, or prepared by a clearly legible copying process. IN R USDCTND L.R. 5-4(a)(1).

  i. Any pleading, motion, brief, affidavit, notice, or proposed order, whether filed electronically or by delivering it to the clerk, must: use at least twelve (12) point type in the body and at least ten (10) point type in footnotes. IN R USDCTND L.R. 5-4(a)(4).

e. *Page numbering.* Any pleading, motion, brief, affidavit, notice, or proposed order, whether filed electronically or by delivering it to the clerk, must: have consecutively numbered pages. IN R USDCTND L.R. 5-4(a)(6).

f. *Caption; Names of parties.* Every pleading must have a caption with the court's name, a title, a file number, and a FRCP 7(a) designation. The title of the complaint must name all the parties; the title of other pleadings, after naming the first party on each side, may refer generally to other parties. FRCP 10(a). Any pleading, motion, brief, affidavit, notice, or proposed order, whether filed electronically or by delivering it to the clerk, must: include a title on the first page. IN R USDCTND L.R. 5-4(a)(7).

  i. *Alternative motions.* Motions must be filed separately, but alternative motions may be filed in a single paper if each is named in the title following the caption. IN R USDCTND L.R. 7-1(a).

g. *Filer's information.* Any pleading, motion, brief, affidavit, notice, or proposed order, whether filed electronically or by delivering it to the clerk, must: except in proposed orders and affidavits, include the filer's name, address, telephone number, fax number (where available), and e-mail address (where available). IN R USDCTND L.R. 5-4(a)(9).

h. *Paragraphs; Separate statements.* A party must state its claims or defenses in numbered paragraphs, each limited as far as practicable to a single set of circumstances. A later pleading may refer by number to a paragraph in an earlier pleading. If doing so would promote clarity, each claim founded on a separate transaction or occurrence—and each defense other than a denial—must be stated in a separate count or defense. FRCP 10(b).

i. *Adoption by reference; Exhibits.* A statement in a pleading may be adopted by reference elsewhere in the same pleading or in any other pleading or motion. A copy of a written instrument that is an exhibit to a pleading is a part of the pleading for all purposes. FRCP 10(c).

j. *Citation of local rules.* The Local Civil Rules of the United States District Court for the Northern District of Indiana may be cited as "N.D. Ind. L.R." IN R USDCTND L.R. 1-1(a)(1).

k. *Acceptance by the clerk.* The clerk must not refuse to file a paper solely because it is not in the form prescribed by the Federal Rules of Civil Procedure or by a local rule or practice. FRCP 5(d)(4).

  i. *Sanctions for formatting errors; Non-compliance.* If a person files a paper that does not comply with the rules governing the format of papers filed with the court, the court may: (1) strike the paper from the record; or (2) fine the person up to one thousand dollars ($1,000). IN R USDCTND L.R. 1-3(a).

    - *Notice.* Before sanctioning a person under IN R USDCTND L.R. 1-3(a)(2), the court must: (1) notify the person that the paper is noncompliant; and (2) give the person the opportunity either to be heard or to revise the paper. IN R USDCTND L.R. 1-3(b).

2. *Form of electronic documents.* Electronically filed documents must meet the same requirements of format and page limits as documents "conventionally filed" (as defined in IN R USDCTND CM/ECF(III)(A))

pursuant to the Federal Rules of Civil Procedure and the Local Civil Rules of the United States District Court for the Northern District of Indiana. IN R USDCTND CM/ECF(II)(A)(2).

a. *PDF format required.* Documents filed in the CM/ECF must be in .pdf format. A document created with almost any word-processing program can be converted to .pdf format. The .pdf program in effect takes a picture of the original document and allows anyone to open the converted document across a broad range of hardware and software, with layout, format, links, and images intact. IN R USDCTND CM/ECF(FN2).

b. *Title of documents.* The person electronically filing a pleading or other document will be responsible for designating a title for the pleading or other document by using one of the categories contained in the events listed in the CM/ECF Menu. IN R USDCTND CM/ECF(II)(G).

c. *Combining documents.* All documents which form part of a single pleading and which are being filed at the same time and by the same party may be electronically filed together under one document number, e.g., the motion and a supporting affidavit, with the exception of memoranda in support. Memoranda in support shall be electronically filed separately and shown as a related document to the motion. IN R USDCTND CM/ECF(II)(A)(4).

d. *Exhibits and attachments.* Filing users must submit in electronic form all documents referenced as exhibits or attachments, unless the court permits conventional filing. A filing user must submit as exhibits or attachments only those excerpts of the referenced documents that are directly germane to the matter under consideration by the court. Excerpted material must be clearly and prominently identified as such. Filing users who file excerpts of documents as exhibits or attachments do so without prejudice to their right to timely file additional excerpts or the complete document. Responding parties may timely file additional excerpts or the complete document that they believe are directly germane. The court may require parties to file additional excerpts or the complete document. IN R USDCTND CM/ECF(II)(A)(6).

e. *Hyperlinks.* Electronically filed documents may contain hyperlink references to an external document as a convenient mechanism for accessing material cited in the document. A hyperlink reference is neither validated for content nor considered a part of the court's records. The court neither endorses the product or organization at the destination of a hyperlink reference, nor does the court exercise any responsibility over the content at the destination. In order to preserve the integrity of the court record, attorneys wishing to insert hyperlinks in court filings shall continue to use the traditional citation method for the cited authority, in addition to the hyperlink. A hyperlink contained in a filing is no more than a convenient mechanism for accessing material cited in the document and a hyperlink reference is extraneous to any filed document and is not part of the court's record. IN R USDCTND CM/ECF(II)(A)(3).

3. *Form of briefs*

   a. *Page limits.* Supporting and response briefs (excluding tables of contents, tables of authorities, and appendices) ordinarily must not exceed twenty-five (25) pages. Reply briefs must not exceed fifteen (15) pages. IN R USDCTND L.R. 7-1(e)(1).

      i. *Exception.* The court may allow a party to file a brief exceeding these page limits for extraordinary and compelling reasons. But if the court permits a brief to exceed twenty-five (25) pages, it must include:

         • A table of contents with page references;

         • An issue statement; and

         • A table of authorities including: (1) all cases (alphabetically arranged), statutes, and other authorities cited in the brief; and (2) references to where the authorities appear in the brief. IN R USDCTND L.R. 7-1(e)(2).

4. *Signing disclosures and discovery requests, responses, and objections.* FRCP 11 does not apply to disclosures and discovery requests, responses, objections, and motions under FRCP 26 through FRCP 37. FRCP 11(d).

   a. *Signature required.* Every disclosure under FRCP 26(a)(1) or FRCP 26(a)(3) and every discovery request, response, or objection must be signed by at least one attorney of record in the attorney's own name—or by the party personally, if unrepresented—and must state the signer's address, e-mail address, and telephone number. FRCP 26(g)(1).

   i. *Signatures on manual filings.* Papers delivered to the clerk for filing must: include the filer's original signature. IN R USDCTND L.R. 5-4(b)(1)(C).

- *Rubber-stamped and faxed signatures.* An original paper with a rubber-stamped or faxed signature is unsigned for purposes of FRCP 11 and FRCP 26(g). IN R USDCTND L.R. 5-4(b)(2).

- *Affidavits.* Only the affiant need sign an affidavit. IN R USDCTND L.R. 5-4(b)(3).

   ii. *Electronic signatures.* Pursuant to FRCP 11, every pleading, motion, and other paper (except lists, schedules, statements or amendments thereto) shall be signed by at least one attorney of record or, if the party is not represented by an attorney, all papers shall be signed by the party. An attorney's/participant's password issued by the court combined with the user's identification, serves as and constitutes the attorney/participant's signature for FRCP 11 and other purposes. IN R USDCTND CM/ECF(I)(C). Documents which must be filed and which must contain original signatures other than those of a participating attorney or which require either verification or an unsworn declaration under any rule or statute, shall be filed electronically, with originally executed copies maintained by the filer. The pleading or other document electronically filed shall contain "s/" signature(s), as noted in IN R USDCTND CM/ECF(II)(E)(3)(b). IN R USDCTND CM/ECF(II)(E)(1).

- *Multiple signatures.* In the case of a stipulation or other document to be signed by two or more attorneys, the following procedure should be used: The filing attorney shall initially confirm that the content of the document is acceptable to all persons required to sign the document and shall obtain the physical signatures of all attorneys on the document. IN R USDCTND CM/ECF(II)(E)(3)(a). The filing attorney then shall file the document electronically, indicating the signatories, e.g., "s/Jane Doe," "s/John Doe," etc. IN R USDCTND CM/ECF(II)(E)(3)(b). The filing attorney shall retain the hard copy of the document containing the original signatures. IN R USDCTND CM/ECF(II)(E)(3)(c).

  b. *Effect of signature.* By signing, an attorney or party certifies that to the best of the person's knowledge, information, and belief formed after a reasonable inquiry:

   i. With respect to a disclosure, it is complete and correct as of the time it is made; and

   ii. With respect to a discovery request, response, or objection, it is:

- Consistent with the Federal Rules of Civil Procedure and warranted by existing law or by a nonfrivolous argument for extending, modifying, or reversing existing law, or for establishing new law;

- Not interposed for any improper purpose, such as to harass, cause unnecessary delay, or needlessly increase the cost of litigation; and

- Neither unreasonable nor unduly burdensome or expensive, considering the needs of the case, prior discovery in the case, the amount in controversy, and the importance of the issues at stake in the action. FRCP 26(g)(1).

  c. *Failure to sign.* Other parties have no duty to act on an unsigned disclosure, request, response, or objection until it is signed, and the court must strike it unless a signature is promptly supplied after the omission is called to the attorney's or party's attention. FRCP 26(g)(2).

  d. *Sanction for improper certification.* If a certification violates FRCP 26(g) without substantial justification, the court, on motion or on its own, must impose an appropriate sanction on the signer, the party on whose behalf the signer was acting, or both. The sanction may include an order to pay the reasonable expenses, including attorney's fees, caused by the violation. FRCP 26(g)(3). Refer to the United States District Court for the Northern District of Indiana KeyRules Motion for Discovery Sanctions document for more information.

5. *Privacy protection for filings made with the court*

  a. *Redacted filings.* Counsel should not include sensitive information in any document filed with the court unless such inclusion is necessary and relevant to the case. IN R USDCTND CM/ECF(VII). Unless the court orders otherwise, in an electronic or paper filing with the court that contains an individual's Social Security number, taxpayer-identification number, or birth date, the name of an individual known to be a minor, or a financial-account number, a party or nonparty making the filing may include only:

    i.   The last four (4) digits of the Social Security number and taxpayer-identification number;

    ii.   The year of the individual's birth;

    iii.   The minor's initials; and

    iv.   The last four (4) digits of the financial-account number. FRCP 5.2(a); IN R USDCTND Order 2005-3.

b.   *Exemptions from the redaction requirement.* The redaction requirement does not apply to the following:

    i.   A financial-account number that identifies the property allegedly subject to forfeiture in a forfeiture proceeding;

    ii.   The record of an administrative or agency proceeding;

    iii.   The official record of a state-court proceeding;

    iv.   The record of a court or tribunal, if that record was not subject to the redaction requirement when originally filed;

    v.   A filing covered by FRCP 5.2(c) or FRCP 5.2(d); and

    vi.   A pro se filing in an action brought under 28 U.S.C.A. § 2241, 28 U.S.C.A. § 2254, or 28 U.S.C.A. § 2255. FRCP 5.2(b).

    vii.   In cases filed under the Social Security Act, 42 U.S.C.A. § 405(g), there is no need for redaction of any information from the documents filed in the case. IN R USDCTND Order 2005-3.

c.   *Limitations on remote access to electronic files; Social Security appeals and immigration cases.* Unless the court orders otherwise, in an action for benefits under the Social Security Act, and in an action or proceeding relating to an order of removal, to relief from removal, or to immigration benefits or detention, access to an electronic file is authorized as follows:

    i.   The parties and their attorneys may have remote electronic access to any part of the case file, including the administrative record;

    ii.   Any other person may have electronic access to the full record at the courthouse, but may have remote electronic access only to:

       • The docket maintained by the court; and

       • An opinion, order, judgment, or other disposition of the court, but not any other part of the case file or the administrative record. FRCP 5.2(c).

d.   *Filings made under seal.* The court may order that a filing be made under seal without redaction. The court may later unseal the filing or order the person who made the filing to file a redacted version for the public record. FRCP 5.2(d). For information on filing documents under seal, refer to IN R USDCTND L.R. 5-3, IN R USDCTND CM/ECF(IV)(A), and IN R USDCTND ECF Order 2004-19.

e.   *Protective orders.* For good cause, the court may by order in a case:

    i.   Require redaction of additional information; or

    ii.   Limit or prohibit a nonparty's remote electronic access to a document filed with the court. FRCP 5.2(e).

f.   *Option for additional unredacted filing under seal.* A person making a redacted filing may also file an unredacted copy under seal. The court must retain the unredacted copy as part of the record. FRCP 5.2(f); IN R USDCTND Order 2005-3.

    i.   The unredacted version of the document or the reference list shall be retained by the court under

seal as part of the record. This paper shall be retained by the court as part of the record. The court may, however, still require the party to file a redacted copy for the public file. IN R USDCTND Order 2005-3.

g. *Option for filing a reference list.* A filing that contains redacted information may be filed together with a reference list that identifies each item of redacted information and specifies an appropriate identifier that uniquely corresponds to each item listed. The list must be filed under seal and may be amended as of right. Any reference in the case to a listed identifier will be construed to refer to the corresponding item of information. FRCP 5.2(g); IN R USDCTND Order 2005-3.

    i. The unredacted version of the document or the reference list shall be retained by the court under seal as part of the record. This paper shall be retained by the court as part of the record. The court may, however, still require the party to file a redacted copy for the public file. IN R USDCTND Order 2005-3.

h. *Responsibility for redaction.* The responsibility for redacting these personal identifiers rests solely with counsel and the parties. The Clerk will not review each paper for compliance with IN R USDCTND Order 2005-3. IN R USDCTND Order 2005-3.

i. *Waiver of protection of identifiers.* A person waives the protection of FRCP 5.2(a) as to the person's own information by filing it without redaction and not under seal. FRCP 5.2(h).

F. Filing and Service Requirements

1. *Filing requirements.* Any paper after the complaint that is required to be served—together with a certificate of service—must be filed within a reasonable time after service. FRCP 5(d)(1). Motions must be filed separately, but alternative motions may be filed in a single paper if each is named in the title following the caption. IN R USDCTND L.R. 7-1(a).

a. *How filing is made; In general.* A paper is filed by delivering it:

    i. To the clerk; or

    ii. To a judge who agrees to accept it for filing, and who must then note the filing date on the paper and promptly send it to the clerk. FRCP 5(d)(2).

       • Papers not filed electronically must be filed with the clerk, not a judge. IN R USDCTND L.R. 5-4(b)(4).

    iii. Parties manually filing a paper that requires the clerk to give others notice, must give the clerk: (1) sufficient copies of the notice; and (2) the name and address of each person entitled to receive the notice. IN R USDCTND L.R. 5-4(b)(8).

b. *Where to file.* Papers not filed electronically must be filed in the division where the case is pending, unless: (1) a person will be prejudiced if the paper is not filed the same day it is tendered; and (2) it includes an adequately sized envelope addressed to the clerk's office in the division where the case is pending and with adequate postage. IN R USDCTND L.R. 5-4(b)(5).

c. *Electronic filing*

    i. *Authorization of electronic filing program.* A court may, by local rule, allow papers to be filed, signed, or verified by electronic means that are consistent with any technical standards established by the Judicial Conference of the United States. A local rule may require electronic filing only if reasonable exceptions are allowed. A paper filed electronically in compliance with a local rule is a written paper for purposes of the Federal Rules of Civil Procedure. FRCP 5(d)(3).

       • Papers must be filed, signed, and verified electronically unless excepted by the court's CM/ECF Civil and Criminal User Manual (IN R USDCTND CM/ECF). IN R USDCTND L.R. 5-1.

    ii. *Mandatory electronic filing.* Unless otherwise permitted by these procedures or otherwise authorized by the assigned judge, all documents submitted for filing in this district in civil and criminal cases, no matter when a case was originally filed, shall be filed electronically using the System. IN R USDCTND CM/ECF(II)(A)(1). The requirement that "all documents" be filed electronically includes briefs, and attachments and exhibits used in support of motions. IN R USDCTND CM/ECF(FN1).

- Sending a document or pleading to the court via e-mail or facsimile does not constitute "electronic filing." IN R USDCTND CM/ECF(I)(A).

   iii. *Conventional filing.* As used in these procedures, a "conventionally" filed or submitted document or pleading is one presented to the Clerk or a party in paper or other non-electronic, tangible format. The following documents shall be filed conventionally and not electronically unless specifically authorized by the Court:

- Exhibits and other documents which cannot be converted to a legible electronic form. Whenever possible, counsel is responsible for converting filings to an electronic form. However, if that is not physically possible, counsel shall electronically file a .pdf document titled Notice of Manual Filing as a notation on the docket sheet that filings are being held in the clerk's office in paper. A sample Notice of Manual Filing is attached as Form 2 (IN R USDCTND CM/ECF(Form 2)). If documents are filed in paper format, counsel must provide an original for the clerk's office, a copy for the judge and a copy must be served on all parties in the case. Large documents which do not exist in an electronic format shall be scanned into .pdf format by counsel, in small batches if necessary, and filed electronically as separate attachments in the System. IN R USDCTND CM/ECF(III)(A)(1).

- Certain documents which are listed in IN R USDCTND CM/ECF(II)(E)(2). IN R US-DCTND CM/ECF(III)(A)(2).

- Documents filed by pro se litigants. IN R USDCTND CM/ECF(III)(A)(3).

   iv. For more information on electronic filing, refer to IN R USDCTND CM/ECF.

2. *Service requirements*

  a. *Service; When required*

    i. *In general.* Unless the Federal Rules of Civil Procedure provide otherwise, each of the following papers must be served on every party:

- An order stating that service is required;

- A pleading filed after the original complaint, unless the court orders otherwise under FRCP 5(c) because there are numerous defendants;

- A discovery paper required to be served on a party, unless the court orders otherwise;

- A written motion, except one that may be heard ex parte; and

- A written notice, appearance, demand, or offer of judgment, or any similar paper. FRCP 5(a)(1).

    ii. *If a party fails to appear.* No service is required on a party who is in default for failing to appear. But a pleading that asserts a new claim for relief against such a party must be served on that party under FRCP 4. FRCP 5(a)(2).

    iii. *Seizing property.* If an action is begun by seizing property and no person is or need be named as a defendant, any service required before the filing of an appearance, answer, or claim must be made on the person who had custody or possession of the property when it was seized. FRCP 5(a)(3).

  b. *Service; How made*

    i. *Serving an attorney.* If a party is represented by an attorney, service under FRCP 5 must be made on the attorney unless the court orders service on the party. FRCP 5(b)(1).

    ii. *Service in general.* A paper is served under FRCP 5 by:

- Handing it to the person;

- Leaving it: (1) at the person's office with a clerk or other person in charge or, if no one is in charge, in a conspicuous place in the office; or (2) if the person has no office or the office is closed, at the person's dwelling or usual place of abode with someone of suitable age and discretion who resides there;

- Mailing it to the person's last known address—in which event service is complete upon mailing;

- Leaving it with the court clerk if the person has no known address;

- Sending it by electronic means if the person consented in writing—in which event service is complete upon transmission, but is not effective if the serving party learns that it did not reach the person to be served; or

- Delivering it by any other means that the person consented to in writing—in which event service is complete when the person making service delivers it to the agency designated to make delivery. FRCP 5(b)(2).

   iii. *Electronic service.* Electronically filed papers may be served electronically if service is consistent with the CM/ECF User Manual (IN R USDCTND CM/ECF). IN R USDCTND L.R. 5-2(a).

- *Waiver of other service.* An attorney's registration will constitute a waiver of conventional service of documents and the attorney agrees to accept service of notice on behalf of the client of the electronic filing by hand, facsimile or authorized email. IN R USDCTND CM/ECF(I)(B)(3).

- *Serving registered persons.* The System will generate a "Notice of Electronic Filing" when any document is filed. This notice represents service of the document on parties who are registered participants with the System. Except as provided in IN R USDCTND CM/ECF(III)(B), the filing party shall not be required to serve any pleading or other documents on any party receiving electronic notice. IN R USDCTND CM/ECF(II)(D)(1). The term "pleading" refers only to those documents listed in FRCP 7(a). IN R USDCTND CM/ECF(FN3).

- *When electronic service is deemed completed.* A person registered to use the court's electronic-filing system is served with an electronically filed paper when a "Notice of Electronic Filing" is transmitted to that person through the court's electronic filing-system. IN R USDCTND L.R. 5-2(b).

- *Serving non-registered persons.* A person who has not registered to use the court's electronic-filing system but who is entitled to service of a paper must be served according to the Local Civil Rules of the United States District Court for the Northern District of Indiana and the Federal Rules of Civil Procedure. IN R USDCTND L.R. 5-2(c); IN R USDCTND CM/ECF(II)(D)(2). If such service of a paper copy is to be made, it shall be done in the manner provided in the Federal Rules of Civil Procedure and the Local Civil Rules of the United States District Court for the Northern District of Indiana. IN R USDCTND CM/ECF(II)(D)(2).

   iv. *Service of conventional filings.* Pleadings or other documents which are filed conventionally rather than electronically shall be served in the manner provided for in the Federal Rules of Civil Procedure and the Local Civil Rules of the United States District Court for the Northern District of Indiana, except as otherwise provided by order of the Court. IN R USDCTND CM/ECF(III)(B).

   v. *Using court facilities.* If a local rule so authorizes, a party may use the court's transmission facilities to make service under FRCP 5(b)(2)(E). FRCP 5(b)(3).

c. *Serving numerous defendants*

   i. *In general.* If an action involves an unusually large number of defendants, the court may, on motion or on its own, order that:

- Defendants' pleadings and replies to them need not be served on other defendants;

- Any crossclaim, counterclaim, avoidance, or affirmative defense in those pleadings and replies to them will be treated as denied or avoided by all other parties; and

- Filing any such pleading and serving it on the plaintiff constitutes notice of the pleading to all parties. FRCP 5(c)(1).

    ii. *Notifying parties.* A copy of every such order must be served on the parties as the court directs. FRCP 5(c)(2).

G. Hearings

1. *Hearings, generally*

    a. *Oral argument.* Due process does not require that oral argument be permitted on a motion and, except as otherwise provided by local rule, the district court has discretion to determine whether it will decide the motion on the papers or hear argument by counsel (and perhaps receive evidence). FPP § 1190; F.D.I.C. v. Deglau, 207 F.3d 153 (3d Cir. 2000).

        i. *Request for oral argument.* A party may request oral argument on a motion by filing and serving a separate document explaining why oral argument is necessary and estimating how long the court should allow for the argument. IN R USDCTND L.R. 7-5(a)(1). Refer to the Documents section of this document for more information.

        ii. *Additional evidence forbidden.* Parties may not present additional evidence at oral argument. IN R USDCTND L.R. 7-5(a)(3).

    b. *Providing a regular schedule for oral hearings.* A court may establish regular times and places for oral hearings on motions. FRCP 78(a).

    c. *Providing for submission on briefs.* By rule or order, the court may provide for submitting and determining motions on briefs, without oral hearings. FRCP 78(b).

    d. *Evidentiary hearings.* A party may request an evidentiary hearing by filing and serving a separate document explaining why the hearing is necessary and estimating how long the court should allow for it. IN R USDCTND L.R. 7-5(b)(2). Refer to the Documents section of this document for more information.

    e. *Court's authority.* The court may: (1) grant or deny a request for oral argument or an evidentiary hearing in its discretion; (2) set oral argument or an evidentiary hearing without a request from a party; or (3) order any oral argument or evidentiary hearing to be held anywhere within the district regardless of where the case will be tried. IN R USDCTND L.R. 7-5(c).

2. *Courtroom and courthouse decorum.* For information on courtroom and courthouse decorum, refer to IN R USDCTND L.R. 83-3.

H. Forms

1. Federal Motion to Compel Discovery Forms

    a. Notice of motion; To compel required disclosure of names and addresses of witnesses and persons having knowledge of the claims involved; Civil proceeding. AMJUR PP DEPOSITION § 6.

    b. Motion; To compel required disclosure of names and addresses of witnesses and persons having knowledge of the claims involved. AMJUR PP DEPOSITION § 7.

    c. Motion; To compel answer to interrogatories; Complete failure to answer. AMJUR PP DEPOSITION § 403.

    d. Affidavit; In opposition of motion to compel psychiatric or physical examinations; By attorney. AMJUR PP DEPOSITION § 645.

    e. Motion; To compel further responses to interrogatories; Various grounds. AMJUR PP DEPOSITION § 713.

    f. Affidavit; In support of motion to compel answers to interrogatories and to impose sanctions. AMJUR PP DEPOSITION § 715.

    g. Opposition; To motion to compel electronic discovery; Federal class action. AMJUR PP DEPOSITION § 721.

    h. Notice of motion; For order to compel compliance with request to permit entry on real property for inspection. AMJUR PP DEPOSITION § 733.

    i.   Motion; To compel production of documents; After rejected request; Request for sanctions. AMJUR PP DEPOSITION § 734.

    j.   Affidavit; In support of motion to compel production of documents; By attorney. AMJUR PP DEPOSITION § 736.

    k.   Motion; To compel doctor's production of medical records for trial. AMJUR PP DEPOSITION § 744.

    l.   Notice of motion to compel party to answer deposition questions. 3B FEDFORMS § 3695.

    m.   Motion to compel deposition, request for sanctions and request for expedited hearing. 3B FEDFORMS § 3698.

    n.   Motion to compel answer to interrogatories. 3B FEDFORMS § 3699.

    o.   Affidavit in support of motion. 3B FEDFORMS § 3702.

    p.   Objection to motion for order requiring witness to answer oral questions on deposition. 3B FEDFORMS § 3705.

    q.   Motion; To compel answers to outstanding discovery requests. FEDPROF § 23:43.

    r.   Motion; To compel required disclosure of names and addresses of witnesses and persons having knowledge of the claims involved. FEDPROF § 23:44.

    s.   Motion; To compel answer to questions asked on oral or written examination. FEDPROF § 23:207.

    t.   Motion; To compel further answers to questions asked on oral or written examination and to award expenses of motion. FEDPROF § 23:208.

    u.   Motion; To compel party to produce witness at deposition. FEDPROF § 23:209.

    v.   Affidavit; By opposing attorney; In opposition to motion to compel answers asked at deposition; Answers tend to incriminate. FEDPROF § 23:212.

    w.   Motion; To compel answer to interrogatories; Complete failure to answer. FEDPROF § 23:375.

    x.   Motion; To compel further responses to interrogatories; Various grounds. FEDPROF § 23:376.

    y.   Motion to compel discovery. GOLDLTGFMS § 21:2.

2. Forms for the Northern District of Indiana

    a.   Certificate of service. IN R USDCTND CM/ECF(Form 1).

    b.   Notice of manual filing. IN R USDCTND CM/ECF(Form 2).

    c.   Declaration that party was unable to file in a timely manner. IN R USDCTND CM/ECF(Form 3).

I. Applicable Rules

1. *Federal rules*

    a.   Serving and filing pleadings and other papers. FRCP 5.

    b.   Constitutional challenge to a statute; Notice, certification, and intervention. FRCP 5.1.

    c.   Privacy protection for filings made with the court. FRCP 5.2.

    d.   Computing and extending time; Time for motion papers. FRCP 6.

    e.   Pleadings allowed; Form of motions and other papers. FRCP 7.

    f.   Form of pleadings. FRCP 10.

    g.   Signing pleadings, motions, and other papers; Representations to the court; Sanctions. FRCP 11.

    h.   Duty to disclose; General provisions governing discovery. FRCP 26.

    i.   Failure to make disclosures or to cooperate in discovery; Sanctions. FRCP 37.

    j.   Taking testimony. FRCP 43.

    k.   Hearing motions; Submission on briefs. FRCP 78.

2. *Local rules*

   a. Citation and scope of the rules. IN R USDCTND L.R. 1-1.

   b. Sanctions for formatting errors. IN R USDCTND L.R. 1-3.

   c. Electronic filing required. IN R USDCTND L.R. 5-1.

   d. Constitutional questions. IN R USDCTND L.R. 5.1-1.

   e. Electronic service. IN R USDCTND L.R. 5-2.

   f. Format of papers. IN R USDCTND L.R. 5-4.

   g. Motion practice. IN R USDCTND L.R. 7-1.

   h. Oral arguments and evidentiary hearings. IN R USDCTND L.R. 7-5.

   i. Pretrial procedure. IN R USDCTND L.R. 16-1.

   j. Alternative dispute resolution. IN R USDCTND L.R. 16-6.

   k. Filing of discovery and other materials. IN R USDCTND L.R. 26-2.

   l. Resolving discovery disputes. IN R USDCTND L.R. 37-1.

   m. Case assignment. IN R USDCTND L.R. 40-1.

   n. Appearance and withdrawal of appearance. IN R USDCTND L.R. 83-8.

   o. CM/ECF civil and criminal user manual. IN R USDCTND CM/ECF.

   p. In re: privacy and public access to civil electronic case files. IN R USDCTND Order 2005-3.

Motions, Oppositions and Replies
Motion for Protective Order

Document Last Updated December 2016

A. **Checklist**

(I) ❑ Matters to be considered by moving party

  (a) ❑ Required documents

    (1) ❑ Notice of motion and motion

    (2) ❑ Certificate of compliance

    (3) ❑ Discovery materials

    (4) ❑ Certificate of service

  (b) ❑ Supplemental documents

    (1) ❑ Brief

    (2) ❑ Supporting evidence

    (3) ❑ Notice of constitutional question

    (4) ❑ Nongovernmental corporate disclosure statement

    (5) ❑ Index of exhibits

    (6) ❑ Request for oral argument

    (7) ❑ Request for evidentiary hearing

    (8) ❑ Copy of authority

    (9) ❑ Proposed order

    (10) ❑ Copy of document with self-addressed envelope

    (11) ❑ Notice of manual filing

       (12) ❑ Courtesy copies

       (13) ❑ Declaration that party was unable to file in a timely manner

   (c) ❑ Timing

       (1) ❑ Although a party or deponent is allowed a reasonable amount of time in which to apply for a protective order, a protective order, as a general rule, must be obtained before the date set for the discovery; motions for a protective order must be made before or on the date the discovery is due

       (2) ❑ A written motion and notice of the hearing must be served at least fourteen (14) days before the time specified for the hearing, with the following exceptions: (i) when the motion may be heard ex parte; (ii) when the Federal Rules of Civil Procedure set a different time; or (iii) when a court order—which a party may, for good cause, apply for ex parte—sets a different time

       (3) ❑ Any affidavit supporting a motion must be served with the motion

(II) ❑ Matters to be considered by opposing party

   (a) ❑ Required documents

       (1) ❑ Response brief

       (2) ❑ Certificate of service

   (b) ❑ Supplemental documents

       (1) ❑ Supporting evidence

       (2) ❑ Notice of constitutional question

       (3) ❑ Index of exhibits

       (4) ❑ Request for oral argument

       (5) ❑ Request for evidentiary hearing

       (6) ❑ Copy of authority

       (7) ❑ Copy of document with self-addressed envelope

       (8) ❑ Notice of manual filing

       (9) ❑ Courtesy copies

       (10) ❑ Declaration that party was unable to file in a timely manner

   (c) ❑ Timing

       (1) ❑ A party must file any response brief to a motion within fourteen (14) days after the motion is served

       (2) ❑ Except as FRCP 59(c) provides otherwise, any opposing affidavit must be served at least seven (7) days before the hearing, unless the court permits service at another time

B. Timing

1. *Motion for protective order.* The express language of FRCP 26(c) does not set out time limits within which a motion for a protective order must be made; yet that requirement remains an implicit condition for obtaining a protective order. FEDPROC § 26:296. Although a party or deponent is allowed a reasonable amount of time in which to apply for a protective order, a protective order, as a general rule, must be obtained before the date set for the discovery. Motions for a protective order must be made before or on the date the discovery is due. FEDPROC § 26:296.

2. *Timing of motions, generally*

   a. *Motion and notice of hearing.* A written motion and notice of the hearing must be served at least fourteen (14) days before the time specified for the hearing, with the following exceptions:

      i. When the motion may be heard ex parte;

      ii. When the Federal Rules of Civil Procedure set a different time; or

      iii.   When a court order—which a party may, for good cause, apply for ex parte—sets a different time. FRCP 6(c)(1).

  b. *Supporting affidavit.* Any affidavit supporting a motion must be served with the motion. FRCP 6(c)(2).

3. *Timing of opposing papers.* A party must file any response brief to a motion within fourteen (14) days after the motion is served. IN R USDCTND L.R. 7-1(d)(2)(A).

  a. *Opposing affidavit.* Except as FRCP 59(c) provides otherwise, any opposing affidavit must be served at least seven (7) days before the hearing, unless the court permits service at another time. FRCP 6(c)(2).

  b. *Extensions.* The court may extend response- and reply-brief deadlines, but only for good cause. IN R USDCTND L.R. 7-1(d)(3).

  c. *Summary rulings.* The court may rule on a motion summarily if an opposing party does not file a response before the deadline. IN R USDCTND L.R. 7-1(d)(4).

4. *Timing of reply papers.* Where the respondent files an answering affidavit setting up a new matter, the moving party ordinarily is allowed a reasonable time to file a reply affidavit since failure to deny the new matter by affidavit may operate as an admission of its truth. AMJUR MOTIONS § 25.

  a. *Reply brief.* The moving party must file any reply brief within seven (7) days after the response brief is served. IN R USDCTND L.R. 7-1(d)(2)(B).

  b. *Extensions.* The court may extend response- and reply-brief deadlines, but only for good cause. IN R USDCTND L.R. 7-1(d)(3).

5. *Computation of time*

  a. *Computing time.* FRCP 6 applies in computing any time period specified in the Federal Rules of Civil Procedure, in any local rule or court order, or in any statute that does not specify a method of computing time. FRCP 6(a).

    i. *Period stated in days or a longer unit.* When the period is stated in days or a longer unit of time:

- Exclude the day of the event that triggers the period;
- Count every day, including intermediate Saturdays, Sundays, and legal holidays; and
- Include the last day of the period, but if the last day is a Saturday, Sunday, or legal holiday, the period continues to run until the end of the next day that is not a Saturday, Sunday, or legal holiday. FRCP 6(a)(1).

    ii. *Period stated in hours.* When the period is stated in hours:

- Begin counting immediately on the occurrence of the event that triggers the period;
- Count every hour, including hours during intermediate Saturdays, Sundays, and legal holidays; and
- If the period would end on a Saturday, Sunday, or legal holiday, the period continues to run until the same time on the next day that is not a Saturday, Sunday, or legal holiday. FRCP 6(a)(2).

    iii. *Inaccessibility of the clerk's office.* Unless the court orders otherwise, if the clerk's office is inaccessible:

- On the last day for filing under FRCP 6(a)(1), then the time for filing is extended to the first accessible day that is not a Saturday, Sunday, or legal holiday; or
- During the last hour for filing under FRCP 6(a)(2), then the time for filing is extended to the same time on the first accessible day that is not a Saturday, Sunday, or legal holiday. FRCP 6(a)(3).

    iv. *"Last day" defined.* Unless a different time is set by a statute, local rule, or court order, the last day ends:

- For electronic filing, at midnight in the court's time zone; and

- For filing by other means, when the clerk's office is scheduled to close. FRCP 6(a)(4).

v. *"Next day" defined.* The "next day" is determined by continuing to count forward when the period is measured after an event and backward when measured before an event. FRCP 6(a)(5).

vi. *"Legal holiday" defined.* "Legal holiday" means:

- The day set aside by statute for observing New Year's Day, Martin Luther King Jr.'s Birthday, Washington's Birthday, Memorial Day, Independence Day, Labor Day, Columbus Day, Veterans' Day, Thanksgiving Day, or Christmas Day;

- Any day declared a holiday by the President or Congress; and

- For periods that are measured after an event, any other day declared a holiday by the state where the district court is located. FRCP 6(a)(6).

b. *Computation of electronic filing deadlines.* Filing documents electronically does not alter any filing deadlines or any time computation pursuant to FRCP 6. The counties of Lake, Porter, LaPorte, Pulaski and Starke are located in the Central time zone and the remaining counties in the Northern District of Indiana are located in the Eastern time zone. Nevertheless, all electronic transmissions of documents must be completed (i.e., received completely by the clerk's office) prior to midnight Eastern Time, (South Bend/Fort Wayne/Lafayette time) in order to be considered timely filed that day, regardless of the local time in the division where the case is pending. Although documents can be filed electronically twenty-four (24) hours a day, filers are strongly encouraged to file all documents during hours when the CM/ECF Help Line is available, from 9:00 a.m. to 4:00 p.m. local time. IN R USDCTND CM/ECF(II)(I).

i. *Technical failures.* If the attorney is unable to file a document in a timely manner due to technical difficulties in the user's system, the attorney must file a document with the court as soon as possible notifying the court of the inability to file the document. A sample document entitled Declaration that Party was Unable to File in a Timely Manner Due to Technical Difficulties is attached hereto as Form 5. IN R USDCTND CM/ECF(VI)(B). [Editor's note: the reference to Form 5 is likely meant to be a reference to Form 3 (IN R USDCTND CM/ECF(Form 3)].

c. *Extending time*

i. *In general.* When an act may or must be done within a specified time, the court may, for good cause, extend the time:

- With or without motion or notice if the court acts, or if a request is made, before the original time or its extension expires; or

- On motion made after the time has expired if the party failed to act because of excusable neglect. FRCP 6(b)(1).

ii. *Exceptions.* A court must not extend the time to act under FRCP 50(b), FRCP 50(d), FRCP 52(b), FRCP 59(b), FRCP 59(d), FRCP 59(e), and FRCP 60(b). FRCP 6(b)(2).

iii. Refer to the United States District Court for the Northern District of Indiana KeyRules Motion for Continuance/Extension of Time document for more information on extending time.

d. *Additional time after certain kinds of service.* When a party may or must act within a specified time after being served and service is made under FRCP 5(b)(2)(C) (mail), FRCP 5(b)(2)(D) (leaving with the clerk), or FRCP 5(b)(2)(F) (other means consented to), three (3) days are added after the period would otherwise expire under FRCP 6(a). FRCP 6(d).

C. General Requirements

1. *Motions, generally*

a. *Requirements.* A request for a court order must be made by motion. The motion must:

i. Be in writing unless made during a hearing or trial;

ii. State with particularity the grounds for seeking the order; and

iii. State the relief sought. FRCP 7(b)(1).

b. *Notice of motion.* A party interested in resisting the relief sought by a motion has a right to notice thereof, and an opportunity to be heard. AMJUR MOTIONS § 12.

    i. In addition to statutory or court rule provisions requiring notice of a motion—the purpose of such a notice requirement having been said to be to prevent a party from being prejudicially surprised by a motion—principles of natural justice dictate that an adverse party generally must be given notice that a motion will be presented to the court. AMJUR MOTIONS § 12.

    ii. "Notice," in this regard, means reasonable notice, including a meaningful opportunity to prepare and to defend against allegations of a motion. AMJUR MOTIONS § 12.

c. *Writing requirement.* The writing requirement is intended to insure that the adverse parties are informed and have a record of both the motion's pendency and the grounds on which the movant seeks an order. FPP § 1191; Feldberg v. Quechee Lakes Corp., 463 F.3d 195 (2d Cir. 2006).

    i. It is sufficient "if the motion is stated in a written notice of the hearing of the motion." FPP § 1191.

d. *Particularity requirement.* The particularity requirement insures that the opposing parties will have notice of their opponent's contentions. FEDPROC § 62:364; Goodman v. 1973 26 Foot Trojan Vessel, Arkansas Registration No. AR1439SN, 859 F.2d 71, 12 Fed.R.Serv.3d 645 (8th Cir. 1988). That requirement ensures that notice of the basis for the motion is provided to the court and to the opposing party so as to avoid prejudice, provide the opponent with a meaningful opportunity to respond, and provide the court with enough information to process the motion correctly. FEDPROC § 62:364; Andreas v. Volkswagen of America, Inc., 336 F.3d 789, 56 Fed.R.Serv.3d 6 (8th Cir. 2003).

    i. Reasonable specification of the grounds for a motion is sufficient. However, where a movant fails to state even one ground for granting the motion in question, the movant has failed to meet the minimal standard of "reasonable specification." FEDPROC § 62:364; Martinez v. Trainor, 556 F.2d 818, 23 Fed.R.Serv.2d 403 (7th Cir. 1977).

    ii. The court may excuse the failure to comply with the particularity requirement if it is inadvertent, and where no prejudice is shown by the opposing party. FEDPROC § 62:364.

e. *Motions must be filed separately.* Motions must be filed separately, but alternative motions may be filed in a single paper if each is named in the title following the caption. IN R USDCTND L.R. 7-1(a).

2. *Motion for protective order.* A party or any person from whom discovery is sought may move for a protective order in the court where the action is pending—or as an alternative on matters relating to a deposition, in the court for the district where the deposition will be taken. FRCP 26(c)(1). FRCP 26(c) was enacted as a safeguard for the protection of parties and witnesses in view of the broad discovery rights authorized by FRCP 26(b). FEDPROC § 26:265; U.S. v. Columbia Broadcasting System, Inc., 666 F.2d 364, 33 Fed.R.Serv.2d 539 (9th Cir. 1982).

a. *Grounds for protective orders.* The court may, for good cause, issue an order to protect a party or person from annoyance, embarrassment, oppression, or undue burden or expense, including one or more of the following:

    i. Forbidding the disclosure or discovery;

    ii. Specifying terms, including time and place or the allocation of expenses, for the disclosure or discovery;

    iii. Prescribing a discovery method other than the one selected by the party seeking discovery;

    iv. Forbidding inquiry into certain matters, or limiting the scope of disclosure or discovery to certain matters;

    v. Designating the persons who may be present while the discovery is conducted;

    vi. Requiring that a deposition be sealed and opened only on court order;

    vii. Requiring that a trade secret or other confidential research, development, or commercial information not be revealed or be revealed only in a specified way; and

    viii. Requiring that the parties simultaneously file specified documents or information in sealed envelopes, to be opened as the court directs. FRCP 26(c)(1).

b. *Third-party protection.* A party may not ask for an order to protect the rights of another party or a witness if that party or witness does not claim protection for himself, but a party may seek an order if it believes its own interest is jeopardized by discovery sought from a third person. FPP § 2035.

c. *Burden.* The party seeking a protective order has the burden of demonstrating that good cause exists for its issuance. FEDPROC § 26:279. The good cause requirement under FRCP 26(c), encompasses a standard of reasonableness. FEDPROC § 26:284.

    i. *Factual demonstration of injury.* The party requesting a protective order must make a specific demonstration of facts in support of the request as opposed to conclusory or speculative statements about the need for a protective order and the harm which will be suffered without one. FEDPROC § 26:282. Such party must demonstrate that failure to issue the order requested will work a clearly defined harm. FEDPROC § 26:282; Cipollone v. Liggett Group, Inc., 822 F.2d 335, 7 Fed.R.Serv.3d 1438 (3d Cir. 1987).

    ii. *Serious injury.* A party seeking a protective order under FRCP 26(c) must demonstrate that failure to issue the order requested will work a very serious injury. FEDPROC § 26:283; Cipollone v. Liggett Group, Inc., 822 F.2d 335, 7 Fed.R.Serv.3d 1438 (3d Cir. 1987).

d. *Application of protective orders.* FRCP 26(c) does not authorize the district court to issue protective orders with respect to data obtained through means other than the court's discovery processes. FEDPROC § 26:271.

    i. *Information not discovered.* FRCP 26(c) does not give the court authority to prohibit disclosure of trade data which was compiled by counsel prior the commencing of a lawsuit. Similarly, material received by one party prior to commencement of an action (and therefore before initiation of any discovery and before a request for protective orders) cannot be made a legitimate part of the corpus of any protective order a court enters. FEDPROC § 26:271.

    ii. *Information discovered in other action.* The trial court lacks the discretion and power to issue a valid protective order to compel the return of documents obtained through discovery in a separate action. FEDPROC § 26:272.

e. *Ordering discovery.* If a motion for a protective order is wholly or partly denied, the court may, on just terms, order that any party or person provide or permit discovery. FRCP 26(c)(2).

f. *Awarding expenses.* FRCP 37(a)(5) applies to the award of expenses. FRCP 26(c)(3). Refer to the United States District Court for the Northern District of Indiana KeyRules Motion for Discovery Sanctions document for more information.

3. *Opposing papers.* The Federal Rules of Civil Procedure do not require any formal answer, return, or reply to a motion, except where the Federal Rules of Civil Procedure or local rules may require affidavits, memoranda, or other papers to be filed in opposition to a motion. Such papers are simply to apprise the court of such opposition and the grounds of that opposition. FEDPROC § 62:359.

a. *Effect of failure to respond to motion.* Although in the absence of statutory provision or court rule, a motion ordinarily does not require a written answer, when a party files a motion and the opposing party fails to respond, the court may construe such failure to respond as nonopposition to the motion or an admission that the motion was meritorious, may take the facts alleged in the motion as true—the rule in some jurisdictions being that the failure to respond to a fact set forth in a motion is deemed an admission—and may grant the motion if the relief requested appears to be justified. AMJUR MOTIONS § 28.

b. *Assent or no opposition not determinative.* However, a motion will not be granted automatically simply because an "assent" or a notation of "no opposition" has been filed; federal judges frequently deny motions that have been assented to when it is thought that justice so dictates. FPP § 1190.

c. *Responsive pleading inappropriate as response to motion.* An attempt to answer or oppose a motion with a responsive pleading usually is not appropriate. FPP § 1190.

4. *Reply papers.* A moving party may be required or permitted to prepare papers in addition to his original motion papers. AMJUR MOTIONS § 25. Papers answering or replying to opposing papers may be appropriate, in the interests of justice, where it appears there is a substantial reason for allowing a reply.

Thus, a court may accept reply papers where a party demonstrates that the papers to which it seeks to file a reply raise new issues that are material to the disposition of the question before the court, or where the court determines, sua sponte, that it wishes further briefing of an issue raised in those papers and orders the submission of additional papers. FEDPROC § 62:360.

a. *Function of reply papers.* The function of a reply affidavit is to answer the arguments made in opposition to the position taken by the movant and not to permit the movant to introduce new arguments in support of the motion. AMJUR MOTIONS § 25.

b. *Issues raised for the first time in a reply document.* However, the view has been followed in some jurisdictions, that as a matter of judicial economy, where there is no prejudice and where the issues could be raised simply by filing a motion to dismiss, the trial court has discretion to consider arguments raised for the first time in a reply memorandum, and that a trial court may grant a motion to strike issues raised for the first time in a reply memorandum. AMJUR MOTIONS § 26.

5. *Appearances.* Attorneys not representing the United States or its agencies must file an appearance when they represent (either in person or by filing a paper) a party. IN R USDCTND L.R. 83-8(a). For more information, refer to IN R USDCTND L.R. 83-8.

6. *Notice of related action.* A party must file a notice of related action as soon as it appears that the party's case and another pending case: (1) arise out of the same transaction or occurrence; (2) involve the same property; or (3) involve the validity or infringement of the same patent, trademark, or copyright. IN R USDCTND L.R. 40-1(d). For more information, refer to IN R USDCTND L.R. 40-1.

7. *Alternative dispute resolution (ADR).* After they confer as required by FRCP 26(f), the parties must advise the court which, if any, alternative-dispute-resolution processes they expect to pursue and when they expect to undertake the process. IN R USDCTND L.R. 16-6(a). For more information on alternative dispute resolution (ADR), refer to IN R USDCTND L.R. 16-6 and IN R USDCTND Order 2003-21.

8. *Settlement or resolution.* The parties must immediately notify the court if they reasonably expect to settle the case or resolve a pending motion. IN R USDCTND L.R. 16-1(g).

9. *Modification or suspension of rules.* The court may, on its own motion or at the request of a party, suspend or modify any rule in a particular case in the interest of justice. IN R USDCTND L.R. 1-1(c).

D. Documents

1. *Documents for moving party*

   a. *Required documents*

      i. *Notice of motion and motion.* The party must not specify a hearing date in the notice of a motion or petition unless the court or the clerk has authorized it. IN R USDCTND L.R. 7-5(b)(2). Refer to the General Requirements section of this document for information on the notice of motion and motion.

      ii. *Certificate of compliance.* A party filing any discovery motion must file a separate certification that the party has conferred in good faith or attempted to confer with other affected parties in an effort to resolve the matter raised in the motion without court action. The certification must include: (1) the date, time, and place of any conference or attempted conference; and (2) the names of the parties participating in the conference. IN R USDCTND L.R. 37-1(a).

         • *Failure to file certification.* The court may deny any motion described in IN R USDCTND L.R. 37-1(a)—except those motions brought by or against a person appearing pro se—if the required certification is not filed. IN R USDCTND L.R. 37-1(b).

      iii. *Discovery materials.* A party who files a motion for relief under FRCP 26(c) or FRCP 37 must file with the motion those parts of the discovery requests or responses that the motion pertains to. IN R USDCTND L.R. 26-2(b).

      iv. *Certificate of service.* FRCP 5(d) requires that the person making service under FRCP 5 certify that service has been effected. FRCP 5(Advisory Committee Notes). Having such information on file may be useful for many purposes, including proof of service if an issue arises concerning the effectiveness of the service. FRCP 5(Advisory Committee Notes).

         • *Certificate of service for electronically-filed documents.* A Certificate of Service is still a requirement when filing documents electronically. A sample Certificate of Service is attached as Form 1 (IN R USDCTND CM/ECF(Form 1)). IN R USDCTND CM/ECF(II)(H).

b. *Supplemental documents*

i. *Brief.* Refer to the Format section of this document for the format of briefs.

ii. *Supporting evidence.* When a motion relies on facts outside the record, the court may hear the matter on affidavits or may hear it wholly or partly on oral testimony or on depositions. FRCP 43(c).

- *Materials necessary for motion.* A party must file those portions of discovery requests or responses (including deposition transcripts) that the party relies on to support a motion that could result in a final order on an issue. IN R USDCTND L.R. 26-2(c).

iii. *Notice of constitutional question.* A party that files a pleading, written motion, or other paper drawing into question the constitutionality of a federal or state statute must promptly:

- *File notice.* File a notice of constitutional question stating the question and identifying the paper that raises it, if: (1) a federal statute is questioned and the parties do not include the United States, one of its agencies, or one of its officers or employees in an official capacity; or (2) a state statute is questioned and the parties do not include the state, one of its agencies, or one of its officers or employees in an official capacity; and

- *Serve notice.* Serve the notice and paper on the Attorney General of the United States if a federal statute is questioned—or on the state attorney general if a state statute is questioned—either by certified or registered mail or by sending it to an electronic address designated by the attorney general for this purpose. FRCP 5.1(a).

- *When to file the notice.* A party required to file a notice of constitutional question under FRCP 5.1 must do so by the later of: (1) the day the parties tender their proposed case-management plan (if one is required); or (2) 21 days after filing the pleading, written motion, or other paper questioning the constitutionality of a federal or state statute. IN R USDCTND L.R. 5.1-1(a).

- *Service on government officials.* The party must also serve the notice and the pleading, written motion, or other paper questioning the constitutionality of a federal or state statute on: (1) the Attorney General of the United States and the United States Attorney for the Northern District of Indiana, if a federal statute is challenged; or (2) the Attorney General for the state if a state statute is challenged. IN R USDCTND L.R. 5.1-1(b). Service required under IN R USDCTND L.R. 5.1-1(b) may be made either by certified or registered mail or by emailing it to an address designated by those officials for this purpose. IN R USDCTND L.R. 5.1-1(c).

- *No forfeiture.* A party's failure to file and serve the notice, or the court's failure to certify, does not forfeit a constitutional claim or defense that is otherwise timely asserted. FRCP 5.1(d).

iv. *Nongovernmental corporate disclosure statement*

- *Contents.* A nongovernmental corporate party must file two (2) copies of a disclosure statement that: (1) identifies any parent corporation and any publicly held corporation owning ten percent (10%) or more of its stock; or (2) states that there is no such corporation. FRCP 7.1(a).

- *Time to file; Supplemental filing.* A party must: (1) file the disclosure statement with its first appearance, pleading, petition, motion, response, or other request addressed to the court; and (2) promptly file a supplemental statement if any required information changes. FRCP 7.1(b).

v. *Index of exhibits.* Any pleading, motion, brief, affidavit, notice, or proposed order, whether filed electronically or by delivering it to the clerk, must: include a separate index identifying and briefly describing each exhibit if there are more than four (4) exhibits. IN R USDCTND L.R. 5-4(a)(8).

vi. *Request for oral argument.* A party may request oral argument on a motion by filing and serving a separate document explaining why oral argument is necessary and estimating how long the court should allow for the argument. IN R USDCTND L.R. 7-5(a)(1). The request must be filed and served with the party's supporting brief, response brief, or reply brief. IN R USDCTND L.R. 7-5(a)(2).

vii. *Request for evidentiary hearing.* A party may request an evidentiary hearing by filing and serving a separate document explaining why the hearing is necessary and estimating how long the court should allow for it. IN R USDCTND L.R. 7-5(b)(1).

viii. *Copy of authority.* A copy of any decision, statute, or regulation cited in a motion or brief must be attached to the paper if—and only if—it is not available on Westlaw or Lexis. But if a copy of a decision, statute, or regulation is only available electronically, a party must provide it to the court or another party upon request. IN R USDCTND L.R. 7-1(f).

ix. *Proposed order.* Parties filing a paper that requires the judge or clerk to enter a routine or uncontested order must include a suitable form of order. IN R USDCTND L.R. 5-4(c).

   • Proposed orders shall not be filed electronically either as a separate document or as an attachment to the main pleading or other document. Instead, all proposed orders must be e-mailed to the chambers of the appropriate judicial officer for the case. The proposed order must be in WordPerfect Format or Rich Text Format (RTF). Proposed orders should be attached to an e-mail and sent to the appropriate judicial officer at the address listed in IN R USDCTND CM/ECF(II)(F). The subject line of the email message should indicate the case title, cause number and document number of the motion, e.g., Smith v. Jones 1:02-cv-1234, motion# ___. IN R USDCTND CM/ECF(II)(F).

x. *Copy of document with self-addressed envelope.* A party who wants a file-stamped copy of a paper must include with the filing an additional copy of the paper and a self-addressed envelope with adequate postage. IN R USDCTND L.R. 5-4(b)(6).

xi. *Notice of manual filing.* However, if that is not physically possible, counsel shall electronically file a .pdf document titled Notice of Manual Filing as a notation on the docket sheet that filings are being held in the clerk's office in paper. A sample Notice of Manual Filing is attached as Form 2 (IN R USDCTND CM/ECF(Form 2)). IN R USDCTND CM/ECF(III)(A)(1).

xii. *Courtesy copies.* If documents are filed in paper format, counsel must provide an original for the clerk's office, a copy for the judge and a copy must be served on all parties in the case. IN R USDCTND CM/ECF(III)(A)(1).

xiii. *Declaration that party was unable to file in a timely manner.* If the attorney is unable to file a document in a timely manner due to technical difficulties in the user's system, the attorney must file a document with the court as soon as possible notifying the court of the inability to file the document. A sample document entitled Declaration that Party was Unable to File in a Timely Manner Due to Technical Difficulties is attached hereto as Form 5. IN R USDCTND CM/ECF(VI)(B). [Editor's note: the reference to Form 5 is likely meant to be a reference to Form 3 (IN R USDCTND CM/ECF(Form 3))].

2. *Documents for opposing party*

   a. *Required documents*

      i. *Response brief.* Refer to the Format section of this document for the format of briefs. Refer to the General Requirements section of this document for information on the opposing papers.

      ii. *Certificate of service.* FRCP 5(d) requires that the person making service under FRCP 5 certify that service has been effected. FRCP 5(Advisory Committee Notes). Having such information on file may be useful for many purposes, including proof of service if an issue arises concerning the effectiveness of the service. FRCP 5(Advisory Committee Notes).

         • *Certificate of service for electronically-filed documents.* A Certificate of Service is still a requirement when filing documents electronically. A sample Certificate of Service is attached as Form 1 (IN R USDCTND CM/ECF(Form 1)). IN R USDCTND CM/ECF(II)(H).

b. *Supplemental documents*

    i. *Supporting evidence.* When a motion relies on facts outside the record, the court may hear the matter on affidavits or may hear it wholly or partly on oral testimony or on depositions. FRCP 43(c).

- *Materials necessary for motion.* A party must file those portions of discovery requests or responses (including deposition transcripts) that the party relies on to support a motion that could result in a final order on an issue. IN R USDCTND L.R. 26-2(c).

    ii. *Notice of constitutional question.* A party that files a pleading, written motion, or other paper drawing into question the constitutionality of a federal or state statute must promptly:

- *File notice.* File a notice of constitutional question stating the question and identifying the paper that raises it, if: (1) a federal statute is questioned and the parties do not include the United States, one of its agencies, or one of its officers or employees in an official capacity; or (2) a state statute is questioned and the parties do not include the state, one of its agencies, or one of its officers or employees in an official capacity; and

- *Serve notice.* Serve the notice and paper on the Attorney General of the United States if a federal statute is questioned—or on the state attorney general if a state statute is questioned—either by certified or registered mail or by sending it to an electronic address designated by the attorney general for this purpose. FRCP 5.1(a).

- *When to file the notice.* A party required to file a notice of constitutional question under FRCP 5.1 must do so by the later of: (1) the day the parties tender their proposed case-management plan (if one is required); or (2) 21 days after filing the pleading, written motion, or other paper questioning the constitutionality of a federal or state statute. IN R USDCTND L.R. 5.1-1(a).

- *Service on government officials.* The party must also serve the notice and the pleading, written motion, or other paper questioning the constitutionality of a federal or state statute on: (1) the Attorney General of the United States and the United States Attorney for the Northern District of Indiana, if a federal statute is challenged; or (2) the Attorney General for the state if a state statute is challenged. IN R USDCTND L.R. 5.1-1(b). Service required under IN R USDCTND L.R. 5.1-1(b) may be made either by certified or registered mail or by emailing it to an address designated by those officials for this purpose. IN R USDCTND L.R. 5.1-1(c).

- *No forfeiture.* A party's failure to file and serve the notice, or the court's failure to certify, does not forfeit a constitutional claim or defense that is otherwise timely asserted. FRCP 5.1(d).

    iii. *Index of exhibits.* Any pleading, motion, brief, affidavit, notice, or proposed order, whether filed electronically or by delivering it to the clerk, must: include a separate index identifying and briefly describing each exhibit if there are more than four (4) exhibits. IN R USDCTND L.R. 5-4(a)(8).

    iv. *Request for oral argument.* A party may request oral argument on a motion by filing and serving a separate document explaining why oral argument is necessary and estimating how long the court should allow for the argument. IN R USDCTND L.R. 7-5(a)(1). The request must be filed and served with the party's supporting brief, response brief, or reply brief. IN R USDCTND L.R. 7-5(a)(2).

    v. *Request for evidentiary hearing.* A party may request an evidentiary hearing by filing and serving a separate document explaining why the hearing is necessary and estimating how long the court should allow for it. IN R USDCTND L.R. 7-5(b)(1).

    vi. *Copy of authority.* A copy of any decision, statute, or regulation cited in a motion or brief must be attached to the paper if—and only if—it is not available on Westlaw or Lexis. But if a copy of a decision, statute, or regulation is only available electronically, a party must provide it to the court or another party upon request. IN R USDCTND L.R. 7-1(f).

    vii. *Copy of document with self-addressed envelope.* A party who wants a file-stamped copy of a paper must include with the filing an additional copy of the paper and a self-addressed envelope with adequate postage. IN R USDCTND L.R. 5-4(b)(6).

viii. *Notice of manual filing.* However, if that is not physically possible, counsel shall electronically file a .pdf document titled Notice of Manual Filing as a notation on the docket sheet that filings are being held in the clerk's office in paper. A sample Notice of Manual Filing is attached as Form 2 (IN R USDCTND CM/ECF(Form 2)). IN R USDCTND CM/ECF(III)(A)(1).

ix. *Courtesy copies.* If documents are filed in paper format, counsel must provide an original for the clerk's office, a copy for the judge and a copy must be served on all parties in the case. IN R USDCTND CM/ECF(III)(A)(1).

x. *Declaration that party was unable to file in a timely manner.* If the attorney is unable to file a document in a timely manner due to technical difficulties in the user's system, the attorney must file a document with the court as soon as possible notifying the court of the inability to file the document. A sample document entitled Declaration that Party was Unable to File in a Timely Manner Due to Technical Difficulties is attached hereto as Form 5. IN R USDCTND CM/ECF(VI)(B). [Editor's note: the reference to Form 5 is likely meant to be a reference to Form 3 (IN R USDCTND CM/ECF(Form 3)].

E. Format

1. *Form of documents.* The rules governing captions and other matters of form in pleadings apply to motions and other papers. FRCP 7(b)(2).

   a. *Paper.* Any pleading, motion, brief, affidavit, notice, or proposed order, whether filed electronically or by delivering it to the clerk, must: use eight and one-half by eleven (8-1/2 x 11) inch pages. IN R USDCTND L.R. 5-4(a)(2).

      i. *Manual filings.* Papers delivered to the clerk for filing must: be flat, unfolded, and on good-quality, white paper. IN R USDCTND L.R. 5-4(b)(1)(A).

         • *Covers or backing.* Papers delivered to the clerk for filing must: not have a cover or a back. IN R USDCTND L.R. 5-4(b)(1)(B).

         • *Recycled paper.* The court encourages using recycled paper. IN R USDCTND L.R. 5-4(b)(7).

   b. *Margins.* Any pleading, motion, brief, affidavit, notice, or proposed order, whether filed electronically or by delivering it to the clerk, must: have at least one (1) inch margins. IN R USDCTND L.R. 5-4(a)(3).

   c. *Spacing.* Any pleading, motion, brief, affidavit, notice, or proposed order, whether filed electronically or by delivering it to the clerk, must: be double spaced (except for headings, footnotes, and quoted material). IN R USDCTND L.R. 5-4(a)(5).

   d. *Text.* Any pleading, motion, brief, affidavit, notice, or proposed order, whether filed electronically or by delivering it to the clerk, must: be plainly typewritten, printed, or prepared by a clearly legible copying process. IN R USDCTND L.R. 5-4(a)(1).

      i. Any pleading, motion, brief, affidavit, notice, or proposed order, whether filed electronically or by delivering it to the clerk, must: use at least twelve (12) point type in the body and at least ten (10) point type in footnotes. IN R USDCTND L.R. 5-4(a)(4).

   e. *Page numbering.* Any pleading, motion, brief, affidavit, notice, or proposed order, whether filed electronically or by delivering it to the clerk, must: have consecutively numbered pages. IN R USDCTND L.R. 5-4(a)(6).

   f. *Caption; Names of parties.* Every pleading must have a caption with the court's name, a title, a file number, and a FRCP 7(a) designation. The title of the complaint must name all the parties; the title of other pleadings, after naming the first party on each side, may refer generally to other parties. FRCP 10(a). Any pleading, motion, brief, affidavit, notice, or proposed order, whether filed electronically or by delivering it to the clerk, must: include a title on the first page. IN R USDCTND L.R. 5-4(a)(7).

      i. *Alternative motions.* Motions must be filed separately, but alternative motions may be filed in a single paper if each is named in the title following the caption. IN R USDCTND L.R. 7-1(a).

g. *Filer's information.* Any pleading, motion, brief, affidavit, notice, or proposed order, whether filed electronically or by delivering it to the clerk, must: except in proposed orders and affidavits, include the filer's name, address, telephone number, fax number (where available), and e-mail address (where available). IN R USDCTND L.R. 5-4(a)(9).

h. *Paragraphs; Separate statements.* A party must state its claims or defenses in numbered paragraphs, each limited as far as practicable to a single set of circumstances. A later pleading may refer by number to a paragraph in an earlier pleading. If doing so would promote clarity, each claim founded on a separate transaction or occurrence—and each defense other than a denial—must be stated in a separate count or defense. FRCP 10(b).

i. *Adoption by reference; Exhibits.* A statement in a pleading may be adopted by reference elsewhere in the same pleading or in any other pleading or motion. A copy of a written instrument that is an exhibit to a pleading is a part of the pleading for all purposes. FRCP 10(c).

j. *Citation of local rules.* The Local Civil Rules of the United States District Court for the Northern District of Indiana may be cited as "N.D. Ind. L.R." IN R USDCTND L.R. 1-1(a)(1).

k. *Acceptance by the clerk.* The clerk must not refuse to file a paper solely because it is not in the form prescribed by the Federal Rules of Civil Procedure or by a local rule or practice. FRCP 5(d)(4).

   i. *Sanctions for formatting errors; Non-compliance.* If a person files a paper that does not comply with the rules governing the format of papers filed with the court, the court may: (1) strike the paper from the record; or (2) fine the person up to one thousand dollars ($1,000). IN R USDCTND L.R. 1-3(a).

   - *Notice.* Before sanctioning a person under IN R USDCTND L.R. 1-3(a)(2), the court must: (1) notify the person that the paper is noncompliant; and (2) give the person the opportunity either to be heard or to revise the paper. IN R USDCTND L.R. 1-3(b).

2. *Form of electronic documents.* Electronically filed documents must meet the same requirements of format and page limits as documents "conventionally filed" (as defined in IN R USDCTND CM/ECF(III)(A)) pursuant to the Federal Rules of Civil Procedure and the Local Civil Rules of the United States District Court for the Northern District of Indiana. IN R USDCTND CM/ECF(II)(A)(2).

   a. *PDF format required.* Documents filed in the CM/ECF must be in .pdf format. A document created with almost any word-processing program can be converted to .pdf format. The .pdf program in effect takes a picture of the original document and allows anyone to open the converted document across a broad range of hardware and software, with layout, format, links, and images intact. IN R USDCTND CM/ECF(FN2).

   b. *Title of documents.* The person electronically filing a pleading or other document will be responsible for designating a title for the pleading or other document by using one of the categories contained in the events listed in the CM/ECF Menu. IN R USDCTND CM/ECF(II)(G).

   c. *Combining documents.* All documents which form part of a single pleading and which are being filed at the same time and by the same party may be electronically filed together under one document number, e.g., the motion and a supporting affidavit, with the exception of memoranda in support. Memoranda in support shall be electronically filed separately and shown as a related document to the motion. IN R USDCTND CM/ECF(II)(A)(4).

   d. *Exhibits and attachments.* Filing users must submit in electronic form all documents referenced as exhibits or attachments, unless the court permits conventional filing. A filing user must submit as exhibits or attachments only those excerpts of the referenced documents that are directly germane to the matter under consideration by the court. Excerpted material must be clearly and prominently identified as such. Filing users who file excerpts of documents as exhibits or attachments do so without prejudice to their right to timely file additional excerpts or the complete document. Responding parties may timely file additional excerpts or the complete document that they believe are directly germane. The court may require parties to file additional excerpts or the complete document. IN R USDCTND CM/ECF(II)(A)(6).

   e. *Hyperlinks.* Electronically filed documents may contain hyperlink references to an external document as a convenient mechanism for accessing material cited in the document. A hyperlink reference is neither validated for content nor considered a part of the court's records. The court neither endorses the product or organization at the destination of a hyperlink reference, nor does the court exercise any responsibility over the content at the destination. In order to preserve the integrity of the court record, attorneys wishing to insert hyperlinks in court filings shall continue to use the traditional citation method for the cited authority, in addition to the hyperlink. A hyperlink contained in a filing is no more than a convenient mechanism for accessing material cited in the document and a hyperlink reference is extraneous to any filed document and is not part of the court's record. IN R USDCTND CM/ECF(II)(A)(3).

3. *Form of briefs*

    a. *Page limits.* Supporting and response briefs (excluding tables of contents, tables of authorities, and appendices) ordinarily must not exceed twenty-five (25) pages. Reply briefs must not exceed fifteen (15) pages. IN R USDCTND L.R. 7-1(e)(1).

        i. *Exception.* The court may allow a party to file a brief exceeding these page limits for extraordinary and compelling reasons. But if the court permits a brief to exceed twenty-five (25) pages, it must include:

            • A table of contents with page references;

            • An issue statement; and

            • A table of authorities including: (1) all cases (alphabetically arranged), statutes, and other authorities cited in the brief; and (2) references to where the authorities appear in the brief. IN R USDCTND L.R. 7-1(e)(2).

4. *Signing disclosures and discovery requests, responses, and objections.* FRCP 11 does not apply to disclosures and discovery requests, responses, objections, and motions under FRCP 26 through FRCP 37. FRCP 11(d).

    a. *Signature required.* Every disclosure under FRCP 26(a)(1) or FRCP 26(a)(3) and every discovery request, response, or objection must be signed by at least one attorney of record in the attorney's own name—or by the party personally, if unrepresented—and must state the signer's address, e-mail address, and telephone number. FRCP 26(g)(1).

        i. *Signatures on manual filings.* Papers delivered to the clerk for filing must: include the filer's original signature. IN R USDCTND L.R. 5-4(b)(1)(C).

            • *Rubber-stamped and faxed signatures.* An original paper with a rubber-stamped or faxed signature is unsigned for purposes of FRCP 11 and FRCP 26(g). IN R USDCTND L.R. 5-4(b)(2).

            • *Affidavits.* Only the affiant need sign an affidavit. IN R USDCTND L.R. 5-4(b)(3).

        ii. *Electronic signatures.* Pursuant to FRCP 11, every pleading, motion, and other paper (except lists, schedules, statements or amendments thereto) shall be signed by at least one attorney of record or, if the party is not represented by an attorney, all papers shall be signed by the party. An attorney's/participant's password issued by the court combined with the user's identification, serves as and constitutes the attorney/participant's signature for FRCP 11 and other purposes. IN R USDCTND CM/ECF(I)(C). Documents which must be filed and which must contain original signatures other than those of a participating attorney or which require either verification or an unsworn declaration under any rule or statute, shall be filed electronically, with originally executed copies maintained by the filer. The pleading or other document electronically filed shall contain "s/" signature(s), as noted in IN R USDCTND CM/ECF(II)(E)(3)(b). IN R USDCTND CM/ECF(II)(E)(1).

            • *Multiple signatures.* In the case of a stipulation or other document to be signed by two or more attorneys, the following procedure should be used: The filing attorney shall initially confirm that the content of the document is acceptable to all persons required to sign the document and shall obtain the physical signatures of all attorneys on the document. IN R USDCTND CM/ECF(II)(E)(3)(a). The filing attorney then shall file the document electronically, indicating the signatories, e.g., "s/Jane Doe," "s/John Doe," etc. IN R US-

DCTND CM/ECF(II)(E)(3)(b). The filing attorney shall retain the hard copy of the document containing the original signatures. IN R USDCTND CM/ECF(II)(E)(3)(c).

b. *Effect of signature.* By signing, an attorney or party certifies that to the best of the person's knowledge, information, and belief formed after a reasonable inquiry:

    i. With respect to a disclosure, it is complete and correct as of the time it is made; and

    ii. With respect to a discovery request, response, or objection, it is:

- Consistent with the Federal Rules of Civil Procedure and warranted by existing law or by a nonfrivolous argument for extending, modifying, or reversing existing law, or for establishing new law;

- Not interposed for any improper purpose, such as to harass, cause unnecessary delay, or needlessly increase the cost of litigation; and

- Neither unreasonable nor unduly burdensome or expensive, considering the needs of the case, prior discovery in the case, the amount in controversy, and the importance of the issues at stake in the action. FRCP 26(g)(1).

c. *Failure to sign.* Other parties have no duty to act on an unsigned disclosure, request, response, or objection until it is signed, and the court must strike it unless a signature is promptly supplied after the omission is called to the attorney's or party's attention. FRCP 26(g)(2).

d. *Sanction for improper certification.* If a certification violates FRCP 26(g) without substantial justification, the court, on motion or on its own, must impose an appropriate sanction on the signer, the party on whose behalf the signer was acting, or both. The sanction may include an order to pay the reasonable expenses, including attorney's fees, caused by the violation. FRCP 26(g)(3). Refer to the United States District Court for the Northern District of Indiana KeyRules Motion for Discovery Sanctions document for more information.

5. *Privacy protection for filings made with the court*

a. *Redacted filings.* Counsel should not include sensitive information in any document filed with the court unless such inclusion is necessary and relevant to the case. IN R USDCTND CM/ECF(VII). Unless the court orders otherwise, in an electronic or paper filing with the court that contains an individual's Social Security number, taxpayer-identification number, or birth date, the name of an individual known to be a minor, or a financial-account number, a party or nonparty making the filing may include only:

    i. The last four (4) digits of the Social Security number and taxpayer-identification number;

    ii. The year of the individual's birth;

    iii. The minor's initials; and

    iv. The last four (4) digits of the financial-account number. FRCP 5.2(a); IN R USDCTND Order 2005-3.

b. *Exemptions from the redaction requirement.* The redaction requirement does not apply to the following:

    i. A financial-account number that identifies the property allegedly subject to forfeiture in a forfeiture proceeding;

    ii. The record of an administrative or agency proceeding;

    iii. The official record of a state-court proceeding;

    iv. The record of a court or tribunal, if that record was not subject to the redaction requirement when originally filed;

    v. A filing covered by FRCP 5.2(c) or FRCP 5.2(d); and

    vi. A pro se filing in an action brought under 28 U.S.C.A. § 2241, 28 U.S.C.A. § 2254, or 28 U.S.C.A. § 2255. FRCP 5.2(b).

    vii. In cases filed under the Social Security Act, 42 U.S.C.A. § 405(g), there is no need for redaction of any information from the documents filed in the case. IN R USDCTND Order 2005-3.

c. *Limitations on remote access to electronic files; Social Security appeals and immigration cases.* Unless the court orders otherwise, in an action for benefits under the Social Security Act, and in an action or proceeding relating to an order of removal, to relief from removal, or to immigration benefits or detention, access to an electronic file is authorized as follows:

    i. The parties and their attorneys may have remote electronic access to any part of the case file, including the administrative record;

    ii. Any other person may have electronic access to the full record at the courthouse, but may have remote electronic access only to:

        • The docket maintained by the court; and

        • An opinion, order, judgment, or other disposition of the court, but not any other part of the case file or the administrative record. FRCP 5.2(c).

d. *Filings made under seal.* The court may order that a filing be made under seal without redaction. The court may later unseal the filing or order the person who made the filing to file a redacted version for the public record. FRCP 5.2(d). For information on filing documents under seal, refer to IN R USDCTND L.R. 5-3, IN R USDCTND CM/ECF(IV)(A), and IN R USDCTND ECF Order 2004-19.

e. *Protective orders.* For good cause, the court may by order in a case:

    i. Require redaction of additional information; or

    ii. Limit or prohibit a nonparty's remote electronic access to a document filed with the court. FRCP 5.2(e).

f. *Option for additional unredacted filing under seal.* A person making a redacted filing may also file an unredacted copy under seal. The court must retain the unredacted copy as part of the record. FRCP 5.2(f); IN R USDCTND Order 2005-3.

    i. The unredacted version of the document or the reference list shall be retained by the court under seal as part of the record. This paper shall be retained by the court as part of the record. The court may, however, still require the party to file a redacted copy for the public file. IN R USDCTND Order 2005-3.

g. *Option for filing a reference list.* A filing that contains redacted information may be filed together with a reference list that identifies each item of redacted information and specifies an appropriate identifier that uniquely corresponds to each item listed. The list must be filed under seal and may be amended as of right. Any reference in the case to a listed identifier will be construed to refer to the corresponding item of information. FRCP 5.2(g); IN R USDCTND Order 2005-3.

    i. The unredacted version of the document or the reference list shall be retained by the court under seal as part of the record. This paper shall be retained by the court as part of the record. The court may, however, still require the party to file a redacted copy for the public file. IN R USDCTND Order 2005-3.

h. *Responsibility for redaction.* The responsibility for redacting these personal identifiers rests solely with counsel and the parties. The Clerk will not review each paper for compliance with IN R USDCTND Order 2005-3. IN R USDCTND Order 2005-3.

i. *Waiver of protection of identifiers.* A person waives the protection of FRCP 5.2(a) as to the person's own information by filing it without redaction and not under seal. FRCP 5.2(h).

F. Filing and Service Requirements

1. *Filing requirements.* Any paper after the complaint that is required to be served—together with a certificate of service—must be filed within a reasonable time after service. FRCP 5(d)(1). Motions must be filed separately, but alternative motions may be filed in a single paper if each is named in the title following the caption. IN R USDCTND L.R. 7-1(a).

    a. *How filing is made; In general.* A paper is filed by delivering it:

        i. To the clerk; or

ii. To a judge who agrees to accept it for filing, and who must then note the filing date on the paper and promptly send it to the clerk. FRCP 5(d)(2).

- Papers not filed electronically must be filed with the clerk, not a judge. IN R USDCTND L.R. 5-4(b)(4).

iii. Parties manually filing a paper that requires the clerk to give others notice, must give the clerk: (1) sufficient copies of the notice; and (2) the name and address of each person entitled to receive the notice. IN R USDCTND L.R. 5-4(b)(8).

b. *Where to file.* Papers not filed electronically must be filed in the division where the case is pending, unless: (1) a person will be prejudiced if the paper is not filed the same day it is tendered; and (2) it includes an adequately sized envelope addressed to the clerk's office in the division where the case is pending and with adequate postage. IN R USDCTND L.R. 5-4(b)(5).

c. *Electronic filing*

i. *Authorization of electronic filing program.* A court may, by local rule, allow papers to be filed, signed, or verified by electronic means that are consistent with any technical standards established by the Judicial Conference of the United States. A local rule may require electronic filing only if reasonable exceptions are allowed. A paper filed electronically in compliance with a local rule is a written paper for purposes of the Federal Rules of Civil Procedure. FRCP 5(d)(3).

- Papers must be filed, signed, and verified electronically unless excepted by the court's CM/ECF Civil and Criminal User Manual (IN R USDCTND CM/ECF). IN R USDCTND L.R. 5-1.

ii. *Mandatory electronic filing.* Unless otherwise permitted by these procedures or otherwise authorized by the assigned judge, all documents submitted for filing in this district in civil and criminal cases, no matter when a case was originally filed, shall be filed electronically using the System. IN R USDCTND CM/ECF(II)(A)(1). The requirement that "all documents" be filed electronically includes briefs, and attachments and exhibits used in support of motions. IN R USDCTND CM/ECF(FN1).

- Sending a document or pleading to the court via e-mail or facsimile does not constitute "electronic filing." IN R USDCTND CM/ECF(I)(A).

iii. *Conventional filing.* As used in these procedures, a "conventionally" filed or submitted document or pleading is one presented to the Clerk or a party in paper or other non-electronic, tangible format. The following documents shall be filed conventionally and not electronically unless specifically authorized by the Court:

- Exhibits and other documents which cannot be converted to a legible electronic form. Whenever possible, counsel is responsible for converting filings to an electronic form. However, if that is not physically possible, counsel shall electronically file a .pdf document titled Notice of Manual Filing as a notation on the docket sheet that filings are being held in the clerk's office in paper. A sample Notice of Manual Filing is attached as Form 2 (IN R USDCTND CM/ECF(Form 2)). If documents are filed in paper format, counsel must provide an original for the clerk's office, a copy for the judge and a copy must be served on all parties in the case. Large documents which do not exist in an electronic format shall be scanned into .pdf format by counsel, in small batches if necessary, and filed electronically as separate attachments in the System. IN R USDCTND CM/ECF(III)(A)(1).

- Certain documents which are listed in IN R USDCTND CM/ECF(II)(E)(2). IN R US-DCTND CM/ECF(III)(A)(2).

- Documents filed by pro se litigants. IN R USDCTND CM/ECF(III)(A)(3).

iv. For more information on electronic filing, refer to IN R USDCTND CM/ECF.

2. *Service requirements*

   a. *Service; When required*

      i. *In general.* Unless the Federal Rules of Civil Procedure provide otherwise, each of the following papers must be served on every party:

- An order stating that service is required;

- A pleading filed after the original complaint, unless the court orders otherwise under FRCP 5(c) because there are numerous defendants;

- A discovery paper required to be served on a party, unless the court orders otherwise;

- A written motion, except one that may be heard ex parte; and

- A written notice, appearance, demand, or offer of judgment, or any similar paper. FRCP 5(a)(1).

      ii. *If a party fails to appear.* No service is required on a party who is in default for failing to appear. But a pleading that asserts a new claim for relief against such a party must be served on that party under FRCP 4. FRCP 5(a)(2).

      iii. *Seizing property.* If an action is begun by seizing property and no person is or need be named as a defendant, any service required before the filing of an appearance, answer, or claim must be made on the person who had custody or possession of the property when it was seized. FRCP 5(a)(3).

   b. *Service; How made*

      i. *Serving an attorney.* If a party is represented by an attorney, service under FRCP 5 must be made on the attorney unless the court orders service on the party. FRCP 5(b)(1).

      ii. *Service in general.* A paper is served under FRCP 5 by:

- Handing it to the person;

- Leaving it: (1) at the person's office with a clerk or other person in charge or, if no one is in charge, in a conspicuous place in the office; or (2) if the person has no office or the office is closed, at the person's dwelling or usual place of abode with someone of suitable age and discretion who resides there;

- Mailing it to the person's last known address—in which event service is complete upon mailing;

- Leaving it with the court clerk if the person has no known address;

- Sending it by electronic means if the person consented in writing—in which event service is complete upon transmission, but is not effective if the serving party learns that it did not reach the person to be served; or

- Delivering it by any other means that the person consented to in writing—in which event service is complete when the person making service delivers it to the agency designated to make delivery. FRCP 5(b)(2).

      iii. *Electronic service.* Electronically filed papers may be served electronically if service is consistent with the CM/ECF User Manual (IN R USDCTND CM/ECF). IN R USDCTND L.R. 5-2(a).

- *Waiver of other service.* An attorney's registration will constitute a waiver of conventional service of documents and the attorney agrees to accept service of notice on behalf of the client of the electronic filing by hand, facsimile or authorized email. IN R USDCTND CM/ECF(I)(B)(3).

- *Serving registered persons.* The System will generate a "Notice of Electronic Filing" when any document is filed. This notice represents service of the document on parties who are registered participants with the System. Except as provided in IN R USDCTND CM/ECF(III)(B), the filing party shall not be required to serve any pleading or other documents on any party receiving electronic notice. IN R USDCTND CM/ECF(II)(D)(1). The term "pleading" refers only to those documents listed in FRCP 7(a). IN R USDCTND CM/ECF(FN3).

- *When electronic service is deemed completed.* A person registered to use the court's electronic-filing system is served with an electronically filed paper when a "Notice of Electronic Filing" is transmitted to that person through the court's electronic filing-system. IN R USDCTND L.R. 5-2(b).

- *Serving non-registered persons.* A person who has not registered to use the court's electronic-filing system but who is entitled to service of a paper must be served according to the Local Civil Rules of the United States District Court for the Northern District of Indiana and the Federal Rules of Civil Procedure. IN R USDCTND L.R. 5-2(c); IN R USDCTND CM/ECF(II)(D)(2). If such service of a paper copy is to be made, it shall be done in the manner provided in the Federal Rules of Civil Procedure and the Local Civil Rules of the United States District Court for the Northern District of Indiana. IN R USDCTND CM/ECF(II)(D)(2).

iv. *Service of conventional filings.* Pleadings or other documents which are filed conventionally rather than electronically shall be served in the manner provided for in the Federal Rules of Civil Procedure and the Local Civil Rules of the United States District Court for the Northern District of Indiana, except as otherwise provided by order of the Court. IN R USDCTND CM/ECF(III)(B).

v. *Using court facilities.* If a local rule so authorizes, a party may use the court's transmission facilities to make service under FRCP 5(b)(2)(E). FRCP 5(b)(3).

c. *Serving numerous defendants*

i. *In general.* If an action involves an unusually large number of defendants, the court may, on motion or on its own, order that:

- Defendants' pleadings and replies to them need not be served on other defendants;

- Any crossclaim, counterclaim, avoidance, or affirmative defense in those pleadings and replies to them will be treated as denied or avoided by all other parties; and

- Filing any such pleading and serving it on the plaintiff constitutes notice of the pleading to all parties. FRCP 5(c)(1).

ii. *Notifying parties.* A copy of every such order must be served on the parties as the court directs. FRCP 5(c)(2).

G. Hearings

1. *Hearings, generally*

a. *Oral argument.* Due process does not require that oral argument be permitted on a motion and, except as otherwise provided by local rule, the district court has discretion to determine whether it will decide the motion on the papers or hear argument by counsel (and perhaps receive evidence). FPP § 1190; F.D.I.C. v. Deglau, 207 F.3d 153 (3d Cir. 2000).

i. *Request for oral argument.* A party may request oral argument on a motion by filing and serving a separate document explaining why oral argument is necessary and estimating how long the court should allow for the argument. IN R USDCTND L.R. 7-5(a)(1). Refer to the Documents section of this document for more information.

ii. *Additional evidence forbidden.* Parties may not present additional evidence at oral argument. IN R USDCTND L.R. 7-5(a)(3).

b. *Providing a regular schedule for oral hearings.* A court may establish regular times and places for oral hearings on motions. FRCP 78(a).

c. *Providing for submission on briefs.* By rule or order, the court may provide for submitting and determining motions on briefs, without oral hearings. FRCP 78(b).

d. *Evidentiary hearings.* A party may request an evidentiary hearing by filing and serving a separate document explaining why the hearing is necessary and estimating how long the court should allow for it. IN R USDCTND L.R. 7-5(b)(2). Refer to the Documents section of this document for more information.

  e. *Court's authority.* The court may: (1) grant or deny a request for oral argument or an evidentiary hearing in its discretion; (2) set oral argument or an evidentiary hearing without a request from a party; or (3) order any oral argument or evidentiary hearing to be held anywhere within the district regardless of where the case will be tried. IN R USDCTND L.R. 7-5(c).

2. *Courtroom and courthouse decorum.* For information on courtroom and courthouse decorum, refer to IN R USDCTND L.R. 83-3.

H. Forms

1. Federal Motion for Protective Order Forms

  a. Notice of motion; For protective order; Preventing deposition of consultant and production of documents; Federal class action. AMJUR PP DEPOSITION § 334.

  b. Motion; For protective order pending court's order on motion to quash deposition notice of plaintiff. AMJUR PP DEPOSITION § 341.

  c. Motion; For protective order; To prevent deposition of consultant and production of documents; Federal class action. AMJUR PP DEPOSITION § 343.

  d. Opposition; By plaintiffs; To motion by defendants for protective order; Prevention of deposition of consultant and production of documents; Federal class action. AMJUR PP DEPOSITION § 370.

  e. Declaration; By plaintiffs' attorney; In support of opposition to defendants' motion for protective order; Federal class action. AMJUR PP DEPOSITION § 371.

  f. Notice of motion; For protective order; To vacate notice to produce documents. AMJUR PP DEPOSITION § 592.

  g. Notice of motion; For protective order; To limit scope of inspection of premises; Premises liability action; Objection to scope of request. AMJUR PP DEPOSITION § 593.

  h. Motion; For protective order; Staying proceedings on production requests; Pending ruling on movant's dispositive motion. AMJUR PP DEPOSITION § 594.

  i. Motion; For protective order; Limiting requests for production; Additional protection of trade secrets. AMJUR PP DEPOSITION § 595.

  j. Motion for protective order limiting scope of oral examination; Privileged material. 3A FEDFORMS § 3264.

  k. Notice of motion and motion for protective order. 3A FEDFORMS § 3265.

  l. Notice of motion and motion for protective order; Prohibiting taking of deposition. 3A FEDFORMS § 3266.

  m. Notice of motion and motion for protective order; To quash notice of taking deposition or for continuance; Late taking of deposition. 3A FEDFORMS § 3267.

  n. Motion for protective order limiting scope of oral examination. 3A FEDFORMS § 3279.

  o. Motion for protective order limiting examination upon written questions. 3A FEDFORMS § 3283.

  p. Answer; To motion for protective order. FEDPROF § 23:196.

  q. Motion; For protective order; Limiting interrogatories. FEDPROF § 23:373.

  r. Motion; For protective order; Staying proceedings on production requests. FEDPROF § 23:422.

  s. Motion; For protective order; Limiting requests for production. FEDPROF § 23:423.

  t. Motion; For protective order staying proceedings on request for admissions. FEDPROF § 23:563.

  u. Notice of motion for protective order. GOLDLTGFMS § 31:2.

  v. Motion for protective order; Federal form. GOLDLTGFMS § 31:5.

  w. Motion for protective order; Deposition not to be taken. GOLDLTGFMS § 31:6.

    x.   Motion for protective order; Retaking depositions. GOLDLTGFMS § 31:7.

    y.   Motion for protective order; Certain matters shall not be inquired into. GOLDLTGFMS § 31:8.

    z.   Motion for protective order; To limit scope of examination. GOLDLTGFMS § 31:10.

2. Forms for the Northern District of Indiana

    a.   Certificate of service. IN R USDCTND CM/ECF(Form 1).

    b.   Notice of manual filing. IN R USDCTND CM/ECF(Form 2).

    c.   Declaration that party was unable to file in a timely manner. IN R USDCTND CM/ECF(Form 3).

I. Applicable Rules

1. *Federal rules*

    a.   Serving and filing pleadings and other papers. FRCP 5.

    b.   Constitutional challenge to a statute; Notice, certification, and intervention. FRCP 5.1.

    c.   Privacy protection for filings made with the court. FRCP 5.2.

    d.   Computing and extending time; Time for motion papers. FRCP 6.

    e.   Pleadings allowed; Form of motions and other papers. FRCP 7.

    f.   Disclosure statement. FRCP 7.1.

    g.   Form of pleadings. FRCP 10.

    h.   Signing pleadings, motions, and other papers; Representations to the court; Sanctions. FRCP 11.

    i.   Duty to disclose; General provisions governing discovery. FRCP 26.

    j.   Taking testimony. FRCP 43.

    k.   Hearing motions; Submission on briefs. FRCP 78.

2. *Local rules*

    a.   Citation and scope of the rules. IN R USDCTND L.R. 1-1.

    b.   Sanctions for formatting errors. IN R USDCTND L.R. 1-3.

    c.   Electronic filing required. IN R USDCTND L.R. 5-1.

    d.   Constitutional questions. IN R USDCTND L.R. 5.1-1.

    e.   Electronic service. IN R USDCTND L.R. 5-2.

    f.   Format of papers. IN R USDCTND L.R. 5-4.

    g.   Motion practice. IN R USDCTND L.R. 7-1.

    h.   Oral arguments and evidentiary hearings. IN R USDCTND L.R. 7-5.

    i.   Pretrial procedure. IN R USDCTND L.R. 16-1.

    j.   Alternative dispute resolution. IN R USDCTND L.R. 16-6.

    k.   Filing of discovery and other materials. IN R USDCTND L.R. 26-2.

    l.   Resolving discovery disputes. IN R USDCTND L.R. 37-1.

    m.   Case assignment. IN R USDCTND L.R. 40-1.

    n.   Appearance and withdrawal of appearance. IN R USDCTND L.R. 83-8.

    o.   CM/ECF civil and criminal user manual. IN R USDCTND CM/ECF.

    p.   In re: privacy and public access to civil electronic case files. IN R USDCTND Order 2005-3.

Motions, Oppositions and Replies
Motion for Discovery Sanctions

Document Last Updated December 2016

A. Checklist

(I) ❏ Matters to be considered by moving party

    (a) ❏ Required documents

        (1) ❏ Notice of motion and motion

        (2) ❏ Certificate of compliance

        (3) ❏ Brief

        (4) ❏ Discovery materials

        (5) ❏ Certificate of service

    (b) ❏ Supplemental documents

        (1) ❏ Supporting evidence

        (2) ❏ Notice of constitutional question

        (3) ❏ Index of exhibits

        (4) ❏ Request for oral argument

        (5) ❏ Request for evidentiary hearing

        (6) ❏ Copy of authority

        (7) ❏ Proposed order

        (8) ❏ Copy of document with self-addressed envelope

        (9) ❏ Notice of manual filing

      (10) ❏ Courtesy copies

      (11) ❏ Declaration that party was unable to file in a timely manner

    (c) ❏ Timing

        (1) ❏ A written motion and notice of the hearing must be served at least fourteen (14) days before the time specified for the hearing, with the following exceptions: (i) when the motion may be heard ex parte; (ii) when the Federal Rules of Civil Procedure set a different time; or (iii) when a court order—which a party may, for good cause, apply for ex parte—sets a different time

        (2) ❏ Any affidavit supporting a motion must be served with the motion

(II) ❏ Matters to be considered by opposing party

    (a) ❏ Required documents

        (1) ❏ Response brief

        (2) ❏ Certificate of service

    (b) ❏ Supplemental documents

        (1) ❏ Supporting evidence

        (2) ❏ Notice of constitutional question

        (3) ❏ Index of exhibits

        (4) ❏ Request for oral argument

        (5) ❏ Request for evidentiary hearing

        (6) ❏ Copy of authority

    (7) ❑ Copy of document with self-addressed envelope

    (8) ❑ Notice of manual filing

    (9) ❑ Courtesy copies

    (10) ❑ Declaration that party was unable to file in a timely manner

(c) ❑ Timing

    (1) ❑ A party must file any response brief to a motion within fourteen (14) days after the motion is served

    (2) ❑ Except as FRCP 59(c) provides otherwise, any opposing affidavit must be served at least seven (7) days before the hearing, unless the court permits service at another time

B. Timing

1. *Motion for discovery sanctions.* There are no specific timing requirements for moving for discovery sanctions.

2. *Timing of motions, generally*

  a. *Motion and notice of hearing.* A written motion and notice of the hearing must be served at least fourteen (14) days before the time specified for the hearing, with the following exceptions:

    i. When the motion may be heard ex parte;

    ii. When the Federal Rules of Civil Procedure set a different time; or

    iii. When a court order—which a party may, for good cause, apply for ex parte—sets a different time. FRCP 6(c)(1).

  b. *Supporting affidavit.* Any affidavit supporting a motion must be served with the motion. FRCP 6(c)(2).

3. *Timing of opposing papers.* A party must file any response brief to a motion within fourteen (14) days after the motion is served. IN R USDCTND L.R. 7-1(d)(2)(A).

  a. *Opposing affidavit.* Except as FRCP 59(c) provides otherwise, any opposing affidavit must be served at least seven (7) days before the hearing, unless the court permits service at another time. FRCP 6(c)(2).

  b. *Extensions.* The court may extend response- and reply-brief deadlines, but only for good cause. IN R USDCTND L.R. 7-1(d)(3).

  c. *Summary rulings.* The court may rule on a motion summarily if an opposing party does not file a response before the deadline. IN R USDCTND L.R. 7-1(d)(4).

4. *Timing of reply papers.* Where the respondent files an answering affidavit setting up a new matter, the moving party ordinarily is allowed a reasonable time to file a reply affidavit since failure to deny the new matter by affidavit may operate as an admission of its truth. AMJUR MOTIONS § 25.

  a. *Reply brief.* The moving party must file any reply brief within seven (7) days after the response brief is served. IN R USDCTND L.R. 7-1(d)(2)(B).

  b. *Extensions.* The court may extend response- and reply-brief deadlines, but only for good cause. IN R USDCTND L.R. 7-1(d)(3).

5. *Computation of time*

  a. *Computing time.* FRCP 6 applies in computing any time period specified in the Federal Rules of Civil Procedure, in any local rule or court order, or in any statute that does not specify a method of computing time. FRCP 6(a).

    i. *Period stated in days or a longer unit.* When the period is stated in days or a longer unit of time:

      • Exclude the day of the event that triggers the period;

      • Count every day, including intermediate Saturdays, Sundays, and legal holidays; and

      • Include the last day of the period, but if the last day is a Saturday, Sunday, or legal holiday, the period continues to run until the end of the next day that is not a Saturday, Sunday, or legal holiday. FRCP 6(a)(1).

ii. *Period stated in hours.* When the period is stated in hours:

   - Begin counting immediately on the occurrence of the event that triggers the period;

   - Count every hour, including hours during intermediate Saturdays, Sundays, and legal holidays; and

   - If the period would end on a Saturday, Sunday, or legal holiday, the period continues to run until the same time on the next day that is not a Saturday, Sunday, or legal holiday. FRCP 6(a)(2).

iii. *Inaccessibility of the clerk's office.* Unless the court orders otherwise, if the clerk's office is inaccessible:

   - On the last day for filing under FRCP 6(a)(1), then the time for filing is extended to the first accessible day that is not a Saturday, Sunday, or legal holiday; or

   - During the last hour for filing under FRCP 6(a)(2), then the time for filing is extended to the same time on the first accessible day that is not a Saturday, Sunday, or legal holiday. FRCP 6(a)(3).

iv. *"Last day" defined.* Unless a different time is set by a statute, local rule, or court order, the last day ends:

   - For electronic filing, at midnight in the court's time zone; and

   - For filing by other means, when the clerk's office is scheduled to close. FRCP 6(a)(4).

v. *"Next day" defined.* The "next day" is determined by continuing to count forward when the period is measured after an event and backward when measured before an event. FRCP 6(a)(5).

vi. *"Legal holiday" defined.* "Legal holiday" means:

   - The day set aside by statute for observing New Year's Day, Martin Luther King Jr.'s Birthday, Washington's Birthday, Memorial Day, Independence Day, Labor Day, Columbus Day, Veterans' Day, Thanksgiving Day, or Christmas Day;

   - Any day declared a holiday by the President or Congress; and

   - For periods that are measured after an event, any other day declared a holiday by the state where the district court is located. FRCP 6(a)(6).

b. *Computation of electronic filing deadlines.* Filing documents electronically does not alter any filing deadlines or any time computation pursuant to FRCP 6. The counties of Lake, Porter, LaPorte, Pulaski and Starke are located in the Central time zone and the remaining counties in the Northern District of Indiana are located in the Eastern time zone. Nevertheless, all electronic transmissions of documents must be completed (i.e., received completely by the clerk's office) prior to midnight Eastern Time, (South Bend/Fort Wayne/Lafayette time) in order to be considered timely filed that day, regardless of the local time in the division where the case is pending. Although documents can be filed electronically twenty-four (24) hours a day, filers are strongly encouraged to file all documents during hours when the CM/ECF Help Line is available, from 9:00 a.m. to 4:00 p.m. local time. IN R USDCTND CM/ECF(II)(I).

i. *Technical failures.* If the attorney is unable to file a document in a timely manner due to technical difficulties in the user's system, the attorney must file a document with the court as soon as possible notifying the court of the inability to file the document. A sample document entitled Declaration that Party was Unable to File in a Timely Manner Due to Technical Difficulties is attached hereto as Form 5. IN R USDCTND CM/ECF(VI)(B). [Editor's note: the reference to Form 5 is likely meant to be a reference to Form 3 (IN R USDCTND CM/ECF(Form 3)].

   c. *Extending time*

      i. *In general.* When an act may or must be done within a specified time, the court may, for good cause, extend the time:

- With or without motion or notice if the court acts, or if a request is made, before the original time or its extension expires; or

- On motion made after the time has expired if the party failed to act because of excusable neglect. FRCP 6(b)(1).

      ii. *Exceptions.* A court must not extend the time to act under FRCP 50(b), FRCP 50(d), FRCP 52(b), FRCP 59(b), FRCP 59(d), FRCP 59(e), and FRCP 60(b). FRCP 6(b)(2).

      iii. Refer to the United States District Court for the Northern District of Indiana KeyRules Motion for Continuance/Extension of Time document for more information on extending time.

   d. *Additional time after certain kinds of service.* When a party may or must act within a specified time after being served and service is made under FRCP 5(b)(2)(C) (mail), FRCP 5(b)(2)(D) (leaving with the clerk), or FRCP 5(b)(2)(F) (other means consented to), three (3) days are added after the period would otherwise expire under FRCP 6(a). FRCP 6(d).

C. General Requirements

1. *Motions, generally*

   a. *Requirements.* A request for a court order must be made by motion. The motion must:

      i. Be in writing unless made during a hearing or trial;

      ii. State with particularity the grounds for seeking the order; and

      iii. State the relief sought. FRCP 7(b)(1).

   b. *Notice of motion.* A party interested in resisting the relief sought by a motion has a right to notice thereof, and an opportunity to be heard. AMJUR MOTIONS § 12.

      i. In addition to statutory or court rule provisions requiring notice of a motion—the purpose of such a notice requirement having been said to be to prevent a party from being prejudicially surprised by a motion—principles of natural justice dictate that an adverse party generally must be given notice that a motion will be presented to the court. AMJUR MOTIONS § 12.

      ii. "Notice," in this regard, means reasonable notice, including a meaningful opportunity to prepare and to defend against allegations of a motion. AMJUR MOTIONS § 12.

   c. *Writing requirement.* The writing requirement is intended to insure that the adverse parties are informed and have a record of both the motion's pendency and the grounds on which the movant seeks an order. FPP § 1191; Feldberg v. Quechee Lakes Corp., 463 F.3d 195 (2d Cir. 2006).

      i. It is sufficient "if the motion is stated in a written notice of the hearing of the motion." FPP § 1191.

   d. *Particularity requirement.* The particularity requirement insures that the opposing parties will have notice of their opponent's contentions. FEDPROC § 62:364; Goodman v. 1973 26 Foot Trojan Vessel, Arkansas Registration No. AR1439SN, 859 F.2d 71, 12 Fed.R.Serv.3d 645 (8th Cir. 1988). That requirement ensures that notice of the basis for the motion is provided to the court and to the opposing party so as to avoid prejudice, provide the opponent with a meaningful opportunity to respond, and provide the court with enough information to process the motion correctly. FEDPROC § 62:364; Andreas v. Volkswagen of America, Inc., 336 F.3d 789, 56 Fed.R.Serv.3d 6 (8th Cir. 2003).

      i. Reasonable specification of the grounds for a motion is sufficient. However, where a movant fails to state even one ground for granting the motion in question, the movant has failed to meet the minimal standard of "reasonable specification." FEDPROC § 62:364; Martinez v. Trainor, 556 F.2d 818, 23 Fed.R.Serv.2d 403 (7th Cir. 1977).

      ii. The court may excuse the failure to comply with the particularity requirement if it is inadvertent, and where no prejudice is shown by the opposing party. FEDPROC § 62:364.

   e. *Motions must be filed separately.* Motions must be filed separately, but alternative motions may be filed in a single paper if each is named in the title following the caption. IN R USDCTND L.R. 7-1(a).

2. *Motion for discovery sanctions*

    a. *Sanctions, generally.* FRCP 37 is flexible. The court is directed to make such orders as are "just" and is not limited in any case of disregard of the discovery rules or court orders under them to a stereotyped response. The sanctions enumerated in FRCP 37 are not exclusive and arbitrary but flexible, selective, and plural. The district court may, within reason, use as many and as varied sanctions as are necessary to hold the scales of justice even. FPP § 2284.

        i. There is one fixed limitation that should be noted. A party may not be imprisoned or otherwise punished for contempt of court for failure to submit to a physical or mental examination, or for failure to produce a person in his or her custody or under his or her control for such an examination. FPP § 2284; Sibbach v. Wilson & Co., 312 U.S. 1, 312 U.S. 655, 61 S.Ct. 422, 85 L.Ed. 479 (1941).

        ii. Although FRCP 37 is very broad, and the courts have considerable discretion in imposing sanctions as authorized by FRCP 37, there are constitutional limits, stemming from the Due Process Clause of U.S.C.A. Const. Amend. V and U.S.C.A. Const. Amend. XIV, on the imposition of sanctions. There are two principal facets of the due process issues:

            • First, the court must ask whether there is a sufficient relationship between the discovery and the merits sought to be foreclosed by the sanction to legitimate depriving a party of the opportunity to litigate the merits. FPP § 2283.

            • Second, before imposing a serious merits sanction the court should determine whether the party guilty of a failure to provide discovery was unable to comply with the discovery. FPP § 2283.

    b. *Sanction for improper certification.* If a certification violates FRCP 26(g) without substantial justification, the court, on motion or on its own, must impose an appropriate sanction on the signer, the party on whose behalf the signer was acting, or both. The sanction may include an order to pay the reasonable expenses, including attorney's fees, caused by the violation. FRCP 26(g)(3).

    c. *Motion to compel discovery; Payment of expenses; Protective orders*

        i. *If the motion is granted (or disclosure or discovery is provided after filing).* If the motion is granted—or if the disclosure or requested discovery is provided after the motion was filed—the court must, after giving an opportunity to be heard, require the party or deponent whose conduct necessitated the motion, the party or attorney advising that conduct, or both to pay the movant's reasonable expenses incurred in making the motion, including attorney's fees. But the court must not order this payment if:

            • The movant filed the motion before attempting in good faith to obtain the disclosure or discovery without court action;

            • The opposing party's nondisclosure, response, or objection was substantially justified; or

            • Other circumstances make an award of expenses unjust. FRCP 37(a)(5)(A).

        ii. *If the motion is denied.* If the motion is denied, the court may issue any protective order authorized under FRCP 26(c) and must, after giving an opportunity to be heard, require the movant, the attorney filing the motion, or both to pay the party or deponent who opposed the motion its reasonable expenses incurred in opposing the motion, including attorney's fees. But the court must not order this payment if the motion was substantially justified or other circumstances make an award of expenses unjust. FRCP 37(a)(5)(B).

        iii. *If the motion is granted in part and denied in part.* If the motion is granted in part and denied in part, the court may issue any protective order authorized under FRCP 26(c) and may, after giving an opportunity to be heard, apportion the reasonable expenses for the motion. FRCP 37(a)(5)(C).

    d. *Failure to comply with a court order*

        i. *Sanctions in the district where the deposition is taken.* If the court where the discovery is taken orders a deponent to be sworn or to answer a question and the deponent fails to obey, the failure may be treated as contempt of court. If a deposition-related motion is transferred to the court where the action is pending, and that court orders a deponent to be sworn or to answer a question and the deponent fails to obey, the failure may be treated as contempt of either the court where the discovery is taken or the court where the action is pending. FRCP 37(b)(1).

ii. *Sanctions in the district where the action is pending; For not obeying a discovery order.* If a party or a party's officer, director, or managing agent—or a witness designated under FRCP 30(b)(6) or FRCP 31(a)(4)—fails to obey an order to provide or permit discovery, including an order under FRCP 26(f), FRCP 35, or FRCP 37(a), the court where the action is pending may issue further just orders. They may include the following:

- Directing that the matters embraced in the order or other designated facts be taken as established for purposes of the action, as the prevailing party claims;
- Prohibiting the disobedient party from supporting or opposing designated claims or defenses, or from introducing designated matters in evidence;
- Striking pleadings in whole or in part;
- Staying further proceedings until the order is obeyed;
- Dismissing the action or proceeding in whole or in part;
- Rendering a default judgment against the disobedient party; or
- Treating as contempt of court the failure to obey any order except an order to submit to a physical or mental examination. FRCP 37(b)(2)(A).

iii. *Sanctions in the district where the action is pending; For not producing a person for examination.* If a party fails to comply with an order under FRCP 35(a) requiring it to produce another person for examination, the court may issue any of the orders listed in FRCP 37(b)(2)(A)(i) through FRCP 37(b)(2)(A)(vi), unless the disobedient party shows that it cannot produce the other person. FRCP 37(b)(2)(B).

iv. *Sanctions in the district where the action is pending; Payment of expenses.* Instead of or in addition to the orders in FRCP 37(b)(2)(A) and FRCP 37(b)(2)(B), the court must order the disobedient party, the attorney advising that party, or both to pay the reasonable expenses, including attorney's fees, caused by the failure, unless the failure was substantially justified or other circumstances make an award of expenses unjust. FRCP 37(b)(2)(C).

e. *Failure to disclose, to supplement an earlier response, or to admit*

i. *Failure to disclose or supplement.* If a party fails to provide information or identify a witness as required by FRCP 26(a) or FRCP 26(e), the party is not allowed to use that information or witness to supply evidence on a motion, at a hearing, or at a trial, unless the failure was substantially justified or is harmless. In addition to or instead of this sanction, the court, on motion and after giving an opportunity to be heard:

- May order payment of the reasonable expenses, including attorney's fees, caused by the failure;
- May inform the jury of the party's failure; and
- May impose other appropriate sanctions, including any of the orders listed in FRCP 37(b)(2)(A)(i) through FRCP 37(b)(2)(A)(vi). FRCP 37(c)(1).

ii. *Failure to admit.* If a party fails to admit what is requested under FRCP 36 and if the requesting party later proves a document to be genuine or the matter true, the requesting party may move that the party who failed to admit pay the reasonable expenses, including attorney's fees, incurred in making that proof. The court must so order unless:

- The request was held objectionable under FRCP 36(a);
- The admission sought was of no substantial importance;
- The party failing to admit had a reasonable ground to believe that it might prevail on the matter; or
- There was other good reason for the failure to admit. FRCP 37(c)(2).

f. *Party's failure to attend its own deposition, serve answers to interrogatories, or respond to a request for inspection*

  i. *Motion; Grounds for sanctions.* The court where the action is pending may, on motion, order sanctions if:

   - A party or a party's officer, director, or managing agent—or a person designated under FRCP 30(b)(6) or FRCP 31(a)(4)—fails, after being served with proper notice, to appear for that person's deposition; or

   - A party, after being properly served with interrogatories under FRCP 33 or a request for inspection under FRCP 34, fails to serve its answers, objections, or written response. FRCP 37(d)(1)(A).

  ii. *Unacceptable excuse for failing to act.* A failure described in FRCP 37(d)(1)(A) is not excused on the ground that the discovery sought was objectionable, unless the party failing to act has a pending motion for a protective order under FRCP 26(c). FRCP 37(d)(2).

  iii. *Types of sanctions.* Sanctions may include any of the orders listed in FRCP 37(b)(2)(A)(i) through FRCP 37(b)(2)(A)(vi). Instead of or in addition to these sanctions, the court must require the party failing to act, the attorney advising that party, or both to pay the reasonable expenses, including attorney's fees, caused by the failure, unless the failure was substantially justified or other circumstances make an award of expenses unjust. FRCP 37(d)(3).

g. *Failure to provide electronically stored information.* If electronically stored information that should have been preserved in the anticipation or conduct of litigation is lost because a party failed to take reasonable steps to preserve it, and it cannot be restored or replaced through additional discovery, the court:

  i. Upon finding prejudice to another party from loss of the information, may order measures no greater than necessary to cure the prejudice; or

  ii. Only upon finding that the party acted with the intent to deprive another party of the information's use in the litigation may: (1) presume that the lost information was unfavorable to the party; (2) instruct the jury that it may or must presume the information was unfavorable to the party; or (3) dismiss the action or enter a default judgment. FRCP 37(e).

h. *Failure to participate in framing a discovery plan.* If a party or its attorney fails to participate in good faith in developing and submitting a proposed discovery plan as required by FRCP 26(f), the court may, after giving an opportunity to be heard, require that party or attorney to pay to any other party the reasonable expenses, including attorney's fees, caused by the failure. FRCP 37(f).

i. *Counsel's liability for excessive costs.* 28 U.S.C.A. § 1927 is a basis for sanctioning attorney misconduct in discovery proceedings. DISCPROFED § 22:3. Any attorney or other person admitted to conduct cases in any court of the United States or any Territory thereof who so multiplies the proceedings in any case unreasonably and vexatiously may be required by the court to satisfy personally the excess costs, expenses, and attorneys' fees reasonably incurred because of such conduct. 28 U.S.C.A. § 1927.

3. *Opposing papers.* The Federal Rules of Civil Procedure do not require any formal answer, return, or reply to a motion, except where the Federal Rules of Civil Procedure or local rules may require affidavits, memoranda, or other papers to be filed in opposition to a motion. Such papers are simply to apprise the court of such opposition and the grounds of that opposition. FEDPROC § 62:359.

a. *Effect of failure to respond to motion.* Although in the absence of statutory provision or court rule, a motion ordinarily does not require a written answer, when a party files a motion and the opposing party fails to respond, the court may construe such failure to respond as nonopposition to the motion or an admission that the motion was meritorious, may take the facts alleged in the motion as true—the rule in some jurisdictions being that the failure to respond to a fact set forth in a motion is deemed an admission—and may grant the motion if the relief requested appears to be justified. AMJUR MOTIONS § 28.

b. *Assent or no opposition not determinative.* However, a motion will not be granted automatically simply because an "assent" or a notation of "no opposition" has been filed; federal judges frequently deny motions that have been assented to when it is thought that justice so dictates. FPP § 1190.

   c. *Responsive pleading inappropriate as response to motion.* An attempt to answer or oppose a motion with a responsive pleading usually is not appropriate. FPP § 1190.

4. *Reply papers.* A moving party may be required or permitted to prepare papers in addition to his original motion papers. AMJUR MOTIONS § 25. Papers answering or replying to opposing papers may be appropriate, in the interests of justice, where it appears there is a substantial reason for allowing a reply. Thus, a court may accept reply papers where a party demonstrates that the papers to which it seeks to file a reply raise new issues that are material to the disposition of the question before the court, or where the court determines, sua sponte, that it wishes further briefing of an issue raised in those papers and orders the submission of additional papers. FEDPROC § 62:360.

   a. *Function of reply papers.* The function of a reply affidavit is to answer the arguments made in opposition to the position taken by the movant and not to permit the movant to introduce new arguments in support of the motion. AMJUR MOTIONS § 25.

   b. *Issues raised for the first time in a reply document.* However, the view has been followed in some jurisdictions, that as a matter of judicial economy, where there is no prejudice and where the issues could be raised simply by filing a motion to dismiss, the trial court has discretion to consider arguments raised for the first time in a reply memorandum, and that a trial court may grant a motion to strike issues raised for the first time in a reply memorandum. AMJUR MOTIONS § 26.

5. *Appearances.* Attorneys not representing the United States or its agencies must file an appearance when they represent (either in person or by filing a paper) a party. IN R USDCTND L.R. 83-8(a). For more information, refer to IN R USDCTND L.R. 83-8.

6. *Notice of related action.* A party must file a notice of related action as soon as it appears that the party's case and another pending case: (1) arise out of the same transaction or occurrence; (2) involve the same property; or (3) involve the validity or infringement of the same patent, trademark, or copyright. IN R USDCTND L.R. 40-1(d). For more information, refer to IN R USDCTND L.R. 40-1.

7. *Alternative dispute resolution (ADR).* After they confer as required by FRCP 26(f), the parties must advise the court which, if any, alternative-dispute-resolution processes they expect to pursue and when they expect to undertake the process. IN R USDCTND L.R. 16-6(a). For more information on alternative dispute resolution (ADR), refer to IN R USDCTND L.R. 16-6 and IN R USDCTND Order 2003-21.

8. *Settlement or resolution.* The parties must immediately notify the court if they reasonably expect to settle the case or resolve a pending motion. IN R USDCTND L.R. 16-1(g).

9. *Modification or suspension of rules.* The court may, on its own motion or at the request of a party, suspend or modify any rule in a particular case in the interest of justice. IN R USDCTND L.R. 1-1(c).

D. Documents

1. *Documents for moving party*

   a. *Required documents*

      i. *Notice of motion and motion.* The party must not specify a hearing date in the notice of a motion or petition unless the court or the clerk has authorized it. IN R USDCTND L.R. 7-5(b)(2). Refer to the General Requirements section of this document for information on the notice of motion and motion.

      ii. *Certificate of compliance.* A party filing any discovery motion must file a separate certification that the party has conferred in good faith or attempted to confer with other affected parties in an effort to resolve the matter raised in the motion without court action. The certification must include: (1) the date, time, and place of any conference or attempted conference; and (2) the names of the parties participating in the conference. IN R USDCTND L.R. 37-1(a). A motion for sanctions for failing to answer or respond must include a certification that the movant has in good faith conferred or attempted to confer with the party failing to act in an effort to obtain the answer or response without court action. FRCP 37(d)(1)(B).

        • *Failure to file certification.* The court may deny any motion described in IN R USDCTND

L.R. 37-1(a)—except those motions brought by or against a person appearing pro se—if the required certification is not filed. IN R USDCTND L.R. 37-1(b).

iii. *Brief.* Parties must file a supporting brief with any motion under: FRCP 37. IN R USDCTND L.R. 7-1(b)(2). Refer to the Format section of this document for the format of briefs.

iv. *Discovery materials.* A party who files a motion for relief under FRCP 26(c) or FRCP 37 must file with the motion those parts of the discovery requests or responses that the motion pertains to. IN R USDCTND L.R. 26-2(b).

v. *Certificate of service.* FRCP 5(d) requires that the person making service under FRCP 5 certify that service has been effected. FRCP 5(Advisory Committee Notes). Having such information on file may be useful for many purposes, including proof of service if an issue arises concerning the effectiveness of the service. FRCP 5(Advisory Committee Notes).

- *Certificate of service for electronically-filed documents.* A Certificate of Service is still a requirement when filing documents electronically. A sample Certificate of Service is attached as Form 1 (IN R USDCTND CM/ECF(Form 1)). IN R USDCTND CM/ECF(II)(H).

b. *Supplemental documents*

i. *Supporting evidence.* When a motion relies on facts outside the record, the court may hear the matter on affidavits or may hear it wholly or partly on oral testimony or on depositions. FRCP 43(c).

- *Materials necessary for motion.* A party must file those portions of discovery requests or responses (including deposition transcripts) that the party relies on to support a motion that could result in a final order on an issue. IN R USDCTND L.R. 26-2(c).

ii. *Notice of constitutional question.* A party that files a pleading, written motion, or other paper drawing into question the constitutionality of a federal or state statute must promptly:

- *File notice.* File a notice of constitutional question stating the question and identifying the paper that raises it, if: (1) a federal statute is questioned and the parties do not include the United States, one of its agencies, or one of its officers or employees in an official capacity; or (2) a state statute is questioned and the parties do not include the state, one of its agencies, or one of its officers or employees in an official capacity; and

- *Serve notice.* Serve the notice and paper on the Attorney General of the United States if a federal statute is questioned—or on the state attorney general if a state statute is questioned—either by certified or registered mail or by sending it to an electronic address designated by the attorney general for this purpose. FRCP 5.1(a).

- *When to file the notice.* A party required to file a notice of constitutional question under FRCP 5.1 must do so by the later of: (1) the day the parties tender their proposed case-management plan (if one is required); or (2) 21 days after filing the pleading, written motion, or other paper questioning the constitutionality of a federal or state statute. IN R USDCTND L.R. 5.1-1(a).

- *Service on government officials.* The party must also serve the notice and the pleading, written motion, or other paper questioning the constitutionality of a federal or state statute on: (1) the Attorney General of the United States and the United States Attorney for the Northern District of Indiana, if a federal statute is challenged; or (2) the Attorney General for the state if a state statute is challenged. IN R USDCTND L.R. 5.1-1(b). Service required under IN R USDCTND L.R. 5.1-1(b) may be made either by certified or registered mail or by emailing it to an address designated by those officials for this purpose. IN R USDCTND L.R. 5.1-1(c).

- *No forfeiture.* A party's failure to file and serve the notice, or the court's failure to certify, does not forfeit a constitutional claim or defense that is otherwise timely asserted. FRCP 5.1(d).

iii. *Index of exhibits.* Any pleading, motion, brief, affidavit, notice, or proposed order, whether filed electronically or by delivering it to the clerk, must: include a separate index identifying and briefly describing each exhibit if there are more than four (4) exhibits. IN R USDCTND L.R. 5-4(a)(8).

iv. *Request for oral argument.* A party may request oral argument on a motion by filing and serving a separate document explaining why oral argument is necessary and estimating how long the court should allow for the argument. IN R USDCTND L.R. 7-5(a)(1). The request must be filed and served with the party's supporting brief, response brief, or reply brief. IN R USDCTND L.R. 7-5(a)(2).

v. *Request for evidentiary hearing.* A party may request an evidentiary hearing by filing and serving a separate document explaining why the hearing is necessary and estimating how long the court should allow for it. IN R USDCTND L.R. 7-5(b)(1).

vi. *Copy of authority.* A copy of any decision, statute, or regulation cited in a motion or brief must be attached to the paper if—and only if—it is not available on Westlaw or Lexis. But if a copy of a decision, statute, or regulation is only available electronically, a party must provide it to the court or another party upon request. IN R USDCTND L.R. 7-1(f).

vii. *Proposed order.* Parties filing a paper that requires the judge or clerk to enter a routine or uncontested order must include a suitable form of order. IN R USDCTND L.R. 5-4(c).

- Proposed orders shall not be filed electronically either as a separate document or as an attachment to the main pleading or other document. Instead, all proposed orders must be e-mailed to the chambers of the appropriate judicial officer for the case. The proposed order must be in WordPerfect Format or Rich Text Format (RTF). Proposed orders should be attached to an e-mail and sent to the appropriate judicial officer at the address listed in IN R USDCTND CM/ECF(II)(F). The subject line of the email message should indicate the case title, cause number and document number of the motion, e.g., Smith v. Jones 1:02-cv-1234, motion# ___. IN R USDCTND CM/ECF(II)(F).

viii. *Copy of document with self-addressed envelope.* A party who wants a file-stamped copy of a paper must include with the filing an additional copy of the paper and a self-addressed envelope with adequate postage. IN R USDCTND L.R. 5-4(b)(6).

ix. *Notice of manual filing.* However, if that is not physically possible, counsel shall electronically file a .pdf document titled Notice of Manual Filing as a notation on the docket sheet that filings are being held in the clerk's office in paper. A sample Notice of Manual Filing is attached as Form 2 (IN R USDCTND CM/ECF(Form 2)). IN R USDCTND CM/ECF(III)(A)(1).

x. *Courtesy copies.* If documents are filed in paper format, counsel must provide an original for the clerk's office, a copy for the judge and a copy must be served on all parties in the case. IN R USDCTND CM/ECF(III)(A)(1).

xi. *Declaration that party was unable to file in a timely manner.* If the attorney is unable to file a document in a timely manner due to technical difficulties in the user's system, the attorney must file a document with the court as soon as possible notifying the court of the inability to file the document. A sample document entitled Declaration that Party was Unable to File in a Timely Manner Due to Technical Difficulties is attached hereto as Form 5. IN R USDCTND CM/ECF(VI)(B). [Editor's note: the reference to Form 5 is likely meant to be a reference to Form 3 (IN R USDCTND CM/ECF(Form 3)].

2. *Documents for opposing party*

 a. *Required documents*

   i. *Response brief.* Refer to the Format section of this document for the format of briefs. Refer to the General Requirements section of this document for information on the opposing papers.

   ii. *Certificate of service.* FRCP 5(d) requires that the person making service under FRCP 5 certify that service has been effected. FRCP 5(Advisory Committee Notes). Having such information on file may be useful for many purposes, including proof of service if an issue arises concerning the effectiveness of the service. FRCP 5(Advisory Committee Notes).

   - *Certificate of service for electronically-filed documents.* A Certificate of Service is still a requirement when filing documents electronically. A sample Certificate of Service is attached as Form 1 (IN R USDCTND CM/ECF(Form 1)). IN R USDCTND CM/ECF(II)(H).

b. *Supplemental documents*

    i.   *Supporting evidence.* When a motion relies on facts outside the record, the court may hear the matter on affidavits or may hear it wholly or partly on oral testimony or on depositions. FRCP 43(c).

- *Materials necessary for motion.* A party must file those portions of discovery requests or responses (including deposition transcripts) that the party relies on to support a motion that could result in a final order on an issue. IN R USDCTND L.R. 26-2(c).

    ii. *Notice of constitutional question.* A party that files a pleading, written motion, or other paper drawing into question the constitutionality of a federal or state statute must promptly:

- *File notice.* File a notice of constitutional question stating the question and identifying the paper that raises it, if: (1) a federal statute is questioned and the parties do not include the United States, one of its agencies, or one of its officers or employees in an official capacity; or (2) a state statute is questioned and the parties do not include the state, one of its agencies, or one of its officers or employees in an official capacity; and

- *Serve notice.* Serve the notice and paper on the Attorney General of the United States if a federal statute is questioned—or on the state attorney general if a state statute is questioned—either by certified or registered mail or by sending it to an electronic address designated by the attorney general for this purpose. FRCP 5.1(a).

- *When to file the notice.* A party required to file a notice of constitutional question under FRCP 5.1 must do so by the later of: (1) the day the parties tender their proposed case-management plan (if one is required); or (2) 21 days after filing the pleading, written motion, or other paper questioning the constitutionality of a federal or state statute. IN R USDCTND L.R. 5.1-1(a).

- *Service on government officials.* The party must also serve the notice and the pleading, written motion, or other paper questioning the constitutionality of a federal or state statute on: (1) the Attorney General of the United States and the United States Attorney for the Northern District of Indiana, if a federal statute is challenged; or (2) the Attorney General for the state if a state statute is challenged. IN R USDCTND L.R. 5.1-1(b). Service required under IN R USDCTND L.R. 5.1-1(b) may be made either by certified or registered mail or by emailing it to an address designated by those officials for this purpose. IN R USDCTND L.R. 5.1-1(c).

- *No forfeiture.* A party's failure to file and serve the notice, or the court's failure to certify, does not forfeit a constitutional claim or defense that is otherwise timely asserted. FRCP 5.1(d).

    iii. *Index of exhibits.* Any pleading, motion, brief, affidavit, notice, or proposed order, whether filed electronically or by delivering it to the clerk, must: include a separate index identifying and briefly describing each exhibit if there are more than four (4) exhibits. IN R USDCTND L.R. 5-4(a)(8).

    iv. *Request for oral argument.* A party may request oral argument on a motion by filing and serving a separate document explaining why oral argument is necessary and estimating how long the court should allow for the argument. IN R USDCTND L.R. 7-5(a)(1). The request must be filed and served with the party's supporting brief, response brief, or reply brief. IN R USDCTND L.R. 7-5(a)(2).

    v. *Request for evidentiary hearing.* A party may request an evidentiary hearing by filing and serving a separate document explaining why the hearing is necessary and estimating how long the court should allow for it. IN R USDCTND L.R. 7-5(b)(1).

    vi. *Copy of authority.* A copy of any decision, statute, or regulation cited in a motion or brief must be attached to the paper if—and only if—it is not available on Westlaw or Lexis. But if a copy of a decision, statute, or regulation is only available electronically, a party must provide it to the court or another party upon request. IN R USDCTND L.R. 7-1(f).

vii. *Copy of document with self-addressed envelope.* A party who wants a file-stamped copy of a paper must include with the filing an additional copy of the paper and a self-addressed envelope with adequate postage. IN R USDCTND L.R. 5-4(b)(6).

viii. *Notice of manual filing.* However, if that is not physically possible, counsel shall electronically file a .pdf document titled Notice of Manual Filing as a notation on the docket sheet that filings are being held in the clerk's office in paper. A sample Notice of Manual Filing is attached as Form 2 (IN R USDCTND CM/ECF(Form 2)). IN R USDCTND CM/ECF(III)(A)(1).

ix. *Courtesy copies.* If documents are filed in paper format, counsel must provide an original for the clerk's office, a copy for the judge and a copy must be served on all parties in the case. IN R USDCTND CM/ECF(III)(A)(1).

x. *Declaration that party was unable to file in a timely manner.* If the attorney is unable to file a document in a timely manner due to technical difficulties in the user's system, the attorney must file a document with the court as soon as possible notifying the court of the inability to file the document. A sample document entitled Declaration that Party was Unable to File in a Timely Manner Due to Technical Difficulties is attached hereto as Form 5. IN R USDCTND CM/ECF(VI)(B). [Editor's note: the reference to Form 5 is likely meant to be a reference to Form 3 (IN R USDCTND CM/ECF(Form 3)].

E. Format

1. *Form of documents.* The rules governing captions and other matters of form in pleadings apply to motions and other papers. FRCP 7(b)(2).

   a. *Paper.* Any pleading, motion, brief, affidavit, notice, or proposed order, whether filed electronically or by delivering it to the clerk, must: use eight and one-half by eleven (8-1/2 x 11) inch pages. IN R USDCTND L.R. 5-4(a)(2).

      i. *Manual filings.* Papers delivered to the clerk for filing must: be flat, unfolded, and on good-quality, white paper. IN R USDCTND L.R. 5-4(b)(1)(A).

         • *Covers or backing.* Papers delivered to the clerk for filing must: not have a cover or a back. IN R USDCTND L.R. 5-4(b)(1)(B).

         • *Recycled paper.* The court encourages using recycled paper. IN R USDCTND L.R. 5-4(b)(7).

   b. *Margins.* Any pleading, motion, brief, affidavit, notice, or proposed order, whether filed electronically or by delivering it to the clerk, must: have at least one (1) inch margins. IN R USDCTND L.R. 5-4(a)(3).

   c. *Spacing.* Any pleading, motion, brief, affidavit, notice, or proposed order, whether filed electronically or by delivering it to the clerk, must: be double spaced (except for headings, footnotes, and quoted material). IN R USDCTND L.R. 5-4(a)(5).

   d. *Text.* Any pleading, motion, brief, affidavit, notice, or proposed order, whether filed electronically or by delivering it to the clerk, must: be plainly typewritten, printed, or prepared by a clearly legible copying process. IN R USDCTND L.R. 5-4(a)(1).

      i. Any pleading, motion, brief, affidavit, notice, or proposed order, whether filed electronically or by delivering it to the clerk, must: use at least twelve (12) point type in the body and at least ten (10) point type in footnotes. IN R USDCTND L.R. 5-4(a)(4).

   e. *Page numbering.* Any pleading, motion, brief, affidavit, notice, or proposed order, whether filed electronically or by delivering it to the clerk, must: have consecutively numbered pages. IN R USDCTND L.R. 5-4(a)(6).

   f. *Caption; Names of parties.* Every pleading must have a caption with the court's name, a title, a file number, and a FRCP 7(a) designation. The title of the complaint must name all the parties; the title of other pleadings, after naming the first party on each side, may refer generally to other parties. FRCP 10(a). Any pleading, motion, brief, affidavit, notice, or proposed order, whether filed electronically or by delivering it to the clerk, must: include a title on the first page. IN R USDCTND L.R. 5-4(a)(7).

    i. *Alternative motions.* Motions must be filed separately, but alternative motions may be filed in a single paper if each is named in the title following the caption. IN R USDCTND L.R. 7-1(a).

g. *Filer's information.* Any pleading, motion, brief, affidavit, notice, or proposed order, whether filed electronically or by delivering it to the clerk, must: except in proposed orders and affidavits, include the filer's name, address, telephone number, fax number (where available), and e-mail address (where available). IN R USDCTND L.R. 5-4(a)(9).

h. *Paragraphs; Separate statements.* A party must state its claims or defenses in numbered paragraphs, each limited as far as practicable to a single set of circumstances. A later pleading may refer by number to a paragraph in an earlier pleading. If doing so would promote clarity, each claim founded on a separate transaction or occurrence—and each defense other than a denial—must be stated in a separate count or defense. FRCP 10(b).

i. *Adoption by reference; Exhibits.* A statement in a pleading may be adopted by reference elsewhere in the same pleading or in any other pleading or motion. A copy of a written instrument that is an exhibit to a pleading is a part of the pleading for all purposes. FRCP 10(c).

j. *Citation of local rules.* The Local Civil Rules of the United States District Court for the Northern District of Indiana may be cited as "N.D. Ind. L.R." IN R USDCTND L.R. 1-1(a)(1).

k. *Acceptance by the clerk.* The clerk must not refuse to file a paper solely because it is not in the form prescribed by the Federal Rules of Civil Procedure or by a local rule or practice. FRCP 5(d)(4).

    i. *Sanctions for formatting errors; Non-compliance.* If a person files a paper that does not comply with the rules governing the format of papers filed with the court, the court may: (1) strike the paper from the record; or (2) fine the person up to one thousand dollars ($1,000). IN R USDCTND L.R. 1-3(a).

        • *Notice.* Before sanctioning a person under IN R USDCTND L.R. 1-3(a)(2), the court must: (1) notify the person that the paper is noncompliant; and (2) give the person the opportunity either to be heard or to revise the paper. IN R USDCTND L.R. 1-3(b).

2. *Form of electronic documents.* Electronically filed documents must meet the same requirements of format and page limits as documents "conventionally filed" (as defined in IN R USDCTND CM/ECF(III)(A)) pursuant to the Federal Rules of Civil Procedure and the Local Civil Rules of the United States District Court for the Northern District of Indiana. IN R USDCTND CM/ECF(II)(A)(2).

a. *PDF format required.* Documents filed in the CM/ECF must be in .pdf format. A document created with almost any word-processing program can be converted to .pdf format. The .pdf program in effect takes a picture of the original document and allows anyone to open the converted document across a broad range of hardware and software, with layout, format, links, and images intact. IN R USDCTND CM/ECF(FN2).

b. *Title of documents.* The person electronically filing a pleading or other document will be responsible for designating a title for the pleading or other document by using one of the categories contained in the events listed in the CM/ECF Menu. IN R USDCTND CM/ECF(II)(G).

c. *Combining documents.* All documents which form part of a single pleading and which are being filed at the same time and by the same party may be electronically filed together under one document number, e.g., the motion and a supporting affidavit, with the exception of memoranda in support. Memoranda in support shall be electronically filed separately and shown as a related document to the motion. IN R USDCTND CM/ECF(II)(A)(4).

d. *Exhibits and attachments.* Filing users must submit in electronic form all documents referenced as exhibits or attachments, unless the court permits conventional filing. A filing user must submit as exhibits or attachments only those excerpts of the referenced documents that are directly germane to the matter under consideration by the court. Excerpted material must be clearly and prominently identified as such. Filing users who file excerpts of documents as exhibits or attachments do so without prejudice to their right to timely file additional excerpts or the complete document. Responding parties may timely file additional excerpts or the complete document that they believe are directly germane. The court may require parties to file additional excerpts or the complete document. IN R USDCTND CM/ECF(II)(A)(6).

e. *Hyperlinks.* Electronically filed documents may contain hyperlink references to an external document as a convenient mechanism for accessing material cited in the document. A hyperlink reference is neither validated for content nor considered a part of the court's records. The court neither endorses the product or organization at the destination of a hyperlink reference, nor does the court exercise any responsibility over the content at the destination. In order to preserve the integrity of the court record, attorneys wishing to insert hyperlinks in court filings shall continue to use the traditional citation method for the cited authority, in addition to the hyperlink. A hyperlink contained in a filing is no more than a convenient mechanism for accessing material cited in the document and a hyperlink reference is extraneous to any filed document and is not part of the court's record. IN R USDCTND CM/ECF(II)(A)(3).

3. *Form of briefs*

a. *Page limits.* Supporting and response briefs (excluding tables of contents, tables of authorities, and appendices) ordinarily must not exceed twenty-five (25) pages. Reply briefs must not exceed fifteen (15) pages. IN R USDCTND L.R. 7-1(e)(1).

   i. *Exception.* The court may allow a party to file a brief exceeding these page limits for extraordinary and compelling reasons. But if the court permits a brief to exceed twenty-five (25) pages, it must include:

   - A table of contents with page references;

   - An issue statement; and

   - A table of authorities including: (1) all cases (alphabetically arranged), statutes, and other authorities cited in the brief; and (2) references to where the authorities appear in the brief. IN R USDCTND L.R. 7-1(e)(2).

4. *Signing disclosures and discovery requests, responses, and objections.* FRCP 11 does not apply to disclosures and discovery requests, responses, objections, and motions under FRCP 26 through FRCP 37. FRCP 11(d).

a. *Signature required.* Every disclosure under FRCP 26(a)(1) or FRCP 26(a)(3) and every discovery request, response, or objection must be signed by at least one attorney of record in the attorney's own name—or by the party personally, if unrepresented—and must state the signer's address, e-mail address, and telephone number. FRCP 26(g)(1).

   i. *Signatures on manual filings.* Papers delivered to the clerk for filing must: include the filer's original signature. IN R USDCTND L.R. 5-4(b)(1)(C).

   - *Rubber-stamped and faxed signatures.* An original paper with a rubber-stamped or faxed signature is unsigned for purposes of FRCP 11 and FRCP 26(g). IN R USDCTND L.R. 5-4(b)(2).

   - *Affidavits.* Only the affiant need sign an affidavit. IN R USDCTND L.R. 5-4(b)(3).

   ii. *Electronic signatures.* Pursuant to FRCP 11, every pleading, motion, and other paper (except lists, schedules, statements or amendments thereto) shall be signed by at least one attorney of record or, if the party is not represented by an attorney, all papers shall be signed by the party. An attorney's/participant's password issued by the court combined with the user's identification, serves as and constitutes the attorney/participant's signature for FRCP 11 and other purposes. IN R USDCTND CM/ECF(I)(C). Documents which must be filed and which must contain original signatures other than those of a participating attorney or which require either verification or an unsworn declaration under any rule or statute, shall be filed electronically, with originally executed copies maintained by the filer. The pleading or other document electronically filed shall contain "s/" signature(s), as noted in IN R USDCTND CM/ECF(II)(E)(3)(b). IN R USDCTND CM/ECF(II)(E)(1).

- *Multiple signatures.* In the case of a stipulation or other document to be signed by two or more attorneys, the following procedure should be used: The filing attorney shall initially confirm that the content of the document is acceptable to all persons required to sign the document and shall obtain the physical signatures of all attorneys on the document. IN R USDCTND CM/ECF(II)(E)(3)(a). The filing attorney then shall file the document electronically, indicating the signatories, e.g., "s/Jane Doe," "s/John Doe," etc. IN R US-DCTND CM/ECF(II)(E)(3)(b). The filing attorney shall retain the hard copy of the document containing the original signatures. IN R USDCTND CM/ECF(II)(E)(3)(c).

b. *Effect of signature.* By signing, an attorney or party certifies that to the best of the person's knowledge, information, and belief formed after a reasonable inquiry:

   i. With respect to a disclosure, it is complete and correct as of the time it is made; and

   ii. With respect to a discovery request, response, or objection, it is:

- Consistent with the Federal Rules of Civil Procedure and warranted by existing law or by a nonfrivolous argument for extending, modifying, or reversing existing law, or for establishing new law;

- Not interposed for any improper purpose, such as to harass, cause unnecessary delay, or needlessly increase the cost of litigation; and

- Neither unreasonable nor unduly burdensome or expensive, considering the needs of the case, prior discovery in the case, the amount in controversy, and the importance of the issues at stake in the action. FRCP 26(g)(1).

c. *Failure to sign.* Other parties have no duty to act on an unsigned disclosure, request, response, or objection until it is signed, and the court must strike it unless a signature is promptly supplied after the omission is called to the attorney's or party's attention. FRCP 26(g)(2).

d. *Sanction for improper certification.* Refer to the General Requirements section of this document for information on the sanction for improper certification.

5. *Privacy protection for filings made with the court*

a. *Redacted filings.* Counsel should not include sensitive information in any document filed with the court unless such inclusion is necessary and relevant to the case. IN R USDCTND CM/ECF(VII). Unless the court orders otherwise, in an electronic or paper filing with the court that contains an individual's Social Security number, taxpayer-identification number, or birth date, the name of an individual known to be a minor, or a financial-account number, a party or nonparty making the filing may include only:

   i. The last four (4) digits of the Social Security number and taxpayer-identification number;

   ii. The year of the individual's birth;

   iii. The minor's initials; and

   iv. The last four (4) digits of the financial-account number. FRCP 5.2(a); IN R USDCTND Order 2005-3.

b. *Exemptions from the redaction requirement.* The redaction requirement does not apply to the following:

   i. A financial-account number that identifies the property allegedly subject to forfeiture in a forfeiture proceeding;

   ii. The record of an administrative or agency proceeding;

   iii. The official record of a state-court proceeding;

   iv. The record of a court or tribunal, if that record was not subject to the redaction requirement when originally filed;

   v. A filing covered by FRCP 5.2(c) or FRCP 5.2(d); and

   vi. A pro se filing in an action brought under 28 U.S.C.A. § 2241, 28 U.S.C.A. § 2254, or 28 U.S.C.A. § 2255. FRCP 5.2(b).

  vii. In cases filed under the Social Security Act, 42 U.S.C.A. § 405(g), there is no need for redaction of any information from the documents filed in the case. IN R USDCTND Order 2005-3.

c. *Limitations on remote access to electronic files; Social Security appeals and immigration cases.* Unless the court orders otherwise, in an action for benefits under the Social Security Act, and in an action or proceeding relating to an order of removal, to relief from removal, or to immigration benefits or detention, access to an electronic file is authorized as follows:

   i. The parties and their attorneys may have remote electronic access to any part of the case file, including the administrative record;

  ii. Any other person may have electronic access to the full record at the courthouse, but may have remote electronic access only to:

   • The docket maintained by the court; and

   • An opinion, order, judgment, or other disposition of the court, but not any other part of the case file or the administrative record. FRCP 5.2(c).

d. *Filings made under seal.* The court may order that a filing be made under seal without redaction. The court may later unseal the filing or order the person who made the filing to file a redacted version for the public record. FRCP 5.2(d). For information on filing documents under seal, refer to IN R USDCTND L.R. 5-3, IN R USDCTND CM/ECF(IV)(A), and IN R USDCTND ECF Order 2004-19.

e. *Protective orders.* For good cause, the court may by order in a case:

   i. Require redaction of additional information; or

  ii. Limit or prohibit a nonparty's remote electronic access to a document filed with the court. FRCP 5.2(e).

f. *Option for additional unredacted filing under seal.* A person making a redacted filing may also file an unredacted copy under seal. The court must retain the unredacted copy as part of the record. FRCP 5.2(f); IN R USDCTND Order 2005-3.

   i. The unredacted version of the document or the reference list shall be retained by the court under seal as part of the record. This paper shall be retained by the court as part of the record. The court may, however, still require the party to file a redacted copy for the public file. IN R USDCTND Order 2005-3.

g. *Option for filing a reference list.* A filing that contains redacted information may be filed together with a reference list that identifies each item of redacted information and specifies an appropriate identifier that uniquely corresponds to each item listed. The list must be filed under seal and may be amended as of right. Any reference in the case to a listed identifier will be construed to refer to the corresponding item of information. FRCP 5.2(g); IN R USDCTND Order 2005-3.

   i. The unredacted version of the document or the reference list shall be retained by the court under seal as part of the record. This paper shall be retained by the court as part of the record. The court may, however, still require the party to file a redacted copy for the public file. IN R USDCTND Order 2005-3.

h. *Responsibility for redaction.* The responsibility for redacting these personal identifiers rests solely with counsel and the parties. The Clerk will not review each paper for compliance with IN R USDCTND Order 2005-3. IN R USDCTND Order 2005-3.

i. *Waiver of protection of identifiers.* A person waives the protection of FRCP 5.2(a) as to the person's own information by filing it without redaction and not under seal. FRCP 5.2(h).

F. Filing and Service Requirements

1. *Filing requirements.* Any paper after the complaint that is required to be served—together with a certificate of service—must be filed within a reasonable time after service. FRCP 5(d)(1). Motions must

be filed separately, but alternative motions may be filed in a single paper if each is named in the title following the caption. IN R USDCTND L.R. 7-1(a).

a. *How filing is made; In general.* A paper is filed by delivering it:

    i. To the clerk; or

    ii. To a judge who agrees to accept it for filing, and who must then note the filing date on the paper and promptly send it to the clerk. FRCP 5(d)(2).

        • Papers not filed electronically must be filed with the clerk, not a judge. IN R USDCTND L.R. 5-4(b)(4).

    iii. Parties manually filing a paper that requires the clerk to give others notice, must give the clerk: (1) sufficient copies of the notice; and (2) the name and address of each person entitled to receive the notice. IN R USDCTND L.R. 5-4(b)(8).

b. *Where to file.* Papers not filed electronically must be filed in the division where the case is pending, unless: (1) a person will be prejudiced if the paper is not filed the same day it is tendered; and (2) it includes an adequately sized envelope addressed to the clerk's office in the division where the case is pending and with adequate postage. IN R USDCTND L.R. 5-4(b)(5).

c. *Electronic filing*

    i. *Authorization of electronic filing program.* A court may, by local rule, allow papers to be filed, signed, or verified by electronic means that are consistent with any technical standards established by the Judicial Conference of the United States. A local rule may require electronic filing only if reasonable exceptions are allowed. A paper filed electronically in compliance with a local rule is a written paper for purposes of the Federal Rules of Civil Procedure. FRCP 5(d)(3).

        • Papers must be filed, signed, and verified electronically unless excepted by the court's CM/ECF Civil and Criminal User Manual (IN R USDCTND CM/ECF). IN R USDCTND L.R. 5-1.

    ii. *Mandatory electronic filing.* Unless otherwise permitted by these procedures or otherwise authorized by the assigned judge, all documents submitted for filing in this district in civil and criminal cases, no matter when a case was originally filed, shall be filed electronically using the System. IN R USDCTND CM/ECF(II)(A)(1). The requirement that "all documents" be filed electronically includes briefs, and attachments and exhibits used in support of motions. IN R USDCTND CM/ECF(FN1).

        • Sending a document or pleading to the court via e-mail or facsimile does not constitute "electronic filing." IN R USDCTND CM/ECF(I)(A).

    iii. *Conventional filing.* As used in these procedures, a "conventionally" filed or submitted document or pleading is one presented to the Clerk or a party in paper or other non-electronic, tangible format. The following documents shall be filed conventionally and not electronically unless specifically authorized by the Court:

        • Exhibits and other documents which cannot be converted to a legible electronic form. Whenever possible, counsel is responsible for converting filings to an electronic form. However, if that is not physically possible, counsel shall electronically file a .pdf document titled Notice of Manual Filing as a notation on the docket sheet that filings are being held in the clerk's office in paper. A sample Notice of Manual Filing is attached as Form 2 (IN R USDCTND CM/ECF(Form 2)). If documents are filed in paper format, counsel must provide an original for the clerk's office, a copy for the judge and a copy must be served on all parties in the case. Large documents which do not exist in an electronic format shall be scanned into .pdf format by counsel, in small batches if necessary, and filed electronically as separate attachments in the System. IN R USDCTND CM/ECF(III)(A)(1).

        • Certain documents which are listed in IN R USDCTND CM/ECF(II)(E)(2). IN R USDCTND CM/ECF(III)(A)(2).

- Documents filed by pro se litigants. IN R USDCTND CM/ECF(III)(A)(3).

 iv. For more information on electronic filing, refer to IN R USDCTND CM/ECF.

2. *Service requirements*

 a. *Service; When required*

  i. *In general.* Unless the Federal Rules of Civil Procedure provide otherwise, each of the following papers must be served on every party:

- An order stating that service is required;
- A pleading filed after the original complaint, unless the court orders otherwise under FRCP 5(c) because there are numerous defendants;
- A discovery paper required to be served on a party, unless the court orders otherwise;
- A written motion, except one that may be heard ex parte; and
- A written notice, appearance, demand, or offer of judgment, or any similar paper. FRCP 5(a)(1).

  ii. *If a party fails to appear.* No service is required on a party who is in default for failing to appear. But a pleading that asserts a new claim for relief against such a party must be served on that party under FRCP 4. FRCP 5(a)(2).

  iii. *Seizing property.* If an action is begun by seizing property and no person is or need be named as a defendant, any service required before the filing of an appearance, answer, or claim must be made on the person who had custody or possession of the property when it was seized. FRCP 5(a)(3).

 b. *Service; How made*

  i. *Serving an attorney.* If a party is represented by an attorney, service under FRCP 5 must be made on the attorney unless the court orders service on the party. FRCP 5(b)(1).

  ii. *Service in general.* A paper is served under FRCP 5 by:

- Handing it to the person;
- Leaving it: (1) at the person's office with a clerk or other person in charge or, if no one is in charge, in a conspicuous place in the office; or (2) if the person has no office or the office is closed, at the person's dwelling or usual place of abode with someone of suitable age and discretion who resides there;
- Mailing it to the person's last known address—in which event service is complete upon mailing;
- Leaving it with the court clerk if the person has no known address;
- Sending it by electronic means if the person consented in writing—in which event service is complete upon transmission, but is not effective if the serving party learns that it did not reach the person to be served; or
- Delivering it by any other means that the person consented to in writing—in which event service is complete when the person making service delivers it to the agency designated to make delivery. FRCP 5(b)(2).

  iii. *Electronic service.* Electronically filed papers may be served electronically if service is consistent with the CM/ECF User Manual (IN R USDCTND CM/ECF). IN R USDCTND L.R. 5-2(a).

- *Waiver of other service.* An attorney's registration will constitute a waiver of conventional service of documents and the attorney agrees to accept service of notice on behalf of the client of the electronic filing by hand, facsimile or authorized email. IN R USDCTND CM/ECF(I)(B)(3).
- *Serving registered persons.* The System will generate a "Notice of Electronic Filing" when any document is filed. This notice represents service of the document on parties who are

registered participants with the System. Except as provided in IN R USDCTND CM/ECF(III)(B), the filing party shall not be required to serve any pleading or other documents on any party receiving electronic notice. IN R USDCTND CM/ECF(II)(D)(1). The term "pleading" refers only to those documents listed in FRCP 7(a). IN R USDCTND CM/ECF(FN3).

- *When electronic service is deemed completed.* A person registered to use the court's electronic-filing system is served with an electronically filed paper when a "Notice of Electronic Filing" is transmitted to that person through the court's electronic filing-system. IN R USDCTND L.R. 5-2(b).

- *Serving non-registered persons.* A person who has not registered to use the court's electronic-filing system but who is entitled to service of a paper must be served according to the Local Civil Rules of the United States District Court for the Northern District of Indiana and the Federal Rules of Civil Procedure. IN R USDCTND L.R. 5-2(c); IN R USDCTND CM/ECF(II)(D)(2). If such service of a paper copy is to be made, it shall be done in the manner provided in the Federal Rules of Civil Procedure and the Local Civil Rules of the United States District Court for the Northern District of Indiana. IN R USDCTND CM/ECF(II)(D)(2).

iv. *Service of conventional filings.* Pleadings or other documents which are filed conventionally rather than electronically shall be served in the manner provided for in the Federal Rules of Civil Procedure and the Local Civil Rules of the United States District Court for the Northern District of Indiana, except as otherwise provided by order of the Court. IN R USDCTND CM/ECF(III)(B).

v. *Using court facilities.* If a local rule so authorizes, a party may use the court's transmission facilities to make service under FRCP 5(b)(2)(E). FRCP 5(b)(3).

c. *Serving numerous defendants*

i. *In general.* If an action involves an unusually large number of defendants, the court may, on motion or on its own, order that:

- Defendants' pleadings and replies to them need not be served on other defendants;

- Any crossclaim, counterclaim, avoidance, or affirmative defense in those pleadings and replies to them will be treated as denied or avoided by all other parties; and

- Filing any such pleading and serving it on the plaintiff constitutes notice of the pleading to all parties. FRCP 5(c)(1).

ii. *Notifying parties.* A copy of every such order must be served on the parties as the court directs. FRCP 5(c)(2).

G. Hearings

1. *Hearings, generally*

a. *Oral argument.* Due process does not require that oral argument be permitted on a motion and, except as otherwise provided by local rule, the district court has discretion to determine whether it will decide the motion on the papers or hear argument by counsel (and perhaps receive evidence). FPP § 1190; F.D.I.C. v. Deglau, 207 F.3d 153 (3d Cir. 2000).

i. *Request for oral argument.* A party may request oral argument on a motion by filing and serving a separate document explaining why oral argument is necessary and estimating how long the court should allow for the argument. IN R USDCTND L.R. 7-5(a)(1). Refer to the Documents section of this document for more information.

ii. *Additional evidence forbidden.* Parties may not present additional evidence at oral argument. IN R USDCTND L.R. 7-5(a)(3).

b. *Providing a regular schedule for oral hearings.* A court may establish regular times and places for oral hearings on motions. FRCP 78(a).

c. *Providing for submission on briefs.* By rule or order, the court may provide for submitting and determining motions on briefs, without oral hearings. FRCP 78(b).

    d.   *Evidentiary hearings.* A party may request an evidentiary hearing by filing and serving a separate document explaining why the hearing is necessary and estimating how long the court should allow for it. IN R USDCTND L.R. 7-5(b)(2). Refer to the Documents section of this document for more information.

    e.   *Court's authority.* The court may: (1) grant or deny a request for oral argument or an evidentiary hearing in its discretion; (2) set oral argument or an evidentiary hearing without a request from a party; or (3) order any oral argument or evidentiary hearing to be held anywhere within the district regardless of where the case will be tried. IN R USDCTND L.R. 7-5(c).

2.   *Courtroom and courthouse decorum.* For information on courtroom and courthouse decorum, refer to IN R USDCTND L.R. 83-3.

H. Forms

1. Federal Motion for Discovery Sanctions Forms

    a.   Motion for contempt. 3B FEDFORMS § 3721.

    b.   Motion for sanctions for failure to appear at deposition. 3B FEDFORMS § 3722.

    c.   Motion that facts be taken as established for failure to answer questions upon deposition. 3B FEDFORMS § 3723.

    d.   Motion for order refusing to allow disobedient party to support or oppose designated claims or defenses. 3B FEDFORMS § 3724.

    e.   Motion for default judgment against defendant for failure to comply with order for production of documents. 3B FEDFORMS § 3725.

    f.   Motion for award of expenses incurred to prove matter opponent failed to admit under FRCP 36. 3B FEDFORMS § 3726.

    g.   Motion to strike answer or dismiss action for failure to comply with order requiring answer to interrogatories. 3B FEDFORMS § 3729.

    h.   Motion to dismiss for failure to comply with previous order requiring answer to interrogatories to party. 3B FEDFORMS § 3732.

    i.   Motion; For order that facts be taken to be established, and/or prohibiting certain claims, defenses, or evidence in opposition thereto. FEDPROF § 23:595.

    j.   Affidavit; By attorney; In support of motion for order that facts be taken to be established, etc; Failure to produce documents for inspection. FEDPROF § 23:596.

    k.   Affidavit; By attorney; In support of motion for order that facts be taken to be established, etc; Failure to obey order to answer questions. FEDPROF § 23:597.

    l.   Motion; For order striking pleadings, and for default judgment or dismissal of action. FEDPROF § 23:599.

    m.   Affidavit; By attorney; In support of motion for default judgment for defendant's failure to obey discovery order. FEDPROF § 23:600.

    n.   Motion; By defendant; For dismissal of action and other sanctions; For failure to comply with orders to complete deposition. FEDPROF § 23:601.

    o.   Motion; By defendant; For dismissal of action or other sanctions; For failure and refusal to comply with order to produce documents. FEDPROF § 23:602.

    p.   Motion; By defendant; For dismissal with prejudice; Failure to answer interrogatories as ordered. FEDPROF § 23:603.

    q.   Motion; For order staying further proceedings until adverse party obeys order compelling discovery. FEDPROF § 23:604.

    r.   Affidavit; By attorney; Opposing motion for order striking pleading and directing entry of default judgment; Good-faith attempt to obey discovery order; Production of documents illegal under foreign law. FEDPROF § 23:605.

s. Motion; For sanctions for failure to comply with examination order. FEDPROF § 23:610.

t. Motion; For order finding person in contempt of court; Refusal, after order, to answer question. FEDPROF § 23:612.

u. Affidavit; By attorney; In support of motion for order finding party in contempt. FEDPROF § 23:613.

v. Affidavit; By plaintiff; In support of motion for order holding defendant in contempt of court; Defendant disobeyed order for production of documents. FEDPROF § 23:614.

w. Motion; For order compelling opposing party to pay expenses incurred in proving facts such party refused to admit. FEDPROF § 23:616.

x. Motion; For sanctions; Failure to attend own deposition, serve answers to interrogatories, or respond to request for inspection. FEDPROF § 23:618.

y. Motion; For order staying proceedings until required response to discovery request is made. FEDPROF § 23:619.

z. Affidavit; By attorney; In support of motion for sanctions; Failure to attend own deposition, serve answers to interrogatories, or respond to request for inspection. FEDPROF § 23:620.

2. Forms for the Northern District of Indiana

a. Certificate of service. IN R USDCTND CM/ECF(Form 1).

b. Notice of manual filing. IN R USDCTND CM/ECF(Form 2).

c. Declaration that party was unable to file in a timely manner. IN R USDCTND CM/ECF(Form 3).

I. Applicable Rules

1. *Federal rules*

a. Counsel's liability for excessive costs. 28 U.S.C.A. § 1927.

b. Serving and filing pleadings and other papers. FRCP 5.

c. Constitutional challenge to a statute; Notice, certification, and intervention. FRCP 5.1.

d. Privacy protection for filings made with the court. FRCP 5.2.

e. Computing and extending time; Time for motion papers. FRCP 6.

f. Pleadings allowed; Form of motions and other papers. FRCP 7.

g. Form of pleadings. FRCP 10.

h. Signing pleadings, motions, and other papers; Representations to the court; Sanctions. FRCP 11.

i. Duty to disclose; General provisions governing discovery. FRCP 26.

j. Failure to make disclosures or to cooperate in discovery; Sanctions. FRCP 37.

k. Taking testimony. FRCP 43.

l. Hearing motions; Submission on briefs. FRCP 78.

2. *Local rules*

a. Citation and scope of the rules. IN R USDCTND L.R. 1-1.

b. Sanctions for formatting errors. IN R USDCTND L.R. 1-3.

c. Electronic filing required. IN R USDCTND L.R. 5-1.

d. Constitutional questions. IN R USDCTND L.R. 5.1-1.

e. Electronic service. IN R USDCTND L.R. 5-2.

f. Format of papers. IN R USDCTND L.R. 5-4.

g. Motion practice. IN R USDCTND L.R. 7-1.

h. Oral arguments and evidentiary hearings. IN R USDCTND L.R. 7-5.

i. Pretrial procedure. IN R USDCTND L.R. 16-1.

j.   Alternative dispute resolution. IN R USDCTND L.R. 16-6.

k.   Filing of discovery and other materials. IN R USDCTND L.R. 26-2.

l.   Resolving discovery disputes. IN R USDCTND L.R. 37-1.

m.   Case assignment. IN R USDCTND L.R. 40-1.

n.   Appearance and withdrawal of appearance. IN R USDCTND L.R. 83-8.

o.   CM/ECF civil and criminal user manual. IN R USDCTND CM/ECF.

p.   In re: privacy and public access to civil electronic case files. IN R USDCTND Order 2005-3.

Motions, Oppositions and Replies
Motion for Preliminary Injunction

Document Last Updated December 2016

A. Checklist

(I)   ❑ Matters to be considered by moving party

   (a)   ❑ Required documents

      (1)   ❑ Notice of motion and motion

      (2)   ❑ Security

      (3)   ❑ Certificate of service

   (b)   ❑ Supplemental documents

      (1)   ❑ Brief

      (2)   ❑ Supporting evidence

      (3)   ❑ Pleadings

      (4)   ❑ Notice of constitutional question

      (5)   ❑ Nongovernmental corporate disclosure statement

      (6)   ❑ Index of exhibits

      (7)   ❑ Request for oral argument

      (8)   ❑ Request for evidentiary hearing

      (9)   ❑ Copy of authority

      (10)   ❑ Proposed order

      (11)   ❑ Copy of document with self-addressed envelope

      (12)   ❑ Notice of manual filing

      (13)   ❑ Courtesy copies

      (14)   ❑ Declaration that party was unable to file in a timely manner

   (c)   ❑ Timing

      (1)   ❑ A written motion and notice of the hearing must be served at least fourteen (14) days before the time specified for the hearing, with the following exceptions: (i) when the motion may be heard ex parte; (ii) when the Federal Rules of Civil Procedure set a different time; or (iii) when a court order—which a party may, for good cause, apply for ex parte—sets a different time

      (2)   ❑ Any affidavit supporting a motion must be served with the motion

(II)   ❑ Matters to be considered by opposing party

   (a)   ❑ Required documents

      (1)   ❑ Response brief

(2) ❑ Certificate of service

(b) ❑ Supplemental documents

    (1) ❑ Supporting evidence

    (2) ❑ Pleadings

    (3) ❑ Notice of constitutional question

    (4) ❑ Nongovernmental corporate disclosure statement

    (5) ❑ Index of exhibits

    (6) ❑ Request for oral argument

    (7) ❑ Request for evidentiary hearing

    (8) ❑ Copy of authority

    (9) ❑ Copy of document with self-addressed envelope

    (10) ❑ Notice of manual filing

    (11) ❑ Courtesy copies

    (12) ❑ Declaration that party was unable to file in a timely manner

(c) ❑ Timing

    (1) ❑ A party must file any response brief to a motion within fourteen (14) days after the motion is served

    (2) ❑ Except as FRCP 59(c) provides otherwise, any opposing affidavit must be served at least seven (7) days before the hearing, unless the court permits service at another time

B. Timing

1. *Motion for preliminary injunction.* FRCP 65 is silent about when notice must be given. FPP § 2949.

2. *Timing of motions, generally*

    a. *Motion and notice of hearing.* A written motion and notice of the hearing must be served at least fourteen (14) days before the time specified for the hearing, with the following exceptions:

        i. When the motion may be heard ex parte;

        ii. When the Federal Rules of Civil Procedure set a different time; or

        iii. When a court order—which a party may, for good cause, apply for ex parte—sets a different time. FRCP 6(c)(1).

    b. *Supporting affidavit.* Any affidavit supporting a motion must be served with the motion. FRCP 6(c)(2).

3. *Timing of opposing papers.* A party must file any response brief to a motion within fourteen (14) days after the motion is served. IN R USDCTND L.R. 7-1(d)(2)(A).

    a. *Opposing affidavit.* Except as FRCP 59(c) provides otherwise, any opposing affidavit must be served at least seven (7) days before the hearing, unless the court permits service at another time. FRCP 6(c)(2).

    b. *Extensions.* The court may extend response- and reply-brief deadlines, but only for good cause. IN R USDCTND L.R. 7-1(d)(3).

    c. *Summary rulings.* The court may rule on a motion summarily if an opposing party does not file a response before the deadline. IN R USDCTND L.R. 7-1(d)(4).

4. *Timing of reply papers.* Where the respondent files an answering affidavit setting up a new matter, the moving party ordinarily is allowed a reasonable time to file a reply affidavit since failure to deny the new matter by affidavit may operate as an admission of its truth. AMJUR MOTIONS § 25.

    a. *Reply brief.* The moving party must file any reply brief within seven (7) days after the response brief is served. IN R USDCTND L.R. 7-1(d)(2)(B).

    b.   *Extensions.* The court may extend response- and reply-brief deadlines, but only for good cause. IN R USDCTND L.R. 7-1(d)(3).

5.   *Computation of time*

    a.   *Computing time.* FRCP 6 applies in computing any time period specified in the Federal Rules of Civil Procedure, in any local rule or court order, or in any statute that does not specify a method of computing time. FRCP 6(a).

        i.   *Period stated in days or a longer unit.* When the period is stated in days or a longer unit of time:

- Exclude the day of the event that triggers the period;
- Count every day, including intermediate Saturdays, Sundays, and legal holidays; and
- Include the last day of the period, but if the last day is a Saturday, Sunday, or legal holiday, the period continues to run until the end of the next day that is not a Saturday, Sunday, or legal holiday. FRCP 6(a)(1).

        ii.   *Period stated in hours.* When the period is stated in hours:

- Begin counting immediately on the occurrence of the event that triggers the period;
- Count every hour, including hours during intermediate Saturdays, Sundays, and legal holidays; and
- If the period would end on a Saturday, Sunday, or legal holiday, the period continues to run until the same time on the next day that is not a Saturday, Sunday, or legal holiday. FRCP 6(a)(2).

        iii.   *Inaccessibility of the clerk's office.* Unless the court orders otherwise, if the clerk's office is inaccessible:

- On the last day for filing under FRCP 6(a)(1), then the time for filing is extended to the first accessible day that is not a Saturday, Sunday, or legal holiday; or
- During the last hour for filing under FRCP 6(a)(2), then the time for filing is extended to the same time on the first accessible day that is not a Saturday, Sunday, or legal holiday. FRCP 6(a)(3).

        iv.   *"Last day" defined.* Unless a different time is set by a statute, local rule, or court order, the last day ends:

- For electronic filing, at midnight in the court's time zone; and
- For filing by other means, when the clerk's office is scheduled to close. FRCP 6(a)(4).

        v.   *"Next day" defined.* The "next day" is determined by continuing to count forward when the period is measured after an event and backward when measured before an event. FRCP 6(a)(5).

        vi.   *"Legal holiday" defined.* "Legal holiday" means:

- The day set aside by statute for observing New Year's Day, Martin Luther King Jr.'s Birthday, Washington's Birthday, Memorial Day, Independence Day, Labor Day, Columbus Day, Veterans' Day, Thanksgiving Day, or Christmas Day;
- Any day declared a holiday by the President or Congress; and
- For periods that are measured after an event, any other day declared a holiday by the state where the district court is located. FRCP 6(a)(6).

    b.   *Computation of electronic filing deadlines.* Filing documents electronically does not alter any filing deadlines or any time computation pursuant to FRCP 6. The counties of Lake, Porter, LaPorte, Pulaski and Starke are located in the Central time zone and the remaining counties in the Northern District of Indiana are located in the Eastern time zone. Nevertheless, all electronic transmissions of documents must be completed (i.e., received completely by the clerk's office) prior to midnight Eastern Time, (South Bend/Fort Wayne/Lafayette time) in order to be considered timely filed that day, regardless of the local time in the division where the case is pending. Although documents can be filed electronically twenty-four (24) hours a day, filers are strongly encouraged to file all

documents during hours when the CM/ECF Help Line is available, from 9:00 a.m. to 4:00 p.m. local time. IN R USDCTND CM/ECF(II)(I).

    i. *Technical failures.* If the attorney is unable to file a document in a timely manner due to technical difficulties in the user's system, the attorney must file a document with the court as soon as possible notifying the court of the inability to file the document. A sample document entitled Declaration that Party was Unable to File in a Timely Manner Due to Technical Difficulties is attached hereto as Form 5. IN R USDCTND CM/ECF(VI)(B). [Editor's note: the reference to Form 5 is likely meant to be a reference to Form 3 (IN R USDCTND CM/ECF(Form 3)].

c. *Extending time*

    i. *In general.* When an act may or must be done within a specified time, the court may, for good cause, extend the time:

- With or without motion or notice if the court acts, or if a request is made, before the original time or its extension expires; or

- On motion made after the time has expired if the party failed to act because of excusable neglect. FRCP 6(b)(1).

    ii. *Exceptions.* A court must not extend the time to act under FRCP 50(b), FRCP 50(d), FRCP 52(b), FRCP 59(b), FRCP 59(d), FRCP 59(e), and FRCP 60(b). FRCP 6(b)(2).

    iii. Refer to the United States District Court for the Northern District of Indiana KeyRules Motion for Continuance/Extension of Time document for more information on extending time.

d. *Additional time after certain kinds of service.* When a party may or must act within a specified time after being served and service is made under FRCP 5(b)(2)(C) (mail), FRCP 5(b)(2)(D) (leaving with the clerk), or FRCP 5(b)(2)(F) (other means consented to), three (3) days are added after the period would otherwise expire under FRCP 6(a). FRCP 6(d).

C. General Requirements

1. *Motions, generally*

a. *Requirements.* A request for a court order must be made by motion. The motion must:

    i. Be in writing unless made during a hearing or trial;

    ii. State with particularity the grounds for seeking the order; and

    iii. State the relief sought. FRCP 7(b)(1).

b. *Notice of motion.* A party interested in resisting the relief sought by a motion has a right to notice thereof, and an opportunity to be heard. AMJUR MOTIONS § 12.

    i. In addition to statutory or court rule provisions requiring notice of a motion—the purpose of such a notice requirement having been said to be to prevent a party from being prejudicially surprised by a motion—principles of natural justice dictate that an adverse party generally must be given notice that a motion will be presented to the court. AMJUR MOTIONS § 12.

    ii. "Notice," in this regard, means reasonable notice, including a meaningful opportunity to prepare and to defend against allegations of a motion. AMJUR MOTIONS § 12.

c. *Writing requirement.* The writing requirement is intended to insure that the adverse parties are informed and have a record of both the motion's pendency and the grounds on which the movant seeks an order. FPP § 1191; Feldberg v. Quechee Lakes Corp., 463 F.3d 195 (2d Cir. 2006).

    i. It is sufficient "if the motion is stated in a written notice of the hearing of the motion." FPP § 1191.

d. *Particularity requirement.* The particularity requirement insures that the opposing parties will have notice of their opponent's contentions. FEDPROC § 62:364; Goodman v. 1973 26 Foot Trojan Vessel, Arkansas Registration No. AR1439SN, 859 F.2d 71, 12 Fed.R.Serv.3d 645 (8th Cir. 1988). That requirement ensures that notice of the basis for the motion is provided to the court and to the opposing party so as to avoid prejudice, provide the opponent with a meaningful opportunity to

respond, and provide the court with enough information to process the motion correctly. FEDPROC § 62:364; Andreas v. Volkswagen of America, Inc., 336 F.3d 789, 56 Fed.R.Serv.3d 6 (8th Cir. 2003).

    i. Reasonable specification of the grounds for a motion is sufficient. However, where a movant fails to state even one ground for granting the motion in question, the movant has failed to meet the minimal standard of "reasonable specification." FEDPROC § 62:364; Martinez v. Trainor, 556 F.2d 818, 23 Fed.R.Serv.2d 403 (7th Cir. 1977).

    ii. The court may excuse the failure to comply with the particularity requirement if it is inadvertent, and where no prejudice is shown by the opposing party. FEDPROC § 62:364.

  e. *Motions must be filed separately.* Motions must be filed separately, but alternative motions may be filed in a single paper if each is named in the title following the caption. IN R USDCTND L.R. 7-1(a).

2. *Motion for preliminary injunction.* The appropriate procedure for requesting a preliminary injunction is by motion, although it also commonly is requested by an order to show cause. FPP § 2949; James Luterbach Constr. Co. v. Adamkus, 781 F.2d 599, 603 (7th Cir. 1986); Studebaker Corp. v. Gittlin, 360 F.2d 692 (2d. Cir. 1966).

  a. *Preliminary injunction.* An interim grant of specific relief is a preliminary injunction that may be issued only on notice to the adverse party. FEDPROC § 47:53; Westar Energy, Inc. v. Lake, 552 F.3d 1215 (10th Cir. 2009). Defined broadly, a preliminary injunction is an injunction that is issued to protect plaintiff from irreparable injury and to preserve the court's power to render a meaningful decision after a trial on the merits. FPP § 2947; Evans v. Buchanan, 555 F.2d 373, 387 (3d Cir. 1977).

    i. *Disfavored injunctions.* There are three types of preliminary injunctions that are disfavored:

- Those that afford the moving party substantially all the relief it might recover after a full trial on the merits;
- Those that disturb the status quo; and
- Those that are mandatory as opposed to prohibitory. FEDPROC § 47:55; Prairie Band of Potawatomi Indians v. Pierce, 253 F.3d 1234, 50 Fed.R.Serv.3d 244 (10th Cir. 2001).

  b. *Notice.* The court may issue a preliminary injunction only on notice to the adverse party. FRCP 65(a)(1). Although FRCP 65(a)(1) does not define what constitutes proper notice, it has been held that providing a copy of the motion and a specification of the time and place of the hearing are adequate. FPP § 2949.

  c. *Security.* The court may issue a preliminary injunction or a temporary restraining order only if the movant gives security in an amount that the court considers proper to pay the costs and damages sustained by any party found to have been wrongfully enjoined or restrained. The United States, its officers, and its agencies are not required to give security. FRCP 65(c).

    i. *Proceedings against a surety.* Whenever the Federal Rules of Civil Procedure (including the Supplemental Rules for Admiralty or Maritime Claims and Asset Forfeiture Actions) require or allow a party to give security, and security is given through a bond or other undertaking with one or more sureties, each surety submits to the court's jurisdiction and irrevocably appoints the court clerk as its agent for receiving service of any papers that affect its liability on the bond or undertaking. The surety's liability may be enforced on motion without an independent action. The motion and any notice that the court orders may be served on the court clerk, who must promptly mail a copy of each to every surety whose address is known. FRCP 65.1.

  d. *Preliminary injunction versus temporary restraining order.* Care should be taken to distinguish preliminary injunctions under FRCP 65(a) from temporary-restraining orders under FRCP 65(b). FPP § 2947.

    i. *Notice and duration.* [Temporary restraining orders] may be issued ex parte without an adversary hearing in order to prevent an immediate, irreparable injury and are of limited duration—they typically remain in effect for a maximum of twenty-eight (28) days. On the other hand, FRCP 65(a)(1) requires that notice be given to the opposing party before a preliminary injunction may be issued. FPP § 2947. Furthermore, a preliminary injunction normally lasts until the completion of the trial on the merits, unless it is dissolved earlier by court order or the consent of the parties. FPP § 2947. Therefore, its duration varies and is controlled by the nature of the situation in which it is utilized. FPP § 2947; Fundicao Tupy S.A. v. U.S., 841 F.2d 1101, 1103 (Fed. Cir. 1988).

ii. *Hearing.* Some type of a hearing also implicitly is required by FRCP 65(a)(2), which was added in 1966 and provides either for the consolidation of the trial on the merits with the preliminary-injunction hearing or the inclusion in the trial record of any evidence received at the FRCP 65(a) hearing. FPP § 2947.

e. *Grounds for granting or denying a preliminary injunction.* The policies that bear on the propriety of granting a preliminary injunction rarely are discussed directly in the cases. Instead they are taken into account by the court considering a number of factors that have been found useful in deciding whether to grant or deny preliminary injunctions in particular cases. A formulation that has become popular in all kinds of cases, although it originally was devised in connection with stays of administrative orders, is that the four most important factors are: (1) the significance of the threat of irreparable harm to plaintiff if the injunction is not granted; (2) the state of the balance between this harm and the injury that granting the injunction would inflict on defendant; (3) the probability that plaintiff will succeed on the merits; and (4) the public interest. FPP § 2948; Pottgen v. Missouri State High School Activities Ass'n, 40 F.3d 926 (8th Cir. 1994).

i. *Irreparable harm.* Perhaps the single most important prerequisite for the issuance of a preliminary injunction is a demonstration that if it is not granted the applicant is likely to suffer irreparable harm before a decision on the merits can be rendered. FPP § 2948.1. Only when the threatened harm would impair the court's ability to grant an effective remedy is there really a need for preliminary relief. FPP § 2948.1.

- There must be a likelihood that irreparable harm will occur. Speculative injury is not sufficient; there must be more than an unfounded fear on the part of the applicant. FPP § 2948.1.

- Thus, a preliminary injunction will not be issued simply to prevent the possibility of some remote future injury. A presently existing actual threat must be shown. However, the injury need not have been inflicted when application is made or be certain to occur; a strong threat of irreparable injury before trial is an adequate basis. FPP § 2948.1.

ii. *Balancing hardship to parties.* The second factor bearing on the court's exercise of its discretion as to whether to grant preliminary relief involves an evaluation of the severity of the impact on defendant should the temporary injunction be granted and the hardship that would occur to plaintiff if the injunction should be denied. Two factors that frequently are considered when balancing the hardship on the respective parties of the grant or denial of relief are whether a preliminary injunction would give plaintiff all or most of the relief to which plaintiff would be entitled if successful at trial and whether mandatory relief is being sought. FPP § 2948.2.

iii. *Likelihood of prevailing on the merits.* The third factor that enters into the preliminary injunction calculus is the likelihood that plaintiff will prevail on the merits. This is relevant because the need for the court to act is, at least in part, a function of the validity of the applicant's claim. The courts use a bewildering variety of formulations of the need for showing some likelihood of success—the most common being that plaintiff must demonstrate a reasonable probability of success. But the verbal differences do not seem to reflect substantive disagreement. All courts agree that plaintiff must present a prima facie case but need not show a certainty of winning. FPP § 2948.3.

iv. *Public interest.* The final major factor bearing on the court's discretion to issue or deny a preliminary injunction is the public interest. Focusing on this factor is another way of inquiring whether there are policy considerations that bear on whether the order should issue. Thus, when granting preliminary relief, courts frequently emphasize that the public interest will be furthered by the injunction. Conversely, preliminary relief will be denied if the court finds that the public interest would be injured were an injunction to be issued. If the court finds there is no public interest supporting preliminary relief, that conclusion also supports denial of any injunction, even if the public interest would not be harmed by one. FPP § 2948.4. Consequently, an evaluation of the public interest should be given considerable weight in determining whether a motion for a preliminary injunction should be granted. FPP § 2948.4; Yakus v. U.S., 321 U.S. 414, 64 S.Ct. 660, 88 L.Ed. 834 (1944).

   f. *Contents and scope of every injunction and restraining order*

      i. *Contents.* Every order granting an injunction and every restraining order must:

- State the reasons why it issued;
- State its terms specifically; and
- Describe in reasonable detail—and not by referring to the complaint or other document— the act or acts restrained or required. FRCP 65(d)(1).

      ii. *Persons bound.* The order binds only the following who receive actual notice of it by personal service or otherwise:

- The parties;
- The parties' officers, agents, servants, employees, and attorneys; and
- Other persons who are in active concert or participation with anyone described in FRCP 65(d)(2)(A) or FRCP 65(d)(2)(B). FRCP 65(d)(2).

   g. *Other laws not modified.* FRCP 65 does not modify the following:

      i. Any federal statute relating to temporary restraining orders or preliminary injunctions in actions affecting employer and employee;

      ii. 28 U.S.C.A. § 2361, which relates to preliminary injunctions in actions of interpleader or in the nature of interpleader; or

      iii. 28 U.S.C.A. § 2284, which relates to actions that must be heard and decided by a three-judge district court. FRCP 65(e).

   h. *Copyright impoundment.* FRCP 65 applies to copyright-impoundment proceedings. FRCP 65(f).

3. *Opposing papers.* The Federal Rules of Civil Procedure do not require any formal answer, return, or reply to a motion, except where the Federal Rules of Civil Procedure or local rules may require affidavits, memoranda, or other papers to be filed in opposition to a motion. Such papers are simply to apprise the court of such opposition and the grounds of that opposition. FEDPROC § 62:359.

   a. *Effect of failure to respond to motion.* Although in the absence of statutory provision or court rule, a motion ordinarily does not require a written answer, when a party files a motion and the opposing party fails to respond, the court may construe such failure to respond as nonopposition to the motion or an admission that the motion was meritorious, may take the facts alleged in the motion as true—the rule in some jurisdictions being that the failure to respond to a fact set forth in a motion is deemed an admission—and may grant the motion if the relief requested appears to be justified. AMJUR MOTIONS § 28.

   b. *Assent or no opposition not determinative.* However, a motion will not be granted automatically simply because an "assent" or a notation of "no opposition" has been filed; federal judges frequently deny motions that have been assented to when it is thought that justice so dictates. FPP § 1190.

   c. *Responsive pleading inappropriate as response to motion.* An attempt to answer or oppose a motion with a responsive pleading usually is not appropriate. FPP § 1190.

4. *Reply papers.* A moving party may be required or permitted to prepare papers in addition to his original motion papers. AMJUR MOTIONS § 25. Papers answering or replying to opposing papers may be appropriate, in the interests of justice, where it appears there is a substantial reason for allowing a reply. Thus, a court may accept reply papers where a party demonstrates that the papers to which it seeks to file a reply raise new issues that are material to the disposition of the question before the court, or where the court determines, sua sponte, that it wishes further briefing of an issue raised in those papers and orders the submission of additional papers. FEDPROC § 62:360.

   a. *Function of reply papers.* The function of a reply affidavit is to answer the arguments made in opposition to the position taken by the movant and not to permit the movant to introduce new arguments in support of the motion. AMJUR MOTIONS § 25.

b. *Issues raised for the first time in a reply document.* However, the view has been followed in some jurisdictions, that as a matter of judicial economy, where there is no prejudice and where the issues could be raised simply by filing a motion to dismiss, the trial court has discretion to consider arguments raised for the first time in a reply memorandum, and that a trial court may grant a motion to strike issues raised for the first time in a reply memorandum. AMJUR MOTIONS § 26.

5. *Appearances.* Attorneys not representing the United States or its agencies must file an appearance when they represent (either in person or by filing a paper) a party. IN R USDCTND L.R. 83-8(a). For more information, refer to IN R USDCTND L.R. 83-8.

6. *Notice of related action.* A party must file a notice of related action as soon as it appears that the party's case and another pending case: (1) arise out of the same transaction or occurrence; (2) involve the same property; or (3) involve the validity or infringement of the same patent, trademark, or copyright. IN R USDCTND L.R. 40-1(d). For more information, refer to IN R USDCTND L.R. 40-1.

7. *Alternative dispute resolution (ADR).* After they confer as required by FRCP 26(f), the parties must advise the court which, if any, alternative-dispute-resolution processes they expect to pursue and when they expect to undertake the process. IN R USDCTND L.R. 16-6(a). For more information on alternative dispute resolution (ADR), refer to IN R USDCTND L.R. 16-6 and IN R USDCTND Order 2003-21.

8. *Settlement or resolution.* The parties must immediately notify the court if they reasonably expect to settle the case or resolve a pending motion. IN R USDCTND L.R. 16-1(g).

9. *Modification or suspension of rules.* The court may, on its own motion or at the request of a party, suspend or modify any rule in a particular case in the interest of justice. IN R USDCTND L.R. 1-1(c).

D. Documents

1. *Documents for moving party*

   a. *Required documents*

      i. *Notice of motion and motion.* The court will consider requests for preliminary injunctions only if the moving party files a separate motion for relief. IN R USDCTND L.R. 65-1(a). The party must not specify a hearing date in the notice of a motion or petition unless the court or the clerk has authorized it. IN R USDCTND L.R. 7-5(b)(2). Refer to the General Requirements section of this document for information on the notice of motion and motion.

      ii. *Security.* Refer to the General Requirements section of this document for information on the security required.

      iii. *Certificate of service.* FRCP 5(d) requires that the person making service under FRCP 5 certify that service has been effected. FRCP 5(Advisory Committee Notes). Having such information on file may be useful for many purposes, including proof of service if an issue arises concerning the effectiveness of the service. FRCP 5(Advisory Committee Notes).

         • *Certificate of service for electronically-filed documents.* A Certificate of Service is still a requirement when filing documents electronically. A sample Certificate of Service is attached as Form 1 (IN R USDCTND CM/ECF(Form 1)). IN R USDCTND CM/ECF(II)(H).

   b. *Supplemental documents*

      i. *Brief.* Refer to the Format section of this document for the format of briefs.

      ii. *Supporting evidence.* When a motion relies on facts outside the record, the court may hear the matter on affidavits or may hear it wholly or partly on oral testimony or on depositions. FRCP 43(c). Evidence that goes beyond the unverified allegations of the pleadings and motion papers must be presented to support or oppose a motion for a preliminary injunction. FPP § 2949.

         • *Materials necessary for motion.* A party must file those portions of discovery requests or responses (including deposition transcripts) that the party relies on to support a motion that could result in a final order on an issue. IN R USDCTND L.R. 26-2(c).

         • *Affidavits.* Affidavits are appropriate on a preliminary injunction motion and typically will be offered by both parties. FPP § 2949. All affidavits should state the facts supporting the litigant's position clearly and specifically. Preliminary injunctions frequently are denied if the affidavits are too vague or conclusory to demonstrate a clear right to relief under FRCP 65. FPP § 2949.

iii. *Pleadings.* Pleadings may be considered if they have been verified. FPP § 2949; K-2 Ski Co. v. Head Ski Co., 467 F.2d 1087 (9th Cir. 1972).

iv. *Notice of constitutional question.* A party that files a pleading, written motion, or other paper drawing into question the constitutionality of a federal or state statute must promptly:

- *File notice.* File a notice of constitutional question stating the question and identifying the paper that raises it, if: (1) a federal statute is questioned and the parties do not include the United States, one of its agencies, or one of its officers or employees in an official capacity; or (2) a state statute is questioned and the parties do not include the state, one of its agencies, or one of its officers or employees in an official capacity; and

- *Serve notice.* Serve the notice and paper on the Attorney General of the United States if a federal statute is questioned—or on the state attorney general if a state statute is questioned—either by certified or registered mail or by sending it to an electronic address designated by the attorney general for this purpose. FRCP 5.1(a).

- *When to file the notice.* A party required to file a notice of constitutional question under FRCP 5.1 must do so by the later of: (1) the day the parties tender their proposed case-management plan (if one is required); or (2) 21 days after filing the pleading, written motion, or other paper questioning the constitutionality of a federal or state statute. IN R USDCTND L.R. 5.1-1(a).

- *Service on government officials.* The party must also serve the notice and the pleading, written motion, or other paper questioning the constitutionality of a federal or state statute on: (1) the Attorney General of the United States and the United States Attorney for the Northern District of Indiana, if a federal statute is challenged; or (2) the Attorney General for the state if a state statute is challenged. IN R USDCTND L.R. 5.1-1(b). Service required under IN R USDCTND L.R. 5.1-1(b) may be made either by certified or registered mail or by emailing it to an address designated by those officials for this purpose. IN R USDCTND L.R. 5.1-1(c).

- *No forfeiture.* A party's failure to file and serve the notice, or the court's failure to certify, does not forfeit a constitutional claim or defense that is otherwise timely asserted. FRCP 5.1(d).

v. *Nongovernmental corporate disclosure statement*

- *Contents.* A nongovernmental corporate party must file two (2) copies of a disclosure statement that: (1) identifies any parent corporation and any publicly held corporation owning ten percent (10%) or more of its stock; or (2) states that there is no such corporation. FRCP 7.1(a).

- *Time to file; Supplemental filing.* A party must: (1) file the disclosure statement with its first appearance, pleading, petition, motion, response, or other request addressed to the court; and (2) promptly file a supplemental statement if any required information changes. FRCP 7.1(b).

vi. *Index of exhibits.* Any pleading, motion, brief, affidavit, notice, or proposed order, whether filed electronically or by delivering it to the clerk, must: include a separate index identifying and briefly describing each exhibit if there are more than four (4) exhibits. IN R USDCTND L.R. 5-4(a)(8).

vii. *Request for oral argument.* A party may request oral argument on a motion by filing and serving a separate document explaining why oral argument is necessary and estimating how long the court should allow for the argument. IN R USDCTND L.R. 7-5(a)(1). The request must be filed and served with the party's supporting brief, response brief, or reply brief. IN R USDCTND L.R. 7-5(a)(2).

viii. *Request for evidentiary hearing.* A party may request an evidentiary hearing by filing and

serving a separate document explaining why the hearing is necessary and estimating how long the court should allow for it. IN R USDCTND L.R. 7-5(b)(1).

ix. *Copy of authority.* A copy of any decision, statute, or regulation cited in a motion or brief must be attached to the paper if—and only if—it is not available on Westlaw or Lexis. But if a copy of a decision, statute, or regulation is only available electronically, a party must provide it to the court or another party upon request. IN R USDCTND L.R. 7-1(f).

x. *Proposed order.* Parties filing a paper that requires the judge or clerk to enter a routine or uncontested order must include a suitable form of order. IN R USDCTND L.R. 5-4(c).

- Proposed orders shall not be filed electronically either as a separate document or as an attachment to the main pleading or other document. Instead, all proposed orders must be e-mailed to the chambers of the appropriate judicial officer for the case. The proposed order must be in WordPerfect Format or Rich Text Format (RTF). Proposed orders should be attached to an e-mail and sent to the appropriate judicial officer at the address listed in IN R USDCTND CM/ECF(II)(F). The subject line of the email message should indicate the case title, cause number and document number of the motion, e.g., Smith v. Jones 1:02-cv-1234, motion# ___. IN R USDCTND CM/ECF(II)(F).

xi. *Copy of document with self-addressed envelope.* A party who wants a file-stamped copy of a paper must include with the filing an additional copy of the paper and a self-addressed envelope with adequate postage. IN R USDCTND L.R. 5-4(b)(6).

xii. *Notice of manual filing.* However, if that is not physically possible, counsel shall electronically file a .pdf document titled Notice of Manual Filing as a notation on the docket sheet that filings are being held in the clerk's office in paper. A sample Notice of Manual Filing is attached as Form 2 (IN R USDCTND CM/ECF(Form 2)). IN R USDCTND CM/ECF(III)(A)(1).

xiii. *Courtesy copies.* If documents are filed in paper format, counsel must provide an original for the clerk's office, a copy for the judge and a copy must be served on all parties in the case. IN R USDCTND CM/ECF(III)(A)(1).

xiv. *Declaration that party was unable to file in a timely manner.* If the attorney is unable to file a document in a timely manner due to technical difficulties in the user's system, the attorney must file a document with the court as soon as possible notifying the court of the inability to file the document. A sample document entitled Declaration that Party was Unable to File in a Timely Manner Due to Technical Difficulties is attached hereto as Form 5. IN R USDCTND CM/ECF(VI)(B). [Editor's note: the reference to Form 5 is likely meant to be a reference to Form 3 (IN R USDCTND CM/ECF(Form 3))].

2. *Documents for opposing party*

a. *Required documents*

i. *Response brief.* Refer to the Format section of this document for the format of briefs. Refer to the General Requirements section of this document for information on the opposing papers.

ii. *Certificate of service.* FRCP 5(d) requires that the person making service under FRCP 5 certify that service has been effected. FRCP 5(Advisory Committee Notes). Having such information on file may be useful for many purposes, including proof of service if an issue arises concerning the effectiveness of the service. FRCP 5(Advisory Committee Notes).

- *Certificate of service for electronically-filed documents.* A Certificate of Service is still a requirement when filing documents electronically. A sample Certificate of Service is attached as Form 1 (IN R USDCTND CM/ECF(Form 1)). IN R USDCTND CM/ECF(II)(H).

b. *Supplemental documents*

i. *Supporting evidence.* When a motion relies on facts outside the record, the court may hear the matter on affidavits or may hear it wholly or partly on oral testimony or on depositions. FRCP 43(c). Evidence that goes beyond the unverified allegations of the pleadings and motion papers must be presented to support or oppose a motion for a preliminary injunction. FPP § 2949.

- *Materials necessary for motion.* A party must file those portions of discovery requests or

responses (including deposition transcripts) that the party relies on to support a motion that could result in a final order on an issue. IN R USDCTND L.R. 26-2(c).

- *Affidavits.* Affidavits are appropriate on a preliminary injunction motion and typically will be offered by both parties. FPP § 2949. All affidavits should state the facts supporting the litigant's position clearly and specifically. Preliminary injunctions frequently are denied if the affidavits are too vague or conclusory to demonstrate a clear right to relief under FRCP 65. FPP § 2949.

ii. *Pleadings.* Pleadings may be considered if they have been verified. FPP § 2949; K-2 Ski Co. v. Head Ski Co., 467 F.2d 1087 (9th Cir. 1972).

iii. *Notice of constitutional question.* A party that files a pleading, written motion, or other paper drawing into question the constitutionality of a federal or state statute must promptly:

- *File notice.* File a notice of constitutional question stating the question and identifying the paper that raises it, if: (1) a federal statute is questioned and the parties do not include the United States, one of its agencies, or one of its officers or employees in an official capacity; or (2) a state statute is questioned and the parties do not include the state, one of its agencies, or one of its officers or employees in an official capacity; and

- *Serve notice.* Serve the notice and paper on the Attorney General of the United States if a federal statute is questioned—or on the state attorney general if a state statute is questioned—either by certified or registered mail or by sending it to an electronic address designated by the attorney general for this purpose. FRCP 5.1(a).

- *When to file the notice.* A party required to file a notice of constitutional question under FRCP 5.1 must do so by the later of: (1) the day the parties tender their proposed case-management plan (if one is required); or (2) 21 days after filing the pleading, written motion, or other paper questioning the constitutionality of a federal or state statute. IN R USDCTND L.R. 5.1-1(a).

- *Service on government officials.* The party must also serve the notice and the pleading, written motion, or other paper questioning the constitutionality of a federal or state statute on: (1) the Attorney General of the United States and the United States Attorney for the Northern District of Indiana, if a federal statute is challenged; or (2) the Attorney General for the state if a state statute is challenged. IN R USDCTND L.R. 5.1-1(b). Service required under IN R USDCTND L.R. 5.1-1(b) may be made either by certified or registered mail or by emailing it to an address designated by those officials for this purpose. IN R USDCTND L.R. 5.1-1(c).

- *No forfeiture.* A party's failure to file and serve the notice, or the court's failure to certify, does not forfeit a constitutional claim or defense that is otherwise timely asserted. FRCP 5.1(d).

iv. *Nongovernmental corporate disclosure statement*

- *Contents.* A nongovernmental corporate party must file two (2) copies of a disclosure statement that: (1) identifies any parent corporation and any publicly held corporation owning ten percent (10%) or more of its stock; or (2) states that there is no such corporation. FRCP 7.1(a).

- *Time to file; Supplemental filing.* A party must: (1) file the disclosure statement with its first appearance, pleading, petition, motion, response, or other request addressed to the court; and (2) promptly file a supplemental statement if any required information changes. FRCP 7.1(b).

v. *Index of exhibits.* Any pleading, motion, brief, affidavit, notice, or proposed order, whether filed electronically or by delivering it to the clerk, must: include a separate index identifying and briefly describing each exhibit if there are more than four (4) exhibits. IN R USDCTND L.R. 5-4(a)(8).

vi. *Request for oral argument.* A party may request oral argument on a motion by filing and serving a separate document explaining why oral argument is necessary and estimating how long the court should allow for the argument. IN R USDCTND L.R. 7-5(a)(1). The request must be filed and served with the party's supporting brief, response brief, or reply brief. IN R USDCTND L.R. 7-5(a)(2).

    vii. *Request for evidentiary hearing.* A party may request an evidentiary hearing by filing and serving a separate document explaining why the hearing is necessary and estimating how long the court should allow for it. IN R USDCTND L.R. 7-5(b)(1).

    viii. *Copy of authority.* A copy of any decision, statute, or regulation cited in a motion or brief must be attached to the paper if—and only if—it is not available on Westlaw or Lexis. But if a copy of a decision, statute, or regulation is only available electronically, a party must provide it to the court or another party upon request. IN R USDCTND L.R. 7-1(f).

    ix. *Copy of document with self-addressed envelope.* A party who wants a file-stamped copy of a paper must include with the filing an additional copy of the paper and a self-addressed envelope with adequate postage. IN R USDCTND L.R. 5-4(b)(6).

    x. *Notice of manual filing.* However, if that is not physically possible, counsel shall electronically file a .pdf document titled Notice of Manual Filing as a notation on the docket sheet that filings are being held in the clerk's office in paper. A sample Notice of Manual Filing is attached as Form 2 (IN R USDCTND CM/ECF(Form 2)). IN R USDCTND CM/ECF(III)(A)(1).

    xi. *Courtesy copies.* If documents are filed in paper format, counsel must provide an original for the clerk's office, a copy for the judge and a copy must be served on all parties in the case. IN R USDCTND CM/ECF(III)(A)(1).

    xii. *Declaration that party was unable to file in a timely manner.* If the attorney is unable to file a document in a timely manner due to technical difficulties in the user's system, the attorney must file a document with the court as soon as possible notifying the court of the inability to file the document. A sample document entitled Declaration that Party was Unable to File in a Timely Manner Due to Technical Difficulties is attached hereto as Form 5. IN R USDCTND CM/ECF(VI)(B). [Editor's note: the reference to Form 5 is likely meant to be a reference to Form 3 (IN R USDCTND CM/ECF(Form 3)].

E. Format

1. *Form of documents.* The rules governing captions and other matters of form in pleadings apply to motions and other papers. FRCP 7(b)(2).

    a. *Paper.* Any pleading, motion, brief, affidavit, notice, or proposed order, whether filed electronically or by delivering it to the clerk, must: use eight and one-half by eleven (8-1/2 x 11) inch pages. IN R USDCTND L.R. 5-4(a)(2).

        i. *Manual filings.* Papers delivered to the clerk for filing must: be flat, unfolded, and on good-quality, white paper. IN R USDCTND L.R. 5-4(b)(1)(A).

        • *Covers or backing.* Papers delivered to the clerk for filing must: not have a cover or a back. IN R USDCTND L.R. 5-4(b)(1)(B).

        • *Recycled paper.* The court encourages using recycled paper. IN R USDCTND L.R. 5-4(b)(7).

    b. *Margins.* Any pleading, motion, brief, affidavit, notice, or proposed order, whether filed electronically or by delivering it to the clerk, must: have at least one (1) inch margins. IN R USDCTND L.R. 5-4(a)(3).

    c. *Spacing.* Any pleading, motion, brief, affidavit, notice, or proposed order, whether filed electronically or by delivering it to the clerk, must: be double spaced (except for headings, footnotes, and quoted material). IN R USDCTND L.R. 5-4(a)(5).

    d. *Text.* Any pleading, motion, brief, affidavit, notice, or proposed order, whether filed electronically or by delivering it to the clerk, must: be plainly typewritten, printed, or prepared by a clearly legible copying process. IN R USDCTND L.R. 5-4(a)(1).

        i. Any pleading, motion, brief, affidavit, notice, or proposed order, whether filed electronically or by delivering it to the clerk, must: use at least twelve (12) point type in the body and at least ten (10) point type in footnotes. IN R USDCTND L.R. 5-4(a)(4).

e. *Page numbering.* Any pleading, motion, brief, affidavit, notice, or proposed order, whether filed electronically or by delivering it to the clerk, must: have consecutively numbered pages. IN R USDCTND L.R. 5-4(a)(6).

f. *Caption; Names of parties.* Every pleading must have a caption with the court's name, a title, a file number, and a FRCP 7(a) designation. The title of the complaint must name all the parties; the title of other pleadings, after naming the first party on each side, may refer generally to other parties. FRCP 10(a). Any pleading, motion, brief, affidavit, notice, or proposed order, whether filed electronically or by delivering it to the clerk, must: include a title on the first page. IN R USDCTND L.R. 5-4(a)(7).

   i. *Alternative motions.* Motions must be filed separately, but alternative motions may be filed in a single paper if each is named in the title following the caption. IN R USDCTND L.R. 7-1(a).

g. *Filer's information.* Any pleading, motion, brief, affidavit, notice, or proposed order, whether filed electronically or by delivering it to the clerk, must: except in proposed orders and affidavits, include the filer's name, address, telephone number, fax number (where available), and e-mail address (where available). IN R USDCTND L.R. 5-4(a)(9).

h. *Paragraphs; Separate statements.* A party must state its claims or defenses in numbered paragraphs, each limited as far as practicable to a single set of circumstances. A later pleading may refer by number to a paragraph in an earlier pleading. If doing so would promote clarity, each claim founded on a separate transaction or occurrence—and each defense other than a denial—must be stated in a separate count or defense. FRCP 10(b).

i. *Adoption by reference; Exhibits.* A statement in a pleading may be adopted by reference elsewhere in the same pleading or in any other pleading or motion. A copy of a written instrument that is an exhibit to a pleading is a part of the pleading for all purposes. FRCP 10(c).

j. *Citation of local rules.* The Local Civil Rules of the United States District Court for the Northern District of Indiana may be cited as "N.D. Ind. L.R." IN R USDCTND L.R. 1-1(a)(1).

k. *Acceptance by the clerk.* The clerk must not refuse to file a paper solely because it is not in the form prescribed by the Federal Rules of Civil Procedure or by a local rule or practice. FRCP 5(d)(4).

   i. *Sanctions for formatting errors; Non-compliance.* If a person files a paper that does not comply with the rules governing the format of papers filed with the court, the court may: (1) strike the paper from the record; or (2) fine the person up to one thousand dollars ($1,000). IN R USDCTND L.R. 1-3(a).

      • *Notice.* Before sanctioning a person under IN R USDCTND L.R. 1-3(a)(2), the court must: (1) notify the person that the paper is noncompliant; and (2) give the person the opportunity either to be heard or to revise the paper. IN R USDCTND L.R. 1-3(b).

2. *Form of electronic documents.* Electronically filed documents must meet the same requirements of format and page limits as documents "conventionally filed" (as defined in IN R USDCTND CM/ECF(III)(A)) pursuant to the Federal Rules of Civil Procedure and the Local Civil Rules of the United States District Court for the Northern District of Indiana. IN R USDCTND CM/ECF(II)(A)(2).

a. *PDF format required.* Documents filed in the CM/ECF must be in .pdf format. A document created with almost any word-processing program can be converted to .pdf format. The .pdf program in effect takes a picture of the original document and allows anyone to open the converted document across a broad range of hardware and software, with layout, format, links, and images intact. IN R USDCTND CM/ECF(FN2).

b. *Title of documents.* The person electronically filing a pleading or other document will be responsible for designating a title for the pleading or other document by using one of the categories contained in the events listed in the CM/ECF Menu. IN R USDCTND CM/ECF(II)(G).

c. *Combining documents.* All documents which form part of a single pleading and which are being filed at the same time and by the same party may be electronically filed together under one document number, e.g., the motion and a supporting affidavit, with the exception of memoranda in support. Memoranda in support shall be electronically filed separately and shown as a related document to the motion. IN R USDCTND CM/ECF(II)(A)(4).

d. *Exhibits and attachments.* Filing users must submit in electronic form all documents referenced as exhibits or attachments, unless the court permits conventional filing. A filing user must submit as exhibits or attachments only those excerpts of the referenced documents that are directly germane to the matter under consideration by the court. Excerpted material must be clearly and prominently identified as such. Filing users who file excerpts of documents as exhibits or attachments do so without prejudice to their right to timely file additional excerpts or the complete document. Responding parties may timely file additional excerpts or the complete document that they believe are directly germane. The court may require parties to file additional excerpts or the complete document. IN R USDCTND CM/ECF(II)(A)(6).

e. *Hyperlinks.* Electronically filed documents may contain hyperlink references to an external document as a convenient mechanism for accessing material cited in the document. A hyperlink reference is neither validated for content nor considered a part of the court's records. The court neither endorses the product or organization at the destination of a hyperlink reference, nor does the court exercise any responsibility over the content at the destination. In order to preserve the integrity of the court record, attorneys wishing to insert hyperlinks in court filings shall continue to use the traditional citation method for the cited authority, in addition to the hyperlink. A hyperlink contained in a filing is no more than a convenient mechanism for accessing material cited in the document and a hyperlink reference is extraneous to any filed document and is not part of the court's record. IN R USDCTND CM/ECF(II)(A)(3).

3. *Form of briefs*

   a. *Page limits.* Supporting and response briefs (excluding tables of contents, tables of authorities, and appendices) ordinarily must not exceed twenty-five (25) pages. Reply briefs must not exceed fifteen (15) pages. IN R USDCTND L.R. 7-1(e)(1).

      i. *Exception.* The court may allow a party to file a brief exceeding these page limits for extraordinary and compelling reasons. But if the court permits a brief to exceed twenty-five (25) pages, it must include:

         • A table of contents with page references;

         • An issue statement; and

         • A table of authorities including: (1) all cases (alphabetically arranged), statutes, and other authorities cited in the brief; and (2) references to where the authorities appear in the brief. IN R USDCTND L.R. 7-1(e)(2).

4. *Signing of pleadings, motions and other papers*

   a. *Signature.* Every pleading, written motion, and other paper must be signed by at least one attorney of record in the attorney's name—or by a party personally if the party is unrepresented. The paper must state the signer's address, e-mail address, and telephone number. FRCP 11(a).

      i. *Signatures on manual filings.* Papers delivered to the clerk for filing must: include the filer's original signature. IN R USDCTND L.R. 5-4(b)(1)(C).

         • *Rubber-stamped and faxed signatures.* An original paper with a rubber-stamped or faxed signature is unsigned for purposes of FRCP 11 and FRCP 26(g). IN R USDCTND L.R. 5-4(b)(2).

         • *Affidavits.* Only the affiant need sign an affidavit. IN R USDCTND L.R. 5-4(b)(3).

      ii. *Electronic signatures.* Pursuant to FRCP 11, every pleading, motion, and other paper (except lists, schedules, statements or amendments thereto) shall be signed by at least one attorney of record or, if the party is not represented by an attorney, all papers shall be signed by the party. An attorney's/participant's password issued by the court combined with the user's identification, serves as and constitutes the attorney/participant's signature for FRCP 11 and other purposes. IN R USDCTND CM/ECF(I)(C). Documents which must be filed and which must contain original signatures other than those of a participating attorney or which require either verification or an unsworn declaration under any rule or statute, shall be filed electronically, with originally executed copies maintained by the filer. The pleading or other document electronically filed shall contain "s/" signature(s), as noted in IN R USDCTND CM/ECF(II)(E)(3)(b). IN R USDCTND CM/ECF(II)(E)(1).

- *Multiple signatures.* In the case of a stipulation or other document to be signed by two or more attorneys, the following procedure should be used: The filing attorney shall initially confirm that the content of the document is acceptable to all persons required to sign the document and shall obtain the physical signatures of all attorneys on the document. IN R USDCTND CM/ECF(II)(E)(3)(a). The filing attorney then shall file the document electronically, indicating the signatories, e.g., "s/Jane Doe," "s/John Doe," etc. IN R US-DCTND CM/ECF(II)(E)(3)(b). The filing attorney shall retain the hard copy of the document containing the original signatures. IN R USDCTND CM/ECF(II)(E)(3)(c).

    iii. *No verification or accompanying affidavit required for pleadings.* Unless a rule or statute specifically states otherwise, a pleading need not be verified or accompanied by an affidavit. FRCP 11(a).

    iv. *Unsigned papers.* The court must strike an unsigned paper unless the omission is promptly corrected after being called to the attorney's or party's attention. FRCP 11(a).

b. *Representations to the court.* By presenting to the court a pleading, written motion, or other paper—whether by signing, filing, submitting, or later advocating it—an attorney or unrepresented party certifies that to the best of the person's knowledge, information, and belief, formed after an inquiry reasonable under the circumstances:

    i. It is not being presented for any improper purpose, such as to harass, cause unnecessary delay, or needlessly increase the cost of litigation;

    ii. The claims, defenses, and other legal contentions are warranted by existing law or by a nonfrivolous argument for extending, modifying, or reversing existing law or for establishing new law;

    iii. The factual contentions have evidentiary support or, if specifically so identified, will likely have evidentiary support after a reasonable opportunity for further investigation or discovery; and

    iv. The denials of factual contentions are warranted on the evidence or, if specifically so identified, are reasonably based on belief or a lack of information. FRCP 11(b).

c. *Sanctions.* If, after notice and a reasonable opportunity to respond, the court determines that FRCP 11(b) has been violated, the court may impose an appropriate sanction on any attorney, law firm, or party that violated FRCP 11(b) or is responsible for the violation. FRCP 11(c)(1). Refer to the United States District Court for the Northern District of Indiana KeyRules Motion for Sanctions document for more information.

5. *Privacy protection for filings made with the court*

a. *Redacted filings.* Counsel should not include sensitive information in any document filed with the court unless such inclusion is necessary and relevant to the case. IN R USDCTND CM/ECF(VII). Unless the court orders otherwise, in an electronic or paper filing with the court that contains an individual's Social Security number, taxpayer-identification number, or birth date, the name of an individual known to be a minor, or a financial-account number, a party or nonparty making the filing may include only:

    i. The last four (4) digits of the Social Security number and taxpayer-identification number;

    ii. The year of the individual's birth;

    iii. The minor's initials; and

    iv. The last four (4) digits of the financial-account number. FRCP 5.2(a); IN R USDCTND Order 2005-3.

b. *Exemptions from the redaction requirement.* The redaction requirement does not apply to the following:

    i.   A financial-account number that identifies the property allegedly subject to forfeiture in a forfeiture proceeding;

    ii.   The record of an administrative or agency proceeding;

    iii.   The official record of a state-court proceeding;

    iv.   The record of a court or tribunal, if that record was not subject to the redaction requirement when originally filed;

    v.   A filing covered by FRCP 5.2(c) or FRCP 5.2(d); and

    vi.   A pro se filing in an action brought under 28 U.S.C.A. § 2241, 28 U.S.C.A. § 2254, or 28 U.S.C.A. § 2255. FRCP 5.2(b).

    vii.   In cases filed under the Social Security Act, 42 U.S.C.A. § 405(g), there is no need for redaction of any information from the documents filed in the case. IN R USDCTND Order 2005-3.

c. *Limitations on remote access to electronic files; Social Security appeals and immigration cases.* Unless the court orders otherwise, in an action for benefits under the Social Security Act, and in an action or proceeding relating to an order of removal, to relief from removal, or to immigration benefits or detention, access to an electronic file is authorized as follows:

    i.   The parties and their attorneys may have remote electronic access to any part of the case file, including the administrative record;

    ii.   Any other person may have electronic access to the full record at the courthouse, but may have remote electronic access only to:

        • The docket maintained by the court; and

        • An opinion, order, judgment, or other disposition of the court, but not any other part of the case file or the administrative record. FRCP 5.2(c).

d. *Filings made under seal.* The court may order that a filing be made under seal without redaction. The court may later unseal the filing or order the person who made the filing to file a redacted version for the public record. FRCP 5.2(d). For information on filing documents under seal, refer to IN R USDCTND L.R. 5-3, IN R USDCTND CM/ECF(IV)(A), and IN R USDCTND ECF Order 2004-19.

e. *Protective orders.* For good cause, the court may by order in a case:

    i.   Require redaction of additional information; or

    ii.   Limit or prohibit a nonparty's remote electronic access to a document filed with the court. FRCP 5.2(e).

f. *Option for additional unredacted filing under seal.* A person making a redacted filing may also file an unredacted copy under seal. The court must retain the unredacted copy as part of the record. FRCP 5.2(f); IN R USDCTND Order 2005-3.

    i.   The unredacted version of the document or the reference list shall be retained by the court under seal as part of the record. This paper shall be retained by the court as part of the record. The court may, however, still require the party to file a redacted copy for the public file. IN R USDCTND Order 2005-3.

g. *Option for filing a reference list.* A filing that contains redacted information may be filed together with a reference list that identifies each item of redacted information and specifies an appropriate identifier that uniquely corresponds to each item listed. The list must be filed under seal and may be amended as of right. Any reference in the case to a listed identifier will be construed to refer to the corresponding item of information. FRCP 5.2(g); IN R USDCTND Order 2005-3.

    i.   The unredacted version of the document or the reference list shall be retained by the court under seal as part of the record. This paper shall be retained by the court as part of the record. The court may, however, still require the party to file a redacted copy for the public file. IN R USDCTND Order 2005-3.

h. *Responsibility for redaction.* The responsibility for redacting these personal identifiers rests solely with counsel and the parties. The Clerk will not review each paper for compliance with IN R USDCTND Order 2005-3. IN R USDCTND Order 2005-3.

i. *Waiver of protection of identifiers.* A person waives the protection of FRCP 5.2(a) as to the person's own information by filing it without redaction and not under seal. FRCP 5.2(h).

F. Filing and Service Requirements

1. *Filing requirements.* Any paper after the complaint that is required to be served—together with a certificate of service—must be filed within a reasonable time after service. FRCP 5(d)(1). Motions must be filed separately, but alternative motions may be filed in a single paper if each is named in the title following the caption. IN R USDCTND L.R. 7-1(a).

   a. *How filing is made; In general.* A paper is filed by delivering it:

      i. To the clerk; or

      ii. To a judge who agrees to accept it for filing, and who must then note the filing date on the paper and promptly send it to the clerk. FRCP 5(d)(2).

      - Papers not filed electronically must be filed with the clerk, not a judge. IN R USDCTND L.R. 5-4(b)(4).

      iii. Parties manually filing a paper that requires the clerk to give others notice, must give the clerk: (1) sufficient copies of the notice; and (2) the name and address of each person entitled to receive the notice. IN R USDCTND L.R. 5-4(b)(8).

   b. *Where to file.* Papers not filed electronically must be filed in the division where the case is pending, unless: (1) a person will be prejudiced if the paper is not filed the same day it is tendered; and (2) it includes an adequately sized envelope addressed to the clerk's office in the division where the case is pending and with adequate postage. IN R USDCTND L.R. 5-4(b)(5).

   c. *Electronic filing*

      i. *Authorization of electronic filing program.* A court may, by local rule, allow papers to be filed, signed, or verified by electronic means that are consistent with any technical standards established by the Judicial Conference of the United States. A local rule may require electronic filing only if reasonable exceptions are allowed. A paper filed electronically in compliance with a local rule is a written paper for purposes of the Federal Rules of Civil Procedure. FRCP 5(d)(3).

         - Papers must be filed, signed, and verified electronically unless excepted by the court's CM/ECF Civil and Criminal User Manual (IN R USDCTND CM/ECF). IN R USDCTND L.R. 5-1.

      ii. *Mandatory electronic filing.* Unless otherwise permitted by these procedures or otherwise authorized by the assigned judge, all documents submitted for filing in this district in civil and criminal cases, no matter when a case was originally filed, shall be filed electronically using the System. IN R USDCTND CM/ECF(II)(A)(1). The requirement that "all documents" be filed electronically includes briefs, and attachments and exhibits used in support of motions. IN R USDCTND CM/ECF(FN1).

         - Sending a document or pleading to the court via e-mail or facsimile does not constitute "electronic filing." IN R USDCTND CM/ECF(I)(A).

      iii. *Conventional filing.* As used in these procedures, a "conventionally" filed or submitted document or pleading is one presented to the Clerk or a party in paper or other non-electronic, tangible format. The following documents shall be filed conventionally and not electronically unless specifically authorized by the Court:

         - Exhibits and other documents which cannot be converted to a legible electronic form. Whenever possible, counsel is responsible for converting filings to an electronic form. However, if that is not physically possible, counsel shall electronically file a .pdf document titled Notice of Manual Filing as a notation on the docket sheet that filings are being held in the clerk's office in paper. A sample Notice of Manual Filing is attached as Form 2 (IN R USDCTND CM/ECF(Form 2)). If documents are filed in paper format, counsel must provide an original for the clerk's office, a copy for the judge and a copy must be served on all parties in the case. Large documents which do not exist in an electronic format shall be scanned into .pdf format by counsel, in small batches if necessary, and filed electronically as separate attachments in the System. IN R USDCTND CM/ECF(III)(A)(1).

- Certain documents which are listed in IN R USDCTND CM/ECF(II)(E)(2). IN R US-DCTND CM/ECF(III)(A)(2).

- Documents filed by pro se litigants. IN R USDCTND CM/ECF(III)(A)(3).

iv.   For more information on electronic filing, refer to IN R USDCTND CM/ECF.

2. *Service requirements*

  a. *Service; When required*

    i. *In general.* Unless the Federal Rules of Civil Procedure provide otherwise, each of the following papers must be served on every party:

- An order stating that service is required;

- A pleading filed after the original complaint, unless the court orders otherwise under FRCP 5(c) because there are numerous defendants;

- A discovery paper required to be served on a party, unless the court orders otherwise;

- A written motion, except one that may be heard ex parte; and

- A written notice, appearance, demand, or offer of judgment, or any similar paper. FRCP 5(a)(1).

    ii. *If a party fails to appear.* No service is required on a party who is in default for failing to appear. But a pleading that asserts a new claim for relief against such a party must be served on that party under FRCP 4. FRCP 5(a)(2).

    iii. *Seizing property.* If an action is begun by seizing property and no person is or need be named as a defendant, any service required before the filing of an appearance, answer, or claim must be made on the person who had custody or possession of the property when it was seized. FRCP 5(a)(3).

  b. *Service; How made*

    i. *Serving an attorney.* If a party is represented by an attorney, service under FRCP 5 must be made on the attorney unless the court orders service on the party. FRCP 5(b)(1).

    ii. *Service in general.* A paper is served under FRCP 5 by:

- Handing it to the person;

- Leaving it: (1) at the person's office with a clerk or other person in charge or, if no one is in charge, in a conspicuous place in the office; or (2) if the person has no office or the office is closed, at the person's dwelling or usual place of abode with someone of suitable age and discretion who resides there;

- Mailing it to the person's last known address—in which event service is complete upon mailing;

- Leaving it with the court clerk if the person has no known address;

- Sending it by electronic means if the person consented in writing—in which event service is complete upon transmission, but is not effective if the serving party learns that it did not reach the person to be served; or

- Delivering it by any other means that the person consented to in writing—in which event service is complete when the person making service delivers it to the agency designated to make delivery. FRCP 5(b)(2).

iii. *Electronic service.* Electronically filed papers may be served electronically if service is consistent with the CM/ECF User Manual (IN R USDCTND CM/ECF). IN R USDCTND L.R. 5-2(a).

- *Waiver of other service.* An attorney's registration will constitute a waiver of conventional service of documents and the attorney agrees to accept service of notice on behalf of the client of the electronic filing by hand, facsimile or authorized email. IN R USDCTND CM/ECF(I)(B)(3).

- *Serving registered persons.* The System will generate a "Notice of Electronic Filing" when any document is filed. This notice represents service of the document on parties who are registered participants with the System. Except as provided in IN R USDCTND CM/ECF(III)(B), the filing party shall not be required to serve any pleading or other documents on any party receiving electronic notice. IN R USDCTND CM/ECF(II)(D)(1). The term "pleading" refers only to those documents listed in FRCP 7(a). IN R USDCTND CM/ECF(FN3).

- *When electronic service is deemed completed.* A person registered to use the court's electronic-filing system is served with an electronically filed paper when a "Notice of Electronic Filing" is transmitted to that person through the court's electronic filing-system. IN R USDCTND L.R. 5-2(b).

- *Serving non-registered persons.* A person who has not registered to use the court's electronic-filing system but who is entitled to service of a paper must be served according to the Local Civil Rules of the United States District Court for the Northern District of Indiana and the Federal Rules of Civil Procedure. IN R USDCTND L.R. 5-2(c); IN R USDCTND CM/ECF(II)(D)(2). If such service of a paper copy is to be made, it shall be done in the manner provided in the Federal Rules of Civil Procedure and the Local Civil Rules of the United States District Court for the Northern District of Indiana. IN R USDCTND CM/ECF(II)(D)(2).

iv. *Service of conventional filings.* Pleadings or other documents which are filed conventionally rather than electronically shall be served in the manner provided for in the Federal Rules of Civil Procedure and the Local Civil Rules of the United States District Court for the Northern District of Indiana, except as otherwise provided by order of the Court. IN R USDCTND CM/ECF(III)(B).

v. *Using court facilities.* If a local rule so authorizes, a party may use the court's transmission facilities to make service under FRCP 5(b)(2)(E). FRCP 5(b)(3).

c. *Serving numerous defendants*

i. *In general.* If an action involves an unusually large number of defendants, the court may, on motion or on its own, order that:

- Defendants' pleadings and replies to them need not be served on other defendants;

- Any crossclaim, counterclaim, avoidance, or affirmative defense in those pleadings and replies to them will be treated as denied or avoided by all other parties; and

- Filing any such pleading and serving it on the plaintiff constitutes notice of the pleading to all parties. FRCP 5(c)(1).

ii. *Notifying parties.* A copy of every such order must be served on the parties as the court directs. FRCP 5(c)(2).

G. Hearings

1. *Hearings, generally*

a. *Oral argument.* Due process does not require that oral argument be permitted on a motion and, except as otherwise provided by local rule, the district court has discretion to determine whether it will decide the motion on the papers or hear argument by counsel (and perhaps receive evidence). FPP § 1190; F.D.I.C. v. Deglau, 207 F.3d 153 (3d Cir. 2000).

i. *Request for oral argument.* A party may request oral argument on a motion by filing and serving a separate document explaining why oral argument is necessary and estimating how long the court should allow for the argument. IN R USDCTND L.R. 7-5(a)(1). Refer to the Documents section of this document for more information.

    ii. *Additional evidence forbidden.* Parties may not present additional evidence at oral argument. IN R USDCTND L.R. 7-5(a)(3).

b. *Providing a regular schedule for oral hearings.* A court may establish regular times and places for oral hearings on motions. FRCP 78(a).

c. *Providing for submission on briefs.* By rule or order, the court may provide for submitting and determining motions on briefs, without oral hearings. FRCP 78(b).

d. *Evidentiary hearings.* A party may request an evidentiary hearing by filing and serving a separate document explaining why the hearing is necessary and estimating how long the court should allow for it. IN R USDCTND L.R. 7-5(b)(2). Refer to the Documents section of this document for more information.

e. *Court's authority.* The court may: (1) grant or deny a request for oral argument or an evidentiary hearing in its discretion; (2) set oral argument or an evidentiary hearing without a request from a party; or (3) order any oral argument or evidentiary hearing to be held anywhere within the district regardless of where the case will be tried. IN R USDCTND L.R. 7-5(c).

2. *Hearing on motion for preliminary injunction*

a. *Consolidating the hearing with the trial on the merits.* Before or after beginning the hearing on a motion for a preliminary injunction, the court may advance the trial on the merits and consolidate it with the hearing. Even when consolidation is not ordered, evidence that is received on the motion and that would be admissible at trial becomes part of the trial record and need not be repeated at trial. But the court must preserve any party's right to a jury trial. FRCP 65(a)(2).

b. *Expediting the hearing after temporary restraining order is issued without notice.* If the order is issued without notice, the motion for a preliminary injunction must be set for hearing at the earliest possible time, taking precedence over all other matters except hearings on older matters of the same character. At the hearing, the party who obtained the order must proceed with the motion; if the party does not, the court must dissolve the order. FRCP 65(b)(3).

3. *Courtroom and courthouse decorum.* For information on courtroom and courthouse decorum, refer to IN R USDCTND L.R. 83-3.

H. Forms

1. Federal Motion for Preliminary Injunction Forms

a. Declaration; In support of motion for preliminary injunction. AMJUR PP INJUNCTION § 38.

b. Memorandum of points and authorities; In support of motion for preliminary injunction. AMJUR PP INJUNCTION § 39.

c. Notice; Motion for preliminary injunction. AMJUR PP INJUNCTION § 40.

d. Motion; For preliminary injunction. AMJUR PP INJUNCTION § 41.

e. Motion; For preliminary injunction; On pleadings and other papers without evidentiary hearing or oral argument. AMJUR PP INJUNCTION § 43.

f. Affidavit; In support of motion for preliminary injunction. AMJUR PP INJUNCTION § 52.

g. Motion for preliminary injunction. 4A FEDFORMS § 5284.

h. Motion enjoining use of information acquired from employment with plaintiff. 4A FEDFORMS § 5287.

i. Motion enjoining interference with public access. 4A FEDFORMS § 5288.

j. Motion enjoining collection of tax assessment. 4A FEDFORMS § 5289.

k. Motion enjoining conducting election or certifying representative. 4A FEDFORMS § 5290.

l. Motion enjoining preventing plaintiff's acting as teacher. 4A FEDFORMS § 5291.

m. Motion enjoining interference with plaintiff's enforcement of judgment in related case. 4A FED-FORMS § 5292.

n. Motion for preliminary injunction in patent infringement action. 4A FEDFORMS § 5293.

o. Motion for preliminary injunction on basis of prayer of complaint and for setting hearing on motion. 4A FEDFORMS § 5294.

p. Notice of motion. 4A FEDFORMS § 5308.

q. Notice of motion and motion. 4A FEDFORMS § 5310.

r. Bond; To obtain preliminary injunction. FEDPROF § 1:701.

s. Opposition; To motion; General form. FEDPROF § 1:750.

t. Brief; Supporting or opposing motion. FEDPROF § 1:752.

u. Motion for temporary restraining order and preliminary injunction. GOLDLTGFMS § 13A:6.

v. Motion for preliminary injunction. GOLDLTGFMS § 13A:18.

w. Motion for preliminary injunction; Based upon pleadings and other papers without evidentiary hearing or oral argument. GOLDLTGFMS § 13A:19.

x. Motion for preliminary injunction; Supporting affidavit. GOLDLTGFMS § 13A:20.

y. Bond. GOLDLTGFMS § 19:2.

z. Bond; In support of injunction. GOLDLTGFMS § 19:3.

2. Forms for the Northern District of Indiana

a. Certificate of service. IN R USDCTND CM/ECF(Form 1).

b. Notice of manual filing. IN R USDCTND CM/ECF(Form 2).

c. Declaration that party was unable to file in a timely manner. IN R USDCTND CM/ECF(Form 3).

I. Applicable Rules

1. *Federal rules*

a. Serving and filing pleadings and other papers. FRCP 5.

b. Constitutional challenge to a statute; Notice, certification, and intervention. FRCP 5.1.

c. Privacy protection for filings made with the court. FRCP 5.2.

d. Computing and extending time; Time for motion papers. FRCP 6.

e. Pleadings allowed; Form of motions and other papers. FRCP 7.

f. Disclosure statement. FRCP 7.1.

g. Form of pleadings. FRCP 10.

h. Signing pleadings, motions, and other papers; Representations to the court; Sanctions. FRCP 11.

i. Taking testimony. FRCP 43.

j. Injunctions and restraining orders. FRCP 65.

k. Proceedings against a surety. FRCP 65.1.

l. Hearing motions; Submission on briefs. FRCP 78.

2. *Local rules*

a. Citation and scope of the rules. IN R USDCTND L.R. 1-1.

b. Sanctions for formatting errors. IN R USDCTND L.R. 1-3.

c. Electronic filing required. IN R USDCTND L.R. 5-1.

d. Constitutional questions. IN R USDCTND L.R. 5.1-1.

e. Electronic service. IN R USDCTND L.R. 5-2.

f. Format of papers. IN R USDCTND L.R. 5-4.

g. Motion practice. IN R USDCTND L.R. 7-1.

h. Oral arguments and evidentiary hearings. IN R USDCTND L.R. 7-5.

i. Pretrial procedure. IN R USDCTND L.R. 16-1.

j. Alternative dispute resolution. IN R USDCTND L.R. 16-6.

k. Filing of discovery and other materials. IN R USDCTND L.R. 26-2.

l. Case assignment. IN R USDCTND L.R. 40-1.

m. Preliminary injunctions and temporary restraining orders. IN R USDCTND L.R. 65-1.

n. Appearance and withdrawal of appearance. IN R USDCTND L.R. 83-8.

o. CM/ECF civil and criminal user manual. IN R USDCTND CM/ECF.

p. In re: privacy and public access to civil electronic case files. IN R USDCTND Order 2005-3.

Motions, Oppositions and Replies
Motion to Dismiss for Failure to State a Claim

Document Last Updated December 2016

A. Checklist

(I) ❑ Matters to be considered by moving party

    (a) ❑ Required documents

        (1) ❑ Notice of motion and motion

        (2) ❑ Brief

        (3) ❑ Certificate of service

    (b) ❑ Supplemental documents

        (1) ❑ Pleading

        (2) ❑ Notice of constitutional question

        (3) ❑ Nongovernmental corporate disclosure statement

        (4) ❑ Index of exhibits

        (5) ❑ Request for oral argument

        (6) ❑ Request for evidentiary hearing

        (7) ❑ Copy of authority

        (8) ❑ Proposed order

        (9) ❑ Copy of document with self-addressed envelope

        (10) ❑ Notice of manual filing

        (11) ❑ Courtesy copies

        (12) ❑ Declaration that party was unable to file in a timely manner

    (c) ❑ Timing

        (1) ❑ Failure to state a claim upon which relief can be granted may be raised in any pleading allowed or ordered under FRCP 7(a); every defense to a claim for relief in any pleading must be asserted in the responsive pleading if one is required

        (2) ❑ A motion asserting any of the defenses in FRCP 12(b) must be made before pleading if a responsive pleading is allowed

        (3) ❑ Failure to state a claim upon which relief can be granted may be raised by a motion under FRCP 12(c); after the pleadings are closed—but early enough not to delay trial—a party may move for judgment on the pleadings

    (4) ❏ Failure to state a claim upon which relief can be granted may be raised at trial; if a pleading sets out a claim for relief that does not require a responsive pleading, an opposing party may assert at trial any defense to that claim

    (5) ❏ A written motion and notice of the hearing must be served at least fourteen (14) days before the time specified for the hearing, with the following exceptions: (i) when the motion may be heard ex parte; (ii) when the Federal Rules of Civil Procedure set a different time; or (iii) when a court order—which a party may, for good cause, apply for ex parte—sets a different time

    (6) ❏ Any affidavit supporting a motion must be served with the motion

(II) ❏ Matters to be considered by opposing party

  (a) ❏ Required documents

    (1) ❏ Response brief

    (2) ❏ Certificate of service

  (b) ❏ Supplemental documents

    (1) ❏ Pleading

    (2) ❏ Notice of constitutional question

    (3) ❏ Index of exhibits

    (4) ❏ Request for oral argument

    (5) ❏ Request for evidentiary hearing

    (6) ❏ Copy of authority

    (7) ❏ Copy of document with self-addressed envelope

    (8) ❏ Notice of manual filing

    (9) ❏ Courtesy copies

   (10) ❏ Declaration that party was unable to file in a timely manner

  (c) ❏ Timing

    (1) ❏ A party must file any response brief to a motion within fourteen (14) days after the motion is served

    (2) ❏ Except as FRCP 59(c) provides otherwise, any opposing affidavit must be served at least seven (7) days before the hearing, unless the court permits service at another time

B. Timing

1. *Motion to dismiss for failure to state a claim*

  a. *In a pleading under FRCP 7(a).* Failure to state a claim upon which relief can be granted may be raised in any pleading allowed or ordered under FRCP 7(a). FRCP 12(h)(2)(A).

    i. *In a responsive pleading.* Every defense to a claim for relief in any pleading must be asserted in the responsive pleading if one is required. FRCP 12(b).

  b. *By motion.* A motion asserting any of the defenses in FRCP 12(b) must be made before pleading if a responsive pleading is allowed. FRCP 12(b). Although FRCP 12(b) encourages the responsive pleader to file a motion to dismiss before filing the answer, nothing in FRCP 12 prohibits the filing of a motion to dismiss with the answer. An untimely motion to dismiss may be considered if the defense asserted in the motion was previously raised in the responsive pleading. FEDPROC § 62:427.

  c. *By motion under FRCP 12(c).* Failure to state a claim upon which relief can be granted may be raised by a motion under FRCP 12(c). FRCP 12(h)(2)(B). After the pleadings are closed—but early enough not to delay trial—a party may move for judgment on the pleadings. FRCP 12(c).

  d. *At trial.* Failure to state a claim upon which relief can be granted may be raised at trial. FRCP

12(h)(2)(C). If a pleading sets out a claim for relief that does not require a responsive pleading, an opposing party may assert at trial any defense to that claim. FRCP 12(b).

2. *Timing of motions, generally*

    a. *Motion and notice of hearing.* A written motion and notice of the hearing must be served at least fourteen (14) days before the time specified for the hearing, with the following exceptions:

        i.   When the motion may be heard ex parte;

        ii. When the Federal Rules of Civil Procedure set a different time; or

        iii. When a court order—which a party may, for good cause, apply for ex parte—sets a different time. FRCP 6(c)(1).

    b. *Supporting affidavit.* Any affidavit supporting a motion must be served with the motion. FRCP 6(c)(2).

3. *Timing of opposing papers.* A party must file any response brief to a motion within fourteen (14) days after the motion is served. IN R USDCTND L.R. 7-1(d)(2)(A).

    a. *Opposing affidavit.* Except as FRCP 59(c) provides otherwise, any opposing affidavit must be served at least seven (7) days before the hearing, unless the court permits service at another time. FRCP 6(c)(2).

    b. *Extensions.* The court may extend response- and reply-brief deadlines, but only for good cause. IN R USDCTND L.R. 7-1(d)(3).

    c. *Summary rulings.* The court may rule on a motion summarily if an opposing party does not file a response before the deadline. IN R USDCTND L.R. 7-1(d)(4).

4. *Timing of reply papers.* Where the respondent files an answering affidavit setting up a new matter, the moving party ordinarily is allowed a reasonable time to file a reply affidavit since failure to deny the new matter by affidavit may operate as an admission of its truth. AMJUR MOTIONS § 25.

    a. *Reply brief.* The moving party must file any reply brief within seven (7) days after the response brief is served. IN R USDCTND L.R. 7-1(d)(2)(B).

    b. *Extensions.* The court may extend response- and reply-brief deadlines, but only for good cause. IN R USDCTND L.R. 7-1(d)(3).

5. *Effect of a FRCP 12 motion on the time to serve a responsive pleading.* Unless the court sets a different time, serving a motion under FRCP 12 alters the periods in FRCP 12(a) as follows:

    a. If the court denies the motion or postpones its disposition until trial, the responsive pleading must be served within fourteen (14) days after notice of the court's action; or

    b. If the court grants a motion for a more definite statement, the responsive pleading must be served within fourteen (14) days after the more definite statement is served. FRCP 12(a)(4).

6. *Computation of time*

    a. *Computing time.* FRCP 6 applies in computing any time period specified in the Federal Rules of Civil Procedure, in any local rule or court order, or in any statute that does not specify a method of computing time. FRCP 6(a).

        i.   *Period stated in days or a longer unit.* When the period is stated in days or a longer unit of time:

             - Exclude the day of the event that triggers the period;

             - Count every day, including intermediate Saturdays, Sundays, and legal holidays; and

             - Include the last day of the period, but if the last day is a Saturday, Sunday, or legal holiday, the period continues to run until the end of the next day that is not a Saturday, Sunday, or legal holiday. FRCP 6(a)(1).

        ii. *Period stated in hours.* When the period is stated in hours:

             - Begin counting immediately on the occurrence of the event that triggers the period;

             - Count every hour, including hours during intermediate Saturdays, Sundays, and legal holidays; and

- If the period would end on a Saturday, Sunday, or legal holiday, the period continues to run until the same time on the next day that is not a Saturday, Sunday, or legal holiday. FRCP 6(a)(2).

iii. *Inaccessibility of the clerk's office.* Unless the court orders otherwise, if the clerk's office is inaccessible:

- On the last day for filing under FRCP 6(a)(1), then the time for filing is extended to the first accessible day that is not a Saturday, Sunday, or legal holiday; or

- During the last hour for filing under FRCP 6(a)(2), then the time for filing is extended to the same time on the first accessible day that is not a Saturday, Sunday, or legal holiday. FRCP 6(a)(3).

iv. *"Last day" defined.* Unless a different time is set by a statute, local rule, or court order, the last day ends:

- For electronic filing, at midnight in the court's time zone; and

- For filing by other means, when the clerk's office is scheduled to close. FRCP 6(a)(4).

v. *"Next day" defined.* The "next day" is determined by continuing to count forward when the period is measured after an event and backward when measured before an event. FRCP 6(a)(5).

vi. *"Legal holiday" defined.* "Legal holiday" means:

- The day set aside by statute for observing New Year's Day, Martin Luther King Jr.'s Birthday, Washington's Birthday, Memorial Day, Independence Day, Labor Day, Columbus Day, Veterans' Day, Thanksgiving Day, or Christmas Day;

- Any day declared a holiday by the President or Congress; and

- For periods that are measured after an event, any other day declared a holiday by the state where the district court is located. FRCP 6(a)(6).

b. *Computation of electronic filing deadlines.* Filing documents electronically does not alter any filing deadlines or any time computation pursuant to FRCP 6. The counties of Lake, Porter, LaPorte, Pulaski and Starke are located in the Central time zone and the remaining counties in the Northern District of Indiana are located in the Eastern time zone. Nevertheless, all electronic transmissions of documents must be completed (i.e., received completely by the clerk's office) prior to midnight Eastern Time, (South Bend/Fort Wayne/Lafayette time) in order to be considered timely filed that day, regardless of the local time in the division where the case is pending. Although documents can be filed electronically twenty-four (24) hours a day, filers are strongly encouraged to file all documents during hours when the CM/ECF Help Line is available, from 9:00 a.m. to 4:00 p.m. local time. IN R USDCTND CM/ECF(II)(I).

i. *Technical failures.* If the attorney is unable to file a document in a timely manner due to technical difficulties in the user's system, the attorney must file a document with the court as soon as possible notifying the court of the inability to file the document. A sample document entitled Declaration that Party was Unable to File in a Timely Manner Due to Technical Difficulties is attached hereto as Form 5. IN R USDCTND CM/ECF(VI)(B). [Editor's note: the reference to Form 5 is likely meant to be a reference to Form 3 (IN R USDCTND CM/ECF(Form 3)].

c. *Extending time*

i. *In general.* When an act may or must be done within a specified time, the court may, for good cause, extend the time:

- With or without motion or notice if the court acts, or if a request is made, before the original time or its extension expires; or

- On motion made after the time has expired if the party failed to act because of excusable neglect. FRCP 6(b)(1).

ii. *Exceptions.* A court must not extend the time to act under FRCP 50(b), FRCP 50(d), FRCP 52(b), FRCP 59(b), FRCP 59(d), FRCP 59(e), and FRCP 60(b). FRCP 6(b)(2).

    iii.   Refer to the United States District Court for the Northern District of Indiana KeyRules Motion for Continuance/Extension of Time document for more information on extending time.

  d. *Additional time after certain kinds of service.* When a party may or must act within a specified time after being served and service is made under FRCP 5(b)(2)(C) (mail), FRCP 5(b)(2)(D) (leaving with the clerk), or FRCP 5(b)(2)(F) (other means consented to), three (3) days are added after the period would otherwise expire under FRCP 6(a). FRCP 6(d).

C. General Requirements

1. *Motions, generally*

  a. *Requirements.* A request for a court order must be made by motion. The motion must:

    i.   Be in writing unless made during a hearing or trial;

    ii. State with particularity the grounds for seeking the order; and

    iii. State the relief sought. FRCP 7(b)(1).

  b. *Notice of motion.* A party interested in resisting the relief sought by a motion has a right to notice thereof, and an opportunity to be heard. AMJUR MOTIONS § 12.

    i.   In addition to statutory or court rule provisions requiring notice of a motion—the purpose of such a notice requirement having been said to be to prevent a party from being prejudicially surprised by a motion—principles of natural justice dictate that an adverse party generally must be given notice that a motion will be presented to the court. AMJUR MOTIONS § 12.

    ii. "Notice," in this regard, means reasonable notice, including a meaningful opportunity to prepare and to defend against allegations of a motion. AMJUR MOTIONS § 12.

  c. *Writing requirement.* The writing requirement is intended to insure that the adverse parties are informed and have a record of both the motion's pendency and the grounds on which the movant seeks an order. FPP § 1191; Feldberg v. Quechee Lakes Corp., 463 F.3d 195 (2d Cir. 2006).

    i.   It is sufficient "if the motion is stated in a written notice of the hearing of the motion." FPP § 1191.

  d. *Particularity requirement.* The particularity requirement insures that the opposing parties will have notice of their opponent's contentions. FEDPROC § 62:364; Goodman v. 1973 26 Foot Trojan Vessel, Arkansas Registration No. AR1439SN, 859 F.2d 71, 12 Fed.R.Serv.3d 645 (8th Cir. 1988). That requirement ensures that notice of the basis for the motion is provided to the court and to the opposing party so as to avoid prejudice, provide the opponent with a meaningful opportunity to respond, and provide the court with enough information to process the motion correctly. FEDPROC § 62:364; Andreas v. Volkswagen of America, Inc., 336 F.3d 789, 56 Fed.R.Serv.3d 6 (8th Cir. 2003).

    i.   Reasonable specification of the grounds for a motion is sufficient. However, where a movant fails to state even one ground for granting the motion in question, the movant has failed to meet the minimal standard of "reasonable specification." FEDPROC § 62:364; Martinez v. Trainor, 556 F.2d 818, 23 Fed.R.Serv.2d 403 (7th Cir. 1977).

    ii. The court may excuse the failure to comply with the particularity requirement if it is inadvertent, and where no prejudice is shown by the opposing party. FEDPROC § 62:364.

  e. *Motions must be filed separately.* Motions must be filed separately, but alternative motions may be filed in a single paper if each is named in the title following the caption. IN R USDCTND L.R. 7-1(a).

2. *Motion to dismiss for failure to state a claim.* A party may assert the defense of failure to state a claim upon which relief can be granted by motion. FRCP 12(b)(6). The court will not rule on a defense under FRCP 12 until the party who raised it files a motion and brief. IN R USDCTND L.R. 7-1(c). The motion under FRCP 12(b)(6) is available to test a claim for relief in any pleading, whether it be in the plaintiff's original complaint, a defendant's counterclaim, a defendant's cross-claim or counterclaim thereto, or a third-party claim or any other FRCP 14 claim. Most commonly, of course, a FRCP 12(b)(6) motion is directed against the plaintiff's complaint. FPP § 1356.

  a. *Applicable standard.* The FRCP 12(b)(6) motion is used to test the sufficiency of the complaint. FEDPROC § 62:461; Petruska v. Gannon University, 462 F.3d 294, 212 Ed.Law.Rep. 598 (3d Cir.

2006). In this regard, the applicable standard is stated in FRCP 8(a)(2), which requires that a pleading setting forth a claim for relief contain a short and plain statement of the claim showing that the pleader is entitled to relief. Thus, a complaint must set forth sufficient information to suggest that there is some recognized legal theory upon which relief can be granted. FEDPROC § 62:461. Only when the plaintiff's complaint fails to meet this liberal pleading standard is it subject to dismissal under FRCP 12(b)(6). FPP § 1356.

    i.   In order to withstand a motion to dismiss filed under FRCP 12(b)(6) in response to claims understood to raise a high risk of abusive litigation, addressed by FRCP 9(b), a plaintiff must state factual allegations with greater particularity than that required by FRCP 8. FEDPROC § 62:470; Bell Atlantic Corp. v. Twombly, 550 U.S. 544, 127 S.Ct. 1955, 167 L.Ed.2d 929, 68 Fed.R.Serv.3d 661 (2007).

    ii.   FRCP 12(b)(6) motions are looked on with disfavor by the courts, and are granted sparingly and with care. FEDPROC § 62:464. Even if it is doubtful that the plaintiff would ultimately prevail, if the plaintiff colorably states facts which, if proven, would entitle him or her to relief, a motion to dismiss for failure to state a claim should not be granted. FEDPROC § 62:464.

  b. *Construction of allegations of complaint (or other pleading).* In considering a FRCP 12(b)(6) motion to dismiss, the complaint is liberally construed and is viewed in the light most favorable to the plaintiff. FEDPROC § 62:467; Bell Atlantic Corp. v. Twombly, 550 U.S. 544, 127 S.Ct. 1955, 167 L.Ed.2d 929, 68 Fed.R.Serv.3d 661 (2007).

    i.   On a motion to dismiss, a federal court presumes that general allegations embrace those specific facts that are necessary to support the claim. FEDPROC § 62:467; Steel Co. v. Citizens for a Better Environment, 523 U.S. 83, 118 S.Ct. 1003, 140 L.Ed.2d 210 (1998).

    ii.   In addition, the well-pleaded allegations of fact contained in the complaint and every inference fairly deducible therefrom are accepted as true for purposes of the motion, including facts alleged on information and belief. FEDPROC § 62:467; Bell Atlantic Corp. v. Twombly, 550 U.S. 544, 127 S.Ct. 1955, 167 L.Ed.2d 929, 68 Fed.R.Serv.3d 661 (2007); Tellabs, Inc. v. Makor Issues & Rights, Ltd., 551 U.S. 308, 127 S.Ct. 2499, 168 L.Ed.2d 179 (2007).

    iii.   However, the court will not accept as true the plaintiff's bare statements of opinions, conclusory allegations, and unwarranted inferences of fact. FEDPROC § 62:467; Leopoldo Fontanillas, Inc. v. Luis Ayala Colon Sucesores, Inc., 283 F.Supp.2d 579 (D.P.R. 2003); Hopkins v. Women's Div., General Bd. of Global Ministries, 238 F.Supp.2d 174 (D.D.C. 2002). Nor will the court accept as true facts which are legally impossible, facts which the court can take judicial notice of as being other than as alleged by the plaintiff, or facts which by the record or by a document attached to the complaint appear to be unfounded. FEDPROC § 62:467; Cohen v. U.S., 129 F.2d 733 (8th Cir. 1942); Henthorn v. Department of Navy, 29 F.3d 682, 29 Fed.R.Serv.3d 1007 (D.C. Cir. 1994).

  c. *Affirmative defenses.* With some exception, it is generally agreed that affirmative defenses can be raised by a FRCP 12(b)(6) motion to dismiss. FEDPROC § 62:471; McCready v. eBay, Inc., 453 F.3d 882 (7th Cir. 2006). However, in order for these defenses to be raised on a FRCP 12(b)(6) motion to dismiss, the complaint must clearly show on its face that the affirmative defense is applicable and bars the action. FEDPROC § 62:471; In re Colonial Mortgage Bankers Corp., 324 F.3d 12 (1st Cir. 2003). Thus, FRCP 12(b)(6) motions may be used to raise the affirmative defenses of: (1) statute of limitations; (2) statute of frauds; (3) res judicata; (4) collateral estoppel; (5) release; (6) waiver; (7) estoppel; (8) sovereign immunity; (9) illegality; and (10) contributory negligence. FEDPROC § 62:471.

  d. *Joining motions*

    i.   *Right to join.* A motion under FRCP 12 may be joined with any other motion allowed by FRCP 12. FRCP 12(g)(1).

    ii.   *Limitation on further motions.* Except as provided in FRCP 12(h)(2) or FRCP 12(h)(3), a party that makes a motion under FRCP 12 must not make another motion under FRCP 12 raising a defense or objection that was available to the party but omitted from its earlier motion. FRCP 12(g)(2).

e. *Waiving and preserving certain defenses.* No defense or objection is waived by joining it with one or more other defenses or objections in a responsive pleading or in a motion. FRCP 12(b).

    i. *When some are waived.* A party waives any defense listed in FRCP 12(b)(2) through FRCP 12(b)(5) by:

- Omitting it from a motion in the circumstances described in FRCP 12(g)(2); or

- Failing to either: (1) make it by motion under FRCP 12; or (2) include it in a responsive pleading or in an amendment allowed by FRCP 15(a)(1) as a matter of course. FRCP 12(h)(1).

    ii. *When to raise others.* Failure to state a claim upon which relief can be granted, to join a person required by FRCP 19(b), or to state a legal defense to a claim may be raised:

- In any pleading allowed or ordered under FRCP 7(a);

- By a motion under FRCP 12(c); or

- At trial. FRCP 12(h)(2).

    iii. *Lack of subject matter jurisdiction.* If the court determines at any time that it lacks subject-matter jurisdiction, the court must dismiss the action. FRCP 12(h)(3).

3. *Opposing papers.* The Federal Rules of Civil Procedure do not require any formal answer, return, or reply to a motion, except where the Federal Rules of Civil Procedure or local rules may require affidavits, memoranda, or other papers to be filed in opposition to a motion. Such papers are simply to apprise the court of such opposition and the grounds of that opposition. FEDPROC § 62:359.

a. *Effect of failure to respond to motion.* Although in the absence of statutory provision or court rule, a motion ordinarily does not require a written answer, when a party files a motion and the opposing party fails to respond, the court may construe such failure to respond as nonopposition to the motion or an admission that the motion was meritorious, may take the facts alleged in the motion as true—the rule in some jurisdictions being that the failure to respond to a fact set forth in a motion is deemed an admission—and may grant the motion if the relief requested appears to be justified. AMJUR MOTIONS § 28.

b. *Assent or no opposition not determinative.* However, a motion will not be granted automatically simply because an "assent" or a notation of "no opposition" has been filed; federal judges frequently deny motions that have been assented to when it is thought that justice so dictates. FPP § 1190.

c. *Responsive pleading inappropriate as response to motion.* An attempt to answer or oppose a motion with a responsive pleading usually is not appropriate. FPP § 1190.

4. *Reply papers.* A moving party may be required or permitted to prepare papers in addition to his original motion papers. AMJUR MOTIONS § 25. Papers answering or replying to opposing papers may be appropriate, in the interests of justice, where it appears there is a substantial reason for allowing a reply. Thus, a court may accept reply papers where a party demonstrates that the papers to which it seeks to file a reply raise new issues that are material to the disposition of the question before the court, or where the court determines, sua sponte, that it wishes further briefing of an issue raised in those papers and orders the submission of additional papers. FEDPROC § 62:360.

a. *Function of reply papers.* The function of a reply affidavit is to answer the arguments made in opposition to the position taken by the movant and not to permit the movant to introduce new arguments in support of the motion. AMJUR MOTIONS § 25.

b. *Issues raised for the first time in a reply document.* However, the view has been followed in some jurisdictions, that as a matter of judicial economy, where there is no prejudice and where the issues could be raised simply by filing a motion to dismiss, the trial court has discretion to consider arguments raised for the first time in a reply memorandum, and that a trial court may grant a motion to strike issues raised for the first time in a reply memorandum. AMJUR MOTIONS § 26.

5. *Appearances.* Attorneys not representing the United States or its agencies must file an appearance when they represent (either in person or by filing a paper) a party. IN R USDCTND L.R. 83-8(a). For more information, refer to IN R USDCTND L.R. 83-8.

6. *Notice of related action.* A party must file a notice of related action as soon as it appears that the party's case and another pending case: (1) arise out of the same transaction or occurrence; (2) involve the same property; or (3) involve the validity or infringement of the same patent, trademark, or copyright. IN R USDCTND L.R. 40-1(d). For more information, refer to IN R USDCTND L.R. 40-1.

7. *Alternative dispute resolution (ADR).* After they confer as required by FRCP 26(f), the parties must advise the court which, if any, alternative-dispute-resolution processes they expect to pursue and when they expect to undertake the process. IN R USDCTND L.R. 16-6(a). For more information on alternative dispute resolution (ADR), refer to IN R USDCTND L.R. 16-6 and IN R USDCTND Order 2003-21.

8. *Settlement or resolution.* The parties must immediately notify the court if they reasonably expect to settle the case or resolve a pending motion. IN R USDCTND L.R. 16-1(g).

9. *Modification or suspension of rules.* The court may, on its own motion or at the request of a party, suspend or modify any rule in a particular case in the interest of justice. IN R USDCTND L.R. 1-1(c).

D. Documents

1. *Documents for moving party*

   a. *Required documents*

      i. *Notice of motion and motion.* The party must not specify a hearing date in the notice of a motion or petition unless the court or the clerk has authorized it. IN R USDCTND L.R. 7-5(b)(2). Refer to the General Requirements section of this document for information on the notice of motion and motion.

      ii. *Brief.* Parties must file a supporting brief with any motion under: FRCP 12. IN R USDCTND L.R. 7-1(b)(1). Refer to the Format section of this document for the format of briefs.

      iii. *Certificate of service.* FRCP 5(d) requires that the person making service under FRCP 5 certify that service has been effected. FRCP 5(Advisory Committee Notes). Having such information on file may be useful for many purposes, including proof of service if an issue arises concerning the effectiveness of the service. FRCP 5(Advisory Committee Notes).

         • *Certificate of service for electronically-filed documents.* A Certificate of Service is still a requirement when filing documents electronically. A sample Certificate of Service is attached as Form 1 (IN R USDCTND CM/ECF(Form 1)). IN R USDCTND CM/ECF(II)(H).

   b. *Supplemental documents*

      i. *Pleading.* As a general rule, the court may only consider the pleading which is attacked by a FRCP 12(b)(6) motion in determining its sufficiency. FEDPROC § 62:466; Armengau v. Cline, 7 Fed.Appx. 336 (6th Cir. 2001). The plaintiff is not entitled to discovery to obtain information relevant to the motion, and the court is not permitted to look at matters outside the record. FEDPROC § 62:466; Cooperativa de Ahorro y Credito Aguada v. Kidder, Peabody & Co., 993 F.2d 269, 37 Fed.R.Evid.Serv. 904, 25 Fed.R.Serv.3d 982 (1st Cir. 1993).

         • *Motion treated as one for summary judgment.* If, on a motion under FRCP 12(b)(6) or FRCP 12(c), matters outside the pleadings are presented to and not excluded by the court, the motion must be treated as one for summary judgment under FRCP 56. All parties must be given a reasonable opportunity to present all the material that is pertinent to the motion. FRCP 12(d).

         • *Documents attached to pleadings.* However, the court may consider documents which are attached to or submitted with the complaint, as well as legal arguments presented in memorandums or briefs and arguments of counsel. FEDPROC § 62:466; Tellabs, Inc. v. Makor Issues & Rights, Ltd., 551 U.S. 308, 127 S.Ct. 2499, 168 L.Ed.2d 179 (2007); E.E.O.C. v. Ohio Edison Co., 7 F.3d 541 (6th Cir. 1993). Documents that the defendant attaches to the motion to dismiss are considered part of the pleadings if they are referred to in the plaintiff's complaint and are central to the claim, and as such may be considered by the court. FEDPROC § 62:466; Hoffman-Pugh v. Ramsey, 312 F.3d 1222 (11th Cir. 2002).

ii. *Notice of constitutional question.* A party that files a pleading, written motion, or other paper drawing into question the constitutionality of a federal or state statute must promptly:

- *File notice.* File a notice of constitutional question stating the question and identifying the paper that raises it, if: (1) a federal statute is questioned and the parties do not include the United States, one of its agencies, or one of its officers or employees in an official capacity; or (2) a state statute is questioned and the parties do not include the state, one of its agencies, or one of its officers or employees in an official capacity; and

- *Serve notice.* Serve the notice and paper on the Attorney General of the United States if a federal statute is questioned—or on the state attorney general if a state statute is questioned—either by certified or registered mail or by sending it to an electronic address designated by the attorney general for this purpose. FRCP 5.1(a).

- *When to file the notice.* A party required to file a notice of constitutional question under FRCP 5.1 must do so by the later of: (1) the day the parties tender their proposed case-management plan (if one is required); or (2) 21 days after filing the pleading, written motion, or other paper questioning the constitutionality of a federal or state statute. IN R USDCTND L.R. 5.1-1(a).

- *Service on government officials.* The party must also serve the notice and the pleading, written motion, or other paper questioning the constitutionality of a federal or state statute on: (1) the Attorney General of the United States and the United States Attorney for the Northern District of Indiana, if a federal statute is challenged; or (2) the Attorney General for the state if a state statute is challenged. IN R USDCTND L.R. 5.1-1(b). Service required under IN R USDCTND L.R. 5.1-1(b) may be made either by certified or registered mail or by emailing it to an address designated by those officials for this purpose. IN R USDCTND L.R. 5.1-1(c).

- *No forfeiture.* A party's failure to file and serve the notice, or the court's failure to certify, does not forfeit a constitutional claim or defense that is otherwise timely asserted. FRCP 5.1(d).

iii. *Nongovernmental corporate disclosure statement*

- *Contents.* A nongovernmental corporate party must file two (2) copies of a disclosure statement that: (1) identifies any parent corporation and any publicly held corporation owning ten percent (10%) or more of its stock; or (2) states that there is no such corporation. FRCP 7.1(a).

- *Time to file; Supplemental filing.* A party must: (1) file the disclosure statement with its first appearance, pleading, petition, motion, response, or other request addressed to the court; and (2) promptly file a supplemental statement if any required information changes. FRCP 7.1(b).

iv. *Index of exhibits.* Any pleading, motion, brief, affidavit, notice, or proposed order, whether filed electronically or by delivering it to the clerk, must: include a separate index identifying and briefly describing each exhibit if there are more than four (4) exhibits. IN R USDCTND L.R. 5-4(a)(8).

v. *Request for oral argument.* A party may request oral argument on a motion by filing and serving a separate document explaining why oral argument is necessary and estimating how long the court should allow for the argument. IN R USDCTND L.R. 7-5(a)(1). The request must be filed and served with the party's supporting brief, response brief, or reply brief. IN R USDCTND L.R. 7-5(a)(2).

vi. *Request for evidentiary hearing.* A party may request an evidentiary hearing by filing and serving a separate document explaining why the hearing is necessary and estimating how long the court should allow for it. IN R USDCTND L.R. 7-5(b)(1).

vii. *Copy of authority.* A copy of any decision, statute, or regulation cited in a motion or brief must be attached to the paper if—and only if—it is not available on Westlaw or Lexis. But if a copy of a decision, statute, or regulation is only available electronically, a party must provide it to the court or another party upon request. IN R USDCTND L.R. 7-1(f).

    viii. *Proposed order.* Parties filing a paper that requires the judge or clerk to enter a routine or uncontested order must include a suitable form of order. IN R USDCTND L.R. 5-4(c).

- Proposed orders shall not be filed electronically either as a separate document or as an attachment to the main pleading or other document. Instead, all proposed orders must be e-mailed to the chambers of the appropriate judicial officer for the case. The proposed order must be in WordPerfect Format or Rich Text Format (RTF). Proposed orders should be attached to an e-mail and sent to the appropriate judicial officer at the address listed in IN R USDCTND CM/ECF(II)(F). The subject line of the email message should indicate the case title, cause number and document number of the motion, e.g., Smith v. Jones 1:02-cv-1234, motion# ___. IN R USDCTND CM/ECF(II)(F).

    ix. *Copy of document with self-addressed envelope.* A party who wants a file-stamped copy of a paper must include with the filing an additional copy of the paper and a self-addressed envelope with adequate postage. IN R USDCTND L.R. 5-4(b)(6).

    x. *Notice of manual filing.* However, if that is not physically possible, counsel shall electronically file a .pdf document titled Notice of Manual Filing as a notation on the docket sheet that filings are being held in the clerk's office in paper. A sample Notice of Manual Filing is attached as Form 2 (IN R USDCTND CM/ECF(Form 2)). IN R USDCTND CM/ECF(III)(A)(1).

    xi. *Courtesy copies.* If documents are filed in paper format, counsel must provide an original for the clerk's office, a copy for the judge and a copy must be served on all parties in the case. IN R USDCTND CM/ECF(III)(A)(1).

    xii. *Declaration that party was unable to file in a timely manner.* If the attorney is unable to file a document in a timely manner due to technical difficulties in the user's system, the attorney must file a document with the court as soon as possible notifying the court of the inability to file the document. A sample document entitled Declaration that Party was Unable to File in a Timely Manner Due to Technical Difficulties is attached hereto as Form 5. IN R USDCTND CM/ECF(VI)(B). [Editor's note: the reference to Form 5 is likely meant to be a reference to Form 3 (IN R USDCTND CM/ECF(Form 3)].

2. *Documents for opposing party*

  a. *Required documents*

    i. *Response brief.* Refer to the Format section of this document for the format of briefs. Refer to the General Requirements section of this document for information on the opposing papers.

    ii. *Certificate of service.* FRCP 5(d) requires that the person making service under FRCP 5 certify that service has been effected. FRCP 5(Advisory Committee Notes). Having such information on file may be useful for many purposes, including proof of service if an issue arises concerning the effectiveness of the service. FRCP 5(Advisory Committee Notes).

- *Certificate of service for electronically-filed documents.* A Certificate of Service is still a requirement when filing documents electronically. A sample Certificate of Service is attached as Form 1 (IN R USDCTND CM/ECF(Form 1)). IN R USDCTND CM/ECF(II)(H).

  b. *Supplemental documents*

    i. *Pleading.* As a general rule, the court may only consider the pleading which is attacked by a FRCP 12(b)(6) motion in determining its sufficiency. FEDPROC § 62:466; Armengau v. Cline, 7 Fed.Appx. 336 (6th Cir. 2001). The plaintiff is not entitled to discovery to obtain information relevant to the motion, and the court is not permitted to look at matters outside the record. FEDPROC § 62:466; Cooperativa de Ahorro y Credito Aguada v. Kidder, Peabody & Co., 993 F.2d 269, 37 Fed.R.Evid.Serv. 904, 25 Fed.R.Serv.3d 982 (1st Cir. 1993).

- *Motion treated as one for summary judgment.* If, on a motion under FRCP 12(b)(6) or FRCP 12(c), matters outside the pleadings are presented to and not excluded by the court, the motion must be treated as one for summary judgment under FRCP 56. All parties must be given a reasonable opportunity to present all the material that is pertinent to the motion. FRCP 12(d).

- *Documents attached to pleadings.* However, the court may consider documents which are attached to or submitted with the complaint, as well as legal arguments presented in memorandums or briefs and arguments of counsel. FEDPROC § 62:466; Tellabs, Inc. v. Makor Issues & Rights, Ltd., 551 U.S. 308, 127 S.Ct. 2499, 168 L.Ed.2d 179 (2007); E.E.O.C. v. Ohio Edison Co., 7 F.3d 541 (6th Cir. 1993). Documents that the defendant attaches to the motion to dismiss are considered part of the pleadings if they are referred to in the plaintiff's complaint and are central to the claim, and as such may be considered by the court. FEDPROC § 62:466; Hoffman-Pugh v. Ramsey, 312 F.3d 1222 (11th Cir. 2002).

ii. *Notice of constitutional question.* A party that files a pleading, written motion, or other paper drawing into question the constitutionality of a federal or state statute must promptly:

- *File notice.* File a notice of constitutional question stating the question and identifying the paper that raises it, if: (1) a federal statute is questioned and the parties do not include the United States, one of its agencies, or one of its officers or employees in an official capacity; or (2) a state statute is questioned and the parties do not include the state, one of its agencies, or one of its officers or employees in an official capacity; and

- *Serve notice.* Serve the notice and paper on the Attorney General of the United States if a federal statute is questioned—or on the state attorney general if a state statute is questioned—either by certified or registered mail or by sending it to an electronic address designated by the attorney general for this purpose. FRCP 5.1(a).

- *When to file the notice.* A party required to file a notice of constitutional question under FRCP 5.1 must do so by the later of: (1) the day the parties tender their proposed case-management plan (if one is required); or (2) 21 days after filing the pleading, written motion, or other paper questioning the constitutionality of a federal or state statute. IN R USDCTND L.R. 5.1-1(a).

- *Service on government officials.* The party must also serve the notice and the pleading, written motion, or other paper questioning the constitutionality of a federal or state statute on: (1) the Attorney General of the United States and the United States Attorney for the Northern District of Indiana, if a federal statute is challenged; or (2) the Attorney General for the state if a state statute is challenged. IN R USDCTND L.R. 5.1-1(b). Service required under IN R USDCTND L.R. 5.1-1(b) may be made either by certified or registered mail or by emailing it to an address designated by those officials for this purpose. IN R USDCTND L.R. 5.1-1(c).

- *No forfeiture.* A party's failure to file and serve the notice, or the court's failure to certify, does not forfeit a constitutional claim or defense that is otherwise timely asserted. FRCP 5.1(d).

iii. *Index of exhibits.* Any pleading, motion, brief, affidavit, notice, or proposed order, whether filed electronically or by delivering it to the clerk, must: include a separate index identifying and briefly describing each exhibit if there are more than four (4) exhibits. IN R USDCTND L.R. 5-4(a)(8).

iv. *Request for oral argument.* A party may request oral argument on a motion by filing and serving a separate document explaining why oral argument is necessary and estimating how long the court should allow for the argument. IN R USDCTND L.R. 7-5(a)(1). The request must be filed and served with the party's supporting brief, response brief, or reply brief. IN R USDCTND L.R. 7-5(a)(2).

v. *Request for evidentiary hearing.* A party may request an evidentiary hearing by filing and serving a separate document explaining why the hearing is necessary and estimating how long the court should allow for it. IN R USDCTND L.R. 7-5(b)(1).

vi. *Copy of authority.* A copy of any decision, statute, or regulation cited in a motion or brief must be attached to the paper if—and only if—it is not available on Westlaw or Lexis. But if a copy of a decision, statute, or regulation is only available electronically, a party must provide it to the court or another party upon request. IN R USDCTND L.R. 7-1(f).

vii. *Copy of document with self-addressed envelope.* A party who wants a file-stamped copy of a paper must include with the filing an additional copy of the paper and a self-addressed envelope with adequate postage. IN R USDCTND L.R. 5-4(b)(6).

viii. *Notice of manual filing.* However, if that is not physically possible, counsel shall electronically file a .pdf document titled Notice of Manual Filing as a notation on the docket sheet that filings are being held in the clerk's office in paper. A sample Notice of Manual Filing is attached as Form 2 (IN R USDCTND CM/ECF(Form 2)). IN R USDCTND CM/ECF(III)(A)(1).

ix. *Courtesy copies.* If documents are filed in paper format, counsel must provide an original for the clerk's office, a copy for the judge and a copy must be served on all parties in the case. IN R USDCTND CM/ECF(III)(A)(1).

x. *Declaration that party was unable to file in a timely manner.* If the attorney is unable to file a document in a timely manner due to technical difficulties in the user's system, the attorney must file a document with the court as soon as possible notifying the court of the inability to file the document. A sample document entitled Declaration that Party was Unable to File in a Timely Manner Due to Technical Difficulties is attached hereto as Form 5. IN R USDCTND CM/ECF(VI)(B). [Editor's note: the reference to Form 5 is likely meant to be a reference to Form 3 (IN R USDCTND CM/ECF(Form 3)].

E. Format

1. *Form of documents.* The rules governing captions and other matters of form in pleadings apply to motions and other papers. FRCP 7(b)(2).

   a. *Paper.* Any pleading, motion, brief, affidavit, notice, or proposed order, whether filed electronically or by delivering it to the clerk, must: use eight and one-half by eleven (8-1/2 x 11) inch pages. IN R USDCTND L.R. 5-4(a)(2).

      i. *Manual filings.* Papers delivered to the clerk for filing must: be flat, unfolded, and on good-quality, white paper. IN R USDCTND L.R. 5-4(b)(1)(A).

         • *Covers or backing.* Papers delivered to the clerk for filing must: not have a cover or a back. IN R USDCTND L.R. 5-4(b)(1)(B).

         • *Recycled paper.* The court encourages using recycled paper. IN R USDCTND L.R. 5-4(b)(7).

   b. *Margins.* Any pleading, motion, brief, affidavit, notice, or proposed order, whether filed electronically or by delivering it to the clerk, must: have at least one (1) inch margins. IN R USDCTND L.R. 5-4(a)(3).

   c. *Spacing.* Any pleading, motion, brief, affidavit, notice, or proposed order, whether filed electronically or by delivering it to the clerk, must: be double spaced (except for headings, footnotes, and quoted material). IN R USDCTND L.R. 5-4(a)(5).

   d. *Text.* Any pleading, motion, brief, affidavit, notice, or proposed order, whether filed electronically or by delivering it to the clerk, must: be plainly typewritten, printed, or prepared by a clearly legible copying process. IN R USDCTND L.R. 5-4(a)(1).

      i. Any pleading, motion, brief, affidavit, notice, or proposed order, whether filed electronically or by delivering it to the clerk, must: use at least twelve (12) point type in the body and at least ten (10) point type in footnotes. IN R USDCTND L.R. 5-4(a)(4).

   e. *Page numbering.* Any pleading, motion, brief, affidavit, notice, or proposed order, whether filed electronically or by delivering it to the clerk, must: have consecutively numbered pages. IN R USDCTND L.R. 5-4(a)(6).

   f. *Caption; Names of parties.* Every pleading must have a caption with the court's name, a title, a file number, and a FRCP 7(a) designation. The title of the complaint must name all the parties; the title of other pleadings, after naming the first party on each side, may refer generally to other parties. FRCP 10(a). Any pleading, motion, brief, affidavit, notice, or proposed order, whether filed electronically or by delivering it to the clerk, must: include a title on the first page. IN R USDCTND L.R. 5-4(a)(7).

    i. *Alternative motions.* Motions must be filed separately, but alternative motions may be filed in a single paper if each is named in the title following the caption. IN R USDCTND L.R. 7-1(a).

g. *Filer's information.* Any pleading, motion, brief, affidavit, notice, or proposed order, whether filed electronically or by delivering it to the clerk, must: except in proposed orders and affidavits, include the filer's name, address, telephone number, fax number (where available), and e-mail address (where available). IN R USDCTND L.R. 5-4(a)(9).

h. *Paragraphs; Separate statements.* A party must state its claims or defenses in numbered paragraphs, each limited as far as practicable to a single set of circumstances. A later pleading may refer by number to a paragraph in an earlier pleading. If doing so would promote clarity, each claim founded on a separate transaction or occurrence—and each defense other than a denial—must be stated in a separate count or defense. FRCP 10(b).

i. *Adoption by reference; Exhibits.* A statement in a pleading may be adopted by reference elsewhere in the same pleading or in any other pleading or motion. A copy of a written instrument that is an exhibit to a pleading is a part of the pleading for all purposes. FRCP 10(c).

j. *Citation of local rules.* The Local Civil Rules of the United States District Court for the Northern District of Indiana may be cited as "N.D. Ind. L.R." IN R USDCTND L.R. 1-1(a)(1).

k. *Acceptance by the clerk.* The clerk must not refuse to file a paper solely because it is not in the form prescribed by the Federal Rules of Civil Procedure or by a local rule or practice. FRCP 5(d)(4).

    i. *Sanctions for formatting errors; Non-compliance.* If a person files a paper that does not comply with the rules governing the format of papers filed with the court, the court may: (1) strike the paper from the record; or (2) fine the person up to one thousand dollars ($1,000). IN R USDCTND L.R. 1-3(a).

        • *Notice.* Before sanctioning a person under IN R USDCTND L.R. 1-3(a)(2), the court must: (1) notify the person that the paper is noncompliant; and (2) give the person the opportunity either to be heard or to revise the paper. IN R USDCTND L.R. 1-3(b).

2. *Form of electronic documents.* Electronically filed documents must meet the same requirements of format and page limits as documents "conventionally filed" (as defined in IN R USDCTND CM/ECF(III)(A)) pursuant to the Federal Rules of Civil Procedure and the Local Civil Rules of the United States District Court for the Northern District of Indiana. IN R USDCTND CM/ECF(II)(A)(2).

a. *PDF format required.* Documents filed in the CM/ECF must be in .pdf format. A document created with almost any word-processing program can be converted to .pdf format. The .pdf program in effect takes a picture of the original document and allows anyone to open the converted document across a broad range of hardware and software, with layout, format, links, and images intact. IN R USDCTND CM/ECF(FN2).

b. *Title of documents.* The person electronically filing a pleading or other document will be responsible for designating a title for the pleading or other document by using one of the categories contained in the events listed in the CM/ECF Menu. IN R USDCTND CM/ECF(II)(G).

c. *Combining documents.* All documents which form part of a single pleading and which are being filed at the same time and by the same party may be electronically filed together under one document number, e.g., the motion and a supporting affidavit, with the exception of memoranda in support. Memoranda in support shall be electronically filed separately and shown as a related document to the motion. IN R USDCTND CM/ECF(II)(A)(4).

d. *Exhibits and attachments.* Filing users must submit in electronic form all documents referenced as exhibits or attachments, unless the court permits conventional filing. A filing user must submit as exhibits or attachments only those excerpts of the referenced documents that are directly germane to the matter under consideration by the court. Excerpted material must be clearly and prominently identified as such. Filing users who file excerpts of documents as exhibits or attachments do so without prejudice to their right to timely file additional excerpts or the complete document.

Responding parties may timely file additional excerpts or the complete document that they believe are directly germane. The court may require parties to file additional excerpts or the complete document. IN R USDCTND CM/ECF(II)(A)(6).

e. *Hyperlinks.* Electronically filed documents may contain hyperlink references to an external document as a convenient mechanism for accessing material cited in the document. A hyperlink reference is neither validated for content nor considered a part of the court's records. The court neither endorses the product or organization at the destination of a hyperlink reference, nor does the court exercise any responsibility over the content at the destination. In order to preserve the integrity of the court record, attorneys wishing to insert hyperlinks in court filings shall continue to use the traditional citation method for the cited authority, in addition to the hyperlink. A hyperlink contained in a filing is no more than a convenient mechanism for accessing material cited in the document and a hyperlink reference is extraneous to any filed document and is not part of the court's record. IN R USDCTND CM/ECF(II)(A)(3).

3. *Form of briefs*

a. *Page limits.* Supporting and response briefs (excluding tables of contents, tables of authorities, and appendices) ordinarily must not exceed twenty-five (25) pages. Reply briefs must not exceed fifteen (15) pages. IN R USDCTND L.R. 7-1(e)(1).

   i. *Exception.* The court may allow a party to file a brief exceeding these page limits for extraordinary and compelling reasons. But if the court permits a brief to exceed twenty-five (25) pages, it must include:

   - A table of contents with page references;

   - An issue statement; and

   - A table of authorities including: (1) all cases (alphabetically arranged), statutes, and other authorities cited in the brief; and (2) references to where the authorities appear in the brief. IN R USDCTND L.R. 7-1(e)(2).

4. *Signing of pleadings, motions and other papers*

a. *Signature.* Every pleading, written motion, and other paper must be signed by at least one attorney of record in the attorney's name—or by a party personally if the party is unrepresented. The paper must state the signer's address, e-mail address, and telephone number. FRCP 11(a).

   i. *Signatures on manual filings.* Papers delivered to the clerk for filing must: include the filer's original signature. IN R USDCTND L.R. 5-4(b)(1)(C).

   - *Rubber-stamped and faxed signatures.* An original paper with a rubber-stamped or faxed signature is unsigned for purposes of FRCP 11 and FRCP 26(g). IN R USDCTND L.R. 5-4(b)(2).

   - *Affidavits.* Only the affiant need sign an affidavit. IN R USDCTND L.R. 5-4(b)(3).

   ii. *Electronic signatures.* Pursuant to FRCP 11, every pleading, motion, and other paper (except lists, schedules, statements or amendments thereto) shall be signed by at least one attorney of record or, if the party is not represented by an attorney, all papers shall be signed by the party. An attorney's/participant's password issued by the court combined with the user's identification, serves as and constitutes the attorney/participant's signature for FRCP 11 and other purposes. IN R USDCTND CM/ECF(I)(C). Documents which must be filed and which must contain original signatures other than those of a participating attorney or which require either verification or an unsworn declaration under any rule or statute, shall be filed electronically, with originally executed copies maintained by the filer. The pleading or other document electronically filed shall contain "s/" signature(s), as noted in IN R USDCTND CM/ECF(II)(E)(3)(b). IN R USDCTND CM/ECF(II)(E)(1).

   - *Multiple signatures.* In the case of a stipulation or other document to be signed by two or more attorneys, the following procedure should be used: The filing attorney shall initially confirm that the content of the document is acceptable to all persons required to sign the document and shall obtain the physical signatures of all attorneys on the document. IN R

USDCTND CM/ECF(II)(E)(3)(a). The filing attorney then shall file the document electronically, indicating the signatories, e.g., "s/Jane Doe," "s/John Doe," etc. IN R USDCTND CM/ECF(II)(E)(3)(b). The filing attorney shall retain the hard copy of the document containing the original signatures. IN R USDCTND CM/ECF(II)(E)(3)(c).

    iii. *No verification or accompanying affidavit required for pleadings.* Unless a rule or statute specifically states otherwise, a pleading need not be verified or accompanied by an affidavit. FRCP 11(a).

    iv. *Unsigned papers.* The court must strike an unsigned paper unless the omission is promptly corrected after being called to the attorney's or party's attention. FRCP 11(a).

b. *Representations to the court.* By presenting to the court a pleading, written motion, or other paper—whether by signing, filing, submitting, or later advocating it—an attorney or unrepresented party certifies that to the best of the person's knowledge, information, and belief, formed after an inquiry reasonable under the circumstances:

    i. It is not being presented for any improper purpose, such as to harass, cause unnecessary delay, or needlessly increase the cost of litigation;

    ii. The claims, defenses, and other legal contentions are warranted by existing law or by a nonfrivolous argument for extending, modifying, or reversing existing law or for establishing new law;

    iii. The factual contentions have evidentiary support or, if specifically so identified, will likely have evidentiary support after a reasonable opportunity for further investigation or discovery; and

    iv. The denials of factual contentions are warranted on the evidence or, if specifically so identified, are reasonably based on belief or a lack of information. FRCP 11(b).

c. *Sanctions.* If, after notice and a reasonable opportunity to respond, the court determines that FRCP 11(b) has been violated, the court may impose an appropriate sanction on any attorney, law firm, or party that violated FRCP 11(b) or is responsible for the violation. FRCP 11(c)(1). Refer to the United States District Court for the Northern District of Indiana KeyRules Motion for Sanctions document for more information.

5. *Privacy protection for filings made with the court*

a. *Redacted filings.* Counsel should not include sensitive information in any document filed with the court unless such inclusion is necessary and relevant to the case. IN R USDCTND CM/ECF(VII). Unless the court orders otherwise, in an electronic or paper filing with the court that contains an individual's Social Security number, taxpayer-identification number, or birth date, the name of an individual known to be a minor, or a financial-account number, a party or nonparty making the filing may include only:

    i. The last four (4) digits of the Social Security number and taxpayer-identification number;

    ii. The year of the individual's birth;

    iii. The minor's initials; and

    iv. The last four (4) digits of the financial-account number. FRCP 5.2(a); IN R USDCTND Order 2005-3.

b. *Exemptions from the redaction requirement.* The redaction requirement does not apply to the following:

    i. A financial-account number that identifies the property allegedly subject to forfeiture in a forfeiture proceeding;

    ii. The record of an administrative or agency proceeding;

    iii. The official record of a state-court proceeding;

    iv. The record of a court or tribunal, if that record was not subject to the redaction requirement when originally filed;

    v. A filing covered by FRCP 5.2(c) or FRCP 5.2(d); and

    vi.   A pro se filing in an action brought under 28 U.S.C.A. § 2241, 28 U.S.C.A. § 2254, or 28 U.S.C.A. § 2255. FRCP 5.2(b).

    vii.   In cases filed under the Social Security Act, 42 U.S.C.A. § 405(g), there is no need for redaction of any information from the documents filed in the case. IN R USDCTND Order 2005-3.

c.   *Limitations on remote access to electronic files; Social Security appeals and immigration cases.* Unless the court orders otherwise, in an action for benefits under the Social Security Act, and in an action or proceeding relating to an order of removal, to relief from removal, or to immigration benefits or detention, access to an electronic file is authorized as follows:

    i.   The parties and their attorneys may have remote electronic access to any part of the case file, including the administrative record;

    ii.   Any other person may have electronic access to the full record at the courthouse, but may have remote electronic access only to:

- The docket maintained by the court; and
- An opinion, order, judgment, or other disposition of the court, but not any other part of the case file or the administrative record. FRCP 5.2(c).

d.   *Filings made under seal.* The court may order that a filing be made under seal without redaction. The court may later unseal the filing or order the person who made the filing to file a redacted version for the public record. FRCP 5.2(d). For information on filing documents under seal, refer to IN R USDCTND L.R. 5-3, IN R USDCTND CM/ECF(IV)(A), and IN R USDCTND ECF Order 2004-19.

e.   *Protective orders.* For good cause, the court may by order in a case:

    i.   Require redaction of additional information; or

    ii.   Limit or prohibit a nonparty's remote electronic access to a document filed with the court. FRCP 5.2(e).

f.   *Option for additional unredacted filing under seal.* A person making a redacted filing may also file an unredacted copy under seal. The court must retain the unredacted copy as part of the record. FRCP 5.2(f); IN R USDCTND Order 2005-3.

    i.   The unredacted version of the document or the reference list shall be retained by the court under seal as part of the record. This paper shall be retained by the court as part of the record. The court may, however, still require the party to file a redacted copy for the public file. IN R USDCTND Order 2005-3.

g.   *Option for filing a reference list.* A filing that contains redacted information may be filed together with a reference list that identifies each item of redacted information and specifies an appropriate identifier that uniquely corresponds to each item listed. The list must be filed under seal and may be amended as of right. Any reference in the case to a listed identifier will be construed to refer to the corresponding item of information. FRCP 5.2(g); IN R USDCTND Order 2005-3.

    i.   The unredacted version of the document or the reference list shall be retained by the court under seal as part of the record. This paper shall be retained by the court as part of the record. The court may, however, still require the party to file a redacted copy for the public file. IN R USDCTND Order 2005-3.

h.   *Responsibility for redaction.* The responsibility for redacting these personal identifiers rests solely with counsel and the parties. The Clerk will not review each paper for compliance with IN R USDCTND Order 2005-3. IN R USDCTND Order 2005-3.

i.   *Waiver of protection of identifiers.* A person waives the protection of FRCP 5.2(a) as to the person's own information by filing it without redaction and not under seal. FRCP 5.2(h).

F. Filing and Service Requirements

1.   *Filing requirements.* Any paper after the complaint that is required to be served—together with a certificate of service—must be filed within a reasonable time after service. FRCP 5(d)(1). Motions must

be filed separately, but alternative motions may be filed in a single paper if each is named in the title following the caption. IN R USDCTND L.R. 7-1(a).

a. *How filing is made; In general.* A paper is filed by delivering it:

    i. To the clerk; or

    ii. To a judge who agrees to accept it for filing, and who must then note the filing date on the paper and promptly send it to the clerk. FRCP 5(d)(2).

- Papers not filed electronically must be filed with the clerk, not a judge. IN R USDCTND L.R. 5-4(b)(4).

    iii. Parties manually filing a paper that requires the clerk to give others notice, must give the clerk: (1) sufficient copies of the notice; and (2) the name and address of each person entitled to receive the notice. IN R USDCTND L.R. 5-4(b)(8).

b. *Where to file.* Papers not filed electronically must be filed in the division where the case is pending, unless: (1) a person will be prejudiced if the paper is not filed the same day it is tendered; and (2) it includes an adequately sized envelope addressed to the clerk's office in the division where the case is pending and with adequate postage. IN R USDCTND L.R. 5-4(b)(5).

c. *Electronic filing*

    i. *Authorization of electronic filing program.* A court may, by local rule, allow papers to be filed, signed, or verified by electronic means that are consistent with any technical standards established by the Judicial Conference of the United States. A local rule may require electronic filing only if reasonable exceptions are allowed. A paper filed electronically in compliance with a local rule is a written paper for purposes of the Federal Rules of Civil Procedure. FRCP 5(d)(3).

- Papers must be filed, signed, and verified electronically unless excepted by the court's CM/ECF Civil and Criminal User Manual (IN R USDCTND CM/ECF). IN R USDCTND L.R. 5-1.

    ii. *Mandatory electronic filing.* Unless otherwise permitted by these procedures or otherwise authorized by the assigned judge, all documents submitted for filing in this district in civil and criminal cases, no matter when a case was originally filed, shall be filed electronically using the System. IN R USDCTND CM/ECF(II)(A)(1). The requirement that "all documents" be filed electronically includes briefs, and attachments and exhibits used in support of motions. IN R USDCTND CM/ECF(FN1).

- Sending a document or pleading to the court via e-mail or facsimile does not constitute "electronic filing." IN R USDCTND CM/ECF(I)(A).

    iii. *Conventional filing.* As used in these procedures, a "conventionally" filed or submitted document or pleading is one presented to the Clerk or a party in paper or other non-electronic, tangible format. The following documents shall be filed conventionally and not electronically unless specifically authorized by the Court:

- Exhibits and other documents which cannot be converted to a legible electronic form. Whenever possible, counsel is responsible for converting filings to an electronic form. However, if that is not physically possible, counsel shall electronically file a .pdf document titled Notice of Manual Filing as a notation on the docket sheet that filings are being held in the clerk's office in paper. A sample Notice of Manual Filing is attached as Form 2 (IN R USDCTND CM/ECF(Form 2)). If documents are filed in paper format, counsel must provide an original for the clerk's office, a copy for the judge and a copy must be served on all parties in the case. Large documents which do not exist in an electronic format shall be scanned into .pdf format by counsel, in small batches if necessary, and filed electronically as separate attachments in the System. IN R USDCTND CM/ECF(III)(A)(1).

- Certain documents which are listed in IN R USDCTND CM/ECF(II)(E)(2). IN R US-DCTND CM/ECF(III)(A)(2).

- Documents filed by pro se litigants. IN R USDCTND CM/ECF(III)(A)(3).

    iv.   For more information on electronic filing, refer to IN R USDCTND CM/ECF.

2. *Service requirements*

   a. *Service; When required*

      i. *In general.* Unless the Federal Rules of Civil Procedure provide otherwise, each of the following papers must be served on every party:

- An order stating that service is required;
- A pleading filed after the original complaint, unless the court orders otherwise under FRCP 5(c) because there are numerous defendants;
- A discovery paper required to be served on a party, unless the court orders otherwise;
- A written motion, except one that may be heard ex parte; and
- A written notice, appearance, demand, or offer of judgment, or any similar paper. FRCP 5(a)(1).

     ii. *If a party fails to appear.* No service is required on a party who is in default for failing to appear. But a pleading that asserts a new claim for relief against such a party must be served on that party under FRCP 4. FRCP 5(a)(2).

    iii. *Seizing property.* If an action is begun by seizing property and no person is or need be named as a defendant, any service required before the filing of an appearance, answer, or claim must be made on the person who had custody or possession of the property when it was seized. FRCP 5(a)(3).

   b. *Service; How made*

      i. *Serving an attorney.* If a party is represented by an attorney, service under FRCP 5 must be made on the attorney unless the court orders service on the party. FRCP 5(b)(1).

     ii. *Service in general.* A paper is served under FRCP 5 by:

- Handing it to the person;
- Leaving it: (1) at the person's office with a clerk or other person in charge or, if no one is in charge, in a conspicuous place in the office; or (2) if the person has no office or the office is closed, at the person's dwelling or usual place of abode with someone of suitable age and discretion who resides there;
- Mailing it to the person's last known address—in which event service is complete upon mailing;
- Leaving it with the court clerk if the person has no known address;
- Sending it by electronic means if the person consented in writing—in which event service is complete upon transmission, but is not effective if the serving party learns that it did not reach the person to be served; or
- Delivering it by any other means that the person consented to in writing—in which event service is complete when the person making service delivers it to the agency designated to make delivery. FRCP 5(b)(2).

    iii. *Electronic service.* Electronically filed papers may be served electronically if service is consistent with the CM/ECF User Manual (IN R USDCTND CM/ECF). IN R USDCTND L.R. 5-2(a).

- *Waiver of other service.* An attorney's registration will constitute a waiver of conventional service of documents and the attorney agrees to accept service of notice on behalf of the client of the electronic filing by hand, facsimile or authorized email. IN R USDCTND CM/ECF(I)(B)(3).
- *Serving registered persons.* The System will generate a "Notice of Electronic Filing" when any document is filed. This notice represents service of the document on parties who are

registered participants with the System. Except as provided in IN R USDCTND CM/ECF(III)(B), the filing party shall not be required to serve any pleading or other documents on any party receiving electronic notice. IN R USDCTND CM/ECF(II)(D)(1). The term "pleading" refers only to those documents listed in FRCP 7(a). IN R USDCTND CM/ECF(FN3).

- *When electronic service is deemed completed.* A person registered to use the court's electronic-filing system is served with an electronically filed paper when a "Notice of Electronic Filing" is transmitted to that person through the court's electronic filing-system. IN R USDCTND L.R. 5-2(b).

- *Serving non-registered persons.* A person who has not registered to use the court's electronic-filing system but who is entitled to service of a paper must be served according to the Local Civil Rules of the United States District Court for the Northern District of Indiana and the Federal Rules of Civil Procedure. IN R USDCTND L.R. 5-2(c); IN R USDCTND CM/ECF(II)(D)(2). If such service of a paper copy is to be made, it shall be done in the manner provided in the Federal Rules of Civil Procedure and the Local Civil Rules of the United States District Court for the Northern District of Indiana. IN R USDCTND CM/ECF(II)(D)(2).

iv. *Service of conventional filings.* Pleadings or other documents which are filed conventionally rather than electronically shall be served in the manner provided for in the Federal Rules of Civil Procedure and the Local Civil Rules of the United States District Court for the Northern District of Indiana, except as otherwise provided by order of the Court. IN R USDCTND CM/ECF(III)(B).

v. *Using court facilities.* If a local rule so authorizes, a party may use the court's transmission facilities to make service under FRCP 5(b)(2)(E). FRCP 5(b)(3).

c. *Serving numerous defendants*

i. *In general.* If an action involves an unusually large number of defendants, the court may, on motion or on its own, order that:

- Defendants' pleadings and replies to them need not be served on other defendants;

- Any crossclaim, counterclaim, avoidance, or affirmative defense in those pleadings and replies to them will be treated as denied or avoided by all other parties; and

- Filing any such pleading and serving it on the plaintiff constitutes notice of the pleading to all parties. FRCP 5(c)(1).

ii. *Notifying parties.* A copy of every such order must be served on the parties as the court directs. FRCP 5(c)(2).

G. Hearings

1. *Hearings, generally*

a. *Oral argument.* Due process does not require that oral argument be permitted on a motion and, except as otherwise provided by local rule, the district court has discretion to determine whether it will decide the motion on the papers or hear argument by counsel (and perhaps receive evidence). FPP § 1190; F.D.I.C. v. Deglau, 207 F.3d 153 (3d Cir. 2000).

i. *Request for oral argument.* A party may request oral argument on a motion by filing and serving a separate document explaining why oral argument is necessary and estimating how long the court should allow for the argument. IN R USDCTND L.R. 7-5(a)(1). Refer to the Documents section of this document for more information.

ii. *Additional evidence forbidden.* Parties may not present additional evidence at oral argument. IN R USDCTND L.R. 7-5(a)(3).

b. *Providing a regular schedule for oral hearings.* A court may establish regular times and places for oral hearings on motions. FRCP 78(a).

c. *Providing for submission on briefs.* By rule or order, the court may provide for submitting and determining motions on briefs, without oral hearings. FRCP 78(b).

d. *Evidentiary hearings.* A party may request an evidentiary hearing by filing and serving a separate document explaining why the hearing is necessary and estimating how long the court should allow for it. IN R USDCTND L.R. 7-5(b)(2). Refer to the Documents section of this document for more information.

e. *Court's authority.* The court may: (1) grant or deny a request for oral argument or an evidentiary hearing in its discretion; (2) set oral argument or an evidentiary hearing without a request from a party; or (3) order any oral argument or evidentiary hearing to be held anywhere within the district regardless of where the case will be tried. IN R USDCTND L.R. 7-5(c).

2. *Hearing on FRCP 12 defenses before trial.* If a party so moves, any defense listed in FRCP 12(b)(1) through FRCP 12(b)(7)—whether made in a pleading or by motion—and a motion under FRCP 12(c) must be heard and decided before trial unless the court orders a deferral until trial. FRCP 12(i).

3. *Courtroom and courthouse decorum.* For information on courtroom and courthouse decorum, refer to IN R USDCTND L.R. 83-3.

H. Forms

1. Federal Motion to Dismiss for Failure to State a Claim Forms

a. Notice in federal court; Motion for involuntary dismissal of action without prejudice; Complaint fails to state a claim on which relief can be granted. AMJUR PP DISMISSAL § 109.

b. Motion; To dismiss; Failure to state a claim on which relief can be granted or facts sufficient to constitute cause of action. AMJUR PP LIMITATION § 100.

c. Motion to dismiss; For failure to state a claim, improper service of process, improper venue, and want of jurisdiction. AMJUR PP MOTIONS § 42.

d. Failure to state a claim upon which relief can be granted. 2C FEDFORMS § 11:80.

e. Failure to state a claim upon which relief can be granted; Long version. 2C FEDFORMS § 11:81.

f. Failure to state a claim upon which relief can be granted; Dismissal of certain allegations. 2C FEDFORMS § 11:82.

g. Failure to state a claim upon which relief can be granted; With supporting reasons. 2C FEDFORMS § 11:83.

h. Failure to state a claim upon which relief can be granted; With supporting reasons; Plaintiff not the real party in interest. 2C FEDFORMS § 11:85.

i. Failure to state a claim upon which relief can be granted; With supporting reasons; Failure to show implied contract. 2C FEDFORMS § 11:86.

j. Failure to state a claim upon which relief can be granted; With supporting reasons; Issue not arbitrable. 2C FEDFORMS § 11:87.

k. Failure to state a claim upon which relief can be granted; With supporting affidavits. 2C FEDFORMS § 11:88.

l. Failure to state a claim upon which relief can be granted; In alternative for summary judgment. 2C FEDFORMS § 11:89.

m. Motion; To dismiss; Failure to state sufficient claim; By one of several defendants. FEDPROF § 1:923.

n. Motion to dismiss; Failure to state sufficient claim; By third-party defendant. FEDPROF § 1:924.

o. Motion to dismiss; Failure to state sufficient claim after successive attempts. FEDPROF § 1:925.

p. Motion to dismiss; By individual defendants. FEDPROF § 1:926.

q. Motion to dismiss; By state agency. FEDPROF § 1:927.

r. Motion to dismiss counterclaim. FEDPROF § 1:931.

s. Allegation; In motion to dismiss; Res judicata. FEDPROF § 1:933.

t. Allegation; In motion to dismiss; Statute of limitations. FEDPROF § 1:935.

u. Allegation; In motion to dismiss; Strict liability claim barred by statute. FEDPROF § 1:936.

v. Allegation; In motion to dismiss; By United States; Absence of consent to suit. FEDPROF § 1:938.

w. Reply; To motion to dismiss for failure to state sufficient claim. FEDPROF § 1:939.

x. Motion to dismiss counterclaim. GOLDLTGFMS § 13:10.

y. Motion to dismiss complaint; General form. GOLDLTGFMS § 20:24.

z. Affidavit in support of motion to dismiss complaint. GOLDLTGFMS § 20:32.

2. Forms for the Northern District of Indiana

a. Certificate of service. IN R USDCTND CM/ECF(Form 1).

b. Notice of manual filing. IN R USDCTND CM/ECF(Form 2).

c. Declaration that party was unable to file in a timely manner. IN R USDCTND CM/ECF(Form 3).

I. Applicable Rules

1. *Federal rules*

a. Serving and filing pleadings and other papers. FRCP 5.

b. Constitutional challenge to a statute; Notice, certification, and intervention. FRCP 5.1.

c. Privacy protection for filings made with the court. FRCP 5.2.

d. Computing and extending time; Time for motion papers. FRCP 6.

e. Pleadings allowed; Form of motions and other papers. FRCP 7.

f. Disclosure statement. FRCP 7.1.

g. Form of pleadings. FRCP 10.

h. Signing pleadings, motions, and other papers; Representations to the court; Sanctions. FRCP 11.

i. Defenses and objections; When and how presented; Motion for judgment on the pleadings; Consolidating motions; Waiving defenses; Pretrial hearing. FRCP 12.

j. Hearing motions; Submission on briefs. FRCP 78.

2. *Local rules*

a. Citation and scope of the rules. IN R USDCTND L.R. 1-1.

b. Sanctions for formatting errors. IN R USDCTND L.R. 1-3.

c. Electronic filing required. IN R USDCTND L.R. 5-1.

d. Constitutional questions. IN R USDCTND L.R. 5.1-1.

e. Electronic service. IN R USDCTND L.R. 5-2.

f. Format of papers. IN R USDCTND L.R. 5-4.

g. Motion practice. IN R USDCTND L.R. 7-1.

h. Oral arguments and evidentiary hearings. IN R USDCTND L.R. 7-5.

i. Pretrial procedure. IN R USDCTND L.R. 16-1.

j. Alternative dispute resolution. IN R USDCTND L.R. 16-6.

k. Case assignment. IN R USDCTND L.R. 40-1.

l. Appearance and withdrawal of appearance. IN R USDCTND L.R. 83-8.

m. CM/ECF civil and criminal user manual. IN R USDCTND CM/ECF.

n. In re: privacy and public access to civil electronic case files. IN R USDCTND Order 2005-3.

Motions, Oppositions and Replies
Motion to Dismiss for Lack of Subject Matter Jurisdiction

Document Last Updated December 2016

A. Checklist

(I) ❑ Matters to be considered by moving party

   (a) ❑ Required documents

     (1) ❑ Notice of motion and motion

     (2) ❑ Brief

     (3) ❑ Certificate of service

   (b) ❑ Supplemental documents

     (1) ❑ Supporting evidence

     (2) ❑ Notice of constitutional question

     (3) ❑ Nongovernmental corporate disclosure statement

     (4) ❑ Index of exhibits

     (5) ❑ Request for oral argument

     (6) ❑ Request for evidentiary hearing

     (7) ❑ Copy of authority

     (8) ❑ Proposed order

     (9) ❑ Copy of document with self-addressed envelope

     (10) ❑ Notice of manual filing

     (11) ❑ Courtesy copies

     (12) ❑ Declaration that party was unable to file in a timely manner

   (c) ❑ Timing

     (1) ❑ The defense of lack of subject matter jurisdiction can be raised at any time

     (2) ❑ Every defense to a claim for relief in any pleading must be asserted in the responsive pleading if one is required

     (3) ❑ A motion asserting any of the defenses in FRCP 12(b) must be made before pleading if a responsive pleading is allowed

     (4) ❑ If a pleading sets out a claim for relief that does not require a responsive pleading, an opposing party may assert at trial any defense to that claim

     (5) ❑ A written motion and notice of the hearing must be served at least fourteen (14) days before the time specified for the hearing, with the following exceptions: (i) when the motion may be heard ex parte; (ii) when the Federal Rules of Civil Procedure set a different time; or (iii) when a court order—which a party may, for good cause, apply for ex parte—sets a different time

     (6) ❑ Any affidavit supporting a motion must be served with the motion

(II) ❑ Matters to be considered by opposing party

   (a) ❑ Required documents

     (1) ❑ Response brief

     (2) ❑ Certificate of service

   (b) ❑ Supplemental documents

     (1) ❑ Supporting evidence

    (2) ❑ Notice of constitutional question

    (3) ❑ Index of exhibits

    (4) ❑ Request for oral argument

    (5) ❑ Request for evidentiary hearing

    (6) ❑ Copy of authority

    (7) ❑ Copy of document with self-addressed envelope

    (8) ❑ Notice of manual filing

    (9) ❑ Courtesy copies

    (10) ❑ Declaration that party was unable to file in a timely manner

(c) ❑ Timing

    (1) ❑ A party must file any response brief to a motion within fourteen (14) days after the motion is served

    (2) ❑ Except as FRCP 59(c) provides otherwise, any opposing affidavit must be served at least seven (7) days before the hearing, unless the court permits service at another time

B. Timing

1. *Motion to dismiss for lack of subject matter jurisdiction.* [The defense of lack of subject matter jurisdiction] can be raised at any time. FEDPROC § 62:434.

    a. *In a responsive pleading.* Every defense to a claim for relief in any pleading must be asserted in the responsive pleading if one is required. FRCP 12(b).

    b. *By motion.* A motion asserting any of the defenses in FRCP 12(b) must be made before pleading if a responsive pleading is allowed. FRCP 12(b). Although FRCP 12(b) encourages the responsive pleader to file a motion to dismiss before filing the answer, nothing in FRCP 12 prohibits the filing of a motion to dismiss with the answer. An untimely motion to dismiss may be considered if the defense asserted in the motion was previously raised in the responsive pleading. FEDPROC § 62:427.

    c. *At trial.* If a pleading sets out a claim for relief that does not require a responsive pleading, an opposing party may assert at trial any defense to that claim. FRCP 12(b).

2. *Timing of motions, generally*

    a. *Motion and notice of hearing.* A written motion and notice of the hearing must be served at least fourteen (14) days before the time specified for the hearing, with the following exceptions:

        i. When the motion may be heard ex parte;

        ii. When the Federal Rules of Civil Procedure set a different time; or

        iii. When a court order—which a party may, for good cause, apply for ex parte—sets a different time. FRCP 6(c)(1).

    b. *Supporting affidavit.* Any affidavit supporting a motion must be served with the motion. FRCP 6(c)(2).

3. *Timing of opposing papers.* A party must file any response brief to a motion within fourteen (14) days after the motion is served. IN R USDCTND L.R. 7-1(d)(2)(A).

    a. *Opposing affidavit.* Except as FRCP 59(c) provides otherwise, any opposing affidavit must be served at least seven (7) days before the hearing, unless the court permits service at another time. FRCP 6(c)(2).

    b. *Extensions.* The court may extend response- and reply-brief deadlines, but only for good cause. IN R USDCTND L.R. 7-1(d)(3).

    c. *Summary rulings.* The court may rule on a motion summarily if an opposing party does not file a response before the deadline. IN R USDCTND L.R. 7-1(d)(4).

4. *Timing of reply papers.* Where the respondent files an answering affidavit setting up a new matter, the

moving party ordinarily is allowed a reasonable time to file a reply affidavit since failure to deny the new matter by affidavit may operate as an admission of its truth. AMJUR MOTIONS § 25.

a. *Reply brief.* The moving party must file any reply brief within seven (7) days after the response brief is served. IN R USDCTND L.R. 7-1(d)(2)(B).

b. *Extensions.* The court may extend response- and reply-brief deadlines, but only for good cause. IN R USDCTND L.R. 7-1(d)(3).

5. *Effect of a FRCP 12 motion on the time to serve a responsive pleading.* Unless the court sets a different time, serving a motion under FRCP 12 alters the periods in FRCP 12(a) as follows:

a. If the court denies the motion or postpones its disposition until trial, the responsive pleading must be served within fourteen (14) days after notice of the court's action; or

b. If the court grants a motion for a more definite statement, the responsive pleading must be served within fourteen (14) days after the more definite statement is served. FRCP 12(a)(4).

6. *Computation of time*

a. *Computing time.* FRCP 6 applies in computing any time period specified in the Federal Rules of Civil Procedure, in any local rule or court order, or in any statute that does not specify a method of computing time. FRCP 6(a).

   i. *Period stated in days or a longer unit.* When the period is stated in days or a longer unit of time:

   - Exclude the day of the event that triggers the period;

   - Count every day, including intermediate Saturdays, Sundays, and legal holidays; and

   - Include the last day of the period, but if the last day is a Saturday, Sunday, or legal holiday, the period continues to run until the end of the next day that is not a Saturday, Sunday, or legal holiday. FRCP 6(a)(1).

   ii. *Period stated in hours.* When the period is stated in hours:

   - Begin counting immediately on the occurrence of the event that triggers the period;

   - Count every hour, including hours during intermediate Saturdays, Sundays, and legal holidays; and

   - If the period would end on a Saturday, Sunday, or legal holiday, the period continues to run until the same time on the next day that is not a Saturday, Sunday, or legal holiday. FRCP 6(a)(2).

   iii. *Inaccessibility of the clerk's office.* Unless the court orders otherwise, if the clerk's office is inaccessible:

   - On the last day for filing under FRCP 6(a)(1), then the time for filing is extended to the first accessible day that is not a Saturday, Sunday, or legal holiday; or

   - During the last hour for filing under FRCP 6(a)(2), then the time for filing is extended to the same time on the first accessible day that is not a Saturday, Sunday, or legal holiday. FRCP 6(a)(3).

   iv. *"Last day" defined.* Unless a different time is set by a statute, local rule, or court order, the last day ends:

   - For electronic filing, at midnight in the court's time zone; and

   - For filing by other means, when the clerk's office is scheduled to close. FRCP 6(a)(4).

   v. *"Next day" defined.* The "next day" is determined by continuing to count forward when the period is measured after an event and backward when measured before an event. FRCP 6(a)(5).

   vi. *"Legal holiday" defined.* "Legal holiday" means:

   - The day set aside by statute for observing New Year's Day, Martin Luther King Jr.'s Birthday, Washington's Birthday, Memorial Day, Independence Day, Labor Day, Columbus Day, Veterans' Day, Thanksgiving Day, or Christmas Day;

- Any day declared a holiday by the President or Congress; and

- For periods that are measured after an event, any other day declared a holiday by the state where the district court is located. FRCP 6(a)(6).

b. *Computation of electronic filing deadlines.* Filing documents electronically does not alter any filing deadlines or any time computation pursuant to FRCP 6. The counties of Lake, Porter, LaPorte, Pulaski and Starke are located in the Central time zone and the remaining counties in the Northern District of Indiana are located in the Eastern time zone. Nevertheless, all electronic transmissions of documents must be completed (i.e., received completely by the clerk's office) prior to midnight Eastern Time, (South Bend/Fort Wayne/Lafayette time) in order to be considered timely filed that day, regardless of the local time in the division where the case is pending. Although documents can be filed electronically twenty-four (24) hours a day, filers are strongly encouraged to file all documents during hours when the CM/ECF Help Line is available, from 9:00 a.m. to 4:00 p.m. local time. IN R USDCTND CM/ECF(II)(I).

   i. *Technical failures.* If the attorney is unable to file a document in a timely manner due to technical difficulties in the user's system, the attorney must file a document with the court as soon as possible notifying the court of the inability to file the document. A sample document entitled Declaration that Party was Unable to File in a Timely Manner Due to Technical Difficulties is attached hereto as Form 5. IN R USDCTND CM/ECF(VI)(B). [Editor's note: the reference to Form 5 is likely meant to be a reference to Form 3 (IN R USDCTND CM/ECF(Form 3)].

c. *Extending time*

   i. *In general.* When an act may or must be done within a specified time, the court may, for good cause, extend the time:

   - With or without motion or notice if the court acts, or if a request is made, before the original time or its extension expires; or

   - On motion made after the time has expired if the party failed to act because of excusable neglect. FRCP 6(b)(1).

   ii. *Exceptions.* A court must not extend the time to act under FRCP 50(b), FRCP 50(d), FRCP 52(b), FRCP 59(b), FRCP 59(d), FRCP 59(e), and FRCP 60(b). FRCP 6(b)(2).

   iii. Refer to the United States District Court for the Northern District of Indiana KeyRules Motion for Continuance/Extension of Time document for more information on extending time.

d. *Additional time after certain kinds of service.* When a party may or must act within a specified time after being served and service is made under FRCP 5(b)(2)(C) (mail), FRCP 5(b)(2)(D) (leaving with the clerk), or FRCP 5(b)(2)(F) (other means consented to), three (3) days are added after the period would otherwise expire under FRCP 6(a). FRCP 6(d).

C. General Requirements

1. *Motions, generally*

a. *Requirements.* A request for a court order must be made by motion. The motion must:

   i. Be in writing unless made during a hearing or trial;

   ii. State with particularity the grounds for seeking the order; and

   iii. State the relief sought. FRCP 7(b)(1).

b. *Notice of motion.* A party interested in resisting the relief sought by a motion has a right to notice thereof, and an opportunity to be heard. AMJUR MOTIONS § 12.

   i. In addition to statutory or court rule provisions requiring notice of a motion—the purpose of such a notice requirement having been said to be to prevent a party from being prejudicially surprised by a motion—principles of natural justice dictate that an adverse party generally must be given notice that a motion will be presented to the court. AMJUR MOTIONS § 12.

   ii. "Notice," in this regard, means reasonable notice, including a meaningful opportunity to prepare and to defend against allegations of a motion. AMJUR MOTIONS § 12.

c. *Writing requirement.* The writing requirement is intended to insure that the adverse parties are informed and have a record of both the motion's pendency and the grounds on which the movant seeks an order. FPP § 1191; Feldberg v. Quechee Lakes Corp., 463 F.3d 195 (2d Cir. 2006).

   i. It is sufficient "if the motion is stated in a written notice of the hearing of the motion." FPP § 1191.

d. *Particularity requirement.* The particularity requirement insures that the opposing parties will have notice of their opponent's contentions. FEDPROC § 62:364; Goodman v. 1973 26 Foot Trojan Vessel, Arkansas Registration No. AR1439SN, 859 F.2d 71, 12 Fed.R.Serv.3d 645 (8th Cir. 1988). That requirement ensures that notice of the basis for the motion is provided to the court and to the opposing party so as to avoid prejudice, provide the opponent with a meaningful opportunity to respond, and provide the court with enough information to process the motion correctly. FEDPROC § 62:364; Andreas v. Volkswagen of America, Inc., 336 F.3d 789, 56 Fed.R.Serv.3d 6 (8th Cir. 2003).

   i. Reasonable specification of the grounds for a motion is sufficient. However, where a movant fails to state even one ground for granting the motion in question, the movant has failed to meet the minimal standard of "reasonable specification." FEDPROC § 62:364; Martinez v. Trainor, 556 F.2d 818, 23 Fed.R.Serv.2d 403 (7th Cir. 1977).

   ii. The court may excuse the failure to comply with the particularity requirement if it is inadvertent, and where no prejudice is shown by the opposing party. FEDPROC § 62:364.

e. *Motions must be filed separately.* Motions must be filed separately, but alternative motions may be filed in a single paper if each is named in the title following the caption. IN R USDCTND L.R. 7-1(a).

2. *Motion to dismiss for lack of subject matter jurisdiction.* A party may assert the defense of lack of subject-matter jurisdiction by motion. FRCP 12(b)(1). The court will not rule on a defense under FRCP 12 until the party who raised it files a motion and brief. IN R USDCTND L.R. 7-1(c). The objection presented by a motion under FRCP 12(b)(1) challenging the court's subject matter jurisdiction is that the district judge has no authority or competence to hear and decide the case before it. A FRCP 12(b)(1) motion most typically is employed when the movant believes that the claim asserted by the plaintiff does not involve a federal question, and there is no diversity of citizenship between the parties or, in a diversity of citizenship case, the amount in controversy does not exceed the required jurisdictional amount. FPP § 1350.

a. *Subject matter jurisdiction.* It always must be remembered that the federal courts are courts of limited jurisdiction and only can adjudicate those cases that fall within Article III of the Constitution (see U.S.C.A. Const. Art. III § 1, et seq.) and a congressional authorization enacted thereunder. FPP § 1350.

   i. *Federal question.* The district courts shall have original jurisdiction of all civil actions arising under the Constitution, laws, or treaties of the United States. 28 U.S.C.A. § 1331.

   ii. *Diversity of citizenship; Amount in controversy.* The district courts shall have original jurisdiction of all civil actions where the matter in controversy exceeds the sum or value of seventy-five thousand dollars ($75,000), exclusive of interest and costs, and is between:

   - Citizens of different States;
   - Citizens of a State and citizens or subjects of a foreign state, except that the district courts shall not have original jurisdiction under 28 U.S.C.A. § 1332 of an action between citizens of a State and citizens or subjects of a foreign state who are lawfully admitted for permanent residence in the United States and are domiciled in the same State;
   - Citizens of different States and in which citizens or subjects of a foreign state are additional parties; and
   - A foreign state, defined in 28 U.S.C.A. § 1603(a), as plaintiff and citizens of a State or of different States. 28 U.S.C.A. § 1332(a).

b. *Types of FRCP 12(b)(1) motions.* There are two separate types of FRCP 12(b)(1) motions to dismiss for lack of subject matter jurisdiction: the "facial attack" and the "factual attack." FEDPROC § 62:440.

   i. *Facial attack.* The facial attack is addressed to the sufficiency of the allegations of the complaint itself. FEDPROC § 62:440; Stalley ex rel. U.S. v. Orlando Regional Healthcare System, Inc., 524 F.3d 1229 (11th Cir. 2008). On such a motion, the court is merely required to determine whether the plaintiff has sufficiently alleged a basis of subject matter jurisdiction, and the factual allegations of the complaint are taken as true. FEDPROC § 62:440; U.S. ex rel. Atkinson v. PA. Shipbuilding Co., 473 F.3d 506 (3d Cir. 2007).

    ii. *Factual attack.* The "factual attack," on the other hand, challenges the existence of subject matter jurisdiction in fact, irrespective of the pleadings, and matters outside the pleadings, such as testimony and affidavits, may be considered by the court. FEDPROC § 62:440; Kligman v. I.R.S., 272 Fed.Appx. 166 (3d Cir. 2008); Paper, Allied-Industrial, Chemical and Energy Workers Intern. Union v. Continental Carbon Co., 428 F.3d 1285 (10th Cir. 2005). The trial court in such a situation is free to weigh the evidence and satisfy itself as to the existence of its power to hear the case; therefore, no presumptive truthfulness attaches to the plaintiff's factual allegations. FEDPROC § 62:440; Land v. Dollar, 330 U.S. 731, 67 S.Ct. 1009, 91 L.Ed. 1209 (1947).

c. *Burden.* With the limited exception of the question whether the amount in controversy requirement in diversity of citizenship cases has been satisfied, the extensive case law on the subject makes clear that the burden of proof on a FRCP 12(b)(1) motion is on the party asserting that subject matter jurisdiction exists, which, of course, typically is the plaintiff. FPP § 1350; Thomson v. Gaskill, 315 U.S. 442, 62 S.Ct. 673, 86 L.Ed. 951 (1942). A plaintiff meets the burden of establishing subject-matter jurisdiction at the pleading stage by pleading sufficient allegations to show the proper basis for the court to assert subject-matter jurisdiction over the action. 2 FEDFORMS § 7:6.

    i. *Federal question.* If subject matter jurisdiction is based on the existence of a federal question, the pleader must show that he or she has alleged a claim for relief arising under federal law and that the claim is not frivolous. FPP § 1350; Baker v. Carr, 369 U.S. 186, 82 S.Ct. 691, 7 L.Ed.2d 663 (1962).

    ii. *Diversity of citizenship.* If jurisdiction is based on diversity of citizenship, on the other hand, the pleader must show that real and complete diversity exists between all of the plaintiffs and all of the defendants, and also that the assertion that the claim exceeds the requisite jurisdictional amount in controversy is made in good faith. FPP § 1350; City of Indianapolis v. Chase Nat. Bank, 314 U.S. 63, 62 S.Ct. 15, 86 L.Ed. 47 (1941). Satisfying this last requirement is a relatively simple task, however, because the claim is deemed to be made in good faith so long as it is not clear to a legal certainty that the claimant could not recover a judgment exceeding the statutorily mandated jurisdictional amount, a matter on which the party challenging the district court's jurisdiction has the burden. FPP § 1350.

d. *Joining motions.* When the motion is based on more than one ground, the cases are legion stating that the district court should consider the FRCP 12(b)(1) challenge first because if it must dismiss the complaint for lack of subject matter jurisdiction, the accompanying defenses and objections become moot and do not need to be determined by the judge. FPP § 1350; Steel Co. v. Citizens for a Better Environment, 523 U.S. 83, 118 S.Ct. 1003, 140 L.Ed.2d 210 (1998). However, there are a number of decisions in which the court has decided one or more defenses in addition to the subject matter jurisdiction question or simply assumed the existence of jurisdiction and gone on to decide another matter. FPP § 1350.

    i. *Right to join.* A motion under FRCP 12 may be joined with any other motion allowed by FRCP 12. FRCP 12(g)(1).

    ii. *Limitation on further motions.* Except as provided in FRCP 12(h)(2) or FRCP 12(h)(3), a party that makes a motion under FRCP 12 must not make another motion under FRCP 12 raising a defense or objection that was available to the party but omitted from its earlier motion. FRCP 12(g)(2).

e. *Waiving and preserving certain defenses.* No defense or objection is waived by joining it with one or more other defenses or objections in a responsive pleading or in a motion. FRCP 12(b).

    i. *Waiver by consent.* The defendant may waive the right to obtain a dismissal prior to trial either by express consent to be sued in a certain district or by some conduct that will be construed as implying consent. FPP § 1352.

    ii. *When some are waived.* A party waives any defense listed in FRCP 12(b)(2) through FRCP 12(b)(5) by:

- Omitting it from a motion in the circumstances described in FRCP 12(g)(2); or
- Failing to either: (1) make it by motion under FRCP 12; or (2) include it in a responsive pleading or in an amendment allowed by FRCP 15(a)(1) as a matter of course. FRCP 12(h)(1).

    iii. *When to raise others.* Failure to state a claim upon which relief can be granted, to join a person required by FRCP 19(b), or to state a legal defense to a claim may be raised:

- In any pleading allowed or ordered under FRCP 7(a);
- By a motion under FRCP 12(c); or
- At trial. FRCP 12(h)(2).

    iv. *Lack of subject matter jurisdiction.* If the court determines at any time that it lacks subject-matter jurisdiction, the court must dismiss the action. FRCP 12(h)(3).

3. *Opposing papers.* The Federal Rules of Civil Procedure do not require any formal answer, return, or reply to a motion, except where the Federal Rules of Civil Procedure or local rules may require affidavits, memoranda, or other papers to be filed in opposition to a motion. Such papers are simply to apprise the court of such opposition and the grounds of that opposition. FEDPROC § 62:359.

    a. *Effect of failure to respond to motion.* Although in the absence of statutory provision or court rule, a motion ordinarily does not require a written answer, when a party files a motion and the opposing party fails to respond, the court may construe such failure to respond as nonopposition to the motion or an admission that the motion was meritorious, may take the facts alleged in the motion as true—the rule in some jurisdictions being that the failure to respond to a fact set forth in a motion is deemed an admission—and may grant the motion if the relief requested appears to be justified. AMJUR MOTIONS § 28.

    b. *Assent or no opposition not determinative.* However, a motion will not be granted automatically simply because an "assent" or a notation of "no opposition" has been filed; federal judges frequently deny motions that have been assented to when it is thought that justice so dictates. FPP § 1190.

    c. *Responsive pleading inappropriate as response to motion.* An attempt to answer or oppose a motion with a responsive pleading usually is not appropriate. FPP § 1190.

4. *Reply papers.* A moving party may be required or permitted to prepare papers in addition to his original motion papers. AMJUR MOTIONS § 25. Papers answering or replying to opposing papers may be appropriate, in the interests of justice, where it appears there is a substantial reason for allowing a reply. Thus, a court may accept reply papers where a party demonstrates that the papers to which it seeks to file a reply raise new issues that are material to the disposition of the question before the court, or where the court determines, sua sponte, that it wishes further briefing of an issue raised in those papers and orders the submission of additional papers. FEDPROC § 62:360.

    a. *Function of reply papers.* The function of a reply affidavit is to answer the arguments made in opposition to the position taken by the movant and not to permit the movant to introduce new arguments in support of the motion. AMJUR MOTIONS § 25.

    b. *Issues raised for the first time in a reply document.* However, the view has been followed in some jurisdictions, that as a matter of judicial economy, where there is no prejudice and where the issues could be raised simply by filing a motion to dismiss, the trial court has discretion to consider arguments raised for the first time in a reply memorandum, and that a trial court may grant a motion to strike issues raised for the first time in a reply memorandum. AMJUR MOTIONS § 26.

5. *Appearances.* Attorneys not representing the United States or its agencies must file an appearance when they represent (either in person or by filing a paper) a party. IN R USDCTND L.R. 83-8(a). For more information, refer to IN R USDCTND L.R. 83-8.

6. *Notice of related action.* A party must file a notice of related action as soon as it appears that the party's case and another pending case: (1) arise out of the same transaction or occurrence; (2) involve the same

property; or (3) involve the validity or infringement of the same patent, trademark, or copyright. IN R USDCTND L.R. 40-1(d). For more information, refer to IN R USDCTND L.R. 40-1.

7. *Alternative dispute resolution (ADR).* After they confer as required by FRCP 26(f), the parties must advise the court which, if any, alternative-dispute-resolution processes they expect to pursue and when they expect to undertake the process. IN R USDCTND L.R. 16-6(a). For more information on alternative dispute resolution (ADR), refer to IN R USDCTND L.R. 16-6 and IN R USDCTND Order 2003-21.

8. *Settlement or resolution.* The parties must immediately notify the court if they reasonably expect to settle the case or resolve a pending motion. IN R USDCTND L.R. 16-1(g).

9. *Modification or suspension of rules.* The court may, on its own motion or at the request of a party, suspend or modify any rule in a particular case in the interest of justice. IN R USDCTND L.R. 1-1(c).

D. Documents

1. *Documents for moving party*

   a. *Required documents*

      i. *Notice of motion and motion.* The party must not specify a hearing date in the notice of a motion or petition unless the court or the clerk has authorized it. IN R USDCTND L.R. 7-5(b)(2). Refer to the General Requirements section of this document for information on the notice of motion and motion.

      ii. *Brief.* Parties must file a supporting brief with any motion under: FRCP 12. IN R USDCTND L.R. 7-1(b)(1). Refer to the Format section of this document for the format of briefs.

      iii. *Certificate of service.* FRCP 5(d) requires that the person making service under FRCP 5 certify that service has been effected. FRCP 5(Advisory Committee Notes). Having such information on file may be useful for many purposes, including proof of service if an issue arises concerning the effectiveness of the service. FRCP 5(Advisory Committee Notes).

         • *Certificate of service for electronically-filed documents.* A Certificate of Service is still a requirement when filing documents electronically. A sample Certificate of Service is attached as Form 1 (IN R USDCTND CM/ECF(Form 1)). IN R USDCTND CM/ECF(II)(H).

   b. *Supplemental documents*

      i. *Supporting evidence.* When a motion relies on facts outside the record, the court may hear the matter on affidavits or may hear it wholly or partly on oral testimony or on depositions. FRCP 43(c).

         • *Materials necessary for motion.* A party must file those portions of discovery requests or responses (including deposition transcripts) that the party relies on to support a motion that could result in a final order on an issue. IN R USDCTND L.R. 26-2(c).

      ii. *Notice of constitutional question.* A party that files a pleading, written motion, or other paper drawing into question the constitutionality of a federal or state statute must promptly:

         • *File notice.* File a notice of constitutional question stating the question and identifying the paper that raises it, if: (1) a federal statute is questioned and the parties do not include the United States, one of its agencies, or one of its officers or employees in an official capacity; or (2) a state statute is questioned and the parties do not include the state, one of its agencies, or one of its officers or employees in an official capacity; and

         • *Serve notice.* Serve the notice and paper on the Attorney General of the United States if a federal statute is questioned—or on the state attorney general if a state statute is questioned—either by certified or registered mail or by sending it to an electronic address designated by the attorney general for this purpose. FRCP 5.1(a).

         • *When to file the notice.* A party required to file a notice of constitutional question under FRCP 5.1 must do so by the later of: (1) the day the parties tender their proposed case-management plan (if one is required); or (2) 21 days after filing the pleading, written motion, or other paper questioning the constitutionality of a federal or state statute. IN R USDCTND L.R. 5.1-1(a).

- *Service on government officials.* The party must also serve the notice and the pleading, written motion, or other paper questioning the constitutionality of a federal or state statute on: (1) the Attorney General of the United States and the United States Attorney for the Northern District of Indiana, if a federal statute is challenged; or (2) the Attorney General for the state if a state statute is challenged. IN R USDCTND L.R. 5.1-1(b). Service required under IN R USDCTND L.R. 5.1-1(b) may be made either by certified or registered mail or by emailing it to an address designated by those officials for this purpose. IN R USDCTND L.R. 5.1-1(c).

- *No forfeiture.* A party's failure to file and serve the notice, or the court's failure to certify, does not forfeit a constitutional claim or defense that is otherwise timely asserted. FRCP 5.1(d).

iii. *Nongovernmental corporate disclosure statement*

- *Contents.* A nongovernmental corporate party must file two (2) copies of a disclosure statement that: (1) identifies any parent corporation and any publicly held corporation owning ten percent (10%) or more of its stock; or (2) states that there is no such corporation. FRCP 7.1(a).

- *Time to file; Supplemental filing.* A party must: (1) file the disclosure statement with its first appearance, pleading, petition, motion, response, or other request addressed to the court; and (2) promptly file a supplemental statement if any required information changes. FRCP 7.1(b).

iv. *Index of exhibits.* Any pleading, motion, brief, affidavit, notice, or proposed order, whether filed electronically or by delivering it to the clerk, must: include a separate index identifying and briefly describing each exhibit if there are more than four (4) exhibits. IN R USDCTND L.R. 5-4(a)(8).

v. *Request for oral argument.* A party may request oral argument on a motion by filing and serving a separate document explaining why oral argument is necessary and estimating how long the court should allow for the argument. IN R USDCTND L.R. 7-5(a)(1). The request must be filed and served with the party's supporting brief, response brief, or reply brief. IN R USDCTND L.R. 7-5(a)(2).

vi. *Request for evidentiary hearing.* A party may request an evidentiary hearing by filing and serving a separate document explaining why the hearing is necessary and estimating how long the court should allow for it. IN R USDCTND L.R. 7-5(b)(1).

vii. *Copy of authority.* A copy of any decision, statute, or regulation cited in a motion or brief must be attached to the paper if—and only if—it is not available on Westlaw or Lexis. But if a copy of a decision, statute, or regulation is only available electronically, a party must provide it to the court or another party upon request. IN R USDCTND L.R. 7-1(f).

viii. *Proposed order.* Parties filing a paper that requires the judge or clerk to enter a routine or uncontested order must include a suitable form of order. IN R USDCTND L.R. 5-4(c).

- Proposed orders shall not be filed electronically either as a separate document or as an attachment to the main pleading or other document. Instead, all proposed orders must be e-mailed to the chambers of the appropriate judicial officer for the case. The proposed order must be in WordPerfect Format or Rich Text Format (RTF). Proposed orders should be attached to an e-mail and sent to the appropriate judicial officer at the address listed in IN R USDCTND CM/ECF(II)(F). The subject line of the email message should indicate the case title, cause number and document number of the motion, e.g., Smith v. Jones 1:02-cv-1234, motion# ___. IN R USDCTND CM/ECF(II)(F).

ix. *Copy of document with self-addressed envelope.* A party who wants a file-stamped copy of a paper must include with the filing an additional copy of the paper and a self-addressed envelope with adequate postage. IN R USDCTND L.R. 5-4(b)(6).

x. *Notice of manual filing.* However, if that is not physically possible, counsel shall electronically file a .pdf document titled Notice of Manual Filing as a notation on the docket sheet that filings are being held in the clerk's office in paper. A sample Notice of Manual Filing is attached as Form 2 (IN R USDCTND CM/ECF(Form 2)). IN R USDCTND CM/ECF(III)(A)(1).

xi. *Courtesy copies.* If documents are filed in paper format, counsel must provide an original for the clerk's office, a copy for the judge and a copy must be served on all parties in the case. IN R USDCTND CM/ECF(III)(A)(1).

xii. *Declaration that party was unable to file in a timely manner.* If the attorney is unable to file a document in a timely manner due to technical difficulties in the user's system, the attorney must file a document with the court as soon as possible notifying the court of the inability to file the document. A sample document entitled Declaration that Party was Unable to File in a Timely Manner Due to Technical Difficulties is attached hereto as Form 5. IN R USDCTND CM/ECF(VI)(B). [Editor's note: the reference to Form 5 is likely meant to be a reference to Form 3 (IN R USDCTND CM/ECF(Form 3)].

2. *Documents for opposing party*

   a. *Required documents*

      i. *Response brief.* Refer to the Format section of this document for the format of briefs. Refer to the General Requirements section of this document for information on the opposing papers.

      ii. *Certificate of service.* FRCP 5(d) requires that the person making service under FRCP 5 certify that service has been effected. FRCP 5(Advisory Committee Notes). Having such information on file may be useful for many purposes, including proof of service if an issue arises concerning the effectiveness of the service. FRCP 5(Advisory Committee Notes).

         • *Certificate of service for electronically-filed documents.* A Certificate of Service is still a requirement when filing documents electronically. A sample Certificate of Service is attached as Form 1 (IN R USDCTND CM/ECF(Form 1)). IN R USDCTND CM/ECF(II)(H).

   b. *Supplemental documents*

      i. *Supporting evidence.* When a motion relies on facts outside the record, the court may hear the matter on affidavits or may hear it wholly or partly on oral testimony or on depositions. FRCP 43(c).

         • *Materials necessary for motion.* A party must file those portions of discovery requests or responses (including deposition transcripts) that the party relies on to support a motion that could result in a final order on an issue. IN R USDCTND L.R. 26-2(c).

      ii. *Notice of constitutional question.* A party that files a pleading, written motion, or other paper drawing into question the constitutionality of a federal or state statute must promptly:

         • *File notice.* File a notice of constitutional question stating the question and identifying the paper that raises it, if: (1) a federal statute is questioned and the parties do not include the United States, one of its agencies, or one of its officers or employees in an official capacity; or (2) a state statute is questioned and the parties do not include the state, one of its agencies, or one of its officers or employees in an official capacity; and

         • *Serve notice.* Serve the notice and paper on the Attorney General of the United States if a federal statute is questioned—or on the state attorney general if a state statute is questioned—either by certified or registered mail or by sending it to an electronic address designated by the attorney general for this purpose. FRCP 5.1(a).

         • *When to file the notice.* A party required to file a notice of constitutional question under FRCP 5.1 must do so by the later of: (1) the day the parties tender their proposed case-management plan (if one is required); or (2) 21 days after filing the pleading, written motion, or other paper questioning the constitutionality of a federal or state statute. IN R USDCTND L.R. 5.1-1(a).

         • *Service on government officials.* The party must also serve the notice and the pleading, written motion, or other paper questioning the constitutionality of a federal or state statute on: (1) the Attorney General of the United States and the United States Attorney for the

Northern District of Indiana, if a federal statute is challenged; or (2) the Attorney General for the state if a state statute is challenged. IN R USDCTND L.R. 5.1-1(b). Service required under IN R USDCTND L.R. 5.1-1(b) may be made either by certified or registered mail or by emailing it to an address designated by those officials for this purpose. IN R USDCTND L.R. 5.1-1(c).

- *No forfeiture.* A party's failure to file and serve the notice, or the court's failure to certify, does not forfeit a constitutional claim or defense that is otherwise timely asserted. FRCP 5.1(d).

iii. *Index of exhibits.* Any pleading, motion, brief, affidavit, notice, or proposed order, whether filed electronically or by delivering it to the clerk, must: include a separate index identifying and briefly describing each exhibit if there are more than four (4) exhibits. IN R USDCTND L.R. 5-4(a)(8).

iv. *Request for oral argument.* A party may request oral argument on a motion by filing and serving a separate document explaining why oral argument is necessary and estimating how long the court should allow for the argument. IN R USDCTND L.R. 7-5(a)(1). The request must be filed and served with the party's supporting brief, response brief, or reply brief. IN R USDCTND L.R. 7-5(a)(2).

v. *Request for evidentiary hearing.* A party may request an evidentiary hearing by filing and serving a separate document explaining why the hearing is necessary and estimating how long the court should allow for it. IN R USDCTND L.R. 7-5(b)(1).

vi. *Copy of authority.* A copy of any decision, statute, or regulation cited in a motion or brief must be attached to the paper if—and only if—it is not available on Westlaw or Lexis. But if a copy of a decision, statute, or regulation is only available electronically, a party must provide it to the court or another party upon request. IN R USDCTND L.R. 7-1(f).

vii. *Copy of document with self-addressed envelope.* A party who wants a file-stamped copy of a paper must include with the filing an additional copy of the paper and a self-addressed envelope with adequate postage. IN R USDCTND L.R. 5-4(b)(6).

viii. *Notice of manual filing.* However, if that is not physically possible, counsel shall electronically file a .pdf document titled Notice of Manual Filing as a notation on the docket sheet that filings are being held in the clerk's office in paper. A sample Notice of Manual Filing is attached as Form 2 (IN R USDCTND CM/ECF(Form 2)). IN R USDCTND CM/ECF(III)(A)(1).

ix. *Courtesy copies.* If documents are filed in paper format, counsel must provide an original for the clerk's office, a copy for the judge and a copy must be served on all parties in the case. IN R USDCTND CM/ECF(III)(A)(1).

x. *Declaration that party was unable to file in a timely manner.* If the attorney is unable to file a document in a timely manner due to technical difficulties in the user's system, the attorney must file a document with the court as soon as possible notifying the court of the inability to file the document. A sample document entitled Declaration that Party was Unable to File in a Timely Manner Due to Technical Difficulties is attached hereto as Form 5. IN R USDCTND CM/ECF(VI)(B). [Editor's note: the reference to Form 5 is likely meant to be a reference to Form 3 (IN R USDCTND CM/ECF(Form 3)].

E. Format

1. *Form of documents.* The rules governing captions and other matters of form in pleadings apply to motions and other papers. FRCP 7(b)(2).

   a. *Paper.* Any pleading, motion, brief, affidavit, notice, or proposed order, whether filed electronically or by delivering it to the clerk, must: use eight and one-half by eleven (8-1/2 x 11) inch pages. IN R USDCTND L.R. 5-4(a)(2).

      i. *Manual filings.* Papers delivered to the clerk for filing must: be flat, unfolded, and on good-quality, white paper. IN R USDCTND L.R. 5-4(b)(1)(A).

      - *Covers or backing.* Papers delivered to the clerk for filing must: not have a cover or a back. IN R USDCTND L.R. 5-4(b)(1)(B).

- *Recycled paper.* The court encourages using recycled paper. IN R USDCTND L.R. 5-4(b)(7).

b. *Margins.* Any pleading, motion, brief, affidavit, notice, or proposed order, whether filed electronically or by delivering it to the clerk, must: have at least one (1) inch margins. IN R USDCTND L.R. 5-4(a)(3).

c. *Spacing.* Any pleading, motion, brief, affidavit, notice, or proposed order, whether filed electronically or by delivering it to the clerk, must: be double spaced (except for headings, footnotes, and quoted material). IN R USDCTND L.R. 5-4(a)(5).

d. *Text.* Any pleading, motion, brief, affidavit, notice, or proposed order, whether filed electronically or by delivering it to the clerk, must: be plainly typewritten, printed, or prepared by a clearly legible copying process. IN R USDCTND L.R. 5-4(a)(1).

  i. Any pleading, motion, brief, affidavit, notice, or proposed order, whether filed electronically or by delivering it to the clerk, must: use at least twelve (12) point type in the body and at least ten (10) point type in footnotes. IN R USDCTND L.R. 5-4(a)(4).

e. *Page numbering.* Any pleading, motion, brief, affidavit, notice, or proposed order, whether filed electronically or by delivering it to the clerk, must: have consecutively numbered pages. IN R USDCTND L.R. 5-4(a)(6).

f. *Caption; Names of parties.* Every pleading must have a caption with the court's name, a title, a file number, and a FRCP 7(a) designation. The title of the complaint must name all the parties; the title of other pleadings, after naming the first party on each side, may refer generally to other parties. FRCP 10(a). Any pleading, motion, brief, affidavit, notice, or proposed order, whether filed electronically or by delivering it to the clerk, must: include a title on the first page. IN R USDCTND L.R. 5-4(a)(7).

  i. *Alternative motions.* Motions must be filed separately, but alternative motions may be filed in a single paper if each is named in the title following the caption. IN R USDCTND L.R. 7-1(a).

g. *Filer's information.* Any pleading, motion, brief, affidavit, notice, or proposed order, whether filed electronically or by delivering it to the clerk, must: except in proposed orders and affidavits, include the filer's name, address, telephone number, fax number (where available), and e-mail address (where available). IN R USDCTND L.R. 5-4(a)(9).

h. *Paragraphs; Separate statements.* A party must state its claims or defenses in numbered paragraphs, each limited as far as practicable to a single set of circumstances. A later pleading may refer by number to a paragraph in an earlier pleading. If doing so would promote clarity, each claim founded on a separate transaction or occurrence—and each defense other than a denial—must be stated in a separate count or defense. FRCP 10(b).

i. *Adoption by reference; Exhibits.* A statement in a pleading may be adopted by reference elsewhere in the same pleading or in any other pleading or motion. A copy of a written instrument that is an exhibit to a pleading is a part of the pleading for all purposes. FRCP 10(c).

j. *Citation of local rules.* The Local Civil Rules of the United States District Court for the Northern District of Indiana may be cited as "N.D. Ind. L.R." IN R USDCTND L.R. 1-1(a)(1).

k. *Acceptance by the clerk.* The clerk must not refuse to file a paper solely because it is not in the form prescribed by the Federal Rules of Civil Procedure or by a local rule or practice. FRCP 5(d)(4).

  i. *Sanctions for formatting errors; Non-compliance.* If a person files a paper that does not comply with the rules governing the format of papers filed with the court, the court may: (1) strike the paper from the record; or (2) fine the person up to one thousand dollars ($1,000). IN R USDCTND L.R. 1-3(a).

    - *Notice.* Before sanctioning a person under IN R USDCTND L.R. 1-3(a)(2), the court must: (1) notify the person that the paper is noncompliant; and (2) give the person the opportunity either to be heard or to revise the paper. IN R USDCTND L.R. 1-3(b).

2. *Form of electronic documents.* Electronically filed documents must meet the same requirements of format and page limits as documents "conventionally filed" (as defined in IN R USDCTND CM/ECF(III)(A))

pursuant to the Federal Rules of Civil Procedure and the Local Civil Rules of the United States District Court for the Northern District of Indiana. IN R USDCTND CM/ECF(II)(A)(2).

a. *PDF format required.* Documents filed in the CM/ECF must be in .pdf format. A document created with almost any word-processing program can be converted to .pdf format. The .pdf program in effect takes a picture of the original document and allows anyone to open the converted document across a broad range of hardware and software, with layout, format, links, and images intact. IN R USDCTND CM/ECF(FN2).

b. *Title of documents.* The person electronically filing a pleading or other document will be responsible for designating a title for the pleading or other document by using one of the categories contained in the events listed in the CM/ECF Menu. IN R USDCTND CM/ECF(II)(G).

c. *Combining documents.* All documents which form part of a single pleading and which are being filed at the same time and by the same party may be electronically filed together under one document number, e.g., the motion and a supporting affidavit, with the exception of memoranda in support. Memoranda in support shall be electronically filed separately and shown as a related document to the motion. IN R USDCTND CM/ECF(II)(A)(4).

d. *Exhibits and attachments.* Filing users must submit in electronic form all documents referenced as exhibits or attachments, unless the court permits conventional filing. A filing user must submit as exhibits or attachments only those excerpts of the referenced documents that are directly germane to the matter under consideration by the court. Excerpted material must be clearly and prominently identified as such. Filing users who file excerpts of documents as exhibits or attachments do so without prejudice to their right to timely file additional excerpts or the complete document. Responding parties may timely file additional excerpts or the complete document that they believe are directly germane. The court may require parties to file additional excerpts or the complete document. IN R USDCTND CM/ECF(II)(A)(6).

e. *Hyperlinks.* Electronically filed documents may contain hyperlink references to an external document as a convenient mechanism for accessing material cited in the document. A hyperlink reference is neither validated for content nor considered a part of the court's records. The court neither endorses the product or organization at the destination of a hyperlink reference, nor does the court exercise any responsibility over the content at the destination. In order to preserve the integrity of the court record, attorneys wishing to insert hyperlinks in court filings shall continue to use the traditional citation method for the cited authority, in addition to the hyperlink. A hyperlink contained in a filing is no more than a convenient mechanism for accessing material cited in the document and a hyperlink reference is extraneous to any filed document and is not part of the court's record. IN R USDCTND CM/ECF(II)(A)(3).

3. *Form of briefs*

   a. *Page limits.* Supporting and response briefs (excluding tables of contents, tables of authorities, and appendices) ordinarily must not exceed twenty-five (25) pages. Reply briefs must not exceed fifteen (15) pages. IN R USDCTND L.R. 7-1(e)(1).

      i. *Exception.* The court may allow a party to file a brief exceeding these page limits for extraordinary and compelling reasons. But if the court permits a brief to exceed twenty-five (25) pages, it must include:

         • A table of contents with page references;

         • An issue statement; and

         • A table of authorities including: (1) all cases (alphabetically arranged), statutes, and other authorities cited in the brief; and (2) references to where the authorities appear in the brief. IN R USDCTND L.R. 7-1(e)(2).

4. *Signing of pleadings, motions and other papers*

   a. *Signature.* Every pleading, written motion, and other paper must be signed by at least one attorney of record in the attorney's name—or by a party personally if the party is unrepresented. The paper must state the signer's address, e-mail address, and telephone number. FRCP 11(a).

   i.   *Signatures on manual filings.* Papers delivered to the clerk for filing must: include the filer's original signature. IN R USDCTND L.R. 5-4(b)(1)(C).

- *Rubber-stamped and faxed signatures.* An original paper with a rubber-stamped or faxed signature is unsigned for purposes of FRCP 11 and FRCP 26(g). IN R USDCTND L.R. 5-4(b)(2).

- *Affidavits.* Only the affiant need sign an affidavit. IN R USDCTND L.R. 5-4(b)(3).

   ii. *Electronic signatures.* Pursuant to FRCP 11, every pleading, motion, and other paper (except lists, schedules, statements or amendments thereto) shall be signed by at least one attorney of record or, if the party is not represented by an attorney, all papers shall be signed by the party. An attorney's/participant's password issued by the court combined with the user's identification, serves as and constitutes the attorney/participant's signature for FRCP 11 and other purposes. IN R USDCTND CM/ECF(I)(C). Documents which must be filed and which must contain original signatures other than those of a participating attorney or which require either verification or an unsworn declaration under any rule or statute, shall be filed electronically, with originally executed copies maintained by the filer. The pleading or other document electronically filed shall contain "s/" signature(s), as noted in IN R USDCTND CM/ECF(II)(E)(3)(b). IN R USDCTND CM/ECF(II)(E)(1).

- *Multiple signatures.* In the case of a stipulation or other document to be signed by two or more attorneys, the following procedure should be used: The filing attorney shall initially confirm that the content of the document is acceptable to all persons required to sign the document and shall obtain the physical signatures of all attorneys on the document. IN R USDCTND CM/ECF(II)(E)(3)(a). The filing attorney then shall file the document electronically, indicating the signatories, e.g., "s/Jane Doe," "s/John Doe," etc. IN R USDCTND CM/ECF(II)(E)(3)(b). The filing attorney shall retain the hard copy of the document containing the original signatures. IN R USDCTND CM/ECF(II)(E)(3)(c).

   iii. *No verification or accompanying affidavit required for pleadings.* Unless a rule or statute specifically states otherwise, a pleading need not be verified or accompanied by an affidavit. FRCP 11(a).

   iv. *Unsigned papers.* The court must strike an unsigned paper unless the omission is promptly corrected after being called to the attorney's or party's attention. FRCP 11(a).

b. *Representations to the court.* By presenting to the court a pleading, written motion, or other paper—whether by signing, filing, submitting, or later advocating it—an attorney or unrepresented party certifies that to the best of the person's knowledge, information, and belief, formed after an inquiry reasonable under the circumstances:

   i.   It is not being presented for any improper purpose, such as to harass, cause unnecessary delay, or needlessly increase the cost of litigation;

   ii. The claims, defenses, and other legal contentions are warranted by existing law or by a nonfrivolous argument for extending, modifying, or reversing existing law or for establishing new law;

   iii. The factual contentions have evidentiary support or, if specifically so identified, will likely have evidentiary support after a reasonable opportunity for further investigation or discovery; and

   iv. The denials of factual contentions are warranted on the evidence or, if specifically so identified, are reasonably based on belief or a lack of information. FRCP 11(b).

c. *Sanctions.* If, after notice and a reasonable opportunity to respond, the court determines that FRCP 11(b) has been violated, the court may impose an appropriate sanction on any attorney, law firm, or party that violated FRCP 11(b) or is responsible for the violation. FRCP 11(c)(1). Refer to the United States District Court for the Northern District of Indiana KeyRules Motion for Sanctions document for more information.

5. *Privacy protection for filings made with the court*

    a. *Redacted filings.* Counsel should not include sensitive information in any document filed with the court unless such inclusion is necessary and relevant to the case. IN R USDCTND CM/ECF(VII). Unless the court orders otherwise, in an electronic or paper filing with the court that contains an individual's Social Security number, taxpayer-identification number, or birth date, the name of an individual known to be a minor, or a financial-account number, a party or nonparty making the filing may include only:

        i.   The last four (4) digits of the Social Security number and taxpayer-identification number;

        ii. The year of the individual's birth;

        iii. The minor's initials; and

        iv. The last four (4) digits of the financial-account number. FRCP 5.2(a); IN R USDCTND Order 2005-3.

    b. *Exemptions from the redaction requirement.* The redaction requirement does not apply to the following:

        i.   A financial-account number that identifies the property allegedly subject to forfeiture in a forfeiture proceeding;

        ii. The record of an administrative or agency proceeding;

        iii. The official record of a state-court proceeding;

        iv. The record of a court or tribunal, if that record was not subject to the redaction requirement when originally filed;

        v.   A filing covered by FRCP 5.2(c) or FRCP 5.2(d); and

        vi. A pro se filing in an action brought under 28 U.S.C.A. § 2241, 28 U.S.C.A. § 2254, or 28 U.S.C.A. § 2255. FRCP 5.2(b).

        vii. In cases filed under the Social Security Act, 42 U.S.C.A. § 405(g), there is no need for redaction of any information from the documents filed in the case. IN R USDCTND Order 2005-3.

    c. *Limitations on remote access to electronic files; Social Security appeals and immigration cases.* Unless the court orders otherwise, in an action for benefits under the Social Security Act, and in an action or proceeding relating to an order of removal, to relief from removal, or to immigration benefits or detention, access to an electronic file is authorized as follows:

        i.   The parties and their attorneys may have remote electronic access to any part of the case file, including the administrative record;

        ii. Any other person may have electronic access to the full record at the courthouse, but may have remote electronic access only to:

             • The docket maintained by the court; and

             • An opinion, order, judgment, or other disposition of the court, but not any other part of the case file or the administrative record. FRCP 5.2(c).

    d. *Filings made under seal.* The court may order that a filing be made under seal without redaction. The court may later unseal the filing or order the person who made the filing to file a redacted version for the public record. FRCP 5.2(d). For information on filing documents under seal, refer to IN R USDCTND L.R. 5-3, IN R USDCTND CM/ECF(IV)(A), and IN R USDCTND ECF Order 2004-19.

    e. *Protective orders.* For good cause, the court may by order in a case:

        i.   Require redaction of additional information; or

        ii. Limit or prohibit a nonparty's remote electronic access to a document filed with the court. FRCP 5.2(e).

    f. *Option for additional unredacted filing under seal.* A person making a redacted filing may also file

an unredacted copy under seal. The court must retain the unredacted copy as part of the record. FRCP 5.2(f); IN R USDCTND Order 2005-3.

    i. The unredacted version of the document or the reference list shall be retained by the court under seal as part of the record. This paper shall be retained by the court as part of the record. The court may, however, still require the party to file a redacted copy for the public file. IN R USDCTND Order 2005-3.

g. *Option for filing a reference list.* A filing that contains redacted information may be filed together with a reference list that identifies each item of redacted information and specifies an appropriate identifier that uniquely corresponds to each item listed. The list must be filed under seal and may be amended as of right. Any reference in the case to a listed identifier will be construed to refer to the corresponding item of information. FRCP 5.2(g); IN R USDCTND Order 2005-3.

    i. The unredacted version of the document or the reference list shall be retained by the court under seal as part of the record. This paper shall be retained by the court as part of the record. The court may, however, still require the party to file a redacted copy for the public file. IN R USDCTND Order 2005-3.

h. *Responsibility for redaction.* The responsibility for redacting these personal identifiers rests solely with counsel and the parties. The Clerk will not review each paper for compliance with IN R USDCTND Order 2005-3. IN R USDCTND Order 2005-3.

i. *Waiver of protection of identifiers.* A person waives the protection of FRCP 5.2(a) as to the person's own information by filing it without redaction and not under seal. FRCP 5.2(h).

F. Filing and Service Requirements

1. *Filing requirements.* Any paper after the complaint that is required to be served—together with a certificate of service—must be filed within a reasonable time after service. FRCP 5(d)(1). Motions must be filed separately, but alternative motions may be filed in a single paper if each is named in the title following the caption. IN R USDCTND L.R. 7-1(a).

a. *How filing is made; In general.* A paper is filed by delivering it:

    i. To the clerk; or

    ii. To a judge who agrees to accept it for filing, and who must then note the filing date on the paper and promptly send it to the clerk. FRCP 5(d)(2).

       • Papers not filed electronically must be filed with the clerk, not a judge. IN R USDCTND L.R. 5-4(b)(4).

    iii. Parties manually filing a paper that requires the clerk to give others notice, must give the clerk: (1) sufficient copies of the notice; and (2) the name and address of each person entitled to receive the notice. IN R USDCTND L.R. 5-4(b)(8).

b. *Where to file.* Papers not filed electronically must be filed in the division where the case is pending, unless: (1) a person will be prejudiced if the paper is not filed the same day it is tendered; and (2) it includes an adequately sized envelope addressed to the clerk's office in the division where the case is pending and with adequate postage. IN R USDCTND L.R. 5-4(b)(5).

c. *Electronic filing*

    i. *Authorization of electronic filing program.* A court may, by local rule, allow papers to be filed, signed, or verified by electronic means that are consistent with any technical standards established by the Judicial Conference of the United States. A local rule may require electronic filing only if reasonable exceptions are allowed. A paper filed electronically in compliance with a local rule is a written paper for purposes of the Federal Rules of Civil Procedure. FRCP 5(d)(3).

       • Papers must be filed, signed, and verified electronically unless excepted by the court's CM/ECF Civil and Criminal User Manual (IN R USDCTND CM/ECF). IN R USDCTND L.R. 5-1.

    ii. *Mandatory electronic filing.* Unless otherwise permitted by these procedures or otherwise authorized by the assigned judge, all documents submitted for filing in this district in civil and criminal cases, no matter when a case was originally filed, shall be filed electronically using the System. IN R USDCTND CM/ECF(II)(A)(1). The requirement that "all documents" be filed electronically includes briefs, and attachments and exhibits used in support of motions. IN R USDCTND CM/ECF(FN1).

- Sending a document or pleading to the court via e-mail or facsimile does not constitute "electronic filing." IN R USDCTND CM/ECF(I)(A).

iii. *Conventional filing.* As used in these procedures, a "conventionally" filed or submitted document or pleading is one presented to the Clerk or a party in paper or other non-electronic, tangible format. The following documents shall be filed conventionally and not electronically unless specifically authorized by the Court:

- Exhibits and other documents which cannot be converted to a legible electronic form. Whenever possible, counsel is responsible for converting filings to an electronic form. However, if that is not physically possible, counsel shall electronically file a .pdf document titled Notice of Manual Filing as a notation on the docket sheet that filings are being held in the clerk's office in paper. A sample Notice of Manual Filing is attached as Form 2 (IN R USDCTND CM/ECF(Form 2)). If documents are filed in paper format, counsel must provide an original for the clerk's office, a copy for the judge and a copy must be served on all parties in the case. Large documents which do not exist in an electronic format shall be scanned into .pdf format by counsel, in small batches if necessary, and filed electronically as separate attachments in the System. IN R USDCTND CM/ECF(III)(A)(1).

- Certain documents which are listed in IN R USDCTND CM/ECF(II)(E)(2). IN R US-DCTND CM/ECF(III)(A)(2).

- Documents filed by pro se litigants. IN R USDCTND CM/ECF(III)(A)(3).

iv. For more information on electronic filing, refer to IN R USDCTND CM/ECF.

2. *Service requirements*

a. *Service; When required*

i. *In general.* Unless the Federal Rules of Civil Procedure provide otherwise, each of the following papers must be served on every party:

- An order stating that service is required;

- A pleading filed after the original complaint, unless the court orders otherwise under FRCP 5(c) because there are numerous defendants;

- A discovery paper required to be served on a party, unless the court orders otherwise;

- A written motion, except one that may be heard ex parte; and

- A written notice, appearance, demand, or offer of judgment, or any similar paper. FRCP 5(a)(1).

ii. *If a party fails to appear.* No service is required on a party who is in default for failing to appear. But a pleading that asserts a new claim for relief against such a party must be served on that party under FRCP 4. FRCP 5(a)(2).

iii. *Seizing property.* If an action is begun by seizing property and no person is or need be named as a defendant, any service required before the filing of an appearance, answer, or claim must be made on the person who had custody or possession of the property when it was seized. FRCP 5(a)(3).

b. *Service; How made*

i. *Serving an attorney.* If a party is represented by an attorney, service under FRCP 5 must be made on the attorney unless the court orders service on the party. FRCP 5(b)(1).

ii. *Service in general.* A paper is served under FRCP 5 by:

- Handing it to the person;

- Leaving it: (1) at the person's office with a clerk or other person in charge or, if no one is in charge, in a conspicuous place in the office; or (2) if the person has no office or the office is closed, at the person's dwelling or usual place of abode with someone of suitable age and discretion who resides there;

- Mailing it to the person's last known address—in which event service is complete upon mailing;

- Leaving it with the court clerk if the person has no known address;

- Sending it by electronic means if the person consented in writing—in which event service is complete upon transmission, but is not effective if the serving party learns that it did not reach the person to be served; or

- Delivering it by any other means that the person consented to in writing—in which event service is complete when the person making service delivers it to the agency designated to make delivery. FRCP 5(b)(2).

iii. *Electronic service.* Electronically filed papers may be served electronically if service is consistent with the CM/ECF User Manual (IN R USDCTND CM/ECF). IN R USDCTND L.R. 5-2(a).

- *Waiver of other service.* An attorney's registration will constitute a waiver of conventional service of documents and the attorney agrees to accept service of notice on behalf of the client of the electronic filing by hand, facsimile or authorized email. IN R USDCTND CM/ECF(I)(B)(3).

- *Serving registered persons.* The System will generate a "Notice of Electronic Filing" when any document is filed. This notice represents service of the document on parties who are registered participants with the System. Except as provided in IN R USDCTND CM/ECF(III)(B), the filing party shall not be required to serve any pleading or other documents on any party receiving electronic notice. IN R USDCTND CM/ECF(II)(D)(1). The term "pleading" refers only to those documents listed in FRCP 7(a). IN R USDCTND CM/ECF(FN3).

- *When electronic service is deemed completed.* A person registered to use the court's electronic-filing system is served with an electronically filed paper when a "Notice of Electronic Filing" is transmitted to that person through the court's electronic filing-system. IN R USDCTND L.R. 5-2(b).

- *Serving non-registered persons.* A person who has not registered to use the court's electronic-filing system but who is entitled to service of a paper must be served according to the Local Civil Rules of the United States District Court for the Northern District of Indiana and the Federal Rules of Civil Procedure. IN R USDCTND L.R. 5-2(c); IN R USDCTND CM/ECF(II)(D)(2). If such service of a paper copy is to be made, it shall be done in the manner provided in the Federal Rules of Civil Procedure and the Local Civil Rules of the United States District Court for the Northern District of Indiana. IN R USDCTND CM/ECF(II)(D)(2).

iv. *Service of conventional filings.* Pleadings or other documents which are filed conventionally rather than electronically shall be served in the manner provided for in the Federal Rules of Civil Procedure and the Local Civil Rules of the United States District Court for the Northern District of Indiana, except as otherwise provided by order of the Court. IN R USDCTND CM/ECF(III)(B).

v. *Using court facilities.* If a local rule so authorizes, a party may use the court's transmission facilities to make service under FRCP 5(b)(2)(E). FRCP 5(b)(3).

c. *Serving numerous defendants*

i. *In general.* If an action involves an unusually large number of defendants, the court may, on motion or on its own, order that:

- Defendants' pleadings and replies to them need not be served on other defendants;

- Any crossclaim, counterclaim, avoidance, or affirmative defense in those pleadings and replies to them will be treated as denied or avoided by all other parties; and

- Filing any such pleading and serving it on the plaintiff constitutes notice of the pleading to all parties. FRCP 5(c)(1).

    ii. *Notifying parties.* A copy of every such order must be served on the parties as the court directs. FRCP 5(c)(2).

G. Hearings

1. *Hearings, generally*

    a. *Oral argument.* Due process does not require that oral argument be permitted on a motion and, except as otherwise provided by local rule, the district court has discretion to determine whether it will decide the motion on the papers or hear argument by counsel (and perhaps receive evidence). FPP § 1190; F.D.I.C. v. Deglau, 207 F.3d 153 (3d Cir. 2000).

        i. *Request for oral argument.* A party may request oral argument on a motion by filing and serving a separate document explaining why oral argument is necessary and estimating how long the court should allow for the argument. IN R USDCTND L.R. 7-5(a)(1). Refer to the Documents section of this document for more information.

        ii. *Additional evidence forbidden.* Parties may not present additional evidence at oral argument. IN R USDCTND L.R. 7-5(a)(3).

    b. *Providing a regular schedule for oral hearings.* A court may establish regular times and places for oral hearings on motions. FRCP 78(a).

    c. *Providing for submission on briefs.* By rule or order, the court may provide for submitting and determining motions on briefs, without oral hearings. FRCP 78(b).

    d. *Evidentiary hearings.* A party may request an evidentiary hearing by filing and serving a separate document explaining why the hearing is necessary and estimating how long the court should allow for it. IN R USDCTND L.R. 7-5(b)(2). Refer to the Documents section of this document for more information.

    e. *Court's authority.* The court may: (1) grant or deny a request for oral argument or an evidentiary hearing in its discretion; (2) set oral argument or an evidentiary hearing without a request from a party; or (3) order any oral argument or evidentiary hearing to be held anywhere within the district regardless of where the case will be tried. IN R USDCTND L.R. 7-5(c).

2. *Hearing on FRCP 12 defenses before trial.* If a party so moves, any defense listed in FRCP 12(b)(1) through FRCP 12(b)(7)—whether made in a pleading or by motion—and a motion under FRCP 12(c) must be heard and decided before trial unless the court orders a deferral until trial. FRCP 12(i).

3. *Hearing on motion to dismiss for lack of subject matter jurisdiction.* It may be error for a court to dismiss a case on the defendant's motion to dismiss for lack of subject matter jurisdiction without first holding a hearing, as FRCP 12(b)(1) requires a preliminary hearing or hearing at trial to determine any disputed facts upon which the motion or opposition to it is predicated. FEDPROC § 62:435.

4. *Courtroom and courthouse decorum.* For information on courtroom and courthouse decorum, refer to IN R USDCTND L.R. 83-3.

H. Forms

1. Federal Motion to Dismiss for Lack of Subject Matter Jurisdiction Forms

    a. Motion to dismiss for lack of subject-matter jurisdiction. 2C FEDFORMS § 11:35.

    b. Motion to dismiss for lack of subject-matter jurisdiction; Want of diversity of citizenship because requisite diversity not alleged. 2C FEDFORMS § 11:37.

    c. Motion to dismiss for lack of subject-matter jurisdiction; Want of diversity on a factual basis and because requisite diversity not alleged. 2C FEDFORMS § 11:38.

    d. Motion to dismiss for lack of subject-matter jurisdiction; Want of diversity of citizenship because state of incorporation and principal place of business of defendant not as alleged. 2C FEDFORMS § 11:39.

e. Motion to dismiss for lack of subject-matter jurisdiction; Want of diversity of citizenship because principal place of business of defendant not as alleged. 2C FEDFORMS § 11:40.

f. Motion to dismiss for lack of subject-matter jurisdiction; Failure to comply with procedural requirements. 2C FEDFORMS § 11:41.

g. Motion to dismiss for lack of subject-matter jurisdiction; Want of diversity upon realignment of parties according to interest. 2C FEDFORMS § 11:42.

h. Motion to dismiss for lack of subject-matter jurisdiction; Want of federal question. 2C FEDFORMS § 11:43.

i. Motion to dismiss for lack of subject-matter jurisdiction; Unsubstantial federal question. 2C FEDFORMS § 11:44.

j. Motion to dismiss for lack of subject-matter jurisdiction; Want of amount in controversy. 2C FEDFORMS § 11:45.

k. Motion to dismiss for lack of subject-matter jurisdiction; Want of amount in controversy; Insurance policy limits do not exceed required jurisdictional amount. 2C FEDFORMS § 11:46.

l. Motion to dismiss for lack of subject-matter jurisdiction; Want of amount in controversy; Claim for damages in excess of jurisdictional amount not made in good faith. 2C FEDFORMS § 11:47.

m. Motion to dismiss for lack of subject-matter jurisdiction; Want of amount in controversy; Made after judgment. 2C FEDFORMS § 11:48.

n. Motion to dismiss for lack of subject-matter jurisdiction; Want of consent by the United States to be sued. 2C FEDFORMS § 11:49.

o. Motion to dismiss for lack of subject-matter jurisdiction; Want of consent by United States to be sued; United States indispensable party. 2C FEDFORMS § 11:50.

p. Affidavit; In opposition to motion to dismiss for lack of diversity; Assignment of claim to plaintiff bona fide. FEDPROF § 1:894.

q. Motion; To dismiss; Plaintiff and defendant citizens of same state when action filed. FEDPROF § 1:888.

r. Motion to dismiss; Assignment to nonresident for purpose of invoking federal jurisdiction sham and ineffective to confer jurisdiction. FEDPROF § 1:889.

s. Motion to dismiss; For lack of diversity in third-party complaint. FEDPROF § 1:890.

t. Affidavit; In support of motion to dismiss for want of diversity of citizenship; Plaintiff and defendant citizens of same state on date action filed. FEDPROF § 1:892.

u. Motion; To dismiss; Insufficiency of amount in controversy. FEDPROF § 1:897.

v. Motion to dismiss; Bad faith in claiming jurisdictional amount. FEDPROF § 1:898.

w. Motion; To dismiss; Lack of jurisdiction over subject matter, generally. FEDPROF § 1:903.

x. Motion to dismiss; Absence of federal question. FEDPROF § 1:904.

y. Motion to dismiss; Absence of federal question; Failure to exhaust state remedies. FEDPROF § 1:905.

z. Affidavit; In opposition to motion to dismiss for absence of jurisdiction over subject matter. FEDPROF § 1:906.

2. **Forms for the Northern District of Indiana**

a. Certificate of service. IN R USDCTND CM/ECF(Form 1).

b. Notice of manual filing. IN R USDCTND CM/ECF(Form 2).

c. Declaration that party was unable to file in a timely manner. IN R USDCTND CM/ECF(Form 3).

I. Applicable Rules

1. *Federal rules*

a. Federal question. 28 U.S.C.A. § 1331.

b. Diversity of citizenship; Amount in controversy; Costs. 28 U.S.C.A. § 1332.

c. Serving and filing pleadings and other papers. FRCP 5.

d. Constitutional challenge to a statute; Notice, certification, and intervention. FRCP 5.1.

e. Privacy protection for filings made with the court. FRCP 5.2.

f. Computing and extending time; Time for motion papers. FRCP 6.

g. Pleadings allowed; Form of motions and other papers. FRCP 7.

h. Disclosure statement. FRCP 7.1.

i. Form of pleadings. FRCP 10.

j. Signing pleadings, motions, and other papers; Representations to the court; Sanctions. FRCP 11.

k. Defenses and objections; When and how presented; Motion for judgment on the pleadings; Consolidating motions; Waiving defenses; Pretrial hearing. FRCP 12.

l. Taking testimony. FRCP 43.

m. Hearing motions; Submission on briefs. FRCP 78.

2. *Local rules*

a. Citation and scope of the rules. IN R USDCTND L.R. 1-1.

b. Sanctions for formatting errors. IN R USDCTND L.R. 1-3.

c. Electronic filing required. IN R USDCTND L.R. 5-1.

d. Constitutional questions. IN R USDCTND L.R. 5.1-1.

e. Electronic service. IN R USDCTND L.R. 5-2.

f. Format of papers. IN R USDCTND L.R. 5-4.

g. Motion practice. IN R USDCTND L.R. 7-1.

h. Oral arguments and evidentiary hearings. IN R USDCTND L.R. 7-5.

i. Pretrial procedure. IN R USDCTND L.R. 16-1.

j. Alternative dispute resolution. IN R USDCTND L.R. 16-6.

k. Filing of discovery and other materials. IN R USDCTND L.R. 26-2.

l. Case assignment. IN R USDCTND L.R. 40-1.

m. Appearance and withdrawal of appearance. IN R USDCTND L.R. 83-8.

n. CM/ECF civil and criminal user manual. IN R USDCTND CM/ECF.

o. In re: privacy and public access to civil electronic case files. IN R USDCTND Order 2005-3.

Motions, Oppositions and Replies
Motion to Dismiss for Lack of Personal Jurisdiction

Document Last Updated December 2016

A. Checklist

(I) ❑ Matters to be considered by moving party

    (a) ❑ Required documents

        (1) ❑ Notice of motion and motion

        (2) ❑ Brief

        (3) ❑ Certificate of service

    (b) ❑ Supplemental documents

        (1) ❑ Supporting evidence

(2) ❑ Notice of constitutional question

(3) ❑ Nongovernmental corporate disclosure statement

(4) ❑ Index of exhibits

(5) ❑ Request for oral argument

(6) ❑ Request for evidentiary hearing

(7) ❑ Copy of authority

(8) ❑ Proposed order

(9) ❑ Copy of document with self-addressed envelope

(10) ❑ Notice of manual filing

(11) ❑ Courtesy copies

(12) ❑ Declaration that party was unable to file in a timely manner

(c) ❑ Timing

    (1) ❑ Every defense to a claim for relief in any pleading must be asserted in the responsive pleading if one is required

    (2) ❑ A motion asserting any of the defenses in FRCP 12(b) must be made before pleading if a responsive pleading is allowed

    (3) ❑ If a pleading sets out a claim for relief that does not require a responsive pleading, an opposing party may assert at trial any defense to that claim

    (4) ❑ A written motion and notice of the hearing must be served at least fourteen (14) days before the time specified for the hearing, with the following exceptions: (i) when the motion may be heard ex parte; (ii) when the Federal Rules of Civil Procedure set a different time; or (iii) when a court order—which a party may, for good cause, apply for ex parte—sets a different time

    (5) ❑ Any affidavit supporting a motion must be served with the motion

(II) ❑ Matters to be considered by opposing party

  (a) ❑ Required documents

    (1) ❑ Response brief

    (2) ❑ Certificate of service

  (b) ❑ Supplemental documents

    (1) ❑ Supporting evidence

    (2) ❑ Notice of constitutional question

    (3) ❑ Index of exhibits

    (4) ❑ Request for oral argument

    (5) ❑ Request for evidentiary hearing

    (6) ❑ Copy of authority

    (7) ❑ Copy of document with self-addressed envelope

    (8) ❑ Notice of manual filing

    (9) ❑ Courtesy copies

    (10) ❑ Declaration that party was unable to file in a timely manner

  (c) ❑ Timing

    (1) ❑ A party must file any response brief to a motion within fourteen (14) days after the motion is served

    (2) ❑ Except as FRCP 59(c) provides otherwise, any opposing affidavit must be served at least seven (7) days before the hearing, unless the court permits service at another time

B. Timing

1. *Motion to dismiss for lack of personal jurisdiction*

    a. *In a responsive pleading.* Every defense to a claim for relief in any pleading must be asserted in the responsive pleading if one is required. FRCP 12(b).

    b. *By motion.* A motion asserting any of the defenses in FRCP 12(b) must be made before pleading if a responsive pleading is allowed. FRCP 12(b). Although FRCP 12(b) encourages the responsive pleader to file a motion to dismiss before filing the answer, nothing in FRCP 12 prohibits the filing of a motion to dismiss with the answer. An untimely motion to dismiss may be considered if the defense asserted in the motion was previously raised in the responsive pleading. FEDPROC § 62:427.

    c. *At trial.* If a pleading sets out a claim for relief that does not require a responsive pleading, an opposing party may assert at trial any defense to that claim. FRCP 12(b).

2. *Timing of motions, generally*

    a. *Motion and notice of hearing.* A written motion and notice of the hearing must be served at least fourteen (14) days before the time specified for the hearing, with the following exceptions:

        i. When the motion may be heard ex parte;

        ii. When the Federal Rules of Civil Procedure set a different time; or

        iii. When a court order—which a party may, for good cause, apply for ex parte—sets a different time. FRCP 6(c)(1).

    b. *Supporting affidavit.* Any affidavit supporting a motion must be served with the motion. FRCP 6(c)(2).

3. *Timing of opposing papers.* A party must file any response brief to a motion within fourteen (14) days after the motion is served. IN R USDCTND L.R. 7-1(d)(2)(A).

    a. *Opposing affidavit.* Except as FRCP 59(c) provides otherwise, any opposing affidavit must be served at least seven (7) days before the hearing, unless the court permits service at another time. FRCP 6(c)(2).

    b. *Extensions.* The court may extend response- and reply-brief deadlines, but only for good cause. IN R USDCTND L.R. 7-1(d)(3).

    c. *Summary rulings.* The court may rule on a motion summarily if an opposing party does not file a response before the deadline. IN R USDCTND L.R. 7-1(d)(4).

4. *Timing of reply papers.* Where the respondent files an answering affidavit setting up a new matter, the moving party ordinarily is allowed a reasonable time to file a reply affidavit since failure to deny the new matter by affidavit may operate as an admission of its truth. AMJUR MOTIONS § 25.

    a. *Reply brief.* The moving party must file any reply brief within seven (7) days after the response brief is served. IN R USDCTND L.R. 7-1(d)(2)(B).

    b. *Extensions.* The court may extend response- and reply-brief deadlines, but only for good cause. IN R USDCTND L.R. 7-1(d)(3).

5. *Effect of a FRCP 12 motion on the time to serve a responsive pleading.* Unless the court sets a different time, serving a motion under FRCP 12 alters the periods in FRCP 12(a) as follows:

    a. If the court denies the motion or postpones its disposition until trial, the responsive pleading must be served within fourteen (14) days after notice of the court's action; or

    b. If the court grants a motion for a more definite statement, the responsive pleading must be served within fourteen (14) days after the more definite statement is served. FRCP 12(a)(4).

6. *Computation of time*

    a. *Computing time.* FRCP 6 applies in computing any time period specified in the Federal Rules of Civil

Procedure, in any local rule or court order, or in any statute that does not specify a method of computing time. FRCP 6(a).

i. *Period stated in days or a longer unit.* When the period is stated in days or a longer unit of time:

- Exclude the day of the event that triggers the period;

- Count every day, including intermediate Saturdays, Sundays, and legal holidays; and

- Include the last day of the period, but if the last day is a Saturday, Sunday, or legal holiday, the period continues to run until the end of the next day that is not a Saturday, Sunday, or legal holiday. FRCP 6(a)(1).

ii. *Period stated in hours.* When the period is stated in hours:

- Begin counting immediately on the occurrence of the event that triggers the period;

- Count every hour, including hours during intermediate Saturdays, Sundays, and legal holidays; and

- If the period would end on a Saturday, Sunday, or legal holiday, the period continues to run until the same time on the next day that is not a Saturday, Sunday, or legal holiday. FRCP 6(a)(2).

iii. *Inaccessibility of the clerk's office.* Unless the court orders otherwise, if the clerk's office is inaccessible:

- On the last day for filing under FRCP 6(a)(1), then the time for filing is extended to the first accessible day that is not a Saturday, Sunday, or legal holiday; or

- During the last hour for filing under FRCP 6(a)(2), then the time for filing is extended to the same time on the first accessible day that is not a Saturday, Sunday, or legal holiday. FRCP 6(a)(3).

iv. *"Last day" defined.* Unless a different time is set by a statute, local rule, or court order, the last day ends:

- For electronic filing, at midnight in the court's time zone; and

- For filing by other means, when the clerk's office is scheduled to close. FRCP 6(a)(4).

v. *"Next day" defined.* The "next day" is determined by continuing to count forward when the period is measured after an event and backward when measured before an event. FRCP 6(a)(5).

vi. *"Legal holiday" defined.* "Legal holiday" means:

- The day set aside by statute for observing New Year's Day, Martin Luther King Jr.'s Birthday, Washington's Birthday, Memorial Day, Independence Day, Labor Day, Columbus Day, Veterans' Day, Thanksgiving Day, or Christmas Day;

- Any day declared a holiday by the President or Congress; and

- For periods that are measured after an event, any other day declared a holiday by the state where the district court is located. FRCP 6(a)(6).

b. *Computation of electronic filing deadlines.* Filing documents electronically does not alter any filing deadlines or any time computation pursuant to FRCP 6. The counties of Lake, Porter, LaPorte, Pulaski and Starke are located in the Central time zone and the remaining counties in the Northern District of Indiana are located in the Eastern time zone. Nevertheless, all electronic transmissions of documents must be completed (i.e., received completely by the clerk's office) prior to midnight Eastern Time, (South Bend/Fort Wayne/Lafayette time) in order to be considered timely filed that day, regardless of the local time in the division where the case is pending. Although documents can be filed electronically twenty-four (24) hours a day, filers are strongly encouraged to file all documents during hours when the CM/ECF Help Line is available, from 9:00 a.m. to 4:00 p.m. local time. IN R USDCTND CM/ECF(II)(I).

i. *Technical failures.* If the attorney is unable to file a document in a timely manner due to technical difficulties in the user's system, the attorney must file a document with the court as

soon as possible notifying the court of the inability to file the document. A sample document entitled Declaration that Party was Unable to File in a Timely Manner Due to Technical Difficulties is attached hereto as Form 5. IN R USDCTND CM/ECF(VI)(B). [Editor's note: the reference to Form 5 is likely meant to be a reference to Form 3 (IN R USDCTND CM/ECF(Form 3)].

   c. *Extending time*

      i. *In general.* When an act may or must be done within a specified time, the court may, for good cause, extend the time:

- With or without motion or notice if the court acts, or if a request is made, before the original time or its extension expires; or

- On motion made after the time has expired if the party failed to act because of excusable neglect. FRCP 6(b)(1).

      ii. *Exceptions.* A court must not extend the time to act under FRCP 50(b), FRCP 50(d), FRCP 52(b), FRCP 59(b), FRCP 59(d), FRCP 59(e), and FRCP 60(b). FRCP 6(b)(2).

      iii. Refer to the United States District Court for the Northern District of Indiana KeyRules Motion for Continuance/Extension of Time document for more information on extending time.

   d. *Additional time after certain kinds of service.* When a party may or must act within a specified time after being served and service is made under FRCP 5(b)(2)(C) (mail), FRCP 5(b)(2)(D) (leaving with the clerk), or FRCP 5(b)(2)(F) (other means consented to), three (3) days are added after the period would otherwise expire under FRCP 6(a). FRCP 6(d).

C. General Requirements

1. *Motions, generally*

   a. *Requirements.* A request for a court order must be made by motion. The motion must:

      i. Be in writing unless made during a hearing or trial;

      ii. State with particularity the grounds for seeking the order; and

      iii. State the relief sought. FRCP 7(b)(1).

   b. *Notice of motion.* A party interested in resisting the relief sought by a motion has a right to notice thereof, and an opportunity to be heard. AMJUR MOTIONS § 12.

      i. In addition to statutory or court rule provisions requiring notice of a motion—the purpose of such a notice requirement having been said to be to prevent a party from being prejudicially surprised by a motion—principles of natural justice dictate that an adverse party generally must be given notice that a motion will be presented to the court. AMJUR MOTIONS § 12.

      ii. "Notice," in this regard, means reasonable notice, including a meaningful opportunity to prepare and to defend against allegations of a motion. AMJUR MOTIONS § 12.

   c. *Writing requirement.* The writing requirement is intended to insure that the adverse parties are informed and have a record of both the motion's pendency and the grounds on which the movant seeks an order. FPP § 1191; Feldberg v. Quechee Lakes Corp., 463 F.3d 195 (2d Cir. 2006).

      i. It is sufficient "if the motion is stated in a written notice of the hearing of the motion." FPP § 1191.

   d. *Particularity requirement.* The particularity requirement insures that the opposing parties will have notice of their opponent's contentions. FEDPROC § 62:364; Goodman v. 1973 26 Foot Trojan Vessel, Arkansas Registration No. AR1439SN, 859 F.2d 71, 12 Fed.R.Serv.3d 645 (8th Cir. 1988). That requirement ensures that notice of the basis for the motion is provided to the court and to the opposing party so as to avoid prejudice, provide the opponent with a meaningful opportunity to respond, and provide the court with enough information to process the motion correctly. FEDPROC § 62:364; Andreas v. Volkswagen of America, Inc., 336 F.3d 789, 56 Fed.R.Serv.3d 6 (8th Cir. 2003).

      i. Reasonable specification of the grounds for a motion is sufficient. However, where a movant fails to state even one ground for granting the motion in question, the movant has failed to meet

the minimal standard of "reasonable specification." FEDPROC § 62:364; Martinez v. Trainor, 556 F.2d 818, 23 Fed.R.Serv.2d 403 (7th Cir. 1977).

    ii. The court may excuse the failure to comply with the particularity requirement if it is inadvertent, and where no prejudice is shown by the opposing party. FEDPROC § 62:364.

  e. *Motions must be filed separately.* Motions must be filed separately, but alternative motions may be filed in a single paper if each is named in the title following the caption. IN R USDCTND L.R. 7-1(a).

2. *Motion to dismiss for lack of personal jurisdiction.* A party may assert the defense of lack of subject-matter jurisdiction by motion. FRCP 12(b)(2). The court will not rule on a defense under FRCP 12 until the party who raised it files a motion and brief. IN R USDCTND L.R. 7-1(c). The most common use of the FRCP 12(b)(2) motion is to challenge the use of a state long-arm statute in a diversity action. FEDPROC § 62:445; Best Van Lines, Inc. v. Walker, 490 F.3d 239 (2d Cir. 2007). A dismissal pursuant to FRCP 12(b)(2) is proper where it appears that the assertion of jurisdiction over the defendant offends traditional notions of fair play and substantial justice—that is, where neither the defendant nor the controversy has a substantial enough connection with the forum state to make the exercise of jurisdiction reasonable. FEDPROC § 62:445; Neogen Corp. v. Neo Gen Screening, Inc., 282 F.3d 883, 2002 Fed.App. 0080P (6th Cir. 2002).

  a. *Personal jurisdiction, generally*

    i. *Due process limitations.* Due process requires that a court obtain jurisdiction over a defendant before it may adjudicate that defendant's personal rights. FEDPROC § 65:1; Omni Capital Intern., Ltd. v. Rudolf Wolff & Co., Ltd., 484 U.S. 97, 108 S.Ct. 404, 98 L.Ed.2d 415, 9 Fed.R.Serv.3d 691 (1987).

- Originally, it was believed that a judgment in personam could only be entered against a defendant found and served within a state, but the increased flow of commerce between the states and the disuse of the writ of capias ad respondendum, which directed the sheriff to secure the defendant's appearance by taking the defendant into custody, in civil cases led to the liberalization of the concept of personal jurisdiction over nonresidents, and the flexible "minimum contacts" test is now followed. FEDPROC § 65:1.

- Today the rule is that no binding judgment may be rendered against an individual or corporate defendant unless the defendant has sufficient contacts, ties, or relations with the jurisdiction. FEDPROC § 65:1; Burger King Corp. v. Rudzewicz, 471 U.S. 462, 105 S.Ct. 2174, 85 L.Ed.2d 528 (1985); International Shoe Co. v. State of Wash., Office of Unemployment Compensation and Placement, 326 U.S. 310, 66 S.Ct. 154, 90 L.Ed. 95, 161 A.L.R. 1057 (1945).

- Moreover, even if the defendant has sufficient contacts with the forum state to satisfy due process, a court nevertheless does not obtain personal jurisdiction over the defendant unless the defendant has notice sufficient to satisfy due process, and, if such notice requires service of a summons, that there is authorization for the type and manner of service used. FEDPROC § 65:1; Omni Capital Intern., Ltd. v. Rudolf Wolff & Co., Ltd., 484 U.S. 97, 108 S.Ct. 404, 98 L.Ed.2d 415, 9 Fed.R.Serv.3d 691 (1987).

- Personal jurisdiction is a prerequisite to the maintenance of an action and must exist even though subject matter jurisdiction and venue are proper. FEDPROC § 65:1; Bookout v. Beck, 354 F.2d 823 (9th Cir. 1965).

- Personal jurisdiction over a nonresident defendant is appropriate under the Due Process Clause only where the defendant has sufficient minimum contacts with the forum state that are more than random, fortuitous, or attenuated contacts made by interacting with other persons affiliated with the state, such that summoning the defendant would not offend traditional notions of fair play and substantial justice. FEDPROC § 65:1; Pecoraro v. Sky Ranch for Boys, Inc., 340 F.3d 558 (8th Cir. 2003).

    ii. *Methods of obtaining jurisdiction over an individual.* There are four basic methods of obtaining jurisdiction over an individual:

- Personal service within the jurisdiction. FEDPROC § 65:22.

- Service on a domiciliary of the forum state who is temporarily outside the jurisdiction, on the theory that the authority of a state over one of its citizens is not terminated by the mere fact of his absence. FEDPROC § 65:22; Milliken v. Meyer, 311 U.S. 457, 61 S.Ct. 339, 85 L.Ed. 278, 132 A.L.R. 1357 (1940).

- Service on a nonresident who has sufficient contacts with the forum state, since the test of International Shoe is applicable to individuals. FEDPROC § 65:22; Kulko v. Superior Court of California In and For City and County of San Francisco, 436 U.S. 84, 98 S.Ct. 1690, 56 L.Ed.2d 132 (1978).

- Service on an agent who has been expressly appointed or appointed by operation of law, such as under a nonresident motorist statute. FEDPROC § 65:22; National Equipment Rental, Limited v. Szukhent, 375 U.S. 311, 84 S.Ct. 411, 11 L.Ed.2d 354, 7 Fed.R.Serv.2d 23 (1964).

   iii. *Territorial limits of effective service*

- *In general.* Serving a summons or filing a waiver of service establishes personal jurisdiction over a defendant: (1) who is subject to the jurisdiction of a court of general jurisdiction in the state where the district court is located; (2) who is a party joined under FRCP 14 or FRCP 19 and is served within a judicial district of the United States and not more than one hundred (100) miles from where the summons was issued; or (3) when authorized by a federal statute. FRCP 4(k)(1).

- *Federal claim outside state-court jurisdiction.* For a claim that arises under federal law, serving a summons or filing a waiver of service establishes personal jurisdiction over a defendant if: (1) the defendant is not subject to jurisdiction in any state's courts of general jurisdiction; and (2) exercising jurisdiction is consistent with the United States Constitution and laws. FRCP 4(k)(2).

b. *Motion based on lack of in rem or quasi-in-rem jurisdiction.* Although FRCP 12(b)(2) only refers to "jurisdiction over the person," the provision presumably is sufficiently elastic to embrace a defense or objection that the district court lacks in rem or quasi-in-rem jurisdiction, admittedly a subject that rarely arises in contemporary practice. FPP § 1351.

c. *Motion based on insufficient process or insufficient service of process.* FRCP 12(b)(2) motions to dismiss are frequently based on the failure to serve the defendant with process or a defective service of process, on the theory that if the defendant was not properly served with process, the court lacks personal jurisdiction over the defendant. FEDPROC § 62:446; Prokopiou v. Long Island R. Co., 2007 WL 1098696 (S.D.N.Y. 2007).

d. *Independent ground for dismissal.* Lack of overall reasonableness in the assertion of personal jurisdiction constitutes an independent ground for dismissal under FRCP 12(b)(2). FEDPROC § 62:448; Federal Ins. Co. v. Lake Shore Inc., 886 F.2d 654 (4th Cir. 1989).

e. *Burden.* On the motion, the plaintiff bears the burden to establish the court's jurisdiction, which normally is not a heavy one, although the standard of proof may vary depending on the procedure used by the court in making its determination and whether the defendant is successful in rebutting the plaintiff's initial showing. Moreover, the Supreme Court has intimated that in the case of a challenge to the constitutional fairness and reasonableness of the chosen forum, the burden is on the defendant. FPP § 1351; Burger King Corp. v. Rudzewicz, 471 U.S. 462, 105 S.Ct. 2174, 85 L.Ed.2d 528 (1985).

   i. The most common formulation found in the judicial opinions is that the plaintiff bears the ultimate burden of demonstrating that the court's personal jurisdiction over the defendant exists by a preponderance of the evidence, but needs only make a prima facie showing when the district judge restricts her review of the FRCP 12(b)(2) motion solely to affidavits and other written evidence. FPP § 1351; Mullins v. TestAmerica, Inc., 564 F.3d 386 (5th Cir. 2009).

   ii. In addition, for purposes of such a review, federal courts will, as they do on other motions under FRCP 12(b), take as true the allegations of the nonmoving party with regard to the jurisdictional issues and resolve all factual disputes in his or her favor. FPP § 1351.

f. *Motion denied.* A party who has unsuccessfully raised an objection under FRCP 12(b)(2) may proceed to trial on the merits without waiving the ability to renew the objection to the court's jurisdiction. FPP § 1351.

g. *Joining motions.* As a general rule, when the court is confronted by a motion raising a combination of FRCP 12(b) defenses, it will pass on the jurisdictional issues before considering whether a claim was stated by the complaint. FPP § 1351.

　　i. *Right to join.* A motion under FRCP 12 may be joined with any other motion allowed by FRCP 12. FRCP 12(g)(1).

　　ii. *Limitation on further motions.* Except as provided in FRCP 12(h)(2) or FRCP 12(h)(3), a party that makes a motion under FRCP 12 must not make another motion under FRCP 12 raising a defense or objection that was available to the party but omitted from its earlier motion. FRCP 12(g)(2).

h. *Waiving and preserving certain defenses.* No defense or objection is waived by joining it with one or more other defenses or objections in a responsive pleading or in a motion. FRCP 12(b).

　　i. *Waiver by consent or stipulation.* A valid consent or a stipulation that the court has jurisdiction prevents the successful assertion of a FRCP 12(b)(2) defense. FPP § 1351.

　　ii. *Waiver by filing permissive counterclaim.* A defendant may be deemed to have waived an objection to personal jurisdiction if he or she files a permissive counterclaim under FRCP 13(b). FPP § 1351.

　　iii. *When some are waived.* A party waives any defense listed in FRCP 12(b)(2) through FRCP 12(b)(5) by:

- Omitting it from a motion in the circumstances described in FRCP 12(g)(2); or
- Failing to either: (1) make it by motion under FRCP 12; or (2) include it in a responsive pleading or in an amendment allowed by FRCP 15(a)(1) as a matter of course. FRCP 12(h)(1).

　　iv. *When to raise others.* Failure to state a claim upon which relief can be granted, to join a person required by FRCP 19(b), or to state a legal defense to a claim may be raised:

- In any pleading allowed or ordered under FRCP 7(a);
- By a motion under FRCP 12(c); or
- At trial. FRCP 12(h)(2).

　　v. *Lack of subject matter jurisdiction.* If the court determines at any time that it lacks subject-matter jurisdiction, the court must dismiss the action. FRCP 12(h)(3).

3. *Opposing papers.* The Federal Rules of Civil Procedure do not require any formal answer, return, or reply to a motion, except where the Federal Rules of Civil Procedure or local rules may require affidavits, memoranda, or other papers to be filed in opposition to a motion. Such papers are simply to apprise the court of such opposition and the grounds of that opposition. FEDPROC § 62:359.

a. *Effect of failure to respond to motion.* Although in the absence of statutory provision or court rule, a motion ordinarily does not require a written answer, when a party files a motion and the opposing party fails to respond, the court may construe such failure to respond as nonopposition to the motion or an admission that the motion was meritorious, may take the facts alleged in the motion as true—the rule in some jurisdictions being that the failure to respond to a fact set forth in a motion is deemed an admission—and may grant the motion if the relief requested appears to be justified. AMJUR MOTIONS § 28.

b. *Assent or no opposition not determinative.* However, a motion will not be granted automatically simply because an "assent" or a notation of "no opposition" has been filed; federal judges frequently deny motions that have been assented to when it is thought that justice so dictates. FPP § 1190.

c. *Responsive pleading inappropriate as response to motion.* An attempt to answer or oppose a motion with a responsive pleading usually is not appropriate. FPP § 1190.

4. *Reply papers.* A moving party may be required or permitted to prepare papers in addition to his original

motion papers. AMJUR MOTIONS § 25. Papers answering or replying to opposing papers may be appropriate, in the interests of justice, where it appears there is a substantial reason for allowing a reply. Thus, a court may accept reply papers where a party demonstrates that the papers to which it seeks to file a reply raise new issues that are material to the disposition of the question before the court, or where the court determines, sua sponte, that it wishes further briefing of an issue raised in those papers and orders the submission of additional papers. FEDPROC § 62:360.

    a. *Function of reply papers.* The function of a reply affidavit is to answer the arguments made in opposition to the position taken by the movant and not to permit the movant to introduce new arguments in support of the motion. AMJUR MOTIONS § 25.

    b. *Issues raised for the first time in a reply document.* However, the view has been followed in some jurisdictions, that as a matter of judicial economy, where there is no prejudice and where the issues could be raised simply by filing a motion to dismiss, the trial court has discretion to consider arguments raised for the first time in a reply memorandum, and that a trial court may grant a motion to strike issues raised for the first time in a reply memorandum. AMJUR MOTIONS § 26.

5. *Appearances.* Attorneys not representing the United States or its agencies must file an appearance when they represent (either in person or by filing a paper) a party. IN R USDCTND L.R. 83-8(a). For more information, refer to IN R USDCTND L.R. 83-8.

6. *Notice of related action.* A party must file a notice of related action as soon as it appears that the party's case and another pending case: (1) arise out of the same transaction or occurrence; (2) involve the same property; or (3) involve the validity or infringement of the same patent, trademark, or copyright. IN R USDCTND L.R. 40-1(d). For more information, refer to IN R USDCTND L.R. 40-1.

7. *Alternative dispute resolution (ADR).* After they confer as required by FRCP 26(f), the parties must advise the court which, if any, alternative-dispute-resolution processes they expect to pursue and when they expect to undertake the process. IN R USDCTND L.R. 16-6(a). For more information on alternative dispute resolution (ADR), refer to IN R USDCTND L.R. 16-6 and IN R USDCTND Order 2003-21.

8. *Settlement or resolution.* The parties must immediately notify the court if they reasonably expect to settle the case or resolve a pending motion. IN R USDCTND L.R. 16-1(g).

9. *Modification or suspension of rules.* The court may, on its own motion or at the request of a party, suspend or modify any rule in a particular case in the interest of justice. IN R USDCTND L.R. 1-1(c).

D. Documents

  1. *Documents for moving party*

    a. *Required documents*

      i. *Notice of motion and motion.* The party must not specify a hearing date in the notice of a motion or petition unless the court or the clerk has authorized it. IN R USDCTND L.R. 7-5(b)(2). Refer to the General Requirements section of this document for information on the notice of motion and motion.

      ii. *Brief.* Parties must file a supporting brief with any motion under: FRCP 12. IN R USDCTND L.R. 7-1(b)(1). Refer to the Format section of this document for the format of briefs.

      iii. *Certificate of service.* FRCP 5(d) requires that the person making service under FRCP 5 certify that service has been effected. FRCP 5(Advisory Committee Notes). Having such information on file may be useful for many purposes, including proof of service if an issue arises concerning the effectiveness of the service. FRCP 5(Advisory Committee Notes).

        • *Certificate of service for electronically-filed documents.* A Certificate of Service is still a requirement when filing documents electronically. A sample Certificate of Service is attached as Form 1 (IN R USDCTND CM/ECF(Form 1)). IN R USDCTND CM/ECF(II)(H).

    b. *Supplemental documents*

      i. *Supporting evidence.* When a motion relies on facts outside the record, the court may hear the

matter on affidavits or may hear it wholly or partly on oral testimony or on depositions. FRCP 43(c).

- *Materials necessary for motion.* A party must file those portions of discovery requests or responses (including deposition transcripts) that the party relies on to support a motion that could result in a final order on an issue. IN R USDCTND L.R. 26-2(c).

ii. *Notice of constitutional question.* A party that files a pleading, written motion, or other paper drawing into question the constitutionality of a federal or state statute must promptly:

- *File notice.* File a notice of constitutional question stating the question and identifying the paper that raises it, if: (1) a federal statute is questioned and the parties do not include the United States, one of its agencies, or one of its officers or employees in an official capacity; or (2) a state statute is questioned and the parties do not include the state, one of its agencies, or one of its officers or employees in an official capacity; and

- *Serve notice.* Serve the notice and paper on the Attorney General of the United States if a federal statute is questioned—or on the state attorney general if a state statute is questioned—either by certified or registered mail or by sending it to an electronic address designated by the attorney general for this purpose. FRCP 5.1(a).

- *When to file the notice.* A party required to file a notice of constitutional question under FRCP 5.1 must do so by the later of: (1) the day the parties tender their proposed case-management plan (if one is required); or (2) 21 days after filing the pleading, written motion, or other paper questioning the constitutionality of a federal or state statute. IN R USDCTND L.R. 5.1-1(a).

- *Service on government officials.* The party must also serve the notice and the pleading, written motion, or other paper questioning the constitutionality of a federal or state statute on: (1) the Attorney General of the United States and the United States Attorney for the Northern District of Indiana, if a federal statute is challenged; or (2) the Attorney General for the state if a state statute is challenged. IN R USDCTND L.R. 5.1-1(b). Service required under IN R USDCTND L.R. 5.1-1(b) may be made either by certified or registered mail or by emailing it to an address designated by those officials for this purpose. IN R USDCTND L.R. 5.1-1(c).

- *No forfeiture.* A party's failure to file and serve the notice, or the court's failure to certify, does not forfeit a constitutional claim or defense that is otherwise timely asserted. FRCP 5.1(d).

iii. *Nongovernmental corporate disclosure statement*

- *Contents.* A nongovernmental corporate party must file two (2) copies of a disclosure statement that: (1) identifies any parent corporation and any publicly held corporation owning ten percent (10%) or more of its stock; or (2) states that there is no such corporation. FRCP 7.1(a).

- *Time to file; Supplemental filing.* A party must: (1) file the disclosure statement with its first appearance, pleading, petition, motion, response, or other request addressed to the court; and (2) promptly file a supplemental statement if any required information changes. FRCP 7.1(b).

iv. *Index of exhibits.* Any pleading, motion, brief, affidavit, notice, or proposed order, whether filed electronically or by delivering it to the clerk, must: include a separate index identifying and briefly describing each exhibit if there are more than four (4) exhibits. IN R USDCTND L.R. 5-4(a)(8).

v. *Request for oral argument.* A party may request oral argument on a motion by filing and serving a separate document explaining why oral argument is necessary and estimating how long the court should allow for the argument. IN R USDCTND L.R. 7-5(a)(1). The request must be filed and served with the party's supporting brief, response brief, or reply brief. IN R USDCTND L.R. 7-5(a)(2).

vi. *Request for evidentiary hearing.* A party may request an evidentiary hearing by filing and

serving a separate document explaining why the hearing is necessary and estimating how long the court should allow for it. IN R USDCTND L.R. 7-5(b)(1).

vii. *Copy of authority.* A copy of any decision, statute, or regulation cited in a motion or brief must be attached to the paper if—and only if—it is not available on Westlaw or Lexis. But if a copy of a decision, statute, or regulation is only available electronically, a party must provide it to the court or another party upon request. IN R USDCTND L.R. 7-1(f).

viii. *Proposed order.* Parties filing a paper that requires the judge or clerk to enter a routine or uncontested order must include a suitable form of order. IN R USDCTND L.R. 5-4(c).

- Proposed orders shall not be filed electronically either as a separate document or as an attachment to the main pleading or other document. Instead, all proposed orders must be e-mailed to the chambers of the appropriate judicial officer for the case. The proposed order must be in WordPerfect Format or Rich Text Format (RTF). Proposed orders should be attached to an e-mail and sent to the appropriate judicial officer at the address listed in IN R USDCTND CM/ECF(II)(F). The subject line of the email message should indicate the case title, cause number and document number of the motion, e.g., Smith v. Jones 1:02-cv-1234, motion# ___. IN R USDCTND CM/ECF(II)(F).

ix. *Copy of document with self-addressed envelope.* A party who wants a file-stamped copy of a paper must include with the filing an additional copy of the paper and a self-addressed envelope with adequate postage. IN R USDCTND L.R. 5-4(b)(6).

x. *Notice of manual filing.* However, if that is not physically possible, counsel shall electronically file a .pdf document titled Notice of Manual Filing as a notation on the docket sheet that filings are being held in the clerk's office in paper. A sample Notice of Manual Filing is attached as Form 2 (IN R USDCTND CM/ECF(Form 2)). IN R USDCTND CM/ECF(III)(A)(1).

xi. *Courtesy copies.* If documents are filed in paper format, counsel must provide an original for the clerk's office, a copy for the judge and a copy must be served on all parties in the case. IN R USDCTND CM/ECF(III)(A)(1).

xii. *Declaration that party was unable to file in a timely manner.* If the attorney is unable to file a document in a timely manner due to technical difficulties in the user's system, the attorney must file a document with the court as soon as possible notifying the court of the inability to file the document. A sample document entitled Declaration that Party was Unable to File in a Timely Manner Due to Technical Difficulties is attached hereto as Form 5. IN R USDCTND CM/ECF(VI)(B). [Editor's note: the reference to Form 5 is likely meant to be a reference to Form 3 (IN R USDCTND CM/ECF(Form 3)].

2. *Documents for opposing party*

   a. *Required documents*

      i. *Response brief.* Refer to the Format section of this document for the format of briefs. Refer to the General Requirements section of this document for information on the opposing papers.

      ii. *Certificate of service.* FRCP 5(d) requires that the person making service under FRCP 5 certify that service has been effected. FRCP 5(Advisory Committee Notes). Having such information on file may be useful for many purposes, including proof of service if an issue arises concerning the effectiveness of the service. FRCP 5(Advisory Committee Notes).

         - *Certificate of service for electronically-filed documents.* A Certificate of Service is still a requirement when filing documents electronically. A sample Certificate of Service is attached as Form 1 (IN R USDCTND CM/ECF(Form 1)). IN R USDCTND CM/ECF(II)(H).

   b. *Supplemental documents*

      i. *Supporting evidence.* When a motion relies on facts outside the record, the court may hear the matter on affidavits or may hear it wholly or partly on oral testimony or on depositions. FRCP 43(c).

         - *Materials necessary for motion.* A party must file those portions of discovery requests or

responses (including deposition transcripts) that the party relies on to support a motion that could result in a final order on an issue. IN R USDCTND L.R. 26-2(c).

ii. *Notice of constitutional question.* A party that files a pleading, written motion, or other paper drawing into question the constitutionality of a federal or state statute must promptly:

- *File notice.* File a notice of constitutional question stating the question and identifying the paper that raises it, if: (1) a federal statute is questioned and the parties do not include the United States, one of its agencies, or one of its officers or employees in an official capacity; or (2) a state statute is questioned and the parties do not include the state, one of its agencies, or one of its officers or employees in an official capacity; and

- *Serve notice.* Serve the notice and paper on the Attorney General of the United States if a federal statute is questioned—or on the state attorney general if a state statute is questioned—either by certified or registered mail or by sending it to an electronic address designated by the attorney general for this purpose. FRCP 5.1(a).

- *When to file the notice.* A party required to file a notice of constitutional question under FRCP 5.1 must do so by the later of: (1) the day the parties tender their proposed case-management plan (if one is required); or (2) 21 days after filing the pleading, written motion, or other paper questioning the constitutionality of a federal or state statute. IN R USDCTND L.R. 5.1-1(a).

- *Service on government officials.* The party must also serve the notice and the pleading, written motion, or other paper questioning the constitutionality of a federal or state statute on: (1) the Attorney General of the United States and the United States Attorney for the Northern District of Indiana, if a federal statute is challenged; or (2) the Attorney General for the state if a state statute is challenged. IN R USDCTND L.R. 5.1-1(b). Service required under IN R USDCTND L.R. 5.1-1(b) may be made either by certified or registered mail or by emailing it to an address designated by those officials for this purpose. IN R USDCTND L.R. 5.1-1(c).

- *No forfeiture.* A party's failure to file and serve the notice, or the court's failure to certify, does not forfeit a constitutional claim or defense that is otherwise timely asserted. FRCP 5.1(d).

iii. *Index of exhibits.* Any pleading, motion, brief, affidavit, notice, or proposed order, whether filed electronically or by delivering it to the clerk, must: include a separate index identifying and briefly describing each exhibit if there are more than four (4) exhibits. IN R USDCTND L.R. 5-4(a)(8).

iv. *Request for oral argument.* A party may request oral argument on a motion by filing and serving a separate document explaining why oral argument is necessary and estimating how long the court should allow for the argument. IN R USDCTND L.R. 7-5(a)(1). The request must be filed and served with the party's supporting brief, response brief, or reply brief. IN R USDCTND L.R. 7-5(a)(2).

v. *Request for evidentiary hearing.* A party may request an evidentiary hearing by filing and serving a separate document explaining why the hearing is necessary and estimating how long the court should allow for it. IN R USDCTND L.R. 7-5(b)(1).

vi. *Copy of authority.* A copy of any decision, statute, or regulation cited in a motion or brief must be attached to the paper if—and only if—it is not available on Westlaw or Lexis. But if a copy of a decision, statute, or regulation is only available electronically, a party must provide it to the court or another party upon request. IN R USDCTND L.R. 7-1(f).

vii. *Copy of document with self-addressed envelope.* A party who wants a file-stamped copy of a paper must include with the filing an additional copy of the paper and a self-addressed envelope with adequate postage. IN R USDCTND L.R. 5-4(b)(6).

viii. *Notice of manual filing.* However, if that is not physically possible, counsel shall electronically file a .pdf document titled Notice of Manual Filing as a notation on the docket sheet that filings are being held in the clerk's office in paper. A sample Notice of Manual Filing is attached as Form 2 (IN R USDCTND CM/ECF(Form 2)). IN R USDCTND CM/ECF(III)(A)(1).

ix. *Courtesy copies.* If documents are filed in paper format, counsel must provide an original for the clerk's office, a copy for the judge and a copy must be served on all parties in the case. IN R USDCTND CM/ECF(III)(A)(1).

x. *Declaration that party was unable to file in a timely manner.* If the attorney is unable to file a document in a timely manner due to technical difficulties in the user's system, the attorney must file a document with the court as soon as possible notifying the court of the inability to file the document. A sample document entitled Declaration that Party was Unable to File in a Timely Manner Due to Technical Difficulties is attached hereto as Form 5. IN R USDCTND CM/ECF(VI)(B). [Editor's note: the reference to Form 5 is likely meant to be a reference to Form 3 (IN R USDCTND CM/ECF(Form 3)].

E. Format

1. *Form of documents.* The rules governing captions and other matters of form in pleadings apply to motions and other papers. FRCP 7(b)(2).

   a. *Paper.* Any pleading, motion, brief, affidavit, notice, or proposed order, whether filed electronically or by delivering it to the clerk, must: use eight and one-half by eleven (8-1/2 x 11) inch pages. IN R USDCTND L.R. 5-4(a)(2).

      i. *Manual filings.* Papers delivered to the clerk for filing must: be flat, unfolded, and on good-quality, white paper. IN R USDCTND L.R. 5-4(b)(1)(A).

         • *Covers or backing.* Papers delivered to the clerk for filing must: not have a cover or a back. IN R USDCTND L.R. 5-4(b)(1)(B).

         • *Recycled paper.* The court encourages using recycled paper. IN R USDCTND L.R. 5-4(b)(7).

   b. *Margins.* Any pleading, motion, brief, affidavit, notice, or proposed order, whether filed electronically or by delivering it to the clerk, must: have at least one (1) inch margins. IN R USDCTND L.R. 5-4(a)(3).

   c. *Spacing.* Any pleading, motion, brief, affidavit, notice, or proposed order, whether filed electronically or by delivering it to the clerk, must: be double spaced (except for headings, footnotes, and quoted material). IN R USDCTND L.R. 5-4(a)(5).

   d. *Text.* Any pleading, motion, brief, affidavit, notice, or proposed order, whether filed electronically or by delivering it to the clerk, must: be plainly typewritten, printed, or prepared by a clearly legible copying process. IN R USDCTND L.R. 5-4(a)(1).

      i. Any pleading, motion, brief, affidavit, notice, or proposed order, whether filed electronically or by delivering it to the clerk, must: use at least twelve (12) point type in the body and at least ten (10) point type in footnotes. IN R USDCTND L.R. 5-4(a)(4).

   e. *Page numbering.* Any pleading, motion, brief, affidavit, notice, or proposed order, whether filed electronically or by delivering it to the clerk, must: have consecutively numbered pages. IN R USDCTND L.R. 5-4(a)(6).

   f. *Caption; Names of parties.* Every pleading must have a caption with the court's name, a title, a file number, and a FRCP 7(a) designation. The title of the complaint must name all the parties; the title of other pleadings, after naming the first party on each side, may refer generally to other parties. FRCP 10(a). Any pleading, motion, brief, affidavit, notice, or proposed order, whether filed electronically or by delivering it to the clerk, must: include a title on the first page. IN R USDCTND L.R. 5-4(a)(7).

      i. *Alternative motions.* Motions must be filed separately, but alternative motions may be filed in a single paper if each is named in the title following the caption. IN R USDCTND L.R. 7-1(a).

   g. *Filer's information.* Any pleading, motion, brief, affidavit, notice, or proposed order, whether filed electronically or by delivering it to the clerk, must: except in proposed orders and affidavits, include the filer's name, address, telephone number, fax number (where available), and e-mail address (where available). IN R USDCTND L.R. 5-4(a)(9).

   h. *Paragraphs; Separate statements.* A party must state its claims or defenses in numbered paragraphs,

each limited as far as practicable to a single set of circumstances. A later pleading may refer by number to a paragraph in an earlier pleading. If doing so would promote clarity, each claim founded on a separate transaction or occurrence—and each defense other than a denial—must be stated in a separate count or defense. FRCP 10(b).

i. *Adoption by reference; Exhibits.* A statement in a pleading may be adopted by reference elsewhere in the same pleading or in any other pleading or motion. A copy of a written instrument that is an exhibit to a pleading is a part of the pleading for all purposes. FRCP 10(c).

j. *Citation of local rules.* The Local Civil Rules of the United States District Court for the Northern District of Indiana may be cited as "N.D. Ind. L.R." IN R USDCTND L.R. 1-1(a)(1).

k. *Acceptance by the clerk.* The clerk must not refuse to file a paper solely because it is not in the form prescribed by the Federal Rules of Civil Procedure or by a local rule or practice. FRCP 5(d)(4).

    i. *Sanctions for formatting errors; Non-compliance.* If a person files a paper that does not comply with the rules governing the format of papers filed with the court, the court may: (1) strike the paper from the record; or (2) fine the person up to one thousand dollars ($1,000). IN R USDCTND L.R. 1-3(a).

        • *Notice.* Before sanctioning a person under IN R USDCTND L.R. 1-3(a)(2), the court must: (1) notify the person that the paper is noncompliant; and (2) give the person the opportunity either to be heard or to revise the paper. IN R USDCTND L.R. 1-3(b).

2. *Form of electronic documents.* Electronically filed documents must meet the same requirements of format and page limits as documents "conventionally filed" (as defined in IN R USDCTND CM/ECF(III)(A)) pursuant to the Federal Rules of Civil Procedure and the Local Civil Rules of the United States District Court for the Northern District of Indiana. IN R USDCTND CM/ECF(II)(A)(2).

a. *PDF format required.* Documents filed in the CM/ECF must be in .pdf format. A document created with almost any word-processing program can be converted to .pdf format. The .pdf program in effect takes a picture of the original document and allows anyone to open the converted document across a broad range of hardware and software, with layout, format, links, and images intact. IN R USDCTND CM/ECF(FN2).

b. *Title of documents.* The person electronically filing a pleading or other document will be responsible for designating a title for the pleading or other document by using one of the categories contained in the events listed in the CM/ECF Menu. IN R USDCTND CM/ECF(II)(G).

c. *Combining documents.* All documents which form part of a single pleading and which are being filed at the same time and by the same party may be electronically filed together under one document number, e.g., the motion and a supporting affidavit, with the exception of memoranda in support. Memoranda in support shall be electronically filed separately and shown as a related document to the motion. IN R USDCTND CM/ECF(II)(A)(4).

d. *Exhibits and attachments.* Filing users must submit in electronic form all documents referenced as exhibits or attachments, unless the court permits conventional filing. A filing user must submit as exhibits or attachments only those excerpts of the referenced documents that are directly germane to the matter under consideration by the court. Excerpted material must be clearly and prominently identified as such. Filing users who file excerpts of documents as exhibits or attachments do so without prejudice to their right to timely file additional excerpts or the complete document. Responding parties may timely file additional excerpts or the complete document that they believe are directly germane. The court may require parties to file additional excerpts or the complete document. IN R USDCTND CM/ECF(II)(A)(6).

e. *Hyperlinks.* Electronically filed documents may contain hyperlink references to an external document as a convenient mechanism for accessing material cited in the document. A hyperlink reference is neither validated for content nor considered a part of the court's records. The court neither endorses the product or organization at the destination of a hyperlink reference, nor does the court exercise any responsibility over the content at the destination. In order to preserve the integrity of the court record, attorneys wishing to insert hyperlinks in court filings shall continue to use the traditional citation method for the cited authority, in addition to the hyperlink. A hyperlink contained in a filing is no more than a convenient mechanism for accessing material cited in the document and a hyperlink reference is extraneous to any filed document and is not part of the court's record. IN R USDCTND CM/ECF(II)(A)(3).

3. *Form of briefs*

    a. *Page limits.* Supporting and response briefs (excluding tables of contents, tables of authorities, and appendices) ordinarily must not exceed twenty-five (25) pages. Reply briefs must not exceed fifteen (15) pages. IN R USDCTND L.R. 7-1(e)(1).

        i. *Exception.* The court may allow a party to file a brief exceeding these page limits for extraordinary and compelling reasons. But if the court permits a brief to exceed twenty-five (25) pages, it must include:

- A table of contents with page references;
- An issue statement; and
- A table of authorities including: (1) all cases (alphabetically arranged), statutes, and other authorities cited in the brief; and (2) references to where the authorities appear in the brief. IN R USDCTND L.R. 7-1(e)(2).

4. *Signing of pleadings, motions and other papers*

    a. *Signature.* Every pleading, written motion, and other paper must be signed by at least one attorney of record in the attorney's name—or by a party personally if the party is unrepresented. The paper must state the signer's address, e-mail address, and telephone number. FRCP 11(a).

        i. *Signatures on manual filings.* Papers delivered to the clerk for filing must: include the filer's original signature. IN R USDCTND L.R. 5-4(b)(1)(C).

- *Rubber-stamped and faxed signatures.* An original paper with a rubber-stamped or faxed signature is unsigned for purposes of FRCP 11 and FRCP 26(g). IN R USDCTND L.R. 5-4(b)(2).
- *Affidavits.* Only the affiant need sign an affidavit. IN R USDCTND L.R. 5-4(b)(3).

        ii. *Electronic signatures.* Pursuant to FRCP 11, every pleading, motion, and other paper (except lists, schedules, statements or amendments thereto) shall be signed by at least one attorney of record or, if the party is not represented by an attorney, all papers shall be signed by the party. An attorney's/participant's password issued by the court combined with the user's identification, serves as and constitutes the attorney/participant's signature for FRCP 11 and other purposes. IN R USDCTND CM/ECF(I)(C). Documents which must be filed and which must contain original signatures other than those of a participating attorney or which require either verification or an unsworn declaration under any rule or statute, shall be filed electronically, with originally executed copies maintained by the filer. The pleading or other document electronically filed shall contain "s/" signature(s), as noted in IN R USDCTND CM/ECF(II)(E)(3)(b). IN R USDCTND CM/ECF(II)(E)(1).

- *Multiple signatures.* In the case of a stipulation or other document to be signed by two or more attorneys, the following procedure should be used: The filing attorney shall initially confirm that the content of the document is acceptable to all persons required to sign the document and shall obtain the physical signatures of all attorneys on the document. IN R USDCTND CM/ECF(II)(E)(3)(a). The filing attorney then shall file the document electronically, indicating the signatories, e.g., "s/Jane Doe," "s/John Doe," etc. IN R US-DCTND CM/ECF(II)(E)(3)(b). The filing attorney shall retain the hard copy of the document containing the original signatures. IN R USDCTND CM/ECF(II)(E)(3)(c).

        iii. *No verification or accompanying affidavit required for pleadings.* Unless a rule or statute specifically states otherwise, a pleading need not be verified or accompanied by an affidavit. FRCP 11(a).

        iv. *Unsigned papers.* The court must strike an unsigned paper unless the omission is promptly corrected after being called to the attorney's or party's attention. FRCP 11(a).

    b. *Representations to the court.* By presenting to the court a pleading, written motion, or other paper—whether by signing, filing, submitting, or later advocating it—an attorney or unrepresented party certifies that to the best of the person's knowledge, information, and belief, formed after an inquiry reasonable under the circumstances:

    i.   It is not being presented for any improper purpose, such as to harass, cause unnecessary delay, or needlessly increase the cost of litigation;

    ii.   The claims, defenses, and other legal contentions are warranted by existing law or by a nonfrivolous argument for extending, modifying, or reversing existing law or for establishing new law;

    iii.   The factual contentions have evidentiary support or, if specifically so identified, will likely have evidentiary support after a reasonable opportunity for further investigation or discovery; and

    iv.   The denials of factual contentions are warranted on the evidence or, if specifically so identified, are reasonably based on belief or a lack of information. FRCP 11(b).

c.   *Sanctions.* If, after notice and a reasonable opportunity to respond, the court determines that FRCP 11(b) has been violated, the court may impose an appropriate sanction on any attorney, law firm, or party that violated FRCP 11(b) or is responsible for the violation. FRCP 11(c)(1). Refer to the United States District Court for the Northern District of Indiana KeyRules Motion for Sanctions document for more information.

5.   *Privacy protection for filings made with the court*

a.   *Redacted filings.* Counsel should not include sensitive information in any document filed with the court unless such inclusion is necessary and relevant to the case. IN R USDCTND CM/ECF(VII). Unless the court orders otherwise, in an electronic or paper filing with the court that contains an individual's Social Security number, taxpayer-identification number, or birth date, the name of an individual known to be a minor, or a financial-account number, a party or nonparty making the filing may include only:

    i.   The last four (4) digits of the Social Security number and taxpayer-identification number;

    ii.   The year of the individual's birth;

    iii.   The minor's initials; and

    iv.   The last four (4) digits of the financial-account number. FRCP 5.2(a); IN R USDCTND Order 2005-3.

b.   *Exemptions from the redaction requirement.* The redaction requirement does not apply to the following:

    i.   A financial-account number that identifies the property allegedly subject to forfeiture in a forfeiture proceeding;

    ii.   The record of an administrative or agency proceeding;

    iii.   The official record of a state-court proceeding;

    iv.   The record of a court or tribunal, if that record was not subject to the redaction requirement when originally filed;

    v.   A filing covered by FRCP 5.2(c) or FRCP 5.2(d); and

    vi.   A pro se filing in an action brought under 28 U.S.C.A. § 2241, 28 U.S.C.A. § 2254, or 28 U.S.C.A. § 2255. FRCP 5.2(b).

    vii.   In cases filed under the Social Security Act, 42 U.S.C.A. § 405(g), there is no need for redaction of any information from the documents filed in the case. IN R USDCTND Order 2005-3.

c.   *Limitations on remote access to electronic files; Social Security appeals and immigration cases.* Unless the court orders otherwise, in an action for benefits under the Social Security Act, and in an action or proceeding relating to an order of removal, to relief from removal, or to immigration benefits or detention, access to an electronic file is authorized as follows:

    i.   The parties and their attorneys may have remote electronic access to any part of the case file, including the administrative record;

    ii.   Any other person may have electronic access to the full record at the courthouse, but may have remote electronic access only to:

- The docket maintained by the court; and

- An opinion, order, judgment, or other disposition of the court, but not any other part of the case file or the administrative record. FRCP 5.2(c).

d.   *Filings made under seal.* The court may order that a filing be made under seal without redaction. The court may later unseal the filing or order the person who made the filing to file a redacted version for the public record. FRCP 5.2(d). For information on filing documents under seal, refer to IN R USDCTND L.R. 5-3, IN R USDCTND CM/ECF(IV)(A), and IN R USDCTND ECF Order 2004-19.

e.   *Protective orders.* For good cause, the court may by order in a case:

    i.   Require redaction of additional information; or

    ii.   Limit or prohibit a nonparty's remote electronic access to a document filed with the court. FRCP 5.2(e).

f.   *Option for additional unredacted filing under seal.* A person making a redacted filing may also file an unredacted copy under seal. The court must retain the unredacted copy as part of the record. FRCP 5.2(f); IN R USDCTND Order 2005-3.

    i.   The unredacted version of the document or the reference list shall be retained by the court under seal as part of the record. This paper shall be retained by the court as part of the record. The court may, however, still require the party to file a redacted copy for the public file. IN R USDCTND Order 2005-3.

g.   *Option for filing a reference list.* A filing that contains redacted information may be filed together with a reference list that identifies each item of redacted information and specifies an appropriate identifier that uniquely corresponds to each item listed. The list must be filed under seal and may be amended as of right. Any reference in the case to a listed identifier will be construed to refer to the corresponding item of information. FRCP 5.2(g); IN R USDCTND Order 2005-3.

    i.   The unredacted version of the document or the reference list shall be retained by the court under seal as part of the record. This paper shall be retained by the court as part of the record. The court may, however, still require the party to file a redacted copy for the public file. IN R USDCTND Order 2005-3.

h.   *Responsibility for redaction.* The responsibility for redacting these personal identifiers rests solely with counsel and the parties. The Clerk will not review each paper for compliance with IN R USDCTND Order 2005-3. IN R USDCTND Order 2005-3.

i.   *Waiver of protection of identifiers.* A person waives the protection of FRCP 5.2(a) as to the person's own information by filing it without redaction and not under seal. FRCP 5.2(h).

F. Filing and Service Requirements

1.   *Filing requirements.* Any paper after the complaint that is required to be served—together with a certificate of service—must be filed within a reasonable time after service. FRCP 5(d)(1). Motions must be filed separately, but alternative motions may be filed in a single paper if each is named in the title following the caption. IN R USDCTND L.R. 7-1(a).

a.   *How filing is made; In general.* A paper is filed by delivering it:

    i.   To the clerk; or

    ii.   To a judge who agrees to accept it for filing, and who must then note the filing date on the paper and promptly send it to the clerk. FRCP 5(d)(2).

- Papers not filed electronically must be filed with the clerk, not a judge. IN R USDCTND L.R. 5-4(b)(4).

    iii.   Parties manually filing a paper that requires the clerk to give others notice, must give the clerk: (1) sufficient copies of the notice; and (2) the name and address of each person entitled to receive the notice. IN R USDCTND L.R. 5-4(b)(8).

b. *Where to file.* Papers not filed electronically must be filed in the division where the case is pending, unless: (1) a person will be prejudiced if the paper is not filed the same day it is tendered; and (2) it includes an adequately sized envelope addressed to the clerk's office in the division where the case is pending and with adequate postage. IN R USDCTND L.R. 5-4(b)(5).

c. *Electronic filing*

    i. *Authorization of electronic filing program.* A court may, by local rule, allow papers to be filed, signed, or verified by electronic means that are consistent with any technical standards established by the Judicial Conference of the United States. A local rule may require electronic filing only if reasonable exceptions are allowed. A paper filed electronically in compliance with a local rule is a written paper for purposes of the Federal Rules of Civil Procedure. FRCP 5(d)(3).

- Papers must be filed, signed, and verified electronically unless excepted by the court's CM/ECF Civil and Criminal User Manual (IN R USDCTND CM/ECF). IN R USDCTND L.R. 5-1.

    ii. *Mandatory electronic filing.* Unless otherwise permitted by these procedures or otherwise authorized by the assigned judge, all documents submitted for filing in this district in civil and criminal cases, no matter when a case was originally filed, shall be filed electronically using the System. IN R USDCTND CM/ECF(II)(A)(1). The requirement that "all documents" be filed electronically includes briefs, and attachments and exhibits used in support of motions. IN R USDCTND CM/ECF(FN1).

- Sending a document or pleading to the court via e-mail or facsimile does not constitute "electronic filing." IN R USDCTND CM/ECF(I)(A).

    iii. *Conventional filing.* As used in these procedures, a "conventionally" filed or submitted document or pleading is one presented to the Clerk or a party in paper or other non-electronic, tangible format. The following documents shall be filed conventionally and not electronically unless specifically authorized by the Court:

- Exhibits and other documents which cannot be converted to a legible electronic form. Whenever possible, counsel is responsible for converting filings to an electronic form. However, if that is not physically possible, counsel shall electronically file a .pdf document titled Notice of Manual Filing as a notation on the docket sheet that filings are being held in the clerk's office in paper. A sample Notice of Manual Filing is attached as Form 2 (IN R USDCTND CM/ECF(Form 2)). If documents are filed in paper format, counsel must provide an original for the clerk's office, a copy for the judge and a copy must be served on all parties in the case. Large documents which do not exist in an electronic format shall be scanned into .pdf format by counsel, in small batches if necessary, and filed electronically as separate attachments in the System. IN R USDCTND CM/ECF(III)(A)(1).

- Certain documents which are listed in IN R USDCTND CM/ECF(II)(E)(2). IN R US-DCTND CM/ECF(III)(A)(2).

- Documents filed by pro se litigants. IN R USDCTND CM/ECF(III)(A)(3).

    iv. For more information on electronic filing, refer to IN R USDCTND CM/ECF.

2. *Service requirements*

a. *Service; When required*

    i. *In general.* Unless the Federal Rules of Civil Procedure provide otherwise, each of the following papers must be served on every party:

- An order stating that service is required;

- A pleading filed after the original complaint, unless the court orders otherwise under FRCP 5(c) because there are numerous defendants;

- A discovery paper required to be served on a party, unless the court orders otherwise;

- A written motion, except one that may be heard ex parte; and

- A written notice, appearance, demand, or offer of judgment, or any similar paper. FRCP 5(a)(1).

   ii. *If a party fails to appear.* No service is required on a party who is in default for failing to appear. But a pleading that asserts a new claim for relief against such a party must be served on that party under FRCP 4. FRCP 5(a)(2).

   iii. *Seizing property.* If an action is begun by seizing property and no person is or need be named as a defendant, any service required before the filing of an appearance, answer, or claim must be made on the person who had custody or possession of the property when it was seized. FRCP 5(a)(3).

b. *Service; How made*

   i. *Serving an attorney.* If a party is represented by an attorney, service under FRCP 5 must be made on the attorney unless the court orders service on the party. FRCP 5(b)(1).

   ii. *Service in general.* A paper is served under FRCP 5 by:

- Handing it to the person;

- Leaving it: (1) at the person's office with a clerk or other person in charge or, if no one is in charge, in a conspicuous place in the office; or (2) if the person has no office or the office is closed, at the person's dwelling or usual place of abode with someone of suitable age and discretion who resides there;

- Mailing it to the person's last known address—in which event service is complete upon mailing;

- Leaving it with the court clerk if the person has no known address;

- Sending it by electronic means if the person consented in writing—in which event service is complete upon transmission, but is not effective if the serving party learns that it did not reach the person to be served; or

- Delivering it by any other means that the person consented to in writing—in which event service is complete when the person making service delivers it to the agency designated to make delivery. FRCP 5(b)(2).

   iii. *Electronic service.* Electronically filed papers may be served electronically if service is consistent with the CM/ECF User Manual (IN R USDCTND CM/ECF). IN R USDCTND L.R. 5-2(a).

- *Waiver of other service.* An attorney's registration will constitute a waiver of conventional service of documents and the attorney agrees to accept service of notice on behalf of the client of the electronic filing by hand, facsimile or authorized email. IN R USDCTND CM/ECF(I)(B)(3).

- *Serving registered persons.* The System will generate a "Notice of Electronic Filing" when any document is filed. This notice represents service of the document on parties who are registered participants with the System. Except as provided in IN R USDCTND CM/ECF(III)(B), the filing party shall not be required to serve any pleading or other documents on any party receiving electronic notice. IN R USDCTND CM/ECF(II)(D)(1). The term "pleading" refers only to those documents listed in FRCP 7(a). IN R USDCTND CM/ECF(FN3).

- *When electronic service is deemed completed.* A person registered to use the court's electronic-filing system is served with an electronically filed paper when a "Notice of Electronic Filing" is transmitted to that person through the court's electronic filing-system. IN R USDCTND L.R. 5-2(b).

- *Serving non-registered persons.* A person who has not registered to use the court's electronic-filing system but who is entitled to service of a paper must be served according to the Local Civil Rules of the United States District Court for the Northern District of

Indiana and the Federal Rules of Civil Procedure. IN R USDCTND L.R. 5-2(c); IN R USDCTND CM/ECF(II)(D)(2). If such service of a paper copy is to be made, it shall be done in the manner provided in the Federal Rules of Civil Procedure and the Local Civil Rules of the United States District Court for the Northern District of Indiana. IN R USDCTND CM/ECF(II)(D)(2).

    iv. *Service of conventional filings.* Pleadings or other documents which are filed conventionally rather than electronically shall be served in the manner provided for in the Federal Rules of Civil Procedure and the Local Civil Rules of the United States District Court for the Northern District of Indiana, except as otherwise provided by order of the Court. IN R USDCTND CM/ECF(III)(B).

    v. *Using court facilities.* If a local rule so authorizes, a party may use the court's transmission facilities to make service under FRCP 5(b)(2)(E). FRCP 5(b)(3).

  c. *Serving numerous defendants*

    i. *In general.* If an action involves an unusually large number of defendants, the court may, on motion or on its own, order that:

- Defendants' pleadings and replies to them need not be served on other defendants;
- Any crossclaim, counterclaim, avoidance, or affirmative defense in those pleadings and replies to them will be treated as denied or avoided by all other parties; and
- Filing any such pleading and serving it on the plaintiff constitutes notice of the pleading to all parties. FRCP 5(c)(1).

    ii. *Notifying parties.* A copy of every such order must be served on the parties as the court directs. FRCP 5(c)(2).

G. Hearings

1. *Hearings, generally*

  a. *Oral argument.* Due process does not require that oral argument be permitted on a motion and, except as otherwise provided by local rule, the district court has discretion to determine whether it will decide the motion on the papers or hear argument by counsel (and perhaps receive evidence). FPP § 1190; F.D.I.C. v. Deglau, 207 F.3d 153 (3d Cir. 2000).

    i. *Request for oral argument.* A party may request oral argument on a motion by filing and serving a separate document explaining why oral argument is necessary and estimating how long the court should allow for the argument. IN R USDCTND L.R. 7-5(a)(1). Refer to the Documents section of this document for more information.

    ii. *Additional evidence forbidden.* Parties may not present additional evidence at oral argument. IN R USDCTND L.R. 7-5(a)(3).

  b. *Providing a regular schedule for oral hearings.* A court may establish regular times and places for oral hearings on motions. FRCP 78(a).

  c. *Providing for submission on briefs.* By rule or order, the court may provide for submitting and determining motions on briefs, without oral hearings. FRCP 78(b).

  d. *Evidentiary hearings.* A party may request an evidentiary hearing by filing and serving a separate document explaining why the hearing is necessary and estimating how long the court should allow for it. IN R USDCTND L.R. 7-5(b)(2). Refer to the Documents section of this document for more information.

  e. *Court's authority.* The court may: (1) grant or deny a request for oral argument or an evidentiary hearing in its discretion; (2) set oral argument or an evidentiary hearing without a request from a party; or (3) order any oral argument or evidentiary hearing to be held anywhere within the district regardless of where the case will be tried. IN R USDCTND L.R. 7-5(c).

2. *Hearing on FRCP 12 defenses before trial.* If a party so moves, any defense listed in FRCP 12(b)(1) through FRCP 12(b)(7)—whether made in a pleading or by motion—and a motion under FRCP 12(c) must be heard and decided before trial unless the court orders a deferral until trial. FRCP 12(i).

3. *Courtroom and courthouse decorum.* For information on courtroom and courthouse decorum, refer to IN R USDCTND L.R. 83-3.

H. Forms

1. Federal Motion to Dismiss for Lack of Personal Jurisdiction Forms

a. Motion and notice; To dismiss; Defendant not present within state where district court is located. AMJUR PP FEDPRAC § 488.

b. Motion and notice; To dismiss; Lack of jurisdiction over person. AMJUR PP FEDPRAC § 489.

c. Motion and notice; To dismiss; Lack of jurisdiction over person; Ineffective service of process on foreign state. AMJUR PP FEDPRAC § 490.

d. Motion and notice; To dismiss; Lack of jurisdiction over person; Consul not agent of country represented for purpose of receiving service of process. AMJUR PP FEDPRAC § 491.

e. Motion and notice; To dismiss; Lack of jurisdiction over corporate defendant. AMJUR PP FEDPRAC § 492.

f. Motion and notice; To dismiss; International organization immune from suit. AMJUR PP FEDPRAC § 493.

g. Motion and notice; To dismiss; Officer or employee of international organization acting within official capacity; Immune from suit. AMJUR PP FEDPRAC § 494.

h. Motion and notice; To dismiss; Family member of member of foreign mission immune from suit. AMJUR PP FEDPRAC § 495.

i. Motion and notice; To dismiss complaint or, in alternative, to quash service of summons; Lack of jurisdiction over corporate defendant. AMJUR PP FEDPRAC § 496.

j. Motion to dismiss; Lack of personal jurisdiction; No minimum contacts. AMJUR PP FEDPRAC § 497.

k. Affidavit; Of Consul General; In support of motion to dismiss; Consular immunity and lack of authority to act as agent for service of process. AMJUR PP FEDPRAC § 498.

l. Motion to dismiss for lack of personal jurisdiction; Corporate defendant. 2C FEDFORMS § 11:52.

m. Motion to dismiss for lack of personal jurisdiction; By corporate defendant; With citation. 2C FEDFORMS § 11:53.

n. Motion to dismiss for lack of personal jurisdiction; By a foreign corporation. 2C FEDFORMS § 11:54.

o. Motion to dismiss for lack of personal jurisdiction; For insufficiency of service. 2C FEDFORMS § 11:55.

p. Motion to dismiss for lack of personal jurisdiction; Insufficiency of process and insufficiency of service of process. 2C FEDFORMS § 11:56.

q. Motion; To dismiss; Lack of jurisdiction over person of defendant. FEDPROF § 1:910.

r. Opposition; To motion; General form. FEDPROF § 1:750.

s. Affidavit; Supporting or opposing motion. FEDPROF § 1:751.

t. Brief; Supporting or opposing motion. FEDPROF § 1:752.

u. Statement of points and authorities; Opposing motion. FEDPROF § 1:753.

v. Motion to dismiss; Lack of jurisdiction over person of defendant; Short form. FEDPROF § 1:911.

w. Motion to dismiss; Lack of jurisdiction over person of defendant; Accident in foreign country and defendants have no contacts with forum state. FEDPROF § 1:911.50.

x. Motion to dismiss; Lack of jurisdiction over corporate defendant. FEDPROF § 1:912.

y. Motion; To dismiss complaint or, in the alternative, to quash service of summons; Lack of jurisdiction over corporate defendant. FEDPROF § 1:913.

z. Motion to dismiss complaint; General form. GOLDLTGFMS § 20:24.

2. Forms for the Northern District of Indiana

    a. Certificate of service. IN R USDCTND CM/ECF(Form 1).

    b. Notice of manual filing. IN R USDCTND CM/ECF(Form 2).

    c. Declaration that party was unable to file in a timely manner. IN R USDCTND CM/ECF(Form 3).

I. Applicable Rules

1. *Federal rules*

    a. Summons. FRCP 4.

    b. Serving and filing pleadings and other papers. FRCP 5.

    c. Constitutional challenge to a statute; Notice, certification, and intervention. FRCP 5.1.

    d. Privacy protection for filings made with the court. FRCP 5.2.

    e. Computing and extending time; Time for motion papers. FRCP 6.

    f. Pleadings allowed; Form of motions and other papers. FRCP 7.

    g. Disclosure statement. FRCP 7.1.

    h. Form of pleadings. FRCP 10.

    i. Signing pleadings, motions, and other papers; Representations to the court; Sanctions. FRCP 11.

    j. Defenses and objections; When and how presented; Motion for judgment on the pleadings; Consolidating motions; Waiving defenses; Pretrial hearing. FRCP 12.

    k. Taking testimony. FRCP 43.

    l. Hearing motions; Submission on briefs. FRCP 78.

2. *Local rules*

    a. Citation and scope of the rules. IN R USDCTND L.R. 1-1.

    b. Sanctions for formatting errors. IN R USDCTND L.R. 1-3.

    c. Electronic filing required. IN R USDCTND L.R. 5-1.

    d. Constitutional questions. IN R USDCTND L.R. 5.1-1.

    e. Electronic service. IN R USDCTND L.R. 5-2.

    f. Format of papers. IN R USDCTND L.R. 5-4.

    g. Motion practice. IN R USDCTND L.R. 7-1.

    h. Oral arguments and evidentiary hearings. IN R USDCTND L.R. 7-5.

    i. Pretrial procedure. IN R USDCTND L.R. 16-1.

    j. Alternative dispute resolution. IN R USDCTND L.R. 16-6.

    k. Filing of discovery and other materials. IN R USDCTND L.R. 26-2.

    l. Case assignment. IN R USDCTND L.R. 40-1.

    m. Appearance and withdrawal of appearance. IN R USDCTND L.R. 83-8.

    n. CM/ECF civil and criminal user manual. IN R USDCTND CM/ECF.

    o. In re: privacy and public access to civil electronic case files. IN R USDCTND Order 2005-3.

Motions, Oppositions and Replies
Motion for Judgment on the Pleadings

Document Last Updated December 2016

A. Checklist

(I) ❑ Matters to be considered by moving party

   (a) ❑ Required documents

      (1) ❑ Notice of motion and motion

      (2) ❑ Brief

      (3) ❑ Certificate of service

   (b) ❑ Supplemental documents

      (1) ❑ Pleadings

      (2) ❑ Notice of constitutional question

      (3) ❑ Nongovernmental corporate disclosure statement

      (4) ❑ Index of exhibits

      (5) ❑ Request for oral argument

      (6) ❑ Request for evidentiary hearing

      (7) ❑ Copy of authority

      (8) ❑ Proposed order

      (9) ❑ Copy of document with self-addressed envelope

     (10) ❑ Notice of manual filing

     (11) ❑ Courtesy copies

     (12) ❑ Declaration that party was unable to file in a timely manner

   (c) ❑ Timing

      (1) ❑ After the pleadings are closed—but early enough not to delay trial—a party may move for judgment on the pleadings

      (2) ❑ A written motion and notice of the hearing must be served at least fourteen (14) days before the time specified for the hearing, with the following exceptions: (i) when the motion may be heard ex parte; (ii) when the Federal Rules of Civil Procedure set a different time; or (iii) when a court order—which a party may, for good cause, apply for ex parte—sets a different time

      (3) ❑ Any affidavit supporting a motion must be served with the motion

(II) ❑ Matters to be considered by opposing party

   (a) ❑ Required documents

      (1) ❑ Response brief

      (2) ❑ Certificate of service

   (b) ❑ Supplemental documents

      (1) ❑ Pleadings

      (2) ❑ Notice of constitutional question

      (3) ❑ Index of exhibits

      (4) ❑ Request for oral argument

      (5) ❑ Request for evidentiary hearing

    (6)   ❏ Copy of authority

    (7)   ❏ Copy of document with self-addressed envelope

    (8)   ❏ Notice of manual filing

    (9)   ❏ Courtesy copies

    (10) ❏ Declaration that party was unable to file in a timely manner

(c) ❏ Timing

    (1)   ❏ A party must file any response brief to a motion within fourteen (14) days after the motion is served

    (2)   ❏ Except as FRCP 59(c) provides otherwise, any opposing affidavit must be served at least seven (7) days before the hearing, unless the court permits service at another time

B. Timing

1. *Motion for judgment on the pleadings.* After the pleadings are closed—but early enough not to delay trial—a party may move for judgment on the pleadings. FRCP 12(c).

   a. *When pleadings are closed.* FRCP 7(a) provides that the pleadings are closed upon the filing of a complaint and an answer (absent a court-ordered reply), unless a counterclaim, cross-claim, or third-party claim is interposed, in which event the filing of a reply to a counterclaim, cross-claim answer, or third-party answer normally will mark the close of the pleadings. FPP § 1367.

   b. *Timeliness and delay.* Ordinarily, a motion for judgment on the pleadings should be made promptly after the close of the pleadings. Generally, however, a FRCP 12(c) motion is considered timely if it is made early enough not to delay trial or cause prejudice to the non-movant. FPP § 1367.

2. *Timing of motions, generally*

   a. *Motion and notice of hearing.* A written motion and notice of the hearing must be served at least fourteen (14) days before the time specified for the hearing, with the following exceptions:

      i.   When the motion may be heard ex parte;

      ii. When the Federal Rules of Civil Procedure set a different time; or

      iii. When a court order—which a party may, for good cause, apply for ex parte—sets a different time. FRCP 6(c)(1).

   b. *Supporting affidavit.* Any affidavit supporting a motion must be served with the motion. FRCP 6(c)(2).

3. *Timing of opposing papers.* A party must file any response brief to a motion within fourteen (14) days after the motion is served. IN R USDCTND L.R. 7-1(d)(2)(A).

   a. *Opposing affidavit.* Except as FRCP 59(c) provides otherwise, any opposing affidavit must be served at least seven (7) days before the hearing, unless the court permits service at another time. FRCP 6(c)(2).

   b. *Extensions.* The court may extend response- and reply-brief deadlines, but only for good cause. IN R USDCTND L.R. 7-1(d)(3).

   c. *Summary rulings.* The court may rule on a motion summarily if an opposing party does not file a response before the deadline. IN R USDCTND L.R. 7-1(d)(4).

4. *Timing of reply papers.* Where the respondent files an answering affidavit setting up a new matter, the moving party ordinarily is allowed a reasonable time to file a reply affidavit since failure to deny the new matter by affidavit may operate as an admission of its truth. AMJUR MOTIONS § 25.

   a. *Reply brief.* The moving party must file any reply brief within seven (7) days after the response brief is served. IN R USDCTND L.R. 7-1(d)(2)(B).

   b. *Extensions.* The court may extend response- and reply-brief deadlines, but only for good cause. IN R USDCTND L.R. 7-1(d)(3).

5. *Effect of a FRCP 12 motion on the time to serve a responsive pleading.* Unless the court sets a different time, serving a motion under FRCP 12 alters the periods in FRCP 12(a) as follows:

   a. If the court denies the motion or postpones its disposition until trial, the responsive pleading must be served within fourteen (14) days after notice of the court's action; or

   b. If the court grants a motion for a more definite statement, the responsive pleading must be served within fourteen (14) days after the more definite statement is served. FRCP 12(a)(4).

6. *Computation of time*

   a. *Computing time.* FRCP 6 applies in computing any time period specified in the Federal Rules of Civil Procedure, in any local rule or court order, or in any statute that does not specify a method of computing time. FRCP 6(a).

      i. *Period stated in days or a longer unit.* When the period is stated in days or a longer unit of time:
         - Exclude the day of the event that triggers the period;
         - Count every day, including intermediate Saturdays, Sundays, and legal holidays; and
         - Include the last day of the period, but if the last day is a Saturday, Sunday, or legal holiday, the period continues to run until the end of the next day that is not a Saturday, Sunday, or legal holiday. FRCP 6(a)(1).

      ii. *Period stated in hours.* When the period is stated in hours:
         - Begin counting immediately on the occurrence of the event that triggers the period;
         - Count every hour, including hours during intermediate Saturdays, Sundays, and legal holidays; and
         - If the period would end on a Saturday, Sunday, or legal holiday, the period continues to run until the same time on the next day that is not a Saturday, Sunday, or legal holiday. FRCP 6(a)(2).

      iii. *Inaccessibility of the clerk's office.* Unless the court orders otherwise, if the clerk's office is inaccessible:
         - On the last day for filing under FRCP 6(a)(1), then the time for filing is extended to the first accessible day that is not a Saturday, Sunday, or legal holiday; or
         - During the last hour for filing under FRCP 6(a)(2), then the time for filing is extended to the same time on the first accessible day that is not a Saturday, Sunday, or legal holiday. FRCP 6(a)(3).

      iv. *"Last day" defined.* Unless a different time is set by a statute, local rule, or court order, the last day ends:
         - For electronic filing, at midnight in the court's time zone; and
         - For filing by other means, when the clerk's office is scheduled to close. FRCP 6(a)(4).

      v. *"Next day" defined.* The "next day" is determined by continuing to count forward when the period is measured after an event and backward when measured before an event. FRCP 6(a)(5).

      vi. *"Legal holiday" defined.* "Legal holiday" means:
         - The day set aside by statute for observing New Year's Day, Martin Luther King Jr.'s Birthday, Washington's Birthday, Memorial Day, Independence Day, Labor Day, Columbus Day, Veterans' Day, Thanksgiving Day, or Christmas Day;
         - Any day declared a holiday by the President or Congress; and
         - For periods that are measured after an event, any other day declared a holiday by the state where the district court is located. FRCP 6(a)(6).

   b. *Computation of electronic filing deadlines.* Filing documents electronically does not alter any filing deadlines or any time computation pursuant to FRCP 6. The counties of Lake, Porter, LaPorte, Pulaski and Starke are located in the Central time zone and the remaining counties in the Northern

District of Indiana are located in the Eastern time zone. Nevertheless, all electronic transmissions of documents must be completed (i.e., received completely by the clerk's office) prior to midnight Eastern Time, (South Bend/Fort Wayne/Lafayette time) in order to be considered timely filed that day, regardless of the local time in the division where the case is pending. Although documents can be filed electronically twenty-four (24) hours a day, filers are strongly encouraged to file all documents during hours when the CM/ECF Help Line is available, from 9:00 a.m. to 4:00 p.m. local time. IN R USDCTND CM/ECF(II)(I).

    i.   *Technical failures.* If the attorney is unable to file a document in a timely manner due to technical difficulties in the user's system, the attorney must file a document with the court as soon as possible notifying the court of the inability to file the document. A sample document entitled Declaration that Party was Unable to File in a Timely Manner Due to Technical Difficulties is attached hereto as Form 5. IN R USDCTND CM/ECF(VI)(B). [Editor's note: the reference to Form 5 is likely meant to be a reference to Form 3 (IN R USDCTND CM/ECF(Form 3)].

  c. *Extending time*

    i.   *In general.* When an act may or must be done within a specified time, the court may, for good cause, extend the time:

- With or without motion or notice if the court acts, or if a request is made, before the original time or its extension expires; or

- On motion made after the time has expired if the party failed to act because of excusable neglect. FRCP 6(b)(1).

    ii. *Exceptions.* A court must not extend the time to act under FRCP 50(b), FRCP 50(d), FRCP 52(b), FRCP 59(b), FRCP 59(d), FRCP 59(e), and FRCP 60(b). FRCP 6(b)(2).

    iii. Refer to the United States District Court for the Northern District of Indiana KeyRules Motion for Continuance/Extension of Time document for more information on extending time.

  d. *Additional time after certain kinds of service.* When a party may or must act within a specified time after being served and service is made under FRCP 5(b)(2)(C) (mail), FRCP 5(b)(2)(D) (leaving with the clerk), or FRCP 5(b)(2)(F) (other means consented to), three (3) days are added after the period would otherwise expire under FRCP 6(a). FRCP 6(d).

C. General Requirements

1. *Motions, generally*

  a. *Requirements.* A request for a court order must be made by motion. The motion must:

    i.   Be in writing unless made during a hearing or trial;

    ii. State with particularity the grounds for seeking the order; and

    iii. State the relief sought. FRCP 7(b)(1).

  b. *Notice of motion.* A party interested in resisting the relief sought by a motion has a right to notice thereof, and an opportunity to be heard. AMJUR MOTIONS § 12.

    i.   In addition to statutory or court rule provisions requiring notice of a motion—the purpose of such a notice requirement having been said to be to prevent a party from being prejudicially surprised by a motion—principles of natural justice dictate that an adverse party generally must be given notice that a motion will be presented to the court. AMJUR MOTIONS § 12.

    ii. "Notice," in this regard, means reasonable notice, including a meaningful opportunity to prepare and to defend against allegations of a motion. AMJUR MOTIONS § 12.

  c. *Writing requirement.* The writing requirement is intended to insure that the adverse parties are informed and have a record of both the motion's pendency and the grounds on which the movant seeks an order. FPP § 1191; Feldberg v. Quechee Lakes Corp., 463 F.3d 195 (2d Cir. 2006).

    i.   It is sufficient "if the motion is stated in a written notice of the hearing of the motion." FPP § 1191.

d. *Particularity requirement.* The particularity requirement insures that the opposing parties will have notice of their opponent's contentions. FEDPROC § 62:364; Goodman v. 1973 26 Foot Trojan Vessel, Arkansas Registration No. AR1439SN, 859 F.2d 71, 12 Fed.R.Serv.3d 645 (8th Cir. 1988). That requirement ensures that notice of the basis for the motion is provided to the court and to the opposing party so as to avoid prejudice, provide the opponent with a meaningful opportunity to respond, and provide the court with enough information to process the motion correctly. FEDPROC § 62:364; Andreas v. Volkswagen of America, Inc., 336 F.3d 789, 56 Fed.R.Serv.3d 6 (8th Cir. 2003).

    i. Reasonable specification of the grounds for a motion is sufficient. However, where a movant fails to state even one ground for granting the motion in question, the movant has failed to meet the minimal standard of "reasonable specification." FEDPROC § 62:364; Martinez v. Trainor, 556 F.2d 818, 23 Fed.R.Serv.2d 403 (7th Cir. 1977).

    ii. The court may excuse the failure to comply with the particularity requirement if it is inadvertent, and where no prejudice is shown by the opposing party. FEDPROC § 62:364.

e. *Motions must be filed separately.* Motions must be filed separately, but alternative motions may be filed in a single paper if each is named in the title following the caption. IN R USDCTND L.R. 7-1(a).

2. *Motion for judgment on the pleadings.* After the pleadings are closed—but early enough not to delay trial—a party may move for judgment on the pleadings. FRCP 12(c).

a. *Relationship to other motions*

    i. *Common law demurrer.* The motion for judgment on the pleadings under FRCP 12(c) has its historical roots in common law practice, which permitted either party, at any point in the proceeding, to demur to his opponent's pleading and secure a dismissal or final judgment on the basis of the pleadings. FPP § 1367.

- The common law demurrer could be used to search the record and raise procedural defects, or it could be employed to resolve the substantive merits of the controversy as disclosed on the face of the pleadings. FPP § 1367.

- In contrast to the common law practice, the FRCP 12(c) judgment on the pleadings procedure primarily is addressed to the latter function of disposing of cases on the basis of the underlying substantive merits of the parties' claims and defenses as they are revealed in the formal pleadings. FPP § 1367. The purpose of FRCP 12(c) is to save time and expense in cases where the ultimate issues of fact are not in dispute, and to prevent the piecemeal process of judicial determination which prevailed under the old common-law practice. FEDPROC § 62:566.

    ii. *Motions to dismiss.* While FRCP 12(b) motions to dismiss and FRCP 12(c) motions for judgment on the pleadings are to some extent merely interchangeable weapons in a party's arsenal of pretrial challenges, there are differences in the scope and effect of the two motions. A FRCP 12(b) motion to dismiss is directed solely toward the defects of the plaintiff's claim for relief, without concern for the merits of the controversy, while a FRCP 12(c) motion for judgment on the pleadings at least theoretically requires some scrutiny of the merits of the controversy. FEDPROC § 62:568.

    iii. *Motion to strike.* The FRCP 12(c) motion also should be contrasted with the motion to strike under FRCP 12(f). The latter motion permits either party to strike redundant, immaterial, impertinent, or scandalous matter from an adversary's pleading and may be used to challenge the sufficiency of defenses asserted by that adversary. The motion serves as a pruning device to eliminate objectionable matter from an opponent's pleadings and, unlike the FRCP 12(c) procedure, it is not directed at gaining a final judgment on the merits, although a FRCP 12(f) motion that succeeds in eliminating the defenses to the action may have that purpose and, in some cases, may have that effect. FPP § 1369.

- If a plaintiff seeks to dispute the legal sufficiency of fewer than all of the defenses raised in the defendant's pleading, he should proceed under FRCP 12(f) rather than under FRCP 12(c) because the latter leads to the entry of a judgment. FPP § 1369.

    iv. *Motion for summary judgment.* In most circumstances a party will find it preferable to proceed under FRCP 56 rather than FRCP 12(c) for a variety of reasons. For example, the summary judgment procedure is available when the defendant fails to file an answer, whereas technically no relief would be available under FRCP 12(c) because the pleadings have not been closed. If a party believes that it will be necessary to introduce evidence outside the formal pleadings in order to demonstrate that no material issue of fact exists and he is clearly entitled to judgment, it is advisable to proceed directly under FRCP 56 rather than taking the circuitous route through FRCP 12(c). Moreover, the FRCP 12(c) path may present certain risks because the court, in its discretion, may refuse to permit the introduction of matters beyond the pleadings and insist on treating the motion as one under FRCP 12(c) or apply the general motion time period set out in FRCP 6(d), rather than the special time provision in FRCP 56. FPP § 1369.

b. *Bringing a FRCP 12(c) motion.* As numerous judicial opinions make clear, a FRCP 12(c) motion is designed to provide a means of disposing of cases when the material facts are not in dispute between the parties and a judgment on the merits can be achieved by focusing on the content of the competing pleadings, exhibits thereto, matters incorporated by reference in the pleadings, whatever is central or integral to the claim for relief or defense, and any facts of which the district court will take judicial notice. FPP § 1367; DiCarlo v. St. Mary Hosp., 530 F.3d 255 (3d Cir. 2008); Buddy Bean Lumber Co. v. Axis Surplus Ins. Co., 715 F.3d 695, 697 (8th Cir. 2013).

  i. The motion for a judgment on the pleadings only has utility when all material allegations of fact are admitted or not controverted in the pleadings and only questions of law remain to be decided by the district court. FPP § 1367; Stafford v. Jewelers Mut. Ins. Co., 554 Fed. Appx. 360, 370 (6th Cir. 2014).

c. *Partial judgment on the pleadings.* Although not provided for by FRCP 12(c), a party may properly move for partial judgment on the pleadings to further the policy goal of efficient resolution of actions when there are no material facts in dispute. This conclusion has been said to be buttressed by FRCP 56(a), which provides that a party may move for summary judgment "on all or part of the claim." FEDPROC § 62:571.

d. *Granting of a motion for judgment on the pleadings.* The federal courts have followed a fairly restrictive standard in ruling on motions for judgment on the pleadings. FPP § 1368. A motion for judgment on the pleadings is a motion for judgment on the merits, and should only be granted if no material issue of fact remains to be resolved and the movant establishes entitlement to judgment as a matter of law. FEDPROC § 62:569; Great Plains Trust Co. v. Morgan Stanley Dean Witter & Co., 313 F.3d 305 (5th Cir. 2002); Sikirica v. Nationwide Ins. Co., 416 F.3d 214 (3d Cir. 2005). A motion for a judgment on the pleadings must be sustained where the undisputed facts appearing in the pleadings, supplemented by any facts of which the court will take judicial notice, show that no relief can be granted. Judgment on the pleadings is not appropriate where the answer raises issues of fact which, if proved, would defeat recovery. FEDPROC § 62:569.

  i. A motion for judgment on the pleadings admits, for purposes of the motion, the truth of all well-pleaded facts in the pleadings of the opposing party, together with all fair inferences to be drawn therefrom, even where the defendant asserts, in the FRCP 12(c) motion, a FRCP 12(b)(6) defense of failure to state a claim upon which relief can be granted. FEDPROC § 62:570; In re World Trade Center Disaster Site Litigation, 521 F.3d 169 (2d Cir. 2008); Massachusetts Nurses Ass'n v. North Adams Regional Hosp., 467 F.3d 27 (1st Cir. 2006). However, all allegations of the moving party which have been denied are taken as false. FEDPROC § 62:570; Volvo Const. Equipment North America, Inc. v. CLM Equipment Company, Inc., 386 F.3d 581 (4th Cir. 2004). In considering a motion for judgment on the pleadings, the trial court is thus required to view the facts presented in the pleadings and inferences to be drawn therefrom in the light most favorable to the nonmoving party. In this fashion the courts hope to insure that the rights of the nonmoving party are decided as fully and fairly on a FRCP 12(c) motion as if there had been a trial. FEDPROC § 62:570.

  ii. On a motion for judgment on the pleadings, the court may consider facts upon the basis of judicial notice. FEDPROC § 62:570; R.G. Financial Corp. v. Vergara-Nunez, 446 F.3d 178 (1st Cir. 2006). However, a motion for judgment on the pleadings does not admit conclusions of law or unwarranted factual inferences. FEDPROC § 62:570; JPMorgan Chase Bank, N.A. v. Winget, 510 F.3d 577 (6th Cir. 2007).

e. *Joining motions*

    i. *Right to join.* A motion under FRCP 12 may be joined with any other motion allowed by FRCP 12. FRCP 12(g)(1).

    ii. *Limitation on further motions.* Except as provided in FRCP 12(h)(2) or FRCP 12(h)(3), a party that makes a motion under FRCP 12 must not make another motion under FRCP 12 raising a defense or objection that was available to the party but omitted from its earlier motion. FRCP 12(g)(2).

f. *Waiving and preserving certain defenses*

    i. *When some are waived.* A party waives any defense listed in FRCP 12(b)(2) through FRCP 12(b)(5) by:

- Omitting it from a motion in the circumstances described in FRCP 12(g)(2); or
- Failing to either: (1) make it by motion under FRCP 12; or (2) include it in a responsive pleading or in an amendment allowed by FRCP 15(a)(1) as a matter of course. FRCP 12(h)(1).

    ii. *When to raise others.* Failure to state a claim upon which relief can be granted, to join a person required by FRCP 19(b), or to state a legal defense to a claim may be raised:

- In any pleading allowed or ordered under FRCP 7(a);
- By a motion under FRCP 12(c); or
- At trial. FRCP 12(h)(2).

    iii. *Lack of subject matter jurisdiction.* If the court determines at any time that it lacks subject-matter jurisdiction, the court must dismiss the action. FRCP 12(h)(3).

3. *Opposing papers.* The Federal Rules of Civil Procedure do not require any formal answer, return, or reply to a motion, except where the Federal Rules of Civil Procedure or local rules may require affidavits, memoranda, or other papers to be filed in opposition to a motion. Such papers are simply to apprise the court of such opposition and the grounds of that opposition. FEDPROC § 62:359.

a. *Effect of failure to respond to motion.* Although in the absence of statutory provision or court rule, a motion ordinarily does not require a written answer, when a party files a motion and the opposing party fails to respond, the court may construe such failure to respond as nonopposition to the motion or an admission that the motion was meritorious, may take the facts alleged in the motion as true—the rule in some jurisdictions being that the failure to respond to a fact set forth in a motion is deemed an admission—and may grant the motion if the relief requested appears to be justified. AMJUR MOTIONS § 28.

b. *Assent or no opposition not determinative.* However, a motion will not be granted automatically simply because an "assent" or a notation of "no opposition" has been filed; federal judges frequently deny motions that have been assented to when it is thought that justice so dictates. FPP § 1190.

c. *Responsive pleading inappropriate as response to motion.* An attempt to answer or oppose a motion with a responsive pleading usually is not appropriate. FPP § 1190.

4. *Reply papers.* A moving party may be required or permitted to prepare papers in addition to his original motion papers. AMJUR MOTIONS § 25. Papers answering or replying to opposing papers may be appropriate, in the interests of justice, where it appears there is a substantial reason for allowing a reply. Thus, a court may accept reply papers where a party demonstrates that the papers to which it seeks to file a reply raise new issues that are material to the disposition of the question before the court, or where the court determines, sua sponte, that it wishes further briefing of an issue raised in those papers and orders the submission of additional papers. FEDPROC § 62:360.

a. *Function of reply papers.* The function of a reply affidavit is to answer the arguments made in opposition to the position taken by the movant and not to permit the movant to introduce new arguments in support of the motion. AMJUR MOTIONS § 25.

b. *Issues raised for the first time in a reply document.* However, the view has been followed in some jurisdictions, that as a matter of judicial economy, where there is no prejudice and where the issues could be raised simply by filing a motion to dismiss, the trial court has discretion to consider arguments raised for the first time in a reply memorandum, and that a trial court may grant a motion to strike issues raised for the first time in a reply memorandum. AMJUR MOTIONS § 26.

5. *Appearances.* Attorneys not representing the United States or its agencies must file an appearance when they represent (either in person or by filing a paper) a party. IN R USDCTND L.R. 83-8(a). For more information, refer to IN R USDCTND L.R. 83-8.

6. *Notice of related action.* A party must file a notice of related action as soon as it appears that the party's case and another pending case: (1) arise out of the same transaction or occurrence; (2) involve the same property; or (3) involve the validity or infringement of the same patent, trademark, or copyright. IN R USDCTND L.R. 40-1(d). For more information, refer to IN R USDCTND L.R. 40-1.

7. *Alternative dispute resolution (ADR).* After they confer as required by FRCP 26(f), the parties must advise the court which, if any, alternative-dispute-resolution processes they expect to pursue and when they expect to undertake the process. IN R USDCTND L.R. 16-6(a). For more information on alternative dispute resolution (ADR), refer to IN R USDCTND L.R. 16-6 and IN R USDCTND Order 2003-21.

8. *Settlement or resolution.* The parties must immediately notify the court if they reasonably expect to settle the case or resolve a pending motion. IN R USDCTND L.R. 16-1(g).

9. *Modification or suspension of rules.* The court may, on its own motion or at the request of a party, suspend or modify any rule in a particular case in the interest of justice. IN R USDCTND L.R. 1-1(c).

D. Documents

1. *Documents for moving party*

   a. *Required documents*

      i. *Notice of motion and motion.* The party must not specify a hearing date in the notice of a motion or petition unless the court or the clerk has authorized it. IN R USDCTND L.R. 7-5(b)(2). Refer to the General Requirements section of this document for information on the notice of motion and motion.

      ii. *Brief.* Parties must file a supporting brief with any motion under: FRCP 12. IN R USDCTND L.R. 7-1(b)(1). Refer to the Format section of this document for the format of briefs.

      iii. *Certificate of service.* FRCP 5(d) requires that the person making service under FRCP 5 certify that service has been effected. FRCP 5(Advisory Committee Notes). Having such information on file may be useful for many purposes, including proof of service if an issue arises concerning the effectiveness of the service. FRCP 5(Advisory Committee Notes).

         • *Certificate of service for electronically-filed documents.* A Certificate of Service is still a requirement when filing documents electronically. A sample Certificate of Service is attached as Form 1 (IN R USDCTND CM/ECF(Form 1)). IN R USDCTND CM/ECF(II)(H).

   b. *Supplemental documents*

      i. *Pleadings.* In considering a motion for judgment on the pleadings, the trial court is. . .required to view the facts presented in the pleadings and inferences to be drawn therefrom in the light most favorable to the nonmoving party. FEDPROC § 62:570.

         • *Motion treated as one for summary judgment.* If, on a motion under FRCP 12(b)(6) or FRCP 12(c), matters outside the pleadings are presented to and not excluded by the court, the motion must be treated as one for summary judgment under FRCP 56. All parties must be given a reasonable opportunity to present all the material that is pertinent to the motion. FRCP 12(d).

      ii. *Notice of constitutional question.* A party that files a pleading, written motion, or other paper drawing into question the constitutionality of a federal or state statute must promptly:

         • *File notice.* File a notice of constitutional question stating the question and identifying the paper that raises it, if: (1) a federal statute is questioned and the parties do not include the United States, one of its agencies, or one of its officers or employees in an official capacity;

or (2) a state statute is questioned and the parties do not include the state, one of its agencies, or one of its officers or employees in an official capacity; and

- *Serve notice.* Serve the notice and paper on the Attorney General of the United States if a federal statute is questioned—or on the state attorney general if a state statute is questioned—either by certified or registered mail or by sending it to an electronic address designated by the attorney general for this purpose. FRCP 5.1(a).

- *When to file the notice.* A party required to file a notice of constitutional question under FRCP 5.1 must do so by the later of: (1) the day the parties tender their proposed case-management plan (if one is required); or (2) 21 days after filing the pleading, written motion, or other paper questioning the constitutionality of a federal or state statute. IN R USDCTND L.R. 5.1-1(a).

- *Service on government officials.* The party must also serve the notice and the pleading, written motion, or other paper questioning the constitutionality of a federal or state statute on: (1) the Attorney General of the United States and the United States Attorney for the Northern District of Indiana, if a federal statute is challenged; or (2) the Attorney General for the state if a state statute is challenged. IN R USDCTND L.R. 5.1-1(b). Service required under IN R USDCTND L.R. 5.1-1(b) may be made either by certified or registered mail or by emailing it to an address designated by those officials for this purpose. IN R USDCTND L.R. 5.1-1(c).

- *No forfeiture.* A party's failure to file and serve the notice, or the court's failure to certify, does not forfeit a constitutional claim or defense that is otherwise timely asserted. FRCP 5.1(d).

iii. *Nongovernmental corporate disclosure statement*

- *Contents.* A nongovernmental corporate party must file two (2) copies of a disclosure statement that: (1) identifies any parent corporation and any publicly held corporation owning ten percent (10%) or more of its stock; or (2) states that there is no such corporation. FRCP 7.1(a).

- *Time to file; Supplemental filing.* A party must: (1) file the disclosure statement with its first appearance, pleading, petition, motion, response, or other request addressed to the court; and (2) promptly file a supplemental statement if any required information changes. FRCP 7.1(b).

iv. *Index of exhibits.* Any pleading, motion, brief, affidavit, notice, or proposed order, whether filed electronically or by delivering it to the clerk, must: include a separate index identifying and briefly describing each exhibit if there are more than four (4) exhibits. IN R USDCTND L.R. 5-4(a)(8).

v. *Request for oral argument.* A party may request oral argument on a motion by filing and serving a separate document explaining why oral argument is necessary and estimating how long the court should allow for the argument. IN R USDCTND L.R. 7-5(a)(1). The request must be filed and served with the party's supporting brief, response brief, or reply brief. IN R USDCTND L.R. 7-5(a)(2).

vi. *Request for evidentiary hearing.* A party may request an evidentiary hearing by filing and serving a separate document explaining why the hearing is necessary and estimating how long the court should allow for it. IN R USDCTND L.R. 7-5(b)(1).

vii. *Copy of authority.* A copy of any decision, statute, or regulation cited in a motion or brief must be attached to the paper if—and only if—it is not available on Westlaw or Lexis. But if a copy of a decision, statute, or regulation is only available electronically, a party must provide it to the court or another party upon request. IN R USDCTND L.R. 7-1(f).

viii. *Proposed order.* Parties filing a paper that requires the judge or clerk to enter a routine or uncontested order must include a suitable form of order. IN R USDCTND L.R. 5-4(c).

- Proposed orders shall not be filed electronically either as a separate document or as an

attachment to the main pleading or other document. Instead, all proposed orders must be e-mailed to the chambers of the appropriate judicial officer for the case. The proposed order must be in WordPerfect Format or Rich Text Format (RTF). Proposed orders should be attached to an e-mail and sent to the appropriate judicial officer at the address listed in IN R USDCTND CM/ECF(II)(F). The subject line of the email message should indicate the case title, cause number and document number of the motion, e.g., Smith v. Jones 1:02-cv-1234, motion# ___. IN R USDCTND CM/ECF(II)(F).

ix. *Copy of document with self-addressed envelope.* A party who wants a file-stamped copy of a paper must include with the filing an additional copy of the paper and a self-addressed envelope with adequate postage. IN R USDCTND L.R. 5-4(b)(6).

x. *Notice of manual filing.* However, if that is not physically possible, counsel shall electronically file a .pdf document titled Notice of Manual Filing as a notation on the docket sheet that filings are being held in the clerk's office in paper. A sample Notice of Manual Filing is attached as Form 2 (IN R USDCTND CM/ECF(Form 2)). IN R USDCTND CM/ECF(III)(A)(1).

xi. *Courtesy copies.* If documents are filed in paper format, counsel must provide an original for the clerk's office, a copy for the judge and a copy must be served on all parties in the case. IN R USDCTND CM/ECF(III)(A)(1).

xii. *Declaration that party was unable to file in a timely manner.* If the attorney is unable to file a document in a timely manner due to technical difficulties in the user's system, the attorney must file a document with the court as soon as possible notifying the court of the inability to file the document. A sample document entitled Declaration that Party was Unable to File in a Timely Manner Due to Technical Difficulties is attached hereto as Form 5. IN R USDCTND CM/ECF(VI)(B). [Editor's note: the reference to Form 5 is likely meant to be a reference to Form 3 (IN R USDCTND CM/ECF(Form 3)].

2. *Documents for opposing party*

  a. *Required documents*

    i. *Response brief.* Refer to the Format section of this document for the format of briefs. Refer to the General Requirements section of this document for information on the opposing papers.

    ii. *Certificate of service.* FRCP 5(d) requires that the person making service under FRCP 5 certify that service has been effected. FRCP 5(Advisory Committee Notes). Having such information on file may be useful for many purposes, including proof of service if an issue arises concerning the effectiveness of the service. FRCP 5(Advisory Committee Notes).

      • *Certificate of service for electronically-filed documents.* A Certificate of Service is still a requirement when filing documents electronically. A sample Certificate of Service is attached as Form 1 (IN R USDCTND CM/ECF(Form 1)). IN R USDCTND CM/ECF(II)(H).

  b. *Supplemental documents*

    i. *Pleadings.* In considering a motion for judgment on the pleadings, the trial court is. . .required to view the facts presented in the pleadings and inferences to be drawn therefrom in the light most favorable to the nonmoving party. FEDPROC § 62:570.

      • *Motion treated as one for summary judgment.* If, on a motion under FRCP 12(b)(6) or FRCP 12(c), matters outside the pleadings are presented to and not excluded by the court, the motion must be treated as one for summary judgment under FRCP 56. All parties must be given a reasonable opportunity to present all the material that is pertinent to the motion. FRCP 12(d).

    ii. *Notice of constitutional question.* A party that files a pleading, written motion, or other paper drawing into question the constitutionality of a federal or state statute must promptly:

      • *File notice.* File a notice of constitutional question stating the question and identifying the paper that raises it, if: (1) a federal statute is questioned and the parties do not include the United States, one of its agencies, or one of its officers or employees in an official capacity;

or (2) a state statute is questioned and the parties do not include the state, one of its agencies, or one of its officers or employees in an official capacity; and

- *Serve notice.* Serve the notice and paper on the Attorney General of the United States if a federal statute is questioned—or on the state attorney general if a state statute is questioned—either by certified or registered mail or by sending it to an electronic address designated by the attorney general for this purpose. FRCP 5.1(a).

- *When to file the notice.* A party required to file a notice of constitutional question under FRCP 5.1 must do so by the later of: (1) the day the parties tender their proposed case-management plan (if one is required); or (2) 21 days after filing the pleading, written motion, or other paper questioning the constitutionality of a federal or state statute. IN R USDCTND L.R. 5.1-1(a).

- *Service on government officials.* The party must also serve the notice and the pleading, written motion, or other paper questioning the constitutionality of a federal or state statute on: (1) the Attorney General of the United States and the United States Attorney for the Northern District of Indiana, if a federal statute is challenged; or (2) the Attorney General for the state if a state statute is challenged. IN R USDCTND L.R. 5.1-1(b). Service required under IN R USDCTND L.R. 5.1-1(b) may be made either by certified or registered mail or by emailing it to an address designated by those officials for this purpose. IN R USDCTND L.R. 5.1-1(c).

- *No forfeiture.* A party's failure to file and serve the notice, or the court's failure to certify, does not forfeit a constitutional claim or defense that is otherwise timely asserted. FRCP 5.1(d).

iii. *Index of exhibits.* Any pleading, motion, brief, affidavit, notice, or proposed order, whether filed electronically or by delivering it to the clerk, must: include a separate index identifying and briefly describing each exhibit if there are more than four (4) exhibits. IN R USDCTND L.R. 5-4(a)(8).

iv. *Request for oral argument.* A party may request oral argument on a motion by filing and serving a separate document explaining why oral argument is necessary and estimating how long the court should allow for the argument. IN R USDCTND L.R. 7-5(a)(1). The request must be filed and served with the party's supporting brief, response brief, or reply brief. IN R USDCTND L.R. 7-5(a)(2).

v. *Request for evidentiary hearing.* A party may request an evidentiary hearing by filing and serving a separate document explaining why the hearing is necessary and estimating how long the court should allow for it. IN R USDCTND L.R. 7-5(b)(1).

vi. *Copy of authority.* A copy of any decision, statute, or regulation cited in a motion or brief must be attached to the paper if—and only if—it is not available on Westlaw or Lexis. But if a copy of a decision, statute, or regulation is only available electronically, a party must provide it to the court or another party upon request. IN R USDCTND L.R. 7-1(f).

vii. *Copy of document with self-addressed envelope.* A party who wants a file-stamped copy of a paper must include with the filing an additional copy of the paper and a self-addressed envelope with adequate postage. IN R USDCTND L.R. 5-4(b)(6).

viii. *Notice of manual filing.* However, if that is not physically possible, counsel shall electronically file a .pdf document titled Notice of Manual Filing as a notation on the docket sheet that filings are being held in the clerk's office in paper. A sample Notice of Manual Filing is attached as Form 2 (IN R USDCTND CM/ECF(Form 2)). IN R USDCTND CM/ECF(III)(A)(1).

ix. *Courtesy copies.* If documents are filed in paper format, counsel must provide an original for the clerk's office, a copy for the judge and a copy must be served on all parties in the case. IN R USDCTND CM/ECF(III)(A)(1).

x. *Declaration that party was unable to file in a timely manner.* If the attorney is unable to file a document in a timely manner due to technical difficulties in the user's system, the attorney must file a document with the court as soon as possible notifying the court of the inability to file the document. A sample document entitled Declaration that Party was Unable to File in a Timely Manner Due to Technical Difficulties is attached hereto as Form 5. IN R USDCTND CM/ECF(VI)(B). [Editor's note: the reference to Form 5 is likely meant to be a reference to Form 3 (IN R USDCTND CM/ECF(Form 3)].

E. Format

1. *Form of documents.* The rules governing captions and other matters of form in pleadings apply to motions and other papers. FRCP 7(b)(2).

   a. *Paper.* Any pleading, motion, brief, affidavit, notice, or proposed order, whether filed electronically or by delivering it to the clerk, must: use eight and one-half by eleven (8-1/2 x 11) inch pages. IN R USDCTND L.R. 5-4(a)(2).

      i. *Manual filings.* Papers delivered to the clerk for filing must: be flat, unfolded, and on good-quality, white paper. IN R USDCTND L.R. 5-4(b)(1)(A).

         • *Covers or backing.* Papers delivered to the clerk for filing must: not have a cover or a back. IN R USDCTND L.R. 5-4(b)(1)(B).

         • *Recycled paper.* The court encourages using recycled paper. IN R USDCTND L.R. 5-4(b)(7).

   b. *Margins.* Any pleading, motion, brief, affidavit, notice, or proposed order, whether filed electronically or by delivering it to the clerk, must: have at least one (1) inch margins. IN R USDCTND L.R. 5-4(a)(3).

   c. *Spacing.* Any pleading, motion, brief, affidavit, notice, or proposed order, whether filed electronically or by delivering it to the clerk, must: be double spaced (except for headings, footnotes, and quoted material). IN R USDCTND L.R. 5-4(a)(5).

   d. *Text.* Any pleading, motion, brief, affidavit, notice, or proposed order, whether filed electronically or by delivering it to the clerk, must: be plainly typewritten, printed, or prepared by a clearly legible copying process. IN R USDCTND L.R. 5-4(a)(1).

      i. Any pleading, motion, brief, affidavit, notice, or proposed order, whether filed electronically or by delivering it to the clerk, must: use at least twelve (12) point type in the body and at least ten (10) point type in footnotes. IN R USDCTND L.R. 5-4(a)(4).

   e. *Page numbering.* Any pleading, motion, brief, affidavit, notice, or proposed order, whether filed electronically or by delivering it to the clerk, must: have consecutively numbered pages. IN R USDCTND L.R. 5-4(a)(6).

   f. *Caption; Names of parties.* Every pleading must have a caption with the court's name, a title, a file number, and a FRCP 7(a) designation. The title of the complaint must name all the parties; the title of other pleadings, after naming the first party on each side, may refer generally to other parties. FRCP 10(a). Any pleading, motion, brief, affidavit, notice, or proposed order, whether filed electronically or by delivering it to the clerk, must: include a title on the first page. IN R USDCTND L.R. 5-4(a)(7).

      i. *Alternative motions.* Motions must be filed separately, but alternative motions may be filed in a single paper if each is named in the title following the caption. IN R USDCTND L.R. 7-1(a).

   g. *Filer's information.* Any pleading, motion, brief, affidavit, notice, or proposed order, whether filed electronically or by delivering it to the clerk, must: except in proposed orders and affidavits, include the filer's name, address, telephone number, fax number (where available), and e-mail address (where available). IN R USDCTND L.R. 5-4(a)(9).

   h. *Paragraphs; Separate statements.* A party must state its claims or defenses in numbered paragraphs, each limited as far as practicable to a single set of circumstances. A later pleading may refer by number to a paragraph in an earlier pleading. If doing so would promote clarity, each claim founded on a separate transaction or occurrence—and each defense other than a denial—must be stated in a separate count or defense. FRCP 10(b).

   i. *Adoption by reference; Exhibits.* A statement in a pleading may be adopted by reference elsewhere in the same pleading or in any other pleading or motion. A copy of a written instrument that is an exhibit to a pleading is a part of the pleading for all purposes. FRCP 10(c).

j. *Citation of local rules.* The Local Civil Rules of the United States District Court for the Northern District of Indiana may be cited as "N.D. Ind. L.R." IN R USDCTND L.R. 1-1(a)(1).

k. *Acceptance by the clerk.* The clerk must not refuse to file a paper solely because it is not in the form prescribed by the Federal Rules of Civil Procedure or by a local rule or practice. FRCP 5(d)(4).

   i. *Sanctions for formatting errors; Non-compliance.* If a person files a paper that does not comply with the rules governing the format of papers filed with the court, the court may: (1) strike the paper from the record; or (2) fine the person up to one thousand dollars ($1,000). IN R USDCTND L.R. 1-3(a).

      • *Notice.* Before sanctioning a person under IN R USDCTND L.R. 1-3(a)(2), the court must: (1) notify the person that the paper is noncompliant; and (2) give the person the opportunity either to be heard or to revise the paper. IN R USDCTND L.R. 1-3(b).

2. *Form of electronic documents.* Electronically filed documents must meet the same requirements of format and page limits as documents "conventionally filed" (as defined in IN R USDCTND CM/ECF(III)(A)) pursuant to the Federal Rules of Civil Procedure and the Local Civil Rules of the United States District Court for the Northern District of Indiana. IN R USDCTND CM/ECF(II)(A)(2).

a. *PDF format required.* Documents filed in the CM/ECF must be in .pdf format. A document created with almost any word-processing program can be converted to .pdf format. The .pdf program in effect takes a picture of the original document and allows anyone to open the converted document across a broad range of hardware and software, with layout, format, links, and images intact. IN R USDCTND CM/ECF(FN2).

b. *Title of documents.* The person electronically filing a pleading or other document will be responsible for designating a title for the pleading or other document by using one of the categories contained in the events listed in the CM/ECF Menu. IN R USDCTND CM/ECF(II)(G).

c. *Combining documents.* All documents which form part of a single pleading and which are being filed at the same time and by the same party may be electronically filed together under one document number, e.g., the motion and a supporting affidavit, with the exception of memoranda in support. Memoranda in support shall be electronically filed separately and shown as a related document to the motion. IN R USDCTND CM/ECF(II)(A)(4).

d. *Exhibits and attachments.* Filing users must submit in electronic form all documents referenced as exhibits or attachments, unless the court permits conventional filing. A filing user must submit as exhibits or attachments only those excerpts of the referenced documents that are directly germane to the matter under consideration by the court. Excerpted material must be clearly and prominently identified as such. Filing users who file excerpts of documents as exhibits or attachments do so without prejudice to their right to timely file additional excerpts or the complete document. Responding parties may timely file additional excerpts or the complete document that they believe are directly germane. The court may require parties to file additional excerpts or the complete document. IN R USDCTND CM/ECF(II)(A)(6).

e. *Hyperlinks.* Electronically filed documents may contain hyperlink references to an external document as a convenient mechanism for accessing material cited in the document. A hyperlink reference is neither validated for content nor considered a part of the court's records. The court neither endorses the product or organization at the destination of a hyperlink reference, nor does the court exercise any responsibility over the content at the destination. In order to preserve the integrity of the court record, attorneys wishing to insert hyperlinks in court filings shall continue to use the traditional citation method for the cited authority, in addition to the hyperlink. A hyperlink contained in a filing is no more than a convenient mechanism for accessing material cited in the document and a hyperlink reference is extraneous to any filed document and is not part of the court's record. IN R USDCTND CM/ECF(II)(A)(3).

3. *Form of briefs*

a. *Page limits.* Supporting and response briefs (excluding tables of contents, tables of authorities, and appendices) ordinarily must not exceed twenty-five (25) pages. Reply briefs must not exceed fifteen (15) pages. IN R USDCTND L.R. 7-1(e)(1).

    i. *Exception.* The court may allow a party to file a brief exceeding these page limits for extraordinary and compelling reasons. But if the court permits a brief to exceed twenty-five (25) pages, it must include:

- A table of contents with page references;
- An issue statement; and
- A table of authorities including: (1) all cases (alphabetically arranged), statutes, and other authorities cited in the brief; and (2) references to where the authorities appear in the brief. IN R USDCTND L.R. 7-1(e)(2).

4. *Signing of pleadings, motions and other papers*

    a. *Signature.* Every pleading, written motion, and other paper must be signed by at least one attorney of record in the attorney's name—or by a party personally if the party is unrepresented. The paper must state the signer's address, e-mail address, and telephone number. FRCP 11(a).

        i. *Signatures on manual filings.* Papers delivered to the clerk for filing must: include the filer's original signature. IN R USDCTND L.R. 5-4(b)(1)(C).

- *Rubber-stamped and faxed signatures.* An original paper with a rubber-stamped or faxed signature is unsigned for purposes of FRCP 11 and FRCP 26(g). IN R USDCTND L.R. 5-4(b)(2).
- *Affidavits.* Only the affiant need sign an affidavit. IN R USDCTND L.R. 5-4(b)(3).

        ii. *Electronic signatures.* Pursuant to FRCP 11, every pleading, motion, and other paper (except lists, schedules, statements or amendments thereto) shall be signed by at least one attorney of record or, if the party is not represented by an attorney, all papers shall be signed by the party. An attorney's/participant's password issued by the court combined with the user's identification, serves as and constitutes the attorney/participant's signature for FRCP 11 and other purposes. IN R USDCTND CM/ECF(I)(C). Documents which must be filed and which must contain original signatures other than those of a participating attorney or which require either verification or an unsworn declaration under any rule or statute, shall be filed electronically, with originally executed copies maintained by the filer. The pleading or other document electronically filed shall contain "s/" signature(s), as noted in IN R USDCTND CM/ECF(II)(E)(3)(b). IN R USDCTND CM/ECF(II)(E)(1).

- *Multiple signatures.* In the case of a stipulation or other document to be signed by two or more attorneys, the following procedure should be used: The filing attorney shall initially confirm that the content of the document is acceptable to all persons required to sign the document and shall obtain the physical signatures of all attorneys on the document. IN R USDCTND CM/ECF(II)(E)(3)(a). The filing attorney then shall file the document electronically, indicating the signatories, e.g., "s/Jane Doe," "s/John Doe," etc. IN R USDCTND CM/ECF(II)(E)(3)(b). The filing attorney shall retain the hard copy of the document containing the original signatures. IN R USDCTND CM/ECF(II)(E)(3)(c).

        iii. *No verification or accompanying affidavit required for pleadings.* Unless a rule or statute specifically states otherwise, a pleading need not be verified or accompanied by an affidavit. FRCP 11(a).

        iv. *Unsigned papers.* The court must strike an unsigned paper unless the omission is promptly corrected after being called to the attorney's or party's attention. FRCP 11(a).

    b. *Representations to the court.* By presenting to the court a pleading, written motion, or other paper—whether by signing, filing, submitting, or later advocating it—an attorney or unrepresented party certifies that to the best of the person's knowledge, information, and belief, formed after an inquiry reasonable under the circumstances:

        i. It is not being presented for any improper purpose, such as to harass, cause unnecessary delay, or needlessly increase the cost of litigation;

    ii.   The claims, defenses, and other legal contentions are warranted by existing law or by a nonfrivolous argument for extending, modifying, or reversing existing law or for establishing new law;

    iii. The factual contentions have evidentiary support or, if specifically so identified, will likely have evidentiary support after a reasonable opportunity for further investigation or discovery; and

    iv. The denials of factual contentions are warranted on the evidence or, if specifically so identified, are reasonably based on belief or a lack of information. FRCP 11(b).

  c. *Sanctions.* If, after notice and a reasonable opportunity to respond, the court determines that FRCP 11(b) has been violated, the court may impose an appropriate sanction on any attorney, law firm, or party that violated FRCP 11(b) or is responsible for the violation. FRCP 11(c)(1). Refer to the United States District Court for the Northern District of Indiana KeyRules Motion for Sanctions document for more information.

5. *Privacy protection for filings made with the court*

  a. *Redacted filings.* Counsel should not include sensitive information in any document filed with the court unless such inclusion is necessary and relevant to the case. IN R USDCTND CM/ECF(VII). Unless the court orders otherwise, in an electronic or paper filing with the court that contains an individual's Social Security number, taxpayer-identification number, or birth date, the name of an individual known to be a minor, or a financial-account number, a party or nonparty making the filing may include only:

    i.   The last four (4) digits of the Social Security number and taxpayer-identification number;

    ii. The year of the individual's birth;

    iii. The minor's initials; and

    iv. The last four (4) digits of the financial-account number. FRCP 5.2(a); IN R USDCTND Order 2005-3.

  b. *Exemptions from the redaction requirement.* The redaction requirement does not apply to the following:

    i.   A financial-account number that identifies the property allegedly subject to forfeiture in a forfeiture proceeding;

    ii. The record of an administrative or agency proceeding;

    iii. The official record of a state-court proceeding;

    iv. The record of a court or tribunal, if that record was not subject to the redaction requirement when originally filed;

    v.   A filing covered by FRCP 5.2(c) or FRCP 5.2(d); and

    vi. A pro se filing in an action brought under 28 U.S.C.A. § 2241, 28 U.S.C.A. § 2254, or 28 U.S.C.A. § 2255. FRCP 5.2(b).

    vii. In cases filed under the Social Security Act, 42 U.S.C.A. § 405(g), there is no need for redaction of any information from the documents filed in the case. IN R USDCTND Order 2005-3.

  c. *Limitations on remote access to electronic files; Social Security appeals and immigration cases.* Unless the court orders otherwise, in an action for benefits under the Social Security Act, and in an action or proceeding relating to an order of removal, to relief from removal, or to immigration benefits or detention, access to an electronic file is authorized as follows:

    i.   The parties and their attorneys may have remote electronic access to any part of the case file, including the administrative record;

    ii. Any other person may have electronic access to the full record at the courthouse, but may have remote electronic access only to:

       • The docket maintained by the court; and

       • An opinion, order, judgment, or other disposition of the court, but not any other part of the case file or the administrative record. FRCP 5.2(c).

d. *Filings made under seal.* The court may order that a filing be made under seal without redaction. The court may later unseal the filing or order the person who made the filing to file a redacted version for the public record. FRCP 5.2(d). For information on filing documents under seal, refer to IN R USDCTND L.R. 5-3, IN R USDCTND CM/ECF(IV)(A), and IN R USDCTND ECF Order 2004-19.

e. *Protective orders.* For good cause, the court may by order in a case:

   i. Require redaction of additional information; or

   ii. Limit or prohibit a nonparty's remote electronic access to a document filed with the court. FRCP 5.2(e).

f. *Option for additional unredacted filing under seal.* A person making a redacted filing may also file an unredacted copy under seal. The court must retain the unredacted copy as part of the record. FRCP 5.2(f); IN R USDCTND Order 2005-3.

   i. The unredacted version of the document or the reference list shall be retained by the court under seal as part of the record. This paper shall be retained by the court as part of the record. The court may, however, still require the party to file a redacted copy for the public file. IN R USDCTND Order 2005-3.

g. *Option for filing a reference list.* A filing that contains redacted information may be filed together with a reference list that identifies each item of redacted information and specifies an appropriate identifier that uniquely corresponds to each item listed. The list must be filed under seal and may be amended as of right. Any reference in the case to a listed identifier will be construed to refer to the corresponding item of information. FRCP 5.2(g); IN R USDCTND Order 2005-3.

   i. The unredacted version of the document or the reference list shall be retained by the court under seal as part of the record. This paper shall be retained by the court as part of the record. The court may, however, still require the party to file a redacted copy for the public file. IN R USDCTND Order 2005-3.

h. *Responsibility for redaction.* The responsibility for redacting these personal identifiers rests solely with counsel and the parties. The Clerk will not review each paper for compliance with IN R USDCTND Order 2005-3. IN R USDCTND Order 2005-3.

i. *Waiver of protection of identifiers.* A person waives the protection of FRCP 5.2(a) as to the person's own information by filing it without redaction and not under seal. FRCP 5.2(h).

F. Filing and Service Requirements

1. *Filing requirements.* Any paper after the complaint that is required to be served—together with a certificate of service—must be filed within a reasonable time after service. FRCP 5(d)(1). Motions must be filed separately, but alternative motions may be filed in a single paper if each is named in the title following the caption. IN R USDCTND L.R. 7-1(a).

a. *How filing is made; In general.* A paper is filed by delivering it:

   i. To the clerk; or

   ii. To a judge who agrees to accept it for filing, and who must then note the filing date on the paper and promptly send it to the clerk. FRCP 5(d)(2).

      • Papers not filed electronically must be filed with the clerk, not a judge. IN R USDCTND L.R. 5-4(b)(4).

   iii. Parties manually filing a paper that requires the clerk to give others notice, must give the clerk: (1) sufficient copies of the notice; and (2) the name and address of each person entitled to receive the notice. IN R USDCTND L.R. 5-4(b)(8).

b. *Where to file.* Papers not filed electronically must be filed in the division where the case is pending, unless: (1) a person will be prejudiced if the paper is not filed the same day it is tendered; and (2) it includes an adequately sized envelope addressed to the clerk's office in the division where the case is pending and with adequate postage. IN R USDCTND L.R. 5-4(b)(5).

c. *Electronic filing*

   i. *Authorization of electronic filing program.* A court may, by local rule, allow papers to be filed,

signed, or verified by electronic means that are consistent with any technical standards established by the Judicial Conference of the United States. A local rule may require electronic filing only if reasonable exceptions are allowed. A paper filed electronically in compliance with a local rule is a written paper for purposes of the Federal Rules of Civil Procedure. FRCP 5(d)(3).

- Papers must be filed, signed, and verified electronically unless excepted by the court's CM/ECF Civil and Criminal User Manual (IN R USDCTND CM/ECF). IN R USDCTND L.R. 5-1.

ii. *Mandatory electronic filing.* Unless otherwise permitted by these procedures or otherwise authorized by the assigned judge, all documents submitted for filing in this district in civil and criminal cases, no matter when a case was originally filed, shall be filed electronically using the System. IN R USDCTND CM/ECF(II)(A)(1). The requirement that "all documents" be filed electronically includes briefs, and attachments and exhibits used in support of motions. IN R USDCTND CM/ECF(FN1).

- Sending a document or pleading to the court via e-mail or facsimile does not constitute "electronic filing." IN R USDCTND CM/ECF(I)(A).

iii. *Conventional filing.* As used in these procedures, a "conventionally" filed or submitted document or pleading is one presented to the Clerk or a party in paper or other non-electronic, tangible format. The following documents shall be filed conventionally and not electronically unless specifically authorized by the Court:

- Exhibits and other documents which cannot be converted to a legible electronic form. Whenever possible, counsel is responsible for converting filings to an electronic form. However, if that is not physically possible, counsel shall electronically file a .pdf document titled Notice of Manual Filing as a notation on the docket sheet that filings are being held in the clerk's office in paper. A sample Notice of Manual Filing is attached as Form 2 (IN R USDCTND CM/ECF(Form 2)). If documents are filed in paper format, counsel must provide an original for the clerk's office, a copy for the judge and a copy must be served on all parties in the case. Large documents which do not exist in an electronic format shall be scanned into .pdf format by counsel, in small batches if necessary, and filed electronically as separate attachments in the System. IN R USDCTND CM/ECF(III)(A)(1).

- Certain documents which are listed in IN R USDCTND CM/ECF(II)(E)(2). IN R USDCTND CM/ECF(III)(A)(2).

- Documents filed by pro se litigants. IN R USDCTND CM/ECF(III)(A)(3).

iv. For more information on electronic filing, refer to IN R USDCTND CM/ECF.

2. *Service requirements*

a. *Service; When required*

i. *In general.* Unless the Federal Rules of Civil Procedure provide otherwise, each of the following papers must be served on every party:

- An order stating that service is required;

- A pleading filed after the original complaint, unless the court orders otherwise under FRCP 5(c) because there are numerous defendants;

- A discovery paper required to be served on a party, unless the court orders otherwise;

- A written motion, except one that may be heard ex parte; and

- A written notice, appearance, demand, or offer of judgment, or any similar paper. FRCP 5(a)(1).

ii. *If a party fails to appear.* No service is required on a party who is in default for failing to appear. But a pleading that asserts a new claim for relief against such a party must be served on that party under FRCP 4. FRCP 5(a)(2).

    iii. *Seizing property.* If an action is begun by seizing property and no person is or need be named as a defendant, any service required before the filing of an appearance, answer, or claim must be made on the person who had custody or possession of the property when it was seized. FRCP 5(a)(3).

  b. *Service; How made*

    i. *Serving an attorney.* If a party is represented by an attorney, service under FRCP 5 must be made on the attorney unless the court orders service on the party. FRCP 5(b)(1).

    ii. *Service in general.* A paper is served under FRCP 5 by:

- Handing it to the person;

- Leaving it: (1) at the person's office with a clerk or other person in charge or, if no one is in charge, in a conspicuous place in the office; or (2) if the person has no office or the office is closed, at the person's dwelling or usual place of abode with someone of suitable age and discretion who resides there;

- Mailing it to the person's last known address—in which event service is complete upon mailing;

- Leaving it with the court clerk if the person has no known address;

- Sending it by electronic means if the person consented in writing—in which event service is complete upon transmission, but is not effective if the serving party learns that it did not reach the person to be served; or

- Delivering it by any other means that the person consented to in writing—in which event service is complete when the person making service delivers it to the agency designated to make delivery. FRCP 5(b)(2).

    iii. *Electronic service.* Electronically filed papers may be served electronically if service is consistent with the CM/ECF User Manual (IN R USDCTND CM/ECF). IN R USDCTND L.R. 5-2(a).

- *Waiver of other service.* An attorney's registration will constitute a waiver of conventional service of documents and the attorney agrees to accept service of notice on behalf of the client of the electronic filing by hand, facsimile or authorized email. IN R USDCTND CM/ECF(I)(B)(3).

- *Serving registered persons.* The System will generate a "Notice of Electronic Filing" when any document is filed. This notice represents service of the document on parties who are registered participants with the System. Except as provided in IN R USDCTND CM/ECF(III)(B), the filing party shall not be required to serve any pleading or other documents on any party receiving electronic notice. IN R USDCTND CM/ECF(II)(D)(1). The term "pleading" refers only to those documents listed in FRCP 7(a). IN R USDCTND CM/ECF(FN3).

- *When electronic service is deemed completed.* A person registered to use the court's electronic-filing system is served with an electronically filed paper when a "Notice of Electronic Filing" is transmitted to that person through the court's electronic filing-system. IN R USDCTND L.R. 5-2(b).

- *Serving non-registered persons.* A person who has not registered to use the court's electronic-filing system but who is entitled to service of a paper must be served according to the Local Civil Rules of the United States District Court for the Northern District of Indiana and the Federal Rules of Civil Procedure. IN R USDCTND L.R. 5-2(c); IN R USDCTND CM/ECF(II)(D)(2). If such service of a paper copy is to be made, it shall be done in the manner provided in the Federal Rules of Civil Procedure and the Local Civil Rules of the United States District Court for the Northern District of Indiana. IN R USDCTND CM/ECF(II)(D)(2).

    iv. *Service of conventional filings.* Pleadings or other documents which are filed conventionally rather than electronically shall be served in the manner provided for in the Federal Rules of

Civil Procedure and the Local Civil Rules of the United States District Court for the Northern District of Indiana, except as otherwise provided by order of the Court. IN R USDCTND CM/ECF(III)(B).

    v. *Using court facilities.* If a local rule so authorizes, a party may use the court's transmission facilities to make service under FRCP 5(b)(2)(E). FRCP 5(b)(3).

  c. *Serving numerous defendants*

    i. *In general.* If an action involves an unusually large number of defendants, the court may, on motion or on its own, order that:

- Defendants' pleadings and replies to them need not be served on other defendants;
- Any crossclaim, counterclaim, avoidance, or affirmative defense in those pleadings and replies to them will be treated as denied or avoided by all other parties; and
- Filing any such pleading and serving it on the plaintiff constitutes notice of the pleading to all parties. FRCP 5(c)(1).

    ii. *Notifying parties.* A copy of every such order must be served on the parties as the court directs. FRCP 5(c)(2).

G. Hearings

1. *Hearings, generally*

  a. *Oral argument.* Due process does not require that oral argument be permitted on a motion and, except as otherwise provided by local rule, the district court has discretion to determine whether it will decide the motion on the papers or hear argument by counsel (and perhaps receive evidence). FPP § 1190; F.D.I.C. v. Deglau, 207 F.3d 153 (3d Cir. 2000).

    i. *Request for oral argument.* A party may request oral argument on a motion by filing and serving a separate document explaining why oral argument is necessary and estimating how long the court should allow for the argument. IN R USDCTND L.R. 7-5(a)(1). Refer to the Documents section of this document for more information.

    ii. *Additional evidence forbidden.* Parties may not present additional evidence at oral argument. IN R USDCTND L.R. 7-5(a)(3).

  b. *Providing a regular schedule for oral hearings.* A court may establish regular times and places for oral hearings on motions. FRCP 78(a).

  c. *Providing for submission on briefs.* By rule or order, the court may provide for submitting and determining motions on briefs, without oral hearings. FRCP 78(b).

  d. *Evidentiary hearings.* A party may request an evidentiary hearing by filing and serving a separate document explaining why the hearing is necessary and estimating how long the court should allow for it. IN R USDCTND L.R. 7-5(b)(2). Refer to the Documents section of this document for more information.

  e. *Court's authority.* The court may: (1) grant or deny a request for oral argument or an evidentiary hearing in its discretion; (2) set oral argument or an evidentiary hearing without a request from a party; or (3) order any oral argument or evidentiary hearing to be held anywhere within the district regardless of where the case will be tried. IN R USDCTND L.R. 7-5(c).

2. *Courtroom and courthouse decorum.* For information on courtroom and courthouse decorum, refer to IN R USDCTND L.R. 83-3.

H. Forms

1. Federal Motion for Judgment on the Pleadings Forms

  a. Motion and notice; For judgment on pleadings. AMJUR PP FEDPRAC § 532.

  b. Countermotion and notice; For judgment on pleadings; By defendants. AMJUR PP FEDPRAC § 533.

  c. Order; For judgment on pleadings; In favor of plaintiff. AMJUR PP FEDPRAC § 534.

    d.   Order; For judgment on pleadings; In favor of defendant. AMJUR PP FEDPRAC § 535.

    e.   Motion for judgment on the pleadings. 2C FEDFORMS § 11:131.

    f.   Motion for judgment on the pleadings; Alternate wording. 2C FEDFORMS § 11:132.

    g.   Motion for judgment on the pleadings; Long version. 2C FEDFORMS § 11:133.

    h.   Motion for judgment on the pleadings; Several grounds. 2C FEDFORMS § 11:134.

    i.   Notice of motion and motion for judgment on the pleadings. 2C FEDFORMS § 11:135.

    j.   Notice of motion for judgment on the pleadings (partial) or for partial summary judgment. 2C FEDFORMS § 11:136.

    k.   Order granting judgment on the pleadings. 2C FEDFORMS § 11:137.

    l.   Order granting judgment on the pleadings; Motion by plaintiff. 2C FEDFORMS § 11:138.

    m.   Judgment on the pleadings. 2C FEDFORMS § 11:139.

    n.   Motion; General form. FEDPROF § 1:746.

    o.   Notice; Of motion; General form. FEDPROF § 1:747.

    p.   Notice; Of motion; With costs of motion. FEDPROF § 1:748.

    q.   Notice; Of motion; Containing motion. FEDPROF § 1:749.

    r.   Opposition; To motion; General form. FEDPROF § 1:750.

    s.   Affidavit; Supporting or opposing motion. FEDPROF § 1:751.

    t.   Brief; Supporting or opposing motion. FEDPROF § 1:752.

    u.   Statement of points and authorities; Opposing motion. FEDPROF § 1:753.

    v.   Motion; For judgment on the pleadings. FEDPROF § 1:1295.

    w.   Order; For judgment on the pleadings; In favor of plaintiff. FEDPROF § 1:1296.

    x.   Order; For judgment on the pleadings; In favor of defendant. FEDPROF § 1:1297.

    y.   Motion for judgment on pleadings; Plaintiff. GOLDLTGFMS § 20:38.

    z.   Motion for judgment on pleadings; Defendant. GOLDLTGFMS § 20:39.

2. Forms for the Northern District of Indiana

    a.   Certificate of service. IN R USDCTND CM/ECF(Form 1).

    b.   Notice of manual filing. IN R USDCTND CM/ECF(Form 2).

    c.   Declaration that party was unable to file in a timely manner. IN R USDCTND CM/ECF(Form 3).

I. Applicable Rules

  1. *Federal rules*

    a.   Serving and filing pleadings and other papers. FRCP 5.

    b.   Constitutional challenge to a statute; Notice, certification, and intervention. FRCP 5.1.

    c.   Privacy protection for filings made with the court. FRCP 5.2.

    d.   Computing and extending time; Time for motion papers. FRCP 6.

    e.   Pleadings allowed; Form of motions and other papers. FRCP 7.

    f.   Disclosure statement. FRCP 7.1.

    g.   Form of pleadings. FRCP 10.

    h.   Signing pleadings, motions, and other papers; Representations to the court; Sanctions. FRCP 11.

    i.   Defenses and objections; When and how presented; Motion for judgment on the pleadings; Consolidating motions; Waiving defenses; Pretrial hearing. FRCP 12.

    j.   Hearing motions; Submission on briefs. FRCP 78.

2. *Local rules*

    a. Citation and scope of the rules. IN R USDCTND L.R. 1-1.

    b. Sanctions for formatting errors. IN R USDCTND L.R. 1-3.

    c. Electronic filing required. IN R USDCTND L.R. 5-1.

    d. Constitutional questions. IN R USDCTND L.R. 5.1-1.

    e. Electronic service. IN R USDCTND L.R. 5-2.

    f. Format of papers. IN R USDCTND L.R. 5-4.

    g. Motion practice. IN R USDCTND L.R. 7-1.

    h. Oral arguments and evidentiary hearings. IN R USDCTND L.R. 7-5.

    i. Pretrial procedure. IN R USDCTND L.R. 16-1.

    j. Alternative dispute resolution. IN R USDCTND L.R. 16-6.

    k. Case assignment. IN R USDCTND L.R. 40-1.

    l. Appearance and withdrawal of appearance. IN R USDCTND L.R. 83-8.

    m. CM/ECF civil and criminal user manual. IN R USDCTND CM/ECF.

    n. In re: privacy and public access to civil electronic case files. IN R USDCTND Order 2005-3.

Motions, Oppositions and Replies
Motion for More Definite Statement

Document Last Updated December 2016

A. Checklist

(I) ❑ Matters to be considered by moving party

    (a) ❑ Required documents

        (1) ❑ Notice of motion and motion

        (2) ❑ Brief

        (3) ❑ Certificate of service

    (b) ❑ Supplemental documents

        (1) ❑ Supporting evidence

        (2) ❑ Notice of constitutional question

        (3) ❑ Nongovernmental corporate disclosure statement

        (4) ❑ Index of exhibits

        (5) ❑ Request for oral argument

        (6) ❑ Request for evidentiary hearing

        (7) ❑ Copy of authority

        (8) ❑ Proposed order

        (9) ❑ Copy of document with self-addressed envelope

        (10) ❑ Notice of manual filing

        (11) ❑ Courtesy copies

        (12) ❑ Declaration that party was unable to file in a timely manner

    (c) ❑ Timing

        (1) ❑ The motion must be made before filing a responsive pleading

     (2)   ❑ A written motion and notice of the hearing must be served at least fourteen (14) days before the time specified for the hearing, with the following exceptions: (i) when the motion may be heard ex parte; (ii) when the Federal Rules of Civil Procedure set a different time; or (iii) when a court order—which a party may, for good cause, apply for ex parte—sets a different time

     (3)   ❑ Any affidavit supporting a motion must be served with the motion

(II)   ❑ Matters to be considered by opposing party

   (a)   ❑ Required documents

     (1)   ❑ Response brief

     (2)   ❑ Certificate of service

   (b)   ❑ Supplemental documents

     (1)   ❑ Supporting evidence

     (2)   ❑ Notice of constitutional question

     (3)   ❑ Index of exhibits

     (4)   ❑ Request for oral argument

     (5)   ❑ Request for evidentiary hearing

     (6)   ❑ Copy of authority

     (7)   ❑ Copy of document with self-addressed envelope

     (8)   ❑ Notice of manual filing

     (9)   ❑ Courtesy copies

     (10)   ❑ Declaration that party was unable to file in a timely manner

   (c)   ❑ Timing

     (1)   ❑ A party must file any response brief to a motion within fourteen (14) days after the motion is served

     (2)   ❑ Except as FRCP 59(c) provides otherwise, any opposing affidavit must be served at least seven (7) days before the hearing, unless the court permits service at another time

B. Timing

1. *Motion for more definite statement.* The motion must be made before filing a responsive pleading. FRCP 12(e). Thus, a motion for a more definite statement must be made before an answer. FEDPROC § 62:386. In several situations, however, the time for moving under FRCP 12(e) is extended well beyond the usual twenty (20) day period for serving a responsive pleading set out in FRCP 12(a). FPP § 1378.

2. *Timing of motions, generally*

   a. *Motion and notice of hearing.* A written motion and notice of the hearing must be served at least fourteen (14) days before the time specified for the hearing, with the following exceptions:

     i.   When the motion may be heard ex parte;

     ii.   When the Federal Rules of Civil Procedure set a different time; or

     iii.   When a court order—which a party may, for good cause, apply for ex parte—sets a different time. FRCP 6(c)(1).

   b. *Supporting affidavit.* Any affidavit supporting a motion must be served with the motion. FRCP 6(c)(2).

3. *Timing of opposing papers.* A party must file any response brief to a motion within fourteen (14) days after the motion is served. IN R USDCTND L.R. 7-1(d)(2)(A).

   a. *Opposing affidavit.* Except as FRCP 59(c) provides otherwise, any opposing affidavit must be served at least seven (7) days before the hearing, unless the court permits service at another time. FRCP 6(c)(2).

    b.   *Extensions.* The court may extend response- and reply-brief deadlines, but only for good cause. IN R USDCTND L.R. 7-1(d)(3).

    c.   *Summary rulings.* The court may rule on a motion summarily if an opposing party does not file a response before the deadline. IN R USDCTND L.R. 7-1(d)(4).

4.   *Timing of reply papers.* Where the respondent files an answering affidavit setting up a new matter, the moving party ordinarily is allowed a reasonable time to file a reply affidavit since failure to deny the new matter by affidavit may operate as an admission of its truth. AMJUR MOTIONS § 25.

    a.   *Reply brief.* The moving party must file any reply brief within seven (7) days after the response brief is served. IN R USDCTND L.R. 7-1(d)(2)(B).

    b.   *Extensions.* The court may extend response- and reply-brief deadlines, but only for good cause. IN R USDCTND L.R. 7-1(d)(3).

5.   *Effect of a FRCP 12 motion on the time to serve a responsive pleading.* Unless the court sets a different time, serving a motion under FRCP 12 alters the periods in FRCP 12(a) as follows:

    a.   If the court denies the motion or postpones its disposition until trial, the responsive pleading must be served within fourteen (14) days after notice of the court's action; or

    b.   If the court grants a motion for a more definite statement, the responsive pleading must be served within fourteen (14) days after the more definite statement is served. FRCP 12(a)(4).

6.   *Computation of time*

    a.   *Computing time.* FRCP 6 applies in computing any time period specified in the Federal Rules of Civil Procedure, in any local rule or court order, or in any statute that does not specify a method of computing time. FRCP 6(a).

        i.   *Period stated in days or a longer unit.* When the period is stated in days or a longer unit of time:

- Exclude the day of the event that triggers the period;
- Count every day, including intermediate Saturdays, Sundays, and legal holidays; and
- Include the last day of the period, but if the last day is a Saturday, Sunday, or legal holiday, the period continues to run until the end of the next day that is not a Saturday, Sunday, or legal holiday. FRCP 6(a)(1).

        ii.   *Period stated in hours.* When the period is stated in hours:

- Begin counting immediately on the occurrence of the event that triggers the period;
- Count every hour, including hours during intermediate Saturdays, Sundays, and legal holidays; and
- If the period would end on a Saturday, Sunday, or legal holiday, the period continues to run until the same time on the next day that is not a Saturday, Sunday, or legal holiday. FRCP 6(a)(2).

        iii.   *Inaccessibility of the clerk's office.* Unless the court orders otherwise, if the clerk's office is inaccessible:

- On the last day for filing under FRCP 6(a)(1), then the time for filing is extended to the first accessible day that is not a Saturday, Sunday, or legal holiday; or
- During the last hour for filing under FRCP 6(a)(2), then the time for filing is extended to the same time on the first accessible day that is not a Saturday, Sunday, or legal holiday. FRCP 6(a)(3).

        iv.   *"Last day" defined.* Unless a different time is set by a statute, local rule, or court order, the last day ends:

- For electronic filing, at midnight in the court's time zone; and
- For filing by other means, when the clerk's office is scheduled to close. FRCP 6(a)(4).

        v.   *"Next day" defined.* The "next day" is determined by continuing to count forward when the period is measured after an event and backward when measured before an event. FRCP 6(a)(5).

vi. *"Legal holiday" defined.* "Legal holiday" means:

- The day set aside by statute for observing New Year's Day, Martin Luther King Jr.'s Birthday, Washington's Birthday, Memorial Day, Independence Day, Labor Day, Columbus Day, Veterans' Day, Thanksgiving Day, or Christmas Day;

- Any day declared a holiday by the President or Congress; and

- For periods that are measured after an event, any other day declared a holiday by the state where the district court is located. FRCP 6(a)(6).

b. *Computation of electronic filing deadlines.* Filing documents electronically does not alter any filing deadlines or any time computation pursuant to FRCP 6. The counties of Lake, Porter, LaPorte, Pulaski and Starke are located in the Central time zone and the remaining counties in the Northern District of Indiana are located in the Eastern time zone. Nevertheless, all electronic transmissions of documents must be completed (i.e., received completely by the clerk's office) prior to midnight Eastern Time, (South Bend/Fort Wayne/Lafayette time) in order to be considered timely filed that day, regardless of the local time in the division where the case is pending. Although documents can be filed electronically twenty-four (24) hours a day, filers are strongly encouraged to file all documents during hours when the CM/ECF Help Line is available, from 9:00 a.m. to 4:00 p.m. local time. IN R USDCTND CM/ECF(II)(I).

i. *Technical failures.* If the attorney is unable to file a document in a timely manner due to technical difficulties in the user's system, the attorney must file a document with the court as soon as possible notifying the court of the inability to file the document. A sample document entitled Declaration that Party was Unable to File in a Timely Manner Due to Technical Difficulties is attached hereto as Form 5. IN R USDCTND CM/ECF(VI)(B). [Editor's note: the reference to Form 5 is likely meant to be a reference to Form 3 (IN R USDCTND CM/ECF(Form 3)].

c. *Extending time*

i. *In general.* When an act may or must be done within a specified time, the court may, for good cause, extend the time:

- With or without motion or notice if the court acts, or if a request is made, before the original time or its extension expires; or

- On motion made after the time has expired if the party failed to act because of excusable neglect. FRCP 6(b)(1).

ii. *Exceptions.* A court must not extend the time to act under FRCP 50(b), FRCP 50(d), FRCP 52(b), FRCP 59(b), FRCP 59(d), FRCP 59(e), and FRCP 60(b). FRCP 6(b)(2).

iii. Refer to the United States District Court for the Northern District of Indiana KeyRules Motion for Continuance/Extension of Time document for more information on extending time.

d. *Additional time after certain kinds of service.* When a party may or must act within a specified time after being served and service is made under FRCP 5(b)(2)(C) (mail), FRCP 5(b)(2)(D) (leaving with the clerk), or FRCP 5(b)(2)(F) (other means consented to), three (3) days are added after the period would otherwise expire under FRCP 6(a). FRCP 6(d).

C. General Requirements

1. *Motions, generally*

a. *Requirements.* A request for a court order must be made by motion. The motion must:

i. Be in writing unless made during a hearing or trial;

ii. State with particularity the grounds for seeking the order; and

iii. State the relief sought. FRCP 7(b)(1).

b. *Notice of motion.* A party interested in resisting the relief sought by a motion has a right to notice thereof, and an opportunity to be heard. AMJUR MOTIONS § 12.

i. In addition to statutory or court rule provisions requiring notice of a motion—the purpose of such a notice requirement having been said to be to prevent a party from being prejudicially surprised by a motion—principles of natural justice dictate that an adverse party generally must be given notice that a motion will be presented to the court. AMJUR MOTIONS § 12.

    ii.   "Notice," in this regard, means reasonable notice, including a meaningful opportunity to prepare and to defend against allegations of a motion. AMJUR MOTIONS § 12.

c.   *Writing requirement.* The writing requirement is intended to insure that the adverse parties are informed and have a record of both the motion's pendency and the grounds on which the movant seeks an order. FPP § 1191; Feldberg v. Quechee Lakes Corp., 463 F.3d 195 (2d Cir. 2006).

    i.   It is sufficient "if the motion is stated in a written notice of the hearing of the motion." FPP § 1191.

d.   *Particularity requirement.* The particularity requirement insures that the opposing parties will have notice of their opponent's contentions. FEDPROC § 62:364; Goodman v. 1973 26 Foot Trojan Vessel, Arkansas Registration No. AR1439SN, 859 F.2d 71, 12 Fed.R.Serv.3d 645 (8th Cir. 1988). That requirement ensures that notice of the basis for the motion is provided to the court and to the opposing party so as to avoid prejudice, provide the opponent with a meaningful opportunity to respond, and provide the court with enough information to process the motion correctly. FEDPROC § 62:364; Andreas v. Volkswagen of America, Inc., 336 F.3d 789, 56 Fed.R.Serv.3d 6 (8th Cir. 2003).

    i.   Reasonable specification of the grounds for a motion is sufficient. However, where a movant fails to state even one ground for granting the motion in question, the movant has failed to meet the minimal standard of "reasonable specification." FEDPROC § 62:364; Martinez v. Trainor, 556 F.2d 818, 23 Fed.R.Serv.2d 403 (7th Cir. 1977).

    ii.   The court may excuse the failure to comply with the particularity requirement if it is inadvertent, and where no prejudice is shown by the opposing party. FEDPROC § 62:364.

e.   *Motions must be filed separately.* Motions must be filed separately, but alternative motions may be filed in a single paper if each is named in the title following the caption. IN R USDCTND L.R. 7-1(a).

2.   *Motion for more definite statement.* A party may move for a more definite statement of a pleading to which a responsive pleading is allowed but which is so vague or ambiguous that the party cannot reasonably prepare a response. FRCP 12(e). A motion for a more definite statement under FRCP 12(e) is inappropriate where a responsive pleading is not required or permitted. FEDPROC § 62:385.

a.   *Contents.* The motion must be made before filing a responsive pleading and must point out the defects complained of and the details desired. FRCP 12(e). A motion for a more definite statement must point out the defects complained of and the details desired, should offer discussion or legal analysis in support of the FRCP 12(e) claim, and will be denied where the motion fails to satisfy this requirement. FEDPROC § 62:387.

    i.   Regardless of whether the plaintiff or the defendant moves under FRCP 12(e), she must identify the deficiencies in the pleading believed to be objectionable, point out the details she desires to have pleaded in a more intelligible form, and assert her inability to prepare a responsive pleading. These requirements are designed to enable the district judge to test the propriety of the motion and formulate an appropriate order in the light of its limited purpose of enabling the framing of a responsive pleading. FPP § 1378.

    ii.   Since FRCP 12(e) must be construed in light of the federal rules relating to liberal pleading, a motion for a more definite statement need not particularize the requested information in great detail and should not request an excessive amount of information. Indeed, if the movant does ask for too much, his motion may be denied on the ground that evidentiary matter is being sought. FPP § 1378.

b.   *Burden.* Most federal courts cast the burden of establishing the need for a more definite statement on the movant. Whether he will succeed in discharging that burden depends on such factors as the availability of information from other sources that may clear up the pleading for the movant and a coparty's ability to answer. FPP § 1378.

c.   *Motion disfavored.* Motions for a more definite statement are not favored by the courts, and thus, are rarely granted, since pleadings in the federal courts are only required to fairly notify the opposing party of the nature of the claim, and since there are ample provisions for discovery under FRCP 26 to FRCP 37 as well as for pretrial procedure under FRCP 16. Generally, motions for more definite statement are disfavored because of their dilatory effect, and the preferred course is to encourage the use of discovery procedures to apprise the parties of the factual basis of the claims made in the pleadings. FEDPROC § 62:388.

    i. *Discretion of court.* A motion for a more definite statement pursuant to FRCP 12(e) is addressed to the discretion of the court. Whether the motion should be granted or denied depends primarily on the facts of each individual case. FEDPROC § 62:388.

d. *Joining motions*

    i. *Right to join.* A motion under FRCP 12 may be joined with any other motion allowed by FRCP 12. FRCP 12(g)(1).

    ii. *Limitation on further motions.* Except as provided in FRCP 12(h)(2) or FRCP 12(h)(3), a party that makes a motion under FRCP 12 must not make another motion under FRCP 12 raising a defense or objection that was available to the party but omitted from its earlier motion. FRCP 12(g)(2).

       • If the movant legitimately is unable to assert his other defenses at the time a motion is made under FRCP 12(e), the movant will not be penalized when he actually does interpose a second motion. FPP § 1378.

e. *Waiving and preserving certain defenses.* No defense or objection is waived by joining it with one or more other defenses or objections in a responsive pleading or in a motion. FRCP 12(b).

    i. *Waiver by consent or stipulation.* A valid consent or a stipulation that the court has jurisdiction prevents the successful assertion of a FRCP 12(b)(2) defense. FPP § 1351.

    ii. *Waiver by filing permissive counterclaim.* A defendant may be deemed to have waived an objection to personal jurisdiction if he or she files a permissive counterclaim under FRCP 13(b). FPP § 1351.

    iii. *When some are waived.* A party waives any defense listed in FRCP 12(b)(2) through FRCP 12(b)(5) by:

       • Omitting it from a motion in the circumstances described in FRCP 12(g)(2); or

       • Failing to either: (1) make it by motion under FRCP 12; or (2) include it in a responsive pleading or in an amendment allowed by FRCP 15(a)(1) as a matter of course. FRCP 12(h)(1).

    iv. *When to raise others.* Failure to state a claim upon which relief can be granted, to join a person required by FRCP 19(b), or to state a legal defense to a claim may be raised:

       • In any pleading allowed or ordered under FRCP 7(a);

       • By a motion under FRCP 12(c); or

       • At trial. FRCP 12(h)(2).

    v. *Lack of subject matter jurisdiction.* If the court determines at any time that it lacks subject-matter jurisdiction, the court must dismiss the action. FRCP 12(h)(3).

f. *General standard for granting motion.* The general standard for granting a motion for a more definite statement is set forth in FRCP 12(e) itself, which provides that a party may move for a more definite statement if a pleading to which a responsive pleading is allowed is so vague or ambiguous that the party cannot reasonably prepare a response. The clear trend of judicial decisions is to deny motions for a more definite statement unless the complaint is so excessively vague and ambiguous as to prejudice the defendant seriously in attempting to answer it. The burden is on the movant to demonstrate that the complaint is so vague or ambiguous that they cannot respond, even with a simple denial, in good faith or without prejudice to himself or herself. FEDPROC § 62:389.

g. *Compliance and enforcement of order.* If the court orders a more definite statement and the order is not obeyed within fourteen (14) days after notice of the order or within the time the court sets, the court may strike the pleading or issue any other appropriate order. FRCP 12(e).

3. *Opposing papers.* The Federal Rules of Civil Procedure do not require any formal answer, return, or reply to a motion, except where the Federal Rules of Civil Procedure or local rules may require affidavits, memoranda, or other papers to be filed in opposition to a motion. Such papers are simply to apprise the court of such opposition and the grounds of that opposition. FEDPROC § 62:359.

   a. *Effect of failure to respond to motion.* Although in the absence of statutory provision or court rule, a motion ordinarily does not require a written answer, when a party files a motion and the opposing party fails to respond, the court may construe such failure to respond as nonopposition to the motion or an admission that the motion was meritorious, may take the facts alleged in the motion as true—the rule in some jurisdictions being that the failure to respond to a fact set forth in a motion is deemed an admission—and may grant the motion if the relief requested appears to be justified. AMJUR MOTIONS § 28.

   b. *Assent or no opposition not determinative.* However, a motion will not be granted automatically simply because an "assent" or a notation of "no opposition" has been filed; federal judges frequently deny motions that have been assented to when it is thought that justice so dictates. FPP § 1190.

   c. *Responsive pleading inappropriate as response to motion.* An attempt to answer or oppose a motion with a responsive pleading usually is not appropriate. FPP § 1190.

4. *Reply papers.* A moving party may be required or permitted to prepare papers in addition to his original motion papers. AMJUR MOTIONS § 25. Papers answering or replying to opposing papers may be appropriate, in the interests of justice, where it appears there is a substantial reason for allowing a reply. Thus, a court may accept reply papers where a party demonstrates that the papers to which it seeks to file a reply raise new issues that are material to the disposition of the question before the court, or where the court determines, sua sponte, that it wishes further briefing of an issue raised in those papers and orders the submission of additional papers. FEDPROC § 62:360.

   a. *Function of reply papers.* The function of a reply affidavit is to answer the arguments made in opposition to the position taken by the movant and not to permit the movant to introduce new arguments in support of the motion. AMJUR MOTIONS § 25.

   b. *Issues raised for the first time in a reply document.* However, the view has been followed in some jurisdictions, that as a matter of judicial economy, where there is no prejudice and where the issues could be raised simply by filing a motion to dismiss, the trial court has discretion to consider arguments raised for the first time in a reply memorandum, and that a trial court may grant a motion to strike issues raised for the first time in a reply memorandum. AMJUR MOTIONS § 26.

5. *Appearances.* Attorneys not representing the United States or its agencies must file an appearance when they represent (either in person or by filing a paper) a party. IN R USDCTND L.R. 83-8(a). For more information, refer to IN R USDCTND L.R. 83-8.

6. *Notice of related action.* A party must file a notice of related action as soon as it appears that the party's case and another pending case: (1) arise out of the same transaction or occurrence; (2) involve the same property; or (3) involve the validity or infringement of the same patent, trademark, or copyright. IN R USDCTND L.R. 40-1(d). For more information, refer to IN R USDCTND L.R. 40-1.

7. *Alternative dispute resolution (ADR).* After they confer as required by FRCP 26(f), the parties must advise the court which, if any, alternative-dispute-resolution processes they expect to pursue and when they expect to undertake the process. IN R USDCTND L.R. 16-6(a). For more information on alternative dispute resolution (ADR), refer to IN R USDCTND L.R. 16-6 and IN R USDCTND Order 2003-21.

8. *Settlement or resolution.* The parties must immediately notify the court if they reasonably expect to settle the case or resolve a pending motion. IN R USDCTND L.R. 16-1(g).

9. *Modification or suspension of rules.* The court may, on its own motion or at the request of a party, suspend or modify any rule in a particular case in the interest of justice. IN R USDCTND L.R. 1-1(c).

D. Documents

1. *Documents for moving party*

   a. *Required documents*

      i. *Notice of motion and motion.* The party must not specify a hearing date in the notice of a motion or petition unless the court or the clerk has authorized it. IN R USDCTND L.R. 7-5(b)(2). Refer to the General Requirements section of this document for information on the notice of motion and motion.

ii. *Brief.* Parties must file a supporting brief with any motion under: FRCP 12. IN R USDCTND L.R. 7-1(b)(1). Refer to the Format section of this document for the format of briefs.

iii. *Certificate of service.* FRCP 5(d) requires that the person making service under FRCP 5 certify that service has been effected. FRCP 5(Advisory Committee Notes). Having such information on file may be useful for many purposes, including proof of service if an issue arises concerning the effectiveness of the service. FRCP 5(Advisory Committee Notes).

- *Certificate of service for electronically-filed documents.* A Certificate of Service is still a requirement when filing documents electronically. A sample Certificate of Service is attached as Form 1 (IN R USDCTND CM/ECF(Form 1)). IN R USDCTND CM/ECF(II)(H).

b. *Supplemental documents*

i. *Supporting evidence.* When a motion relies on facts outside the record, the court may hear the matter on affidavits or may hear it wholly or partly on oral testimony or on depositions. FRCP 43(c).

- *Materials necessary for motion.* A party must file those portions of discovery requests or responses (including deposition transcripts) that the party relies on to support a motion that could result in a final order on an issue. IN R USDCTND L.R. 26-2(c).

- *Supporting affidavit(s).* Good practice for a party seeking relief under FRCP 12(e) is to support the motion by an affidavit showing the necessity for a more definite statement. FEDPROC § 62:387. Courts differ in their attitude toward the use of affidavits on a FRCP 12(e) motion. Some insist on affidavits delineating the ways in which the pleading should be made more definite; others feel that affidavits would be helpful but do not insist upon them; and a few courts, usually when a more definite statement obviously is appropriate, do not seem to require supporting affidavits. FPP § 1378.

ii. *Notice of constitutional question.* A party that files a pleading, written motion, or other paper drawing into question the constitutionality of a federal or state statute must promptly:

- *File notice.* File a notice of constitutional question stating the question and identifying the paper that raises it, if: (1) a federal statute is questioned and the parties do not include the United States, one of its agencies, or one of its officers or employees in an official capacity; or (2) a state statute is questioned and the parties do not include the state, one of its agencies, or one of its officers or employees in an official capacity; and

- *Serve notice.* Serve the notice and paper on the Attorney General of the United States if a federal statute is questioned—or on the state attorney general if a state statute is questioned—either by certified or registered mail or by sending it to an electronic address designated by the attorney general for this purpose. FRCP 5.1(a).

- *When to file the notice.* A party required to file a notice of constitutional question under FRCP 5.1 must do so by the later of: (1) the day the parties tender their proposed case-management plan (if one is required); or (2) 21 days after filing the pleading, written motion, or other paper questioning the constitutionality of a federal or state statute. IN R USDCTND L.R. 5.1-1(a).

- *Service on government officials.* The party must also serve the notice and the pleading, written motion, or other paper questioning the constitutionality of a federal or state statute on: (1) the Attorney General of the United States and the United States Attorney for the Northern District of Indiana, if a federal statute is challenged; or (2) the Attorney General for the state if a state statute is challenged. IN R USDCTND L.R. 5.1-1(b). Service required under IN R USDCTND L.R. 5.1-1(b) may be made either by certified or registered mail or by emailing it to an address designated by those officials for this purpose. IN R USDCTND L.R. 5.1-1(c).

- *No forfeiture.* A party's failure to file and serve the notice, or the court's failure to certify, does not forfeit a constitutional claim or defense that is otherwise timely asserted. FRCP 5.1(d).

iii. *Nongovernmental corporate disclosure statement*

- *Contents.* A nongovernmental corporate party must file two (2) copies of a disclosure statement that: (1) identifies any parent corporation and any publicly held corporation owning ten percent (10%) or more of its stock; or (2) states that there is no such corporation. FRCP 7.1(a).

- *Time to file; Supplemental filing.* A party must: (1) file the disclosure statement with its first appearance, pleading, petition, motion, response, or other request addressed to the court; and (2) promptly file a supplemental statement if any required information changes. FRCP 7.1(b).

iv. *Index of exhibits.* Any pleading, motion, brief, affidavit, notice, or proposed order, whether filed electronically or by delivering it to the clerk, must: include a separate index identifying and briefly describing each exhibit if there are more than four (4) exhibits. IN R USDCTND L.R. 5-4(a)(8).

v. *Request for oral argument.* A party may request oral argument on a motion by filing and serving a separate document explaining why oral argument is necessary and estimating how long the court should allow for the argument. IN R USDCTND L.R. 7-5(a)(1). The request must be filed and served with the party's supporting brief, response brief, or reply brief. IN R USDCTND L.R. 7-5(a)(2).

vi. *Request for evidentiary hearing.* A party may request an evidentiary hearing by filing and serving a separate document explaining why the hearing is necessary and estimating how long the court should allow for it. IN R USDCTND L.R. 7-5(b)(1).

vii. *Copy of authority.* A copy of any decision, statute, or regulation cited in a motion or brief must be attached to the paper if—and only if—it is not available on Westlaw or Lexis. But if a copy of a decision, statute, or regulation is only available electronically, a party must provide it to the court or another party upon request. IN R USDCTND L.R. 7-1(f).

viii. *Proposed order.* Parties filing a paper that requires the judge or clerk to enter a routine or uncontested order must include a suitable form of order. IN R USDCTND L.R. 5-4(c).

- Proposed orders shall not be filed electronically either as a separate document or as an attachment to the main pleading or other document. Instead, all proposed orders must be e-mailed to the chambers of the appropriate judicial officer for the case. The proposed order must be in WordPerfect Format or Rich Text Format (RTF). Proposed orders should be attached to an e-mail and sent to the appropriate judicial officer at the address listed in IN R USDCTND CM/ECF(II)(F). The subject line of the email message should indicate the case title, cause number and document number of the motion, e.g., Smith v. Jones 1:02-cv-1234, motion# ___. IN R USDCTND CM/ECF(II)(F).

ix. *Copy of document with self-addressed envelope.* A party who wants a file-stamped copy of a paper must include with the filing an additional copy of the paper and a self-addressed envelope with adequate postage. IN R USDCTND L.R. 5-4(b)(6).

x. *Notice of manual filing.* However, if that is not physically possible, counsel shall electronically file a .pdf document titled Notice of Manual Filing as a notation on the docket sheet that filings are being held in the clerk's office in paper. A sample Notice of Manual Filing is attached as Form 2 (IN R USDCTND CM/ECF(Form 2)). IN R USDCTND CM/ECF(III)(A)(1).

xi. *Courtesy copies.* If documents are filed in paper format, counsel must provide an original for the clerk's office, a copy for the judge and a copy must be served on all parties in the case. IN R USDCTND CM/ECF(III)(A)(1).

xii. *Declaration that party was unable to file in a timely manner.* If the attorney is unable to file a document in a timely manner due to technical difficulties in the user's system, the attorney must file a document with the court as soon as possible notifying the court of the inability to file the document. A sample document entitled Declaration that Party was Unable to File in a Timely Manner Due to Technical Difficulties is attached hereto as Form 5. IN R USDCTND CM/ECF(VI)(B). [Editor's note: the reference to Form 5 is likely meant to be a reference to Form 3 (IN R USDCTND CM/ECF(Form 3)].

2. *Documents for opposing party*

   a. *Required documents*

      i. *Response brief.* Refer to the Format section of this document for the format of briefs. Refer to the General Requirements section of this document for information on the opposing papers.

      ii. *Certificate of service.* FRCP 5(d) requires that the person making service under FRCP 5 certify that service has been effected. FRCP 5(Advisory Committee Notes). Having such information on file may be useful for many purposes, including proof of service if an issue arises concerning the effectiveness of the service. FRCP 5(Advisory Committee Notes).

         - *Certificate of service for electronically-filed documents.* A Certificate of Service is still a requirement when filing documents electronically. A sample Certificate of Service is attached as Form 1 (IN R USDCTND CM/ECF(Form 1)). IN R USDCTND CM/ECF(II)(H).

   b. *Supplemental documents*

      i. *Supporting evidence.* When a motion relies on facts outside the record, the court may hear the matter on affidavits or may hear it wholly or partly on oral testimony or on depositions. FRCP 43(c).

         - *Materials necessary for motion.* A party must file those portions of discovery requests or responses (including deposition transcripts) that the party relies on to support a motion that could result in a final order on an issue. IN R USDCTND L.R. 26-2(c).

      ii. *Notice of constitutional question.* A party that files a pleading, written motion, or other paper drawing into question the constitutionality of a federal or state statute must promptly:

         - *File notice.* File a notice of constitutional question stating the question and identifying the paper that raises it, if: (1) a federal statute is questioned and the parties do not include the United States, one of its agencies, or one of its officers or employees in an official capacity; or (2) a state statute is questioned and the parties do not include the state, one of its agencies, or one of its officers or employees in an official capacity; and

         - *Serve notice.* Serve the notice and paper on the Attorney General of the United States if a federal statute is questioned—or on the state attorney general if a state statute is questioned—either by certified or registered mail or by sending it to an electronic address designated by the attorney general for this purpose. FRCP 5.1(a).

         - *When to file the notice.* A party required to file a notice of constitutional question under FRCP 5.1 must do so by the later of: (1) the day the parties tender their proposed case-management plan (if one is required); or (2) 21 days after filing the pleading, written motion, or other paper questioning the constitutionality of a federal or state statute. IN R USDCTND L.R. 5.1-1(a).

         - *Service on government officials.* The party must also serve the notice and the pleading, written motion, or other paper questioning the constitutionality of a federal or state statute on: (1) the Attorney General of the United States and the United States Attorney for the Northern District of Indiana, if a federal statute is challenged; or (2) the Attorney General for the state if a state statute is challenged. IN R USDCTND L.R. 5.1-1(b). Service required under IN R USDCTND L.R. 5.1-1(b) may be made either by certified or registered mail or by emailing it to an address designated by those officials for this purpose. IN R USDCTND L.R. 5.1-1(c).

         - *No forfeiture.* A party's failure to file and serve the notice, or the court's failure to certify, does not forfeit a constitutional claim or defense that is otherwise timely asserted. FRCP 5.1(d).

iii. *Index of exhibits.* Any pleading, motion, brief, affidavit, notice, or proposed order, whether filed electronically or by delivering it to the clerk, must: include a separate index identifying and briefly describing each exhibit if there are more than four (4) exhibits. IN R USDCTND L.R. 5-4(a)(8).

iv. *Request for oral argument.* A party may request oral argument on a motion by filing and serving a separate document explaining why oral argument is necessary and estimating how long the court should allow for the argument. IN R USDCTND L.R. 7-5(a)(1). The request must be filed and served with the party's supporting brief, response brief, or reply brief. IN R USDCTND L.R. 7-5(a)(2).

v. *Request for evidentiary hearing.* A party may request an evidentiary hearing by filing and serving a separate document explaining why the hearing is necessary and estimating how long the court should allow for it. IN R USDCTND L.R. 7-5(b)(1).

vi. *Copy of authority.* A copy of any decision, statute, or regulation cited in a motion or brief must be attached to the paper if—and only if—it is not available on Westlaw or Lexis. But if a copy of a decision, statute, or regulation is only available electronically, a party must provide it to the court or another party upon request. IN R USDCTND L.R. 7-1(f).

vii. *Copy of document with self-addressed envelope.* A party who wants a file-stamped copy of a paper must include with the filing an additional copy of the paper and a self-addressed envelope with adequate postage. IN R USDCTND L.R. 5-4(b)(6).

viii. *Notice of manual filing.* However, if that is not physically possible, counsel shall electronically file a .pdf document titled Notice of Manual Filing as a notation on the docket sheet that filings are being held in the clerk's office in paper. A sample Notice of Manual Filing is attached as Form 2 (IN R USDCTND CM/ECF(Form 2)). IN R USDCTND CM/ECF(III)(A)(1).

ix. *Courtesy copies.* If documents are filed in paper format, counsel must provide an original for the clerk's office, a copy for the judge and a copy must be served on all parties in the case. IN R USDCTND CM/ECF(III)(A)(1).

x. *Declaration that party was unable to file in a timely manner.* If the attorney is unable to file a document in a timely manner due to technical difficulties in the user's system, the attorney must file a document with the court as soon as possible notifying the court of the inability to file the document. A sample document entitled Declaration that Party was Unable to File in a Timely Manner Due to Technical Difficulties is attached hereto as Form 5. IN R USDCTND CM/ECF(VI)(B). [Editor's note: the reference to Form 5 is likely meant to be a reference to Form 3 (IN R USDCTND CM/ECF(Form 3)].

E. Format

1. *Form of documents.* The rules governing captions and other matters of form in pleadings apply to motions and other papers. FRCP 7(b)(2).

   a. *Paper.* Any pleading, motion, brief, affidavit, notice, or proposed order, whether filed electronically or by delivering it to the clerk, must: use eight and one-half by eleven (8-1/2 x 11) inch pages. IN R USDCTND L.R. 5-4(a)(2).

      i. *Manual filings.* Papers delivered to the clerk for filing must: be flat, unfolded, and on good-quality, white paper. IN R USDCTND L.R. 5-4(b)(1)(A).

      - *Covers or backing.* Papers delivered to the clerk for filing must: not have a cover or a back. IN R USDCTND L.R. 5-4(b)(1)(B).

      - *Recycled paper.* The court encourages using recycled paper. IN R USDCTND L.R. 5-4(b)(7).

   b. *Margins.* Any pleading, motion, brief, affidavit, notice, or proposed order, whether filed electronically or by delivering it to the clerk, must: have at least one (1) inch margins. IN R USDCTND L.R. 5-4(a)(3).

   c. *Spacing.* Any pleading, motion, brief, affidavit, notice, or proposed order, whether filed electronically or by delivering it to the clerk, must: be double spaced (except for headings, footnotes, and quoted material). IN R USDCTND L.R. 5-4(a)(5).

d. *Text.* Any pleading, motion, brief, affidavit, notice, or proposed order, whether filed electronically or by delivering it to the clerk, must: be plainly typewritten, printed, or prepared by a clearly legible copying process. IN R USDCTND L.R. 5-4(a)(1).

    i. Any pleading, motion, brief, affidavit, notice, or proposed order, whether filed electronically or by delivering it to the clerk, must: use at least twelve (12) point type in the body and at least ten (10) point type in footnotes. IN R USDCTND L.R. 5-4(a)(4).

e. *Page numbering.* Any pleading, motion, brief, affidavit, notice, or proposed order, whether filed electronically or by delivering it to the clerk, must: have consecutively numbered pages. IN R USDCTND L.R. 5-4(a)(6).

f. *Caption; Names of parties.* Every pleading must have a caption with the court's name, a title, a file number, and a FRCP 7(a) designation. The title of the complaint must name all the parties; the title of other pleadings, after naming the first party on each side, may refer generally to other parties. FRCP 10(a). Any pleading, motion, brief, affidavit, notice, or proposed order, whether filed electronically or by delivering it to the clerk, must: include a title on the first page. IN R USDCTND L.R. 5-4(a)(7).

    i. *Alternative motions.* Motions must be filed separately, but alternative motions may be filed in a single paper if each is named in the title following the caption. IN R USDCTND L.R. 7-1(a).

g. *Filer's information.* Any pleading, motion, brief, affidavit, notice, or proposed order, whether filed electronically or by delivering it to the clerk, must: except in proposed orders and affidavits, include the filer's name, address, telephone number, fax number (where available), and e-mail address (where available). IN R USDCTND L.R. 5-4(a)(9).

h. *Paragraphs; Separate statements.* A party must state its claims or defenses in numbered paragraphs, each limited as far as practicable to a single set of circumstances. A later pleading may refer by number to a paragraph in an earlier pleading. If doing so would promote clarity, each claim founded on a separate transaction or occurrence—and each defense other than a denial—must be stated in a separate count or defense. FRCP 10(b).

i. *Adoption by reference; Exhibits.* A statement in a pleading may be adopted by reference elsewhere in the same pleading or in any other pleading or motion. A copy of a written instrument that is an exhibit to a pleading is a part of the pleading for all purposes. FRCP 10(c).

j. *Citation of local rules.* The Local Civil Rules of the United States District Court for the Northern District of Indiana may be cited as "N.D. Ind. L.R." IN R USDCTND L.R. 1-1(a)(1).

k. *Acceptance by the clerk.* The clerk must not refuse to file a paper solely because it is not in the form prescribed by the Federal Rules of Civil Procedure or by a local rule or practice. FRCP 5(d)(4).

    i. *Sanctions for formatting errors; Non-compliance.* If a person files a paper that does not comply with the rules governing the format of papers filed with the court, the court may: (1) strike the paper from the record; or (2) fine the person up to one thousand dollars ($1,000). IN R USDCTND L.R. 1-3(a).

        • *Notice.* Before sanctioning a person under IN R USDCTND L.R. 1-3(a)(2), the court must: (1) notify the person that the paper is noncompliant; and (2) give the person the opportunity either to be heard or to revise the paper. IN R USDCTND L.R. 1-3(b).

2. *Form of electronic documents.* Electronically filed documents must meet the same requirements of format and page limits as documents "conventionally filed" (as defined in IN R USDCTND CM/ECF(III)(A)) pursuant to the Federal Rules of Civil Procedure and the Local Civil Rules of the United States District Court for the Northern District of Indiana. IN R USDCTND CM/ECF(II)(A)(2).

a. *PDF format required.* Documents filed in the CM/ECF must be in .pdf format. A document created with almost any word-processing program can be converted to .pdf format. The .pdf program in effect takes a picture of the original document and allows anyone to open the converted document across a broad range of hardware and software, with layout, format, links, and images intact. IN R USDCTND CM/ECF(FN2).

b. *Title of documents.* The person electronically filing a pleading or other document will be responsible

354

for designating a title for the pleading or other document by using one of the categories contained in the events listed in the CM/ECF Menu. IN R USDCTND CM/ECF(II)(G).

c. *Combining documents.* All documents which form part of a single pleading and which are being filed at the same time and by the same party may be electronically filed together under one document number, e.g., the motion and a supporting affidavit, with the exception of memoranda in support. Memoranda in support shall be electronically filed separately and shown as a related document to the motion. IN R USDCTND CM/ECF(II)(A)(4).

d. *Exhibits and attachments.* Filing users must submit in electronic form all documents referenced as exhibits or attachments, unless the court permits conventional filing. A filing user must submit as exhibits or attachments only those excerpts of the referenced documents that are directly germane to the matter under consideration by the court. Excerpted material must be clearly and prominently identified as such. Filing users who file excerpts of documents as exhibits or attachments do so without prejudice to their right to timely file additional excerpts or the complete document. Responding parties may timely file additional excerpts or the complete document that they believe are directly germane. The court may require parties to file additional excerpts or the complete document. IN R USDCTND CM/ECF(II)(A)(6).

e. *Hyperlinks.* Electronically filed documents may contain hyperlink references to an external document as a convenient mechanism for accessing material cited in the document. A hyperlink reference is neither validated for content nor considered a part of the court's records. The court neither endorses the product or organization at the destination of a hyperlink reference, nor does the court exercise any responsibility over the content at the destination. In order to preserve the integrity of the court record, attorneys wishing to insert hyperlinks in court filings shall continue to use the traditional citation method for the cited authority, in addition to the hyperlink. A hyperlink contained in a filing is no more than a convenient mechanism for accessing material cited in the document and a hyperlink reference is extraneous to any filed document and is not part of the court's record. IN R USDCTND CM/ECF(II)(A)(3).

3. *Form of briefs*

a. *Page limits.* Supporting and response briefs (excluding tables of contents, tables of authorities, and appendices) ordinarily must not exceed twenty-five (25) pages. Reply briefs must not exceed fifteen (15) pages. IN R USDCTND L.R. 7-1(e)(1).

   i. *Exception.* The court may allow a party to file a brief exceeding these page limits for extraordinary and compelling reasons. But if the court permits a brief to exceed twenty-five (25) pages, it must include:

   - A table of contents with page references;

   - An issue statement; and

   - A table of authorities including: (1) all cases (alphabetically arranged), statutes, and other authorities cited in the brief; and (2) references to where the authorities appear in the brief. IN R USDCTND L.R. 7-1(e)(2).

4. *Signing of pleadings, motions and other papers*

a. *Signature.* Every pleading, written motion, and other paper must be signed by at least one attorney of record in the attorney's name—or by a party personally if the party is unrepresented. The paper must state the signer's address, e-mail address, and telephone number. FRCP 11(a).

   i. *Signatures on manual filings.* Papers delivered to the clerk for filing must: include the filer's original signature. IN R USDCTND L.R. 5-4(b)(1)(C).

   - *Rubber-stamped and faxed signatures.* An original paper with a rubber-stamped or faxed signature is unsigned for purposes of FRCP 11 and FRCP 26(g). IN R USDCTND L.R. 5-4(b)(2).

   - *Affidavits.* Only the affiant need sign an affidavit. IN R USDCTND L.R. 5-4(b)(3).

   ii. *Electronic signatures.* Pursuant to FRCP 11, every pleading, motion, and other paper (except lists, schedules, statements or amendments thereto) shall be signed by at least one attorney of record or, if the party is not represented by an attorney, all papers shall be signed by the party. An attorney's/participant's password issued by the court combined with the user's identification, serves as and constitutes the attorney/participant's signature for FRCP 11 and other purposes. IN R USDCTND CM/ECF(I)(C). Documents which must be filed and which must contain original signatures other than those of a participating attorney or which require either verification or an unsworn declaration under any rule or statute, shall be filed electronically, with originally executed copies maintained by the filer. The pleading or other document electronically filed shall contain "s/" signature(s), as noted in IN R USDCTND CM/ECF(II)(E)(3)(b). IN R USDCTND CM/ECF(II)(E)(1).

- *Multiple signatures.* In the case of a stipulation or other document to be signed by two or more attorneys, the following procedure should be used: The filing attorney shall initially confirm that the content of the document is acceptable to all persons required to sign the document and shall obtain the physical signatures of all attorneys on the document. IN R USDCTND CM/ECF(II)(E)(3)(a). The filing attorney then shall file the document electronically, indicating the signatories, e.g., "s/Jane Doe," "s/John Doe," etc. IN R US-DCTND CM/ECF(II)(E)(3)(b). The filing attorney shall retain the hard copy of the document containing the original signatures. IN R USDCTND CM/ECF(II)(E)(3)(c).

   iii. *No verification or accompanying affidavit required for pleadings.* Unless a rule or statute specifically states otherwise, a pleading need not be verified or accompanied by an affidavit. FRCP 11(a).

   iv. *Unsigned papers.* The court must strike an unsigned paper unless the omission is promptly corrected after being called to the attorney's or party's attention. FRCP 11(a).

b. *Representations to the court.* By presenting to the court a pleading, written motion, or other paper—whether by signing, filing, submitting, or later advocating it—an attorney or unrepresented party certifies that to the best of the person's knowledge, information, and belief, formed after an inquiry reasonable under the circumstances:

   i. It is not being presented for any improper purpose, such as to harass, cause unnecessary delay, or needlessly increase the cost of litigation;

   ii. The claims, defenses, and other legal contentions are warranted by existing law or by a nonfrivolous argument for extending, modifying, or reversing existing law or for establishing new law;

   iii. The factual contentions have evidentiary support or, if specifically so identified, will likely have evidentiary support after a reasonable opportunity for further investigation or discovery; and

   iv. The denials of factual contentions are warranted on the evidence or, if specifically so identified, are reasonably based on belief or a lack of information. FRCP 11(b).

c. *Sanctions.* If, after notice and a reasonable opportunity to respond, the court determines that FRCP 11(b) has been violated, the court may impose an appropriate sanction on any attorney, law firm, or party that violated FRCP 11(b) or is responsible for the violation. FRCP 11(c)(1). Refer to the United States District Court for the Northern District of Indiana KeyRules Motion for Sanctions document for more information.

5. *Privacy protection for filings made with the court*

a. *Redacted filings.* Counsel should not include sensitive information in any document filed with the court unless such inclusion is necessary and relevant to the case. IN R USDCTND CM/ECF(VII). Unless the court orders otherwise, in an electronic or paper filing with the court that contains an individual's Social Security number, taxpayer-identification number, or birth date, the name of an individual known to be a minor, or a financial-account number, a party or nonparty making the filing may include only:

   i. The last four (4) digits of the Social Security number and taxpayer-identification number;

   ii. The year of the individual's birth;

   iii. The minor's initials; and

    iv. The last four (4) digits of the financial-account number. FRCP 5.2(a); IN R USDCTND Order 2005-3.

b. *Exemptions from the redaction requirement.* The redaction requirement does not apply to the following:

    i. A financial-account number that identifies the property allegedly subject to forfeiture in a forfeiture proceeding;

    ii. The record of an administrative or agency proceeding;

    iii. The official record of a state-court proceeding;

    iv. The record of a court or tribunal, if that record was not subject to the redaction requirement when originally filed;

    v. A filing covered by FRCP 5.2(c) or FRCP 5.2(d); and

    vi. A pro se filing in an action brought under 28 U.S.C.A. § 2241, 28 U.S.C.A. § 2254, or 28 U.S.C.A. § 2255. FRCP 5.2(b).

    vii. In cases filed under the Social Security Act, 42 U.S.C.A. § 405(g), there is no need for redaction of any information from the documents filed in the case. IN R USDCTND Order 2005-3.

c. *Limitations on remote access to electronic files; Social Security appeals and immigration cases.* Unless the court orders otherwise, in an action for benefits under the Social Security Act, and in an action or proceeding relating to an order of removal, to relief from removal, or to immigration benefits or detention, access to an electronic file is authorized as follows:

    i. The parties and their attorneys may have remote electronic access to any part of the case file, including the administrative record;

    ii. Any other person may have electronic access to the full record at the courthouse, but may have remote electronic access only to:

      • The docket maintained by the court; and

      • An opinion, order, judgment, or other disposition of the court, but not any other part of the case file or the administrative record. FRCP 5.2(c).

d. *Filings made under seal.* The court may order that a filing be made under seal without redaction. The court may later unseal the filing or order the person who made the filing to file a redacted version for the public record. FRCP 5.2(d). For information on filing documents under seal, refer to IN R USDCTND L.R. 5-3, IN R USDCTND CM/ECF(IV)(A), and IN R USDCTND ECF Order 2004-19.

e. *Protective orders.* For good cause, the court may by order in a case:

    i. Require redaction of additional information; or

    ii. Limit or prohibit a nonparty's remote electronic access to a document filed with the court. FRCP 5.2(e).

f. *Option for additional unredacted filing under seal.* A person making a redacted filing may also file an unredacted copy under seal. The court must retain the unredacted copy as part of the record. FRCP 5.2(f); IN R USDCTND Order 2005-3.

    i. The unredacted version of the document or the reference list shall be retained by the court under seal as part of the record. This paper shall be retained by the court as part of the record. The court may, however, still require the party to file a redacted copy for the public file. IN R USDCTND Order 2005-3.

g. *Option for filing a reference list.* A filing that contains redacted information may be filed together with a reference list that identifies each item of redacted information and specifies an appropriate identifier that uniquely corresponds to each item listed. The list must be filed under seal and may be amended as of right. Any reference in the case to a listed identifier will be construed to refer to the corresponding item of information. FRCP 5.2(g); IN R USDCTND Order 2005-3.

    i. The unredacted version of the document or the reference list shall be retained by the court under

seal as part of the record. This paper shall be retained by the court as part of the record. The court may, however, still require the party to file a redacted copy for the public file. IN R USDCTND Order 2005-3.

h. *Responsibility for redaction.* The responsibility for redacting these personal identifiers rests solely with counsel and the parties. The Clerk will not review each paper for compliance with IN R USDCTND Order 2005-3. IN R USDCTND Order 2005-3.

i. *Waiver of protection of identifiers.* A person waives the protection of FRCP 5.2(a) as to the person's own information by filing it without redaction and not under seal. FRCP 5.2(h).

F. Filing and Service Requirements

1. *Filing requirements.* Any paper after the complaint that is required to be served—together with a certificate of service—must be filed within a reasonable time after service. FRCP 5(d)(1). Motions must be filed separately, but alternative motions may be filed in a single paper if each is named in the title following the caption. IN R USDCTND L.R. 7-1(a).

   a. *How filing is made; In general.* A paper is filed by delivering it:

      i. To the clerk; or

      ii. To a judge who agrees to accept it for filing, and who must then note the filing date on the paper and promptly send it to the clerk. FRCP 5(d)(2).

         • Papers not filed electronically must be filed with the clerk, not a judge. IN R USDCTND L.R. 5-4(b)(4).

      iii. Parties manually filing a paper that requires the clerk to give others notice, must give the clerk: (1) sufficient copies of the notice; and (2) the name and address of each person entitled to receive the notice. IN R USDCTND L.R. 5-4(b)(8).

   b. *Where to file.* Papers not filed electronically must be filed in the division where the case is pending, unless: (1) a person will be prejudiced if the paper is not filed the same day it is tendered; and (2) it includes an adequately sized envelope addressed to the clerk's office in the division where the case is pending and with adequate postage. IN R USDCTND L.R. 5-4(b)(5).

   c. *Electronic filing*

      i. *Authorization of electronic filing program.* A court may, by local rule, allow papers to be filed, signed, or verified by electronic means that are consistent with any technical standards established by the Judicial Conference of the United States. A local rule may require electronic filing only if reasonable exceptions are allowed. A paper filed electronically in compliance with a local rule is a written paper for purposes of the Federal Rules of Civil Procedure. FRCP 5(d)(3).

         • Papers must be filed, signed, and verified electronically unless excepted by the court's CM/ECF Civil and Criminal User Manual (IN R USDCTND CM/ECF). IN R USDCTND L.R. 5-1.

      ii. *Mandatory electronic filing.* Unless otherwise permitted by these procedures or otherwise authorized by the assigned judge, all documents submitted for filing in this district in civil and criminal cases, no matter when a case was originally filed, shall be filed electronically using the System. IN R USDCTND CM/ECF(II)(A)(1). The requirement that "all documents" be filed electronically includes briefs, and attachments and exhibits used in support of motions. IN R USDCTND CM/ECF(FN1).

         • Sending a document or pleading to the court via e-mail or facsimile does not constitute "electronic filing." IN R USDCTND CM/ECF(I)(A).

      iii. *Conventional filing.* As used in these procedures, a "conventionally" filed or submitted document or pleading is one presented to the Clerk or a party in paper or other non-electronic, tangible format. The following documents shall be filed conventionally and not electronically unless specifically authorized by the Court:

         • Exhibits and other documents which cannot be converted to a legible electronic form.

Whenever possible, counsel is responsible for converting filings to an electronic form. However, if that is not physically possible, counsel shall electronically file a .pdf document titled Notice of Manual Filing as a notation on the docket sheet that filings are being held in the clerk's office in paper. A sample Notice of Manual Filing is attached as Form 2 (IN R USDCTND CM/ECF(Form 2)). If documents are filed in paper format, counsel must provide an original for the clerk's office, a copy for the judge and a copy must be served on all parties in the case. Large documents which do not exist in an electronic format shall be scanned into .pdf format by counsel, in small batches if necessary, and filed electronically as separate attachments in the System. IN R USDCTND CM/ECF(III)(A)(1).

- Certain documents which are listed in IN R USDCTND CM/ECF(II)(E)(2). IN R US-DCTND CM/ECF(III)(A)(2).

- Documents filed by pro se litigants. IN R USDCTND CM/ECF(III)(A)(3).

iv. For more information on electronic filing, refer to IN R USDCTND CM/ECF.

2. *Service requirements*

a. *Service; When required*

i. *In general.* Unless the Federal Rules of Civil Procedure provide otherwise, each of the following papers must be served on every party:

- An order stating that service is required;

- A pleading filed after the original complaint, unless the court orders otherwise under FRCP 5(c) because there are numerous defendants;

- A discovery paper required to be served on a party, unless the court orders otherwise;

- A written motion, except one that may be heard ex parte; and

- A written notice, appearance, demand, or offer of judgment, or any similar paper. FRCP 5(a)(1).

ii. *If a party fails to appear.* No service is required on a party who is in default for failing to appear. But a pleading that asserts a new claim for relief against such a party must be served on that party under FRCP 4. FRCP 5(a)(2).

iii. *Seizing property.* If an action is begun by seizing property and no person is or need be named as a defendant, any service required before the filing of an appearance, answer, or claim must be made on the person who had custody or possession of the property when it was seized. FRCP 5(a)(3).

b. *Service; How made*

i. *Serving an attorney.* If a party is represented by an attorney, service under FRCP 5 must be made on the attorney unless the court orders service on the party. FRCP 5(b)(1).

ii. *Service in general.* A paper is served under FRCP 5 by:

- Handing it to the person;

- Leaving it: (1) at the person's office with a clerk or other person in charge or, if no one is in charge, in a conspicuous place in the office; or (2) if the person has no office or the office is closed, at the person's dwelling or usual place of abode with someone of suitable age and discretion who resides there;

- Mailing it to the person's last known address—in which event service is complete upon mailing;

- Leaving it with the court clerk if the person has no known address;

- Sending it by electronic means if the person consented in writing—in which event service is complete upon transmission, but is not effective if the serving party learns that it did not reach the person to be served; or

- Delivering it by any other means that the person consented to in writing—in which event service is complete when the person making service delivers it to the agency designated to make delivery. FRCP 5(b)(2).

    iii. *Electronic service.* Electronically filed papers may be served electronically if service is consistent with the CM/ECF User Manual (IN R USDCTND CM/ECF). IN R USDCTND L.R. 5-2(a).

- *Waiver of other service.* An attorney's registration will constitute a waiver of conventional service of documents and the attorney agrees to accept service of notice on behalf of the client of the electronic filing by hand, facsimile or authorized email. IN R USDCTND CM/ECF(I)(B)(3).

- *Serving registered persons.* The System will generate a "Notice of Electronic Filing" when any document is filed. This notice represents service of the document on parties who are registered participants with the System. Except as provided in IN R USDCTND CM/ECF(III)(B), the filing party shall not be required to serve any pleading or other documents on any party receiving electronic notice. IN R USDCTND CM/ECF(II)(D)(1). The term "pleading" refers only to those documents listed in FRCP 7(a). IN R USDCTND CM/ECF(FN3).

- *When electronic service is deemed completed.* A person registered to use the court's electronic-filing system is served with an electronically filed paper when a "Notice of Electronic Filing" is transmitted to that person through the court's electronic filing-system. IN R USDCTND L.R. 5-2(b).

- *Serving non-registered persons.* A person who has not registered to use the court's electronic-filing system but who is entitled to service of a paper must be served according to the Local Civil Rules of the United States District Court for the Northern District of Indiana and the Federal Rules of Civil Procedure. IN R USDCTND L.R. 5-2(c); IN R USDCTND CM/ECF(II)(D)(2). If such service of a paper copy is to be made, it shall be done in the manner provided in the Federal Rules of Civil Procedure and the Local Civil Rules of the United States District Court for the Northern District of Indiana. IN R USDCTND CM/ECF(II)(D)(2).

    iv. *Service of conventional filings.* Pleadings or other documents which are filed conventionally rather than electronically shall be served in the manner provided for in the Federal Rules of Civil Procedure and the Local Civil Rules of the United States District Court for the Northern District of Indiana, except as otherwise provided by order of the Court. IN R USDCTND CM/ECF(III)(B).

    v. *Using court facilities.* If a local rule so authorizes, a party may use the court's transmission facilities to make service under FRCP 5(b)(2)(E). FRCP 5(b)(3).

  c. *Serving numerous defendants*

    i. *In general.* If an action involves an unusually large number of defendants, the court may, on motion or on its own, order that:

- Defendants' pleadings and replies to them need not be served on other defendants;

- Any crossclaim, counterclaim, avoidance, or affirmative defense in those pleadings and replies to them will be treated as denied or avoided by all other parties; and

- Filing any such pleading and serving it on the plaintiff constitutes notice of the pleading to all parties. FRCP 5(c)(1).

    ii. *Notifying parties.* A copy of every such order must be served on the parties as the court directs. FRCP 5(c)(2).

G. Hearings

1. *Hearings, generally*

  a. *Oral argument.* Due process does not require that oral argument be permitted on a motion and, except as otherwise provided by local rule, the district court has discretion to determine whether it will decide the motion on the papers or hear argument by counsel (and perhaps receive evidence). FPP § 1190; F.D.I.C. v. Deglau, 207 F.3d 153 (3d Cir. 2000).

    i.   *Request for oral argument.* A party may request oral argument on a motion by filing and serving a separate document explaining why oral argument is necessary and estimating how long the court should allow for the argument. IN R USDCTND L.R. 7-5(a)(1). Refer to the Documents section of this document for more information.

    ii. *Additional evidence forbidden.* Parties may not present additional evidence at oral argument. IN R USDCTND L.R. 7-5(a)(3).

  b. *Providing a regular schedule for oral hearings.* A court may establish regular times and places for oral hearings on motions. FRCP 78(a).

  c. *Providing for submission on briefs.* By rule or order, the court may provide for submitting and determining motions on briefs, without oral hearings. FRCP 78(b).

  d. *Evidentiary hearings.* A party may request an evidentiary hearing by filing and serving a separate document explaining why the hearing is necessary and estimating how long the court should allow for it. IN R USDCTND L.R. 7-5(b)(2). Refer to the Documents section of this document for more information.

  e. *Court's authority.* The court may: (1) grant or deny a request for oral argument or an evidentiary hearing in its discretion; (2) set oral argument or an evidentiary hearing without a request from a party; or (3) order any oral argument or evidentiary hearing to be held anywhere within the district regardless of where the case will be tried. IN R USDCTND L.R. 7-5(c).

2. *Courtroom and courthouse decorum.* For information on courtroom and courthouse decorum, refer to IN R USDCTND L.R. 83-3.

H. Forms

1. Federal Motion for More Definite Statement Forms

  a. Motion; To strike pleading for failure to comply with order for more definite statement. AMJUR PP FEDPRAC § 443.

  b. Notice of motion; To strike complaint and dismiss action for failure to furnish more definite statement. AMJUR PP FEDPRAC § 445.

  c. Motion and notice; For more definite statement; General form. AMJUR PP FEDPRAC § 541.

  d. Motion and notice; To strike complaint and to dismiss action for failure of plaintiff to furnish more definite statement in compliance with order. AMJUR PP FEDPRAC § 542.

  e. Motion; By multiple defendants; For more definite statement. AMJUR PP FEDPRAC § 543.

  f. More definite statement. AMJUR PP FEDPRAC § 546.

  g. Motion and notice; For more definite statement as to date of transaction alleged in complaint. AMJUR PP FEDPRAC § 1391.

  h. Motion and notice; For more definite statement concerning jurisdictional amount. AMJUR PP FEDPRAC § 1410.

  i. Motion for more definite statement. 2C FEDFORMS § 11:144.

  j. Motion for more definite statement; Describing allegations requiring more definite statement. 2C FEDFORMS § 11:145.

  k. Motion for more definite statement; Damages. 2C FEDFORMS § 11:146.

  l. Motion for more definite statement; Patent case. 2C FEDFORMS § 11:147.

  m. Compliance with order for more definite statement of complaint. 2C FEDFORMS § 11:149.

  n. Motion to strike complaint upon failure of plaintiff to furnish more definite statement ordered by the court. 2C FEDFORMS § 11:150.

  o. Notice; Of motion; Containing motion. FEDPROF § 1:749.

    p.   Opposition; To motion; General form. FEDPROF § 1:750.

    q.   Affidavit; Supporting or opposing motion. FEDPROF § 1:751.

    r.   Brief; Supporting or opposing motion. FEDPROF § 1:752.

    s.   Statement of points and authorities; Opposing motion. FEDPROF § 1:753.

    t.   Motion; For more definite statement; General form. FEDPROF § 1:779.

    u.   Motion; By plaintiff; For more definite statement. FEDPROF § 1:780.

    v.   Motion; By defendant; For more definite statement. FEDPROF § 1:781.

    w.   Motion; By defendant; For more definite statement; By trustee. FEDPROF § 1:782.

    x.   Motion; By multiple defendants; For more definite statement. FEDPROF § 1:783.

    y.   Response; By plaintiff; To motion for more definite statement. FEDPROF § 1:784.

    z.   Notice and motion for more definite statement. GOLDLTGFMS § 20:6.

2. Forms for the Northern District of Indiana

    a.   Certificate of service. IN R USDCTND CM/ECF(Form 1).

    b.   Notice of manual filing. IN R USDCTND CM/ECF(Form 2).

    c.   Declaration that party was unable to file in a timely manner. IN R USDCTND CM/ECF(Form 3).

I. Applicable Rules

1. *Federal rules*

    a.   Serving and filing pleadings and other papers. FRCP 5.

    b.   Constitutional challenge to a statute; Notice, certification, and intervention. FRCP 5.1.

    c.   Privacy protection for filings made with the court. FRCP 5.2.

    d.   Computing and extending time; Time for motion papers. FRCP 6.

    e.   Pleadings allowed; Form of motions and other papers. FRCP 7.

    f.   Disclosure statement. FRCP 7.1.

    g.   Form of pleadings. FRCP 10.

    h.   Signing pleadings, motions, and other papers; Representations to the court; Sanctions. FRCP 11.

    i.   Defenses and objections; When and how presented; Motion for judgment on the pleadings; Consolidating motions; Waiving defenses; Pretrial hearing. FRCP 12.

    j.   Taking testimony. FRCP 43.

    k.   Hearing motions; Submission on briefs. FRCP 78.

2. *Local rules*

    a.   Citation and scope of the rules. IN R USDCTND L.R. 1-1.

    b.   Sanctions for formatting errors. IN R USDCTND L.R. 1-3.

    c.   Electronic filing required. IN R USDCTND L.R. 5-1.

    d.   Constitutional questions. IN R USDCTND L.R. 5.1-1.

    e.   Electronic service. IN R USDCTND L.R. 5-2.

    f.   Format of papers. IN R USDCTND L.R. 5-4.

    g.   Motion practice. IN R USDCTND L.R. 7-1.

    h.   Oral arguments and evidentiary hearings. IN R USDCTND L.R. 7-5.

    i.   Pretrial procedure. IN R USDCTND L.R. 16-1.

    j.   Alternative dispute resolution. IN R USDCTND L.R. 16-6.

    k.   Filing of discovery and other materials. IN R USDCTND L.R. 26-2.

l. Case assignment. IN R USDCTND L.R. 40-1.

m. Appearance and withdrawal of appearance. IN R USDCTND L.R. 83-8.

n. CM/ECF civil and criminal user manual. IN R USDCTND CM/ECF.

o. In re: privacy and public access to civil electronic case files. IN R USDCTND Order 2005-3.

Motions, Oppositions and Replies
Motion for Post-Trial Relief

Document Last Updated December 2016

A. Checklist

(I) ❑ Matters to be considered by moving party

    (a) ❑ Required documents

        (1) ❑ Notice of motion and motion

        (2) ❑ Certificate of service

    (b) ❑ Supplemental documents

        (1) ❑ Brief

        (2) ❑ Supporting evidence

        (3) ❑ Notice of constitutional question

        (4) ❑ Index of exhibits

        (5) ❑ Request for oral argument

        (6) ❑ Request for evidentiary hearing

        (7) ❑ Copy of authority

        (8) ❑ Proposed order

        (9) ❑ Copy of document with self-addressed envelope

        (10) ❑ Notice of manual filing

        (11) ❑ Courtesy copies

        (12) ❑ Declaration that party was unable to file in a timely manner

    (c) ❑ Timing

        (1) ❑ Motion for new trial: a motion for a new trial must be filed no later than twenty-eight (28) days after the entry of judgment

            (i) ❑ When a motion for a new trial is based on affidavits, they must be filed with the motion

        (2) ❑ Motion to alter or amend judgment: a motion to alter or amend a judgment must be filed no later than twenty-eight (28) days after the entry of the judgment

        (3) ❑ Motion for relief from judgment:

            (i) ❑ Clerical mistakes and errors of oversight or omission may be corrected at any time

            (ii) ❑ A motion under FRCP 60(b) must be made within a reasonable time—and for reasons under FRCP 60(b)(1), FRCP 60(b)(2), and FRCP 60(b)(3) no more than a year after the entry of the judgment or order or the date of the proceeding

        (4) ❑ A written motion and notice of the hearing must be served at least fourteen (14) days before the time specified for the hearing, with the following exceptions: (i) when the motion may be heard ex parte; (ii) when the Federal Rules of Civil Procedure set a different time; or (iii) when a court order—which a party may, for good cause, apply for ex parte—sets a different time

(5) ❏ Any affidavit supporting a motion must be served with the motion

(II) ❏ Matters to be considered by opposing party

    (a) ❏ Required documents

        (1) ❏ Response brief

        (2) ❏ Certificate of service

    (b) ❏ Supplemental documents

        (1) ❏ Supporting evidence

        (2) ❏ Notice of constitutional question

        (3) ❏ Index of exhibits

        (4) ❏ Request for oral argument

        (5) ❏ Request for evidentiary hearing

        (6) ❏ Copy of authority

        (7) ❏ Copy of document with self-addressed envelope

        (8) ❏ Notice of manual filing

        (9) ❏ Courtesy copies

      (10) ❏ Declaration that party was unable to file in a timely manner

    (c) ❏ Timing

        (1) ❏ Opposing a motion for new trial: a party must file any response brief to a motion within fourteen (14) days after the motion is served

           (i) ❏ The opposing party has fourteen (14) days after being served to file opposing affidavits

        (2) ❏ Opposing a motion to alter or amend judgment: a party must file any response brief to a motion within fourteen (14) days after the motion is served

           (i) ❏ Except as FRCP 59(c) provides otherwise, any opposing affidavit must be served at least seven (7) days before the hearing, unless the court permits service at another time

        (3) ❏ Opposing a motion for relief from judgment: a party must file any response brief to a motion within fourteen (14) days after the motion is served

           (i) ❏ Except as FRCP 59(c) provides otherwise, any opposing affidavit must be served at least seven (7) days before the hearing, unless the court permits service at another time

B. Timing

1. *Motion for post-trial relief*

    a. *Motion for new trial.* A motion for a new trial must be filed no later than twenty-eight (28) days after the entry of judgment. FRCP 59(b). A motion for a new trial on the ground of newly discovered evidence is subject to the same time limit as any other motion under FRCP 59 and must be made within twenty-eight (28) days after entry of judgment. However, under FRCP 60(b)(2) a party may move for relief from the judgment on this ground within a year of the entry of the judgment. FPP § 2808. The same standard applies for establishing this ground for relief, whether the motion is under FRCP 59 or FRCP 60(b)(2). FPP § 2808; WMS Gaming, Inc. v. International Game Technology, 184 F.3d 1339, 1361 n.10 (Fed. Cir. 1999).

        i. *Supporting affidavit.* When a motion for a new trial is based on affidavits, they must be filed with the motion. FRCP 59(c).

    b. *Motion to alter or amend judgment.* A motion to alter or amend a judgment must be filed no later than twenty-eight (28) days after the entry of the judgment. FRCP 59(e).

    c. *Motion for relief from judgment*

        i. *Correction of clerical mistakes, oversights and omissions in judgment, order, or proceeding.* Clerical mistakes and errors of oversight or omission may be corrected at any time. FPP § 2855.

    ii.   *Relief from judgment, order, or proceeding.* A motion under FRCP 60(b) must be made within a reasonable time—and for reasons under FRCP 60(b)(1), FRCP 60(b)(2), and FRCP 60(b)(3) no more than a year after the entry of the judgment or order or the date of the proceeding. FRCP 60(c)(1).

        ● *Exception for motions under FRCP 60(b)(4).* The time limitations applicable generally to FRCP 60(b) motions ordinarily [do not] apply to motions seeking relief for voidness, and the moving party need not show diligence in seeking to overturn the judgment or a meritorious defense. FEDPROC § 51:150.

2.   *Timing of motions, generally*

    a.   *Motion and notice of hearing.* A written motion and notice of the hearing must be served at least fourteen (14) days before the time specified for the hearing, with the following exceptions:

       i.   When the motion may be heard ex parte;

      ii.   When the Federal Rules of Civil Procedure set a different time; or

     iii.   When a court order—which a party may, for good cause, apply for ex parte—sets a different time. FRCP 6(c)(1).

    b.   *Supporting affidavit.* Any affidavit supporting a motion must be served with the motion. FRCP 6(c)(2).

3.   *Timing of opposing papers*

    a.   *Opposing a motion for new trial.* A party must file any response brief to a motion within fourteen (14) days after the motion is served. IN R USDCTND L.R. 7-1(d)(2)(A).

       i.   *Opposing affidavit.* The opposing party has fourteen (14) days after being served to file opposing affidavits. FRCP 59(c).

    b.   *Opposing a motion to alter or amend judgment.* A party must file any response brief to a motion within fourteen (14) days after the motion is served. IN R USDCTND L.R. 7-1(d)(2)(A).

       i.   *Opposing affidavit.* Except as FRCP 59(c) provides otherwise, any opposing affidavit must be served at least seven (7) days before the hearing, unless the court permits service at another time. FRCP 6(c)(2).

    c.   *Opposing a motion for relief from judgment.* A party must file any response brief to a motion within fourteen (14) days after the motion is served. IN R USDCTND L.R. 7-1(d)(2)(A).

       i.   *Opposing affidavit.* Except as FRCP 59(c) provides otherwise, any opposing affidavit must be served at least seven (7) days before the hearing, unless the court permits service at another time. FRCP 6(c)(2).

    d.   *Extensions.* The court may extend response- and reply-brief deadlines, but only for good cause. IN R USDCTND L.R. 7-1(d)(3).

    e.   *Summary rulings.* The court may rule on a motion summarily if an opposing party does not file a response before the deadline. IN R USDCTND L.R. 7-1(d)(4).

4.   *Timing of reply papers.* Where the respondent files an answering affidavit setting up a new matter, the moving party ordinarily is allowed a reasonable time to file a reply affidavit since failure to deny the new matter by affidavit may operate as an admission of its truth. AMJUR MOTIONS § 25.

    a.   *Reply in support of motion for new trial.* The court may permit reply affidavits. FRCP 59(c). The moving party must file any reply brief within seven (7) days after the response brief is served. IN R USDCTND L.R. 7-1(d)(2)(B).

    b.   *Reply in support of motion to alter or amend judgment.* The moving party must file any reply brief within seven (7) days after the response brief is served. IN R USDCTND L.R. 7-1(d)(2)(B).

    c.   *Reply in support of motion for relief from judgment.* The moving party must file any reply brief within seven (7) days after the response brief is served. IN R USDCTND L.R. 7-1(d)(2)(B).

    d.   *Extensions.* The court may extend response- and reply-brief deadlines, but only for good cause. IN R USDCTND L.R. 7-1(d)(3).

5. *Computation of time*

   a. *Computing time.* FRCP 6 applies in computing any time period specified in the Federal Rules of Civil Procedure, in any local rule or court order, or in any statute that does not specify a method of computing time. FRCP 6(a).

      i. *Period stated in days or a longer unit.* When the period is stated in days or a longer unit of time:
         - Exclude the day of the event that triggers the period;
         - Count every day, including intermediate Saturdays, Sundays, and legal holidays; and
         - Include the last day of the period, but if the last day is a Saturday, Sunday, or legal holiday, the period continues to run until the end of the next day that is not a Saturday, Sunday, or legal holiday. FRCP 6(a)(1).

      ii. *Period stated in hours.* When the period is stated in hours:
         - Begin counting immediately on the occurrence of the event that triggers the period;
         - Count every hour, including hours during intermediate Saturdays, Sundays, and legal holidays; and
         - If the period would end on a Saturday, Sunday, or legal holiday, the period continues to run until the same time on the next day that is not a Saturday, Sunday, or legal holiday. FRCP 6(a)(2).

      iii. *Inaccessibility of the clerk's office.* Unless the court orders otherwise, if the clerk's office is inaccessible:
         - On the last day for filing under FRCP 6(a)(1), then the time for filing is extended to the first accessible day that is not a Saturday, Sunday, or legal holiday; or
         - During the last hour for filing under FRCP 6(a)(2), then the time for filing is extended to the same time on the first accessible day that is not a Saturday, Sunday, or legal holiday. FRCP 6(a)(3).

      iv. *"Last day" defined.* Unless a different time is set by a statute, local rule, or court order, the last day ends:
         - For electronic filing, at midnight in the court's time zone; and
         - For filing by other means, when the clerk's office is scheduled to close. FRCP 6(a)(4).

      v. *"Next day" defined.* The "next day" is determined by continuing to count forward when the period is measured after an event and backward when measured before an event. FRCP 6(a)(5).

      vi. *"Legal holiday" defined.* "Legal holiday" means:
         - The day set aside by statute for observing New Year's Day, Martin Luther King Jr.'s Birthday, Washington's Birthday, Memorial Day, Independence Day, Labor Day, Columbus Day, Veterans' Day, Thanksgiving Day, or Christmas Day;
         - Any day declared a holiday by the President or Congress; and
         - For periods that are measured after an event, any other day declared a holiday by the state where the district court is located. FRCP 6(a)(6).

   b. *Computation of electronic filing deadlines.* Filing documents electronically does not alter any filing deadlines or any time computation pursuant to FRCP 6. The counties of Lake, Porter, LaPorte, Pulaski and Starke are located in the Central time zone and the remaining counties in the Northern District of Indiana are located in the Eastern time zone. Nevertheless, all electronic transmissions of documents must be completed (i.e., received completely by the clerk's office) prior to midnight Eastern Time, (South Bend/Fort Wayne/Lafayette time) in order to be considered timely filed that day, regardless of the local time in the division where the case is pending. Although documents can be filed electronically twenty-four (24) hours a day, filers are strongly encouraged to file all documents during hours when the CM/ECF Help Line is available, from 9:00 a.m. to 4:00 p.m. local time. IN R USDCTND CM/ECF(II)(I).

      i. *Technical failures.* If the attorney is unable to file a document in a timely manner due to

366

technical difficulties in the user's system, the attorney must file a document with the court as soon as possible notifying the court of the inability to file the document. A sample document entitled Declaration that Party was Unable to File in a Timely Manner Due to Technical Difficulties is attached hereto as Form 5. IN R USDCTND CM/ECF(VI)(B). [Editor's note: the reference to Form 5 is likely meant to be a reference to Form 3 (IN R USDCTND CM/ECF(Form 3)].

    c.   *Extending time*

        i.   *In general.* When an act may or must be done within a specified time, the court may, for good cause, extend the time:

- With or without motion or notice if the court acts, or if a request is made, before the original time or its extension expires; or

- On motion made after the time has expired if the party failed to act because of excusable neglect. FRCP 6(b)(1).

       ii.   *Exceptions.* A court must not extend the time to act under FRCP 50(b), FRCP 50(d), FRCP 52(b), FRCP 59(b), FRCP 59(d), FRCP 59(e), and FRCP 60(b). FRCP 6(b)(2).

      iii.   Refer to the United States District Court for the Northern District of Indiana KeyRules Motion for Continuance/Extension of Time document for more information on extending time.

    d.   *Additional time after certain kinds of service.* When a party may or must act within a specified time after being served and service is made under FRCP 5(b)(2)(C) (mail), FRCP 5(b)(2)(D) (leaving with the clerk), or FRCP 5(b)(2)(F) (other means consented to), three (3) days are added after the period would otherwise expire under FRCP 6(a). FRCP 6(d).

C. General Requirements

  1. *Motions, generally*

    a.   *Requirements.* A request for a court order must be made by motion. The motion must:

        i.   Be in writing unless made during a hearing or trial;

       ii.   State with particularity the grounds for seeking the order; and

      iii.   State the relief sought. FRCP 7(b)(1).

    b.   *Notice of motion.* A party interested in resisting the relief sought by a motion has a right to notice thereof, and an opportunity to be heard. AMJUR MOTIONS § 12.

        i.   In addition to statutory or court rule provisions requiring notice of a motion—the purpose of such a notice requirement having been said to be to prevent a party from being prejudicially surprised by a motion—principles of natural justice dictate that an adverse party generally must be given notice that a motion will be presented to the court. AMJUR MOTIONS § 12.

       ii.   "Notice," in this regard, means reasonable notice, including a meaningful opportunity to prepare and to defend against allegations of a motion. AMJUR MOTIONS § 12.

    c.   *Writing requirement.* The writing requirement is intended to insure that the adverse parties are informed and have a record of both the motion's pendency and the grounds on which the movant seeks an order. FPP § 1191; Feldberg v. Quechee Lakes Corp., 463 F.3d 195 (2d Cir. 2006).

        i.   It is sufficient "if the motion is stated in a written notice of the hearing of the motion." FPP § 1191.

    d.   *Particularity requirement.* The particularity requirement insures that the opposing parties will have notice of their opponent's contentions. FEDPROC § 62:364; Goodman v. 1973 26 Foot Trojan Vessel, Arkansas Registration No. AR1439SN, 859 F.2d 71, 12 Fed.R.Serv.3d 645 (8th Cir. 1988). That requirement ensures that notice of the basis for the motion is provided to the court and to the opposing party so as to avoid prejudice, provide the opponent with a meaningful opportunity to respond, and provide the court with enough information to process the motion correctly. FEDPROC § 62:364; Andreas v. Volkswagen of America, Inc., 336 F.3d 789, 56 Fed.R.Serv.3d 6 (8th Cir. 2003).

        i.   Reasonable specification of the grounds for a motion is sufficient. However, where a movant fails to state even one ground for granting the motion in question, the movant has failed to meet the minimal standard of "reasonable specification." FEDPROC § 62:364; Martinez v. Trainor, 556 F.2d 818, 23 Fed.R.Serv.2d 403 (7th Cir. 1977).

ii. The court may excuse the failure to comply with the particularity requirement if it is inadvertent, and where no prejudice is shown by the opposing party. FEDPROC § 62:364.

e. *Motions must be filed separately.* Motions must be filed separately, but alternative motions may be filed in a single paper if each is named in the title following the caption. IN R USDCTND L.R. 7-1(a).

2. *Motion for post-trial relief*

a. *Motion for new trial.* FRCP 59 gives the trial judge ample power to prevent what the judge considers to be a miscarriage of justice. It is the judge's right, and indeed duty, to order a new trial if it is deemed in the interest of justice to do so. FPP § 2803; Juneau Square Corp. v. First Wisconsin Nat. Bank of Milwaukee, 624 F.2d 798, 807 (7th Cir. 1980).

i. *Grounds for new trial.* The court may, on motion, grant a new trial on all or some of the issues—and to any party—as follows: (1) after a jury trial, for any reason for which a new trial has heretofore been granted in an action at law in federal court; or (2) after a nonjury trial, for any reason for which a rehearing has heretofore been granted in a suit in equity in federal court. FRCP 59(a)(1). Any error of law, if prejudicial, is a good ground for a new trial. The other grounds most commonly raised. . .are that the verdict is against the weight of the evidence, that the verdict is too large or too small, that there is newly discovered evidence, that conduct of counsel or of the court has tainted the verdict, or that there has been misconduct affecting the jury. FPP § 2805.

- *Weight of the evidence.* The power of a federal judge to grant a new trial on the ground that the verdict was against the weight of the evidence is clear. FPP § 2806; Byrd v. Blue Ridge Rural Elec. Co-op., Inc., 356 U.S. 525, 540, 78 S.Ct. 893, 902, 2 L.Ed.2d 953 (1958); Montgomery Ward & Co. v. Duncan, 311 U.S. 243, 251, 61 S.Ct. 189, 194, 85 L.Ed. 147 (1940). On a motion for a new trial—unlike a motion for a judgment as a matter of law—the judge may set aside the verdict even though there is substantial evidence to support it. FPP § 2806; ATD Corp. v. Lydall, Inc., 159 F.3d 534, 549 (Fed. Cir. 1998). The judge is not required to take that view of the evidence most favorable to the verdict-winner. FPP § 2806; Bates v. Hensley, 414 F.2d 1006, 1011 (8th Cir. 1969). The mere fact that the evidence is in conflict is not enough to set aside the verdict, however. Indeed the more sharply the evidence conflicts, the more reluctant the judge should be to substitute his judgment for that of the jury. FPP § 2806; Dawson v. Wal-Mart Stores, Inc., 978 F.2d 205 (5th Cir. 1992); Williams v. City of Valdosta, 689 F.2d 964, 974 (11th Cir. 1982). But on a motion for a new trial on the ground that the verdict is against the weight of the evidence, the judge is free to weigh the evidence. FPP § 2806; Uniloc USA, Inc. v. Microsoft Corp., 632 F.3d 1292 (Fed. Cir. 2011). Indeed, it has been said that the granting of a new trial on the ground that the verdict is against the weight of the evidence "involves an element of discretion which goes further than the mere sufficiency of the evidence. It embraces all the reasons which inhere in the integrity of the jury system itself." FPP § 2806; Tidewater Oil Co. v. Waller, 302 F.2d 638, 643 (10th Cir. 1962).

- *Size of the verdict.* A motion under FRCP 59 is an appropriate means to challenge the size of the verdict. The court always may grant relief if the verdict is excessive or inadequate as a matter of law, but this is not the limit of the court's power. FPP § 2807. It also may grant a new trial if the size of the verdict is against the weight of the evidence. FPP § 2807; Sprague v. Boston and Maine Corp., 769 F.2d 26, 28 (1st Cir. 1985). If the court finds that a verdict is unreasonably high, it may condition denial of the motion for a new trial on plaintiff's consent to a remittitur. FPP § 2807. If the verdict is too low, it may not provide for an additur as an alternative to a new trial. FPP § 2807; Dimick v. Schiedt, 293 U.S. 474, 55 S.Ct. 296, 79 L.Ed. 603 (1935).

- *Newly discovered evidence.* Newly discovered evidence must be of facts existing at the time of trial. FPP § 2808; Alicea v. Machete Music, 744 F.3d 773, 781 (1st Cir. 2014). The moving party must have been excusably ignorant of the facts despite using due diligence to learn about them. FPP § 2808; U.S. v. 41 Cases, More or Less, 420 F.2d 1126 (5th Cir. 1970); Huff v. Metropolitan Life Ins. Co., 675 F.2d 119 (6th Cir. 1982). If the facts were known to the party and no excusable ignorance can be shown, a new-trial motion will not be granted. Failure to show due diligence also generally will result in the denial of the motion. FPP § 2808. However, it has been held that a new trial may be granted even though proper diligence was not used if this is necessary to prevent a manifest miscarriage of justice. FPP § 2808; Ferrell v. Trailmobile, Inc., 223 F.2d 697 (5th Cir. 1955).

- *Conduct of counsel and judge.* If a verdict has been unfairly influenced by the misconduct of counsel, a new trial should be granted. Misconduct of counsel that may necessitate a new trial may involve things such as improper comments or arguments to the jury, including presenting arguments about evidence not properly before the court. FPP § 2809. Improper conduct by the trial judge also is a ground for a new trial. Motions raising this ground happily are rare and a new trial is not required if the judge's behavior has not made the trial unfair. The moving party must meet a heavy burden to prevail on the ground of judicial misconduct. FPP § 2809.

- *Misconduct affecting jury.* A common ground for a motion for a new trial is that the jury, or members of it, has not performed in the fashion expected of juries. FPP § 2810. Because of the limitations on the use of testimony by the jurors and because a new trial is required in any event only if conduct affecting the jury has been harmful to the losing party, most motions for a new trial on this ground are denied. It is ground for a new trial if a juror was prejudiced from the start but claims that a juror did not disclose all that he should at voir dire usually fail, unless it can be found that the information omitted would have supported a challenge for cause. Motions for a new trial asserting that the jury did not deliberate for a sufficient length of time also usually fail. FPP § 2810.

ii. *Partial new trial.* FRCP 59(a) provides that a new trial may be granted "on all or some of the issues—and to any party—. . .." Thus it recognizes the court's power to grant a partial new trial. FPP § 2814. If a partial new trial is granted, those portions of the first judgment not set aside become part of the judgment entered following the jury verdict at the new trial. Thus, the end result is a single judgment. FPP § 2814.

iii. *Further action after a nonjury trial.* After a nonjury trial, the court may, on motion for a new trial, open the judgment if one has been entered, take additional testimony, amend findings of fact and conclusions of law or make new ones, and direct the entry of a new judgment. FRCP 59(a)(2).

iv. *New trial on the court's initiate or for reasons not in the motion.* No later than twenty-eight (28) days after the entry of judgment, the court, on its own, may order a new trial for any reason that would justify granting one on a party's motion. After giving the parties notice and an opportunity to be heard, the court may grant a timely motion for a new trial for a reason not stated in the motion. In either event, the court must specify the reasons in its order. FRCP 59(d).

b. *Motion to alter or amend judgment.* FRCP 59(e) authorizes a motion to alter or amend a judgment after its entry. FRCP 59(e) also has been interpreted as permitting a motion to vacate a judgment rather than merely amend it. FPP § 2810.1.

i. *Types of motions covered under FRCP 59(e).* FRCP 59(e) covers a broad range of motions, and the only real limitation on the type of the motion permitted is that it must request a substantive alteration of the judgment, not merely the correction of a clerical error, or relief of a type wholly collateral to the judgment. FPP § 2810.1; Osterneck v. Ernst & Whinney, 489 U.S. 169, 109 S.Ct. 987, 103 L.Ed.2d 146 (1989). The type of relief requested in postjudgment motions for attorney's fees and costs, for instance, is considered collateral unless it is specifically addressed in the judgment, and thus these motions generally do not fall under FRCP 59(e). FPP § 2810.1; Hastert v. Illinois State Bd. of Election Com'rs, 28 F.3d 1430, 1438 n.8 (7th Cir. 1993). FRCP 59(e) does, however, include motions for reconsideration. FPP § 2810.1; U.S. v. $23,000 in U.S. Currency, 356 F.3d 157, 165 n.9 (1st Cir. 2004). A motion under FRCP 59(e) also is appropriate if the court in the original judgment has failed to give relief on a certain claim on which it has found that the party is entitled to relief. Finally, the motion may be used to request an amendment of the judgment to provide for prejudgment interest. The court may not, however, give relief under FRCP 59(e) if this would defeat a party's right to jury trial on an issue. FPP § 2810.1.

    ii.   *Grounds for granting a FRCP 59(e) motion.* There are four basic grounds upon which a FRCP 59(e) motion may be granted. FPP § 2810.1; F.D.I.C. v. World University Inc., 978 F.2d 10 (1st Cir. 1992). First, the movant may demonstrate that the motion is necessary to correct manifest errors of law or fact upon which the judgment is based. Of course, the corollary principle applies and the movant's failure to show any manifest error may result in the motion's denial. FPP § 2810.1. Second, the motion may be granted so that the moving party may present newly discovered or previously unavailable evidence. FPP § 2810.1; GenCorp, Inc. v. American Intern. Underwriters, 178 F.3d 804, 834 (6th Cir. 1999). Third, the motion will be granted if necessary to prevent manifest injustice. Serious misconduct of counsel may justify relief under this theory. Fourth, a FRCP 59(e) motion may be justified by an intervening change in controlling law. FPP § 2810.1.

    iii. *Limitations on a FRCP 59(e) motion.* The FRCP 59(e) motion may not be used to relitigate old matters, or to raise arguments or present evidence that could have been raised prior to the entry of judgment. Also, amendment of the judgment will be denied if it would serve no useful purpose. In practice, because of the narrow purposes for which they are intended, FRCP 59(e) motions typically are denied. FPP § 2810.1.

  c. *Motion for relief from judgment*

    i.   *Corrections based on clerical mistakes; Oversights and omissions.* The court may correct a clerical mistake or a mistake arising from oversight or omission whenever one is found in a judgment, order, or other part of the record. The court may do so on motion or on its own, with or without notice. But after an appeal has been docketed in the appellate court and while it is pending, such a mistake may be corrected only with the appellate court's leave. FRCP 60(a).

- *Correctable mistakes.* A motion under FRCP 60(a) only can be used to make the judgment or record speak the truth and cannot be used to make it say something other than what originally was pronounced. FPP § 2854. FRCP 60(a) is not a vehicle for relitigating matters that already have been litigated and decided, nor to change what has been deliberately done. FPP § 2854. The mistake correctable under FRCP 60(a) need not be committed by the clerk or the court; FRCP 60(a) may be utilized to correct mistakes by the parties as well. FPP § 2854.

- *Substantive changes.* When the change sought is substantive in nature, such as a change in the calculation of interest not originally intended, the addition of an amount to a judgment to compensate for depreciation in stock awarded, or the broadening of a summary-judgment motion to dismiss all claims, relief is not appropriate under FRCP 60(a). FPP § 2854. Errors of a more substantial nature are to be corrected by a motion under FRCP 59(e) or FRCP 60(b). FPP § 2854.

    ii. *Relief from judgment, order, or proceeding.* Relief under FRCP 60(b) ordinarily is obtained by motion in the court that rendered the judgment. FPP § 2865.

- *Grounds for relief from a final judgment, order, or proceeding.* On motion and just terms, the court may relieve a party or its legal representative from a final judgment, order, or proceeding for the following reasons: (1) mistake, inadvertence, surprise, or excusable neglect; (2) newly discovered evidence that, with reasonable diligence, could not have been discovered in time to move for a new trial under FRCP 59(b); (3) fraud (whether previously called intrinsic or extrinsic), misrepresentation, or misconduct by an opposing party; (4) the judgment is void; (5) the judgment has been satisfied, released or discharged; it is based on an earlier judgment that has been reversed or vacated; or applying it prospectively is no longer equitable; or (6) any other reason that justifies relief. FRCP 60(b).

- *Mistake, inadvertence, surprise, or excusable neglect.* Relief will not be granted under

FRCP 60(b)(1) merely because a party is unhappy with the judgment. The party must make some showing justifying the failure to avoid the mistake or inadvertence. Gross carelessness or negligence is not enough. FPP § 2858. A defendant must prove the existence of a meritorious defense as a prerequisite to obtaining relief on these grounds. FEDPROC § 51:132; Augusta Fiberglass Coatings, Inc. v. Fodor Contracting Corp., 843 F.2d 808, 11 Fed.R.Serv.3d 42 (4th Cir. 1988). In all averments of fraud or mistake, the circumstances constituting fraud or mistake must be stated with particularity. This requirement applies with respect to averments of mistake in motion papers under FRCP 60(b)(1). FEDPROC § 51:139. In assessing whether conduct is excusable, several factors must be taken into account, including: (1) the danger of prejudice to the nonmoving party; (2) the length of the delay and its potential impact on judicial proceedings; (3) whether the movant acted in good faith; and (4) the reason for the delay, including whether it was within the reasonable control of the movant. FEDPROC § 51:133; Nara v. Frank, 488 F.3d 187 (3d Cir. 2007).

- *Newly discovered evidence.* The standards for relief from a judgment on the basis of newly discovered evidence are, in summary: (1) the motion must involve legally admissible "evidence" in some technical sense, rather than just factual information of some variety; (2) the evidence must have been in existence at the time of the trial or consists of facts existing at the time of trial; (3) the evidence must be newly-discovered since the trial; (4) the evidence must not have been discoverable by the exercise of due diligence in time for use at the trial or to move for a new trial; (5) the evidence must be material and not merely cumulative or impeaching; and (6) the evidence must be such that, if received, it will probably produce a different result. FEDPROC § 51:141.

- *Fraud, misrepresentation, or other misconduct of opposing party.* Many other cases support the propositions that the burden of proof of fraud is on the moving party and that fraud must be established by clear and convincing evidence. Further, the fraud must have prevented the moving party from fully and fairly presenting his case. It also must be chargeable to an adverse party; the moving party cannot get relief because of the party's own fraud. FPP § 2860. There is some disagreement about the meaning of "fraud" or "misconduct" in this context. One view is that the moving party must show that the adverse party committed a deliberate act that adversely impacted the fairness of the relevant legal proceeding in question. FEDPROC § 51:145; Jordan v. Paccar, Inc., 97 F.3d 1452 (6th Cir. 1996). The prevailing view is broader, however, and allows a motion for relief to be granted regardless of whether the adverse party acted with an evil, innocent or careless purpose. FEDPROC § 51:145.

- *Void judgment.* A judgment is not void merely because it is erroneous. It is void only if the court that rendered it lacked jurisdiction of the subject matter, or of the parties, or if it acted in a manner inconsistent with due process of law. Of course, although a challenge on one of those three grounds can be made under FRCP 60(b)(4), if the court finds that there was subject-matter or personal jurisdiction, or that no due-process violation has occurred, the motion will be denied. FPP § 2862.

- *Judgment satisfied or no longer equitable.* The significant portion of FRCP 60(b)(5) is the final ground, allowing relief if it is no longer equitable for the judgment to be applied prospectively. FPP § 2863. In order to obtain relief on these grounds, the judgment itself must have prospective application and such application must be inequitable due to a change in circumstances since the judgment was rendered. FEDPROC § 51:157. The mere possibility that a judgment has some future effect does not mean that it is "prospective," for purposes of applying FRCP 60(b)(5), because virtually every court order causes at least some reverberations into the future, and has some prospective effect; the essential inquiry into the prospective nature of a judgment revolves around whether it is executory or involves the supervision of changing conduct or conditions. FEDPROC § 51:158; Kalamazoo River Study Group v. Rockwell Intern. Corp., 355 F.3d 574 (6th Cir. 2004); DeWeerth v. Baldinger, 38 F.3d 1266 (2d Cir. 1994). The court's duty when confronted with such a motion is not to examine the correctness of the existing decree at the time it was entered, or even whether it is needed today, but to determine whether, assuming it was needed when entered, intervening changes have eliminated that need. FEDPROC § 51:159; Swift & Co. v. U.S., 367 U.S. 909, 81 S.Ct. 1918, 6 L.Ed.2d 1249 (1961).

- *Any other reason justifying relief.* The broad power granted by FRCP 60(b)(6) is not for the purpose of relieving a party from free, calculated, and deliberate choices the party has made. A party remains under a duty to take legal steps to protect his own interests. FPP § 2864. [Case law] certainly seemed to establish that FRCP 60(b)(6) and the first five clauses are mutually exclusive and that relief cannot be had under FRCP 60(b)(6) if it would have been available under the earlier clauses. FPP § 2864.

- *Effect of motion.* The motion does not affect the judgment's finality or suspend its operation. FRCP 60(c)(2).

- *Other powers to grant relief.* FRCP 60 does not limit a court's power to: (1) entertain an independent action to relieve a party from a judgment, order, or proceeding; (2) grant relief under 28 U.S.C.A. § 1655 to a defendant who was not personally notified of the action; or (3) set aside a judgment for fraud on the court. FRCP 60(d).

    iii. *Bills and writs abolished.* The following are abolished: bills of review, bills in the nature of bills of review, and writs of coram nobis, coram vobis, and audita querela. FRCP 60(e).

3. *Opposing papers.* The Federal Rules of Civil Procedure do not require any formal answer, return, or reply to a motion, except where the Federal Rules of Civil Procedure or local rules may require affidavits, memoranda, or other papers to be filed in opposition to a motion. Such papers are simply to apprise the court of such opposition and the grounds of that opposition. FEDPROC § 62:359.

    a. *Effect of failure to respond to motion.* Although in the absence of statutory provision or court rule, a motion ordinarily does not require a written answer, when a party files a motion and the opposing party fails to respond, the court may construe such failure to respond as nonopposition to the motion or an admission that the motion was meritorious, may take the facts alleged in the motion as true—the rule in some jurisdictions being that the failure to respond to a fact set forth in a motion is deemed an admission—and may grant the motion if the relief requested appears to be justified. AMJUR MOTIONS § 28.

    b. *Assent or no opposition not determinative.* However, a motion will not be granted automatically simply because an "assent" or a notation of "no opposition" has been filed; federal judges frequently deny motions that have been assented to when it is thought that justice so dictates. FPP § 1190.

    c. *Responsive pleading inappropriate as response to motion.* An attempt to answer or oppose a motion with a responsive pleading usually is not appropriate. FPP § 1190.

4. *Reply papers.* A moving party may be required or permitted to prepare papers in addition to his original motion papers. AMJUR MOTIONS § 25. Papers answering or replying to opposing papers may be appropriate, in the interests of justice, where it appears there is a substantial reason for allowing a reply. Thus, a court may accept reply papers where a party demonstrates that the papers to which it seeks to file a reply raise new issues that are material to the disposition of the question before the court, or where the court determines, sua sponte, that it wishes further briefing of an issue raised in those papers and orders the submission of additional papers. FEDPROC § 62:360.

    a. *Function of reply papers.* The function of a reply affidavit is to answer the arguments made in opposition to the position taken by the movant and not to permit the movant to introduce new arguments in support of the motion. AMJUR MOTIONS § 25.

    b. *Issues raised for the first time in a reply document.* However, the view has been followed in some jurisdictions, that as a matter of judicial economy, where there is no prejudice and where the issues could be raised simply by filing a motion to dismiss, the trial court has discretion to consider arguments raised for the first time in a reply memorandum, and that a trial court may grant a motion to strike issues raised for the first time in a reply memorandum. AMJUR MOTIONS § 26.

5. *Appearances.* Attorneys not representing the United States or its agencies must file an appearance when they represent (either in person or by filing a paper) a party. IN R USDCTND L.R. 83-8(a). For more information, refer to IN R USDCTND L.R. 83-8.

6. *Notice of related action.* A party must file a notice of related action as soon as it appears that the party's case and another pending case: (1) arise out of the same transaction or occurrence; (2) involve the same property; or (3) involve the validity or infringement of the same patent, trademark, or copyright. IN R USDCTND L.R. 40-1(d). For more information, refer to IN R USDCTND L.R. 40-1.

7. *Alternative dispute resolution (ADR).* After they confer as required by FRCP 26(f), the parties must advise the court which, if any, alternative-dispute-resolution processes they expect to pursue and when they expect to undertake the process. IN R USDCTND L.R. 16-6(a). For more information on alternative dispute resolution (ADR), refer to IN R USDCTND L.R. 16-6 and IN R USDCTND Order 2003-21.

8. *Settlement or resolution.* The parties must immediately notify the court if they reasonably expect to settle the case or resolve a pending motion. IN R USDCTND L.R. 16-1(g).

9. *Modification or suspension of rules.* The court may, on its own motion or at the request of a party, suspend or modify any rule in a particular case in the interest of justice. IN R USDCTND L.R. 1-1(c).

D. Documents

1. *Documents for moving party*

   a. *Required documents*

      i. *Notice of motion and motion.* The party must not specify a hearing date in the notice of a motion or petition unless the court or the clerk has authorized it. IN R USDCTND L.R. 7-5(b)(2). Refer to the General Requirements section of this document for information on the notice of motion and motion.

      ii. *Certificate of service.* FRCP 5(d) requires that the person making service under FRCP 5 certify that service has been effected. FRCP 5(Advisory Committee Notes). Having such information on file may be useful for many purposes, including proof of service if an issue arises concerning the effectiveness of the service. FRCP 5(Advisory Committee Notes).

      - *Certificate of service for electronically-filed documents.* A Certificate of Service is still a requirement when filing documents electronically. A sample Certificate of Service is attached as Form 1 (IN R USDCTND CM/ECF(Form 1)). IN R USDCTND CM/ECF(II)(H).

   b. *Supplemental documents*

      i. *Brief.* Refer to the Format section of this document for the format of briefs.

      ii. *Supporting evidence.* When a motion relies on facts outside the record, the court may hear the matter on affidavits or may hear it wholly or partly on oral testimony or on depositions. FRCP 43(c).

      - *Materials necessary for motion.* A party must file those portions of discovery requests or responses (including deposition transcripts) that the party relies on to support a motion that could result in a final order on an issue. IN R USDCTND L.R. 26-2(c).

      iii. *Notice of constitutional question.* A party that files a pleading, written motion, or other paper drawing into question the constitutionality of a federal or state statute must promptly:

      - *File notice.* File a notice of constitutional question stating the question and identifying the paper that raises it, if: (1) a federal statute is questioned and the parties do not include the United States, one of its agencies, or one of its officers or employees in an official capacity; or (2) a state statute is questioned and the parties do not include the state, one of its agencies, or one of its officers or employees in an official capacity; and

      - *Serve notice.* Serve the notice and paper on the Attorney General of the United States if a federal statute is questioned—or on the state attorney general if a state statute is questioned—either by certified or registered mail or by sending it to an electronic address designated by the attorney general for this purpose. FRCP 5.1(a).

      - *When to file the notice.* A party required to file a notice of constitutional question under FRCP 5.1 must do so by the later of: (1) the day the parties tender their proposed case-management plan (if one is required); or (2) 21 days after filing the pleading, written

motion, or other paper questioning the constitutionality of a federal or state statute. IN R USDCTND L.R. 5.1-1(a).

- *Service on government officials.* The party must also serve the notice and the pleading, written motion, or other paper questioning the constitutionality of a federal or state statute on: (1) the Attorney General of the United States and the United States Attorney for the Northern District of Indiana, if a federal statute is challenged; or (2) the Attorney General for the state if a state statute is challenged. IN R USDCTND L.R. 5.1-1(b). Service required under IN R USDCTND L.R. 5.1-1(b) may be made either by certified or registered mail or by emailing it to an address designated by those officials for this purpose. IN R USDCTND L.R. 5.1-1(c).

- *No forfeiture.* A party's failure to file and serve the notice, or the court's failure to certify, does not forfeit a constitutional claim or defense that is otherwise timely asserted. FRCP 5.1(d).

iv. *Index of exhibits.* Any pleading, motion, brief, affidavit, notice, or proposed order, whether filed electronically or by delivering it to the clerk, must: include a separate index identifying and briefly describing each exhibit if there are more than four (4) exhibits. IN R USDCTND L.R. 5-4(a)(8).

v. *Request for oral argument.* A party may request oral argument on a motion by filing and serving a separate document explaining why oral argument is necessary and estimating how long the court should allow for the argument. IN R USDCTND L.R. 7-5(a)(1). The request must be filed and served with the party's supporting brief, response brief, or reply brief. IN R USDCTND L.R. 7-5(a)(2).

vi. *Request for evidentiary hearing.* A party may request an evidentiary hearing by filing and serving a separate document explaining why the hearing is necessary and estimating how long the court should allow for it. IN R USDCTND L.R. 7-5(b)(1).

vii. *Copy of authority.* A copy of any decision, statute, or regulation cited in a motion or brief must be attached to the paper if—and only if—it is not available on Westlaw or Lexis. But if a copy of a decision, statute, or regulation is only available electronically, a party must provide it to the court or another party upon request. IN R USDCTND L.R. 7-1(f).

viii. *Proposed order.* Parties filing a paper that requires the judge or clerk to enter a routine or uncontested order must include a suitable form of order. IN R USDCTND L.R. 5-4(c).

- Proposed orders shall not be filed electronically either as a separate document or as an attachment to the main pleading or other document. Instead, all proposed orders must be e-mailed to the chambers of the appropriate judicial officer for the case. The proposed order must be in WordPerfect Format or Rich Text Format (RTF). Proposed orders should be attached to an e-mail and sent to the appropriate judicial officer at the address listed in IN R USDCTND CM/ECF(II)(F). The subject line of the email message should indicate the case title, cause number and document number of the motion, e.g., Smith v. Jones 1:02-cv-1234, motion# ___. IN R USDCTND CM/ECF(II)(F).

ix. *Copy of document with self-addressed envelope.* A party who wants a file-stamped copy of a paper must include with the filing an additional copy of the paper and a self-addressed envelope with adequate postage. IN R USDCTND L.R. 5-4(b)(6).

x. *Notice of manual filing.* However, if that is not physically possible, counsel shall electronically file a .pdf document titled Notice of Manual Filing as a notation on the docket sheet that filings are being held in the clerk's office in paper. A sample Notice of Manual Filing is attached as Form 2 (IN R USDCTND CM/ECF(Form 2)). IN R USDCTND CM/ECF(III)(A)(1).

xi. *Courtesy copies.* If documents are filed in paper format, counsel must provide an original for the clerk's office, a copy for the judge and a copy must be served on all parties in the case. IN R USDCTND CM/ECF(III)(A)(1).

xii. *Declaration that party was unable to file in a timely manner.* If the attorney is unable to file a document in a timely manner due to technical difficulties in the user's system, the attorney must file a document with the court as soon as possible notifying the court of the inability to file the document. A sample document entitled Declaration that Party was Unable to File in a Timely Manner Due to Technical Difficulties is attached hereto as Form 5. IN R USDCTND CM/ECF(VI)(B). [Editor's note: the reference to Form 5 is likely meant to be a reference to Form 3 (IN R USDCTND CM/ECF(Form 3)].

2. *Documents for opposing party*

   a. *Required documents*

      i. *Response brief.* Refer to the Format section of this document for the format of briefs. Refer to the General Requirements section of this document for information on the opposing papers.

      ii. *Certificate of service.* FRCP 5(d) requires that the person making service under FRCP 5 certify that service has been effected. FRCP 5(Advisory Committee Notes). Having such information on file may be useful for many purposes, including proof of service if an issue arises concerning the effectiveness of the service. FRCP 5(Advisory Committee Notes).

- *Certificate of service for electronically-filed documents.* A Certificate of Service is still a requirement when filing documents electronically. A sample Certificate of Service is attached as Form 1 (IN R USDCTND CM/ECF(Form 1)). IN R USDCTND CM/ECF(II)(H).

   b. *Supplemental documents*

      i. *Supporting evidence.* When a motion relies on facts outside the record, the court may hear the matter on affidavits or may hear it wholly or partly on oral testimony or on depositions. FRCP 43(c).

- *Materials necessary for motion.* A party must file those portions of discovery requests or responses (including deposition transcripts) that the party relies on to support a motion that could result in a final order on an issue. IN R USDCTND L.R. 26-2(c).

      ii. *Notice of constitutional question.* A party that files a pleading, written motion, or other paper drawing into question the constitutionality of a federal or state statute must promptly:

- *File notice.* File a notice of constitutional question stating the question and identifying the paper that raises it, if: (1) a federal statute is questioned and the parties do not include the United States, one of its agencies, or one of its officers or employees in an official capacity; or (2) a state statute is questioned and the parties do not include the state, one of its agencies, or one of its officers or employees in an official capacity; and

- *Serve notice.* Serve the notice and paper on the Attorney General of the United States if a federal statute is questioned—or on the state attorney general if a state statute is questioned—either by certified or registered mail or by sending it to an electronic address designated by the attorney general for this purpose. FRCP 5.1(a).

- *When to file the notice.* A party required to file a notice of constitutional question under FRCP 5.1 must do so by the later of: (1) the day the parties tender their proposed case-management plan (if one is required); or (2) 21 days after filing the pleading, written motion, or other paper questioning the constitutionality of a federal or state statute. IN R USDCTND L.R. 5.1-1(a).

- *Service on government officials.* The party must also serve the notice and the pleading, written motion, or other paper questioning the constitutionality of a federal or state statute on: (1) the Attorney General of the United States and the United States Attorney for the Northern District of Indiana, if a federal statute is challenged; or (2) the Attorney General for the state if a state statute is challenged. IN R USDCTND L.R. 5.1-1(b). Service required under IN R USDCTND L.R. 5.1-1(b) may be made either by certified or registered mail or by emailing it to an address designated by those officials for this purpose. IN R USDCTND L.R. 5.1-1(c).

- *No forfeiture.* A party's failure to file and serve the notice, or the court's failure to certify, does not forfeit a constitutional claim or defense that is otherwise timely asserted. FRCP 5.1(d).

iii. *Index of exhibits.* Any pleading, motion, brief, affidavit, notice, or proposed order, whether filed electronically or by delivering it to the clerk, must: include a separate index identifying and briefly describing each exhibit if there are more than four (4) exhibits. IN R USDCTND L.R. 5-4(a)(8).

iv. *Request for oral argument.* A party may request oral argument on a motion by filing and serving a separate document explaining why oral argument is necessary and estimating how long the court should allow for the argument. IN R USDCTND L.R. 7-5(a)(1). The request must be filed and served with the party's supporting brief, response brief, or reply brief. IN R USDCTND L.R. 7-5(a)(2).

v. *Request for evidentiary hearing.* A party may request an evidentiary hearing by filing and serving a separate document explaining why the hearing is necessary and estimating how long the court should allow for it. IN R USDCTND L.R. 7-5(b)(1).

vi. *Copy of authority.* A copy of any decision, statute, or regulation cited in a motion or brief must be attached to the paper if—and only if—it is not available on Westlaw or Lexis. But if a copy of a decision, statute, or regulation is only available electronically, a party must provide it to the court or another party upon request. IN R USDCTND L.R. 7-1(f).

vii. *Copy of document with self-addressed envelope.* A party who wants a file-stamped copy of a paper must include with the filing an additional copy of the paper and a self-addressed envelope with adequate postage. IN R USDCTND L.R. 5-4(b)(6).

viii. *Notice of manual filing.* However, if that is not physically possible, counsel shall electronically file a .pdf document titled Notice of Manual Filing as a notation on the docket sheet that filings are being held in the clerk's office in paper. A sample Notice of Manual Filing is attached as Form 2 (IN R USDCTND CM/ECF(Form 2)). IN R USDCTND CM/ECF(III)(A)(1).

ix. *Courtesy copies.* If documents are filed in paper format, counsel must provide an original for the clerk's office, a copy for the judge and a copy must be served on all parties in the case. IN R USDCTND CM/ECF(III)(A)(1).

x. *Declaration that party was unable to file in a timely manner.* If the attorney is unable to file a document in a timely manner due to technical difficulties in the user's system, the attorney must file a document with the court as soon as possible notifying the court of the inability to file the document. A sample document entitled Declaration that Party was Unable to File in a Timely Manner Due to Technical Difficulties is attached hereto as Form 5. IN R USDCTND CM/ECF(VI)(B). [Editor's note: the reference to Form 5 is likely meant to be a reference to Form 3 (IN R USDCTND CM/ECF(Form 3)].

E. Format

1. *Form of documents.* The rules governing captions and other matters of form in pleadings apply to motions and other papers. FRCP 7(b)(2).

   a. *Paper.* Any pleading, motion, brief, affidavit, notice, or proposed order, whether filed electronically or by delivering it to the clerk, must: use eight and one-half by eleven (8-1/2 x 11) inch pages. IN R USDCTND L.R. 5-4(a)(2).

      i. *Manual filings.* Papers delivered to the clerk for filing must: be flat, unfolded, and on good-quality, white paper. IN R USDCTND L.R. 5-4(b)(1)(A).

         • *Covers or backing.* Papers delivered to the clerk for filing must: not have a cover or a back. IN R USDCTND L.R. 5-4(b)(1)(B).

         • *Recycled paper.* The court encourages using recycled paper. IN R USDCTND L.R. 5-4(b)(7).

   b. *Margins.* Any pleading, motion, brief, affidavit, notice, or proposed order, whether filed electronically or by delivering it to the clerk, must: have at least one (1) inch margins. IN R USDCTND L.R. 5-4(a)(3).

   c. *Spacing.* Any pleading, motion, brief, affidavit, notice, or proposed order, whether filed electronically or by delivering it to the clerk, must: be double spaced (except for headings, footnotes, and quoted material). IN R USDCTND L.R. 5-4(a)(5).

d. *Text.* Any pleading, motion, brief, affidavit, notice, or proposed order, whether filed electronically or by delivering it to the clerk, must: be plainly typewritten, printed, or prepared by a clearly legible copying process. IN R USDCTND L.R. 5-4(a)(1).

   i. Any pleading, motion, brief, affidavit, notice, or proposed order, whether filed electronically or by delivering it to the clerk, must: use at least twelve (12) point type in the body and at least ten (10) point type in footnotes. IN R USDCTND L.R. 5-4(a)(4).

e. *Page numbering.* Any pleading, motion, brief, affidavit, notice, or proposed order, whether filed electronically or by delivering it to the clerk, must: have consecutively numbered pages. IN R USDCTND L.R. 5-4(a)(6).

f. *Caption; Names of parties.* Every pleading must have a caption with the court's name, a title, a file number, and a FRCP 7(a) designation. The title of the complaint must name all the parties; the title of other pleadings, after naming the first party on each side, may refer generally to other parties. FRCP 10(a). Any pleading, motion, brief, affidavit, notice, or proposed order, whether filed electronically or by delivering it to the clerk, must: include a title on the first page. IN R USDCTND L.R. 5-4(a)(7).

   i. *Alternative motions.* Motions must be filed separately, but alternative motions may be filed in a single paper if each is named in the title following the caption. IN R USDCTND L.R. 7-1(a).

g. *Filer's information.* Any pleading, motion, brief, affidavit, notice, or proposed order, whether filed electronically or by delivering it to the clerk, must: except in proposed orders and affidavits, include the filer's name, address, telephone number, fax number (where available), and e-mail address (where available). IN R USDCTND L.R. 5-4(a)(9).

h. *Paragraphs; Separate statements.* A party must state its claims or defenses in numbered paragraphs, each limited as far as practicable to a single set of circumstances. A later pleading may refer by number to a paragraph in an earlier pleading. If doing so would promote clarity, each claim founded on a separate transaction or occurrence—and each defense other than a denial—must be stated in a separate count or defense. FRCP 10(b).

i. *Adoption by reference; Exhibits.* A statement in a pleading may be adopted by reference elsewhere in the same pleading or in any other pleading or motion. A copy of a written instrument that is an exhibit to a pleading is a part of the pleading for all purposes. FRCP 10(c).

j. *Citation of local rules.* The Local Civil Rules of the United States District Court for the Northern District of Indiana may be cited as "N.D. Ind. L.R." IN R USDCTND L.R. 1-1(a)(1).

k. *Acceptance by the clerk.* The clerk must not refuse to file a paper solely because it is not in the form prescribed by the Federal Rules of Civil Procedure or by a local rule or practice. FRCP 5(d)(4).

   i. *Sanctions for formatting errors; Non-compliance.* If a person files a paper that does not comply with the rules governing the format of papers filed with the court, the court may: (1) strike the paper from the record; or (2) fine the person up to one thousand dollars ($1,000). IN R USDCTND L.R. 1-3(a).

      • *Notice.* Before sanctioning a person under IN R USDCTND L.R. 1-3(a)(2), the court must: (1) notify the person that the paper is noncompliant; and (2) give the person the opportunity either to be heard or to revise the paper. IN R USDCTND L.R. 1-3(b).

2. *Form of electronic documents.* Electronically filed documents must meet the same requirements of format and page limits as documents "conventionally filed" (as defined in IN R USDCTND CM/ECF(III)(A)) pursuant to the Federal Rules of Civil Procedure and the Local Civil Rules of the United States District Court for the Northern District of Indiana. IN R USDCTND CM/ECF(II)(A)(2).

a. *PDF format required.* Documents filed in the CM/ECF must be in .pdf format. A document created with almost any word-processing program can be converted to .pdf format. The .pdf program in effect takes a picture of the original document and allows anyone to open the converted document across a broad range of hardware and software, with layout, format, links, and images intact. IN R USDCTND CM/ECF(FN2).

b. *Title of documents.* The person electronically filing a pleading or other document will be responsible for designating a title for the pleading or other document by using one of the categories contained in the events listed in the CM/ECF Menu. IN R USDCTND CM/ECF(II)(G).

c. *Combining documents.* All documents which form part of a single pleading and which are being filed at the same time and by the same party may be electronically filed together under one document number, e.g., the motion and a supporting affidavit, with the exception of memoranda in support. Memoranda in support shall be electronically filed separately and shown as a related document to the motion. IN R USDCTND CM/ECF(II)(A)(4).

d. *Exhibits and attachments.* Filing users must submit in electronic form all documents referenced as exhibits or attachments, unless the court permits conventional filing. A filing user must submit as exhibits or attachments only those excerpts of the referenced documents that are directly germane to the matter under consideration by the court. Excerpted material must be clearly and prominently identified as such. Filing users who file excerpts of documents as exhibits or attachments do so without prejudice to their right to timely file additional excerpts or the complete document. Responding parties may timely file additional excerpts or the complete document that they believe are directly germane. The court may require parties to file additional excerpts or the complete document. IN R USDCTND CM/ECF(II)(A)(6).

e. *Hyperlinks.* Electronically filed documents may contain hyperlink references to an external document as a convenient mechanism for accessing material cited in the document. A hyperlink reference is neither validated for content nor considered a part of the court's records. The court neither endorses the product or organization at the destination of a hyperlink reference, nor does the court exercise any responsibility over the content at the destination. In order to preserve the integrity of the court record, attorneys wishing to insert hyperlinks in court filings shall continue to use the traditional citation method for the cited authority, in addition to the hyperlink. A hyperlink contained in a filing is no more than a convenient mechanism for accessing material cited in the document and a hyperlink reference is extraneous to any filed document and is not part of the court's record. IN R USDCTND CM/ECF(II)(A)(3).

3. *Form of briefs*

a. *Page limits.* Supporting and response briefs (excluding tables of contents, tables of authorities, and appendices) ordinarily must not exceed twenty-five (25) pages. Reply briefs must not exceed fifteen (15) pages. IN R USDCTND L.R. 7-1(e)(1).

   i. *Exception.* The court may allow a party to file a brief exceeding these page limits for extraordinary and compelling reasons. But if the court permits a brief to exceed twenty-five (25) pages, it must include:

   - A table of contents with page references;

   - An issue statement; and

   - A table of authorities including: (1) all cases (alphabetically arranged), statutes, and other authorities cited in the brief; and (2) references to where the authorities appear in the brief. IN R USDCTND L.R. 7-1(e)(2).

4. *Signing of pleadings, motions and other papers*

a. *Signature.* Every pleading, written motion, and other paper must be signed by at least one attorney of record in the attorney's name—or by a party personally if the party is unrepresented. The paper must state the signer's address, e-mail address, and telephone number. FRCP 11(a).

   i. *Signatures on manual filings.* Papers delivered to the clerk for filing must: include the filer's original signature. IN R USDCTND L.R. 5-4(b)(1)(C).

   - *Rubber-stamped and faxed signatures.* An original paper with a rubber-stamped or faxed signature is unsigned for purposes of FRCP 11 and FRCP 26(g). IN R USDCTND L.R. 5-4(b)(2).

   - *Affidavits.* Only the affiant need sign an affidavit. IN R USDCTND L.R. 5-4(b)(3).

   ii. *Electronic signatures.* Pursuant to FRCP 11, every pleading, motion, and other paper (except lists, schedules, statements or amendments thereto) shall be signed by at least one attorney of record or, if the party is not represented by an attorney, all papers shall be signed by the party. An attorney's/participant's password issued by the court combined with the user's identification, serves as and constitutes the attorney/participant's signature for FRCP 11 and other purposes. IN R USDCTND CM/ECF(I)(C). Documents which must be filed and which must contain original signatures other than those of a participating attorney or which require either verification or an unsworn declaration under any rule or statute, shall be filed electronically, with originally executed copies maintained by the filer. The pleading or other document electronically filed shall contain "s/" signature(s), as noted in IN R USDCTND CM/ECF(II)(E)(3)(b). IN R USDCTND CM/ECF(II)(E)(1).

- *Multiple signatures.* In the case of a stipulation or other document to be signed by two or more attorneys, the following procedure should be used: The filing attorney shall initially confirm that the content of the document is acceptable to all persons required to sign the document and shall obtain the physical signatures of all attorneys on the document. IN R USDCTND CM/ECF(II)(E)(3)(a). The filing attorney then shall file the document electronically, indicating the signatories, e.g., "s/Jane Doe," "s/John Doe," etc. IN R USDCTND CM/ECF(II)(E)(3)(b). The filing attorney shall retain the hard copy of the document containing the original signatures. IN R USDCTND CM/ECF(II)(E)(3)(c).

    iii. *No verification or accompanying affidavit required for pleadings.* Unless a rule or statute specifically states otherwise, a pleading need not be verified or accompanied by an affidavit. FRCP 11(a).

    iv. *Unsigned papers.* The court must strike an unsigned paper unless the omission is promptly corrected after being called to the attorney's or party's attention. FRCP 11(a).

b. *Representations to the court.* By presenting to the court a pleading, written motion, or other paper—whether by signing, filing, submitting, or later advocating it—an attorney or unrepresented party certifies that to the best of the person's knowledge, information, and belief, formed after an inquiry reasonable under the circumstances:

    i. It is not being presented for any improper purpose, such as to harass, cause unnecessary delay, or needlessly increase the cost of litigation;

    ii. The claims, defenses, and other legal contentions are warranted by existing law or by a nonfrivolous argument for extending, modifying, or reversing existing law or for establishing new law;

    iii. The factual contentions have evidentiary support or, if specifically so identified, will likely have evidentiary support after a reasonable opportunity for further investigation or discovery; and

    iv. The denials of factual contentions are warranted on the evidence or, if specifically so identified, are reasonably based on belief or a lack of information. FRCP 11(b).

c. *Sanctions.* If, after notice and a reasonable opportunity to respond, the court determines that FRCP 11(b) has been violated, the court may impose an appropriate sanction on any attorney, law firm, or party that violated FRCP 11(b) or is responsible for the violation. FRCP 11(c)(1). Refer to the United States District Court for the Northern District of Indiana KeyRules Motion for Sanctions document for more information.

5. *Privacy protection for filings made with the court*

a. *Redacted filings.* Counsel should not include sensitive information in any document filed with the court unless such inclusion is necessary and relevant to the case. IN R USDCTND CM/ECF(VII). Unless the court orders otherwise, in an electronic or paper filing with the court that contains an individual's Social Security number, taxpayer-identification number, or birth date, the name of an individual known to be a minor, or a financial-account number, a party or nonparty making the filing may include only:

    i. The last four (4) digits of the Social Security number and taxpayer-identification number;

    ii. The year of the individual's birth;

    iii. The minor's initials; and

    iv.   The last four (4) digits of the financial-account number. FRCP 5.2(a); IN R USDCTND Order 2005-3.

b.   *Exemptions from the redaction requirement.* The redaction requirement does not apply to the following:

    i.   A financial-account number that identifies the property allegedly subject to forfeiture in a forfeiture proceeding;

    ii.   The record of an administrative or agency proceeding;

    iii. The official record of a state-court proceeding;

    iv.   The record of a court or tribunal, if that record was not subject to the redaction requirement when originally filed;

    v.   A filing covered by FRCP 5.2(c) or FRCP 5.2(d); and

    vi.   A pro se filing in an action brought under 28 U.S.C.A. § 2241, 28 U.S.C.A. § 2254, or 28 U.S.C.A. § 2255. FRCP 5.2(b).

    vii. In cases filed under the Social Security Act, 42 U.S.C.A. § 405(g), there is no need for redaction of any information from the documents filed in the case. IN R USDCTND Order 2005-3.

c.   *Limitations on remote access to electronic files; Social Security appeals and immigration cases.* Unless the court orders otherwise, in an action for benefits under the Social Security Act, and in an action or proceeding relating to an order of removal, to relief from removal, or to immigration benefits or detention, access to an electronic file is authorized as follows:

    i.   The parties and their attorneys may have remote electronic access to any part of the case file, including the administrative record;

    ii.   Any other person may have electronic access to the full record at the courthouse, but may have remote electronic access only to:

       • The docket maintained by the court; and

       • An opinion, order, judgment, or other disposition of the court, but not any other part of the case file or the administrative record. FRCP 5.2(c).

d.   *Filings made under seal.* The court may order that a filing be made under seal without redaction. The court may later unseal the filing or order the person who made the filing to file a redacted version for the public record. FRCP 5.2(d). For information on filing documents under seal, refer to IN R USDCTND L.R. 5-3, IN R USDCTND CM/ECF(IV)(A), and IN R USDCTND ECF Order 2004-19.

e.   *Protective orders.* For good cause, the court may by order in a case:

    i.   Require redaction of additional information; or

    ii.   Limit or prohibit a nonparty's remote electronic access to a document filed with the court. FRCP 5.2(e).

f.   *Option for additional unredacted filing under seal.* A person making a redacted filing may also file an unredacted copy under seal. The court must retain the unredacted copy as part of the record. FRCP 5.2(f); IN R USDCTND Order 2005-3.

    i.   The unredacted version of the document or the reference list shall be retained by the court under seal as part of the record. This paper shall be retained by the court as part of the record. The court may, however, still require the party to file a redacted copy for the public file. IN R USDCTND Order 2005-3.

g.   *Option for filing a reference list.* A filing that contains redacted information may be filed together with a reference list that identifies each item of redacted information and specifies an appropriate identifier that uniquely corresponds to each item listed. The list must be filed under seal and may be amended as of right. Any reference in the case to a listed identifier will be construed to refer to the corresponding item of information. FRCP 5.2(g); IN R USDCTND Order 2005-3.

    i.   The unredacted version of the document or the reference list shall be retained by the court under

seal as part of the record. This paper shall be retained by the court as part of the record. The court may, however, still require the party to file a redacted copy for the public file. IN R USDCTND Order 2005-3.

h. *Responsibility for redaction.* The responsibility for redacting these personal identifiers rests solely with counsel and the parties. The Clerk will not review each paper for compliance with IN R USDCTND Order 2005-3. IN R USDCTND Order 2005-3.

i. *Waiver of protection of identifiers.* A person waives the protection of FRCP 5.2(a) as to the person's own information by filing it without redaction and not under seal. FRCP 5.2(h).

F. Filing and Service Requirements

1. *Filing requirements.* Any paper after the complaint that is required to be served—together with a certificate of service—must be filed within a reasonable time after service. FRCP 5(d)(1). Motions must be filed separately, but alternative motions may be filed in a single paper if each is named in the title following the caption. IN R USDCTND L.R. 7-1(a).

   a. *How filing is made; In general.* A paper is filed by delivering it:

      i. To the clerk; or

      ii. To a judge who agrees to accept it for filing, and who must then note the filing date on the paper and promptly send it to the clerk. FRCP 5(d)(2).

         • Papers not filed electronically must be filed with the clerk, not a judge. IN R USDCTND L.R. 5-4(b)(4).

      iii. Parties manually filing a paper that requires the clerk to give others notice, must give the clerk: (1) sufficient copies of the notice; and (2) the name and address of each person entitled to receive the notice. IN R USDCTND L.R. 5-4(b)(8).

   b. *Where to file.* Papers not filed electronically must be filed in the division where the case is pending, unless: (1) a person will be prejudiced if the paper is not filed the same day it is tendered; and (2) it includes an adequately sized envelope addressed to the clerk's office in the division where the case is pending and with adequate postage. IN R USDCTND L.R. 5-4(b)(5).

   c. *Electronic filing*

      i. *Authorization of electronic filing program.* A court may, by local rule, allow papers to be filed, signed, or verified by electronic means that are consistent with any technical standards established by the Judicial Conference of the United States. A local rule may require electronic filing only if reasonable exceptions are allowed. A paper filed electronically in compliance with a local rule is a written paper for purposes of the Federal Rules of Civil Procedure. FRCP 5(d)(3).

         • Papers must be filed, signed, and verified electronically unless excepted by the court's CM/ECF Civil and Criminal User Manual (IN R USDCTND CM/ECF). IN R USDCTND L.R. 5-1.

      ii. *Mandatory electronic filing.* Unless otherwise permitted by these procedures or otherwise authorized by the assigned judge, all documents submitted for filing in this district in civil and criminal cases, no matter when a case was originally filed, shall be filed electronically using the System. IN R USDCTND CM/ECF(II)(A)(1). The requirement that "all documents" be filed electronically includes briefs, and attachments and exhibits used in support of motions. IN R USDCTND CM/ECF(FN1).

         • Sending a document or pleading to the court via e-mail or facsimile does not constitute "electronic filing." IN R USDCTND CM/ECF(I)(A).

      iii. *Conventional filing.* As used in these procedures, a "conventionally" filed or submitted document or pleading is one presented to the Clerk or a party in paper or other non-electronic, tangible format. The following documents shall be filed conventionally and not electronically unless specifically authorized by the Court:

         • Exhibits and other documents which cannot be converted to a legible electronic form.

Whenever possible, counsel is responsible for converting filings to an electronic form. However, if that is not physically possible, counsel shall electronically file a .pdf document titled Notice of Manual Filing as a notation on the docket sheet that filings are being held in the clerk's office in paper. A sample Notice of Manual Filing is attached as Form 2 (IN R USDCTND CM/ECF(Form 2)). If documents are filed in paper format, counsel must provide an original for the clerk's office, a copy for the judge and a copy must be served on all parties in the case. Large documents which do not exist in an electronic format shall be scanned into .pdf format by counsel, in small batches if necessary, and filed electronically as separate attachments in the System. IN R USDCTND CM/ECF(III)(A)(1).

- Certain documents which are listed in IN R USDCTND CM/ECF(II)(E)(2). IN R US-DCTND CM/ECF(III)(A)(2).

- Documents filed by pro se litigants. IN R USDCTND CM/ECF(III)(A)(3).

    iv. For more information on electronic filing, refer to IN R USDCTND CM/ECF.

2. *Service requirements*

  a. *Service; When required*

    i. *In general.* Unless the Federal Rules of Civil Procedure provide otherwise, each of the following papers must be served on every party:

- An order stating that service is required;

- A pleading filed after the original complaint, unless the court orders otherwise under FRCP 5(c) because there are numerous defendants;

- A discovery paper required to be served on a party, unless the court orders otherwise;

- A written motion, except one that may be heard ex parte; and

- A written notice, appearance, demand, or offer of judgment, or any similar paper. FRCP 5(a)(1).

    ii. *If a party fails to appear.* No service is required on a party who is in default for failing to appear. But a pleading that asserts a new claim for relief against such a party must be served on that party under FRCP 4. FRCP 5(a)(2).

    iii. *Seizing property.* If an action is begun by seizing property and no person is or need be named as a defendant, any service required before the filing of an appearance, answer, or claim must be made on the person who had custody or possession of the property when it was seized. FRCP 5(a)(3).

  b. *Service; How made*

    i. *Serving an attorney.* If a party is represented by an attorney, service under FRCP 5 must be made on the attorney unless the court orders service on the party. FRCP 5(b)(1).

    ii. *Service in general.* A paper is served under FRCP 5 by:

- Handing it to the person;

- Leaving it: (1) at the person's office with a clerk or other person in charge or, if no one is in charge, in a conspicuous place in the office; or (2) if the person has no office or the office is closed, at the person's dwelling or usual place of abode with someone of suitable age and discretion who resides there;

- Mailing it to the person's last known address—in which event service is complete upon mailing;

- Leaving it with the court clerk if the person has no known address;

- Sending it by electronic means if the person consented in writing—in which event service is complete upon transmission, but is not effective if the serving party learns that it did not reach the person to be served; or

- Delivering it by any other means that the person consented to in writing—in which event service is complete when the person making service delivers it to the agency designated to make delivery. FRCP 5(b)(2).

iii. *Electronic service.* Electronically filed papers may be served electronically if service is consistent with the CM/ECF User Manual (IN R USDCTND CM/ECF). IN R USDCTND L.R. 5-2(a).

- *Waiver of other service.* An attorney's registration will constitute a waiver of conventional service of documents and the attorney agrees to accept service of notice on behalf of the client of the electronic filing by hand, facsimile or authorized email. IN R USDCTND CM/ECF(I)(B)(3).

- *Serving registered persons.* The System will generate a "Notice of Electronic Filing" when any document is filed. This notice represents service of the document on parties who are registered participants with the System. Except as provided in IN R USDCTND CM/ECF(III)(B), the filing party shall not be required to serve any pleading or other documents on any party receiving electronic notice. IN R USDCTND CM/ECF(II)(D)(1). The term "pleading" refers only to those documents listed in FRCP 7(a). IN R USDCTND CM/ECF(FN3).

- *When electronic service is deemed completed.* A person registered to use the court's electronic-filing system is served with an electronically filed paper when a "Notice of Electronic Filing" is transmitted to that person through the court's electronic filing-system. IN R USDCTND L.R. 5-2(b).

- *Serving non-registered persons.* A person who has not registered to use the court's electronic-filing system but who is entitled to service of a paper must be served according to the Local Civil Rules of the United States District Court for the Northern District of Indiana and the Federal Rules of Civil Procedure. IN R USDCTND L.R. 5-2(c); IN R USDCTND CM/ECF(II)(D)(2). If such service of a paper copy is to be made, it shall be done in the manner provided in the Federal Rules of Civil Procedure and the Local Civil Rules of the United States District Court for the Northern District of Indiana. IN R USDCTND CM/ECF(II)(D)(2).

iv. *Service of conventional filings.* Pleadings or other documents which are filed conventionally rather than electronically shall be served in the manner provided for in the Federal Rules of Civil Procedure and the Local Civil Rules of the United States District Court for the Northern District of Indiana, except as otherwise provided by order of the Court. IN R USDCTND CM/ECF(III)(B).

v. *Using court facilities.* If a local rule so authorizes, a party may use the court's transmission facilities to make service under FRCP 5(b)(2)(E). FRCP 5(b)(3).

c. *Serving numerous defendants*

i. *In general.* If an action involves an unusually large number of defendants, the court may, on motion or on its own, order that:

- Defendants' pleadings and replies to them need not be served on other defendants;

- Any crossclaim, counterclaim, avoidance, or affirmative defense in those pleadings and replies to them will be treated as denied or avoided by all other parties; and

- Filing any such pleading and serving it on the plaintiff constitutes notice of the pleading to all parties. FRCP 5(c)(1).

ii. *Notifying parties.* A copy of every such order must be served on the parties as the court directs. FRCP 5(c)(2).

G. Hearings

1. *Hearings, generally*

a. *Oral argument.* Due process does not require that oral argument be permitted on a motion and, except as otherwise provided by local rule, the district court has discretion to determine whether it will decide the motion on the papers or hear argument by counsel (and perhaps receive evidence). FPP § 1190; F.D.I.C. v. Deglau, 207 F.3d 153 (3d Cir. 2000).

    i.   *Request for oral argument.* A party may request oral argument on a motion by filing and serving a separate document explaining why oral argument is necessary and estimating how long the court should allow for the argument. IN R USDCTND L.R. 7-5(a)(1). Refer to the Documents section of this document for more information.

    ii. *Additional evidence forbidden.* Parties may not present additional evidence at oral argument. IN R USDCTND L.R. 7-5(a)(3).

  b. *Providing a regular schedule for oral hearings.* A court may establish regular times and places for oral hearings on motions. FRCP 78(a).

  c. *Providing for submission on briefs.* By rule or order, the court may provide for submitting and determining motions on briefs, without oral hearings. FRCP 78(b).

  d. *Evidentiary hearings.* A party may request an evidentiary hearing by filing and serving a separate document explaining why the hearing is necessary and estimating how long the court should allow for it. IN R USDCTND L.R. 7-5(b)(2). Refer to the Documents section of this document for more information.

  e. *Court's authority.* The court may: (1) grant or deny a request for oral argument or an evidentiary hearing in its discretion; (2) set oral argument or an evidentiary hearing without a request from a party; or (3) order any oral argument or evidentiary hearing to be held anywhere within the district regardless of where the case will be tried. IN R USDCTND L.R. 7-5(c).

2. *Courtroom and courthouse decorum.* For information on courtroom and courthouse decorum, refer to IN R USDCTND L.R. 83-3.

H. Forms

1. Federal Motion for Post-Trial Relief Forms

  a. Notice of motion; To amend or correct judgment. AMJUR PP JUDGMENTS § 38.

  b. Motion for additur or new trial; Plaintiff awarded only medical bills without consideration of pain and suffering; No-fault automobile insurances. AMJUR PP JUDGMENTS § 47.

  c. Motion for judgment; In federal court; By plaintiff; In accordance with motion for directed verdict or for new trial. AMJUR PP JUDGMENTS § 257.

  d. Motion for judgment; By defendant; In accordance with motion for directed verdict or for new trial; In federal court. AMJUR PP JUDGMENTS § 258.

  e. Notice of motion; To vacate judgment. AMJUR PP JUDGMENTS § 344.

  f. Motion for new trial. 4 FEDFORMS § 4840.

  g. Motion for new trial with statement of grounds. 4 FEDFORMS § 4841.

  h. Motion for partial new trial. 4 FEDFORMS § 4844.

  i. Affidavit in support of motion. 4 FEDFORMS § 4860.

  j. Motion for new trial in nonjury action. 4 FEDFORMS § 4873.

  k. Motion for new trial or to amend findings and judgment. 4 FEDFORMS § 4877.

  l. Motion for new trial or to amend judgment. 4 FEDFORMS § 4880.

  m. Motion for new trial and amendment of findings. 4 FEDFORMS § 4881.

  n. Motion to amend judgment. 4 FEDFORMS § 4886.

  o. Notice of motion to amend judgment by correcting amount. 4 FEDFORMS § 4887.

  p. Motion to correct clerical error. 4 FEDFORMS § 4923.

  q. Motion to vacate judgment. 4 FEDFORMS § 4930.

r. Motion to vacate consent decree on ground of excusable neglect, mistake or surprise. 4 FEDFORMS § 4933.

s. Affidavit to vacate judgment; Excusable neglect, mistake, inadvertence or surprise. 4 FEDFORMS § 4935.

t. Motion; Correction of clerical mistake in judgment. FEDPROF § 1:1390.

u. Motion; For relief from judgment; General form. FEDPROF § 1:1391.

v. Motion; For relief from judgment; Newly discovered evidence. FEDPROF § 1:1392.

w. Affidavit; Supporting motion for relief from judgment; Newly discovered evidence. FEDPROF § 1:1395.

x. Motion for new trial; General form. GOLDLTGFMS § 61:3.

y. Motion to vacate judgment; General form. GOLDLTGFMS § 63:2.

z. Motion to vacate judgment; Date of discovery of facts. GOLDLTGFMS § 63:3.

2. Forms for the Northern District of Indiana

a. Certificate of service. IN R USDCTND CM/ECF(Form 1).

b. Notice of manual filing. IN R USDCTND CM/ECF(Form 2).

c. Declaration that party was unable to file in a timely manner. IN R USDCTND CM/ECF(Form 3).

I. Applicable Rules

1. *Federal rules*

a. Serving and filing pleadings and other papers. FRCP 5.

b. Constitutional challenge to a statute; Notice, certification, and intervention. FRCP 5.1.

c. Privacy protection for filings made with the court. FRCP 5.2.

d. Computing and extending time; Time for motion papers. FRCP 6.

e. Pleadings allowed; Form of motions and other papers. FRCP 7.

f. Form of pleadings. FRCP 10.

g. Signing pleadings, motions, and other papers; Representations to the court; Sanctions. FRCP 11.

h. Taking testimony. FRCP 43.

i. New trial; Altering or amending a judgment. FRCP 59.

j. Relief from a judgment or order. FRCP 60.

k. Hearing motions; Submission on briefs. FRCP 78.

2. *Local rules*

a. Citation and scope of the rules. IN R USDCTND L.R. 1-1.

b. Sanctions for formatting errors. IN R USDCTND L.R. 1-3.

c. Electronic filing required. IN R USDCTND L.R. 5-1.

d. Constitutional questions. IN R USDCTND L.R. 5.1-1.

e. Electronic service. IN R USDCTND L.R. 5-2.

f. Format of papers. IN R USDCTND L.R. 5-4.

g. Motion practice. IN R USDCTND L.R. 7-1.

h. Oral arguments and evidentiary hearings. IN R USDCTND L.R. 7-5.

i. Pretrial procedure. IN R USDCTND L.R. 16-1.

j. Alternative dispute resolution. IN R USDCTND L.R. 16-6.

k. Filing of discovery and other materials. IN R USDCTND L.R. 26-2.

l. Case assignment. IN R USDCTND L.R. 40-1.

m. Appearance and withdrawal of appearance. IN R USDCTND L.R. 83-8.

n. CM/ECF civil and criminal user manual. IN R USDCTND CM/ECF.

o. In re: privacy and public access to civil electronic case files. IN R USDCTND Order 2005-3.

Requests, Notices and Applications
Interrogatories

Document Last Updated December 2016

A. **Checklist**

    (I) ❑ Matters to be considered by requesting party

        (a) ❑ Required documents

            (1) ❑ Interrogatories

        (b) ❑ Supplemental documents

            (1) ❑ Certificate of service

        (c) ❑ Timing

            (1) ❑ A party may not seek discovery from any source before the parties have conferred as required by FRCP 26(f), except in a proceeding exempted from initial disclosure under FRCP 26(a)(1)(B), or when authorized by the Federal Rules of Civil Procedure, by stipulation, or by court order

    (II) ❑ Matters to be considered by responding party

        (a) ❑ Required documents

            (1) ❑ Response to interrogatories

        (b) ❑ Supplemental documents

            (1) ❑ Certificate of service

        (c) ❑ Timing

            (1) ❑ The responding party must serve its answers and any objections within thirty (30) days after being served with the interrogatories

B. **Timing**

    1. *Interrogatories.* FRCP 33(a) contains no limit on when interrogatories may first be served. FPP § 2170. FRCP 33 is also silent on how late in a case interrogatories may be served. But FRCP 16(b)(3)(A) provides that the scheduling order in the case "must limit the time to . . . complete discovery." Although the scheduling order requirement does not apply to cases exempted by local rule, ordinarily there should be a scheduling order that sets a discovery cutoff. FPP § 2170.

    2. *Timing of discovery, generally.* A party may not seek discovery from any source before the parties have conferred as required by FRCP 26(f), except in a proceeding exempted from initial disclosure under FRCP 26(a)(1)(B), or when authorized by the Federal Rules of Civil Procedure, by stipulation, or by court order. FRCP 26(d)(1).

    3. *Computation of time*

        a. *Computing time.* FRCP 6 applies in computing any time period specified in the Federal Rules of Civil Procedure, in any local rule or court order, or in any statute that does not specify a method of computing time. FRCP 6(a).

            i. *Period stated in days or a longer unit.* When the period is stated in days or a longer unit of time:

                • Exclude the day of the event that triggers the period;

                • Count every day, including intermediate Saturdays, Sundays, and legal holidays; and

                • Include the last day of the period, but if the last day is a Saturday, Sunday, or legal holiday, the period continues to run until the end of the next day that is not a Saturday, Sunday, or legal holiday. FRCP 6(a)(1).

ii. *Period stated in hours.* When the period is stated in hours:

- Begin counting immediately on the occurrence of the event that triggers the period;

- Count every hour, including hours during intermediate Saturdays, Sundays, and legal holidays; and

- If the period would end on a Saturday, Sunday, or legal holiday, the period continues to run until the same time on the next day that is not a Saturday, Sunday, or legal holiday. FRCP 6(a)(2).

iii. *Inaccessibility of the clerk's office.* Unless the court orders otherwise, if the clerk's office is inaccessible:

- On the last day for filing under FRCP 6(a)(1), then the time for filing is extended to the first accessible day that is not a Saturday, Sunday, or legal holiday; or

- During the last hour for filing under FRCP 6(a)(2), then the time for filing is extended to the same time on the first accessible day that is not a Saturday, Sunday, or legal holiday. FRCP 6(a)(3).

iv. *"Last day" defined.* Unless a different time is set by a statute, local rule, or court order, the last day ends:

- For electronic filing, at midnight in the court's time zone; and

- For filing by other means, when the clerk's office is scheduled to close. FRCP 6(a)(4).

v. *"Next day" defined.* The "next day" is determined by continuing to count forward when the period is measured after an event and backward when measured before an event. FRCP 6(a)(5).

vi. *"Legal holiday" defined.* "Legal holiday" means:

- The day set aside by statute for observing New Year's Day, Martin Luther King Jr.'s Birthday, Washington's Birthday, Memorial Day, Independence Day, Labor Day, Columbus Day, Veterans' Day, Thanksgiving Day, or Christmas Day;

- Any day declared a holiday by the President or Congress; and

- For periods that are measured after an event, any other day declared a holiday by the state where the district court is located. FRCP 6(a)(6).

b. *Computation of electronic filing deadlines.* Filing documents electronically does not alter any filing deadlines or any time computation pursuant to FRCP 6. The counties of Lake, Porter, LaPorte, Pulaski and Starke are located in the Central time zone and the remaining counties in the Northern District of Indiana are located in the Eastern time zone. Nevertheless, all electronic transmissions of documents must be completed (i.e., received completely by the clerk's office) prior to midnight Eastern Time, (South Bend/Fort Wayne/Lafayette time) in order to be considered timely filed that day, regardless of the local time in the division where the case is pending. Although documents can be filed electronically twenty-four (24) hours a day, filers are strongly encouraged to file all documents during hours when the CM/ECF Help Line is available, from 9:00 a.m. to 4:00 p.m. local time. IN R USDCTND CM/ECF(II)(I).

i. *Technical failures.* If the attorney is unable to file a document in a timely manner due to technical difficulties in the user's system, the attorney must file a document with the court as soon as possible notifying the court of the inability to file the document. A sample document entitled Declaration that Party was Unable to File in a Timely Manner Due to Technical Difficulties is attached hereto as Form 5. IN R USDCTND CM/ECF(VI)(B). [Editor's note: the reference to Form 5 is likely meant to be a reference to Form 3 (IN R USDCTND CM/ECF(Form 3)].

   c. *Extending time*

      i. *In general.* When an act may or must be done within a specified time, the court may, for good cause, extend the time:

- With or without motion or notice if the court acts, or if a request is made, before the original time or its extension expires; or

- On motion made after the time has expired if the party failed to act because of excusable neglect. FRCP 6(b)(1).

      ii. *Exceptions.* A court must not extend the time to act under FRCP 50(b), FRCP 50(d), FRCP 52(b), FRCP 59(b), FRCP 59(d), FRCP 59(e), and FRCP 60(b). FRCP 6(b)(2).

      iii. Refer to the United States District Court for the Northern District of Indiana KeyRules Motion for Continuance/Extension of Time document for more information on extending time.

   d. *Additional time after certain kinds of service.* When a party may or must act within a specified time after being served and service is made under FRCP 5(b)(2)(C) (mail), FRCP 5(b)(2)(D) (leaving with the clerk), or FRCP 5(b)(2)(F) (other means consented to), three (3) days are added after the period would otherwise expire under FRCP 6(a). FRCP 6(d).

C. General Requirements

  1. *General provisions governing discovery*

   a. *Discovery scope and limits*

      i. *Scope in general.* Unless otherwise limited by court order, the scope of discovery is as follows: Parties may obtain discovery regarding any nonprivileged matter that is relevant to any party's claim or defense and proportional to the needs of the case, considering the importance of the issues at stake in the action, the amount in controversy, the parties' relative access to relevant information, the parties' resources, the importance of the discovery in resolving the issues, and whether the burden or expense of the proposed discovery outweighs its likely benefit. Information within this scope of discovery need not be admissible in evidence to be discoverable. FRCP 26(b)(1).

      ii. *Limitations on frequency and extent*

- *When permitted.* By order, the court may alter the limits in the Federal Rules of Civil Procedure on the number of depositions and interrogatories or on the length of depositions under FRCP 30. By order or local rule, the court may also limit the number of requests under FRCP 36. FRCP 26(b)(2)(A).

- *Specific limitations on electronically stored information.* A party need not provide discovery of electronically stored information from sources that the party identifies as not reasonably accessible because of undue burden or cost. On motion to compel discovery or for a protective order, the party from whom discovery is sought must show that the information is not reasonably accessible because of undue burden or cost. If that showing is made, the court may nonetheless order discovery from such sources if the requesting party shows good cause, considering the limitations of FRCP 26(b)(2)(C). The court may specify conditions for the discovery. FRCP 26(b)(2)(B).

- *When required.* On motion or on its own, the court must limit the frequency or extent of discovery otherwise allowed by the Federal Rules of Civil Procedure or by local rule if it determines that: (1) the discovery sought is unreasonably cumulative or duplicative, or can be obtained from some other source that is more convenient, less burdensome, or less expensive; (2) the party seeking discovery has had ample opportunity to obtain the information by discovery in the action; or (3) the proposed discovery is outside the scope permitted by FRCP 26(b)(1). FRCP 26(b)(2)(C).

      iii. *Trial preparation; Materials*

- *Documents and tangible things.* Ordinarily, a party may not discover documents and tangible things that are prepared in anticipation of litigation or for trial by or for another party or its representative (including the other party's attorney, consultant, surety, indemnitor, insurer, or agent). But, subject to FRCP 26(b)(4), those materials may be discovered if: (1) they are otherwise discoverable under FRCP 26(b)(1); and (2) the party shows that it has substantial need for the materials to prepare its case and cannot, without undue hardship, obtain their substantial equivalent by other means. FRCP 26(b)(3)(A).

- *Protection against disclosure.* If the court orders discovery of those materials, it must protect against disclosure of the mental impressions, conclusions, opinions, or legal theories of a party's attorney or other representative concerning the litigation. FRCP 26(b)(3)(B).

- *Previous statement.* Any party or other person may, on request and without the required showing, obtain the person's own previous statement about the action or its subject matter. If the request is refused, the person may move for a court order, and FRCP 37(a)(5) applies to the award of expenses. A previous statement is either: (1) a written statement that the person has signed or otherwise adopted or approved; or (2) a contemporaneous stenographic, mechanical, electrical, or other recording—or a transcription of it—that recites substantially verbatim the person's oral statement. FRCP 26(b)(3)(C).

iv. *Trial preparation; Experts*

- *Deposition of an expert who may testify.* A party may depose any person who has been identified as an expert whose opinions may be presented at trial. If FRCP 26(a)(2)(B) requires a report from the expert, the deposition may be conducted only after the report is provided. FRCP 26(b)(4)(A).

- *Trial-preparation protection for draft reports or disclosures.* FRCP 26(b)(3)(A) and FRCP 26(b)(3)(B) protect drafts of any report or disclosure required under FRCP 26(a)(2), regardless of the form in which the draft is recorded. FRCP 26(b)(4)(B).

- *Trial-preparation protection for communications between a party's attorney and expert witnesses.* FRCP 26(b)(3)(A) and FRCP 26(b)(3)(B) protect communications between the party's attorney and any witness required to provide a report under FRCP 26(a)(2)(B), regardless of the form of the communications, except to the extent that the communications: (1) relate to compensation for the expert's study or testimony; (2) identify facts or data that the party's attorney provided and that the expert considered in forming the opinions to be expressed; or (3) identify assumptions that the party's attorney provided and that the expert relied on in forming the opinions to be expressed. FRCP 26(b)(4)(C).

- *Expert employed only for trial preparation.* Ordinarily, a party may not, by interrogatories or deposition, discover facts known or opinions held by an expert who has been retained or specially employed by another party in anticipation of litigation or to prepare for trial and who is not expected to be called as a witness at trial. But a party may do so only: (1) as provided in FRCP 35(b); or (2) on showing exceptional circumstances under which it is impracticable for the party to obtain facts or opinions on the same subject by other means. FRCP 26(b)(4)(D).

- *Payment.* Unless manifest injustice would result, the court must require that the party seeking discovery: (1) pay the expert a reasonable fee for time spent in responding to discovery under FRCP 26(b)(4)(A) or FRCP 26(b)(4)(D); and (2) for discovery under FRCP 26(b)(4)(D), also pay the other party a fair portion of the fees and expenses it reasonably incurred in obtaining the expert's facts and opinions. FRCP 26(b)(4)(E).

v. *Claiming privilege or protecting trial-preparation materials*

- *Information withheld.* When a party withholds information otherwise discoverable by claiming that the information is privileged or subject to protection as trial-preparation material, the party must: (1) expressly make the claim; and (2) describe the nature of the documents, communications, or tangible things not produced or disclosed—and do so in a manner that, without revealing information itself privileged or protected, will enable other parties to assess the claim. FRCP 26(b)(5)(A).

- *Information produced.* If information produced in discovery is subject to a claim of privilege or of protection as trial-preparation material, the party making the claim may notify any party that received the information of the claim and the basis for it. After being notified, a party must promptly return, sequester, or destroy the specified information and any copies it has; must not use or disclose the information until the claim is resolved; must take reasonable steps to retrieve the information if the party disclosed it before being notified; and may promptly present the information to the court under seal for a determination of the claim. The producing party must preserve the information until the claim is resolved. FRCP 26(b)(5)(B).

b. *Protective orders.* A party or any person from whom discovery is sought may move for a protective order in the court where the action is pending—or as an alternative on matters relating to a deposition, in the court for the district where the deposition will be taken. FRCP 26(c)(1). Refer to the United States District Court for the Northern District of Indiana KeyRules Motion for Protective Order document for more information.

c. *Sequence of discovery.* Unless the parties stipulate or the court orders otherwise for the parties' and witnesses' convenience and in the interests of justice: (1) methods of discovery may be used in any sequence; and (2) discovery by one party does not require any other party to delay its discovery. FRCP 26(d)(3).

2. *Interrogatories*

a. *Number.* Unless otherwise stipulated or ordered by the court, a party may serve on any other party no more than twenty-five (25) written interrogatories, including all discrete subparts. Leave to serve additional interrogatories may be granted to the extent consistent with FRCP 26(b)(1) and FRCP 26(b)(2). FRCP 33(a)(1).

b. *Scope.* An interrogatory may relate to any matter that may be inquired into under FRCP 26(b). An interrogatory is not objectionable merely because it asks for an opinion or contention that relates to fact or the application of law to fact, but the court may order that the interrogatory need not be answered until designated discovery is complete, or until a pretrial conference or some other time. FRCP 33(a)(2).

c. *Parties subject to interrogatories.* Depositions may be taken of any person but interrogatories are limited to parties to the litigation. FPP § 2171. Interrogatories may not be directed to the attorney for a party. They must be addressed to the party, who is then required to give all information known to it or its attorney. FPP § 2171; Hickman v. Taylor, 329 U.S. 495, 504, 67 S.Ct. 385, 390, 91 L.Ed. 451 (1947). For more information, refer to FPP § 2171.

d. *Form.* A party propounding written discovery under FRCP 33, FRCP 34, or FRCP 36 must number each interrogatory or request sequentially. IN R USDCTND L.R. 26-1(a). Ideally an interrogatory should be a single direct question phrased in a fashion that will inform the other party what is requested. In fact the courts have given parties considerable latitude in framing interrogatories. Rather general language has been permitted so long as the interrogatory gives the other party a reasonably clear indication of the information to be included in its answer. FPP § 2168.

    i. *Use of definitions.* There is no prohibition against the use of definitions in interrogatories, and definitions may be helpful in clarifying the meaning of obscure terms or avoiding repetitions in a long set of interrogatories. FPP § 2168.

    ii. *Use of standardized form interrogatories.* There have been mixed reactions to the use of standardized form interrogatories. They have been referred to opprobriously as "canned sets of interrogatories of the shotgun variety" and it has been said that their indiscriminate use is an "undesirable practice." FPP § 2168.

e. *Motion to compel.* The party submitting the interrogatories must attempt to confer with the responding party in an effort to secure the information without court action and, if that fails, move for an order under FRCP 37(a) compelling answers. FPP § 2182. Refer to the United States District Court for the Northern District of Indiana KeyRules Motion to Compel Discovery document for more information.

3. *Sanctions for failure to cooperate in discovery.* The court where the action is pending may, on motion, order sanctions if a party, after being properly served with interrogatories under FRCP 33 or a request for inspection under FRCP 34, fails to serve its answers, objections, or written response. FRCP 37(d)(1)(A)(ii). If a motion to compel is granted, the court must, after giving an opportunity to be heard, require the party or deponent whose conduct necessitated the motion, the party or attorney advising that conduct, or both to pay the movant's reasonable expenses incurred in making the motion, including attorney's fees. But the court must not order this payment if the opposing party's nondisclosure, response, or objection was substantially justified. FRCP 37(a)(5)(A)(ii). Refer to the United States District Court for the Northern District of Indiana KeyRules Motion for Discovery Sanctions document for more information.

4. *Stipulations about discovery procedure.* Unless the court orders otherwise, the parties may stipulate that: (1) a deposition may be taken before any person, at any time or place, on any notice, and in the manner specified—in which event it may be used in the same way as any other deposition; and (2) other procedures governing or limiting discovery be modified—but a stipulation extending the time for any form of discovery must have court approval if it would interfere with the time set for completing discovery, for hearing a motion, or for trial. FRCP 29.

5. *Appearances.* Attorneys not representing the United States or its agencies must file an appearance when they represent (either in person or by filing a paper) a party. IN R USDCTND L.R. 83-8(a). For more information, refer to IN R USDCTND L.R. 83-8.

6. *Notice of related action.* A party must file a notice of related action as soon as it appears that the party's case and another pending case: (1) arise out of the same transaction or occurrence; (2) involve the same property; or (3) involve the validity or infringement of the same patent, trademark, or copyright. IN R USDCTND L.R. 40-1(d). For more information, refer to IN R USDCTND L.R. 40-1.

7. *Alternative dispute resolution (ADR).* After they confer as required by FRCP 26(f), the parties must advise the court which, if any, alternative-dispute-resolution processes they expect to pursue and when they expect to undertake the process. IN R USDCTND L.R. 16-6(a). For more information on alternative dispute resolution (ADR), refer to IN R USDCTND L.R. 16-6 and IN R USDCTND Order 2003-21.

8. *Settlement or resolution.* The parties must immediately notify the court if they reasonably expect to settle the case or resolve a pending motion. IN R USDCTND L.R. 16-1(g).

9. *Modification or suspension of rules.* The court may, on its own motion or at the request of a party, suspend or modify any rule in a particular case in the interest of justice. IN R USDCTND L.R. 1-1(c).

D. Documents

1. *Required documents*

   a. *Interrogatories.* Refer to the General Requirements section of this document for information on interrogatories.

2. *Supplemental documents*

   a. *Certificate of service.* FRCP 5(d) requires that the person making service under FRCP 5 certify that service has been effected. FRCP 5(Advisory Committee Notes). Having such information on file may be useful for many purposes, including proof of service if an issue arises concerning the effectiveness of the service. FRCP 5(Advisory Committee Notes).

E. Format

1. *Form of documents.* The rules governing captions and other matters of form in pleadings apply to motions and other papers. FRCP 7(b)(2).

   a. *Paper.* Any pleading, motion, brief, affidavit, notice, or proposed order, whether filed electronically or by delivering it to the clerk, must: use eight and one-half by eleven (8-1/2 x 11) inch pages. IN R USDCTND L.R. 5-4(a)(2).

      i. *Manual filings.* Papers delivered to the clerk for filing must: be flat, unfolded, and on good-quality, white paper. IN R USDCTND L.R. 5-4(b)(1)(A).

         • *Covers or backing.* Papers delivered to the clerk for filing must: not have a cover or a back. IN R USDCTND L.R. 5-4(b)(1)(B).

- *Recycled paper.* The court encourages using recycled paper. IN R USDCTND L.R. 5-4(b)(7).

b. *Margins.* Any pleading, motion, brief, affidavit, notice, or proposed order, whether filed electronically or by delivering it to the clerk, must: have at least one (1) inch margins. IN R USDCTND L.R. 5-4(a)(3).

c. *Spacing.* Any pleading, motion, brief, affidavit, notice, or proposed order, whether filed electronically or by delivering it to the clerk, must: be double spaced (except for headings, footnotes, and quoted material). IN R USDCTND L.R. 5-4(a)(5).

d. *Text.* Any pleading, motion, brief, affidavit, notice, or proposed order, whether filed electronically or by delivering it to the clerk, must: be plainly typewritten, printed, or prepared by a clearly legible copying process. IN R USDCTND L.R. 5-4(a)(1).

   i. Any pleading, motion, brief, affidavit, notice, or proposed order, whether filed electronically or by delivering it to the clerk, must: use at least twelve (12) point type in the body and at least ten (10) point type in footnotes. IN R USDCTND L.R. 5-4(a)(4).

e. *Page numbering.* Any pleading, motion, brief, affidavit, notice, or proposed order, whether filed electronically or by delivering it to the clerk, must: have consecutively numbered pages. IN R USDCTND L.R. 5-4(a)(6).

f. *Caption; Names of parties.* Every pleading must have a caption with the court's name, a title, a file number, and a FRCP 7(a) designation. The title of the complaint must name all the parties; the title of other pleadings, after naming the first party on each side, may refer generally to other parties. FRCP 10(a). Any pleading, motion, brief, affidavit, notice, or proposed order, whether filed electronically or by delivering it to the clerk, must: include a title on the first page. IN R USDCTND L.R. 5-4(a)(7).

g. *Filer's information.* Any pleading, motion, brief, affidavit, notice, or proposed order, whether filed electronically or by delivering it to the clerk, must: except in proposed orders and affidavits, include the filer's name, address, telephone number, fax number (where available), and e-mail address (where available). IN R USDCTND L.R. 5-4(a)(9).

h. *Paragraphs; Separate statements.* A party must state its claims or defenses in numbered paragraphs, each limited as far as practicable to a single set of circumstances. A later pleading may refer by number to a paragraph in an earlier pleading. If doing so would promote clarity, each claim founded on a separate transaction or occurrence—and each defense other than a denial—must be stated in a separate count or defense. FRCP 10(b).

i. *Adoption by reference; Exhibits.* A statement in a pleading may be adopted by reference elsewhere in the same pleading or in any other pleading or motion. A copy of a written instrument that is an exhibit to a pleading is a part of the pleading for all purposes. FRCP 10(c).

j. *Citation of local rules.* The Local Civil Rules of the United States District Court for the Northern District of Indiana may be cited as "N.D. Ind. L.R." IN R USDCTND L.R. 1-1(a)(1).

k. *Acceptance by the clerk.* The clerk must not refuse to file a paper solely because it is not in the form prescribed by the Federal Rules of Civil Procedure or by a local rule or practice. FRCP 5(d)(4).

   i. *Sanctions for formatting errors; Non-compliance.* If a person files a paper that does not comply with the rules governing the format of papers filed with the court, the court may: (1) strike the paper from the record; or (2) fine the person up to one thousand dollars ($1,000). IN R USDCTND L.R. 1-3(a).

      - *Notice.* Before sanctioning a person under IN R USDCTND L.R. 1-3(a)(2), the court must: (1) notify the person that the paper is noncompliant; and (2) give the person the opportunity either to be heard or to revise the paper. IN R USDCTND L.R. 1-3(b).

2. *Form of electronic documents.* Electronically filed documents must meet the same requirements of format and page limits as documents "conventionally filed" (as defined in IN R USDCTND CM/ECF(III)(A)) pursuant to the Federal Rules of Civil Procedure and the Local Civil Rules of the United States District Court for the Northern District of Indiana. IN R USDCTND CM/ECF(II)(A)(2).

a. *PDF format required.* Documents filed in the CM/ECF must be in .pdf format. A document created with almost any word-processing program can be converted to .pdf format. The .pdf program in effect takes a picture of the original document and allows anyone to open the converted document across a broad range of hardware and software, with layout, format, links, and images intact. IN R USDCTND CM/ECF(FN2).

b. *Title of documents.* The person electronically filing a pleading or other document will be responsible for designating a title for the pleading or other document by using one of the categories contained in the events listed in the CM/ECF Menu. IN R USDCTND CM/ECF(II)(G).

c. *Combining documents.* All documents which form part of a single pleading and which are being filed at the same time and by the same party may be electronically filed together under one document number, e.g., the motion and a supporting affidavit, with the exception of memoranda in support. Memoranda in support shall be electronically filed separately and shown as a related document to the motion. IN R USDCTND CM/ECF(II)(A)(4).

d. *Exhibits and attachments.* Filing users must submit in electronic form all documents referenced as exhibits or attachments, unless the court permits conventional filing. A filing user must submit as exhibits or attachments only those excerpts of the referenced documents that are directly germane to the matter under consideration by the court. Excerpted material must be clearly and prominently identified as such. Filing users who file excerpts of documents as exhibits or attachments do so without prejudice to their right to timely file additional excerpts or the complete document. Responding parties may timely file additional excerpts or the complete document that they believe are directly germane. The court may require parties to file additional excerpts or the complete document. IN R USDCTND CM/ECF(II)(A)(6).

e. *Hyperlinks.* Electronically filed documents may contain hyperlink references to an external document as a convenient mechanism for accessing material cited in the document. A hyperlink reference is neither validated for content nor considered a part of the court's records. The court neither endorses the product or organization at the destination of a hyperlink reference, nor does the court exercise any responsibility over the content at the destination. In order to preserve the integrity of the court record, attorneys wishing to insert hyperlinks in court filings shall continue to use the traditional citation method for the cited authority, in addition to the hyperlink. A hyperlink contained in a filing is no more than a convenient mechanism for accessing material cited in the document and a hyperlink reference is extraneous to any filed document and is not part of the court's record. IN R USDCTND CM/ECF(II)(A)(3).

3. *Signing disclosures and discovery requests, responses, and objections.* FRCP 11 does not apply to disclosures and discovery requests, responses, objections, and motions under FRCP 26 through FRCP 37. FRCP 11(d).

a. *Signature required.* Every disclosure under FRCP 26(a)(1) or FRCP 26(a)(3) and every discovery request, response, or objection must be signed by at least one attorney of record in the attorney's own name—or by the party personally, if unrepresented—and must state the signer's address, e-mail address, and telephone number. FRCP 26(g)(1).

   i. *Signatures on manual filings.* Papers delivered to the clerk for filing must: include the filer's original signature. IN R USDCTND L.R. 5-4(b)(1)(C).

      • *Rubber-stamped and faxed signatures.* An original paper with a rubber-stamped or faxed signature is unsigned for purposes of FRCP 11 and FRCP 26(g). IN R USDCTND L.R. 5-4(b)(2).

      • *Affidavits.* Only the affiant need sign an affidavit. IN R USDCTND L.R. 5-4(b)(3).

   ii. *Electronic signatures.* Pursuant to FRCP 11, every pleading, motion, and other paper (except lists, schedules, statements or amendments thereto) shall be signed by at least one attorney of record or, if the party is not represented by an attorney, all papers shall be signed by the party. An attorney's/participant's password issued by the court combined with the user's identification, serves as and constitutes the attorney/participant's signature for FRCP 11 and other purposes. IN R USDCTND CM/ECF(I)(C). Documents which must be filed and which must contain original signatures other than those of a participating attorney or which require either

393

verification or an unsworn declaration under any rule or statute, shall be filed electronically, with originally executed copies maintained by the filer. The pleading or other document electronically filed shall contain "s/" signature(s), as noted in IN R USDCTND CM/ECF(II)(E)(3)(b). IN R USDCTND CM/ECF(II)(E)(1).

- *Multiple signatures.* In the case of a stipulation or other document to be signed by two or more attorneys, the following procedure should be used: The filing attorney shall initially confirm that the content of the document is acceptable to all persons required to sign the document and shall obtain the physical signatures of all attorneys on the document. IN R USDCTND CM/ECF(II)(E)(3)(a). The filing attorney then shall file the document electronically, indicating the signatories, e.g., "s/Jane Doe," "s/John Doe," etc. IN R US-DCTND CM/ECF(II)(E)(3)(b). The filing attorney shall retain the hard copy of the document containing the original signatures. IN R USDCTND CM/ECF(II)(E)(3)(c).

b. *Effect of signature.* By signing, an attorney or party certifies that to the best of the person's knowledge, information, and belief formed after a reasonable inquiry:

   i. With respect to a disclosure, it is complete and correct as of the time it is made; and

   ii. With respect to a discovery request, response, or objection, it is:

- Consistent with the Federal Rules of Civil Procedure and warranted by existing law or by a nonfrivolous argument for extending, modifying, or reversing existing law, or for establishing new law;

- Not interposed for any improper purpose, such as to harass, cause unnecessary delay, or needlessly increase the cost of litigation; and

- Neither unreasonable nor unduly burdensome or expensive, considering the needs of the case, prior discovery in the case, the amount in controversy, and the importance of the issues at stake in the action. FRCP 26(g)(1).

c. *Failure to sign.* Other parties have no duty to act on an unsigned disclosure, request, response, or objection until it is signed, and the court must strike it unless a signature is promptly supplied after the omission is called to the attorney's or party's attention. FRCP 26(g)(2).

d. *Sanction for improper certification.* If a certification violates FRCP 26(g) without substantial justification, the court, on motion or on its own, must impose an appropriate sanction on the signer, the party on whose behalf the signer was acting, or both. The sanction may include an order to pay the reasonable expenses, including attorney's fees, caused by the violation. FRCP 26(g)(3). Refer to the United States District Court for the Northern District of Indiana KeyRules Motion for Discovery Sanctions document for more information.

4. *Privacy protection for filings made with the court*

a. *Redacted filings.* Counsel should not include sensitive information in any document filed with the court unless such inclusion is necessary and relevant to the case. IN R USDCTND CM/ECF(VII). Unless the court orders otherwise, in an electronic or paper filing with the court that contains an individual's Social Security number, taxpayer-identification number, or birth date, the name of an individual known to be a minor, or a financial-account number, a party or nonparty making the filing may include only:

   i. The last four (4) digits of the Social Security number and taxpayer-identification number;

   ii. The year of the individual's birth;

   iii. The minor's initials; and

   iv. The last four (4) digits of the financial-account number. FRCP 5.2(a); IN R USDCTND Order 2005-3.

b. *Exemptions from the redaction requirement.* The redaction requirement does not apply to the following:

   i. A financial-account number that identifies the property allegedly subject to forfeiture in a forfeiture proceeding;

ii.   The record of an administrative or agency proceeding;

iii. The official record of a state-court proceeding;

iv.   The record of a court or tribunal, if that record was not subject to the redaction requirement when originally filed;

v.   A filing covered by FRCP 5.2(c) or FRCP 5.2(d); and

vi.   A pro se filing in an action brought under 28 U.S.C.A. § 2241, 28 U.S.C.A. § 2254, or 28 U.S.C.A. § 2255. FRCP 5.2(b).

vii. In cases filed under the Social Security Act, 42 U.S.C.A. § 405(g), there is no need for redaction of any information from the documents filed in the case. IN R USDCTND Order 2005-3.

c.   *Limitations on remote access to electronic files; Social Security appeals and immigration cases.* Unless the court orders otherwise, in an action for benefits under the Social Security Act, and in an action or proceeding relating to an order of removal, to relief from removal, or to immigration benefits or detention, access to an electronic file is authorized as follows:

i.   The parties and their attorneys may have remote electronic access to any part of the case file, including the administrative record;

ii.   Any other person may have electronic access to the full record at the courthouse, but may have remote electronic access only to:

- The docket maintained by the court; and

- An opinion, order, judgment, or other disposition of the court, but not any other part of the case file or the administrative record. FRCP 5.2(c).

d.   *Filings made under seal.* The court may order that a filing be made under seal without redaction. The court may later unseal the filing or order the person who made the filing to file a redacted version for the public record. FRCP 5.2(d). For information on filing documents under seal, refer to IN R USDCTND L.R. 5-3, IN R USDCTND CM/ECF(IV)(A), and IN R USDCTND ECF Order 2004-19.

e.   *Protective orders.* For good cause, the court may by order in a case:

i.   Require redaction of additional information; or

ii.   Limit or prohibit a nonparty's remote electronic access to a document filed with the court. FRCP 5.2(e).

f.   *Option for additional unredacted filing under seal.* A person making a redacted filing may also file an unredacted copy under seal. The court must retain the unredacted copy as part of the record. FRCP 5.2(f); IN R USDCTND Order 2005-3.

i.   The unredacted version of the document or the reference list shall be retained by the court under seal as part of the record. This paper shall be retained by the court as part of the record. The court may, however, still require the party to file a redacted copy for the public file. IN R USDCTND Order 2005-3.

g.   *Option for filing a reference list.* A filing that contains redacted information may be filed together with a reference list that identifies each item of redacted information and specifies an appropriate identifier that uniquely corresponds to each item listed. The list must be filed under seal and may be amended as of right. Any reference in the case to a listed identifier will be construed to refer to the corresponding item of information. FRCP 5.2(g); IN R USDCTND Order 2005-3.

i.   The unredacted version of the document or the reference list shall be retained by the court under seal as part of the record. This paper shall be retained by the court as part of the record. The court may, however, still require the party to file a redacted copy for the public file. IN R USDCTND Order 2005-3.

h.   *Responsibility for redaction.* The responsibility for redacting these personal identifiers rests solely with counsel and the parties. The Clerk will not review each paper for compliance with IN R USDCTND Order 2005-3. IN R USDCTND Order 2005-3.

i. *Waiver of protection of identifiers.* A person waives the protection of FRCP 5.2(a) as to the person's own information by filing it without redaction and not under seal. FRCP 5.2(h).

F. Filing and Service Requirements

1. *Filing requirements.* Any paper after the complaint that is required to be served—together with a certificate of service—must be filed within a reasonable time after service. But disclosures under FRCP 26(a)(1) or FRCP 26(a)(2) and the following discovery requests and responses must not be filed until they are used in the proceeding or the court orders filing: depositions, interrogatories, requests for documents or tangible things or to permit entry onto land, and requests for admission. FRCP 5(d)(1). Refer to the United States District Court for the Northern District of Indiana KeyRules pleading and motion documents for information on filing with the court.

   a. *Discovery ordinarily not filed.* The party who serves a discovery request or notices a deposition is the custodian of the original discovery response or deposition transcript. Except as required under IN R USDCTND L.R. 26-2(a)(2), parties must not file: (1) disclosures under FRCP 26(a)(1) or FRCP 26(a)(2); (2) deposition notices; (3) deposition transcripts; (4) interrogatories; (5) requests for documents, to permit entry upon land, or for admission; (6) answers to interrogatories; (7) responses to requests for documents, to permit entry upon land, or for admission; or (8) service-of-discovery notices. IN R USDCTND L.R. 26-2(a)(1).

      i. *Exceptions*

         • *Pro se litigation.* All discovery material in cases involving a pro se party must be filed. IN R USDCTND L.R. 26-2(a)(2)(A).

         • *Specific material.* Discovery material must also be filed when: (1) the court orders; or (2) the material is used in a proceeding. IN R USDCTND L.R. 26-2(a)(2)(B).

   b. *When discovery may be filed*

      i. *Filing materials with motion for relief.* A party who files a motion for relief under FRCP 26(c) or FRCP 37 must file with the motion those parts of the discovery requests or responses that the motion pertains to. IN R USDCTND L.R. 26-2(b).

      ii. *Materials necessary for motion.* A party must file those portions of discovery requests or responses (including deposition transcripts) that the party relies on to support a motion that could result in a final order on an issue. IN R USDCTND L.R. 26-2(c).

      iii. *Materials to be used at trial.* A party who reasonably anticipates using discovery requests or responses—including deposition transcripts—at trial must file the relevant portions of the requests or responses with the clerk at the start of the trial. IN R USDCTND L.R. 26-2(d).

2. *Service requirements*

   a. *Service; When required*

      i. *In general.* Unless the Federal Rules of Civil Procedure provide otherwise, each of the following papers must be served on every party:

         • An order stating that service is required;

         • A pleading filed after the original complaint, unless the court orders otherwise under FRCP 5(c) because there are numerous defendants;

         • A discovery paper required to be served on a party, unless the court orders otherwise;

         • A written motion, except one that may be heard ex parte; and

         • A written notice, appearance, demand, or offer of judgment, or any similar paper. FRCP 5(a)(1).

      ii. *If a party fails to appear.* No service is required on a party who is in default for failing to appear. But a pleading that asserts a new claim for relief against such a party must be served on that party under FRCP 4. FRCP 5(a)(2).

      iii. *Seizing property.* If an action is begun by seizing property and no person is or need be named as a defendant, any service required before the filing of an appearance, answer, or claim must be made on the person who had custody or possession of the property when it was seized. FRCP 5(a)(3).

b. *Service; How made*

    i. *Serving an attorney.* If a party is represented by an attorney, service under FRCP 5 must be made on the attorney unless the court orders service on the party. FRCP 5(b)(1).

    ii. *Service in general.* A paper is served under FRCP 5 by:

- Handing it to the person;
- Leaving it: (1) at the person's office with a clerk or other person in charge or, if no one is in charge, in a conspicuous place in the office; or (2) if the person has no office or the office is closed, at the person's dwelling or usual place of abode with someone of suitable age and discretion who resides there;
- Mailing it to the person's last known address—in which event service is complete upon mailing;
- Leaving it with the court clerk if the person has no known address;
- Sending it by electronic means if the person consented in writing—in which event service is complete upon transmission, but is not effective if the serving party learns that it did not reach the person to be served; or
- Delivering it by any other means that the person consented to in writing—in which event service is complete when the person making service delivers it to the agency designated to make delivery. FRCP 5(b)(2).

    iii. *Electronic service.* Electronically filed papers may be served electronically if service is consistent with the CM/ECF User Manual (IN R USDCTND CM/ECF). IN R USDCTND L.R. 5-2(a).

- *Waiver of other service.* An attorney's registration will constitute a waiver of conventional service of documents and the attorney agrees to accept service of notice on behalf of the client of the electronic filing by hand, facsimile or authorized email. IN R USDCTND CM/ECF(I)(B)(3).
- *Serving registered persons.* The System will generate a "Notice of Electronic Filing" when any document is filed. This notice represents service of the document on parties who are registered participants with the System. Except as provided in IN R USDCTND CM/ECF(III)(B), the filing party shall not be required to serve any pleading or other documents on any party receiving electronic notice. IN R USDCTND CM/ECF(II)(D)(1). The term "pleading" refers only to those documents listed in FRCP 7(a). IN R USDCTND CM/ECF(FN3).
- *When electronic service is deemed completed.* A person registered to use the court's electronic-filing system is served with an electronically filed paper when a "Notice of Electronic Filing" is transmitted to that person through the court's electronic filing-system. IN R USDCTND L.R. 5-2(b).
- *Serving non-registered persons.* A person who has not registered to use the court's electronic-filing system but who is entitled to service of a paper must be served according to the Local Civil Rules of the United States District Court for the Northern District of Indiana and the Federal Rules of Civil Procedure. IN R USDCTND L.R. 5-2(c); IN R USDCTND CM/ECF(II)(D)(2). If such service of a paper copy is to be made, it shall be done in the manner provided in the Federal Rules of Civil Procedure and the Local Civil Rules of the United States District Court for the Northern District of Indiana. IN R USDCTND CM/ECF(II)(D)(2).

    iv. *Service of conventional filings.* Pleadings or other documents which are filed conventionally rather than electronically shall be served in the manner provided for in the Federal Rules of Civil Procedure and the Local Civil Rules of the United States District Court for the Northern District of Indiana, except as otherwise provided by order of the Court. IN R USDCTND CM/ECF(III)(B).

    v.   *Using court facilities.* If a local rule so authorizes, a party may use the court's transmission facilities to make service under FRCP 5(b)(2)(E). FRCP 5(b)(3).

  c. *Serving numerous defendants*

    i. *In general.* If an action involves an unusually large number of defendants, the court may, on motion or on its own, order that:

- Defendants' pleadings and replies to them need not be served on other defendants;

- Any crossclaim, counterclaim, avoidance, or affirmative defense in those pleadings and replies to them will be treated as denied or avoided by all other parties; and

- Filing any such pleading and serving it on the plaintiff constitutes notice of the pleading to all parties. FRCP 5(c)(1).

    ii. *Notifying parties.* A copy of every such order must be served on the parties as the court directs. FRCP 5(c)(2).

G. Hearings

1. There is no hearing contemplated in the federal statutes or rules for interrogatories.

H. Forms

1. Federal Interrogatories Forms

  a. Introductory statement; Interrogatories to individual. AMJUR PP DEPOSITION § 405.

  b. Introductory statement; Interrogatories to corporation. AMJUR PP DEPOSITION § 406.

  c. Interrogatories. 3A FEDFORMS § 3488.

  d. Interrogatories; Another form. 3A FEDFORMS § 3489.

  e. Interrogatories by plaintiff; To corporation. 3A FEDFORMS § 3490.

  f. Interrogatories by plaintiff; Complete set. 3A FEDFORMS § 3491.

  g. Interrogatories by plaintiff; Requesting identification of documents and production under FRCP 34. 3A FEDFORMS § 3492.

  h. Interrogatories by plaintiff; With definition of terms used and instructions for answering. 3A FEDFORMS § 3493.

  i. Interrogatories by plaintiff; Employment discrimination case. 3A FEDFORMS § 3494.

  j. Interrogatories by defendant. 3A FEDFORMS § 3495.

  k. Interrogatories by defendant; Complete set. 3A FEDFORMS § 3496.

  l. Interrogatories by defendant; Complete set; Another form. 3A FEDFORMS § 3497.

  m. Interrogatories by defendant; Complete set; Another form. 3A FEDFORMS § 3498.

  n. Interrogatories by defendant; Complete set; Another form. 3A FEDFORMS § 3499.

  o. Interrogatories by defendant; Follow-up interrogatories to plaintiff after lapse of time since first set of interrogatories or deposition. 3A FEDFORMS § 3500.

  p. Certificate of service of interrogatories. 3A FEDFORMS § 3501.

  q. Interrogatories; Outline form. FEDPROF § 23:335.

  r. Interrogatories; To defendant; Trademark action. FEDPROF § 23:347.

  s. Interrogatories; With request for documents; To defendant; Collection of royalties. FEDPROF § 23:348.

  t. Interrogatories; To defendant; Copyright infringement. FEDPROF § 23:350.

  u. Interrogatories; To plaintiff; Products liability. FEDPROF § 23:352.

  v. Interrogatories; To plaintiff; Personal injury. FEDPROF § 23:353.

  w. Interrogatories; To defendant; Premises liability. FEDPROF § 23:356.

x. Interrogatories; To defendant; Medical malpractice. FEDPROF § 23:357.

y. General forms; Standard interrogatories. GOLDLTGFMS § 26:25.

z. General forms; Civil cases. GOLDLTGFMS § 26:26.

I. Applicable Rules

1. *Federal rules*

   a. Serving and filing pleadings and other papers. FRCP 5.

   b. Privacy protection for filings made with the court. FRCP 5.2.

   c. Computing and extending time; Time for motion papers. FRCP 6.

   d. Pleadings allowed; Form of motions and other papers. FRCP 7.

   e. Form of pleadings. FRCP 10.

   f. Signing pleadings, motions, and other papers; Representations to the court; Sanctions. FRCP 11.

   g. Duty to disclose; General provisions governing discovery. FRCP 26.

   h. Stipulations about discovery procedure. FRCP 29.

   i. Interrogatories to parties. FRCP 33.

   j. Failure to make disclosures or to cooperate in discovery; Sanctions. FRCP 37.

2. *Local rules*

   a. Citation and scope of the rules. IN R USDCTND L.R. 1-1.

   b. Sanctions for formatting errors. IN R USDCTND L.R. 1-3.

   c. Electronic service. IN R USDCTND L.R. 5-2.

   d. Format of papers. IN R USDCTND L.R. 5-4.

   e. Pretrial procedure. IN R USDCTND L.R. 16-1.

   f. Alternative dispute resolution. IN R USDCTND L.R. 16-6.

   g. Form of certain discovery documents. IN R USDCTND L.R. 26-1.

   h. Filing of discovery and other materials. IN R USDCTND L.R. 26-2.

   i. Case assignment. IN R USDCTND L.R. 40-1.

   j. Appearance and withdrawal of appearance. IN R USDCTND L.R. 83-8.

   k. CM/ECF civil and criminal user manual. IN R USDCTND CM/ECF.

   l. In re: privacy and public access to civil electronic case files. IN R USDCTND Order 2005-3.

Requests, Notices and Applications
Response to Interrogatories

Document Last Updated December 2016

A. Checklist

(I) ❑ Matters to be considered by requesting party

    (a) ❑ Required documents

        (1) ❑ Interrogatories

    (b) ❑ Supplemental documents

        (1) ❑ Certificate of service

    (c) ❑ Timing

        (1) ❑ A party may not seek discovery from any source before the parties have conferred as

required by FRCP 26(f), except in a proceeding exempted from initial disclosure under FRCP 26(a)(1)(B), or when authorized by the Federal Rules of Civil Procedure, by stipulation, or by court order

(II) ❑ Matters to be considered by responding party

(a) ❑ Required documents

(1) ❑ Response to interrogatories

(b) ❑ Supplemental documents

(1) ❑ Certificate of service

(c) ❑ Timing

(1) ❑ The responding party must serve its answers and any objections within thirty (30) days after being served with the interrogatories

B. Timing

1. *Response to interrogatories.* The responding party must serve its answers and any objections within thirty (30) days after being served with the interrogatories. A shorter or longer time may be stipulated to under FRCP 29 or be ordered by the court. FRCP 33(b)(2).

2. *Automatic initial extension.* The deadline to respond to a pleading or a discovery request—including requests for admission—is automatically extended when an extension notice is filed with the court and: (1) the deadline has not been extended before; (2) the extension is for twenty-eight (28) or fewer days; and (3) the notice states: (A) the original deadline; (B) the new deadline; and (C) that all opposing attorneys the attorney could reach agreed to the extension; or that the party could not reach any other opposing attorneys despite due diligence. IN R USDCTND L.R. 6-1(b).

   a. *Pro se parties.* The automatic initial extension does not apply to pro se parties. IN R USDCTND L.R. 6-1(c).

3. *Computation of time*

   a. *Computing time.* FRCP 6 applies in computing any time period specified in the Federal Rules of Civil Procedure, in any local rule or court order, or in any statute that does not specify a method of computing time. FRCP 6(a).

      i. *Period stated in days or a longer unit.* When the period is stated in days or a longer unit of time:

         • Exclude the day of the event that triggers the period;

         • Count every day, including intermediate Saturdays, Sundays, and legal holidays; and

         • Include the last day of the period, but if the last day is a Saturday, Sunday, or legal holiday, the period continues to run until the end of the next day that is not a Saturday, Sunday, or legal holiday. FRCP 6(a)(1).

      ii. *Period stated in hours.* When the period is stated in hours:

         • Begin counting immediately on the occurrence of the event that triggers the period;

         • Count every hour, including hours during intermediate Saturdays, Sundays, and legal holidays; and

         • If the period would end on a Saturday, Sunday, or legal holiday, the period continues to run until the same time on the next day that is not a Saturday, Sunday, or legal holiday. FRCP 6(a)(2).

      iii. *Inaccessibility of the clerk's office.* Unless the court orders otherwise, if the clerk's office is inaccessible:

         • On the last day for filing under FRCP 6(a)(1), then the time for filing is extended to the first accessible day that is not a Saturday, Sunday, or legal holiday; or

         • During the last hour for filing under FRCP 6(a)(2), then the time for filing is extended to the same time on the first accessible day that is not a Saturday, Sunday, or legal holiday. FRCP 6(a)(3).

iv. *"Last day" defined.* Unless a different time is set by a statute, local rule, or court order, the last day ends:

- For electronic filing, at midnight in the court's time zone; and
- For filing by other means, when the clerk's office is scheduled to close. FRCP 6(a)(4).

v. *"Next day" defined.* The "next day" is determined by continuing to count forward when the period is measured after an event and backward when measured before an event. FRCP 6(a)(5).

vi. *"Legal holiday" defined.* "Legal holiday" means:

- The day set aside by statute for observing New Year's Day, Martin Luther King Jr.'s Birthday, Washington's Birthday, Memorial Day, Independence Day, Labor Day, Columbus Day, Veterans' Day, Thanksgiving Day, or Christmas Day;
- Any day declared a holiday by the President or Congress; and
- For periods that are measured after an event, any other day declared a holiday by the state where the district court is located. FRCP 6(a)(6).

b. *Computation of electronic filing deadlines.* Filing documents electronically does not alter any filing deadlines or any time computation pursuant to FRCP 6. The counties of Lake, Porter, LaPorte, Pulaski and Starke are located in the Central time zone and the remaining counties in the Northern District of Indiana are located in the Eastern time zone. Nevertheless, all electronic transmissions of documents must be completed (i.e., received completely by the clerk's office) prior to midnight Eastern Time, (South Bend/Fort Wayne/Lafayette time) in order to be considered timely filed that day, regardless of the local time in the division where the case is pending. Although documents can be filed electronically twenty-four (24) hours a day, filers are strongly encouraged to file all documents during hours when the CM/ECF Help Line is available, from 9:00 a.m. to 4:00 p.m. local time. IN R USDCTND CM/ECF(II)(I).

i. *Technical failures.* If the attorney is unable to file a document in a timely manner due to technical difficulties in the user's system, the attorney must file a document with the court as soon as possible notifying the court of the inability to file the document. A sample document entitled Declaration that Party was Unable to File in a Timely Manner Due to Technical Difficulties is attached hereto as Form 5. IN R USDCTND CM/ECF(VI)(B). [Editor's note: the reference to Form 5 is likely meant to be a reference to Form 3 (IN R USDCTND CM/ECF(Form 3)].

c. *Extending time*

i. *In general.* When an act may or must be done within a specified time, the court may, for good cause, extend the time:

- With or without motion or notice if the court acts, or if a request is made, before the original time or its extension expires; or
- On motion made after the time has expired if the party failed to act because of excusable neglect. FRCP 6(b)(1).

ii. *Exceptions.* A court must not extend the time to act under FRCP 50(b), FRCP 50(d), FRCP 52(b), FRCP 59(b), FRCP 59(d), FRCP 59(e), and FRCP 60(b). FRCP 6(b)(2).

iii. Refer to the United States District Court for the Northern District of Indiana KeyRules Motion for Continuance/Extension of Time document for more information on extending time.

d. *Additional time after certain kinds of service.* When a party may or must act within a specified time after being served and service is made under FRCP 5(b)(2)(C) (mail), FRCP 5(b)(2)(D) (leaving with the clerk), or FRCP 5(b)(2)(F) (other means consented to), three (3) days are added after the period would otherwise expire under FRCP 6(a). FRCP 6(d).

C. General Requirements

1. *General provisions governing discovery*

a. *Discovery scope and limits*

i. *Scope in general.* Unless otherwise limited by court order, the scope of discovery is as follows:

Parties may obtain discovery regarding any nonprivileged matter that is relevant to any party's claim or defense and proportional to the needs of the case, considering the importance of the issues at stake in the action, the amount in controversy, the parties' relative access to relevant information, the parties' resources, the importance of the discovery in resolving the issues, and whether the burden or expense of the proposed discovery outweighs its likely benefit. Information within this scope of discovery need not be admissible in evidence to be discoverable. FRCP 26(b)(1).

ii. *Limitations on frequency and extent*

- *When permitted.* By order, the court may alter the limits in the Federal Rules of Civil Procedure on the number of depositions and interrogatories or on the length of depositions under FRCP 30. By order or local rule, the court may also limit the number of requests under FRCP 36. FRCP 26(b)(2)(A).

- *Specific limitations on electronically stored information.* A party need not provide discovery of electronically stored information from sources that the party identifies as not reasonably accessible because of undue burden or cost. On motion to compel discovery or for a protective order, the party from whom discovery is sought must show that the information is not reasonably accessible because of undue burden or cost. If that showing is made, the court may nonetheless order discovery from such sources if the requesting party shows good cause, considering the limitations of FRCP 26(b)(2)(C). The court may specify conditions for the discovery. FRCP 26(b)(2)(B).

- *When required.* On motion or on its own, the court must limit the frequency or extent of discovery otherwise allowed by the Federal Rules of Civil Procedure or by local rule if it determines that: (1) the discovery sought is unreasonably cumulative or duplicative, or can be obtained from some other source that is more convenient, less burdensome, or less expensive; (2) the party seeking discovery has had ample opportunity to obtain the information by discovery in the action; or (3) the proposed discovery is outside the scope permitted by FRCP 26(b)(1). FRCP 26(b)(2)(C).

iii. *Trial preparation; Materials*

- *Documents and tangible things.* Ordinarily, a party may not discover documents and tangible things that are prepared in anticipation of litigation or for trial by or for another party or its representative (including the other party's attorney, consultant, surety, indemnitor, insurer, or agent). But, subject to FRCP 26(b)(4), those materials may be discovered if: (1) they are otherwise discoverable under FRCP 26(b)(1); and (2) the party shows that it has substantial need for the materials to prepare its case and cannot, without undue hardship, obtain their substantial equivalent by other means. FRCP 26(b)(3)(A).

- *Protection against disclosure.* If the court orders discovery of those materials, it must protect against disclosure of the mental impressions, conclusions, opinions, or legal theories of a party's attorney or other representative concerning the litigation. FRCP 26(b)(3)(B).

- *Previous statement.* Any party or other person may, on request and without the required showing, obtain the person's own previous statement about the action or its subject matter. If the request is refused, the person may move for a court order, and FRCP 37(a)(5) applies to the award of expenses. A previous statement is either: (1) a written statement that the person has signed or otherwise adopted or approved; or (2) a contemporaneous stenographic, mechanical, electrical, or other recording—or a transcription of it—that recites substantially verbatim the person's oral statement. FRCP 26(b)(3)(C).

iv. *Trial preparation; Experts*

- *Deposition of an expert who may testify.* A party may depose any person who has been identified as an expert whose opinions may be presented at trial. If FRCP 26(a)(2)(B) requires a report from the expert, the deposition may be conducted only after the report is provided. FRCP 26(b)(4)(A).

- *Trial-preparation protection for draft reports or disclosures.* FRCP 26(b)(3)(A) and FRCP 26(b)(3)(B) protect drafts of any report or disclosure required under FRCP 26(a)(2), regardless of the form in which the draft is recorded. FRCP 26(b)(4)(B).

- *Trial-preparation protection for communications between a party's attorney and expert witnesses.* FRCP 26(b)(3)(A) and FRCP 26(b)(3)(B) protect communications between the party's attorney and any witness required to provide a report under FRCP 26(a)(2)(B), regardless of the form of the communications, except to the extent that the communications: (1) relate to compensation for the expert's study or testimony; (2) identify facts or data that the party's attorney provided and that the expert considered in forming the opinions to be expressed; or (3) identify assumptions that the party's attorney provided and that the expert relied on in forming the opinions to be expressed. FRCP 26(b)(4)(C).

- *Expert employed only for trial preparation.* Ordinarily, a party may not, by interrogatories or deposition, discover facts known or opinions held by an expert who has been retained or specially employed by another party in anticipation of litigation or to prepare for trial and who is not expected to be called as a witness at trial. But a party may do so only: (1) as provided in FRCP 35(b); or (2) on showing exceptional circumstances under which it is impracticable for the party to obtain facts or opinions on the same subject by other means. FRCP 26(b)(4)(D).

- *Payment.* Unless manifest injustice would result, the court must require that the party seeking discovery: (1) pay the expert a reasonable fee for time spent in responding to discovery under FRCP 26(b)(4)(A) or FRCP 26(b)(4)(D); and (2) for discovery under FRCP 26(b)(4)(D), also pay the other party a fair portion of the fees and expenses it reasonably incurred in obtaining the expert's facts and opinions. FRCP 26(b)(4)(E).

v. *Claiming privilege or protecting trial-preparation materials*

- *Information withheld.* When a party withholds information otherwise discoverable by claiming that the information is privileged or subject to protection as trial-preparation material, the party must: (1) expressly make the claim; and (2) describe the nature of the documents, communications, or tangible things not produced or disclosed—and do so in a manner that, without revealing information itself privileged or protected, will enable other parties to assess the claim. FRCP 26(b)(5)(A).

- *Information produced.* If information produced in discovery is subject to a claim of privilege or of protection as trial-preparation material, the party making the claim may notify any party that received the information of the claim and the basis for it. After being notified, a party must promptly return, sequester, or destroy the specified information and any copies it has; must not use or disclose the information until the claim is resolved; must take reasonable steps to retrieve the information if the party disclosed it before being notified; and may promptly present the information to the court under seal for a determination of the claim. The producing party must preserve the information until the claim is resolved. FRCP 26(b)(5)(B).

b. *Protective orders.* A party or any person from whom discovery is sought may move for a protective order in the court where the action is pending—or as an alternative on matters relating to a deposition, in the court for the district where the deposition will be taken. FRCP 26(c)(1). Refer to the United States District Court for the Northern District of Indiana KeyRules Motion for Protective Order document for more information.

c. *Sequence of discovery.* Unless the parties stipulate or the court orders otherwise for the parties' and witnesses' convenience and in the interests of justice: (1) methods of discovery may be used in any sequence; and (2) discovery by one party does not require any other party to delay its discovery. FRCP 26(d)(3).

2. *Response to interrogatories*

a. *Form.* A party responding (by answer or objection) to written discovery must: (1) fully quote each interrogatory or request immediately before the party's response; and (2) number each response to correspond with the interrogatory or request being responded to. IN R USDCTND L.R. 26-1(b).

b. *Answers and objections*

    i. *Responding party.* The interrogatories must be answered: (1) by the party to whom they are directed; or (2) if that party is a public or private corporation, a partnership, an association, or a governmental agency, by any officer or agent, who must furnish the information available to the party. FRCP 33(b)(1). It is improper for the party's attorney to answer them, though undoubtedly the common practice is for the attorney to prepare the answers and have the party swear to them. FPP § 2172.

    ii. *Answering each interrogatory.* Each interrogatory must, to the extent it is not objected to, be answered separately and fully in writing under oath. FRCP 33(b)(3). It has been said that interrogatories should be answered directly and without evasion in accordance with information that the answering party possesses after due inquiry. FPP § 2177.

    iii. *Objections.* The grounds for objecting to an interrogatory must be stated with specificity. Any ground not stated in a timely objection is waived unless the court, for good cause, excuses the failure. FRCP 33(b)(4).

        • *Grounds for objections.* Interrogatories may be objected to on the ground that they are not within the scope of discovery as defined in FRCP 26(b), either because they seek information not relevant to the subject matter of the action, or information that is privileged, or information that is protected by the work-product rule and for which the requisite showing has not been made, or information of experts that is not discoverable. FPP § 2174. But this does not exhaust the grounds on which objection can be made. FPP § 2174.

    iv. *Qualifying answers.* If the party to whom the interrogatory is addressed thinks that there is uncertainty in the meaning of the interrogatory, it may qualify its answer if need be. FPP § 2168.

    v. *Signature.* The person who makes the answers must sign them, and the attorney who objects must sign any objections. FRCP 33(b)(5). Refer to the Format section of this document for more information on signing discovery papers.

c. *Use.* An answer to an interrogatory may be used to the extent allowed by the Federal Rules of Evidence. FRCP 33(c).

d. *Option to produce business records.* If the answer to an interrogatory may be determined by examining, auditing, compiling, abstracting, or summarizing a party's business records (including electronically stored information), and if the burden of deriving or ascertaining the answer will be substantially the same for either party, the responding party may answer by:

    i. Specifying the records that must be reviewed, in sufficient detail to enable the interrogating party to locate and identify them as readily as the responding party could; and

    ii. Giving the interrogating party a reasonable opportunity to examine and audit the records and to make copies, compilations, abstracts, or summaries. FRCP 33(d).

3. *Supplementing disclosures and responses.* A party who has made a disclosure under FRCP 26(a)—or who has responded to an interrogatory, request for production, or request for admission—must supplement or correct its disclosure or response: (1) in a timely manner if the party learns that in some material respect the disclosure or response is incomplete or incorrect, and if the additional or corrective information has not otherwise been made known to the other parties during the discovery process or in writing; or (2) as ordered by the court. FRCP 26(e)(1).

4. *Sanctions for failure to cooperate in discovery.* The court where the action is pending may, on motion, order sanctions if a party, after being properly served with interrogatories under FRCP 33 or a request for inspection under FRCP 34, fails to serve its answers, objections, or written response. FRCP 37(d)(1)(A)(ii). If a motion to compel is granted, the court must, after giving an opportunity to be heard, require the party or deponent whose conduct necessitated the motion, the party or attorney advising that conduct, or both to pay the movant's reasonable expenses incurred in making the motion, including attorney's fees. But the court must not order this payment if the opposing party's nondisclosure, response, or objection was substantially justified. FRCP 37(a)(5)(A)(ii). Refer to the United States District Court for the Northern District of Indiana KeyRules Motion for Discovery Sanctions document for more information.

5. *Stipulations about discovery procedure.* Unless the court orders otherwise, the parties may stipulate that: (1) a deposition may be taken before any person, at any time or place, on any notice, and in the manner specified—in which event it may be used in the same way as any other deposition; and (2) other procedures governing or limiting discovery be modified—but a stipulation extending the time for any form of discovery must have court approval if it would interfere with the time set for completing discovery, for hearing a motion, or for trial. FRCP 29.

6. *Appearances.* Attorneys not representing the United States or its agencies must file an appearance when they represent (either in person or by filing a paper) a party. IN R USDCTND L.R. 83-8(a). For more information, refer to IN R USDCTND L.R. 83-8.

7. *Notice of related action.* A party must file a notice of related action as soon as it appears that the party's case and another pending case: (1) arise out of the same transaction or occurrence; (2) involve the same property; or (3) involve the validity or infringement of the same patent, trademark, or copyright. IN R USDCTND L.R. 40-1(d). For more information, refer to IN R USDCTND L.R. 40-1.

8. *Alternative dispute resolution (ADR).* After they confer as required by FRCP 26(f), the parties must advise the court which, if any, alternative-dispute-resolution processes they expect to pursue and when they expect to undertake the process. IN R USDCTND L.R. 16-6(a). For more information on alternative dispute resolution (ADR), refer to IN R USDCTND L.R. 16-6 and IN R USDCTND Order 2003-21.

9. *Settlement or resolution.* The parties must immediately notify the court if they reasonably expect to settle the case or resolve a pending motion. IN R USDCTND L.R. 16-1(g).

10. *Modification or suspension of rules.* The court may, on its own motion or at the request of a party, suspend or modify any rule in a particular case in the interest of justice. IN R USDCTND L.R. 1-1(c).

D. Documents

1. *Required documents*

   a. *Response to interrogatories.* Refer to the General Requirements section of this document for information on the response to interrogatories.

2. *Supplemental documents*

   a. *Certificate of service.* FRCP 5(d) requires that the person making service under FRCP 5 certify that service has been effected. FRCP 5(Advisory Committee Notes). Having such information on file may be useful for many purposes, including proof of service if an issue arises concerning the effectiveness of the service. FRCP 5(Advisory Committee Notes).

E. Format

1. *Form of documents.* The rules governing captions and other matters of form in pleadings apply to motions and other papers. FRCP 7(b)(2).

   a. *Paper.* Any pleading, motion, brief, affidavit, notice, or proposed order, whether filed electronically or by delivering it to the clerk, must: use eight and one-half by eleven (8-1/2 x 11) inch pages. IN R USDCTND L.R. 5-4(a)(2).

      i. *Manual filings.* Papers delivered to the clerk for filing must: be flat, unfolded, and on good-quality, white paper. IN R USDCTND L.R. 5-4(b)(1)(A).

         • *Covers or backing.* Papers delivered to the clerk for filing must: not have a cover or a back. IN R USDCTND L.R. 5-4(b)(1)(B).

         • *Recycled paper.* The court encourages using recycled paper. IN R USDCTND L.R. 5-4(b)(7).

   b. *Margins.* Any pleading, motion, brief, affidavit, notice, or proposed order, whether filed electronically or by delivering it to the clerk, must: have at least one (1) inch margins. IN R USDCTND L.R. 5-4(a)(3).

   c. *Spacing.* Any pleading, motion, brief, affidavit, notice, or proposed order, whether filed electronically or by delivering it to the clerk, must: be double spaced (except for headings, footnotes, and quoted material). IN R USDCTND L.R. 5-4(a)(5).

   d. *Text.* Any pleading, motion, brief, affidavit, notice, or proposed order, whether filed electronically or by delivering it to the clerk, must: be plainly typewritten, printed, or prepared by a clearly legible copying process. IN R USDCTND L.R. 5-4(a)(1).

  i. Any pleading, motion, brief, affidavit, notice, or proposed order, whether filed electronically or by delivering it to the clerk, must: use at least twelve (12) point type in the body and at least ten (10) point type in footnotes. IN R USDCTND L.R. 5-4(a)(4).

e. *Page numbering.* Any pleading, motion, brief, affidavit, notice, or proposed order, whether filed electronically or by delivering it to the clerk, must: have consecutively numbered pages. IN R USDCTND L.R. 5-4(a)(6).

f. *Caption; Names of parties.* Every pleading must have a caption with the court's name, a title, a file number, and a FRCP 7(a) designation. The title of the complaint must name all the parties; the title of other pleadings, after naming the first party on each side, may refer generally to other parties. FRCP 10(a). Any pleading, motion, brief, affidavit, notice, or proposed order, whether filed electronically or by delivering it to the clerk, must: include a title on the first page. IN R USDCTND L.R. 5-4(a)(7).

g. *Filer's information.* Any pleading, motion, brief, affidavit, notice, or proposed order, whether filed electronically or by delivering it to the clerk, must: except in proposed orders and affidavits, include the filer's name, address, telephone number, fax number (where available), and e-mail address (where available). IN R USDCTND L.R. 5-4(a)(9).

h. *Paragraphs; Separate statements.* A party must state its claims or defenses in numbered paragraphs, each limited as far as practicable to a single set of circumstances. A later pleading may refer by number to a paragraph in an earlier pleading. If doing so would promote clarity, each claim founded on a separate transaction or occurrence—and each defense other than a denial—must be stated in a separate count or defense. FRCP 10(b).

i. *Adoption by reference; Exhibits.* A statement in a pleading may be adopted by reference elsewhere in the same pleading or in any other pleading or motion. A copy of a written instrument that is an exhibit to a pleading is a part of the pleading for all purposes. FRCP 10(c).

j. *Citation of local rules.* The Local Civil Rules of the United States District Court for the Northern District of Indiana may be cited as "N.D. Ind. L.R." IN R USDCTND L.R. 1-1(a)(1).

k. *Acceptance by the clerk.* The clerk must not refuse to file a paper solely because it is not in the form prescribed by the Federal Rules of Civil Procedure or by a local rule or practice. FRCP 5(d)(4).

  i. *Sanctions for formatting errors; Non-compliance.* If a person files a paper that does not comply with the rules governing the format of papers filed with the court, the court may: (1) strike the paper from the record; or (2) fine the person up to one thousand dollars ($1,000). IN R USDCTND L.R. 1-3(a).

  • *Notice.* Before sanctioning a person under IN R USDCTND L.R. 1-3(a)(2), the court must: (1) notify the person that the paper is noncompliant; and (2) give the person the opportunity either to be heard or to revise the paper. IN R USDCTND L.R. 1-3(b).

2. *Form of electronic documents.* Electronically filed documents must meet the same requirements of format and page limits as documents "conventionally filed" (as defined in IN R USDCTND CM/ECF(III)(A)) pursuant to the Federal Rules of Civil Procedure and the Local Civil Rules of the United States District Court for the Northern District of Indiana. IN R USDCTND CM/ECF(II)(A)(2).

a. *PDF format required.* Documents filed in the CM/ECF must be in .pdf format. A document created with almost any word-processing program can be converted to .pdf format. The .pdf program in effect takes a picture of the original document and allows anyone to open the converted document across a broad range of hardware and software, with layout, format, links, and images intact. IN R USDCTND CM/ECF(FN2).

b. *Title of documents.* The person electronically filing a pleading or other document will be responsible for designating a title for the pleading or other document by using one of the categories contained in the events listed in the CM/ECF Menu. IN R USDCTND CM/ECF(II)(G).

c. *Combining documents.* All documents which form part of a single pleading and which are being filed

at the same time and by the same party may be electronically filed together under one document number, e.g., the motion and a supporting affidavit, with the exception of memoranda in support. Memoranda in support shall be electronically filed separately and shown as a related document to the motion. IN R USDCTND CM/ECF(II)(A)(4).

d. *Exhibits and attachments.* Filing users must submit in electronic form all documents referenced as exhibits or attachments, unless the court permits conventional filing. A filing user must submit as exhibits or attachments only those excerpts of the referenced documents that are directly germane to the matter under consideration by the court. Excerpted material must be clearly and prominently identified as such. Filing users who file excerpts of documents as exhibits or attachments do so without prejudice to their right to timely file additional excerpts or the complete document. Responding parties may timely file additional excerpts or the complete document that they believe are directly germane. The court may require parties to file additional excerpts or the complete document. IN R USDCTND CM/ECF(II)(A)(6).

e. *Hyperlinks.* Electronically filed documents may contain hyperlink references to an external document as a convenient mechanism for accessing material cited in the document. A hyperlink reference is neither validated for content nor considered a part of the court's records. The court neither endorses the product or organization at the destination of a hyperlink reference, nor does the court exercise any responsibility over the content at the destination. In order to preserve the integrity of the court record, attorneys wishing to insert hyperlinks in court filings shall continue to use the traditional citation method for the cited authority, in addition to the hyperlink. A hyperlink contained in a filing is no more than a convenient mechanism for accessing material cited in the document and a hyperlink reference is extraneous to any filed document and is not part of the court's record. IN R USDCTND CM/ECF(II)(A)(3).

3. *Signing disclosures and discovery requests, responses, and objections.* FRCP 11 does not apply to disclosures and discovery requests, responses, objections, and motions under FRCP 26 through FRCP 37. FRCP 11(d).

a. *Signature required.* Every disclosure under FRCP 26(a)(1) or FRCP 26(a)(3) and every discovery request, response, or objection must be signed by at least one attorney of record in the attorney's own name—or by the party personally, if unrepresented—and must state the signer's address, e-mail address, and telephone number. FRCP 26(g)(1).

 i. *Signatures on manual filings.* Papers delivered to the clerk for filing must: include the filer's original signature. IN R USDCTND L.R. 5-4(b)(1)(C).

 • *Rubber-stamped and faxed signatures.* An original paper with a rubber-stamped or faxed signature is unsigned for purposes of FRCP 11 and FRCP 26(g). IN R USDCTND L.R. 5-4(b)(2).

 • *Affidavits.* Only the affiant need sign an affidavit. IN R USDCTND L.R. 5-4(b)(3).

 ii. *Electronic signatures.* Pursuant to FRCP 11, every pleading, motion, and other paper (except lists, schedules, statements or amendments thereto) shall be signed by at least one attorney of record or, if the party is not represented by an attorney, all papers shall be signed by the party. An attorney's/participant's password issued by the court combined with the user's identification, serves as and constitutes the attorney/participant's signature for FRCP 11 and other purposes. IN R USDCTND CM/ECF(I)(C). Documents which must be filed and which must contain original signatures other than those of a participating attorney or which require either verification or an unsworn declaration under any rule or statute, shall be filed electronically, with originally executed copies maintained by the filer. The pleading or other document electronically filed shall contain "s/" signature(s), as noted in IN R USDCTND CM/ECF(II)(E)(3)(b). IN R USDCTND CM/ECF(II)(E)(1).

 • *Multiple signatures.* In the case of a stipulation or other document to be signed by two or more attorneys, the following procedure should be used: The filing attorney shall initially confirm that the content of the document is acceptable to all persons required to sign the document and shall obtain the physical signatures of all attorneys on the document. IN R USDCTND CM/ECF(II)(E)(3)(a). The filing attorney then shall file the document electronically, indicating the signatories, e.g., "s/Jane Doe," "s/John Doe," etc. IN R US-DCTND CM/ECF(II)(E)(3)(b). The filing attorney shall retain the hard copy of the document containing the original signatures. IN R USDCTND CM/ECF(II)(E)(3)(c).

b. *Effect of signature.* By signing, an attorney or party certifies that to the best of the person's knowledge, information, and belief formed after a reasonable inquiry:

  i. With respect to a disclosure, it is complete and correct as of the time it is made; and

  ii. With respect to a discovery request, response, or objection, it is:

  - Consistent with the Federal Rules of Civil Procedure and warranted by existing law or by a nonfrivolous argument for extending, modifying, or reversing existing law, or for establishing new law;

  - Not interposed for any improper purpose, such as to harass, cause unnecessary delay, or needlessly increase the cost of litigation; and

  - Neither unreasonable nor unduly burdensome or expensive, considering the needs of the case, prior discovery in the case, the amount in controversy, and the importance of the issues at stake in the action. FRCP 26(g)(1).

c. *Failure to sign.* Other parties have no duty to act on an unsigned disclosure, request, response, or objection until it is signed, and the court must strike it unless a signature is promptly supplied after the omission is called to the attorney's or party's attention. FRCP 26(g)(2).

d. *Sanction for improper certification.* If a certification violates FRCP 26(g) without substantial justification, the court, on motion or on its own, must impose an appropriate sanction on the signer, the party on whose behalf the signer was acting, or both. The sanction may include an order to pay the reasonable expenses, including attorney's fees, caused by the violation. FRCP 26(g)(3). Refer to the United States District Court for the Northern District of Indiana KeyRules Motion for Discovery Sanctions document for more information.

4. *Privacy protection for filings made with the court*

a. *Redacted filings.* Counsel should not include sensitive information in any document filed with the court unless such inclusion is necessary and relevant to the case. IN R USDCTND CM/ECF(VII). Unless the court orders otherwise, in an electronic or paper filing with the court that contains an individual's Social Security number, taxpayer-identification number, or birth date, the name of an individual known to be a minor, or a financial-account number, a party or nonparty making the filing may include only:

  i. The last four (4) digits of the Social Security number and taxpayer-identification number;

  ii. The year of the individual's birth;

  iii. The minor's initials; and

  iv. The last four (4) digits of the financial-account number. FRCP 5.2(a); IN R USDCTND Order 2005-3.

b. *Exemptions from the redaction requirement.* The redaction requirement does not apply to the following:

  i. A financial-account number that identifies the property allegedly subject to forfeiture in a forfeiture proceeding;

  ii. The record of an administrative or agency proceeding;

  iii. The official record of a state-court proceeding;

  iv. The record of a court or tribunal, if that record was not subject to the redaction requirement when originally filed;

  v. A filing covered by FRCP 5.2(c) or FRCP 5.2(d); and

  vi. A pro se filing in an action brought under 28 U.S.C.A. § 2241, 28 U.S.C.A. § 2254, or 28 U.S.C.A. § 2255. FRCP 5.2(b).

    vii.   In cases filed under the Social Security Act, 42 U.S.C.A. § 405(g), there is no need for redaction of any information from the documents filed in the case. IN R USDCTND Order 2005-3.

  c. *Limitations on remote access to electronic files; Social Security appeals and immigration cases.* Unless the court orders otherwise, in an action for benefits under the Social Security Act, and in an action or proceeding relating to an order of removal, to relief from removal, or to immigration benefits or detention, access to an electronic file is authorized as follows:

    i.   The parties and their attorneys may have remote electronic access to any part of the case file, including the administrative record;

    ii. Any other person may have electronic access to the full record at the courthouse, but may have remote electronic access only to:

- The docket maintained by the court; and
- An opinion, order, judgment, or other disposition of the court, but not any other part of the case file or the administrative record. FRCP 5.2(c).

  d. *Filings made under seal.* The court may order that a filing be made under seal without redaction. The court may later unseal the filing or order the person who made the filing to file a redacted version for the public record. FRCP 5.2(d). For information on filing documents under seal, refer to IN R USDCTND L.R. 5-3, IN R USDCTND CM/ECF(IV)(A), and IN R USDCTND ECF Order 2004-19.

  e. *Protective orders.* For good cause, the court may by order in a case:

    i.   Require redaction of additional information; or

    ii. Limit or prohibit a nonparty's remote electronic access to a document filed with the court. FRCP 5.2(e).

  f. *Option for additional unredacted filing under seal.* A person making a redacted filing may also file an unredacted copy under seal. The court must retain the unredacted copy as part of the record. FRCP 5.2(f); IN R USDCTND Order 2005-3.

    i.   The unredacted version of the document or the reference list shall be retained by the court under seal as part of the record. This paper shall be retained by the court as part of the record. The court may, however, still require the party to file a redacted copy for the public file. IN R USDCTND Order 2005-3.

  g. *Option for filing a reference list.* A filing that contains redacted information may be filed together with a reference list that identifies each item of redacted information and specifies an appropriate identifier that uniquely corresponds to each item listed. The list must be filed under seal and may be amended as of right. Any reference in the case to a listed identifier will be construed to refer to the corresponding item of information. FRCP 5.2(g); IN R USDCTND Order 2005-3.

    i.   The unredacted version of the document or the reference list shall be retained by the court under seal as part of the record. This paper shall be retained by the court as part of the record. The court may, however, still require the party to file a redacted copy for the public file. IN R USDCTND Order 2005-3.

  h. *Responsibility for redaction.* The responsibility for redacting these personal identifiers rests solely with counsel and the parties. The Clerk will not review each paper for compliance with IN R USDCTND Order 2005-3. IN R USDCTND Order 2005-3.

  i. *Waiver of protection of identifiers.* A person waives the protection of FRCP 5.2(a) as to the person's own information by filing it without redaction and not under seal. FRCP 5.2(h).

F. Filing and Service Requirements

  1. *Filing requirements.* Any paper after the complaint that is required to be served—together with a certificate of service—must be filed within a reasonable time after service. But disclosures under FRCP 26(a)(1) or FRCP 26(a)(2) and the following discovery requests and responses must not be filed until they are used in the proceeding or the court orders filing: depositions, interrogatories, requests for documents or tangible things or to permit entry onto land, and requests for admission. FRCP 5(d)(1). Refer to the

United States District Court for the Northern District of Indiana KeyRules pleading and motion documents for information on filing with the court.

a. *Discovery ordinarily not filed.* The party who serves a discovery request or notices a deposition is the custodian of the original discovery response or deposition transcript. Except as required under IN R USDCTND L.R. 26-2(a)(2), parties must not file: (1) disclosures under FRCP 26(a)(1) or FRCP 26(a)(2); (2) deposition notices; (3) deposition transcripts; (4) interrogatories; (5) requests for documents, to permit entry upon land, or for admission; (6) answers to interrogatories; (7) responses to requests for documents, to permit entry upon land, or for admission; or (8) service-of-discovery notices. IN R USDCTND L.R. 26-2(a)(1).

  i. *Exceptions*

- *Pro se litigation.* All discovery material in cases involving a pro se party must be filed. IN R USDCTND L.R. 26-2(a)(2)(A).

- *Specific material.* Discovery material must also be filed when: (1) the court orders; or (2) the material is used in a proceeding. IN R USDCTND L.R. 26-2(a)(2)(B).

b. *When discovery may be filed*

  i. *Filing materials with motion for relief.* A party who files a motion for relief under FRCP 26(c) or FRCP 37 must file with the motion those parts of the discovery requests or responses that the motion pertains to. IN R USDCTND L.R. 26-2(b).

  ii. *Materials necessary for motion.* A party must file those portions of discovery requests or responses (including deposition transcripts) that the party relies on to support a motion that could result in a final order on an issue. IN R USDCTND L.R. 26-2(c).

  iii. *Materials to be used at trial.* A party who reasonably anticipates using discovery requests or responses—including deposition transcripts—at trial must file the relevant portions of the requests or responses with the clerk at the start of the trial. IN R USDCTND L.R. 26-2(d).

2. *Service requirements*

a. *Service; When required*

  i. *In general.* Unless the Federal Rules of Civil Procedure provide otherwise, each of the following papers must be served on every party:

- An order stating that service is required;

- A pleading filed after the original complaint, unless the court orders otherwise under FRCP 5(c) because there are numerous defendants;

- A discovery paper required to be served on a party, unless the court orders otherwise;

- A written motion, except one that may be heard ex parte; and

- A written notice, appearance, demand, or offer of judgment, or any similar paper. FRCP 5(a)(1).

  ii. *If a party fails to appear.* No service is required on a party who is in default for failing to appear. But a pleading that asserts a new claim for relief against such a party must be served on that party under FRCP 4. FRCP 5(a)(2).

  iii. *Seizing property.* If an action is begun by seizing property and no person is or need be named as a defendant, any service required before the filing of an appearance, answer, or claim must be made on the person who had custody or possession of the property when it was seized. FRCP 5(a)(3).

b. *Service; How made*

  i. *Serving an attorney.* If a party is represented by an attorney, service under FRCP 5 must be made on the attorney unless the court orders service on the party. FRCP 5(b)(1).

  ii. *Service in general.* A paper is served under FRCP 5 by:

- Handing it to the person;

410

- Leaving it: (1) at the person's office with a clerk or other person in charge or, if no one is in charge, in a conspicuous place in the office; or (2) if the person has no office or the office is closed, at the person's dwelling or usual place of abode with someone of suitable age and discretion who resides there;

- Mailing it to the person's last known address—in which event service is complete upon mailing;

- Leaving it with the court clerk if the person has no known address;

- Sending it by electronic means if the person consented in writing—in which event service is complete upon transmission, but is not effective if the serving party learns that it did not reach the person to be served; or

- Delivering it by any other means that the person consented to in writing—in which event service is complete when the person making service delivers it to the agency designated to make delivery. FRCP 5(b)(2).

iii. *Electronic service.* Electronically filed papers may be served electronically if service is consistent with the CM/ECF User Manual (IN R USDCTND CM/ECF). IN R USDCTND L.R. 5-2(a).

- *Waiver of other service.* An attorney's registration will constitute a waiver of conventional service of documents and the attorney agrees to accept service of notice on behalf of the client of the electronic filing by hand, facsimile or authorized email. IN R USDCTND CM/ECF(I)(B)(3).

- *Serving registered persons.* The System will generate a "Notice of Electronic Filing" when any document is filed. This notice represents service of the document on parties who are registered participants with the System. Except as provided in IN R USDCTND CM/ECF(III)(B), the filing party shall not be required to serve any pleading or other documents on any party receiving electronic notice. IN R USDCTND CM/ECF(II)(D)(1). The term "pleading" refers only to those documents listed in FRCP 7(a). IN R USDCTND CM/ECF(FN3).

- *When electronic service is deemed completed.* A person registered to use the court's electronic-filing system is served with an electronically filed paper when a "Notice of Electronic Filing" is transmitted to that person through the court's electronic filing-system. IN R USDCTND L.R. 5-2(b).

- *Serving non-registered persons.* A person who has not registered to use the court's electronic-filing system but who is entitled to service of a paper must be served according to the Local Civil Rules of the United States District Court for the Northern District of Indiana and the Federal Rules of Civil Procedure. IN R USDCTND L.R. 5-2(c); IN R USDCTND CM/ECF(II)(D)(2). If such service of a paper copy is to be made, it shall be done in the manner provided in the Federal Rules of Civil Procedure and the Local Civil Rules of the United States District Court for the Northern District of Indiana. IN R USDCTND CM/ECF(II)(D)(2).

iv. *Service of conventional filings.* Pleadings or other documents which are filed conventionally rather than electronically shall be served in the manner provided for in the Federal Rules of Civil Procedure and the Local Civil Rules of the United States District Court for the Northern District of Indiana, except as otherwise provided by order of the Court. IN R USDCTND CM/ECF(III)(B).

v. *Using court facilities.* If a local rule so authorizes, a party may use the court's transmission facilities to make service under FRCP 5(b)(2)(E). FRCP 5(b)(3).

c. *Serving numerous defendants*

i. *In general.* If an action involves an unusually large number of defendants, the court may, on motion or on its own, order that:

- Defendants' pleadings and replies to them need not be served on other defendants;

411

- Any crossclaim, counterclaim, avoidance, or affirmative defense in those pleadings and replies to them will be treated as denied or avoided by all other parties; and
- Filing any such pleading and serving it on the plaintiff constitutes notice of the pleading to all parties. FRCP 5(c)(1).

    ii. *Notifying parties.* A copy of every such order must be served on the parties as the court directs. FRCP 5(c)(2).

G. Hearings

1. There is no hearing contemplated in the federal statutes or rules for responses to interrogatories.

H. Forms

1. Federal Response to Interrogatories Forms

a. Introductory statement; Answer to interrogatories. AMJUR PP DEPOSITION § 407.

b. Answers to interrogatories; Illustrative form. AMJUR PP DEPOSITION § 408.

c. Response to interrogatories; Illustrative form. AMJUR PP DEPOSITION § 409.

d. Verification; By defendant; Of answers to interrogatories. AMJUR PP DEPOSITION § 410.

e. Answers to interrogatories. 3A FEDFORMS § 3503.

f. Answers to interrogatories; Complete set. 3A FEDFORMS § 3504.

g. Amendments to answers to interrogatories. 3A FEDFORMS § 3505.

h. Supplemental answer to plaintiff's interrogatories. 3A FEDFORMS § 3506.

i. Second supplemental answer to plaintiff's interrogatories. 3A FEDFORMS § 3507.

j. Supplementation of response to interrogatory. 3A FEDFORMS § 3508.

k. Answers by individual. 3A FEDFORMS § 3510.

l. Answers by corporation. 3A FEDFORMS § 3511.

m. Declaration; Answers by individual. 3A FEDFORMS § 3512.

n. Declaration; Answers by corporation. 3A FEDFORMS § 3513.

o. Objections to interrogatories. 3A FEDFORMS § 3514.

p. Objections to interrogatories; Another form. 3A FEDFORMS § 3515.

q. Objections to interrogatories; Another form. 3A FEDFORMS § 3516.

r. Objections to interrogatories; With answers. 3A FEDFORMS § 3517.

s. Statement in answer as to interrogatory to which objection made. 3A FEDFORMS § 3518.

t. Answers; To interrogatories; Outline form. FEDPROF § 23:344.

u. Answers; To interrogatories; By two defendants; Outline form. FEDPROF § 23:345.

v. Objections to interrogatories; Illustrative grounds. FEDPROF § 23:367.

w. Answer to interrogatories. GOLDLTGFMS § 26:72.

x. Answer to interrogatories; Pursuant to civil procedure rules. GOLDLTGFMS § 26:73.

y. Answer to interrogatories; Corporate information as basis for answers. GOLDLTGFMS § 26:74.

z. Answer to interrogatories; Expert not yet selected. GOLDLTGFMS § 26:75.

I. Applicable Rules

1. *Federal rules*

a. Serving and filing pleadings and other papers. FRCP 5.

b. Privacy protection for filings made with the court. FRCP 5.2.

c. Computing and extending time; Time for motion papers. FRCP 6.

d. Pleadings allowed; Form of motions and other papers. FRCP 7.

    e.   Form of pleadings. FRCP 10.

    f.   Signing pleadings, motions, and other papers; Representations to the court; Sanctions. FRCP 11.

    g.   Duty to disclose; General provisions governing discovery. FRCP 26.

    h.   Stipulations about discovery procedure. FRCP 29.

    i.   Interrogatories to parties. FRCP 33.

    j.   Failure to make disclosures or to cooperate in discovery; Sanctions. FRCP 37.

2. *Local rules*

    a.   Citation and scope of the rules. IN R USDCTND L.R. 1-1.

    b.   Sanctions for formatting errors. IN R USDCTND L.R. 1-3.

    c.   Electronic service. IN R USDCTND L.R. 5-2.

    d.   Format of papers. IN R USDCTND L.R. 5-4.

    e.   Extensions of time. IN R USDCTND L.R. 6-1.

    f.   Pretrial procedure. IN R USDCTND L.R. 16-1.

    g.   Alternative dispute resolution. IN R USDCTND L.R. 16-6.

    h.   Form of certain discovery documents. IN R USDCTND L.R. 26-1.

    i.   Filing of discovery and other materials. IN R USDCTND L.R. 26-2.

    j.   Case assignment. IN R USDCTND L.R. 40-1.

    k.   Appearance and withdrawal of appearance. IN R USDCTND L.R. 83-8.

    l.   CM/ECF civil and criminal user manual. IN R USDCTND CM/ECF.

    m.   In re: privacy and public access to civil electronic case files. IN R USDCTND Order 2005-3.

Requests, Notices and Applications
Request for Production of Documents

Document Last Updated December 2016

A. Checklist

(I)   ❑ Matters to be considered by requesting party

    (a) ❑ Required documents

        (1) ❑ Request for production of documents

    (b) ❑ Supplemental documents

        (1) ❑ Subpoena

        (2) ❑ Certificate of service

    (c) ❑ Timing

        (1) ❑ More than twenty-one (21) days after the summons and complaint are served on a party, a request under FRCP 34 may be delivered: (1) to that party by any other party, and (2) by that party to any plaintiff or to any other party that has been served

        (2) ❑ A party may not seek discovery from any source before the parties have conferred as required by FRCP 26(f), except in a proceeding exempted from initial disclosure under FRCP 26(a)(1)(B), or when authorized by the Federal Rules of Civil Procedure, by stipulation, or by court order

(II) ❑ Matters to be considered by responding party

    (a) ❑ Required documents

        (1) ❑ Response to request for production of documents

(b) ❑ Supplemental documents

    (1) ❑ Certificate of service

(c) ❑ Timing

    (1) ❑ The party to whom the request is directed must respond in writing within thirty (30) days after being served or—if the request was delivered under FRCP 26(d)(2)—within thirty (30) days after the parties' first FRCP 26(f) conference

B. Timing

1. *Request for production of documents.* Without leave of court or written stipulation, a request may not be served before the time specified in FRCP 26(d). FEDPROC § 26:632. Of course, discovery under FRCP 34 should ordinarily precede the trial. FEDPROC § 26:632.

   a. *Early FRCP 34 requests*

      i. *Time to deliver.* More than twenty-one (21) days after the summons and complaint are served on a party, a request under FRCP 34 may be delivered:

         • To that party by any other party, and

         • By that party to any plaintiff or to any other party that has been served. FRCP 26(d)(2)(A).

      ii. *When considered served.* The request is considered to have been served at the first FRCP 26(f) conference. FRCP 26(d)(2)(B).

2. *Timing of discovery, generally.* A party may not seek discovery from any source before the parties have conferred as required by FRCP 26(f), except in a proceeding exempted from initial disclosure under FRCP 26(a)(1)(B), or when authorized by the Federal Rules of Civil Procedure, by stipulation, or by court order. FRCP 26(d)(1).

3. *Computation of time*

   a. *Computing time.* FRCP 6 applies in computing any time period specified in the Federal Rules of Civil Procedure, in any local rule or court order, or in any statute that does not specify a method of computing time. FRCP 6(a).

      i. *Period stated in days or a longer unit.* When the period is stated in days or a longer unit of time:

         • Exclude the day of the event that triggers the period;

         • Count every day, including intermediate Saturdays, Sundays, and legal holidays; and

         • Include the last day of the period, but if the last day is a Saturday, Sunday, or legal holiday, the period continues to run until the end of the next day that is not a Saturday, Sunday, or legal holiday. FRCP 6(a)(1).

      ii. *Period stated in hours.* When the period is stated in hours:

         • Begin counting immediately on the occurrence of the event that triggers the period;

         • Count every hour, including hours during intermediate Saturdays, Sundays, and legal holidays; and

         • If the period would end on a Saturday, Sunday, or legal holiday, the period continues to run until the same time on the next day that is not a Saturday, Sunday, or legal holiday. FRCP 6(a)(2).

     iii. *Inaccessibility of the clerk's office.* Unless the court orders otherwise, if the clerk's office is inaccessible:

         • On the last day for filing under FRCP 6(a)(1), then the time for filing is extended to the first accessible day that is not a Saturday, Sunday, or legal holiday; or

         • During the last hour for filing under FRCP 6(a)(2), then the time for filing is extended to the same time on the first accessible day that is not a Saturday, Sunday, or legal holiday. FRCP 6(a)(3).

iv. *"Last day" defined.* Unless a different time is set by a statute, local rule, or court order, the last day ends:

- For electronic filing, at midnight in the court's time zone; and
- For filing by other means, when the clerk's office is scheduled to close. FRCP 6(a)(4).

v. *"Next day" defined.* The "next day" is determined by continuing to count forward when the period is measured after an event and backward when measured before an event. FRCP 6(a)(5).

vi. *"Legal holiday" defined.* "Legal holiday" means:

- The day set aside by statute for observing New Year's Day, Martin Luther King Jr.'s Birthday, Washington's Birthday, Memorial Day, Independence Day, Labor Day, Columbus Day, Veterans' Day, Thanksgiving Day, or Christmas Day;
- Any day declared a holiday by the President or Congress; and
- For periods that are measured after an event, any other day declared a holiday by the state where the district court is located. FRCP 6(a)(6).

b. *Computation of electronic filing deadlines.* Filing documents electronically does not alter any filing deadlines or any time computation pursuant to FRCP 6. The counties of Lake, Porter, LaPorte, Pulaski and Starke are located in the Central time zone and the remaining counties in the Northern District of Indiana are located in the Eastern time zone. Nevertheless, all electronic transmissions of documents must be completed (i.e., received completely by the clerk's office) prior to midnight Eastern Time, (South Bend/Fort Wayne/Lafayette time) in order to be considered timely filed that day, regardless of the local time in the division where the case is pending. Although documents can be filed electronically twenty-four (24) hours a day, filers are strongly encouraged to file all documents during hours when the CM/ECF Help Line is available, from 9:00 a.m. to 4:00 p.m. local time. IN R USDCTND CM/ECF(II)(I).

i. *Technical failures.* If the attorney is unable to file a document in a timely manner due to technical difficulties in the user's system, the attorney must file a document with the court as soon as possible notifying the court of the inability to file the document. A sample document entitled Declaration that Party was Unable to File in a Timely Manner Due to Technical Difficulties is attached hereto as Form 5. IN R USDCTND CM/ECF(VI)(B). [Editor's note: the reference to Form 5 is likely meant to be a reference to Form 3 (IN R USDCTND CM/ECF(Form 3)].

c. *Extending time*

i. *In general.* When an act may or must be done within a specified time, the court may, for good cause, extend the time:

- With or without motion or notice if the court acts, or if a request is made, before the original time or its extension expires; or
- On motion made after the time has expired if the party failed to act because of excusable neglect. FRCP 6(b)(1).

ii. *Exceptions.* A court must not extend the time to act under FRCP 50(b), FRCP 50(d), FRCP 52(b), FRCP 59(b), FRCP 59(d), FRCP 59(e), and FRCP 60(b). FRCP 6(b)(2).

iii. Refer to the United States District Court for the Northern District of Indiana KeyRules Motion for Continuance/Extension of Time document for more information on extending time.

d. *Additional time after certain kinds of service.* When a party may or must act within a specified time after being served and service is made under FRCP 5(b)(2)(C) (mail), FRCP 5(b)(2)(D) (leaving with the clerk), or FRCP 5(b)(2)(F) (other means consented to), three (3) days are added after the period would otherwise expire under FRCP 6(a). FRCP 6(d).

C. General Requirements

1. *General provisions governing discovery*

a. *Discovery scope and limits*

i. *Scope in general.* Unless otherwise limited by court order, the scope of discovery is as follows:

Parties may obtain discovery regarding any nonprivileged matter that is relevant to any party's claim or defense and proportional to the needs of the case, considering the importance of the issues at stake in the action, the amount in controversy, the parties' relative access to relevant information, the parties' resources, the importance of the discovery in resolving the issues, and whether the burden or expense of the proposed discovery outweighs its likely benefit. Information within this scope of discovery need not be admissible in evidence to be discoverable. FRCP 26(b)(1).

ii. *Limitations on frequency and extent*

- *When permitted.* By order, the court may alter the limits in the Federal Rules of Civil Procedure on the number of depositions and interrogatories or on the length of depositions under FRCP 30. By order or local rule, the court may also limit the number of requests under FRCP 36. FRCP 26(b)(2)(A).

- *Specific limitations on electronically stored information.* A party need not provide discovery of electronically stored information from sources that the party identifies as not reasonably accessible because of undue burden or cost. On motion to compel discovery or for a protective order, the party from whom discovery is sought must show that the information is not reasonably accessible because of undue burden or cost. If that showing is made, the court may nonetheless order discovery from such sources if the requesting party shows good cause, considering the limitations of FRCP 26(b)(2)(C). The court may specify conditions for the discovery. FRCP 26(b)(2)(B).

- *When required.* On motion or on its own, the court must limit the frequency or extent of discovery otherwise allowed by the Federal Rules of Civil Procedure or by local rule if it determines that: (1) the discovery sought is unreasonably cumulative or duplicative, or can be obtained from some other source that is more convenient, less burdensome, or less expensive; (2) the party seeking discovery has had ample opportunity to obtain the information by discovery in the action; or (3) the proposed discovery is outside the scope permitted by FRCP 26(b)(1). FRCP 26(b)(2)(C).

iii. *Trial preparation; Materials*

- *Documents and tangible things.* Ordinarily, a party may not discover documents and tangible things that are prepared in anticipation of litigation or for trial by or for another party or its representative (including the other party's attorney, consultant, surety, indemnitor, insurer, or agent). But, subject to FRCP 26(b)(4), those materials may be discovered if: (1) they are otherwise discoverable under FRCP 26(b)(1); and (2) the party shows that it has substantial need for the materials to prepare its case and cannot, without undue hardship, obtain their substantial equivalent by other means. FRCP 26(b)(3)(A).

- *Protection against disclosure.* If the court orders discovery of those materials, it must protect against disclosure of the mental impressions, conclusions, opinions, or legal theories of a party's attorney or other representative concerning the litigation. FRCP 26(b)(3)(B).

- *Previous statement.* Any party or other person may, on request and without the required showing, obtain the person's own previous statement about the action or its subject matter. If the request is refused, the person may move for a court order, and FRCP 37(a)(5) applies to the award of expenses. A previous statement is either: (1) a written statement that the person has signed or otherwise adopted or approved; or (2) a contemporaneous stenographic, mechanical, electrical, or other recording—or a transcription of it—that recites substantially verbatim the person's oral statement. FRCP 26(b)(3)(C).

iv. *Trial preparation; Experts*

- *Deposition of an expert who may testify.* A party may depose any person who has been identified as an expert whose opinions may be presented at trial. If FRCP 26(a)(2)(B) requires a report from the expert, the deposition may be conducted only after the report is provided. FRCP 26(b)(4)(A).

- *Trial-preparation protection for draft reports or disclosures.* FRCP 26(b)(3)(A) and FRCP 26(b)(3)(B) protect drafts of any report or disclosure required under FRCP 26(a)(2), regardless of the form in which the draft is recorded. FRCP 26(b)(4)(B).

- *Trial-preparation protection for communications between a party's attorney and expert witnesses.* FRCP 26(b)(3)(A) and FRCP 26(b)(3)(B) protect communications between the party's attorney and any witness required to provide a report under FRCP 26(a)(2)(B), regardless of the form of the communications, except to the extent that the communications: (1) relate to compensation for the expert's study or testimony; (2) identify facts or data that the party's attorney provided and that the expert considered in forming the opinions to be expressed; or (3) identify assumptions that the party's attorney provided and that the expert relied on in forming the opinions to be expressed. FRCP 26(b)(4)(C).

- *Expert employed only for trial preparation.* Ordinarily, a party may not, by interrogatories or deposition, discover facts known or opinions held by an expert who has been retained or specially employed by another party in anticipation of litigation or to prepare for trial and who is not expected to be called as a witness at trial. But a party may do so only: (1) as provided in FRCP 35(b); or (2) on showing exceptional circumstances under which it is impracticable for the party to obtain facts or opinions on the same subject by other means. FRCP 26(b)(4)(D).

- *Payment.* Unless manifest injustice would result, the court must require that the party seeking discovery: (1) pay the expert a reasonable fee for time spent in responding to discovery under FRCP 26(b)(4)(A) or FRCP 26(b)(4)(D); and (2) for discovery under FRCP 26(b)(4)(D), also pay the other party a fair portion of the fees and expenses it reasonably incurred in obtaining the expert's facts and opinions. FRCP 26(b)(4)(E).

v. *Claiming privilege or protecting trial-preparation materials*

- *Information withheld.* When a party withholds information otherwise discoverable by claiming that the information is privileged or subject to protection as trial-preparation material, the party must: (1) expressly make the claim; and (2) describe the nature of the documents, communications, or tangible things not produced or disclosed—and do so in a manner that, without revealing information itself privileged or protected, will enable other parties to assess the claim. FRCP 26(b)(5)(A).

- *Information produced.* If information produced in discovery is subject to a claim of privilege or of protection as trial-preparation material, the party making the claim may notify any party that received the information of the claim and the basis for it. After being notified, a party must promptly return, sequester, or destroy the specified information and any copies it has; must not use or disclose the information until the claim is resolved; must take reasonable steps to retrieve the information if the party disclosed it before being notified; and may promptly present the information to the court under seal for a determination of the claim. The producing party must preserve the information until the claim is resolved. FRCP 26(b)(5)(B).

b. *Protective orders.* A party or any person from whom discovery is sought may move for a protective order in the court where the action is pending—or as an alternative on matters relating to a deposition, in the court for the district where the deposition will be taken. FRCP 26(c)(1). Refer to the United States District Court for the Northern District of Indiana KeyRules Motion for Protective Order document for more information.

c. *Sequence of discovery.* Unless the parties stipulate or the court orders otherwise for the parties' and witnesses' convenience and in the interests of justice: (1) methods of discovery may be used in any sequence; and (2) discovery by one party does not require any other party to delay its discovery. FRCP 26(d)(3).

2. *Request for production of documents*

    a. *In general.* A party may serve on any other party a request within the scope of FRCP 26(b):

        i. To produce and permit the requesting party or its representative to inspect, copy, test, or sample the following items in the responding party's possession, custody, or control:

- Any designated documents or electronically stored information—including writings, drawings, graphs, charts, photographs, sound recordings, images, and other data or data compilations—stored in any medium from which information can be obtained either directly or, if necessary, after translation by the responding party into a reasonably usable form; or

- Any designated tangible things; or

        ii. To permit entry onto designated land or other property possessed or controlled by the responding party, so that the requesting party may inspect, measure, survey, photograph, test, or sample the property or any designated object or operation on it. FRCP 34(a).

    b. *Form.* A party propounding written discovery under FRCP 33, FRCP 34, or FRCP 36 must number each interrogatory or request sequentially. IN R USDCTND L.R. 26-1(a).

    c. *Contents of the request.* The request: (1) must describe with reasonable particularity each item or category of items to be inspected; (2) must specify a reasonable time, place, and manner for the inspection and for performing the related acts; and (3) may specify the form or forms in which electronically stored information is to be produced. FRCP 34(b)(1).

        i. *Description of items.* Although the phrase "reasonable particularity" eludes precise definition and depends on the facts and circumstances in each case, at least two tests have been suggested:

- The first test is whether the request places a party on "reasonable notice" of what is called for and what is not so that a reasonable person would know what documents or things are called for. FEDPROC § 26:634.

- The second is whether the request gives a court enough information to enable it to rule intelligently on objections. FEDPROC § 26:634.

    d. *Signature.* Though FRCP 34 does not say so, it is sufficient if the request is signed by the attorney for the party seeking discovery. FPP § 2212. Refer to the Format section of this document for more information on signing of discovery papers.

    e. *Other authority on production and inspection*

        i. *Freedom of Information Act.* Although the Freedom of Information Act (FOIA) is fundamentally designed to inform the public about agency action, and not to benefit private litigants, Congress has not acted upon proposals to forbid or limit the use of the FOIA for discovery purposes. FEDPROC § 26:605; National Presto Industries, Inc., 218 Ct.Cl. 696, 1978 WL 8475 (1978). However, a FOIA request may not be used to supplement civil discovery under FRCP 34, as in the case where information is privileged and therefore outside the scope of civil discovery. FEDPROC § 26:605; U.S. v. Weber Aircraft Corp., 465 U.S. 792, 104 S.Ct. 1488, 79 L.Ed.2d 814 (1984).

        ii. *Hague Convention.* Under the Hague Convention, a party seeking evidence abroad must obtain and send a letter of request to the central authority of the country in which the evidence is sought, requesting service of the request on the desired person or entity; if the request complies with the Convention, the central authority will then obtain the desired evidence. FEDPROC § 26:606. [Editor's note: the Hague Convention can be found at T.I.A.S. No. 6638 and is also available in the appendix to FRCP 4].

    f. *Motion to compel.* If a party who has been requested to permit discovery under FRCP 34 makes no response to the request, or if its response objects to all or part of the requested discovery, or if it otherwise fails to permit discovery as requested, the party who submitted the request, if it still wishes the discovery that has been refused, may move under FRCP 37(a) for an order compelling inspection in accordance with the request. FPP § 2214. Refer to the United States District Court for the Northern District of Indiana KeyRules Motion to Compel Discovery document for more information.

3. *Sanctions for failure to cooperate in discovery.* The court where the action is pending may, on motion, order sanctions if a party, after being properly served with interrogatories under FRCP 33 or a request for inspection under FRCP 34, fails to serve its answers, objections, or written response. FRCP 37(d)(1)(A)(ii). If a motion to compel is granted, the court must, after giving an opportunity to be heard, require the party or deponent whose conduct necessitated the motion, the party or attorney advising that conduct, or both to pay the movant's reasonable expenses incurred in making the motion, including attorney's fees. But the court must not order this payment if the opposing party's nondisclosure, response, or objection was substantially justified. FRCP 37(a)(5)(A)(ii). Refer to the United States District Court for the Northern District of Indiana KeyRules Motion for Discovery Sanctions document for more information.

4. *Stipulations about discovery procedure.* Unless the court orders otherwise, the parties may stipulate that: (1) a deposition may be taken before any person, at any time or place, on any notice, and in the manner specified—in which event it may be used in the same way as any other deposition; and (2) other procedures governing or limiting discovery be modified—but a stipulation extending the time for any form of discovery must have court approval if it would interfere with the time set for completing discovery, for hearing a motion, or for trial. FRCP 29.

5. *Appearances.* Attorneys not representing the United States or its agencies must file an appearance when they represent (either in person or by filing a paper) a party. IN R USDCTND L.R. 83-8(a). For more information, refer to IN R USDCTND L.R. 83-8.

6. *Notice of related action.* A party must file a notice of related action as soon as it appears that the party's case and another pending case: (1) arise out of the same transaction or occurrence; (2) involve the same property; or (3) involve the validity or infringement of the same patent, trademark, or copyright. IN R USDCTND L.R. 40-1(d). For more information, refer to IN R USDCTND L.R. 40-1.

7. *Alternative dispute resolution (ADR).* After they confer as required by FRCP 26(f), the parties must advise the court which, if any, alternative-dispute-resolution processes they expect to pursue and when they expect to undertake the process. IN R USDCTND L.R. 16-6(a). For more information on alternative dispute resolution (ADR), refer to IN R USDCTND L.R. 16-6 and IN R USDCTND Order 2003-21.

8. *Settlement or resolution.* The parties must immediately notify the court if they reasonably expect to settle the case or resolve a pending motion. IN R USDCTND L.R. 16-1(g).

9. *Modification or suspension of rules.* The court may, on its own motion or at the request of a party, suspend or modify any rule in a particular case in the interest of justice. IN R USDCTND L.R. 1-1(c).

D. Documents

1. *Required documents*

   a. *Request for production of documents.* Refer to the General Requirements section of this document for information on the request for production of documents.

2. *Supplemental documents*

   a. *Subpoena.* As provided in FRCP 45, a nonparty may be compelled to produce documents and tangible things or to permit an inspection. FRCP 34(c). For information on the form and contents of the subpoena, refer to FRCP 45.

   b. *Certificate of service.* FRCP 5(d) requires that the person making service under FRCP 5 certify that service has been effected. FRCP 5(Advisory Committee Notes). Having such information on file may be useful for many purposes, including proof of service if an issue arises concerning the effectiveness of the service. FRCP 5(Advisory Committee Notes).

E. Format

1. *Form of documents.* The rules governing captions and other matters of form in pleadings apply to motions and other papers. FRCP 7(b)(2).

   a. *Paper.* Any pleading, motion, brief, affidavit, notice, or proposed order, whether filed electronically

or by delivering it to the clerk, must: use eight and one-half by eleven (8-1/2 x 11) inch pages. IN R USDCTND L.R. 5-4(a)(2).

   i. *Manual filings.* Papers delivered to the clerk for filing must: be flat, unfolded, and on good-quality, white paper. IN R USDCTND L.R. 5-4(b)(1)(A).

      • *Covers or backing.* Papers delivered to the clerk for filing must: not have a cover or a back. IN R USDCTND L.R. 5-4(b)(1)(B).

      • *Recycled paper.* The court encourages using recycled paper. IN R USDCTND L.R. 5-4(b)(7).

b. *Margins.* Any pleading, motion, brief, affidavit, notice, or proposed order, whether filed electronically or by delivering it to the clerk, must: have at least one (1) inch margins. IN R USDCTND L.R. 5-4(a)(3).

c. *Spacing.* Any pleading, motion, brief, affidavit, notice, or proposed order, whether filed electronically or by delivering it to the clerk, must: be double spaced (except for headings, footnotes, and quoted material). IN R USDCTND L.R. 5-4(a)(5).

d. *Text.* Any pleading, motion, brief, affidavit, notice, or proposed order, whether filed electronically or by delivering it to the clerk, must: be plainly typewritten, printed, or prepared by a clearly legible copying process. IN R USDCTND L.R. 5-4(a)(1).

   i. Any pleading, motion, brief, affidavit, notice, or proposed order, whether filed electronically or by delivering it to the clerk, must: use at least twelve (12) point type in the body and at least ten (10) point type in footnotes. IN R USDCTND L.R. 5-4(a)(4).

e. *Page numbering.* Any pleading, motion, brief, affidavit, notice, or proposed order, whether filed electronically or by delivering it to the clerk, must: have consecutively numbered pages. IN R USDCTND L.R. 5-4(a)(6).

f. *Caption; Names of parties.* Every pleading must have a caption with the court's name, a title, a file number, and a FRCP 7(a) designation. The title of the complaint must name all the parties; the title of other pleadings, after naming the first party on each side, may refer generally to other parties. FRCP 10(a). Any pleading, motion, brief, affidavit, notice, or proposed order, whether filed electronically or by delivering it to the clerk, must: include a title on the first page. IN R USDCTND L.R. 5-4(a)(7).

g. *Filer's information.* Any pleading, motion, brief, affidavit, notice, or proposed order, whether filed electronically or by delivering it to the clerk, must: except in proposed orders and affidavits, include the filer's name, address, telephone number, fax number (where available), and e-mail address (where available). IN R USDCTND L.R. 5-4(a)(9).

h. *Paragraphs; Separate statements.* A party must state its claims or defenses in numbered paragraphs, each limited as far as practicable to a single set of circumstances. A later pleading may refer by number to a paragraph in an earlier pleading. If doing so would promote clarity, each claim founded on a separate transaction or occurrence—and each defense other than a denial—must be stated in a separate count or defense. FRCP 10(b).

i. *Adoption by reference; Exhibits.* A statement in a pleading may be adopted by reference elsewhere in the same pleading or in any other pleading or motion. A copy of a written instrument that is an exhibit to a pleading is a part of the pleading for all purposes. FRCP 10(c).

j. *Citation of local rules.* The Local Civil Rules of the United States District Court for the Northern District of Indiana may be cited as "N.D. Ind. L.R." IN R USDCTND L.R. 1-1(a)(1).

k. *Acceptance by the clerk.* The clerk must not refuse to file a paper solely because it is not in the form prescribed by the Federal Rules of Civil Procedure or by a local rule or practice. FRCP 5(d)(4).

   i. *Sanctions for formatting errors; Non-compliance.* If a person files a paper that does not comply with the rules governing the format of papers filed with the court, the court may: (1) strike the paper from the record; or (2) fine the person up to one thousand dollars ($1,000). IN R USDCTND L.R. 1-3(a).

      • *Notice.* Before sanctioning a person under IN R USDCTND L.R. 1-3(a)(2), the court must:

(1) notify the person that the paper is noncompliant; and (2) give the person the opportunity either to be heard or to revise the paper. IN R USDCTND L.R. 1-3(b).

2. *Form of electronic documents.* Electronically filed documents must meet the same requirements of format and page limits as documents "conventionally filed" (as defined in IN R USDCTND CM/ECF(III)(A)) pursuant to the Federal Rules of Civil Procedure and the Local Civil Rules of the United States District Court for the Northern District of Indiana. IN R USDCTND CM/ECF(II)(A)(2).

   a. *PDF format required.* Documents filed in the CM/ECF must be in .pdf format. A document created with almost any word-processing program can be converted to .pdf format. The .pdf program in effect takes a picture of the original document and allows anyone to open the converted document across a broad range of hardware and software, with layout, format, links, and images intact. IN R USDCTND CM/ECF(FN2).

   b. *Title of documents.* The person electronically filing a pleading or other document will be responsible for designating a title for the pleading or other document by using one of the categories contained in the events listed in the CM/ECF Menu. IN R USDCTND CM/ECF(II)(G).

   c. *Combining documents.* All documents which form part of a single pleading and which are being filed at the same time and by the same party may be electronically filed together under one document number, e.g., the motion and a supporting affidavit, with the exception of memoranda in support. Memoranda in support shall be electronically filed separately and shown as a related document to the motion. IN R USDCTND CM/ECF(II)(A)(4).

   d. *Exhibits and attachments.* Filing users must submit in electronic form all documents referenced as exhibits or attachments, unless the court permits conventional filing. A filing user must submit as exhibits or attachments only those excerpts of the referenced documents that are directly germane to the matter under consideration by the court. Excerpted material must be clearly and prominently identified as such. Filing users who file excerpts of documents as exhibits or attachments do so without prejudice to their right to timely file additional excerpts or the complete document. Responding parties may timely file additional excerpts or the complete document that they believe are directly germane. The court may require parties to file additional excerpts or the complete document. IN R USDCTND CM/ECF(II)(A)(6).

   e. *Hyperlinks.* Electronically filed documents may contain hyperlink references to an external document as a convenient mechanism for accessing material cited in the document. A hyperlink reference is neither validated for content nor considered a part of the court's records. The court neither endorses the product or organization at the destination of a hyperlink reference, nor does the court exercise any responsibility over the content at the destination. In order to preserve the integrity of the court record, attorneys wishing to insert hyperlinks in court filings shall continue to use the traditional citation method for the cited authority, in addition to the hyperlink. A hyperlink contained in a filing is no more than a convenient mechanism for accessing material cited in the document and a hyperlink reference is extraneous to any filed document and is not part of the court's record. IN R USDCTND CM/ECF(II)(A)(3).

3. *Signing disclosures and discovery requests, responses, and objections.* FRCP 11 does not apply to disclosures and discovery requests, responses, objections, and motions under FRCP 26 through FRCP 37. FRCP 11(d).

   a. *Signature required.* Every disclosure under FRCP 26(a)(1) or FRCP 26(a)(3) and every discovery request, response, or objection must be signed by at least one attorney of record in the attorney's own name—or by the party personally, if unrepresented—and must state the signer's address, e-mail address, and telephone number. FRCP 26(g)(1).

      i. *Signatures on manual filings.* Papers delivered to the clerk for filing must: include the filer's original signature. IN R USDCTND L.R. 5-4(b)(1)(C).

         • *Rubber-stamped and faxed signatures.* An original paper with a rubber-stamped or faxed signature is unsigned for purposes of FRCP 11 and FRCP 26(g). IN R USDCTND L.R. 5-4(b)(2).

         • *Affidavits.* Only the affiant need sign an affidavit. IN R USDCTND L.R. 5-4(b)(3).

ii. *Electronic signatures.* Pursuant to FRCP 11, every pleading, motion, and other paper (except lists, schedules, statements or amendments thereto) shall be signed by at least one attorney of record or, if the party is not represented by an attorney, all papers shall be signed by the party. An attorney's/participant's password issued by the court combined with the user's identification, serves as and constitutes the attorney/participant's signature for FRCP 11 and other purposes. IN R USDCTND CM/ECF(I)(C). Documents which must be filed and which must contain original signatures other than those of a participating attorney or which require either verification or an unsworn declaration under any rule or statute, shall be filed electronically, with originally executed copies maintained by the filer. The pleading or other document electronically filed shall contain "s/" signature(s), as noted in IN R USDCTND CM/ECF(II)(E)(3)(b). IN R USDCTND CM/ECF(II)(E)(1).

- *Multiple signatures.* In the case of a stipulation or other document to be signed by two or more attorneys, the following procedure should be used: The filing attorney shall initially confirm that the content of the document is acceptable to all persons required to sign the document and shall obtain the physical signatures of all attorneys on the document. IN R USDCTND CM/ECF(II)(E)(3)(a). The filing attorney then shall file the document electronically, indicating the signatories, e.g., "s/Jane Doe," "s/John Doe," etc. IN R US-DCTND CM/ECF(II)(E)(3)(b). The filing attorney shall retain the hard copy of the document containing the original signatures. IN R USDCTND CM/ECF(II)(E)(3)(c).

b. *Effect of signature.* By signing, an attorney or party certifies that to the best of the person's knowledge, information, and belief formed after a reasonable inquiry:

  i. With respect to a disclosure, it is complete and correct as of the time it is made; and

  ii. With respect to a discovery request, response, or objection, it is:

  - Consistent with the Federal Rules of Civil Procedure and warranted by existing law or by a nonfrivolous argument for extending, modifying, or reversing existing law, or for establishing new law;

  - Not interposed for any improper purpose, such as to harass, cause unnecessary delay, or needlessly increase the cost of litigation; and

  - Neither unreasonable nor unduly burdensome or expensive, considering the needs of the case, prior discovery in the case, the amount in controversy, and the importance of the issues at stake in the action. FRCP 26(g)(1).

c. *Failure to sign.* Other parties have no duty to act on an unsigned disclosure, request, response, or objection until it is signed, and the court must strike it unless a signature is promptly supplied after the omission is called to the attorney's or party's attention. FRCP 26(g)(2).

d. *Sanction for improper certification.* If a certification violates FRCP 26(g) without substantial justification, the court, on motion or on its own, must impose an appropriate sanction on the signer, the party on whose behalf the signer was acting, or both. The sanction may include an order to pay the reasonable expenses, including attorney's fees, caused by the violation. FRCP 26(g)(3). Refer to the United States District Court for the Northern District of Indiana KeyRules Motion for Discovery Sanctions document for more information.

4. *Privacy protection for filings made with the court*

a. *Redacted filings.* Counsel should not include sensitive information in any document filed with the court unless such inclusion is necessary and relevant to the case. IN R USDCTND CM/ECF(VII). Unless the court orders otherwise, in an electronic or paper filing with the court that contains an individual's Social Security number, taxpayer-identification number, or birth date, the name of an individual known to be a minor, or a financial-account number, a party or nonparty making the filing may include only:

  i. The last four (4) digits of the Social Security number and taxpayer-identification number;

  ii. The year of the individual's birth;

  iii. The minor's initials; and

iv.   The last four (4) digits of the financial-account number. FRCP 5.2(a); IN R USDCTND Order 2005-3.

b.   *Exemptions from the redaction requirement.* The redaction requirement does not apply to the following:

    i.   A financial-account number that identifies the property allegedly subject to forfeiture in a forfeiture proceeding;

    ii.   The record of an administrative or agency proceeding;

    iii.   The official record of a state-court proceeding;

    iv.   The record of a court or tribunal, if that record was not subject to the redaction requirement when originally filed;

    v.   A filing covered by FRCP 5.2(c) or FRCP 5.2(d); and

    vi.   A pro se filing in an action brought under 28 U.S.C.A. § 2241, 28 U.S.C.A. § 2254, or 28 U.S.C.A. § 2255. FRCP 5.2(b).

    vii.   In cases filed under the Social Security Act, 42 U.S.C.A. § 405(g), there is no need for redaction of any information from the documents filed in the case. IN R USDCTND Order 2005-3.

c.   *Limitations on remote access to electronic files; Social Security appeals and immigration cases.* Unless the court orders otherwise, in an action for benefits under the Social Security Act, and in an action or proceeding relating to an order of removal, to relief from removal, or to immigration benefits or detention, access to an electronic file is authorized as follows:

    i.   The parties and their attorneys may have remote electronic access to any part of the case file, including the administrative record;

    ii.   Any other person may have electronic access to the full record at the courthouse, but may have remote electronic access only to:

- The docket maintained by the court; and

- An opinion, order, judgment, or other disposition of the court, but not any other part of the case file or the administrative record. FRCP 5.2(c).

d.   *Filings made under seal.* The court may order that a filing be made under seal without redaction. The court may later unseal the filing or order the person who made the filing to file a redacted version for the public record. FRCP 5.2(d). For information on filing documents under seal, refer to IN R USDCTND L.R. 5-3, IN R USDCTND CM/ECF(IV)(A), and IN R USDCTND ECF Order 2004-19.

e.   *Protective orders.* For good cause, the court may by order in a case:

    i.   Require redaction of additional information; or

    ii.   Limit or prohibit a nonparty's remote electronic access to a document filed with the court. FRCP 5.2(e).

f.   *Option for additional unredacted filing under seal.* A person making a redacted filing may also file an unredacted copy under seal. The court must retain the unredacted copy as part of the record. FRCP 5.2(f); IN R USDCTND Order 2005-3.

    i.   The unredacted version of the document or the reference list shall be retained by the court under seal as part of the record. This paper shall be retained by the court as part of the record. The court may, however, still require the party to file a redacted copy for the public file. IN R USDCTND Order 2005-3.

g.   *Option for filing a reference list.* A filing that contains redacted information may be filed together with a reference list that identifies each item of redacted information and specifies an appropriate identifier that uniquely corresponds to each item listed. The list must be filed under seal and may be amended as of right. Any reference in the case to a listed identifier will be construed to refer to the corresponding item of information. FRCP 5.2(g); IN R USDCTND Order 2005-3.

    i.   The unredacted version of the document or the reference list shall be retained by the court under

seal as part of the record. This paper shall be retained by the court as part of the record. The court may, however, still require the party to file a redacted copy for the public file. IN R USDCTND Order 2005-3.

h. *Responsibility for redaction.* The responsibility for redacting these personal identifiers rests solely with counsel and the parties. The Clerk will not review each paper for compliance with IN R USDCTND Order 2005-3. IN R USDCTND Order 2005-3.

i. *Waiver of protection of identifiers.* A person waives the protection of FRCP 5.2(a) as to the person's own information by filing it without redaction and not under seal. FRCP 5.2(h).

F. Filing and Service Requirements

1. *Filing requirements.* Any paper after the complaint that is required to be served—together with a certificate of service—must be filed within a reasonable time after service. But disclosures under FRCP 26(a)(1) or FRCP 26(a)(2) and the following discovery requests and responses must not be filed until they are used in the proceeding or the court orders filing: depositions, interrogatories, requests for documents or tangible things or to permit entry onto land, and requests for admission. FRCP 5(d)(1). Refer to the United States District Court for the Northern District of Indiana KeyRules pleading and motion documents for information on filing with the court.

   a. *Discovery ordinarily not filed.* The party who serves a discovery request or notices a deposition is the custodian of the original discovery response or deposition transcript. Except as required under IN R USDCTND L.R. 26-2(a)(2), parties must not file: (1) disclosures under FRCP 26(a)(1) or FRCP 26(a)(2); (2) deposition notices; (3) deposition transcripts; (4) interrogatories; (5) requests for documents, to permit entry upon land, or for admission; (6) answers to interrogatories; (7) responses to requests for documents, to permit entry upon land, or for admission; or (8) service-of-discovery notices. IN R USDCTND L.R. 26-2(a)(1).

      i. *Exceptions*

         • *Pro se litigation.* All discovery material in cases involving a pro se party must be filed. IN R USDCTND L.R. 26-2(a)(2)(A).

         • *Specific material.* Discovery material must also be filed when: (1) the court orders; or (2) the material is used in a proceeding. IN R USDCTND L.R. 26-2(a)(2)(B).

   b. *When discovery may be filed*

      i. *Filing materials with motion for relief.* A party who files a motion for relief under FRCP 26(c) or FRCP 37 must file with the motion those parts of the discovery requests or responses that the motion pertains to. IN R USDCTND L.R. 26-2(b).

      ii. *Materials necessary for motion.* A party must file those portions of discovery requests or responses (including deposition transcripts) that the party relies on to support a motion that could result in a final order on an issue. IN R USDCTND L.R. 26-2(c).

      iii. *Materials to be used at trial.* A party who reasonably anticipates using discovery requests or responses—including deposition transcripts—at trial must file the relevant portions of the requests or responses with the clerk at the start of the trial. IN R USDCTND L.R. 26-2(d).

2. *Service requirements*

   a. *Service; When required*

      i. *In general.* Unless the Federal Rules of Civil Procedure provide otherwise, each of the following papers must be served on every party:

         • An order stating that service is required;

         • A pleading filed after the original complaint, unless the court orders otherwise under FRCP 5(c) because there are numerous defendants;

         • A discovery paper required to be served on a party, unless the court orders otherwise;

         • A written motion, except one that may be heard ex parte; and

         • A written notice, appearance, demand, or offer of judgment, or any similar paper. FRCP 5(a)(1).

ii. *If a party fails to appear.* No service is required on a party who is in default for failing to appear. But a pleading that asserts a new claim for relief against such a party must be served on that party under FRCP 4. FRCP 5(a)(2).

iii. *Seizing property.* If an action is begun by seizing property and no person is or need be named as a defendant, any service required before the filing of an appearance, answer, or claim must be made on the person who had custody or possession of the property when it was seized. FRCP 5(a)(3).

b. *Service; How made*

i. *Serving an attorney.* If a party is represented by an attorney, service under FRCP 5 must be made on the attorney unless the court orders service on the party. FRCP 5(b)(1).

ii. *Service in general.* A paper is served under FRCP 5 by:

- Handing it to the person;

- Leaving it: (1) at the person's office with a clerk or other person in charge or, if no one is in charge, in a conspicuous place in the office; or (2) if the person has no office or the office is closed, at the person's dwelling or usual place of abode with someone of suitable age and discretion who resides there;

- Mailing it to the person's last known address—in which event service is complete upon mailing;

- Leaving it with the court clerk if the person has no known address;

- Sending it by electronic means if the person consented in writing—in which event service is complete upon transmission, but is not effective if the serving party learns that it did not reach the person to be served; or

- Delivering it by any other means that the person consented to in writing—in which event service is complete when the person making service delivers it to the agency designated to make delivery. FRCP 5(b)(2).

iii. *Electronic service.* Electronically filed papers may be served electronically if service is consistent with the CM/ECF User Manual (IN R USDCTND CM/ECF). IN R USDCTND L.R. 5-2(a).

- *Waiver of other service.* An attorney's registration will constitute a waiver of conventional service of documents and the attorney agrees to accept service of notice on behalf of the client of the electronic filing by hand, facsimile or authorized email. IN R USDCTND CM/ECF(I)(B)(3).

- *Serving registered persons.* The System will generate a "Notice of Electronic Filing" when any document is filed. This notice represents service of the document on parties who are registered participants with the System. Except as provided in IN R USDCTND CM/ECF(III)(B), the filing party shall not be required to serve any pleading or other documents on any party receiving electronic notice. IN R USDCTND CM/ECF(II)(D)(1). The term "pleading" refers only to those documents listed in FRCP 7(a). IN R USDCTND CM/ECF(FN3).

- *When electronic service is deemed completed.* A person registered to use the court's electronic-filing system is served with an electronically filed paper when a "Notice of Electronic Filing" is transmitted to that person through the court's electronic filing-system. IN R USDCTND L.R. 5-2(b).

- *Serving non-registered persons.* A person who has not registered to use the court's electronic-filing system but who is entitled to service of a paper must be served according to the Local Civil Rules of the United States District Court for the Northern District of Indiana and the Federal Rules of Civil Procedure. IN R USDCTND L.R. 5-2(c); IN R USDCTND CM/ECF(II)(D)(2). If such service of a paper copy is to be made, it shall be done in the manner provided in the Federal Rules of Civil Procedure and the Local Civil Rules of the United States District Court for the Northern District of Indiana. IN R USDCTND CM/ECF(II)(D)(2).

iv. *Service of conventional filings.* Pleadings or other documents which are filed conventionally rather than electronically shall be served in the manner provided for in the Federal Rules of Civil Procedure and the Local Civil Rules of the United States District Court for the Northern District of Indiana, except as otherwise provided by order of the Court. IN R USDCTND CM/ECF(III)(B).

v. *Using court facilities.* If a local rule so authorizes, a party may use the court's transmission facilities to make service under FRCP 5(b)(2)(E). FRCP 5(b)(3).

c. *Serving numerous defendants*

i. *In general.* If an action involves an unusually large number of defendants, the court may, on motion or on its own, order that:

- Defendants' pleadings and replies to them need not be served on other defendants;

- Any crossclaim, counterclaim, avoidance, or affirmative defense in those pleadings and replies to them will be treated as denied or avoided by all other parties; and

- Filing any such pleading and serving it on the plaintiff constitutes notice of the pleading to all parties. FRCP 5(c)(1).

ii. *Notifying parties.* A copy of every such order must be served on the parties as the court directs. FRCP 5(c)(2).

G. Hearings

1. There is no hearing contemplated in the federal statutes or rules for requests for production of documents.

H. Forms

1. Federal Request for Production of Documents Forms

a. Request; Production of documents for inspection and copying. AMJUR PP DEPOSITION § 498.

b. Request for production, inspection and copying of documents, and inspection and photographing of things and real property. 3A FEDFORMS § 3556.

c. Request for production of documents; Business records. 3A FEDFORMS § 3557.

d. Request for production of documents; Patent case. 3A FEDFORMS § 3558.

e. Request for production of documents; Government records and regulations. 3A FEDFORMS § 3559.

f. Request for production of documents; Government personnel files, memoranda, minutes of meetings, and statistics. 3A FEDFORMS § 3560.

g. Request for production of documents; Documents to be identified in physically separate but accompanying interrogatories under FRCP 33. 3A FEDFORMS § 3561.

h. Request for production of documents; Employment discrimination. 3A FEDFORMS § 3562.

i. Letter requesting production of files. 3A FEDFORMS § 3563.

j. Request; Production of documents, records, and objects, under FRCP 34. FEDPROF § 23:394.

k. Request; Production of documents for inspection and copying. FEDPROF § 23:395.

l. Request; Production of documents for inspection and copying; Business records. FEDPROF § 23:396.

m. Request; Production of objects for inspection and sampling. FEDPROF § 23:397.

n. Request; Production of documents for inspection and copying; Government records and files. FEDPROF § 23:398.

o. Request; Production of documents and things; Patent proceeding. FEDPROF § 23:399.

p. Request; Production of documents and things; Trademark action. FEDPROF § 23:400.

q. Request; Production of documents; Trademark action; Likelihood of confusion. FEDPROF § 23:401.

r.   Request; Production of documents; Automobile negligence. FEDPROF § 23:402.

s.   Request; Production of documents; Premises liability. FEDPROF § 23:403.

t.   Request; Production of documents for inspection and copying; Wrongful death due to forklift accident. FEDPROF § 23:404.

u.   Request; Production of documents; Products liability. FEDPROF § 23:405.

v.   Request; Production of documents; Collection of tariff. FEDPROF § 23:406.

w.   Request; Production of medical records. FEDPROF § 23:407.

x.   Request; Production of employment records. FEDPROF § 23:408.

y.   Request; Production of education records. FEDPROF § 23:409.

z.   Request; Production of decedent's records. FEDPROF § 23:410.

I. Applicable Rules

1. *Federal rules*

   a.   Serving and filing pleadings and other papers. FRCP 5.

   b.   Privacy protection for filings made with the court. FRCP 5.2.

   c.   Computing and extending time; Time for motion papers. FRCP 6.

   d.   Pleadings allowed; Form of motions and other papers. FRCP 7.

   e.   Form of pleadings. FRCP 10.

   f.   Signing pleadings, motions, and other papers; Representations to the court; Sanctions. FRCP 11.

   g.   Duty to disclose; General provisions governing discovery. FRCP 26.

   h.   Stipulations about discovery procedure. FRCP 29.

   i.   Producing documents, electronically stored information, and tangible things, or entering onto land, for inspection and other purposes. FRCP 34.

   j.   Failure to make disclosures or to cooperate in discovery; Sanctions. FRCP 37.

2. *Local rules*

   a.   Citation and scope of the rules. IN R USDCTND L.R. 1-1.

   b.   Sanctions for formatting errors. IN R USDCTND L.R. 1-3.

   c.   Electronic service. IN R USDCTND L.R. 5-2.

   d.   Format of papers. IN R USDCTND L.R. 5-4.

   e.   Pretrial procedure. IN R USDCTND L.R. 16-1.

   f.   Alternative dispute resolution. IN R USDCTND L.R. 16-6.

   g.   Form of certain discovery documents. IN R USDCTND L.R. 26-1.

   h.   Filing of discovery and other materials. IN R USDCTND L.R. 26-2.

   i.   Case assignment. IN R USDCTND L.R. 40-1.

   j.   Appearance and withdrawal of appearance. IN R USDCTND L.R. 83-8.

   k.   CM/ECF civil and criminal user manual. IN R USDCTND CM/ECF.

   l.   In re: privacy and public access to civil electronic case files. IN R USDCTND Order 2005-3.

Requests, Notices and Applications
Response to Request for Production of Documents

Document Last Updated December 2016

A. Checklist

(I) ❑ Matters to be considered by requesting party

    (a) ❑ Required documents

        (1) ❑ Request for production of documents

    (b) ❑ Supplemental documents

        (1) ❑ Subpoena

        (2) ❑ Certificate of service

    (c) ❑ Timing

        (1) ❑ More than twenty-one (21) days after the summons and complaint are served on a party, a request under FRCP 34 may be delivered: (1) to that party by any other party, and (2) by that party to any plaintiff or to any other party that has been served

        (2) ❑ A party may not seek discovery from any source before the parties have conferred as required by FRCP 26(f), except in a proceeding exempted from initial disclosure under FRCP 26(a)(1)(B), or when authorized by the Federal Rules of Civil Procedure, by stipulation, or by court order

(II) ❑ Matters to be considered by responding party

    (a) ❑ Required documents

        (1) ❑ Response to request for production of documents

    (b) ❑ Supplemental documents

        (1) ❑ Certificate of service

    (c) ❑ Timing

        (1) ❑ The party to whom the request is directed must respond in writing within thirty (30) days after being served or—if the request was delivered under FRCP 26(d)(2)—within thirty (30) days after the parties' first FRCP 26(f) conference

B. Timing

1. *Response to request for production of documents.* The party to whom the request is directed must respond in writing within thirty (30) days after being served or—if the request was delivered under FRCP 26(d)(2)—within thirty (30) days after the parties' first FRCP 26(f) conference. A shorter or longer time may be stipulated to under FRCP 29 or be ordered by the court. FRCP 34(b)(2)(A).

2. *Automatic initial extension.* The deadline to respond to a pleading or a discovery request—including requests for admission—is automatically extended when an extension notice is filed with the court and: (1) the deadline has not been extended before; (2) the extension is for twenty-eight (28) or fewer days; and (3) the notice states: (A) the original deadline; (B) the new deadline; and (C) that all opposing attorneys the attorney could reach agreed to the extension; or that the party could not reach any other opposing attorneys despite due diligence. IN R USDCTND L.R. 6-1(b).

    a. *Pro se parties.* The automatic initial extension does not apply to pro se parties. IN R USDCTND L.R. 6-1(c).

3. *Computation of time*

    a. *Computing time.* FRCP 6 applies in computing any time period specified in the Federal Rules of Civil

Procedure, in any local rule or court order, or in any statute that does not specify a method of computing time. FRCP 6(a).

i. *Period stated in days or a longer unit.* When the period is stated in days or a longer unit of time:

- Exclude the day of the event that triggers the period;

- Count every day, including intermediate Saturdays, Sundays, and legal holidays; and

- Include the last day of the period, but if the last day is a Saturday, Sunday, or legal holiday, the period continues to run until the end of the next day that is not a Saturday, Sunday, or legal holiday. FRCP 6(a)(1).

ii. *Period stated in hours.* When the period is stated in hours:

- Begin counting immediately on the occurrence of the event that triggers the period;

- Count every hour, including hours during intermediate Saturdays, Sundays, and legal holidays; and

- If the period would end on a Saturday, Sunday, or legal holiday, the period continues to run until the same time on the next day that is not a Saturday, Sunday, or legal holiday. FRCP 6(a)(2).

iii. *Inaccessibility of the clerk's office.* Unless the court orders otherwise, if the clerk's office is inaccessible:

- On the last day for filing under FRCP 6(a)(1), then the time for filing is extended to the first accessible day that is not a Saturday, Sunday, or legal holiday; or

- During the last hour for filing under FRCP 6(a)(2), then the time for filing is extended to the same time on the first accessible day that is not a Saturday, Sunday, or legal holiday. FRCP 6(a)(3).

iv. *"Last day" defined.* Unless a different time is set by a statute, local rule, or court order, the last day ends:

- For electronic filing, at midnight in the court's time zone; and

- For filing by other means, when the clerk's office is scheduled to close. FRCP 6(a)(4).

v. *"Next day" defined.* The "next day" is determined by continuing to count forward when the period is measured after an event and backward when measured before an event. FRCP 6(a)(5).

vi. *"Legal holiday" defined.* "Legal holiday" means:

- The day set aside by statute for observing New Year's Day, Martin Luther King Jr.'s Birthday, Washington's Birthday, Memorial Day, Independence Day, Labor Day, Columbus Day, Veterans' Day, Thanksgiving Day, or Christmas Day;

- Any day declared a holiday by the President or Congress; and

- For periods that are measured after an event, any other day declared a holiday by the state where the district court is located. FRCP 6(a)(6).

b. *Computation of electronic filing deadlines.* Filing documents electronically does not alter any filing deadlines or any time computation pursuant to FRCP 6. The counties of Lake, Porter, LaPorte, Pulaski and Starke are located in the Central time zone and the remaining counties in the Northern District of Indiana are located in the Eastern time zone. Nevertheless, all electronic transmissions of documents must be completed (i.e., received completely by the clerk's office) prior to midnight Eastern Time, (South Bend/Fort Wayne/Lafayette time) in order to be considered timely filed that day, regardless of the local time in the division where the case is pending. Although documents can be filed electronically twenty-four (24) hours a day, filers are strongly encouraged to file all documents during hours when the CM/ECF Help Line is available, from 9:00 a.m. to 4:00 p.m. local time. IN R USDCTND CM/ECF(II)(I).

i. *Technical failures.* If the attorney is unable to file a document in a timely manner due to technical difficulties in the user's system, the attorney must file a document with the court as

soon as possible notifying the court of the inability to file the document. A sample document entitled Declaration that Party was Unable to File in a Timely Manner Due to Technical Difficulties is attached hereto as Form 5. IN R USDCTND CM/ECF(VI)(B). [Editor's note: the reference to Form 5 is likely meant to be a reference to Form 3 (IN R USDCTND CM/ECF(Form 3)].

   c.   *Extending time*

      i.   *In general.* When an act may or must be done within a specified time, the court may, for good cause, extend the time:

- With or without motion or notice if the court acts, or if a request is made, before the original time or its extension expires; or

- On motion made after the time has expired if the party failed to act because of excusable neglect. FRCP 6(b)(1).

      ii.   *Exceptions.* A court must not extend the time to act under FRCP 50(b), FRCP 50(d), FRCP 52(b), FRCP 59(b), FRCP 59(d), FRCP 59(e), and FRCP 60(b). FRCP 6(b)(2).

      iii.   Refer to the United States District Court for the Northern District of Indiana KeyRules Motion for Continuance/Extension of Time document for more information on extending time.

   d.   *Additional time after certain kinds of service.* When a party may or must act within a specified time after being served and service is made under FRCP 5(b)(2)(C) (mail), FRCP 5(b)(2)(D) (leaving with the clerk), or FRCP 5(b)(2)(F) (other means consented to), three (3) days are added after the period would otherwise expire under FRCP 6(a). FRCP 6(d).

C. General Requirements

1.   *General provisions governing discovery*

   a.   *Discovery scope and limits*

      i.   *Scope in general.* Unless otherwise limited by court order, the scope of discovery is as follows: Parties may obtain discovery regarding any nonprivileged matter that is relevant to any party's claim or defense and proportional to the needs of the case, considering the importance of the issues at stake in the action, the amount in controversy, the parties' relative access to relevant information, the parties' resources, the importance of the discovery in resolving the issues, and whether the burden or expense of the proposed discovery outweighs its likely benefit. Information within this scope of discovery need not be admissible in evidence to be discoverable. FRCP 26(b)(1).

      ii.   *Limitations on frequency and extent*

- *When permitted.* By order, the court may alter the limits in the Federal Rules of Civil Procedure on the number of depositions and interrogatories or on the length of depositions under FRCP 30. By order or local rule, the court may also limit the number of requests under FRCP 36. FRCP 26(b)(2)(A).

- *Specific limitations on electronically stored information.* A party need not provide discovery of electronically stored information from sources that the party identifies as not reasonably accessible because of undue burden or cost. On motion to compel discovery or for a protective order, the party from whom discovery is sought must show that the information is not reasonably accessible because of undue burden or cost. If that showing is made, the court may nonetheless order discovery from such sources if the requesting party shows good cause, considering the limitations of FRCP 26(b)(2)(C). The court may specify conditions for the discovery. FRCP 26(b)(2)(B).

- *When required.* On motion or on its own, the court must limit the frequency or extent of discovery otherwise allowed by the Federal Rules of Civil Procedure or by local rule if it determines that: (1) the discovery sought is unreasonably cumulative or duplicative, or can be obtained from some other source that is more convenient, less burdensome, or less expensive; (2) the party seeking discovery has had ample opportunity to obtain the information by discovery in the action; or (3) the proposed discovery is outside the scope permitted by FRCP 26(b)(1). FRCP 26(b)(2)(C).

iii. *Trial preparation; Materials*

- *Documents and tangible things.* Ordinarily, a party may not discover documents and tangible things that are prepared in anticipation of litigation or for trial by or for another party or its representative (including the other party's attorney, consultant, surety, indemnitor, insurer, or agent). But, subject to FRCP 26(b)(4), those materials may be discovered if: (1) they are otherwise discoverable under FRCP 26(b)(1); and (2) the party shows that it has substantial need for the materials to prepare its case and cannot, without undue hardship, obtain their substantial equivalent by other means. FRCP 26(b)(3)(A).

- *Protection against disclosure.* If the court orders discovery of those materials, it must protect against disclosure of the mental impressions, conclusions, opinions, or legal theories of a party's attorney or other representative concerning the litigation. FRCP 26(b)(3)(B).

- *Previous statement.* Any party or other person may, on request and without the required showing, obtain the person's own previous statement about the action or its subject matter. If the request is refused, the person may move for a court order, and FRCP 37(a)(5) applies to the award of expenses. A previous statement is either: (1) a written statement that the person has signed or otherwise adopted or approved; or (2) a contemporaneous stenographic, mechanical, electrical, or other recording—or a transcription of it—that recites substantially verbatim the person's oral statement. FRCP 26(b)(3)(C).

iv. *Trial preparation; Experts*

- *Deposition of an expert who may testify.* A party may depose any person who has been identified as an expert whose opinions may be presented at trial. If FRCP 26(a)(2)(B) requires a report from the expert, the deposition may be conducted only after the report is provided. FRCP 26(b)(4)(A).

- *Trial-preparation protection for draft reports or disclosures.* FRCP 26(b)(3)(A) and FRCP 26(b)(3)(B) protect drafts of any report or disclosure required under FRCP 26(a)(2), regardless of the form in which the draft is recorded. FRCP 26(b)(4)(B).

- *Trial-preparation protection for communications between a party's attorney and expert witnesses.* FRCP 26(b)(3)(A) and FRCP 26(b)(3)(B) protect communications between the party's attorney and any witness required to provide a report under FRCP 26(a)(2)(B), regardless of the form of the communications, except to the extent that the communications: (1) relate to compensation for the expert's study or testimony; (2) identify facts or data that the party's attorney provided and that the expert considered in forming the opinions to be expressed; or (3) identify assumptions that the party's attorney provided and that the expert relied on in forming the opinions to be expressed. FRCP 26(b)(4)(C).

- *Expert employed only for trial preparation.* Ordinarily, a party may not, by interrogatories or deposition, discover facts known or opinions held by an expert who has been retained or specially employed by another party in anticipation of litigation or to prepare for trial and who is not expected to be called as a witness at trial. But a party may do so only: (1) as provided in FRCP 35(b); or (2) on showing exceptional circumstances under which it is impracticable for the party to obtain facts or opinions on the same subject by other means. FRCP 26(b)(4)(D).

- *Payment.* Unless manifest injustice would result, the court must require that the party seeking discovery: (1) pay the expert a reasonable fee for time spent in responding to discovery under FRCP 26(b)(4)(A) or FRCP 26(b)(4)(D); and (2) for discovery under FRCP 26(b)(4)(D), also pay the other party a fair portion of the fees and expenses it reasonably incurred in obtaining the expert's facts and opinions. FRCP 26(b)(4)(E).

v. *Claiming privilege or protecting trial-preparation materials*

- *Information withheld.* When a party withholds information otherwise discoverable by claiming that the information is privileged or subject to protection as trial-preparation material, the party must: (1) expressly make the claim; and (2) describe the nature of the

431

documents, communications, or tangible things not produced or disclosed—and do so in a manner that, without revealing information itself privileged or protected, will enable other parties to assess the claim. FRCP 26(b)(5)(A).

- *Information produced.* If information produced in discovery is subject to a claim of privilege or of protection as trial-preparation material, the party making the claim may notify any party that received the information of the claim and the basis for it. After being notified, a party must promptly return, sequester, or destroy the specified information and any copies it has; must not use or disclose the information until the claim is resolved; must take reasonable steps to retrieve the information if the party disclosed it before being notified; and may promptly present the information to the court under seal for a determination of the claim. The producing party must preserve the information until the claim is resolved. FRCP 26(b)(5)(B).

b. *Protective orders.* A party or any person from whom discovery is sought may move for a protective order in the court where the action is pending—or as an alternative on matters relating to a deposition, in the court for the district where the deposition will be taken. FRCP 26(c)(1). Refer to the United States District Court for the Northern District of Indiana KeyRules Motion for Protective Order document for more information.

c. *Sequence of discovery.* Unless the parties stipulate or the court orders otherwise for the parties' and witnesses' convenience and in the interests of justice: (1) methods of discovery may be used in any sequence; and (2) discovery by one party does not require any other party to delay its discovery. FRCP 26(d)(3).

2. *Response to request for production of documents*

a. *Form.* A party responding (by answer or objection) to written discovery must: (1) fully quote each interrogatory or request immediately before the party's response; and (2) number each response to correspond with the interrogatory or request being responded to. IN R USDCTND L.R. 26-1(b).

b. *Responding to each item.* For each item or category, the response must either state that inspection and related activities will be permitted as requested or state with specificity the grounds for objecting to the request, including the reasons. The responding party may state that it will produce copies of documents or of electronically stored information instead of permitting inspection. The production must then be completed no later than the time for inspection specified in the request or another reasonable time specified in the response. FRCP 34(b)(2)(B).

c. *Objections.* A party may waive its objections to a request for production by failing to object in a timely and effective manner. FEDPROC § 26:645.

   i. An objection must state whether any responsive materials are being withheld on the basis of that objection. An objection to part of a request must specify the part and permit inspection of the rest. FRCP 34(b)(2)(C).

   ii. A response which raises no objection, but simply indicates that the information requested is "unknown" and that the records sought are "not maintained," is evasive and insufficient. FEDPROC § 26:648.

d. *Responding to a request for production of electronically stored information.* The response may state an objection to a requested form for producing electronically stored information. If the responding party objects to a requested form—or if no form was specified in the request—the party must state the form or forms it intends to use. FRCP 34(b)(2)(D).

e. *Producing the documents or electronically stored information.* Unless otherwise stipulated or ordered by the court, these procedures apply to producing documents or electronically stored information:

   i. A party must produce documents as they are kept in the usual course of business or must organize and label them to correspond to the categories in the request;

   ii. If a request does not specify a form for producing electronically stored information, a party must produce it in a form or forms in which it is ordinarily maintained or in a reasonably usable form or forms; and

iii. A party need not produce the same electronically stored information in more than one form. FRCP 34(b)(2)(E).

f. *Documents and things in possession, custody, or control.* FRCP 34 provides. . .that discovery may be had of documents and things that are in the "possession, custody, or control" of a party. FPP § 2210. The concept of "control" is very important in applying FRCP 34, but the application of this concept is often highly fact-specific. Inspection can be had if the party to whom the request is made has the legal right to obtain the document, even though in fact it has no copy. FPP § 2210.

    i. A party may be required to produce documents and things that it possesses even though they belong to a third person who is not a party to the action. FPP § 2210; Societe Internationale Pour Participations Industrielles Et Commerciales, S. A. v. Rogers, 357 U.S. 197, 78 S.Ct. 1087, 2 L.Ed.2d 1255 (1958). And if a party has possession, custody, or control, it must produce documents and things even though the documents and things are themselves beyond the jurisdiction of the court. FPP § 2210.

    ii. If a document or thing does not exist, it cannot be in the possession, custody, or control of a party and therefore cannot be produced for inspection. FEDPROC § 26:623.

    iii. Finally, lack of control may be considered an objection to the discovery request and, like any such objection, it may be waived. FPP § 2210.

g. *Documents made available to all parties.* Documents made available to one party to a suit must be made available to all parties. FEDPROC § 26:637.

h. *Attorney's duty to insure compliance.* An attorney representing a party in connection with a request for the production and inspection of documents pursuant to FRCP 34 has an obligation to verify that his or her client has produced the documents requested, and a further obligation to insure that records are kept indicating which documents have been produced. Failure to comply with these duties has been characterized as careless and inexcusable and has resulted in the imposition of sanctions. FEDPROC § 26:639.

3. *Supplementing disclosures and responses.* A party who has made a disclosure under FRCP 26(a)—or who has responded to an interrogatory, request for production, or request for admission—must supplement or correct its disclosure or response: (1) in a timely manner if the party learns that in some material respect the disclosure or response is incomplete or incorrect, and if the additional or corrective information has not otherwise been made known to the other parties during the discovery process or in writing; or (2) as ordered by the court. FRCP 26(e)(1).

4. *Sanctions for failure to cooperate in discovery.* The court where the action is pending may, on motion, order sanctions if a party, after being properly served with interrogatories under FRCP 33 or a request for inspection under FRCP 34, fails to serve its answers, objections, or written response. FRCP 37(d)(1)(A)(ii). If a motion to compel is granted, the court must, after giving an opportunity to be heard, require the party or deponent whose conduct necessitated the motion, the party or attorney advising that conduct, or both to pay the movant's reasonable expenses incurred in making the motion, including attorney's fees. But the court must not order this payment if the opposing party's nondisclosure, response, or objection was substantially justified. FRCP 37(a)(5)(A)(ii). Refer to the United States District Court for the Northern District of Indiana KeyRules Motion for Discovery Sanctions document for more information.

5. *Stipulations about discovery procedure.* Unless the court orders otherwise, the parties may stipulate that: (1) a deposition may be taken before any person, at any time or place, on any notice, and in the manner specified—in which event it may be used in the same way as any other deposition; and (2) other procedures governing or limiting discovery be modified—but a stipulation extending the time for any form of discovery must have court approval if it would interfere with the time set for completing discovery, for hearing a motion, or for trial. FRCP 29.

6. *Appearances.* Attorneys not representing the United States or its agencies must file an appearance when they represent (either in person or by filing a paper) a party. IN R USDCTND L.R. 83-8(a). For more information, refer to IN R USDCTND L.R. 83-8.

7. *Notice of related action.* A party must file a notice of related action as soon as it appears that the party's

case and another pending case: (1) arise out of the same transaction or occurrence; (2) involve the same property; or (3) involve the validity or infringement of the same patent, trademark, or copyright. IN R USDCTND L.R. 40-1(d). For more information, refer to IN R USDCTND L.R. 40-1.

8. *Alternative dispute resolution (ADR).* After they confer as required by FRCP 26(f), the parties must advise the court which, if any, alternative-dispute-resolution processes they expect to pursue and when they expect to undertake the process. IN R USDCTND L.R. 16-6(a). For more information on alternative dispute resolution (ADR), refer to IN R USDCTND L.R. 16-6 and IN R USDCTND Order 2003-21.

9. *Settlement or resolution.* The parties must immediately notify the court if they reasonably expect to settle the case or resolve a pending motion. IN R USDCTND L.R. 16-1(g).

10. *Modification or suspension of rules.* The court may, on its own motion or at the request of a party, suspend or modify any rule in a particular case in the interest of justice. IN R USDCTND L.R. 1-1(c).

D. Documents

1. *Required documents*

   a. *Response to request for production of documents.* Refer to the General Requirements section of this document for information on the response to request for production of documents.

2. *Supplemental documents*

   a. *Certificate of service.* FRCP 5(d) requires that the person making service under FRCP 5 certify that service has been effected. FRCP 5(Advisory Committee Notes). Having such information on file may be useful for many purposes, including proof of service if an issue arises concerning the effectiveness of the service. FRCP 5(Advisory Committee Notes).

E. Format

1. *Form of documents.* The rules governing captions and other matters of form in pleadings apply to motions and other papers. FRCP 7(b)(2).

   a. *Paper.* Any pleading, motion, brief, affidavit, notice, or proposed order, whether filed electronically or by delivering it to the clerk, must: use eight and one-half by eleven (8-1/2 x 11) inch pages. IN R USDCTND L.R. 5-4(a)(2).

      i. *Manual filings.* Papers delivered to the clerk for filing must: be flat, unfolded, and on good-quality, white paper. IN R USDCTND L.R. 5-4(b)(1)(A).

         • *Covers or backing.* Papers delivered to the clerk for filing must: not have a cover or a back. IN R USDCTND L.R. 5-4(b)(1)(B).

         • *Recycled paper.* The court encourages using recycled paper. IN R USDCTND L.R. 5-4(b)(7).

   b. *Margins.* Any pleading, motion, brief, affidavit, notice, or proposed order, whether filed electronically or by delivering it to the clerk, must: have at least one (1) inch margins. IN R USDCTND L.R. 5-4(a)(3).

   c. *Spacing.* Any pleading, motion, brief, affidavit, notice, or proposed order, whether filed electronically or by delivering it to the clerk, must: be double spaced (except for headings, footnotes, and quoted material). IN R USDCTND L.R. 5-4(a)(5).

   d. *Text.* Any pleading, motion, brief, affidavit, notice, or proposed order, whether filed electronically or by delivering it to the clerk, must: be plainly typewritten, printed, or prepared by a clearly legible copying process. IN R USDCTND L.R. 5-4(a)(1).

      i. Any pleading, motion, brief, affidavit, notice, or proposed order, whether filed electronically or by delivering it to the clerk, must: use at least twelve (12) point type in the body and at least ten (10) point type in footnotes. IN R USDCTND L.R. 5-4(a)(4).

   e. *Page numbering.* Any pleading, motion, brief, affidavit, notice, or proposed order, whether filed electronically or by delivering it to the clerk, must: have consecutively numbered pages. IN R USDCTND L.R. 5-4(a)(6).

   f. *Caption; Names of parties.* Every pleading must have a caption with the court's name, a title, a file number, and a FRCP 7(a) designation. The title of the complaint must name all the parties; the title of other pleadings, after naming the first party on each side, may refer generally to other parties. FRCP 10(a). Any pleading, motion, brief, affidavit, notice, or proposed order, whether filed electronically or by delivering it to the clerk, must: include a title on the first page. IN R USDCTND L.R. 5-4(a)(7).

g. *Filer's information.* Any pleading, motion, brief, affidavit, notice, or proposed order, whether filed electronically or by delivering it to the clerk, must: except in proposed orders and affidavits, include the filer's name, address, telephone number, fax number (where available), and e-mail address (where available). IN R USDCTND L.R. 5-4(a)(9).

h. *Paragraphs; Separate statements.* A party must state its claims or defenses in numbered paragraphs, each limited as far as practicable to a single set of circumstances. A later pleading may refer by number to a paragraph in an earlier pleading. If doing so would promote clarity, each claim founded on a separate transaction or occurrence—and each defense other than a denial—must be stated in a separate count or defense. FRCP 10(b).

i. *Adoption by reference; Exhibits.* A statement in a pleading may be adopted by reference elsewhere in the same pleading or in any other pleading or motion. A copy of a written instrument that is an exhibit to a pleading is a part of the pleading for all purposes. FRCP 10(c).

j. *Citation of local rules.* The Local Civil Rules of the United States District Court for the Northern District of Indiana may be cited as "N.D. Ind. L.R." IN R USDCTND L.R. 1-1(a)(1).

k. *Acceptance by the clerk.* The clerk must not refuse to file a paper solely because it is not in the form prescribed by the Federal Rules of Civil Procedure or by a local rule or practice. FRCP 5(d)(4).

   i. *Sanctions for formatting errors; Non-compliance.* If a person files a paper that does not comply with the rules governing the format of papers filed with the court, the court may: (1) strike the paper from the record; or (2) fine the person up to one thousand dollars ($1,000). IN R USDCTND L.R. 1-3(a).

      • *Notice.* Before sanctioning a person under IN R USDCTND L.R. 1-3(a)(2), the court must: (1) notify the person that the paper is noncompliant; and (2) give the person the opportunity either to be heard or to revise the paper. IN R USDCTND L.R. 1-3(b).

2. *Form of electronic documents.* Electronically filed documents must meet the same requirements of format and page limits as documents "conventionally filed" (as defined in IN R USDCTND CM/ECF(III)(A)) pursuant to the Federal Rules of Civil Procedure and the Local Civil Rules of the United States District Court for the Northern District of Indiana. IN R USDCTND CM/ECF(II)(A)(2).

a. *PDF format required.* Documents filed in the CM/ECF must be in .pdf format. A document created with almost any word-processing program can be converted to .pdf format. The .pdf program in effect takes a picture of the original document and allows anyone to open the converted document across a broad range of hardware and software, with layout, format, links, and images intact. IN R USDCTND CM/ECF(FN2).

b. *Title of documents.* The person electronically filing a pleading or other document will be responsible for designating a title for the pleading or other document by using one of the categories contained in the events listed in the CM/ECF Menu. IN R USDCTND CM/ECF(II)(G).

c. *Combining documents.* All documents which form part of a single pleading and which are being filed at the same time and by the same party may be electronically filed together under one document number, e.g., the motion and a supporting affidavit, with the exception of memoranda in support. Memoranda in support shall be electronically filed separately and shown as a related document to the motion. IN R USDCTND CM/ECF(II)(A)(4).

d. *Exhibits and attachments.* Filing users must submit in electronic form all documents referenced as exhibits or attachments, unless the court permits conventional filing. A filing user must submit as exhibits or attachments only those excerpts of the referenced documents that are directly germane to the matter under consideration by the court. Excerpted material must be clearly and prominently identified as such. Filing users who file excerpts of documents as exhibits or attachments do so without prejudice to their right to timely file additional excerpts or the complete document.

Responding parties may timely file additional excerpts or the complete document that they believe are directly germane. The court may require parties to file additional excerpts or the complete document. IN R USDCTND CM/ECF(II)(A)(6).

e. *Hyperlinks.* Electronically filed documents may contain hyperlink references to an external document as a convenient mechanism for accessing material cited in the document. A hyperlink reference is neither validated for content nor considered a part of the court's records. The court neither endorses the product or organization at the destination of a hyperlink reference, nor does the court exercise any responsibility over the content at the destination. In order to preserve the integrity of the court record, attorneys wishing to insert hyperlinks in court filings shall continue to use the traditional citation method for the cited authority, in addition to the hyperlink. A hyperlink contained in a filing is no more than a convenient mechanism for accessing material cited in the document and a hyperlink reference is extraneous to any filed document and is not part of the court's record. IN R USDCTND CM/ECF(II)(A)(3).

3. *Signing disclosures and discovery requests, responses, and objections.* FRCP 11 does not apply to disclosures and discovery requests, responses, objections, and motions under FRCP 26 through FRCP 37. FRCP 11(d).

  a. *Signature required.* Every disclosure under FRCP 26(a)(1) or FRCP 26(a)(3) and every discovery request, response, or objection must be signed by at least one attorney of record in the attorney's own name—or by the party personally, if unrepresented—and must state the signer's address, e-mail address, and telephone number. FRCP 26(g)(1).

   i. *Signatures on manual filings.* Papers delivered to the clerk for filing must: include the filer's original signature. IN R USDCTND L.R. 5-4(b)(1)(C).

     - *Rubber-stamped and faxed signatures.* An original paper with a rubber-stamped or faxed signature is unsigned for purposes of FRCP 11 and FRCP 26(g). IN R USDCTND L.R. 5-4(b)(2).

     - *Affidavits.* Only the affiant need sign an affidavit. IN R USDCTND L.R. 5-4(b)(3).

   ii. *Electronic signatures.* Pursuant to FRCP 11, every pleading, motion, and other paper (except lists, schedules, statements or amendments thereto) shall be signed by at least one attorney of record or, if the party is not represented by an attorney, all papers shall be signed by the party. An attorney's/participant's password issued by the court combined with the user's identification, serves as and constitutes the attorney/participant's signature for FRCP 11 and other purposes. IN R USDCTND CM/ECF(I)(C). Documents which must be filed and which must contain original signatures other than those of a participating attorney or which require either verification or an unsworn declaration under any rule or statute, shall be filed electronically, with originally executed copies maintained by the filer. The pleading or other document electronically filed shall contain "s/" signature(s), as noted in IN R USDCTND CM/ECF(II)(E)(3)(b). IN R USDCTND CM/ECF(II)(E)(1).

     - *Multiple signatures.* In the case of a stipulation or other document to be signed by two or more attorneys, the following procedure should be used: The filing attorney shall initially confirm that the content of the document is acceptable to all persons required to sign the document and shall obtain the physical signatures of all attorneys on the document. IN R USDCTND CM/ECF(II)(E)(3)(a). The filing attorney then shall file the document electronically, indicating the signatories, e.g., "s/Jane Doe," "s/John Doe," etc. IN R USDCTND CM/ECF(II)(E)(3)(b). The filing attorney shall retain the hard copy of the document containing the original signatures. IN R USDCTND CM/ECF(II)(E)(3)(c).

  b. *Effect of signature.* By signing, an attorney or party certifies that to the best of the person's knowledge, information, and belief formed after a reasonable inquiry:

   i. With respect to a disclosure, it is complete and correct as of the time it is made; and

   ii. With respect to a discovery request, response, or objection, it is:

     - Consistent with the Federal Rules of Civil Procedure and warranted by existing law or by a nonfrivolous argument for extending, modifying, or reversing existing law, or for establishing new law;

- Not interposed for any improper purpose, such as to harass, cause unnecessary delay, or needlessly increase the cost of litigation; and

- Neither unreasonable nor unduly burdensome or expensive, considering the needs of the case, prior discovery in the case, the amount in controversy, and the importance of the issues at stake in the action. FRCP 26(g)(1).

c. *Failure to sign.* Other parties have no duty to act on an unsigned disclosure, request, response, or objection until it is signed, and the court must strike it unless a signature is promptly supplied after the omission is called to the attorney's or party's attention. FRCP 26(g)(2).

d. *Sanction for improper certification.* If a certification violates FRCP 26(g) without substantial justification, the court, on motion or on its own, must impose an appropriate sanction on the signer, the party on whose behalf the signer was acting, or both. The sanction may include an order to pay the reasonable expenses, including attorney's fees, caused by the violation. FRCP 26(g)(3). Refer to the United States District Court for the Northern District of Indiana KeyRules Motion for Discovery Sanctions document for more information.

4. *Privacy protection for filings made with the court*

a. *Redacted filings.* Counsel should not include sensitive information in any document filed with the court unless such inclusion is necessary and relevant to the case. IN R USDCTND CM/ECF(VII). Unless the court orders otherwise, in an electronic or paper filing with the court that contains an individual's Social Security number, taxpayer-identification number, or birth date, the name of an individual known to be a minor, or a financial-account number, a party or nonparty making the filing may include only:

i. The last four (4) digits of the Social Security number and taxpayer-identification number;

ii. The year of the individual's birth;

iii. The minor's initials; and

iv. The last four (4) digits of the financial-account number. FRCP 5.2(a); IN R USDCTND Order 2005-3.

b. *Exemptions from the redaction requirement.* The redaction requirement does not apply to the following:

i. A financial-account number that identifies the property allegedly subject to forfeiture in a forfeiture proceeding;

ii. The record of an administrative or agency proceeding;

iii. The official record of a state-court proceeding;

iv. The record of a court or tribunal, if that record was not subject to the redaction requirement when originally filed;

v. A filing covered by FRCP 5.2(c) or FRCP 5.2(d); and

vi. A pro se filing in an action brought under 28 U.S.C.A. § 2241, 28 U.S.C.A. § 2254, or 28 U.S.C.A. § 2255. FRCP 5.2(b).

vii. In cases filed under the Social Security Act, 42 U.S.C.A. § 405(g), there is no need for redaction of any information from the documents filed in the case. IN R USDCTND Order 2005-3.

c. *Limitations on remote access to electronic files; Social Security appeals and immigration cases.* Unless the court orders otherwise, in an action for benefits under the Social Security Act, and in an action or proceeding relating to an order of removal, to relief from removal, or to immigration benefits or detention, access to an electronic file is authorized as follows:

i. The parties and their attorneys may have remote electronic access to any part of the case file, including the administrative record;

ii. Any other person may have electronic access to the full record at the courthouse, but may have remote electronic access only to:

- The docket maintained by the court; and

- An opinion, order, judgment, or other disposition of the court, but not any other part of the case file or the administrative record. FRCP 5.2(c).

d. *Filings made under seal.* The court may order that a filing be made under seal without redaction. The court may later unseal the filing or order the person who made the filing to file a redacted version for the public record. FRCP 5.2(d). For information on filing documents under seal, refer to IN R USDCTND L.R. 5-3, IN R USDCTND CM/ECF(IV)(A), and IN R USDCTND ECF Order 2004-19.

e. *Protective orders.* For good cause, the court may by order in a case:

   i. Require redaction of additional information; or

   ii. Limit or prohibit a nonparty's remote electronic access to a document filed with the court. FRCP 5.2(e).

f. *Option for additional unredacted filing under seal.* A person making a redacted filing may also file an unredacted copy under seal. The court must retain the unredacted copy as part of the record. FRCP 5.2(f); IN R USDCTND Order 2005-3.

   i. The unredacted version of the document or the reference list shall be retained by the court under seal as part of the record. This paper shall be retained by the court as part of the record. The court may, however, still require the party to file a redacted copy for the public file. IN R USDCTND Order 2005-3.

g. *Option for filing a reference list.* A filing that contains redacted information may be filed together with a reference list that identifies each item of redacted information and specifies an appropriate identifier that uniquely corresponds to each item listed. The list must be filed under seal and may be amended as of right. Any reference in the case to a listed identifier will be construed to refer to the corresponding item of information. FRCP 5.2(g); IN R USDCTND Order 2005-3.

   i. The unredacted version of the document or the reference list shall be retained by the court under seal as part of the record. This paper shall be retained by the court as part of the record. The court may, however, still require the party to file a redacted copy for the public file. IN R USDCTND Order 2005-3.

h. *Responsibility for redaction.* The responsibility for redacting these personal identifiers rests solely with counsel and the parties. The Clerk will not review each paper for compliance with IN R USDCTND Order 2005-3. IN R USDCTND Order 2005-3.

i. *Waiver of protection of identifiers.* A person waives the protection of FRCP 5.2(a) as to the person's own information by filing it without redaction and not under seal. FRCP 5.2(h).

F. Filing and Service Requirements

1. *Filing requirements.* Any paper after the complaint that is required to be served—together with a certificate of service—must be filed within a reasonable time after service. But disclosures under FRCP 26(a)(1) or FRCP 26(a)(2) and the following discovery requests and responses must not be filed until they are used in the proceeding or the court orders filing: depositions, interrogatories, requests for documents or tangible things or to permit entry onto land, and requests for admission. FRCP 5(d)(1). Refer to the United States District Court for the Northern District of Indiana KeyRules pleading and motion documents for information on filing with the court.

a. *Discovery ordinarily not filed.* The party who serves a discovery request or notices a deposition is the custodian of the original discovery response or deposition transcript. Except as required under IN R USDCTND L.R. 26-2(a)(2), parties must not file: (1) disclosures under FRCP 26(a)(1) or FRCP 26(a)(2); (2) deposition notices; (3) deposition transcripts; (4) interrogatories; (5) requests for documents, to permit entry upon land, or for admission; (6) answers to interrogatories; (7) responses to requests for documents, to permit entry upon land, or for admission; or (8) service-of-discovery notices. IN R USDCTND L.R. 26-2(a)(1).

   i. *Exceptions*

      - *Pro se litigation.* All discovery material in cases involving a pro se party must be filed. IN R USDCTND L.R. 26-2(a)(2)(A).

- *Specific material.* Discovery material must also be filed when: (1) the court orders; or (2) the material is used in a proceeding. IN R USDCTND L.R. 26-2(a)(2)(B).

b. *When discovery may be filed*

    i. *Filing materials with motion for relief.* A party who files a motion for relief under FRCP 26(c) or FRCP 37 must file with the motion those parts of the discovery requests or responses that the motion pertains to. IN R USDCTND L.R. 26-2(b).

    ii. *Materials necessary for motion.* A party must file those portions of discovery requests or responses (including deposition transcripts) that the party relies on to support a motion that could result in a final order on an issue. IN R USDCTND L.R. 26-2(c).

    iii. *Materials to be used at trial.* A party who reasonably anticipates using discovery requests or responses—including deposition transcripts—at trial must file the relevant portions of the requests or responses with the clerk at the start of the trial. IN R USDCTND L.R. 26-2(d).

2. *Service requirements.* The response must be served on all the parties to the action, unless the court otherwise orders, rather than only on the requesting party. FPP § 2213.

a. *Service; When required*

    i. *In general.* Unless the Federal Rules of Civil Procedure provide otherwise, each of the following papers must be served on every party:

- An order stating that service is required;
- A pleading filed after the original complaint, unless the court orders otherwise under FRCP 5(c) because there are numerous defendants;
- A discovery paper required to be served on a party, unless the court orders otherwise;
- A written motion, except one that may be heard ex parte; and
- A written notice, appearance, demand, or offer of judgment, or any similar paper. FRCP 5(a)(1).

    ii. *If a party fails to appear.* No service is required on a party who is in default for failing to appear. But a pleading that asserts a new claim for relief against such a party must be served on that party under FRCP 4. FRCP 5(a)(2).

    iii. *Seizing property.* If an action is begun by seizing property and no person is or need be named as a defendant, any service required before the filing of an appearance, answer, or claim must be made on the person who had custody or possession of the property when it was seized. FRCP 5(a)(3).

b. *Service; How made*

    i. *Serving an attorney.* If a party is represented by an attorney, service under FRCP 5 must be made on the attorney unless the court orders service on the party. FRCP 5(b)(1).

    ii. *Service in general.* A paper is served under FRCP 5 by:

- Handing it to the person;
- Leaving it: (1) at the person's office with a clerk or other person in charge or, if no one is in charge, in a conspicuous place in the office; or (2) if the person has no office or the office is closed, at the person's dwelling or usual place of abode with someone of suitable age and discretion who resides there;
- Mailing it to the person's last known address—in which event service is complete upon mailing;
- Leaving it with the court clerk if the person has no known address;
- Sending it by electronic means if the person consented in writing—in which event service is complete upon transmission, but is not effective if the serving party learns that it did not reach the person to be served; or
- Delivering it by any other means that the person consented to in writing—in which event

service is complete when the person making service delivers it to the agency designated to make delivery. FRCP 5(b)(2).

iii. *Electronic service.* Electronically filed papers may be served electronically if service is consistent with the CM/ECF User Manual (IN R USDCTND CM/ECF). IN R USDCTND L.R. 5-2(a).

- *Waiver of other service.* An attorney's registration will constitute a waiver of conventional service of documents and the attorney agrees to accept service of notice on behalf of the client of the electronic filing by hand, facsimile or authorized email. IN R USDCTND CM/ECF(I)(B)(3).

- *Serving registered persons.* The System will generate a "Notice of Electronic Filing" when any document is filed. This notice represents service of the document on parties who are registered participants with the System. Except as provided in IN R USDCTND CM/ECF(III)(B), the filing party shall not be required to serve any pleading or other documents on any party receiving electronic notice. IN R USDCTND CM/ECF(II)(D)(1). The term "pleading" refers only to those documents listed in FRCP 7(a). IN R USDCTND CM/ECF(FN3).

- *When electronic service is deemed completed.* A person registered to use the court's electronic-filing system is served with an electronically filed paper when a "Notice of Electronic Filing" is transmitted to that person through the court's electronic filing-system. IN R USDCTND L.R. 5-2(b).

- *Serving non-registered persons.* A person who has not registered to use the court's electronic-filing system but who is entitled to service of a paper must be served according to the Local Civil Rules of the United States District Court for the Northern District of Indiana and the Federal Rules of Civil Procedure. IN R USDCTND L.R. 5-2(c); IN R USDCTND CM/ECF(II)(D)(2). If such service of a paper copy is to be made, it shall be done in the manner provided in the Federal Rules of Civil Procedure and the Local Civil Rules of the United States District Court for the Northern District of Indiana. IN R USDCTND CM/ECF(II)(D)(2).

iv. *Service of conventional filings.* Pleadings or other documents which are filed conventionally rather than electronically shall be served in the manner provided for in the Federal Rules of Civil Procedure and the Local Civil Rules of the United States District Court for the Northern District of Indiana, except as otherwise provided by order of the Court. IN R USDCTND CM/ECF(III)(B).

v. *Using court facilities.* If a local rule so authorizes, a party may use the court's transmission facilities to make service under FRCP 5(b)(2)(E). FRCP 5(b)(3).

c. *Serving numerous defendants*

i. *In general.* If an action involves an unusually large number of defendants, the court may, on motion or on its own, order that:

- Defendants' pleadings and replies to them need not be served on other defendants;

- Any crossclaim, counterclaim, avoidance, or affirmative defense in those pleadings and replies to them will be treated as denied or avoided by all other parties; and

- Filing any such pleading and serving it on the plaintiff constitutes notice of the pleading to all parties. FRCP 5(c)(1).

ii. *Notifying parties.* A copy of every such order must be served on the parties as the court directs. FRCP 5(c)(2).

G. Hearings

1. There is no hearing contemplated in the federal statutes or rules for responses to requests for production of documents.

H. Forms

1. Federal Response to Request for Production of Documents Forms

a. Response; To request for production of documents and other items. AMJUR PP DEPOSITION § 523.

b. Response; To request for production and inspection of documents and other items. AMJUR PP DEPOSITION § 524.

c. Verification; By defendant; Of response to request for production of documents and other items. AMJUR PP DEPOSITION § 525.

d. Response; To request for inspection. AMJUR PP DEPOSITION § 526.

e. Response; To request for production of documents; Objection; Documents not within objecting party's possession. AMJUR PP DEPOSITION § 597.

f. Response; To request for production of documents; Objection; Documents within attorney-client privilege. AMJUR PP DEPOSITION § 598.

g. Response; To request for production of documents prepared in anticipation of litigation; Objection; Requestor may easily obtain information elsewhere. AMJUR PP DEPOSITION § 599.

h. Response to request for production. 3A FEDFORMS § 3564.

i. Response to request for production of documents; Government personnel files, memoranda, minutes of meetings and statistics. 3A FEDFORMS § 3565.

j. Response; To request for production of documents and things. FEDPROF § 23:414.

k. Response; To request for production of documents; With various objections. FEDPROF § 23:415.

l. Response to request for production of documents and things; Government records. FEDPROF § 23:416.

m. Objection; To request for production of documents; Documents not within objecting party's possession. FEDPROF § 23:417.

n. Objection; To request for production of documents; Documents within attorney-client privilege. FEDPROF § 23:418.

o. Objection; To request for production of documents prepared in anticipation of litigation; Requestor may easily obtain information elsewhere. FEDPROF § 23:419.

p. Objection; To request for production of documents; Documents do not exist. FEDPROF § 23:420.

q. First notice for production; Response. GOLDLTGFMS § 28:30.

I. Applicable Rules

1. *Federal rules*

   a. Serving and filing pleadings and other papers. FRCP 5.

   b. Privacy protection for filings made with the court. FRCP 5.2.

   c. Computing and extending time; Time for motion papers. FRCP 6.

   d. Pleadings allowed; Form of motions and other papers. FRCP 7.

   e. Form of pleadings. FRCP 10.

   f. Signing pleadings, motions, and other papers; Representations to the court; Sanctions. FRCP 11.

   g. Duty to disclose; General provisions governing discovery. FRCP 26.

   h. Stipulations about discovery procedure. FRCP 29.

   i. Producing documents, electronically stored information, and tangible things, or entering onto land, for inspection and other purposes. FRCP 34.

   j. Failure to make disclosures or to cooperate in discovery; Sanctions. FRCP 37.

2. *Local rules*

   a. Citation and scope of the rules. IN R USDCTND L.R. 1-1.

b. Sanctions for formatting errors. IN R USDCTND L.R. 1-3.

c. Electronic service. IN R USDCTND L.R. 5-2.

d. Format of papers. IN R USDCTND L.R. 5-4.

e. Extensions of time. IN R USDCTND L.R. 6-1.

f. Pretrial procedure. IN R USDCTND L.R. 16-1.

g. Alternative dispute resolution. IN R USDCTND L.R. 16-6.

h. Form of certain discovery documents. IN R USDCTND L.R. 26-1.

i. Filing of discovery and other materials. IN R USDCTND L.R. 26-2.

j. Case assignment. IN R USDCTND L.R. 40-1.

k. Appearance and withdrawal of appearance. IN R USDCTND L.R. 83-8.

l. CM/ECF civil and criminal user manual. IN R USDCTND CM/ECF.

m. In re: privacy and public access to civil electronic case files. IN R USDCTND Order 2005-3.

Requests, Notices and Applications
Request for Admissions

Document Last Updated December 2016

A. Checklist

(I) ❑ Matters to be considered by requesting party

    (a) ❑ Required documents

        (1) ❑ Request for admissions

    (b) ❑ Supplemental documents

        (1) ❑ Document(s)

        (2) ❑ Certificate of service

    (c) ❑ Timing

        (1) ❑ A party may not seek discovery from any source before the parties have conferred as required by FRCP 26(f), except in a proceeding exempted from initial disclosure under FRCP 26(a)(1)(B), or when authorized by the Federal Rules of Civil Procedure, by stipulation, or by court order

(II) ❑ Matters to be considered by responding party

    (a) ❑ Required documents

        (1) ❑ Response to request for admissions

    (b) ❑ Supplemental documents

        (1) ❑ Certificate of service

    (c) ❑ Timing

        (1) ❑ A matter is admitted unless, within thirty (30) days after being served, the party to whom the request is directed serves on the requesting party a written answer or objection addressed to the matter and signed by the party or its attorney

B. Timing

1. *Request for admissions.* Without leave of court or written stipulation, requests for admission may not be served before the time specified in FRCP 26(d). FEDPROC § 26:706.

2. *Timing of discovery, generally.* A party may not seek discovery from any source before the parties have conferred as required by FRCP 26(f), except in a proceeding exempted from initial disclosure under

FRCP 26(a)(1)(B), or when authorized by the Federal Rules of Civil Procedure, by stipulation, or by court order. FRCP 26(d)(1).

3. *Computation of time*

    a. *Computing time.* FRCP 6 applies in computing any time period specified in the Federal Rules of Civil Procedure, in any local rule or court order, or in any statute that does not specify a method of computing time. FRCP 6(a).

        i. *Period stated in days or a longer unit.* When the period is stated in days or a longer unit of time:

- Exclude the day of the event that triggers the period;
- Count every day, including intermediate Saturdays, Sundays, and legal holidays; and
- Include the last day of the period, but if the last day is a Saturday, Sunday, or legal holiday, the period continues to run until the end of the next day that is not a Saturday, Sunday, or legal holiday. FRCP 6(a)(1).

        ii. *Period stated in hours.* When the period is stated in hours:

- Begin counting immediately on the occurrence of the event that triggers the period;
- Count every hour, including hours during intermediate Saturdays, Sundays, and legal holidays; and
- If the period would end on a Saturday, Sunday, or legal holiday, the period continues to run until the same time on the next day that is not a Saturday, Sunday, or legal holiday. FRCP 6(a)(2).

        iii. *Inaccessibility of the clerk's office.* Unless the court orders otherwise, if the clerk's office is inaccessible:

- On the last day for filing under FRCP 6(a)(1), then the time for filing is extended to the first accessible day that is not a Saturday, Sunday, or legal holiday; or
- During the last hour for filing under FRCP 6(a)(2), then the time for filing is extended to the same time on the first accessible day that is not a Saturday, Sunday, or legal holiday. FRCP 6(a)(3).

        iv. *"Last day" defined.* Unless a different time is set by a statute, local rule, or court order, the last day ends:

- For electronic filing, at midnight in the court's time zone; and
- For filing by other means, when the clerk's office is scheduled to close. FRCP 6(a)(4).

        v. *"Next day" defined.* The "next day" is determined by continuing to count forward when the period is measured after an event and backward when measured before an event. FRCP 6(a)(5).

        vi. *"Legal holiday" defined.* "Legal holiday" means:

- The day set aside by statute for observing New Year's Day, Martin Luther King Jr.'s Birthday, Washington's Birthday, Memorial Day, Independence Day, Labor Day, Columbus Day, Veterans' Day, Thanksgiving Day, or Christmas Day;
- Any day declared a holiday by the President or Congress; and
- For periods that are measured after an event, any other day declared a holiday by the state where the district court is located. FRCP 6(a)(6).

    b. *Computation of electronic filing deadlines.* Filing documents electronically does not alter any filing deadlines or any time computation pursuant to FRCP 6. The counties of Lake, Porter, LaPorte, Pulaski and Starke are located in the Central time zone and the remaining counties in the Northern District of Indiana are located in the Eastern time zone. Nevertheless, all electronic transmissions of documents must be completed (i.e., received completely by the clerk's office) prior to midnight Eastern Time, (South Bend/Fort Wayne/Lafayette time) in order to be considered timely filed that day, regardless of the local time in the division where the case is pending. Although documents can be filed electronically twenty-four (24) hours a day, filers are strongly encouraged to file all

documents during hours when the CM/ECF Help Line is available, from 9:00 a.m. to 4:00 p.m. local time. IN R USDCTND CM/ECF(II)(I).

    i. *Technical failures.* If the attorney is unable to file a document in a timely manner due to technical difficulties in the user's system, the attorney must file a document with the court as soon as possible notifying the court of the inability to file the document. A sample document entitled Declaration that Party was Unable to File in a Timely Manner Due to Technical Difficulties is attached hereto as Form 5. IN R USDCTND CM/ECF(VI)(B). [Editor's note: the reference to Form 5 is likely meant to be a reference to Form 3 (IN R USDCTND CM/ECF(Form 3)].

  c. *Extending time*

    i. *In general.* When an act may or must be done within a specified time, the court may, for good cause, extend the time:

- With or without motion or notice if the court acts, or if a request is made, before the original time or its extension expires; or

- On motion made after the time has expired if the party failed to act because of excusable neglect. FRCP 6(b)(1).

    ii. *Exceptions.* A court must not extend the time to act under FRCP 50(b), FRCP 50(d), FRCP 52(b), FRCP 59(b), FRCP 59(d), FRCP 59(e), and FRCP 60(b). FRCP 6(b)(2).

    iii. Refer to the United States District Court for the Northern District of Indiana KeyRules Motion for Continuance/Extension of Time document for more information on extending time.

  d. *Additional time after certain kinds of service.* When a party may or must act within a specified time after being served and service is made under FRCP 5(b)(2)(C) (mail), FRCP 5(b)(2)(D) (leaving with the clerk), or FRCP 5(b)(2)(F) (other means consented to), three (3) days are added after the period would otherwise expire under FRCP 6(a). FRCP 6(d).

C. General Requirements

1. *General provisions governing discovery*

  a. *Discovery scope and limits*

    i. *Scope in general.* Unless otherwise limited by court order, the scope of discovery is as follows: Parties may obtain discovery regarding any nonprivileged matter that is relevant to any party's claim or defense and proportional to the needs of the case, considering the importance of the issues at stake in the action, the amount in controversy, the parties' relative access to relevant information, the parties' resources, the importance of the discovery in resolving the issues, and whether the burden or expense of the proposed discovery outweighs its likely benefit. Information within this scope of discovery need not be admissible in evidence to be discoverable. FRCP 26(b)(1).

    ii. *Limitations on frequency and extent*

- *When permitted.* By order, the court may alter the limits in the Federal Rules of Civil Procedure on the number of depositions and interrogatories or on the length of depositions under FRCP 30. By order or local rule, the court may also limit the number of requests under FRCP 36. FRCP 26(b)(2)(A).

- *Specific limitations on electronically stored information.* A party need not provide discovery of electronically stored information from sources that the party identifies as not reasonably accessible because of undue burden or cost. On motion to compel discovery or for a protective order, the party from whom discovery is sought must show that the information is not reasonably accessible because of undue burden or cost. If that showing is made, the court may nonetheless order discovery from such sources if the requesting party shows good cause, considering the limitations of FRCP 26(b)(2)(C). The court may specify conditions for the discovery. FRCP 26(b)(2)(B).

- *When required.* On motion or on its own, the court must limit the frequency or extent of discovery otherwise allowed by the Federal Rules of Civil Procedure or by local rule if it determines that: (1) the discovery sought is unreasonably cumulative or duplicative, or can be obtained from some other source that is more convenient, less burdensome, or less expensive; (2) the party seeking discovery has had ample opportunity to obtain the information by discovery in the action; or (3) the proposed discovery is outside the scope permitted by FRCP 26(b)(1). FRCP 26(b)(2)(C).

iii. *Trial preparation; Materials*

- *Documents and tangible things.* Ordinarily, a party may not discover documents and tangible things that are prepared in anticipation of litigation or for trial by or for another party or its representative (including the other party's attorney, consultant, surety, indemnitor, insurer, or agent). But, subject to FRCP 26(b)(4), those materials may be discovered if: (1) they are otherwise discoverable under FRCP 26(b)(1); and (2) the party shows that it has substantial need for the materials to prepare its case and cannot, without undue hardship, obtain their substantial equivalent by other means. FRCP 26(b)(3)(A).

- *Protection against disclosure.* If the court orders discovery of those materials, it must protect against disclosure of the mental impressions, conclusions, opinions, or legal theories of a party's attorney or other representative concerning the litigation. FRCP 26(b)(3)(B).

- *Previous statement.* Any party or other person may, on request and without the required showing, obtain the person's own previous statement about the action or its subject matter. If the request is refused, the person may move for a court order, and FRCP 37(a)(5) applies to the award of expenses. A previous statement is either: (1) a written statement that the person has signed or otherwise adopted or approved; or (2) a contemporaneous stenographic, mechanical, electrical, or other recording—or a transcription of it—that recites substantially verbatim the person's oral statement. FRCP 26(b)(3)(C).

iv. *Trial preparation; Experts*

- *Deposition of an expert who may testify.* A party may depose any person who has been identified as an expert whose opinions may be presented at trial. If FRCP 26(a)(2)(B) requires a report from the expert, the deposition may be conducted only after the report is provided. FRCP 26(b)(4)(A).

- *Trial-preparation protection for draft reports or disclosures.* FRCP 26(b)(3)(A) and FRCP 26(b)(3)(B) protect drafts of any report or disclosure required under FRCP 26(a)(2), regardless of the form in which the draft is recorded. FRCP 26(b)(4)(B).

- *Trial-preparation protection for communications between a party's attorney and expert witnesses.* FRCP 26(b)(3)(A) and FRCP 26(b)(3)(B) protect communications between the party's attorney and any witness required to provide a report under FRCP 26(a)(2)(B), regardless of the form of the communications, except to the extent that the communications: (1) relate to compensation for the expert's study or testimony; (2) identify facts or data that the party's attorney provided and that the expert considered in forming the opinions to be expressed; or (3) identify assumptions that the party's attorney provided and that the expert relied on in forming the opinions to be expressed. FRCP 26(b)(4)(C).

- *Expert employed only for trial preparation.* Ordinarily, a party may not, by interrogatories or deposition, discover facts known or opinions held by an expert who has been retained or specially employed by another party in anticipation of litigation or to prepare for trial and who is not expected to be called as a witness at trial. But a party may do so only: (1) as provided in FRCP 35(b); or (2) on showing exceptional circumstances under which it is impracticable for the party to obtain facts or opinions on the same subject by other means. FRCP 26(b)(4)(D).

- *Payment.* Unless manifest injustice would result, the court must require that the party seeking discovery: (1) pay the expert a reasonable fee for time spent in responding to discovery under FRCP 26(b)(4)(A) or FRCP 26(b)(4)(D); and (2) for discovery under

FRCP 26(b)(4)(D), also pay the other party a fair portion of the fees and expenses it reasonably incurred in obtaining the expert's facts and opinions. FRCP 26(b)(4)(E).

v. *Claiming privilege or protecting trial-preparation materials*

- *Information withheld.* When a party withholds information otherwise discoverable by claiming that the information is privileged or subject to protection as trial-preparation material, the party must: (1) expressly make the claim; and (2) describe the nature of the documents, communications, or tangible things not produced or disclosed—and do so in a manner that, without revealing information itself privileged or protected, will enable other parties to assess the claim. FRCP 26(b)(5)(A).

- *Information produced.* If information produced in discovery is subject to a claim of privilege or of protection as trial-preparation material, the party making the claim may notify any party that received the information of the claim and the basis for it. After being notified, a party must promptly return, sequester, or destroy the specified information and any copies it has; must not use or disclose the information until the claim is resolved; must take reasonable steps to retrieve the information if the party disclosed it before being notified; and may promptly present the information to the court under seal for a determination of the claim. The producing party must preserve the information until the claim is resolved. FRCP 26(b)(5)(B).

b. *Protective orders.* A party or any person from whom discovery is sought may move for a protective order in the court where the action is pending—or as an alternative on matters relating to a deposition, in the court for the district where the deposition will be taken. FRCP 26(c)(1). Refer to the United States District Court for the Northern District of Indiana KeyRules Motion for Protective Order document for more information.

c. *Sequence of discovery.* Unless the parties stipulate or the court orders otherwise for the parties' and witnesses' convenience and in the interests of justice: (1) methods of discovery may be used in any sequence; and (2) discovery by one party does not require any other party to delay its discovery. FRCP 26(d)(3).

2. *Request for admissions*

a. *Scope.* A party may serve on any other party a written request to admit, for purposes of the pending action only, the truth of any matters within the scope of FRCP 26(b)(1) relating to: (1) facts, the application of law to fact, or opinions about either; and (2) the genuineness of any described documents. FRCP 36(a)(1).

   i. A party may serve a request for admission even though the party has the burden of proving the matters asserted therein because FRCP 36 permits requests for admission to address claims of the party seeking discovery, and generally, the party asserting a claim bears the burden of proof thereon. FEDPROC § 26:715.

b. *Number.* FRCP 36 does not limit a party to a single request, or set of requests, for admissions. But FRCP 26(b)(2)(A) authorizes courts to limit the number of requests by order or local rule. In addition, the court has power to protect a party from harassment by repeated requests for admissions, but will not bar such repeated requests when the circumstances of the case justify them. Even a second request about the same fact or the genuineness of the same document is permissible if circumstances warrant a renewed request. FPP § 2258.

   i. *Limit on requests for admission.* Ordinarily, a party may not serve more than thirty (30) requests for admission on another party (not counting requests that relate to the authenticity of a document). A party wanting to serve more requests must file a motion setting forth the proposed additional requests and why they are necessary. IN R USDCTND L.R. 26-1(c).

c. *Form.* A party propounding written discovery under FRCP 33, FRCP 34, or FRCP 36 must number each interrogatory or request sequentially. IN R USDCTND L.R. 26-1(a). Each matter must be separately stated. FRCP 36(a)(2). The party called upon to respond should not be required to go through a document and assume the responsibility of determining what facts it is being requested to admit. FPP § 2258. Each request for an admission should be phrased simply and directly so that it can be admitted or denied without explanation. FPP § 2258; United Coal Cos. v. Powell Const. Co., 839 F.2d 958, 968 (3d Cir. 1988).

    i.   A request for an admission need not state the source of information about the matter for which the request is made. FPP § 2258.

d.   *Effect of an admission; Withdrawing or amending it.* A matter admitted under FRCP 36 is conclusively established unless the court, on motion, permits the admission to be withdrawn or amended. Subject to FRCP 16(e), the court may permit withdrawal or amendment if it would promote the presentation of the merits of the action and if the court is not persuaded that it would prejudice the requesting party in maintaining or defending the action on the merits. An admission under FRCP 36 is not an admission for any other purpose and cannot be used against the party in any other proceeding. FRCP 36(b).

e.   *Motion to compel.* The motion to compel discovery provided by FRCP 37(a) does not apply to a failure to respond to a request for admissions. The automatic admission from a failure to respond is a sufficient remedy for the party who made the request. If, however, a request is objected to, or the requesting party thinks that a response to a request is insufficient, it may move under FRCP 36(a)(6) to determine the sufficiency of the answers or objections. FPP § 2265.

f.   *Motion regarding the sufficiency of an answer or objection.* The requesting party may move to determine the sufficiency of an answer or objection. Unless the court finds an objection justified, it must order that an answer be served. On finding that an answer does not comply with FRCP 36, the court may order either that the matter is admitted or that an amended answer be served. The court may defer its final decision until a pretrial conference or a specified time before trial. FRCP 37(a)(5) applies to an award of expenses. FRCP 36(a)(6). Refer to the United States District Court for the Northern District of Indiana KeyRules Motion for Discovery Sanctions document for more information on sanctions.

3.   *Sanctions for failure to cooperate in discovery.* The pattern of sanctions for FRCP 36 is somewhat different from that for the other discovery rules. The most important sanctions are two:

    a.   A failure to respond to a request is deemed an admission of the matter to which the request is directed; and

    b.   A party who, without good reason, refuses to admit a matter will be required to pay the costs incurred in proving that matter. FPP § 2265. If a party fails to admit what is requested under FRCP 36 and if the requesting party later proves a document to be genuine or the matter true, the requesting party may move that the party who failed to admit pay the reasonable expenses, including attorney's fees, incurred in making that proof. The court must so order unless:

       i.   The request was held objectionable under FRCP 36(a);

       ii.   The admission sought was of no substantial importance;

       iii.   The party failing to admit had a reasonable ground to believe that it might prevail on the matter; or

       iv.   There was other good reason for the failure to admit. FRCP 37(c)(2).

    c.   Refer to the United States District Court for the Northern District of Indiana KeyRules Motion for Discovery Sanctions document for more information on sanctions.

4.   *Stipulations about discovery procedure.* Unless the court orders otherwise, the parties may stipulate that: (1) a deposition may be taken before any person, at any time or place, on any notice, and in the manner specified—in which event it may be used in the same way as any other deposition; and (2) other procedures governing or limiting discovery be modified—but a stipulation extending the time for any form of discovery must have court approval if it would interfere with the time set for completing discovery, for hearing a motion, or for trial. FRCP 29.

5.   *Appearances.* Attorneys not representing the United States or its agencies must file an appearance when they represent (either in person or by filing a paper) a party. IN R USDCTND L.R. 83-8(a). For more information, refer to IN R USDCTND L.R. 83-8.

6.   *Notice of related action.* A party must file a notice of related action as soon as it appears that the party's

case and another pending case: (1) arise out of the same transaction or occurrence; (2) involve the same property; or (3) involve the validity or infringement of the same patent, trademark, or copyright. IN R USDCTND L.R. 40-1(d). For more information, refer to IN R USDCTND L.R. 40-1.

7. *Alternative dispute resolution (ADR).* After they confer as required by FRCP 26(f), the parties must advise the court which, if any, alternative-dispute-resolution processes they expect to pursue and when they expect to undertake the process. IN R USDCTND L.R. 16-6(a). For more information on alternative dispute resolution (ADR), refer to IN R USDCTND L.R. 16-6 and IN R USDCTND Order 2003-21.

8. *Settlement or resolution.* The parties must immediately notify the court if they reasonably expect to settle the case or resolve a pending motion. IN R USDCTND L.R. 16-1(g).

9. *Modification or suspension of rules.* The court may, on its own motion or at the request of a party, suspend or modify any rule in a particular case in the interest of justice. IN R USDCTND L.R. 1-1(c).

D. Documents

1. *Required documents*

   a. *Request for admissions.* Refer to the General Requirements section of this document for information on the request for admissions.

2. *Supplemental documents*

   a. *Document(s).* A request to admit the genuineness of a document must be accompanied by a copy of the document unless it is, or has been, otherwise furnished or made available for inspection and copying. FRCP 36(a)(2).

   b. *Certificate of service.* FRCP 5(d) requires that the person making service under FRCP 5 certify that service has been effected. FRCP 5(Advisory Committee Notes). Having such information on file may be useful for many purposes, including proof of service if an issue arises concerning the effectiveness of the service. FRCP 5(Advisory Committee Notes).

E. Format

1. *Form of documents.* The rules governing captions and other matters of form in pleadings apply to motions and other papers. FRCP 7(b)(2).

   a. *Paper.* Any pleading, motion, brief, affidavit, notice, or proposed order, whether filed electronically or by delivering it to the clerk, must: use eight and one-half by eleven (8-1/2 x 11) inch pages. IN R USDCTND L.R. 5-4(a)(2).

      i. *Manual filings.* Papers delivered to the clerk for filing must: be flat, unfolded, and on good-quality, white paper. IN R USDCTND L.R. 5-4(b)(1)(A).

         - *Covers or backing.* Papers delivered to the clerk for filing must: not have a cover or a back. IN R USDCTND L.R. 5-4(b)(1)(B).

         - *Recycled paper.* The court encourages using recycled paper. IN R USDCTND L.R. 5-4(b)(7).

   b. *Margins.* Any pleading, motion, brief, affidavit, notice, or proposed order, whether filed electronically or by delivering it to the clerk, must: have at least one (1) inch margins. IN R USDCTND L.R. 5-4(a)(3).

   c. *Spacing.* Any pleading, motion, brief, affidavit, notice, or proposed order, whether filed electronically or by delivering it to the clerk, must: be double spaced (except for headings, footnotes, and quoted material). IN R USDCTND L.R. 5-4(a)(5).

   d. *Text.* Any pleading, motion, brief, affidavit, notice, or proposed order, whether filed electronically or by delivering it to the clerk, must: be plainly typewritten, printed, or prepared by a clearly legible copying process. IN R USDCTND L.R. 5-4(a)(1).

      i. Any pleading, motion, brief, affidavit, notice, or proposed order, whether filed electronically or by delivering it to the clerk, must: use at least twelve (12) point type in the body and at least ten (10) point type in footnotes. IN R USDCTND L.R. 5-4(a)(4).

   e. *Page numbering.* Any pleading, motion, brief, affidavit, notice, or proposed order, whether filed electronically or by delivering it to the clerk, must: have consecutively numbered pages. IN R USDCTND L.R. 5-4(a)(6).

f.   *Caption; Names of parties.* Every pleading must have a caption with the court's name, a title, a file number, and a FRCP 7(a) designation. The title of the complaint must name all the parties; the title of other pleadings, after naming the first party on each side, may refer generally to other parties. FRCP 10(a). Any pleading, motion, brief, affidavit, notice, or proposed order, whether filed electronically or by delivering it to the clerk, must: include a title on the first page. IN R USDCTND L.R. 5-4(a)(7).

g.   *Filer's information.* Any pleading, motion, brief, affidavit, notice, or proposed order, whether filed electronically or by delivering it to the clerk, must: except in proposed orders and affidavits, include the filer's name, address, telephone number, fax number (where available), and e-mail address (where available). IN R USDCTND L.R. 5-4(a)(9).

h.   *Paragraphs; Separate statements.* A party must state its claims or defenses in numbered paragraphs, each limited as far as practicable to a single set of circumstances. A later pleading may refer by number to a paragraph in an earlier pleading. If doing so would promote clarity, each claim founded on a separate transaction or occurrence—and each defense other than a denial—must be stated in a separate count or defense. FRCP 10(b).

i.   *Adoption by reference; Exhibits.* A statement in a pleading may be adopted by reference elsewhere in the same pleading or in any other pleading or motion. A copy of a written instrument that is an exhibit to a pleading is a part of the pleading for all purposes. FRCP 10(c).

j.   *Citation of local rules.* The Local Civil Rules of the United States District Court for the Northern District of Indiana may be cited as "N.D. Ind. L.R." IN R USDCTND L.R. 1-1(a)(1).

k.   *Acceptance by the clerk.* The clerk must not refuse to file a paper solely because it is not in the form prescribed by the Federal Rules of Civil Procedure or by a local rule or practice. FRCP 5(d)(4).

  i.   *Sanctions for formatting errors; Non-compliance.* If a person files a paper that does not comply with the rules governing the format of papers filed with the court, the court may: (1) strike the paper from the record; or (2) fine the person up to one thousand dollars ($1,000). IN R USDCTND L.R. 1-3(a).

   • *Notice.* Before sanctioning a person under IN R USDCTND L.R. 1-3(a)(2), the court must: (1) notify the person that the paper is noncompliant; and (2) give the person the opportunity either to be heard or to revise the paper. IN R USDCTND L.R. 1-3(b).

2.   *Form of electronic documents.* Electronically filed documents must meet the same requirements of format and page limits as documents "conventionally filed" (as defined in IN R USDCTND CM/ECF(III)(A)) pursuant to the Federal Rules of Civil Procedure and the Local Civil Rules of the United States District Court for the Northern District of Indiana. IN R USDCTND CM/ECF(II)(A)(2).

a.   *PDF format required.* Documents filed in the CM/ECF must be in .pdf format. A document created with almost any word-processing program can be converted to .pdf format. The .pdf program in effect takes a picture of the original document and allows anyone to open the converted document across a broad range of hardware and software, with layout, format, links, and images intact. IN R USDCTND CM/ECF(FN2).

b.   *Title of documents.* The person electronically filing a pleading or other document will be responsible for designating a title for the pleading or other document by using one of the categories contained in the events listed in the CM/ECF Menu. IN R USDCTND CM/ECF(II)(G).

c.   *Combining documents.* All documents which form part of a single pleading and which are being filed at the same time and by the same party may be electronically filed together under one document number, e.g., the motion and a supporting affidavit, with the exception of memoranda in support. Memoranda in support shall be electronically filed separately and shown as a related document to the motion. IN R USDCTND CM/ECF(II)(A)(4).

d.   *Exhibits and attachments.* Filing users must submit in electronic form all documents referenced as exhibits or attachments, unless the court permits conventional filing. A filing user must submit as

exhibits or attachments only those excerpts of the referenced documents that are directly germane to the matter under consideration by the court. Excerpted material must be clearly and prominently identified as such. Filing users who file excerpts of documents as exhibits or attachments do so without prejudice to their right to timely file additional excerpts or the complete document. Responding parties may timely file additional excerpts or the complete document that they believe are directly germane. The court may require parties to file additional excerpts or the complete document. IN R USDCTND CM/ECF(II)(A)(6).

e. *Hyperlinks.* Electronically filed documents may contain hyperlink references to an external document as a convenient mechanism for accessing material cited in the document. A hyperlink reference is neither validated for content nor considered a part of the court's records. The court neither endorses the product or organization at the destination of a hyperlink reference, nor does the court exercise any responsibility over the content at the destination. In order to preserve the integrity of the court record, attorneys wishing to insert hyperlinks in court filings shall continue to use the traditional citation method for the cited authority, in addition to the hyperlink. A hyperlink contained in a filing is no more than a convenient mechanism for accessing material cited in the document and a hyperlink reference is extraneous to any filed document and is not part of the court's record. IN R USDCTND CM/ECF(II)(A)(3).

3. *Signing disclosures and discovery requests, responses, and objections.* FRCP 11 does not apply to disclosures and discovery requests, responses, objections, and motions under FRCP 26 through FRCP 37. FRCP 11(d).

    a. *Signature required.* Every disclosure under FRCP 26(a)(1) or FRCP 26(a)(3) and every discovery request, response, or objection must be signed by at least one attorney of record in the attorney's own name—or by the party personally, if unrepresented—and must state the signer's address, e-mail address, and telephone number. FRCP 26(g)(1).

        i. *Signatures on manual filings.* Papers delivered to the clerk for filing must: include the filer's original signature. IN R USDCTND L.R. 5-4(b)(1)(C).

- *Rubber-stamped and faxed signatures.* An original paper with a rubber-stamped or faxed signature is unsigned for purposes of FRCP 11 and FRCP 26(g). IN R USDCTND L.R. 5-4(b)(2).

- *Affidavits.* Only the affiant need sign an affidavit. IN R USDCTND L.R. 5-4(b)(3).

        ii. *Electronic signatures.* Pursuant to FRCP 11, every pleading, motion, and other paper (except lists, schedules, statements or amendments thereto) shall be signed by at least one attorney of record or, if the party is not represented by an attorney, all papers shall be signed by the party. An attorney's/participant's password issued by the court combined with the user's identification, serves as and constitutes the attorney/participant's signature for FRCP 11 and other purposes. IN R USDCTND CM/ECF(I)(C). Documents which must be filed and which must contain original signatures other than those of a participating attorney or which require either verification or an unsworn declaration under any rule or statute, shall be filed electronically, with originally executed copies maintained by the filer. The pleading or other document electronically filed shall contain "s/" signature(s), as noted in IN R USDCTND CM/ECF(II)(E)(3)(b). IN R USDCTND CM/ECF(II)(E)(1).

- *Multiple signatures.* In the case of a stipulation or other document to be signed by two or more attorneys, the following procedure should be used: The filing attorney shall initially confirm that the content of the document is acceptable to all persons required to sign the document and shall obtain the physical signatures of all attorneys on the document. IN R USDCTND CM/ECF(II)(E)(3)(a). The filing attorney then shall file the document electronically, indicating the signatories, e.g., "s/Jane Doe," "s/John Doe," etc. IN R US-DCTND CM/ECF(II)(E)(3)(b). The filing attorney shall retain the hard copy of the document containing the original signatures. IN R USDCTND CM/ECF(II)(E)(3)(c).

    b. *Effect of signature.* By signing, an attorney or party certifies that to the best of the person's knowledge, information, and belief formed after a reasonable inquiry:

        i. With respect to a disclosure, it is complete and correct as of the time it is made; and

ii. With respect to a discovery request, response, or objection, it is:

- Consistent with the Federal Rules of Civil Procedure and warranted by existing law or by a nonfrivolous argument for extending, modifying, or reversing existing law, or for establishing new law;

- Not interposed for any improper purpose, such as to harass, cause unnecessary delay, or needlessly increase the cost of litigation; and

- Neither unreasonable nor unduly burdensome or expensive, considering the needs of the case, prior discovery in the case, the amount in controversy, and the importance of the issues at stake in the action. FRCP 26(g)(1).

c. *Failure to sign.* Other parties have no duty to act on an unsigned disclosure, request, response, or objection until it is signed, and the court must strike it unless a signature is promptly supplied after the omission is called to the attorney's or party's attention. FRCP 26(g)(2).

d. *Sanction for improper certification.* If a certification violates FRCP 26(g) without substantial justification, the court, on motion or on its own, must impose an appropriate sanction on the signer, the party on whose behalf the signer was acting, or both. The sanction may include an order to pay the reasonable expenses, including attorney's fees, caused by the violation. FRCP 26(g)(3). Refer to the United States District Court for the Northern District of Indiana KeyRules Motion for Discovery Sanctions document for more information.

4. *Privacy protection for filings made with the court*

a. *Redacted filings.* Counsel should not include sensitive information in any document filed with the court unless such inclusion is necessary and relevant to the case. IN R USDCTND CM/ECF(VII). Unless the court orders otherwise, in an electronic or paper filing with the court that contains an individual's Social Security number, taxpayer-identification number, or birth date, the name of an individual known to be a minor, or a financial-account number, a party or nonparty making the filing may include only:

i. The last four (4) digits of the Social Security number and taxpayer-identification number;

ii. The year of the individual's birth;

iii. The minor's initials; and

iv. The last four (4) digits of the financial-account number. FRCP 5.2(a); IN R USDCTND Order 2005-3.

b. *Exemptions from the redaction requirement.* The redaction requirement does not apply to the following:

i. A financial-account number that identifies the property allegedly subject to forfeiture in a forfeiture proceeding;

ii. The record of an administrative or agency proceeding;

iii. The official record of a state-court proceeding;

iv. The record of a court or tribunal, if that record was not subject to the redaction requirement when originally filed;

v. A filing covered by FRCP 5.2(c) or FRCP 5.2(d); and

vi. A pro se filing in an action brought under 28 U.S.C.A. § 2241, 28 U.S.C.A. § 2254, or 28 U.S.C.A. § 2255. FRCP 5.2(b).

vii. In cases filed under the Social Security Act, 42 U.S.C.A. § 405(g), there is no need for redaction of any information from the documents filed in the case. IN R USDCTND Order 2005-3.

c. *Limitations on remote access to electronic files; Social Security appeals and immigration cases.* Unless the court orders otherwise, in an action for benefits under the Social Security Act, and in an action or proceeding relating to an order of removal, to relief from removal, or to immigration benefits or detention, access to an electronic file is authorized as follows:

i. The parties and their attorneys may have remote electronic access to any part of the case file, including the administrative record;

    ii.   Any other person may have electronic access to the full record at the courthouse, but may have remote electronic access only to:

- The docket maintained by the court; and

- An opinion, order, judgment, or other disposition of the court, but not any other part of the case file or the administrative record. FRCP 5.2(c).

d.   *Filings made under seal.* The court may order that a filing be made under seal without redaction. The court may later unseal the filing or order the person who made the filing to file a redacted version for the public record. FRCP 5.2(d). For information on filing documents under seal, refer to IN R USDCTND L.R. 5-3, IN R USDCTND CM/ECF(IV)(A), and IN R USDCTND ECF Order 2004-19.

e.   *Protective orders.* For good cause, the court may by order in a case:

    i.   Require redaction of additional information; or

    ii.   Limit or prohibit a nonparty's remote electronic access to a document filed with the court. FRCP 5.2(e).

f.   *Option for additional unredacted filing under seal.* A person making a redacted filing may also file an unredacted copy under seal. The court must retain the unredacted copy as part of the record. FRCP 5.2(f); IN R USDCTND Order 2005-3.

    i.   The unredacted version of the document or the reference list shall be retained by the court under seal as part of the record. This paper shall be retained by the court as part of the record. The court may, however, still require the party to file a redacted copy for the public file. IN R USDCTND Order 2005-3.

g.   *Option for filing a reference list.* A filing that contains redacted information may be filed together with a reference list that identifies each item of redacted information and specifies an appropriate identifier that uniquely corresponds to each item listed. The list must be filed under seal and may be amended as of right. Any reference in the case to a listed identifier will be construed to refer to the corresponding item of information. FRCP 5.2(g); IN R USDCTND Order 2005-3.

    i.   The unredacted version of the document or the reference list shall be retained by the court under seal as part of the record. This paper shall be retained by the court as part of the record. The court may, however, still require the party to file a redacted copy for the public file. IN R USDCTND Order 2005-3.

h.   *Responsibility for redaction.* The responsibility for redacting these personal identifiers rests solely with counsel and the parties. The Clerk will not review each paper for compliance with IN R USDCTND Order 2005-3. IN R USDCTND Order 2005-3.

i.   *Waiver of protection of identifiers.* A person waives the protection of FRCP 5.2(a) as to the person's own information by filing it without redaction and not under seal. FRCP 5.2(h).

F. Filing and Service Requirements

1.   *Filing requirements.* Any paper after the complaint that is required to be served—together with a certificate of service—must be filed within a reasonable time after service. But disclosures under FRCP 26(a)(1) or FRCP 26(a)(2) and the following discovery requests and responses must not be filed until they are used in the proceeding or the court orders filing: depositions, interrogatories, requests for documents or tangible things or to permit entry onto land, and requests for admission. FRCP 5(d)(1). Refer to the United States District Court for the Northern District of Indiana KeyRules pleading and motion documents for information on filing with the court.

    a.   *Discovery ordinarily not filed.* The party who serves a discovery request or notices a deposition is the custodian of the original discovery response or deposition transcript. Except as required under IN R USDCTND L.R. 26-2(a)(2), parties must not file: (1) disclosures under FRCP 26(a)(1) or FRCP 26(a)(2); (2) deposition notices; (3) deposition transcripts; (4) interrogatories; (5) requests for documents, to permit entry upon land, or for admission; (6) answers to interrogatories; (7) responses to requests for documents, to permit entry upon land, or for admission; or (8) service-of-discovery notices. IN R USDCTND L.R. 26-2(a)(1).

   i. *Exceptions*

- *Pro se litigation.* All discovery material in cases involving a pro se party must be filed. IN R USDCTND L.R. 26-2(a)(2)(A).

- *Specific material.* Discovery material must also be filed when: (1) the court orders; or (2) the material is used in a proceeding. IN R USDCTND L.R. 26-2(a)(2)(B).

b. *When discovery may be filed*

   i. *Filing materials with motion for relief.* A party who files a motion for relief under FRCP 26(c) or FRCP 37 must file with the motion those parts of the discovery requests or responses that the motion pertains to. IN R USDCTND L.R. 26-2(b).

   ii. *Materials necessary for motion.* A party must file those portions of discovery requests or responses (including deposition transcripts) that the party relies on to support a motion that could result in a final order on an issue. IN R USDCTND L.R. 26-2(c).

   iii. *Materials to be used at trial.* A party who reasonably anticipates using discovery requests or responses—including deposition transcripts—at trial must file the relevant portions of the requests or responses with the clerk at the start of the trial. IN R USDCTND L.R. 26-2(d).

2. *Service requirements.* [A request for an admission] must be served on the party from whom the admission is requested and, unless the court has otherwise ordered, a copy of the request must be served on every other party. FPP § 2258.

a. *Service; When required*

   i. *In general.* Unless the Federal Rules of Civil Procedure provide otherwise, each of the following papers must be served on every party:

- An order stating that service is required;

- A pleading filed after the original complaint, unless the court orders otherwise under FRCP 5(c) because there are numerous defendants;

- A discovery paper required to be served on a party, unless the court orders otherwise;

- A written motion, except one that may be heard ex parte; and

- A written notice, appearance, demand, or offer of judgment, or any similar paper. FRCP 5(a)(1).

   ii. *If a party fails to appear.* No service is required on a party who is in default for failing to appear. But a pleading that asserts a new claim for relief against such a party must be served on that party under FRCP 4. FRCP 5(a)(2).

   iii. *Seizing property.* If an action is begun by seizing property and no person is or need be named as a defendant, any service required before the filing of an appearance, answer, or claim must be made on the person who had custody or possession of the property when it was seized. FRCP 5(a)(3).

b. *Service; How made*

   i. *Serving an attorney.* If a party is represented by an attorney, service under FRCP 5 must be made on the attorney unless the court orders service on the party. FRCP 5(b)(1).

   ii. *Service in general.* A paper is served under FRCP 5 by:

- Handing it to the person;

- Leaving it: (1) at the person's office with a clerk or other person in charge or, if no one is in charge, in a conspicuous place in the office; or (2) if the person has no office or the office is closed, at the person's dwelling or usual place of abode with someone of suitable age and discretion who resides there;

- Mailing it to the person's last known address—in which event service is complete upon mailing;

453

- Leaving it with the court clerk if the person has no known address;

- Sending it by electronic means if the person consented in writing—in which event service is complete upon transmission, but is not effective if the serving party learns that it did not reach the person to be served; or

- Delivering it by any other means that the person consented to in writing—in which event service is complete when the person making service delivers it to the agency designated to make delivery. FRCP 5(b)(2).

iii. *Electronic service.* Electronically filed papers may be served electronically if service is consistent with the CM/ECF User Manual (IN R USDCTND CM/ECF). IN R USDCTND L.R. 5-2(a).

- *Waiver of other service.* An attorney's registration will constitute a waiver of conventional service of documents and the attorney agrees to accept service of notice on behalf of the client of the electronic filing by hand, facsimile or authorized email. IN R USDCTND CM/ECF(I)(B)(3).

- *Serving registered persons.* The System will generate a "Notice of Electronic Filing" when any document is filed. This notice represents service of the document on parties who are registered participants with the System. Except as provided in IN R USDCTND CM/ECF(III)(B), the filing party shall not be required to serve any pleading or other documents on any party receiving electronic notice. IN R USDCTND CM/ECF(II)(D)(1). The term "pleading" refers only to those documents listed in FRCP 7(a). IN R USDCTND CM/ECF(FN3).

- *When electronic service is deemed completed.* A person registered to use the court's electronic-filing system is served with an electronically filed paper when a "Notice of Electronic Filing" is transmitted to that person through the court's electronic filing-system. IN R USDCTND L.R. 5-2(b).

- *Serving non-registered persons.* A person who has not registered to use the court's electronic-filing system but who is entitled to service of a paper must be served according to the Local Civil Rules of the United States District Court for the Northern District of Indiana and the Federal Rules of Civil Procedure. IN R USDCTND L.R. 5-2(c); IN R USDCTND CM/ECF(II)(D)(2). If such service of a paper copy is to be made, it shall be done in the manner provided in the Federal Rules of Civil Procedure and the Local Civil Rules of the United States District Court for the Northern District of Indiana. IN R USDCTND CM/ECF(II)(D)(2).

iv. *Service of conventional filings.* Pleadings or other documents which are filed conventionally rather than electronically shall be served in the manner provided for in the Federal Rules of Civil Procedure and the Local Civil Rules of the United States District Court for the Northern District of Indiana, except as otherwise provided by order of the Court. IN R USDCTND CM/ECF(III)(B).

v. *Using court facilities.* If a local rule so authorizes, a party may use the court's transmission facilities to make service under FRCP 5(b)(2)(E). FRCP 5(b)(3).

c. *Serving numerous defendants*

i. *In general.* If an action involves an unusually large number of defendants, the court may, on motion or on its own, order that:

- Defendants' pleadings and replies to them need not be served on other defendants;

- Any crossclaim, counterclaim, avoidance, or affirmative defense in those pleadings and replies to them will be treated as denied or avoided by all other parties; and

- Filing any such pleading and serving it on the plaintiff constitutes notice of the pleading to all parties. FRCP 5(c)(1).

ii. *Notifying parties.* A copy of every such order must be served on the parties as the court directs. FRCP 5(c)(2).

G. Hearings

    1.   There is no hearing contemplated in the federal statutes or rules for requests for admissions.

H. Forms

    1. Federal Request for Admissions Forms

        a.   Request; For admission of facts and genuineness of documents. AMJUR PP DEPOSITION § 674.

        b.   Plaintiff's request for admission. 3B FEDFORMS § 3650.

        c.   Plaintiff's request for admission; Another form. 3B FEDFORMS § 3651.

        d.   Plaintiff's request for admission; Statements in documents. 3B FEDFORMS § 3652.

        e.   Plaintiff's request for admission; Statements in documents; Another form. 3B FEDFORMS § 3653.

        f.   Plaintiff's request for admission; Specific facts. 3B FEDFORMS § 3654.

        g.   Plaintiff's request for admission; Specific facts; Another form. 3B FEDFORMS § 3655.

        h.   Plaintiff's request for admission; Specific documents and facts. 3B FEDFORMS § 3656.

        i.   Plaintiff's request for admission; Specific documents and facts; Another form. 3B FEDFORMS § 3657.

        j.   Plaintiff's request for admission; True copies, filing and operational effect of government documents. 3B FEDFORMS § 3658.

        k.   Plaintiff's request for additional admission. 3B FEDFORMS § 3659.

        l.   Defendant's request for admission of genuineness; Specific document. 3B FEDFORMS § 3660.

        m.   Defendant's request for admission of genuineness; Specific document; Another form. 3B FEDFORMS § 3661.

        n.   Defendant's request for admission of genuineness; Specific document; Another form. 3B FEDFORMS § 3662.

        o.   Defendant's request for admission; Truth of statement. 3B FEDFORMS § 3663.

        p.   Request for admissions under FRCP 36. FEDPROF § 23:535.

        q.   Request for admissions; General form. FEDPROF § 23:536.

        r.   Request for admissions; Action to collect royalties. FEDPROF § 23:537.

        s.   Request for admissions; Trademark action. FEDPROF § 23:538.

        t.   Request for admissions; Automobile negligence action. FEDPROF § 23:539.

        u.   Request for admissions; Motor vehicle action. FEDPROF § 23:540.

        v.   Request for admissions; Premises liability action. FEDPROF § 23:541.

        w.   Request for admissions; Products liability action. FEDPROF § 23:542.

        x.   Request for admissions; Medical malpractice action. FEDPROF § 23:543.

        y.   Request for admissions; Genuineness of documents. FEDPROF § 23:544.

        z.   Request for admissions; Wrongful death due to forklift accident. FEDPROF § 23:545.

I. Applicable Rules

    1.   *Federal rules*

        a.   Serving and filing pleadings and other papers. FRCP 5.

        b.   Privacy protection for filings made with the court. FRCP 5.2.

        c.   Computing and extending time; Time for motion papers. FRCP 6.

        d.   Pleadings allowed; Form of motions and other papers. FRCP 7.

        e.   Form of pleadings. FRCP 10.

        f.   Signing pleadings, motions, and other papers; Representations to the court; Sanctions. FRCP 11.

g.   Duty to disclose; General provisions governing discovery. FRCP 26.

h.   Stipulations about discovery procedure. FRCP 29.

i.   Requests for admission. FRCP 36.

j.   Failure to make disclosures or to cooperate in discovery; Sanctions. FRCP 37.

2.   *Local rules*

a.   Citation and scope of the rules. IN R USDCTND L.R. 1-1.

b.   Sanctions for formatting errors. IN R USDCTND L.R. 1-3.

c.   Electronic service. IN R USDCTND L.R. 5-2.

d.   Format of papers. IN R USDCTND L.R. 5-4.

e.   Pretrial procedure. IN R USDCTND L.R. 16-1.

f.   Alternative dispute resolution. IN R USDCTND L.R. 16-6.

g.   Form of certain discovery documents. IN R USDCTND L.R. 26-1.

h.   Filing of discovery and other materials. IN R USDCTND L.R. 26-2.

i.   Case assignment. IN R USDCTND L.R. 40-1.

j.   Appearance and withdrawal of appearance. IN R USDCTND L.R. 83-8.

k.   CM/ECF civil and criminal user manual. IN R USDCTND CM/ECF.

l.   In re: privacy and public access to civil electronic case files. IN R USDCTND Order 2005-3.

Requests, Notices and Applications
Response to Request for Admissions

Document Last Updated December 2016

A.   Checklist

(I)   ❑ Matters to be considered by requesting party

   (a)   ❑ Required documents

      (1)   ❑ Request for admissions

   (b)   ❑ Supplemental documents

      (1)   ❑ Document(s)

      (2)   ❑ Certificate of service

   (c)   ❑ Timing

      (1)   ❑ A party may not seek discovery from any source before the parties have conferred as required by FRCP 26(f), except in a proceeding exempted from initial disclosure under FRCP 26(a)(1)(B), or when authorized by the Federal Rules of Civil Procedure, by stipulation, or by court order

(II)   ❑ Matters to be considered by responding party

   (a)   ❑ Required documents

      (1)   ❑ Response to request for admissions

   (b)   ❑ Supplemental documents

      (1)   ❑ Certificate of service

   (c)   ❑ Timing

      (1)   ❑ A matter is admitted unless, within thirty (30) days after being served, the party to whom the request is directed serves on the requesting party a written answer or objection addressed to the matter and signed by the party or its attorney

B. Timing

1. *Response to request for admissions.* A matter is admitted unless, within thirty (30) days after being served, the party to whom the request is directed serves on the requesting party a written answer or objection addressed to the matter and signed by the party or its attorney. A shorter or longer time for responding may be stipulated to under FRCP 29 or be ordered by the court. FRCP 36(a)(3).

2. *Automatic initial extension.* The deadline to respond to a pleading or a discovery request—including requests for admission—is automatically extended when an extension notice is filed with the court and: (1) the deadline has not been extended before; (2) the extension is for twenty-eight (28) or fewer days; and (3) the notice states: (A) the original deadline; (B) the new deadline; and (C) that all opposing attorneys the attorney could reach agreed to the extension; or that the party could not reach any other opposing attorneys despite due diligence. IN R USDCTND L.R. 6-1(b).

   a. *Pro se parties.* The automatic initial extension does not apply to pro se parties. IN R USDCTND L.R. 6-1(c).

3. *Computation of time*

   a. *Computing time.* FRCP 6 applies in computing any time period specified in the Federal Rules of Civil Procedure, in any local rule or court order, or in any statute that does not specify a method of computing time. FRCP 6(a).

      i. *Period stated in days or a longer unit.* When the period is stated in days or a longer unit of time:

         - Exclude the day of the event that triggers the period;
         - Count every day, including intermediate Saturdays, Sundays, and legal holidays; and
         - Include the last day of the period, but if the last day is a Saturday, Sunday, or legal holiday, the period continues to run until the end of the next day that is not a Saturday, Sunday, or legal holiday. FRCP 6(a)(1).

      ii. *Period stated in hours.* When the period is stated in hours:

         - Begin counting immediately on the occurrence of the event that triggers the period;
         - Count every hour, including hours during intermediate Saturdays, Sundays, and legal holidays; and
         - If the period would end on a Saturday, Sunday, or legal holiday, the period continues to run until the same time on the next day that is not a Saturday, Sunday, or legal holiday. FRCP 6(a)(2).

      iii. *Inaccessibility of the clerk's office.* Unless the court orders otherwise, if the clerk's office is inaccessible:

         - On the last day for filing under FRCP 6(a)(1), then the time for filing is extended to the first accessible day that is not a Saturday, Sunday, or legal holiday; or
         - During the last hour for filing under FRCP 6(a)(2), then the time for filing is extended to the same time on the first accessible day that is not a Saturday, Sunday, or legal holiday. FRCP 6(a)(3).

      iv. *"Last day" defined.* Unless a different time is set by a statute, local rule, or court order, the last day ends:

         - For electronic filing, at midnight in the court's time zone; and
         - For filing by other means, when the clerk's office is scheduled to close. FRCP 6(a)(4).

      v. *"Next day" defined.* The "next day" is determined by continuing to count forward when the period is measured after an event and backward when measured before an event. FRCP 6(a)(5).

      vi. *"Legal holiday" defined.* "Legal holiday" means:

         - The day set aside by statute for observing New Year's Day, Martin Luther King Jr.'s Birthday, Washington's Birthday, Memorial Day, Independence Day, Labor Day, Columbus Day, Veterans' Day, Thanksgiving Day, or Christmas Day;

- Any day declared a holiday by the President or Congress; and
- For periods that are measured after an event, any other day declared a holiday by the state where the district court is located. FRCP 6(a)(6).

b. *Computation of electronic filing deadlines.* Filing documents electronically does not alter any filing deadlines or any time computation pursuant to FRCP 6. The counties of Lake, Porter, LaPorte, Pulaski and Starke are located in the Central time zone and the remaining counties in the Northern District of Indiana are located in the Eastern time zone. Nevertheless, all electronic transmissions of documents must be completed (i.e., received completely by the clerk's office) prior to midnight Eastern Time, (South Bend/Fort Wayne/Lafayette time) in order to be considered timely filed that day, regardless of the local time in the division where the case is pending. Although documents can be filed electronically twenty-four (24) hours a day, filers are strongly encouraged to file all documents during hours when the CM/ECF Help Line is available, from 9:00 a.m. to 4:00 p.m. local time. IN R USDCTND CM/ECF(II)(I).

   i. *Technical failures.* If the attorney is unable to file a document in a timely manner due to technical difficulties in the user's system, the attorney must file a document with the court as soon as possible notifying the court of the inability to file the document. A sample document entitled Declaration that Party was Unable to File in a Timely Manner Due to Technical Difficulties is attached hereto as Form 5. IN R USDCTND CM/ECF(VI)(B). [Editor's note: the reference to Form 5 is likely meant to be a reference to Form 3 (IN R USDCTND CM/ECF(Form 3)].

c. *Extending time*

   i. *In general.* When an act may or must be done within a specified time, the court may, for good cause, extend the time:

      - With or without motion or notice if the court acts, or if a request is made, before the original time or its extension expires; or
      - On motion made after the time has expired if the party failed to act because of excusable neglect. FRCP 6(b)(1).

   ii. *Exceptions.* A court must not extend the time to act under FRCP 50(b), FRCP 50(d), FRCP 52(b), FRCP 59(b), FRCP 59(d), FRCP 59(e), and FRCP 60(b). FRCP 6(b)(2).

   iii. Refer to the United States District Court for the Northern District of Indiana KeyRules Motion for Continuance/Extension of Time document for more information on extending time.

d. *Additional time after certain kinds of service.* When a party may or must act within a specified time after being served and service is made under FRCP 5(b)(2)(C) (mail), FRCP 5(b)(2)(D) (leaving with the clerk), or FRCP 5(b)(2)(F) (other means consented to), three (3) days are added after the period would otherwise expire under FRCP 6(a). FRCP 6(d).

C. General Requirements

1. *General provisions governing discovery*

   a. *Discovery scope and limits*

      i. *Scope in general.* Unless otherwise limited by court order, the scope of discovery is as follows: Parties may obtain discovery regarding any nonprivileged matter that is relevant to any party's claim or defense and proportional to the needs of the case, considering the importance of the issues at stake in the action, the amount in controversy, the parties' relative access to relevant information, the parties' resources, the importance of the discovery in resolving the issues, and whether the burden or expense of the proposed discovery outweighs its likely benefit. Information within this scope of discovery need not be admissible in evidence to be discoverable. FRCP 26(b)(1).

      ii. *Limitations on frequency and extent*

         - *When permitted.* By order, the court may alter the limits in the Federal Rules of Civil Procedure on the number of depositions and interrogatories or on the length of depositions under FRCP 30. By order or local rule, the court may also limit the number of requests under FRCP 36. FRCP 26(b)(2)(A).

- *Specific limitations on electronically stored information.* A party need not provide discovery of electronically stored information from sources that the party identifies as not reasonably accessible because of undue burden or cost. On motion to compel discovery or for a protective order, the party from whom discovery is sought must show that the information is not reasonably accessible because of undue burden or cost. If that showing is made, the court may nonetheless order discovery from such sources if the requesting party shows good cause, considering the limitations of FRCP 26(b)(2)(C). The court may specify conditions for the discovery. FRCP 26(b)(2)(B).

- *When required.* On motion or on its own, the court must limit the frequency or extent of discovery otherwise allowed by the Federal Rules of Civil Procedure or by local rule if it determines that: (1) the discovery sought is unreasonably cumulative or duplicative, or can be obtained from some other source that is more convenient, less burdensome, or less expensive; (2) the party seeking discovery has had ample opportunity to obtain the information by discovery in the action; or (3) the proposed discovery is outside the scope permitted by FRCP 26(b)(1). FRCP 26(b)(2)(C).

iii. *Trial preparation; Materials*

- *Documents and tangible things.* Ordinarily, a party may not discover documents and tangible things that are prepared in anticipation of litigation or for trial by or for another party or its representative (including the other party's attorney, consultant, surety, indemnitor, insurer, or agent). But, subject to FRCP 26(b)(4), those materials may be discovered if: (1) they are otherwise discoverable under FRCP 26(b)(1); and (2) the party shows that it has substantial need for the materials to prepare its case and cannot, without undue hardship, obtain their substantial equivalent by other means. FRCP 26(b)(3)(A).

- *Protection against disclosure.* If the court orders discovery of those materials, it must protect against disclosure of the mental impressions, conclusions, opinions, or legal theories of a party's attorney or other representative concerning the litigation. FRCP 26(b)(3)(B).

- *Previous statement.* Any party or other person may, on request and without the required showing, obtain the person's own previous statement about the action or its subject matter. If the request is refused, the person may move for a court order, and FRCP 37(a)(5) applies to the award of expenses. A previous statement is either: (1) a written statement that the person has signed or otherwise adopted or approved; or (2) a contemporaneous stenographic, mechanical, electrical, or other recording—or a transcription of it—that recites substantially verbatim the person's oral statement. FRCP 26(b)(3)(C).

iv. *Trial preparation; Experts*

- *Deposition of an expert who may testify.* A party may depose any person who has been identified as an expert whose opinions may be presented at trial. If FRCP 26(a)(2)(B) requires a report from the expert, the deposition may be conducted only after the report is provided. FRCP 26(b)(4)(A).

- *Trial-preparation protection for draft reports or disclosures.* FRCP 26(b)(3)(A) and FRCP 26(b)(3)(B) protect drafts of any report or disclosure required under FRCP 26(a)(2), regardless of the form in which the draft is recorded. FRCP 26(b)(4)(B).

- *Trial-preparation protection for communications between a party's attorney and expert witnesses.* FRCP 26(b)(3)(A) and FRCP 26(b)(3)(B) protect communications between the party's attorney and any witness required to provide a report under FRCP 26(a)(2)(B), regardless of the form of the communications, except to the extent that the communications: (1) relate to compensation for the expert's study or testimony; (2) identify facts or data that the party's attorney provided and that the expert considered in forming the opinions to be expressed; or (3) identify assumptions that the party's attorney provided and that the expert relied on in forming the opinions to be expressed. FRCP 26(b)(4)(C).

- *Expert employed only for trial preparation.* Ordinarily, a party may not, by interrogatories or deposition, discover facts known or opinions held by an expert who has been retained or specially employed by another party in anticipation of litigation or to prepare for trial and who is not expected to be called as a witness at trial. But a party may do so only: (1) as provided in FRCP 35(b); or (2) on showing exceptional circumstances under which it is impracticable for the party to obtain facts or opinions on the same subject by other means. FRCP 26(b)(4)(D).

- *Payment.* Unless manifest injustice would result, the court must require that the party seeking discovery: (1) pay the expert a reasonable fee for time spent in responding to discovery under FRCP 26(b)(4)(A) or FRCP 26(b)(4)(D); and (2) for discovery under FRCP 26(b)(4)(D), also pay the other party a fair portion of the fees and expenses it reasonably incurred in obtaining the expert's facts and opinions. FRCP 26(b)(4)(E).

   v. *Claiming privilege or protecting trial-preparation materials*

- *Information withheld.* When a party withholds information otherwise discoverable by claiming that the information is privileged or subject to protection as trial-preparation material, the party must: (1) expressly make the claim; and (2) describe the nature of the documents, communications, or tangible things not produced or disclosed—and do so in a manner that, without revealing information itself privileged or protected, will enable other parties to assess the claim. FRCP 26(b)(5)(A).

- *Information produced.* If information produced in discovery is subject to a claim of privilege or of protection as trial-preparation material, the party making the claim may notify any party that received the information of the claim and the basis for it. After being notified, a party must promptly return, sequester, or destroy the specified information and any copies it has; must not use or disclose the information until the claim is resolved; must take reasonable steps to retrieve the information if the party disclosed it before being notified; and may promptly present the information to the court under seal for a determination of the claim. The producing party must preserve the information until the claim is resolved. FRCP 26(b)(5)(B).

b. *Protective orders.* A party or any person from whom discovery is sought may move for a protective order in the court where the action is pending—or as an alternative on matters relating to a deposition, in the court for the district where the deposition will be taken. FRCP 26(c)(1). Refer to the United States District Court for the Northern District of Indiana KeyRules Motion for Protective Order document for more information.

c. *Sequence of discovery.* Unless the parties stipulate or the court orders otherwise for the parties' and witnesses' convenience and in the interests of justice: (1) methods of discovery may be used in any sequence; and (2) discovery by one party does not require any other party to delay its discovery. FRCP 26(d)(3).

2. *Response to request for admissions*

a. *Form.* A party responding (by answer or objection) to written discovery must: (1) fully quote each interrogatory or request immediately before the party's response; and (2) number each response to correspond with the interrogatory or request being responded to. IN R USDCTND L.R. 26-1(b). The response to a request for admissions must be in writing and signed by the party or its attorney. FPP § 2259. The response should be a single document, in which the various requests are listed in order and an admission, a denial, an objection, or a statement of inability to admit or deny made to each of the requests as is appropriate. FPP § 2259.

b. *Answer.* If a matter is not admitted, the answer must specifically deny it or state in detail why the answering party cannot truthfully admit or deny it. FRCP 36(a)(4).

   i. *Denial.* A denial must fairly respond to the substance of the matter; and when good faith requires that a party qualify an answer or deny only a part of a matter, the answer must specify the part admitted and qualify or deny the rest. FRCP 36(a)(4). It is expected that denials will be forthright, specific, and unconditional. If a response is thought insufficient as a denial, the court may treat it as an admission. FPP § 2260.

    ii.   *Lack of knowledge or information.* The answering party may assert lack of knowledge or information as a reason for failing to admit or deny only if the party states that it has made reasonable inquiry and that the information it knows or can readily obtain is insufficient to enable it to admit or deny. FRCP 36(a)(4). A general statement that it can neither admit nor deny, unaccompanied by reasons, will be held an insufficient response, and the court may either take the matter as admitted or order a further answer. FPP § 2261.

  c.   *Objections.* Objections must be made in writing within the time allowed for answering the request. If some requests are to be answered and others objected to, the answers and objections should be contained in a single document. FPP § 2262. The grounds for objecting to a request must be stated. A party must not object solely on the ground that the request presents a genuine issue for trial. FRCP 36(a)(5). Failure to object to a request waives the objection. FPP § 2262.

  d.   *Motion regarding the sufficiency of an answer or objection.* The requesting party may move to determine the sufficiency of an answer or objection. Unless the court finds an objection justified, it must order that an answer be served. On finding that an answer does not comply with FRCP 36, the court may order either that the matter is admitted or that an amended answer be served. The court may defer its final decision until a pretrial conference or a specified time before trial. FRCP 37(a)(5) applies to an award of expenses. FRCP 36(a)(6). Refer to the United States District Court for the Northern District of Indiana KeyRules Motion for Discovery Sanctions document for more information on sanctions.

  e.   *Effect of an admission; Withdrawing or amending it.* A matter admitted under FRCP 36 is conclusively established unless the court, on motion, permits the admission to be withdrawn or amended. Subject to FRCP 16(e), the court may permit withdrawal or amendment if it would promote the presentation of the merits of the action and if the court is not persuaded that it would prejudice the requesting party in maintaining or defending the action on the merits. An admission under FRCP 36 is not an admission for any other purpose and cannot be used against the party in any other proceeding. FRCP 36(b).

3.   *Supplementing disclosures and responses.* A party who has made a disclosure under FRCP 26(a)—or who has responded to an interrogatory, request for production, or request for admission—must supplement or correct its disclosure or response: (1) in a timely manner if the party learns that in some material respect the disclosure or response is incomplete or incorrect, and if the additional or corrective information has not otherwise been made known to the other parties during the discovery process or in writing; or (2) as ordered by the court. FRCP 26(e)(1).

4.   *Sanctions for failure to cooperate in discovery.* The pattern of sanctions for FRCP 36 is somewhat different from that for the other discovery rules. The most important sanctions are two:

  a.   A failure to respond to a request is deemed an admission of the matter to which the request is directed; and

  b.   A party who, without good reason, refuses to admit a matter will be required to pay the costs incurred in proving that matter. FPP § 2265. If a party fails to admit what is requested under FRCP 36 and if the requesting party later proves a document to be genuine or the matter true, the requesting party may move that the party who failed to admit pay the reasonable expenses, including attorney's fees, incurred in making that proof. The court must so order unless:

    i.   The request was held objectionable under FRCP 36(a);

    ii.   The admission sought was of no substantial importance;

    iii.   The party failing to admit had a reasonable ground to believe that it might prevail on the matter; or

    iv.   There was other good reason for the failure to admit. FRCP 37(c)(2).

  c.   Refer to the United States District Court for the Northern District of Indiana KeyRules Motion for Discovery Sanctions document for more information on sanctions.

5.   *Stipulations about discovery procedure.* Unless the court orders otherwise, the parties may stipulate that: (1) a deposition may be taken before any person, at any time or place, on any notice, and in the manner

specified—in which event it may be used in the same way as any other deposition; and (2) other procedures governing or limiting discovery be modified—but a stipulation extending the time for any form of discovery must have court approval if it would interfere with the time set for completing discovery, for hearing a motion, or for trial. FRCP 29.

6. *Appearances.* Attorneys not representing the United States or its agencies must file an appearance when they represent (either in person or by filing a paper) a party. IN R USDCTND L.R. 83-8(a). For more information, refer to IN R USDCTND L.R. 83-8.

7. *Notice of related action.* A party must file a notice of related action as soon as it appears that the party's case and another pending case: (1) arise out of the same transaction or occurrence; (2) involve the same property; or (3) involve the validity or infringement of the same patent, trademark, or copyright. IN R USDCTND L.R. 40-1(d). For more information, refer to IN R USDCTND L.R. 40-1.

8. *Alternative dispute resolution (ADR).* After they confer as required by FRCP 26(f), the parties must advise the court which, if any, alternative-dispute-resolution processes they expect to pursue and when they expect to undertake the process. IN R USDCTND L.R. 16-6(a). For more information on alternative dispute resolution (ADR), refer to IN R USDCTND L.R. 16-6 and IN R USDCTND Order 2003-21.

9. *Settlement or resolution.* The parties must immediately notify the court if they reasonably expect to settle the case or resolve a pending motion. IN R USDCTND L.R. 16-1(g).

10. *Modification or suspension of rules.* The court may, on its own motion or at the request of a party, suspend or modify any rule in a particular case in the interest of justice. IN R USDCTND L.R. 1-1(c).

D. Documents

1. *Required documents*

   a. *Response to request for admissions.* Refer to the General Requirements section of this document for information on the response to request for admissions.

2. *Supplemental documents*

   a. *Certificate of service.* FRCP 5(d) requires that the person making service under FRCP 5 certify that service has been effected. FRCP 5(Advisory Committee Notes). Having such information on file may be useful for many purposes, including proof of service if an issue arises concerning the effectiveness of the service. FRCP 5(Advisory Committee Notes).

E. Format

1. *Form of documents.* The rules governing captions and other matters of form in pleadings apply to motions and other papers. FRCP 7(b)(2).

   a. *Paper.* Any pleading, motion, brief, affidavit, notice, or proposed order, whether filed electronically or by delivering it to the clerk, must: use eight and one-half by eleven (8-1/2 x 11) inch pages. IN R USDCTND L.R. 5-4(a)(2).

      i. *Manual filings.* Papers delivered to the clerk for filing must: be flat, unfolded, and on good-quality, white paper. IN R USDCTND L.R. 5-4(b)(1)(A).

         • *Covers or backing.* Papers delivered to the clerk for filing must: not have a cover or a back. IN R USDCTND L.R. 5-4(b)(1)(B).

         • *Recycled paper.* The court encourages using recycled paper. IN R USDCTND L.R. 5-4(b)(7).

   b. *Margins.* Any pleading, motion, brief, affidavit, notice, or proposed order, whether filed electronically or by delivering it to the clerk, must: have at least one (1) inch margins. IN R USDCTND L.R. 5-4(a)(3).

   c. *Spacing.* Any pleading, motion, brief, affidavit, notice, or proposed order, whether filed electronically or by delivering it to the clerk, must: be double spaced (except for headings, footnotes, and quoted material). IN R USDCTND L.R. 5-4(a)(5).

   d. *Text.* Any pleading, motion, brief, affidavit, notice, or proposed order, whether filed electronically or by delivering it to the clerk, must: be plainly typewritten, printed, or prepared by a clearly legible copying process. IN R USDCTND L.R. 5-4(a)(1).

    i.   Any pleading, motion, brief, affidavit, notice, or proposed order, whether filed electronically or by delivering it to the clerk, must: use at least twelve (12) point type in the body and at least ten (10) point type in footnotes. IN R USDCTND L.R. 5-4(a)(4).

e.   *Page numbering.* Any pleading, motion, brief, affidavit, notice, or proposed order, whether filed electronically or by delivering it to the clerk, must: have consecutively numbered pages. IN R USDCTND L.R. 5-4(a)(6).

f.   *Caption; Names of parties.* Every pleading must have a caption with the court's name, a title, a file number, and a FRCP 7(a) designation. The title of the complaint must name all the parties; the title of other pleadings, after naming the first party on each side, may refer generally to other parties. FRCP 10(a). Any pleading, motion, brief, affidavit, notice, or proposed order, whether filed electronically or by delivering it to the clerk, must: include a title on the first page. IN R USDCTND L.R. 5-4(a)(7).

g.   *Filer's information.* Any pleading, motion, brief, affidavit, notice, or proposed order, whether filed electronically or by delivering it to the clerk, must: except in proposed orders and affidavits, include the filer's name, address, telephone number, fax number (where available), and e-mail address (where available). IN R USDCTND L.R. 5-4(a)(9).

h.   *Paragraphs; Separate statements.* A party must state its claims or defenses in numbered paragraphs, each limited as far as practicable to a single set of circumstances. A later pleading may refer by number to a paragraph in an earlier pleading. If doing so would promote clarity, each claim founded on a separate transaction or occurrence—and each defense other than a denial—must be stated in a separate count or defense. FRCP 10(b).

i.   *Adoption by reference; Exhibits.* A statement in a pleading may be adopted by reference elsewhere in the same pleading or in any other pleading or motion. A copy of a written instrument that is an exhibit to a pleading is a part of the pleading for all purposes. FRCP 10(c).

j.   *Citation of local rules.* The Local Civil Rules of the United States District Court for the Northern District of Indiana may be cited as "N.D. Ind. L.R." IN R USDCTND L.R. 1-1(a)(1).

k.   *Acceptance by the clerk.* The clerk must not refuse to file a paper solely because it is not in the form prescribed by the Federal Rules of Civil Procedure or by a local rule or practice. FRCP 5(d)(4).

    i.   *Sanctions for formatting errors; Non-compliance.* If a person files a paper that does not comply with the rules governing the format of papers filed with the court, the court may: (1) strike the paper from the record; or (2) fine the person up to one thousand dollars ($1,000). IN R USDCTND L.R. 1-3(a).

       •   *Notice.* Before sanctioning a person under IN R USDCTND L.R. 1-3(a)(2), the court must: (1) notify the person that the paper is noncompliant; and (2) give the person the opportunity either to be heard or to revise the paper. IN R USDCTND L.R. 1-3(b).

2.   *Form of electronic documents.* Electronically filed documents must meet the same requirements of format and page limits as documents "conventionally filed" (as defined in IN R USDCTND CM/ECF(III)(A)) pursuant to the Federal Rules of Civil Procedure and the Local Civil Rules of the United States District Court for the Northern District of Indiana. IN R USDCTND CM/ECF(II)(A)(2).

a.   *PDF format required.* Documents filed in the CM/ECF must be in .pdf format. A document created with almost any word-processing program can be converted to .pdf format. The .pdf program in effect takes a picture of the original document and allows anyone to open the converted document across a broad range of hardware and software, with layout, format, links, and images intact. IN R USDCTND CM/ECF(FN2).

b.   *Title of documents.* The person electronically filing a pleading or other document will be responsible for designating a title for the pleading or other document by using one of the categories contained in the events listed in the CM/ECF Menu. IN R USDCTND CM/ECF(II)(G).

c.   *Combining documents.* All documents which form part of a single pleading and which are being filed

at the same time and by the same party may be electronically filed together under one document number, e.g., the motion and a supporting affidavit, with the exception of memoranda in support. Memoranda in support shall be electronically filed separately and shown as a related document to the motion. IN R USDCTND CM/ECF(II)(A)(4).

d. *Exhibits and attachments.* Filing users must submit in electronic form all documents referenced as exhibits or attachments, unless the court permits conventional filing. A filing user must submit as exhibits or attachments only those excerpts of the referenced documents that are directly germane to the matter under consideration by the court. Excerpted material must be clearly and prominently identified as such. Filing users who file excerpts of documents as exhibits or attachments do so without prejudice to their right to timely file additional excerpts or the complete document. Responding parties may timely file additional excerpts or the complete document that they believe are directly germane. The court may require parties to file additional excerpts or the complete document. IN R USDCTND CM/ECF(II)(A)(6).

e. *Hyperlinks.* Electronically filed documents may contain hyperlink references to an external document as a convenient mechanism for accessing material cited in the document. A hyperlink reference is neither validated for content nor considered a part of the court's records. The court neither endorses the product or organization at the destination of a hyperlink reference, nor does the court exercise any responsibility over the content at the destination. In order to preserve the integrity of the court record, attorneys wishing to insert hyperlinks in court filings shall continue to use the traditional citation method for the cited authority, in addition to the hyperlink. A hyperlink contained in a filing is no more than a convenient mechanism for accessing material cited in the document and a hyperlink reference is extraneous to any filed document and is not part of the court's record. IN R USDCTND CM/ECF(II)(A)(3).

3. *Signing disclosures and discovery requests, responses, and objections.* FRCP 11 does not apply to disclosures and discovery requests, responses, objections, and motions under FRCP 26 through FRCP 37. FRCP 11(d).

   a. *Signature required.* Every disclosure under FRCP 26(a)(1) or FRCP 26(a)(3) and every discovery request, response, or objection must be signed by at least one attorney of record in the attorney's own name—or by the party personally, if unrepresented—and must state the signer's address, e-mail address, and telephone number. FRCP 26(g)(1).

      i. *Signatures on manual filings.* Papers delivered to the clerk for filing must: include the filer's original signature. IN R USDCTND L.R. 5-4(b)(1)(C).

         - *Rubber-stamped and faxed signatures.* An original paper with a rubber-stamped or faxed signature is unsigned for purposes of FRCP 11 and FRCP 26(g). IN R USDCTND L.R. 5-4(b)(2).

         - *Affidavits.* Only the affiant need sign an affidavit. IN R USDCTND L.R. 5-4(b)(3).

      ii. *Electronic signatures.* Pursuant to FRCP 11, every pleading, motion, and other paper (except lists, schedules, statements or amendments thereto) shall be signed by at least one attorney of record or, if the party is not represented by an attorney, all papers shall be signed by the party. An attorney's/participant's password issued by the court combined with the user's identification, serves as and constitutes the attorney/participant's signature for FRCP 11 and other purposes. IN R USDCTND CM/ECF(I)(C). Documents which must be filed and which must contain original signatures other than those of a participating attorney or which require either verification or an unsworn declaration under any rule or statute, shall be filed electronically, with originally executed copies maintained by the filer. The pleading or other document electronically filed shall contain "s/" signature(s), as noted in IN R USDCTND CM/ECF(II)(E)(3)(b). IN R USDCTND CM/ECF(II)(E)(1).

         - *Multiple signatures.* In the case of a stipulation or other document to be signed by two or more attorneys, the following procedure should be used: The filing attorney shall initially confirm that the content of the document is acceptable to all persons required to sign the document and shall obtain the physical signatures of all attorneys on the document. IN R USDCTND CM/ECF(II)(E)(3)(a). The filing attorney then shall file the document electronically, indicating the signatories, e.g., "s/Jane Doe," "s/John Doe," etc. IN R US-DCTND CM/ECF(II)(E)(3)(b). The filing attorney shall retain the hard copy of the document containing the original signatures. IN R USDCTND CM/ECF(II)(E)(3)(c).

b. *Effect of signature.* By signing, an attorney or party certifies that to the best of the person's knowledge, information, and belief formed after a reasonable inquiry:

   i. With respect to a disclosure, it is complete and correct as of the time it is made; and

   ii. With respect to a discovery request, response, or objection, it is:

- Consistent with the Federal Rules of Civil Procedure and warranted by existing law or by a nonfrivolous argument for extending, modifying, or reversing existing law, or for establishing new law;

- Not interposed for any improper purpose, such as to harass, cause unnecessary delay, or needlessly increase the cost of litigation; and

- Neither unreasonable nor unduly burdensome or expensive, considering the needs of the case, prior discovery in the case, the amount in controversy, and the importance of the issues at stake in the action. FRCP 26(g)(1).

c. *Failure to sign.* Other parties have no duty to act on an unsigned disclosure, request, response, or objection until it is signed, and the court must strike it unless a signature is promptly supplied after the omission is called to the attorney's or party's attention. FRCP 26(g)(2).

d. *Sanction for improper certification.* If a certification violates FRCP 26(g) without substantial justification, the court, on motion or on its own, must impose an appropriate sanction on the signer, the party on whose behalf the signer was acting, or both. The sanction may include an order to pay the reasonable expenses, including attorney's fees, caused by the violation. FRCP 26(g)(3). Refer to the United States District Court for the Northern District of Indiana KeyRules Motion for Discovery Sanctions document for more information.

4. *Privacy protection for filings made with the court*

a. *Redacted filings.* Counsel should not include sensitive information in any document filed with the court unless such inclusion is necessary and relevant to the case. IN R USDCTND CM/ECF(VII). Unless the court orders otherwise, in an electronic or paper filing with the court that contains an individual's Social Security number, taxpayer-identification number, or birth date, the name of an individual known to be a minor, or a financial-account number, a party or nonparty making the filing may include only:

   i. The last four (4) digits of the Social Security number and taxpayer-identification number;

   ii. The year of the individual's birth;

   iii. The minor's initials; and

   iv. The last four (4) digits of the financial-account number. FRCP 5.2(a); IN R USDCTND Order 2005-3.

b. *Exemptions from the redaction requirement.* The redaction requirement does not apply to the following:

   i. A financial-account number that identifies the property allegedly subject to forfeiture in a forfeiture proceeding;

   ii. The record of an administrative or agency proceeding;

   iii. The official record of a state-court proceeding;

   iv. The record of a court or tribunal, if that record was not subject to the redaction requirement when originally filed;

   v. A filing covered by FRCP 5.2(c) or FRCP 5.2(d); and

   vi. A pro se filing in an action brought under 28 U.S.C.A. § 2241, 28 U.S.C.A. § 2254, or 28 U.S.C.A. § 2255. FRCP 5.2(b).

vii. In cases filed under the Social Security Act, 42 U.S.C.A. § 405(g), there is no need for redaction of any information from the documents filed in the case. IN R USDCTND Order 2005-3.

c. *Limitations on remote access to electronic files; Social Security appeals and immigration cases.* Unless the court orders otherwise, in an action for benefits under the Social Security Act, and in an action or proceeding relating to an order of removal, to relief from removal, or to immigration benefits or detention, access to an electronic file is authorized as follows:

i. The parties and their attorneys may have remote electronic access to any part of the case file, including the administrative record;

ii. Any other person may have electronic access to the full record at the courthouse, but may have remote electronic access only to:

- The docket maintained by the court; and
- An opinion, order, judgment, or other disposition of the court, but not any other part of the case file or the administrative record. FRCP 5.2(c).

d. *Filings made under seal.* The court may order that a filing be made under seal without redaction. The court may later unseal the filing or order the person who made the filing to file a redacted version for the public record. FRCP 5.2(d). For information on filing documents under seal, refer to IN R USDCTND L.R. 5-3, IN R USDCTND CM/ECF(IV)(A), and IN R USDCTND ECF Order 2004-19.

e. *Protective orders.* For good cause, the court may by order in a case:

i. Require redaction of additional information; or

ii. Limit or prohibit a nonparty's remote electronic access to a document filed with the court. FRCP 5.2(e).

f. *Option for additional unredacted filing under seal.* A person making a redacted filing may also file an unredacted copy under seal. The court must retain the unredacted copy as part of the record. FRCP 5.2(f); IN R USDCTND Order 2005-3.

i. The unredacted version of the document or the reference list shall be retained by the court under seal as part of the record. This paper shall be retained by the court as part of the record. The court may, however, still require the party to file a redacted copy for the public file. IN R USDCTND Order 2005-3.

g. *Option for filing a reference list.* A filing that contains redacted information may be filed together with a reference list that identifies each item of redacted information and specifies an appropriate identifier that uniquely corresponds to each item listed. The list must be filed under seal and may be amended as of right. Any reference in the case to a listed identifier will be construed to refer to the corresponding item of information. FRCP 5.2(g); IN R USDCTND Order 2005-3.

i. The unredacted version of the document or the reference list shall be retained by the court under seal as part of the record. This paper shall be retained by the court as part of the record. The court may, however, still require the party to file a redacted copy for the public file. IN R USDCTND Order 2005-3.

h. *Responsibility for redaction.* The responsibility for redacting these personal identifiers rests solely with counsel and the parties. The Clerk will not review each paper for compliance with IN R USDCTND Order 2005-3. IN R USDCTND Order 2005-3.

i. *Waiver of protection of identifiers.* A person waives the protection of FRCP 5.2(a) as to the person's own information by filing it without redaction and not under seal. FRCP 5.2(h).

F. Filing and Service Requirements

1. *Filing requirements.* Any paper after the complaint that is required to be served—together with a certificate of service—must be filed within a reasonable time after service. But disclosures under FRCP 26(a)(1) or FRCP 26(a)(2) and the following discovery requests and responses must not be filed until they are used in the proceeding or the court orders filing: depositions, interrogatories, requests for documents or tangible things or to permit entry onto land, and requests for admission. FRCP 5(d)(1). Refer to the

United States District Court for the Northern District of Indiana KeyRules pleading and motion documents for information on filing with the court.

a. *Discovery ordinarily not filed.* The party who serves a discovery request or notices a deposition is the custodian of the original discovery response or deposition transcript. Except as required under IN R USDCTND L.R. 26-2(a)(2), parties must not file: (1) disclosures under FRCP 26(a)(1) or FRCP 26(a)(2); (2) deposition notices; (3) deposition transcripts; (4) interrogatories; (5) requests for documents, to permit entry upon land, or for admission; (6) answers to interrogatories; (7) responses to requests for documents, to permit entry upon land, or for admission; or (8) service-of-discovery notices. IN R USDCTND L.R. 26-2(a)(1).

   i. *Exceptions*

   - *Pro se litigation.* All discovery material in cases involving a pro se party must be filed. IN R USDCTND L.R. 26-2(a)(2)(A).

   - *Specific material.* Discovery material must also be filed when: (1) the court orders; or (2) the material is used in a proceeding. IN R USDCTND L.R. 26-2(a)(2)(B).

b. *When discovery may be filed*

   i. *Filing materials with motion for relief.* A party who files a motion for relief under FRCP 26(c) or FRCP 37 must file with the motion those parts of the discovery requests or responses that the motion pertains to. IN R USDCTND L.R. 26-2(b).

   ii. *Materials necessary for motion.* A party must file those portions of discovery requests or responses (including deposition transcripts) that the party relies on to support a motion that could result in a final order on an issue. IN R USDCTND L.R. 26-2(c).

   iii. *Materials to be used at trial.* A party who reasonably anticipates using discovery requests or responses—including deposition transcripts—at trial must file the relevant portions of the requests or responses with the clerk at the start of the trial. IN R USDCTND L.R. 26-2(d).

2. *Service requirements.* A copy of the response must be served upon the party making the request. A copy of the response must also be served on all other parties to the action unless the court has ordered to the contrary. FPP § 2259.

a. *Service; When required*

   i. *In general.* Unless the Federal Rules of Civil Procedure provide otherwise, each of the following papers must be served on every party:

   - An order stating that service is required;

   - A pleading filed after the original complaint, unless the court orders otherwise under FRCP 5(c) because there are numerous defendants;

   - A discovery paper required to be served on a party, unless the court orders otherwise;

   - A written motion, except one that may be heard ex parte; and

   - A written notice, appearance, demand, or offer of judgment, or any similar paper. FRCP 5(a)(1).

   ii. *If a party fails to appear.* No service is required on a party who is in default for failing to appear. But a pleading that asserts a new claim for relief against such a party must be served on that party under FRCP 4. FRCP 5(a)(2).

   iii. *Seizing property.* If an action is begun by seizing property and no person is or need be named as a defendant, any service required before the filing of an appearance, answer, or claim must be made on the person who had custody or possession of the property when it was seized. FRCP 5(a)(3).

b. *Service; How made*

   i. *Serving an attorney.* If a party is represented by an attorney, service under FRCP 5 must be made on the attorney unless the court orders service on the party. FRCP 5(b)(1).

ii. *Service in general.* A paper is served under FRCP 5 by:

- Handing it to the person;

- Leaving it: (1) at the person's office with a clerk or other person in charge or, if no one is in charge, in a conspicuous place in the office; or (2) if the person has no office or the office is closed, at the person's dwelling or usual place of abode with someone of suitable age and discretion who resides there;

- Mailing it to the person's last known address—in which event service is complete upon mailing;

- Leaving it with the court clerk if the person has no known address;

- Sending it by electronic means if the person consented in writing—in which event service is complete upon transmission, but is not effective if the serving party learns that it did not reach the person to be served; or

- Delivering it by any other means that the person consented to in writing—in which event service is complete when the person making service delivers it to the agency designated to make delivery. FRCP 5(b)(2).

iii. *Electronic service.* Electronically filed papers may be served electronically if service is consistent with the CM/ECF User Manual (IN R USDCTND CM/ECF). IN R USDCTND L.R. 5-2(a).

- *Waiver of other service.* An attorney's registration will constitute a waiver of conventional service of documents and the attorney agrees to accept service of notice on behalf of the client of the electronic filing by hand, facsimile or authorized email. IN R USDCTND CM/ECF(I)(B)(3).

- *Serving registered persons.* The System will generate a "Notice of Electronic Filing" when any document is filed. This notice represents service of the document on parties who are registered participants with the System. Except as provided in IN R USDCTND CM/ECF(III)(B), the filing party shall not be required to serve any pleading or other documents on any party receiving electronic notice. IN R USDCTND CM/ECF(II)(D)(1). The term "pleading" refers only to those documents listed in FRCP 7(a). IN R USDCTND CM/ECF(FN3).

- *When electronic service is deemed completed.* A person registered to use the court's electronic-filing system is served with an electronically filed paper when a "Notice of Electronic Filing" is transmitted to that person through the court's electronic filing-system. IN R USDCTND L.R. 5-2(b).

- *Serving non-registered persons.* A person who has not registered to use the court's electronic-filing system but who is entitled to service of a paper must be served according to the Local Civil Rules of the United States District Court for the Northern District of Indiana and the Federal Rules of Civil Procedure. IN R USDCTND L.R. 5-2(c); IN R USDCTND CM/ECF(II)(D)(2). If such service of a paper copy is to be made, it shall be done in the manner provided in the Federal Rules of Civil Procedure and the Local Civil Rules of the United States District Court for the Northern District of Indiana. IN R USDCTND CM/ECF(II)(D)(2).

iv. *Service of conventional filings.* Pleadings or other documents which are filed conventionally rather than electronically shall be served in the manner provided for in the Federal Rules of Civil Procedure and the Local Civil Rules of the United States District Court for the Northern District of Indiana, except as otherwise provided by order of the Court. IN R USDCTND CM/ECF(III)(B).

v. *Using court facilities.* If a local rule so authorizes, a party may use the court's transmission facilities to make service under FRCP 5(b)(2)(E). FRCP 5(b)(3).

    c. *Serving numerous defendants*

        i. *In general.* If an action involves an unusually large number of defendants, the court may, on motion or on its own, order that:

- Defendants' pleadings and replies to them need not be served on other defendants;

- Any crossclaim, counterclaim, avoidance, or affirmative defense in those pleadings and replies to them will be treated as denied or avoided by all other parties; and

- Filing any such pleading and serving it on the plaintiff constitutes notice of the pleading to all parties. FRCP 5(c)(1).

        ii. *Notifying parties.* A copy of every such order must be served on the parties as the court directs. FRCP 5(c)(2).

G. Hearings

1. There is no hearing contemplated in the federal statutes or rules for responses to requests for admissions.

H. Forms

1. Federal Response to Request for Admissions Forms

    a. Reply; To request for admission of facts. AMJUR PP DEPOSITION § 684.

    b. Reply; To request for admission of facts; With verification. AMJUR PP DEPOSITION § 685.

    c. Reply; To request for admissions of fact and genuineness of documents; Refusal to answer on ground of privilege. AMJUR PP DEPOSITION § 686.

    d. Answer; To demand for admissions; Admission or denial not required under governing statute or rule. AMJUR PP DEPOSITION § 687.

    e. Reply; Objection to request for admissions; Irrelevancy and immateriality; Answer already made in response to interrogatories. AMJUR PP DEPOSITION § 688.

    f. Response to request for admission. 3B FEDFORMS § 3664.

    g. Response to request for admission; Admissions, qualified admissions, denials. 3B FEDFORMS § 3665.

    h. Response to request for admission; Denials and admissions of specific facts and explanatory statement of inability to admit or deny. 3B FEDFORMS § 3666.

    i. Response to request for admission; Denials and admissions of specific facts and explanatory statement of inability to admit or deny; Another form. 3B FEDFORMS § 3667.

    j. Objections to requests for admissions. 3B FEDFORMS § 3668.

    k. Objections to request for admissions; Privileged. 3B FEDFORMS § 3668.50.

    l. Amended response to request for admission. 3B FEDFORMS § 3669.

    m. Answer; To request for admissions; General form. FEDPROF § 23:550.

    n. Answer; To request for admissions; Insurance claim. FEDPROF § 23:551.

    o. Objections; To request for admissions. FEDPROF § 23:552.

    p. Objections to request. GOLDLTGFMS § 30:12.

    q. Reply to request for admissions. GOLDLTGFMS § 30:15.

    r. Response to request; General form. GOLDLTGFMS § 30:16.

    s. Response to request; Denials. GOLDLTGFMS § 30:17.

    t. Response to request; Admission of genuineness of document. GOLDLTGFMS § 30:18.

    u. Response to request; Admission of facts. GOLDLTGFMS § 30:19.

    v. Reply and objections to request for admissions. GOLDLTGFMS § 30:20.

I. Applicable Rules

1. *Federal rules*

   a. Serving and filing pleadings and other papers. FRCP 5.

   b. Privacy protection for filings made with the court. FRCP 5.2.

   c. Computing and extending time; Time for motion papers. FRCP 6.

   d. Pleadings allowed; Form of motions and other papers. FRCP 7.

   e. Form of pleadings. FRCP 10.

   f. Signing pleadings, motions, and other papers; Representations to the court; Sanctions. FRCP 11.

   g. Duty to disclose; General provisions governing discovery. FRCP 26.

   h. Stipulations about discovery procedure. FRCP 29.

   i. Requests for admission. FRCP 36.

   j. Failure to make disclosures or to cooperate in discovery; Sanctions. FRCP 37.

2. *Local rules*

   a. Citation and scope of the rules. IN R USDCTND L.R. 1-1.

   b. Sanctions for formatting errors. IN R USDCTND L.R. 1-3.

   c. Electronic service. IN R USDCTND L.R. 5-2.

   d. Format of papers. IN R USDCTND L.R. 5-4.

   e. Extensions of time. IN R USDCTND L.R. 6-1.

   f. Pretrial procedure. IN R USDCTND L.R. 16-1.

   g. Alternative dispute resolution. IN R USDCTND L.R. 16-6.

   h. Form of certain discovery documents. IN R USDCTND L.R. 26-1.

   i. Filing of discovery and other materials. IN R USDCTND L.R. 26-2.

   j. Case assignment. IN R USDCTND L.R. 40-1.

   k. Appearance and withdrawal of appearance. IN R USDCTND L.R. 83-8.

   l. CM/ECF civil and criminal user manual. IN R USDCTND CM/ECF.

   m. In re: privacy and public access to civil electronic case files. IN R USDCTND Order 2005-3.

Requests, Notices and Applications
Notice of Deposition

Document Last Updated December 2016

A. Checklist

(I) ❑ Matters to be considered by deposing party for depositions by oral examination

    (a) ❑ Required documents

        (1) ❑ Notice of deposition

    (b) ❑ Supplemental documents

        (1) ❑ Subpoena

        (2) ❑ Subpoena duces tecum

        (3) ❑ Request for production of documents

        (4) ❑ Certificate of service

    (c) ❑ Timing

        (1) ❑ A party may, by oral questions, depose any person, including a party, without leave of court except as provided in FRCP 30(a)(2)

        (2) ❑ A party must obtain leave of court, and the court must grant leave to the extent consistent with FRCP 26(b)(1) and FRCP 26(b)(2):

            (i) ❑ If the parties have not stipulated to the deposition and: (1) the deposition would result in more than ten (10) depositions being taken under FRCP 30 or FRCP 31 by the plaintiffs, or by the defendants, or by the third-party defendants; (2) the deponent has already been deposed in the case; or (3) the party seeks to take the deposition before the time specified in FRCP 26(d), unless the party certifies in the notice, with supporting facts, that the deponent is expected to leave the United States and be unavailable for examination in this country after that time; or

           (ii) ❑ If the deponent is confined in prison

        (3) ❑ A party who wants to depose a person by oral questions must give reasonable written notice to every other party

            (i) ❑ Attorneys must schedule depositions with at least fourteen (14) days' notice, unless opposing counsel agrees to shorter notice or the court orders otherwise

(II) ❑ Matters to be considered by deposing party for depositions by written questions

    (a) ❑ Required documents

        (1) ❑ Notice of deposition

        (2) ❑ Written questions

    (b) ❑ Supplemental documents

        (1) ❑ Subpoena

        (2) ❑ Certificate of service

    (c) ❑ Timing

        (1) ❑ A party may, by written questions, depose any person, including a party, without leave of court except as provided in FRCP 31(a)(2)

        (2) ❑ A party must obtain leave of court, and the court must grant leave to the extent consistent with FRCP 26(b)(1) and FRCP 26(b)(2):

            (i) ❑ If the parties have not stipulated to the deposition and: (1) the deposition would result in more than ten (10) depositions being taken under FRCP 31 or FRCP 30 by the plaintiffs, or by the defendants, or by the third-party defendants; (2) the deponent has already been deposed in the case; or (3) the party seeks to take a deposition before the time specified in FRCP 26(d); or

           (ii) ❑ If the deponent is confined in prison

        (3) ❑ A party who wants to depose a person by written questions must serve them on every other party, with a notice

B. Timing

  1. *Depositions by oral examination*

    a. *Without leave.* A party may, by oral questions, depose any person, including a party, without leave of court except as provided in FRCP 30(a)(2). FRCP 30(a)(1).

    b. *With leave.* A party must obtain leave of court, and the court must grant leave to the extent consistent with FRCP 26(b)(1) and FRCP 26(b)(2):

      i. If the parties have not stipulated to the deposition and: (1) the deposition would result in more than ten (10) depositions being taken under FRCP 30 or FRCP 31 by the plaintiffs, or by the defendants, or by the third-party defendants; (2) the deponent has already been deposed in the case; or (3) the party seeks to take the deposition before the time specified in FRCP 26(d), unless the party certifies in the notice, with supporting facts, that the deponent is expected to leave the United States and be unavailable for examination in this country after that time; or

    ii.   If the deponent is confined in prison. FRCP 30(a)(2).

  c. *Notice of deposition.* A party who wants to depose a person by oral questions must give reasonable written notice to every other party. FRCP 30(b)(1).

    i.   Attorneys must schedule depositions with at least fourteen (14) days' notice, unless opposing counsel agrees to shorter notice or the court orders otherwise. IN R USDCTND L.R. 30-1(b).

2. *Depositions by written questions*

  a. *Without leave.* A party may, by written questions, depose any person, including a party, without leave of court except as provided in FRCP 31(a)(2). FRCP 31(a)(1).

  b. *With leave.* A party must obtain leave of court, and the court must grant leave to the extent consistent with FRCP 26(b)(1) and FRCP 26(b)(2):

    i.   If the parties have not stipulated to the deposition and: (1) the deposition would result in more than ten (10) depositions being taken under FRCP 31 or FRCP 30 by the plaintiffs, or by the defendants, or by the third-party defendants; (2) the deponent has already been deposed in the case; or (3) the party seeks to take a deposition before the time specified in FRCP 26(d); or

    ii.   If the deponent is confined in prison. FRCP 31(a)(2).

  c. *Notice of deposition with written questions.* A party who wants to depose a person by written questions must serve them on every other party, with a notice. FRCP 31(a)(3). Refer to the General Requirements section of this document for the contents of the notice.

  d. *Questions from other parties.* Any questions to the deponent from other parties must be served on all parties as follows:

    i.   *Cross-questions.* Cross-questions, within fourteen (14) days after being served with the notice and direct questions;

    ii.   *Redirect questions.* Redirect questions, within seven (7) days after being served with cross-questions; and

    iii.   *Recross-questions.* Recross-questions, within seven (7) days after being served with redirect questions. FRCP 31(a)(5).

    iv.   *Modification of timing requirements.* The court may, for good cause, extend or shorten these times. FRCP 31(a)(5).

3. *Timing of discovery, generally.* A party may not seek discovery from any source before the parties have conferred as required by FRCP 26(f), except in a proceeding exempted from initial disclosure under FRCP 26(a)(1)(B), or when authorized by the Federal Rules of Civil Procedure, by stipulation, or by court order. FRCP 26(d)(1).

4. *Computation of time*

  a. *Computing time.* FRCP 6 applies in computing any time period specified in the Federal Rules of Civil Procedure, in any local rule or court order, or in any statute that does not specify a method of computing time. FRCP 6(a).

    i.   *Period stated in days or a longer unit.* When the period is stated in days or a longer unit of time:

       • Exclude the day of the event that triggers the period;

       • Count every day, including intermediate Saturdays, Sundays, and legal holidays; and

       • Include the last day of the period, but if the last day is a Saturday, Sunday, or legal holiday, the period continues to run until the end of the next day that is not a Saturday, Sunday, or legal holiday. FRCP 6(a)(1).

    ii.   *Period stated in hours.* When the period is stated in hours:

       • Begin counting immediately on the occurrence of the event that triggers the period;

- Count every hour, including hours during intermediate Saturdays, Sundays, and legal holidays; and

- If the period would end on a Saturday, Sunday, or legal holiday, the period continues to run until the same time on the next day that is not a Saturday, Sunday, or legal holiday. FRCP 6(a)(2).

iii. *Inaccessibility of the clerk's office.* Unless the court orders otherwise, if the clerk's office is inaccessible:

- On the last day for filing under FRCP 6(a)(1), then the time for filing is extended to the first accessible day that is not a Saturday, Sunday, or legal holiday; or

- During the last hour for filing under FRCP 6(a)(2), then the time for filing is extended to the same time on the first accessible day that is not a Saturday, Sunday, or legal holiday. FRCP 6(a)(3).

iv. *"Last day" defined.* Unless a different time is set by a statute, local rule, or court order, the last day ends:

- For electronic filing, at midnight in the court's time zone; and

- For filing by other means, when the clerk's office is scheduled to close. FRCP 6(a)(4).

v. *"Next day" defined.* The "next day" is determined by continuing to count forward when the period is measured after an event and backward when measured before an event. FRCP 6(a)(5).

vi. *"Legal holiday" defined.* "Legal holiday" means:

- The day set aside by statute for observing New Year's Day, Martin Luther King Jr.'s Birthday, Washington's Birthday, Memorial Day, Independence Day, Labor Day, Columbus Day, Veterans' Day, Thanksgiving Day, or Christmas Day;

- Any day declared a holiday by the President or Congress; and

- For periods that are measured after an event, any other day declared a holiday by the state where the district court is located. FRCP 6(a)(6).

b. *Computation of electronic filing deadlines.* Filing documents electronically does not alter any filing deadlines or any time computation pursuant to FRCP 6. The counties of Lake, Porter, LaPorte, Pulaski and Starke are located in the Central time zone and the remaining counties in the Northern District of Indiana are located in the Eastern time zone. Nevertheless, all electronic transmissions of documents must be completed (i.e., received completely by the clerk's office) prior to midnight Eastern Time, (South Bend/Fort Wayne/Lafayette time) in order to be considered timely filed that day, regardless of the local time in the division where the case is pending. Although documents can be filed electronically twenty-four (24) hours a day, filers are strongly encouraged to file all documents during hours when the CM/ECF Help Line is available, from 9:00 a.m. to 4:00 p.m. local time. IN R USDCTND CM/ECF(II)(I).

i. *Technical failures.* If the attorney is unable to file a document in a timely manner due to technical difficulties in the user's system, the attorney must file a document with the court as soon as possible notifying the court of the inability to file the document. A sample document entitled Declaration that Party was Unable to File in a Timely Manner Due to Technical Difficulties is attached hereto as Form 5. IN R USDCTND CM/ECF(VI)(B). [Editor's note: the reference to Form 5 is likely meant to be a reference to Form 3 (IN R USDCTND CM/ECF(Form 3)].

c. *Extending time*

i. *In general.* When an act may or must be done within a specified time, the court may, for good cause, extend the time:

- With or without motion or notice if the court acts, or if a request is made, before the original time or its extension expires; or

- On motion made after the time has expired if the party failed to act because of excusable neglect. FRCP 6(b)(1).

    ii. *Exceptions.* A court must not extend the time to act under FRCP 50(b), FRCP 50(d), FRCP 52(b), FRCP 59(b), FRCP 59(d), FRCP 59(e), and FRCP 60(b). FRCP 6(b)(2).

    iii. Refer to the United States District Court for the Northern District of Indiana KeyRules Motion for Continuance/Extension of Time document for more information on extending time.

  d. *Additional time after certain kinds of service.* When a party may or must act within a specified time after being served and service is made under FRCP 5(b)(2)(C) (mail), FRCP 5(b)(2)(D) (leaving with the clerk), or FRCP 5(b)(2)(F) (other means consented to), three (3) days are added after the period would otherwise expire under FRCP 6(a). FRCP 6(d).

C. General Requirements

1. *General provisions governing discovery*

  a. *Discovery scope and limits*

    i. *Scope in general.* Unless otherwise limited by court order, the scope of discovery is as follows: Parties may obtain discovery regarding any nonprivileged matter that is relevant to any party's claim or defense and proportional to the needs of the case, considering the importance of the issues at stake in the action, the amount in controversy, the parties' relative access to relevant information, the parties' resources, the importance of the discovery in resolving the issues, and whether the burden or expense of the proposed discovery outweighs its likely benefit. Information within this scope of discovery need not be admissible in evidence to be discoverable. FRCP 26(b)(1).

    ii. *Limitations on frequency and extent*

- *When permitted.* By order, the court may alter the limits in the Federal Rules of Civil Procedure on the number of depositions and interrogatories or on the length of depositions under FRCP 30. By order or local rule, the court may also limit the number of requests under FRCP 36. FRCP 26(b)(2)(A).

- *Specific limitations on electronically stored information.* A party need not provide discovery of electronically stored information from sources that the party identifies as not reasonably accessible because of undue burden or cost. On motion to compel discovery or for a protective order, the party from whom discovery is sought must show that the information is not reasonably accessible because of undue burden or cost. If that showing is made, the court may nonetheless order discovery from such sources if the requesting party shows good cause, considering the limitations of FRCP 26(b)(2)(C). The court may specify conditions for the discovery. FRCP 26(b)(2)(B).

- *When required.* On motion or on its own, the court must limit the frequency or extent of discovery otherwise allowed by the Federal Rules of Civil Procedure or by local rule if it determines that: (1) the discovery sought is unreasonably cumulative or duplicative, or can be obtained from some other source that is more convenient, less burdensome, or less expensive; (2) the party seeking discovery has had ample opportunity to obtain the information by discovery in the action; or (3) the proposed discovery is outside the scope permitted by FRCP 26(b)(1). FRCP 26(b)(2)(C).

    iii. *Trial preparation; Materials*

- *Documents and tangible things.* Ordinarily, a party may not discover documents and tangible things that are prepared in anticipation of litigation or for trial by or for another party or its representative (including the other party's attorney, consultant, surety, indemnitor, insurer, or agent). But, subject to FRCP 26(b)(4), those materials may be discovered if: (1) they are otherwise discoverable under FRCP 26(b)(1); and (2) the party shows that it has substantial need for the materials to prepare its case and cannot, without undue hardship, obtain their substantial equivalent by other means. FRCP 26(b)(3)(A).

- *Protection against disclosure.* If the court orders discovery of those materials, it must protect against disclosure of the mental impressions, conclusions, opinions, or legal theories of a party's attorney or other representative concerning the litigation. FRCP 26(b)(3)(B).

- *Previous statement.* Any party or other person may, on request and without the required showing, obtain the person's own previous statement about the action or its subject matter. If the request is refused, the person may move for a court order, and FRCP 37(a)(5) applies to the award of expenses. A previous statement is either: (1) a written statement that the person has signed or otherwise adopted or approved; or (2) a contemporaneous stenographic, mechanical, electrical, or other recording—or a transcription of it—that recites substantially verbatim the person's oral statement. FRCP 26(b)(3)(C).

iv. *Trial preparation; Experts*

- *Deposition of an expert who may testify.* A party may depose any person who has been identified as an expert whose opinions may be presented at trial. If FRCP 26(a)(2)(B) requires a report from the expert, the deposition may be conducted only after the report is provided. FRCP 26(b)(4)(A).

- *Trial-preparation protection for draft reports or disclosures.* FRCP 26(b)(3)(A) and FRCP 26(b)(3)(B) protect drafts of any report or disclosure required under FRCP 26(a)(2), regardless of the form in which the draft is recorded. FRCP 26(b)(4)(B).

- *Trial-preparation protection for communications between a party's attorney and expert witnesses.* FRCP 26(b)(3)(A) and FRCP 26(b)(3)(B) protect communications between the party's attorney and any witness required to provide a report under FRCP 26(a)(2)(B), regardless of the form of the communications, except to the extent that the communications: (1) relate to compensation for the expert's study or testimony; (2) identify facts or data that the party's attorney provided and that the expert considered in forming the opinions to be expressed; or (3) identify assumptions that the party's attorney provided and that the expert relied on in forming the opinions to be expressed. FRCP 26(b)(4)(C).

- *Expert employed only for trial preparation.* Ordinarily, a party may not, by interrogatories or deposition, discover facts known or opinions held by an expert who has been retained or specially employed by another party in anticipation of litigation or to prepare for trial and who is not expected to be called as a witness at trial. But a party may do so only: (1) as provided in FRCP 35(b); or (2) on showing exceptional circumstances under which it is impracticable for the party to obtain facts or opinions on the same subject by other means. FRCP 26(b)(4)(D).

- *Payment.* Unless manifest injustice would result, the court must require that the party seeking discovery: (1) pay the expert a reasonable fee for time spent in responding to discovery under FRCP 26(b)(4)(A) or FRCP 26(b)(4)(D); and (2) for discovery under FRCP 26(b)(4)(D), also pay the other party a fair portion of the fees and expenses it reasonably incurred in obtaining the expert's facts and opinions. FRCP 26(b)(4)(E).

v. *Claiming privilege or protecting trial-preparation materials*

- *Information withheld.* When a party withholds information otherwise discoverable by claiming that the information is privileged or subject to protection as trial-preparation material, the party must: (1) expressly make the claim; and (2) describe the nature of the documents, communications, or tangible things not produced or disclosed—and do so in a manner that, without revealing information itself privileged or protected, will enable other parties to assess the claim. FRCP 26(b)(5)(A).

- *Information produced.* If information produced in discovery is subject to a claim of privilege or of protection as trial-preparation material, the party making the claim may notify any party that received the information of the claim and the basis for it. After being notified, a party must promptly return, sequester, or destroy the specified information and any copies it has; must not use or disclose the information until the claim is resolved; must take reasonable steps to retrieve the information if the party disclosed it before being notified; and may promptly present the information to the court under seal for a determination of the claim. The producing party must preserve the information until the claim is resolved. FRCP 26(b)(5)(B).

b. *Protective orders.* A party or any person from whom discovery is sought may move for a protective order in the court where the action is pending—or as an alternative on matters relating to a deposition, in the court for the district where the deposition will be taken. FRCP 26(c)(1). Refer to the United States District Court for the Northern District of Indiana KeyRules Motion for Protective Order document for more information.

c. *Sequence of discovery.* Unless the parties stipulate or the court orders otherwise for the parties' and witnesses' convenience and in the interests of justice: (1) methods of discovery may be used in any sequence; and (2) discovery by one party does not require any other party to delay its discovery. FRCP 26(d)(3).

2. *Persons before whom depositions may be taken*

a. *Within the United States.* Within the United States or a territory or insular possession subject to United States jurisdiction, a deposition must be taken before: (1) an officer authorized to administer oaths either by federal law or by the law in the place of examination; or (2) a person appointed by the court where the action is pending to administer oaths and take testimony. FRCP 28(a)(1).

 i. *Definition of "officer".* The term "officer" in FRCP 30, FRCP 31, and FRCP 32 includes a person appointed by the court under FRCP 28 or designated by the parties under FRCP 29(a). FRCP 28(a)(2).

b. *In a foreign country.* A deposition may be taken in a foreign country: (1) under an applicable treaty or convention; (2) under a letter of request, whether or not captioned a "letter rogatory"; (3) on notice, before a person authorized to administer oaths either by federal law or by the law in the place of examination; or (4) before a person commissioned by the court to administer any necessary oath and take testimony. FRCP 28(b)(1).

 i. *Issuing a letter of request or a commission.* A letter of request, a commission, or both may be issued: (1) on appropriate terms after an application and notice of it; and (2) without a showing that taking the deposition in another manner is impracticable or inconvenient. FRCP 28(b)(2).

 ii. *Form of a request, notice, or commission.* When a letter of request or any other device is used according to a treaty or convention, it must be captioned in the form prescribed by that treaty or convention. A letter of request may be addressed "To the Appropriate Authority in [name of country]." A deposition notice or a commission must designate by name or descriptive title the person before whom the deposition is to be taken. FRCP 28(b)(3).

 iii. *Letter of request; Admitting evidence.* Evidence obtained in response to a letter of request need not be excluded merely because it is not a verbatim transcript, because the testimony was not taken under oath, or because of any similar departure from the requirements for depositions taken within the United States. FRCP 28(b)(4).

c. *Disqualification.* A deposition must not be taken before a person who is any party's relative, employee, or attorney; who is related to or employed by any party's attorney; or who is financially interested in the action. FRCP 28(c).

3. *Depositions by oral examination*

a. *Scheduling; Avoiding conflicts.* Attorneys must try in good faith to schedule depositions to avoid calendar conflicts. IN R USDCTND L.R. 30-1(a).

b. *Notice of the deposition.* A party who wants to depose a person by oral questions must give reasonable written notice to every other party. The notice must state the time and place of the deposition and, if known, the deponent's name and address. If the name is unknown, the notice must provide a general description sufficient to identify the person or the particular class or group to which the person belongs. FRCP 30(b)(1).

 i. *Notice or subpoena directed to an organization.* In its notice or subpoena, a party may name as the deponent a public or private corporation, a partnership, an association, a governmental agency, or other entity and must describe with reasonable particularity the matters for examination. The named organization must then designate one or more officers, directors, or managing agents, or designate other persons who consent to testify on its behalf; and it may set out the matters on which each person designated will testify. A subpoena must advise a nonparty organization of its duty to make this designation. The persons designated must testify about information known or reasonably available to the organization. FRCP 30(b)(6) does not preclude a deposition by any other procedure allowed by the Federal Rules of Civil Procedure. FRCP 30(b)(6).

c. *Method of recording*

    i. *Method stated in the notice.* The party who notices the deposition must state in the notice the method for recording the testimony. Unless the court orders otherwise, testimony may be recorded by audio, audiovisual, or stenographic means. The noticing party bears the recording costs. Any party may arrange to transcribe a deposition. FRCP 30(b)(3)(A).

    ii. *Additional method.* With prior notice to the deponent and other parties, any party may designate another method for recording the testimony in addition to that specified in the original notice. That party bears the expense of the additional record or transcript unless the court orders otherwise. FRCP 30(b)(3)(B).

d. *By remote means.* The parties may stipulate—or the court may on motion order—that a deposition be taken by telephone or other remote means. For the purpose of FRCP 30 and FRCP 28(a), FRCP 37(a)(2), and FRCP 37(b)(1), the deposition takes place where the deponent answers the questions. FRCP 30(b)(4).

e. *Officer's duties*

    i. *Before the deposition.* Unless the parties stipulate otherwise, a deposition must be conducted before an officer appointed or designated under FRCP 28. The officer must begin the deposition with an on-the-record statement that includes: (1) the officer's name and business address; (2) the date, time, and place of the deposition; (3) the deponent's name; (4) the officer's administration of the oath or affirmation to the deponent; and (5) the identity of all persons present. FRCP 30(b)(5)(A).

    ii. *Conducting the deposition; Avoiding distortion.* If the deposition is recorded non-stenographically, the officer must repeat the items in FRCP 30(b)(5)(A)(i) through FRCP 30(b)(5)(A)(iii) at the beginning of each unit of the recording medium. The deponent's and attorneys' appearance or demeanor must not be distorted through recording techniques. FRCP 30(b)(5)(B).

    iii. *After the deposition.* At the end of a deposition, the officer must state on the record that the deposition is complete and must set out any stipulations made by the attorneys about custody of the transcript or recording and of the exhibits, or about any other pertinent matters. FRCP 30(b)(5)(C).

f. *Examination and cross-examination.* The examination and cross-examination of a deponent proceed as they would at trial under the Federal Rules of Evidence, except FRE 103 and FRE 615. FRCP 30(c)(1).

    i. *Record of the examination.* After putting the deponent under oath or affirmation, the officer must record the testimony by the method designated under FRCP 30(b)(3)(A). The testimony must be recorded by the officer personally or by a person acting in the presence and under the direction of the officer. FRCP 30(c)(1).

    ii. *Objections.* An objection at the time of the examination—whether to evidence, to a party's conduct, to the officer's qualifications, to the manner of taking the deposition, or to any other aspect of the deposition—must be noted on the record, but the examination still proceeds; the testimony is taken subject to any objection. An objection must be stated concisely in a nonargumentative and nonsuggestive manner. A person may instruct a deponent not to answer only when necessary to preserve a privilege, to enforce a limitation ordered by the court, or to present a motion under FRCP 30(d)(3). FRCP 30(c)(2).

    iii. *Dealing with objections during depositions*

       • *Attempt to resolve dispute.* Before contacting the court for a ruling on an objection during a deposition, all parties must confer in good faith or attempt to confer in an effort to resolve the matter without court action. IN R USDCTND L.R. 37-3(a).

- *Raising objections with the court.* A party may recess a deposition to submit an objection by phone to a judge if: (1) a judge is available and willing to address the objection; and (2) the objection: (A) could cause the deposition to be adjourned; and (B) can be resolved without submitting written materials to the court. IN R USDCTND L.R. 37-3(b).

    iv. *Participating through written questions.* Instead of participating in the oral examination, a party may serve written questions in a sealed envelope on the party noticing the deposition, who must deliver them to the officer. The officer must ask the deponent those questions and record the answers verbatim. FRCP 30(c)(3).

g. *Duration.* Unless otherwise stipulated or ordered by the court, a deposition is limited to one (1) day of seven (7) hours. The court must allow additional time consistent with FRCP 26(b)(1) and FRCP 26(b)(2) if needed to fairly examine the deponent or if the deponent, another person, or any other circumstance impedes or delays the examination. FRCP 30(d)(1).

h. *Sanction.* The court may impose an appropriate sanction—including the reasonable expenses and attorney's fees incurred by any party—on a person who impedes, delays, or frustrates the fair examination of the deponent. FRCP 30(d)(2). Refer to the United States District Court for the Northern District of Indiana KeyRules Motion for Discovery Sanctions document for more information on sanctions.

i. *Motion to terminate or limit.* At any time during a deposition, the deponent or a party may move to terminate or limit it on the ground that it is being conducted in bad faith or in a manner that unreasonably annoys, embarrasses, or oppresses the deponent or party. The motion may be filed in the court where the action is pending or the deposition is being taken. If the objecting deponent or party so demands, the deposition must be suspended for the time necessary to obtain an order. FRCP 30(d)(3)(A).

    i. *Order.* The court may order that the deposition be terminated or may limit its scope and manner as provided in FRCP 26(c). If terminated, the deposition may be resumed only by order of the court where the action is pending. FRCP 30(d)(3)(B).

    ii. *Award of expenses.* FRCP 37(a)(5) applies to the award of expenses. FRCP 30(d)(3)(C). Refer to the United States District Court for the Northern District of Indiana KeyRules Motion for Discovery Sanctions document for more information on sanctions.

j. *Review by the witness; Statement of changes.* On request by the deponent or a party before the deposition is completed, the deponent must be allowed thirty (30) days after being notified by the officer that the transcript or recording is available in which: (1) to review the transcript or recording; and (2) if there are changes in form or substance, to sign a statement listing the changes and the reasons for making them. FRCP 30(e)(1).

    i. *Changes indicated in the officer's certificate.* The officer must note in the certificate prescribed by FRCP 30(f)(1) whether a review was requested and, if so, must attach any changes the deponent makes during the thirty (30) day period. FRCP 30(e)(2).

k. *Certification and delivery.* The officer must certify in writing that the witness was duly sworn and that the deposition accurately records the witness's testimony. The certificate must accompany the record of the deposition. Unless the court orders otherwise, the officer must seal the deposition in an envelope or package bearing the title of the action and marked "Deposition of [witness's name]" and must promptly send it to the attorney who arranged for the transcript or recording. The attorney must store it under conditions that will protect it against loss, destruction, tampering, or deterioration. FRCP 30(f)(1).

l. *Documents and tangible things.* Documents and tangible things produced for inspection during a deposition must, on a party's request, be marked for identification and attached to the deposition. Any party may inspect and copy them. But if the person who produced them wants to keep the originals, the person may: (1) offer copies to be marked, attached to the deposition, and then used as originals—after giving all parties a fair opportunity to verify the copies by comparing them with the originals; or (2) give all parties a fair opportunity to inspect and copy the originals after they are marked—in which event the originals may be used as if attached to the deposition. FRCP 30(f)(2)(A).

    i. *Order regarding the originals.* Any party may move for an order that the originals be attached to the deposition pending final disposition of the case. FRCP 30(f)(2)(B).

m. *Copies of the transcript or recording.* Unless otherwise stipulated or ordered by the court, the officer must retain the stenographic notes of a deposition taken stenographically or a copy of the recording of a deposition taken by another method. When paid reasonable charges, the officer must furnish a copy of the transcript or recording to any party or the deponent. FRCP 30(f)(3).

    i. Motions to publish deposition transcripts are not required. IN R USDCTND L.R. 26-2.

n. *Failure to attend a deposition or serve a subpoena; Expenses.* A party who, expecting a deposition to be taken, attends in person or by an attorney may recover reasonable expenses for attending, including attorney's fees, if the noticing party failed to: (1) attend and proceed with the deposition; or (2) serve a subpoena on a nonparty deponent, who consequently did not attend. FRCP 30(g). Refer to the United States District Court for the Northern District of Indiana KeyRules Motion for Discovery Sanctions document for more information on sanctions.

4. *Depositions by written questions*

a. *Notice of deposition.* A party who wants to depose a person by written questions must serve them on every other party, with a notice stating, if known, the deponent's name and address. If the name is unknown, the notice must provide a general description sufficient to identify the person or the particular class or group to which the person belongs. The notice must also state the name or descriptive title and the address of the officer before whom the deposition will be taken. FRCP 31(a)(3).

b. *Questions directed to an organization.* A public or private corporation, a partnership, an association, or a governmental agency may be deposed by written questions in accordance with FRCP 30(b)(6). FRCP 31(a)(4).

c. *Delivery to the officer; Officer's duties.* The party who noticed the deposition must deliver to the officer a copy of all the questions served and of the notice. The officer must promptly proceed in the manner provided in FRCP 30(c), FRCP 30(e), and FRCP 30(f) to:

    i. Take the deponent's testimony in response to the questions;

    ii. Prepare and certify the deposition; and

    iii. Send it to the party, attaching a copy of the questions and of the notice. FRCP 31(b).

d. *Notice of completion.* The party who noticed the deposition must notify all other parties when it is completed. FRCP 31(c)(1).

5. *Depositions to perpetuate testimony.* For information on depositions to perpetuate testimony, refer to FRCP 27.

6. *Stipulations about discovery procedure.* Unless the court orders otherwise, the parties may stipulate that: (1) a deposition may be taken before any person, at any time or place, on any notice, and in the manner specified—in which event it may be used in the same way as any other deposition; and (2) other procedures governing or limiting discovery be modified—but a stipulation extending the time for any form of discovery must have court approval if it would interfere with the time set for completing discovery, for hearing a motion, or for trial. FRCP 29.

7. *Appearances.* Attorneys not representing the United States or its agencies must file an appearance when they represent (either in person or by filing a paper) a party. IN R USDCTND L.R. 83-8(a). For more information, refer to IN R USDCTND L.R. 83-8.

8. *Notice of related action.* A party must file a notice of related action as soon as it appears that the party's case and another pending case: (1) arise out of the same transaction or occurrence; (2) involve the same property; or (3) involve the validity or infringement of the same patent, trademark, or copyright. IN R USDCTND L.R. 40-1(d). For more information, refer to IN R USDCTND L.R. 40-1.

9. *Alternative dispute resolution (ADR).* After they confer as required by FRCP 26(f), the parties must advise

the court which, if any, alternative-dispute-resolution processes they expect to pursue and when they expect to undertake the process. IN R USDCTND L.R. 16-6(a). For more information on alternative dispute resolution (ADR), refer to IN R USDCTND L.R. 16-6 and IN R USDCTND Order 2003-21.

10. *Settlement or resolution.* The parties must immediately notify the court if they reasonably expect to settle the case or resolve a pending motion. IN R USDCTND L.R. 16-1(g).

11. *Modification or suspension of rules.* The court may, on its own motion or at the request of a party, suspend or modify any rule in a particular case in the interest of justice. IN R USDCTND L.R. 1-1(c).

D. Documents

1. *Depositions by oral examination*

   a. *Required documents*

      i. *Notice of deposition.* Refer to the General Requirements section of this document for the form and contents of the notice of deposition.

   b. *Supplemental documents*

      i. *Subpoena.* The deponent's attendance may be compelled by subpoena under FRCP 45. FRCP 30(a)(1). For more information on subpoenas, refer to FRCP 45.

      ii. *Subpoena duces tecum.* If a subpoena duces tecum is to be served on the deponent, the materials designated for production, as set out in the subpoena, must be listed in the notice or in an attachment. FRCP 30(b)(2). For more information on subpoenas duces tecum, refer to FRCP 45.

      iii. *Request for production of documents.* The notice to a party deponent may be accompanied by a request under FRCP 34 to produce documents and tangible things at the deposition. FRCP 30(b)(2). Refer to the United States District Court for the Northern District of Indiana KeyRules Request for Production of Documents document for more information.

      iv. *Certificate of service.* FRCP 5(d) requires that the person making service under FRCP 5 certify that service has been effected. FRCP 5(Advisory Committee Notes). Having such information on file may be useful for many purposes, including proof of service if an issue arises concerning the effectiveness of the service. FRCP 5(Advisory Committee Notes).

2. *Depositions by written questions*

   a. *Required documents*

      i. *Notice of deposition.* Refer to the General Requirements section of this document for the form and contents of the notice of deposition.

      ii. *Written questions.* A party who wants to depose a person by written questions must serve them on every other party, with a notice. FRCP 31(a)(3).

   b. *Supplemental documents*

      i. *Subpoena.* The deponent's attendance may be compelled by subpoena under FRCP 45. FRCP 31(a)(1). For more information on subpoenas, refer to FRCP 45.

      ii. *Certificate of service.* FRCP 5(d) requires that the person making service under FRCP 5 certify that service has been effected. FRCP 5(Advisory Committee Notes). Having such information on file may be useful for many purposes, including proof of service if an issue arises concerning the effectiveness of the service. FRCP 5(Advisory Committee Notes).

E. Format

1. *Form of documents.* The rules governing captions and other matters of form in pleadings apply to motions and other papers. FRCP 7(b)(2).

   a. *Paper.* Any pleading, motion, brief, affidavit, notice, or proposed order, whether filed electronically

or by delivering it to the clerk, must: use eight and one-half by eleven (8-1/2 x 11) inch pages. IN R USDCTND L.R. 5-4(a)(2).

   i. *Manual filings.* Papers delivered to the clerk for filing must: be flat, unfolded, and on good-quality, white paper. IN R USDCTND L.R. 5-4(b)(1)(A).

- *Covers or backing.* Papers delivered to the clerk for filing must: not have a cover or a back. IN R USDCTND L.R. 5-4(b)(1)(B).
- *Recycled paper.* The court encourages using recycled paper. IN R USDCTND L.R. 5-4(b)(7).

b. *Margins.* Any pleading, motion, brief, affidavit, notice, or proposed order, whether filed electronically or by delivering it to the clerk, must: have at least one (1) inch margins. IN R USDCTND L.R. 5-4(a)(3).

c. *Spacing.* Any pleading, motion, brief, affidavit, notice, or proposed order, whether filed electronically or by delivering it to the clerk, must: be double spaced (except for headings, footnotes, and quoted material). IN R USDCTND L.R. 5-4(a)(5).

d. *Text.* Any pleading, motion, brief, affidavit, notice, or proposed order, whether filed electronically or by delivering it to the clerk, must: be plainly typewritten, printed, or prepared by a clearly legible copying process. IN R USDCTND L.R. 5-4(a)(1).

   i. Any pleading, motion, brief, affidavit, notice, or proposed order, whether filed electronically or by delivering it to the clerk, must: use at least twelve (12) point type in the body and at least ten (10) point type in footnotes. IN R USDCTND L.R. 5-4(a)(4).

e. *Page numbering.* Any pleading, motion, brief, affidavit, notice, or proposed order, whether filed electronically or by delivering it to the clerk, must: have consecutively numbered pages. IN R USDCTND L.R. 5-4(a)(6).

f. *Caption; Names of parties.* Every pleading must have a caption with the court's name, a title, a file number, and a FRCP 7(a) designation. The title of the complaint must name all the parties; the title of other pleadings, after naming the first party on each side, may refer generally to other parties. FRCP 10(a). Any pleading, motion, brief, affidavit, notice, or proposed order, whether filed electronically or by delivering it to the clerk, must: include a title on the first page. IN R USDCTND L.R. 5-4(a)(7).

g. *Filer's information.* Any pleading, motion, brief, affidavit, notice, or proposed order, whether filed electronically or by delivering it to the clerk, must: except in proposed orders and affidavits, include the filer's name, address, telephone number, fax number (where available), and e-mail address (where available). IN R USDCTND L.R. 5-4(a)(9).

h. *Paragraphs; Separate statements.* A party must state its claims or defenses in numbered paragraphs, each limited as far as practicable to a single set of circumstances. A later pleading may refer by number to a paragraph in an earlier pleading. If doing so would promote clarity, each claim founded on a separate transaction or occurrence—and each defense other than a denial—must be stated in a separate count or defense. FRCP 10(b).

i. *Adoption by reference; Exhibits.* A statement in a pleading may be adopted by reference elsewhere in the same pleading or in any other pleading or motion. A copy of a written instrument that is an exhibit to a pleading is a part of the pleading for all purposes. FRCP 10(c).

j. *Citation of local rules.* The Local Civil Rules of the United States District Court for the Northern District of Indiana may be cited as "N.D. Ind. L.R." IN R USDCTND L.R. 1-1(a)(1).

k. *Acceptance by the clerk.* The clerk must not refuse to file a paper solely because it is not in the form prescribed by the Federal Rules of Civil Procedure or by a local rule or practice. FRCP 5(d)(4).

   i. *Sanctions for formatting errors; Non-compliance.* If a person files a paper that does not comply with the rules governing the format of papers filed with the court, the court may: (1) strike the paper from the record; or (2) fine the person up to one thousand dollars ($1,000). IN R USDCTND L.R. 1-3(a).

- *Notice.* Before sanctioning a person under IN R USDCTND L.R. 1-3(a)(2), the court must:

(1) notify the person that the paper is noncompliant; and (2) give the person the opportunity either to be heard or to revise the paper. IN R USDCTND L.R. 1-3(b).

2. *Form of electronic documents.* Electronically filed documents must meet the same requirements of format and page limits as documents "conventionally filed" (as defined in IN R USDCTND CM/ECF(III)(A)) pursuant to the Federal Rules of Civil Procedure and the Local Civil Rules of the United States District Court for the Northern District of Indiana. IN R USDCTND CM/ECF(II)(A)(2).

   a. *PDF format required.* Documents filed in the CM/ECF must be in .pdf format. A document created with almost any word-processing program can be converted to .pdf format. The .pdf program in effect takes a picture of the original document and allows anyone to open the converted document across a broad range of hardware and software, with layout, format, links, and images intact. IN R USDCTND CM/ECF(FN2).

   b. *Title of documents.* The person electronically filing a pleading or other document will be responsible for designating a title for the pleading or other document by using one of the categories contained in the events listed in the CM/ECF Menu. IN R USDCTND CM/ECF(II)(G).

   c. *Combining documents.* All documents which form part of a single pleading and which are being filed at the same time and by the same party may be electronically filed together under one document number, e.g., the motion and a supporting affidavit, with the exception of memoranda in support. Memoranda in support shall be electronically filed separately and shown as a related document to the motion. IN R USDCTND CM/ECF(II)(A)(4).

   d. *Exhibits and attachments.* Filing users must submit in electronic form all documents referenced as exhibits or attachments, unless the court permits conventional filing. A filing user must submit as exhibits or attachments only those excerpts of the referenced documents that are directly germane to the matter under consideration by the court. Excerpted material must be clearly and prominently identified as such. Filing users who file excerpts of documents as exhibits or attachments do so without prejudice to their right to timely file additional excerpts or the complete document. Responding parties may timely file additional excerpts or the complete document that they believe are directly germane. The court may require parties to file additional excerpts or the complete document. IN R USDCTND CM/ECF(II)(A)(6).

   e. *Hyperlinks.* Electronically filed documents may contain hyperlink references to an external document as a convenient mechanism for accessing material cited in the document. A hyperlink reference is neither validated for content nor considered a part of the court's records. The court neither endorses the product or organization at the destination of a hyperlink reference, nor does the court exercise any responsibility over the content at the destination. In order to preserve the integrity of the court record, attorneys wishing to insert hyperlinks in court filings shall continue to use the traditional citation method for the cited authority, in addition to the hyperlink. A hyperlink contained in a filing is no more than a convenient mechanism for accessing material cited in the document and a hyperlink reference is extraneous to any filed document and is not part of the court's record. IN R USDCTND CM/ECF(II)(A)(3).

3. *Signing disclosures and discovery requests, responses, and objections.* FRCP 11 does not apply to disclosures and discovery requests, responses, objections, and motions under FRCP 26 through FRCP 37. FRCP 11(d).

   a. *Signature required.* Every disclosure under FRCP 26(a)(1) or FRCP 26(a)(3) and every discovery request, response, or objection must be signed by at least one attorney of record in the attorney's own name—or by the party personally, if unrepresented—and must state the signer's address, e-mail address, and telephone number. FRCP 26(g)(1).

      i. *Signatures on manual filings.* Papers delivered to the clerk for filing must: include the filer's original signature. IN R USDCTND L.R. 5-4(b)(1)(C).

         • *Rubber-stamped and faxed signatures.* An original paper with a rubber-stamped or faxed signature is unsigned for purposes of FRCP 11 and FRCP 26(g). IN R USDCTND L.R. 5-4(b)(2).

         • *Affidavits.* Only the affiant need sign an affidavit. IN R USDCTND L.R. 5-4(b)(3).

ii. *Electronic signatures.* Pursuant to FRCP 11, every pleading, motion, and other paper (except lists, schedules, statements or amendments thereto) shall be signed by at least one attorney of record or, if the party is not represented by an attorney, all papers shall be signed by the party. An attorney's/participant's password issued by the court combined with the user's identification, serves as and constitutes the attorney/participant's signature for FRCP 11 and other purposes. IN R USDCTND CM/ECF(I)(C). Documents which must be filed and which must contain original signatures other than those of a participating attorney or which require either verification or an unsworn declaration under any rule or statute, shall be filed electronically, with originally executed copies maintained by the filer. The pleading or other document electronically filed shall contain "s/" signature(s), as noted in IN R USDCTND CM/ECF(II)(E)(3)(b). IN R USDCTND CM/ECF(II)(E)(1).

- *Multiple signatures.* In the case of a stipulation or other document to be signed by two or more attorneys, the following procedure should be used: The filing attorney shall initially confirm that the content of the document is acceptable to all persons required to sign the document and shall obtain the physical signatures of all attorneys on the document. IN R USDCTND CM/ECF(II)(E)(3)(a). The filing attorney then shall file the document electronically, indicating the signatories, e.g., "s/Jane Doe," "s/John Doe," etc. IN R US-DCTND CM/ECF(II)(E)(3)(b). The filing attorney shall retain the hard copy of the document containing the original signatures. IN R USDCTND CM/ECF(II)(E)(3)(c).

b. *Effect of signature.* By signing, an attorney or party certifies that to the best of the person's knowledge, information, and belief formed after a reasonable inquiry:

   i. With respect to a disclosure, it is complete and correct as of the time it is made; and

   ii. With respect to a discovery request, response, or objection, it is:

   - Consistent with the Federal Rules of Civil Procedure and warranted by existing law or by a nonfrivolous argument for extending, modifying, or reversing existing law, or for establishing new law;

   - Not interposed for any improper purpose, such as to harass, cause unnecessary delay, or needlessly increase the cost of litigation; and

   - Neither unreasonable nor unduly burdensome or expensive, considering the needs of the case, prior discovery in the case, the amount in controversy, and the importance of the issues at stake in the action. FRCP 26(g)(1).

c. *Failure to sign.* Other parties have no duty to act on an unsigned disclosure, request, response, or objection until it is signed, and the court must strike it unless a signature is promptly supplied after the omission is called to the attorney's or party's attention. FRCP 26(g)(2).

d. *Sanction for improper certification.* If a certification violates FRCP 26(g) without substantial justification, the court, on motion or on its own, must impose an appropriate sanction on the signer, the party on whose behalf the signer was acting, or both. The sanction may include an order to pay the reasonable expenses, including attorney's fees, caused by the violation. FRCP 26(g)(3). Refer to the United States District Court for the Northern District of Indiana KeyRules Motion for Discovery Sanctions document for more information.

4. *Privacy protection for filings made with the court*

   a. *Redacted filings.* Counsel should not include sensitive information in any document filed with the court unless such inclusion is necessary and relevant to the case. IN R USDCTND CM/ECF(VII). Unless the court orders otherwise, in an electronic or paper filing with the court that contains an individual's Social Security number, taxpayer-identification number, or birth date, the name of an individual known to be a minor, or a financial-account number, a party or nonparty making the filing may include only:

      i. The last four (4) digits of the Social Security number and taxpayer-identification number;

      ii. The year of the individual's birth;

      iii. The minor's initials; and

iv. The last four (4) digits of the financial-account number. FRCP 5.2(a); IN R USDCTND Order 2005-3.

b. *Exemptions from the redaction requirement.* The redaction requirement does not apply to the following:

    i. A financial-account number that identifies the property allegedly subject to forfeiture in a forfeiture proceeding;

    ii. The record of an administrative or agency proceeding;

    iii. The official record of a state-court proceeding;

    iv. The record of a court or tribunal, if that record was not subject to the redaction requirement when originally filed;

    v. A filing covered by FRCP 5.2(c) or FRCP 5.2(d); and

    vi. A pro se filing in an action brought under 28 U.S.C.A. § 2241, 28 U.S.C.A. § 2254, or 28 U.S.C.A. § 2255. FRCP 5.2(b).

    vii. In cases filed under the Social Security Act, 42 U.S.C.A. § 405(g), there is no need for redaction of any information from the documents filed in the case. IN R USDCTND Order 2005-3.

c. *Limitations on remote access to electronic files; Social Security appeals and immigration cases.* Unless the court orders otherwise, in an action for benefits under the Social Security Act, and in an action or proceeding relating to an order of removal, to relief from removal, or to immigration benefits or detention, access to an electronic file is authorized as follows:

    i. The parties and their attorneys may have remote electronic access to any part of the case file, including the administrative record;

    ii. Any other person may have electronic access to the full record at the courthouse, but may have remote electronic access only to:

        • The docket maintained by the court; and

        • An opinion, order, judgment, or other disposition of the court, but not any other part of the case file or the administrative record. FRCP 5.2(c).

d. *Filings made under seal.* The court may order that a filing be made under seal without redaction. The court may later unseal the filing or order the person who made the filing to file a redacted version for the public record. FRCP 5.2(d). For information on filing documents under seal, refer to IN R USDCTND L.R. 5-3, IN R USDCTND CM/ECF(IV)(A), and IN R USDCTND ECF Order 2004-19.

e. *Protective orders.* For good cause, the court may by order in a case:

    i. Require redaction of additional information; or

    ii. Limit or prohibit a nonparty's remote electronic access to a document filed with the court. FRCP 5.2(e).

f. *Option for additional unredacted filing under seal.* A person making a redacted filing may also file an unredacted copy under seal. The court must retain the unredacted copy as part of the record. FRCP 5.2(f); IN R USDCTND Order 2005-3.

    i. The unredacted version of the document or the reference list shall be retained by the court under seal as part of the record. This paper shall be retained by the court as part of the record. The court may, however, still require the party to file a redacted copy for the public file. IN R USDCTND Order 2005-3.

g. *Option for filing a reference list.* A filing that contains redacted information may be filed together with a reference list that identifies each item of redacted information and specifies an appropriate identifier that uniquely corresponds to each item listed. The list must be filed under seal and may be amended as of right. Any reference in the case to a listed identifier will be construed to refer to the corresponding item of information. FRCP 5.2(g); IN R USDCTND Order 2005-3.

    i. The unredacted version of the document or the reference list shall be retained by the court under

seal as part of the record. This paper shall be retained by the court as part of the record. The court may, however, still require the party to file a redacted copy for the public file. IN R USDCTND Order 2005-3.

h. *Responsibility for redaction.* The responsibility for redacting these personal identifiers rests solely with counsel and the parties. The Clerk will not review each paper for compliance with IN R USDCTND Order 2005-3. IN R USDCTND Order 2005-3.

i. *Waiver of protection of identifiers.* A person waives the protection of FRCP 5.2(a) as to the person's own information by filing it without redaction and not under seal. FRCP 5.2(h).

F. Filing and Service Requirements

1. *Filing requirements.* Any paper after the complaint that is required to be served—together with a certificate of service—must be filed within a reasonable time after service. But disclosures under FRCP 26(a)(1) or FRCP 26(a)(2) and the following discovery requests and responses must not be filed until they are used in the proceeding or the court orders filing: depositions, interrogatories, requests for documents or tangible things or to permit entry onto land, and requests for admission. FRCP 5(d)(1). Refer to the United States District Court for the Northern District of Indiana KeyRules pleading and motion documents for information on filing with the court.

   a. *Discovery ordinarily not filed.* The party who serves a discovery request or notices a deposition is the custodian of the original discovery response or deposition transcript. Except as required under IN R USDCTND L.R. 26-2(a)(2), parties must not file: (1) disclosures under FRCP 26(a)(1) or FRCP 26(a)(2); (2) deposition notices; (3) deposition transcripts; (4) interrogatories; (5) requests for documents, to permit entry upon land, or for admission; (6) answers to interrogatories; (7) responses to requests for documents, to permit entry upon land, or for admission; or (8) service-of-discovery notices. IN R USDCTND L.R. 26-2(a)(1).

      i. *Exceptions*

         - *Pro se litigation.* All discovery material in cases involving a pro se party must be filed. IN R USDCTND L.R. 26-2(a)(2)(A).

         - *Specific material.* Discovery material must also be filed when: (1) the court orders; or (2) the material is used in a proceeding. IN R USDCTND L.R. 26-2(a)(2)(B).

   b. *When discovery may be filed*

      i. *Filing materials with motion for relief.* A party who files a motion for relief under FRCP 26(c) or FRCP 37 must file with the motion those parts of the discovery requests or responses that the motion pertains to. IN R USDCTND L.R. 26-2(b).

      ii. *Materials necessary for motion.* A party must file those portions of discovery requests or responses (including deposition transcripts) that the party relies on to support a motion that could result in a final order on an issue. IN R USDCTND L.R. 26-2(c).

      iii. *Materials to be used at trial.* A party who reasonably anticipates using discovery requests or responses—including deposition transcripts—at trial must file the relevant portions of the requests or responses with the clerk at the start of the trial. IN R USDCTND L.R. 26-2(d).

   c. *Notice of filing*

      i. *Depositions by oral examination.* A party who files the deposition must promptly notify all other parties of the filing. FRCP 30(f)(4).

      ii. *Depositions by written questions.* A party who files the deposition must promptly notify all other parties of the filing. FRCP 31(c)(2).

2. *Service requirements*

   a. *Service; When required*

      i. *In general.* Unless the Federal Rules of Civil Procedure provide otherwise, each of the following papers must be served on every party:

         - An order stating that service is required;

485

- A pleading filed after the original complaint, unless the court orders otherwise under FRCP 5(c) because there are numerous defendants;

- A discovery paper required to be served on a party, unless the court orders otherwise;

- A written motion, except one that may be heard ex parte; and

- A written notice, appearance, demand, or offer of judgment, or any similar paper. FRCP 5(a)(1).

    ii.   *If a party fails to appear.* No service is required on a party who is in default for failing to appear. But a pleading that asserts a new claim for relief against such a party must be served on that party under FRCP 4. FRCP 5(a)(2).

    iii.   *Seizing property.* If an action is begun by seizing property and no person is or need be named as a defendant, any service required before the filing of an appearance, answer, or claim must be made on the person who had custody or possession of the property when it was seized. FRCP 5(a)(3).

  b. *Service; How made*

    i.   *Serving an attorney.* If a party is represented by an attorney, service under FRCP 5 must be made on the attorney unless the court orders service on the party. FRCP 5(b)(1).

    ii.   *Service in general.* A paper is served under FRCP 5 by:

- Handing it to the person;

- Leaving it: (1) at the person's office with a clerk or other person in charge or, if no one is in charge, in a conspicuous place in the office; or (2) if the person has no office or the office is closed, at the person's dwelling or usual place of abode with someone of suitable age and discretion who resides there;

- Mailing it to the person's last known address—in which event service is complete upon mailing;

- Leaving it with the court clerk if the person has no known address;

- Sending it by electronic means if the person consented in writing—in which event service is complete upon transmission, but is not effective if the serving party learns that it did not reach the person to be served; or

- Delivering it by any other means that the person consented to in writing—in which event service is complete when the person making service delivers it to the agency designated to make delivery. FRCP 5(b)(2).

    iii.   *Electronic service.* Electronically filed papers may be served electronically if service is consistent with the CM/ECF User Manual (IN R USDCTND CM/ECF). IN R USDCTND L.R. 5-2(a).

- *Waiver of other service.* An attorney's registration will constitute a waiver of conventional service of documents and the attorney agrees to accept service of notice on behalf of the client of the electronic filing by hand, facsimile or authorized email. IN R USDCTND CM/ECF(I)(B)(3).

- *Serving registered persons.* The System will generate a "Notice of Electronic Filing" when any document is filed. This notice represents service of the document on parties who are registered participants with the System. Except as provided in IN R USDCTND CM/ECF(III)(B), the filing party shall not be required to serve any pleading or other documents on any party receiving electronic notice. IN R USDCTND CM/ECF(II)(D)(1). The term "pleading" refers only to those documents listed in FRCP 7(a). IN R USDCTND CM/ECF(FN3).

- *When electronic service is deemed completed.* A person registered to use the court's electronic-filing system is served with an electronically filed paper when a "Notice of Electronic Filing" is transmitted to that person through the court's electronic filing-system. IN R USDCTND L.R. 5-2(b).

- *Serving non-registered persons.* A person who has not registered to use the court's electronic-filing system but who is entitled to service of a paper must be served according to the Local Civil Rules of the United States District Court for the Northern District of Indiana and the Federal Rules of Civil Procedure. IN R USDCTND L.R. 5-2(c); IN R USDCTND CM/ECF(II)(D)(2). If such service of a paper copy is to be made, it shall be done in the manner provided in the Federal Rules of Civil Procedure and the Local Civil Rules of the United States District Court for the Northern District of Indiana. IN R USDCTND CM/ECF(II)(D)(2).

iv. *Service of conventional filings.* Pleadings or other documents which are filed conventionally rather than electronically shall be served in the manner provided for in the Federal Rules of Civil Procedure and the Local Civil Rules of the United States District Court for the Northern District of Indiana, except as otherwise provided by order of the Court. IN R USDCTND CM/ECF(III)(B).

v. *Using court facilities.* If a local rule so authorizes, a party may use the court's transmission facilities to make service under FRCP 5(b)(2)(E). FRCP 5(b)(3).

c. *Serving numerous defendants*

i. *In general.* If an action involves an unusually large number of defendants, the court may, on motion or on its own, order that:

- Defendants' pleadings and replies to them need not be served on other defendants;

- Any crossclaim, counterclaim, avoidance, or affirmative defense in those pleadings and replies to them will be treated as denied or avoided by all other parties; and

- Filing any such pleading and serving it on the plaintiff constitutes notice of the pleading to all parties. FRCP 5(c)(1).

ii. *Notifying parties.* A copy of every such order must be served on the parties as the court directs. FRCP 5(c)(2).

G. Hearings

1. There is no hearing contemplated in the federal statutes or rules for the notice of deposition.

H. Forms

1. Federal Notice of Deposition Forms

a. Notice to take deposition to perpetuate testimony. 3A FEDFORMS § 3339.

b. Notice of taking of deposition to perpetuate testimony pending appeal. 3A FEDFORMS § 3345.

c. Notice of taking deposition upon oral examination. 3A FEDFORMS § 3422.

d. Notice of taking deposition upon oral examination; Party. 3A FEDFORMS § 3423.

e. Notice of taking deposition upon oral examination; Naming and describing person not a party. 3A FEDFORMS § 3424.

f. Notice of taking deposition upon oral examination; Describing deponents whose names are unknown. 3A FEDFORMS § 3425.

g. Notice of taking deposition upon oral examination; Pursuant to order granting leave to take deposition. 3A FEDFORMS § 3426.

h. Notice of taking of deposition of party with notice to produce documents. 3A FEDFORMS § 3427.

i. Notice of taking of deposition of witness; Including designation of materials in related subpoena duces tecum. 3A FEDFORMS § 3428.

j. Notice of taking deposition of witness; Including reference to materials designated in attached subpoena. 3A FEDFORMS § 3429.

k. Notice of taking deposition upon written questions served with notice. 3A FEDFORMS § 3449.

l. Questions to be attached to notice or served with it. 3A FEDFORMS § 3450.

m. Notice of return and filing of deposition taken upon written questions. 3A FEDFORMS § 3456.

n. Notice; Taking of deposition on oral examination. FEDPROF § 23:136.

o. Notice; Taking of deposition on oral examination; Patent proceedings. FEDPROF § 23:137.

p. Notice; Taking of deposition on oral examination; Corporate officer. FEDPROF § 23:138.

q. Notice; Taking of deposition on oral examination; Corporate officers to be designated by corporation. FEDPROF § 23:139.

r. Notice; Taking of deposition on written questions. FEDPROF § 23:140.

s. Notice; Taking of deposition on oral examination or on written questions; Pursuant to court order. FEDPROF § 23:141.

t. Notice; In connection with deposition on written questions; Of cross, redirect, or recross questions. FEDPROF § 23:142.

u. Attachment to notice; Taking of deposition on written questions; Questions to be propounded. FEDPROF § 23:143.

v. Attachment to notice; Cross, redirect, or recross questions to be propounded. FEDPROF § 23:144.

w. Notice; To party taking deposition; Written questions submitted in lieu of participation in oral examination. FEDPROF § 23:145.

x. Notice of taking deposition; Expert witness; Request for production of supporting documents. FEDPROF § 23:151.

y. Subpoena; To testify at taking of deposition and to produce documents or things (form AO 88). FEDPROF § 23:152.

z. Provision in subpoena; Advice to nonparty organization of its duty to designate witness. FEDPROF § 23:155.

I. Applicable Rules

1. *Federal rules*

    a. Serving and filing pleadings and other papers. FRCP 5.

    b. Privacy protection for filings made with the court. FRCP 5.2.

    c. Computing and extending time; Time for motion papers. FRCP 6.

    d. Pleadings allowed; Form of motions and other papers. FRCP 7.

    e. Form of pleadings. FRCP 10.

    f. Signing pleadings, motions, and other papers; Representations to the court; Sanctions. FRCP 11.

    g. Duty to disclose; General provisions governing discovery. FRCP 26.

    h. Persons before whom depositions may be taken. FRCP 28.

    i. Stipulations about discovery procedure. FRCP 29.

    j. Depositions by oral examination. FRCP 30.

    k. Depositions by written questions. FRCP 31.

    l. Failure to make disclosures or to cooperate in discovery; Sanctions. FRCP 37.

2. *Local rules*

    a. Citation and scope of the rules. IN R USDCTND L.R. 1-1.

    b. Sanctions for formatting errors. IN R USDCTND L.R. 1-3.

    c. Electronic service. IN R USDCTND L.R. 5-2.

    d. Format of papers. IN R USDCTND L.R. 5-4.

    e. Pretrial procedure. IN R USDCTND L.R. 16-1.

    f. Alternative dispute resolution. IN R USDCTND L.R. 16-6.

g. Filing of discovery and other materials. IN R USDCTND L.R. 26-2.

h. Scheduling depositions. IN R USDCTND L.R. 30-1.

i. Dealing with objections during depositions. IN R USDCTND L.R. 37-3.

j. Case assignment. IN R USDCTND L.R. 40-1.

k. Appearance and withdrawal of appearance. IN R USDCTND L.R. 83-8.

l. CM/ECF civil and criminal user manual. IN R USDCTND CM/ECF.

m. In re: privacy and public access to civil electronic case files. IN R USDCTND Order 2005-3.

Requests, Notices and Applications
Application for Temporary Restraining Order

Document Last Updated December 2016

A. Checklist

(I) ❑ Matters to be considered by party applying (with notice)

   (a) ❑ Required documents

      (1) ❑ Notice of motion and motion

      (2) ❑ Brief

      (3) ❑ Security

      (4) ❑ Certificate of service

   (b) ❑ Supplemental documents

      (1) ❑ Supporting evidence

      (2) ❑ Notice of constitutional question

      (3) ❑ Nongovernmental corporate disclosure statement

      (4) ❑ Index of exhibits

      (5) ❑ Request for oral argument

      (6) ❑ Request for evidentiary hearing

      (7) ❑ Copy of authority

      (8) ❑ Proposed order

      (9) ❑ Copy of document with self-addressed envelope

      (10) ❑ Notice of manual filing

      (11) ❑ Courtesy copies

      (12) ❑ Declaration that party was unable to file in a timely manner

   (c) ❑ Timing

      (1) ❑ A written motion and notice of the hearing must be served at least fourteen (14) days before the time specified for the hearing, with the following exceptions: (i) when the motion may be heard ex parte; (ii) when the Federal Rules of Civil Procedure set a different time; or (iii) when a court order—which a party may, for good cause, apply for ex parte—sets a different time

      (2) ❑ Any affidavit supporting a motion must be served with the motion

(II) ❑ Matters to be considered by party applying (without notice, or "ex parte")

   (a) ❑ Required documents

      (1) ❑ Motion

(2) ❑ Brief

(3) ❑ Affidavit or verified complaint

(4) ❑ Certificate of attorney

(5) ❑ Security

(b) ❑ Supplemental documents

(1) ❑ Supporting evidence

(2) ❑ Notice of constitutional question

(3) ❑ Nongovernmental corporate disclosure statement

(4) ❑ Index of exhibits

(5) ❑ Request for oral argument

(6) ❑ Request for evidentiary hearing

(7) ❑ Copy of authority

(8) ❑ Proposed order

(9) ❑ Copy of document with self-addressed envelope

(10) ❑ Notice of manual filing

(11) ❑ Courtesy copies

(12) ❑ Declaration that party was unable to file in a timely manner

(c) ❑ Timing

(1) ❑ There are no specific timing requirements for applying for a temporary restraining order without notice

(2) ❑ Any affidavit supporting a motion must be served with the motion

B. Timing

1. *Application for temporary restraining order*

   a. *With notice.* There are no specific timing requirements for applying for a temporary restraining order with notice.

   b. *Without notice, or "ex parte."* There are no specific timing requirements for applying for a temporary restraining order without notice, or "ex parte."

2. *Motion to dissolve or modify.* On two (2) days' notice to the party who obtained the order without notice—or on shorter notice set by the court—the adverse party may appear and move to dissolve or modify the order. The court must then hear and decide the motion as promptly as justice requires. FRCP 65(b)(4).

3. *Timing of motions, generally*

   a. *Motion and notice of hearing.* A written motion and notice of the hearing must be served at least fourteen (14) days before the time specified for the hearing, with the following exceptions:

      i. When the motion may be heard ex parte;

      ii. When the Federal Rules of Civil Procedure set a different time; or

      iii. When a court order—which a party may, for good cause, apply for ex parte—sets a different time. FRCP 6(c)(1).

   b. *Supporting affidavit.* Any affidavit supporting a motion must be served with the motion. FRCP 6(c)(2).

4. *Computation of time*

   a. *Computing time.* FRCP 6 applies in computing any time period specified in the Federal Rules of Civil

Procedure, in any local rule or court order, or in any statute that does not specify a method of computing time. FRCP 6(a).

    i.   *Period stated in days or a longer unit.* When the period is stated in days or a longer unit of time:

- Exclude the day of the event that triggers the period;
- Count every day, including intermediate Saturdays, Sundays, and legal holidays; and
- Include the last day of the period, but if the last day is a Saturday, Sunday, or legal holiday, the period continues to run until the end of the next day that is not a Saturday, Sunday, or legal holiday. FRCP 6(a)(1).

    ii.   *Period stated in hours.* When the period is stated in hours:

- Begin counting immediately on the occurrence of the event that triggers the period;
- Count every hour, including hours during intermediate Saturdays, Sundays, and legal holidays; and
- If the period would end on a Saturday, Sunday, or legal holiday, the period continues to run until the same time on the next day that is not a Saturday, Sunday, or legal holiday. FRCP 6(a)(2).

    iii.   *Inaccessibility of the clerk's office.* Unless the court orders otherwise, if the clerk's office is inaccessible:

- On the last day for filing under FRCP 6(a)(1), then the time for filing is extended to the first accessible day that is not a Saturday, Sunday, or legal holiday; or
- During the last hour for filing under FRCP 6(a)(2), then the time for filing is extended to the same time on the first accessible day that is not a Saturday, Sunday, or legal holiday. FRCP 6(a)(3).

    iv.   *"Last day" defined.* Unless a different time is set by a statute, local rule, or court order, the last day ends:

- For electronic filing, at midnight in the court's time zone; and
- For filing by other means, when the clerk's office is scheduled to close. FRCP 6(a)(4).

    v.   *"Next day" defined.* The "next day" is determined by continuing to count forward when the period is measured after an event and backward when measured before an event. FRCP 6(a)(5).

    vi.   *"Legal holiday" defined.* "Legal holiday" means:

- The day set aside by statute for observing New Year's Day, Martin Luther King Jr.'s Birthday, Washington's Birthday, Memorial Day, Independence Day, Labor Day, Columbus Day, Veterans' Day, Thanksgiving Day, or Christmas Day;
- Any day declared a holiday by the President or Congress; and
- For periods that are measured after an event, any other day declared a holiday by the state where the district court is located. FRCP 6(a)(6).

  b. *Computation of electronic filing deadlines.* Filing documents electronically does not alter any filing deadlines or any time computation pursuant to FRCP 6. The counties of Lake, Porter, LaPorte, Pulaski and Starke are located in the Central time zone and the remaining counties in the Northern District of Indiana are located in the Eastern time zone. Nevertheless, all electronic transmissions of documents must be completed (i.e., received completely by the clerk's office) prior to midnight Eastern Time, (South Bend/Fort Wayne/Lafayette time) in order to be considered timely filed that day, regardless of the local time in the division where the case is pending. Although documents can be filed electronically twenty-four (24) hours a day, filers are strongly encouraged to file all documents during hours when the CM/ECF Help Line is available, from 9:00 a.m. to 4:00 p.m. local time. IN R USDCTND CM/ECF(II)(I).

    i.   *Technical failures.* If the attorney is unable to file a document in a timely manner due to technical difficulties in the user's system, the attorney must file a document with the court as

soon as possible notifying the court of the inability to file the document. A sample document entitled Declaration that Party was Unable to File in a Timely Manner Due to Technical Difficulties is attached hereto as Form 5. IN R USDCTND CM/ECF(VI)(B). [Editor's note: the reference to Form 5 is likely meant to be a reference to Form 3 (IN R USDCTND CM/ECF(Form 3)].

   c. *Extending time*

     i. *In general.* When an act may or must be done within a specified time, the court may, for good cause, extend the time:

- With or without motion or notice if the court acts, or if a request is made, before the original time or its extension expires; or

- On motion made after the time has expired if the party failed to act because of excusable neglect. FRCP 6(b)(1).

     ii. *Exceptions.* A court must not extend the time to act under FRCP 50(b), FRCP 50(d), FRCP 52(b), FRCP 59(b), FRCP 59(d), FRCP 59(e), and FRCP 60(b). FRCP 6(b)(2).

     iii. Refer to the United States District Court for the Northern District of Indiana KeyRules Motion for Continuance/Extension of Time document for more information on extending time.

   d. *Additional time after certain kinds of service.* When a party may or must act within a specified time after being served and service is made under FRCP 5(b)(2)(C) (mail), FRCP 5(b)(2)(D) (leaving with the clerk), or FRCP 5(b)(2)(F) (other means consented to), three (3) days are added after the period would otherwise expire under FRCP 6(a). FRCP 6(d).

C. General Requirements

1. *Motions, generally*

   a. *Requirements.* A request for a court order must be made by motion. The motion must:

     i. Be in writing unless made during a hearing or trial;

     ii. State with particularity the grounds for seeking the order; and

     iii. State the relief sought. FRCP 7(b)(1).

   b. *Notice of motion.* A party interested in resisting the relief sought by a motion has a right to notice thereof, and an opportunity to be heard. AMJUR MOTIONS § 12.

     i. In addition to statutory or court rule provisions requiring notice of a motion—the purpose of such a notice requirement having been said to be to prevent a party from being prejudicially surprised by a motion—principles of natural justice dictate that an adverse party generally must be given notice that a motion will be presented to the court. AMJUR MOTIONS § 12.

     ii. "Notice," in this regard, means reasonable notice, including a meaningful opportunity to prepare and to defend against allegations of a motion. AMJUR MOTIONS § 12.

   c. *Writing requirement.* The writing requirement is intended to insure that the adverse parties are informed and have a record of both the motion's pendency and the grounds on which the movant seeks an order. FPP § 1191; Feldberg v. Quechee Lakes Corp., 463 F.3d 195 (2d Cir. 2006).

     i. It is sufficient "if the motion is stated in a written notice of the hearing of the motion." FPP § 1191.

   d. *Particularity requirement.* The particularity requirement insures that the opposing parties will have notice of their opponent's contentions. FEDPROC § 62:364; Goodman v. 1973 26 Foot Trojan Vessel, Arkansas Registration No. AR1439SN, 859 F.2d 71, 12 Fed.R.Serv.3d 645 (8th Cir. 1988). That requirement ensures that notice of the basis for the motion is provided to the court and to the opposing party so as to avoid prejudice, provide the opponent with a meaningful opportunity to respond, and provide the court with enough information to process the motion correctly. FEDPROC § 62:364; Andreas v. Volkswagen of America, Inc., 336 F.3d 789, 56 Fed.R.Serv.3d 6 (8th Cir. 2003).

     i. Reasonable specification of the grounds for a motion is sufficient. However, where a movant fails to state even one ground for granting the motion in question, the movant has failed to meet

the minimal standard of "reasonable specification." FEDPROC § 62:364; Martinez v. Trainor, 556 F.2d 818, 23 Fed.R.Serv.2d 403 (7th Cir. 1977).

    ii.   The court may excuse the failure to comply with the particularity requirement if it is inadvertent, and where no prejudice is shown by the opposing party. FEDPROC § 62:364.

  e. *Motions must be filed separately.* Motions must be filed separately, but alternative motions may be filed in a single paper if each is named in the title following the caption. IN R USDCTND L.R. 7-1(a).

2. *Application for temporary restraining order.* Applicants for injunctive relief occasionally are faced with the possibility that irreparable injury will occur before the hearing for a preliminary injunction required by FRCP 65(a) can be held. In that event a temporary restraining order may be available under FRCP 65(b). FPP § 2951. The order is designed to preserve the status quo until there is an opportunity to hold a hearing on the application for a preliminary injunction and may be issued with or without notice to the adverse party. FPP § 2951; Granny Goose Foods, Inc. v. Brotherhood of Teamsters & Auto Truck Drivers Local No. 70 of Alameda County, 415 U.S. 423, 94 S.Ct. 1113, 39 L.Ed.2d 435 (1974).

  a. *Requirements.* The court will consider requests for temporary restraining orders only if the moving party: (1) files a separate motion for relief; (2) files a supporting brief; and (3) complies with FRCP 65(b). IN R USDCTND L.R. 65-1(b).

  b. *Issuing with notice.* When the opposing party actually receives notice of the application for a restraining order, the procedure that is followed does not differ functionally from that on an application for a preliminary injunction and the proceeding is not subject to any special requirements. FPP § 2951; Dilworth v. Riner, 343 F.2d 226 (5th Cir. 1965).

    i.   *Duration.* By its terms FRCP 65(b) only governs restraining orders issued without notice or a hearing. But. . .it has been argued that its provisions, at least with regard to the duration of a restraining order, apply even to an order granted when notice has been given to the adverse party but there has been no hearing. FPP § 2951.

  c. *Issuing without notice*

    i.   *When available.* The court may issue a temporary restraining order without written or oral notice to the adverse party or its attorney only if:

- Specific facts in an affidavit or a verified complaint clearly show that immediate and irreparable injury, loss, or damage will result to the movant before the adverse party can be heard in opposition; and

- The movant's attorney certifies in writing any efforts made to give notice and the reasons why it should not be required. FRCP 65(b)(1).

    ii.   *Contents.* Every temporary restraining order issued without notice must state the date and hour it was issued; describe the injury and state why it is irreparable; state why the order was issued without notice; and be promptly filed in the clerk's office and entered in the record. FRCP 65(b)(2).

    iii.   *Expiration.* The order expires at the time after entry—not to exceed fourteen (14) days—that the court sets, unless before that time the court, for good cause, extends it for a like period or the adverse party consents to a longer extension. The reasons for an extension must be entered in the record. FRCP 65(b)(2).

  d. *Temporary restraining order versus preliminary injunction.* A temporary restraining order differs from a preliminary injunction, the core reasons being that a temporary restraining order is of limited duration and it may issue without notice to the opposing party before the adverse party can be heard in opposition. FEDPROC § 47:80.

  e. *Factors considered.* As in the case of an application for a preliminary injunction, four factors must be considered in determining whether a temporary restraining order is to be granted, which are whether the moving party has established: (1) a substantial likelihood of success on the merits; (2) that irreparable injury will be suffered if the relief is not granted; (3) that the threatened injury outweighs the harm the relief would inflict on the nonmoving party; and (4) that entry of the relief would serve the public interest. FEDPROC § 47:84; Schiavo ex rel. Schindler v. Schiavo, 403 F.3d 1223 (11th Cir. 2005).

    i.   Plaintiffs are not required to prevail on each of these factors, rather, the factors must be viewed as a continuum, with more of one factor compensating for less of another. In each case, however, all of the factors must be considered to determine whether on balance they weigh toward granting relief. FEDPROC § 47:84.

    ii. In the context of a temporary restraining order, it is particularly important for the moving party to demonstrate a substantial likelihood of success on the merits, because otherwise, there would be no justification for the court's intrusion into the ordinary processes of administration and judicial review. FEDPROC § 47:84.

    iii. Refer to the United States District Court for the Northern District of Indiana KeyRules Motion for Preliminary Injunction document for more information on the factors considered in moving for a preliminary injunction.

f.   *Burden.* As with a preliminary injunction, the burden is on the moving party to establish that relief is appropriate. FEDPROC § 47:84.

g.   *Security.* The court may issue a preliminary injunction or a temporary restraining order only if the movant gives security in an amount that the court considers proper to pay the costs and damages sustained by any party found to have been wrongfully enjoined or restrained. The United States, its officers, and its agencies are not required to give security. FRCP 65(c).

    i.   *Proceedings against a surety.* Whenever the Federal Rules of Civil Procedure (including the Supplemental Rules for Admiralty or Maritime Claims and Asset Forfeiture Actions) require or allow a party to give security, and security is given through a bond or other undertaking with one or more sureties, each surety submits to the court's jurisdiction and irrevocably appoints the court clerk as its agent for receiving service of any papers that affect its liability on the bond or undertaking. The surety's liability may be enforced on motion without an independent action. The motion and any notice that the court orders may be served on the court clerk, who must promptly mail a copy of each to every surety whose address is known. FRCP 65.1.

h.   *Contents and scope of every injunction and restraining order*

    i.   *Contents.* Every order granting an injunction and every restraining order must:

- State the reasons why it issued;
- State its terms specifically; and
- Describe in reasonable detail—and not by referring to the complaint or other document—the act or acts restrained or required. FRCP 65(d)(1).

    ii. *Persons bound.* The order binds only the following who receive actual notice of it by personal service or otherwise:

- The parties;
- The parties' officers, agents, servants, employees, and attorneys; and
- Other persons who are in active concert or participation with anyone described in FRCP 65(d)(2)(A) or FRCP 65(d)(2)(B). FRCP 65(d)(2).

i.   *Other laws not modified.* FRCP 65 does not modify the following:

    i.   Any federal statute relating to temporary restraining orders or preliminary injunctions in actions affecting employer and employee;

    ii. 28 U.S.C.A. § 2361, which relates to preliminary injunctions in actions of interpleader or in the nature of interpleader; or

    iii. 28 U.S.C.A. § 2284, which relates to actions that must be heard and decided by a three-judge district court. FRCP 65(e).

j.   *Copyright impoundment.* FRCP 65 applies to copyright-impoundment proceedings. FRCP 65(f).

3. *Appearances.* Attorneys not representing the United States or its agencies must file an appearance when

they represent (either in person or by filing a paper) a party. IN R USDCTND L.R. 83-8(a). For more information, refer to IN R USDCTND L.R. 83-8.

4. *Notice of related action.* A party must file a notice of related action as soon as it appears that the party's case and another pending case: (1) arise out of the same transaction or occurrence; (2) involve the same property; or (3) involve the validity or infringement of the same patent, trademark, or copyright. IN R USDCTND L.R. 40-1(d). For more information, refer to IN R USDCTND L.R. 40-1.

5. *Alternative dispute resolution (ADR).* After they confer as required by FRCP 26(f), the parties must advise the court which, if any, alternative-dispute-resolution processes they expect to pursue and when they expect to undertake the process. IN R USDCTND L.R. 16-6(a). For more information on alternative dispute resolution (ADR), refer to IN R USDCTND L.R. 16-6 and IN R USDCTND Order 2003-21.

6. *Settlement or resolution.* The parties must immediately notify the court if they reasonably expect to settle the case or resolve a pending motion. IN R USDCTND L.R. 16-1(g).

7. *Modification or suspension of rules.* The court may, on its own motion or at the request of a party, suspend or modify any rule in a particular case in the interest of justice. IN R USDCTND L.R. 1-1(c).

D. Documents

1. *Application for temporary restraining order (with notice)*

   a. *Required documents*

      i. *Notice of motion and motion.* The court will consider requests for temporary restraining orders only if the moving party: files a separate motion for relief. IN R USDCTND L.R. 65-1(b)(1). The party must not specify a hearing date in the notice of a motion or petition unless the court or the clerk has authorized it. IN R USDCTND L.R. 7-5(b)(2). Refer to the General Requirements section of this document for information on the notice of motion and motion.

      ii. *Brief.* Parties must file a supporting brief with any motion under: FRCP 65(b). IN R USDCTND L.R. 7-1(b)(4). The court will consider requests for temporary restraining orders only if the moving party: files a supporting brief. IN R USDCTND L.R. 65-1(b)(2). Refer to the Format section of this document for the format of briefs.

      iii. *Security.* Refer to the General Requirements section of this document for information on the security required.

      iv. *Certificate of service.* FRCP 5(d) requires that the person making service under FRCP 5 certify that service has been effected. FRCP 5(Advisory Committee Notes). Having such information on file may be useful for many purposes, including proof of service if an issue arises concerning the effectiveness of the service. FRCP 5(Advisory Committee Notes).

         - *Certificate of service for electronically-filed documents.* A Certificate of Service is still a requirement when filing documents electronically. A sample Certificate of Service is attached as Form 1 (IN R USDCTND CM/ECF(Form 1)). IN R USDCTND CM/ECF(II)(H).

   b. *Supplemental documents*

      i. *Supporting evidence.* When a motion relies on facts outside the record, the court may hear the matter on affidavits or may hear it wholly or partly on oral testimony or on depositions. FRCP 43(c).

         - *Materials necessary for motion.* A party must file those portions of discovery requests or responses (including deposition transcripts) that the party relies on to support a motion that could result in a final order on an issue. IN R USDCTND L.R. 26-2(c).

      ii. *Notice of constitutional question.* A party that files a pleading, written motion, or other paper drawing into question the constitutionality of a federal or state statute must promptly:

         - *File notice.* File a notice of constitutional question stating the question and identifying the paper that raises it, if: (1) a federal statute is questioned and the parties do not include the United States, one of its agencies, or one of its officers or employees in an official capacity; or (2) a state statute is questioned and the parties do not include the state, one of its agencies, or one of its officers or employees in an official capacity; and

- *Serve notice.* Serve the notice and paper on the Attorney General of the United States if a federal statute is questioned—or on the state attorney general if a state statute is questioned—either by certified or registered mail or by sending it to an electronic address designated by the attorney general for this purpose. FRCP 5.1(a).

- *When to file the notice.* A party required to file a notice of constitutional question under FRCP 5.1 must do so by the later of: (1) the day the parties tender their proposed case-management plan (if one is required); or (2) 21 days after filing the pleading, written motion, or other paper questioning the constitutionality of a federal or state statute. IN R USDCTND L.R. 5.1-1(a).

- *Service on government officials.* The party must also serve the notice and the pleading, written motion, or other paper questioning the constitutionality of a federal or state statute on: (1) the Attorney General of the United States and the United States Attorney for the Northern District of Indiana, if a federal statute is challenged; or (2) the Attorney General for the state if a state statute is challenged. IN R USDCTND L.R. 5.1-1(b). Service required under IN R USDCTND L.R. 5.1-1(b) may be made either by certified or registered mail or by emailing it to an address designated by those officials for this purpose. IN R USDCTND L.R. 5.1-1(c).

- *No forfeiture.* A party's failure to file and serve the notice, or the court's failure to certify, does not forfeit a constitutional claim or defense that is otherwise timely asserted. FRCP 5.1(d).

iii. *Nongovernmental corporate disclosure statement*

- *Contents.* A nongovernmental corporate party must file two (2) copies of a disclosure statement that: (1) identifies any parent corporation and any publicly held corporation owning ten percent (10%) or more of its stock; or (2) states that there is no such corporation. FRCP 7.1(a).

- *Time to file; Supplemental filing.* A party must: (1) file the disclosure statement with its first appearance, pleading, petition, motion, response, or other request addressed to the court; and (2) promptly file a supplemental statement if any required information changes. FRCP 7.1(b).

iv. *Index of exhibits.* Any pleading, motion, brief, affidavit, notice, or proposed order, whether filed electronically or by delivering it to the clerk, must: include a separate index identifying and briefly describing each exhibit if there are more than four (4) exhibits. IN R USDCTND L.R. 5-4(a)(8).

v. *Request for oral argument.* A party may request oral argument on a motion by filing and serving a separate document explaining why oral argument is necessary and estimating how long the court should allow for the argument. IN R USDCTND L.R. 7-5(a)(1). The request must be filed and served with the party's supporting brief, response brief, or reply brief. IN R USDCTND L.R. 7-5(a)(2).

vi. *Request for evidentiary hearing.* A party may request an evidentiary hearing by filing and serving a separate document explaining why the hearing is necessary and estimating how long the court should allow for it. IN R USDCTND L.R. 7-5(b)(1).

vii. *Copy of authority.* A copy of any decision, statute, or regulation cited in a motion or brief must be attached to the paper if—and only if—it is not available on Westlaw or Lexis. But if a copy of a decision, statute, or regulation is only available electronically, a party must provide it to the court or another party upon request. IN R USDCTND L.R. 7-1(f).

viii. *Proposed order.* Parties filing a paper that requires the judge or clerk to enter a routine or uncontested order must include a suitable form of order. IN R USDCTND L.R. 5-4(c).

- Proposed orders shall not be filed electronically either as a separate document or as an attachment to the main pleading or other document. Instead, all proposed orders must be e-mailed to the chambers of the appropriate judicial officer for the case. The proposed order must be in WordPerfect Format or Rich Text Format (RTF). Proposed orders should be attached to an e-mail and sent to the appropriate judicial officer at the address listed in IN R USDCTND CM/ECF(II)(F). The subject line of the email message should indicate the case title, cause number and document number of the motion, e.g., Smith v. Jones 1:02-cv-1234, motion# ___. IN R USDCTND CM/ECF(II)(F).

ix. *Copy of document with self-addressed envelope.* A party who wants a file-stamped copy of a paper must include with the filing an additional copy of the paper and a self-addressed envelope with adequate postage. IN R USDCTND L.R. 5-4(b)(6).

x. *Notice of manual filing.* However, if that is not physically possible, counsel shall electronically file a .pdf document titled Notice of Manual Filing as a notation on the docket sheet that filings are being held in the clerk's office in paper. A sample Notice of Manual Filing is attached as Form 2 (IN R USDCTND CM/ECF(Form 2)). IN R USDCTND CM/ECF(III)(A)(1).

xi. *Courtesy copies.* If documents are filed in paper format, counsel must provide an original for the clerk's office, a copy for the judge and a copy must be served on all parties in the case. IN R USDCTND CM/ECF(III)(A)(1).

xii. *Declaration that party was unable to file in a timely manner.* If the attorney is unable to file a document in a timely manner due to technical difficulties in the user's system, the attorney must file a document with the court as soon as possible notifying the court of the inability to file the document. A sample document entitled Declaration that Party was Unable to File in a Timely Manner Due to Technical Difficulties is attached hereto as Form 5. IN R USDCTND CM/ECF(VI)(B). [Editor's note: the reference to Form 5 is likely meant to be a reference to Form 3 (IN R USDCTND CM/ECF(Form 3)].

2. *Application for temporary restraining order (without notice, or "ex parte")*

   a. *Required documents*

      i. *Motion.* The court will consider requests for temporary restraining orders only if the moving party: files a separate motion for relief. IN R USDCTND L.R. 65-1(b)(1). Refer to the General Requirements section of this document for information on the motion.

      ii. *Brief.* Parties must file a supporting brief with any motion under: FRCP 65(b). IN R USDCTND L.R. 7-1(b)(4). The court will consider requests for temporary restraining orders only if the moving party: files a supporting brief. IN R USDCTND L.R. 65-1(b)(2). Refer to the Format section of this document for the format of briefs.

      iii. *Affidavit or verified complaint.* The applicant for an ex parte restraining order must present to the court, in an affidavit or a verified complaint, facts that clearly show irreparable injury. FPP § 2952.

      iv. *Certificate of attorney.* The applicant's attorney must certify in writing any efforts made to give notice and the reasons why it should not be required. FEDPROC § 47:81.

      v. *Security.* Refer to the General Requirements section of this document for information on the security required.

   b. *Supplemental documents*

      i. *Supporting evidence.* When a motion relies on facts outside the record, the court may hear the matter on affidavits or may hear it wholly or partly on oral testimony or on depositions. FRCP 43(c).

         • *Materials necessary for motion.* A party must file those portions of discovery requests or responses (including deposition transcripts) that the party relies on to support a motion that could result in a final order on an issue. IN R USDCTND L.R. 26-2(c).

      ii. *Notice of constitutional question.* A party that files a pleading, written motion, or other paper drawing into question the constitutionality of a federal or state statute must promptly:

         • *File notice.* File a notice of constitutional question stating the question and identifying the paper that raises it, if: (1) a federal statute is questioned and the parties do not include the United States, one of its agencies, or one of its officers or employees in an official capacity;

or (2) a state statute is questioned and the parties do not include the state, one of its agencies, or one of its officers or employees in an official capacity; and

- *Serve notice.* Serve the notice and paper on the Attorney General of the United States if a federal statute is questioned—or on the state attorney general if a state statute is questioned—either by certified or registered mail or by sending it to an electronic address designated by the attorney general for this purpose. FRCP 5.1(a).

- *When to file the notice.* A party required to file a notice of constitutional question under FRCP 5.1 must do so by the later of: (1) the day the parties tender their proposed case-management plan (if one is required); or (2) 21 days after filing the pleading, written motion, or other paper questioning the constitutionality of a federal or state statute. IN R USDCTND L.R. 5.1-1(a).

- *Service on government officials.* The party must also serve the notice and the pleading, written motion, or other paper questioning the constitutionality of a federal or state statute on: (1) the Attorney General of the United States and the United States Attorney for the Northern District of Indiana, if a federal statute is challenged; or (2) the Attorney General for the state if a state statute is challenged. IN R USDCTND L.R. 5.1-1(b). Service required under IN R USDCTND L.R. 5.1-1(b) may be made either by certified or registered mail or by emailing it to an address designated by those officials for this purpose. IN R USDCTND L.R. 5.1-1(c).

- *No forfeiture.* A party's failure to file and serve the notice, or the court's failure to certify, does not forfeit a constitutional claim or defense that is otherwise timely asserted. FRCP 5.1(d).

iii. *Nongovernmental corporate disclosure statement*

- *Contents.* A nongovernmental corporate party must file two (2) copies of a disclosure statement that: (1) identifies any parent corporation and any publicly held corporation owning ten percent (10%) or more of its stock; or (2) states that there is no such corporation. FRCP 7.1(a).

- *Time to file; Supplemental filing.* A party must: (1) file the disclosure statement with its first appearance, pleading, petition, motion, response, or other request addressed to the court; and (2) promptly file a supplemental statement if any required information changes. FRCP 7.1(b).

iv. *Index of exhibits.* Any pleading, motion, brief, affidavit, notice, or proposed order, whether filed electronically or by delivering it to the clerk, must: include a separate index identifying and briefly describing each exhibit if there are more than four (4) exhibits. IN R USDCTND L.R. 5-4(a)(8).

v. *Request for oral argument.* A party may request oral argument on a motion by filing and serving a separate document explaining why oral argument is necessary and estimating how long the court should allow for the argument. IN R USDCTND L.R. 7-5(a)(1). The request must be filed and served with the party's supporting brief, response brief, or reply brief. IN R USDCTND L.R. 7-5(a)(2).

vi. *Request for evidentiary hearing.* A party may request an evidentiary hearing by filing and serving a separate document explaining why the hearing is necessary and estimating how long the court should allow for it. IN R USDCTND L.R. 7-5(b)(1).

vii. *Copy of authority.* A copy of any decision, statute, or regulation cited in a motion or brief must be attached to the paper if—and only if—it is not available on Westlaw or Lexis. But if a copy of a decision, statute, or regulation is only available electronically, a party must provide it to the court or another party upon request. IN R USDCTND L.R. 7-1(f).

viii. *Proposed order.* Parties filing a paper that requires the judge or clerk to enter a routine or uncontested order must include a suitable form of order. IN R USDCTND L.R. 5-4(c).

- Proposed orders shall not be filed electronically either as a separate document or as an

attachment to the main pleading or other document. Instead, all proposed orders must be e-mailed to the chambers of the appropriate judicial officer for the case. The proposed order must be in WordPerfect Format or Rich Text Format (RTF). Proposed orders should be attached to an e-mail and sent to the appropriate judicial officer at the address listed in IN R USDCTND CM/ECF(II)(F). The subject line of the email message should indicate the case title, cause number and document number of the motion, e.g., Smith v. Jones 1:02-cv-1234, motion# ___. IN R USDCTND CM/ECF(II)(F).

ix. *Copy of document with self-addressed envelope.* A party who wants a file-stamped copy of a paper must include with the filing an additional copy of the paper and a self-addressed envelope with adequate postage. IN R USDCTND L.R. 5-4(b)(6).

x. *Notice of manual filing.* However, if that is not physically possible, counsel shall electronically file a .pdf document titled Notice of Manual Filing as a notation on the docket sheet that filings are being held in the clerk's office in paper. A sample Notice of Manual Filing is attached as Form 2 (IN R USDCTND CM/ECF(Form 2)). IN R USDCTND CM/ECF(III)(A)(1).

xi. *Courtesy copies.* If documents are filed in paper format, counsel must provide an original for the clerk's office, a copy for the judge and a copy must be served on all parties in the case. IN R USDCTND CM/ECF(III)(A)(1).

xii. *Declaration that party was unable to file in a timely manner.* If the attorney is unable to file a document in a timely manner due to technical difficulties in the user's system, the attorney must file a document with the court as soon as possible notifying the court of the inability to file the document. A sample document entitled Declaration that Party was Unable to File in a Timely Manner Due to Technical Difficulties is attached hereto as Form 5. IN R USDCTND CM/ECF(VI)(B). [Editor's note: the reference to Form 5 is likely meant to be a reference to Form 3 (IN R USDCTND CM/ECF(Form 3)].

E. Format

1. *Form of documents.* The rules governing captions and other matters of form in pleadings apply to motions and other papers. FRCP 7(b)(2).

   a. *Paper.* Any pleading, motion, brief, affidavit, notice, or proposed order, whether filed electronically or by delivering it to the clerk, must: use eight and one-half by eleven (8-1/2 x 11) inch pages. IN R USDCTND L.R. 5-4(a)(2).

      i. *Manual filings.* Papers delivered to the clerk for filing must: be flat, unfolded, and on good-quality, white paper. IN R USDCTND L.R. 5-4(b)(1)(A).

         • *Covers or backing.* Papers delivered to the clerk for filing must: not have a cover or a back. IN R USDCTND L.R. 5-4(b)(1)(B).

         • *Recycled paper.* The court encourages using recycled paper. IN R USDCTND L.R. 5-4(b)(7).

   b. *Margins.* Any pleading, motion, brief, affidavit, notice, or proposed order, whether filed electronically or by delivering it to the clerk, must: have at least one (1) inch margins. IN R USDCTND L.R. 5-4(a)(3).

   c. *Spacing.* Any pleading, motion, brief, affidavit, notice, or proposed order, whether filed electronically or by delivering it to the clerk, must: be double spaced (except for headings, footnotes, and quoted material). IN R USDCTND L.R. 5-4(a)(5).

   d. *Text.* Any pleading, motion, brief, affidavit, notice, or proposed order, whether filed electronically or by delivering it to the clerk, must: be plainly typewritten, printed, or prepared by a clearly legible copying process. IN R USDCTND L.R. 5-4(a)(1).

      i. Any pleading, motion, brief, affidavit, notice, or proposed order, whether filed electronically or by delivering it to the clerk, must: use at least twelve (12) point type in the body and at least ten (10) point type in footnotes. IN R USDCTND L.R. 5-4(a)(4).

   e. *Page numbering.* Any pleading, motion, brief, affidavit, notice, or proposed order, whether filed electronically or by delivering it to the clerk, must: have consecutively numbered pages. IN R USDCTND L.R. 5-4(a)(6).

f. *Caption; Names of parties.* Every pleading must have a caption with the court's name, a title, a file number, and a FRCP 7(a) designation. The title of the complaint must name all the parties; the title of other pleadings, after naming the first party on each side, may refer generally to other parties. FRCP 10(a). Any pleading, motion, brief, affidavit, notice, or proposed order, whether filed electronically or by delivering it to the clerk, must: include a title on the first page. IN R USDCTND L.R. 5-4(a)(7).

   i. *Alternative motions.* Motions must be filed separately, but alternative motions may be filed in a single paper if each is named in the title following the caption. IN R USDCTND L.R. 7-1(a).

g. *Filer's information.* Any pleading, motion, brief, affidavit, notice, or proposed order, whether filed electronically or by delivering it to the clerk, must: except in proposed orders and affidavits, include the filer's name, address, telephone number, fax number (where available), and e-mail address (where available). IN R USDCTND L.R. 5-4(a)(9).

h. *Paragraphs; Separate statements.* A party must state its claims or defenses in numbered paragraphs, each limited as far as practicable to a single set of circumstances. A later pleading may refer by number to a paragraph in an earlier pleading. If doing so would promote clarity, each claim founded on a separate transaction or occurrence—and each defense other than a denial—must be stated in a separate count or defense. FRCP 10(b).

i. *Adoption by reference; Exhibits.* A statement in a pleading may be adopted by reference elsewhere in the same pleading or in any other pleading or motion. A copy of a written instrument that is an exhibit to a pleading is a part of the pleading for all purposes. FRCP 10(c).

j. *Citation of local rules.* The Local Civil Rules of the United States District Court for the Northern District of Indiana may be cited as "N.D. Ind. L.R." IN R USDCTND L.R. 1-1(a)(1).

k. *Acceptance by the clerk.* The clerk must not refuse to file a paper solely because it is not in the form prescribed by the Federal Rules of Civil Procedure or by a local rule or practice. FRCP 5(d)(4).

   i. *Sanctions for formatting errors; Non-compliance.* If a person files a paper that does not comply with the rules governing the format of papers filed with the court, the court may: (1) strike the paper from the record; or (2) fine the person up to one thousand dollars ($1,000). IN R USDCTND L.R. 1-3(a).

      • *Notice.* Before sanctioning a person under IN R USDCTND L.R. 1-3(a)(2), the court must: (1) notify the person that the paper is noncompliant; and (2) give the person the opportunity either to be heard or to revise the paper. IN R USDCTND L.R. 1-3(b).

2. *Form of electronic documents.* Electronically filed documents must meet the same requirements of format and page limits as documents "conventionally filed" (as defined in IN R USDCTND CM/ECF(III)(A)) pursuant to the Federal Rules of Civil Procedure and the Local Civil Rules of the United States District Court for the Northern District of Indiana. IN R USDCTND CM/ECF(II)(A)(2).

a. *PDF format required.* Documents filed in the CM/ECF must be in .pdf format. A document created with almost any word-processing program can be converted to .pdf format. The .pdf program in effect takes a picture of the original document and allows anyone to open the converted document across a broad range of hardware and software, with layout, format, links, and images intact. IN R USDCTND CM/ECF(FN2).

b. *Title of documents.* The person electronically filing a pleading or other document will be responsible for designating a title for the pleading or other document by using one of the categories contained in the events listed in the CM/ECF Menu. IN R USDCTND CM/ECF(II)(G).

c. *Combining documents.* All documents which form part of a single pleading and which are being filed at the same time and by the same party may be electronically filed together under one document number, e.g., the motion and a supporting affidavit, with the exception of memoranda in support. Memoranda in support shall be electronically filed separately and shown as a related document to the motion. IN R USDCTND CM/ECF(II)(A)(4).

d. *Exhibits and attachments.* Filing users must submit in electronic form all documents referenced as exhibits or attachments, unless the court permits conventional filing. A filing user must submit as

exhibits or attachments only those excerpts of the referenced documents that are directly germane to the matter under consideration by the court. Excerpted material must be clearly and prominently identified as such. Filing users who file excerpts of documents as exhibits or attachments do so without prejudice to their right to timely file additional excerpts or the complete document. Responding parties may timely file additional excerpts or the complete document that they believe are directly germane. The court may require parties to file additional excerpts or the complete document. IN R USDCTND CM/ECF(II)(A)(6).

e. *Hyperlinks.* Electronically filed documents may contain hyperlink references to an external document as a convenient mechanism for accessing material cited in the document. A hyperlink reference is neither validated for content nor considered a part of the court's records. The court neither endorses the product or organization at the destination of a hyperlink reference, nor does the court exercise any responsibility over the content at the destination. In order to preserve the integrity of the court record, attorneys wishing to insert hyperlinks in court filings shall continue to use the traditional citation method for the cited authority, in addition to the hyperlink. A hyperlink contained in a filing is no more than a convenient mechanism for accessing material cited in the document and a hyperlink reference is extraneous to any filed document and is not part of the court's record. IN R USDCTND CM/ECF(II)(A)(3).

3. *Form of briefs*

   a. *Page limits.* Supporting and response briefs (excluding tables of contents, tables of authorities, and appendices) ordinarily must not exceed twenty-five (25) pages. Reply briefs must not exceed fifteen (15) pages. IN R USDCTND L.R. 7-1(e)(1).

      i. *Exception.* The court may allow a party to file a brief exceeding these page limits for extraordinary and compelling reasons. But if the court permits a brief to exceed twenty-five (25) pages, it must include:

         • A table of contents with page references;

         • An issue statement; and

         • A table of authorities including: (1) all cases (alphabetically arranged), statutes, and other authorities cited in the brief; and (2) references to where the authorities appear in the brief. IN R USDCTND L.R. 7-1(e)(2).

4. *Signing of pleadings, motions and other papers*

   a. *Signature.* Every pleading, written motion, and other paper must be signed by at least one attorney of record in the attorney's name—or by a party personally if the party is unrepresented. The paper must state the signer's address, e-mail address, and telephone number. FRCP 11(a).

      i. *Signatures on manual filings.* Papers delivered to the clerk for filing must: include the filer's original signature. IN R USDCTND L.R. 5-4(b)(1)(C).

         • *Rubber-stamped and faxed signatures.* An original paper with a rubber-stamped or faxed signature is unsigned for purposes of FRCP 11 and FRCP 26(g). IN R USDCTND L.R. 5-4(b)(2).

         • *Affidavits.* Only the affiant need sign an affidavit. IN R USDCTND L.R. 5-4(b)(3).

      ii. *Electronic signatures.* Pursuant to FRCP 11, every pleading, motion, and other paper (except lists, schedules, statements or amendments thereto) shall be signed by at least one attorney of record or, if the party is not represented by an attorney, all papers shall be signed by the party. An attorney's/participant's password issued by the court combined with the user's identification, serves as and constitutes the attorney/participant's signature for FRCP 11 and other purposes. IN R USDCTND CM/ECF(I)(C). Documents which must be filed and which must contain original signatures other than those of a participating attorney or which require either verification or an unsworn declaration under any rule or statute, shall be filed electronically, with originally executed copies maintained by the filer. The pleading or other document electronically filed shall contain "s/" signature(s), as noted in IN R USDCTND CM/ECF(II)(E)(3)(b). IN R USDCTND CM/ECF(II)(E)(1).

         • *Multiple signatures.* In the case of a stipulation or other document to be signed by two or

more attorneys, the following procedure should be used: The filing attorney shall initially confirm that the content of the document is acceptable to all persons required to sign the document and shall obtain the physical signatures of all attorneys on the document. IN R USDCTND CM/ECF(II)(E)(3)(a). The filing attorney then shall file the document electronically, indicating the signatories, e.g., "s/Jane Doe," "s/John Doe," etc. IN R US-DCTND CM/ECF(II)(E)(3)(b). The filing attorney shall retain the hard copy of the document containing the original signatures. IN R USDCTND CM/ECF(II)(E)(3)(c).

    iii. *No verification or accompanying affidavit required for pleadings.* Unless a rule or statute specifically states otherwise, a pleading need not be verified or accompanied by an affidavit. FRCP 11(a).

    iv. *Unsigned papers.* The court must strike an unsigned paper unless the omission is promptly corrected after being called to the attorney's or party's attention. FRCP 11(a).

  b. *Representations to the court.* By presenting to the court a pleading, written motion, or other paper—whether by signing, filing, submitting, or later advocating it—an attorney or unrepresented party certifies that to the best of the person's knowledge, information, and belief, formed after an inquiry reasonable under the circumstances:

    i. It is not being presented for any improper purpose, such as to harass, cause unnecessary delay, or needlessly increase the cost of litigation;

    ii. The claims, defenses, and other legal contentions are warranted by existing law or by a nonfrivolous argument for extending, modifying, or reversing existing law or for establishing new law;

    iii. The factual contentions have evidentiary support or, if specifically so identified, will likely have evidentiary support after a reasonable opportunity for further investigation or discovery; and

    iv. The denials of factual contentions are warranted on the evidence or, if specifically so identified, are reasonably based on belief or a lack of information. FRCP 11(b).

  c. *Sanctions.* If, after notice and a reasonable opportunity to respond, the court determines that FRCP 11(b) has been violated, the court may impose an appropriate sanction on any attorney, law firm, or party that violated FRCP 11(b) or is responsible for the violation. FRCP 11(c)(1). Refer to the United States District Court for the Northern District of Indiana KeyRules Motion for Sanctions document for more information.

5. *Privacy protection for filings made with the court*

  a. *Redacted filings.* Counsel should not include sensitive information in any document filed with the court unless such inclusion is necessary and relevant to the case. IN R USDCTND CM/ECF(VII). Unless the court orders otherwise, in an electronic or paper filing with the court that contains an individual's Social Security number, taxpayer-identification number, or birth date, the name of an individual known to be a minor, or a financial-account number, a party or nonparty making the filing may include only:

    i. The last four (4) digits of the Social Security number and taxpayer-identification number;

    ii. The year of the individual's birth;

    iii. The minor's initials; and

    iv. The last four (4) digits of the financial-account number. FRCP 5.2(a); IN R USDCTND Order 2005-3.

  b. *Exemptions from the redaction requirement.* The redaction requirement does not apply to the following:

    i. A financial-account number that identifies the property allegedly subject to forfeiture in a forfeiture proceeding;

    ii. The record of an administrative or agency proceeding;

    iii. The official record of a state-court proceeding;

    iv. The record of a court or tribunal, if that record was not subject to the redaction requirement when originally filed;

    v.   A filing covered by FRCP 5.2(c) or FRCP 5.2(d); and

    vi.   A pro se filing in an action brought under 28 U.S.C.A. § 2241, 28 U.S.C.A. § 2254, or 28 U.S.C.A. § 2255. FRCP 5.2(b).

    vii.   In cases filed under the Social Security Act, 42 U.S.C.A. § 405(g), there is no need for redaction of any information from the documents filed in the case. IN R USDCTND Order 2005-3.

c. *Limitations on remote access to electronic files; Social Security appeals and immigration cases.* Unless the court orders otherwise, in an action for benefits under the Social Security Act, and in an action or proceeding relating to an order of removal, to relief from removal, or to immigration benefits or detention, access to an electronic file is authorized as follows:

    i.   The parties and their attorneys may have remote electronic access to any part of the case file, including the administrative record;

    ii.   Any other person may have electronic access to the full record at the courthouse, but may have remote electronic access only to:

        • The docket maintained by the court; and

        • An opinion, order, judgment, or other disposition of the court, but not any other part of the case file or the administrative record. FRCP 5.2(c).

d. *Filings made under seal.* The court may order that a filing be made under seal without redaction. The court may later unseal the filing or order the person who made the filing to file a redacted version for the public record. FRCP 5.2(d). For information on filing documents under seal, refer to IN R USDCTND L.R. 5-3, IN R USDCTND CM/ECF(IV)(A), and IN R USDCTND ECF Order 2004-19.

e. *Protective orders.* For good cause, the court may by order in a case:

    i.   Require redaction of additional information; or

    ii.   Limit or prohibit a nonparty's remote electronic access to a document filed with the court. FRCP 5.2(e).

f. *Option for additional unredacted filing under seal.* A person making a redacted filing may also file an unredacted copy under seal. The court must retain the unredacted copy as part of the record. FRCP 5.2(f); IN R USDCTND Order 2005-3.

    i.   The unredacted version of the document or the reference list shall be retained by the court under seal as part of the record. This paper shall be retained by the court as part of the record. The court may, however, still require the party to file a redacted copy for the public file. IN R USDCTND Order 2005-3.

g. *Option for filing a reference list.* A filing that contains redacted information may be filed together with a reference list that identifies each item of redacted information and specifies an appropriate identifier that uniquely corresponds to each item listed. The list must be filed under seal and may be amended as of right. Any reference in the case to a listed identifier will be construed to refer to the corresponding item of information. FRCP 5.2(g); IN R USDCTND Order 2005-3.

    i.   The unredacted version of the document or the reference list shall be retained by the court under seal as part of the record. This paper shall be retained by the court as part of the record. The court may, however, still require the party to file a redacted copy for the public file. IN R USDCTND Order 2005-3.

h. *Responsibility for redaction.* The responsibility for redacting these personal identifiers rests solely with counsel and the parties. The Clerk will not review each paper for compliance with IN R USDCTND Order 2005-3. IN R USDCTND Order 2005-3.

i. *Waiver of protection of identifiers.* A person waives the protection of FRCP 5.2(a) as to the person's own information by filing it without redaction and not under seal. FRCP 5.2(h).

F. Filing and Service Requirements

1. *Filing requirements.* Any paper after the complaint that is required to be served—together with a

certificate of service—must be filed within a reasonable time after service. FRCP 5(d)(1). Motions must be filed separately, but alternative motions may be filed in a single paper if each is named in the title following the caption. IN R USDCTND L.R. 7-1(a). To file. . .a document ex parte in a civil case, a party must file it electronically as required by the CM/ECF User Manual (IN R USDCTND CM/ECF). IN R USDCTND L.R. 5-3(c)(1). Ex parte motions and ex parte documents in non-sealed civil cases shall be filed electronically in the CM/ECF system using the appropriate civil event, either "Ex Parte Motion" or "Ex Parte Document". IN R USDCTND CM/ECF(IV)(A)(3).

a. *How filing is made; In general.* A paper is filed by delivering it:

   i. To the clerk; or

   ii. To a judge who agrees to accept it for filing, and who must then note the filing date on the paper and promptly send it to the clerk. FRCP 5(d)(2).

- Papers not filed electronically must be filed with the clerk, not a judge. IN R USDCTND L.R. 5-4(b)(4).

   iii. Parties manually filing a paper that requires the clerk to give others notice, must give the clerk: (1) sufficient copies of the notice; and (2) the name and address of each person entitled to receive the notice. IN R USDCTND L.R. 5-4(b)(8).

b. *Where to file.* Papers not filed electronically must be filed in the division where the case is pending, unless: (1) a person will be prejudiced if the paper is not filed the same day it is tendered; and (2) it includes an adequately sized envelope addressed to the clerk's office in the division where the case is pending and with adequate postage. IN R USDCTND L.R. 5-4(b)(5).

c. *Electronic filing*

   i. *Authorization of electronic filing program.* A court may, by local rule, allow papers to be filed, signed, or verified by electronic means that are consistent with any technical standards established by the Judicial Conference of the United States. A local rule may require electronic filing only if reasonable exceptions are allowed. A paper filed electronically in compliance with a local rule is a written paper for purposes of the Federal Rules of Civil Procedure. FRCP 5(d)(3).

- Papers must be filed, signed, and verified electronically unless excepted by the court's CM/ECF Civil and Criminal User Manual (IN R USDCTND CM/ECF). IN R USDCTND L.R. 5-1.

   ii. *Mandatory electronic filing.* Unless otherwise permitted by these procedures or otherwise authorized by the assigned judge, all documents submitted for filing in this district in civil and criminal cases, no matter when a case was originally filed, shall be filed electronically using the System. IN R USDCTND CM/ECF(II)(A)(1). The requirement that "all documents" be filed electronically includes briefs, and attachments and exhibits used in support of motions. IN R USDCTND CM/ECF(FN1).

- Sending a document or pleading to the court via e-mail or facsimile does not constitute "electronic filing." IN R USDCTND CM/ECF(I)(A).

   iii. *Conventional filing.* As used in these procedures, a "conventionally" filed or submitted document or pleading is one presented to the Clerk or a party in paper or other non-electronic, tangible format. The following documents shall be filed conventionally and not electronically unless specifically authorized by the Court:

- Exhibits and other documents which cannot be converted to a legible electronic form. Whenever possible, counsel is responsible for converting filings to an electronic form. However, if that is not physically possible, counsel shall electronically file a .pdf document titled Notice of Manual Filing as a notation on the docket sheet that filings are being held in the clerk's office in paper. A sample Notice of Manual Filing is attached as Form 2 (IN R USDCTND CM/ECF(Form 2)). If documents are filed in paper format, counsel must provide an original for the clerk's office, a copy for the judge and a copy must be served on all parties in the case. Large documents which do not exist in an electronic format shall be scanned into .pdf format by counsel, in small batches if necessary, and filed electronically as separate attachments in the System. IN R USDCTND CM/ECF(III)(A)(1).

- Certain documents which are listed in IN R USDCTND CM/ECF(II)(E)(2). IN R US-DCTND CM/ECF(III)(A)(2).
- Documents filed by pro se litigants. IN R USDCTND CM/ECF(III)(A)(3).

    iv. For more information on electronic filing, refer to IN R USDCTND CM/ECF.

2. *Service requirements*

   a. *Service; When required*

     i. *In general.* Unless the Federal Rules of Civil Procedure provide otherwise, each of the following papers must be served on every party:

- An order stating that service is required;
- A pleading filed after the original complaint, unless the court orders otherwise under FRCP 5(c) because there are numerous defendants;
- A discovery paper required to be served on a party, unless the court orders otherwise;
- A written motion, except one that may be heard ex parte; and
- A written notice, appearance, demand, or offer of judgment, or any similar paper. FRCP 5(a)(1).

     ii. *If a party fails to appear.* No service is required on a party who is in default for failing to appear. But a pleading that asserts a new claim for relief against such a party must be served on that party under FRCP 4. FRCP 5(a)(2).

     iii. *Seizing property.* If an action is begun by seizing property and no person is or need be named as a defendant, any service required before the filing of an appearance, answer, or claim must be made on the person who had custody or possession of the property when it was seized. FRCP 5(a)(3).

   b. *Service; How made*

     i. *Serving an attorney.* If a party is represented by an attorney, service under FRCP 5 must be made on the attorney unless the court orders service on the party. FRCP 5(b)(1).

     ii. *Service in general.* A paper is served under FRCP 5 by:

- Handing it to the person;
- Leaving it: (1) at the person's office with a clerk or other person in charge or, if no one is in charge, in a conspicuous place in the office; or (2) if the person has no office or the office is closed, at the person's dwelling or usual place of abode with someone of suitable age and discretion who resides there;
- Mailing it to the person's last known address—in which event service is complete upon mailing;
- Leaving it with the court clerk if the person has no known address;
- Sending it by electronic means if the person consented in writing—in which event service is complete upon transmission, but is not effective if the serving party learns that it did not reach the person to be served; or
- Delivering it by any other means that the person consented to in writing—in which event service is complete when the person making service delivers it to the agency designated to make delivery. FRCP 5(b)(2).

     iii. *Electronic service.* Electronically filed papers may be served electronically if service is consistent with the CM/ECF User Manual (IN R USDCTND CM/ECF). IN R USDCTND L.R. 5-2(a).

- *Waiver of other service.* An attorney's registration will constitute a waiver of conventional service of documents and the attorney agrees to accept service of notice on behalf of the client of the electronic filing by hand, facsimile or authorized email. IN R USDCTND CM/ECF(I)(B)(3).

- *Serving registered persons.* The System will generate a "Notice of Electronic Filing" when any document is filed. This notice represents service of the document on parties who are registered participants with the System. Except as provided in IN R USDCTND CM/ECF(III)(B), the filing party shall not be required to serve any pleading or other documents on any party receiving electronic notice. IN R USDCTND CM/ECF(II)(D)(1). The term "pleading" refers only to those documents listed in FRCP 7(a). IN R USDCTND CM/ECF(FN3).

- *When electronic service is deemed completed.* A person registered to use the court's electronic-filing system is served with an electronically filed paper when a "Notice of Electronic Filing" is transmitted to that person through the court's electronic filing-system. IN R USDCTND L.R. 5-2(b).

- *Serving non-registered persons.* A person who has not registered to use the court's electronic-filing system but who is entitled to service of a paper must be served according to the Local Civil Rules of the United States District Court for the Northern District of Indiana and the Federal Rules of Civil Procedure. IN R USDCTND L.R. 5-2(c); IN R USDCTND CM/ECF(II)(D)(2). If such service of a paper copy is to be made, it shall be done in the manner provided in the Federal Rules of Civil Procedure and the Local Civil Rules of the United States District Court for the Northern District of Indiana. IN R USDCTND CM/ECF(II)(D)(2).

iv. *Service of conventional filings.* Pleadings or other documents which are filed conventionally rather than electronically shall be served in the manner provided for in the Federal Rules of Civil Procedure and the Local Civil Rules of the United States District Court for the Northern District of Indiana, except as otherwise provided by order of the Court. IN R USDCTND CM/ECF(III)(B).

v. *Using court facilities.* If a local rule so authorizes, a party may use the court's transmission facilities to make service under FRCP 5(b)(2)(E). FRCP 5(b)(3).

c. *Serving numerous defendants*

i. *In general.* If an action involves an unusually large number of defendants, the court may, on motion or on its own, order that:

- Defendants' pleadings and replies to them need not be served on other defendants;

- Any crossclaim, counterclaim, avoidance, or affirmative defense in those pleadings and replies to them will be treated as denied or avoided by all other parties; and

- Filing any such pleading and serving it on the plaintiff constitutes notice of the pleading to all parties. FRCP 5(c)(1).

ii. *Notifying parties.* A copy of every such order must be served on the parties as the court directs. FRCP 5(c)(2).

G. Hearings

1. *Hearings, generally*

a. *Oral argument.* Due process does not require that oral argument be permitted on a motion and, except as otherwise provided by local rule, the district court has discretion to determine whether it will decide the motion on the papers or hear argument by counsel (and perhaps receive evidence). FPP § 1190; F.D.I.C. v. Deglau, 207 F.3d 153 (3d Cir. 2000).

i. *Request for oral argument.* A party may request oral argument on a motion by filing and serving a separate document explaining why oral argument is necessary and estimating how long the court should allow for the argument. IN R USDCTND L.R. 7-5(a)(1). Refer to the Documents section of this document for more information.

ii. *Additional evidence forbidden.* Parties may not present additional evidence at oral argument. IN R USDCTND L.R. 7-5(a)(3).

b. *Providing a regular schedule for oral hearings.* A court may establish regular times and places for oral hearings on motions. FRCP 78(a).

c. *Providing for submission on briefs.* By rule or order, the court may provide for submitting and determining motions on briefs, without oral hearings. FRCP 78(b).

d. *Evidentiary hearings.* A party may request an evidentiary hearing by filing and serving a separate document explaining why the hearing is necessary and estimating how long the court should allow for it. IN R USDCTND L.R. 7-5(b)(2). Refer to the Documents section of this document for more information.

e. *Court's authority.* The court may: (1) grant or deny a request for oral argument or an evidentiary hearing in its discretion; (2) set oral argument or an evidentiary hearing without a request from a party; or (3) order any oral argument or evidentiary hearing to be held anywhere within the district regardless of where the case will be tried. IN R USDCTND L.R. 7-5(c).

2. *Hearing on motion for preliminary injunction after temporary restraining order is issued without notice*

   a. *Expediting the preliminary injunction hearing.* If the order is issued without notice, the motion for a preliminary injunction must be set for hearing at the earliest possible time, taking precedence over all other matters except hearings on older matters of the same character. At the hearing, the party who obtained the order must proceed with the motion; if the party does not, the court must dissolve the order. FRCP 65(b)(3). Refer to the United States District Court for the Northern District of Indiana KeyRules Motion for Preliminary Injunction document for more information on the hearing on the motion for preliminary injunction.

3. *Courtroom and courthouse decorum.* For information on courtroom and courthouse decorum, refer to IN R USDCTND L.R. 83-3.

H. Forms

1. Federal Application for Temporary Restraining Order Forms

a. Ex parte motion; For temporary restraining order and order to show cause; Interference with property rights. AMJUR PP INJUNCTION § 42.

b. Affidavit; In support of ex parte motion for temporary restraining order. AMJUR PP INJUNCTION § 48.

c. Certificate of attorney; In support of ex parte motion for temporary restraining order. AMJUR PP INJUNCTION § 50.

d. Affidavit; In support of ex parte motion for temporary restraining order; Interference with property rights. AMJUR PP INJUNCTION § 51.

e. Motion. 4A FEDFORMS § 5344.

f. Motion; Another form. 4A FEDFORMS § 5345.

g. Motion; Another form. 4A FEDFORMS § 5346.

h. Motion without notice. 4A FEDFORMS § 5347.

i. Motion without notice; Another form. 4A FEDFORMS § 5348.

j. Motion without notice; Another form. 4A FEDFORMS § 5349.

k. Motion without notice; Another form. 4A FEDFORMS § 5350.

l. Motion without notice; Another form. 4A FEDFORMS § 5351.

m. Motion without notice; Another form. 4A FEDFORMS § 5352.

n. Certificate of attorney's efforts to give notice. 4A FEDFORMS § 5353.

o. Certificate of attorney's efforts to give notice; Another form. 4A FEDFORMS § 5354.

p. Certificate of attorney's efforts to give notice; Another form. 4A FEDFORMS § 5355.

q. Certificate of attorney's efforts to give notice; Another form. 4A FEDFORMS § 5356.

r. Motion requesting expedited hearing. 4A FEDFORMS § 5357.

    s.   Motion seeking temporary restraining order. 4A FEDFORMS § 5359.

    t.   Motion to dissolve or modify temporary restraining order. 4A FEDFORMS § 5361.

    u.   Motion for temporary restraining order and preliminary injunction. GOLDLTGFMS § 13A:6.

    v.   Motion for temporary restraining order; General form. GOLDLTGFMS § 13A:11.

    w.   Motion for temporary restraining order; Ex parte application. GOLDLTGFMS § 13A:12.

    x.   Motion for temporary restraining order; Ex parte application; Supporting affidavit by party. GOLDLTGFMS § 13A:13.

    y.   Motion for temporary restraining order; Ex parte application; Supporting affidavit by party; Copyright infringement. GOLDLTGFMS § 13A:14.

    z.   Motion for temporary restraining order; Ex parte application; Certificate by counsel. GOLDLTGFMS § 13A:15.

2. Forms for the Northern District of Indiana

    a.   Certificate of service. IN R USDCTND CM/ECF(Form 1).

    b.   Notice of manual filing. IN R USDCTND CM/ECF(Form 2).

    c.   Declaration that party was unable to file in a timely manner. IN R USDCTND CM/ECF(Form 3).

I. Applicable Rules

  1. *Federal rules*

    a.   Serving and filing pleadings and other papers. FRCP 5.

    b.   Constitutional challenge to a statute; Notice, certification, and intervention. FRCP 5.1.

    c.   Privacy protection for filings made with the court. FRCP 5.2.

    d.   Computing and extending time; Time for motion papers. FRCP 6.

    e.   Pleadings allowed; Form of motions and other papers. FRCP 7.

    f.   Disclosure statement. FRCP 7.1.

    g.   Form of pleadings. FRCP 10.

    h.   Signing pleadings, motions, and other papers; Representations to the court; Sanctions. FRCP 11.

    i.   Taking testimony. FRCP 43.

    j.   Injunctions and restraining orders. FRCP 65.

    k.   Proceedings against a surety. FRCP 65.1.

    l.   Hearing motions; Submission on briefs. FRCP 78.

  2. *Local rules*

    a.   Citation and scope of the rules. IN R USDCTND L.R. 1-1.

    b.   Sanctions for formatting errors. IN R USDCTND L.R. 1-3.

    c.   Electronic filing required. IN R USDCTND L.R. 5-1.

    d.   Constitutional questions. IN R USDCTND L.R. 5.1-1.

    e.   Electronic service. IN R USDCTND L.R. 5-2.

    f.   Filing under seal or ex parte. IN R USDCTND L.R. 5-3.

    g.   Format of papers. IN R USDCTND L.R. 5-4.

    h.   Motion practice. IN R USDCTND L.R. 7-1.

    i.   Oral arguments and evidentiary hearings. IN R USDCTND L.R. 7-5.

    j.   Pretrial procedure. IN R USDCTND L.R. 16-1.

    k.   Alternative dispute resolution. IN R USDCTND L.R. 16-6.

    l.   Filing of discovery and other materials. IN R USDCTND L.R. 26-2.

m.   Case assignment. IN R USDCTND L.R. 40-1.

n.   Preliminary injunctions and temporary restraining orders. IN R USDCTND L.R. 65-1.

o.   Appearance and withdrawal of appearance. IN R USDCTND L.R. 83-8.

p.   CM/ECF civil and criminal user manual. IN R USDCTND CM/ECF.

q.   In re: privacy and public access to civil electronic case files. IN R USDCTND Order 2005-3.

Requests, Notices and Applications
Pretrial Conferences, Scheduling, Management

Document Last Updated December 2016

A.   Checklist

(I)   ❏ Matters to be considered by parties for the pretrial conference

   (a)   ❏ Documents to consider

      (1)   ❏ Pretrial memorandum or statement

      (2)   ❏ Notice of constitutional question

      (3)   ❏ Index of exhibits

      (4)   ❏ Copy of document with self-addressed envelope

      (5)   ❏ Notice of manual filing

      (6)   ❏ Courtesy copies

      (7)   ❏ Declaration that party was unable to file in a timely manner

   (b)   ❏ Timing

      (1)   ❏ The court determines at what stage in the action to hold a pretrial conference

(II)   ❏ Matters to be considered by parties for the scheduling conference

   (a)   ❏ Documents to consider

      (1)   ❏ Request for scheduling conference

      (2)   ❏ Proposed scheduling order

      (3)   ❏ Notice of constitutional question

      (4)   ❏ Index of exhibits

      (5)   ❏ Copy of document with self-addressed envelope

      (6)   ❏ Notice of manual filing

      (7)   ❏ Courtesy copies

      (8)   ❏ Declaration that party was unable to file in a timely manner

   (b)   ❏ Timing

      (1)   ❏ If a scheduling conference is called, it is important to recognize that, unlike the ordinary pretrial conference, the scheduling conference occurs before the substantive issues have been defined and is directed toward organizing the processing of the action by setting deadlines for the completion of the various pretrial phases

(III)   ❏ Matters to be considered by parties for the final pretrial conference

   (a)   ❏ Documents to consider

      (1)   ❏ Proposed final pretrial order

      (2)   ❏ Notice of constitutional question

      (3)   ❏ Index of exhibits

    (4) ❑ Copy of document with self-addressed envelope

    (5) ❑ Notice of manual filing

    (6) ❑ Courtesy copies

    (7) ❑ Declaration that party was unable to file in a timely manner

  (b) ❑ Timing

    (1) ❑ There are no specific timing requirements for the final pretrial conference or the proposed final pretrial order

(IV) ❑ Matters to be considered by parties for the discovery planning conference

  (a) ❑ Required documents

    (1) ❑ Written report outlining proposed discovery plan

  (b) ❑ Supplemental documents

    (1) ❑ Notice of constitutional question

    (2) ❑ Index of exhibits

    (3) ❑ Copy of document with self-addressed envelope

    (4) ❑ Notice of manual filing

    (5) ❑ Courtesy copies

    (6) ❑ Declaration that party was unable to file in a timely manner

  (c) ❑ Timing

    (1) ❑ Except in a proceeding exempted from initial disclosure under FRCP 26(a)(1)(B) or when the court orders otherwise, the parties must confer as soon as practicable—and in any event at least twenty-one (21) days before a scheduling conference is to be held or a scheduling order is due under FRCP 16(b)

    (2) ❑ Within fourteen (14) days after the conference, the attorneys of record are responsible for submitting a written report outlining the plan

B. Timing

1. *Pretrial conferences, generally.* The court determines at what stage in the action to hold a pretrial conference. When only one conference is involved, the most favored practice seems to be to wait until after the case has been prepared for trial. FPP § 1524. Although there rarely will be any need to hold a conference in a relatively simple case until after the preliminary motions have been disposed of, the only inherently logical limitation on the court's discretion as to when to hold a conference is that it should not be held before all the necessary and indispensable parties are served. FPP § 1524.

2. *Scheduling conference.* If a scheduling conference is called, it is important to recognize that, unlike the ordinary pretrial conference, the scheduling conference occurs before the substantive issues have been defined and is directed toward organizing the processing of the action by setting deadlines for the completion of the various pretrial phases. FPP § 1522.1.

3. *Final pretrial conference.* There are no specific timing requirements for the final pretrial conference or the proposed final pretrial order.

4. *Discovery planning conference.* Except in a proceeding exempted from initial disclosure under FRCP 26(a)(1)(B) or when the court orders otherwise, the parties must confer as soon as practicable—and in any event at least twenty-one (21) days before a scheduling conference is to be held or a scheduling order is due under FRCP 16(b). FRCP 26(f)(1).

  a. *Submission of written report outlining proposed discovery plan.* The attorneys of record and all unrepresented parties that have appeared in the case are jointly responsible for arranging the conference, for attempting in good faith to agree on the proposed discovery plan, and for submitting to the court within fourteen (14) days after the conference a written report outlining the plan. FRCP 26(f)(2).

b. *Expedited schedule.* If necessary to comply with its expedited schedule for FRCP 16(b) conferences, a court may by local rule: (1) require the parties' conference to occur less than twenty-one (21) days before the scheduling conference is held or a scheduling order is due under FRCP 16(b); and (2) require the written report outlining the discovery plan to be filed less than fourteen (14) days after the parties' conference, or excuse the parties from submitting a written report and permit them to report orally on their discovery plan at the FRCP 16(b) conference. FRCP 26(f)(4).

5. *Computation of time*

    a. *Computing time.* FRCP 6 applies in computing any time period specified in the Federal Rules of Civil Procedure, in any local rule or court order, or in any statute that does not specify a method of computing time. FRCP 6(a).

        i. *Period stated in days or a longer unit.* When the period is stated in days or a longer unit of time:

- Exclude the day of the event that triggers the period;
- Count every day, including intermediate Saturdays, Sundays, and legal holidays; and
- Include the last day of the period, but if the last day is a Saturday, Sunday, or legal holiday, the period continues to run until the end of the next day that is not a Saturday, Sunday, or legal holiday. FRCP 6(a)(1).

        ii. *Period stated in hours.* When the period is stated in hours:

- Begin counting immediately on the occurrence of the event that triggers the period;
- Count every hour, including hours during intermediate Saturdays, Sundays, and legal holidays; and
- If the period would end on a Saturday, Sunday, or legal holiday, the period continues to run until the same time on the next day that is not a Saturday, Sunday, or legal holiday. FRCP 6(a)(2).

        iii. *Inaccessibility of the clerk's office.* Unless the court orders otherwise, if the clerk's office is inaccessible:

- On the last day for filing under FRCP 6(a)(1), then the time for filing is extended to the first accessible day that is not a Saturday, Sunday, or legal holiday; or
- During the last hour for filing under FRCP 6(a)(2), then the time for filing is extended to the same time on the first accessible day that is not a Saturday, Sunday, or legal holiday. FRCP 6(a)(3).

        iv. *"Last day" defined.* Unless a different time is set by a statute, local rule, or court order, the last day ends:

- For electronic filing, at midnight in the court's time zone; and
- For filing by other means, when the clerk's office is scheduled to close. FRCP 6(a)(4).

        v. *"Next day" defined.* The "next day" is determined by continuing to count forward when the period is measured after an event and backward when measured before an event. FRCP 6(a)(5).

        vi. *"Legal holiday" defined.* "Legal holiday" means:

- The day set aside by statute for observing New Year's Day, Martin Luther King Jr.'s Birthday, Washington's Birthday, Memorial Day, Independence Day, Labor Day, Columbus Day, Veterans' Day, Thanksgiving Day, or Christmas Day;
- Any day declared a holiday by the President or Congress; and
- For periods that are measured after an event, any other day declared a holiday by the state where the district court is located. FRCP 6(a)(6).

    b. *Computation of electronic filing deadlines.* Filing documents electronically does not alter any filing deadlines or any time computation pursuant to FRCP 6. The counties of Lake, Porter, LaPorte, Pulaski and Starke are located in the Central time zone and the remaining counties in the Northern District of Indiana are located in the Eastern time zone. Nevertheless, all electronic transmissions of documents must be completed (i.e., received completely by the clerk's office) prior to midnight Eastern Time, (South Bend/Fort Wayne/Lafayette time) in order to be considered timely filed that day, regardless of the local time in the division where the case is pending. Although documents can be filed electronically twenty-four (24) hours a day, filers are strongly encouraged to file all documents during hours when the CM/ECF Help Line is available, from 9:00 a.m. to 4:00 p.m. local time. IN R USDCTND CM/ECF(II)(I).

    i. *Technical failures.* If the attorney is unable to file a document in a timely manner due to technical difficulties in the user's system, the attorney must file a document with the court as soon as possible notifying the court of the inability to file the document. A sample document entitled Declaration that Party was Unable to File in a Timely Manner Due to Technical Difficulties is attached hereto as Form 5. IN R USDCTND CM/ECF(VI)(B). [Editor's note: the reference to Form 5 is likely meant to be a reference to Form 3 (IN R USDCTND CM/ECF(Form 3)].

  c. *Extending time*

    i. *In general.* When an act may or must be done within a specified time, the court may, for good cause, extend the time:

- With or without motion or notice if the court acts, or if a request is made, before the original time or its extension expires; or

- On motion made after the time has expired if the party failed to act because of excusable neglect. FRCP 6(b)(1).

    ii. *Exceptions.* A court must not extend the time to act under FRCP 50(b), FRCP 50(d), FRCP 52(b), FRCP 59(b), FRCP 59(d), FRCP 59(e), and FRCP 60(b). FRCP 6(b)(2).

    iii. Refer to the United States District Court for the Northern District of Indiana KeyRules Motion for Continuance/Extension of Time document for more information on extending time.

  d. *Additional time after certain kinds of service.* When a party may or must act within a specified time after being served and service is made under FRCP 5(b)(2)(C) (mail), FRCP 5(b)(2)(D) (leaving with the clerk), or FRCP 5(b)(2)(F) (other means consented to), three (3) days are added after the period would otherwise expire under FRCP 6(a). FRCP 6(d).

C. General Requirements

1. *Pretrial conferences, generally*

  a. *Purposes of a pretrial conference.* FRCP 16 provides an important mechanism for carrying out one of the basic policies of the Federal Rules of Civil Procedure—the determination of disputes on their merits rather than on the basis of procedural niceties or tactical advantage. FPP § 1522. In any action, the court may order the attorneys and any unrepresented parties to appear for one or more pretrial conferences for such purposes as:

    i. Expediting disposition of the action;

    ii. Establishing early and continuing control so that the case will not be protracted because of lack of management;

    iii. Discouraging wasteful pretrial activities;

    iv. Improving the quality of the trial through more thorough preparation; and

    v. Facilitating settlement. FRCP 16(a).

  b. *When appropriate.* FRCP 16 specifically provides that the court "may order the attorneys and any unrepresented parties to appear for one or more pretrial conferences." This language makes it clear that the utilization of the pretrial conference procedure lies within the discretion of the district court both as a matter of general policy and in terms of whether and when the rule should be invoked in a particular case. FPP § 1523; Mizwicki v. Helwig, 196 F.3d 828 (7th Cir. 1999). There is no requirement that any pretrial conferences be held or not held in certain types of actions. FPP § 1523.

    i. *Notice from clerk.* A clerk-issued notice directing the parties to prepare for and attend a pretrial conference is a court order for purposes of FRCP 16(a). IN R USDCTND L.R. 16-1(a).

c. *Attendance at a pretrial conference.* A represented party must authorize at least one of its attorneys to make stipulations and admissions about all matters that can reasonably be anticipated for discussion at a pretrial conference. If appropriate, the court may require that a party or its representative be present or reasonably available by other means to consider possible settlement. FRCP 16(c)(1).

d. *Preparation for pretrial conferences.* Parties must confer before each pretrial conference and must be prepared to address the following matters at the conference:

   i. Case-management plan issues;

   ii. Alternative-dispute-resolution processes, including mediation, early neutral evaluation, and mini-trial;

   iii. Settlement, including their present positions on settlement;

   iv. Trial readiness; and

   v. Any other matters specifically directed by the court. IN R USDCTND L.R. 16-1(e).

e. *Matters for consideration at a pretrial conference.* At any pretrial conference, the court may consider and take appropriate action on the following matters:

   i. Formulating and simplifying the issues, and eliminating frivolous claims or defenses;

   ii. Amending the pleadings if necessary or desirable;

   iii. Obtaining admissions and stipulations about facts and documents to avoid unnecessary proof, and ruling in advance on the admissibility of evidence;

   iv. Avoiding unnecessary proof and cumulative evidence, and limiting the use of testimony under FRE 702;

   v. Determining the appropriateness and timing of summary adjudication under FRCP 56;

   vi. Controlling and scheduling discovery, including orders affecting disclosures and discovery under FRCP 26 and FRCP 29 through FRCP 37;

   vii. Identifying witnesses and documents, scheduling the filing and exchange of any pretrial briefs, and setting dates for further conferences and for trial;

   viii. Referring matters to a magistrate judge or a master;

   ix. Settling the case and using special procedures to assist in resolving the dispute when authorized by statute or local rule;

   x. Determining the form and content of the pretrial order;

   xi. Disposing of pending motions;

   xii. Adopting special procedures for managing potentially difficult or protracted actions that may involve complex issues, multiple parties, difficult legal questions, or unusual proof problems;

   xiii. Ordering a separate trial under FRCP 42(b) of a claim, counterclaim, crossclaim, third-party claim, or particular issue;

   xiv. Ordering the presentation of evidence early in the trial on a manageable issue that might, on the evidence, be the basis for a judgment as a matter of law under FRCP 50(a) or a judgment on partial findings under FRCP 52(c);

   xv. Establishing a reasonable limit on the time allowed to present evidence; and

   xvi. Facilitating in other ways the just, speedy, and inexpensive disposition of the action. FRCP 16(c)(2).

f. *Settlement negotiations*

   i. *Facilitation at pretrial conferences.* The court may facilitate settlement negotiations at any pretrial conference after an initial conference. Accordingly, attorneys attending a pretrial conference after the initial conference must: (1) know their settlement authority; and (2) be prepared to negotiate in good faith at the conference. IN R USDCTND L.R. 16-1(f)(1).

    ii.   *Attendance by parties.* To assist settlement discussions, the court may require a party, a corporate party's agent, or an insurance-company representative to appear at a pretrial conference. IN R USDCTND L.R. 16-1(f)(2).

    iii.   *Disclosure prohibited.* The court may not disclose the details of any negotiations at a pretrial conference in an order or docket entry. IN R USDCTND L.R. 16-1(f)(3).

g.   *Pretrial orders.* After any conference under FRCP 16, the court should issue an order reciting the action taken. This order controls the course of the action unless the court modifies it. FRCP 16(d).

h.   *Sanctions.* On motion or on its own, the court may issue any just orders, including those authorized by FRCP 37(b)(2)(A)(ii) through FRCP 37(b)(2)(A)(vii), if a party or its attorney: (1) fails to appear at a scheduling or other pretrial conference; (2) is substantially unprepared to participate—or does not participate in good faith—in the conference; or (3) fails to obey a scheduling or other pretrial order. FRCP 16(f)(1).

    i.   *Imposing fees and costs.* Instead of or in addition to any other sanction, the court must order the party, its attorney, or both to pay the reasonable expenses—including attorney's fees—incurred because of any noncompliance with FRCP 16, unless the noncompliance was substantially justified or other circumstances make an award of expenses unjust. FRCP 16(f)(2).

2.   *Scheduling conference.* A scheduling conference may be requested by the judge or by the parties, but it is not mandatory. FPP § 1522.1.

a.   *Scheduling order.* Except in categories of actions exempted by local rule, the district judge—or a magistrate judge when authorized by local rule—must issue a scheduling order: (1) after receiving the parties' report under FRCP 26(f); or (2) after consulting with the parties' attorneys and any unrepresented parties at a scheduling conference. FRCP 16(b)(1).

    i.   *Exemptions.* The following categories of actions are exempted from the requirements of FRCP 16(b):

- An action for review on an administrative record;
- A forfeiture action in rem arising from a federal statute;
- A petition for habeas corpus or any other proceeding to challenge a criminal conviction or sentence;
- An action to enforce or quash an administrative summons or subpoena;
- An action by the United States to recover benefits payments;
- An action by the United States to collect on a student loan guaranteed by the United States;
- A proceeding ancillary to a proceeding in another court;
- An action to enforce an arbitration award; and
- An action for mortgage foreclosure if the United States is a party. IN R USDCTND L.R. 16-1(c).

    ii.   *Required contents of the order.* The scheduling order must limit the time to join other parties, amend the pleadings, complete discovery, and file motions. FRCP 16(b)(3)(A).

    iii.   *Permitted contents of the order.* The scheduling order may:

- Modify the timing of disclosures under FRCP 26(a) and FRCP 26(e)(1);
- Modify the extent of discovery;
- Provide for disclosure, discovery, or preservation of electronically stored information;
- Include any agreements the parties reach for asserting claims of privilege or of protection as trial-preparation material after information is produced, including agreements reached under FRE 502;
- Direct that before moving for an order relating to discovery, the movant must request a conference with the court;
- Set dates for pretrial conferences and for trial; and

- Include other appropriate matters. FRCP 16(b)(3)(B).

- Following the consideration of that proposed ADR Process which the parties wish to employ, if any, as well as when that process should be undertaken, the Court shall, if the Court approves, incorporate the process in the Court's scheduling order entered in accordance with FRCP 16(b)(6) and FRCP 16(c)(9). If the Court disapproves of the ADR Process proposed by the parties, or upon consideration determines that no ADR Process is to be employed in the case, the Court shall make specific findings on the record establishing good cause therefore. IN R USDCTND Order 2003-21. [Editor's note: the reference to FRCP 16(b)(6) is likely meant to be a reference to FRCP 16(b)(1), and the reference to FRCP 16(c)(9) is likely meant to be a reference to FRCP 16(c)(2)(I)].

b. *Time to issue.* The judge must issue the scheduling order as soon as practicable, but unless the judge finds good cause for delay, the judge must issue it within the earlier of ninety (90) days after any defendant has been served with the complaint or sixty (60) days after any defendant has appeared. FRCP 16(b)(2).

c. *Modifying a schedule.* A schedule may be modified only for good cause and with the judge's consent. FRCP 16(b)(4).

d. *Actions with unrepresented parties.* In actions where a party is unrepresented, the court may issue a scheduling order after consulting with the parties' attorneys and the unrepresented parties at a scheduling conference or by telephone, mail, or other means. IN R USDCTND L.R. 16-1(b).

3. *Final pretrial conference.* The court may hold a final pretrial conference to formulate a trial plan, including a plan to facilitate the admission of evidence. FRCP 16(e).

a. *Timing and attendance.* The conference must be held as close to the start of trial as is reasonable, and must be attended by at least one attorney who will conduct the trial for each party and by any unrepresented party. FRCP 16(e).

b. *Modification of final pretrial order.* The court may modify the order issued after a final pretrial conference only to prevent manifest injustice. FRCP 16(e).

4. *Discovery planning conference*

a. *Conference content.* In conferring, the parties must consider the nature and basis of their claims and defenses and the possibilities for promptly settling or resolving the case; make or arrange for the disclosures required by FRCP 26(a)(1); discuss any issues about preserving discoverable information; and develop a proposed discovery plan. FRCP 26(f)(2).

b. *Parties' responsibilities.* The attorneys of record and all unrepresented parties that have appeared in the case are jointly responsible for arranging the conference, for attempting in good faith to agree on the proposed discovery plan, and for submitting to the court within fourteen (14) days after the conference a written report outlining the plan. The court may order the parties or attorneys to attend the conference in person. FRCP 26(f)(2).

   i. When the court orders an initial pretrial conference, the parties must file a Report of the Parties' Planning Meeting following their FRCP 26(f) planning meeting. The report must be consistent with the form on the court's website. The court may adopt all or some of the report as part of its scheduling order. IN R USDCTND L.R. 16-1(d).

c. *Discovery plan.* A discovery plan must state the parties' views and proposals on:

   i. What changes should be made in the timing, form, or requirement for disclosures under FRCP 26(a), including a statement of when initial disclosures were made or will be made;

   ii. The subjects on which discovery may be needed, when discovery should be completed, and whether discovery should be conducted in phases or be limited to or focused on particular issues;

   iii. Any issues about disclosure, discovery, or preservation of electronically stored information, including the form or forms in which it should be produced;

   iv. Any issues about claims of privilege or of protection as trial-preparation materials,

515

including—if the parties agree on a procedure to assert these claims after production—whether to ask the court to include their agreement in an order under FRE 502;

v.   What changes should be made in the limitations on discovery imposed under the Federal Rules of Civil Procedure or by local rule, and what other limitations should be imposed; and

vi. Any other orders that the court should issue under FRCP 26(c) or under FRCP 16(b) and FRCP 26(c). FRCP 26(f)(3).

d. *Sanctions.* If a party or its attorney fails to participate in good faith in developing and submitting a proposed discovery plan as required by FRCP 26(f), the court may, after giving an opportunity to be heard, require that party or attorney to pay to any other party the reasonable expenses, including attorney's fees, caused by the failure. FRCP 37(f).

5. *Appearances.* Attorneys not representing the United States or its agencies must file an appearance when they represent (either in person or by filing a paper) a party. IN R USDCTND L.R. 83-8(a). For more information, refer to IN R USDCTND L.R. 83-8.

6. *Notice of related action.* A party must file a notice of related action as soon as it appears that the party's case and another pending case: (1) arise out of the same transaction or occurrence; (2) involve the same property; or (3) involve the validity or infringement of the same patent, trademark, or copyright. IN R USDCTND L.R. 40-1(d). For more information, refer to IN R USDCTND L.R. 40-1.

7. *Alternative dispute resolution (ADR).* After they confer as required by FRCP 26(f), the parties must advise the court which, if any, alternative-dispute-resolution processes they expect to pursue and when they expect to undertake the process. IN R USDCTND L.R. 16-6(a). For more information on alternative dispute resolution (ADR), refer to IN R USDCTND L.R. 16-6 and IN R USDCTND Order 2003-21.

8. *Settlement or resolution.* The parties must immediately notify the court if they reasonably expect to settle the case or resolve a pending motion. IN R USDCTND L.R. 16-1(g).

9. *Modification or suspension of rules.* The court may, on its own motion or at the request of a party, suspend or modify any rule in a particular case in the interest of justice. IN R USDCTND L.R. 1-1(c).

D. Documents

1. *Pretrial conference*

    a. *Documents to consider*

        i. *Pretrial memorandum or statement.* Even though it is not specifically mentioned in FRCP 16, most courts require the attorney for each side to file a pretrial memorandum or statement prior to the conference, which, if adopted by the court, may be binding at trial. FPP § 1524. The purpose of the memorandum is to reveal the lawyer's theory of the case and the issues counsel believes are in contention in order to aid the court in determining what matters should be considered at the conference itself. FPP § 1524; Manbeck v. Ostrowski, 384 F.2d 970 (D.C. Cir. 1967).

        ii. *Notice of constitutional question.* A party that files a pleading, written motion, or other paper drawing into question the constitutionality of a federal or state statute must promptly:

            • *File notice.* File a notice of constitutional question stating the question and identifying the paper that raises it, if: (1) a federal statute is questioned and the parties do not include the United States, one of its agencies, or one of its officers or employees in an official capacity; or (2) a state statute is questioned and the parties do not include the state, one of its agencies, or one of its officers or employees in an official capacity; and

            • *Serve notice.* Serve the notice and paper on the Attorney General of the United States if a federal statute is questioned—or on the state attorney general if a state statute is questioned—either by certified or registered mail or by sending it to an electronic address designated by the attorney general for this purpose. FRCP 5.1(a).

            • *When to file the notice.* A party required to file a notice of constitutional question under FRCP 5.1 must do so by the later of: (1) the day the parties tender their proposed case-management plan (if one is required); or (2) 21 days after filing the pleading, written

motion, or other paper questioning the constitutionality of a federal or state statute. IN R USDCTND L.R. 5.1-1(a).

- *Service on government officials.* The party must also serve the notice and the pleading, written motion, or other paper questioning the constitutionality of a federal or state statute on: (1) the Attorney General of the United States and the United States Attorney for the Northern District of Indiana, if a federal statute is challenged; or (2) the Attorney General for the state if a state statute is challenged. IN R USDCTND L.R. 5.1-1(b). Service required under IN R USDCTND L.R. 5.1-1(b) may be made either by certified or registered mail or by emailing it to an address designated by those officials for this purpose. IN R USDCTND L.R. 5.1-1(c).

- *No forfeiture.* A party's failure to file and serve the notice, or the court's failure to certify, does not forfeit a constitutional claim or defense that is otherwise timely asserted. FRCP 5.1(d).

iii. *Index of exhibits.* Any pleading, motion, brief, affidavit, notice, or proposed order, whether filed electronically or by delivering it to the clerk, must: include a separate index identifying and briefly describing each exhibit if there are more than four (4) exhibits. IN R USDCTND L.R. 5-4(a)(8).

iv. *Copy of document with self-addressed envelope.* A party who wants a file-stamped copy of a paper must include with the filing an additional copy of the paper and a self-addressed envelope with adequate postage. IN R USDCTND L.R. 5-4(b)(6).

v. *Notice of manual filing.* However, if that is not physically possible, counsel shall electronically file a .pdf document titled Notice of Manual Filing as a notation on the docket sheet that filings are being held in the clerk's office in paper. A sample Notice of Manual Filing is attached as Form 2 (IN R USDCTND CM/ECF(Form 2)). IN R USDCTND CM/ECF(III)(A)(1).

vi. *Courtesy copies.* If documents are filed in paper format, counsel must provide an original for the clerk's office, a copy for the judge and a copy must be served on all parties in the case. IN R USDCTND CM/ECF(III)(A)(1).

vii. *Declaration that party was unable to file in a timely manner.* If the attorney is unable to file a document in a timely manner due to technical difficulties in the user's system, the attorney must file a document with the court as soon as possible notifying the court of the inability to file the document. A sample document entitled Declaration that Party was Unable to File in a Timely Manner Due to Technical Difficulties is attached hereto as Form 5. IN R USDCTND CM/ECF(VI)(B). [Editor's note: the reference to Form 5 is likely meant to be a reference to Form 3 (IN R USDCTND CM/ECF(Form 3)].

2. *Scheduling conference*

   a. *Documents to consider*

      i. *Request for scheduling conference.* A scheduling conference may be requested by the judge or by the parties, but it is not mandatory. FPP § 1522.1.

      ii. *Proposed scheduling order.* Parties filing a paper that requires the judge or clerk to enter a routine or uncontested order must include a suitable form of order. IN R USDCTND L.R. 5-4(c).

         - Unlike proposed orders, Proposed Discovery Plans/Scheduling Orders and proposed Final Pretrial Orders should not contain a signature line for the Judge. The attorney filing these documents shall initially confirm that the content of the document is acceptable to all persons required to sign the document and shall obtain the physical signatures of all attorneys on the document. The filing attorney then shall file the document electronically, indicating the signatories, e.g., "s/Jane Doe," "s/John Doe," etc. The filing attorney shall retain the hard copy of the document containing the original signatures. IN R USDCTND CM/ECF(II)(F).

iii. *Notice of constitutional question.* A party that files a pleading, written motion, or other paper drawing into question the constitutionality of a federal or state statute must promptly:

- *File notice.* File a notice of constitutional question stating the question and identifying the paper that raises it, if: (1) a federal statute is questioned and the parties do not include the United States, one of its agencies, or one of its officers or employees in an official capacity; or (2) a state statute is questioned and the parties do not include the state, one of its agencies, or one of its officers or employees in an official capacity; and

- *Serve notice.* Serve the notice and paper on the Attorney General of the United States if a federal statute is questioned—or on the state attorney general if a state statute is questioned—either by certified or registered mail or by sending it to an electronic address designated by the attorney general for this purpose. FRCP 5.1(a).

- *When to file the notice.* A party required to file a notice of constitutional question under FRCP 5.1 must do so by the later of: (1) the day the parties tender their proposed case-management plan (if one is required); or (2) 21 days after filing the pleading, written motion, or other paper questioning the constitutionality of a federal or state statute. IN R USDCTND L.R. 5.1-1(a).

- *Service on government officials.* The party must also serve the notice and the pleading, written motion, or other paper questioning the constitutionality of a federal or state statute on: (1) the Attorney General of the United States and the United States Attorney for the Northern District of Indiana, if a federal statute is challenged; or (2) the Attorney General for the state if a state statute is challenged. IN R USDCTND L.R. 5.1-1(b). Service required under IN R USDCTND L.R. 5.1-1(b) may be made either by certified or registered mail or by emailing it to an address designated by those officials for this purpose. IN R USDCTND L.R. 5.1-1(c).

- *No forfeiture.* A party's failure to file and serve the notice, or the court's failure to certify, does not forfeit a constitutional claim or defense that is otherwise timely asserted. FRCP 5.1(d).

iv. *Index of exhibits.* Any pleading, motion, brief, affidavit, notice, or proposed order, whether filed electronically or by delivering it to the clerk, must: include a separate index identifying and briefly describing each exhibit if there are more than four (4) exhibits. IN R USDCTND L.R. 5-4(a)(8).

v. *Copy of document with self-addressed envelope.* A party who wants a file-stamped copy of a paper must include with the filing an additional copy of the paper and a self-addressed envelope with adequate postage. IN R USDCTND L.R. 5-4(b)(6).

vi. *Notice of manual filing.* However, if that is not physically possible, counsel shall electronically file a .pdf document titled Notice of Manual Filing as a notation on the docket sheet that filings are being held in the clerk's office in paper. A sample Notice of Manual Filing is attached as Form 2 (IN R USDCTND CM/ECF(Form 2)). IN R USDCTND CM/ECF(III)(A)(1).

vii. *Courtesy copies.* If documents are filed in paper format, counsel must provide an original for the clerk's office, a copy for the judge and a copy must be served on all parties in the case. IN R USDCTND CM/ECF(III)(A)(1).

viii. *Declaration that party was unable to file in a timely manner.* If the attorney is unable to file a document in a timely manner due to technical difficulties in the user's system, the attorney must file a document with the court as soon as possible notifying the court of the inability to file the document. A sample document entitled Declaration that Party was Unable to File in a Timely Manner Due to Technical Difficulties is attached hereto as Form 5. IN R USDCTND CM/ECF(VI)(B). [Editor's note: the reference to Form 5 is likely meant to be a reference to Form 3 (IN R USDCTND CM/ECF(Form 3)].

3. *Final pretrial conference*

 a. *Documents to consider*

  i. *Proposed final pretrial order.* Parties filing a paper that requires the judge or clerk to enter a routine or uncontested order must include a suitable form of order. IN R USDCTND L.R. 5-4(c).

- Unlike proposed orders, Proposed Discovery Plans/Scheduling Orders and proposed Final Pretrial Orders should not contain a signature line for the Judge. The attorney filing these documents shall initially confirm that the content of the document is acceptable to all persons required to sign the document and shall obtain the physical signatures of all attorneys on the document. The filing attorney then shall file the document electronically, indicating the signatories, e.g., "s/Jane Doe," "s/John Doe," etc. The filing attorney shall retain the hard copy of the document containing the original signatures. IN R USDCTND CM/ECF(II)(F).

ii. *Notice of constitutional question.* A party that files a pleading, written motion, or other paper drawing into question the constitutionality of a federal or state statute must promptly:

- *File notice.* File a notice of constitutional question stating the question and identifying the paper that raises it, if: (1) a federal statute is questioned and the parties do not include the United States, one of its agencies, or one of its officers or employees in an official capacity; or (2) a state statute is questioned and the parties do not include the state, one of its agencies, or one of its officers or employees in an official capacity; and

- *Serve notice.* Serve the notice and paper on the Attorney General of the United States if a federal statute is questioned—or on the state attorney general if a state statute is questioned—either by certified or registered mail or by sending it to an electronic address designated by the attorney general for this purpose. FRCP 5.1(a).

- *When to file the notice.* A party required to file a notice of constitutional question under FRCP 5.1 must do so by the later of: (1) the day the parties tender their proposed case-management plan (if one is required); or (2) 21 days after filing the pleading, written motion, or other paper questioning the constitutionality of a federal or state statute. IN R USDCTND L.R. 5.1-1(a).

- *Service on government officials.* The party must also serve the notice and the pleading, written motion, or other paper questioning the constitutionality of a federal or state statute on: (1) the Attorney General of the United States and the United States Attorney for the Northern District of Indiana, if a federal statute is challenged; or (2) the Attorney General for the state if a state statute is challenged. IN R USDCTND L.R. 5.1-1(b). Service required under IN R USDCTND L.R. 5.1-1(b) may be made either by certified or registered mail or by emailing it to an address designated by those officials for this purpose. IN R USDCTND L.R. 5.1-1(c).

- *No forfeiture.* A party's failure to file and serve the notice, or the court's failure to certify, does not forfeit a constitutional claim or defense that is otherwise timely asserted. FRCP 5.1(d).

iii. *Index of exhibits.* Any pleading, motion, brief, affidavit, notice, or proposed order, whether filed electronically or by delivering it to the clerk, must: include a separate index identifying and briefly describing each exhibit if there are more than four (4) exhibits. IN R USDCTND L.R. 5-4(a)(8).

iv. *Copy of document with self-addressed envelope.* A party who wants a file-stamped copy of a paper must include with the filing an additional copy of the paper and a self-addressed envelope with adequate postage. IN R USDCTND L.R. 5-4(b)(6).

v. *Notice of manual filing.* However, if that is not physically possible, counsel shall electronically file a .pdf document titled Notice of Manual Filing as a notation on the docket sheet that filings are being held in the clerk's office in paper. A sample Notice of Manual Filing is attached as Form 2 (IN R USDCTND CM/ECF(Form 2)). IN R USDCTND CM/ECF(III)(A)(1).

vi. *Courtesy copies.* If documents are filed in paper format, counsel must provide an original for the clerk's office, a copy for the judge and a copy must be served on all parties in the case. IN R USDCTND CM/ECF(III)(A)(1).

vii. *Declaration that party was unable to file in a timely manner.* If the attorney is unable to file a document in a timely manner due to technical difficulties in the user's system, the attorney must file a document with the court as soon as possible notifying the court of the inability to file the document. A sample document entitled Declaration that Party was Unable to File in a Timely Manner Due to Technical Difficulties is attached hereto as Form 5. IN R USDCTND CM/ECF(VI)(B). [Editor's note: the reference to Form 5 is likely meant to be a reference to Form 3 (IN R USDCTND CM/ECF(Form 3)].

4. *Discovery planning conference*

   a. *Required documents*

      i. *Written report outlining proposed discovery plan.* Parties filing a paper that requires the judge or clerk to enter a routine or uncontested order must include a suitable form of order. IN R USDCTND L.R. 5-4(c). The report must be consistent with the form on the court's website. IN R USDCTND L.R. 16-1(d). Refer to the General Requirements section of this document for information on the parties' responsibilities for submitting a written report outlining the proposed discovery plan.

      - Unlike proposed orders, Proposed Discovery Plans/Scheduling Orders and proposed Final Pretrial Orders should not contain a signature line for the Judge. The attorney filing these documents shall initially confirm that the content of the document is acceptable to all persons required to sign the document and shall obtain the physical signatures of all attorneys on the document. The filing attorney then shall file the document electronically, indicating the signatories, e.g., "s/Jane Doe," "s/John Doe," etc. The filing attorney shall retain the hard copy of the document containing the original signatures. IN R USDCTND CM/ECF(II)(F).

   b. *Supplemental documents*

      i. *Notice of constitutional question.* A party that files a pleading, written motion, or other paper drawing into question the constitutionality of a federal or state statute must promptly:

         - *File notice.* File a notice of constitutional question stating the question and identifying the paper that raises it, if: (1) a federal statute is questioned and the parties do not include the United States, one of its agencies, or one of its officers or employees in an official capacity; or (2) a state statute is questioned and the parties do not include the state, one of its agencies, or one of its officers or employees in an official capacity; and

         - *Serve notice.* Serve the notice and paper on the Attorney General of the United States if a federal statute is questioned—or on the state attorney general if a state statute is questioned—either by certified or registered mail or by sending it to an electronic address designated by the attorney general for this purpose. FRCP 5.1(a).

         - *When to file the notice.* A party required to file a notice of constitutional question under FRCP 5.1 must do so by the later of: (1) the day the parties tender their proposed case-management plan (if one is required); or (2) 21 days after filing the pleading, written motion, or other paper questioning the constitutionality of a federal or state statute. IN R USDCTND L.R. 5.1-1(a).

         - *Service on government officials.* The party must also serve the notice and the pleading, written motion, or other paper questioning the constitutionality of a federal or state statute on: (1) the Attorney General of the United States and the United States Attorney for the Northern District of Indiana, if a federal statute is challenged; or (2) the Attorney General for the state if a state statute is challenged. IN R USDCTND L.R. 5.1-1(b). Service required under IN R USDCTND L.R. 5.1-1(b) may be made either by certified or registered mail or by emailing it to an address designated by those officials for this purpose. IN R USDCTND L.R. 5.1-1(c).

         - *No forfeiture.* A party's failure to file and serve the notice, or the court's failure to certify, does not forfeit a constitutional claim or defense that is otherwise timely asserted. FRCP 5.1(d).

ii. *Index of exhibits.* Any pleading, motion, brief, affidavit, notice, or proposed order, whether filed electronically or by delivering it to the clerk, must: include a separate index identifying and briefly describing each exhibit if there are more than four (4) exhibits. IN R USDCTND L.R. 5-4(a)(8).

iii. *Copy of document with self-addressed envelope.* A party who wants a file-stamped copy of a paper must include with the filing an additional copy of the paper and a self-addressed envelope with adequate postage. IN R USDCTND L.R. 5-4(b)(6).

iv. *Notice of manual filing.* However, if that is not physically possible, counsel shall electronically file a .pdf document titled Notice of Manual Filing as a notation on the docket sheet that filings are being held in the clerk's office in paper. A sample Notice of Manual Filing is attached as Form 2 (IN R USDCTND CM/ECF(Form 2)). IN R USDCTND CM/ECF(III)(A)(1).

v. *Courtesy copies.* If documents are filed in paper format, counsel must provide an original for the clerk's office, a copy for the judge and a copy must be served on all parties in the case. IN R USDCTND CM/ECF(III)(A)(1).

vi. *Declaration that party was unable to file in a timely manner.* If the attorney is unable to file a document in a timely manner due to technical difficulties in the user's system, the attorney must file a document with the court as soon as possible notifying the court of the inability to file the document. A sample document entitled Declaration that Party was Unable to File in a Timely Manner Due to Technical Difficulties is attached hereto as Form 5. IN R USDCTND CM/ECF(VI)(B). [Editor's note: the reference to Form 5 is likely meant to be a reference to Form 3 (IN R USDCTND CM/ECF(Form 3)].

E. Format

1. *Form of documents.* The rules governing captions and other matters of form in pleadings apply to motions and other papers. FRCP 7(b)(2).

   a. *Paper.* Any pleading, motion, brief, affidavit, notice, or proposed order, whether filed electronically or by delivering it to the clerk, must: use eight and one-half by eleven (8-1/2 x 11) inch pages. IN R USDCTND L.R. 5-4(a)(2).

      i. *Manual filings.* Papers delivered to the clerk for filing must: be flat, unfolded, and on good-quality, white paper. IN R USDCTND L.R. 5-4(b)(1)(A).

         - *Covers or backing.* Papers delivered to the clerk for filing must: not have a cover or a back. IN R USDCTND L.R. 5-4(b)(1)(B).
         - *Recycled paper.* The court encourages using recycled paper. IN R USDCTND L.R. 5-4(b)(7).

   b. *Margins.* Any pleading, motion, brief, affidavit, notice, or proposed order, whether filed electronically or by delivering it to the clerk, must: have at least one (1) inch margins. IN R USDCTND L.R. 5-4(a)(3).

   c. *Spacing.* Any pleading, motion, brief, affidavit, notice, or proposed order, whether filed electronically or by delivering it to the clerk, must: be double spaced (except for headings, footnotes, and quoted material). IN R USDCTND L.R. 5-4(a)(5).

   d. *Text.* Any pleading, motion, brief, affidavit, notice, or proposed order, whether filed electronically or by delivering it to the clerk, must: be plainly typewritten, printed, or prepared by a clearly legible copying process. IN R USDCTND L.R. 5-4(a)(1).

      i. Any pleading, motion, brief, affidavit, notice, or proposed order, whether filed electronically or by delivering it to the clerk, must: use at least twelve (12) point type in the body and at least ten (10) point type in footnotes. IN R USDCTND L.R. 5-4(a)(4).

   e. *Page numbering.* Any pleading, motion, brief, affidavit, notice, or proposed order, whether filed electronically or by delivering it to the clerk, must: have consecutively numbered pages. IN R USDCTND L.R. 5-4(a)(6).

   f. *Caption; Names of parties.* Every pleading must have a caption with the court's name, a title, a file number, and a FRCP 7(a) designation. The title of the complaint must name all the parties; the title of other pleadings, after naming the first party on each side, may refer generally to other parties. FRCP 10(a). Any pleading, motion, brief, affidavit, notice, or proposed order, whether filed electronically or by delivering it to the clerk, must: include a title on the first page. IN R USDCTND L.R. 5-4(a)(7).

g. *Filer's information.* Any pleading, motion, brief, affidavit, notice, or proposed order, whether filed electronically or by delivering it to the clerk, must: except in proposed orders and affidavits, include the filer's name, address, telephone number, fax number (where available), and e-mail address (where available). IN R USDCTND L.R. 5-4(a)(9).

h. *Paragraphs; Separate statements.* A party must state its claims or defenses in numbered paragraphs, each limited as far as practicable to a single set of circumstances. A later pleading may refer by number to a paragraph in an earlier pleading. If doing so would promote clarity, each claim founded on a separate transaction or occurrence—and each defense other than a denial—must be stated in a separate count or defense. FRCP 10(b).

i. *Adoption by reference; Exhibits.* A statement in a pleading may be adopted by reference elsewhere in the same pleading or in any other pleading or motion. A copy of a written instrument that is an exhibit to a pleading is a part of the pleading for all purposes. FRCP 10(c).

j. *Citation of local rules.* The Local Civil Rules of the United States District Court for the Northern District of Indiana may be cited as "N.D. Ind. L.R." IN R USDCTND L.R. 1-1(a)(1).

k. *Acceptance by the clerk.* The clerk must not refuse to file a paper solely because it is not in the form prescribed by the Federal Rules of Civil Procedure or by a local rule or practice. FRCP 5(d)(4).

    i. *Sanctions for formatting errors; Non-compliance.* If a person files a paper that does not comply with the rules governing the format of papers filed with the court, the court may: (1) strike the paper from the record; or (2) fine the person up to one thousand dollars ($1,000). IN R USDCTND L.R. 1-3(a).

        • *Notice.* Before sanctioning a person under IN R USDCTND L.R. 1-3(a)(2), the court must: (1) notify the person that the paper is noncompliant; and (2) give the person the opportunity either to be heard or to revise the paper. IN R USDCTND L.R. 1-3(b).

2. *Form of electronic documents.* Electronically filed documents must meet the same requirements of format and page limits as documents "conventionally filed" (as defined in IN R USDCTND CM/ECF(III)(A)) pursuant to the Federal Rules of Civil Procedure and the Local Civil Rules of the United States District Court for the Northern District of Indiana. IN R USDCTND CM/ECF(II)(A)(2).

a. *PDF format required.* Documents filed in the CM/ECF must be in .pdf format. A document created with almost any word-processing program can be converted to .pdf format. The .pdf program in effect takes a picture of the original document and allows anyone to open the converted document across a broad range of hardware and software, with layout, format, links, and images intact. IN R USDCTND CM/ECF(FN2).

b. *Title of documents.* The person electronically filing a pleading or other document will be responsible for designating a title for the pleading or other document by using one of the categories contained in the events listed in the CM/ECF Menu. IN R USDCTND CM/ECF(II)(G).

c. *Combining documents.* All documents which form part of a single pleading and which are being filed at the same time and by the same party may be electronically filed together under one document number, e.g., the motion and a supporting affidavit, with the exception of memoranda in support. Memoranda in support shall be electronically filed separately and shown as a related document to the motion. IN R USDCTND CM/ECF(II)(A)(4).

d. *Exhibits and attachments.* Filing users must submit in electronic form all documents referenced as exhibits or attachments, unless the court permits conventional filing. A filing user must submit as exhibits or attachments only those excerpts of the referenced documents that are directly germane to the matter under consideration by the court. Excerpted material must be clearly and prominently identified as such. Filing users who file excerpts of documents as exhibits or attachments do so without prejudice to their right to timely file additional excerpts or the complete document.

Responding parties may timely file additional excerpts or the complete document that they believe are directly germane. The court may require parties to file additional excerpts or the complete document. IN R USDCTND CM/ECF(II)(A)(6).

e. *Hyperlinks.* Electronically filed documents may contain hyperlink references to an external document as a convenient mechanism for accessing material cited in the document. A hyperlink reference is neither validated for content nor considered a part of the court's records. The court neither endorses the product or organization at the destination of a hyperlink reference, nor does the court exercise any responsibility over the content at the destination. In order to preserve the integrity of the court record, attorneys wishing to insert hyperlinks in court filings shall continue to use the traditional citation method for the cited authority, in addition to the hyperlink. A hyperlink contained in a filing is no more than a convenient mechanism for accessing material cited in the document and a hyperlink reference is extraneous to any filed document and is not part of the court's record. IN R USDCTND CM/ECF(II)(A)(3).

3. *Signing of pleadings, motions and other papers*

a. *Signature.* Every pleading, written motion, and other paper must be signed by at least one attorney of record in the attorney's name—or by a party personally if the party is unrepresented. The paper must state the signer's address, e-mail address, and telephone number. FRCP 11(a).

 i. *Signatures on manual filings.* Papers delivered to the clerk for filing must: include the filer's original signature. IN R USDCTND L.R. 5-4(b)(1)(C).

  • *Rubber-stamped and faxed signatures.* An original paper with a rubber-stamped or faxed signature is unsigned for purposes of FRCP 11 and FRCP 26(g). IN R USDCTND L.R. 5-4(b)(2).

  • *Affidavits.* Only the affiant need sign an affidavit. IN R USDCTND L.R. 5-4(b)(3).

 ii. *Electronic signatures.* Pursuant to FRCP 11, every pleading, motion, and other paper (except lists, schedules, statements or amendments thereto) shall be signed by at least one attorney of record or, if the party is not represented by an attorney, all papers shall be signed by the party. An attorney's/participant's password issued by the court combined with the user's identification, serves as and constitutes the attorney/participant's signature for FRCP 11 and other purposes. IN R USDCTND CM/ECF(I)(C). Documents which must be filed and which must contain original signatures other than those of a participating attorney or which require either verification or an unsworn declaration under any rule or statute, shall be filed electronically, with originally executed copies maintained by the filer. The pleading or other document electronically filed shall contain "s/" signature(s), as noted in IN R USDCTND CM/ECF(II)(E)(3)(b). IN R USDCTND CM/ECF(II)(E)(1).

  • *Multiple signatures.* In the case of a stipulation or other document to be signed by two or more attorneys, the following procedure should be used: The filing attorney shall initially confirm that the content of the document is acceptable to all persons required to sign the document and shall obtain the physical signatures of all attorneys on the document. IN R USDCTND CM/ECF(II)(E)(3)(a). The filing attorney then shall file the document electronically, indicating the signatories, e.g., "s/Jane Doe," "s/John Doe," etc. IN R USDCTND CM/ECF(II)(E)(3)(b). The filing attorney shall retain the hard copy of the document containing the original signatures. IN R USDCTND CM/ECF(II)(E)(3)(c).

 iii. *No verification or accompanying affidavit required for pleadings.* Unless a rule or statute specifically states otherwise, a pleading need not be verified or accompanied by an affidavit. FRCP 11(a).

 iv. *Unsigned papers.* The court must strike an unsigned paper unless the omission is promptly corrected after being called to the attorney's or party's attention. FRCP 11(a).

b. *Representations to the court.* By presenting to the court a pleading, written motion, or other paper—whether by signing, filing, submitting, or later advocating it—an attorney or unrepresented party certifies that to the best of the person's knowledge, information, and belief, formed after an inquiry reasonable under the circumstances:

    i.   It is not being presented for any improper purpose, such as to harass, cause unnecessary delay, or needlessly increase the cost of litigation;

    ii.   The claims, defenses, and other legal contentions are warranted by existing law or by a nonfrivolous argument for extending, modifying, or reversing existing law or for establishing new law;

    iii.   The factual contentions have evidentiary support or, if specifically so identified, will likely have evidentiary support after a reasonable opportunity for further investigation or discovery; and

    iv.   The denials of factual contentions are warranted on the evidence or, if specifically so identified, are reasonably based on belief or a lack of information. FRCP 11(b).

  c. *Sanctions.* If, after notice and a reasonable opportunity to respond, the court determines that FRCP 11(b) has been violated, the court may impose an appropriate sanction on any attorney, law firm, or party that violated FRCP 11(b) or is responsible for the violation. FRCP 11(c)(1). Refer to the United States District Court for the Northern District of Indiana KeyRules Motion for Sanctions document for more information.

4. *Privacy protection for filings made with the court*

  a. *Redacted filings.* Counsel should not include sensitive information in any document filed with the court unless such inclusion is necessary and relevant to the case. IN R USDCTND CM/ECF(VII). Unless the court orders otherwise, in an electronic or paper filing with the court that contains an individual's Social Security number, taxpayer-identification number, or birth date, the name of an individual known to be a minor, or a financial-account number, a party or nonparty making the filing may include only:

    i.   The last four (4) digits of the Social Security number and taxpayer-identification number;

    ii.   The year of the individual's birth;

    iii.   The minor's initials; and

    iv.   The last four (4) digits of the financial-account number. FRCP 5.2(a); IN R USDCTND Order 2005-3.

  b. *Exemptions from the redaction requirement.* The redaction requirement does not apply to the following:

    i.   A financial-account number that identifies the property allegedly subject to forfeiture in a forfeiture proceeding;

    ii.   The record of an administrative or agency proceeding;

    iii.   The official record of a state-court proceeding;

    iv.   The record of a court or tribunal, if that record was not subject to the redaction requirement when originally filed;

    v.   A filing covered by FRCP 5.2(c) or FRCP 5.2(d); and

    vi.   A pro se filing in an action brought under 28 U.S.C.A. § 2241, 28 U.S.C.A. § 2254, or 28 U.S.C.A. § 2255. FRCP 5.2(b).

    vii.   In cases filed under the Social Security Act, 42 U.S.C.A. § 405(g), there is no need for redaction of any information from the documents filed in the case. IN R USDCTND Order 2005-3.

  c. *Limitations on remote access to electronic files; Social Security appeals and immigration cases.* Unless the court orders otherwise, in an action for benefits under the Social Security Act, and in an action or proceeding relating to an order of removal, to relief from removal, or to immigration benefits or detention, access to an electronic file is authorized as follows:

    i.   The parties and their attorneys may have remote electronic access to any part of the case file, including the administrative record;

    ii.   Any other person may have electronic access to the full record at the courthouse, but may have remote electronic access only to:

- The docket maintained by the court; and

- An opinion, order, judgment, or other disposition of the court, but not any other part of the case file or the administrative record. FRCP 5.2(c).

d.   *Filings made under seal.* The court may order that a filing be made under seal without redaction. The court may later unseal the filing or order the person who made the filing to file a redacted version for the public record. FRCP 5.2(d). For information on filing documents under seal, refer to IN R USDCTND L.R. 5-3, IN R USDCTND CM/ECF(IV)(A), and IN R USDCTND ECF Order 2004-19.

e.   *Protective orders.* For good cause, the court may by order in a case:

    i.   Require redaction of additional information; or

    ii.   Limit or prohibit a nonparty's remote electronic access to a document filed with the court. FRCP 5.2(e).

f.   *Option for additional unredacted filing under seal.* A person making a redacted filing may also file an unredacted copy under seal. The court must retain the unredacted copy as part of the record. FRCP 5.2(f); IN R USDCTND Order 2005-3.

    i.   The unredacted version of the document or the reference list shall be retained by the court under seal as part of the record. This paper shall be retained by the court as part of the record. The court may, however, still require the party to file a redacted copy for the public file. IN R USDCTND Order 2005-3.

g.   *Option for filing a reference list.* A filing that contains redacted information may be filed together with a reference list that identifies each item of redacted information and specifies an appropriate identifier that uniquely corresponds to each item listed. The list must be filed under seal and may be amended as of right. Any reference in the case to a listed identifier will be construed to refer to the corresponding item of information. FRCP 5.2(g); IN R USDCTND Order 2005-3.

    i.   The unredacted version of the document or the reference list shall be retained by the court under seal as part of the record. This paper shall be retained by the court as part of the record. The court may, however, still require the party to file a redacted copy for the public file. IN R USDCTND Order 2005-3.

h.   *Responsibility for redaction.* The responsibility for redacting these personal identifiers rests solely with counsel and the parties. The Clerk will not review each paper for compliance with IN R USDCTND Order 2005-3. IN R USDCTND Order 2005-3.

i.   *Waiver of protection of identifiers.* A person waives the protection of FRCP 5.2(a) as to the person's own information by filing it without redaction and not under seal. FRCP 5.2(h).

F. Filing and Service Requirements

1.   *Filing requirements.* Any paper after the complaint that is required to be served—together with a certificate of service—must be filed within a reasonable time after service. FRCP 5(d)(1).

a.   *How filing is made; In general.* A paper is filed by delivering it:

    i.   To the clerk; or

    ii.   To a judge who agrees to accept it for filing, and who must then note the filing date on the paper and promptly send it to the clerk. FRCP 5(d)(2).

- Papers not filed electronically must be filed with the clerk, not a judge. IN R USDCTND L.R. 5-4(b)(4).

    iii.   Parties manually filing a paper that requires the clerk to give others notice, must give the clerk: (1) sufficient copies of the notice; and (2) the name and address of each person entitled to receive the notice. IN R USDCTND L.R. 5-4(b)(8).

b.   *Where to file.* Papers not filed electronically must be filed in the division where the case is pending, unless: (1) a person will be prejudiced if the paper is not filed the same day it is tendered; and (2) it includes an adequately sized envelope addressed to the clerk's office in the division where the case is pending and with adequate postage. IN R USDCTND L.R. 5-4(b)(5).

   c. *Electronic filing*

      i. *Authorization of electronic filing program.* A court may, by local rule, allow papers to be filed, signed, or verified by electronic means that are consistent with any technical standards established by the Judicial Conference of the United States. A local rule may require electronic filing only if reasonable exceptions are allowed. A paper filed electronically in compliance with a local rule is a written paper for purposes of the Federal Rules of Civil Procedure. FRCP 5(d)(3).

- Papers must be filed, signed, and verified electronically unless excepted by the court's CM/ECF Civil and Criminal User Manual (IN R USDCTND CM/ECF). IN R USDCTND L.R. 5-1.

      ii. *Mandatory electronic filing.* Unless otherwise permitted by these procedures or otherwise authorized by the assigned judge, all documents submitted for filing in this district in civil and criminal cases, no matter when a case was originally filed, shall be filed electronically using the System. IN R USDCTND CM/ECF(II)(A)(1). The requirement that "all documents" be filed electronically includes briefs, and attachments and exhibits used in support of motions. IN R USDCTND CM/ECF(FN1).

- Sending a document or pleading to the court via e-mail or facsimile does not constitute "electronic filing." IN R USDCTND CM/ECF(I)(A).

      iii. *Conventional filing.* As used in these procedures, a "conventionally" filed or submitted document or pleading is one presented to the Clerk or a party in paper or other non-electronic, tangible format. The following documents shall be filed conventionally and not electronically unless specifically authorized by the Court:

- Exhibits and other documents which cannot be converted to a legible electronic form. Whenever possible, counsel is responsible for converting filings to an electronic form. However, if that is not physically possible, counsel shall electronically file a .pdf document titled Notice of Manual Filing as a notation on the docket sheet that filings are being held in the clerk's office in paper. A sample Notice of Manual Filing is attached as Form 2 (IN R USDCTND CM/ECF(Form 2)). If documents are filed in paper format, counsel must provide an original for the clerk's office, a copy for the judge and a copy must be served on all parties in the case. Large documents which do not exist in an electronic format shall be scanned into .pdf format by counsel, in small batches if necessary, and filed electronically as separate attachments in the System. IN R USDCTND CM/ECF(III)(A)(1).

- Certain documents which are listed in IN R USDCTND CM/ECF(II)(E)(2). IN R USDCTND CM/ECF(III)(A)(2).

- Documents filed by pro se litigants. IN R USDCTND CM/ECF(III)(A)(3).

      iv. For more information on electronic filing, refer to IN R USDCTND CM/ECF.

2. *Service requirements*

   a. *Service; When required*

      i. *In general.* Unless the Federal Rules of Civil Procedure provide otherwise, each of the following papers must be served on every party:

- An order stating that service is required;

- A pleading filed after the original complaint, unless the court orders otherwise under FRCP 5(c) because there are numerous defendants;

- A discovery paper required to be served on a party, unless the court orders otherwise;

- A written motion, except one that may be heard ex parte; and

- A written notice, appearance, demand, or offer of judgment, or any similar paper. FRCP 5(a)(1).

ii. *If a party fails to appear.* No service is required on a party who is in default for failing to appear. But a pleading that asserts a new claim for relief against such a party must be served on that party under FRCP 4. FRCP 5(a)(2).

iii. *Seizing property.* If an action is begun by seizing property and no person is or need be named as a defendant, any service required before the filing of an appearance, answer, or claim must be made on the person who had custody or possession of the property when it was seized. FRCP 5(a)(3).

b. *Service; How made*

i. *Serving an attorney.* If a party is represented by an attorney, service under FRCP 5 must be made on the attorney unless the court orders service on the party. FRCP 5(b)(1).

ii. *Service in general.* A paper is served under FRCP 5 by:

- Handing it to the person;

- Leaving it: (1) at the person's office with a clerk or other person in charge or, if no one is in charge, in a conspicuous place in the office; or (2) if the person has no office or the office is closed, at the person's dwelling or usual place of abode with someone of suitable age and discretion who resides there;

- Mailing it to the person's last known address—in which event service is complete upon mailing;

- Leaving it with the court clerk if the person has no known address;

- Sending it by electronic means if the person consented in writing—in which event service is complete upon transmission, but is not effective if the serving party learns that it did not reach the person to be served; or

- Delivering it by any other means that the person consented to in writing—in which event service is complete when the person making service delivers it to the agency designated to make delivery. FRCP 5(b)(2).

iii. *Electronic service.* Electronically filed papers may be served electronically if service is consistent with the CM/ECF User Manual (IN R USDCTND CM/ECF). IN R USDCTND L.R. 5-2(a).

- *Waiver of other service.* An attorney's registration will constitute a waiver of conventional service of documents and the attorney agrees to accept service of notice on behalf of the client of the electronic filing by hand, facsimile or authorized email. IN R USDCTND CM/ECF(I)(B)(3).

- *Serving registered persons.* The System will generate a "Notice of Electronic Filing" when any document is filed. This notice represents service of the document on parties who are registered participants with the System. Except as provided in IN R USDCTND CM/ECF(III)(B), the filing party shall not be required to serve any pleading or other documents on any party receiving electronic notice. IN R USDCTND CM/ECF(II)(D)(1). The term "pleading" refers only to those documents listed in FRCP 7(a). IN R USDCTND CM/ECF(FN3).

- *When electronic service is deemed completed.* A person registered to use the court's electronic-filing system is served with an electronically filed paper when a "Notice of Electronic Filing" is transmitted to that person through the court's electronic filing-system. IN R USDCTND L.R. 5-2(b).

- *Serving non-registered persons.* A person who has not registered to use the court's electronic-filing system but who is entitled to service of a paper must be served according to the Local Civil Rules of the United States District Court for the Northern District of Indiana and the Federal Rules of Civil Procedure. IN R USDCTND L.R. 5-2(c); IN R

USDCTND CM/ECF(II)(D)(2). If such service of a paper copy is to be made, it shall be done in the manner provided in the Federal Rules of Civil Procedure and the Local Civil Rules of the United States District Court for the Northern District of Indiana. IN R USDCTND CM/ECF(II)(D)(2).

    iv. *Service of conventional filings.* Pleadings or other documents which are filed conventionally rather than electronically shall be served in the manner provided for in the Federal Rules of Civil Procedure and the Local Civil Rules of the United States District Court for the Northern District of Indiana, except as otherwise provided by order of the Court. IN R USDCTND CM/ECF(III)(B).

    v. *Using court facilities.* If a local rule so authorizes, a party may use the court's transmission facilities to make service under FRCP 5(b)(2)(E). FRCP 5(b)(3).

  c. *Serving numerous defendants*

    i. *In general.* If an action involves an unusually large number of defendants, the court may, on motion or on its own, order that:

- Defendants' pleadings and replies to them need not be served on other defendants;
- Any crossclaim, counterclaim, avoidance, or affirmative defense in those pleadings and replies to them will be treated as denied or avoided by all other parties; and
- Filing any such pleading and serving it on the plaintiff constitutes notice of the pleading to all parties. FRCP 5(c)(1).

    ii. *Notifying parties.* A copy of every such order must be served on the parties as the court directs. FRCP 5(c)(2).

G. Hearings

1. Refer to the General Requirements section of this document for information on pretrial conferences, scheduling conferences, and discovery planning conferences.

H. Forms

1. Federal Pretrial Conferences, Scheduling, Management Forms

  a. Plaintiff's informal summary of status of case to judge prior to pretrial conference in complex case. 2C FEDFORMS § 2807.

  b. Joint pretrial report. 2C FEDFORMS § 2807.10.

  c. Joint statement of undisputed facts. 2C FEDFORMS § 2807.20.

  d. Joint statement of disputed facts. 2C FEDFORMS § 2807.30.

  e. Joint report of counsel prior to pretrial conference. 2C FEDFORMS § 2807.40.

  f. Plaintiff's pretrial conference statement; Insurance case. 2C FEDFORMS § 2807.50.

  g. Defendant's pretrial conference statement; Insurance case. 2C FEDFORMS § 2807.60.

  h. Plaintiff's list of exhibits to be offered at trial. 2C FEDFORMS § 2811.

  i. Defendant's list of prospective witnesses. 2C FEDFORMS § 2811.10.

  j. Designation of witnesses whom plaintiff intends to call at trial pursuant to pretrial conference oral stipulation. 2C FEDFORMS § 2811.20.

  k. Defendant's list of prospective exhibits. 2C FEDFORMS § 2811.40.

  l. Report of parties' planning meeting. 3A FEDFORMS § 3314.

  m. Report of parties' discovery conference; Another form. 3A FEDFORMS § 3315.

  n. Report of parties' discovery conference; Another form. 3A FEDFORMS § 3316.

  o. Joint scheduling report. 3A FEDFORMS § 3316.5.

  p. Stipulation and order regarding discovery conference discussions. 3A FEDFORMS § 3316.6.

  q. Pretrial statement; By plaintiff; Automobile collision involving corporate defendant. FEDPROF § 1:658.

r. Pretrial statement; By defendant; Automobile collision. FEDPROF § 1:659.

s. Pretrial statement; By parties jointly; Automobile collision. FEDPROF § 1:660.

t. Pretrial statement; Provision; Waiver of abandoned claims or defenses. FEDPROF § 1:661.

u. Status report. GOLDLTGFMS § 34:2.

v. Preliminary pretrial checklist. GOLDLTGFMS § 34:3.

w. Pretrial memorandum. GOLDLTGFMS § 34:4.

x. Pretrial memorandum; Short form. GOLDLTGFMS § 34:5.

y. Pretrial memorandum; Civil action. GOLDLTGFMS § 34:6.

z. Pretrial memorandum; Worker's compensation case. GOLDLTGFMS § 34:7.

2. Forms for the Northern District of Indiana

a. Sample pre-trial order. IN R USDCTND App. A.

b. Notice of manual filing. IN R USDCTND CM/ECF(Form 2).

c. Declaration that party was unable to file in a timely manner. IN R USDCTND CM/ECF(Form 3).

I. Applicable Rules

1. *Federal rules*

a. Serving and filing pleadings and other papers. FRCP 5.

b. Constitutional challenge to a statute; Notice, certification, and intervention. FRCP 5.1.

c. Privacy protection for filings made with the court. FRCP 5.2.

d. Computing and extending time; Time for motion papers. FRCP 6.

e. Pleadings allowed; Form of motions and other papers. FRCP 7.

f. Form of pleadings. FRCP 10.

g. Signing pleadings, motions, and other papers; Representations to the court; Sanctions. FRCP 11.

h. Pretrial conferences; Scheduling; Management. FRCP 16.

i. Duty to disclose; General provisions governing discovery. FRCP 26.

j. Failure to make disclosures or to cooperate in discovery; Sanctions. FRCP 37.

2. *Local rules*

a. Citation and scope of the rules. IN R USDCTND L.R. 1-1.

b. Sanctions for formatting errors. IN R USDCTND L.R. 1-3.

c. Electronic filing required. IN R USDCTND L.R. 5-1.

d. Constitutional questions. IN R USDCTND L.R. 5.1-1.

e. Electronic service. IN R USDCTND L.R. 5-2.

f. Format of papers. IN R USDCTND L.R. 5-4.

g. Pretrial procedure. IN R USDCTND L.R. 16-1.

h. Alternative dispute resolution. IN R USDCTND L.R. 16-6.

i. Case assignment. IN R USDCTND L.R. 40-1.

j. Appearance and withdrawal of appearance. IN R USDCTND L.R. 83-8.

k. CM/ECF civil and criminal user manual. IN R USDCTND CM/ECF.

l. In re: privacy and public access to civil electronic case files. IN R USDCTND Order 2005-3.

m. In re: a general order of the court [alternative dispute resolution]. IN R USDCTND Order 2003-21.

SOUTHERN DISTRICT OF INDIANA

Pleadings
Complaint

Document Last Updated December 2016

A. Checklist

(I) ❑ Matters to be considered by plaintiff

    (a) ❑ Required documents

        (1) ❑ Civil cover sheet

        (2) ❑ Complaint

        (3) ❑ Summons

        (4) ❑ Filing fee

        (5) ❑ Affidavit proving service

    (b) ❑ Supplemental documents

        (1) ❑ Notice and request for waiver of service

        (2) ❑ Notice of constitutional question

        (3) ❑ Notice of issue concerning foreign law

        (4) ❑ Nongovernmental corporate disclosure statement

        (5) ❑ Request for three-judge court

        (6) ❑ Index of exhibits

        (7) ❑ Copy of document with self-address envelope

        (8) ❑ Notice of manual filing

        (9) ❑ Courtesy copies

        (10) ❑ Copies for three-judge court

        (11) ❑ Declaration that party was unable to file in a timely manner due to technical difficulties

    (c) ❑ Timing

        (1) ❑ A civil action is commenced by filing a complaint with the court

        (2) ❑ If a defendant is not served within ninety (90) days after the complaint is filed, the court—on motion or on its own after notice to the plaintiff—must dismiss the action without prejudice against that defendant or order that service be made within a specified time

        (3) ❑ When a party who is not exempt from the electronic filing requirement files a document directly with the clerk, the party must present the document to the clerk within one (1) business day after filing the notice of manual filing

        (4) ❑ Unless the court orders otherwise, the [untimely] document and declaration [that party was unable to file in a timely manner due to technical difficulties] must be filed no later than 12:00 noon of the first day on which the court is open for business following the original filing deadline

(II) ❑ Matters to be considered by defendant

    (a) ❑ Required documents

        (1) ❑ Answer

        (2) ❑ Certificate of service

(b) ❑ Supplemental documents

    (1) ❑ Waiver of the service of summons

    (2) ❑ Notice of constitutional question

    (3) ❑ Notice of issue concerning foreign law

    (4) ❑ Nongovernmental corporate disclosure statement

    (5) ❑ Request for three-judge court

    (6) ❑ Index of exhibits

    (7) ❑ Copy of document with self-address envelope

    (8) ❑ Notice of manual filing

    (9) ❑ Courtesy copies

  (10) ❑ Copies for three-judge court

  (11) ❑ Declaration that party was unable to file in a timely manner due to technical difficulties

(c) ❑ Timing

    (1) ❑ A defendant must serve an answer:

        (i) ❑ Within twenty-one (21) days after being served with the summons and complaint; or

        (ii) ❑ If it has timely waived service under FRCP 4(d), within sixty (60) days after the request for a waiver was sent, or within ninety (90) days after it was sent to the defendant outside any judicial district of the United States

    (2) ❑ The United States, a United States agency, or a United States officer or employee sued only in an official capacity must serve an answer to a complaint, counterclaim, or crossclaim within sixty (60) days after service on the United States attorney

    (3) ❑ A United States officer or employee sued in an individual capacity for an act or omission occurring in connection with duties performed on the United States' behalf must serve an answer to a complaint, counterclaim, or crossclaim within sixty (60) days after service on the officer or employee or service on the United States attorney, whichever is later

    (4) ❑ Unless the court sets a different time, serving a motion under FRCP 12 alters these periods as follows:

        (i) ❑ If the court denies the motion or postpones its disposition until trial, the responsive pleading must be served within fourteen (14) days after notice of the court's action; or

        (ii) ❑ If the court grants a motion for a more definite statement, the responsive pleading must be served within fourteen (14) days after the more definite statement is served

    (5) ❑ Defendant is given a reasonable time of at least thirty (30) days after a waiver of service request is sent—or at least sixty (60) days if sent to defendant outside any judicial district of the United States—to return the waiver

    (6) ❑ When a party who is not exempt from the electronic filing requirement files a document directly with the clerk, the party must present the document to the clerk within one (1) business day after filing the notice of manual filing

    (7) ❑ Unless the court orders otherwise, the [untimely] document and declaration [that party was unable to file in a timely manner due to technical difficulties] must be filed no later than 12:00 noon of the first day on which the court is open for business following the original filing deadline

B. Timing

1. *Commencing an action.* A civil action is commenced by filing a complaint with the court. FRCP 3.

    a. *Statute of limitations.* An action will be barred if it is not commenced within the period set forth in the applicable statute of limitations. Under the Federal Rules of Civil Procedure (FRCP), an action is commenced by filing a complaint with the court. Thus, in a suit on a right created by federal law, filing a complaint suffices to satisfy the statute of limitations. FEDPROF § 61:2.

   i. *Federal question cases.* Absent a specific statutory provision for tolling the statute of limitations, in federal question cases, the filing of the complaint will toll the statute, even if not all filing fees have been paid, although some courts have added the requirement of reasonable diligence in effecting service. FEDPROF § 61:2.

   ii. *Diversity cases.* In diversity actions the matter is less clear. In the landmark Ragan case, the Supreme Court held in construing FRCP 3 that if, under local law, an action is not commenced until the defendant has been served, the statute is not tolled until service has been accomplished. FEDPROF § 61:2; Ragan v. Merchants Transfer & Warehouse Co., 337 U.S. 530, 69 S.Ct. 1233, 93 L.Ed. 1520 (1949). However, in a subsequent case, the Supreme Court distinguished Ragan in holding that the provision of FRCP 4 governing methods of service prevails over a conflicting state rule requiring personal service. FEDPROF § 61:2; Hanna v. Plumer, 380 U.S. 460, 85 S.Ct. 1136, 14 L.Ed.2d 8 (1965). The court reaffirmed Ragan and held that (1) a state law mandating actual service of a summons to toll the statute of limitations must be followed in a diversity case, and (2) FRCP 3 only governs other timing requirements in the federal rules. FEDPROF § 61:2; Walker v. Armco Steel Corp., 446 U.S. 740, 100 S.Ct. 1978, 64 L.Ed.2d 659 (1980).

2. *Service of summons and complaint.* If a defendant is not served within ninety (90) days after the complaint is filed, the court—on motion or on its own after notice to the plaintiff—must dismiss the action without prejudice against that defendant or order that service be made within a specified time. But if the plaintiff shows good cause for the failure, the court must extend the time for service for an appropriate period. FRCP 4(m) does not apply to service in a foreign country under FRCP 4(f), FRCP 4(h)(2), or FRCP 4(j)(1). FRCP 4(m).

3. *Document filing by non-exempt party.* When a party who is not exempt from the electronic filing requirement files a document directly with the clerk, the party must: present the document to the clerk within one (1) business day after filing the notice of manual filing. IN R USDCTSD L.R. 5-2(d)(2).

4. *Declaration that party was unable to file in a timely manner due to technical difficulties.* Unless the Court orders otherwise, the [untimely] document and declaration [that party was unable to file in a timely manner due to technical difficulties] must be filed no later than 12:00 noon of the first day on which the Court is open for business following the original filing deadline. IN R USDCTSD ECF Procedures(16).

5. *Computation of time*

   a. *Computing time.* FRCP 6 applies in computing any time period specified in the Federal Rules of Civil Procedure, in any local rule or court order, or in any statute that does not specify a method of computing time. FRCP 6(a).

      i. *Period stated in days or a longer unit.* When the period is stated in days or a longer unit of time:

      - Exclude the day of the event that triggers the period;

      - Count every day, including intermediate Saturdays, Sundays, and legal holidays; and

      - Include the last day of the period, but if the last day is a Saturday, Sunday, or legal holiday, the period continues to run until the end of the next day that is not a Saturday, Sunday, or legal holiday. FRCP 6(a)(1).

      ii. *Period stated in hours.* When the period is stated in hours:

      - Begin counting immediately on the occurrence of the event that triggers the period;

      - Count every hour, including hours during intermediate Saturdays, Sundays, and legal holidays; and

      - If the period would end on a Saturday, Sunday, or legal holiday, the period continues to run until the same time on the next day that is not a Saturday, Sunday, or legal holiday. FRCP 6(a)(2).

iii. *Inaccessibility of the clerk's office.* Unless the court orders otherwise, if the clerk's office is inaccessible:

- On the last day for filing under FRCP 6(a)(1), then the time for filing is extended to the first accessible day that is not a Saturday, Sunday, or legal holiday; or

- During the last hour for filing under FRCP 6(a)(2), then the time for filing is extended to the same time on the first accessible day that is not a Saturday, Sunday, or legal holiday. FRCP 6(a)(3).

iv. *"Last day" defined.* Unless a different time is set by a statute, local rule, or court order, the last day ends:

- For electronic filing, at midnight in the court's time zone; and

- For filing by other means, when the clerk's office is scheduled to close. FRCP 6(a)(4).

v. *"Next day" defined.* The "next day" is determined by continuing to count forward when the period is measured after an event and backward when measured before an event. FRCP 6(a)(5).

vi. *"Legal holiday" defined.* "Legal holiday" means:

- The day set aside by statute for observing New Year's Day, Martin Luther King Jr.'s Birthday, Washington's Birthday, Memorial Day, Independence Day, Labor Day, Columbus Day, Veterans' Day, Thanksgiving Day, or Christmas Day;

- Any day declared a holiday by the President or Congress; and

- For periods that are measured after an event, any other day declared a holiday by the state where the district court is located. FRCP 6(a)(6).

b. *Computation of electronic filing deadlines.* Filing documents electronically does not alter filing deadlines. IN R USDCTSD ECF Procedures(7). A document due on a particular day must be filed before midnight local time of the division where the case is pending. IN R USDCTSD L.R. 5-4(a). All electronic transmissions of documents must be completed (i.e. received completely by the Clerk's Office) prior to midnight of the local time of the division in which the case is pending in order to be considered timely filed that day (NOTE: time will be noted in Eastern Time on the Court's docket. If you have filed a document prior to midnight local time of the division in which the case is pending and the document is due that date, but the electronic receipt and docket reflect the following calendar day, please contact the Court). IN R USDCTSD ECF Procedures(7). Although attorneys may file documents electronically twenty-four (24) hours a day, seven (7) days a week, attorneys are encouraged to file all documents during the normal working hours of the Clerk's Office (Monday through Friday, 8:30 a.m. to 4:30 p.m.) when technical support is available. IN R USDCTSD ECF Procedures(7); IN R USDCTSD ECF Procedures(9).

i. *Technical difficulties.* Parties are encouraged to file documents electronically during normal business hours, in case a problem is encountered. In the event a technical failure occurs and a document cannot be filed electronically despite the best efforts of the filing party, the party should print (if possible) a copy of the error message received. In addition, as soon as practically possible, the party should file a "Declaration that Party was Unable to File in a Timely Manner Due to Technical Difficulties." A model form is provided as Appendix D (IN R USDCTSD ECF Procedures(Appendix D)). IN R USDCTSD ECF Procedures(16).

- If a party is unable to file electronically and, as a result, may miss a filing deadline, the party must contact the Clerk's Office at the number listed in IN R USDCTSD ECF Procedures(15) to inform the court's staff of the difficulty. If a party misses a filing deadline due to an inability to file electronically, the party may submit the untimely filed document, accompanied by a declaration stating the reason(s) for missing the deadline. Unless the Court orders otherwise, the document and declaration must be filed no later than 12:00 noon of the first day on which the Court is open for business following the original filing deadline. IN R USDCTSD ECF Procedures(16).

   c. *Extending time*

      i. *In general.* When an act may or must be done within a specified time, the court may, for good cause, extend the time:

- With or without motion or notice if the court acts, or if a request is made, before the original time or its extension expires; or

- On motion made after the time has expired if the party failed to act because of excusable neglect. FRCP 6(b)(1).

      ii. *Exceptions.* A court must not extend the time to act under FRCP 50(b), FRCP 50(d), FRCP 52(b), FRCP 59(b), FRCP 59(d), FRCP 59(e), and FRCP 60(b). FRCP 6(b)(2).

      iii. Refer to the United States District Court for the Southern District of Indiana KeyRules Motion for Continuance/Extension of Time document for more information on extending time.

C. General Requirements

1. *Pleading, generally*

   a. *Pleadings allowed.* Only these pleadings are allowed: (1) a complaint; (2) an answer to a complaint; (3) an answer to a counterclaim designated as a counterclaim; (4) an answer to a crossclaim; (5) a third-party complaint; (6) an answer to a third-party complaint; and (7) if the court orders one, a reply to an answer. FRCP 7(a).

   b. *Pleading to be concise and direct.* Each allegation must be simple, concise, and direct. No technical form is required. FRCP 8(d)(1).

   c. *Alternative statements of a claim or defense.* A party may set out two or more statements of a claim or defense alternatively or hypothetically, either in a single count or defense or in separate ones. If a party makes alternative statements, the pleading is sufficient if any one of them is sufficient. FRCP 8(d)(2).

   d. *Inconsistent claims or defenses.* A party may state as many separate claims or defenses as it has, regardless of consistency. FRCP 8(d)(3).

   e. *Construing pleadings.* Pleadings must be construed so as to do justice. FRCP 8(e).

2. *Pleading special matters*

   a. *Capacity or authority to sue; Legal existence*

      i. *In general.* Except when required to show that the court has jurisdiction, a pleading need not allege:

- A party's capacity to sue or be sued;

- A party's authority to sue or be sued in a representative capacity; or

- The legal existence of an organized association of persons that is made a party. FRCP 9(a)(1).

      ii. *Raising those issues.* To raise any of those issues, a party must do so by a specific denial, which must state any supporting facts that are peculiarly within the party's knowledge. FRCP 9(a)(2).

   b. *Fraud or mistake; Conditions of mind.* In alleging fraud or mistake, a party must state with particularity the circumstances constituting fraud or mistake. Malice, intent, knowledge, and other conditions of a person's mind may be alleged generally. FRCP 9(b).

   c. *Conditions precedent.* In pleading conditions precedent, it suffices to allege generally that all conditions precedent have occurred or been performed. But when denying that a condition precedent has occurred or been performed, a party must do so with particularity. FRCP 9(c).

   d. *Official document or act.* In pleading an official document or official act, it suffices to allege that the document was legally issued or the act legally done. FRCP 9(d).

   e. *Judgment.* In pleading a judgment or decision of a domestic or foreign court, a judicial or quasi-judicial tribunal, or a board or officer, it suffices to plead the judgment or decision without showing jurisdiction to render it. FRCP 9(e).

f. *Time and place.* An allegation of time or place is material when testing the sufficiency of a pleading. FRCP 9(f).

g. *Special damages.* If an item of special damage is claimed, it must be specifically stated. FRCP 9(g).

h. *Admiralty or maritime claim*

    i. *How designated.* If a claim for relief is within the admiralty or maritime jurisdiction and also within the court's subject-matter jurisdiction on some other ground, the pleading may designate the claim as an admiralty or maritime claim for purposes of FRCP 14(c), FRCP 38(e), and FRCP 82 and the Supplemental Rules for Admiralty or Maritime Claims and Asset Forfeiture Actions. A claim cognizable only in the admiralty or maritime jurisdiction is an admiralty or maritime claim for those purposes, whether or not so designated. FRCP 9(h)(1).

    ii. *Designation for appeal.* A case that includes an admiralty or maritime claim within FRCP 9(h) is an admiralty case within 28 U.S.C.A. § 1292(a)(3). FRCP 9(h)(2).

3. *Complaint.* A pleading that states a claim for relief must contain: (1) a short and plain statement of the grounds for the court's jurisdiction, unless the court already has jurisdiction and the claim needs no new jurisdictional support; (2) a short and plain statement of the claim showing that the pleader is entitled to relief; and (3) a demand for the relief sought, which may include relief in the alternative or different types of relief. FRCP 8(a).

    a. *Statement of jurisdiction.* Federal courts are courts of limited jurisdiction, and it is presumed that they are without jurisdiction unless the contrary affirmatively appears. FEDPROC § 62:38; Kirkland Masonry, Inc. v. C.I.R., 614 F.2d 532 (5th Cir. 1980). Therefore, in order for a complaint to comply with the requirement that it contain a short and plain statement of the grounds upon which the court's jurisdiction depends, the jurisdictional basis must be alleged affirmatively and distinctly on the face of the complaint. FEDPROC § 62:38; Spain v. U.S. Through Atomic Nuclear Regulatory Commission Through U.S. Atomic Safety and Licensing Bd., 397 F.Supp. 15 (M.D.La. 1975).

        i. Although it has been said that the jurisdictional statement requirement contemplates reference to a federal statute, a sufficient jurisdictional statement is not made by simply citing a federal statute without alleging facts which bring the plaintiff within the purview of the statute. FEDPROC § 62:38; Atkins v. School Bd. of Halifax County, 379 F.Supp. 1060 (W.D.Va. 1974); Sims v. Mercy Hospital of Monroe, 451 F.2d 171 (6th Cir. 1971).

        ii. Improper venue is an affirmative defense, and a complaint need not include allegations showing venue to be proper. FEDPROC § 62:38; Ripperger v. A.C. Allyn & Co., 113 F.2d 332 (2d Cir. 1940).

    b. *Statement of claim*

        i. *Notice pleading.* Because the only function left exclusively to the pleadings by the Federal Rules of Civil Procedure is that of giving notice, federal courts frequently have said that the Federal Rules of Civil Procedure have adopted a system of "notice pleading." FPP § 1202; Swierkiewicz v. Sorema N.A., 534 U.S. 506, 122 S.Ct. 992, 152 L.Ed.2d 1 (2002). To comply with the requirement that a complaint contain a short and plain statement of the claim, a pleading must give the opposing party fair notice of the nature of a claim and of the basis or grounds for it, so that the defendant will at least be notified as to which of its actions gave rise to the claim upon which the complaint is based. FEDPROC § 62:45.

          • *Plausibility standard.* Bell Atlantic Corporation v. Twombly and Ashcroft v. Iqbal have paved the way for a heightened "plausibility" pleading standard that requires plaintiffs to provide greater factual development in their complaints in order to survive a FRCP 12(b)(6) motion to dismiss. FPP § 1202; Bell Atlantic Corp. v. Twombly, 550 U.S. 544, 127 S.Ct. 1955, 167 L.Ed.2d 929, 68 Fed.R.Serv.3d 661 (2007); Ashcroft v. Iqbal, 556 U.S. 662, 129 S.Ct. 1937, 173 L.Ed.2d 868 (2009). In discussing what appears to be the new plausibility standard, the Court [in Bell Atlantic Corp. v. Twombly] stated: "While a complaint attacked by a Rule 12(b)(6) motion to dismiss does not need detailed factual allegations. . .a plaintiff's obligation to provide the 'grounds' of his 'entitle[ment] to relief' requires more than labels and conclusions, and a formulaic recitation of the elements of a cause of action will not do. . .Factual allegations must be enough to raise a right to relief above the speculative level." FPP § 1216; Bell Atlantic Corp. v. Twombly, 550 U.S. 544, 127 S.Ct. 1955, 167 L.Ed.2d 929, 68 Fed.R.Serv.3d 661 (2007).

ii. *Facts and evidence.* The complaint need only state enough facts to raise a reasonable expectation that discovery will reveal evidence of the necessary elements. FEDPROC § 62:52; Phillips v. County of Allegheny, 515 F.3d 224 (3d Cir. 2008). A complaint is not intended to formulate issues or fully summarize the facts involved. FEDPROC § 62:52; Hill v. MCI WorldCom Communications, Inc., 141 F.Supp.2d 1205 (S.D.Iowa 2001). Under notice pleading, the full development of the facts and the narrowing of contested issues are accomplished through discovery and other pretrial procedures. FEDPROC § 62:52.

iii. *Particularity.* The claim should be particularized sufficiently for the defendant to prepare an adequate defense, file a responsive pleading, determine whether the defense of res judicata is appropriate, and commence discovery, and should insure that the court is sufficiently informed to determine the issue presented and to decide whether the complaint states a claim upon which relief can be had. FEDPROC § 62:45; Kelly v. Schmidberger, 806 F.2d 44, 6 Fed.R.Serv.3d 798 (2d Cir. 1986); Frank v. Mracek, 58 F.R.D. 365 (M.D.Ala. 1973); Barlow v. Pep Boys, Inc., 625 F.Supp. 130 (E.D.Pa. 1985); Philadelphia Dressed Beef Co. v. Wilson & Co., 19 F.R.D. 198 (E.D.Pa. 1956); Luckett v. Cohen, 145 F.Supp. 155 (S.D.N.Y. 1956).

c. *Pro se complaints.* Parties representing themselves must file the following types of complaints on forms that the clerk supplies:

i. Complaints alleging claims under The Civil Rights Act, 42 U.S.C.A. § 1983. IN R USDCTSD L.R. 8-1.

ii. Complaints alleging claims under The Social Security Act, 42 U.S.C.A. § 405(g). IN R USDCTSD L.R. 8-1.

iii. Complaints alleging employment discrimination under a federal statute. IN R USDCTSD L.R. 8-1.

d. *Demand for relief sought.* FRCP 8(a)(3) does not require a party to frame the demand for judgment according to a prescribed form or set of particular words; any concise statement identifying the remedies and the parties against whom relief is sought will be sufficient. FPP § 1255; Chandler v. McKee Foods Corp., 2009 WL 210858 (W.D.Va. 2009). Moreover, the pleader need only make one demand for relief regardless of the number of claims that are asserted. FPP § 1255; Liberty Mut. Ins. Co. v. Wetzel, 424 U.S. 737, 96 S.Ct. 1202, 47 L.Ed.2d 435 (1976).

i. Relief must be requested as to each defendant. FEDPROC § 62:58; RKO-Stanley Warner Theatres, Inc. v. Mellon Nat. Bank & Trust Co., 436 F.2d 1297 (3d Cir. 1970).

4. *Joinder*

a. *Joinder of claims.* A party asserting a claim, counterclaim, crossclaim, or third-party claim may join, as independent or alternative claims, as many claims as it has against an opposing party. FRCP 18(a).

i. *Joinder of contingent claims.* A party may join two claims even though one of them is contingent on the disposition of the other; but the court may grant relief only in accordance with the parties' relative substantive rights. In particular, a plaintiff may state a claim for money and a claim to set aside a conveyance that is fraudulent as to that plaintiff, without first obtaining a judgment for the money. FRCP 18(b).

b. *Joinder of parties; Required*

i. *Persons required to be joined if feasible; Required party.* A person who is subject to service of process and whose joinder will not deprive the court of subject-matter jurisdiction must be joined as a party if:

- In that person's absence, the court cannot accord complete relief among existing parties; or

- That person claims an interest relating to the subject of the action and is so situated that disposing of the action in the person's absence may: (1) as a practical matter impair or impede the person's ability to protect the interest; or (2) leave an existing party subject to a substantial risk of incurring double, multiple, or otherwise inconsistent obligations because of the interest. FRCP 19(a)(1).

ii. *Joinder of parties by court order.* If a person has not been joined as required, the court must order that the person be made a party. A person who refuses to join as a plaintiff may be made either a defendant or, in a proper case, an involuntary plaintiff. FRCP 19(a)(2).

iii. *Venue.* If a joined party objects to venue and the joinder would make venue improper, the court must dismiss that party. FRCP 19(a)(3).

iv. *When joinder of parties is not feasible.* If a person who is required to be joined if feasible cannot be joined, the court must determine whether, in equity and good conscience, the action should proceed among the existing parties or should be dismissed. FRCP 19(b). For a list of the factors for the court to consider in determining whether joinder of parties is feasible, refer to FRCP 19(b)(1) through FRCP 19(b)(4).

v. *Pleading the reasons for nonjoinder.* When asserting a claim for relief, a party must state:

- The name, if known, of any person who is required to be joined if feasible but is not joined; and

- The reasons for not joining that person. FRCP 19(c).

vi. *Exception for class actions.* FRCP 19 is subject to FRCP 23. FRCP 19(d). For information on class actions, refer to FRCP 23.

c. *Joinder of parties; Permissible*

i. *Persons who may join or be joined*

- *Plaintiffs.* Persons may join in one action as plaintiffs if: (1) they assert any right to relief jointly, severally, or in the alternative with respect to or arising out of the same transaction, occurrence, or series of transactions or occurrences; and (2) any question of law or fact common to all plaintiffs will arise in the action. FRCP 20(a)(1).

- *Defendants.* Persons—as well as a vessel, cargo, or other property subject to admiralty process in rem—may be joined in one action as defendants if: (1) any right to relief is asserted against them jointly, severally, or in the alternative with respect to or arising out of the same transaction, occurrence, or series of transactions or occurrences; and (2) any question of law or fact common to all defendants will arise in the action. FRCP 20(a)(2).

- *Extent of relief.* Neither a plaintiff nor a defendant need be interested in obtaining or defending against all the relief demanded. The court may grant judgment to one or more plaintiffs according to their rights, and against one or more defendants according to their liabilities. FRCP 20(a)(3).

ii. *Protective measures.* The court may issue orders—including an order for separate trials—to protect a party against embarrassment, delay, expense, or other prejudice that arises from including a person against whom the party asserts no claim and who asserts no claim against the party. FRCP 20(b).

d. *Misjoinder and nonjoinder of parties.* Misjoinder of parties is not a ground for dismissing an action. On motion or on its own, the court may at any time, on just terms, add or drop a party. The court may also sever any claim against a party. FRCP 21.

5. *Right to a jury trial; Demand*

a. *Right preserved.* The right of trial by jury as declared by U.S.C.A. Const. Amend. VII, or as provided by a federal statute, is preserved to the parties inviolate. FRCP 38(a).

b. *Demand.* On any issue triable of right by a jury, a party may demand a jury trial by:

i. Serving the other parties with a written demand—which may be included in a pleading—no later than fourteen (14) days after the last pleading directed to the issue is served; and

ii. Filing the demand in accordance with FRCP 5(d). FRCP 38(b).

    c.   *Specifying issues.* In its demand, a party may specify the issues that it wishes to have tried by a jury; otherwise, it is considered to have demanded a jury trial on all the issues so triable. If the party has demanded a jury trial on only some issues, any other party may—within fourteen (14) days after being served with the demand or within a shorter time ordered by the court—serve a demand for a jury trial on any other or all factual issues triable by jury. FRCP 38(c).

    d.   *Waiver; Withdrawal.* A party waives a jury trial unless its demand is properly served and filed. A proper demand may be withdrawn only if the parties consent. FRCP 38(d).

    e.   *Admiralty and maritime claims.* The rules in FRCP 38 do not create a right to a jury trial on issues in a claim that is an admiralty or maritime claim under FRCP 9(h). FRCP 38(e).

6.   *Appearances.* Every attorney who represents a party or who files a document on a party's behalf must file an appearance for that party. IN R USDCTSD L.R. 83-7. The filing of a Notice of Appearance shall act to establish the filing attorney as an attorney of record representing a designated party or parties in a particular cause of action. As a result, it is necessary for each attorney to file a separate Notice of Appearance when entering an appearance in a case. A joint appearance on behalf of multiple attorneys may be filed electronically only if it is filed separately for each attorney, using his/her ECF login. IN R USDCTSD ECF Procedures(12). Only those attorneys who have filed an appearance in a pending action are entitled to be served with case documents under FRCP 5(a). IN R USDCTSD L.R. 83-7. For more information, refer to IN R USDCTSD L.R. 83-7 and IN R USDCTSD ECF Procedures(12).

7.   *Notice of related action.* A party must file a notice of related action: as soon as it appears that the party's case and another pending case: (1) arise out of the same transaction or occurrence; (2) involve the same property; or (3) involve the validity or infringement or the same patent, trademark, or copyright. IN R USDCTSD L.R. 40-1(d)(2). For more information, refer to IN R USDCTSD L.R. 40-1.

8.   *Alternative dispute resolution (ADR)*

    a.   *Application.* Unless limited by specific provisions, or unless there are other applicable specific statutory, common law, or constitutional procedures, the Local Alternative Dispute Resolution Rules of the United States District Court for the Southern District of Indiana shall apply in all civil litigation filed in the U.S. District Court for the Southern District of Indiana, except in the following cases and proceedings:

        i.   Applications for writs of habeas corpus under 28 U.S.C.A. § 2254;

        ii.   Forfeiture cases;

        iii.   Non-adversary proceedings in bankruptcy;

        iv.   Social Security administrative review cases; and

        v.   Such other matters as specified by order of the Court; for example, matters involving important public policy issues, constitutional law, or the establishment of new law. IN R USDCTSD A.D.R. Rule 1.2.

    b.   *Mediation.* Mediation under this section (IN R USDCTSD A.D.R. Rule 2.1, et seq.) involves the confidential process by which a person acting as a Mediator, selected by the parties or appointed by the Court, assists the litigants in reaching a mutually acceptable agreement. It is an informal and nonadversarial process. The role of the Mediator is to assist in identifying the issues, reducing misunderstandings, clarifying priorities, exploring areas of compromise, and finding points of agreement as well as legitimate points of disagreement. Final decision-making authority rests with the parties, not the Mediator. IN R USDCTSD A.D.R. Rule 2.1. It is anticipated that an agreement may not resolve all of the disputed issues, but the process, nonetheless, can reduce points of contention. Parties and their representatives are required to mediate in good faith, but are not compelled to reach an agreement. IN R USDCTSD A.D.R. Rule 2.1.

        i.   *Case selection.* The Court with the agreement of the parties may refer a civil case for mediation. Unless otherwise ordered or as specifically provided in IN R USDCTSD A.D.R. Rule 2.8, referral to mediation does not abate or suspend the action, and no scheduled dates shall be delayed or deferred, including the date of trial. IN R USDCTSD A.D.R. Rule 2.2.

        ii.   For more information on mediation, refer to IN R USDCTSD A.D.R. Rule 2.1, et seq.

    c. *Other methods of dispute resolution.* The Local Alternative Dispute Resolution Rules of the United States District Court for the Southern District of Indiana shall not preclude the parties from utilizing any other reasonable method or technique of alternative dispute resolution to resolve disputes to which the parties agree. However, any use of arbitration by the parties will be governed by and comply with the requirements of 28 U.S.C.A. § 654 through 28 U.S.C.A. § 657. IN R USDCTSD A.D.R. Rule 1.5.

    d. For more information on alternative dispute resolution (ADR), refer to IN R USDCTSD A.D.R. Rule 1.1, et seq.

9. *Notice of settlement or resolution.* The parties must immediately notify the court if they reasonably anticipate settling their case or resolving a pending motion. IN R USDCTSD L.R. 7-1(h).

10. *Modification or suspension of rules.* The court may, on its own motion or at the request of a party, suspend or modify any rule in a particular case in the interest of justice. IN R USDCTSD L.R. 1-1(c).

D. Documents

1. *Required documents*

    a. *Civil cover sheet.* A civil cover sheet is submitted with each civil complaint filed in the district court. Copies of the cover sheet may be obtained from the Clerk of Court. 2 FEDFORMS § 3:29(Comment).

    b. *Complaint.* Refer to the General Requirements section of this document for the form and contents of the complaint.

    c. *Summons.* A summons must be served with a copy of the complaint. FRCP 4(c)(1). A summons must:

        i. Name the court and the parties;

        ii. Be directed to the defendant;

        iii. State the name and address of the plaintiff's attorney or—if unrepresented—of the plaintiff;

        iv. State the time within which the defendant must appear and defend;

        v. Notify the defendant that a failure to appear and defend will result in a default judgment against the defendant for the relief demanded in the complaint;

        vi. Be signed by the clerk; and

        vii. Bear the court's seal. FRCP 4(a)(1).

    d. *Filing fee.* The clerk of each district court shall require the parties instituting any civil action, suit or proceeding in such court, whether by original process, removal or otherwise, to pay a filing fee. 28 U.S.C.A. § 1914(a). Each district court by rule or standing order may require advance payment of fees. 28 U.S.C.A. § 1914(c). For information on filing fees and the District Court Miscellaneous Fee Schedule, refer to 28 U.S.C.A. § 1914.

    e. *Affidavit proving service.* Unless service is waived, proof of service must be made to the court. Except for service by a United States marshal or deputy marshal, proof must be by the server's affidavit. FRCP 4(l)(1). Refer to the Filing and Service Requirements section of this document for more information.

2. *Supplemental documents*

    a. *Notice and request for waiver of service.* An individual, corporation, or association that is subject to service under FRCP 4(e), FRCP 4(f), or FRCP 4(h) has a duty to avoid unnecessary expenses of serving the summons. The plaintiff may notify such a defendant that an action has been commenced and request that the defendant waive service of a summons. The notice and request must:

        i. Be in writing and be addressed:

            • To the individual defendant; or

            • For a defendant subject to service under FRCP 4(h), to an officer, a managing or general agent, or any other agent authorized by appointment or by law to receive service of process;

    ii.   Name the court where the complaint was filed;

    iii. Be accompanied by a copy of the complaint, two (2) copies of a waiver form appended to FRCP 4, and a prepaid means for returning the form;

    iv. Inform the defendant, using the form appended to FRCP 4, of the consequences of waiving and not waiving service;

    v.   State the date when the request is sent;

    vi. Give the defendant a reasonable time of at least thirty (30) days after the request was sent—or at least sixty (60) days if sent to the defendant outside any judicial district of the United States—to return the waiver; and

    vii. Be sent by first-class mail or other reliable means. FRCP 4(d)(1).

b. *Notice of constitutional question.* A party that files a pleading, written motion, or other paper drawing into question the constitutionality of a federal or state statute must promptly:

    i. *File notice.* File a notice of constitutional question stating the question and identifying the paper that raises it, if:

- A federal statute is questioned and the parties do not include the United States, one of its agencies, or one of its officers or employees in an official capacity; or

- A state statute is questioned and the parties do not include the state, one of its agencies, or one of its officers or employees in an official capacity; and

    ii. *Serve notice.* Serve the notice and paper on the Attorney General of the United States if a federal statute is questioned—or on the state attorney general if a state statute is questioned—either by certified or registered mail or by sending it to an electronic address designated by the attorney general for this purpose. FRCP 5.1(a).

    iii. *Time for filing.* A notice of constitutional challenge to a statute filed in accordance with FRCP 5.1 must be filed at the same time the parties tender their proposed case management plan, if one is required, or within twenty-one (21) days of the filing drawing into question the constitutionality of a federal or state statute, whichever occurs later. IN R USDCTSD L.R. 5.1-1(a).

    iv. *Additional service requirements.* If a federal statute is challenged, in addition to the service requirements of FRCP 5.1(a), the party filing the notice of constitutional challenge must serve the notice and documents on the United States Attorney for the Southern District of Indiana, either by certified or registered mail or by sending it to an electronic address designated for that purpose by that official. IN R USDCTSD L.R. 5.1-1(b).

    v. *No forfeiture.* A party's failure to file and serve the notice, or the court's failure to certify, does not forfeit a constitutional claim or defense that is otherwise timely asserted. FRCP 5.1(d).

c. *Notice of issue concerning foreign law.* A party who intends to raise an issue about a foreign country's law must give notice by a pleading or other writing. In determining foreign law, the court may consider any relevant material or source, including testimony, whether or not submitted by a party or admissible under the Federal Rules of Evidence. The court's determination must be treated as a ruling on a question of law. FRCP 44.1.

d. *Nongovernmental corporate disclosure statement*

    i. *Contents.* A nongovernmental corporate party must file two (2) copies of a disclosure statement that:

- Identifies any parent corporation and any publicly held corporation owning ten percent (10%) or more of its stock; or

- States that there is no such corporation. FRCP 7.1(a).

    ii. *Time to file; Supplemental filing.* A party must:

- File the disclosure statement with its first appearance, pleading, petition, motion, response, or other request addressed to the court; and

- Promptly file a supplemental statement if any required information changes. FRCP 7.1(b).

e. *Request for three-judge court.* To request a three-judge court in a case, a party must: (1) print "Three-Judge District Court Requested" or the equivalent immediately following the title on the first pleading the party files; and (2) set forth the basis for the request in the pleading or in a brief statement attached to the pleading, unless the basis is apparent from the pleading. IN R USDCTSD L.R. 9-2(a). The words "Three-Judge District Court Requested" or the equivalent on a pleading is a sufficient request under 28 U.S.C.A. § 2284. IN R USDCTSD L.R. 9-2(b).

f. *Index of exhibits.* Any pleading, motion, brief, affidavit, notice, or proposed order filed with the court, whether electronically or with the clerk, must: if it has four (4) or more exhibits, include a separate index that identifies and briefly describes each exhibit. IN R USDCTSD L.R. 5-1(b).

g. *Copy of document with self-address envelope.* To receive a file-stamped copy of a document filed directly with the clerk, a party must include with the original document an additional copy and a self-addressed envelope. The envelope must be big enough to hold the copy and have enough postage on it to send the copy via regular first-class mail. IN R USDCTSD L.R. 5-10(b).

h. *Notice of manual filing.* When a party who is not exempt from the electronic filing requirement files a document directly with the clerk, the party must: electronically file a notice of manual filing that explains why the document cannot be filed electronically. IN R USDCTSD L.R. 5-2(d)(1). Refer to the Filing and Service Requirements section of this document for more information.

  i. Where an individual component cannot be included in an electronic filing (e.g. the component cannot be converted to electronic format), the filer shall electronically file the prescribed Notice of Manual Filing in place of that component. A model form is provided as Appendix C (IN R USDCTSD ECF Procedures(Appendix C)). IN R USDCTSD ECF Procedures(13).

  ii. Before making a manual filing of a component, the filing party shall first electronically file a Notice of Manual Filing (See IN R USDCTSD ECF Procedures(Appendix C)). The filer shall initiate the electronic filing process as if filing the actual component but shall instead attach to the filing the Notice of Manual Filing setting forth the reason(s) why the component cannot be filed electronically. The manual filing should be accompanied by a copy of the previously filed Notice of Manual Filing. A party may seek to have a component excluded from electronic filing pursuant to applicable Federal and Local Rules (e.g., FRCP 26(c)). IN R USDCTSD ECF Procedures(15).

i. *Courtesy copies.* District Judges and Magistrate Judges regularly receive documents filed by all parties. Therefore, parties shall not bring "courtesy copies" to any chambers unless specifically directed to do so by the Court. IN R USDCTSD Case Mgt(General Instructions For All Cases).

j. *Copies for three-judge court.* Parties in a case where a three-judge court has been requested must file an original and three copies of any document filed directly with the clerk (instead of electronically) until the court: (1) denies the request; (2) dissolves the three-judge court; or (3) allows the parties to file fewer copies. IN R USDCTSD L.R. 9-2(c).

k. *Declaration that party was unable to file in a timely manner due to technical difficulties.* If a party misses a filing deadline due to an inability to file electronically, the party may submit the untimely filed document, accompanied by a declaration stating the reason(s) for missing the deadline. IN R USDCTSD ECF Procedures(16). A model form is provided as Appendix D (IN R USDCTSD ECF Procedures(Appendix D)). IN R USDCTSD ECF Procedures(16).

E. Format

1. *Form of documents*

   a. *Paper (manual filings only).* Any document that is not filed electronically must: be flat, unfolded, and on good-quality, eight and one-half by eleven (8-1/2 x 11) inch white paper. IN R USDCTSD L.R. 5-1(d)(1). Any document that is not filed electronically must: be single-sided. IN R USDCTSD L.R. 5-1(d)(1).

      i. *Covers or backing.* Any document that is not filed electronically must: not have a cover or a back. IN R USDCTSD L.R. 5-1(d)(1).

      ii. *Fastening.* Any document that is not filed electronically must: be (if consisting of more than one

(1) page) fastened by paperclip or binder clip and may not be stapled. IN R USDCTSD L.R. 5-1(d)(1).

- *Request for nonconforming fastening.* If a document cannot be fastened or bound as required by IN R USDCTSD L.R. 5-1(d), a party may ask the clerk for permission to fasten it in another manner. The party must make such a request before attempting to file the document with nonconforming fastening. IN R USDCTSD L.R. 5-1(d)(2).

iii. *Hole punching.* Any document that is not filed electronically must: be two-hole punched at the top with the holes two and three-quarter (2-3/4) inches apart and appropriately centered. IN R USDCTSD L.R. 5-1(d)(1).

b. *Margins.* Any pleading, motion, brief, affidavit, notice, or proposed order filed with the court, whether electronically or with the clerk, must: have at least one (1) inch margins. IN R USDCTSD L.R. 5-1(b).

c. *Spacing.* Any pleading, motion, brief, affidavit, notice, or proposed order filed with the court, whether electronically or with the clerk, must: be double spaced (except for headings, footnotes, and quoted material). IN R USDCTSD L.R. 5-1(b).

d. *Text.* Any pleading, motion, brief, affidavit, notice, or proposed order filed with the court, whether electronically or with the clerk, must: be plainly typewritten, printed, or prepared by a clearly legible copying process. IN R USDCTSD L.R. 5-1(b).

e. *Font size.* Any pleading, motion, brief, affidavit, notice, or proposed order filed with the court, whether electronically or with the clerk, must: use at least 12-point type in the body of the document and at least 10-point type in footnotes. IN R USDCTSD L.R. 5-1(b).

f. *Page numbering.* Any pleading, motion, brief, affidavit, notice, or proposed order filed with the court, whether electronically or with the clerk, must: have consecutively numbered pages. IN R USDCTSD L.R. 5-1(b).

g. *Caption; Names of parties.* Every pleading must have a caption with the court's name, a title, a file number, and a FRCP 7(a) designation. The title of the complaint must name all the parties; the title of other pleadings, after naming the first party on each side, may refer generally to other parties. FRCP 10(a). Any pleading, motion, brief, affidavit, notice, or proposed order filed with the court, whether electronically or with the clerk, must: include a title on the first page. IN R USDCTSD L.R. 5-1(b).

i. *Jury demand.* A party demanding a jury trial in a pleading as permitted by FRCP 38(b) must include the demand in the title by way of a notation placed on the front page of the pleading, immediately following the title of the pleading, stating "Demand for Jury Trial." Failure to do so will not result in a waiver under FRCP 38(d) if a jury demand is otherwise properly filed and served under FRCP 38(b). IN R USDCTSD L.R. 38-1.

ii. *Request for three-judge court.* To request a three-judge court in a case, a party must: (1) print "Three-Judge District Court Requested" or the equivalent immediately following the title on the first pleading the party files. IN R USDCTSD L.R. 9-2(a)(1). Refer to the Documents section of this document for more information.

iii. *Class actions.* A party seeking to maintain a case as a class action (whether for or against a class) must include in the complaint, crossclaim, or counterclaim: (1) the words "Class Action" in the document's title; and (2) a reference to each part of FRCP 23 that the party relies on in seeking to maintain the case as a class action. IN R USDCTSD L.R. 23-1(a). The provisions of IN R USDCTSD L.R. 23-1 will apply, with appropriate adaptations, to any counterclaim or crossclaim alleged to be brought for or against a class. IN R USDCTSD L.R. 23-1(b).

h. *Filer's information.* Any pleading, motion, brief, affidavit, notice, or proposed order filed with the court, whether electronically or with the clerk, must: in the case of pleadings, motions, legal briefs, and notices, include the name, complete address, telephone number, facsimile number (where available), and e-mail address (where available) of the pro se litigant or attorney who files it. IN R USDCTSD L.R. 5-1(b).

i. *Paragraphs; Separate statements.* A party must state its claims or defenses in numbered paragraphs,

each limited as far as practicable to a single set of circumstances. A later pleading may refer by number to a paragraph in an earlier pleading. If doing so would promote clarity, each claim founded on a separate transaction or occurrence—and each defense other than a denial—must be stated in a separate count or defense. FRCP 10(b).

j. *Adoption by reference; Exhibits.* A statement in a pleading may be adopted by reference elsewhere in the same pleading or in any other pleading or motion. A copy of a written instrument that is an exhibit to a pleading is a part of the pleading for all purposes. FRCP 10(c).

k. *Citations*

    i. *Local rules.* The Local Rules of the United States District Court for the Southern District of Indiana may be cited as "S.D. Ind. L.R." IN R USDCTSD L.R. 1-1(a).

    ii. *Local alternative dispute resolution rules.* These Rules shall be known as the Local Alternative Dispute Resolution Rules of the United States District Court for the Southern District of Indiana. They shall be cited as "S.D.Ind. Local A.D.R. Rule _____." IN R USDCTSD A.D.R. Rule 1.1.

l. *Acceptance by the clerk.* The clerk must not refuse to file a paper solely because it is not in the form prescribed by the Federal Rules of Civil Procedure or by a local rule or practice. FRCP 5(d)(4). The clerk will accept a document that violates IN R USDCTSD L.R. 5-1, but the court may exclude the document from the official record. IN R USDCTSD L.R. 5-1(e).

    i. *Sanctions for errors as to form.* The court may strike from the record any document that does not comply with the rules governing the form of documents filed with the court, such as rules that regulate document size or the number of copies to be filed or that require a special designation in the caption. The court may also sanction an attorney or party who files a non-compliant document. IN R USDCTSD L.R. 1-3.

2. *Form of electronic documents.* Any document submitted via the court's electronic case filing (ECF) system must be: otherwise prepared and filed in a manner consistent with the CM/ECF Policies and Procedures Manual (IN R USDCTSD ECF Procedures). IN R USDCTSD L.R. 5-1(c). Electronically filed documents must meet the requirements of FRCP 10 (Form of Pleadings), IN R USDCTSD L.R. 5-1 (Format of Papers Presented for Filing), and FRCP 5.2 (Privacy Protection for Filings Made with the Court), as if they had been submitted on paper. Documents filed electronically are also subject to any page limitations set forth by Court Order, by IN R USDCTSD L.R. 7-1 (Motion Practice), or IN R USDCTSD L.R. 56-1 (Summary Judgment Practice), as applicable. IN R USDCTSD ECF Procedures(13).

a. *PDF format required.* Any document submitted via the court's electronic case filing (ECF) system must be: in .pdf format. IN R USDCTSD L.R. 5-1(c); IN R USDCTSD ECF Procedures(7). Any document submitted via the court's electronic case filing (ECF) system must be: converted to a .pdf file directly from a word processing program, unless it exists only in paper format (in which case it may be scanned to create a .pdf document). IN R USDCTSD L.R. 5-1(c); IN R USDCTSD ECF Procedures(13).

    i. An exhibit may be scanned into PDF format, at a recommended 300 dpi resolution or higher, only if it does not already exist in electronic format. The filing attorney is responsible for reviewing all PDF documents for legibility before submitting them through the Court's Electronic Case Filing system. For technical guidance in creating PDF documents, please contact the Clerk's Office. IN R USDCTSD ECF Procedures(13).

b. *File size limitations.* Any document submitted via the court's electronic case filing (ECF) system must be: submitted as one or more .pdf files that do not exceed ten megabytes (10 MB) each (consistent with the CM/ECF Policies and Procedures Manual (IN R USDCTSD ECF Procedures)). IN R USDCTSD L.R. 5-1(c); IN R USDCTSD ECF Procedures(13).

    i. To electronically file a document or attachment that exceeds ten megabytes (10 MB), the document must first be broken down into two or more smaller files. For example, if Exhibit A is a twelve megabyte (12 MB) PDF file, it should be divided into 2 equal parts prior to electronic filing. Each component part of the exhibit would be filed as an attachment to the main document and described appropriately as "Exhibit A (part 1 of 2)" and "Exhibit A (part 2 of 2)." IN R USDCTSD ECF Procedures(13).

ii. The supporting items mentioned in IN R USDCTSD ECF Procedures(13) should not be confused with memorandums or briefs in support of motions as outlined in IN R USDCTSD L.R. 7-1 or IN R USDCTSD L.R. 56-1. These memorandums or briefs in support are to be filed as entirely separate documents pursuant to the appropriate rule. Additionally, no motion shall be embodied in the text of a response or reply brief/memorandum unless otherwise ordered by the Court. IN R USDCTSD ECF Procedures(13).

c. *Separate component parts.* A key objective of the electronic filing system is to ensure that as much of the case as possible is managed electronically. To facilitate electronic filing and retrieval, documents to be filed electronically are to be reasonably broken into their separate component parts. By way of example, most filings include a foundation document (e.g., motion) and other supporting items (e.g., exhibits, proposed orders, proposed amended pleadings). The foundation document, as well as the supporting items, are each separate components of the filing; supporting items must be filed as attachments to the foundation document. These exhibits or attachments should include only those excerpts of the referenced documents that are directly germane to the matter under consideration. IN R USDCTSD ECF Procedures(13).

i. Where an individual component cannot be included in an electronic filing (e.g. the component cannot be converted to electronic format), the filer shall electronically file the prescribed Notice of Manual Filing in place of that component. A model form is provided as Appendix C (IN R USDCTSD ECF Procedures(Appendix C)). IN R USDCTSD ECF Procedures(13).

d. *Exhibits.* Each electronically filed exhibit to a main document must be: (1) created as a separate .pdf file; (2) submitted as an attachment to the main document and given a title which describes its content; and (3) limited to excerpts that are directly germane to the main document's subject matter. IN R USDCTSD L.R. 5-6(a).

i. When uploading attachments during the electronic filing process, exhibits must be uploaded in a logical sequence and a brief description must be entered for each individual PDF file. The description must include not only the exhibit number or letter, but also a brief description of the document. This information may be entered in CM/ECF using a combination of the Category drop-down menu, the Description text box, or both (see IN R USDCTSD ECF Procedures(13)(Figure 1)). The information that is provided in each box will be combined to create a description of the document as it appears on the case docket (see IN R USDCTSD ECF Procedures(13)(Figure 2)). IN R USDCTSD ECF Procedures(13). For an example, refer to IN R USDCTSD ECF Procedures(13).

e. *Excerpts.* A party filing an exhibit that consists of excerpts from a larger document must clearly and prominently identify the exhibit as containing excerpted material. Either party will have the right to timely file additional excerpts or the complete document to the extent they are or become directly germane to the main document's subject matter. IN R USDCTSD L.R. 5-6(b).

f. For an example illustrating the application of IN R USDCTSD ECF Procedures(13), refer to IN R USDCTSD ECF Procedures(13).

3. *Signing of pleadings, motions and other papers*

a. *Signature.* Every pleading, written motion, and other paper must be signed by at least one attorney of record in the attorney's name—or by a party personally if the party is unrepresented. The paper must state the signer's address, e-mail address, and telephone number. FRCP 11(a).

i. *Signatures on manual filings.* Any document that is not filed electronically must: include the original signature of the pro se litigant or attorney who files it. IN R USDCTSD L.R. 5-1(d)(1).

ii. *Electronic signatures.* Use of the attorney's login and password when filing documents electronically serves in part as the attorney's signature for purposes of FRCP 11, the Local Rules of the United States District Court for the Southern District of Indiana, and any other purpose for which a signature is required in connection with proceedings before the Court. IN R USDCTSD ECF Procedures(14); IN R USDCTSD ECF Procedures(10). A pleading, motion, brief, or notice filed electronically under an attorney's ECF log-in and password must be signed by that attorney. IN R USDCTSD L.R. 5-7(a). A signature on a document other than a document filed as provided under IN R USDCTSD L.R. 5-7(a) must be an original handwritten signature and must be scanned into .pdf format for electronic filing. IN R USDCTSD L.R. 5-7(c); IN R USDCTSD ECF Procedures(14).

- *Form of electronic signature.* If a document is converted directly from a word processing application to .pdf (as opposed to scanning), the name of the Filing User under whose log-in and password the document is submitted must be preceded by a "s/" and typed on the signature line where the Filing User's handwritten signature would otherwise appear. IN R USDCTSD L.R. 5-7(b). All documents filed electronically shall include a signature block and include the filing attorney's typewritten name, address, telephone number, facsimile number and e-mail address. In addition, the name of the filing attorney under whose ECF login the document will be filed should be preceded by a "s/" and typed in the space where the attorney's handwritten signature would otherwise appear. IN R US-DCTSD ECF Procedures(14). For a sample format, refer to IN R USDCTSD ECF Procedures(14).

- *Effect of electronic signature.* Filing an electronically signed document under an attorney's ECF log-in and password constitutes the attorney's signature on the document under the Federal Rules of Civil Procedure, under the Local Rules of the United States District Court for the Southern District of Indiana, and for any other reason a signature is required in connection with the court's activities. IN R USDCTSD L.R. 5-7(d).

- *Documents with multiple attorneys' signatures.* Documents requiring signatures of more than one attorney shall be filed either by: (1) obtaining consent from the other attorney, then typing the "s/ [Name]" signature of the other attorney on the signature line where the other attorney's signature would otherwise appear; (2) identifying in the signature section the name of the other attorney whose signature is required and by the submission of a Notice of Endorsement (see IN R USDCTSD ECF Procedures(Appendix B)) by the other attorney no later than three (3) business days after filing; (3) submitting a scanned document containing all handwritten signatures; or (4) in any other manner approved by the Court. IN R USDCTSD ECF Procedures(14); IN R USDCTSD L.R. 5-7(e).

iii. *No verification or accompanying affidavit required for pleadings.* Unless a rule or statute specifically states otherwise, a pleading need not be verified or accompanied by an affidavit. FRCP 11(a).

iv. *Unsigned papers.* The court must strike an unsigned paper unless the omission is promptly corrected after being called to the attorney's or party's attention. FRCP 11(a). The court will strike any document filed directly with the clerk that is not signed by an attorney of record or the pro se litigant filing it, but the court may do so only after giving the attorney or pro se litigant notice of the omission and reasonable time to correct it. Rubber-stamp or facsimile signatures are not original signatures and the court will deem documents containing them to be unsigned for purposes of FRCP 11 and FRCP 26(g) and IN R USDCTSD L.R. 5-10. IN R USDCTSD L.R. 5-10(g).

b. *Representations to the court.* By presenting to the court a pleading, written motion, or other paper—whether by signing, filing, submitting, or later advocating it—an attorney or unrepresented party certifies that to the best of the person's knowledge, information, and belief, formed after an inquiry reasonable under the circumstances:

i. It is not being presented for any improper purpose, such as to harass, cause unnecessary delay, or needlessly increase the cost of litigation;

ii. The claims, defenses, and other legal contentions are warranted by existing law or by a nonfrivolous argument for extending, modifying, or reversing existing law or for establishing new law;

iii. The factual contentions have evidentiary support or, if specifically so identified, will likely have evidentiary support after a reasonable opportunity for further investigation or discovery; and

iv. The denials of factual contentions are warranted on the evidence or, if specifically so identified, are reasonably based on belief or a lack of information. FRCP 11(b).

c. *Sanctions.* If, after notice and a reasonable opportunity to respond, the court determines that FRCP 11(b) has been violated, the court may impose an appropriate sanction on any attorney, law firm, or party that violated FRCP 11(b) or is responsible for the violation. FRCP 11(c)(1). Refer to the United States District Court for the Southern District of Indiana KeyRules Motion for Sanctions document for more information.

4. *Privacy protection for filings made with the court.* Electronically filed documents must meet the requirements of. . .FRCP 5.2 (Privacy Protection for Filings Made with the Court), as if they had been submitted on paper. IN R USDCTSD ECF Procedures(13).

a. *Redacted filings.* Unless the court orders otherwise, in an electronic or paper filing with the court that contains an individual's Social Security number, taxpayer-identification number, or birth date, the name of an individual known to be a minor, or a financial-account number, a party or nonparty making the filing may include only:

   i. The last four (4) digits of the Social Security number and taxpayer-identification number;

   ii. The year of the individual's birth;

   iii. The minor's initials; and

   iv. The last four (4) digits of the financial-account number. FRCP 5.2(a).

b. *Exemptions from the redaction requirement.* The redaction requirement does not apply to the following:

   i. A financial-account number that identifies the property allegedly subject to forfeiture in a forfeiture proceeding;

   ii. The record of an administrative or agency proceeding;

   iii. The official record of a state-court proceeding;

   iv. The record of a court or tribunal, if that record was not subject to the redaction requirement when originally filed;

   v. A filing covered by FRCP 5.2(c) or FRCP 5.2(d); and

   vi. A pro se filing in an action brought under 28 U.S.C.A. § 2241, 28 U.S.C.A. § 2254, or 28 U.S.C.A. § 2255. FRCP 5.2(b).

c. *Limitations on remote access to electronic files; Social Security appeals and immigration cases.* Unless the court orders otherwise, in an action for benefits under the Social Security Act, and in an action or proceeding relating to an order of removal, to relief from removal, or to immigration benefits or detention, access to an electronic file is authorized as follows:

   i. The parties and their attorneys may have remote electronic access to any part of the case file, including the administrative record;

   ii. Any other person may have electronic access to the full record at the courthouse, but may have remote electronic access only to:

   - The docket maintained by the court; and

   - An opinion, order, judgment, or other disposition of the court, but not any other part of the case file or the administrative record. FRCP 5.2(c).

d. *Filings made under seal.* The court may order that a filing be made under seal without redaction. The court may later unseal the filing or order the person who made the filing to file a redacted version for the public record. FRCP 5.2(d). For more information on filing under seal, refer to IN R USDCTSD L.R. 5-11 and IN R USDCTSD ECF Procedures(18).

e. *Protective orders.* For good cause, the court may by order in a case:

   i. Require redaction of additional information; or

   ii. Limit or prohibit a nonparty's remote electronic access to a document filed with the court. FRCP 5.2(e).

f. *Option for additional unredacted filing under seal.* A person making a redacted filing may also file

an unredacted copy under seal. The court must retain the unredacted copy as part of the record. FRCP 5.2(f).

g. *Option for filing a reference list.* A filing that contains redacted information may be filed together with a reference list that identifies each item of redacted information and specifies an appropriate identifier that uniquely corresponds to each item listed. The list must be filed under seal and may be amended as of right. Any reference in the case to a listed identifier will be construed to refer to the corresponding item of information. FRCP 5.2(g).

h. *Waiver of protection of identifiers.* A person waives the protection of FRCP 5.2(a) as to the person's own information by filing it without redaction and not under seal. FRCP 5.2(h).

F. Filing and Service Requirements

1. *Filing requirements.* A civil action is commenced by filing a complaint with the court. FRCP 3. The first step in a civil action in a United States district court is the filing of the complaint with the clerk or the judge. FPP § 1052. Filing a complaint requires nothing more than delivery of the document to a court officer authorized to receive it. FPP § 1052; Central States, Southeast & Southwest Areas Pension Fund v. Paramount Liquor Co., 34 F.Supp.2d 1092 (N.D.Ill. 1999). The initial pleading and accompanying documents, including the complaint and issuance of the summons, may be filed either in paper form or electronically through the court's ECF system. IN R USDCTSD L.R. 5-2(b); IN R USDCTSD ECF Procedures(6). All subsequent documents must be filed electronically except as provided in the Local Rules of the United States District Court for the Southern District of Indiana or as ordered by the court. IN R USDCTSD L.R. 5-2(b); IN R USDCTSD ECF Procedures(6). If a party files a document directly with the clerk that requires the clerk to give others notice, the party must provide the clerk with sufficient copies of the notice and the names and addresses of each person who is to receive the notice. IN R USDCTSD L.R. 5-10(d).

   a. *How filing is made; In general.* In certain instances, the court will direct the parties to submit items directly to chambers (e.g., confidential settlement statements). However, absent specific prior authorization, counsel and litigants should not submit letters or documents directly to chambers, and such materials should be filed with the clerk. IN R USDCTSD L.R. 5-1(Local Rules Advisory Committee Comment).

      i. A document or item submitted in relation to a matter within the court's jurisdiction is deemed filed upon delivery to the office of the clerk in a manner prescribed by the Local Rules of the United States District Court for the Southern District of Indiana or the Federal Rules of Civil Procedure or authorized by the court. Any submission directed to a Judge or Judge's staff, the office of the clerk or any employee thereof, in a manner that is not contemplated by IN R USDCTSD L.R. 5-1 and without prior court authorization is prohibited. IN R USDCTSD L.R. 5-1(a).

   b. *Non-electronic filing.* Any document that is exempt from electronic filing must be filed directly with the clerk and served on other parties in the case as required by those Federal Rules of Civil Procedure and Local Rules of the United States District Court for the Southern District of Indiana that apply to the service of non-electronic documents. IN R USDCTSD L.R. 5-2(c).

      i. *When completed.* A document or other item that is not required to be filed electronically is deemed filed:

         • Upon delivery in person, by courier, or via U.S. Mail or other mail delivery service to the clerk's office during business hours;

         • When the courtroom deputy clerk accepts it, if the document or item is filed in open court; or

         • Upon completion of any other manner of filing that the court authorizes. IN R USDCTSD L.R. 5-10(a).

      ii. *Document filing by non-exempt party.* When a party who is not exempt from the electronic filing requirement files a document directly with the clerk, the party must:

         • Electronically file a notice of manual filing that explains why the document cannot be filed electronically;

- Present the document to the clerk within one (1) business day after filing the notice of manual filing; and

- Present the clerk with a copy of the notice of manual filing when the party files the document with the clerk. IN R USDCTSD L.R. 5-2(d).

c. *Pro se incarcerated litigants.* Individuals who are incarcerated and are filing their legal documents pro se may benefit from a special "mailbox rule," which fixes the time of commencement of an action at the point when the complaint enters the prison mail system, rather than when it reaches the court clerk. FPP § 1052; Houston v. Lack, 487 U.S. 266, 276, 108 S.Ct. 2379, 2385, 101 L.Ed.2d 245 (1988).

d. *Electronic filing*

    i. *Authorization of electronic filing program.* A court may, by local rule, allow papers to be filed, signed, or verified by electronic means that are consistent with any technical standards established by the Judicial Conference of the United States. A local rule may require electronic filing only if reasonable exceptions are allowed. A paper filed electronically in compliance with a local rule is a written paper for purposes of the Federal Rules of Civil Procedure. FRCP 5(d)(3).

- IN R USDCTSD L.R. 5-2 requires electronic filing, as allowed by FRCP 5(d)(3). The policies and procedures in IN R USDCTSD ECF Procedures govern electronic filing in this district unless, due to circumstances in a particular case, a judicial officer determines that these policies and procedures (IN R USDCTSD ECF Procedures) should be modified. IN R USDCTSD ECF Procedures(1).

- Unless modified by order of the Court, all Federal Rules of Civil Procedure and Local Rules of the United States District Court for the Southern District of Indiana shall continue to apply to cases maintained in the Court's Case Management/Electronic Case Filing System (CM/ECF). IN R USDCTSD ECF Procedures(3).

    ii. *Mandatory electronic filing.* Unless exempted pursuant to IN R USDCTSD L.R. 5-3(e), attorneys admitted to the court's bar (including those admitted pro hac vice) or authorized to represent the United States must use the court's ECF system to file documents. IN R USDCTSD L.R. 5-3(a). Electronic filing by attorneys is required for eligible documents filed in civil and criminal cases pending with the Court, unless specifically exempted by Local Rule or Court Order. IN R USDCTSD ECF Procedures(4).

- *Exceptions.* All civil cases (other than those cases the court specifically exempts) must be maintained in the court's electronic case filing (ECF) system. Accordingly, as allowed by FRCP 5(d)(3), every document filed in this court (including exhibits) must be transmitted to the clerk's office via the ECF system consistent with IN R USDCTSD L.R. 5-2 through IN R USDCTSD L.R. 5-11 except: (1) documents filed by pro se litigants; (2) transcripts in cases filed by claimants under the Social Security Act (and related statutes); (3) exhibits in a format that does not readily permit electronic filing (such as videos and large maps and charts); (4) documents that are illegible when scanned into .pdf format; (5) documents filed in cases not maintained on the ECF system; and (6) any other documents that the court or the Local Rules of the United States District Court for the Southern District of Indiana specifically allow to be filed directly with the clerk. IN R USDCTSD L.R. 5-2(a). Parties otherwise participating in the electronic filing system may be excused from filing a particular component electronically under certain limited circumstances, such as when the component cannot be reduced to an electronic format. Such components shall not be filed electronically, but instead shall be manually filed with the Clerk of Court and served upon the parties in accordance with the applicable Federal Rules of Civil Procedure and the Local Rules of the United States District Court for the Southern District of Indiana for filing and service of non-electronic documents. IN R USDCTSD ECF Procedures(15).

- *Exemption from participation.* The court may exempt attorneys from using the ECF system in a particular case for good cause. An attorney must file a petition for ECF exemption and a CM/ECF technical requirements exemption questionnaire in each case in

which the attorney seeks an exemption. (The CM/ECF technical requirements exemption questionnaire is available on the court's website). IN R USDCTSD L.R. 5-3(e).

iii. *Consequences of electronic filing.* Electronic transmission of a document consistent with the procedures adopted by the Court shall, upon the complete receipt of the same by the Clerk of Court, constitute filing of the document for all purposes of the Federal Rules of Civil and Criminal Procedure and the Local Rules of the United States District Court for the Southern District of Indiana, and shall constitute entry of that document onto the docket maintained by the Clerk pursuant to FRCP 58 and FRCP 79. IN R USDCTSD ECF Procedures(7); IN R USDCTSD L.R. 5-4(c)(1). When a document has been filed electronically: the document, as filed, binds the filing party. IN R USDCTSD L.R. 5-4(c)(3).

- A Notice of Electronic Filing (NEF) acknowledging that the document has been filed will immediately appear on the filer's screen after the document has been submitted. Attorneys are strongly encouraged to print or electronically save a copy of the NEF. Attorneys can also verify the filing of documents by inspecting the Court's electronic docket sheet through the use of a PACER login. IN R USDCTSD ECF Procedures(7). When a document has been filed electronically: the notice of electronic filing for the document serves as the court's date-stamp and proof of filing. IN R USDCTSD L.R. 5-4(c)(4).

- The Court may, upon the motion of a party or upon its own motion, strike any inappropriately filed document. IN R USDCTSD ECF Procedures(7).

iv. For more information on electronic filing, refer to IN R USDCTSD ECF Procedures.

e. *Fax filing.* The clerk may not file a faxed document without court authorization. The court may not authorize the clerk to file faxed documents without finding that compelling circumstances justify it. A party must submit a copy of the document that otherwise complies with IN R USDCTSD L.R. 5-10 to replace the faxed copy within seven (7) days after faxing the document. IN R USDCTSD L.R. 5-10(e).

2. *Issuance of summons.* On or after filing the complaint, the plaintiff may present a summons to the clerk for signature and seal. If the summons is properly completed, the clerk must sign, seal, and issue it to the plaintiff for service on the defendant. A summons—or a copy of a summons that is addressed to multiple defendants—must be issued for each defendant to be served. FRCP 4(b).

a. *Amendments.* The court may permit a summons to be amended. FRCP 4(a)(2).

3. *Service requirements.* A summons must be served with a copy of the complaint. The plaintiff is responsible for having the summons and complaint served within the time allowed by FRCP 4(m) and must furnish the necessary copies to the person who makes service. FRCP 4(c)(1). Case initiating documents must be served in the traditional manner on paper. IN R USDCTSD L.R. 5-2(b); IN R USDCTSD ECF Procedures(6).

a. *By whom served.* Any person who is at least 18 years old and not a party may serve a summons and complaint. FRCP 4(c)(2).

i. *By a marshal or someone specially appointed.* At the plaintiff's request, the court may order that service be made by a United States marshal or deputy marshal or by a person specially appointed by the court. The court must so order if the plaintiff is authorized to proceed in forma pauperis under 28 U.S.C.A. § 1915 or as a seaman under 28 U.S.C.A. § 1916. FRCP 4(c)(3).

b. *Serving an individual within a judicial district of the United States.* Unless federal law provides otherwise, an individual—other than a minor, an incompetent person, or a person whose waiver has been filed—may be served in a judicial district of the United States by:

i. Following state law for serving a summons in an action brought in courts of general jurisdiction in the state where the district court is located or where service is made; or

ii. Doing any of the following:

- Delivering a copy of the summons and of the complaint to the individual personally;

- Leaving a copy of each at the individual's dwelling or usual place of abode with someone of suitable age and discretion who resides there; or

- Delivering a copy of each to an agent authorized by appointment or by law to receive service of process. FRCP 4(e).

c.   *Serving an individual in a foreign country.* Unless federal law provides otherwise, an individual— other than a minor, an incompetent person, or a person whose waiver has been filed—may be served at a place not within any judicial district of the United States:

   i.   By any internationally agreed means of service that is reasonably calculated to give notice, such as those authorized by the Hague Convention on the Service Abroad of Judicial and Extrajudicial Documents;

   ii. If there is no internationally agreed means, or if an international agreement allows but does not specify other means, by a method that is reasonably calculated to give notice:

- As prescribed by the foreign country's law for service in that country in an action in its courts of general jurisdiction;

- As the foreign authority directs in response to a letter rogatory or letter of request; or

- Unless prohibited by the foreign country's law, by: (1) delivering a copy of the summons and of the complaint to the individual personally; or (2) using any form of mail that the clerk addresses and sends to the individual and that requires a signed receipt; or

- By other means not prohibited by international agreement, as the court orders. FRCP 4(f).

d.   *Serving a minor or an incompetent person.* A minor or an incompetent person in a judicial district of the United States must be served by following state law for serving a summons or like process on such a defendant in an action brought in the courts of general jurisdiction of the state where service is made. A minor or an incompetent person who is not within any judicial district of the United States must be served in the manner prescribed by FRCP 4(f)(2)(A), FRCP 4(f)(2)(B), or FRCP 4(f)(3). FRCP 4(g).

e.   *Serving a corporation, partnership, or association.* Unless federal law provides otherwise or the defendant's waiver has been filed, a domestic or foreign corporation, or a partnership or other unincorporated association that is subject to suit under a common name, must be served:

   i.   In a judicial district of the United States:

- In the manner prescribed by FRCP 4(e)(1) for serving an individual; or

- By delivering a copy of the summons and of the complaint to an officer, a managing or general agent, or any other agent authorized by appointment or by law to receive service of process and—if the agent is one authorized by statute and the statute so requires—by also mailing a copy of each to the defendant; or

   ii. At a place not within any judicial district of the United States, in any manner prescribed by FRCP 4(f) for serving an individual, except personal delivery under FRCP 4(f)(2)(C)(i). FRCP 4(h).

f.   *Serving the United States and its agencies, corporations, officers, or employees*

   i.   *United States.* To serve the United States, a party must:

- Deliver a copy of the summons and of the complaint to the United States attorney for the district where the action is brought—or to an assistant United States attorney or clerical employee whom the United States attorney designates in a writing filed with the court clerk—or send a copy of each by registered or certified mail to the civil-process clerk at the United States attorney's office;

- Send a copy of each by registered or certified mail to the Attorney General of the United States at Washington, D.C.; and

- If the action challenges an order of a nonparty agency or officer of the United States, send a copy of each by registered or certified mail to the agency or officer. FRCP 4(i)(1).

   ii. *Agency; Corporation; Officer or employee sued in an official capacity.* To serve a United States agency or corporation, or a United States officer or employee sued only in an official capacity, a party must serve the United States and also send a copy of the summons and of the complaint by registered or certified mail to the agency, corporation, officer, or employee. FRCP 4(i)(2).

iii. *Officer or employee sued individually.* To serve a United States officer or employee sued in an individual capacity for an act or omission occurring in connection with duties performed on the United States' behalf (whether or not the officer or employee is also sued in an official capacity), a party must serve the United States and also serve the officer or employee under FRCP 4(e), FRCP 4(f), or FRCP 4(g). FRCP 4(i)(3).

iv. *Extending time.* The court must allow a party a reasonable time to cure its failure to:

- Serve a person required to be served under FRCP 4(i)(2), if the party has served either the United States attorney or the Attorney General of the United States; or
- Serve the United States under FRCP 4(i)(3), if the party has served the United States officer or employee. FRCP 4(i)(4).

g. *Serving a foreign, state, or local government*

i. *Foreign state.* A foreign state or its political subdivision, agency, or instrumentality must be served in accordance with 28 U.S.C.A. § 1608. FRCP 4(j)(1).

ii. *State or local government.* A state, a municipal corporation, or any other state-created governmental organization that is subject to suit must be served by:

- Delivering a copy of the summons and of the complaint to its chief executive officer; or
- Serving a copy of each in the manner prescribed by that state's law for serving a summons or like process on such a defendant. FRCP 4(j)(2).

h. *Notice by publication.* The clerk must send notices required to be published to the party originating the notice. The party must deliver the notice to the appropriate newspapers for publication. IN R USDCTSD L.R. 5-10(f).

i. *Territorial limits of effective service*

i. *In general.* Serving a summons or filing a waiver of service establishes personal jurisdiction over a defendant:

- Who is subject to the jurisdiction of a court of general jurisdiction in the state where the district court is located;
- Who is a party joined under FRCP 14 or FRCP 19 and is served within a judicial district of the United States and not more than one hundred (100) miles from where the summons was issued; or
- When authorized by a federal statute. FRCP 4(k)(1).

ii. *Federal claim outside state-court jurisdiction.* For a claim that arises under federal law, serving a summons or filing a waiver of service establishes personal jurisdiction over a defendant if:

- The defendant is not subject to jurisdiction in any state's courts of general jurisdiction; and
- Exercising jurisdiction is consistent with the United States Constitution and laws. FRCP 4(k)(2).

j. *Asserting jurisdiction over property or assets*

i. *Federal law.* The court may assert jurisdiction over property if authorized by a federal statute. Notice to claimants of the property must be given as provided in the statute or by serving a summons under FRCP 4. FRCP 4(n)(1).

ii. *State law.* On a showing that personal jurisdiction over a defendant cannot be obtained in the district where the action is brought by reasonable efforts to serve a summons under FRCP 4, the court may assert jurisdiction over the defendant's assets found in the district. Jurisdiction is acquired by seizing the assets under the circumstances and in the manner provided by state law in that district. FRCP 4(n)(2).

k. *Proving service*

i. *Affidavit required.* Unless service is waived, proof of service must be made to the court. Except for service by a United States marshal or deputy marshal, proof must be by the server's affidavit. FRCP 4(l)(1).

ii. *Service outside the United States.* Service not within any judicial district of the United States must be proved as follows:

- If made under FRCP 4(f)(1), as provided in the applicable treaty or convention; or

- If made under FRCP 4(f)(2) or FRCP 4(f)(3), by a receipt signed by the addressee, or by other evidence satisfying the court that the summons and complaint were delivered to the addressee. FRCP 4(l)(2).

iii. *Validity of service; Amending proof.* Failure to prove service does not affect the validity of service. The court may permit proof of service to be amended. FRCP 4(l)(3).

iv. *Results of filing a waiver of service.* When the plaintiff files a waiver, proof of service is not required and FRCP 4 applies as if a summons and complaint had been served at the time of filing the waiver. FRCP 4(d)(4).

l. *Service of other process.* For information on service of other process, refer to FRCP 4.1.

G. Hearings

1. There is no hearing contemplated in the federal statutes or rules for the complaint and summons.

H. Forms

1. Official Federal Complaint and Summons Forms

a. Rule 4 notice of a lawsuit and request to waive service of summons. FRCP 4.

2. Federal Complaint and Summons Forms

a. Summons. 2 FEDFORMS § 3:23.

b. Summons; With proof of service. 2 FEDFORMS § 3:24.

c. Summons; Suit against officers of the United States. 2 FEDFORMS § 3:26.

d. Request for summons. 2 FEDFORMS § 3:27.

e. Civil cover sheet. 2 FEDFORMS § 3:29.

f. Motion for appointment of person to serve process. 2 FEDFORMS § 3:30.

g. Motion for appointment of United States marshal to serve process. 2 FEDFORMS § 3:34.

h. Notice of lawsuit and request for waiver of service of summons and waiver of summons. 2 FEDFORMS § 3:36.

i. Motion for payment of costs of personal service. 2 FEDFORMS § 3:37.

j. Affidavit of personal service; Delivery to individual. 2 FEDFORMS § 3:54.

k. Declaration of service; Delivery to individual. 2 FEDFORMS § 3:55.

l. Declaration of service; Delivery at usual place of abode or residence. 2 FEDFORMS § 3:56.

m. Declaration of service; Service on corporation; Delivery to officer. 2 FEDFORMS § 3:57.

n. Declaration of service; Service on United States. 2 FEDFORMS § 3:69.

o. Declaration of service; Service on officer of United States. 2 FEDFORMS § 3:71.

p. Complaint. 2 FEDFORMS § 7:14.

q. Introductory clause; Single claim stated. 2 FEDFORMS § 7:16.

r. Introductory clause; Several claims stated in separate counts. 2 FEDFORMS § 7:18.

s. Allegations on information and belief. 2 FEDFORMS § 7:19.

t. General prayer for relief. 2 FEDFORMS § 7:21.

u. Disparate treatment; Sex discrimination; Sexual harassment and constructive discharge. 2A FEDFORMS § 7:143.

v. Against manufacturer for negligent design and manufacture. 2B FEDFORMS § 7:426.

w. Complaint; Single count. FEDPROF § 1:68.

x. Complaint; Multiple counts; With same jurisdictional basis. FEDPROF § 1:69.

y. Complaint; Multiple counts; With different jurisdictional basis for each. FEDPROF § 1:70.

z. Civil cover sheet; General form (form JS-44). FEDPROF § 1:144.

3. Forms for the Southern District of Indiana

a. Notice of endorsement. IN R USDCTSD ECF Procedures(Appendix B).

b. Notice of manual filing. IN R USDCTSD ECF Procedures(Appendix C).

c. Declaration that party was unable to file in a timely manner due to technical difficulties. IN R USDCTSD ECF Procedures(Appendix D).

I. Applicable Rules

1. *Federal rules*

a. District court; Filing and miscellaneous fees; Rules of court. 28 U.S.C.A. § 1914.

b. Commencing an action. FRCP 3.

c. Summons. FRCP 4.

d. Serving and filing pleadings and other papers. FRCP 5.

e. Constitutional challenge to a statute; Notice, certification, and intervention. FRCP 5.1.

f. Privacy protection for filings made with the court. FRCP 5.2.

g. Computing and extending time; Time for motion papers. FRCP 6.

h. Pleadings allowed; Form of motions and other papers. FRCP 7.

i. Disclosure statement. FRCP 7.1.

j. General rules of pleading. FRCP 8.

k. Pleading special matters. FRCP 9.

l. Form of pleadings. FRCP 10.

m. Signing pleadings, motions, and other papers; Representations to the court; Sanctions. FRCP 11.

n. Joinder of claims. FRCP 18.

o. Required joinder of parties. FRCP 19.

p. Permissive joinder of parties. FRCP 20.

q. Misjoinder and nonjoinder of parties. FRCP 21.

r. Right to a jury trial; Demand. FRCP 38.

s. Determining foreign law. FRCP 44.1.

2. *Local rules*

a. Scope of the rules. IN R USDCTSD L.R. 1-1.

b. Sanctions for errors as to form. IN R USDCTSD L.R. 1-3.

c. Format of documents presented for filing. IN R USDCTSD L.R. 5-1.

d. Constitutional challenge to a statute; Notice. IN R USDCTSD L.R. 5.1-1.

e. Filing of documents electronically required. IN R USDCTSD L.R. 5-2.

f. Eligibility, registration, passwords for electronic filing; Exemption from electronic filing. IN R USDCTSD L.R. 5-3.

g. Timing and consequences of electronic filing. IN R USDCTSD L.R. 5-4.

h. Attachments and exhibits in cases filed electronically. IN R USDCTSD L.R. 5-6.

i. Signatures in cases filed electronically. IN R USDCTSD L.R. 5-7.

j. Non-electronic filings. IN R USDCTSD L.R. 5-10.

k. Motion practice. [IN R USDCTSD L.R. 7-1, as amended by IN ORDER 16-2319, effective December 1, 2016].

l. Pro se complaints. IN R USDCTSD L.R. 8-1.

m. Request for three-judge court. IN R USDCTSD L.R. 9-2.

n. Designation of "class action" in the caption. IN R USDCTSD L.R. 23-1.

o. Jury demand. IN R USDCTSD L.R. 38-1.

p. Assignment of cases. IN R USDCTSD L.R. 40-1.

q. Alternative dispute resolution. IN R USDCTSD A.D.R. Rule 1.1; IN R USDCTSD A.D.R. Rule 1.2; IN R USDCTSD A.D.R. Rule 1.5; IN R USDCTSD A.D.R. Rule 2.1; IN R USDCTSD A.D.R. Rule 2.2.

r. Instructions for preparing case management plan. IN R USDCTSD Case Mgt.

s. Electronic case filing policies and procedures manual. IN R USDCTSD ECF Procedures.

Pleadings
Answer

Document Last Updated December 2016

A. **Checklist**

(I) ❏ Matters to be considered by plaintiff

  (a) ❏ Required documents

    (1) ❏ Civil cover sheet

    (2) ❏ Complaint

    (3) ❏ Summons

    (4) ❏ Filing fee

    (5) ❏ Affidavit proving service

  (b) ❏ Supplemental documents

    (1) ❏ Notice and request for waiver of service

    (2) ❏ Notice of constitutional question

    (3) ❏ Notice of issue concerning foreign law

    (4) ❏ Nongovernmental corporate disclosure statement

    (5) ❏ Request for three-judge court

    (6) ❏ Index of exhibits

    (7) ❏ Copy of document with self-address envelope

    (8) ❏ Notice of manual filing

    (9) ❏ Courtesy copies

    (10) ❏ Copies for three-judge court

    (11) ❏ Declaration that party was unable to file in a timely manner due to technical difficulties

  (c) ❏ Timing

    (1) ❏ A civil action is commenced by filing a complaint with the court

    (2) ❏ If a defendant is not served within ninety (90) days after the complaint is filed, the court—on

motion or on its own after notice to the plaintiff—must dismiss the action without prejudice against that defendant or order that service be made within a specified time

    (3) ❏ When a party who is not exempt from the electronic filing requirement files a document directly with the clerk, the party must present the document to the clerk within one (1) business day after filing the notice of manual filing

    (4) ❏ Unless the court orders otherwise, the [untimely] document and declaration [that party was unable to file in a timely manner due to technical difficulties] must be filed no later than 12:00 noon of the first day on which the court is open for business following the original filing deadline

(II) ❏ Matters to be considered by defendant

  (a) ❏ Required documents

    (1) ❏ Answer

    (2) ❏ Certificate of service

  (b) ❏ Supplemental documents

    (1) ❏ Waiver of the service of summons

    (2) ❏ Notice of constitutional question

    (3) ❏ Notice of issue concerning foreign law

    (4) ❏ Nongovernmental corporate disclosure statement

    (5) ❏ Request for three-judge court

    (6) ❏ Index of exhibits

    (7) ❏ Copy of document with self-address envelope

    (8) ❏ Notice of manual filing

    (9) ❏ Courtesy copies

    (10) ❏ Copies for three-judge court

    (11) ❏ Declaration that party was unable to file in a timely manner due to technical difficulties

  (c) ❏ Timing

    (1) ❏ A defendant must serve an answer:

      (i) ❏ Within twenty-one (21) days after being served with the summons and complaint; or

      (ii) ❏ If it has timely waived service under FRCP 4(d), within sixty (60) days after the request for a waiver was sent, or within ninety (90) days after it was sent to the defendant outside any judicial district of the United States

    (2) ❏ The United States, a United States agency, or a United States officer or employee sued only in an official capacity must serve an answer to a complaint, counterclaim, or crossclaim within sixty (60) days after service on the United States attorney

    (3) ❏ A United States officer or employee sued in an individual capacity for an act or omission occurring in connection with duties performed on the United States' behalf must serve an answer to a complaint, counterclaim, or crossclaim within sixty (60) days after service on the officer or employee or service on the United States attorney, whichever is later

    (4) ❏ Unless the court sets a different time, serving a motion under FRCP 12 alters these periods as follows:

      (i) ❏ If the court denies the motion or postpones its disposition until trial, the responsive pleading must be served within fourteen (14) days after notice of the court's action; or

      (ii) ❏ If the court grants a motion for a more definite statement, the responsive pleading must be served within fourteen (14) days after the more definite statement is served

    (5) ❏ Defendant is given a reasonable time of at least thirty (30) days after a waiver of service

request is sent—or at least sixty (60) days if sent to defendant outside any judicial district of the United States—to return the waiver

(6) ❑ When a party who is not exempt from the electronic filing requirement files a document directly with the clerk, the party must present the document to the clerk within one (1) business day after filing the notice of manual filing

(7) ❑ Unless the court orders otherwise, the [untimely] document and declaration [that party was unable to file in a timely manner due to technical difficulties] must be filed no later than 12:00 noon of the first day on which the court is open for business following the original filing deadline

B. Timing

1. *Answer.* Unless another time is specified by FRCP 12 or a federal statute. . .a defendant must serve an answer: (1) within twenty-one (21) days after being served with the summons and complaint; or (2) if it has timely waived service under FRCP 4(d), within sixty (60) days after the request for a waiver was sent, or within ninety (90) days after it was sent to the defendant outside any judicial district of the United States. FRCP 12(a)(1)(A).

   a. *Time to serve other responsive pleadings.* Unless another time is specified by FRCP 12 or a federal statute, the time for serving a responsive pleading is as follows:

      i. *Answer to counterclaim or crossclaim.* A party must serve an answer to a counterclaim or crossclaim within twenty-one (21) days after being served with the pleading that states the counterclaim or crossclaim. FRCP 12(a)(1)(B).

      ii. *Reply to an answer.* A party must serve a reply to an answer within twenty-one (21) days after being served with an order to reply, unless the order specifies a different time. FRCP 12(a)(1)(C).

   b. *United States and its agencies, officers, or employees sued in an official capacity.* The United States, a United States agency, or a United States officer or employee sued only in an official capacity must serve an answer to a complaint, counterclaim, or crossclaim within sixty (60) days after service on the United States attorney. FRCP 12(a)(2).

   c. *United States officers or employees sued in an individual capacity.* A United States officer or employee sued in an individual capacity for an act or omission occurring in connection with duties performed on the United States' behalf must serve an answer to a complaint, counterclaim, or crossclaim within sixty (60) days after service on the officer or employee or service on the United States attorney, whichever is later. FRCP 12(a)(3).

   d. *Effect of a FRCP 12 motion on the time to serve a responsive pleading.* Unless the court sets a different time, serving a motion under FRCP 12 alters the periods in FRCP 12(a) as follows:

      i. If the court denies the motion or postpones its disposition until trial, the responsive pleading must be served within fourteen (14) days after notice of the court's action; or

      ii. If the court grants a motion for a more definite statement, the responsive pleading must be served within fourteen (14) days after the more definite statement is served. FRCP 12(a)(4).

2. *Waiver of service.* The notice and request for waiver must give the defendant a reasonable time of at least thirty (30) days after the request was sent—or at least sixty (60) days if sent to defendant outside any judicial district of the United States—to return the waiver. FRCP 4(d)(1)(F).

   a. *Time to answer after a waiver.* A defendant who, before being served with process, timely returns a waiver need not serve an answer to the complaint until sixty (60) days after the request was sent—or until ninety (90) days after it was sent to the defendant outside any judicial district of the United States. FRCP 4(d)(3).

3. *Document filing by non-exempt party.* When a party who is not exempt from the electronic filing requirement files a document directly with the clerk, the party must: present the document to the clerk within one (1) business day after filing the notice of manual filing. IN R USDCTSD L.R. 5-2(d)(2).

4. *Declaration that party was unable to file in a timely manner due to technical difficulties.* Unless the Court

orders otherwise, the [untimely] document and declaration [that party was unable to file in a timely manner due to technical difficulties] must be filed no later than 12:00 noon of the first day on which the Court is open for business following the original filing deadline. IN R USDCTSD ECF Procedures(16).

5. *Automatic initial extension.* The deadline for filing a response to a pleading or to any written request for discovery or admissions will automatically be extended upon filing a notice of the extension with the court that states: (1) the deadline has not been previously extended; (2) the extension is for twenty-eight (28) or fewer days; (3) the extension does not interfere with the Case Management Plan, scheduled hearings, or other case deadlines; (4) the original deadline and extended deadline; (5) that all opposing counsel the filing attorney could reach agreed to the extension; or that the filing attorney could not reach any opposing counsel, and providing the dates, times and manner of all attempts to reach opposing counsel. IN R USDCTSD L.R. 6-1(b).

    a. *Pro se parties.* The automatic initial extension does not apply to pro se parties. IN R USDCTSD L.R. 6-1(c).

6. *Computation of time*

    a. *Computing time.* FRCP 6 applies in computing any time period specified in the Federal Rules of Civil Procedure, in any local rule or court order, or in any statute that does not specify a method of computing time. FRCP 6(a).

        i. *Period stated in days or a longer unit.* When the period is stated in days or a longer unit of time:

- Exclude the day of the event that triggers the period;
- Count every day, including intermediate Saturdays, Sundays, and legal holidays; and
- Include the last day of the period, but if the last day is a Saturday, Sunday, or legal holiday, the period continues to run until the end of the day that is not a Saturday, Sunday, or legal holiday. FRCP 6(a)(1).

        ii. *Period stated in hours.* When the period is stated in hours:

- Begin counting immediately on the occurrence of the event that triggers the period;
- Count every hour, including hours during intermediate Saturdays, Sundays, and legal holidays; and
- If the period would end on a Saturday, Sunday, or legal holiday, the period continues to run until the same time on the next day that is not a Saturday, Sunday, or legal holiday. FRCP 6(a)(2).

        iii. *Inaccessibility of the clerk's office.* Unless the court orders otherwise, if the clerk's office is inaccessible:

- On the last day for filing under FRCP 6(a)(1), then the time for filing is extended to the first accessible day that is not a Saturday, Sunday, or legal holiday; or
- During the last hour for filing under FRCP 6(a)(2), then the time for filing is extended to the same time on the first accessible day that is not a Saturday, Sunday, or legal holiday. FRCP 6(a)(3).

        iv. *"Last day" defined.* Unless a different time is set by a statute, local rule, or court order, the last day ends:

- For electronic filing, at midnight in the court's time zone; and
- For filing by other means, when the clerk's office is scheduled to close. FRCP 6(a)(4).

        v. *"Next day" defined.* The "next day" is determined by continuing to count forward when the period is measured after an event and backward when measured before an event. FRCP 6(a)(5).

        vi. *"Legal holiday" defined.* "Legal holiday" means:

- The day set aside by statute for observing New Year's Day, Martin Luther King Jr.'s Birthday, Washington's Birthday, Memorial Day, Independence Day, Labor Day, Columbus Day, Veterans' Day, Thanksgiving Day, or Christmas Day;

- Any day declared a holiday by the President or Congress; and
- For periods that are measured after an event, any other day declared a holiday by the state where the district court is located. FRCP 6(a)(6).

b. *Computation of electronic filing deadlines.* Filing documents electronically does not alter filing deadlines. IN R USDCTSD ECF Procedures(7). A document due on a particular day must be filed before midnight local time of the division where the case is pending. IN R USDCTSD L.R. 5-4(a). All electronic transmissions of documents must be completed (i.e. received completely by the Clerk's Office) prior to midnight of the local time of the division in which the case is pending in order to be considered timely filed that day (NOTE: time will be noted in Eastern Time on the Court's docket. If you have filed a document prior to midnight local time of the division in which the case is pending and the document is due that date, but the electronic receipt and docket reflect the following calendar day, please contact the Court). IN R USDCTSD ECF Procedures(7). Although attorneys may file documents electronically twenty-four (24) hours a day, seven (7) days a week, attorneys are encouraged to file all documents during the normal working hours of the Clerk's Office (Monday through Friday, 8:30 a.m. to 4:30 p.m.) when technical support is available. IN R USDCTSD ECF Procedures(7); IN R USDCTSD ECF Procedures(9).

   i. *Technical difficulties.* Parties are encouraged to file documents electronically during normal business hours, in case a problem is encountered. In the event a technical failure occurs and a document cannot be filed electronically despite the best efforts of the filing party, the party should print (if possible) a copy of the error message received. In addition, as soon as practically possible, the party should file a "Declaration that Party was Unable to File in a Timely Manner Due to Technical Difficulties." A model form is provided as Appendix D (IN R USDCTSD ECF Procedures(Appendix D)). IN R USDCTSD ECF Procedures(16).

   - If a party is unable to file electronically and, as a result, may miss a filing deadline, the party must contact the Clerk's Office at the number listed in IN R USDCTSD ECF Procedures(15) to inform the court's staff of the difficulty. If a party misses a filing deadline due to an inability to file electronically, the party may submit the untimely filed document, accompanied by a declaration stating the reason(s) for missing the deadline. Unless the Court orders otherwise, the document and declaration must be filed no later than 12:00 noon of the first day on which the Court is open for business following the original filing deadline. IN R USDCTSD ECF Procedures(16).

c. *Extending time*

   i. *In general.* When an act may or must be done within a specified time, the court may, for good cause, extend the time:

   - With or without motion or notice if the court acts, or if a request is made, before the original time or its extension expires; or

   - On motion made after the time has expired if the party failed to act because of excusable neglect. FRCP 6(b)(1).

   ii. *Exceptions.* A court must not extend the time to act under FRCP 50(b), FRCP 50(d), FRCP 52(b), FRCP 59(b), FRCP 59(d), FRCP 59(e), and FRCP 60(b). FRCP 6(b)(2).

   iii. Refer to the United States District Court for the Southern District of Indiana KeyRules Motion for Continuance/Extension of Time document for more information on extending time.

d. *Additional time after certain kinds of service.* When a party may or must act within a specified time after being served and service is made under FRCP 5(b)(2)(C) (mail), FRCP 5(b)(2)(D) (leaving with the clerk), or FRCP 5(b)(2)(F) (other means consented to), three (3) days are added after the period would otherwise expire under FRCP 6(a). FRCP 6(d). Service by electronic mail shall constitute service pursuant to FRCP 5(b)(2)(E) and shall entitle the party being served to the additional three (3) days provided by FRCP 6(d). IN R USDCTSD ECF Procedures(11).

C. General Requirements

1. *Pleading, generally*

   a. *Pleadings allowed.* Only these pleadings are allowed: (1) a complaint; (2) an answer to a complaint;

(3) an answer to a counterclaim designated as a counterclaim; (4) an answer to a crossclaim; (5) a third-party complaint; (6) an answer to a third-party complaint; and (7) if the court orders one, a reply to an answer. FRCP 7(a).

b. *Pleading to be concise and direct.* Each allegation must be simple, concise, and direct. No technical form is required. FRCP 8(d)(1).

c. *Alternative statements of a claim or defense.* A party may set out two or more statements of a claim or defense alternatively or hypothetically, either in a single count or defense or in separate ones. If a party makes alternative statements, the pleading is sufficient if any one of them is sufficient. FRCP 8(d)(2).

d. *Inconsistent claims or defenses.* A party may state as many separate claims or defenses as it has, regardless of consistency. FRCP 8(d)(3).

e. *Construing pleadings.* Pleadings must be construed so as to do justice. FRCP 8(e).

2. *Pleading special matters*

   a. *Capacity or authority to sue; Legal existence*

      i. *In general.* Except when required to show that the court has jurisdiction, a pleading need not allege:

         - A party's capacity to sue or be sued;
         - A party's authority to sue or be sued in a representative capacity; or
         - The legal existence of an organized association of persons that is made a party. FRCP 9(a)(1).

      ii. *Raising those issues.* To raise any of those issues, a party must do so by a specific denial, which must state any supporting facts that are peculiarly within the party's knowledge. FRCP 9(a)(2).

   b. *Fraud or mistake; Conditions of mind.* In alleging fraud or mistake, a party must state with particularity the circumstances constituting fraud or mistake. Malice, intent, knowledge, and other conditions of a person's mind may be alleged generally. FRCP 9(b).

   c. *Conditions precedent.* In pleading conditions precedent, it suffices to allege generally that all conditions precedent have occurred or been performed. But when denying that a condition precedent has occurred or been performed, a party must do so with particularity. FRCP 9(c).

   d. *Official document or act.* In pleading an official document or official act, it suffices to allege that the document was legally issued or the act legally done. FRCP 9(d).

   e. *Judgment.* In pleading a judgment or decision of a domestic or foreign court, a judicial or quasi-judicial tribunal, or a board or officer, it suffices to plead the judgment or decision without showing jurisdiction to render it. FRCP 9(e).

   f. *Time and place.* An allegation of time or place is material when testing the sufficiency of a pleading. FRCP 9(f).

   g. *Special damages.* If an item of special damage is claimed, it must be specifically stated. FRCP 9(g).

   h. *Admiralty or maritime claim*

      i. *How designated.* If a claim for relief is within the admiralty or maritime jurisdiction and also within the court's subject-matter jurisdiction on some other ground, the pleading may designate the claim as an admiralty or maritime claim for purposes of FRCP 14(c), FRCP 38(e), and FRCP 82 and the Supplemental Rules for Admiralty or Maritime Claims and Asset Forfeiture Actions. A claim cognizable only in the admiralty or maritime jurisdiction is an admiralty or maritime claim for those purposes, whether or not so designated. FRCP 9(h)(1).

      ii. *Designation for appeal.* A case that includes an admiralty or maritime claim within FRCP 9(h) is an admiralty case within 28 U.S.C.A. § 1292(a)(3). FRCP 9(h)(2).

3. *Answer*

   a. *Defenses; Admissions and denials*

      i. *In general.* In responding to a pleading, a party must: (1) state in short and plain terms its defenses to each claim asserted against it; and (2) admit or deny the allegations asserted against it by an opposing party. FRCP 8(b)(1).

- The purpose of an answer is to formulate issues by means of defenses addressed to the allegations of the complaint, and to give the plaintiff notice of the defenses he or she will be called upon to meet. FEDPROC § 62:70; Lopez v. U.S. Fidelity & Guaranty Co., 15 Alaska 633, 18 F.R.D. 59 (1955); Moriarty v. Curran, 18 F.R.D. 461 (S.D.N.Y. 1956).

- An answer is adequate where it accomplishes these purposes, even if it contains general and specific denials and at the same time asserts additional facts by way of justification or explanation, and even if it sets forth conclusions of law. FEDPROC § 62:70; Johnston v. Jones, 178 F.2d 481 (3d Cir. 1949); Burke v. Mesta Mach. Co., 5 F.R.D. 134 (W.D.Pa. 1946).

ii. *Denials; Responding to the substance.* A denial must fairly respond to the substance of the allegation. FRCP 8(b)(2).

iii. *General and specific denials.* A party that intends in good faith to deny all the allegations of a pleading—including the jurisdictional grounds—may do so by a general denial. A party that does not intend to deny all the allegations must either specifically deny designated allegations or generally deny all except those specifically admitted. FRCP 8(b)(3).

iv. *Denying part of an allegation.* A party that intends in good faith to deny only part of an allegation must admit the part that is true and deny the rest. FRCP 8(b)(4).

v. *Lacking knowledge or information.* A party that lacks knowledge or information sufficient to form a belief about the truth of an allegation must so state, and the statement has the effect of a denial. FRCP 8(b)(5).

- An answer merely stating that the defendant lacks knowledge to form a belief as to the plaintiff's allegations, and making no statement as to his or her lack of information, has been held to be insufficient, the court suggesting that the phrase might be used in an attempt to mask the defendant's inability to make a good-faith denial of the allegations. FEDPROC § 62:73; Gilbert v. Johnston, 127 F.R.D. 145 (N.D.Ill. 1989).

vi. *Effect of failing to deny.* An allegation—other than one relating to the amount of damages—is admitted if a responsive pleading is required and the allegation is not denied. If a responsive pleading is not required, an allegation is considered denied or avoided. FRCP 8(b)(6).

b. *Affirmative defenses.* In responding to a pleading, a party must affirmatively state any avoidance or affirmative defense, including: (1) accord and satisfaction; (2) arbitration and award; (3) assumption of risk; (4) contributory negligence; (5) duress; (6) estoppel; (7) failure of consideration; (8) fraud; (9) illegality; (10) injury by fellow servant; (11) laches; (12) license; (13) payment; (14) release; (15) res judicata; (16) statute of frauds; (17) statute of limitations; and (18) waiver. FRCP 8(c)(1).

i. *Mistaken designation.* If a party mistakenly designates a defense as a counterclaim, or a counterclaim as a defense, the court must, if justice requires, treat the pleading as though it were correctly designated, and may impose terms for doing so. FRCP 8(c)(2).

c. *How to present defenses.* Every defense to a claim for relief in any pleading must be asserted in the responsive pleading if one is required. But a party may assert the following defenses by motion: (1) lack of subject-matter jurisdiction; (2) lack of personal jurisdiction; (3) improper venue; (4) insufficient process; (5) insufficient service of process; (6) failure to state a claim upon which relief can be granted; and (7) failure to join a party under FRCP 19. FRCP 12(b).

i. A motion asserting any of these defenses must be made before pleading if a responsive pleading is allowed. If a pleading sets out a claim for relief that does not require a responsive pleading, an opposing party may assert at trial any defense to that claim. FRCP 12(b).

ii. Refer to the United States District Court for the Southern District of Indiana KeyRules Motion to Dismiss for Lack of Subject Matter Jurisdiction, Motion to Dismiss for Lack of Personal Jurisdiction, Motion to Dismiss for Improper Venue, and Motion to Dismiss for Failure to State a Claim documents for more information on motions under FRCP 12(b)(1), FRCP 12(b)(2), FRCP 12(b)(3), and FRCP 12(b)(6).

d. *Waiving and preserving certain defenses.* No defense or objection is waived by joining it with one or more other defenses or objections in a responsive pleading or in a motion. FRCP 12(b).

   i. *When some are waived.* A party waives any defense listed in FRCP 12(b)(2) through FRCP 12(b)(5) by:

- Omitting it from a motion in the circumstances described in FRCP 12(g)(2); or

- Failing to either: (1) make it by motion under FRCP 12; or (2) include it in a responsive pleading or in an amendment allowed by FRCP 15(a)(1) as a matter of course. FRCP 12(h)(1).

   ii. *When to raise others.* Failure to state a claim upon which relief can be granted, to join a person required by FRCP 19(b), or to state a legal defense to a claim may be raised:

- In any pleading allowed or ordered under FRCP 7(a);

- By a motion under FRCP 12(c); or

- At trial. FRCP 12(h)(2).

   iii. *Lack of subject matter jurisdiction.* If the court determines at any time that it lacks subject-matter jurisdiction, the court must dismiss the action. FRCP 12(h)(3).

4. *Counterclaim and crossclaim*

  a. *Compulsory counterclaim*

   i. *In general.* A pleading must state as a counterclaim any claim that—at the time of its service—the pleader has against an opposing party if the claim:

- Arises out of the transaction or occurrence that is the subject matter of the opposing party's claim; and

- Does not require adding another party over whom the court cannot acquire jurisdiction. FRCP 13(a)(1).

   ii. *Exceptions.* The pleader need not state the claim if:

- When the action was commenced, the claim was the subject of another pending action; or

- The opposing party sued on its claim by attachment or other process that did not establish personal jurisdiction over the pleader on that claim, and the pleader does not assert any counterclaim under FRCP 13. FRCP 13(a)(2).

  b. *Permissive counterclaim.* A pleading may state as a counterclaim against an opposing party any claim that is not compulsory. FRCP 13(b).

  c. *Relief sought in a counterclaim.* A counterclaim need not diminish or defeat the recovery sought by the opposing party. It may request relief that exceeds in amount or differs in kind from the relief sought by the opposing party. FRCP 13(c).

  d. *Counterclaim against the United States.* The Federal Rules of Civil Procedure do not expand the right to assert a counterclaim—or to claim a credit—against the United States or a United States officer or agency. FRCP 13(d).

  e. *Counterclaim maturing or acquired after pleading.* The court may permit a party to file a supplemental pleading asserting a counterclaim that matured or was acquired by the party after serving an earlier pleading. FRCP 13(e).

  f. *Crossclaim against a coparty.* A pleading may state as a crossclaim any claim by one party against a coparty if the claim arises out of the transaction or occurrence that is the subject matter of the original action or of a counterclaim, or if the claim relates to any property that is the subject matter of the original action. The crossclaim may include a claim that the coparty is or may be liable to the cross-claimant for all or part of a claim asserted in the action against the cross-claimant. FRCP 13(g).

  g. *Joining additional parties.* FRCP 19 and FRCP 20 govern the addition of a person as a party to a counterclaim or crossclaim. FRCP 13(h).

  h. *Separate trials; Separate judgments.* If the court orders separate trials under FRCP 42(b), it may enter judgment on a counterclaim or crossclaim under FRCP 54(b) when it has jurisdiction to do so, even if the opposing party's claims have been dismissed or otherwise resolved. FRCP 13(i).

5. *Third-party practice*

a. *Timing of the summons and complaint.* A defending party may, as third-party plaintiff, serve a summons and complaint on a nonparty who is or may be liable to it for all or part of the claim against it. But the third-party plaintiff must, by motion, obtain the court's leave if it files the third-party complaint more than fourteen (14) days after serving its original answer. FRCP 14(a)(1).

b. *Third-party defendant's claims and defenses.* The person served with the summons and third-party complaint—the "third-party defendant":

   i. Must assert any defense against the third-party plaintiff's claim under FRCP 12;

   ii. Must assert any counterclaim against the third-party plaintiff under FRCP 13(a), and may assert any counterclaim against the third-party plaintiff under FRCP 13(b) or any crossclaim against another third-party defendant under FRCP 13(g);

   iii. May assert against the plaintiff any defense that the third-party plaintiff has to the plaintiff's claim; and

   iv. May also assert against the plaintiff any claim arising out of the transaction or occurrence that is the subject matter of the plaintiff's claim against the third-party plaintiff. FRCP 14(a)(2).

c. For more information on third-party practice, refer to FRCP 14.

6. *Right to a jury trial; Demand*

a. *Right preserved.* The right of trial by jury as declared by U.S.C.A. Const. Amend. VII, or as provided by a federal statute, is preserved to the parties inviolate. FRCP 38(a).

b. *Demand.* On any issue triable of right by a jury, a party may demand a jury trial by:

   i. Serving the other parties with a written demand—which may be included in a pleading—no later than fourteen (14) days after the last pleading directed to the issue is served; and

   ii. Filing the demand in accordance with FRCP 5(d). FRCP 38(b).

c. *Specifying issues.* In its demand, a party may specify the issues that it wishes to have tried by a jury; otherwise, it is considered to have demanded a jury trial on all the issues so triable. If the party has demanded a jury trial on only some issues, any other party may—within fourteen (14) days after being served with the demand or within a shorter time ordered by the court—serve a demand for a jury trial on any other or all factual issues triable by jury. FRCP 38(c).

d. *Waiver; Withdrawal.* A party waives a jury trial unless its demand is properly served and filed. A proper demand may be withdrawn only if the parties consent. FRCP 38(d).

e. *Admiralty and maritime claims.* The rules in FRCP 38 do not create a right to a jury trial on issues in a claim that is an admiralty or maritime claim under FRCP 9(h). FRCP 38(e).

7. *Appearances.* Every attorney who represents a party or who files a document on a party's behalf must file an appearance for that party. IN R USDCTSD L.R. 83-7. The filing of a Notice of Appearance shall act to establish the filing attorney as an attorney of record representing a designated party or parties in a particular cause of action. As a result, it is necessary for each attorney to file a separate Notice of Appearance when entering an appearance in a case. A joint appearance on behalf of multiple attorneys may be filed electronically only if it is filed separately for each attorney, using his/her ECF login. IN R USDCTSD ECF Procedures(12). Only those attorneys who have filed an appearance in a pending action are entitled to be served with case documents under FRCP 5(a). IN R USDCTSD L.R. 83-7. For more information, refer to IN R USDCTSD L.R. 83-7 and IN R USDCTSD ECF Procedures(12).

8. *Notice of related action.* A party must file a notice of related action: as soon as it appears that the party's case and another pending case: (1) arise out of the same transaction or occurrence; (2) involve the same property; or (3) involve the validity or infringement or the same patent, trademark, or copyright. IN R USDCTSD L.R. 40-1(d)(2). For more information, refer to IN R USDCTSD L.R. 40-1.

9. *Alternative dispute resolution (ADR)*

a. *Application.* Unless limited by specific provisions, or unless there are other applicable specific

statutory, common law, or constitutional procedures, the Local Alternative Dispute Resolution Rules of the United States District Court for the Southern District of Indiana shall apply in all civil litigation filed in the U.S. District Court for the Southern District of Indiana, except in the following cases and proceedings:

    i. Applications for writs of habeas corpus under 28 U.S.C.A. § 2254;

    ii. Forfeiture cases;

    iii. Non-adversary proceedings in bankruptcy;

    iv. Social Security administrative review cases; and

    v. Such other matters as specified by order of the Court; for example, matters involving important public policy issues, constitutional law, or the establishment of new law. IN R USDCTSD A.D.R. Rule 1.2.

b. *Mediation.* Mediation under this section (IN R USDCTSD A.D.R. Rule 2.1, et seq.) involves the confidential process by which a person acting as a Mediator, selected by the parties or appointed by the Court, assists the litigants in reaching a mutually acceptable agreement. It is an informal and nonadversarial process. The role of the Mediator is to assist in identifying the issues, reducing misunderstandings, clarifying priorities, exploring areas of compromise, and finding points of agreement as well as legitimate points of disagreement. Final decision-making authority rests with the parties, not the Mediator. IN R USDCTSD A.D.R. Rule 2.1. It is anticipated that an agreement may not resolve all of the disputed issues, but the process, nonetheless, can reduce points of contention. Parties and their representatives are required to mediate in good faith, but are not compelled to reach an agreement. IN R USDCTSD A.D.R. Rule 2.1.

    i. *Case selection.* The Court with the agreement of the parties may refer a civil case for mediation. Unless otherwise ordered or as specifically provided in IN R USDCTSD A.D.R. Rule 2.8, referral to mediation does not abate or suspend the action, and no scheduled dates shall be delayed or deferred, including the date of trial. IN R USDCTSD A.D.R. Rule 2.2.

    ii. For more information on mediation, refer to IN R USDCTSD A.D.R. Rule 2.1, et seq.

c. *Other methods of dispute resolution.* The Local Alternative Dispute Resolution Rules of the United States District Court for the Southern District of Indiana shall not preclude the parties from utilizing any other reasonable method or technique of alternative dispute resolution to resolve disputes to which the parties agree. However, any use of arbitration by the parties will be governed by and comply with the requirements of 28 U.S.C.A. § 654 through 28 U.S.C.A. § 657. IN R USDCTSD A.D.R. Rule 1.5.

d. For more information on alternative dispute resolution (ADR), refer to IN R USDCTSD A.D.R. Rule 1.1, et seq.

10. *Notice of settlement or resolution.* The parties must immediately notify the court if they reasonably anticipate settling their case or resolving a pending motion. IN R USDCTSD L.R. 7-1(h).

11. *Modification or suspension of rules.* The court may, on its own motion or at the request of a party, suspend or modify any rule in a particular case in the interest of justice. IN R USDCTSD L.R. 1-1(c).

D. Documents

1. *Required documents*

    a. *Answer.* Refer to the General Requirements section of this document for information on the form and contents of the answer.

    b. *Certificate of service.* FRCP 5(d) requires that the person making service under FRCP 5 certify that service has been effected. FRCP 5(Advisory Committee Notes). Having such information on file may be useful for many purposes, including proof of service if an issue arises concerning the effectiveness of the service. FRCP 5(Advisory Committee Notes).

        i. *Certificate of service for electronically-filed documents.* A certificate of service must be included with all documents filed electronically. Such certificate shall indicate that service was accomplished pursuant to the Court's electronic filing procedures. IN R USDCTSD ECF

Procedures(11). For the suggested format for a certificate of service for electronic filing, refer to IN R USDCTSD ECF Procedures(11).

2. *Supplemental documents*

   a. *Waiver of the service of summons.* An individual, corporation, or association that is subject to service under FRCP 4(e), FRCP 4(f), or FRCP 4(h) has a duty to avoid unnecessary expenses of serving the summons. FRCP 4(d)(1). Waiving service of a summons does not waive any objection to personal jurisdiction or to venue. FRCP 4(d)(5). If a defendant located within the United States fails, without good cause, to sign and return a waiver requested by a plaintiff located within the United States, the court must impose on the defendant:

      i. The expenses later incurred in making service; and

      ii. The reasonable expenses, including attorney's fees, of any motion required to collect those service expenses. FRCP 4(d)(2).

   b. *Notice of constitutional question.* A party that files a pleading, written motion, or other paper drawing into question the constitutionality of a federal or state statute must promptly:

      i. *File notice.* File a notice of constitutional question stating the question and identifying the paper that raises it, if:

- A federal statute is questioned and the parties do not include the United States, one of its agencies, or one of its officers or employees in an official capacity; or

- A state statute is questioned and the parties do not include the state, one of its agencies, or one of its officers or employees in an official capacity; and

      ii. *Serve notice.* Serve the notice and paper on the Attorney General of the United States if a federal statute is questioned—or on the state attorney general if a state statute is questioned—either by certified or registered mail or by sending it to an electronic address designated by the attorney general for this purpose. FRCP 5.1(a).

      iii. *Time for filing.* A notice of constitutional challenge to a statute filed in accordance with FRCP 5.1 must be filed at the same time the parties tender their proposed case management plan, if one is required, or within twenty-one (21) days of the filing drawing into question the constitutionality of a federal or state statute, whichever occurs later. IN R USDCTSD L.R. 5.1-1(a).

      iv. *Additional service requirements.* If a federal statute is challenged, in addition to the service requirements of FRCP 5.1(a), the party filing the notice of constitutional challenge must serve the notice and documents on the United States Attorney for the Southern District of Indiana, either by certified or registered mail or by sending it to an electronic address designated for that purpose by that official. IN R USDCTSD L.R. 5.1-1(b).

      v. *No forfeiture.* A party's failure to file and serve the notice, or the court's failure to certify, does not forfeit a constitutional claim or defense that is otherwise timely asserted. FRCP 5.1(d).

   c. *Notice of issue concerning foreign law.* A party who intends to raise an issue about a foreign country's law must give notice by a pleading or other writing. In determining foreign law, the court may consider any relevant material or source, including testimony, whether or not submitted by a party or admissible under the Federal Rules of Evidence. The court's determination must be treated as a ruling on a question of law. FRCP 44.1.

   d. *Nongovernmental corporate disclosure statement*

      i. *Contents.* A nongovernmental corporate party must file two (2) copies of a disclosure statement that:

- Identifies any parent corporation and any publicly held corporation owning ten percent (10%) or more of its stock; or

- States that there is no such corporation. FRCP 7.1(a).

      ii. *Time to file; Supplemental filing.* A party must:

- File the disclosure statement with its first appearance, pleading, petition, motion, response, or other request addressed to the court; and

- Promptly file a supplemental statement if any required information changes. FRCP 7.1(b).

e. *Request for three-judge court.* To request a three-judge court in a case, a party must: (1) print "Three-Judge District Court Requested" or the equivalent immediately following the title on the first pleading the party files; and (2) set forth the basis for the request in the pleading or in a brief statement attached to the pleading, unless the basis is apparent from the pleading. IN R USDCTSD L.R. 9-2(a). The words "Three-Judge District Court Requested" or the equivalent on a pleading is a sufficient request under 28 U.S.C.A. § 2284. IN R USDCTSD L.R. 9-2(b).

f. *Index of exhibits.* Any pleading, motion, brief, affidavit, notice, or proposed order filed with the court, whether electronically or with the clerk, must: if it has four (4) or more exhibits, include a separate index that identifies and briefly describes each exhibit. IN R USDCTSD L.R. 5-1(b).

g. *Copy of document with self-address envelope.* To receive a file-stamped copy of a document filed directly with the clerk, a party must include with the original document an additional copy and a self-addressed envelope. The envelope must be big enough to hold the copy and have enough postage on it to send the copy via regular first-class mail. IN R USDCTSD L.R. 5-10(b).

h. *Notice of manual filing.* When a party who is not exempt from the electronic filing requirement files a document directly with the clerk, the party must: electronically file a notice of manual filing that explains why the document cannot be filed electronically. IN R USDCTSD L.R. 5-2(d)(1). Refer to the Filing and Service Requirements section of this document for more information.

  i. Where an individual component cannot be included in an electronic filing (e.g. the component cannot be converted to electronic format), the filer shall electronically file the prescribed Notice of Manual Filing in place of that component. A model form is provided as Appendix C (IN R USDCTSD ECF Procedures(Appendix C)). IN R USDCTSD ECF Procedures(13).

  ii. Before making a manual filing of a component, the filing party shall first electronically file a Notice of Manual Filing (See IN R USDCTSD ECF Procedures(Appendix C)). The filer shall initiate the electronic filing process as if filing the actual component but shall instead attach to the filing the Notice of Manual Filing setting forth the reason(s) why the component cannot be filed electronically. The manual filing should be accompanied by a copy of the previously filed Notice of Manual Filing. A party may seek to have a component excluded from electronic filing pursuant to applicable Federal and Local Rules (e.g., FRCP 26(c)). IN R USDCTSD ECF Procedures(15).

i. *Courtesy copies.* District Judges and Magistrate Judges regularly receive documents filed by all parties. Therefore, parties shall not bring "courtesy copies" to any chambers unless specifically directed to do so by the Court. IN R USDCTSD Case Mgt(General Instructions For All Cases).

j. *Copies for three-judge court.* Parties in a case where a three-judge court has been requested must file an original and three copies of any document filed directly with the clerk (instead of electronically) until the court: (1) denies the request; (2) dissolves the three-judge court; or (3) allows the parties to file fewer copies. IN R USDCTSD L.R. 9-2(c).

k. *Declaration that party was unable to file in a timely manner due to technical difficulties.* If a party misses a filing deadline due to an inability to file electronically, the party may submit the untimely filed document, accompanied by a declaration stating the reason(s) for missing the deadline. IN R USDCTSD ECF Procedures(16). A model form is provided as Appendix D (IN R USDCTSD ECF Procedures(Appendix D)). IN R USDCTSD ECF Procedures(16).

E. Format

1. *Form of documents*

   a. *Paper (manual filings only).* Any document that is not filed electronically must: be flat, unfolded, and on good-quality, eight and one-half by eleven (8-1/2 x 11) inch white paper. IN R USDCTSD L.R. 5-1(d)(1). Any document that is not filed electronically must: be single-sided. IN R USDCTSD L.R. 5-1(d)(1).

      i. *Covers or backing.* Any document that is not filed electronically must: not have a cover or a back. IN R USDCTSD L.R. 5-1(d)(1).

    ii.   *Fastening.* Any document that is not filed electronically must: be (if consisting of more than one (1) page) fastened by paperclip or binder clip and may not be stapled. IN R USDCTSD L.R. 5-1(d)(1).

- *Request for nonconforming fastening.* If a document cannot be fastened or bound as required by IN R USDCTSD L.R. 5-1(d), a party may ask the clerk for permission to fasten it in another manner. The party must make such a request before attempting to file the document with nonconforming fastening. IN R USDCTSD L.R. 5-1(d)(2).

    iii.   *Hole punching.* Any document that is not filed electronically must: be two-hole punched at the top with the holes two and three-quarter (2-3/4) inches apart and appropriately centered. IN R USDCTSD L.R. 5-1(d)(1).

b. *Margins.* Any pleading, motion, brief, affidavit, notice, or proposed order filed with the court, whether electronically or with the clerk, must: have at least one (1) inch margins. IN R USDCTSD L.R. 5-1(b).

c. *Spacing.* Any pleading, motion, brief, affidavit, notice, or proposed order filed with the court, whether electronically or with the clerk, must: be double spaced (except for headings, footnotes, and quoted material). IN R USDCTSD L.R. 5-1(b).

d. *Text.* Any pleading, motion, brief, affidavit, notice, or proposed order filed with the court, whether electronically or with the clerk, must: be plainly typewritten, printed, or prepared by a clearly legible copying process. IN R USDCTSD L.R. 5-1(b).

e. *Font size.* Any pleading, motion, brief, affidavit, notice, or proposed order filed with the court, whether electronically or with the clerk, must: use at least 12-point type in the body of the document and at least 10-point type in footnotes. IN R USDCTSD L.R. 5-1(b).

f. *Page numbering.* Any pleading, motion, brief, affidavit, notice, or proposed order filed with the court, whether electronically or with the clerk, must: have consecutively numbered pages. IN R USDCTSD L.R. 5-1(b).

g. *Caption; Names of parties.* Every pleading must have a caption with the court's name, a title, a file number, and a FRCP 7(a) designation. The title of the complaint must name all the parties; the title of other pleadings, after naming the first party on each side, may refer generally to other parties. FRCP 10(a). Any pleading, motion, brief, affidavit, notice, or proposed order filed with the court, whether electronically or with the clerk, must: include a title on the first page. IN R USDCTSD L.R. 5-1(b).

    i.   *Jury demand.* A party demanding a jury trial in a pleading as permitted by FRCP 38(b) must include the demand in the title by way of a notation placed on the front page of the pleading, immediately following the title of the pleading, stating "Demand for Jury Trial." Failure to do so will not result in a waiver under FRCP 38(d) if a jury demand is otherwise properly filed and served under FRCP 38(b). IN R USDCTSD L.R. 38-1.

    ii.   *Request for three-judge court.* To request a three-judge court in a case, a party must: (1) print "Three-Judge District Court Requested" or the equivalent immediately following the title on the first pleading the party files. IN R USDCTSD L.R. 9-2(a)(1). Refer to the Documents section of this document for more information.

    iii.   *Class actions.* A party seeking to maintain a case as a class action (whether for or against a class) must include in the complaint, crossclaim, or counterclaim: (1) the words "Class Action" in the document's title; and (2) a reference to each part of FRCP 23 that the party relies on in seeking to maintain the case as a class action. IN R USDCTSD L.R. 23-1(a). The provisions of IN R USDCTSD L.R. 23-1 will apply, with appropriate adaptations, to any counterclaim or crossclaim alleged to be brought for or against a class. IN R USDCTSD L.R. 23-1(b).

h. *Filer's information.* Any pleading, motion, brief, affidavit, notice, or proposed order filed with the court, whether electronically or with the clerk, must: in the case of pleadings, motions, legal briefs, and notices, include the name, complete address, telephone number, facsimile number (where available), and e-mail address (where available) of the pro se litigant or attorney who files it. IN R USDCTSD L.R. 5-1(b).

i. *Paragraphs; Separate statements.* A party must state its claims or defenses in numbered paragraphs, each limited as far as practicable to a single set of circumstances. A later pleading may refer by number to a paragraph in an earlier pleading. If doing so would promote clarity, each claim founded on a separate transaction or occurrence—and each defense other than a denial—must be stated in a separate count or defense. FRCP 10(b).

j. *Adoption by reference; Exhibits.* A statement in a pleading may be adopted by reference elsewhere in the same pleading or in any other pleading or motion. A copy of a written instrument that is an exhibit to a pleading is a part of the pleading for all purposes. FRCP 10(c).

k. *Citations*

    i. *Local rules.* The Local Rules of the United States District Court for the Southern District of Indiana may be cited as "S.D. Ind. L.R." IN R USDCTSD L.R. 1-1(a).

    ii. *Local alternative dispute resolution rules.* These Rules shall be known as the Local Alternative Dispute Resolution Rules of the United States District Court for the Southern District of Indiana. They shall be cited as "S.D.Ind. Local A.D.R. Rule _____." IN R USDCTSD A.D.R. Rule 1.1.

l. *Acceptance by the clerk.* The clerk must not refuse to file a paper solely because it is not in the form prescribed by the Federal Rules of Civil Procedure or by a local rule or practice. FRCP 5(d)(4). The clerk will accept a document that violates IN R USDCTSD L.R. 5-1, but the court may exclude the document from the official record. IN R USDCTSD L.R. 5-1(e).

    i. *Sanctions for errors as to form.* The court may strike from the record any document that does not comply with the rules governing the form of documents filed with the court, such as rules that regulate document size or the number of copies to be filed or that require a special designation in the caption. The court may also sanction an attorney or party who files a non-compliant document. IN R USDCTSD L.R. 1-3.

2. *Form of electronic documents.* Any document submitted via the court's electronic case filing (ECF) system must be: otherwise prepared and filed in a manner consistent with the CM/ECF Policies and Procedures Manual (IN R USDCTSD ECF Procedures). IN R USDCTSD L.R. 5-1(c). Electronically filed documents must meet the requirements of FRCP 10 (Form of Pleadings), IN R USDCTSD L.R. 5-1 (Format of Papers Presented for Filing), and FRCP 5.2 (Privacy Protection for Filings Made with the Court), as if they had been submitted on paper. Documents filed electronically are also subject to any page limitations set forth by Court Order, by IN R USDCTSD L.R. 7-1 (Motion Practice), or IN R USDCTSD L.R. 56-1 (Summary Judgment Practice), as applicable. IN R USDCTSD ECF Procedures(13).

a. *PDF format required.* Any document submitted via the court's electronic case filing (ECF) system must be: in .pdf format. IN R USDCTSD L.R. 5-1(c); IN R USDCTSD ECF Procedures(7). Any document submitted via the court's electronic case filing (ECF) system must be: converted to a .pdf file directly from a word processing program, unless it exists only in paper format (in which case it may be scanned to create a .pdf document). IN R USDCTSD L.R. 5-1(c); IN R USDCTSD ECF Procedures(13).

    i. An exhibit may be scanned into PDF format, at a recommended 300 dpi resolution or higher, only if it does not already exist in electronic format. The filing attorney is responsible for reviewing all PDF documents for legibility before submitting them through the Court's Electronic Case Filing system. For technical guidance in creating PDF documents, please contact the Clerk's Office. IN R USDCTSD ECF Procedures(13).

b. *File size limitations.* Any document submitted via the court's electronic case filing (ECF) system must be: submitted as one or more .pdf files that do not exceed ten megabytes (10 MB) each (consistent with the CM/ECF Policies and Procedures Manual (IN R USDCTSD ECF Procedures)). IN R USDCTSD L.R. 5-1(c); IN R USDCTSD ECF Procedures(13).

    i. To electronically file a document or attachment that exceeds ten megabytes (10 MB), the document must first be broken down into two or more smaller files. For example, if Exhibit A is a twelve megabyte (12 MB) PDF file, it should be divided into 2 equal parts prior to electronic filing. Each component part of the exhibit would be filed as an attachment to the main document and described appropriately as "Exhibit A (part 1 of 2)" and "Exhibit A (part 2 of 2)." IN R USDCTSD ECF Procedures(13).

ii. The supporting items mentioned in IN R USDCTSD ECF Procedures(13) should not be confused with memorandums or briefs in support of motions as outlined in IN R USDCTSD L.R. 7-1 or IN R USDCTSD L.R. 56-1. These memorandums or briefs in support are to be filed as entirely separate documents pursuant to the appropriate rule. Additionally, no motion shall be embodied in the text of a response or reply brief/memorandum unless otherwise ordered by the Court. IN R USDCTSD ECF Procedures(13).

c. *Separate component parts.* A key objective of the electronic filing system is to ensure that as much of the case as possible is managed electronically. To facilitate electronic filing and retrieval, documents to be filed electronically are to be reasonably broken into their separate component parts. By way of example, most filings include a foundation document (e.g., motion) and other supporting items (e.g., exhibits, proposed orders, proposed amended pleadings). The foundation document, as well as the supporting items, are each separate components of the filing; supporting items must be filed as attachments to the foundation document. These exhibits or attachments should include only those excerpts of the referenced documents that are directly germane to the matter under consideration. IN R USDCTSD ECF Procedures(13).

i. Where an individual component cannot be included in an electronic filing (e.g. the component cannot be converted to electronic format), the filer shall electronically file the prescribed Notice of Manual Filing in place of that component. A model form is provided as Appendix C (IN R USDCTSD ECF Procedures(Appendix C)). IN R USDCTSD ECF Procedures(13).

d. *Exhibits.* Each electronically filed exhibit to a main document must be: (1) created as a separate .pdf file; (2) submitted as an attachment to the main document and given a title which describes its content; and (3) limited to excerpts that are directly germane to the main document's subject matter. IN R USDCTSD L.R. 5-6(a).

i. When uploading attachments during the electronic filing process, exhibits must be uploaded in a logical sequence and a brief description must be entered for each individual PDF file. The description must include not only the exhibit number or letter, but also a brief description of the document. This information may be entered in CM/ECF using a combination of the Category drop-down menu, the Description text box, or both (see IN R USDCTSD ECF Procedures(13)(Figure 1)). The information that is provided in each box will be combined to create a description of the document as it appears on the case docket (see IN R USDCTSD ECF Procedures(13)(Figure 2)). IN R USDCTSD ECF Procedures(13). For an example, refer to IN R USDCTSD ECF Procedures(13).

e. *Excerpts.* A party filing an exhibit that consists of excerpts from a larger document must clearly and prominently identify the exhibit as containing excerpted material. Either party will have the right to timely file additional excerpts or the complete document to the extent they are or become directly germane to the main document's subject matter. IN R USDCTSD L.R. 5-6(b).

f. For an example illustrating the application of IN R USDCTSD ECF Procedures(13), refer to IN R USDCTSD ECF Procedures(13).

3. *Signing of pleadings, motions and other papers*

a. *Signature.* Every pleading, written motion, and other paper must be signed by at least one attorney of record in the attorney's name—or by a party personally if the party is unrepresented. The paper must state the signer's address, e-mail address, and telephone number. FRCP 11(a).

i. *Signatures on manual filings.* Any document that is not filed electronically must: include the original signature of the pro se litigant or attorney who files it. IN R USDCTSD L.R. 5-1(d)(1).

ii. *Electronic signatures.* Use of the attorney's login and password when filing documents electronically serves in part as the attorney's signature for purposes of FRCP 11, the Local Rules of the United States District Court for the Southern District of Indiana, and any other purpose for which a signature is required in connection with proceedings before the Court. IN R USDCTSD ECF Procedures(14); IN R USDCTSD ECF Procedures(10). A pleading, motion, brief, or notice filed electronically under an attorney's ECF log-in and password must be signed by that attorney. IN R USDCTSD L.R. 5-7(a). A signature on a document other than a document filed as provided under IN R USDCTSD L.R. 5-7(a) must be an original handwritten signature and must be scanned into .pdf format for electronic filing. IN R USDCTSD L.R. 5-7(c); IN R USDCTSD ECF Procedures(14).

- *Form of electronic signature.* If a document is converted directly from a word processing application to .pdf (as opposed to scanning), the name of the Filing User under whose log-in and password the document is submitted must be preceded by a "s/" and typed on the signature line where the Filing User's handwritten signature would otherwise appear. IN R USDCTSD L.R. 5-7(b). All documents filed electronically shall include a signature block and include the filing attorney's typewritten name, address, telephone number, facsimile number and e-mail address. In addition, the name of the filing attorney under whose ECF login the document will be filed should be preceded by a "s/" and typed in the space where the attorney's handwritten signature would otherwise appear. IN R US-DCTSD ECF Procedures(14). For a sample format, refer to IN R USDCTSD ECF Procedures(14).

- *Effect of electronic signature.* Filing an electronically signed document under an attorney's ECF log-in and password constitutes the attorney's signature on the document under the Federal Rules of Civil Procedure, under the Local Rules of the United States District Court for the Southern District of Indiana, and for any other reason a signature is required in connection with the court's activities. IN R USDCTSD L.R. 5-7(d).

- *Documents with multiple attorneys' signatures.* Documents requiring signatures of more than one attorney shall be filed either by: (1) obtaining consent from the other attorney, then typing the "s/ [Name]" signature of the other attorney on the signature line where the other attorney's signature would otherwise appear; (2) identifying in the signature section the name of the other attorney whose signature is required and by the submission of a Notice of Endorsement (see IN R USDCTSD ECF Procedures(Appendix B)) by the other attorney no later than three (3) business days after filing; (3) submitting a scanned document containing all handwritten signatures; or (4) in any other manner approved by the Court. IN R USDCTSD ECF Procedures(14); IN R USDCTSD L.R. 5-7(e).

iii. *No verification or accompanying affidavit required for pleadings.* Unless a rule or statute specifically states otherwise, a pleading need not be verified or accompanied by an affidavit. FRCP 11(a).

iv. *Unsigned papers.* The court must strike an unsigned paper unless the omission is promptly corrected after being called to the attorney's or party's attention. FRCP 11(a). The court will strike any document filed directly with the clerk that is not signed by an attorney of record or the pro se litigant filing it, but the court may do so only after giving the attorney or pro se litigant notice of the omission and reasonable time to correct it. Rubber-stamp or facsimile signatures are not original signatures and the court will deem documents containing them to be unsigned for purposes of FRCP 11 and FRCP 26(g) and IN R USDCTSD L.R. 5-10. IN R USDCTSD L.R. 5-10(g).

b. *Representations to the court.* By presenting to the court a pleading, written motion, or other paper—whether by signing, filing, submitting, or later advocating it—an attorney or unrepresented party certifies that to the best of the person's knowledge, information, and belief, formed after an inquiry reasonable under the circumstances:

i. It is not being presented for any improper purpose, such as to harass, cause unnecessary delay, or needlessly increase the cost of litigation;

ii. The claims, defenses, and other legal contentions are warranted by existing law or by a nonfrivolous argument for extending, modifying, or reversing existing law or for establishing new law;

iii. The factual contentions have evidentiary support or, if specifically so identified, will likely have evidentiary support after a reasonable opportunity for further investigation or discovery; and

iv. The denials of factual contentions are warranted on the evidence or, if specifically so identified, are reasonably based on belief or a lack of information. FRCP 11(b).

c. *Sanctions.* If, after notice and a reasonable opportunity to respond, the court determines that FRCP 11(b) has been violated, the court may impose an appropriate sanction on any attorney, law firm, or party that violated FRCP 11(b) or is responsible for the violation. FRCP 11(c)(1). Refer to the United States District Court for the Southern District of Indiana KeyRules Motion for Sanctions document for more information.

4. *Privacy protection for filings made with the court.* Electronically filed documents must meet the requirements of. . .FRCP 5.2 (Privacy Protection for Filings Made with the Court), as if they had been submitted on paper. IN R USDCTSD ECF Procedures(13).

a. *Redacted filings.* Unless the court orders otherwise, in an electronic or paper filing with the court that contains an individual's Social Security number, taxpayer-identification number, or birth date, the name of an individual known to be a minor, or a financial-account number, a party or nonparty making the filing may include only:

i. The last four (4) digits of the Social Security number and taxpayer-identification number;

ii. The year of the individual's birth;

iii. The minor's initials; and

iv. The last four (4) digits of the financial-account number. FRCP 5.2(a).

b. *Exemptions from the redaction requirement.* The redaction requirement does not apply to the following:

i. A financial-account number that identifies the property allegedly subject to forfeiture in a forfeiture proceeding;

ii. The record of an administrative or agency proceeding;

iii. The official record of a state-court proceeding;

iv. The record of a court or tribunal, if that record was not subject to the redaction requirement when originally filed;

v. A filing covered by FRCP 5.2(c) or FRCP 5.2(d); and

vi. A pro se filing in an action brought under 28 U.S.C.A. § 2241, 28 U.S.C.A. § 2254, or 28 U.S.C.A. § 2255. FRCP 5.2(b).

c. *Limitations on remote access to electronic files; Social Security appeals and immigration cases.* Unless the court orders otherwise, in an action for benefits under the Social Security Act, and in an action or proceeding relating to an order of removal, to relief from removal, or to immigration benefits or detention, access to an electronic file is authorized as follows:

i. The parties and their attorneys may have remote electronic access to any part of the case file, including the administrative record;

ii. Any other person may have electronic access to the full record at the courthouse, but may have remote electronic access only to:

- The docket maintained by the court; and

- An opinion, order, judgment, or other disposition of the court, but not any other part of the case file or the administrative record. FRCP 5.2(c).

d. *Filings made under seal.* The court may order that a filing be made under seal without redaction. The court may later unseal the filing or order the person who made the filing to file a redacted version for the public record. FRCP 5.2(d). For more information on filing under seal, refer to IN R USDCTSD L.R. 5-11 and IN R USDCTSD ECF Procedures(18).

e. *Protective orders.* For good cause, the court may by order in a case:

i. Require redaction of additional information; or

ii. Limit or prohibit a nonparty's remote electronic access to a document filed with the court. FRCP 5.2(e).

f. *Option for additional unredacted filing under seal.* A person making a redacted filing may also file an unredacted copy under seal. The court must retain the unredacted copy as part of the record. FRCP 5.2(f).

g. *Option for filing a reference list.* A filing that contains redacted information may be filed together with a reference list that identifies each item of redacted information and specifies an appropriate identifier that uniquely corresponds to each item listed. The list must be filed under seal and may be amended as of right. Any reference in the case to a listed identifier will be construed to refer to the corresponding item of information. FRCP 5.2(g).

h. *Waiver of protection of identifiers.* A person waives the protection of FRCP 5.2(a) as to the person's own information by filing it without redaction and not under seal. FRCP 5.2(h).

F. Filing and Service Requirements

1. *Filing requirements.* Any paper after the complaint that is required to be served—together with a certificate of service—must be filed within a reasonable time after service. FRCP 5(d)(1).

    a. *How filing is made; In general.* A paper is filed by delivering it:

        i. To the clerk; or

        ii. To a judge who agrees to accept it for filing, and who must then note the filing date on the paper and promptly send it to the clerk. FRCP 5(d)(2).

        - In certain instances, the court will direct the parties to submit items directly to chambers (e.g., confidential settlement statements). However, absent specific prior authorization, counsel and litigants should not submit letters or documents directly to chambers, and such materials should be filed with the clerk. IN R USDCTSD L.R. 5-1(Local Rules Advisory Committee Comment).

        iii. A document or item submitted in relation to a matter within the court's jurisdiction is deemed filed upon delivery to the office of the clerk in a manner prescribed by the Local Rules of the United States District Court for the Southern District of Indiana or the Federal Rules of Civil Procedure or authorized by the court. Any submission directed to a Judge or Judge's staff, the office of the clerk or any employee thereof, in a manner that is not contemplated by IN R USDCTSD L.R. 5-1 and without prior court authorization is prohibited. IN R USDCTSD L.R. 5-1(a).

    b. *Non-electronic filing.* Any document that is exempt from electronic filing must be filed directly with the clerk and served on other parties in the case as required by those Federal Rules of Civil Procedure and Local Rules of the United States District Court for the Southern District of Indiana that apply to the service of non-electronic documents. IN R USDCTSD L.R. 5-2(c).

        i. *When completed.* A document or other item that is not required to be filed electronically is deemed filed:

        - Upon delivery in person, by courier, or via U.S. Mail or other mail delivery service to the clerk's office during business hours;

        - When the courtroom deputy clerk accepts it, if the document or item is filed in open court; or

        - Upon completion of any other manner of filing that the court authorizes. IN R USDCTSD L.R. 5-10(a).

        ii. *Document filing by non-exempt party.* When a party who is not exempt from the electronic filing requirement files a document directly with the clerk, the party must:

        - Electronically file a notice of manual filing that explains why the document cannot be filed electronically;

        - Present the document to the clerk within one (1) business day after filing the notice of manual filing; and

        - Present the clerk with a copy of the notice of manual filing when the party files the document with the clerk. IN R USDCTSD L.R. 5-2(d).

c. *Electronic filing*

    i. *Authorization of electronic filing program.* A court may, by local rule, allow papers to be filed, signed, or verified by electronic means that are consistent with any technical standards established by the Judicial Conference of the United States. A local rule may require electronic filing only if reasonable exceptions are allowed. A paper filed electronically in compliance with a local rule is a written paper for purposes of the Federal Rules of Civil Procedure. FRCP 5(d)(3).

- IN R USDCTSD L.R. 5-2 requires electronic filing, as allowed by FRCP 5(d)(3). The policies and procedures in IN R USDCTSD ECF Procedures govern electronic filing in this district unless, due to circumstances in a particular case, a judicial officer determines that these policies and procedures (IN R USDCTSD ECF Procedures) should be modified. IN R USDCTSD ECF Procedures(1).

- Unless modified by order of the Court, all Federal Rules of Civil Procedure and Local Rules of the United States District Court for the Southern District of Indiana shall continue to apply to cases maintained in the Court's Case Management/Electronic Case Filing System (CM/ECF). IN R USDCTSD ECF Procedures(3).

    ii. *Mandatory electronic filing.* Unless exempted pursuant to IN R USDCTSD L.R. 5-3(e), attorneys admitted to the court's bar (including those admitted pro hac vice) or authorized to represent the United States must use the court's ECF system to file documents. IN R USDCTSD L.R. 5-3(a). Electronic filing by attorneys is required for eligible documents filed in civil and criminal cases pending with the Court, unless specifically exempted by Local Rule or Court Order. IN R USDCTSD ECF Procedures(4).

- *Exceptions.* All civil cases (other than those cases the court specifically exempts) must be maintained in the court's electronic case filing (ECF) system. Accordingly, as allowed by FRCP 5(d)(3), every document filed in this court (including exhibits) must be transmitted to the clerk's office via the ECF system consistent with IN R USDCTSD L.R. 5-2 through IN R USDCTSD L.R. 5-11 except: (1) documents filed by pro se litigants; (2) transcripts in cases filed by claimants under the Social Security Act (and related statutes); (3) exhibits in a format that does not readily permit electronic filing (such as videos and large maps and charts); (4) documents that are illegible when scanned into .pdf format; (5) documents filed in cases not maintained on the ECF system; and (6) any other documents that the court or the Local Rules of the United States District Court for the Southern District of Indiana specifically allow to be filed directly with the clerk. IN R USDCTSD L.R. 5-2(a). Parties otherwise participating in the electronic filing system may be excused from filing a particular component electronically under certain limited circumstances, such as when the component cannot be reduced to an electronic format. Such components shall not be filed electronically, but instead shall be manually filed with the Clerk of Court and served upon the parties in accordance with the applicable Federal Rules of Civil Procedure and the Local Rules of the United States District Court for the Southern District of Indiana for filing and service of non-electronic documents. IN R USDCTSD ECF Procedures(15).

- *Exemption from participation.* The court may exempt attorneys from using the ECF system in a particular case for good cause. An attorney must file a petition for ECF exemption and a CM/ECF technical requirements exemption questionnaire in each case in which the attorney seeks an exemption. (The CM/ECF technical requirements exemption questionnaire is available on the court's website). IN R USDCTSD L.R. 5-3(e).

    iii. *Consequences of electronic filing.* Electronic transmission of a document consistent with the procedures adopted by the Court shall, upon the complete receipt of the same by the Clerk of Court, constitute filing of the document for all purposes of the Federal Rules of Civil and Criminal Procedure and the Local Rules of the United States District Court for the Southern District of Indiana, and shall constitute entry of that document onto the docket maintained by the Clerk pursuant to FRCP 58 and FRCP 79. IN R USDCTSD ECF Procedures(7); IN R USDCTSD L.R. 5-4(c)(1). When a document has been filed electronically: the document, as filed, binds the filing party. IN R USDCTSD L.R. 5-4(c)(3).

- A Notice of Electronic Filing (NEF) acknowledging that the document has been filed will immediately appear on the filer's screen after the document has been submitted. Attorneys are strongly encouraged to print or electronically save a copy of the NEF. Attorneys can also verify the filing of documents by inspecting the Court's electronic docket sheet through the use of a PACER login. IN R USDCTSD ECF Procedures(7). When a document has been filed electronically: the notice of electronic filing for the document serves as the court's date-stamp and proof of filing. IN R USDCTSD L.R. 5-4(c)(4).

- The Court may, upon the motion of a party or upon its own motion, strike any inappropriately filed document. IN R USDCTSD ECF Procedures(7).

iv. For more information on electronic filing, refer to IN R USDCTSD ECF Procedures.

d. *Fax filing.* The clerk may not file a faxed document without court authorization. The court may not authorize the clerk to file faxed documents without finding that compelling circumstances justify it. A party must submit a copy of the document that otherwise complies with IN R USDCTSD L.R. 5-10 to replace the faxed copy within seven (7) days after faxing the document. IN R USDCTSD L.R. 5-10(e).

2. *Service requirements*

a. *Service; When required*

i. *In general.* Unless the Federal Rules of Civil Procedure provide otherwise, each of the following papers must be served on every party:

- An order stating that service is required;
- A pleading filed after the original complaint, unless the court orders otherwise under FRCP 5(c) because there are numerous defendants;
- A discovery paper required to be served on a party, unless the court orders otherwise;
- A written motion, except one that may be heard ex parte; and
- A written notice, appearance, demand, or offer of judgment, or any similar paper. FRCP 5(a)(1).

ii. *If a party fails to appear.* No service is required on a party who is in default for failing to appear. But a pleading that asserts a new claim for relief against such a party must be served on that party under FRCP 4. FRCP 5(a)(2).

iii. *Seizing property.* If an action is begun by seizing property and no person is or need be named as a defendant, any service required before the filing of an appearance, answer, or claim must be made on the person who had custody or possession of the property when it was seized. FRCP 5(a)(3).

b. *Service; How made*

i. *Serving an attorney.* If a party is represented by an attorney, service under FRCP 5 must be made on the attorney unless the court orders service on the party. FRCP 5(b)(1).

ii. *Service in general.* A paper is served under FRCP 5 by:

- Handing it to the person;
- Leaving it: (1) at the person's office with a clerk or other person in charge or, if no one is in charge, in a conspicuous place in the office; or (2) if the person has no office or the office is closed, at the person's dwelling or usual place of abode with someone of suitable age and discretion who resides there;
- Mailing it to the person's last known address—in which event service is complete upon mailing;
- Leaving it with the court clerk if the person has no known address;
- Sending it by electronic means if the person consented in writing—in which event service is complete upon transmission, but is not effective if the serving party learns that it did not reach the person to be served; or

- Delivering it by any other means that the person consented to in writing—in which event service is complete when the person making service delivers it to the agency designated to make delivery. FRCP 5(b)(2).

iii. *Electronic service*

- *Consent.* By registering to use the ECF system, attorneys consent to electronic service of documents filed in cases maintained on the ECF system. IN R USDCTSD L.R. 5-3(d). By participating in the Electronic Case Filing Program, attorneys consent to the electronic service of documents, and shall make available electronic mail addresses for service. IN R USDCTSD ECF Procedures(11).

- *Service on registered parties.* Upon the filing of a document by a party, an e-mail message will be automatically generated by the electronic filing system and sent via electronic mail to the e-mail addresses of all registered attorneys who have appeared in the case. The Notice of Electronic Filing will contain a document hyperlink which will provide recipients with one "free look" at the electronically filed document. Recipients are encouraged to print and/or save a copy of the document during the "free look" to avoid incurring PACER charges for future viewings of the document. IN R USDCTSD ECF Procedures(11). When a document has been filed electronically: transmission of the notice of electronic filing generated by the ECF system to an attorney's e-mail address constitutes service of the document on that attorney. IN R USDCTSD L.R. 5-4(c)(5). The party effectuates service on all registered attorneys by filing electronically. IN R USDCTSD ECF Procedures(11). When a document has been filed electronically: no other attempted service will constitute electronic service of the document. IN R USDCTSD L.R. 5-4(c)(6).

- *Service on exempt parties.* A filer must serve a copy of the document consistent with FRCP 5 on any party or attorney who is exempt from participating in electronic filing. IN R USDCTSD L.R. 5-4(d). It is the responsibility of the filing attorney to conventionally serve all parties who do not receive electronic service (the identity of these parties will be indicated on the filing receipt generated by the ECF system). IN R USDCTSD ECF Procedures(11).

- *Service on parties excused from electronic filing.* Parties otherwise participating in the electronic filing system may be excused from filing a particular component electronically under certain limited circumstances, such as when the component cannot be reduced to an electronic format. Such components shall not be filed electronically, but instead shall be manually filed with the Clerk of Court and served upon the parties in accordance with the applicable Federal Rules of Civil Procedure and the Local Rules of the United States District Court for the Southern District of Indiana for filing and service of non-electronic documents. IN R USDCTSD ECF Procedures(15).

- *Service of exempt documents.* Any document that is exempt from electronic filing must be filed directly with the clerk and served on other parties in the case as required by those Federal Rules of Civil Procedure and Local Rules of the United States District Court for the Southern District of Indiana that apply to the service of non-electronic documents. IN R USDCTSD L.R. 5-2(c).

iv. *Using court facilities.* If a local rule so authorizes, a party may use the court's transmission facilities to make service under FRCP 5(b)(2)(E). FRCP 5(b)(3).

c. *Serving numerous defendants*

i. *In general.* If an action involves an unusually large number of defendants, the court may, on motion or on its own, order that:

- Defendants' pleadings and replies to them need not be served on other defendants;

- Any crossclaim, counterclaim, avoidance, or affirmative defense in those pleadings and replies to them will be treated as denied or avoided by all other parties; and

- Filing any such pleading and serving it on the plaintiff constitutes notice of the pleading to all parties. FRCP 5(c)(1).

ii. *Notifying parties.* A copy of every such order must be served on the parties as the court directs. FRCP 5(c)(2).

G. Hearings

1. *Hearing on FRCP 12 defenses before trial.* If a party so moves, any defense listed in FRCP 12(b)(1) through FRCP 12(b)(7)—whether made in a pleading or by motion—and a motion under FRCP 12(c) must be heard and decided before trial unless the court orders a deferral until trial. FRCP 12(i).

H. Forms

1. Official Federal Answer Forms

a. Rule 4 waiver of the service of summons. FRCP 4.

2. Federal Answer Forms

a. Generally. 2B FEDFORMS § 8:10.

b. Introduction to separate defenses. 2B FEDFORMS § 8:11.

c. Presenting defenses. 2B FEDFORMS § 8:12.

d. With counterclaim for interpleader. 2B FEDFORMS § 8:13.

e. Denials and admissions. 2B FEDFORMS § 8:14.

f. Denials, admissions and affirmative defenses. 2B FEDFORMS § 8:15.

g. Separate answer of two defendants; Duty of fair representation. 2B FEDFORMS § 8:16.

h. Separate answer of third defendant. 2B FEDFORMS § 8:17.

i. Reciting paragraphs and subparagraphs of complaint; Account malpractice. 2B FEDFORMS § 8:18.

j. One of multiple defendants. 2B FEDFORMS § 8:21.

k. Answer to complaint for employment discrimination. 2B FEDFORMS § 8:22.

l. Denial of particular averment. 2B FEDFORMS § 8:24.

m. Admission of particular averment. 2B FEDFORMS § 8:25.

n. Denial of all averments of paragraph. 2B FEDFORMS § 8:26.

o. Admission of all averments of paragraph. 2B FEDFORMS § 8:27.

p. Denial in part and admission in part of paragraph. 2B FEDFORMS § 8:28.

q. General denial. 2B FEDFORMS § 8:29.

r. Qualified general denial. 2B FEDFORMS § 8:30.

s. Denial of knowledge or information sufficient to form a belief. 2B FEDFORMS § 8:31.

t. Denial of jurisdictional allegations; Jurisdictional amount. 2B FEDFORMS § 8:32.

u. Denial of jurisdictional allegations; Federal question. 2B FEDFORMS § 8:34.

v. Denial of jurisdictional allegations; Diversity of citizenship. 2B FEDFORMS § 8:37.

w. Contributory negligence. 2B FEDFORMS § 8:58.

x. Fraud. 2B FEDFORMS § 8:74.

y. Mistake. 2B FEDFORMS § 8:85.

z. Statute of limitations. 2B FEDFORMS § 8:103.

3. Forms for the Southern District of Indiana

a. Notice of endorsement. IN R USDCTSD ECF Procedures(Appendix B).

b. Notice of manual filing. IN R USDCTSD ECF Procedures(Appendix C).

c. Declaration that party was unable to file in a timely manner due to technical difficulties. IN R USDCTSD ECF Procedures(Appendix D).

I. Applicable Rules

1. *Federal rules*

   a. Summons. FRCP 4.

   b. Serving and filing pleadings and other papers. FRCP 5.

   c. Constitutional challenge to a statute; Notice, certification, and intervention. FRCP 5.1.

   d. Privacy protection for filings made with the court. FRCP 5.2.

   e. Computing and extending time; Time for motion papers. FRCP 6.

   f. Pleadings allowed; Form of motions and other papers. FRCP 7.

   g. Disclosure statement. FRCP 7.1.

   h. General rules of pleading. FRCP 8.

   i. Pleading special matters. FRCP 9.

   j. Form of pleadings. FRCP 10.

   k. Signing pleadings, motions, and other papers; Representations to the court; Sanctions. FRCP 11.

   l. Defenses and objections; When and how presented; Motion for judgment on the pleadings; Consolidating motions; Waiving defenses; Pretrial hearing. FRCP 12.

   m. Counterclaim and crossclaim. FRCP 13.

   n. Third-party practice. FRCP 14.

   o. Right to a jury trial; Demand. FRCP 38.

   p. Determining foreign law. FRCP 44.1.

2. *Local rules*

   a. Scope of the rules. IN R USDCTSD L.R. 1-1.

   b. Sanctions for errors as to form. IN R USDCTSD L.R. 1-3.

   c. Format of documents presented for filing. IN R USDCTSD L.R. 5-1.

   d. Constitutional challenge to a statute; Notice. IN R USDCTSD L.R. 5.1-1.

   e. Filing of documents electronically required. IN R USDCTSD L.R. 5-2.

   f. Eligibility, registration, passwords for electronic filing; Exemption from electronic filing. IN R USDCTSD L.R. 5-3.

   g. Timing and consequences of electronic filing. IN R USDCTSD L.R. 5-4.

   h. Attachments and exhibits in cases filed electronically. IN R USDCTSD L.R. 5-6.

   i. Signatures in cases filed electronically. IN R USDCTSD L.R. 5-7.

   j. Non-electronic filings. IN R USDCTSD L.R. 5-10.

   k. Extensions of time. IN R USDCTSD L.R. 6-1.

   l. Motion practice. [IN R USDCTSD L.R. 7-1, as amended by IN ORDER 16-2319, effective December 1, 2016].

   m. Request for three-judge court. IN R USDCTSD L.R. 9-2.

   n. Designation of "class action" in the caption. IN R USDCTSD L.R. 23-1.

   o. Jury demand. IN R USDCTSD L.R. 38-1.

   p. Assignment of cases. IN R USDCTSD L.R. 40-1.

   q. Alternative dispute resolution. IN R USDCTSD A.D.R. Rule 1.1; IN R USDCTSD A.D.R. Rule 1.2; IN R USDCTSD A.D.R. Rule 1.5; IN R USDCTSD A.D.R. Rule 2.1; IN R USDCTSD A.D.R. Rule 2.2.

   r. Instructions for preparing case management plan. IN R USDCTSD Case Mgt.

s. Electronic case filing policies and procedures manual. IN R USDCTSD ECF Procedures.

Pleadings
Amended Pleading

Document Last Updated December 2016

A. Checklist

(I) ❑ Matters to be considered by plaintiff or defendant

   (a) ❑ Required documents

      (1) ❑ Amended pleading

      (2) ❑ Certificate of service

   (b) ❑ Supplemental documents

      (1) ❑ Notice of constitutional question

      (2) ❑ Notice of issue concerning foreign law

      (3) ❑ Index of exhibits

      (4) ❑ Copy of document with self-address envelope

      (5) ❑ Notice of manual filing

      (6) ❑ Courtesy copies

      (7) ❑ Copies for three-judge court

      (8) ❑ Declaration that party was unable to file in a timely manner due to technical difficulties

   (c) ❑ Timing

      (1) ❑ A party may amend its pleading once as a matter of course within:

         (i) ❑ Twenty-one (21) days after serving it, or

         (ii) ❑ If the pleading is one to which a responsive pleading is required, twenty-one (21) days after service of a responsive pleading or twenty-one (21) days after service of a motion under FRCP 12(b), FRCP 12(e), or FRCP 12(f), whichever is earlier

      (2) ❑ When a party who is not exempt from the electronic filing requirement files a document directly with the clerk, the party must present the document to the clerk within one (1) business day after filing the notice of manual filing

      (3) ❑ Unless the court orders otherwise, the [untimely] document and declaration [that party was unable to file in a timely manner due to technical difficulties] must be filed no later than 12:00 noon of the first day on which the court is open for business following the original filing deadline

B. Timing

1. *Amended pleading*

   a. *Amending as a matter of course.* A party may amend its pleading once as a matter of course within:

     i. Twenty-one (21) days after serving it, or

     ii. If the pleading is one to which a responsive pleading is required, twenty-one (21) days after service of a responsive pleading or twenty-one (21) days after service of a motion under FRCP 12(b), FRCP 12(e), or FRCP 12(f), whichever is earlier. FRCP 15(a)(1).

   b. *Extension of time.* If the time for serving the responsive pleading is extended by a motion for enlargement of time under FRCP 6(b), or by a stipulation, the period for amending as of right also may be enlarged. FPP § 1480.

   c. *Other amendments.* In all other cases, a party may amend its pleading only with the opposing party's written consent or the court's leave. The court should freely give leave when justice so requires. FRCP 15(a)(2). Refer to the United States District Court for the Southern District of Indiana KeyRules Motion for Leave to Amend document for more information.

2. *Time to respond to an amended pleading.* Unless the court orders otherwise, any required response to an amended pleading must be made within the time remaining to respond to the original pleading or within fourteen (14) days after service of the amended pleading, whichever is later. FRCP 15(a)(3).

3. *Document filing by non-exempt party.* When a party who is not exempt from the electronic filing requirement files a document directly with the clerk, the party must: present the document to the clerk within one (1) business day after filing the notice of manual filing. IN R USDCTSD L.R. 5-2(d)(2).

4. *Declaration that party was unable to file in a timely manner due to technical difficulties.* Unless the Court orders otherwise, the [untimely] document and declaration [that party was unable to file in a timely manner due to technical difficulties] must be filed no later than 12:00 noon of the first day on which the Court is open for business following the original filing deadline. IN R USDCTSD ECF Procedures(16).

5. *Automatic initial extension.* The deadline for filing a response to a pleading or to any written request for discovery or admissions will automatically be extended upon filing a notice of the extension with the court that states: (1) the deadline has not been previously extended; (2) the extension is for twenty-eight (28) or fewer days; (3) the extension does not interfere with the Case Management Plan, scheduled hearings, or other case deadlines; (4) the original deadline and extended deadline; (5) that all opposing counsel the filing attorney could reach agreed to the extension; or that the filing attorney could not reach any opposing counsel, and providing the dates, times and manner of all attempts to reach opposing counsel. IN R USDCTSD L.R. 6-1(b).

   a. *Pro se parties.* The automatic initial extension does not apply to pro se parties. IN R USDCTSD L.R. 6-1(c).

6. *Computation of time*

   a. *Computing time.* FRCP 6 applies in computing any time period specified in the Federal Rules of Civil Procedure, in any local rule or court order, or in any statute that does not specify a method of computing time. FRCP 6(a).

      i. *Period stated in days or a longer unit.* When the period is stated in days or a longer unit of time:
         - Exclude the day of the event that triggers the period;
         - Count every day, including intermediate Saturdays, Sundays, and legal holidays; and
         - Include the last day of the period, but if the last day is a Saturday, Sunday, or legal holiday, the period continues to run until the end of the next day that is not a Saturday, Sunday, or legal holiday. FRCP 6(a)(1).

      ii. *Period stated in hours.* When the period is stated in hours:
         - Begin counting immediately on the occurrence of the event that triggers the period;
         - Count every hour, including hours during intermediate Saturdays, Sundays, and legal holidays; and
         - If the period would end on a Saturday, Sunday, or legal holiday, the period continues to run until the same time on the next day that is not a Saturday, Sunday, or legal holiday. FRCP 6(a)(2).

      iii. *Inaccessibility of the clerk's office.* Unless the court orders otherwise, if the clerk's office is inaccessible:
         - On the last day for filing under FRCP 6(a)(1), then the time for filing is extended to the first accessible day that is not a Saturday, Sunday, or legal holiday; or
         - During the last hour for filing under FRCP 6(a)(2), then the time for filing is extended to the same time on the first accessible day that is not a Saturday, Sunday, or legal holiday. FRCP 6(a)(3).

iv. *"Last day" defined.* Unless a different time is set by a statute, local rule, or court order, the last day ends:

- For electronic filing, at midnight in the court's time zone; and

- For filing by other means, when the clerk's office is scheduled to close. FRCP 6(a)(4).

v. *"Next day" defined.* The "next day" is determined by continuing to count forward when the period is measured after an event and backward when measured before an event. FRCP 6(a)(5).

vi. *"Legal holiday" defined.* "Legal holiday" means:

- The day set aside by statute for observing New Year's Day, Martin Luther King Jr.'s Birthday, Washington's Birthday, Memorial Day, Independence Day, Labor Day, Columbus Day, Veterans' Day, Thanksgiving Day, or Christmas Day;

- Any day declared a holiday by the President or Congress; and

- For periods that are measured after an event, any other day declared a holiday by the state where the district court is located. FRCP 6(a)(6).

b. *Computation of electronic filing deadlines.* Filing documents electronically does not alter filing deadlines. IN R USDCTSD ECF Procedures(7). A document due on a particular day must be filed before midnight local time of the division where the case is pending. IN R USDCTSD L.R. 5-4(a). All electronic transmissions of documents must be completed (i.e. received completely by the Clerk's Office) prior to midnight of the local time of the division in which the case is pending in order to be considered timely filed that day (NOTE: time will be noted in Eastern Time on the Court's docket. If you have filed a document prior to midnight local time of the division in which the case is pending and the document is due that date, but the electronic receipt and docket reflect the following calendar day, please contact the Court). IN R USDCTSD ECF Procedures(7). Although attorneys may file documents electronically twenty-four (24) hours a day, seven (7) days a week, attorneys are encouraged to file all documents during the normal working hours of the Clerk's Office (Monday through Friday, 8:30 a.m. to 4:30 p.m.) when technical support is available. IN R USDCTSD ECF Procedures(7); IN R USDCTSD ECF Procedures(9).

i. *Technical difficulties.* Parties are encouraged to file documents electronically during normal business hours, in case a problem is encountered. In the event a technical failure occurs and a document cannot be filed electronically despite the best efforts of the filing party, the party should print (if possible) a copy of the error message received. In addition, as soon as practically possible, the party should file a "Declaration that Party was Unable to File in a Timely Manner Due to Technical Difficulties." A model form is provided as Appendix D (IN R USDCTSD ECF Procedures(Appendix D)). IN R USDCTSD ECF Procedures(16).

- If a party is unable to file electronically and, as a result, may miss a filing deadline, the party must contact the Clerk's Office at the number listed in IN R USDCTSD ECF Procedures(15) to inform the court's staff of the difficulty. If a party misses a filing deadline due to an inability to file electronically, the party may submit the untimely filed document, accompanied by a declaration stating the reason(s) for missing the deadline. Unless the Court orders otherwise, the document and declaration must be filed no later than 12:00 noon of the first day on which the Court is open for business following the original filing deadline. IN R USDCTSD ECF Procedures(16).

c. *Extending time*

i. *In general.* When an act may or must be done within a specified time, the court may, for good cause, extend the time:

- With or without motion or notice if the court acts, or if a request is made, before the original time or its extension expires; or

- On motion made after the time has expired if the party failed to act because of excusable neglect. FRCP 6(b)(1).

ii. *Exceptions.* A court must not extend the time to act under FRCP 50(b), FRCP 50(d), FRCP 52(b), FRCP 59(b), FRCP 59(d), FRCP 59(e), and FRCP 60(b). FRCP 6(b)(2).

iii. Refer to the United States District Court for the Southern District of Indiana KeyRules Motion for Continuance/Extension of Time document for more information on extending time.

d. *Additional time after certain kinds of service.* When a party may or must act within a specified time after being served and service is made under FRCP 5(b)(2)(C) (mail), FRCP 5(b)(2)(D) (leaving with the clerk), or FRCP 5(b)(2)(F) (other means consented to), three (3) days are added after the period would otherwise expire under FRCP 6(a). FRCP 6(d). Service by electronic mail shall constitute service pursuant to FRCP 5(b)(2)(E) and shall entitle the party being served to the additional three (3) days provided by FRCP 6(d). IN R USDCTSD ECF Procedures(11).

C. General Requirements

1. *Pleading, generally*

   a. *Pleadings allowed.* Only these pleadings are allowed: (1) a complaint; (2) an answer to a complaint; (3) an answer to a counterclaim designated as a counterclaim; (4) an answer to a crossclaim; (5) a third-party complaint; (6) an answer to a third-party complaint; and (7) if the court orders one, a reply to an answer. FRCP 7(a).

   b. *Pleading to be concise and direct.* Each allegation must be simple, concise, and direct. No technical form is required. FRCP 8(d)(1).

   c. *Alternative statements of a claim or defense.* A party may set out two or more statements of a claim or defense alternatively or hypothetically, either in a single count or defense or in separate ones. If a party makes alternative statements, the pleading is sufficient if any one of them is sufficient. FRCP 8(d)(2).

   d. *Inconsistent claims or defenses.* A party may state as many separate claims or defenses as it has, regardless of consistency. FRCP 8(d)(3).

   e. *Construing pleadings.* Pleadings must be construed so as to do justice. FRCP 8(e).

2. *Pleading special matters*

   a. *Capacity or authority to sue; Legal existence*

      i. *In general.* Except when required to show that the court has jurisdiction, a pleading need not allege:

         • A party's capacity to sue or be sued;

         • A party's authority to sue or be sued in a representative capacity; or

         • The legal existence of an organized association of persons that is made a party. FRCP 9(a)(1).

      ii. *Raising those issues.* To raise any of those issues, a party must do so by a specific denial, which must state any supporting facts that are peculiarly within the party's knowledge. FRCP 9(a)(2).

   b. *Fraud or mistake; Conditions of mind.* In alleging fraud or mistake, a party must state with particularity the circumstances constituting fraud or mistake. Malice, intent, knowledge, and other conditions of a person's mind may be alleged generally. FRCP 9(b).

   c. *Conditions precedent.* In pleading conditions precedent, it suffices to allege generally that all conditions precedent have occurred or been performed. But when denying that a condition precedent has occurred or been performed, a party must do so with particularity. FRCP 9(c).

   d. *Official document or act.* In pleading an official document or official act, it suffices to allege that the document was legally issued or the act legally done. FRCP 9(d).

   e. *Judgment.* In pleading a judgment or decision of a domestic or foreign court, a judicial or quasi-judicial tribunal, or a board or officer, it suffices to plead the judgment or decision without showing jurisdiction to render it. FRCP 9(e).

   f. *Time and place.* An allegation of time or place is material when testing the sufficiency of a pleading. FRCP 9(f).

   g. *Special damages.* If an item of special damage is claimed, it must be specifically stated. FRCP 9(g).

h. *Admiralty or maritime claim*

    i. *How designated.* If a claim for relief is within the admiralty or maritime jurisdiction and also within the court's subject-matter jurisdiction on some other ground, the pleading may designate the claim as an admiralty or maritime claim for purposes of FRCP 14(c), FRCP 38(e), and FRCP 82 and the Supplemental Rules for Admiralty or Maritime Claims and Asset Forfeiture Actions. A claim cognizable only in the admiralty or maritime jurisdiction is an admiralty or maritime claim for those purposes, whether or not so designated. FRCP 9(h)(1).

    ii. *Designation for appeal.* A case that includes an admiralty or maritime claim within FRCP 9(h) is an admiralty case within 28 U.S.C.A. § 1292(a)(3). FRCP 9(h)(2).

3. *Amended pleading*

a. *Amendments before trial.* The function of FRCP 15(a), which provides generally for the amendment of pleadings, is to enable a party to assert matters that were overlooked or were unknown at the time the party interposed the original complaint or answer. FPP § 1473; Smiga v. Dean Witter Reynolds, Inc., 766 F.2d 698, 703 (2d Cir. 1985).

    i. *Matters contained in amended pleading under FRCP 15(a).* Although FRCP 15(a) does not expressly state that an amendment must contain only matters that occurred within a particular time period, FRCP 15(d) provides that any "transaction, occurrence, or event that happened after the date of the pleading" should be set forth in a supplemental pleading. FPP § 1473. Thus, impliedly, an amended pleading, whether prepared with or without leave of court, only should relate to matters that have taken place prior to the date of the earlier pleading. FPP § 1473; Ford Motor Co. v. U.S., 19 C.I.T. 946, 896 F.Supp. 1224, 1230 (1995).

    ii. *Amending as a matter of course.* The right to amend as of course is not restricted to any particular litigant or pleading. FPP § 1480. It is a right conferred on all of the parties to an action and thus extends to persons who were not original parties to the litigation, but are brought into the action by way of counterclaim, crossclaim, third-party claim, or defensive interpleader. FPP § 1480; Johnson v. Walsh, 65 F.Supp. 157 (W.D.Mo. 1946).

        • *Amending a complaint with multiple defendants.* When a number of defendants are involved in an action, some of whom have answered and some of whom have filed no responsive pleading, the plaintiff can amend as a matter of course as to those defendants who have not answered. FEDPROC § 62:267; Pallant v. Sinatra, 7 F.R.D. 293 (S.D.N.Y. 1945). On the other hand, a plaintiff may not file an amended complaint as of right against those defendants who have not yet answered, if he or she has amended the complaint once already as a matter of course. FEDPROC § 62:267; Glaros v. Perse, 628 F.2d 679 (1st Cir. 1980).

    iii. *Amending with leave of court.* Refer to the United States District Court for the Southern District of Indiana KeyRules Motion for Leave to Amend document for information on amending the pleadings with leave of court.

    iv. *Types of amendments permitted under FRCP 15(a)*

        • *Cure a defective pleading.* Perhaps the most common use of FRCP 15(a) is by a party seeking to amend in order to cure a defective pleading. FPP § 1474.

        • *Correct insufficiently stated claims or defenses.* A more common use of FRCP 15(a) amendments is to correct insufficiently stated claims or defenses. Typically, amendments of this character involve either adding a necessary allegation in order to state a claim for relief or correcting a misnomer of a party to the action. FPP § 1474.

        • *Change nature or theory of claim or capacity of party.* Courts also have allowed a party to amend in order to change the nature or theory of the party's claim or the capacity in which the party is bringing the action. FPP § 1474.

        • *State additional claims or defenses or drop claims or defenses.* Plaintiffs and defendants also have been permitted to amend their pleadings to state additional claims, to assert additional defenses, or to drop claims or defenses. FPP § 1474; Weinberger v. Retail Credit Co., 498 F.2d 552, 554, n.4 (4th Cir. 1974).

- *Increase amount of damages or elect a different remedy.* A FRCP 15(a) amendment also is appropriate for increasing the amount of damages sought, or for electing a different remedy than the one originally requested. FPP § 1474; McFadden v. Sanchez, 710 F.2d 907 (2d Cir. 1983).

- *Add, substitute, or drop parties.* Finally, a party may make a FRCP 15(a) amendment to add, substitute, or drop parties to the action. FPP § 1474.

b. *Amendments during and after trial*

   i. *Based on an objection at trial.* If, at trial, a party objects that evidence is not within the issues raised in the pleadings, the court may permit the pleadings to be amended. The court should freely permit an amendment when doing so will aid in presenting the merits and the objecting party fails to satisfy the court that the evidence would prejudice that party's action or defense on the merits. The court may grant a continuance to enable the objecting party to meet the evidence. FRCP 15(b)(1).

   ii. *For issues tried by consent.* When an issue not raised by the pleadings is tried by the parties' express or implied consent, it must be treated in all respects as if raised in the pleadings. A party may move—at any time, even after judgment—to amend the pleadings to conform them to the evidence and to raise an unpleaded issue. But failure to amend does not affect the result of the trial of that issue. FRCP 15(b)(2).

   iii. Refer to the United States District Court for the Southern District of Indiana KeyRules Motion for Leave to Amend document for more information on moving to amend the pleadings.

c. *Relation back of amendments*

   i. *When an amendment relates back.* An amendment to a pleading relates back to the date of the original pleading when:

      - The law that provides the applicable statute of limitations allows relation back;

      - The amendment asserts a claim or defense that arose out of the conduct, transaction, or occurrence set out—or attempted to be set out—in the original pleading; or

      - The amendment changes the party or the naming of the party against whom a claim is asserted, if FRCP 15(c)(1)(B) is satisfied and if, within the period provided by FRCP 4(m) for serving the summons and complaint, the party to be brought in by amendment: (1) received such notice of the action that it will not be prejudiced in defending on the merits; and (2) knew or should have known that the action would have been brought against it, but for a mistake concerning the proper party's identity. FRCP 15(c)(1).

   ii. *Notice to the United States.* When the United States or a United States officer or agency is added as a defendant by amendment, the notice requirements of FRCP 15(c)(1)(C)(i) and FRCP 15(c)(1)(C)(ii) are satisfied if, during the stated period, process was delivered or mailed to the United States attorney or the United States attorney's designee, to the Attorney General of the United States, or to the officer or agency. FRCP 15(c)(2).

d. *Effect of an amended pleading.* A pleading that has been amended under FRCP 15(a) supersedes the pleading it modifies and remains in effect throughout the action unless it subsequently is modified. FPP § 1476. Once an amended pleading is interposed, the original pleading no longer performs any function in the case and any subsequent motion made by an opposing party should be directed at the amended pleading. FPP § 1476; Ferdik v. Bonzelet, 963 F.2d 1258, 1262 (9th Cir. 1992); Davis v. TXO Production Corp., 929 F.2d 1515, 1517 (10th Cir. 1991).

4. *Amended complaint.* Refer to the United States District Court for the Southern District of Indiana KeyRules Complaint document for the requirements specific to the amended complaint.

5. *Amended answer.* Refer to the United States District Court for the Southern District of Indiana KeyRules Answer document for the requirements specific to the amended answer.

6. *Right to a jury trial; Demand*

   a. *Right preserved.* The right of trial by jury as declared by U.S.C.A. Const. Amend. VII, or as provided by a federal statute, is preserved to the parties inviolate. FRCP 38(a).

b. *Demand.* On any issue triable of right by a jury, a party may demand a jury trial by:

   i. Serving the other parties with a written demand—which may be included in a pleading—no later than fourteen (14) days after the last pleading directed to the issue is served; and

   ii. Filing the demand in accordance with FRCP 5(d). FRCP 38(b).

c. *Specifying issues.* In its demand, a party may specify the issues that it wishes to have tried by a jury; otherwise, it is considered to have demanded a jury trial on all the issues so triable. If the party has demanded a jury trial on only some issues, any other party may—within fourteen (14) days after being served with the demand or within a shorter time ordered by the court—serve a demand for a jury trial on any other or all factual issues triable by jury. FRCP 38(c).

d. *Waiver; Withdrawal.* A party waives a jury trial unless its demand is properly served and filed. A proper demand may be withdrawn only if the parties consent. FRCP 38(d).

e. *Admiralty and maritime claims.* The rules in FRCP 38 do not create a right to a jury trial on issues in a claim that is an admiralty or maritime claim under FRCP 9(h). FRCP 38(e).

7. *Appearances.* Every attorney who represents a party or who files a document on a party's behalf must file an appearance for that party. IN R USDCTSD L.R. 83-7. The filing of a Notice of Appearance shall act to establish the filing attorney as an attorney of record representing a designated party or parties in a particular cause of action. As a result, it is necessary for each attorney to file a separate Notice of Appearance when entering an appearance in a case. A joint appearance on behalf of multiple attorneys may be filed electronically only if it is filed separately for each attorney, using his/her ECF login. IN R USDCTSD ECF Procedures(12). Only those attorneys who have filed an appearance in a pending action are entitled to be served with case documents under FRCP 5(a). IN R USDCTSD L.R. 83-7. For more information, refer to IN R USDCTSD L.R. 83-7 and IN R USDCTSD ECF Procedures(12).

8. *Notice of related action.* A party must file a notice of related action: as soon as it appears that the party's case and another pending case: (1) arise out of the same transaction or occurrence; (2) involve the same property; or (3) involve the validity or infringement or the same patent, trademark, or copyright. IN R USDCTSD L.R. 40-1(d)(2). For more information, refer to IN R USDCTSD L.R. 40-1.

9. *Alternative dispute resolution (ADR)*

a. *Application.* Unless limited by specific provisions, or unless there are other applicable specific statutory, common law, or constitutional procedures, the Local Alternative Dispute Resolution Rules of the United States District Court for the Southern District of Indiana shall apply in all civil litigation filed in the U.S. District Court for the Southern District of Indiana, except in the following cases and proceedings:

   i. Applications for writs of habeas corpus under 28 U.S.C.A. § 2254;

   ii. Forfeiture cases;

   iii. Non-adversary proceedings in bankruptcy;

   iv. Social Security administrative review cases; and

   v. Such other matters as specified by order of the Court; for example, matters involving important public policy issues, constitutional law, or the establishment of new law. IN R USDCTSD A.D.R. Rule 1.2.

b. *Mediation.* Mediation under this section (IN R USDCTSD A.D.R. Rule 2.1, et seq.) involves the confidential process by which a person acting as a Mediator, selected by the parties or appointed by the Court, assists the litigants in reaching a mutually acceptable agreement. It is an informal and nonadversarial process. The role of the Mediator is to assist in identifying the issues, reducing misunderstandings, clarifying priorities, exploring areas of compromise, and finding points of agreement as well as legitimate points of disagreement. Final decision-making authority rests with the parties, not the Mediator. IN R USDCTSD A.D.R. Rule 2.1. It is anticipated that an agreement may not resolve all of the disputed issues, but the process, nonetheless, can reduce points of contention. Parties and their representatives are required to mediate in good faith, but are not compelled to reach an agreement. IN R USDCTSD A.D.R. Rule 2.1.

   i. *Case selection.* The Court with the agreement of the parties may refer a civil case for mediation.

Unless otherwise ordered or as specifically provided in IN R USDCTSD A.D.R. Rule 2.8, referral to mediation does not abate or suspend the action, and no scheduled dates shall be delayed or deferred, including the date of trial. IN R USDCTSD A.D.R. Rule 2.2.

ii. For more information on mediation, refer to IN R USDCTSD A.D.R. Rule 2.1, et seq.

c. *Other methods of dispute resolution.* The Local Alternative Dispute Resolution Rules of the United States District Court for the Southern District of Indiana shall not preclude the parties from utilizing any other reasonable method or technique of alternative dispute resolution to resolve disputes to which the parties agree. However, any use of arbitration by the parties will be governed by and comply with the requirements of 28 U.S.C.A. § 654 through 28 U.S.C.A. § 657. IN R USDCTSD A.D.R. Rule 1.5.

d. For more information on alternative dispute resolution (ADR), refer to IN R USDCTSD A.D.R. Rule 1.1, et seq.

10. *Notice of settlement or resolution.* The parties must immediately notify the court if they reasonably anticipate settling their case or resolving a pending motion. IN R USDCTSD L.R. 7-1(h).

11. *Modification or suspension of rules.* The court may, on its own motion or at the request of a party, suspend or modify any rule in a particular case in the interest of justice. IN R USDCTSD L.R. 1-1(c).

D. Documents

1. *Required documents*

a. *Amended pleading.* Refer to the General Requirements section of this document for the form and contents of the amended pleading.

b. *Certificate of service.* FRCP 5(d) requires that the person making service under FRCP 5 certify that service has been effected. FRCP 5(Advisory Committee Notes). Having such information on file may be useful for many purposes, including proof of service if an issue arises concerning the effectiveness of the service. FRCP 5(Advisory Committee Notes).

i. *Certificate of service for electronically-filed documents.* A certificate of service must be included with all documents filed electronically. Such certificate shall indicate that service was accomplished pursuant to the Court's electronic filing procedures. IN R USDCTSD ECF Procedures(11). For the suggested format for a certificate of service for electronic filing, refer to IN R USDCTSD ECF Procedures(11).

2. *Supplemental documents*

a. *Notice of constitutional question.* A party that files a pleading, written motion, or other paper drawing into question the constitutionality of a federal or state statute must promptly:

i. *File notice.* File a notice of constitutional question stating the question and identifying the paper that raises it, if:

- A federal statute is questioned and the parties do not include the United States, one of its agencies, or one of its officers or employees in an official capacity; or

- A state statute is questioned and the parties do not include the state, one of its agencies, or one of its officers or employees in an official capacity; and

ii. *Serve notice.* Serve the notice and paper on the Attorney General of the United States if a federal statute is questioned—or on the state attorney general if a state statute is questioned—either by certified or registered mail or by sending it to an electronic address designated by the attorney general for this purpose. FRCP 5.1(a).

iii. *Time for filing.* A notice of constitutional challenge to a statute filed in accordance with FRCP 5.1 must be filed at the same time the parties tender their proposed case management plan, if one is required, or within twenty-one (21) days of the filing drawing into question the constitutionality of a federal or state statute, whichever occurs later. IN R USDCTSD L.R. 5.1-1(a).

iv. *Additional service requirements.* If a federal statute is challenged, in addition to the service requirements of FRCP 5.1(a), the party filing the notice of constitutional challenge must serve the notice and documents on the United States Attorney for the Southern District of Indiana, either by certified or registered mail or by sending it to an electronic address designated for that purpose by that official. IN R USDCTSD L.R. 5.1-1(b).

    v. *No forfeiture.* A party's failure to file and serve the notice, or the court's failure to certify, does not forfeit a constitutional claim or defense that is otherwise timely asserted. FRCP 5.1(d).

b. *Notice of issue concerning foreign law.* A party who intends to raise an issue about a foreign country's law must give notice by a pleading or other writing. In determining foreign law, the court may consider any relevant material or source, including testimony, whether or not submitted by a party or admissible under the Federal Rules of Evidence. The court's determination must be treated as a ruling on a question of law. FRCP 44.1.

c. *Index of exhibits.* Any pleading, motion, brief, affidavit, notice, or proposed order filed with the court, whether electronically or with the clerk, must: if it has four (4) or more exhibits, include a separate index that identifies and briefly describes each exhibit. IN R USDCTSD L.R. 5-1(b).

d. *Copy of document with self-address envelope.* To receive a file-stamped copy of a document filed directly with the clerk, a party must include with the original document an additional copy and a self-addressed envelope. The envelope must be big enough to hold the copy and have enough postage on it to send the copy via regular first-class mail. IN R USDCTSD L.R. 5-10(b).

e. *Notice of manual filing.* When a party who is not exempt from the electronic filing requirement files a document directly with the clerk, the party must: electronically file a notice of manual filing that explains why the document cannot be filed electronically. IN R USDCTSD L.R. 5-2(d)(1). Refer to the Filing and Service Requirements section of this document for more information.

    i. Where an individual component cannot be included in an electronic filing (e.g. the component cannot be converted to electronic format), the filer shall electronically file the prescribed Notice of Manual Filing in place of that component. A model form is provided as Appendix C (IN R USDCTSD ECF Procedures(Appendix C)). IN R USDCTSD ECF Procedures(13).

    ii. Before making a manual filing of a component, the filing party shall first electronically file a Notice of Manual Filing (See IN R USDCTSD ECF Procedures(Appendix C)). The filer shall initiate the electronic filing process as if filing the actual component but shall instead attach to the filing the Notice of Manual Filing setting forth the reason(s) why the component cannot be filed electronically. The manual filing should be accompanied by a copy of the previously filed Notice of Manual Filing. A party may seek to have a component excluded from electronic filing pursuant to applicable Federal and Local Rules (e.g., FRCP 26(c)). IN R USDCTSD ECF Procedures(15).

f. *Courtesy copies.* District Judges and Magistrate Judges regularly receive documents filed by all parties. Therefore, parties shall not bring "courtesy copies" to any chambers unless specifically directed to do so by the Court. IN R USDCTSD Case Mgt(General Instructions For All Cases).

g. *Copies for three-judge court.* Parties in a case where a three-judge court has been requested must file an original and three copies of any document filed directly with the clerk (instead of electronically) until the court: (1) denies the request; (2) dissolves the three-judge court; or (3) allows the parties to file fewer copies. IN R USDCTSD L.R. 9-2(c).

h. *Declaration that party was unable to file in a timely manner due to technical difficulties.* If a party misses a filing deadline due to an inability to file electronically, the party may submit the untimely filed document, accompanied by a declaration stating the reason(s) for missing the deadline. IN R USDCTSD ECF Procedures(16). A model form is provided as Appendix D (IN R USDCTSD ECF Procedures(Appendix D)). IN R USDCTSD ECF Procedures(16).

3. *Documents required for an amended complaint adding a new claim for relief or new party.* Refer to the United States District Court for the Southern District of Indiana KeyRules Complaint document for the documents for an amended complaint adding a new claim for relief or being filed and served against a new party.

E. Format

1. *Form of documents*

a. *Paper (manual filings only).* Any document that is not filed electronically must: be flat, unfolded, and

on good-quality, eight and one-half by eleven (8-1/2 x 11) inch white paper. IN R USDCTSD L.R. 5-1(d)(1). Any document that is not filed electronically must: be single-sided. IN R USDCTSD L.R. 5-1(d)(1).

   i. *Covers or backing.* Any document that is not filed electronically must: not have a cover or a back. IN R USDCTSD L.R. 5-1(d)(1).

   ii. *Fastening.* Any document that is not filed electronically must: be (if consisting of more than one (1) page) fastened by paperclip or binder clip and may not be stapled. IN R USDCTSD L.R. 5-1(d)(1).

      • *Request for nonconforming fastening.* If a document cannot be fastened or bound as required by IN R USDCTSD L.R. 5-1(d), a party may ask the clerk for permission to fasten it in another manner. The party must make such a request before attempting to file the document with nonconforming fastening. IN R USDCTSD L.R. 5-1(d)(2).

   iii. *Hole punching.* Any document that is not filed electronically must: be two-hole punched at the top with the holes two and three-quarter (2-3/4) inches apart and appropriately centered. IN R USDCTSD L.R. 5-1(d)(1).

b. *Margins.* Any pleading, motion, brief, affidavit, notice, or proposed order filed with the court, whether electronically or with the clerk, must: have at least one (1) inch margins. IN R USDCTSD L.R. 5-1(b).

c. *Spacing.* Any pleading, motion, brief, affidavit, notice, or proposed order filed with the court, whether electronically or with the clerk, must: be double spaced (except for headings, footnotes, and quoted material). IN R USDCTSD L.R. 5-1(b).

d. *Text.* Any pleading, motion, brief, affidavit, notice, or proposed order filed with the court, whether electronically or with the clerk, must: be plainly typewritten, printed, or prepared by a clearly legible copying process. IN R USDCTSD L.R. 5-1(b).

e. *Font size.* Any pleading, motion, brief, affidavit, notice, or proposed order filed with the court, whether electronically or with the clerk, must: use at least 12-point type in the body of the document and at least 10-point type in footnotes. IN R USDCTSD L.R. 5-1(b).

f. *Page numbering.* Any pleading, motion, brief, affidavit, notice, or proposed order filed with the court, whether electronically or with the clerk, must: have consecutively numbered pages. IN R USDCTSD L.R. 5-1(b).

g. *Caption; Names of parties.* Every pleading must have a caption with the court's name, a title, a file number, and a FRCP 7(a) designation. The title of the complaint must name all the parties; the title of other pleadings, after naming the first party on each side, may refer generally to other parties. FRCP 10(a). Any pleading, motion, brief, affidavit, notice, or proposed order filed with the court, whether electronically or with the clerk, must: include a title on the first page. IN R USDCTSD L.R. 5-1(b).

   i. *Jury demand.* A party demanding a jury trial in a pleading as permitted by FRCP 38(b) must include the demand in the title by way of a notation placed on the front page of the pleading, immediately following the title of the pleading, stating "Demand for Jury Trial." Failure to do so will not result in a waiver under FRCP 38(d) if a jury demand is otherwise properly filed and served under FRCP 38(b). IN R USDCTSD L.R. 38-1.

h. *Filer's information.* Any pleading, motion, brief, affidavit, notice, or proposed order filed with the court, whether electronically or with the clerk, must: in the case of pleadings, motions, legal briefs, and notices, include the name, complete address, telephone number, facsimile number (where available), and e-mail address (where available) of the pro se litigant or attorney who files it. IN R USDCTSD L.R. 5-1(b).

i. *Paragraphs; Separate statements.* A party must state its claims or defenses in numbered paragraphs, each limited as far as practicable to a single set of circumstances. A later pleading may refer by number to a paragraph in an earlier pleading. If doing so would promote clarity, each claim founded on a separate transaction or occurrence—and each defense other than a denial—must be stated in a separate count or defense. FRCP 10(b).

j. *Adoption by reference; Exhibits.* A statement in a pleading may be adopted by reference elsewhere in the same pleading or in any other pleading or motion. A copy of a written instrument that is an exhibit to a pleading is a part of the pleading for all purposes. FRCP 10(c).

k. *Citations*

    i. *Local rules.* The Local Rules of the United States District Court for the Southern District of Indiana may be cited as "S.D. Ind. L.R." IN R USDCTSD L.R. 1-1(a).

    ii. *Local alternative dispute resolution rules.* These Rules shall be known as the Local Alternative Dispute Resolution Rules of the United States District Court for the Southern District of Indiana. They shall be cited as "S.D.Ind. Local A.D.R. Rule _____." IN R USDCTSD A.D.R. Rule 1.1.

l. *Acceptance by the clerk.* The clerk must not refuse to file a paper solely because it is not in the form prescribed by the Federal Rules of Civil Procedure or by a local rule or practice. FRCP 5(d)(4). The clerk will accept a document that violates IN R USDCTSD L.R. 5-1, but the court may exclude the document from the official record. IN R USDCTSD L.R. 5-1(e).

    i. *Sanctions for errors as to form.* The court may strike from the record any document that does not comply with the rules governing the form of documents filed with the court, such as rules that regulate document size or the number of copies to be filed or that require a special designation in the caption. The court may also sanction an attorney or party who files a non-compliant document. IN R USDCTSD L.R. 1-3.

2. *Form of electronic documents.* Any document submitted via the court's electronic case filing (ECF) system must be: otherwise prepared and filed in a manner consistent with the CM/ECF Policies and Procedures Manual (IN R USDCTSD ECF Procedures). IN R USDCTSD L.R. 5-1(c). Electronically filed documents must meet the requirements of FRCP 10 (Form of Pleadings), IN R USDCTSD L.R. 5-1 (Format of Papers Presented for Filing), and FRCP 5.2 (Privacy Protection for Filings Made with the Court), as if they had been submitted on paper. Documents filed electronically are also subject to any page limitations set forth by Court Order, by IN R USDCTSD L.R. 7-1 (Motion Practice), or IN R USDCTSD L.R. 56-1 (Summary Judgment Practice), as applicable. IN R USDCTSD ECF Procedures(13).

a. *PDF format required.* Any document submitted via the court's electronic case filing (ECF) system must be: in .pdf format. IN R USDCTSD L.R. 5-1(c); IN R USDCTSD ECF Procedures(7). Any document submitted via the court's electronic case filing (ECF) system must be: converted to a .pdf file directly from a word processing program, unless it exists only in paper format (in which case it may be scanned to create a .pdf document). IN R USDCTSD L.R. 5-1(c); IN R USDCTSD ECF Procedures(13).

    i. An exhibit may be scanned into PDF format, at a recommended 300 dpi resolution or higher, only if it does not already exist in electronic format. The filing attorney is responsible for reviewing all PDF documents for legibility before submitting them through the Court's Electronic Case Filing system. For technical guidance in creating PDF documents, please contact the Clerk's Office. IN R USDCTSD ECF Procedures(13).

b. *File size limitations.* Any document submitted via the court's electronic case filing (ECF) system must be: submitted as one or more .pdf files that do not exceed ten megabytes (10 MB) each (consistent with the CM/ECF Policies and Procedures Manual (IN R USDCTSD ECF Procedures)). IN R USDCTSD L.R. 5-1(c); IN R USDCTSD ECF Procedures(13).

    i. To electronically file a document or attachment that exceeds ten megabytes (10 MB), the document must first be broken down into two or more smaller files. For example, if Exhibit A is a twelve megabyte (12 MB) PDF file, it should be divided into 2 equal parts prior to electronic filing. Each component part of the exhibit would be filed as an attachment to the main document and described appropriately as "Exhibit A (part 1 of 2)" and "Exhibit A (part 2 of 2)." IN R USDCTSD ECF Procedures(13).

    ii. The supporting items mentioned in IN R USDCTSD ECF Procedures(13) should not be confused with memorandums or briefs in support of motions as outlined in IN R USDCTSD L.R. 7-1 or IN R USDCTSD L.R. 56-1. These memorandums or briefs in support are to be filed as entirely separate documents pursuant to the appropriate rule. Additionally, no motion shall be embodied in the text of a response or reply brief/memorandum unless otherwise ordered by the Court. IN R USDCTSD ECF Procedures(13).

c. *Separate component parts.* A key objective of the electronic filing system is to ensure that as much of the case as possible is managed electronically. To facilitate electronic filing and retrieval, documents to be filed electronically are to be reasonably broken into their separate component parts. By way of example, most filings include a foundation document (e.g., motion) and other supporting items (e.g., exhibits, proposed orders, proposed amended pleadings). The foundation document, as well as the supporting items, are each separate components of the filing; supporting items must be filed as attachments to the foundation document. These exhibits or attachments should include only those excerpts of the referenced documents that are directly germane to the matter under consideration. IN R USDCTSD ECF Procedures(13).

    i. Where an individual component cannot be included in an electronic filing (e.g. the component cannot be converted to electronic format), the filer shall electronically file the prescribed Notice of Manual Filing in place of that component. A model form is provided as Appendix C (IN R USDCTSD ECF Procedures(Appendix C)). IN R USDCTSD ECF Procedures(13).

d. *Exhibits.* Each electronically filed exhibit to a main document must be: (1) created as a separate .pdf file; (2) submitted as an attachment to the main document and given a title which describes its content; and (3) limited to excerpts that are directly germane to the main document's subject matter. IN R USDCTSD L.R. 5-6(a).

    i. When uploading attachments during the electronic filing process, exhibits must be uploaded in a logical sequence and a brief description must be entered for each individual PDF file. The description must include not only the exhibit number or letter, but also a brief description of the document. This information may be entered in CM/ECF using a combination of the Category drop-down menu, the Description text box, or both (see IN R USDCTSD ECF Procedures(13)(Figure 1)). The information that is provided in each box will be combined to create a description of the document as it appears on the case docket (see IN R USDCTSD ECF Procedures(13)(Figure 2)). IN R USDCTSD ECF Procedures(13). For an example, refer to IN R USDCTSD ECF Procedures(13).

e. *Excerpts.* A party filing an exhibit that consists of excerpts from a larger document must clearly and prominently identify the exhibit as containing excerpted material. Either party will have the right to timely file additional excerpts or the complete document to the extent they are or become directly germane to the main document's subject matter. IN R USDCTSD L.R. 5-6(b).

f. For an example illustrating the application of IN R USDCTSD ECF Procedures(13), refer to IN R USDCTSD ECF Procedures(13).

3. *Signing of pleadings, motions and other papers*

a. *Signature.* Every pleading, written motion, and other paper must be signed by at least one attorney of record in the attorney's name—or by a party personally if the party is unrepresented. The paper must state the signer's address, e-mail address, and telephone number. FRCP 11(a).

    i. *Signatures on manual filings.* Any document that is not filed electronically must: include the original signature of the pro se litigant or attorney who files it. IN R USDCTSD L.R. 5-1(d)(1).

    ii. *Electronic signatures.* Use of the attorney's login and password when filing documents electronically serves in part as the attorney's signature for purposes of FRCP 11, the Local Rules of the United States District Court for the Southern District of Indiana, and any other purpose for which a signature is required in connection with proceedings before the Court. IN R USDCTSD ECF Procedures(14); IN R USDCTSD ECF Procedures(10). A pleading, motion, brief, or notice filed electronically under an attorney's ECF log-in and password must be signed by that attorney. IN R USDCTSD L.R. 5-7(a). A signature on a document other than a document filed as provided under IN R USDCTSD L.R. 5-7(a) must be an original handwritten signature and must be scanned into .pdf format for electronic filing. IN R USDCTSD L.R. 5-7(c); IN R USDCTSD ECF Procedures(14).

       • *Form of electronic signature.* If a document is converted directly from a word processing application to .pdf (as opposed to scanning), the name of the Filing User under whose log-in and password the document is submitted must be preceded by a "s/" and typed on the signature line where the Filing User's handwritten signature would otherwise appear. IN R USDCTSD L.R. 5-7(b). All documents filed electronically shall include a signature block and include the filing attorney's typewritten name, address, telephone number, facsimile number and e-mail address. In addition, the name of the filing attorney under whose ECF login the document will be filed should be preceded by a "s/" and typed in the space where the attorney's handwritten signature would otherwise appear. IN R US-DCTSD ECF Procedures(14). For a sample format, refer to IN R USDCTSD ECF Procedures(14).

- *Effect of electronic signature.* Filing an electronically signed document under an attorney's ECF log-in and password constitutes the attorney's signature on the document under the Federal Rules of Civil Procedure, under the Local Rules of the United States District Court for the Southern District of Indiana, and for any other reason a signature is required in connection with the court's activities. IN R USDCTSD L.R. 5-7(d).

- *Documents with multiple attorneys' signatures.* Documents requiring signatures of more than one attorney shall be filed either by: (1) obtaining consent from the other attorney, then typing the "s/ [Name]" signature of the other attorney on the signature line where the other attorney's signature would otherwise appear; (2) identifying in the signature section the name of the other attorney whose signature is required and by the submission of a Notice of Endorsement (see IN R USDCTSD ECF Procedures(Appendix B)) by the other attorney no later than three (3) business days after filing; (3) submitting a scanned document containing all handwritten signatures; or (4) in any other manner approved by the Court. IN R USDCTSD ECF Procedures(14); IN R USDCTSD L.R. 5-7(e).

iii. *No verification or accompanying affidavit required for pleadings.* Unless a rule or statute specifically states otherwise, a pleading need not be verified or accompanied by an affidavit. FRCP 11(a).

iv. *Unsigned papers.* The court must strike an unsigned paper unless the omission is promptly corrected after being called to the attorney's or party's attention. FRCP 11(a). The court will strike any document filed directly with the clerk that is not signed by an attorney of record or the pro se litigant filing it, but the court may do so only after giving the attorney or pro se litigant notice of the omission and reasonable time to correct it. Rubber-stamp or facsimile signatures are not original signatures and the court will deem documents containing them to be unsigned for purposes of FRCP 11 and FRCP 26(g) and IN R USDCTSD L.R. 5-10. IN R USDCTSD L.R. 5-10(g).

b. *Representations to the court.* By presenting to the court a pleading, written motion, or other paper—whether by signing, filing, submitting, or later advocating it—an attorney or unrepresented party certifies that to the best of the person's knowledge, information, and belief, formed after an inquiry reasonable under the circumstances:

i. It is not being presented for any improper purpose, such as to harass, cause unnecessary delay, or needlessly increase the cost of litigation;

ii. The claims, defenses, and other legal contentions are warranted by existing law or by a nonfrivolous argument for extending, modifying, or reversing existing law or for establishing new law;

iii. The factual contentions have evidentiary support or, if specifically so identified, will likely have evidentiary support after a reasonable opportunity for further investigation or discovery; and

iv. The denials of factual contentions are warranted on the evidence or, if specifically so identified, are reasonably based on belief or a lack of information. FRCP 11(b).

c. *Sanctions.* If, after notice and a reasonable opportunity to respond, the court determines that FRCP 11(b) has been violated, the court may impose an appropriate sanction on any attorney, law firm, or party that violated FRCP 11(b) or is responsible for the violation. FRCP 11(c)(1). Refer to the United

States District Court for the Southern District of Indiana KeyRules Motion for Sanctions document for more information.

4. *Privacy protection for filings made with the court.* Electronically filed documents must meet the requirements of. . .FRCP 5.2 (Privacy Protection for Filings Made with the Court), as if they had been submitted on paper. IN R USDCTSD ECF Procedures(13).

a. *Redacted filings.* Unless the court orders otherwise, in an electronic or paper filing with the court that contains an individual's Social Security number, taxpayer-identification number, or birth date, the name of an individual known to be a minor, or a financial-account number, a party or nonparty making the filing may include only:

   i. The last four (4) digits of the Social Security number and taxpayer-identification number;

   ii. The year of the individual's birth;

   iii. The minor's initials; and

   iv. The last four (4) digits of the financial-account number. FRCP 5.2(a).

b. *Exemptions from the redaction requirement.* The redaction requirement does not apply to the following:

   i. A financial-account number that identifies the property allegedly subject to forfeiture in a forfeiture proceeding;

   ii. The record of an administrative or agency proceeding;

   iii. The official record of a state-court proceeding;

   iv. The record of a court or tribunal, if that record was not subject to the redaction requirement when originally filed;

   v. A filing covered by FRCP 5.2(c) or FRCP 5.2(d); and

   vi. A pro se filing in an action brought under 28 U.S.C.A. § 2241, 28 U.S.C.A. § 2254, or 28 U.S.C.A. § 2255. FRCP 5.2(b).

c. *Limitations on remote access to electronic files; Social Security appeals and immigration cases.* Unless the court orders otherwise, in an action for benefits under the Social Security Act, and in an action or proceeding relating to an order of removal, to relief from removal, or to immigration benefits or detention, access to an electronic file is authorized as follows:

   i. The parties and their attorneys may have remote electronic access to any part of the case file, including the administrative record;

   ii. Any other person may have electronic access to the full record at the courthouse, but may have remote electronic access only to:

   - The docket maintained by the court; and

   - An opinion, order, judgment, or other disposition of the court, but not any other part of the case file or the administrative record. FRCP 5.2(c).

d. *Filings made under seal.* The court may order that a filing be made under seal without redaction. The court may later unseal the filing or order the person who made the filing to file a redacted version for the public record. FRCP 5.2(d). For more information on filing under seal, refer to IN R USDCTSD L.R. 5-11 and IN R USDCTSD ECF Procedures(18).

e. *Protective orders.* For good cause, the court may by order in a case:

   i. Require redaction of additional information; or

   ii. Limit or prohibit a nonparty's remote electronic access to a document filed with the court. FRCP 5.2(e).

f. *Option for additional unredacted filing under seal.* A person making a redacted filing may also file an unredacted copy under seal. The court must retain the unredacted copy as part of the record. FRCP 5.2(f).

g. *Option for filing a reference list.* A filing that contains redacted information may be filed together with a reference list that identifies each item of redacted information and specifies an appropriate identifier that uniquely corresponds to each item listed. The list must be filed under seal and may be amended as of right. Any reference in the case to a listed identifier will be construed to refer to the corresponding item of information. FRCP 5.2(g).

h. *Waiver of protection of identifiers.* A person waives the protection of FRCP 5.2(a) as to the person's own information by filing it without redaction and not under seal. FRCP 5.2(h).

F. Filing and Service Requirements

1. *Filing requirements.* Any paper after the complaint that is required to be served—together with a certificate of service—must be filed within a reasonable time after service. FRCP 5(d)(1).

    a. *How filing is made; In general.* A paper is filed by delivering it:

        i. To the clerk; or

        ii. To a judge who agrees to accept it for filing, and who must then note the filing date on the paper and promptly send it to the clerk. FRCP 5(d)(2).

            • In certain instances, the court will direct the parties to submit items directly to chambers (e.g., confidential settlement statements). However, absent specific prior authorization, counsel and litigants should not submit letters or documents directly to chambers, and such materials should be filed with the clerk. IN R USDCTSD L.R. 5-1(Local Rules Advisory Committee Comment).

        iii. A document or item submitted in relation to a matter within the court's jurisdiction is deemed filed upon delivery to the office of the clerk in a manner prescribed by the Local Rules of the United States District Court for the Southern District of Indiana or the Federal Rules of Civil Procedure or authorized by the court. Any submission directed to a Judge or Judge's staff, the office of the clerk or any employee thereof, in a manner that is not contemplated by IN R USDCTSD L.R. 5-1 and without prior court authorization is prohibited. IN R USDCTSD L.R. 5-1(a).

    b. *Non-electronic filing.* Any document that is exempt from electronic filing must be filed directly with the clerk and served on other parties in the case as required by those Federal Rules of Civil Procedure and Local Rules of the United States District Court for the Southern District of Indiana that apply to the service of non-electronic documents. IN R USDCTSD L.R. 5-2(c).

        i. *When completed.* A document or other item that is not required to be filed electronically is deemed filed:

            • Upon delivery in person, by courier, or via U.S. Mail or other mail delivery service to the clerk's office during business hours;

            • When the courtroom deputy clerk accepts it, if the document or item is filed in open court; or

            • Upon completion of any other manner of filing that the court authorizes. IN R USDCTSD L.R. 5-10(a).

        ii. *Document filing by non-exempt party.* When a party who is not exempt from the electronic filing requirement files a document directly with the clerk, the party must:

            • Electronically file a notice of manual filing that explains why the document cannot be filed electronically;

            • Present the document to the clerk within one (1) business day after filing the notice of manual filing; and

            • Present the clerk with a copy of the notice of manual filing when the party files the document with the clerk. IN R USDCTSD L.R. 5-2(d).

    c. *Electronic filing*

        i. *Authorization of electronic filing program.* A court may, by local rule, allow papers to be filed, signed, or verified by electronic means that are consistent with any technical standards established by the Judicial Conference of the United States. A local rule may require electronic filing only if reasonable exceptions are allowed. A paper filed electronically in compliance with a local rule is a written paper for purposes of the Federal Rules of Civil Procedure. FRCP 5(d)(3).

- IN R USDCTSD L.R. 5-2 requires electronic filing, as allowed by FRCP 5(d)(3). The policies and procedures in IN R USDCTSD ECF Procedures govern electronic filing in this district unless, due to circumstances in a particular case, a judicial officer determines that these policies and procedures (IN R USDCTSD ECF Procedures) should be modified. IN R USDCTSD ECF Procedures(1).

- Unless modified by order of the Court, all Federal Rules of Civil Procedure and Local Rules of the United States District Court for the Southern District of Indiana shall continue to apply to cases maintained in the Court's Case Management/Electronic Case Filing System (CM/ECF). IN R USDCTSD ECF Procedures(3).

ii. *Mandatory electronic filing.* Unless exempted pursuant to IN R USDCTSD L.R. 5-3(e), attorneys admitted to the court's bar (including those admitted pro hac vice) or authorized to represent the United States must use the court's ECF system to file documents. IN R USDCTSD L.R. 5-3(a). Electronic filing by attorneys is required for eligible documents filed in civil and criminal cases pending with the Court, unless specifically exempted by Local Rule or Court Order. IN R USDCTSD ECF Procedures(4).

- *Exceptions.* All civil cases (other than those cases the court specifically exempts) must be maintained in the court's electronic case filing (ECF) system. Accordingly, as allowed by FRCP 5(d)(3), every document filed in this court (including exhibits) must be transmitted to the clerk's office via the ECF system consistent with IN R USDCTSD L.R. 5-2 through IN R USDCTSD L.R. 5-11 except: (1) documents filed by pro se litigants; (2) transcripts in cases filed by claimants under the Social Security Act (and related statutes); (3) exhibits in a format that does not readily permit electronic filing (such as videos and large maps and charts); (4) documents that are illegible when scanned into .pdf format; (5) documents filed in cases not maintained on the ECF system; and (6) any other documents that the court or the Local Rules of the United States District Court for the Southern District of Indiana specifically allow to be filed directly with the clerk. IN R USDCTSD L.R. 5-2(a). Parties otherwise participating in the electronic filing system may be excused from filing a particular component electronically under certain limited circumstances, such as when the component cannot be reduced to an electronic format. Such components shall not be filed electronically, but instead shall be manually filed with the Clerk of Court and served upon the parties in accordance with the applicable Federal Rules of Civil Procedure and the Local Rules of the United States District Court for the Southern District of Indiana for filing and service of non-electronic documents. IN R USDCTSD ECF Procedures(15).

- *Exemption from participation.* The court may exempt attorneys from using the ECF system in a particular case for good cause. An attorney must file a petition for ECF exemption and a CM/ECF technical requirements exemption questionnaire in each case in which the attorney seeks an exemption. (The CM/ECF technical requirements exemption questionnaire is available on the court's website). IN R USDCTSD L.R. 5-3(e).

iii. *Consequences of electronic filing.* Electronic transmission of a document consistent with the procedures adopted by the Court shall, upon the complete receipt of the same by the Clerk of Court, constitute filing of the document for all purposes of the Federal Rules of Civil and Criminal Procedure and the Local Rules of the United States District Court for the Southern District of Indiana, and shall constitute entry of that document onto the docket maintained by the Clerk pursuant to FRCP 58 and FRCP 79. IN R USDCTSD ECF Procedures(7); IN R USDCTSD L.R. 5-4(c)(1). When a document has been filed electronically: the document, as filed, binds the filing party. IN R USDCTSD L.R. 5-4(c)(3).

- A Notice of Electronic Filing (NEF) acknowledging that the document has been filed will immediately appear on the filer's screen after the document has been submitted. Attorneys are strongly encouraged to print or electronically save a copy of the NEF. Attorneys can also verify the filing of documents by inspecting the Court's electronic docket sheet through the use of a PACER login. IN R USDCTSD ECF Procedures(7). When a document has been filed electronically: the notice of electronic filing for the document serves as the court's date-stamp and proof of filing. IN R USDCTSD L.R. 5-4(c)(4).

- The Court may, upon the motion of a party or upon its own motion, strike any inappropriately filed document. IN R USDCTSD ECF Procedures(7).

iv. For more information on electronic filing, refer to IN R USDCTSD ECF Procedures.

d. *Fax filing.* The clerk may not file a faxed document without court authorization. The court may not authorize the clerk to file faxed documents without finding that compelling circumstances justify it. A party must submit a copy of the document that otherwise complies with IN R USDCTSD L.R. 5-10 to replace the faxed copy within seven (7) days after faxing the document. IN R USDCTSD L.R. 5-10(e).

2. *Service requirements*

a. *Service; When required*

i. *In general.* Unless the Federal Rules of Civil Procedure provide otherwise, each of the following papers must be served on every party:

- An order stating that service is required;

- A pleading filed after the original complaint, unless the court orders otherwise under FRCP 5(c) because there are numerous defendants;

- A discovery paper required to be served on a party, unless the court orders otherwise;

- A written motion, except one that may be heard ex parte; and

- A written notice, appearance, demand, or offer of judgment, or any similar paper. FRCP 5(a)(1).

ii. *If a party fails to appear.* No service is required on a party who is in default for failing to appear. But a pleading that asserts a new claim for relief against such a party must be served on that party under FRCP 4. FRCP 5(a)(2).

iii. *Seizing property.* If an action is begun by seizing property and no person is or need be named as a defendant, any service required before the filing of an appearance, answer, or claim must be made on the person who had custody or possession of the property when it was seized. FRCP 5(a)(3).

b. *Service; How made*

i. *Serving an attorney.* If a party is represented by an attorney, service under FRCP 5 must be made on the attorney unless the court orders service on the party. FRCP 5(b)(1).

ii. *Service in general.* A paper is served under FRCP 5 by:

- Handing it to the person;

- Leaving it: (1) at the person's office with a clerk or other person in charge or, if no one is in charge, in a conspicuous place in the office; or (2) if the person has no office or the office is closed, at the person's dwelling or usual place of abode with someone of suitable age and discretion who resides there;

- Mailing it to the person's last known address—in which event service is complete upon mailing;

- Leaving it with the court clerk if the person has no known address;

- Sending it by electronic means if the person consented in writing—in which event service is complete upon transmission, but is not effective if the serving party learns that it did not reach the person to be served; or

- Delivering it by any other means that the person consented to in writing—in which event service is complete when the person making service delivers it to the agency designated to make delivery. FRCP 5(b)(2).

iii. *Electronic service*

- *Consent.* By registering to use the ECF system, attorneys consent to electronic service of documents filed in cases maintained on the ECF system. IN R USDCTSD L.R. 5-3(d). By participating in the Electronic Case Filing Program, attorneys consent to the electronic service of documents, and shall make available electronic mail addresses for service. IN R USDCTSD ECF Procedures(11).

- *Service on registered parties.* Upon the filing of a document by a party, an e-mail message will be automatically generated by the electronic filing system and sent via electronic mail to the e-mail addresses of all registered attorneys who have appeared in the case. The Notice of Electronic Filing will contain a document hyperlink which will provide recipients with one "free look" at the electronically filed document. Recipients are encouraged to print and/or save a copy of the document during the "free look" to avoid incurring PACER charges for future viewings of the document. IN R USDCTSD ECF Procedures(11). When a document has been filed electronically: transmission of the notice of electronic filing generated by the ECF system to an attorney's e-mail address constitutes service of the document on that attorney. IN R USDCTSD L.R. 5-4(c)(5). The party effectuates service on all registered attorneys by filing electronically. IN R USDCTSD ECF Procedures(11). When a document has been filed electronically: no other attempted service will constitute electronic service of the document. IN R USDCTSD L.R. 5-4(c)(6).

- *Service on exempt parties.* A filer must serve a copy of the document consistent with FRCP 5 on any party or attorney who is exempt from participating in electronic filing. IN R USDCTSD L.R. 5-4(d). It is the responsibility of the filing attorney to conventionally serve all parties who do not receive electronic service (the identity of these parties will be indicated on the filing receipt generated by the ECF system). IN R USDCTSD ECF Procedures(11).

- *Service on parties excused from electronic filing.* Parties otherwise participating in the electronic filing system may be excused from filing a particular component electronically under certain limited circumstances, such as when the component cannot be reduced to an electronic format. Such components shall not be filed electronically, but instead shall be manually filed with the Clerk of Court and served upon the parties in accordance with the applicable Federal Rules of Civil Procedure and the Local Rules of the United States District Court for the Southern District of Indiana for filing and service of non-electronic documents. IN R USDCTSD ECF Procedures(15).

- *Service of exempt documents.* Any document that is exempt from electronic filing must be filed directly with the clerk and served on other parties in the case as required by those Federal Rules of Civil Procedure and Local Rules of the United States District Court for the Southern District of Indiana that apply to the service of non-electronic documents. IN R USDCTSD L.R. 5-2(c).

iv. *Using court facilities.* If a local rule so authorizes, a party may use the court's transmission facilities to make service under FRCP 5(b)(2)(E). FRCP 5(b)(3).

c. *Serving numerous defendants*

i. *In general.* If an action involves an unusually large number of defendants, the court may, on motion or on its own, order that:

- Defendants' pleadings and replies to them need not be served on other defendants;

- Any crossclaim, counterclaim, avoidance, or affirmative defense in those pleadings and replies to them will be treated as denied or avoided by all other parties; and

- Filing any such pleading and serving it on the plaintiff constitutes notice of the pleading to all parties. FRCP 5(c)(1).

ii. *Notifying parties.* A copy of every such order must be served on the parties as the court directs. FRCP 5(c)(2).

3. *Service requirements of an amended complaint asserting new or additional claims for relief.* The service

of amended pleadings is generally governed by FRCP 5. Thus, except for an amended pleading against a defaulting party that does not assert new or additional claims for relief, an amended pleading must be served in accordance with FRCP 5. FEDPROC § 62:263; International Controls Corp. v. Vesco, 556 F.2d 665, 23 Fed.R.Serv.2d 923 (2d Cir. 1977). However, while FRCP 5 permits service of an amended complaint on counsel, where the amended complaint contains an entirely different cause of action that could not have been properly served originally by the method used in serving the original complaint, the amended complaint must be served in accordance with the terms of FRCP 4. FEDPROC § 62:263; Lasch v. Antkies, 161 F.Supp. 851 (E.D.Pa. 1958). Refer to the United States District Court for the Southern District of Indiana KeyRules Complaint document for more information on serving the amended complaint in accordance with FRCP 4.

G. Hearings

1. *Hearings, generally.* Generally, there is no hearing contemplated in the federal statutes or rules for the amended pleading.

   a. *Amended answer; Hearing on FRCP 12 defenses before trial.* If a party so moves, any defense listed in FRCP 12(b)(1) through FRCP 12(b)(7)—whether made in a pleading or by motion—and a motion under FRCP 12(c) must be heard and decided before trial unless the court orders a deferral until trial. FRCP 12(i).

H. Forms

1. Federal Amended Pleading Forms

   a. Notice; Of filing amended pleading as of course. AMJUR PP FEDPRAC § 153.

   b. Amendment; Of pleading as of course. AMJUR PP FEDPRAC § 154.

   c. Civil cover sheet. 2 FEDFORMS § 3:29.

   d. Notice of lawsuit and request for waiver of service of summons and waiver of summons. 2 FEDFORMS § 3:36.

   e. Complaint. 2 FEDFORMS § 7:14.

   f. Generally. 2B FEDFORMS § 8:10.

   g. Presenting defenses; Official form. 2B FEDFORMS § 8:12.

   h. Denials, admissions and affirmative defenses. 2B FEDFORMS § 8:15.

   i. Denial of particular averment. 2B FEDFORMS § 8:24.

   j. Admission of particular averment. 2B FEDFORMS § 8:25.

   k. Denial of all averments of paragraph. 2B FEDFORMS § 8:26.

   l. Admission of all averments of paragraph. 2B FEDFORMS § 8:27.

   m. Denial in part and admission in part of paragraph. 2B FEDFORMS § 8:28.

   n. Notice of amended complaint. 2C FEDFORMS § 14:10.

   o. Amendment to complaint. 2C FEDFORMS § 14:47.

   p. Amendment to complaint; Short version. 2C FEDFORMS § 14:48.

   q. Amendment to complaint; As of course. 2C FEDFORMS § 14:49.

   r. Complaint; Single count. FEDPROF § 1:68.

   s. Complaint; Multiple counts; With same jurisdictional basis. FEDPROF § 1:69.

   t. Amendment of pleading; As matter of course. FEDPROF § 1:220.

   u. Notice of filing amended pleading; Where amendment is matter of course. FEDPROF § 1:221.

   v. Amendment of pleading; Particular clauses. FEDPROF § 1:224.

   w. Amendment of pleading; Clause; Change in title of action. FEDPROF § 1:225.

   x. Amendment of pleading; Clause; To show amount in controversy. FEDPROF § 1:227.

   y. Amendment of pleading; Clause; To show diversity of citizenship. FEDPROF § 1:228.

z.   Amendment of pleading; Clause; Prayer for relief. FEDPROF § 1:229.

2.   Forms for the Southern District of Indiana

a.   Notice of endorsement. IN R USDCTSD ECF Procedures(Appendix B).

b.   Notice of manual filing. IN R USDCTSD ECF Procedures(Appendix C).

c.   Declaration that party was unable to file in a timely manner due to technical difficulties. IN R USDCTSD ECF Procedures(Appendix D).

I.   Applicable Rules

1.   *Federal rules*

a.   Serving and filing pleadings and other papers. FRCP 5.

b.   Constitutional challenge to a statute; Notice, certification, and intervention. FRCP 5.1.

c.   Privacy protection for filings made with the court. FRCP 5.2.

d.   Computing and extending time; Time for motion papers. FRCP 6.

e.   Pleadings allowed; Form of motions and other papers. FRCP 7.

f.   General rules of pleading. FRCP 8.

g.   Pleading special matters. FRCP 9.

h.   Form of pleadings. FRCP 10.

i.   Signing pleadings, motions, and other papers; Representations to the court; Sanctions. FRCP 11.

j.   Defenses and objections; When and how presented; Motion for judgment on the pleadings; Consolidating motions; Waiving defenses; Pretrial hearing. FRCP 12.

k.   Amended and supplemental pleadings. FRCP 15.

l.   Right to a jury trial; Demand. FRCP 38.

m.   Determining foreign law. FRCP 44.1.

2.   *Local rules*

a.   Scope of the rules. IN R USDCTSD L.R. 1-1.

b.   Sanctions for errors as to form. IN R USDCTSD L.R. 1-3.

c.   Format of documents presented for filing. IN R USDCTSD L.R. 5-1.

d.   Constitutional challenge to a statute; Notice. IN R USDCTSD L.R. 5.1-1.

e.   Filing of documents electronically required. IN R USDCTSD L.R. 5-2.

f.   Eligibility, registration, passwords for electronic filing; Exemption from electronic filing. IN R USDCTSD L.R. 5-3.

g.   Timing and consequences of electronic filing. IN R USDCTSD L.R. 5-4.

h.   Attachments and exhibits in cases filed electronically. IN R USDCTSD L.R. 5-6.

i.   Signatures in cases filed electronically. IN R USDCTSD L.R. 5-7.

j.   Non-electronic filings. IN R USDCTSD L.R. 5-10.

k.   Extensions of time. IN R USDCTSD L.R. 6-1.

l.   Motion practice. [IN R USDCTSD L.R. 7-1, as amended by IN ORDER 16-2319, effective December 1, 2016].

m.   Request for three-judge court. IN R USDCTSD L.R. 9-2.

n.   Jury demand. IN R USDCTSD L.R. 38-1.

o.   Assignment of cases. IN R USDCTSD L.R. 40-1.

p.   Alternative dispute resolution. IN R USDCTSD A.D.R. Rule 1.1; IN R USDCTSD A.D.R. Rule 1.2; IN R USDCTSD A.D.R. Rule 1.5; IN R USDCTSD A.D.R. Rule 2.1; IN R USDCTSD A.D.R. Rule 2.2.

q. Instructions for preparing case management plan. IN R USDCTSD Case Mgt.

r. Electronic case filing policies and procedures manual. IN R USDCTSD ECF Procedures.

Motions, Oppositions and Replies
Motion to Strike

Document Last Updated December 2016

A. **Checklist**

  (I) ❏ Matters to be considered by moving party

    (a) ❏ Required documents

      (1) ❏ Notice of motion and motion

      (2) ❏ Certificate of service

    (b) ❏ Supplemental documents

      (1) ❏ Brief

      (2) ❏ Deposition

      (3) ❏ Notice of constitutional question

      (4) ❏ Nongovernmental corporate disclosure statement

      (5) ❏ Index of exhibits

      (6) ❏ Request for oral argument

      (7) ❏ Request for evidentiary hearing

      (8) ❏ Copy of authority

      (9) ❏ Proposed order

      (10) ❏ Copy of document with self-address envelope

      (11) ❏ Notice of manual filing

      (12) ❏ Courtesy copies

      (13) ❏ Copies for three-judge court

      (14) ❏ Declaration that party was unable to file in a timely manner due to technical difficulties

    (c) ❏ Timing

      (1) ❏ The court may act on motion made by a party either before responding to the pleading or, if a response is not allowed, within twenty-one (21) days after being served with the pleading

      (2) ❏ A written motion and notice of the hearing must be served at least fourteen (14) days before the time specified for the hearing, with the following exceptions: (i) when the motion may be heard ex parte; (ii) when the Federal Rules of Civil Procedure set a different time; or (iii) when a court order—which a party may, for good cause, apply for ex parte—sets a different time

      (3) ❏ Any affidavit supporting a motion must be served with the motion

      (4) ❏ When a party who is not exempt from the electronic filing requirement files a document directly with the clerk, the party must present the document to the clerk within one (1) business day after filing the notice of manual filing

      (5) ❏ Unless the court orders otherwise, the [untimely] document and declaration [that party was unable to file in a timely manner due to technical difficulties] must be filed no later than 12:00 noon of the first day on which the court is open for business following the original filing deadline

(II) ❑ Matters to be considered by opposing party

    (a) ❑ Required documents

        (1) ❑ Response brief

        (2) ❑ Certificate of service

    (b) ❑ Supplemental documents

        (1) ❑ Deposition

        (2) ❑ Notice of constitutional question

        (3) ❑ Index of exhibits

        (4) ❑ Request for oral argument

        (5) ❑ Request for evidentiary hearing

        (6) ❑ Copy of authority

        (7) ❑ Copy of document with self-address envelope

        (8) ❑ Notice of manual filing

        (9) ❑ Courtesy copies

        (10) ❑ Copies for three-judge court

        (11) ❑ Declaration that party was unable to file in a timely manner due to technical difficulties

    (c) ❑ Timing

        (1) ❑ Any response is due within fourteen (14) days after service of the motion

        (2) ❑ Except as FRCP 59(c) provides otherwise, any opposing affidavit must be served at least seven (7) days before the hearing, unless the court permits service at another time

        (3) ❑ When a party who is not exempt from the electronic filing requirement files a document directly with the clerk, the party must present the document to the clerk within one (1) business day after filing the notice of manual filing

        (4) ❑ Unless the court orders otherwise, the [untimely] document and declaration [that party was unable to file in a timely manner due to technical difficulties] must be filed no later than 12:00 noon of the first day on which the court is open for business following the original filing deadline

B. Timing

1. *Motion to strike.* The court may act on motion made by a party either before responding to the pleading or, if a response is not allowed, within twenty-one (21) days after being served with the pleading. FRCP 12(f)(2).

2. *Timing of motions, generally*

    a. *Motion and notice of hearing.* A written motion and notice of the hearing must be served at least fourteen (14) days before the time specified for the hearing, with the following exceptions:

        i. When the motion may be heard ex parte;

        ii. When the Federal Rules of Civil Procedure set a different time; or

        iii. When a court order—which a party may, for good cause, apply for ex parte—sets a different time. FRCP 6(c)(1).

    b. *Supporting affidavit.* Any affidavit supporting a motion must be served with the motion. FRCP 6(c)(2).

3. *Timing of opposing papers.* Any response is due within fourteen (14) days after service of the motion. IN R USDCTSD L.R. 7-1(c)(2)(A).

    a. *Opposing affidavit.* Except as FRCP 59(c) provides otherwise, any opposing affidavit must be served at least seven (7) days before the hearing, unless the court permits service at another time. FRCP 6(c)(2).

b. *Extensions.* The court may extend response and reply deadlines, but only for good cause. IN R USDCTSD L.R. 7-1(c)(3).

c. *Summary ruling on failure to respond.* The court may summarily rule on a motion if an opposing party does not file a response within the deadline. IN R USDCTSD L.R. 7-1(c)(4).

4. *Timing of reply papers.* Where the respondent files an answering affidavit setting up a new matter, the moving party ordinarily is allowed a reasonable time to file a reply affidavit since failure to deny the new matter by affidavit may operate as an admission of its truth. AMJUR MOTIONS § 25.

   a. *Reply brief.* Any reply is due within seven (7) days after service of the response. IN R USDCTSD L.R. 7-1(c)(2)(B).

   b. *Extensions.* The court may extend response and reply deadlines, but only for good cause. IN R USDCTSD L.R. 7-1(c)(3).

5. *Effect of a FRCP 12 motion on the time to serve a responsive pleading.* Unless the court sets a different time, serving a motion under FRCP 12 alters the periods in FRCP 12(a) as follows:

   a. If the court denies the motion or postpones its disposition until trial, the responsive pleading must be served within fourteen (14) days after notice of the court's action; or

   b. If the court grants a motion for a more definite statement, the responsive pleading must be served within fourteen (14) days after the more definite statement is served. FRCP 12(a)(4).

6. *Document filing by non-exempt party.* When a party who is not exempt from the electronic filing requirement files a document directly with the clerk, the party must: present the document to the clerk within one (1) business day after filing the notice of manual filing. IN R USDCTSD L.R. 5-2(d)(2).

7. *Declaration that party was unable to file in a timely manner due to technical difficulties.* Unless the Court orders otherwise, the [untimely] document and declaration [that party was unable to file in a timely manner due to technical difficulties] must be filed no later than 12:00 noon of the first day on which the Court is open for business following the original filing deadline. IN R USDCTSD ECF Procedures(16).

8. *Computation of time*

   a. *Computing time.* FRCP 6 applies in computing any time period specified in the Federal Rules of Civil Procedure, in any local rule or court order, or in any statute that does not specify a method of computing time. FRCP 6(a).

      i. *Period stated in days or a longer unit.* When the period is stated in days or a longer unit of time:

         - Exclude the day of the event that triggers the period;

         - Count every day, including intermediate Saturdays, Sundays, and legal holidays; and

         - Include the last day of the period, but if the last day is a Saturday, Sunday, or legal holiday, the period continues to run until the end of the next day that is not a Saturday, Sunday, or legal holiday. FRCP 6(a)(1).

      ii. *Period stated in hours.* When the period is stated in hours:

         - Begin counting immediately on the occurrence of the event that triggers the period;

         - Count every hour, including hours during intermediate Saturdays, Sundays, and legal holidays; and

         - If the period would end on a Saturday, Sunday, or legal holiday, the period continues to run until the same time on the next day that is not a Saturday, Sunday, or legal holiday. FRCP 6(a)(2).

      iii. *Inaccessibility of the clerk's office.* Unless the court orders otherwise, if the clerk's office is inaccessible:

         - On the last day for filing under FRCP 6(a)(1), then the time for filing is extended to the first accessible day that is not a Saturday, Sunday, or legal holiday; or

         - During the last hour for filing under FRCP 6(a)(2), then the time for filing is extended to the same time on the first accessible day that is not a Saturday, Sunday, or legal holiday. FRCP 6(a)(3).

iv. *"Last day" defined.* Unless a different time is set by a statute, local rule, or court order, the last day ends:

- For electronic filing, at midnight in the court's time zone; and
- For filing by other means, when the clerk's office is scheduled to close. FRCP 6(a)(4).

v. *"Next day" defined.* The "next day" is determined by continuing to count forward when the period is measured after an event and backward when measured before an event. FRCP 6(a)(5).

vi. *"Legal holiday" defined.* "Legal holiday" means:

- The day set aside by statute for observing New Year's Day, Martin Luther King Jr.'s Birthday, Washington's Birthday, Memorial Day, Independence Day, Labor Day, Columbus Day, Veterans' Day, Thanksgiving Day, or Christmas Day;
- Any day declared a holiday by the President or Congress; and
- For periods that are measured after an event, any other day declared a holiday by the state where the district court is located. FRCP 6(a)(6).

b. *Computation of electronic filing deadlines.* Filing documents electronically does not alter filing deadlines. IN R USDCTSD ECF Procedures(7). A document due on a particular day must be filed before midnight local time of the division where the case is pending. IN R USDCTSD L.R. 5-4(a). All electronic transmissions of documents must be completed (i.e. received completely by the Clerk's Office) prior to midnight of the local time of the division in which the case is pending in order to be considered timely filed that day (NOTE: time will be noted in Eastern Time on the Court's docket. If you have filed a document prior to midnight local time of the division in which the case is pending and the document is due that date, but the electronic receipt and docket reflect the following calendar day, please contact the Court). IN R USDCTSD ECF Procedures(7). Although attorneys may file documents electronically twenty-four (24) hours a day, seven (7) days a week, attorneys are encouraged to file all documents during the normal working hours of the Clerk's Office (Monday through Friday, 8:30 a.m. to 4:30 p.m.) when technical support is available. IN R USDCTSD ECF Procedures(7); IN R USDCTSD ECF Procedures(9).

i. *Technical difficulties.* Parties are encouraged to file documents electronically during normal business hours, in case a problem is encountered. In the event a technical failure occurs and a document cannot be filed electronically despite the best efforts of the filing party, the party should print (if possible) a copy of the error message received. In addition, as soon as practically possible, the party should file a "Declaration that Party was Unable to File in a Timely Manner Due to Technical Difficulties." A model form is provided as Appendix D (IN R USDCTSD ECF Procedures(Appendix D)). IN R USDCTSD ECF Procedures(16).

- If a party is unable to file electronically and, as a result, may miss a filing deadline, the party must contact the Clerk's Office at the number listed in IN R USDCTSD ECF Procedures(15) to inform the court's staff of the difficulty. If a party misses a filing deadline due to an inability to file electronically, the party may submit the untimely filed document, accompanied by a declaration stating the reason(s) for missing the deadline. Unless the Court orders otherwise, the document and declaration must be filed no later than 12:00 noon of the first day on which the Court is open for business following the original filing deadline. IN R USDCTSD ECF Procedures(16).

c. *Extending time*

i. *In general.* When an act may or must be done within a specified time, the court may, for good cause, extend the time:

- With or without motion or notice if the court acts, or if a request is made, before the original time or its extension expires; or
- On motion made after the time has expired if the party failed to act because of excusable neglect. FRCP 6(b)(1).

ii. *Exceptions.* A court must not extend the time to act under FRCP 50(b), FRCP 50(d), FRCP 52(b), FRCP 59(b), FRCP 59(d), FRCP 59(e), and FRCP 60(b). FRCP 6(b)(2).

      iii.   Refer to the United States District Court for the Southern District of Indiana KeyRules Motion for Continuance/Extension of Time document for more information on extending time.

  d. *Additional time after certain kinds of service.* When a party may or must act within a specified time after being served and service is made under FRCP 5(b)(2)(C) (mail), FRCP 5(b)(2)(D) (leaving with the clerk), or FRCP 5(b)(2)(F) (other means consented to), three (3) days are added after the period would otherwise expire under FRCP 6(a). FRCP 6(d). Service by electronic mail shall constitute service pursuant to FRCP 5(b)(2)(E) and shall entitle the party being served to the additional three (3) days provided by FRCP 6(d). IN R USDCTSD ECF Procedures(11).

C. General Requirements

1. *Motions, generally*

  a. *Requirements.* A request for a court order must be made by motion. The motion must:

      i.   Be in writing unless made during a hearing or trial;

      ii.   State with particularity the grounds for seeking the order; and

      iii.   State the relief sought. FRCP 7(b)(1).

  b. *Notice of motion.* A party interested in resisting the relief sought by a motion has a right to notice thereof, and an opportunity to be heard. AMJUR MOTIONS § 12.

      i.   In addition to statutory or court rule provisions requiring notice of a motion—the purpose of such a notice requirement having been said to be to prevent a party from being prejudicially surprised by a motion—principles of natural justice dictate that an adverse party generally must be given notice that a motion will be presented to the court. AMJUR MOTIONS § 12.

      ii.   "Notice," in this regard, means reasonable notice, including a meaningful opportunity to prepare and to defend against allegations of a motion. AMJUR MOTIONS § 12.

  c. *Writing requirement.* The writing requirement is intended to insure that the adverse parties are informed and have a record of both the motion's pendency and the grounds on which the movant seeks an order. FPP § 1191; Feldberg v. Quechee Lakes Corp., 463 F.3d 195 (2d Cir. 2006).

      i.   It is sufficient "if the motion is stated in a written notice of the hearing of the motion." FPP § 1191.

  d. *Particularity requirement.* The particularity requirement insures that the opposing parties will have notice of their opponent's contentions. FEDPROC § 62:364; Goodman v. 1973 26 Foot Trojan Vessel, Arkansas Registration No. AR1439SN, 859 F.2d 71, 12 Fed.R.Serv.3d 645 (8th Cir. 1988). That requirement ensures that notice of the basis for the motion is provided to the court and to the opposing party so as to avoid prejudice, provide the opponent with a meaningful opportunity to respond, and provide the court with enough information to process the motion correctly. FEDPROC § 62:364; Andreas v. Volkswagen of America, Inc., 336 F.3d 789, 56 Fed.R.Serv.3d 6 (8th Cir. 2003).

      i.   Reasonable specification of the grounds for a motion is sufficient. However, where a movant fails to state even one ground for granting the motion in question, the movant has failed to meet the minimal standard of "reasonable specification." FEDPROC § 62:364; Martinez v. Trainor, 556 F.2d 818, 23 Fed.R.Serv.2d 403 (7th Cir. 1977).

      ii.   The court may excuse the failure to comply with the particularity requirement if it is inadvertent, and where no prejudice is shown by the opposing party. FEDPROC § 62:364.

  e. *Motions must be filed separately.* Motions must be filed separately, but alternative motions may be filed in a single document if each is named in the title. A motion must not be contained within a brief, response, or reply to a previously filed motion, unless ordered by the court. IN R USDCTSD L.R. 7-1(a).

  f. *Routine or uncontested motions.* The court may rule upon a routine or uncontested motion before the response deadline passes, unless: (1) the motion indicates that an opposing party objects to it; or (2) the court otherwise believes that a response will be filed. IN R USDCTSD L.R. 7-1(d).

2. *Informal conference to resolve disputes involving non-dispositive issues.* In addition to those conferences required by IN R USDCTSD L.R. 37-1, counsel are encouraged to hold informal conferences in person

or by phone to resolve any disputes involving non-dispositive issues that may otherwise require submission of a motion to the Court. This requirement does not apply to cases involving pro se parties. Therefore, prior to filing any non-dispositive motion (including motions for extension of time), the moving party must contact opposing counsel to determine whether there is an objection to any non-dispositive motion (including motions for extension of time), and state in the motion whether opposing counsel objects to the motion. IN R USDCTSD Case Mgt(General Instructions For All Cases). Refer to the Documents section of this document for more information on the contents of the motion.

3. *Motion to strike.* The court may strike from a pleading an insufficient defense or any redundant, immaterial, impertinent, or scandalous matter. The court may act: (1) on its own; or (2) on motion made by a party either before responding to the pleading or, if a response is not allowed, within twenty-one (21) days after being served with the pleading. FRCP 12(f). FRCP 12(f) also is designed to reinforce the requirement in FRCP 8(e) that pleadings be simple, concise, and direct. However, as the cases make clear, it is neither an authorized nor a proper way to procure the dismissal of all or a part of a complaint, or a counterclaim, or to strike an opponent's affidavits. FPP § 1380.

 a. *Practice on a motion to strike.* All well-pleaded facts are taken as admitted on a motion to strike but conclusions of law or conclusions drawn from the facts do not have to be treated in that fashion by the district judge. FPP § 1380. Both because striking a portion of a pleading is a drastic remedy and because it often is sought by the movant simply as a dilatory or harassing tactic, numerous judicial decisions make it clear that motions under FRCP 12(f) are viewed with disfavor by the federal courts and are infrequently granted. FPP § 1380.

 b. *Striking an insufficient defense.* Only if a defense is insufficient as a matter of law will it be stricken. If a defense cannot succeed under any set of circumstances alleged, the defense may be deemed insufficient as a matter of law. In other words, a defense may be stricken if, on the face of the pleadings, it is patently frivolous, or if it is clearly invalid as a matter of law. FEDPROC § 62:412.

  i. A defense will be stricken if it could not possibly prevent recovery by the plaintiff on its claim. FEDPROC § 62:413. In addition, a defense may be stricken if:

   • The defense requires separate statements;

   • The defense has been previously advanced and rejected; or

   • The defense cannot be waived. FEDPROC § 62:413.

 c. *Striking immaterial or impertinent matter.* Immaterial or impertinent matter will be stricken from a pleading if it is clear that it can have no possible bearing upon the subject matter of the litigation, and that its inclusion will prejudice the movant. If there is any doubt as to whether under any contingency the matter may raise an issue, the motion should be denied. FEDPROC § 62:415.

  i. "Immaterial matter," for purposes of FRCP 12(f), is matter which has no essential or important relationship to the claim for relief or the defenses being pleaded. FEDPROC § 62:414. A statement of unnecessary particulars in connection with and descriptive of that which is material may be stricken as immaterial matter. FEDPROC § 62:416.

  ii. "Impertinent matter," for purposes of FRCP 12(f), consists of statements that do not pertain, and are not necessary, to the issues in question. FEDPROC § 62:414.

 d. *Striking redundant matter.* "Redundant matter," for purposes of FRCP 12(f), consists of allegations that constitute a needless repetition of other averments or which are wholly foreign to the issue to be decided. However, even if allegations are redundant, they need not be stricken if their presence in the pleading cannot prejudice the moving party. FEDPROC § 62:417.

  i. Merely duplicative remedies do not necessarily make claims "redundant," within the meaning of FRCP 12(f), if the claims otherwise require proof of different elements, but a claim that merely recasts the same elements under the guise of a different theory may be stricken as redundant. FEDPROC § 62:417.

 e. *Striking scandalous matter.* A matter is deemed scandalous, for purposes of FRCP 12(f), when it improperly casts a derogatory light on someone, usually a party to the action. Scandalous matter also consists of any unnecessary allegation which reflects cruelly upon the moral character of an individual, or states anything in repulsive language which detracts from the dignity of the court. To be scandalous, degrading charges must be irrelevant, or, if relevant, must go into in unnecessary detail. FEDPROC § 62:418.

    i.   Allegations may be stricken as scandalous if the matter bears no possible relation to the controversy or may cause the objecting party prejudice. FEDPROC § 62:418.

    ii.   But there are several limitations on the court's willingness to strike scandalous allegations. For example, it is not enough that the matter offends the sensibilities of the objecting party or the person who is the subject of the statements in the pleading, if the challenged allegations describe acts or events that are relevant to the action. FPP § 1382.

f.   *Striking sham or false matter.* FRCP 12(f) does not authorize a motion to strike part or all of a pleading on the ground that it is sham, and the grounds for a motion to strike similarly do not include falsity of the matter alleged. FEDPROC § 62:419; PAE Government Services, Inc. v. MPRI, Inc., 514 F.3d 856 (9th Cir. 2007). However, it has been said that a court will strike a pleading according to FRCP 12(f) when it appears beyond peradventure that it is a sham and false and that its allegations are devoid of factual basis. FEDPROC § 62:419.

g.   *Striking conclusions of law.* Unwarranted conclusions of law may be stricken from a pleading pursuant to FRCP 12(f), but ordinarily an allegation is not subject to being stricken merely because it is a conclusion of law. To the contrary, the Federal Rules of Civil Procedure do not condemn conclusions of law, but rather encourage them as at times the clearest and simplest way of stating a claim for relief. Conclusions of law must be unwarranted enough to justify a motion to strike, such as when a plaintiff states causes of action under a federal statute which provides no explicit private right of action. FEDPROC § 62:420.

h.   *Striking other particular matter.* Under FRCP 12(f), which permits a court to order stricken from any pleading any redundant, immaterial, impertinent, or scandalous matter, courts have the authority to strike a prayer for relief seeking damages that are not recoverable as a matter of law. A motion to strike may be used to remove an excessive or unauthorized claim for damages. Furthermore, a motion to strike a demand for punitive damages under FRCP 12(f) may be proper if such damages are clearly not collectible, such as in an ordinary breach of contract action. However, there are other ways to raise this issue, and in a particular case, one of these other methods may be more appropriate, such as a motion to dismiss for failure to state a claim pursuant to FRCP 12(b)(6). FEDPROC § 62:421.

i.   *Form.* On a motion to strike portions of a pleading, the movant must indicate what paragraphs are being challenged in order to fulfill the particularity requirement; the movant cannot merely state the conclusion that the allegations are too indefinite and insufficient to state a claim or defense. FPP § 1192.

j.   *Joining motions*

    i.   *Right to join.* A motion under FRCP 12 may be joined with any other motion allowed by FRCP 12. FRCP 12(g)(1).

    ii.   *Limitation on further motions.* Except as provided in FRCP 12(h)(2) or FRCP 12(h)(3), a party that makes a motion under FRCP 12 must not make another motion under FRCP 12 raising a defense or objection that was available to the party but omitted from its earlier motion. FRCP 12(g)(2).

4.   *Opposing papers.* The Federal Rules of Civil Procedure do not require any formal answer, return, or reply to a motion, except where the Federal Rules of Civil Procedure or local rules may require affidavits, memoranda, or other papers to be filed in opposition to a motion. Such papers are simply to apprise the court of such opposition and the grounds of that opposition. FEDPROC § 62:359.

a.   *Effect of failure to respond to motion.* Although in the absence of statutory provision or court rule, a motion ordinarily does not require a written answer, when a party files a motion and the opposing party fails to respond, the court may construe such failure to respond as nonopposition to the motion or an admission that the motion was meritorious, may take the facts alleged in the motion as true—the rule in some jurisdictions being that the failure to respond to a fact set forth in a motion is deemed an admission—and may grant the motion if the relief requested appears to be justified. AMJUR MOTIONS § 28.

 b. *Assent or no opposition not determinative.* However, a motion will not be granted automatically simply because an "assent" or a notation of "no opposition" has been filed; federal judges frequently deny motions that have been assented to when it is thought that justice so dictates. FPP § 1190.

 c. *Responsive pleading inappropriate as response to motion.* An attempt to answer or oppose a motion with a responsive pleading usually is not appropriate. FPP § 1190.

5. *Reply papers.* A moving party may be required or permitted to prepare papers in addition to his original motion papers. AMJUR MOTIONS § 25. Papers answering or replying to opposing papers may be appropriate, in the interests of justice, where it appears there is a substantial reason for allowing a reply. Thus, a court may accept reply papers where a party demonstrates that the papers to which it seeks to file a reply raise new issues that are material to the disposition of the question before the court, or where the court determines, sua sponte, that it wishes further briefing of an issue raised in those papers and orders the submission of additional papers. FEDPROC § 62:360.

 a. *Function of reply papers.* The function of a reply affidavit is to answer the arguments made in opposition to the position taken by the movant and not to permit the movant to introduce new arguments in support of the motion. AMJUR MOTIONS § 25.

 b. *Issues raised for the first time in a reply document.* However, the view has been followed in some jurisdictions, that as a matter of judicial economy, where there is no prejudice and where the issues could be raised simply by filing a motion to dismiss, the trial court has discretion to consider arguments raised for the first time in a reply memorandum, and that a trial court may grant a motion to strike issues raised for the first time in a reply memorandum. AMJUR MOTIONS § 26.

6. *Appearances.* Every attorney who represents a party or who files a document on a party's behalf must file an appearance for that party. IN R USDCTSD L.R. 83-7. The filing of a Notice of Appearance shall act to establish the filing attorney as an attorney of record representing a designated party or parties in a particular cause of action. As a result, it is necessary for each attorney to file a separate Notice of Appearance when entering an appearance in a case. A joint appearance on behalf of multiple attorneys may be filed electronically only if it is filed separately for each attorney, using his/her ECF login. IN R USDCTSD ECF Procedures(12). Only those attorneys who have filed an appearance in a pending action are entitled to be served with case documents under FRCP 5(a). IN R USDCTSD L.R. 83-7. For more information, refer to IN R USDCTSD L.R. 83-7 and IN R USDCTSD ECF Procedures(12).

7. *Notice of related action.* A party must file a notice of related action: as soon as it appears that the party's case and another pending case: (1) arise out of the same transaction or occurrence; (2) involve the same property; or (3) involve the validity or infringement or the same patent, trademark, or copyright. IN R USDCTSD L.R. 40-1(d)(2). For more information, refer to IN R USDCTSD L.R. 40-1.

8. *Alternative dispute resolution (ADR)*

 a. *Application.* Unless limited by specific provisions, or unless there are other applicable specific statutory, common law, or constitutional procedures, the Local Alternative Dispute Resolution Rules of the United States District Court for the Southern District of Indiana shall apply in all civil litigation filed in the U.S. District Court for the Southern District of Indiana, except in the following cases and proceedings:

  i. Applications for writs of habeas corpus under 28 U.S.C.A. § 2254;

  ii. Forfeiture cases;

  iii. Non-adversary proceedings in bankruptcy;

  iv. Social Security administrative review cases; and

  v. Such other matters as specified by order of the Court; for example, matters involving important public policy issues, constitutional law, or the establishment of new law. IN R USDCTSD A.D.R. Rule 1.2.

 b. *Mediation.* Mediation under this section (IN R USDCTSD A.D.R. Rule 2.1, et seq.) involves the confidential process by which a person acting as a Mediator, selected by the parties or appointed by the Court, assists the litigants in reaching a mutually acceptable agreement. It is an informal and nonadversarial process. The role of the Mediator is to assist in identifying the issues, reducing misunderstandings, clarifying priorities, exploring areas of compromise, and finding points of agreement as well as legitimate points of disagreement. Final decision-making authority rests with the parties, not the Mediator. IN R USDCTSD A.D.R. Rule 2.1. It is anticipated that an agreement may not resolve all of the disputed issues, but the process, nonetheless, can reduce points of contention. Parties and their representatives are required to mediate in good faith, but are not compelled to reach an agreement. IN R USDCTSD A.D.R. Rule 2.1.

    i. *Case selection.* The Court with the agreement of the parties may refer a civil case for mediation. Unless otherwise ordered or as specifically provided in IN R USDCTSD A.D.R. Rule 2.8, referral to mediation does not abate or suspend the action, and no scheduled dates shall be delayed or deferred, including the date of trial. IN R USDCTSD A.D.R. Rule 2.2.

    ii. For more information on mediation, refer to IN R USDCTSD A.D.R. Rule 2.1, et seq.

  c. *Other methods of dispute resolution.* The Local Alternative Dispute Resolution Rules of the United States District Court for the Southern District of Indiana shall not preclude the parties from utilizing any other reasonable method or technique of alternative dispute resolution to resolve disputes to which the parties agree. However, any use of arbitration by the parties will be governed by and comply with the requirements of 28 U.S.C.A. § 654 through 28 U.S.C.A. § 657. IN R USDCTSD A.D.R. Rule 1.5.

  d. For more information on alternative dispute resolution (ADR), refer to IN R USDCTSD A.D.R. Rule 1.1, et seq.

9. *Notice of settlement or resolution.* The parties must immediately notify the court if they reasonably anticipate settling their case or resolving a pending motion. IN R USDCTSD L.R. 7-1(h).

10. *Modification or suspension of rules.* The court may, on its own motion or at the request of a party, suspend or modify any rule in a particular case in the interest of justice. IN R USDCTSD L.R. 1-1(c).

D. Documents

1. *Documents for moving party*

  a. *Required documents*

    i. *Notice of motion and motion.* [P]rior to filing any non-dispositive motion (including motions for extension of time), the moving party must contact opposing counsel to determine whether there is an objection to any non-dispositive motion (including motions for extension of time), and state in the motion whether opposing counsel objects to the motion. If an objection cannot be resolved by counsel, the opposing counsel's position shall be stated within the motion. The motion should also indicate whether opposing counsel plans to file a written objection to the motion and the date by which the Court can expect to receive the objection (within the time limits set in IN R USDCTSD L.R. 7-1). If after a reasonable effort, opposing counsel cannot be reached, the moving party shall recite in the motion the dates and times that messages were left for opposing counsel. IN R USDCTSD Case Mgt(General Instructions For All Cases). Refer to the General Requirements section of this document for information on the notice of motion and motion.

    ii. *Certificate of service.* FRCP 5(d) requires that the person making service under FRCP 5 certify that service has been effected. FRCP 5(Advisory Committee Notes). Having such information on file may be useful for many purposes, including proof of service if an issue arises concerning the effectiveness of the service. FRCP 5(Advisory Committee Notes).

      • *Certificate of service for electronically-filed documents.* A certificate of service must be included with all documents filed electronically. Such certificate shall indicate that service was accomplished pursuant to the Court's electronic filing procedures. IN R USDCTSD ECF Procedures(11). For the suggested format for a certificate of service for electronic filing, refer to IN R USDCTSD ECF Procedures(11).

  b. *Supplemental documents.* Matter outside the pleadings normally is not considered on a FRCP 12(f) motion; for example, affidavits in support of or in opposition to the motion typically may not be used. FPP § 1380.

i.   *Brief.* Refer to the Format section of this document for the format of briefs.

ii. *Deposition.* Notwithstanding the general rule that matters outside the pleadings should ordinarily not be considered in passing upon a motion to strike under FRCP 12(f), a court may consider a deposition in deciding a FRCP 12(f) motion if the attorneys for both the plaintiff and the defendant, in their respective briefs, refer to the deposition and to the testimony contained therein. FEDPROC § 62:407.

- *Materials necessary for motion.* A party seeking relief under FRCP 26(c) or FRCP 37, or by way of a pretrial motion that could result in a final order on an issue, must file with the motion those parts of the discovery materials relevant to the motion. IN R USDCTSD L.R. 26-2(a).

iii. *Notice of constitutional question.* A party that files a pleading, written motion, or other paper drawing into question the constitutionality of a federal or state statute must promptly:

- *File notice.* File a notice of constitutional question stating the question and identifying the paper that raises it, if: (1) a federal statute is questioned and the parties do not include the United States, one of its agencies, or one of its officers or employees in an official capacity; or (2) a state statute is questioned and the parties do not include the state, one of its agencies, or one of its officers or employees in an official capacity; and

- *Serve notice.* Serve the notice and paper on the Attorney General of the United States if a federal statute is questioned—or on the state attorney general if a state statute is questioned—either by certified or registered mail or by sending it to an electronic address designated by the attorney general for this purpose. FRCP 5.1(a).

- *Time for filing.* A notice of constitutional challenge to a statute filed in accordance with FRCP 5.1 must be filed at the same time the parties tender their proposed case management plan, if one is required, or within twenty-one (21) days of the filing drawing into question the constitutionality of a federal or state statute, whichever occurs later. IN R USDCTSD L.R. 5.1-1(a).

- *Additional service requirements.* If a federal statute is challenged, in addition to the service requirements of FRCP 5.1(a), the party filing the notice of constitutional challenge must serve the notice and documents on the United States Attorney for the Southern District of Indiana, either by certified or registered mail or by sending it to an electronic address designated for that purpose by that official. IN R USDCTSD L.R. 5.1-1(b).

- *No forfeiture.* A party's failure to file and serve the notice, or the court's failure to certify, does not forfeit a constitutional claim or defense that is otherwise timely asserted. FRCP 5.1(d).

iv. *Nongovernmental corporate disclosure statement*

- *Contents.* A nongovernmental corporate party must file two (2) copies of a disclosure statement that: (1) identifies any parent corporation and any publicly held corporation owning ten percent (10%) or more of its stock; or (2) states that there is no such corporation. FRCP 7.1(a).

- *Time to file; Supplemental filing.* A party must: (1) file the disclosure statement with its first appearance, pleading, petition, motion, response, or other request addressed to the court; and (2) promptly file a supplemental statement if any required information changes. FRCP 7.1(b).

v.   *Index of exhibits.* Any pleading, motion, brief, affidavit, notice, or proposed order filed with the court, whether electronically or with the clerk, must: if it has four (4) or more exhibits, include a separate index that identifies and briefly describes each exhibit. IN R USDCTSD L.R. 5-1(b).

vi. *Request for oral argument.* A party may request oral argument by filing a separate motion explaining why oral argument is necessary and estimating how long the court should allow for the argument. The request must be filed and served with the supporting brief, response brief, or reply brief. IN R USDCTSD L.R. 7-5(a).

vii. *Request for evidentiary hearing.* A party may request an evidentiary hearing on a motion or petition by serving and filing a separate motion explaining why the hearing is necessary and estimating how long the court should allow for the hearing. IN R USDCTSD L.R. 7-5(c).

viii. *Copy of authority.* Generally, copies of cited authorities may not be attached to court filings. However, a party must attach to the party's motion or brief a copy of any cited authority if it is not available on Westlaw or Lexis. Upon request, a party must provide copies of any cited authority that is only available through electronic means to the court or the other parties. IN R USDCTSD L.R. 7-1(f).

ix.   *Proposed order.* A party must include a suitable form of order with any document that requests the judge or the clerk to enter a routine or uncontested order. IN R USDCTSD L.R. 5-5(b); IN R USDCTSD L.R. 5-10(c); IN R USDCTSD L.R. 7-1(d).

- A service statement and/or list must be included on each proposed order, as required by IN R USDCTSD L.R. 5-5(d). IN R USDCTSD ECF Procedures(11). Any pleading, motion, brief, affidavit, notice, or proposed order filed with the court, whether electronically or with the clerk, must: if it is a form of order, include a statement of service, in the format required by IN R USDCTSD L.R. 5-5(d) in the lower left corner of the document. IN R USDCTSD L.R. 5-1(b).

- A party electronically filing a proposed order—whether voluntarily or because required by IN R USDCTSD L.R. 5-5—must convert the order directly from a word processing program and file it as an attachment to the document it relates to. Proposed orders must include in the lower left-hand corner of the signature page a statement that service will be made electronically on all ECF-registered counsel of record via email generated by the court's ECF system, without listing all such counsel. A service list including the name and postal address of any pro se litigant or non-registered attorney of record must follow, stating that service on the listed individuals will be made in the traditional paper manner, via first-class U.S. Mail. IN R USDCTSD L.R. 5-5(d).

x.   *Copy of document with self-address envelope.* To receive a file-stamped copy of a document filed directly with the clerk, a party must include with the original document an additional copy and a self-addressed envelope. The envelope must be big enough to hold the copy and have enough postage on it to send the copy via regular first-class mail. IN R USDCTSD L.R. 5-10(b).

xi.   *Notice of manual filing.* When a party who is not exempt from the electronic filing requirement files a document directly with the clerk, the party must: electronically file a notice of manual filing that explains why the document cannot be filed electronically. IN R USDCTSD L.R. 5-2(d)(1). Refer to the Filing and Service Requirements section of this document for more information.

- Where an individual component cannot be included in an electronic filing (e.g. the component cannot be converted to electronic format), the filer shall electronically file the prescribed Notice of Manual Filing in place of that component. A model form is provided as Appendix C (IN R USDCTSD ECF Procedures(Appendix C)). IN R USDCTSD ECF Procedures(13).

- Before making a manual filing of a component, the filing party shall first electronically file a Notice of Manual Filing (See IN R USDCTSD ECF Procedures(Appendix C)). The filer shall initiate the electronic filing process as if filing the actual component but shall instead attach to the filing the Notice of Manual Filing setting forth the reason(s) why the component cannot be filed electronically. The manual filing should be accompanied by a copy of the previously filed Notice of Manual Filing. A party may seek to have a component excluded from electronic filing pursuant to applicable Federal and Local Rules (e.g., FRCP 26(c)). IN R USDCTSD ECF Procedures(15).

xii. *Courtesy copies.* District Judges and Magistrate Judges regularly receive documents filed by all parties. Therefore, parties shall not bring "courtesy copies" to any chambers unless specifically directed to do so by the Court. IN R USDCTSD Case Mgt(General Instructions For All Cases).

xiii. *Copies for three-judge court.* Parties in a case where a three-judge court has been requested must file an original and three copies of any document filed directly with the clerk (instead of electronically) until the court: (1) denies the request; (2) dissolves the three-judge court; or (3) allows the parties to file fewer copies. IN R USDCTSD L.R. 9-2(c).

xiv. *Declaration that party was unable to file in a timely manner due to technical difficulties.* If a party misses a filing deadline due to an inability to file electronically, the party may submit the untimely filed document, accompanied by a declaration stating the reason(s) for missing the deadline. IN R USDCTSD ECF Procedures(16). A model form is provided as Appendix D (IN R USDCTSD ECF Procedures(Appendix D)). IN R USDCTSD ECF Procedures(16).

2. *Documents for opposing party*

  a. *Required documents*

    i. *Response brief.* Refer to the Format section of this document for the format of briefs. Refer to the General Requirements section of this document for information on the opposing papers.

    ii. *Certificate of service.* FRCP 5(d) requires that the person making service under FRCP 5 certify that service has been effected. FRCP 5(Advisory Committee Notes). Having such information on file may be useful for many purposes, including proof of service if an issue arises concerning the effectiveness of the service. FRCP 5(Advisory Committee Notes).

      • *Certificate of service for electronically-filed documents.* A certificate of service must be included with all documents filed electronically. Such certificate shall indicate that service was accomplished pursuant to the Court's electronic filing procedures. IN R USDCTSD ECF Procedures(11). For the suggested format for a certificate of service for electronic filing, refer to IN R USDCTSD ECF Procedures(11).

  b. *Supplemental documents.* Matter outside the pleadings normally is not considered on a FRCP 12(f) motion; for example, affidavits in support of or in opposition to the motion typically may not be used. FPP § 1380.

    i. *Deposition.* Notwithstanding the general rule that matters outside the pleadings should ordinarily not be considered in passing upon a motion to strike under FRCP 12(f), a court may consider a deposition in deciding a FRCP 12(f) motion if the attorneys for both the plaintiff and the defendant, in their respective briefs, refer to the deposition and to the testimony contained therein. FEDPROC § 62:407.

      • *Materials necessary for motion.* A party seeking relief under FRCP 26(c) or FRCP 37, or by way of a pretrial motion that could result in a final order on an issue, must file with the motion those parts of the discovery materials relevant to the motion. IN R USDCTSD L.R. 26-2(a).

    ii. *Notice of constitutional question.* A party that files a pleading, written motion, or other paper drawing into question the constitutionality of a federal or state statute must promptly:

      • *File notice.* File a notice of constitutional question stating the question and identifying the paper that raises it, if: (1) a federal statute is questioned and the parties do not include the United States, one of its agencies, or one of its officers or employees in an official capacity; or (2) a state statute is questioned and the parties do not include the state, one of its agencies, or one of its officers or employees in an official capacity; and

      • *Serve notice.* Serve the notice and paper on the Attorney General of the United States if a federal statute is questioned—or on the state attorney general if a state statute is questioned—either by certified or registered mail or by sending it to an electronic address designated by the attorney general for this purpose. FRCP 5.1(a).

      • *Time for filing.* A notice of constitutional challenge to a statute filed in accordance with FRCP 5.1 must be filed at the same time the parties tender their proposed case management plan, if one is required, or within twenty-one (21) days of the filing drawing into question the constitutionality of a federal or state statute, whichever occurs later. IN R USDCTSD L.R. 5.1-1(a).

- *Additional service requirements.* If a federal statute is challenged, in addition to the service requirements of FRCP 5.1(a), the party filing the notice of constitutional challenge must serve the notice and documents on the United States Attorney for the Southern District of Indiana, either by certified or registered mail or by sending it to an electronic address designated for that purpose by that official. IN R USDCTSD L.R. 5.1-1(b).

- *No forfeiture.* A party's failure to file and serve the notice, or the court's failure to certify, does not forfeit a constitutional claim or defense that is otherwise timely asserted. FRCP 5.1(d).

iii. *Index of exhibits.* Any pleading, motion, brief, affidavit, notice, or proposed order filed with the court, whether electronically or with the clerk, must: if it has four (4) or more exhibits, include a separate index that identifies and briefly describes each exhibit. IN R USDCTSD L.R. 5-1(b).

iv. *Request for oral argument.* A party may request oral argument by filing a separate motion explaining why oral argument is necessary and estimating how long the court should allow for the argument. The request must be filed and served with the supporting brief, response brief, or reply brief. IN R USDCTSD L.R. 7-5(a).

v. *Request for evidentiary hearing.* A party may request an evidentiary hearing on a motion or petition by serving and filing a separate motion explaining why the hearing is necessary and estimating how long the court should allow for the hearing. IN R USDCTSD L.R. 7-5(c).

vi. *Copy of authority.* Generally, copies of cited authorities may not be attached to court filings. However, a party must attach to the party's motion or brief a copy of any cited authority if it is not available on Westlaw or Lexis. Upon request, a party must provide copies of any cited authority that is only available through electronic means to the court or the other parties. IN R USDCTSD L.R. 7-1(f).

vii. *Copy of document with self-address envelope.* To receive a file-stamped copy of a document filed directly with the clerk, a party must include with the original document an additional copy and a self-addressed envelope. The envelope must be big enough to hold the copy and have enough postage on it to send the copy via regular first-class mail. IN R USDCTSD L.R. 5-10(b).

viii. *Notice of manual filing.* When a party who is not exempt from the electronic filing requirement files a document directly with the clerk, the party must: electronically file a notice of manual filing that explains why the document cannot be filed electronically. IN R USDCTSD L.R. 5-2(d)(1). Refer to the Filing and Service Requirements section of this document for more information.

- Where an individual component cannot be included in an electronic filing (e.g. the component cannot be converted to electronic format), the filer shall electronically file the prescribed Notice of Manual Filing in place of that component. A model form is provided as Appendix C (IN R USDCTSD ECF Procedures(Appendix C)). IN R USDCTSD ECF Procedures(13).

- Before making a manual filing of a component, the filing party shall first electronically file a Notice of Manual Filing (See IN R USDCTSD ECF Procedures(Appendix C)). The filer shall initiate the electronic filing process as if filing the actual component but shall instead attach to the filing the Notice of Manual Filing setting forth the reason(s) why the component cannot be filed electronically. The manual filing should be accompanied by a copy of the previously filed Notice of Manual Filing. A party may seek to have a component excluded from electronic filing pursuant to applicable Federal and Local Rules (e.g., FRCP 26(c)). IN R USDCTSD ECF Procedures(15).

ix. *Courtesy copies.* District Judges and Magistrate Judges regularly receive documents filed by all parties. Therefore, parties shall not bring "courtesy copies" to any chambers unless specifically directed to do so by the Court. IN R USDCTSD Case Mgt(General Instructions For All Cases).

x. *Copies for three-judge court.* Parties in a case where a three-judge court has been requested must file an original and three copies of any document filed directly with the clerk (instead of electronically) until the court: (1) denies the request; (2) dissolves the three-judge court; or (3) allows the parties to file fewer copies. IN R USDCTSD L.R. 9-2(c).

xi. *Declaration that party was unable to file in a timely manner due to technical difficulties.* If a party misses a filing deadline due to an inability to file electronically, the party may submit the untimely filed document, accompanied by a declaration stating the reason(s) for missing the deadline. IN R USDCTSD ECF Procedures(16). A model form is provided as Appendix D (IN R USDCTSD ECF Procedures(Appendix D)). IN R USDCTSD ECF Procedures(16).

E. Format

1. *Form of documents.* The rules governing captions and other matters of form in pleadings apply to motions and other papers. FRCP 7(b)(2).

   a. *Paper (manual filings only).* Any document that is not filed electronically must: be flat, unfolded, and on good-quality, eight and one-half by eleven (8-1/2 x 11) inch white paper. IN R USDCTSD L.R. 5-1(d)(1). Any document that is not filed electronically must: be single-sided. IN R USDCTSD L.R. 5-1(d)(1).

      i. *Covers or backing.* Any document that is not filed electronically must: not have a cover or a back. IN R USDCTSD L.R. 5-1(d)(1).

      ii. *Fastening.* Any document that is not filed electronically must: be (if consisting of more than one (1) page) fastened by paperclip or binder clip and may not be stapled. IN R USDCTSD L.R. 5-1(d)(1).

         • *Request for nonconforming fastening.* If a document cannot be fastened or bound as required by IN R USDCTSD L.R. 5-1(d), a party may ask the clerk for permission to fasten it in another manner. The party must make such a request before attempting to file the document with nonconforming fastening. IN R USDCTSD L.R. 5-1(d)(2).

      iii. *Hole punching.* Any document that is not filed electronically must: be two-hole punched at the top with the holes two and three-quarter (2-3/4) inches apart and appropriately centered. IN R USDCTSD L.R. 5-1(d)(1).

   b. *Margins.* Any pleading, motion, brief, affidavit, notice, or proposed order filed with the court, whether electronically or with the clerk, must: have at least one (1) inch margins. IN R USDCTSD L.R. 5-1(b).

   c. *Spacing.* Any pleading, motion, brief, affidavit, notice, or proposed order filed with the court, whether electronically or with the clerk, must: be double spaced (except for headings, footnotes, and quoted material). IN R USDCTSD L.R. 5-1(b).

   d. *Text.* Any pleading, motion, brief, affidavit, notice, or proposed order filed with the court, whether electronically or with the clerk, must: be plainly typewritten, printed, or prepared by a clearly legible copying process. IN R USDCTSD L.R. 5-1(b).

   e. *Font size.* Any pleading, motion, brief, affidavit, notice, or proposed order filed with the court, whether electronically or with the clerk, must: use at least 12-point type in the body of the document and at least 10-point type in footnotes. IN R USDCTSD L.R. 5-1(b).

   f. *Page numbering.* Any pleading, motion, brief, affidavit, notice, or proposed order filed with the court, whether electronically or with the clerk, must: have consecutively numbered pages. IN R USDCTSD L.R. 5-1(b).

   g. *Caption; Names of parties.* Every pleading must have a caption with the court's name, a title, a file number, and a FRCP 7(a) designation. The title of the complaint must name all the parties; the title of other pleadings, after naming the first party on each side, may refer generally to other parties. FRCP 10(a). Any pleading, motion, brief, affidavit, notice, or proposed order filed with the court, whether electronically or with the clerk, must: include a title on the first page. IN R USDCTSD L.R. 5-1(b).

      i. *Alternative motions.* Motions must be filed separately, but alternative motions may be filed in a single document if each is named in the title. IN R USDCTSD L.R. 7-1(a).

h. *Filer's information.* Any pleading, motion, brief, affidavit, notice, or proposed order filed with the court, whether electronically or with the clerk, must: in the case of pleadings, motions, legal briefs, and notices, include the name, complete address, telephone number, facsimile number (where available), and e-mail address (where available) of the pro se litigant or attorney who files it. IN R USDCTSD L.R. 5-1(b).

i. *Paragraphs; Separate statements.* A party must state its claims or defenses in numbered paragraphs, each limited as far as practicable to a single set of circumstances. A later pleading may refer by number to a paragraph in an earlier pleading. If doing so would promote clarity, each claim founded on a separate transaction or occurrence—and each defense other than a denial—must be stated in a separate count or defense. FRCP 10(b).

j. *Adoption by reference; Exhibits.* A statement in a pleading may be adopted by reference elsewhere in the same pleading or in any other pleading or motion. A copy of a written instrument that is an exhibit to a pleading is a part of the pleading for all purposes. FRCP 10(c).

k. *Citations*

    i. *Local rules.* The Local Rules of the United States District Court for the Southern District of Indiana may be cited as "S.D. Ind. L.R." IN R USDCTSD L.R. 1-1(a).

    ii. *Local alternative dispute resolution rules.* These Rules shall be known as the Local Alternative Dispute Resolution Rules of the United States District Court for the Southern District of Indiana. They shall be cited as "S.D.Ind. Local A.D.R. Rule _____." IN R USDCTSD A.D.R. Rule 1.1.

l. *Acceptance by the clerk.* The clerk must not refuse to file a paper solely because it is not in the form prescribed by the Federal Rules of Civil Procedure or by a local rule or practice. FRCP 5(d)(4). The clerk will accept a document that violates IN R USDCTSD L.R. 5-1, but the court may exclude the document from the official record. IN R USDCTSD L.R. 5-1(e).

    i. *Sanctions for errors as to form.* The court may strike from the record any document that does not comply with the rules governing the form of documents filed with the court, such as rules that regulate document size or the number of copies to be filed or that require a special designation in the caption. The court may also sanction an attorney or party who files a non-compliant document. IN R USDCTSD L.R. 1-3.

2. *Form of electronic documents.* Any document submitted via the court's electronic case filing (ECF) system must be: otherwise prepared and filed in a manner consistent with the CM/ECF Policies and Procedures Manual (IN R USDCTSD ECF Procedures). IN R USDCTSD L.R. 5-1(c). Electronically filed documents must meet the requirements of FRCP 10 (Form of Pleadings), IN R USDCTSD L.R. 5-1 (Format of Papers Presented for Filing), and FRCP 5.2 (Privacy Protection for Filings Made with the Court), as if they had been submitted on paper. Documents filed electronically are also subject to any page limitations set forth by Court Order, by IN R USDCTSD L.R. 7-1 (Motion Practice), or IN R USDCTSD L.R. 56-1 (Summary Judgment Practice), as applicable. IN R USDCTSD ECF Procedures(13).

a. *PDF format required.* Any document submitted via the court's electronic case filing (ECF) system must be: in .pdf format. IN R USDCTSD L.R. 5-1(c); IN R USDCTSD ECF Procedures(7). Any document submitted via the court's electronic case filing (ECF) system must be: converted to a .pdf file directly from a word processing program, unless it exists only in paper format (in which case it may be scanned to create a .pdf document). IN R USDCTSD L.R. 5-1(c); IN R USDCTSD ECF Procedures(13).

    i. An exhibit may be scanned into PDF format, at a recommended 300 dpi resolution or higher, only if it does not already exist in electronic format. The filing attorney is responsible for reviewing all PDF documents for legibility before submitting them through the Court's Electronic Case Filing system. For technical guidance in creating PDF documents, please contact the Clerk's Office. IN R USDCTSD ECF Procedures(13).

b. *File size limitations.* Any document submitted via the court's electronic case filing (ECF) system must be: submitted as one or more .pdf files that do not exceed ten megabytes (10 MB) each (consistent with the CM/ECF Policies and Procedures Manual (IN R USDCTSD ECF Procedures)). IN R USDCTSD L.R. 5-1(c); IN R USDCTSD ECF Procedures(13).

   i. To electronically file a document or attachment that exceeds ten megabytes (10 MB), the document must first be broken down into two or more smaller files. For example, if Exhibit A is a twelve megabyte (12 MB) PDF file, it should be divided into 2 equal parts prior to electronic filing. Each component part of the exhibit would be filed as an attachment to the main document and described appropriately as "Exhibit A (part 1 of 2)" and "Exhibit A (part 2 of 2)." IN R USDCTSD ECF Procedures(13).

   ii. The supporting items mentioned in IN R USDCTSD ECF Procedures(13) should not be confused with memorandums or briefs in support of motions as outlined in IN R USDCTSD L.R. 7-1 or IN R USDCTSD L.R. 56-1. These memorandums or briefs in support are to be filed as entirely separate documents pursuant to the appropriate rule. Additionally, no motion shall be embodied in the text of a response or reply brief/memorandum unless otherwise ordered by the Court. IN R USDCTSD ECF Procedures(13).

  c. *Separate component parts.* A key objective of the electronic filing system is to ensure that as much of the case as possible is managed electronically. To facilitate electronic filing and retrieval, documents to be filed electronically are to be reasonably broken into their separate component parts. By way of example, most filings include a foundation document (e.g., motion) and other supporting items (e.g., exhibits, proposed orders, proposed amended pleadings). The foundation document, as well as the supporting items, are each separate components of the filing; supporting items must be filed as attachments to the foundation document. These exhibits or attachments should include only those excerpts of the referenced documents that are directly germane to the matter under consideration. IN R USDCTSD ECF Procedures(13).

   i. Where an individual component cannot be included in an electronic filing (e.g. the component cannot be converted to electronic format), the filer shall electronically file the prescribed Notice of Manual Filing in place of that component. A model form is provided as Appendix C (IN R USDCTSD ECF Procedures(Appendix C)). IN R USDCTSD ECF Procedures(13).

  d. *Exhibits.* Each electronically filed exhibit to a main document must be: (1) created as a separate .pdf file; (2) submitted as an attachment to the main document and given a title which describes its content; and (3) limited to excerpts that are directly germane to the main document's subject matter. IN R USDCTSD L.R. 5-6(a).

   i. When uploading attachments during the electronic filing process, exhibits must be uploaded in a logical sequence and a brief description must be entered for each individual PDF file. The description must include not only the exhibit number or letter, but also a brief description of the document. This information may be entered in CM/ECF using a combination of the Category drop-down menu, the Description text box, or both (see IN R USDCTSD ECF Procedures(13)(Figure 1)). The information that is provided in each box will be combined to create a description of the document as it appears on the case docket (see IN R USDCTSD ECF Procedures(13)(Figure 2)). IN R USDCTSD ECF Procedures(13). For an example, refer to IN R USDCTSD ECF Procedures(13).

  e. *Excerpts.* A party filing an exhibit that consists of excerpts from a larger document must clearly and prominently identify the exhibit as containing excerpted material. Either party will have the right to timely file additional excerpts or the complete document to the extent they are or become directly germane to the main document's subject matter. IN R USDCTSD L.R. 5-6(b).

  f. For an example illustrating the application of IN R USDCTSD ECF Procedures(13), refer to IN R USDCTSD ECF Procedures(13).

3. *Form of briefs*

  a. *Page limits.* Supporting and response briefs (excluding tables of contents, tables of authorities, appendices, and certificates of service) may not exceed thirty-five (35) pages. Reply briefs may not exceed twenty (20) pages. IN R USDCTSD L.R. 7-1(e)(1).

   i. *Permission to exceed limits.* The court may allow a party to file a brief exceeding these page limits for extraordinary and compelling reasons. IN R USDCTSD L.R. 7-1(e)(2).

    ii. *Supporting and response briefs exceeding limits.* If the court allows a party to file a brief or response exceeding thirty-five (35) pages, the document must include:

- A table of contents with page references;
- A statement of issues; and
- A table of authorities including: (1) all cases (alphabetically arranged), statutes, and other authorities cited in the brief; and (2) page numbers where the authorities are cited in the brief. IN R USDCTSD L.R. 7-1(e)(3).

4. *Signing of pleadings, motions and other papers*

  a. *Signature.* Every pleading, written motion, and other paper must be signed by at least one attorney of record in the attorney's name—or by a party personally if the party is unrepresented. The paper must state the signer's address, e-mail address, and telephone number. FRCP 11(a).

    i. *Signatures on manual filings.* Any document that is not filed electronically must: include the original signature of the pro se litigant or attorney who files it. IN R USDCTSD L.R. 5-1(d)(1).

    ii. *Electronic signatures.* Use of the attorney's login and password when filing documents electronically serves in part as the attorney's signature for purposes of FRCP 11, the Local Rules of the United States District Court for the Southern District of Indiana, and any other purpose for which a signature is required in connection with proceedings before the Court. IN R USDCTSD ECF Procedures(14); IN R USDCTSD ECF Procedures(10). A pleading, motion, brief, or notice filed electronically under an attorney's ECF log-in and password must be signed by that attorney. IN R USDCTSD L.R. 5-7(a). A signature on a document other than a document filed as provided under IN R USDCTSD L.R. 5-7(a) must be an original handwritten signature and must be scanned into .pdf format for electronic filing. IN R USDCTSD L.R. 5-7(c); IN R USDCTSD ECF Procedures(14).

- *Form of electronic signature.* If a document is converted directly from a word processing application to .pdf (as opposed to scanning), the name of the Filing User under whose log-in and password the document is submitted must be preceded by a "s/" and typed on the signature line where the Filing User's handwritten signature would otherwise appear. IN R USDCTSD L.R. 5-7(b). All documents filed electronically shall include a signature block and include the filing attorney's typewritten name, address, telephone number, facsimile number and e-mail address. In addition, the name of the filing attorney under whose ECF login the document will be filed should be preceded by a "s/" and typed in the space where the attorney's handwritten signature would otherwise appear. IN R US-DCTSD ECF Procedures(14). For a sample format, refer to IN R USDCTSD ECF Procedures(14).

- *Effect of electronic signature.* Filing an electronically signed document under an attorney's ECF log-in and password constitutes the attorney's signature on the document under the Federal Rules of Civil Procedure, under the Local Rules of the United States District Court for the Southern District of Indiana, and for any other reason a signature is required in connection with the court's activities. IN R USDCTSD L.R. 5-7(d).

- *Documents with multiple attorneys' signatures.* Documents requiring signatures of more than one attorney shall be filed either by: (1) obtaining consent from the other attorney, then typing the "s/ [Name]" signature of the other attorney on the signature line where the other attorney's signature would otherwise appear; (2) identifying in the signature section the name of the other attorney whose signature is required and by the submission of a Notice of Endorsement (see IN R USDCTSD ECF Procedures(Appendix B)) by the other attorney no later than three (3) business days after filing; (3) submitting a scanned document containing all handwritten signatures; or (4) in any other manner approved by the Court. IN R USDCTSD ECF Procedures(14); IN R USDCTSD L.R. 5-7(e).

    iii. *No verification or accompanying affidavit required for pleadings.* Unless a rule or statute specifically states otherwise, a pleading need not be verified or accompanied by an affidavit. FRCP 11(a).

      iv.   *Unsigned papers.* The court must strike an unsigned paper unless the omission is promptly corrected after being called to the attorney's or party's attention. FRCP 11(a). The court will strike any document filed directly with the clerk that is not signed by an attorney of record or the pro se litigant filing it, but the court may do so only after giving the attorney or pro se litigant notice of the omission and reasonable time to correct it. Rubber-stamp or facsimile signatures are not original signatures and the court will deem documents containing them to be unsigned for purposes of FRCP 11 and FRCP 26(g) and IN R USDCTSD L.R. 5-10. IN R USDCTSD L.R. 5-10(g).

  b. *Representations to the court.* By presenting to the court a pleading, written motion, or other paper—whether by signing, filing, submitting, or later advocating it—an attorney or unrepresented party certifies that to the best of the person's knowledge, information, and belief, formed after an inquiry reasonable under the circumstances:

      i.   It is not being presented for any improper purpose, such as to harass, cause unnecessary delay, or needlessly increase the cost of litigation;

      ii.   The claims, defenses, and other legal contentions are warranted by existing law or by a nonfrivolous argument for extending, modifying, or reversing existing law or for establishing new law;

      iii.   The factual contentions have evidentiary support or, if specifically so identified, will likely have evidentiary support after a reasonable opportunity for further investigation or discovery; and

      iv.   The denials of factual contentions are warranted on the evidence or, if specifically so identified, are reasonably based on belief or a lack of information. FRCP 11(b).

  c. *Sanctions.* If, after notice and a reasonable opportunity to respond, the court determines that FRCP 11(b) has been violated, the court may impose an appropriate sanction on any attorney, law firm, or party that violated FRCP 11(b) or is responsible for the violation. FRCP 11(c)(1). Refer to the United States District Court for the Southern District of Indiana KeyRules Motion for Sanctions document for more information.

5. *Privacy protection for filings made with the court.* Electronically filed documents must meet the requirements of. . .FRCP 5.2 (Privacy Protection for Filings Made with the Court), as if they had been submitted on paper. IN R USDCTSD ECF Procedures(13).

  a. *Redacted filings.* Unless the court orders otherwise, in an electronic or paper filing with the court that contains an individual's Social Security number, taxpayer-identification number, or birth date, the name of an individual known to be a minor, or a financial-account number, a party or nonparty making the filing may include only:

      i.   The last four (4) digits of the Social Security number and taxpayer-identification number;

      ii.   The year of the individual's birth;

      iii.   The minor's initials; and

      iv.   The last four (4) digits of the financial-account number. FRCP 5.2(a).

  b. *Exemptions from the redaction requirement.* The redaction requirement does not apply to the following:

      i.   A financial-account number that identifies the property allegedly subject to forfeiture in a forfeiture proceeding;

      ii.   The record of an administrative or agency proceeding;

      iii.   The official record of a state-court proceeding;

      iv.   The record of a court or tribunal, if that record was not subject to the redaction requirement when originally filed;

      v.   A filing covered by FRCP 5.2(c) or FRCP 5.2(d); and

      vi.   A pro se filing in an action brought under 28 U.S.C.A. § 2241, 28 U.S.C.A. § 2254, or 28 U.S.C.A. § 2255. FRCP 5.2(b).

c. *Limitations on remote access to electronic files; Social Security appeals and immigration cases.* Unless the court orders otherwise, in an action for benefits under the Social Security Act, and in an action or proceeding relating to an order of removal, to relief from removal, or to immigration benefits or detention, access to an electronic file is authorized as follows:

   i. The parties and their attorneys may have remote electronic access to any part of the case file, including the administrative record;

   ii. Any other person may have electronic access to the full record at the courthouse, but may have remote electronic access only to:

   - The docket maintained by the court; and

   - An opinion, order, judgment, or other disposition of the court, but not any other part of the case file or the administrative record. FRCP 5.2(c).

d. *Filings made under seal.* The court may order that a filing be made under seal without redaction. The court may later unseal the filing or order the person who made the filing to file a redacted version for the public record. FRCP 5.2(d). For more information on filing under seal, refer to IN R USDCTSD L.R. 5-11 and IN R USDCTSD ECF Procedures(18).

e. *Protective orders.* For good cause, the court may by order in a case:

   i. Require redaction of additional information; or

   ii. Limit or prohibit a nonparty's remote electronic access to a document filed with the court. FRCP 5.2(e).

f. *Option for additional unredacted filing under seal.* A person making a redacted filing may also file an unredacted copy under seal. The court must retain the unredacted copy as part of the record. FRCP 5.2(f).

g. *Option for filing a reference list.* A filing that contains redacted information may be filed together with a reference list that identifies each item of redacted information and specifies an appropriate identifier that uniquely corresponds to each item listed. The list must be filed under seal and may be amended as of right. Any reference in the case to a listed identifier will be construed to refer to the corresponding item of information. FRCP 5.2(g).

h. *Waiver of protection of identifiers.* A person waives the protection of FRCP 5.2(a) as to the person's own information by filing it without redaction and not under seal. FRCP 5.2(h).

F. Filing and Service Requirements

1. *Filing requirements.* Any paper after the complaint that is required to be served—together with a certificate of service—must be filed within a reasonable time after service. FRCP 5(d)(1). Motions must be filed separately, but alternative motions may be filed in a single document if each is named in the title. IN R USDCTSD L.R. 7-1(a).

   a. *How filing is made; In general.* A paper is filed by delivering it:

      i. To the clerk; or

      ii. To a judge who agrees to accept it for filing, and who must then note the filing date on the paper and promptly send it to the clerk. FRCP 5(d)(2).

         - In certain instances, the court will direct the parties to submit items directly to chambers (e.g., confidential settlement statements). However, absent specific prior authorization, counsel and litigants should not submit letters or documents directly to chambers, and such materials should be filed with the clerk. IN R USDCTSD L.R. 5-1(Local Rules Advisory Committee Comment).

      iii. A document or item submitted in relation to a matter within the court's jurisdiction is deemed filed upon delivery to the office of the clerk in a manner prescribed by the Local Rules of the United States District Court for the Southern District of Indiana or the Federal Rules of Civil Procedure or authorized by the court. Any submission directed to a Judge or Judge's staff, the office of the clerk or any employee thereof, in a manner that is not contemplated by IN R USDCTSD L.R. 5-1 and without prior court authorization is prohibited. IN R USDCTSD L.R. 5-1(a).

b. *Non-electronic filing.* Any document that is exempt from electronic filing must be filed directly with the clerk and served on other parties in the case as required by those Federal Rules of Civil Procedure and Local Rules of the United States District Court for the Southern District of Indiana that apply to the service of non-electronic documents. IN R USDCTSD L.R. 5-2(c).

   i. *When completed.* A document or other item that is not required to be filed electronically is deemed filed:

- Upon delivery in person, by courier, or via U.S. Mail or other mail delivery service to the clerk's office during business hours;

- When the courtroom deputy clerk accepts it, if the document or item is filed in open court; or

- Upon completion of any other manner of filing that the court authorizes. IN R USDCTSD L.R. 5-10(a).

   ii. *Document filing by non-exempt party.* When a party who is not exempt from the electronic filing requirement files a document directly with the clerk, the party must:

- Electronically file a notice of manual filing that explains why the document cannot be filed electronically;

- Present the document to the clerk within one (1) business day after filing the notice of manual filing; and

- Present the clerk with a copy of the notice of manual filing when the party files the document with the clerk. IN R USDCTSD L.R. 5-2(d).

c. *Electronic filing*

   i. *Authorization of electronic filing program.* A court may, by local rule, allow papers to be filed, signed, or verified by electronic means that are consistent with any technical standards established by the Judicial Conference of the United States. A local rule may require electronic filing only if reasonable exceptions are allowed. A paper filed electronically in compliance with a local rule is a written paper for purposes of the Federal Rules of Civil Procedure. FRCP 5(d)(3).

- IN R USDCTSD L.R. 5-2 requires electronic filing, as allowed by FRCP 5(d)(3). The policies and procedures in IN R USDCTSD ECF Procedures govern electronic filing in this district unless, due to circumstances in a particular case, a judicial officer determines that these policies and procedures (IN R USDCTSD ECF Procedures) should be modified. IN R USDCTSD ECF Procedures(1).

- Unless modified by order of the Court, all Federal Rules of Civil Procedure and Local Rules of the United States District Court for the Southern District of Indiana shall continue to apply to cases maintained in the Court's Case Management/Electronic Case Filing System (CM/ECF). IN R USDCTSD ECF Procedures(3).

   ii. *Mandatory electronic filing.* Unless exempted pursuant to IN R USDCTSD L.R. 5-3(e), attorneys admitted to the court's bar (including those admitted pro hac vice) or authorized to represent the United States must use the court's ECF system to file documents. IN R USDCTSD L.R. 5-3(a). Electronic filing by attorneys is required for eligible documents filed in civil and criminal cases pending with the Court, unless specifically exempted by Local Rule or Court Order. IN R USDCTSD ECF Procedures(4).

- *Exceptions.* All civil cases (other than those cases the court specifically exempts) must be maintained in the court's electronic case filing (ECF) system. Accordingly, as allowed by FRCP 5(d)(3), every document filed in this court (including exhibits) must be transmitted to the clerk's office via the ECF system consistent with IN R USDCTSD L.R. 5-2 through IN R USDCTSD L.R. 5-11 except: (1) documents filed by pro se litigants; (2) transcripts in cases filed by claimants under the Social Security Act (and related statutes); (3) exhibits in a format that does not readily permit electronic filing (such as videos and large maps and charts); (4) documents that are illegible when scanned into .pdf format; (5) documents filed in cases not maintained on the ECF system; and (6) any other documents that the court or the Local Rules of the United States District Court for the Southern District of Indiana specifically allow to be filed directly with the clerk. IN R USDCTSD L.R. 5-2(a). Parties otherwise participating in the electronic filing system may be excused from filing a particular component electronically under certain limited circumstances, such as when the component cannot be reduced to an electronic format. Such components shall not be filed electronically, but instead shall be manually filed with the Clerk of Court and served upon the parties in accordance with the applicable Federal Rules of Civil Procedure and the Local Rules of the United States District Court for the Southern District of Indiana for filing and service of non-electronic documents. IN R USDCTSD ECF Procedures(15).

- *Exemption from participation.* The court may exempt attorneys from using the ECF system in a particular case for good cause. An attorney must file a petition for ECF exemption and a CM/ECF technical requirements exemption questionnaire in each case in which the attorney seeks an exemption. (The CM/ECF technical requirements exemption questionnaire is available on the court's website). IN R USDCTSD L.R. 5-3(e).

iii. *Consequences of electronic filing.* Electronic transmission of a document consistent with the procedures adopted by the Court shall, upon the complete receipt of the same by the Clerk of Court, constitute filing of the document for all purposes of the Federal Rules of Civil and Criminal Procedure and the Local Rules of the United States District Court for the Southern District of Indiana, and shall constitute entry of that document onto the docket maintained by the Clerk pursuant to FRCP 58 and FRCP 79. IN R USDCTSD ECF Procedures(7); IN R USDCTSD L.R. 5-4(c)(1). When a document has been filed electronically: the document, as filed, binds the filing party. IN R USDCTSD L.R. 5-4(c)(3).

- A Notice of Electronic Filing (NEF) acknowledging that the document has been filed will immediately appear on the filer's screen after the document has been submitted. Attorneys are strongly encouraged to print or electronically save a copy of the NEF. Attorneys can also verify the filing of documents by inspecting the Court's electronic docket sheet through the use of a PACER login. IN R USDCTSD ECF Procedures(7). When a document has been filed electronically: the notice of electronic filing for the document serves as the court's date-stamp and proof of filing. IN R USDCTSD L.R. 5-4(c)(4).

- The Court may, upon the motion of a party or upon its own motion, strike any inappropriately filed document. IN R USDCTSD ECF Procedures(7).

iv. For more information on electronic filing, refer to IN R USDCTSD ECF Procedures.

d. *Fax filing.* The clerk may not file a faxed document without court authorization. The court may not authorize the clerk to file faxed documents without finding that compelling circumstances justify it. A party must submit a copy of the document that otherwise complies with IN R USDCTSD L.R. 5-10 to replace the faxed copy within seven (7) days after faxing the document. IN R USDCTSD L.R. 5-10(e).

2. *Service requirements*

a. *Service; When required*

i. *In general.* Unless the Federal Rules of Civil Procedure provide otherwise, each of the following papers must be served on every party:

- An order stating that service is required;

- A pleading filed after the original complaint, unless the court orders otherwise under FRCP 5(c) because there are numerous defendants;

- A discovery paper required to be served on a party, unless the court orders otherwise;

- A written motion, except one that may be heard ex parte; and

- A written notice, appearance, demand, or offer of judgment, or any similar paper. FRCP 5(a)(1).

ii. *If a party fails to appear.* No service is required on a party who is in default for failing to appear.

But a pleading that asserts a new claim for relief against such a party must be served on that party under FRCP 4. FRCP 5(a)(2).

    iii. *Seizing property.* If an action is begun by seizing property and no person is or need be named as a defendant, any service required before the filing of an appearance, answer, or claim must be made on the person who had custody or possession of the property when it was seized. FRCP 5(a)(3).

b. *Service; How made*

    i. *Serving an attorney.* If a party is represented by an attorney, service under FRCP 5 must be made on the attorney unless the court orders service on the party. FRCP 5(b)(1).

    ii. *Service in general.* A paper is served under FRCP 5 by:

- Handing it to the person;

- Leaving it: (1) at the person's office with a clerk or other person in charge or, if no one is in charge, in a conspicuous place in the office; or (2) if the person has no office or the office is closed, at the person's dwelling or usual place of abode with someone of suitable age and discretion who resides there;

- Mailing it to the person's last known address—in which event service is complete upon mailing;

- Leaving it with the court clerk if the person has no known address;

- Sending it by electronic means if the person consented in writing—in which event service is complete upon transmission, but is not effective if the serving party learns that it did not reach the person to be served; or

- Delivering it by any other means that the person consented to in writing—in which event service is complete when the person making service delivers it to the agency designated to make delivery. FRCP 5(b)(2).

    iii. *Electronic service*

- *Consent.* By registering to use the ECF system, attorneys consent to electronic service of documents filed in cases maintained on the ECF system. IN R USDCTSD L.R. 5-3(d). By participating in the Electronic Case Filing Program, attorneys consent to the electronic service of documents, and shall make available electronic mail addresses for service. IN R USDCTSD ECF Procedures(11).

- *Service on registered parties.* Upon the filing of a document by a party, an e-mail message will be automatically generated by the electronic filing system and sent via electronic mail to the e-mail addresses of all registered attorneys who have appeared in the case. The Notice of Electronic Filing will contain a document hyperlink which will provide recipients with one "free look" at the electronically filed document. Recipients are encouraged to print and/or save a copy of the document during the "free look" to avoid incurring PACER charges for future viewings of the document. IN R USDCTSD ECF Procedures(11). When a document has been filed electronically: transmission of the notice of electronic filing generated by the ECF system to an attorney's e-mail address constitutes service of the document on that attorney. IN R USDCTSD L.R. 5-4(c)(5). The party effectuates service on all registered attorneys by filing electronically. IN R USDCTSD ECF Procedures(11). When a document has been filed electronically: no other attempted service will constitute electronic service of the document. IN R USDCTSD L.R. 5-4(c)(6).

- *Service on exempt parties.* A filer must serve a copy of the document consistent with FRCP 5 on any party or attorney who is exempt from participating in electronic filing. IN R USDCTSD L.R. 5-4(d). It is the responsibility of the filing attorney to conventionally serve all parties who do not receive electronic service (the identity of these parties will be indicated on the filing receipt generated by the ECF system). IN R USDCTSD ECF Procedures(11).

- *Service on parties excused from electronic filing.* Parties otherwise participating in the electronic filing system may be excused from filing a particular component electronically under certain limited circumstances, such as when the component cannot be reduced to an electronic format. Such components shall not be filed electronically, but instead shall be manually filed with the Clerk of Court and served upon the parties in accordance with the applicable Federal Rules of Civil Procedure and the Local Rules of the United States District Court for the Southern District of Indiana for filing and service of non-electronic documents. IN R USDCTSD ECF Procedures(15).

- *Service of exempt documents.* Any document that is exempt from electronic filing must be filed directly with the clerk and served on other parties in the case as required by those Federal Rules of Civil Procedure and Local Rules of the United States District Court for the Southern District of Indiana that apply to the service of non-electronic documents. IN R USDCTSD L.R. 5-2(c).

    iv. *Using court facilities.* If a local rule so authorizes, a party may use the court's transmission facilities to make service under FRCP 5(b)(2)(E). FRCP 5(b)(3).

  c. *Serving numerous defendants*

    i. *In general.* If an action involves an unusually large number of defendants, the court may, on motion or on its own, order that:

- Defendants' pleadings and replies to them need not be served on other defendants;

- Any crossclaim, counterclaim, avoidance, or affirmative defense in those pleadings and replies to them will be treated as denied or avoided by all other parties; and

- Filing any such pleading and serving it on the plaintiff constitutes notice of the pleading to all parties. FRCP 5(c)(1).

    ii. *Notifying parties.* A copy of every such order must be served on the parties as the court directs. FRCP 5(c)(2).

G. Hearings

1. *Hearings, generally*

  a. *Oral argument.* Due process does not require that oral argument be permitted on a motion and, except as otherwise provided by local rule, the district court has discretion to determine whether it will decide the motion on the papers or hear argument by counsel (and perhaps receive evidence). FPP § 1190; F.D.I.C. v. Deglau, 207 F.3d 153 (3d Cir. 2000).

    i. *Request for oral argument.* A party may request oral argument by filing a separate motion explaining why oral argument is necessary and estimating how long the court should allow for the argument. IN R USDCTSD L.R. 7-5(a). Refer to the Documents section of this document for more information.

    ii. *No additional evidence at oral argument.* Parties may not present additional evidence at oral argument. IN R USDCTSD L.R. 7-5(b).

  b. *Providing a regular schedule for oral hearings.* A court may establish regular times and places for oral hearings on motions. FRCP 78(a).

  c. *Providing for submission on briefs.* By rule or order, the court may provide for submitting and determining motions on briefs, without oral hearings. FRCP 78(b).

  d. *Request for evidentiary hearing.* A party may request an evidentiary hearing on a motion or petition by serving and filing a separate motion explaining why the hearing is necessary and estimating how long the court should allow for the hearing. IN R USDCTSD L.R. 7-5(c).

  e. *Directed by the court.* The court may: (1) grant or deny a request for oral argument or an evidentiary hearing in its sole discretion; (2) set oral argument or an evidentiary hearing without a request from a party; and (3) order any oral argument or evidentiary hearing to be held anywhere within the district regardless of where the case will be tried. IN R USDCTSD L.R. 7-5(d).

2. *Courtroom and courthouse decorum.* For information on courtroom and courthouse decorum, refer to IN R USDCTSD L.R. 83-3.

H. Forms

1. Federal Motion to Strike Forms

a. Motion; By plaintiff; To strike insufficient defense from answer. AMJUR PP FEDPRAC § 441.

b. Motion; To strike redundant, immaterial, impertinent, or scandalous matter from pleading. AMJUR PP FEDPRAC § 442.

c. Motion; To strike portions of complaint. AMJUR PP FEDPRAC § 444.

d. Motion to strike insufficient affirmative defenses. 2C FEDFORMS § 11:151.

e. Motion to strike insufficient defense in answer; Stating particular reason. 2C FEDFORMS § 11:153.

f. Notice of motion and motion to strike insufficient affirmative defense. 2C FEDFORMS § 11:155.

g. Motion to strike impertinence and scandal. 2C FEDFORMS § 11:157.

h. Motion to strike impertinence and immateriality. 2C FEDFORMS § 11:158.

i. Motion to strike redundancy and scandal. 2C FEDFORMS § 11:159.

j. Motion to strike immaterial defense. 2C FEDFORMS § 11:160.

k. Motion to strike for immateriality. 2C FEDFORMS § 11:161.

l. Motion to strike counterclaim for lack of evidence. 2C FEDFORMS § 11:162.

m. Opposition; To motion; General form. FEDPROF § 1:750.

n. Affidavit; Supporting or opposing motion. FEDPROF § 1:751.

o. Brief; Supporting or opposing motion. FEDPROF § 1:752.

p. Statement of points and authorities; Opposing motion. FEDPROF § 1:753.

q. Motion; To strike material outside statute of limitations. FEDPROF § 1:773.

r. Opposition to motion; Material not contained in pleading. FEDPROF § 1:774.

s. General form. GOLDLTGFMS § 20:8.

t. General form; Federal form. GOLDLTGFMS § 20:10.

u. Notice and motion to strike immaterial, redundant or scandalous matter. GOLDLTGFMS § 20:13.

v. Motion to strike complaint and dismiss action as to one defendant. GOLDLTGFMS § 20:14.

w. Defendant's motion to strike. GOLDLTGFMS § 20:16.

x. Defendant's motion to strike; Plaintiff's response. GOLDLTGFMS § 20:17.

y. Motion to strike answer. GOLDLTGFMS § 20:19.

z. Objections to motion to strike. GOLDLTGFMS § 20:20.

2. Forms for the Southern District of Indiana

a. Notice of endorsement. IN R USDCTSD ECF Procedures(Appendix B).

b. Notice of manual filing. IN R USDCTSD ECF Procedures(Appendix C).

c. Declaration that party was unable to file in a timely manner due to technical difficulties. IN R USDCTSD ECF Procedures(Appendix D).

I. Applicable Rules

1. *Federal rules*

a. Serving and filing pleadings and other papers. FRCP 5.

b. Constitutional challenge to a statute; Notice, certification, and intervention. FRCP 5.1.

c. Privacy protection for filings made with the court. FRCP 5.2.

d. Computing and extending time; Time for motion papers. FRCP 6.

e. Pleadings allowed; Form of motions and other papers. FRCP 7.

    f.   Disclosure statement. FRCP 7.1.

    g.   Form of pleadings. FRCP 10.

    h.   Signing pleadings, motions, and other papers; Representations to the court; Sanctions. FRCP 11.

    i.   Defenses and objections; When and how presented; Motion for judgment on the pleadings; Consolidating motions; Waiving defenses; Pretrial hearing. FRCP 12.

    j.   Hearing motions; Submission on briefs. FRCP 78.

2. *Local rules*

    a.   Scope of the rules. IN R USDCTSD L.R. 1-1.

    b.   Sanctions for errors as to form. IN R USDCTSD L.R. 1-3.

    c.   Format of documents presented for filing. IN R USDCTSD L.R. 5-1.

    d.   Constitutional challenge to a statute; Notice. IN R USDCTSD L.R. 5.1-1.

    e.   Filing of documents electronically required. IN R USDCTSD L.R. 5-2.

    f.   Eligibility, registration, passwords for electronic filing; Exemption from electronic filing. IN R USDCTSD L.R. 5-3.

    g.   Timing and consequences of electronic filing. IN R USDCTSD L.R. 5-4.

    h.   Attachments and exhibits in cases filed electronically. IN R USDCTSD L.R. 5-6.

    i.   Signatures in cases filed electronically. IN R USDCTSD L.R. 5-7.

    j.   Non-electronic filings. IN R USDCTSD L.R. 5-10.

    k.   Motion practice. [IN R USDCTSD L.R. 7-1, as amended by IN ORDER 16-2319, effective December 1, 2016].

    l.   Oral arguments and hearings. IN R USDCTSD L.R. 7-5.

    m.   Request for three-judge court. IN R USDCTSD L.R. 9-2.

    n.   Filing of discovery materials. IN R USDCTSD L.R. 26-2.

    o.   Assignment of cases. IN R USDCTSD L.R. 40-1.

    p.   Alternative dispute resolution. IN R USDCTSD A.D.R. Rule 1.1; IN R USDCTSD A.D.R. Rule 1.2; IN R USDCTSD A.D.R. Rule 1.5; IN R USDCTSD A.D.R. Rule 2.1; IN R USDCTSD A.D.R. Rule 2.2.

    q.   Instructions for preparing case management plan. IN R USDCTSD Case Mgt.

    r.   Electronic case filing policies and procedures manual. IN R USDCTSD ECF Procedures.

Motions, Oppositions and Replies
Motion to Dismiss for Improper Venue

Document Last Updated December 2016

A. Checklist

(I) ❑ Matters to be considered by moving party

    (a) ❑ Required documents

        (1) ❑ Notice of motion and motion

        (2) ❑ Brief

        (3) ❑ Certificate of service

    (b) ❑ Supplemental documents

        (1) ❑ Supporting evidence

        (2) ❑ Notice of constitutional question

   (3) ❑ Nongovernmental corporate disclosure statement

   (4) ❑ Index of exhibits

   (5) ❑ Request for oral argument

   (6) ❑ Request for evidentiary hearing

   (7) ❑ Copy of authority

   (8) ❑ Proposed order

   (9) ❑ Copy of document with self-address envelope

   (10) ❑ Notice of manual filing

   (11) ❑ Courtesy copies

   (12) ❑ Copies for three-judge court

   (13) ❑ Declaration that party was unable to file in a timely manner due to technical difficulties

 (c) ❑ Timing

   (1) ❑ Every defense to a claim for relief in any pleading must be asserted in the responsive pleading if one is required

   (2) ❑ A motion asserting any of the defenses in FRCP 12(b) must be made before pleading if a responsive pleading is allowed

   (3) ❑ If a pleading sets out a claim for relief that does not require a responsive pleading, an opposing party may assert at trial any defense to that claim

   (4) ❑ A written motion and notice of the hearing must be served at least fourteen (14) days before the time specified for the hearing, with the following exceptions: (i) when the motion may be heard ex parte; (ii) when the Federal Rules of Civil Procedure set a different time; or (iii) when a court order—which a party may, for good cause, apply for ex parte—sets a different time

   (5) ❑ Any affidavit supporting a motion must be served with the motion

   (6) ❑ When a party who is not exempt from the electronic filing requirement files a document directly with the clerk, the party must present the document to the clerk within one (1) business day after filing the notice of manual filing

   (7) ❑ Unless the court orders otherwise, the [untimely] document and declaration [that party was unable to file in a timely manner due to technical difficulties] must be filed no later than 12:00 noon of the first day on which the court is open for business following the original filing deadline

(II) ❑ Matters to be considered by opposing party

 (a) ❑ Required documents

   (1) ❑ Response brief

   (2) ❑ Certificate of service

 (b) ❑ Supplemental documents

   (1) ❑ Supporting evidence

   (2) ❑ Notice of constitutional question

   (3) ❑ Index of exhibits

   (4) ❑ Request for oral argument

   (5) ❑ Request for evidentiary hearing

   (6) ❑ Copy of authority

   (7) ❑ Copy of document with self-address envelope

   (8) ❑ Notice of manual filing

(9) ❑ Courtesy copies

(10) ❑ Copies for three-judge court

(11) ❑ Declaration that party was unable to file in a timely manner due to technical difficulties

(c) ❑ Timing

(1) ❑ Any response is due within fourteen (14) days after service of the motion

(2) ❑ Except as FRCP 59(c) provides otherwise, any opposing affidavit must be served at least seven (7) days before the hearing, unless the court permits service at another time

(3) ❑ When a party who is not exempt from the electronic filing requirement files a document directly with the clerk, the party must present the document to the clerk within one (1) business day after filing the notice of manual filing

(4) ❑ Unless the court orders otherwise, the [untimely] document and declaration [that party was unable to file in a timely manner due to technical difficulties] must be filed no later than 12:00 noon of the first day on which the court is open for business following the original filing deadline

B. Timing

1. *Motion to dismiss for improper venue*

   a. *In a responsive pleading.* Every defense to a claim for relief in any pleading must be asserted in the responsive pleading if one is required. FRCP 12(b).

   b. *By motion.* A motion asserting any of the defenses in FRCP 12(b) must be made before pleading if a responsive pleading is allowed. FRCP 12(b). Although FRCP 12(b) encourages the responsive pleader to file a motion to dismiss before filing the answer, nothing in FRCP 12 prohibits the filing of a motion to dismiss with the answer. An untimely motion to dismiss may be considered if the defense asserted in the motion was previously raised in the responsive pleading. FEDPROC § 62:427.

   c. *At trial.* If a pleading sets out a claim for relief that does not require a responsive pleading, an opposing party may assert at trial any defense to that claim. FRCP 12(b).

2. *Timing of motions, generally*

   a. *Motion and notice of hearing.* A written motion and notice of the hearing must be served at least fourteen (14) days before the time specified for the hearing, with the following exceptions:

      i. When the motion may be heard ex parte;

      ii. When the Federal Rules of Civil Procedure set a different time; or

      iii. When a court order—which a party may, for good cause, apply for ex parte—sets a different time. FRCP 6(c)(1).

   b. *Supporting affidavit.* Any affidavit supporting a motion must be served with the motion. FRCP 6(c)(2).

3. *Timing of opposing papers.* Any response is due within fourteen (14) days after service of the motion. IN R USDCTSD L.R. 7-1(c)(2)(A).

   a. *Opposing affidavit.* Except as FRCP 59(c) provides otherwise, any opposing affidavit must be served at least seven (7) days before the hearing, unless the court permits service at another time. FRCP 6(c)(2).

   b. *Extensions.* The court may extend response and reply deadlines, but only for good cause. IN R USDCTSD L.R. 7-1(c)(3).

   c. *Summary ruling on failure to respond.* The court may summarily rule on a motion if an opposing party does not file a response within the deadline. IN R USDCTSD L.R. 7-1(c)(4).

4. *Timing of reply papers.* Where the respondent files an answering affidavit setting up a new matter, the

moving party ordinarily is allowed a reasonable time to file a reply affidavit since failure to deny the new matter by affidavit may operate as an admission of its truth. AMJUR MOTIONS § 25.

a. *Reply brief.* Any reply is due within seven (7) days after service of the response. IN R USDCTSD L.R. 7-1(c)(2)(B).

b. *Extensions.* The court may extend response and reply deadlines, but only for good cause. IN R USDCTSD L.R. 7-1(c)(3).

5. *Effect of a FRCP 12 motion on the time to serve a responsive pleading.* Unless the court sets a different time, serving a motion under FRCP 12 alters the periods in FRCP 12(a) as follows:

a. If the court denies the motion or postpones its disposition until trial, the responsive pleading must be served within fourteen (14) days after notice of the court's action; or

b. If the court grants a motion for a more definite statement, the responsive pleading must be served within fourteen (14) days after the more definite statement is served. FRCP 12(a)(4).

6. *Document filing by non-exempt party.* When a party who is not exempt from the electronic filing requirement files a document directly with the clerk, the party must: present the document to the clerk within one (1) business day after filing the notice of manual filing. IN R USDCTSD L.R. 5-2(d)(2).

7. *Declaration that party was unable to file in a timely manner due to technical difficulties.* Unless the Court orders otherwise, the [untimely] document and declaration [that party was unable to file in a timely manner due to technical difficulties] must be filed no later than 12:00 noon of the first day on which the Court is open for business following the original filing deadline. IN R USDCTSD ECF Procedures(16).

8. *Computation of time*

a. *Computing time.* FRCP 6 applies in computing any time period specified in the Federal Rules of Civil Procedure, in any local rule or court order, or in any statute that does not specify a method of computing time. FRCP 6(a).

   i. *Period stated in days or a longer unit.* When the period is stated in days or a longer unit of time:

- Exclude the day of the event that triggers the period;

- Count every day, including intermediate Saturdays, Sundays, and legal holidays; and

- Include the last day of the period, but if the last day is a Saturday, Sunday, or legal holiday, the period continues to run until the end of the next day that is not a Saturday, Sunday, or legal holiday. FRCP 6(a)(1).

   ii. *Period stated in hours.* When the period is stated in hours:

- Begin counting immediately on the occurrence of the event that triggers the period;

- Count every hour, including hours during intermediate Saturdays, Sundays, and legal holidays; and

- If the period would end on a Saturday, Sunday, or legal holiday, the period continues to run until the same time on the next day that is not a Saturday, Sunday, or legal holiday. FRCP 6(a)(2).

   iii. *Inaccessibility of the clerk's office.* Unless the court orders otherwise, if the clerk's office is inaccessible:

- On the last day for filing under FRCP 6(a)(1), then the time for filing is extended to the first accessible day that is not a Saturday, Sunday, or legal holiday; or

- During the last hour for filing under FRCP 6(a)(2), then the time for filing is extended to the same time on the first accessible day that is not a Saturday, Sunday, or legal holiday. FRCP 6(a)(3).

   iv. *"Last day" defined.* Unless a different time is set by a statute, local rule, or court order, the last day ends:

- For electronic filing, at midnight in the court's time zone; and

- For filing by other means, when the clerk's office is scheduled to close. FRCP 6(a)(4).

    v.   *"Next day" defined.* The "next day" is determined by continuing to count forward when the period is measured after an event and backward when measured before an event. FRCP 6(a)(5).

    vi.   *"Legal holiday" defined.* "Legal holiday" means:

- The day set aside by statute for observing New Year's Day, Martin Luther King Jr.'s Birthday, Washington's Birthday, Memorial Day, Independence Day, Labor Day, Columbus Day, Veterans' Day, Thanksgiving Day, or Christmas Day;

- Any day declared a holiday by the President or Congress; and

- For periods that are measured after an event, any other day declared a holiday by the state where the district court is located. FRCP 6(a)(6).

b.   *Computation of electronic filing deadlines.* Filing documents electronically does not alter filing deadlines. IN R USDCTSD ECF Procedures(7). A document due on a particular day must be filed before midnight local time of the division where the case is pending. IN R USDCTSD L.R. 5-4(a). All electronic transmissions of documents must be completed (i.e. received completely by the Clerk's Office) prior to midnight of the local time of the division in which the case is pending in order to be considered timely filed that day (NOTE: time will be noted in Eastern Time on the Court's docket. If you have filed a document prior to midnight local time of the division in which the case is pending and the document is due that date, but the electronic receipt and docket reflect the following calendar day, please contact the Court). IN R USDCTSD ECF Procedures(7). Although attorneys may file documents electronically twenty-four (24) hours a day, seven (7) days a week, attorneys are encouraged to file all documents during the normal working hours of the Clerk's Office (Monday through Friday, 8:30 a.m. to 4:30 p.m.) when technical support is available. IN R USDCTSD ECF Procedures(7); IN R USDCTSD ECF Procedures(9).

    i.   *Technical difficulties.* Parties are encouraged to file documents electronically during normal business hours, in case a problem is encountered. In the event a technical failure occurs and a document cannot be filed electronically despite the best efforts of the filing party, the party should print (if possible) a copy of the error message received. In addition, as soon as practically possible, the party should file a "Declaration that Party was Unable to File in a Timely Manner Due to Technical Difficulties." A model form is provided as Appendix D (IN R USDCTSD ECF Procedures(Appendix D)). IN R USDCTSD ECF Procedures(16).

- If a party is unable to file electronically and, as a result, may miss a filing deadline, the party must contact the Clerk's Office at the number listed in IN R USDCTSD ECF Procedures(15) to inform the court's staff of the difficulty. If a party misses a filing deadline due to an inability to file electronically, the party may submit the untimely filed document, accompanied by a declaration stating the reason(s) for missing the deadline. Unless the Court orders otherwise, the document and declaration must be filed no later than 12:00 noon of the first day on which the Court is open for business following the original filing deadline. IN R USDCTSD ECF Procedures(16).

c.   *Extending time*

    i.   *In general.* When an act may or must be done within a specified time, the court may, for good cause, extend the time:

- With or without motion or notice if the court acts, or if a request is made, before the original time or its extension expires; or

- On motion made after the time has expired if the party failed to act because of excusable neglect. FRCP 6(b)(1).

    ii.   *Exceptions.* A court must not extend the time to act under FRCP 50(b), FRCP 50(d), FRCP 52(b), FRCP 59(b), FRCP 59(d), FRCP 59(e), and FRCP 60(b). FRCP 6(b)(2).

    iii.   Refer to the United States District Court for the Southern District of Indiana KeyRules Motion for Continuance/Extension of Time document for more information on extending time.

d.   *Additional time after certain kinds of service.* When a party may or must act within a specified time after being served and service is made under FRCP 5(b)(2)(C) (mail), FRCP 5(b)(2)(D) (leaving with the clerk), or FRCP 5(b)(2)(F) (other means consented to), three (3) days are added after the period would otherwise expire under FRCP 6(a). FRCP 6(d). Service by electronic mail shall constitute service pursuant to FRCP 5(b)(2)(E) and shall entitle the party being served to the additional three (3) days provided by FRCP 6(d). IN R USDCTSD ECF Procedures(11).

C. General Requirements

1. *Motions, generally*

    a. *Requirements.* A request for a court order must be made by motion. The motion must:

        i.   Be in writing unless made during a hearing or trial;

        ii. State with particularity the grounds for seeking the order; and

        iii. State the relief sought. FRCP 7(b)(1).

    b. *Notice of motion.* A party interested in resisting the relief sought by a motion has a right to notice thereof, and an opportunity to be heard. AMJUR MOTIONS § 12.

        i. In addition to statutory or court rule provisions requiring notice of a motion—the purpose of such a notice requirement having been said to be to prevent a party from being prejudicially surprised by a motion—principles of natural justice dictate that an adverse party generally must be given notice that a motion will be presented to the court. AMJUR MOTIONS § 12.

        ii. "Notice," in this regard, means reasonable notice, including a meaningful opportunity to prepare and to defend against allegations of a motion. AMJUR MOTIONS § 12.

    c. *Writing requirement.* The writing requirement is intended to insure that the adverse parties are informed and have a record of both the motion's pendency and the grounds on which the movant seeks an order. FPP § 1191; Feldberg v. Quechee Lakes Corp., 463 F.3d 195 (2d Cir. 2006).

        i. It is sufficient "if the motion is stated in a written notice of the hearing of the motion." FPP § 1191.

    d. *Particularity requirement.* The particularity requirement insures that the opposing parties will have notice of their opponent's contentions. FEDPROC § 62:364; Goodman v. 1973 26 Foot Trojan Vessel, Arkansas Registration No. AR1439SN, 859 F.2d 71, 12 Fed.R.Serv.3d 645 (8th Cir. 1988). That requirement ensures that notice of the basis for the motion is provided to the court and to the opposing party so as to avoid prejudice, provide the opponent with a meaningful opportunity to respond, and provide the court with enough information to process the motion correctly. FEDPROC § 62:364; Andreas v. Volkswagen of America, Inc., 336 F.3d 789, 56 Fed.R.Serv.3d 6 (8th Cir. 2003).

        i. Reasonable specification of the grounds for a motion is sufficient. However, where a movant fails to state even one ground for granting the motion in question, the movant has failed to meet the minimal standard of "reasonable specification." FEDPROC § 62:364; Martinez v. Trainor, 556 F.2d 818, 23 Fed.R.Serv.2d 403 (7th Cir. 1977).

        ii. The court may excuse the failure to comply with the particularity requirement if it is inadvertent, and where no prejudice is shown by the opposing party. FEDPROC § 62:364.

    e. *Motions must be filed separately.* Motions must be filed separately, but alternative motions may be filed in a single document if each is named in the title. A motion must not be contained within a brief, response, or reply to a previously filed motion, unless ordered by the court. IN R USDCTSD L.R. 7-1(a).

    f. *Routine or uncontested motions.* The court may rule upon a routine or uncontested motion before the response deadline passes, unless: (1) the motion indicates that an opposing party objects to it; or (2) the court otherwise believes that a response will be filed. IN R USDCTSD L.R. 7-1(d).

2. *Motion to dismiss for improper venue.* A party may assert the defense of improper venue by motion. FRCP 12(b)(3). Objections to venue typically stem from a failure to adhere to the requirements specified in the general venue statute, 28 U.S.C.A. § 1391, or some other statutory venue provision. FPP § 1352.

    a. *Forum selection clauses.* In recent years, however, there have been what appears to be an increasing number of venue motions based on the enforcement of forum selection clauses in contracts. FPP § 1352; Tropp v. Corp. of Lloyd's, 385 Fed.Appx. 36, 37 (2d Cir. 2010). The courts of appeal are split as to whether dismissal of the action is proper pursuant to FRCP 12(b)(3) or FRCP 12(b)(6) when it is based on one of these forum selection clauses rather than on noncompliance with a federal venue statute; most of the decided cases use the former rule as the basis, however. FPP § 1352.

    i.   The Supreme Court resolved this split in its 2013 decision Atlantic Marine Construction Co. Inc. v. United States District Court for the Western District of Texas by holding that the appropriate method for enforcing a valid forum-selection clause is the use of transfer to the contractually selected forum under 28 U.S.C.A. § 1404(a). FPP § 1352; Atlantic Marine Construction Co. Inc. v. United States District Court for the Western District of Texas, 134 S.Ct. 568, 187 L.Ed.2d 487 (2013); Martinez v. Bloomberg LP, 740 F.3d 211, 216 (2d Cir. 2014).

    ii.   Forum-selection clauses cannot make venue "wrong" or "improper" within the meaning of 28 U.S.C.A. § 1406(a) or FRCP 12(b)(3), which is why FRCP 12(b)(3) is no longer an appropriate method for enforcing forum selection clauses. FPP § 1352; Atlantic Marine Construction Co. Inc. v. United States District Court for the Western District of Texas, 134 S.Ct. 568, 579, 187 L.Ed.2d 487 (2013).

b.   *Burden.* On a motion under FRCP 12(b)(3), facts must be shown that will defeat the plaintiff's assertion of venue. FPP § 1352; Pierce v. Shorty Small's of Branson Inc., 137 F.3d 1190 (10th Cir. 1998). Courts have not agreed as to which party has the burden of proof on a motion for improper venue. FEDPROC § 62:450.

    i.   *On defendant.* A number of federal courts have concluded that the burden of doing so is on the defendant, since venue is a "personal privilege" that can be waived and a lack of venue should be established by the party asserting it. FPP § 1352; Myers v. American Dental Ass'n, 695 F.2d 716 (3d Cir. 1982).

    ii.   *On plaintiff.* On the other hand, an equal (perhaps a larger) number of federal courts have imposed the burden on the plaintiff in keeping with the rule applied in the context of subject matter and personal jurisdiction defenses. FPP § 1352. The latter view seems correct inasmuch as it is the plaintiff's obligation to institute his action in a permissible forum, both in terms of jurisdiction and venue. FPP § 1352; Pierce v. Shorty Small's of Branson Inc., 137 F.3d 1190 (10th Cir. 1998).

        •   If the court chooses to rely on pleadings and affidavits, the plaintiff need only make a prima facie showing of venue, but if the court holds an evidentiary hearing, the plaintiff must demonstrate venue by a preponderance of the evidence. FEDPROF § 1:830; Gulf Ins. Co. v. Glasbrenner, 417 F.3d 353, 62 Fed.R.Serv.3d 592 (2d Cir. 2005).

c.   *Form.* A motion to dismiss for lack of venue must be denied as insufficient where it is not apparent which venue provision the moving party wishes to invoke or, assuming that the general venue statute 28 U.S.C.A. § 1391 is contemplated, which paragraph is considered controlling. FEDPROC § 62:449.

d.   *Practice on a FRCP 12(b)(3) motion.* All well-pleaded allegations in the complaint bearing on the venue question generally are taken as true, unless contradicted by the defendant's affidavits. A district court may examine facts outside the complaint to determine whether its venue is proper. FPP § 1352; Ambraco, Inc. v. Bossclip B.V., 570 F.3d 233 (5th Cir. 2009). And, as is consistent with practice in other contexts, such as construing the complaint, the court must draw all reasonable inferences and resolve all factual conflicts in favor of the plaintiff. FPP § 1352.

e.   *Dismissal versus transfer.* The chances of a motion to dismiss for improper venue being successful have been diminished even further by the liberal attitude of the courts in permitting venue defects to be cured. FPP § 1352.

    i.   A motion to dismiss for improper venue under FRCP 12(b)(3) no longer is necessary in order to object to an inconvenient forum. FPP § 1352. With the enactment of 28 U.S.C.A. § 1404(a) as part of the 1948 revision of the Judicial Code, the district courts now have authority to transfer any case to a more convenient forum if the transfer is in the interest of justice. FPP § 1352; Norwood v. Kirkpatrick, 349 U.S. 29, 75 S.Ct. 544, 99 L.Ed. 789 (1955). Consideration of a dismissal for improper venue must take into account 28 U.S.C.A. § 1406(a) as well as FRCP 12(b)(3). FEDPROC § 62:452.

        •   The district court of a district in which is filed a case laying venue in the wrong division or district shall dismiss, or if it be in the interest of justice, transfer such case to any district or division in which it could have been brought. 28 U.S.C.A. § 1406(a).

- For the convenience of parties and witnesses, in the interest of justice, a district court may transfer any civil action to any other district or division where it might have been brought or to any district or division to which all parties have consented. 28 U.S.C.A. § 1404(a).

    ii.   Technically speaking, motions to transfer are made pursuant to a motion under 28 U.S.C.A. § 1404(a) rather than under FRCP 12(b)(3), although little, other than the possible application of the consolidation requirement in FRCP 12(g), turns on this distinction. FPP § 1352.

f.   *Joining motions*

    i.   *Right to join.* A motion under FRCP 12 may be joined with any other motion allowed by FRCP 12. FRCP 12(g)(1).

    ii.   *Limitation on further motions.* Except as provided in FRCP 12(h)(2) or FRCP 12(h)(3), a party that makes a motion under FRCP 12 must not make another motion under FRCP 12 raising a defense or objection that was available to the party but omitted from its earlier motion. FRCP 12(g)(2).

g.   *Waiving and preserving certain defenses.* No defense or objection is waived by joining it with one or more other defenses or objections in a responsive pleading or in a motion. FRCP 12(b).

    i.   *Waiver by consent.* The defendant may waive the right to obtain a dismissal prior to trial either by express consent to be sued in a certain district or by some conduct that will be construed as implying consent. FPP § 1352.

    ii.   *When some are waived.* A party waives any defense listed in FRCP 12(b)(2) through FRCP 12(b)(5) by:

- Omitting it from a motion in the circumstances described in FRCP 12(g)(2); or

- Failing to either: (1) make it by motion under FRCP 12; or (2) include it in a responsive pleading or in an amendment allowed by FRCP 15(a)(1) as a matter of course. FRCP 12(h)(1).

    iii.   *When to raise others.* Failure to state a claim upon which relief can be granted, to join a person required by FRCP 19(b), or to state a legal defense to a claim may be raised:

- In any pleading allowed or ordered under FRCP 7(a);

- By a motion under FRCP 12(c); or

- At trial. FRCP 12(h)(2).

    iv.   *Lack of subject matter jurisdiction.* If the court determines at any time that it lacks subject-matter jurisdiction, the court must dismiss the action. FRCP 12(h)(3).

3.   *Venue, generally*

a.   *Applicability of 28 U.S.C.A. § 1391.* Except as otherwise provided by law:

    i.   28 U.S.C.A. § 1391 shall govern the venue of all civil actions brought in district courts of the United States; and

    ii.   The proper venue for a civil action shall be determined without regard to whether the action is local or transitory in nature. 28 U.S.C.A. § 1391(a).

b.   *Venue in general.* A civil action may be brought in:

    i.   A judicial district in which any defendant resides, if all defendants are residents of the State in which the district is located;

    ii.   A judicial district in which a substantial part of the events or omissions giving rise to the claim occurred, or a substantial part of property that is the subject of the action is situated; or

    iii.   If there is no district in which an action may otherwise be brought as provided in 28 U.S.C.A. § 1391, any judicial district in which any defendant is subject to the court's personal jurisdiction with respect to such action. 28 U.S.C.A. § 1391(b).

c. *Residency.* For all venue purposes:

    i. A natural person, including an alien lawfully admitted for permanent residence in the United States, shall be deemed to reside in the judicial district in which that person is domiciled;

    ii. An entity with the capacity to sue and be sued in its common name under applicable law, whether or not incorporated, shall be deemed to reside, if a defendant, in any judicial district in which such defendant is subject to the court's personal jurisdiction with respect to the civil action in question and, if a plaintiff, only in the judicial district in which it maintains its principal place of business; and

    iii. A defendant not resident in the United States may be sued in any judicial district, and the joinder of such a defendant shall be disregarded in determining where the action may be brought with respect to other defendants. 28 U.S.C.A. § 1391(c).

d. *Residency of corporations in states with multiple districts.* For purposes of venue Chapter 87 of the United States Code (28 U.S.C.A. § 1390, et seq.), in a State which has more than one judicial district and in which a defendant that is a corporation is subject to personal jurisdiction at the time an action is commenced, such corporation shall be deemed to reside in any district in that State within which its contacts would be sufficient to subject it to personal jurisdiction if that district were a separate State, and, if there is no such district, the corporation shall be deemed to reside in the district within which it has the most significant contacts. 28 U.S.C.A. § 1391(d).

e. *Actions where defendant is officer or employee of the United States*

    i. *In general.* A civil action in which a defendant is an officer or employee of the United States or any agency thereof acting in his official capacity or under color of legal authority, or an agency of the United States, or the United States, may, except as otherwise provided by law, be brought in any judicial district in which: (1) a defendant in the action resides, (2) a substantial part of the events or omissions giving rise to the claim occurred, or a substantial part of property that is the subject of the action is situated, or (3) the plaintiff resides if no real property is involved in the action. Additional persons may be joined as parties to any such action in accordance with the Federal Rules of Civil Procedure and with such other venue requirements as would be applicable if the United States or one of its officers, employees, or agencies were not a party. 28 U.S.C.A. § 1391(e)(1).

    ii. *Service.* The summons and complaint in such an action shall be served as provided by the Federal Rules of Civil Procedure except that the delivery of the summons and complaint to the officer or agency as required by the Federal Rules of Civil Procedure may be made by certified mail beyond the territorial limits of the district in which the action is brought. 28 U.S.C.A. § 1391(e)(2).

f. *Civil actions against a foreign state.* A civil action against a foreign state as defined in 28 U.S.C.A. § 1603(a) may be brought:

    i. In any judicial district in which a substantial part of the events or omissions giving rise to the claim occurred, or a substantial part of property that is the subject of the action is situated;

    ii. In any judicial district in which the vessel or cargo of a foreign state is situated, if the claim is asserted under 28 U.S.C.A. § 1605(b);

    iii. In any judicial district in which the agency or instrumentality is licensed to do business or is doing business, if the action is brought against an agency or instrumentality of a foreign state as defined in 28 U.S.C.A. § 1603(b); or

    iv. In the United States District Court for the District of Columbia if the action is brought against a foreign state or political subdivision thereof. 28 U.S.C.A. § 1391(f).

g. *Multiparty, multiforum litigation.* A civil action in which jurisdiction of the district court is based upon 28 U.S.C.A. § 1369 may be brought in any district in which any defendant resides or in which a substantial part of the accident giving rise to the action took place. 28 U.S.C.A. § 1391(g).

4. *Opposing papers.* The Federal Rules of Civil Procedure do not require any formal answer, return, or reply to a motion, except where the Federal Rules of Civil Procedure or local rules may require affidavits,

memoranda, or other papers to be filed in opposition to a motion. Such papers are simply to apprise the court of such opposition and the grounds of that opposition. FEDPROC § 62:359.

a. *Effect of failure to respond to motion.* Although in the absence of statutory provision or court rule, a motion ordinarily does not require a written answer, when a party files a motion and the opposing party fails to respond, the court may construe such failure to respond as nonopposition to the motion or an admission that the motion was meritorious, may take the facts alleged in the motion as true—the rule in some jurisdictions being that the failure to respond to a fact set forth in a motion is deemed an admission—and may grant the motion if the relief requested appears to be justified. AMJUR MOTIONS § 28.

b. *Assent or no opposition not determinative.* However, a motion will not be granted automatically simply because an "assent" or a notation of "no opposition" has been filed; federal judges frequently deny motions that have been assented to when it is thought that justice so dictates. FPP § 1190.

c. *Responsive pleading inappropriate as response to motion.* An attempt to answer or oppose a motion with a responsive pleading usually is not appropriate. FPP § 1190.

5. *Reply papers.* A moving party may be required or permitted to prepare papers in addition to his original motion papers. AMJUR MOTIONS § 25. Papers answering or replying to opposing papers may be appropriate, in the interests of justice, where it appears there is a substantial reason for allowing a reply. Thus, a court may accept reply papers where a party demonstrates that the papers to which it seeks to file a reply raise new issues that are material to the disposition of the question before the court, or where the court determines, sua sponte, that it wishes further briefing of an issue raised in those papers and orders the submission of additional papers. FEDPROC § 62:360.

a. *Function of reply papers.* The function of a reply affidavit is to answer the arguments made in opposition to the position taken by the movant and not to permit the movant to introduce new arguments in support of the motion. AMJUR MOTIONS § 25.

b. *Issues raised for the first time in a reply document.* However, the view has been followed in some jurisdictions, that as a matter of judicial economy, where there is no prejudice and where the issues could be raised simply by filing a motion to dismiss, the trial court has discretion to consider arguments raised for the first time in a reply memorandum, and that a trial court may grant a motion to strike issues raised for the first time in a reply memorandum. AMJUR MOTIONS § 26.

6. *Appearances.* Every attorney who represents a party or who files a document on a party's behalf must file an appearance for that party. IN R USDCTSD L.R. 83-7. The filing of a Notice of Appearance shall act to establish the filing attorney as an attorney of record representing a designated party or parties in a particular cause of action. As a result, it is necessary for each attorney to file a separate Notice of Appearance when entering an appearance in a case. A joint appearance on behalf of multiple attorneys may be filed electronically only if it is filed separately for each attorney, using his/her ECF login. IN R USDCTSD ECF Procedures(12). Only those attorneys who have filed an appearance in a pending action are entitled to be served with case documents under FRCP 5(a). IN R USDCTSD L.R. 83-7. For more information, refer to IN R USDCTSD L.R. 83-7 and IN R USDCTSD ECF Procedures(12).

7. *Notice of related action.* A party must file a notice of related action: as soon as it appears that the party's case and another pending case: (1) arise out of the same transaction or occurrence; (2) involve the same property; or (3) involve the validity or infringement or the same patent, trademark, or copyright. IN R USDCTSD L.R. 40-1(d)(2). For more information, refer to IN R USDCTSD L.R. 40-1.

8. *Alternative dispute resolution (ADR)*

a. *Application.* Unless limited by specific provisions, or unless there are other applicable specific statutory, common law, or constitutional procedures, the Local Alternative Dispute Resolution Rules of the United States District Court for the Southern District of Indiana shall apply in all civil litigation filed in the U.S. District Court for the Southern District of Indiana, except in the following cases and proceedings:

   i. Applications for writs of habeas corpus under 28 U.S.C.A. § 2254;

   ii. Forfeiture cases;

   iii. Non-adversary proceedings in bankruptcy;

      iv. Social Security administrative review cases; and

      v. Such other matters as specified by order of the Court; for example, matters involving important public policy issues, constitutional law, or the establishment of new law. IN R USDCTSD A.D.R. Rule 1.2.

  b. *Mediation.* Mediation under this section (IN R USDCTSD A.D.R. Rule 2.1, et seq.) involves the confidential process by which a person acting as a Mediator, selected by the parties or appointed by the Court, assists the litigants in reaching a mutually acceptable agreement. It is an informal and nonadversarial process. The role of the Mediator is to assist in identifying the issues, reducing misunderstandings, clarifying priorities, exploring areas of compromise, and finding points of agreement as well as legitimate points of disagreement. Final decision-making authority rests with the parties, not the Mediator. IN R USDCTSD A.D.R. Rule 2.1. It is anticipated that an agreement may not resolve all of the disputed issues, but the process, nonetheless, can reduce points of contention. Parties and their representatives are required to mediate in good faith, but are not compelled to reach an agreement. IN R USDCTSD A.D.R. Rule 2.1.

      i. *Case selection.* The Court with the agreement of the parties may refer a civil case for mediation. Unless otherwise ordered or as specifically provided in IN R USDCTSD A.D.R. Rule 2.8, referral to mediation does not abate or suspend the action, and no scheduled dates shall be delayed or deferred, including the date of trial. IN R USDCTSD A.D.R. Rule 2.2.

      ii. For more information on mediation, refer to IN R USDCTSD A.D.R. Rule 2.1, et seq.

  c. *Other methods of dispute resolution.* The Local Alternative Dispute Resolution Rules of the United States District Court for the Southern District of Indiana shall not preclude the parties from utilizing any other reasonable method or technique of alternative dispute resolution to resolve disputes to which the parties agree. However, any use of arbitration by the parties will be governed by and comply with the requirements of 28 U.S.C.A. § 654 through 28 U.S.C.A. § 657. IN R USDCTSD A.D.R. Rule 1.5.

  d. For more information on alternative dispute resolution (ADR), refer to IN R USDCTSD A.D.R. Rule 1.1, et seq.

9. *Notice of settlement or resolution.* The parties must immediately notify the court if they reasonably anticipate settling their case or resolving a pending motion. IN R USDCTSD L.R. 7-1(h).

10. *Modification or suspension of rules.* The court may, on its own motion or at the request of a party, suspend or modify any rule in a particular case in the interest of justice. IN R USDCTSD L.R. 1-1(c).

D. Documents

1. *Documents for moving party*

  a. *Required documents*

      i. *Notice of motion and motion.* Refer to the General Requirements section of this document for information on the notice of motion and motion.

      ii. *Brief.* The following motion must also be accompanied by a supporting brief: a motion to dismiss. IN R USDCTSD L.R. 7-1(b)(1). Refer to the Format section of this document for the format of briefs.

      iii. *Certificate of service.* FRCP 5(d) requires that the person making service under FRCP 5 certify that service has been effected. FRCP 5(Advisory Committee Notes). Having such information on file may be useful for many purposes, including proof of service if an issue arises concerning the effectiveness of the service. FRCP 5(Advisory Committee Notes).

        • *Certificate of service for electronically-filed documents.* A certificate of service must be included with all documents filed electronically. Such certificate shall indicate that service was accomplished pursuant to the Court's electronic filing procedures. IN R USDCTSD ECF Procedures(11). For the suggested format for a certificate of service for electronic filing, refer to IN R USDCTSD ECF Procedures(11).

  b. *Supplemental documents*

      i. *Supporting evidence.* When a motion relies on facts outside the record, the court may hear the

matter on affidavits or may hear it wholly or partly on oral testimony or on depositions. FRCP 43(c).

- *Materials necessary for motion.* A party seeking relief under FRCP 26(c) or FRCP 37, or by way of a pretrial motion that could result in a final order on an issue, must file with the motion those parts of the discovery materials relevant to the motion. IN R USDCTSD L.R. 26-2(a).

ii. *Notice of constitutional question.* A party that files a pleading, written motion, or other paper drawing into question the constitutionality of a federal or state statute must promptly:

- *File notice.* File a notice of constitutional question stating the question and identifying the paper that raises it, if: (1) a federal statute is questioned and the parties do not include the United States, one of its agencies, or one of its officers or employees in an official capacity; or (2) a state statute is questioned and the parties do not include the state, one of its agencies, or one of its officers or employees in an official capacity; and

- *Serve notice.* Serve the notice and paper on the Attorney General of the United States if a federal statute is questioned—or on the state attorney general if a state statute is questioned—either by certified or registered mail or by sending it to an electronic address designated by the attorney general for this purpose. FRCP 5.1(a).

- *Time for filing.* A notice of constitutional challenge to a statute filed in accordance with FRCP 5.1 must be filed at the same time the parties tender their proposed case management plan, if one is required, or within twenty-one (21) days of the filing drawing into question the constitutionality of a federal or state statute, whichever occurs later. IN R USDCTSD L.R. 5.1-1(a).

- *Additional service requirements.* If a federal statute is challenged, in addition to the service requirements of FRCP 5.1(a), the party filing the notice of constitutional challenge must serve the notice and documents on the United States Attorney for the Southern District of Indiana, either by certified or registered mail or by sending it to an electronic address designated for that purpose by that official. IN R USDCTSD L.R. 5.1-1(b).

- *No forfeiture.* A party's failure to file and serve the notice, or the court's failure to certify, does not forfeit a constitutional claim or defense that is otherwise timely asserted. FRCP 5.1(d).

iii. *Nongovernmental corporate disclosure statement*

- *Contents.* A nongovernmental corporate party must file two (2) copies of a disclosure statement that: (1) identifies any parent corporation and any publicly held corporation owning ten percent (10%) or more of its stock; or (2) states that there is no such corporation. FRCP 7.1(a).

- *Time to file; Supplemental filing.* A party must: (1) file the disclosure statement with its first appearance, pleading, petition, motion, response, or other request addressed to the court; and (2) promptly file a supplemental statement if any required information changes. FRCP 7.1(b).

iv. *Index of exhibits.* Any pleading, motion, brief, affidavit, notice, or proposed order filed with the court, whether electronically or with the clerk, must: if it has four (4) or more exhibits, include a separate index that identifies and briefly describes each exhibit. IN R USDCTSD L.R. 5-1(b).

v. *Request for oral argument.* A party may request oral argument by filing a separate motion explaining why oral argument is necessary and estimating how long the court should allow for the argument. The request must be filed and served with the supporting brief, response brief, or reply brief. IN R USDCTSD L.R. 7-5(a).

vi. *Request for evidentiary hearing.* A party may request an evidentiary hearing on a motion or petition by serving and filing a separate motion explaining why the hearing is necessary and estimating how long the court should allow for the hearing. IN R USDCTSD L.R. 7-5(c).

vii. *Copy of authority.* Generally, copies of cited authorities may not be attached to court filings.

However, a party must attach to the party's motion or brief a copy of any cited authority if it is not available on Westlaw or Lexis. Upon request, a party must provide copies of any cited authority that is only available through electronic means to the court or the other parties. IN R USDCTSD L.R. 7-1(f).

viii. *Proposed order.* A party must include a suitable form of order with any document that requests the judge or the clerk to enter a routine or uncontested order. IN R USDCTSD L.R. 5-5(b); IN R USDCTSD L.R. 5-10(c); IN R USDCTSD L.R. 7-1(d).

- A service statement and/or list must be included on each proposed order, as required by IN R USDCTSD L.R. 5-5(d). IN R USDCTSD ECF Procedures(11). Any pleading, motion, brief, affidavit, notice, or proposed order filed with the court, whether electronically or with the clerk, must: if it is a form of order, include a statement of service, in the format required by IN R USDCTSD L.R. 5-5(d) in the lower left corner of the document. IN R USDCTSD L.R. 5-1(b).

- A party electronically filing a proposed order—whether voluntarily or because required by IN R USDCTSD L.R. 5-5—must convert the order directly from a word processing program and file it as an attachment to the document it relates to. Proposed orders must include in the lower left-hand corner of the signature page a statement that service will be made electronically on all ECF-registered counsel of record via email generated by the court's ECF system, without listing all such counsel. A service list including the name and postal address of any pro se litigant or non-registered attorney of record must follow, stating that service on the listed individuals will be made in the traditional paper manner, via first-class U.S. Mail. IN R USDCTSD L.R. 5-5(d).

ix. *Copy of document with self-address envelope.* To receive a file-stamped copy of a document filed directly with the clerk, a party must include with the original document an additional copy and a self-addressed envelope. The envelope must be big enough to hold the copy and have enough postage on it to send the copy via regular first-class mail. IN R USDCTSD L.R. 5-10(b).

x. *Notice of manual filing.* When a party who is not exempt from the electronic filing requirement files a document directly with the clerk, the party must: electronically file a notice of manual filing that explains why the document cannot be filed electronically. IN R USDCTSD L.R. 5-2(d)(1). Refer to the Filing and Service Requirements section of this document for more information.

- Where an individual component cannot be included in an electronic filing (e.g. the component cannot be converted to electronic format), the filer shall electronically file the prescribed Notice of Manual Filing in place of that component. A model form is provided as Appendix C (IN R USDCTSD ECF Procedures(Appendix C)). IN R USDCTSD ECF Procedures(13).

- Before making a manual filing of a component, the filing party shall first electronically file a Notice of Manual Filing (See IN R USDCTSD ECF Procedures(Appendix C)). The filer shall initiate the electronic filing process as if filing the actual component but shall instead attach to the filing the Notice of Manual Filing setting forth the reason(s) why the component cannot be filed electronically. The manual filing should be accompanied by a copy of the previously filed Notice of Manual Filing. A party may seek to have a component excluded from electronic filing pursuant to applicable Federal and Local Rules (e.g., FRCP 26(c)). IN R USDCTSD ECF Procedures(15).

xi. *Courtesy copies.* District Judges and Magistrate Judges regularly receive documents filed by all parties. Therefore, parties shall not bring "courtesy copies" to any chambers unless specifically directed to do so by the Court. IN R USDCTSD Case Mgt(General Instructions For All Cases).

xii. *Copies for three-judge court.* Parties in a case where a three-judge court has been requested must file an original and three copies of any document filed directly with the clerk (instead of electronically) until the court: (1) denies the request; (2) dissolves the three-judge court; or (3) allows the parties to file fewer copies. IN R USDCTSD L.R. 9-2(c).

xiii. *Declaration that party was unable to file in a timely manner due to technical difficulties.* If a party misses a filing deadline due to an inability to file electronically, the party may submit the untimely filed document, accompanied by a declaration stating the reason(s) for missing the deadline. IN R USDCTSD ECF Procedures(16). A model form is provided as Appendix D (IN R USDCTSD ECF Procedures(Appendix D)). IN R USDCTSD ECF Procedures(16).

2. *Documents for opposing party*

   a. *Required documents*

      i. *Response brief.* Refer to the Format section of this document for the format of briefs. Refer to the General Requirements section of this document for information on the opposing papers.

      ii. *Certificate of service.* FRCP 5(d) requires that the person making service under FRCP 5 certify that service has been effected. FRCP 5(Advisory Committee Notes). Having such information on file may be useful for many purposes, including proof of service if an issue arises concerning the effectiveness of the service. FRCP 5(Advisory Committee Notes).

         • *Certificate of service for electronically-filed documents.* A certificate of service must be included with all documents filed electronically. Such certificate shall indicate that service was accomplished pursuant to the Court's electronic filing procedures. IN R USDCTSD ECF Procedures(11). For the suggested format for a certificate of service for electronic filing, refer to IN R USDCTSD ECF Procedures(11).

   b. *Supplemental documents*

      i. *Supporting evidence.* When a motion relies on facts outside the record, the court may hear the matter on affidavits or may hear it wholly or partly on oral testimony or on depositions. FRCP 43(c).

         • *Materials necessary for motion.* A party seeking relief under FRCP 26(c) or FRCP 37, or by way of a pretrial motion that could result in a final order on an issue, must file with the motion those parts of the discovery materials relevant to the motion. IN R USDCTSD L.R. 26-2(a).

      ii. *Notice of constitutional question.* A party that files a pleading, written motion, or other paper drawing into question the constitutionality of a federal or state statute must promptly:

         • *File notice.* File a notice of constitutional question stating the question and identifying the paper that raises it, if: (1) a federal statute is questioned and the parties do not include the United States, one of its agencies, or one of its officers or employees in an official capacity; or (2) a state statute is questioned and the parties do not include the state, one of its agencies, or one of its officers or employees in an official capacity; and

         • *Serve notice.* Serve the notice and paper on the Attorney General of the United States if a federal statute is questioned—or on the state attorney general if a state statute is questioned—either by certified or registered mail or by sending it to an electronic address designated by the attorney general for this purpose. FRCP 5.1(a).

         • *Time for filing.* A notice of constitutional challenge to a statute filed in accordance with FRCP 5.1 must be filed at the same time the parties tender their proposed case management plan, if one is required, or within twenty-one (21) days of the filing drawing into question the constitutionality of a federal or state statute, whichever occurs later. IN R USDCTSD L.R. 5.1-1(a).

         • *Additional service requirements.* If a federal statute is challenged, in addition to the service requirements of FRCP 5.1(a), the party filing the notice of constitutional challenge must serve the notice and documents on the United States Attorney for the Southern District of Indiana, either by certified or registered mail or by sending it to an electronic address designated for that purpose by that official. IN R USDCTSD L.R. 5.1-1(b).

         • *No forfeiture.* A party's failure to file and serve the notice, or the court's failure to certify, does not forfeit a constitutional claim or defense that is otherwise timely asserted. FRCP 5.1(d).

      iii. *Index of exhibits.* Any pleading, motion, brief, affidavit, notice, or proposed order filed with the court, whether electronically or with the clerk, must: if it has four (4) or more exhibits, include a separate index that identifies and briefly describes each exhibit. IN R USDCTSD L.R. 5-1(b).

iv. *Request for oral argument.* A party may request oral argument by filing a separate motion explaining why oral argument is necessary and estimating how long the court should allow for the argument. The request must be filed and served with the supporting brief, response brief, or reply brief. IN R USDCTSD L.R. 7-5(a).

v. *Request for evidentiary hearing.* A party may request an evidentiary hearing on a motion or petition by serving and filing a separate motion explaining why the hearing is necessary and estimating how long the court should allow for the hearing. IN R USDCTSD L.R. 7-5(c).

vi. *Copy of authority.* Generally, copies of cited authorities may not be attached to court filings. However, a party must attach to the party's motion or brief a copy of any cited authority if it is not available on Westlaw or Lexis. Upon request, a party must provide copies of any cited authority that is only available through electronic means to the court or the other parties. IN R USDCTSD L.R. 7-1(f).

vii. *Copy of document with self-address envelope.* To receive a file-stamped copy of a document filed directly with the clerk, a party must include with the original document an additional copy and a self-addressed envelope. The envelope must be big enough to hold the copy and have enough postage on it to send the copy via regular first-class mail. IN R USDCTSD L.R. 5-10(b).

viii. *Notice of manual filing.* When a party who is not exempt from the electronic filing requirement files a document directly with the clerk, the party must: electronically file a notice of manual filing that explains why the document cannot be filed electronically. IN R USDCTSD L.R. 5-2(d)(1). Refer to the Filing and Service Requirements section of this document for more information.

- Where an individual component cannot be included in an electronic filing (e.g. the component cannot be converted to electronic format), the filer shall electronically file the prescribed Notice of Manual Filing in place of that component. A model form is provided as Appendix C (IN R USDCTSD ECF Procedures(Appendix C)). IN R USDCTSD ECF Procedures(13).

- Before making a manual filing of a component, the filing party shall first electronically file a Notice of Manual Filing (See IN R USDCTSD ECF Procedures(Appendix C)). The filer shall initiate the electronic filing process as if filing the actual component but shall instead attach to the filing the Notice of Manual Filing setting forth the reason(s) why the component cannot be filed electronically. The manual filing should be accompanied by a copy of the previously filed Notice of Manual Filing. A party may seek to have a component excluded from electronic filing pursuant to applicable Federal and Local Rules (e.g., FRCP 26(c)). IN R USDCTSD ECF Procedures(15).

ix. *Courtesy copies.* District Judges and Magistrate Judges regularly receive documents filed by all parties. Therefore, parties shall not bring "courtesy copies" to any chambers unless specifically directed to do so by the Court. IN R USDCTSD Case Mgt(General Instructions For All Cases).

x. *Copies for three-judge court.* Parties in a case where a three-judge court has been requested must file an original and three copies of any document filed directly with the clerk (instead of electronically) until the court: (1) denies the request; (2) dissolves the three-judge court; or (3) allows the parties to file fewer copies. IN R USDCTSD L.R. 9-2(c).

xi. *Declaration that party was unable to file in a timely manner due to technical difficulties.* If a party misses a filing deadline due to an inability to file electronically, the party may submit the untimely filed document, accompanied by a declaration stating the reason(s) for missing the deadline. IN R USDCTSD ECF Procedures(16). A model form is provided as Appendix D (IN R USDCTSD ECF Procedures(Appendix D)). IN R USDCTSD ECF Procedures(16).

E. Format

1. *Form of documents.* The rules governing captions and other matters of form in pleadings apply to motions and other papers. FRCP 7(b)(2).

   a. *Paper (manual filings only).* Any document that is not filed electronically must: be flat, unfolded, and

on good-quality, eight and one-half by eleven (8-1/2 x 11) inch white paper. IN R USDCTSD L.R. 5-1(d)(1). Any document that is not filed electronically must: be single-sided. IN R USDCTSD L.R. 5-1(d)(1).

   i. *Covers or backing.* Any document that is not filed electronically must: not have a cover or a back. IN R USDCTSD L.R. 5-1(d)(1).

   ii. *Fastening.* Any document that is not filed electronically must: be (if consisting of more than one (1) page) fastened by paperclip or binder clip and may not be stapled. IN R USDCTSD L.R. 5-1(d)(1).

   • *Request for nonconforming fastening.* If a document cannot be fastened or bound as required by IN R USDCTSD L.R. 5-1(d), a party may ask the clerk for permission to fasten it in another manner. The party must make such a request before attempting to file the document with nonconforming fastening. IN R USDCTSD L.R. 5-1(d)(2).

   iii. *Hole punching.* Any document that is not filed electronically must: be two-hole punched at the top with the holes two and three-quarter (2-3/4) inches apart and appropriately centered. IN R USDCTSD L.R. 5-1(d)(1).

b. *Margins.* Any pleading, motion, brief, affidavit, notice, or proposed order filed with the court, whether electronically or with the clerk, must: have at least one (1) inch margins. IN R USDCTSD L.R. 5-1(b).

c. *Spacing.* Any pleading, motion, brief, affidavit, notice, or proposed order filed with the court, whether electronically or with the clerk, must: be double spaced (except for headings, footnotes, and quoted material). IN R USDCTSD L.R. 5-1(b).

d. *Text.* Any pleading, motion, brief, affidavit, notice, or proposed order filed with the court, whether electronically or with the clerk, must: be plainly typewritten, printed, or prepared by a clearly legible copying process. IN R USDCTSD L.R. 5-1(b).

e. *Font size.* Any pleading, motion, brief, affidavit, notice, or proposed order filed with the court, whether electronically or with the clerk, must: use at least 12-point type in the body of the document and at least 10-point type in footnotes. IN R USDCTSD L.R. 5-1(b).

f. *Page numbering.* Any pleading, motion, brief, affidavit, notice, or proposed order filed with the court, whether electronically or with the clerk, must: have consecutively numbered pages. IN R USDCTSD L.R. 5-1(b).

g. *Caption; Names of parties.* Every pleading must have a caption with the court's name, a title, a file number, and a FRCP 7(a) designation. The title of the complaint must name all the parties; the title of other pleadings, after naming the first party on each side, may refer generally to other parties. FRCP 10(a). Any pleading, motion, brief, affidavit, notice, or proposed order filed with the court, whether electronically or with the clerk, must: include a title on the first page. IN R USDCTSD L.R. 5-1(b).

   i. *Alternative motions.* Motions must be filed separately, but alternative motions may be filed in a single document if each is named in the title. IN R USDCTSD L.R. 7-1(a).

h. *Filer's information.* Any pleading, motion, brief, affidavit, notice, or proposed order filed with the court, whether electronically or with the clerk, must: in the case of pleadings, motions, legal briefs, and notices, include the name, complete address, telephone number, facsimile number (where available), and e-mail address (where available) of the pro se litigant or attorney who files it. IN R USDCTSD L.R. 5-1(b).

i. *Paragraphs; Separate statements.* A party must state its claims or defenses in numbered paragraphs, each limited as far as practicable to a single set of circumstances. A later pleading may refer by number to a paragraph in an earlier pleading. If doing so would promote clarity, each claim founded on a separate transaction or occurrence—and each defense other than a denial—must be stated in a separate count or defense. FRCP 10(b).

j. *Adoption by reference; Exhibits.* A statement in a pleading may be adopted by reference elsewhere in the same pleading or in any other pleading or motion. A copy of a written instrument that is an exhibit to a pleading is a part of the pleading for all purposes. FRCP 10(c).

k. *Citations*

    i. *Local rules.* The Local Rules of the United States District Court for the Southern District of Indiana may be cited as "S.D. Ind. L.R." IN R USDCTSD L.R. 1-1(a).

    ii. *Local alternative dispute resolution rules.* These Rules shall be known as the Local Alternative Dispute Resolution Rules of the United States District Court for the Southern District of Indiana. They shall be cited as "S.D.Ind. Local A.D.R. Rule _____." IN R USDCTSD A.D.R. Rule 1.1.

l. *Acceptance by the clerk.* The clerk must not refuse to file a paper solely because it is not in the form prescribed by the Federal Rules of Civil Procedure or by a local rule or practice. FRCP 5(d)(4). The clerk will accept a document that violates IN R USDCTSD L.R. 5-1, but the court may exclude the document from the official record. IN R USDCTSD L.R. 5-1(e).

    i. *Sanctions for errors as to form.* The court may strike from the record any document that does not comply with the rules governing the form of documents filed with the court, such as rules that regulate document size or the number of copies to be filed or that require a special designation in the caption. The court may also sanction an attorney or party who files a non-compliant document. IN R USDCTSD L.R. 1-3.

2. *Form of electronic documents.* Any document submitted via the court's electronic case filing (ECF) system must be: otherwise prepared and filed in a manner consistent with the CM/ECF Policies and Procedures Manual (IN R USDCTSD ECF Procedures). IN R USDCTSD L.R. 5-1(c). Electronically filed documents must meet the requirements of FRCP 10 (Form of Pleadings), IN R USDCTSD L.R. 5-1 (Format of Papers Presented for Filing), and FRCP 5.2 (Privacy Protection for Filings Made with the Court), as if they had been submitted on paper. Documents filed electronically are also subject to any page limitations set forth by Court Order, by IN R USDCTSD L.R. 7-1 (Motion Practice), or IN R USDCTSD L.R. 56-1 (Summary Judgment Practice), as applicable. IN R USDCTSD ECF Procedures(13).

a. *PDF format required.* Any document submitted via the court's electronic case filing (ECF) system must be: in .pdf format. IN R USDCTSD L.R. 5-1(c); IN R USDCTSD ECF Procedures(7). Any document submitted via the court's electronic case filing (ECF) system must be: converted to a .pdf file directly from a word processing program, unless it exists only in paper format (in which case it may be scanned to create a .pdf document). IN R USDCTSD L.R. 5-1(c); IN R USDCTSD ECF Procedures(13).

    i. An exhibit may be scanned into PDF format, at a recommended 300 dpi resolution or higher, only if it does not already exist in electronic format. The filing attorney is responsible for reviewing all PDF documents for legibility before submitting them through the Court's Electronic Case Filing system. For technical guidance in creating PDF documents, please contact the Clerk's Office. IN R USDCTSD ECF Procedures(13).

b. *File size limitations.* Any document submitted via the court's electronic case filing (ECF) system must be: submitted as one or more .pdf files that do not exceed ten megabytes (10 MB) each (consistent with the CM/ECF Policies and Procedures Manual (IN R USDCTSD ECF Procedures)). IN R USDCTSD L.R. 5-1(c); IN R USDCTSD ECF Procedures(13).

    i. To electronically file a document or attachment that exceeds ten megabytes (10 MB), the document must first be broken down into two or more smaller files. For example, if Exhibit A is a twelve megabyte (12 MB) PDF file, it should be divided into 2 equal parts prior to electronic filing. Each component part of the exhibit would be filed as an attachment to the main document and described appropriately as "Exhibit A (part 1 of 2)" and "Exhibit A (part 2 of 2)." IN R USDCTSD ECF Procedures(13).

    ii. The supporting items mentioned in IN R USDCTSD ECF Procedures(13) should not be confused with memorandums or briefs in support of motions as outlined in IN R USDCTSD L.R. 7-1 or IN R USDCTSD L.R. 56-1. These memorandums or briefs in support are to be filed as entirely separate documents pursuant to the appropriate rule. Additionally, no motion shall be embodied in the text of a response or reply brief/memorandum unless otherwise ordered by the Court. IN R USDCTSD ECF Procedures(13).

c. *Separate component parts.* A key objective of the electronic filing system is to ensure that as much of the case as possible is managed electronically. To facilitate electronic filing and retrieval, documents to be filed electronically are to be reasonably broken into their separate component parts. By way of example, most filings include a foundation document (e.g., motion) and other supporting items (e.g., exhibits, proposed orders, proposed amended pleadings). The foundation document, as well as the supporting items, are each separate components of the filing; supporting items must be filed as attachments to the foundation document. These exhibits or attachments should include only those excerpts of the referenced documents that are directly germane to the matter under consideration. IN R USDCTSD ECF Procedures(13).

  i. Where an individual component cannot be included in an electronic filing (e.g. the component cannot be converted to electronic format), the filer shall electronically file the prescribed Notice of Manual Filing in place of that component. A model form is provided as Appendix C (IN R USDCTSD ECF Procedures(Appendix C)). IN R USDCTSD ECF Procedures(13).

d. *Exhibits.* Each electronically filed exhibit to a main document must be: (1) created as a separate .pdf file; (2) submitted as an attachment to the main document and given a title which describes its content; and (3) limited to excerpts that are directly germane to the main document's subject matter. IN R USDCTSD L.R. 5-6(a).

  i. When uploading attachments during the electronic filing process, exhibits must be uploaded in a logical sequence and a brief description must be entered for each individual PDF file. The description must include not only the exhibit number or letter, but also a brief description of the document. This information may be entered in CM/ECF using a combination of the Category drop-down menu, the Description text box, or both (see IN R USDCTSD ECF Procedures(13)(Figure 1)). The information that is provided in each box will be combined to create a description of the document as it appears on the case docket (see IN R USDCTSD ECF Procedures(13)(Figure 2)). IN R USDCTSD ECF Procedures(13). For an example, refer to IN R USDCTSD ECF Procedures(13).

e. *Excerpts.* A party filing an exhibit that consists of excerpts from a larger document must clearly and prominently identify the exhibit as containing excerpted material. Either party will have the right to timely file additional excerpts or the complete document to the extent they are or become directly germane to the main document's subject matter. IN R USDCTSD L.R. 5-6(b).

f. For an example illustrating the application of IN R USDCTSD ECF Procedures(13), refer to IN R USDCTSD ECF Procedures(13).

3. *Form of briefs*

a. *Page limits.* Supporting and response briefs (excluding tables of contents, tables of authorities, appendices, and certificates of service) may not exceed thirty-five (35) pages. Reply briefs may not exceed twenty (20) pages. IN R USDCTSD L.R. 7-1(e)(1).

  i. *Permission to exceed limits.* The court may allow a party to file a brief exceeding these page limits for extraordinary and compelling reasons. IN R USDCTSD L.R. 7-1(e)(2).

  ii. *Supporting and response briefs exceeding limits.* If the court allows a party to file a brief or response exceeding thirty-five (35) pages, the document must include:

  - A table of contents with page references;
  - A statement of issues; and
  - A table of authorities including: (1) all cases (alphabetically arranged), statutes, and other authorities cited in the brief; and (2) page numbers where the authorities are cited in the brief. IN R USDCTSD L.R. 7-1(e)(3).

4. *Signing of pleadings, motions and other papers*

a. *Signature.* Every pleading, written motion, and other paper must be signed by at least one attorney of record in the attorney's name—or by a party personally if the party is unrepresented. The paper must state the signer's address, e-mail address, and telephone number. FRCP 11(a).

  i. *Signatures on manual filings.* Any document that is not filed electronically must: include the original signature of the pro se litigant or attorney who files it. IN R USDCTSD L.R. 5-1(d)(1).

    ii.   *Electronic signatures.* Use of the attorney's login and password when filing documents electronically serves in part as the attorney's signature for purposes of FRCP 11, the Local Rules of the United States District Court for the Southern District of Indiana, and any other purpose for which a signature is required in connection with proceedings before the Court. IN R USDCTSD ECF Procedures(14); IN R USDCTSD ECF Procedures(10). A pleading, motion, brief, or notice filed electronically under an attorney's ECF log-in and password must be signed by that attorney. IN R USDCTSD L.R. 5-7(a). A signature on a document other than a document filed as provided under IN R USDCTSD L.R. 5-7(a) must be an original handwritten signature and must be scanned into .pdf format for electronic filing. IN R USDCTSD L.R. 5-7(c); IN R USDCTSD ECF Procedures(14).

- *Form of electronic signature.* If a document is converted directly from a word processing application to .pdf (as opposed to scanning), the name of the Filing User under whose log-in and password the document is submitted must be preceded by a "s/" and typed on the signature line where the Filing User's handwritten signature would otherwise appear. IN R USDCTSD L.R. 5-7(b). All documents filed electronically shall include a signature block and include the filing attorney's typewritten name, address, telephone number, facsimile number and e-mail address. In addition, the name of the filing attorney under whose ECF login the document will be filed should be preceded by a "s/" and typed in the space where the attorney's handwritten signature would otherwise appear. IN R USDCTSD ECF Procedures(14). For a sample format, refer to IN R USDCTSD ECF Procedures(14).

- *Effect of electronic signature.* Filing an electronically signed document under an attorney's ECF log-in and password constitutes the attorney's signature on the document under the Federal Rules of Civil Procedure, under the Local Rules of the United States District Court for the Southern District of Indiana, and for any other reason a signature is required in connection with the court's activities. IN R USDCTSD L.R. 5-7(d).

- *Documents with multiple attorneys' signatures.* Documents requiring signatures of more than one attorney shall be filed either by: (1) obtaining consent from the other attorney, then typing the "s/ [Name]" signature of the other attorney on the signature line where the other attorney's signature would otherwise appear; (2) identifying in the signature section the name of the other attorney whose signature is required and by the submission of a Notice of Endorsement (see IN R USDCTSD ECF Procedures(Appendix B)) by the other attorney no later than three (3) business days after filing; (3) submitting a scanned document containing all handwritten signatures; or (4) in any other manner approved by the Court. IN R USDCTSD ECF Procedures(14); IN R USDCTSD L.R. 5-7(e).

    iii. *No verification or accompanying affidavit required for pleadings.* Unless a rule or statute specifically states otherwise, a pleading need not be verified or accompanied by an affidavit. FRCP 11(a).

    iv. *Unsigned papers.* The court must strike an unsigned paper unless the omission is promptly corrected after being called to the attorney's or party's attention. FRCP 11(a). The court will strike any document filed directly with the clerk that is not signed by an attorney of record or the pro se litigant filing it, but the court may do so only after giving the attorney or pro se litigant notice of the omission and reasonable time to correct it. Rubber-stamp or facsimile signatures are not original signatures and the court will deem documents containing them to be unsigned for purposes of FRCP 11 and FRCP 26(g) and IN R USDCTSD L.R. 5-10. IN R USDCTSD L.R. 5-10(g).

b. *Representations to the court.* By presenting to the court a pleading, written motion, or other paper—whether by signing, filing, submitting, or later advocating it—an attorney or unrepresented party certifies that to the best of the person's knowledge, information, and belief, formed after an inquiry reasonable under the circumstances:

    i. It is not being presented for any improper purpose, such as to harass, cause unnecessary delay, or needlessly increase the cost of litigation;

    ii. The claims, defenses, and other legal contentions are warranted by existing law or by a nonfrivolous argument for extending, modifying, or reversing existing law or for establishing new law;

iii. The factual contentions have evidentiary support or, if specifically so identified, will likely have evidentiary support after a reasonable opportunity for further investigation or discovery; and

iv. The denials of factual contentions are warranted on the evidence or, if specifically so identified, are reasonably based on belief or a lack of information. FRCP 11(b).

c. *Sanctions.* If, after notice and a reasonable opportunity to respond, the court determines that FRCP 11(b) has been violated, the court may impose an appropriate sanction on any attorney, law firm, or party that violated FRCP 11(b) or is responsible for the violation. FRCP 11(c)(1). Refer to the United States District Court for the Southern District of Indiana KeyRules Motion for Sanctions document for more information.

5. *Privacy protection for filings made with the court.* Electronically filed documents must meet the requirements of. . .FRCP 5.2 (Privacy Protection for Filings Made with the Court), as if they had been submitted on paper. IN R USDCTSD ECF Procedures(13).

a. *Redacted filings.* Unless the court orders otherwise, in an electronic or paper filing with the court that contains an individual's Social Security number, taxpayer-identification number, or birth date, the name of an individual known to be a minor, or a financial-account number, a party or nonparty making the filing may include only:

i. The last four (4) digits of the Social Security number and taxpayer-identification number;

ii. The year of the individual's birth;

iii. The minor's initials; and

iv. The last four (4) digits of the financial-account number. FRCP 5.2(a).

b. *Exemptions from the redaction requirement.* The redaction requirement does not apply to the following:

i. A financial-account number that identifies the property allegedly subject to forfeiture in a forfeiture proceeding;

ii. The record of an administrative or agency proceeding;

iii. The official record of a state-court proceeding;

iv. The record of a court or tribunal, if that record was not subject to the redaction requirement when originally filed;

v. A filing covered by FRCP 5.2(c) or FRCP 5.2(d); and

vi. A pro se filing in an action brought under 28 U.S.C.A. § 2241, 28 U.S.C.A. § 2254, or 28 U.S.C.A. § 2255. FRCP 5.2(b).

c. *Limitations on remote access to electronic files; Social Security appeals and immigration cases.* Unless the court orders otherwise, in an action for benefits under the Social Security Act, and in an action or proceeding relating to an order of removal, to relief from removal, or to immigration benefits or detention, access to an electronic file is authorized as follows:

i. The parties and their attorneys may have remote electronic access to any part of the case file, including the administrative record;

ii. Any other person may have electronic access to the full record at the courthouse, but may have remote electronic access only to:

- The docket maintained by the court; and

- An opinion, order, judgment, or other disposition of the court, but not any other part of the case file or the administrative record. FRCP 5.2(c).

d. *Filings made under seal.* The court may order that a filing be made under seal without redaction. The court may later unseal the filing or order the person who made the filing to file a redacted version for the public record. FRCP 5.2(d). For more information on filing under seal, refer to IN R USDCTSD L.R. 5-11 and IN R USDCTSD ECF Procedures(18).

e. *Protective orders.* For good cause, the court may by order in a case:

    i. Require redaction of additional information; or

    ii. Limit or prohibit a nonparty's remote electronic access to a document filed with the court. FRCP 5.2(e).

f. *Option for additional unredacted filing under seal.* A person making a redacted filing may also file an unredacted copy under seal. The court must retain the unredacted copy as part of the record. FRCP 5.2(f).

g. *Option for filing a reference list.* A filing that contains redacted information may be filed together with a reference list that identifies each item of redacted information and specifies an appropriate identifier that uniquely corresponds to each item listed. The list must be filed under seal and may be amended as of right. Any reference in the case to a listed identifier will be construed to refer to the corresponding item of information. FRCP 5.2(g).

h. *Waiver of protection of identifiers.* A person waives the protection of FRCP 5.2(a) as to the person's own information by filing it without redaction and not under seal. FRCP 5.2(h).

F. Filing and Service Requirements

1. *Filing requirements.* Any paper after the complaint that is required to be served—together with a certificate of service—must be filed within a reasonable time after service. FRCP 5(d)(1). Motions must be filed separately, but alternative motions may be filed in a single document if each is named in the title. IN R USDCTSD L.R. 7-1(a).

a. *How filing is made; In general.* A paper is filed by delivering it:

    i. To the clerk; or

    ii. To a judge who agrees to accept it for filing, and who must then note the filing date on the paper and promptly send it to the clerk. FRCP 5(d)(2).

        • In certain instances, the court will direct the parties to submit items directly to chambers (e.g., confidential settlement statements). However, absent specific prior authorization, counsel and litigants should not submit letters or documents directly to chambers, and such materials should be filed with the clerk. IN R USDCTSD L.R. 5-1(Local Rules Advisory Committee Comment).

    iii. A document or item submitted in relation to a matter within the court's jurisdiction is deemed filed upon delivery to the office of the clerk in a manner prescribed by the Local Rules of the United States District Court for the Southern District of Indiana or the Federal Rules of Civil Procedure or authorized by the court. Any submission directed to a Judge or Judge's staff, the office of the clerk or any employee thereof, in a manner that is not contemplated by IN R USDCTSD L.R. 5-1 and without prior court authorization is prohibited. IN R USDCTSD L.R. 5-1(a).

b. *Non-electronic filing.* Any document that is exempt from electronic filing must be filed directly with the clerk and served on other parties in the case as required by those Federal Rules of Civil Procedure and Local Rules of the United States District Court for the Southern District of Indiana that apply to the service of non-electronic documents. IN R USDCTSD L.R. 5-2(c).

    i. *When completed.* A document or other item that is not required to be filed electronically is deemed filed:

        • Upon delivery in person, by courier, or via U.S. Mail or other mail delivery service to the clerk's office during business hours;

        • When the courtroom deputy clerk accepts it, if the document or item is filed in open court; or

        • Upon completion of any other manner of filing that the court authorizes. IN R USDCTSD L.R. 5-10(a).

ii. *Document filing by non-exempt party.* When a party who is not exempt from the electronic filing requirement files a document directly with the clerk, the party must:

- Electronically file a notice of manual filing that explains why the document cannot be filed electronically;

- Present the document to the clerk within one (1) business day after filing the notice of manual filing; and

- Present the clerk with a copy of the notice of manual filing when the party files the document with the clerk. IN R USDCTSD L.R. 5-2(d).

c. *Electronic filing*

i. *Authorization of electronic filing program.* A court may, by local rule, allow papers to be filed, signed, or verified by electronic means that are consistent with any technical standards established by the Judicial Conference of the United States. A local rule may require electronic filing only if reasonable exceptions are allowed. A paper filed electronically in compliance with a local rule is a written paper for purposes of the Federal Rules of Civil Procedure. FRCP 5(d)(3).

- IN R USDCTSD L.R. 5-2 requires electronic filing, as allowed by FRCP 5(d)(3). The policies and procedures in IN R USDCTSD ECF Procedures govern electronic filing in this district unless, due to circumstances in a particular case, a judicial officer determines that these policies and procedures (IN R USDCTSD ECF Procedures) should be modified. IN R USDCTSD ECF Procedures(1).

- Unless modified by order of the Court, all Federal Rules of Civil Procedure and Local Rules of the United States District Court for the Southern District of Indiana shall continue to apply to cases maintained in the Court's Case Management/Electronic Case Filing System (CM/ECF). IN R USDCTSD ECF Procedures(3).

ii. *Mandatory electronic filing.* Unless exempted pursuant to IN R USDCTSD L.R. 5-3(e), attorneys admitted to the court's bar (including those admitted pro hac vice) or authorized to represent the United States must use the court's ECF system to file documents. IN R USDCTSD L.R. 5-3(a). Electronic filing by attorneys is required for eligible documents filed in civil and criminal cases pending with the Court, unless specifically exempted by Local Rule or Court Order. IN R USDCTSD ECF Procedures(4).

- *Exceptions.* All civil cases (other than those cases the court specifically exempts) must be maintained in the court's electronic case filing (ECF) system. Accordingly, as allowed by FRCP 5(d)(3), every document filed in this court (including exhibits) must be transmitted to the clerk's office via the ECF system consistent with IN R USDCTSD L.R. 5-2 through IN R USDCTSD L.R. 5-11 except: (1) documents filed by pro se litigants; (2) transcripts in cases filed by claimants under the Social Security Act (and related statutes); (3) exhibits in a format that does not readily permit electronic filing (such as videos and large maps and charts); (4) documents that are illegible when scanned into .pdf format; (5) documents filed in cases not maintained on the ECF system; and (6) any other documents that the court or the Local Rules of the United States District Court for the Southern District of Indiana specifically allow to be filed directly with the clerk. IN R USDCTSD L.R. 5-2(a). Parties otherwise participating in the electronic filing system may be excused from filing a particular component electronically under certain limited circumstances, such as when the component cannot be reduced to an electronic format. Such components shall not be filed electronically, but instead shall be manually filed with the Clerk of Court and served upon the parties in accordance with the applicable Federal Rules of Civil Procedure and the Local Rules of the United States District Court for the Southern District of Indiana for filing and service of non-electronic documents. IN R USDCTSD ECF Procedures(15).

- *Exemption from participation.* The court may exempt attorneys from using the ECF system in a particular case for good cause. An attorney must file a petition for ECF exemption and a CM/ECF technical requirements exemption questionnaire in each case in

which the attorney seeks an exemption. (The CM/ECF technical requirements exemption questionnaire is available on the court's website). IN R USDCTSD L.R. 5-3(e).

    iii. *Consequences of electronic filing.* Electronic transmission of a document consistent with the procedures adopted by the Court shall, upon the complete receipt of the same by the Clerk of Court, constitute filing of the document for all purposes of the Federal Rules of Civil and Criminal Procedure and the Local Rules of the United States District Court for the Southern District of Indiana, and shall constitute entry of that document onto the docket maintained by the Clerk pursuant to FRCP 58 and FRCP 79. IN R USDCTSD ECF Procedures(7); IN R USDCTSD L.R. 5-4(c)(1). When a document has been filed electronically: the document, as filed, binds the filing party. IN R USDCTSD L.R. 5-4(c)(3).

- A Notice of Electronic Filing (NEF) acknowledging that the document has been filed will immediately appear on the filer's screen after the document has been submitted. Attorneys are strongly encouraged to print or electronically save a copy of the NEF. Attorneys can also verify the filing of documents by inspecting the Court's electronic docket sheet through the use of a PACER login. IN R USDCTSD ECF Procedures(7). When a document has been filed electronically: the notice of electronic filing for the document serves as the court's date-stamp and proof of filing. IN R USDCTSD L.R. 5-4(c)(4).

- The Court may, upon the motion of a party or upon its own motion, strike any inappropriately filed document. IN R USDCTSD ECF Procedures(7).

    iv. For more information on electronic filing, refer to IN R USDCTSD ECF Procedures.

  d. *Fax filing.* The clerk may not file a faxed document without court authorization. The court may not authorize the clerk to file faxed documents without finding that compelling circumstances justify it. A party must submit a copy of the document that otherwise complies with IN R USDCTSD L.R. 5-10 to replace the faxed copy within seven (7) days after faxing the document. IN R USDCTSD L.R. 5-10(e).

2. *Service requirements*

  a. *Service; When required*

    i. *In general.* Unless the Federal Rules of Civil Procedure provide otherwise, each of the following papers must be served on every party:

- An order stating that service is required;

- A pleading filed after the original complaint, unless the court orders otherwise under FRCP 5(c) because there are numerous defendants;

- A discovery paper required to be served on a party, unless the court orders otherwise;

- A written motion, except one that may be heard ex parte; and

- A written notice, appearance, demand, or offer of judgment, or any similar paper. FRCP 5(a)(1).

    ii. *If a party fails to appear.* No service is required on a party who is in default for failing to appear. But a pleading that asserts a new claim for relief against such a party must be served on that party under FRCP 4. FRCP 5(a)(2).

    iii. *Seizing property.* If an action is begun by seizing property and no person is or need be named as a defendant, any service required before the filing of an appearance, answer, or claim must be made on the person who had custody or possession of the property when it was seized. FRCP 5(a)(3).

  b. *Service; How made*

    i. *Serving an attorney.* If a party is represented by an attorney, service under FRCP 5 must be made on the attorney unless the court orders service on the party. FRCP 5(b)(1).

    ii. *Service in general.* A paper is served under FRCP 5 by:

- Handing it to the person;

- Leaving it: (1) at the person's office with a clerk or other person in charge or, if no one is in charge, in a conspicuous place in the office; or (2) if the person has no office or the office is closed, at the person's dwelling or usual place of abode with someone of suitable age and discretion who resides there;

- Mailing it to the person's last known address—in which event service is complete upon mailing;

- Leaving it with the court clerk if the person has no known address;

- Sending it by electronic means if the person consented in writing—in which event service is complete upon transmission, but is not effective if the serving party learns that it did not reach the person to be served; or

- Delivering it by any other means that the person consented to in writing—in which event service is complete when the person making service delivers it to the agency designated to make delivery. FRCP 5(b)(2).

iii. *Electronic service*

- *Consent.* By registering to use the ECF system, attorneys consent to electronic service of documents filed in cases maintained on the ECF system. IN R USDCTSD L.R. 5-3(d). By participating in the Electronic Case Filing Program, attorneys consent to the electronic service of documents, and shall make available electronic mail addresses for service. IN R USDCTSD ECF Procedures(11).

- *Service on registered parties.* Upon the filing of a document by a party, an e-mail message will be automatically generated by the electronic filing system and sent via electronic mail to the e-mail addresses of all registered attorneys who have appeared in the case. The Notice of Electronic Filing will contain a document hyperlink which will provide recipients with one "free look" at the electronically filed document. Recipients are encouraged to print and/or save a copy of the document during the "free look" to avoid incurring PACER charges for future viewings of the document. IN R USDCTSD ECF Procedures(11). When a document has been filed electronically: transmission of the notice of electronic filing generated by the ECF system to an attorney's e-mail address constitutes service of the document on that attorney. IN R USDCTSD L.R. 5-4(c)(5). The party effectuates service on all registered attorneys by filing electronically. IN R USDCTSD ECF Procedures(11). When a document has been filed electronically: no other attempted service will constitute electronic service of the document. IN R USDCTSD L.R. 5-4(c)(6).

- *Service on exempt parties.* A filer must serve a copy of the document consistent with FRCP 5 on any party or attorney who is exempt from participating in electronic filing. IN R USDCTSD L.R. 5-4(d). It is the responsibility of the filing attorney to conventionally serve all parties who do not receive electronic service (the identity of these parties will be indicated on the filing receipt generated by the ECF system). IN R USDCTSD ECF Procedures(11).

- *Service on parties excused from electronic filing.* Parties otherwise participating in the electronic filing system may be excused from filing a particular component electronically under certain limited circumstances, such as when the component cannot be reduced to an electronic format. Such components shall not be filed electronically, but instead shall be manually filed with the Clerk of Court and served upon the parties in accordance with the applicable Federal Rules of Civil Procedure and the Local Rules of the United States District Court for the Southern District of Indiana for filing and service of non-electronic documents. IN R USDCTSD ECF Procedures(15).

- *Service of exempt documents.* Any document that is exempt from electronic filing must be filed directly with the clerk and served on other parties in the case as required by those Federal Rules of Civil Procedure and Local Rules of the United States District Court for the Southern District of Indiana that apply to the service of non-electronic documents. IN R USDCTSD L.R. 5-2(c).

iv. *Using court facilities.* If a local rule so authorizes, a party may use the court's transmission facilities to make service under FRCP 5(b)(2)(E). FRCP 5(b)(3).

c. *Serving numerous defendants*

i. *In general.* If an action involves an unusually large number of defendants, the court may, on motion or on its own, order that:

- Defendants' pleadings and replies to them need not be served on other defendants;

- Any crossclaim, counterclaim, avoidance, or affirmative defense in those pleadings and replies to them will be treated as denied or avoided by all other parties; and

- Filing any such pleading and serving it on the plaintiff constitutes notice of the pleading to all parties. FRCP 5(c)(1).

ii. *Notifying parties.* A copy of every such order must be served on the parties as the court directs. FRCP 5(c)(2).

G. Hearings

1. *Hearings, generally*

a. *Oral argument.* Due process does not require that oral argument be permitted on a motion and, except as otherwise provided by local rule, the district court has discretion to determine whether it will decide the motion on the papers or hear argument by counsel (and perhaps receive evidence). FPP § 1190; F.D.I.C. v. Deglau, 207 F.3d 153 (3d Cir. 2000).

i. *Request for oral argument.* A party may request oral argument by filing a separate motion explaining why oral argument is necessary and estimating how long the court should allow for the argument. IN R USDCTSD L.R. 7-5(a). Refer to the Documents section of this document for more information.

ii. *No additional evidence at oral argument.* Parties may not present additional evidence at oral argument. IN R USDCTSD L.R. 7-5(b).

b. *Providing a regular schedule for oral hearings.* A court may establish regular times and places for oral hearings on motions. FRCP 78(a).

c. *Providing for submission on briefs.* By rule or order, the court may provide for submitting and determining motions on briefs, without oral hearings. FRCP 78(b).

d. *Request for evidentiary hearing.* A party may request an evidentiary hearing on a motion or petition by serving and filing a separate motion explaining why the hearing is necessary and estimating how long the court should allow for the hearing. IN R USDCTSD L.R. 7-5(c).

e. *Directed by the court.* The court may: (1) grant or deny a request for oral argument or an evidentiary hearing in its sole discretion; (2) set oral argument or an evidentiary hearing without a request from a party; and (3) order any oral argument or evidentiary hearing to be held anywhere within the district regardless of where the case will be tried. IN R USDCTSD L.R. 7-5(d).

2. *Hearing on FRCP 12 defenses before trial.* If a party so moves, any defense listed in FRCP 12(b)(1) through FRCP 12(b)(7)—whether made in a pleading or by motion—and a motion under FRCP 12(c) must be heard and decided before trial unless the court orders a deferral until trial. FRCP 12(i).

3. *Courtroom and courthouse decorum.* For information on courtroom and courthouse decorum, refer to IN R USDCTSD L.R. 83-3.

H. Forms

1. Federal Motion to Dismiss for Improper Venue Forms

a. Defense; Improper venue; Defendant resident of another district. FEDPROF § 1:184.

b. Motion; For dismissal or transfer of action on grounds of improper venue; Diversity case. FEDPROF § 1:371.

c. Motion; For dismissal; Improper venue; Lack of personal jurisdiction. FEDPROF § 1:371.50.

d. Motion; General form. FEDPROF § 1:746.

e. Notice; Of motion; General form. FEDPROF § 1:747.

f. Notice; Of motion; With costs of motion. FEDPROF § 1:748.

g. Notice; Of motion; Containing motion. FEDPROF § 1:749.

h. Opposition; To motion; General form. FEDPROF § 1:750.

i. Affidavit; Supporting or opposing motion. FEDPROF § 1:751.

j. Brief; Supporting or opposing motion. FEDPROF § 1:752.

k. Statement of points and authorities; Opposing motion. FEDPROF § 1:753.

l. Motion; To dismiss; Improper venue; Diversity action. FEDPROF § 1:916.

m. Motion to dismiss; Improper venue; Action not founded solely on diversity. FEDPROF § 1:917.

n. Motion to dismiss; Improper venue; Corporate defendant not subject to personal jurisdiction in district. FEDPROF § 1:918.

o. Motion to dismiss; Improper venue; Action of local nature. FEDPROF § 1:919.

p. Motion; To dismiss or, alternatively, to transfer action; Improper venue. FEDPROF § 1:920.

q. Affidavit; In support of motion to dismiss for improper venue; Corporate defendant not subject to personal jurisdiction in district. FEDPROF § 1:921.

r. Motion; To dismiss action for improper venue. FEDPROF § 22:56.

s. Motion to dismiss complaint; General form. GOLDLTGFMS § 20:24.

t. Affidavit in support of motion to dismiss complaint. GOLDLTGFMS § 20:32.

u. Motion; Federal form. GOLDLTGFMS § 45:4.

v. Affidavit in support of motion; Improper venue. GOLDLTGFMS § 45:15.

2. **Forms for the Southern District of Indiana**

a. Notice of endorsement. IN R USDCTSD ECF Procedures(Appendix B).

b. Notice of manual filing. IN R USDCTSD ECF Procedures(Appendix C).

c. Declaration that party was unable to file in a timely manner due to technical difficulties. IN R USDCTSD ECF Procedures(Appendix D).

I. Applicable Rules

1. *Federal rules*

a. Venue generally. 28 U.S.C.A. § 1391.

b. Serving and filing pleadings and other papers. FRCP 5.

c. Constitutional challenge to a statute; Notice, certification, and intervention. FRCP 5.1.

d. Privacy protection for filings made with the court. FRCP 5.2.

e. Computing and extending time; Time for motion papers. FRCP 6.

f. Pleadings allowed; Form of motions and other papers. FRCP 7.

g. Disclosure statement. FRCP 7.1.

h. Form of pleadings. FRCP 10.

i. Signing pleadings, motions, and other papers; Representations to the court; Sanctions. FRCP 11.

j. Defenses and objections; When and how presented; Motion for judgment on the pleadings; Consolidating motions; Waiving defenses; Pretrial hearing. FRCP 12.

k. Taking testimony. FRCP 43.

l. Hearing motions; Submission on briefs. FRCP 78.

2. *Local rules*

a. Scope of the rules. IN R USDCTSD L.R. 1-1.

b. Sanctions for errors as to form. IN R USDCTSD L.R. 1-3.

c. Format of documents presented for filing. IN R USDCTSD L.R. 5-1.

d. Constitutional challenge to a statute; Notice. IN R USDCTSD L.R. 5.1-1.

e. Filing of documents electronically required. IN R USDCTSD L.R. 5-2.

f. Eligibility, registration, passwords for electronic filing; Exemption from electronic filing. IN R USDCTSD L.R. 5-3.

g. Timing and consequences of electronic filing. IN R USDCTSD L.R. 5-4.

h. Attachments and exhibits in cases filed electronically. IN R USDCTSD L.R. 5-6.

i. Signatures in cases filed electronically. IN R USDCTSD L.R. 5-7.

j. Non-electronic filings. IN R USDCTSD L.R. 5-10.

k. Motion practice. [IN R USDCTSD L.R. 7-1, as amended by IN ORDER 16-2319, effective December 1, 2016].

l. Oral arguments and hearings. IN R USDCTSD L.R. 7-5.

m. Request for three-judge court. IN R USDCTSD L.R. 9-2.

n. Filing of discovery materials. IN R USDCTSD L.R. 26-2.

o. Assignment of cases. IN R USDCTSD L.R. 40-1.

p. Alternative dispute resolution. IN R USDCTSD A.D.R. Rule 1.1; IN R USDCTSD A.D.R. Rule 1.2; IN R USDCTSD A.D.R. Rule 1.5; IN R USDCTSD A.D.R. Rule 2.1; IN R USDCTSD A.D.R. Rule 2.2.

q. Instructions for preparing case management plan. IN R USDCTSD Case Mgt.

r. Electronic case filing policies and procedures manual. IN R USDCTSD ECF Procedures.

Motions, Oppositions and Replies
Motion for Leave to Amend

Document Last Updated December 2016

A. **Checklist**

(I) ❏ Matters to be considered by moving party

   (a) ❏ Required documents

      (1) ❏ Notice of motion and motion

      (2) ❏ Proposed amended pleading

      (3) ❏ Proposed order

      (4) ❏ Certificate of service

   (b) ❏ Supplemental documents

      (1) ❏ Brief

      (2) ❏ Supporting evidence

      (3) ❏ Notice of constitutional question

      (4) ❏ Index of exhibits

      (5) ❏ Request for oral argument

      (6) ❏ Request for evidentiary hearing

      (7) ❏ Copy of authority

      (8) ❏ Copy of document with self-address envelope

(9) ❑ Notice of manual filing

(10) ❑ Courtesy copies

(11) ❑ Copies for three-judge court

(12) ❑ Declaration that party was unable to file in a timely manner due to technical difficulties

(c) ❑ Timing

    (1) ❑ Unlike amendments as of course, amendments under FRCP 15(a)(2) may be made at any stage of the litigation

    (2) ❑ A party may move—at any time, even after judgment—to amend the pleadings to conform them to the evidence and to raise an unpleaded issue

    (3) ❑ A written motion and notice of the hearing must be served at least fourteen (14) days before the time specified for the hearing, with the following exceptions: (i) when the motion may be heard ex parte; (ii) when the Federal Rules of Civil Procedure set a different time; or (iii) when a court order—which a party may, for good cause, apply for ex parte—sets a different time

    (4) ❑ Any affidavit supporting a motion must be served with the motion

    (5) ❑ When a party who is not exempt from the electronic filing requirement files a document directly with the clerk, the party must present the document to the clerk within one (1) business day after filing the notice of manual filing

    (6) ❑ Unless the court orders otherwise, the [untimely] document and declaration [that party was unable to file in a timely manner due to technical difficulties] must be filed no later than 12:00 noon of the first day on which the court is open for business following the original filing deadline

(II) ❑ Matters to be considered by opposing party

(a) ❑ Required documents

    (1) ❑ Response brief

    (2) ❑ Certificate of service

(b) ❑ Supplemental documents

    (1) ❑ Supporting evidence

    (2) ❑ Notice of constitutional question

    (3) ❑ Index of exhibits

    (4) ❑ Request for oral argument

    (5) ❑ Request for evidentiary hearing

    (6) ❑ Copy of authority

    (7) ❑ Copy of document with self-address envelope

    (8) ❑ Notice of manual filing

    (9) ❑ Courtesy copies

    (10) ❑ Copies for three-judge court

    (11) ❑ Declaration that party was unable to file in a timely manner due to technical difficulties

(c) ❑ Timing

    (1) ❑ Any response is due within fourteen (14) days after service of the motion

    (2) ❑ Except as FRCP 59(c) provides otherwise, any opposing affidavit must be served at least seven (7) days before the hearing, unless the court permits service at another time

    (3) ❑ When a party who is not exempt from the electronic filing requirement files a document directly with the clerk, the party must present the document to the clerk within one (1) business day after filing the notice of manual filing

(4) ☐ Unless the court orders otherwise, the [untimely] document and declaration [that party was unable to file in a timely manner due to technical difficulties] must be filed no later than 12:00 noon of the first day on which the court is open for business following the original filing deadline

B. Timing

1. *Motion for leave to amend.* Unlike amendments as of course, amendments under FRCP 15(a)(2) may be made at any stage of the litigation. FPP § 1484.

    a. *Amendments to conform to the evidence.* A party may move—at any time, even after judgment—to amend the pleadings to conform them to the evidence and to raise an unpleaded issue. FRCP 15(b)(2).

    b. *Time to respond to an amended pleading.* Unless the court orders otherwise, any required response to an amended pleading must be made within the time remaining to respond to the original pleading or within fourteen (14) days after service of the amended pleading, whichever is later. FRCP 15(a)(3).

2. *Timing of motions, generally*

    a. *Motion and notice of hearing.* A written motion and notice of the hearing must be served at least fourteen (14) days before the time specified for the hearing, with the following exceptions:

        i. When the motion may be heard ex parte;

        ii. When the Federal Rules of Civil Procedure set a different time; or

        iii. When a court order—which a party may, for good cause, apply for ex parte—sets a different time. FRCP 6(c)(1).

    b. *Supporting affidavit.* Any affidavit supporting a motion must be served with the motion. FRCP 6(c)(2).

3. *Timing of opposing papers.* Any response is due within fourteen (14) days after service of the motion. IN R USDCTSD L.R. 7-1(c)(2)(A).

    a. *Opposing affidavit.* Except as FRCP 59(c) provides otherwise, any opposing affidavit must be served at least seven (7) days before the hearing, unless the court permits service at another time. FRCP 6(c)(2).

    b. *Extensions.* The court may extend response and reply deadlines, but only for good cause. IN R USDCTSD L.R. 7-1(c)(3).

    c. *Summary ruling on failure to respond.* The court may summarily rule on a motion if an opposing party does not file a response within the deadline. IN R USDCTSD L.R. 7-1(c)(4).

4. *Timing of reply papers.* Where the respondent files an answering affidavit setting up a new matter, the moving party ordinarily is allowed a reasonable time to file a reply affidavit since failure to deny the new matter by affidavit may operate as an admission of its truth. AMJUR MOTIONS § 25.

    a. *Reply brief.* Any reply is due within seven (7) days after service of the response. IN R USDCTSD L.R. 7-1(c)(2)(B).

    b. *Extensions.* The court may extend response and reply deadlines, but only for good cause. IN R USDCTSD L.R. 7-1(c)(3).

5. *Document filing by non-exempt party.* When a party who is not exempt from the electronic filing requirement files a document directly with the clerk, the party must: present the document to the clerk within one (1) business day after filing the notice of manual filing. IN R USDCTSD L.R. 5-2(d)(2).

6. *Declaration that party was unable to file in a timely manner due to technical difficulties.* Unless the Court orders otherwise, the [untimely] document and declaration [that party was unable to file in a timely manner due to technical difficulties] must be filed no later than 12:00 noon of the first day on which the Court is open for business following the original filing deadline. IN R USDCTSD ECF Procedures(16).

7. *Computation of time*

    a. *Computing time.* FRCP 6 applies in computing any time period specified in the Federal Rules of Civil

Procedure, in any local rule or court order, or in any statute that does not specify a method of computing time. FRCP 6(a).

    i.   *Period stated in days or a longer unit.* When the period is stated in days or a longer unit of time:

- Exclude the day of the event that triggers the period;
- Count every day, including intermediate Saturdays, Sundays, and legal holidays; and
- Include the last day of the period, but if the last day is a Saturday, Sunday, or legal holiday, the period continues to run until the end of the next day that is not a Saturday, Sunday, or legal holiday. FRCP 6(a)(1).

    ii.   *Period stated in hours.* When the period is stated in hours:

- Begin counting immediately on the occurrence of the event that triggers the period;
- Count every hour, including hours during intermediate Saturdays, Sundays, and legal holidays; and
- If the period would end on a Saturday, Sunday, or legal holiday, the period continues to run until the same time on the next day that is not a Saturday, Sunday, or legal holiday. FRCP 6(a)(2).

    iii.   *Inaccessibility of the clerk's office.* Unless the court orders otherwise, if the clerk's office is inaccessible:

- On the last day for filing under FRCP 6(a)(1), then the time for filing is extended to the first accessible day that is not a Saturday, Sunday, or legal holiday; or
- During the last hour for filing under FRCP 6(a)(2), then the time for filing is extended to the same time on the first accessible day that is not a Saturday, Sunday, or legal holiday. FRCP 6(a)(3).

    iv.   *"Last day" defined.* Unless a different time is set by a statute, local rule, or court order, the last day ends:

- For electronic filing, at midnight in the court's time zone; and
- For filing by other means, when the clerk's office is scheduled to close. FRCP 6(a)(4).

    v.   *"Next day" defined.* The "next day" is determined by continuing to count forward when the period is measured after an event and backward when measured before an event. FRCP 6(a)(5).

    vi.   *"Legal holiday" defined.* "Legal holiday" means:

- The day set aside by statute for observing New Year's Day, Martin Luther King Jr.'s Birthday, Washington's Birthday, Memorial Day, Independence Day, Labor Day, Columbus Day, Veterans' Day, Thanksgiving Day, or Christmas Day;
- Any day declared a holiday by the President or Congress; and
- For periods that are measured after an event, any other day declared a holiday by the state where the district court is located. FRCP 6(a)(6).

  b. *Computation of electronic filing deadlines.* Filing documents electronically does not alter filing deadlines. IN R USDCTSD ECF Procedures(7). A document due on a particular day must be filed before midnight local time of the division where the case is pending. IN R USDCTSD L.R. 5-4(a). All electronic transmissions of documents must be completed (i.e. received completely by the Clerk's Office) prior to midnight of the local time of the division in which the case is pending in order to be considered timely filed that day (NOTE: time will be noted in Eastern Time on the Court's docket. If you have filed a document prior to midnight local time of the division in which the case is pending and the document is due that date, but the electronic receipt and docket reflect the following calendar day, please contact the Court). IN R USDCTSD ECF Procedures(7). Although attorneys may file documents electronically twenty-four (24) hours a day, seven (7) days a week, attorneys are encouraged to file all documents during the normal working hours of the Clerk's Office (Monday through Friday, 8:30 a.m. to 4:30 p.m.) when technical support is available. IN R USDCTSD ECF Procedures(7); IN R USDCTSD ECF Procedures(9).

    i.   *Technical difficulties.* Parties are encouraged to file documents electronically during normal business hours, in case a problem is encountered. In the event a technical failure occurs and a document cannot be filed electronically despite the best efforts of the filing party, the party should print (if possible) a copy of the error message received. In addition, as soon as practically possible, the party should file a "Declaration that Party was Unable to File in a Timely Manner Due to Technical Difficulties." A model form is provided as Appendix D (IN R USDCTSD ECF Procedures(Appendix D)). IN R USDCTSD ECF Procedures(16).

- If a party is unable to file electronically and, as a result, may miss a filing deadline, the party must contact the Clerk's Office at the number listed in IN R USDCTSD ECF Procedures(15) to inform the court's staff of the difficulty. If a party misses a filing deadline due to an inability to file electronically, the party may submit the untimely filed document, accompanied by a declaration stating the reason(s) for missing the deadline. Unless the Court orders otherwise, the document and declaration must be filed no later than 12:00 noon of the first day on which the Court is open for business following the original filing deadline. IN R USDCTSD ECF Procedures(16).

c. *Extending time*

    i. *In general.* When an act may or must be done within a specified time, the court may, for good cause, extend the time:

- With or without motion or notice if the court acts, or if a request is made, before the original time or its extension expires; or
- On motion made after the time has expired if the party failed to act because of excusable neglect. FRCP 6(b)(1).

    ii. *Exceptions.* A court must not extend the time to act under FRCP 50(b), FRCP 50(d), FRCP 52(b), FRCP 59(b), FRCP 59(d), FRCP 59(e), and FRCP 60(b). FRCP 6(b)(2).

    iii. Refer to the United States District Court for the Southern District of Indiana KeyRules Motion for Continuance/Extension of Time document for more information on extending time.

d. *Additional time after certain kinds of service.* When a party may or must act within a specified time after being served and service is made under FRCP 5(b)(2)(C) (mail), FRCP 5(b)(2)(D) (leaving with the clerk), or FRCP 5(b)(2)(F) (other means consented to), three (3) days are added after the period would otherwise expire under FRCP 6(a). FRCP 6(d). Service by electronic mail shall constitute service pursuant to FRCP 5(b)(2)(E) and shall entitle the party being served to the additional three (3) days provided by FRCP 6(d). IN R USDCTSD ECF Procedures(11).

C. General Requirements

1. *Motions, generally*

a. *Requirements.* A request for a court order must be made by motion. The motion must:

    i. Be in writing unless made during a hearing or trial;

    ii. State with particularity the grounds for seeking the order; and

    iii. State the relief sought. FRCP 7(b)(1).

b. *Notice of motion.* A party interested in resisting the relief sought by a motion has a right to notice thereof, and an opportunity to be heard. AMJUR MOTIONS § 12.

    i. In addition to statutory or court rule provisions requiring notice of a motion—the purpose of such a notice requirement having been said to be to prevent a party from being prejudicially surprised by a motion—principles of natural justice dictate that an adverse party generally must be given notice that a motion will be presented to the court. AMJUR MOTIONS § 12.

    ii. "Notice," in this regard, means reasonable notice, including a meaningful opportunity to prepare and to defend against allegations of a motion. AMJUR MOTIONS § 12.

c. *Writing requirement.* The writing requirement is intended to insure that the adverse parties are informed and have a record of both the motion's pendency and the grounds on which the movant seeks an order. FPP § 1191; Feldberg v. Quechee Lakes Corp., 463 F.3d 195 (2d Cir. 2006).

    i. It is sufficient "if the motion is stated in a written notice of the hearing of the motion." FPP § 1191.

d. *Particularity requirement.* The particularity requirement insures that the opposing parties will have notice of their opponent's contentions. FEDPROC § 62:364; Goodman v. 1973 26 Foot Trojan Vessel, Arkansas Registration No. AR1439SN, 859 F.2d 71, 12 Fed.R.Serv.3d 645 (8th Cir. 1988). That requirement ensures that notice of the basis for the motion is provided to the court and to the opposing party so as to avoid prejudice, provide the opponent with a meaningful opportunity to respond, and provide the court with enough information to process the motion correctly. FEDPROC § 62:364; Andreas v. Volkswagen of America, Inc., 336 F.3d 789, 56 Fed.R.Serv.3d 6 (8th Cir. 2003).

    i. Reasonable specification of the grounds for a motion is sufficient. However, where a movant fails to state even one ground for granting the motion in question, the movant has failed to meet the minimal standard of "reasonable specification." FEDPROC § 62:364; Martinez v. Trainor, 556 F.2d 818, 23 Fed.R.Serv.2d 403 (7th Cir. 1977).

    ii. The court may excuse the failure to comply with the particularity requirement if it is inadvertent, and where no prejudice is shown by the opposing party. FEDPROC § 62:364.

e. *Motions must be filed separately.* Motions must be filed separately, but alternative motions may be filed in a single document if each is named in the title. A motion must not be contained within a brief, response, or reply to a previously filed motion, unless ordered by the court. IN R USDCTSD L.R. 7-1(a).

f. *Routine or uncontested motions.* The court may rule upon a routine or uncontested motion before the response deadline passes, unless: (1) the motion indicates that an opposing party objects to it; or (2) the court otherwise believes that a response will be filed. IN R USDCTSD L.R. 7-1(d).

2. *Informal conference to resolve disputes involving non-dispositive issues.* In addition to those conferences required by IN R USDCTSD L.R. 37-1, counsel are encouraged to hold informal conferences in person or by phone to resolve any disputes involving non-dispositive issues that may otherwise require submission of a motion to the Court. This requirement does not apply to cases involving pro se parties. Therefore, prior to filing any non-dispositive motion (including motions for extension of time), the moving party must contact opposing counsel to determine whether there is an objection to any non-dispositive motion (including motions for extension of time), and state in the motion whether opposing counsel objects to the motion. IN R USDCTSD Case Mgt(General Instructions For All Cases). Refer to the Documents section of this document for more information on the contents of the motion.

3. *Motion for leave to amend.* FRCP 15(a)(2) provides that after a party has amended a pleading once as of course or the time for amendments of that type has expired, a party may amend only by obtaining leave of the court or if the adverse party consents to it. FPP § 1484; In re Cessna Distributorship Antitrust Litigation, 532 F.2d 64 (8th Cir. 1976). FRCP 15(a) does not set forth any specific procedure for obtaining leave to amend. Typically, it is sought by a motion addressed to the court's discretion. FPP § 1485.

a. *Pleadings to be amended.* As in the case of amendments as of course under FRCP 15(a)(1), any of the pleadings enumerated in FRCP 7(a) may be amended with the court's leave and FRCP 15 does not restrict the purposes for which an amendment may be made or its character. FPP § 1484.

b. *Prerequisites for leave to amend.* The only prerequisites are that the district court have jurisdiction over the case and an appeal must not be pending. FPP § 1484. If these two conditions are met, the court will proceed to examine the effect and the timing of the proposed amendments to determine whether they would prejudice the rights of any of the other parties to the suit. FPP § 1484; Nilsen v. City of Moss Point, Miss., 674 F.2d 379, 388 (5th Cir. 1982).

c. *When leave or consent is not obtained.* In general, if an amendment that cannot be made as of right is served without obtaining the court's leave or the opposing party's consent, it is without legal effect and any new matter it contains will not be considered unless the amendment is resubmitted for the court's approval. Some courts have held, however, that an untimely amended pleading served without judicial permission may be considered as properly introduced when leave to amend would have been granted had it been sought and when it does not appear that any of the parties will be prejudiced by allowing the change. FPP § 1484.

d. *Form.* A motion to amend under FRCP 15(a), as is true of motions generally, is subject to the requirements of FRCP 7(b), and must set forth with particularity the relief or order requested and the grounds supporting the application. In order to satisfy these prerequisites a copy of the amendment should be submitted with the motion so that the court and the adverse party know the precise nature of the pleading changes being proposed. FPP § 1485.

e. *Oral motion for leave to amend.* Courts have held that an oral request to amend a pleading that is made before the court in the presence of opposing party's counsel may be sufficient if the adverse party is put on notice of the nature and purpose of the request and is given the same opportunity to present objections to the proposed amendment as would have occurred if a formal motion had been made. FPP § 1485.

f. *Conditions imposed on leave to amend.* While FRCP 15(a) does not specifically authorize the district court to impose conditions on its granting of leave to amend, it is well settled that the court may impose such conditions to avoid or minimize any prejudice to the opposing party. FEDPROC § 62:276. Conditions frequently are imposed because the amending party knew of the facts sought to be asserted in the amendment but failed to assert such facts until later, to the prejudice of the opposing party. Conversely, the court may decline to impose conditions where the amendment was asserted with relative promptness. FEDPROC § 62:276.

   i. The moving party's refusal to comply with the conditions imposed by the court normally will result in a denial of the right to amend. FPP § 1486.

g. *When leave to amend may be granted.* If the underlying facts or circumstances relied upon by a plaintiff may be a proper subject of relief, he ought to be afforded an opportunity to test his claim on the merits. In the absence of any apparent or declared reason—such as undue delay, bad faith or dilatory motive on the part of the movant, repeated failure to cure deficiencies by amendments previously allowed, undue prejudice to the opposing party by virtue of allowance of the amendment, futility of amendment, etc.—the leave sought should, as the rules require, be "freely given." FPP § 1487; Foman v. Davis, 371 U.S. 178, 182, 83 S.Ct. 227, 230, 9 L.Ed.2d 222 (1962).

4. *Amendments, generally*

a. *Amendments before trial.* The function of FRCP 15(a), which provides generally for the amendment of pleadings, is to enable a party to assert matters that were overlooked or were unknown at the time the party interposed the original complaint or answer. FPP § 1473; Smiga v. Dean Witter Reynolds, Inc., 766 F.2d 698, 703 (2d Cir. 1985).

   i. *Matters contained in amended pleading under FRCP 15(a).* Although FRCP 15(a) does not expressly state that an amendment must contain only matters that occurred within a particular time period, FRCP 15(d) provides that any "transaction, occurrence, or event that happened after the date of the pleading" should be set forth in a supplemental pleading. FPP § 1473. Thus, impliedly, an amended pleading, whether prepared with or without leave of court, only should relate to matters that have taken place prior to the date of the earlier pleading. FPP § 1473; Ford Motor Co. v. U.S., 19 C.I.T. 946, 896 F.Supp. 1224, 1230 (1995).

   ii. *Amending as a matter of course.* A party may amend its pleading once as a matter of course within: (1) twenty-one (21) days after serving it, or if the pleading is one to which a responsive pleading is required, twenty-one (21) days after service of a responsive pleading or twenty-one (21) days after service of a motion under FRCP 12(b), FRCP 12(e), or FRCP 12(f), whichever is earlier. FRCP 15(a)(1). Refer to the United States District Court for the Southern District of Indiana KeyRules Amended Pleading document for more information on amending as a matter of course.

   iii. *Other amendments.* In all other cases, a party may amend its pleading only with the opposing party's written consent or the court's leave. The court should freely give leave when justice so requires. FRCP 15(a)(2).

   iv. *Types of amendments permitted under FRCP 15(a)*

      • *Cure a defective pleading.* Perhaps the most common use of FRCP 15(a) is by a party seeking to amend in order to cure a defective pleading. FPP § 1474.

      • *Correct insufficiently stated claims or defenses.* A more common use of FRCP 15(a) amendments is to correct insufficiently stated claims or defenses. Typically, amendments of this character involve either adding a necessary allegation in order to state a claim for relief or correcting a misnomer of a party to the action. FPP § 1474.

- *Change nature or theory of claim or capacity of party.* Courts also have allowed a party to amend in order to change the nature or theory of the party's claim or the capacity in which the party is bringing the action. FPP § 1474.

- *State additional claims or defenses or drop claims or defenses.* Plaintiffs and defendants also have been permitted to amend their pleadings to state additional claims, to assert additional defenses, or to drop claims or defenses. FPP § 1474; Weinberger v. Retail Credit Co., 498 F.2d 552, 554, n.4 (4th Cir. 1974).

- *Increase amount of damages or elect a different remedy.* A FRCP 15(a) amendment also is appropriate for increasing the amount of damages sought, or for electing a different remedy than the one originally requested. FPP § 1474; McFadden v. Sanchez, 710 F.2d 907 (2d Cir. 1983).

- *Add, substitute, or drop parties.* Finally, a party may make a FRCP 15(a) amendment to add, substitute, or drop parties to the action. FPP § 1474.

b. *Amendments during and after trial*

   i. *Based on an objection at trial.* If, at trial, a party objects that evidence is not within the issues raised in the pleadings, the court may permit the pleadings to be amended. The court should freely permit an amendment when doing so will aid in presenting the merits and the objecting party fails to satisfy the court that the evidence would prejudice that party's action or defense on the merits. The court may grant a continuance to enable the objecting party to meet the evidence. FRCP 15(b)(1).

   ii. *For issues tried by consent.* When an issue not raised by the pleadings is tried by the parties' express or implied consent, it must be treated in all respects as if raised in the pleadings. A party may move—at any time, even after judgment—to amend the pleadings to conform them to the evidence and to raise an unpleaded issue. But failure to amend does not affect the result of the trial of that issue. FRCP 15(b)(2).

c. *Relation back of amendments*

   i. *When an amendment relates back.* An amendment to a pleading relates back to the date of the original pleading when:

- The law that provides the applicable statute of limitations allows relation back;

- The amendment asserts a claim or defense that arose out of the conduct, transaction, or occurrence set out—or attempted to be set out—in the original pleading; or

- The amendment changes the party or the naming of the party against whom a claim is asserted, if FRCP 15(c)(1)(B) is satisfied and if, within the period provided by FRCP 4(m) for serving the summons and complaint, the party to be brought in by amendment: (1) received such notice of the action that it will not be prejudiced in defending on the merits; and (2) knew or should have known that the action would have been brought against it, but for a mistake concerning the proper party's identity. FRCP 15(c)(1).

   ii. *Notice to the United States.* When the United States or a United States officer or agency is added as a defendant by amendment, the notice requirements of FRCP 15(c)(1)(C)(i) and FRCP 15(c)(1)(C)(ii) are satisfied if, during the stated period, process was delivered or mailed to the United States attorney or the United States attorney's designee, to the Attorney General of the United States, or to the officer or agency. FRCP 15(c)(2).

d. *Effect of an amended pleading.* A pleading that has been amended under FRCP 15(a) supersedes the pleading it modifies and remains in effect throughout the action unless it subsequently is modified. FPP § 1476. Once an amended pleading is interposed, the original pleading no longer performs any function in the case and any subsequent motion made by an opposing party should be directed at the amended pleading. FPP § 1476; Ferdik v. Bonzelet, 963 F.2d 1258, 1262 (9th Cir. 1992); Davis v. TXO Production Corp., 929 F.2d 1515, 1517 (10th Cir. 1991).

5. *Opposing papers.* The Federal Rules of Civil Procedure do not require any formal answer, return, or reply to a motion, except where the Federal Rules of Civil Procedure or local rules may require affidavits, memoranda, or other papers to be filed in opposition to a motion. Such papers are simply to apprise the court of such opposition and the grounds of that opposition. FEDPROC § 62:359.

   a. *Effect of failure to respond to motion.* Although in the absence of statutory provision or court rule, a motion ordinarily does not require a written answer, when a party files a motion and the opposing party fails to respond, the court may construe such failure to respond as nonopposition to the motion or an admission that the motion was meritorious, may take the facts alleged in the motion as true—the rule in some jurisdictions being that the failure to respond to a fact set forth in a motion is deemed an admission—and may grant the motion if the relief requested appears to be justified. AMJUR MOTIONS § 28.

   b. *Assent or no opposition not determinative.* However, a motion will not be granted automatically simply because an "assent" or a notation of "no opposition" has been filed; federal judges frequently deny motions that have been assented to when it is thought that justice so dictates. FPP § 1190.

   c. *Responsive pleading inappropriate as response to motion.* An attempt to answer or oppose a motion with a responsive pleading usually is not appropriate. FPP § 1190.

6. *Reply papers.* A moving party may be required or permitted to prepare papers in addition to his original motion papers. AMJUR MOTIONS § 25. Papers answering or replying to opposing papers may be appropriate, in the interests of justice, where it appears there is a substantial reason for allowing a reply. Thus, a court may accept reply papers where a party demonstrates that the papers to which it seeks to file a reply raise new issues that are material to the disposition of the question before the court, or where the court determines, sua sponte, that it wishes further briefing of an issue raised in those papers and orders the submission of additional papers. FEDPROC § 62:360.

   a. *Function of reply papers.* The function of a reply affidavit is to answer the arguments made in opposition to the position taken by the movant and not to permit the movant to introduce new arguments in support of the motion. AMJUR MOTIONS § 25.

   b. *Issues raised for the first time in a reply document.* However, the view has been followed in some jurisdictions, that as a matter of judicial economy, where there is no prejudice and where the issues could be raised simply by filing a motion to dismiss, the trial court has discretion to consider arguments raised for the first time in a reply memorandum, and that a trial court may grant a motion to strike issues raised for the first time in a reply memorandum. AMJUR MOTIONS § 26.

7. *Appearances.* Every attorney who represents a party or who files a document on a party's behalf must file an appearance for that party. IN R USDCTSD L.R. 83-7. The filing of a Notice of Appearance shall act to establish the filing attorney as an attorney of record representing a designated party or parties in a particular cause of action. As a result, it is necessary for each attorney to file a separate Notice of Appearance when entering an appearance in a case. A joint appearance on behalf of multiple attorneys may be filed electronically only if it is filed separately for each attorney, using his/her ECF login. IN R USDCTSD ECF Procedures(12). Only those attorneys who have filed an appearance in a pending action are entitled to be served with case documents under FRCP 5(a). IN R USDCTSD L.R. 83-7. For more information, refer to IN R USDCTSD L.R. 83-7 and IN R USDCTSD ECF Procedures(12).

8. *Notice of related action.* A party must file a notice of related action: as soon as it appears that the party's case and another pending case: (1) arise out of the same transaction or occurrence; (2) involve the same property; or (3) involve the validity or infringement or the same patent, trademark, or copyright. IN R USDCTSD L.R. 40-1(d)(2). For more information, refer to IN R USDCTSD L.R. 40-1.

9. *Alternative dispute resolution (ADR)*

   a. *Application.* Unless limited by specific provisions, or unless there are other applicable specific statutory, common law, or constitutional procedures, the Local Alternative Dispute Resolution Rules of the United States District Court for the Southern District of Indiana shall apply in all civil litigation filed in the U.S. District Court for the Southern District of Indiana, except in the following cases and proceedings:

      i. Applications for writs of habeas corpus under 28 U.S.C.A. § 2254;

     ii.   Forfeiture cases;

     iii.   Non-adversary proceedings in bankruptcy;

     iv.   Social Security administrative review cases; and

     v.   Such other matters as specified by order of the Court; for example, matters involving important public policy issues, constitutional law, or the establishment of new law. IN R USDCTSD A.D.R. Rule 1.2.

b.   *Mediation.* Mediation under this section (IN R USDCTSD A.D.R. Rule 2.1, et seq.) involves the confidential process by which a person acting as a Mediator, selected by the parties or appointed by the Court, assists the litigants in reaching a mutually acceptable agreement. It is an informal and nonadversarial process. The role of the Mediator is to assist in identifying the issues, reducing misunderstandings, clarifying priorities, exploring areas of compromise, and finding points of agreement as well as legitimate points of disagreement. Final decision-making authority rests with the parties, not the Mediator. IN R USDCTSD A.D.R. Rule 2.1. It is anticipated that an agreement may not resolve all of the disputed issues, but the process, nonetheless, can reduce points of contention. Parties and their representatives are required to mediate in good faith, but are not compelled to reach an agreement. IN R USDCTSD A.D.R. Rule 2.1.

     i.   *Case selection.* The Court with the agreement of the parties may refer a civil case for mediation. Unless otherwise ordered or as specifically provided in IN R USDCTSD A.D.R. Rule 2.8, referral to mediation does not abate or suspend the action, and no scheduled dates shall be delayed or deferred, including the date of trial. IN R USDCTSD A.D.R. Rule 2.2.

     ii.   For more information on mediation, refer to IN R USDCTSD A.D.R. Rule 2.1, et seq.

c.   *Other methods of dispute resolution.* The Local Alternative Dispute Resolution Rules of the United States District Court for the Southern District of Indiana shall not preclude the parties from utilizing any other reasonable method or technique of alternative dispute resolution to resolve disputes to which the parties agree. However, any use of arbitration by the parties will be governed by and comply with the requirements of 28 U.S.C.A. § 654 through 28 U.S.C.A. § 657. IN R USDCTSD A.D.R. Rule 1.5.

d.   For more information on alternative dispute resolution (ADR), refer to IN R USDCTSD A.D.R. Rule 1.1, et seq.

10.   *Notice of settlement or resolution.* The parties must immediately notify the court if they reasonably anticipate settling their case or resolving a pending motion. IN R USDCTSD L.R. 7-1(h).

11.   *Modification or suspension of rules.* The court may, on its own motion or at the request of a party, suspend or modify any rule in a particular case in the interest of justice. IN R USDCTSD L.R. 1-1(c).

D. Documents

1.   *Documents for moving party*

   a.   *Required documents*

     i.   *Notice of motion and motion.* [P]rior to filing any non-dispositive motion (including motions for extension of time), the moving party must contact opposing counsel to determine whether there is an objection to any non-dispositive motion (including motions for extension of time), and state in the motion whether opposing counsel objects to the motion. If an objection cannot be resolved by counsel, the opposing counsel's position shall be stated within the motion. The motion should also indicate whether opposing counsel plans to file a written objection to the motion and the date by which the Court can expect to receive the objection (within the time limits set in IN R USDCTSD L.R. 7-1). If after a reasonable effort, opposing counsel cannot be reached, the moving party shall recite in the motion the dates and times that messages were left for opposing counsel. IN R USDCTSD Case Mgt(General Instructions For All Cases). Refer to the General Requirements section of this document for information on the notice of motion and motion.

     ii.   *Proposed amended pleading.* A motion to amend a pleading must: (1) if it is filed electronically, include as attachments the signed proposed amended pleading and a proposed order; or (2) if it is filed directly with the clerk, be accompanied by a proposed order and one (1) signed original and one (1) copy of the proposed amended pleading. IN R USDCTSD L.R. 15-1(a). Amendments to a pleading must reproduce the entire pleading as amended. IN R USDCTSD L.R. 15-1(b). In order to satisfy the prerequisites of FRCP 7(b), a copy of the amendment should be submitted with the motion so that the court and the adverse party know the precise nature of the pleading changes being proposed. FPP § 1485. The amending party should submit a copy of the proposed amendment at least by the date of the hearing on the motion for leave to amend. FEDPROC § 62:274; Grombach v. Oerlikon Tool & Arms Corp. of America, 276 F.2d 155 (4th Cir. 1960).

- The documents accompanying the motion for leave to amend may be an appropriate substitute for a formally proposed amendment, if the documents sufficiently indicate the gist of the amendment. FEDPROC § 62:274.

iii. *Proposed order.* A motion to amend a pleading must: (1) if it is filed electronically, include as attachments the signed proposed amended pleading and a proposed order; or (2) if it is filed directly with the clerk, be accompanied by a proposed order and one (1) signed original and one (1) copy of the proposed amended pleading. IN R USDCTSD L.R. 15-1(a). A party must include a suitable form of order with any document that requests the judge or the clerk to enter a routine or uncontested order. IN R USDCTSD L.R. 5-5(b); IN R USDCTSD L.R. 5-10(c); IN R USDCTSD L.R. 7-1(d).

- A service statement and/or list must be included on each proposed order, as required by IN R USDCTSD L.R. 5-5(d). IN R USDCTSD ECF Procedures(11). Any pleading, motion, brief, affidavit, notice, or proposed order filed with the court, whether electronically or with the clerk, must: if it is a form of order, include a statement of service, in the format required by IN R USDCTSD L.R. 5-5(d) in the lower left corner of the document. IN R USDCTSD L.R. 5-1(b).

- A party electronically filing a proposed order—whether voluntarily or because required by IN R USDCTSD L.R. 5-5—must convert the order directly from a word processing program and file it as an attachment to the document it relates to. Proposed orders must include in the lower left-hand corner of the signature page a statement that service will be made electronically on all ECF-registered counsel of record via email generated by the court's ECF system, without listing all such counsel. A service list including the name and postal address of any pro se litigant or non-registered attorney of record must follow, stating that service on the listed individuals will be made in the traditional paper manner, via first-class U.S. Mail. IN R USDCTSD L.R. 5-5(d).

iv. *Certificate of service.* FRCP 5(d) requires that the person making service under FRCP 5 certify that service has been effected. FRCP 5(Advisory Committee Notes). Having such information on file may be useful for many purposes, including proof of service if an issue arises concerning the effectiveness of the service. FRCP 5(Advisory Committee Notes).

- *Certificate of service for electronically-filed documents.* A certificate of service must be included with all documents filed electronically. Such certificate shall indicate that service was accomplished pursuant to the Court's electronic filing procedures. IN R USDCTSD ECF Procedures(11). For the suggested format for a certificate of service for electronic filing, refer to IN R USDCTSD ECF Procedures(11).

b. *Supplemental documents*

i. *Brief.* Refer to the Format section of this document for the format of briefs.

ii. *Supporting evidence.* When a motion relies on facts outside the record, the court may hear the matter on affidavits or may hear it wholly or partly on oral testimony or on depositions. FRCP 43(c).

- *Materials necessary for motion.* A party seeking relief under FRCP 26(c) or FRCP 37, or by way of a pretrial motion that could result in a final order on an issue, must file with the motion those parts of the discovery materials relevant to the motion. IN R USDCTSD L.R. 26-2(a).

iii. *Notice of constitutional question.* A party that files a pleading, written motion, or other paper drawing into question the constitutionality of a federal or state statute must promptly:

- *File notice.* File a notice of constitutional question stating the question and identifying the paper that raises it, if: (1) a federal statute is questioned and the parties do not include the United States, one of its agencies, or one of its officers or employees in an official capacity; or (2) a state statute is questioned and the parties do not include the state, one of its agencies, or one of its officers or employees in an official capacity; and

- *Serve notice.* Serve the notice and paper on the Attorney General of the United States if a federal statute is questioned—or on the state attorney general if a state statute is questioned—either by certified or registered mail or by sending it to an electronic address designated by the attorney general for this purpose. FRCP 5.1(a).

- *Time for filing.* A notice of constitutional challenge to a statute filed in accordance with FRCP 5.1 must be filed at the same time the parties tender their proposed case management plan, if one is required, or within twenty-one (21) days of the filing drawing into question the constitutionality of a federal or state statute, whichever occurs later. IN R USDCTSD L.R. 5.1-1(a).

- *Additional service requirements.* If a federal statute is challenged, in addition to the service requirements of FRCP 5.1(a), the party filing the notice of constitutional challenge must serve the notice and documents on the United States Attorney for the Southern District of Indiana, either by certified or registered mail or by sending it to an electronic address designated for that purpose by that official. IN R USDCTSD L.R. 5.1-1(b).

- *No forfeiture.* A party's failure to file and serve the notice, or the court's failure to certify, does not forfeit a constitutional claim or defense that is otherwise timely asserted. FRCP 5.1(d).

iv. *Index of exhibits.* Any pleading, motion, brief, affidavit, notice, or proposed order filed with the court, whether electronically or with the clerk, must: if it has four (4) or more exhibits, include a separate index that identifies and briefly describes each exhibit. IN R USDCTSD L.R. 5-1(b).

v. *Request for oral argument.* A party may request oral argument by filing a separate motion explaining why oral argument is necessary and estimating how long the court should allow for the argument. The request must be filed and served with the supporting brief, response brief, or reply brief. IN R USDCTSD L.R. 7-5(a).

vi. *Request for evidentiary hearing.* A party may request an evidentiary hearing on a motion or petition by serving and filing a separate motion explaining why the hearing is necessary and estimating how long the court should allow for the hearing. IN R USDCTSD L.R. 7-5(c).

vii. *Copy of authority.* Generally, copies of cited authorities may not be attached to court filings. However, a party must attach to the party's motion or brief a copy of any cited authority if it is not available on Westlaw or Lexis. Upon request, a party must provide copies of any cited authority that is only available through electronic means to the court or the other parties. IN R USDCTSD L.R. 7-1(f).

viii. *Copy of document with self-address envelope.* To receive a file-stamped copy of a document filed directly with the clerk, a party must include with the original document an additional copy and a self-addressed envelope. The envelope must be big enough to hold the copy and have enough postage on it to send the copy via regular first-class mail. IN R USDCTSD L.R. 5-10(b).

ix. *Notice of manual filing.* When a party who is not exempt from the electronic filing requirement files a document directly with the clerk, the party must: electronically file a notice of manual filing that explains why the document cannot be filed electronically. IN R USDCTSD L.R. 5-2(d)(1). Refer to the Filing and Service Requirements section of this document for more information.

- Where an individual component cannot be included in an electronic filing (e.g. the component cannot be converted to electronic format), the filer shall electronically file the prescribed Notice of Manual Filing in place of that component. A model form is provided as Appendix C (IN R USDCTSD ECF Procedures(Appendix C)). IN R USDCTSD ECF Procedures(13).

- Before making a manual filing of a component, the filing party shall first electronically file a Notice of Manual Filing (See IN R USDCTSD ECF Procedures(Appendix C)). The filer shall initiate the electronic filing process as if filing the actual component but shall instead attach to the filing the Notice of Manual Filing setting forth the reason(s) why the component cannot be filed electronically. The manual filing should be accompanied by a copy of the previously filed Notice of Manual Filing. A party may seek to have a component excluded from electronic filing pursuant to applicable Federal and Local Rules (e.g., FRCP 26(c)). IN R USDCTSD ECF Procedures(15).

x. *Courtesy copies.* District Judges and Magistrate Judges regularly receive documents filed by all parties. Therefore, parties shall not bring "courtesy copies" to any chambers unless specifically directed to do so by the Court. IN R USDCTSD Case Mgt(General Instructions For All Cases).

xi. *Copies for three-judge court.* Parties in a case where a three-judge court has been requested must file an original and three copies of any document filed directly with the clerk (instead of electronically) until the court: (1) denies the request; (2) dissolves the three-judge court; or (3) allows the parties to file fewer copies. IN R USDCTSD L.R. 9-2(c).

xii. *Declaration that party was unable to file in a timely manner due to technical difficulties.* If a party misses a filing deadline due to an inability to file electronically, the party may submit the untimely filed document, accompanied by a declaration stating the reason(s) for missing the deadline. IN R USDCTSD ECF Procedures(16). A model form is provided as Appendix D (IN R USDCTSD ECF Procedures(Appendix D)). IN R USDCTSD ECF Procedures(16).

2. *Documents for opposing party*

a. *Required documents*

i. *Response brief.* Refer to the Format section of this document for the format of briefs. Refer to the General Requirements section of this document for information on the opposing papers.

ii. *Certificate of service.* FRCP 5(d) requires that the person making service under FRCP 5 certify that service has been effected. FRCP 5(Advisory Committee Notes). Having such information on file may be useful for many purposes, including proof of service if an issue arises concerning the effectiveness of the service. FRCP 5(Advisory Committee Notes).

- *Certificate of service for electronically-filed documents.* A certificate of service must be included with all documents filed electronically. Such certificate shall indicate that service was accomplished pursuant to the Court's electronic filing procedures. IN R USDCTSD ECF Procedures(11). For the suggested format for a certificate of service for electronic filing, refer to IN R USDCTSD ECF Procedures(11).

b. *Supplemental documents*

i. *Supporting evidence.* When a motion relies on facts outside the record, the court may hear the matter on affidavits or may hear it wholly or partly on oral testimony or on depositions. FRCP 43(c).

- *Materials necessary for motion.* A party seeking relief under FRCP 26(c) or FRCP 37, or by way of a pretrial motion that could result in a final order on an issue, must file with the motion those parts of the discovery materials relevant to the motion. IN R USDCTSD L.R. 26-2(a).

ii. *Notice of constitutional question.* A party that files a pleading, written motion, or other paper drawing into question the constitutionality of a federal or state statute must promptly:

- *File notice.* File a notice of constitutional question stating the question and identifying the paper that raises it, if: (1) a federal statute is questioned and the parties do not include the United States, one of its agencies, or one of its officers or employees in an official capacity; or (2) a state statute is questioned and the parties do not include the state, one of its agencies, or one of its officers or employees in an official capacity; and

- *Serve notice.* Serve the notice and paper on the Attorney General of the United States if a federal statute is questioned—or on the state attorney general if a state statute is questioned—either by certified or registered mail or by sending it to an electronic address designated by the attorney general for this purpose. FRCP 5.1(a).

- *Time for filing.* A notice of constitutional challenge to a statute filed in accordance with FRCP 5.1 must be filed at the same time the parties tender their proposed case management plan, if one is required, or within twenty-one (21) days of the filing drawing into question the constitutionality of a federal or state statute, whichever occurs later. IN R USDCTSD L.R. 5.1-1(a).

- *Additional service requirements.* If a federal statute is challenged, in addition to the service requirements of FRCP 5.1(a), the party filing the notice of constitutional challenge must serve the notice and documents on the United States Attorney for the Southern District of Indiana, either by certified or registered mail or by sending it to an electronic address designated for that purpose by that official. IN R USDCTSD L.R. 5.1-1(b).

- *No forfeiture.* A party's failure to file and serve the notice, or the court's failure to certify, does not forfeit a constitutional claim or defense that is otherwise timely asserted. FRCP 5.1(d).

iii. *Index of exhibits.* Any pleading, motion, brief, affidavit, notice, or proposed order filed with the court, whether electronically or with the clerk, must: if it has four (4) or more exhibits, include a separate index that identifies and briefly describes each exhibit. IN R USDCTSD L.R. 5-1(b).

iv. *Request for oral argument.* A party may request oral argument by filing a separate motion explaining why oral argument is necessary and estimating how long the court should allow for the argument. The request must be filed and served with the supporting brief, response brief, or reply brief. IN R USDCTSD L.R. 7-5(a).

v. *Request for evidentiary hearing.* A party may request an evidentiary hearing on a motion or petition by serving and filing a separate motion explaining why the hearing is necessary and estimating how long the court should allow for the hearing. IN R USDCTSD L.R. 7-5(c).

vi. *Copy of authority.* Generally, copies of cited authorities may not be attached to court filings. However, a party must attach to the party's motion or brief a copy of any cited authority if it is not available on Westlaw or Lexis. Upon request, a party must provide copies of any cited authority that is only available through electronic means to the court or the other parties. IN R USDCTSD L.R. 7-1(f).

vii. *Copy of document with self-address envelope.* To receive a file-stamped copy of a document filed directly with the clerk, a party must include with the original document an additional copy and a self-addressed envelope. The envelope must be big enough to hold the copy and have enough postage on it to send the copy via regular first-class mail. IN R USDCTSD L.R. 5-10(b).

viii. *Notice of manual filing.* When a party who is not exempt from the electronic filing requirement files a document directly with the clerk, the party must: electronically file a notice of manual filing that explains why the document cannot be filed electronically. IN R USDCTSD L.R. 5-2(d)(1). Refer to the Filing and Service Requirements section of this document for more information.

- Where an individual component cannot be included in an electronic filing (e.g. the component cannot be converted to electronic format), the filer shall electronically file the prescribed Notice of Manual Filing in place of that component. A model form is provided as Appendix C (IN R USDCTSD ECF Procedures(Appendix C)). IN R USDCTSD ECF Procedures(13).

- Before making a manual filing of a component, the filing party shall first electronically file a Notice of Manual Filing (See IN R USDCTSD ECF Procedures(Appendix C)). The filer shall initiate the electronic filing process as if filing the actual component but shall instead attach to the filing the Notice of Manual Filing setting forth the reason(s) why the component cannot be filed electronically. The manual filing should be accompanied by a copy of the previously filed Notice of Manual Filing. A party may seek to have a component excluded from electronic filing pursuant to applicable Federal and Local Rules (e.g., FRCP 26(c)). IN R USDCTSD ECF Procedures(15).

ix. *Courtesy copies.* District Judges and Magistrate Judges regularly receive documents filed by all parties. Therefore, parties shall not bring "courtesy copies" to any chambers unless specifically directed to do so by the Court. IN R USDCTSD Case Mgt(General Instructions For All Cases).

x. *Copies for three-judge court.* Parties in a case where a three-judge court has been requested must file an original and three copies of any document filed directly with the clerk (instead of electronically) until the court: (1) denies the request; (2) dissolves the three-judge court; or (3) allows the parties to file fewer copies. IN R USDCTSD L.R. 9-2(c).

xi. *Declaration that party was unable to file in a timely manner due to technical difficulties.* If a party misses a filing deadline due to an inability to file electronically, the party may submit the untimely filed document, accompanied by a declaration stating the reason(s) for missing the deadline. IN R USDCTSD ECF Procedures(16). A model form is provided as Appendix D (IN R USDCTSD ECF Procedures(Appendix D)). IN R USDCTSD ECF Procedures(16).

E. Format

1. *Form of documents.* The rules governing captions and other matters of form in pleadings apply to motions and other papers. FRCP 7(b)(2).

   a. *Paper (manual filings only).* Any document that is not filed electronically must: be flat, unfolded, and on good-quality, eight and one-half by eleven (8-1/2 x 11) inch white paper. IN R USDCTSD L.R. 5-1(d)(1). Any document that is not filed electronically must: be single-sided. IN R USDCTSD L.R. 5-1(d)(1).

      i. *Covers or backing.* Any document that is not filed electronically must: not have a cover or a back. IN R USDCTSD L.R. 5-1(d)(1).

      ii. *Fastening.* Any document that is not filed electronically must: be (if consisting of more than one (1) page) fastened by paperclip or binder clip and may not be stapled. IN R USDCTSD L.R. 5-1(d)(1).

      - *Request for nonconforming fastening.* If a document cannot be fastened or bound as required by IN R USDCTSD L.R. 5-1(d), a party may ask the clerk for permission to fasten it in another manner. The party must make such a request before attempting to file the document with nonconforming fastening. IN R USDCTSD L.R. 5-1(d)(2).

      iii. *Hole punching.* Any document that is not filed electronically must: be two-hole punched at the top with the holes two and three-quarter (2-3/4) inches apart and appropriately centered. IN R USDCTSD L.R. 5-1(d)(1).

   b. *Margins.* Any pleading, motion, brief, affidavit, notice, or proposed order filed with the court, whether electronically or with the clerk, must: have at least one (1) inch margins. IN R USDCTSD L.R. 5-1(b).

   c. *Spacing.* Any pleading, motion, brief, affidavit, notice, or proposed order filed with the court, whether electronically or with the clerk, must: be double spaced (except for headings, footnotes, and quoted material). IN R USDCTSD L.R. 5-1(b).

   d. *Text.* Any pleading, motion, brief, affidavit, notice, or proposed order filed with the court, whether electronically or with the clerk, must: be plainly typewritten, printed, or prepared by a clearly legible copying process. IN R USDCTSD L.R. 5-1(b).

   e. *Font size.* Any pleading, motion, brief, affidavit, notice, or proposed order filed with the court, whether electronically or with the clerk, must: use at least 12-point type in the body of the document and at least 10-point type in footnotes. IN R USDCTSD L.R. 5-1(b).

   f. *Page numbering.* Any pleading, motion, brief, affidavit, notice, or proposed order filed with the court, whether electronically or with the clerk, must: have consecutively numbered pages. IN R USDCTSD L.R. 5-1(b).

   g. *Caption; Names of parties.* Every pleading must have a caption with the court's name, a title, a file number, and a FRCP 7(a) designation. The title of the complaint must name all the parties; the title of other pleadings, after naming the first party on each side, may refer generally to other parties. FRCP 10(a). Any pleading, motion, brief, affidavit, notice, or proposed order filed with the court, whether electronically or with the clerk, must: include a title on the first page. IN R USDCTSD L.R. 5-1(b).

    i. *Alternative motions.* Motions must be filed separately, but alternative motions may be filed in a single document if each is named in the title. IN R USDCTSD L.R. 7-1(a).

h. *Filer's information.* Any pleading, motion, brief, affidavit, notice, or proposed order filed with the court, whether electronically or with the clerk, must: in the case of pleadings, motions, legal briefs, and notices, include the name, complete address, telephone number, facsimile number (where available), and e-mail address (where available) of the pro se litigant or attorney who files it. IN R USDCTSD L.R. 5-1(b).

i. *Paragraphs; Separate statements.* A party must state its claims or defenses in numbered paragraphs, each limited as far as practicable to a single set of circumstances. A later pleading may refer by number to a paragraph in an earlier pleading. If doing so would promote clarity, each claim founded on a separate transaction or occurrence—and each defense other than a denial—must be stated in a separate count or defense. FRCP 10(b).

j. *Adoption by reference; Exhibits.* A statement in a pleading may be adopted by reference elsewhere in the same pleading or in any other pleading or motion. A copy of a written instrument that is an exhibit to a pleading is a part of the pleading for all purposes. FRCP 10(c).

k. *Citations*

    i. *Local rules.* The Local Rules of the United States District Court for the Southern District of Indiana may be cited as "S.D. Ind. L.R." IN R USDCTSD L.R. 1-1(a).

    ii. *Local alternative dispute resolution rules.* These Rules shall be known as the Local Alternative Dispute Resolution Rules of the United States District Court for the Southern District of Indiana. They shall be cited as "S.D.Ind. Local A.D.R. Rule _____." IN R USDCTSD A.D.R. Rule 1.1.

l. *Acceptance by the clerk.* The clerk must not refuse to file a paper solely because it is not in the form prescribed by the Federal Rules of Civil Procedure or by a local rule or practice. FRCP 5(d)(4). The clerk will accept a document that violates IN R USDCTSD L.R. 5-1, but the court may exclude the document from the official record. IN R USDCTSD L.R. 5-1(e).

    i. *Sanctions for errors as to form.* The court may strike from the record any document that does not comply with the rules governing the form of documents filed with the court, such as rules that regulate document size or the number of copies to be filed or that require a special designation in the caption. The court may also sanction an attorney or party who files a non-compliant document. IN R USDCTSD L.R. 1-3.

2. *Form of electronic documents.* Any document submitted via the court's electronic case filing (ECF) system must be: otherwise prepared and filed in a manner consistent with the CM/ECF Policies and Procedures Manual (IN R USDCTSD ECF Procedures). IN R USDCTSD L.R. 5-1(c). Electronically filed documents must meet the requirements of FRCP 10 (Form of Pleadings), IN R USDCTSD L.R. 5-1 (Format of Papers Presented for Filing), and FRCP 5.2 (Privacy Protection for Filings Made with the Court), as if they had been submitted on paper. Documents filed electronically are also subject to any page limitations set forth by Court Order, by IN R USDCTSD L.R. 7-1 (Motion Practice), or IN R USDCTSD L.R. 56-1 (Summary Judgment Practice), as applicable. IN R USDCTSD ECF Procedures(13).

a. *PDF format required.* Any document submitted via the court's electronic case filing (ECF) system must be: in .pdf format. IN R USDCTSD L.R. 5-1(c); IN R USDCTSD ECF Procedures(7). Any document submitted via the court's electronic case filing (ECF) system must be: converted to a .pdf file directly from a word processing program, unless it exists only in paper format (in which case it may be scanned to create a .pdf document). IN R USDCTSD L.R. 5-1(c); IN R USDCTSD ECF Procedures(13).

    i. An exhibit may be scanned into PDF format, at a recommended 300 dpi resolution or higher, only if it does not already exist in electronic format. The filing attorney is responsible for reviewing all PDF documents for legibility before submitting them through the Court's Electronic Case Filing system. For technical guidance in creating PDF documents, please contact the Clerk's Office. IN R USDCTSD ECF Procedures(13).

b. *File size limitations.* Any document submitted via the court's electronic case filing (ECF) system must be: submitted as one or more .pdf files that do not exceed ten megabytes (10 MB) each (consistent with the CM/ECF Policies and Procedures Manual (IN R USDCTSD ECF Procedures)). IN R USDCTSD L.R. 5-1(c); IN R USDCTSD ECF Procedures(13).

    i. To electronically file a document or attachment that exceeds ten megabytes (10 MB), the document must first be broken down into two or more smaller files. For example, if Exhibit A is a twelve megabyte (12 MB) PDF file, it should be divided into 2 equal parts prior to electronic filing. Each component part of the exhibit would be filed as an attachment to the main document and described appropriately as "Exhibit A (part 1 of 2)" and "Exhibit A (part 2 of 2)." IN R USDCTSD ECF Procedures(13).

    ii. The supporting items mentioned in IN R USDCTSD ECF Procedures(13) should not be confused with memorandums or briefs in support of motions as outlined in IN R USDCTSD L.R. 7-1 or IN R USDCTSD L.R. 56-1. These memorandums or briefs in support are to be filed as entirely separate documents pursuant to the appropriate rule. Additionally, no motion shall be embodied in the text of a response or reply brief/memorandum unless otherwise ordered by the Court. IN R USDCTSD ECF Procedures(13).

c. *Separate component parts.* A key objective of the electronic filing system is to ensure that as much of the case as possible is managed electronically. To facilitate electronic filing and retrieval, documents to be filed electronically are to be reasonably broken into their separate component parts. By way of example, most filings include a foundation document (e.g., motion) and other supporting items (e.g., exhibits, proposed orders, proposed amended pleadings). The foundation document, as well as the supporting items, are each separate components of the filing; supporting items must be filed as attachments to the foundation document. These exhibits or attachments should include only those excerpts of the referenced documents that are directly germane to the matter under consideration. IN R USDCTSD ECF Procedures(13).

    i. Where an individual component cannot be included in an electronic filing (e.g. the component cannot be converted to electronic format), the filer shall electronically file the prescribed Notice of Manual Filing in place of that component. A model form is provided as Appendix C (IN R USDCTSD ECF Procedures(Appendix C)). IN R USDCTSD ECF Procedures(13).

d. *Exhibits.* Each electronically filed exhibit to a main document must be: (1) created as a separate .pdf file; (2) submitted as an attachment to the main document and given a title which describes its content; and (3) limited to excerpts that are directly germane to the main document's subject matter. IN R USDCTSD L.R. 5-6(a).

    i. When uploading attachments during the electronic filing process, exhibits must be uploaded in a logical sequence and a brief description must be entered for each individual PDF file. The description must include not only the exhibit number or letter, but also a brief description of the document. This information may be entered in CM/ECF using a combination of the Category drop-down menu, the Description text box, or both (see IN R USDCTSD ECF Procedures(13)(Figure 1)). The information that is provided in each box will be combined to create a description of the document as it appears on the case docket (see IN R USDCTSD ECF Procedures(13)(Figure 2)). IN R USDCTSD ECF Procedures(13). For an example, refer to IN R USDCTSD ECF Procedures(13).

e. *Excerpts.* A party filing an exhibit that consists of excerpts from a larger document must clearly and prominently identify the exhibit as containing excerpted material. Either party will have the right to timely file additional excerpts or the complete document to the extent they are or become directly germane to the main document's subject matter. IN R USDCTSD L.R. 5-6(b).

f. For an example illustrating the application of IN R USDCTSD ECF Procedures(13), refer to IN R USDCTSD ECF Procedures(13).

3. *Form of briefs*

    a. *Page limits.* Supporting and response briefs (excluding tables of contents, tables of authorities, appendices, and certificates of service) may not exceed thirty-five (35) pages. Reply briefs may not exceed twenty (20) pages. IN R USDCTSD L.R. 7-1(e)(1).

        i. *Permission to exceed limits.* The court may allow a party to file a brief exceeding these page limits for extraordinary and compelling reasons. IN R USDCTSD L.R. 7-1(e)(2).

        ii. *Supporting and response briefs exceeding limits.* If the court allows a party to file a brief or response exceeding thirty-five (35) pages, the document must include:

- A table of contents with page references;

- A statement of issues; and

- A table of authorities including: (1) all cases (alphabetically arranged), statutes, and other authorities cited in the brief; and (2) page numbers where the authorities are cited in the brief. IN R USDCTSD L.R. 7-1(e)(3).

4. *Signing of pleadings, motions and other papers*

    a. *Signature.* Every pleading, written motion, and other paper must be signed by at least one attorney of record in the attorney's name—or by a party personally if the party is unrepresented. The paper must state the signer's address, e-mail address, and telephone number. FRCP 11(a).

        i. *Signatures on manual filings.* Any document that is not filed electronically must: include the original signature of the pro se litigant or attorney who files it. IN R USDCTSD L.R. 5-1(d)(1).

        ii. *Electronic signatures.* Use of the attorney's login and password when filing documents electronically serves in part as the attorney's signature for purposes of FRCP 11, the Local Rules of the United States District Court for the Southern District of Indiana, and any other purpose for which a signature is required in connection with proceedings before the Court. IN R USDCTSD ECF Procedures(14); IN R USDCTSD ECF Procedures(10). A pleading, motion, brief, or notice filed electronically under an attorney's ECF log-in and password must be signed by that attorney. IN R USDCTSD L.R. 5-7(a). A signature on a document other than a document filed as provided under IN R USDCTSD L.R. 5-7(a) must be an original handwritten signature and must be scanned into .pdf format for electronic filing. IN R USDCTSD L.R. 5-7(c); IN R USDCTSD ECF Procedures(14).

- *Form of electronic signature.* If a document is converted directly from a word processing application to .pdf (as opposed to scanning), the name of the Filing User under whose log-in and password the document is submitted must be preceded by a "s/" and typed on the signature line where the Filing User's handwritten signature would otherwise appear. IN R USDCTSD L.R. 5-7(b). All documents filed electronically shall include a signature block and include the filing attorney's typewritten name, address, telephone number, facsimile number and e-mail address. In addition, the name of the filing attorney under whose ECF login the document will be filed should be preceded by a "s/" and typed in the space where the attorney's handwritten signature would otherwise appear. IN R US-DCTSD ECF Procedures(14). For a sample format, refer to IN R USDCTSD ECF Procedures(14).

- *Effect of electronic signature.* Filing an electronically signed document under an attorney's ECF log-in and password constitutes the attorney's signature on the document under the Federal Rules of Civil Procedure, under the Local Rules of the United States District Court for the Southern District of Indiana, and for any other reason a signature is required in connection with the court's activities. IN R USDCTSD L.R. 5-7(d).

- *Documents with multiple attorneys' signatures.* Documents requiring signatures of more than one attorney shall be filed either by: (1) obtaining consent from the other attorney, then typing the "s/ [Name]" signature of the other attorney on the signature line where the other attorney's signature would otherwise appear; (2) identifying in the signature section the name of the other attorney whose signature is required and by the submission of a

Notice of Endorsement (see IN R USDCTSD ECF Procedures(Appendix B)) by the other attorney no later than three (3) business days after filing; (3) submitting a scanned document containing all handwritten signatures; or (4) in any other manner approved by the Court. IN R USDCTSD ECF Procedures(14); IN R USDCTSD L.R. 5-7(e).

iii. *No verification or accompanying affidavit required for pleadings.* Unless a rule or statute specifically states otherwise, a pleading need not be verified or accompanied by an affidavit. FRCP 11(a).

iv. *Unsigned papers.* The court must strike an unsigned paper unless the omission is promptly corrected after being called to the attorney's or party's attention. FRCP 11(a). The court will strike any document filed directly with the clerk that is not signed by an attorney of record or the pro se litigant filing it, but the court may do so only after giving the attorney or pro se litigant notice of the omission and reasonable time to correct it. Rubber-stamp or facsimile signatures are not original signatures and the court will deem documents containing them to be unsigned for purposes of FRCP 11 and FRCP 26(g) and IN R USDCTSD L.R. 5-10. IN R USDCTSD L.R. 5-10(g).

b. *Representations to the court.* By presenting to the court a pleading, written motion, or other paper—whether by signing, filing, submitting, or later advocating it—an attorney or unrepresented party certifies that to the best of the person's knowledge, information, and belief, formed after an inquiry reasonable under the circumstances:

i. It is not being presented for any improper purpose, such as to harass, cause unnecessary delay, or needlessly increase the cost of litigation;

ii. The claims, defenses, and other legal contentions are warranted by existing law or by a nonfrivolous argument for extending, modifying, or reversing existing law or for establishing new law;

iii. The factual contentions have evidentiary support or, if specifically so identified, will likely have evidentiary support after a reasonable opportunity for further investigation or discovery; and

iv. The denials of factual contentions are warranted on the evidence or, if specifically so identified, are reasonably based on belief or a lack of information. FRCP 11(b).

c. *Sanctions.* If, after notice and a reasonable opportunity to respond, the court determines that FRCP 11(b) has been violated, the court may impose an appropriate sanction on any attorney, law firm, or party that violated FRCP 11(b) or is responsible for the violation. FRCP 11(c)(1). Refer to the United States District Court for the Southern District of Indiana KeyRules Motion for Sanctions document for more information.

5. *Privacy protection for filings made with the court.* Electronically filed documents must meet the requirements of. . .FRCP 5.2 (Privacy Protection for Filings Made with the Court), as if they had been submitted on paper. IN R USDCTSD ECF Procedures(13).

a. *Redacted filings.* Unless the court orders otherwise, in an electronic or paper filing with the court that contains an individual's Social Security number, taxpayer-identification number, or birth date, the name of an individual known to be a minor, or a financial-account number, a party or nonparty making the filing may include only:

i. The last four (4) digits of the Social Security number and taxpayer-identification number;

ii. The year of the individual's birth;

iii. The minor's initials; and

iv. The last four (4) digits of the financial-account number. FRCP 5.2(a).

b. *Exemptions from the redaction requirement.* The redaction requirement does not apply to the following:

i. A financial-account number that identifies the property allegedly subject to forfeiture in a forfeiture proceeding;

ii. The record of an administrative or agency proceeding;

    iii.   The official record of a state-court proceeding;

    iv.   The record of a court or tribunal, if that record was not subject to the redaction requirement when originally filed;

    v.   A filing covered by FRCP 5.2(c) or FRCP 5.2(d); and

    vi.   A pro se filing in an action brought under 28 U.S.C.A. § 2241, 28 U.S.C.A. § 2254, or 28 U.S.C.A. § 2255. FRCP 5.2(b).

c.   *Limitations on remote access to electronic files; Social Security appeals and immigration cases.* Unless the court orders otherwise, in an action for benefits under the Social Security Act, and in an action or proceeding relating to an order of removal, to relief from removal, or to immigration benefits or detention, access to an electronic file is authorized as follows:

    i.   The parties and their attorneys may have remote electronic access to any part of the case file, including the administrative record;

    ii.   Any other person may have electronic access to the full record at the courthouse, but may have remote electronic access only to:

        • The docket maintained by the court; and

        • An opinion, order, judgment, or other disposition of the court, but not any other part of the case file or the administrative record. FRCP 5.2(c).

d.   *Filings made under seal.* The court may order that a filing be made under seal without redaction. The court may later unseal the filing or order the person who made the filing to file a redacted version for the public record. FRCP 5.2(d). For more information on filing under seal, refer to IN R USDCTSD L.R. 5-11 and IN R USDCTSD ECF Procedures(18).

e.   *Protective orders.* For good cause, the court may by order in a case:

    i.   Require redaction of additional information; or

    ii.   Limit or prohibit a nonparty's remote electronic access to a document filed with the court. FRCP 5.2(e).

f.   *Option for additional unredacted filing under seal.* A person making a redacted filing may also file an unredacted copy under seal. The court must retain the unredacted copy as part of the record. FRCP 5.2(f).

g.   *Option for filing a reference list.* A filing that contains redacted information may be filed together with a reference list that identifies each item of redacted information and specifies an appropriate identifier that uniquely corresponds to each item listed. The list must be filed under seal and may be amended as of right. Any reference in the case to a listed identifier will be construed to refer to the corresponding item of information. FRCP 5.2(g).

h.   *Waiver of protection of identifiers.* A person waives the protection of FRCP 5.2(a) as to the person's own information by filing it without redaction and not under seal. FRCP 5.2(h).

F. Filing and Service Requirements

1.   *Filing requirements.* Any paper after the complaint that is required to be served—together with a certificate of service—must be filed within a reasonable time after service. FRCP 5(d)(1). Motions must be filed separately, but alternative motions may be filed in a single document if each is named in the title. IN R USDCTSD L.R. 7-1(a).

    a.   *How filing is made; In general.* A paper is filed by delivering it:

        i.   To the clerk; or

        ii.   To a judge who agrees to accept it for filing, and who must then note the filing date on the paper and promptly send it to the clerk. FRCP 5(d)(2).

            • In certain instances, the court will direct the parties to submit items directly to chambers (e.g., confidential settlement statements). However, absent specific prior authorization, counsel and litigants should not submit letters or documents directly to chambers, and such materials should be filed with the clerk. IN R USDCTSD L.R. 5-1(Local Rules Advisory Committee Comment).

    iii.   A document or item submitted in relation to a matter within the court's jurisdiction is deemed filed upon delivery to the office of the clerk in a manner prescribed by the Local Rules of the United States District Court for the Southern District of Indiana or the Federal Rules of Civil Procedure or authorized by the court. Any submission directed to a Judge or Judge's staff, the office of the clerk or any employee thereof, in a manner that is not contemplated by IN R USDCTSD L.R. 5-1 and without prior court authorization is prohibited. IN R USDCTSD L.R. 5-1(a).

b.   *Non-electronic filing.* Any document that is exempt from electronic filing must be filed directly with the clerk and served on other parties in the case as required by those Federal Rules of Civil Procedure and Local Rules of the United States District Court for the Southern District of Indiana that apply to the service of non-electronic documents. IN R USDCTSD L.R. 5-2(c).

    i.   *When completed.* A document or other item that is not required to be filed electronically is deemed filed:

- Upon delivery in person, by courier, or via U.S. Mail or other mail delivery service to the clerk's office during business hours;
- When the courtroom deputy clerk accepts it, if the document or item is filed in open court; or
- Upon completion of any other manner of filing that the court authorizes. IN R USDCTSD L.R. 5-10(a).

    ii.   *Document filing by non-exempt party.* When a party who is not exempt from the electronic filing requirement files a document directly with the clerk, the party must:

- Electronically file a notice of manual filing that explains why the document cannot be filed electronically;
- Present the document to the clerk within one (1) business day after filing the notice of manual filing; and
- Present the clerk with a copy of the notice of manual filing when the party files the document with the clerk. IN R USDCTSD L.R. 5-2(d).

c.   *Electronic filing*

    i.   *Authorization of electronic filing program.* A court may, by local rule, allow papers to be filed, signed, or verified by electronic means that are consistent with any technical standards established by the Judicial Conference of the United States. A local rule may require electronic filing only if reasonable exceptions are allowed. A paper filed electronically in compliance with a local rule is a written paper for purposes of the Federal Rules of Civil Procedure. FRCP 5(d)(3).

- IN R USDCTSD L.R. 5-2 requires electronic filing, as allowed by FRCP 5(d)(3). The policies and procedures in IN R USDCTSD ECF Procedures govern electronic filing in this district unless, due to circumstances in a particular case, a judicial officer determines that these policies and procedures (IN R USDCTSD ECF Procedures) should be modified. IN R USDCTSD ECF Procedures(1).
- Unless modified by order of the Court, all Federal Rules of Civil Procedure and Local Rules of the United States District Court for the Southern District of Indiana shall continue to apply to cases maintained in the Court's Case Management/Electronic Case Filing System (CM/ECF). IN R USDCTSD ECF Procedures(3).

    ii.   *Mandatory electronic filing.* Unless exempted pursuant to IN R USDCTSD L.R. 5-3(e), attorneys admitted to the court's bar (including those admitted pro hac vice) or authorized to represent the United States must use the court's ECF system to file documents. IN R USDCTSD L.R. 5-3(a). Electronic filing by attorneys is required for eligible documents filed in civil and

criminal cases pending with the Court, unless specifically exempted by Local Rule or Court Order. IN R USDCTSD ECF Procedures(4).

- *Exceptions.* All civil cases (other than those cases the court specifically exempts) must be maintained in the court's electronic case filing (ECF) system. Accordingly, as allowed by FRCP 5(d)(3), every document filed in this court (including exhibits) must be transmitted to the clerk's office via the ECF system consistent with IN R USDCTSD L.R. 5-2 through IN R USDCTSD L.R. 5-11 except: (1) documents filed by pro se litigants; (2) transcripts in cases filed by claimants under the Social Security Act (and related statutes); (3) exhibits in a format that does not readily permit electronic filing (such as videos and large maps and charts); (4) documents that are illegible when scanned into .pdf format; (5) documents filed in cases not maintained on the ECF system; and (6) any other documents that the court or the Local Rules of the United States District Court for the Southern District of Indiana specifically allow to be filed directly with the clerk. IN R USDCTSD L.R. 5-2(a). Parties otherwise participating in the electronic filing system may be excused from filing a particular component electronically under certain limited circumstances, such as when the component cannot be reduced to an electronic format. Such components shall not be filed electronically, but instead shall be manually filed with the Clerk of Court and served upon the parties in accordance with the applicable Federal Rules of Civil Procedure and the Local Rules of the United States District Court for the Southern District of Indiana for filing and service of non-electronic documents. IN R USDCTSD ECF Procedures(15).

- *Exemption from participation.* The court may exempt attorneys from using the ECF system in a particular case for good cause. An attorney must file a petition for ECF exemption and a CM/ECF technical requirements exemption questionnaire in each case in which the attorney seeks an exemption. (The CM/ECF technical requirements exemption questionnaire is available on the court's website). IN R USDCTSD L.R. 5-3(e).

iii. *Consequences of electronic filing.* Electronic transmission of a document consistent with the procedures adopted by the Court shall, upon the complete receipt of the same by the Clerk of Court, constitute filing of the document for all purposes of the Federal Rules of Civil and Criminal Procedure and the Local Rules of the United States District Court for the Southern District of Indiana, and shall constitute entry of that document onto the docket maintained by the Clerk pursuant to FRCP 58 and FRCP 79. IN R USDCTSD ECF Procedures(7); IN R USDCTSD L.R. 5-4(c)(1). When a document has been filed electronically: the document, as filed, binds the filing party. IN R USDCTSD L.R. 5-4(c)(3).

- A Notice of Electronic Filing (NEF) acknowledging that the document has been filed will immediately appear on the filer's screen after the document has been submitted. Attorneys are strongly encouraged to print or electronically save a copy of the NEF. Attorneys can also verify the filing of documents by inspecting the Court's electronic docket sheet through the use of a PACER login. IN R USDCTSD ECF Procedures(7). When a document has been filed electronically: the notice of electronic filing for the document serves as the court's date-stamp and proof of filing. IN R USDCTSD L.R. 5-4(c)(4).

- The Court may, upon the motion of a party or upon its own motion, strike any inappropriately filed document. IN R USDCTSD ECF Procedures(7).

iv. For more information on electronic filing, refer to IN R USDCTSD ECF Procedures.

d. *Fax filing.* The clerk may not file a faxed document without court authorization. The court may not authorize the clerk to file faxed documents without finding that compelling circumstances justify it. A party must submit a copy of the document that otherwise complies with IN R USDCTSD L.R. 5-10 to replace the faxed copy within seven (7) days after faxing the document. IN R USDCTSD L.R. 5-10(e).

2. *Service requirements*

a. *Service; When required*

i. *In general.* Unless the Federal Rules of Civil Procedure provide otherwise, each of the following papers must be served on every party:

- An order stating that service is required;

- A pleading filed after the original complaint, unless the court orders otherwise under FRCP 5(c) because there are numerous defendants;
- A discovery paper required to be served on a party, unless the court orders otherwise;
- A written motion, except one that may be heard ex parte; and
- A written notice, appearance, demand, or offer of judgment, or any similar paper. FRCP 5(a)(1).

    ii.   *If a party fails to appear.* No service is required on a party who is in default for failing to appear. But a pleading that asserts a new claim for relief against such a party must be served on that party under FRCP 4. FRCP 5(a)(2).

    iii.   *Seizing property.* If an action is begun by seizing property and no person is or need be named as a defendant, any service required before the filing of an appearance, answer, or claim must be made on the person who had custody or possession of the property when it was seized. FRCP 5(a)(3).

  b. *Service; How made*

    i.   *Serving an attorney.* If a party is represented by an attorney, service under FRCP 5 must be made on the attorney unless the court orders service on the party. FRCP 5(b)(1).

    ii.   *Service in general.* A paper is served under FRCP 5 by:

- Handing it to the person;
- Leaving it: (1) at the person's office with a clerk or other person in charge or, if no one is in charge, in a conspicuous place in the office; or (2) if the person has no office or the office is closed, at the person's dwelling or usual place of abode with someone of suitable age and discretion who resides there;
- Mailing it to the person's last known address—in which event service is complete upon mailing;
- Leaving it with the court clerk if the person has no known address;
- Sending it by electronic means if the person consented in writing—in which event service is complete upon transmission, but is not effective if the serving party learns that it did not reach the person to be served; or
- Delivering it by any other means that the person consented to in writing—in which event service is complete when the person making service delivers it to the agency designated to make delivery. FRCP 5(b)(2).

    iii.   *Electronic service*

- *Consent.* By registering to use the ECF system, attorneys consent to electronic service of documents filed in cases maintained on the ECF system. IN R USDCTSD L.R. 5-3(d). By participating in the Electronic Case Filing Program, attorneys consent to the electronic service of documents, and shall make available electronic mail addresses for service. IN R USDCTSD ECF Procedures(11).

- *Service on registered parties.* Upon the filing of a document by a party, an e-mail message will be automatically generated by the electronic filing system and sent via electronic mail to the e-mail addresses of all registered attorneys who have appeared in the case. The Notice of Electronic Filing will contain a document hyperlink which will provide recipients with one "free look" at the electronically filed document. Recipients are encouraged to print and/or save a copy of the document during the "free look" to avoid incurring PACER charges for future viewings of the document. IN R USDCTSD ECF Procedures(11). When a document has been filed electronically: transmission of the notice of electronic filing generated by the ECF system to an attorney's e-mail address constitutes service of the document on that attorney. IN R USDCTSD L.R. 5-4(c)(5). The party effectuates service on all registered attorneys by filing electronically. IN R USDCTSD ECF Procedures(11). When a document has been filed electronically: no other attempted service will constitute electronic service of the document. IN R USDCTSD L.R. 5-4(c)(6).

- *Service on exempt parties.* A filer must serve a copy of the document consistent with FRCP 5 on any party or attorney who is exempt from participating in electronic filing. IN R USDCTSD L.R. 5-4(d). It is the responsibility of the filing attorney to conventionally serve all parties who do not receive electronic service (the identity of these parties will be indicated on the filing receipt generated by the ECF system). IN R USDCTSD ECF Procedures(11).

- *Service on parties excused from electronic filing.* Parties otherwise participating in the electronic filing system may be excused from filing a particular component electronically under certain limited circumstances, such as when the component cannot be reduced to an electronic format. Such components shall not be filed electronically, but instead shall be manually filed with the Clerk of Court and served upon the parties in accordance with the applicable Federal Rules of Civil Procedure and the Local Rules of the United States District Court for the Southern District of Indiana for filing and service of non-electronic documents. IN R USDCTSD ECF Procedures(15).

- *Service of exempt documents.* Any document that is exempt from electronic filing must be filed directly with the clerk and served on other parties in the case as required by those Federal Rules of Civil Procedure and Local Rules of the United States District Court for the Southern District of Indiana that apply to the service of non-electronic documents. IN R USDCTSD L.R. 5-2(c).

iv. *Using court facilities.* If a local rule so authorizes, a party may use the court's transmission facilities to make service under FRCP 5(b)(2)(E). FRCP 5(b)(3).

c. *Serving numerous defendants*

   i. *In general.* If an action involves an unusually large number of defendants, the court may, on motion or on its own, order that:

   - Defendants' pleadings and replies to them need not be served on other defendants;

   - Any crossclaim, counterclaim, avoidance, or affirmative defense in those pleadings and replies to them will be treated as denied or avoided by all other parties; and

   - Filing any such pleading and serving it on the plaintiff constitutes notice of the pleading to all parties. FRCP 5(c)(1).

   ii. *Notifying parties.* A copy of every such order must be served on the parties as the court directs. FRCP 5(c)(2).

G. Hearings

1. *Hearings, generally*

   a. *Oral argument.* Due process does not require that oral argument be permitted on a motion and, except as otherwise provided by local rule, the district court has discretion to determine whether it will decide the motion on the papers or hear argument by counsel (and perhaps receive evidence). FPP § 1190; F.D.I.C. v. Deglau, 207 F.3d 153 (3d Cir. 2000).

   i. *Request for oral argument.* A party may request oral argument by filing a separate motion explaining why oral argument is necessary and estimating how long the court should allow for the argument. IN R USDCTSD L.R. 7-5(a). Refer to the Documents section of this document for more information.

   ii. *No additional evidence at oral argument.* Parties may not present additional evidence at oral argument. IN R USDCTSD L.R. 7-5(b).

   b. *Providing a regular schedule for oral hearings.* A court may establish regular times and places for oral hearings on motions. FRCP 78(a).

   c. *Providing for submission on briefs.* By rule or order, the court may provide for submitting and determining motions on briefs, without oral hearings. FRCP 78(b).

   d. *Request for evidentiary hearing.* A party may request an evidentiary hearing on a motion or petition by serving and filing a separate motion explaining why the hearing is necessary and estimating how long the court should allow for the hearing. IN R USDCTSD L.R. 7-5(c).

e.   *Directed by the court.* The court may: (1) grant or deny a request for oral argument or an evidentiary hearing in its sole discretion; (2) set oral argument or an evidentiary hearing without a request from a party; and (3) order any oral argument or evidentiary hearing to be held anywhere within the district regardless of where the case will be tried. IN R USDCTSD L.R. 7-5(d).

2.   *Courtroom and courthouse decorum.* For information on courtroom and courthouse decorum, refer to IN R USDCTSD L.R. 83-3.

H.   Forms

1.   Federal Motion for Leave to Amend Forms

a.   Leave to amend complaint; Attaching copy of amendment. 2C FEDFORMS § 14:18.

b.   Leave to amend complaint; Inserting amendment. 2C FEDFORMS § 14:19.

c.   Leave to amend complaint; Interlineation. 2C FEDFORMS § 14:20.

d.   Leave to amend complaint; Responding to motion to dismiss complaint. 2C FEDFORMS § 14:21.

e.   Leave to amend complaint; Close to trial. 2C FEDFORMS § 14:22.

f.   Leave to amend complaint; Adding new count. 2C FEDFORMS § 14:24.

g.   Leave to amend complaint; Asserting lack of knowledge of facts at time of original complaint. 2C FEDFORMS § 14:25.

h.   Leave to amend complaint; Seeking fourth amendment. 2C FEDFORMS § 14:26.

i.   Leave to amend complaint; Substituting plaintiff and dropping defendant. 2C FEDFORMS § 14:27.

j.   Leave to amend answer. 2C FEDFORMS § 14:30.

k.   Leave to amend answer; With leave endorsed. 2C FEDFORMS § 14:31.

l.   Leave to amend answer; Correcting errors, deleting and interlining. 2C FEDFORMS § 14:32.

m.   Leave to amend answer; Adding paragraph. 2C FEDFORMS § 14:33.

n.   Leave to amend answer; Adding defense. 2C FEDFORMS § 14:34.

o.   Leave to amend answer; During trial. 2C FEDFORMS § 14:35.

p.   Defendant's response to motion for leave to amend complaint a fourth time. 2C FEDFORMS § 14:36.

q.   Motion and notice; For leave to file amended pleading. FEDPROF § 1:222.

r.   Motion; To amend pleading to conform to findings of master. FEDPROF § 1:223.

s.   Affidavit; In support of motion for amendment of pleading. FEDPROF § 1:230.

t.   Opposition; To motion; General form. FEDPROF § 1:750.

u.   Affidavit; Supporting or opposing motion. FEDPROF § 1:751.

v.   Brief; Supporting or opposing motion. FEDPROF § 1:752.

w.   Statement of points and authorities; Opposing motion. FEDPROF § 1:753.

x.   Motion for leave to amend pleading. GOLDLTGFMS § 14:3.

y.   Motion to file second amended complaint on ground of newly discovered evidence. GOLDLTGFMS § 14:20.

z.   Motion for leave to file amended answer. GOLDLTGFMS § 14:22.

2.   Forms for the Southern District of Indiana

a.   Notice of endorsement. IN R USDCTSD ECF Procedures(Appendix B).

b.   Notice of manual filing. IN R USDCTSD ECF Procedures(Appendix C).

c.   Declaration that party was unable to file in a timely manner due to technical difficulties. IN R USDCTSD ECF Procedures(Appendix D).

I. Applicable Rules

1. *Federal rules*

   a. Serving and filing pleadings and other papers. FRCP 5.

   b. Constitutional challenge to a statute; Notice, certification, and intervention. FRCP 5.1.

   c. Privacy protection for filings made with the court. FRCP 5.2.

   d. Computing and extending time; Time for motion papers. FRCP 6.

   e. Pleadings allowed; Form of motions and other papers. FRCP 7.

   f. Form of pleadings. FRCP 10.

   g. Signing pleadings, motions, and other papers; Representations to the court; Sanctions. FRCP 11.

   h. Amended and supplemental pleadings. FRCP 15.

   i. Taking testimony. FRCP 43.

   j. Hearing motions; Submission on briefs. FRCP 78.

2. *Local rules*

   a. Scope of the rules. IN R USDCTSD L.R. 1-1.

   b. Sanctions for errors as to form. IN R USDCTSD L.R. 1-3.

   c. Format of documents presented for filing. IN R USDCTSD L.R. 5-1.

   d. Constitutional challenge to a statute; Notice. IN R USDCTSD L.R. 5.1-1.

   e. Filing of documents electronically required. IN R USDCTSD L.R. 5-2.

   f. Eligibility, registration, passwords for electronic filing; Exemption from electronic filing. IN R USDCTSD L.R. 5-3.

   g. Timing and consequences of electronic filing. IN R USDCTSD L.R. 5-4.

   h. Attachments and exhibits in cases filed electronically. IN R USDCTSD L.R. 5-6.

   i. Signatures in cases filed electronically. IN R USDCTSD L.R. 5-7.

   j. Non-electronic filings. IN R USDCTSD L.R. 5-10.

   k. Motion practice. [IN R USDCTSD L.R. 7-1, as amended by IN ORDER 16-2319, effective December 1, 2016].

   l. Oral arguments and hearings. IN R USDCTSD L.R. 7-5.

   m. Request for three-judge court. IN R USDCTSD L.R. 9-2.

   n. Motions to amend pleadings. IN R USDCTSD L.R. 15-1.

   o. Filing of discovery materials. IN R USDCTSD L.R. 26-2.

   p. Assignment of cases. IN R USDCTSD L.R. 40-1.

   q. Alternative dispute resolution. IN R USDCTSD A.D.R. Rule 1.1; IN R USDCTSD A.D.R. Rule 1.2; IN R USDCTSD A.D.R. Rule 1.5; IN R USDCTSD A.D.R. Rule 2.1; IN R USDCTSD A.D.R. Rule 2.2.

   r. Instructions for preparing case management plan. IN R USDCTSD Case Mgt.

   s. Electronic case filing policies and procedures manual. IN R USDCTSD ECF Procedures.

Motions, Oppositions and Replies
Motion for Continuance/Extension of Time

Document Last Updated December 2016

A. Checklist

(I) ❑ Matters to be considered by moving party

    (a) ❑ Required documents

        (1) ❑ Notice of motion and motion

        (2) ❑ Certificate of service

    (b) ❑ Supplemental documents

        (1) ❑ Brief

        (2) ❑ Supporting evidence

        (3) ❑ Notice of constitutional question

        (4) ❑ Nongovernmental corporate disclosure statement

        (5) ❑ Index of exhibits

        (6) ❑ Request for oral argument

        (7) ❑ Request for evidentiary hearing

        (8) ❑ Copy of authority

        (9) ❑ Proposed order

        (10) ❑ Copy of document with self-address envelope

        (11) ❑ Notice of manual filing

        (12) ❑ Courtesy copies

        (13) ❑ Copies for three-judge court

        (14) ❑ Declaration that party was unable to file in a timely manner due to technical difficulties

    (c) ❑ Timing

        (1) ❑ Continuance: there are no specific timing requirements for moving for a continuance

        (2) ❑ Extension of time: when an act may or must be done within a specified time, the court may, for good cause, extend the time:

            (i) ❑ With or without motion or notice if the court acts, or if a request is made, before the original time or its extension expires; or

            (ii) ❑ On motion made after the time has expired if the party failed to act because of excusable neglect

        (3) ❑ A written motion and notice of the hearing must be served at least fourteen (14) days before the time specified for the hearing, with the following exceptions: (i) when the motion may be heard ex parte; (ii) when the Federal Rules of Civil Procedure set a different time; or (iii) when a court order—which a party may, for good cause, apply for ex parte—sets a different time

        (4) ❑ Any affidavit supporting a motion must be served with the motion

        (5) ❑ When a party who is not exempt from the electronic filing requirement files a document directly with the clerk, the party must present the document to the clerk within one (1) business day after filing the notice of manual filing

        (6) ❑ Unless the court orders otherwise, the [untimely] document and declaration [that party was unable to file in a timely manner due to technical difficulties] must be filed no later than 12:00 noon of the first day on which the court is open for business following the original filing deadline

(II)   ❑ Matters to be considered by opposing party

    (a)   ❑ Required documents

        (1)   ❑ Response brief

        (2)   ❑ Certificate of service

    (b)   ❑ Supplemental documents

        (1)   ❑ Supporting evidence

        (2)   ❑ Notice of constitutional question

        (3)   ❑ Index of exhibits

        (4)   ❑ Request for oral argument

        (5)   ❑ Request for evidentiary hearing

        (6)   ❑ Copy of authority

        (7)   ❑ Copy of document with self-address envelope

        (8)   ❑ Notice of manual filing

        (9)   ❑ Courtesy copies

        (10)   ❑ Copies for three-judge court

        (11)   ❑ Declaration that party was unable to file in a timely manner due to technical difficulties

    (c)   ❑ Timing

        (1)   ❑ Any response is due within fourteen (14) days after service of the motion

        (2)   ❑ Except as FRCP 59(c) provides otherwise, any opposing affidavit must be served at least seven (7) days before the hearing, unless the court permits service at another time

        (3)   ❑ When a party who is not exempt from the electronic filing requirement files a document directly with the clerk, the party must present the document to the clerk within one (1) business day after filing the notice of manual filing

        (4)   ❑ Unless the court orders otherwise, the [untimely] document and declaration [that party was unable to file in a timely manner due to technical difficulties] must be filed no later than 12:00 noon of the first day on which the court is open for business following the original filing deadline

B. Timing

1. *Motion for continuance/extension of time*

    a. *Continuance.* There are no specific timing requirements for moving for a continuance.

    b. *Extension of time.* When an act may or must be done within a specified time, the court may, for good cause, extend the time:

        i. With or without motion or notice if the court acts, or if a request is made, before the original time or its extension expires; or

        ii. On motion made after the time has expired if the party failed to act because of excusable neglect. FRCP 6(b)(1).

2. *Timing of motions, generally*

    a. *Motion and notice of hearing.* A written motion and notice of the hearing must be served at least fourteen (14) days before the time specified for the hearing, with the following exceptions:

        i. When the motion may be heard ex parte;

        ii. When the Federal Rules of Civil Procedure set a different time; or

        iii. When a court order—which a party may, for good cause, apply for ex parte—sets a different time. FRCP 6(c)(1).

    b. *Supporting affidavit.* Any affidavit supporting a motion must be served with the motion. FRCP 6(c)(2).

3. *Timing of opposing papers.* Any response is due within fourteen (14) days after service of the motion. IN R USDCTSD L.R. 7-1(c)(2)(A).

    a. *Opposing affidavit.* Except as FRCP 59(c) provides otherwise, any opposing affidavit must be served at least seven (7) days before the hearing, unless the court permits service at another time. FRCP 6(c)(2).

    b. *Extensions.* The court may extend response and reply deadlines, but only for good cause. IN R USDCTSD L.R. 7-1(c)(3).

    c. *Summary ruling on failure to respond.* The court may summarily rule on a motion if an opposing party does not file a response within the deadline. IN R USDCTSD L.R. 7-1(c)(4).

4. *Timing of reply papers.* Where the respondent files an answering affidavit setting up a new matter, the moving party ordinarily is allowed a reasonable time to file a reply affidavit since failure to deny the new matter by affidavit may operate as an admission of its truth. AMJUR MOTIONS § 25.

    a. *Reply brief.* Any reply is due within seven (7) days after service of the response. IN R USDCTSD L.R. 7-1(c)(2)(B).

    b. *Extensions.* The court may extend response and reply deadlines, but only for good cause. IN R USDCTSD L.R. 7-1(c)(3).

5. *Document filing by non-exempt party.* When a party who is not exempt from the electronic filing requirement files a document directly with the clerk, the party must: present the document to the clerk within one (1) business day after filing the notice of manual filing. IN R USDCTSD L.R. 5-2(d)(2).

6. *Declaration that party was unable to file in a timely manner due to technical difficulties.* Unless the Court orders otherwise, the [untimely] document and declaration [that party was unable to file in a timely manner due to technical difficulties] must be filed no later than 12:00 noon of the first day on which the Court is open for business following the original filing deadline. IN R USDCTSD ECF Procedures(16).

7. *Computation of time*

    a. *Computing time.* FRCP 6 applies in computing any time period specified in the Federal Rules of Civil Procedure, in any local rule or court order, or in any statute that does not specify a method of computing time. FRCP 6(a).

        i. *Period stated in days or a longer unit.* When the period is stated in days or a longer unit of time:

            • Exclude the day of the event that triggers the period;

            • Count every day, including intermediate Saturdays, Sundays, and legal holidays; and

            • Include the last day of the period, but if the last day is a Saturday, Sunday, or legal holiday, the period continues to run until the end of the next day that is not a Saturday, Sunday, or legal holiday. FRCP 6(a)(1).

        ii. *Period stated in hours.* When the period is stated in hours:

            • Begin counting immediately on the occurrence of the event that triggers the period;

            • Count every hour, including hours during intermediate Saturdays, Sundays, and legal holidays; and

            • If the period would end on a Saturday, Sunday, or legal holiday, the period continues to run until the same time on the next day that is not a Saturday, Sunday, or legal holiday. FRCP 6(a)(2).

        iii. *Inaccessibility of the clerk's office.* Unless the court orders otherwise, if the clerk's office is inaccessible:

            • On the last day for filing under FRCP 6(a)(1), then the time for filing is extended to the first accessible day that is not a Saturday, Sunday, or legal holiday; or

            • During the last hour for filing under FRCP 6(a)(2), then the time for filing is extended to the same time on the first accessible day that is not a Saturday, Sunday, or legal holiday. FRCP 6(a)(3).

iv. *"Last day" defined.* Unless a different time is set by a statute, local rule, or court order, the last day ends:

- For electronic filing, at midnight in the court's time zone; and

- For filing by other means, when the clerk's office is scheduled to close. FRCP 6(a)(4).

v. *"Next day" defined.* The "next day" is determined by continuing to count forward when the period is measured after an event and backward when measured before an event. FRCP 6(a)(5).

vi. *"Legal holiday" defined.* "Legal holiday" means:

- The day set aside by statute for observing New Year's Day, Martin Luther King Jr.'s Birthday, Washington's Birthday, Memorial Day, Independence Day, Labor Day, Columbus Day, Veterans' Day, Thanksgiving Day, or Christmas Day;

- Any day declared a holiday by the President or Congress; and

- For periods that are measured after an event, any other day declared a holiday by the state where the district court is located. FRCP 6(a)(6).

b. *Computation of electronic filing deadlines.* Filing documents electronically does not alter filing deadlines. IN R USDCTSD ECF Procedures(7). A document due on a particular day must be filed before midnight local time of the division where the case is pending. IN R USDCTSD L.R. 5-4(a). All electronic transmissions of documents must be completed (i.e. received completely by the Clerk's Office) prior to midnight of the local time of the division in which the case is pending in order to be considered timely filed that day (NOTE: time will be noted in Eastern Time on the Court's docket. If you have filed a document prior to midnight local time of the division in which the case is pending and the document is due that date, but the electronic receipt and docket reflect the following calendar day, please contact the Court). IN R USDCTSD ECF Procedures(7). Although attorneys may file documents electronically twenty-four (24) hours a day, seven (7) days a week, attorneys are encouraged to file all documents during the normal working hours of the Clerk's Office (Monday through Friday, 8:30 a.m. to 4:30 p.m.) when technical support is available. IN R USDCTSD ECF Procedures(7); IN R USDCTSD ECF Procedures(9).

i. *Technical difficulties.* Parties are encouraged to file documents electronically during normal business hours, in case a problem is encountered. In the event a technical failure occurs and a document cannot be filed electronically despite the best efforts of the filing party, the party should print (if possible) a copy of the error message received. In addition, as soon as practically possible, the party should file a "Declaration that Party was Unable to File in a Timely Manner Due to Technical Difficulties." A model form is provided as Appendix D (IN R USDCTSD ECF Procedures(Appendix D)). IN R USDCTSD ECF Procedures(16).

- If a party is unable to file electronically and, as a result, may miss a filing deadline, the party must contact the Clerk's Office at the number listed in IN R USDCTSD ECF Procedures(15) to inform the court's staff of the difficulty. If a party misses a filing deadline due to an inability to file electronically, the party may submit the untimely filed document, accompanied by a declaration stating the reason(s) for missing the deadline. Unless the Court orders otherwise, the document and declaration must be filed no later than 12:00 noon of the first day on which the Court is open for business following the original filing deadline. IN R USDCTSD ECF Procedures(16).

c. *Extending time.* Refer to the General Requirements section of this document for information on extending time.

d. *Additional time after certain kinds of service.* When a party may or must act within a specified time after being served and service is made under FRCP 5(b)(2)(C) (mail), FRCP 5(b)(2)(D) (leaving with the clerk), or FRCP 5(b)(2)(F) (other means consented to), three (3) days are added after the period would otherwise expire under FRCP 6(a). FRCP 6(d). Service by electronic mail shall constitute service pursuant to FRCP 5(b)(2)(E) and shall entitle the party being served to the additional three (3) days provided by FRCP 6(d). IN R USDCTSD ECF Procedures(11).

C. General Requirements

1. *Motions, generally*

   a. *Requirements.* A request for a court order must be made by motion. The motion must:

      i. Be in writing unless made during a hearing or trial;

      ii. State with particularity the grounds for seeking the order; and

      iii. State the relief sought. FRCP 7(b)(1).

   b. *Notice of motion.* A party interested in resisting the relief sought by a motion has a right to notice thereof, and an opportunity to be heard. AMJUR MOTIONS § 12.

      i. In addition to statutory or court rule provisions requiring notice of a motion—the purpose of such a notice requirement having been said to be to prevent a party from being prejudicially surprised by a motion—principles of natural justice dictate that an adverse party generally must be given notice that a motion will be presented to the court. AMJUR MOTIONS § 12.

      ii. "Notice," in this regard, means reasonable notice, including a meaningful opportunity to prepare and to defend against allegations of a motion. AMJUR MOTIONS § 12.

   c. *Writing requirement.* The writing requirement is intended to insure that the adverse parties are informed and have a record of both the motion's pendency and the grounds on which the movant seeks an order. FPP § 1191; Feldberg v. Quechee Lakes Corp., 463 F.3d 195 (2d Cir. 2006).

      i. It is sufficient "if the motion is stated in a written notice of the hearing of the motion." FPP § 1191.

   d. *Particularity requirement.* The particularity requirement insures that the opposing parties will have notice of their opponent's contentions. FEDPROC § 62:364; Goodman v. 1973 26 Foot Trojan Vessel, Arkansas Registration No. AR1439SN, 859 F.2d 71, 12 Fed.R.Serv.3d 645 (8th Cir. 1988). That requirement ensures that notice of the basis for the motion is provided to the court and to the opposing party so as to avoid prejudice, provide the opponent with a meaningful opportunity to respond, and provide the court with enough information to process the motion correctly. FEDPROC § 62:364; Andreas v. Volkswagen of America, Inc., 336 F.3d 789, 56 Fed.R.Serv.3d 6 (8th Cir. 2003).

      i. Reasonable specification of the grounds for a motion is sufficient. However, where a movant fails to state even one ground for granting the motion in question, the movant has failed to meet the minimal standard of "reasonable specification." FEDPROC § 62:364; Martinez v. Trainor, 556 F.2d 818, 23 Fed.R.Serv.2d 403 (7th Cir. 1977).

      ii. The court may excuse the failure to comply with the particularity requirement if it is inadvertent, and where no prejudice is shown by the opposing party. FEDPROC § 62:364.

   e. *Motions must be filed separately.* Motions must be filed separately, but alternative motions may be filed in a single document if each is named in the title. A motion must not be contained within a brief, response, or reply to a previously filed motion, unless ordered by the court. IN R USDCTSD L.R. 7-1(a).

   f. *Routine or uncontested motions.* The court may rule upon a routine or uncontested motion before the response deadline passes, unless: (1) the motion indicates that an opposing party objects to it; or (2) the court otherwise believes that a response will be filed. IN R USDCTSD L.R. 7-1(d).

2. *Informal conference to resolve disputes involving non-dispositive issues.* In addition to those conferences required by IN R USDCTSD L.R. 37-1, counsel are encouraged to hold informal conferences in person or by phone to resolve any disputes involving non-dispositive issues that may otherwise require submission of a motion to the Court. This requirement does not apply to cases involving pro se parties. Therefore, prior to filing any non-dispositive motion (including motions for extension of time), the moving party must contact opposing counsel to determine whether there is an objection to any non-dispositive motion (including motions for extension of time), and state in the motion whether opposing counsel objects to the motion. IN R USDCTSD Case Mgt(General Instructions For All Cases). Refer to the Documents section of this document for more information on the contents of the motion.

3. *Motion for continuance/extension of time*

   a. *Continuance.* The court may continue proceedings in a civil case on its own or on the motion of one or more parties. IN R USDCTSD L.R. 16-3(a). Attorneys must consult with their clients before asking the court to continue a trial. IN R USDCTSD L.R. 16-3(b). Absent a controlling statute, the grant or denial of a continuance rests in the discretion of the trial judge to whom application is made, taking into consideration not only the facts of the particular case but also all of the demands on counsel's time and the court's. FEDPROC § 77:28; Star Financial Services, Inc. v. AASTAR Mortg. Corp., 89 F.3d 5 (1st Cir. 1996); Streber v. Hunter, 221 F.3d 701, 55 Fed.R.Evid.Serv. 376 (5th Cir. 2000). The court may order a party seeking a continuance to reimburse other parties for their actual expenses caused by the delay. IN R USDCTSD L.R. 16-3(e). The grounds upon which a continuance is sought may include the following:

i. Unpreparedness of a party. FEDPROC § 77:29; U.S. v. 110 Bars of Silver, 3 Crucibles of Silver, 11 Bags of Silver Coins, 508 F.2d 799 (5th Cir. 1975).

ii. Absence of a party. FEDPROC § 77:29. Since it is generally recognized that a party to a civil action ordinarily has a right to attend the trial, an illness severe enough to prevent a party from appearing in court is always a legitimate ground for asking for a continuance. FEDPROC § 77:30; Davis v. Operation Amigo, Inc., 378 F.2d 101 (10th Cir. 1967). However, the failure of the moving party to produce any competent medical evidence of the reasons and necessities for the party's unavailability will result in the denial of the continuance. FEDPROC § 77:30; Weisman v. Alleco, Inc., 925 F.2d 77 (4th Cir. 1991). Some courts, moreover, require a showing that the party has some particular contribution to make to the trial as a material witness or otherwise before granting a continuance due to the party's illness. FEDPROC § 77:30; Johnston v. Harris County Flood Control Dist., 869 F.2d 1565 (5th Cir. 1989).

iii. Absence of counsel. FEDPROC § 77:29. The courts have shown greater leniency when the illness of counsel is the ground for the continuance, especially where the case presents complex issues. FEDPROC § 77:31; Smith-Weik Machinery Corp. v. Murdock Mach. & Engineering Co., 423 F.2d 842 (5th Cir. 1970). However, many courts do not favor the granting of a continuance where counsel is unavailable due to a claimed engagement elsewhere or where it is not clear that counsel's illness was genuine. FEDPROC § 77:31; Community Nat. Life Ins. Co. v. Parker Square Sav. & Loan Ass'n, 406 F.2d 603 (10th Cir. 1969); Williams v. Johanns, 518 F.Supp.2d 205 (D.D.C. 2007).

iv. Absence of a witness or evidence. FEDPROC § 77:29. The moving party must show. . .that the witness's testimony would be competent and material and that there are no other witnesses who can establish the same facts. FEDPROC § 77:32; Krodel v. Houghtaling, 468 F.2d 887 (4th Cir. 1972); Vitarelle v. Long Island R. Co., 415 F.2d 302 (2d Cir. 1969).

- *Stipulation to absent evidence.* The court may not continue a trial because evidence is unavailable if all parties stipulate to the content of the unavailable evidence. Despite the stipulation, the parties may contest the stipulated evidence as if it had been available at trial. IN R USDCTSD L.R. 16-3(d).

v. Surprise and prejudice. FEDPROC § 77:29. The action complained of should not be one which could have been anticipated by due diligence or of which the movant had actual notice. FEDPROC § 77:33; Communications Maintenance, Inc. v. Motorola, Inc., 761 F.2d 1202, 2 Fed.R.Serv.3d 126 (7th Cir. 1985). Surprise and prejudice are often claimed as a result of the court allowing the other party to amend its pleadings under FRCP 15(b). FEDPROC § 77:29.

vi. In determining whether to grant a continuance, the court will consider a variety of factors, including:

- Good faith on the part of the moving party;

- Due diligence of the moving party;

- The likelihood that the need prompting the request for a continuance will be met if the continuance is granted;

- Inconvenience to the court and the nonmoving party, including the witnesses, if the continuance is granted;

- Possible harm to the moving party if the continuance is denied;

- Prior delays in the proceedings;

- The court's prior refusal to grant the opposing party a continuance;

- Judicial economy. FEDPROC § 77:29; Amarin Plastics, Inc. v. Maryland Cup Corp., 946 F.2d 147, 34 Fed.R.Evid.Serv. 528 (1st Cir. 1991); Lewis v. Rawson, 564 F.3d 569 (2d Cir. 2009); U.S. v. 2.61 Acres of Land, More or Less, Situated in Mariposa County, State of Cal., 791 F.2d 666 (9th Cir. 1985); In re Homestore.com, Inc. Securities Litigation, 347 F.Supp.2d 814 (C.D.Cal. 2004).

b. *Extension of time.* Ordinarily, a request for an extension of time not made in open court or at a conference must: (1) be made by written motion; (2) state the original deadline and the requested deadline; (3) provide the reasons why an extension is requested; and (4) if all parties are represented by counsel, either: (A) state that there is no objection to the extension; or (B) describe all attempts made to obtain an agreement to the extension and state whether opposing counsel objects to it. IN R USDCTSD L.R. 6-1(a). When an act may or must be done within a specified time, the court may, for good cause, extend the time:

   i. *Before original time or its extension expires.* With or without motion or notice if the court acts, or if a request is made, before the original time or its extension expires. FRCP 6(b)(1)(A).

      - An application for the enlargement of time under FRCP 6(b)(1)(A) normally will be granted in the absence of bad faith on the part of the party seeking relief or prejudice to the adverse party. FPP § 1165.

      - Neither a formal motion for enlargement nor notice to the adverse party is expressly required by FRCP 6(b). FPP § 1165.

   ii. *After the time has expired.* On motion made after the time has expired if the party failed to act because of excusable neglect. FRCP 6(b)(1)(B).

      - *Excusable neglect.* Excusable neglect is intended and has proven to be quite elastic in its application. In essence it is an equitable concept that must take account of all relevant circumstances of the party's failure to act within the required time. FPP § 1165.

      - *Burden.* The burden is on the movant to establish that the failure to act in a timely manner was the result of excusable neglect. FEDPROC § 77:5. Common sense indicates that among the most important factors are the possibility of prejudice to the other parties, the length of the applicant's delay and its impact on the proceeding, the reason for the delay and whether it was within the control of the movant, and whether the movant has acted in good faith. FPP § 1165; Kettle Range Conservation Group v. U.S. Forest Service, 8 Fed.Appx. 729 (9th Cir. 2001).

      - *Motion required.* No relief may be granted under FRCP 6(b)(1)(B) after the expiration of the specified period, even though the failure to act may have been the result of excusable neglect, if no motion is made by the party who failed to act. FEDPROC § 77:3.

   iii. *Exceptions.* A court must not extend the time to act under FRCP 50(b), FRCP 50(d), FRCP 52(b), FRCP 59(b), FRCP 59(d), FRCP 59(e), and FRCP 60(b). FRCP 6(b)(2). FRCP 6(b) does not require the district courts to extend a time period where the extension would contravene a local court rule and does not apply to periods of time that are definitely fixed by statute. FEDPROC § 77:4; Truncale v. Universal Pictures Co., 82 F.Supp. 576 (S.D.N.Y. 1949); Lusk v. Lyon Metal Products, 9 F.R.D. 250 (W.D.Mo. 1949).

   iv. *Automatic initial extension.* The deadline for filing a response to a pleading or to any written request for discovery or admissions will automatically be extended upon filing a notice of the extension with the court that states: (1) the deadline has not been previously extended; (2) the extension is for twenty-eight (28) or fewer days; (3) the extension does not interfere with the Case Management Plan, scheduled hearings, or other case deadlines; (4) the original deadline and extended deadline; (5) that all opposing counsel the filing attorney could reach agreed to the extension; or that the filing attorney could not reach any opposing counsel, and providing the

679

dates, times and manner of all attempts to reach opposing counsel. IN R USDCTSD L.R. 6-1(b).

- *Pro se parties.* The automatic initial extension does not apply to pro se parties. IN R USDCTSD L.R. 6-1(c).

4. *Opposing papers.* The Federal Rules of Civil Procedure do not require any formal answer, return, or reply to a motion, except where the Federal Rules of Civil Procedure or local rules may require affidavits, memoranda, or other papers to be filed in opposition to a motion. Such papers are simply to apprise the court of such opposition and the grounds of that opposition. FEDPROC § 62:359.

   a. *Effect of failure to respond to motion.* Although in the absence of statutory provision or court rule, a motion ordinarily does not require a written answer, when a party files a motion and the opposing party fails to respond, the court may construe such failure to respond as nonopposition to the motion or an admission that the motion was meritorious, may take the facts alleged in the motion as true—the rule in some jurisdictions being that the failure to respond to a fact set forth in a motion is deemed an admission—and may grant the motion if the relief requested appears to be justified. AMJUR MOTIONS § 28.

   b. *Assent or no opposition not determinative.* However, a motion will not be granted automatically simply because an "assent" or a notation of "no opposition" has been filed; federal judges frequently deny motions that have been assented to when it is thought that justice so dictates. FPP § 1190.

   c. *Responsive pleading inappropriate as response to motion.* An attempt to answer or oppose a motion with a responsive pleading usually is not appropriate. FPP § 1190.

5. *Reply papers.* A moving party may be required or permitted to prepare papers in addition to his original motion papers. AMJUR MOTIONS § 25. Papers answering or replying to opposing papers may be appropriate, in the interests of justice, where it appears there is a substantial reason for allowing a reply. Thus, a court may accept reply papers where a party demonstrates that the papers to which it seeks to file a reply raise new issues that are material to the disposition of the question before the court, or where the court determines, sua sponte, that it wishes further briefing of an issue raised in those papers and orders the submission of additional papers. FEDPROC § 62:360.

   a. *Function of reply papers.* The function of a reply affidavit is to answer the arguments made in opposition to the position taken by the movant and not to permit the movant to introduce new arguments in support of the motion. AMJUR MOTIONS § 25.

   b. *Issues raised for the first time in a reply document.* However, the view has been followed in some jurisdictions, that as a matter of judicial economy, where there is no prejudice and where the issues could be raised simply by filing a motion to dismiss, the trial court has discretion to consider arguments raised for the first time in a reply memorandum, and that a trial court may grant a motion to strike issues raised for the first time in a reply memorandum. AMJUR MOTIONS § 26.

6. *Appearances.* Every attorney who represents a party or who files a document on a party's behalf must file an appearance for that party. IN R USDCTSD L.R. 83-7. The filing of a Notice of Appearance shall act to establish the filing attorney as an attorney of record representing a designated party or parties in a particular cause of action. As a result, it is necessary for each attorney to file a separate Notice of Appearance when entering an appearance in a case. A joint appearance on behalf of multiple attorneys may be filed electronically only if it is filed separately for each attorney, using his/her ECF login. IN R USDCTSD ECF Procedures(12). Only those attorneys who have filed an appearance in a pending action are entitled to be served with case documents under FRCP 5(a). IN R USDCTSD L.R. 83-7. For more information, refer to IN R USDCTSD L.R. 83-7 and IN R USDCTSD ECF Procedures(12).

7. *Notice of related action.* A party must file a notice of related action: as soon as it appears that the party's case and another pending case: (1) arise out of the same transaction or occurrence; (2) involve the same property; or (3) involve the validity or infringement or the same patent, trademark, or copyright. IN R USDCTSD L.R. 40-1(d)(2). For more information, refer to IN R USDCTSD L.R. 40-1.

8. *Alternative dispute resolution (ADR)*

   a. *Application.* Unless limited by specific provisions, or unless there are other applicable specific statutory, common law, or constitutional procedures, the Local Alternative Dispute Resolution Rules of the United States District Court for the Southern District of Indiana shall apply in all civil litigation filed in the U.S. District Court for the Southern District of Indiana, except in the following cases and proceedings:

    i.   Applications for writs of habeas corpus under 28 U.S.C.A. § 2254;

    ii.   Forfeiture cases;

    iii.   Non-adversary proceedings in bankruptcy;

    iv.   Social Security administrative review cases; and

    v.   Such other matters as specified by order of the Court; for example, matters involving important public policy issues, constitutional law, or the establishment of new law. IN R USDCTSD A.D.R. Rule 1.2.

b. *Mediation.* Mediation under this section (IN R USDCTSD A.D.R. Rule 2.1, et seq.) involves the confidential process by which a person acting as a Mediator, selected by the parties or appointed by the Court, assists the litigants in reaching a mutually acceptable agreement. It is an informal and nonadversarial process. The role of the Mediator is to assist in identifying the issues, reducing misunderstandings, clarifying priorities, exploring areas of compromise, and finding points of agreement as well as legitimate points of disagreement. Final decision-making authority rests with the parties, not the Mediator. IN R USDCTSD A.D.R. Rule 2.1. It is anticipated that an agreement may not resolve all of the disputed issues, but the process, nonetheless, can reduce points of contention. Parties and their representatives are required to mediate in good faith, but are not compelled to reach an agreement. IN R USDCTSD A.D.R. Rule 2.1.

    i.   *Case selection.* The Court with the agreement of the parties may refer a civil case for mediation. Unless otherwise ordered or as specifically provided in IN R USDCTSD A.D.R. Rule 2.8, referral to mediation does not abate or suspend the action, and no scheduled dates shall be delayed or deferred, including the date of trial. IN R USDCTSD A.D.R. Rule 2.2.

    ii.   For more information on mediation, refer to IN R USDCTSD A.D.R. Rule 2.1, et seq.

c. *Other methods of dispute resolution.* The Local Alternative Dispute Resolution Rules of the United States District Court for the Southern District of Indiana shall not preclude the parties from utilizing any other reasonable method or technique of alternative dispute resolution to resolve disputes to which the parties agree. However, any use of arbitration by the parties will be governed by and comply with the requirements of 28 U.S.C.A. § 654 through 28 U.S.C.A. § 657. IN R USDCTSD A.D.R. Rule 1.5.

d. For more information on alternative dispute resolution (ADR), refer to IN R USDCTSD A.D.R. Rule 1.1, et seq.

9. *Notice of settlement or resolution.* The parties must immediately notify the court if they reasonably anticipate settling their case or resolving a pending motion. IN R USDCTSD L.R. 7-1(h).

10. *Modification or suspension of rules.* The court may, on its own motion or at the request of a party, suspend or modify any rule in a particular case in the interest of justice. IN R USDCTSD L.R. 1-1(c).

D. Documents

1. *Documents for moving party*

    a. *Required documents*

        i. *Notice of motion and motion.* [P]rior to filing any non-dispositive motion (including motions for extension of time), the moving party must contact opposing counsel to determine whether there is an objection to any non-dispositive motion (including motions for extension of time), and state in the motion whether opposing counsel objects to the motion. If an objection cannot be resolved by counsel, the opposing counsel's position shall be stated within the motion. The motion should also indicate whether opposing counsel plans to file a written objection to the motion and the date by which the Court can expect to receive the objection (within the time limits set in IN R USDCTSD L.R. 7-1). If after a reasonable effort, opposing counsel cannot be reached, the moving party shall recite in the motion the dates and times that messages were left for opposing counsel. IN R USDCTSD Case Mgt(General Instructions For All Cases). Refer to the General Requirements section of this document for information on the notice of motion and motion.

ii. *Certificate of service.* FRCP 5(d) requires that the person making service under FRCP 5 certify that service has been effected. FRCP 5(Advisory Committee Notes). Having such information on file may be useful for many purposes, including proof of service if an issue arises concerning the effectiveness of the service. FRCP 5(Advisory Committee Notes).

- *Certificate of service for electronically-filed documents.* A certificate of service must be included with all documents filed electronically. Such certificate shall indicate that service was accomplished pursuant to the Court's electronic filing procedures. IN R USDCTSD ECF Procedures(11). For the suggested format for a certificate of service for electronic filing, refer to IN R USDCTSD ECF Procedures(11).

b. *Supplemental documents*

i. *Brief.* Refer to the Format section of this document for the format of briefs.

ii. *Supporting evidence.* When a motion relies on facts outside the record, the court may hear the matter on affidavits or may hear it wholly or partly on oral testimony or on depositions. FRCP 43(c).

- *Materials necessary for motion.* A party seeking relief under FRCP 26(c) or FRCP 37, or by way of a pretrial motion that could result in a final order on an issue, must file with the motion those parts of the discovery materials relevant to the motion. IN R USDCTSD L.R. 26-2(a).

- *Unavailable evidence.* A party seeking to continue a trial because evidence is unavailable must include with the motion an affidavit showing: (1) how the evidence is material; (2) that the party has used due diligence to obtain the evidence; (3) where the party believes the evidence is; and (4) if the evidence is the testimony of an absent witness, (A) the name and residence of the witness, if known; (B) the likelihood of procuring the testimony within a reasonable time; (C) that neither the party nor anyone at the party's request or with the party's knowledge procured the witness's absence; (D) the facts the party believes the witness will truthfully testify to; and (E) that the party cannot prove the facts by any other witness whose testimony can be readily procured. IN R USDCTSD L.R. 16-3(c).

iii. *Notice of constitutional question.* A party that files a pleading, written motion, or other paper drawing into question the constitutionality of a federal or state statute must promptly:

- *File notice.* File a notice of constitutional question stating the question and identifying the paper that raises it, if: (1) a federal statute is questioned and the parties do not include the United States, one of its agencies, or one of its officers or employees in an official capacity; or (2) a state statute is questioned and the parties do not include the state, one of its agencies, or one of its officers or employees in an official capacity; and

- *Serve notice.* Serve the notice and paper on the Attorney General of the United States if a federal statute is questioned—or on the state attorney general if a state statute is questioned—either by certified or registered mail or by sending it to an electronic address designated by the attorney general for this purpose. FRCP 5.1(a).

- *Time for filing.* A notice of constitutional challenge to a statute filed in accordance with FRCP 5.1 must be filed at the same time the parties tender their proposed case management plan, if one is required, or within twenty-one (21) days of the filing drawing into question the constitutionality of a federal or state statute, whichever occurs later. IN R USDCTSD L.R. 5.1-1(a).

- *Additional service requirements.* If a federal statute is challenged, in addition to the service requirements of FRCP 5.1(a), the party filing the notice of constitutional challenge must serve the notice and documents on the United States Attorney for the Southern District of Indiana, either by certified or registered mail or by sending it to an electronic address designated for that purpose by that official. IN R USDCTSD L.R. 5.1-1(b).

- *No forfeiture.* A party's failure to file and serve the notice, or the court's failure to certify, does not forfeit a constitutional claim or defense that is otherwise timely asserted. FRCP 5.1(d).

iv. *Nongovernmental corporate disclosure statement*

- *Contents.* A nongovernmental corporate party must file two (2) copies of a disclosure statement that: (1) identifies any parent corporation and any publicly held corporation owning ten percent (10%) or more of its stock; or (2) states that there is no such corporation. FRCP 7.1(a).

- *Time to file; Supplemental filing.* A party must: (1) file the disclosure statement with its first appearance, pleading, petition, motion, response, or other request addressed to the court; and (2) promptly file a supplemental statement if any required information changes. FRCP 7.1(b).

v. *Request for oral argument.* A party may request oral argument by filing a separate motion explaining why oral argument is necessary and estimating how long the court should allow for the argument. The request must be filed and served with the supporting brief, response brief, or reply brief. IN R USDCTSD L.R. 7-5(a).

vi. *Request for evidentiary hearing.* A party may request an evidentiary hearing on a motion or petition by serving and filing a separate motion explaining why the hearing is necessary and estimating how long the court should allow for the hearing. IN R USDCTSD L.R. 7-5(c).

vii. *Copy of authority.* Generally, copies of cited authorities may not be attached to court filings. However, a party must attach to the party's motion or brief a copy of any cited authority if it is not available on Westlaw or Lexis. Upon request, a party must provide copies of any cited authority that is only available through electronic means to the court or the other parties. IN R USDCTSD L.R. 7-1(f).

viii. *Proposed order.* A party must include a suitable form of order with any document that requests the judge or the clerk to enter a routine or uncontested order. IN R USDCTSD L.R. 5-5(b); IN R USDCTSD L.R. 5-10(c); IN R USDCTSD L.R. 7-1(d).

- A service statement and/or list must be included on each proposed order, as required by IN R USDCTSD L.R. 5-5(d). IN R USDCTSD ECF Procedures(11). Any pleading, motion, brief, affidavit, notice, or proposed order filed with the court, whether electronically or with the clerk, must: if it is a form of order, include a statement of service, in the format required by IN R USDCTSD L.R. 5-5(d) in the lower left corner of the document. IN R USDCTSD L.R. 5-1(b).

- A party electronically filing a proposed order—whether voluntarily or because required by IN R USDCTSD L.R. 5-5—must convert the order directly from a word processing program and file it as an attachment to the document it relates to. Proposed orders must include in the lower left-hand corner of the signature page a statement that service will be made electronically on all ECF-registered counsel of record via email generated by the court's ECF system, without listing all such counsel. A service list including the name and postal address of any pro se litigant or non-registered attorney of record must follow, stating that service on the listed individuals will be made in the traditional paper manner, via first-class U.S. Mail. IN R USDCTSD L.R. 5-5(d).

ix. *Index of exhibits.* Any pleading, motion, brief, affidavit, notice, or proposed order filed with the court, whether electronically or with the clerk, must: if it has four (4) or more exhibits, include a separate index that identifies and briefly describes each exhibit. IN R USDCTSD L.R. 5-1(b).

x. *Copy of document with self-address envelope.* To receive a file-stamped copy of a document filed directly with the clerk, a party must include with the original document an additional copy and a self-addressed envelope. The envelope must be big enough to hold the copy and have enough postage on it to send the copy via regular first-class mail. IN R USDCTSD L.R. 5-10(b).

xi. *Notice of manual filing.* When a party who is not exempt from the electronic filing requirement files a document directly with the clerk, the party must: electronically file a notice of manual filing that explains why the document cannot be filed electronically. IN R USDCTSD L.R. 5-2(d)(1). Refer to the Filing and Service Requirements section of this document for more information.

- Where an individual component cannot be included in an electronic filing (e.g. the component cannot be converted to electronic format), the filer shall electronically file the prescribed Notice of Manual Filing in place of that component. A model form is provided as Appendix C (IN R USDCTSD ECF Procedures(Appendix C)). IN R USDCTSD ECF Procedures(13).

- Before making a manual filing of a component, the filing party shall first electronically file a Notice of Manual Filing (See IN R USDCTSD ECF Procedures(Appendix C)). The filer shall initiate the electronic filing process as if filing the actual component but shall instead attach to the filing the Notice of Manual Filing setting forth the reason(s) why the component cannot be filed electronically. The manual filing should be accompanied by a copy of the previously filed Notice of Manual Filing. A party may seek to have a component excluded from electronic filing pursuant to applicable Federal and Local Rules (e.g., FRCP 26(c)). IN R USDCTSD ECF Procedures(15).

xii. *Courtesy copies.* District Judges and Magistrate Judges regularly receive documents filed by all parties. Therefore, parties shall not bring "courtesy copies" to any chambers unless specifically directed to do so by the Court. IN R USDCTSD Case Mgt(General Instructions For All Cases).

xiii. *Copies for three-judge court.* Parties in a case where a three-judge court has been requested must file an original and three copies of any document filed directly with the clerk (instead of electronically) until the court: (1) denies the request; (2) dissolves the three-judge court; or (3) allows the parties to file fewer copies. IN R USDCTSD L.R. 9-2(c).

xiv. *Declaration that party was unable to file in a timely manner due to technical difficulties.* If a party misses a filing deadline due to an inability to file electronically, the party may submit the untimely filed document, accompanied by a declaration stating the reason(s) for missing the deadline. IN R USDCTSD ECF Procedures(16). A model form is provided as Appendix D (IN R USDCTSD ECF Procedures(Appendix D)). IN R USDCTSD ECF Procedures(16).

2. *Documents for opposing party*

   a. *Required documents*

      i. *Response brief.* Refer to the Format section of this document for the format of briefs. Refer to the General Requirements section of this document for information on the opposing papers.

      ii. *Certificate of service.* FRCP 5(d) requires that the person making service under FRCP 5 certify that service has been effected. FRCP 5(Advisory Committee Notes). Having such information on file may be useful for many purposes, including proof of service if an issue arises concerning the effectiveness of the service. FRCP 5(Advisory Committee Notes).

         - *Certificate of service for electronically-filed documents.* A certificate of service must be included with all documents filed electronically. Such certificate shall indicate that service was accomplished pursuant to the Court's electronic filing procedures. IN R USDCTSD ECF Procedures(11). For the suggested format for a certificate of service for electronic filing, refer to IN R USDCTSD ECF Procedures(11).

   b. *Supplemental documents*

      i. *Supporting evidence.* When a motion relies on facts outside the record, the court may hear the matter on affidavits or may hear it wholly or partly on oral testimony or on depositions. FRCP 43(c).

         - *Materials necessary for motion.* A party seeking relief under FRCP 26(c) or FRCP 37, or by way of a pretrial motion that could result in a final order on an issue, must file with the motion those parts of the discovery materials relevant to the motion. IN R USDCTSD L.R. 26-2(a).

ii. *Notice of constitutional question.* A party that files a pleading, written motion, or other paper drawing into question the constitutionality of a federal or state statute must promptly:

- *File notice.* File a notice of constitutional question stating the question and identifying the paper that raises it, if: (1) a federal statute is questioned and the parties do not include the United States, one of its agencies, or one of its officers or employees in an official capacity; or (2) a state statute is questioned and the parties do not include the state, one of its agencies, or one of its officers or employees in an official capacity; and

- *Serve notice.* Serve the notice and paper on the Attorney General of the United States if a federal statute is questioned—or on the state attorney general if a state statute is questioned—either by certified or registered mail or by sending it to an electronic address designated by the attorney general for this purpose. FRCP 5.1(a).

- *Time for filing.* A notice of constitutional challenge to a statute filed in accordance with FRCP 5.1 must be filed at the same time the parties tender their proposed case management plan, if one is required, or within twenty-one (21) days of the filing drawing into question the constitutionality of a federal or state statute, whichever occurs later. IN R USDCTSD L.R. 5.1-1(a).

- *Additional service requirements.* If a federal statute is challenged, in addition to the service requirements of FRCP 5.1(a), the party filing the notice of constitutional challenge must serve the notice and documents on the United States Attorney for the Southern District of Indiana, either by certified or registered mail or by sending it to an electronic address designated for that purpose by that official. IN R USDCTSD L.R. 5.1-1(b).

- *No forfeiture.* A party's failure to file and serve the notice, or the court's failure to certify, does not forfeit a constitutional claim or defense that is otherwise timely asserted. FRCP 5.1(d).

iii. *Index of exhibits.* Any pleading, motion, brief, affidavit, notice, or proposed order filed with the court, whether electronically or with the clerk, must: if it has four (4) or more exhibits, include a separate index that identifies and briefly describes each exhibit. IN R USDCTSD L.R. 5-1(b).

iv. *Request for oral argument.* A party may request oral argument by filing a separate motion explaining why oral argument is necessary and estimating how long the court should allow for the argument. The request must be filed and served with the supporting brief, response brief, or reply brief. IN R USDCTSD L.R. 7-5(a).

v. *Request for evidentiary hearing.* A party may request an evidentiary hearing on a motion or petition by serving and filing a separate motion explaining why the hearing is necessary and estimating how long the court should allow for the hearing. IN R USDCTSD L.R. 7-5(c).

vi. *Copy of authority.* Generally, copies of cited authorities may not be attached to court filings. However, a party must attach to the party's motion or brief a copy of any cited authority if it is not available on Westlaw or Lexis. Upon request, a party must provide copies of any cited authority that is only available through electronic means to the court or the other parties. IN R USDCTSD L.R. 7-1(f).

vii. *Copy of document with self-address envelope.* To receive a file-stamped copy of a document filed directly with the clerk, a party must include with the original document an additional copy and a self-addressed envelope. The envelope must be big enough to hold the copy and have enough postage on it to send the copy via regular first-class mail. IN R USDCTSD L.R. 5-10(b).

viii. *Notice of manual filing.* When a party who is not exempt from the electronic filing requirement files a document directly with the clerk, the party must: electronically file a notice of manual filing that explains why the document cannot be filed electronically. IN R USDCTSD L.R. 5-2(d)(1). Refer to the Filing and Service Requirements section of this document for more information.

- Where an individual component cannot be included in an electronic filing (e.g. the component cannot be converted to electronic format), the filer shall electronically file the prescribed Notice of Manual Filing in place of that component. A model form is provided as Appendix C (IN R USDCTSD ECF Procedures(Appendix C)). IN R USDCTSD ECF Procedures(13).

- Before making a manual filing of a component, the filing party shall first electronically file a Notice of Manual Filing (See IN R USDCTSD ECF Procedures(Appendix C)). The filer shall initiate the electronic filing process as if filing the actual component but shall instead attach to the filing the Notice of Manual Filing setting forth the reason(s) why the component cannot be filed electronically. The manual filing should be accompanied by a copy of the previously filed Notice of Manual Filing. A party may seek to have a component excluded from electronic filing pursuant to applicable Federal and Local Rules (e.g., FRCP 26(c)). IN R USDCTSD ECF Procedures(15).

ix. *Courtesy copies.* District Judges and Magistrate Judges regularly receive documents filed by all parties. Therefore, parties shall not bring "courtesy copies" to any chambers unless specifically directed to do so by the Court. IN R USDCTSD Case Mgt(General Instructions For All Cases).

x. *Copies for three-judge court.* Parties in a case where a three-judge court has been requested must file an original and three copies of any document filed directly with the clerk (instead of electronically) until the court: (1) denies the request; (2) dissolves the three-judge court; or (3) allows the parties to file fewer copies. IN R USDCTSD L.R. 9-2(c).

xi. *Declaration that party was unable to file in a timely manner due to technical difficulties.* If a party misses a filing deadline due to an inability to file electronically, the party may submit the untimely filed document, accompanied by a declaration stating the reason(s) for missing the deadline. IN R USDCTSD ECF Procedures(16). A model form is provided as Appendix D (IN R USDCTSD ECF Procedures(Appendix D)). IN R USDCTSD ECF Procedures(16).

E. Format

1. *Form of documents.* The rules governing captions and other matters of form in pleadings apply to motions and other papers. FRCP 7(b)(2).

   a. *Paper (manual filings only).* Any document that is not filed electronically must: be flat, unfolded, and on good-quality, eight and one-half by eleven (8-1/2 x 11) inch white paper. IN R USDCTSD L.R. 5-1(d)(1). Any document that is not filed electronically must: be single-sided. IN R USDCTSD L.R. 5-1(d)(1).

      i. *Covers or backing.* Any document that is not filed electronically must: not have a cover or a back. IN R USDCTSD L.R. 5-1(d)(1).

      ii. *Fastening.* Any document that is not filed electronically must: be (if consisting of more than one (1) page) fastened by paperclip or binder clip and may not be stapled. IN R USDCTSD L.R. 5-1(d)(1).

         - *Request for nonconforming fastening.* If a document cannot be fastened or bound as required by IN R USDCTSD L.R. 5-1(d), a party may ask the clerk for permission to fasten it in another manner. The party must make such a request before attempting to file the document with nonconforming fastening. IN R USDCTSD L.R. 5-1(d)(2).

      iii. *Hole punching.* Any document that is not filed electronically must: be two-hole punched at the top with the holes two and three-quarter (2-3/4) inches apart and appropriately centered. IN R USDCTSD L.R. 5-1(d)(1).

   b. *Margins.* Any pleading, motion, brief, affidavit, notice, or proposed order filed with the court, whether electronically or with the clerk, must: have at least one (1) inch margins. IN R USDCTSD L.R. 5-1(b).

   c. *Spacing.* Any pleading, motion, brief, affidavit, notice, or proposed order filed with the court, whether electronically or with the clerk, must: be double spaced (except for headings, footnotes, and quoted material). IN R USDCTSD L.R. 5-1(b).

   d. *Text.* Any pleading, motion, brief, affidavit, notice, or proposed order filed with the court, whether electronically or with the clerk, must: be plainly typewritten, printed, or prepared by a clearly legible copying process. IN R USDCTSD L.R. 5-1(b).

e. *Font size.* Any pleading, motion, brief, affidavit, notice, or proposed order filed with the court, whether electronically or with the clerk, must: use at least 12-point type in the body of the document and at least 10-point type in footnotes. IN R USDCTSD L.R. 5-1(b).

f. *Page numbering.* Any pleading, motion, brief, affidavit, notice, or proposed order filed with the court, whether electronically or with the clerk, must: have consecutively numbered pages. IN R USDCTSD L.R. 5-1(b).

g. *Caption; Names of parties.* Every pleading must have a caption with the court's name, a title, a file number, and a FRCP 7(a) designation. The title of the complaint must name all the parties; the title of other pleadings, after naming the first party on each side, may refer generally to other parties. FRCP 10(a). Any pleading, motion, brief, affidavit, notice, or proposed order filed with the court, whether electronically or with the clerk, must: include a title on the first page. IN R USDCTSD L.R. 5-1(b).

    i. *Alternative motions.* Motions must be filed separately, but alternative motions may be filed in a single document if each is named in the title. IN R USDCTSD L.R. 7-1(a).

h. *Filer's information.* Any pleading, motion, brief, affidavit, notice, or proposed order filed with the court, whether electronically or with the clerk, must: in the case of pleadings, motions, legal briefs, and notices, include the name, complete address, telephone number, facsimile number (where available), and e-mail address (where available) of the pro se litigant or attorney who files it. IN R USDCTSD L.R. 5-1(b).

i. *Paragraphs; Separate statements.* A party must state its claims or defenses in numbered paragraphs, each limited as far as practicable to a single set of circumstances. A later pleading may refer by number to a paragraph in an earlier pleading. If doing so would promote clarity, each claim founded on a separate transaction or occurrence—and each defense other than a denial—must be stated in a separate count or defense. FRCP 10(b).

j. *Adoption by reference; Exhibits.* A statement in a pleading may be adopted by reference elsewhere in the same pleading or in any other pleading or motion. A copy of a written instrument that is an exhibit to a pleading is a part of the pleading for all purposes. FRCP 10(c).

k. *Citations*

    i. *Local rules.* The Local Rules of the United States District Court for the Southern District of Indiana may be cited as "S.D. Ind. L.R." IN R USDCTSD L.R. 1-1(a).

    ii. *Local alternative dispute resolution rules.* These Rules shall be known as the Local Alternative Dispute Resolution Rules of the United States District Court for the Southern District of Indiana. They shall be cited as "S.D.Ind. Local A.D.R. Rule _____." IN R USDCTSD A.D.R. Rule 1.1.

l. *Acceptance by the clerk.* The clerk must not refuse to file a paper solely because it is not in the form prescribed by the Federal Rules of Civil Procedure or by a local rule or practice. FRCP 5(d)(4). The clerk will accept a document that violates IN R USDCTSD L.R. 5-1, but the court may exclude the document from the official record. IN R USDCTSD L.R. 5-1(e).

    i. *Sanctions for errors as to form.* The court may strike from the record any document that does not comply with the rules governing the form of documents filed with the court, such as rules that regulate document size or the number of copies to be filed or that require a special designation in the caption. The court may also sanction an attorney or party who files a non-compliant document. IN R USDCTSD L.R. 1-3.

2. *Form of electronic documents.* Any document submitted via the court's electronic case filing (ECF) system must be: otherwise prepared and filed in a manner consistent with the CM/ECF Policies and Procedures Manual (IN R USDCTSD ECF Procedures). IN R USDCTSD L.R. 5-1(c). Electronically filed documents must meet the requirements of FRCP 10 (Form of Pleadings), IN R USDCTSD L.R. 5-1 (Format of Papers Presented for Filing), and FRCP 5.2 (Privacy Protection for Filings Made with the Court), as if they had been submitted on paper. Documents filed electronically are also subject to any page limitations set forth by Court Order, by IN R USDCTSD L.R. 7-1 (Motion Practice), or IN R USDCTSD L.R. 56-1 (Summary Judgment Practice), as applicable. IN R USDCTSD ECF Procedures(13).

a. *PDF format required.* Any document submitted via the court's electronic case filing (ECF) system must be: in .pdf format. IN R USDCTSD L.R. 5-1(c); IN R USDCTSD ECF Procedures(7). Any document submitted via the court's electronic case filing (ECF) system must be: converted to a .pdf file directly from a word processing program, unless it exists only in paper format (in which case it may be scanned to create a .pdf document). IN R USDCTSD L.R. 5-1(c); IN R USDCTSD ECF Procedures(13).

    i.   An exhibit may be scanned into PDF format, at a recommended 300 dpi resolution or higher, only if it does not already exist in electronic format. The filing attorney is responsible for reviewing all PDF documents for legibility before submitting them through the Court's Electronic Case Filing system. For technical guidance in creating PDF documents, please contact the Clerk's Office. IN R USDCTSD ECF Procedures(13).

b.   *File size limitations.* Any document submitted via the court's electronic case filing (ECF) system must be: submitted as one or more .pdf files that do not exceed ten megabytes (10 MB) each (consistent with the CM/ECF Policies and Procedures Manual (IN R USDCTSD ECF Procedures)). IN R USDCTSD L.R. 5-1(c); IN R USDCTSD ECF Procedures(13).

    i.   To electronically file a document or attachment that exceeds ten megabytes (10 MB), the document must first be broken down into two or more smaller files. For example, if Exhibit A is a twelve megabyte (12 MB) PDF file, it should be divided into 2 equal parts prior to electronic filing. Each component part of the exhibit would be filed as an attachment to the main document and described appropriately as "Exhibit A (part 1 of 2)" and "Exhibit A (part 2 of 2)." IN R USDCTSD ECF Procedures(13).

    ii.   The supporting items mentioned in IN R USDCTSD ECF Procedures(13) should not be confused with memorandums or briefs in support of motions as outlined in IN R USDCTSD L.R. 7-1 or IN R USDCTSD L.R. 56-1. These memorandums or briefs in support are to be filed as entirely separate documents pursuant to the appropriate rule. Additionally, no motion shall be embodied in the text of a response or reply brief/memorandum unless otherwise ordered by the Court. IN R USDCTSD ECF Procedures(13).

c.   *Separate component parts.* A key objective of the electronic filing system is to ensure that as much of the case as possible is managed electronically. To facilitate electronic filing and retrieval, documents to be filed electronically are to be reasonably broken into their separate component parts. By way of example, most filings include a foundation document (e.g., motion) and other supporting items (e.g., exhibits, proposed orders, proposed amended pleadings). The foundation document, as well as the supporting items, are each separate components of the filing; supporting items must be filed as attachments to the foundation document. These exhibits or attachments should include only those excerpts of the referenced documents that are directly germane to the matter under consideration. IN R USDCTSD ECF Procedures(13).

    i.   Where an individual component cannot be included in an electronic filing (e.g. the component cannot be converted to electronic format), the filer shall electronically file the prescribed Notice of Manual Filing in place of that component. A model form is provided as Appendix C (IN R USDCTSD ECF Procedures(Appendix C)). IN R USDCTSD ECF Procedures(13).

d.   *Exhibits.* Each electronically filed exhibit to a main document must be: (1) created as a separate .pdf file; (2) submitted as an attachment to the main document and given a title which describes its content; and (3) limited to excerpts that are directly germane to the main document's subject matter. IN R USDCTSD L.R. 5-6(a).

    i.   When uploading attachments during the electronic filing process, exhibits must be uploaded in a logical sequence and a brief description must be entered for each individual PDF file. The description must include not only the exhibit number or letter, but also a brief description of the document. This information may be entered in CM/ECF using a combination of the Category drop-down menu, the Description text box, or both (see IN R USDCTSD ECF Procedures(13)(Figure 1)). The information that is provided in each box will be combined to create a description of the document as it appears on the case docket (see IN R USDCTSD ECF Procedures(13)(Figure 2)). IN R USDCTSD ECF Procedures(13). For an example, refer to IN R USDCTSD ECF Procedures(13).

e. *Excerpts.* A party filing an exhibit that consists of excerpts from a larger document must clearly and prominently identify the exhibit as containing excerpted material. Either party will have the right to timely file additional excerpts or the complete document to the extent they are or become directly germane to the main document's subject matter. IN R USDCTSD L.R. 5-6(b).

f. For an example illustrating the application of IN R USDCTSD ECF Procedures(13), refer to IN R USDCTSD ECF Procedures(13).

3. *Form of briefs*

a. *Page limits.* Supporting and response briefs (excluding tables of contents, tables of authorities, appendices, and certificates of service) may not exceed thirty-five (35) pages. Reply briefs may not exceed twenty (20) pages. IN R USDCTSD L.R. 7-1(e)(1).

   i. *Permission to exceed limits.* The court may allow a party to file a brief exceeding these page limits for extraordinary and compelling reasons. IN R USDCTSD L.R. 7-1(e)(2).

   ii. *Supporting and response briefs exceeding limits.* If the court allows a party to file a brief or response exceeding thirty-five (35) pages, the document must include:

   • A table of contents with page references;

   • A statement of issues; and

   • A table of authorities including: (1) all cases (alphabetically arranged), statutes, and other authorities cited in the brief; and (2) page numbers where the authorities are cited in the brief. IN R USDCTSD L.R. 7-1(e)(3).

4. *Signing of pleadings, motions and other papers*

a. *Signature.* Every pleading, written motion, and other paper must be signed by at least one attorney of record in the attorney's name—or by a party personally if the party is unrepresented. The paper must state the signer's address, e-mail address, and telephone number. FRCP 11(a).

   i. *Signatures on manual filings.* Any document that is not filed electronically must: include the original signature of the pro se litigant or attorney who files it. IN R USDCTSD L.R. 5-1(d)(1).

   ii. *Electronic signatures.* Use of the attorney's login and password when filing documents electronically serves in part as the attorney's signature for purposes of FRCP 11, the Local Rules of the United States District Court for the Southern District of Indiana, and any other purpose for which a signature is required in connection with proceedings before the Court. IN R USDCTSD ECF Procedures(14); IN R USDCTSD ECF Procedures(10). A pleading, motion, brief, or notice filed electronically under an attorney's ECF log-in and password must be signed by that attorney. IN R USDCTSD L.R. 5-7(a). A signature on a document other than a document filed as provided under IN R USDCTSD L.R. 5-7(a) must be an original handwritten signature and must be scanned into .pdf format for electronic filing. IN R USDCTSD L.R. 5-7(c); IN R USDCTSD ECF Procedures(14).

   • *Form of electronic signature.* If a document is converted directly from a word processing application to .pdf (as opposed to scanning), the name of the Filing User under whose log-in and password the document is submitted must be preceded by a "s/" and typed on the signature line where the Filing User's handwritten signature would otherwise appear. IN R USDCTSD L.R. 5-7(b). All documents filed electronically shall include a signature block and include the filing attorney's typewritten name, address, telephone number, facsimile number and e-mail address. In addition, the name of the filing attorney under whose ECF login the document will be filed should be preceded by a "s/" and typed in the space where the attorney's handwritten signature would otherwise appear. IN R US-DCTSD ECF Procedures(14). For a sample format, refer to IN R USDCTSD ECF Procedures(14).

   • *Effect of electronic signature.* Filing an electronically signed document under an attorney's ECF log-in and password constitutes the attorney's signature on the document under the Federal Rules of Civil Procedure, under the Local Rules of the United States District Court for the Southern District of Indiana, and for any other reason a signature is required in connection with the court's activities. IN R USDCTSD L.R. 5-7(d).

- *Documents with multiple attorneys' signatures.* Documents requiring signatures of more than one attorney shall be filed either by: (1) obtaining consent from the other attorney, then typing the "s/ [Name]" signature of the other attorney on the signature line where the other attorney's signature would otherwise appear; (2) identifying in the signature section the name of the other attorney whose signature is required and by the submission of a Notice of Endorsement (see IN R USDCTSD ECF Procedures(Appendix B)) by the other attorney no later than three (3) business days after filing; (3) submitting a scanned document containing all handwritten signatures; or (4) in any other manner approved by the Court. IN R USDCTSD ECF Procedures(14); IN R USDCTSD L.R. 5-7(e).

iii. *No verification or accompanying affidavit required for pleadings.* Unless a rule or statute specifically states otherwise, a pleading need not be verified or accompanied by an affidavit. FRCP 11(a).

iv. *Unsigned papers.* The court must strike an unsigned paper unless the omission is promptly corrected after being called to the attorney's or party's attention. FRCP 11(a). The court will strike any document filed directly with the clerk that is not signed by an attorney of record or the pro se litigant filing it, but the court may do so only after giving the attorney or pro se litigant notice of the omission and reasonable time to correct it. Rubber-stamp or facsimile signatures are not original signatures and the court will deem documents containing them to be unsigned for purposes of FRCP 11 and FRCP 26(g) and IN R USDCTSD L.R. 5-10. IN R USDCTSD L.R. 5-10(g).

b. *Representations to the court.* By presenting to the court a pleading, written motion, or other paper—whether by signing, filing, submitting, or later advocating it—an attorney or unrepresented party certifies that to the best of the person's knowledge, information, and belief, formed after an inquiry reasonable under the circumstances:

   i. It is not being presented for any improper purpose, such as to harass, cause unnecessary delay, or needlessly increase the cost of litigation;

   ii. The claims, defenses, and other legal contentions are warranted by existing law or by a nonfrivolous argument for extending, modifying, or reversing existing law or for establishing new law;

   iii. The factual contentions have evidentiary support or, if specifically so identified, will likely have evidentiary support after a reasonable opportunity for further investigation or discovery; and

   iv. The denials of factual contentions are warranted on the evidence or, if specifically so identified, are reasonably based on belief or a lack of information. FRCP 11(b).

c. *Sanctions.* If, after notice and a reasonable opportunity to respond, the court determines that FRCP 11(b) has been violated, the court may impose an appropriate sanction on any attorney, law firm, or party that violated FRCP 11(b) or is responsible for the violation. FRCP 11(c)(1). Refer to the United States District Court for the Southern District of Indiana KeyRules Motion for Sanctions document for more information.

5. *Privacy protection for filings made with the court.* Electronically filed documents must meet the requirements of. . .FRCP 5.2 (Privacy Protection for Filings Made with the Court), as if they had been submitted on paper. IN R USDCTSD ECF Procedures(13).

   a. *Redacted filings.* Unless the court orders otherwise, in an electronic or paper filing with the court that contains an individual's Social Security number, taxpayer-identification number, or birth date, the name of an individual known to be a minor, or a financial-account number, a party or nonparty making the filing may include only:

      i. The last four (4) digits of the Social Security number and taxpayer-identification number;

      ii. The year of the individual's birth;

      iii. The minor's initials; and

      iv. The last four (4) digits of the financial-account number. FRCP 5.2(a).

    b. *Exemptions from the redaction requirement.* The redaction requirement does not apply to the following:

        i. A financial-account number that identifies the property allegedly subject to forfeiture in a forfeiture proceeding;

        ii. The record of an administrative or agency proceeding;

        iii. The official record of a state-court proceeding;

        iv. The record of a court or tribunal, if that record was not subject to the redaction requirement when originally filed;

        v. A filing covered by FRCP 5.2(c) or FRCP 5.2(d); and

        vi. A pro se filing in an action brought under 28 U.S.C.A. § 2241, 28 U.S.C.A. § 2254, or 28 U.S.C.A. § 2255. FRCP 5.2(b).

    c. *Limitations on remote access to electronic files; Social Security appeals and immigration cases.* Unless the court orders otherwise, in an action for benefits under the Social Security Act, and in an action or proceeding relating to an order of removal, to relief from removal, or to immigration benefits or detention, access to an electronic file is authorized as follows:

        i. The parties and their attorneys may have remote electronic access to any part of the case file, including the administrative record;

        ii. Any other person may have electronic access to the full record at the courthouse, but may have remote electronic access only to:

            • The docket maintained by the court; and

            • An opinion, order, judgment, or other disposition of the court, but not any other part of the case file or the administrative record. FRCP 5.2(c).

    d. *Filings made under seal.* The court may order that a filing be made under seal without redaction. The court may later unseal the filing or order the person who made the filing to file a redacted version for the public record. FRCP 5.2(d). For more information on filing under seal, refer to IN R USDCTSD L.R. 5-11 and IN R USDCTSD ECF Procedures(18).

    e. *Protective orders.* For good cause, the court may by order in a case:

        i. Require redaction of additional information; or

        ii. Limit or prohibit a nonparty's remote electronic access to a document filed with the court. FRCP 5.2(e).

    f. *Option for additional unredacted filing under seal.* A person making a redacted filing may also file an unredacted copy under seal. The court must retain the unredacted copy as part of the record. FRCP 5.2(f).

    g. *Option for filing a reference list.* A filing that contains redacted information may be filed together with a reference list that identifies each item of redacted information and specifies an appropriate identifier that uniquely corresponds to each item listed. The list must be filed under seal and may be amended as of right. Any reference in the case to a listed identifier will be construed to refer to the corresponding item of information. FRCP 5.2(g).

    h. *Waiver of protection of identifiers.* A person waives the protection of FRCP 5.2(a) as to the person's own information by filing it without redaction and not under seal. FRCP 5.2(h).

F. Filing and Service Requirements

  1. *Filing requirements.* Any paper after the complaint that is required to be served—together with a certificate of service—must be filed within a reasonable time after service. FRCP 5(d)(1). Motions must be filed separately, but alternative motions may be filed in a single document if each is named in the title. IN R USDCTSD L.R. 7-1(a).

    a. *How filing is made; In general.* A paper is filed by delivering it:

        i. To the clerk; or

ii. To a judge who agrees to accept it for filing, and who must then note the filing date on the paper and promptly send it to the clerk. FRCP 5(d)(2).

- In certain instances, the court will direct the parties to submit items directly to chambers (e.g., confidential settlement statements). However, absent specific prior authorization, counsel and litigants should not submit letters or documents directly to chambers, and such materials should be filed with the clerk. IN R USDCTSD L.R. 5-1(Local Rules Advisory Committee Comment).

iii. A document or item submitted in relation to a matter within the court's jurisdiction is deemed filed upon delivery to the office of the clerk in a manner prescribed by the Local Rules of the United States District Court for the Southern District of Indiana or the Federal Rules of Civil Procedure or authorized by the court. Any submission directed to a Judge or Judge's staff, the office of the clerk or any employee thereof, in a manner that is not contemplated by IN R USDCTSD L.R. 5-1 and without prior court authorization is prohibited. IN R USDCTSD L.R. 5-1(a).

b. *Non-electronic filing.* Any document that is exempt from electronic filing must be filed directly with the clerk and served on other parties in the case as required by those Federal Rules of Civil Procedure and Local Rules of the United States District Court for the Southern District of Indiana that apply to the service of non-electronic documents. IN R USDCTSD L.R. 5-2(c).

i. *When completed.* A document or other item that is not required to be filed electronically is deemed filed:

- Upon delivery in person, by courier, or via U.S. Mail or other mail delivery service to the clerk's office during business hours;

- When the courtroom deputy clerk accepts it, if the document or item is filed in open court; or

- Upon completion of any other manner of filing that the court authorizes. IN R USDCTSD L.R. 5-10(a).

ii. *Document filing by non-exempt party.* When a party who is not exempt from the electronic filing requirement files a document directly with the clerk, the party must:

- Electronically file a notice of manual filing that explains why the document cannot be filed electronically;

- Present the document to the clerk within one (1) business day after filing the notice of manual filing; and

- Present the clerk with a copy of the notice of manual filing when the party files the document with the clerk. IN R USDCTSD L.R. 5-2(d).

c. *Electronic filing*

i. *Authorization of electronic filing program.* A court may, by local rule, allow papers to be filed, signed, or verified by electronic means that are consistent with any technical standards established by the Judicial Conference of the United States. A local rule may require electronic filing only if reasonable exceptions are allowed. A paper filed electronically in compliance with a local rule is a written paper for purposes of the Federal Rules of Civil Procedure. FRCP 5(d)(3).

- IN R USDCTSD L.R. 5-2 requires electronic filing, as allowed by FRCP 5(d)(3). The policies and procedures in IN R USDCTSD ECF Procedures govern electronic filing in this district unless, due to circumstances in a particular case, a judicial officer determines that these policies and procedures (IN R USDCTSD ECF Procedures) should be modified. IN R USDCTSD ECF Procedures(1).

- Unless modified by order of the Court, all Federal Rules of Civil Procedure and Local Rules of the United States District Court for the Southern District of Indiana shall continue to apply to cases maintained in the Court's Case Management/Electronic Case Filing System (CM/ECF). IN R USDCTSD ECF Procedures(3).

ii. *Mandatory electronic filing.* Unless exempted pursuant to IN R USDCTSD L.R. 5-3(e), attorneys admitted to the court's bar (including those admitted pro hac vice) or authorized to represent the United States must use the court's ECF system to file documents. IN R USDCTSD L.R. 5-3(a). Electronic filing by attorneys is required for eligible documents filed in civil and criminal cases pending with the Court, unless specifically exempted by Local Rule or Court Order. IN R USDCTSD ECF Procedures(4).

- *Exceptions.* All civil cases (other than those cases the court specifically exempts) must be maintained in the court's electronic case filing (ECF) system. Accordingly, as allowed by FRCP 5(d)(3), every document filed in this court (including exhibits) must be transmitted to the clerk's office via the ECF system consistent with IN R USDCTSD L.R. 5-2 through IN R USDCTSD L.R. 5-11 except: (1) documents filed by pro se litigants; (2) transcripts in cases filed by claimants under the Social Security Act (and related statutes); (3) exhibits in a format that does not readily permit electronic filing (such as videos and large maps and charts); (4) documents that are illegible when scanned into .pdf format; (5) documents filed in cases not maintained on the ECF system; and (6) any other documents that the court or the Local Rules of the United States District Court for the Southern District of Indiana specifically allow to be filed directly with the clerk. IN R USDCTSD L.R. 5-2(a). Parties otherwise participating in the electronic filing system may be excused from filing a particular component electronically under certain limited circumstances, such as when the component cannot be reduced to an electronic format. Such components shall not be filed electronically, but instead shall be manually filed with the Clerk of Court and served upon the parties in accordance with the applicable Federal Rules of Civil Procedure and the Local Rules of the United States District Court for the Southern District of Indiana for filing and service of non-electronic documents. IN R USDCTSD ECF Procedures(15).

- *Exemption from participation.* The court may exempt attorneys from using the ECF system in a particular case for good cause. An attorney must file a petition for ECF exemption and a CM/ECF technical requirements exemption questionnaire in each case in which the attorney seeks an exemption. (The CM/ECF technical requirements exemption questionnaire is available on the court's website). IN R USDCTSD L.R. 5-3(e).

iii. *Consequences of electronic filing.* Electronic transmission of a document consistent with the procedures adopted by the Court shall, upon the complete receipt of the same by the Clerk of Court, constitute filing of the document for all purposes of the Federal Rules of Civil and Criminal Procedure and the Local Rules of the United States District Court for the Southern District of Indiana, and shall constitute entry of that document onto the docket maintained by the Clerk pursuant to FRCP 58 and FRCP 79. IN R USDCTSD ECF Procedures(7); IN R USDCTSD L.R. 5-4(c)(1). When a document has been filed electronically: the document, as filed, binds the filing party. IN R USDCTSD L.R. 5-4(c)(3).

- A Notice of Electronic Filing (NEF) acknowledging that the document has been filed will immediately appear on the filer's screen after the document has been submitted. Attorneys are strongly encouraged to print or electronically save a copy of the NEF. Attorneys can also verify the filing of documents by inspecting the Court's electronic docket sheet through the use of a PACER login. IN R USDCTSD ECF Procedures(7). When a document has been filed electronically: the notice of electronic filing for the document serves as the court's date-stamp and proof of filing. IN R USDCTSD L.R. 5-4(c)(4).

- The Court may, upon the motion of a party or upon its own motion, strike any inappropriately filed document. IN R USDCTSD ECF Procedures(7).

iv. For more information on electronic filing, refer to IN R USDCTSD ECF Procedures.

d. *Fax filing.* The clerk may not file a faxed document without court authorization. The court may not authorize the clerk to file faxed documents without finding that compelling circumstances justify it. A party must submit a copy of the document that otherwise complies with IN R USDCTSD L.R. 5-10 to replace the faxed copy within seven (7) days after faxing the document. IN R USDCTSD L.R. 5-10(e).

2. *Service requirements*

  a. *Service; When required*

    i. *In general.* Unless the Federal Rules of Civil Procedure provide otherwise, each of the following papers must be served on every party:

- An order stating that service is required;

- A pleading filed after the original complaint, unless the court orders otherwise under FRCP 5(c) because there are numerous defendants;

- A discovery paper required to be served on a party, unless the court orders otherwise;

- A written motion, except one that may be heard ex parte; and

- A written notice, appearance, demand, or offer of judgment, or any similar paper. FRCP 5(a)(1).

    ii. *If a party fails to appear.* No service is required on a party who is in default for failing to appear. But a pleading that asserts a new claim for relief against such a party must be served on that party under FRCP 4. FRCP 5(a)(2).

    iii. *Seizing property.* If an action is begun by seizing property and no person is or need be named as a defendant, any service required before the filing of an appearance, answer, or claim must be made on the person who had custody or possession of the property when it was seized. FRCP 5(a)(3).

  b. *Service; How made*

    i. *Serving an attorney.* If a party is represented by an attorney, service under FRCP 5 must be made on the attorney unless the court orders service on the party. FRCP 5(b)(1).

    ii. *Service in general.* A paper is served under FRCP 5 by:

- Handing it to the person;

- Leaving it: (1) at the person's office with a clerk or other person in charge or, if no one is in charge, in a conspicuous place in the office; or (2) if the person has no office or the office is closed, at the person's dwelling or usual place of abode with someone of suitable age and discretion who resides there;

- Mailing it to the person's last known address—in which event service is complete upon mailing;

- Leaving it with the court clerk if the person has no known address;

- Sending it by electronic means if the person consented in writing—in which event service is complete upon transmission, but is not effective if the serving party learns that it did not reach the person to be served; or

- Delivering it by any other means that the person consented to in writing—in which event service is complete when the person making service delivers it to the agency designated to make delivery. FRCP 5(b)(2).

    iii. *Electronic service*

- *Consent.* By registering to use the ECF system, attorneys consent to electronic service of documents filed in cases maintained on the ECF system. IN R USDCTSD L.R. 5-3(d). By participating in the Electronic Case Filing Program, attorneys consent to the electronic service of documents, and shall make available electronic mail addresses for service. IN R USDCTSD ECF Procedures(11).

- *Service on registered parties.* Upon the filing of a document by a party, an e-mail message will be automatically generated by the electronic filing system and sent via electronic mail to the e-mail addresses of all registered attorneys who have appeared in the case. The Notice of Electronic Filing will contain a document hyperlink which will provide recipients with one "free look" at the electronically filed document. Recipients are encouraged to print and/or save a copy of the document during the "free look" to avoid incurring PACER charges for future viewings of the document. IN R USDCTSD ECF Procedures(11). When a document has been filed electronically: transmission of the notice of electronic filing generated by the ECF system to an attorney's e-mail address constitutes service of the document on that attorney. IN R USDCTSD L.R. 5-4(c)(5). The party effectuates service on all registered attorneys by filing electronically. IN R USDCTSD ECF Procedures(11). When a document has been filed electronically: no other attempted service will constitute electronic service of the document. IN R USDCTSD L.R. 5-4(c)(6).

- *Service on exempt parties.* A filer must serve a copy of the document consistent with FRCP 5 on any party or attorney who is exempt from participating in electronic filing. IN R USDCTSD L.R. 5-4(d). It is the responsibility of the filing attorney to conventionally serve all parties who do not receive electronic service (the identity of these parties will be indicated on the filing receipt generated by the ECF system). IN R USDCTSD ECF Procedures(11).

- *Service on parties excused from electronic filing.* Parties otherwise participating in the electronic filing system may be excused from filing a particular component electronically under certain limited circumstances, such as when the component cannot be reduced to an electronic format. Such components shall not be filed electronically, but instead shall be manually filed with the Clerk of Court and served upon the parties in accordance with the applicable Federal Rules of Civil Procedure and the Local Rules of the United States District Court for the Southern District of Indiana for filing and service of non-electronic documents. IN R USDCTSD ECF Procedures(15).

- *Service of exempt documents.* Any document that is exempt from electronic filing must be filed directly with the clerk and served on other parties in the case as required by those Federal Rules of Civil Procedure and Local Rules of the United States District Court for the Southern District of Indiana that apply to the service of non-electronic documents. IN R USDCTSD L.R. 5-2(c).

iv. *Using court facilities.* If a local rule so authorizes, a party may use the court's transmission facilities to make service under FRCP 5(b)(2)(E). FRCP 5(b)(3).

c. *Serving numerous defendants*

   i. *In general.* If an action involves an unusually large number of defendants, the court may, on motion or on its own, order that:

- Defendants' pleadings and replies to them need not be served on other defendants;

- Any crossclaim, counterclaim, avoidance, or affirmative defense in those pleadings and replies to them will be treated as denied or avoided by all other parties; and

- Filing any such pleading and serving it on the plaintiff constitutes notice of the pleading to all parties. FRCP 5(c)(1).

   ii. *Notifying parties.* A copy of every such order must be served on the parties as the court directs. FRCP 5(c)(2).

G. Hearings

1. *Hearings, generally*

a. *Oral argument.* Due process does not require that oral argument be permitted on a motion and, except as otherwise provided by local rule, the district court has discretion to determine whether it will decide the motion on the papers or hear argument by counsel (and perhaps receive evidence). FPP § 1190; F.D.I.C. v. Deglau, 207 F.3d 153 (3d Cir. 2000).

   i. *Request for oral argument.* A party may request oral argument by filing a separate motion explaining why oral argument is necessary and estimating how long the court should allow for the argument. IN R USDCTSD L.R. 7-5(a). Refer to the Documents section of this document for more information.

   ii. *No additional evidence at oral argument.* Parties may not present additional evidence at oral argument. IN R USDCTSD L.R. 7-5(b).

b. *Providing a regular schedule for oral hearings.* A court may establish regular times and places for oral hearings on motions. FRCP 78(a).

c. *Providing for submission on briefs.* By rule or order, the court may provide for submitting and determining motions on briefs, without oral hearings. FRCP 78(b).

d. *Request for evidentiary hearing.* A party may request an evidentiary hearing on a motion or petition by serving and filing a separate motion explaining why the hearing is necessary and estimating how long the court should allow for the hearing. IN R USDCTSD L.R. 7-5(c).

e. *Directed by the court.* The court may: (1) grant or deny a request for oral argument or an evidentiary hearing in its sole discretion; (2) set oral argument or an evidentiary hearing without a request from a party; and (3) order any oral argument or evidentiary hearing to be held anywhere within the district regardless of where the case will be tried. IN R USDCTSD L.R. 7-5(d).

2. *Courtroom and courthouse decorum.* For information on courtroom and courthouse decorum, refer to IN R USDCTSD L.R. 83-3.

H. Forms

1. Federal Motion for Continuance/Extension of Time Forms

a. Opposition in federal district court; To motion for continuance; On ground of additional time required to prepare for trial; No excusable neglect shown. AMJUR PP CONTIN § 79.

b. Affidavit in opposition to motion for continuance; By plaintiff's attorney; Lack of due diligence in discovery of documents. AMJUR PP CONTIN § 80.

c. Affidavit in opposition to motion for continuance; By plaintiff's attorney; Defendant's absent witness previously absent; Lack of due diligence in compelling attendance of witness. AMJUR PP CONTIN § 81.

d. Affidavit in opposition to motion for continuance; By plaintiff; Admission that absent witness of defendant would testify according to affidavit. AMJUR PP CONTIN § 83.

e. Affidavit in opposition to defendant's motion for continuance; By plaintiff's counsel; Testimony of absent witness merely cumulative. AMJUR PP CONTIN § 85.

f. Motion for enlargement of time. 2 FEDFORMS § 5:11.

g. Motion for enlargement of time; By plaintiff. 2 FEDFORMS § 5:12.

h. Motion for enlargement of time; To answer motion. 2 FEDFORMS § 5:14.

i. Motion for continuance. 2 FEDFORMS § 5:36.

j. Motion for continuance; Reciting supporting facts; New allegations in amended answer. 2 FEDFORMS § 5:37.

k. Motion for continuance; Reciting supporting facts; Absence of witness. 2 FEDFORMS § 5:38.

l. Motion for continuance; Reciting supporting facts; Absence of witness; Witness outside the country. 2 FEDFORMS § 5:39.

m. Motion for continuance or in the alternative for change of venue; Hostility against defendant. 2 FEDFORMS § 5:40.

n. Notice; Of motion; Containing motion. FEDPROF § 1:749.

o. Brief; Supporting or opposing motion. FEDPROF § 1:752.

p. Opposition to motion; For continuance; No excusable neglect. FEDPROF § 1:808.

q. Affidavit; Opposing motion for continuance; Offer to stipulate to testimony of unavailable witness. FEDPROF § 1:813.

r. Reply to motion for extension of time. GOLDLTGFMS § 10:40.

s. Motions; Extension of time to file jury demand. GOLDLTGFMS § 12:6.

t. Motion for extension of time. GOLDLTGFMS § 25:37.

u. Motion for extension of time to answer. GOLDLTGFMS § 26:13.

v.   Motion to extend time for serving answers. GOLDLTGFMS § 26:14.

w.   Motion for continuance. GOLDLTGFMS § 43:2.

x.   Motion for continuance; Lawyer unavailable. GOLDLTGFMS § 43:3.

y.   Motion for continuance; Witness unavailable. GOLDLTGFMS § 43:4.

z.   Motion for continuance; Party in military service. GOLDLTGFMS § 43:6.

2. Forms for the Southern District of Indiana

a.   Notice of endorsement. IN R USDCTSD ECF Procedures(Appendix B).

b.   Notice of manual filing. IN R USDCTSD ECF Procedures(Appendix C).

c.   Declaration that party was unable to file in a timely manner due to technical difficulties. IN R USDCTSD ECF Procedures(Appendix D).

I. Applicable Rules

1. *Federal rules*

a.   Serving and filing pleadings and other papers. FRCP 5.

b.   Constitutional challenge to a statute; Notice, certification, and intervention. FRCP 5.1.

c.   Privacy protection for filings made with the court. FRCP 5.2.

d.   Computing and extending time; Time for motion papers. FRCP 6.

e.   Pleadings allowed; Form of motions and other papers. FRCP 7.

f.   Disclosure statement. FRCP 7.1.

g.   Form of pleadings. FRCP 10.

h.   Signing pleadings, motions, and other papers; Representations to the court; Sanctions. FRCP 11.

i.   Taking testimony. FRCP 43.

j.   Hearing motions; Submission on briefs. FRCP 78.

2. *Local rules*

a.   Scope of the rules. IN R USDCTSD L.R. 1-1.

b.   Sanctions for errors as to form. IN R USDCTSD L.R. 1-3.

c.   Format of documents presented for filing. IN R USDCTSD L.R. 5-1.

d.   Constitutional challenge to a statute; Notice. IN R USDCTSD L.R. 5.1-1.

e.   Filing of documents electronically required. IN R USDCTSD L.R. 5-2.

f.   Eligibility, registration, passwords for electronic filing; Exemption from electronic filing. IN R USDCTSD L.R. 5-3.

g.   Timing and consequences of electronic filing. IN R USDCTSD L.R. 5-4.

h.   Attachments and exhibits in cases filed electronically. IN R USDCTSD L.R. 5-6.

i.   Signatures in cases filed electronically. IN R USDCTSD L.R. 5-7.

j.   Non-electronic filings. IN R USDCTSD L.R. 5-10.

k.   Extensions of time. IN R USDCTSD L.R. 6-1.

l.   Motion practice. [IN R USDCTSD L.R. 7-1, as amended by IN ORDER 16-2319, effective December 1, 2016].

m.   Oral arguments and hearings. IN R USDCTSD L.R. 7-5.

n.   Request for three-judge court. IN R USDCTSD L.R. 9-2.

o.   Continuances in civil cases. IN R USDCTSD L.R. 16-3.

p.   Filing of discovery materials. IN R USDCTSD L.R. 26-2.

q.   Assignment of cases. IN R USDCTSD L.R. 40-1.

r. Alternative dispute resolution. IN R USDCTSD A.D.R. Rule 1.1; IN R USDCTSD A.D.R. Rule 1.2; IN R USDCTSD A.D.R. Rule 1.5; IN R USDCTSD A.D.R. Rule 2.1; IN R USDCTSD A.D.R. Rule 2.2.

s. Instructions for preparing case management plan. IN R USDCTSD Case Mgt.

t. Electronic case filing policies and procedures manual. IN R USDCTSD ECF Procedures.

Motions, Oppositions and Replies
Motion for Summary Judgment

Document Last Updated December 2016

A. Checklist

(I) ❑ Matters to be considered by moving party

    (a) ❑ Required documents

        (1) ❑ Notice of motion and motion

        (2) ❑ Brief

        (3) ❑ Certificate of service

    (b) ❑ Supplemental documents

        (1) ❑ Supporting evidence

        (2) ❑ Notice of constitutional question

        (3) ❑ Nongovernmental corporate disclosure statement

        (4) ❑ Index of exhibits

        (5) ❑ Notice to pro se litigant

        (6) ❑ Request for oral argument

        (7) ❑ Request for evidentiary hearing

        (8) ❑ Copy of authority

        (9) ❑ Proposed order

        (10) ❑ Copy of document with self-address envelope

        (11) ❑ Notice of manual filing

        (12) ❑ Courtesy copies

        (13) ❑ Copies for three-judge court

        (14) ❑ Declaration that party was unable to file in a timely manner due to technical difficulties

    (c) ❑ Timing

        (1) ❑ Unless a different time is set by local rule or the court orders otherwise, a party may file a motion for summary judgment at any time until thirty (30) days after the close of all discovery

        (2) ❑ A written motion and notice of the hearing must be served at least fourteen (14) days before the time specified for the hearing, with the following exceptions: (i) when the motion may be heard ex parte; (ii) when the Federal Rules of Civil Procedure set a different time; or (iii) when a court order—which a party may, for good cause, apply for ex parte—sets a different time

        (3) ❑ Any affidavit supporting a motion must be served with the motion

        (4) ❑ When a party who is not exempt from the electronic filing requirement files a document directly with the clerk, the party must present the document to the clerk within one (1) business day after filing the notice of manual filing

(5) ❑ Unless the court orders otherwise, the [untimely] document and declaration [that party was unable to file in a timely manner due to technical difficulties] must be filed no later than 12:00 noon of the first day on which the court is open for business following the original filing deadline

(II) ❑ Matters to be considered by opposing party

    (a) ❑ Required documents

        (1) ❑ Response brief

        (2) ❑ Certificate of service

    (b) ❑ Supplemental documents

        (1) ❑ Supporting evidence

        (2) ❑ Notice of constitutional question

        (3) ❑ Index of exhibits

        (4) ❑ Request for oral argument

        (5) ❑ Request for evidentiary hearing

        (6) ❑ Copy of authority

        (7) ❑ Copy of document with self-address envelope

        (8) ❑ Notice of manual filing

        (9) ❑ Courtesy copies

       (10) ❑ Copies for three-judge court

       (11) ❑ Declaration that party was unable to file in a timely manner due to technical difficulties

    (c) ❑ Timing

        (1) ❑ A party opposing a summary judgment motion must, within twenty-eight (28) days after the movant serves the motion, file and serve a response brief and any evidence (that is not already in the record) that the party relies on to oppose the motion

        (2) ❑ Except as FRCP 59(c) provides otherwise, any opposing affidavit must be served at least seven (7) days before the hearing, unless the court permits service at another time

        (3) ❑ When a party who is not exempt from the electronic filing requirement files a document directly with the clerk, the party must present the document to the clerk within one (1) business day after filing the notice of manual filing

        (4) ❑ Unless the court orders otherwise, the [untimely] document and declaration [that party was unable to file in a timely manner due to technical difficulties] must be filed no later than 12:00 noon of the first day on which the court is open for business following the original filing deadline

B. Timing

1. *Motion for summary judgment.* Unless a different time is set by local rule or the court orders otherwise, a party may file a motion for summary judgment at any time until thirty (30) days after the close of all discovery. FRCP 56(b).

2. *Timing of motions, generally*

    a. *Motion and notice of hearing.* A written motion and notice of the hearing must be served at least fourteen (14) days before the time specified for the hearing, with the following exceptions:

        i. When the motion may be heard ex parte;

        ii. When the Federal Rules of Civil Procedure set a different time; or

        iii. When a court order—which a party may, for good cause, apply for ex parte—sets a different time. FRCP 6(c)(1).

    b. *Supporting affidavit.* Any affidavit supporting a motion must be served with the motion. FRCP 6(c)(2).

3. *Timing of opposing papers.* Summary judgment motions are subject to the deadlines in IN R USDCTSD L.R. 56-1. IN R USDCTSD L.R. 7-1(c)(1). A party opposing a summary judgment motion must, within twenty-eight (28) days after the movant serves the motion, file and serve a response brief and any evidence (that is not already in the record) that the party relies on to oppose the motion. IN R USDCTSD L.R. 56-1(b).

   a. *Opposing affidavit.* Except as FRCP 59(c) provides otherwise, any opposing affidavit must be served at least seven (7) days before the hearing, unless the court permits service at another time. FRCP 6(c)(2).

   b. *Extensions.* The court may extend response and reply deadlines, but only for good cause. IN R USDCTSD L.R. 7-1(c)(3).

   c. *Summary ruling on failure to respond.* The court may summarily rule on a motion if an opposing party does not file a response within the deadline. IN R USDCTSD L.R. 7-1(c)(4).

4. *Timing of reply papers.* Where the respondent files an answering affidavit setting up a new matter, the moving party ordinarily is allowed a reasonable time to file a reply affidavit since failure to deny the new matter by affidavit may operate as an admission of its truth. AMJUR MOTIONS § 25.

   a. *Reply brief.* Summary judgment motions are subject to the deadlines in IN R USDCTSD L.R. 56-1. IN R USDCTSD L.R. 7-1(c)(1). The movant may file a reply brief within fourteen (14) days after a response is served. IN R USDCTSD L.R. 56-1(c).

   b. *Extensions.* The court may extend response and reply deadlines, but only for good cause. IN R USDCTSD L.R. 7-1(c)(3).

5. *Timing of surreply papers.* The surreply must be filed within seven (7) days after the movant serves the reply and must be limited to the new evidence and objections. IN R USDCTSD L.R. 56-1(d).

6. *Document filing by non-exempt party.* When a party who is not exempt from the electronic filing requirement files a document directly with the clerk, the party must: present the document to the clerk within one (1) business day after filing the notice of manual filing. IN R USDCTSD L.R. 5-2(d)(2).

7. *Declaration that party was unable to file in a timely manner due to technical difficulties.* Unless the Court orders otherwise, the [untimely] document and declaration [that party was unable to file in a timely manner due to technical difficulties] must be filed no later than 12:00 noon of the first day on which the Court is open for business following the original filing deadline. IN R USDCTSD ECF Procedures(16).

8. *Computation of time*

   a. *Computing time.* FRCP 6 applies in computing any time period specified in the Federal Rules of Civil Procedure, in any local rule or court order, or in any statute that does not specify a method of computing time. FRCP 6(a).

      i. *Period stated in days or a longer unit.* When the period is stated in days or a longer unit of time:
      - Exclude the day of the event that triggers the period;
      - Count every day, including intermediate Saturdays, Sundays, and legal holidays; and
      - Include the last day of the period, but if the last day is a Saturday, Sunday, or legal holiday, the period continues to run until the end of the next day that is not a Saturday, Sunday, or legal holiday. FRCP 6(a)(1).

      ii. *Period stated in hours.* When the period is stated in hours:
      - Begin counting immediately on the occurrence of the event that triggers the period;
      - Count every hour, including hours during intermediate Saturdays, Sundays, and legal holidays; and
      - If the period would end on a Saturday, Sunday, or legal holiday, the period continues to run until the same time on the next day that is not a Saturday, Sunday, or legal holiday. FRCP 6(a)(2).

iii. *Inaccessibility of the clerk's office.* Unless the court orders otherwise, if the clerk's office is inaccessible:

- On the last day for filing under FRCP 6(a)(1), then the time for filing is extended to the first accessible day that is not a Saturday, Sunday, or legal holiday; or

- During the last hour for filing under FRCP 6(a)(2), then the time for filing is extended to the same time on the first accessible day that is not a Saturday, Sunday, or legal holiday. FRCP 6(a)(3).

iv. *"Last day" defined.* Unless a different time is set by a statute, local rule, or court order, the last day ends:

- For electronic filing, at midnight in the court's time zone; and

- For filing by other means, when the clerk's office is scheduled to close. FRCP 6(a)(4).

v. *"Next day" defined.* The "next day" is determined by continuing to count forward when the period is measured after an event and backward when measured before an event. FRCP 6(a)(5).

vi. *"Legal holiday" defined.* "Legal holiday" means:

- The day set aside by statute for observing New Year's Day, Martin Luther King Jr.'s Birthday, Washington's Birthday, Memorial Day, Independence Day, Labor Day, Columbus Day, Veterans' Day, Thanksgiving Day, or Christmas Day;

- Any day declared a holiday by the President or Congress; and

- For periods that are measured after an event, any other day declared a holiday by the state where the district court is located. FRCP 6(a)(6).

b. *Computation of electronic filing deadlines.* Filing documents electronically does not alter filing deadlines. IN R USDCTSD ECF Procedures(7). A document due on a particular day must be filed before midnight local time of the division where the case is pending. IN R USDCTSD L.R. 5-4(a). All electronic transmissions of documents must be completed (i.e. received completely by the Clerk's Office) prior to midnight of the local time of the division in which the case is pending in order to be considered timely filed that day (NOTE: time will be noted in Eastern Time on the Court's docket. If you have filed a document prior to midnight local time of the division in which the case is pending and the document is due that date, but the electronic receipt and docket reflect the following calendar day, please contact the Court). IN R USDCTSD ECF Procedures(7). Although attorneys may file documents electronically twenty-four (24) hours a day, seven (7) days a week, attorneys are encouraged to file all documents during the normal working hours of the Clerk's Office (Monday through Friday, 8:30 a.m. to 4:30 p.m.) when technical support is available. IN R USDCTSD ECF Procedures(7); IN R USDCTSD ECF Procedures(9).

i. *Technical difficulties.* Parties are encouraged to file documents electronically during normal business hours, in case a problem is encountered. In the event a technical failure occurs and a document cannot be filed electronically despite the best efforts of the filing party, the party should print (if possible) a copy of the error message received. In addition, as soon as practically possible, the party should file a "Declaration that Party was Unable to File in a Timely Manner Due to Technical Difficulties." A model form is provided as Appendix D (IN R USDCTSD ECF Procedures(Appendix D)). IN R USDCTSD ECF Procedures(16).

- If a party is unable to file electronically and, as a result, may miss a filing deadline, the party must contact the Clerk's Office at the number listed in IN R USDCTSD ECF Procedures(15) to inform the court's staff of the difficulty. If a party misses a filing deadline due to an inability to file electronically, the party may submit the untimely filed document, accompanied by a declaration stating the reason(s) for missing the deadline. Unless the Court orders otherwise, the document and declaration must be filed no later than 12:00 noon of the first day on which the Court is open for business following the original filing deadline. IN R USDCTSD ECF Procedures(16).

    c. *Extending time*

        i. *In general.* When an act may or must be done within a specified time, the court may, for good cause, extend the time:

- With or without motion or notice if the court acts, or if a request is made, before the original time or its extension expires; or

- On motion made after the time has expired if the party failed to act because of excusable neglect. FRCP 6(b)(1).

        ii. *Exceptions.* A court must not extend the time to act under FRCP 50(b), FRCP 50(d), FRCP 52(b), FRCP 59(b), FRCP 59(d), FRCP 59(e), and FRCP 60(b). FRCP 6(b)(2).

        iii. Refer to the United States District Court for the Southern District of Indiana KeyRules Motion for Continuance/Extension of Time document for more information on extending time.

    d. *Additional time after certain kinds of service.* When a party may or must act within a specified time after being served and service is made under FRCP 5(b)(2)(C) (mail), FRCP 5(b)(2)(D) (leaving with the clerk), or FRCP 5(b)(2)(F) (other means consented to), three (3) days are added after the period would otherwise expire under FRCP 6(a). FRCP 6(d). Service by electronic mail shall constitute service pursuant to FRCP 5(b)(2)(E) and shall entitle the party being served to the additional three (3) days provided by FRCP 6(d). IN R USDCTSD ECF Procedures(11).

C. General Requirements

1. *Motions, generally*

    a. *Requirements.* A request for a court order must be made by motion. The motion must:

        i. Be in writing unless made during a hearing or trial;

        ii. State with particularity the grounds for seeking the order; and

        iii. State the relief sought. FRCP 7(b)(1).

    b. *Notice of motion.* A party interested in resisting the relief sought by a motion has a right to notice thereof, and an opportunity to be heard. AMJUR MOTIONS § 12.

        i. In addition to statutory or court rule provisions requiring notice of a motion—the purpose of such a notice requirement having been said to be to prevent a party from being prejudicially surprised by a motion—principles of natural justice dictate that an adverse party generally must be given notice that a motion will be presented to the court. AMJUR MOTIONS § 12.

        ii. "Notice," in this regard, means reasonable notice, including a meaningful opportunity to prepare and to defend against allegations of a motion. AMJUR MOTIONS § 12.

    c. *Writing requirement.* The writing requirement is intended to insure that the adverse parties are informed and have a record of both the motion's pendency and the grounds on which the movant seeks an order. FPP § 1191; Feldberg v. Quechee Lakes Corp., 463 F.3d 195 (2d Cir. 2006).

        i. It is sufficient "if the motion is stated in a written notice of the hearing of the motion." FPP § 1191.

    d. *Particularity requirement.* The particularity requirement insures that the opposing parties will have notice of their opponent's contentions. FEDPROC § 62:364; Goodman v. 1973 26 Foot Trojan Vessel, Arkansas Registration No. AR1439SN, 859 F.2d 71, 12 Fed.R.Serv.3d 645 (8th Cir. 1988). That requirement ensures that notice of the basis for the motion is provided to the court and to the opposing party so as to avoid prejudice, provide the opponent with a meaningful opportunity to respond, and provide the court with enough information to process the motion correctly. FEDPROC § 62:364; Andreas v. Volkswagen of America, Inc., 336 F.3d 789, 56 Fed.R.Serv.3d 6 (8th Cir. 2003).

        i. Reasonable specification of the grounds for a motion is sufficient. However, where a movant fails to state even one ground for granting the motion in question, the movant has failed to meet the minimal standard of "reasonable specification." FEDPROC § 62:364; Martinez v. Trainor, 556 F.2d 818, 23 Fed.R.Serv.2d 403 (7th Cir. 1977).

        ii. The court may excuse the failure to comply with the particularity requirement if it is inadvertent, and where no prejudice is shown by the opposing party. FEDPROC § 62:364.

e. *Motions must be filed separately.* Motions must be filed separately, but alternative motions may be filed in a single document if each is named in the title. A motion must not be contained within a brief, response, or reply to a previously filed motion, unless ordered by the court. IN R USDCTSD L.R. 7-1(a).

f. *Routine or uncontested motions.* The court may rule upon a routine or uncontested motion before the response deadline passes, unless: (1) the motion indicates that an opposing party objects to it; or (2) the court otherwise believes that a response will be filed. IN R USDCTSD L.R. 7-1(d).

2. *Motion for summary judgment.* A party may move for summary judgment, identifying each claim or defense—or the part of each claim or defense—on which summary judgment is sought. The court shall grant summary judgment if the movant shows that there is no genuine dispute as to any material fact and the movant is entitled to judgment as a matter of law. The court should state on the record the reasons for granting or denying the motion. FRCP 56(a).

a. *Burden of proof and presumptions*

   i. *Movant's burden.* It is well-settled that the party moving for summary judgment has the burden of demonstrating that the FRCP 56(c) test—"no genuine issue as to any material fact"—is satisfied and that the movant is entitled to judgment as a matter of law. FPP § 2727; Adickes v. S. H. Kress & Co., 398 U.S. 144, 157, 90 S.Ct. 1598, 1608, 26 L.Ed.2d 142 (1970).

- The movant is held to a stringent standard. FPP § 2727. Before summary judgment will be granted it must be clear what the truth is and any doubt as to the existence of a genuine dispute of material fact will be resolved against the movant. FPP § 2727; Poller v. Columbia Broadcasting Sys., Inc., 368 U.S. 464, 82 S.Ct. 486, 7 L.Ed.2d 458 (1962); Adickes v. S. H. Kress & Co., 398 U.S. 144, 90 S.Ct. 1598, 26 L.Ed.2d 142 (1970).

- Because the burden is on the movant, the evidence presented to the court always is construed in favor of the party opposing the motion and the opponent is given the benefit of all favorable inferences that can be drawn from it. FPP § 2727; Scott v. Harris, 550 U.S. 372, 127 S.Ct. 1769, 167 L.Ed.2d 686 (2007).

- Finally, facts asserted by the party opposing the motion, if supported by affidavits or other evidentiary material, are regarded as true. FPP § 2727; McLaughlin v. Liu, 849 F.2d 1205, 1208 (9th Cir. 1988).

   ii. *Opponent's burden.* If the summary-judgment movant makes out a prima facie case that would entitle him to a judgment as a matter of law if uncontroverted at trial, summary judgment will be granted unless the opposing party offers some competent evidence that could be presented at trial showing that there is a genuine dispute as to a material fact. FPP § 2727.2; Scott v. Harris, 550 U.S. 372, 127 S.Ct. 1769, 167 L.Ed.2d 686 (2007). In this way the burden of producing evidence is shifted to the party opposing the motion. FPP § 2727.2; Celotex Corp. v. Catrett, 477 U.S. 317, 331, 106 S.Ct. 2548, 2557, 91 L.Ed.2d 265 (1986).

- The burden on the nonmoving party is not a heavy one; the nonmoving party simply is required to show specific facts, as opposed to general allegations, that present a genuine issue worthy of trial. FPP § 2727.2; Lujan v. Defenders of Wildlife, 504 U.S. 555, 112 S.Ct. 2130, 119 L.Ed.2d 351 (1992).

- The nonmoving party has two options once the moving party has met its burden of production of evidence demonstrating the absence of a genuine issue of material fact: either come forward with countervailing evidence showing that a genuine issue does exist, or submit an affidavit under FRCP 56(f) demonstrating that more time or further discovery are necessary to enable it to oppose the summary judgment motion. FEDPROC § 62:589.

b. *Court's assumptions about facts.* In deciding a summary judgment motion, the court will assume that:

   i. The facts as claimed and supported by admissible evidence by the movant are admitted without controversy except to the extent that:

- The non-movant specifically controverts the facts in that party's "Statement of Material Facts in Dispute" with admissible evidence; or

- It is shown that the movant's facts are not supported by admissible evidence; or

- The facts, alone or in conjunction with other admissible evidence, allow the court to draw reasonable inferences in the non-movant's favor sufficient to preclude summary judgment. IN R USDCTSD L.R. 56-1(f)(1).

    ii. Facts that a non-movant asserts are true to the extent admissible evidence supports them. IN R USDCTSD L.R. 56-1(f)(2).

c. *Stipulation to facts.* The parties may stipulate to facts in the summary judgment process, and may state that their stipulations are entered only for the purpose of the motion for summary judgment and are not intended to be otherwise binding. IN R USDCTSD L.R. 56-1(g).

d. *Failing to properly support or address a fact.* If a party fails to properly support an assertion of fact or fails to properly address another party's assertion of fact as required by FRCP 56(c), the court may:

    i. Give an opportunity to properly support or address the fact;

    ii. Consider the fact undisputed for purposes of the motion;

    iii. Grant summary judgment if the motion and supporting materials—including the facts considered undisputed—show that the movant is entitled to it; or

    iv. Issue any other appropriate order. FRCP 56(e).

e. *Judgment independent of the motion.* After giving notice and a reasonable time to respond, the court may:

    i. Grant summary judgment for a nonmovant;

    ii. Grant the motion on grounds not raised by a party; or

    iii. Consider summary judgment on its own after identifying for the parties material facts that may not be genuinely in dispute. FRCP 56(f).

f. *Failing to grant all the requested relief.* If the court does not grant all the relief requested by the motion, it may enter an order stating any material fact—including an item of damages or other relief—that is not genuinely in dispute and treating the fact as established in the case. FRCP 56(g).

g. *Affidavit or declaration submitted in bad faith.* If satisfied that an affidavit or declaration under FRCP 56 is submitted in bad faith or solely for delay, the court—after notice and a reasonable time to respond—may order the submitting party to pay the other party the reasonable expenses, including attorney's fees, it incurred as a result. An offending party or attorney may also be held in contempt or subjected to other appropriate sanctions. FRCP 56(h).

h. *Conversion of motions under FRCP 12(b)(6) and FRCP 12(c).* If, on a motion under FRCP 12(b)(6) or FRCP 12(c), matters outside the pleadings are presented to and not excluded by the court, the motion must be treated as one for summary judgment under FRCP 56. FRCP 12(d).

i. *Compliance with IN R USDCTSD L.R. 56-1.* The court may, in the interest of justice or for good cause, excuse failure to comply strictly with IN R USDCTSD L.R. 56-1. IN R USDCTSD L.R. 56-1(l).

3. *Opposing papers*

a. *Opposing papers, generally.* The Federal Rules of Civil Procedure do not require any formal answer, return, or reply to a motion, except where the Federal Rules of Civil Procedure or local rules may require affidavits, memoranda, or other papers to be filed in opposition to a motion. Such papers are simply to apprise the court of such opposition and the grounds of that opposition. FEDPROC § 62:359.

    i. *Effect of failure to respond to motion.* Although in the absence of statutory provision or court rule, a motion ordinarily does not require a written answer, when a party files a motion and the opposing party fails to respond, the court may construe such failure to respond as nonopposition to the motion or an admission that the motion was meritorious, may take the facts alleged in the motion as true—the rule in some jurisdictions being that the failure to respond to a fact set forth in a motion is deemed an admission—and may grant the motion if the relief requested appears to be justified. AMJUR MOTIONS § 28.

    ii.   *Assent or no opposition not determinative.* However, a motion will not be granted automatically simply because an "assent" or a notation of "no opposition" has been filed; federal judges frequently deny motions that have been assented to when it is thought that justice so dictates. FPP § 1190.

    iii.   *Responsive pleading inappropriate as response to motion.* An attempt to answer or oppose a motion with a responsive pleading usually is not appropriate. FPP § 1190.

  b.   *Opposition to motion for summary judgment.* The party opposing summary judgment does not have a duty to present evidence in opposition to a motion under FRCP 56 in all circumstances. FPP § 2727.2; Jaroma v. Massey, 873 F.2d 17 (1st Cir. 1989).

    i.   *When facts are unavailable to the nonmovant.* If a nonmovant shows by affidavit or declaration that, for specified reasons, it cannot present facts essential to justify its opposition, the court may:

- Defer considering the motion or deny it;
- Allow time to obtain affidavits or declarations or to take discovery; or
- Issue any other appropriate order. FRCP 56(d).

4.   *Reply papers.* A moving party may be required or permitted to prepare papers in addition to his original motion papers. AMJUR MOTIONS § 25. Papers answering or replying to opposing papers may be appropriate, in the interests of justice, where it appears there is a substantial reason for allowing a reply. Thus, a court may accept reply papers where a party demonstrates that the papers to which it seeks to file a reply raise new issues that are material to the disposition of the question before the court, or where the court determines, sua sponte, that it wishes further briefing of an issue raised in those papers and orders the submission of additional papers. FEDPROC § 62:360.

  a.   *Function of reply papers.* The function of a reply affidavit is to answer the arguments made in opposition to the position taken by the movant and not to permit the movant to introduce new arguments in support of the motion. AMJUR MOTIONS § 25.

  b.   *Issues raised for the first time in a reply document.* However, the view has been followed in some jurisdictions, that as a matter of judicial economy, where there is no prejudice and where the issues could be raised simply by filing a motion to dismiss, the trial court has discretion to consider arguments raised for the first time in a reply memorandum, and that a trial court may grant a motion to strike issues raised for the first time in a reply memorandum. AMJUR MOTIONS § 26.

5.   *Surreply.* A party opposing a summary judgment motion may file a surreply brief only if the movant cites new evidence in the reply or objects to the admissibility of the evidence cited in the response. IN R USDCTSD L.R. 56-1(d).

6.   *Appearances.* Every attorney who represents a party or who files a document on a party's behalf must file an appearance for that party. IN R USDCTSD L.R. 83-7. The filing of a Notice of Appearance shall act to establish the filing attorney as an attorney of record representing a designated party or parties in a particular cause of action. As a result, it is necessary for each attorney to file a separate Notice of Appearance when entering an appearance in a case. A joint appearance on behalf of multiple attorneys may be filed electronically only if it is filed separately for each attorney, using his/her ECF login. IN R USDCTSD ECF Procedures(12). Only those attorneys who have filed an appearance in a pending action are entitled to be served with case documents under FRCP 5(a). IN R USDCTSD L.R. 83-7. For more information, refer to IN R USDCTSD L.R. 83-7 and IN R USDCTSD ECF Procedures(12).

7.   *Notice of related action.* A party must file a notice of related action: as soon as it appears that the party's case and another pending case: (1) arise out of the same transaction or occurrence; (2) involve the same property; or (3) involve the validity or infringement or the same patent, trademark, or copyright. IN R USDCTSD L.R. 40-1(d)(2). For more information, refer to IN R USDCTSD L.R. 40-1.

8.   *Alternative dispute resolution (ADR)*

  a.   *Application.* Unless limited by specific provisions, or unless there are other applicable specific

statutory, common law, or constitutional procedures, the Local Alternative Dispute Resolution Rules of the United States District Court for the Southern District of Indiana shall apply in all civil litigation filed in the U.S. District Court for the Southern District of Indiana, except in the following cases and proceedings:

    i. Applications for writs of habeas corpus under 28 U.S.C.A. § 2254;

    ii. Forfeiture cases;

    iii. Non-adversary proceedings in bankruptcy;

    iv. Social Security administrative review cases; and

    v. Such other matters as specified by order of the Court; for example, matters involving important public policy issues, constitutional law, or the establishment of new law. IN R USDCTSD A.D.R. Rule 1.2.

  b. *Mediation.* Mediation under this section (IN R USDCTSD A.D.R. Rule 2.1, et seq.) involves the confidential process by which a person acting as a Mediator, selected by the parties or appointed by the Court, assists the litigants in reaching a mutually acceptable agreement. It is an informal and nonadversarial process. The role of the Mediator is to assist in identifying the issues, reducing misunderstandings, clarifying priorities, exploring areas of compromise, and finding points of agreement as well as legitimate points of disagreement. Final decision-making authority rests with the parties, not the Mediator. IN R USDCTSD A.D.R. Rule 2.1. It is anticipated that an agreement may not resolve all of the disputed issues, but the process, nonetheless, can reduce points of contention. Parties and their representatives are required to mediate in good faith, but are not compelled to reach an agreement. IN R USDCTSD A.D.R. Rule 2.1.

    i. *Case selection.* The Court with the agreement of the parties may refer a civil case for mediation. Unless otherwise ordered or as specifically provided in IN R USDCTSD A.D.R. Rule 2.8, referral to mediation does not abate or suspend the action, and no scheduled dates shall be delayed or deferred, including the date of trial. IN R USDCTSD A.D.R. Rule 2.2.

    ii. For more information on mediation, refer to IN R USDCTSD A.D.R. Rule 2.1, et seq.

  c. *Other methods of dispute resolution.* The Local Alternative Dispute Resolution Rules of the United States District Court for the Southern District of Indiana shall not preclude the parties from utilizing any other reasonable method or technique of alternative dispute resolution to resolve disputes to which the parties agree. However, any use of arbitration by the parties will be governed by and comply with the requirements of 28 U.S.C.A. § 654 through 28 U.S.C.A. § 657. IN R USDCTSD A.D.R. Rule 1.5.

  d. For more information on alternative dispute resolution (ADR), refer to IN R USDCTSD A.D.R. Rule 1.1, et seq.

  9. *Notice of settlement or resolution.* The parties must immediately notify the court if they reasonably anticipate settling their case or resolving a pending motion. IN R USDCTSD L.R. 7-1(h).

  10. *Modification or suspension of rules.* The court may, on its own motion or at the request of a party, suspend or modify any rule in a particular case in the interest of justice. IN R USDCTSD L.R. 1-1(c).

D. Documents

  1. *Documents for moving party*

    a. *Required documents*

      i. *Notice of motion and motion.* Refer to the General Requirements section of this document for information on the notice of motion and motion.

      ii. *Brief.* The following motion must also be accompanied by a supporting brief: a motion for summary judgment under FRCP 56. IN R USDCTSD L.R. 7-1(b)(3). A party seeking summary judgment must file and serve a supporting brief and any evidence (that is not already in the record) that the party relies on to support the motion. IN R USDCTSD L.R. 56-1(a). Refer to the Format section of this document for the format of briefs.

        • *Statement of material facts not in dispute.* The brief must include a section labeled

706

"Statement of Material Facts Not in Dispute" containing the facts: (1) that are potentially determinative of the motion; and (2) as to which the movant contends there is no genuine issue. IN R USDCTSD L.R. 56-1(a).

- *Citations to supporting facts.* A party must support each fact the party asserts in a brief with a citation to a discovery response, a deposition, an affidavit, or other admissible evidence. The evidence must be in the record or in an appendix to the brief. The citation must refer to a page or paragraph number or otherwise similarly specify where the relevant information can be found in the supporting evidence. IN R USDCTSD L.R. 56-1(e). The court has no duty to search or consider any part of the record not specifically cited in the manner described in IN R USDCTSD L.R. 56-1(e). IN R USDCTSD L.R. 56-1(h).

- Refer to the General Requirements section of this document for more information about facts.

iii. *Certificate of service.* FRCP 5(d) requires that the person making service under FRCP 5 certify that service has been effected. FRCP 5(Advisory Committee Notes). Having such information on file may be useful for many purposes, including proof of service if an issue arises concerning the effectiveness of the service. FRCP 5(Advisory Committee Notes).

- *Certificate of service for electronically-filed documents.* A certificate of service must be included with all documents filed electronically. Such certificate shall indicate that service was accomplished pursuant to the Court's electronic filing procedures. IN R USDCTSD ECF Procedures(11). For the suggested format for a certificate of service for electronic filing, refer to IN R USDCTSD ECF Procedures(11).

b. *Supplemental documents*

i. *Supporting evidence.* When a motion relies on facts outside the record, the court may hear the matter on affidavits or may hear it wholly or partly on oral testimony or on depositions. FRCP 43(c).

- *Materials necessary for motion.* A party seeking relief under FRCP 26(c) or FRCP 37, or by way of a pretrial motion that could result in a final order on an issue, must file with the motion those parts of the discovery materials relevant to the motion. IN R USDCTSD L.R. 26-2(a).

- *Supporting factual positions.* A party asserting that a fact cannot be or is genuinely disputed must support the assertion by: (1) citing to particular parts of materials in the record, including depositions, documents, electronically stored information, affidavits or declarations, stipulations (including those made for purposes of the motion only), admissions, interrogatory answers, or other materials; or (2) showing that the materials cited do not establish the absence or presence of a genuine dispute, or that an adverse party cannot produce admissible evidence to support the fact. FRCP 56(c)(1).

- *Objection that a fact is not supported by admissible evidence.* A party may object that the material cited to support or dispute a fact cannot be presented in a form that would be admissible in evidence. FRCP 56(c)(2).

- *Materials not cited.* The court need consider only the cited materials, but it may consider other materials in the record. FRCP 56(c)(3).

- *Affidavits or declarations.* An affidavit or declaration used to support or oppose a motion must be made on personal knowledge, set out facts that would be admissible in evidence, and show that the affiant or declarant is competent to testify on the matters stated. FRCP 56(c)(4).

ii. *Notice of constitutional question.* A party that files a pleading, written motion, or other paper drawing into question the constitutionality of a federal or state statute must promptly:

- *File notice.* File a notice of constitutional question stating the question and identifying the paper that raises it, if: (1) a federal statute is questioned and the parties do not include the United States, one of its agencies, or one of its officers or employees in an official capacity;

707

or (2) a state statute is questioned and the parties do not include the state, one of its agencies, or one of its officers or employees in an official capacity; and

- *Serve notice.* Serve the notice and paper on the Attorney General of the United States if a federal statute is questioned—or on the state attorney general if a state statute is questioned—either by certified or registered mail or by sending it to an electronic address designated by the attorney general for this purpose. FRCP 5.1(a).

- *Time for filing.* A notice of constitutional challenge to a statute filed in accordance with FRCP 5.1 must be filed at the same time the parties tender their proposed case management plan, if one is required, or within twenty-one (21) days of the filing drawing into question the constitutionality of a federal or state statute, whichever occurs later. IN R USDCTSD L.R. 5.1-1(a).

- *Additional service requirements.* If a federal statute is challenged, in addition to the service requirements of FRCP 5.1(a), the party filing the notice of constitutional challenge must serve the notice and documents on the United States Attorney for the Southern District of Indiana, either by certified or registered mail or by sending it to an electronic address designated for that purpose by that official. IN R USDCTSD L.R. 5.1-1(b).

- *No forfeiture.* A party's failure to file and serve the notice, or the court's failure to certify, does not forfeit a constitutional claim or defense that is otherwise timely asserted. FRCP 5.1(d).

iii. *Nongovernmental corporate disclosure statement*

- *Contents.* A nongovernmental corporate party must file two (2) copies of a disclosure statement that: (1) identifies any parent corporation and any publicly held corporation owning ten percent (10%) or more of its stock; or (2) states that there is no such corporation. FRCP 7.1(a).

- *Time to file; Supplemental filing.* A party must: (1) file the disclosure statement with its first appearance, pleading, petition, motion, response, or other request addressed to the court; and (2) promptly file a supplemental statement if any required information changes. FRCP 7.1(b).

iv. *Index of exhibits.* Any pleading, motion, brief, affidavit, notice, or proposed order filed with the court, whether electronically or with the clerk, must: if it has four (4) or more exhibits, include a separate index that identifies and briefly describes each exhibit. IN R USDCTSD L.R. 5-1(b).

v. *Notice to pro se litigant.* A party seeking summary judgment against an unrepresented party must file and serve the notice contained in Appendix A (IN R USDCTSD App. A). IN R USDCTSD L.R. 56-1(k).

vi. *Request for oral argument.* A party may request oral argument by filing a separate motion explaining why oral argument is necessary and estimating how long the court should allow for the argument. The request must be filed and served with the supporting brief, response brief, or reply brief. IN R USDCTSD L.R. 7-5(a).

vii. *Request for evidentiary hearing.* A party may request an evidentiary hearing on a motion or petition by serving and filing a separate motion explaining why the hearing is necessary and estimating how long the court should allow for the hearing. IN R USDCTSD L.R. 7-5(c).

viii. *Copy of authority.* Generally, copies of cited authorities may not be attached to court filings. However, a party must attach to the party's motion or brief a copy of any cited authority if it is not available on Westlaw or Lexis. Upon request, a party must provide copies of any cited authority that is only available through electronic means to the court or the other parties. IN R USDCTSD L.R. 7-1(f).

ix. *Proposed order.* A party must include a suitable form of order with any document that requests the judge or the clerk to enter a routine or uncontested order. IN R USDCTSD L.R. 5-5(b); IN R USDCTSD L.R. 5-10(c); IN R USDCTSD L.R. 7-1(d).

- A service statement and/or list must be included on each proposed order, as required by IN

R USDCTSD L.R. 5-5(d). IN R USDCTSD ECF Procedures(11). Any pleading, motion, brief, affidavit, notice, or proposed order filed with the court, whether electronically or with the clerk, must: if it is a form of order, include a statement of service, in the format required by IN R USDCTSD L.R. 5-5(d) in the lower left corner of the document. IN R USDCTSD L.R. 5-1(b).

- A party electronically filing a proposed order—whether voluntarily or because required by IN R USDCTSD L.R. 5-5—must convert the order directly from a word processing program and file it as an attachment to the document it relates to. Proposed orders must include in the lower left-hand corner of the signature page a statement that service will be made electronically on all ECF-registered counsel of record via email generated by the court's ECF system, without listing all such counsel. A service list including the name and postal address of any pro se litigant or non-registered attorney of record must follow, stating that service on the listed individuals will be made in the traditional paper manner, via first-class U.S. Mail. IN R USDCTSD L.R. 5-5(d).

x. *Copy of document with self-address envelope.* To receive a file-stamped copy of a document filed directly with the clerk, a party must include with the original document an additional copy and a self-addressed envelope. The envelope must be big enough to hold the copy and have enough postage on it to send the copy via regular first-class mail. IN R USDCTSD L.R. 5-10(b).

xi. *Notice of manual filing.* When a party who is not exempt from the electronic filing requirement files a document directly with the clerk, the party must: electronically file a notice of manual filing that explains why the document cannot be filed electronically. IN R USDCTSD L.R. 5-2(d)(1). Refer to the Filing and Service Requirements section of this document for more information.

- Where an individual component cannot be included in an electronic filing (e.g. the component cannot be converted to electronic format), the filer shall electronically file the prescribed Notice of Manual Filing in place of that component. A model form is provided as Appendix C (IN R USDCTSD ECF Procedures(Appendix C)). IN R USDCTSD ECF Procedures(13).

- Before making a manual filing of a component, the filing party shall first electronically file a Notice of Manual Filing (See IN R USDCTSD ECF Procedures(Appendix C)). The filer shall initiate the electronic filing process as if filing the actual component but shall instead attach to the filing the Notice of Manual Filing setting forth the reason(s) why the component cannot be filed electronically. The manual filing should be accompanied by a copy of the previously filed Notice of Manual Filing. A party may seek to have a component excluded from electronic filing pursuant to applicable Federal and Local Rules (e.g., FRCP 26(c)). IN R USDCTSD ECF Procedures(15).

xii. *Courtesy copies.* District Judges and Magistrate Judges regularly receive documents filed by all parties. Therefore, parties shall not bring "courtesy copies" to any chambers unless specifically directed to do so by the Court. IN R USDCTSD Case Mgt(General Instructions For All Cases).

xiii. *Copies for three-judge court.* Parties in a case where a three-judge court has been requested must file an original and three copies of any document filed directly with the clerk (instead of electronically) until the court: (1) denies the request; (2) dissolves the three-judge court; or (3) allows the parties to file fewer copies. IN R USDCTSD L.R. 9-2(c).

xiv. *Declaration that party was unable to file in a timely manner due to technical difficulties.* If a party misses a filing deadline due to an inability to file electronically, the party may submit the untimely filed document, accompanied by a declaration stating the reason(s) for missing the deadline. IN R USDCTSD ECF Procedures(16). A model form is provided as Appendix D (IN R USDCTSD ECF Procedures(Appendix D)). IN R USDCTSD ECF Procedures(16).

2. *Documents for opposing party*

a. *Required documents*

i. *Response brief.* A party opposing a summary judgment motion must, within twenty-eight (28) days after the movant serves the motion, file and serve a response brief and any evidence (that is not already in the record) that the party relies on to oppose the motion. IN R USDCTSD L.R. 56-1(b). Refer to the Format section of this document for the format of briefs. Refer to the General Requirements section of this document for information on the opposing papers.

- *Statement of material facts in dispute.* The response must include a section labeled "Statement of Material Facts in Dispute" that identifies the potentially determinative facts and factual disputes that the party contends demonstrate a dispute of fact precluding summary judgment. IN R USDCTSD L.R. 56-1(b).

- *Citations to supporting facts.* A party must support each fact the party asserts in a brief with a citation to a discovery response, a deposition, an affidavit, or other admissible evidence. The evidence must be in the record or in an appendix to the brief. The citation must refer to a page or paragraph number or otherwise similarly specify where the relevant information can be found in the supporting evidence. IN R USDCTSD L.R. 56-1(e). The court has no duty to search or consider any part of the record not specifically cited in the manner described in IN R USDCTSD L.R. 56-1(e). IN R USDCTSD L.R. 56-1(h).

- *Dispute over admissibility or effect of evidence.* The court disfavors collateral motions—such as motions to strike—in the summary judgment process. Any dispute over the admissibility or effect of evidence must be raised through an objection within a party's brief. IN R USDCTSD L.R. 56-1(i).

- Refer to the General Requirements section of this document for more information about facts.

ii. *Certificate of service.* FRCP 5(d) requires that the person making service under FRCP 5 certify that service has been effected. FRCP 5(Advisory Committee Notes). Having such information on file may be useful for many purposes, including proof of service if an issue arises concerning the effectiveness of the service. FRCP 5(Advisory Committee Notes).

- *Certificate of service for electronically-filed documents.* A certificate of service must be included with all documents filed electronically. Such certificate shall indicate that service was accomplished pursuant to the Court's electronic filing procedures. IN R USDCTSD ECF Procedures(11). For the suggested format for a certificate of service for electronic filing, refer to IN R USDCTSD ECF Procedures(11).

b. *Supplemental documents*

i. *Supporting evidence.* When a motion relies on facts outside the record, the court may hear the matter on affidavits or may hear it wholly or partly on oral testimony or on depositions. FRCP 43(c).

- *Materials necessary for motion.* A party seeking relief under FRCP 26(c) or FRCP 37, or by way of a pretrial motion that could result in a final order on an issue, must file with the motion those parts of the discovery materials relevant to the motion. IN R USDCTSD L.R. 26-2(a).

- *Supporting factual positions.* A party asserting that a fact cannot be or is genuinely disputed must support the assertion by: (1) citing to particular parts of materials in the record, including depositions, documents, electronically stored information, affidavits or declarations, stipulations (including those made for purposes of the motion only), admissions, interrogatory answers, or other materials; or (2) showing that the materials cited do not establish the absence or presence of a genuine dispute, or that an adverse party cannot produce admissible evidence to support the fact. FRCP 56(c)(1).

- *Objection that a fact is not supported by admissible evidence.* A party may object that the material cited to support or dispute a fact cannot be presented in a form that would be admissible in evidence. FRCP 56(c)(2).

- *Materials not cited.* The court need consider only the cited materials, but it may consider other materials in the record. FRCP 56(c)(3).

- *Affidavits or declarations.* An affidavit or declaration used to support or oppose a motion must be made on personal knowledge, set out facts that would be admissible in evidence, and show that the affiant or declarant is competent to testify on the matters stated. FRCP 56(c)(4).

ii. *Notice of constitutional question.* A party that files a pleading, written motion, or other paper drawing into question the constitutionality of a federal or state statute must promptly:

- *File notice.* File a notice of constitutional question stating the question and identifying the paper that raises it, if: (1) a federal statute is questioned and the parties do not include the United States, one of its agencies, or one of its officers or employees in an official capacity; or (2) a state statute is questioned and the parties do not include the state, one of its agencies, or one of its officers or employees in an official capacity; and

- *Serve notice.* Serve the notice and paper on the Attorney General of the United States if a federal statute is questioned—or on the state attorney general if a state statute is questioned—either by certified or registered mail or by sending it to an electronic address designated by the attorney general for this purpose. FRCP 5.1(a).

- *Time for filing.* A notice of constitutional challenge to a statute filed in accordance with FRCP 5.1 must be filed at the same time the parties tender their proposed case management plan, if one is required, or within twenty-one (21) days of the filing drawing into question the constitutionality of a federal or state statute, whichever occurs later. IN R USDCTSD L.R. 5.1-1(a).

- *Additional service requirements.* If a federal statute is challenged, in addition to the service requirements of FRCP 5.1(a), the party filing the notice of constitutional challenge must serve the notice and documents on the United States Attorney for the Southern District of Indiana, either by certified or registered mail or by sending it to an electronic address designated for that purpose by that official. IN R USDCTSD L.R. 5.1-1(b).

- *No forfeiture.* A party's failure to file and serve the notice, or the court's failure to certify, does not forfeit a constitutional claim or defense that is otherwise timely asserted. FRCP 5.1(d).

iii. *Index of exhibits.* Any pleading, motion, brief, affidavit, notice, or proposed order filed with the court, whether electronically or with the clerk, must: if it has four (4) or more exhibits, include a separate index that identifies and briefly describes each exhibit. IN R USDCTSD L.R. 5-1(b).

iv. *Request for oral argument.* A party may request oral argument by filing a separate motion explaining why oral argument is necessary and estimating how long the court should allow for the argument. The request must be filed and served with the supporting brief, response brief, or reply brief. IN R USDCTSD L.R. 7-5(a).

v. *Request for evidentiary hearing.* A party may request an evidentiary hearing on a motion or petition by serving and filing a separate motion explaining why the hearing is necessary and estimating how long the court should allow for the hearing. IN R USDCTSD L.R. 7-5(c).

vi. *Copy of authority.* Generally, copies of cited authorities may not be attached to court filings. However, a party must attach to the party's motion or brief a copy of any cited authority if it is not available on Westlaw or Lexis. Upon request, a party must provide copies of any cited authority that is only available through electronic means to the court or the other parties. IN R USDCTSD L.R. 7-1(f).

vii. *Copy of document with self-address envelope.* To receive a file-stamped copy of a document filed directly with the clerk, a party must include with the original document an additional copy and a self-addressed envelope. The envelope must be big enough to hold the copy and have enough postage on it to send the copy via regular first-class mail. IN R USDCTSD L.R. 5-10(b).

viii. *Notice of manual filing.* When a party who is not exempt from the electronic filing requirement files a document directly with the clerk, the party must: electronically file a notice of manual filing that explains why the document cannot be filed electronically. IN R USDCTSD L.R. 5-2(d)(1). Refer to the Filing and Service Requirements section of this document for more information.

- Where an individual component cannot be included in an electronic filing (e.g. the

component cannot be converted to electronic format), the filer shall electronically file the prescribed Notice of Manual Filing in place of that component. A model form is provided as Appendix C (IN R USDCTSD ECF Procedures(Appendix C)). IN R USDCTSD ECF Procedures(13).

- Before making a manual filing of a component, the filing party shall first electronically file a Notice of Manual Filing (See IN R USDCTSD ECF Procedures(Appendix C)). The filer shall initiate the electronic filing process as if filing the actual component but shall instead attach to the filing the Notice of Manual Filing setting forth the reason(s) why the component cannot be filed electronically. The manual filing should be accompanied by a copy of the previously filed Notice of Manual Filing. A party may seek to have a component excluded from electronic filing pursuant to applicable Federal and Local Rules (e.g., FRCP 26(c)). IN R USDCTSD ECF Procedures(15).

  ix. *Courtesy copies.* District Judges and Magistrate Judges regularly receive documents filed by all parties. Therefore, parties shall not bring "courtesy copies" to any chambers unless specifically directed to do so by the Court. IN R USDCTSD Case Mgt(General Instructions For All Cases).

  x. *Copies for three-judge court.* Parties in a case where a three-judge court has been requested must file an original and three copies of any document filed directly with the clerk (instead of electronically) until the court: (1) denies the request; (2) dissolves the three-judge court; or (3) allows the parties to file fewer copies. IN R USDCTSD L.R. 9-2(c).

  xi. *Declaration that party was unable to file in a timely manner due to technical difficulties.* If a party misses a filing deadline due to an inability to file electronically, the party may submit the untimely filed document, accompanied by a declaration stating the reason(s) for missing the deadline. IN R USDCTSD ECF Procedures(16). A model form is provided as Appendix D (IN R USDCTSD ECF Procedures(Appendix D)). IN R USDCTSD ECF Procedures(16).

E. Format

1. *Form of documents.* The rules governing captions and other matters of form in pleadings apply to motions and other papers. FRCP 7(b)(2).

  a. *Paper (manual filings only).* Any document that is not filed electronically must: be flat, unfolded, and on good-quality, eight and one-half by eleven (8-1/2 x 11) inch white paper. IN R USDCTSD L.R. 5-1(d)(1). Any document that is not filed electronically must: be single-sided. IN R USDCTSD L.R. 5-1(d)(1).

    i. *Covers or backing.* Any document that is not filed electronically must: not have a cover or a back. IN R USDCTSD L.R. 5-1(d)(1).

    ii. *Fastening.* Any document that is not filed electronically must: be (if consisting of more than one (1) page) fastened by paperclip or binder clip and may not be stapled. IN R USDCTSD L.R. 5-1(d)(1).

- *Request for nonconforming fastening.* If a document cannot be fastened or bound as required by IN R USDCTSD L.R. 5-1(d), a party may ask the clerk for permission to fasten it in another manner. The party must make such a request before attempting to file the document with nonconforming fastening. IN R USDCTSD L.R. 5-1(d)(2).

    iii. *Hole punching.* Any document that is not filed electronically must: be two-hole punched at the top with the holes two and three-quarter (2-3/4) inches apart and appropriately centered. IN R USDCTSD L.R. 5-1(d)(1).

  b. *Margins.* Any pleading, motion, brief, affidavit, notice, or proposed order filed with the court, whether electronically or with the clerk, must: have at least one (1) inch margins. IN R USDCTSD L.R. 5-1(b).

  c. *Spacing.* Any pleading, motion, brief, affidavit, notice, or proposed order filed with the court, whether electronically or with the clerk, must: be double spaced (except for headings, footnotes, and quoted material). IN R USDCTSD L.R. 5-1(b).

  d. *Text.* Any pleading, motion, brief, affidavit, notice, or proposed order filed with the court, whether electronically or with the clerk, must: be plainly typewritten, printed, or prepared by a clearly legible copying process. IN R USDCTSD L.R. 5-1(b).

e. *Font size.* Any pleading, motion, brief, affidavit, notice, or proposed order filed with the court, whether electronically or with the clerk, must: use at least 12-point type in the body of the document and at least 10-point type in footnotes. IN R USDCTSD L.R. 5-1(b).

f. *Page numbering.* Any pleading, motion, brief, affidavit, notice, or proposed order filed with the court, whether electronically or with the clerk, must: have consecutively numbered pages. IN R USDCTSD L.R. 5-1(b).

g. *Caption; Names of parties.* Every pleading must have a caption with the court's name, a title, a file number, and a FRCP 7(a) designation. The title of the complaint must name all the parties; the title of other pleadings, after naming the first party on each side, may refer generally to other parties. FRCP 10(a). Any pleading, motion, brief, affidavit, notice, or proposed order filed with the court, whether electronically or with the clerk, must: include a title on the first page. IN R USDCTSD L.R. 5-1(b).

   i. *Alternative motions.* Motions must be filed separately, but alternative motions may be filed in a single document if each is named in the title. IN R USDCTSD L.R. 7-1(a).

h. *Filer's information.* Any pleading, motion, brief, affidavit, notice, or proposed order filed with the court, whether electronically or with the clerk, must: in the case of pleadings, motions, legal briefs, and notices, include the name, complete address, telephone number, facsimile number (where available), and e-mail address (where available) of the pro se litigant or attorney who files it. IN R USDCTSD L.R. 5-1(b).

i. *Paragraphs; Separate statements.* A party must state its claims or defenses in numbered paragraphs, each limited as far as practicable to a single set of circumstances. A later pleading may refer by number to a paragraph in an earlier pleading. If doing so would promote clarity, each claim founded on a separate transaction or occurrence—and each defense other than a denial—must be stated in a separate count or defense. FRCP 10(b).

j. *Adoption by reference; Exhibits.* A statement in a pleading may be adopted by reference elsewhere in the same pleading or in any other pleading or motion. A copy of a written instrument that is an exhibit to a pleading is a part of the pleading for all purposes. FRCP 10(c).

k. *Citations*

   i. *Local rules.* The Local Rules of the United States District Court for the Southern District of Indiana may be cited as "S.D. Ind. L.R." IN R USDCTSD L.R. 1-1(a).

   ii. *Local alternative dispute resolution rules.* These Rules shall be known as the Local Alternative Dispute Resolution Rules of the United States District Court for the Southern District of Indiana. They shall be cited as "S.D.Ind. Local A.D.R. Rule _____." IN R USDCTSD A.D.R. Rule 1.1.

l. *Acceptance by the clerk.* The clerk must not refuse to file a paper solely because it is not in the form prescribed by the Federal Rules of Civil Procedure or by a local rule or practice. FRCP 5(d)(4). The clerk will accept a document that violates IN R USDCTSD L.R. 5-1, but the court may exclude the document from the official record. IN R USDCTSD L.R. 5-1(e).

   i. *Sanctions for errors as to form.* The court may strike from the record any document that does not comply with the rules governing the form of documents filed with the court, such as rules that regulate document size or the number of copies to be filed or that require a special designation in the caption. The court may also sanction an attorney or party who files a non-compliant document. IN R USDCTSD L.R. 1-3.

2. *Form of electronic documents.* Any document submitted via the court's electronic case filing (ECF) system must be: otherwise prepared and filed in a manner consistent with the CM/ECF Policies and Procedures Manual (IN R USDCTSD ECF Procedures). IN R USDCTSD L.R. 5-1(c). Electronically filed documents must meet the requirements of FRCP 10 (Form of Pleadings), IN R USDCTSD L.R. 5-1 (Format of Papers Presented for Filing), and FRCP 5.2 (Privacy Protection for Filings Made with the

Court), as if they had been submitted on paper. Documents filed electronically are also subject to any page limitations set forth by Court Order, by IN R USDCTSD L.R. 7-1 (Motion Practice), or IN R USDCTSD L.R. 56-1 (Summary Judgment Practice), as applicable. IN R USDCTSD ECF Procedures(13).

a. *PDF format required.* Any document submitted via the court's electronic case filing (ECF) system must be: in .pdf format. IN R USDCTSD L.R. 5-1(c); IN R USDCTSD ECF Procedures(7). Any document submitted via the court's electronic case filing (ECF) system must be: converted to a .pdf file directly from a word processing program, unless it exists only in paper format (in which case it may be scanned to create a .pdf document). IN R USDCTSD L.R. 5-1(c); IN R USDCTSD ECF Procedures(13).

   i. An exhibit may be scanned into PDF format, at a recommended 300 dpi resolution or higher, only if it does not already exist in electronic format. The filing attorney is responsible for reviewing all PDF documents for legibility before submitting them through the Court's Electronic Case Filing system. For technical guidance in creating PDF documents, please contact the Clerk's Office. IN R USDCTSD ECF Procedures(13).

b. *File size limitations.* Any document submitted via the court's electronic case filing (ECF) system must be: submitted as one or more .pdf files that do not exceed ten megabytes (10 MB) each (consistent with the CM/ECF Policies and Procedures Manual (IN R USDCTSD ECF Procedures)). IN R USDCTSD L.R. 5-1(c); IN R USDCTSD ECF Procedures(13).

   i. To electronically file a document or attachment that exceeds ten megabytes (10 MB), the document must first be broken down into two or more smaller files. For example, if Exhibit A is a twelve megabyte (12 MB) PDF file, it should be divided into 2 equal parts prior to electronic filing. Each component part of the exhibit would be filed as an attachment to the main document and described appropriately as "Exhibit A (part 1 of 2)" and "Exhibit A (part 2 of 2)." IN R USDCTSD ECF Procedures(13).

   ii. The supporting items mentioned in IN R USDCTSD ECF Procedures(13) should not be confused with memorandums or briefs in support of motions as outlined in IN R USDCTSD L.R. 7-1 or IN R USDCTSD L.R. 56-1. These memorandums or briefs in support are to be filed as entirely separate documents pursuant to the appropriate rule. Additionally, no motion shall be embodied in the text of a response or reply brief/memorandum unless otherwise ordered by the Court. IN R USDCTSD ECF Procedures(13).

c. *Separate component parts.* A key objective of the electronic filing system is to ensure that as much of the case as possible is managed electronically. To facilitate electronic filing and retrieval, documents to be filed electronically are to be reasonably broken into their separate component parts. By way of example, most filings include a foundation document (e.g., motion) and other supporting items (e.g., exhibits, proposed orders, proposed amended pleadings). The foundation document, as well as the supporting items, are each separate components of the filing; supporting items must be filed as attachments to the foundation document. These exhibits or attachments should include only those excerpts of the referenced documents that are directly germane to the matter under consideration. IN R USDCTSD ECF Procedures(13).

   i. Where an individual component cannot be included in an electronic filing (e.g. the component cannot be converted to electronic format), the filer shall electronically file the prescribed Notice of Manual Filing in place of that component. A model form is provided as Appendix C (IN R USDCTSD ECF Procedures(Appendix C)). IN R USDCTSD ECF Procedures(13).

d. *Exhibits.* Each electronically filed exhibit to a main document must be: (1) created as a separate .pdf file; (2) submitted as an attachment to the main document and given a title which describes its content; and (3) limited to excerpts that are directly germane to the main document's subject matter. IN R USDCTSD L.R. 5-6(a).

   i. When uploading attachments during the electronic filing process, exhibits must be uploaded in a logical sequence and a brief description must be entered for each individual PDF file. The description must include not only the exhibit number or letter, but also a brief description of the document. This information may be entered in CM/ECF using a combination of the Category drop-down menu, the Description text box, or both (see IN R USDCTSD ECF

Procedures(13)(Figure 1)). The information that is provided in each box will be combined to create a description of the document as it appears on the case docket (see IN R USDCTSD ECF Procedures(13)(Figure 2)). IN R USDCTSD ECF Procedures(13). For an example, refer to IN R USDCTSD ECF Procedures(13).

e. *Excerpts.* A party filing an exhibit that consists of excerpts from a larger document must clearly and prominently identify the exhibit as containing excerpted material. Either party will have the right to timely file additional excerpts or the complete document to the extent they are or become directly germane to the main document's subject matter. IN R USDCTSD L.R. 5-6(b).

f. For an example illustrating the application of IN R USDCTSD ECF Procedures(13), refer to IN R USDCTSD ECF Procedures(13).

3. *Form of briefs*

a. *Page limits.* Supporting and response briefs (excluding tables of contents, tables of authorities, appendices, and certificates of service) may not exceed thirty-five (35) pages. Reply briefs may not exceed twenty (20) pages. IN R USDCTSD L.R. 7-1(e)(1).

    i. *Permission to exceed limits.* The court may allow a party to file a brief exceeding these page limits for extraordinary and compelling reasons. IN R USDCTSD L.R. 7-1(e)(2).

    ii. *Supporting and response briefs exceeding limits.* If the court allows a party to file a brief or response exceeding thirty-five (35) pages, the document must include:

- A table of contents with page references;

- A statement of issues; and

- A table of authorities including: (1) all cases (alphabetically arranged), statutes, and other authorities cited in the brief; and (2) page numbers where the authorities are cited in the brief. IN R USDCTSD L.R. 7-1(e)(3).

4. *Signing of pleadings, motions and other papers*

a. *Signature.* Every pleading, written motion, and other paper must be signed by at least one attorney of record in the attorney's name—or by a party personally if the party is unrepresented. The paper must state the signer's address, e-mail address, and telephone number. FRCP 11(a).

    i. *Signatures on manual filings.* Any document that is not filed electronically must: include the original signature of the pro se litigant or attorney who files it. IN R USDCTSD L.R. 5-1(d)(1).

    ii. *Electronic signatures.* Use of the attorney's login and password when filing documents electronically serves in part as the attorney's signature for purposes of FRCP 11, the Local Rules of the United States District Court for the Southern District of Indiana, and any other purpose for which a signature is required in connection with proceedings before the Court. IN R USDCTSD ECF Procedures(14); IN R USDCTSD ECF Procedures(10). A pleading, motion, brief, or notice filed electronically under an attorney's ECF log-in and password must be signed by that attorney. IN R USDCTSD L.R. 5-7(a). A signature on a document other than a document filed as provided under IN R USDCTSD L.R. 5-7(a) must be an original handwritten signature and must be scanned into .pdf format for electronic filing. IN R USDCTSD L.R. 5-7(c); IN R USDCTSD ECF Procedures(14).

- *Form of electronic signature.* If a document is converted directly from a word processing application to .pdf (as opposed to scanning), the name of the Filing User under whose log-in and password the document is submitted must be preceded by a "s/" and typed on the signature line where the Filing User's handwritten signature would otherwise appear. IN R USDCTSD L.R. 5-7(b). All documents filed electronically shall include a signature block and include the filing attorney's typewritten name, address, telephone number, facsimile number and e-mail address. In addition, the name of the filing attorney under whose ECF login the document will be filed should be preceded by a "s/" and typed in the space where the attorney's handwritten signature would otherwise appear. IN R US-DCTSD ECF Procedures(14). For a sample format, refer to IN R USDCTSD ECF Procedures(14).

- *Effect of electronic signature.* Filing an electronically signed document under an attorney's ECF log-in and password constitutes the attorney's signature on the document under the Federal Rules of Civil Procedure, under the Local Rules of the United States District Court for the Southern District of Indiana, and for any other reason a signature is required in connection with the court's activities. IN R USDCTSD L.R. 5-7(d).

- *Documents with multiple attorneys' signatures.* Documents requiring signatures of more than one attorney shall be filed either by: (1) obtaining consent from the other attorney, then typing the "s/ [Name]" signature of the other attorney on the signature line where the other attorney's signature would otherwise appear; (2) identifying in the signature section the name of the other attorney whose signature is required and by the submission of a Notice of Endorsement (see IN R USDCTSD ECF Procedures(Appendix B)) by the other attorney no later than three (3) business days after filing; (3) submitting a scanned document containing all handwritten signatures; or (4) in any other manner approved by the Court. IN R USDCTSD ECF Procedures(14); IN R USDCTSD L.R. 5-7(e).

  iii. *No verification or accompanying affidavit required for pleadings.* Unless a rule or statute specifically states otherwise, a pleading need not be verified or accompanied by an affidavit. FRCP 11(a).

  iv. *Unsigned papers.* The court must strike an unsigned paper unless the omission is promptly corrected after being called to the attorney's or party's attention. FRCP 11(a). The court will strike any document filed directly with the clerk that is not signed by an attorney of record or the pro se litigant filing it, but the court may do so only after giving the attorney or pro se litigant notice of the omission and reasonable time to correct it. Rubber-stamp or facsimile signatures are not original signatures and the court will deem documents containing them to be unsigned for purposes of FRCP 11 and FRCP 26(g) and IN R USDCTSD L.R. 5-10. IN R USDCTSD L.R. 5-10(g).

b. *Representations to the court.* By presenting to the court a pleading, written motion, or other paper—whether by signing, filing, submitting, or later advocating it—an attorney or unrepresented party certifies that to the best of the person's knowledge, information, and belief, formed after an inquiry reasonable under the circumstances:

  i. It is not being presented for any improper purpose, such as to harass, cause unnecessary delay, or needlessly increase the cost of litigation;

  ii. The claims, defenses, and other legal contentions are warranted by existing law or by a nonfrivolous argument for extending, modifying, or reversing existing law or for establishing new law;

  iii. The factual contentions have evidentiary support or, if specifically so identified, will likely have evidentiary support after a reasonable opportunity for further investigation or discovery; and

  iv. The denials of factual contentions are warranted on the evidence or, if specifically so identified, are reasonably based on belief or a lack of information. FRCP 11(b).

c. *Sanctions.* If, after notice and a reasonable opportunity to respond, the court determines that FRCP 11(b) has been violated, the court may impose an appropriate sanction on any attorney, law firm, or party that violated FRCP 11(b) or is responsible for the violation. FRCP 11(c)(1). Refer to the United States District Court for the Southern District of Indiana KeyRules Motion for Sanctions document for more information.

5. *Privacy protection for filings made with the court.* Electronically filed documents must meet the requirements of. . .FRCP 5.2 (Privacy Protection for Filings Made with the Court), as if they had been submitted on paper. IN R USDCTSD ECF Procedures(13).

a. *Redacted filings.* Unless the court orders otherwise, in an electronic or paper filing with the court that contains an individual's Social Security number, taxpayer-identification number, or birth date, the name of an individual known to be a minor, or a financial-account number, a party or nonparty making the filing may include only:

  i. The last four (4) digits of the Social Security number and taxpayer-identification number;

    ii.   The year of the individual's birth;

    iii.   The minor's initials; and

    iv.   The last four (4) digits of the financial-account number. FRCP 5.2(a).

b. *Exemptions from the redaction requirement.* The redaction requirement does not apply to the following:

    i.   A financial-account number that identifies the property allegedly subject to forfeiture in a forfeiture proceeding;

    ii.   The record of an administrative or agency proceeding;

    iii.   The official record of a state-court proceeding;

    iv.   The record of a court or tribunal, if that record was not subject to the redaction requirement when originally filed;

    v.   A filing covered by FRCP 5.2(c) or FRCP 5.2(d); and

    vi.   A pro se filing in an action brought under 28 U.S.C.A. § 2241, 28 U.S.C.A. § 2254, or 28 U.S.C.A. § 2255. FRCP 5.2(b).

c. *Limitations on remote access to electronic files; Social Security appeals and immigration cases.* Unless the court orders otherwise, in an action for benefits under the Social Security Act, and in an action or proceeding relating to an order of removal, to relief from removal, or to immigration benefits or detention, access to an electronic file is authorized as follows:

    i.   The parties and their attorneys may have remote electronic access to any part of the case file, including the administrative record;

    ii.   Any other person may have electronic access to the full record at the courthouse, but may have remote electronic access only to:

        • The docket maintained by the court; and

        • An opinion, order, judgment, or other disposition of the court, but not any other part of the case file or the administrative record. FRCP 5.2(c).

d. *Filings made under seal.* The court may order that a filing be made under seal without redaction. The court may later unseal the filing or order the person who made the filing to file a redacted version for the public record. FRCP 5.2(d). For more information on filing under seal, refer to IN R USDCTSD L.R. 5-11 and IN R USDCTSD ECF Procedures(18).

e. *Protective orders.* For good cause, the court may by order in a case:

    i.   Require redaction of additional information; or

    ii.   Limit or prohibit a nonparty's remote electronic access to a document filed with the court. FRCP 5.2(e).

f. *Option for additional unredacted filing under seal.* A person making a redacted filing may also file an unredacted copy under seal. The court must retain the unredacted copy as part of the record. FRCP 5.2(f).

g. *Option for filing a reference list.* A filing that contains redacted information may be filed together with a reference list that identifies each item of redacted information and specifies an appropriate identifier that uniquely corresponds to each item listed. The list must be filed under seal and may be amended as of right. Any reference in the case to a listed identifier will be construed to refer to the corresponding item of information. FRCP 5.2(g).

h. *Waiver of protection of identifiers.* A person waives the protection of FRCP 5.2(a) as to the person's own information by filing it without redaction and not under seal. FRCP 5.2(h).

F. Filing and Service Requirements

1. *Filing requirements.* Any paper after the complaint that is required to be served—together with a certificate of service—must be filed within a reasonable time after service. FRCP 5(d)(1). Motions must

be filed separately, but alternative motions may be filed in a single document if each is named in the title. IN R USDCTSD L.R. 7-1(a).

a. *How filing is made; In general.* A paper is filed by delivering it:

    i. To the clerk; or

    ii. To a judge who agrees to accept it for filing, and who must then note the filing date on the paper and promptly send it to the clerk. FRCP 5(d)(2).

- In certain instances, the court will direct the parties to submit items directly to chambers (e.g., confidential settlement statements). However, absent specific prior authorization, counsel and litigants should not submit letters or documents directly to chambers, and such materials should be filed with the clerk. IN R USDCTSD L.R. 5-1(Local Rules Advisory Committee Comment).

    iii. A document or item submitted in relation to a matter within the court's jurisdiction is deemed filed upon delivery to the office of the clerk in a manner prescribed by the Local Rules of the United States District Court for the Southern District of Indiana or the Federal Rules of Civil Procedure or authorized by the court. Any submission directed to a Judge or Judge's staff, the office of the clerk or any employee thereof, in a manner that is not contemplated by IN R USDCTSD L.R. 5-1 and without prior court authorization is prohibited. IN R USDCTSD L.R. 5-1(a).

b. *Non-electronic filing.* Any document that is exempt from electronic filing must be filed directly with the clerk and served on other parties in the case as required by those Federal Rules of Civil Procedure and Local Rules of the United States District Court for the Southern District of Indiana that apply to the service of non-electronic documents. IN R USDCTSD L.R. 5-2(c).

    i. *When completed.* A document or other item that is not required to be filed electronically is deemed filed:

- Upon delivery in person, by courier, or via U.S. Mail or other mail delivery service to the clerk's office during business hours;

- When the courtroom deputy clerk accepts it, if the document or item is filed in open court; or

- Upon completion of any other manner of filing that the court authorizes. IN R USDCTSD L.R. 5-10(a).

    ii. *Document filing by non-exempt party.* When a party who is not exempt from the electronic filing requirement files a document directly with the clerk, the party must:

- Electronically file a notice of manual filing that explains why the document cannot be filed electronically;

- Present the document to the clerk within one (1) business day after filing the notice of manual filing; and

- Present the clerk with a copy of the notice of manual filing when the party files the document with the clerk. IN R USDCTSD L.R. 5-2(d).

c. *Electronic filing*

    i. *Authorization of electronic filing program.* A court may, by local rule, allow papers to be filed, signed, or verified by electronic means that are consistent with any technical standards established by the Judicial Conference of the United States. A local rule may require electronic filing only if reasonable exceptions are allowed. A paper filed electronically in compliance with a local rule is a written paper for purposes of the Federal Rules of Civil Procedure. FRCP 5(d)(3).

- IN R USDCTSD L.R. 5-2 requires electronic filing, as allowed by FRCP 5(d)(3). The policies and procedures in IN R USDCTSD ECF Procedures govern electronic filing in this district unless, due to circumstances in a particular case, a judicial officer determines that these policies and procedures (IN R USDCTSD ECF Procedures) should be modified. IN R USDCTSD ECF Procedures(1).

- Unless modified by order of the Court, all Federal Rules of Civil Procedure and Local Rules of the United States District Court for the Southern District of Indiana shall continue to apply to cases maintained in the Court's Case Management/Electronic Case Filing System (CM/ECF). IN R USDCTSD ECF Procedures(3).

ii. *Mandatory electronic filing.* Unless exempted pursuant to IN R USDCTSD L.R. 5-3(e), attorneys admitted to the court's bar (including those admitted pro hac vice) or authorized to represent the United States must use the court's ECF system to file documents. IN R USDCTSD L.R. 5-3(a). Electronic filing by attorneys is required for eligible documents filed in civil and criminal cases pending with the Court, unless specifically exempted by Local Rule or Court Order. IN R USDCTSD ECF Procedures(4).

- *Exceptions.* All civil cases (other than those cases the court specifically exempts) must be maintained in the court's electronic case filing (ECF) system. Accordingly, as allowed by FRCP 5(d)(3), every document filed in this court (including exhibits) must be transmitted to the clerk's office via the ECF system consistent with IN R USDCTSD L.R. 5-2 through IN R USDCTSD L.R. 5-11 except: (1) documents filed by pro se litigants; (2) transcripts in cases filed by claimants under the Social Security Act (and related statutes); (3) exhibits in a format that does not readily permit electronic filing (such as videos and large maps and charts); (4) documents that are illegible when scanned into .pdf format; (5) documents filed in cases not maintained on the ECF system; and (6) any other documents that the court or the Local Rules of the United States District Court for the Southern District of Indiana specifically allow to be filed directly with the clerk. IN R USDCTSD L.R. 5-2(a). Parties otherwise participating in the electronic filing system may be excused from filing a particular component electronically under certain limited circumstances, such as when the component cannot be reduced to an electronic format. Such components shall not be filed electronically, but instead shall be manually filed with the Clerk of Court and served upon the parties in accordance with the applicable Federal Rules of Civil Procedure and the Local Rules of the United States District Court for the Southern District of Indiana for filing and service of non-electronic documents. IN R USDCTSD ECF Procedures(15).

- *Exemption from participation.* The court may exempt attorneys from using the ECF system in a particular case for good cause. An attorney must file a petition for ECF exemption and a CM/ECF technical requirements exemption questionnaire in each case in which the attorney seeks an exemption. (The CM/ECF technical requirements exemption questionnaire is available on the court's website). IN R USDCTSD L.R. 5-3(e).

iii. *Consequences of electronic filing.* Electronic transmission of a document consistent with the procedures adopted by the Court shall, upon the complete receipt of the same by the Clerk of Court, constitute filing of the document for all purposes of the Federal Rules of Civil and Criminal Procedure and the Local Rules of the United States District Court for the Southern District of Indiana, and shall constitute entry of that document onto the docket maintained by the Clerk pursuant to FRCP 58 and FRCP 79. IN R USDCTSD ECF Procedures(7); IN R USDCTSD L.R. 5-4(c)(1). When a document has been filed electronically: the document, as filed, binds the filing party. IN R USDCTSD L.R. 5-4(c)(3).

- A Notice of Electronic Filing (NEF) acknowledging that the document has been filed will immediately appear on the filer's screen after the document has been submitted. Attorneys are strongly encouraged to print or electronically save a copy of the NEF. Attorneys can also verify the filing of documents by inspecting the Court's electronic docket sheet through the use of a PACER login. IN R USDCTSD ECF Procedures(7). When a document has been filed electronically: the notice of electronic filing for the document serves as the court's date-stamp and proof of filing. IN R USDCTSD L.R. 5-4(c)(4).

- The Court may, upon the motion of a party or upon its own motion, strike any inappropriately filed document. IN R USDCTSD ECF Procedures(7).

iv. For more information on electronic filing, refer to IN R USDCTSD ECF Procedures.

d. *Fax filing.* The clerk may not file a faxed document without court authorization. The court may not authorize the clerk to file faxed documents without finding that compelling circumstances justify it. A party must submit a copy of the document that otherwise complies with IN R USDCTSD L.R. 5-10 to replace the faxed copy within seven (7) days after faxing the document. IN R USDCTSD L.R. 5-10(e).

2. *Service requirements*

   a. *Service; When required*

      i. *In general.* Unless the Federal Rules of Civil Procedure provide otherwise, each of the following papers must be served on every party:

- An order stating that service is required;

- A pleading filed after the original complaint, unless the court orders otherwise under FRCP 5(c) because there are numerous defendants;

- A discovery paper required to be served on a party, unless the court orders otherwise;

- A written motion, except one that may be heard ex parte; and

- A written notice, appearance, demand, or offer of judgment, or any similar paper. FRCP 5(a)(1).

      ii. *If a party fails to appear.* No service is required on a party who is in default for failing to appear. But a pleading that asserts a new claim for relief against such a party must be served on that party under FRCP 4. FRCP 5(a)(2).

      iii. *Seizing property.* If an action is begun by seizing property and no person is or need be named as a defendant, any service required before the filing of an appearance, answer, or claim must be made on the person who had custody or possession of the property when it was seized. FRCP 5(a)(3).

   b. *Service; How made*

      i. *Serving an attorney.* If a party is represented by an attorney, service under FRCP 5 must be made on the attorney unless the court orders service on the party. FRCP 5(b)(1).

      ii. *Service in general.* A paper is served under FRCP 5 by:

- Handing it to the person;

- Leaving it: (1) at the person's office with a clerk or other person in charge or, if no one is in charge, in a conspicuous place in the office; or (2) if the person has no office or the office is closed, at the person's dwelling or usual place of abode with someone of suitable age and discretion who resides there;

- Mailing it to the person's last known address—in which event service is complete upon mailing;

- Leaving it with the court clerk if the person has no known address;

- Sending it by electronic means if the person consented in writing—in which event service is complete upon transmission, but is not effective if the serving party learns that it did not reach the person to be served; or

- Delivering it by any other means that the person consented to in writing—in which event service is complete when the person making service delivers it to the agency designated to make delivery. FRCP 5(b)(2).

      iii. *Electronic service*

- *Consent.* By registering to use the ECF system, attorneys consent to electronic service of documents filed in cases maintained on the ECF system. IN R USDCTSD L.R. 5-3(d). By participating in the Electronic Case Filing Program, attorneys consent to the electronic service of documents, and shall make available electronic mail addresses for service. IN R USDCTSD ECF Procedures(11).

- *Service on registered parties.* Upon the filing of a document by a party, an e-mail message will be automatically generated by the electronic filing system and sent via electronic mail to the e-mail addresses of all registered attorneys who have appeared in the case. The Notice of Electronic Filing will contain a document hyperlink which will provide recipients with one "free look" at the electronically filed document. Recipients are encouraged to print and/or save a copy of the document during the "free look" to avoid incurring PACER charges for future viewings of the document. IN R USDCTSD ECF Procedures(11). When a document has been filed electronically: transmission of the notice of electronic filing generated by the ECF system to an attorney's e-mail address constitutes service of the document on that attorney. IN R USDCTSD L.R. 5-4(c)(5). The party effectuates service on all registered attorneys by filing electronically. IN R USDCTSD ECF Procedures(11). When a document has been filed electronically: no other attempted service will constitute electronic service of the document. IN R USDCTSD L.R. 5-4(c)(6).

- *Service on exempt parties.* A filer must serve a copy of the document consistent with FRCP 5 on any party or attorney who is exempt from participating in electronic filing. IN R USDCTSD L.R. 5-4(d). It is the responsibility of the filing attorney to conventionally serve all parties who do not receive electronic service (the identity of these parties will be indicated on the filing receipt generated by the ECF system). IN R USDCTSD ECF Procedures(11).

- *Service on parties excused from electronic filing.* Parties otherwise participating in the electronic filing system may be excused from filing a particular component electronically under certain limited circumstances, such as when the component cannot be reduced to an electronic format. Such components shall not be filed electronically, but instead shall be manually filed with the Clerk of Court and served upon the parties in accordance with the applicable Federal Rules of Civil Procedure and the Local Rules of the United States District Court for the Southern District of Indiana for filing and service of non-electronic documents. IN R USDCTSD ECF Procedures(15).

- *Service of exempt documents.* Any document that is exempt from electronic filing must be filed directly with the clerk and served on other parties in the case as required by those Federal Rules of Civil Procedure and Local Rules of the United States District Court for the Southern District of Indiana that apply to the service of non-electronic documents. IN R USDCTSD L.R. 5-2(c).

iv. *Using court facilities.* If a local rule so authorizes, a party may use the court's transmission facilities to make service under FRCP 5(b)(2)(E). FRCP 5(b)(3).

c. *Serving numerous defendants*

i. *In general.* If an action involves an unusually large number of defendants, the court may, on motion or on its own, order that:

- Defendants' pleadings and replies to them need not be served on other defendants;

- Any crossclaim, counterclaim, avoidance, or affirmative defense in those pleadings and replies to them will be treated as denied or avoided by all other parties; and

- Filing any such pleading and serving it on the plaintiff constitutes notice of the pleading to all parties. FRCP 5(c)(1).

ii. *Notifying parties.* A copy of every such order must be served on the parties as the court directs. FRCP 5(c)(2).

G. Hearings

1. *Hearings, generally*

a. *Oral argument.* Due process does not require that oral argument be permitted on a motion and, except as otherwise provided by local rule, the district court has discretion to determine whether it will decide the motion on the papers or hear argument by counsel (and perhaps receive evidence). FPP § 1190; F.D.I.C. v. Deglau, 207 F.3d 153 (3d Cir. 2000).

i. *Request for oral argument.* A party may request oral argument by filing a separate motion

explaining why oral argument is necessary and estimating how long the court should allow for the argument. IN R USDCTSD L.R. 7-5(a). Refer to the Documents section of this document for more information.

ii. *No additional evidence at oral argument.* Parties may not present additional evidence at oral argument. IN R USDCTSD L.R. 7-5(b).

b. *Providing a regular schedule for oral hearings.* A court may establish regular times and places for oral hearings on motions. FRCP 78(a).

c. *Providing for submission on briefs.* By rule or order, the court may provide for submitting and determining motions on briefs, without oral hearings. FRCP 78(b).

d. *Request for evidentiary hearing.* A party may request an evidentiary hearing on a motion or petition by serving and filing a separate motion explaining why the hearing is necessary and estimating how long the court should allow for the hearing. IN R USDCTSD L.R. 7-5(c).

e. *Directed by the court.* The court may: (1) grant or deny a request for oral argument or an evidentiary hearing in its sole discretion; (2) set oral argument or an evidentiary hearing without a request from a party; and (3) order any oral argument or evidentiary hearing to be held anywhere within the district regardless of where the case will be tried. IN R USDCTSD L.R. 7-5(d).

2. *Hearing on motion for summary judgment.* Even though FRCP 56(c) makes reference to a hearing on the motion for summary judgment, FRCP 56 confers no right to an oral hearing on the summary judgment motion, nor is a hearing required by due process considerations. FEDPROC § 62:673; Forjan v. Leprino Foods, Inc., 209 Fed.Appx. 8, 2006 WL 3623496 (2d Cir. 2006).

a. *Oral argument.* The court will decide summary judgment motions without oral argument or hearing unless the court otherwise directs or grants a request under IN R USDCTSD L.R. 7-5. IN R USDCTSD L.R. 56-1(j). Oral argument on a motion for summary judgment may be considered ordinarily appropriate, so that as a general rule, a district court should grant a request for oral argument on all but frivolous summary judgment motions, or a nonmovant's request for oral argument must be granted unless summary judgment is also denied, according to some courts. FEDPROC § 62:674; Season-All Industries, Inc. v. Turkiye Sise Ve Cam Fabrikalari, A. S., 425 F.2d 34 (3d Cir. 1970); Houston v. Bryan, 725 F.2d 516 (9th Cir. 1984); Fernhoff v. Tahoe Regional Planning Agency, 803 F.2d 979 (9th Cir. 1986).

i. Oral argument on a summary judgment motion may be deemed waived where the opposing party does not request it. FEDPROC § 62:674; McCormack v. Citibank, N.A., 100 F.3d 532, 30 UCC Rep.Serv.2d 1175 (8th Cir. 1996).

3. *Courtroom and courthouse decorum.* For information on courtroom and courthouse decorum, refer to IN R USDCTSD L.R. 83-3.

H. Forms

1. Federal Motion for Summary Judgment Forms

a. Answer; To plaintiff's motion for summary judgment. AMJUR PP SUMMARY § 56.

b. Affidavit opposing defendant's motion for summary judgment; By plaintiff. AMJUR PP SUMMARY § 64.

c. Affidavit opposing motion for summary judgment; By party; Dispute as to issues of fact. AMJUR PP SUMMARY § 73.

d. Affidavit opposing motion for summary judgment; By party; Inability to present facts. AMJUR PP SUMMARY § 74.

e. Affidavit opposing motion for summary judgment; By party; Good defense to part of claim. AMJUR PP SUMMARY § 77.

f. Statement of disputed and undisputed material facts; In opposition to motion for summary judgment. AMJUR PP SUMMARY § 89.

g. Motion and notice of motion for summary judgment. 4 FEDFORMS § 4708.

h. Motion for summary judgment by plaintiff. 4 FEDFORMS § 4709.

i. Motion for summary judgment by defendant. 4 FEDFORMS § 4713.

j. Motion for summary judgment by defendant; Claims of plaintiff and counterclaims of defendant. 4 FEDFORMS § 4717.

k. Motion for summary judgment by defendant; Interpleader against another claimant. 4 FEDFORMS § 4718.

l. Motion for summary judgment by defendant; Failure of plaintiff to produce evidence. 4 FEDFORMS § 4719.

m. Motion for summary judgment by defendant; Statute of limitations. 4 FEDFORMS § 4720.

n. Notice of motion for summary judgment. 4 FEDFORMS § 4744.

o. Affidavit in support of motion for summary judgment. 4 FEDFORMS § 4773.

p. Movant's contention there are no genuine issues of material facts. 4 FEDFORMS § 4776.

q. Opposition to statement of uncontested material facts. 4 FEDFORMS § 4777.

r. Response to movant's contention there are no genuine issues with respect to listed material facts. 4 FEDFORMS § 4778.

s. Motion; For summary judgment; By claimant. FEDPROF § 1:1298.

t. Motion; For summary judgment; By defending party. FEDPROF § 1:1302.

u. Motion; By plaintiff; For partial summary judgment. FEDPROF § 1:1305.

v. Notice of cross motion; For summary judgment; By defending party. FEDPROF § 1:1306.

w. Statement of material facts; In support of summary judgment motion. FEDPROF § 1:1311.

x. Statement in support of defendant's summary judgment motion; By codefendant. FEDPROF § 1:1312.

y. Affidavit; Opposing claimant's motion for summary judgment; Witnesses unavailable. FEDPROF § 1:1316.

z. Affidavit; Opposing part of claim. FEDPROF § 1:1317.

2. Forms for the Southern District of Indiana

a. Notice regarding right to respond to and submit evidence in opposition to motion for summary judgment. IN R USDCTSD App. A.

b. Notice of endorsement. IN R USDCTSD ECF Procedures(Appendix B).

c. Notice of manual filing. IN R USDCTSD ECF Procedures(Appendix C).

d. Declaration that party was unable to file in a timely manner due to technical difficulties. IN R USDCTSD ECF Procedures(Appendix D).

I. Applicable Rules

1. *Federal rules*

a. Serving and filing pleadings and other papers. FRCP 5.

b. Constitutional challenge to a statute; Notice, certification, and intervention. FRCP 5.1.

c. Privacy protection for filings made with the court. FRCP 5.2.

d. Computing and extending time; Time for motion papers. FRCP 6.

e. Pleadings allowed; Form of motions and other papers. FRCP 7.

f. Disclosure statement. FRCP 7.1.

g. Form of pleadings. FRCP 10.

h. Signing pleadings, motions, and other papers; Representations to the court; Sanctions. FRCP 11.

i. Defenses and objections; When and how presented; Motion for judgment on the pleadings; Consolidating motions; Waiving defenses; Pretrial hearing. FRCP 12.

j. Taking testimony. FRCP 43.

k. Summary judgment. FRCP 56.

l. Hearing motions; Submission on briefs. FRCP 78.

2. *Local rules*

a. Scope of the rules. IN R USDCTSD L.R. 1-1.

b. Sanctions for errors as to form. IN R USDCTSD L.R. 1-3.

c. Format of documents presented for filing. IN R USDCTSD L.R. 5-1.

d. Constitutional challenge to a statute; Notice. IN R USDCTSD L.R. 5.1-1.

e. Filing of documents electronically required. IN R USDCTSD L.R. 5-2.

f. Eligibility, registration, passwords for electronic filing; Exemption from electronic filing. IN R USDCTSD L.R. 5-3.

g. Timing and consequences of electronic filing. IN R USDCTSD L.R. 5-4.

h. Attachments and exhibits in cases filed electronically. IN R USDCTSD L.R. 5-6.

i. Signatures in cases filed electronically. IN R USDCTSD L.R. 5-7.

j. Non-electronic filings. IN R USDCTSD L.R. 5-10.

k. Motion practice. [IN R USDCTSD L.R. 7-1, as amended by IN ORDER 16-2319, effective December 1, 2016].

l. Oral arguments and hearings. IN R USDCTSD L.R. 7-5.

m. Request for three-judge court. IN R USDCTSD L.R. 9-2.

n. Filing of discovery materials. IN R USDCTSD L.R. 26-2.

o. Assignment of cases. IN R USDCTSD L.R. 40-1.

p. Summary judgment procedure. IN R USDCTSD L.R. 56-1.

q. Alternative dispute resolution. IN R USDCTSD A.D.R. Rule 1.1; IN R USDCTSD A.D.R. Rule 1.2; IN R USDCTSD A.D.R. Rule 1.5; IN R USDCTSD A.D.R. Rule 2.1; IN R USDCTSD A.D.R. Rule 2.2.

r. Instructions for preparing case management plan. IN R USDCTSD Case Mgt.

s. Electronic case filing policies and procedures manual. IN R USDCTSD ECF Procedures.

Motions, Oppositions and Replies
Motion for Sanctions

Document Last Updated December 2016

A. Checklist

(I) ❑ Matters to be considered by moving party

  (a) ❑ Required documents

    (1) ❑ Notice of motion and motion

    (2) ❑ Statement regarding efforts

    (3) ❑ Certificate of service

  (b) ❑ Supplemental documents

    (1) ❑ Brief

    (2) ❑ Supporting evidence

    (3) ❑ Notice of constitutional question

    (4) ❑ Nongovernmental corporate disclosure statement

    (5) ❑ Index of exhibits

    (6) ❑ Request for oral argument

    (7) ❑ Request for evidentiary hearing

    (8) ❑ Copy of authority

    (9) ❑ Proposed order

    (10) ❑ Copy of document with self-address envelope

    (11) ❑ Notice of manual filing

    (12) ❑ Courtesy copies

    (13) ❑ Copies for three-judge court

    (14) ❑ Declaration that party was unable to file in a timely manner due to technical difficulties

  (c) ❑ Timing

    (1) ❑ A party who is aware of a FRCP 11 violation should act promptly; however, motions for sanctions can be timely even when filed well after the original pleadings

        (i) ❑ It must not be filed or be presented to the court if the challenged paper, claim, defense, contention, or denial is withdrawn or appropriately corrected within twenty-one (21) days after service or within another time the court sets

    (2) ❑ A written motion and notice of the hearing must be served at least fourteen (14) days before the time specified for the hearing, with the following exceptions: (i) when the motion may be heard ex parte; (ii) when the Federal Rules of Civil Procedure set a different time; or (iii) when a court order—which a party may, for good cause, apply for ex parte—sets a different time

    (3) ❑ Any affidavit supporting a motion must be served with the motion

    (4) ❑ When a party who is not exempt from the electronic filing requirement files a document directly with the clerk, the party must present the document to the clerk within one (1) business day after filing the notice of manual filing

    (5) ❑ Unless the court orders otherwise, the [untimely] document and declaration [that party was unable to file in a timely manner due to technical difficulties] must be filed no later than 12:00 noon of the first day on which the court is open for business following the original filing deadline

(II) ❑ Matters to be considered by opposing party

  (a) ❑ Required documents

    (1) ❑ Response brief

    (2) ❑ Certificate of service

  (b) ❑ Supplemental documents

    (1) ❑ Supporting evidence

    (2) ❑ Notice of constitutional question

    (3) ❑ Index of exhibits

    (4) ❑ Request for oral argument

    (5) ❑ Request for evidentiary hearing

    (6) ❑ Copy of authority

    (7) ❑ Copy of document with self-address envelope

    (8) ❑ Notice of manual filing

    (9) ❑ Courtesy copies

(10) ❑ Copies for three-judge court

(11) ❑ Declaration that party was unable to file in a timely manner due to technical difficulties

(c) ❑ Timing

   (1) ❑ Any response is due within fourteen (14) days after service of the motion

   (2) ❑ Except as FRCP 59(c) provides otherwise, any opposing affidavit must be served at least seven (7) days before the hearing, unless the court permits service at another time

   (3) ❑ When a party who is not exempt from the electronic filing requirement files a document directly with the clerk, the party must present the document to the clerk within one (1) business day after filing the notice of manual filing

   (4) ❑ Unless the court orders otherwise, the [untimely] document and declaration [that party was unable to file in a timely manner due to technical difficulties] must be filed no later than 12:00 noon of the first day on which the court is open for business following the original filing deadline

B. Timing

1. *Motion for sanctions.* The deterrent purpose of FRCP 11 can best be served by imposing sanctions at or near the time of the violation. FEDPROC § 62:777. Accordingly, a party who is aware of a FRCP 11 violation should act promptly. FEDPROC § 62:777; Oliveri v. Thompson, 803 F.2d 1265, 5 Fed.R.Serv.3d 761 (2d Cir. 1986). However, whether a case is well-grounded in fact will often not be evident until a plaintiff has been given a chance to conduct discovery. Therefore, motions for sanctions can be timely even when filed well after the original pleadings. FEDPROC § 62:777; Runfola & Associates, Inc. v. Spectrum Reporting II, Inc., 88 F.3d 368, 35 Fed.R.Serv.3d 434, 1996 Fed.App. 0198P (6th Cir. 1996).

   a. *Safe harbor provision.* The motion must be served under FRCP 5, but it must not be filed or be presented to the court if the challenged paper, claim, defense, contention, or denial is withdrawn or appropriately corrected within twenty-one (21) days after service or within another time the court sets. FRCP 11(c)(2).

2. *Timing of motions, generally*

   a. *Motion and notice of hearing.* A written motion and notice of the hearing must be served at least fourteen (14) days before the time specified for the hearing, with the following exceptions:

      i. When the motion may be heard ex parte;

      ii. When the Federal Rules of Civil Procedure set a different time; or

      iii. When a court order—which a party may, for good cause, apply for ex parte—sets a different time. FRCP 6(c)(1).

   b. *Supporting affidavit.* Any affidavit supporting a motion must be served with the motion. FRCP 6(c)(2).

3. *Timing of opposing papers.* Any response is due within fourteen (14) days after service of the motion. IN R USDCTSD L.R. 7-1(c)(2)(A).

   a. *Opposing affidavit.* Except as FRCP 59(c) provides otherwise, any opposing affidavit must be served at least seven (7) days before the hearing, unless the court permits service at another time. FRCP 6(c)(2).

   b. *Extensions.* The court may extend response and reply deadlines, but only for good cause. IN R USDCTSD L.R. 7-1(c)(3).

   c. *Summary ruling on failure to respond.* The court may summarily rule on a motion if an opposing party does not file a response within the deadline. IN R USDCTSD L.R. 7-1(c)(4).

4. *Timing of reply papers.* Where the respondent files an answering affidavit setting up a new matter, the moving party ordinarily is allowed a reasonable time to file a reply affidavit since failure to deny the new matter by affidavit may operate as an admission of its truth. AMJUR MOTIONS § 25.

   a. *Reply brief.* Any reply is due within seven (7) days after service of the response. IN R USDCTSD L.R. 7-1(c)(2)(B).

b. *Extensions.* The court may extend response and reply deadlines, but only for good cause. IN R USDCTSD L.R. 7-1(c)(3).

5. *Document filing by non-exempt party.* When a party who is not exempt from the electronic filing requirement files a document directly with the clerk, the party must: present the document to the clerk within one (1) business day after filing the notice of manual filing. IN R USDCTSD L.R. 5-2(d)(2).

6. *Declaration that party was unable to file in a timely manner due to technical difficulties.* Unless the Court orders otherwise, the [untimely] document and declaration [that party was unable to file in a timely manner due to technical difficulties] must be filed no later than 12:00 noon of the first day on which the Court is open for business following the original filing deadline. IN R USDCTSD ECF Procedures(16).

7. *Computation of time*

   a. *Computing time.* FRCP 6 applies in computing any time period specified in the Federal Rules of Civil Procedure, in any local rule or court order, or in any statute that does not specify a method of computing time. FRCP 6(a).

      i. *Period stated in days or a longer unit.* When the period is stated in days or a longer unit of time:

         • Exclude the day of the event that triggers the period;

         • Count every day, including intermediate Saturdays, Sundays, and legal holidays; and

         • Include the last day of the period, but if the last day is a Saturday, Sunday, or legal holiday, the period continues to run until the end of the next day that is not a Saturday, Sunday, or legal holiday. FRCP 6(a)(1).

      ii. *Period stated in hours.* When the period is stated in hours:

         • Begin counting immediately on the occurrence of the event that triggers the period;

         • Count every hour, including hours during intermediate Saturdays, Sundays, and legal holidays; and

         • If the period would end on a Saturday, Sunday, or legal holiday, the period continues to run until the same time on the next day that is not a Saturday, Sunday, or legal holiday. FRCP 6(a)(2).

      iii. *Inaccessibility of the clerk's office.* Unless the court orders otherwise, if the clerk's office is inaccessible:

         • On the last day for filing under FRCP 6(a)(1), then the time for filing is extended to the first accessible day that is not a Saturday, Sunday, or legal holiday; or

         • During the last hour for filing under FRCP 6(a)(2), then the time for filing is extended to the same time on the first accessible day that is not a Saturday, Sunday, or legal holiday. FRCP 6(a)(3).

      iv. *"Last day" defined.* Unless a different time is set by a statute, local rule, or court order, the last day ends:

         • For electronic filing, at midnight in the court's time zone; and

         • For filing by other means, when the clerk's office is scheduled to close. FRCP 6(a)(4).

      v. *"Next day" defined.* The "next day" is determined by continuing to count forward when the period is measured after an event and backward when measured before an event. FRCP 6(a)(5).

      vi. *"Legal holiday" defined.* "Legal holiday" means:

         • The day set aside by statute for observing New Year's Day, Martin Luther King Jr.'s Birthday, Washington's Birthday, Memorial Day, Independence Day, Labor Day, Columbus Day, Veterans' Day, Thanksgiving Day, or Christmas Day;

         • Any day declared a holiday by the President or Congress; and

         • For periods that are measured after an event, any other day declared a holiday by the state where the district court is located. FRCP 6(a)(6).

   b. *Computation of electronic filing deadlines.* Filing documents electronically does not alter filing deadlines. IN R USDCTSD ECF Procedures(7). A document due on a particular day must be filed before midnight local time of the division where the case is pending. IN R USDCTSD L.R. 5-4(a). All electronic transmissions of documents must be completed (i.e. received completely by the Clerk's Office) prior to midnight of the local time of the division in which the case is pending in order to be considered timely filed that day (NOTE: time will be noted in Eastern Time on the Court's docket. If you have filed a document prior to midnight local time of the division in which the case is pending and the document is due that date, but the electronic receipt and docket reflect the following calendar day, please contact the Court). IN R USDCTSD ECF Procedures(7). Although attorneys may file documents electronically twenty-four (24) hours a day, seven (7) days a week, attorneys are encouraged to file all documents during the normal working hours of the Clerk's Office (Monday through Friday, 8:30 a.m. to 4:30 p.m.) when technical support is available. IN R USDCTSD ECF Procedures(7); IN R USDCTSD ECF Procedures(9).

    i. *Technical difficulties.* Parties are encouraged to file documents electronically during normal business hours, in case a problem is encountered. In the event a technical failure occurs and a document cannot be filed electronically despite the best efforts of the filing party, the party should print (if possible) a copy of the error message received. In addition, as soon as practically possible, the party should file a "Declaration that Party was Unable to File in a Timely Manner Due to Technical Difficulties." A model form is provided as Appendix D (IN R USDCTSD ECF Procedures(Appendix D)). IN R USDCTSD ECF Procedures(16).

- If a party is unable to file electronically and, as a result, may miss a filing deadline, the party must contact the Clerk's Office at the number listed in IN R USDCTSD ECF Procedures(15) to inform the court's staff of the difficulty. If a party misses a filing deadline due to an inability to file electronically, the party may submit the untimely filed document, accompanied by a declaration stating the reason(s) for missing the deadline. Unless the Court orders otherwise, the document and declaration must be filed no later than 12:00 noon of the first day on which the Court is open for business following the original filing deadline. IN R USDCTSD ECF Procedures(16).

  c. *Extending time*

    i. *In general.* When an act may or must be done within a specified time, the court may, for good cause, extend the time:

- With or without motion or notice if the court acts, or if a request is made, before the original time or its extension expires; or

- On motion made after the time has expired if the party failed to act because of excusable neglect. FRCP 6(b)(1).

    ii. *Exceptions.* A court must not extend the time to act under FRCP 50(b), FRCP 50(d), FRCP 52(b), FRCP 59(b), FRCP 59(d), FRCP 59(e), and FRCP 60(b). FRCP 6(b)(2).

    iii. Refer to the United States District Court for the Southern District of Indiana KeyRules Motion for Continuance/Extension of Time document for more information on extending time.

  d. *Additional time after certain kinds of service.* When a party may or must act within a specified time after being served and service is made under FRCP 5(b)(2)(C) (mail), FRCP 5(b)(2)(D) (leaving with the clerk), or FRCP 5(b)(2)(F) (other means consented to), three (3) days are added after the period would otherwise expire under FRCP 6(a). FRCP 6(d). Service by electronic mail shall constitute service pursuant to FRCP 5(b)(2)(E) and shall entitle the party being served to the additional three (3) days provided by FRCP 6(d). IN R USDCTSD ECF Procedures(11).

C. General Requirements

1. *Motions, generally*

  a. *Requirements.* A request for a court order must be made by motion. The motion must:

    i. Be in writing unless made during a hearing or trial;

    ii. State with particularity the grounds for seeking the order; and

    iii. State the relief sought. FRCP 7(b)(1).

b. *Notice of motion.* A party interested in resisting the relief sought by a motion has a right to notice thereof, and an opportunity to be heard. AMJUR MOTIONS § 12.

    i. In addition to statutory or court rule provisions requiring notice of a motion—the purpose of such a notice requirement having been said to be to prevent a party from being prejudicially surprised by a motion—principles of natural justice dictate that an adverse party generally must be given notice that a motion will be presented to the court. AMJUR MOTIONS § 12.

    ii. "Notice," in this regard, means reasonable notice, including a meaningful opportunity to prepare and to defend against allegations of a motion. AMJUR MOTIONS § 12.

c. *Writing requirement.* The writing requirement is intended to insure that the adverse parties are informed and have a record of both the motion's pendency and the grounds on which the movant seeks an order. FPP § 1191; Feldberg v. Quechee Lakes Corp., 463 F.3d 195 (2d Cir. 2006).

    i. It is sufficient "if the motion is stated in a written notice of the hearing of the motion." FPP § 1191.

d. *Particularity requirement.* The particularity requirement insures that the opposing parties will have notice of their opponent's contentions. FEDPROC § 62:364; Goodman v. 1973 26 Foot Trojan Vessel, Arkansas Registration No. AR1439SN, 859 F.2d 71, 12 Fed.R.Serv.3d 645 (8th Cir. 1988). That requirement ensures that notice of the basis for the motion is provided to the court and to the opposing party so as to avoid prejudice, provide the opponent with a meaningful opportunity to respond, and provide the court with enough information to process the motion correctly. FEDPROC § 62:364; Andreas v. Volkswagen of America, Inc., 336 F.3d 789, 56 Fed.R.Serv.3d 6 (8th Cir. 2003).

    i. Reasonable specification of the grounds for a motion is sufficient. However, where a movant fails to state even one ground for granting the motion in question, the movant has failed to meet the minimal standard of "reasonable specification." FEDPROC § 62:364; Martinez v. Trainor, 556 F.2d 818, 23 Fed.R.Serv.2d 403 (7th Cir. 1977).

    ii. The court may excuse the failure to comply with the particularity requirement if it is inadvertent, and where no prejudice is shown by the opposing party. FEDPROC § 62:364.

e. *Motions must be filed separately.* Motions must be filed separately, but alternative motions may be filed in a single document if each is named in the title. A motion must not be contained within a brief, response, or reply to a previously filed motion, unless ordered by the court. IN R USDCTSD L.R. 7-1(a).

f. *Routine or uncontested motions.* The court may rule upon a routine or uncontested motion before the response deadline passes, unless: (1) the motion indicates that an opposing party objects to it; or (2) the court otherwise believes that a response will be filed. IN R USDCTSD L.R. 7-1(d).

2. *Informal conference to resolve disputes involving non-dispositive issues.* In addition to those conferences required by IN R USDCTSD L.R. 37-1, counsel are encouraged to hold informal conferences in person or by phone to resolve any disputes involving non-dispositive issues that may otherwise require submission of a motion to the Court. This requirement does not apply to cases involving pro se parties. Therefore, prior to filing any non-dispositive motion (including motions for extension of time), the moving party must contact opposing counsel to determine whether there is an objection to any non-dispositive motion (including motions for extension of time), and state in the motion whether opposing counsel objects to the motion. IN R USDCTSD Case Mgt(General Instructions For All Cases). Refer to the Documents section of this document for more information on the contents of the motion.

3. *Reasonable efforts to resolve dispute.* The court may not grant the following motion unless the movant's attorney files with the motion a statement showing that the attorney made reasonable efforts to confer with opposing counsel and resolve the matters raised in the motion: motion for sanctions under FRCP 11. IN R USDCTSD L.R. 7-1(g)(1)(B). Refer to the Documents section of this document for more information.

a. *Refusal or delay of conference.* The court may take action appropriate to avoid unreasonable delay if any party's attorney advises the court in writing that any opposing counsel has refused to meet or otherwise delayed efforts to resolve the matters raised in the motion. IN R USDCTSD L.R. 7-1(g)(3).

4. *Motion for sanctions.* A motion for sanctions under FRCP 11 may be filed by either the plaintiff or the

defendant. FEDPROC § 62:774. Only parties and other "participants" in an action have standing to seek sanctions, however. FEDPROC § 62:774; New York News, Inc. v. Kheel, 972 F.2d 482, 23 Fed.R.Serv.3d 317 (2d Cir. 1992).

a. *Basis for motion for sanctions.* FRCP 11(c) authorizes sanctions for misconduct relating to representations to the court. These representations are based on misconduct relating to the presentation (whether by signing, filing, submitting, or later advocating) of a pleading, written motion, or other paper to the court. Improper conduct includes, but is not limited to: (1) the filing of a frivolous suit or document; (2) the filing of a document or lawsuit for an improper purpose; and (3) the filing of actions that needlessly increase the cost or length of litigation. LITGTORT § 20:7. Refer to the Format section of this document for more information on representations to the court.

b. *Informal notice.* In most cases, counsel should be expected to give informal notice to the other party, whether in person or by a telephone call or letter, of a potential violation before proceeding to prepare and serve a FRCP 11 motion. FRCP 11(Advisory Committee Notes).

c. *Safe harbor provision.* A motion for sanctions must be made separately from any other motion and must describe the specific conduct that allegedly violates FRCP 11(b). The motion must be served under FRCP 5, but it must not be filed or be presented to the court if the challenged paper, claim, defense, contention, or denial is withdrawn or appropriately corrected within twenty-one (21) days after service or within another time the court sets. If warranted, the court may award to the prevailing party the reasonable expenses, including attorney's fees, incurred for the motion. FRCP 11(c)(2).

   i. These provisions are intended to provide a type of "safe harbor" against motions under FRCP 11 in that a party will not be subject to sanctions on the basis of another party's motion unless, after receiving the motion, it refuses to withdraw that position or to acknowledge candidly that it does not currently have evidence to support a specified allegation. FRCP 11(Advisory Committee Notes).

d. *Imposition of sanctions.* If, after notice and a reasonable opportunity to respond, the court determines that FRCP 11(b) has been violated, the court may impose an appropriate sanction on any attorney, law firm, or party that violated FRCP 11(b) or is responsible for the violation. Absent exceptional circumstances, a law firm must be held jointly responsible for a violation committed by its partner, associate, or employee. FRCP 11(c)(1).

   i. *Government agencies and their counsel.* FRCP 11 applies to government agencies and their counsel as well as private parties. Thus, the United States is bound by FRCP 11 just as are private parties, and must have reasonable grounds to make allegations within its complaint or answer. FEDPROC § 62:769.

   ii. *Pro se litigants.* In applying FRCP 11, the court may consider the special circumstances of pro se litigants. FEDPROC § 62:771; Maduakolam v. Columbia University, 866 F.2d 53, 51 Ed.Law.Rep. 441, 12 Fed.R.Serv.3d 1271 (2d Cir. 1989). Pro se litigants are held to a more lenient standard than professional counsel, with FRCP 11's application determined on a sliding scale according to the litigant's level of sophistication. FEDPROC § 62:771.

e. *Nature of a sanction.* A sanction imposed under FRCP 11 must be limited to what suffices to deter repetition of the conduct or comparable conduct by others similarly situated. The sanction may include nonmonetary directives; an order to pay a penalty into court; or, if imposed on motion and warranted for effective deterrence, an order directing payment to the movant of part or all of the reasonable attorney's fees and other expenses directly resulting from the violation. FRCP 11(c)(4).

f. *Counsel's liability for excessive costs.* Any attorney or other person admitted to conduct cases in any court of the United States or any Territory thereof who so multiplies the proceedings in any case unreasonably and vexatiously may be required by the court to satisfy personally the excess costs, expenses, and attorneys' fees reasonably incurred because of such conduct. 28 U.S.C.A. § 1927.

g. *Limitations on monetary sanctions.* The court must not impose a monetary sanction:

   i. Against a represented party for violating FRCP 11(b)(2); or

   ii. On its own, unless it issued the show-cause order under FRCP 11(c)(3) before voluntary dismissal or settlement of the claims made by or against the party that is, or whose attorneys are, to be sanctioned. FRCP 11(c)(5).

h. *Requirements for an order.* An order imposing a sanction must describe the sanctioned conduct and explain the basis for the sanction. FRCP 11(c)(6).

    i. *On the court's initiative.* On its own, the court may order an attorney, law firm, or party to show cause why conduct specifically described in the order has not violated FRCP 11(b). FRCP 11(c)(3).

5. *Opposing papers.* The Federal Rules of Civil Procedure do not require any formal answer, return, or reply to a motion, except where the Federal Rules of Civil Procedure or local rules may require affidavits, memoranda, or other papers to be filed in opposition to a motion. Such papers are simply to apprise the court of such opposition and the grounds of that opposition. FEDPROC § 62:359.

a. *Effect of failure to respond to motion.* Although in the absence of statutory provision or court rule, a motion ordinarily does not require a written answer, when a party files a motion and the opposing party fails to respond, the court may construe such failure to respond as nonopposition to the motion or an admission that the motion was meritorious, may take the facts alleged in the motion as true—the rule in some jurisdictions being that the failure to respond to a fact set forth in a motion is deemed an admission—and may grant the motion if the relief requested appears to be justified. AMJUR MOTIONS § 28.

b. *Assent or no opposition not determinative.* However, a motion will not be granted automatically simply because an "assent" or a notation of "no opposition" has been filed; federal judges frequently deny motions that have been assented to when it is thought that justice so dictates. FPP § 1190.

c. *Responsive pleading inappropriate as response to motion.* An attempt to answer or oppose a motion with a responsive pleading usually is not appropriate. FPP § 1190.

6. *Reply papers.* A moving party may be required or permitted to prepare papers in addition to his original motion papers. AMJUR MOTIONS § 25. Papers answering or replying to opposing papers may be appropriate, in the interests of justice, where it appears there is a substantial reason for allowing a reply. Thus, a court may accept reply papers where a party demonstrates that the papers to which it seeks to file a reply raise new issues that are material to the disposition of the question before the court, or where the court determines, sua sponte, that it wishes further briefing of an issue raised in those papers and orders the submission of additional papers. FEDPROC § 62:360.

a. *Function of reply papers.* The function of a reply affidavit is to answer the arguments made in opposition to the position taken by the movant and not to permit the movant to introduce new arguments in support of the motion. AMJUR MOTIONS § 25.

b. *Issues raised for the first time in a reply document.* However, the view has been followed in some jurisdictions, that as a matter of judicial economy, where there is no prejudice and where the issues could be raised simply by filing a motion to dismiss, the trial court has discretion to consider arguments raised for the first time in a reply memorandum, and that a trial court may grant a motion to strike issues raised for the first time in a reply memorandum. AMJUR MOTIONS § 26.

7. *Appearances.* Every attorney who represents a party or who files a document on a party's behalf must file an appearance for that party. IN R USDCTSD L.R. 83-7. The filing of a Notice of Appearance shall act to establish the filing attorney as an attorney of record representing a designated party or parties in a particular cause of action. As a result, it is necessary for each attorney to file a separate Notice of Appearance when entering an appearance in a case. A joint appearance on behalf of multiple attorneys may be filed electronically only if it is filed separately for each attorney, using his/her ECF login. IN R USDCTSD ECF Procedures(12). Only those attorneys who have filed an appearance in a pending action are entitled to be served with case documents under FRCP 5(a). IN R USDCTSD L.R. 83-7. For more information, refer to IN R USDCTSD L.R. 83-7 and IN R USDCTSD ECF Procedures(12).

8. *Notice of related action.* A party must file a notice of related action: as soon as it appears that the party's case and another pending case: (1) arise out of the same transaction or occurrence; (2) involve the same property; or (3) involve the validity or infringement or the same patent, trademark, or copyright. IN R USDCTSD L.R. 40-1(d)(2). For more information, refer to IN R USDCTSD L.R. 40-1.

9. *Alternative dispute resolution (ADR)*

a. *Application.* Unless limited by specific provisions, or unless there are other applicable specific

statutory, common law, or constitutional procedures, the Local Alternative Dispute Resolution Rules of the United States District Court for the Southern District of Indiana shall apply in all civil litigation filed in the U.S. District Court for the Southern District of Indiana, except in the following cases and proceedings:

   i.   Applications for writs of habeas corpus under 28 U.S.C.A. § 2254;

   ii. Forfeiture cases;

   iii. Non-adversary proceedings in bankruptcy;

   iv. Social Security administrative review cases; and

   v.   Such other matters as specified by order of the Court; for example, matters involving important public policy issues, constitutional law, or the establishment of new law. IN R USDCTSD A.D.R. Rule 1.2.

   b. *Mediation.* Mediation under this section (IN R USDCTSD A.D.R. Rule 2.1, et seq.) involves the confidential process by which a person acting as a Mediator, selected by the parties or appointed by the Court, assists the litigants in reaching a mutually acceptable agreement. It is an informal and nonadversarial process. The role of the Mediator is to assist in identifying the issues, reducing misunderstandings, clarifying priorities, exploring areas of compromise, and finding points of agreement as well as legitimate points of disagreement. Final decision-making authority rests with the parties, not the Mediator. IN R USDCTSD A.D.R. Rule 2.1. It is anticipated that an agreement may not resolve all of the disputed issues, but the process, nonetheless, can reduce points of contention. Parties and their representatives are required to mediate in good faith, but are not compelled to reach an agreement. IN R USDCTSD A.D.R. Rule 2.1.

      i. *Case selection.* The Court with the agreement of the parties may refer a civil case for mediation. Unless otherwise ordered or as specifically provided in IN R USDCTSD A.D.R. Rule 2.8, referral to mediation does not abate or suspend the action, and no scheduled dates shall be delayed or deferred, including the date of trial. IN R USDCTSD A.D.R. Rule 2.2.

      ii. For more information on mediation, refer to IN R USDCTSD A.D.R. Rule 2.1, et seq.

   c. *Other methods of dispute resolution.* The Local Alternative Dispute Resolution Rules of the United States District Court for the Southern District of Indiana shall not preclude the parties from utilizing any other reasonable method or technique of alternative dispute resolution to resolve disputes to which the parties agree. However, any use of arbitration by the parties will be governed by and comply with the requirements of 28 U.S.C.A. § 654 through 28 U.S.C.A. § 657. IN R USDCTSD A.D.R. Rule 1.5.

   d. For more information on alternative dispute resolution (ADR), refer to IN R USDCTSD A.D.R. Rule 1.1, et seq.

10. *Notice of settlement or resolution.* The parties must immediately notify the court if they reasonably anticipate settling their case or resolving a pending motion. IN R USDCTSD L.R. 7-1(h).

11. *Modification or suspension of rules.* The court may, on its own motion or at the request of a party, suspend or modify any rule in a particular case in the interest of justice. IN R USDCTSD L.R. 1-1(c).

D. Documents

1. *Documents for moving party*

   a. *Required documents*

      i. *Notice of motion and motion.* [P]rior to filing any non-dispositive motion (including motions for extension of time), the moving party must contact opposing counsel to determine whether there is an objection to any non-dispositive motion (including motions for extension of time), and state in the motion whether opposing counsel objects to the motion. If an objection cannot be resolved by counsel, the opposing counsel's position shall be stated within the motion. The motion should also indicate whether opposing counsel plans to file a written objection to the motion and the date by which the Court can expect to receive the objection (within the time limits set in IN R USDCTSD L.R. 7-1). If after a reasonable effort, opposing counsel cannot be reached, the moving party shall recite in the motion the dates and times that messages were left for opposing counsel. IN R USDCTSD Case Mgt(General Instructions For All Cases). Refer to the General Requirements section of this document for information on the notice of motion and motion.

    ii.   *Statement regarding efforts.* The court may not grant the following motion unless the movant's attorney files with the motion a statement showing that the attorney made reasonable efforts to confer with opposing counsel and resolve the matters raised in the motion: motion for sanctions under FRCP 11. IN R USDCTSD L.R. 7-1(g)(1)(B). The statement required by IN R US-DCTSD L.R. 7-1(g)(1) must include: (1) the date, time, and place of all conferences; and (2) the names of all conference participants. IN R USDCTSD L.R. 7-1(g)(2).

    iii.   *Certificate of service.* FRCP 5(d) requires that the person making service under FRCP 5 certify that service has been effected. FRCP 5(Advisory Committee Notes). Having such information on file may be useful for many purposes, including proof of service if an issue arises concerning the effectiveness of the service. FRCP 5(Advisory Committee Notes).

> • *Certificate of service for electronically-filed documents.* A certificate of service must be included with all documents filed electronically. Such certificate shall indicate that service was accomplished pursuant to the Court's electronic filing procedures. IN R USDCTSD ECF Procedures(11). For the suggested format for a certificate of service for electronic filing, refer to IN R USDCTSD ECF Procedures(11).

  b. *Supplemental documents*

    i.   *Brief.* Refer to the Format section of this document for the format of briefs.

    ii.   *Supporting evidence.* When a motion relies on facts outside the record, the court may hear the matter on affidavits or may hear it wholly or partly on oral testimony or on depositions. FRCP 43(c).

> • *Materials necessary for motion.* A party seeking relief under FRCP 26(c) or FRCP 37, or by way of a pretrial motion that could result in a final order on an issue, must file with the motion those parts of the discovery materials relevant to the motion. IN R USDCTSD L.R. 26-2(a).

    iii.   *Notice of constitutional question.* A party that files a pleading, written motion, or other paper drawing into question the constitutionality of a federal or state statute must promptly:

> • *File notice.* File a notice of constitutional question stating the question and identifying the paper that raises it, if: (1) a federal statute is questioned and the parties do not include the United States, one of its agencies, or one of its officers or employees in an official capacity; or (2) a state statute is questioned and the parties do not include the state, one of its agencies, or one of its officers or employees in an official capacity; and

> • *Serve notice.* Serve the notice and paper on the Attorney General of the United States if a federal statute is questioned—or on the state attorney general if a state statute is questioned—either by certified or registered mail or by sending it to an electronic address designated by the attorney general for this purpose. FRCP 5.1(a).

> • *Time for filing.* A notice of constitutional challenge to a statute filed in accordance with FRCP 5.1 must be filed at the same time the parties tender their proposed case management plan, if one is required, or within twenty-one (21) days of the filing drawing into question the constitutionality of a federal or state statute, whichever occurs later. IN R USDCTSD L.R. 5.1-1(a).

> • *Additional service requirements.* If a federal statute is challenged, in addition to the service requirements of FRCP 5.1(a), the party filing the notice of constitutional challenge must serve the notice and documents on the United States Attorney for the Southern District of Indiana, either by certified or registered mail or by sending it to an electronic address designated for that purpose by that official. IN R USDCTSD L.R. 5.1-1(b).

> • *No forfeiture.* A party's failure to file and serve the notice, or the court's failure to certify,

does not forfeit a constitutional claim or defense that is otherwise timely asserted. FRCP 5.1(d).

iv. *Nongovernmental corporate disclosure statement*

- *Contents.* A nongovernmental corporate party must file two (2) copies of a disclosure statement that: (1) identifies any parent corporation and any publicly held corporation owning ten percent (10%) or more of its stock; or (2) states that there is no such corporation. FRCP 7.1(a).

- *Time to file; Supplemental filing.* A party must: (1) file the disclosure statement with its first appearance, pleading, petition, motion, response, or other request addressed to the court; and (2) promptly file a supplemental statement if any required information changes. FRCP 7.1(b).

v. *Index of exhibits.* Any pleading, motion, brief, affidavit, notice, or proposed order filed with the court, whether electronically or with the clerk, must: if it has four (4) or more exhibits, include a separate index that identifies and briefly describes each exhibit. IN R USDCTSD L.R. 5-1(b).

vi. *Request for oral argument.* A party may request oral argument by filing a separate motion explaining why oral argument is necessary and estimating how long the court should allow for the argument. The request must be filed and served with the supporting brief, response brief, or reply brief. IN R USDCTSD L.R. 7-5(a).

vii. *Request for evidentiary hearing.* A party may request an evidentiary hearing on a motion or petition by serving and filing a separate motion explaining why the hearing is necessary and estimating how long the court should allow for the hearing. IN R USDCTSD L.R. 7-5(c).

viii. *Copy of authority.* Generally, copies of cited authorities may not be attached to court filings. However, a party must attach to the party's motion or brief a copy of any cited authority if it is not available on Westlaw or Lexis. Upon request, a party must provide copies of any cited authority that is only available through electronic means to the court or the other parties. IN R USDCTSD L.R. 7-1(f).

ix. *Proposed order.* A party must include a suitable form of order with any document that requests the judge or the clerk to enter a routine or uncontested order. IN R USDCTSD L.R. 5-5(b); IN R USDCTSD L.R. 5-10(c); IN R USDCTSD L.R. 7-1(d).

- A service statement and/or list must be included on each proposed order, as required by IN R USDCTSD L.R. 5-5(d). IN R USDCTSD ECF Procedures(11). Any pleading, motion, brief, affidavit, notice, or proposed order filed with the court, whether electronically or with the clerk, must: if it is a form of order, include a statement of service, in the format required by IN R USDCTSD L.R. 5-5(d) in the lower left corner of the document. IN R USDCTSD L.R. 5-1(b).

- A party electronically filing a proposed order—whether voluntarily or because required by IN R USDCTSD L.R. 5-5—must convert the order directly from a word processing program and file it as an attachment to the document it relates to. Proposed orders must include in the lower left-hand corner of the signature page a statement that service will be made electronically on all ECF-registered counsel of record via email generated by the court's ECF system, without listing all such counsel. A service list including the name and postal address of any pro se litigant or non-registered attorney of record must follow, stating that service on the listed individuals will be made in the traditional paper manner, via first-class U.S. Mail. IN R USDCTSD L.R. 5-5(d).

x. *Copy of document with self-address envelope.* To receive a file-stamped copy of a document filed directly with the clerk, a party must include with the original document an additional copy and a self-addressed envelope. The envelope must be big enough to hold the copy and have enough postage on it to send the copy via regular first-class mail. IN R USDCTSD L.R. 5-10(b).

xi. *Notice of manual filing.* When a party who is not exempt from the electronic filing requirement files a document directly with the clerk, the party must: electronically file a notice of manual filing that explains why the document cannot be filed electronically. IN R USDCTSD L.R.

5-2(d)(1). Refer to the Filing and Service Requirements section of this document for more information.

- Where an individual component cannot be included in an electronic filing (e.g. the component cannot be converted to electronic format), the filer shall electronically file the prescribed Notice of Manual Filing in place of that component. A model form is provided as Appendix C (IN R USDCTSD ECF Procedures(Appendix C)). IN R USDCTSD ECF Procedures(13).

- Before making a manual filing of a component, the filing party shall first electronically file a Notice of Manual Filing (See IN R USDCTSD ECF Procedures(Appendix C)). The filer shall initiate the electronic filing process as if filing the actual component but shall instead attach to the filing the Notice of Manual Filing setting forth the reason(s) why the component cannot be filed electronically. The manual filing should be accompanied by a copy of the previously filed Notice of Manual Filing. A party may seek to have a component excluded from electronic filing pursuant to applicable Federal and Local Rules (e.g., FRCP 26(c)). IN R USDCTSD ECF Procedures(15).

xii. *Courtesy copies.* District Judges and Magistrate Judges regularly receive documents filed by all parties. Therefore, parties shall not bring "courtesy copies" to any chambers unless specifically directed to do so by the Court. IN R USDCTSD Case Mgt(General Instructions For All Cases).

xiii. *Copies for three-judge court.* Parties in a case where a three-judge court has been requested must file an original and three copies of any document filed directly with the clerk (instead of electronically) until the court: (1) denies the request; (2) dissolves the three-judge court; or (3) allows the parties to file fewer copies. IN R USDCTSD L.R. 9-2(c).

xiv. *Declaration that party was unable to file in a timely manner due to technical difficulties.* If a party misses a filing deadline due to an inability to file electronically, the party may submit the untimely filed document, accompanied by a declaration stating the reason(s) for missing the deadline. IN R USDCTSD ECF Procedures(16). A model form is provided as Appendix D (IN R USDCTSD ECF Procedures(Appendix D)). IN R USDCTSD ECF Procedures(16).

2. *Documents for opposing party*

   a. *Required documents*

      i. *Response brief.* Refer to the Format section of this document for the format of briefs. Refer to the General Requirements section of this document for information on the opposing papers.

      ii. *Certificate of service.* FRCP 5(d) requires that the person making service under FRCP 5 certify that service has been effected. FRCP 5(Advisory Committee Notes). Having such information on file may be useful for many purposes, including proof of service if an issue arises concerning the effectiveness of the service. FRCP 5(Advisory Committee Notes).

         - *Certificate of service for electronically-filed documents.* A certificate of service must be included with all documents filed electronically. Such certificate shall indicate that service was accomplished pursuant to the Court's electronic filing procedures. IN R USDCTSD ECF Procedures(11). For the suggested format for a certificate of service for electronic filing, refer to IN R USDCTSD ECF Procedures(11).

   b. *Supplemental documents*

      i. *Supporting evidence.* When a motion relies on facts outside the record, the court may hear the matter on affidavits or may hear it wholly or partly on oral testimony or on depositions. FRCP 43(c).

         - *Materials necessary for motion.* A party seeking relief under FRCP 26(c) or FRCP 37, or by way of a pretrial motion that could result in a final order on an issue, must file with the motion those parts of the discovery materials relevant to the motion. IN R USDCTSD L.R. 26-2(a).

      ii. *Notice of constitutional question.* A party that files a pleading, written motion, or other paper drawing into question the constitutionality of a federal or state statute must promptly:

         - *File notice.* File a notice of constitutional question stating the question and identifying the

paper that raises it, if: (1) a federal statute is questioned and the parties do not include the United States, one of its agencies, or one of its officers or employees in an official capacity; or (2) a state statute is questioned and the parties do not include the state, one of its agencies, or one of its officers or employees in an official capacity; and

- *Serve notice.* Serve the notice and paper on the Attorney General of the United States if a federal statute is questioned—or on the state attorney general if a state statute is questioned—either by certified or registered mail or by sending it to an electronic address designated by the attorney general for this purpose. FRCP 5.1(a).

- *Time for filing.* A notice of constitutional challenge to a statute filed in accordance with FRCP 5.1 must be filed at the same time the parties tender their proposed case management plan, if one is required, or within twenty-one (21) days of the filing drawing into question the constitutionality of a federal or state statute, whichever occurs later. IN R USDCTSD L.R. 5.1-1(a).

- *Additional service requirements.* If a federal statute is challenged, in addition to the service requirements of FRCP 5.1(a), the party filing the notice of constitutional challenge must serve the notice and documents on the United States Attorney for the Southern District of Indiana, either by certified or registered mail or by sending it to an electronic address designated for that purpose by that official. IN R USDCTSD L.R. 5.1-1(b).

- *No forfeiture.* A party's failure to file and serve the notice, or the court's failure to certify, does not forfeit a constitutional claim or defense that is otherwise timely asserted. FRCP 5.1(d).

iii. *Index of exhibits.* Any pleading, motion, brief, affidavit, notice, or proposed order filed with the court, whether electronically or with the clerk, must: if it has four (4) or more exhibits, include a separate index that identifies and briefly describes each exhibit. IN R USDCTSD L.R. 5-1(b).

iv. *Request for oral argument.* A party may request oral argument by filing a separate motion explaining why oral argument is necessary and estimating how long the court should allow for the argument. The request must be filed and served with the supporting brief, response brief, or reply brief. IN R USDCTSD L.R. 7-5(a).

v. *Request for evidentiary hearing.* A party may request an evidentiary hearing on a motion or petition by serving and filing a separate motion explaining why the hearing is necessary and estimating how long the court should allow for the hearing. IN R USDCTSD L.R. 7-5(c).

vi. *Copy of authority.* Generally, copies of cited authorities may not be attached to court filings. However, a party must attach to the party's motion or brief a copy of any cited authority if it is not available on Westlaw or Lexis. Upon request, a party must provide copies of any cited authority that is only available through electronic means to the court or the other parties. IN R USDCTSD L.R. 7-1(f).

vii. *Copy of document with self-address envelope.* To receive a file-stamped copy of a document filed directly with the clerk, a party must include with the original document an additional copy and a self-addressed envelope. The envelope must be big enough to hold the copy and have enough postage on it to send the copy via regular first-class mail. IN R USDCTSD L.R. 5-10(b).

viii. *Notice of manual filing.* When a party who is not exempt from the electronic filing requirement files a document directly with the clerk, the party must: electronically file a notice of manual filing that explains why the document cannot be filed electronically. IN R USDCTSD L.R. 5-2(d)(1). Refer to the Filing and Service Requirements section of this document for more information.

- Where an individual component cannot be included in an electronic filing (e.g. the component cannot be converted to electronic format), the filer shall electronically file the prescribed Notice of Manual Filing in place of that component. A model form is provided as Appendix C (IN R USDCTSD ECF Procedures(Appendix C)). IN R USDCTSD ECF Procedures(13).

- Before making a manual filing of a component, the filing party shall first electronically file a Notice of Manual Filing (See IN R USDCTSD ECF Procedures(Appendix C)). The filer shall initiate the electronic filing process as if filing the actual component but shall instead attach to the filing the Notice of Manual Filing setting forth the reason(s) why the component cannot be filed electronically. The manual filing should be accompanied by a copy of the previously filed Notice of Manual Filing. A party may seek to have a component excluded from electronic filing pursuant to applicable Federal and Local Rules (e.g., FRCP 26(c)). IN R USDCTSD ECF Procedures(15).

ix. *Courtesy copies.* District Judges and Magistrate Judges regularly receive documents filed by all parties. Therefore, parties shall not bring "courtesy copies" to any chambers unless specifically directed to do so by the Court. IN R USDCTSD Case Mgt(General Instructions For All Cases).

x. *Copies for three-judge court.* Parties in a case where a three-judge court has been requested must file an original and three copies of any document filed directly with the clerk (instead of electronically) until the court: (1) denies the request; (2) dissolves the three-judge court; or (3) allows the parties to file fewer copies. IN R USDCTSD L.R. 9-2(c).

xi. *Declaration that party was unable to file in a timely manner due to technical difficulties.* If a party misses a filing deadline due to an inability to file electronically, the party may submit the untimely filed document, accompanied by a declaration stating the reason(s) for missing the deadline. IN R USDCTSD ECF Procedures(16). A model form is provided as Appendix D (IN R USDCTSD ECF Procedures(Appendix D)). IN R USDCTSD ECF Procedures(16).

E. Format

1. *Form of documents.* The rules governing captions and other matters of form in pleadings apply to motions and other papers. FRCP 7(b)(2).

a. *Paper (manual filings only).* Any document that is not filed electronically must: be flat, unfolded, and on good-quality, eight and one-half by eleven (8-1/2 x 11) inch white paper. IN R USDCTSD L.R. 5-1(d)(1). Any document that is not filed electronically must: be single-sided. IN R USDCTSD L.R. 5-1(d)(1).

   i. *Covers or backing.* Any document that is not filed electronically must: not have a cover or a back. IN R USDCTSD L.R. 5-1(d)(1).

   ii. *Fastening.* Any document that is not filed electronically must: be (if consisting of more than one (1) page) fastened by paperclip or binder clip and may not be stapled. IN R USDCTSD L.R. 5-1(d)(1).

      • *Request for nonconforming fastening.* If a document cannot be fastened or bound as required by IN R USDCTSD L.R. 5-1(d), a party may ask the clerk for permission to fasten it in another manner. The party must make such a request before attempting to file the document with nonconforming fastening. IN R USDCTSD L.R. 5-1(d)(2).

   iii. *Hole punching.* Any document that is not filed electronically must: be two-hole punched at the top with the holes two and three-quarter (2-3/4) inches apart and appropriately centered. IN R USDCTSD L.R. 5-1(d)(1).

b. *Margins.* Any pleading, motion, brief, affidavit, notice, or proposed order filed with the court, whether electronically or with the clerk, must: have at least one (1) inch margins. IN R USDCTSD L.R. 5-1(b).

c. *Spacing.* Any pleading, motion, brief, affidavit, notice, or proposed order filed with the court, whether electronically or with the clerk, must: be double spaced (except for headings, footnotes, and quoted material). IN R USDCTSD L.R. 5-1(b).

d. *Text.* Any pleading, motion, brief, affidavit, notice, or proposed order filed with the court, whether electronically or with the clerk, must: be plainly typewritten, printed, or prepared by a clearly legible copying process. IN R USDCTSD L.R. 5-1(b).

e. *Font size.* Any pleading, motion, brief, affidavit, notice, or proposed order filed with the court, whether electronically or with the clerk, must: use at least 12-point type in the body of the document and at least 10-point type in footnotes. IN R USDCTSD L.R. 5-1(b).

f. *Page numbering.* Any pleading, motion, brief, affidavit, notice, or proposed order filed with the court, whether electronically or with the clerk, must: have consecutively numbered pages. IN R USDCTSD L.R. 5-1(b).

g. *Caption; Names of parties.* Every pleading must have a caption with the court's name, a title, a file number, and a FRCP 7(a) designation. The title of the complaint must name all the parties; the title of other pleadings, after naming the first party on each side, may refer generally to other parties. FRCP 10(a). Any pleading, motion, brief, affidavit, notice, or proposed order filed with the court, whether electronically or with the clerk, must: include a title on the first page. IN R USDCTSD L.R. 5-1(b).

   i. *Alternative motions.* Motions must be filed separately, but alternative motions may be filed in a single document if each is named in the title. IN R USDCTSD L.R. 7-1(a).

h. *Filer's information.* Any pleading, motion, brief, affidavit, notice, or proposed order filed with the court, whether electronically or with the clerk, must: in the case of pleadings, motions, legal briefs, and notices, include the name, complete address, telephone number, facsimile number (where available), and e-mail address (where available) of the pro se litigant or attorney who files it. IN R USDCTSD L.R. 5-1(b).

i. *Paragraphs; Separate statements.* A party must state its claims or defenses in numbered paragraphs, each limited as far as practicable to a single set of circumstances. A later pleading may refer by number to a paragraph in an earlier pleading. If doing so would promote clarity, each claim founded on a separate transaction or occurrence—and each defense other than a denial—must be stated in a separate count or defense. FRCP 10(b).

j. *Adoption by reference; Exhibits.* A statement in a pleading may be adopted by reference elsewhere in the same pleading or in any other pleading or motion. A copy of a written instrument that is an exhibit to a pleading is a part of the pleading for all purposes. FRCP 10(c).

k. *Citations*

   i. *Local rules.* The Local Rules of the United States District Court for the Southern District of Indiana may be cited as "S.D. Ind. L.R." IN R USDCTSD L.R. 1-1(a).

   ii. *Local alternative dispute resolution rules.* These Rules shall be known as the Local Alternative Dispute Resolution Rules of the United States District Court for the Southern District of Indiana. They shall be cited as "S.D.Ind. Local A.D.R. Rule _____." IN R USDCTSD A.D.R. Rule 1.1.

l. *Acceptance by the clerk.* The clerk must not refuse to file a paper solely because it is not in the form prescribed by the Federal Rules of Civil Procedure or by a local rule or practice. FRCP 5(d)(4). The clerk will accept a document that violates IN R USDCTSD L.R. 5-1, but the court may exclude the document from the official record. IN R USDCTSD L.R. 5-1(e).

   i. *Sanctions for errors as to form.* The court may strike from the record any document that does not comply with the rules governing the form of documents filed with the court, such as rules that regulate document size or the number of copies to be filed or that require a special designation in the caption. The court may also sanction an attorney or party who files a non-compliant document. IN R USDCTSD L.R. 1-3.

2. *Form of electronic documents.* Any document submitted via the court's electronic case filing (ECF) system must be: otherwise prepared and filed in a manner consistent with the CM/ECF Policies and Procedures Manual (IN R USDCTSD ECF Procedures). IN R USDCTSD L.R. 5-1(c). Electronically filed documents must meet the requirements of FRCP 10 (Form of Pleadings), IN R USDCTSD L.R. 5-1 (Format of Papers Presented for Filing), and FRCP 5.2 (Privacy Protection for Filings Made with the Court), as if they had been submitted on paper. Documents filed electronically are also subject to any page limitations set forth by Court Order, by IN R USDCTSD L.R. 7-1 (Motion Practice), or IN R USDCTSD L.R. 56-1 (Summary Judgment Practice), as applicable. IN R USDCTSD ECF Procedures(13).

a. *PDF format required.* Any document submitted via the court's electronic case filing (ECF) system must be: in .pdf format. IN R USDCTSD L.R. 5-1(c); IN R USDCTSD ECF Procedures(7). Any document submitted via the court's electronic case filing (ECF) system must be: converted to a .pdf file directly from a word processing program, unless it exists only in paper format (in which case it may be scanned to create a .pdf document). IN R USDCTSD L.R. 5-1(c); IN R USDCTSD ECF Procedures(13).

    i.   An exhibit may be scanned into PDF format, at a recommended 300 dpi resolution or higher, only if it does not already exist in electronic format. The filing attorney is responsible for reviewing all PDF documents for legibility before submitting them through the Court's Electronic Case Filing system. For technical guidance in creating PDF documents, please contact the Clerk's Office. IN R USDCTSD ECF Procedures(13).

b.   *File size limitations.* Any document submitted via the court's electronic case filing (ECF) system must be: submitted as one or more .pdf files that do not exceed ten megabytes (10 MB) each (consistent with the CM/ECF Policies and Procedures Manual (IN R USDCTSD ECF Procedures)). IN R USDCTSD L.R. 5-1(c); IN R USDCTSD ECF Procedures(13).

    i.   To electronically file a document or attachment that exceeds ten megabytes (10 MB), the document must first be broken down into two or more smaller files. For example, if Exhibit A is a twelve megabyte (12 MB) PDF file, it should be divided into 2 equal parts prior to electronic filing. Each component part of the exhibit would be filed as an attachment to the main document and described appropriately as "Exhibit A (part 1 of 2)" and "Exhibit A (part 2 of 2)." IN R USDCTSD ECF Procedures(13).

    ii.   The supporting items mentioned in IN R USDCTSD ECF Procedures(13) should not be confused with memorandums or briefs in support of motions as outlined in IN R USDCTSD L.R. 7-1 or IN R USDCTSD L.R. 56-1. These memorandums or briefs in support are to be filed as entirely separate documents pursuant to the appropriate rule. Additionally, no motion shall be embodied in the text of a response or reply brief/memorandum unless otherwise ordered by the Court. IN R USDCTSD ECF Procedures(13).

c.   *Separate component parts.* A key objective of the electronic filing system is to ensure that as much of the case as possible is managed electronically. To facilitate electronic filing and retrieval, documents to be filed electronically are to be reasonably broken into their separate component parts. By way of example, most filings include a foundation document (e.g., motion) and other supporting items (e.g., exhibits, proposed orders, proposed amended pleadings). The foundation document, as well as the supporting items, are each separate components of the filing; supporting items must be filed as attachments to the foundation document. These exhibits or attachments should include only those excerpts of the referenced documents that are directly germane to the matter under consideration. IN R USDCTSD ECF Procedures(13).

    i.   Where an individual component cannot be included in an electronic filing (e.g. the component cannot be converted to electronic format), the filer shall electronically file the prescribed Notice of Manual Filing in place of that component. A model form is provided as Appendix C (IN R USDCTSD ECF Procedures(Appendix C)). IN R USDCTSD ECF Procedures(13).

d.   *Exhibits.* Each electronically filed exhibit to a main document must be: (1) created as a separate .pdf file; (2) submitted as an attachment to the main document and given a title which describes its content; and (3) limited to excerpts that are directly germane to the main document's subject matter. IN R USDCTSD L.R. 5-6(a).

    i.   When uploading attachments during the electronic filing process, exhibits must be uploaded in a logical sequence and a brief description must be entered for each individual PDF file. The description must include not only the exhibit number or letter, but also a brief description of the document. This information may be entered in CM/ECF using a combination of the Category drop-down menu, the Description text box, or both (see IN R USDCTSD ECF Procedures(13)(Figure 1)). The information that is provided in each box will be combined to create a description of the document as it appears on the case docket (see IN R USDCTSD ECF Procedures(13)(Figure 2)). IN R USDCTSD ECF Procedures(13). For an example, refer to IN R USDCTSD ECF Procedures(13).

e.   *Excerpts.* A party filing an exhibit that consists of excerpts from a larger document must clearly and prominently identify the exhibit as containing excerpted material. Either party will have the right to timely file additional excerpts or the complete document to the extent they are or become directly germane to the main document's subject matter. IN R USDCTSD L.R. 5-6(b).

    f. For an example illustrating the application of IN R USDCTSD ECF Procedures(13), refer to IN R USDCTSD ECF Procedures(13).

3. *Form of briefs*

    a. *Page limits.* Supporting and response briefs (excluding tables of contents, tables of authorities, appendices, and certificates of service) may not exceed thirty-five (35) pages. Reply briefs may not exceed twenty (20) pages. IN R USDCTSD L.R. 7-1(e)(1).

        i. *Permission to exceed limits.* The court may allow a party to file a brief exceeding these page limits for extraordinary and compelling reasons. IN R USDCTSD L.R. 7-1(e)(2).

        ii. *Supporting and response briefs exceeding limits.* If the court allows a party to file a brief or response exceeding thirty-five (35) pages, the document must include:

- A table of contents with page references;

- A statement of issues; and

- A table of authorities including: (1) all cases (alphabetically arranged), statutes, and other authorities cited in the brief; and (2) page numbers where the authorities are cited in the brief. IN R USDCTSD L.R. 7-1(e)(3).

4. *Signing of pleadings, motions and other papers*

    a. *Signature.* Every pleading, written motion, and other paper must be signed by at least one attorney of record in the attorney's name—or by a party personally if the party is unrepresented. The paper must state the signer's address, e-mail address, and telephone number. FRCP 11(a).

        i. *Signatures on manual filings.* Any document that is not filed electronically must: include the original signature of the pro se litigant or attorney who files it. IN R USDCTSD L.R. 5-1(d)(1).

        ii. *Electronic signatures.* Use of the attorney's login and password when filing documents electronically serves in part as the attorney's signature for purposes of FRCP 11, the Local Rules of the United States District Court for the Southern District of Indiana, and any other purpose for which a signature is required in connection with proceedings before the Court. IN R USDCTSD ECF Procedures(14); IN R USDCTSD ECF Procedures(10). A pleading, motion, brief, or notice filed electronically under an attorney's ECF log-in and password must be signed by that attorney. IN R USDCTSD L.R. 5-7(a). A signature on a document other than a document filed as provided under IN R USDCTSD L.R. 5-7(a) must be an original handwritten signature and must be scanned into .pdf format for electronic filing. IN R USDCTSD L.R. 5-7(c); IN R USDCTSD ECF Procedures(14).

- *Form of electronic signature.* If a document is converted directly from a word processing application to .pdf (as opposed to scanning), the name of the Filing User under whose log-in and password the document is submitted must be preceded by a "s/" and typed on the signature line where the Filing User's handwritten signature would otherwise appear. IN R USDCTSD L.R. 5-7(b). All documents filed electronically shall include a signature block and include the filing attorney's typewritten name, address, telephone number, facsimile number and e-mail address. In addition, the name of the filing attorney under whose ECF login the document will be filed should be preceded by a "s/" and typed in the space where the attorney's handwritten signature would otherwise appear. IN R US-DCTSD ECF Procedures(14). For a sample format, refer to IN R USDCTSD ECF Procedures(14).

- *Effect of electronic signature.* Filing an electronically signed document under an attorney's ECF log-in and password constitutes the attorney's signature on the document under the Federal Rules of Civil Procedure, under the Local Rules of the United States District Court for the Southern District of Indiana, and for any other reason a signature is required in connection with the court's activities. IN R USDCTSD L.R. 5-7(d).

- *Documents with multiple attorneys' signatures.* Documents requiring signatures of more than one attorney shall be filed either by: (1) obtaining consent from the other attorney, then typing the "s/ [Name]" signature of the other attorney on the signature line where the other attorney's signature would otherwise appear; (2) identifying in the signature section the name of the other attorney whose signature is required and by the submission of a Notice of Endorsement (see IN R USDCTSD ECF Procedures(Appendix B)) by the other attorney no later than three (3) business days after filing; (3) submitting a scanned document containing all handwritten signatures; or (4) in any other manner approved by the Court. IN R USDCTSD ECF Procedures(14); IN R USDCTSD L.R. 5-7(e).

    iii. *No verification or accompanying affidavit required for pleadings.* Unless a rule or statute specifically states otherwise, a pleading need not be verified or accompanied by an affidavit. FRCP 11(a).

    iv. *Unsigned papers.* The court must strike an unsigned paper unless the omission is promptly corrected after being called to the attorney's or party's attention. FRCP 11(a). The court will strike any document filed directly with the clerk that is not signed by an attorney of record or the pro se litigant filing it, but the court may do so only after giving the attorney or pro se litigant notice of the omission and reasonable time to correct it. Rubber-stamp or facsimile signatures are not original signatures and the court will deem documents containing them to be unsigned for purposes of FRCP 11 and FRCP 26(g) and IN R USDCTSD L.R. 5-10. IN R USDCTSD L.R. 5-10(g).

  b. *Representations to the court.* By presenting to the court a pleading, written motion, or other paper—whether by signing, filing, submitting, or later advocating it—an attorney or unrepresented party certifies that to the best of the person's knowledge, information, and belief, formed after an inquiry reasonable under the circumstances:

    i. It is not being presented for any improper purpose, such as to harass, cause unnecessary delay, or needlessly increase the cost of litigation;

    ii. The claims, defenses, and other legal contentions are warranted by existing law or by a nonfrivolous argument for extending, modifying, or reversing existing law or for establishing new law;

    iii. The factual contentions have evidentiary support or, if specifically so identified, will likely have evidentiary support after a reasonable opportunity for further investigation or discovery; and

    iv. The denials of factual contentions are warranted on the evidence or, if specifically so identified, are reasonably based on belief or a lack of information. FRCP 11(b).

  c. *Sanctions.* Refer to the General Requirements section of this document for information on sanctions.

5. *Privacy protection for filings made with the court.* Electronically filed documents must meet the requirements of. . .FRCP 5.2 (Privacy Protection for Filings Made with the Court), as if they had been submitted on paper. IN R USDCTSD ECF Procedures(13).

  a. *Redacted filings.* Unless the court orders otherwise, in an electronic or paper filing with the court that contains an individual's Social Security number, taxpayer-identification number, or birth date, the name of an individual known to be a minor, or a financial-account number, a party or nonparty making the filing may include only:

    i. The last four (4) digits of the Social Security number and taxpayer-identification number;

    ii. The year of the individual's birth;

    iii. The minor's initials; and

    iv. The last four (4) digits of the financial-account number. FRCP 5.2(a).

  b. *Exemptions from the redaction requirement.* The redaction requirement does not apply to the following:

    i. A financial-account number that identifies the property allegedly subject to forfeiture in a forfeiture proceeding;

    ii. The record of an administrative or agency proceeding;

iii. The official record of a state-court proceeding;

iv. The record of a court or tribunal, if that record was not subject to the redaction requirement when originally filed;

v. A filing covered by FRCP 5.2(c) or FRCP 5.2(d); and

vi. A pro se filing in an action brought under 28 U.S.C.A. § 2241, 28 U.S.C.A. § 2254, or 28 U.S.C.A. § 2255. FRCP 5.2(b).

c. *Limitations on remote access to electronic files; Social Security appeals and immigration cases.* Unless the court orders otherwise, in an action for benefits under the Social Security Act, and in an action or proceeding relating to an order of removal, to relief from removal, or to immigration benefits or detention, access to an electronic file is authorized as follows:

i. The parties and their attorneys may have remote electronic access to any part of the case file, including the administrative record;

ii. Any other person may have electronic access to the full record at the courthouse, but may have remote electronic access only to:

- The docket maintained by the court; and

- An opinion, order, judgment, or other disposition of the court, but not any other part of the case file or the administrative record. FRCP 5.2(c).

d. *Filings made under seal.* The court may order that a filing be made under seal without redaction. The court may later unseal the filing or order the person who made the filing to file a redacted version for the public record. FRCP 5.2(d). For more information on filing under seal, refer to IN R USDCTSD L.R. 5-11 and IN R USDCTSD ECF Procedures(18).

e. *Protective orders.* For good cause, the court may by order in a case:

i. Require redaction of additional information; or

ii. Limit or prohibit a nonparty's remote electronic access to a document filed with the court. FRCP 5.2(e).

f. *Option for additional unredacted filing under seal.* A person making a redacted filing may also file an unredacted copy under seal. The court must retain the unredacted copy as part of the record. FRCP 5.2(f).

g. *Option for filing a reference list.* A filing that contains redacted information may be filed together with a reference list that identifies each item of redacted information and specifies an appropriate identifier that uniquely corresponds to each item listed. The list must be filed under seal and may be amended as of right. Any reference in the case to a listed identifier will be construed to refer to the corresponding item of information. FRCP 5.2(g).

h. *Waiver of protection of identifiers.* A person waives the protection of FRCP 5.2(a) as to the person's own information by filing it without redaction and not under seal. FRCP 5.2(h).

F. Filing and Service Requirements

1. *Filing requirements.* Any paper after the complaint that is required to be served—together with a certificate of service—must be filed within a reasonable time after service. FRCP 5(d)(1). Motions must be filed separately, but alternative motions may be filed in a single document if each is named in the title. IN R USDCTSD L.R. 7-1(a).

a. *How filing is made; In general.* A paper is filed by delivering it:

i. To the clerk; or

ii. To a judge who agrees to accept it for filing, and who must then note the filing date on the paper and promptly send it to the clerk. FRCP 5(d)(2).

- In certain instances, the court will direct the parties to submit items directly to chambers (e.g., confidential settlement statements). However, absent specific prior authorization, counsel and litigants should not submit letters or documents directly to chambers, and such materials should be filed with the clerk. IN R USDCTSD L.R. 5-1(Local Rules Advisory Committee Comment).

    iii. A document or item submitted in relation to a matter within the court's jurisdiction is deemed filed upon delivery to the office of the clerk in a manner prescribed by the Local Rules of the United States District Court for the Southern District of Indiana or the Federal Rules of Civil Procedure or authorized by the court. Any submission directed to a Judge or Judge's staff, the office of the clerk or any employee thereof, in a manner that is not contemplated by IN R USDCTSD L.R. 5-1 and without prior court authorization is prohibited. IN R USDCTSD L.R. 5-1(a).

b. *Non-electronic filing.* Any document that is exempt from electronic filing must be filed directly with the clerk and served on other parties in the case as required by those Federal Rules of Civil Procedure and Local Rules of the United States District Court for the Southern District of Indiana that apply to the service of non-electronic documents. IN R USDCTSD L.R. 5-2(c).

    i. *When completed.* A document or other item that is not required to be filed electronically is deemed filed:

- Upon delivery in person, by courier, or via U.S. Mail or other mail delivery service to the clerk's office during business hours;
- When the courtroom deputy clerk accepts it, if the document or item is filed in open court; or
- Upon completion of any other manner of filing that the court authorizes. IN R USDCTSD L.R. 5-10(a).

    ii. *Document filing by non-exempt party.* When a party who is not exempt from the electronic filing requirement files a document directly with the clerk, the party must:

- Electronically file a notice of manual filing that explains why the document cannot be filed electronically;
- Present the document to the clerk within one (1) business day after filing the notice of manual filing; and
- Present the clerk with a copy of the notice of manual filing when the party files the document with the clerk. IN R USDCTSD L.R. 5-2(d).

c. *Electronic filing*

    i. *Authorization of electronic filing program.* A court may, by local rule, allow papers to be filed, signed, or verified by electronic means that are consistent with any technical standards established by the Judicial Conference of the United States. A local rule may require electronic filing only if reasonable exceptions are allowed. A paper filed electronically in compliance with a local rule is a written paper for purposes of the Federal Rules of Civil Procedure. FRCP 5(d)(3).

- IN R USDCTSD L.R. 5-2 requires electronic filing, as allowed by FRCP 5(d)(3). The policies and procedures in IN R USDCTSD ECF Procedures govern electronic filing in this district unless, due to circumstances in a particular case, a judicial officer determines that these policies and procedures (IN R USDCTSD ECF Procedures) should be modified. IN R USDCTSD ECF Procedures(1).
- Unless modified by order of the Court, all Federal Rules of Civil Procedure and Local Rules of the United States District Court for the Southern District of Indiana shall continue to apply to cases maintained in the Court's Case Management/Electronic Case Filing System (CM/ECF). IN R USDCTSD ECF Procedures(3).

    ii. *Mandatory electronic filing.* Unless exempted pursuant to IN R USDCTSD L.R. 5-3(e), attorneys admitted to the court's bar (including those admitted pro hac vice) or authorized to represent the United States must use the court's ECF system to file documents. IN R USDCTSD L.R. 5-3(a). Electronic filing by attorneys is required for eligible documents filed in civil and

criminal cases pending with the Court, unless specifically exempted by Local Rule or Court Order. IN R USDCTSD ECF Procedures(4).

- *Exceptions.* All civil cases (other than those cases the court specifically exempts) must be maintained in the court's electronic case filing (ECF) system. Accordingly, as allowed by FRCP 5(d)(3), every document filed in this court (including exhibits) must be transmitted to the clerk's office via the ECF system consistent with IN R USDCTSD L.R. 5-2 through IN R USDCTSD L.R. 5-11 except: (1) documents filed by pro se litigants; (2) transcripts in cases filed by claimants under the Social Security Act (and related statutes); (3) exhibits in a format that does not readily permit electronic filing (such as videos and large maps and charts); (4) documents that are illegible when scanned into .pdf format; (5) documents filed in cases not maintained on the ECF system; and (6) any other documents that the court or the Local Rules of the United States District Court for the Southern District of Indiana specifically allow to be filed directly with the clerk. IN R USDCTSD L.R. 5-2(a). Parties otherwise participating in the electronic filing system may be excused from filing a particular component electronically under certain limited circumstances, such as when the component cannot be reduced to an electronic format. Such components shall not be filed electronically, but instead shall be manually filed with the Clerk of Court and served upon the parties in accordance with the applicable Federal Rules of Civil Procedure and the Local Rules of the United States District Court for the Southern District of Indiana for filing and service of non-electronic documents. IN R USDCTSD ECF Procedures(15).

- *Exemption from participation.* The court may exempt attorneys from using the ECF system in a particular case for good cause. An attorney must file a petition for ECF exemption and a CM/ECF technical requirements exemption questionnaire in each case in which the attorney seeks an exemption. (The CM/ECF technical requirements exemption questionnaire is available on the court's website). IN R USDCTSD L.R. 5-3(e).

iii. *Consequences of electronic filing.* Electronic transmission of a document consistent with the procedures adopted by the Court shall, upon the complete receipt of the same by the Clerk of Court, constitute filing of the document for all purposes of the Federal Rules of Civil and Criminal Procedure and the Local Rules of the United States District Court for the Southern District of Indiana, and shall constitute entry of that document onto the docket maintained by the Clerk pursuant to FRCP 58 and FRCP 79. IN R USDCTSD ECF Procedures(7); IN R USDCTSD L.R. 5-4(c)(1). When a document has been filed electronically: the document, as filed, binds the filing party. IN R USDCTSD L.R. 5-4(c)(3).

- A Notice of Electronic Filing (NEF) acknowledging that the document has been filed will immediately appear on the filer's screen after the document has been submitted. Attorneys are strongly encouraged to print or electronically save a copy of the NEF. Attorneys can also verify the filing of documents by inspecting the Court's electronic docket sheet through the use of a PACER login. IN R USDCTSD ECF Procedures(7). When a document has been filed electronically: the notice of electronic filing for the document serves as the court's date-stamp and proof of filing. IN R USDCTSD L.R. 5-4(c)(4).

- The Court may, upon the motion of a party or upon its own motion, strike any inappropriately filed document. IN R USDCTSD ECF Procedures(7).

iv. For more information on electronic filing, refer to IN R USDCTSD ECF Procedures.

d. *Fax filing.* The clerk may not file a faxed document without court authorization. The court may not authorize the clerk to file faxed documents without finding that compelling circumstances justify it. A party must submit a copy of the document that otherwise complies with IN R USDCTSD L.R. 5-10 to replace the faxed copy within seven (7) days after faxing the document. IN R USDCTSD L.R. 5-10(e).

2. *Service requirements*

a. *Service; When required*

i. *In general.* Unless the Federal Rules of Civil Procedure provide otherwise, each of the following papers must be served on every party:

- An order stating that service is required;

- A pleading filed after the original complaint, unless the court orders otherwise under FRCP 5(c) because there are numerous defendants;

- A discovery paper required to be served on a party, unless the court orders otherwise;

- A written motion, except one that may be heard ex parte; and

- A written notice, appearance, demand, or offer of judgment, or any similar paper. FRCP 5(a)(1).

ii. *If a party fails to appear.* No service is required on a party who is in default for failing to appear. But a pleading that asserts a new claim for relief against such a party must be served on that party under FRCP 4. FRCP 5(a)(2).

iii. *Seizing property.* If an action is begun by seizing property and no person is or need be named as a defendant, any service required before the filing of an appearance, answer, or claim must be made on the person who had custody or possession of the property when it was seized. FRCP 5(a)(3).

b. *Service; How made*

i. *Serving an attorney.* If a party is represented by an attorney, service under FRCP 5 must be made on the attorney unless the court orders service on the party. FRCP 5(b)(1).

ii. *Service in general.* A paper is served under FRCP 5 by:

- Handing it to the person;

- Leaving it: (1) at the person's office with a clerk or other person in charge or, if no one is in charge, in a conspicuous place in the office; or (2) if the person has no office or the office is closed, at the person's dwelling or usual place of abode with someone of suitable age and discretion who resides there;

- Mailing it to the person's last known address—in which event service is complete upon mailing;

- Leaving it with the court clerk if the person has no known address;

- Sending it by electronic means if the person consented in writing—in which event service is complete upon transmission, but is not effective if the serving party learns that it did not reach the person to be served; or

- Delivering it by any other means that the person consented to in writing—in which event service is complete when the person making service delivers it to the agency designated to make delivery. FRCP 5(b)(2).

iii. *Electronic service*

- *Consent.* By registering to use the ECF system, attorneys consent to electronic service of documents filed in cases maintained on the ECF system. IN R USDCTSD L.R. 5-3(d). By participating in the Electronic Case Filing Program, attorneys consent to the electronic service of documents, and shall make available electronic mail addresses for service. IN R USDCTSD ECF Procedures(11).

- *Service on registered parties.* Upon the filing of a document by a party, an e-mail message will be automatically generated by the electronic filing system and sent via electronic mail to the e-mail addresses of all registered attorneys who have appeared in the case. The Notice of Electronic Filing will contain a document hyperlink which will provide recipients with one "free look" at the electronically filed document. Recipients are encouraged to print and/or save a copy of the document during the "free look" to avoid incurring PACER charges for future viewings of the document. IN R USDCTSD ECF Procedures(11). When a document has been filed electronically: transmission of the notice of electronic filing generated by the ECF system to an attorney's e-mail address constitutes service of the document on that attorney. IN R USDCTSD L.R. 5-4(c)(5). The party effectuates service on all registered attorneys by filing electronically. IN R USDCTSD ECF Procedures(11). When a document has been filed electronically: no other attempted service will constitute electronic service of the document. IN R USDCTSD L.R. 5-4(c)(6).

- *Service on exempt parties.* A filer must serve a copy of the document consistent with FRCP 5 on any party or attorney who is exempt from participating in electronic filing. IN R USDCTSD L.R. 5-4(d). It is the responsibility of the filing attorney to conventionally serve all parties who do not receive electronic service (the identity of these parties will be indicated on the filing receipt generated by the ECF system). IN R USDCTSD ECF Procedures(11).

- *Service on parties excused from electronic filing.* Parties otherwise participating in the electronic filing system may be excused from filing a particular component electronically under certain limited circumstances, such as when the component cannot be reduced to an electronic format. Such components shall not be filed electronically, but instead shall be manually filed with the Clerk of Court and served upon the parties in accordance with the applicable Federal Rules of Civil Procedure and the Local Rules of the United States District Court for the Southern District of Indiana for filing and service of non-electronic documents. IN R USDCTSD ECF Procedures(15).

- *Service of exempt documents.* Any document that is exempt from electronic filing must be filed directly with the clerk and served on other parties in the case as required by those Federal Rules of Civil Procedure and Local Rules of the United States District Court for the Southern District of Indiana that apply to the service of non-electronic documents. IN R USDCTSD L.R. 5-2(c).

    iv. *Using court facilities.* If a local rule so authorizes, a party may use the court's transmission facilities to make service under FRCP 5(b)(2)(E). FRCP 5(b)(3).

  c. *Serving numerous defendants*

    i. *In general.* If an action involves an unusually large number of defendants, the court may, on motion or on its own, order that:

- Defendants' pleadings and replies to them need not be served on other defendants;

- Any crossclaim, counterclaim, avoidance, or affirmative defense in those pleadings and replies to them will be treated as denied or avoided by all other parties; and

- Filing any such pleading and serving it on the plaintiff constitutes notice of the pleading to all parties. FRCP 5(c)(1).

    ii. *Notifying parties.* A copy of every such order must be served on the parties as the court directs. FRCP 5(c)(2).

G. Hearings

1. *Hearings, generally*

  a. *Oral argument.* Due process does not require that oral argument be permitted on a motion and, except as otherwise provided by local rule, the district court has discretion to determine whether it will decide the motion on the papers or hear argument by counsel (and perhaps receive evidence). FPP § 1190; F.D.I.C. v. Deglau, 207 F.3d 153 (3d Cir. 2000).

    i. *Request for oral argument.* A party may request oral argument by filing a separate motion explaining why oral argument is necessary and estimating how long the court should allow for the argument. IN R USDCTSD L.R. 7-5(a). Refer to the Documents section of this document for more information.

    ii. *No additional evidence at oral argument.* Parties may not present additional evidence at oral argument. IN R USDCTSD L.R. 7-5(b).

  b. *Providing a regular schedule for oral hearings.* A court may establish regular times and places for oral hearings on motions. FRCP 78(a).

  c. *Providing for submission on briefs.* By rule or order, the court may provide for submitting and determining motions on briefs, without oral hearings. FRCP 78(b).

  d. *Request for evidentiary hearing.* A party may request an evidentiary hearing on a motion or petition by serving and filing a separate motion explaining why the hearing is necessary and estimating how long the court should allow for the hearing. IN R USDCTSD L.R. 7-5(c).

e. *Directed by the court.* The court may: (1) grant or deny a request for oral argument or an evidentiary hearing in its sole discretion; (2) set oral argument or an evidentiary hearing without a request from a party; and (3) order any oral argument or evidentiary hearing to be held anywhere within the district regardless of where the case will be tried. IN R USDCTSD L.R. 7-5(d).

2. *Courtroom and courthouse decorum.* For information on courtroom and courthouse decorum, refer to IN R USDCTSD L.R. 83-3.

H. Forms

1. Federal Motion for Sanctions Forms

a. Motion; For order imposing sanctions pursuant to FRCP 11; Notice of removal frivolous, not well grounded in fact, or interposed for purpose of causing unnecessary delay and needlessly to increase cost of litigation. AMJUR PP FEDPRAC § 364.

b. Notice of motion for sanctions. 2C FEDFORMS § 10:74.

c. Notice of motion and motion for sanctions. 2C FEDFORMS § 10:75.

d. Notice of motion and motion for sanctions; Including motion for sanctions under FRCP 37(c). 2C FEDFORMS § 10:76.

e. Motion for sanctions; Including sanctions under FRCP 37(d). 2C FEDFORMS § 10:77.

f. Defendant's summary of attorney fees. 2C FEDFORMS § 10:78.

g. Motion; General form. FEDPROF § 1:746.

h. Notice; Of motion; General form. FEDPROF § 1:747.

i. Notice; Of motion; With costs of motion. FEDPROF § 1:748.

j. Notice; Of motion; Containing motion. FEDPROF § 1:749.

k. Opposition; To motion; General form. FEDPROF § 1:750.

l. Affidavit; Supporting or opposing motion. FEDPROF § 1:751.

m. Brief; Supporting or opposing motion. FEDPROF § 1:752.

n. Statement of points and authorities; Opposing motion. FEDPROF § 1:753.

o. Illustrative forms; FRCP 11; Notice and motion for sanctions. LITGTORT § 20:36.

p. Illustrative forms; FRCP 11; Memorandum in support of motion. LITGTORT § 20:37.

q. Illustrative forms; FRCP 11; Declaration in support of motion. LITGTORT § 20:38.

r. Illustrative forms; FRCP 11 and 28 U.S.C.A. § 1927; Notice of motion and motion for sanctions. LITGTORT § 20:39.

s. Illustrative forms; FRCP 11 and 28 U.S.C.A. § 1927; Brief in support of motion. LITGTORT § 20:40.

2. Forms for the Southern District of Indiana

a. Notice of endorsement. IN R USDCTSD ECF Procedures(Appendix B).

b. Notice of manual filing. IN R USDCTSD ECF Procedures(Appendix C).

c. Declaration that party was unable to file in a timely manner due to technical difficulties. IN R USDCTSD ECF Procedures(Appendix D).

I. Applicable Rules

1. *Federal rules*

a. Counsel's liability for excessive costs. 28 U.S.C.A. § 1927.

b. Serving and filing pleadings and other papers. FRCP 5.

c. Constitutional challenge to a statute; Notice, certification, and intervention. FRCP 5.1.

d. Privacy protection for filings made with the court. FRCP 5.2.

e. Computing and extending time; Time for motion papers. FRCP 6.

f. Pleadings allowed; Form of motions and other papers. FRCP 7.

g. Disclosure statement. FRCP 7.1.

h. Form of pleadings. FRCP 10.

i. Signing pleadings, motions, and other papers; Representations to the court; Sanctions. FRCP 11.

j. Taking testimony. FRCP 43.

k. Hearing motions; Submission on briefs. FRCP 78.

2. *Local rules*

a. Scope of the rules. IN R USDCTSD L.R. 1-1.

b. Sanctions for errors as to form. IN R USDCTSD L.R. 1-3.

c. Format of documents presented for filing. IN R USDCTSD L.R. 5-1.

d. Constitutional challenge to a statute; Notice. IN R USDCTSD L.R. 5.1-1.

e. Filing of documents electronically required. IN R USDCTSD L.R. 5-2.

f. Eligibility, registration, passwords for electronic filing; Exemption from electronic filing. IN R USDCTSD L.R. 5-3.

g. Timing and consequences of electronic filing. IN R USDCTSD L.R. 5-4.

h. Attachments and exhibits in cases filed electronically. IN R USDCTSD L.R. 5-6.

i. Signatures in cases filed electronically. IN R USDCTSD L.R. 5-7.

j. Non-electronic filings. IN R USDCTSD L.R. 5-10.

k. Motion practice. [IN R USDCTSD L.R. 7-1, as amended by IN ORDER 16-2319, effective December 1, 2016].

l. Oral arguments and hearings. IN R USDCTSD L.R. 7-5.

m. Request for three-judge court. IN R USDCTSD L.R. 9-2.

n. Filing of discovery materials. IN R USDCTSD L.R. 26-2.

o. Assignment of cases. IN R USDCTSD L.R. 40-1.

p. Alternative dispute resolution. IN R USDCTSD A.D.R. Rule 1.1; IN R USDCTSD A.D.R. Rule 1.2; IN R USDCTSD A.D.R. Rule 1.5; IN R USDCTSD A.D.R. Rule 2.1; IN R USDCTSD A.D.R. Rule 2.2.

q. Instructions for preparing case management plan. IN R USDCTSD Case Mgt.

r. Electronic case filing policies and procedures manual. IN R USDCTSD ECF Procedures.

Motions, Oppositions and Replies
Motion to Compel Discovery

Document Last Updated December 2016

A. Checklist

(I)   ❑ Matters to be considered by moving party

(a)   ❑ Required documents

(1)   ❑ Notice of motion and motion

(2)   ❑ Certificate of compliance

(3)   ❑ Brief

(4)   ❑ Discovery materials

    (5) ❑ Certificate of service

(b) ❑ Supplemental documents

    (1) ❑ Supporting evidence

    (2) ❑ Notice of constitutional question

    (3) ❑ Index of exhibits

    (4) ❑ Request for oral argument

    (5) ❑ Request for evidentiary hearing

    (6) ❑ Copy of authority

    (7) ❑ Proposed order

    (8) ❑ Copy of document with self-address envelope

    (9) ❑ Notice of manual filing

  (10) ❑ Courtesy copies

  (11) ❑ Copies for three-judge court

  (12) ❑ Declaration that party was unable to file in a timely manner due to technical difficulties

(c) ❑ Timing

    (1) ❑ A motion must simply be submitted within a reasonable time; however, a motion to compel discovery filed under FRCP 37(a) is premature if it is filed before any request for discovery is made

    (2) ❑ A written motion and notice of the hearing must be served at least fourteen (14) days before the time specified for the hearing, with the following exceptions: (i) when the motion may be heard ex parte; (ii) when the Federal Rules of Civil Procedure set a different time; or (iii) when a court order—which a party may, for good cause, apply for ex parte—sets a different time

    (3) ❑ Any affidavit supporting a motion must be served with the motion

    (4) ❑ When a party who is not exempt from the electronic filing requirement files a document directly with the clerk, the party must present the document to the clerk within one (1) business day after filing the notice of manual filing

    (5) ❑ Unless the court orders otherwise, the [untimely] document and declaration [that party was unable to file in a timely manner due to technical difficulties] must be filed no later than 12:00 noon of the first day on which the court is open for business following the original filing deadline

(II) ❑ Matters to be considered by opposing party

(a) ❑ Required documents

    (1) ❑ Response brief

    (2) ❑ Certificate of service

(b) ❑ Supplemental documents

    (1) ❑ Supporting evidence

    (2) ❑ Notice of constitutional question

    (3) ❑ Index of exhibits

    (4) ❑ Request for oral argument

    (5) ❑ Request for evidentiary hearing

    (6) ❑ Copy of authority

    (7) ❑ Copy of document with self-address envelope

    (8) ❑ Notice of manual filing

(9) ❑ Courtesy copies

(10) ❑ Copies for three-judge court

(11) ❑ Declaration that party was unable to file in a timely manner due to technical difficulties

(c) ❑ Timing

(1) ❑ Any response is due within fourteen (14) days after service of the motion

(2) ❑ Except as FRCP 59(c) provides otherwise, any opposing affidavit must be served at least seven (7) days before the hearing, unless the court permits service at another time

(3) ❑ When a party who is not exempt from the electronic filing requirement files a document directly with the clerk, the party must present the document to the clerk within one (1) business day after filing the notice of manual filing

(4) ❑ Unless the court orders otherwise, the [untimely] document and declaration [that party was unable to file in a timely manner due to technical difficulties] must be filed no later than 12:00 noon of the first day on which the court is open for business following the original filing deadline

B. Timing

1. *Motion to compel discovery.* There is no specific time limit for a motion to compel discovery under FRCP 37(a); rather, a motion must simply be submitted within a reasonable time. FEDPROC § 26:779. However, a motion to compel discovery filed under FRCP 37(a) is premature if it is filed before any request for discovery is made. FEDPROC § 26:779; Bermudez v. Duenas, 936 F.2d 1064, 19 Fed.R.Serv.3d 1443 (9th Cir. 1991).

2. *Timing of motions, generally*

   a. *Motion and notice of hearing.* A written motion and notice of the hearing must be served at least fourteen (14) days before the time specified for the hearing, with the following exceptions:

      i.   When the motion may be heard ex parte;

      ii. When the Federal Rules of Civil Procedure set a different time; or

      iii. When a court order—which a party may, for good cause, apply for ex parte—sets a different time. FRCP 6(c)(1).

   b. *Supporting affidavit.* Any affidavit supporting a motion must be served with the motion. FRCP 6(c)(2).

3. *Timing of opposing papers.* Any response is due within fourteen (14) days after service of the motion. IN R USDCTSD L.R. 7-1(c)(2)(A).

   a. *Opposing affidavit.* Except as FRCP 59(c) provides otherwise, any opposing affidavit must be served at least seven (7) days before the hearing, unless the court permits service at another time. FRCP 6(c)(2).

   b. *Extensions.* The court may extend response and reply deadlines, but only for good cause. IN R USDCTSD L.R. 7-1(c)(3).

   c. *Summary ruling on failure to respond.* The court may summarily rule on a motion if an opposing party does not file a response within the deadline. IN R USDCTSD L.R. 7-1(c)(4).

4. *Timing of reply papers.* Where the respondent files an answering affidavit setting up a new matter, the moving party ordinarily is allowed a reasonable time to file a reply affidavit since failure to deny the new matter by affidavit may operate as an admission of its truth. AMJUR MOTIONS § 25.

   a. *Reply brief.* Any reply is due within seven (7) days after service of the response. IN R USDCTSD L.R. 7-1(c)(2)(B).

   b. *Extensions.* The court may extend response and reply deadlines, but only for good cause. IN R USDCTSD L.R. 7-1(c)(3).

5. *Document filing by non-exempt party.* When a party who is not exempt from the electronic filing requirement files a document directly with the clerk, the party must: present the document to the clerk within one (1) business day after filing the notice of manual filing. IN R USDCTSD L.R. 5-2(d)(2).

6. *Declaration that party was unable to file in a timely manner due to technical difficulties.* Unless the Court orders otherwise, the [untimely] document and declaration [that party was unable to file in a timely manner due to technical difficulties] must be filed no later than 12:00 noon of the first day on which the Court is open for business following the original filing deadline. IN R USDCTSD ECF Procedures(16).

7. *Computation of time*

   a. *Computing time.* FRCP 6 applies in computing any time period specified in the Federal Rules of Civil Procedure, in any local rule or court order, or in any statute that does not specify a method of computing time. FRCP 6(a).

      i. *Period stated in days or a longer unit.* When the period is stated in days or a longer unit of time:

         • Exclude the day of the event that triggers the period;

         • Count every day, including intermediate Saturdays, Sundays, and legal holidays; and

         • Include the last day of the period, but if the last day is a Saturday, Sunday, or legal holiday, the period continues to run until the end of the next day that is not a Saturday, Sunday, or legal holiday. FRCP 6(a)(1).

      ii. *Period stated in hours.* When the period is stated in hours:

         • Begin counting immediately on the occurrence of the event that triggers the period;

         • Count every hour, including hours during intermediate Saturdays, Sundays, and legal holidays; and

         • If the period would end on a Saturday, Sunday, or legal holiday, the period continues to run until the same time on the next day that is not a Saturday, Sunday, or legal holiday. FRCP 6(a)(2).

      iii. *Inaccessibility of the clerk's office.* Unless the court orders otherwise, if the clerk's office is inaccessible:

         • On the last day for filing under FRCP 6(a)(1), then the time for filing is extended to the first accessible day that is not a Saturday, Sunday, or legal holiday; or

         • During the last hour for filing under FRCP 6(a)(2), then the time for filing is extended to the same time on the first accessible day that is not a Saturday, Sunday, or legal holiday. FRCP 6(a)(3).

      iv. *"Last day" defined.* Unless a different time is set by a statute, local rule, or court order, the last day ends:

         • For electronic filing, at midnight in the court's time zone; and

         • For filing by other means, when the clerk's office is scheduled to close. FRCP 6(a)(4).

      v. *"Next day" defined.* The "next day" is determined by continuing to count forward when the period is measured after an event and backward when measured before an event. FRCP 6(a)(5).

      vi. *"Legal holiday" defined.* "Legal holiday" means:

         • The day set aside by statute for observing New Year's Day, Martin Luther King Jr.'s Birthday, Washington's Birthday, Memorial Day, Independence Day, Labor Day, Columbus Day, Veterans' Day, Thanksgiving Day, or Christmas Day;

         • Any day declared a holiday by the President or Congress; and

         • For periods that are measured after an event, any other day declared a holiday by the state where the district court is located. FRCP 6(a)(6).

   b. *Computation of electronic filing deadlines.* Filing documents electronically does not alter filing deadlines. IN R USDCTSD ECF Procedures(7). A document due on a particular day must be filed before midnight local time of the division where the case is pending. IN R USDCTSD L.R. 5-4(a). All electronic transmissions of documents must be completed (i.e. received completely by the Clerk's Office) prior to midnight of the local time of the division in which the case is pending in order to be considered timely filed that day (NOTE: time will be noted in Eastern Time on the Court's docket. If you have filed a document prior to midnight local time of the division in which the case is pending and the document is due that date, but the electronic receipt and docket reflect the following calendar day, please contact the Court). IN R USDCTSD ECF Procedures(7). Although attorneys may file documents electronically twenty-four (24) hours a day, seven (7) days a week, attorneys are encouraged to file all documents during the normal working hours of the Clerk's Office (Monday through Friday, 8:30 a.m. to 4:30 p.m.) when technical support is available. IN R USDCTSD ECF Procedures(7); IN R USDCTSD ECF Procedures(9).

    i. *Technical difficulties.* Parties are encouraged to file documents electronically during normal business hours, in case a problem is encountered. In the event a technical failure occurs and a document cannot be filed electronically despite the best efforts of the filing party, the party should print (if possible) a copy of the error message received. In addition, as soon as practically possible, the party should file a "Declaration that Party was Unable to File in a Timely Manner Due to Technical Difficulties." A model form is provided as Appendix D (IN R USDCTSD ECF Procedures(Appendix D)). IN R USDCTSD ECF Procedures(16).

- If a party is unable to file electronically and, as a result, may miss a filing deadline, the party must contact the Clerk's Office at the number listed in IN R USDCTSD ECF Procedures(15) to inform the court's staff of the difficulty. If a party misses a filing deadline due to an inability to file electronically, the party may submit the untimely filed document, accompanied by a declaration stating the reason(s) for missing the deadline. Unless the Court orders otherwise, the document and declaration must be filed no later than 12:00 noon of the first day on which the Court is open for business following the original filing deadline. IN R USDCTSD ECF Procedures(16).

  c. *Extending time*

    i. *In general.* When an act may or must be done within a specified time, the court may, for good cause, extend the time:

- With or without motion or notice if the court acts, or if a request is made, before the original time or its extension expires; or

- On motion made after the time has expired if the party failed to act because of excusable neglect. FRCP 6(b)(1).

    ii. *Exceptions.* A court must not extend the time to act under FRCP 50(b), FRCP 50(d), FRCP 52(b), FRCP 59(b), FRCP 59(d), FRCP 59(e), and FRCP 60(b). FRCP 6(b)(2).

    iii. Refer to the United States District Court for the Southern District of Indiana KeyRules Motion for Continuance/Extension of Time document for more information on extending time.

  d. *Additional time after certain kinds of service.* When a party may or must act within a specified time after being served and service is made under FRCP 5(b)(2)(C) (mail), FRCP 5(b)(2)(D) (leaving with the clerk), or FRCP 5(b)(2)(F) (other means consented to), three (3) days are added after the period would otherwise expire under FRCP 6(a). FRCP 6(d). Service by electronic mail shall constitute service pursuant to FRCP 5(b)(2)(E) and shall entitle the party being served to the additional three (3) days provided by FRCP 6(d). IN R USDCTSD ECF Procedures(11).

C. General Requirements

1. *Motions, generally*

  a. *Requirements.* A request for a court order must be made by motion. The motion must:

    i. Be in writing unless made during a hearing or trial;

    ii. State with particularity the grounds for seeking the order; and

    iii. State the relief sought. FRCP 7(b)(1).

  b. *Notice of motion.* A party interested in resisting the relief sought by a motion has a right to notice thereof, and an opportunity to be heard. AMJUR MOTIONS § 12.

    i. In addition to statutory or court rule provisions requiring notice of a motion—the purpose of such a notice requirement having been said to be to prevent a party from being prejudicially surprised by a motion—principles of natural justice dictate that an adverse party generally must be given notice that a motion will be presented to the court. AMJUR MOTIONS § 12.

    ii. "Notice," in this regard, means reasonable notice, including a meaningful opportunity to prepare and to defend against allegations of a motion. AMJUR MOTIONS § 12.

  c. *Writing requirement.* The writing requirement is intended to insure that the adverse parties are informed and have a record of both the motion's pendency and the grounds on which the movant seeks an order. FPP § 1191; Feldberg v. Quechee Lakes Corp., 463 F.3d 195 (2d Cir. 2006).

    i. It is sufficient "if the motion is stated in a written notice of the hearing of the motion." FPP § 1191.

  d. *Particularity requirement.* The particularity requirement insures that the opposing parties will have notice of their opponent's contentions. FEDPROC § 62:364; Goodman v. 1973 26 Foot Trojan Vessel, Arkansas Registration No. AR1439SN, 859 F.2d 71, 12 Fed.R.Serv.3d 645 (8th Cir. 1988). That requirement ensures that notice of the basis for the motion is provided to the court and to the opposing party so as to avoid prejudice, provide the opponent with a meaningful opportunity to respond, and provide the court with enough information to process the motion correctly. FEDPROC § 62:364; Andreas v. Volkswagen of America, Inc., 336 F.3d 789, 56 Fed.R.Serv.3d 6 (8th Cir. 2003).

    i. Reasonable specification of the grounds for a motion is sufficient. However, where a movant fails to state even one ground for granting the motion in question, the movant has failed to meet the minimal standard of "reasonable specification." FEDPROC § 62:364; Martinez v. Trainor, 556 F.2d 818, 23 Fed.R.Serv.2d 403 (7th Cir. 1977).

    ii. The court may excuse the failure to comply with the particularity requirement if it is inadvertent, and where no prejudice is shown by the opposing party. FEDPROC § 62:364.

  e. *Motions must be filed separately.* Motions must be filed separately, but alternative motions may be filed in a single document if each is named in the title. A motion must not be contained within a brief, response, or reply to a previously filed motion, unless ordered by the court. IN R USDCTSD L.R. 7-1(a).

  f. *Routine or uncontested motions.* The court may rule upon a routine or uncontested motion before the response deadline passes, unless: (1) the motion indicates that an opposing party objects to it; or (2) the court otherwise believes that a response will be filed. IN R USDCTSD L.R. 7-1(d).

2. *Informal conference to resolve disputes involving non-dispositive issues.* In addition to those conferences required by IN R USDCTSD L.R. 37-1, counsel are encouraged to hold informal conferences in person or by phone to resolve any disputes involving non-dispositive issues that may otherwise require submission of a motion to the Court. This requirement does not apply to cases involving pro se parties. Therefore, prior to filing any non-dispositive motion (including motions for extension of time), the moving party must contact opposing counsel to determine whether there is an objection to any non-dispositive motion (including motions for extension of time), and state in the motion whether opposing counsel objects to the motion. IN R USDCTSD Case Mgt(General Instructions For All Cases). Refer to the Documents section of this document for more information on the contents of the motion.

3. *Required actions prior to court involvement.* Prior to involving the court in any discovery dispute, including disputes involving depositions, counsel must confer in a good faith attempt to resolve the dispute. If any such dispute cannot be resolved in this manner, counsel are encouraged to contact the chambers of the assigned Magistrate Judge to determine whether the Magistrate Judge is available to resolve the discovery dispute by way of a telephone conference or other proceeding prior to counsel filing a formal discovery motion. When the dispute involves an objection raised during a deposition that threatens to prevent completion of the deposition, any party may recess the deposition to contact the Magistrate Judge's chambers. IN R USDCTSD L.R. 37-1(a). Discovery disputes involving pro se parties are not subject to IN R USDCTSD L.R. 37-1. IN R USDCTSD L.R. 37-1(c). Refer to the Documents section of this document for more information.

4. *Motion to compel discovery.* On notice to other parties and all affected persons, a party may move for an order compelling disclosure or discovery. FRCP 37(a)(1). A party must request the specific documents in

issue from the opposing party before filing a motion to compel the production of documents. FEDPROC § 26:778.

   a. *Appropriate court.* A motion for an order to a party must be made in the court where the action is pending. A motion for an order to a nonparty must be made in the court where the discovery is or will be taken. FRCP 37(a)(2).

   b. *Specific motions*

      i. *To compel disclosure.* If a party fails to make a disclosure required by FRCP 26(a), any other party may move to compel disclosure and for appropriate sanctions. FRCP 37(a)(3)(A). Refer to the United States District Court for the Southern District of Indiana KeyRules Motion for Discovery Sanctions document for more information on sanctions.

      ii. *To compel a discovery response.* A party seeking discovery may move for an order compelling an answer, designation, production, or inspection. This motion may be made if:

- A deponent fails to answer a question asked under FRCP 30 or FRCP 31;

- A corporation or other entity fails to make a designation under FRCP 30(b)(6) or FRCP 31(a)(4);

- A party fails to answer an interrogatory submitted under FRCP 33; or

- A party fails to produce documents or fails to respond that inspection will be permitted—or fails to permit inspection—as requested under FRCP 34. FRCP 37(a)(3)(B).

      iii. *Related to a deposition.* When taking an oral deposition, the party asking a question may complete or adjourn the examination before moving for an order. FRCP 37(a)(3)(C).

      iv. *Evasive or incomplete disclosure, answer, or response.* For purposes of FRCP 37(a), an evasive or incomplete disclosure, answer, or response must be treated as a failure to disclose, answer, or respond. FRCP 37(a)(4).

   c. *Payment of expenses; Protective orders*

      i. *If the motion is granted (or disclosure or discovery is provided after filing).* If the motion is granted—or if the disclosure or requested discovery is provided after the motion was filed—the court must, after giving an opportunity to be heard, require the party or deponent whose conduct necessitated the motion, the party or attorney advising that conduct, or both to pay the movant's reasonable expenses incurred in making the motion, including attorney's fees. But the court must not order this payment if:

- The movant filed the motion before attempting in good faith to obtain the disclosure or discovery without court action;

- The opposing party's nondisclosure, response, or objection was substantially justified; or

- Other circumstances make an award of expenses unjust. FRCP 37(a)(5)(A).

      ii. *If the motion is denied.* If the motion is denied, the court may issue any protective order authorized under FRCP 26(c) and must, after giving an opportunity to be heard, require the movant, the attorney filing the motion, or both to pay the party or deponent who opposed the motion its reasonable expenses incurred in opposing the motion, including attorney's fees. But the court must not order this payment if the motion was substantially justified or other circumstances make an award of expenses unjust. FRCP 37(a)(5)(B).

      iii. *If the motion is granted in part and denied in part.* If the motion is granted in part and denied in part, the court may issue any protective order authorized under FRCP 26(c) and may, after giving an opportunity to be heard, apportion the reasonable expenses for the motion. FRCP 37(a)(5)(C).

5. *Opposing papers.* The Federal Rules of Civil Procedure do not require any formal answer, return, or reply to a motion, except where the Federal Rules of Civil Procedure or local rules may require affidavits, memoranda, or other papers to be filed in opposition to a motion. Such papers are simply to apprise the court of such opposition and the grounds of that opposition. FEDPROC § 62:359.

   a. *Effect of failure to respond to motion.* Although in the absence of statutory provision or court rule, a motion ordinarily does not require a written answer, when a party files a motion and the opposing party fails to respond, the court may construe such failure to respond as nonopposition to the motion or an admission that the motion was meritorious, may take the facts alleged in the motion as true—the rule in some jurisdictions being that the failure to respond to a fact set forth in a motion is deemed an admission—and may grant the motion if the relief requested appears to be justified. AMJUR MOTIONS § 28.

b. *Assent or no opposition not determinative.* However, a motion will not be granted automatically simply because an "assent" or a notation of "no opposition" has been filed; federal judges frequently deny motions that have been assented to when it is thought that justice so dictates. FPP § 1190.

c. *Responsive pleading inappropriate as response to motion.* An attempt to answer or oppose a motion with a responsive pleading usually is not appropriate. FPP § 1190.

6. *Reply papers.* A moving party may be required or permitted to prepare papers in addition to his original motion papers. AMJUR MOTIONS § 25. Papers answering or replying to opposing papers may be appropriate, in the interests of justice, where it appears there is a substantial reason for allowing a reply. Thus, a court may accept reply papers where a party demonstrates that the papers to which it seeks to file a reply raise new issues that are material to the disposition of the question before the court, or where the court determines, sua sponte, that it wishes further briefing of an issue raised in those papers and orders the submission of additional papers. FEDPROC § 62:360.

a. *Function of reply papers.* The function of a reply affidavit is to answer the arguments made in opposition to the position taken by the movant and not to permit the movant to introduce new arguments in support of the motion. AMJUR MOTIONS § 25.

b. *Issues raised for the first time in a reply document.* However, the view has been followed in some jurisdictions, that as a matter of judicial economy, where there is no prejudice and where the issues could be raised simply by filing a motion to dismiss, the trial court has discretion to consider arguments raised for the first time in a reply memorandum, and that a trial court may grant a motion to strike issues raised for the first time in a reply memorandum. AMJUR MOTIONS § 26.

7. *Appearances.* Every attorney who represents a party or who files a document on a party's behalf must file an appearance for that party. IN R USDCTSD L.R. 83-7. The filing of a Notice of Appearance shall act to establish the filing attorney as an attorney of record representing a designated party or parties in a particular cause of action. As a result, it is necessary for each attorney to file a separate Notice of Appearance when entering an appearance in a case. A joint appearance on behalf of multiple attorneys may be filed electronically only if it is filed separately for each attorney, using his/her ECF login. IN R USDCTSD ECF Procedures(12). Only those attorneys who have filed an appearance in a pending action are entitled to be served with case documents under FRCP 5(a). IN R USDCTSD L.R. 83-7. For more information, refer to IN R USDCTSD L.R. 83-7 and IN R USDCTSD ECF Procedures(12).

8. *Notice of related action.* A party must file a notice of related action: as soon as it appears that the party's case and another pending case: (1) arise out of the same transaction or occurrence; (2) involve the same property; or (3) involve the validity or infringement or the same patent, trademark, or copyright. IN R USDCTSD L.R. 40-1(d)(2). For more information, refer to IN R USDCTSD L.R. 40-1.

9. *Alternative dispute resolution (ADR)*

a. *Application.* Unless limited by specific provisions, or unless there are other applicable specific statutory, common law, or constitutional procedures, the Local Alternative Dispute Resolution Rules of the United States District Court for the Southern District of Indiana shall apply in all civil litigation filed in the U.S. District Court for the Southern District of Indiana, except in the following cases and proceedings:

i. Applications for writs of habeas corpus under 28 U.S.C.A. § 2254;

ii. Forfeiture cases;

iii. Non-adversary proceedings in bankruptcy;

iv. Social Security administrative review cases; and

v. Such other matters as specified by order of the Court; for example, matters involving important public policy issues, constitutional law, or the establishment of new law. IN R USDCTSD A.D.R. Rule 1.2.

b.   *Mediation.* Mediation under this section (IN R USDCTSD A.D.R. Rule 2.1, et seq.) involves the confidential process by which a person acting as a Mediator, selected by the parties or appointed by the Court, assists the litigants in reaching a mutually acceptable agreement. It is an informal and nonadversarial process. The role of the Mediator is to assist in identifying the issues, reducing misunderstandings, clarifying priorities, exploring areas of compromise, and finding points of agreement as well as legitimate points of disagreement. Final decision-making authority rests with the parties, not the Mediator. IN R USDCTSD A.D.R. Rule 2.1. It is anticipated that an agreement may not resolve all of the disputed issues, but the process, nonetheless, can reduce points of contention. Parties and their representatives are required to mediate in good faith, but are not compelled to reach an agreement. IN R USDCTSD A.D.R. Rule 2.1.

   i.   *Case selection.* The Court with the agreement of the parties may refer a civil case for mediation. Unless otherwise ordered or as specifically provided in IN R USDCTSD A.D.R. Rule 2.8, referral to mediation does not abate or suspend the action, and no scheduled dates shall be delayed or deferred, including the date of trial. IN R USDCTSD A.D.R. Rule 2.2.

   ii.   For more information on mediation, refer to IN R USDCTSD A.D.R. Rule 2.1, et seq.

c.   *Other methods of dispute resolution.* The Local Alternative Dispute Resolution Rules of the United States District Court for the Southern District of Indiana shall not preclude the parties from utilizing any other reasonable method or technique of alternative dispute resolution to resolve disputes to which the parties agree. However, any use of arbitration by the parties will be governed by and comply with the requirements of 28 U.S.C.A. § 654 through 28 U.S.C.A. § 657. IN R USDCTSD A.D.R. Rule 1.5.

d.   For more information on alternative dispute resolution (ADR), refer to IN R USDCTSD A.D.R. Rule 1.1, et seq.

10.   *Notice of settlement or resolution.* The parties must immediately notify the court if they reasonably anticipate settling their case or resolving a pending motion. IN R USDCTSD L.R. 7-1(h).

11.   *Modification or suspension of rules.* The court may, on its own motion or at the request of a party, suspend or modify any rule in a particular case in the interest of justice. IN R USDCTSD L.R. 1-1(c).

D.   Documents

1.   *Documents for moving party*

   a.   *Required documents*

      i.   *Notice of motion and motion.* [P]rior to filing any non-dispositive motion (including motions for extension of time), the moving party must contact opposing counsel to determine whether there is an objection to any non-dispositive motion (including motions for extension of time), and state in the motion whether opposing counsel objects to the motion. If an objection cannot be resolved by counsel, the opposing counsel's position shall be stated within the motion. The motion should also indicate whether opposing counsel plans to file a written objection to the motion and the date by which the Court can expect to receive the objection (within the time limits set in IN R USDCTSD L.R. 7-1). If after a reasonable effort, opposing counsel cannot be reached, the moving party shall recite in the motion the dates and times that messages were left for opposing counsel. IN R USDCTSD Case Mgt(General Instructions For All Cases). Refer to the General Requirements section of this document for information on the notice of motion and motion.

      ii.   *Certificate of compliance.* In the event that the discovery dispute is not resolved at the conference, counsel may file a motion to compel or other motion raising the dispute. Any motion raising a discovery dispute must contain a statement setting forth the efforts taken to resolve the dispute, including the date, time, and place of any discovery conference and the names of all participating parties. The court may deny any motion raising a discovery dispute that does not contain such a statement. IN R USDCTSD L.R. 37-1(b). Discovery disputes involving pro se parties are not subject to IN R USDCTSD L.R. 37-1. IN R USDCTSD L.R.

37-1(c). The motion must include a certification that the movant has in good faith conferred or attempted to confer with the person or party failing to make disclosure or discovery in an effort to obtain it without court action. FRCP 37(a)(1).

iii. *Brief.* The following motion must also be accompanied by a supporting brief: any motion made under FRCP 37. IN R USDCTSD L.R. 7-1(b)(2). Refer to the Format section of this document for the format of briefs.

iv. *Discovery materials.* A party seeking relief under FRCP 26(c) or FRCP 37, or by way of a pretrial motion that could result in a final order on an issue, must file with the motion those parts of the discovery materials relevant to the motion. IN R USDCTSD L.R. 26-2(a).

v. *Certificate of service.* FRCP 5(d) requires that the person making service under FRCP 5 certify that service has been effected. FRCP 5(Advisory Committee Notes). Having such information on file may be useful for many purposes, including proof of service if an issue arises concerning the effectiveness of the service. FRCP 5(Advisory Committee Notes).

- *Certificate of service for electronically-filed documents.* A certificate of service must be included with all documents filed electronically. Such certificate shall indicate that service was accomplished pursuant to the Court's electronic filing procedures. IN R USDCTSD ECF Procedures(11). For the suggested format for a certificate of service for electronic filing, refer to IN R USDCTSD ECF Procedures(11).

b. *Supplemental documents*

i. *Supporting evidence.* When a motion relies on facts outside the record, the court may hear the matter on affidavits or may hear it wholly or partly on oral testimony or on depositions. FRCP 43(c).

- *Materials necessary for motion.* A party seeking relief under FRCP 26(c) or FRCP 37, or by way of a pretrial motion that could result in a final order on an issue, must file with the motion those parts of the discovery materials relevant to the motion. IN R USDCTSD L.R. 26-2(a).

ii. *Notice of constitutional question.* A party that files a pleading, written motion, or other paper drawing into question the constitutionality of a federal or state statute must promptly:

- *File notice.* File a notice of constitutional question stating the question and identifying the paper that raises it, if: (1) a federal statute is questioned and the parties do not include the United States, one of its agencies, or one of its officers or employees in an official capacity; or (2) a state statute is questioned and the parties do not include the state, one of its agencies, or one of its officers or employees in an official capacity; and

- *Serve notice.* Serve the notice and paper on the Attorney General of the United States if a federal statute is questioned—or on the state attorney general if a state statute is questioned—either by certified or registered mail or by sending it to an electronic address designated by the attorney general for this purpose. FRCP 5.1(a).

- *Time for filing.* A notice of constitutional challenge to a statute filed in accordance with FRCP 5.1 must be filed at the same time the parties tender their proposed case management plan, if one is required, or within twenty-one (21) days of the filing drawing into question the constitutionality of a federal or state statute, whichever occurs later. IN R USDCTSD L.R. 5.1-1(a).

- *Additional service requirements.* If a federal statute is challenged, in addition to the service requirements of FRCP 5.1(a), the party filing the notice of constitutional challenge must serve the notice and documents on the United States Attorney for the Southern District of Indiana, either by certified or registered mail or by sending it to an electronic address designated for that purpose by that official. IN R USDCTSD L.R. 5.1-1(b).

- *No forfeiture.* A party's failure to file and serve the notice, or the court's failure to certify, does not forfeit a constitutional claim or defense that is otherwise timely asserted. FRCP 5.1(d).

iii. *Index of exhibits.* Any pleading, motion, brief, affidavit, notice, or proposed order filed with the court, whether electronically or with the clerk, must: if it has four (4) or more exhibits, include a separate index that identifies and briefly describes each exhibit. IN R USDCTSD L.R. 5-1(b).

iv. *Request for oral argument.* A party may request oral argument by filing a separate motion explaining why oral argument is necessary and estimating how long the court should allow for the argument. The request must be filed and served with the supporting brief, response brief, or reply brief. IN R USDCTSD L.R. 7-5(a).

v. *Request for evidentiary hearing.* A party may request an evidentiary hearing on a motion or petition by serving and filing a separate motion explaining why the hearing is necessary and estimating how long the court should allow for the hearing. IN R USDCTSD L.R. 7-5(c).

vi. *Copy of authority.* Generally, copies of cited authorities may not be attached to court filings. However, a party must attach to the party's motion or brief a copy of any cited authority if it is not available on Westlaw or Lexis. Upon request, a party must provide copies of any cited authority that is only available through electronic means to the court or the other parties. IN R USDCTSD L.R. 7-1(f).

vii. *Proposed order.* A party must include a suitable form of order with any document that requests the judge or the clerk to enter a routine or uncontested order. IN R USDCTSD L.R. 5-5(b); IN R USDCTSD L.R. 5-10(c); IN R USDCTSD L.R. 7-1(d).

- A service statement and/or list must be included on each proposed order, as required by IN R USDCTSD L.R. 5-5(d). IN R USDCTSD ECF Procedures(11). Any pleading, motion, brief, affidavit, notice, or proposed order filed with the court, whether electronically or with the clerk, must: if it is a form of order, include a statement of service, in the format required by IN R USDCTSD L.R. 5-5(d) in the lower left corner of the document. IN R USDCTSD L.R. 5-1(b).

- A party electronically filing a proposed order—whether voluntarily or because required by IN R USDCTSD L.R. 5-5—must convert the order directly from a word processing program and file it as an attachment to the document it relates to. Proposed orders must include in the lower left-hand corner of the signature page a statement that service will be made electronically on all ECF-registered counsel of record via email generated by the court's ECF system, without listing all such counsel. A service list including the name and postal address of any pro se litigant or non-registered attorney of record must follow, stating that service on the listed individuals will be made in the traditional paper manner, via first-class U.S. Mail. IN R USDCTSD L.R. 5-5(d).

viii. *Copy of document with self-address envelope.* To receive a file-stamped copy of a document filed directly with the clerk, a party must include with the original document an additional copy and a self-addressed envelope. The envelope must be big enough to hold the copy and have enough postage on it to send the copy via regular first-class mail. IN R USDCTSD L.R. 5-10(b).

ix. *Notice of manual filing.* When a party who is not exempt from the electronic filing requirement files a document directly with the clerk, the party must: electronically file a notice of manual filing that explains why the document cannot be filed electronically. IN R USDCTSD L.R. 5-2(d)(1). Refer to the Filing and Service Requirements section of this document for more information.

- Where an individual component cannot be included in an electronic filing (e.g. the component cannot be converted to electronic format), the filer shall electronically file the prescribed Notice of Manual Filing in place of that component. A model form is provided as Appendix C (IN R USDCTSD ECF Procedures(Appendix C)). IN R USDCTSD ECF Procedures(13).

- Before making a manual filing of a component, the filing party shall first electronically file a Notice of Manual Filing (See IN R USDCTSD ECF Procedures(Appendix C)). The filer shall initiate the electronic filing process as if filing the actual component but shall instead attach to the filing the Notice of Manual Filing setting forth the reason(s) why the component cannot be filed electronically. The manual filing should be accompanied by a copy of the previously filed Notice of Manual Filing. A party may seek to have a component excluded from electronic filing pursuant to applicable Federal and Local Rules (e.g., FRCP 26(c)). IN R USDCTSD ECF Procedures(15).

x. *Courtesy copies.* District Judges and Magistrate Judges regularly receive documents filed by all parties. Therefore, parties shall not bring "courtesy copies" to any chambers unless specifically directed to do so by the Court. IN R USDCTSD Case Mgt(General Instructions For All Cases).

xi. *Copies for three-judge court.* Parties in a case where a three-judge court has been requested must file an original and three copies of any document filed directly with the clerk (instead of electronically) until the court: (1) denies the request; (2) dissolves the three-judge court; or (3) allows the parties to file fewer copies. IN R USDCTSD L.R. 9-2(c).

xii. *Declaration that party was unable to file in a timely manner due to technical difficulties.* If a party misses a filing deadline due to an inability to file electronically, the party may submit the untimely filed document, accompanied by a declaration stating the reason(s) for missing the deadline. IN R USDCTSD ECF Procedures(16). A model form is provided as Appendix D (IN R USDCTSD ECF Procedures(Appendix D)). IN R USDCTSD ECF Procedures(16).

2. *Documents for opposing party*

   a. *Required documents*

      i. *Response brief.* Refer to the Format section of this document for the format of briefs. Refer to the General Requirements section of this document for information on the opposing papers.

      ii. *Certificate of service.* FRCP 5(d) requires that the person making service under FRCP 5 certify that service has been effected. FRCP 5(Advisory Committee Notes). Having such information on file may be useful for many purposes, including proof of service if an issue arises concerning the effectiveness of the service. FRCP 5(Advisory Committee Notes).

         • *Certificate of service for electronically-filed documents.* A certificate of service must be included with all documents filed electronically. Such certificate shall indicate that service was accomplished pursuant to the Court's electronic filing procedures. IN R USDCTSD ECF Procedures(11). For the suggested format for a certificate of service for electronic filing, refer to IN R USDCTSD ECF Procedures(11).

   b. *Supplemental documents*

      i. *Supporting evidence.* When a motion relies on facts outside the record, the court may hear the matter on affidavits or may hear it wholly or partly on oral testimony or on depositions. FRCP 43(c).

         • *Materials necessary for motion.* A party seeking relief under FRCP 26(c) or FRCP 37, or by way of a pretrial motion that could result in a final order on an issue, must file with the motion those parts of the discovery materials relevant to the motion. IN R USDCTSD L.R. 26-2(a).

      ii. *Notice of constitutional question.* A party that files a pleading, written motion, or other paper drawing into question the constitutionality of a federal or state statute must promptly:

         • *File notice.* File a notice of constitutional question stating the question and identifying the paper that raises it, if: (1) a federal statute is questioned and the parties do not include the United States, one of its agencies, or one of its officers or employees in an official capacity; or (2) a state statute is questioned and the parties do not include the state, one of its agencies, or one of its officers or employees in an official capacity; and

         • *Serve notice.* Serve the notice and paper on the Attorney General of the United States if a federal statute is questioned—or on the state attorney general if a state statute is questioned—either by certified or registered mail or by sending it to an electronic address designated by the attorney general for this purpose. FRCP 5.1(a).

         • *Time for filing.* A notice of constitutional challenge to a statute filed in accordance with FRCP 5.1 must be filed at the same time the parties tender their proposed case management plan, if one is required, or within twenty-one (21) days of the filing drawing into question the constitutionality of a federal or state statute, whichever occurs later. IN R USDCTSD L.R. 5.1-1(a).

- *Additional service requirements.* If a federal statute is challenged, in addition to the service requirements of FRCP 5.1(a), the party filing the notice of constitutional challenge must serve the notice and documents on the United States Attorney for the Southern District of Indiana, either by certified or registered mail or by sending it to an electronic address designated for that purpose by that official. IN R USDCTSD L.R. 5.1-1(b).

- *No forfeiture.* A party's failure to file and serve the notice, or the court's failure to certify, does not forfeit a constitutional claim or defense that is otherwise timely asserted. FRCP 5.1(d).

iii. *Index of exhibits.* Any pleading, motion, brief, affidavit, notice, or proposed order filed with the court, whether electronically or with the clerk, must: if it has four (4) or more exhibits, include a separate index that identifies and briefly describes each exhibit. IN R USDCTSD L.R. 5-1(b).

iv. *Request for oral argument.* A party may request oral argument by filing a separate motion explaining why oral argument is necessary and estimating how long the court should allow for the argument. The request must be filed and served with the supporting brief, response brief, or reply brief. IN R USDCTSD L.R. 7-5(a).

v. *Request for evidentiary hearing.* A party may request an evidentiary hearing on a motion or petition by serving and filing a separate motion explaining why the hearing is necessary and estimating how long the court should allow for the hearing. IN R USDCTSD L.R. 7-5(c).

vi. *Copy of authority.* Generally, copies of cited authorities may not be attached to court filings. However, a party must attach to the party's motion or brief a copy of any cited authority if it is not available on Westlaw or Lexis. Upon request, a party must provide copies of any cited authority that is only available through electronic means to the court or the other parties. IN R USDCTSD L.R. 7-1(f).

vii. *Copy of document with self-address envelope.* To receive a file-stamped copy of a document filed directly with the clerk, a party must include with the original document an additional copy and a self-addressed envelope. The envelope must be big enough to hold the copy and have enough postage on it to send the copy via regular first-class mail. IN R USDCTSD L.R. 5-10(b).

viii. *Notice of manual filing.* When a party who is not exempt from the electronic filing requirement files a document directly with the clerk, the party must: electronically file a notice of manual filing that explains why the document cannot be filed electronically. IN R USDCTSD L.R. 5-2(d)(1). Refer to the Filing and Service Requirements section of this document for more information.

- Where an individual component cannot be included in an electronic filing (e.g. the component cannot be converted to electronic format), the filer shall electronically file the prescribed Notice of Manual Filing in place of that component. A model form is provided as Appendix C (IN R USDCTSD ECF Procedures(Appendix C)). IN R USDCTSD ECF Procedures(13).

- Before making a manual filing of a component, the filing party shall first electronically file a Notice of Manual Filing (See IN R USDCTSD ECF Procedures(Appendix C)). The filer shall initiate the electronic filing process as if filing the actual component but shall instead attach to the filing the Notice of Manual Filing setting forth the reason(s) why the component cannot be filed electronically. The manual filing should be accompanied by a copy of the previously filed Notice of Manual Filing. A party may seek to have a component excluded from electronic filing pursuant to applicable Federal and Local Rules (e.g., FRCP 26(c)). IN R USDCTSD ECF Procedures(15).

ix. *Courtesy copies.* District Judges and Magistrate Judges regularly receive documents filed by ll parties. Therefore, parties shall not bring "courtesy copies" to any chambers unless specifically directed to do so by the Court. IN R USDCTSD Case Mgt(General Instructions For All Cases).

    x. *Copies for three-judge court.* Parties in a case where a three-judge court has been requested must file an original and three copies of any document filed directly with the clerk (instead of electronically) until the court: (1) denies the request; (2) dissolves the three-judge court; or (3) allows the parties to file fewer copies. IN R USDCTSD L.R. 9-2(c).

    xi. *Declaration that party was unable to file in a timely manner due to technical difficulties.* If a party misses a filing deadline due to an inability to file electronically, the party may submit the untimely filed document, accompanied by a declaration stating the reason(s) for missing the deadline. IN R USDCTSD ECF Procedures(16). A model form is provided as Appendix D (IN R USDCTSD ECF Procedures(Appendix D)). IN R USDCTSD ECF Procedures(16).

E. Format

1. *Form of documents.* The rules governing captions and other matters of form in pleadings apply to motions and other papers. FRCP 7(b)(2).

    a. *Paper (manual filings only).* Any document that is not filed electronically must: be flat, unfolded, and on good-quality, eight and one-half by eleven (8-1/2 x 11) inch white paper. IN R USDCTSD L.R. 5-1(d)(1). Any document that is not filed electronically must: be single-sided. IN R USDCTSD L.R. 5-1(d)(1).

        i. *Covers or backing.* Any document that is not filed electronically must: not have a cover or a back. IN R USDCTSD L.R. 5-1(d)(1).

        ii. *Fastening.* Any document that is not filed electronically must: be (if consisting of more than one (1) page) fastened by paperclip or binder clip and may not be stapled. IN R USDCTSD L.R. 5-1(d)(1).

          • *Request for nonconforming fastening.* If a document cannot be fastened or bound as required by IN R USDCTSD L.R. 5-1(d), a party may ask the clerk for permission to fasten it in another manner. The party must make such a request before attempting to file the document with nonconforming fastening. IN R USDCTSD L.R. 5-1(d)(2).

        iii. *Hole punching.* Any document that is not filed electronically must: be two-hole punched at the top with the holes two and three-quarter (2-3/4) inches apart and appropriately centered. IN R USDCTSD L.R. 5-1(d)(1).

    b. *Margins.* Any pleading, motion, brief, affidavit, notice, or proposed order filed with the court, whether electronically or with the clerk, must: have at least one (1) inch margins. IN R USDCTSD L.R. 5-1(b).

    c. *Spacing.* Any pleading, motion, brief, affidavit, notice, or proposed order filed with the court, whether electronically or with the clerk, must: be double spaced (except for headings, footnotes, and quoted material). IN R USDCTSD L.R. 5-1(b).

    d. *Text.* Any pleading, motion, brief, affidavit, notice, or proposed order filed with the court, whether electronically or with the clerk, must: be plainly typewritten, printed, or prepared by a clearly legible copying process. IN R USDCTSD L.R. 5-1(b).

    e. *Font size.* Any pleading, motion, brief, affidavit, notice, or proposed order filed with the court, whether electronically or with the clerk, must: use at least 12-point type in the body of the document and at least 10-point type in footnotes. IN R USDCTSD L.R. 5-1(b).

    f. *Page numbering.* Any pleading, motion, brief, affidavit, notice, or proposed order filed with the court, whether electronically or with the clerk, must: have consecutively numbered pages. IN R USDCTSD L.R. 5-1(b).

    g. *Caption; Names of parties.* Every pleading must have a caption with the court's name, a title, a file number, and a FRCP 7(a) designation. The title of the complaint must name all the parties; the title of other pleadings, after naming the first party on each side, may refer generally to other parties. FRCP 10(a). Any pleading, motion, brief, affidavit, notice, or proposed order filed with the court, whether electronically or with the clerk, must: include a title on the first page. IN R USDCTSD L.R. 5-1(b).

        i. *Alternative motions.* Motions must be filed separately, but alternative motions may be filed in a single document if each is named in the title. IN R USDCTSD L.R. 7-1(a).

h. *Filer's information.* Any pleading, motion, brief, affidavit, notice, or proposed order filed with the court, whether electronically or with the clerk, must: in the case of pleadings, motions, legal briefs, and notices, include the name, complete address, telephone number, facsimile number (where available), and e-mail address (where available) of the pro se litigant or attorney who files it. IN R USDCTSD L.R. 5-1(b).

i. *Paragraphs; Separate statements.* A party must state its claims or defenses in numbered paragraphs, each limited as far as practicable to a single set of circumstances. A later pleading may refer by number to a paragraph in an earlier pleading. If doing so would promote clarity, each claim founded on a separate transaction or occurrence—and each defense other than a denial—must be stated in a separate count or defense. FRCP 10(b).

j. *Adoption by reference; Exhibits.* A statement in a pleading may be adopted by reference elsewhere in the same pleading or in any other pleading or motion. A copy of a written instrument that is an exhibit to a pleading is a part of the pleading for all purposes. FRCP 10(c).

k. *Citations*

   i. *Local rules.* The Local Rules of the United States District Court for the Southern District of Indiana may be cited as "S.D. Ind. L.R." IN R USDCTSD L.R. 1-1(a).

   ii. *Local alternative dispute resolution rules.* These Rules shall be known as the Local Alternative Dispute Resolution Rules of the United States District Court for the Southern District of Indiana. They shall be cited as "S.D.Ind. Local A.D.R. Rule _____." IN R USDCTSD A.D.R. Rule 1.1.

l. *Acceptance by the clerk.* The clerk must not refuse to file a paper solely because it is not in the form prescribed by the Federal Rules of Civil Procedure or by a local rule or practice. FRCP 5(d)(4). The clerk will accept a document that violates IN R USDCTSD L.R. 5-1, but the court may exclude the document from the official record. IN R USDCTSD L.R. 5-1(e).

   i. *Sanctions for errors as to form.* The court may strike from the record any document that does not comply with the rules governing the form of documents filed with the court, such as rules that regulate document size or the number of copies to be filed or that require a special designation in the caption. The court may also sanction an attorney or party who files a non-compliant document. IN R USDCTSD L.R. 1-3.

2. *Form of electronic documents.* Any document submitted via the court's electronic case filing (ECF) system must be: otherwise prepared and filed in a manner consistent with the CM/ECF Policies and Procedures Manual (IN R USDCTSD ECF Procedures). IN R USDCTSD L.R. 5-1(c). Electronically filed documents must meet the requirements of FRCP 10 (Form of Pleadings), IN R USDCTSD L.R. 5-1 (Format of Papers Presented for Filing), and FRCP 5.2 (Privacy Protection for Filings Made with the Court), as if they had been submitted on paper. Documents filed electronically are also subject to any page limitations set forth by Court Order, by IN R USDCTSD L.R. 7-1 (Motion Practice), or IN R USDCTSD L.R. 56-1 (Summary Judgment Practice), as applicable. IN R USDCTSD ECF Procedures(13).

a. *PDF format required.* Any document submitted via the court's electronic case filing (ECF) system must be: in .pdf format. IN R USDCTSD L.R. 5-1(c); IN R USDCTSD ECF Procedures(7). Any document submitted via the court's electronic case filing (ECF) system must be: converted to a .pdf file directly from a word processing program, unless it exists only in paper format (in which case it may be scanned to create a .pdf document). IN R USDCTSD L.R. 5-1(c); IN R USDCTSD ECF Procedures(13).

   i. An exhibit may be scanned into PDF format, at a recommended 300 dpi resolution or higher, only if it does not already exist in electronic format. The filing attorney is responsible for reviewing all PDF documents for legibility before submitting them through the Court's Electronic Case Filing system. For technical guidance in creating PDF documents, please contact the Clerk's Office. IN R USDCTSD ECF Procedures(13).

b. *File size limitations.* Any document submitted via the court's electronic case filing (ECF) system must be: submitted as one or more .pdf files that do not exceed ten megabytes (10 MB) each (consistent with the CM/ECF Policies and Procedures Manual (IN R USDCTSD ECF Procedures)). IN R USDCTSD L.R. 5-1(c); IN R USDCTSD ECF Procedures(13).

    i.   To electronically file a document or attachment that exceeds ten megabytes (10 MB), the document must first be broken down into two or more smaller files. For example, if Exhibit A is a twelve megabyte (12 MB) PDF file, it should be divided into 2 equal parts prior to electronic filing. Each component part of the exhibit would be filed as an attachment to the main document and described appropriately as "Exhibit A (part 1 of 2)" and "Exhibit A (part 2 of 2)." IN R USDCTSD ECF Procedures(13).

    ii.   The supporting items mentioned in IN R USDCTSD ECF Procedures(13) should not be confused with memorandums or briefs in support of motions as outlined in IN R USDCTSD L.R. 7-1 or IN R USDCTSD L.R. 56-1. These memorandums or briefs in support are to be filed as entirely separate documents pursuant to the appropriate rule. Additionally, no motion shall be embodied in the text of a response or reply brief/memorandum unless otherwise ordered by the Court. IN R USDCTSD ECF Procedures(13).

c.   *Separate component parts.* A key objective of the electronic filing system is to ensure that as much of the case as possible is managed electronically. To facilitate electronic filing and retrieval, documents to be filed electronically are to be reasonably broken into their separate component parts. By way of example, most filings include a foundation document (e.g., motion) and other supporting items (e.g., exhibits, proposed orders, proposed amended pleadings). The foundation document, as well as the supporting items, are each separate components of the filing; supporting items must be filed as attachments to the foundation document. These exhibits or attachments should include only those excerpts of the referenced documents that are directly germane to the matter under consideration. IN R USDCTSD ECF Procedures(13).

    i.   Where an individual component cannot be included in an electronic filing (e.g. the component cannot be converted to electronic format), the filer shall electronically file the prescribed Notice of Manual Filing in place of that component. A model form is provided as Appendix C (IN R USDCTSD ECF Procedures(Appendix C)). IN R USDCTSD ECF Procedures(13).

d.   *Exhibits.* Each electronically filed exhibit to a main document must be: (1) created as a separate .pdf file; (2) submitted as an attachment to the main document and given a title which describes its content; and (3) limited to excerpts that are directly germane to the main document's subject matter. IN R USDCTSD L.R. 5-6(a).

    i.   When uploading attachments during the electronic filing process, exhibits must be uploaded in a logical sequence and a brief description must be entered for each individual PDF file. The description must include not only the exhibit number or letter, but also a brief description of the document. This information may be entered in CM/ECF using a combination of the Category drop-down menu, the Description text box, or both (see IN R USDCTSD ECF Procedures(13)(Figure 1)). The information that is provided in each box will be combined to create a description of the document as it appears on the case docket (see IN R USDCTSD ECF Procedures(13)(Figure 2)). IN R USDCTSD ECF Procedures(13). For an example, refer to IN R USDCTSD ECF Procedures(13).

e.   *Excerpts.* A party filing an exhibit that consists of excerpts from a larger document must clearly and prominently identify the exhibit as containing excerpted material. Either party will have the right to timely file additional excerpts or the complete document to the extent they are or become directly germane to the main document's subject matter. IN R USDCTSD L.R. 5-6(b).

f.   For an example illustrating the application of IN R USDCTSD ECF Procedures(13), refer to IN R USDCTSD ECF Procedures(13).

3.   *Form of briefs*

a.   *Page limits.* Supporting and response briefs (excluding tables of contents, tables of authorities, appendices, and certificates of service) may not exceed thirty-five (35) pages. Reply briefs may not exceed twenty (20) pages. IN R USDCTSD L.R. 7-1(e)(1).

    i.   *Permission to exceed limits.* The court may allow a party to file a brief exceeding these page limits for extraordinary and compelling reasons. IN R USDCTSD L.R. 7-1(e)(2).

ii. *Supporting and response briefs exceeding limits.* If the court allows a party to file a brief or response exceeding thirty-five (35) pages, the document must include:

- A table of contents with page references;
- A statement of issues; and
- A table of authorities including: (1) all cases (alphabetically arranged), statutes, and other authorities cited in the brief; and (2) page numbers where the authorities are cited in the brief. IN R USDCTSD L.R. 7-1(e)(3).

4. *Signing disclosures and discovery requests, responses, and objections.* FRCP 11 does not apply to disclosures and discovery requests, responses, objections, and motions under FRCP 26 through FRCP 37. FRCP 11(d).

   a. *Signature required.* Every disclosure under FRCP 26(a)(1) or FRCP 26(a)(3) and every discovery request, response, or objection must be signed by at least one attorney of record in the attorney's own name—or by the party personally, if unrepresented—and must state the signer's address, e-mail address, and telephone number. FRCP 26(g)(1).

   i. *Signatures on manual filings.* Any document that is not filed electronically must: include the original signature of the pro se litigant or attorney who files it. IN R USDCTSD L.R. 5-1(d)(1).

   ii. *Electronic signatures.* Use of the attorney's login and password when filing documents electronically serves in part as the attorney's signature for purposes of FRCP 11, the Local Rules of the United States District Court for the Southern District of Indiana, and any other purpose for which a signature is required in connection with proceedings before the Court. IN R USDCTSD ECF Procedures(14); IN R USDCTSD ECF Procedures(10). A pleading, motion, brief, or notice filed electronically under an attorney's ECF log-in and password must be signed by that attorney. IN R USDCTSD L.R. 5-7(a). A signature on a document other than a document filed as provided under IN R USDCTSD L.R. 5-7(a) must be an original handwritten signature and must be scanned into .pdf format for electronic filing. IN R USDCTSD L.R. 5-7(c); IN R USDCTSD ECF Procedures(14).

   - *Form of electronic signature.* If a document is converted directly from a word processing application to .pdf (as opposed to scanning), the name of the Filing User under whose log-in and password the document is submitted must be preceded by a "s/" and typed on the signature line where the Filing User's handwritten signature would otherwise appear. IN R USDCTSD L.R. 5-7(b). All documents filed electronically shall include a signature block and include the filing attorney's typewritten name, address, telephone number, facsimile number and e-mail address. In addition, the name of the filing attorney under whose ECF login the document will be filed should be preceded by a "s/" and typed in the space where the attorney's handwritten signature would otherwise appear. IN R US-DCTSD ECF Procedures(14). For a sample format, refer to IN R USDCTSD ECF Procedures(14).

   - *Effect of electronic signature.* Filing an electronically signed document under an attorney's ECF log-in and password constitutes the attorney's signature on the document under the Federal Rules of Civil Procedure, under the Local Rules of the United States District Court for the Southern District of Indiana, and for any other reason a signature is required in connection with the court's activities. IN R USDCTSD L.R. 5-7(d).

   - *Documents with multiple attorneys' signatures.* Documents requiring signatures of more than one attorney shall be filed either by: (1) obtaining consent from the other attorney, then typing the "s/ [Name]" signature of the other attorney on the signature line where the other attorney's signature would otherwise appear; (2) identifying in the signature section the name of the other attorney whose signature is required and by the submission of a Notice of Endorsement (see IN R USDCTSD ECF Procedures(Appendix B)) by the other attorney no later than three (3) business days after filing; (3) submitting a scanned document containing all handwritten signatures; or (4) in any other manner approved by the Court. IN R USDCTSD ECF Procedures(14); IN R USDCTSD L.R. 5-7(e).

   b.   *Effect of signature.* By signing, an attorney or party certifies that to the best of the person's knowledge, information, and belief formed after a reasonable inquiry:

      i.   With respect to a disclosure, it is complete and correct as of the time it is made; and

      ii.   With respect to a discovery request, response, or objection, it is:

- Consistent with the Federal Rules of Civil Procedure and warranted by existing law or by a nonfrivolous argument for extending, modifying, or reversing existing law, or for establishing new law;

- Not interposed for any improper purpose, such as to harass, cause unnecessary delay, or needlessly increase the cost of litigation; and

- Neither unreasonable nor unduly burdensome or expensive, considering the needs of the case, prior discovery in the case, the amount in controversy, and the importance of the issues at stake in the action. FRCP 26(g)(1).

   c.   *Failure to sign.* Other parties have no duty to act on an unsigned disclosure, request, response, or objection until it is signed, and the court must strike it unless a signature is promptly supplied after the omission is called to the attorney's or party's attention. FRCP 26(g)(2). The court will strike any document filed directly with the clerk that is not signed by an attorney of record or the pro se litigant filing it, but the court may do so only after giving the attorney or pro se litigant notice of the omission and reasonable time to correct it. Rubber-stamp or facsimile signatures are not original signatures and the court will deem documents containing them to be unsigned for purposes of FRCP 11 and FRCP 26(g) and IN R USDCTSD L.R. 5-10. IN R USDCTSD L.R. 5-10(g).

   d.   *Sanction for improper certification.* If a certification violates FRCP 26(g) without substantial justification, the court, on motion or on its own, must impose an appropriate sanction on the signer, the party on whose behalf the signer was acting, or both. The sanction may include an order to pay the reasonable expenses, including attorney's fees, caused by the violation. FRCP 26(g)(3). Refer to the United States District Court for the Southern District of Indiana KeyRules Motion for Discovery Sanctions document for more information.

5.   *Privacy protection for filings made with the court.* Electronically filed documents must meet the requirements of. . .FRCP 5.2 (Privacy Protection for Filings Made with the Court), as if they had been submitted on paper. IN R USDCTSD ECF Procedures(13).

   a.   *Redacted filings.* Unless the court orders otherwise, in an electronic or paper filing with the court that contains an individual's Social Security number, taxpayer-identification number, or birth date, the name of an individual known to be a minor, or a financial-account number, a party or nonparty making the filing may include only:

      i.   The last four (4) digits of the Social Security number and taxpayer-identification number;

      ii.   The year of the individual's birth;

      iii.   The minor's initials; and

      iv.   The last four (4) digits of the financial-account number. FRCP 5.2(a).

   b.   *Exemptions from the redaction requirement.* The redaction requirement does not apply to the following:

      i.   A financial-account number that identifies the property allegedly subject to forfeiture in a forfeiture proceeding;

      ii.   The record of an administrative or agency proceeding;

      iii.   The official record of a state-court proceeding;

      iv.   The record of a court or tribunal, if that record was not subject to the redaction requirement when originally filed;

      v.   A filing covered by FRCP 5.2(c) or FRCP 5.2(d); and

      vi.   A pro se filing in an action brought under 28 U.S.C.A. § 2241, 28 U.S.C.A. § 2254, or 28 U.S.C.A. § 2255. FRCP 5.2(b).

c. *Limitations on remote access to electronic files; Social Security appeals and immigration cases.* Unless the court orders otherwise, in an action for benefits under the Social Security Act, and in an action or proceeding relating to an order of removal, to relief from removal, or to immigration benefits or detention, access to an electronic file is authorized as follows:

  i. The parties and their attorneys may have remote electronic access to any part of the case file, including the administrative record;

  ii. Any other person may have electronic access to the full record at the courthouse, but may have remote electronic access only to:

  • The docket maintained by the court; and

  • An opinion, order, judgment, or other disposition of the court, but not any other part of the case file or the administrative record. FRCP 5.2(c).

d. *Filings made under seal.* The court may order that a filing be made under seal without redaction. The court may later unseal the filing or order the person who made the filing to file a redacted version for the public record. FRCP 5.2(d). For more information on filing under seal, refer to IN R USDCTSD L.R. 5-11 and IN R USDCTSD ECF Procedures(18).

e. *Protective orders.* For good cause, the court may by order in a case:

  i. Require redaction of additional information; or

  ii. Limit or prohibit a nonparty's remote electronic access to a document filed with the court. FRCP 5.2(e).

f. *Option for additional unredacted filing under seal.* A person making a redacted filing may also file an unredacted copy under seal. The court must retain the unredacted copy as part of the record. FRCP 5.2(f).

g. *Option for filing a reference list.* A filing that contains redacted information may be filed together with a reference list that identifies each item of redacted information and specifies an appropriate identifier that uniquely corresponds to each item listed. The list must be filed under seal and may be amended as of right. Any reference in the case to a listed identifier will be construed to refer to the corresponding item of information. FRCP 5.2(g).

h. *Waiver of protection of identifiers.* A person waives the protection of FRCP 5.2(a) as to the person's own information by filing it without redaction and not under seal. FRCP 5.2(h).

F. Filing and Service Requirements

1. *Filing requirements.* Any paper after the complaint that is required to be served—together with a certificate of service—must be filed within a reasonable time after service. FRCP 5(d)(1). Motions must be filed separately, but alternative motions may be filed in a single document if each is named in the title. IN R USDCTSD L.R. 7-1(a).

  a. *How filing is made; In general.* A paper is filed by delivering it:

   i. To the clerk; or

   ii. To a judge who agrees to accept it for filing, and who must then note the filing date on the paper and promptly send it to the clerk. FRCP 5(d)(2).

   • In certain instances, the court will direct the parties to submit items directly to chambers (e.g., confidential settlement statements). However, absent specific prior authorization, counsel and litigants should not submit letters or documents directly to chambers, and such materials should be filed with the clerk. IN R USDCTSD L.R. 5-1(Local Rules Advisory Committee Comment).

   iii. A document or item submitted in relation to a matter within the court's jurisdiction is deemed filed upon delivery to the office of the clerk in a manner prescribed by the Local Rules of the United States District Court for the Southern District of Indiana or the Federal Rules of Civil Procedure or authorized by the court. Any submission directed to a Judge or Judge's staff, the office of the clerk or any employee thereof, in a manner that is not contemplated by IN R USDCTSD L.R. 5-1 and without prior court authorization is prohibited. IN R USDCTSD L.R. 5-1(a).

b. *Non-electronic filing.* Any document that is exempt from electronic filing must be filed directly with the clerk and served on other parties in the case as required by those Federal Rules of Civil Procedure and Local Rules of the United States District Court for the Southern District of Indiana that apply to the service of non-electronic documents. IN R USDCTSD L.R. 5-2(c).

    i. *When completed.* A document or other item that is not required to be filed electronically is deemed filed:

- Upon delivery in person, by courier, or via U.S. Mail or other mail delivery service to the clerk's office during business hours;

- When the courtroom deputy clerk accepts it, if the document or item is filed in open court; or

- Upon completion of any other manner of filing that the court authorizes. IN R USDCTSD L.R. 5-10(a).

    ii. *Document filing by non-exempt party.* When a party who is not exempt from the electronic filing requirement files a document directly with the clerk, the party must:

- Electronically file a notice of manual filing that explains why the document cannot be filed electronically;

- Present the document to the clerk within one (1) business day after filing the notice of manual filing; and

- Present the clerk with a copy of the notice of manual filing when the party files the document with the clerk. IN R USDCTSD L.R. 5-2(d).

c. *Electronic filing*

    i. *Authorization of electronic filing program.* A court may, by local rule, allow papers to be filed, signed, or verified by electronic means that are consistent with any technical standards established by the Judicial Conference of the United States. A local rule may require electronic filing only if reasonable exceptions are allowed. A paper filed electronically in compliance with a local rule is a written paper for purposes of the Federal Rules of Civil Procedure. FRCP 5(d)(3).

- IN R USDCTSD L.R. 5-2 requires electronic filing, as allowed by FRCP 5(d)(3). The policies and procedures in IN R USDCTSD ECF Procedures govern electronic filing in this district unless, due to circumstances in a particular case, a judicial officer determines that these policies and procedures (IN R USDCTSD ECF Procedures) should be modified. IN R USDCTSD ECF Procedures(1).

- Unless modified by order of the Court, all Federal Rules of Civil Procedure and Local Rules of the United States District Court for the Southern District of Indiana shall continue to apply to cases maintained in the Court's Case Management/Electronic Case Filing System (CM/ECF). IN R USDCTSD ECF Procedures(3).

    ii. *Mandatory electronic filing.* Unless exempted pursuant to IN R USDCTSD L.R. 5-3(e), attorneys admitted to the court's bar (including those admitted pro hac vice) or authorized to represent the United States must use the court's ECF system to file documents. IN R USDCTSD L.R. 5-3(a). Electronic filing by attorneys is required for eligible documents filed in civil and criminal cases pending with the Court, unless specifically exempted by Local Rule or Court Order. IN R USDCTSD ECF Procedures(4).

- *Exceptions.* All civil cases (other than those cases the court specifically exempts) must be maintained in the court's electronic case filing (ECF) system. Accordingly, as allowed by FRCP 5(d)(3), every document filed in this court (including exhibits) must be transmitted to the clerk's office via the ECF system consistent with IN R USDCTSD L.R. 5-2 through IN R USDCTSD L.R. 5-11 except: (1) documents filed by pro se litigants; (2) transcripts in cases filed by claimants under the Social Security Act (and related statutes); (3) exhibits in a format that does not readily permit electronic filing (such as videos and large maps and charts); (4) documents that are illegible when scanned into .pdf format; (5) documents filed in cases not maintained on the ECF system; and (6) any other documents that the court or the Local Rules of the United States District Court for the Southern District of Indiana specifically allow to be filed directly with the clerk. IN R USDCTSD L.R. 5-2(a). Parties otherwise participating in the electronic filing system may be excused from filing a particular component electronically under certain limited circumstances, such as when the component cannot be reduced to an electronic format. Such components shall not be filed electronically, but instead shall be manually filed with the Clerk of Court and served upon the parties in accordance with the applicable Federal Rules of Civil Procedure and the Local Rules of the United States District Court for the Southern District of Indiana for filing and service of non-electronic documents. IN R USDCTSD ECF Procedures(15).

- *Exemption from participation.* The court may exempt attorneys from using the ECF system in a particular case for good cause. An attorney must file a petition for ECF exemption and a CM/ECF technical requirements exemption questionnaire in each case in which the attorney seeks an exemption. (The CM/ECF technical requirements exemption questionnaire is available on the court's website). IN R USDCTSD L.R. 5-3(e).

iii. *Consequences of electronic filing.* Electronic transmission of a document consistent with the procedures adopted by the Court shall, upon the complete receipt of the same by the Clerk of Court, constitute filing of the document for all purposes of the Federal Rules of Civil and Criminal Procedure and the Local Rules of the United States District Court for the Southern District of Indiana, and shall constitute entry of that document onto the docket maintained by the Clerk pursuant to FRCP 58 and FRCP 79. IN R USDCTSD ECF Procedures(7); IN R USDCTSD L.R. 5-4(c)(1). When a document has been filed electronically: the document, as filed, binds the filing party. IN R USDCTSD L.R. 5-4(c)(3).

- A Notice of Electronic Filing (NEF) acknowledging that the document has been filed will immediately appear on the filer's screen after the document has been submitted. Attorneys are strongly encouraged to print or electronically save a copy of the NEF. Attorneys can also verify the filing of documents by inspecting the Court's electronic docket sheet through the use of a PACER login. IN R USDCTSD ECF Procedures(7). When a document has been filed electronically: the notice of electronic filing for the document serves as the court's date-stamp and proof of filing. IN R USDCTSD L.R. 5-4(c)(4).

- The Court may, upon the motion of a party or upon its own motion, strike any inappropriately filed document. IN R USDCTSD ECF Procedures(7).

iv. For more information on electronic filing, refer to IN R USDCTSD ECF Procedures.

d. *Fax filing.* The clerk may not file a faxed document without court authorization. The court may not authorize the clerk to file faxed documents without finding that compelling circumstances justify it. A party must submit a copy of the document that otherwise complies with IN R USDCTSD L.R. 5-10 to replace the faxed copy within seven (7) days after faxing the document. IN R USDCTSD L.R. 5-10(e).

2. *Service requirements*

a. *Service; When required*

i. *In general.* Unless the Federal Rules of Civil Procedure provide otherwise, each of the following papers must be served on every party:

- An order stating that service is required;

- A pleading filed after the original complaint, unless the court orders otherwise under FRCP 5(c) because there are numerous defendants;

- A discovery paper required to be served on a party, unless the court orders otherwise;

- A written motion, except one that may be heard ex parte; and

- A written notice, appearance, demand, or offer of judgment, or any similar paper. FRCP 5(a)(1).

ii. *If a party fails to appear.* No service is required on a party who is in default for failing to appear.

But a pleading that asserts a new claim for relief against such a party must be served on that party under FRCP 4. FRCP 5(a)(2).

    iii. *Seizing property.* If an action is begun by seizing property and no person is or need be named as a defendant, any service required before the filing of an appearance, answer, or claim must be made on the person who had custody or possession of the property when it was seized. FRCP 5(a)(3).

b. *Service; How made*

    i. *Serving an attorney.* If a party is represented by an attorney, service under FRCP 5 must be made on the attorney unless the court orders service on the party. FRCP 5(b)(1).

    ii. *Service in general.* A paper is served under FRCP 5 by:

- Handing it to the person;
- Leaving it: (1) at the person's office with a clerk or other person in charge or, if no one is in charge, in a conspicuous place in the office; or (2) if the person has no office or the office is closed, at the person's dwelling or usual place of abode with someone of suitable age and discretion who resides there;
- Mailing it to the person's last known address—in which event service is complete upon mailing;
- Leaving it with the court clerk if the person has no known address;
- Sending it by electronic means if the person consented in writing—in which event service is complete upon transmission, but is not effective if the serving party learns that it did not reach the person to be served; or
- Delivering it by any other means that the person consented to in writing—in which event service is complete when the person making service delivers it to the agency designated to make delivery. FRCP 5(b)(2).

    iii. *Electronic service*

- *Consent.* By registering to use the ECF system, attorneys consent to electronic service of documents filed in cases maintained on the ECF system. IN R USDCTSD L.R. 5-3(d). By participating in the Electronic Case Filing Program, attorneys consent to the electronic service of documents, and shall make available electronic mail addresses for service. IN R USDCTSD ECF Procedures(11).

- *Service on registered parties.* Upon the filing of a document by a party, an e-mail message will be automatically generated by the electronic filing system and sent via electronic mail to the e-mail addresses of all registered attorneys who have appeared in the case. The Notice of Electronic Filing will contain a document hyperlink which will provide recipients with one "free look" at the electronically filed document. Recipients are encouraged to print and/or save a copy of the document during the "free look" to avoid incurring PACER charges for future viewings of the document. IN R USDCTSD ECF Procedures(11). When a document has been filed electronically: transmission of the notice of electronic filing generated by the ECF system to an attorney's e-mail address constitutes service of the document on that attorney. IN R USDCTSD L.R. 5-4(c)(5). The party effectuates service on all registered attorneys by filing electronically. IN R USDCTSD ECF Procedures(11). When a document has been filed electronically: no other attempted service will constitute electronic service of the document. IN R USDCTSD L.R. 5-4(c)(6).

- *Service on exempt parties.* A filer must serve a copy of the document consistent with FRCP 5 on any party or attorney who is exempt from participating in electronic filing. IN R USDCTSD L.R. 5-4(d). It is the responsibility of the filing attorney to conventionally serve all parties who do not receive electronic service (the identity of these parties will be indicated on the filing receipt generated by the ECF system). IN R USDCTSD ECF Procedures(11).

- *Service on parties excused from electronic filing.* Parties otherwise participating in the electronic filing system may be excused from filing a particular component electronically under certain limited circumstances, such as when the component cannot be reduced to an electronic format. Such components shall not be filed electronically, but instead shall be manually filed with the Clerk of Court and served upon the parties in accordance with the applicable Federal Rules of Civil Procedure and the Local Rules of the United States District Court for the Southern District of Indiana for filing and service of non-electronic documents. IN R USDCTSD ECF Procedures(15).

- *Service of exempt documents.* Any document that is exempt from electronic filing must be filed directly with the clerk and served on other parties in the case as required by those Federal Rules of Civil Procedure and Local Rules of the United States District Court for the Southern District of Indiana that apply to the service of non-electronic documents. IN R USDCTSD L.R. 5-2(c).

iv. *Using court facilities.* If a local rule so authorizes, a party may use the court's transmission facilities to make service under FRCP 5(b)(2)(E). FRCP 5(b)(3).

c. *Serving numerous defendants*

i. *In general.* If an action involves an unusually large number of defendants, the court may, on motion or on its own, order that:

- Defendants' pleadings and replies to them need not be served on other defendants;

- Any crossclaim, counterclaim, avoidance, or affirmative defense in those pleadings and replies to them will be treated as denied or avoided by all other parties; and

- Filing any such pleading and serving it on the plaintiff constitutes notice of the pleading to all parties. FRCP 5(c)(1).

ii. *Notifying parties.* A copy of every such order must be served on the parties as the court directs. FRCP 5(c)(2).

G. Hearings

1. *Hearings, generally*

a. *Oral argument.* Due process does not require that oral argument be permitted on a motion and, except as otherwise provided by local rule, the district court has discretion to determine whether it will decide the motion on the papers or hear argument by counsel (and perhaps receive evidence). FPP § 1190; F.D.I.C. v. Deglau, 207 F.3d 153 (3d Cir. 2000).

i. *Request for oral argument.* A party may request oral argument by filing a separate motion explaining why oral argument is necessary and estimating how long the court should allow for the argument. IN R USDCTSD L.R. 7-5(a). Refer to the Documents section of this document for more information.

ii. *No additional evidence at oral argument.* Parties may not present additional evidence at oral argument. IN R USDCTSD L.R. 7-5(b).

b. *Providing a regular schedule for oral hearings.* A court may establish regular times and places for oral hearings on motions. FRCP 78(a).

c. *Providing for submission on briefs.* By rule or order, the court may provide for submitting and determining motions on briefs, without oral hearings. FRCP 78(b).

d. *Request for evidentiary hearing.* A party may request an evidentiary hearing on a motion or petition by serving and filing a separate motion explaining why the hearing is necessary and estimating how long the court should allow for the hearing. IN R USDCTSD L.R. 7-5(c).

e. *Directed by the court.* The court may: (1) grant or deny a request for oral argument or an evidentiary hearing in its sole discretion; (2) set oral argument or an evidentiary hearing without a request from a party; and (3) order any oral argument or evidentiary hearing to be held anywhere within the district regardless of where the case will be tried. IN R USDCTSD L.R. 7-5(d).

2. *Courtroom and courthouse decorum.* For information on courtroom and courthouse decorum, refer to IN R USDCTSD L.R. 83-3.

H. Forms

1. Federal Motion to Compel Discovery Forms

a. Notice of motion; To compel required disclosure of names and addresses of witnesses and persons having knowledge of the claims involved; Civil proceeding. AMJUR PP DEPOSITION § 6.

b. Motion; To compel required disclosure of names and addresses of witnesses and persons having knowledge of the claims involved. AMJUR PP DEPOSITION § 7.

c. Motion; To compel answer to interrogatories; Complete failure to answer. AMJUR PP DEPOSITION § 403.

d. Affidavit; In opposition of motion to compel psychiatric or physical examinations; By attorney. AMJUR PP DEPOSITION § 645.

e. Motion; To compel further responses to interrogatories; Various grounds. AMJUR PP DEPOSITION § 713.

f. Affidavit; In support of motion to compel answers to interrogatories and to impose sanctions. AMJUR PP DEPOSITION § 715.

g. Opposition; To motion to compel electronic discovery; Federal class action. AMJUR PP DEPOSITION § 721.

h. Notice of motion; For order to compel compliance with request to permit entry on real property for inspection. AMJUR PP DEPOSITION § 733.

i. Motion; To compel production of documents; After rejected request; Request for sanctions. AMJUR PP DEPOSITION § 734.

j. Affidavit; In support of motion to compel production of documents; By attorney. AMJUR PP DEPOSITION § 736.

k. Motion; To compel doctor's production of medical records for trial. AMJUR PP DEPOSITION § 744.

l. Notice of motion to compel party to answer deposition questions. 3B FEDFORMS § 3695.

m. Motion to compel deposition, request for sanctions and request for expedited hearing. 3B FEDFORMS § 3698.

n. Motion to compel answer to interrogatories. 3B FEDFORMS § 3699.

o. Affidavit in support of motion. 3B FEDFORMS § 3702.

p. Objection to motion for order requiring witness to answer oral questions on deposition. 3B FEDFORMS § 3705.

q. Motion; To compel answers to outstanding discovery requests. FEDPROF § 23:43.

r. Motion; To compel required disclosure of names and addresses of witnesses and persons having knowledge of the claims involved. FEDPROF § 23:44.

s. Motion; To compel answer to questions asked on oral or written examination. FEDPROF § 23:207.

t. Motion; To compel further answers to questions asked on oral or written examination and to award expenses of motion. FEDPROF § 23:208.

u. Motion; To compel party to produce witness at deposition. FEDPROF § 23:209.

v. Affidavit; By opposing attorney; In opposition to motion to compel answers asked at deposition; Answers tend to incriminate. FEDPROF § 23:212.

w. Motion; To compel answer to interrogatories; Complete failure to answer. FEDPROF § 23:375.

x. Motion; To compel further responses to interrogatories; Various grounds. FEDPROF § 23:376.

y. Motion to compel discovery. GOLDLTGFMS § 21:2.

2. Forms for the Southern District of Indiana

a. Notice of endorsement. IN R USDCTSD ECF Procedures(Appendix B).

    b. Notice of manual filing. IN R USDCTSD ECF Procedures(Appendix C).

    c. Declaration that party was unable to file in a timely manner due to technical difficulties. IN R USDCTSD ECF Procedures(Appendix D).

I. Applicable Rules

1. *Federal rules*

    a. Serving and filing pleadings and other papers. FRCP 5.

    b. Constitutional challenge to a statute; Notice, certification, and intervention. FRCP 5.1.

    c. Privacy protection for filings made with the court. FRCP 5.2.

    d. Computing and extending time; Time for motion papers. FRCP 6.

    e. Pleadings allowed; Form of motions and other papers. FRCP 7.

    f. Form of pleadings. FRCP 10.

    g. Signing pleadings, motions, and other papers; Representations to the court; Sanctions. FRCP 11.

    h. Duty to disclose; General provisions governing discovery. FRCP 26.

    i. Failure to make disclosures or to cooperate in discovery; Sanctions. FRCP 37.

    j. Taking testimony. FRCP 43.

    k. Hearing motions; Submission on briefs. FRCP 78.

2. *Local rules*

    a. Scope of the rules. IN R USDCTSD L.R. 1-1.

    b. Sanctions for errors as to form. IN R USDCTSD L.R. 1-3.

    c. Format of documents presented for filing. IN R USDCTSD L.R. 5-1.

    d. Constitutional challenge to a statute; Notice. IN R USDCTSD L.R. 5.1-1.

    e. Filing of documents electronically required. IN R USDCTSD L.R. 5-2.

    f. Eligibility, registration, passwords for electronic filing; Exemption from electronic filing. IN R USDCTSD L.R. 5-3.

    g. Timing and consequences of electronic filing. IN R USDCTSD L.R. 5-4.

    h. Attachments and exhibits in cases filed electronically. IN R USDCTSD L.R. 5-6.

    i. Signatures in cases filed electronically. IN R USDCTSD L.R. 5-7.

    j. Non-electronic filings. IN R USDCTSD L.R. 5-10.

    k. Motion practice. [IN R USDCTSD L.R. 7-1, as amended by IN ORDER 16-2319, effective December 1, 2016].

    l. Oral arguments and hearings. IN R USDCTSD L.R. 7-5.

    m. Request for three-judge court. IN R USDCTSD L.R. 9-2.

    n. Filing of discovery materials. IN R USDCTSD L.R. 26-2.

    o. Discovery disputes. IN R USDCTSD L.R. 37-1.

    p. Assignment of cases. IN R USDCTSD L.R. 40-1.

    q. Alternative dispute resolution. IN R USDCTSD A.D.R. Rule 1.1; IN R USDCTSD A.D.R. Rule 1.2; IN R USDCTSD A.D.R. Rule 1.5; IN R USDCTSD A.D.R. Rule 2.1; IN R USDCTSD A.D.R. Rule 2.2.

    r. Instructions for preparing case management plan. IN R USDCTSD Case Mgt.

    s. Electronic case filing policies and procedures manual. IN R USDCTSD ECF Procedures.

Motions, Oppositions and Replies
Motion for Protective Order

Document Last Updated December 2016

A. Checklist

(I) ❑ Matters to be considered by moving party

    (a) ❑ Required documents

        (1) ❑ Notice of motion and motion

        (2) ❑ Certificate of compliance

        (3) ❑ Discovery materials

        (4) ❑ Certificate of service

    (b) ❑ Supplemental documents

        (1) ❑ Brief

        (2) ❑ Supporting evidence

        (3) ❑ Notice of constitutional question

        (4) ❑ Nongovernmental corporate disclosure statement

        (5) ❑ Index of exhibits

        (6) ❑ Request for oral argument

        (7) ❑ Request for evidentiary hearing

        (8) ❑ Copy of authority

        (9) ❑ Proposed order

        (10) ❑ Copy of document with self-address envelope

        (11) ❑ Notice of manual filing

        (12) ❑ Courtesy copies

        (13) ❑ Copies for three-judge court

        (14) ❑ Declaration that party was unable to file in a timely manner due to technical difficulties

    (c) ❑ Timing

        (1) ❑ Although a party or deponent is allowed a reasonable amount of time in which to apply for a protective order, a protective order, as a general rule, must be obtained before the date set for the discovery; motions for a protective order must be made before or on the date the discovery is due

        (2) ❑ A written motion and notice of the hearing must be served at least fourteen (14) days before the time specified for the hearing, with the following exceptions: (i) when the motion may be heard ex parte; (ii) when the Federal Rules of Civil Procedure set a different time; or (iii) when a court order—which a party may, for good cause, apply for ex parte—sets a different time

        (3) ❑ Any affidavit supporting a motion must be served with the motion

        (4) ❑ When a party who is not exempt from the electronic filing requirement files a document directly with the clerk, the party must present the document to the clerk within one (1) business day after filing the notice of manual filing

        (5) ❑ Unless the court orders otherwise, the [untimely] document and declaration [that party was unable to file in a timely manner due to technical difficulties] must be filed no later than 12:00 noon of the first day on which the court is open for business following the original filing deadline

(II) ❑ Matters to be considered by opposing party

    (a) ❑ Required documents

        (1) ❑ Response brief

        (2) ❑ Certificate of service

    (b) ❑ Supplemental documents

        (1) ❑ Supporting evidence

        (2) ❑ Notice of constitutional question

        (3) ❑ Index of exhibits

        (4) ❑ Request for oral argument

        (5) ❑ Request for evidentiary hearing

        (6) ❑ Copy of authority

        (7) ❑ Copy of document with self-address envelope

        (8) ❑ Notice of manual filing

        (9) ❑ Courtesy copies

       (10) ❑ Copies for three-judge court

       (11) ❑ Declaration that party was unable to file in a timely manner due to technical difficulties

    (c) ❑ Timing

        (1) ❑ Any response is due within fourteen (14) days after service of the motion

        (2) ❑ Except as FRCP 59(c) provides otherwise, any opposing affidavit must be served at least seven (7) days before the hearing, unless the court permits service at another time

        (3) ❑ When a party who is not exempt from the electronic filing requirement files a document directly with the clerk, the party must present the document to the clerk within one (1) business day after filing the notice of manual filing

        (4) ❑ Unless the court orders otherwise, the [untimely] document and declaration [that party was unable to file in a timely manner due to technical difficulties] must be filed no later than 12:00 noon of the first day on which the court is open for business following the original filing deadline

B. Timing

1. *Motion for protective order.* The express language of FRCP 26(c) does not set out time limits within which a motion for a protective order must be made; yet that requirement remains an implicit condition for obtaining a protective order. FEDPROC § 26:296. Although a party or deponent is allowed a reasonable amount of time in which to apply for a protective order, a protective order, as a general rule, must be obtained before the date set for the discovery. Motions for a protective order must be made before or on the date the discovery is due. FEDPROC § 26:296.

2. *Timing of motions, generally*

    a. *Motion and notice of hearing.* A written motion and notice of the hearing must be served at least fourteen (14) days before the time specified for the hearing, with the following exceptions:

        i. When the motion may be heard ex parte;

        ii. When the Federal Rules of Civil Procedure set a different time; or

        iii. When a court order—which a party may, for good cause, apply for ex parte—sets a different time. FRCP 6(c)(1).

    b. *Supporting affidavit.* Any affidavit supporting a motion must be served with the motion. FRCP 6(c)(2).

3. *Timing of opposing papers.* Any response is due within fourteen (14) days after service of the motion. IN R USDCTSD L.R. 7-1(c)(2)(A).

   a. *Opposing affidavit.* Except as FRCP 59(c) provides otherwise, any opposing affidavit must be served at least seven (7) days before the hearing, unless the court permits service at another time. FRCP 6(c)(2).

   b. *Extensions.* The court may extend response and reply deadlines, but only for good cause. IN R USDCTSD L.R. 7-1(c)(3).

   c. *Summary ruling on failure to respond.* The court may summarily rule on a motion if an opposing party does not file a response within the deadline. IN R USDCTSD L.R. 7-1(c)(4).

4. *Timing of reply papers.* Where the respondent files an answering affidavit setting up a new matter, the moving party ordinarily is allowed a reasonable time to file a reply affidavit since failure to deny the new matter by affidavit may operate as an admission of its truth. AMJUR MOTIONS § 25.

   a. *Reply brief.* Any reply is due within seven (7) days after service of the response. IN R USDCTSD L.R. 7-1(c)(2)(B).

   b. *Extensions.* The court may extend response and reply deadlines, but only for good cause. IN R USDCTSD L.R. 7-1(c)(3).

5. *Document filing by non-exempt party.* When a party who is not exempt from the electronic filing requirement files a document directly with the clerk, the party must: present the document to the clerk within one (1) business day after filing the notice of manual filing. IN R USDCTSD L.R. 5-2(d)(2).

6. *Declaration that party was unable to file in a timely manner due to technical difficulties.* Unless the Court orders otherwise, the [untimely] document and declaration [that party was unable to file in a timely manner due to technical difficulties] must be filed no later than 12:00 noon of the first day on which the Court is open for business following the original filing deadline. IN R USDCTSD ECF Procedures(16).

7. *Computation of time*

   a. *Computing time.* FRCP 6 applies in computing any time period specified in the Federal Rules of Civil Procedure, in any local rule or court order, or in any statute that does not specify a method of computing time. FRCP 6(a).

      i. *Period stated in days or a longer unit.* When the period is stated in days or a longer unit of time:
         - Exclude the day of the event that triggers the period;
         - Count every day, including intermediate Saturdays, Sundays, and legal holidays; and
         - Include the last day of the period, but if the last day is a Saturday, Sunday, or legal holiday, the period continues to run until the end of the next day that is not a Saturday, Sunday, or legal holiday. FRCP 6(a)(1).

      ii. *Period stated in hours.* When the period is stated in hours:
         - Begin counting immediately on the occurrence of the event that triggers the period;
         - Count every hour, including hours during intermediate Saturdays, Sundays, and legal holidays; and
         - If the period would end on a Saturday, Sunday, or legal holiday, the period continues to run until the same time on the next day that is not a Saturday, Sunday, or legal holiday. FRCP 6(a)(2).

      iii. *Inaccessibility of the clerk's office.* Unless the court orders otherwise, if the clerk's office is inaccessible:
         - On the last day for filing under FRCP 6(a)(1), then the time for filing is extended to the first accessible day that is not a Saturday, Sunday, or legal holiday; or
         - During the last hour for filing under FRCP 6(a)(2), then the time for filing is extended to the same time on the first accessible day that is not a Saturday, Sunday, or legal holiday. FRCP 6(a)(3).

iv. *"Last day" defined.* Unless a different time is set by a statute, local rule, or court order, the last day ends:

- For electronic filing, at midnight in the court's time zone; and

- For filing by other means, when the clerk's office is scheduled to close. FRCP 6(a)(4).

v. *"Next day" defined.* The "next day" is determined by continuing to count forward when the period is measured after an event and backward when measured before an event. FRCP 6(a)(5).

vi. *"Legal holiday" defined.* "Legal holiday" means:

- The day set aside by statute for observing New Year's Day, Martin Luther King Jr.'s Birthday, Washington's Birthday, Memorial Day, Independence Day, Labor Day, Columbus Day, Veterans' Day, Thanksgiving Day, or Christmas Day;

- Any day declared a holiday by the President or Congress; and

- For periods that are measured after an event, any other day declared a holiday by the state where the district court is located. FRCP 6(a)(6).

b. *Computation of electronic filing deadlines.* Filing documents electronically does not alter filing deadlines. IN R USDCTSD ECF Procedures(7). A document due on a particular day must be filed before midnight local time of the division where the case is pending. IN R USDCTSD L.R. 5-4(a). All electronic transmissions of documents must be completed (i.e. received completely by the Clerk's Office) prior to midnight of the local time of the division in which the case is pending in order to be considered timely filed that day (NOTE: time will be noted in Eastern Time on the Court's docket. If you have filed a document prior to midnight local time of the division in which the case is pending and the document is due that date, but the electronic receipt and docket reflect the following calendar day, please contact the Court). IN R USDCTSD ECF Procedures(7). Although attorneys may file documents electronically twenty-four (24) hours a day, seven (7) days a week, attorneys are encouraged to file all documents during the normal working hours of the Clerk's Office (Monday through Friday, 8:30 a.m. to 4:30 p.m.) when technical support is available. IN R USDCTSD ECF Procedures(7); IN R USDCTSD ECF Procedures(9).

i. *Technical difficulties.* Parties are encouraged to file documents electronically during normal business hours, in case a problem is encountered. In the event a technical failure occurs and a document cannot be filed electronically despite the best efforts of the filing party, the party should print (if possible) a copy of the error message received. In addition, as soon as practically possible, the party should file a "Declaration that Party was Unable to File in a Timely Manner Due to Technical Difficulties." A model form is provided as Appendix D (IN R USDCTSD ECF Procedures(Appendix D)). IN R USDCTSD ECF Procedures(16).

- If a party is unable to file electronically and, as a result, may miss a filing deadline, the party must contact the Clerk's Office at the number listed in IN R USDCTSD ECF Procedures(15) to inform the court's staff of the difficulty. If a party misses a filing deadline due to an inability to file electronically, the party may submit the untimely filed document, accompanied by a declaration stating the reason(s) for missing the deadline. Unless the Court orders otherwise, the document and declaration must be filed no later than 12:00 noon of the first day on which the Court is open for business following the original filing deadline. IN R USDCTSD ECF Procedures(16).

c. *Extending time*

i. *In general.* When an act may or must be done within a specified time, the court may, for good cause, extend the time:

- With or without motion or notice if the court acts, or if a request is made, before the original time or its extension expires; or

- On motion made after the time has expired if the party failed to act because of excusable neglect. FRCP 6(b)(1).

ii. *Exceptions.* A court must not extend the time to act under FRCP 50(b), FRCP 50(d), FRCP 52(b), FRCP 59(b), FRCP 59(d), FRCP 59(e), and FRCP 60(b). FRCP 6(b)(2).

      iii.   Refer to the United States District Court for the Southern District of Indiana KeyRules Motion for Continuance/Extension of Time document for more information on extending time.

   d. *Additional time after certain kinds of service.* When a party may or must act within a specified time after being served and service is made under FRCP 5(b)(2)(C) (mail), FRCP 5(b)(2)(D) (leaving with the clerk), or FRCP 5(b)(2)(F) (other means consented to), three (3) days are added after the period would otherwise expire under FRCP 6(a). FRCP 6(d). Service by electronic mail shall constitute service pursuant to FRCP 5(b)(2)(E) and shall entitle the party being served to the additional three (3) days provided by FRCP 6(d). IN R USDCTSD ECF Procedures(11).

C. General Requirements

1. *Motions, generally*

   a. *Requirements.* A request for a court order must be made by motion. The motion must:

      i.   Be in writing unless made during a hearing or trial;

      ii. State with particularity the grounds for seeking the order; and

      iii. State the relief sought. FRCP 7(b)(1).

   b. *Notice of motion.* A party interested in resisting the relief sought by a motion has a right to notice thereof, and an opportunity to be heard. AMJUR MOTIONS § 12.

      i.   In addition to statutory or court rule provisions requiring notice of a motion—the purpose of such a notice requirement having been said to be to prevent a party from being prejudicially surprised by a motion—principles of natural justice dictate that an adverse party generally must be given notice that a motion will be presented to the court. AMJUR MOTIONS § 12.

      ii. "Notice," in this regard, means reasonable notice, including a meaningful opportunity to prepare and to defend against allegations of a motion. AMJUR MOTIONS § 12.

   c. *Writing requirement.* The writing requirement is intended to insure that the adverse parties are informed and have a record of both the motion's pendency and the grounds on which the movant seeks an order. FPP § 1191; Feldberg v. Quechee Lakes Corp., 463 F.3d 195 (2d Cir. 2006).

      i.   It is sufficient "if the motion is stated in a written notice of the hearing of the motion." FPP § 1191.

   d. *Particularity requirement.* The particularity requirement insures that the opposing parties will have notice of their opponent's contentions. FEDPROC § 62:364; Goodman v. 1973 26 Foot Trojan Vessel, Arkansas Registration No. AR1439SN, 859 F.2d 71, 12 Fed.R.Serv.3d 645 (8th Cir. 1988). That requirement ensures that notice of the basis for the motion is provided to the court and to the opposing party so as to avoid prejudice, provide the opponent with a meaningful opportunity to respond, and provide the court with enough information to process the motion correctly. FEDPROC § 62:364; Andreas v. Volkswagen of America, Inc., 336 F.3d 789, 56 Fed.R.Serv.3d 6 (8th Cir. 2003).

      i.   Reasonable specification of the grounds for a motion is sufficient. However, where a movant fails to state even one ground for granting the motion in question, the movant has failed to meet the minimal standard of "reasonable specification." FEDPROC § 62:364; Martinez v. Trainor, 556 F.2d 818, 23 Fed.R.Serv.2d 403 (7th Cir. 1977).

      ii. The court may excuse the failure to comply with the particularity requirement if it is inadvertent, and where no prejudice is shown by the opposing party. FEDPROC § 62:364.

   e. *Motions must be filed separately.* Motions must be filed separately, but alternative motions may be filed in a single document if each is named in the title. A motion must not be contained within a brief, response, or reply to a previously filed motion, unless ordered by the court. IN R USDCTSD L.R. 7-1(a).

   f. *Routine or uncontested motions.* The court may rule upon a routine or uncontested motion before the response deadline passes, unless: (1) the motion indicates that an opposing party objects to it; or (2) the court otherwise believes that a response will be filed. IN R USDCTSD L.R. 7-1(d).

2. *Informal conference to resolve disputes involving non-dispositive issues.* In addition to those conferences required by IN R USDCTSD L.R. 37-1, counsel are encouraged to hold informal conferences in person

or by phone to resolve any disputes involving non-dispositive issues that may otherwise require submission of a motion to the Court. This requirement does not apply to cases involving pro se parties. Therefore, prior to filing any non-dispositive motion (including motions for extension of time), the moving party must contact opposing counsel to determine whether there is an objection to any non-dispositive motion (including motions for extension of time), and state in the motion whether opposing counsel objects to the motion. IN R USDCTSD Case Mgt(General Instructions For All Cases). Refer to the Documents section of this document for more information on the contents of the motion.

3. *Required actions prior to court involvement.* Prior to involving the court in any discovery dispute, including disputes involving depositions, counsel must confer in a good faith attempt to resolve the dispute. If any such dispute cannot be resolved in this manner, counsel are encouraged to contact the chambers of the assigned Magistrate Judge to determine whether the Magistrate Judge is available to resolve the discovery dispute by way of a telephone conference or other proceeding prior to counsel filing a formal discovery motion. When the dispute involves an objection raised during a deposition that threatens to prevent completion of the deposition, any party may recess the deposition to contact the Magistrate Judge's chambers. IN R USDCTSD L.R. 37-1(a). Discovery disputes involving pro se parties are not subject to IN R USDCTSD L.R. 37-1. IN R USDCTSD L.R. 37-1(c). Refer to the Documents section of this document for more information.

4. *Motion for protective order.* A party or any person from whom discovery is sought may move for a protective order in the court where the action is pending—or as an alternative on matters relating to a deposition, in the court for the district where the deposition will be taken. FRCP 26(c)(1). FRCP 26(c) was enacted as a safeguard for the protection of parties and witnesses in view of the broad discovery rights authorized by FRCP 26(b). FEDPROC § 26:265; U.S. v. Columbia Broadcasting System, Inc., 666 F.2d 364, 33 Fed.R.Serv.2d 539 (9th Cir. 1982).

   a. *Grounds for protective orders.* The court may, for good cause, issue an order to protect a party or person from annoyance, embarrassment, oppression, or undue burden or expense, including one or more of the following:

      i. Forbidding the disclosure or discovery;

      ii. Specifying terms, including time and place or the allocation of expenses, for the disclosure or discovery;

      iii. Prescribing a discovery method other than the one selected by the party seeking discovery;

      iv. Forbidding inquiry into certain matters, or limiting the scope of disclosure or discovery to certain matters;

      v. Designating the persons who may be present while the discovery is conducted;

      vi. Requiring that a deposition be sealed and opened only on court order;

      vii. Requiring that a trade secret or other confidential research, development, or commercial information not be revealed or be revealed only in a specified way; and

      viii. Requiring that the parties simultaneously file specified documents or information in sealed envelopes, to be opened as the court directs. FRCP 26(c)(1).

   b. *Third-party protection.* A party may not ask for an order to protect the rights of another party or a witness if that party or witness does not claim protection for himself, but a party may seek an order if it believes its own interest is jeopardized by discovery sought from a third person. FPP § 2035.

   c. *Burden.* The party seeking a protective order has the burden of demonstrating that good cause exists for its issuance. FEDPROC § 26:279. The good cause requirement under FRCP 26(c), encompasses a standard of reasonableness. FEDPROC § 26:284.

      i. *Factual demonstration of injury.* The party requesting a protective order must make a specific demonstration of facts in support of the request as opposed to conclusory or speculative statements about the need for a protective order and the harm which will be suffered without one. FEDPROC § 26:282. Such party must demonstrate that failure to issue the order requested will work a clearly defined harm. FEDPROC § 26:282; Cipollone v. Liggett Group, Inc., 822 F.2d 335, 7 Fed.R.Serv.3d 1438 (3d Cir. 1987).

    ii.   *Serious injury.* A party seeking a protective order under FRCP 26(c) must demonstrate that failure to issue the order requested will work a very serious injury. FEDPROC § 26:283; Cipollone v. Liggett Group, Inc., 822 F.2d 335, 7 Fed.R.Serv.3d 1438 (3d Cir. 1987).

  d. *Application of protective orders.* FRCP 26(c) does not authorize the district court to issue protective orders with respect to data obtained through means other than the court's discovery processes. FEDPROC § 26:271.

    i.   *Information not discovered.* FRCP 26(c) does not give the court authority to prohibit disclosure of trade data which was compiled by counsel prior the commencing of a lawsuit. Similarly, material received by one party prior to commencement of an action (and therefore before initiation of any discovery and before a request for protective orders) cannot be made a legitimate part of the corpus of any protective order a court enters. FEDPROC § 26:271.

    ii.   *Information discovered in other action.* The trial court lacks the discretion and power to issue a valid protective order to compel the return of documents obtained through discovery in a separate action. FEDPROC § 26:272.

  e. *Ordering discovery.* If a motion for a protective order is wholly or partly denied, the court may, on just terms, order that any party or person provide or permit discovery. FRCP 26(c)(2).

  f. *Awarding expenses.* FRCP 37(a)(5) applies to the award of expenses. FRCP 26(c)(3). Refer to the United States District Court for the Southern District of Indiana KeyRules Motion for Discovery Sanctions document for more information.

5. *Opposing papers.* The Federal Rules of Civil Procedure do not require any formal answer, return, or reply to a motion, except where the Federal Rules of Civil Procedure or local rules may require affidavits, memoranda, or other papers to be filed in opposition to a motion. Such papers are simply to apprise the court of such opposition and the grounds of that opposition. FEDPROC § 62:359.

  a. *Effect of failure to respond to motion.* Although in the absence of statutory provision or court rule, a motion ordinarily does not require a written answer, when a party files a motion and the opposing party fails to respond, the court may construe such failure to respond as nonopposition to the motion or an admission that the motion was meritorious, may take the facts alleged in the motion as true—the rule in some jurisdictions being that the failure to respond to a fact set forth in a motion is deemed an admission—and may grant the motion if the relief requested appears to be justified. AMJUR MOTIONS § 28.

  b. *Assent or no opposition not determinative.* However, a motion will not be granted automatically simply because an "assent" or a notation of "no opposition" has been filed; federal judges frequently deny motions that have been assented to when it is thought that justice so dictates. FPP § 1190.

  c. *Responsive pleading inappropriate as response to motion.* An attempt to answer or oppose a motion with a responsive pleading usually is not appropriate. FPP § 1190.

6. *Reply papers.* A moving party may be required or permitted to prepare papers in addition to his original motion papers. AMJUR MOTIONS § 25. Papers answering or replying to opposing papers may be appropriate, in the interests of justice, where it appears there is a substantial reason for allowing a reply. Thus, a court may accept reply papers where a party demonstrates that the papers to which it seeks to file a reply raise new issues that are material to the disposition of the question before the court, or where the court determines, sua sponte, that it wishes further briefing of an issue raised in those papers and orders the submission of additional papers. FEDPROC § 62:360.

  a. *Function of reply papers.* The function of a reply affidavit is to answer the arguments made in opposition to the position taken by the movant and not to permit the movant to introduce new arguments in support of the motion. AMJUR MOTIONS § 25.

  b. *Issues raised for the first time in a reply document.* However, the view has been followed in some jurisdictions, that as a matter of judicial economy, where there is no prejudice and where the issues could be raised simply by filing a motion to dismiss, the trial court has discretion to consider arguments raised for the first time in a reply memorandum, and that a trial court may grant a motion to strike issues raised for the first time in a reply memorandum. AMJUR MOTIONS § 26.

7. *Appearances.* Every attorney who represents a party or who files a document on a party's behalf must file

an appearance for that party. IN R USDCTSD L.R. 83-7. The filing of a Notice of Appearance shall act to establish the filing attorney as an attorney of record representing a designated party or parties in a particular cause of action. As a result, it is necessary for each attorney to file a separate Notice of Appearance when entering an appearance in a case. A joint appearance on behalf of multiple attorneys may be filed electronically only if it is filed separately for each attorney, using his/her ECF login. IN R USDCTSD ECF Procedures(12). Only those attorneys who have filed an appearance in a pending action are entitled to be served with case documents under FRCP 5(a). IN R USDCTSD L.R. 83-7. For more information, refer to IN R USDCTSD L.R. 83-7 and IN R USDCTSD ECF Procedures(12).

8. *Notice of related action.* A party must file a notice of related action: as soon as it appears that the party's case and another pending case: (1) arise out of the same transaction or occurrence; (2) involve the same property; or (3) involve the validity or infringement or the same patent, trademark, or copyright. IN R USDCTSD L.R. 40-1(d)(2). For more information, refer to IN R USDCTSD L.R. 40-1.

9. *Alternative dispute resolution (ADR)*

   a. *Application.* Unless limited by specific provisions, or unless there are other applicable specific statutory, common law, or constitutional procedures, the Local Alternative Dispute Resolution Rules of the United States District Court for the Southern District of Indiana shall apply in all civil litigation filed in the U.S. District Court for the Southern District of Indiana, except in the following cases and proceedings:

      i. Applications for writs of habeas corpus under 28 U.S.C.A. § 2254;

      ii. Forfeiture cases;

      iii. Non-adversary proceedings in bankruptcy;

      iv. Social Security administrative review cases; and

      v. Such other matters as specified by order of the Court; for example, matters involving important public policy issues, constitutional law, or the establishment of new law. IN R USDCTSD A.D.R. Rule 1.2.

   b. *Mediation.* Mediation under this section (IN R USDCTSD A.D.R. Rule 2.1, et seq.) involves the confidential process by which a person acting as a Mediator, selected by the parties or appointed by the Court, assists the litigants in reaching a mutually acceptable agreement. It is an informal and nonadversarial process. The role of the Mediator is to assist in identifying the issues, reducing misunderstandings, clarifying priorities, exploring areas of compromise, and finding points of agreement as well as legitimate points of disagreement. Final decision-making authority rests with the parties, not the Mediator. IN R USDCTSD A.D.R. Rule 2.1. It is anticipated that an agreement may not resolve all of the disputed issues, but the process, nonetheless, can reduce points of contention. Parties and their representatives are required to mediate in good faith, but are not compelled to reach an agreement. IN R USDCTSD A.D.R. Rule 2.1.

      i. *Case selection.* The Court with the agreement of the parties may refer a civil case for mediation. Unless otherwise ordered or as specifically provided in IN R USDCTSD A.D.R. Rule 2.8, referral to mediation does not abate or suspend the action, and no scheduled dates shall be delayed or deferred, including the date of trial. IN R USDCTSD A.D.R. Rule 2.2.

      ii. For more information on mediation, refer to IN R USDCTSD A.D.R. Rule 2.1, et seq.

   c. *Other methods of dispute resolution.* The Local Alternative Dispute Resolution Rules of the United States District Court for the Southern District of Indiana shall not preclude the parties from utilizing any other reasonable method or technique of alternative dispute resolution to resolve disputes to which the parties agree. However, any use of arbitration by the parties will be governed by and comply with the requirements of 28 U.S.C.A. § 654 through 28 U.S.C.A. § 657. IN R USDCTSD A.D.R. Rule 1.5.

   d. For more information on alternative dispute resolution (ADR), refer to IN R USDCTSD A.D.R. Rule 1.1, et seq.

10. *Notice of settlement or resolution.* The parties must immediately notify the court if they reasonably anticipate settling their case or resolving a pending motion. IN R USDCTSD L.R. 7-1(h).

11. *Modification or suspension of rules.* The court may, on its own motion or at the request of a party, suspend or modify any rule in a particular case in the interest of justice. IN R USDCTSD L.R. 1-1(c).

D. Documents

1. *Documents for moving party*

   a. *Required documents*

      i. *Notice of motion and motion.* [P]rior to filing any non-dispositive motion (including motions for extension of time), the moving party must contact opposing counsel to determine whether there is an objection to any non-dispositive motion (including motions for extension of time), and state in the motion whether opposing counsel objects to the motion. If an objection cannot be resolved by counsel, the opposing counsel's position shall be stated within the motion. The motion should also indicate whether opposing counsel plans to file a written objection to the motion and the date by which the Court can expect to receive the objection (within the time limits set in IN R USDCTSD L.R. 7-1). If after a reasonable effort, opposing counsel cannot be reached, the moving party shall recite in the motion the dates and times that messages were left for opposing counsel. IN R USDCTSD Case Mgt(General Instructions For All Cases). Refer to the General Requirements section of this document for information on the notice of motion and motion.

      ii. *Certificate of compliance.* In the event that the discovery dispute is not resolved at the conference, counsel may file a motion to compel or other motion raising the dispute. Any motion raising a discovery dispute must contain a statement setting forth the efforts taken to resolve the dispute, including the date, time, and place of any discovery conference and the names of all participating parties. The court may deny any motion raising a discovery dispute that does not contain such a statement. IN R USDCTSD L.R. 37-1(b). Discovery disputes involving pro se parties are not subject to IN R USDCTSD L.R. 37-1. IN R USDCTSD L.R. 37-1(c).

      iii. *Discovery materials.* A party seeking relief under FRCP 26(c) or FRCP 37, or by way of a pretrial motion that could result in a final order on an issue, must file with the motion those parts of the discovery materials relevant to the motion. IN R USDCTSD L.R. 26-2(a).

      iv. *Certificate of service.* FRCP 5(d) requires that the person making service under FRCP 5 certify that service has been effected. FRCP 5(Advisory Committee Notes). Having such information on file may be useful for many purposes, including proof of service if an issue arises concerning the effectiveness of the service. FRCP 5(Advisory Committee Notes).

         • *Certificate of service for electronically-filed documents.* A certificate of service must be included with all documents filed electronically. Such certificate shall indicate that service was accomplished pursuant to the Court's electronic filing procedures. IN R USDCTSD ECF Procedures(11). For the suggested format for a certificate of service for electronic filing, refer to IN R USDCTSD ECF Procedures(11).

   b. *Supplemental documents*

      i. *Brief.* Refer to the Format section of this document for the format of briefs.

      ii. *Supporting evidence.* When a motion relies on facts outside the record, the court may hear the matter on affidavits or may hear it wholly or partly on oral testimony or on depositions. FRCP 43(c).

         • *Materials necessary for motion.* A party seeking relief under FRCP 26(c) or FRCP 37, or by way of a pretrial motion that could result in a final order on an issue, must file with the motion those parts of the discovery materials relevant to the motion. IN R USDCTSD L.R. 26-2(a).

      iii. *Notice of constitutional question.* A party that files a pleading, written motion, or other paper drawing into question the constitutionality of a federal or state statute must promptly:

         • *File notice.* File a notice of constitutional question stating the question and identifying the paper that raises it, if: (1) a federal statute is questioned and the parties do not include the

United States, one of its agencies, or one of its officers or employees in an official capacity; or (2) a state statute is questioned and the parties do not include the state, one of its agencies, or one of its officers or employees in an official capacity; and

- *Serve notice.* Serve the notice and paper on the Attorney General of the United States if a federal statute is questioned—or on the state attorney general if a state statute is questioned—either by certified or registered mail or by sending it to an electronic address designated by the attorney general for this purpose. FRCP 5.1(a).

- *Time for filing.* A notice of constitutional challenge to a statute filed in accordance with FRCP 5.1 must be filed at the same time the parties tender their proposed case management plan, if one is required, or within twenty-one (21) days of the filing drawing into question the constitutionality of a federal or state statute, whichever occurs later. IN R USDCTSD L.R. 5.1-1(a).

- *Additional service requirements.* If a federal statute is challenged, in addition to the service requirements of FRCP 5.1(a), the party filing the notice of constitutional challenge must serve the notice and documents on the United States Attorney for the Southern District of Indiana, either by certified or registered mail or by sending it to an electronic address designated for that purpose by that official. IN R USDCTSD L.R. 5.1-1(b).

- *No forfeiture.* A party's failure to file and serve the notice, or the court's failure to certify, does not forfeit a constitutional claim or defense that is otherwise timely asserted. FRCP 5.1(d).

iv. *Nongovernmental corporate disclosure statement*

- *Contents.* A nongovernmental corporate party must file two (2) copies of a disclosure statement that: (1) identifies any parent corporation and any publicly held corporation owning ten percent (10%) or more of its stock; or (2) states that there is no such corporation. FRCP 7.1(a).

- *Time to file; Supplemental filing.* A party must: (1) file the disclosure statement with its first appearance, pleading, petition, motion, response, or other request addressed to the court; and (2) promptly file a supplemental statement if any required information changes. FRCP 7.1(b).

v. *Index of exhibits.* Any pleading, motion, brief, affidavit, notice, or proposed order filed with the court, whether electronically or with the clerk, must: if it has four (4) or more exhibits, include a separate index that identifies and briefly describes each exhibit. IN R USDCTSD L.R. 5-1(b).

vi. *Request for oral argument.* A party may request oral argument by filing a separate motion explaining why oral argument is necessary and estimating how long the court should allow for the argument. The request must be filed and served with the supporting brief, response brief, or reply brief. IN R USDCTSD L.R. 7-5(a).

vii. *Request for evidentiary hearing.* A party may request an evidentiary hearing on a motion or petition by serving and filing a separate motion explaining why the hearing is necessary and estimating how long the court should allow for the hearing. IN R USDCTSD L.R. 7-5(c).

viii. *Copy of authority.* Generally, copies of cited authorities may not be attached to court filings. However, a party must attach to the party's motion or brief a copy of any cited authority if it is not available on Westlaw or Lexis. Upon request, a party must provide copies of any cited authority that is only available through electronic means to the court or the other parties. IN R USDCTSD L.R. 7-1(f).

ix. *Proposed order.* A party must include a suitable form of order with any document that requests the judge or the clerk to enter a routine or uncontested order. IN R USDCTSD L.R. 5-5(b); IN R USDCTSD L.R. 5-10(c); IN R USDCTSD L.R. 7-1(d).

- A service statement and/or list must be included on each proposed order, as required by IN R USDCTSD L.R. 5-5(d). IN R USDCTSD ECF Procedures(11). Any pleading, motion, brief, affidavit, notice, or proposed order filed with the court, whether electronically or with the clerk, must: if it is a form of order, include a statement of service, in the format required by IN R USDCTSD L.R. 5-5(d) in the lower left corner of the document. IN R USDCTSD L.R. 5-1(b).

- A party electronically filing a proposed order—whether voluntarily or because required by IN R USDCTSD L.R. 5-5—must convert the order directly from a word processing program and file it as an attachment to the document it relates to. Proposed orders must include in the lower left-hand corner of the signature page a statement that service will be made electronically on all ECF-registered counsel of record via email generated by the court's ECF system, without listing all such counsel. A service list including the name and postal address of any pro se litigant or non-registered attorney of record must follow, stating that service on the listed individuals will be made in the traditional paper manner, via first-class U.S. Mail. IN R USDCTSD L.R. 5-5(d).

x. *Copy of document with self-address envelope.* To receive a file-stamped copy of a document filed directly with the clerk, a party must include with the original document an additional copy and a self-addressed envelope. The envelope must be big enough to hold the copy and have enough postage on it to send the copy via regular first-class mail. IN R USDCTSD L.R. 5-10(b).

xi. *Notice of manual filing.* When a party who is not exempt from the electronic filing requirement files a document directly with the clerk, the party must: electronically file a notice of manual filing that explains why the document cannot be filed electronically. IN R USDCTSD L.R. 5-2(d)(1). Refer to the Filing and Service Requirements section of this document for more information.

- Where an individual component cannot be included in an electronic filing (e.g. the component cannot be converted to electronic format), the filer shall electronically file the prescribed Notice of Manual Filing in place of that component. A model form is provided as Appendix C (IN R USDCTSD ECF Procedures(Appendix C)). IN R USDCTSD ECF Procedures(13).

- Before making a manual filing of a component, the filing party shall first electronically file a Notice of Manual Filing (See IN R USDCTSD ECF Procedures(Appendix C)). The filer shall initiate the electronic filing process as if filing the actual component but shall instead attach to the filing the Notice of Manual Filing setting forth the reason(s) why the component cannot be filed electronically. The manual filing should be accompanied by a copy of the previously filed Notice of Manual Filing. A party may seek to have a component excluded from electronic filing pursuant to applicable Federal and Local Rules (e.g., FRCP 26(c)). IN R USDCTSD ECF Procedures(15).

xii. *Courtesy copies.* District Judges and Magistrate Judges regularly receive documents filed by all parties. Therefore, parties shall not bring "courtesy copies" to any chambers unless specifically directed to do so by the Court. IN R USDCTSD Case Mgt(General Instructions For All Cases).

xiii. *Copies for three-judge court.* Parties in a case where a three-judge court has been requested must file an original and three copies of any document filed directly with the clerk (instead of electronically) until the court: (1) denies the request; (2) dissolves the three-judge court; or (3) allows the parties to file fewer copies. IN R USDCTSD L.R. 9-2(c).

xiv. *Declaration that party was unable to file in a timely manner due to technical difficulties.* If a party misses a filing deadline due to an inability to file electronically, the party may submit the untimely filed document, accompanied by a declaration stating the reason(s) for missing the deadline. IN R USDCTSD ECF Procedures(16). A model form is provided as Appendix D (IN R USDCTSD ECF Procedures(Appendix D)). IN R USDCTSD ECF Procedures(16).

2. *Documents for opposing party*

    a. *Required documents*

        i. *Response brief.* Refer to the Format section of this document for the format of briefs. Refer to the General Requirements section of this document for information on the opposing papers.

        ii. *Certificate of service.* FRCP 5(d) requires that the person making service under FRCP 5 certify that service has been effected. FRCP 5(Advisory Committee Notes). Having such information on file may be useful for many purposes, including proof of service if an issue arises concerning the effectiveness of the service. FRCP 5(Advisory Committee Notes).

- *Certificate of service for electronically-filed documents.* A certificate of service must be included with all documents filed electronically. Such certificate shall indicate that service was accomplished pursuant to the Court's electronic filing procedures. IN R USDCTSD ECF Procedures(11). For the suggested format for a certificate of service for electronic filing, refer to IN R USDCTSD ECF Procedures(11).

b. *Supplemental documents*

   i. *Supporting evidence.* When a motion relies on facts outside the record, the court may hear the matter on affidavits or may hear it wholly or partly on oral testimony or on depositions. FRCP 43(c).

      - *Materials necessary for motion.* A party seeking relief under FRCP 26(c) or FRCP 37, or by way of a pretrial motion that could result in a final order on an issue, must file with the motion those parts of the discovery materials relevant to the motion. IN R USDCTSD L.R. 26-2(a).

   ii. *Notice of constitutional question.* A party that files a pleading, written motion, or other paper drawing into question the constitutionality of a federal or state statute must promptly:

      - *File notice.* File a notice of constitutional question stating the question and identifying the paper that raises it, if: (1) a federal statute is questioned and the parties do not include the United States, one of its agencies, or one of its officers or employees in an official capacity; or (2) a state statute is questioned and the parties do not include the state, one of its agencies, or one of its officers or employees in an official capacity; and

      - *Serve notice.* Serve the notice and paper on the Attorney General of the United States if a federal statute is questioned—or on the state attorney general if a state statute is questioned—either by certified or registered mail or by sending it to an electronic address designated by the attorney general for this purpose. FRCP 5.1(a).

      - *Time for filing.* A notice of constitutional challenge to a statute filed in accordance with FRCP 5.1 must be filed at the same time the parties tender their proposed case management plan, if one is required, or within twenty-one (21) days of the filing drawing into question the constitutionality of a federal or state statute, whichever occurs later. IN R USDCTSD L.R. 5.1-1(a).

      - *Additional service requirements.* If a federal statute is challenged, in addition to the service requirements of FRCP 5.1(a), the party filing the notice of constitutional challenge must serve the notice and documents on the United States Attorney for the Southern District of Indiana, either by certified or registered mail or by sending it to an electronic address designated for that purpose by that official. IN R USDCTSD L.R. 5.1-1(b).

      - *No forfeiture.* A party's failure to file and serve the notice, or the court's failure to certify, does not forfeit a constitutional claim or defense that is otherwise timely asserted. FRCP 5.1(d).

   iii. *Index of exhibits.* Any pleading, motion, brief, affidavit, notice, or proposed order filed with the court, whether electronically or with the clerk, must: if it has four (4) or more exhibits, include a separate index that identifies and briefly describes each exhibit. IN R USDCTSD L.R. 5-1(b).

   iv. *Request for oral argument.* A party may request oral argument by filing a separate motion explaining why oral argument is necessary and estimating how long the court should allow for the argument. The request must be filed and served with the supporting brief, response brief, or reply brief. IN R USDCTSD L.R. 7-5(a).

   v. *Request for evidentiary hearing.* A party may request an evidentiary hearing on a motion or petition by serving and filing a separate motion explaining why the hearing is necessary and estimating how long the court should allow for the hearing. IN R USDCTSD L.R. 7-5(c).

vi. *Copy of authority.* Generally, copies of cited authorities may not be attached to court filings. However, a party must attach to the party's motion or brief a copy of any cited authority if it is not available on Westlaw or Lexis. Upon request, a party must provide copies of any cited authority that is only available through electronic means to the court or the other parties. IN R USDCTSD L.R. 7-1(f).

vii. *Copy of document with self-address envelope.* To receive a file-stamped copy of a document filed directly with the clerk, a party must include with the original document an additional copy and a self-addressed envelope. The envelope must be big enough to hold the copy and have enough postage on it to send the copy via regular first-class mail. IN R USDCTSD L.R. 5-10(b).

viii. *Notice of manual filing.* When a party who is not exempt from the electronic filing requirement files a document directly with the clerk, the party must: electronically file a notice of manual filing that explains why the document cannot be filed electronically. IN R USDCTSD L.R. 5-2(d)(1). Refer to the Filing and Service Requirements section of this document for more information.

- Where an individual component cannot be included in an electronic filing (e.g. the component cannot be converted to electronic format), the filer shall electronically file the prescribed Notice of Manual Filing in place of that component. A model form is provided as Appendix C (IN R USDCTSD ECF Procedures(Appendix C)). IN R USDCTSD ECF Procedures(13).

- Before making a manual filing of a component, the filing party shall first electronically file a Notice of Manual Filing (See IN R USDCTSD ECF Procedures(Appendix C)). The filer shall initiate the electronic filing process as if filing the actual component but shall instead attach to the filing the Notice of Manual Filing setting forth the reason(s) why the component cannot be filed electronically. The manual filing should be accompanied by a copy of the previously filed Notice of Manual Filing. A party may seek to have a component excluded from electronic filing pursuant to applicable Federal and Local Rules (e.g., FRCP 26(c)). IN R USDCTSD ECF Procedures(15).

ix. *Courtesy copies.* District Judges and Magistrate Judges regularly receive documents filed by all parties. Therefore, parties shall not bring "courtesy copies" to any chambers unless specifically directed to do so by the Court. IN R USDCTSD Case Mgt(General Instructions For All Cases).

x. *Copies for three-judge court.* Parties in a case where a three-judge court has been requested must file an original and three copies of any document filed directly with the clerk (instead of electronically) until the court: (1) denies the request; (2) dissolves the three-judge court; or (3) allows the parties to file fewer copies. IN R USDCTSD L.R. 9-2(c).

xi. *Declaration that party was unable to file in a timely manner due to technical difficulties.* If a party misses a filing deadline due to an inability to file electronically, the party may submit the untimely filed document, accompanied by a declaration stating the reason(s) for missing the deadline. IN R USDCTSD ECF Procedures(16). A model form is provided as Appendix D (IN R USDCTSD ECF Procedures(Appendix D)). IN R USDCTSD ECF Procedures(16).

E. Format

1. *Form of documents.* The rules governing captions and other matters of form in pleadings apply to motions and other papers. FRCP 7(b)(2).

   a. *Paper (manual filings only).* Any document that is not filed electronically must: be flat, unfolded, and on good-quality, eight and one-half by eleven (8-1/2 x 11) inch white paper. IN R USDCTSD L.R. 5-1(d)(1). Any document that is not filed electronically must: be single-sided. IN R USDCTSD L.R. 5-1(d)(1).

      i. *Covers or backing.* Any document that is not filed electronically must: not have a cover or a back. IN R USDCTSD L.R. 5-1(d)(1).

      ii. *Fastening.* Any document that is not filed electronically must: be (if consisting of more than one (1) page) fastened by paperclip or binder clip and may not be stapled. IN R USDCTSD L.R. 5-1(d)(1).

      - *Request for nonconforming fastening.* If a document cannot be fastened or bound as

required by IN R USDCTSD L.R. 5-1(d), a party may ask the clerk for permission to fasten it in another manner. The party must make such a request before attempting to file the document with nonconforming fastening. IN R USDCTSD L.R. 5-1(d)(2).

    iii. *Hole punching.* Any document that is not filed electronically must: be two-hole punched at the top with the holes two and three-quarter (2-3/4) inches apart and appropriately centered. IN R USDCTSD L.R. 5-1(d)(1).

b. *Margins.* Any pleading, motion, brief, affidavit, notice, or proposed order filed with the court, whether electronically or with the clerk, must: have at least one (1) inch margins. IN R USDCTSD L.R. 5-1(b).

c. *Spacing.* Any pleading, motion, brief, affidavit, notice, or proposed order filed with the court, whether electronically or with the clerk, must: be double spaced (except for headings, footnotes, and quoted material). IN R USDCTSD L.R. 5-1(b).

d. *Text.* Any pleading, motion, brief, affidavit, notice, or proposed order filed with the court, whether electronically or with the clerk, must: be plainly typewritten, printed, or prepared by a clearly legible copying process. IN R USDCTSD L.R. 5-1(b).

e. *Font size.* Any pleading, motion, brief, affidavit, notice, or proposed order filed with the court, whether electronically or with the clerk, must: use at least 12-point type in the body of the document and at least 10-point type in footnotes. IN R USDCTSD L.R. 5-1(b).

f. *Page numbering.* Any pleading, motion, brief, affidavit, notice, or proposed order filed with the court, whether electronically or with the clerk, must: have consecutively numbered pages. IN R USDCTSD L.R. 5-1(b).

g. *Caption; Names of parties.* Every pleading must have a caption with the court's name, a title, a file number, and a FRCP 7(a) designation. The title of the complaint must name all the parties; the title of other pleadings, after naming the first party on each side, may refer generally to other parties. FRCP 10(a). Any pleading, motion, brief, affidavit, notice, or proposed order filed with the court, whether electronically or with the clerk, must: include a title on the first page. IN R USDCTSD L.R. 5-1(b).

    i. *Alternative motions.* Motions must be filed separately, but alternative motions may be filed in a single document if each is named in the title. IN R USDCTSD L.R. 7-1(a).

h. *Filer's information.* Any pleading, motion, brief, affidavit, notice, or proposed order filed with the court, whether electronically or with the clerk, must: in the case of pleadings, motions, legal briefs, and notices, include the name, complete address, telephone number, facsimile number (where available), and e-mail address (where available) of the pro se litigant or attorney who files it. IN R USDCTSD L.R. 5-1(b).

i. *Paragraphs; Separate statements.* A party must state its claims or defenses in numbered paragraphs, each limited as far as practicable to a single set of circumstances. A later pleading may refer by number to a paragraph in an earlier pleading. If doing so would promote clarity, each claim founded on a separate transaction or occurrence—and each defense other than a denial—must be stated in a separate count or defense. FRCP 10(b).

j. *Adoption by reference; Exhibits.* A statement in a pleading may be adopted by reference elsewhere in the same pleading or in any other pleading or motion. A copy of a written instrument that is an exhibit to a pleading is a part of the pleading for all purposes. FRCP 10(c).

k. *Citations*

    i. *Local rules.* The Local Rules of the United States District Court for the Southern District of Indiana may be cited as "S.D. Ind. L.R." IN R USDCTSD L.R. 1-1(a).

    ii. *Local alternative dispute resolution rules.* These Rules shall be known as the Local Alternative Dispute Resolution Rules of the United States District Court for the Southern District of Indiana. They shall be cited as "S.D.Ind. Local A.D.R. Rule _____." IN R USDCTSD A.D.R. Rule 1.1.

l. *Acceptance by the clerk.* The clerk must not refuse to file a paper solely because it is not in the form prescribed by the Federal Rules of Civil Procedure or by a local rule or practice. FRCP 5(d)(4). The clerk will accept a document that violates IN R USDCTSD L.R. 5-1, but the court may exclude the document from the official record. IN R USDCTSD L.R. 5-1(e).

    i. *Sanctions for errors as to form.* The court may strike from the record any document that does not comply with the rules governing the form of documents filed with the court, such as rules that regulate document size or the number of copies to be filed or that require a special designation in the caption. The court may also sanction an attorney or party who files a non-compliant document. IN R USDCTSD L.R. 1-3.

2. *Form of electronic documents.* Any document submitted via the court's electronic case filing (ECF) system must be: otherwise prepared and filed in a manner consistent with the CM/ECF Policies and Procedures Manual (IN R USDCTSD ECF Procedures). IN R USDCTSD L.R. 5-1(c). Electronically filed documents must meet the requirements of FRCP 10 (Form of Pleadings), IN R USDCTSD L.R. 5-1 (Format of Papers Presented for Filing), and FRCP 5.2 (Privacy Protection for Filings Made with the Court), as if they had been submitted on paper. Documents filed electronically are also subject to any page limitations set forth by Court Order, by IN R USDCTSD L.R. 7-1 (Motion Practice), or IN R USDCTSD L.R. 56-1 (Summary Judgment Practice), as applicable. IN R USDCTSD ECF Procedures(13).

  a. *PDF format required.* Any document submitted via the court's electronic case filing (ECF) system must be: in .pdf format. IN R USDCTSD L.R. 5-1(c); IN R USDCTSD ECF Procedures(7). Any document submitted via the court's electronic case filing (ECF) system must be: converted to a .pdf file directly from a word processing program, unless it exists only in paper format (in which case it may be scanned to create a .pdf document). IN R USDCTSD L.R. 5-1(c); IN R USDCTSD ECF Procedures(13).

    i. An exhibit may be scanned into PDF format, at a recommended 300 dpi resolution or higher, only if it does not already exist in electronic format. The filing attorney is responsible for reviewing all PDF documents for legibility before submitting them through the Court's Electronic Case Filing system. For technical guidance in creating PDF documents, please contact the Clerk's Office. IN R USDCTSD ECF Procedures(13).

  b. *File size limitations.* Any document submitted via the court's electronic case filing (ECF) system must be: submitted as one or more .pdf files that do not exceed ten megabytes (10 MB) each (consistent with the CM/ECF Policies and Procedures Manual (IN R USDCTSD ECF Procedures)). IN R USDCTSD L.R. 5-1(c); IN R USDCTSD ECF Procedures(13).

    i. To electronically file a document or attachment that exceeds ten megabytes (10 MB), the document must first be broken down into two or more smaller files. For example, if Exhibit A is a twelve megabyte (12 MB) PDF file, it should be divided into 2 equal parts prior to electronic filing. Each component part of the exhibit would be filed as an attachment to the main document and described appropriately as "Exhibit A (part 1 of 2)" and "Exhibit A (part 2 of 2)." IN R USDCTSD ECF Procedures(13).

    ii. The supporting items mentioned in IN R USDCTSD ECF Procedures(13) should not be confused with memorandums or briefs in support of motions as outlined in IN R USDCTSD L.R. 7-1 or IN R USDCTSD L.R. 56-1. These memorandums or briefs in support are to be filed as entirely separate documents pursuant to the appropriate rule. Additionally, no motion shall be embodied in the text of a response or reply brief/memorandum unless otherwise ordered by the Court. IN R USDCTSD ECF Procedures(13).

  c. *Separate component parts.* A key objective of the electronic filing system is to ensure that as much of the case as possible is managed electronically. To facilitate electronic filing and retrieval, documents to be filed electronically are to be reasonably broken into their separate component parts. By way of example, most filings include a foundation document (e.g., motion) and other supporting items (e.g., exhibits, proposed orders, proposed amended pleadings). The foundation document, as well as the supporting items, are each separate components of the filing; supporting items must be filed as attachments to the foundation document. These exhibits or attachments should include only those excerpts of the referenced documents that are directly germane to the matter under consideration. IN R USDCTSD ECF Procedures(13).

    i. Where an individual component cannot be included in an electronic filing (e.g. the component

cannot be converted to electronic format), the filer shall electronically file the prescribed Notice of Manual Filing in place of that component. A model form is provided as Appendix C (IN R USDCTSD ECF Procedures(Appendix C)). IN R USDCTSD ECF Procedures(13).

d. *Exhibits.* Each electronically filed exhibit to a main document must be: (1) created as a separate .pdf file; (2) submitted as an attachment to the main document and given a title which describes its content; and (3) limited to excerpts that are directly germane to the main document's subject matter. IN R USDCTSD L.R. 5-6(a).

    i. When uploading attachments during the electronic filing process, exhibits must be uploaded in a logical sequence and a brief description must be entered for each individual PDF file. The description must include not only the exhibit number or letter, but also a brief description of the document. This information may be entered in CM/ECF using a combination of the Category drop-down menu, the Description text box, or both (see IN R USDCTSD ECF Procedures(13)(Figure 1)). The information that is provided in each box will be combined to create a description of the document as it appears on the case docket (see IN R USDCTSD ECF Procedures(13)(Figure 2)). IN R USDCTSD ECF Procedures(13). For an example, refer to IN R USDCTSD ECF Procedures(13).

e. *Excerpts.* A party filing an exhibit that consists of excerpts from a larger document must clearly and prominently identify the exhibit as containing excerpted material. Either party will have the right to timely file additional excerpts or the complete document to the extent they are or become directly germane to the main document's subject matter. IN R USDCTSD L.R. 5-6(b).

f. For an example illustrating the application of IN R USDCTSD ECF Procedures(13), refer to IN R USDCTSD ECF Procedures(13).

3. *Form of briefs*

a. *Page limits.* Supporting and response briefs (excluding tables of contents, tables of authorities, appendices, and certificates of service) may not exceed thirty-five (35) pages. Reply briefs may not exceed twenty (20) pages. IN R USDCTSD L.R. 7-1(e)(1).

    i. *Permission to exceed limits.* The court may allow a party to file a brief exceeding these page limits for extraordinary and compelling reasons. IN R USDCTSD L.R. 7-1(e)(2).

    ii. *Supporting and response briefs exceeding limits.* If the court allows a party to file a brief or response exceeding thirty-five (35) pages, the document must include:

        • A table of contents with page references;

        • A statement of issues; and

        • A table of authorities including: (1) all cases (alphabetically arranged), statutes, and other authorities cited in the brief; and (2) page numbers where the authorities are cited in the brief. IN R USDCTSD L.R. 7-1(e)(3).

4. *Signing disclosures and discovery requests, responses, and objections.* FRCP 11 does not apply to disclosures and discovery requests, responses, objections, and motions under FRCP 26 through FRCP 37. FRCP 11(d).

a. *Signature required.* Every disclosure under FRCP 26(a)(1) or FRCP 26(a)(3) and every discovery request, response, or objection must be signed by at least one attorney of record in the attorney's own name—or by the party personally, if unrepresented—and must state the signer's address, e-mail address, and telephone number. FRCP 26(g)(1).

    i. *Signatures on manual filings.* Any document that is not filed electronically must: include the original signature of the pro se litigant or attorney who files it. IN R USDCTSD L.R. 5-1(d)(1).

    ii. *Electronic signatures.* Use of the attorney's login and password when filing documents electronically serves in part as the attorney's signature for purposes of FRCP 11, the Local Rules of the United States District Court for the Southern District of Indiana, and any other purpose for which a signature is required in connection with proceedings before the Court. IN R USDCTSD ECF Procedures(14); IN R USDCTSD ECF Procedures(10). A pleading, motion, brief, or notice filed electronically under an attorney's ECF log-in and password must be signed by that attorney. IN R USDCTSD L.R. 5-7(a). A signature on a document other than a document filed as provided under IN R USDCTSD L.R. 5-7(a) must be an original handwritten signature and must be scanned into .pdf format for electronic filing. IN R USDCTSD L.R. 5-7(c); IN R USDCTSD ECF Procedures(14).

- *Form of electronic signature.* If a document is converted directly from a word processing application to .pdf (as opposed to scanning), the name of the Filing User under whose log-in and password the document is submitted must be preceded by a "s/" and typed on the signature line where the Filing User's handwritten signature would otherwise appear. IN R USDCTSD L.R. 5-7(b). All documents filed electronically shall include a signature block and include the filing attorney's typewritten name, address, telephone number, facsimile number and e-mail address. In addition, the name of the filing attorney under whose ECF login the document will be filed should be preceded by a "s/" and typed in the space where the attorney's handwritten signature would otherwise appear. IN R US-DCTSD ECF Procedures(14). For a sample format, refer to IN R USDCTSD ECF Procedures(14).

- *Effect of electronic signature.* Filing an electronically signed document under an attorney's ECF log-in and password constitutes the attorney's signature on the document under the Federal Rules of Civil Procedure, under the Local Rules of the United States District Court for the Southern District of Indiana, and for any other reason a signature is required in connection with the court's activities. IN R USDCTSD L.R. 5-7(d).

- *Documents with multiple attorneys' signatures.* Documents requiring signatures of more than one attorney shall be filed either by: (1) obtaining consent from the other attorney, then typing the "s/ [Name]" signature of the other attorney on the signature line where the other attorney's signature would otherwise appear; (2) identifying in the signature section the name of the other attorney whose signature is required and by the submission of a Notice of Endorsement (see IN R USDCTSD ECF Procedures(Appendix B)) by the other attorney no later than three (3) business days after filing; (3) submitting a scanned document containing all handwritten signatures; or (4) in any other manner approved by the Court. IN R USDCTSD ECF Procedures(14); IN R USDCTSD L.R. 5-7(e).

b. *Effect of signature.* By signing, an attorney or party certifies that to the best of the person's knowledge, information, and belief formed after a reasonable inquiry:

   i. With respect to a disclosure, it is complete and correct as of the time it is made; and

   ii. With respect to a discovery request, response, or objection, it is:

- Consistent with the Federal Rules of Civil Procedure and warranted by existing law or by a nonfrivolous argument for extending, modifying, or reversing existing law, or for establishing new law;

- Not interposed for any improper purpose, such as to harass, cause unnecessary delay, or needlessly increase the cost of litigation; and

- Neither unreasonable nor unduly burdensome or expensive, considering the needs of the case, prior discovery in the case, the amount in controversy, and the importance of the issues at stake in the action. FRCP 26(g)(1).

c. *Failure to sign.* Other parties have no duty to act on an unsigned disclosure, request, response, or objection until it is signed, and the court must strike it unless a signature is promptly supplied after the omission is called to the attorney's or party's attention. FRCP 26(g)(2). The court will strike any document filed directly with the clerk that is not signed by an attorney of record or the pro se litigant filing it, but the court may do so only after giving the attorney or pro se litigant notice of the omission and reasonable time to correct it. Rubber-stamp or facsimile signatures are not original signatures and the court will deem documents containing them to be unsigned for purposes of FRCP 11 and FRCP 26(g) and IN R USDCTSD L.R. 5-10. IN R USDCTSD L.R. 5-10(g).

d. *Sanction for improper certification.* If a certification violates FRCP 26(g) without substantial justification, the court, on motion or on its own, must impose an appropriate sanction on the signer, the party on whose behalf the signer was acting, or both. The sanction may include an order to pay the reasonable expenses, including attorney's fees, caused by the violation. FRCP 26(g)(3). Refer to the United States District Court for the Southern District of Indiana KeyRules Motion for Discovery Sanctions document for more information.

5. *Privacy protection for filings made with the court.* Electronically filed documents must meet the requirements of. . .FRCP 5.2 (Privacy Protection for Filings Made with the Court), as if they had been submitted on paper. IN R USDCTSD ECF Procedures(13).

   a. *Redacted filings.* Unless the court orders otherwise, in an electronic or paper filing with the court that contains an individual's Social Security number, taxpayer-identification number, or birth date, the name of an individual known to be a minor, or a financial-account number, a party or nonparty making the filing may include only:

      i. The last four (4) digits of the Social Security number and taxpayer-identification number;

      ii. The year of the individual's birth;

      iii. The minor's initials; and

      iv. The last four (4) digits of the financial-account number. FRCP 5.2(a).

   b. *Exemptions from the redaction requirement.* The redaction requirement does not apply to the following:

      i. A financial-account number that identifies the property allegedly subject to forfeiture in a forfeiture proceeding;

      ii. The record of an administrative or agency proceeding;

      iii. The official record of a state-court proceeding;

      iv. The record of a court or tribunal, if that record was not subject to the redaction requirement when originally filed;

      v. A filing covered by FRCP 5.2(c) or FRCP 5.2(d); and

      vi. A pro se filing in an action brought under 28 U.S.C.A. § 2241, 28 U.S.C.A. § 2254, or 28 U.S.C.A. § 2255. FRCP 5.2(b).

   c. *Limitations on remote access to electronic files; Social Security appeals and immigration cases.* Unless the court orders otherwise, in an action for benefits under the Social Security Act, and in an action or proceeding relating to an order of removal, to relief from removal, or to immigration benefits or detention, access to an electronic file is authorized as follows:

      i. The parties and their attorneys may have remote electronic access to any part of the case file, including the administrative record;

      ii. Any other person may have electronic access to the full record at the courthouse, but may have remote electronic access only to:

         • The docket maintained by the court; and

         • An opinion, order, judgment, or other disposition of the court, but not any other part of the case file or the administrative record. FRCP 5.2(c).

   d. *Filings made under seal.* The court may order that a filing be made under seal without redaction. The court may later unseal the filing or order the person who made the filing to file a redacted version for the public record. FRCP 5.2(d). For more information on filing under seal, refer to IN R USDCTSD L.R. 5-11 and IN R USDCTSD ECF Procedures(18).

   e. *Protective orders.* For good cause, the court may by order in a case:

      i. Require redaction of additional information; or

      ii. Limit or prohibit a nonparty's remote electronic access to a document filed with the court. FRCP 5.2(e).

   f. *Option for additional unredacted filing under seal.* A person making a redacted filing may also file an unredacted copy under seal. The court must retain the unredacted copy as part of the record. FRCP 5.2(f).

g. *Option for filing a reference list.* A filing that contains redacted information may be filed together with a reference list that identifies each item of redacted information and specifies an appropriate identifier that uniquely corresponds to each item listed. The list must be filed under seal and may be amended as of right. Any reference in the case to a listed identifier will be construed to refer to the corresponding item of information. FRCP 5.2(g).

h. *Waiver of protection of identifiers.* A person waives the protection of FRCP 5.2(a) as to the person's own information by filing it without redaction and not under seal. FRCP 5.2(h).

F. Filing and Service Requirements

1. *Filing requirements.* Any paper after the complaint that is required to be served—together with a certificate of service—must be filed within a reasonable time after service. FRCP 5(d)(1). Motions must be filed separately, but alternative motions may be filed in a single document if each is named in the title. IN R USDCTSD L.R. 7-1(a).

   a. *How filing is made; In general.* A paper is filed by delivering it:

      i. To the clerk; or

      ii. To a judge who agrees to accept it for filing, and who must then note the filing date on the paper and promptly send it to the clerk. FRCP 5(d)(2).

         • In certain instances, the court will direct the parties to submit items directly to chambers (e.g., confidential settlement statements). However, absent specific prior authorization, counsel and litigants should not submit letters or documents directly to chambers, and such materials should be filed with the clerk. IN R USDCTSD L.R. 5-1(Local Rules Advisory Committee Comment).

      iii. A document or item submitted in relation to a matter within the court's jurisdiction is deemed filed upon delivery to the office of the clerk in a manner prescribed by the Local Rules of the United States District Court for the Southern District of Indiana or the Federal Rules of Civil Procedure or authorized by the court. Any submission directed to a Judge or Judge's staff, the office of the clerk or any employee thereof, in a manner that is not contemplated by IN R USDCTSD L.R. 5-1 and without prior court authorization is prohibited. IN R USDCTSD L.R. 5-1(a).

   b. *Non-electronic filing.* Any document that is exempt from electronic filing must be filed directly with the clerk and served on other parties in the case as required by those Federal Rules of Civil Procedure and Local Rules of the United States District Court for the Southern District of Indiana that apply to the service of non-electronic documents. IN R USDCTSD L.R. 5-2(c).

      i. *When completed.* A document or other item that is not required to be filed electronically is deemed filed:

         • Upon delivery in person, by courier, or via U.S. Mail or other mail delivery service to the clerk's office during business hours;

         • When the courtroom deputy clerk accepts it, if the document or item is filed in open court; or

         • Upon completion of any other manner of filing that the court authorizes. IN R USDCTSD L.R. 5-10(a).

      ii. *Document filing by non-exempt party.* When a party who is not exempt from the electronic filing requirement files a document directly with the clerk, the party must:

         • Electronically file a notice of manual filing that explains why the document cannot be filed electronically;

         • Present the document to the clerk within one (1) business day after filing the notice of manual filing; and

         • Present the clerk with a copy of the notice of manual filing when the party files the document with the clerk. IN R USDCTSD L.R. 5-2(d).

   c. *Electronic filing*

      i. *Authorization of electronic filing program.* A court may, by local rule, allow papers to be filed,

signed, or verified by electronic means that are consistent with any technical standards established by the Judicial Conference of the United States. A local rule may require electronic filing only if reasonable exceptions are allowed. A paper filed electronically in compliance with a local rule is a written paper for purposes of the Federal Rules of Civil Procedure. FRCP 5(d)(3).

- IN R USDCTSD L.R. 5-2 requires electronic filing, as allowed by FRCP 5(d)(3). The policies and procedures in IN R USDCTSD ECF Procedures govern electronic filing in this district unless, due to circumstances in a particular case, a judicial officer determines that these policies and procedures (IN R USDCTSD ECF Procedures) should be modified. IN R USDCTSD ECF Procedures(1).

- Unless modified by order of the Court, all Federal Rules of Civil Procedure and Local Rules of the United States District Court for the Southern District of Indiana shall continue to apply to cases maintained in the Court's Case Management/Electronic Case Filing System (CM/ECF). IN R USDCTSD ECF Procedures(3).

ii. *Mandatory electronic filing.* Unless exempted pursuant to IN R USDCTSD L.R. 5-3(e), attorneys admitted to the court's bar (including those admitted pro hac vice) or authorized to represent the United States must use the court's ECF system to file documents. IN R USDCTSD L.R. 5-3(a). Electronic filing by attorneys is required for eligible documents filed in civil and criminal cases pending with the Court, unless specifically exempted by Local Rule or Court Order. IN R USDCTSD ECF Procedures(4).

- *Exceptions.* All civil cases (other than those cases the court specifically exempts) must be maintained in the court's electronic case filing (ECF) system. Accordingly, as allowed by FRCP 5(d)(3), every document filed in this court (including exhibits) must be transmitted to the clerk's office via the ECF system consistent with IN R USDCTSD L.R. 5-2 through IN R USDCTSD L.R. 5-11 except: (1) documents filed by pro se litigants; (2) transcripts in cases filed by claimants under the Social Security Act (and related statutes); (3) exhibits in a format that does not readily permit electronic filing (such as videos and large maps and charts); (4) documents that are illegible when scanned into .pdf format; (5) documents filed in cases not maintained on the ECF system; and (6) any other documents that the court or the Local Rules of the United States District Court for the Southern District of Indiana specifically allow to be filed directly with the clerk. IN R USDCTSD L.R. 5-2(a). Parties otherwise participating in the electronic filing system may be excused from filing a particular component electronically under certain limited circumstances, such as when the component cannot be reduced to an electronic format. Such components shall not be filed electronically, but instead shall be manually filed with the Clerk of Court and served upon the parties in accordance with the applicable Federal Rules of Civil Procedure and the Local Rules of the United States District Court for the Southern District of Indiana for filing and service of non-electronic documents. IN R USDCTSD ECF Procedures(15).

- *Exemption from participation.* The court may exempt attorneys from using the ECF system in a particular case for good cause. An attorney must file a petition for ECF exemption and a CM/ECF technical requirements exemption questionnaire in each case in which the attorney seeks an exemption. (The CM/ECF technical requirements exemption questionnaire is available on the court's website). IN R USDCTSD L.R. 5-3(e).

iii. *Consequences of electronic filing.* Electronic transmission of a document consistent with the procedures adopted by the Court shall, upon the complete receipt of the same by the Clerk of Court, constitute filing of the document for all purposes of the Federal Rules of Civil and Criminal Procedure and the Local Rules of the United States District Court for the Southern District of Indiana, and shall constitute entry of that document onto the docket maintained by the Clerk pursuant to FRCP 58 and FRCP 79. IN R USDCTSD ECF Procedures(7); IN R USDCTSD L.R. 5-4(c)(1). When a document has been filed electronically: the document, as filed, binds the filing party. IN R USDCTSD L.R. 5-4(c)(3).

- A Notice of Electronic Filing (NEF) acknowledging that the document has been filed will immediately appear on the filer's screen after the document has been submitted. Attorneys are strongly encouraged to print or electronically save a copy of the NEF. Attorneys can also verify the filing of documents by inspecting the Court's electronic docket sheet through the use of a PACER login. IN R USDCTSD ECF Procedures(7). When a document has been filed electronically: the notice of electronic filing for the document serves as the court's date-stamp and proof of filing. IN R USDCTSD L.R. 5-4(c)(4).

- The Court may, upon the motion of a party or upon its own motion, strike any inappropriately filed document. IN R USDCTSD ECF Procedures(7).

iv. For more information on electronic filing, refer to IN R USDCTSD ECF Procedures.

d. *Fax filing.* The clerk may not file a faxed document without court authorization. The court may not authorize the clerk to file faxed documents without finding that compelling circumstances justify it. A party must submit a copy of the document that otherwise complies with IN R USDCTSD L.R. 5-10 to replace the faxed copy within seven (7) days after faxing the document. IN R USDCTSD L.R. 5-10(e).

2. *Service requirements*

a. *Service; When required*

i. *In general.* Unless the Federal Rules of Civil Procedure provide otherwise, each of the following papers must be served on every party:

- An order stating that service is required;

- A pleading filed after the original complaint, unless the court orders otherwise under FRCP 5(c) because there are numerous defendants;

- A discovery paper required to be served on a party, unless the court orders otherwise;

- A written motion, except one that may be heard ex parte; and

- A written notice, appearance, demand, or offer of judgment, or any similar paper. FRCP 5(a)(1).

ii. *If a party fails to appear.* No service is required on a party who is in default for failing to appear. But a pleading that asserts a new claim for relief against such a party must be served on that party under FRCP 4. FRCP 5(a)(2).

iii. *Seizing property.* If an action is begun by seizing property and no person is or need be named as a defendant, any service required before the filing of an appearance, answer, or claim must be made on the person who had custody or possession of the property when it was seized. FRCP 5(a)(3).

b. *Service; How made*

i. *Serving an attorney.* If a party is represented by an attorney, service under FRCP 5 must be made on the attorney unless the court orders service on the party. FRCP 5(b)(1).

ii. *Service in general.* A paper is served under FRCP 5 by:

- Handing it to the person;

- Leaving it: (1) at the person's office with a clerk or other person in charge or, if no one is in charge, in a conspicuous place in the office; or (2) if the person has no office or the office is closed, at the person's dwelling or usual place of abode with someone of suitable age and discretion who resides there;

- Mailing it to the person's last known address—in which event service is complete upon mailing;

- Leaving it with the court clerk if the person has no known address;

- Sending it by electronic means if the person consented in writing—in which event service is complete upon transmission, but is not effective if the serving party learns that it did not reach the person to be served; or

- Delivering it by any other means that the person consented to in writing—in which event service is complete when the person making service delivers it to the agency designated to make delivery. FRCP 5(b)(2).

iii. *Electronic service*

- *Consent.* By registering to use the ECF system, attorneys consent to electronic service of documents filed in cases maintained on the ECF system. IN R USDCTSD L.R. 5-3(d). By participating in the Electronic Case Filing Program, attorneys consent to the electronic service of documents, and shall make available electronic mail addresses for service. IN R USDCTSD ECF Procedures(11).

- *Service on registered parties.* Upon the filing of a document by a party, an e-mail message will be automatically generated by the electronic filing system and sent via electronic mail to the e-mail addresses of all registered attorneys who have appeared in the case. The Notice of Electronic Filing will contain a document hyperlink which will provide recipients with one "free look" at the electronically filed document. Recipients are encouraged to print and/or save a copy of the document during the "free look" to avoid incurring PACER charges for future viewings of the document. IN R USDCTSD ECF Procedures(11). When a document has been filed electronically: transmission of the notice of electronic filing generated by the ECF system to an attorney's e-mail address constitutes service of the document on that attorney. IN R USDCTSD L.R. 5-4(c)(5). The party effectuates service on all registered attorneys by filing electronically. IN R USDCTSD ECF Procedures(11). When a document has been filed electronically: no other attempted service will constitute electronic service of the document. IN R USDCTSD L.R. 5-4(c)(6).

- *Service on exempt parties.* A filer must serve a copy of the document consistent with FRCP 5 on any party or attorney who is exempt from participating in electronic filing. IN R USDCTSD L.R. 5-4(d). It is the responsibility of the filing attorney to conventionally serve all parties who do not receive electronic service (the identity of these parties will be indicated on the filing receipt generated by the ECF system). IN R USDCTSD ECF Procedures(11).

- *Service on parties excused from electronic filing.* Parties otherwise participating in the electronic filing system may be excused from filing a particular component electronically under certain limited circumstances, such as when the component cannot be reduced to an electronic format. Such components shall not be filed electronically, but instead shall be manually filed with the Clerk of Court and served upon the parties in accordance with the applicable Federal Rules of Civil Procedure and the Local Rules of the United States District Court for the Southern District of Indiana for filing and service of non-electronic documents. IN R USDCTSD ECF Procedures(15).

- *Service of exempt documents.* Any document that is exempt from electronic filing must be filed directly with the clerk and served on other parties in the case as required by those Federal Rules of Civil Procedure and Local Rules of the United States District Court for the Southern District of Indiana that apply to the service of non-electronic documents. IN R USDCTSD L.R. 5-2(c).

iv. *Using court facilities.* If a local rule so authorizes, a party may use the court's transmission facilities to make service under FRCP 5(b)(2)(E). FRCP 5(b)(3).

c. *Serving numerous defendants*

i. *In general.* If an action involves an unusually large number of defendants, the court may, on motion or on its own, order that:

- Defendants' pleadings and replies to them need not be served on other defendants;

- Any crossclaim, counterclaim, avoidance, or affirmative defense in those pleadings and replies to them will be treated as denied or avoided by all other parties; and

- Filing any such pleading and serving it on the plaintiff constitutes notice of the pleading to all parties. FRCP 5(c)(1).

ii. *Notifying parties.* A copy of every such order must be served on the parties as the court directs. FRCP 5(c)(2).

G. Hearings

1. *Hearings, generally*

   a. *Oral argument.* Due process does not require that oral argument be permitted on a motion and, except as otherwise provided by local rule, the district court has discretion to determine whether it will decide the motion on the papers or hear argument by counsel (and perhaps receive evidence). FPP § 1190; F.D.I.C. v. Deglau, 207 F.3d 153 (3d Cir. 2000).

      i. *Request for oral argument.* A party may request oral argument by filing a separate motion explaining why oral argument is necessary and estimating how long the court should allow for the argument. IN R USDCTSD L.R. 7-5(a). Refer to the Documents section of this document for more information.

      ii. *No additional evidence at oral argument.* Parties may not present additional evidence at oral argument. IN R USDCTSD L.R. 7-5(b).

   b. *Providing a regular schedule for oral hearings.* A court may establish regular times and places for oral hearings on motions. FRCP 78(a).

   c. *Providing for submission on briefs.* By rule or order, the court may provide for submitting and determining motions on briefs, without oral hearings. FRCP 78(b).

   d. *Request for evidentiary hearing.* A party may request an evidentiary hearing on a motion or petition by serving and filing a separate motion explaining why the hearing is necessary and estimating how long the court should allow for the hearing. IN R USDCTSD L.R. 7-5(c).

   e. *Directed by the court.* The court may: (1) grant or deny a request for oral argument or an evidentiary hearing in its sole discretion; (2) set oral argument or an evidentiary hearing without a request from a party; and (3) order any oral argument or evidentiary hearing to be held anywhere within the district regardless of where the case will be tried. IN R USDCTSD L.R. 7-5(d).

2. *Courtroom and courthouse decorum.* For information on courtroom and courthouse decorum, refer to IN R USDCTSD L.R. 83-3.

H. Forms

1. Federal Motion for Protective Order Forms

   a. Notice of motion; For protective order; Preventing deposition of consultant and production of documents; Federal class action. AMJUR PP DEPOSITION § 334.

   b. Motion; For protective order pending court's order on motion to quash deposition notice of plaintiff. AMJUR PP DEPOSITION § 341.

   c. Motion; For protective order; To prevent deposition of consultant and production of documents; Federal class action. AMJUR PP DEPOSITION § 343.

   d. Opposition; By plaintiffs; To motion by defendants for protective order; Prevention of deposition of consultant and production of documents; Federal class action. AMJUR PP DEPOSITION § 370.

   e. Declaration; By plaintiffs' attorney; In support of opposition to defendants' motion for protective order; Federal class action. AMJUR PP DEPOSITION § 371.

   f. Notice of motion; For protective order; To vacate notice to produce documents. AMJUR PP DEPOSITION § 592.

   g. Notice of motion; For protective order; To limit scope of inspection of premises; Premises liability action; Objection to scope of request. AMJUR PP DEPOSITION § 593.

   h. Motion; For protective order; Staying proceedings on production requests; Pending ruling on movant's dispositive motion. AMJUR PP DEPOSITION § 594.

   i. Motion; For protective order; Limiting requests for production; Additional protection of trade secrets. AMJUR PP DEPOSITION § 595.

   j. Motion for protective order limiting scope of oral examination; Privileged material. 3A FED-FORMS § 3264.

k. Notice of motion and motion for protective order. 3A FEDFORMS § 3265.

l. Notice of motion and motion for protective order; Prohibiting taking of deposition. 3A FEDFORMS § 3266.

m. Notice of motion and motion for protective order; To quash notice of taking deposition or for continuance; Late taking of deposition. 3A FEDFORMS § 3267.

n. Motion for protective order limiting scope of oral examination. 3A FEDFORMS § 3279.

o. Motion for protective order limiting examination upon written questions. 3A FEDFORMS § 3283.

p. Answer; To motion for protective order. FEDPROF § 23:196.

q. Motion; For protective order; Limiting interrogatories. FEDPROF § 23:373.

r. Motion; For protective order; Staying proceedings on production requests. FEDPROF § 23:422.

s. Motion; For protective order; Limiting requests for production. FEDPROF § 23:423.

t. Motion; For protective order staying proceedings on request for admissions. FEDPROF § 23:563.

u. Notice of motion for protective order. GOLDLTGFMS § 31:2.

v. Motion for protective order; Federal form. GOLDLTGFMS § 31:5.

w. Motion for protective order; Deposition not to be taken. GOLDLTGFMS § 31:6.

x. Motion for protective order; Retaking depositions. GOLDLTGFMS § 31:7.

y. Motion for protective order; Certain matters shall not be inquired into. GOLDLTGFMS § 31:8.

z. Motion for protective order; To limit scope of examination. GOLDLTGFMS § 31:10.

2. Forms for the Southern District of Indiana

a. Uniform stipulated protective order. IN R USDCTSD Uniform Protective Order(Uniform Stipulated Protective Order).

b. Notice of endorsement. IN R USDCTSD ECF Procedures(Appendix B).

c. Notice of manual filing. IN R USDCTSD ECF Procedures(Appendix C).

d. Declaration that party was unable to file in a timely manner due to technical difficulties. IN R USDCTSD ECF Procedures(Appendix D).

I. Applicable Rules

1. *Federal rules*

a. Serving and filing pleadings and other papers. FRCP 5.

b. Constitutional challenge to a statute; Notice, certification, and intervention. FRCP 5.1.

c. Privacy protection for filings made with the court. FRCP 5.2.

d. Computing and extending time; Time for motion papers. FRCP 6.

e. Pleadings allowed; Form of motions and other papers. FRCP 7.

f. Disclosure statement. FRCP 7.1.

g. Form of pleadings. FRCP 10.

h. Signing pleadings, motions, and other papers; Representations to the court; Sanctions. FRCP 11.

i. Duty to disclose; General provisions governing discovery. FRCP 26.

j. Taking testimony. FRCP 43.

k. Hearing motions; Submission on briefs. FRCP 78.

2. *Local rules*

a. Scope of the rules. IN R USDCTSD L.R. 1-1.

b. Sanctions for errors as to form. IN R USDCTSD L.R. 1-3.

c. Format of documents presented for filing. IN R USDCTSD L.R. 5-1.

d. Constitutional challenge to a statute; Notice. IN R USDCTSD L.R. 5.1-1.

e. Filing of documents electronically required. IN R USDCTSD L.R. 5-2.

f. Eligibility, registration, passwords for electronic filing; Exemption from electronic filing. IN R USDCTSD L.R. 5-3.

g. Timing and consequences of electronic filing. IN R USDCTSD L.R. 5-4.

h. Attachments and exhibits in cases filed electronically. IN R USDCTSD L.R. 5-6.

i. Signatures in cases filed electronically. IN R USDCTSD L.R. 5-7.

j. Non-electronic filings. IN R USDCTSD L.R. 5-10.

k. Motion practice. [IN R USDCTSD L.R. 7-1, as amended by IN ORDER 16-2319, effective December 1, 2016].

l. Oral arguments and hearings. IN R USDCTSD L.R. 7-5.

m. Request for three-judge court. IN R USDCTSD L.R. 9-2.

n. Filing of discovery materials. IN R USDCTSD L.R. 26-2.

o. Discovery disputes. IN R USDCTSD L.R. 37-1.

p. Assignment of cases. IN R USDCTSD L.R. 40-1.

q. Alternative dispute resolution. IN R USDCTSD A.D.R. Rule 1.1; IN R USDCTSD A.D.R. Rule 1.2; IN R USDCTSD A.D.R. Rule 1.5; IN R USDCTSD A.D.R. Rule 2.1; IN R USDCTSD A.D.R. Rule 2.2.

r. Instructions for preparing case management plan. IN R USDCTSD Case Mgt.

s. Electronic case filing policies and procedures manual. IN R USDCTSD ECF Procedures.

Motions, Oppositions and Replies
Motion for Discovery Sanctions

Document Last Updated December 2016

A. **Checklist**

(I) ❏ Matters to be considered by moving party

    (a) ❏ Required documents

        (1) ❏ Notice of motion and motion

        (2) ❏ Certificate of compliance

        (3) ❏ Brief

        (4) ❏ Discovery materials

        (5) ❏ Certificate of service

    (b) ❏ Supplemental documents

        (1) ❏ Supporting evidence

        (2) ❏ Notice of constitutional question

        (3) ❏ Index of exhibits

        (4) ❏ Request for oral argument

        (5) ❏ Request for evidentiary hearing

        (6) ❏ Copy of authority

        (7) ❏ Proposed order

        (8) ❏ Copy of document with self-address envelope

(9) ❏ Notice of manual filing

(10) ❏ Courtesy copies

(11) ❏ Copies for three-judge court

(12) ❏ Declaration that party was unable to file in a timely manner due to technical difficulties

(c) ❏ Timing

(1) ❏ A written motion and notice of the hearing must be served at least fourteen (14) days before the time specified for the hearing, with the following exceptions: (i) when the motion may be heard ex parte; (ii) when the Federal Rules of Civil Procedure set a different time; or (iii) when a court order—which a party may, for good cause, apply for ex parte—sets a different time

(2) ❏ Any affidavit supporting a motion must be served with the motion

(3) ❏ When a party who is not exempt from the electronic filing requirement files a document directly with the clerk, the party must present the document to the clerk within one (1) business day after filing the notice of manual filing

(4) ❏ Unless the court orders otherwise, the [untimely] document and declaration [that party was unable to file in a timely manner due to technical difficulties] must be filed no later than 12:00 noon of the first day on which the court is open for business following the original filing deadline

(II) ❏ Matters to be considered by opposing party

(a) ❏ Required documents

(1) ❏ Response brief

(2) ❏ Certificate of service

(b) ❏ Supplemental documents

(1) ❏ Supporting evidence

(2) ❏ Notice of constitutional question

(3) ❏ Index of exhibits

(4) ❏ Request for oral argument

(5) ❏ Request for evidentiary hearing

(6) ❏ Copy of authority

(7) ❏ Copy of document with self-address envelope

(8) ❏ Notice of manual filing

(9) ❏ Courtesy copies

(10) ❏ Copies for three-judge court

(11) ❏ Declaration that party was unable to file in a timely manner due to technical difficulties

(c) ❏ Timing

(1) ❏ Any response is due within fourteen (14) days after service of the motion

(2) ❏ Except as FRCP 59(c) provides otherwise, any opposing affidavit must be served at least seven (7) days before the hearing, unless the court permits service at another time

(3) ❏ When a party who is not exempt from the electronic filing requirement files a document directly with the clerk, the party must present the document to the clerk within one (1) business day after filing the notice of manual filing

(4) ❏ Unless the court orders otherwise, the [untimely] document and declaration [that party was unable to file in a timely manner due to technical difficulties] must be filed no later than 12:00 noon of the first day on which the court is open for business following the original filing deadline

B. Timing

1. *Motion for discovery sanctions.* There are no specific timing requirements for moving for discovery sanctions.

2. *Timing of motions, generally*

   a. *Motion and notice of hearing.* A written motion and notice of the hearing must be served at least fourteen (14) days before the time specified for the hearing, with the following exceptions:

      i.   When the motion may be heard ex parte;

      ii. When the Federal Rules of Civil Procedure set a different time; or

      iii. When a court order—which a party may, for good cause, apply for ex parte—sets a different time. FRCP 6(c)(1).

   b. *Supporting affidavit.* Any affidavit supporting a motion must be served with the motion. FRCP 6(c)(2).

3. *Timing of opposing papers.* Any response is due within fourteen (14) days after service of the motion. IN R USDCTSD L.R. 7-1(c)(2)(A).

   a. *Opposing affidavit.* Except as FRCP 59(c) provides otherwise, any opposing affidavit must be served at least seven (7) days before the hearing, unless the court permits service at another time. FRCP 6(c)(2).

   b. *Extensions.* The court may extend response and reply deadlines, but only for good cause. IN R USDCTSD L.R. 7-1(c)(3).

   c. *Summary ruling on failure to respond.* The court may summarily rule on a motion if an opposing party does not file a response within the deadline. IN R USDCTSD L.R. 7-1(c)(4).

4. *Timing of reply papers.* Where the respondent files an answering affidavit setting up a new matter, the moving party ordinarily is allowed a reasonable time to file a reply affidavit since failure to deny the new matter by affidavit may operate as an admission of its truth. AMJUR MOTIONS § 25.

   a. *Reply brief.* Any reply is due within seven (7) days after service of the response. IN R USDCTSD L.R. 7-1(c)(2)(B).

   b. *Extensions.* The court may extend response and reply deadlines, but only for good cause. IN R USDCTSD L.R. 7-1(c)(3).

5. *Document filing by non-exempt party.* When a party who is not exempt from the electronic filing requirement files a document directly with the clerk, the party must: present the document to the clerk within one (1) business day after filing the notice of manual filing. IN R USDCTSD L.R. 5-2(d)(2).

6. *Declaration that party was unable to file in a timely manner due to technical difficulties.* Unless the Court orders otherwise, the [untimely] document and declaration [that party was unable to file in a timely manner due to technical difficulties] must be filed no later than 12:00 noon of the first day on which the Court is open for business following the original filing deadline. IN R USDCTSD ECF Procedures(16).

7. *Computation of time*

   a. *Computing time.* FRCP 6 applies in computing any time period specified in the Federal Rules of Civil Procedure, in any local rule or court order, or in any statute that does not specify a method of computing time. FRCP 6(a).

      i. *Period stated in days or a longer unit.* When the period is stated in days or a longer unit of time:

      • Exclude the day of the event that triggers the period;

      • Count every day, including intermediate Saturdays, Sundays, and legal holidays; and

      • Include the last day of the period, but if the last day is a Saturday, Sunday, or legal holiday, the period continues to run until the end of the next day that is not a Saturday, Sunday, or legal holiday. FRCP 6(a)(1).

      ii. *Period stated in hours.* When the period is stated in hours:

      • Begin counting immediately on the occurrence of the event that triggers the period;

- Count every hour, including hours during intermediate Saturdays, Sundays, and legal holidays; and

- If the period would end on a Saturday, Sunday, or legal holiday, the period continues to run until the same time on the next day that is not a Saturday, Sunday, or legal holiday. FRCP 6(a)(2).

iii. *Inaccessibility of the clerk's office.* Unless the court orders otherwise, if the clerk's office is inaccessible:

- On the last day for filing under FRCP 6(a)(1), then the time for filing is extended to the first accessible day that is not a Saturday, Sunday, or legal holiday; or

- During the last hour for filing under FRCP 6(a)(2), then the time for filing is extended to the same time on the first accessible day that is not a Saturday, Sunday, or legal holiday. FRCP 6(a)(3).

iv. *"Last day" defined.* Unless a different time is set by a statute, local rule, or court order, the last day ends:

- For electronic filing, at midnight in the court's time zone; and

- For filing by other means, when the clerk's office is scheduled to close. FRCP 6(a)(4).

v. *"Next day" defined.* The "next day" is determined by continuing to count forward when the period is measured after an event and backward when measured before an event. FRCP 6(a)(5).

vi. *"Legal holiday" defined.* "Legal holiday" means:

- The day set aside by statute for observing New Year's Day, Martin Luther King Jr.'s Birthday, Washington's Birthday, Memorial Day, Independence Day, Labor Day, Columbus Day, Veterans' Day, Thanksgiving Day, or Christmas Day;

- Any day declared a holiday by the President or Congress; and

- For periods that are measured after an event, any other day declared a holiday by the state where the district court is located. FRCP 6(a)(6).

b. *Computation of electronic filing deadlines.* Filing documents electronically does not alter filing deadlines. IN R USDCTSD ECF Procedures(7). A document due on a particular day must be filed before midnight local time of the division where the case is pending. IN R USDCTSD L.R. 5-4(a). All electronic transmissions of documents must be completed (i.e. received completely by the Clerk's Office) prior to midnight of the local time of the division in which the case is pending in order to be considered timely filed that day (NOTE: time will be noted in Eastern Time on the Court's docket. If you have filed a document prior to midnight local time of the division in which the case is pending and the document is due that date, but the electronic receipt and docket reflect the following calendar day, please contact the Court). IN R USDCTSD ECF Procedures(7). Although attorneys may file documents electronically twenty-four (24) hours a day, seven (7) days a week, attorneys are encouraged to file all documents during the normal working hours of the Clerk's Office (Monday through Friday, 8:30 a.m. to 4:30 p.m.) when technical support is available. IN R USDCTSD ECF Procedures(7); IN R USDCTSD ECF Procedures(9).

i. *Technical difficulties.* Parties are encouraged to file documents electronically during normal business hours, in case a problem is encountered. In the event a technical failure occurs and a document cannot be filed electronically despite the best efforts of the filing party, the party should print (if possible) a copy of the error message received. In addition, as soon as practically possible, the party should file a "Declaration that Party was Unable to File in a Timely Manner Due to Technical Difficulties." A model form is provided as Appendix D (IN R USDCTSD ECF Procedures(Appendix D)). IN R USDCTSD ECF Procedures(16).

- If a party is unable to file electronically and, as a result, may miss a filing deadline, the party must contact the Clerk's Office at the number listed in IN R USDCTSD ECF Procedures(15) to inform the court's staff of the difficulty. If a party misses a filing deadline due to an inability to file electronically, the party may submit the untimely filed document, accompanied by a declaration stating the reason(s) for missing the deadline.

Unless the Court orders otherwise, the document and declaration must be filed no later than 12:00 noon of the first day on which the Court is open for business following the original filing deadline. IN R USDCTSD ECF Procedures(16).

   c. *Extending time*

      i. *In general.* When an act may or must be done within a specified time, the court may, for good cause, extend the time:

- With or without motion or notice if the court acts, or if a request is made, before the original time or its extension expires; or

- On motion made after the time has expired if the party failed to act because of excusable neglect. FRCP 6(b)(1).

      ii. *Exceptions.* A court must not extend the time to act under FRCP 50(b), FRCP 50(d), FRCP 52(b), FRCP 59(b), FRCP 59(d), FRCP 59(e), and FRCP 60(b). FRCP 6(b)(2).

      iii. Refer to the United States District Court for the Southern District of Indiana KeyRules Motion for Continuance/Extension of Time document for more information on extending time.

   d. *Additional time after certain kinds of service.* When a party may or must act within a specified time after being served and service is made under FRCP 5(b)(2)(C) (mail), FRCP 5(b)(2)(D) (leaving with the clerk), or FRCP 5(b)(2)(F) (other means consented to), three (3) days are added after the period would otherwise expire under FRCP 6(a). FRCP 6(d). Service by electronic mail shall constitute service pursuant to FRCP 5(b)(2)(E) and shall entitle the party being served to the additional three (3) days provided by FRCP 6(d). IN R USDCTSD ECF Procedures(11).

C. General Requirements

1. *Motions, generally*

   a. *Requirements.* A request for a court order must be made by motion. The motion must:

      i. Be in writing unless made during a hearing or trial;

      ii. State with particularity the grounds for seeking the order; and

      iii. State the relief sought. FRCP 7(b)(1).

   b. *Notice of motion.* A party interested in resisting the relief sought by a motion has a right to notice thereof, and an opportunity to be heard. AMJUR MOTIONS § 12.

      i. In addition to statutory or court rule provisions requiring notice of a motion—the purpose of such a notice requirement having been said to be to prevent a party from being prejudicially surprised by a motion—principles of natural justice dictate that an adverse party generally must be given notice that a motion will be presented to the court. AMJUR MOTIONS § 12.

      ii. "Notice," in this regard, means reasonable notice, including a meaningful opportunity to prepare and to defend against allegations of a motion. AMJUR MOTIONS § 12.

   c. *Writing requirement.* The writing requirement is intended to insure that the adverse parties are informed and have a record of both the motion's pendency and the grounds on which the movant seeks an order. FPP § 1191; Feldberg v. Quechee Lakes Corp., 463 F.3d 195 (2d Cir. 2006).

      i. It is sufficient "if the motion is stated in a written notice of the hearing of the motion." FPP § 1191.

   d. *Particularity requirement.* The particularity requirement insures that the opposing parties will have notice of their opponent's contentions. FEDPROC § 62:364; Goodman v. 1973 26 Foot Trojan Vessel, Arkansas Registration No. AR1439SN, 859 F.2d 71, 12 Fed.R.Serv.3d 645 (8th Cir. 1988). That requirement ensures that notice of the basis for the motion is provided to the court and to the opposing party so as to avoid prejudice, provide the opponent with a meaningful opportunity to respond, and provide the court with enough information to process the motion correctly. FEDPROC § 62:364; Andreas v. Volkswagen of America, Inc., 336 F.3d 789, 56 Fed.R.Serv.3d 6 (8th Cir. 2003).

      i. Reasonable specification of the grounds for a motion is sufficient. However, where a movant fails to state even one ground for granting the motion in question, the movant has failed to meet

the minimal standard of "reasonable specification." FEDPROC § 62:364; Martinez v. Trainor, 556 F.2d 818, 23 Fed.R.Serv.2d 403 (7th Cir. 1977).

    ii.   The court may excuse the failure to comply with the particularity requirement if it is inadvertent, and where no prejudice is shown by the opposing party. FEDPROC § 62:364.

   e.   *Motions must be filed separately.* Motions must be filed separately, but alternative motions may be filed in a single document if each is named in the title. A motion must not be contained within a brief, response, or reply to a previously filed motion, unless ordered by the court. IN R USDCTSD L.R. 7-1(a).

   f.   *Routine or uncontested motions.* The court may rule upon a routine or uncontested motion before the response deadline passes, unless: (1) the motion indicates that an opposing party objects to it; or (2) the court otherwise believes that a response will be filed. IN R USDCTSD L.R. 7-1(d).

2.   *Informal conference to resolve disputes involving non-dispositive issues.* In addition to those conferences required by IN R USDCTSD L.R. 37-1, counsel are encouraged to hold informal conferences in person or by phone to resolve any disputes involving non-dispositive issues that may otherwise require submission of a motion to the Court. This requirement does not apply to cases involving pro se parties. Therefore, prior to filing any non-dispositive motion (including motions for extension of time), the moving party must contact opposing counsel to determine whether there is an objection to any non-dispositive motion (including motions for extension of time), and state in the motion whether opposing counsel objects to the motion. IN R USDCTSD Case Mgt(General Instructions For All Cases). Refer to the Documents section of this document for more information on the contents of the motion.

3.   *Required actions prior to court involvement.* Prior to involving the court in any discovery dispute, including disputes involving depositions, counsel must confer in a good faith attempt to resolve the dispute. If any such dispute cannot be resolved in this manner, counsel are encouraged to contact the chambers of the assigned Magistrate Judge to determine whether the Magistrate Judge is available to resolve the discovery dispute by way of a telephone conference or other proceeding prior to counsel filing a formal discovery motion. When the dispute involves an objection raised during a deposition that threatens to prevent completion of the deposition, any party may recess the deposition to contact the Magistrate Judge's chambers. IN R USDCTSD L.R. 37-1(a). Discovery disputes involving pro se parties are not subject to IN R USDCTSD L.R. 37-1. IN R USDCTSD L.R. 37-1(c). Refer to the Documents section of this document for more information.

4.   *Motion for discovery sanctions*

   a.   *Sanctions, generally.* FRCP 37 is flexible. The court is directed to make such orders as are "just" and is not limited in any case of disregard of the discovery rules or court orders under them to a stereotyped response. The sanctions enumerated in FRCP 37 are not exclusive and arbitrary but flexible, selective, and plural. The district court may, within reason, use as many and as varied sanctions as are necessary to hold the scales of justice even. FPP § 2284.

    i.   There is one fixed limitation that should be noted. A party may not be imprisoned or otherwise punished for contempt of court for failure to submit to a physical or mental examination, or for failure to produce a person in his or her custody or under his or her control for such an examination. FPP § 2284; Sibbach v. Wilson & Co., 312 U.S. 1, 312 U.S. 655, 61 S.Ct. 422, 85 L.Ed. 479 (1941).

    ii.   Although FRCP 37 is very broad, and the courts have considerable discretion in imposing sanctions as authorized by FRCP 37, there are constitutional limits, stemming from the Due Process Clause of U.S.C.A. Const. Amend. V and U.S.C.A. Const. Amend. XIV, on the imposition of sanctions. There are two principal facets of the due process issues:

       •   First, the court must ask whether there is a sufficient relationship between the discovery and the merits sought to be foreclosed by the sanction to legitimate depriving a party of the opportunity to litigate the merits. FPP § 2283.

       •   Second, before imposing a serious merits sanction the court should determine whether the party guilty of a failure to provide discovery was unable to comply with the discovery. FPP § 2283.

b.   *Sanction for improper certification.* If a certification violates FRCP 26(g) without substantial justification, the court, on motion or on its own, must impose an appropriate sanction on the signer, the party on whose behalf the signer was acting, or both. The sanction may include an order to pay the reasonable expenses, including attorney's fees, caused by the violation. FRCP 26(g)(3).

c.   *Motion to compel discovery; Payment of expenses; Protective orders*

   i.   *If the motion is granted (or disclosure or discovery is provided after filing).* If the motion is granted—or if the disclosure or requested discovery is provided after the motion was filed—the court must, after giving an opportunity to be heard, require the party or deponent whose conduct necessitated the motion, the party or attorney advising that conduct, or both to pay the movant's reasonable expenses incurred in making the motion, including attorney's fees. But the court must not order this payment if:

   • The movant filed the motion before attempting in good faith to obtain the disclosure or discovery without court action;

   • The opposing party's nondisclosure, response, or objection was substantially justified; or

   • Other circumstances make an award of expenses unjust. FRCP 37(a)(5)(A).

   ii. *If the motion is denied.* If the motion is denied, the court may issue any protective order authorized under FRCP 26(c) and must, after giving an opportunity to be heard, require the movant, the attorney filing the motion, or both to pay the party or deponent who opposed the motion its reasonable expenses incurred in opposing the motion, including attorney's fees. But the court must not order this payment if the motion was substantially justified or other circumstances make an award of expenses unjust. FRCP 37(a)(5)(B).

   iii. *If the motion is granted in part and denied in part.* If the motion is granted in part and denied in part, the court may issue any protective order authorized under FRCP 26(c) and may, after giving an opportunity to be heard, apportion the reasonable expenses for the motion. FRCP 37(a)(5)(C).

d.   *Failure to comply with a court order*

   i.   *Sanctions in the district where the deposition is taken.* If the court where the discovery is taken orders a deponent to be sworn or to answer a question and the deponent fails to obey, the failure may be treated as contempt of court. If a deposition-related motion is transferred to the court where the action is pending, and that court orders a deponent to be sworn or to answer a question and the deponent fails to obey, the failure may be treated as contempt of either the court where the discovery is taken or the court where the action is pending. FRCP 37(b)(1).

   ii. *Sanctions in the district where the action is pending; For not obeying a discovery order.* If a party or a party's officer, director, or managing agent—or a witness designated under FRCP 30(b)(6) or FRCP 31(a)(4)—fails to obey an order to provide or permit discovery, including an order under FRCP 26(f), FRCP 35, or FRCP 37(a), the court where the action is pending may issue further just orders. They may include the following:

   • Directing that the matters embraced in the order or other designated facts be taken as established for purposes of the action, as the prevailing party claims;

   • Prohibiting the disobedient party from supporting or opposing designated claims or defenses, or from introducing designated matters in evidence;

   • Striking pleadings in whole or in part;

   • Staying further proceedings until the order is obeyed;

   • Dismissing the action or proceeding in whole or in part;

   • Rendering a default judgment against the disobedient party; or

   • Treating as contempt of court the failure to obey any order except an order to submit to a physical or mental examination. FRCP 37(b)(2)(A).

   iii. *Sanctions in the district where the action is pending; For not producing a person for examination.* If a party fails to comply with an order under FRCP 35(a) requiring it to produce another person for examination, the court may issue any of the orders listed in FRCP 37(b)(2)(A)(i) through FRCP 37(b)(2)(A)(vi), unless the disobedient party shows that it cannot produce the other person. FRCP 37(b)(2)(B).

    iv. *Sanctions in the district where the action is pending; Payment of expenses.* Instead of or in addition to the orders in FRCP 37(b)(2)(A) and FRCP 37(b)(2)(B), the court must order the disobedient party, the attorney advising that party, or both to pay the reasonable expenses, including attorney's fees, caused by the failure, unless the failure was substantially justified or other circumstances make an award of expenses unjust. FRCP 37(b)(2)(C).

e.   *Failure to disclose, to supplement an earlier response, or to admit*

    i. *Failure to disclose or supplement.* If a party fails to provide information or identify a witness as required by FRCP 26(a) or FRCP 26(e), the party is not allowed to use that information or witness to supply evidence on a motion, at a hearing, or at a trial, unless the failure was substantially justified or is harmless. In addition to or instead of this sanction, the court, on motion and after giving an opportunity to be heard:

- May order payment of the reasonable expenses, including attorney's fees, caused by the failure;

- May inform the jury of the party's failure; and

- May impose other appropriate sanctions, including any of the orders listed in FRCP 37(b)(2)(A)(i) through FRCP 37(b)(2)(A)(vi). FRCP 37(c)(1).

    ii. *Failure to admit.* If a party fails to admit what is requested under FRCP 36 and if the requesting party later proves a document to be genuine or the matter true, the requesting party may move that the party who failed to admit pay the reasonable expenses, including attorney's fees, incurred in making that proof. The court must so order unless:

- The request was held objectionable under FRCP 36(a);

- The admission sought was of no substantial importance;

- The party failing to admit had a reasonable ground to believe that it might prevail on the matter; or

- There was other good reason for the failure to admit. FRCP 37(c)(2).

f.   *Party's failure to attend its own deposition, serve answers to interrogatories, or respond to a request for inspection*

    i. *Motion; Grounds for sanctions.* The court where the action is pending may, on motion, order sanctions if:

- A party or a party's officer, director, or managing agent—or a person designated under FRCP 30(b)(6) or FRCP 31(a)(4)—fails, after being served with proper notice, to appear for that person's deposition; or

- A party, after being properly served with interrogatories under FRCP 33 or a request for inspection under FRCP 34, fails to serve its answers, objections, or written response. FRCP 37(d)(1)(A).

    ii. *Unacceptable excuse for failing to act.* A failure described in FRCP 37(d)(1)(A) is not excused on the ground that the discovery sought was objectionable, unless the party failing to act has a pending motion for a protective order under FRCP 26(c). FRCP 37(d)(2).

    iii. *Types of sanctions.* Sanctions may include any of the orders listed in FRCP 37(b)(2)(A)(i) through FRCP 37(b)(2)(A)(vi). Instead of or in addition to these sanctions, the court must require the party failing to act, the attorney advising that party, or both to pay the reasonable expenses, including attorney's fees, caused by the failure, unless the failure was substantially justified or other circumstances make an award of expenses unjust. FRCP 37(d)(3).

g.   *Failure to provide electronically stored information.* If electronically stored information that should have been preserved in the anticipation or conduct of litigation is lost because a party failed to take reasonable steps to preserve it, and it cannot be restored or replaced through additional discovery, the court:

    i. Upon finding prejudice to another party from loss of the information, may order measures no greater than necessary to cure the prejudice; or

    ii. Only upon finding that the party acted with the intent to deprive another party of the information's use in the litigation may: (1) presume that the lost information was unfavorable to the party; (2) instruct the jury that it may or must presume the information was unfavorable to the party; or (3) dismiss the action or enter a default judgment. FRCP 37(e).

  h. *Failure to participate in framing a discovery plan.* If a party or its attorney fails to participate in good faith in developing and submitting a proposed discovery plan as required by FRCP 26(f), the court may, after giving an opportunity to be heard, require that party or attorney to pay to any other party the reasonable expenses, including attorney's fees, caused by the failure. FRCP 37(f).

  i. *Counsel's liability for excessive costs.* 28 U.S.C.A. § 1927 is a basis for sanctioning attorney misconduct in discovery proceedings. DISCPROFED § 22:3. Any attorney or other person admitted to conduct cases in any court of the United States or any Territory thereof who so multiplies the proceedings in any case unreasonably and vexatiously may be required by the court to satisfy personally the excess costs, expenses, and attorneys' fees reasonably incurred because of such conduct. 28 U.S.C.A. § 1927.

5. *Opposing papers.* The Federal Rules of Civil Procedure do not require any formal answer, return, or reply to a motion, except where the Federal Rules of Civil Procedure or local rules may require affidavits, memoranda, or other papers to be filed in opposition to a motion. Such papers are simply to apprise the court of such opposition and the grounds of that opposition. FEDPROC § 62:359.

  a. *Effect of failure to respond to motion.* Although in the absence of statutory provision or court rule, a motion ordinarily does not require a written answer, when a party files a motion and the opposing party fails to respond, the court may construe such failure to respond as nonopposition to the motion or an admission that the motion was meritorious, may take the facts alleged in the motion as true—the rule in some jurisdictions being that the failure to respond to a fact set forth in a motion is deemed an admission—and may grant the motion if the relief requested appears to be justified. AMJUR MOTIONS § 28.

  b. *Assent or no opposition not determinative.* However, a motion will not be granted automatically simply because an "assent" or a notation of "no opposition" has been filed; federal judges frequently deny motions that have been assented to when it is thought that justice so dictates. FPP § 1190.

  c. *Responsive pleading inappropriate as response to motion.* An attempt to answer or oppose a motion with a responsive pleading usually is not appropriate. FPP § 1190.

6. *Reply papers.* A moving party may be required or permitted to prepare papers in addition to his original motion papers. AMJUR MOTIONS § 25. Papers answering or replying to opposing papers may be appropriate, in the interests of justice, where it appears there is a substantial reason for allowing a reply. Thus, a court may accept reply papers where a party demonstrates that the papers to which it seeks to file a reply raise new issues that are material to the disposition of the question before the court, or where the court determines, sua sponte, that it wishes further briefing of an issue raised in those papers and orders the submission of additional papers. FEDPROC § 62:360.

  a. *Function of reply papers.* The function of a reply affidavit is to answer the arguments made in opposition to the position taken by the movant and not to permit the movant to introduce new arguments in support of the motion. AMJUR MOTIONS § 25.

  b. *Issues raised for the first time in a reply document.* However, the view has been followed in some jurisdictions, that as a matter of judicial economy, where there is no prejudice and where the issues could be raised simply by filing a motion to dismiss, the trial court has discretion to consider arguments raised for the first time in a reply memorandum, and that a trial court may grant a motion to strike issues raised for the first time in a reply memorandum. AMJUR MOTIONS § 26.

7. *Appearances.* Every attorney who represents a party or who files a document on a party's behalf must file an appearance for that party. IN R USDCTSD L.R. 83-7. The filing of a Notice of Appearance shall act to

establish the filing attorney as an attorney of record representing a designated party or parties in a particular cause of action. As a result, it is necessary for each attorney to file a separate Notice of Appearance when entering an appearance in a case. A joint appearance on behalf of multiple attorneys may be filed electronically only if it is filed separately for each attorney, using his/her ECF login. IN R USDCTSD ECF Procedures(12). Only those attorneys who have filed an appearance in a pending action are entitled to be served with case documents under FRCP 5(a). IN R USDCTSD L.R. 83-7. For more information, refer to IN R USDCTSD L.R. 83-7 and IN R USDCTSD ECF Procedures(12).

8. *Notice of related action.* A party must file a notice of related action: as soon as it appears that the party's case and another pending case: (1) arise out of the same transaction or occurrence; (2) involve the same property; or (3) involve the validity or infringement or the same patent, trademark, or copyright. IN R USDCTSD L.R. 40-1(d)(2). For more information, refer to IN R USDCTSD L.R. 40-1.

9. *Alternative dispute resolution (ADR)*

    a. *Application.* Unless limited by specific provisions, or unless there are other applicable specific statutory, common law, or constitutional procedures, the Local Alternative Dispute Resolution Rules of the United States District Court for the Southern District of Indiana shall apply in all civil litigation filed in the U.S. District Court for the Southern District of Indiana, except in the following cases and proceedings:

        i.   Applications for writs of habeas corpus under 28 U.S.C.A. § 2254;

        ii. Forfeiture cases;

        iii. Non-adversary proceedings in bankruptcy;

        iv. Social Security administrative review cases; and

        v.   Such other matters as specified by order of the Court; for example, matters involving important public policy issues, constitutional law, or the establishment of new law. IN R USDCTSD A.D.R. Rule 1.2.

    b. *Mediation.* Mediation under this section (IN R USDCTSD A.D.R. Rule 2.1, et seq.) involves the confidential process by which a person acting as a Mediator, selected by the parties or appointed by the Court, assists the litigants in reaching a mutually acceptable agreement. It is an informal and nonadversarial process. The role of the Mediator is to assist in identifying the issues, reducing misunderstandings, clarifying priorities, exploring areas of compromise, and finding points of agreement as well as legitimate points of disagreement. Final decision-making authority rests with the parties, not the Mediator. IN R USDCTSD A.D.R. Rule 2.1. It is anticipated that an agreement may not resolve all of the disputed issues, but the process, nonetheless, can reduce points of contention. Parties and their representatives are required to mediate in good faith, but are not compelled to reach an agreement. IN R USDCTSD A.D.R. Rule 2.1.

        i.   *Case selection.* The Court with the agreement of the parties may refer a civil case for mediation. Unless otherwise ordered or as specifically provided in IN R USDCTSD A.D.R. Rule 2.8, referral to mediation does not abate or suspend the action, and no scheduled dates shall be delayed or deferred, including the date of trial. IN R USDCTSD A.D.R. Rule 2.2.

        ii. For more information on mediation, refer to IN R USDCTSD A.D.R. Rule 2.1, et seq.

    c. *Other methods of dispute resolution.* The Local Alternative Dispute Resolution Rules of the United States District Court for the Southern District of Indiana shall not preclude the parties from utilizing any other reasonable method or technique of alternative dispute resolution to resolve disputes to which the parties agree. However, any use of arbitration by the parties will be governed by and comply with the requirements of 28 U.S.C.A. § 654 through 28 U.S.C.A. § 657. IN R USDCTSD A.D.R. Rule 1.5.

    d. For more information on alternative dispute resolution (ADR), refer to IN R USDCTSD A.D.R. Rule 1.1, et seq.

10. *Notice of settlement or resolution.* The parties must immediately notify the court if they reasonably anticipate settling their case or resolving a pending motion. IN R USDCTSD L.R. 7-1(h).

11. *Modification or suspension of rules.* The court may, on its own motion or at the request of a party, suspend or modify any rule in a particular case in the interest of justice. IN R USDCTSD L.R. 1-1(c).

D. Documents

1. *Documents for moving party*

   a. *Required documents*

      i. *Notice of motion and motion.* [P]rior to filing any non-dispositive motion (including motions for extension of time), the moving party must contact opposing counsel to determine whether there is an objection to any non-dispositive motion (including motions for extension of time), and state in the motion whether opposing counsel objects to the motion. If an objection cannot be resolved by counsel, the opposing counsel's position shall be stated within the motion. The motion should also indicate whether opposing counsel plans to file a written objection to the motion and the date by which the Court can expect to receive the objection (within the time limits set in IN R USDCTSD L.R. 7-1). If after a reasonable effort, opposing counsel cannot be reached, the moving party shall recite in the motion the dates and times that messages were left for opposing counsel. IN R USDCTSD Case Mgt(General Instructions For All Cases). Refer to the General Requirements section of this document for information on the notice of motion and motion.

      ii. *Certificate of compliance.* In the event that the discovery dispute is not resolved at the conference, counsel may file a motion to compel or other motion raising the dispute. Any motion raising a discovery dispute must contain a statement setting forth the efforts taken to resolve the dispute, including the date, time, and place of any discovery conference and the names of all participating parties. The court may deny any motion raising a discovery dispute that does not contain such a statement. IN R USDCTSD L.R. 37-1(b). Discovery disputes involving pro se parties are not subject to IN R USDCTSD L.R. 37-1. IN R USDCTSD L.R. 37-1(c). A motion for sanctions for failing to answer or respond must include a certification that the movant has in good faith conferred or attempted to confer with the party failing to act in an effort to obtain the answer or response without court action. FRCP 37(d)(1)(B).

      iii. *Brief.* The following motion must also be accompanied by a supporting brief: any motion made under FRCP 37. IN R USDCTSD L.R. 7-1(b)(2). Refer to the Format section of this document for the format of briefs.

      iv. *Discovery materials.* A party seeking relief under FRCP 26(c) or FRCP 37, or by way of a pretrial motion that could result in a final order on an issue, must file with the motion those parts of the discovery materials relevant to the motion. IN R USDCTSD L.R. 26-2(a).

      v. *Certificate of service.* FRCP 5(d) requires that the person making service under FRCP 5 certify that service has been effected. FRCP 5(Advisory Committee Notes). Having such information on file may be useful for many purposes, including proof of service if an issue arises concerning the effectiveness of the service. FRCP 5(Advisory Committee Notes).

         - *Certificate of service for electronically-filed documents.* A certificate of service must be included with all documents filed electronically. Such certificate shall indicate that service was accomplished pursuant to the Court's electronic filing procedures. IN R USDCTSD ECF Procedures(11). For the suggested format for a certificate of service for electronic filing, refer to IN R USDCTSD ECF Procedures(11).

   b. *Supplemental documents*

      i. *Supporting evidence.* When a motion relies on facts outside the record, the court may hear the matter on affidavits or may hear it wholly or partly on oral testimony or on depositions. FRCP 43(c).

         - *Materials necessary for motion.* A party seeking relief under FRCP 26(c) or FRCP 37, or by way of a pretrial motion that could result in a final order on an issue, must file with the motion those parts of the discovery materials relevant to the motion. IN R USDCTSD L.R. 26-2(a).

      ii. *Notice of constitutional question.* A party that files a pleading, written motion, or other paper drawing into question the constitutionality of a federal or state statute must promptly:

         - *File notice.* File a notice of constitutional question stating the question and identifying the

paper that raises it, if: (1) a federal statute is questioned and the parties do not include the United States, one of its agencies, or one of its officers or employees in an official capacity; or (2) a state statute is questioned and the parties do not include the state, one of its agencies, or one of its officers or employees in an official capacity; and

- *Serve notice.* Serve the notice and paper on the Attorney General of the United States if a federal statute is questioned—or on the state attorney general if a state statute is questioned—either by certified or registered mail or by sending it to an electronic address designated by the attorney general for this purpose. FRCP 5.1(a).

- *Time for filing.* A notice of constitutional challenge to a statute filed in accordance with FRCP 5.1 must be filed at the same time the parties tender their proposed case management plan, if one is required, or within twenty-one (21) days of the filing drawing into question the constitutionality of a federal or state statute, whichever occurs later. IN R USDCTSD L.R. 5.1-1(a).

- *Additional service requirements.* If a federal statute is challenged, in addition to the service requirements of FRCP 5.1(a), the party filing the notice of constitutional challenge must serve the notice and documents on the United States Attorney for the Southern District of Indiana, either by certified or registered mail or by sending it to an electronic address designated for that purpose by that official. IN R USDCTSD L.R. 5.1-1(b).

- *No forfeiture.* A party's failure to file and serve the notice, or the court's failure to certify, does not forfeit a constitutional claim or defense that is otherwise timely asserted. FRCP 5.1(d).

iii. *Index of exhibits.* Any pleading, motion, brief, affidavit, notice, or proposed order filed with the court, whether electronically or with the clerk, must: if it has four (4) or more exhibits, include a separate index that identifies and briefly describes each exhibit. IN R USDCTSD L.R. 5-1(b).

iv. *Request for oral argument.* A party may request oral argument by filing a separate motion explaining why oral argument is necessary and estimating how long the court should allow for the argument. The request must be filed and served with the supporting brief, response brief, or reply brief. IN R USDCTSD L.R. 7-5(a).

v. *Request for evidentiary hearing.* A party may request an evidentiary hearing on a motion or petition by serving and filing a separate motion explaining why the hearing is necessary and estimating how long the court should allow for the hearing. IN R USDCTSD L.R. 7-5(c).

vi. *Copy of authority.* Generally, copies of cited authorities may not be attached to court filings. However, a party must attach to the party's motion or brief a copy of any cited authority if it is not available on Westlaw or Lexis. Upon request, a party must provide copies of any cited authority that is only available through electronic means to the court or the other parties. IN R USDCTSD L.R. 7-1(f).

vii. *Proposed order.* A party must include a suitable form of order with any document that requests the judge or the clerk to enter a routine or uncontested order. IN R USDCTSD L.R. 5-5(b); IN R USDCTSD L.R. 5-10(c); IN R USDCTSD L.R. 7-1(d).

- A service statement and/or list must be included on each proposed order, as required by IN R USDCTSD L.R. 5-5(d). IN R USDCTSD ECF Procedures(11). Any pleading, motion, brief, affidavit, notice, or proposed order filed with the court, whether electronically or with the clerk, must: if it is a form of order, include a statement of service, in the format required by IN R USDCTSD L.R. 5-5(d) in the lower left corner of the document. IN R USDCTSD L.R. 5-1(b).

- A party electronically filing a proposed order—whether voluntarily or because required by IN R USDCTSD L.R. 5-5—must convert the order directly from a word processing program and file it as an attachment to the document it relates to. Proposed orders must include in the lower left-hand corner of the signature page a statement that service will be made electronically on all ECF-registered counsel of record via email generated by the court's ECF system, without listing all such counsel. A service list including the name and postal address of any pro se litigant or non-registered attorney of record must follow, stating that service on the listed individuals will be made in the traditional paper manner, via first-class U.S. Mail. IN R USDCTSD L.R. 5-5(d).

viii. *Copy of document with self-address envelope.* To receive a file-stamped copy of a document filed directly with the clerk, a party must include with the original document an additional copy and a self-addressed envelope. The envelope must be big enough to hold the copy and have enough postage on it to send the copy via regular first-class mail. IN R USDCTSD L.R. 5-10(b).

ix. *Notice of manual filing.* When a party who is not exempt from the electronic filing requirement files a document directly with the clerk, the party must: electronically file a notice of manual filing that explains why the document cannot be filed electronically. IN R USDCTSD L.R. 5-2(d)(1). Refer to the Filing and Service Requirements section of this document for more information.

- Where an individual component cannot be included in an electronic filing (e.g. the component cannot be converted to electronic format), the filer shall electronically file the prescribed Notice of Manual Filing in place of that component. A model form is provided as Appendix C (IN R USDCTSD ECF Procedures(Appendix C)). IN R USDCTSD ECF Procedures(13).

- Before making a manual filing of a component, the filing party shall first electronically file a Notice of Manual Filing (See IN R USDCTSD ECF Procedures(Appendix C)). The filer shall initiate the electronic filing process as if filing the actual component but shall instead attach to the filing the Notice of Manual Filing setting forth the reason(s) why the component cannot be filed electronically. The manual filing should be accompanied by a copy of the previously filed Notice of Manual Filing. A party may seek to have a component excluded from electronic filing pursuant to applicable Federal and Local Rules (e.g., FRCP 26(c)). IN R USDCTSD ECF Procedures(15).

x. *Courtesy copies.* District Judges and Magistrate Judges regularly receive documents filed by all parties. Therefore, parties shall not bring "courtesy copies" to any chambers unless specifically directed to do so by the Court. IN R USDCTSD Case Mgt(General Instructions For All Cases).

xi. *Copies for three-judge court.* Parties in a case where a three-judge court has been requested must file an original and three copies of any document filed directly with the clerk (instead of electronically) until the court: (1) denies the request; (2) dissolves the three-judge court; or (3) allows the parties to file fewer copies. IN R USDCTSD L.R. 9-2(c).

xii. *Declaration that party was unable to file in a timely manner due to technical difficulties.* If a party misses a filing deadline due to an inability to file electronically, the party may submit the untimely filed document, accompanied by a declaration stating the reason(s) for missing the deadline. IN R USDCTSD ECF Procedures(16). A model form is provided as Appendix D (IN R USDCTSD ECF Procedures(Appendix D)). IN R USDCTSD ECF Procedures(16).

2. *Documents for opposing party*

a. *Required documents*

i. *Response brief.* Refer to the Format section of this document for the format of briefs. Refer to the General Requirements section of this document for information on the opposing papers.

ii. *Certificate of service.* FRCP 5(d) requires that the person making service under FRCP 5 certify that service has been effected. FRCP 5(Advisory Committee Notes). Having such information on file may be useful for many purposes, including proof of service if an issue arises concerning the effectiveness of the service. FRCP 5(Advisory Committee Notes).

- *Certificate of service for electronically-filed documents.* A certificate of service must be included with all documents filed electronically. Such certificate shall indicate that service was accomplished pursuant to the Court's electronic filing procedures. IN R USDCTSD ECF Procedures(11). For the suggested format for a certificate of service for electronic filing, refer to IN R USDCTSD ECF Procedures(11).

b. *Supplemental documents*

    i. *Supporting evidence.* When a motion relies on facts outside the record, the court may hear the matter on affidavits or may hear it wholly or partly on oral testimony or on depositions. FRCP 43(c).

        • *Materials necessary for motion.* A party seeking relief under FRCP 26(c) or FRCP 37, or by way of a pretrial motion that could result in a final order on an issue, must file with the motion those parts of the discovery materials relevant to the motion. IN R USDCTSD L.R. 26-2(a).

    ii. *Notice of constitutional question.* A party that files a pleading, written motion, or other paper drawing into question the constitutionality of a federal or state statute must promptly:

        • *File notice.* File a notice of constitutional question stating the question and identifying the paper that raises it, if: (1) a federal statute is questioned and the parties do not include the United States, one of its agencies, or one of its officers or employees in an official capacity; or (2) a state statute is questioned and the parties do not include the state, one of its agencies, or one of its officers or employees in an official capacity; and

        • *Serve notice.* Serve the notice and paper on the Attorney General of the United States if a federal statute is questioned—or on the state attorney general if a state statute is questioned—either by certified or registered mail or by sending it to an electronic address designated by the attorney general for this purpose. FRCP 5.1(a).

        • *Time for filing.* A notice of constitutional challenge to a statute filed in accordance with FRCP 5.1 must be filed at the same time the parties tender their proposed case management plan, if one is required, or within twenty-one (21) days of the filing drawing into question the constitutionality of a federal or state statute, whichever occurs later. IN R USDCTSD L.R. 5.1-1(a).

        • *Additional service requirements.* If a federal statute is challenged, in addition to the service requirements of FRCP 5.1(a), the party filing the notice of constitutional challenge must serve the notice and documents on the United States Attorney for the Southern District of Indiana, either by certified or registered mail or by sending it to an electronic address designated for that purpose by that official. IN R USDCTSD L.R. 5.1-1(b).

        • *No forfeiture.* A party's failure to file and serve the notice, or the court's failure to certify, does not forfeit a constitutional claim or defense that is otherwise timely asserted. FRCP 5.1(d).

    iii. *Index of exhibits.* Any pleading, motion, brief, affidavit, notice, or proposed order filed with the court, whether electronically or with the clerk, must: if it has four (4) or more exhibits, include a separate index that identifies and briefly describes each exhibit. IN R USDCTSD L.R. 5-1(b).

    iv. *Request for oral argument.* A party may request oral argument by filing a separate motion explaining why oral argument is necessary and estimating how long the court should allow for the argument. The request must be filed and served with the supporting brief, response brief, or reply brief. IN R USDCTSD L.R. 7-5(a).

    v. *Request for evidentiary hearing.* A party may request an evidentiary hearing on a motion or petition by serving and filing a separate motion explaining why the hearing is necessary and estimating how long the court should allow for the hearing. IN R USDCTSD L.R. 7-5(c).

    vi. *Copy of authority.* Generally, copies of cited authorities may not be attached to court filings. However, a party must attach to the party's motion or brief a copy of any cited authority if it is not available on Westlaw or Lexis. Upon request, a party must provide copies of any cited authority that is only available through electronic means to the court or the other parties. IN R USDCTSD L.R. 7-1(f).

    vii. *Copy of document with self-address envelope.* To receive a file-stamped copy of a document filed directly with the clerk, a party must include with the original document an additional copy and a self-addressed envelope. The envelope must be big enough to hold the copy and have enough postage on it to send the copy via regular first-class mail. IN R USDCTSD L.R. 5-10(b).

viii. *Notice of manual filing.* When a party who is not exempt from the electronic filing requirement files a document directly with the clerk, the party must: electronically file a notice of manual filing that explains why the document cannot be filed electronically. IN R USDCTSD L.R. 5-2(d)(1). Refer to the Filing and Service Requirements section of this document for more information.

- Where an individual component cannot be included in an electronic filing (e.g. the component cannot be converted to electronic format), the filer shall electronically file the prescribed Notice of Manual Filing in place of that component. A model form is provided as Appendix C (IN R USDCTSD ECF Procedures(Appendix C)). IN R USDCTSD ECF Procedures(13).

- Before making a manual filing of a component, the filing party shall first electronically file a Notice of Manual Filing (See IN R USDCTSD ECF Procedures(Appendix C)). The filer shall initiate the electronic filing process as if filing the actual component but shall instead attach to the filing the Notice of Manual Filing setting forth the reason(s) why the component cannot be filed electronically. The manual filing should be accompanied by a copy of the previously filed Notice of Manual Filing. A party may seek to have a component excluded from electronic filing pursuant to applicable Federal and Local Rules (e.g., FRCP 26(c)). IN R USDCTSD ECF Procedures(15).

ix. *Courtesy copies.* District Judges and Magistrate Judges regularly receive documents filed by all parties. Therefore, parties shall not bring "courtesy copies" to any chambers unless specifically directed to do so by the Court. IN R USDCTSD Case Mgt(General Instructions For All Cases).

x. *Copies for three-judge court.* Parties in a case where a three-judge court has been requested must file an original and three copies of any document filed directly with the clerk (instead of electronically) until the court: (1) denies the request; (2) dissolves the three-judge court; or (3) allows the parties to file fewer copies. IN R USDCTSD L.R. 9-2(c).

xi. *Declaration that party was unable to file in a timely manner due to technical difficulties.* If a party misses a filing deadline due to an inability to file electronically, the party may submit the untimely filed document, accompanied by a declaration stating the reason(s) for missing the deadline. IN R USDCTSD ECF Procedures(16). A model form is provided as Appendix D (IN R USDCTSD ECF Procedures(Appendix D)). IN R USDCTSD ECF Procedures(16).

E. Format

1. *Form of documents.* The rules governing captions and other matters of form in pleadings apply to motions and other papers. FRCP 7(b)(2).

   a. *Paper (manual filings only).* Any document that is not filed electronically must: be flat, unfolded, and on good-quality, eight and one-half by eleven (8-1/2 x 11) inch white paper. IN R USDCTSD L.R. 5-1(d)(1). Any document that is not filed electronically must: be single-sided. IN R USDCTSD L.R. 5-1(d)(1).

      i. *Covers or backing.* Any document that is not filed electronically must: not have a cover or a back. IN R USDCTSD L.R. 5-1(d)(1).

      ii. *Fastening.* Any document that is not filed electronically must: be (if consisting of more than one (1) page) fastened by paperclip or binder clip and may not be stapled. IN R USDCTSD L.R. 5-1(d)(1).

         - *Request for nonconforming fastening.* If a document cannot be fastened or bound as required by IN R USDCTSD L.R. 5-1(d), a party may ask the clerk for permission to fasten it in another manner. The party must make such a request before attempting to file the document with nonconforming fastening. IN R USDCTSD L.R. 5-1(d)(2).

      iii. *Hole punching.* Any document that is not filed electronically must: be two-hole punched at the top with the holes two and three-quarter (2-3/4) inches apart and appropriately centered. IN R USDCTSD L.R. 5-1(d)(1).

   b. *Margins.* Any pleading, motion, brief, affidavit, notice, or proposed order filed with the court, whether electronically or with the clerk, must: have at least one (1) inch margins. IN R USDCTSD L.R. 5-1(b).

c. *Spacing.* Any pleading, motion, brief, affidavit, notice, or proposed order filed with the court, whether electronically or with the clerk, must: be double spaced (except for headings, footnotes, and quoted material). IN R USDCTSD L.R. 5-1(b).

d. *Text.* Any pleading, motion, brief, affidavit, notice, or proposed order filed with the court, whether electronically or with the clerk, must: be plainly typewritten, printed, or prepared by a clearly legible copying process. IN R USDCTSD L.R. 5-1(b).

e. *Font size.* Any pleading, motion, brief, affidavit, notice, or proposed order filed with the court, whether electronically or with the clerk, must: use at least 12-point type in the body of the document and at least 10-point type in footnotes. IN R USDCTSD L.R. 5-1(b).

f. *Page numbering.* Any pleading, motion, brief, affidavit, notice, or proposed order filed with the court, whether electronically or with the clerk, must: have consecutively numbered pages. IN R USDCTSD L.R. 5-1(b).

g. *Caption; Names of parties.* Every pleading must have a caption with the court's name, a title, a file number, and a FRCP 7(a) designation. The title of the complaint must name all the parties; the title of other pleadings, after naming the first party on each side, may refer generally to other parties. FRCP 10(a). Any pleading, motion, brief, affidavit, notice, or proposed order filed with the court, whether electronically or with the clerk, must: include a title on the first page. IN R USDCTSD L.R. 5-1(b).

   i. *Alternative motions.* Motions must be filed separately, but alternative motions may be filed in a single document if each is named in the title. IN R USDCTSD L.R. 7-1(a).

h. *Filer's information.* Any pleading, motion, brief, affidavit, notice, or proposed order filed with the court, whether electronically or with the clerk, must: in the case of pleadings, motions, legal briefs, and notices, include the name, complete address, telephone number, facsimile number (where available), and e-mail address (where available) of the pro se litigant or attorney who files it. IN R USDCTSD L.R. 5-1(b).

i. *Paragraphs; Separate statements.* A party must state its claims or defenses in numbered paragraphs, each limited as far as practicable to a single set of circumstances. A later pleading may refer by number to a paragraph in an earlier pleading. If doing so would promote clarity, each claim founded on a separate transaction or occurrence—and each defense other than a denial—must be stated in a separate count or defense. FRCP 10(b).

j. *Adoption by reference; Exhibits.* A statement in a pleading may be adopted by reference elsewhere in the same pleading or in any other pleading or motion. A copy of a written instrument that is an exhibit to a pleading is a part of the pleading for all purposes. FRCP 10(c).

k. *Citations*

   i. *Local rules.* The Local Rules of the United States District Court for the Southern District of Indiana may be cited as "S.D. Ind. L.R." IN R USDCTSD L.R. 1-1(a).

   ii. *Local alternative dispute resolution rules.* These Rules shall be known as the Local Alternative Dispute Resolution Rules of the United States District Court for the Southern District of Indiana. They shall be cited as "S.D.Ind. Local A.D.R. Rule _____." IN R USDCTSD A.D.R. Rule 1.1.

l. *Acceptance by the clerk.* The clerk must not refuse to file a paper solely because it is not in the form prescribed by the Federal Rules of Civil Procedure or by a local rule or practice. FRCP 5(d)(4). The clerk will accept a document that violates IN R USDCTSD L.R. 5-1, but the court may exclude the document from the official record. IN R USDCTSD L.R. 5-1(e).

   i. *Sanctions for errors as to form.* The court may strike from the record any document that does not comply with the rules governing the form of documents filed with the court, such as rules that regulate document size or the number of copies to be filed or that require a special designation in the caption. The court may also sanction an attorney or party who files a non-compliant document. IN R USDCTSD L.R. 1-3.

2. *Form of electronic documents.* Any document submitted via the court's electronic case filing (ECF) system must be: otherwise prepared and filed in a manner consistent with the CM/ECF Policies and Procedures Manual (IN R USDCTSD ECF Procedures). IN R USDCTSD L.R. 5-1(c). Electronically filed documents must meet the requirements of FRCP 10 (Form of Pleadings), IN R USDCTSD L.R. 5-1 (Format of Papers Presented for Filing), and FRCP 5.2 (Privacy Protection for Filings Made with the Court), as if they had been submitted on paper. Documents filed electronically are also subject to any page limitations set forth by Court Order, by IN R USDCTSD L.R. 7-1 (Motion Practice), or IN R USDCTSD L.R. 56-1 (Summary Judgment Practice), as applicable. IN R USDCTSD ECF Procedures(13).

    a. *PDF format required.* Any document submitted via the court's electronic case filing (ECF) system must be: in .pdf format. IN R USDCTSD L.R. 5-1(c); IN R USDCTSD ECF Procedures(7). Any document submitted via the court's electronic case filing (ECF) system must be: converted to a .pdf file directly from a word processing program, unless it exists only in paper format (in which case it may be scanned to create a .pdf document). IN R USDCTSD L.R. 5-1(c); IN R USDCTSD ECF Procedures(13).

        i. An exhibit may be scanned into PDF format, at a recommended 300 dpi resolution or higher, only if it does not already exist in electronic format. The filing attorney is responsible for reviewing all PDF documents for legibility before submitting them through the Court's Electronic Case Filing system. For technical guidance in creating PDF documents, please contact the Clerk's Office. IN R USDCTSD ECF Procedures(13).

    b. *File size limitations.* Any document submitted via the court's electronic case filing (ECF) system must be: submitted as one or more .pdf files that do not exceed ten megabytes (10 MB) each (consistent with the CM/ECF Policies and Procedures Manual (IN R USDCTSD ECF Procedures)). IN R USDCTSD L.R. 5-1(c); IN R USDCTSD ECF Procedures(13).

        i. To electronically file a document or attachment that exceeds ten megabytes (10 MB), the document must first be broken down into two or more smaller files. For example, if Exhibit A is a twelve megabyte (12 MB) PDF file, it should be divided into 2 equal parts prior to electronic filing. Each component part of the exhibit would be filed as an attachment to the main document and described appropriately as "Exhibit A (part 1 of 2)" and "Exhibit A (part 2 of 2)." IN R USDCTSD ECF Procedures(13).

        ii. The supporting items mentioned in IN R USDCTSD ECF Procedures(13) should not be confused with memorandums or briefs in support of motions as outlined in IN R USDCTSD L.R. 7-1 or IN R USDCTSD L.R. 56-1. These memorandums or briefs in support are to be filed as entirely separate documents pursuant to the appropriate rule. Additionally, no motion shall be embodied in the text of a response or reply brief/memorandum unless otherwise ordered by the Court. IN R USDCTSD ECF Procedures(13).

    c. *Separate component parts.* A key objective of the electronic filing system is to ensure that as much of the case as possible is managed electronically. To facilitate electronic filing and retrieval, documents to be filed electronically are to be reasonably broken into their separate component parts. By way of example, most filings include a foundation document (e.g., motion) and other supporting items (e.g., exhibits, proposed orders, proposed amended pleadings). The foundation document, as well as the supporting items, are each separate components of the filing; supporting items must be filed as attachments to the foundation document. These exhibits or attachments should include only those excerpts of the referenced documents that are directly germane to the matter under consideration. IN R USDCTSD ECF Procedures(13).

        i. Where an individual component cannot be included in an electronic filing (e.g. the component cannot be converted to electronic format), the filer shall electronically file the prescribed Notice of Manual Filing in place of that component. A model form is provided as Appendix C (IN R USDCTSD ECF Procedures(Appendix C)). IN R USDCTSD ECF Procedures(13).

    d. *Exhibits.* Each electronically filed exhibit to a main document must be: (1) created as a separate .pdf file; (2) submitted as an attachment to the main document and given a title which describes its content; and (3) limited to excerpts that are directly germane to the main document's subject matter. IN R USDCTSD L.R. 5-6(a).

        i. When uploading attachments during the electronic filing process, exhibits must be uploaded in

a logical sequence and a brief description must be entered for each individual PDF file. The description must include not only the exhibit number or letter, but also a brief description of the document. This information may be entered in CM/ECF using a combination of the Category drop-down menu, the Description text box, or both (see IN R USDCTSD ECF Procedures(13)(Figure 1)). The information that is provided in each box will be combined to create a description of the document as it appears on the case docket (see IN R USDCTSD ECF Procedures(13)(Figure 2)). IN R USDCTSD ECF Procedures(13). For an example, refer to IN R USDCTSD ECF Procedures(13).

e. *Excerpts.* A party filing an exhibit that consists of excerpts from a larger document must clearly and prominently identify the exhibit as containing excerpted material. Either party will have the right to timely file additional excerpts or the complete document to the extent they are or become directly germane to the main document's subject matter. IN R USDCTSD L.R. 5-6(b).

f. For an example illustrating the application of IN R USDCTSD ECF Procedures(13), refer to IN R USDCTSD ECF Procedures(13).

3. *Form of briefs*

a. *Page limits.* Supporting and response briefs (excluding tables of contents, tables of authorities, appendices, and certificates of service) may not exceed thirty-five (35) pages. Reply briefs may not exceed twenty (20) pages. IN R USDCTSD L.R. 7-1(e)(1).

   i. *Permission to exceed limits.* The court may allow a party to file a brief exceeding these page limits for extraordinary and compelling reasons. IN R USDCTSD L.R. 7-1(e)(2).

   ii. *Supporting and response briefs exceeding limits.* If the court allows a party to file a brief or response exceeding thirty-five (35) pages, the document must include:

- A table of contents with page references;
- A statement of issues; and
- A table of authorities including: (1) all cases (alphabetically arranged), statutes, and other authorities cited in the brief; and (2) page numbers where the authorities are cited in the brief. IN R USDCTSD L.R. 7-1(e)(3).

4. *Signing disclosures and discovery requests, responses, and objections.* FRCP 11 does not apply to disclosures and discovery requests, responses, objections, and motions under FRCP 26 through FRCP 37. FRCP 11(d).

a. *Signature required.* Every disclosure under FRCP 26(a)(1) or FRCP 26(a)(3) and every discovery request, response, or objection must be signed by at least one attorney of record in the attorney's own name—or by the party personally, if unrepresented—and must state the signer's address, e-mail address, and telephone number. FRCP 26(g)(1).

   i. *Signatures on manual filings.* Any document that is not filed electronically must: include the original signature of the pro se litigant or attorney who files it. IN R USDCTSD L.R. 5-1(d)(1).

   ii. *Electronic signatures.* Use of the attorney's login and password when filing documents electronically serves in part as the attorney's signature for purposes of FRCP 11, the Local Rules of the United States District Court for the Southern District of Indiana, and any other purpose for which a signature is required in connection with proceedings before the Court. IN R USDCTSD ECF Procedures(14); IN R USDCTSD ECF Procedures(10). A pleading, motion, brief, or notice filed electronically under an attorney's ECF log-in and password must be signed by that attorney. IN R USDCTSD L.R. 5-7(a). A signature on a document other than a document filed as provided under IN R USDCTSD L.R. 5-7(a) must be an original handwritten signature and must be scanned into .pdf format for electronic filing. IN R USDCTSD L.R. 5-7(c); IN R USDCTSD ECF Procedures(14).

- *Form of electronic signature.* If a document is converted directly from a word processing application to .pdf (as opposed to scanning), the name of the Filing User under whose log-in and password the document is submitted must be preceded by a "s/" and typed on the signature line where the Filing User's handwritten signature would otherwise appear.

IN R USDCTSD L.R. 5-7(b). All documents filed electronically shall include a signature block and include the filing attorney's typewritten name, address, telephone number, facsimile number and e-mail address. In addition, the name of the filing attorney under whose ECF login the document will be filed should be preceded by a "s/" and typed in the space where the attorney's handwritten signature would otherwise appear. IN R US-DCTSD ECF Procedures(14). For a sample format, refer to IN R USDCTSD ECF Procedures(14).

- *Effect of electronic signature.* Filing an electronically signed document under an attorney's ECF log-in and password constitutes the attorney's signature on the document under the Federal Rules of Civil Procedure, under the Local Rules of the United States District Court for the Southern District of Indiana, and for any other reason a signature is required in connection with the court's activities. IN R USDCTSD L.R. 5-7(d).

- *Documents with multiple attorneys' signatures.* Documents requiring signatures of more than one attorney shall be filed either by: (1) obtaining consent from the other attorney, then typing the "s/ [Name]" signature of the other attorney on the signature line where the other attorney's signature would otherwise appear; (2) identifying in the signature section the name of the other attorney whose signature is required and by the submission of a Notice of Endorsement (see IN R USDCTSD ECF Procedures(Appendix B)) by the other attorney no later than three (3) business days after filing; (3) submitting a scanned document containing all handwritten signatures; or (4) in any other manner approved by the Court. IN R USDCTSD ECF Procedures(14); IN R USDCTSD L.R. 5-7(e).

b. *Effect of signature.* By signing, an attorney or party certifies that to the best of the person's knowledge, information, and belief formed after a reasonable inquiry:

   i. With respect to a disclosure, it is complete and correct as of the time it is made; and

   ii. With respect to a discovery request, response, or objection, it is:

- Consistent with the Federal Rules of Civil Procedure and warranted by existing law or by a nonfrivolous argument for extending, modifying, or reversing existing law, or for establishing new law;

- Not interposed for any improper purpose, such as to harass, cause unnecessary delay, or needlessly increase the cost of litigation; and

- Neither unreasonable nor unduly burdensome or expensive, considering the needs of the case, prior discovery in the case, the amount in controversy, and the importance of the issues at stake in the action. FRCP 26(g)(1).

c. *Failure to sign.* Other parties have no duty to act on an unsigned disclosure, request, response, or objection until it is signed, and the court must strike it unless a signature is promptly supplied after the omission is called to the attorney's or party's attention. FRCP 26(g)(2). The court will strike any document filed directly with the clerk that is not signed by an attorney of record or the pro se litigant filing it, but the court may do so only after giving the attorney or pro se litigant notice of the omission and reasonable time to correct it. Rubber-stamp or facsimile signatures are not original signatures and the court will deem documents containing them to be unsigned for purposes of FRCP 11 and FRCP 26(g) and IN R USDCTSD L.R. 5-10. IN R USDCTSD L.R. 5-10(g).

d. *Sanction for improper certification.* Refer to the General Requirements section of this document for information on the sanction for improper certification.

5. *Privacy protection for filings made with the court.* Electronically filed documents must meet the requirements of. . .FRCP 5.2 (Privacy Protection for Filings Made with the Court), as if they had been submitted on paper. IN R USDCTSD ECF Procedures(13).

  a. *Redacted filings.* Unless the court orders otherwise, in an electronic or paper filing with the court that contains an individual's Social Security number, taxpayer-identification number, or birth date, the name of an individual known to be a minor, or a financial-account number, a party or nonparty making the filing may include only:

   i. The last four (4) digits of the Social Security number and taxpayer-identification number;

    ii.   The year of the individual's birth;

    iii.   The minor's initials; and

    iv.   The last four (4) digits of the financial-account number. FRCP 5.2(a).

  b. *Exemptions from the redaction requirement.* The redaction requirement does not apply to the following:

    i.   A financial-account number that identifies the property allegedly subject to forfeiture in a forfeiture proceeding;

    ii.   The record of an administrative or agency proceeding;

    iii.   The official record of a state-court proceeding;

    iv.   The record of a court or tribunal, if that record was not subject to the redaction requirement when originally filed;

    v.   A filing covered by FRCP 5.2(c) or FRCP 5.2(d); and

    vi.   A pro se filing in an action brought under 28 U.S.C.A. § 2241, 28 U.S.C.A. § 2254, or 28 U.S.C.A. § 2255. FRCP 5.2(b).

  c. *Limitations on remote access to electronic files; Social Security appeals and immigration cases.* Unless the court orders otherwise, in an action for benefits under the Social Security Act, and in an action or proceeding relating to an order of removal, to relief from removal, or to immigration benefits or detention, access to an electronic file is authorized as follows:

    i.   The parties and their attorneys may have remote electronic access to any part of the case file, including the administrative record;

    ii.   Any other person may have electronic access to the full record at the courthouse, but may have remote electronic access only to:

        • The docket maintained by the court; and

        • An opinion, order, judgment, or other disposition of the court, but not any other part of the case file or the administrative record. FRCP 5.2(c).

  d. *Filings made under seal.* The court may order that a filing be made under seal without redaction. The court may later unseal the filing or order the person who made the filing to file a redacted version for the public record. FRCP 5.2(d). For more information on filing under seal, refer to IN R USDCTSD L.R. 5-11 and IN R USDCTSD ECF Procedures(18).

  e. *Protective orders.* For good cause, the court may by order in a case:

    i.   Require redaction of additional information; or

    ii.   Limit or prohibit a nonparty's remote electronic access to a document filed with the court. FRCP 5.2(e).

  f. *Option for additional unredacted filing under seal.* A person making a redacted filing may also file an unredacted copy under seal. The court must retain the unredacted copy as part of the record. FRCP 5.2(f).

  g. *Option for filing a reference list.* A filing that contains redacted information may be filed together with a reference list that identifies each item of redacted information and specifies an appropriate identifier that uniquely corresponds to each item listed. The list must be filed under seal and may be amended as of right. Any reference in the case to a listed identifier will be construed to refer to the corresponding item of information. FRCP 5.2(g).

  h. *Waiver of protection of identifiers.* A person waives the protection of FRCP 5.2(a) as to the person's own information by filing it without redaction and not under seal. FRCP 5.2(h).

F. Filing and Service Requirements

  1. *Filing requirements.* Any paper after the complaint that is required to be served—together with a certificate of service—must be filed within a reasonable time after service. FRCP 5(d)(1). Motions must

be filed separately, but alternative motions may be filed in a single document if each is named in the title. IN R USDCTSD L.R. 7-1(a).

a. *How filing is made; In general.* A paper is filed by delivering it:

   i. To the clerk; or

   ii. To a judge who agrees to accept it for filing, and who must then note the filing date on the paper and promptly send it to the clerk. FRCP 5(d)(2).

- In certain instances, the court will direct the parties to submit items directly to chambers (e.g., confidential settlement statements). However, absent specific prior authorization, counsel and litigants should not submit letters or documents directly to chambers, and such materials should be filed with the clerk. IN R USDCTSD L.R. 5-1(Local Rules Advisory Committee Comment).

   iii. A document or item submitted in relation to a matter within the court's jurisdiction is deemed filed upon delivery to the office of the clerk in a manner prescribed by the Local Rules of the United States District Court for the Southern District of Indiana or the Federal Rules of Civil Procedure or authorized by the court. Any submission directed to a Judge or Judge's staff, the office of the clerk or any employee thereof, in a manner that is not contemplated by IN R USDCTSD L.R. 5-1 and without prior court authorization is prohibited. IN R USDCTSD L.R. 5-1(a).

b. *Non-electronic filing.* Any document that is exempt from electronic filing must be filed directly with the clerk and served on other parties in the case as required by those Federal Rules of Civil Procedure and Local Rules of the United States District Court for the Southern District of Indiana that apply to the service of non-electronic documents. IN R USDCTSD L.R. 5-2(c).

   i. *When completed.* A document or other item that is not required to be filed electronically is deemed filed:

- Upon delivery in person, by courier, or via U.S. Mail or other mail delivery service to the clerk's office during business hours;
- When the courtroom deputy clerk accepts it, if the document or item is filed in open court; or
- Upon completion of any other manner of filing that the court authorizes. IN R USDCTSD L.R. 5-10(a).

   ii. *Document filing by non-exempt party.* When a party who is not exempt from the electronic filing requirement files a document directly with the clerk, the party must:

- Electronically file a notice of manual filing that explains why the document cannot be filed electronically;
- Present the document to the clerk within one (1) business day after filing the notice of manual filing; and
- Present the clerk with a copy of the notice of manual filing when the party files the document with the clerk. IN R USDCTSD L.R. 5-2(d).

c. *Electronic filing*

   i. *Authorization of electronic filing program.* A court may, by local rule, allow papers to be filed, signed, or verified by electronic means that are consistent with any technical standards established by the Judicial Conference of the United States. A local rule may require electronic filing only if reasonable exceptions are allowed. A paper filed electronically in compliance with a local rule is a written paper for purposes of the Federal Rules of Civil Procedure. FRCP 5(d)(3).

- IN R USDCTSD L.R. 5-2 requires electronic filing, as allowed by FRCP 5(d)(3). The policies and procedures in IN R USDCTSD ECF Procedures govern electronic filing in this district unless, due to circumstances in a particular case, a judicial officer determines that these policies and procedures (IN R USDCTSD ECF Procedures) should be modified. IN R USDCTSD ECF Procedures(1).

- Unless modified by order of the Court, all Federal Rules of Civil Procedure and Local Rules of the United States District Court for the Southern District of Indiana shall continue to apply to cases maintained in the Court's Case Management/Electronic Case Filing System (CM/ECF). IN R USDCTSD ECF Procedures(3).

ii. *Mandatory electronic filing.* Unless exempted pursuant to IN R USDCTSD L.R. 5-3(e), attorneys admitted to the court's bar (including those admitted pro hac vice) or authorized to represent the United States must use the court's ECF system to file documents. IN R USDCTSD L.R. 5-3(a). Electronic filing by attorneys is required for eligible documents filed in civil and criminal cases pending with the Court, unless specifically exempted by Local Rule or Court Order. IN R USDCTSD ECF Procedures(4).

- *Exceptions.* All civil cases (other than those cases the court specifically exempts) must be maintained in the court's electronic case filing (ECF) system. Accordingly, as allowed by FRCP 5(d)(3), every document filed in this court (including exhibits) must be transmitted to the clerk's office via the ECF system consistent with IN R USDCTSD L.R. 5-2 through IN R USDCTSD L.R. 5-11 except: (1) documents filed by pro se litigants; (2) transcripts in cases filed by claimants under the Social Security Act (and related statutes); (3) exhibits in a format that does not readily permit electronic filing (such as videos and large maps and charts); (4) documents that are illegible when scanned into .pdf format; (5) documents filed in cases not maintained on the ECF system; and (6) any other documents that the court or the Local Rules of the United States District Court for the Southern District of Indiana specifically allow to be filed directly with the clerk. IN R USDCTSD L.R. 5-2(a). Parties otherwise participating in the electronic filing system may be excused from filing a particular component electronically under certain limited circumstances, such as when the component cannot be reduced to an electronic format. Such components shall not be filed electronically, but instead shall be manually filed with the Clerk of Court and served upon the parties in accordance with the applicable Federal Rules of Civil Procedure and the Local Rules of the United States District Court for the Southern District of Indiana for filing and service of non-electronic documents. IN R USDCTSD ECF Procedures(15).

- *Exemption from participation.* The court may exempt attorneys from using the ECF system in a particular case for good cause. An attorney must file a petition for ECF exemption and a CM/ECF technical requirements exemption questionnaire in each case in which the attorney seeks an exemption. (The CM/ECF technical requirements exemption questionnaire is available on the court's website). IN R USDCTSD L.R. 5-3(e).

iii. *Consequences of electronic filing.* Electronic transmission of a document consistent with the procedures adopted by the Court shall, upon the complete receipt of the same by the Clerk of Court, constitute filing of the document for all purposes of the Federal Rules of Civil and Criminal Procedure and the Local Rules of the United States District Court for the Southern District of Indiana, and shall constitute entry of that document onto the docket maintained by the Clerk pursuant to FRCP 58 and FRCP 79. IN R USDCTSD ECF Procedures(7); IN R USDCTSD L.R. 5-4(c)(1). When a document has been filed electronically: the document, as filed, binds the filing party. IN R USDCTSD L.R. 5-4(c)(3).

- A Notice of Electronic Filing (NEF) acknowledging that the document has been filed will immediately appear on the filer's screen after the document has been submitted. Attorneys are strongly encouraged to print or electronically save a copy of the NEF. Attorneys can also verify the filing of documents by inspecting the Court's electronic docket sheet through the use of a PACER login. IN R USDCTSD ECF Procedures(7). When a document has been filed electronically: the notice of electronic filing for the document serves as the court's date-stamp and proof of filing. IN R USDCTSD L.R. 5-4(c)(4).

- The Court may, upon the motion of a party or upon its own motion, strike any inappropriately filed document. IN R USDCTSD ECF Procedures(7).

iv. For more information on electronic filing, refer to IN R USDCTSD ECF Procedures.

d. *Fax filing.* The clerk may not file a faxed document without court authorization. The court may not authorize the clerk to file faxed documents without finding that compelling circumstances justify it. A party must submit a copy of the document that otherwise complies with IN R USDCTSD L.R. 5-10 to replace the faxed copy within seven (7) days after faxing the document. IN R USDCTSD L.R. 5-10(e).

2. *Service requirements*

 a. *Service; When required*

 .i. *In general.* Unless the Federal Rules of Civil Procedure provide otherwise, each of the following papers must be served on every party:

 - An order stating that service is required;

 - A pleading filed after the original complaint, unless the court orders otherwise under FRCP 5(c) because there are numerous defendants;

 - A discovery paper required to be served on a party, unless the court orders otherwise;

 - A written motion, except one that may be heard ex parte; and

 - A written notice, appearance, demand, or offer of judgment, or any similar paper. FRCP 5(a)(1).

 ii. *If a party fails to appear.* No service is required on a party who is in default for failing to appear. But a pleading that asserts a new claim for relief against such a party must be served on that party under FRCP 4. FRCP 5(a)(2).

 iii. *Seizing property.* If an action is begun by seizing property and no person is or need be named as a defendant, any service required before the filing of an appearance, answer, or claim must be made on the person who had custody or possession of the property when it was seized. FRCP 5(a)(3).

 b. *Service; How made*

 i. *Serving an attorney.* If a party is represented by an attorney, service under FRCP 5 must be made on the attorney unless the court orders service on the party. FRCP 5(b)(1).

 ii. *Service in general.* A paper is served under FRCP 5 by:

 - Handing it to the person;

 - Leaving it: (1) at the person's office with a clerk or other person in charge or, if no one is in charge, in a conspicuous place in the office; or (2) if the person has no office or the office is closed, at the person's dwelling or usual place of abode with someone of suitable age and discretion who resides there;

 - Mailing it to the person's last known address—in which event service is complete upon mailing;

 - Leaving it with the court clerk if the person has no known address;

 - Sending it by electronic means if the person consented in writing—in which event service is complete upon transmission, but is not effective if the serving party learns that it did not reach the person to be served; or

 - Delivering it by any other means that the person consented to in writing—in which event service is complete when the person making service delivers it to the agency designated to make delivery. FRCP 5(b)(2).

 iii. *Electronic service*

 - *Consent.* By registering to use the ECF system, attorneys consent to electronic service of documents filed in cases maintained on the ECF system. IN R USDCTSD L.R. 5-3(d). By participating in the Electronic Case Filing Program, attorneys consent to the electronic service of documents, and shall make available electronic mail addresses for service. IN R USDCTSD ECF Procedures(11).

 - *Service on registered parties.* Upon the filing of a document by a party, an e-mail message will be automatically generated by the electronic filing system and sent via electronic mail to the e-mail addresses of all registered attorneys who have appeared in the case. The Notice of Electronic Filing will contain a document hyperlink which will provide recipients with one "free look" at the electronically filed document. Recipients are encouraged to print and/or save a copy of the document during the "free look" to avoid incurring PACER charges for future viewings of the document. IN R USDCTSD ECF Procedures(11). When a document has been filed electronically: transmission of the notice of electronic filing generated by the ECF system to an attorney's e-mail address constitutes service of the document on that attorney. IN R USDCTSD L.R. 5-4(c)(5). The party effectuates service on all registered attorneys by filing electronically. IN R USDCTSD ECF Procedures(11). When a document has been filed electronically: no other attempted service will constitute electronic service of the document. IN R USDCTSD L.R. 5-4(c)(6).

- *Service on exempt parties.* A filer must serve a copy of the document consistent with FRCP 5 on any party or attorney who is exempt from participating in electronic filing. IN R USDCTSD L.R. 5-4(d). It is the responsibility of the filing attorney to conventionally serve all parties who do not receive electronic service (the identity of these parties will be indicated on the filing receipt generated by the ECF system). IN R USDCTSD ECF Procedures(11).

- *Service on parties excused from electronic filing.* Parties otherwise participating in the electronic filing system may be excused from filing a particular component electronically under certain limited circumstances, such as when the component cannot be reduced to an electronic format. Such components shall not be filed electronically, but instead shall be manually filed with the Clerk of Court and served upon the parties in accordance with the applicable Federal Rules of Civil Procedure and the Local Rules of the United States District Court for the Southern District of Indiana for filing and service of non-electronic documents. IN R USDCTSD ECF Procedures(15).

- *Service of exempt documents.* Any document that is exempt from electronic filing must be filed directly with the clerk and served on other parties in the case as required by those Federal Rules of Civil Procedure and Local Rules of the United States District Court for the Southern District of Indiana that apply to the service of non-electronic documents. IN R USDCTSD L.R. 5-2(c).

   iv. *Using court facilities.* If a local rule so authorizes, a party may use the court's transmission facilities to make service under FRCP 5(b)(2)(E). FRCP 5(b)(3).

  c. *Serving numerous defendants*

    i. *In general.* If an action involves an unusually large number of defendants, the court may, on motion or on its own, order that:

- Defendants' pleadings and replies to them need not be served on other defendants;

- Any crossclaim, counterclaim, avoidance, or affirmative defense in those pleadings and replies to them will be treated as denied or avoided by all other parties; and

- Filing any such pleading and serving it on the plaintiff constitutes notice of the pleading to all parties. FRCP 5(c)(1).

    ii. *Notifying parties.* A copy of every such order must be served on the parties as the court directs. FRCP 5(c)(2).

G. Hearings

1. *Hearings, generally*

  a. *Oral argument.* Due process does not require that oral argument be permitted on a motion and, except as otherwise provided by local rule, the district court has discretion to determine whether it will decide the motion on the papers or hear argument by counsel (and perhaps receive evidence). FPP § 1190; F.D.I.C. v. Deglau, 207 F.3d 153 (3d Cir. 2000).

    i. *Request for oral argument.* A party may request oral argument by filing a separate motion

explaining why oral argument is necessary and estimating how long the court should allow for the argument. IN R USDCTSD L.R. 7-5(a). Refer to the Documents section of this document for more information.

    ii. *No additional evidence at oral argument.* Parties may not present additional evidence at oral argument. IN R USDCTSD L.R. 7-5(b).

b. *Providing a regular schedule for oral hearings.* A court may establish regular times and places for oral hearings on motions. FRCP 78(a).

c. *Providing for submission on briefs.* By rule or order, the court may provide for submitting and determining motions on briefs, without oral hearings. FRCP 78(b).

d. *Request for evidentiary hearing.* A party may request an evidentiary hearing on a motion or petition by serving and filing a separate motion explaining why the hearing is necessary and estimating how long the court should allow for the hearing. IN R USDCTSD L.R. 7-5(c).

e. *Directed by the court.* The court may: (1) grant or deny a request for oral argument or an evidentiary hearing in its sole discretion; (2) set oral argument or an evidentiary hearing without a request from a party; and (3) order any oral argument or evidentiary hearing to be held anywhere within the district regardless of where the case will be tried. IN R USDCTSD L.R. 7-5(d).

2. *Courtroom and courthouse decorum.* For information on courtroom and courthouse decorum, refer to IN R USDCTSD L.R. 83-3.

H. Forms

1. Federal Motion for Discovery Sanctions Forms

a. Motion for contempt. 3B FEDFORMS § 3721.

b. Motion for sanctions for failure to appear at deposition. 3B FEDFORMS § 3722.

c. Motion that facts be taken as established for failure to answer questions upon deposition. 3B FEDFORMS § 3723.

d. Motion for order refusing to allow disobedient party to support or oppose designated claims or defenses. 3B FEDFORMS § 3724.

e. Motion for default judgment against defendant for failure to comply with order for production of documents. 3B FEDFORMS § 3725.

f. Motion for award of expenses incurred to prove matter opponent failed to admit under FRCP 36. 3B FEDFORMS § 3726.

g. Motion to strike answer or dismiss action for failure to comply with order requiring answer to interrogatories. 3B FEDFORMS § 3729.

h. Motion to dismiss for failure to comply with previous order requiring answer to interrogatories to party. 3B FEDFORMS § 3732.

i. Motion; For order that facts be taken to be established, and/or prohibiting certain claims, defenses, or evidence in opposition thereto. FEDPROF § 23:595.

j. Affidavit; By attorney; In support of motion for order that facts be taken to be established, etc; Failure to produce documents for inspection. FEDPROF § 23:596.

k. Affidavit; By attorney; In support of motion for order that facts be taken to be established, etc; Failure to obey order to answer questions. FEDPROF § 23:597.

l. Motion; For order striking pleadings, and for default judgment or dismissal of action. FEDPROF § 23:599.

m. Affidavit; By attorney; In support of motion for default judgment for defendant's failure to obey discovery order. FEDPROF § 23:600.

n. Motion; By defendant; For dismissal of action and other sanctions; For failure to comply with orders to complete deposition. FEDPROF § 23:601.

o. Motion; By defendant; For dismissal of action or other sanctions; For failure and refusal to comply with order to produce documents. FEDPROF § 23:602.

p. Motion; By defendant; For dismissal with prejudice; Failure to answer interrogatories as ordered. FEDPROF § 23:603.

q. Motion; For order staying further proceedings until adverse party obeys order compelling discovery. FEDPROF § 23:604.

r. Affidavit; By attorney; Opposing motion for order striking pleading and directing entry of default judgment; Good-faith attempt to obey discovery order; Production of documents illegal under foreign law. FEDPROF § 23:605.

s. Motion; For sanctions for failure to comply with examination order. FEDPROF § 23:610.

t. Motion; For order finding person in contempt of court; Refusal, after order, to answer question. FEDPROF § 23:612.

u. Affidavit; By attorney; In support of motion for order finding party in contempt. FEDPROF § 23:613.

v. Affidavit; By plaintiff; In support of motion for order holding defendant in contempt of court; Defendant disobeyed order for production of documents. FEDPROF § 23:614.

w. Motion; For order compelling opposing party to pay expenses incurred in proving facts such party refused to admit. FEDPROF § 23:616.

x. Motion; For sanctions; Failure to attend own deposition, serve answers to interrogatories, or respond to request for inspection. FEDPROF § 23:618.

y. Motion; For order staying proceedings until required response to discovery request is made. FEDPROF § 23:619.

z. Affidavit; By attorney; In support of motion for sanctions; Failure to attend own deposition, serve answers to interrogatories, or respond to request for inspection. FEDPROF § 23:620.

2. Forms for the Southern District of Indiana

a. Notice of endorsement. IN R USDCTSD ECF Procedures(Appendix B).

b. Notice of manual filing. IN R USDCTSD ECF Procedures(Appendix C).

c. Declaration that party was unable to file in a timely manner due to technical difficulties. IN R USDCTSD ECF Procedures(Appendix D).

I. Applicable Rules

1. *Federal rules*

a. Counsel's liability for excessive costs. 28 U.S.C.A. § 1927.

b. Serving and filing pleadings and other papers. FRCP 5.

c. Constitutional challenge to a statute; Notice, certification, and intervention. FRCP 5.1.

d. Privacy protection for filings made with the court. FRCP 5.2.

e. Computing and extending time; Time for motion papers. FRCP 6.

f. Pleadings allowed; Form of motions and other papers. FRCP 7.

g. Form of pleadings. FRCP 10.

h. Signing pleadings, motions, and other papers; Representations to the court; Sanctions. FRCP 11.

i. Duty to disclose; General provisions governing discovery. FRCP 26.

j. Failure to make disclosures or to cooperate in discovery; Sanctions. FRCP 37.

k. Taking testimony. FRCP 43.

l. Hearing motions; Submission on briefs. FRCP 78.

2. *Local rules*

a. Scope of the rules. IN R USDCTSD L.R. 1-1.

b. Sanctions for errors as to form. IN R USDCTSD L.R. 1-3.

c. Format of documents presented for filing. IN R USDCTSD L.R. 5-1.

d. Constitutional challenge to a statute; Notice. IN R USDCTSD L.R. 5.1-1.

e. Filing of documents electronically required. IN R USDCTSD L.R. 5-2.

f. Eligibility, registration, passwords for electronic filing; Exemption from electronic filing. IN R USDCTSD L.R. 5-3.

g. Timing and consequences of electronic filing. IN R USDCTSD L.R. 5-4.

h. Attachments and exhibits in cases filed electronically. IN R USDCTSD L.R. 5-6.

i. Signatures in cases filed electronically. IN R USDCTSD L.R. 5-7.

j. Non-electronic filings. IN R USDCTSD L.R. 5-10.

k. Motion practice. [IN R USDCTSD L.R. 7-1, as amended by IN ORDER 16-2319, effective December 1, 2016].

l. Oral arguments and hearings. IN R USDCTSD L.R. 7-5.

m. Request for three-judge court. IN R USDCTSD L.R. 9-2.

n. Filing of discovery materials. IN R USDCTSD L.R. 26-2.

o. Discovery disputes. IN R USDCTSD L.R. 37-1.

p. Assignment of cases. IN R USDCTSD L.R. 40-1.

q. Alternative dispute resolution. IN R USDCTSD A.D.R. Rule 1.1; IN R USDCTSD A.D.R. Rule 1.2; IN R USDCTSD A.D.R. Rule 1.5; IN R USDCTSD A.D.R. Rule 2.1; IN R USDCTSD A.D.R. Rule 2.2.

r. Instructions for preparing case management plan. IN R USDCTSD Case Mgt.

s. Electronic case filing policies and procedures manual. IN R USDCTSD ECF Procedures.

Motions, Oppositions and Replies
Motion for Preliminary Injunction

Document Last Updated December 2016

A. Checklist

(I) ❑ Matters to be considered by moving party

    (a) ❑ Required documents

        (1) ❑ Notice of motion and motion

        (2) ❑ Security

        (3) ❑ Certificate of service

    (b) ❑ Supplemental documents

        (1) ❑ Brief

        (2) ❑ Supporting evidence

        (3) ❑ Pleadings

        (4) ❑ Notice of constitutional question

        (5) ❑ Nongovernmental corporate disclosure statement

        (6) ❑ Index of exhibits

        (7) ❑ Request for oral argument

        (8) ❑ Request for evidentiary hearing

        (9) ❑ Copy of authority

(10) ❑ Proposed order

(11) ❑ Copy of document with self-address envelope

(12) ❑ Notice of manual filing

(13) ❑ Courtesy copies

(14) ❑ Copies for three-judge court

(15) ❑ Declaration that party was unable to file in a timely manner due to technical difficulties

(c) ❑ Timing

    (1) ❑ A written motion and notice of the hearing must be served at least fourteen (14) days before the time specified for the hearing, with the following exceptions: (i) when the motion may be heard ex parte; (ii) when the Federal Rules of Civil Procedure set a different time; or (iii) when a court order—which a party may, for good cause, apply for ex parte—sets a different time

    (2) ❑ Any affidavit supporting a motion must be served with the motion

    (3) ❑ When a party who is not exempt from the electronic filing requirement files a document directly with the clerk, the party must present the document to the clerk within one (1) business day after filing the notice of manual filing

    (4) ❑ Unless the court orders otherwise, the [untimely] document and declaration [that party was unable to file in a timely manner due to technical difficulties] must be filed no later than 12:00 noon of the first day on which the court is open for business following the original filing deadline

(II) ❑ Matters to be considered by opposing party

(a) ❑ Required documents

    (1) ❑ Response brief

    (2) ❑ Certificate of service

(b) ❑ Supplemental documents

    (1) ❑ Supporting evidence

    (2) ❑ Pleadings

    (3) ❑ Notice of constitutional question

    (4) ❑ Nongovernmental corporate disclosure statement

    (5) ❑ Index of exhibits

    (6) ❑ Request for oral argument

    (7) ❑ Request for evidentiary hearing

    (8) ❑ Copy of authority

    (9) ❑ Copy of document with self-address envelope

    (10) ❑ Notice of manual filing

    (11) ❑ Courtesy copies

    (12) ❑ Copies for three-judge court

    (13) ❑ Declaration that party was unable to file in a timely manner due to technical difficulties

(c) ❑ Timing

    (1) ❑ Any response is due within fourteen (14) days after service of the motion

    (2) ❑ Except as FRCP 59(c) provides otherwise, any opposing affidavit must be served at least seven (7) days before the hearing, unless the court permits service at another time

    (3) ❑ When a party who is not exempt from the electronic filing requirement files a document

directly with the clerk, the party must present the document to the clerk within one (1) business day after filing the notice of manual filing

(4) ❑ Unless the court orders otherwise, the [untimely] document and declaration [that party was unable to file in a timely manner due to technical difficulties] must be filed no later than 12:00 noon of the first day on which the court is open for business following the original filing deadline

B. Timing

1. *Motion for preliminary injunction.* FRCP 65 is silent about when notice must be given. FPP § 2949.

2. *Timing of motions, generally*

   a. *Motion and notice of hearing.* A written motion and notice of the hearing must be served at least fourteen (14) days before the time specified for the hearing, with the following exceptions:

      i. When the motion may be heard ex parte;

      ii. When the Federal Rules of Civil Procedure set a different time; or

      iii. When a court order—which a party may, for good cause, apply for ex parte—sets a different time. FRCP 6(c)(1).

   b. *Supporting affidavit.* Any affidavit supporting a motion must be served with the motion. FRCP 6(c)(2).

3. *Timing of opposing papers.* Any response is due within fourteen (14) days after service of the motion. IN R USDCTSD L.R. 7-1(c)(2)(A).

   a. *Opposing affidavit.* Except as FRCP 59(c) provides otherwise, any opposing affidavit must be served at least seven (7) days before the hearing, unless the court permits service at another time. FRCP 6(c)(2).

   b. *Extensions.* The court may extend response and reply deadlines, but only for good cause. IN R USDCTSD L.R. 7-1(c)(3).

   c. *Summary ruling on failure to respond.* The court may summarily rule on a motion if an opposing party does not file a response within the deadline. IN R USDCTSD L.R. 7-1(c)(4).

4. *Timing of reply papers.* Where the respondent files an answering affidavit setting up a new matter, the moving party ordinarily is allowed a reasonable time to file a reply affidavit since failure to deny the new matter by affidavit may operate as an admission of its truth. AMJUR MOTIONS § 25.

   a. *Reply brief.* Any reply is due within seven (7) days after service of the response. IN R USDCTSD L.R. 7-1(c)(2)(B).

   b. *Extensions.* The court may extend response and reply deadlines, but only for good cause. IN R USDCTSD L.R. 7-1(c)(3).

5. *Document filing by non-exempt party.* When a party who is not exempt from the electronic filing requirement files a document directly with the clerk, the party must: present the document to the clerk within one (1) business day after filing the notice of manual filing. IN R USDCTSD L.R. 5-2(d)(2).

6. *Declaration that party was unable to file in a timely manner due to technical difficulties.* Unless the Court orders otherwise, the [untimely] document and declaration [that party was unable to file in a timely manner due to technical difficulties] must be filed no later than 12:00 noon of the first day on which the Court is open for business following the original filing deadline. IN R USDCTSD ECF Procedures(16).

7. *Computation of time*

   a. *Computing time.* FRCP 6 applies in computing any time period specified in the Federal Rules of Civil Procedure, in any local rule or court order, or in any statute that does not specify a method of computing time. FRCP 6(a).

      i. *Period stated in days or a longer unit.* When the period is stated in days or a longer unit of time:

         • Exclude the day of the event that triggers the period;

         • Count every day, including intermediate Saturdays, Sundays, and legal holidays; and

- Include the last day of the period, but if the last day is a Saturday, Sunday, or legal holiday, the period continues to run until the end of the next day that is not a Saturday, Sunday, or legal holiday. FRCP 6(a)(1).

ii. *Period stated in hours.* When the period is stated in hours:

- Begin counting immediately on the occurrence of the event that triggers the period;

- Count every hour, including hours during intermediate Saturdays, Sundays, and legal holidays; and

- If the period would end on a Saturday, Sunday, or legal holiday, the period continues to run until the same time on the next day that is not a Saturday, Sunday, or legal holiday. FRCP 6(a)(2).

iii. *Inaccessibility of the clerk's office.* Unless the court orders otherwise, if the clerk's office is inaccessible:

- On the last day for filing under FRCP 6(a)(1), then the time for filing is extended to the first accessible day that is not a Saturday, Sunday, or legal holiday; or

- During the last hour for filing under FRCP 6(a)(2), then the time for filing is extended to the same time on the first accessible day that is not a Saturday, Sunday, or legal holiday. FRCP 6(a)(3).

iv. *"Last day" defined.* Unless a different time is set by a statute, local rule, or court order, the last day ends:

- For electronic filing, at midnight in the court's time zone; and

- For filing by other means, when the clerk's office is scheduled to close. FRCP 6(a)(4).

v. *"Next day" defined.* The "next day" is determined by continuing to count forward when the period is measured after an event and backward when measured before an event. FRCP 6(a)(5).

vi. *"Legal holiday" defined.* "Legal holiday" means:

- The day set aside by statute for observing New Year's Day, Martin Luther King Jr.'s Birthday, Washington's Birthday, Memorial Day, Independence Day, Labor Day, Columbus Day, Veterans' Day, Thanksgiving Day, or Christmas Day;

- Any day declared a holiday by the President or Congress; and

- For periods that are measured after an event, any other day declared a holiday by the state where the district court is located. FRCP 6(a)(6).

b. *Computation of electronic filing deadlines.* Filing documents electronically does not alter filing deadlines. IN R USDCTSD ECF Procedures(7). A document due on a particular day must be filed before midnight local time of the division where the case is pending. IN R USDCTSD L.R. 5-4(a). All electronic transmissions of documents must be completed (i.e. received completely by the Clerk's Office) prior to midnight of the local time of the division in which the case is pending in order to be considered timely filed that day (NOTE: time will be noted in Eastern Time on the Court's docket. If you have filed a document prior to midnight local time of the division in which the case is pending and the document is due that date, but the electronic receipt and docket reflect the following calendar day, please contact the Court). IN R USDCTSD ECF Procedures(7). Although attorneys may file documents electronically twenty-four (24) hours a day, seven (7) days a week, attorneys are encouraged to file all documents during the normal working hours of the Clerk's Office (Monday through Friday, 8:30 a.m. to 4:30 p.m.) when technical support is available. IN R USDCTSD ECF Procedures(7); IN R USDCTSD ECF Procedures(9).

i. *Technical difficulties.* Parties are encouraged to file documents electronically during normal business hours, in case a problem is encountered. In the event a technical failure occurs and a document cannot be filed electronically despite the best efforts of the filing party, the party should print (if possible) a copy of the error message received. In addition, as soon as practically possible, the party should file a "Declaration that Party was Unable to File in a Timely Manner

826

Due to Technical Difficulties." A model form is provided as Appendix D (IN R USDCTSD ECF Procedures(Appendix D)). IN R USDCTSD ECF Procedures(16).

- If a party is unable to file electronically and, as a result, may miss a filing deadline, the party must contact the Clerk's Office at the number listed in IN R USDCTSD ECF Procedures(15) to inform the court's staff of the difficulty. If a party misses a filing deadline due to an inability to file electronically, the party may submit the untimely filed document, accompanied by a declaration stating the reason(s) for missing the deadline. Unless the Court orders otherwise, the document and declaration must be filed no later than 12:00 noon of the first day on which the Court is open for business following the original filing deadline. IN R USDCTSD ECF Procedures(16).

c. *Extending time*

   i. *In general.* When an act may or must be done within a specified time, the court may, for good cause, extend the time:

- With or without motion or notice if the court acts, or if a request is made, before the original time or its extension expires; or

- On motion made after the time has expired if the party failed to act because of excusable neglect. FRCP 6(b)(1).

   ii. *Exceptions.* A court must not extend the time to act under FRCP 50(b), FRCP 50(d), FRCP 52(b), FRCP 59(b), FRCP 59(d), FRCP 59(e), and FRCP 60(b). FRCP 6(b)(2).

   iii. Refer to the United States District Court for the Southern District of Indiana KeyRules Motion for Continuance/Extension of Time document for more information on extending time.

d. *Additional time after certain kinds of service.* When a party may or must act within a specified time after being served and service is made under FRCP 5(b)(2)(C) (mail), FRCP 5(b)(2)(D) (leaving with the clerk), or FRCP 5(b)(2)(F) (other means consented to), three (3) days are added after the period would otherwise expire under FRCP 6(a). FRCP 6(d). Service by electronic mail shall constitute service pursuant to FRCP 5(b)(2)(E) and shall entitle the party being served to the additional three (3) days provided by FRCP 6(d). IN R USDCTSD ECF Procedures(11).

C. General Requirements

1. *Motions, generally*

a. *Requirements.* A request for a court order must be made by motion. The motion must:

   i. Be in writing unless made during a hearing or trial;

   ii. State with particularity the grounds for seeking the order; and

   iii. State the relief sought. FRCP 7(b)(1).

b. *Notice of motion.* A party interested in resisting the relief sought by a motion has a right to notice thereof, and an opportunity to be heard. AMJUR MOTIONS § 12.

   i. In addition to statutory or court rule provisions requiring notice of a motion—the purpose of such a notice requirement having been said to be to prevent a party from being prejudicially surprised by a motion—principles of natural justice dictate that an adverse party generally must be given notice that a motion will be presented to the court. AMJUR MOTIONS § 12.

   ii. "Notice," in this regard, means reasonable notice, including a meaningful opportunity to prepare and to defend against allegations of a motion. AMJUR MOTIONS § 12.

c. *Writing requirement.* The writing requirement is intended to insure that the adverse parties are informed and have a record of both the motion's pendency and the grounds on which the movant seeks an order. FPP § 1191; Feldberg v. Quechee Lakes Corp., 463 F.3d 195 (2d Cir. 2006).

   i. It is sufficient "if the motion is stated in a written notice of the hearing of the motion." FPP § 1191.

d. *Particularity requirement.* The particularity requirement insures that the opposing parties will have notice of their opponent's contentions. FEDPROC § 62:364; Goodman v. 1973 26 Foot Trojan

Vessel, Arkansas Registration No. AR1439SN, 859 F.2d 71, 12 Fed.R.Serv.3d 645 (8th Cir. 1988). That requirement ensures that notice of the basis for the motion is provided to the court and to the opposing party so as to avoid prejudice, provide the opponent with a meaningful opportunity to respond, and provide the court with enough information to process the motion correctly. FEDPROC § 62:364; Andreas v. Volkswagen of America, Inc., 336 F.3d 789, 56 Fed.R.Serv.3d 6 (8th Cir. 2003).

    i. Reasonable specification of the grounds for a motion is sufficient. However, where a movant fails to state even one ground for granting the motion in question, the movant has failed to meet the minimal standard of "reasonable specification." FEDPROC § 62:364; Martinez v. Trainor, 556 F.2d 818, 23 Fed.R.Serv.2d 403 (7th Cir. 1977).

    ii. The court may excuse the failure to comply with the particularity requirement if it is inadvertent, and where no prejudice is shown by the opposing party. FEDPROC § 62:364.

e. *Motions must be filed separately.* Motions must be filed separately, but alternative motions may be filed in a single document if each is named in the title. A motion must not be contained within a brief, response, or reply to a previously filed motion, unless ordered by the court. IN R USDCTSD L.R. 7-1(a).

f. *Routine or uncontested motions.* The court may rule upon a routine or uncontested motion before the response deadline passes, unless: (1) the motion indicates that an opposing party objects to it; or (2) the court otherwise believes that a response will be filed. IN R USDCTSD L.R. 7-1(d).

2. *Informal conference to resolve disputes involving non-dispositive issues.* In addition to those conferences required by IN R USDCTSD L.R. 37-1, counsel are encouraged to hold informal conferences in person or by phone to resolve any disputes involving non-dispositive issues that may otherwise require submission of a motion to the Court. This requirement does not apply to cases involving pro se parties. Therefore, prior to filing any non-dispositive motion (including motions for extension of time), the moving party must contact opposing counsel to determine whether there is an objection to any non-dispositive motion (including motions for extension of time), and state in the motion whether opposing counsel objects to the motion. IN R USDCTSD Case Mgt(General Instructions For All Cases). Refer to the Documents section of this document for more information on the contents of the motion.

3. *Motion for preliminary injunction.* The appropriate procedure for requesting a preliminary injunction is by motion, although it also commonly is requested by an order to show cause. FPP § 2949; James Luterbach Constr. Co. v. Adamkus, 781 F.2d 599, 603 (7th Cir. 1986); Studebaker Corp. v. Gittlin, 360 F.2d 692 (2d. Cir. 1966).

a. *Preliminary injunction.* An interim grant of specific relief is a preliminary injunction that may be issued only on notice to the adverse party. FEDPROC § 47:53; Westar Energy, Inc. v. Lake, 552 F.3d 1215 (10th Cir. 2009). Defined broadly, a preliminary injunction is an injunction that is issued to protect plaintiff from irreparable injury and to preserve the court's power to render a meaningful decision after a trial on the merits. FPP § 2947; Evans v. Buchanan, 555 F.2d 373, 387 (3d Cir. 1977).

    i. *Disfavored injunctions.* There are three types of preliminary injunctions that are disfavored:

- Those that afford the moving party substantially all the relief it might recover after a full trial on the merits;

- Those that disturb the status quo; and

- Those that are mandatory as opposed to prohibitory. FEDPROC § 47:55; Prairie Band of Potawatomi Indians v. Pierce, 253 F.3d 1234, 50 Fed.R.Serv.3d 244 (10th Cir. 2001).

b. *Notice.* The court may issue a preliminary injunction only on notice to the adverse party. FRCP 65(a)(1). Although FRCP 65(a)(1) does not define what constitutes proper notice, it has been held that providing a copy of the motion and a specification of the time and place of the hearing are adequate. FPP § 2949.

c. *Security.* The court may issue a preliminary injunction or a temporary restraining order only if the movant gives security in an amount that the court considers proper to pay the costs and damages sustained by any party found to have been wrongfully enjoined or restrained. The United States, its officers, and its agencies are not required to give security. FRCP 65(c).

    i. *Proceedings against a surety.* Whenever the Federal Rules of Civil Procedure (including the

Supplemental Rules for Admiralty or Maritime Claims and Asset Forfeiture Actions) require or allow a party to give security, and security is given through a bond or other undertaking with one or more sureties, each surety submits to the court's jurisdiction and irrevocably appoints the court clerk as its agent for receiving service of any papers that affect its liability on the bond or undertaking. The surety's liability may be enforced on motion without an independent action. The motion and any notice that the court orders may be served on the court clerk, who must promptly mail a copy of each to every surety whose address is known. FRCP 65.1.

d. *Preliminary injunction versus temporary restraining order.* Care should be taken to distinguish preliminary injunctions under FRCP 65(a) from temporary-restraining orders under FRCP 65(b). FPP § 2947.

    i. *Notice and duration.* [Temporary restraining orders] may be issued ex parte without an adversary hearing in order to prevent an immediate, irreparable injury and are of limited duration—they typically remain in effect for a maximum of twenty-eight (28) days. On the other hand, FRCP 65(a)(1) requires that notice be given to the opposing party before a preliminary injunction may be issued. FPP § 2947. Furthermore, a preliminary injunction normally lasts until the completion of the trial on the merits, unless it is dissolved earlier by court order or the consent of the parties. FPP § 2947. Therefore, its duration varies and is controlled by the nature of the situation in which it is utilized. FPP § 2947; Fundicao Tupy S.A. v. U.S., 841 F.2d 1101, 1103 (Fed. Cir. 1988).

    ii. *Hearing.* Some type of a hearing also implicitly is required by FRCP 65(a)(2), which was added in 1966 and provides either for the consolidation of the trial on the merits with the preliminary-injunction hearing or the inclusion in the trial record of any evidence received at the FRCP 65(a) hearing. FPP § 2947.

e. *Grounds for granting or denying a preliminary injunction.* The policies that bear on the propriety of granting a preliminary injunction rarely are discussed directly in the cases. Instead they are taken into account by the court considering a number of factors that have been found useful in deciding whether to grant or deny preliminary injunctions in particular cases. A formulation that has become popular in all kinds of cases, although it originally was devised in connection with stays of administrative orders, is that the four most important factors are: (1) the significance of the threat of irreparable harm to plaintiff if the injunction is not granted; (2) the state of the balance between this harm and the injury that granting the injunction would inflict on defendant; (3) the probability that plaintiff will succeed on the merits; and (4) the public interest. FPP § 2948; Pottgen v. Missouri State High School Activities Ass'n, 40 F.3d 926 (8th Cir. 1994).

    i. *Irreparable harm.* Perhaps the single most important prerequisite for the issuance of a preliminary injunction is a demonstration that if it is not granted the applicant is likely to suffer irreparable harm before a decision on the merits can be rendered. FPP § 2948.1. Only when the threatened harm would impair the court's ability to grant an effective remedy is there really a need for preliminary relief. FPP § 2948.1.

        • There must be a likelihood that irreparable harm will occur. Speculative injury is not sufficient; there must be more than an unfounded fear on the part of the applicant. FPP § 2948.1.

        • Thus, a preliminary injunction will not be issued simply to prevent the possibility of some remote future injury. A presently existing actual threat must be shown. However, the injury need not have been inflicted when application is made or be certain to occur; a strong threat of irreparable injury before trial is an adequate basis. FPP § 2948.1.

    ii. *Balancing hardship to parties.* The second factor bearing on the court's exercise of its discretion as to whether to grant preliminary relief involves an evaluation of the severity of the impact on defendant should the temporary injunction be granted and the hardship that would occur to plaintiff if the injunction should be denied. Two factors that frequently are considered when balancing the hardship on the respective parties of the grant or denial of relief are whether a preliminary injunction would give plaintiff all or most of the relief to which plaintiff would be entitled if successful at trial and whether mandatory relief is being sought. FPP § 2948.2.

iii. *Likelihood of prevailing on the merits.* The third factor that enters into the preliminary injunction calculus is the likelihood that plaintiff will prevail on the merits. This is relevant because the need for the court to act is, at least in part, a function of the validity of the applicant's claim. The courts use a bewildering variety of formulations of the need for showing some likelihood of success—the most common being that plaintiff must demonstrate a reasonable probability of success. But the verbal differences do not seem to reflect substantive disagreement. All courts agree that plaintiff must present a prima facie case but need not show a certainty of winning. FPP § 2948.3.

iv. *Public interest.* The final major factor bearing on the court's discretion to issue or deny a preliminary injunction is the public interest. Focusing on this factor is another way of inquiring whether there are policy considerations that bear on whether the order should issue. Thus, when granting preliminary relief, courts frequently emphasize that the public interest will be furthered by the injunction. Conversely, preliminary relief will be denied if the court finds that the public interest would be injured were an injunction to be issued. If the court finds there is no public interest supporting preliminary relief, that conclusion also supports denial of any injunction, even if the public interest would not be harmed by one. FPP § 2948.4. Consequently, an evaluation of the public interest should be given considerable weight in determining whether a motion for a preliminary injunction should be granted. FPP § 2948.4; Yakus v. U.S., 321 U.S. 414, 64 S.Ct. 660, 88 L.Ed. 834 (1944).

f. *Contents and scope of every injunction and restraining order*

   i. *Contents.* Every order granting an injunction and every restraining order must:

   - State the reasons why it issued;

   - State its terms specifically; and

   - Describe in reasonable detail—and not by referring to the complaint or other document— the act or acts restrained or required. FRCP 65(d)(1).

   ii. *Persons bound.* The order binds only the following who receive actual notice of it by personal service or otherwise:

   - The parties;

   - The parties' officers, agents, servants, employees, and attorneys; and

   - Other persons who are in active concert or participation with anyone described in FRCP 65(d)(2)(A) or FRCP 65(d)(2)(B). FRCP 65(d)(2).

g. *Other laws not modified.* FRCP 65 does not modify the following:

   i. Any federal statute relating to temporary restraining orders or preliminary injunctions in actions affecting employer and employee;

   ii. 28 U.S.C.A. § 2361, which relates to preliminary injunctions in actions of interpleader or in the nature of interpleader; or

   iii. 28 U.S.C.A. § 2284, which relates to actions that must be heard and decided by a three-judge district court. FRCP 65(e).

h. *Copyright impoundment.* FRCP 65 applies to copyright-impoundment proceedings. FRCP 65(f).

4. *Opposing papers.* The Federal Rules of Civil Procedure do not require any formal answer, return, or reply to a motion, except where the Federal Rules of Civil Procedure or local rules may require affidavits, memoranda, or other papers to be filed in opposition to a motion. Such papers are simply to apprise the court of such opposition and the grounds of that opposition. FEDPROC § 62:359.

a. *Effect of failure to respond to motion.* Although in the absence of statutory provision or court rule, a motion ordinarily does not require a written answer, when a party files a motion and the opposing party fails to respond, the court may construe such failure to respond as nonopposition to the motion or an admission that the motion was meritorious, may take the facts alleged in the motion as true—the rule in some jurisdictions being that the failure to respond to a fact set forth in a motion is deemed an admission—and may grant the motion if the relief requested appears to be justified. AMJUR MOTIONS § 28.

    b.   *Assent or no opposition not determinative.* However, a motion will not be granted automatically simply because an "assent" or a notation of "no opposition" has been filed; federal judges frequently deny motions that have been assented to when it is thought that justice so dictates. FPP § 1190.

    c.   *Responsive pleading inappropriate as response to motion.* An attempt to answer or oppose a motion with a responsive pleading usually is not appropriate. FPP § 1190.

5.   *Reply papers.* A moving party may be required or permitted to prepare papers in addition to his original motion papers. AMJUR MOTIONS § 25. Papers answering or replying to opposing papers may be appropriate, in the interests of justice, where it appears there is a substantial reason for allowing a reply. Thus, a court may accept reply papers where a party demonstrates that the papers to which it seeks to file a reply raise new issues that are material to the disposition of the question before the court, or where the court determines, sua sponte, that it wishes further briefing of an issue raised in those papers and orders the submission of additional papers. FEDPROC § 62:360.

    a.   *Function of reply papers.* The function of a reply affidavit is to answer the arguments made in opposition to the position taken by the movant and not to permit the movant to introduce new arguments in support of the motion. AMJUR MOTIONS § 25.

    b.   *Issues raised for the first time in a reply document.* However, the view has been followed in some jurisdictions, that as a matter of judicial economy, where there is no prejudice and where the issues could be raised simply by filing a motion to dismiss, the trial court has discretion to consider arguments raised for the first time in a reply memorandum, and that a trial court may grant a motion to strike issues raised for the first time in a reply memorandum. AMJUR MOTIONS § 26.

6.   *Appearances.* Every attorney who represents a party or who files a document on a party's behalf must file an appearance for that party. IN R USDCTSD L.R. 83-7. The filing of a Notice of Appearance shall act to establish the filing attorney as an attorney of record representing a designated party or parties in a particular cause of action. As a result, it is necessary for each attorney to file a separate Notice of Appearance when entering an appearance in a case. A joint appearance on behalf of multiple attorneys may be filed electronically only if it is filed separately for each attorney, using his/her ECF login. IN R USDCTSD ECF Procedures(12). Only those attorneys who have filed an appearance in a pending action are entitled to be served with case documents under FRCP 5(a). IN R USDCTSD L.R. 83-7. For more information, refer to IN R USDCTSD L.R. 83-7 and IN R USDCTSD ECF Procedures(12).

7.   *Notice of related action.* A party must file a notice of related action: as soon as it appears that the party's case and another pending case: (1) arise out of the same transaction or occurrence; (2) involve the same property; or (3) involve the validity or infringement or the same patent, trademark, or copyright. IN R USDCTSD L.R. 40-1(d)(2). For more information, refer to IN R USDCTSD L.R. 40-1.

8.   *Alternative dispute resolution (ADR)*

    a.   *Application.* Unless limited by specific provisions, or unless there are other applicable specific statutory, common law, or constitutional procedures, the Local Alternative Dispute Resolution Rules of the United States District Court for the Southern District of Indiana shall apply in all civil litigation filed in the U.S. District Court for the Southern District of Indiana, except in the following cases and proceedings:

        i.   Applications for writs of habeas corpus under 28 U.S.C.A. § 2254;

        ii.   Forfeiture cases;

        iii.   Non-adversary proceedings in bankruptcy;

        iv.   Social Security administrative review cases; and

        v.   Such other matters as specified by order of the Court; for example, matters involving important public policy issues, constitutional law, or the establishment of new law. IN R USDCTSD A.D.R. Rule 1.2.

    b.   *Mediation.* Mediation under this section (IN R USDCTSD A.D.R. Rule 2.1, et seq.) involves the confidential process by which a person acting as a Mediator, selected by the parties or appointed by the Court, assists the litigants in reaching a mutually acceptable agreement. It is an informal and nonadversarial process. The role of the Mediator is to assist in identifying the issues, reducing misunderstandings, clarifying priorities, exploring areas of compromise, and finding points of agreement as well as legitimate points of disagreement. Final decision-making authority rests with the parties, not the Mediator. IN R USDCTSD A.D.R. Rule 2.1. It is anticipated that an agreement may not resolve all of the disputed issues, but the process, nonetheless, can reduce points of contention. Parties and their representatives are required to mediate in good faith, but are not compelled to reach an agreement. IN R USDCTSD A.D.R. Rule 2.1.

   i. *Case selection.* The Court with the agreement of the parties may refer a civil case for mediation. Unless otherwise ordered or as specifically provided in IN R USDCTSD A.D.R. Rule 2.8, referral to mediation does not abate or suspend the action, and no scheduled dates shall be delayed or deferred, including the date of trial. IN R USDCTSD A.D.R. Rule 2.2.

   ii. For more information on mediation, refer to IN R USDCTSD A.D.R. Rule 2.1, et seq.

  c. *Other methods of dispute resolution.* The Local Alternative Dispute Resolution Rules of the United States District Court for the Southern District of Indiana shall not preclude the parties from utilizing any other reasonable method or technique of alternative dispute resolution to resolve disputes to which the parties agree. However, any use of arbitration by the parties will be governed by and comply with the requirements of 28 U.S.C.A. § 654 through 28 U.S.C.A. § 657. IN R USDCTSD A.D.R. Rule 1.5.

  d. For more information on alternative dispute resolution (ADR), refer to IN R USDCTSD A.D.R. Rule 1.1, et seq.

9. *Notice of settlement or resolution.* The parties must immediately notify the court if they reasonably anticipate settling their case or resolving a pending motion. IN R USDCTSD L.R. 7-1(h).

10. *Modification or suspension of rules.* The court may, on its own motion or at the request of a party, suspend or modify any rule in a particular case in the interest of justice. IN R USDCTSD L.R. 1-1(c).

D. Documents

1. *Documents for moving party*

  a. *Required documents*

    i. *Notice of motion and motion.* The court will consider a request for preliminary injunction only if the movant files a separate motion for relief and complies with FRCP 65(a). IN R USDCTSD L.R. 65-2(a). [P]rior to filing any non-dispositive motion (including motions for extension of time), the moving party must contact opposing counsel to determine whether there is an objection to any non-dispositive motion (including motions for extension of time), and state in the motion whether opposing counsel objects to the motion. If an objection cannot be resolved by counsel, the opposing counsel's position shall be stated within the motion. The motion should also indicate whether opposing counsel plans to file a written objection to the motion and the date by which the Court can expect to receive the objection (within the time limits set in IN R USDCTSD L.R. 7-1). If after a reasonable effort, opposing counsel cannot be reached, the moving party shall recite in the motion the dates and times that messages were left for opposing counsel. IN R USDCTSD Case Mgt(General Instructions For All Cases). Refer to the General Requirements section of this document for information on the notice of motion and motion.

    ii. *Security.* Refer to the General Requirements section of this document for information on the security required.

    iii. *Certificate of service.* FRCP 5(d) requires that the person making service under FRCP 5 certify that service has been effected. FRCP 5(Advisory Committee Notes). Having such information on file may be useful for many purposes, including proof of service if an issue arises concerning the effectiveness of the service. FRCP 5(Advisory Committee Notes).

      • *Certificate of service for electronically-filed documents.* A certificate of service must be included with all documents filed electronically. Such certificate shall indicate that service was accomplished pursuant to the Court's electronic filing procedures. IN R USDCTSD ECF Procedures(11). For the suggested format for a certificate of service for electronic filing, refer to IN R USDCTSD ECF Procedures(11).

b. *Supplemental documents*

    i. *Brief.* Supporting and response briefs are not required, but the court may request them. IN R USDCTSD L.R. 65-2(a). Refer to the Format section of this document for the format of briefs.

    ii. *Supporting evidence.* When a motion relies on facts outside the record, the court may hear the matter on affidavits or may hear it wholly or partly on oral testimony or on depositions. FRCP 43(c). Evidence that goes beyond the unverified allegations of the pleadings and motion papers must be presented to support or oppose a motion for a preliminary injunction. FPP § 2949.

- *Materials necessary for motion.* A party seeking relief under FRCP 26(c) or FRCP 37, or by way of a pretrial motion that could result in a final order on an issue, must file with the motion those parts of the discovery materials relevant to the motion. IN R USDCTSD L.R. 26-2(a).

- *Affidavits.* Affidavits are appropriate on a preliminary injunction motion and typically will be offered by both parties. FPP § 2949. All affidavits should state the facts supporting the litigant's position clearly and specifically. Preliminary injunctions frequently are denied if the affidavits are too vague or conclusory to demonstrate a clear right to relief under FRCP 65. FPP § 2949.

    iii. *Pleadings.* Pleadings may be considered if they have been verified. FPP § 2949; K-2 Ski Co. v. Head Ski Co., 467 F.2d 1087 (9th Cir. 1972).

    iv. *Notice of constitutional question.* A party that files a pleading, written motion, or other paper drawing into question the constitutionality of a federal or state statute must promptly:

- *File notice.* File a notice of constitutional question stating the question and identifying the paper that raises it, if: (1) a federal statute is questioned and the parties do not include the United States, one of its agencies, or one of its officers or employees in an official capacity; or (2) a state statute is questioned and the parties do not include the state, one of its agencies, or one of its officers or employees in an official capacity; and

- *Serve notice.* Serve the notice and paper on the Attorney General of the United States if a federal statute is questioned—or on the state attorney general if a state statute is questioned—either by certified or registered mail or by sending it to an electronic address designated by the attorney general for this purpose. FRCP 5.1(a).

- *Time for filing.* A notice of constitutional challenge to a statute filed in accordance with FRCP 5.1 must be filed at the same time the parties tender their proposed case management plan, if one is required, or within twenty-one (21) days of the filing drawing into question the constitutionality of a federal or state statute, whichever occurs later. IN R USDCTSD L.R. 5.1-1(a).

- *Additional service requirements.* If a federal statute is challenged, in addition to the service requirements of FRCP 5.1(a), the party filing the notice of constitutional challenge must serve the notice and documents on the United States Attorney for the Southern District of Indiana, either by certified or registered mail or by sending it to an electronic address designated for that purpose by that official. IN R USDCTSD L.R. 5.1-1(b).

- *No forfeiture.* A party's failure to file and serve the notice, or the court's failure to certify, does not forfeit a constitutional claim or defense that is otherwise timely asserted. FRCP 5.1(d).

    v. *Nongovernmental corporate disclosure statement*

- *Contents.* A nongovernmental corporate party must file two (2) copies of a disclosure statement that: (1) identifies any parent corporation and any publicly held corporation owning ten percent (10%) or more of its stock; or (2) states that there is no such corporation. FRCP 7.1(a).

- *Time to file; Supplemental filing.* A party must: (1) file the disclosure statement with its first appearance, pleading, petition, motion, response, or other request addressed to the court; and (2) promptly file a supplemental statement if any required information changes. FRCP 7.1(b).

vi. *Index of exhibits.* Any pleading, motion, brief, affidavit, notice, or proposed order filed with the court, whether electronically or with the clerk, must: if it has four (4) or more exhibits, include a separate index that identifies and briefly describes each exhibit. IN R USDCTSD L.R. 5-1(b).

vii. *Request for oral argument.* A party may request oral argument by filing a separate motion explaining why oral argument is necessary and estimating how long the court should allow for the argument. The request must be filed and served with the supporting brief, response brief, or reply brief. IN R USDCTSD L.R. 7-5(a).

viii. *Request for evidentiary hearing.* A party may request an evidentiary hearing on a motion or petition by serving and filing a separate motion explaining why the hearing is necessary and estimating how long the court should allow for the hearing. IN R USDCTSD L.R. 7-5(c).

ix. *Copy of authority.* Generally, copies of cited authorities may not be attached to court filings. However, a party must attach to the party's motion or brief a copy of any cited authority if it is not available on Westlaw or Lexis. Upon request, a party must provide copies of any cited authority that is only available through electronic means to the court or the other parties. IN R USDCTSD L.R. 7-1(f).

x. *Proposed order.* A party must include a suitable form of order with any document that requests the judge or the clerk to enter a routine or uncontested order. IN R USDCTSD L.R. 5-5(b); IN R USDCTSD L.R. 5-10(c); IN R USDCTSD L.R. 7-1(d).

- A service statement and/or list must be included on each proposed order, as required by IN R USDCTSD L.R. 5-5(d). IN R USDCTSD ECF Procedures(11). Any pleading, motion, brief, affidavit, notice, or proposed order filed with the court, whether electronically or with the clerk, must: if it is a form of order, include a statement of service, in the format required by IN R USDCTSD L.R. 5-5(d) in the lower left corner of the document. IN R USDCTSD L.R. 5-1(b).

- A party electronically filing a proposed order—whether voluntarily or because required by IN R USDCTSD L.R. 5-5—must convert the order directly from a word processing program and file it as an attachment to the document it relates to. Proposed orders must include in the lower left-hand corner of the signature page a statement that service will be made electronically on all ECF-registered counsel of record via email generated by the court's ECF system, without listing all such counsel. A service list including the name and postal address of any pro se litigant or non-registered attorney of record must follow, stating that service on the listed individuals will be made in the traditional paper manner, via first-class U.S. Mail. IN R USDCTSD L.R. 5-5(d).

xi. *Copy of document with self-address envelope.* To receive a file-stamped copy of a document filed directly with the clerk, a party must include with the original document an additional copy and a self-addressed envelope. The envelope must be big enough to hold the copy and have enough postage on it to send the copy via regular first-class mail. IN R USDCTSD L.R. 5-10(b).

xii. *Notice of manual filing.* When a party who is not exempt from the electronic filing requirement files a document directly with the clerk, the party must: electronically file a notice of manual filing that explains why the document cannot be filed electronically. IN R USDCTSD L.R. 5-2(d)(1). Refer to the Filing and Service Requirements section of this document for more information.

- Where an individual component cannot be included in an electronic filing (e.g. the component cannot be converted to electronic format), the filer shall electronically file the prescribed Notice of Manual Filing in place of that component. A model form is provided as Appendix C (IN R USDCTSD ECF Procedures(Appendix C)). IN R USDCTSD ECF Procedures(13).

- Before making a manual filing of a component, the filing party shall first electronically file a Notice of Manual Filing (See IN R USDCTSD ECF Procedures(Appendix C)). The filer shall initiate the electronic filing process as if filing the actual component but shall instead attach to the filing the Notice of Manual Filing setting forth the reason(s) why the component cannot be filed electronically. The manual filing should be accompanied by a copy of the previously filed Notice of Manual Filing. A party may seek to have a component excluded from electronic filing pursuant to applicable Federal and Local Rules (e.g., FRCP 26(c)). IN R USDCTSD ECF Procedures(15).

xiii. *Courtesy copies.* District Judges and Magistrate Judges regularly receive documents filed by all parties. Therefore, parties shall not bring "courtesy copies" to any chambers unless specifically directed to do so by the Court. IN R USDCTSD Case Mgt(General Instructions For All Cases).

xiv. *Copies for three-judge court.* Parties in a case where a three-judge court has been requested must file an original and three copies of any document filed directly with the clerk (instead of electronically) until the court: (1) denies the request; (2) dissolves the three-judge court; or (3) allows the parties to file fewer copies. IN R USDCTSD L.R. 9-2(c).

xv. *Declaration that party was unable to file in a timely manner due to technical difficulties.* If a party misses a filing deadline due to an inability to file electronically, the party may submit the untimely filed document, accompanied by a declaration stating the reason(s) for missing the deadline. IN R USDCTSD ECF Procedures(16). A model form is provided as Appendix D (IN R USDCTSD ECF Procedures(Appendix D)). IN R USDCTSD ECF Procedures(16).

2. *Documents for opposing party*

   a. *Required documents*

      i. *Response brief.* Supporting and response briefs are not required, but the court may request them. IN R USDCTSD L.R. 65-2(a). Refer to the Format section of this document for the format of briefs. Refer to the General Requirements section of this document for information on the opposing papers.

      ii. *Certificate of service.* FRCP 5(d) requires that the person making service under FRCP 5 certify that service has been effected. FRCP 5(Advisory Committee Notes). Having such information on file may be useful for many purposes, including proof of service if an issue arises concerning the effectiveness of the service. FRCP 5(Advisory Committee Notes).

         • *Certificate of service for electronically-filed documents.* A certificate of service must be included with all documents filed electronically. Such certificate shall indicate that service was accomplished pursuant to the Court's electronic filing procedures. IN R USDCTSD ECF Procedures(11). For the suggested format for a certificate of service for electronic filing, refer to IN R USDCTSD ECF Procedures(11).

   b. *Supplemental documents*

      i. *Supporting evidence.* When a motion relies on facts outside the record, the court may hear the matter on affidavits or may hear it wholly or partly on oral testimony or on depositions. FRCP 43(c). Evidence that goes beyond the unverified allegations of the pleadings and motion papers must be presented to support or oppose a motion for a preliminary injunction. FPP § 2949.

         • *Materials necessary for motion.* A party seeking relief under FRCP 26(c) or FRCP 37, or by way of a pretrial motion that could result in a final order on an issue, must file with the motion those parts of the discovery materials relevant to the motion. IN R USDCTSD L.R. 26-2(a).

         • *Affidavits.* Affidavits are appropriate on a preliminary injunction motion and typically will be offered by both parties. FPP § 2949. All affidavits should state the facts supporting the litigant's position clearly and specifically. Preliminary injunctions frequently are denied if the affidavits are too vague or conclusory to demonstrate a clear right to relief under FRCP 65. FPP § 2949.

      ii. *Pleadings.* Pleadings may be considered if they have been verified. FPP § 2949; K-2 Ski Co. v. Head Ski Co., 467 F.2d 1087 (9th Cir. 1972).

      iii. *Notice of constitutional question.* A party that files a pleading, written motion, or other paper drawing into question the constitutionality of a federal or state statute must promptly:

         • *File notice.* File a notice of constitutional question stating the question and identifying the

paper that raises it, if: (1) a federal statute is questioned and the parties do not include the United States, one of its agencies, or one of its officers or employees in an official capacity; or (2) a state statute is questioned and the parties do not include the state, one of its agencies, or one of its officers or employees in an official capacity; and

- *Serve notice.* Serve the notice and paper on the Attorney General of the United States if a federal statute is questioned—or on the state attorney general if a state statute is questioned—either by certified or registered mail or by sending it to an electronic address designated by the attorney general for this purpose. FRCP 5.1(a).

- *Time for filing.* A notice of constitutional challenge to a statute filed in accordance with FRCP 5.1 must be filed at the same time the parties tender their proposed case management plan, if one is required, or within twenty-one (21) days of the filing drawing into question the constitutionality of a federal or state statute, whichever occurs later. IN R USDCTSD L.R. 5.1-1(a).

- *Additional service requirements.* If a federal statute is challenged, in addition to the service requirements of FRCP 5.1(a), the party filing the notice of constitutional challenge must serve the notice and documents on the United States Attorney for the Southern District of Indiana, either by certified or registered mail or by sending it to an electronic address designated for that purpose by that official. IN R USDCTSD L.R. 5.1-1(b).

- *No forfeiture.* A party's failure to file and serve the notice, or the court's failure to certify, does not forfeit a constitutional claim or defense that is otherwise timely asserted. FRCP 5.1(d).

iv. *Nongovernmental corporate disclosure statement*

- *Contents.* A nongovernmental corporate party must file two (2) copies of a disclosure statement that: (1) identifies any parent corporation and any publicly held corporation owning ten percent (10%) or more of its stock; or (2) states that there is no such corporation. FRCP 7.1(a).

- *Time to file; Supplemental filing.* A party must: (1) file the disclosure statement with its first appearance, pleading, petition, motion, response, or other request addressed to the court; and (2) promptly file a supplemental statement if any required information changes. FRCP 7.1(b).

v. *Index of exhibits.* Any pleading, motion, brief, affidavit, notice, or proposed order filed with the court, whether electronically or with the clerk, must: if it has four (4) or more exhibits, include a separate index that identifies and briefly describes each exhibit. IN R USDCTSD L.R. 5-1(b).

vi. *Request for oral argument.* A party may request oral argument by filing a separate motion explaining why oral argument is necessary and estimating how long the court should allow for the argument. The request must be filed and served with the supporting brief, response brief, or reply brief. IN R USDCTSD L.R. 7-5(a).

vii. *Request for evidentiary hearing.* A party may request an evidentiary hearing on a motion or petition by serving and filing a separate motion explaining why the hearing is necessary and estimating how long the court should allow for the hearing. IN R USDCTSD L.R. 7-5(c).

viii. *Copy of authority.* Generally, copies of cited authorities may not be attached to court filings. However, a party must attach to the party's motion or brief a copy of any cited authority if it is not available on Westlaw or Lexis. Upon request, a party must provide copies of any cited authority that is only available through electronic means to the court or the other parties. IN R USDCTSD L.R. 7-1(f).

ix. *Copy of document with self-address envelope.* To receive a file-stamped copy of a document filed directly with the clerk, a party must include with the original document an additional copy and a self-addressed envelope. The envelope must be big enough to hold the copy and have enough postage on it to send the copy via regular first-class mail. IN R USDCTSD L.R. 5-10(b).

x. *Notice of manual filing.* When a party who is not exempt from the electronic filing requirement

files a document directly with the clerk, the party must: electronically file a notice of manual filing that explains why the document cannot be filed electronically. IN R USDCTSD L.R. 5-2(d)(1). Refer to the Filing and Service Requirements section of this document for more information.

- Where an individual component cannot be included in an electronic filing (e.g. the component cannot be converted to electronic format), the filer shall electronically file the prescribed Notice of Manual Filing in place of that component. A model form is provided as Appendix C (IN R USDCTSD ECF Procedures(Appendix C)). IN R USDCTSD ECF Procedures(13).

- Before making a manual filing of a component, the filing party shall first electronically file a Notice of Manual Filing (See IN R USDCTSD ECF Procedures(Appendix C)). The filer shall initiate the electronic filing process as if filing the actual component but shall instead attach to the filing the Notice of Manual Filing setting forth the reason(s) why the component cannot be filed electronically. The manual filing should be accompanied by a copy of the previously filed Notice of Manual Filing. A party may seek to have a component excluded from electronic filing pursuant to applicable Federal and Local Rules (e.g., FRCP 26(c)). IN R USDCTSD ECF Procedures(15).

xi. *Courtesy copies.* District Judges and Magistrate Judges regularly receive documents filed by all parties. Therefore, parties shall not bring "courtesy copies" to any chambers unless specifically directed to do so by the Court. IN R USDCTSD Case Mgt(General Instructions For All Cases).

xii. *Copies for three-judge court.* Parties in a case where a three-judge court has been requested must file an original and three copies of any document filed directly with the clerk (instead of electronically) until the court: (1) denies the request; (2) dissolves the three-judge court; or (3) allows the parties to file fewer copies. IN R USDCTSD L.R. 9-2(c).

xiii. *Declaration that party was unable to file in a timely manner due to technical difficulties.* If a party misses a filing deadline due to an inability to file electronically, the party may submit the untimely filed document, accompanied by a declaration stating the reason(s) for missing the deadline. IN R USDCTSD ECF Procedures(16). A model form is provided as Appendix D (IN R USDCTSD ECF Procedures(Appendix D)). IN R USDCTSD ECF Procedures(16).

E. Format

1. *Form of documents.* The rules governing captions and other matters of form in pleadings apply to motions and other papers. FRCP 7(b)(2).

   a. *Paper (manual filings only).* Any document that is not filed electronically must: be flat, unfolded, and on good-quality, eight and one-half by eleven (8-1/2 x 11) inch white paper. IN R USDCTSD L.R. 5-1(d)(1). Any document that is not filed electronically must: be single-sided. IN R USDCTSD L.R. 5-1(d)(1).

      i. *Covers or backing.* Any document that is not filed electronically must: not have a cover or a back. IN R USDCTSD L.R. 5-1(d)(1).

      ii. *Fastening.* Any document that is not filed electronically must: be (if consisting of more than one (1) page) fastened by paperclip or binder clip and may not be stapled. IN R USDCTSD L.R. 5-1(d)(1).

         - *Request for nonconforming fastening.* If a document cannot be fastened or bound as required by IN R USDCTSD L.R. 5-1(d), a party may ask the clerk for permission to fasten it in another manner. The party must make such a request before attempting to file the document with nonconforming fastening. IN R USDCTSD L.R. 5-1(d)(2).

      iii. *Hole punching.* Any document that is not filed electronically must: be two-hole punched at the top with the holes two and three-quarter (2-3/4) inches apart and appropriately centered. IN R USDCTSD L.R. 5-1(d)(1).

   b. *Margins.* Any pleading, motion, brief, affidavit, notice, or proposed order filed with the court, whether electronically or with the clerk, must: have at least one (1) inch margins. IN R USDCTSD L.R. 5-1(b).

c. *Spacing.* Any pleading, motion, brief, affidavit, notice, or proposed order filed with the court, whether electronically or with the clerk, must: be double spaced (except for headings, footnotes, and quoted material). IN R USDCTSD L.R. 5-1(b).

d. *Text.* Any pleading, motion, brief, affidavit, notice, or proposed order filed with the court, whether electronically or with the clerk, must: be plainly typewritten, printed, or prepared by a clearly legible copying process. IN R USDCTSD L.R. 5-1(b).

e. *Font size.* Any pleading, motion, brief, affidavit, notice, or proposed order filed with the court, whether electronically or with the clerk, must: use at least 12-point type in the body of the document and at least 10-point type in footnotes. IN R USDCTSD L.R. 5-1(b).

f. *Page numbering.* Any pleading, motion, brief, affidavit, notice, or proposed order filed with the court, whether electronically or with the clerk, must: have consecutively numbered pages. IN R USDCTSD L.R. 5-1(b).

g. *Caption; Names of parties.* Every pleading must have a caption with the court's name, a title, a file number, and a FRCP 7(a) designation. The title of the complaint must name all the parties; the title of other pleadings, after naming the first party on each side, may refer generally to other parties. FRCP 10(a). Any pleading, motion, brief, affidavit, notice, or proposed order filed with the court, whether electronically or with the clerk, must: include a title on the first page. IN R USDCTSD L.R. 5-1(b).

    i. *Alternative motions.* Motions must be filed separately, but alternative motions may be filed in a single document if each is named in the title. IN R USDCTSD L.R. 7-1(a).

h. *Filer's information.* Any pleading, motion, brief, affidavit, notice, or proposed order filed with the court, whether electronically or with the clerk, must: in the case of pleadings, motions, legal briefs, and notices, include the name, complete address, telephone number, facsimile number (where available), and e-mail address (where available) of the pro se litigant or attorney who files it. IN R USDCTSD L.R. 5-1(b).

i. *Paragraphs; Separate statements.* A party must state its claims or defenses in numbered paragraphs, each limited as far as practicable to a single set of circumstances. A later pleading may refer by number to a paragraph in an earlier pleading. If doing so would promote clarity, each claim founded on a separate transaction or occurrence—and each defense other than a denial—must be stated in a separate count or defense. FRCP 10(b).

j. *Adoption by reference; Exhibits.* A statement in a pleading may be adopted by reference elsewhere in the same pleading or in any other pleading or motion. A copy of a written instrument that is an exhibit to a pleading is a part of the pleading for all purposes. FRCP 10(c).

k. *Citations*

    i. *Local rules.* The Local Rules of the United States District Court for the Southern District of Indiana may be cited as "S.D. Ind. L.R." IN R USDCTSD L.R. 1-1(a).

    ii. *Local alternative dispute resolution rules.* These Rules shall be known as the Local Alternative Dispute Resolution Rules of the United States District Court for the Southern District of Indiana. They shall be cited as "S.D.Ind. Local A.D.R. Rule _____." IN R USDCTSD A.D.R. Rule 1.1.

l. *Acceptance by the clerk.* The clerk must not refuse to file a paper solely because it is not in the form prescribed by the Federal Rules of Civil Procedure or by a local rule or practice. FRCP 5(d)(4). The clerk will accept a document that violates IN R USDCTSD L.R. 5-1, but the court may exclude the document from the official record. IN R USDCTSD L.R. 5-1(e).

    i. *Sanctions for errors as to form.* The court may strike from the record any document that does not comply with the rules governing the form of documents filed with the court, such as rules that regulate document size or the number of copies to be filed or that require a special designation in the caption. The court may also sanction an attorney or party who files a non-compliant document. IN R USDCTSD L.R. 1-3.

2. *Form of electronic documents.* Any document submitted via the court's electronic case filing (ECF)

system must be: otherwise prepared and filed in a manner consistent with the CM/ECF Policies and Procedures Manual (IN R USDCTSD ECF Procedures). IN R USDCTSD L.R. 5-1(c). Electronically filed documents must meet the requirements of FRCP 10 (Form of Pleadings), IN R USDCTSD L.R. 5-1 (Format of Papers Presented for Filing), and FRCP 5.2 (Privacy Protection for Filings Made with the Court), as if they had been submitted on paper. Documents filed electronically are also subject to any page limitations set forth by Court Order, by IN R USDCTSD L.R. 7-1 (Motion Practice), or IN R USDCTSD L.R. 56-1 (Summary Judgment Practice), as applicable. IN R USDCTSD ECF Procedures(13).

a. *PDF format required.* Any document submitted via the court's electronic case filing (ECF) system must be: in .pdf format. IN R USDCTSD L.R. 5-1(c); IN R USDCTSD ECF Procedures(7). Any document submitted via the court's electronic case filing (ECF) system must be: converted to a .pdf file directly from a word processing program, unless it exists only in paper format (in which case it may be scanned to create a .pdf document). IN R USDCTSD L.R. 5-1(c); IN R USDCTSD ECF Procedures(13).

    i. An exhibit may be scanned into PDF format, at a recommended 300 dpi resolution or higher, only if it does not already exist in electronic format. The filing attorney is responsible for reviewing all PDF documents for legibility before submitting them through the Court's Electronic Case Filing system. For technical guidance in creating PDF documents, please contact the Clerk's Office. IN R USDCTSD ECF Procedures(13).

b. *File size limitations.* Any document submitted via the court's electronic case filing (ECF) system must be: submitted as one or more .pdf files that do not exceed ten megabytes (10 MB) each (consistent with the CM/ECF Policies and Procedures Manual (IN R USDCTSD ECF Procedures)). IN R USDCTSD L.R. 5-1(c); IN R USDCTSD ECF Procedures(13).

    i. To electronically file a document or attachment that exceeds ten megabytes (10 MB), the document must first be broken down into two or more smaller files. For example, if Exhibit A is a twelve megabyte (12 MB) PDF file, it should be divided into 2 equal parts prior to electronic filing. Each component part of the exhibit would be filed as an attachment to the main document and described appropriately as "Exhibit A (part 1 of 2)" and "Exhibit A (part 2 of 2)." IN R USDCTSD ECF Procedures(13).

    ii. The supporting items mentioned in IN R USDCTSD ECF Procedures(13) should not be confused with memorandums or briefs in support of motions as outlined in IN R USDCTSD L.R. 7-1 or IN R USDCTSD L.R. 56-1. These memorandums or briefs in support are to be filed as entirely separate documents pursuant to the appropriate rule. Additionally, no motion shall be embodied in the text of a response or reply brief/memorandum unless otherwise ordered by the Court. IN R USDCTSD ECF Procedures(13).

c. *Separate component parts.* A key objective of the electronic filing system is to ensure that as much of the case as possible is managed electronically. To facilitate electronic filing and retrieval, documents to be filed electronically are to be reasonably broken into their separate component parts. By way of example, most filings include a foundation document (e.g., motion) and other supporting items (e.g., exhibits, proposed orders, proposed amended pleadings). The foundation document, as well as the supporting items, are each separate components of the filing; supporting items must be filed as attachments to the foundation document. These exhibits or attachments should include only those excerpts of the referenced documents that are directly germane to the matter under consideration. IN R USDCTSD ECF Procedures(13).

    i. Where an individual component cannot be included in an electronic filing (e.g. the component cannot be converted to electronic format), the filer shall electronically file the prescribed Notice of Manual Filing in place of that component. A model form is provided as Appendix C (IN R USDCTSD ECF Procedures(Appendix C)). IN R USDCTSD ECF Procedures(13).

d. *Exhibits.* Each electronically filed exhibit to a main document must be: (1) created as a separate .pdf file; (2) submitted as an attachment to the main document and given a title which describes its content; and (3) limited to excerpts that are directly germane to the main document's subject matter. IN R USDCTSD L.R. 5-6(a).

    i. When uploading attachments during the electronic filing process, exhibits must be uploaded in

a logical sequence and a brief description must be entered for each individual PDF file. The description must include not only the exhibit number or letter, but also a brief description of the document. This information may be entered in CM/ECF using a combination of the Category drop-down menu, the Description text box, or both (see IN R USDCTSD ECF Procedures(13)(Figure 1)). The information that is provided in each box will be combined to create a description of the document as it appears on the case docket (see IN R USDCTSD ECF Procedures(13)(Figure 2)). IN R USDCTSD ECF Procedures(13). For an example, refer to IN R USDCTSD ECF Procedures(13).

e. *Excerpts.* A party filing an exhibit that consists of excerpts from a larger document must clearly and prominently identify the exhibit as containing excerpted material. Either party will have the right to timely file additional excerpts or the complete document to the extent they are or become directly germane to the main document's subject matter. IN R USDCTSD L.R. 5-6(b).

f. For an example illustrating the application of IN R USDCTSD ECF Procedures(13), refer to IN R USDCTSD ECF Procedures(13).

3. *Form of briefs*

a. *Page limits.* Supporting and response briefs (excluding tables of contents, tables of authorities, appendices, and certificates of service) may not exceed thirty-five (35) pages. Reply briefs may not exceed twenty (20) pages. IN R USDCTSD L.R. 7-1(e)(1).

   i. *Permission to exceed limits.* The court may allow a party to file a brief exceeding these page limits for extraordinary and compelling reasons. IN R USDCTSD L.R. 7-1(e)(2).

   ii. *Supporting and response briefs exceeding limits.* If the court allows a party to file a brief or response exceeding thirty-five (35) pages, the document must include:

- A table of contents with page references;
- A statement of issues; and
- A table of authorities including: (1) all cases (alphabetically arranged), statutes, and other authorities cited in the brief; and (2) page numbers where the authorities are cited in the brief. IN R USDCTSD L.R. 7-1(e)(3).

4. *Signing of pleadings, motions and other papers*

a. *Signature.* Every pleading, written motion, and other paper must be signed by at least one attorney of record in the attorney's name—or by a party personally if the party is unrepresented. The paper must state the signer's address, e-mail address, and telephone number. FRCP 11(a).

   i. *Signatures on manual filings.* Any document that is not filed electronically must: include the original signature of the pro se litigant or attorney who files it. IN R USDCTSD L.R. 5-1(d)(1).

   ii. *Electronic signatures.* Use of the attorney's login and password when filing documents electronically serves in part as the attorney's signature for purposes of FRCP 11, the Local Rules of the United States District Court for the Southern District of Indiana, and any other purpose for which a signature is required in connection with proceedings before the Court. IN R USDCTSD ECF Procedures(14); IN R USDCTSD ECF Procedures(10). A pleading, motion, brief, or notice filed electronically under an attorney's ECF log-in and password must be signed by that attorney. IN R USDCTSD L.R. 5-7(a). A signature on a document other than a document filed as provided under IN R USDCTSD L.R. 5-7(a) must be an original handwritten signature and must be scanned into .pdf format for electronic filing. IN R USDCTSD L.R. 5-7(c); IN R USDCTSD ECF Procedures(14).

- *Form of electronic signature.* If a document is converted directly from a word processing application to .pdf (as opposed to scanning), the name of the Filing User under whose log-in and password the document is submitted must be preceded by a "s/" and typed on the signature line where the Filing User's handwritten signature would otherwise appear. IN R USDCTSD L.R. 5-7(b). All documents filed electronically shall include a signature block and include the filing attorney's typewritten name, address, telephone number, facsimile number and e-mail address. In addition, the name of the filing attorney under

whose ECF login the document will be filed should be preceded by a "s/" and typed in the space where the attorney's handwritten signature would otherwise appear. IN R US-DCTSD ECF Procedures(14). For a sample format, refer to IN R USDCTSD ECF Procedures(14).

- *Effect of electronic signature.* Filing an electronically signed document under an attorney's ECF log-in and password constitutes the attorney's signature on the document under the Federal Rules of Civil Procedure, under the Local Rules of the United States District Court for the Southern District of Indiana, and for any other reason a signature is required in connection with the court's activities. IN R USDCTSD L.R. 5-7(d).

- *Documents with multiple attorneys' signatures.* Documents requiring signatures of more than one attorney shall be filed either by: (1) obtaining consent from the other attorney, then typing the "s/ [Name]" signature of the other attorney on the signature line where the other attorney's signature would otherwise appear; (2) identifying in the signature section the name of the other attorney whose signature is required and by the submission of a Notice of Endorsement (see IN R USDCTSD ECF Procedures(Appendix B)) by the other attorney no later than three (3) business days after filing; (3) submitting a scanned document containing all handwritten signatures; or (4) in any other manner approved by the Court. IN R USDCTSD ECF Procedures(14); IN R USDCTSD L.R. 5-7(e).

iii. *No verification or accompanying affidavit required for pleadings.* Unless a rule or statute specifically states otherwise, a pleading need not be verified or accompanied by an affidavit. FRCP 11(a).

iv. *Unsigned papers.* The court must strike an unsigned paper unless the omission is promptly corrected after being called to the attorney's or party's attention. FRCP 11(a). The court will strike any document filed directly with the clerk that is not signed by an attorney of record or the pro se litigant filing it, but the court may do so only after giving the attorney or pro se litigant notice of the omission and reasonable time to correct it. Rubber-stamp or facsimile signatures are not original signatures and the court will deem documents containing them to be unsigned for purposes of FRCP 11 and FRCP 26(g) and IN R USDCTSD L.R. 5-10. IN R USDCTSD L.R. 5-10(g).

b. *Representations to the court.* By presenting to the court a pleading, written motion, or other paper—whether by signing, filing, submitting, or later advocating it—an attorney or unrepresented party certifies that to the best of the person's knowledge, information, and belief, formed after an inquiry reasonable under the circumstances:

i. It is not being presented for any improper purpose, such as to harass, cause unnecessary delay, or needlessly increase the cost of litigation;

ii. The claims, defenses, and other legal contentions are warranted by existing law or by a nonfrivolous argument for extending, modifying, or reversing existing law or for establishing new law;

iii. The factual contentions have evidentiary support or, if specifically so identified, will likely have evidentiary support after a reasonable opportunity for further investigation or discovery; and

iv. The denials of factual contentions are warranted on the evidence or, if specifically so identified, are reasonably based on belief or a lack of information. FRCP 11(b).

c. *Sanctions.* If, after notice and a reasonable opportunity to respond, the court determines that FRCP 11(b) has been violated, the court may impose an appropriate sanction on any attorney, law firm, or party that violated FRCP 11(b) or is responsible for the violation. FRCP 11(c)(1). Refer to the United States District Court for the Southern District of Indiana KeyRules Motion for Sanctions document for more information.

5. *Privacy protection for filings made with the court.* Electronically filed documents must meet the requirements of. . .FRCP 5.2 (Privacy Protection for Filings Made with the Court), as if they had been submitted on paper. IN R USDCTSD ECF Procedures(13).

a. *Redacted filings.* Unless the court orders otherwise, in an electronic or paper filing with the court that

contains an individual's Social Security number, taxpayer-identification number, or birth date, the name of an individual known to be a minor, or a financial-account number, a party or nonparty making the filing may include only:

    i. The last four (4) digits of the Social Security number and taxpayer-identification number;

    ii. The year of the individual's birth;

    iii. The minor's initials; and

    iv. The last four (4) digits of the financial-account number. FRCP 5.2(a).

b. *Exemptions from the redaction requirement.* The redaction requirement does not apply to the following:

    i. A financial-account number that identifies the property allegedly subject to forfeiture in a forfeiture proceeding;

    ii. The record of an administrative or agency proceeding;

    iii. The official record of a state-court proceeding;

    iv. The record of a court or tribunal, if that record was not subject to the redaction requirement when originally filed;

    v. A filing covered by FRCP 5.2(c) or FRCP 5.2(d); and

    vi. A pro se filing in an action brought under 28 U.S.C.A. § 2241, 28 U.S.C.A. § 2254, or 28 U.S.C.A. § 2255. FRCP 5.2(b).

c. *Limitations on remote access to electronic files; Social Security appeals and immigration cases.* Unless the court orders otherwise, in an action for benefits under the Social Security Act, and in an action or proceeding relating to an order of removal, to relief from removal, or to immigration benefits or detention, access to an electronic file is authorized as follows:

    i. The parties and their attorneys may have remote electronic access to any part of the case file, including the administrative record;

    ii. Any other person may have electronic access to the full record at the courthouse, but may have remote electronic access only to:

        • The docket maintained by the court; and

        • An opinion, order, judgment, or other disposition of the court, but not any other part of the case file or the administrative record. FRCP 5.2(c).

d. *Filings made under seal.* The court may order that a filing be made under seal without redaction. The court may later unseal the filing or order the person who made the filing to file a redacted version for the public record. FRCP 5.2(d). For more information on filing under seal, refer to IN R USDCTSD L.R. 5-11 and IN R USDCTSD ECF Procedures(18).

e. *Protective orders.* For good cause, the court may by order in a case:

    i. Require redaction of additional information; or

    ii. Limit or prohibit a nonparty's remote electronic access to a document filed with the court. FRCP 5.2(e).

f. *Option for additional unredacted filing under seal.* A person making a redacted filing may also file an unredacted copy under seal. The court must retain the unredacted copy as part of the record. FRCP 5.2(f).

g. *Option for filing a reference list.* A filing that contains redacted information may be filed together with a reference list that identifies each item of redacted information and specifies an appropriate identifier that uniquely corresponds to each item listed. The list must be filed under seal and may be amended as of right. Any reference in the case to a listed identifier will be construed to refer to the corresponding item of information. FRCP 5.2(g).

h. *Waiver of protection of identifiers.* A person waives the protection of FRCP 5.2(a) as to the person's own information by filing it without redaction and not under seal. FRCP 5.2(h).

F. Filing and Service Requirements

1. *Filing requirements.* Any paper after the complaint that is required to be served—together with a certificate of service—must be filed within a reasonable time after service. FRCP 5(d)(1). Motions must be filed separately, but alternative motions may be filed in a single document if each is named in the title. IN R USDCTSD L.R. 7-1(a).

   a. *How filing is made; In general.* A paper is filed by delivering it:

      i. To the clerk; or

      ii. To a judge who agrees to accept it for filing, and who must then note the filing date on the paper and promptly send it to the clerk. FRCP 5(d)(2).

      - In certain instances, the court will direct the parties to submit items directly to chambers (e.g., confidential settlement statements). However, absent specific prior authorization, counsel and litigants should not submit letters or documents directly to chambers, and such materials should be filed with the clerk. IN R USDCTSD L.R. 5-1(Local Rules Advisory Committee Comment).

      iii. A document or item submitted in relation to a matter within the court's jurisdiction is deemed filed upon delivery to the office of the clerk in a manner prescribed by the Local Rules of the United States District Court for the Southern District of Indiana or the Federal Rules of Civil Procedure or authorized by the court. Any submission directed to a Judge or Judge's staff, the office of the clerk or any employee thereof, in a manner that is not contemplated by IN R USDCTSD L.R. 5-1 and without prior court authorization is prohibited. IN R USDCTSD L.R. 5-1(a).

   b. *Non-electronic filing.* Any document that is exempt from electronic filing must be filed directly with the clerk and served on other parties in the case as required by those Federal Rules of Civil Procedure and Local Rules of the United States District Court for the Southern District of Indiana that apply to the service of non-electronic documents. IN R USDCTSD L.R. 5-2(c).

      i. *When completed.* A document or other item that is not required to be filed electronically is deemed filed:

      - Upon delivery in person, by courier, or via U.S. Mail or other mail delivery service to the clerk's office during business hours;

      - When the courtroom deputy clerk accepts it, if the document or item is filed in open court; or

      - Upon completion of any other manner of filing that the court authorizes. IN R USDCTSD L.R. 5-10(a).

      ii. *Document filing by non-exempt party.* When a party who is not exempt from the electronic filing requirement files a document directly with the clerk, the party must:

      - Electronically file a notice of manual filing that explains why the document cannot be filed electronically;

      - Present the document to the clerk within one (1) business day after filing the notice of manual filing; and

      - Present the clerk with a copy of the notice of manual filing when the party files the document with the clerk. IN R USDCTSD L.R. 5-2(d).

   c. *Electronic filing*

      i. *Authorization of electronic filing program.* A court may, by local rule, allow papers to be filed, signed, or verified by electronic means that are consistent with any technical standards established by the Judicial Conference of the United States. A local rule may require electronic filing only if reasonable exceptions are allowed. A paper filed electronically in compliance with a local rule is a written paper for purposes of the Federal Rules of Civil Procedure. FRCP 5(d)(3).

      - IN R USDCTSD L.R. 5-2 requires electronic filing, as allowed by FRCP 5(d)(3). The

policies and procedures in IN R USDCTSD ECF Procedures govern electronic filing in this district unless, due to circumstances in a particular case, a judicial officer determines that these policies and procedures (IN R USDCTSD ECF Procedures) should be modified. IN R USDCTSD ECF Procedures(1).

- Unless modified by order of the Court, all Federal Rules of Civil Procedure and Local Rules of the United States District Court for the Southern District of Indiana shall continue to apply to cases maintained in the Court's Case Management/Electronic Case Filing System (CM/ECF). IN R USDCTSD ECF Procedures(3).

ii. *Mandatory electronic filing.* Unless exempted pursuant to IN R USDCTSD L.R. 5-3(e), attorneys admitted to the court's bar (including those admitted pro hac vice) or authorized to represent the United States must use the court's ECF system to file documents. IN R USDCTSD L.R. 5-3(a). Electronic filing by attorneys is required for eligible documents filed in civil and criminal cases pending with the Court, unless specifically exempted by Local Rule or Court Order. IN R USDCTSD ECF Procedures(4).

- *Exceptions.* All civil cases (other than those cases the court specifically exempts) must be maintained in the court's electronic case filing (ECF) system. Accordingly, as allowed by FRCP 5(d)(3), every document filed in this court (including exhibits) must be transmitted to the clerk's office via the ECF system consistent with IN R USDCTSD L.R. 5-2 through IN R USDCTSD L.R. 5-11 except: (1) documents filed by pro se litigants; (2) transcripts in cases filed by claimants under the Social Security Act (and related statutes); (3) exhibits in a format that does not readily permit electronic filing (such as videos and large maps and charts); (4) documents that are illegible when scanned into .pdf format; (5) documents filed in cases not maintained on the ECF system; and (6) any other documents that the court or the Local Rules of the United States District Court for the Southern District of Indiana specifically allow to be filed directly with the clerk. IN R USDCTSD L.R. 5-2(a). Parties otherwise participating in the electronic filing system may be excused from filing a particular component electronically under certain limited circumstances, such as when the component cannot be reduced to an electronic format. Such components shall not be filed electronically, but instead shall be manually filed with the Clerk of Court and served upon the parties in accordance with the applicable Federal Rules of Civil Procedure and the Local Rules of the United States District Court for the Southern District of Indiana for filing and service of non-electronic documents. IN R USDCTSD ECF Procedures(15).

- *Exemption from participation.* The court may exempt attorneys from using the ECF system in a particular case for good cause. An attorney must file a petition for ECF exemption and a CM/ECF technical requirements exemption questionnaire in each case in which the attorney seeks an exemption. (The CM/ECF technical requirements exemption questionnaire is available on the court's website). IN R USDCTSD L.R. 5-3(e).

iii. *Consequences of electronic filing.* Electronic transmission of a document consistent with the procedures adopted by the Court shall, upon the complete receipt of the same by the Clerk of Court, constitute filing of the document for all purposes of the Federal Rules of Civil and Criminal Procedure and the Local Rules of the United States District Court for the Southern District of Indiana, and shall constitute entry of that document onto the docket maintained by the Clerk pursuant to FRCP 58 and FRCP 79. IN R USDCTSD ECF Procedures(7); IN R USDCTSD L.R. 5-4(c)(1). When a document has been filed electronically: the document, as filed, binds the filing party. IN R USDCTSD L.R. 5-4(c)(3).

- A Notice of Electronic Filing (NEF) acknowledging that the document has been filed will immediately appear on the filer's screen after the document has been submitted. Attorneys are strongly encouraged to print or electronically save a copy of the NEF. Attorneys can also verify the filing of documents by inspecting the Court's electronic docket sheet through the use of a PACER login. IN R USDCTSD ECF Procedures(7). When a document has been filed electronically: the notice of electronic filing for the document serves as the court's date-stamp and proof of filing. IN R USDCTSD L.R. 5-4(c)(4).

- The Court may, upon the motion of a party or upon its own motion, strike any inappropriately filed document. IN R USDCTSD ECF Procedures(7).

iv. For more information on electronic filing, refer to IN R USDCTSD ECF Procedures.

d. *Fax filing.* The clerk may not file a faxed document without court authorization. The court may not authorize the clerk to file faxed documents without finding that compelling circumstances justify it. A party must submit a copy of the document that otherwise complies with IN R USDCTSD L.R. 5-10 to replace the faxed copy within seven (7) days after faxing the document. IN R USDCTSD L.R. 5-10(e).

2. *Service requirements*

a. *Service; When required*

i. *In general.* Unless the Federal Rules of Civil Procedure provide otherwise, each of the following papers must be served on every party:

- An order stating that service is required;
- A pleading filed after the original complaint, unless the court orders otherwise under FRCP 5(c) because there are numerous defendants;
- A discovery paper required to be served on a party, unless the court orders otherwise;
- A written motion, except one that may be heard ex parte; and
- A written notice, appearance, demand, or offer of judgment, or any similar paper. FRCP 5(a)(1).

ii. *If a party fails to appear.* No service is required on a party who is in default for failing to appear. But a pleading that asserts a new claim for relief against such a party must be served on that party under FRCP 4. FRCP 5(a)(2).

iii. *Seizing property.* If an action is begun by seizing property and no person is or need be named as a defendant, any service required before the filing of an appearance, answer, or claim must be made on the person who had custody or possession of the property when it was seized. FRCP 5(a)(3).

b. *Service; How made*

i. *Serving an attorney.* If a party is represented by an attorney, service under FRCP 5 must be made on the attorney unless the court orders service on the party. FRCP 5(b)(1).

ii. *Service in general.* A paper is served under FRCP 5 by:

- Handing it to the person;
- Leaving it: (1) at the person's office with a clerk or other person in charge or, if no one is in charge, in a conspicuous place in the office; or (2) if the person has no office or the office is closed, at the person's dwelling or usual place of abode with someone of suitable age and discretion who resides there;
- Mailing it to the person's last known address—in which event service is complete upon mailing;
- Leaving it with the court clerk if the person has no known address;
- Sending it by electronic means if the person consented in writing—in which event service is complete upon transmission, but is not effective if the serving party learns that it did not reach the person to be served; or
- Delivering it by any other means that the person consented to in writing—in which event service is complete when the person making service delivers it to the agency designated to make delivery. FRCP 5(b)(2).

iii. *Electronic service*

- *Consent.* By registering to use the ECF system, attorneys consent to electronic service of documents filed in cases maintained on the ECF system. IN R USDCTSD L.R. 5-3(d). By participating in the Electronic Case Filing Program, attorneys consent to the electronic service of documents, and shall make available electronic mail addresses for service. IN R USDCTSD ECF Procedures(11).

- *Service on registered parties.* Upon the filing of a document by a party, an e-mail message will be automatically generated by the electronic filing system and sent via electronic mail to the e-mail addresses of all registered attorneys who have appeared in the case. The Notice of Electronic Filing will contain a document hyperlink which will provide recipients with one "free look" at the electronically filed document. Recipients are encouraged to print and/or save a copy of the document during the "free look" to avoid incurring PACER charges for future viewings of the document. IN R USDCTSD ECF Procedures(11). When a document has been filed electronically: transmission of the notice of electronic filing generated by the ECF system to an attorney's e-mail address constitutes service of the document on that attorney. IN R USDCTSD L.R. 5-4(c)(5). The party effectuates service on all registered attorneys by filing electronically. IN R USDCTSD ECF Procedures(11). When a document has been filed electronically: no other attempted service will constitute electronic service of the document. IN R USDCTSD L.R. 5-4(c)(6).

- *Service on exempt parties.* A filer must serve a copy of the document consistent with FRCP 5 on any party or attorney who is exempt from participating in electronic filing. IN R USDCTSD L.R. 5-4(d). It is the responsibility of the filing attorney to conventionally serve all parties who do not receive electronic service (the identity of these parties will be indicated on the filing receipt generated by the ECF system). IN R USDCTSD ECF Procedures(11).

- *Service on parties excused from electronic filing.* Parties otherwise participating in the electronic filing system may be excused from filing a particular component electronically under certain limited circumstances, such as when the component cannot be reduced to an electronic format. Such components shall not be filed electronically, but instead shall be manually filed with the Clerk of Court and served upon the parties in accordance with the applicable Federal Rules of Civil Procedure and the Local Rules of the United States District Court for the Southern District of Indiana for filing and service of non-electronic documents. IN R USDCTSD ECF Procedures(15).

- *Service of exempt documents.* Any document that is exempt from electronic filing must be filed directly with the clerk and served on other parties in the case as required by those Federal Rules of Civil Procedure and Local Rules of the United States District Court for the Southern District of Indiana that apply to the service of non-electronic documents. IN R USDCTSD L.R. 5-2(c).

iv. *Using court facilities.* If a local rule so authorizes, a party may use the court's transmission facilities to make service under FRCP 5(b)(2)(E). FRCP 5(b)(3).

c. *Serving numerous defendants*

i. *In general.* If an action involves an unusually large number of defendants, the court may, on motion or on its own, order that:

- Defendants' pleadings and replies to them need not be served on other defendants;

- Any crossclaim, counterclaim, avoidance, or affirmative defense in those pleadings and replies to them will be treated as denied or avoided by all other parties; and

- Filing any such pleading and serving it on the plaintiff constitutes notice of the pleading to all parties. FRCP 5(c)(1).

ii. *Notifying parties.* A copy of every such order must be served on the parties as the court directs. FRCP 5(c)(2).

G. Hearings

1. *Hearings, generally*

a. *Oral argument.* Due process does not require that oral argument be permitted on a motion and, except as otherwise provided by local rule, the district court has discretion to determine whether it will decide the motion on the papers or hear argument by counsel (and perhaps receive evidence). FPP § 1190; F.D.I.C. v. Deglau, 207 F.3d 153 (3d Cir. 2000).

i. *Request for oral argument.* A party may request oral argument by filing a separate motion

explaining why oral argument is necessary and estimating how long the court should allow for the argument. IN R USDCTSD L.R. 7-5(a). Refer to the Documents section of this document for more information.

    ii. *No additional evidence at oral argument.* Parties may not present additional evidence at oral argument. IN R USDCTSD L.R. 7-5(b).

  b. *Providing a regular schedule for oral hearings.* A court may establish regular times and places for oral hearings on motions. FRCP 78(a).

  c. *Providing for submission on briefs.* By rule or order, the court may provide for submitting and determining motions on briefs, without oral hearings. FRCP 78(b).

  d. *Request for evidentiary hearing.* A party may request an evidentiary hearing on a motion or petition by serving and filing a separate motion explaining why the hearing is necessary and estimating how long the court should allow for the hearing. IN R USDCTSD L.R. 7-5(c).

  e. *Directed by the court.* The court may: (1) grant or deny a request for oral argument or an evidentiary hearing in its sole discretion; (2) set oral argument or an evidentiary hearing without a request from a party; and (3) order any oral argument or evidentiary hearing to be held anywhere within the district regardless of where the case will be tried. IN R USDCTSD L.R. 7-5(d).

2. *Hearing on motion for preliminary injunction*

  a. *Consolidating the hearing with the trial on the merits.* Before or after beginning the hearing on a motion for a preliminary injunction, the court may advance the trial on the merits and consolidate it with the hearing. Even when consolidation is not ordered, evidence that is received on the motion and that would be admissible at trial becomes part of the trial record and need not be repeated at trial. But the court must preserve any party's right to a jury trial. FRCP 65(a)(2).

  b. *Expediting the hearing after temporary restraining order is issued without notice.* If the order is issued without notice, the motion for a preliminary injunction must be set for hearing at the earliest possible time, taking precedence over all other matters except hearings on older matters of the same character. At the hearing, the party who obtained the order must proceed with the motion; if the party does not, the court must dissolve the order. FRCP 65(b)(3).

3. *Courtroom and courthouse decorum.* For information on courtroom and courthouse decorum, refer to IN R USDCTSD L.R. 83-3.

H. Forms

1. Federal Motion for Preliminary Injunction Forms

  a. Declaration; In support of motion for preliminary injunction. AMJUR PP INJUNCTION § 38.

  b. Memorandum of points and authorities; In support of motion for preliminary injunction. AMJUR PP INJUNCTION § 39.

  c. Notice; Motion for preliminary injunction. AMJUR PP INJUNCTION § 40.

  d. Motion; For preliminary injunction. AMJUR PP INJUNCTION § 41.

  e. Motion; For preliminary injunction; On pleadings and other papers without evidentiary hearing or oral argument. AMJUR PP INJUNCTION § 43.

  f. Affidavit; In support of motion for preliminary injunction. AMJUR PP INJUNCTION § 52.

  g. Motion for preliminary injunction. 4A FEDFORMS § 5284.

  h. Motion enjoining use of information acquired from employment with plaintiff. 4A FEDFORMS § 5287.

  i. Motion enjoining interference with public access. 4A FEDFORMS § 5288.

  j. Motion enjoining collection of tax assessment. 4A FEDFORMS § 5289.

  k. Motion enjoining conducting election or certifying representative. 4A FEDFORMS § 5290.

  l. Motion enjoining preventing plaintiff's acting as teacher. 4A FEDFORMS § 5291.

  m. Motion enjoining interference with plaintiff's enforcement of judgment in related case. 4A FEDFORMS § 5292.

n.   Motion for preliminary injunction in patent infringement action. 4A FEDFORMS § 5293.

o.   Motion for preliminary injunction on basis of prayer of complaint and for setting hearing on motion. 4A FEDFORMS § 5294.

p.   Notice of motion. 4A FEDFORMS § 5308.

q.   Notice of motion and motion. 4A FEDFORMS § 5310.

r.   Bond; To obtain preliminary injunction. FEDPROF § 1:701.

s.   Opposition; To motion; General form. FEDPROF § 1:750.

t.   Brief; Supporting or opposing motion. FEDPROF § 1:752.

u.   Motion for temporary restraining order and preliminary injunction. GOLDLTGFMS § 13A:6.

v.   Motion for preliminary injunction. GOLDLTGFMS § 13A:18.

w.   Motion for preliminary injunction; Based upon pleadings and other papers without evidentiary hearing or oral argument. GOLDLTGFMS § 13A:19.

x.   Motion for preliminary injunction; Supporting affidavit. GOLDLTGFMS § 13A:20.

y.   Bond. GOLDLTGFMS § 19:2.

z.   Bond; In support of injunction. GOLDLTGFMS § 19:3.

2.   Forms for the Southern District of Indiana

a.   Notice of endorsement. IN R USDCTSD ECF Procedures(Appendix B).

b.   Notice of manual filing. IN R USDCTSD ECF Procedures(Appendix C).

c.   Declaration that party was unable to file in a timely manner due to technical difficulties. IN R USDCTSD ECF Procedures(Appendix D).

I. Applicable Rules

1. *Federal rules*

a.   Serving and filing pleadings and other papers. FRCP 5.

b.   Constitutional challenge to a statute; Notice, certification, and intervention. FRCP 5.1.

c.   Privacy protection for filings made with the court. FRCP 5.2.

d.   Computing and extending time; Time for motion papers. FRCP 6.

e.   Pleadings allowed; Form of motions and other papers. FRCP 7.

f.   Disclosure statement. FRCP 7.1.

g.   Form of pleadings. FRCP 10.

h.   Signing pleadings, motions, and other papers; Representations to the court; Sanctions. FRCP 11.

i.   Taking testimony. FRCP 43.

j.   Injunctions and restraining orders. FRCP 65.

k.   Proceedings against a surety. FRCP 65.1.

l.   Hearing motions; Submission on briefs. FRCP 78.

2. *Local rules*

a.   Scope of the rules. IN R USDCTSD L.R. 1-1.

b.   Sanctions for errors as to form. IN R USDCTSD L.R. 1-3.

c.   Format of documents presented for filing. IN R USDCTSD L.R. 5-1.

d.   Constitutional challenge to a statute; Notice. IN R USDCTSD L.R. 5.1-1.

e.   Filing of documents electronically required. IN R USDCTSD L.R. 5-2.

f.   Eligibility, registration, passwords for electronic filing; Exemption from electronic filing. IN R USDCTSD L.R. 5-3.

g. Timing and consequences of electronic filing. IN R USDCTSD L.R. 5-4.

h. Attachments and exhibits in cases filed electronically. IN R USDCTSD L.R. 5-6.

i. Signatures in cases filed electronically. IN R USDCTSD L.R. 5-7.

j. Non-electronic filings. IN R USDCTSD L.R. 5-10.

k. Motion practice. [IN R USDCTSD L.R. 7-1, as amended by IN ORDER 16-2319, effective December 1, 2016].

l. Oral arguments and hearings. IN R USDCTSD L.R. 7-5.

m. Request for three-judge court. IN R USDCTSD L.R. 9-2.

n. Filing of discovery materials. IN R USDCTSD L.R. 26-2.

o. Assignment of cases. IN R USDCTSD L.R. 40-1.

p. Motions for preliminary injunctions and temporary restraining orders. IN R USDCTSD L.R. 65-2.

q. Alternative dispute resolution. IN R USDCTSD A.D.R. Rule 1.1; IN R USDCTSD A.D.R. Rule 1.2; IN R USDCTSD A.D.R. Rule 1.5; IN R USDCTSD A.D.R. Rule 2.1; IN R USDCTSD A.D.R. Rule 2.2.

r. Instructions for preparing case management plan. IN R USDCTSD Case Mgt.

s. Electronic case filing policies and procedures manual. IN R USDCTSD ECF Procedures.

Motions, Oppositions and Replies
Motion to Dismiss for Failure to State a Claim

Document Last Updated December 2016

A. Checklist

(I) ❑ Matters to be considered by moving party

    (a) ❑ Required documents

        (1) ❑ Notice of motion and motion

        (2) ❑ Brief

        (3) ❑ Certificate of service

    (b) ❑ Supplemental documents

        (1) ❑ Pleading

        (2) ❑ Notice of constitutional question

        (3) ❑ Nongovernmental corporate disclosure statement

        (4) ❑ Index of exhibits

        (5) ❑ Request for oral argument

        (6) ❑ Request for evidentiary hearing

        (7) ❑ Copy of authority

        (8) ❑ Proposed order

        (9) ❑ Copy of document with self-address envelope

        (10) ❑ Notice of manual filing

        (11) ❑ Courtesy copies

        (12) ❑ Copies for three-judge court

        (13) ❑ Declaration that party was unable to file in a timely manner due to technical difficulties

    (c) ❑ Timing

        (1) ❑ Failure to state a claim upon which relief can be granted may be raised in any pleading

allowed or ordered under FRCP 7(a); every defense to a claim for relief in any pleading must be asserted in the responsive pleading if one is required

(2) ❏ A motion asserting any of the defenses in FRCP 12(b) must be made before pleading if a responsive pleading is allowed

(3) ❏ Failure to state a claim upon which relief can be granted may be raised by a motion under FRCP 12(c); after the pleadings are closed—but early enough not to delay trial—a party may move for judgment on the pleadings

(4) ❏ Failure to state a claim upon which relief can be granted may be raised at trial; if a pleading sets out a claim for relief that does not require a responsive pleading, an opposing party may assert at trial any defense to that claim

(5) ❏ A written motion and notice of the hearing must be served at least fourteen (14) days before the time specified for the hearing, with the following exceptions: (i) when the motion may be heard ex parte; (ii) when the Federal Rules of Civil Procedure set a different time; or (iii) when a court order—which a party may, for good cause, apply for ex parte—sets a different time

(6) ❏ Any affidavit supporting a motion must be served with the motion

(7) ❏ When a party who is not exempt from the electronic filing requirement files a document directly with the clerk, the party must present the document to the clerk within one (1) business day after filing the notice of manual filing

(8) ❏ Unless the court orders otherwise, the [untimely] document and declaration [that party was unable to file in a timely manner due to technical difficulties] must be filed no later than 12:00 noon of the first day on which the court is open for business following the original filing deadline

(II) ❏ Matters to be considered by opposing party
  (a) ❏ Required documents
    (1) ❏ Response brief
    (2) ❏ Certificate of service
  (b) ❏ Supplemental documents
    (1) ❏ Pleading
    (2) ❏ Notice of constitutional question
    (3) ❏ Index of exhibits
    (4) ❏ Request for oral argument
    (5) ❏ Request for evidentiary hearing
    (6) ❏ Copy of authority
    (7) ❏ Copy of document with self-address envelope
    (8) ❏ Notice of manual filing
    (9) ❏ Courtesy copies
    (10) ❏ Copies for three-judge court
    (11) ❏ Declaration that party was unable to file in a timely manner due to technical difficulties
  (c) ❏ Timing
    (1) ❏ Any response is due within fourteen (14) days after service of the motion
    (2) ❏ Except as FRCP 59(c) provides otherwise, any opposing affidavit must be served at least seven (7) days before the hearing, unless the court permits service at another time
    (3) ❏ When a party who is not exempt from the electronic filing requirement files a document directly with the clerk, the party must present the document to the clerk within one (1) business day after filing the notice of manual filing

(4) ❏ Unless the court orders otherwise, the [untimely] document and declaration [that party was unable to file in a timely manner due to technical difficulties] must be filed no later than 12:00 noon of the first day on which the court is open for business following the original filing deadline

B. Timing

1. *Motion to dismiss for failure to state a claim*

   a. *In a pleading under FRCP 7(a).* Failure to state a claim upon which relief can be granted may be raised in any pleading allowed or ordered under FRCP 7(a). FRCP 12(h)(2)(A).

      i. *In a responsive pleading.* Every defense to a claim for relief in any pleading must be asserted in the responsive pleading if one is required. FRCP 12(b).

   b. *By motion.* A motion asserting any of the defenses in FRCP 12(b) must be made before pleading if a responsive pleading is allowed. FRCP 12(b). Although FRCP 12(b) encourages the responsive pleader to file a motion to dismiss before filing the answer, nothing in FRCP 12 prohibits the filing of a motion to dismiss with the answer. An untimely motion to dismiss may be considered if the defense asserted in the motion was previously raised in the responsive pleading. FEDPROC § 62:427.

   c. *By motion under FRCP 12(c).* Failure to state a claim upon which relief can be granted may be raised by a motion under FRCP 12(c). FRCP 12(h)(2)(B). After the pleadings are closed—but early enough not to delay trial—a party may move for judgment on the pleadings. FRCP 12(c).

   d. *At trial.* Failure to state a claim upon which relief can be granted may be raised at trial. FRCP 12(h)(2)(C). If a pleading sets out a claim for relief that does not require a responsive pleading, an opposing party may assert at trial any defense to that claim. FRCP 12(b).

2. *Timing of motions, generally*

   a. *Motion and notice of hearing.* A written motion and notice of the hearing must be served at least fourteen (14) days before the time specified for the hearing, with the following exceptions:

      i. When the motion may be heard ex parte;

      ii. When the Federal Rules of Civil Procedure set a different time; or

      iii. When a court order—which a party may, for good cause, apply for ex parte—sets a different time. FRCP 6(c)(1).

   b. *Supporting affidavit.* Any affidavit supporting a motion must be served with the motion. FRCP 6(c)(2).

3. *Timing of opposing papers.* Any response is due within fourteen (14) days after service of the motion. IN R USDCTSD L.R. 7-1(c)(2)(A).

   a. *Opposing affidavit.* Except as FRCP 59(c) provides otherwise, any opposing affidavit must be served at least seven (7) days before the hearing, unless the court permits service at another time. FRCP 6(c)(2).

   b. *Extensions.* The court may extend response and reply deadlines, but only for good cause. IN R USDCTSD L.R. 7-1(c)(3).

   c. *Summary ruling on failure to respond.* The court may summarily rule on a motion if an opposing party does not file a response within the deadline. IN R USDCTSD L.R. 7-1(c)(4).

4. *Timing of reply papers.* Where the respondent files an answering affidavit setting up a new matter, the moving party ordinarily is allowed a reasonable time to file a reply affidavit since failure to deny the new matter by affidavit may operate as an admission of its truth. AMJUR MOTIONS § 25.

   a. *Reply brief.* Any reply is due within seven (7) days after service of the response. IN R USDCTSD L.R. 7-1(c)(2)(B).

   b. *Extensions.* The court may extend response and reply deadlines, but only for good cause. IN R USDCTSD L.R. 7-1(c)(3).

5. *Effect of a FRCP 12 motion on the time to serve a responsive pleading.* Unless the court sets a different time, serving a motion under FRCP 12 alters the periods in FRCP 12(a) as follows:

   a. If the court denies the motion or postpones its disposition until trial, the responsive pleading must be served within fourteen (14) days after notice of the court's action; or

   b. If the court grants a motion for a more definite statement, the responsive pleading must be served within fourteen (14) days after the more definite statement is served. FRCP 12(a)(4).

6. *Document filing by non-exempt party.* When a party who is not exempt from the electronic filing requirement files a document directly with the clerk, the party must: present the document to the clerk within one (1) business day after filing the notice of manual filing. IN R USDCTSD L.R. 5-2(d)(2).

7. *Declaration that party was unable to file in a timely manner due to technical difficulties.* Unless the Court orders otherwise, the [untimely] document and declaration [that party was unable to file in a timely manner due to technical difficulties] must be filed no later than 12:00 noon of the first day on which the Court is open for business following the original filing deadline. IN R USDCTSD ECF Procedures(16).

8. *Computation of time*

   a. *Computing time.* FRCP 6 applies in computing any time period specified in the Federal Rules of Civil Procedure, in any local rule or court order, or in any statute that does not specify a method of computing time. FRCP 6(a).

      i. *Period stated in days or a longer unit.* When the period is stated in days or a longer unit of time:

         • Exclude the day of the event that triggers the period;

         • Count every day, including intermediate Saturdays, Sundays, and legal holidays; and

         • Include the last day of the period, but if the last day is a Saturday, Sunday, or legal holiday, the period continues to run until the end of the next day that is not a Saturday, Sunday, or legal holiday. FRCP 6(a)(1).

      ii. *Period stated in hours.* When the period is stated in hours:

         • Begin counting immediately on the occurrence of the event that triggers the period;

         • Count every hour, including hours during intermediate Saturdays, Sundays, and legal holidays; and

         • If the period would end on a Saturday, Sunday, or legal holiday, the period continues to run until the same time on the next day that is not a Saturday, Sunday, or legal holiday. FRCP 6(a)(2).

      iii. *Inaccessibility of the clerk's office.* Unless the court orders otherwise, if the clerk's office is inaccessible:

         • On the last day for filing under FRCP 6(a)(1), then the time for filing is extended to the first accessible day that is not a Saturday, Sunday, or legal holiday; or

         • During the last hour for filing under FRCP 6(a)(2), then the time for filing is extended to the same time on the first accessible day that is not a Saturday, Sunday, or legal holiday. FRCP 6(a)(3).

      iv. *"Last day" defined.* Unless a different time is set by a statute, local rule, or court order, the last day ends:

         • For electronic filing, at midnight in the court's time zone; and

         • For filing by other means, when the clerk's office is scheduled to close. FRCP 6(a)(4).

      v. *"Next day" defined.* The "next day" is determined by continuing to count forward when the period is measured after an event and backward when measured before an event. FRCP 6(a)(5).

      vi. *"Legal holiday" defined.* "Legal holiday" means:

         • The day set aside by statute for observing New Year's Day, Martin Luther King Jr.'s Birthday, Washington's Birthday, Memorial Day, Independence Day, Labor Day, Columbus Day, Veterans' Day, Thanksgiving Day, or Christmas Day;

- Any day declared a holiday by the President or Congress; and

- For periods that are measured after an event, any other day declared a holiday by the state where the district court is located. FRCP 6(a)(6).

b. *Computation of electronic filing deadlines.* Filing documents electronically does not alter filing deadlines. IN R USDCTSD ECF Procedures(7). A document due on a particular day must be filed before midnight local time of the division where the case is pending. IN R USDCTSD L.R. 5-4(a). All electronic transmissions of documents must be completed (i.e. received completely by the Clerk's Office) prior to midnight of the local time of the division in which the case is pending in order to be considered timely filed that day (NOTE: time will be noted in Eastern Time on the Court's docket. If you have filed a document prior to midnight local time of the division in which the case is pending and the document is due that date, but the electronic receipt and docket reflect the following calendar day, please contact the Court). IN R USDCTSD ECF Procedures(7). Although attorneys may file documents electronically twenty-four (24) hours a day, seven (7) days a week, attorneys are encouraged to file all documents during the normal working hours of the Clerk's Office (Monday through Friday, 8:30 a.m. to 4:30 p.m.) when technical support is available. IN R USDCTSD ECF Procedures(7); IN R USDCTSD ECF Procedures(9).

  i. *Technical difficulties.* Parties are encouraged to file documents electronically during normal business hours, in case a problem is encountered. In the event a technical failure occurs and a document cannot be filed electronically despite the best efforts of the filing party, the party should print (if possible) a copy of the error message received. In addition, as soon as practically possible, the party should file a "Declaration that Party was Unable to File in a Timely Manner Due to Technical Difficulties." A model form is provided as Appendix D (IN R USDCTSD ECF Procedures(Appendix D)). IN R USDCTSD ECF Procedures(16).

    - If a party is unable to file electronically and, as a result, may miss a filing deadline, the party must contact the Clerk's Office at the number listed in IN R USDCTSD ECF Procedures(15) to inform the court's staff of the difficulty. If a party misses a filing deadline due to an inability to file electronically, the party may submit the untimely filed document, accompanied by a declaration stating the reason(s) for missing the deadline. Unless the Court orders otherwise, the document and declaration must be filed no later than 12:00 noon of the first day on which the Court is open for business following the original filing deadline. IN R USDCTSD ECF Procedures(16).

c. *Extending time*

  i. *In general.* When an act may or must be done within a specified time, the court may, for good cause, extend the time:

    - With or without motion or notice if the court acts, or if a request is made, before the original time or its extension expires; or

    - On motion made after the time has expired if the party failed to act because of excusable neglect. FRCP 6(b)(1).

  ii. *Exceptions.* A court must not extend the time to act under FRCP 50(b), FRCP 50(d), FRCP 52(b), FRCP 59(b), FRCP 59(d), FRCP 59(e), and FRCP 60(b). FRCP 6(b)(2).

  iii. Refer to the United States District Court for the Southern District of Indiana KeyRules Motion for Continuance/Extension of Time document for more information on extending time.

d. *Additional time after certain kinds of service.* When a party may or must act within a specified time after being served and service is made under FRCP 5(b)(2)(C) (mail), FRCP 5(b)(2)(D) (leaving with the clerk), or FRCP 5(b)(2)(F) (other means consented to), three (3) days are added after the period would otherwise expire under FRCP 6(a). FRCP 6(d). Service by electronic mail shall constitute service pursuant to FRCP 5(b)(2)(E) and shall entitle the party being served to the additional three (3) days provided by FRCP 6(d). IN R USDCTSD ECF Procedures(11).

C. General Requirements

1. *Motions, generally*

   a. *Requirements.* A request for a court order must be made by motion. The motion must:

      i. Be in writing unless made during a hearing or trial;

      ii. State with particularity the grounds for seeking the order; and

      iii. State the relief sought. FRCP 7(b)(1).

   b. *Notice of motion.* A party interested in resisting the relief sought by a motion has a right to notice thereof, and an opportunity to be heard. AMJUR MOTIONS § 12.

      i. In addition to statutory or court rule provisions requiring notice of a motion—the purpose of such a notice requirement having been said to be to prevent a party from being prejudicially surprised by a motion—principles of natural justice dictate that an adverse party generally must be given notice that a motion will be presented to the court. AMJUR MOTIONS § 12.

      ii. "Notice," in this regard, means reasonable notice, including a meaningful opportunity to prepare and to defend against allegations of a motion. AMJUR MOTIONS § 12.

   c. *Writing requirement.* The writing requirement is intended to insure that the adverse parties are informed and have a record of both the motion's pendency and the grounds on which the movant seeks an order. FPP § 1191; Feldberg v. Quechee Lakes Corp., 463 F.3d 195 (2d Cir. 2006).

      i. It is sufficient "if the motion is stated in a written notice of the hearing of the motion." FPP § 1191.

   d. *Particularity requirement.* The particularity requirement insures that the opposing parties will have notice of their opponent's contentions. FEDPROC § 62:364; Goodman v. 1973 26 Foot Trojan Vessel, Arkansas Registration No. AR1439SN, 859 F.2d 71, 12 Fed.R.Serv.3d 645 (8th Cir. 1988). That requirement ensures that notice of the basis for the motion is provided to the court and to the opposing party so as to avoid prejudice, provide the opponent with a meaningful opportunity to respond, and provide the court with enough information to process the motion correctly. FEDPROC § 62:364; Andreas v. Volkswagen of America, Inc., 336 F.3d 789, 56 Fed.R.Serv.3d 6 (8th Cir. 2003).

      i. Reasonable specification of the grounds for a motion is sufficient. However, where a movant fails to state even one ground for granting the motion in question, the movant has failed to meet the minimal standard of "reasonable specification." FEDPROC § 62:364; Martinez v. Trainor, 556 F.2d 818, 23 Fed.R.Serv.2d 403 (7th Cir. 1977).

      ii. The court may excuse the failure to comply with the particularity requirement if it is inadvertent, and where no prejudice is shown by the opposing party. FEDPROC § 62:364.

   e. *Motions must be filed separately.* Motions must be filed separately, but alternative motions may be filed in a single document if each is named in the title. A motion must not be contained within a brief, response, or reply to a previously filed motion, unless ordered by the court. IN R USDCTSD L.R. 7-1(a).

   f. *Routine or uncontested motions.* The court may rule upon a routine or uncontested motion before the response deadline passes, unless: (1) the motion indicates that an opposing party objects to it; or (2) the court otherwise believes that a response will be filed. IN R USDCTSD L.R. 7-1(d).

2. *Motion to dismiss for failure to state a claim.* A party may assert the defense of failure to state a claim upon which relief can be granted by motion. FRCP 12(b)(6). The motion under FRCP 12(b)(6) is available to test a claim for relief in any pleading, whether it be in the plaintiff's original complaint, a defendant's counterclaim, a defendant's cross-claim or counterclaim thereto, or a third-party claim or any other FRCP 14 claim. Most commonly, of course, a FRCP 12(b)(6) motion is directed against the plaintiff's complaint. FPP § 1356.

   a. *Applicable standard.* The FRCP 12(b)(6) motion is used to test the sufficiency of the complaint. FEDPROC § 62:461; Petruska v. Gannon University, 462 F.3d 294, 212 Ed.Law.Rep. 598 (3d Cir. 2006). In this regard, the applicable standard is stated in FRCP 8(a)(2), which requires that a pleading setting forth a claim for relief contain a short and plain statement of the claim showing that the pleader is entitled to relief. Thus, a complaint must set forth sufficient information to suggest that there is some recognized legal theory upon which relief can be granted. FEDPROC § 62:461. Only when the plaintiff's complaint fails to meet this liberal pleading standard is it subject to dismissal under FRCP 12(b)(6). FPP § 1356.

    i. In order to withstand a motion to dismiss filed under FRCP 12(b)(6) in response to claims understood to raise a high risk of abusive litigation, addressed by FRCP 9(b), a plaintiff must state factual allegations with greater particularity than that required by FRCP 8. FEDPROC § 62:470; Bell Atlantic Corp. v. Twombly, 550 U.S. 544, 127 S.Ct. 1955, 167 L.Ed.2d 929, 68 Fed.R.Serv.3d 661 (2007).

    ii. FRCP 12(b)(6) motions are looked on with disfavor by the courts, and are granted sparingly and with care. FEDPROC § 62:464. Even if it is doubtful that the plaintiff would ultimately prevail, if the plaintiff colorably states facts which, if proven, would entitle him or her to relief, a motion to dismiss for failure to state a claim should not be granted. FEDPROC § 62:464.

b. *Construction of allegations of complaint (or other pleading).* In considering a FRCP 12(b)(6) motion to dismiss, the complaint is liberally construed and is viewed in the light most favorable to the plaintiff. FEDPROC § 62:467; Bell Atlantic Corp. v. Twombly, 550 U.S. 544, 127 S.Ct. 1955, 167 L.Ed.2d 929, 68 Fed.R.Serv.3d 661 (2007).

    i. On a motion to dismiss, a federal court presumes that general allegations embrace those specific facts that are necessary to support the claim. FEDPROC § 62:467; Steel Co. v. Citizens for a Better Environment, 523 U.S. 83, 118 S.Ct. 1003, 140 L.Ed.2d 210 (1998).

    ii. In addition, the well-pleaded allegations of fact contained in the complaint and every inference fairly deducible therefrom are accepted as true for purposes of the motion, including facts alleged on information and belief. FEDPROC § 62:467; Bell Atlantic Corp. v. Twombly, 550 U.S. 544, 127 S.Ct. 1955, 167 L.Ed.2d 929, 68 Fed.R.Serv.3d 661 (2007); Tellabs, Inc. v. Makor Issues & Rights, Ltd., 551 U.S. 308, 127 S.Ct. 2499, 168 L.Ed.2d 179 (2007).

    iii. However, the court will not accept as true the plaintiff's bare statements of opinions, conclusory allegations, and unwarranted inferences of fact. FEDPROC § 62:467; Leopoldo Fontanillas, Inc. v. Luis Ayala Colon Sucesores, Inc., 283 F.Supp.2d 579 (D.P.R. 2003); Hopkins v. Women's Div., General Bd. of Global Ministries, 238 F.Supp.2d 174 (D.D.C. 2002). Nor will the court accept as true facts which are legally impossible, facts which the court can take judicial notice of as being other than as alleged by the plaintiff, or facts which by the record or by a document attached to the complaint appear to be unfounded. FEDPROC § 62:467; Cohen v. U.S., 129 F.2d 733 (8th Cir. 1942); Henthorn v. Department of Navy, 29 F.3d 682, 29 Fed.R.Serv.3d 1007 (D.C. Cir. 1994).

c. *Affirmative defenses.* With some exception, it is generally agreed that affirmative defenses can be raised by a FRCP 12(b)(6) motion to dismiss. FEDPROC § 62:471; McCready v. eBay, Inc., 453 F.3d 882 (7th Cir. 2006). However, in order for these defenses to be raised on a FRCP 12(b)(6) motion to dismiss, the complaint must clearly show on its face that the affirmative defense is applicable and bars the action. FEDPROC § 62:471; In re Colonial Mortgage Bankers Corp., 324 F.3d 12 (1st Cir. 2003). Thus, FRCP 12(b)(6) motions may be used to raise the affirmative defenses of: (1) statute of limitations; (2) statute of frauds; (3) res judicata; (4) collateral estoppel; (5) release; (6) waiver; (7) estoppel; (8) sovereign immunity; (9) illegality; and (10) contributory negligence. FEDPROC § 62:471.

d. *Joining motions*

    i. *Right to join.* A motion under FRCP 12 may be joined with any other motion allowed by FRCP 12. FRCP 12(g)(1).

    ii. *Limitation on further motions.* Except as provided in FRCP 12(h)(2) or FRCP 12(h)(3), a party that makes a motion under FRCP 12 must not make another motion under FRCP 12 raising a defense or objection that was available to the party but omitted from its earlier motion. FRCP 12(g)(2).

e.   *Waiving and preserving certain defenses.* No defense or objection is waived by joining it with one or more other defenses or objections in a responsive pleading or in a motion. FRCP 12(b).

   i.   *When some are waived.* A party waives any defense listed in FRCP 12(b)(2) through FRCP 12(b)(5) by:

   • Omitting it from a motion in the circumstances described in FRCP 12(g)(2); or

   • Failing to either: (1) make it by motion under FRCP 12; or (2) include it in a responsive pleading or in an amendment allowed by FRCP 15(a)(1) as a matter of course. FRCP 12(h)(1).

   ii.   *When to raise others.* Failure to state a claim upon which relief can be granted, to join a person required by FRCP 19(b), or to state a legal defense to a claim may be raised:

   • In any pleading allowed or ordered under FRCP 7(a);

   • By a motion under FRCP 12(c); or

   • At trial. FRCP 12(h)(2).

   iii.   *Lack of subject matter jurisdiction.* If the court determines at any time that it lacks subject-matter jurisdiction, the court must dismiss the action. FRCP 12(h)(3).

3.   *Opposing papers.* The Federal Rules of Civil Procedure do not require any formal answer, return, or reply to a motion, except where the Federal Rules of Civil Procedure or local rules may require affidavits, memoranda, or other papers to be filed in opposition to a motion. Such papers are simply to apprise the court of such opposition and the grounds of that opposition. FEDPROC § 62:359.

   a.   *Effect of failure to respond to motion.* Although in the absence of statutory provision or court rule, a motion ordinarily does not require a written answer, when a party files a motion and the opposing party fails to respond, the court may construe such failure to respond as nonopposition to the motion or an admission that the motion was meritorious, may take the facts alleged in the motion as true—the rule in some jurisdictions being that the failure to respond to a fact set forth in a motion is deemed an admission—and may grant the motion if the relief requested appears to be justified. AMJUR MOTIONS § 28.

   b.   *Assent or no opposition not determinative.* However, a motion will not be granted automatically simply because an "assent" or a notation of "no opposition" has been filed; federal judges frequently deny motions that have been assented to when it is thought that justice so dictates. FPP § 1190.

   c.   *Responsive pleading inappropriate as response to motion.* An attempt to answer or oppose a motion with a responsive pleading usually is not appropriate. FPP § 1190.

4.   *Reply papers.* A moving party may be required or permitted to prepare papers in addition to his original motion papers. AMJUR MOTIONS § 25. Papers answering or replying to opposing papers may be appropriate, in the interests of justice, where it appears there is a substantial reason for allowing a reply. Thus, a court may accept reply papers where a party demonstrates that the papers to which it seeks to file a reply raise new issues that are material to the disposition of the question before the court, or where the court determines, sua sponte, that it wishes further briefing of an issue raised in those papers and orders the submission of additional papers. FEDPROC § 62:360.

   a.   *Function of reply papers.* The function of a reply affidavit is to answer the arguments made in opposition to the position taken by the movant and not to permit the movant to introduce new arguments in support of the motion. AMJUR MOTIONS § 25.

   b.   *Issues raised for the first time in a reply document.* However, the view has been followed in some jurisdictions, that as a matter of judicial economy, where there is no prejudice and where the issues could be raised simply by filing a motion to dismiss, the trial court has discretion to consider arguments raised for the first time in a reply memorandum, and that a trial court may grant a motion to strike issues raised for the first time in a reply memorandum. AMJUR MOTIONS § 26.

5.   *Appearances.* Every attorney who represents a party or who files a document on a party's behalf must file an appearance for that party. IN R USDCTSD L.R. 83-7. The filing of a Notice of Appearance shall act to establish the filing attorney as an attorney of record representing a designated party or parties in a

particular cause of action. As a result, it is necessary for each attorney to file a separate Notice of Appearance when entering an appearance in a case. A joint appearance on behalf of multiple attorneys may be filed electronically only if it is filed separately for each attorney, using his/her ECF login. IN R USDCTSD ECF Procedures(12). Only those attorneys who have filed an appearance in a pending action are entitled to be served with case documents under FRCP 5(a). IN R USDCTSD L.R. 83-7. For more information, refer to IN R USDCTSD L.R. 83-7 and IN R USDCTSD ECF Procedures(12).

6. *Notice of related action.* A party must file a notice of related action: as soon as it appears that the party's case and another pending case: (1) arise out of the same transaction or occurrence; (2) involve the same property; or (3) involve the validity or infringement or the same patent, trademark, or copyright. IN R USDCTSD L.R. 40-1(d)(2). For more information, refer to IN R USDCTSD L.R. 40-1.

7. *Alternative dispute resolution (ADR)*

   a. *Application.* Unless limited by specific provisions, or unless there are other applicable specific statutory, common law, or constitutional procedures, the Local Alternative Dispute Resolution Rules of the United States District Court for the Southern District of Indiana shall apply in all civil litigation filed in the U.S. District Court for the Southern District of Indiana, except in the following cases and proceedings:

      i. Applications for writs of habeas corpus under 28 U.S.C.A. § 2254;

      ii. Forfeiture cases;

      iii. Non-adversary proceedings in bankruptcy;

      iv. Social Security administrative review cases; and

      v. Such other matters as specified by order of the Court; for example, matters involving important public policy issues, constitutional law, or the establishment of new law. IN R USDCTSD A.D.R. Rule 1.2.

   b. *Mediation.* Mediation under this section (IN R USDCTSD A.D.R. Rule 2.1, et seq.) involves the confidential process by which a person acting as a Mediator, selected by the parties or appointed by the Court, assists the litigants in reaching a mutually acceptable agreement. It is an informal and nonadversarial process. The role of the Mediator is to assist in identifying the issues, reducing misunderstandings, clarifying priorities, exploring areas of compromise, and finding points of agreement as well as legitimate points of disagreement. Final decision-making authority rests with the parties, not the Mediator. IN R USDCTSD A.D.R. Rule 2.1. It is anticipated that an agreement may not resolve all of the disputed issues, but the process, nonetheless, can reduce points of contention. Parties and their representatives are required to mediate in good faith, but are not compelled to reach an agreement. IN R USDCTSD A.D.R. Rule 2.1.

      i. *Case selection.* The Court with the agreement of the parties may refer a civil case for mediation. Unless otherwise ordered or as specifically provided in IN R USDCTSD A.D.R. Rule 2.8, referral to mediation does not abate or suspend the action, and no scheduled dates shall be delayed or deferred, including the date of trial. IN R USDCTSD A.D.R. Rule 2.2.

      ii. For more information on mediation, refer to IN R USDCTSD A.D.R. Rule 2.1, et seq.

   c. *Other methods of dispute resolution.* The Local Alternative Dispute Resolution Rules of the United States District Court for the Southern District of Indiana shall not preclude the parties from utilizing any other reasonable method or technique of alternative dispute resolution to resolve disputes to which the parties agree. However, any use of arbitration by the parties will be governed by and comply with the requirements of 28 U.S.C.A. § 654 through 28 U.S.C.A. § 657. IN R USDCTSD A.D.R. Rule 1.5.

   d. For more information on alternative dispute resolution (ADR), refer to IN R USDCTSD A.D.R. Rule 1.1, et seq.

8. *Notice of settlement or resolution.* The parties must immediately notify the court if they reasonably anticipate settling their case or resolving a pending motion. IN R USDCTSD L.R. 7-1(h).

9. *Modification or suspension of rules.* The court may, on its own motion or at the request of a party, suspend or modify any rule in a particular case in the interest of justice. IN R USDCTSD L.R. 1-1(c).

D. Documents

1. *Documents for moving party*

   a. *Required documents*

      i. *Notice of motion and motion.* Refer to the General Requirements section of this document for information on the notice of motion and motion.

      ii. *Brief.* The following motion must also be accompanied by a supporting brief: a motion to dismiss. IN R USDCTSD L.R. 7-1(b)(1). Refer to the Format section of this document for the format of briefs.

      iii. *Certificate of service.* FRCP 5(d) requires that the person making service under FRCP 5 certify that service has been effected. FRCP 5(Advisory Committee Notes). Having such information on file may be useful for many purposes, including proof of service if an issue arises concerning the effectiveness of the service. FRCP 5(Advisory Committee Notes).

         - *Certificate of service for electronically-filed documents.* A certificate of service must be included with all documents filed electronically. Such certificate shall indicate that service was accomplished pursuant to the Court's electronic filing procedures. IN R USDCTSD ECF Procedures(11). For the suggested format for a certificate of service for electronic filing, refer to IN R USDCTSD ECF Procedures(11).

   b. *Supplemental documents*

      i. *Pleading.* As a general rule, the court may only consider the pleading which is attacked by a FRCP 12(b)(6) motion in determining its sufficiency. FEDPROC § 62:466; Armengau v. Cline, 7 Fed.Appx. 336 (6th Cir. 2001). The plaintiff is not entitled to discovery to obtain information relevant to the motion, and the court is not permitted to look at matters outside the record. FEDPROC § 62:466; Cooperativa de Ahorro y Credito Aguada v. Kidder, Peabody & Co., 993 F.2d 269, 37 Fed.R.Evid.Serv. 904, 25 Fed.R.Serv.3d 982 (1st Cir. 1993).

         - *Motion treated as one for summary judgment.* If, on a motion under FRCP 12(b)(6) or FRCP 12(c), matters outside the pleadings are presented to and not excluded by the court, the motion must be treated as one for summary judgment under FRCP 56. All parties must be given a reasonable opportunity to present all the material that is pertinent to the motion. FRCP 12(d).

         - *Documents attached to pleadings.* However, the court may consider documents which are attached to or submitted with the complaint, as well as legal arguments presented in memorandums or briefs and arguments of counsel. FEDPROC § 62:466; Tellabs, Inc. v. Makor Issues & Rights, Ltd., 551 U.S. 308, 127 S.Ct. 2499, 168 L.Ed.2d 179 (2007); E.E.O.C. v. Ohio Edison Co., 7 F.3d 541 (6th Cir. 1993). Documents that the defendant attaches to the motion to dismiss are considered part of the pleadings if they are referred to in the plaintiff's complaint and are central to the claim, and as such may be considered by the court. FEDPROC § 62:466; Hoffman-Pugh v. Ramsey, 312 F.3d 1222 (11th Cir. 2002).

      ii. *Notice of constitutional question.* A party that files a pleading, written motion, or other paper drawing into question the constitutionality of a federal or state statute must promptly:

         - *File notice.* File a notice of constitutional question stating the question and identifying the paper that raises it, if: (1) a federal statute is questioned and the parties do not include the United States, one of its agencies, or one of its officers or employees in an official capacity; or (2) a state statute is questioned and the parties do not include the state, one of its agencies, or one of its officers or employees in an official capacity; and

         - *Serve notice.* Serve the notice and paper on the Attorney General of the United States if a federal statute is questioned—or on the state attorney general if a state statute is questioned—either by certified or registered mail or by sending it to an electronic address designated by the attorney general for this purpose. FRCP 5.1(a).

         - *Time for filing.* A notice of constitutional challenge to a statute filed in accordance with FRCP 5.1 must be filed at the same time the parties tender their proposed case management plan, if one is required, or within twenty-one (21) days of the filing drawing into question the constitutionality of a federal or state statute, whichever occurs later. IN R USDCTSD L.R. 5.1-1(a).

- *Additional service requirements.* If a federal statute is challenged, in addition to the service requirements of FRCP 5.1(a), the party filing the notice of constitutional challenge must serve the notice and documents on the United States Attorney for the Southern District of Indiana, either by certified or registered mail or by sending it to an electronic address designated for that purpose by that official. IN R USDCTSD L.R. 5.1-1(b).

- *No forfeiture.* A party's failure to file and serve the notice, or the court's failure to certify, does not forfeit a constitutional claim or defense that is otherwise timely asserted. FRCP 5.1(d).

iii. *Nongovernmental corporate disclosure statement*

- *Contents.* A nongovernmental corporate party must file two (2) copies of a disclosure statement that: (1) identifies any parent corporation and any publicly held corporation owning ten percent (10%) or more of its stock; or (2) states that there is no such corporation. FRCP 7.1(a).

- *Time to file; Supplemental filing.* A party must: (1) file the disclosure statement with its first appearance, pleading, petition, motion, response, or other request addressed to the court; and (2) promptly file a supplemental statement if any required information changes. FRCP 7.1(b).

iv. *Index of exhibits.* Any pleading, motion, brief, affidavit, notice, or proposed order filed with the court, whether electronically or with the clerk, must: if it has four (4) or more exhibits, include a separate index that identifies and briefly describes each exhibit. IN R USDCTSD L.R. 5-1(b).

v. *Request for oral argument.* A party may request oral argument by filing a separate motion explaining why oral argument is necessary and estimating how long the court should allow for the argument. The request must be filed and served with the supporting brief, response brief, or reply brief. IN R USDCTSD L.R. 7-5(a).

vi. *Request for evidentiary hearing.* A party may request an evidentiary hearing on a motion or petition by serving and filing a separate motion explaining why the hearing is necessary and estimating how long the court should allow for the hearing. IN R USDCTSD L.R. 7-5(c).

vii. *Copy of authority.* Generally, copies of cited authorities may not be attached to court filings. However, a party must attach to the party's motion or brief a copy of any cited authority if it is not available on Westlaw or Lexis. Upon request, a party must provide copies of any cited authority that is only available through electronic means to the court or the other parties. IN R USDCTSD L.R. 7-1(f).

viii. *Proposed order.* A party must include a suitable form of order with any document that requests the judge or the clerk to enter a routine or uncontested order. IN R USDCTSD L.R. 5-5(b); IN R USDCTSD L.R. 5-10(c); IN R USDCTSD L.R. 7-1(d).

- A service statement and/or list must be included on each proposed order, as required by IN R USDCTSD L.R. 5-5(d). IN R USDCTSD ECF Procedures(11). Any pleading, motion, brief, affidavit, notice, or proposed order filed with the court, whether electronically or with the clerk, must: if it is a form of order, include a statement of service, in the format required by IN R USDCTSD L.R. 5-5(d) in the lower left corner of the document. IN R USDCTSD L.R. 5-1(b).

- A party electronically filing a proposed order—whether voluntarily or because required by IN R USDCTSD L.R. 5-5—must convert the order directly from a word processing program and file it as an attachment to the document it relates to. Proposed orders must include in the lower left-hand corner of the signature page a statement that service will be made electronically on all ECF-registered counsel of record via email generated by the court's ECF system, without listing all such counsel. A service list including the name and postal address of any pro se litigant or non-registered attorney of record must follow, stating that service on the listed individuals will be made in the traditional paper manner, via first-class U.S. Mail. IN R USDCTSD L.R. 5-5(d).

ix. *Copy of document with self-address envelope.* To receive a file-stamped copy of a document filed directly with the clerk, a party must include with the original document an additional copy and a self-addressed envelope. The envelope must be big enough to hold the copy and have enough postage on it to send the copy via regular first-class mail. IN R USDCTSD L.R. 5-10(b).

x. *Notice of manual filing.* When a party who is not exempt from the electronic filing requirement files a document directly with the clerk, the party must: electronically file a notice of manual filing that explains why the document cannot be filed electronically. IN R USDCTSD L.R. 5-2(d)(1). Refer to the Filing and Service Requirements section of this document for more information.

- Where an individual component cannot be included in an electronic filing (e.g. the component cannot be converted to electronic format), the filer shall electronically file the prescribed Notice of Manual Filing in place of that component. A model form is provided as Appendix C (IN R USDCTSD ECF Procedures(Appendix C)). IN R USDCTSD ECF Procedures(13).

- Before making a manual filing of a component, the filing party shall first electronically file a Notice of Manual Filing (See IN R USDCTSD ECF Procedures(Appendix C)). The filer shall initiate the electronic filing process as if filing the actual component but shall instead attach to the filing the Notice of Manual Filing setting forth the reason(s) why the component cannot be filed electronically. The manual filing should be accompanied by a copy of the previously filed Notice of Manual Filing. A party may seek to have a component excluded from electronic filing pursuant to applicable Federal and Local Rules (e.g., FRCP 26(c)). IN R USDCTSD ECF Procedures(15).

xi. *Courtesy copies.* District Judges and Magistrate Judges regularly receive documents filed by all parties. Therefore, parties shall not bring "courtesy copies" to any chambers unless specifically directed to do so by the Court. IN R USDCTSD Case Mgt(General Instructions For All Cases).

xii. *Copies for three-judge court.* Parties in a case where a three-judge court has been requested must file an original and three copies of any document filed directly with the clerk (instead of electronically) until the court: (1) denies the request; (2) dissolves the three-judge court; or (3) allows the parties to file fewer copies. IN R USDCTSD L.R. 9-2(c).

xiii. *Declaration that party was unable to file in a timely manner due to technical difficulties.* If a party misses a filing deadline due to an inability to file electronically, the party may submit the untimely filed document, accompanied by a declaration stating the reason(s) for missing the deadline. IN R USDCTSD ECF Procedures(16). A model form is provided as Appendix D (IN R USDCTSD ECF Procedures(Appendix D)). IN R USDCTSD ECF Procedures(16).

2. *Documents for opposing party*

  a. *Required documents*

    i. *Response brief.* Refer to the Format section of this document for the format of briefs. Refer to the General Requirements section of this document for information on the opposing papers.

    ii. *Certificate of service.* FRCP 5(d) requires that the person making service under FRCP 5 certify that service has been effected. FRCP 5(Advisory Committee Notes). Having such information on file may be useful for many purposes, including proof of service if an issue arises concerning the effectiveness of the service. FRCP 5(Advisory Committee Notes).

      - *Certificate of service for electronically-filed documents.* A certificate of service must be included with all documents filed electronically. Such certificate shall indicate that service was accomplished pursuant to the Court's electronic filing procedures. IN R USDCTSD ECF Procedures(11). For the suggested format for a certificate of service for electronic filing, refer to IN R USDCTSD ECF Procedures(11).

  b. *Supplemental documents*

    i. *Pleading.* As a general rule, the court may only consider the pleading which is attacked by a

FRCP 12(b)(6) motion in determining its sufficiency. FEDPROC § 62:466; Armengau v. Cline, 7 Fed.Appx. 336 (6th Cir. 2001). The plaintiff is not entitled to discovery to obtain information relevant to the motion, and the court is not permitted to look at matters outside the record. FEDPROC § 62:466; Cooperativa de Ahorro y Credito Aguada v. Kidder, Peabody & Co., 993 F.2d 269, 37 Fed.R.Evid.Serv. 904, 25 Fed.R.Serv.3d 982 (1st Cir. 1993).

- *Motion treated as one for summary judgment.* If, on a motion under FRCP 12(b)(6) or FRCP 12(c), matters outside the pleadings are presented to and not excluded by the court, the motion must be treated as one for summary judgment under FRCP 56. All parties must be given a reasonable opportunity to present all the material that is pertinent to the motion. FRCP 12(d).

- *Documents attached to pleadings.* However, the court may consider documents which are attached to or submitted with the complaint, as well as legal arguments presented in memorandums or briefs and arguments of counsel. FEDPROC § 62:466; Tellabs, Inc. v. Makor Issues & Rights, Ltd., 551 U.S. 308, 127 S.Ct. 2499, 168 L.Ed.2d 179 (2007); E.E.O.C. v. Ohio Edison Co., 7 F.3d 541 (6th Cir. 1993). Documents that the defendant attaches to the motion to dismiss are considered part of the pleadings if they are referred to in the plaintiff's complaint and are central to the claim, and as such may be considered by the court. FEDPROC § 62:466; Hoffman-Pugh v. Ramsey, 312 F.3d 1222 (11th Cir. 2002).

ii. *Notice of constitutional question.* A party that files a pleading, written motion, or other paper drawing into question the constitutionality of a federal or state statute must promptly:

- *File notice.* File a notice of constitutional question stating the question and identifying the paper that raises it, if: (1) a federal statute is questioned and the parties do not include the United States, one of its agencies, or one of its officers or employees in an official capacity; or (2) a state statute is questioned and the parties do not include the state, one of its agencies, or one of its officers or employees in an official capacity; and

- *Serve notice.* Serve the notice and paper on the Attorney General of the United States if a federal statute is questioned—or on the state attorney general if a state statute is questioned—either by certified or registered mail or by sending it to an electronic address designated by the attorney general for this purpose. FRCP 5.1(a).

- *Time for filing.* A notice of constitutional challenge to a statute filed in accordance with FRCP 5.1 must be filed at the same time the parties tender their proposed case management plan, if one is required, or within twenty-one (21) days of the filing drawing into question the constitutionality of a federal or state statute, whichever occurs later. IN R USDCTSD L.R. 5.1-1(a).

- *Additional service requirements.* If a federal statute is challenged, in addition to the service requirements of FRCP 5.1(a), the party filing the notice of constitutional challenge must serve the notice and documents on the United States Attorney for the Southern District of Indiana, either by certified or registered mail or by sending it to an electronic address designated for that purpose by that official. IN R USDCTSD L.R. 5.1-1(b).

- *No forfeiture.* A party's failure to file and serve the notice, or the court's failure to certify, does not forfeit a constitutional claim or defense that is otherwise timely asserted. FRCP 5.1(d).

iii. *Index of exhibits.* Any pleading, motion, brief, affidavit, notice, or proposed order filed with the court, whether electronically or with the clerk, must: if it has four (4) or more exhibits, include a separate index that identifies and briefly describes each exhibit. IN R USDCTSD L.R. 5-1(b).

iv. *Request for oral argument.* A party may request oral argument by filing a separate motion explaining why oral argument is necessary and estimating how long the court should allow for the argument. The request must be filed and served with the supporting brief, response brief, or reply brief. IN R USDCTSD L.R. 7-5(a).

v. *Request for evidentiary hearing.* A party may request an evidentiary hearing on a motion or petition by serving and filing a separate motion explaining why the hearing is necessary and estimating how long the court should allow for the hearing. IN R USDCTSD L.R. 7-5(c).

vi. *Copy of authority.* Generally, copies of cited authorities may not be attached to court filings. However, a party must attach to the party's motion or brief a copy of any cited authority if it is not available on Westlaw or Lexis. Upon request, a party must provide copies of any cited authority that is only available through electronic means to the court or the other parties. IN R USDCTSD L.R. 7-1(f).

vii. *Copy of document with self-address envelope.* To receive a file-stamped copy of a document filed directly with the clerk, a party must include with the original document an additional copy and a self-addressed envelope. The envelope must be big enough to hold the copy and have enough postage on it to send the copy via regular first-class mail. IN R USDCTSD L.R. 5-10(b).

viii. *Notice of manual filing.* When a party who is not exempt from the electronic filing requirement files a document directly with the clerk, the party must: electronically file a notice of manual filing that explains why the document cannot be filed electronically. IN R USDCTSD L.R. 5-2(d)(1). Refer to the Filing and Service Requirements section of this document for more information.

- Where an individual component cannot be included in an electronic filing (e.g. the component cannot be converted to electronic format), the filer shall electronically file the prescribed Notice of Manual Filing in place of that component. A model form is provided as Appendix C (IN R USDCTSD ECF Procedures(Appendix C)). IN R USDCTSD ECF Procedures(13).

- Before making a manual filing of a component, the filing party shall first electronically file a Notice of Manual Filing (See IN R USDCTSD ECF Procedures(Appendix C)). The filer shall initiate the electronic filing process as if filing the actual component but shall instead attach to the filing the Notice of Manual Filing setting forth the reason(s) why the component cannot be filed electronically. The manual filing should be accompanied by a copy of the previously filed Notice of Manual Filing. A party may seek to have a component excluded from electronic filing pursuant to applicable Federal and Local Rules (e.g., FRCP 26(c)). IN R USDCTSD ECF Procedures(15).

ix. *Courtesy copies.* District Judges and Magistrate Judges regularly receive documents filed by all parties. Therefore, parties shall not bring "courtesy copies" to any chambers unless specifically directed to do so by the Court. IN R USDCTSD Case Mgt(General Instructions For All Cases).

x. *Copies for three-judge court.* Parties in a case where a three-judge court has been requested must file an original and three copies of any document filed directly with the clerk (instead of electronically) until the court: (1) denies the request; (2) dissolves the three-judge court; or (3) allows the parties to file fewer copies. IN R USDCTSD L.R. 9-2(c).

xi. *Declaration that party was unable to file in a timely manner due to technical difficulties.* If a party misses a filing deadline due to an inability to file electronically, the party may submit the untimely filed document, accompanied by a declaration stating the reason(s) for missing the deadline. IN R USDCTSD ECF Procedures(16). A model form is provided as Appendix D (IN R USDCTSD ECF Procedures(Appendix D)). IN R USDCTSD ECF Procedures(16).

E. Format

1. *Form of documents.* The rules governing captions and other matters of form in pleadings apply to motions and other papers. FRCP 7(b)(2).

  a. *Paper (manual filings only).* Any document that is not filed electronically must: be flat, unfolded, and on good-quality, eight and one-half by eleven (8-1/2 x 11) inch white paper. IN R USDCTSD L.R. 5-1(d)(1). Any document that is not filed electronically must: be single-sided. IN R USDCTSD L.R. 5-1(d)(1).

    i. *Covers or backing.* Any document that is not filed electronically must: not have a cover or a back. IN R USDCTSD L.R. 5-1(d)(1).

    ii. *Fastening.* Any document that is not filed electronically must: be (if consisting of more than one (1) page) fastened by paperclip or binder clip and may not be stapled. IN R USDCTSD L.R. 5-1(d)(1).

      - *Request for nonconforming fastening.* If a document cannot be fastened or bound as

required by IN R USDCTSD L.R. 5-1(d), a party may ask the clerk for permission to fasten it in another manner. The party must make such a request before attempting to file the document with nonconforming fastening. IN R USDCTSD L.R. 5-1(d)(2).

    iii. *Hole punching.* Any document that is not filed electronically must: be two-hole punched at the top with the holes two and three-quarter (2-3/4) inches apart and appropriately centered. IN R USDCTSD L.R. 5-1(d)(1).

b. *Margins.* Any pleading, motion, brief, affidavit, notice, or proposed order filed with the court, whether electronically or with the clerk, must: have at least one (1) inch margins. IN R USDCTSD L.R. 5-1(b).

c. *Spacing.* Any pleading, motion, brief, affidavit, notice, or proposed order filed with the court, whether electronically or with the clerk, must: be double spaced (except for headings, footnotes, and quoted material). IN R USDCTSD L.R. 5-1(b).

d. *Text.* Any pleading, motion, brief, affidavit, notice, or proposed order filed with the court, whether electronically or with the clerk, must: be plainly typewritten, printed, or prepared by a clearly legible copying process. IN R USDCTSD L.R. 5-1(b).

e. *Font size.* Any pleading, motion, brief, affidavit, notice, or proposed order filed with the court, whether electronically or with the clerk, must: use at least 12-point type in the body of the document and at least 10-point type in footnotes. IN R USDCTSD L.R. 5-1(b).

f. *Page numbering.* Any pleading, motion, brief, affidavit, notice, or proposed order filed with the court, whether electronically or with the clerk, must: have consecutively numbered pages. IN R USDCTSD L.R. 5-1(b).

g. *Caption; Names of parties.* Every pleading must have a caption with the court's name, a title, a file number, and a FRCP 7(a) designation. The title of the complaint must name all the parties; the title of other pleadings, after naming the first party on each side, may refer generally to other parties. FRCP 10(a). Any pleading, motion, brief, affidavit, notice, or proposed order filed with the court, whether electronically or with the clerk, must: include a title on the first page. IN R USDCTSD L.R. 5-1(b).

    i. *Alternative motions.* Motions must be filed separately, but alternative motions may be filed in a single document if each is named in the title. IN R USDCTSD L.R. 7-1(a).

h. *Filer's information.* Any pleading, motion, brief, affidavit, notice, or proposed order filed with the court, whether electronically or with the clerk, must: in the case of pleadings, motions, legal briefs, and notices, include the name, complete address, telephone number, facsimile number (where available), and e-mail address (where available) of the pro se litigant or attorney who files it. IN R USDCTSD L.R. 5-1(b).

i. *Paragraphs; Separate statements.* A party must state its claims or defenses in numbered paragraphs, each limited as far as practicable to a single set of circumstances. A later pleading may refer by number to a paragraph in an earlier pleading. If doing so would promote clarity, each claim founded on a separate transaction or occurrence—and each defense other than a denial—must be stated in a separate count or defense. FRCP 10(b).

j. *Adoption by reference; Exhibits.* A statement in a pleading may be adopted by reference elsewhere in the same pleading or in any other pleading or motion. A copy of a written instrument that is an exhibit to a pleading is a part of the pleading for all purposes. FRCP 10(c).

k. *Citations*

    i. *Local rules.* The Local Rules of the United States District Court for the Southern District of Indiana may be cited as "S.D. Ind. L.R." IN R USDCTSD L.R. 1-1(a).

    ii. *Local alternative dispute resolution rules.* These Rules shall be known as the Local Alternative Dispute Resolution Rules of the United States District Court for the Southern District of Indiana. They shall be cited as "S.D.Ind. Local A.D.R. Rule _____." IN R USDCTSD A.D.R. Rule 1.1.

l. *Acceptance by the clerk.* The clerk must not refuse to file a paper solely because it is not in the form prescribed by the Federal Rules of Civil Procedure or by a local rule or practice. FRCP 5(d)(4). The clerk will accept a document that violates IN R USDCTSD L.R. 5-1, but the court may exclude the document from the official record. IN R USDCTSD L.R. 5-1(e).

    i.   *Sanctions for errors as to form.* The court may strike from the record any document that does not comply with the rules governing the form of documents filed with the court, such as rules that regulate document size or the number of copies to be filed or that require a special designation in the caption. The court may also sanction an attorney or party who files a non-compliant document. IN R USDCTSD L.R. 1-3.

2. *Form of electronic documents.* Any document submitted via the court's electronic case filing (ECF) system must be: otherwise prepared and filed in a manner consistent with the CM/ECF Policies and Procedures Manual (IN R USDCTSD ECF Procedures). IN R USDCTSD L.R. 5-1(c). Electronically filed documents must meet the requirements of FRCP 10 (Form of Pleadings), IN R USDCTSD L.R. 5-1 (Format of Papers Presented for Filing), and FRCP 5.2 (Privacy Protection for Filings Made with the Court), as if they had been submitted on paper. Documents filed electronically are also subject to any page limitations set forth by Court Order, by IN R USDCTSD L.R. 7-1 (Motion Practice), or IN R USDCTSD L.R. 56-1 (Summary Judgment Practice), as applicable. IN R USDCTSD ECF Procedures(13).

  a. *PDF format required.* Any document submitted via the court's electronic case filing (ECF) system must be: in .pdf format. IN R USDCTSD L.R. 5-1(c); IN R USDCTSD ECF Procedures(7). Any document submitted via the court's electronic case filing (ECF) system must be: converted to a .pdf file directly from a word processing program, unless it exists only in paper format (in which case it may be scanned to create a .pdf document). IN R USDCTSD L.R. 5-1(c); IN R USDCTSD ECF Procedures(13).

    i.   An exhibit may be scanned into PDF format, at a recommended 300 dpi resolution or higher, only if it does not already exist in electronic format. The filing attorney is responsible for reviewing all PDF documents for legibility before submitting them through the Court's Electronic Case Filing system. For technical guidance in creating PDF documents, please contact the Clerk's Office. IN R USDCTSD ECF Procedures(13).

  b. *File size limitations.* Any document submitted via the court's electronic case filing (ECF) system must be: submitted as one or more .pdf files that do not exceed ten megabytes (10 MB) each (consistent with the CM/ECF Policies and Procedures Manual (IN R USDCTSD ECF Procedures)). IN R USDCTSD L.R. 5-1(c); IN R USDCTSD ECF Procedures(13).

    i.   To electronically file a document or attachment that exceeds ten megabytes (10 MB), the document must first be broken down into two or more smaller files. For example, if Exhibit A is a twelve megabyte (12 MB) PDF file, it should be divided into 2 equal parts prior to electronic filing. Each component part of the exhibit would be filed as an attachment to the main document and described appropriately as "Exhibit A (part 1 of 2)" and "Exhibit A (part 2 of 2)." IN R USDCTSD ECF Procedures(13).

    ii. The supporting items mentioned in IN R USDCTSD ECF Procedures(13) should not be confused with memorandums or briefs in support of motions as outlined in IN R USDCTSD L.R. 7-1 or IN R USDCTSD L.R. 56-1. These memorandums or briefs in support are to be filed as entirely separate documents pursuant to the appropriate rule. Additionally, no motion shall be embodied in the text of a response or reply brief/memorandum unless otherwise ordered by the Court. IN R USDCTSD ECF Procedures(13).

  c. *Separate component parts.* A key objective of the electronic filing system is to ensure that as much of the case as possible is managed electronically. To facilitate electronic filing and retrieval, documents to be filed electronically are to be reasonably broken into their separate component parts. By way of example, most filings include a foundation document (e.g., motion) and other supporting items (e.g., exhibits, proposed orders, proposed amended pleadings). The foundation document, as well as the supporting items, are each separate components of the filing; supporting items must be filed as attachments to the foundation document. These exhibits or attachments should include only those excerpts of the referenced documents that are directly germane to the matter under consideration. IN R USDCTSD ECF Procedures(13).

    i.   Where an individual component cannot be included in an electronic filing (e.g. the component

cannot be converted to electronic format), the filer shall electronically file the prescribed Notice of Manual Filing in place of that component. A model form is provided as Appendix C (IN R USDCTSD ECF Procedures(Appendix C)). IN R USDCTSD ECF Procedures(13).

d. *Exhibits.* Each electronically filed exhibit to a main document must be: (1) created as a separate .pdf file; (2) submitted as an attachment to the main document and given a title which describes its content; and (3) limited to excerpts that are directly germane to the main document's subject matter. IN R USDCTSD L.R. 5-6(a).

    i. When uploading attachments during the electronic filing process, exhibits must be uploaded in a logical sequence and a brief description must be entered for each individual PDF file. The description must include not only the exhibit number or letter, but also a brief description of the document. This information may be entered in CM/ECF using a combination of the Category drop-down menu, the Description text box, or both (see IN R USDCTSD ECF Procedures(13)(Figure 1)). The information that is provided in each box will be combined to create a description of the document as it appears on the case docket (see IN R USDCTSD ECF Procedures(13)(Figure 2)). IN R USDCTSD ECF Procedures(13). For an example, refer to IN R USDCTSD ECF Procedures(13).

e. *Excerpts.* A party filing an exhibit that consists of excerpts from a larger document must clearly and prominently identify the exhibit as containing excerpted material. Either party will have the right to timely file additional excerpts or the complete document to the extent they are or become directly germane to the main document's subject matter. IN R USDCTSD L.R. 5-6(b).

f. For an example illustrating the application of IN R USDCTSD ECF Procedures(13), refer to IN R USDCTSD ECF Procedures(13).

3. *Form of briefs*

a. *Page limits.* Supporting and response briefs (excluding tables of contents, tables of authorities, appendices, and certificates of service) may not exceed thirty-five (35) pages. Reply briefs may not exceed twenty (20) pages. IN R USDCTSD L.R. 7-1(e)(1).

    i. *Permission to exceed limits.* The court may allow a party to file a brief exceeding these page limits for extraordinary and compelling reasons. IN R USDCTSD L.R. 7-1(e)(2).

    ii. *Supporting and response briefs exceeding limits.* If the court allows a party to file a brief or response exceeding thirty-five (35) pages, the document must include:

- A table of contents with page references;
- A statement of issues; and
- A table of authorities including: (1) all cases (alphabetically arranged), statutes, and other authorities cited in the brief; and (2) page numbers where the authorities are cited in the brief. IN R USDCTSD L.R. 7-1(e)(3).

4. *Signing of pleadings, motions and other papers*

a. *Signature.* Every pleading, written motion, and other paper must be signed by at least one attorney of record in the attorney's name—or by a party personally if the party is unrepresented. The paper must state the signer's address, e-mail address, and telephone number. FRCP 11(a).

    i. *Signatures on manual filings.* Any document that is not filed electronically must: include the original signature of the pro se litigant or attorney who files it. IN R USDCTSD L.R. 5-1(d)(1).

    ii. *Electronic signatures.* Use of the attorney's login and password when filing documents electronically serves in part as the attorney's signature for purposes of FRCP 11, the Local Rules of the United States District Court for the Southern District of Indiana, and any other purpose for which a signature is required in connection with proceedings before the Court. IN R USDCTSD ECF Procedures(14); IN R USDCTSD ECF Procedures(10). A pleading, motion, brief, or notice filed electronically under an attorney's ECF log-in and password must be signed by that attorney. IN R USDCTSD L.R. 5-7(a). A signature on a document other than a document filed as provided under IN R USDCTSD L.R. 5-7(a) must be an original handwritten signature and must be scanned into .pdf format for electronic filing. IN R USDCTSD L.R. 5-7(c); IN R USDCTSD ECF Procedures(14).

- *Form of electronic signature.* If a document is converted directly from a word processing application to .pdf (as opposed to scanning), the name of the Filing User under whose log-in and password the document is submitted must be preceded by a "s/" and typed on the signature line where the Filing User's handwritten signature would otherwise appear. IN R USDCTSD L.R. 5-7(b). All documents filed electronically shall include a signature block and include the filing attorney's typewritten name, address, telephone number, facsimile number and e-mail address. In addition, the name of the filing attorney under whose ECF login the document will be filed should be preceded by a "s/" and typed in the space where the attorney's handwritten signature would otherwise appear. IN R US-DCTSD ECF Procedures(14). For a sample format, refer to IN R USDCTSD ECF Procedures(14).

- *Effect of electronic signature.* Filing an electronically signed document under an attorney's ECF log-in and password constitutes the attorney's signature on the document under the Federal Rules of Civil Procedure, under the Local Rules of the United States District Court for the Southern District of Indiana, and for any other reason a signature is required in connection with the court's activities. IN R USDCTSD L.R. 5-7(d).

- *Documents with multiple attorneys' signatures.* Documents requiring signatures of more than one attorney shall be filed either by: (1) obtaining consent from the other attorney, then typing the "s/ [Name]" signature of the other attorney on the signature line where the other attorney's signature would otherwise appear; (2) identifying in the signature section the name of the other attorney whose signature is required and by the submission of a Notice of Endorsement (see IN R USDCTSD ECF Procedures(Appendix B)) by the other attorney no later than three (3) business days after filing; (3) submitting a scanned document containing all handwritten signatures; or (4) in any other manner approved by the Court. IN R USDCTSD ECF Procedures(14); IN R USDCTSD L.R. 5-7(e).

iii. *No verification or accompanying affidavit required for pleadings.* Unless a rule or statute specifically states otherwise, a pleading need not be verified or accompanied by an affidavit. FRCP 11(a).

iv. *Unsigned papers.* The court must strike an unsigned paper unless the omission is promptly corrected after being called to the attorney's or party's attention. FRCP 11(a). The court will strike any document filed directly with the clerk that is not signed by an attorney of record or the pro se litigant filing it, but the court may do so only after giving the attorney or pro se litigant notice of the omission and reasonable time to correct it. Rubber-stamp or facsimile signatures are not original signatures and the court will deem documents containing them to be unsigned for purposes of FRCP 11 and FRCP 26(g) and IN R USDCTSD L.R. 5-10. IN R USDCTSD L.R. 5-10(g).

b. *Representations to the court.* By presenting to the court a pleading, written motion, or other paper—whether by signing, filing, submitting, or later advocating it—an attorney or unrepresented party certifies that to the best of the person's knowledge, information, and belief, formed after an inquiry reasonable under the circumstances:

i. It is not being presented for any improper purpose, such as to harass, cause unnecessary delay, or needlessly increase the cost of litigation;

ii. The claims, defenses, and other legal contentions are warranted by existing law or by a nonfrivolous argument for extending, modifying, or reversing existing law or for establishing new law;

iii. The factual contentions have evidentiary support or, if specifically so identified, will likely have evidentiary support after a reasonable opportunity for further investigation or discovery; and

iv. The denials of factual contentions are warranted on the evidence or, if specifically so identified, are reasonably based on belief or a lack of information. FRCP 11(b).

c. *Sanctions.* If, after notice and a reasonable opportunity to respond, the court determines that FRCP 11(b) has been violated, the court may impose an appropriate sanction on any attorney, law firm, or party that violated FRCP 11(b) or is responsible for the violation. FRCP 11(c)(1). Refer to the United States District Court for the Southern District of Indiana KeyRules Motion for Sanctions document for more information.

5. *Privacy protection for filings made with the court.* Electronically filed documents must meet the requirements of. . .FRCP 5.2 (Privacy Protection for Filings Made with the Court), as if they had been submitted on paper. IN R USDCTSD ECF Procedures(13).

a. *Redacted filings.* Unless the court orders otherwise, in an electronic or paper filing with the court that contains an individual's Social Security number, taxpayer-identification number, or birth date, the name of an individual known to be a minor, or a financial-account number, a party or nonparty making the filing may include only:

    i. The last four (4) digits of the Social Security number and taxpayer-identification number;

    ii. The year of the individual's birth;

    iii. The minor's initials; and

    iv. The last four (4) digits of the financial-account number. FRCP 5.2(a).

b. *Exemptions from the redaction requirement.* The redaction requirement does not apply to the following:

    i. A financial-account number that identifies the property allegedly subject to forfeiture in a forfeiture proceeding;

    ii. The record of an administrative or agency proceeding;

    iii. The official record of a state-court proceeding;

    iv. The record of a court or tribunal, if that record was not subject to the redaction requirement when originally filed;

    v. A filing covered by FRCP 5.2(c) or FRCP 5.2(d); and

    vi. A pro se filing in an action brought under 28 U.S.C.A. § 2241, 28 U.S.C.A. § 2254, or 28 U.S.C.A. § 2255. FRCP 5.2(b).

c. *Limitations on remote access to electronic files; Social Security appeals and immigration cases.* Unless the court orders otherwise, in an action for benefits under the Social Security Act, and in an action or proceeding relating to an order of removal, to relief from removal, or to immigration benefits or detention, access to an electronic file is authorized as follows:

    i. The parties and their attorneys may have remote electronic access to any part of the case file, including the administrative record;

    ii. Any other person may have electronic access to the full record at the courthouse, but may have remote electronic access only to:

        • The docket maintained by the court; and

        • An opinion, order, judgment, or other disposition of the court, but not any other part of the case file or the administrative record. FRCP 5.2(c).

d. *Filings made under seal.* The court may order that a filing be made under seal without redaction. The court may later unseal the filing or order the person who made the filing to file a redacted version for the public record. FRCP 5.2(d). For more information on filing under seal, refer to IN R USDCTSD L.R. 5-11 and IN R USDCTSD ECF Procedures(18).

e. *Protective orders.* For good cause, the court may by order in a case:

    i. Require redaction of additional information; or

    ii. Limit or prohibit a nonparty's remote electronic access to a document filed with the court. FRCP 5.2(e).

f. *Option for additional unredacted filing under seal.* A person making a redacted filing may also file

an unredacted copy under seal. The court must retain the unredacted copy as part of the record. FRCP 5.2(f).

g. *Option for filing a reference list.* A filing that contains redacted information may be filed together with a reference list that identifies each item of redacted information and specifies an appropriate identifier that uniquely corresponds to each item listed. The list must be filed under seal and may be amended as of right. Any reference in the case to a listed identifier will be construed to refer to the corresponding item of information. FRCP 5.2(g).

h. *Waiver of protection of identifiers.* A person waives the protection of FRCP 5.2(a) as to the person's own information by filing it without redaction and not under seal. FRCP 5.2(h).

F. Filing and Service Requirements

1. *Filing requirements.* Any paper after the complaint that is required to be served—together with a certificate of service—must be filed within a reasonable time after service. FRCP 5(d)(1). Motions must be filed separately, but alternative motions may be filed in a single document if each is named in the title. IN R USDCTSD L.R. 7-1(a).

   a. *How filing is made; In general.* A paper is filed by delivering it:

      i. To the clerk; or

      ii. To a judge who agrees to accept it for filing, and who must then note the filing date on the paper and promptly send it to the clerk. FRCP 5(d)(2).

         • In certain instances, the court will direct the parties to submit items directly to chambers (e.g., confidential settlement statements). However, absent specific prior authorization, counsel and litigants should not submit letters or documents directly to chambers, and such materials should be filed with the clerk. IN R USDCTSD L.R. 5-1(Local Rules Advisory Committee Comment).

      iii. A document or item submitted in relation to a matter within the court's jurisdiction is deemed filed upon delivery to the office of the clerk in a manner prescribed by the Local Rules of the United States District Court for the Southern District of Indiana or the Federal Rules of Civil Procedure or authorized by the court. Any submission directed to a Judge or Judge's staff, the office of the clerk or any employee thereof, in a manner that is not contemplated by IN R USDCTSD L.R. 5-1 and without prior court authorization is prohibited. IN R USDCTSD L.R. 5-1(a).

   b. *Non-electronic filing.* Any document that is exempt from electronic filing must be filed directly with the clerk and served on other parties in the case as required by those Federal Rules of Civil Procedure and Local Rules of the United States District Court for the Southern District of Indiana that apply to the service of non-electronic documents. IN R USDCTSD L.R. 5-2(c).

      i. *When completed.* A document or other item that is not required to be filed electronically is deemed filed:

         • Upon delivery in person, by courier, or via U.S. Mail or other mail delivery service to the clerk's office during business hours;

         • When the courtroom deputy clerk accepts it, if the document or item is filed in open court; or

         • Upon completion of any other manner of filing that the court authorizes. IN R USDCTSD L.R. 5-10(a).

      ii. *Document filing by non-exempt party.* When a party who is not exempt from the electronic filing requirement files a document directly with the clerk, the party must:

         • Electronically file a notice of manual filing that explains why the document cannot be filed electronically;

         • Present the document to the clerk within one (1) business day after filing the notice of manual filing; and

         • Present the clerk with a copy of the notice of manual filing when the party files the document with the clerk. IN R USDCTSD L.R. 5-2(d).

c. *Electronic filing*

    i. *Authorization of electronic filing program.* A court may, by local rule, allow papers to be filed, signed, or verified by electronic means that are consistent with any technical standards established by the Judicial Conference of the United States. A local rule may require electronic filing only if reasonable exceptions are allowed. A paper filed electronically in compliance with a local rule is a written paper for purposes of the Federal Rules of Civil Procedure. FRCP 5(d)(3).

- IN R USDCTSD L.R. 5-2 requires electronic filing, as allowed by FRCP 5(d)(3). The policies and procedures in IN R USDCTSD ECF Procedures govern electronic filing in this district unless, due to circumstances in a particular case, a judicial officer determines that these policies and procedures (IN R USDCTSD ECF Procedures) should be modified. IN R USDCTSD ECF Procedures(1).

- Unless modified by order of the Court, all Federal Rules of Civil Procedure and Local Rules of the United States District Court for the Southern District of Indiana shall continue to apply to cases maintained in the Court's Case Management/Electronic Case Filing System (CM/ECF). IN R USDCTSD ECF Procedures(3).

    ii. *Mandatory electronic filing.* Unless exempted pursuant to IN R USDCTSD L.R. 5-3(e), attorneys admitted to the court's bar (including those admitted pro hac vice) or authorized to represent the United States must use the court's ECF system to file documents. IN R USDCTSD L.R. 5-3(a). Electronic filing by attorneys is required for eligible documents filed in civil and criminal cases pending with the Court, unless specifically exempted by Local Rule or Court Order. IN R USDCTSD ECF Procedures(4).

- *Exceptions.* All civil cases (other than those cases the court specifically exempts) must be maintained in the court's electronic case filing (ECF) system. Accordingly, as allowed by FRCP 5(d)(3), every document filed in this court (including exhibits) must be transmitted to the clerk's office via the ECF system consistent with IN R USDCTSD L.R. 5-2 through IN R USDCTSD L.R. 5-11 except: (1) documents filed by pro se litigants; (2) transcripts in cases filed by claimants under the Social Security Act (and related statutes); (3) exhibits in a format that does not readily permit electronic filing (such as videos and large maps and charts); (4) documents that are illegible when scanned into .pdf format; (5) documents filed in cases not maintained on the ECF system; and (6) any other documents that the court or the Local Rules of the United States District Court for the Southern District of Indiana specifically allow to be filed directly with the clerk. IN R USDCTSD L.R. 5-2(a). Parties otherwise participating in the electronic filing system may be excused from filing a particular component electronically under certain limited circumstances, such as when the component cannot be reduced to an electronic format. Such components shall not be filed electronically, but instead shall be manually filed with the Clerk of Court and served upon the parties in accordance with the applicable Federal Rules of Civil Procedure and the Local Rules of the United States District Court for the Southern District of Indiana for filing and service of non-electronic documents. IN R USDCTSD ECF Procedures(15).

- *Exemption from participation.* The court may exempt attorneys from using the ECF system in a particular case for good cause. An attorney must file a petition for ECF exemption and a CM/ECF technical requirements exemption questionnaire in each case in which the attorney seeks an exemption. (The CM/ECF technical requirements exemption questionnaire is available on the court's website). IN R USDCTSD L.R. 5-3(e).

    iii. *Consequences of electronic filing.* Electronic transmission of a document consistent with the procedures adopted by the Court shall, upon the complete receipt of the same by the Clerk of Court, constitute filing of the document for all purposes of the Federal Rules of Civil and Criminal Procedure and the Local Rules of the United States District Court for the Southern District of Indiana, and shall constitute entry of that document onto the docket maintained by the Clerk pursuant to FRCP 58 and FRCP 79. IN R USDCTSD ECF Procedures(7); IN R USDCTSD L.R. 5-4(c)(1). When a document has been filed electronically: the document, as filed, binds the filing party. IN R USDCTSD L.R. 5-4(c)(3).

- A Notice of Electronic Filing (NEF) acknowledging that the document has been filed will immediately appear on the filer's screen after the document has been submitted. Attorneys are strongly encouraged to print or electronically save a copy of the NEF. Attorneys can also verify the filing of documents by inspecting the Court's electronic docket sheet through the use of a PACER login. IN R USDCTSD ECF Procedures(7). When a document has been filed electronically: the notice of electronic filing for the document serves as the court's date-stamp and proof of filing. IN R USDCTSD L.R. 5-4(c)(4).

- The Court may, upon the motion of a party or upon its own motion, strike any inappropriately filed document. IN R USDCTSD ECF Procedures(7).

iv. For more information on electronic filing, refer to IN R USDCTSD ECF Procedures.

d. *Fax filing.* The clerk may not file a faxed document without court authorization. The court may not authorize the clerk to file faxed documents without finding that compelling circumstances justify it. A party must submit a copy of the document that otherwise complies with IN R USDCTSD L.R. 5-10 to replace the faxed copy within seven (7) days after faxing the document. IN R USDCTSD L.R. 5-10(e).

2. *Service requirements*

a. *Service; When required*

i. *In general.* Unless the Federal Rules of Civil Procedure provide otherwise, each of the following papers must be served on every party:

- An order stating that service is required;

- A pleading filed after the original complaint, unless the court orders otherwise under FRCP 5(c) because there are numerous defendants;

- A discovery paper required to be served on a party, unless the court orders otherwise;

- A written motion, except one that may be heard ex parte; and

- A written notice, appearance, demand, or offer of judgment, or any similar paper. FRCP 5(a)(1).

ii. *If a party fails to appear.* No service is required on a party who is in default for failing to appear. But a pleading that asserts a new claim for relief against such a party must be served on that party under FRCP 4. FRCP 5(a)(2).

iii. *Seizing property.* If an action is begun by seizing property and no person is or need be named as a defendant, any service required before the filing of an appearance, answer, or claim must be made on the person who had custody or possession of the property when it was seized. FRCP 5(a)(3).

b. *Service; How made*

i. *Serving an attorney.* If a party is represented by an attorney, service under FRCP 5 must be made on the attorney unless the court orders service on the party. FRCP 5(b)(1).

ii. *Service in general.* A paper is served under FRCP 5 by:

- Handing it to the person;

- Leaving it: (1) at the person's office with a clerk or other person in charge or, if no one is in charge, in a conspicuous place in the office; or (2) if the person has no office or the office is closed, at the person's dwelling or usual place of abode with someone of suitable age and discretion who resides there;

- Mailing it to the person's last known address—in which event service is complete upon mailing;

- Leaving it with the court clerk if the person has no known address;

- Sending it by electronic means if the person consented in writing—in which event service is complete upon transmission, but is not effective if the serving party learns that it did not reach the person to be served; or

- Delivering it by any other means that the person consented to in writing—in which event service is complete when the person making service delivers it to the agency designated to make delivery. FRCP 5(b)(2).

iii. *Electronic service*

- *Consent.* By registering to use the ECF system, attorneys consent to electronic service of documents filed in cases maintained on the ECF system. IN R USDCTSD L.R. 5-3(d). By participating in the Electronic Case Filing Program, attorneys consent to the electronic service of documents, and shall make available electronic mail addresses for service. IN R USDCTSD ECF Procedures(11).

- *Service on registered parties.* Upon the filing of a document by a party, an e-mail message will be automatically generated by the electronic filing system and sent via electronic mail to the e-mail addresses of all registered attorneys who have appeared in the case. The Notice of Electronic Filing will contain a document hyperlink which will provide recipients with one "free look" at the electronically filed document. Recipients are encouraged to print and/or save a copy of the document during the "free look" to avoid incurring PACER charges for future viewings of the document. IN R USDCTSD ECF Procedures(11). When a document has been filed electronically: transmission of the notice of electronic filing generated by the ECF system to an attorney's e-mail address constitutes service of the document on that attorney. IN R USDCTSD L.R. 5-4(c)(5). The party effectuates service on all registered attorneys by filing electronically. IN R USDCTSD ECF Procedures(11). When a document has been filed electronically: no other attempted service will constitute electronic service of the document. IN R USDCTSD L.R. 5-4(c)(6).

- *Service on exempt parties.* A filer must serve a copy of the document consistent with FRCP 5 on any party or attorney who is exempt from participating in electronic filing. IN R USDCTSD L.R. 5-4(d). It is the responsibility of the filing attorney to conventionally serve all parties who do not receive electronic service (the identity of these parties will be indicated on the filing receipt generated by the ECF system). IN R USDCTSD ECF Procedures(11).

- *Service on parties excused from electronic filing.* Parties otherwise participating in the electronic filing system may be excused from filing a particular component electronically under certain limited circumstances, such as when the component cannot be reduced to an electronic format. Such components shall not be filed electronically, but instead shall be manually filed with the Clerk of Court and served upon the parties in accordance with the applicable Federal Rules of Civil Procedure and the Local Rules of the United States District Court for the Southern District of Indiana for filing and service of non-electronic documents. IN R USDCTSD ECF Procedures(15).

- *Service of exempt documents.* Any document that is exempt from electronic filing must be filed directly with the clerk and served on other parties in the case as required by those Federal Rules of Civil Procedure and Local Rules of the United States District Court for the Southern District of Indiana that apply to the service of non-electronic documents. IN R USDCTSD L.R. 5-2(c).

iv. *Using court facilities.* If a local rule so authorizes, a party may use the court's transmission facilities to make service under FRCP 5(b)(2)(E). FRCP 5(b)(3).

c. *Serving numerous defendants*

i. *In general.* If an action involves an unusually large number of defendants, the court may, on motion or on its own, order that:

- Defendants' pleadings and replies to them need not be served on other defendants;

- Any crossclaim, counterclaim, avoidance, or affirmative defense in those pleadings and replies to them will be treated as denied or avoided by all other parties; and

- Filing any such pleading and serving it on the plaintiff constitutes notice of the pleading to all parties. FRCP 5(c)(1).

    ii. *Notifying parties.* A copy of every such order must be served on the parties as the court directs. FRCP 5(c)(2).

G. Hearings

1. *Hearings, generally*

    a. *Oral argument.* Due process does not require that oral argument be permitted on a motion and, except as otherwise provided by local rule, the district court has discretion to determine whether it will decide the motion on the papers or hear argument by counsel (and perhaps receive evidence). FPP § 1190; F.D.I.C. v. Deglau, 207 F.3d 153 (3d Cir. 2000).

        i. *Request for oral argument.* A party may request oral argument by filing a separate motion explaining why oral argument is necessary and estimating how long the court should allow for the argument. IN R USDCTSD L.R. 7-5(a). Refer to the Documents section of this document for more information.

        ii. *No additional evidence at oral argument.* Parties may not present additional evidence at oral argument. IN R USDCTSD L.R. 7-5(b).

    b. *Providing a regular schedule for oral hearings.* A court may establish regular times and places for oral hearings on motions. FRCP 78(a).

    c. *Providing for submission on briefs.* By rule or order, the court may provide for submitting and determining motions on briefs, without oral hearings. FRCP 78(b).

    d. *Request for evidentiary hearing.* A party may request an evidentiary hearing on a motion or petition by serving and filing a separate motion explaining why the hearing is necessary and estimating how long the court should allow for the hearing. IN R USDCTSD L.R. 7-5(c).

    e. *Directed by the court.* The court may: (1) grant or deny a request for oral argument or an evidentiary hearing in its sole discretion; (2) set oral argument or an evidentiary hearing without a request from a party; and (3) order any oral argument or evidentiary hearing to be held anywhere within the district regardless of where the case will be tried. IN R USDCTSD L.R. 7-5(d).

2. *Hearing on FRCP 12 defenses before trial.* If a party so moves, any defense listed in FRCP 12(b)(1) through FRCP 12(b)(7)—whether made in a pleading or by motion—and a motion under FRCP 12(c) must be heard and decided before trial unless the court orders a deferral until trial. FRCP 12(i).

3. *Courtroom and courthouse decorum.* For information on courtroom and courthouse decorum, refer to IN R USDCTSD L.R. 83-3.

H. Forms

1. Federal Motion to Dismiss for Failure to State a Claim Forms

    a. Notice in federal court; Motion for involuntary dismissal of action without prejudice; Complaint fails to state a claim on which relief can be granted. AMJUR PP DISMISSAL § 109.

    b. Motion; To dismiss; Failure to state a claim on which relief can be granted or facts sufficient to constitute cause of action. AMJUR PP LIMITATION § 100.

    c. Motion to dismiss; For failure to state a claim, improper service of process, improper venue, and want of jurisdiction. AMJUR PP MOTIONS § 42.

    d. Failure to state a claim upon which relief can be granted. 2C FEDFORMS § 11:80.

    e. Failure to state a claim upon which relief can be granted; Long version. 2C FEDFORMS § 11:81.

    f. Failure to state a claim upon which relief can be granted; Dismissal of certain allegations. 2C FEDFORMS § 11:82.

    g. Failure to state a claim upon which relief can be granted; With supporting reasons. 2C FEDFORMS § 11:83.

    h. Failure to state a claim upon which relief can be granted; With supporting reasons; Plaintiff not the real party in interest. 2C FEDFORMS § 11:85.

    i. Failure to state a claim upon which relief can be granted; With supporting reasons; Failure to show implied contract. 2C FEDFORMS § 11:86.

j. Failure to state a claim upon which relief can be granted; With supporting reasons; Issue not arbitrable. 2C FEDFORMS § 11:87.

k. Failure to state a claim upon which relief can be granted; With supporting affidavits. 2C FED-FORMS § 11:88.

l. Failure to state a claim upon which relief can be granted; In alternative for summary judgment. 2C FEDFORMS § 11:89.

m. Motion; To dismiss; Failure to state sufficient claim; By one of several defendants. FEDPROF § 1:923.

n. Motion to dismiss; Failure to state sufficient claim; By third-party defendant. FEDPROF § 1:924.

o. Motion to dismiss; Failure to state sufficient claim after successive attempts. FEDPROF § 1:925.

p. Motion to dismiss; By individual defendants. FEDPROF § 1:926.

q. Motion to dismiss; By state agency. FEDPROF § 1:927.

r. Motion to dismiss counterclaim. FEDPROF § 1:931.

s. Allegation; In motion to dismiss; Res judicata. FEDPROF § 1:933.

t. Allegation; In motion to dismiss; Statute of limitations. FEDPROF § 1:935.

u. Allegation; In motion to dismiss; Strict liability claim barred by statute. FEDPROF § 1:936.

v. Allegation; In motion to dismiss; By United States; Absence of consent to suit. FEDPROF § 1:938.

w. Reply; To motion to dismiss for failure to state sufficient claim. FEDPROF § 1:939.

x. Motion to dismiss counterclaim. GOLDLTGFMS § 13:10.

y. Motion to dismiss complaint; General form. GOLDLTGFMS § 20:24.

z. Affidavit in support of motion to dismiss complaint. GOLDLTGFMS § 20:32.

2. **Forms for the Southern District of Indiana**

a. Notice of endorsement. IN R USDCTSD ECF Procedures(Appendix B).

b. Notice of manual filing. IN R USDCTSD ECF Procedures(Appendix C).

c. Declaration that party was unable to file in a timely manner due to technical difficulties. IN R USDCTSD ECF Procedures(Appendix D).

I. Applicable Rules

1. *Federal rules*

a. Serving and filing pleadings and other papers. FRCP 5.

b. Constitutional challenge to a statute; Notice, certification, and intervention. FRCP 5.1.

c. Privacy protection for filings made with the court. FRCP 5.2.

d. Computing and extending time; Time for motion papers. FRCP 6.

e. Pleadings allowed; Form of motions and other papers. FRCP 7.

f. Disclosure statement. FRCP 7.1.

g. Form of pleadings. FRCP 10.

h. Signing pleadings, motions, and other papers; Representations to the court; Sanctions. FRCP 11.

i. Defenses and objections; When and how presented; Motion for judgment on the pleadings; Consolidating motions; Waiving defenses; Pretrial hearing. FRCP 12.

j. Hearing motions; Submission on briefs. FRCP 78.

2. *Local rules*

a. Scope of the rules. IN R USDCTSD L.R. 1-1.

b. Sanctions for errors as to form. IN R USDCTSD L.R. 1-3.

c. Format of documents presented for filing. IN R USDCTSD L.R. 5-1.

d. Constitutional challenge to a statute; Notice. IN R USDCTSD L.R. 5.1-1.

e. Filing of documents electronically required. IN R USDCTSD L.R. 5-2.

f. Eligibility, registration, passwords for electronic filing; Exemption from electronic filing. IN R USDCTSD L.R. 5-3.

g. Timing and consequences of electronic filing. IN R USDCTSD L.R. 5-4.

h. Attachments and exhibits in cases filed electronically. IN R USDCTSD L.R. 5-6.

i. Signatures in cases filed electronically. IN R USDCTSD L.R. 5-7.

j. Non-electronic filings. IN R USDCTSD L.R. 5-10.

k. Motion practice. [IN R USDCTSD L.R. 7-1, as amended by IN ORDER 16-2319, effective December 1, 2016].

l. Oral arguments and hearings. IN R USDCTSD L.R. 7-5.

m. Request for three-judge court. IN R USDCTSD L.R. 9-2.

n. Assignment of cases. IN R USDCTSD L.R. 40-1.

o. Alternative dispute resolution. IN R USDCTSD A.D.R. Rule 1.1; IN R USDCTSD A.D.R. Rule 1.2; IN R USDCTSD A.D.R. Rule 1.5; IN R USDCTSD A.D.R. Rule 2.1; IN R USDCTSD A.D.R. Rule 2.2.

p. Instructions for preparing case management plan. IN R USDCTSD Case Mgt.

q. Electronic case filing policies and procedures manual. IN R USDCTSD ECF Procedures.

Motions, Oppositions and Replies
Motion to Dismiss for Lack of Subject Matter Jurisdiction

Document Last Updated December 2016

A. Checklist

(I) ❏ Matters to be considered by moving party

   (a) ❏ Required documents

      (1) ❏ Notice of motion and motion

      (2) ❏ Brief

      (3) ❏ Certificate of service

   (b) ❏ Supplemental documents

      (1) ❏ Supporting evidence

      (2) ❏ Notice of constitutional question

      (3) ❏ Nongovernmental corporate disclosure statement

      (4) ❏ Index of exhibits

      (5) ❏ Request for oral argument

      (6) ❏ Request for evidentiary hearing

      (7) ❏ Copy of authority

      (8) ❏ Proposed order

      (9) ❏ Copy of document with self-address envelope

     (10) ❏ Notice of manual filing

     (11) ❏ Courtesy copies

(12) ❑ Copies for three-judge court

(13) ❑ Declaration that party was unable to file in a timely manner due to technical difficulties

(c) ❑ Timing

    (1) ❑ The defense of lack of subject matter jurisdiction can be raised at any time

    (2) ❑ Every defense to a claim for relief in any pleading must be asserted in the responsive pleading if one is required

    (3) ❑ A motion asserting any of the defenses in FRCP 12(b) must be made before pleading if a responsive pleading is allowed

    (4) ❑ If a pleading sets out a claim for relief that does not require a responsive pleading, an opposing party may assert at trial any defense to that claim

    (5) ❑ A written motion and notice of the hearing must be served at least fourteen (14) days before the time specified for the hearing, with the following exceptions: (i) when the motion may be heard ex parte; (ii) when the Federal Rules of Civil Procedure set a different time; or (iii) when a court order—which a party may, for good cause, apply for ex parte—sets a different time

    (6) ❑ Any affidavit supporting a motion must be served with the motion

    (7) ❑ When a party who is not exempt from the electronic filing requirement files a document directly with the clerk, the party must present the document to the clerk within one (1) business day after filing the notice of manual filing

    (8) ❑ Unless the court orders otherwise, the [untimely] document and declaration [that party was unable to file in a timely manner due to technical difficulties] must be filed no later than 12:00 noon of the first day on which the court is open for business following the original filing deadline

(II) ❑ Matters to be considered by opposing party

(a) ❑ Required documents

    (1) ❑ Response brief

    (2) ❑ Certificate of service

(b) ❑ Supplemental documents

    (1) ❑ Supporting evidence

    (2) ❑ Notice of constitutional question

    (3) ❑ Index of exhibits

    (4) ❑ Request for oral argument

    (5) ❑ Request for evidentiary hearing

    (6) ❑ Copy of authority

    (7) ❑ Copy of document with self-address envelope

    (8) ❑ Notice of manual filing

    (9) ❑ Courtesy copies

    (10) ❑ Copies for three-judge court

    (11) ❑ Declaration that party was unable to file in a timely manner due to technical difficulties

(c) ❑ Timing

    (1) ❑ Any response is due within fourteen (14) days after service of the motion

    (2) ❑ Except as FRCP 59(c) provides otherwise, any opposing affidavit must be served at least seven (7) days before the hearing, unless the court permits service at another time

    (3) ❑ When a party who is not exempt from the electronic filing requirement files a document

directly with the clerk, the party must present the document to the clerk within one (1) business day after filing the notice of manual filing

(4) ❑ Unless the court orders otherwise, the [untimely] document and declaration [that party was unable to file in a timely manner due to technical difficulties] must be filed no later than 12:00 noon of the first day on which the court is open for business following the original filing deadline

B. Timing

1. *Motion to dismiss for lack of subject matter jurisdiction.* [The defense of lack of subject matter jurisdiction] can be raised at any time. FEDPROC § 62:434.

   a. *In a responsive pleading.* Every defense to a claim for relief in any pleading must be asserted in the responsive pleading if one is required. FRCP 12(b).

   b. *By motion.* A motion asserting any of the defenses in FRCP 12(b) must be made before pleading if a responsive pleading is allowed. FRCP 12(b). Although FRCP 12(b) encourages the responsive pleader to file a motion to dismiss before filing the answer, nothing in FRCP 12 prohibits the filing of a motion to dismiss with the answer. An untimely motion to dismiss may be considered if the defense asserted in the motion was previously raised in the responsive pleading. FEDPROC § 62:427.

   c. *At trial.* If a pleading sets out a claim for relief that does not require a responsive pleading, an opposing party may assert at trial any defense to that claim. FRCP 12(b).

2. *Timing of motions, generally*

   a. *Motion and notice of hearing.* A written motion and notice of the hearing must be served at least fourteen (14) days before the time specified for the hearing, with the following exceptions:

      i. When the motion may be heard ex parte;

      ii. When the Federal Rules of Civil Procedure set a different time; or

      iii. When a court order—which a party may, for good cause, apply for ex parte—sets a different time. FRCP 6(c)(1).

   b. *Supporting affidavit.* Any affidavit supporting a motion must be served with the motion. FRCP 6(c)(2).

3. *Timing of opposing papers.* Any response is due within fourteen (14) days after service of the motion. IN R USDCTSD L.R. 7-1(c)(2)(A).

   a. *Opposing affidavit.* Except as FRCP 59(c) provides otherwise, any opposing affidavit must be served at least seven (7) days before the hearing, unless the court permits service at another time. FRCP 6(c)(2).

   b. *Extensions.* The court may extend response and reply deadlines, but only for good cause. IN R USDCTSD L.R. 7-1(c)(3).

   c. *Summary ruling on failure to respond.* The court may summarily rule on a motion if an opposing party does not file a response within the deadline. IN R USDCTSD L.R. 7-1(c)(4).

4. *Timing of reply papers.* Where the respondent files an answering affidavit setting up a new matter, the moving party ordinarily is allowed a reasonable time to file a reply affidavit since failure to deny the new matter by affidavit may operate as an admission of its truth. AMJUR MOTIONS § 25.

   a. *Reply brief.* Any reply is due within seven (7) days after service of the response. IN R USDCTSD L.R. 7-1(c)(2)(B).

   b. *Extensions.* The court may extend response and reply deadlines, but only for good cause. IN R USDCTSD L.R. 7-1(c)(3).

5. *Effect of a FRCP 12 motion on the time to serve a responsive pleading.* Unless the court sets a different time, serving a motion under FRCP 12 alters the periods in FRCP 12(a) as follows:

   a. If the court denies the motion or postpones its disposition until trial, the responsive pleading must be served within fourteen (14) days after notice of the court's action; or

    b.   If the court grants a motion for a more definite statement, the responsive pleading must be served within fourteen (14) days after the more definite statement is served. FRCP 12(a)(4).

6.   *Document filing by non-exempt party.* When a party who is not exempt from the electronic filing requirement files a document directly with the clerk, the party must: present the document to the clerk within one (1) business day after filing the notice of manual filing. IN R USDCTSD L.R. 5-2(d)(2).

7.   *Declaration that party was unable to file in a timely manner due to technical difficulties.* Unless the Court orders otherwise, the [untimely] document and declaration [that party was unable to file in a timely manner due to technical difficulties] must be filed no later than 12:00 noon of the first day on which the Court is open for business following the original filing deadline. IN R USDCTSD ECF Procedures(16).

8.   *Computation of time*

    a.   *Computing time.* FRCP 6 applies in computing any time period specified in the Federal Rules of Civil Procedure, in any local rule or court order, or in any statute that does not specify a method of computing time. FRCP 6(a).

        i.   *Period stated in days or a longer unit.* When the period is stated in days or a longer unit of time:

- Exclude the day of the event that triggers the period;
- Count every day, including intermediate Saturdays, Sundays, and legal holidays; and
- Include the last day of the period, but if the last day is a Saturday, Sunday, or legal holiday, the period continues to run until the end of the next day that is not a Saturday, Sunday, or legal holiday. FRCP 6(a)(1).

        ii.   *Period stated in hours.* When the period is stated in hours:

- Begin counting immediately on the occurrence of the event that triggers the period;
- Count every hour, including hours during intermediate Saturdays, Sundays, and legal holidays; and
- If the period would end on a Saturday, Sunday, or legal holiday, the period continues to run until the same time on the next day that is not a Saturday, Sunday, or legal holiday. FRCP 6(a)(2).

        iii.   *Inaccessibility of the clerk's office.* Unless the court orders otherwise, if the clerk's office is inaccessible:

- On the last day for filing under FRCP 6(a)(1), then the time for filing is extended to the first accessible day that is not a Saturday, Sunday, or legal holiday; or
- During the last hour for filing under FRCP 6(a)(2), then the time for filing is extended to the same time on the first accessible day that is not a Saturday, Sunday, or legal holiday. FRCP 6(a)(3).

        iv.   *"Last day" defined.* Unless a different time is set by a statute, local rule, or court order, the last day ends:

- For electronic filing, at midnight in the court's time zone; and
- For filing by other means, when the clerk's office is scheduled to close. FRCP 6(a)(4).

        v.   *"Next day" defined.* The "next day" is determined by continuing to count forward when the period is measured after an event and backward when measured before an event. FRCP 6(a)(5).

        vi.   *"Legal holiday" defined.* "Legal holiday" means:

- The day set aside by statute for observing New Year's Day, Martin Luther King Jr.'s Birthday, Washington's Birthday, Memorial Day, Independence Day, Labor Day, Columbus Day, Veterans' Day, Thanksgiving Day, or Christmas Day;
- Any day declared a holiday by the President or Congress; and
- For periods that are measured after an event, any other day declared a holiday by the state where the district court is located. FRCP 6(a)(6).

    b.   *Computation of electronic filing deadlines.* Filing documents electronically does not alter filing deadlines. IN R USDCTSD ECF Procedures(7). A document due on a particular day must be filed before midnight local time of the division where the case is pending. IN R USDCTSD L.R. 5-4(a). All electronic transmissions of documents must be completed (i.e. received completely by the Clerk's Office) prior to midnight of the local time of the division in which the case is pending in order to be considered timely filed that day (NOTE: time will be noted in Eastern Time on the Court's docket. If you have filed a document prior to midnight local time of the division in which the case is pending and the document is due that date, but the electronic receipt and docket reflect the following calendar day, please contact the Court). IN R USDCTSD ECF Procedures(7). Although attorneys may file documents electronically twenty-four (24) hours a day, seven (7) days a week, attorneys are encouraged to file all documents during the normal working hours of the Clerk's Office (Monday through Friday, 8:30 a.m. to 4:30 p.m.) when technical support is available. IN R USDCTSD ECF Procedures(7); IN R USDCTSD ECF Procedures(9).

    i. *Technical difficulties.* Parties are encouraged to file documents electronically during normal business hours, in case a problem is encountered. In the event a technical failure occurs and a document cannot be filed electronically despite the best efforts of the filing party, the party should print (if possible) a copy of the error message received. In addition, as soon as practically possible, the party should file a "Declaration that Party was Unable to File in a Timely Manner Due to Technical Difficulties." A model form is provided as Appendix D (IN R USDCTSD ECF Procedures(Appendix D)). IN R USDCTSD ECF Procedures(16).

- If a party is unable to file electronically and, as a result, may miss a filing deadline, the party must contact the Clerk's Office at the number listed in IN R USDCTSD ECF Procedures(15) to inform the court's staff of the difficulty. If a party misses a filing deadline due to an inability to file electronically, the party may submit the untimely filed document, accompanied by a declaration stating the reason(s) for missing the deadline. Unless the Court orders otherwise, the document and declaration must be filed no later than 12:00 noon of the first day on which the Court is open for business following the original filing deadline. IN R USDCTSD ECF Procedures(16).

  c. *Extending time*

    i. *In general.* When an act may or must be done within a specified time, the court may, for good cause, extend the time:

- With or without motion or notice if the court acts, or if a request is made, before the original time or its extension expires; or

- On motion made after the time has expired if the party failed to act because of excusable neglect. FRCP 6(b)(1).

    ii. *Exceptions.* A court must not extend the time to act under FRCP 50(b), FRCP 50(d), FRCP 52(b), FRCP 59(b), FRCP 59(d), FRCP 59(e), and FRCP 60(b). FRCP 6(b)(2).

    iii. Refer to the United States District Court for the Southern District of Indiana KeyRules Motion for Continuance/Extension of Time document for more information on extending time.

  d. *Additional time after certain kinds of service.* When a party may or must act within a specified time after being served and service is made under FRCP 5(b)(2)(C) (mail), FRCP 5(b)(2)(D) (leaving with the clerk), or FRCP 5(b)(2)(F) (other means consented to), three (3) days are added after the period would otherwise expire under FRCP 6(a). FRCP 6(d). Service by electronic mail shall constitute service pursuant to FRCP 5(b)(2)(E) and shall entitle the party being served to the additional three (3) days provided by FRCP 6(d). IN R USDCTSD ECF Procedures(11).

C. General Requirements

1. *Motions, generally*

  a. *Requirements.* A request for a court order must be made by motion. The motion must:

    i. Be in writing unless made during a hearing or trial;

    ii. State with particularity the grounds for seeking the order; and

    iii. State the relief sought. FRCP 7(b)(1).

b. *Notice of motion.* A party interested in resisting the relief sought by a motion has a right to notice thereof, and an opportunity to be heard. AMJUR MOTIONS § 12.

    i. In addition to statutory or court rule provisions requiring notice of a motion—the purpose of such a notice requirement having been said to be to prevent a party from being prejudicially surprised by a motion—principles of natural justice dictate that an adverse party generally must be given notice that a motion will be presented to the court. AMJUR MOTIONS § 12.

    ii. "Notice," in this regard, means reasonable notice, including a meaningful opportunity to prepare and to defend against allegations of a motion. AMJUR MOTIONS § 12.

c. *Writing requirement.* The writing requirement is intended to insure that the adverse parties are informed and have a record of both the motion's pendency and the grounds on which the movant seeks an order. FPP § 1191; Feldberg v. Quechee Lakes Corp., 463 F.3d 195 (2d Cir. 2006).

    i. It is sufficient "if the motion is stated in a written notice of the hearing of the motion." FPP § 1191.

d. *Particularity requirement.* The particularity requirement insures that the opposing parties will have notice of their opponent's contentions. FEDPROC § 62:364; Goodman v. 1973 26 Foot Trojan Vessel, Arkansas Registration No. AR1439SN, 859 F.2d 71, 12 Fed.R.Serv.3d 645 (8th Cir. 1988). That requirement ensures that notice of the basis for the motion is provided to the court and to the opposing party so as to avoid prejudice, provide the opponent with a meaningful opportunity to respond, and provide the court with enough information to process the motion correctly. FEDPROC § 62:364; Andreas v. Volkswagen of America, Inc., 336 F.3d 789, 56 Fed.R.Serv.3d 6 (8th Cir. 2003).

    i. Reasonable specification of the grounds for a motion is sufficient. However, where a movant fails to state even one ground for granting the motion in question, the movant has failed to meet the minimal standard of "reasonable specification." FEDPROC § 62:364; Martinez v. Trainor, 556 F.2d 818, 23 Fed.R.Serv.2d 403 (7th Cir. 1977).

    ii. The court may excuse the failure to comply with the particularity requirement if it is inadvertent, and where no prejudice is shown by the opposing party. FEDPROC § 62:364.

e. *Motions must be filed separately.* Motions must be filed separately, but alternative motions may be filed in a single document if each is named in the title. A motion must not be contained within a brief, response, or reply to a previously filed motion, unless ordered by the court. IN R USDCTSD L.R. 7-1(a).

f. *Routine or uncontested motions.* The court may rule upon a routine or uncontested motion before the response deadline passes, unless: (1) the motion indicates that an opposing party objects to it; or (2) the court otherwise believes that a response will be filed. IN R USDCTSD L.R. 7-1(d).

2. *Motion to dismiss for lack of subject matter jurisdiction.* A party may assert the defense of lack of subject-matter jurisdiction by motion. FRCP 12(b)(1). The objection presented by a motion under FRCP 12(b)(1) challenging the court's subject matter jurisdiction is that the district judge has no authority or competence to hear and decide the case before it. A FRCP 12(b)(1) motion most typically is employed when the movant believes that the claim asserted by the plaintiff does not involve a federal question, and there is no diversity of citizenship between the parties or, in a diversity of citizenship case, the amount in controversy does not exceed the required jurisdictional amount. FPP § 1350.

    a. *Subject matter jurisdiction.* It always must be remembered that the federal courts are courts of limited jurisdiction and only can adjudicate those cases that fall within Article III of the Constitution (see U.S.C.A. Const. Art. III § 1, et seq.) and a congressional authorization enacted thereunder. FPP § 1350.

        i. *Federal question.* The district courts shall have original jurisdiction of all civil actions arising under the Constitution, laws, or treaties of the United States. 28 U.S.C.A. § 1331.

        ii. *Diversity of citizenship; Amount in controversy.* The district courts shall have original jurisdiction of all civil actions where the matter in controversy exceeds the sum or value of seventy-five thousand dollars ($75,000), exclusive of interest and costs, and is between:

            • Citizens of different States;

- Citizens of a State and citizens or subjects of a foreign state, except that the district courts shall not have original jurisdiction under 28 U.S.C.A. § 1332 of an action between citizens of a State and citizens or subjects of a foreign state who are lawfully admitted for permanent residence in the United States and are domiciled in the same State;
- Citizens of different States and in which citizens or subjects of a foreign state are additional parties; and
- A foreign state, defined in 28 U.S.C.A. § 1603(a), as plaintiff and citizens of a State or of different States. 28 U.S.C.A. § 1332(a).

b. *Types of FRCP 12(b)(1) motions.* There are two separate types of FRCP 12(b)(1) motions to dismiss for lack of subject matter jurisdiction: the "facial attack" and the "factual attack." FEDPROC § 62:440.

  i. *Facial attack.* The facial attack is addressed to the sufficiency of the allegations of the complaint itself. FEDPROC § 62:440; Stalley ex rel. U.S. v. Orlando Regional Healthcare System, Inc., 524 F.3d 1229 (11th Cir. 2008). On such a motion, the court is merely required to determine whether the plaintiff has sufficiently alleged a basis of subject matter jurisdiction, and the factual allegations of the complaint are taken as true. FEDPROC § 62:440; U.S. ex rel. Atkinson v. PA. Shipbuilding Co., 473 F.3d 506 (3d Cir. 2007).

  ii. *Factual attack.* The "factual attack," on the other hand, challenges the existence of subject matter jurisdiction in fact, irrespective of the pleadings, and matters outside the pleadings, such as testimony and affidavits, may be considered by the court. FEDPROC § 62:440; Kligman v. I.R.S., 272 Fed.Appx. 166 (3d Cir. 2008); Paper, Allied-Industrial, Chemical and Energy Workers Intern. Union v. Continental Carbon Co., 428 F.3d 1285 (10th Cir. 2005). The trial court in such a situation is free to weigh the evidence and satisfy itself as to the existence of its power to hear the case; therefore, no presumptive truthfulness attaches to the plaintiff's factual allegations. FEDPROC § 62:440; Land v. Dollar, 330 U.S. 731, 67 S.Ct. 1009, 91 L.Ed. 1209 (1947).

c. *Burden.* With the limited exception of the question whether the amount in controversy requirement in diversity of citizenship cases has been satisfied, the extensive case law on the subject makes clear that the burden of proof on a FRCP 12(b)(1) motion is on the party asserting that subject matter jurisdiction exists, which, of course, typically is the plaintiff. FPP § 1350; Thomson v. Gaskill, 315 U.S. 442, 62 S.Ct. 673, 86 L.Ed. 951 (1942). A plaintiff meets the burden of establishing subject-matter jurisdiction at the pleading stage by pleading sufficient allegations to show the proper basis for the court to assert subject-matter jurisdiction over the action. 2 FEDFORMS § 7:6.

  i. *Federal question.* If subject matter jurisdiction is based on the existence of a federal question, the pleader must show that he or she has alleged a claim for relief arising under federal law and that the claim is not frivolous. FPP § 1350; Baker v. Carr, 369 U.S. 186, 82 S.Ct. 691, 7 L.Ed.2d 663 (1962).

  ii. *Diversity of citizenship.* If jurisdiction is based on diversity of citizenship, on the other hand, the pleader must show that real and complete diversity exists between all of the plaintiffs and all of the defendants, and also that the assertion that the claim exceeds the requisite jurisdictional amount in controversy is made in good faith. FPP § 1350; City of Indianapolis v. Chase Nat. Bank, 314 U.S. 63, 62 S.Ct. 15, 86 L.Ed. 47 (1941). Satisfying this last requirement is a relatively simple task, however, because the claim is deemed to be made in good faith so long as it is not clear to a legal certainty that the claimant could not recover a judgment exceeding the statutorily mandated jurisdictional amount, a matter on which the party challenging the district court's jurisdiction has the burden. FPP § 1350.

d. *Joining motions.* When the motion is based on more than one ground, the cases are legion stating that the district court should consider the FRCP 12(b)(1) challenge first because if it must dismiss the complaint for lack of subject matter jurisdiction, the accompanying defenses and objections become moot and do not need to be determined by the judge. FPP § 1350; Steel Co. v. Citizens for a Better Environment, 523 U.S. 83, 118 S.Ct. 1003, 140 L.Ed.2d 210 (1998). However, there are a number of decisions in which the court has decided one or more defenses in addition to the subject matter jurisdiction question or simply assumed the existence of jurisdiction and gone on to decide another matter. FPP § 1350.

    i.   *Right to join.* A motion under FRCP 12 may be joined with any other motion allowed by FRCP 12. FRCP 12(g)(1).

    ii.   *Limitation on further motions.* Except as provided in FRCP 12(h)(2) or FRCP 12(h)(3), a party that makes a motion under FRCP 12 must not make another motion under FRCP 12 raising a defense or objection that was available to the party but omitted from its earlier motion. FRCP 12(g)(2).

e.   *Waiving and preserving certain defenses.* No defense or objection is waived by joining it with one or more other defenses or objections in a responsive pleading or in a motion. FRCP 12(b).

    i.   *Waiver by consent.* The defendant may waive the right to obtain a dismissal prior to trial either by express consent to be sued in a certain district or by some conduct that will be construed as implying consent. FPP § 1352.

    ii.   *When some are waived.* A party waives any defense listed in FRCP 12(b)(2) through FRCP 12(b)(5) by:

- Omitting it from a motion in the circumstances described in FRCP 12(g)(2); or
- Failing to either: (1) make it by motion under FRCP 12; or (2) include it in a responsive pleading or in an amendment allowed by FRCP 15(a)(1) as a matter of course. FRCP 12(h)(1).

    iii.   *When to raise others.* Failure to state a claim upon which relief can be granted, to join a person required by FRCP 19(b), or to state a legal defense to a claim may be raised:

- In any pleading allowed or ordered under FRCP 7(a);
- By a motion under FRCP 12(c); or
- At trial. FRCP 12(h)(2).

    iv.   *Lack of subject matter jurisdiction.* If the court determines at any time that it lacks subject-matter jurisdiction, the court must dismiss the action. FRCP 12(h)(3).

3.   *Opposing papers.* The Federal Rules of Civil Procedure do not require any formal answer, return, or reply to a motion, except where the Federal Rules of Civil Procedure or local rules may require affidavits, memoranda, or other papers to be filed in opposition to a motion. Such papers are simply to apprise the court of such opposition and the grounds of that opposition. FEDPROC § 62:359.

a.   *Effect of failure to respond to motion.* Although in the absence of statutory provision or court rule, a motion ordinarily does not require a written answer, when a party files a motion and the opposing party fails to respond, the court may construe such failure to respond as nonopposition to the motion or an admission that the motion was meritorious, may take the facts alleged in the motion as true—the rule in some jurisdictions being that the failure to respond to a fact set forth in a motion is deemed an admission—and may grant the motion if the relief requested appears to be justified. AMJUR MOTIONS § 28.

b.   *Assent or no opposition not determinative.* However, a motion will not be granted automatically simply because an "assent" or a notation of "no opposition" has been filed; federal judges frequently deny motions that have been assented to when it is thought that justice so dictates. FPP § 1190.

c.   *Responsive pleading inappropriate as response to motion.* An attempt to answer or oppose a motion with a responsive pleading usually is not appropriate. FPP § 1190.

4.   *Reply papers.* A moving party may be required or permitted to prepare papers in addition to his original motion papers. AMJUR MOTIONS § 25. Papers answering or replying to opposing papers may be appropriate, in the interests of justice, where it appears there is a substantial reason for allowing a reply. Thus, a court may accept reply papers where a party demonstrates that the papers to which it seeks to file a reply raise new issues that are material to the disposition of the question before the court, or where the court determines, sua sponte, that it wishes further briefing of an issue raised in those papers and orders the submission of additional papers. FEDPROC § 62:360.

a.   *Function of reply papers.* The function of a reply affidavit is to answer the arguments made in opposition to the position taken by the movant and not to permit the movant to introduce new arguments in support of the motion. AMJUR MOTIONS § 25.

b. *Issues raised for the first time in a reply document.* However, the view has been followed in some jurisdictions, that as a matter of judicial economy, where there is no prejudice and where the issues could be raised simply by filing a motion to dismiss, the trial court has discretion to consider arguments raised for the first time in a reply memorandum, and that a trial court may grant a motion to strike issues raised for the first time in a reply memorandum. AMJUR MOTIONS § 26.

5. *Appearances.* Every attorney who represents a party or who files a document on a party's behalf must file an appearance for that party. IN R USDCTSD L.R. 83-7. The filing of a Notice of Appearance shall act to establish the filing attorney as an attorney of record representing a designated party or parties in a particular cause of action. As a result, it is necessary for each attorney to file a separate Notice of Appearance when entering an appearance in a case. A joint appearance on behalf of multiple attorneys may be filed electronically only if it is filed separately for each attorney, using his/her ECF login. IN R USDCTSD ECF Procedures(12). Only those attorneys who have filed an appearance in a pending action are entitled to be served with case documents under FRCP 5(a). IN R USDCTSD L.R. 83-7. For more information, refer to IN R USDCTSD L.R. 83-7 and IN R USDCTSD ECF Procedures(12).

6. *Notice of related action.* A party must file a notice of related action: as soon as it appears that the party's case and another pending case: (1) arise out of the same transaction or occurrence; (2) involve the same property; or (3) involve the validity or infringement or the same patent, trademark, or copyright. IN R USDCTSD L.R. 40-1(d)(2). For more information, refer to IN R USDCTSD L.R. 40-1.

7. *Alternative dispute resolution (ADR)*

a. *Application.* Unless limited by specific provisions, or unless there are other applicable specific statutory, common law, or constitutional procedures, the Local Alternative Dispute Resolution Rules of the United States District Court for the Southern District of Indiana shall apply in all civil litigation filed in the U.S. District Court for the Southern District of Indiana, except in the following cases and proceedings:

   i. Applications for writs of habeas corpus under 28 U.S.C.A. § 2254;

   ii. Forfeiture cases;

   iii. Non-adversary proceedings in bankruptcy;

   iv. Social Security administrative review cases; and

   v. Such other matters as specified by order of the Court; for example, matters involving important public policy issues, constitutional law, or the establishment of new law. IN R USDCTSD A.D.R. Rule 1.2.

b. *Mediation.* Mediation under this section (IN R USDCTSD A.D.R. Rule 2.1, et seq.) involves the confidential process by which a person acting as a Mediator, selected by the parties or appointed by the Court, assists the litigants in reaching a mutually acceptable agreement. It is an informal and nonadversarial process. The role of the Mediator is to assist in identifying the issues, reducing misunderstandings, clarifying priorities, exploring areas of compromise, and finding points of agreement as well as legitimate points of disagreement. Final decision-making authority rests with the parties, not the Mediator. IN R USDCTSD A.D.R. Rule 2.1. It is anticipated that an agreement may not resolve all of the disputed issues, but the process, nonetheless, can reduce points of contention. Parties and their representatives are required to mediate in good faith, but are not compelled to reach an agreement. IN R USDCTSD A.D.R. Rule 2.1.

   i. *Case selection.* The Court with the agreement of the parties may refer a civil case for mediation. Unless otherwise ordered or as specifically provided in IN R USDCTSD A.D.R. Rule 2.8, referral to mediation does not abate or suspend the action, and no scheduled dates shall be delayed or deferred, including the date of trial. IN R USDCTSD A.D.R. Rule 2.2.

   ii. For more information on mediation, refer to IN R USDCTSD A.D.R. Rule 2.1, et seq.

c. *Other methods of dispute resolution.* The Local Alternative Dispute Resolution Rules of the United States District Court for the Southern District of Indiana shall not preclude the parties from utilizing any other reasonable method or technique of alternative dispute resolution to resolve disputes to which the parties agree. However, any use of arbitration by the parties will be governed by and comply with the requirements of 28 U.S.C.A. § 654 through 28 U.S.C.A. § 657. IN R USDCTSD A.D.R. Rule 1.5.

    d. For more information on alternative dispute resolution (ADR), refer to IN R USDCTSD A.D.R. Rule 1.1, et seq.

8. *Notice of settlement or resolution.* The parties must immediately notify the court if they reasonably anticipate settling their case or resolving a pending motion. IN R USDCTSD L.R. 7-1(h).

9. *Modification or suspension of rules.* The court may, on its own motion or at the request of a party, suspend or modify any rule in a particular case in the interest of justice. IN R USDCTSD L.R. 1-1(c).

D. Documents

1. *Documents for moving party*

  a. *Required documents*

    i. *Notice of motion and motion.* Refer to the General Requirements section of this document for information on the notice of motion and motion.

    ii. *Brief.* The following motion must also be accompanied by a supporting brief: a motion to dismiss. IN R USDCTSD L.R. 7-1(b)(1). Refer to the Format section of this document for the format of briefs.

    iii. *Certificate of service.* FRCP 5(d) requires that the person making service under FRCP 5 certify that service has been effected. FRCP 5(Advisory Committee Notes). Having such information on file may be useful for many purposes, including proof of service if an issue arises concerning the effectiveness of the service. FRCP 5(Advisory Committee Notes).

      • *Certificate of service for electronically-filed documents.* A certificate of service must be included with all documents filed electronically. Such certificate shall indicate that service was accomplished pursuant to the Court's electronic filing procedures. IN R USDCTSD ECF Procedures(11). For the suggested format for a certificate of service for electronic filing, refer to IN R USDCTSD ECF Procedures(11).

  b. *Supplemental documents*

    i. *Supporting evidence.* When a motion relies on facts outside the record, the court may hear the matter on affidavits or may hear it wholly or partly on oral testimony or on depositions. FRCP 43(c).

      • *Materials necessary for motion.* A party seeking relief under FRCP 26(c) or FRCP 37, or by way of a pretrial motion that could result in a final order on an issue, must file with the motion those parts of the discovery materials relevant to the motion. IN R USDCTSD L.R. 26-2(a).

    ii. *Notice of constitutional question.* A party that files a pleading, written motion, or other paper drawing into question the constitutionality of a federal or state statute must promptly:

      • *File notice.* File a notice of constitutional question stating the question and identifying the paper that raises it, if: (1) a federal statute is questioned and the parties do not include the United States, one of its agencies, or one of its officers or employees in an official capacity; or (2) a state statute is questioned and the parties do not include the state, one of its agencies, or one of its officers or employees in an official capacity; and

      • *Serve notice.* Serve the notice and paper on the Attorney General of the United States if a federal statute is questioned—or on the state attorney general if a state statute is questioned—either by certified or registered mail or by sending it to an electronic address designated by the attorney general for this purpose. FRCP 5.1(a).

      • *Time for filing.* A notice of constitutional challenge to a statute filed in accordance with FRCP 5.1 must be filed at the same time the parties tender their proposed case management plan, if one is required, or within twenty-one (21) days of the filing drawing into question the constitutionality of a federal or state statute, whichever occurs later. IN R USDCTSD L.R. 5.1-1(a).

- *Additional service requirements.* If a federal statute is challenged, in addition to the service requirements of FRCP 5.1(a), the party filing the notice of constitutional challenge must serve the notice and documents on the United States Attorney for the Southern District of Indiana, either by certified or registered mail or by sending it to an electronic address designated for that purpose by that official. IN R USDCTSD L.R. 5.1-1(b).

- *No forfeiture.* A party's failure to file and serve the notice, or the court's failure to certify, does not forfeit a constitutional claim or defense that is otherwise timely asserted. FRCP 5.1(d).

iii. *Nongovernmental corporate disclosure statement*

- *Contents.* A nongovernmental corporate party must file two (2) copies of a disclosure statement that: (1) identifies any parent corporation and any publicly held corporation owning ten percent (10%) or more of its stock; or (2) states that there is no such corporation. FRCP 7.1(a).

- *Time to file; Supplemental filing.* A party must: (1) file the disclosure statement with its first appearance, pleading, petition, motion, response, or other request addressed to the court; and (2) promptly file a supplemental statement if any required information changes. FRCP 7.1(b).

iv. *Index of exhibits.* Any pleading, motion, brief, affidavit, notice, or proposed order filed with the court, whether electronically or with the clerk, must: if it has four (4) or more exhibits, include a separate index that identifies and briefly describes each exhibit. IN R USDCTSD L.R. 5-1(b).

v. *Request for oral argument.* A party may request oral argument by filing a separate motion explaining why oral argument is necessary and estimating how long the court should allow for the argument. The request must be filed and served with the supporting brief, response brief, or reply brief. IN R USDCTSD L.R. 7-5(a).

vi. *Request for evidentiary hearing.* A party may request an evidentiary hearing on a motion or petition by serving and filing a separate motion explaining why the hearing is necessary and estimating how long the court should allow for the hearing. IN R USDCTSD L.R. 7-5(c).

vii. *Copy of authority.* Generally, copies of cited authorities may not be attached to court filings. However, a party must attach to the party's motion or brief a copy of any cited authority if it is not available on Westlaw or Lexis. Upon request, a party must provide copies of any cited authority that is only available through electronic means to the court or the other parties. IN R USDCTSD L.R. 7-1(f).

viii. *Proposed order.* A party must include a suitable form of order with any document that requests the judge or the clerk to enter a routine or uncontested order. IN R USDCTSD L.R. 5-5(b); IN R USDCTSD L.R. 5-10(c); IN R USDCTSD L.R. 7-1(d).

- A service statement and/or list must be included on each proposed order, as required by IN R USDCTSD L.R. 5-5(d). IN R USDCTSD ECF Procedures(11). Any pleading, motion, brief, affidavit, notice, or proposed order filed with the court, whether electronically or with the clerk, must: if it is a form of order, include a statement of service, in the format required by IN R USDCTSD L.R. 5-5(d) in the lower left corner of the document. IN R USDCTSD L.R. 5-1(b).

- A party electronically filing a proposed order—whether voluntarily or because required by IN R USDCTSD L.R. 5-5—must convert the order directly from a word processing program and file it as an attachment to the document it relates to. Proposed orders must include in the lower left-hand corner of the signature page a statement that service will be made electronically on all ECF-registered counsel of record via email generated by the court's ECF system, without listing all such counsel. A service list including the name and postal address of any pro se litigant or non-registered attorney of record must follow, stating that service on the listed individuals will be made in the traditional paper manner, via first-class U.S. Mail. IN R USDCTSD L.R. 5-5(d).

ix. *Copy of document with self-address envelope.* To receive a file-stamped copy of a document filed directly with the clerk, a party must include with the original document an additional copy and a self-addressed envelope. The envelope must be big enough to hold the copy and have enough postage on it to send the copy via regular first-class mail. IN R USDCTSD L.R. 5-10(b).

x. *Notice of manual filing.* When a party who is not exempt from the electronic filing requirement files a document directly with the clerk, the party must: electronically file a notice of manual filing that explains why the document cannot be filed electronically. IN R USDCTSD L.R. 5-2(d)(1). Refer to the Filing and Service Requirements section of this document for more information.

- Where an individual component cannot be included in an electronic filing (e.g. the component cannot be converted to electronic format), the filer shall electronically file the prescribed Notice of Manual Filing in place of that component. A model form is provided as Appendix C (IN R USDCTSD ECF Procedures(Appendix C)). IN R USDCTSD ECF Procedures(13).

- Before making a manual filing of a component, the filing party shall first electronically file a Notice of Manual Filing (See IN R USDCTSD ECF Procedures(Appendix C)). The filer shall initiate the electronic filing process as if filing the actual component but shall instead attach to the filing the Notice of Manual Filing setting forth the reason(s) why the component cannot be filed electronically. The manual filing should be accompanied by a copy of the previously filed Notice of Manual Filing. A party may seek to have a component excluded from electronic filing pursuant to applicable Federal and Local Rules (e.g., FRCP 26(c)). IN R USDCTSD ECF Procedures(15).

xi. *Courtesy copies.* District Judges and Magistrate Judges regularly receive documents filed by all parties. Therefore, parties shall not bring "courtesy copies" to any chambers unless specifically directed to do so by the Court. IN R USDCTSD Case Mgt(General Instructions For All Cases).

xii. *Copies for three-judge court.* Parties in a case where a three-judge court has been requested must file an original and three copies of any document filed directly with the clerk (instead of electronically) until the court: (1) denies the request; (2) dissolves the three-judge court; or (3) allows the parties to file fewer copies. IN R USDCTSD L.R. 9-2(c).

xiii. *Declaration that party was unable to file in a timely manner due to technical difficulties.* If a party misses a filing deadline due to an inability to file electronically, the party may submit the untimely filed document, accompanied by a declaration stating the reason(s) for missing the deadline. IN R USDCTSD ECF Procedures(16). A model form is provided as Appendix D (IN R USDCTSD ECF Procedures(Appendix D)). IN R USDCTSD ECF Procedures(16).

2. *Documents for opposing party*

   a. *Required documents*

      i. *Response brief.* Refer to the Format section of this document for the format of briefs. Refer to the General Requirements section of this document for information on the opposing papers.

      ii. *Certificate of service.* FRCP 5(d) requires that the person making service under FRCP 5 certify that service has been effected. FRCP 5(Advisory Committee Notes). Having such information on file may be useful for many purposes, including proof of service if an issue arises concerning the effectiveness of the service. FRCP 5(Advisory Committee Notes).

      - *Certificate of service for electronically-filed documents.* A certificate of service must be included with all documents filed electronically. Such certificate shall indicate that service was accomplished pursuant to the Court's electronic filing procedures. IN R USDCTSD ECF Procedures(11). For the suggested format for a certificate of service for electronic filing, refer to IN R USDCTSD ECF Procedures(11).

   b. *Supplemental documents*

      i. *Supporting evidence.* When a motion relies on facts outside the record, the court may hear the

matter on affidavits or may hear it wholly or partly on oral testimony or on depositions. FRCP 43(c).

- *Materials necessary for motion.* A party seeking relief under FRCP 26(c) or FRCP 37, or by way of a pretrial motion that could result in a final order on an issue, must file with the motion those parts of the discovery materials relevant to the motion. IN R USDCTSD L.R. 26-2(a).

ii. *Notice of constitutional question.* A party that files a pleading, written motion, or other paper drawing into question the constitutionality of a federal or state statute must promptly:

- *File notice.* File a notice of constitutional question stating the question and identifying the paper that raises it, if: (1) a federal statute is questioned and the parties do not include the United States, one of its agencies, or one of its officers or employees in an official capacity; or (2) a state statute is questioned and the parties do not include the state, one of its agencies, or one of its officers or employees in an official capacity; and

- *Serve notice.* Serve the notice and paper on the Attorney General of the United States if a federal statute is questioned—or on the state attorney general if a state statute is questioned—either by certified or registered mail or by sending it to an electronic address designated by the attorney general for this purpose. FRCP 5.1(a).

- *Time for filing.* A notice of constitutional challenge to a statute filed in accordance with FRCP 5.1 must be filed at the same time the parties tender their proposed case management plan, if one is required, or within twenty-one (21) days of the filing drawing into question the constitutionality of a federal or state statute, whichever occurs later. IN R USDCTSD L.R. 5.1-1(a).

- *Additional service requirements.* If a federal statute is challenged, in addition to the service requirements of FRCP 5.1(a), the party filing the notice of constitutional challenge must serve the notice and documents on the United States Attorney for the Southern District of Indiana, either by certified or registered mail or by sending it to an electronic address designated for that purpose by that official. IN R USDCTSD L.R. 5.1-1(b).

- *No forfeiture.* A party's failure to file and serve the notice, or the court's failure to certify, does not forfeit a constitutional claim or defense that is otherwise timely asserted. FRCP 5.1(d).

iii. *Index of exhibits.* Any pleading, motion, brief, affidavit, notice, or proposed order filed with the court, whether electronically or with the clerk, must: if it has four (4) or more exhibits, include a separate index that identifies and briefly describes each exhibit. IN R USDCTSD L.R. 5-1(b).

iv. *Request for oral argument.* A party may request oral argument by filing a separate motion explaining why oral argument is necessary and estimating how long the court should allow for the argument. The request must be filed and served with the supporting brief, response brief, or reply brief. IN R USDCTSD L.R. 7-5(a).

v. *Request for evidentiary hearing.* A party may request an evidentiary hearing on a motion or petition by serving and filing a separate motion explaining why the hearing is necessary and estimating how long the court should allow for the hearing. IN R USDCTSD L.R. 7-5(c).

vi. *Copy of authority.* Generally, copies of cited authorities may not be attached to court filings. However, a party must attach to the party's motion or brief a copy of any cited authority if it is not available on Westlaw or Lexis. Upon request, a party must provide copies of any cited authority that is only available through electronic means to the court or the other parties. IN R USDCTSD L.R. 7-1(f).

vii. *Copy of document with self-address envelope.* To receive a file-stamped copy of a document filed directly with the clerk, a party must include with the original document an additional copy and a self-addressed envelope. The envelope must be big enough to hold the copy and have enough postage on it to send the copy via regular first-class mail. IN R USDCTSD L.R. 5-10(b).

viii. *Notice of manual filing.* When a party who is not exempt from the electronic filing requirement

files a document directly with the clerk, the party must: electronically file a notice of manual filing that explains why the document cannot be filed electronically. IN R USDCTSD L.R. 5-2(d)(1). Refer to the Filing and Service Requirements section of this document for more information.

- Where an individual component cannot be included in an electronic filing (e.g. the component cannot be converted to electronic format), the filer shall electronically file the prescribed Notice of Manual Filing in place of that component. A model form is provided as Appendix C (IN R USDCTSD ECF Procedures(Appendix C)). IN R USDCTSD ECF Procedures(13).

- Before making a manual filing of a component, the filing party shall first electronically file a Notice of Manual Filing (See IN R USDCTSD ECF Procedures(Appendix C)). The filer shall initiate the electronic filing process as if filing the actual component but shall instead attach to the filing the Notice of Manual Filing setting forth the reason(s) why the component cannot be filed electronically. The manual filing should be accompanied by a copy of the previously filed Notice of Manual Filing. A party may seek to have a component excluded from electronic filing pursuant to applicable Federal and Local Rules (e.g., FRCP 26(c)). IN R USDCTSD ECF Procedures(15).

ix. *Courtesy copies.* District Judges and Magistrate Judges regularly receive documents filed by all parties. Therefore, parties shall not bring "courtesy copies" to any chambers unless specifically directed to do so by the Court. IN R USDCTSD Case Mgt(General Instructions For All Cases).

x. *Copies for three-judge court.* Parties in a case where a three-judge court has been requested must file an original and three copies of any document filed directly with the clerk (instead of electronically) until the court: (1) denies the request; (2) dissolves the three-judge court; or (3) allows the parties to file fewer copies. IN R USDCTSD L.R. 9-2(c).

xi. *Declaration that party was unable to file in a timely manner due to technical difficulties.* If a party misses a filing deadline due to an inability to file electronically, the party may submit the untimely filed document, accompanied by a declaration stating the reason(s) for missing the deadline. IN R USDCTSD ECF Procedures(16). A model form is provided as Appendix D (IN R USDCTSD ECF Procedures(Appendix D)). IN R USDCTSD ECF Procedures(16).

E. Format

1. *Form of documents.* The rules governing captions and other matters of form in pleadings apply to motions and other papers. FRCP 7(b)(2).

   a. *Paper (manual filings only).* Any document that is not filed electronically must: be flat, unfolded, and on good-quality, eight and one-half by eleven (8-1/2 x 11) inch white paper. IN R USDCTSD L.R. 5-1(d)(1). Any document that is not filed electronically must: be single-sided. IN R USDCTSD L.R. 5-1(d)(1).

      i. *Covers or backing.* Any document that is not filed electronically must: not have a cover or a back. IN R USDCTSD L.R. 5-1(d)(1).

      ii. *Fastening.* Any document that is not filed electronically must: be (if consisting of more than one (1) page) fastened by paperclip or binder clip and may not be stapled. IN R USDCTSD L.R. 5-1(d)(1).

         - *Request for nonconforming fastening.* If a document cannot be fastened or bound as required by IN R USDCTSD L.R. 5-1(d), a party may ask the clerk for permission to fasten it in another manner. The party must make such a request before attempting to file the document with nonconforming fastening. IN R USDCTSD L.R. 5-1(d)(2).

      iii. *Hole punching.* Any document that is not filed electronically must: be two-hole punched at the top with the holes two and three-quarter (2-3/4) inches apart and appropriately centered. IN R USDCTSD L.R. 5-1(d)(1).

   b. *Margins.* Any pleading, motion, brief, affidavit, notice, or proposed order filed with the court, whether electronically or with the clerk, must: have at least one (1) inch margins. IN R USDCTSD L.R. 5-1(b).

c. *Spacing.* Any pleading, motion, brief, affidavit, notice, or proposed order filed with the court, whether electronically or with the clerk, must: be double spaced (except for headings, footnotes, and quoted material). IN R USDCTSD L.R. 5-1(b).

d. *Text.* Any pleading, motion, brief, affidavit, notice, or proposed order filed with the court, whether electronically or with the clerk, must: be plainly typewritten, printed, or prepared by a clearly legible copying process. IN R USDCTSD L.R. 5-1(b).

e. *Font size.* Any pleading, motion, brief, affidavit, notice, or proposed order filed with the court, whether electronically or with the clerk, must: use at least 12-point type in the body of the document and at least 10-point type in footnotes. IN R USDCTSD L.R. 5-1(b).

f. *Page numbering.* Any pleading, motion, brief, affidavit, notice, or proposed order filed with the court, whether electronically or with the clerk, must: have consecutively numbered pages. IN R USDCTSD L.R. 5-1(b).

g. *Caption; Names of parties.* Every pleading must have a caption with the court's name, a title, a file number, and a FRCP 7(a) designation. The title of the complaint must name all the parties; the title of other pleadings, after naming the first party on each side, may refer generally to other parties. FRCP 10(a). Any pleading, motion, brief, affidavit, notice, or proposed order filed with the court, whether electronically or with the clerk, must: include a title on the first page. IN R USDCTSD L.R. 5-1(b).

   i. *Alternative motions.* Motions must be filed separately, but alternative motions may be filed in a single document if each is named in the title. IN R USDCTSD L.R. 7-1(a).

h. *Filer's information.* Any pleading, motion, brief, affidavit, notice, or proposed order filed with the court, whether electronically or with the clerk, must: in the case of pleadings, motions, legal briefs, and notices, include the name, complete address, telephone number, facsimile number (where available), and e-mail address (where available) of the pro se litigant or attorney who files it. IN R USDCTSD L.R. 5-1(b).

i. *Paragraphs; Separate statements.* A party must state its claims or defenses in numbered paragraphs, each limited as far as practicable to a single set of circumstances. A later pleading may refer by number to a paragraph in an earlier pleading. If doing so would promote clarity, each claim founded on a separate transaction or occurrence—and each defense other than a denial—must be stated in a separate count or defense. FRCP 10(b).

j. *Adoption by reference; Exhibits.* A statement in a pleading may be adopted by reference elsewhere in the same pleading or in any other pleading or motion. A copy of a written instrument that is an exhibit to a pleading is a part of the pleading for all purposes. FRCP 10(c).

k. *Citations*

   i. *Local rules.* The Local Rules of the United States District Court for the Southern District of Indiana may be cited as "S.D. Ind. L.R." IN R USDCTSD L.R. 1-1(a).

   ii. *Local alternative dispute resolution rules.* These Rules shall be known as the Local Alternative Dispute Resolution Rules of the United States District Court for the Southern District of Indiana. They shall be cited as "S.D.Ind. Local A.D.R. Rule _____." IN R USDCTSD A.D.R. Rule 1.1.

l. *Acceptance by the clerk.* The clerk must not refuse to file a paper solely because it is not in the form prescribed by the Federal Rules of Civil Procedure or by a local rule or practice. FRCP 5(d)(4). The clerk will accept a document that violates IN R USDCTSD L.R. 5-1, but the court may exclude the document from the official record. IN R USDCTSD L.R. 5-1(e).

   i. *Sanctions for errors as to form.* The court may strike from the record any document that does not comply with the rules governing the form of documents filed with the court, such as rules that regulate document size or the number of copies to be filed or that require a special designation in the caption. The court may also sanction an attorney or party who files a non-compliant document. IN R USDCTSD L.R. 1-3.

2. *Form of electronic documents.* Any document submitted via the court's electronic case filing (ECF)

system must be: otherwise prepared and filed in a manner consistent with the CM/ECF Policies and Procedures Manual (IN R USDCTSD ECF Procedures). IN R USDCTSD L.R. 5-1(c). Electronically filed documents must meet the requirements of FRCP 10 (Form of Pleadings), IN R USDCTSD L.R. 5-1 (Format of Papers Presented for Filing), and FRCP 5.2 (Privacy Protection for Filings Made with the Court), as if they had been submitted on paper. Documents filed electronically are also subject to any page limitations set forth by Court Order, by IN R USDCTSD L.R. 7-1 (Motion Practice), or IN R USDCTSD L.R. 56-1 (Summary Judgment Practice), as applicable. IN R USDCTSD ECF Procedures(13).

a. *PDF format required.* Any document submitted via the court's electronic case filing (ECF) system must be: in .pdf format. IN R USDCTSD L.R. 5-1(c); IN R USDCTSD ECF Procedures(7). Any document submitted via the court's electronic case filing (ECF) system must be: converted to a .pdf file directly from a word processing program, unless it exists only in paper format (in which case it may be scanned to create a .pdf document). IN R USDCTSD L.R. 5-1(c); IN R USDCTSD ECF Procedures(13).

 i. An exhibit may be scanned into PDF format, at a recommended 300 dpi resolution or higher, only if it does not already exist in electronic format. The filing attorney is responsible for reviewing all PDF documents for legibility before submitting them through the Court's Electronic Case Filing system. For technical guidance in creating PDF documents, please contact the Clerk's Office. IN R USDCTSD ECF Procedures(13).

b. *File size limitations.* Any document submitted via the court's electronic case filing (ECF) system must be: submitted as one or more .pdf files that do not exceed ten megabytes (10 MB) each (consistent with the CM/ECF Policies and Procedures Manual (IN R USDCTSD ECF Procedures)). IN R USDCTSD L.R. 5-1(c); IN R USDCTSD ECF Procedures(13).

 i. To electronically file a document or attachment that exceeds ten megabytes (10 MB), the document must first be broken down into two or more smaller files. For example, if Exhibit A is a twelve megabyte (12 MB) PDF file, it should be divided into 2 equal parts prior to electronic filing. Each component part of the exhibit would be filed as an attachment to the main document and described appropriately as "Exhibit A (part 1 of 2)" and "Exhibit A (part 2 of 2)." IN R USDCTSD ECF Procedures(13).

 ii. The supporting items mentioned in IN R USDCTSD ECF Procedures(13) should not be confused with memorandums or briefs in support of motions as outlined in IN R USDCTSD L.R. 7-1 or IN R USDCTSD L.R. 56-1. These memorandums or briefs in support are to be filed as entirely separate documents pursuant to the appropriate rule. Additionally, no motion shall be embodied in the text of a response or reply brief/memorandum unless otherwise ordered by the Court. IN R USDCTSD ECF Procedures(13).

c. *Separate component parts.* A key objective of the electronic filing system is to ensure that as much of the case as possible is managed electronically. To facilitate electronic filing and retrieval, documents to be filed electronically are to be reasonably broken into their separate component parts. By way of example, most filings include a foundation document (e.g., motion) and other supporting items (e.g., exhibits, proposed orders, proposed amended pleadings). The foundation document, as well as the supporting items, are each separate components of the filing; supporting items must be filed as attachments to the foundation document. These exhibits or attachments should include only those excerpts of the referenced documents that are directly germane to the matter under consideration. IN R USDCTSD ECF Procedures(13).

 i. Where an individual component cannot be included in an electronic filing (e.g. the component cannot be converted to electronic format), the filer shall electronically file the prescribed Notice of Manual Filing in place of that component. A model form is provided as Appendix C (IN R USDCTSD ECF Procedures(Appendix C)). IN R USDCTSD ECF Procedures(13).

d. *Exhibits.* Each electronically filed exhibit to a main document must be: (1) created as a separate .pdf file; (2) submitted as an attachment to the main document and given a title which describes its content; and (3) limited to excerpts that are directly germane to the main document's subject matter. IN R USDCTSD L.R. 5-6(a).

 i. When uploading attachments during the electronic filing process, exhibits must be uploaded in

a logical sequence and a brief description must be entered for each individual PDF file. The description must include not only the exhibit number or letter, but also a brief description of the document. This information may be entered in CM/ECF using a combination of the Category drop-down menu, the Description text box, or both (see IN R USDCTSD ECF Procedures(13)(Figure 1)). The information that is provided in each box will be combined to create a description of the document as it appears on the case docket (see IN R USDCTSD ECF Procedures(13)(Figure 2)). IN R USDCTSD ECF Procedures(13). For an example, refer to IN R USDCTSD ECF Procedures(13).

   e. *Excerpts.* A party filing an exhibit that consists of excerpts from a larger document must clearly and prominently identify the exhibit as containing excerpted material. Either party will have the right to timely file additional excerpts or the complete document to the extent they are or become directly germane to the main document's subject matter. IN R USDCTSD L.R. 5-6(b).

   f. For an example illustrating the application of IN R USDCTSD ECF Procedures(13), refer to IN R USDCTSD ECF Procedures(13).

3. *Form of briefs*

   a. *Page limits.* Supporting and response briefs (excluding tables of contents, tables of authorities, appendices, and certificates of service) may not exceed thirty-five (35) pages. Reply briefs may not exceed twenty (20) pages. IN R USDCTSD L.R. 7-1(e)(1).

     i. *Permission to exceed limits.* The court may allow a party to file a brief exceeding these page limits for extraordinary and compelling reasons. IN R USDCTSD L.R. 7-1(e)(2).

     ii. *Supporting and response briefs exceeding limits.* If the court allows a party to file a brief or response exceeding thirty-five (35) pages, the document must include:

- A table of contents with page references;
- A statement of issues; and
- A table of authorities including: (1) all cases (alphabetically arranged), statutes, and other authorities cited in the brief; and (2) page numbers where the authorities are cited in the brief. IN R USDCTSD L.R. 7-1(e)(3).

4. *Signing of pleadings, motions and other papers*

   a. *Signature.* Every pleading, written motion, and other paper must be signed by at least one attorney of record in the attorney's name—or by a party personally if the party is unrepresented. The paper must state the signer's address, e-mail address, and telephone number. FRCP 11(a).

     i. *Signatures on manual filings.* Any document that is not filed electronically must: include the original signature of the pro se litigant or attorney who files it. IN R USDCTSD L.R. 5-1(d)(1).

     ii. *Electronic signatures.* Use of the attorney's login and password when filing documents electronically serves in part as the attorney's signature for purposes of FRCP 11, the Local Rules of the United States District Court for the Southern District of Indiana, and any other purpose for which a signature is required in connection with proceedings before the Court. IN R USDCTSD ECF Procedures(14); IN R USDCTSD ECF Procedures(10). A pleading, motion, brief, or notice filed electronically under an attorney's ECF log-in and password must be signed by that attorney. IN R USDCTSD L.R. 5-7(a). A signature on a document other than a document filed as provided under IN R USDCTSD L.R. 5-7(a) must be an original handwritten signature and must be scanned into .pdf format for electronic filing. IN R USDCTSD L.R. 5-7(c); IN R USDCTSD ECF Procedures(14).

- *Form of electronic signature.* If a document is converted directly from a word processing application to .pdf (as opposed to scanning), the name of the Filing User under whose log-in and password the document is submitted must be preceded by a "s/" and typed on the signature line where the Filing User's handwritten signature would otherwise appear. IN R USDCTSD L.R. 5-7(b). All documents filed electronically shall include a signature block and include the filing attorney's typewritten name, address, telephone number, facsimile number and e-mail address. In addition, the name of the filing attorney under

whose ECF login the document will be filed should be preceded by a "s/" and typed in the space where the attorney's handwritten signature would otherwise appear. IN R US-DCTSD ECF Procedures(14). For a sample format, refer to IN R USDCTSD ECF Procedures(14).

- *Effect of electronic signature.* Filing an electronically signed document under an attorney's ECF log-in and password constitutes the attorney's signature on the document under the Federal Rules of Civil Procedure, under the Local Rules of the United States District Court for the Southern District of Indiana, and for any other reason a signature is required in connection with the court's activities. IN R USDCTSD L.R. 5-7(d).

- *Documents with multiple attorneys' signatures.* Documents requiring signatures of more than one attorney shall be filed either by: (1) obtaining consent from the other attorney, then typing the "s/ [Name]" signature of the other attorney on the signature line where the other attorney's signature would otherwise appear; (2) identifying in the signature section the name of the other attorney whose signature is required and by the submission of a Notice of Endorsement (see IN R USDCTSD ECF Procedures(Appendix B)) by the other attorney no later than three (3) business days after filing; (3) submitting a scanned document containing all handwritten signatures; or (4) in any other manner approved by the Court. IN R USDCTSD ECF Procedures(14); IN R USDCTSD L.R. 5-7(e).

iii. *No verification or accompanying affidavit required for pleadings.* Unless a rule or statute specifically states otherwise, a pleading need not be verified or accompanied by an affidavit. FRCP 11(a).

iv. *Unsigned papers.* The court must strike an unsigned paper unless the omission is promptly corrected after being called to the attorney's or party's attention. FRCP 11(a). The court will strike any document filed directly with the clerk that is not signed by an attorney of record or the pro se litigant filing it, but the court may do so only after giving the attorney or pro se litigant notice of the omission and reasonable time to correct it. Rubber-stamp or facsimile signatures are not original signatures and the court will deem documents containing them to be unsigned for purposes of FRCP 11 and FRCP 26(g) and IN R USDCTSD L.R. 5-10. IN R USDCTSD L.R. 5-10(g).

b. *Representations to the court.* By presenting to the court a pleading, written motion, or other paper—whether by signing, filing, submitting, or later advocating it—an attorney or unrepresented party certifies that to the best of the person's knowledge, information, and belief, formed after an inquiry reasonable under the circumstances:

i. It is not being presented for any improper purpose, such as to harass, cause unnecessary delay, or needlessly increase the cost of litigation;

ii. The claims, defenses, and other legal contentions are warranted by existing law or by a nonfrivolous argument for extending, modifying, or reversing existing law or for establishing new law;

iii. The factual contentions have evidentiary support or, if specifically so identified, will likely have evidentiary support after a reasonable opportunity for further investigation or discovery; and

iv. The denials of factual contentions are warranted on the evidence or, if specifically so identified, are reasonably based on belief or a lack of information. FRCP 11(b).

c. *Sanctions.* If, after notice and a reasonable opportunity to respond, the court determines that FRCP 11(b) has been violated, the court may impose an appropriate sanction on any attorney, law firm, or party that violated FRCP 11(b) or is responsible for the violation. FRCP 11(c)(1). Refer to the United States District Court for the Southern District of Indiana KeyRules Motion for Sanctions document for more information.

5. *Privacy protection for filings made with the court.* Electronically filed documents must meet the requirements of. . .FRCP 5.2 (Privacy Protection for Filings Made with the Court), as if they had been submitted on paper. IN R USDCTSD ECF Procedures(13).

a. *Redacted filings.* Unless the court orders otherwise, in an electronic or paper filing with the court that

contains an individual's Social Security number, taxpayer-identification number, or birth date, the name of an individual known to be a minor, or a financial-account number, a party or nonparty making the filing may include only:

    i.   The last four (4) digits of the Social Security number and taxpayer-identification number;

    ii.   The year of the individual's birth;

    iii.   The minor's initials; and

    iv.   The last four (4) digits of the financial-account number. FRCP 5.2(a).

b. *Exemptions from the redaction requirement.* The redaction requirement does not apply to the following:

    i.   A financial-account number that identifies the property allegedly subject to forfeiture in a forfeiture proceeding;

    ii.   The record of an administrative or agency proceeding;

    iii.   The official record of a state-court proceeding;

    iv.   The record of a court or tribunal, if that record was not subject to the redaction requirement when originally filed;

    v.   A filing covered by FRCP 5.2(c) or FRCP 5.2(d); and

    vi.   A pro se filing in an action brought under 28 U.S.C.A. § 2241, 28 U.S.C.A. § 2254, or 28 U.S.C.A. § 2255. FRCP 5.2(b).

c. *Limitations on remote access to electronic files; Social Security appeals and immigration cases.* Unless the court orders otherwise, in an action for benefits under the Social Security Act, and in an action or proceeding relating to an order of removal, to relief from removal, or to immigration benefits or detention, access to an electronic file is authorized as follows:

    i.   The parties and their attorneys may have remote electronic access to any part of the case file, including the administrative record;

    ii.   Any other person may have electronic access to the full record at the courthouse, but may have remote electronic access only to:

       • The docket maintained by the court; and

       • An opinion, order, judgment, or other disposition of the court, but not any other part of the case file or the administrative record. FRCP 5.2(c).

d. *Filings made under seal.* The court may order that a filing be made under seal without redaction. The court may later unseal the filing or order the person who made the filing to file a redacted version for the public record. FRCP 5.2(d). For more information on filing under seal, refer to IN R USDCTSD L.R. 5-11 and IN R USDCTSD ECF Procedures(18).

e. *Protective orders.* For good cause, the court may by order in a case:

    i.   Require redaction of additional information; or

    ii.   Limit or prohibit a nonparty's remote electronic access to a document filed with the court. FRCP 5.2(e).

f. *Option for additional unredacted filing under seal.* A person making a redacted filing may also file an unredacted copy under seal. The court must retain the unredacted copy as part of the record. FRCP 5.2(f).

g. *Option for filing a reference list.* A filing that contains redacted information may be filed together with a reference list that identifies each item of redacted information and specifies an appropriate identifier that uniquely corresponds to each item listed. The list must be filed under seal and may be amended as of right. Any reference in the case to a listed identifier will be construed to refer to the corresponding item of information. FRCP 5.2(g).

h. *Waiver of protection of identifiers.* A person waives the protection of FRCP 5.2(a) as to the person's own information by filing it without redaction and not under seal. FRCP 5.2(h).

F. Filing and Service Requirements

1. *Filing requirements.* Any paper after the complaint that is required to be served—together with a certificate of service—must be filed within a reasonable time after service. FRCP 5(d)(1). Motions must be filed separately, but alternative motions may be filed in a single document if each is named in the title. IN R USDCTSD L.R. 7-1(a).

   a. *How filing is made; In general.* A paper is filed by delivering it:

      i. To the clerk; or

      ii. To a judge who agrees to accept it for filing, and who must then note the filing date on the paper and promptly send it to the clerk. FRCP 5(d)(2).

         ● In certain instances, the court will direct the parties to submit items directly to chambers (e.g., confidential settlement statements). However, absent specific prior authorization, counsel and litigants should not submit letters or documents directly to chambers, and such materials should be filed with the clerk. IN R USDCTSD L.R. 5-1(Local Rules Advisory Committee Comment).

      iii. A document or item submitted in relation to a matter within the court's jurisdiction is deemed filed upon delivery to the office of the clerk in a manner prescribed by the Local Rules of the United States District Court for the Southern District of Indiana or the Federal Rules of Civil Procedure or authorized by the court. Any submission directed to a Judge or Judge's staff, the office of the clerk or any employee thereof, in a manner that is not contemplated by IN R USDCTSD L.R. 5-1 and without prior court authorization is prohibited. IN R USDCTSD L.R. 5-1(a).

   b. *Non-electronic filing.* Any document that is exempt from electronic filing must be filed directly with the clerk and served on other parties in the case as required by those Federal Rules of Civil Procedure and Local Rules of the United States District Court for the Southern District of Indiana that apply to the service of non-electronic documents. IN R USDCTSD L.R. 5-2(c).

      i. *When completed.* A document or other item that is not required to be filed electronically is deemed filed:

         ● Upon delivery in person, by courier, or via U.S. Mail or other mail delivery service to the clerk's office during business hours;

         ● When the courtroom deputy clerk accepts it, if the document or item is filed in open court; or

         ● Upon completion of any other manner of filing that the court authorizes. IN R USDCTSD L.R. 5-10(a).

      ii. *Document filing by non-exempt party.* When a party who is not exempt from the electronic filing requirement files a document directly with the clerk, the party must:

         ● Electronically file a notice of manual filing that explains why the document cannot be filed electronically;

         ● Present the document to the clerk within one (1) business day after filing the notice of manual filing; and

         ● Present the clerk with a copy of the notice of manual filing when the party files the document with the clerk. IN R USDCTSD L.R. 5-2(d).

   c. *Electronic filing*

      i. *Authorization of electronic filing program.* A court may, by local rule, allow papers to be filed, signed, or verified by electronic means that are consistent with any technical standards established by the Judicial Conference of the United States. A local rule may require electronic filing only if reasonable exceptions are allowed. A paper filed electronically in compliance with a local rule is a written paper for purposes of the Federal Rules of Civil Procedure. FRCP 5(d)(3).

         ● IN R USDCTSD L.R. 5-2 requires electronic filing, as allowed by FRCP 5(d)(3). The

policies and procedures in IN R USDCTSD ECF Procedures govern electronic filing in this district unless, due to circumstances in a particular case, a judicial officer determines that these policies and procedures (IN R USDCTSD ECF Procedures) should be modified. IN R USDCTSD ECF Procedures(1).

- Unless modified by order of the Court, all Federal Rules of Civil Procedure and Local Rules of the United States District Court for the Southern District of Indiana shall continue to apply to cases maintained in the Court's Case Management/Electronic Case Filing System (CM/ECF). IN R USDCTSD ECF Procedures(3).

ii. *Mandatory electronic filing.* Unless exempted pursuant to IN R USDCTSD L.R. 5-3(e), attorneys admitted to the court's bar (including those admitted pro hac vice) or authorized to represent the United States must use the court's ECF system to file documents. IN R USDCTSD L.R. 5-3(a). Electronic filing by attorneys is required for eligible documents filed in civil and criminal cases pending with the Court, unless specifically exempted by Local Rule or Court Order. IN R USDCTSD ECF Procedures(4).

- *Exceptions.* All civil cases (other than those cases the court specifically exempts) must be maintained in the court's electronic case filing (ECF) system. Accordingly, as allowed by FRCP 5(d)(3), every document filed in this court (including exhibits) must be transmitted to the clerk's office via the ECF system consistent with IN R USDCTSD L.R. 5-2 through IN R USDCTSD L.R. 5-11 except: (1) documents filed by pro se litigants; (2) transcripts in cases filed by claimants under the Social Security Act (and related statutes); (3) exhibits in a format that does not readily permit electronic filing (such as videos and large maps and charts); (4) documents that are illegible when scanned into .pdf format; (5) documents filed in cases not maintained on the ECF system; and (6) any other documents that the court or the Local Rules of the United States District Court for the Southern District of Indiana specifically allow to be filed directly with the clerk. IN R USDCTSD L.R. 5-2(a). Parties otherwise participating in the electronic filing system may be excused from filing a particular component electronically under certain limited circumstances, such as when the component cannot be reduced to an electronic format. Such components shall not be filed electronically, but instead shall be manually filed with the Clerk of Court and served upon the parties in accordance with the applicable Federal Rules of Civil Procedure and the Local Rules of the United States District Court for the Southern District of Indiana for filing and service of non-electronic documents. IN R USDCTSD ECF Procedures(15).

- *Exemption from participation.* The court may exempt attorneys from using the ECF system in a particular case for good cause. An attorney must file a petition for ECF exemption and a CM/ECF technical requirements exemption questionnaire in each case in which the attorney seeks an exemption. (The CM/ECF technical requirements exemption questionnaire is available on the court's website). IN R USDCTSD L.R. 5-3(e).

iii. *Consequences of electronic filing.* Electronic transmission of a document consistent with the procedures adopted by the Court shall, upon the complete receipt of the same by the Clerk of Court, constitute filing of the document for all purposes of the Federal Rules of Civil and Criminal Procedure and the Local Rules of the United States District Court for the Southern District of Indiana, and shall constitute entry of that document onto the docket maintained by the Clerk pursuant to FRCP 58 and FRCP 79. IN R USDCTSD ECF Procedures(7); IN R USDCTSD L.R. 5-4(c)(1). When a document has been filed electronically: the document, as filed, binds the filing party. IN R USDCTSD L.R. 5-4(c)(3).

- A Notice of Electronic Filing (NEF) acknowledging that the document has been filed will immediately appear on the filer's screen after the document has been submitted. Attorneys are strongly encouraged to print or electronically save a copy of the NEF. Attorneys can also verify the filing of documents by inspecting the Court's electronic docket sheet through the use of a PACER login. IN R USDCTSD ECF Procedures(7). When a document has been filed electronically: the notice of electronic filing for the document serves as the court's date-stamp and proof of filing. IN R USDCTSD L.R. 5-4(c)(4).

- The Court may, upon the motion of a party or upon its own motion, strike any inappropriately filed document. IN R USDCTSD ECF Procedures(7).

      iv. For more information on electronic filing, refer to IN R USDCTSD ECF Procedures.

  d. *Fax filing.* The clerk may not file a faxed document without court authorization. The court may not authorize the clerk to file faxed documents without finding that compelling circumstances justify it. A party must submit a copy of the document that otherwise complies with IN R USDCTSD L.R. 5-10 to replace the faxed copy within seven (7) days after faxing the document. IN R USDCTSD L.R. 5-10(e).

2. *Service requirements*

  a. *Service; When required*

      i. *In general.* Unless the Federal Rules of Civil Procedure provide otherwise, each of the following papers must be served on every party:

- An order stating that service is required;
- A pleading filed after the original complaint, unless the court orders otherwise under FRCP 5(c) because there are numerous defendants;
- A discovery paper required to be served on a party, unless the court orders otherwise;
- A written motion, except one that may be heard ex parte; and
- A written notice, appearance, demand, or offer of judgment, or any similar paper. FRCP 5(a)(1).

      ii. *If a party fails to appear.* No service is required on a party who is in default for failing to appear. But a pleading that asserts a new claim for relief against such a party must be served on that party under FRCP 4. FRCP 5(a)(2).

      iii. *Seizing property.* If an action is begun by seizing property and no person is or need be named as a defendant, any service required before the filing of an appearance, answer, or claim must be made on the person who had custody or possession of the property when it was seized. FRCP 5(a)(3).

  b. *Service; How made*

      i. *Serving an attorney.* If a party is represented by an attorney, service under FRCP 5 must be made on the attorney unless the court orders service on the party. FRCP 5(b)(1).

      ii. *Service in general.* A paper is served under FRCP 5 by:

- Handing it to the person;
- Leaving it: (1) at the person's office with a clerk or other person in charge or, if no one is in charge, in a conspicuous place in the office; or (2) if the person has no office or the office is closed, at the person's dwelling or usual place of abode with someone of suitable age and discretion who resides there;
- Mailing it to the person's last known address—in which event service is complete upon mailing;
- Leaving it with the court clerk if the person has no known address;
- Sending it by electronic means if the person consented in writing—in which event service is complete upon transmission, but is not effective if the serving party learns that it did not reach the person to be served; or
- Delivering it by any other means that the person consented to in writing—in which event service is complete when the person making service delivers it to the agency designated to make delivery. FRCP 5(b)(2).

      iii. *Electronic service*

- *Consent.* By registering to use the ECF system, attorneys consent to electronic service of documents filed in cases maintained on the ECF system. IN R USDCTSD L.R. 5-3(d). By participating in the Electronic Case Filing Program, attorneys consent to the electronic service of documents, and shall make available electronic mail addresses for service. IN R USDCTSD ECF Procedures(11).

- *Service on registered parties.* Upon the filing of a document by a party, an e-mail message will be automatically generated by the electronic filing system and sent via electronic mail to the e-mail addresses of all registered attorneys who have appeared in the case. The Notice of Electronic Filing will contain a document hyperlink which will provide recipients with one "free look" at the electronically filed document. Recipients are encouraged to print and/or save a copy of the document during the "free look" to avoid incurring PACER charges for future viewings of the document. IN R USDCTSD ECF Procedures(11). When a document has been filed electronically: transmission of the notice of electronic filing generated by the ECF system to an attorney's e-mail address constitutes service of the document on that attorney. IN R USDCTSD L.R. 5-4(c)(5). The party effectuates service on all registered attorneys by filing electronically. IN R USDCTSD ECF Procedures(11). When a document has been filed electronically: no other attempted service will constitute electronic service of the document. IN R USDCTSD L.R. 5-4(c)(6).

- *Service on exempt parties.* A filer must serve a copy of the document consistent with FRCP 5 on any party or attorney who is exempt from participating in electronic filing. IN R USDCTSD L.R. 5-4(d). It is the responsibility of the filing attorney to conventionally serve all parties who do not receive electronic service (the identity of these parties will be indicated on the filing receipt generated by the ECF system). IN R USDCTSD ECF Procedures(11).

- *Service on parties excused from electronic filing.* Parties otherwise participating in the electronic filing system may be excused from filing a particular component electronically under certain limited circumstances, such as when the component cannot be reduced to an electronic format. Such components shall not be filed electronically, but instead shall be manually filed with the Clerk of Court and served upon the parties in accordance with the applicable Federal Rules of Civil Procedure and the Local Rules of the United States District Court for the Southern District of Indiana for filing and service of non-electronic documents. IN R USDCTSD ECF Procedures(15).

- *Service of exempt documents.* Any document that is exempt from electronic filing must be filed directly with the clerk and served on other parties in the case as required by those Federal Rules of Civil Procedure and Local Rules of the United States District Court for the Southern District of Indiana that apply to the service of non-electronic documents. IN R USDCTSD L.R. 5-2(c).

    iv. *Using court facilities.* If a local rule so authorizes, a party may use the court's transmission facilities to make service under FRCP 5(b)(2)(E). FRCP 5(b)(3).

  c. *Serving numerous defendants*

    i. *In general.* If an action involves an unusually large number of defendants, the court may, on motion or on its own, order that:

- Defendants' pleadings and replies to them need not be served on other defendants;

- Any crossclaim, counterclaim, avoidance, or affirmative defense in those pleadings and replies to them will be treated as denied or avoided by all other parties; and

- Filing any such pleading and serving it on the plaintiff constitutes notice of the pleading to all parties. FRCP 5(c)(1).

    ii. *Notifying parties.* A copy of every such order must be served on the parties as the court directs. FRCP 5(c)(2).

G. Hearings

1. *Hearings, generally*

  a. *Oral argument.* Due process does not require that oral argument be permitted on a motion and, except as otherwise provided by local rule, the district court has discretion to determine whether it will decide the motion on the papers or hear argument by counsel (and perhaps receive evidence). FPP § 1190; F.D.I.C. v. Deglau, 207 F.3d 153 (3d Cir. 2000).

    i. *Request for oral argument.* A party may request oral argument by filing a separate motion

explaining why oral argument is necessary and estimating how long the court should allow for the argument. IN R USDCTSD L.R. 7-5(a). Refer to the Documents section of this document for more information.

 ii. *No additional evidence at oral argument.* Parties may not present additional evidence at oral argument. IN R USDCTSD L.R. 7-5(b).

 b. *Providing a regular schedule for oral hearings.* A court may establish regular times and places for oral hearings on motions. FRCP 78(a).

 c. *Providing for submission on briefs.* By rule or order, the court may provide for submitting and determining motions on briefs, without oral hearings. FRCP 78(b).

 d. *Request for evidentiary hearing.* A party may request an evidentiary hearing on a motion or petition by serving and filing a separate motion explaining why the hearing is necessary and estimating how long the court should allow for the hearing. IN R USDCTSD L.R. 7-5(c).

 e. *Directed by the court.* The court may: (1) grant or deny a request for oral argument or an evidentiary hearing in its sole discretion; (2) set oral argument or an evidentiary hearing without a request from a party; and (3) order any oral argument or evidentiary hearing to be held anywhere within the district regardless of where the case will be tried. IN R USDCTSD L.R. 7-5(d).

2. *Hearing on FRCP 12 defenses before trial.* If a party so moves, any defense listed in FRCP 12(b)(1) through FRCP 12(b)(7)—whether made in a pleading or by motion—and a motion under FRCP 12(c) must be heard and decided before trial unless the court orders a deferral until trial. FRCP 12(i).

3. *Hearing on motion to dismiss for lack of subject matter jurisdiction.* It may be error for a court to dismiss a case on the defendant's motion to dismiss for lack of subject matter jurisdiction without first holding a hearing, as FRCP 12(b)(1) requires a preliminary hearing or hearing at trial to determine any disputed facts upon which the motion or opposition to it is predicated. FEDPROC § 62:435.

4. *Courtroom and courthouse decorum.* For information on courtroom and courthouse decorum, refer to IN R USDCTSD L.R. 83-3.

H. Forms

1. Federal Motion to Dismiss for Lack of Subject Matter Jurisdiction Forms

 a. Motion to dismiss for lack of subject-matter jurisdiction. 2C FEDFORMS § 11:35.

 b. Motion to dismiss for lack of subject-matter jurisdiction; Want of diversity of citizenship because requisite diversity not alleged. 2C FEDFORMS § 11:37.

 c. Motion to dismiss for lack of subject-matter jurisdiction; Want of diversity on a factual basis and because requisite diversity not alleged. 2C FEDFORMS § 11:38.

 d. Motion to dismiss for lack of subject-matter jurisdiction; Want of diversity of citizenship because state of incorporation and principal place of business of defendant not as alleged. 2C FEDFORMS § 11:39.

 e. Motion to dismiss for lack of subject-matter jurisdiction; Want of diversity of citizenship because principal place of business of defendant not as alleged. 2C FEDFORMS § 11:40.

 f. Motion to dismiss for lack of subject-matter jurisdiction; Failure to comply with procedural requirements. 2C FEDFORMS § 11:41.

 g. Motion to dismiss for lack of subject-matter jurisdiction; Want of diversity upon realignment of parties according to interest. 2C FEDFORMS § 11:42.

 h. Motion to dismiss for lack of subject-matter jurisdiction; Want of federal question. 2C FEDFORMS § 11:43.

 i. Motion to dismiss for lack of subject-matter jurisdiction; Unsubstantial federal question. 2C FEDFORMS § 11:44.

 j. Motion to dismiss for lack of subject-matter jurisdiction; Want of amount in controversy. 2C FEDFORMS § 11:45.

 k. Motion to dismiss for lack of subject-matter jurisdiction; Want of amount in controversy; Insurance policy limits do not exceed required jurisdictional amount. 2C FEDFORMS § 11:46.

l. Motion to dismiss for lack of subject-matter jurisdiction; Want of amount in controversy; Claim for damages in excess of jurisdictional amount not made in good faith. 2C FEDFORMS § 11:47.

m. Motion to dismiss for lack of subject-matter jurisdiction; Want of amount in controversy; Made after judgment. 2C FEDFORMS § 11:48.

n. Motion to dismiss for lack of subject-matter jurisdiction; Want of consent by the United States to be sued. 2C FEDFORMS § 11:49.

o. Motion to dismiss for lack of subject-matter jurisdiction; Want of consent by United States to be sued; United States indispensable party. 2C FEDFORMS § 11:50.

p. Affidavit; In opposition to motion to dismiss for lack of diversity; Assignment of claim to plaintiff bona fide. FEDPROF § 1:894.

q. Motion; To dismiss; Plaintiff and defendant citizens of same state when action filed. FEDPROF § 1:888.

r. Motion to dismiss; Assignment to nonresident for purpose of invoking federal jurisdiction sham and ineffective to confer jurisdiction. FEDPROF § 1:889.

s. Motion to dismiss; For lack of diversity in third-party complaint. FEDPROF § 1:890.

t. Affidavit; In support of motion to dismiss for want of diversity of citizenship; Plaintiff and defendant citizens of same state on date action filed. FEDPROF § 1:892.

u. Motion; To dismiss; Insufficiency of amount in controversy. FEDPROF § 1:897.

v. Motion to dismiss; Bad faith in claiming jurisdictional amount. FEDPROF § 1:898.

w. Motion; To dismiss; Lack of jurisdiction over subject matter, generally. FEDPROF § 1:903.

x. Motion to dismiss; Absence of federal question. FEDPROF § 1:904.

y. Motion to dismiss; Absence of federal question; Failure to exhaust state remedies. FEDPROF § 1:905.

z. Affidavit; In opposition to motion to dismiss for absence of jurisdiction over subject matter. FEDPROF § 1:906.

2. Forms for the Southern District of Indiana

a. Notice of endorsement. IN R USDCTSD ECF Procedures(Appendix B).

b. Notice of manual filing. IN R USDCTSD ECF Procedures(Appendix C).

c. Declaration that party was unable to file in a timely manner due to technical difficulties. IN R USDCTSD ECF Procedures(Appendix D).

I. Applicable Rules

1. *Federal rules*

a. Federal question. 28 U.S.C.A. § 1331.

b. Diversity of citizenship; Amount in controversy; Costs. 28 U.S.C.A. § 1332.

c. Serving and filing pleadings and other papers. FRCP 5.

d. Constitutional challenge to a statute; Notice, certification, and intervention. FRCP 5.1.

e. Privacy protection for filings made with the court. FRCP 5.2.

f. Computing and extending time; Time for motion papers. FRCP 6.

g. Pleadings allowed; Form of motions and other papers. FRCP 7.

h. Disclosure statement. FRCP 7.1.

i. Form of pleadings. FRCP 10.

j. Signing pleadings, motions, and other papers; Representations to the court; Sanctions. FRCP 11.

k. Defenses and objections; When and how presented; Motion for judgment on the pleadings; Consolidating motions; Waiving defenses; Pretrial hearing. FRCP 12.

    l.   Taking testimony. FRCP 43.

    m. Hearing motions; Submission on briefs. FRCP 78.

2. *Local rules*

    a.   Scope of the rules. IN R USDCTSD L.R. 1-1.

    b.   Sanctions for errors as to form. IN R USDCTSD L.R. 1-3.

    c.   Format of documents presented for filing. IN R USDCTSD L.R. 5-1.

    d.   Constitutional challenge to a statute; Notice. IN R USDCTSD L.R. 5.1-1.

    e.   Filing of documents electronically required. IN R USDCTSD L.R. 5-2.

    f.   Eligibility, registration, passwords for electronic filing; Exemption from electronic filing. IN R USDCTSD L.R. 5-3.

    g.   Timing and consequences of electronic filing. IN R USDCTSD L.R. 5-4.

    h.   Attachments and exhibits in cases filed electronically. IN R USDCTSD L.R. 5-6.

    i.   Signatures in cases filed electronically. IN R USDCTSD L.R. 5-7.

    j.   Non-electronic filings. IN R USDCTSD L.R. 5-10.

    k.   Motion practice. [IN R USDCTSD L.R. 7-1, as amended by IN ORDER 16-2319, effective December 1, 2016].

    l.   Oral arguments and hearings. IN R USDCTSD L.R. 7-5.

    m. Request for three-judge court. IN R USDCTSD L.R. 9-2.

    n.   Filing of discovery materials. IN R USDCTSD L.R. 26-2.

    o.   Assignment of cases. IN R USDCTSD L.R. 40-1.

    p.   Alternative dispute resolution. IN R USDCTSD A.D.R. Rule 1.1; IN R USDCTSD A.D.R. Rule 1.2; IN R USDCTSD A.D.R. Rule 1.5; IN R USDCTSD A.D.R. Rule 2.1; IN R USDCTSD A.D.R. Rule 2.2.

    q.   Instructions for preparing case management plan. IN R USDCTSD Case Mgt.

    r.   Electronic case filing policies and procedures manual. IN R USDCTSD ECF Procedures.

Motions, Oppositions and Replies
Motion to Dismiss for Lack of Personal Jurisdiction

Document Last Updated December 2016

A. Checklist

  (I) ❏ Matters to be considered by moving party

    (a) ❏ Required documents

      (1) ❏ Notice of motion and motion

      (2) ❏ Brief

      (3) ❏ Certificate of service

    (b) ❏ Supplemental documents

      (1) ❏ Supporting evidence

      (2) ❏ Notice of constitutional question

      (3) ❏ Nongovernmental corporate disclosure statement

      (4) ❏ Index of exhibits

      (5) ❏ Request for oral argument

    (6) ❑ Request for evidentiary hearing

    (7) ❑ Copy of authority

    (8) ❑ Proposed order

    (9) ❑ Copy of document with self-address envelope

    (10) ❑ Notice of manual filing

    (11) ❑ Courtesy copies

    (12) ❑ Copies for three-judge court

    (13) ❑ Declaration that party was unable to file in a timely manner due to technical difficulties

(c) ❑ Timing

    (1) ❑ Every defense to a claim for relief in any pleading must be asserted in the responsive pleading if one is required

    (2) ❑ A motion asserting any of the defenses in FRCP 12(b) must be made before pleading if a responsive pleading is allowed

    (3) ❑ If a pleading sets out a claim for relief that does not require a responsive pleading, an opposing party may assert at trial any defense to that claim

    (4) ❑ A written motion and notice of the hearing must be served at least fourteen (14) days before the time specified for the hearing, with the following exceptions: (i) when the motion may be heard ex parte; (ii) when the Federal Rules of Civil Procedure set a different time; or (iii) when a court order—which a party may, for good cause, apply for ex parte—sets a different time

    (5) ❑ Any affidavit supporting a motion must be served with the motion

    (6) ❑ When a party who is not exempt from the electronic filing requirement files a document directly with the clerk, the party must present the document to the clerk within one (1) business day after filing the notice of manual filing

    (7) ❑ Unless the court orders otherwise, the [untimely] document and declaration [that party was unable to file in a timely manner due to technical difficulties] must be filed no later than 12:00 noon of the first day on which the court is open for business following the original filing deadline

(II) ❑ Matters to be considered by opposing party

  (a) ❑ Required documents

    (1) ❑ Response brief

    (2) ❑ Certificate of service

  (b) ❑ Supplemental documents

    (1) ❑ Supporting evidence

    (2) ❑ Notice of constitutional question

    (3) ❑ Index of exhibits

    (4) ❑ Request for oral argument

    (5) ❑ Request for evidentiary hearing

    (6) ❑ Copy of authority

    (7) ❑ Copy of document with self-address envelope

    (8) ❑ Notice of manual filing

    (9) ❑ Courtesy copies

    (10) ❑ Copies for three-judge court

    (11) ❑ Declaration that party was unable to file in a timely manner due to technical difficulties

(c) ❑ Timing

    (1) ❑ Any response is due within fourteen (14) days after service of the motion

    (2) ❑ Except as FRCP 59(c) provides otherwise, any opposing affidavit must be served at least seven (7) days before the hearing, unless the court permits service at another time

    (3) ❑ When a party who is not exempt from the electronic filing requirement files a document directly with the clerk, the party must present the document to the clerk within one (1) business day after filing the notice of manual filing

    (4) ❑ Unless the court orders otherwise, the [untimely] document and declaration [that party was unable to file in a timely manner due to technical difficulties] must be filed no later than 12:00 noon of the first day on which the court is open for business following the original filing deadline

B. Timing

1. *Motion to dismiss for lack of personal jurisdiction*

    a. *In a responsive pleading.* Every defense to a claim for relief in any pleading must be asserted in the responsive pleading if one is required. FRCP 12(b).

    b. *By motion.* A motion asserting any of the defenses in FRCP 12(b) must be made before pleading if a responsive pleading is allowed. FRCP 12(b). Although FRCP 12(b) encourages the responsive pleader to file a motion to dismiss before filing the answer, nothing in FRCP 12 prohibits the filing of a motion to dismiss with the answer. An untimely motion to dismiss may be considered if the defense asserted in the motion was previously raised in the responsive pleading. FEDPROC § 62:427.

    c. *At trial.* If a pleading sets out a claim for relief that does not require a responsive pleading, an opposing party may assert at trial any defense to that claim. FRCP 12(b).

2. *Timing of motions, generally*

    a. *Motion and notice of hearing.* A written motion and notice of the hearing must be served at least fourteen (14) days before the time specified for the hearing, with the following exceptions:

        i. When the motion may be heard ex parte;

        ii. When the Federal Rules of Civil Procedure set a different time; or

        iii. When a court order—which a party may, for good cause, apply for ex parte—sets a different time. FRCP 6(c)(1).

    b. *Supporting affidavit.* Any affidavit supporting a motion must be served with the motion. FRCP 6(c)(2).

3. *Timing of opposing papers.* Any response is due within fourteen (14) days after service of the motion. IN R USDCTSD L.R. 7-1(c)(2)(A).

    a. *Opposing affidavit.* Except as FRCP 59(c) provides otherwise, any opposing affidavit must be served at least seven (7) days before the hearing, unless the court permits service at another time. FRCP 6(c)(2).

    b. *Extensions.* The court may extend response and reply deadlines, but only for good cause. IN R USDCTSD L.R. 7-1(c)(3).

    c. *Summary ruling on failure to respond.* The court may summarily rule on a motion if an opposing party does not file a response within the deadline. IN R USDCTSD L.R. 7-1(c)(4).

4. *Timing of reply papers.* Where the respondent files an answering affidavit setting up a new matter, the moving party ordinarily is allowed a reasonable time to file a reply affidavit since failure to deny the new matter by affidavit may operate as an admission of its truth. AMJUR MOTIONS § 25.

    a. *Reply brief.* Any reply is due within seven (7) days after service of the response. IN R USDCTSD L.R. 7-1(c)(2)(B).

    b. *Extensions.* The court may extend response and reply deadlines, but only for good cause. IN R USDCTSD L.R. 7-1(c)(3).

5. *Effect of a FRCP 12 motion on the time to serve a responsive pleading.* Unless the court sets a different time, serving a motion under FRCP 12 alters the periods in FRCP 12(a) as follows:

   a. If the court denies the motion or postpones its disposition until trial, the responsive pleading must be served within fourteen (14) days after notice of the court's action; or

   b. If the court grants a motion for a more definite statement, the responsive pleading must be served within fourteen (14) days after the more definite statement is served. FRCP 12(a)(4).

6. *Document filing by non-exempt party.* When a party who is not exempt from the electronic filing requirement files a document directly with the clerk, the party must: present the document to the clerk within one (1) business day after filing the notice of manual filing. IN R USDCTSD L.R. 5-2(d)(2).

7. *Declaration that party was unable to file in a timely manner due to technical difficulties.* Unless the Court orders otherwise, the [untimely] document and declaration [that party was unable to file in a timely manner due to technical difficulties] must be filed no later than 12:00 noon of the first day on which the Court is open for business following the original filing deadline. IN R USDCTSD ECF Procedures(16).

8. *Computation of time*

   a. *Computing time.* FRCP 6 applies in computing any time period specified in the Federal Rules of Civil Procedure, in any local rule or court order, or in any statute that does not specify a method of computing time. FRCP 6(a).

      i. *Period stated in days or a longer unit.* When the period is stated in days or a longer unit of time:

         - Exclude the day of the event that triggers the period;

         - Count every day, including intermediate Saturdays, Sundays, and legal holidays; and

         - Include the last day of the period, but if the last day is a Saturday, Sunday, or legal holiday, the period continues to run until the end of the next day that is not a Saturday, Sunday, or legal holiday. FRCP 6(a)(1).

      ii. *Period stated in hours.* When the period is stated in hours:

         - Begin counting immediately on the occurrence of the event that triggers the period;

         - Count every hour, including hours during intermediate Saturdays, Sundays, and legal holidays; and

         - If the period would end on a Saturday, Sunday, or legal holiday, the period continues to run until the same time on the next day that is not a Saturday, Sunday, or legal holiday. FRCP 6(a)(2).

      iii. *Inaccessibility of the clerk's office.* Unless the court orders otherwise, if the clerk's office is inaccessible:

         - On the last day for filing under FRCP 6(a)(1), then the time for filing is extended to the first accessible day that is not a Saturday, Sunday, or legal holiday; or

         - During the last hour for filing under FRCP 6(a)(2), then the time for filing is extended to the same time on the first accessible day that is not a Saturday, Sunday, or legal holiday. FRCP 6(a)(3).

      iv. *"Last day" defined.* Unless a different time is set by a statute, local rule, or court order, the last day ends:

         - For electronic filing, at midnight in the court's time zone; and

         - For filing by other means, when the clerk's office is scheduled to close. FRCP 6(a)(4).

      v. *"Next day" defined.* The "next day" is determined by continuing to count forward when the period is measured after an event and backward when measured before an event. FRCP 6(a)(5).

      vi. *"Legal holiday" defined.* "Legal holiday" means:

         - The day set aside by statute for observing New Year's Day, Martin Luther King Jr.'s Birthday, Washington's Birthday, Memorial Day, Independence Day, Labor Day, Columbus Day, Veterans' Day, Thanksgiving Day, or Christmas Day;

- Any day declared a holiday by the President or Congress; and
- For periods that are measured after an event, any other day declared a holiday by the state where the district court is located. FRCP 6(a)(6).

b. *Computation of electronic filing deadlines.* Filing documents electronically does not alter filing deadlines. IN R USDCTSD ECF Procedures(7). A document due on a particular day must be filed before midnight local time of the division where the case is pending. IN R USDCTSD L.R. 5-4(a). All electronic transmissions of documents must be completed (i.e. received completely by the Clerk's Office) prior to midnight of the local time of the division in which the case is pending in order to be considered timely filed that day (NOTE: time will be noted in Eastern Time on the Court's docket. If you have filed a document prior to midnight local time of the division in which the case is pending and the document is due that date, but the electronic receipt and docket reflect the following calendar day, please contact the Court). IN R USDCTSD ECF Procedures(7). Although attorneys may file documents electronically twenty-four (24) hours a day, seven (7) days a week, attorneys are encouraged to file all documents during the normal working hours of the Clerk's Office (Monday through Friday, 8:30 a.m. to 4:30 p.m.) when technical support is available. IN R USDCTSD ECF Procedures(7); IN R USDCTSD ECF Procedures(9).

   i. *Technical difficulties.* Parties are encouraged to file documents electronically during normal business hours, in case a problem is encountered. In the event a technical failure occurs and a document cannot be filed electronically despite the best efforts of the filing party, the party should print (if possible) a copy of the error message received. In addition, as soon as practically possible, the party should file a "Declaration that Party was Unable to File in a Timely Manner Due to Technical Difficulties." A model form is provided as Appendix D (IN R USDCTSD ECF Procedures(Appendix D)). IN R USDCTSD ECF Procedures(16).

   - If a party is unable to file electronically and, as a result, may miss a filing deadline, the party must contact the Clerk's Office at the number listed in IN R USDCTSD ECF Procedures(15) to inform the court's staff of the difficulty. If a party misses a filing deadline due to an inability to file electronically, the party may submit the untimely filed document, accompanied by a declaration stating the reason(s) for missing the deadline. Unless the Court orders otherwise, the document and declaration must be filed no later than 12:00 noon of the first day on which the Court is open for business following the original filing deadline. IN R USDCTSD ECF Procedures(16).

c. *Extending time*

   i. *In general.* When an act may or must be done within a specified time, the court may, for good cause, extend the time:

   - With or without motion or notice if the court acts, or if a request is made, before the original time or its extension expires; or
   - On motion made after the time has expired if the party failed to act because of excusable neglect. FRCP 6(b)(1).

   ii. *Exceptions.* A court must not extend the time to act under FRCP 50(b), FRCP 50(d), FRCP 52(b), FRCP 59(b), FRCP 59(d), FRCP 59(e), and FRCP 60(b). FRCP 6(b)(2).

   iii. Refer to the United States District Court for the Southern District of Indiana KeyRules Motion for Continuance/Extension of Time document for more information on extending time.

d. *Additional time after certain kinds of service.* When a party may or must act within a specified time after being served and service is made under FRCP 5(b)(2)(C) (mail), FRCP 5(b)(2)(D) (leaving with the clerk), or FRCP 5(b)(2)(F) (other means consented to), three (3) days are added after the period would otherwise expire under FRCP 6(a). FRCP 6(d). Service by electronic mail shall constitute service pursuant to FRCP 5(b)(2)(E) and shall entitle the party being served to the additional three (3) days provided by FRCP 6(d). IN R USDCTSD ECF Procedures(11).

C. General Requirements

1. *Motions, generally*

   a. *Requirements.* A request for a court order must be made by motion. The motion must:

      i. Be in writing unless made during a hearing or trial;

      ii. State with particularity the grounds for seeking the order; and

      iii. State the relief sought. FRCP 7(b)(1).

   b. *Notice of motion.* A party interested in resisting the relief sought by a motion has a right to notice thereof, and an opportunity to be heard. AMJUR MOTIONS § 12.

      i. In addition to statutory or court rule provisions requiring notice of a motion—the purpose of such a notice requirement having been said to be to prevent a party from being prejudicially surprised by a motion—principles of natural justice dictate that an adverse party generally must be given notice that a motion will be presented to the court. AMJUR MOTIONS § 12.

      ii. "Notice," in this regard, means reasonable notice, including a meaningful opportunity to prepare and to defend against allegations of a motion. AMJUR MOTIONS § 12.

   c. *Writing requirement.* The writing requirement is intended to insure that the adverse parties are informed and have a record of both the motion's pendency and the grounds on which the movant seeks an order. FPP § 1191; Feldberg v. Quechee Lakes Corp., 463 F.3d 195 (2d Cir. 2006).

      i. It is sufficient "if the motion is stated in a written notice of the hearing of the motion." FPP § 1191.

   d. *Particularity requirement.* The particularity requirement insures that the opposing parties will have notice of their opponent's contentions. FEDPROC § 62:364; Goodman v. 1973 26 Foot Trojan Vessel, Arkansas Registration No. AR1439SN, 859 F.2d 71, 12 Fed.R.Serv.3d 645 (8th Cir. 1988). That requirement ensures that notice of the basis for the motion is provided to the court and to the opposing party so as to avoid prejudice, provide the opponent with a meaningful opportunity to respond, and provide the court with enough information to process the motion correctly. FEDPROC § 62:364; Andreas v. Volkswagen of America, Inc., 336 F.3d 789, 56 Fed.R.Serv.3d 6 (8th Cir. 2003).

      i. Reasonable specification of the grounds for a motion is sufficient. However, where a movant fails to state even one ground for granting the motion in question, the movant has failed to meet the minimal standard of "reasonable specification." FEDPROC § 62:364; Martinez v. Trainor, 556 F.2d 818, 23 Fed.R.Serv.2d 403 (7th Cir. 1977).

      ii. The court may excuse the failure to comply with the particularity requirement if it is inadvertent, and where no prejudice is shown by the opposing party. FEDPROC § 62:364.

   e. *Motions must be filed separately.* Motions must be filed separately, but alternative motions may be filed in a single document if each is named in the title. A motion must not be contained within a brief, response, or reply to a previously filed motion, unless ordered by the court. IN R USDCTSD L.R. 7-1(a).

   f. *Routine or uncontested motions.* The court may rule upon a routine or uncontested motion before the response deadline passes, unless: (1) the motion indicates that an opposing party objects to it; or (2) the court otherwise believes that a response will be filed. IN R USDCTSD L.R. 7-1(d).

2. *Motion to dismiss for lack of personal jurisdiction.* A party may assert the defense of lack of subject-matter jurisdiction by motion. FRCP 12(b)(2). The most common use of the FRCP 12(b)(2) motion is to challenge the use of a state long-arm statute in a diversity action. FEDPROC § 62:445; Best Van Lines, Inc. v. Walker, 490 F.3d 239 (2d Cir. 2007). A dismissal pursuant to FRCP 12(b)(2) is proper where it appears that the assertion of jurisdiction over the defendant offends traditional notions of fair play and substantial justice—that is, where neither the defendant nor the controversy has a substantial enough connection with the forum state to make the exercise of jurisdiction reasonable. FEDPROC § 62:445; Neogen Corp. v. Neo Gen Screening, Inc., 282 F.3d 883, 2002 Fed.App. 0080P (6th Cir. 2002).

   a. *Personal jurisdiction, generally*

      i. *Due process limitations.* Due process requires that a court obtain jurisdiction over a defendant before it may adjudicate that defendant's personal rights. FEDPROC § 65:1; Omni Capital Intern., Ltd. v. Rudolf Wolff & Co., Ltd., 484 U.S. 97, 108 S.Ct. 404, 98 L.Ed.2d 415, 9 Fed.R.Serv.3d 691 (1987).

- Originally, it was believed that a judgment in personam could only be entered against a defendant found and served within a state, but the increased flow of commerce between the states and the disuse of the writ of capias ad respondendum, which directed the sheriff to secure the defendant's appearance by taking the defendant into custody, in civil cases led to the liberalization of the concept of personal jurisdiction over nonresidents, and the flexible "minimum contacts" test is now followed. FEDPROC § 65:1.

- Today the rule is that no binding judgment may be rendered against an individual or corporate defendant unless the defendant has sufficient contacts, ties, or relations with the jurisdiction. FEDPROC § 65:1; Burger King Corp. v. Rudzewicz, 471 U.S. 462, 105 S.Ct. 2174, 85 L.Ed.2d 528 (1985); International Shoe Co. v. State of Wash., Office of Unemployment Compensation and Placement, 326 U.S. 310, 66 S.Ct. 154, 90 L.Ed. 95, 161 A.L.R. 1057 (1945).

- Moreover, even if the defendant has sufficient contacts with the forum state to satisfy due process, a court nevertheless does not obtain personal jurisdiction over the defendant unless the defendant has notice sufficient to satisfy due process, and, if such notice requires service of a summons, that there is authorization for the type and manner of service used. FEDPROC § 65:1; Omni Capital Intern., Ltd. v. Rudolf Wolff & Co., Ltd., 484 U.S. 97, 108 S.Ct. 404, 98 L.Ed.2d 415, 9 Fed.R.Serv.3d 691 (1987).

- Personal jurisdiction is a prerequisite to the maintenance of an action and must exist even though subject matter jurisdiction and venue are proper. FEDPROC § 65:1; Bookout v. Beck, 354 F.2d 823 (9th Cir. 1965).

- Personal jurisdiction over a nonresident defendant is appropriate under the Due Process Clause only where the defendant has sufficient minimum contacts with the forum state that are more than random, fortuitous, or attenuated contacts made by interacting with other persons affiliated with the state, such that summoning the defendant would not offend traditional notions of fair play and substantial justice. FEDPROC § 65:1; Pecoraro v. Sky Ranch for Boys, Inc., 340 F.3d 558 (8th Cir. 2003).

ii. *Methods of obtaining jurisdiction over an individual.* There are four basic methods of obtaining jurisdiction over an individual:

- Personal service within the jurisdiction. FEDPROC § 65:22.

- Service on a domiciliary of the forum state who is temporarily outside the jurisdiction, on the theory that the authority of a state over one of its citizens is not terminated by the mere fact of his absence. FEDPROC § 65:22; Milliken v. Meyer, 311 U.S. 457, 61 S.Ct. 339, 85 L.Ed. 278, 132 A.L.R. 1357 (1940).

- Service on a nonresident who has sufficient contacts with the forum state, since the test of International Shoe is applicable to individuals. FEDPROC § 65:22; Kulko v. Superior Court of California In and For City and County of San Francisco, 436 U.S. 84, 98 S.Ct. 1690, 56 L.Ed.2d 132 (1978).

- Service on an agent who has been expressly appointed or appointed by operation of law, such as under a nonresident motorist statute. FEDPROC § 65:22; National Equipment Rental, Limited v. Szukhent, 375 U.S. 311, 84 S.Ct. 411, 11 L.Ed.2d 354, 7 Fed.R.Serv.2d 23 (1964).

iii. *Territorial limits of effective service*

- *In general.* Serving a summons or filing a waiver of service establishes personal jurisdiction over a defendant: (1) who is subject to the jurisdiction of a court of general jurisdiction in the state where the district court is located; (2) who is a party joined under FRCP 14 or FRCP 19 and is served within a judicial district of the United States and not more than one hundred (100) miles from where the summons was issued; or (3) when authorized by a federal statute. FRCP 4(k)(1).

- *Federal claim outside state-court jurisdiction.* For a claim that arises under federal law, serving a summons or filing a waiver of service establishes personal jurisdiction over a defendant if: (1) the defendant is not subject to jurisdiction in any state's courts of general jurisdiction; and (2) exercising jurisdiction is consistent with the United States Constitution and laws. FRCP 4(k)(2).

b. *Motion based on lack of in rem or quasi-in-rem jurisdiction.* Although FRCP 12(b)(2) only refers to "jurisdiction over the person," the provision presumably is sufficiently elastic to embrace a defense or objection that the district court lacks in rem or quasi-in-rem jurisdiction, admittedly a subject that rarely arises in contemporary practice. FPP § 1351.

c. *Motion based on insufficient process or insufficient service of process.* FRCP 12(b)(2) motions to dismiss are frequently based on the failure to serve the defendant with process or a defective service of process, on the theory that if the defendant was not properly served with process, the court lacks personal jurisdiction over the defendant. FEDPROC § 62:446; Prokopiou v. Long Island R. Co., 2007 WL 1098696 (S.D.N.Y. 2007).

d. *Independent ground for dismissal.* Lack of overall reasonableness in the assertion of personal jurisdiction constitutes an independent ground for dismissal under FRCP 12(b)(2). FEDPROC § 62:448; Federal Ins. Co. v. Lake Shore Inc., 886 F.2d 654 (4th Cir. 1989).

e. *Burden.* On the motion, the plaintiff bears the burden to establish the court's jurisdiction, which normally is not a heavy one, although the standard of proof may vary depending on the procedure used by the court in making its determination and whether the defendant is successful in rebutting the plaintiff's initial showing. Moreover, the Supreme Court has intimated that in the case of a challenge to the constitutional fairness and reasonableness of the chosen forum, the burden is on the defendant. FPP § 1351; Burger King Corp. v. Rudzewicz, 471 U.S. 462, 105 S.Ct. 2174, 85 L.Ed.2d 528 (1985).

   i. The most common formulation found in the judicial opinions is that the plaintiff bears the ultimate burden of demonstrating that the court's personal jurisdiction over the defendant exists by a preponderance of the evidence, but needs only make a prima facie showing when the district judge restricts her review of the FRCP 12(b)(2) motion solely to affidavits and other written evidence. FPP § 1351; Mullins v. TestAmerica, Inc., 564 F.3d 386 (5th Cir. 2009).

   ii. In addition, for purposes of such a review, federal courts will, as they do on other motions under FRCP 12(b), take as true the allegations of the nonmoving party with regard to the jurisdictional issues and resolve all factual disputes in his or her favor. FPP § 1351.

f. *Motion denied.* A party who has unsuccessfully raised an objection under FRCP 12(b)(2) may proceed to trial on the merits without waiving the ability to renew the objection to the court's jurisdiction. FPP § 1351.

g. *Joining motions.* As a general rule, when the court is confronted by a motion raising a combination of FRCP 12(b) defenses, it will pass on the jurisdictional issues before considering whether a claim was stated by the complaint. FPP § 1351.

   i. *Right to join.* A motion under FRCP 12 may be joined with any other motion allowed by FRCP 12. FRCP 12(g)(1).

   ii. *Limitation on further motions.* Except as provided in FRCP 12(h)(2) or FRCP 12(h)(3), a party that makes a motion under FRCP 12 must not make another motion under FRCP 12 raising a defense or objection that was available to the party but omitted from its earlier motion. FRCP 12(g)(2).

h. *Waiving and preserving certain defenses.* No defense or objection is waived by joining it with one or more other defenses or objections in a responsive pleading or in a motion. FRCP 12(b).

   i. *Waiver by consent or stipulation.* A valid consent or a stipulation that the court has jurisdiction prevents the successful assertion of a FRCP 12(b)(2) defense. FPP § 1351.

   ii. *Waiver by filing permissive counterclaim.* A defendant may be deemed to have waived an objection to personal jurisdiction if he or she files a permissive counterclaim under FRCP 13(b). FPP § 1351.

    iii. *When some are waived.* A party waives any defense listed in FRCP 12(b)(2) through FRCP 12(b)(5) by:

- Omitting it from a motion in the circumstances described in FRCP 12(g)(2); or

- Failing to either: (1) make it by motion under FRCP 12; or (2) include it in a responsive pleading or in an amendment allowed by FRCP 15(a)(1) as a matter of course. FRCP 12(h)(1).

    iv. *When to raise others.* Failure to state a claim upon which relief can be granted, to join a person required by FRCP 19(b), or to state a legal defense to a claim may be raised:

- In any pleading allowed or ordered under FRCP 7(a);

- By a motion under FRCP 12(c); or

- At trial. FRCP 12(h)(2).

    v. *Lack of subject matter jurisdiction.* If the court determines at any time that it lacks subject-matter jurisdiction, the court must dismiss the action. FRCP 12(h)(3).

3. *Opposing papers.* The Federal Rules of Civil Procedure do not require any formal answer, return, or reply to a motion, except where the Federal Rules of Civil Procedure or local rules may require affidavits, memoranda, or other papers to be filed in opposition to a motion. Such papers are simply to apprise the court of such opposition and the grounds of that opposition. FEDPROC § 62:359.

    a. *Effect of failure to respond to motion.* Although in the absence of statutory provision or court rule, a motion ordinarily does not require a written answer, when a party files a motion and the opposing party fails to respond, the court may construe such failure to respond as nonopposition to the motion or an admission that the motion was meritorious, may take the facts alleged in the motion as true—the rule in some jurisdictions being that the failure to respond to a fact set forth in a motion is deemed an admission—and may grant the motion if the relief requested appears to be justified. AMJUR MOTIONS § 28.

    b. *Assent or no opposition not determinative.* However, a motion will not be granted automatically simply because an "assent" or a notation of "no opposition" has been filed; federal judges frequently deny motions that have been assented to when it is thought that justice so dictates. FPP § 1190.

    c. *Responsive pleading inappropriate as response to motion.* An attempt to answer or oppose a motion with a responsive pleading usually is not appropriate. FPP § 1190.

4. *Reply papers.* A moving party may be required or permitted to prepare papers in addition to his original motion papers. AMJUR MOTIONS § 25. Papers answering or replying to opposing papers may be appropriate, in the interests of justice, where it appears there is a substantial reason for allowing a reply. Thus, a court may accept reply papers where a party demonstrates that the papers to which it seeks to file a reply raise new issues that are material to the disposition of the question before the court, or where the court determines, sua sponte, that it wishes further briefing of an issue raised in those papers and orders the submission of additional papers. FEDPROC § 62:360.

    a. *Function of reply papers.* The function of a reply affidavit is to answer the arguments made in opposition to the position taken by the movant and not to permit the movant to introduce new arguments in support of the motion. AMJUR MOTIONS § 25.

    b. *Issues raised for the first time in a reply document.* However, the view has been followed in some jurisdictions, that as a matter of judicial economy, where there is no prejudice and where the issues could be raised simply by filing a motion to dismiss, the trial court has discretion to consider arguments raised for the first time in a reply memorandum, and that a trial court may grant a motion to strike issues raised for the first time in a reply memorandum. AMJUR MOTIONS § 26.

5. *Appearances.* Every attorney who represents a party or who files a document on a party's behalf must file an appearance for that party. IN R USDCTSD L.R. 83-7. The filing of a Notice of Appearance shall act to establish the filing attorney as an attorney of record representing a designated party or parties in a particular cause of action. As a result, it is necessary for each attorney to file a separate Notice of Appearance when entering an appearance in a case. A joint appearance on behalf of multiple attorneys may be filed electronically only if it is filed separately for each attorney, using his/her ECF login. IN R

USDCTSD ECF Procedures(12). Only those attorneys who have filed an appearance in a pending action are entitled to be served with case documents under FRCP 5(a). IN R USDCTSD L.R. 83-7. For more information, refer to IN R USDCTSD L.R. 83-7 and IN R USDCTSD ECF Procedures(12).

6. *Notice of related action.* A party must file a notice of related action: as soon as it appears that the party's case and another pending case: (1) arise out of the same transaction or occurrence; (2) involve the same property; or (3) involve the validity or infringement or the same patent, trademark, or copyright. IN R USDCTSD L.R. 40-1(d)(2). For more information, refer to IN R USDCTSD L.R. 40-1.

7. *Alternative dispute resolution (ADR)*

   a. *Application.* Unless limited by specific provisions, or unless there are other applicable specific statutory, common law, or constitutional procedures, the Local Alternative Dispute Resolution Rules of the United States District Court for the Southern District of Indiana shall apply in all civil litigation filed in the U.S. District Court for the Southern District of Indiana, except in the following cases and proceedings:

      i. Applications for writs of habeas corpus under 28 U.S.C.A. § 2254;

      ii. Forfeiture cases;

      iii. Non-adversary proceedings in bankruptcy;

      iv. Social Security administrative review cases; and

      v. Such other matters as specified by order of the Court; for example, matters involving important public policy issues, constitutional law, or the establishment of new law. IN R USDCTSD A.D.R. Rule 1.2.

   b. *Mediation.* Mediation under this section (IN R USDCTSD A.D.R. Rule 2.1, et seq.) involves the confidential process by which a person acting as a Mediator, selected by the parties or appointed by the Court, assists the litigants in reaching a mutually acceptable agreement. It is an informal and nonadversarial process. The role of the Mediator is to assist in identifying the issues, reducing misunderstandings, clarifying priorities, exploring areas of compromise, and finding points of agreement as well as legitimate points of disagreement. Final decision-making authority rests with the parties, not the Mediator. IN R USDCTSD A.D.R. Rule 2.1. It is anticipated that an agreement may not resolve all of the disputed issues, but the process, nonetheless, can reduce points of contention. Parties and their representatives are required to mediate in good faith, but are not compelled to reach an agreement. IN R USDCTSD A.D.R. Rule 2.1.

      i. *Case selection.* The Court with the agreement of the parties may refer a civil case for mediation. Unless otherwise ordered or as specifically provided in IN R USDCTSD A.D.R. Rule 2.8, referral to mediation does not abate or suspend the action, and no scheduled dates shall be delayed or deferred, including the date of trial. IN R USDCTSD A.D.R. Rule 2.2.

      ii. For more information on mediation, refer to IN R USDCTSD A.D.R. Rule 2.1, et seq.

   c. *Other methods of dispute resolution.* The Local Alternative Dispute Resolution Rules of the United States District Court for the Southern District of Indiana shall not preclude the parties from utilizing any other reasonable method or technique of alternative dispute resolution to resolve disputes to which the parties agree. However, any use of arbitration by the parties will be governed by and comply with the requirements of 28 U.S.C.A. § 654 through 28 U.S.C.A. § 657. IN R USDCTSD A.D.R. Rule 1.5.

   d. For more information on alternative dispute resolution (ADR), refer to IN R USDCTSD A.D.R. Rule 1.1, et seq.

8. *Notice of settlement or resolution.* The parties must immediately notify the court if they reasonably anticipate settling their case or resolving a pending motion. IN R USDCTSD L.R. 7-1(h).

9. *Modification or suspension of rules.* The court may, on its own motion or at the request of a party, suspend or modify any rule in a particular case in the interest of justice. IN R USDCTSD L.R. 1-1(c).

D. Documents

1. *Documents for moving party*

   a. *Required documents*

      i. *Notice of motion and motion.* Refer to the General Requirements section of this document for information on the notice of motion and motion.

      ii. *Brief.* The following motion must also be accompanied by a supporting brief: a motion to dismiss. IN R USDCTSD L.R. 7-1(b)(1). Refer to the Format section of this document for the format of briefs.

      iii. *Certificate of service.* FRCP 5(d) requires that the person making service under FRCP 5 certify that service has been effected. FRCP 5(Advisory Committee Notes). Having such information on file may be useful for many purposes, including proof of service if an issue arises concerning the effectiveness of the service. FRCP 5(Advisory Committee Notes).

         - *Certificate of service for electronically-filed documents.* A certificate of service must be included with all documents filed electronically. Such certificate shall indicate that service was accomplished pursuant to the Court's electronic filing procedures. IN R USDCTSD ECF Procedures(11). For the suggested format for a certificate of service for electronic filing, refer to IN R USDCTSD ECF Procedures(11).

   b. *Supplemental documents*

      i. *Supporting evidence.* When a motion relies on facts outside the record, the court may hear the matter on affidavits or may hear it wholly or partly on oral testimony or on depositions. FRCP 43(c).

         - *Materials necessary for motion.* A party seeking relief under FRCP 26(c) or FRCP 37, or by way of a pretrial motion that could result in a final order on an issue, must file with the motion those parts of the discovery materials relevant to the motion. IN R USDCTSD L.R. 26-2(a).

      ii. *Notice of constitutional question.* A party that files a pleading, written motion, or other paper drawing into question the constitutionality of a federal or state statute must promptly:

         - *File notice.* File a notice of constitutional question stating the question and identifying the paper that raises it, if: (1) a federal statute is questioned and the parties do not include the United States, one of its agencies, or one of its officers or employees in an official capacity; or (2) a state statute is questioned and the parties do not include the state, one of its agencies, or one of its officers or employees in an official capacity; and

         - *Serve notice.* Serve the notice and paper on the Attorney General of the United States if a federal statute is questioned—or on the state attorney general if a state statute is questioned—either by certified or registered mail or by sending it to an electronic address designated by the attorney general for this purpose. FRCP 5.1(a).

         - *Time for filing.* A notice of constitutional challenge to a statute filed in accordance with FRCP 5.1 must be filed at the same time the parties tender their proposed case management plan, if one is required, or within twenty-one (21) days of the filing drawing into question the constitutionality of a federal or state statute, whichever occurs later. IN R USDCTSD L.R. 5.1-1(a).

         - *Additional service requirements.* If a federal statute is challenged, in addition to the service requirements of FRCP 5.1(a), the party filing the notice of constitutional challenge must serve the notice and documents on the United States Attorney for the Southern District of Indiana, either by certified or registered mail or by sending it to an electronic address designated for that purpose by that official. IN R USDCTSD L.R. 5.1-1(b).

         - *No forfeiture.* A party's failure to file and serve the notice, or the court's failure to certify, does not forfeit a constitutional claim or defense that is otherwise timely asserted. FRCP 5.1(d).

iii. *Nongovernmental corporate disclosure statement*

- *Contents.* A nongovernmental corporate party must file two (2) copies of a disclosure statement that: (1) identifies any parent corporation and any publicly held corporation owning ten percent (10%) or more of its stock; or (2) states that there is no such corporation. FRCP 7.1(a).

- *Time to file; Supplemental filing.* A party must: (1) file the disclosure statement with its first appearance, pleading, petition, motion, response, or other request addressed to the court; and (2) promptly file a supplemental statement if any required information changes. FRCP 7.1(b).

iv. *Index of exhibits.* Any pleading, motion, brief, affidavit, notice, or proposed order filed with the court, whether electronically or with the clerk, must: if it has four (4) or more exhibits, include a separate index that identifies and briefly describes each exhibit. IN R USDCTSD L.R. 5-1(b).

v. *Request for oral argument.* A party may request oral argument by filing a separate motion explaining why oral argument is necessary and estimating how long the court should allow for the argument. The request must be filed and served with the supporting brief, response brief, or reply brief. IN R USDCTSD L.R. 7-5(a).

vi. *Request for evidentiary hearing.* A party may request an evidentiary hearing on a motion or petition by serving and filing a separate motion explaining why the hearing is necessary and estimating how long the court should allow for the hearing. IN R USDCTSD L.R. 7-5(c).

vii. *Copy of authority.* Generally, copies of cited authorities may not be attached to court filings. However, a party must attach to the party's motion or brief a copy of any cited authority if it is not available on Westlaw or Lexis. Upon request, a party must provide copies of any cited authority that is only available through electronic means to the court or the other parties. IN R USDCTSD L.R. 7-1(f).

viii. *Proposed order.* A party must include a suitable form of order with any document that requests the judge or the clerk to enter a routine or uncontested order. IN R USDCTSD L.R. 5-5(b); IN R USDCTSD L.R. 5-10(c); IN R USDCTSD L.R. 7-1(d).

- A service statement and/or list must be included on each proposed order, as required by IN R USDCTSD L.R. 5-5(d). IN R USDCTSD ECF Procedures(11). Any pleading, motion, brief, affidavit, notice, or proposed order filed with the court, whether electronically or with the clerk, must: if it is a form of order, include a statement of service, in the format required by IN R USDCTSD L.R. 5-5(d) in the lower left corner of the document. IN R USDCTSD L.R. 5-1(b).

- A party electronically filing a proposed order—whether voluntarily or because required by IN R USDCTSD L.R. 5-5—must convert the order directly from a word processing program and file it as an attachment to the document it relates to. Proposed orders must include in the lower left-hand corner of the signature page a statement that service will be made electronically on all ECF-registered counsel of record via email generated by the court's ECF system, without listing all such counsel. A service list including the name and postal address of any pro se litigant or non-registered attorney of record must follow, stating that service on the listed individuals will be made in the traditional paper manner, via first-class U.S. Mail. IN R USDCTSD L.R. 5-5(d).

ix. *Copy of document with self-address envelope.* To receive a file-stamped copy of a document filed directly with the clerk, a party must include with the original document an additional copy and a self-addressed envelope. The envelope must be big enough to hold the copy and have enough postage on it to send the copy via regular first-class mail. IN R USDCTSD L.R. 5-10(b).

x. *Notice of manual filing.* When a party who is not exempt from the electronic filing requirement files a document directly with the clerk, the party must: electronically file a notice of manual filing that explains why the document cannot be filed electronically. IN R USDCTSD L.R. 5-2(d)(1). Refer to the Filing and Service Requirements section of this document for more information.

- Where an individual component cannot be included in an electronic filing (e.g. the

component cannot be converted to electronic format), the filer shall electronically file the prescribed Notice of Manual Filing in place of that component. A model form is provided as Appendix C (IN R USDCTSD ECF Procedures(Appendix C)). IN R USDCTSD ECF Procedures(13).

- Before making a manual filing of a component, the filing party shall first electronically file a Notice of Manual Filing (See IN R USDCTSD ECF Procedures(Appendix C)). The filer shall initiate the electronic filing process as if filing the actual component but shall instead attach to the filing the Notice of Manual Filing setting forth the reason(s) why the component cannot be filed electronically. The manual filing should be accompanied by a copy of the previously filed Notice of Manual Filing. A party may seek to have a component excluded from electronic filing pursuant to applicable Federal and Local Rules (e.g., FRCP 26(c)). IN R USDCTSD ECF Procedures(15).

xi. *Courtesy copies.* District Judges and Magistrate Judges regularly receive documents filed by all parties. Therefore, parties shall not bring "courtesy copies" to any chambers unless specifically directed to do so by the Court. IN R USDCTSD Case Mgt(General Instructions For All Cases).

xii. *Copies for three-judge court.* Parties in a case where a three-judge court has been requested must file an original and three copies of any document filed directly with the clerk (instead of electronically) until the court: (1) denies the request; (2) dissolves the three-judge court; or (3) allows the parties to file fewer copies. IN R USDCTSD L.R. 9-2(c).

xiii. *Declaration that party was unable to file in a timely manner due to technical difficulties.* If a party misses a filing deadline due to an inability to file electronically, the party may submit the untimely filed document, accompanied by a declaration stating the reason(s) for missing the deadline. IN R USDCTSD ECF Procedures(16). A model form is provided as Appendix D (IN R USDCTSD ECF Procedures(Appendix D)). IN R USDCTSD ECF Procedures(16).

2. *Documents for opposing party*

   a. *Required documents*

      i. *Response brief.* Refer to the Format section of this document for the format of briefs. Refer to the General Requirements section of this document for information on the opposing papers.

      ii. *Certificate of service.* FRCP 5(d) requires that the person making service under FRCP 5 certify that service has been effected. FRCP 5(Advisory Committee Notes). Having such information on file may be useful for many purposes, including proof of service if an issue arises concerning the effectiveness of the service. FRCP 5(Advisory Committee Notes).

         - *Certificate of service for electronically-filed documents.* A certificate of service must be included with all documents filed electronically. Such certificate shall indicate that service was accomplished pursuant to the Court's electronic filing procedures. IN R USDCTSD ECF Procedures(11). For the suggested format for a certificate of service for electronic filing, refer to IN R USDCTSD ECF Procedures(11).

   b. *Supplemental documents*

      i. *Supporting evidence.* When a motion relies on facts outside the record, the court may hear the matter on affidavits or may hear it wholly or partly on oral testimony or on depositions. FRCP 43(c).

         - *Materials necessary for motion.* A party seeking relief under FRCP 26(c) or FRCP 37, or by way of a pretrial motion that could result in a final order on an issue, must file with the motion those parts of the discovery materials relevant to the motion. IN R USDCTSD L.R. 26-2(a).

      ii. *Notice of constitutional question.* A party that files a pleading, written motion, or other paper drawing into question the constitutionality of a federal or state statute must promptly:

         - *File notice.* File a notice of constitutional question stating the question and identifying the paper that raises it, if: (1) a federal statute is questioned and the parties do not include the United States, one of its agencies, or one of its officers or employees in an official capacity;

or (2) a state statute is questioned and the parties do not include the state, one of its agencies, or one of its officers or employees in an official capacity; and

- *Serve notice.* Serve the notice and paper on the Attorney General of the United States if a federal statute is questioned—or on the state attorney general if a state statute is questioned—either by certified or registered mail or by sending it to an electronic address designated by the attorney general for this purpose. FRCP 5.1(a).

- *Time for filing.* A notice of constitutional challenge to a statute filed in accordance with FRCP 5.1 must be filed at the same time the parties tender their proposed case management plan, if one is required, or within twenty-one (21) days of the filing drawing into question the constitutionality of a federal or state statute, whichever occurs later. IN R USDCTSD L.R. 5.1-1(a).

- *Additional service requirements.* If a federal statute is challenged, in addition to the service requirements of FRCP 5.1(a), the party filing the notice of constitutional challenge must serve the notice and documents on the United States Attorney for the Southern District of Indiana, either by certified or registered mail or by sending it to an electronic address designated for that purpose by that official. IN R USDCTSD L.R. 5.1-1(b).

- *No forfeiture.* A party's failure to file and serve the notice, or the court's failure to certify, does not forfeit a constitutional claim or defense that is otherwise timely asserted. FRCP 5.1(d).

iii.   *Index of exhibits.* Any pleading, motion, brief, affidavit, notice, or proposed order filed with the court, whether electronically or with the clerk, must: if it has four (4) or more exhibits, include a separate index that identifies and briefly describes each exhibit. IN R USDCTSD L.R. 5-1(b).

iv.   *Request for oral argument.* A party may request oral argument by filing a separate motion explaining why oral argument is necessary and estimating how long the court should allow for the argument. The request must be filed and served with the supporting brief, response brief, or reply brief. IN R USDCTSD L.R. 7-5(a).

v.   *Request for evidentiary hearing.* A party may request an evidentiary hearing on a motion or petition by serving and filing a separate motion explaining why the hearing is necessary and estimating how long the court should allow for the hearing. IN R USDCTSD L.R. 7-5(c).

vi.   *Copy of authority.* Generally, copies of cited authorities may not be attached to court filings. However, a party must attach to the party's motion or brief a copy of any cited authority if it is not available on Westlaw or Lexis. Upon request, a party must provide copies of any cited authority that is only available through electronic means to the court or the other parties. IN R USDCTSD L.R. 7-1(f).

vii.   *Copy of document with self-address envelope.* To receive a file-stamped copy of a document filed directly with the clerk, a party must include with the original document an additional copy and a self-addressed envelope. The envelope must be big enough to hold the copy and have enough postage on it to send the copy via regular first-class mail. IN R USDCTSD L.R. 5-10(b).

viii.   *Notice of manual filing.* When a party who is not exempt from the electronic filing requirement files a document directly with the clerk, the party must: electronically file a notice of manual filing that explains why the document cannot be filed electronically. IN R USDCTSD L.R. 5-2(d)(1). Refer to the Filing and Service Requirements section of this document for more information.

- Where an individual component cannot be included in an electronic filing (e.g. the component cannot be converted to electronic format), the filer shall electronically file the prescribed Notice of Manual Filing in place of that component. A model form is provided as Appendix C (IN R USDCTSD ECF Procedures(Appendix C)). IN R USDCTSD ECF Procedures(13).

- Before making a manual filing of a component, the filing party shall first electronically file a Notice of Manual Filing (See IN R USDCTSD ECF Procedures(Appendix C)). The filer shall initiate the electronic filing process as if filing the actual component but shall instead attach to the filing the Notice of Manual Filing setting forth the reason(s) why the component cannot be filed electronically. The manual filing should be accompanied by a copy of the previously filed Notice of Manual Filing. A party may seek to have a component excluded from electronic filing pursuant to applicable Federal and Local Rules (e.g., FRCP 26(c)). IN R USDCTSD ECF Procedures(15).

ix. *Courtesy copies.* District Judges and Magistrate Judges regularly receive documents filed by all parties. Therefore, parties shall not bring "courtesy copies" to any chambers unless specifically directed to do so by the Court. IN R USDCTSD Case Mgt(General Instructions For All Cases).

x. *Copies for three-judge court.* Parties in a case where a three-judge court has been requested must file an original and three copies of any document filed directly with the clerk (instead of electronically) until the court: (1) denies the request; (2) dissolves the three-judge court; or (3) allows the parties to file fewer copies. IN R USDCTSD L.R. 9-2(c).

xi. *Declaration that party was unable to file in a timely manner due to technical difficulties.* If a party misses a filing deadline due to an inability to file electronically, the party may submit the untimely filed document, accompanied by a declaration stating the reason(s) for missing the deadline. IN R USDCTSD ECF Procedures(16). A model form is provided as Appendix D (IN R USDCTSD ECF Procedures(Appendix D)). IN R USDCTSD ECF Procedures(16).

E. Format

1. *Form of documents.* The rules governing captions and other matters of form in pleadings apply to motions and other papers. FRCP 7(b)(2).

   a. *Paper (manual filings only).* Any document that is not filed electronically must: be flat, unfolded, and on good-quality, eight and one-half by eleven (8-1/2 x 11) inch white paper. IN R USDCTSD L.R. 5-1(d)(1). Any document that is not filed electronically must: be single-sided. IN R USDCTSD L.R. 5-1(d)(1).

      i. *Covers or backing.* Any document that is not filed electronically must: not have a cover or a back. IN R USDCTSD L.R. 5-1(d)(1).

      ii. *Fastening.* Any document that is not filed electronically must: be (if consisting of more than one (1) page) fastened by paperclip or binder clip and may not be stapled. IN R USDCTSD L.R. 5-1(d)(1).

      • *Request for nonconforming fastening.* If a document cannot be fastened or bound as required by IN R USDCTSD L.R. 5-1(d), a party may ask the clerk for permission to fasten it in another manner. The party must make such a request before attempting to file the document with nonconforming fastening. IN R USDCTSD L.R. 5-1(d)(2).

      iii. *Hole punching.* Any document that is not filed electronically must: be two-hole punched at the top with the holes two and three-quarter (2-3/4) inches apart and appropriately centered. IN R USDCTSD L.R. 5-1(d)(1).

   b. *Margins.* Any pleading, motion, brief, affidavit, notice, or proposed order filed with the court, whether electronically or with the clerk, must: have at least one (1) inch margins. IN R USDCTSD L.R. 5-1(b).

   c. *Spacing.* Any pleading, motion, brief, affidavit, notice, or proposed order filed with the court, whether electronically or with the clerk, must: be double spaced (except for headings, footnotes, and quoted material). IN R USDCTSD L.R. 5-1(b).

   d. *Text.* Any pleading, motion, brief, affidavit, notice, or proposed order filed with the court, whether electronically or with the clerk, must: be plainly typewritten, printed, or prepared by a clearly legible copying process. IN R USDCTSD L.R. 5-1(b).

   e. *Font size.* Any pleading, motion, brief, affidavit, notice, or proposed order filed with the court, whether electronically or with the clerk, must: use at least 12-point type in the body of the document and at least 10-point type in footnotes. IN R USDCTSD L.R. 5-1(b).

   f. *Page numbering.* Any pleading, motion, brief, affidavit, notice, or proposed order filed with the court, whether electronically or with the clerk, must: have consecutively numbered pages. IN R USDCTSD L.R. 5-1(b).

g. *Caption; Names of parties.* Every pleading must have a caption with the court's name, a title, a file number, and a FRCP 7(a) designation. The title of the complaint must name all the parties; the title of other pleadings, after naming the first party on each side, may refer generally to other parties. FRCP 10(a). Any pleading, motion, brief, affidavit, notice, or proposed order filed with the court, whether electronically or with the clerk, must: include a title on the first page. IN R USDCTSD L.R. 5-1(b).

    i. *Alternative motions.* Motions must be filed separately, but alternative motions may be filed in a single document if each is named in the title. IN R USDCTSD L.R. 7-1(a).

h. *Filer's information.* Any pleading, motion, brief, affidavit, notice, or proposed order filed with the court, whether electronically or with the clerk, must: in the case of pleadings, motions, legal briefs, and notices, include the name, complete address, telephone number, facsimile number (where available), and e-mail address (where available) of the pro se litigant or attorney who files it. IN R USDCTSD L.R. 5-1(b).

i. *Paragraphs; Separate statements.* A party must state its claims or defenses in numbered paragraphs, each limited as far as practicable to a single set of circumstances. A later pleading may refer by number to a paragraph in an earlier pleading. If doing so would promote clarity, each claim founded on a separate transaction or occurrence—and each defense other than a denial—must be stated in a separate count or defense. FRCP 10(b).

j. *Adoption by reference; Exhibits.* A statement in a pleading may be adopted by reference elsewhere in the same pleading or in any other pleading or motion. A copy of a written instrument that is an exhibit to a pleading is a part of the pleading for all purposes. FRCP 10(c).

k. *Citations*

    i. *Local rules.* The Local Rules of the United States District Court for the Southern District of Indiana may be cited as "S.D. Ind. L.R." IN R USDCTSD L.R. 1-1(a).

    ii. *Local alternative dispute resolution rules.* These Rules shall be known as the Local Alternative Dispute Resolution Rules of the United States District Court for the Southern District of Indiana. They shall be cited as "S.D.Ind. Local A.D.R. Rule _____." IN R USDCTSD A.D.R. Rule 1.1.

l. *Acceptance by the clerk.* The clerk must not refuse to file a paper solely because it is not in the form prescribed by the Federal Rules of Civil Procedure or by a local rule or practice. FRCP 5(d)(4). The clerk will accept a document that violates IN R USDCTSD L.R. 5-1, but the court may exclude the document from the official record. IN R USDCTSD L.R. 5-1(e).

    i. *Sanctions for errors as to form.* The court may strike from the record any document that does not comply with the rules governing the form of documents filed with the court, such as rules that regulate document size or the number of copies to be filed or that require a special designation in the caption. The court may also sanction an attorney or party who files a non-compliant document. IN R USDCTSD L.R. 1-3.

2. *Form of electronic documents.* Any document submitted via the court's electronic case filing (ECF) system must be: otherwise prepared and filed in a manner consistent with the CM/ECF Policies and Procedures Manual (IN R USDCTSD ECF Procedures). IN R USDCTSD L.R. 5-1(c). Electronically filed documents must meet the requirements of FRCP 10 (Form of Pleadings), IN R USDCTSD L.R. 5-1 (Format of Papers Presented for Filing), and FRCP 5.2 (Privacy Protection for Filings Made with the Court), as if they had been submitted on paper. Documents filed electronically are also subject to any page limitations set forth by Court Order, by IN R USDCTSD L.R. 7-1 (Motion Practice), or IN R USDCTSD L.R. 56-1 (Summary Judgment Practice), as applicable. IN R USDCTSD ECF Procedures(13).

a. *PDF format required.* Any document submitted via the court's electronic case filing (ECF) system must be: in .pdf format. IN R USDCTSD L.R. 5-1(c); IN R USDCTSD ECF Procedures(7). Any document submitted via the court's electronic case filing (ECF) system must be: converted to a .pdf file directly from a word processing program, unless it exists only in paper format (in which case it may be scanned to create a .pdf document). IN R USDCTSD L.R. 5-1(c); IN R USDCTSD ECF Procedures(13).

    i. An exhibit may be scanned into PDF format, at a recommended 300 dpi resolution or higher, only if it does not already exist in electronic format. The filing attorney is responsible for reviewing all PDF documents for legibility before submitting them through the Court's Electronic Case Filing system. For technical guidance in creating PDF documents, please contact the Clerk's Office. IN R USDCTSD ECF Procedures(13).

b. *File size limitations.* Any document submitted via the court's electronic case filing (ECF) system must be: submitted as one or more .pdf files that do not exceed ten megabytes (10 MB) each (consistent with the CM/ECF Policies and Procedures Manual (IN R USDCTSD ECF Procedures)). IN R USDCTSD L.R. 5-1(c); IN R USDCTSD ECF Procedures(13).

    i. To electronically file a document or attachment that exceeds ten megabytes (10 MB), the document must first be broken down into two or more smaller files. For example, if Exhibit A is a twelve megabyte (12 MB) PDF file, it should be divided into 2 equal parts prior to electronic filing. Each component part of the exhibit would be filed as an attachment to the main document and described appropriately as "Exhibit A (part 1 of 2)" and "Exhibit A (part 2 of 2)." IN R USDCTSD ECF Procedures(13).

    ii. The supporting items mentioned in IN R USDCTSD ECF Procedures(13) should not be confused with memorandums or briefs in support of motions as outlined in IN R USDCTSD L.R. 7-1 or IN R USDCTSD L.R. 56-1. These memorandums or briefs in support are to be filed as entirely separate documents pursuant to the appropriate rule. Additionally, no motion shall be embodied in the text of a response or reply brief/memorandum unless otherwise ordered by the Court. IN R USDCTSD ECF Procedures(13).

c. *Separate component parts.* A key objective of the electronic filing system is to ensure that as much of the case as possible is managed electronically. To facilitate electronic filing and retrieval, documents to be filed electronically are to be reasonably broken into their separate component parts. By way of example, most filings include a foundation document (e.g., motion) and other supporting items (e.g., exhibits, proposed orders, proposed amended pleadings). The foundation document, as well as the supporting items, are each separate components of the filing; supporting items must be filed as attachments to the foundation document. These exhibits or attachments should include only those excerpts of the referenced documents that are directly germane to the matter under consideration. IN R USDCTSD ECF Procedures(13).

    i. Where an individual component cannot be included in an electronic filing (e.g. the component cannot be converted to electronic format), the filer shall electronically file the prescribed Notice of Manual Filing in place of that component. A model form is provided as Appendix C (IN R USDCTSD ECF Procedures(Appendix C)). IN R USDCTSD ECF Procedures(13).

d. *Exhibits.* Each electronically filed exhibit to a main document must be: (1) created as a separate .pdf file; (2) submitted as an attachment to the main document and given a title which describes its content; and (3) limited to excerpts that are directly germane to the main document's subject matter. IN R USDCTSD L.R. 5-6(a).

    i. When uploading attachments during the electronic filing process, exhibits must be uploaded in a logical sequence and a brief description must be entered for each individual PDF file. The description must include not only the exhibit number or letter, but also a brief description of the document. This information may be entered in CM/ECF using a combination of the Category drop-down menu, the Description text box, or both (see IN R USDCTSD ECF Procedures(13)(Figure 1)). The information that is provided in each box will be combined to create a description of the document as it appears on the case docket (see IN R USDCTSD ECF Procedures(13)(Figure 2)). IN R USDCTSD ECF Procedures(13). For an example, refer to IN R USDCTSD ECF Procedures(13).

e. *Excerpts.* A party filing an exhibit that consists of excerpts from a larger document must clearly and prominently identify the exhibit as containing excerpted material. Either party will have the right to timely file additional excerpts or the complete document to the extent they are or become directly germane to the main document's subject matter. IN R USDCTSD L.R. 5-6(b).

f. For an example illustrating the application of IN R USDCTSD ECF Procedures(13), refer to IN R USDCTSD ECF Procedures(13).

3. *Form of briefs*

   a. *Page limits.* Supporting and response briefs (excluding tables of contents, tables of authorities, appendices, and certificates of service) may not exceed thirty-five (35) pages. Reply briefs may not exceed twenty (20) pages. IN R USDCTSD L.R. 7-1(e)(1).

      i. *Permission to exceed limits.* The court may allow a party to file a brief exceeding these page limits for extraordinary and compelling reasons. IN R USDCTSD L.R. 7-1(e)(2).

      ii. *Supporting and response briefs exceeding limits.* If the court allows a party to file a brief or response exceeding thirty-five (35) pages, the document must include:

      - A table of contents with page references;

      - A statement of issues; and

      - A table of authorities including: (1) all cases (alphabetically arranged), statutes, and other authorities cited in the brief; and (2) page numbers where the authorities are cited in the brief. IN R USDCTSD L.R. 7-1(e)(3).

4. *Signing of pleadings, motions and other papers*

   a. *Signature.* Every pleading, written motion, and other paper must be signed by at least one attorney of record in the attorney's name—or by a party personally if the party is unrepresented. The paper must state the signer's address, e-mail address, and telephone number. FRCP 11(a).

      i. *Signatures on manual filings.* Any document that is not filed electronically must: include the original signature of the pro se litigant or attorney who files it. IN R USDCTSD L.R. 5-1(d)(1).

      ii. *Electronic signatures.* Use of the attorney's login and password when filing documents electronically serves in part as the attorney's signature for purposes of FRCP 11, the Local Rules of the United States District Court for the Southern District of Indiana, and any other purpose for which a signature is required in connection with proceedings before the Court. IN R USDCTSD ECF Procedures(14); IN R USDCTSD ECF Procedures(10). A pleading, motion, brief, or notice filed electronically under an attorney's ECF log-in and password must be signed by that attorney. IN R USDCTSD L.R. 5-7(a). A signature on a document other than a document filed as provided under IN R USDCTSD L.R. 5-7(a) must be an original handwritten signature and must be scanned into .pdf format for electronic filing. IN R USDCTSD L.R. 5-7(c); IN R USDCTSD ECF Procedures(14).

         - *Form of electronic signature.* If a document is converted directly from a word processing application to .pdf (as opposed to scanning), the name of the Filing User under whose log-in and password the document is submitted must be preceded by a "s/" and typed on the signature line where the Filing User's handwritten signature would otherwise appear. IN R USDCTSD L.R. 5-7(b). All documents filed electronically shall include a signature block and include the filing attorney's typewritten name, address, telephone number, facsimile number and e-mail address. In addition, the name of the filing attorney under whose ECF login the document will be filed should be preceded by a "s/" and typed in the space where the attorney's handwritten signature would otherwise appear. IN R US-DCTSD ECF Procedures(14). For a sample format, refer to IN R USDCTSD ECF Procedures(14).

         - *Effect of electronic signature.* Filing an electronically signed document under an attorney's ECF log-in and password constitutes the attorney's signature on the document under the Federal Rules of Civil Procedure, under the Local Rules of the United States District Court for the Southern District of Indiana, and for any other reason a signature is required in connection with the court's activities. IN R USDCTSD L.R. 5-7(d).

         - *Documents with multiple attorneys' signatures.* Documents requiring signatures of more than one attorney shall be filed either by: (1) obtaining consent from the other attorney, then typing the "s/ [Name]" signature of the other attorney on the signature line where the other attorney's signature would otherwise appear; (2) identifying in the signature section the name of the other attorney whose signature is required and by the submission of a

Notice of Endorsement (see IN R USDCTSD ECF Procedures(Appendix B)) by the other attorney no later than three (3) business days after filing; (3) submitting a scanned document containing all handwritten signatures; or (4) in any other manner approved by the Court. IN R USDCTSD ECF Procedures(14); IN R USDCTSD L.R. 5-7(e).

iii. *No verification or accompanying affidavit required for pleadings.* Unless a rule or statute specifically states otherwise, a pleading need not be verified or accompanied by an affidavit. FRCP 11(a).

iv. *Unsigned papers.* The court must strike an unsigned paper unless the omission is promptly corrected after being called to the attorney's or party's attention. FRCP 11(a). The court will strike any document filed directly with the clerk that is not signed by an attorney of record or the pro se litigant filing it, but the court may do so only after giving the attorney or pro se litigant notice of the omission and reasonable time to correct it. Rubber-stamp or facsimile signatures are not original signatures and the court will deem documents containing them to be unsigned for purposes of FRCP 11 and FRCP 26(g) and IN R USDCTSD L.R. 5-10. IN R USDCTSD L.R. 5-10(g).

b. *Representations to the court.* By presenting to the court a pleading, written motion, or other paper—whether by signing, filing, submitting, or later advocating it—an attorney or unrepresented party certifies that to the best of the person's knowledge, information, and belief, formed after an inquiry reasonable under the circumstances:

i. It is not being presented for any improper purpose, such as to harass, cause unnecessary delay, or needlessly increase the cost of litigation;

ii. The claims, defenses, and other legal contentions are warranted by existing law or by a nonfrivolous argument for extending, modifying, or reversing existing law or for establishing new law;

iii. The factual contentions have evidentiary support or, if specifically so identified, will likely have evidentiary support after a reasonable opportunity for further investigation or discovery; and

iv. The denials of factual contentions are warranted on the evidence or, if specifically so identified, are reasonably based on belief or a lack of information. FRCP 11(b).

c. *Sanctions.* If, after notice and a reasonable opportunity to respond, the court determines that FRCP 11(b) has been violated, the court may impose an appropriate sanction on any attorney, law firm, or party that violated FRCP 11(b) or is responsible for the violation. FRCP 11(c)(1). Refer to the United States District Court for the Southern District of Indiana KeyRules Motion for Sanctions document for more information.

5. *Privacy protection for filings made with the court.* Electronically filed documents must meet the requirements of. . .FRCP 5.2 (Privacy Protection for Filings Made with the Court), as if they had been submitted on paper. IN R USDCTSD ECF Procedures(13).

a. *Redacted filings.* Unless the court orders otherwise, in an electronic or paper filing with the court that contains an individual's Social Security number, taxpayer-identification number, or birth date, the name of an individual known to be a minor, or a financial-account number, a party or nonparty making the filing may include only:

i. The last four (4) digits of the Social Security number and taxpayer-identification number;

ii. The year of the individual's birth;

iii. The minor's initials; and

iv. The last four (4) digits of the financial-account number. FRCP 5.2(a).

b. *Exemptions from the redaction requirement.* The redaction requirement does not apply to the following:

i. A financial-account number that identifies the property allegedly subject to forfeiture in a forfeiture proceeding;

ii. The record of an administrative or agency proceeding;

   iii.   The official record of a state-court proceeding;

   iv.   The record of a court or tribunal, if that record was not subject to the redaction requirement when originally filed;

   v.   A filing covered by FRCP 5.2(c) or FRCP 5.2(d); and

   vi.   A pro se filing in an action brought under 28 U.S.C.A. § 2241, 28 U.S.C.A. § 2254, or 28 U.S.C.A. § 2255. FRCP 5.2(b).

c.   *Limitations on remote access to electronic files; Social Security appeals and immigration cases.* Unless the court orders otherwise, in an action for benefits under the Social Security Act, and in an action or proceeding relating to an order of removal, to relief from removal, or to immigration benefits or detention, access to an electronic file is authorized as follows:

   i.   The parties and their attorneys may have remote electronic access to any part of the case file, including the administrative record;

   ii.   Any other person may have electronic access to the full record at the courthouse, but may have remote electronic access only to:

      • The docket maintained by the court; and

      • An opinion, order, judgment, or other disposition of the court, but not any other part of the case file or the administrative record. FRCP 5.2(c).

d.   *Filings made under seal.* The court may order that a filing be made under seal without redaction. The court may later unseal the filing or order the person who made the filing to file a redacted version for the public record. FRCP 5.2(d). For more information on filing under seal, refer to IN R USDCTSD L.R. 5-11 and IN R USDCTSD ECF Procedures(18).

e.   *Protective orders.* For good cause, the court may by order in a case:

   i.   Require redaction of additional information; or

   ii.   Limit or prohibit a nonparty's remote electronic access to a document filed with the court. FRCP 5.2(e).

f.   *Option for additional unredacted filing under seal.* A person making a redacted filing may also file an unredacted copy under seal. The court must retain the unredacted copy as part of the record. FRCP 5.2(f).

g.   *Option for filing a reference list.* A filing that contains redacted information may be filed together with a reference list that identifies each item of redacted information and specifies an appropriate identifier that uniquely corresponds to each item listed. The list must be filed under seal and may be amended as of right. Any reference in the case to a listed identifier will be construed to refer to the corresponding item of information. FRCP 5.2(g).

h.   *Waiver of protection of identifiers.* A person waives the protection of FRCP 5.2(a) as to the person's own information by filing it without redaction and not under seal. FRCP 5.2(h).

F. Filing and Service Requirements

1.   *Filing requirements.* Any paper after the complaint that is required to be served—together with a certificate of service—must be filed within a reasonable time after service. FRCP 5(d)(1). Motions must be filed separately, but alternative motions may be filed in a single document if each is named in the title. IN R USDCTSD L.R. 7-1(a).

a.   *How filing is made; In general.* A paper is filed by delivering it:

   i.   To the clerk; or

   ii.   To a judge who agrees to accept it for filing, and who must then note the filing date on the paper and promptly send it to the clerk. FRCP 5(d)(2).

      • In certain instances, the court will direct the parties to submit items directly to chambers (e.g., confidential settlement statements). However, absent specific prior authorization, counsel and litigants should not submit letters or documents directly to chambers, and

> such materials should be filed with the clerk. IN R USDCTSD L.R. 5-1(Local Rules Advisory Committee Comment).

   iii. A document or item submitted in relation to a matter within the court's jurisdiction is deemed filed upon delivery to the office of the clerk in a manner prescribed by the Local Rules of the United States District Court for the Southern District of Indiana or the Federal Rules of Civil Procedure or authorized by the court. Any submission directed to a Judge or Judge's staff, the office of the clerk or any employee thereof, in a manner that is not contemplated by IN R USDCTSD L.R. 5-1 and without prior court authorization is prohibited. IN R USDCTSD L.R. 5-1(a).

b. *Non-electronic filing.* Any document that is exempt from electronic filing must be filed directly with the clerk and served on other parties in the case as required by those Federal Rules of Civil Procedure and Local Rules of the United States District Court for the Southern District of Indiana that apply to the service of non-electronic documents. IN R USDCTSD L.R. 5-2(c).

   i. *When completed.* A document or other item that is not required to be filed electronically is deemed filed:

- Upon delivery in person, by courier, or via U.S. Mail or other mail delivery service to the clerk's office during business hours;
- When the courtroom deputy clerk accepts it, if the document or item is filed in open court; or
- Upon completion of any other manner of filing that the court authorizes. IN R USDCTSD L.R. 5-10(a).

   ii. *Document filing by non-exempt party.* When a party who is not exempt from the electronic filing requirement files a document directly with the clerk, the party must:

- Electronically file a notice of manual filing that explains why the document cannot be filed electronically;
- Present the document to the clerk within one (1) business day after filing the notice of manual filing; and
- Present the clerk with a copy of the notice of manual filing when the party files the document with the clerk. IN R USDCTSD L.R. 5-2(d).

c. *Electronic filing*

   i. *Authorization of electronic filing program.* A court may, by local rule, allow papers to be filed, signed, or verified by electronic means that are consistent with any technical standards established by the Judicial Conference of the United States. A local rule may require electronic filing only if reasonable exceptions are allowed. A paper filed electronically in compliance with a local rule is a written paper for purposes of the Federal Rules of Civil Procedure. FRCP 5(d)(3).

- IN R USDCTSD L.R. 5-2 requires electronic filing, as allowed by FRCP 5(d)(3). The policies and procedures in IN R USDCTSD ECF Procedures govern electronic filing in this district unless, due to circumstances in a particular case, a judicial officer determines that these policies and procedures (IN R USDCTSD ECF Procedures) should be modified. IN R USDCTSD ECF Procedures(1).
- Unless modified by order of the Court, all Federal Rules of Civil Procedure and Local Rules of the United States District Court for the Southern District of Indiana shall continue to apply to cases maintained in the Court's Case Management/Electronic Case Filing System (CM/ECF). IN R USDCTSD ECF Procedures(3).

   ii. *Mandatory electronic filing.* Unless exempted pursuant to IN R USDCTSD L.R. 5-3(e), attorneys admitted to the court's bar (including those admitted pro hac vice) or authorized to represent the United States must use the court's ECF system to file documents. IN R USDCTSD L.R. 5-3(a). Electronic filing by attorneys is required for eligible documents filed in civil and

criminal cases pending with the Court, unless specifically exempted by Local Rule or Court Order. IN R USDCTSD ECF Procedures(4).

- *Exceptions.* All civil cases (other than those cases the court specifically exempts) must be maintained in the court's electronic case filing (ECF) system. Accordingly, as allowed by FRCP 5(d)(3), every document filed in this court (including exhibits) must be transmitted to the clerk's office via the ECF system consistent with IN R USDCTSD L.R. 5-2 through IN R USDCTSD L.R. 5-11 except: (1) documents filed by pro se litigants; (2) transcripts in cases filed by claimants under the Social Security Act (and related statutes); (3) exhibits in a format that does not readily permit electronic filing (such as videos and large maps and charts); (4) documents that are illegible when scanned into .pdf format; (5) documents filed in cases not maintained on the ECF system; and (6) any other documents that the court or the Local Rules of the United States District Court for the Southern District of Indiana specifically allow to be filed directly with the clerk. IN R USDCTSD L.R. 5-2(a). Parties otherwise participating in the electronic filing system may be excused from filing a particular component electronically under certain limited circumstances, such as when the component cannot be reduced to an electronic format. Such components shall not be filed electronically, but instead shall be manually filed with the Clerk of Court and served upon the parties in accordance with the applicable Federal Rules of Civil Procedure and the Local Rules of the United States District Court for the Southern District of Indiana for filing and service of non-electronic documents. IN R USDCTSD ECF Procedures(15).

- *Exemption from participation.* The court may exempt attorneys from using the ECF system in a particular case for good cause. An attorney must file a petition for ECF exemption and a CM/ECF technical requirements exemption questionnaire in each case in which the attorney seeks an exemption. (The CM/ECF technical requirements exemption questionnaire is available on the court's website). IN R USDCTSD L.R. 5-3(e).

iii. *Consequences of electronic filing.* Electronic transmission of a document consistent with the procedures adopted by the Court shall, upon the complete receipt of the same by the Clerk of Court, constitute filing of the document for all purposes of the Federal Rules of Civil and Criminal Procedure and the Local Rules of the United States District Court for the Southern District of Indiana, and shall constitute entry of that document onto the docket maintained by the Clerk pursuant to FRCP 58 and FRCP 79. IN R USDCTSD ECF Procedures(7); IN R USDCTSD L.R. 5-4(c)(1). When a document has been filed electronically: the document, as filed, binds the filing party. IN R USDCTSD L.R. 5-4(c)(3).

- A Notice of Electronic Filing (NEF) acknowledging that the document has been filed will immediately appear on the filer's screen after the document has been submitted. Attorneys are strongly encouraged to print or electronically save a copy of the NEF. Attorneys can also verify the filing of documents by inspecting the Court's electronic docket sheet through the use of a PACER login. IN R USDCTSD ECF Procedures(7). When a document has been filed electronically: the notice of electronic filing for the document serves as the court's date-stamp and proof of filing. IN R USDCTSD L.R. 5-4(c)(4).

- The Court may, upon the motion of a party or upon its own motion, strike any inappropriately filed document. IN R USDCTSD ECF Procedures(7).

iv. For more information on electronic filing, refer to IN R USDCTSD ECF Procedures.

d. *Fax filing.* The clerk may not file a faxed document without court authorization. The court may not authorize the clerk to file faxed documents without finding that compelling circumstances justify it. A party must submit a copy of the document that otherwise complies with IN R USDCTSD L.R. 5-10 to replace the faxed copy within seven (7) days after faxing the document. IN R USDCTSD L.R. 5-10(e).

2. *Service requirements*

a. *Service; When required*

i. *In general.* Unless the Federal Rules of Civil Procedure provide otherwise, each of the following papers must be served on every party:

- An order stating that service is required;

- A pleading filed after the original complaint, unless the court orders otherwise under FRCP 5(c) because there are numerous defendants;

- A discovery paper required to be served on a party, unless the court orders otherwise;

- A written motion, except one that may be heard ex parte; and

- A written notice, appearance, demand, or offer of judgment, or any similar paper. FRCP 5(a)(1).

ii. *If a party fails to appear.* No service is required on a party who is in default for failing to appear. But a pleading that asserts a new claim for relief against such a party must be served on that party under FRCP 4. FRCP 5(a)(2).

iii. *Seizing property.* If an action is begun by seizing property and no person is or need be named as a defendant, any service required before the filing of an appearance, answer, or claim must be made on the person who had custody or possession of the property when it was seized. FRCP 5(a)(3).

b. *Service; How made*

i. *Serving an attorney.* If a party is represented by an attorney, service under FRCP 5 must be made on the attorney unless the court orders service on the party. FRCP 5(b)(1).

ii. *Service in general.* A paper is served under FRCP 5 by:

- Handing it to the person;

- Leaving it: (1) at the person's office with a clerk or other person in charge or, if no one is in charge, in a conspicuous place in the office; or (2) if the person has no office or the office is closed, at the person's dwelling or usual place of abode with someone of suitable age and discretion who resides there;

- Mailing it to the person's last known address—in which event service is complete upon mailing;

- Leaving it with the court clerk if the person has no known address;

- Sending it by electronic means if the person consented in writing—in which event service is complete upon transmission, but is not effective if the serving party learns that it did not reach the person to be served; or

- Delivering it by any other means that the person consented to in writing—in which event service is complete when the person making service delivers it to the agency designated to make delivery. FRCP 5(b)(2).

iii. *Electronic service*

- *Consent.* By registering to use the ECF system, attorneys consent to electronic service of documents filed in cases maintained on the ECF system. IN R USDCTSD L.R. 5-3(d). By participating in the Electronic Case Filing Program, attorneys consent to the electronic service of documents, and shall make available electronic mail addresses for service. IN R USDCTSD ECF Procedures(11).

- *Service on registered parties.* Upon the filing of a document by a party, an e-mail message will be automatically generated by the electronic filing system and sent via electronic mail to the e-mail addresses of all registered attorneys who have appeared in the case. The Notice of Electronic Filing will contain a document hyperlink which will provide recipients with one "free look" at the electronically filed document. Recipients are encouraged to print and/or save a copy of the document during the "free look" to avoid incurring PACER charges for future viewings of the document. IN R USDCTSD ECF Procedures(11). When a document has been filed electronically: transmission of the notice of electronic filing generated by the ECF system to an attorney's e-mail address constitutes service of the document on that attorney. IN R USDCTSD L.R. 5-4(c)(5). The party effectuates service on all registered attorneys by filing electronically. IN R USDCTSD ECF Procedures(11). When a document has been filed electronically: no other attempted service will constitute electronic service of the document. IN R USDCTSD L.R. 5-4(c)(6).

- *Service on exempt parties.* A filer must serve a copy of the document consistent with FRCP 5 on any party or attorney who is exempt from participating in electronic filing. IN R USDCTSD L.R. 5-4(d). It is the responsibility of the filing attorney to conventionally serve all parties who do not receive electronic service (the identity of these parties will be indicated on the filing receipt generated by the ECF system). IN R USDCTSD ECF Procedures(11).

- *Service on parties excused from electronic filing.* Parties otherwise participating in the electronic filing system may be excused from filing a particular component electronically under certain limited circumstances, such as when the component cannot be reduced to an electronic format. Such components shall not be filed electronically, but instead shall be manually filed with the Clerk of Court and served upon the parties in accordance with the applicable Federal Rules of Civil Procedure and the Local Rules of the United States District Court for the Southern District of Indiana for filing and service of non-electronic documents. IN R USDCTSD ECF Procedures(15).

- *Service of exempt documents.* Any document that is exempt from electronic filing must be filed directly with the clerk and served on other parties in the case as required by those Federal Rules of Civil Procedure and Local Rules of the United States District Court for the Southern District of Indiana that apply to the service of non-electronic documents. IN R USDCTSD L.R. 5-2(c).

iv. *Using court facilities.* If a local rule so authorizes, a party may use the court's transmission facilities to make service under FRCP 5(b)(2)(E). FRCP 5(b)(3).

c. *Serving numerous defendants*

    i. *In general.* If an action involves an unusually large number of defendants, the court may, on motion or on its own, order that:

- Defendants' pleadings and replies to them need not be served on other defendants;

- Any crossclaim, counterclaim, avoidance, or affirmative defense in those pleadings and replies to them will be treated as denied or avoided by all other parties; and

- Filing any such pleading and serving it on the plaintiff constitutes notice of the pleading to all parties. FRCP 5(c)(1).

    ii. *Notifying parties.* A copy of every such order must be served on the parties as the court directs. FRCP 5(c)(2).

G. Hearings

1. *Hearings, generally*

a. *Oral argument.* Due process does not require that oral argument be permitted on a motion and, except as otherwise provided by local rule, the district court has discretion to determine whether it will decide the motion on the papers or hear argument by counsel (and perhaps receive evidence). FPP § 1190; F.D.I.C. v. Deglau, 207 F.3d 153 (3d Cir. 2000).

    i. *Request for oral argument.* A party may request oral argument by filing a separate motion explaining why oral argument is necessary and estimating how long the court should allow for the argument. IN R USDCTSD L.R. 7-5(a). Refer to the Documents section of this document for more information.

    ii. *No additional evidence at oral argument.* Parties may not present additional evidence at oral argument. IN R USDCTSD L.R. 7-5(b).

b. *Providing a regular schedule for oral hearings.* A court may establish regular times and places for oral hearings on motions. FRCP 78(a).

c. *Providing for submission on briefs.* By rule or order, the court may provide for submitting and determining motions on briefs, without oral hearings. FRCP 78(b).

d. *Request for evidentiary hearing.* A party may request an evidentiary hearing on a motion or petition by serving and filing a separate motion explaining why the hearing is necessary and estimating how long the court should allow for the hearing. IN R USDCTSD L.R. 7-5(c).

e.   *Directed by the court.* The court may: (1) grant or deny a request for oral argument or an evidentiary hearing in its sole discretion; (2) set oral argument or an evidentiary hearing without a request from a party; and (3) order any oral argument or evidentiary hearing to be held anywhere within the district regardless of where the case will be tried. IN R USDCTSD L.R. 7-5(d).

2.   *Hearing on FRCP 12 defenses before trial.* If a party so moves, any defense listed in FRCP 12(b)(1) through FRCP 12(b)(7)—whether made in a pleading or by motion—and a motion under FRCP 12(c) must be heard and decided before trial unless the court orders a deferral until trial. FRCP 12(i).

3.   *Courtroom and courthouse decorum.* For information on courtroom and courthouse decorum, refer to IN R USDCTSD L.R. 83-3.

H.   Forms

1.   Federal Motion to Dismiss for Lack of Personal Jurisdiction Forms

a.   Motion and notice; To dismiss; Defendant not present within state where district court is located. AMJUR PP FEDPRAC § 488.

b.   Motion and notice; To dismiss; Lack of jurisdiction over person. AMJUR PP FEDPRAC § 489.

c.   Motion and notice; To dismiss; Lack of jurisdiction over person; Ineffective service of process on foreign state. AMJUR PP FEDPRAC § 490.

d.   Motion and notice; To dismiss; Lack of jurisdiction over person; Consul not agent of country represented for purpose of receiving service of process. AMJUR PP FEDPRAC § 491.

e.   Motion and notice; To dismiss; Lack of jurisdiction over corporate defendant. AMJUR PP FEDPRAC § 492.

f.   Motion and notice; To dismiss; International organization immune from suit. AMJUR PP FEDPRAC § 493.

g.   Motion and notice; To dismiss; Officer or employee of international organization acting within official capacity; Immune from suit. AMJUR PP FEDPRAC § 494.

h.   Motion and notice; To dismiss; Family member of member of foreign mission immune from suit. AMJUR PP FEDPRAC § 495.

i.   Motion and notice; To dismiss complaint or, in alternative, to quash service of summons; Lack of jurisdiction over corporate defendant. AMJUR PP FEDPRAC § 496.

j.   Motion to dismiss; Lack of personal jurisdiction; No minimum contacts. AMJUR PP FEDPRAC § 497.

k.   Affidavit; Of Consul General; In support of motion to dismiss; Consular immunity and lack of authority to act as agent for service of process. AMJUR PP FEDPRAC § 498.

l.   Motion to dismiss for lack of personal jurisdiction; Corporate defendant. 2C FEDFORMS § 11:52.

m.   Motion to dismiss for lack of personal jurisdiction; By corporate defendant; With citation. 2C FEDFORMS § 11:53.

n.   Motion to dismiss for lack of personal jurisdiction; By a foreign corporation. 2C FEDFORMS § 11:54.

o.   Motion to dismiss for lack of personal jurisdiction; For insufficiency of service. 2C FEDFORMS § 11:55.

p.   Motion to dismiss for lack of personal jurisdiction; Insufficiency of process and insufficiency of service of process. 2C FEDFORMS § 11:56.

q.   Motion; To dismiss; Lack of jurisdiction over person of defendant. FEDPROF § 1:910.

r.   Opposition; To motion; General form. FEDPROF § 1:750.

s.   Affidavit; Supporting or opposing motion. FEDPROF § 1:751.

t.   Brief; Supporting or opposing motion. FEDPROF § 1:752.

u.   Statement of points and authorities; Opposing motion. FEDPROF § 1:753.

v. Motion to dismiss; Lack of jurisdiction over person of defendant; Short form. FEDPROF § 1:911.

w. Motion to dismiss; Lack of jurisdiction over person of defendant; Accident in foreign country and defendants have no contacts with forum state. FEDPROF § 1:911.50.

x. Motion to dismiss; Lack of jurisdiction over corporate defendant. FEDPROF § 1:912.

y. Motion; To dismiss complaint or, in the alternative, to quash service of summons; Lack of jurisdiction over corporate defendant. FEDPROF § 1:913.

z. Motion to dismiss complaint; General form. GOLDLTGFMS § 20:24.

2. Forms for the Southern District of Indiana

a. Notice of endorsement. IN R USDCTSD ECF Procedures(Appendix B).

b. Notice of manual filing. IN R USDCTSD ECF Procedures(Appendix C).

c. Declaration that party was unable to file in a timely manner due to technical difficulties. IN R USDCTSD ECF Procedures(Appendix D).

I. Applicable Rules

1. *Federal rules*

a. Summons. FRCP 4.

b. Serving and filing pleadings and other papers. FRCP 5.

c. Constitutional challenge to a statute; Notice, certification, and intervention. FRCP 5.1.

d. Privacy protection for filings made with the court. FRCP 5.2.

e. Computing and extending time; Time for motion papers. FRCP 6.

f. Pleadings allowed; Form of motions and other papers. FRCP 7.

g. Disclosure statement. FRCP 7.1.

h. Form of pleadings. FRCP 10.

i. Signing pleadings, motions, and other papers; Representations to the court; Sanctions. FRCP 11.

j. Defenses and objections; When and how presented; Motion for judgment on the pleadings; Consolidating motions; Waiving defenses; Pretrial hearing. FRCP 12.

k. Taking testimony. FRCP 43.

l. Hearing motions; Submission on briefs. FRCP 78.

2. *Local rules*

a. Scope of the rules. IN R USDCTSD L.R. 1-1.

b. Sanctions for errors as to form. IN R USDCTSD L.R. 1-3.

c. Format of documents presented for filing. IN R USDCTSD L.R. 5-1.

d. Constitutional challenge to a statute; Notice. IN R USDCTSD L.R. 5.1-1.

e. Filing of documents electronically required. IN R USDCTSD L.R. 5-2.

f. Eligibility, registration, passwords for electronic filing; Exemption from electronic filing. IN R USDCTSD L.R. 5-3.

g. Timing and consequences of electronic filing. IN R USDCTSD L.R. 5-4.

h. Attachments and exhibits in cases filed electronically. IN R USDCTSD L.R. 5-6.

i. Signatures in cases filed electronically. IN R USDCTSD L.R. 5-7.

j. Non-electronic filings. IN R USDCTSD L.R. 5-10.

k. Motion practice. [IN R USDCTSD L.R. 7-1, as amended by IN ORDER 16-2319, effective December 1, 2016].

l. Oral arguments and hearings. IN R USDCTSD L.R. 7-5.

m. Request for three-judge court. IN R USDCTSD L.R. 9-2.

n. Filing of discovery materials. IN R USDCTSD L.R. 26-2.

o. Assignment of cases. IN R USDCTSD L.R. 40-1.

p. Alternative dispute resolution. IN R USDCTSD A.D.R. Rule 1.1; IN R USDCTSD A.D.R. Rule 1.2; IN R USDCTSD A.D.R. Rule 1.5; IN R USDCTSD A.D.R. Rule 2.1; IN R USDCTSD A.D.R. Rule 2.2.

q. Instructions for preparing case management plan. IN R USDCTSD Case Mgt.

r. Electronic case filing policies and procedures manual. IN R USDCTSD ECF Procedures.

Motions, Oppositions and Replies
Motion for Judgment on the Pleadings

Document Last Updated December 2016

A. Checklist

(I) ❏ Matters to be considered by moving party

  (a) ❏ Required documents

    (1) ❏ Notice of motion and motion

    (2) ❏ Brief

    (3) ❏ Certificate of service

  (b) ❏ Supplemental documents

    (1) ❏ Pleadings

    (2) ❏ Notice of constitutional question

    (3) ❏ Nongovernmental corporate disclosure statement

    (4) ❏ Index of exhibits

    (5) ❏ Request for oral argument

    (6) ❏ Request for evidentiary hearing

    (7) ❏ Copy of authority

    (8) ❏ Proposed order

    (9) ❏ Copy of document with self-address envelope

    (10) ❏ Notice of manual filing

    (11) ❏ Courtesy copies

    (12) ❏ Copies for three-judge court

    (13) ❏ Declaration that party was unable to file in a timely manner due to technical difficulties

  (c) ❏ Timing

    (1) ❏ After the pleadings are closed—but early enough not to delay trial—a party may move for judgment on the pleadings

    (2) ❏ A written motion and notice of the hearing must be served at least fourteen (14) days before the time specified for the hearing, with the following exceptions: (i) when the motion may be heard ex parte; (ii) when the Federal Rules of Civil Procedure set a different time; or (iii) when a court order—which a party may, for good cause, apply for ex parte—sets a different time

    (3) ❏ Any affidavit supporting a motion must be served with the motion

    (4) ❏ When a party who is not exempt from the electronic filing requirement files a document

directly with the clerk, the party must present the document to the clerk within one (1) business day after filing the notice of manual filing

(5) ❑ Unless the court orders otherwise, the [untimely] document and declaration [that party was unable to file in a timely manner due to technical difficulties] must be filed no later than 12:00 noon of the first day on which the court is open for business following the original filing deadline

(II) ❑ Matters to be considered by opposing party

  (a) ❑ Required documents

    (1) ❑ Response brief

    (2) ❑ Certificate of service

  (b) ❑ Supplemental documents

    (1) ❑ Pleadings

    (2) ❑ Notice of constitutional question

    (3) ❑ Index of exhibits

    (4) ❑ Request for oral argument

    (5) ❑ Request for evidentiary hearing

    (6) ❑ Copy of authority

    (7) ❑ Copy of document with self-address envelope

    (8) ❑ Notice of manual filing

    (9) ❑ Courtesy copies

    (10) ❑ Copies for three-judge court

    (11) ❑ Declaration that party was unable to file in a timely manner due to technical difficulties

  (c) ❑ Timing

    (1) ❑ Any response is due within fourteen (14) days after service of the motion

    (2) ❑ Except as FRCP 59(c) provides otherwise, any opposing affidavit must be served at least seven (7) days before the hearing, unless the court permits service at another time

    (3) ❑ When a party who is not exempt from the electronic filing requirement files a document directly with the clerk, the party must present the document to the clerk within one (1) business day after filing the notice of manual filing

    (4) ❑ Unless the court orders otherwise, the [untimely] document and declaration [that party was unable to file in a timely manner due to technical difficulties] must be filed no later than 12:00 noon of the first day on which the court is open for business following the original filing deadline

B. Timing

1. *Motion for judgment on the pleadings.* After the pleadings are closed—but early enough not to delay trial—a party may move for judgment on the pleadings. FRCP 12(c).

  a. *When pleadings are closed.* FRCP 7(a) provides that the pleadings are closed upon the filing of a complaint and an answer (absent a court-ordered reply), unless a counterclaim, cross-claim, or third-party claim is interposed, in which event the filing of a reply to a counterclaim, cross-claim answer, or third-party answer normally will mark the close of the pleadings. FPP § 1367.

  b. *Timeliness and delay.* Ordinarily, a motion for judgment on the pleadings should be made promptly after the close of the pleadings. Generally, however, a FRCP 12(c) motion is considered timely if it is made early enough not to delay trial or cause prejudice to the non-movant. FPP § 1367.

2. *Timing of motions, generally*

    a. *Motion and notice of hearing.* A written motion and notice of the hearing must be served at least fourteen (14) days before the time specified for the hearing, with the following exceptions:

        i. When the motion may be heard ex parte;

        ii. When the Federal Rules of Civil Procedure set a different time; or

        iii. When a court order—which a party may, for good cause, apply for ex parte—sets a different time. FRCP 6(c)(1).

    b. *Supporting affidavit.* Any affidavit supporting a motion must be served with the motion. FRCP 6(c)(2).

3. *Timing of opposing papers.* Any response is due within fourteen (14) days after service of the motion. IN R USDCTSD L.R. 7-1(c)(2)(A).

    a. *Opposing affidavit.* Except as FRCP 59(c) provides otherwise, any opposing affidavit must be served at least seven (7) days before the hearing, unless the court permits service at another time. FRCP 6(c)(2).

    b. *Extensions.* The court may extend response and reply deadlines, but only for good cause. IN R USDCTSD L.R. 7-1(c)(3).

    c. *Summary ruling on failure to respond.* The court may summarily rule on a motion if an opposing party does not file a response within the deadline. IN R USDCTSD L.R. 7-1(c)(4).

4. *Timing of reply papers.* Where the respondent files an answering affidavit setting up a new matter, the moving party ordinarily is allowed a reasonable time to file a reply affidavit since failure to deny the new matter by affidavit may operate as an admission of its truth. AMJUR MOTIONS § 25.

    a. *Reply brief.* Any reply is due within seven (7) days after service of the response. IN R USDCTSD L.R. 7-1(c)(2)(B).

    b. *Extensions.* The court may extend response and reply deadlines, but only for good cause. IN R USDCTSD L.R. 7-1(c)(3).

5. *Effect of a FRCP 12 motion on the time to serve a responsive pleading.* Unless the court sets a different time, serving a motion under FRCP 12 alters the periods in FRCP 12(a) as follows:

    a. If the court denies the motion or postpones its disposition until trial, the responsive pleading must be served within fourteen (14) days after notice of the court's action; or

    b. If the court grants a motion for a more definite statement, the responsive pleading must be served within fourteen (14) days after the more definite statement is served. FRCP 12(a)(4).

6. *Document filing by non-exempt party.* When a party who is not exempt from the electronic filing requirement files a document directly with the clerk, the party must: present the document to the clerk within one (1) business day after filing the notice of manual filing. IN R USDCTSD L.R. 5-2(d)(2).

7. *Declaration that party was unable to file in a timely manner due to technical difficulties.* Unless the Court orders otherwise, the [untimely] document and declaration [that party was unable to file in a timely manner due to technical difficulties] must be filed no later than 12:00 noon of the first day on which the Court is open for business following the original filing deadline. IN R USDCTSD ECF Procedures(16).

8. *Computation of time*

    a. *Computing time.* FRCP 6 applies in computing any time period specified in the Federal Rules of Civil Procedure, in any local rule or court order, or in any statute that does not specify a method of computing time. FRCP 6(a).

        i. *Period stated in days or a longer unit.* When the period is stated in days or a longer unit of time:

          • Exclude the day of the event that triggers the period;

          • Count every day, including intermediate Saturdays, Sundays, and legal holidays; and

          • Include the last day of the period, but if the last day is a Saturday, Sunday, or legal holiday, the period continues to run until the end of the next day that is not a Saturday, Sunday, or legal holiday. FRCP 6(a)(1).

ii. *Period stated in hours.* When the period is stated in hours:

- Begin counting immediately on the occurrence of the event that triggers the period;

- Count every hour, including hours during intermediate Saturdays, Sundays, and legal holidays; and

- If the period would end on a Saturday, Sunday, or legal holiday, the period continues to run until the same time on the next day that is not a Saturday, Sunday, or legal holiday. FRCP 6(a)(2).

iii. *Inaccessibility of the clerk's office.* Unless the court orders otherwise, if the clerk's office is inaccessible:

- On the last day for filing under FRCP 6(a)(1), then the time for filing is extended to the first accessible day that is not a Saturday, Sunday, or legal holiday; or

- During the last hour for filing under FRCP 6(a)(2), then the time for filing is extended to the same time on the first accessible day that is not a Saturday, Sunday, or legal holiday. FRCP 6(a)(3).

iv. *"Last day" defined.* Unless a different time is set by a statute, local rule, or court order, the last day ends:

- For electronic filing, at midnight in the court's time zone; and

- For filing by other means, when the clerk's office is scheduled to close. FRCP 6(a)(4).

v. *"Next day" defined.* The "next day" is determined by continuing to count forward when the period is measured after an event and backward when measured before an event. FRCP 6(a)(5).

vi. *"Legal holiday" defined.* "Legal holiday" means:

- The day set aside by statute for observing New Year's Day, Martin Luther King Jr.'s Birthday, Washington's Birthday, Memorial Day, Independence Day, Labor Day, Columbus Day, Veterans' Day, Thanksgiving Day, or Christmas Day;

- Any day declared a holiday by the President or Congress; and

- For periods that are measured after an event, any other day declared a holiday by the state where the district court is located. FRCP 6(a)(6).

b. *Computation of electronic filing deadlines.* Filing documents electronically does not alter filing deadlines. IN R USDCTSD ECF Procedures(7). A document due on a particular day must be filed before midnight local time of the division where the case is pending. IN R USDCTSD L.R. 5-4(a). All electronic transmissions of documents must be completed (i.e. received completely by the Clerk's Office) prior to midnight of the local time of the division in which the case is pending in order to be considered timely filed that day (NOTE: time will be noted in Eastern Time on the Court's docket. If you have filed a document prior to midnight local time of the division in which the case is pending and the document is due that date, but the electronic receipt and docket reflect the following calendar day, please contact the Court). IN R USDCTSD ECF Procedures(7). Although attorneys may file documents electronically twenty-four (24) hours a day, seven (7) days a week, attorneys are encouraged to file all documents during the normal working hours of the Clerk's Office (Monday through Friday, 8:30 a.m. to 4:30 p.m.) when technical support is available. IN R USDCTSD ECF Procedures(7); IN R USDCTSD ECF Procedures(9).

i. *Technical difficulties.* Parties are encouraged to file documents electronically during normal business hours, in case a problem is encountered. In the event a technical failure occurs and a document cannot be filed electronically despite the best efforts of the filing party, the party should print (if possible) a copy of the error message received. In addition, as soon as practically possible, the party should file a "Declaration that Party was Unable to File in a Timely Manner Due to Technical Difficulties." A model form is provided as Appendix D (IN R USDCTSD ECF Procedures(Appendix D)). IN R USDCTSD ECF Procedures(16).

- If a party is unable to file electronically and, as a result, may miss a filing deadline, the party must contact the Clerk's Office at the number listed in IN R USDCTSD ECF

Procedures(15) to inform the court's staff of the difficulty. If a party misses a filing deadline due to an inability to file electronically, the party may submit the untimely filed document, accompanied by a declaration stating the reason(s) for missing the deadline. Unless the Court orders otherwise, the document and declaration must be filed no later than 12:00 noon of the first day on which the Court is open for business following the original filing deadline. IN R USDCTSD ECF Procedures(16).

   c. *Extending time*

      i. *In general.* When an act may or must be done within a specified time, the court may, for good cause, extend the time:

- With or without motion or notice if the court acts, or if a request is made, before the original time or its extension expires; or

- On motion made after the time has expired if the party failed to act because of excusable neglect. FRCP 6(b)(1).

      ii. *Exceptions.* A court must not extend the time to act under FRCP 50(b), FRCP 50(d), FRCP 52(b), FRCP 59(b), FRCP 59(d), FRCP 59(e), and FRCP 60(b). FRCP 6(b)(2).

      iii. Refer to the United States District Court for the Southern District of Indiana KeyRules Motion for Continuance/Extension of Time document for more information on extending time.

   d. *Additional time after certain kinds of service.* When a party may or must act within a specified time after being served and service is made under FRCP 5(b)(2)(C) (mail), FRCP 5(b)(2)(D) (leaving with the clerk), or FRCP 5(b)(2)(F) (other means consented to), three (3) days are added after the period would otherwise expire under FRCP 6(a). FRCP 6(d). Service by electronic mail shall constitute service pursuant to FRCP 5(b)(2)(E) and shall entitle the party being served to the additional three (3) days provided by FRCP 6(d). IN R USDCTSD ECF Procedures(11).

C. General Requirements

1. *Motions, generally*

   a. *Requirements.* A request for a court order must be made by motion. The motion must:

      i. Be in writing unless made during a hearing or trial;

      ii. State with particularity the grounds for seeking the order; and

      iii. State the relief sought. FRCP 7(b)(1).

   b. *Notice of motion.* A party interested in resisting the relief sought by a motion has a right to notice thereof, and an opportunity to be heard. AMJUR MOTIONS § 12.

      i. In addition to statutory or court rule provisions requiring notice of a motion—the purpose of such a notice requirement having been said to be to prevent a party from being prejudicially surprised by a motion—principles of natural justice dictate that an adverse party generally must be given notice that a motion will be presented to the court. AMJUR MOTIONS § 12.

      ii. "Notice," in this regard, means reasonable notice, including a meaningful opportunity to prepare and to defend against allegations of a motion. AMJUR MOTIONS § 12.

   c. *Writing requirement.* The writing requirement is intended to insure that the adverse parties are informed and have a record of both the motion's pendency and the grounds on which the movant seeks an order. FPP § 1191; Feldberg v. Quechee Lakes Corp., 463 F.3d 195 (2d Cir. 2006).

      i. It is sufficient "if the motion is stated in a written notice of the hearing of the motion." FPP § 1191.

   d. *Particularity requirement.* The particularity requirement insures that the opposing parties will have notice of their opponent's contentions. FEDPROC § 62:364; Goodman v. 1973 26 Foot Trojan Vessel, Arkansas Registration No. AR1439SN, 859 F.2d 71, 12 Fed.R.Serv.3d 645 (8th Cir. 1988). That requirement ensures that notice of the basis for the motion is provided to the court and to the opposing party so as to avoid prejudice, provide the opponent with a meaningful opportunity to

respond, and provide the court with enough information to process the motion correctly. FEDPROC § 62:364; Andreas v. Volkswagen of America, Inc., 336 F.3d 789, 56 Fed.R.Serv.3d 6 (8th Cir. 2003).

    i.   Reasonable specification of the grounds for a motion is sufficient. However, where a movant fails to state even one ground for granting the motion in question, the movant has failed to meet the minimal standard of "reasonable specification." FEDPROC § 62:364; Martinez v. Trainor, 556 F.2d 818, 23 Fed.R.Serv.2d 403 (7th Cir. 1977).

    ii.   The court may excuse the failure to comply with the particularity requirement if it is inadvertent, and where no prejudice is shown by the opposing party. FEDPROC § 62:364.

  e. *Motions must be filed separately.* Motions must be filed separately, but alternative motions may be filed in a single document if each is named in the title. A motion must not be contained within a brief, response, or reply to a previously filed motion, unless ordered by the court. IN R USDCTSD L.R. 7-1(a).

  f. *Routine or uncontested motions.* The court may rule upon a routine or uncontested motion before the response deadline passes, unless: (1) the motion indicates that an opposing party objects to it; or (2) the court otherwise believes that a response will be filed. IN R USDCTSD L.R. 7-1(d).

2. *Motion for judgment on the pleadings.* After the pleadings are closed—but early enough not to delay trial—a party may move for judgment on the pleadings. FRCP 12(c).

  a. *Relationship to other motions*

    i.   *Common law demurrer.* The motion for judgment on the pleadings under FRCP 12(c) has its historical roots in common law practice, which permitted either party, at any point in the proceeding, to demur to his opponent's pleading and secure a dismissal or final judgment on the basis of the pleadings. FPP § 1367.

       • The common law demurrer could be used to search the record and raise procedural defects, or it could be employed to resolve the substantive merits of the controversy as disclosed on the face of the pleadings. FPP § 1367.

       • In contrast to the common law practice, the FRCP 12(c) judgment on the pleadings procedure primarily is addressed to the latter function of disposing of cases on the basis of the underlying substantive merits of the parties' claims and defenses as they are revealed in the formal pleadings. FPP § 1367. The purpose of FRCP 12(c) is to save time and expense in cases where the ultimate issues of fact are not in dispute, and to prevent the piecemeal process of judicial determination which prevailed under the old common-law practice. FEDPROC § 62:566.

    ii. *Motions to dismiss.* While FRCP 12(b) motions to dismiss and FRCP 12(c) motions for judgment on the pleadings are to some extent merely interchangeable weapons in a party's arsenal of pretrial challenges, there are differences in the scope and effect of the two motions. A FRCP 12(b) motion to dismiss is directed solely toward the defects of the plaintiff's claim for relief, without concern for the merits of the controversy, while a FRCP 12(c) motion for judgment on the pleadings at least theoretically requires some scrutiny of the merits of the controversy. FEDPROC § 62:568.

    iii. *Motion to strike.* The FRCP 12(c) motion also should be contrasted with the motion to strike under FRCP 12(f). The latter motion permits either party to strike redundant, immaterial, impertinent, or scandalous matter from an adversary's pleading and may be used to challenge the sufficiency of defenses asserted by that adversary. The motion serves as a pruning device to eliminate objectionable matter from an opponent's pleadings and, unlike the FRCP 12(c) procedure, it is not directed at gaining a final judgment on the merits, although a FRCP 12(f) motion that succeeds in eliminating the defenses to the action may have that purpose and, in some cases, may have that effect. FPP § 1369.

       • If a plaintiff seeks to dispute the legal sufficiency of fewer than all of the defenses raised in the defendant's pleading, he should proceed under FRCP 12(f) rather than under FRCP 12(c) because the latter leads to the entry of a judgment. FPP § 1369.

    iv. *Motion for summary judgment.* In most circumstances a party will find it preferable to proceed under FRCP 56 rather than FRCP 12(c) for a variety of reasons. For example, the summary judgment procedure is available when the defendant fails to file an answer, whereas technically no relief would be available under FRCP 12(c) because the pleadings have not been closed. If a party believes that it will be necessary to introduce evidence outside the formal pleadings in order to demonstrate that no material issue of fact exists and he is clearly entitled to judgment, it is advisable to proceed directly under FRCP 56 rather than taking the circuitous route through FRCP 12(c). Moreover, the FRCP 12(c) path may present certain risks because the court, in its discretion, may refuse to permit the introduction of matters beyond the pleadings and insist on treating the motion as one under FRCP 12(c) or apply the general motion time period set out in FRCP 6(d), rather than the special time provision in FRCP 56. FPP § 1369.

b. *Bringing a FRCP 12(c) motion.* As numerous judicial opinions make clear, a FRCP 12(c) motion is designed to provide a means of disposing of cases when the material facts are not in dispute between the parties and a judgment on the merits can be achieved by focusing on the content of the competing pleadings, exhibits thereto, matters incorporated by reference in the pleadings, whatever is central or integral to the claim for relief or defense, and any facts of which the district court will take judicial notice. FPP § 1367; DiCarlo v. St. Mary Hosp., 530 F.3d 255 (3d Cir. 2008); Buddy Bean Lumber Co. v. Axis Surplus Ins. Co., 715 F.3d 695, 697 (8th Cir. 2013).

  i. The motion for a judgment on the pleadings only has utility when all material allegations of fact are admitted or not controverted in the pleadings and only questions of law remain to be decided by the district court. FPP § 1367; Stafford v. Jewelers Mut. Ins. Co., 554 Fed. Appx. 360, 370 (6th Cir. 2014).

c. *Partial judgment on the pleadings.* Although not provided for by FRCP 12(c), a party may properly move for partial judgment on the pleadings to further the policy goal of efficient resolution of actions when there are no material facts in dispute. This conclusion has been said to be buttressed by FRCP 56(a), which provides that a party may move for summary judgment "on all or part of the claim." FEDPROC § 62:571.

d. *Granting of a motion for judgment on the pleadings.* The federal courts have followed a fairly restrictive standard in ruling on motions for judgment on the pleadings. FPP § 1368. A motion for judgment on the pleadings is a motion for judgment on the merits, and should only be granted if no material issue of fact remains to be resolved and the movant establishes entitlement to judgment as a matter of law. FEDPROC § 62:569; Great Plains Trust Co. v. Morgan Stanley Dean Witter & Co., 313 F.3d 305 (5th Cir. 2002); Sikirica v. Nationwide Ins. Co., 416 F.3d 214 (3d Cir. 2005). A motion for a judgment on the pleadings must be sustained where the undisputed facts appearing in the pleadings, supplemented by any facts of which the court will take judicial notice, show that no relief can be granted. Judgment on the pleadings is not appropriate where the answer raises issues of fact which, if proved, would defeat recovery. FEDPROC § 62:569.

  i. A motion for judgment on the pleadings admits, for purposes of the motion, the truth of all well-pleaded facts in the pleadings of the opposing party, together with all fair inferences to be drawn therefrom, even where the defendant asserts, in the FRCP 12(c) motion, a FRCP 12(b)(6) defense of failure to state a claim upon which relief can be granted. FEDPROC § 62:570; In re World Trade Center Disaster Site Litigation, 521 F.3d 169 (2d Cir. 2008); Massachusetts Nurses Ass'n v. North Adams Regional Hosp., 467 F.3d 27 (1st Cir. 2006). However, all allegations of the moving party which have been denied are taken as false. FEDPROC § 62:570; Volvo Const. Equipment North America, Inc. v. CLM Equipment Company, Inc., 386 F.3d 581 (4th Cir. 2004). In considering a motion for judgment on the pleadings, the trial court is thus required to view the facts presented in the pleadings and inferences to be drawn therefrom in the light most favorable to the nonmoving party. In this fashion the courts hope to insure that the rights of the nonmoving party are decided as fully and fairly on a FRCP 12(c) motion as if there had been a trial. FEDPROC § 62:570.

  ii. On a motion for judgment on the pleadings, the court may consider facts upon the basis of judicial notice. FEDPROC § 62:570; R.G. Financial Corp. v. Vergara-Nunez, 446 F.3d 178 (1st Cir. 2006). However, a motion for judgment on the pleadings does not admit conclusions of law or unwarranted factual inferences. FEDPROC § 62:570; JPMorgan Chase Bank, N.A. v. Winget, 510 F.3d 577 (6th Cir. 2007).

e. *Joining motions*

    i. *Right to join.* A motion under FRCP 12 may be joined with any other motion allowed by FRCP 12. FRCP 12(g)(1).

    ii. *Limitation on further motions.* Except as provided in FRCP 12(h)(2) or FRCP 12(h)(3), a party that makes a motion under FRCP 12 must not make another motion under FRCP 12 raising a defense or objection that was available to the party but omitted from its earlier motion. FRCP 12(g)(2).

f. *Waiving and preserving certain defenses*

    i. *When some are waived.* A party waives any defense listed in FRCP 12(b)(2) through FRCP 12(b)(5) by:

- Omitting it from a motion in the circumstances described in FRCP 12(g)(2); or

- Failing to either: (1) make it by motion under FRCP 12; or (2) include it in a responsive pleading or in an amendment allowed by FRCP 15(a)(1) as a matter of course. FRCP 12(h)(1).

    ii. *When to raise others.* Failure to state a claim upon which relief can be granted, to join a person required by FRCP 19(b), or to state a legal defense to a claim may be raised:

- In any pleading allowed or ordered under FRCP 7(a);

- By a motion under FRCP 12(c); or

- At trial. FRCP 12(h)(2).

    iii. *Lack of subject matter jurisdiction.* If the court determines at any time that it lacks subject-matter jurisdiction, the court must dismiss the action. FRCP 12(h)(3).

3. *Opposing papers.* The Federal Rules of Civil Procedure do not require any formal answer, return, or reply to a motion, except where the Federal Rules of Civil Procedure or local rules may require affidavits, memoranda, or other papers to be filed in opposition to a motion. Such papers are simply to apprise the court of such opposition and the grounds of that opposition. FEDPROC § 62:359.

a. *Effect of failure to respond to motion.* Although in the absence of statutory provision or court rule, a motion ordinarily does not require a written answer, when a party files a motion and the opposing party fails to respond, the court may construe such failure to respond as nonopposition to the motion or an admission that the motion was meritorious, may take the facts alleged in the motion as true—the rule in some jurisdictions being that the failure to respond to a fact set forth in a motion is deemed an admission—and may grant the motion if the relief requested appears to be justified. AMJUR MOTIONS § 28.

b. *Assent or no opposition not determinative.* However, a motion will not be granted automatically simply because an "assent" or a notation of "no opposition" has been filed; federal judges frequently deny motions that have been assented to when it is thought that justice so dictates. FPP § 1190.

c. *Responsive pleading inappropriate as response to motion.* An attempt to answer or oppose a motion with a responsive pleading usually is not appropriate. FPP § 1190.

4. *Reply papers.* A moving party may be required or permitted to prepare papers in addition to his original motion papers. AMJUR MOTIONS § 25. Papers answering or replying to opposing papers may be appropriate, in the interests of justice, where it appears there is a substantial reason for allowing a reply. Thus, a court may accept reply papers where a party demonstrates that the papers to which it seeks to file a reply raise new issues that are material to the disposition of the question before the court, or where the court determines, sua sponte, that it wishes further briefing of an issue raised in those papers and orders the submission of additional papers. FEDPROC § 62:360.

a. *Function of reply papers.* The function of a reply affidavit is to answer the arguments made in opposition to the position taken by the movant and not to permit the movant to introduce new arguments in support of the motion. AMJUR MOTIONS § 25.

b. *Issues raised for the first time in a reply document.* However, the view has been followed in some jurisdictions, that as a matter of judicial economy, where there is no prejudice and where the issues could be raised simply by filing a motion to dismiss, the trial court has discretion to consider arguments raised for the first time in a reply memorandum, and that a trial court may grant a motion to strike issues raised for the first time in a reply memorandum. AMJUR MOTIONS § 26.

5. *Appearances.* Every attorney who represents a party or who files a document on a party's behalf must file an appearance for that party. IN R USDCTSD L.R. 83-7. The filing of a Notice of Appearance shall act to establish the filing attorney as an attorney of record representing a designated party or parties in a particular cause of action. As a result, it is necessary for each attorney to file a separate Notice of Appearance when entering an appearance in a case. A joint appearance on behalf of multiple attorneys may be filed electronically only if it is filed separately for each attorney, using his/her ECF login. IN R USDCTSD ECF Procedures(12). Only those attorneys who have filed an appearance in a pending action are entitled to be served with case documents under FRCP 5(a). IN R USDCTSD L.R. 83-7. For more information, refer to IN R USDCTSD L.R. 83-7 and IN R USDCTSD ECF Procedures(12).

6. *Notice of related action.* A party must file a notice of related action: as soon as it appears that the party's case and another pending case: (1) arise out of the same transaction or occurrence; (2) involve the same property; or (3) involve the validity or infringement or the same patent, trademark, or copyright. IN R USDCTSD L.R. 40-1(d)(2). For more information, refer to IN R USDCTSD L.R. 40-1.

7. *Alternative dispute resolution (ADR)*

   a. *Application.* Unless limited by specific provisions, or unless there are other applicable specific statutory, common law, or constitutional procedures, the Local Alternative Dispute Resolution Rules of the United States District Court for the Southern District of Indiana shall apply in all civil litigation filed in the U.S. District Court for the Southern District of Indiana, except in the following cases and proceedings:

      i. Applications for writs of habeas corpus under 28 U.S.C.A. § 2254;

      ii. Forfeiture cases;

      iii. Non-adversary proceedings in bankruptcy;

      iv. Social Security administrative review cases; and

      v. Such other matters as specified by order of the Court; for example, matters involving important public policy issues, constitutional law, or the establishment of new law. IN R USDCTSD A.D.R. Rule 1.2.

   b. *Mediation.* Mediation under this section (IN R USDCTSD A.D.R. Rule 2.1, et seq.) involves the confidential process by which a person acting as a Mediator, selected by the parties or appointed by the Court, assists the litigants in reaching a mutually acceptable agreement. It is an informal and nonadversarial process. The role of the Mediator is to assist in identifying the issues, reducing misunderstandings, clarifying priorities, exploring areas of compromise, and finding points of agreement as well as legitimate points of disagreement. Final decision-making authority rests with the parties, not the Mediator. IN R USDCTSD A.D.R. Rule 2.1. It is anticipated that an agreement may not resolve all of the disputed issues, but the process, nonetheless, can reduce points of contention. Parties and their representatives are required to mediate in good faith, but are not compelled to reach an agreement. IN R USDCTSD A.D.R. Rule 2.1.

      i. *Case selection.* The Court with the agreement of the parties may refer a civil case for mediation. Unless otherwise ordered or as specifically provided in IN R USDCTSD A.D.R. Rule 2.8, referral to mediation does not abate or suspend the action, and no scheduled dates shall be delayed or deferred, including the date of trial. IN R USDCTSD A.D.R. Rule 2.2.

      ii. For more information on mediation, refer to IN R USDCTSD A.D.R. Rule 2.1, et seq.

   c. *Other methods of dispute resolution.* The Local Alternative Dispute Resolution Rules of the United States District Court for the Southern District of Indiana shall not preclude the parties from utilizing any other reasonable method or technique of alternative dispute resolution to resolve disputes to which the parties agree. However, any use of arbitration by the parties will be governed by and comply with the requirements of 28 U.S.C.A. § 654 through 28 U.S.C.A. § 657. IN R USDCTSD A.D.R. Rule 1.5.

    d.   For more information on alternative dispute resolution (ADR), refer to IN R USDCTSD A.D.R. Rule 1.1, et seq.

8.   *Notice of settlement or resolution.* The parties must immediately notify the court if they reasonably anticipate settling their case or resolving a pending motion. IN R USDCTSD L.R. 7-1(h).

9.   *Modification or suspension of rules.* The court may, on its own motion or at the request of a party, suspend or modify any rule in a particular case in the interest of justice. IN R USDCTSD L.R. 1-1(c).

D. Documents

1.   *Documents for moving party*

    a.   *Required documents*

        i.   *Notice of motion and motion.* Refer to the General Requirements section of this document for information on the notice of motion and motion.

        ii.   *Brief.* The following motion must also be accompanied by a supporting brief: for judgment on the pleadings. IN R USDCTSD L.R. 7-1(b)(1). Refer to the Format section of this document for the format of briefs.

        iii.   *Certificate of service.* FRCP 5(d) requires that the person making service under FRCP 5 certify that service has been effected. FRCP 5(Advisory Committee Notes). Having such information on file may be useful for many purposes, including proof of service if an issue arises concerning the effectiveness of the service. FRCP 5(Advisory Committee Notes).

           •   *Certificate of service for electronically-filed documents.* A certificate of service must be included with all documents filed electronically. Such certificate shall indicate that service was accomplished pursuant to the Court's electronic filing procedures. IN R USDCTSD ECF Procedures(11). For the suggested format for a certificate of service for electronic filing, refer to IN R USDCTSD ECF Procedures(11).

    b.   *Supplemental documents*

        i.   *Pleadings.* In considering a motion for judgment on the pleadings, the trial court is. . .required to view the facts presented in the pleadings and inferences to be drawn therefrom in the light most favorable to the nonmoving party. FEDPROC § 62:570.

           •   *Motion treated as one for summary judgment.* If, on a motion under FRCP 12(b)(6) or FRCP 12(c), matters outside the pleadings are presented to and not excluded by the court, the motion must be treated as one for summary judgment under FRCP 56. All parties must be given a reasonable opportunity to present all the material that is pertinent to the motion. FRCP 12(d).

        ii.   *Notice of constitutional question.* A party that files a pleading, written motion, or other paper drawing into question the constitutionality of a federal or state statute must promptly:

           •   *File notice.* File a notice of constitutional question stating the question and identifying the paper that raises it, if: (1) a federal statute is questioned and the parties do not include the United States, one of its agencies, or one of its officers or employees in an official capacity; or (2) a state statute is questioned and the parties do not include the state, one of its agencies, or one of its officers or employees in an official capacity; and

           •   *Serve notice.* Serve the notice and paper on the Attorney General of the United States if a federal statute is questioned—or on the state attorney general if a state statute is questioned—either by certified or registered mail or by sending it to an electronic address designated by the attorney general for this purpose. FRCP 5.1(a).

           •   *Time for filing.* A notice of constitutional challenge to a statute filed in accordance with FRCP 5.1 must be filed at the same time the parties tender their proposed case management plan, if one is required, or within twenty-one (21) days of the filing drawing into question the constitutionality of a federal or state statute, whichever occurs later. IN R USDCTSD L.R. 5.1-1(a).

           •   *Additional service requirements.* If a federal statute is challenged, in addition to the service requirements of FRCP 5.1(a), the party filing the notice of constitutional challenge must serve the notice and documents on the United States Attorney for the Southern District of Indiana, either by certified or registered mail or by sending it to an electronic address designated for that purpose by that official. IN R USDCTSD L.R. 5.1-1(b).

- *No forfeiture.* A party's failure to file and serve the notice, or the court's failure to certify, does not forfeit a constitutional claim or defense that is otherwise timely asserted. FRCP 5.1(d).

iii. *Nongovernmental corporate disclosure statement*

- *Contents.* A nongovernmental corporate party must file two (2) copies of a disclosure statement that: (1) identifies any parent corporation and any publicly held corporation owning ten percent (10%) or more of its stock; or (2) states that there is no such corporation. FRCP 7.1(a).

- *Time to file; Supplemental filing.* A party must: (1) file the disclosure statement with its first appearance, pleading, petition, motion, response, or other request addressed to the court; and (2) promptly file a supplemental statement if any required information changes. FRCP 7.1(b).

iv. *Index of exhibits.* Any pleading, motion, brief, affidavit, notice, or proposed order filed with the court, whether electronically or with the clerk, must: if it has four (4) or more exhibits, include a separate index that identifies and briefly describes each exhibit. IN R USDCTSD L.R. 5-1(b).

v. *Request for oral argument.* A party may request oral argument by filing a separate motion explaining why oral argument is necessary and estimating how long the court should allow for the argument. The request must be filed and served with the supporting brief, response brief, or reply brief. IN R USDCTSD L.R. 7-5(a).

vi. *Request for evidentiary hearing.* A party may request an evidentiary hearing on a motion or petition by serving and filing a separate motion explaining why the hearing is necessary and estimating how long the court should allow for the hearing. IN R USDCTSD L.R. 7-5(c).

vii. *Copy of authority.* Generally, copies of cited authorities may not be attached to court filings. However, a party must attach to the party's motion or brief a copy of any cited authority if it is not available on Westlaw or Lexis. Upon request, a party must provide copies of any cited authority that is only available through electronic means to the court or the other parties. IN R USDCTSD L.R. 7-1(f).

viii. *Proposed order.* A party must include a suitable form of order with any document that requests the judge or the clerk to enter a routine or uncontested order. IN R USDCTSD L.R. 5-5(b); IN R USDCTSD L.R. 5-10(c); IN R USDCTSD L.R. 7-1(d).

- A service statement and/or list must be included on each proposed order, as required by IN R USDCTSD L.R. 5-5(d). IN R USDCTSD ECF Procedures(11). Any pleading, motion, brief, affidavit, notice, or proposed order filed with the court, whether electronically or with the clerk, must: if it is a form of order, include a statement of service, in the format required by IN R USDCTSD L.R. 5-5(d) in the lower left corner of the document. IN R USDCTSD L.R. 5-1(b).

- A party electronically filing a proposed order—whether voluntarily or because required by IN R USDCTSD L.R. 5-5—must convert the order directly from a word processing program and file it as an attachment to the document it relates to. Proposed orders must include in the lower left-hand corner of the signature page a statement that service will be made electronically on all ECF-registered counsel of record via email generated by the court's ECF system, without listing all such counsel. A service list including the name and postal address of any pro se litigant or non-registered attorney of record must follow, stating that service on the listed individuals will be made in the traditional paper manner, via first-class U.S. Mail. IN R USDCTSD L.R. 5-5(d).

ix. *Copy of document with self-address envelope.* To receive a file-stamped copy of a document filed directly with the clerk, a party must include with the original document an additional copy and a self-addressed envelope. The envelope must be big enough to hold the copy and have enough postage on it to send the copy via regular first-class mail. IN R USDCTSD L.R. 5-10(b).

   x. *Notice of manual filing.* When a party who is not exempt from the electronic filing requirement files a document directly with the clerk, the party must: electronically file a notice of manual filing that explains why the document cannot be filed electronically. IN R USDCTSD L.R. 5-2(d)(1). Refer to the Filing and Service Requirements section of this document for more information.

- Where an individual component cannot be included in an electronic filing (e.g. the component cannot be converted to electronic format), the filer shall electronically file the prescribed Notice of Manual Filing in place of that component. A model form is provided as Appendix C (IN R USDCTSD ECF Procedures(Appendix C)). IN R USDCTSD ECF Procedures(13).

- Before making a manual filing of a component, the filing party shall first electronically file a Notice of Manual Filing (See IN R USDCTSD ECF Procedures(Appendix C)). The filer shall initiate the electronic filing process as if filing the actual component but shall instead attach to the filing the Notice of Manual Filing setting forth the reason(s) why the component cannot be filed electronically. The manual filing should be accompanied by a copy of the previously filed Notice of Manual Filing. A party may seek to have a component excluded from electronic filing pursuant to applicable Federal and Local Rules (e.g., FRCP 26(c)). IN R USDCTSD ECF Procedures(15).

   xi. *Courtesy copies.* District Judges and Magistrate Judges regularly receive documents filed by all parties. Therefore, parties shall not bring "courtesy copies" to any chambers unless specifically directed to do so by the Court. IN R USDCTSD Case Mgt(General Instructions For All Cases).

   xii. *Copies for three-judge court.* Parties in a case where a three-judge court has been requested must file an original and three copies of any document filed directly with the clerk (instead of electronically) until the court: (1) denies the request; (2) dissolves the three-judge court; or (3) allows the parties to file fewer copies. IN R USDCTSD L.R. 9-2(c).

   xiii. *Declaration that party was unable to file in a timely manner due to technical difficulties.* If a party misses a filing deadline due to an inability to file electronically, the party may submit the untimely filed document, accompanied by a declaration stating the reason(s) for missing the deadline. IN R USDCTSD ECF Procedures(16). A model form is provided as Appendix D (IN R USDCTSD ECF Procedures(Appendix D)). IN R USDCTSD ECF Procedures(16).

2. *Documents for opposing party*

  a. *Required documents*

    i. *Response brief.* Refer to the Format section of this document for the format of briefs. Refer to the General Requirements section of this document for information on the opposing papers.

    ii. *Certificate of service.* FRCP 5(d) requires that the person making service under FRCP 5 certify that service has been effected. FRCP 5(Advisory Committee Notes). Having such information on file may be useful for many purposes, including proof of service if an issue arises concerning the effectiveness of the service. FRCP 5(Advisory Committee Notes).

- *Certificate of service for electronically-filed documents.* A certificate of service must be included with all documents filed electronically. Such certificate shall indicate that service was accomplished pursuant to the Court's electronic filing procedures. IN R USDCTSD ECF Procedures(11). For the suggested format for a certificate of service for electronic filing, refer to IN R USDCTSD ECF Procedures(11).

  b. *Supplemental documents*

    i. *Pleadings.* In considering a motion for judgment on the pleadings, the trial court is. . .required to view the facts presented in the pleadings and inferences to be drawn therefrom in the light most favorable to the nonmoving party. FEDPROC § 62:570.

- *Motion treated as one for summary judgment.* If, on a motion under FRCP 12(b)(6) or

FRCP 12(c), matters outside the pleadings are presented to and not excluded by the court, the motion must be treated as one for summary judgment under FRCP 56. All parties must be given a reasonable opportunity to present all the material that is pertinent to the motion. FRCP 12(d).

ii. *Notice of constitutional question.* A party that files a pleading, written motion, or other paper drawing into question the constitutionality of a federal or state statute must promptly:

- *File notice.* File a notice of constitutional question stating the question and identifying the paper that raises it, if: (1) a federal statute is questioned and the parties do not include the United States, one of its agencies, or one of its officers or employees in an official capacity; or (2) a state statute is questioned and the parties do not include the state, one of its agencies, or one of its officers or employees in an official capacity; and

- *Serve notice.* Serve the notice and paper on the Attorney General of the United States if a federal statute is questioned—or on the state attorney general if a state statute is questioned—either by certified or registered mail or by sending it to an electronic address designated by the attorney general for this purpose. FRCP 5.1(a).

- *Time for filing.* A notice of constitutional challenge to a statute filed in accordance with FRCP 5.1 must be filed at the same time the parties tender their proposed case management plan, if one is required, or within twenty-one (21) days of the filing drawing into question the constitutionality of a federal or state statute, whichever occurs later. IN R USDCTSD L.R. 5.1-1(a).

- *Additional service requirements.* If a federal statute is challenged, in addition to the service requirements of FRCP 5.1(a), the party filing the notice of constitutional challenge must serve the notice and documents on the United States Attorney for the Southern District of Indiana, either by certified or registered mail or by sending it to an electronic address designated for that purpose by that official. IN R USDCTSD L.R. 5.1-1(b).

- *No forfeiture.* A party's failure to file and serve the notice, or the court's failure to certify, does not forfeit a constitutional claim or defense that is otherwise timely asserted. FRCP 5.1(d).

iii. *Index of exhibits.* Any pleading, motion, brief, affidavit, notice, or proposed order filed with the court, whether electronically or with the clerk, must: if it has four (4) or more exhibits, include a separate index that identifies and briefly describes each exhibit. IN R USDCTSD L.R. 5-1(b).

iv. *Request for oral argument.* A party may request oral argument by filing a separate motion explaining why oral argument is necessary and estimating how long the court should allow for the argument. The request must be filed and served with the supporting brief, response brief, or reply brief. IN R USDCTSD L.R. 7-5(a).

v. *Request for evidentiary hearing.* A party may request an evidentiary hearing on a motion or petition by serving and filing a separate motion explaining why the hearing is necessary and estimating how long the court should allow for the hearing. IN R USDCTSD L.R. 7-5(c).

vi. *Copy of authority.* Generally, copies of cited authorities may not be attached to court filings. However, a party must attach to the party's motion or brief a copy of any cited authority if it is not available on Westlaw or Lexis. Upon request, a party must provide copies of any cited authority that is only available through electronic means to the court or the other parties. IN R USDCTSD L.R. 7-1(f).

vii. *Copy of document with self-address envelope.* To receive a file-stamped copy of a document filed directly with the clerk, a party must include with the original document an additional copy and a self-addressed envelope. The envelope must be big enough to hold the copy and have enough postage on it to send the copy via regular first-class mail. IN R USDCTSD L.R. 5-10(b).

viii. *Notice of manual filing.* When a party who is not exempt from the electronic filing requirement files a document directly with the clerk, the party must: electronically file a notice of manual filing that explains why the document cannot be filed electronically. IN R USDCTSD L.R.

5-2(d)(1). Refer to the Filing and Service Requirements section of this document for more information.

- Where an individual component cannot be included in an electronic filing (e.g. the component cannot be converted to electronic format), the filer shall electronically file the prescribed Notice of Manual Filing in place of that component. A model form is provided as Appendix C (IN R USDCTSD ECF Procedures(Appendix C)). IN R USDCTSD ECF Procedures(13).

- Before making a manual filing of a component, the filing party shall first electronically file a Notice of Manual Filing (See IN R USDCTSD ECF Procedures(Appendix C)). The filer shall initiate the electronic filing process as if filing the actual component but shall instead attach to the filing the Notice of Manual Filing setting forth the reason(s) why the component cannot be filed electronically. The manual filing should be accompanied by a copy of the previously filed Notice of Manual Filing. A party may seek to have a component excluded from electronic filing pursuant to applicable Federal and Local Rules (e.g., FRCP 26(c)). IN R USDCTSD ECF Procedures(15).

ix. *Courtesy copies.* District Judges and Magistrate Judges regularly receive documents filed by all parties. Therefore, parties shall not bring "courtesy copies" to any chambers unless specifically directed to do so by the Court. IN R USDCTSD Case Mgt(General Instructions For All Cases).

x. *Copies for three-judge court.* Parties in a case where a three-judge court has been requested must file an original and three copies of any document filed directly with the clerk (instead of electronically) until the court: (1) denies the request; (2) dissolves the three-judge court; or (3) allows the parties to file fewer copies. IN R USDCTSD L.R. 9-2(c).

xi. *Declaration that party was unable to file in a timely manner due to technical difficulties.* If a party misses a filing deadline due to an inability to file electronically, the party may submit the untimely filed document, accompanied by a declaration stating the reason(s) for missing the deadline. IN R USDCTSD ECF Procedures(16). A model form is provided as Appendix D (IN R USDCTSD ECF Procedures(Appendix D)). IN R USDCTSD ECF Procedures(16).

E. Format

1. *Form of documents.* The rules governing captions and other matters of form in pleadings apply to motions and other papers. FRCP 7(b)(2).

    a. *Paper (manual filings only).* Any document that is not filed electronically must: be flat, unfolded, and on good-quality, eight and one-half by eleven (8-1/2 x 11) inch white paper. IN R USDCTSD L.R. 5-1(d)(1). Any document that is not filed electronically must: be single-sided. IN R USDCTSD L.R. 5-1(d)(1).

        i. *Covers or backing.* Any document that is not filed electronically must: not have a cover or a back. IN R USDCTSD L.R. 5-1(d)(1).

        ii. *Fastening.* Any document that is not filed electronically must: be (if consisting of more than one (1) page) fastened by paperclip or binder clip and may not be stapled. IN R USDCTSD L.R. 5-1(d)(1).

        - *Request for nonconforming fastening.* If a document cannot be fastened or bound as required by IN R USDCTSD L.R. 5-1(d), a party may ask the clerk for permission to fasten it in another manner. The party must make such a request before attempting to file the document with nonconforming fastening. IN R USDCTSD L.R. 5-1(d)(2).

        iii. *Hole punching.* Any document that is not filed electronically must: be two-hole punched at the top with the holes two and three-quarter (2-3/4) inches apart and appropriately centered. IN R USDCTSD L.R. 5-1(d)(1).

    b. *Margins.* Any pleading, motion, brief, affidavit, notice, or proposed order filed with the court, whether electronically or with the clerk, must: have at least one (1) inch margins. IN R USDCTSD L.R. 5-1(b).

    c. *Spacing.* Any pleading, motion, brief, affidavit, notice, or proposed order filed with the court, whether electronically or with the clerk, must: be double spaced (except for headings, footnotes, and quoted material). IN R USDCTSD L.R. 5-1(b).

d. *Text.* Any pleading, motion, brief, affidavit, notice, or proposed order filed with the court, whether electronically or with the clerk, must: be plainly typewritten, printed, or prepared by a clearly legible copying process. IN R USDCTSD L.R. 5-1(b).

e. *Font size.* Any pleading, motion, brief, affidavit, notice, or proposed order filed with the court, whether electronically or with the clerk, must: use at least 12-point type in the body of the document and at least 10-point type in footnotes. IN R USDCTSD L.R. 5-1(b).

f. *Page numbering.* Any pleading, motion, brief, affidavit, notice, or proposed order filed with the court, whether electronically or with the clerk, must: have consecutively numbered pages. IN R USDCTSD L.R. 5-1(b).

g. *Caption; Names of parties.* Every pleading must have a caption with the court's name, a title, a file number, and a FRCP 7(a) designation. The title of the complaint must name all the parties; the title of other pleadings, after naming the first party on each side, may refer generally to other parties. FRCP 10(a). Any pleading, motion, brief, affidavit, notice, or proposed order filed with the court, whether electronically or with the clerk, must: include a title on the first page. IN R USDCTSD L.R. 5-1(b).

    i. *Alternative motions.* Motions must be filed separately, but alternative motions may be filed in a single document if each is named in the title. IN R USDCTSD L.R. 7-1(a).

h. *Filer's information.* Any pleading, motion, brief, affidavit, notice, or proposed order filed with the court, whether electronically or with the clerk, must: in the case of pleadings, motions, legal briefs, and notices, include the name, complete address, telephone number, facsimile number (where available), and e-mail address (where available) of the pro se litigant or attorney who files it. IN R USDCTSD L.R. 5-1(b).

i. *Paragraphs; Separate statements.* A party must state its claims or defenses in numbered paragraphs, each limited as far as practicable to a single set of circumstances. A later pleading may refer by number to a paragraph in an earlier pleading. If doing so would promote clarity, each claim founded on a separate transaction or occurrence—and each defense other than a denial—must be stated in a separate count or defense. FRCP 10(b).

j. *Adoption by reference; Exhibits.* A statement in a pleading may be adopted by reference elsewhere in the same pleading or in any other pleading or motion. A copy of a written instrument that is an exhibit to a pleading is a part of the pleading for all purposes. FRCP 10(c).

k. *Citations*

    i. *Local rules.* The Local Rules of the United States District Court for the Southern District of Indiana may be cited as "S.D. Ind. L.R." IN R USDCTSD L.R. 1-1(a).

    ii. *Local alternative dispute resolution rules.* These Rules shall be known as the Local Alternative Dispute Resolution Rules of the United States District Court for the Southern District of Indiana. They shall be cited as "S.D.Ind. Local A.D.R. Rule _____." IN R USDCTSD A.D.R. Rule 1.1.

l. *Acceptance by the clerk.* The clerk must not refuse to file a paper solely because it is not in the form prescribed by the Federal Rules of Civil Procedure or by a local rule or practice. FRCP 5(d)(4). The clerk will accept a document that violates IN R USDCTSD L.R. 5-1, but the court may exclude the document from the official record. IN R USDCTSD L.R. 5-1(e).

    i. *Sanctions for errors as to form.* The court may strike from the record any document that does not comply with the rules governing the form of documents filed with the court, such as rules that regulate document size or the number of copies to be filed or that require a special designation in the caption. The court may also sanction an attorney or party who files a non-compliant document. IN R USDCTSD L.R. 1-3.

2. *Form of electronic documents.* Any document submitted via the court's electronic case filing (ECF) system must be: otherwise prepared and filed in a manner consistent with the CM/ECF Policies and

Procedures Manual (IN R USDCTSD ECF Procedures). IN R USDCTSD L.R. 5-1(c). Electronically filed documents must meet the requirements of FRCP 10 (Form of Pleadings), IN R USDCTSD L.R. 5-1 (Format of Papers Presented for Filing), and FRCP 5.2 (Privacy Protection for Filings Made with the Court), as if they had been submitted on paper. Documents filed electronically are also subject to any page limitations set forth by Court Order, by IN R USDCTSD L.R. 7-1 (Motion Practice), or IN R USDCTSD L.R. 56-1 (Summary Judgment Practice), as applicable. IN R USDCTSD ECF Procedures(13).

a. *PDF format required.* Any document submitted via the court's electronic case filing (ECF) system must be: in .pdf format. IN R USDCTSD L.R. 5-1(c); IN R USDCTSD ECF Procedures(7). Any document submitted via the court's electronic case filing (ECF) system must be: converted to a .pdf file directly from a word processing program, unless it exists only in paper format (in which case it may be scanned to create a .pdf document). IN R USDCTSD L.R. 5-1(c); IN R USDCTSD ECF Procedures(13).

    i. An exhibit may be scanned into PDF format, at a recommended 300 dpi resolution or higher, only if it does not already exist in electronic format. The filing attorney is responsible for reviewing all PDF documents for legibility before submitting them through the Court's Electronic Case Filing system. For technical guidance in creating PDF documents, please contact the Clerk's Office. IN R USDCTSD ECF Procedures(13).

b. *File size limitations.* Any document submitted via the court's electronic case filing (ECF) system must be: submitted as one or more .pdf files that do not exceed ten megabytes (10 MB) each (consistent with the CM/ECF Policies and Procedures Manual (IN R USDCTSD ECF Procedures)). IN R USDCTSD L.R. 5-1(c); IN R USDCTSD ECF Procedures(13).

    i. To electronically file a document or attachment that exceeds ten megabytes (10 MB), the document must first be broken down into two or more smaller files. For example, if Exhibit A is a twelve megabyte (12 MB) PDF file, it should be divided into 2 equal parts prior to electronic filing. Each component part of the exhibit would be filed as an attachment to the main document and described appropriately as "Exhibit A (part 1 of 2)" and "Exhibit A (part 2 of 2)." IN R USDCTSD ECF Procedures(13).

    ii. The supporting items mentioned in IN R USDCTSD ECF Procedures(13) should not be confused with memorandums or briefs in support of motions as outlined in IN R USDCTSD L.R. 7-1 or IN R USDCTSD L.R. 56-1. These memorandums or briefs in support are to be filed as entirely separate documents pursuant to the appropriate rule. Additionally, no motion shall be embodied in the text of a response or reply brief/memorandum unless otherwise ordered by the Court. IN R USDCTSD ECF Procedures(13).

c. *Separate component parts.* A key objective of the electronic filing system is to ensure that as much of the case as possible is managed electronically. To facilitate electronic filing and retrieval, documents to be filed electronically are to be reasonably broken into their separate component parts. By way of example, most filings include a foundation document (e.g., motion) and other supporting items (e.g., exhibits, proposed orders, proposed amended pleadings). The foundation document, as well as the supporting items, are each separate components of the filing; supporting items must be filed as attachments to the foundation document. These exhibits or attachments should include only those excerpts of the referenced documents that are directly germane to the matter under consideration. IN R USDCTSD ECF Procedures(13).

    i. Where an individual component cannot be included in an electronic filing (e.g. the component cannot be converted to electronic format), the filer shall electronically file the prescribed Notice of Manual Filing in place of that component. A model form is provided as Appendix C (IN R USDCTSD ECF Procedures(Appendix C)). IN R USDCTSD ECF Procedures(13).

d. *Exhibits.* Each electronically filed exhibit to a main document must be: (1) created as a separate .pdf file; (2) submitted as an attachment to the main document and given a title which describes its content; and (3) limited to excerpts that are directly germane to the main document's subject matter. IN R USDCTSD L.R. 5-6(a).

    i. When uploading attachments during the electronic filing process, exhibits must be uploaded in a logical sequence and a brief description must be entered for each individual PDF file. The description must include not only the exhibit number or letter, but also a brief description of the document. This information may be entered in CM/ECF using a combination of the Category drop-down menu, the Description text box, or both (see IN R USDCTSD ECF Procedures(13)(Figure 1)). The information that is provided in each box will be combined to create a description of the document as it appears on the case docket (see IN R USDCTSD ECF Procedures(13)(Figure 2)). IN R USDCTSD ECF Procedures(13). For an example, refer to IN R USDCTSD ECF Procedures(13).

e. *Excerpts.* A party filing an exhibit that consists of excerpts from a larger document must clearly and prominently identify the exhibit as containing excerpted material. Either party will have the right to timely file additional excerpts or the complete document to the extent they are or become directly germane to the main document's subject matter. IN R USDCTSD L.R. 5-6(b).

f. For an example illustrating the application of IN R USDCTSD ECF Procedures(13), refer to IN R USDCTSD ECF Procedures(13).

3. *Form of briefs*

   a. *Page limits.* Supporting and response briefs (excluding tables of contents, tables of authorities, appendices, and certificates of service) may not exceed thirty-five (35) pages. Reply briefs may not exceed twenty (20) pages. IN R USDCTSD L.R. 7-1(e)(1).

      i. *Permission to exceed limits.* The court may allow a party to file a brief exceeding these page limits for extraordinary and compelling reasons. IN R USDCTSD L.R. 7-1(e)(2).

      ii. *Supporting and response briefs exceeding limits.* If the court allows a party to file a brief or response exceeding thirty-five (35) pages, the document must include:

         • A table of contents with page references;

         • A statement of issues; and

         • A table of authorities including: (1) all cases (alphabetically arranged), statutes, and other authorities cited in the brief; and (2) page numbers where the authorities are cited in the brief. IN R USDCTSD L.R. 7-1(e)(3).

4. *Signing of pleadings, motions and other papers*

   a. *Signature.* Every pleading, written motion, and other paper must be signed by at least one attorney of record in the attorney's name—or by a party personally if the party is unrepresented. The paper must state the signer's address, e-mail address, and telephone number. FRCP 11(a).

      i. *Signatures on manual filings.* Any document that is not filed electronically must: include the original signature of the pro se litigant or attorney who files it. IN R USDCTSD L.R. 5-1(d)(1).

      ii. *Electronic signatures.* Use of the attorney's login and password when filing documents electronically serves in part as the attorney's signature for purposes of FRCP 11, the Local Rules of the United States District Court for the Southern District of Indiana, and any other purpose for which a signature is required in connection with proceedings before the Court. IN R USDCTSD ECF Procedures(14); IN R USDCTSD ECF Procedures(10). A pleading, motion, brief, or notice filed electronically under an attorney's ECF log-in and password must be signed by that attorney. IN R USDCTSD L.R. 5-7(a). A signature on a document other than a document filed as provided under IN R USDCTSD L.R. 5-7(a) must be an original handwritten signature and must be scanned into .pdf format for electronic filing. IN R USDCTSD L.R. 5-7(c); IN R USDCTSD ECF Procedures(14).

         • *Form of electronic signature.* If a document is converted directly from a word processing application to .pdf (as opposed to scanning), the name of the Filing User under whose log-in and password the document is submitted must be preceded by a "s/" and typed on the signature line where the Filing User's handwritten signature would otherwise appear. IN R USDCTSD L.R. 5-7(b). All documents filed electronically shall include a signature block and include the filing attorney's typewritten name, address, telephone number, facsimile number and e-mail address. In addition, the name of the filing attorney under whose ECF login the document will be filed should be preceded by a "s/" and typed in the space where the attorney's handwritten signature would otherwise appear. IN R US-DCTSD ECF Procedures(14). For a sample format, refer to IN R USDCTSD ECF Procedures(14).

- *Effect of electronic signature.* Filing an electronically signed document under an attorney's ECF log-in and password constitutes the attorney's signature on the document under the Federal Rules of Civil Procedure, under the Local Rules of the United States District Court for the Southern District of Indiana, and for any other reason a signature is required in connection with the court's activities. IN R USDCTSD L.R. 5-7(d).

- *Documents with multiple attorneys' signatures.* Documents requiring signatures of more than one attorney shall be filed either by: (1) obtaining consent from the other attorney, then typing the "s/ [Name]" signature of the other attorney on the signature line where the other attorney's signature would otherwise appear; (2) identifying in the signature section the name of the other attorney whose signature is required and by the submission of a Notice of Endorsement (see IN R USDCTSD ECF Procedures(Appendix B)) by the other attorney no later than three (3) business days after filing; (3) submitting a scanned document containing all handwritten signatures; or (4) in any other manner approved by the Court. IN R USDCTSD ECF Procedures(14); IN R USDCTSD L.R. 5-7(e).

iii. *No verification or accompanying affidavit required for pleadings.* Unless a rule or statute specifically states otherwise, a pleading need not be verified or accompanied by an affidavit. FRCP 11(a).

iv. *Unsigned papers.* The court must strike an unsigned paper unless the omission is promptly corrected after being called to the attorney's or party's attention. FRCP 11(a). The court will strike any document filed directly with the clerk that is not signed by an attorney of record or the pro se litigant filing it, but the court may do so only after giving the attorney or pro se litigant notice of the omission and reasonable time to correct it. Rubber-stamp or facsimile signatures are not original signatures and the court will deem documents containing them to be unsigned for purposes of FRCP 11 and FRCP 26(g) and IN R USDCTSD L.R. 5-10. IN R USDCTSD L.R. 5-10(g).

b. *Representations to the court.* By presenting to the court a pleading, written motion, or other paper—whether by signing, filing, submitting, or later advocating it—an attorney or unrepresented party certifies that to the best of the person's knowledge, information, and belief, formed after an inquiry reasonable under the circumstances:

i. It is not being presented for any improper purpose, such as to harass, cause unnecessary delay, or needlessly increase the cost of litigation;

ii. The claims, defenses, and other legal contentions are warranted by existing law or by a nonfrivolous argument for extending, modifying, or reversing existing law or for establishing new law;

iii. The factual contentions have evidentiary support or, if specifically so identified, will likely have evidentiary support after a reasonable opportunity for further investigation or discovery; and

iv. The denials of factual contentions are warranted on the evidence or, if specifically so identified, are reasonably based on belief or a lack of information. FRCP 11(b).

c. *Sanctions.* If, after notice and a reasonable opportunity to respond, the court determines that FRCP 11(b) has been violated, the court may impose an appropriate sanction on any attorney, law firm, or party that violated FRCP 11(b) or is responsible for the violation. FRCP 11(c)(1). Refer to the United States District Court for the Southern District of Indiana KeyRules Motion for Sanctions document for more information.

5. *Privacy protection for filings made with the court.* Electronically filed documents must meet the requirements of. . .FRCP 5.2 (Privacy Protection for Filings Made with the Court), as if they had been submitted on paper. IN R USDCTSD ECF Procedures(13).

a. *Redacted filings.* Unless the court orders otherwise, in an electronic or paper filing with the court that contains an individual's Social Security number, taxpayer-identification number, or birth date, the name of an individual known to be a minor, or a financial-account number, a party or nonparty making the filing may include only:

    i.   The last four (4) digits of the Social Security number and taxpayer-identification number;

    ii.   The year of the individual's birth;

    iii.   The minor's initials; and

    iv.   The last four (4) digits of the financial-account number. FRCP 5.2(a).

b. *Exemptions from the redaction requirement.* The redaction requirement does not apply to the following:

    i.   A financial-account number that identifies the property allegedly subject to forfeiture in a forfeiture proceeding;

    ii.   The record of an administrative or agency proceeding;

    iii.   The official record of a state-court proceeding;

    iv.   The record of a court or tribunal, if that record was not subject to the redaction requirement when originally filed;

    v.   A filing covered by FRCP 5.2(c) or FRCP 5.2(d); and

    vi.   A pro se filing in an action brought under 28 U.S.C.A. § 2241, 28 U.S.C.A. § 2254, or 28 U.S.C.A. § 2255. FRCP 5.2(b).

c. *Limitations on remote access to electronic files; Social Security appeals and immigration cases.* Unless the court orders otherwise, in an action for benefits under the Social Security Act, and in an action or proceeding relating to an order of removal, to relief from removal, or to immigration benefits or detention, access to an electronic file is authorized as follows:

    i.   The parties and their attorneys may have remote electronic access to any part of the case file, including the administrative record;

    ii.   Any other person may have electronic access to the full record at the courthouse, but may have remote electronic access only to:

        • The docket maintained by the court; and

        • An opinion, order, judgment, or other disposition of the court, but not any other part of the case file or the administrative record. FRCP 5.2(c).

d. *Filings made under seal.* The court may order that a filing be made under seal without redaction. The court may later unseal the filing or order the person who made the filing to file a redacted version for the public record. FRCP 5.2(d). For more information on filing under seal, refer to IN R USDCTSD L.R. 5-11 and IN R USDCTSD ECF Procedures(18).

e. *Protective orders.* For good cause, the court may by order in a case:

    i.   Require redaction of additional information; or

    ii.   Limit or prohibit a nonparty's remote electronic access to a document filed with the court. FRCP 5.2(e).

f. *Option for additional unredacted filing under seal.* A person making a redacted filing may also file an unredacted copy under seal. The court must retain the unredacted copy as part of the record. FRCP 5.2(f).

g. *Option for filing a reference list.* A filing that contains redacted information may be filed together with a reference list that identifies each item of redacted information and specifies an appropriate identifier that uniquely corresponds to each item listed. The list must be filed under seal and may be amended as of right. Any reference in the case to a listed identifier will be construed to refer to the corresponding item of information. FRCP 5.2(g).

h. *Waiver of protection of identifiers.* A person waives the protection of FRCP 5.2(a) as to the person's own information by filing it without redaction and not under seal. FRCP 5.2(h).

F. Filing and Service Requirements

1. *Filing requirements.* Any paper after the complaint that is required to be served—together with a certificate of service—must be filed within a reasonable time after service. FRCP 5(d)(1). Motions must be filed separately, but alternative motions may be filed in a single document if each is named in the title. IN R USDCTSD L.R. 7-1(a).

    a. *How filing is made; In general.* A paper is filed by delivering it:

        i.   To the clerk; or

        ii. To a judge who agrees to accept it for filing, and who must then note the filing date on the paper and promptly send it to the clerk. FRCP 5(d)(2).

             *   In certain instances, the court will direct the parties to submit items directly to chambers (e.g., confidential settlement statements). However, absent specific prior authorization, counsel and litigants should not submit letters or documents directly to chambers, and such materials should be filed with the clerk. IN R USDCTSD L.R. 5-1(Local Rules Advisory Committee Comment).

        iii. A document or item submitted in relation to a matter within the court's jurisdiction is deemed filed upon delivery to the office of the clerk in a manner prescribed by the Local Rules of the United States District Court for the Southern District of Indiana or the Federal Rules of Civil Procedure or authorized by the court. Any submission directed to a Judge or Judge's staff, the office of the clerk or any employee thereof, in a manner that is not contemplated by IN R USDCTSD L.R. 5-1 and without prior court authorization is prohibited. IN R USDCTSD L.R. 5-1(a).

    b. *Non-electronic filing.* Any document that is exempt from electronic filing must be filed directly with the clerk and served on other parties in the case as required by those Federal Rules of Civil Procedure and Local Rules of the United States District Court for the Southern District of Indiana that apply to the service of non-electronic documents. IN R USDCTSD L.R. 5-2(c).

        i.   *When completed.* A document or other item that is not required to be filed electronically is deemed filed:

             *   Upon delivery in person, by courier, or via U.S. Mail or other mail delivery service to the clerk's office during business hours;

             *   When the courtroom deputy clerk accepts it, if the document or item is filed in open court; or

             *   Upon completion of any other manner of filing that the court authorizes. IN R USDCTSD L.R. 5-10(a).

        ii. *Document filing by non-exempt party.* When a party who is not exempt from the electronic filing requirement files a document directly with the clerk, the party must:

             *   Electronically file a notice of manual filing that explains why the document cannot be filed electronically;

             *   Present the document to the clerk within one (1) business day after filing the notice of manual filing; and

             *   Present the clerk with a copy of the notice of manual filing when the party files the document with the clerk. IN R USDCTSD L.R. 5-2(d).

    c. *Electronic filing*

        i.   *Authorization of electronic filing program.* A court may, by local rule, allow papers to be filed, signed, or verified by electronic means that are consistent with any technical standards established by the Judicial Conference of the United States. A local rule may require electronic filing only if reasonable exceptions are allowed. A paper filed electronically in compliance with a local rule is a written paper for purposes of the Federal Rules of Civil Procedure. FRCP 5(d)(3).

             *   IN R USDCTSD L.R. 5-2 requires electronic filing, as allowed by FRCP 5(d)(3). The

policies and procedures in IN R USDCTSD ECF Procedures govern electronic filing in this district unless, due to circumstances in a particular case, a judicial officer determines that these policies and procedures (IN R USDCTSD ECF Procedures) should be modified. IN R USDCTSD ECF Procedures(1).

- Unless modified by order of the Court, all Federal Rules of Civil Procedure and Local Rules of the United States District Court for the Southern District of Indiana shall continue to apply to cases maintained in the Court's Case Management/Electronic Case Filing System (CM/ECF). IN R USDCTSD ECF Procedures(3).

ii. *Mandatory electronic filing.* Unless exempted pursuant to IN R USDCTSD L.R. 5-3(e), attorneys admitted to the court's bar (including those admitted pro hac vice) or authorized to represent the United States must use the court's ECF system to file documents. IN R USDCTSD L.R. 5-3(a). Electronic filing by attorneys is required for eligible documents filed in civil and criminal cases pending with the Court, unless specifically exempted by Local Rule or Court Order. IN R USDCTSD ECF Procedures(4).

  - *Exceptions.* All civil cases (other than those cases the court specifically exempts) must be maintained in the court's electronic case filing (ECF) system. Accordingly, as allowed by FRCP 5(d)(3), every document filed in this court (including exhibits) must be transmitted to the clerk's office via the ECF system consistent with IN R USDCTSD L.R. 5-2 through IN R USDCTSD L.R. 5-11 except: (1) documents filed by pro se litigants; (2) transcripts in cases filed by claimants under the Social Security Act (and related statutes); (3) exhibits in a format that does not readily permit electronic filing (such as videos and large maps and charts); (4) documents that are illegible when scanned into .pdf format; (5) documents filed in cases not maintained on the ECF system; and (6) any other documents that the court or the Local Rules of the United States District Court for the Southern District of Indiana specifically allow to be filed directly with the clerk. IN R USDCTSD L.R. 5-2(a). Parties otherwise participating in the electronic filing system may be excused from filing a particular component electronically under certain limited circumstances, such as when the component cannot be reduced to an electronic format. Such components shall not be filed electronically, but instead shall be manually filed with the Clerk of Court and served upon the parties in accordance with the applicable Federal Rules of Civil Procedure and the Local Rules of the United States District Court for the Southern District of Indiana for filing and service of non-electronic documents. IN R USDCTSD ECF Procedures(15).

  - *Exemption from participation.* The court may exempt attorneys from using the ECF system in a particular case for good cause. An attorney must file a petition for ECF exemption and a CM/ECF technical requirements exemption questionnaire in each case in which the attorney seeks an exemption. (The CM/ECF technical requirements exemption questionnaire is available on the court's website). IN R USDCTSD L.R. 5-3(e).

iii. *Consequences of electronic filing.* Electronic transmission of a document consistent with the procedures adopted by the Court shall, upon the complete receipt of the same by the Clerk of Court, constitute filing of the document for all purposes of the Federal Rules of Civil and Criminal Procedure and the Local Rules of the United States District Court for the Southern District of Indiana, and shall constitute entry of that document onto the docket maintained by the Clerk pursuant to FRCP 58 and FRCP 79. IN R USDCTSD ECF Procedures(7); IN R USDCTSD L.R. 5-4(c)(1). When a document has been filed electronically: the document, as filed, binds the filing party. IN R USDCTSD L.R. 5-4(c)(3).

  - A Notice of Electronic Filing (NEF) acknowledging that the document has been filed will immediately appear on the filer's screen after the document has been submitted. Attorneys are strongly encouraged to print or electronically save a copy of the NEF. Attorneys can also verify the filing of documents by inspecting the Court's electronic docket sheet through the use of a PACER login. IN R USDCTSD ECF Procedures(7). When a document has been filed electronically: the notice of electronic filing for the document serves as the court's date-stamp and proof of filing. IN R USDCTSD L.R. 5-4(c)(4).

  - The Court may, upon the motion of a party or upon its own motion, strike any inappropriately filed document. IN R USDCTSD ECF Procedures(7).

iv. For more information on electronic filing, refer to IN R USDCTSD ECF Procedures.

d. *Fax filing.* The clerk may not file a faxed document without court authorization. The court may not authorize the clerk to file faxed documents without finding that compelling circumstances justify it. A party must submit a copy of the document that otherwise complies with IN R USDCTSD L.R. 5-10 to replace the faxed copy within seven (7) days after faxing the document. IN R USDCTSD L.R. 5-10(e).

2. *Service requirements*

a. *Service; When required*

   i. *In general.* Unless the Federal Rules of Civil Procedure provide otherwise, each of the following papers must be served on every party:

- An order stating that service is required;
- A pleading filed after the original complaint, unless the court orders otherwise under FRCP 5(c) because there are numerous defendants;
- A discovery paper required to be served on a party, unless the court orders otherwise;
- A written motion, except one that may be heard ex parte; and
- A written notice, appearance, demand, or offer of judgment, or any similar paper. FRCP 5(a)(1).

   ii. *If a party fails to appear.* No service is required on a party who is in default for failing to appear. But a pleading that asserts a new claim for relief against such a party must be served on that party under FRCP 4. FRCP 5(a)(2).

   iii. *Seizing property.* If an action is begun by seizing property and no person is or need be named as a defendant, any service required before the filing of an appearance, answer, or claim must be made on the person who had custody or possession of the property when it was seized. FRCP 5(a)(3).

b. *Service; How made*

   i. *Serving an attorney.* If a party is represented by an attorney, service under FRCP 5 must be made on the attorney unless the court orders service on the party. FRCP 5(b)(1).

   ii. *Service in general.* A paper is served under FRCP 5 by:

- Handing it to the person;
- Leaving it: (1) at the person's office with a clerk or other person in charge or, if no one is in charge, in a conspicuous place in the office; or (2) if the person has no office or the office is closed, at the person's dwelling or usual place of abode with someone of suitable age and discretion who resides there;
- Mailing it to the person's last known address—in which event service is complete upon mailing;
- Leaving it with the court clerk if the person has no known address;
- Sending it by electronic means if the person consented in writing—in which event service is complete upon transmission, but is not effective if the serving party learns that it did not reach the person to be served; or
- Delivering it by any other means that the person consented to in writing—in which event service is complete when the person making service delivers it to the agency designated to make delivery. FRCP 5(b)(2).

   iii. *Electronic service*

- *Consent.* By registering to use the ECF system, attorneys consent to electronic service of documents filed in cases maintained on the ECF system. IN R USDCTSD L.R. 5-3(d). By participating in the Electronic Case Filing Program, attorneys consent to the electronic service of documents, and shall make available electronic mail addresses for service. IN R USDCTSD ECF Procedures(11).

- *Service on registered parties.* Upon the filing of a document by a party, an e-mail message will be automatically generated by the electronic filing system and sent via electronic mail to the e-mail addresses of all registered attorneys who have appeared in the case. The Notice of Electronic Filing will contain a document hyperlink which will provide recipients with one "free look" at the electronically filed document. Recipients are encouraged to print and/or save a copy of the document during the "free look" to avoid incurring PACER charges for future viewings of the document. IN R USDCTSD ECF Procedures(11). When a document has been filed electronically: transmission of the notice of electronic filing generated by the ECF system to an attorney's e-mail address constitutes service of the document on that attorney. IN R USDCTSD L.R. 5-4(c)(5). The party effectuates service on all registered attorneys by filing electronically. IN R USDCTSD ECF Procedures(11). When a document has been filed electronically: no other attempted service will constitute electronic service of the document. IN R USDCTSD L.R. 5-4(c)(6).

- *Service on exempt parties.* A filer must serve a copy of the document consistent with FRCP 5 on any party or attorney who is exempt from participating in electronic filing. IN R USDCTSD L.R. 5-4(d). It is the responsibility of the filing attorney to conventionally serve all parties who do not receive electronic service (the identity of these parties will be indicated on the filing receipt generated by the ECF system). IN R USDCTSD ECF Procedures(11).

- *Service on parties excused from electronic filing.* Parties otherwise participating in the electronic filing system may be excused from filing a particular component electronically under certain limited circumstances, such as when the component cannot be reduced to an electronic format. Such components shall not be filed electronically, but instead shall be manually filed with the Clerk of Court and served upon the parties in accordance with the applicable Federal Rules of Civil Procedure and the Local Rules of the United States District Court for the Southern District of Indiana for filing and service of non-electronic documents. IN R USDCTSD ECF Procedures(15).

- *Service of exempt documents.* Any document that is exempt from electronic filing must be filed directly with the clerk and served on other parties in the case as required by those Federal Rules of Civil Procedure and Local Rules of the United States District Court for the Southern District of Indiana that apply to the service of non-electronic documents. IN R USDCTSD L.R. 5-2(c).

iv. *Using court facilities.* If a local rule so authorizes, a party may use the court's transmission facilities to make service under FRCP 5(b)(2)(E). FRCP 5(b)(3).

c. *Serving numerous defendants*

    i. *In general.* If an action involves an unusually large number of defendants, the court may, on motion or on its own, order that:

- Defendants' pleadings and replies to them need not be served on other defendants;

- Any crossclaim, counterclaim, avoidance, or affirmative defense in those pleadings and replies to them will be treated as denied or avoided by all other parties; and

- Filing any such pleading and serving it on the plaintiff constitutes notice of the pleading to all parties. FRCP 5(c)(1).

    ii. *Notifying parties.* A copy of every such order must be served on the parties as the court directs. FRCP 5(c)(2).

G. Hearings

1. *Hearings, generally*

    a. *Oral argument.* Due process does not require that oral argument be permitted on a motion and, except as otherwise provided by local rule, the district court has discretion to determine whether it will decide the motion on the papers or hear argument by counsel (and perhaps receive evidence). FPP § 1190; F.D.I.C. v. Deglau, 207 F.3d 153 (3d Cir. 2000).

       i. *Request for oral argument.* A party may request oral argument by filing a separate motion

explaining why oral argument is necessary and estimating how long the court should allow for the argument. IN R USDCTSD L.R. 7-5(a). Refer to the Documents section of this document for more information.

   ii. *No additional evidence at oral argument.* Parties may not present additional evidence at oral argument. IN R USDCTSD L.R. 7-5(b).

b. *Providing a regular schedule for oral hearings.* A court may establish regular times and places for oral hearings on motions. FRCP 78(a).

c. *Providing for submission on briefs.* By rule or order, the court may provide for submitting and determining motions on briefs, without oral hearings. FRCP 78(b).

d. *Request for evidentiary hearing.* A party may request an evidentiary hearing on a motion or petition by serving and filing a separate motion explaining why the hearing is necessary and estimating how long the court should allow for the hearing. IN R USDCTSD L.R. 7-5(c).

e. *Directed by the court.* The court may: (1) grant or deny a request for oral argument or an evidentiary hearing in its sole discretion; (2) set oral argument or an evidentiary hearing without a request from a party; and (3) order any oral argument or evidentiary hearing to be held anywhere within the district regardless of where the case will be tried. IN R USDCTSD L.R. 7-5(d).

2. *Courtroom and courthouse decorum.* For information on courtroom and courthouse decorum, refer to IN R USDCTSD L.R. 83-3.

H. Forms

1. Federal Motion for Judgment on the Pleadings Forms

a. Motion and notice; For judgment on pleadings. AMJUR PP FEDPRAC § 532.

b. Countermotion and notice; For judgment on pleadings; By defendants. AMJUR PP FEDPRAC § 533.

c. Order; For judgment on pleadings; In favor of plaintiff. AMJUR PP FEDPRAC § 534.

d. Order; For judgment on pleadings; In favor of defendant. AMJUR PP FEDPRAC § 535.

e. Motion for judgment on the pleadings. 2C FEDFORMS § 11:131.

f. Motion for judgment on the pleadings; Alternate wording. 2C FEDFORMS § 11:132.

g. Motion for judgment on the pleadings; Long version. 2C FEDFORMS § 11:133.

h. Motion for judgment on the pleadings; Several grounds. 2C FEDFORMS § 11:134.

i. Notice of motion and motion for judgment on the pleadings. 2C FEDFORMS § 11:135.

j. Notice of motion for judgment on the pleadings (partial) or for partial summary judgment. 2C FEDFORMS § 11:136.

k. Order granting judgment on the pleadings. 2C FEDFORMS § 11:137.

l. Order granting judgment on the pleadings; Motion by plaintiff. 2C FEDFORMS § 11:138.

m. Judgment on the pleadings. 2C FEDFORMS § 11:139.

n. Motion; General form. FEDPROF § 1:746.

o. Notice; Of motion; General form. FEDPROF § 1:747.

p. Notice; Of motion; With costs of motion. FEDPROF § 1:748.

q. Notice; Of motion; Containing motion. FEDPROF § 1:749.

r. Opposition; To motion; General form. FEDPROF § 1:750.

s. Affidavit; Supporting or opposing motion. FEDPROF § 1:751.

t. Brief; Supporting or opposing motion. FEDPROF § 1:752.

u. Statement of points and authorities; Opposing motion. FEDPROF § 1:753.

v. Motion; For judgment on the pleadings. FEDPROF § 1:1295.

w. Order; For judgment on the pleadings; In favor of plaintiff. FEDPROF § 1:1296.

x. Order; For judgment on the pleadings; In favor of defendant. FEDPROF § 1:1297.

y. Motion for judgment on pleadings; Plaintiff. GOLDLTGFMS § 20:38.

z. Motion for judgment on pleadings; Defendant. GOLDLTGFMS § 20:39.

2. Forms for the Southern District of Indiana

a. Notice of endorsement. IN R USDCTSD ECF Procedures(Appendix B).

b. Notice of manual filing. IN R USDCTSD ECF Procedures(Appendix C).

c. Declaration that party was unable to file in a timely manner due to technical difficulties. IN R USDCTSD ECF Procedures(Appendix D).

I. Applicable Rules

1. *Federal rules*

a. Serving and filing pleadings and other papers. FRCP 5.

b. Constitutional challenge to a statute; Notice, certification, and intervention. FRCP 5.1.

c. Privacy protection for filings made with the court. FRCP 5.2.

d. Computing and extending time; Time for motion papers. FRCP 6.

e. Pleadings allowed; Form of motions and other papers. FRCP 7.

f. Disclosure statement. FRCP 7.1.

g. Form of pleadings. FRCP 10.

h. Signing pleadings, motions, and other papers; Representations to the court; Sanctions. FRCP 11.

i. Defenses and objections; When and how presented; Motion for judgment on the pleadings; Consolidating motions; Waiving defenses; Pretrial hearing. FRCP 12.

j. Hearing motions; Submission on briefs. FRCP 78.

2. *Local rules*

a. Scope of the rules. IN R USDCTSD L.R. 1-1.

b. Sanctions for errors as to form. IN R USDCTSD L.R. 1-3.

c. Format of documents presented for filing. IN R USDCTSD L.R. 5-1.

d. Constitutional challenge to a statute; Notice. IN R USDCTSD L.R. 5.1-1.

e. Filing of documents electronically required. IN R USDCTSD L.R. 5-2.

f. Eligibility, registration, passwords for electronic filing; Exemption from electronic filing. IN R USDCTSD L.R. 5-3.

g. Timing and consequences of electronic filing. IN R USDCTSD L.R. 5-4.

h. Attachments and exhibits in cases filed electronically. IN R USDCTSD L.R. 5-6.

i. Signatures in cases filed electronically. IN R USDCTSD L.R. 5-7.

j. Non-electronic filings. IN R USDCTSD L.R. 5-10.

k. Motion practice. [IN R USDCTSD L.R. 7-1, as amended by IN ORDER 16-2319, effective December 1, 2016].

l. Oral arguments and hearings. IN R USDCTSD L.R. 7-5.

m. Request for three-judge court. IN R USDCTSD L.R. 9-2.

n. Assignment of cases. IN R USDCTSD L.R. 40-1.

o. Alternative dispute resolution. IN R USDCTSD A.D.R. Rule 1.1; IN R USDCTSD A.D.R. Rule 1.2; IN R USDCTSD A.D.R. Rule 1.5; IN R USDCTSD A.D.R. Rule 2.1; IN R USDCTSD A.D.R. Rule 2.2.

p.   Instructions for preparing case management plan. IN R USDCTSD Case Mgt.

q.   Electronic case filing policies and procedures manual. IN R USDCTSD ECF Procedures.

Motions, Oppositions and Replies
Motion for More Definite Statement

Document Last Updated December 2016

A. Checklist

(I)   ❑ Matters to be considered by moving party

  (a)   ❑ Required documents

   (1)   ❑ Notice of motion and motion

   (2)   ❑ Brief

   (3)   ❑ Certificate of service

  (b)   ❑ Supplemental documents

   (1)   ❑ Supporting evidence

   (2)   ❑ Notice of constitutional question

   (3)   ❑ Nongovernmental corporate disclosure statement

   (4)   ❑ Index of exhibits

   (5)   ❑ Request for oral argument

   (6)   ❑ Request for evidentiary hearing

   (7)   ❑ Copy of authority

   (8)   ❑ Proposed order

   (9)   ❑ Copy of document with self-address envelope

   (10)   ❑ Notice of manual filing

   (11)   ❑ Courtesy copies

   (12)   ❑ Copies for three-judge court

   (13)   ❑ Declaration that party was unable to file in a timely manner due to technical difficulties

  (c)   ❑ Timing

   (1)   ❑ The motion must be made before filing a responsive pleading

   (2)   ❑ A written motion and notice of the hearing must be served at least fourteen (14) days before the time specified for the hearing, with the following exceptions: (i) when the motion may be heard ex parte; (ii) when the Federal Rules of Civil Procedure set a different time; or (iii) when a court order—which a party may, for good cause, apply for ex parte—sets a different time

   (3)   ❑ Any affidavit supporting a motion must be served with the motion

   (4)   ❑ When a party who is not exempt from the electronic filing requirement files a document directly with the clerk, the party must present the document to the clerk within one (1) business day after filing the notice of manual filing

   (5)   ❑ Unless the court orders otherwise, the [untimely] document and declaration [that party was unable to file in a timely manner due to technical difficulties] must be filed no later than 12:00 noon of the first day on which the court is open for business following the original filing deadline

(II) ❏ Matters to be considered by opposing party

    (a) ❏ Required documents

        (1) ❏ Response brief

        (2) ❏ Certificate of service

    (b) ❏ Supplemental documents

        (1) ❏ Supporting evidence

        (2) ❏ Notice of constitutional question

        (3) ❏ Index of exhibits

        (4) ❏ Request for oral argument

        (5) ❏ Request for evidentiary hearing

        (6) ❏ Copy of authority

        (7) ❏ Copy of document with self-address envelope

        (8) ❏ Notice of manual filing

        (9) ❏ Courtesy copies

        (10) ❏ Copies for three-judge court

        (11) ❏ Declaration that party was unable to file in a timely manner due to technical difficulties

    (c) ❏ Timing

        (1) ❏ Any response is due within fourteen (14) days after service of the motion

        (2) ❏ Except as FRCP 59(c) provides otherwise, any opposing affidavit must be served at least seven (7) days before the hearing, unless the court permits service at another time

        (3) ❏ When a party who is not exempt from the electronic filing requirement files a document directly with the clerk, the party must present the document to the clerk within one (1) business day after filing the notice of manual filing

        (4) ❏ Unless the court orders otherwise, the [untimely] document and declaration [that party was unable to file in a timely manner due to technical difficulties] must be filed no later than 12:00 noon of the first day on which the court is open for business following the original filing deadline

B. Timing

1. *Motion for more definite statement.* The motion must be made before filing a responsive pleading. FRCP 12(e). Thus, a motion for a more definite statement must be made before an answer. FEDPROC § 62:386. In several situations, however, the time for moving under FRCP 12(e) is extended well beyond the usual twenty (20) day period for serving a responsive pleading set out in FRCP 12(a). FPP § 1378.

2. *Timing of motions, generally*

    a. *Motion and notice of hearing.* A written motion and notice of the hearing must be served at least fourteen (14) days before the time specified for the hearing, with the following exceptions:

        i. When the motion may be heard ex parte;

        ii. When the Federal Rules of Civil Procedure set a different time; or

        iii. When a court order—which a party may, for good cause, apply for ex parte—sets a different time. FRCP 6(c)(1).

    b. *Supporting affidavit.* Any affidavit supporting a motion must be served with the motion. FRCP 6(c)(2).

3. *Timing of opposing papers.* Any response is due within fourteen (14) days after service of the motion. IN R USDCTSD L.R. 7-1(c)(2)(A).

    a. *Opposing affidavit.* Except as FRCP 59(c) provides otherwise, any opposing affidavit must be served at least seven (7) days before the hearing, unless the court permits service at another time. FRCP 6(c)(2).

    b.   *Extensions.* The court may extend response and reply deadlines, but only for good cause. IN R USDCTSD L.R. 7-1(c)(3).

    c.   *Summary ruling on failure to respond.* The court may summarily rule on a motion if an opposing party does not file a response within the deadline. IN R USDCTSD L.R. 7-1(c)(4).

4.   *Timing of reply papers.* Where the respondent files an answering affidavit setting up a new matter, the moving party ordinarily is allowed a reasonable time to file a reply affidavit since failure to deny the new matter by affidavit may operate as an admission of its truth. AMJUR MOTIONS § 25.

    a.   *Reply brief.* Any reply is due within seven (7) days after service of the response. IN R USDCTSD L.R. 7-1(c)(2)(B).

    b.   *Extensions.* The court may extend response and reply deadlines, but only for good cause. IN R USDCTSD L.R. 7-1(c)(3).

5.   *Effect of a FRCP 12 motion on the time to serve a responsive pleading.* Unless the court sets a different time, serving a motion under FRCP 12 alters the periods in FRCP 12(a) as follows:

    a.   If the court denies the motion or postpones its disposition until trial, the responsive pleading must be served within fourteen (14) days after notice of the court's action; or

    b.   If the court grants a motion for a more definite statement, the responsive pleading must be served within fourteen (14) days after the more definite statement is served. FRCP 12(a)(4).

6.   *Document filing by non-exempt party.* When a party who is not exempt from the electronic filing requirement files a document directly with the clerk, the party must: present the document to the clerk within one (1) business day after filing the notice of manual filing. IN R USDCTSD L.R. 5-2(d)(2).

7.   *Declaration that party was unable to file in a timely manner due to technical difficulties.* Unless the Court orders otherwise, the [untimely] document and declaration [that party was unable to file in a timely manner due to technical difficulties] must be filed no later than 12:00 noon of the first day on which the Court is open for business following the original filing deadline. IN R USDCTSD ECF Procedures(16).

8.   *Computation of time*

    a.   *Computing time.* FRCP 6 applies in computing any time period specified in the Federal Rules of Civil Procedure, in any local rule or court order, or in any statute that does not specify a method of computing time. FRCP 6(a).

        i.   *Period stated in days or a longer unit.* When the period is stated in days or a longer unit of time:

- Exclude the day of the event that triggers the period;
- Count every day, including intermediate Saturdays, Sundays, and legal holidays; and
- Include the last day of the period, but if the last day is a Saturday, Sunday, or legal holiday, the period continues to run until the end of the next day that is not a Saturday, Sunday, or legal holiday. FRCP 6(a)(1).

        ii.   *Period stated in hours.* When the period is stated in hours:

- Begin counting immediately on the occurrence of the event that triggers the period;
- Count every hour, including hours during intermediate Saturdays, Sundays, and legal holidays; and
- If the period would end on a Saturday, Sunday, or legal holiday, the period continues to run until the same time on the next day that is not a Saturday, Sunday, or legal holiday. FRCP 6(a)(2).

        iii.   *Inaccessibility of the clerk's office.* Unless the court orders otherwise, if the clerk's office is inaccessible:

- On the last day for filing under FRCP 6(a)(1), then the time for filing is extended to the first accessible day that is not a Saturday, Sunday, or legal holiday; or

- During the last hour for filing under FRCP 6(a)(2), then the time for filing is extended to the same time on the first accessible day that is not a Saturday, Sunday, or legal holiday. FRCP 6(a)(3).

iv. *"Last day" defined.* Unless a different time is set by a statute, local rule, or court order, the last day ends:

- For electronic filing, at midnight in the court's time zone; and

- For filing by other means, when the clerk's office is scheduled to close. FRCP 6(a)(4).

v. *"Next day" defined.* The "next day" is determined by continuing to count forward when the period is measured after an event and backward when measured before an event. FRCP 6(a)(5).

vi. *"Legal holiday" defined.* "Legal holiday" means:

- The day set aside by statute for observing New Year's Day, Martin Luther King Jr.'s Birthday, Washington's Birthday, Memorial Day, Independence Day, Labor Day, Columbus Day, Veterans' Day, Thanksgiving Day, or Christmas Day;

- Any day declared a holiday by the President or Congress; and

- For periods that are measured after an event, any other day declared a holiday by the state where the district court is located. FRCP 6(a)(6).

b. *Computation of electronic filing deadlines.* Filing documents electronically does not alter filing deadlines. IN R USDCTSD ECF Procedures(7). A document due on a particular day must be filed before midnight local time of the division where the case is pending. IN R USDCTSD L.R. 5-4(a). All electronic transmissions of documents must be completed (i.e. received completely by the Clerk's Office) prior to midnight of the local time of the division in which the case is pending in order to be considered timely filed that day (NOTE: time will be noted in Eastern Time on the Court's docket. If you have filed a document prior to midnight local time of the division in which the case is pending and the document is due that date, but the electronic receipt and docket reflect the following calendar day, please contact the Court). IN R USDCTSD ECF Procedures(7). Although attorneys may file documents electronically twenty-four (24) hours a day, seven (7) days a week, attorneys are encouraged to file all documents during the normal working hours of the Clerk's Office (Monday through Friday, 8:30 a.m. to 4:30 p.m.) when technical support is available. IN R USDCTSD ECF Procedures(7); IN R USDCTSD ECF Procedures(9).

i. *Technical difficulties.* Parties are encouraged to file documents electronically during normal business hours, in case a problem is encountered. In the event a technical failure occurs and a document cannot be filed electronically despite the best efforts of the filing party, the party should print (if possible) a copy of the error message received. In addition, as soon as practically possible, the party should file a "Declaration that Party was Unable to File in a Timely Manner Due to Technical Difficulties." A model form is provided as Appendix D (IN R USDCTSD ECF Procedures(Appendix D)). IN R USDCTSD ECF Procedures(16).

- If a party is unable to file electronically and, as a result, may miss a filing deadline, the party must contact the Clerk's Office at the number listed in IN R USDCTSD ECF Procedures(15) to inform the court's staff of the difficulty. If a party misses a filing deadline due to an inability to file electronically, the party may submit the untimely filed document, accompanied by a declaration stating the reason(s) for missing the deadline. Unless the Court orders otherwise, the document and declaration must be filed no later than 12:00 noon of the first day on which the Court is open for business following the original filing deadline. IN R USDCTSD ECF Procedures(16).

c. *Extending time*

i. *In general.* When an act may or must be done within a specified time, the court may, for good cause, extend the time:

- With or without motion or notice if the court acts, or if a request is made, before the original time or its extension expires; or

- On motion made after the time has expired if the party failed to act because of excusable neglect. FRCP 6(b)(1).

ii. *Exceptions.* A court must not extend the time to act under FRCP 50(b), FRCP 50(d), FRCP 52(b), FRCP 59(b), FRCP 59(d), FRCP 59(e), and FRCP 60(b). FRCP 6(b)(2).

iii. Refer to the United States District Court for the Southern District of Indiana KeyRules Motion for Continuance/Extension of Time document for more information on extending time.

d. *Additional time after certain kinds of service.* When a party may or must act within a specified time after being served and service is made under FRCP 5(b)(2)(C) (mail), FRCP 5(b)(2)(D) (leaving with the clerk), or FRCP 5(b)(2)(F) (other means consented to), three (3) days are added after the period would otherwise expire under FRCP 6(a). FRCP 6(d). Service by electronic mail shall constitute service pursuant to FRCP 5(b)(2)(E) and shall entitle the party being served to the additional three (3) days provided by FRCP 6(d). IN R USDCTSD ECF Procedures(11).

C. General Requirements

1. *Motions, generally*

   a. *Requirements.* A request for a court order must be made by motion. The motion must:

      i. Be in writing unless made during a hearing or trial;

      ii. State with particularity the grounds for seeking the order; and

      iii. State the relief sought. FRCP 7(b)(1).

   b. *Notice of motion.* A party interested in resisting the relief sought by a motion has a right to notice thereof, and an opportunity to be heard. AMJUR MOTIONS § 12.

      i. In addition to statutory or court rule provisions requiring notice of a motion—the purpose of such a notice requirement having been said to be to prevent a party from being prejudicially surprised by a motion—principles of natural justice dictate that an adverse party generally must be given notice that a motion will be presented to the court. AMJUR MOTIONS § 12.

      ii. "Notice," in this regard, means reasonable notice, including a meaningful opportunity to prepare and to defend against allegations of a motion. AMJUR MOTIONS § 12.

   c. *Writing requirement.* The writing requirement is intended to insure that the adverse parties are informed and have a record of both the motion's pendency and the grounds on which the movant seeks an order. FPP § 1191; Feldberg v. Quechee Lakes Corp., 463 F.3d 195 (2d Cir. 2006).

      i. It is sufficient "if the motion is stated in a written notice of the hearing of the motion." FPP § 1191.

   d. *Particularity requirement.* The particularity requirement insures that the opposing parties will have notice of their opponent's contentions. FEDPROC § 62:364; Goodman v. 1973 26 Foot Trojan Vessel, Arkansas Registration No. AR1439SN, 859 F.2d 71, 12 Fed.R.Serv.3d 645 (8th Cir. 1988). That requirement ensures that notice of the basis for the motion is provided to the court and to the opposing party so as to avoid prejudice, provide the opponent with a meaningful opportunity to respond, and provide the court with enough information to process the motion correctly. FEDPROC § 62:364; Andreas v. Volkswagen of America, Inc., 336 F.3d 789, 56 Fed.R.Serv.3d 6 (8th Cir. 2003).

      i. Reasonable specification of the grounds for a motion is sufficient. However, where a movant fails to state even one ground for granting the motion in question, the movant has failed to meet the minimal standard of "reasonable specification." FEDPROC § 62:364; Martinez v. Trainor, 556 F.2d 818, 23 Fed.R.Serv.2d 403 (7th Cir. 1977).

      ii. The court may excuse the failure to comply with the particularity requirement if it is inadvertent, and where no prejudice is shown by the opposing party. FEDPROC § 62:364.

   e. *Motions must be filed separately.* Motions must be filed separately, but alternative motions may be filed in a single document if each is named in the title. A motion must not be contained within a brief, response, or reply to a previously filed motion, unless ordered by the court. IN R USDCTSD L.R. 7-1(a).

   f. *Routine or uncontested motions.* The court may rule upon a routine or uncontested motion before the response deadline passes, unless: (1) the motion indicates that an opposing party objects to it; or (2) the court otherwise believes that a response will be filed. IN R USDCTSD L.R. 7-1(d).

2. *Informal conference to resolve disputes involving non-dispositive issues.* In addition to those conferences required by IN R USDCTSD L.R. 37-1, counsel are encouraged to hold informal conferences in person or by phone to resolve any disputes involving non-dispositive issues that may otherwise require submission of a motion to the Court. This requirement does not apply to cases involving pro se parties. Therefore, prior to filing any non-dispositive motion (including motions for extension of time), the moving party must contact opposing counsel to determine whether there is an objection to any non-dispositive motion (including motions for extension of time), and state in the motion whether opposing counsel objects to the motion. IN R USDCTSD Case Mgt(General Instructions For All Cases). Refer to the Documents section of this document for more information on the contents of the motion.

3. *Motion for more definite statement.* A party may move for a more definite statement of a pleading to which a responsive pleading is allowed but which is so vague or ambiguous that the party cannot reasonably prepare a response. FRCP 12(e). A motion for a more definite statement under FRCP 12(e) is inappropriate where a responsive pleading is not required or permitted. FEDPROC § 62:385.

   a. *Contents.* The motion must be made before filing a responsive pleading and must point out the defects complained of and the details desired. FRCP 12(e). A motion for a more definite statement must point out the defects complained of and the details desired, should offer discussion or legal analysis in support of the FRCP 12(e) claim, and will be denied where the motion fails to satisfy this requirement. FEDPROC § 62:387.

      i. Regardless of whether the plaintiff or the defendant moves under FRCP 12(e), she must identify the deficiencies in the pleading believed to be objectionable, point out the details she desires to have pleaded in a more intelligible form, and assert her inability to prepare a responsive pleading. These requirements are designed to enable the district judge to test the propriety of the motion and formulate an appropriate order in the light of its limited purpose of enabling the framing of a responsive pleading. FPP § 1378.

      ii. Since FRCP 12(e) must be construed in light of the federal rules relating to liberal pleading, a motion for a more definite statement need not particularize the requested information in great detail and should not request an excessive amount of information. Indeed, if the movant does ask for too much, his motion may be denied on the ground that evidentiary matter is being sought. FPP § 1378.

   b. *Burden.* Most federal courts cast the burden of establishing the need for a more definite statement on the movant. Whether he will succeed in discharging that burden depends on such factors as the availability of information from other sources that may clear up the pleading for the movant and a coparty's ability to answer. FPP § 1378.

   c. *Motion disfavored.* Motions for a more definite statement are not favored by the courts, and thus, are rarely granted, since pleadings in the federal courts are only required to fairly notify the opposing party of the nature of the claim, and since there are ample provisions for discovery under FRCP 26 to FRCP 37 as well as for pretrial procedure under FRCP 16. Generally, motions for more definite statement are disfavored because of their dilatory effect, and the preferred course is to encourage the use of discovery procedures to apprise the parties of the factual basis of the claims made in the pleadings. FEDPROC § 62:388.

      i. *Discretion of court.* A motion for a more definite statement pursuant to FRCP 12(e) is addressed to the discretion of the court. Whether the motion should be granted or denied depends primarily on the facts of each individual case. FEDPROC § 62:388.

   d. *Joining motions*

      i. *Right to join.* A motion under FRCP 12 may be joined with any other motion allowed by FRCP 12. FRCP 12(g)(1).

      ii. *Limitation on further motions.* Except as provided in FRCP 12(h)(2) or FRCP 12(h)(3), a party that makes a motion under FRCP 12 must not make another motion under FRCP 12 raising a defense or objection that was available to the party but omitted from its earlier motion. FRCP 12(g)(2).

         • If the movant legitimately is unable to assert his other defenses at the time a motion is made under FRCP 12(e), the movant will not be penalized when he actually does interpose a second motion. FPP § 1378.

e. *Waiving and preserving certain defenses.* No defense or objection is waived by joining it with one or more other defenses or objections in a responsive pleading or in a motion. FRCP 12(b).

  i. *Waiver by consent or stipulation.* A valid consent or a stipulation that the court has jurisdiction prevents the successful assertion of a FRCP 12(b)(2) defense. FPP § 1351.

  ii. *Waiver by filing permissive counterclaim.* A defendant may be deemed to have waived an objection to personal jurisdiction if he or she files a permissive counterclaim under FRCP 13(b). FPP § 1351.

  iii. *When some are waived.* A party waives any defense listed in FRCP 12(b)(2) through FRCP 12(b)(5) by:

   • Omitting it from a motion in the circumstances described in FRCP 12(g)(2); or

   • Failing to either: (1) make it by motion under FRCP 12; or (2) include it in a responsive pleading or in an amendment allowed by FRCP 15(a)(1) as a matter of course. FRCP 12(h)(1).

  iv. *When to raise others.* Failure to state a claim upon which relief can be granted, to join a person required by FRCP 19(b), or to state a legal defense to a claim may be raised:

   • In any pleading allowed or ordered under FRCP 7(a);

   • By a motion under FRCP 12(c); or

   • At trial. FRCP 12(h)(2).

  v. *Lack of subject matter jurisdiction.* If the court determines at any time that it lacks subject-matter jurisdiction, the court must dismiss the action. FRCP 12(h)(3).

f. *General standard for granting motion.* The general standard for granting a motion for a more definite statement is set forth in FRCP 12(e) itself, which provides that a party may move for a more definite statement if a pleading to which a responsive pleading is allowed is so vague or ambiguous that the party cannot reasonably prepare a response. The clear trend of judicial decisions is to deny motions for a more definite statement unless the complaint is so excessively vague and ambiguous as to prejudice the defendant seriously in attempting to answer it. The burden is on the movant to demonstrate that the complaint is so vague or ambiguous that they cannot respond, even with a simple denial, in good faith or without prejudice to himself or herself. FEDPROC § 62:389.

g. *Compliance and enforcement of order.* If the court orders a more definite statement and the order is not obeyed within fourteen (14) days after notice of the order or within the time the court sets, the court may strike the pleading or issue any other appropriate order. FRCP 12(e).

4. *Opposing papers.* The Federal Rules of Civil Procedure do not require any formal answer, return, or reply to a motion, except where the Federal Rules of Civil Procedure or local rules may require affidavits, memoranda, or other papers to be filed in opposition to a motion. Such papers are simply to apprise the court of such opposition and the grounds of that opposition. FEDPROC § 62:359.

a. *Effect of failure to respond to motion.* Although in the absence of statutory provision or court rule, a motion ordinarily does not require a written answer, when a party files a motion and the opposing party fails to respond, the court may construe such failure to respond as nonopposition to the motion or an admission that the motion was meritorious, may take the facts alleged in the motion as true—the rule in some jurisdictions being that the failure to respond to a fact set forth in a motion is deemed an admission—and may grant the motion if the relief requested appears to be justified. AMJUR MOTIONS § 28.

b. *Assent or no opposition not determinative.* However, a motion will not be granted automatically simply because an "assent" or a notation of "no opposition" has been filed; federal judges frequently deny motions that have been assented to when it is thought that justice so dictates. FPP § 1190.

c. *Responsive pleading inappropriate as response to motion.* An attempt to answer or oppose a motion with a responsive pleading usually is not appropriate. FPP § 1190.

5. *Reply papers.* A moving party may be required or permitted to prepare papers in addition to his original motion papers. AMJUR MOTIONS § 25. Papers answering or replying to opposing papers may be appropriate, in the interests of justice, where it appears there is a substantial reason for allowing a reply. Thus, a court may accept reply papers where a party demonstrates that the papers to which it seeks to file a reply raise new issues that are material to the disposition of the question before the court, or where the court determines, sua sponte, that it wishes further briefing of an issue raised in those papers and orders the submission of additional papers. FEDPROC § 62:360.

   a. *Function of reply papers.* The function of a reply affidavit is to answer the arguments made in opposition to the position taken by the movant and not to permit the movant to introduce new arguments in support of the motion. AMJUR MOTIONS § 25.

   b. *Issues raised for the first time in a reply document.* However, the view has been followed in some jurisdictions, that as a matter of judicial economy, where there is no prejudice and where the issues could be raised simply by filing a motion to dismiss, the trial court has discretion to consider arguments raised for the first time in a reply memorandum, and that a trial court may grant a motion to strike issues raised for the first time in a reply memorandum. AMJUR MOTIONS § 26.

6. *Appearances.* Every attorney who represents a party or who files a document on a party's behalf must file an appearance for that party. IN R USDCTSD L.R. 83-7. The filing of a Notice of Appearance shall act to establish the filing attorney as an attorney of record representing a designated party or parties in a particular cause of action. As a result, it is necessary for each attorney to file a separate Notice of Appearance when entering an appearance in a case. A joint appearance on behalf of multiple attorneys may be filed electronically only if it is filed separately for each attorney, using his/her ECF login. IN R USDCTSD ECF Procedures(12). Only those attorneys who have filed an appearance in a pending action are entitled to be served with case documents under FRCP 5(a). IN R USDCTSD L.R. 83-7. For more information, refer to IN R USDCTSD L.R. 83-7 and IN R USDCTSD ECF Procedures(12).

7. *Notice of related action.* A party must file a notice of related action: as soon as it appears that the party's case and another pending case: (1) arise out of the same transaction or occurrence; (2) involve the same property; or (3) involve the validity or infringement or the same patent, trademark, or copyright. IN R USDCTSD L.R. 40-1(d)(2). For more information, refer to IN R USDCTSD L.R. 40-1.

8. *Alternative dispute resolution (ADR)*

   a. *Application.* Unless limited by specific provisions, or unless there are other applicable specific statutory, common law, or constitutional procedures, the Local Alternative Dispute Resolution Rules of the United States District Court for the Southern District of Indiana shall apply in all civil litigation filed in the U.S. District Court for the Southern District of Indiana, except in the following cases and proceedings:

      i. Applications for writs of habeas corpus under 28 U.S.C.A. § 2254;

      ii. Forfeiture cases;

      iii. Non-adversary proceedings in bankruptcy;

      iv. Social Security administrative review cases; and

      v. Such other matters as specified by order of the Court; for example, matters involving important public policy issues, constitutional law, or the establishment of new law. IN R USDCTSD A.D.R. Rule 1.2.

   b. *Mediation.* Mediation under this section (IN R USDCTSD A.D.R. Rule 2.1, et seq.) involves the confidential process by which a person acting as a Mediator, selected by the parties or appointed by the Court, assists the litigants in reaching a mutually acceptable agreement. It is an informal and nonadversarial process. The role of the Mediator is to assist in identifying the issues, reducing misunderstandings, clarifying priorities, exploring areas of compromise, and finding points of agreement as well as legitimate points of disagreement. Final decision-making authority rests with the parties, not the Mediator. IN R USDCTSD A.D.R. Rule 2.1. It is anticipated that an agreement may not resolve all of the disputed issues, but the process, nonetheless, can reduce points of contention. Parties and their representatives are required to mediate in good faith, but are not compelled to reach an agreement. IN R USDCTSD A.D.R. Rule 2.1.

      i. *Case selection.* The Court with the agreement of the parties may refer a civil case for mediation.

Unless otherwise ordered or as specifically provided in IN R USDCTSD A.D.R. Rule 2.8, referral to mediation does not abate or suspend the action, and no scheduled dates shall be delayed or deferred, including the date of trial. IN R USDCTSD A.D.R. Rule 2.2.

    ii.   For more information on mediation, refer to IN R USDCTSD A.D.R. Rule 2.1, et seq.

  c. *Other methods of dispute resolution.* The Local Alternative Dispute Resolution Rules of the United States District Court for the Southern District of Indiana shall not preclude the parties from utilizing any other reasonable method or technique of alternative dispute resolution to resolve disputes to which the parties agree. However, any use of arbitration by the parties will be governed by and comply with the requirements of 28 U.S.C.A. § 654 through 28 U.S.C.A. § 657. IN R USDCTSD A.D.R. Rule 1.5.

  d. For more information on alternative dispute resolution (ADR), refer to IN R USDCTSD A.D.R. Rule 1.1, et seq.

9. *Notice of settlement or resolution.* The parties must immediately notify the court if they reasonably anticipate settling their case or resolving a pending motion. IN R USDCTSD L.R. 7-1(h).

10. *Modification or suspension of rules.* The court may, on its own motion or at the request of a party, suspend or modify any rule in a particular case in the interest of justice. IN R USDCTSD L.R. 1-1(c).

D. Documents

1. *Documents for moving party*

  a. *Required documents*

    i.   *Notice of motion and motion.* [P]rior to filing any non-dispositive motion (including motions for extension of time), the moving party must contact opposing counsel to determine whether there is an objection to any non-dispositive motion (including motions for extension of time), and state in the motion whether opposing counsel objects to the motion. If an objection cannot be resolved by counsel, the opposing counsel's position shall be stated within the motion. The motion should also indicate whether opposing counsel plans to file a written objection to the motion and the date by which the Court can expect to receive the objection (within the time limits set in IN R USDCTSD L.R. 7-1). If after a reasonable effort, opposing counsel cannot be reached, the moving party shall recite in the motion the dates and times that messages were left for opposing counsel. IN R USDCTSD Case Mgt(General Instructions For All Cases). Refer to the General Requirements section of this document for information on the notice of motion and motion.

    ii. *Brief.* The following motion must also be accompanied by a supporting brief: for more definite statement under FRCP 12. IN R USDCTSD L.R. 7-1(b)(1). Refer to the Format section of this document for the format of briefs.

    iii. *Certificate of service.* FRCP 5(d) requires that the person making service under FRCP 5 certify that service has been effected. FRCP 5(Advisory Committee Notes). Having such information on file may be useful for many purposes, including proof of service if an issue arises concerning the effectiveness of the service. FRCP 5(Advisory Committee Notes).

      • *Certificate of service for electronically-filed documents.* A certificate of service must be included with all documents filed electronically. Such certificate shall indicate that service was accomplished pursuant to the Court's electronic filing procedures. IN R USDCTSD ECF Procedures(11). For the suggested format for a certificate of service for electronic filing, refer to IN R USDCTSD ECF Procedures(11).

  b. *Supplemental documents*

    i.   *Supporting evidence.* When a motion relies on facts outside the record, the court may hear the matter on affidavits or may hear it wholly or partly on oral testimony or on depositions. FRCP 43(c).

      • *Materials necessary for motion.* A party seeking relief under FRCP 26(c) or FRCP 37, or by way of a pretrial motion that could result in a final order on an issue, must file with the motion those parts of the discovery materials relevant to the motion. IN R USDCTSD L.R. 26-2(a).

- *Supporting affidavit(s).* Good practice for a party seeking relief under FRCP 12(e) is to support the motion by an affidavit showing the necessity for a more definite statement. FEDPROC § 62:387. Courts differ in their attitude toward the use of affidavits on a FRCP 12(e) motion. Some insist on affidavits delineating the ways in which the pleading should be made more definite; others feel that affidavits would be helpful but do not insist upon them; and a few courts, usually when a more definite statement obviously is appropriate, do not seem to require supporting affidavits. FPP § 1378.

ii. *Notice of constitutional question.* A party that files a pleading, written motion, or other paper drawing into question the constitutionality of a federal or state statute must promptly:

- *File notice.* File a notice of constitutional question stating the question and identifying the paper that raises it, if: (1) a federal statute is questioned and the parties do not include the United States, one of its agencies, or one of its officers or employees in an official capacity; or (2) a state statute is questioned and the parties do not include the state, one of its agencies, or one of its officers or employees in an official capacity; and

- *Serve notice.* Serve the notice and paper on the Attorney General of the United States if a federal statute is questioned—or on the state attorney general if a state statute is questioned—either by certified or registered mail or by sending it to an electronic address designated by the attorney general for this purpose. FRCP 5.1(a).

- *Time for filing.* A notice of constitutional challenge to a statute filed in accordance with FRCP 5.1 must be filed at the same time the parties tender their proposed case management plan, if one is required, or within twenty-one (21) days of the filing drawing into question the constitutionality of a federal or state statute, whichever occurs later. IN R USDCTSD L.R. 5.1-1(a).

- *Additional service requirements.* If a federal statute is challenged, in addition to the service requirements of FRCP 5.1(a), the party filing the notice of constitutional challenge must serve the notice and documents on the United States Attorney for the Southern District of Indiana, either by certified or registered mail or by sending it to an electronic address designated for that purpose by that official. IN R USDCTSD L.R. 5.1-1(b).

- *No forfeiture.* A party's failure to file and serve the notice, or the court's failure to certify, does not forfeit a constitutional claim or defense that is otherwise timely asserted. FRCP 5.1(d).

iii. *Nongovernmental corporate disclosure statement*

- *Contents.* A nongovernmental corporate party must file two (2) copies of a disclosure statement that: (1) identifies any parent corporation and any publicly held corporation owning ten percent (10%) or more of its stock; or (2) states that there is no such corporation. FRCP 7.1(a).

- *Time to file; Supplemental filing.* A party must: (1) file the disclosure statement with its first appearance, pleading, petition, motion, response, or other request addressed to the court; and (2) promptly file a supplemental statement if any required information changes. FRCP 7.1(b).

iv. *Index of exhibits.* Any pleading, motion, brief, affidavit, notice, or proposed order filed with the court, whether electronically or with the clerk, must: if it has four (4) or more exhibits, include a separate index that identifies and briefly describes each exhibit. IN R USDCTSD L.R. 5-1(b).

v. *Request for oral argument.* A party may request oral argument by filing a separate motion explaining why oral argument is necessary and estimating how long the court should allow for the argument. The request must be filed and served with the supporting brief, response brief, or reply brief. IN R USDCTSD L.R. 7-5(a).

vi. *Request for evidentiary hearing.* A party may request an evidentiary hearing on a motion or petition by serving and filing a separate motion explaining why the hearing is necessary and estimating how long the court should allow for the hearing. IN R USDCTSD L.R. 7-5(c).

vii. *Copy of authority.* Generally, copies of cited authorities may not be attached to court filings.

However, a party must attach to the party's motion or brief a copy of any cited authority if it is not available on Westlaw or Lexis. Upon request, a party must provide copies of any cited authority that is only available through electronic means to the court or the other parties. IN R USDCTSD L.R. 7-1(f).

viii. *Proposed order.* A party must include a suitable form of order with any document that requests the judge or the clerk to enter a routine or uncontested order. IN R USDCTSD L.R. 5-5(b); IN R USDCTSD L.R. 5-10(c); IN R USDCTSD L.R. 7-1(d).

- A service statement and/or list must be included on each proposed order, as required by IN R USDCTSD L.R. 5-5(d). IN R USDCTSD ECF Procedures(11). Any pleading, motion, brief, affidavit, notice, or proposed order filed with the court, whether electronically or with the clerk, must: if it is a form of order, include a statement of service, in the format required by IN R USDCTSD L.R. 5-5(d) in the lower left corner of the document. IN R USDCTSD L.R. 5-1(b).

- A party electronically filing a proposed order—whether voluntarily or because required by IN R USDCTSD L.R. 5-5—must convert the order directly from a word processing program and file it as an attachment to the document it relates to. Proposed orders must include in the lower left-hand corner of the signature page a statement that service will be made electronically on all ECF-registered counsel of record via email generated by the court's ECF system, without listing all such counsel. A service list including the name and postal address of any pro se litigant or non-registered attorney of record must follow, stating that service on the listed individuals will be made in the traditional paper manner, via first-class U.S. Mail. IN R USDCTSD L.R. 5-5(d).

ix. *Copy of document with self-address envelope.* To receive a file-stamped copy of a document filed directly with the clerk, a party must include with the original document an additional copy and a self-addressed envelope. The envelope must be big enough to hold the copy and have enough postage on it to send the copy via regular first-class mail. IN R USDCTSD L.R. 5-10(b).

x. *Notice of manual filing.* When a party who is not exempt from the electronic filing requirement files a document directly with the clerk, the party must: electronically file a notice of manual filing that explains why the document cannot be filed electronically. IN R USDCTSD L.R. 5-2(d)(1). Refer to the Filing and Service Requirements section of this document for more information.

- Where an individual component cannot be included in an electronic filing (e.g. the component cannot be converted to electronic format), the filer shall electronically file the prescribed Notice of Manual Filing in place of that component. A model form is provided as Appendix C (IN R USDCTSD ECF Procedures(Appendix C)). IN R USDCTSD ECF Procedures(13).

- Before making a manual filing of a component, the filing party shall first electronically file a Notice of Manual Filing (See IN R USDCTSD ECF Procedures(Appendix C)). The filer shall initiate the electronic filing process as if filing the actual component but shall instead attach to the filing the Notice of Manual Filing setting forth the reason(s) why the component cannot be filed electronically. The manual filing should be accompanied by a copy of the previously filed Notice of Manual Filing. A party may seek to have a component excluded from electronic filing pursuant to applicable Federal and Local Rules (e.g., FRCP 26(c)). IN R USDCTSD ECF Procedures(15).

xi. *Courtesy copies.* District Judges and Magistrate Judges regularly receive documents filed by all parties. Therefore, parties shall not bring "courtesy copies" to any chambers unless specifically directed to do so by the Court. IN R USDCTSD Case Mgt(General Instructions For All Cases).

xii. *Copies for three-judge court.* Parties in a case where a three-judge court has been requested must file an original and three copies of any document filed directly with the clerk (instead of electronically) until the court: (1) denies the request; (2) dissolves the three-judge court; or (3) allows the parties to file fewer copies. IN R USDCTSD L.R. 9-2(c).

xiii. *Declaration that party was unable to file in a timely manner due to technical difficulties.* If a party misses a filing deadline due to an inability to file electronically, the party may submit the untimely filed document, accompanied by a declaration stating the reason(s) for missing the deadline. IN R USDCTSD ECF Procedures(16). A model form is provided as Appendix D (IN R USDCTSD ECF Procedures(Appendix D)). IN R USDCTSD ECF Procedures(16).

2. *Documents for opposing party*

   a. *Required documents*

      i. *Response brief.* Refer to the Format section of this document for the format of briefs. Refer to the General Requirements section of this document for information on the opposing papers.

      ii. *Certificate of service.* FRCP 5(d) requires that the person making service under FRCP 5 certify that service has been effected. FRCP 5(Advisory Committee Notes). Having such information on file may be useful for many purposes, including proof of service if an issue arises concerning the effectiveness of the service. FRCP 5(Advisory Committee Notes).

         • *Certificate of service for electronically-filed documents.* A certificate of service must be included with all documents filed electronically. Such certificate shall indicate that service was accomplished pursuant to the Court's electronic filing procedures. IN R USDCTSD ECF Procedures(11). For the suggested format for a certificate of service for electronic filing, refer to IN R USDCTSD ECF Procedures(11).

   b. *Supplemental documents*

      i. *Supporting evidence.* When a motion relies on facts outside the record, the court may hear the matter on affidavits or may hear it wholly or partly on oral testimony or on depositions. FRCP 43(c).

         • *Materials necessary for motion.* A party seeking relief under FRCP 26(c) or FRCP 37, or by way of a pretrial motion that could result in a final order on an issue, must file with the motion those parts of the discovery materials relevant to the motion. IN R USDCTSD L.R. 26-2(a).

      ii. *Notice of constitutional question.* A party that files a pleading, written motion, or other paper drawing into question the constitutionality of a federal or state statute must promptly:

         • *File notice.* File a notice of constitutional question stating the question and identifying the paper that raises it, if: (1) a federal statute is questioned and the parties do not include the United States, one of its agencies, or one of its officers or employees in an official capacity; or (2) a state statute is questioned and the parties do not include the state, one of its agencies, or one of its officers or employees in an official capacity; and

         • *Serve notice.* Serve the notice and paper on the Attorney General of the United States if a federal statute is questioned—or on the state attorney general if a state statute is questioned—either by certified or registered mail or by sending it to an electronic address designated by the attorney general for this purpose. FRCP 5.1(a).

         • *Time for filing.* A notice of constitutional challenge to a statute filed in accordance with FRCP 5.1 must be filed at the same time the parties tender their proposed case management plan, if one is required, or within twenty-one (21) days of the filing drawing into question the constitutionality of a federal or state statute, whichever occurs later. IN R USDCTSD L.R. 5.1-1(a).

         • *Additional service requirements.* If a federal statute is challenged, in addition to the service requirements of FRCP 5.1(a), the party filing the notice of constitutional challenge must serve the notice and documents on the United States Attorney for the Southern District of Indiana, either by certified or registered mail or by sending it to an electronic address designated for that purpose by that official. IN R USDCTSD L.R. 5.1-1(b).

         • *No forfeiture.* A party's failure to file and serve the notice, or the court's failure to certify, does not forfeit a constitutional claim or defense that is otherwise timely asserted. FRCP 5.1(d).

      iii. *Index of exhibits.* Any pleading, motion, brief, affidavit, notice, or proposed order filed with the court, whether electronically or with the clerk, must: if it has four (4) or more exhibits, include a separate index that identifies and briefly describes each exhibit. IN R USDCTSD L.R. 5-1(b).

iv. *Request for oral argument.* A party may request oral argument by filing a separate motion explaining why oral argument is necessary and estimating how long the court should allow for the argument. The request must be filed and served with the supporting brief, response brief, or reply brief. IN R USDCTSD L.R. 7-5(a).

v. *Request for evidentiary hearing.* A party may request an evidentiary hearing on a motion or petition by serving and filing a separate motion explaining why the hearing is necessary and estimating how long the court should allow for the hearing. IN R USDCTSD L.R. 7-5(c).

vi. *Copy of authority.* Generally, copies of cited authorities may not be attached to court filings. However, a party must attach to the party's motion or brief a copy of any cited authority if it is not available on Westlaw or Lexis. Upon request, a party must provide copies of any cited authority that is only available through electronic means to the court or the other parties. IN R USDCTSD L.R. 7-1(f).

vii. *Copy of document with self-address envelope.* To receive a file-stamped copy of a document filed directly with the clerk, a party must include with the original document an additional copy and a self-addressed envelope. The envelope must be big enough to hold the copy and have enough postage on it to send the copy via regular first-class mail. IN R USDCTSD L.R. 5-10(b).

viii. *Notice of manual filing.* When a party who is not exempt from the electronic filing requirement files a document directly with the clerk, the party must: electronically file a notice of manual filing that explains why the document cannot be filed electronically. IN R USDCTSD L.R. 5-2(d)(1). Refer to the Filing and Service Requirements section of this document for more information.

- Where an individual component cannot be included in an electronic filing (e.g. the component cannot be converted to electronic format), the filer shall electronically file the prescribed Notice of Manual Filing in place of that component. A model form is provided as Appendix C (IN R USDCTSD ECF Procedures(Appendix C)). IN R USDCTSD ECF Procedures(13).

- Before making a manual filing of a component, the filing party shall first electronically file a Notice of Manual Filing (See IN R USDCTSD ECF Procedures(Appendix C)). The filer shall initiate the electronic filing process as if filing the actual component but shall instead attach to the filing the Notice of Manual Filing setting forth the reason(s) why the component cannot be filed electronically. The manual filing should be accompanied by a copy of the previously filed Notice of Manual Filing. A party may seek to have a component excluded from electronic filing pursuant to applicable Federal and Local Rules (e.g., FRCP 26(c)). IN R USDCTSD ECF Procedures(15).

ix. *Courtesy copies.* District Judges and Magistrate Judges regularly receive documents filed by all parties. Therefore, parties shall not bring "courtesy copies" to any chambers unless specifically directed to do so by the Court. IN R USDCTSD Case Mgt(General Instructions For All Cases).

x. *Copies for three-judge court.* Parties in a case where a three-judge court has been requested must file an original and three copies of any document filed directly with the clerk (instead of electronically) until the court: (1) denies the request; (2) dissolves the three-judge court; or (3) allows the parties to file fewer copies. IN R USDCTSD L.R. 9-2(c).

xi. *Declaration that party was unable to file in a timely manner due to technical difficulties.* If a party misses a filing deadline due to an inability to file electronically, the party may submit the untimely filed document, accompanied by a declaration stating the reason(s) for missing the deadline. IN R USDCTSD ECF Procedures(16). A model form is provided as Appendix D (IN R USDCTSD ECF Procedures(Appendix D)). IN R USDCTSD ECF Procedures(16).

E. Format

1. *Form of documents.* The rules governing captions and other matters of form in pleadings apply to motions and other papers. FRCP 7(b)(2).

   a. *Paper (manual filings only).* Any document that is not filed electronically must: be flat, unfolded, and

on good-quality, eight and one-half by eleven (8-1/2 x 11) inch white paper. IN R USDCTSD L.R. 5-1(d)(1). Any document that is not filed electronically must: be single-sided. IN R USDCTSD L.R. 5-1(d)(1).

    i. *Covers or backing.* Any document that is not filed electronically must: not have a cover or a back. IN R USDCTSD L.R. 5-1(d)(1).

    ii. *Fastening.* Any document that is not filed electronically must: be (if consisting of more than one (1) page) fastened by paperclip or binder clip and may not be stapled. IN R USDCTSD L.R. 5-1(d)(1).

- *Request for nonconforming fastening.* If a document cannot be fastened or bound as required by IN R USDCTSD L.R. 5-1(d), a party may ask the clerk for permission to fasten it in another manner. The party must make such a request before attempting to file the document with nonconforming fastening. IN R USDCTSD L.R. 5-1(d)(2).

    iii. *Hole punching.* Any document that is not filed electronically must: be two-hole punched at the top with the holes two and three-quarter (2-3/4) inches apart and appropriately centered. IN R USDCTSD L.R. 5-1(d)(1).

b. *Margins.* Any pleading, motion, brief, affidavit, notice, or proposed order filed with the court, whether electronically or with the clerk, must: have at least one (1) inch margins. IN R USDCTSD L.R. 5-1(b).

c. *Spacing.* Any pleading, motion, brief, affidavit, notice, or proposed order filed with the court, whether electronically or with the clerk, must: be double spaced (except for headings, footnotes, and quoted material). IN R USDCTSD L.R. 5-1(b).

d. *Text.* Any pleading, motion, brief, affidavit, notice, or proposed order filed with the court, whether electronically or with the clerk, must: be plainly typewritten, printed, or prepared by a clearly legible copying process. IN R USDCTSD L.R. 5-1(b).

e. *Font size.* Any pleading, motion, brief, affidavit, notice, or proposed order filed with the court, whether electronically or with the clerk, must: use at least 12-point type in the body of the document and at least 10-point type in footnotes. IN R USDCTSD L.R. 5-1(b).

f. *Page numbering.* Any pleading, motion, brief, affidavit, notice, or proposed order filed with the court, whether electronically or with the clerk, must: have consecutively numbered pages. IN R USDCTSD L.R. 5-1(b).

g. *Caption; Names of parties.* Every pleading must have a caption with the court's name, a title, a file number, and a FRCP 7(a) designation. The title of the complaint must name all the parties; the title of other pleadings, after naming the first party on each side, may refer generally to other parties. FRCP 10(a). Any pleading, motion, brief, affidavit, notice, or proposed order filed with the court, whether electronically or with the clerk, must: include a title on the first page. IN R USDCTSD L.R. 5-1(b).

    i. *Alternative motions.* Motions must be filed separately, but alternative motions may be filed in a single document if each is named in the title. IN R USDCTSD L.R. 7-1(a).

h. *Filer's information.* Any pleading, motion, brief, affidavit, notice, or proposed order filed with the court, whether electronically or with the clerk, must: in the case of pleadings, motions, legal briefs, and notices, include the name, complete address, telephone number, facsimile number (where available), and e-mail address (where available) of the pro se litigant or attorney who files it. IN R USDCTSD L.R. 5-1(b).

i. *Paragraphs; Separate statements.* A party must state its claims or defenses in numbered paragraphs, each limited as far as practicable to a single set of circumstances. A later pleading may refer by number to a paragraph in an earlier pleading. If doing so would promote clarity, each claim founded on a separate transaction or occurrence—and each defense other than a denial—must be stated in a separate count or defense. FRCP 10(b).

j. *Adoption by reference; Exhibits.* A statement in a pleading may be adopted by reference elsewhere in the same pleading or in any other pleading or motion. A copy of a written instrument that is an exhibit to a pleading is a part of the pleading for all purposes. FRCP 10(c).

k. *Citations*

    i. *Local rules.* The Local Rules of the United States District Court for the Southern District of Indiana may be cited as "S.D. Ind. L.R." IN R USDCTSD L.R. 1-1(a).

    ii. *Local alternative dispute resolution rules.* These Rules shall be known as the Local Alternative Dispute Resolution Rules of the United States District Court for the Southern District of Indiana. They shall be cited as "S.D.Ind. Local A.D.R. Rule _____." IN R USDCTSD A.D.R. Rule 1.1.

l. *Acceptance by the clerk.* The clerk must not refuse to file a paper solely because it is not in the form prescribed by the Federal Rules of Civil Procedure or by a local rule or practice. FRCP 5(d)(4). The clerk will accept a document that violates IN R USDCTSD L.R. 5-1, but the court may exclude the document from the official record. IN R USDCTSD L.R. 5-1(e).

    i. *Sanctions for errors as to form.* The court may strike from the record any document that does not comply with the rules governing the form of documents filed with the court, such as rules that regulate document size or the number of copies to be filed or that require a special designation in the caption. The court may also sanction an attorney or party who files a non-compliant document. IN R USDCTSD L.R. 1-3.

2. *Form of electronic documents.* Any document submitted via the court's electronic case filing (ECF) system must be: otherwise prepared and filed in a manner consistent with the CM/ECF Policies and Procedures Manual (IN R USDCTSD ECF Procedures). IN R USDCTSD L.R. 5-1(c). Electronically filed documents must meet the requirements of FRCP 10 (Form of Pleadings), IN R USDCTSD L.R. 5-1 (Format of Papers Presented for Filing), and FRCP 5.2 (Privacy Protection for Filings Made with the Court), as if they had been submitted on paper. Documents filed electronically are also subject to any page limitations set forth by Court Order, by IN R USDCTSD L.R. 7-1 (Motion Practice), or IN R USDCTSD L.R. 56-1 (Summary Judgment Practice), as applicable. IN R USDCTSD ECF Procedures(13).

a. *PDF format required.* Any document submitted via the court's electronic case filing (ECF) system must be: in .pdf format. IN R USDCTSD L.R. 5-1(c); IN R USDCTSD ECF Procedures(7). Any document submitted via the court's electronic case filing (ECF) system must be: converted to a .pdf file directly from a word processing program, unless it exists only in paper format (in which case it may be scanned to create a .pdf document). IN R USDCTSD L.R. 5-1(c); IN R USDCTSD ECF Procedures(13).

    i. An exhibit may be scanned into PDF format, at a recommended 300 dpi resolution or higher, only if it does not already exist in electronic format. The filing attorney is responsible for reviewing all PDF documents for legibility before submitting them through the Court's Electronic Case Filing system. For technical guidance in creating PDF documents, please contact the Clerk's Office. IN R USDCTSD ECF Procedures(13).

b. *File size limitations.* Any document submitted via the court's electronic case filing (ECF) system must be: submitted as one or more .pdf files that do not exceed ten megabytes (10 MB) each (consistent with the CM/ECF Policies and Procedures Manual (IN R USDCTSD ECF Procedures)). IN R USDCTSD L.R. 5-1(c); IN R USDCTSD ECF Procedures(13).

    i. To electronically file a document or attachment that exceeds ten megabytes (10 MB), the document must first be broken down into two or more smaller files. For example, if Exhibit A is a twelve megabyte (12 MB) PDF file, it should be divided into 2 equal parts prior to electronic filing. Each component part of the exhibit would be filed as an attachment to the main document and described appropriately as "Exhibit A (part 1 of 2)" and "Exhibit A (part 2 of 2)." IN R USDCTSD ECF Procedures(13).

    ii. The supporting items mentioned in IN R USDCTSD ECF Procedures(13) should not be confused with memorandums or briefs in support of motions as outlined in IN R USDCTSD L.R. 7-1 or IN R USDCTSD L.R. 56-1. These memorandums or briefs in support are to be filed as entirely separate documents pursuant to the appropriate rule. Additionally, no motion shall be embodied in the text of a response or reply brief/memorandum unless otherwise ordered by the Court. IN R USDCTSD ECF Procedures(13).

c. *Separate component parts.* A key objective of the electronic filing system is to ensure that as much of the case as possible is managed electronically. To facilitate electronic filing and retrieval, documents to be filed electronically are to be reasonably broken into their separate component parts. By way of example, most filings include a foundation document (e.g., motion) and other supporting items (e.g., exhibits, proposed orders, proposed amended pleadings). The foundation document, as well as the supporting items, are each separate components of the filing; supporting items must be filed as attachments to the foundation document. These exhibits or attachments should include only those excerpts of the referenced documents that are directly germane to the matter under consideration. IN R USDCTSD ECF Procedures(13).

   i. Where an individual component cannot be included in an electronic filing (e.g. the component cannot be converted to electronic format), the filer shall electronically file the prescribed Notice of Manual Filing in place of that component. A model form is provided as Appendix C (IN R USDCTSD ECF Procedures(Appendix C)). IN R USDCTSD ECF Procedures(13).

d. *Exhibits.* Each electronically filed exhibit to a main document must be: (1) created as a separate .pdf file; (2) submitted as an attachment to the main document and given a title which describes its content; and (3) limited to excerpts that are directly germane to the main document's subject matter. IN R USDCTSD L.R. 5-6(a).

   i. When uploading attachments during the electronic filing process, exhibits must be uploaded in a logical sequence and a brief description must be entered for each individual PDF file. The description must include not only the exhibit number or letter, but also a brief description of the document. This information may be entered in CM/ECF using a combination of the Category drop-down menu, the Description text box, or both (see IN R USDCTSD ECF Procedures(13)(Figure 1)). The information that is provided in each box will be combined to create a description of the document as it appears on the case docket (see IN R USDCTSD ECF Procedures(13)(Figure 2)). IN R USDCTSD ECF Procedures(13). For an example, refer to IN R USDCTSD ECF Procedures(13).

e. *Excerpts.* A party filing an exhibit that consists of excerpts from a larger document must clearly and prominently identify the exhibit as containing excerpted material. Either party will have the right to timely file additional excerpts or the complete document to the extent they are or become directly germane to the main document's subject matter. IN R USDCTSD L.R. 5-6(b).

f. For an example illustrating the application of IN R USDCTSD ECF Procedures(13), refer to IN R USDCTSD ECF Procedures(13).

3. *Form of briefs*

   a. *Page limits.* Supporting and response briefs (excluding tables of contents, tables of authorities, appendices, and certificates of service) may not exceed thirty-five (35) pages. Reply briefs may not exceed twenty (20) pages. IN R USDCTSD L.R. 7-1(e)(1).

      i. *Permission to exceed limits.* The court may allow a party to file a brief exceeding these page limits for extraordinary and compelling reasons. IN R USDCTSD L.R. 7-1(e)(2).

      ii. *Supporting and response briefs exceeding limits.* If the court allows a party to file a brief or response exceeding thirty-five (35) pages, the document must include:

         • A table of contents with page references;

         • A statement of issues; and

         • A table of authorities including: (1) all cases (alphabetically arranged), statutes, and other authorities cited in the brief; and (2) page numbers where the authorities are cited in the brief. IN R USDCTSD L.R. 7-1(e)(3).

4. *Signing of pleadings, motions and other papers*

   a. *Signature.* Every pleading, written motion, and other paper must be signed by at least one attorney of record in the attorney's name—or by a party personally if the party is unrepresented. The paper must state the signer's address, e-mail address, and telephone number. FRCP 11(a).

      i. *Signatures on manual filings.* Any document that is not filed electronically must: include the original signature of the pro se litigant or attorney who files it. IN R USDCTSD L.R. 5-1(d)(1).

ii. *Electronic signatures.* Use of the attorney's login and password when filing documents electronically serves in part as the attorney's signature for purposes of FRCP 11, the Local Rules of the United States District Court for the Southern District of Indiana, and any other purpose for which a signature is required in connection with proceedings before the Court. IN R USDCTSD ECF Procedures(14); IN R USDCTSD ECF Procedures(10). A pleading, motion, brief, or notice filed electronically under an attorney's ECF log-in and password must be signed by that attorney. IN R USDCTSD L.R. 5-7(a). A signature on a document other than a document filed as provided under IN R USDCTSD L.R. 5-7(a) must be an original handwritten signature and must be scanned into .pdf format for electronic filing. IN R USDCTSD L.R. 5-7(c); IN R USDCTSD ECF Procedures(14).

- *Form of electronic signature.* If a document is converted directly from a word processing application to .pdf (as opposed to scanning), the name of the Filing User under whose log-in and password the document is submitted must be preceded by a "s/" and typed on the signature line where the Filing User's handwritten signature would otherwise appear. IN R USDCTSD L.R. 5-7(b). All documents filed electronically shall include a signature block and include the filing attorney's typewritten name, address, telephone number, facsimile number and e-mail address. In addition, the name of the filing attorney under whose ECF login the document will be filed should be preceded by a "s/" and typed in the space where the attorney's handwritten signature would otherwise appear. IN R US-DCTSD ECF Procedures(14). For a sample format, refer to IN R USDCTSD ECF Procedures(14).

- *Effect of electronic signature.* Filing an electronically signed document under an attorney's ECF log-in and password constitutes the attorney's signature on the document under the Federal Rules of Civil Procedure, under the Local Rules of the United States District Court for the Southern District of Indiana, and for any other reason a signature is required in connection with the court's activities. IN R USDCTSD L.R. 5-7(d).

- *Documents with multiple attorneys' signatures.* Documents requiring signatures of more than one attorney shall be filed either by: (1) obtaining consent from the other attorney, then typing the "s/ [Name]" signature of the other attorney on the signature line where the other attorney's signature would otherwise appear; (2) identifying in the signature section the name of the other attorney whose signature is required and by the submission of a Notice of Endorsement (see IN R USDCTSD ECF Procedures(Appendix B)) by the other attorney no later than three (3) business days after filing; (3) submitting a scanned document containing all handwritten signatures; or (4) in any other manner approved by the Court. IN R USDCTSD ECF Procedures(14); IN R USDCTSD L.R. 5-7(e).

iii. *No verification or accompanying affidavit required for pleadings.* Unless a rule or statute specifically states otherwise, a pleading need not be verified or accompanied by an affidavit. FRCP 11(a).

iv. *Unsigned papers.* The court must strike an unsigned paper unless the omission is promptly corrected after being called to the attorney's or party's attention. FRCP 11(a). The court will strike any document filed directly with the clerk that is not signed by an attorney of record or the pro se litigant filing it, but the court may do so only after giving the attorney or pro se litigant notice of the omission and reasonable time to correct it. Rubber-stamp or facsimile signatures are not original signatures and the court will deem documents containing them to be unsigned for purposes of FRCP 11 and FRCP 26(g) and IN R USDCTSD L.R. 5-10. IN R USDCTSD L.R. 5-10(g).

b. *Representations to the court.* By presenting to the court a pleading, written motion, or other paper—whether by signing, filing, submitting, or later advocating it—an attorney or unrepresented party certifies that to the best of the person's knowledge, information, and belief, formed after an inquiry reasonable under the circumstances:

i. It is not being presented for any improper purpose, such as to harass, cause unnecessary delay, or needlessly increase the cost of litigation;

ii. The claims, defenses, and other legal contentions are warranted by existing law or by a

> nonfrivolous argument for extending, modifying, or reversing existing law or for establishing new law;

    iii.   The factual contentions have evidentiary support or, if specifically so identified, will likely have evidentiary support after a reasonable opportunity for further investigation or discovery; and

    iv.   The denials of factual contentions are warranted on the evidence or, if specifically so identified, are reasonably based on belief or a lack of information. FRCP 11(b).

   c. *Sanctions.* If, after notice and a reasonable opportunity to respond, the court determines that FRCP 11(b) has been violated, the court may impose an appropriate sanction on any attorney, law firm, or party that violated FRCP 11(b) or is responsible for the violation. FRCP 11(c)(1). Refer to the United States District Court for the Southern District of Indiana KeyRules Motion for Sanctions document for more information.

5. *Privacy protection for filings made with the court.* Electronically filed documents must meet the requirements of. . .FRCP 5.2 (Privacy Protection for Filings Made with the Court), as if they had been submitted on paper. IN R USDCTSD ECF Procedures(13).

   a. *Redacted filings.* Unless the court orders otherwise, in an electronic or paper filing with the court that contains an individual's Social Security number, taxpayer-identification number, or birth date, the name of an individual known to be a minor, or a financial-account number, a party or nonparty making the filing may include only:

    i.   The last four (4) digits of the Social Security number and taxpayer-identification number;

    ii.   The year of the individual's birth;

    iii.   The minor's initials; and

    iv.   The last four (4) digits of the financial-account number. FRCP 5.2(a).

   b. *Exemptions from the redaction requirement.* The redaction requirement does not apply to the following:

    i.   A financial-account number that identifies the property allegedly subject to forfeiture in a forfeiture proceeding;

    ii.   The record of an administrative or agency proceeding;

    iii.   The official record of a state-court proceeding;

    iv.   The record of a court or tribunal, if that record was not subject to the redaction requirement when originally filed;

    v.   A filing covered by FRCP 5.2(c) or FRCP 5.2(d); and

    vi.   A pro se filing in an action brought under 28 U.S.C.A. § 2241, 28 U.S.C.A. § 2254, or 28 U.S.C.A. § 2255. FRCP 5.2(b).

   c. *Limitations on remote access to electronic files; Social Security appeals and immigration cases.* Unless the court orders otherwise, in an action for benefits under the Social Security Act, and in an action or proceeding relating to an order of removal, to relief from removal, or to immigration benefits or detention, access to an electronic file is authorized as follows:

    i.   The parties and their attorneys may have remote electronic access to any part of the case file, including the administrative record;

    ii.   Any other person may have electronic access to the full record at the courthouse, but may have remote electronic access only to:

      • The docket maintained by the court; and

      • An opinion, order, judgment, or other disposition of the court, but not any other part of the case file or the administrative record. FRCP 5.2(c).

   d. *Filings made under seal.* The court may order that a filing be made under seal without redaction. The court may later unseal the filing or order the person who made the filing to file a redacted version for the public record. FRCP 5.2(d). For more information on filing under seal, refer to IN R USDCTSD L.R. 5-11 and IN R USDCTSD ECF Procedures(18).

e. *Protective orders.* For good cause, the court may by order in a case:

    i. Require redaction of additional information; or

    ii. Limit or prohibit a nonparty's remote electronic access to a document filed with the court. FRCP 5.2(e).

f. *Option for additional unredacted filing under seal.* A person making a redacted filing may also file an unredacted copy under seal. The court must retain the unredacted copy as part of the record. FRCP 5.2(f).

g. *Option for filing a reference list.* A filing that contains redacted information may be filed together with a reference list that identifies each item of redacted information and specifies an appropriate identifier that uniquely corresponds to each item listed. The list must be filed under seal and may be amended as of right. Any reference in the case to a listed identifier will be construed to refer to the corresponding item of information. FRCP 5.2(g).

h. *Waiver of protection of identifiers.* A person waives the protection of FRCP 5.2(a) as to the person's own information by filing it without redaction and not under seal. FRCP 5.2(h).

F. Filing and Service Requirements

1. *Filing requirements.* Any paper after the complaint that is required to be served—together with a certificate of service—must be filed within a reasonable time after service. FRCP 5(d)(1). Motions must be filed separately, but alternative motions may be filed in a single document if each is named in the title. IN R USDCTSD L.R. 7-1(a).

    a. *How filing is made; In general.* A paper is filed by delivering it:

        i. To the clerk; or

        ii. To a judge who agrees to accept it for filing, and who must then note the filing date on the paper and promptly send it to the clerk. FRCP 5(d)(2).

            • In certain instances, the court will direct the parties to submit items directly to chambers (e.g., confidential settlement statements). However, absent specific prior authorization, counsel and litigants should not submit letters or documents directly to chambers, and such materials should be filed with the clerk. IN R USDCTSD L.R. 5-1(Local Rules Advisory Committee Comment).

        iii. A document or item submitted in relation to a matter within the court's jurisdiction is deemed filed upon delivery to the office of the clerk in a manner prescribed by the Local Rules of the United States District Court for the Southern District of Indiana or the Federal Rules of Civil Procedure or authorized by the court. Any submission directed to a Judge or Judge's staff, the office of the clerk or any employee thereof, in a manner that is not contemplated by IN R USDCTSD L.R. 5-1 and without prior court authorization is prohibited. IN R USDCTSD L.R. 5-1(a).

    b. *Non-electronic filing.* Any document that is exempt from electronic filing must be filed directly with the clerk and served on other parties in the case as required by those Federal Rules of Civil Procedure and Local Rules of the United States District Court for the Southern District of Indiana that apply to the service of non-electronic documents. IN R USDCTSD L.R. 5-2(c).

        i. *When completed.* A document or other item that is not required to be filed electronically is deemed filed:

            • Upon delivery in person, by courier, or via U.S. Mail or other mail delivery service to the clerk's office during business hours;

            • When the courtroom deputy clerk accepts it, if the document or item is filed in open court; or

            • Upon completion of any other manner of filing that the court authorizes. IN R USDCTSD L.R. 5-10(a).

    ii. *Document filing by non-exempt party.* When a party who is not exempt from the electronic filing requirement files a document directly with the clerk, the party must:

- Electronically file a notice of manual filing that explains why the document cannot be filed electronically;

- Present the document to the clerk within one (1) business day after filing the notice of manual filing; and

- Present the clerk with a copy of the notice of manual filing when the party files the document with the clerk. IN R USDCTSD L.R. 5-2(d).

  c. *Electronic filing*

    i. *Authorization of electronic filing program.* A court may, by local rule, allow papers to be filed, signed, or verified by electronic means that are consistent with any technical standards established by the Judicial Conference of the United States. A local rule may require electronic filing only if reasonable exceptions are allowed. A paper filed electronically in compliance with a local rule is a written paper for purposes of the Federal Rules of Civil Procedure. FRCP 5(d)(3).

- IN R USDCTSD L.R. 5-2 requires electronic filing, as allowed by FRCP 5(d)(3). The policies and procedures in IN R USDCTSD ECF Procedures govern electronic filing in this district unless, due to circumstances in a particular case, a judicial officer determines that these policies and procedures (IN R USDCTSD ECF Procedures) should be modified. IN R USDCTSD ECF Procedures(1).

- Unless modified by order of the Court, all Federal Rules of Civil Procedure and Local Rules of the United States District Court for the Southern District of Indiana shall continue to apply to cases maintained in the Court's Case Management/Electronic Case Filing System (CM/ECF). IN R USDCTSD ECF Procedures(3).

    ii. *Mandatory electronic filing.* Unless exempted pursuant to IN R USDCTSD L.R. 5-3(e), attorneys admitted to the court's bar (including those admitted pro hac vice) or authorized to represent the United States must use the court's ECF system to file documents. IN R USDCTSD L.R. 5-3(a). Electronic filing by attorneys is required for eligible documents filed in civil and criminal cases pending with the Court, unless specifically exempted by Local Rule or Court Order. IN R USDCTSD ECF Procedures(4).

- *Exceptions.* All civil cases (other than those cases the court specifically exempts) must be maintained in the court's electronic case filing (ECF) system. Accordingly, as allowed by FRCP 5(d)(3), every document filed in this court (including exhibits) must be transmitted to the clerk's office via the ECF system consistent with IN R USDCTSD L.R. 5-2 through IN R USDCTSD L.R. 5-11 except: (1) documents filed by pro se litigants; (2) transcripts in cases filed by claimants under the Social Security Act (and related statutes); (3) exhibits in a format that does not readily permit electronic filing (such as videos and large maps and charts); (4) documents that are illegible when scanned into .pdf format; (5) documents filed in cases not maintained on the ECF system; and (6) any other documents that the court or the Local Rules of the United States District Court for the Southern District of Indiana specifically allow to be filed directly with the clerk. IN R USDCTSD L.R. 5-2(a). Parties otherwise participating in the electronic filing system may be excused from filing a particular component electronically under certain limited circumstances, such as when the component cannot be reduced to an electronic format. Such components shall not be filed electronically, but instead shall be manually filed with the Clerk of Court and served upon the parties in accordance with the applicable Federal Rules of Civil Procedure and the Local Rules of the United States District Court for the Southern District of Indiana for filing and service of non-electronic documents. IN R USDCTSD ECF Procedures(15).

- *Exemption from participation.* The court may exempt attorneys from using the ECF system in a particular case for good cause. An attorney must file a petition for ECF exemption and a CM/ECF technical requirements exemption questionnaire in each case in

which the attorney seeks an exemption. (The CM/ECF technical requirements exemption questionnaire is available on the court's website). IN R USDCTSD L.R. 5-3(e).

iii. *Consequences of electronic filing.* Electronic transmission of a document consistent with the procedures adopted by the Court shall, upon the complete receipt of the same by the Clerk of Court, constitute filing of the document for all purposes of the Federal Rules of Civil and Criminal Procedure and the Local Rules of the United States District Court for the Southern District of Indiana, and shall constitute entry of that document onto the docket maintained by the Clerk pursuant to FRCP 58 and FRCP 79. IN R USDCTSD ECF Procedures(7); IN R USDCTSD L.R. 5-4(c)(1). When a document has been filed electronically: the document, as filed, binds the filing party. IN R USDCTSD L.R. 5-4(c)(3).

- A Notice of Electronic Filing (NEF) acknowledging that the document has been filed will immediately appear on the filer's screen after the document has been submitted. Attorneys are strongly encouraged to print or electronically save a copy of the NEF. Attorneys can also verify the filing of documents by inspecting the Court's electronic docket sheet through the use of a PACER login. IN R USDCTSD ECF Procedures(7). When a document has been filed electronically: the notice of electronic filing for the document serves as the court's date-stamp and proof of filing. IN R USDCTSD L.R. 5-4(c)(4).

- The Court may, upon the motion of a party or upon its own motion, strike any inappropriately filed document. IN R USDCTSD ECF Procedures(7).

iv. For more information on electronic filing, refer to IN R USDCTSD ECF Procedures.

d. *Fax filing.* The clerk may not file a faxed document without court authorization. The court may not authorize the clerk to file faxed documents without finding that compelling circumstances justify it. A party must submit a copy of the document that otherwise complies with IN R USDCTSD L.R. 5-10 to replace the faxed copy within seven (7) days after faxing the document. IN R USDCTSD L.R. 5-10(e).

2. *Service requirements*

a. *Service; When required*

i. *In general.* Unless the Federal Rules of Civil Procedure provide otherwise, each of the following papers must be served on every party:

- An order stating that service is required;

- A pleading filed after the original complaint, unless the court orders otherwise under FRCP 5(c) because there are numerous defendants;

- A discovery paper required to be served on a party, unless the court orders otherwise;

- A written motion, except one that may be heard ex parte; and

- A written notice, appearance, demand, or offer of judgment, or any similar paper. FRCP 5(a)(1).

ii. *If a party fails to appear.* No service is required on a party who is in default for failing to appear. But a pleading that asserts a new claim for relief against such a party must be served on that party under FRCP 4. FRCP 5(a)(2).

iii. *Seizing property.* If an action is begun by seizing property and no person is or need be named as a defendant, any service required before the filing of an appearance, answer, or claim must be made on the person who had custody or possession of the property when it was seized. FRCP 5(a)(3).

b. *Service; How made*

i. *Serving an attorney.* If a party is represented by an attorney, service under FRCP 5 must be made on the attorney unless the court orders service on the party. FRCP 5(b)(1).

ii. *Service in general.* A paper is served under FRCP 5 by:

- Handing it to the person;

- Leaving it: (1) at the person's office with a clerk or other person in charge or, if no one is in charge, in a conspicuous place in the office; or (2) if the person has no office or the office is closed, at the person's dwelling or usual place of abode with someone of suitable age and discretion who resides there;

- Mailing it to the person's last known address—in which event service is complete upon mailing;

- Leaving it with the court clerk if the person has no known address;

- Sending it by electronic means if the person consented in writing—in which event service is complete upon transmission, but is not effective if the serving party learns that it did not reach the person to be served; or

- Delivering it by any other means that the person consented to in writing—in which event service is complete when the person making service delivers it to the agency designated to make delivery. FRCP 5(b)(2).

iii. *Electronic service*

- *Consent.* By registering to use the ECF system, attorneys consent to electronic service of documents filed in cases maintained on the ECF system. IN R USDCTSD L.R. 5-3(d). By participating in the Electronic Case Filing Program, attorneys consent to the electronic service of documents, and shall make available electronic mail addresses for service. IN R USDCTSD ECF Procedures(11).

- *Service on registered parties.* Upon the filing of a document by a party, an e-mail message will be automatically generated by the electronic filing system and sent via electronic mail to the e-mail addresses of all registered attorneys who have appeared in the case. The Notice of Electronic Filing will contain a document hyperlink which will provide recipients with one "free look" at the electronically filed document. Recipients are encouraged to print and/or save a copy of the document during the "free look" to avoid incurring PACER charges for future viewings of the document. IN R USDCTSD ECF Procedures(11). When a document has been filed electronically: transmission of the notice of electronic filing generated by the ECF system to an attorney's e-mail address constitutes service of the document on that attorney. IN R USDCTSD L.R. 5-4(c)(5). The party effectuates service on all registered attorneys by filing electronically. IN R USDCTSD ECF Procedures(11). When a document has been filed electronically: no other attempted service will constitute electronic service of the document. IN R USDCTSD L.R. 5-4(c)(6).

- *Service on exempt parties.* A filer must serve a copy of the document consistent with FRCP 5 on any party or attorney who is exempt from participating in electronic filing. IN R USDCTSD L.R. 5-4(d). It is the responsibility of the filing attorney to conventionally serve all parties who do not receive electronic service (the identity of these parties will be indicated on the filing receipt generated by the ECF system). IN R USDCTSD ECF Procedures(11).

- *Service on parties excused from electronic filing.* Parties otherwise participating in the electronic filing system may be excused from filing a particular component electronically under certain limited circumstances, such as when the component cannot be reduced to an electronic format. Such components shall not be filed electronically, but instead shall be manually filed with the Clerk of Court and served upon the parties in accordance with the applicable Federal Rules of Civil Procedure and the Local Rules of the United States District Court for the Southern District of Indiana for filing and service of non-electronic documents. IN R USDCTSD ECF Procedures(15).

- *Service of exempt documents.* Any document that is exempt from electronic filing must be filed directly with the clerk and served on other parties in the case as required by those Federal Rules of Civil Procedure and Local Rules of the United States District Court for the Southern District of Indiana that apply to the service of non-electronic documents. IN R USDCTSD L.R. 5-2(c).

iv. *Using court facilities.* If a local rule so authorizes, a party may use the court's transmission facilities to make service under FRCP 5(b)(2)(E). FRCP 5(b)(3).

c. *Serving numerous defendants*

i. *In general.* If an action involves an unusually large number of defendants, the court may, on motion or on its own, order that:

- Defendants' pleadings and replies to them need not be served on other defendants;
- Any crossclaim, counterclaim, avoidance, or affirmative defense in those pleadings and replies to them will be treated as denied or avoided by all other parties; and
- Filing any such pleading and serving it on the plaintiff constitutes notice of the pleading to all parties. FRCP 5(c)(1).

ii. *Notifying parties.* A copy of every such order must be served on the parties as the court directs. FRCP 5(c)(2).

G. Hearings

1. *Hearings, generally*

a. *Oral argument.* Due process does not require that oral argument be permitted on a motion and, except as otherwise provided by local rule, the district court has discretion to determine whether it will decide the motion on the papers or hear argument by counsel (and perhaps receive evidence). FPP § 1190; F.D.I.C. v. Deglau, 207 F.3d 153 (3d Cir. 2000).

i. *Request for oral argument.* A party may request oral argument by filing a separate motion explaining why oral argument is necessary and estimating how long the court should allow for the argument. IN R USDCTSD L.R. 7-5(a). Refer to the Documents section of this document for more information.

ii. *No additional evidence at oral argument.* Parties may not present additional evidence at oral argument. IN R USDCTSD L.R. 7-5(b).

b. *Providing a regular schedule for oral hearings.* A court may establish regular times and places for oral hearings on motions. FRCP 78(a).

c. *Providing for submission on briefs.* By rule or order, the court may provide for submitting and determining motions on briefs, without oral hearings. FRCP 78(b).

d. *Request for evidentiary hearing.* A party may request an evidentiary hearing on a motion or petition by serving and filing a separate motion explaining why the hearing is necessary and estimating how long the court should allow for the hearing. IN R USDCTSD L.R. 7-5(c).

e. *Directed by the court.* The court may: (1) grant or deny a request for oral argument or an evidentiary hearing in its sole discretion; (2) set oral argument or an evidentiary hearing without a request from a party; and (3) order any oral argument or evidentiary hearing to be held anywhere within the district regardless of where the case will be tried. IN R USDCTSD L.R. 7-5(d).

2. *Courtroom and courthouse decorum.* For information on courtroom and courthouse decorum, refer to IN R USDCTSD L.R. 83-3.

H. Forms

1. Federal Motion for More Definite Statement Forms

a. Motion; To strike pleading for failure to comply with order for more definite statement. AMJUR PP FEDPRAC § 443.

b. Notice of motion; To strike complaint and dismiss action for failure to furnish more definite statement. AMJUR PP FEDPRAC § 445.

c. Motion and notice; For more definite statement; General form. AMJUR PP FEDPRAC § 541.

d. Motion and notice; To strike complaint and to dismiss action for failure of plaintiff to furnish more definite statement in compliance with order. AMJUR PP FEDPRAC § 542.

e. Motion; By multiple defendants; For more definite statement. AMJUR PP FEDPRAC § 543.

f. More definite statement. AMJUR PP FEDPRAC § 546.

g. Motion and notice; For more definite statement as to date of transaction alleged in complaint. AMJUR PP FEDPRAC § 1391.

h. Motion and notice; For more definite statement concerning jurisdictional amount. AMJUR PP FEDPRAC § 1410.

i. Motion for more definite statement. 2C FEDFORMS § 11:144.

j. Motion for more definite statement; Describing allegations requiring more definite statement. 2C FEDFORMS § 11:145.

k. Motion for more definite statement; Damages. 2C FEDFORMS § 11:146.

l. Motion for more definite statement; Patent case. 2C FEDFORMS § 11:147.

m. Compliance with order for more definite statement of complaint. 2C FEDFORMS § 11:149.

n. Motion to strike complaint upon failure of plaintiff to furnish more definite statement ordered by the court. 2C FEDFORMS § 11:150.

o. Notice; Of motion; Containing motion. FEDPROF § 1:749.

p. Opposition; To motion; General form. FEDPROF § 1:750.

q. Affidavit; Supporting or opposing motion. FEDPROF § 1:751.

r. Brief; Supporting or opposing motion. FEDPROF § 1:752.

s. Statement of points and authorities; Opposing motion. FEDPROF § 1:753.

t. Motion; For more definite statement; General form. FEDPROF § 1:779.

u. Motion; By plaintiff; For more definite statement. FEDPROF § 1:780.

v. Motion; By defendant; For more definite statement. FEDPROF § 1:781.

w. Motion; By defendant; For more definite statement; By trustee. FEDPROF § 1:782.

x. Motion; By multiple defendants; For more definite statement. FEDPROF § 1:783.

y. Response; By plaintiff; To motion for more definite statement. FEDPROF § 1:784.

z. Notice and motion for more definite statement. GOLDLTGFMS § 20:6.

2. **Forms for the Southern District of Indiana**

a. Notice of endorsement. IN R USDCTSD ECF Procedures(Appendix B).

b. Notice of manual filing. IN R USDCTSD ECF Procedures(Appendix C).

c. Declaration that party was unable to file in a timely manner due to technical difficulties. IN R USDCTSD ECF Procedures(Appendix D).

I. Applicable Rules

1. *Federal rules*

a. Serving and filing pleadings and other papers. FRCP 5.

b. Constitutional challenge to a statute; Notice, certification, and intervention. FRCP 5.1.

c. Privacy protection for filings made with the court. FRCP 5.2.

d. Computing and extending time; Time for motion papers. FRCP 6.

e. Pleadings allowed; Form of motions and other papers. FRCP 7.

f. Disclosure statement. FRCP 7.1.

g. Form of pleadings. FRCP 10.

h. Signing pleadings, motions, and other papers; Representations to the court; Sanctions. FRCP 11.

i. Defenses and objections; When and how presented; Motion for judgment on the pleadings; Consolidating motions; Waiving defenses; Pretrial hearing. FRCP 12.

      j.   Taking testimony. FRCP 43.

      k.   Hearing motions; Submission on briefs. FRCP 78.

2. *Local rules*

      a.   Scope of the rules. IN R USDCTSD L.R. 1-1.

      b.   Sanctions for errors as to form. IN R USDCTSD L.R. 1-3.

      c.   Format of documents presented for filing. IN R USDCTSD L.R. 5-1.

      d.   Constitutional challenge to a statute; Notice. IN R USDCTSD L.R. 5.1-1.

      e.   Filing of documents electronically required. IN R USDCTSD L.R. 5-2.

      f.   Eligibility, registration, passwords for electronic filing; Exemption from electronic filing. IN R USDCTSD L.R. 5-3.

      g.   Timing and consequences of electronic filing. IN R USDCTSD L.R. 5-4.

      h.   Attachments and exhibits in cases filed electronically. IN R USDCTSD L.R. 5-6.

      i.   Signatures in cases filed electronically. IN R USDCTSD L.R. 5-7.

      j.   Non-electronic filings. IN R USDCTSD L.R. 5-10.

      k.   Motion practice. [IN R USDCTSD L.R. 7-1, as amended by IN ORDER 16-2319, effective December 1, 2016].

      l.   Oral arguments and hearings. IN R USDCTSD L.R. 7-5.

      m.   Request for three-judge court. IN R USDCTSD L.R. 9-2.

      n.   Filing of discovery materials. IN R USDCTSD L.R. 26-2.

      o.   Assignment of cases. IN R USDCTSD L.R. 40-1.

      p.   Alternative dispute resolution. IN R USDCTSD A.D.R. Rule 1.1; IN R USDCTSD A.D.R. Rule 1.2; IN R USDCTSD A.D.R. Rule 1.5; IN R USDCTSD A.D.R. Rule 2.1; IN R USDCTSD A.D.R. Rule 2.2.

      q.   Instructions for preparing case management plan. IN R USDCTSD Case Mgt.

      r.   Electronic case filing policies and procedures manual. IN R USDCTSD ECF Procedures.

Motions, Oppositions and Replies
Motion for Post-Trial Relief

Document Last Updated December 2016

A. Checklist

(I) ❑ Matters to be considered by moving party

    (a) ❑ Required documents

        (1) ❑ Notice of motion and motion

        (2) ❑ Certificate of service

    (b) ❑ Supplemental documents

        (1) ❑ Brief

        (2) ❑ Supporting evidence

        (3) ❑ Notice of constitutional question

        (4) ❑ Index of exhibits

        (5) ❑ Request for oral argument

        (6) ❑ Request for evidentiary hearing

(7) ❏ Copy of authority

(8) ❏ Proposed order

(9) ❏ Copy of document with self-address envelope

(10) ❏ Notice of manual filing

(11) ❏ Courtesy copies

(12) ❏ Copies for three-judge court

(13) ❏ Declaration that party was unable to file in a timely manner due to technical difficulties

(c) ❏ Timing

    (1) ❏ Motion for new trial: a motion for a new trial must be filed no later than twenty-eight (28) days after the entry of judgment

        (i) ❏ When a motion for a new trial is based on affidavits, they must be filed with the motion

    (2) ❏ Motion to alter or amend judgment: a motion to alter or amend a judgment must be filed no later than twenty-eight (28) days after the entry of the judgment

    (3) ❏ Motion for relief from judgment:

        (i) ❏ Clerical mistakes and errors of oversight or omission may be corrected at any time

        (ii) ❏ A motion under FRCP 60(b) must be made within a reasonable time—and for reasons under FRCP 60(b)(1), FRCP 60(b)(2), and FRCP 60(b)(3) no more than a year after the entry of the judgment or order or the date of the proceeding

    (4) ❏ A written motion and notice of the hearing must be served at least fourteen (14) days before the time specified for the hearing, with the following exceptions: (i) when the motion may be heard ex parte; (ii) when the Federal Rules of Civil Procedure set a different time; or (iii) when a court order—which a party may, for good cause, apply for ex parte—sets a different time

    (5) ❏ Any affidavit supporting a motion must be served with the motion

    (6) ❏ When a party who is not exempt from the electronic filing requirement files a document directly with the clerk, the party must present the document to the clerk within one (1) business day after filing the notice of manual filing

    (7) ❏ Unless the court orders otherwise, the [untimely] document and declaration [that party was unable to file in a timely manner due to technical difficulties] must be filed no later than 12:00 noon of the first day on which the court is open for business following the original filing deadline

(II) ❏ Matters to be considered by opposing party

(a) ❏ Required documents

    (1) ❏ Response brief

    (2) ❏ Certificate of service

(b) ❏ Supplemental documents

    (1) ❏ Supporting evidence

    (2) ❏ Notice of constitutional question

    (3) ❏ Index of exhibits

    (4) ❏ Request for oral argument

    (5) ❏ Request for evidentiary hearing

    (6) ❏ Copy of authority

    (7) ❏ Copy of document with self-address envelope

    (8) ❏ Notice of manual filing

(9) ❑ Courtesy copies

(10) ❑ Copies for three-judge court

(11) ❑ Declaration that party was unable to file in a timely manner due to technical difficulties

(c) ❑ Timing

(1) ❑ Opposing a motion for new trial: any response is due within fourteen (14) days after service of the motion

(i) ❑ The opposing party has fourteen (14) days after being served to file opposing affidavits

(2) ❑ Opposing a motion to alter or amend judgment: any response is due within fourteen (14) days after service of the motion

(i) ❑ Except as FRCP 59(c) provides otherwise, any opposing affidavit must be served at least seven (7) days before the hearing, unless the court permits service at another time

(3) ❑ Opposing a motion for relief from judgment: any response is due within fourteen (14) days after service of the motion

(i) ❑ Except as FRCP 59(c) provides otherwise, any opposing affidavit must be served at least seven (7) days before the hearing, unless the court permits service at another time

(4) ❑ When a party who is not exempt from the electronic filing requirement files a document directly with the clerk, the party must present the document to the clerk within one (1) business day after filing the notice of manual filing

(5) ❑ Unless the court orders otherwise, the [untimely] document and declaration [that party was unable to file in a timely manner due to technical difficulties] must be filed no later than 12:00 noon of the first day on which the court is open for business following the original filing deadline

B. Timing

1. *Motion for post-trial relief*

   a. *Motion for new trial.* A motion for a new trial must be filed no later than twenty-eight (28) days after the entry of judgment. FRCP 59(b). A motion for a new trial on the ground of newly discovered evidence is subject to the same time limit as any other motion under FRCP 59 and must be made within twenty-eight (28) days after entry of judgment. However, under FRCP 60(b)(2) a party may move for relief from the judgment on this ground within a year of the entry of the judgment. FPP § 2808. The same standard applies for establishing this ground for relief, whether the motion is under FRCP 59 or FRCP 60(b)(2). FPP § 2808; WMS Gaming, Inc. v. International Game Technology, 184 F.3d 1339, 1361 n.10 (Fed. Cir. 1999).

      i. *Supporting affidavit.* When a motion for a new trial is based on affidavits, they must be filed with the motion. FRCP 59(c).

   b. *Motion to alter or amend judgment.* A motion to alter or amend a judgment must be filed no later than twenty-eight (28) days after the entry of the judgment. FRCP 59(e).

   c. *Motion for relief from judgment*

      i. *Correction of clerical mistakes, oversights and omissions in judgment, order, or proceeding.* Clerical mistakes and errors of oversight or omission may be corrected at any time. FPP § 2855.

      ii. *Relief from judgment, order, or proceeding.* A motion under FRCP 60(b) must be made within a reasonable time—and for reasons under FRCP 60(b)(1), FRCP 60(b)(2), and FRCP 60(b)(3) no more than a year after the entry of the judgment or order or the date of the proceeding. FRCP 60(c)(1).

         • *Exception for motions under FRCP 60(b)(4).* The time limitations applicable generally to FRCP 60(b) motions ordinarily [do not] apply to motions seeking relief for voidness, and the moving party need not show diligence in seeking to overturn the judgment or a meritorious defense. FEDPROC § 51:150.

2. *Timing of motions, generally*

    a. *Motion and notice of hearing.* A written motion and notice of the hearing must be served at least fourteen (14) days before the time specified for the hearing, with the following exceptions:

        i. When the motion may be heard ex parte;

        ii. When the Federal Rules of Civil Procedure set a different time; or

        iii. When a court order—which a party may, for good cause, apply for ex parte—sets a different time. FRCP 6(c)(1).

    b. *Supporting affidavit.* Any affidavit supporting a motion must be served with the motion. FRCP 6(c)(2).

3. *Timing of opposing papers*

    a. *Opposing a motion for new trial.* Any response is due within fourteen (14) days after service of the motion. IN R USDCTSD L.R. 7-1(c)(2)(A).

        i. *Opposing affidavit.* The opposing party has fourteen (14) days after being served to file opposing affidavits. FRCP 59(c).

    b. *Opposing a motion to alter or amend judgment.* Any response is due within fourteen (14) days after service of the motion. IN R USDCTSD L.R. 7-1(c)(2)(A).

        i. *Opposing affidavit.* Except as FRCP 59(c) provides otherwise, any opposing affidavit must be served at least seven (7) days before the hearing, unless the court permits service at another time. FRCP 6(c)(2).

    c. *Opposing a motion for relief from judgment.* Any response is due within fourteen (14) days after service of the motion. IN R USDCTSD L.R. 7-1(c)(2)(A).

        i. *Opposing affidavit.* Except as FRCP 59(c) provides otherwise, any opposing affidavit must be served at least seven (7) days before the hearing, unless the court permits service at another time. FRCP 6(c)(2).

    d. *Extensions.* The court may extend response and reply deadlines, but only for good cause. IN R USDCTSD L.R. 7-1(c)(3).

    e. *Summary ruling on failure to respond.* The court may summarily rule on a motion if an opposing party does not file a response within the deadline. IN R USDCTSD L.R. 7-1(c)(4).

4. *Timing of reply papers.* Where the respondent files an answering affidavit setting up a new matter, the moving party ordinarily is allowed a reasonable time to file a reply affidavit since failure to deny the new matter by affidavit may operate as an admission of its truth. AMJUR MOTIONS § 25.

    a. *Reply in support of motion for new trial.* The court may permit reply affidavits. FRCP 59(c). Any reply is due within seven (7) days after service of the response. IN R USDCTSD L.R. 7-1(c)(2)(B).

    b. *Reply in support of motion to alter or amend judgment.* Any reply is due within seven (7) days after service of the response. IN R USDCTSD L.R. 7-1(c)(2)(B).

    c. *Reply in support of motion for relief from judgment.* Any reply is due within seven (7) days after service of the response. IN R USDCTSD L.R. 7-1(c)(2)(B).

    d. *Extensions.* The court may extend response and reply deadlines, but only for good cause. IN R USDCTSD L.R. 7-1(c)(3).

5. *Document filing by non-exempt party.* When a party who is not exempt from the electronic filing requirement files a document directly with the clerk, the party must: present the document to the clerk within one (1) business day after filing the notice of manual filing. IN R USDCTSD L.R. 5-2(d)(2).

6. *Declaration that party was unable to file in a timely manner due to technical difficulties.* Unless the Court orders otherwise, the [untimely] document and declaration [that party was unable to file in a timely manner due to technical difficulties] must be filed no later than 12:00 noon of the first day on which the Court is open for business following the original filing deadline. IN R USDCTSD ECF Procedures(16).

7. *Computation of time*

    a. *Computing time.* FRCP 6 applies in computing any time period specified in the Federal Rules of Civil

Procedure, in any local rule or court order, or in any statute that does not specify a method of computing time. FRCP 6(a).

    i.   *Period stated in days or a longer unit.* When the period is stated in days or a longer unit of time:

- Exclude the day of the event that triggers the period;

- Count every day, including intermediate Saturdays, Sundays, and legal holidays; and

- Include the last day of the period, but if the last day is a Saturday, Sunday, or legal holiday, the period continues to run until the end of the next day that is not a Saturday, Sunday, or legal holiday. FRCP 6(a)(1).

    ii.   *Period stated in hours.* When the period is stated in hours:

- Begin counting immediately on the occurrence of the event that triggers the period;

- Count every hour, including hours during intermediate Saturdays, Sundays, and legal holidays; and

- If the period would end on a Saturday, Sunday, or legal holiday, the period continues to run until the same time on the next day that is not a Saturday, Sunday, or legal holiday. FRCP 6(a)(2).

    iii.   *Inaccessibility of the clerk's office.* Unless the court orders otherwise, if the clerk's office is inaccessible:

- On the last day for filing under FRCP 6(a)(1), then the time for filing is extended to the first accessible day that is not a Saturday, Sunday, or legal holiday; or

- During the last hour for filing under FRCP 6(a)(2), then the time for filing is extended to the same time on the first accessible day that is not a Saturday, Sunday, or legal holiday. FRCP 6(a)(3).

    iv.   *"Last day" defined.* Unless a different time is set by a statute, local rule, or court order, the last day ends:

- For electronic filing, at midnight in the court's time zone; and

- For filing by other means, when the clerk's office is scheduled to close. FRCP 6(a)(4).

    v.   *"Next day" defined.* The "next day" is determined by continuing to count forward when the period is measured after an event and backward when measured before an event. FRCP 6(a)(5).

    vi.   *"Legal holiday" defined.* "Legal holiday" means:

- The day set aside by statute for observing New Year's Day, Martin Luther King Jr.'s Birthday, Washington's Birthday, Memorial Day, Independence Day, Labor Day, Columbus Day, Veterans' Day, Thanksgiving Day, or Christmas Day;

- Any day declared a holiday by the President or Congress; and

- For periods that are measured after an event, any other day declared a holiday by the state where the district court is located. FRCP 6(a)(6).

b.   *Computation of electronic filing deadlines.* Filing documents electronically does not alter filing deadlines. IN R USDCTSD ECF Procedures(7). A document due on a particular day must be filed before midnight local time of the division where the case is pending. IN R USDCTSD L.R. 5-4(a). All electronic transmissions of documents must be completed (i.e. received completely by the Clerk's Office) prior to midnight of the local time of the division in which the case is pending in order to be considered timely filed that day (NOTE: time will be noted in Eastern Time on the Court's docket. If you have filed a document prior to midnight local time of the division in which the case is pending and the document is due that date, but the electronic receipt and docket reflect the following calendar day, please contact the Court). IN R USDCTSD ECF Procedures(7). Although attorneys may file documents electronically twenty-four (24) hours a day, seven (7) days a week, attorneys are encouraged to file all documents during the normal working hours of the Clerk's Office (Monday through Friday, 8:30 a.m. to 4:30 p.m.) when technical support is available. IN R USDCTSD ECF Procedures(7); IN R USDCTSD ECF Procedures(9).

    i.   *Technical difficulties.* Parties are encouraged to file documents electronically during normal business hours, in case a problem is encountered. In the event a technical failure occurs and a document cannot be filed electronically despite the best efforts of the filing party, the party should print (if possible) a copy of the error message received. In addition, as soon as practically possible, the party should file a "Declaration that Party was Unable to File in a Timely Manner Due to Technical Difficulties." A model form is provided as Appendix D (IN R USDCTSD ECF Procedures(Appendix D)). IN R USDCTSD ECF Procedures(16).

- If a party is unable to file electronically and, as a result, may miss a filing deadline, the party must contact the Clerk's Office at the number listed in IN R USDCTSD ECF Procedures(15) to inform the court's staff of the difficulty. If a party misses a filing deadline due to an inability to file electronically, the party may submit the untimely filed document, accompanied by a declaration stating the reason(s) for missing the deadline. Unless the Court orders otherwise, the document and declaration must be filed no later than 12:00 noon of the first day on which the Court is open for business following the original filing deadline. IN R USDCTSD ECF Procedures(16).

   c. *Extending time*

      i. *In general.* When an act may or must be done within a specified time, the court may, for good cause, extend the time:

- With or without motion or notice if the court acts, or if a request is made, before the original time or its extension expires; or

- On motion made after the time has expired if the party failed to act because of excusable neglect. FRCP 6(b)(1).

      ii. *Exceptions.* A court must not extend the time to act under FRCP 50(b), FRCP 50(d), FRCP 52(b), FRCP 59(b), FRCP 59(d), FRCP 59(e), and FRCP 60(b). FRCP 6(b)(2).

      iii. Refer to the United States District Court for the Southern District of Indiana KeyRules Motion for Continuance/Extension of Time document for more information on extending time.

   d. *Additional time after certain kinds of service.* When a party may or must act within a specified time after being served and service is made under FRCP 5(b)(2)(C) (mail), FRCP 5(b)(2)(D) (leaving with the clerk), or FRCP 5(b)(2)(F) (other means consented to), three (3) days are added after the period would otherwise expire under FRCP 6(a). FRCP 6(d). Service by electronic mail shall constitute service pursuant to FRCP 5(b)(2)(E) and shall entitle the party being served to the additional three (3) days provided by FRCP 6(d). IN R USDCTSD ECF Procedures(11).

C. General Requirements

1. *Motions, generally*

   a. *Requirements.* A request for a court order must be made by motion. The motion must:

      i. Be in writing unless made during a hearing or trial;

      ii. State with particularity the grounds for seeking the order; and

      iii. State the relief sought. FRCP 7(b)(1).

   b. *Notice of motion.* A party interested in resisting the relief sought by a motion has a right to notice thereof, and an opportunity to be heard. AMJUR MOTIONS § 12.

      i. In addition to statutory or court rule provisions requiring notice of a motion—the purpose of such a notice requirement having been said to be to prevent a party from being prejudicially surprised by a motion—principles of natural justice dictate that an adverse party generally must be given notice that a motion will be presented to the court. AMJUR MOTIONS § 12.

      ii. "Notice," in this regard, means reasonable notice, including a meaningful opportunity to prepare and to defend against allegations of a motion. AMJUR MOTIONS § 12.

   c. *Writing requirement.* The writing requirement is intended to insure that the adverse parties are informed and have a record of both the motion's pendency and the grounds on which the movant seeks an order. FPP § 1191; Feldberg v. Quechee Lakes Corp., 463 F.3d 195 (2d Cir. 2006).

      i. It is sufficient "if the motion is stated in a written notice of the hearing of the motion." FPP § 1191.

d. *Particularity requirement.* The particularity requirement insures that the opposing parties will have notice of their opponent's contentions. FEDPROC § 62:364; Goodman v. 1973 26 Foot Trojan Vessel, Arkansas Registration No. AR1439SN, 859 F.2d 71, 12 Fed.R.Serv.3d 645 (8th Cir. 1988). That requirement ensures that notice of the basis for the motion is provided to the court and to the opposing party so as to avoid prejudice, provide the opponent with a meaningful opportunity to respond, and provide the court with enough information to process the motion correctly. FEDPROC § 62:364; Andreas v. Volkswagen of America, Inc., 336 F.3d 789, 56 Fed.R.Serv.3d 6 (8th Cir. 2003).

    i. Reasonable specification of the grounds for a motion is sufficient. However, where a movant fails to state even one ground for granting the motion in question, the movant has failed to meet the minimal standard of "reasonable specification." FEDPROC § 62:364; Martinez v. Trainor, 556 F.2d 818, 23 Fed.R.Serv.2d 403 (7th Cir. 1977).

    ii. The court may excuse the failure to comply with the particularity requirement if it is inadvertent, and where no prejudice is shown by the opposing party. FEDPROC § 62:364.

e. *Motions must be filed separately.* Motions must be filed separately, but alternative motions may be filed in a single document if each is named in the title. A motion must not be contained within a brief, response, or reply to a previously filed motion, unless ordered by the court. IN R USDCTSD L.R. 7-1(a).

f. *Routine or uncontested motions.* The court may rule upon a routine or uncontested motion before the response deadline passes, unless: (1) the motion indicates that an opposing party objects to it; or (2) the court otherwise believes that a response will be filed. IN R USDCTSD L.R. 7-1(d).

2. *Informal conference to resolve disputes involving non-dispositive issues.* In addition to those conferences required by IN R USDCTSD L.R. 37-1, counsel are encouraged to hold informal conferences in person or by phone to resolve any disputes involving non-dispositive issues that may otherwise require submission of a motion to the Court. This requirement does not apply to cases involving pro se parties. Therefore, prior to filing any non-dispositive motion (including motions for extension of time), the moving party must contact opposing counsel to determine whether there is an objection to any non-dispositive motion (including motions for extension of time), and state in the motion whether opposing counsel objects to the motion. IN R USDCTSD Case Mgt(General Instructions For All Cases). Refer to the Documents section of this document for more information on the contents of the motion.

3. *Motion for post-trial relief*

a. *Motion for new trial.* FRCP 59 gives the trial judge ample power to prevent what the judge considers to be a miscarriage of justice. It is the judge's right, and indeed duty, to order a new trial if it is deemed in the interest of justice to do so. FPP § 2803; Juneau Square Corp. v. First Wisconsin Nat. Bank of Milwaukee, 624 F.2d 798, 807 (7th Cir. 1980).

    i. *Grounds for new trial.* The court may, on motion, grant a new trial on all or some of the issues—and to any party—as follows: (1) after a jury trial, for any reason for which a new trial has heretofore been granted in an action at law in federal court; or (2) after a nonjury trial, for any reason for which a rehearing has heretofore been granted in a suit in equity in federal court. FRCP 59(a)(1). Any error of law, if prejudicial, is a good ground for a new trial. The other grounds most commonly raised. . .are that the verdict is against the weight of the evidence, that the verdict is too large or too small, that there is newly discovered evidence, that conduct of counsel or of the court has tainted the verdict, or that there has been misconduct affecting the jury. FPP § 2805.

        • *Weight of the evidence.* The power of a federal judge to grant a new trial on the ground that the verdict was against the weight of the evidence is clear. FPP § 2806; Byrd v. Blue Ridge Rural Elec. Co-op., Inc., 356 U.S. 525, 540, 78 S.Ct. 893, 902, 2 L.Ed.2d 953 (1958); Montgomery Ward & Co. v. Duncan, 311 U.S. 243, 251, 61 S.Ct. 189, 194, 85 L.Ed. 147 (1940). On a motion for a new trial—unlike a motion for a judgment as a matter of law—the judge may set aside the verdict even though there is substantial evidence to support it. FPP § 2806; ATD Corp. v. Lydall, Inc., 159 F.3d 534, 549 (Fed. Cir. 1998). The judge is not required to take that view of the evidence most favorable to the verdict-winner. FPP § 2806; Bates v. Hensley, 414 F.2d 1006, 1011 (8th Cir. 1969). The mere fact that the evidence is in conflict is not enough to set aside the verdict, however. Indeed the more sharply the evidence conflicts, the more reluctant the judge should be to substitute his judgment for that of the jury. FPP § 2806; Dawson v. Wal-Mart Stores, Inc., 978 F.2d 205 (5th Cir. 1992); Williams v. City of Valdosta, 689 F.2d 964, 974 (11th Cir. 1982). But on a motion for a new trial on the ground that the verdict is against the weight of the evidence, the judge is free to weigh the evidence. FPP § 2806; Uniloc USA, Inc. v. Microsoft Corp., 632 F.3d 1292 (Fed. Cir. 2011). Indeed, it has been said that the granting of a new trial on the ground that the verdict is against the weight of the evidence "involves an element of discretion which goes further than the mere sufficiency of the evidence. It embraces all the reasons which inhere in the integrity of the jury system itself." FPP § 2806; Tidewater Oil Co. v. Waller, 302 F.2d 638, 643 (10th Cir. 1962).

- *Size of the verdict.* A motion under FRCP 59 is an appropriate means to challenge the size of the verdict. The court always may grant relief if the verdict is excessive or inadequate as a matter of law, but this is not the limit of the court's power. FPP § 2807. It also may grant a new trial if the size of the verdict is against the weight of the evidence. FPP § 2807; Sprague v. Boston and Maine Corp., 769 F.2d 26, 28 (1st Cir. 1985). If the court finds that a verdict is unreasonably high, it may condition denial of the motion for a new trial on plaintiff's consent to a remittitur. FPP § 2807. If the verdict is too low, it may not provide for an additur as an alternative to a new trial. FPP § 2807; Dimick v. Schiedt, 293 U.S. 474, 55 S.Ct. 296, 79 L.Ed. 603 (1935).

- *Newly discovered evidence.* Newly discovered evidence must be of facts existing at the time of trial. FPP § 2808; Alicea v. Machete Music, 744 F.3d 773, 781 (1st Cir. 2014). The moving party must have been excusably ignorant of the facts despite using due diligence to learn about them. FPP § 2808; U.S. v. 41 Cases, More or Less, 420 F.2d 1126 (5th Cir. 1970); Huff v. Metropolitan Life Ins. Co., 675 F.2d 119 (6th Cir. 1982). If the facts were known to the party and no excusable ignorance can be shown, a new-trial motion will not be granted. Failure to show due diligence also generally will result in the denial of the motion. FPP § 2808. However, it has been held that a new trial may be granted even though proper diligence was not used if this is necessary to prevent a manifest miscarriage of justice. FPP § 2808; Ferrell v. Trailmobile, Inc., 223 F.2d 697 (5th Cir. 1955).

- *Conduct of counsel and judge.* If a verdict has been unfairly influenced by the misconduct of counsel, a new trial should be granted. Misconduct of counsel that may necessitate a new trial may involve things such as improper comments or arguments to the jury, including presenting arguments about evidence not properly before the court. FPP § 2809. Improper conduct by the trial judge also is a ground for a new trial. Motions raising this ground happily are rare and a new trial is not required if the judge's behavior has not made the trial unfair. The moving party must meet a heavy burden to prevail on the ground of judicial misconduct. FPP § 2809.

- *Misconduct affecting jury.* A common ground for a motion for a new trial is that the jury, or members of it, has not performed in the fashion expected of juries. FPP § 2810. Because of the limitations on the use of testimony by the jurors and because a new trial is required in any event only if conduct affecting the jury has been harmful to the losing party, most motions for a new trial on this ground are denied. It is ground for a new trial if a juror was prejudiced from the start but claims that a juror did not disclose all that he should at voir dire usually fail, unless it can be found that the information omitted would have supported a challenge for cause. Motions for a new trial asserting that the jury did not deliberate for a sufficient length of time also usually fail. FPP § 2810.

ii. *Partial new trial.* FRCP 59(a) provides that a new trial may be granted "on all or some of the issues—and to any party—. . . .." Thus it recognizes the court's power to grant a partial new trial. FPP § 2814. If a partial new trial is granted, those portions of the first judgment not set aside become part of the judgment entered following the jury verdict at the new trial. Thus, the end result is a single judgment. FPP § 2814.

iii. *Further action after a nonjury trial.* After a nonjury trial, the court may, on motion for a new trial, open the judgment if one has been entered, take additional testimony, amend findings of fact and conclusions of law or make new ones, and direct the entry of a new judgment. FRCP 59(a)(2).

    iv. *New trial on the court's initiate or for reasons not in the motion.* No later than twenty-eight (28) days after the entry of judgment, the court, on its own, may order a new trial for any reason that would justify granting one on a party's motion. After giving the parties notice and an opportunity to be heard, the court may grant a timely motion for a new trial for a reason not stated in the motion. In either event, the court must specify the reasons in its order. FRCP 59(d).

b. *Motion to alter or amend judgment.* FRCP 59(e) authorizes a motion to alter or amend a judgment after its entry. FRCP 59(e) also has been interpreted as permitting a motion to vacate a judgment rather than merely amend it. FPP § 2810.1.

    i. *Types of motions covered under FRCP 59(e).* FRCP 59(e) covers a broad range of motions, and the only real limitation on the type of the motion permitted is that it must request a substantive alteration of the judgment, not merely the correction of a clerical error, or relief of a type wholly collateral to the judgment. FPP § 2810.1; Osterneck v. Ernst & Whinney, 489 U.S. 169, 109 S.Ct. 987, 103 L.Ed.2d 146 (1989). The type of relief requested in postjudgment motions for attorney's fees and costs, for instance, is considered collateral unless it is specifically addressed in the judgment, and thus these motions generally do not fall under FRCP 59(e). FPP § 2810.1; Hastert v. Illinois State Bd. of Election Com'rs, 28 F.3d 1430, 1438 n.8 (7th Cir. 1993). FRCP 59(e) does, however, include motions for reconsideration. FPP § 2810.1; U.S. v. $23,000 in U.S. Currency, 356 F.3d 157, 165 n.9 (1st Cir. 2004). A motion under FRCP 59(e) also is appropriate if the court in the original judgment has failed to give relief on a certain claim on which it has found that the party is entitled to relief. Finally, the motion may be used to request an amendment of the judgment to provide for prejudgment interest. The court may not, however, give relief under FRCP 59(e) if this would defeat a party's right to jury trial on an issue. FPP § 2810.1.

    ii. *Grounds for granting a FRCP 59(e) motion.* There are four basic grounds upon which a FRCP 59(e) motion may be granted. FPP § 2810.1; F.D.I.C. v. World University Inc., 978 F.2d 10 (1st Cir. 1992). First, the movant may demonstrate that the motion is necessary to correct manifest errors of law or fact upon which the judgment is based. Of course, the corollary principle applies and the movant's failure to show any manifest error may result in the motion's denial. FPP § 2810.1. Second, the motion may be granted so that the moving party may present newly discovered or previously unavailable evidence. FPP § 2810.1; GenCorp, Inc. v. American Intern. Underwriters, 178 F.3d 804, 834 (6th Cir. 1999). Third, the motion will be granted if necessary to prevent manifest injustice. Serious misconduct of counsel may justify relief under this theory. Fourth, a FRCP 59(e) motion may be justified by an intervening change in controlling law. FPP § 2810.1.

    iii. *Limitations on a FRCP 59(e) motion.* The FRCP 59(e) motion may not be used to relitigate old matters, or to raise arguments or present evidence that could have been raised prior to the entry of judgment. Also, amendment of the judgment will be denied if it would serve no useful purpose. In practice, because of the narrow purposes for which they are intended, FRCP 59(e) motions typically are denied. FPP § 2810.1.

c. *Motion for relief from judgment*

    i. *Corrections based on clerical mistakes; Oversights and omissions.* The court may correct a clerical mistake or a mistake arising from oversight or omission whenever one is found in a judgment, order, or other part of the record. The court may do so on motion or on its own, with or without notice. But after an appeal has been docketed in the appellate court and while it is pending, such a mistake may be corrected only with the appellate court's leave. FRCP 60(a).

        • *Correctable mistakes.* A motion under FRCP 60(a) only can be used to make the judgment or record speak the truth and cannot be used to make it say something other than what originally was pronounced. FPP § 2854. FRCP 60(a) is not a vehicle for relitigating matters that already have been litigated and decided, nor to change what has been deliberately done. FPP § 2854. The mistake correctable under FRCP 60(a) need not be committed by the clerk or the court; FRCP 60(a) may be utilized to correct mistakes by the parties as well. FPP § 2854.

- *Substantive changes.* When the change sought is substantive in nature, such as a change in the calculation of interest not originally intended, the addition of an amount to a judgment to compensate for depreciation in stock awarded, or the broadening of a summary-judgment motion to dismiss all claims, relief is not appropriate under FRCP 60(a). FPP § 2854. Errors of a more substantial nature are to be corrected by a motion under FRCP 59(e) or FRCP 60(b). FPP § 2854.

ii. *Relief from judgment, order, or proceeding.* Relief under FRCP 60(b) ordinarily is obtained by motion in the court that rendered the judgment. FPP § 2865.

- *Grounds for relief from a final judgment, order, or proceeding.* On motion and just terms, the court may relieve a party or its legal representative from a final judgment, order, or proceeding for the following reasons: (1) mistake, inadvertence, surprise, or excusable neglect; (2) newly discovered evidence that, with reasonable diligence, could not have been discovered in time to move for a new trial under FRCP 59(b); (3) fraud (whether previously called intrinsic or extrinsic), misrepresentation, or misconduct by an opposing party; (4) the judgment is void; (5) the judgment has been satisfied, released or discharged; it is based on an earlier judgment that has been reversed or vacated; or applying it prospectively is no longer equitable; or (6) any other reason that justifies relief. FRCP 60(b).

- *Mistake, inadvertence, surprise, or excusable neglect.* Relief will not be granted under FRCP 60(b)(1) merely because a party is unhappy with the judgment. The party must make some showing justifying the failure to avoid the mistake or inadvertence. Gross carelessness or negligence is not enough. FPP § 2858. A defendant must prove the existence of a meritorious defense as a prerequisite to obtaining relief on these grounds. FEDPROC § 51:132; Augusta Fiberglass Coatings, Inc. v. Fodor Contracting Corp., 843 F.2d 808, 11 Fed.R.Serv.3d 42 (4th Cir. 1988). In all averments of fraud or mistake, the circumstances constituting fraud or mistake must be stated with particularity. This requirement applies with respect to averments of mistake in motion papers under FRCP 60(b)(1). FEDPROC § 51:139. In assessing whether conduct is excusable, several factors must be taken into account, including: (1) the danger of prejudice to the nonmoving party; (2) the length of the delay and its potential impact on judicial proceedings; (3) whether the movant acted in good faith; and (4) the reason for the delay, including whether it was within the reasonable control of the movant. FEDPROC § 51:133; Nara v. Frank, 488 F.3d 187 (3d Cir. 2007).

- *Newly discovered evidence.* The standards for relief from a judgment on the basis of newly discovered evidence are, in summary: (1) the motion must involve legally admissible "evidence" in some technical sense, rather than just factual information of some variety; (2) the evidence must have been in existence at the time of the trial or consists of facts existing at the time of trial; (3) the evidence must be newly-discovered since the trial; (4) the evidence must not have been discoverable by the exercise of due diligence in time for use at the trial or to move for a new trial; (5) the evidence must be material and not merely cumulative or impeaching; and (6) the evidence must be such that, if received, it will probably produce a different result. FEDPROC § 51:141.

- *Fraud, misrepresentation, or other misconduct of opposing party.* Many other cases support the propositions that the burden of proof of fraud is on the moving party and that fraud must be established by clear and convincing evidence. Further, the fraud must have prevented the moving party from fully and fairly presenting his case. It also must be chargeable to an adverse party; the moving party cannot get relief because of the party's own fraud. FPP § 2860. There is some disagreement about the meaning of "fraud" or "misconduct" in this context. One view is that the moving party must show that the adverse party committed a deliberate act that adversely impacted the fairness of the relevant legal proceeding in question. FEDPROC § 51:145; Jordan v. Paccar, Inc., 97 F.3d 1452 (6th Cir. 1996). The prevailing view is broader, however, and allows a motion for relief to be granted regardless of whether the adverse party acted with an evil, innocent or careless purpose. FEDPROC § 51:145.

- *Void judgment.* A judgment is not void merely because it is erroneous. It is void only if the court that rendered it lacked jurisdiction of the subject matter, or of the parties, or if it acted in a manner inconsistent with due process of law. Of course, although a challenge on one of those three grounds can be made under FRCP 60(b)(4), if the court finds that there was subject-matter or personal jurisdiction, or that no due-process violation has occurred, the motion will be denied. FPP § 2862.

- *Judgment satisfied or no longer equitable.* The significant portion of FRCP 60(b)(5) is the final ground, allowing relief if it is no longer equitable for the judgment to be applied prospectively. FPP § 2863. In order to obtain relief on these grounds, the judgment itself must have prospective application and such application must be inequitable due to a change in circumstances since the judgment was rendered. FEDPROC § 51:157. The mere possibility that a judgment has some future effect does not mean that it is "prospective," for purposes of applying FRCP 60(b)(5), because virtually every court order causes at least some reverberations into the future, and has some prospective effect; the essential inquiry into the prospective nature of a judgment revolves around whether it is executory or involves the supervision of changing conduct or conditions. FEDPROC § 51:158; Kalamazoo River Study Group v. Rockwell Intern. Corp., 355 F.3d 574 (6th Cir. 2004); DeWeerth v. Baldinger, 38 F.3d 1266 (2d Cir. 1994). The court's duty when confronted with such a motion is not to examine the correctness of the existing decree at the time it was entered, or even whether it is needed today, but to determine whether, assuming it was needed when entered, intervening changes have eliminated that need. FEDPROC § 51:159; Swift & Co. v. U.S., 367 U.S. 909, 81 S.Ct. 1918, 6 L.Ed.2d 1249 (1961).

- *Any other reason justifying relief.* The broad power granted by FRCP 60(b)(6) is not for the purpose of relieving a party from free, calculated, and deliberate choices the party has made. A party remains under a duty to take legal steps to protect his own interests. FPP § 2864. [Case law] certainly seemed to establish that FRCP 60(b)(6) and the first five clauses are mutually exclusive and that relief cannot be had under FRCP 60(b)(6) if it would have been available under the earlier clauses. FPP § 2864.

- *Effect of motion.* The motion does not affect the judgment's finality or suspend its operation. FRCP 60(c)(2).

- *Other powers to grant relief.* FRCP 60 does not limit a court's power to: (1) entertain an independent action to relieve a party from a judgment, order, or proceeding; (2) grant relief under 28 U.S.C.A. § 1655 to a defendant who was not personally notified of the action; or (3) set aside a judgment for fraud on the court. FRCP 60(d).

iii. *Bills and writs abolished.* The following are abolished: bills of review, bills in the nature of bills of review, and writs of coram nobis, coram vobis, and audita querela. FRCP 60(e).

4. *Opposing papers.* The Federal Rules of Civil Procedure do not require any formal answer, return, or reply to a motion, except where the Federal Rules of Civil Procedure or local rules may require affidavits, memoranda, or other papers to be filed in opposition to a motion. Such papers are simply to apprise the court of such opposition and the grounds of that opposition. FEDPROC § 62:359.

a. *Effect of failure to respond to motion.* Although in the absence of statutory provision or court rule, a motion ordinarily does not require a written answer, when a party files a motion and the opposing party fails to respond, the court may construe such failure to respond as nonopposition to the motion or an admission that the motion was meritorious, may take the facts alleged in the motion as true—the rule in some jurisdictions being that the failure to respond to a fact set forth in a motion is deemed an admission—and may grant the motion if the relief requested appears to be justified. AMJUR MOTIONS § 28.

b. *Assent or no opposition not determinative.* However, a motion will not be granted automatically simply because an "assent" or a notation of "no opposition" has been filed; federal judges frequently deny motions that have been assented to when it is thought that justice so dictates. FPP § 1190.

   c. *Responsive pleading inappropriate as response to motion.* An attempt to answer or oppose a motion with a responsive pleading usually is not appropriate. FPP § 1190.

5. *Reply papers.* A moving party may be required or permitted to prepare papers in addition to his original motion papers. AMJUR MOTIONS § 25. Papers answering or replying to opposing papers may be appropriate, in the interests of justice, where it appears there is a substantial reason for allowing a reply. Thus, a court may accept reply papers where a party demonstrates that the papers to which it seeks to file a reply raise new issues that are material to the disposition of the question before the court, or where the court determines, sua sponte, that it wishes further briefing of an issue raised in those papers and orders the submission of additional papers. FEDPROC § 62:360.

   a. *Function of reply papers.* The function of a reply affidavit is to answer the arguments made in opposition to the position taken by the movant and not to permit the movant to introduce new arguments in support of the motion. AMJUR MOTIONS § 25.

   b. *Issues raised for the first time in a reply document.* However, the view has been followed in some jurisdictions, that as a matter of judicial economy, where there is no prejudice and where the issues could be raised simply by filing a motion to dismiss, the trial court has discretion to consider arguments raised for the first time in a reply memorandum, and that a trial court may grant a motion to strike issues raised for the first time in a reply memorandum. AMJUR MOTIONS § 26.

6. *Appearances.* Every attorney who represents a party or who files a document on a party's behalf must file an appearance for that party. IN R USDCTSD L.R. 83-7. The filing of a Notice of Appearance shall act to establish the filing attorney as an attorney of record representing a designated party or parties in a particular cause of action. As a result, it is necessary for each attorney to file a separate Notice of Appearance when entering an appearance in a case. A joint appearance on behalf of multiple attorneys may be filed electronically only if it is filed separately for each attorney, using his/her ECF login. IN R USDCTSD ECF Procedures(12). Only those attorneys who have filed an appearance in a pending action are entitled to be served with case documents under FRCP 5(a). IN R USDCTSD L.R. 83-7. For more information, refer to IN R USDCTSD L.R. 83-7 and IN R USDCTSD ECF Procedures(12).

7. *Notice of related action.* A party must file a notice of related action: as soon as it appears that the party's case and another pending case: (1) arise out of the same transaction or occurrence; (2) involve the same property; or (3) involve the validity or infringement or the same patent, trademark, or copyright. IN R USDCTSD L.R. 40-1(d)(2). For more information, refer to IN R USDCTSD L.R. 40-1.

8. *Alternative dispute resolution (ADR)*

   a. *Application.* Unless limited by specific provisions, or unless there are other applicable specific statutory, common law, or constitutional procedures, the Local Alternative Dispute Resolution Rules of the United States District Court for the Southern District of Indiana shall apply in all civil litigation filed in the U.S. District Court for the Southern District of Indiana, except in the following cases and proceedings:

      i.   Applications for writs of habeas corpus under 28 U.S.C.A. § 2254;

      ii. Forfeiture cases;

      iii. Non-adversary proceedings in bankruptcy;

      iv. Social Security administrative review cases; and

      v. Such other matters as specified by order of the Court; for example, matters involving important public policy issues, constitutional law, or the establishment of new law. IN R USDCTSD A.D.R. Rule 1.2.

   b. *Mediation.* Mediation under this section (IN R USDCTSD A.D.R. Rule 2.1, et seq.) involves the confidential process by which a person acting as a Mediator, selected by the parties or appointed by the Court, assists the litigants in reaching a mutually acceptable agreement. It is an informal and nonadversarial process. The role of the Mediator is to assist in identifying the issues, reducing misunderstandings, clarifying priorities, exploring areas of compromise, and finding points of agreement as well as legitimate points of disagreement. Final decision-making authority rests with the parties, not the Mediator. IN R USDCTSD A.D.R. Rule 2.1. It is anticipated that an agreement may not resolve all of the disputed issues, but the process, nonetheless, can reduce points of contention. Parties and their representatives are required to mediate in good faith, but are not compelled to reach an agreement. IN R USDCTSD A.D.R. Rule 2.1.

 i. *Case selection.* The Court with the agreement of the parties may refer a civil case for mediation. Unless otherwise ordered or as specifically provided in IN R USDCTSD A.D.R. Rule 2.8, referral to mediation does not abate or suspend the action, and no scheduled dates shall be delayed or deferred, including the date of trial. IN R USDCTSD A.D.R. Rule 2.2.

 ii. For more information on mediation, refer to IN R USDCTSD A.D.R. Rule 2.1, et seq.

 c. *Other methods of dispute resolution.* The Local Alternative Dispute Resolution Rules of the United States District Court for the Southern District of Indiana shall not preclude the parties from utilizing any other reasonable method or technique of alternative dispute resolution to resolve disputes to which the parties agree. However, any use of arbitration by the parties will be governed by and comply with the requirements of 28 U.S.C.A. § 654 through 28 U.S.C.A. § 657. IN R USDCTSD A.D.R. Rule 1.5.

 d. For more information on alternative dispute resolution (ADR), refer to IN R USDCTSD A.D.R. Rule 1.1, et seq.

9. *Notice of settlement or resolution.* The parties must immediately notify the court if they reasonably anticipate settling their case or resolving a pending motion. IN R USDCTSD L.R. 7-1(h).

10. *Modification or suspension of rules.* The court may, on its own motion or at the request of a party, suspend or modify any rule in a particular case in the interest of justice. IN R USDCTSD L.R. 1-1(c).

D. Documents

1. *Documents for moving party*

 a. *Required documents*

  i. *Notice of motion and motion.* [P]rior to filing any non-dispositive motion (including motions for extension of time), the moving party must contact opposing counsel to determine whether there is an objection to any non-dispositive motion (including motions for extension of time), and state in the motion whether opposing counsel objects to the motion. If an objection cannot be resolved by counsel, the opposing counsel's position shall be stated within the motion. The motion should also indicate whether opposing counsel plans to file a written objection to the motion and the date by which the Court can expect to receive the objection (within the time limits set in IN R USDCTSD L.R. 7-1). If after a reasonable effort, opposing counsel cannot be reached, the moving party shall recite in the motion the dates and times that messages were left for opposing counsel. IN R USDCTSD Case Mgt(General Instructions For All Cases). Refer to the General Requirements section of this document for information on the notice of motion and motion.

  ii. *Certificate of service.* FRCP 5(d) requires that the person making service under FRCP 5 certify that service has been effected. FRCP 5(Advisory Committee Notes). Having such information on file may be useful for many purposes, including proof of service if an issue arises concerning the effectiveness of the service. FRCP 5(Advisory Committee Notes).

   • *Certificate of service for electronically-filed documents.* A certificate of service must be included with all documents filed electronically. Such certificate shall indicate that service was accomplished pursuant to the Court's electronic filing procedures. IN R USDCTSD ECF Procedures(11). For the suggested format for a certificate of service for electronic filing, refer to IN R USDCTSD ECF Procedures(11).

 b. *Supplemental documents*

  i. *Brief.* Refer to the Format section of this document for the format of briefs.

  ii. *Supporting evidence.* When a motion relies on facts outside the record, the court may hear the matter on affidavits or may hear it wholly or partly on oral testimony or on depositions. FRCP 43(c).

iii. *Notice of constitutional question.* A party that files a pleading, written motion, or other paper drawing into question the constitutionality of a federal or state statute must promptly:

- *File notice.* File a notice of constitutional question stating the question and identifying the paper that raises it, if: (1) a federal statute is questioned and the parties do not include the United States, one of its agencies, or one of its officers or employees in an official capacity; or (2) a state statute is questioned and the parties do not include the state, one of its agencies, or one of its officers or employees in an official capacity; and

- *Serve notice.* Serve the notice and paper on the Attorney General of the United States if a federal statute is questioned—or on the state attorney general if a state statute is questioned—either by certified or registered mail or by sending it to an electronic address designated by the attorney general for this purpose. FRCP 5.1(a).

- *Time for filing.* A notice of constitutional challenge to a statute filed in accordance with FRCP 5.1 must be filed at the same time the parties tender their proposed case management plan, if one is required, or within twenty-one (21) days of the filing drawing into question the constitutionality of a federal or state statute, whichever occurs later. IN R USDCTSD L.R. 5.1-1(a).

- *Additional service requirements.* If a federal statute is challenged, in addition to the service requirements of FRCP 5.1(a), the party filing the notice of constitutional challenge must serve the notice and documents on the United States Attorney for the Southern District of Indiana, either by certified or registered mail or by sending it to an electronic address designated for that purpose by that official. IN R USDCTSD L.R. 5.1-1(b).

- *No forfeiture.* A party's failure to file and serve the notice, or the court's failure to certify, does not forfeit a constitutional claim or defense that is otherwise timely asserted. FRCP 5.1(d).

iv. *Index of exhibits.* Any pleading, motion, brief, affidavit, notice, or proposed order filed with the court, whether electronically or with the clerk, must: if it has four (4) or more exhibits, include a separate index that identifies and briefly describes each exhibit. IN R USDCTSD L.R. 5-1(b).

v. *Request for oral argument.* A party may request oral argument by filing a separate motion explaining why oral argument is necessary and estimating how long the court should allow for the argument. The request must be filed and served with the supporting brief, response brief, or reply brief. IN R USDCTSD L.R. 7-5(a).

vi. *Request for evidentiary hearing.* A party may request an evidentiary hearing on a motion or petition by serving and filing a separate motion explaining why the hearing is necessary and estimating how long the court should allow for the hearing. IN R USDCTSD L.R. 7-5(c).

vii. *Copy of authority.* Generally, copies of cited authorities may not be attached to court filings. However, a party must attach to the party's motion or brief a copy of any cited authority if it is not available on Westlaw or Lexis. Upon request, a party must provide copies of any cited authority that is only available through electronic means to the court or the other parties. IN R USDCTSD L.R. 7-1(f).

viii. *Proposed order.* A party must include a suitable form of order with any document that requests the judge or the clerk to enter a routine or uncontested order. IN R USDCTSD L.R. 5-5(b); IN R USDCTSD L.R. 5-10(c); IN R USDCTSD L.R. 7-1(d).

- A service statement and/or list must be included on each proposed order, as required by IN R USDCTSD L.R. 5-5(d). IN R USDCTSD ECF Procedures(11). Any pleading, motion, brief, affidavit, notice, or proposed order filed with the court, whether electronically or with the clerk, must: if it is a form of order, include a statement of service, in the format required by IN R USDCTSD L.R. 5-5(d) in the lower left corner of the document. IN R USDCTSD L.R. 5-1(b).

- A party electronically filing a proposed order—whether voluntarily or because required by IN R USDCTSD L.R. 5-5—must convert the order directly from a word processing program and file it as an attachment to the document it relates to. Proposed orders must include in the lower left-hand corner of the signature page a statement that service will be made electronically on all ECF-registered counsel of record via email generated by the court's ECF system, without listing all such counsel. A service list including the name and postal address of any pro se litigant or non-registered attorney of record must follow, stating that service on the listed individuals will be made in the traditional paper manner, via first-class U.S. Mail. IN R USDCTSD L.R. 5-5(d).

ix. *Copy of document with self-address envelope.* To receive a file-stamped copy of a document filed directly with the clerk, a party must include with the original document an additional copy and a self-addressed envelope. The envelope must be big enough to hold the copy and have enough postage on it to send the copy via regular first-class mail. IN R USDCTSD L.R. 5-10(b).

x. *Notice of manual filing.* When a party who is not exempt from the electronic filing requirement files a document directly with the clerk, the party must: electronically file a notice of manual filing that explains why the document cannot be filed electronically. IN R USDCTSD L.R. 5-2(d)(1). Refer to the Filing and Service Requirements section of this document for more information.

- Where an individual component cannot be included in an electronic filing (e.g. the component cannot be converted to electronic format), the filer shall electronically file the prescribed Notice of Manual Filing in place of that component. A model form is provided as Appendix C (IN R USDCTSD ECF Procedures(Appendix C)). IN R USDCTSD ECF Procedures(13).

- Before making a manual filing of a component, the filing party shall first electronically file a Notice of Manual Filing (See IN R USDCTSD ECF Procedures(Appendix C)). The filer shall initiate the electronic filing process as if filing the actual component but shall instead attach to the filing the Notice of Manual Filing setting forth the reason(s) why the component cannot be filed electronically. The manual filing should be accompanied by a copy of the previously filed Notice of Manual Filing. A party may seek to have a component excluded from electronic filing pursuant to applicable Federal and Local Rules (e.g., FRCP 26(c)). IN R USDCTSD ECF Procedures(15).

xi. *Courtesy copies.* District Judges and Magistrate Judges regularly receive documents filed by all parties. Therefore, parties shall not bring "courtesy copies" to any chambers unless specifically directed to do so by the Court. IN R USDCTSD Case Mgt(General Instructions For All Cases).

xii. *Copies for three-judge court.* Parties in a case where a three-judge court has been requested must file an original and three copies of any document filed directly with the clerk (instead of electronically) until the court: (1) denies the request; (2) dissolves the three-judge court; or (3) allows the parties to file fewer copies. IN R USDCTSD L.R. 9-2(c).

xiii. *Declaration that party was unable to file in a timely manner due to technical difficulties.* If a party misses a filing deadline due to an inability to file electronically, the party may submit the untimely filed document, accompanied by a declaration stating the reason(s) for missing the deadline. IN R USDCTSD ECF Procedures(16). A model form is provided as Appendix D (IN R USDCTSD ECF Procedures(Appendix D)). IN R USDCTSD ECF Procedures(16).

2. *Documents for opposing party*

   a. *Required documents*

      i. *Response brief.* Refer to the Format section of this document for the format of briefs. Refer to the General Requirements section of this document for information on the opposing papers.

      ii. *Certificate of service.* FRCP 5(d) requires that the person making service under FRCP 5 certify that service has been effected. FRCP 5(Advisory Committee Notes). Having such information on file may be useful for many purposes, including proof of service if an issue arises concerning the effectiveness of the service. FRCP 5(Advisory Committee Notes).

         - *Certificate of service for electronically-filed documents.* A certificate of service must be included with all documents filed electronically. Such certificate shall indicate that service was accomplished pursuant to the Court's electronic filing procedures. IN R USDCTSD

ECF Procedures(11). For the suggested format for a certificate of service for electronic filing, refer to IN R USDCTSD ECF Procedures(11).

b. *Supplemental documents*

   i. *Supporting evidence.* When a motion relies on facts outside the record, the court may hear the matter on affidavits or may hear it wholly or partly on oral testimony or on depositions. FRCP 43(c).

   ii. *Notice of constitutional question.* A party that files a pleading, written motion, or other paper drawing into question the constitutionality of a federal or state statute must promptly:

   - *File notice.* File a notice of constitutional question stating the question and identifying the paper that raises it, if: (1) a federal statute is questioned and the parties do not include the United States, one of its agencies, or one of its officers or employees in an official capacity; or (2) a state statute is questioned and the parties do not include the state, one of its agencies, or one of its officers or employees in an official capacity; and

   - *Serve notice.* Serve the notice and paper on the Attorney General of the United States if a federal statute is questioned—or on the state attorney general if a state statute is questioned—either by certified or registered mail or by sending it to an electronic address designated by the attorney general for this purpose. FRCP 5.1(a).

   - *Time for filing.* A notice of constitutional challenge to a statute filed in accordance with FRCP 5.1 must be filed at the same time the parties tender their proposed case management plan, if one is required, or within twenty-one (21) days of the filing drawing into question the constitutionality of a federal or state statute, whichever occurs later. IN R USDCTSD L.R. 5.1-1(a).

   - *Additional service requirements.* If a federal statute is challenged, in addition to the service requirements of FRCP 5.1(a), the party filing the notice of constitutional challenge must serve the notice and documents on the United States Attorney for the Southern District of Indiana, either by certified or registered mail or by sending it to an electronic address designated for that purpose by that official. IN R USDCTSD L.R. 5.1-1(b).

   - *No forfeiture.* A party's failure to file and serve the notice, or the court's failure to certify, does not forfeit a constitutional claim or defense that is otherwise timely asserted. FRCP 5.1(d).

   iii. *Index of exhibits.* Any pleading, motion, brief, affidavit, notice, or proposed order filed with the court, whether electronically or with the clerk, must: if it has four (4) or more exhibits, include a separate index that identifies and briefly describes each exhibit. IN R USDCTSD L.R. 5-1(b).

   iv. *Request for oral argument.* A party may request oral argument by filing a separate motion explaining why oral argument is necessary and estimating how long the court should allow for the argument. The request must be filed and served with the supporting brief, response brief, or reply brief. IN R USDCTSD L.R. 7-5(a).

   v. *Request for evidentiary hearing.* A party may request an evidentiary hearing on a motion or petition by serving and filing a separate motion explaining why the hearing is necessary and estimating how long the court should allow for the hearing. IN R USDCTSD L.R. 7-5(c).

   vi. *Copy of authority.* Generally, copies of cited authorities may not be attached to court filings. However, a party must attach to the party's motion or brief a copy of any cited authority if it is not available on Westlaw or Lexis. Upon request, a party must provide copies of any cited authority that is only available through electronic means to the court or the other parties. IN R USDCTSD L.R. 7-1(f).

   vii. *Copy of document with self-address envelope.* To receive a file-stamped copy of a document filed directly with the clerk, a party must include with the original document an additional copy and a self-addressed envelope. The envelope must be big enough to hold the copy and have enough postage on it to send the copy via regular first-class mail. IN R USDCTSD L.R. 5-10(b).

   viii. *Notice of manual filing.* When a party who is not exempt from the electronic filing requirement

files a document directly with the clerk, the party must: electronically file a notice of manual filing that explains why the document cannot be filed electronically. IN R USDCTSD L.R. 5-2(d)(1). Refer to the Filing and Service Requirements section of this document for more information.

- Where an individual component cannot be included in an electronic filing (e.g. the component cannot be converted to electronic format), the filer shall electronically file the prescribed Notice of Manual Filing in place of that component. A model form is provided as Appendix C (IN R USDCTSD ECF Procedures(Appendix C)). IN R USDCTSD ECF Procedures(13).

- Before making a manual filing of a component, the filing party shall first electronically file a Notice of Manual Filing (See IN R USDCTSD ECF Procedures(Appendix C)). The filer shall initiate the electronic filing process as if filing the actual component but shall instead attach to the filing the Notice of Manual Filing setting forth the reason(s) why the component cannot be filed electronically. The manual filing should be accompanied by a copy of the previously filed Notice of Manual Filing. A party may seek to have a component excluded from electronic filing pursuant to applicable Federal and Local Rules (e.g., FRCP 26(c)). IN R USDCTSD ECF Procedures(15).

ix. *Courtesy copies.* District Judges and Magistrate Judges regularly receive documents filed by all parties. Therefore, parties shall not bring "courtesy copies" to any chambers unless specifically directed to do so by the Court. IN R USDCTSD Case Mgt(General Instructions For All Cases).

x. *Copies for three-judge court.* Parties in a case where a three-judge court has been requested must file an original and three copies of any document filed directly with the clerk (instead of electronically) until the court: (1) denies the request; (2) dissolves the three-judge court; or (3) allows the parties to file fewer copies. IN R USDCTSD L.R. 9-2(c).

xi. *Declaration that party was unable to file in a timely manner due to technical difficulties.* If a party misses a filing deadline due to an inability to file electronically, the party may submit the untimely filed document, accompanied by a declaration stating the reason(s) for missing the deadline. IN R USDCTSD ECF Procedures(16). A model form is provided as Appendix D (IN R USDCTSD ECF Procedures(Appendix D)). IN R USDCTSD ECF Procedures(16).

E. Format

1. *Form of documents.* The rules governing captions and other matters of form in pleadings apply to motions and other papers. FRCP 7(b)(2).

   a. *Paper (manual filings only).* Any document that is not filed electronically must: be flat, unfolded, and on good-quality, eight and one-half by eleven (8-1/2 x 11) inch white paper. IN R USDCTSD L.R. 5-1(d)(1). Any document that is not filed electronically must: be single-sided. IN R USDCTSD L.R. 5-1(d)(1).

      i. *Covers or backing.* Any document that is not filed electronically must: not have a cover or a back. IN R USDCTSD L.R. 5-1(d)(1).

      ii. *Fastening.* Any document that is not filed electronically must: be (if consisting of more than one (1) page) fastened by paperclip or binder clip and may not be stapled. IN R USDCTSD L.R. 5-1(d)(1).

         - *Request for nonconforming fastening.* If a document cannot be fastened or bound as required by IN R USDCTSD L.R. 5-1(d), a party may ask the clerk for permission to fasten it in another manner. The party must make such a request before attempting to file the document with nonconforming fastening. IN R USDCTSD L.R. 5-1(d)(2).

      iii. *Hole punching.* Any document that is not filed electronically must: be two-hole punched at the top with the holes two and three-quarter (2-3/4) inches apart and appropriately centered. IN R USDCTSD L.R. 5-1(d)(1).

   b. *Margins.* Any pleading, motion, brief, affidavit, notice, or proposed order filed with the court, whether electronically or with the clerk, must: have at least one (1) inch margins. IN R USDCTSD L.R. 5-1(b).

c. *Spacing.* Any pleading, motion, brief, affidavit, notice, or proposed order filed with the court, whether electronically or with the clerk, must: be double spaced (except for headings, footnotes, and quoted material). IN R USDCTSD L.R. 5-1(b).

d. *Text.* Any pleading, motion, brief, affidavit, notice, or proposed order filed with the court, whether electronically or with the clerk, must: be plainly typewritten, printed, or prepared by a clearly legible copying process. IN R USDCTSD L.R. 5-1(b).

e. *Font size.* Any pleading, motion, brief, affidavit, notice, or proposed order filed with the court, whether electronically or with the clerk, must: use at least 12-point type in the body of the document and at least 10-point type in footnotes. IN R USDCTSD L.R. 5-1(b).

f. *Page numbering.* Any pleading, motion, brief, affidavit, notice, or proposed order filed with the court, whether electronically or with the clerk, must: have consecutively numbered pages. IN R USDCTSD L.R. 5-1(b).

g. *Caption; Names of parties.* Every pleading must have a caption with the court's name, a title, a file number, and a FRCP 7(a) designation. The title of the complaint must name all the parties; the title of other pleadings, after naming the first party on each side, may refer generally to other parties. FRCP 10(a). Any pleading, motion, brief, affidavit, notice, or proposed order filed with the court, whether electronically or with the clerk, must: include a title on the first page. IN R USDCTSD L.R. 5-1(b).

   i. *Alternative motions.* Motions must be filed separately, but alternative motions may be filed in a single document if each is named in the title. IN R USDCTSD L.R. 7-1(a).

h. *Filer's information.* Any pleading, motion, brief, affidavit, notice, or proposed order filed with the court, whether electronically or with the clerk, must: in the case of pleadings, motions, legal briefs, and notices, include the name, complete address, telephone number, facsimile number (where available), and e-mail address (where available) of the pro se litigant or attorney who files it. IN R USDCTSD L.R. 5-1(b).

i. *Paragraphs; Separate statements.* A party must state its claims or defenses in numbered paragraphs, each limited as far as practicable to a single set of circumstances. A later pleading may refer by number to a paragraph in an earlier pleading. If doing so would promote clarity, each claim founded on a separate transaction or occurrence—and each defense other than a denial—must be stated in a separate count or defense. FRCP 10(b).

j. *Adoption by reference; Exhibits.* A statement in a pleading may be adopted by reference elsewhere in the same pleading or in any other pleading or motion. A copy of a written instrument that is an exhibit to a pleading is a part of the pleading for all purposes. FRCP 10(c).

k. *Citations*

   i. *Local rules.* The Local Rules of the United States District Court for the Southern District of Indiana may be cited as "S.D. Ind. L.R." IN R USDCTSD L.R. 1-1(a).

   ii. *Local alternative dispute resolution rules.* These Rules shall be known as the Local Alternative Dispute Resolution Rules of the United States District Court for the Southern District of Indiana. They shall be cited as "S.D.Ind. Local A.D.R. Rule _____." IN R USDCTSD A.D.R. Rule 1.1.

l. *Acceptance by the clerk.* The clerk must not refuse to file a paper solely because it is not in the form prescribed by the Federal Rules of Civil Procedure or by a local rule or practice. FRCP 5(d)(4). The clerk will accept a document that violates IN R USDCTSD L.R. 5-1, but the court may exclude the document from the official record. IN R USDCTSD L.R. 5-1(e).

   i. *Sanctions for errors as to form.* The court may strike from the record any document that does not comply with the rules governing the form of documents filed with the court, such as rules that regulate document size or the number of copies to be filed or that require a special designation in the caption. The court may also sanction an attorney or party who files a non-compliant document. IN R USDCTSD L.R. 1-3.

2. *Form of electronic documents.* Any document submitted via the court's electronic case filing (ECF)

system must be: otherwise prepared and filed in a manner consistent with the CM/ECF Policies and Procedures Manual (IN R USDCTSD ECF Procedures). IN R USDCTSD L.R. 5-1(c). Electronically filed documents must meet the requirements of FRCP 10 (Form of Pleadings), IN R USDCTSD L.R. 5-1 (Format of Papers Presented for Filing), and FRCP 5.2 (Privacy Protection for Filings Made with the Court), as if they had been submitted on paper. Documents filed electronically are also subject to any page limitations set forth by Court Order, by IN R USDCTSD L.R. 7-1 (Motion Practice), or IN R USDCTSD L.R. 56-1 (Summary Judgment Practice), as applicable. IN R USDCTSD ECF Procedures(13).

a. *PDF format required.* Any document submitted via the court's electronic case filing (ECF) system must be: in .pdf format. IN R USDCTSD L.R. 5-1(c); IN R USDCTSD ECF Procedures(7). Any document submitted via the court's electronic case filing (ECF) system must be: converted to a .pdf file directly from a word processing program, unless it exists only in paper format (in which case it may be scanned to create a .pdf document). IN R USDCTSD L.R. 5-1(c); IN R USDCTSD ECF Procedures(13).

   i. An exhibit may be scanned into PDF format, at a recommended 300 dpi resolution or higher, only if it does not already exist in electronic format. The filing attorney is responsible for reviewing all PDF documents for legibility before submitting them through the Court's Electronic Case Filing system. For technical guidance in creating PDF documents, please contact the Clerk's Office. IN R USDCTSD ECF Procedures(13).

b. *File size limitations.* Any document submitted via the court's electronic case filing (ECF) system must be: submitted as one or more .pdf files that do not exceed ten megabytes (10 MB) each (consistent with the CM/ECF Policies and Procedures Manual (IN R USDCTSD ECF Procedures)). IN R USDCTSD L.R. 5-1(c); IN R USDCTSD ECF Procedures(13).

   i. To electronically file a document or attachment that exceeds ten megabytes (10 MB), the document must first be broken down into two or more smaller files. For example, if Exhibit A is a twelve megabyte (12 MB) PDF file, it should be divided into 2 equal parts prior to electronic filing. Each component part of the exhibit would be filed as an attachment to the main document and described appropriately as "Exhibit A (part 1 of 2)" and "Exhibit A (part 2 of 2)." IN R USDCTSD ECF Procedures(13).

   ii. The supporting items mentioned in IN R USDCTSD ECF Procedures(13) should not be confused with memorandums or briefs in support of motions as outlined in IN R USDCTSD L.R. 7-1 or IN R USDCTSD L.R. 56-1. These memorandums or briefs in support are to be filed as entirely separate documents pursuant to the appropriate rule. Additionally, no motion shall be embodied in the text of a response or reply brief/memorandum unless otherwise ordered by the Court. IN R USDCTSD ECF Procedures(13).

c. *Separate component parts.* A key objective of the electronic filing system is to ensure that as much of the case as possible is managed electronically. To facilitate electronic filing and retrieval, documents to be filed electronically are to be reasonably broken into their separate component parts. By way of example, most filings include a foundation document (e.g., motion) and other supporting items (e.g., exhibits, proposed orders, proposed amended pleadings). The foundation document, as well as the supporting items, are each separate components of the filing; supporting items must be filed as attachments to the foundation document. These exhibits or attachments should include only those excerpts of the referenced documents that are directly germane to the matter under consideration. IN R USDCTSD ECF Procedures(13).

   i. Where an individual component cannot be included in an electronic filing (e.g. the component cannot be converted to electronic format), the filer shall electronically file the prescribed Notice of Manual Filing in place of that component. A model form is provided as Appendix C (IN R USDCTSD ECF Procedures(Appendix C)). IN R USDCTSD ECF Procedures(13).

d. *Exhibits.* Each electronically filed exhibit to a main document must be: (1) created as a separate .pdf file; (2) submitted as an attachment to the main document and given a title which describes its content; and (3) limited to excerpts that are directly germane to the main document's subject matter. IN R USDCTSD L.R. 5-6(a).

   i. When uploading attachments during the electronic filing process, exhibits must be uploaded in

a logical sequence and a brief description must be entered for each individual PDF file. The description must include not only the exhibit number or letter, but also a brief description of the document. This information may be entered in CM/ECF using a combination of the Category drop-down menu, the Description text box, or both (see IN R USDCTSD ECF Procedures(13)(Figure 1)). The information that is provided in each box will be combined to create a description of the document as it appears on the case docket (see IN R USDCTSD ECF Procedures(13)(Figure 2)). IN R USDCTSD ECF Procedures(13). For an example, refer to IN R USDCTSD ECF Procedures(13).

e. *Excerpts.* A party filing an exhibit that consists of excerpts from a larger document must clearly and prominently identify the exhibit as containing excerpted material. Either party will have the right to timely file additional excerpts or the complete document to the extent they are or become directly germane to the main document's subject matter. IN R USDCTSD L.R. 5-6(b).

f. For an example illustrating the application of IN R USDCTSD ECF Procedures(13), refer to IN R USDCTSD ECF Procedures(13).

3. *Form of briefs*

   a. *Page limits.* Supporting and response briefs (excluding tables of contents, tables of authorities, appendices, and certificates of service) may not exceed thirty-five (35) pages. Reply briefs may not exceed twenty (20) pages. IN R USDCTSD L.R. 7-1(e)(1).

      i. *Permission to exceed limits.* The court may allow a party to file a brief exceeding these page limits for extraordinary and compelling reasons. IN R USDCTSD L.R. 7-1(e)(2).

      ii. *Supporting and response briefs exceeding limits.* If the court allows a party to file a brief or response exceeding thirty-five (35) pages, the document must include:

      • A table of contents with page references;

      • A statement of issues; and

      • A table of authorities including: (1) all cases (alphabetically arranged), statutes, and other authorities cited in the brief; and (2) page numbers where the authorities are cited in the brief. IN R USDCTSD L.R. 7-1(e)(3).

4. *Signing of pleadings, motions and other papers*

   a. *Signature.* Every pleading, written motion, and other paper must be signed by at least one attorney of record in the attorney's name—or by a party personally if the party is unrepresented. The paper must state the signer's address, e-mail address, and telephone number. FRCP 11(a).

      i. *Signatures on manual filings.* Any document that is not filed electronically must: include the original signature of the pro se litigant or attorney who files it. IN R USDCTSD L.R. 5-1(d)(1).

      ii. *Electronic signatures.* Use of the attorney's login and password when filing documents electronically serves in part as the attorney's signature for purposes of FRCP 11, the Local Rules of the United States District Court for the Southern District of Indiana, and any other purpose for which a signature is required in connection with proceedings before the Court. IN R USDCTSD ECF Procedures(14); IN R USDCTSD ECF Procedures(10). A pleading, motion, brief, or notice filed electronically under an attorney's ECF log-in and password must be signed by that attorney. IN R USDCTSD L.R. 5-7(a). A signature on a document other than a document filed as provided under IN R USDCTSD L.R. 5-7(a) must be an original handwritten signature and must be scanned into .pdf format for electronic filing. IN R USDCTSD L.R. 5-7(c); IN R USDCTSD ECF Procedures(14).

      • *Form of electronic signature.* If a document is converted directly from a word processing application to .pdf (as opposed to scanning), the name of the Filing User under whose log-in and password the document is submitted must be preceded by a "s/" and typed on the signature line where the Filing User's handwritten signature would otherwise appear. IN R USDCTSD L.R. 5-7(b). All documents filed electronically shall include a signature block and include the filing attorney's typewritten name, address, telephone number, facsimile number and e-mail address. In addition, the name of the filing attorney under

whose ECF login the document will be filed should be preceded by a "s/" and typed in the space where the attorney's handwritten signature would otherwise appear. IN R US-DCTSD ECF Procedures(14). For a sample format, refer to IN R USDCTSD ECF Procedures(14).

- *Effect of electronic signature.* Filing an electronically signed document under an attorney's ECF log-in and password constitutes the attorney's signature on the document under the Federal Rules of Civil Procedure, under the Local Rules of the United States District Court for the Southern District of Indiana, and for any other reason a signature is required in connection with the court's activities. IN R USDCTSD L.R. 5-7(d).

- *Documents with multiple attorneys' signatures.* Documents requiring signatures of more than one attorney shall be filed either by: (1) obtaining consent from the other attorney, then typing the "s/ [Name]" signature of the other attorney on the signature line where the other attorney's signature would otherwise appear; (2) identifying in the signature section the name of the other attorney whose signature is required and by the submission of a Notice of Endorsement (see IN R USDCTSD ECF Procedures(Appendix B)) by the other attorney no later than three (3) business days after filing; (3) submitting a scanned document containing all handwritten signatures; or (4) in any other manner approved by the Court. IN R USDCTSD ECF Procedures(14); IN R USDCTSD L.R. 5-7(e).

iii. *No verification or accompanying affidavit required for pleadings.* Unless a rule or statute specifically states otherwise, a pleading need not be verified or accompanied by an affidavit. FRCP 11(a).

iv. *Unsigned papers.* The court must strike an unsigned paper unless the omission is promptly corrected after being called to the attorney's or party's attention. FRCP 11(a). The court will strike any document filed directly with the clerk that is not signed by an attorney of record or the pro se litigant filing it, but the court may do so only after giving the attorney or pro se litigant notice of the omission and reasonable time to correct it. Rubber-stamp or facsimile signatures are not original signatures and the court will deem documents containing them to be unsigned for purposes of FRCP 11 and FRCP 26(g) and IN R USDCTSD L.R. 5-10. IN R USDCTSD L.R. 5-10(g).

b. *Representations to the court.* By presenting to the court a pleading, written motion, or other paper—whether by signing, filing, submitting, or later advocating it—an attorney or unrepresented party certifies that to the best of the person's knowledge, information, and belief, formed after an inquiry reasonable under the circumstances:

i. It is not being presented for any improper purpose, such as to harass, cause unnecessary delay, or needlessly increase the cost of litigation;

ii. The claims, defenses, and other legal contentions are warranted by existing law or by a nonfrivolous argument for extending, modifying, or reversing existing law or for establishing new law;

iii. The factual contentions have evidentiary support or, if specifically so identified, will likely have evidentiary support after a reasonable opportunity for further investigation or discovery; and

iv. The denials of factual contentions are warranted on the evidence or, if specifically so identified, are reasonably based on belief or a lack of information. FRCP 11(b).

c. *Sanctions.* If, after notice and a reasonable opportunity to respond, the court determines that FRCP 11(b) has been violated, the court may impose an appropriate sanction on any attorney, law firm, or party that violated FRCP 11(b) or is responsible for the violation. FRCP 11(c)(1). Refer to the United States District Court for the Southern District of Indiana KeyRules Motion for Sanctions document for more information.

5. *Privacy protection for filings made with the court.* Electronically filed documents must meet the requirements of. . .FRCP 5.2 (Privacy Protection for Filings Made with the Court), as if they had been submitted on paper. IN R USDCTSD ECF Procedures(13).

a. *Redacted filings.* Unless the court orders otherwise, in an electronic or paper filing with the court that

contains an individual's Social Security number, taxpayer-identification number, or birth date, the name of an individual known to be a minor, or a financial-account number, a party or nonparty making the filing may include only:

    i.   The last four (4) digits of the Social Security number and taxpayer-identification number;

    ii.   The year of the individual's birth;

    iii.   The minor's initials; and

    iv.   The last four (4) digits of the financial-account number. FRCP 5.2(a).

b. *Exemptions from the redaction requirement.* The redaction requirement does not apply to the following:

    i.   A financial-account number that identifies the property allegedly subject to forfeiture in a forfeiture proceeding;

    ii.   The record of an administrative or agency proceeding;

    iii.   The official record of a state-court proceeding;

    iv.   The record of a court or tribunal, if that record was not subject to the redaction requirement when originally filed;

    v.   A filing covered by FRCP 5.2(c) or FRCP 5.2(d); and

    vi.   A pro se filing in an action brought under 28 U.S.C.A. § 2241, 28 U.S.C.A. § 2254, or 28 U.S.C.A. § 2255. FRCP 5.2(b).

c. *Limitations on remote access to electronic files; Social Security appeals and immigration cases.* Unless the court orders otherwise, in an action for benefits under the Social Security Act, and in an action or proceeding relating to an order of removal, to relief from removal, or to immigration benefits or detention, access to an electronic file is authorized as follows:

    i.   The parties and their attorneys may have remote electronic access to any part of the case file, including the administrative record;

    ii.   Any other person may have electronic access to the full record at the courthouse, but may have remote electronic access only to:

        • The docket maintained by the court; and

        • An opinion, order, judgment, or other disposition of the court, but not any other part of the case file or the administrative record. FRCP 5.2(c).

d. *Filings made under seal.* The court may order that a filing be made under seal without redaction. The court may later unseal the filing or order the person who made the filing to file a redacted version for the public record. FRCP 5.2(d). For more information on filing under seal, refer to IN R USDCTSD L.R. 5-11 and IN R USDCTSD ECF Procedures(18).

e. *Protective orders.* For good cause, the court may by order in a case:

    i.   Require redaction of additional information; or

    ii.   Limit or prohibit a nonparty's remote electronic access to a document filed with the court. FRCP 5.2(e).

f. *Option for additional unredacted filing under seal.* A person making a redacted filing may also file an unredacted copy under seal. The court must retain the unredacted copy as part of the record. FRCP 5.2(f).

g. *Option for filing a reference list.* A filing that contains redacted information may be filed together with a reference list that identifies each item of redacted information and specifies an appropriate identifier that uniquely corresponds to each item listed. The list must be filed under seal and may be amended as of right. Any reference in the case to a listed identifier will be construed to refer to the corresponding item of information. FRCP 5.2(g).

h. *Waiver of protection of identifiers.* A person waives the protection of FRCP 5.2(a) as to the person's own information by filing it without redaction and not under seal. FRCP 5.2(h).

F. Filing and Service Requirements

1. *Filing requirements.* Any paper after the complaint that is required to be served—together with a certificate of service—must be filed within a reasonable time after service. FRCP 5(d)(1). Motions must be filed separately, but alternative motions may be filed in a single document if each is named in the title. IN R USDCTSD L.R. 7-1(a).

   a. *How filing is made; In general.* A paper is filed by delivering it:

      i. To the clerk; or

      ii. To a judge who agrees to accept it for filing, and who must then note the filing date on the paper and promptly send it to the clerk. FRCP 5(d)(2).

         • In certain instances, the court will direct the parties to submit items directly to chambers (e.g., confidential settlement statements). However, absent specific prior authorization, counsel and litigants should not submit letters or documents directly to chambers, and such materials should be filed with the clerk. IN R USDCTSD L.R. 5-1(Local Rules Advisory Committee Comment).

      iii. A document or item submitted in relation to a matter within the court's jurisdiction is deemed filed upon delivery to the office of the clerk in a manner prescribed by the Local Rules of the United States District Court for the Southern District of Indiana or the Federal Rules of Civil Procedure or authorized by the court. Any submission directed to a Judge or Judge's staff, the office of the clerk or any employee thereof, in a manner that is not contemplated by IN R USDCTSD L.R. 5-1 and without prior court authorization is prohibited. IN R USDCTSD L.R. 5-1(a).

   b. *Non-electronic filing.* Any document that is exempt from electronic filing must be filed directly with the clerk and served on other parties in the case as required by those Federal Rules of Civil Procedure and Local Rules of the United States District Court for the Southern District of Indiana that apply to the service of non-electronic documents. IN R USDCTSD L.R. 5-2(c).

      i. *When completed.* A document or other item that is not required to be filed electronically is deemed filed:

         • Upon delivery in person, by courier, or via U.S. Mail or other mail delivery service to the clerk's office during business hours;

         • When the courtroom deputy clerk accepts it, if the document or item is filed in open court; or

         • Upon completion of any other manner of filing that the court authorizes. IN R USDCTSD L.R. 5-10(a).

      ii. *Document filing by non-exempt party.* When a party who is not exempt from the electronic filing requirement files a document directly with the clerk, the party must:

         • Electronically file a notice of manual filing that explains why the document cannot be filed electronically;

         • Present the document to the clerk within one (1) business day after filing the notice of manual filing; and

         • Present the clerk with a copy of the notice of manual filing when the party files the document with the clerk. IN R USDCTSD L.R. 5-2(d).

   c. *Electronic filing*

      i. *Authorization of electronic filing program.* A court may, by local rule, allow papers to be filed, signed, or verified by electronic means that are consistent with any technical standards established by the Judicial Conference of the United States. A local rule may require electronic filing only if reasonable exceptions are allowed. A paper filed electronically in compliance with a local rule is a written paper for purposes of the Federal Rules of Civil Procedure. FRCP 5(d)(3).

         • IN R USDCTSD L.R. 5-2 requires electronic filing, as allowed by FRCP 5(d)(3). The

policies and procedures in IN R USDCTSD ECF Procedures govern electronic filing in this district unless, due to circumstances in a particular case, a judicial officer determines that these policies and procedures (IN R USDCTSD ECF Procedures) should be modified. IN R USDCTSD ECF Procedures(1).

- Unless modified by order of the Court, all Federal Rules of Civil Procedure and Local Rules of the United States District Court for the Southern District of Indiana shall continue to apply to cases maintained in the Court's Case Management/Electronic Case Filing System (CM/ECF). IN R USDCTSD ECF Procedures(3).

ii. *Mandatory electronic filing.* Unless exempted pursuant to IN R USDCTSD L.R. 5-3(e), attorneys admitted to the court's bar (including those admitted pro hac vice) or authorized to represent the United States must use the court's ECF system to file documents. IN R USDCTSD L.R. 5-3(a). Electronic filing by attorneys is required for eligible documents filed in civil and criminal cases pending with the Court, unless specifically exempted by Local Rule or Court Order. IN R USDCTSD ECF Procedures(4).

- *Exceptions.* All civil cases (other than those cases the court specifically exempts) must be maintained in the court's electronic case filing (ECF) system. Accordingly, as allowed by FRCP 5(d)(3), every document filed in this court (including exhibits) must be transmitted to the clerk's office via the ECF system consistent with IN R USDCTSD L.R. 5-2 through IN R USDCTSD L.R. 5-11 except: (1) documents filed by pro se litigants; (2) transcripts in cases filed by claimants under the Social Security Act (and related statutes); (3) exhibits in a format that does not readily permit electronic filing (such as videos and large maps and charts); (4) documents that are illegible when scanned into .pdf format; (5) documents filed in cases not maintained on the ECF system; and (6) any other documents that the court or the Local Rules of the United States District Court for the Southern District of Indiana specifically allow to be filed directly with the clerk. IN R USDCTSD L.R. 5-2(a). Parties otherwise participating in the electronic filing system may be excused from filing a particular component electronically under certain limited circumstances, such as when the component cannot be reduced to an electronic format. Such components shall not be filed electronically, but instead shall be manually filed with the Clerk of Court and served upon the parties in accordance with the applicable Federal Rules of Civil Procedure and the Local Rules of the United States District Court for the Southern District of Indiana for filing and service of non-electronic documents. IN R USDCTSD ECF Procedures(15).

- *Exemption from participation.* The court may exempt attorneys from using the ECF system in a particular case for good cause. An attorney must file a petition for ECF exemption and a CM/ECF technical requirements exemption questionnaire in each case in which the attorney seeks an exemption. (The CM/ECF technical requirements exemption questionnaire is available on the court's website). IN R USDCTSD L.R. 5-3(e).

iii. *Consequences of electronic filing.* Electronic transmission of a document consistent with the procedures adopted by the Court shall, upon the complete receipt of the same by the Clerk of Court, constitute filing of the document for all purposes of the Federal Rules of Civil and Criminal Procedure and the Local Rules of the United States District Court for the Southern District of Indiana, and shall constitute entry of that document onto the docket maintained by the Clerk pursuant to FRCP 58 and FRCP 79. IN R USDCTSD ECF Procedures(7); IN R USDCTSD L.R. 5-4(c)(1). When a document has been filed electronically: the document, as filed, binds the filing party. IN R USDCTSD L.R. 5-4(c)(3).

- A Notice of Electronic Filing (NEF) acknowledging that the document has been filed will immediately appear on the filer's screen after the document has been submitted. Attorneys are strongly encouraged to print or electronically save a copy of the NEF. Attorneys can also verify the filing of documents by inspecting the Court's electronic docket sheet through the use of a PACER login. IN R USDCTSD ECF Procedures(7). When a document has been filed electronically: the notice of electronic filing for the document serves as the court's date-stamp and proof of filing. IN R USDCTSD L.R. 5-4(c)(4).

- The Court may, upon the motion of a party or upon its own motion, strike any inappropriately filed document. IN R USDCTSD ECF Procedures(7).

SOUTHERN DISTRICT OF INDIANA

iv. For more information on electronic filing, refer to IN R USDCTSD ECF Procedures.

d. *Fax filing.* The clerk may not file a faxed document without court authorization. The court may not authorize the clerk to file faxed documents without finding that compelling circumstances justify it. A party must submit a copy of the document that otherwise complies with IN R USDCTSD L.R. 5-10 to replace the faxed copy within seven (7) days after faxing the document. IN R USDCTSD L.R. 5-10(e).

2. *Service requirements*

a. *Service; When required*

i. *In general.* Unless the Federal Rules of Civil Procedure provide otherwise, each of the following papers must be served on every party:

- An order stating that service is required;

- A pleading filed after the original complaint, unless the court orders otherwise under FRCP 5(c) because there are numerous defendants;

- A discovery paper required to be served on a party, unless the court orders otherwise;

- A written motion, except one that may be heard ex parte; and

- A written notice, appearance, demand, or offer of judgment, or any similar paper. FRCP 5(a)(1).

ii. *If a party fails to appear.* No service is required on a party who is in default for failing to appear. But a pleading that asserts a new claim for relief against such a party must be served on that party under FRCP 4. FRCP 5(a)(2).

iii. *Seizing property.* If an action is begun by seizing property and no person is or need be named as a defendant, any service required before the filing of an appearance, answer, or claim must be made on the person who had custody or possession of the property when it was seized. FRCP 5(a)(3).

b. *Service; How made*

i. *Serving an attorney.* If a party is represented by an attorney, service under FRCP 5 must be made on the attorney unless the court orders service on the party. FRCP 5(b)(1).

ii. *Service in general.* A paper is served under FRCP 5 by:

- Handing it to the person;

- Leaving it: (1) at the person's office with a clerk or other person in charge or, if no one is in charge, in a conspicuous place in the office; or (2) if the person has no office or the office is closed, at the person's dwelling or usual place of abode with someone of suitable age and discretion who resides there;

- Mailing it to the person's last known address—in which event service is complete upon mailing;

- Leaving it with the court clerk if the person has no known address;

- Sending it by electronic means if the person consented in writing—in which event service is complete upon transmission, but is not effective if the serving party learns that it did not reach the person to be served; or

- Delivering it by any other means that the person consented to in writing—in which event service is complete when the person making service delivers it to the agency designated to make delivery. FRCP 5(b)(2).

iii. *Electronic service*

- *Consent.* By registering to use the ECF system, attorneys consent to electronic service of documents filed in cases maintained on the ECF system. IN R USDCTSD L.R. 5-3(d). By participating in the Electronic Case Filing Program, attorneys consent to the electronic service of documents, and shall make available electronic mail addresses for service. IN R USDCTSD ECF Procedures(11).

998

- *Service on registered parties.* Upon the filing of a document by a party, an e-mail message will be automatically generated by the electronic filing system and sent via electronic mail to the e-mail addresses of all registered attorneys who have appeared in the case. The Notice of Electronic Filing will contain a document hyperlink which will provide recipients with one "free look" at the electronically filed document. Recipients are encouraged to print and/or save a copy of the document during the "free look" to avoid incurring PACER charges for future viewings of the document. IN R USDCTSD ECF Procedures(11). When a document has been filed electronically: transmission of the notice of electronic filing generated by the ECF system to an attorney's e-mail address constitutes service of the document on that attorney. IN R USDCTSD L.R. 5-4(c)(5). The party effectuates service on all registered attorneys by filing electronically. IN R USDCTSD ECF Procedures(11). When a document has been filed electronically: no other attempted service will constitute electronic service of the document. IN R USDCTSD L.R. 5-4(c)(6).

- *Service on exempt parties.* A filer must serve a copy of the document consistent with FRCP 5 on any party or attorney who is exempt from participating in electronic filing. IN R USDCTSD L.R. 5-4(d). It is the responsibility of the filing attorney to conventionally serve all parties who do not receive electronic service (the identity of these parties will be indicated on the filing receipt generated by the ECF system). IN R USDCTSD ECF Procedures(11).

- *Service on parties excused from electronic filing.* Parties otherwise participating in the electronic filing system may be excused from filing a particular component electronically under certain limited circumstances, such as when the component cannot be reduced to an electronic format. Such components shall not be filed electronically, but instead shall be manually filed with the Clerk of Court and served upon the parties in accordance with the applicable Federal Rules of Civil Procedure and the Local Rules of the United States District Court for the Southern District of Indiana for filing and service of non-electronic documents. IN R USDCTSD ECF Procedures(15).

- *Service of exempt documents.* Any document that is exempt from electronic filing must be filed directly with the clerk and served on other parties in the case as required by those Federal Rules of Civil Procedure and Local Rules of the United States District Court for the Southern District of Indiana that apply to the service of non-electronic documents. IN R USDCTSD L.R. 5-2(c).

iv. *Using court facilities.* If a local rule so authorizes, a party may use the court's transmission facilities to make service under FRCP 5(b)(2)(E). FRCP 5(b)(3).

c. *Serving numerous defendants*

   i. *In general.* If an action involves an unusually large number of defendants, the court may, on motion or on its own, order that:

   - Defendants' pleadings and replies to them need not be served on other defendants;

   - Any crossclaim, counterclaim, avoidance, or affirmative defense in those pleadings and replies to them will be treated as denied or avoided by all other parties; and

   - Filing any such pleading and serving it on the plaintiff constitutes notice of the pleading to all parties. FRCP 5(c)(1).

   ii. *Notifying parties.* A copy of every such order must be served on the parties as the court directs. FRCP 5(c)(2).

G. Hearings

1. *Hearings, generally*

   a. *Oral argument.* Due process does not require that oral argument be permitted on a motion and, except as otherwise provided by local rule, the district court has discretion to determine whether it will decide the motion on the papers or hear argument by counsel (and perhaps receive evidence). FPP § 1190; F.D.I.C. v. Deglau, 207 F.3d 153 (3d Cir. 2000).

      i. *Request for oral argument.* A party may request oral argument by filing a separate motion

explaining why oral argument is necessary and estimating how long the court should allow for the argument. IN R USDCTSD L.R. 7-5(a). Refer to the Documents section of this document for more information.

    ii. *No additional evidence at oral argument.* Parties may not present additional evidence at oral argument. IN R USDCTSD L.R. 7-5(b).

b. *Providing a regular schedule for oral hearings.* A court may establish regular times and places for oral hearings on motions. FRCP 78(a).

c. *Providing for submission on briefs.* By rule or order, the court may provide for submitting and determining motions on briefs, without oral hearings. FRCP 78(b).

d. *Request for evidentiary hearing.* A party may request an evidentiary hearing on a motion or petition by serving and filing a separate motion explaining why the hearing is necessary and estimating how long the court should allow for the hearing. IN R USDCTSD L.R. 7-5(c).

e. *Directed by the court.* The court may: (1) grant or deny a request for oral argument or an evidentiary hearing in its sole discretion; (2) set oral argument or an evidentiary hearing without a request from a party; and (3) order any oral argument or evidentiary hearing to be held anywhere within the district regardless of where the case will be tried. IN R USDCTSD L.R. 7-5(d).

2. *Courtroom and courthouse decorum.* For information on courtroom and courthouse decorum, refer to IN R USDCTSD L.R. 83-3.

H. Forms

1. Federal Motion for Post-Trial Relief Forms

a. Notice of motion; To amend or correct judgment. AMJUR PP JUDGMENTS § 38.

b. Motion for additur or new trial; Plaintiff awarded only medical bills without consideration of pain and suffering; No-fault automobile insurances. AMJUR PP JUDGMENTS § 47.

c. Motion for judgment; In federal court; By plaintiff; In accordance with motion for directed verdict or for new trial. AMJUR PP JUDGMENTS § 257.

d. Motion for judgment; By defendant; In accordance with motion for directed verdict or for new trial; In federal court. AMJUR PP JUDGMENTS § 258.

e. Notice of motion; To vacate judgment. AMJUR PP JUDGMENTS § 344.

f. Motion for new trial. 4 FEDFORMS § 4840.

g. Motion for new trial with statement of grounds. 4 FEDFORMS § 4841.

h. Motion for partial new trial. 4 FEDFORMS § 4844.

i. Affidavit in support of motion. 4 FEDFORMS § 4860.

j. Motion for new trial in nonjury action. 4 FEDFORMS § 4873.

k. Motion for new trial or to amend findings and judgment. 4 FEDFORMS § 4877.

l. Motion for new trial or to amend judgment. 4 FEDFORMS § 4880.

m. Motion for new trial and amendment of findings. 4 FEDFORMS § 4881.

n. Motion to amend judgment. 4 FEDFORMS § 4886.

o. Notice of motion to amend judgment by correcting amount. 4 FEDFORMS § 4887.

p. Motion to correct clerical error. 4 FEDFORMS § 4923.

q. Motion to vacate judgment. 4 FEDFORMS § 4930.

r. Motion to vacate consent decree on ground of excusable neglect, mistake or surprise. 4 FEDFORMS § 4933.

s. Affidavit to vacate judgment; Excusable neglect, mistake, inadvertence or surprise. 4 FEDFORMS § 4935.

t. Motion; Correction of clerical mistake in judgment. FEDPROF § 1:1390.

u. Motion; For relief from judgment; General form. FEDPROF § 1:1391.

v. Motion; For relief from judgment; Newly discovered evidence. FEDPROF § 1:1392.

w. Affidavit; Supporting motion for relief from judgment; Newly discovered evidence. FEDPROF § 1:1395.

x. Motion for new trial; General form. GOLDLTGFMS § 61:3.

y. Motion to vacate judgment; General form. GOLDLTGFMS § 63:2.

z. Motion to vacate judgment; Date of discovery of facts. GOLDLTGFMS § 63:3.

2. Forms for the Southern District of Indiana

a. Notice of endorsement. IN R USDCTSD ECF Procedures(Appendix B).

b. Notice of manual filing. IN R USDCTSD ECF Procedures(Appendix C).

c. Declaration that party was unable to file in a timely manner due to technical difficulties. IN R USDCTSD ECF Procedures(Appendix D).

I. Applicable Rules

1. *Federal rules*

a. Serving and filing pleadings and other papers. FRCP 5.

b. Constitutional challenge to a statute; Notice, certification, and intervention. FRCP 5.1.

c. Privacy protection for filings made with the court. FRCP 5.2.

d. Computing and extending time; Time for motion papers. FRCP 6.

e. Pleadings allowed; Form of motions and other papers. FRCP 7.

f. Form of pleadings. FRCP 10.

g. Signing pleadings, motions, and other papers; Representations to the court; Sanctions. FRCP 11.

h. Taking testimony. FRCP 43.

i. New trial; Altering or amending a judgment. FRCP 59.

j. Relief from a judgment or order. FRCP 60.

k. Hearing motions; Submission on briefs. FRCP 78.

2. *Local rules*

a. Scope of the rules. IN R USDCTSD L.R. 1-1.

b. Sanctions for errors as to form. IN R USDCTSD L.R. 1-3.

c. Format of documents presented for filing. IN R USDCTSD L.R. 5-1.

d. Constitutional challenge to a statute; Notice. IN R USDCTSD L.R. 5.1-1.

e. Filing of documents electronically required. IN R USDCTSD L.R. 5-2.

f. Eligibility, registration, passwords for electronic filing; Exemption from electronic filing. IN R USDCTSD L.R. 5-3.

g. Timing and consequences of electronic filing. IN R USDCTSD L.R. 5-4.

h. Attachments and exhibits in cases filed electronically. IN R USDCTSD L.R. 5-6.

i. Signatures in cases filed electronically. IN R USDCTSD L.R. 5-7.

j. Non-electronic filings. IN R USDCTSD L.R. 5-10.

k. Motion practice. [IN R USDCTSD L.R. 7-1, as amended by IN ORDER 16-2319, effective December 1, 2016].

l. Oral arguments and hearings. IN R USDCTSD L.R. 7-5.

m. Request for three-judge court. IN R USDCTSD L.R. 9-2.

n. Assignment of cases. IN R USDCTSD L.R. 40-1.

o. Alternative dispute resolution. IN R USDCTSD A.D.R. Rule 1.1; IN R USDCTSD A.D.R. Rule 1.2; IN R USDCTSD A.D.R. Rule 1.5; IN R USDCTSD A.D.R. Rule 2.1; IN R USDCTSD A.D.R. Rule 2.2.

p. Instructions for preparing case management plan. IN R USDCTSD Case Mgt.

q. Electronic case filing policies and procedures manual. IN R USDCTSD ECF Procedures.

Requests, Notices and Applications
Interrogatories

Document Last Updated December 2016

A. Checklist

(I) ❑ Matters to be considered by requesting party

    (a) ❑ Required documents

        (1) ❑ Interrogatories

    (b) ❑ Supplemental documents

        (1) ❑ Certificate of service

    (c) ❑ Timing

        (1) ❑ A party may not seek discovery from any source before the parties have conferred as required by FRCP 26(f), except in a proceeding exempted from initial disclosure under FRCP 26(a)(1)(B), or when authorized by the Federal Rules of Civil Procedure, by stipulation, or by court order

(II) ❑ Matters to be considered by responding party

    (a) ❑ Required documents

        (1) ❑ Response to interrogatories

    (b) ❑ Supplemental documents

        (1) ❑ Certificate of service

    (c) ❑ Timing

        (1) ❑ The responding party must serve its answers and any objections within thirty (30) days after being served with the interrogatories

B. Timing

1. *Interrogatories.* FRCP 33(a) contains no limit on when interrogatories may first be served. FPP § 2170. FRCP 33 is also silent on how late in a case interrogatories may be served. But FRCP 16(b)(3)(A) provides that the scheduling order in the case "must limit the time to . . . complete discovery." Although the scheduling order requirement does not apply to cases exempted by local rule, ordinarily there should be a scheduling order that sets a discovery cutoff. FPP § 2170.

2. *Timing of discovery, generally.* A party may not seek discovery from any source before the parties have conferred as required by FRCP 26(f), except in a proceeding exempted from initial disclosure under FRCP 26(a)(1)(B), or when authorized by the Federal Rules of Civil Procedure, by stipulation, or by court order. FRCP 26(d)(1).

3. *Computation of time*

    a. *Computing time.* FRCP 6 applies in computing any time period specified in the Federal Rules of Civil Procedure, in any local rule or court order, or in any statute that does not specify a method of computing time. FRCP 6(a).

        i. *Period stated in days or a longer unit.* When the period is stated in days or a longer unit of time:

            • Exclude the day of the event that triggers the period;

- Count every day, including intermediate Saturdays, Sundays, and legal holidays; and
- Include the last day of the period, but if the last day is a Saturday, Sunday, or legal holiday, the period continues to run until the end of the next day that is not a Saturday, Sunday, or legal holiday. FRCP 6(a)(1).

ii. *Period stated in hours.* When the period is stated in hours:

- Begin counting immediately on the occurrence of the event that triggers the period;
- Count every hour, including hours during intermediate Saturdays, Sundays, and legal holidays; and
- If the period would end on a Saturday, Sunday, or legal holiday, the period continues to run until the same time on the next day that is not a Saturday, Sunday, or legal holiday. FRCP 6(a)(2).

iii. *Inaccessibility of the clerk's office.* Unless the court orders otherwise, if the clerk's office is inaccessible:

- On the last day for filing under FRCP 6(a)(1), then the time for filing is extended to the first accessible day that is not a Saturday, Sunday, or legal holiday; or
- During the last hour for filing under FRCP 6(a)(2), then the time for filing is extended to the same time on the first accessible day that is not a Saturday, Sunday, or legal holiday. FRCP 6(a)(3).

iv. *"Last day" defined.* Unless a different time is set by a statute, local rule, or court order, the last day ends:

- For electronic filing, at midnight in the court's time zone; and
- For filing by other means, when the clerk's office is scheduled to close. FRCP 6(a)(4).

v. *"Next day" defined.* The "next day" is determined by continuing to count forward when the period is measured after an event and backward when measured before an event. FRCP 6(a)(5).

vi. *"Legal holiday" defined.* "Legal holiday" means:

- The day set aside by statute for observing New Year's Day, Martin Luther King Jr.'s Birthday, Washington's Birthday, Memorial Day, Independence Day, Labor Day, Columbus Day, Veterans' Day, Thanksgiving Day, or Christmas Day;
- Any day declared a holiday by the President or Congress; and
- For periods that are measured after an event, any other day declared a holiday by the state where the district court is located. FRCP 6(a)(6).

b. *Computation of electronic filing deadlines.* Filing documents electronically does not alter filing deadlines. IN R USDCTSD ECF Procedures(7). A document due on a particular day must be filed before midnight local time of the division where the case is pending. IN R USDCTSD L.R. 5-4(a). All electronic transmissions of documents must be completed (i.e. received completely by the Clerk's Office) prior to midnight of the local time of the division in which the case is pending in order to be considered timely filed that day (NOTE: time will be noted in Eastern Time on the Court's docket. If you have filed a document prior to midnight local time of the division in which the case is pending and the document is due that date, but the electronic receipt and docket reflect the following calendar day, please contact the Court). IN R USDCTSD ECF Procedures(7). Although attorneys may file documents electronically twenty-four (24) hours a day, seven (7) days a week, attorneys are encouraged to file all documents during the normal working hours of the Clerk's Office (Monday through Friday, 8:30 a.m. to 4:30 p.m.) when technical support is available. IN R USDCTSD ECF Procedures(7); IN R USDCTSD ECF Procedures(9).

i. *Technical difficulties.* Parties are encouraged to file documents electronically during normal business hours, in case a problem is encountered. In the event a technical failure occurs and a document cannot be filed electronically despite the best efforts of the filing party, the party should print (if possible) a copy of the error message received. In addition, as soon as practically possible, the party should file a "Declaration that Party was Unable to File in a Timely Manner

Due to Technical Difficulties." A model form is provided as Appendix D (IN R USDCTSD ECF Procedures(Appendix D)). IN R USDCTSD ECF Procedures(16).

- If a party is unable to file electronically and, as a result, may miss a filing deadline, the party must contact the Clerk's Office at the number listed in IN R USDCTSD ECF Procedures(15) to inform the court's staff of the difficulty. If a party misses a filing deadline due to an inability to file electronically, the party may submit the untimely filed document, accompanied by a declaration stating the reason(s) for missing the deadline. Unless the Court orders otherwise, the document and declaration must be filed no later than 12:00 noon of the first day on which the Court is open for business following the original filing deadline. IN R USDCTSD ECF Procedures(16).

c. *Extending time*

  i. *In general.* When an act may or must be done within a specified time, the court may, for good cause, extend the time:

- With or without motion or notice if the court acts, or if a request is made, before the original time or its extension expires; or

- On motion made after the time has expired if the party failed to act because of excusable neglect. FRCP 6(b)(1).

  ii. *Exceptions.* A court must not extend the time to act under FRCP 50(b), FRCP 50(d), FRCP 52(b), FRCP 59(b), FRCP 59(d), FRCP 59(e), and FRCP 60(b). FRCP 6(b)(2).

  iii. Refer to the United States District Court for the Southern District of Indiana KeyRules Motion for Continuance/Extension of Time document for more information on extending time.

d. *Additional time after certain kinds of service.* When a party may or must act within a specified time after being served and service is made under FRCP 5(b)(2)(C) (mail), FRCP 5(b)(2)(D) (leaving with the clerk), or FRCP 5(b)(2)(F) (other means consented to), three (3) days are added after the period would otherwise expire under FRCP 6(a). FRCP 6(d). Service by electronic mail shall constitute service pursuant to FRCP 5(b)(2)(E) and shall entitle the party being served to the additional three (3) days provided by FRCP 6(d). IN R USDCTSD ECF Procedures(11).

C. General Requirements

1. *General provisions governing discovery*

a. *Discovery scope and limits*

  i. *Scope in general.* Unless otherwise limited by court order, the scope of discovery is as follows: Parties may obtain discovery regarding any nonprivileged matter that is relevant to any party's claim or defense and proportional to the needs of the case, considering the importance of the issues at stake in the action, the amount in controversy, the parties' relative access to relevant information, the parties' resources, the importance of the discovery in resolving the issues, and whether the burden or expense of the proposed discovery outweighs its likely benefit. Information within this scope of discovery need not be admissible in evidence to be discoverable. FRCP 26(b)(1).

  ii. *Limitations on frequency and extent*

- *When permitted.* By order, the court may alter the limits in the Federal Rules of Civil Procedure on the number of depositions and interrogatories or on the length of depositions under FRCP 30. By order or local rule, the court may also limit the number of requests under FRCP 36. FRCP 26(b)(2)(A).

- *Specific limitations on electronically stored information.* A party need not provide discovery of electronically stored information from sources that the party identifies as not reasonably accessible because of undue burden or cost. On motion to compel discovery or for a protective order, the party from whom discovery is sought must show that the information is not reasonably accessible because of undue burden or cost. If that showing is made, the court may nonetheless order discovery from such sources if the requesting party shows good cause, considering the limitations of FRCP 26(b)(2)(C). The court may specify conditions for the discovery. FRCP 26(b)(2)(B).

- *When required.* On motion or on its own, the court must limit the frequency or extent of discovery otherwise allowed by the Federal Rules of Civil Procedure or by local rule if it determines that: (1) the discovery sought is unreasonably cumulative or duplicative, or can be obtained from some other source that is more convenient, less burdensome, or less expensive; (2) the party seeking discovery has had ample opportunity to obtain the information by discovery in the action; or (3) the proposed discovery is outside the scope permitted by FRCP 26(b)(1). FRCP 26(b)(2)(C).

iii. *Trial preparation; Materials*

- *Documents and tangible things.* Ordinarily, a party may not discover documents and tangible things that are prepared in anticipation of litigation or for trial by or for another party or its representative (including the other party's attorney, consultant, surety, indemnitor, insurer, or agent). But, subject to FRCP 26(b)(4), those materials may be discovered if: (1) they are otherwise discoverable under FRCP 26(b)(1); and (2) the party shows that it has substantial need for the materials to prepare its case and cannot, without undue hardship, obtain their substantial equivalent by other means. FRCP 26(b)(3)(A).

- *Protection against disclosure.* If the court orders discovery of those materials, it must protect against disclosure of the mental impressions, conclusions, opinions, or legal theories of a party's attorney or other representative concerning the litigation. FRCP 26(b)(3)(B).

- *Previous statement.* Any party or other person may, on request and without the required showing, obtain the person's own previous statement about the action or its subject matter. If the request is refused, the person may move for a court order, and FRCP 37(a)(5) applies to the award of expenses. A previous statement is either: (1) a written statement that the person has signed or otherwise adopted or approved; or (2) a contemporaneous stenographic, mechanical, electrical, or other recording—or a transcription of it—that recites substantially verbatim the person's oral statement. FRCP 26(b)(3)(C).

iv. *Trial preparation; Experts*

- *Deposition of an expert who may testify.* A party may depose any person who has been identified as an expert whose opinions may be presented at trial. If FRCP 26(a)(2)(B) requires a report from the expert, the deposition may be conducted only after the report is provided. FRCP 26(b)(4)(A).

- *Trial-preparation protection for draft reports or disclosures.* FRCP 26(b)(3)(A) and FRCP 26(b)(3)(B) protect drafts of any report or disclosure required under FRCP 26(a)(2), regardless of the form in which the draft is recorded. FRCP 26(b)(4)(B).

- *Trial-preparation protection for communications between a party's attorney and expert witnesses.* FRCP 26(b)(3)(A) and FRCP 26(b)(3)(B) protect communications between the party's attorney and any witness required to provide a report under FRCP 26(a)(2)(B), regardless of the form of the communications, except to the extent that the communications: (1) relate to compensation for the expert's study or testimony; (2) identify facts or data that the party's attorney provided and that the expert considered in forming the opinions to be expressed; or (3) identify assumptions that the party's attorney provided and that the expert relied on in forming the opinions to be expressed. FRCP 26(b)(4)(C).

- *Expert employed only for trial preparation.* Ordinarily, a party may not, by interrogatories or deposition, discover facts known or opinions held by an expert who has been retained or specially employed by another party in anticipation of litigation or to prepare for trial and who is not expected to be called as a witness at trial. But a party may do so only: (1) as provided in FRCP 35(b); or (2) on showing exceptional circumstances under which it is impracticable for the party to obtain facts or opinions on the same subject by other means. FRCP 26(b)(4)(D).

- *Payment.* Unless manifest injustice would result, the court must require that the party seeking discovery: (1) pay the expert a reasonable fee for time spent in responding to discovery under FRCP 26(b)(4)(A) or FRCP 26(b)(4)(D); and (2) for discovery under FRCP 26(b)(4)(D), also pay the other party a fair portion of the fees and expenses it reasonably incurred in obtaining the expert's facts and opinions. FRCP 26(b)(4)(E).

    v. *Claiming privilege or protecting trial-preparation materials*

- *Information withheld.* When a party withholds information otherwise discoverable by claiming that the information is privileged or subject to protection as trial-preparation material, the party must: (1) expressly make the claim; and (2) describe the nature of the documents, communications, or tangible things not produced or disclosed—and do so in a manner that, without revealing information itself privileged or protected, will enable other parties to assess the claim. FRCP 26(b)(5)(A).

- *Information produced.* If information produced in discovery is subject to a claim of privilege or of protection as trial-preparation material, the party making the claim may notify any party that received the information of the claim and the basis for it. After being notified, a party must promptly return, sequester, or destroy the specified information and any copies it has; must not use or disclose the information until the claim is resolved; must take reasonable steps to retrieve the information if the party disclosed it before being notified; and may promptly present the information to the court under seal for a determination of the claim. The producing party must preserve the information until the claim is resolved. FRCP 26(b)(5)(B).

  b. *Protective orders.* A party or any person from whom discovery is sought may move for a protective order in the court where the action is pending—or as an alternative on matters relating to a deposition, in the court for the district where the deposition will be taken. FRCP 26(c)(1). Refer to the United States District Court for the Southern District of Indiana KeyRules Motion for Protective Order document for more information.

  c. *Sequence of discovery.* Unless the parties stipulate or the court orders otherwise for the parties' and witnesses' convenience and in the interests of justice: (1) methods of discovery may be used in any sequence; and (2) discovery by one party does not require any other party to delay its discovery. FRCP 26(d)(3).

2. *Interrogatories*

  a. *Number.* Unless otherwise stipulated or ordered by the court, a party may serve on any other party no more than twenty-five (25) written interrogatories, including all discrete subparts. Leave to serve additional interrogatories may be granted to the extent consistent with FRCP 26(b)(1) and FRCP 26(b)(2). FRCP 33(a)(1).

  b. *Scope.* An interrogatory may relate to any matter that may be inquired into under FRCP 26(b). An interrogatory is not objectionable merely because it asks for an opinion or contention that relates to fact or the application of law to fact, but the court may order that the interrogatory need not be answered until designated discovery is complete, or until a pretrial conference or some other time. FRCP 33(a)(2).

  c. *Parties subject to interrogatories.* Depositions may be taken of any person but interrogatories are limited to parties to the litigation. FPP § 2171. Interrogatories may not be directed to the attorney for a party. They must be addressed to the party, who is then required to give all information known to it or its attorney. FPP § 2171; Hickman v. Taylor, 329 U.S. 495, 504, 67 S.Ct. 385, 390, 91 L.Ed. 451 (1947). For more information, refer to FPP § 2171.

  d. *Form.* A party propounding written discovery under FRCP 33, FRCP 34, or FRCP 36 must number each interrogatory or request sequentially and, upon request, supply the written discovery to the responding party in an editable word processing format. IN R USDCTSD L.R. 26-1(a). Ideally an interrogatory should be a single direct question phrased in a fashion that will inform the other party what is requested. In fact the courts have given parties considerable latitude in framing interrogatories. Rather general language has been permitted so long as the interrogatory gives the other party a reasonably clear indication of the information to be included in its answer. FPP § 2168.

    i. *Use of definitions.* There is no prohibition against the use of definitions in interrogatories, and definitions may be helpful in clarifying the meaning of obscure terms or avoiding repetitions in a long set of interrogatories. FPP § 2168.

    ii. *Use of standardized form interrogatories.* There have been mixed reactions to the use of standardized form interrogatories. They have been referred to opprobriously as "canned sets of interrogatories of the shotgun variety" and it has been said that their indiscriminate use is an "undesirable practice." FPP § 2168.

  e. *Motion to compel.* The party submitting the interrogatories must attempt to confer with the responding party in an effort to secure the information without court action and, if that fails, move for an order under FRCP 37(a) compelling answers. FPP § 2182. Refer to the United States District Court for the Southern District of Indiana KeyRules Motion to Compel Discovery document for more information.

3. *Sanctions for failure to cooperate in discovery.* The court where the action is pending may, on motion, order sanctions if a party, after being properly served with interrogatories under FRCP 33 or a request for inspection under FRCP 34, fails to serve its answers, objections, or written response. FRCP 37(d)(1)(A)(ii). If a motion to compel is granted, the court must, after giving an opportunity to be heard, require the party or deponent whose conduct necessitated the motion, the party or attorney advising that conduct, or both to pay the movant's reasonable expenses incurred in making the motion, including attorney's fees. But the court must not order this payment if the opposing party's nondisclosure, response, or objection was substantially justified. FRCP 37(a)(5)(A)(ii). Refer to the United States District Court for the Southern District of Indiana KeyRules Motion for Discovery Sanctions document for more information.

4. *Stipulations about discovery procedure.* Unless the court orders otherwise, the parties may stipulate that: (1) a deposition may be taken before any person, at any time or place, on any notice, and in the manner specified—in which event it may be used in the same way as any other deposition; and (2) other procedures governing or limiting discovery be modified—but a stipulation extending the time for any form of discovery must have court approval if it would interfere with the time set for completing discovery, for hearing a motion, or for trial. FRCP 29.

5. *Appearances.* Every attorney who represents a party or who files a document on a party's behalf must file an appearance for that party. IN R USDCTSD L.R. 83-7. The filing of a Notice of Appearance shall act to establish the filing attorney as an attorney of record representing a designated party or parties in a particular cause of action. As a result, it is necessary for each attorney to file a separate Notice of Appearance when entering an appearance in a case. A joint appearance on behalf of multiple attorneys may be filed electronically only if it is filed separately for each attorney, using his/her ECF login. IN R USDCTSD ECF Procedures(12). Only those attorneys who have filed an appearance in a pending action are entitled to be served with case documents under FRCP 5(a). IN R USDCTSD L.R. 83-7. For more information, refer to IN R USDCTSD L.R. 83-7 and IN R USDCTSD ECF Procedures(12).

6. *Notice of related action.* A party must file a notice of related action: as soon as it appears that the party's case and another pending case: (1) arise out of the same transaction or occurrence; (2) involve the same property; or (3) involve the validity or infringement or the same patent, trademark, or copyright. IN R USDCTSD L.R. 40-1(d)(2). For more information, refer to IN R USDCTSD L.R. 40-1.

7. *Alternative dispute resolution (ADR)*

  a. *Application.* Unless limited by specific provisions, or unless there are other applicable specific statutory, common law, or constitutional procedures, the Local Alternative Dispute Resolution Rules of the United States District Court for the Southern District of Indiana shall apply in all civil litigation filed in the U.S. District Court for the Southern District of Indiana, except in the following cases and proceedings:

    i. Applications for writs of habeas corpus under 28 U.S.C.A. § 2254;

    ii. Forfeiture cases;

    iii. Non-adversary proceedings in bankruptcy;

    iv. Social Security administrative review cases; and

    v. Such other matters as specified by order of the Court; for example, matters involving important public policy issues, constitutional law, or the establishment of new law. IN R USDCTSD A.D.R. Rule 1.2.

b. *Mediation.* Mediation under this section (IN R USDCTSD A.D.R. Rule 2.1, et seq.) involves the confidential process by which a person acting as a Mediator, selected by the parties or appointed by the Court, assists the litigants in reaching a mutually acceptable agreement. It is an informal and nonadversarial process. The role of the Mediator is to assist in identifying the issues, reducing misunderstandings, clarifying priorities, exploring areas of compromise, and finding points of agreement as well as legitimate points of disagreement. Final decision-making authority rests with the parties, not the Mediator. IN R USDCTSD A.D.R. Rule 2.1. It is anticipated that an agreement may not resolve all of the disputed issues, but the process, nonetheless, can reduce points of contention. Parties and their representatives are required to mediate in good faith, but are not compelled to reach an agreement. IN R USDCTSD A.D.R. Rule 2.1.

    i. *Case selection.* The Court with the agreement of the parties may refer a civil case for mediation. Unless otherwise ordered or as specifically provided in IN R USDCTSD A.D.R. Rule 2.8, referral to mediation does not abate or suspend the action, and no scheduled dates shall be delayed or deferred, including the date of trial. IN R USDCTSD A.D.R. Rule 2.2.

    ii. For more information on mediation, refer to IN R USDCTSD A.D.R. Rule 2.1, et seq.

c. *Other methods of dispute resolution.* The Local Alternative Dispute Resolution Rules of the United States District Court for the Southern District of Indiana shall not preclude the parties from utilizing any other reasonable method or technique of alternative dispute resolution to resolve disputes to which the parties agree. However, any use of arbitration by the parties will be governed by and comply with the requirements of 28 U.S.C.A. § 654 through 28 U.S.C.A. § 657. IN R USDCTSD A.D.R. Rule 1.5.

d. For more information on alternative dispute resolution (ADR), refer to IN R USDCTSD A.D.R. Rule 1.1, et seq.

8. *Notice of settlement or resolution.* The parties must immediately notify the court if they reasonably anticipate settling their case or resolving a pending motion. IN R USDCTSD L.R. 7-1(h).

9. *Modification or suspension of rules.* The court may, on its own motion or at the request of a party, suspend or modify any rule in a particular case in the interest of justice. IN R USDCTSD L.R. 1-1(c).

D. Documents

1. *Required documents*

a. *Interrogatories.* Refer to the General Requirements section of this document for information on interrogatories.

2. *Supplemental documents*

a. *Certificate of service.* FRCP 5(d) requires that the person making service under FRCP 5 certify that service has been effected. FRCP 5(Advisory Committee Notes). Having such information on file may be useful for many purposes, including proof of service if an issue arises concerning the effectiveness of the service. FRCP 5(Advisory Committee Notes).

E. Format

1. *Form of documents.* The rules governing captions and other matters of form in pleadings apply to motions and other papers. FRCP 7(b)(2).

a. *Paper (manual filings only).* Any document that is not filed electronically must: be flat, unfolded, and on good-quality, eight and one-half by eleven (8-1/2 x 11) inch white paper. IN R USDCTSD L.R. 5-1(d)(1). Any document that is not filed electronically must: be single-sided. IN R USDCTSD L.R. 5-1(d)(1).

    i. *Covers or backing.* Any document that is not filed electronically must: not have a cover or a back. IN R USDCTSD L.R. 5-1(d)(1).

    ii. *Fastening.* Any document that is not filed electronically must: be (if consisting of more than one

(1) page) fastened by paperclip or binder clip and may not be stapled. IN R USDCTSD L.R. 5-1(d)(1).

- *Request for nonconforming fastening.* If a document cannot be fastened or bound as required by IN R USDCTSD L.R. 5-1(d), a party may ask the clerk for permission to fasten it in another manner. The party must make such a request before attempting to file the document with nonconforming fastening. IN R USDCTSD L.R. 5-1(d)(2).

 iii. *Hole punching.* Any document that is not filed electronically must: be two-hole punched at the top with the holes two and three-quarter (2-3/4) inches apart and appropriately centered. IN R USDCTSD L.R. 5-1(d)(1).

b. *Margins.* Any pleading, motion, brief, affidavit, notice, or proposed order filed with the court, whether electronically or with the clerk, must: have at least one (1) inch margins. IN R USDCTSD L.R. 5-1(b).

c. *Spacing.* Any pleading, motion, brief, affidavit, notice, or proposed order filed with the court, whether electronically or with the clerk, must: be double spaced (except for headings, footnotes, and quoted material). IN R USDCTSD L.R. 5-1(b).

d. *Text.* Any pleading, motion, brief, affidavit, notice, or proposed order filed with the court, whether electronically or with the clerk, must: be plainly typewritten, printed, or prepared by a clearly legible copying process. IN R USDCTSD L.R. 5-1(b).

e. *Font size.* Any pleading, motion, brief, affidavit, notice, or proposed order filed with the court, whether electronically or with the clerk, must: use at least 12-point type in the body of the document and at least 10-point type in footnotes. IN R USDCTSD L.R. 5-1(b).

f. *Page numbering.* Any pleading, motion, brief, affidavit, notice, or proposed order filed with the court, whether electronically or with the clerk, must: have consecutively numbered pages. IN R USDCTSD L.R. 5-1(b).

g. *Caption; Names of parties.* Every pleading must have a caption with the court's name, a title, a file number, and a FRCP 7(a) designation. The title of the complaint must name all the parties; the title of other pleadings, after naming the first party on each side, may refer generally to other parties. FRCP 10(a). Any pleading, motion, brief, affidavit, notice, or proposed order filed with the court, whether electronically or with the clerk, must: include a title on the first page. IN R USDCTSD L.R. 5-1(b).

h. *Filer's information.* Any pleading, motion, brief, affidavit, notice, or proposed order filed with the court, whether electronically or with the clerk, must: in the case of pleadings, motions, legal briefs, and notices, include the name, complete address, telephone number, facsimile number (where available), and e-mail address (where available) of the pro se litigant or attorney who files it. IN R USDCTSD L.R. 5-1(b).

i. *Paragraphs; Separate statements.* A party must state its claims or defenses in numbered paragraphs, each limited as far as practicable to a single set of circumstances. A later pleading may refer by number to a paragraph in an earlier pleading. If doing so would promote clarity, each claim founded on a separate transaction or occurrence—and each defense other than a denial—must be stated in a separate count or defense. FRCP 10(b).

j. *Adoption by reference; Exhibits.* A statement in a pleading may be adopted by reference elsewhere in the same pleading or in any other pleading or motion. A copy of a written instrument that is an exhibit to a pleading is a part of the pleading for all purposes. FRCP 10(c).

k. *Citations*

 i. *Local rules.* The Local Rules of the United States District Court for the Southern District of Indiana may be cited as "S.D. Ind. L.R." IN R USDCTSD L.R. 1-1(a).

 ii. *Local alternative dispute resolution rules.* These Rules shall be known as the Local Alternative Dispute Resolution Rules of the United States District Court for the Southern District of Indiana. They shall be cited as "S.D.Ind. Local A.D.R. Rule _____." IN R USDCTSD A.D.R. Rule 1.1.

l. *Acceptance by the clerk.* The clerk must not refuse to file a paper solely because it is not in the form prescribed by the Federal Rules of Civil Procedure or by a local rule or practice. FRCP 5(d)(4). The clerk will accept a document that violates IN R USDCTSD L.R. 5-1, but the court may exclude the document from the official record. IN R USDCTSD L.R. 5-1(e).

    i. *Sanctions for errors as to form.* The court may strike from the record any document that does not comply with the rules governing the form of documents filed with the court, such as rules that regulate document size or the number of copies to be filed or that require a special designation in the caption. The court may also sanction an attorney or party who files a non-compliant document. IN R USDCTSD L.R. 1-3.

2. *Form of electronic documents.* Any document submitted via the court's electronic case filing (ECF) system must be: otherwise prepared and filed in a manner consistent with the CM/ECF Policies and Procedures Manual (IN R USDCTSD ECF Procedures). IN R USDCTSD L.R. 5-1(c). Electronically filed documents must meet the requirements of FRCP 10 (Form of Pleadings), IN R USDCTSD L.R. 5-1 (Format of Papers Presented for Filing), and FRCP 5.2 (Privacy Protection for Filings Made with the Court), as if they had been submitted on paper. Documents filed electronically are also subject to any page limitations set forth by Court Order, by IN R USDCTSD L.R. 7-1 (Motion Practice), or IN R USDCTSD L.R. 56-1 (Summary Judgment Practice), as applicable. IN R USDCTSD ECF Procedures(13).

    a. *PDF format required.* Any document submitted via the court's electronic case filing (ECF) system must be: in .pdf format. IN R USDCTSD L.R. 5-1(c); IN R USDCTSD ECF Procedures(7). Any document submitted via the court's electronic case filing (ECF) system must be: converted to a .pdf file directly from a word processing program, unless it exists only in paper format (in which case it may be scanned to create a .pdf document). IN R USDCTSD L.R. 5-1(c); IN R USDCTSD ECF Procedures(13).

        i. An exhibit may be scanned into PDF format, at a recommended 300 dpi resolution or higher, only if it does not already exist in electronic format. The filing attorney is responsible for reviewing all PDF documents for legibility before submitting them through the Court's Electronic Case Filing system. For technical guidance in creating PDF documents, please contact the Clerk's Office. IN R USDCTSD ECF Procedures(13).

    b. *File size limitations.* Any document submitted via the court's electronic case filing (ECF) system must be: submitted as one or more .pdf files that do not exceed ten megabytes (10 MB) each (consistent with the CM/ECF Policies and Procedures Manual (IN R USDCTSD ECF Procedures)). IN R USDCTSD L.R. 5-1(c); IN R USDCTSD ECF Procedures(13).

        i. To electronically file a document or attachment that exceeds ten megabytes (10 MB), the document must first be broken down into two or more smaller files. For example, if Exhibit A is a twelve megabyte (12 MB) PDF file, it should be divided into 2 equal parts prior to electronic filing. Each component part of the exhibit would be filed as an attachment to the main document and described appropriately as "Exhibit A (part 1 of 2)" and "Exhibit A (part 2 of 2)." IN R USDCTSD ECF Procedures(13).

        ii. The supporting items mentioned in IN R USDCTSD ECF Procedures(13) should not be confused with memorandums or briefs in support of motions as outlined in IN R USDCTSD L.R. 7-1 or IN R USDCTSD L.R. 56-1. These memorandums or briefs in support are to be filed as entirely separate documents pursuant to the appropriate rule. Additionally, no motion shall be embodied in the text of a response or reply brief/memorandum unless otherwise ordered by the Court. IN R USDCTSD ECF Procedures(13).

    c. *Separate component parts.* A key objective of the electronic filing system is to ensure that as much of the case as possible is managed electronically. To facilitate electronic filing and retrieval, documents to be filed electronically are to be reasonably broken into their separate component parts. By way of example, most filings include a foundation document (e.g., motion) and other supporting items (e.g., exhibits, proposed orders, proposed amended pleadings). The foundation document, as well as the supporting items, are each separate components of the filing; supporting items must be filed as attachments to the foundation document. These exhibits or attachments should include only those excerpts of the referenced documents that are directly germane to the matter under consideration. IN R USDCTSD ECF Procedures(13).

    i.   Where an individual component cannot be included in an electronic filing (e.g. the component cannot be converted to electronic format), the filer shall electronically file the prescribed Notice of Manual Filing in place of that component. A model form is provided as Appendix C (IN R USDCTSD ECF Procedures(Appendix C)). IN R USDCTSD ECF Procedures(13).

  d. *Exhibits.* Each electronically filed exhibit to a main document must be: (1) created as a separate .pdf file; (2) submitted as an attachment to the main document and given a title which describes its content; and (3) limited to excerpts that are directly germane to the main document's subject matter. IN R USDCTSD L.R. 5-6(a).

    i.   When uploading attachments during the electronic filing process, exhibits must be uploaded in a logical sequence and a brief description must be entered for each individual PDF file. The description must include not only the exhibit number or letter, but also a brief description of the document. This information may be entered in CM/ECF using a combination of the Category drop-down menu, the Description text box, or both (see IN R USDCTSD ECF Procedures(13)(Figure 1)). The information that is provided in each box will be combined to create a description of the document as it appears on the case docket (see IN R USDCTSD ECF Procedures(13)(Figure 2)). IN R USDCTSD ECF Procedures(13). For an example, refer to IN R USDCTSD ECF Procedures(13).

  e. *Excerpts.* A party filing an exhibit that consists of excerpts from a larger document must clearly and prominently identify the exhibit as containing excerpted material. Either party will have the right to timely file additional excerpts or the complete document to the extent they are or become directly germane to the main document's subject matter. IN R USDCTSD L.R. 5-6(b).

  f. For an example illustrating the application of IN R USDCTSD ECF Procedures(13), refer to IN R USDCTSD ECF Procedures(13).

3. *Signing disclosures and discovery requests, responses, and objections.* FRCP 11 does not apply to disclosures and discovery requests, responses, objections, and motions under FRCP 26 through FRCP 37. FRCP 11(d).

  a. *Signature required.* Every disclosure under FRCP 26(a)(1) or FRCP 26(a)(3) and every discovery request, response, or objection must be signed by at least one attorney of record in the attorney's own name—or by the party personally, if unrepresented—and must state the signer's address, e-mail address, and telephone number. FRCP 26(g)(1).

    i.   *Signatures on manual filings.* Any document that is not filed electronically must: include the original signature of the pro se litigant or attorney who files it. IN R USDCTSD L.R. 5-1(d)(1).

    ii.   *Electronic signatures.* Use of the attorney's login and password when filing documents electronically serves in part as the attorney's signature for purposes of FRCP 11, the Local Rules of the United States District Court for the Southern District of Indiana, and any other purpose for which a signature is required in connection with proceedings before the Court. IN R USDCTSD ECF Procedures(14); IN R USDCTSD ECF Procedures(10). A pleading, motion, brief, or notice filed electronically under an attorney's ECF log-in and password must be signed by that attorney. IN R USDCTSD L.R. 5-7(a). A signature on a document other than a document filed as provided under IN R USDCTSD L.R. 5-7(a) must be an original handwritten signature and must be scanned into .pdf format for electronic filing. IN R USDCTSD L.R. 5-7(c); IN R USDCTSD ECF Procedures(14).

       ● *Form of electronic signature.* If a document is converted directly from a word processing application to .pdf (as opposed to scanning), the name of the Filing User under whose log-in and password the document is submitted must be preceded by a "s/" and typed on the signature line where the Filing User's handwritten signature would otherwise appear. IN R USDCTSD L.R. 5-7(b). All documents filed electronically shall include a signature block and include the filing attorney's typewritten name, address, telephone number, facsimile number and e-mail address. In addition, the name of the filing attorney under

whose ECF login the document will be filed should be preceded by a "s/" and typed in the space where the attorney's handwritten signature would otherwise appear. IN R US-DCTSD ECF Procedures(14). For a sample format, refer to IN R USDCTSD ECF Procedures(14).

- *Effect of electronic signature.* Filing an electronically signed document under an attorney's ECF log-in and password constitutes the attorney's signature on the document under the Federal Rules of Civil Procedure, under the Local Rules of the United States District Court for the Southern District of Indiana, and for any other reason a signature is required in connection with the court's activities. IN R USDCTSD L.R. 5-7(d).

- *Documents with multiple attorneys' signatures.* Documents requiring signatures of more than one attorney shall be filed either by: (1) obtaining consent from the other attorney, then typing the "s/ [Name]" signature of the other attorney on the signature line where the other attorney's signature would otherwise appear; (2) identifying in the signature section the name of the other attorney whose signature is required and by the submission of a Notice of Endorsement (see IN R USDCTSD ECF Procedures(Appendix B)) by the other attorney no later than three (3) business days after filing; (3) submitting a scanned document containing all handwritten signatures; or (4) in any other manner approved by the Court. IN R USDCTSD ECF Procedures(14); IN R USDCTSD L.R. 5-7(e).

b. *Effect of signature.* By signing, an attorney or party certifies that to the best of the person's knowledge, information, and belief formed after a reasonable inquiry:

    i. With respect to a disclosure, it is complete and correct as of the time it is made; and

    ii. With respect to a discovery request, response, or objection, it is:

- Consistent with the Federal Rules of Civil Procedure and warranted by existing law or by a nonfrivolous argument for extending, modifying, or reversing existing law, or for establishing new law;

- Not interposed for any improper purpose, such as to harass, cause unnecessary delay, or needlessly increase the cost of litigation; and

- Neither unreasonable nor unduly burdensome or expensive, considering the needs of the case, prior discovery in the case, the amount in controversy, and the importance of the issues at stake in the action. FRCP 26(g)(1).

c. *Failure to sign.* Other parties have no duty to act on an unsigned disclosure, request, response, or objection until it is signed, and the court must strike it unless a signature is promptly supplied after the omission is called to the attorney's or party's attention. FRCP 26(g)(2). The court will strike any document filed directly with the clerk that is not signed by an attorney of record or the pro se litigant filing it, but the court may do so only after giving the attorney or pro se litigant notice of the omission and reasonable time to correct it. Rubber-stamp or facsimile signatures are not original signatures and the court will deem documents containing them to be unsigned for purposes of FRCP 11 and FRCP 26(g) and IN R USDCTSD L.R. 5-10. IN R USDCTSD L.R. 5-10(g).

d. *Sanction for improper certification.* If a certification violates FRCP 26(g) without substantial justification, the court, on motion or on its own, must impose an appropriate sanction on the signer, the party on whose behalf the signer was acting, or both. The sanction may include an order to pay the reasonable expenses, including attorney's fees, caused by the violation. FRCP 26(g)(3). Refer to the United States District Court for the Southern District of Indiana KeyRules Motion for Discovery Sanctions document for more information.

4. *Privacy protection for filings made with the court.* Electronically filed documents must meet the requirements of. . .FRCP 5.2 (Privacy Protection for Filings Made with the Court), as if they had been submitted on paper. IN R USDCTSD ECF Procedures(13).

a. *Redacted filings.* Unless the court orders otherwise, in an electronic or paper filing with the court that contains an individual's Social Security number, taxpayer-identification number, or birth date, the name of an individual known to be a minor, or a financial-account number, a party or nonparty making the filing may include only:

    i. The last four (4) digits of the Social Security number and taxpayer-identification number;

      ii.   The year of the individual's birth;

     iii.   The minor's initials; and

     iv.   The last four (4) digits of the financial-account number. FRCP 5.2(a).

b.   *Exemptions from the redaction requirement.* The redaction requirement does not apply to the following:

      i.   A financial-account number that identifies the property allegedly subject to forfeiture in a forfeiture proceeding;

      ii.   The record of an administrative or agency proceeding;

     iii.   The official record of a state-court proceeding;

     iv.   The record of a court or tribunal, if that record was not subject to the redaction requirement when originally filed;

      v.   A filing covered by FRCP 5.2(c) or FRCP 5.2(d); and

     vi.   A pro se filing in an action brought under 28 U.S.C.A. § 2241, 28 U.S.C.A. § 2254, or 28 U.S.C.A. § 2255. FRCP 5.2(b).

c.   *Limitations on remote access to electronic files; Social Security appeals and immigration cases.* Unless the court orders otherwise, in an action for benefits under the Social Security Act, and in an action or proceeding relating to an order of removal, to relief from removal, or to immigration benefits or detention, access to an electronic file is authorized as follows:

      i.   The parties and their attorneys may have remote electronic access to any part of the case file, including the administrative record;

      ii.   Any other person may have electronic access to the full record at the courthouse, but may have remote electronic access only to:

          • The docket maintained by the court; and

          • An opinion, order, judgment, or other disposition of the court, but not any other part of the case file or the administrative record. FRCP 5.2(c).

d.   *Filings made under seal.* The court may order that a filing be made under seal without redaction. The court may later unseal the filing or order the person who made the filing to file a redacted version for the public record. FRCP 5.2(d). For more information on filing under seal, refer to IN R USDCTSD L.R. 5-11 and IN R USDCTSD ECF Procedures(18).

e.   *Protective orders.* For good cause, the court may by order in a case:

      i.   Require redaction of additional information; or

      ii.   Limit or prohibit a nonparty's remote electronic access to a document filed with the court. FRCP 5.2(e).

f.   *Option for additional unredacted filing under seal.* A person making a redacted filing may also file an unredacted copy under seal. The court must retain the unredacted copy as part of the record. FRCP 5.2(f).

g.   *Option for filing a reference list.* A filing that contains redacted information may be filed together with a reference list that identifies each item of redacted information and specifies an appropriate identifier that uniquely corresponds to each item listed. The list must be filed under seal and may be amended as of right. Any reference in the case to a listed identifier will be construed to refer to the corresponding item of information. FRCP 5.2(g).

h.   *Waiver of protection of identifiers.* A person waives the protection of FRCP 5.2(a) as to the person's own information by filing it without redaction and not under seal. FRCP 5.2(h).

F. Filing and Service Requirements

1.   *Filing requirements.* Any paper after the complaint that is required to be served—together with a certificate of service—must be filed within a reasonable time after service. But disclosures under FRCP 26(a)(1) or FRCP 26(a)(2) and the following discovery requests and responses must not be filed until they

are used in the proceeding or the court orders filing: depositions, interrogatories, requests for documents or tangible things or to permit entry onto land, and requests for admission. FRCP 5(d)(1). Refer to the United States District Court for the Southern District of Indiana KeyRules pleading and motion documents for information on filing with the court.

    a. *When discovery may be filed.* Discovery materials (whether discovery requests, responses, or deposition transcripts) may not be filed with the court except in the following circumstances:

        i. *Relevant to certain motions.* A party seeking relief under FRCP 26(c) or FRCP 37, or by way of a pretrial motion that could result in a final order on an issue, must file with the motion those parts of the discovery materials relevant to the motion. IN R USDCTSD L.R. 26-2(a).

        ii. *For anticipated use at trial.* When a party can reasonably anticipate using discovery materials at trial, the party must file the relevant portions at the start of the trial. IN R USDCTSD L.R. 26-2(b).

        iii. *Materials necessary for appeal.* A party seeking for purposes of appeal to supplement the record with discovery materials not previously filed may do so by stipulation of the parties or by court order approving the filing. IN R USDCTSD L.R. 26-2(c).

2. *Service requirements*

    a. *Service; When required*

        i. *In general.* Unless the Federal Rules of Civil Procedure provide otherwise, each of the following papers must be served on every party:

- An order stating that service is required;
- A pleading filed after the original complaint, unless the court orders otherwise under FRCP 5(c) because there are numerous defendants;
- A discovery paper required to be served on a party, unless the court orders otherwise;
- A written motion, except one that may be heard ex parte; and
- A written notice, appearance, demand, or offer of judgment, or any similar paper. FRCP 5(a)(1).

        ii. *If a party fails to appear.* No service is required on a party who is in default for failing to appear. But a pleading that asserts a new claim for relief against such a party must be served on that party under FRCP 4. FRCP 5(a)(2).

        iii. *Seizing property.* If an action is begun by seizing property and no person is or need be named as a defendant, any service required before the filing of an appearance, answer, or claim must be made on the person who had custody or possession of the property when it was seized. FRCP 5(a)(3).

    b. *Service; How made*

        i. *Serving an attorney.* If a party is represented by an attorney, service under FRCP 5 must be made on the attorney unless the court orders service on the party. FRCP 5(b)(1).

        ii. *Service in general.* A paper is served under FRCP 5 by:

- Handing it to the person;
- Leaving it: (1) at the person's office with a clerk or other person in charge or, if no one is in charge, in a conspicuous place in the office; or (2) if the person has no office or the office is closed, at the person's dwelling or usual place of abode with someone of suitable age and discretion who resides there;
- Mailing it to the person's last known address—in which event service is complete upon mailing;
- Leaving it with the court clerk if the person has no known address;
- Sending it by electronic means if the person consented in writing—in which event service is complete upon transmission, but is not effective if the serving party learns that it did not reach the person to be served; or

- Delivering it by any other means that the person consented to in writing—in which event service is complete when the person making service delivers it to the agency designated to make delivery. FRCP 5(b)(2).

iii. *Electronic service*

- *Consent.* By registering to use the ECF system, attorneys consent to electronic service of documents filed in cases maintained on the ECF system. IN R USDCTSD L.R. 5-3(d). By participating in the Electronic Case Filing Program, attorneys consent to the electronic service of documents, and shall make available electronic mail addresses for service. IN R USDCTSD ECF Procedures(11).

- *Service on registered parties.* Upon the filing of a document by a party, an e-mail message will be automatically generated by the electronic filing system and sent via electronic mail to the e-mail addresses of all registered attorneys who have appeared in the case. The Notice of Electronic Filing will contain a document hyperlink which will provide recipients with one "free look" at the electronically filed document. Recipients are encouraged to print and/or save a copy of the document during the "free look" to avoid incurring PACER charges for future viewings of the document. IN R USDCTSD ECF Procedures(11). When a document has been filed electronically: transmission of the notice of electronic filing generated by the ECF system to an attorney's e-mail address constitutes service of the document on that attorney. IN R USDCTSD L.R. 5-4(c)(5). The party effectuates service on all registered attorneys by filing electronically. IN R USDCTSD ECF Procedures(11). When a document has been filed electronically: no other attempted service will constitute electronic service of the document. IN R USDCTSD L.R. 5-4(c)(6).

- *Service on exempt parties.* A filer must serve a copy of the document consistent with FRCP 5 on any party or attorney who is exempt from participating in electronic filing. IN R USDCTSD L.R. 5-4(d). It is the responsibility of the filing attorney to conventionally serve all parties who do not receive electronic service (the identity of these parties will be indicated on the filing receipt generated by the ECF system). IN R USDCTSD ECF Procedures(11).

- *Service on parties excused from electronic filing.* Parties otherwise participating in the electronic filing system may be excused from filing a particular component electronically under certain limited circumstances, such as when the component cannot be reduced to an electronic format. Such components shall not be filed electronically, but instead shall be manually filed with the Clerk of Court and served upon the parties in accordance with the applicable Federal Rules of Civil Procedure and the Local Rules of the United States District Court for the Southern District of Indiana for filing and service of non-electronic documents. IN R USDCTSD ECF Procedures(15).

- *Service of exempt documents.* Any document that is exempt from electronic filing must be filed directly with the clerk and served on other parties in the case as required by those Federal Rules of Civil Procedure and Local Rules of the United States District Court for the Southern District of Indiana that apply to the service of non-electronic documents. IN R USDCTSD L.R. 5-2(c).

iv. *Using court facilities.* If a local rule so authorizes, a party may use the court's transmission facilities to make service under FRCP 5(b)(2)(E). FRCP 5(b)(3).

c. *Serving numerous defendants*

i. *In general.* If an action involves an unusually large number of defendants, the court may, on motion or on its own, order that:

- Defendants' pleadings and replies to them need not be served on other defendants;

- Any crossclaim, counterclaim, avoidance, or affirmative defense in those pleadings and replies to them will be treated as denied or avoided by all other parties; and

- Filing any such pleading and serving it on the plaintiff constitutes notice of the pleading to all parties. FRCP 5(c)(1).

      ii. *Notifying parties.* A copy of every such order must be served on the parties as the court directs. FRCP 5(c)(2).

G. Hearings

1. There is no hearing contemplated in the federal statutes or rules for interrogatories.

H. Forms

1. Federal Interrogatories Forms

    a. Introductory statement; Interrogatories to individual. AMJUR PP DEPOSITION § 405.

    b. Introductory statement; Interrogatories to corporation. AMJUR PP DEPOSITION § 406.

    c. Interrogatories. 3A FEDFORMS § 3488.

    d. Interrogatories; Another form. 3A FEDFORMS § 3489.

    e. Interrogatories by plaintiff; To corporation. 3A FEDFORMS § 3490.

    f. Interrogatories by plaintiff; Complete set. 3A FEDFORMS § 3491.

    g. Interrogatories by plaintiff; Requesting identification of documents and production under FRCP 34. 3A FEDFORMS § 3492.

    h. Interrogatories by plaintiff; With definition of terms used and instructions for answering. 3A FEDFORMS § 3493.

    i. Interrogatories by plaintiff; Employment discrimination case. 3A FEDFORMS § 3494.

    j. Interrogatories by defendant. 3A FEDFORMS § 3495.

    k. Interrogatories by defendant; Complete set. 3A FEDFORMS § 3496.

    l. Interrogatories by defendant; Complete set; Another form. 3A FEDFORMS § 3497.

    m. Interrogatories by defendant; Complete set; Another form. 3A FEDFORMS § 3498.

    n. Interrogatories by defendant; Complete set; Another form. 3A FEDFORMS § 3499.

    o. Interrogatories by defendant; Follow-up interrogatories to plaintiff after lapse of time since first set of interrogatories or deposition. 3A FEDFORMS § 3500.

    p. Certificate of service of interrogatories. 3A FEDFORMS § 3501.

    q. Interrogatories; Outline form. FEDPROF § 23:335.

    r. Interrogatories; To defendant; Trademark action. FEDPROF § 23:347.

    s. Interrogatories; With request for documents; To defendant; Collection of royalties. FEDPROF § 23:348.

    t. Interrogatories; To defendant; Copyright infringement. FEDPROF § 23:350.

    u. Interrogatories; To plaintiff; Products liability. FEDPROF § 23:352.

    v. Interrogatories; To plaintiff; Personal injury. FEDPROF § 23:353.

    w. Interrogatories; To defendant; Premises liability. FEDPROF § 23:356.

    x. Interrogatories; To defendant; Medical malpractice. FEDPROF § 23:357.

    y. General forms; Standard interrogatories. GOLDLTGFMS § 26:25.

    z. General forms; Civil cases. GOLDLTGFMS § 26:26.

I. Applicable Rules

1. *Federal rules*

    a. Serving and filing pleadings and other papers. FRCP 5.

    b. Privacy protection for filings made with the court. FRCP 5.2.

    c. Computing and extending time; Time for motion papers. FRCP 6.

    d. Pleadings allowed; Form of motions and other papers. FRCP 7.

    e.   Form of pleadings. FRCP 10.

    f.   Signing pleadings, motions, and other papers; Representations to the court; Sanctions. FRCP 11.

    g.   Duty to disclose; General provisions governing discovery. FRCP 26.

    h.   Stipulations about discovery procedure. FRCP 29.

    i.   Interrogatories to parties. FRCP 33.

    j.   Failure to make disclosures or to cooperate in discovery; Sanctions. FRCP 37.

2. *Local rules*

    a.   Scope of the rules. IN R USDCTSD L.R. 1-1.

    b.   Sanctions for errors as to form. IN R USDCTSD L.R. 1-3.

    c.   Format of documents presented for filing. IN R USDCTSD L.R. 5-1.

    d.   Filing of documents electronically required. IN R USDCTSD L.R. 5-2.

    e.   Eligibility, registration, passwords for electronic filing; Exemption from electronic filing. IN R USDCTSD L.R. 5-3.

    f.   Timing and consequences of electronic filing. IN R USDCTSD L.R. 5-4.

    g.   Attachments and exhibits in cases filed electronically. IN R USDCTSD L.R. 5-6.

    h.   Signatures in cases filed electronically. IN R USDCTSD L.R. 5-7.

    i.   Non-electronic filings. IN R USDCTSD L.R. 5-10.

    j.   Motion practice. [IN R USDCTSD L.R. 7-1, as amended by IN ORDER 16-2319, effective December 1, 2016].

    k.   Form of certain discovery requests. IN R USDCTSD L.R. 26-1.

    l.   Filing of discovery materials. IN R USDCTSD L.R. 26-2.

    m.   Assignment of cases. IN R USDCTSD L.R. 40-1.

    n.   Alternative dispute resolution. IN R USDCTSD A.D.R. Rule 1.1; IN R USDCTSD A.D.R. Rule 1.2; IN R USDCTSD A.D.R. Rule 1.5; IN R USDCTSD A.D.R. Rule 2.1; IN R USDCTSD A.D.R. Rule 2.2.

    o.   Electronic case filing policies and procedures manual. IN R USDCTSD ECF Procedures.

Requests, Notices and Applications
Response to Interrogatories

Document Last Updated December 2016

A. Checklist

  (I) ❑ Matters to be considered by requesting party

    (a) ❑ Required documents

      (1) ❑ Interrogatories

    (b) ❑ Supplemental documents

      (1) ❑ Certificate of service

    (c) ❑ Timing

      (1) ❑ A party may not seek discovery from any source before the parties have conferred as required by FRCP 26(f), except in a proceeding exempted from initial disclosure under FRCP 26(a)(1)(B), or when authorized by the Federal Rules of Civil Procedure, by stipulation, or by court order

(II) ❑ Matters to be considered by responding party

    (a) ❑ Required documents

        (1) ❑ Response to interrogatories

    (b) ❑ Supplemental documents

        (1) ❑ Certificate of service

    (c) ❑ Timing

        (1) ❑ The responding party must serve its answers and any objections within thirty (30) days after being served with the interrogatories

B. Timing

1. *Response to interrogatories.* The responding party must serve its answers and any objections within thirty (30) days after being served with the interrogatories. A shorter or longer time may be stipulated to under FRCP 29 or be ordered by the court. FRCP 33(b)(2).

2. *Automatic initial extension.* The deadline for filing a response to a pleading or to any written request for discovery or admissions will automatically be extended upon filing a notice of the extension with the court that states: (1) the deadline has not been previously extended; (2) the extension is for twenty-eight (28) or fewer days; (3) the extension does not interfere with the Case Management Plan, scheduled hearings, or other case deadlines; (4) the original deadline and extended deadline; (5) that all opposing counsel the filing attorney could reach agreed to the extension; or that the filing attorney could not reach any opposing counsel, and providing the dates, times and manner of all attempts to reach opposing counsel. IN R USDCTSD L.R. 6-1(b).

    a. *Pro se parties.* The automatic initial extension does not apply to pro se parties. IN R USDCTSD L.R. 6-1(c).

3. *Computation of time*

    a. *Computing time.* FRCP 6 applies in computing any time period specified in the Federal Rules of Civil Procedure, in any local rule or court order, or in any statute that does not specify a method of computing time. FRCP 6(a).

        i. *Period stated in days or a longer unit.* When the period is stated in days or a longer unit of time:

- Exclude the day of the event that triggers the period;

- Count every day, including intermediate Saturdays, Sundays, and legal holidays; and

- Include the last day of the period, but if the last day is a Saturday, Sunday, or legal holiday, the period continues to run until the end of the next day that is not a Saturday, Sunday, or legal holiday. FRCP 6(a)(1).

        ii. *Period stated in hours.* When the period is stated in hours:

- Begin counting immediately on the occurrence of the event that triggers the period;

- Count every hour, including hours during intermediate Saturdays, Sundays, and legal holidays; and

- If the period would end on a Saturday, Sunday, or legal holiday, the period continues to run until the same time on the next day that is not a Saturday, Sunday, or legal holiday. FRCP 6(a)(2).

        iii. *Inaccessibility of the clerk's office.* Unless the court orders otherwise, if the clerk's office is inaccessible:

- On the last day for filing under FRCP 6(a)(1), then the time for filing is extended to the first accessible day that is not a Saturday, Sunday, or legal holiday; or

- During the last hour for filing under FRCP 6(a)(2), then the time for filing is extended to the same time on the first accessible day that is not a Saturday, Sunday, or legal holiday. FRCP 6(a)(3).

    iv. *"Last day" defined.* Unless a different time is set by a statute, local rule, or court order, the last day ends:

- For electronic filing, at midnight in the court's time zone; and
- For filing by other means, when the clerk's office is scheduled to close. FRCP 6(a)(4).

    v. *"Next day" defined.* The "next day" is determined by continuing to count forward when the period is measured after an event and backward when measured before an event. FRCP 6(a)(5).

    vi. *"Legal holiday" defined.* "Legal holiday" means:

- The day set aside by statute for observing New Year's Day, Martin Luther King Jr.'s Birthday, Washington's Birthday, Memorial Day, Independence Day, Labor Day, Columbus Day, Veterans' Day, Thanksgiving Day, or Christmas Day;
- Any day declared a holiday by the President or Congress; and
- For periods that are measured after an event, any other day declared a holiday by the state where the district court is located. FRCP 6(a)(6).

  b. *Computation of electronic filing deadlines.* Filing documents electronically does not alter filing deadlines. IN R USDCTSD ECF Procedures(7). A document due on a particular day must be filed before midnight local time of the division where the case is pending. IN R USDCTSD L.R. 5-4(a). All electronic transmissions of documents must be completed (i.e. received completely by the Clerk's Office) prior to midnight of the local time of the division in which the case is pending in order to be considered timely filed that day (NOTE: time will be noted in Eastern Time on the Court's docket. If you have filed a document prior to midnight local time of the division in which the case is pending and the document is due that date, but the electronic receipt and docket reflect the following calendar day, please contact the Court). IN R USDCTSD ECF Procedures(7). Although attorneys may file documents electronically twenty-four (24) hours a day, seven (7) days a week, attorneys are encouraged to file all documents during the normal working hours of the Clerk's Office (Monday through Friday, 8:30 a.m. to 4:30 p.m.) when technical support is available. IN R USDCTSD ECF Procedures(7); IN R USDCTSD ECF Procedures(9).

    i. *Technical difficulties.* Parties are encouraged to file documents electronically during normal business hours, in case a problem is encountered. In the event a technical failure occurs and a document cannot be filed electronically despite the best efforts of the filing party, the party should print (if possible) a copy of the error message received. In addition, as soon as practically possible, the party should file a "Declaration that Party was Unable to File in a Timely Manner Due to Technical Difficulties." A model form is provided as Appendix D (IN R USDCTSD ECF Procedures(Appendix D)). IN R USDCTSD ECF Procedures(16).

- If a party is unable to file electronically and, as a result, may miss a filing deadline, the party must contact the Clerk's Office at the number listed in IN R USDCTSD ECF Procedures(15) to inform the court's staff of the difficulty. If a party misses a filing deadline due to an inability to file electronically, the party may submit the untimely filed document, accompanied by a declaration stating the reason(s) for missing the deadline. Unless the Court orders otherwise, the document and declaration must be filed no later than 12:00 noon of the first day on which the Court is open for business following the original filing deadline. IN R USDCTSD ECF Procedures(16).

  c. *Extending time*

    i. *In general.* When an act may or must be done within a specified time, the court may, for good cause, extend the time:

- With or without motion or notice if the court acts, or if a request is made, before the original time or its extension expires; or
- On motion made after the time has expired if the party failed to act because of excusable neglect. FRCP 6(b)(1).

    ii. *Exceptions.* A court must not extend the time to act under FRCP 50(b), FRCP 50(d), FRCP 52(b), FRCP 59(b), FRCP 59(d), FRCP 59(e), and FRCP 60(b). FRCP 6(b)(2).

    iii.   Refer to the United States District Court for the Southern District of Indiana KeyRules Motion for Continuance/Extension of Time document for more information on extending time.

  d. *Additional time after certain kinds of service.* When a party may or must act within a specified time after being served and service is made under FRCP 5(b)(2)(C) (mail), FRCP 5(b)(2)(D) (leaving with the clerk), or FRCP 5(b)(2)(F) (other means consented to), three (3) days are added after the period would otherwise expire under FRCP 6(a). FRCP 6(d). Service by electronic mail shall constitute service pursuant to FRCP 5(b)(2)(E) and shall entitle the party being served to the additional three (3) days provided by FRCP 6(d). IN R USDCTSD ECF Procedures(11).

C. General Requirements

1. *General provisions governing discovery*

  a. *Discovery scope and limits*

    i.   *Scope in general.* Unless otherwise limited by court order, the scope of discovery is as follows: Parties may obtain discovery regarding any nonprivileged matter that is relevant to any party's claim or defense and proportional to the needs of the case, considering the importance of the issues at stake in the action, the amount in controversy, the parties' relative access to relevant information, the parties' resources, the importance of the discovery in resolving the issues, and whether the burden or expense of the proposed discovery outweighs its likely benefit. Information within this scope of discovery need not be admissible in evidence to be discoverable. FRCP 26(b)(1).

    ii. *Limitations on frequency and extent*

      • *When permitted.* By order, the court may alter the limits in the Federal Rules of Civil Procedure on the number of depositions and interrogatories or on the length of depositions under FRCP 30. By order or local rule, the court may also limit the number of requests under FRCP 36. FRCP 26(b)(2)(A).

      • *Specific limitations on electronically stored information.* A party need not provide discovery of electronically stored information from sources that the party identifies as not reasonably accessible because of undue burden or cost. On motion to compel discovery or for a protective order, the party from whom discovery is sought must show that the information is not reasonably accessible because of undue burden or cost. If that showing is made, the court may nonetheless order discovery from such sources if the requesting party shows good cause, considering the limitations of FRCP 26(b)(2)(C). The court may specify conditions for the discovery. FRCP 26(b)(2)(B).

      • *When required.* On motion or on its own, the court must limit the frequency or extent of discovery otherwise allowed by the Federal Rules of Civil Procedure or by local rule if it determines that: (1) the discovery sought is unreasonably cumulative or duplicative, or can be obtained from some other source that is more convenient, less burdensome, or less expensive; (2) the party seeking discovery has had ample opportunity to obtain the information by discovery in the action; or (3) the proposed discovery is outside the scope permitted by FRCP 26(b)(1). FRCP 26(b)(2)(C).

    iii. *Trial preparation; Materials*

      • *Documents and tangible things.* Ordinarily, a party may not discover documents and tangible things that are prepared in anticipation of litigation or for trial by or for another party or its representative (including the other party's attorney, consultant, surety, indemnitor, insurer, or agent). But, subject to FRCP 26(b)(4), those materials may be discovered if: (1) they are otherwise discoverable under FRCP 26(b)(1); and (2) the party shows that it has substantial need for the materials to prepare its case and cannot, without undue hardship, obtain their substantial equivalent by other means. FRCP 26(b)(3)(A).

      • *Protection against disclosure.* If the court orders discovery of those materials, it must protect against disclosure of the mental impressions, conclusions, opinions, or legal theories of a party's attorney or other representative concerning the litigation. FRCP 26(b)(3)(B).

- *Previous statement.* Any party or other person may, on request and without the required showing, obtain the person's own previous statement about the action or its subject matter. If the request is refused, the person may move for a court order, and FRCP 37(a)(5) applies to the award of expenses. A previous statement is either: (1) a written statement that the person has signed or otherwise adopted or approved; or (2) a contemporaneous steno-graphic, mechanical, electrical, or other recording—or a transcription of it—that recites substantially verbatim the person's oral statement. FRCP 26(b)(3)(C).

iv. *Trial preparation; Experts*

- *Deposition of an expert who may testify.* A party may depose any person who has been identified as an expert whose opinions may be presented at trial. If FRCP 26(a)(2)(B) requires a report from the expert, the deposition may be conducted only after the report is provided. FRCP 26(b)(4)(A).

- *Trial-preparation protection for draft reports or disclosures.* FRCP 26(b)(3)(A) and FRCP 26(b)(3)(B) protect drafts of any report or disclosure required under FRCP 26(a)(2), regardless of the form in which the draft is recorded. FRCP 26(b)(4)(B).

- *Trial-preparation protection for communications between a party's attorney and expert witnesses.* FRCP 26(b)(3)(A) and FRCP 26(b)(3)(B) protect communications between the party's attorney and any witness required to provide a report under FRCP 26(a)(2)(B), regardless of the form of the communications, except to the extent that the communica-tions: (1) relate to compensation for the expert's study or testimony; (2) identify facts or data that the party's attorney provided and that the expert considered in forming the opinions to be expressed; or (3) identify assumptions that the party's attorney provided and that the expert relied on in forming the opinions to be expressed. FRCP 26(b)(4)(C).

- *Expert employed only for trial preparation.* Ordinarily, a party may not, by interrogatories or deposition, discover facts known or opinions held by an expert who has been retained or specially employed by another party in anticipation of litigation or to prepare for trial and who is not expected to be called as a witness at trial. But a party may do so only: (1) as provided in FRCP 35(b); or (2) on showing exceptional circumstances under which it is impracticable for the party to obtain facts or opinions on the same subject by other means. FRCP 26(b)(4)(D).

- *Payment.* Unless manifest injustice would result, the court must require that the party seeking discovery: (1) pay the expert a reasonable fee for time spent in responding to discovery under FRCP 26(b)(4)(A) or FRCP 26(b)(4)(D); and (2) for discovery under FRCP 26(b)(4)(D), also pay the other party a fair portion of the fees and expenses it reasonably incurred in obtaining the expert's facts and opinions. FRCP 26(b)(4)(E).

v. *Claiming privilege or protecting trial-preparation materials*

- *Information withheld.* When a party withholds information otherwise discoverable by claiming that the information is privileged or subject to protection as trial-preparation material, the party must: (1) expressly make the claim; and (2) describe the nature of the documents, communications, or tangible things not produced or disclosed—and do so in a manner that, without revealing information itself privileged or protected, will enable other parties to assess the claim. FRCP 26(b)(5)(A).

- *Information produced.* If information produced in discovery is subject to a claim of privilege or of protection as trial-preparation material, the party making the claim may notify any party that received the information of the claim and the basis for it. After being notified, a party must promptly return, sequester, or destroy the specified information and any copies it has; must not use or disclose the information until the claim is resolved; must take reasonable steps to retrieve the information if the party disclosed it before being notified; and may promptly present the information to the court under seal for a determi-nation of the claim. The producing party must preserve the information until the claim is resolved. FRCP 26(b)(5)(B).

b. *Protective orders.* A party or any person from whom discovery is sought may move for a protective order in the court where the action is pending—or as an alternative on matters relating to a deposition, in the court for the district where the deposition will be taken. FRCP 26(c)(1). Refer to the United States District Court for the Southern District of Indiana KeyRules Motion for Protective Order document for more information.

c. *Sequence of discovery.* Unless the parties stipulate or the court orders otherwise for the parties' and witnesses' convenience and in the interests of justice: (1) methods of discovery may be used in any sequence; and (2) discovery by one party does not require any other party to delay its discovery. FRCP 26(d)(3).

2. *Response to interrogatories*

a. *Form.* A party responding (by answer or objection) to written discovery must fully quote each interrogatory or request immediately before each response and number each response to correspond with the interrogatory or request. IN R USDCTSD L.R. 26-1(b).

b. *Answers and objections*

i. *Responding party.* The interrogatories must be answered: (1) by the party to whom they are directed; or (2) if that party is a public or private corporation, a partnership, an association, or a governmental agency, by any officer or agent, who must furnish the information available to the party. FRCP 33(b)(1). It is improper for the party's attorney to answer them, though undoubtedly the common practice is for the attorney to prepare the answers and have the party swear to them. FPP § 2172.

ii. *Answering each interrogatory.* Each interrogatory must, to the extent it is not objected to, be answered separately and fully in writing under oath. FRCP 33(b)(3). It has been said that interrogatories should be answered directly and without evasion in accordance with information that the answering party possesses after due inquiry. FPP § 2177.

iii. *Objections.* The grounds for objecting to an interrogatory must be stated with specificity. Any ground not stated in a timely objection is waived unless the court, for good cause, excuses the failure. FRCP 33(b)(4).

- *Grounds for objections.* Interrogatories may be objected to on the ground that they are not within the scope of discovery as defined in FRCP 26(b), either because they seek information not relevant to the subject matter of the action, or information that is privileged, or information that is protected by the work-product rule and for which the requisite showing has not been made, or information of experts that is not discoverable. FPP § 2174. But this does not exhaust the grounds on which objection can be made. FPP § 2174.

iv. *Qualifying answers.* If the party to whom the interrogatory is addressed thinks that there is uncertainty in the meaning of the interrogatory, it may qualify its answer if need be. FPP § 2168.

v. *Signature.* The person who makes the answers must sign them, and the attorney who objects must sign any objections. FRCP 33(b)(5). Refer to the Format section of this document for more information on signing discovery papers.

c. *Use.* An answer to an interrogatory may be used to the extent allowed by the Federal Rules of Evidence. FRCP 33(c).

d. *Option to produce business records.* If the answer to an interrogatory may be determined by examining, auditing, compiling, abstracting, or summarizing a party's business records (including electronically stored information), and if the burden of deriving or ascertaining the answer will be substantially the same for either party, the responding party may answer by:

i. Specifying the records that must be reviewed, in sufficient detail to enable the interrogating party to locate and identify them as readily as the responding party could; and

ii. Giving the interrogating party a reasonable opportunity to examine and audit the records and to make copies, compilations, abstracts, or summaries. FRCP 33(d).

3. *Supplementing disclosures and responses.* A party who has made a disclosure under FRCP 26(a)—or who has responded to an interrogatory, request for production, or request for admission—must supplement or

correct its disclosure or response: (1) in a timely manner if the party learns that in some material respect the disclosure or response is incomplete or incorrect, and if the additional or corrective information has not otherwise been made known to the other parties during the discovery process or in writing; or (2) as ordered by the court. FRCP 26(e)(1).

4. *Sanctions for failure to cooperate in discovery.* The court where the action is pending may, on motion, order sanctions if a party, after being properly served with interrogatories under FRCP 33 or a request for inspection under FRCP 34, fails to serve its answers, objections, or written response. FRCP 37(d)(1)(A)(ii). If a motion to compel is granted, the court must, after giving an opportunity to be heard, require the party or deponent whose conduct necessitated the motion, the party or attorney advising that conduct, or both to pay the movant's reasonable expenses incurred in making the motion, including attorney's fees. But the court must not order this payment if the opposing party's nondisclosure, response, or objection was substantially justified. FRCP 37(a)(5)(A)(ii). Refer to the United States District Court for the Southern District of Indiana KeyRules Motion for Discovery Sanctions document for more information.

5. *Stipulations about discovery procedure.* Unless the court orders otherwise, the parties may stipulate that: (1) a deposition may be taken before any person, at any time or place, on any notice, and in the manner specified—in which event it may be used in the same way as any other deposition; and (2) other procedures governing or limiting discovery be modified—but a stipulation extending the time for any form of discovery must have court approval if it would interfere with the time set for completing discovery, for hearing a motion, or for trial. FRCP 29.

6. *Appearances.* Every attorney who represents a party or who files a document on a party's behalf must file an appearance for that party. IN R USDCTSD L.R. 83-7. The filing of a Notice of Appearance shall act to establish the filing attorney as an attorney of record representing a designated party or parties in a particular cause of action. As a result, it is necessary for each attorney to file a separate Notice of Appearance when entering an appearance in a case. A joint appearance on behalf of multiple attorneys may be filed electronically only if it is filed separately for each attorney, using his/her ECF login. IN R USDCTSD ECF Procedures(12). Only those attorneys who have filed an appearance in a pending action are entitled to be served with case documents under FRCP 5(a). IN R USDCTSD L.R. 83-7. For more information, refer to IN R USDCTSD L.R. 83-7 and IN R USDCTSD ECF Procedures(12).

7. *Notice of related action.* A party must file a notice of related action: as soon as it appears that the party's case and another pending case: (1) arise out of the same transaction or occurrence; (2) involve the same property; or (3) involve the validity or infringement or the same patent, trademark, or copyright. IN R USDCTSD L.R. 40-1(d)(2). For more information, refer to IN R USDCTSD L.R. 40-1.

8. *Alternative dispute resolution (ADR)*

   a. *Application.* Unless limited by specific provisions, or unless there are other applicable specific statutory, common law, or constitutional procedures, the Local Alternative Dispute Resolution Rules of the United States District Court for the Southern District of Indiana shall apply in all civil litigation filed in the U.S. District Court for the Southern District of Indiana, except in the following cases and proceedings:

      i. Applications for writs of habeas corpus under 28 U.S.C.A. § 2254;

      ii. Forfeiture cases;

      iii. Non-adversary proceedings in bankruptcy;

      iv. Social Security administrative review cases; and

      v. Such other matters as specified by order of the Court; for example, matters involving important public policy issues, constitutional law, or the establishment of new law. IN R USDCTSD A.D.R. Rule 1.2.

   b. *Mediation.* Mediation under this section (IN R USDCTSD A.D.R. Rule 2.1, et seq.) involves the confidential process by which a person acting as a Mediator, selected by the parties or appointed by the Court, assists the litigants in reaching a mutually acceptable agreement. It is an informal and nonadversarial process. The role of the Mediator is to assist in identifying the issues, reducing misunderstandings, clarifying priorities, exploring areas of compromise, and finding points of agreement as well as legitimate points of disagreement. Final decision-making authority rests with the parties, not the Mediator. IN R USDCTSD A.D.R. Rule 2.1. It is anticipated that an agreement may not resolve all of the disputed issues, but the process, nonetheless, can reduce points of contention. Parties and their representatives are required to mediate in good faith, but are not compelled to reach an agreement. IN R USDCTSD A.D.R. Rule 2.1.

    i. *Case selection.* The Court with the agreement of the parties may refer a civil case for mediation. Unless otherwise ordered or as specifically provided in IN R USDCTSD A.D.R. Rule 2.8, referral to mediation does not abate or suspend the action, and no scheduled dates shall be delayed or deferred, including the date of trial. IN R USDCTSD A.D.R. Rule 2.2.

    ii. For more information on mediation, refer to IN R USDCTSD A.D.R. Rule 2.1, et seq.

  c. *Other methods of dispute resolution.* The Local Alternative Dispute Resolution Rules of the United States District Court for the Southern District of Indiana shall not preclude the parties from utilizing any other reasonable method or technique of alternative dispute resolution to resolve disputes to which the parties agree. However, any use of arbitration by the parties will be governed by and comply with the requirements of 28 U.S.C.A. § 654 through 28 U.S.C.A. § 657. IN R USDCTSD A.D.R. Rule 1.5.

  d. For more information on alternative dispute resolution (ADR), refer to IN R USDCTSD A.D.R. Rule 1.1, et seq.

9. *Notice of settlement or resolution.* The parties must immediately notify the court if they reasonably anticipate settling their case or resolving a pending motion. IN R USDCTSD L.R. 7-1(h).

10. *Modification or suspension of rules.* The court may, on its own motion or at the request of a party, suspend or modify any rule in a particular case in the interest of justice. IN R USDCTSD L.R. 1-1(c).

D. Documents

1. *Required documents*

  a. *Response to interrogatories.* Refer to the General Requirements section of this document for information on the response to interrogatories.

2. *Supplemental documents*

  a. *Certificate of service.* FRCP 5(d) requires that the person making service under FRCP 5 certify that service has been effected. FRCP 5(Advisory Committee Notes). Having such information on file may be useful for many purposes, including proof of service if an issue arises concerning the effectiveness of the service. FRCP 5(Advisory Committee Notes).

E. Format

1. *Form of documents.* The rules governing captions and other matters of form in pleadings apply to motions and other papers. FRCP 7(b)(2).

  a. *Paper (manual filings only).* Any document that is not filed electronically must: be flat, unfolded, and on good-quality, eight and one-half by eleven (8-1/2 x 11) inch white paper. IN R USDCTSD L.R. 5-1(d)(1). Any document that is not filed electronically must: be single-sided. IN R USDCTSD L.R. 5-1(d)(1).

    i. *Covers or backing.* Any document that is not filed electronically must: not have a cover or a back. IN R USDCTSD L.R. 5-1(d)(1).

    ii. *Fastening.* Any document that is not filed electronically must: be (if consisting of more than one (1) page) fastened by paperclip or binder clip and may not be stapled. IN R USDCTSD L.R. 5-1(d)(1).

      • *Request for nonconforming fastening.* If a document cannot be fastened or bound as required by IN R USDCTSD L.R. 5-1(d), a party may ask the clerk for permission to fasten it in another manner. The party must make such a request before attempting to file the document with nonconforming fastening. IN R USDCTSD L.R. 5-1(d)(2).

    iii. *Hole punching.* Any document that is not filed electronically must: be two-hole punched at the top with the holes two and three-quarter (2-3/4) inches apart and appropriately centered. IN R USDCTSD L.R. 5-1(d)(1).

b. *Margins.* Any pleading, motion, brief, affidavit, notice, or proposed order filed with the court, whether electronically or with the clerk, must: have at least one (1) inch margins. IN R USDCTSD L.R. 5-1(b).

c. *Spacing.* Any pleading, motion, brief, affidavit, notice, or proposed order filed with the court, whether electronically or with the clerk, must: be double spaced (except for headings, footnotes, and quoted material). IN R USDCTSD L.R. 5-1(b).

d. *Text.* Any pleading, motion, brief, affidavit, notice, or proposed order filed with the court, whether electronically or with the clerk, must: be plainly typewritten, printed, or prepared by a clearly legible copying process. IN R USDCTSD L.R. 5-1(b).

e. *Font size.* Any pleading, motion, brief, affidavit, notice, or proposed order filed with the court, whether electronically or with the clerk, must: use at least 12-point type in the body of the document and at least 10-point type in footnotes. IN R USDCTSD L.R. 5-1(b).

f. *Page numbering.* Any pleading, motion, brief, affidavit, notice, or proposed order filed with the court, whether electronically or with the clerk, must: have consecutively numbered pages. IN R USDCTSD L.R. 5-1(b).

g. *Caption; Names of parties.* Every pleading must have a caption with the court's name, a title, a file number, and a FRCP 7(a) designation. The title of the complaint must name all the parties; the title of other pleadings, after naming the first party on each side, may refer generally to other parties. FRCP 10(a). Any pleading, motion, brief, affidavit, notice, or proposed order filed with the court, whether electronically or with the clerk, must: include a title on the first page. IN R USDCTSD L.R. 5-1(b).

h. *Filer's information.* Any pleading, motion, brief, affidavit, notice, or proposed order filed with the court, whether electronically or with the clerk, must: in the case of pleadings, motions, legal briefs, and notices, include the name, complete address, telephone number, facsimile number (where available), and e-mail address (where available) of the pro se litigant or attorney who files it. IN R USDCTSD L.R. 5-1(b).

i. *Paragraphs; Separate statements.* A party must state its claims or defenses in numbered paragraphs, each limited as far as practicable to a single set of circumstances. A later pleading may refer by number to a paragraph in an earlier pleading. If doing so would promote clarity, each claim founded on a separate transaction or occurrence—and each defense other than a denial—must be stated in a separate count or defense. FRCP 10(b).

j. *Adoption by reference; Exhibits.* A statement in a pleading may be adopted by reference elsewhere in the same pleading or in any other pleading or motion. A copy of a written instrument that is an exhibit to a pleading is a part of the pleading for all purposes. FRCP 10(c).

k. *Citations*

  i. *Local rules.* The Local Rules of the United States District Court for the Southern District of Indiana may be cited as "S.D. Ind. L.R." IN R USDCTSD L.R. 1-1(a).

  ii. *Local alternative dispute resolution rules.* These Rules shall be known as the Local Alternative Dispute Resolution Rules of the United States District Court for the Southern District of Indiana. They shall be cited as "S.D.Ind. Local A.D.R. Rule _____." IN R USDCTSD A.D.R. Rule 1.1.

l. *Acceptance by the clerk.* The clerk must not refuse to file a paper solely because it is not in the form prescribed by the Federal Rules of Civil Procedure or by a local rule or practice. FRCP 5(d)(4). The clerk will accept a document that violates IN R USDCTSD L.R. 5-1, but the court may exclude the document from the official record. IN R USDCTSD L.R. 5-1(e).

  i. *Sanctions for errors as to form.* The court may strike from the record any document that does not comply with the rules governing the form of documents filed with the court, such as rules that regulate document size or the number of copies to be filed or that require a special designation in the caption. The court may also sanction an attorney or party who files a non-compliant document. IN R USDCTSD L.R. 1-3.

2. *Form of electronic documents.* Any document submitted via the court's electronic case filing (ECF) system must be: otherwise prepared and filed in a manner consistent with the CM/ECF Policies and Procedures Manual (IN R USDCTSD ECF Procedures). IN R USDCTSD L.R. 5-1(c). Electronically filed documents must meet the requirements of FRCP 10 (Form of Pleadings), IN R USDCTSD L.R. 5-1 (Format of Papers Presented for Filing), and FRCP 5.2 (Privacy Protection for Filings Made with the Court), as if they had been submitted on paper. Documents filed electronically are also subject to any page limitations set forth by Court Order, by IN R USDCTSD L.R. 7-1 (Motion Practice), or IN R USDCTSD L.R. 56-1 (Summary Judgment Practice), as applicable. IN R USDCTSD ECF Procedures(13).

   a. *PDF format required.* Any document submitted via the court's electronic case filing (ECF) system must be: in .pdf format. IN R USDCTSD L.R. 5-1(c); IN R USDCTSD ECF Procedures(7). Any document submitted via the court's electronic case filing (ECF) system must be: converted to a .pdf file directly from a word processing program, unless it exists only in paper format (in which case it may be scanned to create a .pdf document). IN R USDCTSD L.R. 5-1(c); IN R USDCTSD ECF Procedures(13).

      i. An exhibit may be scanned into PDF format, at a recommended 300 dpi resolution or higher, only if it does not already exist in electronic format. The filing attorney is responsible for reviewing all PDF documents for legibility before submitting them through the Court's Electronic Case Filing system. For technical guidance in creating PDF documents, please contact the Clerk's Office. IN R USDCTSD ECF Procedures(13).

   b. *File size limitations.* Any document submitted via the court's electronic case filing (ECF) system must be: submitted as one or more .pdf files that do not exceed ten megabytes (10 MB) each (consistent with the CM/ECF Policies and Procedures Manual (IN R USDCTSD ECF Procedures)). IN R USDCTSD L.R. 5-1(c); IN R USDCTSD ECF Procedures(13).

      i. To electronically file a document or attachment that exceeds ten megabytes (10 MB), the document must first be broken down into two or more smaller files. For example, if Exhibit A is a twelve megabyte (12 MB) PDF file, it should be divided into 2 equal parts prior to electronic filing. Each component part of the exhibit would be filed as an attachment to the main document and described appropriately as "Exhibit A (part 1 of 2)" and "Exhibit A (part 2 of 2)." IN R USDCTSD ECF Procedures(13).

      ii. The supporting items mentioned in IN R USDCTSD ECF Procedures(13) should not be confused with memorandums or briefs in support of motions as outlined in IN R USDCTSD L.R. 7-1 or IN R USDCTSD L.R. 56-1. These memorandums or briefs in support are to be filed as entirely separate documents pursuant to the appropriate rule. Additionally, no motion shall be embodied in the text of a response or reply brief/memorandum unless otherwise ordered by the Court. IN R USDCTSD ECF Procedures(13).

   c. *Separate component parts.* A key objective of the electronic filing system is to ensure that as much of the case as possible is managed electronically. To facilitate electronic filing and retrieval, documents to be filed electronically are to be reasonably broken into their separate component parts. By way of example, most filings include a foundation document (e.g., motion) and other supporting items (e.g., exhibits, proposed orders, proposed amended pleadings). The foundation document, as well as the supporting items, are each separate components of the filing; supporting items must be filed as attachments to the foundation document. These exhibits or attachments should include only those excerpts of the referenced documents that are directly germane to the matter under consideration. IN R USDCTSD ECF Procedures(13).

      i. Where an individual component cannot be included in an electronic filing (e.g. the component cannot be converted to electronic format), the filer shall electronically file the prescribed Notice of Manual Filing in place of that component. A model form is provided as Appendix C (IN R USDCTSD ECF Procedures(Appendix C)). IN R USDCTSD ECF Procedures(13).

   d. *Exhibits.* Each electronically filed exhibit to a main document must be: (1) created as a separate .pdf file; (2) submitted as an attachment to the main document and given a title which describes its content; and (3) limited to excerpts that are directly germane to the main document's subject matter. IN R USDCTSD L.R. 5-6(a).

      i. When uploading attachments during the electronic filing process, exhibits must be uploaded in

a logical sequence and a brief description must be entered for each individual PDF file. The description must include not only the exhibit number or letter, but also a brief description of the document. This information may be entered in CM/ECF using a combination of the Category drop-down menu, the Description text box, or both (see IN R USDCTSD ECF Procedures(13)(Figure 1)). The information that is provided in each box will be combined to create a description of the document as it appears on the case docket (see IN R USDCTSD ECF Procedures(13)(Figure 2)). IN R USDCTSD ECF Procedures(13). For an example, refer to IN R USDCTSD ECF Procedures(13).

e. *Excerpts.* A party filing an exhibit that consists of excerpts from a larger document must clearly and prominently identify the exhibit as containing excerpted material. Either party will have the right to timely file additional excerpts or the complete document to the extent they are or become directly germane to the main document's subject matter. IN R USDCTSD L.R. 5-6(b).

f. For an example illustrating the application of IN R USDCTSD ECF Procedures(13), refer to IN R USDCTSD ECF Procedures(13).

3. *Signing disclosures and discovery requests, responses, and objections.* FRCP 11 does not apply to disclosures and discovery requests, responses, objections, and motions under FRCP 26 through FRCP 37. FRCP 11(d).

a. *Signature required.* Every disclosure under FRCP 26(a)(1) or FRCP 26(a)(3) and every discovery request, response, or objection must be signed by at least one attorney of record in the attorney's own name—or by the party personally, if unrepresented—and must state the signer's address, e-mail address, and telephone number. FRCP 26(g)(1).

   i. *Signatures on manual filings.* Any document that is not filed electronically must: include the original signature of the pro se litigant or attorney who files it. IN R USDCTSD L.R. 5-1(d)(1).

   ii. *Electronic signatures.* Use of the attorney's login and password when filing documents electronically serves in part as the attorney's signature for purposes of FRCP 11, the Local Rules of the United States District Court for the Southern District of Indiana, and any other purpose for which a signature is required in connection with proceedings before the Court. IN R USDCTSD ECF Procedures(14); IN R USDCTSD ECF Procedures(10). A pleading, motion, brief, or notice filed electronically under an attorney's ECF log-in and password must be signed by that attorney. IN R USDCTSD L.R. 5-7(a). A signature on a document other than a document filed as provided under IN R USDCTSD L.R. 5-7(a) must be an original handwritten signature and must be scanned into .pdf format for electronic filing. IN R USDCTSD L.R. 5-7(c); IN R USDCTSD ECF Procedures(14).

      - *Form of electronic signature.* If a document is converted directly from a word processing application to .pdf (as opposed to scanning), the name of the Filing User under whose log-in and password the document is submitted must be preceded by a "s/" and typed on the signature line where the Filing User's handwritten signature would otherwise appear. IN R USDCTSD L.R. 5-7(b). All documents filed electronically shall include a signature block and include the filing attorney's typewritten name, address, telephone number, facsimile number and e-mail address. In addition, the name of the filing attorney under whose ECF login the document will be filed should be preceded by a "s/" and typed in the space where the attorney's handwritten signature would otherwise appear. IN R US-DCTSD ECF Procedures(14). For a sample format, refer to IN R USDCTSD ECF Procedures(14).

      - *Effect of electronic signature.* Filing an electronically signed document under an attorney's ECF log-in and password constitutes the attorney's signature on the document under the Federal Rules of Civil Procedure, under the Local Rules of the United States District Court for the Southern District of Indiana, and for any other reason a signature is required in connection with the court's activities. IN R USDCTSD L.R. 5-7(d).

      - *Documents with multiple attorneys' signatures.* Documents requiring signatures of more than one attorney shall be filed either by: (1) obtaining consent from the other attorney, then typing the "s/ [Name]" signature of the other attorney on the signature line where the other attorney's signature would otherwise appear; (2) identifying in the signature section the name of the other attorney whose signature is required and by the submission of a Notice of Endorsement (see IN R USDCTSD ECF Procedures(Appendix B)) by the other attorney no later than three (3) business days after filing; (3) submitting a scanned document containing all handwritten signatures; or (4) in any other manner approved by the Court. IN R USDCTSD ECF Procedures(14); IN R USDCTSD L.R. 5-7(e).

b. *Effect of signature.* By signing, an attorney or party certifies that to the best of the person's knowledge, information, and belief formed after a reasonable inquiry:

   i. With respect to a disclosure, it is complete and correct as of the time it is made; and

   ii. With respect to a discovery request, response, or objection, it is:

- Consistent with the Federal Rules of Civil Procedure and warranted by existing law or by a nonfrivolous argument for extending, modifying, or reversing existing law, or for establishing new law;

- Not interposed for any improper purpose, such as to harass, cause unnecessary delay, or needlessly increase the cost of litigation; and

- Neither unreasonable nor unduly burdensome or expensive, considering the needs of the case, prior discovery in the case, the amount in controversy, and the importance of the issues at stake in the action. FRCP 26(g)(1).

c. *Failure to sign.* Other parties have no duty to act on an unsigned disclosure, request, response, or objection until it is signed, and the court must strike it unless a signature is promptly supplied after the omission is called to the attorney's or party's attention. FRCP 26(g)(2). The court will strike any document filed directly with the clerk that is not signed by an attorney of record or the pro se litigant filing it, but the court may do so only after giving the attorney or pro se litigant notice of the omission and reasonable time to correct it. Rubber-stamp or facsimile signatures are not original signatures and the court will deem documents containing them to be unsigned for purposes of FRCP 11 and FRCP 26(g) and IN R USDCTSD L.R. 5-10. IN R USDCTSD L.R. 5-10(g).

d. *Sanction for improper certification.* If a certification violates FRCP 26(g) without substantial justification, the court, on motion or on its own, must impose an appropriate sanction on the signer, the party on whose behalf the signer was acting, or both. The sanction may include an order to pay the reasonable expenses, including attorney's fees, caused by the violation. FRCP 26(g)(3). Refer to the United States District Court for the Southern District of Indiana KeyRules Motion for Discovery Sanctions document for more information.

4. *Privacy protection for filings made with the court.* Electronically filed documents must meet the requirements of. . .FRCP 5.2 (Privacy Protection for Filings Made with the Court), as if they had been submitted on paper. IN R USDCTSD ECF Procedures(13).

a. *Redacted filings.* Unless the court orders otherwise, in an electronic or paper filing with the court that contains an individual's Social Security number, taxpayer-identification number, or birth date, the name of an individual known to be a minor, or a financial-account number, a party or nonparty making the filing may include only:

   i. The last four (4) digits of the Social Security number and taxpayer-identification number;

   ii. The year of the individual's birth;

   iii. The minor's initials; and

   iv. The last four (4) digits of the financial-account number. FRCP 5.2(a).

b. *Exemptions from the redaction requirement.* The redaction requirement does not apply to the following:

   i. A financial-account number that identifies the property allegedly subject to forfeiture in a forfeiture proceeding;

   ii. The record of an administrative or agency proceeding;

   iii. The official record of a state-court proceeding;

    iv. The record of a court or tribunal, if that record was not subject to the redaction requirement when originally filed;

    v. A filing covered by FRCP 5.2(c) or FRCP 5.2(d); and

    vi. A pro se filing in an action brought under 28 U.S.C.A. § 2241, 28 U.S.C.A. § 2254, or 28 U.S.C.A. § 2255. FRCP 5.2(b).

c. *Limitations on remote access to electronic files; Social Security appeals and immigration cases.* Unless the court orders otherwise, in an action for benefits under the Social Security Act, and in an action or proceeding relating to an order of removal, to relief from removal, or to immigration benefits or detention, access to an electronic file is authorized as follows:

    i. The parties and their attorneys may have remote electronic access to any part of the case file, including the administrative record;

    ii. Any other person may have electronic access to the full record at the courthouse, but may have remote electronic access only to:

- The docket maintained by the court; and
- An opinion, order, judgment, or other disposition of the court, but not any other part of the case file or the administrative record. FRCP 5.2(c).

d. *Filings made under seal.* The court may order that a filing be made under seal without redaction. The court may later unseal the filing or order the person who made the filing to file a redacted version for the public record. FRCP 5.2(d). For more information on filing under seal, refer to IN R USDCTSD L.R. 5-11 and IN R USDCTSD ECF Procedures(18).

e. *Protective orders.* For good cause, the court may by order in a case:

    i. Require redaction of additional information; or

    ii. Limit or prohibit a nonparty's remote electronic access to a document filed with the court. FRCP 5.2(e).

f. *Option for additional unredacted filing under seal.* A person making a redacted filing may also file an unredacted copy under seal. The court must retain the unredacted copy as part of the record. FRCP 5.2(f).

g. *Option for filing a reference list.* A filing that contains redacted information may be filed together with a reference list that identifies each item of redacted information and specifies an appropriate identifier that uniquely corresponds to each item listed. The list must be filed under seal and may be amended as of right. Any reference in the case to a listed identifier will be construed to refer to the corresponding item of information. FRCP 5.2(g).

h. *Waiver of protection of identifiers.* A person waives the protection of FRCP 5.2(a) as to the person's own information by filing it without redaction and not under seal. FRCP 5.2(h).

F. Filing and Service Requirements

1. *Filing requirements.* Any paper after the complaint that is required to be served—together with a certificate of service—must be filed within a reasonable time after service. But disclosures under FRCP 26(a)(1) or FRCP 26(a)(2) and the following discovery requests and responses must not be filed until they are used in the proceeding or the court orders filing: depositions, interrogatories, requests for documents or tangible things or to permit entry onto land, and requests for admission. FRCP 5(d)(1). Refer to the United States District Court for the Southern District of Indiana KeyRules pleading and motion documents for information on filing with the court.

a. *When discovery may be filed.* Discovery materials (whether discovery requests, responses, or deposition transcripts) may not be filed with the court except in the following circumstances:

    i. *Relevant to certain motions.* A party seeking relief under FRCP 26(c) or FRCP 37, or by way of a pretrial motion that could result in a final order on an issue, must file with the motion those parts of the discovery materials relevant to the motion. IN R USDCTSD L.R. 26-2(a).

    ii. *For anticipated use at trial.* When a party can reasonably anticipate using discovery materials at trial, the party must file the relevant portions at the start of the trial. IN R USDCTSD L.R. 26-2(b).

iii. *Materials necessary for appeal.* A party seeking for purposes of appeal to supplement the record with discovery materials not previously filed may do so by stipulation of the parties or by court order approving the filing. IN R USDCTSD L.R. 26-2(c).

2. *Service requirements*

a. *Service; When required*

i. *In general.* Unless the Federal Rules of Civil Procedure provide otherwise, each of the following papers must be served on every party:

- An order stating that service is required;
- A pleading filed after the original complaint, unless the court orders otherwise under FRCP 5(c) because there are numerous defendants;
- A discovery paper required to be served on a party, unless the court orders otherwise;
- A written motion, except one that may be heard ex parte; and
- A written notice, appearance, demand, or offer of judgment, or any similar paper. FRCP 5(a)(1).

ii. *If a party fails to appear.* No service is required on a party who is in default for failing to appear. But a pleading that asserts a new claim for relief against such a party must be served on that party under FRCP 4. FRCP 5(a)(2).

iii. *Seizing property.* If an action is begun by seizing property and no person is or need be named as a defendant, any service required before the filing of an appearance, answer, or claim must be made on the person who had custody or possession of the property when it was seized. FRCP 5(a)(3).

b. *Service; How made*

i. *Serving an attorney.* If a party is represented by an attorney, service under FRCP 5 must be made on the attorney unless the court orders service on the party. FRCP 5(b)(1).

ii. *Service in general.* A paper is served under FRCP 5 by:

- Handing it to the person;
- Leaving it: (1) at the person's office with a clerk or other person in charge or, if no one is in charge, in a conspicuous place in the office; or (2) if the person has no office or the office is closed, at the person's dwelling or usual place of abode with someone of suitable age and discretion who resides there;
- Mailing it to the person's last known address—in which event service is complete upon mailing;
- Leaving it with the court clerk if the person has no known address;
- Sending it by electronic means if the person consented in writing—in which event service is complete upon transmission, but is not effective if the serving party learns that it did not reach the person to be served; or
- Delivering it by any other means that the person consented to in writing—in which event service is complete when the person making service delivers it to the agency designated to make delivery. FRCP 5(b)(2).

iii. *Electronic service*

- *Consent.* By registering to use the ECF system, attorneys consent to electronic service of documents filed in cases maintained on the ECF system. IN R USDCTSD L.R. 5-3(d). By participating in the Electronic Case Filing Program, attorneys consent to the electronic service of documents, and shall make available electronic mail addresses for service. IN R USDCTSD ECF Procedures(11).

- *Service on registered parties.* Upon the filing of a document by a party, an e-mail message will be automatically generated by the electronic filing system and sent via electronic mail to the e-mail addresses of all registered attorneys who have appeared in the case. The Notice of Electronic Filing will contain a document hyperlink which will provide recipients with one "free look" at the electronically filed document. Recipients are encouraged to print and/or save a copy of the document during the "free look" to avoid incurring PACER charges for future viewings of the document. IN R USDCTSD ECF Procedures(11). When a document has been filed electronically: transmission of the notice of electronic filing generated by the ECF system to an attorney's e-mail address constitutes service of the document on that attorney. IN R USDCTSD L.R. 5-4(c)(5). The party effectuates service on all registered attorneys by filing electronically. IN R USDCTSD ECF Procedures(11). When a document has been filed electronically: no other attempted service will constitute electronic service of the document. IN R USDCTSD L.R. 5-4(c)(6).

- *Service on exempt parties.* A filer must serve a copy of the document consistent with FRCP 5 on any party or attorney who is exempt from participating in electronic filing. IN R USDCTSD L.R. 5-4(d). It is the responsibility of the filing attorney to conventionally serve all parties who do not receive electronic service (the identity of these parties will be indicated on the filing receipt generated by the ECF system). IN R USDCTSD ECF Procedures(11).

- *Service on parties excused from electronic filing.* Parties otherwise participating in the electronic filing system may be excused from filing a particular component electronically under certain limited circumstances, such as when the component cannot be reduced to an electronic format. Such components shall not be filed electronically, but instead shall be manually filed with the Clerk of Court and served upon the parties in accordance with the applicable Federal Rules of Civil Procedure and the Local Rules of the United States District Court for the Southern District of Indiana for filing and service of non-electronic documents. IN R USDCTSD ECF Procedures(15).

- *Service of exempt documents.* Any document that is exempt from electronic filing must be filed directly with the clerk and served on other parties in the case as required by those Federal Rules of Civil Procedure and Local Rules of the United States District Court for the Southern District of Indiana that apply to the service of non-electronic documents. IN R USDCTSD L.R. 5-2(c).

 iv. *Using court facilities.* If a local rule so authorizes, a party may use the court's transmission facilities to make service under FRCP 5(b)(2)(E). FRCP 5(b)(3).

c. *Serving numerous defendants*

 i. *In general.* If an action involves an unusually large number of defendants, the court may, on motion or on its own, order that:

- Defendants' pleadings and replies to them need not be served on other defendants;

- Any crossclaim, counterclaim, avoidance, or affirmative defense in those pleadings and replies to them will be treated as denied or avoided by all other parties; and

- Filing any such pleading and serving it on the plaintiff constitutes notice of the pleading to all parties. FRCP 5(c)(1).

 ii. *Notifying parties.* A copy of every such order must be served on the parties as the court directs. FRCP 5(c)(2).

G. Hearings

1. There is no hearing contemplated in the federal statutes or rules for responses to interrogatories.

H. Forms

1. Federal Response to Interrogatories Forms

a. Introductory statement; Answer to interrogatories. AMJUR PP DEPOSITION § 407.

b. Answers to interrogatories; Illustrative form. AMJUR PP DEPOSITION § 408.

  c. Response to interrogatories; Illustrative form. AMJUR PP DEPOSITION § 409.

  d. Verification; By defendant; Of answers to interrogatories. AMJUR PP DEPOSITION § 410.

  e. Answers to interrogatories. 3A FEDFORMS § 3503.

  f. Answers to interrogatories; Complete set. 3A FEDFORMS § 3504.

  g. Amendments to answers to interrogatories. 3A FEDFORMS § 3505.

  h. Supplemental answer to plaintiff's interrogatories. 3A FEDFORMS § 3506.

  i. Second supplemental answer to plaintiff's interrogatories. 3A FEDFORMS § 3507.

  j. Supplementation of response to interrogatory. 3A FEDFORMS § 3508.

  k. Answers by individual. 3A FEDFORMS § 3510.

  l. Answers by corporation. 3A FEDFORMS § 3511.

  m. Declaration; Answers by individual. 3A FEDFORMS § 3512.

  n. Declaration; Answers by corporation. 3A FEDFORMS § 3513.

  o. Objections to interrogatories. 3A FEDFORMS § 3514.

  p. Objections to interrogatories; Another form. 3A FEDFORMS § 3515.

  q. Objections to interrogatories; Another form. 3A FEDFORMS § 3516.

  r. Objections to interrogatories; With answers. 3A FEDFORMS § 3517.

  s. Statement in answer as to interrogatory to which objection made. 3A FEDFORMS § 3518.

  t. Answers; To interrogatories; Outline form. FEDPROF § 23:344.

  u. Answers; To interrogatories; By two defendants; Outline form. FEDPROF § 23:345.

  v. Objections to interrogatories; Illustrative grounds. FEDPROF § 23:367.

  w. Answer to interrogatories. GOLDLTGFMS § 26:72.

  x. Answer to interrogatories; Pursuant to civil procedure rules. GOLDLTGFMS § 26:73.

  y. Answer to interrogatories; Corporate information as basis for answers. GOLDLTGFMS § 26:74.

  z. Answer to interrogatories; Expert not yet selected. GOLDLTGFMS § 26:75.

I. Applicable Rules

  1. *Federal rules*

    a. Serving and filing pleadings and other papers. FRCP 5.

    b. Privacy protection for filings made with the court. FRCP 5.2.

    c. Computing and extending time; Time for motion papers. FRCP 6.

    d. Pleadings allowed; Form of motions and other papers. FRCP 7.

    e. Form of pleadings. FRCP 10.

    f. Signing pleadings, motions, and other papers; Representations to the court; Sanctions. FRCP 11.

    g. Duty to disclose; General provisions governing discovery. FRCP 26.

    h. Stipulations about discovery procedure. FRCP 29.

    i. Interrogatories to parties. FRCP 33.

    j. Failure to make disclosures or to cooperate in discovery; Sanctions. FRCP 37.

  2. *Local rules*

    a. Scope of the rules. IN R USDCTSD L.R. 1-1.

    b. Sanctions for errors as to form. IN R USDCTSD L.R. 1-3.

    c. Format of documents presented for filing. IN R USDCTSD L.R. 5-1.

    d. Filing of documents electronically required. IN R USDCTSD L.R. 5-2.

e. Eligibility, registration, passwords for electronic filing; Exemption from electronic filing. IN R USDCTSD L.R. 5-3.

f. Timing and consequences of electronic filing. IN R USDCTSD L.R. 5-4.

g. Attachments and exhibits in cases filed electronically. IN R USDCTSD L.R. 5-6.

h. Signatures in cases filed electronically. IN R USDCTSD L.R. 5-7.

i. Non-electronic filings. IN R USDCTSD L.R. 5-10.

j. Extensions of time. IN R USDCTSD L.R. 6-1.

k. Motion practice. [IN R USDCTSD L.R. 7-1, as amended by IN ORDER 16-2319, effective December 1, 2016].

l. Form of certain discovery requests. IN R USDCTSD L.R. 26-1.

m. Filing of discovery materials. IN R USDCTSD L.R. 26-2.

n. Assignment of cases. IN R USDCTSD L.R. 40-1.

o. Alternative dispute resolution. IN R USDCTSD A.D.R. Rule 1.1; IN R USDCTSD A.D.R. Rule 1.2; IN R USDCTSD A.D.R. Rule 1.5; IN R USDCTSD A.D.R. Rule 2.1; IN R USDCTSD A.D.R. Rule 2.2.

p. Electronic case filing policies and procedures manual. IN R USDCTSD ECF Procedures.

Requests, Notices and Applications
Request for Production of Documents

Document Last Updated December 2016

A. Checklist

(I) ❑ Matters to be considered by requesting party

  (a) ❑ Required documents

    (1) ❑ Request for production of documents

  (b) ❑ Supplemental documents

    (1) ❑ Subpoena

    (2) ❑ Certificate of service

  (c) ❑ Timing

    (1) ❑ More than twenty-one (21) days after the summons and complaint are served on a party, a request under FRCP 34 may be delivered: (1) to that party by any other party, and (2) by that party to any plaintiff or to any other party that has been served

    (2) ❑ A party may not seek discovery from any source before the parties have conferred as required by FRCP 26(f), except in a proceeding exempted from initial disclosure under FRCP 26(a)(1)(B), or when authorized by the Federal Rules of Civil Procedure, by stipulation, or by court order

    (3) ❑ If a subpoena to produce or permit is to be served upon a nonparty, a copy of the proposed subpoena must be served on all other parties at least seven (7) days prior to service of the subpoena on the nonparty, unless the parties agree to a different time frame or the case management plan provides otherwise; provided, however, that if such subpoena relates to a matter set for hearing within such seven (7) day period or arises out of a bona fide emergency, such subpoena may be served upon a nonparty one (1) day after a notice and copy of the subpoena is served on each party

(II) ❑ Matters to be considered by responding party

  (a) ❑ Required documents

    (1) ❑ Response to request for production of documents

    (b) ❑ Supplemental documents

        (1) ❑ Certificate of service

    (c) ❑ Timing

        (1) ❑ The party to whom the request is directed must respond in writing within thirty (30) days after being served or—if the request was delivered under FRCP 26(d)(2)—within thirty (30) days after the parties' first FRCP 26(f) conference

B. Timing

1. *Request for production of documents.* Without leave of court or written stipulation, a request may not be served before the time specified in FRCP 26(d). FEDPROC § 26:632. Of course, discovery under FRCP 34 should ordinarily precede the trial. FEDPROC § 26:632.

    a. *Early FRCP 34 requests*

        i. *Time to deliver.* More than twenty-one (21) days after the summons and complaint are served on a party, a request under FRCP 34 may be delivered:

- To that party by any other party, and

- By that party to any plaintiff or to any other party that has been served. FRCP 26(d)(2)(A).

        ii. *When considered served.* The request is considered to have been served at the first FRCP 26(f) conference. FRCP 26(d)(2)(B).

    b. *Service of subpoena on non-parties.* If a subpoena to produce or permit is to be served upon a nonparty, a copy of the proposed subpoena must be served on all other parties at least seven (7) days prior to service of the subpoena on the nonparty, unless the parties agree to a different time frame or the case management plan provides otherwise. Provided, however, that if such subpoena relates to a matter set for hearing within such seven (7) day period or arises out of a bona fide emergency, such subpoena may be served upon a nonparty one (1) day after a notice and copy of the subpoena is served on each party. IN R USDCTSD L.R. 45-1.

2. *Timing of discovery, generally.* A party may not seek discovery from any source before the parties have conferred as required by FRCP 26(f), except in a proceeding exempted from initial disclosure under FRCP 26(a)(1)(B), or when authorized by the Federal Rules of Civil Procedure, by stipulation, or by court order. FRCP 26(d)(1).

3. *Computation of time*

    a. *Computing time.* FRCP 6 applies in computing any time period specified in the Federal Rules of Civil Procedure, in any local rule or court order, or in any statute that does not specify a method of computing time. FRCP 6(a).

        i. *Period stated in days or a longer unit.* When the period is stated in days or a longer unit of time:

- Exclude the day of the event that triggers the period;

- Count every day, including intermediate Saturdays, Sundays, and legal holidays; and

- Include the last day of the period, but if the last day is a Saturday, Sunday, or legal holiday, the period continues to run until the end of the next day that is not a Saturday, Sunday, or legal holiday. FRCP 6(a)(1).

        ii. *Period stated in hours.* When the period is stated in hours:

- Begin counting immediately on the occurrence of the event that triggers the period;

- Count every hour, including hours during intermediate Saturdays, Sundays, and legal holidays; and

- If the period would end on a Saturday, Sunday, or legal holiday, the period continues to run until the same time on the next day that is not a Saturday, Sunday, or legal holiday. FRCP 6(a)(2).

iii. *Inaccessibility of the clerk's office.* Unless the court orders otherwise, if the clerk's office is inaccessible:

- On the last day for filing under FRCP 6(a)(1), then the time for filing is extended to the first accessible day that is not a Saturday, Sunday, or legal holiday; or

- During the last hour for filing under FRCP 6(a)(2), then the time for filing is extended to the same time on the first accessible day that is not a Saturday, Sunday, or legal holiday. FRCP 6(a)(3).

iv. *"Last day" defined.* Unless a different time is set by a statute, local rule, or court order, the last day ends:

- For electronic filing, at midnight in the court's time zone; and

- For filing by other means, when the clerk's office is scheduled to close. FRCP 6(a)(4).

v. *"Next day" defined.* The "next day" is determined by continuing to count forward when the period is measured after an event and backward when measured before an event. FRCP 6(a)(5).

vi. *"Legal holiday" defined.* "Legal holiday" means:

- The day set aside by statute for observing New Year's Day, Martin Luther King Jr.'s Birthday, Washington's Birthday, Memorial Day, Independence Day, Labor Day, Columbus Day, Veterans' Day, Thanksgiving Day, or Christmas Day;

- Any day declared a holiday by the President or Congress; and

- For periods that are measured after an event, any other day declared a holiday by the state where the district court is located. FRCP 6(a)(6).

b. *Computation of electronic filing deadlines.* Filing documents electronically does not alter filing deadlines. IN R USDCTSD ECF Procedures(7). A document due on a particular day must be filed before midnight local time of the division where the case is pending. IN R USDCTSD L.R. 5-4(a). All electronic transmissions of documents must be completed (i.e. received completely by the Clerk's Office) prior to midnight of the local time of the division in which the case is pending in order to be considered timely filed that day (NOTE: time will be noted in Eastern Time on the Court's docket. If you have filed a document prior to midnight local time of the division in which the case is pending and the document is due that date, but the electronic receipt and docket reflect the following calendar day, please contact the Court). IN R USDCTSD ECF Procedures(7). Although attorneys may file documents electronically twenty-four (24) hours a day, seven (7) days a week, attorneys are encouraged to file all documents during the normal working hours of the Clerk's Office (Monday through Friday, 8:30 a.m. to 4:30 p.m.) when technical support is available. IN R USDCTSD ECF Procedures(7); IN R USDCTSD ECF Procedures(9).

i. *Technical difficulties.* Parties are encouraged to file documents electronically during normal business hours, in case a problem is encountered. In the event a technical failure occurs and a document cannot be filed electronically despite the best efforts of the filing party, the party should print (if possible) a copy of the error message received. In addition, as soon as practically possible, the party should file a "Declaration that Party was Unable to File in a Timely Manner Due to Technical Difficulties." A model form is provided as Appendix D (IN R USDCTSD ECF Procedures(Appendix D)). IN R USDCTSD ECF Procedures(16).

- If a party is unable to file electronically and, as a result, may miss a filing deadline, the party must contact the Clerk's Office at the number listed in IN R USDCTSD ECF Procedures(15) to inform the court's staff of the difficulty. If a party misses a filing deadline due to an inability to file electronically, the party may submit the untimely filed document, accompanied by a declaration stating the reason(s) for missing the deadline. Unless the Court orders otherwise, the document and declaration must be filed no later than 12:00 noon of the first day on which the Court is open for business following the original filing deadline. IN R USDCTSD ECF Procedures(16).

c. *Extending time*

  i. *In general.* When an act may or must be done within a specified time, the court may, for good cause, extend the time:

  - With or without motion or notice if the court acts, or if a request is made, before the original time or its extension expires; or

  - On motion made after the time has expired if the party failed to act because of excusable neglect. FRCP 6(b)(1).

  ii. *Exceptions.* A court must not extend the time to act under FRCP 50(b), FRCP 50(d), FRCP 52(b), FRCP 59(b), FRCP 59(d), FRCP 59(e), and FRCP 60(b). FRCP 6(b)(2).

  iii. Refer to the United States District Court for the Southern District of Indiana KeyRules Motion for Continuance/Extension of Time document for more information on extending time.

d. *Additional time after certain kinds of service.* When a party may or must act within a specified time after being served and service is made under FRCP 5(b)(2)(C) (mail), FRCP 5(b)(2)(D) (leaving with the clerk), or FRCP 5(b)(2)(F) (other means consented to), three (3) days are added after the period would otherwise expire under FRCP 6(a). FRCP 6(d). Service by electronic mail shall constitute service pursuant to FRCP 5(b)(2)(E) and shall entitle the party being served to the additional three (3) days provided by FRCP 6(d). IN R USDCTSD ECF Procedures(11).

C. General Requirements

1. *General provisions governing discovery*

a. *Discovery scope and limits*

  i. *Scope in general.* Unless otherwise limited by court order, the scope of discovery is as follows: Parties may obtain discovery regarding any nonprivileged matter that is relevant to any party's claim or defense and proportional to the needs of the case, considering the importance of the issues at stake in the action, the amount in controversy, the parties' relative access to relevant information, the parties' resources, the importance of the discovery in resolving the issues, and whether the burden or expense of the proposed discovery outweighs its likely benefit. Information within this scope of discovery need not be admissible in evidence to be discoverable. FRCP 26(b)(1).

  ii. *Limitations on frequency and extent*

  - *When permitted.* By order, the court may alter the limits in the Federal Rules of Civil Procedure on the number of depositions and interrogatories or on the length of depositions under FRCP 30. By order or local rule, the court may also limit the number of requests under FRCP 36. FRCP 26(b)(2)(A).

  - *Specific limitations on electronically stored information.* A party need not provide discovery of electronically stored information from sources that the party identifies as not reasonably accessible because of undue burden or cost. On motion to compel discovery or for a protective order, the party from whom discovery is sought must show that the information is not reasonably accessible because of undue burden or cost. If that showing is made, the court may nonetheless order discovery from such sources if the requesting party shows good cause, considering the limitations of FRCP 26(b)(2)(C). The court may specify conditions for the discovery. FRCP 26(b)(2)(B).

  - *When required.* On motion or on its own, the court must limit the frequency or extent of discovery otherwise allowed by the Federal Rules of Civil Procedure or by local rule if it determines that: (1) the discovery sought is unreasonably cumulative or duplicative, or can be obtained from some other source that is more convenient, less burdensome, or less expensive; (2) the party seeking discovery has had ample opportunity to obtain the information by discovery in the action; or (3) the proposed discovery is outside the scope permitted by FRCP 26(b)(1). FRCP 26(b)(2)(C).

  iii. *Trial preparation; Materials*

  - *Documents and tangible things.* Ordinarily, a party may not discover documents and tangible things that are prepared in anticipation of litigation or for trial by or for another party or its representative (including the other party's attorney, consultant, surety, indemnitor, insurer, or agent). But, subject to FRCP 26(b)(4), those materials may be discovered if: (1) they are otherwise discoverable under FRCP 26(b)(1); and (2) the party shows that it has substantial need for the materials to prepare its case and cannot, without undue hardship, obtain their substantial equivalent by other means. FRCP 26(b)(3)(A).

- *Protection against disclosure.* If the court orders discovery of those materials, it must protect against disclosure of the mental impressions, conclusions, opinions, or legal theories of a party's attorney or other representative concerning the litigation. FRCP 26(b)(3)(B).

- *Previous statement.* Any party or other person may, on request and without the required showing, obtain the person's own previous statement about the action or its subject matter. If the request is refused, the person may move for a court order, and FRCP 37(a)(5) applies to the award of expenses. A previous statement is either: (1) a written statement that the person has signed or otherwise adopted or approved; or (2) a contemporaneous stenographic, mechanical, electrical, or other recording—or a transcription of it—that recites substantially verbatim the person's oral statement. FRCP 26(b)(3)(C).

iv. *Trial preparation; Experts*

- *Deposition of an expert who may testify.* A party may depose any person who has been identified as an expert whose opinions may be presented at trial. If FRCP 26(a)(2)(B) requires a report from the expert, the deposition may be conducted only after the report is provided. FRCP 26(b)(4)(A).

- *Trial-preparation protection for draft reports or disclosures.* FRCP 26(b)(3)(A) and FRCP 26(b)(3)(B) protect drafts of any report or disclosure required under FRCP 26(a)(2), regardless of the form in which the draft is recorded. FRCP 26(b)(4)(B).

- *Trial-preparation protection for communications between a party's attorney and expert witnesses.* FRCP 26(b)(3)(A) and FRCP 26(b)(3)(B) protect communications between the party's attorney and any witness required to provide a report under FRCP 26(a)(2)(B), regardless of the form of the communications, except to the extent that the communications: (1) relate to compensation for the expert's study or testimony; (2) identify facts or data that the party's attorney provided and that the expert considered in forming the opinions to be expressed; or (3) identify assumptions that the party's attorney provided and that the expert relied on in forming the opinions to be expressed. FRCP 26(b)(4)(C).

- *Expert employed only for trial preparation.* Ordinarily, a party may not, by interrogatories or deposition, discover facts known or opinions held by an expert who has been retained or specially employed by another party in anticipation of litigation or to prepare for trial and who is not expected to be called as a witness at trial. But a party may do so only: (1) as provided in FRCP 35(b); or (2) on showing exceptional circumstances under which it is impracticable for the party to obtain facts or opinions on the same subject by other means. FRCP 26(b)(4)(D).

- *Payment.* Unless manifest injustice would result, the court must require that the party seeking discovery: (1) pay the expert a reasonable fee for time spent in responding to discovery under FRCP 26(b)(4)(A) or FRCP 26(b)(4)(D); and (2) for discovery under FRCP 26(b)(4)(D), also pay the other party a fair portion of the fees and expenses it reasonably incurred in obtaining the expert's facts and opinions. FRCP 26(b)(4)(E).

v. *Claiming privilege or protecting trial-preparation materials*

- *Information withheld.* When a party withholds information otherwise discoverable by claiming that the information is privileged or subject to protection as trial-preparation material, the party must: (1) expressly make the claim; and (2) describe the nature of the documents, communications, or tangible things not produced or disclosed—and do so in a manner that, without revealing information itself privileged or protected, will enable other parties to assess the claim. FRCP 26(b)(5)(A).

- *Information produced.* If information produced in discovery is subject to a claim of privilege or of protection as trial-preparation material, the party making the claim may notify any party that received the information of the claim and the basis for it. After being notified, a party must promptly return, sequester, or destroy the specified information and any copies it has; must not use or disclose the information until the claim is resolved; must take reasonable steps to retrieve the information if the party disclosed it before being notified; and may promptly present the information to the court under seal for a determination of the claim. The producing party must preserve the information until the claim is resolved. FRCP 26(b)(5)(B).

b. *Protective orders.* A party or any person from whom discovery is sought may move for a protective order in the court where the action is pending—or as an alternative on matters relating to a deposition, in the court for the district where the deposition will be taken. FRCP 26(c)(1). Refer to the United States District Court for the Southern District of Indiana KeyRules Motion for Protective Order document for more information.

c. *Sequence of discovery.* Unless the parties stipulate or the court orders otherwise for the parties' and witnesses' convenience and in the interests of justice: (1) methods of discovery may be used in any sequence; and (2) discovery by one party does not require any other party to delay its discovery. FRCP 26(d)(3).

2. *Request for production of documents*

   a. *In general.* A party may serve on any other party a request within the scope of FRCP 26(b):

      i. To produce and permit the requesting party or its representative to inspect, copy, test, or sample the following items in the responding party's possession, custody, or control:

         - Any designated documents or electronically stored information—including writings, drawings, graphs, charts, photographs, sound recordings, images, and other data or data compilations—stored in any medium from which information can be obtained either directly or, if necessary, after translation by the responding party into a reasonably usable form; or

         - Any designated tangible things; or

      ii. To permit entry onto designated land or other property possessed or controlled by the responding party, so that the requesting party may inspect, measure, survey, photograph, test, or sample the property or any designated object or operation on it. FRCP 34(a).

   b. *Form.* A party propounding written discovery under FRCP 33, FRCP 34, or FRCP 36 must number each interrogatory or request sequentially and, upon request, supply the written discovery to the responding party in an editable word processing format. IN R USDCTSD L.R. 26-1(a).

   c. *Contents of the request.* The request: (1) must describe with reasonable particularity each item or category of items to be inspected; (2) must specify a reasonable time, place, and manner for the inspection and for performing the related acts; and (3) may specify the form or forms in which electronically stored information is to be produced. FRCP 34(b)(1).

      i. *Description of items.* Although the phrase "reasonable particularity" eludes precise definition and depends on the facts and circumstances in each case, at least two tests have been suggested:

         - The first test is whether the request places a party on "reasonable notice" of what is called for and what is not so that a reasonable person would know what documents or things are called for. FEDPROC § 26:634.

         - The second is whether the request gives a court enough information to enable it to rule intelligently on objections. FEDPROC § 26:634.

   d. *Signature.* Though FRCP 34 does not say so, it is sufficient if the request is signed by the attorney for the party seeking discovery. FPP § 2212. Refer to the Format section of this document for more information on signing of discovery papers.

   e. *Other authority on production and inspection*

      i. *Freedom of Information Act.* Although the Freedom of Information Act (FOIA) is fundamentally designed to inform the public about agency action, and not to benefit private litigants, Congress has not acted upon proposals to forbid or limit the use of the FOIA for discovery purposes. FEDPROC § 26:605; National Presto Industries, Inc., 218 Ct.Cl. 696, 1978 WL 8475 (1978). However, a FOIA request may not be used to supplement civil discovery under FRCP 34, as in the case where information is privileged and therefore outside the scope of civil discovery. FEDPROC § 26:605; U.S. v. Weber Aircraft Corp., 465 U.S. 792, 104 S.Ct. 1488, 79 L.Ed.2d 814 (1984).

    ii. *Hague Convention.* Under the Hague Convention, a party seeking evidence abroad must obtain and send a letter of request to the central authority of the country in which the evidence is sought, requesting service of the request on the desired person or entity; if the request complies with the Convention, the central authority will then obtain the desired evidence. FEDPROC § 26:606. [Editor's note: the Hague Convention can be found at T.I.A.S. No. 6638 and is also available in the appendix to FRCP 4].

    f. *Motion to compel.* If a party who has been requested to permit discovery under FRCP 34 makes no response to the request, or if its response objects to all or part of the requested discovery, or if it otherwise fails to permit discovery as requested, the party who submitted the request, if it still wishes the discovery that has been refused, may move under FRCP 37(a) for an order compelling inspection in accordance with the request. FPP § 2214. Refer to the United States District Court for the Southern District of Indiana KeyRules Motion to Compel Discovery document for more information.

3. *Sanctions for failure to cooperate in discovery.* The court where the action is pending may, on motion, order sanctions if a party, after being properly served with interrogatories under FRCP 33 or a request for inspection under FRCP 34, fails to serve its answers, objections, or written response. FRCP 37(d)(1)(A)(ii). If a motion to compel is granted, the court must, after giving an opportunity to be heard, require the party or deponent whose conduct necessitated the motion, the party or attorney advising that conduct, or both to pay the movant's reasonable expenses incurred in making the motion, including attorney's fees. But the court must not order this payment if the opposing party's nondisclosure, response, or objection was substantially justified. FRCP 37(a)(5)(A)(ii). Refer to the United States District Court for the Southern District of Indiana KeyRules Motion for Discovery Sanctions document for more information.

4. *Stipulations about discovery procedure.* Unless the court orders otherwise, the parties may stipulate that: (1) a deposition may be taken before any person, at any time or place, on any notice, and in the manner specified—in which event it may be used in the same way as any other deposition; and (2) other procedures governing or limiting discovery be modified—but a stipulation extending the time for any form of discovery must have court approval if it would interfere with the time set for completing discovery, for hearing a motion, or for trial. FRCP 29.

5. *Appearances.* Every attorney who represents a party or who files a document on a party's behalf must file an appearance for that party. IN R USDCTSD L.R. 83-7. The filing of a Notice of Appearance shall act to establish the filing attorney as an attorney of record representing a designated party or parties in a particular cause of action. As a result, it is necessary for each attorney to file a separate Notice of Appearance when entering an appearance in a case. A joint appearance on behalf of multiple attorneys may be filed electronically only if it is filed separately for each attorney, using his/her ECF login. IN R USDCTSD ECF Procedures(12). Only those attorneys who have filed an appearance in a pending action are entitled to be served with case documents under FRCP 5(a). IN R USDCTSD L.R. 83-7. For more information, refer to IN R USDCTSD L.R. 83-7 and IN R USDCTSD ECF Procedures(12).

6. *Notice of related action.* A party must file a notice of related action: as soon as it appears that the party's case and another pending case: (1) arise out of the same transaction or occurrence; (2) involve the same property; or (3) involve the validity or infringement or the same patent, trademark, or copyright. IN R USDCTSD L.R. 40-1(d)(2). For more information, refer to IN R USDCTSD L.R. 40-1.

7. *Alternative dispute resolution (ADR)*

    a. *Application.* Unless limited by specific provisions, or unless there are other applicable specific statutory, common law, or constitutional procedures, the Local Alternative Dispute Resolution Rules of the United States District Court for the Southern District of Indiana shall apply in all civil litigation filed in the U.S. District Court for the Southern District of Indiana, except in the following cases and proceedings:

    i.   Applications for writs of habeas corpus under 28 U.S.C.A. § 2254;

    ii.   Forfeiture cases;

    iii.   Non-adversary proceedings in bankruptcy;

    iv.   Social Security administrative review cases; and

    v.   Such other matters as specified by order of the Court; for example, matters involving important public policy issues, constitutional law, or the establishment of new law. IN R USDCTSD A.D.R. Rule 1.2.

  b. *Mediation.* Mediation under this section (IN R USDCTSD A.D.R. Rule 2.1, et seq.) involves the confidential process by which a person acting as a Mediator, selected by the parties or appointed by the Court, assists the litigants in reaching a mutually acceptable agreement. It is an informal and nonadversarial process. The role of the Mediator is to assist in identifying the issues, reducing misunderstandings, clarifying priorities, exploring areas of compromise, and finding points of agreement as well as legitimate points of disagreement. Final decision-making authority rests with the parties, not the Mediator. IN R USDCTSD A.D.R. Rule 2.1. It is anticipated that an agreement may not resolve all of the disputed issues, but the process, nonetheless, can reduce points of contention. Parties and their representatives are required to mediate in good faith, but are not compelled to reach an agreement. IN R USDCTSD A.D.R. Rule 2.1.

    i.   *Case selection.* The Court with the agreement of the parties may refer a civil case for mediation. Unless otherwise ordered or as specifically provided in IN R USDCTSD A.D.R. Rule 2.8, referral to mediation does not abate or suspend the action, and no scheduled dates shall be delayed or deferred, including the date of trial. IN R USDCTSD A.D.R. Rule 2.2.

    ii.   For more information on mediation, refer to IN R USDCTSD A.D.R. Rule 2.1, et seq.

  c. *Other methods of dispute resolution.* The Local Alternative Dispute Resolution Rules of the United States District Court for the Southern District of Indiana shall not preclude the parties from utilizing any other reasonable method or technique of alternative dispute resolution to resolve disputes to which the parties agree. However, any use of arbitration by the parties will be governed by and comply with the requirements of 28 U.S.C.A. § 654 through 28 U.S.C.A. § 657. IN R USDCTSD A.D.R. Rule 1.5.

  d. For more information on alternative dispute resolution (ADR), refer to IN R USDCTSD A.D.R. Rule 1.1, et seq.

8. *Notice of settlement or resolution.* The parties must immediately notify the court if they reasonably anticipate settling their case or resolving a pending motion. IN R USDCTSD L.R. 7-1(h).

9. *Modification or suspension of rules.* The court may, on its own motion or at the request of a party, suspend or modify any rule in a particular case in the interest of justice. IN R USDCTSD L.R. 1-1(c).

D. Documents

1. *Required documents*

  a. *Request for production of documents.* Refer to the General Requirements section of this document for information on the request for production of documents.

2. *Supplemental documents*

  a. *Subpoena.* As provided in FRCP 45, a nonparty may be compelled to produce documents and tangible things or to permit an inspection. FRCP 34(c). If a subpoena to produce or permit is to be served upon a nonparty, a copy of the proposed subpoena must be served on all other parties. IN R USDCTSD L.R. 45-1. For information on the form and contents of the subpoena, refer to FRCP 45.

  b. *Certificate of service.* FRCP 5(d) requires that the person making service under FRCP 5 certify that service has been effected. FRCP 5(Advisory Committee Notes). Having such information on file may be useful for many purposes, including proof of service if an issue arises concerning the effectiveness of the service. FRCP 5(Advisory Committee Notes).

E. Format

1. *Form of documents.* The rules governing captions and other matters of form in pleadings apply to motions and other papers. FRCP 7(b)(2).

    a. *Paper (manual filings only).* Any document that is not filed electronically must: be flat, unfolded, and on good-quality, eight and one-half by eleven (8-1/2 x 11) inch white paper. IN R USDCTSD L.R. 5-1(d)(1). Any document that is not filed electronically must: be single-sided. IN R USDCTSD L.R. 5-1(d)(1).

        i. *Covers or backing.* Any document that is not filed electronically must: not have a cover or a back. IN R USDCTSD L.R. 5-1(d)(1).

        ii. *Fastening.* Any document that is not filed electronically must: be (if consisting of more than one (1) page) fastened by paperclip or binder clip and may not be stapled. IN R USDCTSD L.R. 5-1(d)(1).

            • *Request for nonconforming fastening.* If a document cannot be fastened or bound as required by IN R USDCTSD L.R. 5-1(d), a party may ask the clerk for permission to fasten it in another manner. The party must make such a request before attempting to file the document with nonconforming fastening. IN R USDCTSD L.R. 5-1(d)(2).

        iii. *Hole punching.* Any document that is not filed electronically must: be two-hole punched at the top with the holes two and three-quarter (2-3/4) inches apart and appropriately centered. IN R USDCTSD L.R. 5-1(d)(1).

    b. *Margins.* Any pleading, motion, brief, affidavit, notice, or proposed order filed with the court, whether electronically or with the clerk, must: have at least one (1) inch margins. IN R USDCTSD L.R. 5-1(b).

    c. *Spacing.* Any pleading, motion, brief, affidavit, notice, or proposed order filed with the court, whether electronically or with the clerk, must: be double spaced (except for headings, footnotes, and quoted material). IN R USDCTSD L.R. 5-1(b).

    d. *Text.* Any pleading, motion, brief, affidavit, notice, or proposed order filed with the court, whether electronically or with the clerk, must: be plainly typewritten, printed, or prepared by a clearly legible copying process. IN R USDCTSD L.R. 5-1(b).

    e. *Font size.* Any pleading, motion, brief, affidavit, notice, or proposed order filed with the court, whether electronically or with the clerk, must: use at least 12-point type in the body of the document and at least 10-point type in footnotes. IN R USDCTSD L.R. 5-1(b).

    f. *Page numbering.* Any pleading, motion, brief, affidavit, notice, or proposed order filed with the court, whether electronically or with the clerk, must: have consecutively numbered pages. IN R USDCTSD L.R. 5-1(b).

    g. *Caption; Names of parties.* Every pleading must have a caption with the court's name, a title, a file number, and a FRCP 7(a) designation. The title of the complaint must name all the parties; the title of other pleadings, after naming the first party on each side, may refer generally to other parties. FRCP 10(a). Any pleading, motion, brief, affidavit, notice, or proposed order filed with the court, whether electronically or with the clerk, must: include a title on the first page. IN R USDCTSD L.R. 5-1(b).

    h. *Filer's information.* Any pleading, motion, brief, affidavit, notice, or proposed order filed with the court, whether electronically or with the clerk, must: in the case of pleadings, motions, legal briefs, and notices, include the name, complete address, telephone number, facsimile number (where available), and e-mail address (where available) of the pro se litigant or attorney who files it. IN R USDCTSD L.R. 5-1(b).

    i. *Paragraphs; Separate statements.* A party must state its claims or defenses in numbered paragraphs, each limited as far as practicable to a single set of circumstances. A later pleading may refer by number to a paragraph in an earlier pleading. If doing so would promote clarity, each claim founded on a separate transaction or occurrence—and each defense other than a denial—must be stated in a separate count or defense. FRCP 10(b).

j. *Adoption by reference; Exhibits.* A statement in a pleading may be adopted by reference elsewhere in the same pleading or in any other pleading or motion. A copy of a written instrument that is an exhibit to a pleading is a part of the pleading for all purposes. FRCP 10(c).

k. *Citations*

   i. *Local rules.* The Local Rules of the United States District Court for the Southern District of Indiana may be cited as "S.D. Ind. L.R." IN R USDCTSD L.R. 1-1(a).

   ii. *Local alternative dispute resolution rules.* These Rules shall be known as the Local Alternative Dispute Resolution Rules of the United States District Court for the Southern District of Indiana. They shall be cited as "S.D.Ind. Local A.D.R. Rule _____." IN R USDCTSD A.D.R. Rule 1.1.

l. *Acceptance by the clerk.* The clerk must not refuse to file a paper solely because it is not in the form prescribed by the Federal Rules of Civil Procedure or by a local rule or practice. FRCP 5(d)(4). The clerk will accept a document that violates IN R USDCTSD L.R. 5-1, but the court may exclude the document from the official record. IN R USDCTSD L.R. 5-1(e).

   i. *Sanctions for errors as to form.* The court may strike from the record any document that does not comply with the rules governing the form of documents filed with the court, such as rules that regulate document size or the number of copies to be filed or that require a special designation in the caption. The court may also sanction an attorney or party who files a non-compliant document. IN R USDCTSD L.R. 1-3.

2. *Form of electronic documents.* Any document submitted via the court's electronic case filing (ECF) system must be: otherwise prepared and filed in a manner consistent with the CM/ECF Policies and Procedures Manual (IN R USDCTSD ECF Procedures). IN R USDCTSD L.R. 5-1(c). Electronically filed documents must meet the requirements of FRCP 10 (Form of Pleadings), IN R USDCTSD L.R. 5-1 (Format of Papers Presented for Filing), and FRCP 5.2 (Privacy Protection for Filings Made with the Court), as if they had been submitted on paper. Documents filed electronically are also subject to any page limitations set forth by Court Order, by IN R USDCTSD L.R. 7-1 (Motion Practice), or IN R USDCTSD L.R. 56-1 (Summary Judgment Practice), as applicable. IN R USDCTSD ECF Procedures(13).

a. *PDF format required.* Any document submitted via the court's electronic case filing (ECF) system must be: in .pdf format. IN R USDCTSD L.R. 5-1(c); IN R USDCTSD ECF Procedures(7). Any document submitted via the court's electronic case filing (ECF) system must be: converted to a .pdf file directly from a word processing program, unless it exists only in paper format (in which case it may be scanned to create a .pdf document). IN R USDCTSD L.R. 5-1(c); IN R USDCTSD ECF Procedures(13).

   i. An exhibit may be scanned into PDF format, at a recommended 300 dpi resolution or higher, only if it does not already exist in electronic format. The filing attorney is responsible for reviewing all PDF documents for legibility before submitting them through the Court's Electronic Case Filing system. For technical guidance in creating PDF documents, please contact the Clerk's Office. IN R USDCTSD ECF Procedures(13).

b. *File size limitations.* Any document submitted via the court's electronic case filing (ECF) system must be: submitted as one or more .pdf files that do not exceed ten megabytes (10 MB) each (consistent with the CM/ECF Policies and Procedures Manual (IN R USDCTSD ECF Procedures)). IN R USDCTSD L.R. 5-1(c); IN R USDCTSD ECF Procedures(13).

   i. To electronically file a document or attachment that exceeds ten megabytes (10 MB), the document must first be broken down into two or more smaller files. For example, if Exhibit A is a twelve megabyte (12 MB) PDF file, it should be divided into 2 equal parts prior to electronic filing. Each component part of the exhibit would be filed as an attachment to the main document and described appropriately as "Exhibit A (part 1 of 2)" and "Exhibit A (part 2 of 2)." IN R USDCTSD ECF Procedures(13).

   ii. The supporting items mentioned in IN R USDCTSD ECF Procedures(13) should not be confused with memorandums or briefs in support of motions as outlined in IN R USDCTSD L.R. 7-1 or IN R USDCTSD L.R. 56-1. These memorandums or briefs in support are to be filed as entirely separate documents pursuant to the appropriate rule. Additionally, no motion shall be embodied in the text of a response or reply brief/memorandum unless otherwise ordered by the Court. IN R USDCTSD ECF Procedures(13).

c. *Separate component parts.* A key objective of the electronic filing system is to ensure that as much of the case as possible is managed electronically. To facilitate electronic filing and retrieval, documents to be filed electronically are to be reasonably broken into their separate component parts. By way of example, most filings include a foundation document (e.g., motion) and other supporting items (e.g., exhibits, proposed orders, proposed amended pleadings). The foundation document, as well as the supporting items, are each separate components of the filing; supporting items must be filed as attachments to the foundation document. These exhibits or attachments should include only those excerpts of the referenced documents that are directly germane to the matter under consideration. IN R USDCTSD ECF Procedures(13).

   i. Where an individual component cannot be included in an electronic filing (e.g. the component cannot be converted to electronic format), the filer shall electronically file the prescribed Notice of Manual Filing in place of that component. A model form is provided as Appendix C (IN R USDCTSD ECF Procedures(Appendix C)). IN R USDCTSD ECF Procedures(13).

d. *Exhibits.* Each electronically filed exhibit to a main document must be: (1) created as a separate .pdf file; (2) submitted as an attachment to the main document and given a title which describes its content; and (3) limited to excerpts that are directly germane to the main document's subject matter. IN R USDCTSD L.R. 5-6(a).

   i. When uploading attachments during the electronic filing process, exhibits must be uploaded in a logical sequence and a brief description must be entered for each individual PDF file. The description must include not only the exhibit number or letter, but also a brief description of the document. This information may be entered in CM/ECF using a combination of the Category drop-down menu, the Description text box, or both (see IN R USDCTSD ECF Procedures(13)(Figure 1)). The information that is provided in each box will be combined to create a description of the document as it appears on the case docket (see IN R USDCTSD ECF Procedures(13)(Figure 2)). IN R USDCTSD ECF Procedures(13). For an example, refer to IN R USDCTSD ECF Procedures(13).

e. *Excerpts.* A party filing an exhibit that consists of excerpts from a larger document must clearly and prominently identify the exhibit as containing excerpted material. Either party will have the right to timely file additional excerpts or the complete document to the extent they are or become directly germane to the main document's subject matter. IN R USDCTSD L.R. 5-6(b).

f. For an example illustrating the application of IN R USDCTSD ECF Procedures(13), refer to IN R USDCTSD ECF Procedures(13).

3. *Signing disclosures and discovery requests, responses, and objections.* FRCP 11 does not apply to disclosures and discovery requests, responses, objections, and motions under FRCP 26 through FRCP 37. FRCP 11(d).

a. *Signature required.* Every disclosure under FRCP 26(a)(1) or FRCP 26(a)(3) and every discovery request, response, or objection must be signed by at least one attorney of record in the attorney's own name—or by the party personally, if unrepresented—and must state the signer's address, e-mail address, and telephone number. FRCP 26(g)(1).

   i. *Signatures on manual filings.* Any document that is not filed electronically must: include the original signature of the pro se litigant or attorney who files it. IN R USDCTSD L.R. 5-1(d)(1).

   ii. *Electronic signatures.* Use of the attorney's login and password when filing documents electronically serves in part as the attorney's signature for purposes of FRCP 11, the Local Rules of the United States District Court for the Southern District of Indiana, and any other purpose for which a signature is required in connection with proceedings before the Court. IN R USDCTSD ECF Procedures(14); IN R USDCTSD ECF Procedures(10). A pleading, motion, brief, or notice filed electronically under an attorney's ECF log-in and password must be signed by that attorney. IN R USDCTSD L.R. 5-7(a). A signature on a document other than a document filed as provided under IN R USDCTSD L.R. 5-7(a) must be an original handwritten signature and must be scanned into .pdf format for electronic filing. IN R USDCTSD L.R. 5-7(c); IN R USDCTSD ECF Procedures(14).

- *Form of electronic signature.* If a document is converted directly from a word processing application to .pdf (as opposed to scanning), the name of the Filing User under whose log-in and password the document is submitted must be preceded by a "s/" and typed on the signature line where the Filing User's handwritten signature would otherwise appear. IN R USDCTSD L.R. 5-7(b). All documents filed electronically shall include a signature block and include the filing attorney's typewritten name, address, telephone number, facsimile number and e-mail address. In addition, the name of the filing attorney under whose ECF login the document will be filed should be preceded by a "s/" and typed in the space where the attorney's handwritten signature would otherwise appear. IN R US-DCTSD ECF Procedures(14). For a sample format, refer to IN R USDCTSD ECF Procedures(14).

- *Effect of electronic signature.* Filing an electronically signed document under an attorney's ECF log-in and password constitutes the attorney's signature on the document under the Federal Rules of Civil Procedure, under the Local Rules of the United States District Court for the Southern District of Indiana, and for any other reason a signature is required in connection with the court's activities. IN R USDCTSD L.R. 5-7(d).

- *Documents with multiple attorneys' signatures.* Documents requiring signatures of more than one attorney shall be filed either by: (1) obtaining consent from the other attorney, then typing the "s/ [Name]" signature of the other attorney on the signature line where the other attorney's signature would otherwise appear; (2) identifying in the signature section the name of the other attorney whose signature is required and by the submission of a Notice of Endorsement (see IN R USDCTSD ECF Procedures(Appendix B)) by the other attorney no later than three (3) business days after filing; (3) submitting a scanned document containing all handwritten signatures; or (4) in any other manner approved by the Court. IN R USDCTSD ECF Procedures(14); IN R USDCTSD L.R. 5-7(e).

b. *Effect of signature.* By signing, an attorney or party certifies that to the best of the person's knowledge, information, and belief formed after a reasonable inquiry:

   i. With respect to a disclosure, it is complete and correct as of the time it is made; and

   ii. With respect to a discovery request, response, or objection, it is:

- Consistent with the Federal Rules of Civil Procedure and warranted by existing law or by a nonfrivolous argument for extending, modifying, or reversing existing law, or for establishing new law;

- Not interposed for any improper purpose, such as to harass, cause unnecessary delay, or needlessly increase the cost of litigation; and

- Neither unreasonable nor unduly burdensome or expensive, considering the needs of the case, prior discovery in the case, the amount in controversy, and the importance of the issues at stake in the action. FRCP 26(g)(1).

c. *Failure to sign.* Other parties have no duty to act on an unsigned disclosure, request, response, or objection until it is signed, and the court must strike it unless a signature is promptly supplied after the omission is called to the attorney's or party's attention. FRCP 26(g)(2). The court will strike any document filed directly with the clerk that is not signed by an attorney of record or the pro se litigant filing it, but the court may do so only after giving the attorney or pro se litigant notice of the omission and reasonable time to correct it. Rubber-stamp or facsimile signatures are not original signatures and the court will deem documents containing them to be unsigned for purposes of FRCP 11 and FRCP 26(g) and IN R USDCTSD L.R. 5-10. IN R USDCTSD L.R. 5-10(g).

d. *Sanction for improper certification.* If a certification violates FRCP 26(g) without substantial justification, the court, on motion or on its own, must impose an appropriate sanction on the signer, the party on whose behalf the signer was acting, or both. The sanction may include an order to pay the reasonable expenses, including attorney's fees, caused by the violation. FRCP 26(g)(3). Refer to the United States District Court for the Southern District of Indiana KeyRules Motion for Discovery Sanctions document for more information.

4. *Privacy protection for filings made with the court.* Electronically filed documents must meet the requirements of. . .FRCP 5.2 (Privacy Protection for Filings Made with the Court), as if they had been submitted on paper. IN R USDCTSD ECF Procedures(13).

 a. *Redacted filings.* Unless the court orders otherwise, in an electronic or paper filing with the court that contains an individual's Social Security number, taxpayer-identification number, or birth date, the name of an individual known to be a minor, or a financial-account number, a party or nonparty making the filing may include only:

 i. The last four (4) digits of the Social Security number and taxpayer-identification number;

 ii. The year of the individual's birth;

 iii. The minor's initials; and

 iv. The last four (4) digits of the financial-account number. FRCP 5.2(a).

 b. *Exemptions from the redaction requirement.* The redaction requirement does not apply to the following:

 i. A financial-account number that identifies the property allegedly subject to forfeiture in a forfeiture proceeding;

 ii. The record of an administrative or agency proceeding;

 iii. The official record of a state-court proceeding;

 iv. The record of a court or tribunal, if that record was not subject to the redaction requirement when originally filed;

 v. A filing covered by FRCP 5.2(c) or FRCP 5.2(d); and

 vi. A pro se filing in an action brought under 28 U.S.C.A. § 2241, 28 U.S.C.A. § 2254, or 28 U.S.C.A. § 2255. FRCP 5.2(b).

 c. *Limitations on remote access to electronic files; Social Security appeals and immigration cases.* Unless the court orders otherwise, in an action for benefits under the Social Security Act, and in an action or proceeding relating to an order of removal, to relief from removal, or to immigration benefits or detention, access to an electronic file is authorized as follows:

 i. The parties and their attorneys may have remote electronic access to any part of the case file, including the administrative record;

 ii. Any other person may have electronic access to the full record at the courthouse, but may have remote electronic access only to:

 • The docket maintained by the court; and

 • An opinion, order, judgment, or other disposition of the court, but not any other part of the case file or the administrative record. FRCP 5.2(c).

 d. *Filings made under seal.* The court may order that a filing be made under seal without redaction. The court may later unseal the filing or order the person who made the filing to file a redacted version for the public record. FRCP 5.2(d). For more information on filing under seal, refer to IN R USDCTSD L.R. 5-11 and IN R USDCTSD ECF Procedures(18).

 e. *Protective orders.* For good cause, the court may by order in a case:

 i. Require redaction of additional information; or

 ii. Limit or prohibit a nonparty's remote electronic access to a document filed with the court. FRCP 5.2(e).

 f. *Option for additional unredacted filing under seal.* A person making a redacted filing may also file an unredacted copy under seal. The court must retain the unredacted copy as part of the record. FRCP 5.2(f).

g. *Option for filing a reference list.* A filing that contains redacted information may be filed together with a reference list that identifies each item of redacted information and specifies an appropriate identifier that uniquely corresponds to each item listed. The list must be filed under seal and may be amended as of right. Any reference in the case to a listed identifier will be construed to refer to the corresponding item of information. FRCP 5.2(g).

h. *Waiver of protection of identifiers.* A person waives the protection of FRCP 5.2(a) as to the person's own information by filing it without redaction and not under seal. FRCP 5.2(h).

F. Filing and Service Requirements

1. *Filing requirements.* Any paper after the complaint that is required to be served—together with a certificate of service—must be filed within a reasonable time after service. But disclosures under FRCP 26(a)(1) or FRCP 26(a)(2) and the following discovery requests and responses must not be filed until they are used in the proceeding or the court orders filing: depositions, interrogatories, requests for documents or tangible things or to permit entry onto land, and requests for admission. FRCP 5(d)(1). Refer to the United States District Court for the Southern District of Indiana KeyRules pleading and motion documents for information on filing with the court.

   a. *When discovery may be filed.* Discovery materials (whether discovery requests, responses, or deposition transcripts) may not be filed with the court except in the following circumstances:

      i. *Relevant to certain motions.* A party seeking relief under FRCP 26(c) or FRCP 37, or by way of a pretrial motion that could result in a final order on an issue, must file with the motion those parts of the discovery materials relevant to the motion. IN R USDCTSD L.R. 26-2(a).

      ii. *For anticipated use at trial.* When a party can reasonably anticipate using discovery materials at trial, the party must file the relevant portions at the start of the trial. IN R USDCTSD L.R. 26-2(b).

      iii. *Materials necessary for appeal.* A party seeking for purposes of appeal to supplement the record with discovery materials not previously filed may do so by stipulation of the parties or by court order approving the filing. IN R USDCTSD L.R. 26-2(c).

2. *Service requirements*

   a. *Service; When required*

      i. *In general.* Unless the Federal Rules of Civil Procedure provide otherwise, each of the following papers must be served on every party:

         • An order stating that service is required;

         • A pleading filed after the original complaint, unless the court orders otherwise under FRCP 5(c) because there are numerous defendants;

         • A discovery paper required to be served on a party, unless the court orders otherwise;

         • A written motion, except one that may be heard ex parte; and

         • A written notice, appearance, demand, or offer of judgment, or any similar paper. FRCP 5(a)(1).

      ii. *If a party fails to appear.* No service is required on a party who is in default for failing to appear. But a pleading that asserts a new claim for relief against such a party must be served on that party under FRCP 4. FRCP 5(a)(2).

      iii. *Seizing property.* If an action is begun by seizing property and no person is or need be named as a defendant, any service required before the filing of an appearance, answer, or claim must be made on the person who had custody or possession of the property when it was seized. FRCP 5(a)(3).

   b. *Service; How made*

      i. *Serving an attorney.* If a party is represented by an attorney, service under FRCP 5 must be made on the attorney unless the court orders service on the party. FRCP 5(b)(1).

      ii. *Service in general.* A paper is served under FRCP 5 by:

         • Handing it to the person;

- Leaving it: (1) at the person's office with a clerk or other person in charge or, if no one is in charge, in a conspicuous place in the office; or (2) if the person has no office or the office is closed, at the person's dwelling or usual place of abode with someone of suitable age and discretion who resides there;

- Mailing it to the person's last known address—in which event service is complete upon mailing;

- Leaving it with the court clerk if the person has no known address;

- Sending it by electronic means if the person consented in writing—in which event service is complete upon transmission, but is not effective if the serving party learns that it did not reach the person to be served; or

- Delivering it by any other means that the person consented to in writing—in which event service is complete when the person making service delivers it to the agency designated to make delivery. FRCP 5(b)(2).

iii. *Electronic service*

- *Consent.* By registering to use the ECF system, attorneys consent to electronic service of documents filed in cases maintained on the ECF system. IN R USDCTSD L.R. 5-3(d). By participating in the Electronic Case Filing Program, attorneys consent to the electronic service of documents, and shall make available electronic mail addresses for service. IN R USDCTSD ECF Procedures(11).

- *Service on registered parties.* Upon the filing of a document by a party, an e-mail message will be automatically generated by the electronic filing system and sent via electronic mail to the e-mail addresses of all registered attorneys who have appeared in the case. The Notice of Electronic Filing will contain a document hyperlink which will provide recipients with one "free look" at the electronically filed document. Recipients are encouraged to print and/or save a copy of the document during the "free look" to avoid incurring PACER charges for future viewings of the document. IN R USDCTSD ECF Procedures(11). When a document has been filed electronically: transmission of the notice of electronic filing generated by the ECF system to an attorney's e-mail address constitutes service of the document on that attorney. IN R USDCTSD L.R. 5-4(c)(5). The party effectuates service on all registered attorneys by filing electronically. IN R USDCTSD ECF Procedures(11). When a document has been filed electronically: no other attempted service will constitute electronic service of the document. IN R USDCTSD L.R. 5-4(c)(6).

- *Service on exempt parties.* A filer must serve a copy of the document consistent with FRCP 5 on any party or attorney who is exempt from participating in electronic filing. IN R USDCTSD L.R. 5-4(d). It is the responsibility of the filing attorney to conventionally serve all parties who do not receive electronic service (the identity of these parties will be indicated on the filing receipt generated by the ECF system). IN R USDCTSD ECF Procedures(11).

- *Service on parties excused from electronic filing.* Parties otherwise participating in the electronic filing system may be excused from filing a particular component electronically under certain limited circumstances, such as when the component cannot be reduced to an electronic format. Such components shall not be filed electronically, but instead shall be manually filed with the Clerk of Court and served upon the parties in accordance with the applicable Federal Rules of Civil Procedure and the Local Rules of the United States District Court for the Southern District of Indiana for filing and service of non-electronic documents. IN R USDCTSD ECF Procedures(15).

- *Service of exempt documents.* Any document that is exempt from electronic filing must be filed directly with the clerk and served on other parties in the case as required by those Federal Rules of Civil Procedure and Local Rules of the United States District Court for the Southern District of Indiana that apply to the service of non-electronic documents. IN R USDCTSD L.R. 5-2(c).

iv. *Using court facilities.* If a local rule so authorizes, a party may use the court's transmission facilities to make service under FRCP 5(b)(2)(E). FRCP 5(b)(3).

c. *Serving numerous defendants*

i. *In general.* If an action involves an unusually large number of defendants, the court may, on motion or on its own, order that:

- Defendants' pleadings and replies to them need not be served on other defendants;

- Any crossclaim, counterclaim, avoidance, or affirmative defense in those pleadings and replies to them will be treated as denied or avoided by all other parties; and

- Filing any such pleading and serving it on the plaintiff constitutes notice of the pleading to all parties. FRCP 5(c)(1).

ii. *Notifying parties.* A copy of every such order must be served on the parties as the court directs. FRCP 5(c)(2).

G. Hearings

1. There is no hearing contemplated in the federal statutes or rules for requests for production of documents.

H. Forms

1. Federal Request for Production of Documents Forms

a. Request; Production of documents for inspection and copying. AMJUR PP DEPOSITION § 498.

b. Request for production, inspection and copying of documents, and inspection and photographing of things and real property. 3A FEDFORMS § 3556.

c. Request for production of documents; Business records. 3A FEDFORMS § 3557.

d. Request for production of documents; Patent case. 3A FEDFORMS § 3558.

e. Request for production of documents; Government records and regulations. 3A FEDFORMS § 3559.

f. Request for production of documents; Government personnel files, memoranda, minutes of meetings, and statistics. 3A FEDFORMS § 3560.

g. Request for production of documents; Documents to be identified in physically separate but accompanying interrogatories under FRCP 33. 3A FEDFORMS § 3561.

h. Request for production of documents; Employment discrimination. 3A FEDFORMS § 3562.

i. Letter requesting production of files. 3A FEDFORMS § 3563.

j. Request; Production of documents, records, and objects, under FRCP 34. FEDPROF § 23:394.

k. Request; Production of documents for inspection and copying. FEDPROF § 23:395.

l. Request; Production of documents for inspection and copying; Business records. FEDPROF § 23:396.

m. Request; Production of objects for inspection and sampling. FEDPROF § 23:397.

n. Request; Production of documents for inspection and copying; Government records and files. FEDPROF § 23:398.

o. Request; Production of documents and things; Patent proceeding. FEDPROF § 23:399.

p. Request; Production of documents and things; Trademark action. FEDPROF § 23:400.

q. Request; Production of documents; Trademark action; Likelihood of confusion. FEDPROF § 23:401.

r. Request; Production of documents; Automobile negligence. FEDPROF § 23:402.

s. Request; Production of documents; Premises liability. FEDPROF § 23:403.

t. Request; Production of documents for inspection and copying; Wrongful death due to forklift accident. FEDPROF § 23:404.

u. Request; Production of documents; Products liability. FEDPROF § 23:405.

v. Request; Production of documents; Collection of tariff. FEDPROF § 23:406.

w. Request; Production of medical records. FEDPROF § 23:407.

x. Request; Production of employment records. FEDPROF § 23:408.

y. Request; Production of education records. FEDPROF § 23:409.

z. Request; Production of decedent's records. FEDPROF § 23:410.

I. Applicable Rules

1. *Federal rules*

   a. Serving and filing pleadings and other papers. FRCP 5.

   b. Privacy protection for filings made with the court. FRCP 5.2.

   c. Computing and extending time; Time for motion papers. FRCP 6.

   d. Pleadings allowed; Form of motions and other papers. FRCP 7.

   e. Form of pleadings. FRCP 10.

   f. Signing pleadings, motions, and other papers; Representations to the court; Sanctions. FRCP 11.

   g. Duty to disclose; General provisions governing discovery. FRCP 26.

   h. Stipulations about discovery procedure. FRCP 29.

   i. Producing documents, electronically stored information, and tangible things, or entering onto land, for inspection and other purposes. FRCP 34.

   j. Failure to make disclosures or to cooperate in discovery; Sanctions. FRCP 37.

2. *Local rules*

   a. Scope of the rules. IN R USDCTSD L.R. 1-1.

   b. Sanctions for errors as to form. IN R USDCTSD L.R. 1-3.

   c. Format of documents presented for filing. IN R USDCTSD L.R. 5-1.

   d. Filing of documents electronically required. IN R USDCTSD L.R. 5-2.

   e. Eligibility, registration, passwords for electronic filing; Exemption from electronic filing. IN R USDCTSD L.R. 5-3.

   f. Timing and consequences of electronic filing. IN R USDCTSD L.R. 5-4.

   g. Attachments and exhibits in cases filed electronically. IN R USDCTSD L.R. 5-6.

   h. Signatures in cases filed electronically. IN R USDCTSD L.R. 5-7.

   i. Non-electronic filings. IN R USDCTSD L.R. 5-10.

   j. Motion practice. [IN R USDCTSD L.R. 7-1, as amended by IN ORDER 16-2319, effective December 1, 2016].

   k. Form of certain discovery requests. IN R USDCTSD L.R. 26-1.

   l. Filing of discovery materials. IN R USDCTSD L.R. 26-2.

   m. Assignment of cases. IN R USDCTSD L.R. 40-1.

   n. Service of subpoena on non-parties; Notice requirement. IN R USDCTSD L.R. 45-1.

   o. Alternative dispute resolution. IN R USDCTSD A.D.R. Rule 1.1; IN R USDCTSD A.D.R. Rule 1.2; IN R USDCTSD A.D.R. Rule 1.5; IN R USDCTSD A.D.R. Rule 2.1; IN R USDCTSD A.D.R. Rule 2.2.

   p. Electronic case filing policies and procedures manual. IN R USDCTSD ECF Procedures.

Requests, Notices and Applications
Response to Request for Production of Documents

Document Last Updated December 2016

A. Checklist

(I) ❑ Matters to be considered by requesting party

    (a) ❑ Required documents

        (1) ❑ Request for production of documents

    (b) ❑ Supplemental documents

        (1) ❑ Subpoena

        (2) ❑ Certificate of service

    (c) ❑ Timing

        (1) ❑ More than twenty-one (21) days after the summons and complaint are served on a party, a request under FRCP 34 may be delivered: (1) to that party by any other party, and (2) by that party to any plaintiff or to any other party that has been served

        (2) ❑ A party may not seek discovery from any source before the parties have conferred as required by FRCP 26(f), except in a proceeding exempted from initial disclosure under FRCP 26(a)(1)(B), or when authorized by the Federal Rules of Civil Procedure, by stipulation, or by court order

        (3) ❑ If a subpoena to produce or permit is to be served upon a nonparty, a copy of the proposed subpoena must be served on all other parties at least seven (7) days prior to service of the subpoena on the nonparty, unless the parties agree to a different time frame or the case management plan provides otherwise; provided, however, that if such subpoena relates to a matter set for hearing within such seven (7) day period or arises out of a bona fide emergency, such subpoena may be served upon a nonparty one (1) day after a notice and copy of the subpoena is served on each party

(II) ❑ Matters to be considered by responding party

    (a) ❑ Required documents

        (1) ❑ Response to request for production of documents

    (b) ❑ Supplemental documents

        (1) ❑ Certificate of service

    (c) ❑ Timing

        (1) ❑ The party to whom the request is directed must respond in writing within thirty (30) days after being served or—if the request was delivered under FRCP 26(d)(2)—within thirty (30) days after the parties' first FRCP 26(f) conference

B. Timing

1. *Response to request for production of documents.* The party to whom the request is directed must respond in writing within thirty (30) days after being served or—if the request was delivered under FRCP 26(d)(2)—within thirty (30) days after the parties' first FRCP 26(f) conference. A shorter or longer time may be stipulated to under FRCP 29 or be ordered by the court. FRCP 34(b)(2)(A).

2. *Automatic initial extension.* The deadline for filing a response to a pleading or to any written request for discovery or admissions will automatically be extended upon filing a notice of the extension with the court that states: (1) the deadline has not been previously extended; (2) the extension is for twenty-eight (28) or fewer days; (3) the extension does not interfere with the Case Management Plan, scheduled hearings, or other case deadlines; (4) the original deadline and extended deadline; (5) that all opposing counsel the filing attorney could reach agreed to the extension; or that the filing attorney could not reach any opposing

counsel, and providing the dates, times and manner of all attempts to reach opposing counsel. IN R USDCTSD L.R. 6-1(b).

    a.   *Pro se parties.* The automatic initial extension does not apply to pro se parties. IN R USDCTSD L.R. 6-1(c).

3. *Computation of time*

    a.   *Computing time.* FRCP 6 applies in computing any time period specified in the Federal Rules of Civil Procedure, in any local rule or court order, or in any statute that does not specify a method of computing time. FRCP 6(a).

        i.   *Period stated in days or a longer unit.* When the period is stated in days or a longer unit of time:

- Exclude the day of the event that triggers the period;
- Count every day, including intermediate Saturdays, Sundays, and legal holidays; and
- Include the last day of the period, but if the last day is a Saturday, Sunday, or legal holiday, the period continues to run until the end of the next day that is not a Saturday, Sunday, or legal holiday. FRCP 6(a)(1).

        ii.   *Period stated in hours.* When the period is stated in hours:

- Begin counting immediately on the occurrence of the event that triggers the period;
- Count every hour, including hours during intermediate Saturdays, Sundays, and legal holidays; and
- If the period would end on a Saturday, Sunday, or legal holiday, the period continues to run until the same time on the next day that is not a Saturday, Sunday, or legal holiday. FRCP 6(a)(2).

        iii.   *Inaccessibility of the clerk's office.* Unless the court orders otherwise, if the clerk's office is inaccessible:

- On the last day for filing under FRCP 6(a)(1), then the time for filing is extended to the first accessible day that is not a Saturday, Sunday, or legal holiday; or
- During the last hour for filing under FRCP 6(a)(2), then the time for filing is extended to the same time on the first accessible day that is not a Saturday, Sunday, or legal holiday. FRCP 6(a)(3).

        iv.   *"Last day" defined.* Unless a different time is set by a statute, local rule, or court order, the last day ends:

- For electronic filing, at midnight in the court's time zone; and
- For filing by other means, when the clerk's office is scheduled to close. FRCP 6(a)(4).

        v.   *"Next day" defined.* The "next day" is determined by continuing to count forward when the period is measured after an event and backward when measured before an event. FRCP 6(a)(5).

        vi.   *"Legal holiday" defined.* "Legal holiday" means:

- The day set aside by statute for observing New Year's Day, Martin Luther King Jr.'s Birthday, Washington's Birthday, Memorial Day, Independence Day, Labor Day, Columbus Day, Veterans' Day, Thanksgiving Day, or Christmas Day;
- Any day declared a holiday by the President or Congress; and
- For periods that are measured after an event, any other day declared a holiday by the state where the district court is located. FRCP 6(a)(6).

    b.   *Computation of electronic filing deadlines.* Filing documents electronically does not alter filing deadlines. IN R USDCTSD ECF Procedures(7). A document due on a particular day must be filed before midnight local time of the division where the case is pending. IN R USDCTSD L.R. 5-4(a). All electronic transmissions of documents must be completed (i.e. received completely by the Clerk's Office) prior to midnight of the local time of the division in which the case is pending in order to be considered timely filed that day (NOTE: time will be noted in Eastern Time on the Court's docket. If you have filed a document prior to midnight local time of the division in which the case is pending and the document is due that date, but the electronic receipt and docket reflect the following calendar day, please contact the Court). IN R USDCTSD ECF Procedures(7). Although attorneys may file documents electronically twenty-four (24) hours a day, seven (7) days a week, attorneys are encouraged to file all documents during the normal working hours of the Clerk's Office (Monday through Friday, 8:30 a.m. to 4:30 p.m.) when technical support is available. IN R USDCTSD ECF Procedures(7); IN R USDCTSD ECF Procedures(9).

    i. *Technical difficulties.* Parties are encouraged to file documents electronically during normal business hours, in case a problem is encountered. In the event a technical failure occurs and a document cannot be filed electronically despite the best efforts of the filing party, the party should print (if possible) a copy of the error message received. In addition, as soon as practically possible, the party should file a "Declaration that Party was Unable to File in a Timely Manner Due to Technical Difficulties." A model form is provided as Appendix D (IN R USDCTSD ECF Procedures(Appendix D)). IN R USDCTSD ECF Procedures(16).

- If a party is unable to file electronically and, as a result, may miss a filing deadline, the party must contact the Clerk's Office at the number listed in IN R USDCTSD ECF Procedures(15) to inform the court's staff of the difficulty. If a party misses a filing deadline due to an inability to file electronically, the party may submit the untimely filed document, accompanied by a declaration stating the reason(s) for missing the deadline. Unless the Court orders otherwise, the document and declaration must be filed no later than 12:00 noon of the first day on which the Court is open for business following the original filing deadline. IN R USDCTSD ECF Procedures(16).

  c. *Extending time*

    i. *In general.* When an act may or must be done within a specified time, the court may, for good cause, extend the time:

- With or without motion or notice if the court acts, or if a request is made, before the original time or its extension expires; or

- On motion made after the time has expired if the party failed to act because of excusable neglect. FRCP 6(b)(1).

    ii. *Exceptions.* A court must not extend the time to act under FRCP 50(b), FRCP 50(d), FRCP 52(b), FRCP 59(b), FRCP 59(d), FRCP 59(e), and FRCP 60(b). FRCP 6(b)(2).

    iii. Refer to the United States District Court for the Southern District of Indiana KeyRules Motion for Continuance/Extension of Time document for more information on extending time.

  d. *Additional time after certain kinds of service.* When a party may or must act within a specified time after being served and service is made under FRCP 5(b)(2)(C) (mail), FRCP 5(b)(2)(D) (leaving with the clerk), or FRCP 5(b)(2)(F) (other means consented to), three (3) days are added after the period would otherwise expire under FRCP 6(a). FRCP 6(d). Service by electronic mail shall constitute service pursuant to FRCP 5(b)(2)(E) and shall entitle the party being served to the additional three (3) days provided by FRCP 6(d). IN R USDCTSD ECF Procedures(11).

C. General Requirements

1. *General provisions governing discovery*

  a. *Discovery scope and limits*

    i. *Scope in general.* Unless otherwise limited by court order, the scope of discovery is as follows: Parties may obtain discovery regarding any nonprivileged matter that is relevant to any party's claim or defense and proportional to the needs of the case, considering the importance of the issues at stake in the action, the amount in controversy, the parties' relative access to relevant information, the parties' resources, the importance of the discovery in resolving the issues, and whether the burden or expense of the proposed discovery outweighs its likely benefit. Information within this scope of discovery need not be admissible in evidence to be discoverable. FRCP 26(b)(1).

ii. *Limitations on frequency and extent*

- *When permitted.* By order, the court may alter the limits in the Federal Rules of Civil Procedure on the number of depositions and interrogatories or on the length of depositions under FRCP 30. By order or local rule, the court may also limit the number of requests under FRCP 36. FRCP 26(b)(2)(A).

- *Specific limitations on electronically stored information.* A party need not provide discovery of electronically stored information from sources that the party identifies as not reasonably accessible because of undue burden or cost. On motion to compel discovery or for a protective order, the party from whom discovery is sought must show that the information is not reasonably accessible because of undue burden or cost. If that showing is made, the court may nonetheless order discovery from such sources if the requesting party shows good cause, considering the limitations of FRCP 26(b)(2)(C). The court may specify conditions for the discovery. FRCP 26(b)(2)(B).

- *When required.* On motion or on its own, the court must limit the frequency or extent of discovery otherwise allowed by the Federal Rules of Civil Procedure or by local rule if it determines that: (1) the discovery sought is unreasonably cumulative or duplicative, or can be obtained from some other source that is more convenient, less burdensome, or less expensive; (2) the party seeking discovery has had ample opportunity to obtain the information by discovery in the action; or (3) the proposed discovery is outside the scope permitted by FRCP 26(b)(1). FRCP 26(b)(2)(C).

iii. *Trial preparation; Materials*

- *Documents and tangible things.* Ordinarily, a party may not discover documents and tangible things that are prepared in anticipation of litigation or for trial by or for another party or its representative (including the other party's attorney, consultant, surety, indemnitor, insurer, or agent). But, subject to FRCP 26(b)(4), those materials may be discovered if: (1) they are otherwise discoverable under FRCP 26(b)(1); and (2) the party shows that it has substantial need for the materials to prepare its case and cannot, without undue hardship, obtain their substantial equivalent by other means. FRCP 26(b)(3)(A).

- *Protection against disclosure.* If the court orders discovery of those materials, it must protect against disclosure of the mental impressions, conclusions, opinions, or legal theories of a party's attorney or other representative concerning the litigation. FRCP 26(b)(3)(B).

- *Previous statement.* Any party or other person may, on request and without the required showing, obtain the person's own previous statement about the action or its subject matter. If the request is refused, the person may move for a court order, and FRCP 37(a)(5) applies to the award of expenses. A previous statement is either: (1) a written statement that the person has signed or otherwise adopted or approved; or (2) a contemporaneous stenographic, mechanical, electrical, or other recording—or a transcription of it—that recites substantially verbatim the person's oral statement. FRCP 26(b)(3)(C).

iv. *Trial preparation; Experts*

- *Deposition of an expert who may testify.* A party may depose any person who has been identified as an expert whose opinions may be presented at trial. If FRCP 26(a)(2)(B) requires a report from the expert, the deposition may be conducted only after the report is provided. FRCP 26(b)(4)(A).

- *Trial-preparation protection for draft reports or disclosures.* FRCP 26(b)(3)(A) and FRCP 26(b)(3)(B) protect drafts of any report or disclosure required under FRCP 26(a)(2), regardless of the form in which the draft is recorded. FRCP 26(b)(4)(B).

- *Trial-preparation protection for communications between a party's attorney and expert witnesses.* FRCP 26(b)(3)(A) and FRCP 26(b)(3)(B) protect communications between the party's attorney and any witness required to provide a report under FRCP 26(a)(2)(B), regardless of the form of the communications, except to the extent that the communica-

1053

tions: (1) relate to compensation for the expert's study or testimony; (2) identify facts or data that the party's attorney provided and that the expert considered in forming the opinions to be expressed; or (3) identify assumptions that the party's attorney provided and that the expert relied on in forming the opinions to be expressed. FRCP 26(b)(4)(C).

- *Expert employed only for trial preparation.* Ordinarily, a party may not, by interrogatories or deposition, discover facts known or opinions held by an expert who has been retained or specially employed by another party in anticipation of litigation or to prepare for trial and who is not expected to be called as a witness at trial. But a party may do so only: (1) as provided in FRCP 35(b); or (2) on showing exceptional circumstances under which it is impracticable for the party to obtain facts or opinions on the same subject by other means. FRCP 26(b)(4)(D).

- *Payment.* Unless manifest injustice would result, the court must require that the party seeking discovery: (1) pay the expert a reasonable fee for time spent in responding to discovery under FRCP 26(b)(4)(A) or FRCP 26(b)(4)(D); and (2) for discovery under FRCP 26(b)(4)(D), also pay the other party a fair portion of the fees and expenses it reasonably incurred in obtaining the expert's facts and opinions. FRCP 26(b)(4)(E).

v. *Claiming privilege or protecting trial-preparation materials*

- *Information withheld.* When a party withholds information otherwise discoverable by claiming that the information is privileged or subject to protection as trial-preparation material, the party must: (1) expressly make the claim; and (2) describe the nature of the documents, communications, or tangible things not produced or disclosed—and do so in a manner that, without revealing information itself privileged or protected, will enable other parties to assess the claim. FRCP 26(b)(5)(A).

- *Information produced.* If information produced in discovery is subject to a claim of privilege or of protection as trial-preparation material, the party making the claim may notify any party that received the information of the claim and the basis for it. After being notified, a party must promptly return, sequester, or destroy the specified information and any copies it has; must not use or disclose the information until the claim is resolved; must take reasonable steps to retrieve the information if the party disclosed it before being notified; and may promptly present the information to the court under seal for a determination of the claim. The producing party must preserve the information until the claim is resolved. FRCP 26(b)(5)(B).

b. *Protective orders.* A party or any person from whom discovery is sought may move for a protective order in the court where the action is pending—or as an alternative on matters relating to a deposition, in the court for the district where the deposition will be taken. FRCP 26(c)(1). Refer to the United States District Court for the Southern District of Indiana KeyRules Motion for Protective Order document for more information.

c. *Sequence of discovery.* Unless the parties stipulate or the court orders otherwise for the parties' and witnesses' convenience and in the interests of justice: (1) methods of discovery may be used in any sequence; and (2) discovery by one party does not require any other party to delay its discovery. FRCP 26(d)(3).

2. *Response to request for production of documents*

a. *Form.* A party responding (by answer or objection) to written discovery must fully quote each interrogatory or request immediately before each response and number each response to correspond with the interrogatory or request. IN R USDCTSD L.R. 26-1(b).

b. *Responding to each item.* For each item or category, the response must either state that inspection and related activities will be permitted as requested or state with specificity the grounds for objecting to the request, including the reasons. The responding party may state that it will produce copies of documents or of electronically stored information instead of permitting inspection. The production must then be completed no later than the time for inspection specified in the request or another reasonable time specified in the response. FRCP 34(b)(2)(B).

c. *Objections.* A party may waive its objections to a request for production by failing to object in a timely and effective manner. FEDPROC § 26:645.

 i. An objection must state whether any responsive materials are being withheld on the basis of that objection. An objection to part of a request must specify the part and permit inspection of the rest. FRCP 34(b)(2)(C).

 ii. A response which raises no objection, but simply indicates that the information requested is "unknown" and that the records sought are "not maintained," is evasive and insufficient. FEDPROC § 26:648.

d. *Responding to a request for production of electronically stored information.* The response may state an objection to a requested form for producing electronically stored information. If the responding party objects to a requested form—or if no form was specified in the request—the party must state the form or forms it intends to use. FRCP 34(b)(2)(D).

e. *Producing the documents or electronically stored information.* Unless otherwise stipulated or ordered by the court, these procedures apply to producing documents or electronically stored information:

 i. A party must produce documents as they are kept in the usual course of business or must organize and label them to correspond to the categories in the request;

 ii. If a request does not specify a form for producing electronically stored information, a party must produce it in a form or forms in which it is ordinarily maintained or in a reasonably usable form or forms; and

 iii. A party need not produce the same electronically stored information in more than one form. FRCP 34(b)(2)(E).

f. *Documents and things in possession, custody, or control.* FRCP 34 provides. . .that discovery may be had of documents and things that are in the "possession, custody, or control" of a party. FPP § 2210. The concept of "control" is very important in applying FRCP 34, but the application of this concept is often highly fact-specific. Inspection can be had if the party to whom the request is made has the legal right to obtain the document, even though in fact it has no copy. FPP § 2210.

 i. A party may be required to produce documents and things that it possesses even though they belong to a third person who is not a party to the action. FPP § 2210; Societe Internationale Pour Participations Industrielles Et Commerciales, S. A. v. Rogers, 357 U.S. 197, 78 S.Ct. 1087, 2 L.Ed.2d 1255 (1958). And if a party has possession, custody, or control, it must produce documents and things even though the documents and things are themselves beyond the jurisdiction of the court. FPP § 2210.

 ii. If a document or thing does not exist, it cannot be in the possession, custody, or control of a party and therefore cannot be produced for inspection. FEDPROC § 26:623.

 iii. Finally, lack of control may be considered an objection to the discovery request and, like any such objection, it may be waived. FPP § 2210.

g. *Documents made available to all parties.* Documents made available to one party to a suit must be made available to all parties. FEDPROC § 26:637.

h. *Attorney's duty to insure compliance.* An attorney representing a party in connection with a request for the production and inspection of documents pursuant to FRCP 34 has an obligation to verify that his or her client has produced the documents requested, and a further obligation to insure that records are kept indicating which documents have been produced. Failure to comply with these duties has been characterized as careless and inexcusable and has resulted in the imposition of sanctions. FEDPROC § 26:639.

3. *Supplementing disclosures and responses.* A party who has made a disclosure under FRCP 26(a)—or who has responded to an interrogatory, request for production, or request for admission—must supplement or correct its disclosure or response: (1) in a timely manner if the party learns that in some material respect the disclosure or response is incomplete or incorrect, and if the additional or corrective information has not otherwise been made known to the other parties during the discovery process or in writing; or (2) as ordered by the court. FRCP 26(e)(1).

4. *Sanctions for failure to cooperate in discovery.* The court where the action is pending may, on motion, order sanctions if a party, after being properly served with interrogatories under FRCP 33 or a request for inspection under FRCP 34, fails to serve its answers, objections, or written response. FRCP 37(d)(1)(A)(ii). If a motion to compel is granted, the court must, after giving an opportunity to be heard, require the party or deponent whose conduct necessitated the motion, the party or attorney advising that conduct, or both to pay the movant's reasonable expenses incurred in making the motion, including attorney's fees. But the court must not order this payment if the opposing party's nondisclosure, response, or objection was substantially justified. FRCP 37(a)(5)(A)(ii). Refer to the United States District Court for the Southern District of Indiana KeyRules Motion for Discovery Sanctions document for more information.

5. *Stipulations about discovery procedure.* Unless the court orders otherwise, the parties may stipulate that: (1) a deposition may be taken before any person, at any time or place, on any notice, and in the manner specified—in which event it may be used in the same way as any other deposition; and (2) other procedures governing or limiting discovery be modified—but a stipulation extending the time for any form of discovery must have court approval if it would interfere with the time set for completing discovery, for hearing a motion, or for trial. FRCP 29.

6. *Appearances.* Every attorney who represents a party or who files a document on a party's behalf must file an appearance for that party. IN R USDCTSD L.R. 83-7. The filing of a Notice of Appearance shall act to establish the filing attorney as an attorney of record representing a designated party or parties in a particular cause of action. As a result, it is necessary for each attorney to file a separate Notice of Appearance when entering an appearance in a case. A joint appearance on behalf of multiple attorneys may be filed electronically only if it is filed separately for each attorney, using his/her ECF login. IN R USDCTSD ECF Procedures(12). Only those attorneys who have filed an appearance in a pending action are entitled to be served with case documents under FRCP 5(a). IN R USDCTSD L.R. 83-7. For more information, refer to IN R USDCTSD L.R. 83-7 and IN R USDCTSD ECF Procedures(12).

7. *Notice of related action.* A party must file a notice of related action: as soon as it appears that the party's case and another pending case: (1) arise out of the same transaction or occurrence; (2) involve the same property; or (3) involve the validity or infringement or the same patent, trademark, or copyright. IN R USDCTSD L.R. 40-1(d)(2). For more information, refer to IN R USDCTSD L.R. 40-1.

8. *Alternative dispute resolution (ADR)*

   a. *Application.* Unless limited by specific provisions, or unless there are other applicable specific statutory, common law, or constitutional procedures, the Local Alternative Dispute Resolution Rules of the United States District Court for the Southern District of Indiana shall apply in all civil litigation filed in the U.S. District Court for the Southern District of Indiana, except in the following cases and proceedings:

      i. Applications for writs of habeas corpus under 28 U.S.C.A. § 2254;

      ii. Forfeiture cases;

      iii. Non-adversary proceedings in bankruptcy;

      iv. Social Security administrative review cases; and

      v. Such other matters as specified by order of the Court; for example, matters involving important public policy issues, constitutional law, or the establishment of new law. IN R USDCTSD A.D.R. Rule 1.2.

   b. *Mediation.* Mediation under this section (IN R USDCTSD A.D.R. Rule 2.1, et seq.) involves the confidential process by which a person acting as a Mediator, selected by the parties or appointed by the Court, assists the litigants in reaching a mutually acceptable agreement. It is an informal and nonadversarial process. The role of the Mediator is to assist in identifying the issues, reducing misunderstandings, clarifying priorities, exploring areas of compromise, and finding points of agreement as well as legitimate points of disagreement. Final decision-making authority rests with the parties, not the Mediator. IN R USDCTSD A.D.R. Rule 2.1. It is anticipated that an agreement may not resolve all of the disputed issues, but the process, nonetheless, can reduce points of contention. Parties and their representatives are required to mediate in good faith, but are not compelled to reach an agreement. IN R USDCTSD A.D.R. Rule 2.1.

    i. *Case selection.* The Court with the agreement of the parties may refer a civil case for mediation. Unless otherwise ordered or as specifically provided in IN R USDCTSD A.D.R. Rule 2.8, referral to mediation does not abate or suspend the action, and no scheduled dates shall be delayed or deferred, including the date of trial. IN R USDCTSD A.D.R. Rule 2.2.

    ii. For more information on mediation, refer to IN R USDCTSD A.D.R. Rule 2.1, et seq.

  c. *Other methods of dispute resolution.* The Local Alternative Dispute Resolution Rules of the United States District Court for the Southern District of Indiana shall not preclude the parties from utilizing any other reasonable method or technique of alternative dispute resolution to resolve disputes to which the parties agree. However, any use of arbitration by the parties will be governed by and comply with the requirements of 28 U.S.C.A. § 654 through 28 U.S.C.A. § 657. IN R USDCTSD A.D.R. Rule 1.5.

  d. For more information on alternative dispute resolution (ADR), refer to IN R USDCTSD A.D.R. Rule 1.1, et seq.

9. *Notice of settlement or resolution.* The parties must immediately notify the court if they reasonably anticipate settling their case or resolving a pending motion. IN R USDCTSD L.R. 7-1(h).

10. *Modification or suspension of rules.* The court may, on its own motion or at the request of a party, suspend or modify any rule in a particular case in the interest of justice. IN R USDCTSD L.R. 1-1(c).

D. Documents

1. *Required documents*

  a. *Response to request for production of documents.* Refer to the General Requirements section of this document for information on the response to request for production of documents.

2. *Supplemental documents*

  a. *Certificate of service.* FRCP 5(d) requires that the person making service under FRCP 5 certify that service has been effected. FRCP 5(Advisory Committee Notes). Having such information on file may be useful for many purposes, including proof of service if an issue arises concerning the effectiveness of the service. FRCP 5(Advisory Committee Notes).

E. Format

1. *Form of documents.* The rules governing captions and other matters of form in pleadings apply to motions and other papers. FRCP 7(b)(2).

  a. *Paper (manual filings only).* Any document that is not filed electronically must: be flat, unfolded, and on good-quality, eight and one-half by eleven (8-1/2 x 11) inch white paper. IN R USDCTSD L.R. 5-1(d)(1). Any document that is not filed electronically must: be single-sided. IN R USDCTSD L.R. 5-1(d)(1).

    i. *Covers or backing.* Any document that is not filed electronically must: not have a cover or a back. IN R USDCTSD L.R. 5-1(d)(1).

    ii. *Fastening.* Any document that is not filed electronically must: be (if consisting of more than one (1) page) fastened by paperclip or binder clip and may not be stapled. IN R USDCTSD L.R. 5-1(d)(1).

      • *Request for nonconforming fastening.* If a document cannot be fastened or bound as required by IN R USDCTSD L.R. 5-1(d), a party may ask the clerk for permission to fasten it in another manner. The party must make such a request before attempting to file the document with nonconforming fastening. IN R USDCTSD L.R. 5-1(d)(2).

    iii. *Hole punching.* Any document that is not filed electronically must: be two-hole punched at the top with the holes two and three-quarter (2-3/4) inches apart and appropriately centered. IN R USDCTSD L.R. 5-1(d)(1).

  b. *Margins.* Any pleading, motion, brief, affidavit, notice, or proposed order filed with the court, whether electronically or with the clerk, must: have at least one (1) inch margins. IN R USDCTSD L.R. 5-1(b).

c. *Spacing.* Any pleading, motion, brief, affidavit, notice, or proposed order filed with the court, whether electronically or with the clerk, must: be double spaced (except for headings, footnotes, and quoted material). IN R USDCTSD L.R. 5-1(b).

d. *Text.* Any pleading, motion, brief, affidavit, notice, or proposed order filed with the court, whether electronically or with the clerk, must: be plainly typewritten, printed, or prepared by a clearly legible copying process. IN R USDCTSD L.R. 5-1(b).

e. *Font size.* Any pleading, motion, brief, affidavit, notice, or proposed order filed with the court, whether electronically or with the clerk, must: use at least 12-point type in the body of the document and at least 10-point type in footnotes. IN R USDCTSD L.R. 5-1(b).

f. *Page numbering.* Any pleading, motion, brief, affidavit, notice, or proposed order filed with the court, whether electronically or with the clerk, must: have consecutively numbered pages. IN R USDCTSD L.R. 5-1(b).

g. *Caption; Names of parties.* Every pleading must have a caption with the court's name, a title, a file number, and a FRCP 7(a) designation. The title of the complaint must name all the parties; the title of other pleadings, after naming the first party on each side, may refer generally to other parties. FRCP 10(a). Any pleading, motion, brief, affidavit, notice, or proposed order filed with the court, whether electronically or with the clerk, must: include a title on the first page. IN R USDCTSD L.R. 5-1(b).

h. *Filer's information.* Any pleading, motion, brief, affidavit, notice, or proposed order filed with the court, whether electronically or with the clerk, must: in the case of pleadings, motions, legal briefs, and notices, include the name, complete address, telephone number, facsimile number (where available), and e-mail address (where available) of the pro se litigant or attorney who files it. IN R USDCTSD L.R. 5-1(b).

i. *Paragraphs; Separate statements.* A party must state its claims or defenses in numbered paragraphs, each limited as far as practicable to a single set of circumstances. A later pleading may refer by number to a paragraph in an earlier pleading. If doing so would promote clarity, each claim founded on a separate transaction or occurrence—and each defense other than a denial—must be stated in a separate count or defense. FRCP 10(b).

j. *Adoption by reference; Exhibits.* A statement in a pleading may be adopted by reference elsewhere in the same pleading or in any other pleading or motion. A copy of a written instrument that is an exhibit to a pleading is a part of the pleading for all purposes. FRCP 10(c).

k. *Citations*

    i. *Local rules.* The Local Rules of the United States District Court for the Southern District of Indiana may be cited as "S.D. Ind. L.R." IN R USDCTSD L.R. 1-1(a).

    ii. *Local alternative dispute resolution rules.* These Rules shall be known as the Local Alternative Dispute Resolution Rules of the United States District Court for the Southern District of Indiana. They shall be cited as "S.D.Ind. Local A.D.R. Rule _____." IN R USDCTSD A.D.R. Rule 1.1.

l. *Acceptance by the clerk.* The clerk must not refuse to file a paper solely because it is not in the form prescribed by the Federal Rules of Civil Procedure or by a local rule or practice. FRCP 5(d)(4). The clerk will accept a document that violates IN R USDCTSD L.R. 5-1, but the court may exclude the document from the official record. IN R USDCTSD L.R. 5-1(e).

    i. *Sanctions for errors as to form.* The court may strike from the record any document that does not comply with the rules governing the form of documents filed with the court, such as rules that regulate document size or the number of copies to be filed or that require a special designation in the caption. The court may also sanction an attorney or party who files a non-compliant document. IN R USDCTSD L.R. 1-3.

2. *Form of electronic documents.* Any document submitted via the court's electronic case filing (ECF)

system must be: otherwise prepared and filed in a manner consistent with the CM/ECF Policies and Procedures Manual (IN R USDCTSD ECF Procedures). IN R USDCTSD L.R. 5-1(c). Electronically filed documents must meet the requirements of FRCP 10 (Form of Pleadings), IN R USDCTSD L.R. 5-1 (Format of Papers Presented for Filing), and FRCP 5.2 (Privacy Protection for Filings Made with the Court), as if they had been submitted on paper. Documents filed electronically are also subject to any page limitations set forth by Court Order, by IN R USDCTSD L.R. 7-1 (Motion Practice), or IN R USDCTSD L.R. 56-1 (Summary Judgment Practice), as applicable. IN R USDCTSD ECF Procedures(13).

a. *PDF format required.* Any document submitted via the court's electronic case filing (ECF) system must be: in .pdf format. IN R USDCTSD L.R. 5-1(c); IN R USDCTSD ECF Procedures(7). Any document submitted via the court's electronic case filing (ECF) system must be: converted to a .pdf file directly from a word processing program, unless it exists only in paper format (in which case it may be scanned to create a .pdf document). IN R USDCTSD L.R. 5-1(c); IN R USDCTSD ECF Procedures(13).

    i. An exhibit may be scanned into PDF format, at a recommended 300 dpi resolution or higher, only if it does not already exist in electronic format. The filing attorney is responsible for reviewing all PDF documents for legibility before submitting them through the Court's Electronic Case Filing system. For technical guidance in creating PDF documents, please contact the Clerk's Office. IN R USDCTSD ECF Procedures(13).

b. *File size limitations.* Any document submitted via the court's electronic case filing (ECF) system must be: submitted as one or more .pdf files that do not exceed ten megabytes (10 MB) each (consistent with the CM/ECF Policies and Procedures Manual (IN R USDCTSD ECF Procedures)). IN R USDCTSD L.R. 5-1(c); IN R USDCTSD ECF Procedures(13).

    i. To electronically file a document or attachment that exceeds ten megabytes (10 MB), the document must first be broken down into two or more smaller files. For example, if Exhibit A is a twelve megabyte (12 MB) PDF file, it should be divided into 2 equal parts prior to electronic filing. Each component part of the exhibit would be filed as an attachment to the main document and described appropriately as "Exhibit A (part 1 of 2)" and "Exhibit A (part 2 of 2)." IN R USDCTSD ECF Procedures(13).

    ii. The supporting items mentioned in IN R USDCTSD ECF Procedures(13) should not be confused with memorandums or briefs in support of motions as outlined in IN R USDCTSD L.R. 7-1 or IN R USDCTSD L.R. 56-1. These memorandums or briefs in support are to be filed as entirely separate documents pursuant to the appropriate rule. Additionally, no motion shall be embodied in the text of a response or reply brief/memorandum unless otherwise ordered by the Court. IN R USDCTSD ECF Procedures(13).

c. *Separate component parts.* A key objective of the electronic filing system is to ensure that as much of the case as possible is managed electronically. To facilitate electronic filing and retrieval, documents to be filed electronically are to be reasonably broken into their separate component parts. By way of example, most filings include a foundation document (e.g., motion) and other supporting items (e.g., exhibits, proposed orders, proposed amended pleadings). The foundation document, as well as the supporting items, are each separate components of the filing; supporting items must be filed as attachments to the foundation document. These exhibits or attachments should include only those excerpts of the referenced documents that are directly germane to the matter under consideration. IN R USDCTSD ECF Procedures(13).

    i. Where an individual component cannot be included in an electronic filing (e.g. the component cannot be converted to electronic format), the filer shall electronically file the prescribed Notice of Manual Filing in place of that component. A model form is provided as Appendix C (IN R USDCTSD ECF Procedures(Appendix C)). IN R USDCTSD ECF Procedures(13).

d. *Exhibits.* Each electronically filed exhibit to a main document must be: (1) created as a separate .pdf file; (2) submitted as an attachment to the main document and given a title which describes its content; and (3) limited to excerpts that are directly germane to the main document's subject matter. IN R USDCTSD L.R. 5-6(a).

    i. When uploading attachments during the electronic filing process, exhibits must be uploaded in

a logical sequence and a brief description must be entered for each individual PDF file. The description must include not only the exhibit number or letter, but also a brief description of the document. This information may be entered in CM/ECF using a combination of the Category drop-down menu, the Description text box, or both (see IN R USDCTSD ECF Procedures(13)(Figure 1)). The information that is provided in each box will be combined to create a description of the document as it appears on the case docket (see IN R USDCTSD ECF Procedures(13)(Figure 2)). IN R USDCTSD ECF Procedures(13). For an example, refer to IN R USDCTSD ECF Procedures(13).

e. *Excerpts.* A party filing an exhibit that consists of excerpts from a larger document must clearly and prominently identify the exhibit as containing excerpted material. Either party will have the right to timely file additional excerpts or the complete document to the extent they are or become directly germane to the main document's subject matter. IN R USDCTSD L.R. 5-6(b).

f. For an example illustrating the application of IN R USDCTSD ECF Procedures(13), refer to IN R USDCTSD ECF Procedures(13).

3. *Signing disclosures and discovery requests, responses, and objections.* FRCP 11 does not apply to disclosures and discovery requests, responses, objections, and motions under FRCP 26 through FRCP 37. FRCP 11(d).

a. *Signature required.* Every disclosure under FRCP 26(a)(1) or FRCP 26(a)(3) and every discovery request, response, or objection must be signed by at least one attorney of record in the attorney's own name—or by the party personally, if unrepresented—and must state the signer's address, e-mail address, and telephone number. FRCP 26(g)(1).

i. *Signatures on manual filings.* Any document that is not filed electronically must: include the original signature of the pro se litigant or attorney who files it. IN R USDCTSD L.R. 5-1(d)(1).

ii. *Electronic signatures.* Use of the attorney's login and password when filing documents electronically serves in part as the attorney's signature for purposes of FRCP 11, the Local Rules of the United States District Court for the Southern District of Indiana, and any other purpose for which a signature is required in connection with proceedings before the Court. IN R USDCTSD ECF Procedures(14); IN R USDCTSD ECF Procedures(10). A pleading, motion, brief, or notice filed electronically under an attorney's ECF log-in and password must be signed by that attorney. IN R USDCTSD L.R. 5-7(a). A signature on a document other than a document filed as provided under IN R USDCTSD L.R. 5-7(a) must be an original handwritten signature and must be scanned into .pdf format for electronic filing. IN R USDCTSD L.R. 5-7(c); IN R USDCTSD ECF Procedures(14).

• *Form of electronic signature.* If a document is converted directly from a word processing application to .pdf (as opposed to scanning), the name of the Filing User under whose log-in and password the document is submitted must be preceded by a "s/" and typed on the signature line where the Filing User's handwritten signature would otherwise appear. IN R USDCTSD L.R. 5-7(b). All documents filed electronically shall include a signature block and include the filing attorney's typewritten name, address, telephone number, facsimile number and e-mail address. In addition, the name of the filing attorney under whose ECF login the document will be filed should be preceded by a "s/" and typed in the space where the attorney's handwritten signature would otherwise appear. IN R US-DCTSD ECF Procedures(14). For a sample format, refer to IN R USDCTSD ECF Procedures(14).

• *Effect of electronic signature.* Filing an electronically signed document under an attorney's ECF log-in and password constitutes the attorney's signature on the document under the Federal Rules of Civil Procedure, under the Local Rules of the United States District Court for the Southern District of Indiana, and for any other reason a signature is required in connection with the court's activities. IN R USDCTSD L.R. 5-7(d).

• *Documents with multiple attorneys' signatures.* Documents requiring signatures of more than one attorney shall be filed either by: (1) obtaining consent from the other attorney, then typing the "s/ [Name]" signature of the other attorney on the signature line where the other attorney's signature would otherwise appear; (2) identifying in the signature section the name of the other attorney whose signature is required and by the submission of a Notice of Endorsement (see IN R USDCTSD ECF Procedures(Appendix B)) by the other attorney no later than three (3) business days after filing; (3) submitting a scanned document containing all handwritten signatures; or (4) in any other manner approved by the Court. IN R USDCTSD ECF Procedures(14); IN R USDCTSD L.R. 5-7(e).

b. *Effect of signature.* By signing, an attorney or party certifies that to the best of the person's knowledge, information, and belief formed after a reasonable inquiry:

    i. With respect to a disclosure, it is complete and correct as of the time it is made; and

    ii. With respect to a discovery request, response, or objection, it is:

- Consistent with the Federal Rules of Civil Procedure and warranted by existing law or by a nonfrivolous argument for extending, modifying, or reversing existing law, or for establishing new law;

- Not interposed for any improper purpose, such as to harass, cause unnecessary delay, or needlessly increase the cost of litigation; and

- Neither unreasonable nor unduly burdensome or expensive, considering the needs of the case, prior discovery in the case, the amount in controversy, and the importance of the issues at stake in the action. FRCP 26(g)(1).

c. *Failure to sign.* Other parties have no duty to act on an unsigned disclosure, request, response, or objection until it is signed, and the court must strike it unless a signature is promptly supplied after the omission is called to the attorney's or party's attention. FRCP 26(g)(2). The court will strike any document filed directly with the clerk that is not signed by an attorney of record or the pro se litigant filing it, but the court may do so only after giving the attorney or pro se litigant notice of the omission and reasonable time to correct it. Rubber-stamp or facsimile signatures are not original signatures and the court will deem documents containing them to be unsigned for purposes of FRCP 11 and FRCP 26(g) and IN R USDCTSD L.R. 5-10. IN R USDCTSD L.R. 5-10(g).

d. *Sanction for improper certification.* If a certification violates FRCP 26(g) without substantial justification, the court, on motion or on its own, must impose an appropriate sanction on the signer, the party on whose behalf the signer was acting, or both. The sanction may include an order to pay the reasonable expenses, including attorney's fees, caused by the violation. FRCP 26(g)(3). Refer to the United States District Court for the Southern District of Indiana KeyRules Motion for Discovery Sanctions document for more information.

4. *Privacy protection for filings made with the court.* Electronically filed documents must meet the requirements of. . .FRCP 5.2 (Privacy Protection for Filings Made with the Court), as if they had been submitted on paper. IN R USDCTSD ECF Procedures(13).

a. *Redacted filings.* Unless the court orders otherwise, in an electronic or paper filing with the court that contains an individual's Social Security number, taxpayer-identification number, or birth date, the name of an individual known to be a minor, or a financial-account number, a party or nonparty making the filing may include only:

    i. The last four (4) digits of the Social Security number and taxpayer-identification number;

    ii. The year of the individual's birth;

    iii. The minor's initials; and

    iv. The last four (4) digits of the financial-account number. FRCP 5.2(a).

b. *Exemptions from the redaction requirement.* The redaction requirement does not apply to the following:

    i. A financial-account number that identifies the property allegedly subject to forfeiture in a forfeiture proceeding;

    ii. The record of an administrative or agency proceeding;

    iii. The official record of a state-court proceeding;

iv. The record of a court or tribunal, if that record was not subject to the redaction requirement when originally filed;

v. A filing covered by FRCP 5.2(c) or FRCP 5.2(d); and

vi. A pro se filing in an action brought under 28 U.S.C.A. § 2241, 28 U.S.C.A. § 2254, or 28 U.S.C.A. § 2255. FRCP 5.2(b).

c. *Limitations on remote access to electronic files; Social Security appeals and immigration cases.* Unless the court orders otherwise, in an action for benefits under the Social Security Act, and in an action or proceeding relating to an order of removal, to relief from removal, or to immigration benefits or detention, access to an electronic file is authorized as follows:

i. The parties and their attorneys may have remote electronic access to any part of the case file, including the administrative record;

ii. Any other person may have electronic access to the full record at the courthouse, but may have remote electronic access only to:

- The docket maintained by the court; and

- An opinion, order, judgment, or other disposition of the court, but not any other part of the case file or the administrative record. FRCP 5.2(c).

d. *Filings made under seal.* The court may order that a filing be made under seal without redaction. The court may later unseal the filing or order the person who made the filing to file a redacted version for the public record. FRCP 5.2(d). For more information on filing under seal, refer to IN R USDCTSD L.R. 5-11 and IN R USDCTSD ECF Procedures(18).

e. *Protective orders.* For good cause, the court may by order in a case:

i. Require redaction of additional information; or

ii. Limit or prohibit a nonparty's remote electronic access to a document filed with the court. FRCP 5.2(e).

f. *Option for additional unredacted filing under seal.* A person making a redacted filing may also file an unredacted copy under seal. The court must retain the unredacted copy as part of the record. FRCP 5.2(f).

g. *Option for filing a reference list.* A filing that contains redacted information may be filed together with a reference list that identifies each item of redacted information and specifies an appropriate identifier that uniquely corresponds to each item listed. The list must be filed under seal and may be amended as of right. Any reference in the case to a listed identifier will be construed to refer to the corresponding item of information. FRCP 5.2(g).

h. *Waiver of protection of identifiers.* A person waives the protection of FRCP 5.2(a) as to the person's own information by filing it without redaction and not under seal. FRCP 5.2(h).

F. Filing and Service Requirements

1. *Filing requirements.* Any paper after the complaint that is required to be served—together with a certificate of service—must be filed within a reasonable time after service. But disclosures under FRCP 26(a)(1) or FRCP 26(a)(2) and the following discovery requests and responses must not be filed until they are used in the proceeding or the court orders filing: depositions, interrogatories, requests for documents or tangible things or to permit entry onto land, and requests for admission. FRCP 5(d)(1). Refer to the United States District Court for the Southern District of Indiana KeyRules pleading and motion documents for information on filing with the court.

a. *When discovery may be filed.* Discovery materials (whether discovery requests, responses, or deposition transcripts) may not be filed with the court except in the following circumstances:

i. *Relevant to certain motions.* A party seeking relief under FRCP 26(c) or FRCP 37, or by way of a pretrial motion that could result in a final order on an issue, must file with the motion those parts of the discovery materials relevant to the motion. IN R USDCTSD L.R. 26-2(a).

ii. *For anticipated use at trial.* When a party can reasonably anticipate using discovery materials at trial, the party must file the relevant portions at the start of the trial. IN R USDCTSD L.R. 26-2(b).

    iii. *Materials necessary for appeal.* A party seeking for purposes of appeal to supplement the record with discovery materials not previously filed may do so by stipulation of the parties or by court order approving the filing. IN R USDCTSD L.R. 26-2(c).

2. *Service requirements.* The response must be served on all the parties to the action, unless the court otherwise orders, rather than only on the requesting party. FPP § 2213.

  a. *Service; When required*

    i. *In general.* Unless the Federal Rules of Civil Procedure provide otherwise, each of the following papers must be served on every party:

- An order stating that service is required;
- A pleading filed after the original complaint, unless the court orders otherwise under FRCP 5(c) because there are numerous defendants;
- A discovery paper required to be served on a party, unless the court orders otherwise;
- A written motion, except one that may be heard ex parte; and
- A written notice, appearance, demand, or offer of judgment, or any similar paper. FRCP 5(a)(1).

    ii. *If a party fails to appear.* No service is required on a party who is in default for failing to appear. But a pleading that asserts a new claim for relief against such a party must be served on that party under FRCP 4. FRCP 5(a)(2).

    iii. *Seizing property.* If an action is begun by seizing property and no person is or need be named as a defendant, any service required before the filing of an appearance, answer, or claim must be made on the person who had custody or possession of the property when it was seized. FRCP 5(a)(3).

  b. *Service; How made*

    i. *Serving an attorney.* If a party is represented by an attorney, service under FRCP 5 must be made on the attorney unless the court orders service on the party. FRCP 5(b)(1).

    ii. *Service in general.* A paper is served under FRCP 5 by:

- Handing it to the person;
- Leaving it: (1) at the person's office with a clerk or other person in charge or, if no one is in charge, in a conspicuous place in the office; or (2) if the person has no office or the office is closed, at the person's dwelling or usual place of abode with someone of suitable age and discretion who resides there;
- Mailing it to the person's last known address—in which event service is complete upon mailing;
- Leaving it with the court clerk if the person has no known address;
- Sending it by electronic means if the person consented in writing—in which event service is complete upon transmission, but is not effective if the serving party learns that it did not reach the person to be served; or
- Delivering it by any other means that the person consented to in writing—in which event service is complete when the person making service delivers it to the agency designated to make delivery. FRCP 5(b)(2).

    iii. *Electronic service*

- *Consent.* By registering to use the ECF system, attorneys consent to electronic service of documents filed in cases maintained on the ECF system. IN R USDCTSD L.R. 5-3(d). By participating in the Electronic Case Filing Program, attorneys consent to the electronic service of documents, and shall make available electronic mail addresses for service. IN R USDCTSD ECF Procedures(11).

- *Service on registered parties.* Upon the filing of a document by a party, an e-mail message will be automatically generated by the electronic filing system and sent via electronic mail to the e-mail addresses of all registered attorneys who have appeared in the case. The Notice of Electronic Filing will contain a document hyperlink which will provide recipients with one "free look" at the electronically filed document. Recipients are encouraged to print and/or save a copy of the document during the "free look" to avoid incurring PACER charges for future viewings of the document. IN R USDCTSD ECF Procedures(11). When a document has been filed electronically: transmission of the notice of electronic filing generated by the ECF system to an attorney's e-mail address constitutes service of the document on that attorney. IN R USDCTSD L.R. 5-4(c)(5). The party effectuates service on all registered attorneys by filing electronically. IN R USDCTSD ECF Procedures(11). When a document has been filed electronically: no other attempted service will constitute electronic service of the document. IN R USDCTSD L.R. 5-4(c)(6).

- *Service on exempt parties.* A filer must serve a copy of the document consistent with FRCP 5 on any party or attorney who is exempt from participating in electronic filing. IN R USDCTSD L.R. 5-4(d). It is the responsibility of the filing attorney to conventionally serve all parties who do not receive electronic service (the identity of these parties will be indicated on the filing receipt generated by the ECF system). IN R USDCTSD ECF Procedures(11).

- *Service on parties excused from electronic filing.* Parties otherwise participating in the electronic filing system may be excused from filing a particular component electronically under certain limited circumstances, such as when the component cannot be reduced to an electronic format. Such components shall not be filed electronically, but instead shall be manually filed with the Clerk of Court and served upon the parties in accordance with the applicable Federal Rules of Civil Procedure and the Local Rules of the United States District Court for the Southern District of Indiana for filing and service of non-electronic documents. IN R USDCTSD ECF Procedures(15).

- *Service of exempt documents.* Any document that is exempt from electronic filing must be filed directly with the clerk and served on other parties in the case as required by those Federal Rules of Civil Procedure and Local Rules of the United States District Court for the Southern District of Indiana that apply to the service of non-electronic documents. IN R USDCTSD L.R. 5-2(c).

iv. *Using court facilities.* If a local rule so authorizes, a party may use the court's transmission facilities to make service under FRCP 5(b)(2)(E). FRCP 5(b)(3).

c. *Serving numerous defendants*

i. *In general.* If an action involves an unusually large number of defendants, the court may, on motion or on its own, order that:

- Defendants' pleadings and replies to them need not be served on other defendants;

- Any crossclaim, counterclaim, avoidance, or affirmative defense in those pleadings and replies to them will be treated as denied or avoided by all other parties; and

- Filing any such pleading and serving it on the plaintiff constitutes notice of the pleading to all parties. FRCP 5(c)(1).

ii. *Notifying parties.* A copy of every such order must be served on the parties as the court directs. FRCP 5(c)(2).

G. Hearings

1. There is no hearing contemplated in the federal statutes or rules for responses to requests for production of documents.

H. Forms

1. Federal Response to Request for Production of Documents Forms

a. Response; To request for production of documents and other items. AMJUR PP DEPOSITION § 523.

b. Response; To request for production and inspection of documents and other items. AMJUR PP DEPOSITION § 524.

c. Verification; By defendant; Of response to request for production of documents and other items. AMJUR PP DEPOSITION § 525.

d. Response; To request for inspection. AMJUR PP DEPOSITION § 526.

e. Response; To request for production of documents; Objection; Documents not within objecting party's possession. AMJUR PP DEPOSITION § 597.

f. Response; To request for production of documents; Objection; Documents within attorney-client privilege. AMJUR PP DEPOSITION § 598.

g. Response; To request for production of documents prepared in anticipation of litigation; Objection; Requestor may easily obtain information elsewhere. AMJUR PP DEPOSITION § 599.

h. Response to request for production. 3A FEDFORMS § 3564.

i. Response to request for production of documents; Government personnel files, memoranda, minutes of meetings and statistics. 3A FEDFORMS § 3565.

j. Response; To request for production of documents and things. FEDPROF § 23:414.

k. Response; To request for production of documents; With various objections. FEDPROF § 23:415.

l. Response to request for production of documents and things; Government records. FEDPROF § 23:416.

m. Objection; To request for production of documents; Documents not within objecting party's possession. FEDPROF § 23:417.

n. Objection; To request for production of documents; Documents within attorney-client privilege. FEDPROF § 23:418.

o. Objection; To request for production of documents prepared in anticipation of litigation; Requestor may easily obtain information elsewhere. FEDPROF § 23:419.

p. Objection; To request for production of documents; Documents do not exist. FEDPROF § 23:420.

q. First notice for production; Response. GOLDLTGFMS § 28:30.

I. Applicable Rules

1. *Federal rules*

   a. Serving and filing pleadings and other papers. FRCP 5.

   b. Privacy protection for filings made with the court. FRCP 5.2.

   c. Computing and extending time; Time for motion papers. FRCP 6.

   d. Pleadings allowed; Form of motions and other papers. FRCP 7.

   e. Form of pleadings. FRCP 10.

   f. Signing pleadings, motions, and other papers; Representations to the court; Sanctions. FRCP 11.

   g. Duty to disclose; General provisions governing discovery. FRCP 26.

   h. Stipulations about discovery procedure. FRCP 29.

   i. Producing documents, electronically stored information, and tangible things, or entering onto land, for inspection and other purposes. FRCP 34.

   j. Failure to make disclosures or to cooperate in discovery; Sanctions. FRCP 37.

2. *Local rules*

   a. Scope of the rules. IN R USDCTSD L.R. 1-1.

   b. Sanctions for errors as to form. IN R USDCTSD L.R. 1-3.

   c. Format of documents presented for filing. IN R USDCTSD L.R. 5-1.

   d. Filing of documents electronically required. IN R USDCTSD L.R. 5-2.

e. Eligibility, registration, passwords for electronic filing; Exemption from electronic filing. IN R USDCTSD L.R. 5-3.

f. Timing and consequences of electronic filing. IN R USDCTSD L.R. 5-4.

g. Attachments and exhibits in cases filed electronically. IN R USDCTSD L.R. 5-6.

h. Signatures in cases filed electronically. IN R USDCTSD L.R. 5-7.

i. Non-electronic filings. IN R USDCTSD L.R. 5-10.

j. Extensions of time. IN R USDCTSD L.R. 6-1.

k. Motion practice. [IN R USDCTSD L.R. 7-1, as amended by IN ORDER 16-2319, effective December 1, 2016].

l. Form of certain discovery requests. IN R USDCTSD L.R. 26-1.

m. Filing of discovery materials. IN R USDCTSD L.R. 26-2.

n. Assignment of cases. IN R USDCTSD L.R. 40-1.

o. Alternative dispute resolution. IN R USDCTSD A.D.R. Rule 1.1; IN R USDCTSD A.D.R. Rule 1.2; IN R USDCTSD A.D.R. Rule 1.5; IN R USDCTSD A.D.R. Rule 2.1; IN R USDCTSD A.D.R. Rule 2.2.

p. Electronic case filing policies and procedures manual. IN R USDCTSD ECF Procedures.

Requests, Notices and Applications
Request for Admissions

Document Last Updated December 2016

A. Checklist

(I) ❑ Matters to be considered by requesting party

    (a) ❑ Required documents

        (1) ❑ Request for admissions

    (b) ❑ Supplemental documents

        (1) ❑ Document(s)

        (2) ❑ Certificate of service

    (c) ❑ Timing

        (1) ❑ A party may not seek discovery from any source before the parties have conferred as required by FRCP 26(f), except in a proceeding exempted from initial disclosure under FRCP 26(a)(1)(B), or when authorized by the Federal Rules of Civil Procedure, by stipulation, or by court order

(II) ❑ Matters to be considered by responding party

    (a) ❑ Required documents

        (1) ❑ Response to request for admissions

    (b) ❑ Supplemental documents

        (1) ❑ Certificate of service

    (c) ❑ Timing

        (1) ❑ A matter is admitted unless, within thirty (30) days after being served, the party to whom the request is directed serves on the requesting party a written answer or objection addressed to the matter and signed by the party or its attorney

B. Timing

1. *Request for admissions.* Without leave of court or written stipulation, requests for admission may not be served before the time specified in FRCP 26(d). FEDPROC § 26:706.

2. *Timing of discovery, generally.* A party may not seek discovery from any source before the parties have conferred as required by FRCP 26(f), except in a proceeding exempted from initial disclosure under FRCP 26(a)(1)(B), or when authorized by the Federal Rules of Civil Procedure, by stipulation, or by court order. FRCP 26(d)(1).

3. *Computation of time*

   a. *Computing time.* FRCP 6 applies in computing any time period specified in the Federal Rules of Civil Procedure, in any local rule or court order, or in any statute that does not specify a method of computing time. FRCP 6(a).

      i. *Period stated in days or a longer unit.* When the period is stated in days or a longer unit of time:
         - Exclude the day of the event that triggers the period;
         - Count every day, including intermediate Saturdays, Sundays, and legal holidays; and
         - Include the last day of the period, but if the last day is a Saturday, Sunday, or legal holiday, the period continues to run until the end of the next day that is not a Saturday, Sunday, or legal holiday. FRCP 6(a)(1).

      ii. *Period stated in hours.* When the period is stated in hours:
         - Begin counting immediately on the occurrence of the event that triggers the period;
         - Count every hour, including hours during intermediate Saturdays, Sundays, and legal holidays; and
         - If the period would end on a Saturday, Sunday, or legal holiday, the period continues to run until the same time on the next day that is not a Saturday, Sunday, or legal holiday. FRCP 6(a)(2).

      iii. *Inaccessibility of the clerk's office.* Unless the court orders otherwise, if the clerk's office is inaccessible:
         - On the last day for filing under FRCP 6(a)(1), then the time for filing is extended to the first accessible day that is not a Saturday, Sunday, or legal holiday; or
         - During the last hour for filing under FRCP 6(a)(2), then the time for filing is extended to the same time on the first accessible day that is not a Saturday, Sunday, or legal holiday. FRCP 6(a)(3).

      iv. *"Last day" defined.* Unless a different time is set by a statute, local rule, or court order, the last day ends:
         - For electronic filing, at midnight in the court's time zone; and
         - For filing by other means, when the clerk's office is scheduled to close. FRCP 6(a)(4).

      v. *"Next day" defined.* The "next day" is determined by continuing to count forward when the period is measured after an event and backward when measured before an event. FRCP 6(a)(5).

      vi. *"Legal holiday" defined.* "Legal holiday" means:
         - The day set aside by statute for observing New Year's Day, Martin Luther King Jr.'s Birthday, Washington's Birthday, Memorial Day, Independence Day, Labor Day, Columbus Day, Veterans' Day, Thanksgiving Day, or Christmas Day;
         - Any day declared a holiday by the President or Congress; and
         - For periods that are measured after an event, any other day declared a holiday by the state where the district court is located. FRCP 6(a)(6).

   b. *Computation of electronic filing deadlines.* Filing documents electronically does not alter filing deadlines. IN R USDCTSD ECF Procedures(7). A document due on a particular day must be filed before midnight local time of the division where the case is pending. IN R USDCTSD L.R. 5-4(a). All electronic transmissions of documents must be completed (i.e. received completely by the Clerk's Office) prior to midnight of the local time of the division in which the case is pending in order to be considered timely filed that day (NOTE: time will be noted in Eastern Time on the Court's docket. If you have filed a document prior to midnight local time of the division in which the case is pending and the document is due that date, but the electronic receipt and docket reflect the following calendar day, please contact the Court). IN R USDCTSD ECF Procedures(7). Although attorneys may file documents electronically twenty-four (24) hours a day, seven (7) days a week, attorneys are encouraged to file all documents during the normal working hours of the Clerk's Office (Monday through Friday, 8:30 a.m. to 4:30 p.m.) when technical support is available. IN R USDCTSD ECF Procedures(7); IN R USDCTSD ECF Procedures(9).

    i. *Technical difficulties.* Parties are encouraged to file documents electronically during normal business hours, in case a problem is encountered. In the event a technical failure occurs and a document cannot be filed electronically despite the best efforts of the filing party, the party should print (if possible) a copy of the error message received. In addition, as soon as practically possible, the party should file a "Declaration that Party was Unable to File in a Timely Manner Due to Technical Difficulties." A model form is provided as Appendix D (IN R USDCTSD ECF Procedures(Appendix D)). IN R USDCTSD ECF Procedures(16).

- If a party is unable to file electronically and, as a result, may miss a filing deadline, the party must contact the Clerk's Office at the number listed in IN R USDCTSD ECF Procedures(15) to inform the court's staff of the difficulty. If a party misses a filing deadline due to an inability to file electronically, the party may submit the untimely filed document, accompanied by a declaration stating the reason(s) for missing the deadline. Unless the Court orders otherwise, the document and declaration must be filed no later than 12:00 noon of the first day on which the Court is open for business following the original filing deadline. IN R USDCTSD ECF Procedures(16).

  c. *Extending time*

    i. *In general.* When an act may or must be done within a specified time, the court may, for good cause, extend the time:

- With or without motion or notice if the court acts, or if a request is made, before the original time or its extension expires; or

- On motion made after the time has expired if the party failed to act because of excusable neglect. FRCP 6(b)(1).

    ii. *Exceptions.* A court must not extend the time to act under FRCP 50(b), FRCP 50(d), FRCP 52(b), FRCP 59(b), FRCP 59(d), FRCP 59(e), and FRCP 60(b). FRCP 6(b)(2).

    iii. Refer to the United States District Court for the Southern District of Indiana KeyRules Motion for Continuance/Extension of Time document for more information on extending time.

  d. *Additional time after certain kinds of service.* When a party may or must act within a specified time after being served and service is made under FRCP 5(b)(2)(C) (mail), FRCP 5(b)(2)(D) (leaving with the clerk), or FRCP 5(b)(2)(F) (other means consented to), three (3) days are added after the period would otherwise expire under FRCP 6(a). FRCP 6(d). Service by electronic mail shall constitute service pursuant to FRCP 5(b)(2)(E) and shall entitle the party being served to the additional three (3) days provided by FRCP 6(d). IN R USDCTSD ECF Procedures(11).

C. General Requirements

1. *General provisions governing discovery*

  a. *Discovery scope and limits*

    i. *Scope in general.* Unless otherwise limited by court order, the scope of discovery is as follows: Parties may obtain discovery regarding any nonprivileged matter that is relevant to any party's claim or defense and proportional to the needs of the case, considering the importance of the issues at stake in the action, the amount in controversy, the parties' relative access to relevant information, the parties' resources, the importance of the discovery in resolving the issues, and whether the burden or expense of the proposed discovery outweighs its likely benefit. Information within this scope of discovery need not be admissible in evidence to be discoverable. FRCP 26(b)(1).

ii. *Limitations on frequency and extent*

- *When permitted.* By order, the court may alter the limits in the Federal Rules of Civil Procedure on the number of depositions and interrogatories or on the length of depositions under FRCP 30. By order or local rule, the court may also limit the number of requests under FRCP 36. FRCP 26(b)(2)(A).

- *Specific limitations on electronically stored information.* A party need not provide discovery of electronically stored information from sources that the party identifies as not reasonably accessible because of undue burden or cost. On motion to compel discovery or for a protective order, the party from whom discovery is sought must show that the information is not reasonably accessible because of undue burden or cost. If that showing is made, the court may nonetheless order discovery from such sources if the requesting party shows good cause, considering the limitations of FRCP 26(b)(2)(C). The court may specify conditions for the discovery. FRCP 26(b)(2)(B).

- *When required.* On motion or on its own, the court must limit the frequency or extent of discovery otherwise allowed by the Federal Rules of Civil Procedure or by local rule if it determines that: (1) the discovery sought is unreasonably cumulative or duplicative, or can be obtained from some other source that is more convenient, less burdensome, or less expensive; (2) the party seeking discovery has had ample opportunity to obtain the information by discovery in the action; or (3) the proposed discovery is outside the scope permitted by FRCP 26(b)(1). FRCP 26(b)(2)(C).

iii. *Trial preparation; Materials*

- *Documents and tangible things.* Ordinarily, a party may not discover documents and tangible things that are prepared in anticipation of litigation or for trial by or for another party or its representative (including the other party's attorney, consultant, surety, indemnitor, insurer, or agent). But, subject to FRCP 26(b)(4), those materials may be discovered if: (1) they are otherwise discoverable under FRCP 26(b)(1); and (2) the party shows that it has substantial need for the materials to prepare its case and cannot, without undue hardship, obtain their substantial equivalent by other means. FRCP 26(b)(3)(A).

- *Protection against disclosure.* If the court orders discovery of those materials, it must protect against disclosure of the mental impressions, conclusions, opinions, or legal theories of a party's attorney or other representative concerning the litigation. FRCP 26(b)(3)(B).

- *Previous statement.* Any party or other person may, on request and without the required showing, obtain the person's own previous statement about the action or its subject matter. If the request is refused, the person may move for a court order, and FRCP 37(a)(5) applies to the award of expenses. A previous statement is either: (1) a written statement that the person has signed or otherwise adopted or approved; or (2) a contemporaneous stenographic, mechanical, electrical, or other recording—or a transcription of it—that recites substantially verbatim the person's oral statement. FRCP 26(b)(3)(C).

iv. *Trial preparation; Experts*

- *Deposition of an expert who may testify.* A party may depose any person who has been identified as an expert whose opinions may be presented at trial. If FRCP 26(a)(2)(B) requires a report from the expert, the deposition may be conducted only after the report is provided. FRCP 26(b)(4)(A).

- *Trial-preparation protection for draft reports or disclosures.* FRCP 26(b)(3)(A) and FRCP 26(b)(3)(B) protect drafts of any report or disclosure required under FRCP 26(a)(2), regardless of the form in which the draft is recorded. FRCP 26(b)(4)(B).

- *Trial-preparation protection for communications between a party's attorney and expert witnesses.* FRCP 26(b)(3)(A) and FRCP 26(b)(3)(B) protect communications between the party's attorney and any witness required to provide a report under FRCP 26(a)(2)(B), regardless of the form of the communications, except to the extent that the communications: (1) relate to compensation for the expert's study or testimony; (2) identify facts or data that the party's attorney provided and that the expert considered in forming the opinions to be expressed; or (3) identify assumptions that the party's attorney provided and that the expert relied on in forming the opinions to be expressed. FRCP 26(b)(4)(C).

- *Expert employed only for trial preparation.* Ordinarily, a party may not, by interrogatories or deposition, discover facts known or opinions held by an expert who has been retained or specially employed by another party in anticipation of litigation or to prepare for trial and who is not expected to be called as a witness at trial. But a party may do so only: (1) as provided in FRCP 35(b); or (2) on showing exceptional circumstances under which it is impracticable for the party to obtain facts or opinions on the same subject by other means. FRCP 26(b)(4)(D).

- *Payment.* Unless manifest injustice would result, the court must require that the party seeking discovery: (1) pay the expert a reasonable fee for time spent in responding to discovery under FRCP 26(b)(4)(A) or FRCP 26(b)(4)(D); and (2) for discovery under FRCP 26(b)(4)(D), also pay the other party a fair portion of the fees and expenses it reasonably incurred in obtaining the expert's facts and opinions. FRCP 26(b)(4)(E).

   v. *Claiming privilege or protecting trial-preparation materials*

- *Information withheld.* When a party withholds information otherwise discoverable by claiming that the information is privileged or subject to protection as trial-preparation material, the party must: (1) expressly make the claim; and (2) describe the nature of the documents, communications, or tangible things not produced or disclosed—and do so in a manner that, without revealing information itself privileged or protected, will enable other parties to assess the claim. FRCP 26(b)(5)(A).

- *Information produced.* If information produced in discovery is subject to a claim of privilege or of protection as trial-preparation material, the party making the claim may notify any party that received the information of the claim and the basis for it. After being notified, a party must promptly return, sequester, or destroy the specified information and any copies it has; must not use or disclose the information until the claim is resolved; must take reasonable steps to retrieve the information if the party disclosed it before being notified; and may promptly present the information to the court under seal for a determination of the claim. The producing party must preserve the information until the claim is resolved. FRCP 26(b)(5)(B).

  b. *Protective orders.* A party or any person from whom discovery is sought may move for a protective order in the court where the action is pending—or as an alternative on matters relating to a deposition, in the court for the district where the deposition will be taken. FRCP 26(c)(1). Refer to the United States District Court for the Southern District of Indiana KeyRules Motion for Protective Order document for more information.

  c. *Sequence of discovery.* Unless the parties stipulate or the court orders otherwise for the parties' and witnesses' convenience and in the interests of justice: (1) methods of discovery may be used in any sequence; and (2) discovery by one party does not require any other party to delay its discovery. FRCP 26(d)(3).

2. *Request for admissions*

  a. *Scope.* A party may serve on any other party a written request to admit, for purposes of the pending action only, the truth of any matters within the scope of FRCP 26(b)(1) relating to: (1) facts, the application of law to fact, or opinions about either; and (2) the genuineness of any described documents. FRCP 36(a)(1).

    i. A party may serve a request for admission even though the party has the burden of proving the matters asserted therein because FRCP 36 permits requests for admission to address claims of the party seeking discovery, and generally, the party asserting a claim bears the burden of proof thereon. FEDPROC § 26:715.

b. *Number.* FRCP 36 does not limit a party to a single request, or set of requests, for admissions. But FRCP 26(b)(2)(A) authorizes courts to limit the number of requests by order or local rule. In addition, the court has power to protect a party from harassment by repeated requests for admissions, but will not bar such repeated requests when the circumstances of the case justify them. Even a second request about the same fact or the genuineness of the same document is permissible if circumstances warrant a renewed request. FPP § 2258.

   i. *Limit on requests for admission.* No party may serve on any other party more than twenty-five (25) requests for admission without leave of court. Requests relating to the authenticity or genuineness of documents are not subject to this limitation. Any party desiring to serve additional requests for admission must file a written motion setting forth the proposed additional requests for admission and the reason(s) for their use. IN R USDCTSD L.R. 36-1.

c. *Form.* A party propounding written discovery under FRCP 33, FRCP 34, or FRCP 36 must number each interrogatory or request sequentially and, upon request, supply the written discovery to the responding party in an editable word processing format. IN R USDCTSD L.R. 26-1(a). Each matter must be separately stated. FRCP 36(a)(2). The party called upon to respond should not be required to go through a document and assume the responsibility of determining what facts it is being requested to admit. FPP § 2258. Each request for an admission should be phrased simply and directly so that it can be admitted or denied without explanation. FPP § 2258; United Coal Cos. v. Powell Const. Co., 839 F.2d 958, 968 (3d Cir. 1988).

   i. A request for an admission need not state the source of information about the matter for which the request is made. FPP § 2258.

d. *Effect of an admission; Withdrawing or amending it.* A matter admitted under FRCP 36 is conclusively established unless the court, on motion, permits the admission to be withdrawn or amended. Subject to FRCP 16(e), the court may permit withdrawal or amendment if it would promote the presentation of the merits of the action and if the court is not persuaded that it would prejudice the requesting party in maintaining or defending the action on the merits. An admission under FRCP 36 is not an admission for any other purpose and cannot be used against the party in any other proceeding. FRCP 36(b).

e. *Motion to compel.* The motion to compel discovery provided by FRCP 37(a) does not apply to a failure to respond to a request for admissions. The automatic admission from a failure to respond is a sufficient remedy for the party who made the request. If, however, a request is objected to, or the requesting party thinks that a response to a request is insufficient, it may move under FRCP 36(a)(6) to determine the sufficiency of the answers or objections. FPP § 2265.

f. *Motion regarding the sufficiency of an answer or objection.* The requesting party may move to determine the sufficiency of an answer or objection. Unless the court finds an objection justified, it must order that an answer be served. On finding that an answer does not comply with FRCP 36, the court may order either that the matter is admitted or that an amended answer be served. The court may defer its final decision until a pretrial conference or a specified time before trial. FRCP 37(a)(5) applies to an award of expenses. FRCP 36(a)(6). Refer to the United States District Court for the Southern District of Indiana KeyRules Motion for Discovery Sanctions document for more information on sanctions.

3. *Sanctions for failure to cooperate in discovery.* The pattern of sanctions for FRCP 36 is somewhat different from that for the other discovery rules. The most important sanctions are two:

   a. A failure to respond to a request is deemed an admission of the matter to which the request is directed; and

   b. A party who, without good reason, refuses to admit a matter will be required to pay the costs incurred in proving that matter. FPP § 2265. If a party fails to admit what is requested under FRCP 36 and if the requesting party later proves a document to be genuine or the matter true, the requesting party may move that the party who failed to admit pay the reasonable expenses, including attorney's fees, incurred in making that proof. The court must so order unless:

    i.   The request was held objectionable under FRCP 36(a);

    ii.   The admission sought was of no substantial importance;

    iii.   The party failing to admit had a reasonable ground to believe that it might prevail on the matter; or

    iv.   There was other good reason for the failure to admit. FRCP 37(c)(2).

  c. Refer to the United States District Court for the Southern District of Indiana KeyRules Motion for Discovery Sanctions document for more information on sanctions.

4. *Stipulations about discovery procedure.* Unless the court orders otherwise, the parties may stipulate that: (1) a deposition may be taken before any person, at any time or place, on any notice, and in the manner specified—in which event it may be used in the same way as any other deposition; and (2) other procedures governing or limiting discovery be modified—but a stipulation extending the time for any form of discovery must have court approval if it would interfere with the time set for completing discovery, for hearing a motion, or for trial. FRCP 29.

5. *Appearances.* Every attorney who represents a party or who files a document on a party's behalf must file an appearance for that party. IN R USDCTSD L.R. 83-7. The filing of a Notice of Appearance shall act to establish the filing attorney as an attorney of record representing a designated party or parties in a particular cause of action. As a result, it is necessary for each attorney to file a separate Notice of Appearance when entering an appearance in a case. A joint appearance on behalf of multiple attorneys may be filed electronically only if it is filed separately for each attorney, using his/her ECF login. IN R USDCTSD ECF Procedures(12). Only those attorneys who have filed an appearance in a pending action are entitled to be served with case documents under FRCP 5(a). IN R USDCTSD L.R. 83-7. For more information, refer to IN R USDCTSD L.R. 83-7 and IN R USDCTSD ECF Procedures(12).

6. *Notice of related action.* A party must file a notice of related action: as soon as it appears that the party's case and another pending case: (1) arise out of the same transaction or occurrence; (2) involve the same property; or (3) involve the validity or infringement or the same patent, trademark, or copyright. IN R USDCTSD L.R. 40-1(d)(2). For more information, refer to IN R USDCTSD L.R. 40-1.

7. *Alternative dispute resolution (ADR)*

  a. *Application.* Unless limited by specific provisions, or unless there are other applicable specific statutory, common law, or constitutional procedures, the Local Alternative Dispute Resolution Rules of the United States District Court for the Southern District of Indiana shall apply in all civil litigation filed in the U.S. District Court for the Southern District of Indiana, except in the following cases and proceedings:

    i.   Applications for writs of habeas corpus under 28 U.S.C.A. § 2254;

    ii.   Forfeiture cases;

    iii.   Non-adversary proceedings in bankruptcy;

    iv.   Social Security administrative review cases; and

    v.   Such other matters as specified by order of the Court; for example, matters involving important public policy issues, constitutional law, or the establishment of new law. IN R USDCTSD A.D.R. Rule 1.2.

  b. *Mediation.* Mediation under this section (IN R USDCTSD A.D.R. Rule 2.1, et seq.) involves the confidential process by which a person acting as a Mediator, selected by the parties or appointed by the Court, assists the litigants in reaching a mutually acceptable agreement. It is an informal and nonadversarial process. The role of the Mediator is to assist in identifying the issues, reducing misunderstandings, clarifying priorities, exploring areas of compromise, and finding points of agreement as well as legitimate points of disagreement. Final decision-making authority rests with the parties, not the Mediator. IN R USDCTSD A.D.R. Rule 2.1. It is anticipated that an agreement may not resolve all of the disputed issues, but the process, nonetheless, can reduce points of contention. Parties and their representatives are required to mediate in good faith, but are not compelled to reach an agreement. IN R USDCTSD A.D.R. Rule 2.1.

    i. *Case selection.* The Court with the agreement of the parties may refer a civil case for mediation. Unless otherwise ordered or as specifically provided in IN R USDCTSD A.D.R. Rule 2.8, referral to mediation does not abate or suspend the action, and no scheduled dates shall be delayed or deferred, including the date of trial. IN R USDCTSD A.D.R. Rule 2.2.

    ii. For more information on mediation, refer to IN R USDCTSD A.D.R. Rule 2.1, et seq.

  c. *Other methods of dispute resolution.* The Local Alternative Dispute Resolution Rules of the United States District Court for the Southern District of Indiana shall not preclude the parties from utilizing any other reasonable method or technique of alternative dispute resolution to resolve disputes to which the parties agree. However, any use of arbitration by the parties will be governed by and comply with the requirements of 28 U.S.C.A. § 654 through 28 U.S.C.A. § 657. IN R USDCTSD A.D.R. Rule 1.5.

  d. For more information on alternative dispute resolution (ADR), refer to IN R USDCTSD A.D.R. Rule 1.1, et seq.

8. *Notice of settlement or resolution.* The parties must immediately notify the court if they reasonably anticipate settling their case or resolving a pending motion. IN R USDCTSD L.R. 7-1(h).

9. *Modification or suspension of rules.* The court may, on its own motion or at the request of a party, suspend or modify any rule in a particular case in the interest of justice. IN R USDCTSD L.R. 1-1(c).

D. Documents

1. *Required documents*

  a. *Request for admissions.* Refer to the General Requirements section of this document for information on the request for admissions.

2. *Supplemental documents*

  a. *Document(s).* A request to admit the genuineness of a document must be accompanied by a copy of the document unless it is, or has been, otherwise furnished or made available for inspection and copying. FRCP 36(a)(2).

  b. *Certificate of service.* FRCP 5(d) requires that the person making service under FRCP 5 certify that service has been effected. FRCP 5(Advisory Committee Notes). Having such information on file may be useful for many purposes, including proof of service if an issue arises concerning the effectiveness of the service. FRCP 5(Advisory Committee Notes).

E. Format

1. *Form of documents.* The rules governing captions and other matters of form in pleadings apply to motions and other papers. FRCP 7(b)(2).

  a. *Paper (manual filings only).* Any document that is not filed electronically must: be flat, unfolded, and on good-quality, eight and one-half by eleven (8-1/2 x 11) inch white paper. IN R USDCTSD L.R. 5-1(d)(1). Any document that is not filed electronically must: be single-sided. IN R USDCTSD L.R. 5-1(d)(1).

    i. *Covers or backing.* Any document that is not filed electronically must: not have a cover or a back. IN R USDCTSD L.R. 5-1(d)(1).

    ii. *Fastening.* Any document that is not filed electronically must: be (if consisting of more than one (1) page) fastened by paperclip or binder clip and may not be stapled. IN R USDCTSD L.R. 5-1(d)(1).

      • *Request for nonconforming fastening.* If a document cannot be fastened or bound as required by IN R USDCTSD L.R. 5-1(d), a party may ask the clerk for permission to fasten it in another manner. The party must make such a request before attempting to file the document with nonconforming fastening. IN R USDCTSD L.R. 5-1(d)(2).

    iii. *Hole punching.* Any document that is not filed electronically must: be two-hole punched at the top with the holes two and three-quarter (2-3/4) inches apart and appropriately centered. IN R USDCTSD L.R. 5-1(d)(1).

b. *Margins.* Any pleading, motion, brief, affidavit, notice, or proposed order filed with the court, whether electronically or with the clerk, must: have at least one (1) inch margins. IN R USDCTSD L.R. 5-1(b).

c. *Spacing.* Any pleading, motion, brief, affidavit, notice, or proposed order filed with the court, whether electronically or with the clerk, must: be double spaced (except for headings, footnotes, and quoted material). IN R USDCTSD L.R. 5-1(b).

d. *Text.* Any pleading, motion, brief, affidavit, notice, or proposed order filed with the court, whether electronically or with the clerk, must: be plainly typewritten, printed, or prepared by a clearly legible copying process. IN R USDCTSD L.R. 5-1(b).

e. *Font size.* Any pleading, motion, brief, affidavit, notice, or proposed order filed with the court, whether electronically or with the clerk, must: use at least 12-point type in the body of the document and at least 10-point type in footnotes. IN R USDCTSD L.R. 5-1(b).

f. *Page numbering.* Any pleading, motion, brief, affidavit, notice, or proposed order filed with the court, whether electronically or with the clerk, must: have consecutively numbered pages. IN R USDCTSD L.R. 5-1(b).

g. *Caption; Names of parties.* Every pleading must have a caption with the court's name, a title, a file number, and a FRCP 7(a) designation. The title of the complaint must name all the parties; the title of other pleadings, after naming the first party on each side, may refer generally to other parties. FRCP 10(a). Any pleading, motion, brief, affidavit, notice, or proposed order filed with the court, whether electronically or with the clerk, must: include a title on the first page. IN R USDCTSD L.R. 5-1(b).

h. *Filer's information.* Any pleading, motion, brief, affidavit, notice, or proposed order filed with the court, whether electronically or with the clerk, must: in the case of pleadings, motions, legal briefs, and notices, include the name, complete address, telephone number, facsimile number (where available), and e-mail address (where available) of the pro se litigant or attorney who files it. IN R USDCTSD L.R. 5-1(b).

i. *Paragraphs; Separate statements.* A party must state its claims or defenses in numbered paragraphs, each limited as far as practicable to a single set of circumstances. A later pleading may refer by number to a paragraph in an earlier pleading. If doing so would promote clarity, each claim founded on a separate transaction or occurrence—and each defense other than a denial—must be stated in a separate count or defense. FRCP 10(b).

j. *Adoption by reference; Exhibits.* A statement in a pleading may be adopted by reference elsewhere in the same pleading or in any other pleading or motion. A copy of a written instrument that is an exhibit to a pleading is a part of the pleading for all purposes. FRCP 10(c).

k. *Citations*

   i. *Local rules.* The Local Rules of the United States District Court for the Southern District of Indiana may be cited as "S.D. Ind. L.R." IN R USDCTSD L.R. 1-1(a).

   ii. *Local alternative dispute resolution rules.* These Rules shall be known as the Local Alternative Dispute Resolution Rules of the United States District Court for the Southern District of Indiana. They shall be cited as "S.D.Ind. Local A.D.R. Rule _____." IN R USDCTSD A.D.R. Rule 1.1.

l. *Acceptance by the clerk.* The clerk must not refuse to file a paper solely because it is not in the form prescribed by the Federal Rules of Civil Procedure or by a local rule or practice. FRCP 5(d)(4). The clerk will accept a document that violates IN R USDCTSD L.R. 5-1, but the court may exclude the document from the official record. IN R USDCTSD L.R. 5-1(e).

   i. *Sanctions for errors as to form.* The court may strike from the record any document that does not comply with the rules governing the form of documents filed with the court, such as rules that regulate document size or the number of copies to be filed or that require a special designation in the caption. The court may also sanction an attorney or party who files a non-compliant document. IN R USDCTSD L.R. 1-3.

2. *Form of electronic documents.* Any document submitted via the court's electronic case filing (ECF) system must be: otherwise prepared and filed in a manner consistent with the CM/ECF Policies and Procedures Manual (IN R USDCTSD ECF Procedures). IN R USDCTSD L.R. 5-1(c). Electronically filed documents must meet the requirements of FRCP 10 (Form of Pleadings), IN R USDCTSD L.R. 5-1 (Format of Papers Presented for Filing), and FRCP 5.2 (Privacy Protection for Filings Made with the Court), as if they had been submitted on paper. Documents filed electronically are also subject to any page limitations set forth by Court Order, by IN R USDCTSD L.R. 7-1 (Motion Practice), or IN R USDCTSD L.R. 56-1 (Summary Judgment Practice), as applicable. IN R USDCTSD ECF Procedures(13).

   a. *PDF format required.* Any document submitted via the court's electronic case filing (ECF) system must be: in .pdf format. IN R USDCTSD L.R. 5-1(c); IN R USDCTSD ECF Procedures(7). Any document submitted via the court's electronic case filing (ECF) system must be: converted to a .pdf file directly from a word processing program, unless it exists only in paper format (in which case it may be scanned to create a .pdf document). IN R USDCTSD L.R. 5-1(c); IN R USDCTSD ECF Procedures(13).

      i. An exhibit may be scanned into PDF format, at a recommended 300 dpi resolution or higher, only if it does not already exist in electronic format. The filing attorney is responsible for reviewing all PDF documents for legibility before submitting them through the Court's Electronic Case Filing system. For technical guidance in creating PDF documents, please contact the Clerk's Office. IN R USDCTSD ECF Procedures(13).

   b. *File size limitations.* Any document submitted via the court's electronic case filing (ECF) system must be: submitted as one or more .pdf files that do not exceed ten megabytes (10 MB) each (consistent with the CM/ECF Policies and Procedures Manual (IN R USDCTSD ECF Procedures)). IN R USDCTSD L.R. 5-1(c); IN R USDCTSD ECF Procedures(13).

      i. To electronically file a document or attachment that exceeds ten megabytes (10 MB), the document must first be broken down into two or more smaller files. For example, if Exhibit A is a twelve megabyte (12 MB) PDF file, it should be divided into 2 equal parts prior to electronic filing. Each component part of the exhibit would be filed as an attachment to the main document and described appropriately as "Exhibit A (part 1 of 2)" and "Exhibit A (part 2 of 2)." IN R USDCTSD ECF Procedures(13).

      ii. The supporting items mentioned in IN R USDCTSD ECF Procedures(13) should not be confused with memorandums or briefs in support of motions as outlined in IN R USDCTSD L.R. 7-1 or IN R USDCTSD L.R. 56-1. These memorandums or briefs in support are to be filed as entirely separate documents pursuant to the appropriate rule. Additionally, no motion shall be embodied in the text of a response or reply brief/memorandum unless otherwise ordered by the Court. IN R USDCTSD ECF Procedures(13).

   c. *Separate component parts.* A key objective of the electronic filing system is to ensure that as much of the case as possible is managed electronically. To facilitate electronic filing and retrieval, documents to be filed electronically are to be reasonably broken into their separate component parts. By way of example, most filings include a foundation document (e.g., motion) and other supporting items (e.g., exhibits, proposed orders, proposed amended pleadings). The foundation document, as well as the supporting items, are each separate components of the filing; supporting items must be filed as attachments to the foundation document. These exhibits or attachments should include only those excerpts of the referenced documents that are directly germane to the matter under consideration. IN R USDCTSD ECF Procedures(13).

      i. Where an individual component cannot be included in an electronic filing (e.g. the component cannot be converted to electronic format), the filer shall electronically file the prescribed Notice of Manual Filing in place of that component. A model form is provided as Appendix C (IN R USDCTSD ECF Procedures(Appendix C)). IN R USDCTSD ECF Procedures(13).

   d. *Exhibits.* Each electronically filed exhibit to a main document must be: (1) created as a separate .pdf file; (2) submitted as an attachment to the main document and given a title which describes its content; and (3) limited to excerpts that are directly germane to the main document's subject matter. IN R USDCTSD L.R. 5-6(a).

    i. When uploading attachments during the electronic filing process, exhibits must be uploaded in a logical sequence and a brief description must be entered for each individual PDF file. The description must include not only the exhibit number or letter, but also a brief description of the document. This information may be entered in CM/ECF using a combination of the Category drop-down menu, the Description text box, or both (see IN R USDCTSD ECF Procedures(13)(Figure 1)). The information that is provided in each box will be combined to create a description of the document as it appears on the case docket (see IN R USDCTSD ECF Procedures(13)(Figure 2)). IN R USDCTSD ECF Procedures(13). For an example, refer to IN R USDCTSD ECF Procedures(13).

e. *Excerpts.* A party filing an exhibit that consists of excerpts from a larger document must clearly and prominently identify the exhibit as containing excerpted material. Either party will have the right to timely file additional excerpts or the complete document to the extent they are or become directly germane to the main document's subject matter. IN R USDCTSD L.R. 5-6(b).

f. For an example illustrating the application of IN R USDCTSD ECF Procedures(13), refer to IN R USDCTSD ECF Procedures(13).

3. *Signing disclosures and discovery requests, responses, and objections.* FRCP 11 does not apply to disclosures and discovery requests, responses, objections, and motions under FRCP 26 through FRCP 37. FRCP 11(d).

a. *Signature required.* Every disclosure under FRCP 26(a)(1) or FRCP 26(a)(3) and every discovery request, response, or objection must be signed by at least one attorney of record in the attorney's own name—or by the party personally, if unrepresented—and must state the signer's address, e-mail address, and telephone number. FRCP 26(g)(1).

    i. *Signatures on manual filings.* Any document that is not filed electronically must: include the original signature of the pro se litigant or attorney who files it. IN R USDCTSD L.R. 5-1(d)(1).

    ii. *Electronic signatures.* Use of the attorney's login and password when filing documents electronically serves in part as the attorney's signature for purposes of FRCP 11, the Local Rules of the United States District Court for the Southern District of Indiana, and any other purpose for which a signature is required in connection with proceedings before the Court. IN R USDCTSD ECF Procedures(14); IN R USDCTSD ECF Procedures(10). A pleading, motion, brief, or notice filed electronically under an attorney's ECF log-in and password must be signed by that attorney. IN R USDCTSD L.R. 5-7(a). A signature on a document other than a document filed as provided under IN R USDCTSD L.R. 5-7(a) must be an original handwritten signature and must be scanned into .pdf format for electronic filing. IN R USDCTSD L.R. 5-7(c); IN R USDCTSD ECF Procedures(14).

        • *Form of electronic signature.* If a document is converted directly from a word processing application to .pdf (as opposed to scanning), the name of the Filing User under whose log-in and password the document is submitted must be preceded by a "s/" and typed on the signature line where the Filing User's handwritten signature would otherwise appear. IN R USDCTSD L.R. 5-7(b). All documents filed electronically shall include a signature block and include the filing attorney's typewritten name, address, telephone number, facsimile number and e-mail address. In addition, the name of the filing attorney under whose ECF login the document will be filed should be preceded by a "s/" and typed in the space where the attorney's handwritten signature would otherwise appear. IN R US-DCTSD ECF Procedures(14). For a sample format, refer to IN R USDCTSD ECF Procedures(14).

        • *Effect of electronic signature.* Filing an electronically signed document under an attorney's ECF log-in and password constitutes the attorney's signature on the document under the Federal Rules of Civil Procedure, under the Local Rules of the United States District Court for the Southern District of Indiana, and for any other reason a signature is required in connection with the court's activities. IN R USDCTSD L.R. 5-7(d).

- *Documents with multiple attorneys' signatures.* Documents requiring signatures of more than one attorney shall be filed either by: (1) obtaining consent from the other attorney, then typing the "s/ [Name]" signature of the other attorney on the signature line where the other attorney's signature would otherwise appear; (2) identifying in the signature section the name of the other attorney whose signature is required and by the submission of a Notice of Endorsement (see IN R USDCTSD ECF Procedures(Appendix B)) by the other attorney no later than three (3) business days after filing; (3) submitting a scanned document containing all handwritten signatures; or (4) in any other manner approved by the Court. IN R USDCTSD ECF Procedures(14); IN R USDCTSD L.R. 5-7(e).

b. *Effect of signature.* By signing, an attorney or party certifies that to the best of the person's knowledge, information, and belief formed after a reasonable inquiry:

    i. With respect to a disclosure, it is complete and correct as of the time it is made; and

    ii. With respect to a discovery request, response, or objection, it is:

- Consistent with the Federal Rules of Civil Procedure and warranted by existing law or by a nonfrivolous argument for extending, modifying, or reversing existing law, or for establishing new law;

- Not interposed for any improper purpose, such as to harass, cause unnecessary delay, or needlessly increase the cost of litigation; and

- Neither unreasonable nor unduly burdensome or expensive, considering the needs of the case, prior discovery in the case, the amount in controversy, and the importance of the issues at stake in the action. FRCP 26(g)(1).

c. *Failure to sign.* Other parties have no duty to act on an unsigned disclosure, request, response, or objection until it is signed, and the court must strike it unless a signature is promptly supplied after the omission is called to the attorney's or party's attention. FRCP 26(g)(2). The court will strike any document filed directly with the clerk that is not signed by an attorney of record or the pro se litigant filing it, but the court may do so only after giving the attorney or pro se litigant notice of the omission and reasonable time to correct it. Rubber-stamp or facsimile signatures are not original signatures and the court will deem documents containing them to be unsigned for purposes of FRCP 11 and FRCP 26(g) and IN R USDCTSD L.R. 5-10. IN R USDCTSD L.R. 5-10(g).

d. *Sanction for improper certification.* If a certification violates FRCP 26(g) without substantial justification, the court, on motion or on its own, must impose an appropriate sanction on the signer, the party on whose behalf the signer was acting, or both. The sanction may include an order to pay the reasonable expenses, including attorney's fees, caused by the violation. FRCP 26(g)(3). Refer to the United States District Court for the Southern District of Indiana KeyRules Motion for Discovery Sanctions document for more information.

4. *Privacy protection for filings made with the court.* Electronically filed documents must meet the requirements of. . .FRCP 5.2 (Privacy Protection for Filings Made with the Court), as if they had been submitted on paper. IN R USDCTSD ECF Procedures(13).

a. *Redacted filings.* Unless the court orders otherwise, in an electronic or paper filing with the court that contains an individual's Social Security number, taxpayer-identification number, or birth date, the name of an individual known to be a minor, or a financial-account number, a party or nonparty making the filing may include only:

    i. The last four (4) digits of the Social Security number and taxpayer-identification number;

    ii. The year of the individual's birth;

    iii. The minor's initials; and

    iv. The last four (4) digits of the financial-account number. FRCP 5.2(a).

b. *Exemptions from the redaction requirement.* The redaction requirement does not apply to the following:

    i. A financial-account number that identifies the property allegedly subject to forfeiture in a forfeiture proceeding;

ii. The record of an administrative or agency proceeding;

iii. The official record of a state-court proceeding;

iv. The record of a court or tribunal, if that record was not subject to the redaction requirement when originally filed;

v. A filing covered by FRCP 5.2(c) or FRCP 5.2(d); and

vi. A pro se filing in an action brought under 28 U.S.C.A. § 2241, 28 U.S.C.A. § 2254, or 28 U.S.C.A. § 2255. FRCP 5.2(b).

c. *Limitations on remote access to electronic files; Social Security appeals and immigration cases.* Unless the court orders otherwise, in an action for benefits under the Social Security Act, and in an action or proceeding relating to an order of removal, to relief from removal, or to immigration benefits or detention, access to an electronic file is authorized as follows:

i. The parties and their attorneys may have remote electronic access to any part of the case file, including the administrative record;

ii. Any other person may have electronic access to the full record at the courthouse, but may have remote electronic access only to:

- The docket maintained by the court; and

- An opinion, order, judgment, or other disposition of the court, but not any other part of the case file or the administrative record. FRCP 5.2(c).

d. *Filings made under seal.* The court may order that a filing be made under seal without redaction. The court may later unseal the filing or order the person who made the filing to file a redacted version for the public record. FRCP 5.2(d). For more information on filing under seal, refer to IN R USDCTSD L.R. 5-11 and IN R USDCTSD ECF Procedures(18).

e. *Protective orders.* For good cause, the court may by order in a case:

i. Require redaction of additional information; or

ii. Limit or prohibit a nonparty's remote electronic access to a document filed with the court. FRCP 5.2(e).

f. *Option for additional unredacted filing under seal.* A person making a redacted filing may also file an unredacted copy under seal. The court must retain the unredacted copy as part of the record. FRCP 5.2(f).

g. *Option for filing a reference list.* A filing that contains redacted information may be filed together with a reference list that identifies each item of redacted information and specifies an appropriate identifier that uniquely corresponds to each item listed. The list must be filed under seal and may be amended as of right. Any reference in the case to a listed identifier will be construed to refer to the corresponding item of information. FRCP 5.2(g).

h. *Waiver of protection of identifiers.* A person waives the protection of FRCP 5.2(a) as to the person's own information by filing it without redaction and not under seal. FRCP 5.2(h).

F. Filing and Service Requirements

1. *Filing requirements.* Any paper after the complaint that is required to be served—together with a certificate of service—must be filed within a reasonable time after service. But disclosures under FRCP 26(a)(1) or FRCP 26(a)(2) and the following discovery requests and responses must not be filed until they are used in the proceeding or the court orders filing: depositions, interrogatories, requests for documents or tangible things or to permit entry onto land, and requests for admission. FRCP 5(d)(1). Refer to the United States District Court for the Southern District of Indiana KeyRules pleading and motion documents for information on filing with the court.

a. *When discovery may be filed.* Discovery materials (whether discovery requests, responses, or deposition transcripts) may not be filed with the court except in the following circumstances:

i. *Relevant to certain motions.* A party seeking relief under FRCP 26(c) or FRCP 37, or by way of a pretrial motion that could result in a final order on an issue, must file with the motion those parts of the discovery materials relevant to the motion. IN R USDCTSD L.R. 26-2(a).

ii. *For anticipated use at trial.* When a party can reasonably anticipate using discovery materials at trial, the party must file the relevant portions at the start of the trial. IN R USDCTSD L.R. 26-2(b).

iii. *Materials necessary for appeal.* A party seeking for purposes of appeal to supplement the record with discovery materials not previously filed may do so by stipulation of the parties or by court order approving the filing. IN R USDCTSD L.R. 26-2(c).

2. *Service requirements.* [A request for an admission] must be served on the party from whom the admission is requested and, unless the court has otherwise ordered, a copy of the request must be served on every other party. FPP § 2258.

   a. *Service; When required*

      i. *In general.* Unless the Federal Rules of Civil Procedure provide otherwise, each of the following papers must be served on every party:

         • An order stating that service is required;

         • A pleading filed after the original complaint, unless the court orders otherwise under FRCP 5(c) because there are numerous defendants;

         • A discovery paper required to be served on a party, unless the court orders otherwise;

         • A written motion, except one that may be heard ex parte; and

         • A written notice, appearance, demand, or offer of judgment, or any similar paper. FRCP 5(a)(1).

      ii. *If a party fails to appear.* No service is required on a party who is in default for failing to appear. But a pleading that asserts a new claim for relief against such a party must be served on that party under FRCP 4. FRCP 5(a)(2).

      iii. *Seizing property.* If an action is begun by seizing property and no person is or need be named as a defendant, any service required before the filing of an appearance, answer, or claim must be made on the person who had custody or possession of the property when it was seized. FRCP 5(a)(3).

   b. *Service; How made*

      i. *Serving an attorney.* If a party is represented by an attorney, service under FRCP 5 must be made on the attorney unless the court orders service on the party. FRCP 5(b)(1).

      ii. *Service in general.* A paper is served under FRCP 5 by:

         • Handing it to the person;

         • Leaving it: (1) at the person's office with a clerk or other person in charge or, if no one is in charge, in a conspicuous place in the office; or (2) if the person has no office or the office is closed, at the person's dwelling or usual place of abode with someone of suitable age and discretion who resides there;

         • Mailing it to the person's last known address—in which event service is complete upon mailing;

         • Leaving it with the court clerk if the person has no known address;

         • Sending it by electronic means if the person consented in writing—in which event service is complete upon transmission, but is not effective if the serving party learns that it did not reach the person to be served; or

         • Delivering it by any other means that the person consented to in writing—in which event service is complete when the person making service delivers it to the agency designated to make delivery. FRCP 5(b)(2).

      iii. *Electronic service*

         • *Consent.* By registering to use the ECF system, attorneys consent to electronic service of documents filed in cases maintained on the ECF system. IN R USDCTSD L.R. 5-3(d). By participating in the Electronic Case Filing Program, attorneys consent to the electronic service of documents, and shall make available electronic mail addresses for service. IN R USDCTSD ECF Procedures(11).

- *Service on registered parties.* Upon the filing of a document by a party, an e-mail message will be automatically generated by the electronic filing system and sent via electronic mail to the e-mail addresses of all registered attorneys who have appeared in the case. The Notice of Electronic Filing will contain a document hyperlink which will provide recipients with one "free look" at the electronically filed document. Recipients are encouraged to print and/or save a copy of the document during the "free look" to avoid incurring PACER charges for future viewings of the document. IN R USDCTSD ECF Procedures(11). When a document has been filed electronically: transmission of the notice of electronic filing generated by the ECF system to an attorney's e-mail address constitutes service of the document on that attorney. IN R USDCTSD L.R. 5-4(c)(5). The party effectuates service on all registered attorneys by filing electronically. IN R USDCTSD ECF Procedures(11). When a document has been filed electronically: no other attempted service will constitute electronic service of the document. IN R USDCTSD L.R. 5-4(c)(6).

- *Service on exempt parties.* A filer must serve a copy of the document consistent with FRCP 5 on any party or attorney who is exempt from participating in electronic filing. IN R USDCTSD L.R. 5-4(d). It is the responsibility of the filing attorney to conventionally serve all parties who do not receive electronic service (the identity of these parties will be indicated on the filing receipt generated by the ECF system). IN R USDCTSD ECF Procedures(11).

- *Service on parties excused from electronic filing.* Parties otherwise participating in the electronic filing system may be excused from filing a particular component electronically under certain limited circumstances, such as when the component cannot be reduced to an electronic format. Such components shall not be filed electronically, but instead shall be manually filed with the Clerk of Court and served upon the parties in accordance with the applicable Federal Rules of Civil Procedure and the Local Rules of the United States District Court for the Southern District of Indiana for filing and service of non-electronic documents. IN R USDCTSD ECF Procedures(15).

- *Service of exempt documents.* Any document that is exempt from electronic filing must be filed directly with the clerk and served on other parties in the case as required by those Federal Rules of Civil Procedure and Local Rules of the United States District Court for the Southern District of Indiana that apply to the service of non-electronic documents. IN R USDCTSD L.R. 5-2(c).

iv. *Using court facilities.* If a local rule so authorizes, a party may use the court's transmission facilities to make service under FRCP 5(b)(2)(E). FRCP 5(b)(3).

c. *Serving numerous defendants*

   i. *In general.* If an action involves an unusually large number of defendants, the court may, on motion or on its own, order that:

- Defendants' pleadings and replies to them need not be served on other defendants;

- Any crossclaim, counterclaim, avoidance, or affirmative defense in those pleadings and replies to them will be treated as denied or avoided by all other parties; and

- Filing any such pleading and serving it on the plaintiff constitutes notice of the pleading to all parties. FRCP 5(c)(1).

   ii. *Notifying parties.* A copy of every such order must be served on the parties as the court directs. FRCP 5(c)(2).

G. Hearings

1. There is no hearing contemplated in the federal statutes or rules for requests for admissions.

H. Forms

1. Federal Request for Admissions Forms

a. Request; For admission of facts and genuineness of documents. AMJUR PP DEPOSITION § 674.

b. Plaintiff's request for admission. 3B FEDFORMS § 3650.

c. Plaintiff's request for admission; Another form. 3B FEDFORMS § 3651.

d. Plaintiff's request for admission; Statements in documents. 3B FEDFORMS § 3652.

e. Plaintiff's request for admission; Statements in documents; Another form. 3B FEDFORMS § 3653.

f. Plaintiff's request for admission; Specific facts. 3B FEDFORMS § 3654.

g. Plaintiff's request for admission; Specific facts; Another form. 3B FEDFORMS § 3655.

h. Plaintiff's request for admission; Specific documents and facts. 3B FEDFORMS § 3656.

i. Plaintiff's request for admission; Specific documents and facts; Another form. 3B FEDFORMS § 3657.

j. Plaintiff's request for admission; True copies, filing and operational effect of government documents. 3B FEDFORMS § 3658.

k. Plaintiff's request for additional admission. 3B FEDFORMS § 3659.

l. Defendant's request for admission of genuineness; Specific document. 3B FEDFORMS § 3660.

m. Defendant's request for admission of genuineness; Specific document; Another form. 3B FED-FORMS § 3661.

n. Defendant's request for admission of genuineness; Specific document; Another form. 3B FED-FORMS § 3662.

o. Defendant's request for admission; Truth of statement. 3B FEDFORMS § 3663.

p. Request for admissions under FRCP 36. FEDPROF § 23:535.

q. Request for admissions; General form. FEDPROF § 23:536.

r. Request for admissions; Action to collect royalties. FEDPROF § 23:537.

s. Request for admissions; Trademark action. FEDPROF § 23:538.

t. Request for admissions; Automobile negligence action. FEDPROF § 23:539.

u. Request for admissions; Motor vehicle action. FEDPROF § 23:540.

v. Request for admissions; Premises liability action. FEDPROF § 23:541.

w. Request for admissions; Products liability action. FEDPROF § 23:542.

x. Request for admissions; Medical malpractice action. FEDPROF § 23:543.

y. Request for admissions; Genuineness of documents. FEDPROF § 23:544.

z. Request for admissions; Wrongful death due to forklift accident. FEDPROF § 23:545.

I. Applicable Rules

1. *Federal rules*

a. Serving and filing pleadings and other papers. FRCP 5.

b. Privacy protection for filings made with the court. FRCP 5.2.

c. Computing and extending time; Time for motion papers. FRCP 6.

d. Pleadings allowed; Form of motions and other papers. FRCP 7.

e. Form of pleadings. FRCP 10.

f. Signing pleadings, motions, and other papers; Representations to the court; Sanctions. FRCP 11.

g. Duty to disclose; General provisions governing discovery. FRCP 26.

h. Stipulations about discovery procedure. FRCP 29.

i. Requests for admission. FRCP 36.

j. Failure to make disclosures or to cooperate in discovery; Sanctions. FRCP 37.

2. *Local rules*

a. Scope of the rules. IN R USDCTSD L.R. 1-1.

b. Sanctions for errors as to form. IN R USDCTSD L.R. 1-3.

c. Format of documents presented for filing. IN R USDCTSD L.R. 5-1.

d. Filing of documents electronically required. IN R USDCTSD L.R. 5-2.

e. Eligibility, registration, passwords for electronic filing; Exemption from electronic filing. IN R USDCTSD L.R. 5-3.

f. Timing and consequences of electronic filing. IN R USDCTSD L.R. 5-4.

g. Attachments and exhibits in cases filed electronically. IN R USDCTSD L.R. 5-6.

h. Signatures in cases filed electronically. IN R USDCTSD L.R. 5-7.

i. Non-electronic filings. IN R USDCTSD L.R. 5-10.

j. Motion practice. [IN R USDCTSD L.R. 7-1, as amended by IN ORDER 16-2319, effective December 1, 2016].

k. Form of certain discovery requests. IN R USDCTSD L.R. 26-1.

l. Filing of discovery materials. IN R USDCTSD L.R. 26-2.

m. Requests for admissions. IN R USDCTSD L.R. 36-1.

n. Assignment of cases. IN R USDCTSD L.R. 40-1.

o. Alternative dispute resolution. IN R USDCTSD A.D.R. Rule 1.1; IN R USDCTSD A.D.R. Rule 1.2; IN R USDCTSD A.D.R. Rule 1.5; IN R USDCTSD A.D.R. Rule 2.1; IN R USDCTSD A.D.R. Rule 2.2.

p. Electronic case filing policies and procedures manual. IN R USDCTSD ECF Procedures.

Requests, Notices and Applications
Response to Request for Admissions

Document Last Updated December 2016

A. Checklist

(I) ❑ Matters to be considered by requesting party

  (a) ❑ Required documents

    (1) ❑ Request for admissions

  (b) ❑ Supplemental documents

    (1) ❑ Document(s)

    (2) ❑ Certificate of service

  (c) ❑ Timing

    (1) ❑ A party may not seek discovery from any source before the parties have conferred as required by FRCP 26(f), except in a proceeding exempted from initial disclosure under FRCP 26(a)(1)(B), or when authorized by the Federal Rules of Civil Procedure, by stipulation, or by court order

(II) ❑ Matters to be considered by responding party

  (a) ❑ Required documents

    (1) ❑ Response to request for admissions

    (b) ❑ Supplemental documents

        (1) ❑ Certificate of service

    (c) ❑ Timing

        (1) ❑ A matter is admitted unless, within thirty (30) days after being served, the party to whom the request is directed serves on the requesting party a written answer or objection addressed to the matter and signed by the party or its attorney

B. Timing

1. *Response to request for admissions.* A matter is admitted unless, within thirty (30) days after being served, the party to whom the request is directed serves on the requesting party a written answer or objection addressed to the matter and signed by the party or its attorney. A shorter or longer time for responding may be stipulated to under FRCP 29 or be ordered by the court. FRCP 36(a)(3).

2. *Automatic initial extension.* The deadline for filing a response to a pleading or to any written request for discovery or admissions will automatically be extended upon filing a notice of the extension with the court that states: (1) the deadline has not been previously extended; (2) the extension is for twenty-eight (28) or fewer days; (3) the extension does not interfere with the Case Management Plan, scheduled hearings, or other case deadlines; (4) the original deadline and extended deadline; (5) that all opposing counsel the filing attorney could reach agreed to the extension; or that the filing attorney could not reach any opposing counsel, and providing the dates, times and manner of all attempts to reach opposing counsel. IN R USDCTSD L.R. 6-1(b).

    a. *Pro se parties.* The automatic initial extension does not apply to pro se parties. IN R USDCTSD L.R. 6-1(c).

3. *Computation of time*

    a. *Computing time.* FRCP 6 applies in computing any time period specified in the Federal Rules of Civil Procedure, in any local rule or court order, or in any statute that does not specify a method of computing time. FRCP 6(a).

        i. *Period stated in days or a longer unit.* When the period is stated in days or a longer unit of time:

- Exclude the day of the event that triggers the period;
- Count every day, including intermediate Saturdays, Sundays, and legal holidays; and
- Include the last day of the period, but if the last day is a Saturday, Sunday, or legal holiday, the period continues to run until the end of the next day that is not a Saturday, Sunday, or legal holiday. FRCP 6(a)(1).

        ii. *Period stated in hours.* When the period is stated in hours:

- Begin counting immediately on the occurrence of the event that triggers the period;
- Count every hour, including hours during intermediate Saturdays, Sundays, and legal holidays; and
- If the period would end on a Saturday, Sunday, or legal holiday, the period continues to run until the same time on the next day that is not a Saturday, Sunday, or legal holiday. FRCP 6(a)(2).

        iii. *Inaccessibility of the clerk's office.* Unless the court orders otherwise, if the clerk's office is inaccessible:

- On the last day for filing under FRCP 6(a)(1), then the time for filing is extended to the first accessible day that is not a Saturday, Sunday, or legal holiday; or
- During the last hour for filing under FRCP 6(a)(2), then the time for filing is extended to the same time on the first accessible day that is not a Saturday, Sunday, or legal holiday. FRCP 6(a)(3).

        iv. *"Last day" defined.* Unless a different time is set by a statute, local rule, or court order, the last day ends:

- For electronic filing, at midnight in the court's time zone; and

- For filing by other means, when the clerk's office is scheduled to close. FRCP 6(a)(4).

v. *"Next day" defined.* The "next day" is determined by continuing to count forward when the period is measured after an event and backward when measured before an event. FRCP 6(a)(5).

vi. *"Legal holiday" defined.* "Legal holiday" means:

- The day set aside by statute for observing New Year's Day, Martin Luther King Jr.'s Birthday, Washington's Birthday, Memorial Day, Independence Day, Labor Day, Columbus Day, Veterans' Day, Thanksgiving Day, or Christmas Day;

- Any day declared a holiday by the President or Congress; and

- For periods that are measured after an event, any other day declared a holiday by the state where the district court is located. FRCP 6(a)(6).

b. *Computation of electronic filing deadlines.* Filing documents electronically does not alter filing deadlines. IN R USDCTSD ECF Procedures(7). A document due on a particular day must be filed before midnight local time of the division where the case is pending. IN R USDCTSD L.R. 5-4(a). All electronic transmissions of documents must be completed (i.e. received completely by the Clerk's Office) prior to midnight of the local time of the division in which the case is pending in order to be considered timely filed that day (NOTE: time will be noted in Eastern Time on the Court's docket. If you have filed a document prior to midnight local time of the division in which the case is pending and the document is due that date, but the electronic receipt and docket reflect the following calendar day, please contact the Court). IN R USDCTSD ECF Procedures(7). Although attorneys may file documents electronically twenty-four (24) hours a day, seven (7) days a week, attorneys are encouraged to file all documents during the normal working hours of the Clerk's Office (Monday through Friday, 8:30 a.m. to 4:30 p.m.) when technical support is available. IN R USDCTSD ECF Procedures(7); IN R USDCTSD ECF Procedures(9).

i. *Technical difficulties.* Parties are encouraged to file documents electronically during normal business hours, in case a problem is encountered. In the event a technical failure occurs and a document cannot be filed electronically despite the best efforts of the filing party, the party should print (if possible) a copy of the error message received. In addition, as soon as practically possible, the party should file a "Declaration that Party was Unable to File in a Timely Manner Due to Technical Difficulties." A model form is provided as Appendix D (IN R USDCTSD ECF Procedures(Appendix D)). IN R USDCTSD ECF Procedures(16).

- If a party is unable to file electronically and, as a result, may miss a filing deadline, the party must contact the Clerk's Office at the number listed in IN R USDCTSD ECF Procedures(15) to inform the court's staff of the difficulty. If a party misses a filing deadline due to an inability to file electronically, the party may submit the untimely filed document, accompanied by a declaration stating the reason(s) for missing the deadline. Unless the Court orders otherwise, the document and declaration must be filed no later than 12:00 noon of the first day on which the Court is open for business following the original filing deadline. IN R USDCTSD ECF Procedures(16).

c. *Extending time*

i. *In general.* When an act may or must be done within a specified time, the court may, for good cause, extend the time:

- With or without motion or notice if the court acts, or if a request is made, before the original time or its extension expires; or

- On motion made after the time has expired if the party failed to act because of excusable neglect. FRCP 6(b)(1).

ii. *Exceptions.* A court must not extend the time to act under FRCP 50(b), FRCP 50(d), FRCP 52(b), FRCP 59(b), FRCP 59(d), FRCP 59(e), and FRCP 60(b). FRCP 6(b)(2).

iii. Refer to the United States District Court for the Southern District of Indiana KeyRules Motion for Continuance/Extension of Time document for more information on extending time.

d. *Additional time after certain kinds of service.* When a party may or must act within a specified time after being served and service is made under FRCP 5(b)(2)(C) (mail), FRCP 5(b)(2)(D) (leaving with the clerk), or FRCP 5(b)(2)(F) (other means consented to), three (3) days are added after the period would otherwise expire under FRCP 6(a). FRCP 6(d). Service by electronic mail shall constitute service pursuant to FRCP 5(b)(2)(E) and shall entitle the party being served to the additional three (3) days provided by FRCP 6(d). IN R USDCTSD ECF Procedures(11).

C. General Requirements

1. *General provisions governing discovery*

   a. *Discovery scope and limits*

      i. *Scope in general.* Unless otherwise limited by court order, the scope of discovery is as follows: Parties may obtain discovery regarding any nonprivileged matter that is relevant to any party's claim or defense and proportional to the needs of the case, considering the importance of the issues at stake in the action, the amount in controversy, the parties' relative access to relevant information, the parties' resources, the importance of the discovery in resolving the issues, and whether the burden or expense of the proposed discovery outweighs its likely benefit. Information within this scope of discovery need not be admissible in evidence to be discoverable. FRCP 26(b)(1).

      ii. *Limitations on frequency and extent*

         • *When permitted.* By order, the court may alter the limits in the Federal Rules of Civil Procedure on the number of depositions and interrogatories or on the length of depositions under FRCP 30. By order or local rule, the court may also limit the number of requests under FRCP 36. FRCP 26(b)(2)(A).

         • *Specific limitations on electronically stored information.* A party need not provide discovery of electronically stored information from sources that the party identifies as not reasonably accessible because of undue burden or cost. On motion to compel discovery or for a protective order, the party from whom discovery is sought must show that the information is not reasonably accessible because of undue burden or cost. If that showing is made, the court may nonetheless order discovery from such sources if the requesting party shows good cause, considering the limitations of FRCP 26(b)(2)(C). The court may specify conditions for the discovery. FRCP 26(b)(2)(B).

         • *When required.* On motion or on its own, the court must limit the frequency or extent of discovery otherwise allowed by the Federal Rules of Civil Procedure or by local rule if it determines that: (1) the discovery sought is unreasonably cumulative or duplicative, or can be obtained from some other source that is more convenient, less burdensome, or less expensive; (2) the party seeking discovery has had ample opportunity to obtain the information by discovery in the action; or (3) the proposed discovery is outside the scope permitted by FRCP 26(b)(1). FRCP 26(b)(2)(C).

      iii. *Trial preparation; Materials*

         • *Documents and tangible things.* Ordinarily, a party may not discover documents and tangible things that are prepared in anticipation of litigation or for trial by or for another party or its representative (including the other party's attorney, consultant, surety, indemnitor, insurer, or agent). But, subject to FRCP 26(b)(4), those materials may be discovered if: (1) they are otherwise discoverable under FRCP 26(b)(1); and (2) the party shows that it has substantial need for the materials to prepare its case and cannot, without undue hardship, obtain their substantial equivalent by other means. FRCP 26(b)(3)(A).

         • *Protection against disclosure.* If the court orders discovery of those materials, it must protect against disclosure of the mental impressions, conclusions, opinions, or legal theories of a party's attorney or other representative concerning the litigation. FRCP 26(b)(3)(B).

         • *Previous statement.* Any party or other person may, on request and without the required showing, obtain the person's own previous statement about the action or its subject matter. If the request is refused, the person may move for a court order, and FRCP 37(a)(5) applies to the award of expenses. A previous statement is either: (1) a written statement that the person has signed or otherwise adopted or approved; or (2) a contemporaneous steno-graphic, mechanical, electrical, or other recording—or a transcription of it—that recites substantially verbatim the person's oral statement. FRCP 26(b)(3)(C).

iv. *Trial preparation; Experts*

- *Deposition of an expert who may testify.* A party may depose any person who has been identified as an expert whose opinions may be presented at trial. If FRCP 26(a)(2)(B) requires a report from the expert, the deposition may be conducted only after the report is provided. FRCP 26(b)(4)(A).

- *Trial-preparation protection for draft reports or disclosures.* FRCP 26(b)(3)(A) and FRCP 26(b)(3)(B) protect drafts of any report or disclosure required under FRCP 26(a)(2), regardless of the form in which the draft is recorded. FRCP 26(b)(4)(B).

- *Trial-preparation protection for communications between a party's attorney and expert witnesses.* FRCP 26(b)(3)(A) and FRCP 26(b)(3)(B) protect communications between the party's attorney and any witness required to provide a report under FRCP 26(a)(2)(B), regardless of the form of the communications, except to the extent that the communica-tions: (1) relate to compensation for the expert's study or testimony; (2) identify facts or data that the party's attorney provided and that the expert considered in forming the opinions to be expressed; or (3) identify assumptions that the party's attorney provided and that the expert relied on in forming the opinions to be expressed. FRCP 26(b)(4)(C).

- *Expert employed only for trial preparation.* Ordinarily, a party may not, by interrogatories or deposition, discover facts known or opinions held by an expert who has been retained or specially employed by another party in anticipation of litigation or to prepare for trial and who is not expected to be called as a witness at trial. But a party may do so only: (1) as provided in FRCP 35(b); or (2) on showing exceptional circumstances under which it is impracticable for the party to obtain facts or opinions on the same subject by other means. FRCP 26(b)(4)(D).

- *Payment.* Unless manifest injustice would result, the court must require that the party seeking discovery: (1) pay the expert a reasonable fee for time spent in responding to discovery under FRCP 26(b)(4)(A) or FRCP 26(b)(4)(D); and (2) for discovery under FRCP 26(b)(4)(D), also pay the other party a fair portion of the fees and expenses it reasonably incurred in obtaining the expert's facts and opinions. FRCP 26(b)(4)(E).

v. *Claiming privilege or protecting trial-preparation materials*

- *Information withheld.* When a party withholds information otherwise discoverable by claiming that the information is privileged or subject to protection as trial-preparation material, the party must: (1) expressly make the claim; and (2) describe the nature of the documents, communications, or tangible things not produced or disclosed—and do so in a manner that, without revealing information itself privileged or protected, will enable other parties to assess the claim. FRCP 26(b)(5)(A).

- *Information produced.* If information produced in discovery is subject to a claim of privilege or of protection as trial-preparation material, the party making the claim may notify any party that received the information of the claim and the basis for it. After being notified, a party must promptly return, sequester, or destroy the specified information and any copies it has; must not use or disclose the information until the claim is resolved; must take reasonable steps to retrieve the information if the party disclosed it before being notified; and may promptly present the information to the court under seal for a determi-nation of the claim. The producing party must preserve the information until the claim is resolved. FRCP 26(b)(5)(B).

b. *Protective orders.* A party or any person from whom discovery is sought may move for a protective order in the court where the action is pending—or as an alternative on matters relating to a deposition, in the court for the district where the deposition will be taken. FRCP 26(c)(1). Refer to the United States District Court for the Southern District of Indiana KeyRules Motion for Protective Order document for more information.

    c.   *Sequence of discovery.* Unless the parties stipulate or the court orders otherwise for the parties' and witnesses' convenience and in the interests of justice: (1) methods of discovery may be used in any sequence; and (2) discovery by one party does not require any other party to delay its discovery. FRCP 26(d)(3).

2.   *Response to request for admissions*

    a.   *Form.* A party responding (by answer or objection) to written discovery must fully quote each interrogatory or request immediately before each response and number each response to correspond with the interrogatory or request. IN R USDCTSD L.R. 26-1(b). The response to a request for admissions must be in writing and signed by the party or its attorney. FPP § 2259. The response should be a single document, in which the various requests are listed in order and an admission, a denial, an objection, or a statement of inability to admit or deny made to each of the requests as is appropriate. FPP § 2259.

    b.   *Answer.* If a matter is not admitted, the answer must specifically deny it or state in detail why the answering party cannot truthfully admit or deny it. FRCP 36(a)(4).

        i.   *Denial.* A denial must fairly respond to the substance of the matter; and when good faith requires that a party qualify an answer or deny only a part of a matter, the answer must specify the part admitted and qualify or deny the rest. FRCP 36(a)(4). It is expected that denials will be forthright, specific, and unconditional. If a response is thought insufficient as a denial, the court may treat it as an admission. FPP § 2260.

       ii.   *Lack of knowledge or information.* The answering party may assert lack of knowledge or information as a reason for failing to admit or deny only if the party states that it has made reasonable inquiry and that the information it knows or can readily obtain is insufficient to enable it to admit or deny. FRCP 36(a)(4). A general statement that it can neither admit nor deny, unaccompanied by reasons, will be held an insufficient response, and the court may either take the matter as admitted or order a further answer. FPP § 2261.

    c.   *Objections.* Objections must be made in writing within the time allowed for answering the request. If some requests are to be answered and others objected to, the answers and objections should be contained in a single document. FPP § 2262. The grounds for objecting to a request must be stated. A party must not object solely on the ground that the request presents a genuine issue for trial. FRCP 36(a)(5). Failure to object to a request waives the objection. FPP § 2262.

    d.   *Motion regarding the sufficiency of an answer or objection.* The requesting party may move to determine the sufficiency of an answer or objection. Unless the court finds an objection justified, it must order that an answer be served. On finding that an answer does not comply with FRCP 36, the court may order either that the matter is admitted or that an amended answer be served. The court may defer its final decision until a pretrial conference or a specified time before trial. FRCP 37(a)(5) applies to an award of expenses. FRCP 36(a)(6). Refer to the United States District Court for the Southern District of Indiana KeyRules Motion for Discovery Sanctions document for more information on sanctions.

    e.   *Effect of an admission; Withdrawing or amending it.* A matter admitted under FRCP 36 is conclusively established unless the court, on motion, permits the admission to be withdrawn or amended. Subject to FRCP 16(e), the court may permit withdrawal or amendment if it would promote the presentation of the merits of the action and if the court is not persuaded that it would prejudice the requesting party in maintaining or defending the action on the merits. An admission under FRCP 36 is not an admission for any other purpose and cannot be used against the party in any other proceeding. FRCP 36(b).

3.   *Supplementing disclosures and responses.* A party who has made a disclosure under FRCP 26(a)—or who has responded to an interrogatory, request for production, or request for admission—must supplement or correct its disclosure or response: (1) in a timely manner if the party learns that in some material respect the disclosure or response is incomplete or incorrect, and if the additional or corrective information has

not otherwise been made known to the other parties during the discovery process or in writing; or (2) as ordered by the court. FRCP 26(e)(1).

4. *Sanctions for failure to cooperate in discovery.* The pattern of sanctions for FRCP 36 is somewhat different from that for the other discovery rules. The most important sanctions are two:

   a. A failure to respond to a request is deemed an admission of the matter to which the request is directed; and

   b. A party who, without good reason, refuses to admit a matter will be required to pay the costs incurred in proving that matter. FPP § 2265. If a party fails to admit what is requested under FRCP 36 and if the requesting party later proves a document to be genuine or the matter true, the requesting party may move that the party who failed to admit pay the reasonable expenses, including attorney's fees, incurred in making that proof. The court must so order unless:

      i. The request was held objectionable under FRCP 36(a);

      ii. The admission sought was of no substantial importance;

      iii. The party failing to admit had a reasonable ground to believe that it might prevail on the matter; or

      iv. There was other good reason for the failure to admit. FRCP 37(c)(2).

   c. Refer to the United States District Court for the Southern District of Indiana KeyRules Motion for Discovery Sanctions document for more information on sanctions.

5. *Stipulations about discovery procedure.* Unless the court orders otherwise, the parties may stipulate that: (1) a deposition may be taken before any person, at any time or place, on any notice, and in the manner specified—in which event it may be used in the same way as any other deposition; and (2) other procedures governing or limiting discovery be modified—but a stipulation extending the time for any form of discovery must have court approval if it would interfere with the time set for completing discovery, for hearing a motion, or for trial. FRCP 29.

6. *Appearances.* Every attorney who represents a party or who files a document on a party's behalf must file an appearance for that party. IN R USDCTSD L.R. 83-7. The filing of a Notice of Appearance shall act to establish the filing attorney as an attorney of record representing a designated party or parties in a particular cause of action. As a result, it is necessary for each attorney to file a separate Notice of Appearance when entering an appearance in a case. A joint appearance on behalf of multiple attorneys may be filed electronically only if it is filed separately for each attorney, using his/her ECF login. IN R USDCTSD ECF Procedures(12). Only those attorneys who have filed an appearance in a pending action are entitled to be served with case documents under FRCP 5(a). IN R USDCTSD L.R. 83-7. For more information, refer to IN R USDCTSD L.R. 83-7 and IN R USDCTSD ECF Procedures(12).

7. *Notice of related action.* A party must file a notice of related action: as soon as it appears that the party's case and another pending case: (1) arise out of the same transaction or occurrence; (2) involve the same property; or (3) involve the validity or infringement or the same patent, trademark, or copyright. IN R USDCTSD L.R. 40-1(d)(2). For more information, refer to IN R USDCTSD L.R. 40-1.

8. *Alternative dispute resolution (ADR)*

   a. *Application.* Unless limited by specific provisions, or unless there are other applicable specific statutory, common law, or constitutional procedures, the Local Alternative Dispute Resolution Rules of the United States District Court for the Southern District of Indiana shall apply in all civil litigation filed in the U.S. District Court for the Southern District of Indiana, except in the following cases and proceedings:

      i. Applications for writs of habeas corpus under 28 U.S.C.A. § 2254;

      ii. Forfeiture cases;

      iii. Non-adversary proceedings in bankruptcy;

      iv. Social Security administrative review cases; and

      v. Such other matters as specified by order of the Court; for example, matters involving important public policy issues, constitutional law, or the establishment of new law. IN R USDCTSD A.D.R. Rule 1.2.

b. *Mediation.* Mediation under this section (IN R USDCTSD A.D.R. Rule 2.1, et seq.) involves the confidential process by which a person acting as a Mediator, selected by the parties or appointed by the Court, assists the litigants in reaching a mutually acceptable agreement. It is an informal and nonadversarial process. The role of the Mediator is to assist in identifying the issues, reducing misunderstandings, clarifying priorities, exploring areas of compromise, and finding points of agreement as well as legitimate points of disagreement. Final decision-making authority rests with the parties, not the Mediator. IN R USDCTSD A.D.R. Rule 2.1. It is anticipated that an agreement may not resolve all of the disputed issues, but the process, nonetheless, can reduce points of contention. Parties and their representatives are required to mediate in good faith, but are not compelled to reach an agreement. IN R USDCTSD A.D.R. Rule 2.1.

   i. *Case selection.* The Court with the agreement of the parties may refer a civil case for mediation. Unless otherwise ordered or as specifically provided in IN R USDCTSD A.D.R. Rule 2.8, referral to mediation does not abate or suspend the action, and no scheduled dates shall be delayed or deferred, including the date of trial. IN R USDCTSD A.D.R. Rule 2.2.

   ii. For more information on mediation, refer to IN R USDCTSD A.D.R. Rule 2.1, et seq.

c. *Other methods of dispute resolution.* The Local Alternative Dispute Resolution Rules of the United States District Court for the Southern District of Indiana shall not preclude the parties from utilizing any other reasonable method or technique of alternative dispute resolution to resolve disputes to which the parties agree. However, any use of arbitration by the parties will be governed by and comply with the requirements of 28 U.S.C.A. § 654 through 28 U.S.C.A. § 657. IN R USDCTSD A.D.R. Rule 1.5.

d. For more information on alternative dispute resolution (ADR), refer to IN R USDCTSD A.D.R. Rule 1.1, et seq.

9. *Notice of settlement or resolution.* The parties must immediately notify the court if they reasonably anticipate settling their case or resolving a pending motion. IN R USDCTSD L.R. 7-1(h).

10. *Modification or suspension of rules.* The court may, on its own motion or at the request of a party, suspend or modify any rule in a particular case in the interest of justice. IN R USDCTSD L.R. 1-1(c).

D. Documents

1. *Required documents*

   a. *Response to request for admissions.* Refer to the General Requirements section of this document for information on the response to request for admissions.

2. *Supplemental documents*

   a. *Certificate of service.* FRCP 5(d) requires that the person making service under FRCP 5 certify that service has been effected. FRCP 5(Advisory Committee Notes). Having such information on file may be useful for many purposes, including proof of service if an issue arises concerning the effectiveness of the service. FRCP 5(Advisory Committee Notes).

E. Format

1. *Form of documents.* The rules governing captions and other matters of form in pleadings apply to motions and other papers. FRCP 7(b)(2).

   a. *Paper (manual filings only).* Any document that is not filed electronically must: be flat, unfolded, and on good-quality, eight and one-half by eleven (8-1/2 x 11) inch white paper. IN R USDCTSD L.R. 5-1(d)(1). Any document that is not filed electronically must: be single-sided. IN R USDCTSD L.R. 5-1(d)(1).

      i. *Covers or backing.* Any document that is not filed electronically must: not have a cover or a back. IN R USDCTSD L.R. 5-1(d)(1).

      ii. *Fastening.* Any document that is not filed electronically must: be (if consisting of more than one (1) page) fastened by paperclip or binder clip and may not be stapled. IN R USDCTSD L.R. 5-1(d)(1).

         • *Request for nonconforming fastening.* If a document cannot be fastened or bound as

required by IN R USDCTSD L.R. 5-1(d), a party may ask the clerk for permission to fasten it in another manner. The party must make such a request before attempting to file the document with nonconforming fastening. IN R USDCTSD L.R. 5-1(d)(2).

iii. *Hole punching.* Any document that is not filed electronically must: be two-hole punched at the top with the holes two and three-quarter (2-3/4) inches apart and appropriately centered. IN R USDCTSD L.R. 5-1(d)(1).

b. *Margins.* Any pleading, motion, brief, affidavit, notice, or proposed order filed with the court, whether electronically or with the clerk, must: have at least one (1) inch margins. IN R USDCTSD L.R. 5-1(b).

c. *Spacing.* Any pleading, motion, brief, affidavit, notice, or proposed order filed with the court, whether electronically or with the clerk, must: be double spaced (except for headings, footnotes, and quoted material). IN R USDCTSD L.R. 5-1(b).

d. *Text.* Any pleading, motion, brief, affidavit, notice, or proposed order filed with the court, whether electronically or with the clerk, must: be plainly typewritten, printed, or prepared by a clearly legible copying process. IN R USDCTSD L.R. 5-1(b).

e. *Font size.* Any pleading, motion, brief, affidavit, notice, or proposed order filed with the court, whether electronically or with the clerk, must: use at least 12-point type in the body of the document and at least 10-point type in footnotes. IN R USDCTSD L.R. 5-1(b).

f. *Page numbering.* Any pleading, motion, brief, affidavit, notice, or proposed order filed with the court, whether electronically or with the clerk, must: have consecutively numbered pages. IN R USDCTSD L.R. 5-1(b).

g. *Caption; Names of parties.* Every pleading must have a caption with the court's name, a title, a file number, and a FRCP 7(a) designation. The title of the complaint must name all the parties; the title of other pleadings, after naming the first party on each side, may refer generally to other parties. FRCP 10(a). Any pleading, motion, brief, affidavit, notice, or proposed order filed with the court, whether electronically or with the clerk, must: include a title on the first page. IN R USDCTSD L.R. 5-1(b).

h. *Filer's information.* Any pleading, motion, brief, affidavit, notice, or proposed order filed with the court, whether electronically or with the clerk, must: in the case of pleadings, motions, legal briefs, and notices, include the name, complete address, telephone number, facsimile number (where available), and e-mail address (where available) of the pro se litigant or attorney who files it. IN R USDCTSD L.R. 5-1(b).

i. *Paragraphs; Separate statements.* A party must state its claims or defenses in numbered paragraphs, each limited as far as practicable to a single set of circumstances. A later pleading may refer by number to a paragraph in an earlier pleading. If doing so would promote clarity, each claim founded on a separate transaction or occurrence—and each defense other than a denial—must be stated in a separate count or defense. FRCP 10(b).

j. *Adoption by reference; Exhibits.* A statement in a pleading may be adopted by reference elsewhere in the same pleading or in any other pleading or motion. A copy of a written instrument that is an exhibit to a pleading is a part of the pleading for all purposes. FRCP 10(c).

k. *Citations*

i. *Local rules.* The Local Rules of the United States District Court for the Southern District of Indiana may be cited as "S.D. Ind. L.R." IN R USDCTSD L.R. 1-1(a).

ii. *Local alternative dispute resolution rules.* These Rules shall be known as the Local Alternative Dispute Resolution Rules of the United States District Court for the Southern District of Indiana. They shall be cited as "S.D.Ind. Local A.D.R. Rule _____." IN R USDCTSD A.D.R. Rule 1.1.

l. *Acceptance by the clerk.* The clerk must not refuse to file a paper solely because it is not in the form prescribed by the Federal Rules of Civil Procedure or by a local rule or practice. FRCP 5(d)(4). The clerk will accept a document that violates IN R USDCTSD L.R. 5-1, but the court may exclude the document from the official record. IN R USDCTSD L.R. 5-1(e).

    i.   *Sanctions for errors as to form.* The court may strike from the record any document that does not comply with the rules governing the form of documents filed with the court, such as rules that regulate document size or the number of copies to be filed or that require a special designation in the caption. The court may also sanction an attorney or party who files a non-compliant document. IN R USDCTSD L.R. 1-3.

2. *Form of electronic documents.* Any document submitted via the court's electronic case filing (ECF) system must be: otherwise prepared and filed in a manner consistent with the CM/ECF Policies and Procedures Manual (IN R USDCTSD ECF Procedures). IN R USDCTSD L.R. 5-1(c). Electronically filed documents must meet the requirements of FRCP 10 (Form of Pleadings), IN R USDCTSD L.R. 5-1 (Format of Papers Presented for Filing), and FRCP 5.2 (Privacy Protection for Filings Made with the Court), as if they had been submitted on paper. Documents filed electronically are also subject to any page limitations set forth by Court Order, by IN R USDCTSD L.R. 7-1 (Motion Practice), or IN R USDCTSD L.R. 56-1 (Summary Judgment Practice), as applicable. IN R USDCTSD ECF Procedures(13).

  a. *PDF format required.* Any document submitted via the court's electronic case filing (ECF) system must be: in .pdf format. IN R USDCTSD L.R. 5-1(c); IN R USDCTSD ECF Procedures(7). Any document submitted via the court's electronic case filing (ECF) system must be: converted to a .pdf file directly from a word processing program, unless it exists only in paper format (in which case it may be scanned to create a .pdf document). IN R USDCTSD L.R. 5-1(c); IN R USDCTSD ECF Procedures(13).

    i.   An exhibit may be scanned into PDF format, at a recommended 300 dpi resolution or higher, only if it does not already exist in electronic format. The filing attorney is responsible for reviewing all PDF documents for legibility before submitting them through the Court's Electronic Case Filing system. For technical guidance in creating PDF documents, please contact the Clerk's Office. IN R USDCTSD ECF Procedures(13).

  b. *File size limitations.* Any document submitted via the court's electronic case filing (ECF) system must be: submitted as one or more .pdf files that do not exceed ten megabytes (10 MB) each (consistent with the CM/ECF Policies and Procedures Manual (IN R USDCTSD ECF Procedures)). IN R USDCTSD L.R. 5-1(c); IN R USDCTSD ECF Procedures(13).

    i.   To electronically file a document or attachment that exceeds ten megabytes (10 MB), the document must first be broken down into two or more smaller files. For example, if Exhibit A is a twelve megabyte (12 MB) PDF file, it should be divided into 2 equal parts prior to electronic filing. Each component part of the exhibit would be filed as an attachment to the main document and described appropriately as "Exhibit A (part 1 of 2)" and "Exhibit A (part 2 of 2)." IN R USDCTSD ECF Procedures(13).

    ii. The supporting items mentioned in IN R USDCTSD ECF Procedures(13) should not be confused with memorandums or briefs in support of motions as outlined in IN R USDCTSD L.R. 7-1 or IN R USDCTSD L.R. 56-1. These memorandums or briefs in support are to be filed as entirely separate documents pursuant to the appropriate rule. Additionally, no motion shall be embodied in the text of a response or reply brief/memorandum unless otherwise ordered by the Court. IN R USDCTSD ECF Procedures(13).

  c. *Separate component parts.* A key objective of the electronic filing system is to ensure that as much of the case as possible is managed electronically. To facilitate electronic filing and retrieval, documents to be filed electronically are to be reasonably broken into their separate component parts. By way of example, most filings include a foundation document (e.g., motion) and other supporting items (e.g., exhibits, proposed orders, proposed amended pleadings). The foundation document, as well as the supporting items, are each separate components of the filing; supporting items must be filed as attachments to the foundation document. These exhibits or attachments should include only those excerpts of the referenced documents that are directly germane to the matter under consideration. IN R USDCTSD ECF Procedures(13).

    i.   Where an individual component cannot be included in an electronic filing (e.g. the component

cannot be converted to electronic format), the filer shall electronically file the prescribed Notice of Manual Filing in place of that component. A model form is provided as Appendix C (IN R USDCTSD ECF Procedures(Appendix C)). IN R USDCTSD ECF Procedures(13).

d. *Exhibits.* Each electronically filed exhibit to a main document must be: (1) created as a separate .pdf file; (2) submitted as an attachment to the main document and given a title which describes its content; and (3) limited to excerpts that are directly germane to the main document's subject matter. IN R USDCTSD L.R. 5-6(a).

    i. When uploading attachments during the electronic filing process, exhibits must be uploaded in a logical sequence and a brief description must be entered for each individual PDF file. The description must include not only the exhibit number or letter, but also a brief description of the document. This information may be entered in CM/ECF using a combination of the Category drop-down menu, the Description text box, or both (see IN R USDCTSD ECF Procedures(13)(Figure 1)). The information that is provided in each box will be combined to create a description of the document as it appears on the case docket (see IN R USDCTSD ECF Procedures(13)(Figure 2)). IN R USDCTSD ECF Procedures(13). For an example, refer to IN R USDCTSD ECF Procedures(13).

e. *Excerpts.* A party filing an exhibit that consists of excerpts from a larger document must clearly and prominently identify the exhibit as containing excerpted material. Either party will have the right to timely file additional excerpts or the complete document to the extent they are or become directly germane to the main document's subject matter. IN R USDCTSD L.R. 5-6(b).

f. For an example illustrating the application of IN R USDCTSD ECF Procedures(13), refer to IN R USDCTSD ECF Procedures(13).

3. *Signing disclosures and discovery requests, responses, and objections.* FRCP 11 does not apply to disclosures and discovery requests, responses, objections, and motions under FRCP 26 through FRCP 37. FRCP 11(d).

a. *Signature required.* Every disclosure under FRCP 26(a)(1) or FRCP 26(a)(3) and every discovery request, response, or objection must be signed by at least one attorney of record in the attorney's own name—or by the party personally, if unrepresented—and must state the signer's address, e-mail address, and telephone number. FRCP 26(g)(1).

    i. *Signatures on manual filings.* Any document that is not filed electronically must: include the original signature of the pro se litigant or attorney who files it. IN R USDCTSD L.R. 5-1(d)(1).

    ii. *Electronic signatures.* Use of the attorney's login and password when filing documents electronically serves in part as the attorney's signature for purposes of FRCP 11, the Local Rules of the United States District Court for the Southern District of Indiana, and any other purpose for which a signature is required in connection with proceedings before the Court. IN R USDCTSD ECF Procedures(14); IN R USDCTSD ECF Procedures(10). A pleading, motion, brief, or notice filed electronically under an attorney's ECF log-in and password must be signed by that attorney. IN R USDCTSD L.R. 5-7(a). A signature on a document other than a document filed as provided under IN R USDCTSD L.R. 5-7(a) must be an original handwritten signature and must be scanned into .pdf format for electronic filing. IN R USDCTSD L.R. 5-7(c); IN R USDCTSD ECF Procedures(14).

        • *Form of electronic signature.* If a document is converted directly from a word processing application to .pdf (as opposed to scanning), the name of the Filing User under whose log-in and password the document is submitted must be preceded by a "s/" and typed on the signature line where the Filing User's handwritten signature would otherwise appear. IN R USDCTSD L.R. 5-7(b). All documents filed electronically shall include a signature block and include the filing attorney's typewritten name, address, telephone number, facsimile number and e-mail address. In addition, the name of the filing attorney under whose ECF login the document will be filed should be preceded by a "s/" and typed in the space where the attorney's handwritten signature would otherwise appear. IN R US-DCTSD ECF Procedures(14). For a sample format, refer to IN R USDCTSD ECF Procedures(14).

- *Effect of electronic signature.* Filing an electronically signed document under an attorney's ECF log-in and password constitutes the attorney's signature on the document under the Federal Rules of Civil Procedure, under the Local Rules of the United States District Court for the Southern District of Indiana, and for any other reason a signature is required in connection with the court's activities. IN R USDCTSD L.R. 5-7(d).

- *Documents with multiple attorneys' signatures.* Documents requiring signatures of more than one attorney shall be filed either by: (1) obtaining consent from the other attorney, then typing the "s/ [Name]" signature of the other attorney on the signature line where the other attorney's signature would otherwise appear; (2) identifying in the signature section the name of the other attorney whose signature is required and by the submission of a Notice of Endorsement (see IN R USDCTSD ECF Procedures(Appendix B)) by the other attorney no later than three (3) business days after filing; (3) submitting a scanned document containing all handwritten signatures; or (4) in any other manner approved by the Court. IN R USDCTSD ECF Procedures(14); IN R USDCTSD L.R. 5-7(e).

b. *Effect of signature.* By signing, an attorney or party certifies that to the best of the person's knowledge, information, and belief formed after a reasonable inquiry:

   i.   With respect to a disclosure, it is complete and correct as of the time it is made; and

   ii.   With respect to a discovery request, response, or objection, it is:

- Consistent with the Federal Rules of Civil Procedure and warranted by existing law or by a nonfrivolous argument for extending, modifying, or reversing existing law, or for establishing new law;

- Not interposed for any improper purpose, such as to harass, cause unnecessary delay, or needlessly increase the cost of litigation; and

- Neither unreasonable nor unduly burdensome or expensive, considering the needs of the case, prior discovery in the case, the amount in controversy, and the importance of the issues at stake in the action. FRCP 26(g)(1).

c. *Failure to sign.* Other parties have no duty to act on an unsigned disclosure, request, response, or objection until it is signed, and the court must strike it unless a signature is promptly supplied after the omission is called to the attorney's or party's attention. FRCP 26(g)(2). The court will strike any document filed directly with the clerk that is not signed by an attorney of record or the pro se litigant filing it, but the court may do so only after giving the attorney or pro se litigant notice of the omission and reasonable time to correct it. Rubber-stamp or facsimile signatures are not original signatures and the court will deem documents containing them to be unsigned for purposes of FRCP 11 and FRCP 26(g) and IN R USDCTSD L.R. 5-10. IN R USDCTSD L.R. 5-10(g).

d. *Sanction for improper certification.* If a certification violates FRCP 26(g) without substantial justification, the court, on motion or on its own, must impose an appropriate sanction on the signer, the party on whose behalf the signer was acting, or both. The sanction may include an order to pay the reasonable expenses, including attorney's fees, caused by the violation. FRCP 26(g)(3). Refer to the United States District Court for the Southern District of Indiana KeyRules Motion for Discovery Sanctions document for more information.

4. *Privacy protection for filings made with the court.* Electronically filed documents must meet the requirements of. . .FRCP 5.2 (Privacy Protection for Filings Made with the Court), as if they had been submitted on paper. IN R USDCTSD ECF Procedures(13).

a. *Redacted filings.* Unless the court orders otherwise, in an electronic or paper filing with the court that contains an individual's Social Security number, taxpayer-identification number, or birth date, the name of an individual known to be a minor, or a financial-account number, a party or nonparty making the filing may include only:

   i.   The last four (4) digits of the Social Security number and taxpayer-identification number;

   ii.   The year of the individual's birth;

   iii.   The minor's initials; and

    iv.   The last four (4) digits of the financial-account number. FRCP 5.2(a).

  b. *Exemptions from the redaction requirement.* The redaction requirement does not apply to the following:

    i.   A financial-account number that identifies the property allegedly subject to forfeiture in a forfeiture proceeding;

    ii.   The record of an administrative or agency proceeding;

    iii.   The official record of a state-court proceeding;

    iv.   The record of a court or tribunal, if that record was not subject to the redaction requirement when originally filed;

    v.   A filing covered by FRCP 5.2(c) or FRCP 5.2(d); and

    vi.   A pro se filing in an action brought under 28 U.S.C.A. § 2241, 28 U.S.C.A. § 2254, or 28 U.S.C.A. § 2255. FRCP 5.2(b).

  c. *Limitations on remote access to electronic files; Social Security appeals and immigration cases.* Unless the court orders otherwise, in an action for benefits under the Social Security Act, and in an action or proceeding relating to an order of removal, to relief from removal, or to immigration benefits or detention, access to an electronic file is authorized as follows:

    i.   The parties and their attorneys may have remote electronic access to any part of the case file, including the administrative record;

    ii.   Any other person may have electronic access to the full record at the courthouse, but may have remote electronic access only to:

       • The docket maintained by the court; and

       • An opinion, order, judgment, or other disposition of the court, but not any other part of the case file or the administrative record. FRCP 5.2(c).

  d. *Filings made under seal.* The court may order that a filing be made under seal without redaction. The court may later unseal the filing or order the person who made the filing to file a redacted version for the public record. FRCP 5.2(d). For more information on filing under seal, refer to IN R USDCTSD L.R. 5-11 and IN R USDCTSD ECF Procedures(18).

  e. *Protective orders.* For good cause, the court may by order in a case:

    i.   Require redaction of additional information; or

    ii.   Limit or prohibit a nonparty's remote electronic access to a document filed with the court. FRCP 5.2(e).

  f. *Option for additional unredacted filing under seal.* A person making a redacted filing may also file an unredacted copy under seal. The court must retain the unredacted copy as part of the record. FRCP 5.2(f).

  g. *Option for filing a reference list.* A filing that contains redacted information may be filed together with a reference list that identifies each item of redacted information and specifies an appropriate identifier that uniquely corresponds to each item listed. The list must be filed under seal and may be amended as of right. Any reference in the case to a listed identifier will be construed to refer to the corresponding item of information. FRCP 5.2(g).

  h. *Waiver of protection of identifiers.* A person waives the protection of FRCP 5.2(a) as to the person's own information by filing it without redaction and not under seal. FRCP 5.2(h).

F. Filing and Service Requirements

  1. *Filing requirements.* Any paper after the complaint that is required to be served—together with a certificate of service—must be filed within a reasonable time after service. But disclosures under FRCP 26(a)(1) or FRCP 26(a)(2) and the following discovery requests and responses must not be filed until they are used in the proceeding or the court orders filing: depositions, interrogatories, requests for documents or tangible things or to permit entry onto land, and requests for admission. FRCP 5(d)(1). Refer to the

United States District Court for the Southern District of Indiana KeyRules pleading and motion documents for information on filing with the court.

a. *When discovery may be filed.* Discovery materials (whether discovery requests, responses, or deposition transcripts) may not be filed with the court except in the following circumstances:

   i. *Relevant to certain motions.* A party seeking relief under FRCP 26(c) or FRCP 37, or by way of a pretrial motion that could result in a final order on an issue, must file with the motion those parts of the discovery materials relevant to the motion. IN R USDCTSD L.R. 26-2(a).

   ii. *For anticipated use at trial.* When a party can reasonably anticipate using discovery materials at trial, the party must file the relevant portions at the start of the trial. IN R USDCTSD L.R. 26-2(b).

   iii. *Materials necessary for appeal.* A party seeking for purposes of appeal to supplement the record with discovery materials not previously filed may do so by stipulation of the parties or by court order approving the filing. IN R USDCTSD L.R. 26-2(c).

2. *Service requirements.* A copy of the response must be served upon the party making the request. A copy of the response must also be served on all other parties to the action unless the court has ordered to the contrary. FPP § 2259.

a. *Service; When required*

   i. *In general.* Unless the Federal Rules of Civil Procedure provide otherwise, each of the following papers must be served on every party:

- An order stating that service is required;
- A pleading filed after the original complaint, unless the court orders otherwise under FRCP 5(c) because there are numerous defendants;
- A discovery paper required to be served on a party, unless the court orders otherwise;
- A written motion, except one that may be heard ex parte; and
- A written notice, appearance, demand, or offer of judgment, or any similar paper. FRCP 5(a)(1).

   ii. *If a party fails to appear.* No service is required on a party who is in default for failing to appear. But a pleading that asserts a new claim for relief against such a party must be served on that party under FRCP 4. FRCP 5(a)(2).

   iii. *Seizing property.* If an action is begun by seizing property and no person is or need be named as a defendant, any service required before the filing of an appearance, answer, or claim must be made on the person who had custody or possession of the property when it was seized. FRCP 5(a)(3).

b. *Service; How made*

   i. *Serving an attorney.* If a party is represented by an attorney, service under FRCP 5 must be made on the attorney unless the court orders service on the party. FRCP 5(b)(1).

   ii. *Service in general.* A paper is served under FRCP 5 by:

- Handing it to the person;
- Leaving it: (1) at the person's office with a clerk or other person in charge or, if no one is in charge, in a conspicuous place in the office; or (2) if the person has no office or the office is closed, at the person's dwelling or usual place of abode with someone of suitable age and discretion who resides there;
- Mailing it to the person's last known address—in which event service is complete upon mailing;
- Leaving it with the court clerk if the person has no known address;
- Sending it by electronic means if the person consented in writing—in which event service is complete upon transmission, but is not effective if the serving party learns that it did not reach the person to be served; or

- Delivering it by any other means that the person consented to in writing—in which event service is complete when the person making service delivers it to the agency designated to make delivery. FRCP 5(b)(2).

iii. *Electronic service*

- *Consent.* By registering to use the ECF system, attorneys consent to electronic service of documents filed in cases maintained on the ECF system. IN R USDCTSD L.R. 5-3(d). By participating in the Electronic Case Filing Program, attorneys consent to the electronic service of documents, and shall make available electronic mail addresses for service. IN R USDCTSD ECF Procedures(11).

- *Service on registered parties.* Upon the filing of a document by a party, an e-mail message will be automatically generated by the electronic filing system and sent via electronic mail to the e-mail addresses of all registered attorneys who have appeared in the case. The Notice of Electronic Filing will contain a document hyperlink which will provide recipients with one "free look" at the electronically filed document. Recipients are encouraged to print and/or save a copy of the document during the "free look" to avoid incurring PACER charges for future viewings of the document. IN R USDCTSD ECF Procedures(11). When a document has been filed electronically: transmission of the notice of electronic filing generated by the ECF system to an attorney's e-mail address constitutes service of the document on that attorney. IN R USDCTSD L.R. 5-4(c)(5). The party effectuates service on all registered attorneys by filing electronically. IN R USDCTSD ECF Procedures(11). When a document has been filed electronically: no other attempted service will constitute electronic service of the document. IN R USDCTSD L.R. 5-4(c)(6).

- *Service on exempt parties.* A filer must serve a copy of the document consistent with FRCP 5 on any party or attorney who is exempt from participating in electronic filing. IN R USDCTSD L.R. 5-4(d). It is the responsibility of the filing attorney to conventionally serve all parties who do not receive electronic service (the identity of these parties will be indicated on the filing receipt generated by the ECF system). IN R USDCTSD ECF Procedures(11).

- *Service on parties excused from electronic filing.* Parties otherwise participating in the electronic filing system may be excused from filing a particular component electronically under certain limited circumstances, such as when the component cannot be reduced to an electronic format. Such components shall not be filed electronically, but instead shall be manually filed with the Clerk of Court and served upon the parties in accordance with the applicable Federal Rules of Civil Procedure and the Local Rules of the United States District Court for the Southern District of Indiana for filing and service of non-electronic documents. IN R USDCTSD ECF Procedures(15).

- *Service of exempt documents.* Any document that is exempt from electronic filing must be filed directly with the clerk and served on other parties in the case as required by those Federal Rules of Civil Procedure and Local Rules of the United States District Court for the Southern District of Indiana that apply to the service of non-electronic documents. IN R USDCTSD L.R. 5-2(c).

iv. *Using court facilities.* If a local rule so authorizes, a party may use the court's transmission facilities to make service under FRCP 5(b)(2)(E). FRCP 5(b)(3).

c. *Serving numerous defendants*

i. *In general.* If an action involves an unusually large number of defendants, the court may, on motion or on its own, order that:

- Defendants' pleadings and replies to them need not be served on other defendants;

- Any crossclaim, counterclaim, avoidance, or affirmative defense in those pleadings and replies to them will be treated as denied or avoided by all other parties; and

- Filing any such pleading and serving it on the plaintiff constitutes notice of the pleading to all parties. FRCP 5(c)(1).

       ii.   *Notifying parties.* A copy of every such order must be served on the parties as the court directs. FRCP 5(c)(2).

G. Hearings

    1.   There is no hearing contemplated in the federal statutes or rules for responses to requests for admissions.

H. Forms

1. Federal Response to Request for Admissions Forms

      a.   Reply; To request for admission of facts. AMJUR PP DEPOSITION § 684.

      b.   Reply; To request for admission of facts; With verification. AMJUR PP DEPOSITION § 685.

      c.   Reply; To request for admissions of fact and genuineness of documents; Refusal to answer on ground of privilege. AMJUR PP DEPOSITION § 686.

      d.   Answer; To demand for admissions; Admission or denial not required under governing statute or rule. AMJUR PP DEPOSITION § 687.

      e.   Reply; Objection to request for admissions; Irrelevancy and immateriality; Answer already made in response to interrogatories. AMJUR PP DEPOSITION § 688.

      f.   Response to request for admission. 3B FEDFORMS § 3664.

      g.   Response to request for admission; Admissions, qualified admissions, denials. 3B FEDFORMS § 3665.

      h.   Response to request for admission; Denials and admissions of specific facts and explanatory statement of inability to admit or deny. 3B FEDFORMS § 3666.

      i.   Response to request for admission; Denials and admissions of specific facts and explanatory statement of inability to admit or deny; Another form. 3B FEDFORMS § 3667.

      j.   Objections to requests for admissions. 3B FEDFORMS § 3668.

      k.   Objections to request for admissions; Privileged. 3B FEDFORMS § 3668.50.

      l.   Amended response to request for admission. 3B FEDFORMS § 3669.

     m.   Answer; To request for admissions; General form. FEDPROF § 23:550.

      n.   Answer; To request for admissions; Insurance claim. FEDPROF § 23:551.

      o.   Objections; To request for admissions. FEDPROF § 23:552.

      p.   Objections to request. GOLDLTGFMS § 30:12.

      q.   Reply to request for admissions. GOLDLTGFMS § 30:15.

      r.   Response to request; General form. GOLDLTGFMS § 30:16.

      s.   Response to request; Denials. GOLDLTGFMS § 30:17.

      t.   Response to request; Admission of genuineness of document. GOLDLTGFMS § 30:18.

      u.   Response to request; Admission of facts. GOLDLTGFMS § 30:19.

      v.   Reply and objections to request for admissions. GOLDLTGFMS § 30:20.

I. Applicable Rules

    1.   *Federal rules*

      a.   Serving and filing pleadings and other papers. FRCP 5.

      b.   Privacy protection for filings made with the court. FRCP 5.2.

      c.   Computing and extending time; Time for motion papers. FRCP 6.

      d.   Pleadings allowed; Form of motions and other papers. FRCP 7.

      e.   Form of pleadings. FRCP 10.

      f.   Signing pleadings, motions, and other papers; Representations to the court; Sanctions. FRCP 11.

      g.   Duty to disclose; General provisions governing discovery. FRCP 26.

    h.   Stipulations about discovery procedure. FRCP 29.

    i.   Requests for admission. FRCP 36.

    j.   Failure to make disclosures or to cooperate in discovery; Sanctions. FRCP 37.

2. *Local rules*

    a.   Scope of the rules. IN R USDCTSD L.R. 1-1.

    b.   Sanctions for errors as to form. IN R USDCTSD L.R. 1-3.

    c.   Format of documents presented for filing. IN R USDCTSD L.R. 5-1.

    d.   Filing of documents electronically required. IN R USDCTSD L.R. 5-2.

    e.   Eligibility, registration, passwords for electronic filing; Exemption from electronic filing. IN R USDCTSD L.R. 5-3.

    f.   Timing and consequences of electronic filing. IN R USDCTSD L.R. 5-4.

    g.   Attachments and exhibits in cases filed electronically. IN R USDCTSD L.R. 5-6.

    h.   Signatures in cases filed electronically. IN R USDCTSD L.R. 5-7.

    i.   Non-electronic filings. IN R USDCTSD L.R. 5-10.

    j.   Extensions of time. IN R USDCTSD L.R. 6-1.

    k.   Motion practice. [IN R USDCTSD L.R. 7-1, as amended by IN ORDER 16-2319, effective December 1, 2016].

    l.   Form of certain discovery requests. IN R USDCTSD L.R. 26-1.

    m.   Filing of discovery materials. IN R USDCTSD L.R. 26-2.

    n.   Assignment of cases. IN R USDCTSD L.R. 40-1.

    o.   Alternative dispute resolution. IN R USDCTSD A.D.R. Rule 1.1; IN R USDCTSD A.D.R. Rule 1.2; IN R USDCTSD A.D.R. Rule 1.5; IN R USDCTSD A.D.R. Rule 2.1; IN R USDCTSD A.D.R. Rule 2.2.

    p.   Electronic case filing policies and procedures manual. IN R USDCTSD ECF Procedures.

Requests, Notices and Applications
Notice of Deposition

Document Last Updated December 2016

A. Checklist

(I) ❑ Matters to be considered by deposing party for depositions by oral examination

    (a) ❑ Required documents

        (1) ❑ Notice of deposition

    (b) ❑ Supplemental documents

        (1) ❑ Subpoena

        (2) ❑ Subpoena duces tecum

        (3) ❑ Request for production of documents

        (4) ❑ Certificate of service

    (c) ❑ Timing

        (1) ❑ A party may, by oral questions, depose any person, including a party, without leave of court except as provided in FRCP 30(a)(2)

(2) ❑ A party must obtain leave of court, and the court must grant leave to the extent consistent with FRCP 26(b)(1) and FRCP 26(b)(2):

    (i) ❑ If the parties have not stipulated to the deposition and: (1) the deposition would result in more than ten (10) depositions being taken under FRCP 30 or FRCP 31 by the plaintiffs, or by the defendants, or by the third-party defendants; (2) the deponent has already been deposed in the case; or (3) the party seeks to take the deposition before the time specified in FRCP 26(d), unless the party certifies in the notice, with supporting facts, that the deponent is expected to leave the United States and be unavailable for examination in this country after that time; or

    (ii) ❑ If the deponent is confined in prison

(3) ❑ A party who wants to depose a person by oral questions must give reasonable written notice to every other party

    (i) ❑ Unless agreed by counsel or otherwise ordered by the court, no deposition will be scheduled on less than fourteen (14) days notice

(II) ❑ Matters to be considered by deposing party for depositions by written questions

  (a) ❑ Required documents

    (1) ❑ Notice of deposition

    (2) ❑ Written questions

  (b) ❑ Supplemental documents

    (1) ❑ Subpoena

    (2) ❑ Certificate of service

  (c) ❑ Timing

    (1) ❑ A party may, by written questions, depose any person, including a party, without leave of court except as provided in FRCP 31(a)(2)

    (2) ❑ A party must obtain leave of court, and the court must grant leave to the extent consistent with FRCP 26(b)(1) and FRCP 26(b)(2):

        (i) ❑ If the parties have not stipulated to the deposition and: (1) the deposition would result in more than ten (10) depositions being taken under FRCP 31 or FRCP 30 by the plaintiffs, or by the defendants, or by the third-party defendants; (2) the deponent has already been deposed in the case; or (3) the party seeks to take a deposition before the time specified in FRCP 26(d); or

        (ii) ❑ If the deponent is confined in prison

    (3) ❑ A party who wants to depose a person by written questions must serve them on every other party, with a notice

B. Timing

1. *Depositions by oral examination*

  a. *Without leave.* A party may, by oral questions, depose any person, including a party, without leave of court except as provided in FRCP 30(a)(2). FRCP 30(a)(1).

  b. *With leave.* A party must obtain leave of court, and the court must grant leave to the extent consistent with FRCP 26(b)(1) and FRCP 26(b)(2):

    i. If the parties have not stipulated to the deposition and: (1) the deposition would result in more than ten (10) depositions being taken under FRCP 30 or FRCP 31 by the plaintiffs, or by the defendants, or by the third-party defendants; (2) the deponent has already been deposed in the case; or (3) the party seeks to take the deposition before the time specified in FRCP 26(d), unless the party certifies in the notice, with supporting facts, that the deponent is expected to leave the United States and be unavailable for examination in this country after that time; or

    ii. If the deponent is confined in prison. FRCP 30(a)(2).

    c. *Notice of deposition.* A party who wants to depose a person by oral questions must give reasonable written notice to every other party. FRCP 30(b)(1).

        i. Unless agreed by counsel or otherwise ordered by the court, no deposition will be scheduled on less than fourteen (14) days notice. IN R USDCTSD L.R. 30-1(d).

2. *Depositions by written questions*

    a. *Without leave.* A party may, by written questions, depose any person, including a party, without leave of court except as provided in FRCP 31(a)(2). FRCP 31(a)(1).

    b. *With leave.* A party must obtain leave of court, and the court must grant leave to the extent consistent with FRCP 26(b)(1) and FRCP 26(b)(2):

        i. If the parties have not stipulated to the deposition and: (1) the deposition would result in more than ten (10) depositions being taken under FRCP 31 or FRCP 30 by the plaintiffs, or by the defendants, or by the third-party defendants; (2) the deponent has already been deposed in the case; or (3) the party seeks to take a deposition before the time specified in FRCP 26(d); or

        ii. If the deponent is confined in prison. FRCP 31(a)(2).

    c. *Notice of deposition with written questions.* A party who wants to depose a person by written questions must serve them on every other party, with a notice. FRCP 31(a)(3). Refer to the General Requirements section of this document for the contents of the notice.

    d. *Questions from other parties.* Any questions to the deponent from other parties must be served on all parties as follows:

        i. *Cross-questions.* Cross-questions, within fourteen (14) days after being served with the notice and direct questions;

        ii. *Redirect questions.* Redirect questions, within seven (7) days after being served with cross-questions; and

        iii. *Recross-questions.* Recross-questions, within seven (7) days after being served with redirect questions. FRCP 31(a)(5).

        iv. *Modification of timing requirements.* The court may, for good cause, extend or shorten these times. FRCP 31(a)(5).

3. *Timing of discovery, generally.* A party may not seek discovery from any source before the parties have conferred as required by FRCP 26(f), except in a proceeding exempted from initial disclosure under FRCP 26(a)(1)(B), or when authorized by the Federal Rules of Civil Procedure, by stipulation, or by court order. FRCP 26(d)(1).

4. *Computation of time*

    a. *Computing time.* FRCP 6 applies in computing any time period specified in the Federal Rules of Civil Procedure, in any local rule or court order, or in any statute that does not specify a method of computing time. FRCP 6(a).

        i. *Period stated in days or a longer unit.* When the period is stated in days or a longer unit of time:

- Exclude the day of the event that triggers the period;
- Count every day, including intermediate Saturdays, Sundays, and legal holidays; and
- Include the last day of the period, but if the last day is a Saturday, Sunday, or legal holiday, the period continues to run until the end of the next day that is not a Saturday, Sunday, or legal holiday. FRCP 6(a)(1).

        ii. *Period stated in hours.* When the period is stated in hours:

- Begin counting immediately on the occurrence of the event that triggers the period;
- Count every hour, including hours during intermediate Saturdays, Sundays, and legal holidays; and
- If the period would end on a Saturday, Sunday, or legal holiday, the period continues to run until the same time on the next day that is not a Saturday, Sunday, or legal holiday. FRCP 6(a)(2).

iii. *Inaccessibility of the clerk's office.* Unless the court orders otherwise, if the clerk's office is inaccessible:

- On the last day for filing under FRCP 6(a)(1), then the time for filing is extended to the first accessible day that is not a Saturday, Sunday, or legal holiday; or

- During the last hour for filing under FRCP 6(a)(2), then the time for filing is extended to the same time on the first accessible day that is not a Saturday, Sunday, or legal holiday. FRCP 6(a)(3).

iv. *"Last day" defined.* Unless a different time is set by a statute, local rule, or court order, the last day ends:

- For electronic filing, at midnight in the court's time zone; and

- For filing by other means, when the clerk's office is scheduled to close. FRCP 6(a)(4).

v. *"Next day" defined.* The "next day" is determined by continuing to count forward when the period is measured after an event and backward when measured before an event. FRCP 6(a)(5).

vi. *"Legal holiday" defined.* "Legal holiday" means:

- The day set aside by statute for observing New Year's Day, Martin Luther King Jr.'s Birthday, Washington's Birthday, Memorial Day, Independence Day, Labor Day, Columbus Day, Veterans' Day, Thanksgiving Day, or Christmas Day;

- Any day declared a holiday by the President or Congress; and

- For periods that are measured after an event, any other day declared a holiday by the state where the district court is located. FRCP 6(a)(6).

b. *Computation of electronic filing deadlines.* Filing documents electronically does not alter filing deadlines. IN R USDCTSD ECF Procedures(7). A document due on a particular day must be filed before midnight local time of the division where the case is pending. IN R USDCTSD L.R. 5-4(a). All electronic transmissions of documents must be completed (i.e. received completely by the Clerk's Office) prior to midnight of the local time of the division in which the case is pending in order to be considered timely filed that day (NOTE: time will be noted in Eastern Time on the Court's docket. If you have filed a document prior to midnight local time of the division in which the case is pending and the document is due that date, but the electronic receipt and docket reflect the following calendar day, please contact the Court). IN R USDCTSD ECF Procedures(7). Although attorneys may file documents electronically twenty-four (24) hours a day, seven (7) days a week, attorneys are encouraged to file all documents during the normal working hours of the Clerk's Office (Monday through Friday, 8:30 a.m. to 4:30 p.m.) when technical support is available. IN R USDCTSD ECF Procedures(7); IN R USDCTSD ECF Procedures(9).

i. *Technical difficulties.* Parties are encouraged to file documents electronically during normal business hours, in case a problem is encountered. In the event a technical failure occurs and a document cannot be filed electronically despite the best efforts of the filing party, the party should print (if possible) a copy of the error message received. In addition, as soon as practically possible, the party should file a "Declaration that Party was Unable to File in a Timely Manner Due to Technical Difficulties." A model form is provided as Appendix D (IN R USDCTSD ECF Procedures(Appendix D)). IN R USDCTSD ECF Procedures(16).

- If a party is unable to file electronically and, as a result, may miss a filing deadline, the party must contact the Clerk's Office at the number listed in IN R USDCTSD ECF Procedures(15) to inform the court's staff of the difficulty. If a party misses a filing deadline due to an inability to file electronically, the party may submit the untimely filed document, accompanied by a declaration stating the reason(s) for missing the deadline. Unless the Court orders otherwise, the document and declaration must be filed no later than 12:00 noon of the first day on which the Court is open for business following the original filing deadline. IN R USDCTSD ECF Procedures(16).

   c. *Extending time*

      i. *In general.* When an act may or must be done within a specified time, the court may, for good cause, extend the time:

- With or without motion or notice if the court acts, or if a request is made, before the original time or its extension expires; or

- On motion made after the time has expired if the party failed to act because of excusable neglect. FRCP 6(b)(1).

      ii. *Exceptions.* A court must not extend the time to act under FRCP 50(b), FRCP 50(d), FRCP 52(b), FRCP 59(b), FRCP 59(d), FRCP 59(e), and FRCP 60(b). FRCP 6(b)(2).

      iii. Refer to the United States District Court for the Southern District of Indiana KeyRules Motion for Continuance/Extension of Time document for more information on extending time.

   d. *Additional time after certain kinds of service.* When a party may or must act within a specified time after being served and service is made under FRCP 5(b)(2)(C) (mail), FRCP 5(b)(2)(D) (leaving with the clerk), or FRCP 5(b)(2)(F) (other means consented to), three (3) days are added after the period would otherwise expire under FRCP 6(a). FRCP 6(d). Service by electronic mail shall constitute service pursuant to FRCP 5(b)(2)(E) and shall entitle the party being served to the additional three (3) days provided by FRCP 6(d). IN R USDCTSD ECF Procedures(11).

C. General Requirements

1. *General provisions governing discovery*

   a. *Discovery scope and limits*

      i. *Scope in general.* Unless otherwise limited by court order, the scope of discovery is as follows: Parties may obtain discovery regarding any nonprivileged matter that is relevant to any party's claim or defense and proportional to the needs of the case, considering the importance of the issues at stake in the action, the amount in controversy, the parties' relative access to relevant information, the parties' resources, the importance of the discovery in resolving the issues, and whether the burden or expense of the proposed discovery outweighs its likely benefit. Information within this scope of discovery need not be admissible in evidence to be discoverable. FRCP 26(b)(1).

      ii. *Limitations on frequency and extent*

- *When permitted.* By order, the court may alter the limits in the Federal Rules of Civil Procedure on the number of depositions and interrogatories or on the length of depositions under FRCP 30. By order or local rule, the court may also limit the number of requests under FRCP 36. FRCP 26(b)(2)(A).

- *Specific limitations on electronically stored information.* A party need not provide discovery of electronically stored information from sources that the party identifies as not reasonably accessible because of undue burden or cost. On motion to compel discovery or for a protective order, the party from whom discovery is sought must show that the information is not reasonably accessible because of undue burden or cost. If that showing is made, the court may nonetheless order discovery from such sources if the requesting party shows good cause, considering the limitations of FRCP 26(b)(2)(C). The court may specify conditions for the discovery. FRCP 26(b)(2)(B).

- *When required.* On motion or on its own, the court must limit the frequency or extent of discovery otherwise allowed by the Federal Rules of Civil Procedure or by local rule if it determines that: (1) the discovery sought is unreasonably cumulative or duplicative, or can be obtained from some other source that is more convenient, less burdensome, or less expensive; (2) the party seeking discovery has had ample opportunity to obtain the information by discovery in the action; or (3) the proposed discovery is outside the scope permitted by FRCP 26(b)(1). FRCP 26(b)(2)(C).

      iii. *Trial preparation; Materials*

- *Documents and tangible things.* Ordinarily, a party may not discover documents and tangible things that are prepared in anticipation of litigation or for trial by or for another party or its representative (including the other party's attorney, consultant, surety, indemnitor, insurer, or agent). But, subject to FRCP 26(b)(4), those materials may be discovered if: (1) they are otherwise discoverable under FRCP 26(b)(1); and (2) the party shows that it has substantial need for the materials to prepare its case and cannot, without undue hardship, obtain their substantial equivalent by other means. FRCP 26(b)(3)(A).

- *Protection against disclosure.* If the court orders discovery of those materials, it must protect against disclosure of the mental impressions, conclusions, opinions, or legal theories of a party's attorney or other representative concerning the litigation. FRCP 26(b)(3)(B).

- *Previous statement.* Any party or other person may, on request and without the required showing, obtain the person's own previous statement about the action or its subject matter. If the request is refused, the person may move for a court order, and FRCP 37(a)(5) applies to the award of expenses. A previous statement is either: (1) a written statement that the person has signed or otherwise adopted or approved; or (2) a contemporaneous stenographic, mechanical, electrical, or other recording—or a transcription of it—that recites substantially verbatim the person's oral statement. FRCP 26(b)(3)(C).

iv. *Trial preparation; Experts*

- *Deposition of an expert who may testify.* A party may depose any person who has been identified as an expert whose opinions may be presented at trial. If FRCP 26(a)(2)(B) requires a report from the expert, the deposition may be conducted only after the report is provided. FRCP 26(b)(4)(A).

- *Trial-preparation protection for draft reports or disclosures.* FRCP 26(b)(3)(A) and FRCP 26(b)(3)(B) protect drafts of any report or disclosure required under FRCP 26(a)(2), regardless of the form in which the draft is recorded. FRCP 26(b)(4)(B).

- *Trial-preparation protection for communications between a party's attorney and expert witnesses.* FRCP 26(b)(3)(A) and FRCP 26(b)(3)(B) protect communications between the party's attorney and any witness required to provide a report under FRCP 26(a)(2)(B), regardless of the form of the communications, except to the extent that the communications: (1) relate to compensation for the expert's study or testimony; (2) identify facts or data that the party's attorney provided and that the expert considered in forming the opinions to be expressed; or (3) identify assumptions that the party's attorney provided and that the expert relied on in forming the opinions to be expressed. FRCP 26(b)(4)(C).

- *Expert employed only for trial preparation.* Ordinarily, a party may not, by interrogatories or deposition, discover facts known or opinions held by an expert who has been retained or specially employed by another party in anticipation of litigation or to prepare for trial and who is not expected to be called as a witness at trial. But a party may do so only: (1) as provided in FRCP 35(b); or (2) on showing exceptional circumstances under which it is impracticable for the party to obtain facts or opinions on the same subject by other means. FRCP 26(b)(4)(D).

- *Payment.* Unless manifest injustice would result, the court must require that the party seeking discovery: (1) pay the expert a reasonable fee for time spent in responding to discovery under FRCP 26(b)(4)(A) or FRCP 26(b)(4)(D); and (2) for discovery under FRCP 26(b)(4)(D), also pay the other party a fair portion of the fees and expenses it reasonably incurred in obtaining the expert's facts and opinions. FRCP 26(b)(4)(E).

v. *Claiming privilege or protecting trial-preparation materials*

- *Information withheld.* When a party withholds information otherwise discoverable by claiming that the information is privileged or subject to protection as trial-preparation material, the party must: (1) expressly make the claim; and (2) describe the nature of the documents, communications, or tangible things not produced or disclosed—and do so in a manner that, without revealing information itself privileged or protected, will enable other parties to assess the claim. FRCP 26(b)(5)(A).

- *Information produced.* If information produced in discovery is subject to a claim of privilege or of protection as trial-preparation material, the party making the claim may notify any party that received the information of the claim and the basis for it. After being notified, a party must promptly return, sequester, or destroy the specified information and any copies it has; must not use or disclose the information until the claim is resolved; must take reasonable steps to retrieve the information if the party disclosed it before being notified; and may promptly present the information to the court under seal for a determination of the claim. The producing party must preserve the information until the claim is resolved. FRCP 26(b)(5)(B).

b. *Protective orders.* A party or any person from whom discovery is sought may move for a protective order in the court where the action is pending—or as an alternative on matters relating to a deposition, in the court for the district where the deposition will be taken. FRCP 26(c)(1). Refer to the United States District Court for the Southern District of Indiana KeyRules Motion for Protective Order document for more information.

c. *Sequence of discovery.* Unless the parties stipulate or the court orders otherwise for the parties' and witnesses' convenience and in the interests of justice: (1) methods of discovery may be used in any sequence; and (2) discovery by one party does not require any other party to delay its discovery. FRCP 26(d)(3).

2. *Persons before whom depositions may be taken*

a. *Within the United States.* Within the United States or a territory or insular possession subject to United States jurisdiction, a deposition must be taken before: (1) an officer authorized to administer oaths either by federal law or by the law in the place of examination; or (2) a person appointed by the court where the action is pending to administer oaths and take testimony. FRCP 28(a)(1).

i. *Definition of "officer".* The term "officer" in FRCP 30, FRCP 31, and FRCP 32 includes a person appointed by the court under FRCP 28 or designated by the parties under FRCP 29(a). FRCP 28(a)(2).

b. *In a foreign country.* A deposition may be taken in a foreign country: (1) under an applicable treaty or convention; (2) under a letter of request, whether or not captioned a "letter rogatory"; (3) on notice, before a person authorized to administer oaths either by federal law or by the law in the place of examination; or (4) before a person commissioned by the court to administer any necessary oath and take testimony. FRCP 28(b)(1).

i. *Issuing a letter of request or a commission.* A letter of request, a commission, or both may be issued: (1) on appropriate terms after an application and notice of it; and (2) without a showing that taking the deposition in another manner is impracticable or inconvenient. FRCP 28(b)(2).

ii. *Form of a request, notice, or commission.* When a letter of request or any other device is used according to a treaty or convention, it must be captioned in the form prescribed by that treaty or convention. A letter of request may be addressed "To the Appropriate Authority in [name of country]." A deposition notice or a commission must designate by name or descriptive title the person before whom the deposition is to be taken. FRCP 28(b)(3).

iii. *Letter of request; Admitting evidence.* Evidence obtained in response to a letter of request need not be excluded merely because it is not a verbatim transcript, because the testimony was not taken under oath, or because of any similar departure from the requirements for depositions taken within the United States. FRCP 28(b)(4).

c. *Disqualification.* A deposition must not be taken before a person who is any party's relative, employee, or attorney; who is related to or employed by any party's attorney; or who is financially interested in the action. FRCP 28(c).

3. *Depositions by oral examination*

a. *Scheduling; Avoiding conflicts.* Under the Standards for Professional Conduct within the Seventh Federal Judicial Circuit, Lawyers Duty to Other Counsel, paragraph 14, (CTA7 Atty Conduct(Lawyers Duty to Other Counsel)(14)), attorneys will make a good faith effort to schedule depositions in a manner that avoids scheduling conflicts. IN R USDCTSD L.R. 30-1(d).

b. *Notice of the deposition.* A party who wants to depose a person by oral questions must give reasonable written notice to every other party. The notice must state the time and place of the deposition and, if known, the deponent's name and address. If the name is unknown, the notice must provide a general description sufficient to identify the person or the particular class or group to which the person belongs. FRCP 30(b)(1).

   i. *Notice or subpoena directed to an organization.* In its notice or subpoena, a party may name as the deponent a public or private corporation, a partnership, an association, a governmental agency, or other entity and must describe with reasonable particularity the matters for examination. The named organization must then designate one or more officers, directors, or managing agents, or designate other persons who consent to testify on its behalf; and it may set out the matters on which each person designated will testify. A subpoena must advise a nonparty organization of its duty to make this designation. The persons designated must testify about information known or reasonably available to the organization. FRCP 30(b)(6) does not preclude a deposition by any other procedure allowed by the Federal Rules of Civil Procedure. FRCP 30(b)(6).

c. *Method of recording*

   i. *Method stated in the notice.* The party who notices the deposition must state in the notice the method for recording the testimony. Unless the court orders otherwise, testimony may be recorded by audio, audiovisual, or stenographic means. The noticing party bears the recording costs. Any party may arrange to transcribe a deposition. FRCP 30(b)(3)(A).

   ii. *Additional method.* With prior notice to the deponent and other parties, any party may designate another method for recording the testimony in addition to that specified in the original notice. That party bears the expense of the additional record or transcript unless the court orders otherwise. FRCP 30(b)(3)(B).

d. *By remote means.* The parties may stipulate—or the court may on motion order—that a deposition be taken by telephone or other remote means. For the purpose of FRCP 30 and FRCP 28(a), FRCP 37(a)(2), and FRCP 37(b)(1), the deposition takes place where the deponent answers the questions. FRCP 30(b)(4).

e. *Officer's duties*

   i. *Before the deposition.* Unless the parties stipulate otherwise, a deposition must be conducted before an officer appointed or designated under FRCP 28. The officer must begin the deposition with an on-the-record statement that includes: (1) the officer's name and business address; (2) the date, time, and place of the deposition; (3) the deponent's name; (4) the officer's administration of the oath or affirmation to the deponent; and (5) the identity of all persons present. FRCP 30(b)(5)(A).

   ii. *Conducting the deposition; Avoiding distortion.* If the deposition is recorded non-stenographically, the officer must repeat the items in FRCP 30(b)(5)(A)(i) through FRCP 30(b)(5)(A)(iii) at the beginning of each unit of the recording medium. The deponent's and attorneys' appearance or demeanor must not be distorted through recording techniques. FRCP 30(b)(5)(B).

   iii. *After the deposition.* At the end of a deposition, the officer must state on the record that the deposition is complete and must set out any stipulations made by the attorneys about custody of the transcript or recording and of the exhibits, or about any other pertinent matters. FRCP 30(b)(5)(C).

f. *Examination and cross-examination.* The examination and cross-examination of a deponent proceed as they would at trial under the Federal Rules of Evidence, except FRE 103 and FRE 615. FRCP 30(c)(1).

   i. *Record of the examination.* After putting the deponent under oath or affirmation, the officer must record the testimony by the method designated under FRCP 30(b)(3)(A). The testimony must be recorded by the officer personally or by a person acting in the presence and under the direction of the officer. FRCP 30(c)(1).

ii. *Objections.* An objection at the time of the examination—whether to evidence, to a party's conduct, to the officer's qualifications, to the manner of taking the deposition, or to any other aspect of the deposition—must be noted on the record, but the examination still proceeds; the testimony is taken subject to any objection. An objection must be stated concisely in a nonargumentative and nonsuggestive manner. A person may instruct a deponent not to answer only when necessary to preserve a privilege, to enforce a limitation ordered by the court, or to present a motion under FRCP 30(d)(3). FRCP 30(c)(2).

- *Raising objections with the court.* A party may recess a deposition to submit an objection by phone to a judicial officer if the objection: (1) could cause the deposition to be terminated; and (2) can be resolved without submitting written materials to the court. IN R USDCTSD L.R. 30-1(c).

iii. *Questions about an asserted privilege.* An attorney may question a deponent who refuses to answer a question on the basis of privilege about information related to the appropriateness of the privilege, including whether: (1) the privilege applies under the circumstances; (2) the privilege has been waived; and (3) circumstances exist to overcome a claim of qualified privilege. IN R USDCTSD L.R. 30-1(a).

iv. *Private conference regarding a pending question.* A deponent's attorney may not initiate a private conference with the deponent during the deposition about a pending question except to determine whether to assert a claim of privilege. IN R USDCTSD L.R. 30-1(b).

v. *Participating through written questions.* Instead of participating in the oral examination, a party may serve written questions in a sealed envelope on the party noticing the deposition, who must deliver them to the officer. The officer must ask the deponent those questions and record the answers verbatim. FRCP 30(c)(3).

g. *Duration.* Unless otherwise stipulated or ordered by the court, a deposition is limited to one (1) day of seven (7) hours. The court must allow additional time consistent with FRCP 26(b)(1) and FRCP 26(b)(2) if needed to fairly examine the deponent or if the deponent, another person, or any other circumstance impedes or delays the examination. FRCP 30(d)(1).

h. *Sanction.* The court may impose an appropriate sanction—including the reasonable expenses and attorney's fees incurred by any party—on a person who impedes, delays, or frustrates the fair examination of the deponent. FRCP 30(d)(2). Refer to the United States District Court for the Southern District of Indiana KeyRules Motion for Discovery Sanctions document for more information on sanctions.

i. *Motion to terminate or limit.* At any time during a deposition, the deponent or a party may move to terminate or limit it on the ground that it is being conducted in bad faith or in a manner that unreasonably annoys, embarrasses, or oppresses the deponent or party. The motion may be filed in the court where the action is pending or the deposition is being taken. If the objecting deponent or party so demands, the deposition must be suspended for the time necessary to obtain an order. FRCP 30(d)(3)(A).

i. *Order.* The court may order that the deposition be terminated or may limit its scope and manner as provided in FRCP 26(c). If terminated, the deposition may be resumed only by order of the court where the action is pending. FRCP 30(d)(3)(B).

ii. *Award of expenses.* FRCP 37(a)(5) applies to the award of expenses. FRCP 30(d)(3)(C). Refer to the United States District Court for the Southern District of Indiana KeyRules Motion for Discovery Sanctions document for more information on sanctions.

j. *Review by the witness; Statement of changes.* On request by the deponent or a party before the deposition is completed, the deponent must be allowed thirty (30) days after being notified by the officer that the transcript or recording is available in which: (1) to review the transcript or recording; and (2) if there are changes in form or substance, to sign a statement listing the changes and the reasons for making them. FRCP 30(e)(1).

i. *Changes indicated in the officer's certificate.* The officer must note in the certificate prescribed by FRCP 30(f)(1) whether a review was requested and, if so, must attach any changes the deponent makes during the thirty (30) day period. FRCP 30(e)(2).

k. *Certification and delivery.* The officer must certify in writing that the witness was duly sworn and that the deposition accurately records the witness's testimony. The certificate must accompany the record of the deposition. Unless the court orders otherwise, the officer must seal the deposition in an envelope or package bearing the title of the action and marked "Deposition of [witness's name]" and must promptly send it to the attorney who arranged for the transcript or recording. The attorney must store it under conditions that will protect it against loss, destruction, tampering, or deterioration. FRCP 30(f)(1).

l. *Documents and tangible things.* Documents and tangible things produced for inspection during a deposition must, on a party's request, be marked for identification and attached to the deposition. Any party may inspect and copy them. But if the person who produced them wants to keep the originals, the person may: (1) offer copies to be marked, attached to the deposition, and then used as originals—after giving all parties a fair opportunity to verify the copies by comparing them with the originals; or (2) give all parties a fair opportunity to inspect and copy the originals after they are marked—in which event the originals may be used as if attached to the deposition. FRCP 30(f)(2)(A).

    i. *Order regarding the originals.* Any party may move for an order that the originals be attached to the deposition pending final disposition of the case. FRCP 30(f)(2)(B).

m. *Copies of the transcript or recording.* Unless otherwise stipulated or ordered by the court, the officer must retain the stenographic notes of a deposition taken stenographically or a copy of the recording of a deposition taken by another method. When paid reasonable charges, the officer must furnish a copy of the transcript or recording to any party or the deponent. FRCP 30(f)(3).

n. *Failure to attend a deposition or serve a subpoena; Expenses.* A party who, expecting a deposition to be taken, attends in person or by an attorney may recover reasonable expenses for attending, including attorney's fees, if the noticing party failed to: (1) attend and proceed with the deposition; or (2) serve a subpoena on a nonparty deponent, who consequently did not attend. FRCP 30(g). Refer to the United States District Court for the Southern District of Indiana KeyRules Motion for Discovery Sanctions document for more information on sanctions.

4. *Depositions by written questions*

    a. *Notice of deposition.* A party who wants to depose a person by written questions must serve them on every other party, with a notice stating, if known, the deponent's name and address. If the name is unknown, the notice must provide a general description sufficient to identify the person or the particular class or group to which the person belongs. The notice must also state the name or descriptive title and the address of the officer before whom the deposition will be taken. FRCP 31(a)(3).

    b. *Questions directed to an organization.* A public or private corporation, a partnership, an association, or a governmental agency may be deposed by written questions in accordance with FRCP 30(b)(6). FRCP 31(a)(4).

    c. *Delivery to the officer; Officer's duties.* The party who noticed the deposition must deliver to the officer a copy of all the questions served and of the notice. The officer must promptly proceed in the manner provided in FRCP 30(c), FRCP 30(e), and FRCP 30(f) to:

        i.   Take the deponent's testimony in response to the questions;

        ii. Prepare and certify the deposition; and

        iii. Send it to the party, attaching a copy of the questions and of the notice. FRCP 31(b).

    d. *Notice of completion.* The party who noticed the deposition must notify all other parties when it is completed. FRCP 31(c)(1).

5. *Depositions to perpetuate testimony.* For information on depositions to perpetuate testimony, refer to FRCP 27.

6. *Stipulations about discovery procedure.* Unless the court orders otherwise, the parties may stipulate that: (1) a deposition may be taken before any person, at any time or place, on any notice, and in the manner specified—in which event it may be used in the same way as any other deposition; and (2) other

procedures governing or limiting discovery be modified—but a stipulation extending the time for any form of discovery must have court approval if it would interfere with the time set for completing discovery, for hearing a motion, or for trial. FRCP 29.

7. *Appearances.* Every attorney who represents a party or who files a document on a party's behalf must file an appearance for that party. IN R USDCTSD L.R. 83-7. The filing of a Notice of Appearance shall act to establish the filing attorney as an attorney of record representing a designated party or parties in a particular cause of action. As a result, it is necessary for each attorney to file a separate Notice of Appearance when entering an appearance in a case. A joint appearance on behalf of multiple attorneys may be filed electronically only if it is filed separately for each attorney, using his/her ECF login. IN R USDCTSD ECF Procedures(12). Only those attorneys who have filed an appearance in a pending action are entitled to be served with case documents under FRCP 5(a). IN R USDCTSD L.R. 83-7. For more information, refer to IN R USDCTSD L.R. 83-7 and IN R USDCTSD ECF Procedures(12).

8. *Notice of related action.* A party must file a notice of related action: as soon as it appears that the party's case and another pending case: (1) arise out of the same transaction or occurrence; (2) involve the same property; or (3) involve the validity or infringement or the same patent, trademark, or copyright. IN R USDCTSD L.R. 40-1(d)(2). For more information, refer to IN R USDCTSD L.R. 40-1.

9. *Alternative dispute resolution (ADR)*

   a. *Application.* Unless limited by specific provisions, or unless there are other applicable specific statutory, common law, or constitutional procedures, the Local Alternative Dispute Resolution Rules of the United States District Court for the Southern District of Indiana shall apply in all civil litigation filed in the U.S. District Court for the Southern District of Indiana, except in the following cases and proceedings:

      i. Applications for writs of habeas corpus under 28 U.S.C.A. § 2254;

      ii. Forfeiture cases;

      iii. Non-adversary proceedings in bankruptcy;

      iv. Social Security administrative review cases; and

      v. Such other matters as specified by order of the Court; for example, matters involving important public policy issues, constitutional law, or the establishment of new law. IN R USDCTSD A.D.R. Rule 1.2.

   b. *Mediation.* Mediation under this section (IN R USDCTSD A.D.R. Rule 2.1, et seq.) involves the confidential process by which a person acting as a Mediator, selected by the parties or appointed by the Court, assists the litigants in reaching a mutually acceptable agreement. It is an informal and nonadversarial process. The role of the Mediator is to assist in identifying the issues, reducing misunderstandings, clarifying priorities, exploring areas of compromise, and finding points of agreement as well as legitimate points of disagreement. Final decision-making authority rests with the parties, not the Mediator. IN R USDCTSD A.D.R. Rule 2.1. It is anticipated that an agreement may not resolve all of the disputed issues, but the process, nonetheless, can reduce points of contention. Parties and their representatives are required to mediate in good faith, but are not compelled to reach an agreement. IN R USDCTSD A.D.R. Rule 2.1.

      i. *Case selection.* The Court with the agreement of the parties may refer a civil case for mediation. Unless otherwise ordered or as specifically provided in IN R USDCTSD A.D.R. Rule 2.8, referral to mediation does not abate or suspend the action, and no scheduled dates shall be delayed or deferred, including the date of trial. IN R USDCTSD A.D.R. Rule 2.2.

      ii. For more information on mediation, refer to IN R USDCTSD A.D.R. Rule 2.1, et seq.

   c. *Other methods of dispute resolution.* The Local Alternative Dispute Resolution Rules of the United States District Court for the Southern District of Indiana shall not preclude the parties from utilizing any other reasonable method or technique of alternative dispute resolution to resolve disputes to which the parties agree. However, any use of arbitration by the parties will be governed by and comply with the requirements of 28 U.S.C.A. § 654 through 28 U.S.C.A. § 657. IN R USDCTSD A.D.R. Rule 1.5.

d. For more information on alternative dispute resolution (ADR), refer to IN R USDCTSD A.D.R. Rule 1.1, et seq.

10. *Notice of settlement or resolution.* The parties must immediately notify the court if they reasonably anticipate settling their case or resolving a pending motion. IN R USDCTSD L.R. 7-1(h).

11. *Modification or suspension of rules.* The court may, on its own motion or at the request of a party, suspend or modify any rule in a particular case in the interest of justice. IN R USDCTSD L.R. 1-1(c).

D. Documents

1. *Depositions by oral examination*

   a. *Required documents*

      i. *Notice of deposition.* Refer to the General Requirements section of this document for the form and contents of the notice of deposition.

   b. *Supplemental documents*

      i. *Subpoena.* The deponent's attendance may be compelled by subpoena under FRCP 45. FRCP 30(a)(1). For more information on subpoenas, refer to FRCP 45.

      ii. *Subpoena duces tecum.* If a subpoena duces tecum is to be served on the deponent, the materials designated for production, as set out in the subpoena, must be listed in the notice or in an attachment. FRCP 30(b)(2). If a subpoena to produce or permit is to be served upon a nonparty, a copy of the proposed subpoena must be served on all other parties. IN R USDCTSD L.R. 45-1. For more information on subpoenas duces tecum, refer to FRCP 45 and IN R USDCTSD L.R. 45-1.

      iii. *Request for production of documents.* The notice to a party deponent may be accompanied by a request under FRCP 34 to produce documents and tangible things at the deposition. FRCP 30(b)(2). Refer to the United States District Court for the Southern District of Indiana KeyRules Request for Production of Documents document for more information.

      iv. *Certificate of service.* FRCP 5(d) requires that the person making service under FRCP 5 certify that service has been effected. FRCP 5(Advisory Committee Notes). Having such information on file may be useful for many purposes, including proof of service if an issue arises concerning the effectiveness of the service. FRCP 5(Advisory Committee Notes).

2. *Depositions by written questions*

   a. *Required documents*

      i. *Notice of deposition.* Refer to the General Requirements section of this document for the form and contents of the notice of deposition.

      ii. *Written questions.* A party who wants to depose a person by written questions must serve them on every other party, with a notice. FRCP 31(a)(3).

   b. *Supplemental documents*

      i. *Subpoena.* The deponent's attendance may be compelled by subpoena under FRCP 45. FRCP 31(a)(1). For more information on subpoenas, refer to FRCP 45.

      ii. *Certificate of service.* FRCP 5(d) requires that the person making service under FRCP 5 certify that service has been effected. FRCP 5(Advisory Committee Notes). Having such information on file may be useful for many purposes, including proof of service if an issue arises concerning the effectiveness of the service. FRCP 5(Advisory Committee Notes).

E. Format

1. *Form of documents.* The rules governing captions and other matters of form in pleadings apply to motions and other papers. FRCP 7(b)(2).

   a. *Paper (manual filings only).* Any document that is not filed electronically must: be flat, unfolded, and on good-quality, eight and one-half by eleven (8-1/2 x 11) inch white paper. IN R USDCTSD L.R.

5-1(d)(1). Any document that is not filed electronically must: be single-sided. IN R USDCTSD L.R. 5-1(d)(1).

   i. *Covers or backing.* Any document that is not filed electronically must: not have a cover or a back. IN R USDCTSD L.R. 5-1(d)(1).

   ii. *Fastening.* Any document that is not filed electronically must: be (if consisting of more than one (1) page) fastened by paperclip or binder clip and may not be stapled. IN R USDCTSD L.R. 5-1(d)(1).

- *Request for nonconforming fastening.* If a document cannot be fastened or bound as required by IN R USDCTSD L.R. 5-1(d), a party may ask the clerk for permission to fasten it in another manner. The party must make such a request before attempting to file the document with nonconforming fastening. IN R USDCTSD L.R. 5-1(d)(2).

   iii. *Hole punching.* Any document that is not filed electronically must: be two-hole punched at the top with the holes two and three-quarter (2-3/4) inches apart and appropriately centered. IN R USDCTSD L.R. 5-1(d)(1).

b. *Margins.* Any pleading, motion, brief, affidavit, notice, or proposed order filed with the court, whether electronically or with the clerk, must: have at least one (1) inch margins. IN R USDCTSD L.R. 5-1(b).

c. *Spacing.* Any pleading, motion, brief, affidavit, notice, or proposed order filed with the court, whether electronically or with the clerk, must: be double spaced (except for headings, footnotes, and quoted material). IN R USDCTSD L.R. 5-1(b).

d. *Text.* Any pleading, motion, brief, affidavit, notice, or proposed order filed with the court, whether electronically or with the clerk, must: be plainly typewritten, printed, or prepared by a clearly legible copying process. IN R USDCTSD L.R. 5-1(b).

e. *Font size.* Any pleading, motion, brief, affidavit, notice, or proposed order filed with the court, whether electronically or with the clerk, must: use at least 12-point type in the body of the document and at least 10-point type in footnotes. IN R USDCTSD L.R. 5-1(b).

f. *Page numbering.* Any pleading, motion, brief, affidavit, notice, or proposed order filed with the court, whether electronically or with the clerk, must: have consecutively numbered pages. IN R USDCTSD L.R. 5-1(b).

g. *Caption; Names of parties.* Every pleading must have a caption with the court's name, a title, a file number, and a FRCP 7(a) designation. The title of the complaint must name all the parties; the title of other pleadings, after naming the first party on each side, may refer generally to other parties. FRCP 10(a). Any pleading, motion, brief, affidavit, notice, or proposed order filed with the court, whether electronically or with the clerk, must: include a title on the first page. IN R USDCTSD L.R. 5-1(b).

h. *Filer's information.* Any pleading, motion, brief, affidavit, notice, or proposed order filed with the court, whether electronically or with the clerk, must: in the case of pleadings, motions, legal briefs, and notices, include the name, complete address, telephone number, facsimile number (where available), and e-mail address (where available) of the pro se litigant or attorney who files it. IN R USDCTSD L.R. 5-1(b).

i. *Paragraphs; Separate statements.* A party must state its claims or defenses in numbered paragraphs, each limited as far as practicable to a single set of circumstances. A later pleading may refer by number to a paragraph in an earlier pleading. If doing so would promote clarity, each claim founded on a separate transaction or occurrence—and each defense other than a denial—must be stated in a separate count or defense. FRCP 10(b).

j. *Adoption by reference; Exhibits.* A statement in a pleading may be adopted by reference elsewhere in the same pleading or in any other pleading or motion. A copy of a written instrument that is an exhibit to a pleading is a part of the pleading for all purposes. FRCP 10(c).

k. *Citations*

   i. *Local rules.* The Local Rules of the United States District Court for the Southern District of Indiana may be cited as "S.D. Ind. L.R." IN R USDCTSD L.R. 1-1(a).

  ii. *Local alternative dispute resolution rules.* These Rules shall be known as the Local Alternative Dispute Resolution Rules of the United States District Court for the Southern District of Indiana. They shall be cited as "S.D.Ind. Local A.D.R. Rule _____." IN R USDCTSD A.D.R. Rule 1.1.

 l. *Acceptance by the clerk.* The clerk must not refuse to file a paper solely because it is not in the form prescribed by the Federal Rules of Civil Procedure or by a local rule or practice. FRCP 5(d)(4). The clerk will accept a document that violates IN R USDCTSD L.R. 5-1, but the court may exclude the document from the official record. IN R USDCTSD L.R. 5-1(e).

  i. *Sanctions for errors as to form.* The court may strike from the record any document that does not comply with the rules governing the form of documents filed with the court, such as rules that regulate document size or the number of copies to be filed or that require a special designation in the caption. The court may also sanction an attorney or party who files a non-compliant document. IN R USDCTSD L.R. 1-3.

2. *Form of electronic documents.* Any document submitted via the court's electronic case filing (ECF) system must be: otherwise prepared and filed in a manner consistent with the CM/ECF Policies and Procedures Manual (IN R USDCTSD ECF Procedures). IN R USDCTSD L.R. 5-1(c). Electronically filed documents must meet the requirements of FRCP 10 (Form of Pleadings), IN R USDCTSD L.R. 5-1 (Format of Papers Presented for Filing), and FRCP 5.2 (Privacy Protection for Filings Made with the Court), as if they had been submitted on paper. Documents filed electronically are also subject to any page limitations set forth by Court Order, by IN R USDCTSD L.R. 7-1 (Motion Practice), or IN R USDCTSD L.R. 56-1 (Summary Judgment Practice), as applicable. IN R USDCTSD ECF Procedures(13).

 a. *PDF format required.* Any document submitted via the court's electronic case filing (ECF) system must be: in .pdf format. IN R USDCTSD L.R. 5-1(c); IN R USDCTSD ECF Procedures(7). Any document submitted via the court's electronic case filing (ECF) system must be: converted to a .pdf file directly from a word processing program, unless it exists only in paper format (in which case it may be scanned to create a .pdf document). IN R USDCTSD L.R. 5-1(c); IN R USDCTSD ECF Procedures(13).

  i. An exhibit may be scanned into PDF format, at a recommended 300 dpi resolution or higher, only if it does not already exist in electronic format. The filing attorney is responsible for reviewing all PDF documents for legibility before submitting them through the Court's Electronic Case Filing system. For technical guidance in creating PDF documents, please contact the Clerk's Office. IN R USDCTSD ECF Procedures(13).

 b. *File size limitations.* Any document submitted via the court's electronic case filing (ECF) system must be: submitted as one or more .pdf files that do not exceed ten megabytes (10 MB) each (consistent with the CM/ECF Policies and Procedures Manual (IN R USDCTSD ECF Procedures)). IN R USDCTSD L.R. 5-1(c); IN R USDCTSD ECF Procedures(13).

  i. To electronically file a document or attachment that exceeds ten megabytes (10 MB), the document must first be broken down into two or more smaller files. For example, if Exhibit A is a twelve megabyte (12 MB) PDF file, it should be divided into 2 equal parts prior to electronic filing. Each component part of the exhibit would be filed as an attachment to the main document and described appropriately as "Exhibit A (part 1 of 2)" and "Exhibit A (part 2 of 2)." IN R USDCTSD ECF Procedures(13).

  ii. The supporting items mentioned in IN R USDCTSD ECF Procedures(13) should not be confused with memorandums or briefs in support of motions as outlined in IN R USDCTSD L.R. 7-1 or IN R USDCTSD L.R. 56-1. These memorandums or briefs in support are to be filed as entirely separate documents pursuant to the appropriate rule. Additionally, no motion shall be embodied in the text of a response or reply brief/memorandum unless otherwise ordered by the Court. IN R USDCTSD ECF Procedures(13).

 c. *Separate component parts.* A key objective of the electronic filing system is to ensure that as much of the case as possible is managed electronically. To facilitate electronic filing and retrieval, documents to be filed electronically are to be reasonably broken into their separate component parts. By way of example, most filings include a foundation document (e.g., motion) and other supporting items (e.g., exhibits, proposed orders, proposed amended pleadings). The foundation document, as well as the supporting items, are each separate components of the filing; supporting items must be filed as attachments to the foundation document. These exhibits or attachments should include only those excerpts of the referenced documents that are directly germane to the matter under consideration. IN R USDCTSD ECF Procedures(13).

 i. Where an individual component cannot be included in an electronic filing (e.g. the component cannot be converted to electronic format), the filer shall electronically file the prescribed Notice of Manual Filing in place of that component. A model form is provided as Appendix C (IN R USDCTSD ECF Procedures(Appendix C)). IN R USDCTSD ECF Procedures(13).

d. *Exhibits.* Each electronically filed exhibit to a main document must be: (1) created as a separate .pdf file; (2) submitted as an attachment to the main document and given a title which describes its content; and (3) limited to excerpts that are directly germane to the main document's subject matter. IN R USDCTSD L.R. 5-6(a).

 i. When uploading attachments during the electronic filing process, exhibits must be uploaded in a logical sequence and a brief description must be entered for each individual PDF file. The description must include not only the exhibit number or letter, but also a brief description of the document. This information may be entered in CM/ECF using a combination of the Category drop-down menu, the Description text box, or both (see IN R USDCTSD ECF Procedures(13)(Figure 1)). The information that is provided in each box will be combined to create a description of the document as it appears on the case docket (see IN R USDCTSD ECF Procedures(13)(Figure 2)). IN R USDCTSD ECF Procedures(13). For an example, refer to IN R USDCTSD ECF Procedures(13).

e. *Excerpts.* A party filing an exhibit that consists of excerpts from a larger document must clearly and prominently identify the exhibit as containing excerpted material. Either party will have the right to timely file additional excerpts or the complete document to the extent they are or become directly germane to the main document's subject matter. IN R USDCTSD L.R. 5-6(b).

f. For an example illustrating the application of IN R USDCTSD ECF Procedures(13), refer to IN R USDCTSD ECF Procedures(13).

3. *Signing disclosures and discovery requests, responses, and objections.* FRCP 11 does not apply to disclosures and discovery requests, responses, objections, and motions under FRCP 26 through FRCP 37. FRCP 11(d).

a. *Signature required.* Every disclosure under FRCP 26(a)(1) or FRCP 26(a)(3) and every discovery request, response, or objection must be signed by at least one attorney of record in the attorney's own name—or by the party personally, if unrepresented—and must state the signer's address, e-mail address, and telephone number. FRCP 26(g)(1).

 i. *Signatures on manual filings.* Any document that is not filed electronically must: include the original signature of the pro se litigant or attorney who files it. IN R USDCTSD L.R. 5-1(d)(1).

 ii. *Electronic signatures.* Use of the attorney's login and password when filing documents electronically serves in part as the attorney's signature for purposes of FRCP 11, the Local Rules of the United States District Court for the Southern District of Indiana, and any other purpose for which a signature is required in connection with proceedings before the Court. IN R USDCTSD ECF Procedures(14); IN R USDCTSD ECF Procedures(10). A pleading, motion, brief, or notice filed electronically under an attorney's ECF log-in and password must be signed by that attorney. IN R USDCTSD L.R. 5-7(a). A signature on a document other than a document filed as provided under IN R USDCTSD L.R. 5-7(a) must be an original handwritten signature and must be scanned into .pdf format for electronic filing. IN R USDCTSD L.R. 5-7(c); IN R USDCTSD ECF Procedures(14).

  • *Form of electronic signature.* If a document is converted directly from a word processing application to .pdf (as opposed to scanning), the name of the Filing User under whose log-in and password the document is submitted must be preceded by a "s/" and typed on the signature line where the Filing User's handwritten signature would otherwise appear.

IN R USDCTSD L.R. 5-7(b). All documents filed electronically shall include a signature block and include the filing attorney's typewritten name, address, telephone number, facsimile number and e-mail address. In addition, the name of the filing attorney under whose ECF login the document will be filed should be preceded by a "s/" and typed in the space where the attorney's handwritten signature would otherwise appear. IN R US-DCTSD ECF Procedures(14). For a sample format, refer to IN R USDCTSD ECF Procedures(14).

- *Effect of electronic signature.* Filing an electronically signed document under an attorney's ECF log-in and password constitutes the attorney's signature on the document under the Federal Rules of Civil Procedure, under the Local Rules of the United States District Court for the Southern District of Indiana, and for any other reason a signature is required in connection with the court's activities. IN R USDCTSD L.R. 5-7(d).

- *Documents with multiple attorneys' signatures.* Documents requiring signatures of more than one attorney shall be filed either by: (1) obtaining consent from the other attorney, then typing the "s/ [Name]" signature of the other attorney on the signature line where the other attorney's signature would otherwise appear; (2) identifying in the signature section the name of the other attorney whose signature is required and by the submission of a Notice of Endorsement (see IN R USDCTSD ECF Procedures(Appendix B)) by the other attorney no later than three (3) business days after filing; (3) submitting a scanned document containing all handwritten signatures; or (4) in any other manner approved by the Court. IN R USDCTSD ECF Procedures(14); IN R USDCTSD L.R. 5-7(e).

b. *Effect of signature.* By signing, an attorney or party certifies that to the best of the person's knowledge, information, and belief formed after a reasonable inquiry:

   i. With respect to a disclosure, it is complete and correct as of the time it is made; and

   ii. With respect to a discovery request, response, or objection, it is:

- Consistent with the Federal Rules of Civil Procedure and warranted by existing law or by a nonfrivolous argument for extending, modifying, or reversing existing law, or for establishing new law;

- Not interposed for any improper purpose, such as to harass, cause unnecessary delay, or needlessly increase the cost of litigation; and

- Neither unreasonable nor unduly burdensome or expensive, considering the needs of the case, prior discovery in the case, the amount in controversy, and the importance of the issues at stake in the action. FRCP 26(g)(1).

c. *Failure to sign.* Other parties have no duty to act on an unsigned disclosure, request, response, or objection until it is signed, and the court must strike it unless a signature is promptly supplied after the omission is called to the attorney's or party's attention. FRCP 26(g)(2). The court will strike any document filed directly with the clerk that is not signed by an attorney of record or the pro se litigant filing it, but the court may do so only after giving the attorney or pro se litigant notice of the omission and reasonable time to correct it. Rubber-stamp or facsimile signatures are not original signatures and the court will deem documents containing them to be unsigned for purposes of FRCP 11 and FRCP 26(g) and IN R USDCTSD L.R. 5-10. IN R USDCTSD L.R. 5-10(g).

d. *Sanction for improper certification.* If a certification violates FRCP 26(g) without substantial justification, the court, on motion or on its own, must impose an appropriate sanction on the signer, the party on whose behalf the signer was acting, or both. The sanction may include an order to pay the reasonable expenses, including attorney's fees, caused by the violation. FRCP 26(g)(3). Refer to the United States District Court for the Southern District of Indiana KeyRules Motion for Discovery Sanctions document for more information.

4. *Privacy protection for filings made with the court.* Electronically filed documents must meet the requirements of. . .FRCP 5.2 (Privacy Protection for Filings Made with the Court), as if they had been submitted on paper. IN R USDCTSD ECF Procedures(13).

   a. *Redacted filings.* Unless the court orders otherwise, in an electronic or paper filing with the court that

contains an individual's Social Security number, taxpayer-identification number, or birth date, the name of an individual known to be a minor, or a financial-account number, a party or nonparty making the filing may include only:

    i.   The last four (4) digits of the Social Security number and taxpayer-identification number;

    ii.   The year of the individual's birth;

    iii.   The minor's initials; and

    iv.   The last four (4) digits of the financial-account number. FRCP 5.2(a).

b.   *Exemptions from the redaction requirement.* The redaction requirement does not apply to the following:

    i.   A financial-account number that identifies the property allegedly subject to forfeiture in a forfeiture proceeding;

    ii.   The record of an administrative or agency proceeding;

    iii.   The official record of a state-court proceeding;

    iv.   The record of a court or tribunal, if that record was not subject to the redaction requirement when originally filed;

    v.   A filing covered by FRCP 5.2(c) or FRCP 5.2(d); and

    vi.   A pro se filing in an action brought under 28 U.S.C.A. § 2241, 28 U.S.C.A. § 2254, or 28 U.S.C.A. § 2255. FRCP 5.2(b).

c.   *Limitations on remote access to electronic files; Social Security appeals and immigration cases.* Unless the court orders otherwise, in an action for benefits under the Social Security Act, and in an action or proceeding relating to an order of removal, to relief from removal, or to immigration benefits or detention, access to an electronic file is authorized as follows:

    i.   The parties and their attorneys may have remote electronic access to any part of the case file, including the administrative record;

    ii.   Any other person may have electronic access to the full record at the courthouse, but may have remote electronic access only to:

        •   The docket maintained by the court; and

        •   An opinion, order, judgment, or other disposition of the court, but not any other part of the case file or the administrative record. FRCP 5.2(c).

d.   *Filings made under seal.* The court may order that a filing be made under seal without redaction. The court may later unseal the filing or order the person who made the filing to file a redacted version for the public record. FRCP 5.2(d). For more information on filing under seal, refer to IN R USDCTSD L.R. 5-11 and IN R USDCTSD ECF Procedures(18).

e.   *Protective orders.* For good cause, the court may by order in a case:

    i.   Require redaction of additional information; or

    ii.   Limit or prohibit a nonparty's remote electronic access to a document filed with the court. FRCP 5.2(e).

f.   *Option for additional unredacted filing under seal.* A person making a redacted filing may also file an unredacted copy under seal. The court must retain the unredacted copy as part of the record. FRCP 5.2(f).

g.   *Option for filing a reference list.* A filing that contains redacted information may be filed together with a reference list that identifies each item of redacted information and specifies an appropriate identifier that uniquely corresponds to each item listed. The list must be filed under seal and may be amended as of right. Any reference in the case to a listed identifier will be construed to refer to the corresponding item of information. FRCP 5.2(g).

h.   *Waiver of protection of identifiers.* A person waives the protection of FRCP 5.2(a) as to the person's own information by filing it without redaction and not under seal. FRCP 5.2(h).

F. Filing and Service Requirements

1. *Filing requirements.* Any paper after the complaint that is required to be served—together with a certificate of service—must be filed within a reasonable time after service. But disclosures under FRCP 26(a)(1) or FRCP 26(a)(2) and the following discovery requests and responses must not be filed until they are used in the proceeding or the court orders filing: depositions, interrogatories, requests for documents or tangible things or to permit entry onto land, and requests for admission. FRCP 5(d)(1). Refer to the United States District Court for the Southern District of Indiana KeyRules pleading and motion documents for information on filing with the court.

   a. *When discovery may be filed.* Discovery materials (whether discovery requests, responses, or deposition transcripts) may not be filed with the court except in the following circumstances:

      i. *Relevant to certain motions.* A party seeking relief under FRCP 26(c) or FRCP 37, or by way of a pretrial motion that could result in a final order on an issue, must file with the motion those parts of the discovery materials relevant to the motion. IN R USDCTSD L.R. 26-2(a).

      ii. *For anticipated use at trial.* When a party can reasonably anticipate using discovery materials at trial, the party must file the relevant portions at the start of the trial. IN R USDCTSD L.R. 26-2(b).

      iii. *Materials necessary for appeal.* A party seeking for purposes of appeal to supplement the record with discovery materials not previously filed may do so by stipulation of the parties or by court order approving the filing. IN R USDCTSD L.R. 26-2(c).

   b. *Notice of filing*

      i. *Depositions by oral examination.* A party who files the deposition must promptly notify all other parties of the filing. FRCP 30(f)(4).

      ii. *Depositions by written questions.* A party who files the deposition must promptly notify all other parties of the filing. FRCP 31(c)(2).

2. *Service requirements*

   a. *Service; When required*

      i. *In general.* Unless the Federal Rules of Civil Procedure provide otherwise, each of the following papers must be served on every party:

         • An order stating that service is required;

         • A pleading filed after the original complaint, unless the court orders otherwise under FRCP 5(c) because there are numerous defendants;

         • A discovery paper required to be served on a party, unless the court orders otherwise;

         • A written motion, except one that may be heard ex parte; and

         • A written notice, appearance, demand, or offer of judgment, or any similar paper. FRCP 5(a)(1).

      ii. *If a party fails to appear.* No service is required on a party who is in default for failing to appear. But a pleading that asserts a new claim for relief against such a party must be served on that party under FRCP 4. FRCP 5(a)(2).

      iii. *Seizing property.* If an action is begun by seizing property and no person is or need be named as a defendant, any service required before the filing of an appearance, answer, or claim must be made on the person who had custody or possession of the property when it was seized. FRCP 5(a)(3).

   b. *Service; How made*

      i. *Serving an attorney.* If a party is represented by an attorney, service under FRCP 5 must be made on the attorney unless the court orders service on the party. FRCP 5(b)(1).

      ii. *Service in general.* A paper is served under FRCP 5 by:

         • Handing it to the person;

- Leaving it: (1) at the person's office with a clerk or other person in charge or, if no one is in charge, in a conspicuous place in the office; or (2) if the person has no office or the office is closed, at the person's dwelling or usual place of abode with someone of suitable age and discretion who resides there;

- Mailing it to the person's last known address—in which event service is complete upon mailing;

- Leaving it with the court clerk if the person has no known address;

- Sending it by electronic means if the person consented in writing—in which event service is complete upon transmission, but is not effective if the serving party learns that it did not reach the person to be served; or

- Delivering it by any other means that the person consented to in writing—in which event service is complete when the person making service delivers it to the agency designated to make delivery. FRCP 5(b)(2).

iii. *Electronic service*

- *Consent.* By registering to use the ECF system, attorneys consent to electronic service of documents filed in cases maintained on the ECF system. IN R USDCTSD L.R. 5-3(d). By participating in the Electronic Case Filing Program, attorneys consent to the electronic service of documents, and shall make available electronic mail addresses for service. IN R USDCTSD ECF Procedures(11).

- *Service on registered parties.* Upon the filing of a document by a party, an e-mail message will be automatically generated by the electronic filing system and sent via electronic mail to the e-mail addresses of all registered attorneys who have appeared in the case. The Notice of Electronic Filing will contain a document hyperlink which will provide recipients with one "free look" at the electronically filed document. Recipients are encouraged to print and/or save a copy of the document during the "free look" to avoid incurring PACER charges for future viewings of the document. IN R USDCTSD ECF Procedures(11). When a document has been filed electronically: transmission of the notice of electronic filing generated by the ECF system to an attorney's e-mail address constitutes service of the document on that attorney. IN R USDCTSD L.R. 5-4(c)(5). The party effectuates service on all registered attorneys by filing electronically. IN R USDCTSD ECF Procedures(11). When a document has been filed electronically: no other attempted service will constitute electronic service of the document. IN R USDCTSD L.R. 5-4(c)(6).

- *Service on exempt parties.* A filer must serve a copy of the document consistent with FRCP 5 on any party or attorney who is exempt from participating in electronic filing. IN R USDCTSD L.R. 5-4(d). It is the responsibility of the filing attorney to conventionally serve all parties who do not receive electronic service (the identity of these parties will be indicated on the filing receipt generated by the ECF system). IN R USDCTSD ECF Procedures(11).

- *Service on parties excused from electronic filing.* Parties otherwise participating in the electronic filing system may be excused from filing a particular component electronically under certain limited circumstances, such as when the component cannot be reduced to an electronic format. Such components shall not be filed electronically, but instead shall be manually filed with the Clerk of Court and served upon the parties in accordance with the applicable Federal Rules of Civil Procedure and the Local Rules of the United States District Court for the Southern District of Indiana for filing and service of non-electronic documents. IN R USDCTSD ECF Procedures(15).

- *Service of exempt documents.* Any document that is exempt from electronic filing must be filed directly with the clerk and served on other parties in the case as required by those Federal Rules of Civil Procedure and Local Rules of the United States District Court for the Southern District of Indiana that apply to the service of non-electronic documents. IN R USDCTSD L.R. 5-2(c).

iv. *Using court facilities.* If a local rule so authorizes, a party may use the court's transmission facilities to make service under FRCP 5(b)(2)(E). FRCP 5(b)(3).

c. *Serving numerous defendants*

    i. *In general.* If an action involves an unusually large number of defendants, the court may, on motion or on its own, order that:

- Defendants' pleadings and replies to them need not be served on other defendants;
- Any crossclaim, counterclaim, avoidance, or affirmative defense in those pleadings and replies to them will be treated as denied or avoided by all other parties; and
- Filing any such pleading and serving it on the plaintiff constitutes notice of the pleading to all parties. FRCP 5(c)(1).

    ii. *Notifying parties.* A copy of every such order must be served on the parties as the court directs. FRCP 5(c)(2).

G. Hearings

1. There is no hearing contemplated in the federal statutes or rules for the notice of deposition.

H. Forms

1. Federal Notice of Deposition Forms

a. Notice to take deposition to perpetuate testimony. 3A FEDFORMS § 3339.

b. Notice of taking of deposition to perpetuate testimony pending appeal. 3A FEDFORMS § 3345.

c. Notice of taking deposition upon oral examination. 3A FEDFORMS § 3422.

d. Notice of taking deposition upon oral examination; Party. 3A FEDFORMS § 3423.

e. Notice of taking deposition upon oral examination; Naming and describing person not a party. 3A FEDFORMS § 3424.

f. Notice of taking deposition upon oral examination; Describing deponents whose names are unknown. 3A FEDFORMS § 3425.

g. Notice of taking deposition upon oral examination; Pursuant to order granting leave to take deposition. 3A FEDFORMS § 3426.

h. Notice of taking of deposition of party with notice to produce documents. 3A FEDFORMS § 3427.

i. Notice of taking of deposition of witness; Including designation of materials in related subpoena duces tecum. 3A FEDFORMS § 3428.

j. Notice of taking deposition of witness; Including reference to materials designated in attached subpoena. 3A FEDFORMS § 3429.

k. Notice of taking deposition upon written questions served with notice. 3A FEDFORMS § 3449.

l. Questions to be attached to notice or served with it. 3A FEDFORMS § 3450.

m. Notice of return and filing of deposition taken upon written questions. 3A FEDFORMS § 3456.

n. Notice; Taking of deposition on oral examination. FEDPROF § 23:136.

o. Notice; Taking of deposition on oral examination; Patent proceedings. FEDPROF § 23:137.

p. Notice; Taking of deposition on oral examination; Corporate officer. FEDPROF § 23:138.

q. Notice; Taking of deposition on oral examination; Corporate officers to be designated by corporation. FEDPROF § 23:139.

r. Notice; Taking of deposition on written questions. FEDPROF § 23:140.

s. Notice; Taking of deposition on oral examination or on written questions; Pursuant to court order. FEDPROF § 23:141.

t. Notice; In connection with deposition on written questions; Of cross, redirect, or recross questions. FEDPROF § 23:142.

u. Attachment to notice; Taking of deposition on written questions; Questions to be propounded. FEDPROF § 23:143.

v. Attachment to notice; Cross, redirect, or recross questions to be propounded. FEDPROF § 23:144.

w. Notice; To party taking deposition; Written questions submitted in lieu of participation in oral examination. FEDPROF § 23:145.

x. Notice of taking deposition; Expert witness; Request for production of supporting documents. FEDPROF § 23:151.

y. Subpoena; To testify at taking of deposition and to produce documents or things (form AO 88). FEDPROF § 23:152.

z. Provision in subpoena; Advice to nonparty organization of its duty to designate witness. FEDPROF § 23:155.

I. Applicable Rules

1. *Federal rules*

   a. Serving and filing pleadings and other papers. FRCP 5.

   b. Privacy protection for filings made with the court. FRCP 5.2.

   c. Computing and extending time; Time for motion papers. FRCP 6.

   d. Pleadings allowed; Form of motions and other papers. FRCP 7.

   e. Form of pleadings. FRCP 10.

   f. Signing pleadings, motions, and other papers; Representations to the court; Sanctions. FRCP 11.

   g. Duty to disclose; General provisions governing discovery. FRCP 26.

   h. Persons before whom depositions may be taken. FRCP 28.

   i. Stipulations about discovery procedure. FRCP 29.

   j. Depositions by oral examination. FRCP 30.

   k. Depositions by written questions. FRCP 31.

   l. Failure to make disclosures or to cooperate in discovery; Sanctions. FRCP 37.

2. *Local rules*

   a. Scope of the rules. IN R USDCTSD L.R. 1-1.

   b. Sanctions for errors as to form. IN R USDCTSD L.R. 1-3.

   c. Format of documents presented for filing. IN R USDCTSD L.R. 5-1.

   d. Filing of documents electronically required. IN R USDCTSD L.R. 5-2.

   e. Eligibility, registration, passwords for electronic filing; Exemption from electronic filing. IN R USDCTSD L.R. 5-3.

   f. Timing and consequences of electronic filing. IN R USDCTSD L.R. 5-4.

   g. Attachments and exhibits in cases filed electronically. IN R USDCTSD L.R. 5-6.

   h. Signatures in cases filed electronically. IN R USDCTSD L.R. 5-7.

   i. Non-electronic filings. IN R USDCTSD L.R. 5-10.

   j. Motion practice. [IN R USDCTSD L.R. 7-1, as amended by IN ORDER 16-2319, effective December 1, 2016].

   k. Filing of discovery materials. IN R USDCTSD L.R. 26-2.

   l. Conduct of depositions. IN R USDCTSD L.R. 30-1.

   m. Assignment of cases. IN R USDCTSD L.R. 40-1.

   n. Service of subpoena on non-parties; Notice requirement. IN R USDCTSD L.R. 45-1.

   o. Alternative dispute resolution. IN R USDCTSD A.D.R. Rule 1.1; IN R USDCTSD A.D.R. Rule 1.2;

IN R USDCTSD A.D.R. Rule 1.5; IN R USDCTSD A.D.R. Rule 2.1; IN R USDCTSD A.D.R. Rule 2.2.

p.   Electronic case filing policies and procedures manual. IN R USDCTSD ECF Procedures.

Requests, Notices and Applications
Application for Temporary Restraining Order

Document Last Updated December 2016

A. Checklist

(I)   ❏ Matters to be considered by party applying (with notice)

    (a)   ❏ Required documents

        (1)   ❏ Notice of motion and motion

        (2)   ❏ Brief

        (3)   ❏ Security

        (4)   ❏ Certificate of service

    (b)   ❏ Supplemental documents

        (1)   ❏ Supporting evidence

        (2)   ❏ Notice of constitutional question

        (3)   ❏ Nongovernmental corporate disclosure statement

        (4)   ❏ Index of exhibits

        (5)   ❏ Request for oral argument

        (6)   ❏ Request for evidentiary hearing

        (7)   ❏ Copy of authority

        (8)   ❏ Proposed order

        (9)   ❏ Copy of document with self-address envelope

        (10)   ❏ Notice of manual filing

        (11)   ❏ Courtesy copies

        (12)   ❏ Copies for three-judge court

        (13)   ❏ Declaration that party was unable to file in a timely manner due to technical difficulties

    (c)   ❏ Timing

        (1)   ❏ A written motion and notice of the hearing must be served at least fourteen (14) days before the time specified for the hearing, with the following exceptions: (i) when the motion may be heard ex parte; (ii) when the Federal Rules of Civil Procedure set a different time; or (iii) when a court order—which a party may, for good cause, apply for ex parte—sets a different time

        (2)   ❏ Any affidavit supporting a motion must be served with the motion

        (3)   ❏ When a party who is not exempt from the electronic filing requirement files a document directly with the clerk, the party must present the document to the clerk within one (1) business day after filing the notice of manual filing

        (4)   ❏ Unless the court orders otherwise, the [untimely] document and declaration [that party was unable to file in a timely manner due to technical difficulties] must be filed no later than 12:00 noon of the first day on which the court is open for business following the original filing deadline

(II) ❑ Matters to be considered by party applying (without notice, or "ex parte")

    (a) ❑ Required documents

        (1) ❑ Motion

        (2) ❑ Brief

        (3) ❑ Affidavit or verified complaint

        (4) ❑ Certificate of attorney

        (5) ❑ Security

    (b) ❑ Supplemental documents

        (1) ❑ Supporting evidence

        (2) ❑ Notice of constitutional question

        (3) ❑ Nongovernmental corporate disclosure statement

        (4) ❑ Index of exhibits

        (5) ❑ Request for oral argument

        (6) ❑ Request for evidentiary hearing

        (7) ❑ Copy of authority

        (8) ❑ Proposed order

        (9) ❑ Copy of document with self-address envelope

        (10) ❑ Notice of manual filing

        (11) ❑ Courtesy copies

        (12) ❑ Copies for three-judge court

        (13) ❑ Declaration that party was unable to file in a timely manner due to technical difficulties

    (c) ❑ Timing

        (1) ❑ There are no specific timing requirements for applying for a temporary restraining order without notice

        (2) ❑ Any affidavit supporting a motion must be served with the motion

        (3) ❑ When a party who is not exempt from the electronic filing requirement files a document directly with the clerk, the party must present the document to the clerk within one (1) business day after filing the notice of manual filing

        (4) ❑ Unless the court orders otherwise, the [untimely] document and declaration [that party was unable to file in a timely manner due to technical difficulties] must be filed no later than 12:00 noon of the first day on which the court is open for business following the original filing deadline

B. Timing

1. *Application for temporary restraining order*

    a. *With notice.* There are no specific timing requirements for applying for a temporary restraining order with notice.

    b. *Without notice, or "ex parte."* There are no specific timing requirements for applying for a temporary restraining order without notice, or "ex parte."

2. *Motion to dissolve or modify.* On two (2) days' notice to the party who obtained the order without notice—or on shorter notice set by the court—the adverse party may appear and move to dissolve or modify the order. The court must then hear and decide the motion as promptly as justice requires. FRCP 65(b)(4).

3. *Timing of motions, generally*

   a. *Motion and notice of hearing.* A written motion and notice of the hearing must be served at least fourteen (14) days before the time specified for the hearing, with the following exceptions:

      i. When the motion may be heard ex parte;

      ii. When the Federal Rules of Civil Procedure set a different time; or

      iii. When a court order—which a party may, for good cause, apply for ex parte—sets a different time. FRCP 6(c)(1).

   b. *Supporting affidavit.* Any affidavit supporting a motion must be served with the motion. FRCP 6(c)(2).

4. *Document filing by non-exempt party.* When a party who is not exempt from the electronic filing requirement files a document directly with the clerk, the party must: present the document to the clerk within one (1) business day after filing the notice of manual filing. IN R USDCTSD L.R. 5-2(d)(2).

5. *Declaration that party was unable to file in a timely manner due to technical difficulties.* Unless the Court orders otherwise, the [untimely] document and declaration [that party was unable to file in a timely manner due to technical difficulties] must be filed no later than 12:00 noon of the first day on which the Court is open for business following the original filing deadline. IN R USDCTSD ECF Procedures(16).

6. *Computation of time*

   a. *Computing time.* FRCP 6 applies in computing any time period specified in the Federal Rules of Civil Procedure, in any local rule or court order, or in any statute that does not specify a method of computing time. FRCP 6(a).

      i. *Period stated in days or a longer unit.* When the period is stated in days or a longer unit of time:

         • Exclude the day of the event that triggers the period;

         • Count every day, including intermediate Saturdays, Sundays, and legal holidays; and

         • Include the last day of the period, but if the last day is a Saturday, Sunday, or legal holiday, the period continues to run until the end of the next day that is not a Saturday, Sunday, or legal holiday. FRCP 6(a)(1).

      ii. *Period stated in hours.* When the period is stated in hours:

         • Begin counting immediately on the occurrence of the event that triggers the period;

         • Count every hour, including hours during intermediate Saturdays, Sundays, and legal holidays; and

         • If the period would end on a Saturday, Sunday, or legal holiday, the period continues to run until the same time on the next day that is not a Saturday, Sunday, or legal holiday. FRCP 6(a)(2).

      iii. *Inaccessibility of the clerk's office.* Unless the court orders otherwise, if the clerk's office is inaccessible:

         • On the last day for filing under FRCP 6(a)(1), then the time for filing is extended to the first accessible day that is not a Saturday, Sunday, or legal holiday; or

         • During the last hour for filing under FRCP 6(a)(2), then the time for filing is extended to the same time on the first accessible day that is not a Saturday, Sunday, or legal holiday. FRCP 6(a)(3).

      iv. *"Last day" defined.* Unless a different time is set by a statute, local rule, or court order, the last day ends:

         • For electronic filing, at midnight in the court's time zone; and

         • For filing by other means, when the clerk's office is scheduled to close. FRCP 6(a)(4).

      v. *"Next day" defined.* The "next day" is determined by continuing to count forward when the period is measured after an event and backward when measured before an event. FRCP 6(a)(5).

    vi.   *"Legal holiday" defined.* "Legal holiday" means:

- The day set aside by statute for observing New Year's Day, Martin Luther King Jr.'s Birthday, Washington's Birthday, Memorial Day, Independence Day, Labor Day, Columbus Day, Veterans' Day, Thanksgiving Day, or Christmas Day;

- Any day declared a holiday by the President or Congress; and

- For periods that are measured after an event, any other day declared a holiday by the state where the district court is located. FRCP 6(a)(6).

b.   *Computation of electronic filing deadlines.* Filing documents electronically does not alter filing deadlines. IN R USDCTSD ECF Procedures(7). A document due on a particular day must be filed before midnight local time of the division where the case is pending. IN R USDCTSD L.R. 5-4(a). All electronic transmissions of documents must be completed (i.e. received completely by the Clerk's Office) prior to midnight of the local time of the division in which the case is pending in order to be considered timely filed that day (NOTE: time will be noted in Eastern Time on the Court's docket. If you have filed a document prior to midnight local time of the division in which the case is pending and the document is due that date, but the electronic receipt and docket reflect the following calendar day, please contact the Court). IN R USDCTSD ECF Procedures(7). Although attorneys may file documents electronically twenty-four (24) hours a day, seven (7) days a week, attorneys are encouraged to file all documents during the normal working hours of the Clerk's Office (Monday through Friday, 8:30 a.m. to 4:30 p.m.) when technical support is available. IN R USDCTSD ECF Procedures(7); IN R USDCTSD ECF Procedures(9).

    i.   *Technical difficulties.* Parties are encouraged to file documents electronically during normal business hours, in case a problem is encountered. In the event a technical failure occurs and a document cannot be filed electronically despite the best efforts of the filing party, the party should print (if possible) a copy of the error message received. In addition, as soon as practically possible, the party should file a "Declaration that Party was Unable to File in a Timely Manner Due to Technical Difficulties." A model form is provided as Appendix D (IN R USDCTSD ECF Procedures(Appendix D)). IN R USDCTSD ECF Procedures(16).

- If a party is unable to file electronically and, as a result, may miss a filing deadline, the party must contact the Clerk's Office at the number listed in IN R USDCTSD ECF Procedures(15) to inform the court's staff of the difficulty. If a party misses a filing deadline due to an inability to file electronically, the party may submit the untimely filed document, accompanied by a declaration stating the reason(s) for missing the deadline. Unless the Court orders otherwise, the document and declaration must be filed no later than 12:00 noon of the first day on which the Court is open for business following the original filing deadline. IN R USDCTSD ECF Procedures(16).

c.   *Extending time*

    i.   *In general.* When an act may or must be done within a specified time, the court may, for good cause, extend the time:

- With or without motion or notice if the court acts, or if a request is made, before the original time or its extension expires; or

- On motion made after the time has expired if the party failed to act because of excusable neglect. FRCP 6(b)(1).

    ii.   *Exceptions.* A court must not extend the time to act under FRCP 50(b), FRCP 50(d), FRCP 52(b), FRCP 59(b), FRCP 59(d), FRCP 59(e), and FRCP 60(b). FRCP 6(b)(2).

    iii.   Refer to the United States District Court for the Southern District of Indiana KeyRules Motion for Continuance/Extension of Time document for more information on extending time.

d.   *Additional time after certain kinds of service.* When a party may or must act within a specified time after being served and service is made under FRCP 5(b)(2)(C) (mail), FRCP 5(b)(2)(D) (leaving with the clerk), or FRCP 5(b)(2)(F) (other means consented to), three (3) days are added after the period would otherwise expire under FRCP 6(a). FRCP 6(d). Service by electronic mail shall constitute service pursuant to FRCP 5(b)(2)(E) and shall entitle the party being served to the additional three (3) days provided by FRCP 6(d). IN R USDCTSD ECF Procedures(11).

C. General Requirements

1. *Motions, generally*

   a. *Requirements.* A request for a court order must be made by motion. The motion must:

      i. Be in writing unless made during a hearing or trial;

      ii. State with particularity the grounds for seeking the order; and

      iii. State the relief sought. FRCP 7(b)(1).

   b. *Notice of motion.* A party interested in resisting the relief sought by a motion has a right to notice thereof, and an opportunity to be heard. AMJUR MOTIONS § 12.

      i. In addition to statutory or court rule provisions requiring notice of a motion—the purpose of such a notice requirement having been said to be to prevent a party from being prejudicially surprised by a motion—principles of natural justice dictate that an adverse party generally must be given notice that a motion will be presented to the court. AMJUR MOTIONS § 12.

      ii. "Notice," in this regard, means reasonable notice, including a meaningful opportunity to prepare and to defend against allegations of a motion. AMJUR MOTIONS § 12.

   c. *Writing requirement.* The writing requirement is intended to insure that the adverse parties are informed and have a record of both the motion's pendency and the grounds on which the movant seeks an order. FPP § 1191; Feldberg v. Quechee Lakes Corp., 463 F.3d 195 (2d Cir. 2006).

      i. It is sufficient "if the motion is stated in a written notice of the hearing of the motion." FPP § 1191.

   d. *Particularity requirement.* The particularity requirement insures that the opposing parties will have notice of their opponent's contentions. FEDPROC § 62:364; Goodman v. 1973 26 Foot Trojan Vessel, Arkansas Registration No. AR1439SN, 859 F.2d 71, 12 Fed.R.Serv.3d 645 (8th Cir. 1988). That requirement ensures that notice of the basis for the motion is provided to the court and to the opposing party so as to avoid prejudice, provide the opponent with a meaningful opportunity to respond, and provide the court with enough information to process the motion correctly. FEDPROC § 62:364; Andreas v. Volkswagen of America, Inc., 336 F.3d 789, 56 Fed.R.Serv.3d 6 (8th Cir. 2003).

      i. Reasonable specification of the grounds for a motion is sufficient. However, where a movant fails to state even one ground for granting the motion in question, the movant has failed to meet the minimal standard of "reasonable specification." FEDPROC § 62:364; Martinez v. Trainor, 556 F.2d 818, 23 Fed.R.Serv.2d 403 (7th Cir. 1977).

      ii. The court may excuse the failure to comply with the particularity requirement if it is inadvertent, and where no prejudice is shown by the opposing party. FEDPROC § 62:364.

   e. *Motions must be filed separately.* Motions must be filed separately, but alternative motions may be filed in a single document if each is named in the title. A motion must not be contained within a brief, response, or reply to a previously filed motion, unless ordered by the court. IN R USDCTSD L.R. 7-1(a).

   f. *Routine or uncontested motions.* The court may rule upon a routine or uncontested motion before the response deadline passes, unless: (1) the motion indicates that an opposing party objects to it; or (2) the court otherwise believes that a response will be filed. IN R USDCTSD L.R. 7-1(d).

2. *Informal conference to resolve disputes involving non-dispositive issues.* In addition to those conferences required by IN R USDCTSD L.R. 37-1, counsel are encouraged to hold informal conferences in person or by phone to resolve any disputes involving non-dispositive issues that may otherwise require submission of a motion to the Court. This requirement does not apply to cases involving pro se parties. Therefore, prior to filing any non-dispositive motion (including motions for extension of time), the moving party must contact opposing counsel to determine whether there is an objection to any non-dispositive motion (including motions for extension of time), and state in the motion whether opposing counsel objects to the motion. IN R USDCTSD Case Mgt(General Instructions For All Cases). Refer to the Documents section of this document for more information on the contents of the motion.

3. *Application for temporary restraining order.* Applicants for injunctive relief occasionally are faced with the possibility that irreparable injury will occur before the hearing for a preliminary injunction required by FRCP 65(a) can be held. In that event a temporary restraining order may be available under FRCP 65(b). FPP § 2951. The order is designed to preserve the status quo until there is an opportunity to hold a hearing on the application for a preliminary injunction and may be issued with or without notice to the adverse party. FPP § 2951; Granny Goose Foods, Inc. v. Brotherhood of Teamsters & Auto Truck Drivers Local No. 70 of Alameda County, 415 U.S. 423, 94 S.Ct. 1113, 39 L.Ed.2d 435 (1974).

    a. *Issuing with notice.* When the opposing party actually receives notice of the application for a restraining order, the procedure that is followed does not differ functionally from that on an application for a preliminary injunction and the proceeding is not subject to any special requirements. FPP § 2951; Dilworth v. Riner, 343 F.2d 226 (5th Cir. 1965).

        i. *Duration.* By its terms FRCP 65(b) only governs restraining orders issued without notice or a hearing. But. . .it has been argued that its provisions, at least with regard to the duration of a restraining order, apply even to an order granted when notice has been given to the adverse party but there has been no hearing. FPP § 2951.

    b. *Issuing without notice*

        i. *When available.* The court may issue a temporary restraining order without written or oral notice to the adverse party or its attorney only if:

- Specific facts in an affidavit or a verified complaint clearly show that immediate and irreparable injury, loss, or damage will result to the movant before the adverse party can be heard in opposition; and

- The movant's attorney certifies in writing any efforts made to give notice and the reasons why it should not be required. FRCP 65(b)(1).

        ii. *Contents.* Every temporary restraining order issued without notice must state the date and hour it was issued; describe the injury and state why it is irreparable; state why the order was issued without notice; and be promptly filed in the clerk's office and entered in the record. FRCP 65(b)(2).

        iii. *Expiration.* The order expires at the time after entry—not to exceed fourteen (14) days—that the court sets, unless before that time the court, for good cause, extends it for a like period or the adverse party consents to a longer extension. The reasons for an extension must be entered in the record. FRCP 65(b)(2).

    c. *Temporary restraining order versus preliminary injunction.* A temporary restraining order differs from a preliminary injunction, the core reasons being that a temporary restraining order is of limited duration and it may issue without notice to the opposing party before the adverse party can be heard in opposition. FEDPROC § 47:80.

    d. *Factors considered.* As in the case of an application for a preliminary injunction, four factors must be considered in determining whether a temporary restraining order is to be granted, which are whether the moving party has established: (1) a substantial likelihood of success on the merits; (2) that irreparable injury will be suffered if the relief is not granted; (3) that the threatened injury outweighs the harm the relief would inflict on the nonmoving party; and (4) that entry of the relief would serve the public interest. FEDPROC § 47:84; Schiavo ex rel. Schindler v. Schiavo, 403 F.3d 1223 (11th Cir. 2005).

        i. Plaintiffs are not required to prevail on each of these factors, rather, the factors must be viewed as a continuum, with more of one factor compensating for less of another. In each case, however, all of the factors must be considered to determine whether on balance they weigh toward granting relief. FEDPROC § 47:84.

        ii. In the context of a temporary restraining order, it is particularly important for the moving party to demonstrate a substantial likelihood of success on the merits, because otherwise, there would be no justification for the court's intrusion into the ordinary processes of administration and judicial review. FEDPROC § 47:84.

        iii. Refer to the United States District Court for the Southern District of Indiana KeyRules Motion for Preliminary Injunction document for more information on the factors considered in moving for a preliminary injunction.

e. *Burden.* As with a preliminary injunction, the burden is on the moving party to establish that relief is appropriate. FEDPROC § 47:84.

f. *Security.* The court may issue a preliminary injunction or a temporary restraining order only if the movant gives security in an amount that the court considers proper to pay the costs and damages sustained by any party found to have been wrongfully enjoined or restrained. The United States, its officers, and its agencies are not required to give security. FRCP 65(c).

   i. *Proceedings against a surety.* Whenever the Federal Rules of Civil Procedure (including the Supplemental Rules for Admiralty or Maritime Claims and Asset Forfeiture Actions) require or allow a party to give security, and security is given through a bond or other undertaking with one or more sureties, each surety submits to the court's jurisdiction and irrevocably appoints the court clerk as its agent for receiving service of any papers that affect its liability on the bond or undertaking. The surety's liability may be enforced on motion without an independent action. The motion and any notice that the court orders may be served on the court clerk, who must promptly mail a copy of each to every surety whose address is known. FRCP 65.1.

g. *Contents and scope of every injunction and restraining order*

   i. *Contents.* Every order granting an injunction and every restraining order must:

   - State the reasons why it issued;
   - State its terms specifically; and
   - Describe in reasonable detail—and not by referring to the complaint or other document—the act or acts restrained or required. FRCP 65(d)(1).

   ii. *Persons bound.* The order binds only the following who receive actual notice of it by personal service or otherwise:

   - The parties;
   - The parties' officers, agents, servants, employees, and attorneys; and
   - Other persons who are in active concert or participation with anyone described in FRCP 65(d)(2)(A) or FRCP 65(d)(2)(B). FRCP 65(d)(2).

h. *Other laws not modified.* FRCP 65 does not modify the following:

   i. Any federal statute relating to temporary restraining orders or preliminary injunctions in actions affecting employer and employee;

   ii. 28 U.S.C.A. § 2361, which relates to preliminary injunctions in actions of interpleader or in the nature of interpleader; or

   iii. 28 U.S.C.A. § 2284, which relates to actions that must be heard and decided by a three-judge district court. FRCP 65(e).

i. *Copyright impoundment.* FRCP 65 applies to copyright-impoundment proceedings. FRCP 65(f).

4. *Appearances.* Every attorney who represents a party or who files a document on a party's behalf must file an appearance for that party. IN R USDCTSD L.R. 83-7. The filing of a Notice of Appearance shall act to establish the filing attorney as an attorney of record representing a designated party or parties in a particular cause of action. As a result, it is necessary for each attorney to file a separate Notice of Appearance when entering an appearance in a case. A joint appearance on behalf of multiple attorneys may be filed electronically only if it is filed separately for each attorney, using his/her ECF login. IN R USDCTSD ECF Procedures(12). Only those attorneys who have filed an appearance in a pending action are entitled to be served with case documents under FRCP 5(a). IN R USDCTSD L.R. 83-7. For more information, refer to IN R USDCTSD L.R. 83-7 and IN R USDCTSD ECF Procedures(12).

5. *Notice of related action.* A party must file a notice of related action: as soon as it appears that the party's case and another pending case: (1) arise out of the same transaction or occurrence; (2) involve the same property; or (3) involve the validity or infringement or the same patent, trademark, or copyright. IN R USDCTSD L.R. 40-1(d)(2). For more information, refer to IN R USDCTSD L.R. 40-1.

6. *Alternative dispute resolution (ADR)*

    a. *Application.* Unless limited by specific provisions, or unless there are other applicable specific statutory, common law, or constitutional procedures, the Local Alternative Dispute Resolution Rules of the United States District Court for the Southern District of Indiana shall apply in all civil litigation filed in the U.S. District Court for the Southern District of Indiana, except in the following cases and proceedings:

        i. Applications for writs of habeas corpus under 28 U.S.C.A. § 2254;

        ii. Forfeiture cases;

        iii. Non-adversary proceedings in bankruptcy;

        iv. Social Security administrative review cases; and

        v. Such other matters as specified by order of the Court; for example, matters involving important public policy issues, constitutional law, or the establishment of new law. IN R USDCTSD A.D.R. Rule 1.2.

    b. *Mediation.* Mediation under this section (IN R USDCTSD A.D.R. Rule 2.1, et seq.) involves the confidential process by which a person acting as a Mediator, selected by the parties or appointed by the Court, assists the litigants in reaching a mutually acceptable agreement. It is an informal and nonadversarial process. The role of the Mediator is to assist in identifying the issues, reducing misunderstandings, clarifying priorities, exploring areas of compromise, and finding points of agreement as well as legitimate points of disagreement. Final decision-making authority rests with the parties, not the Mediator. IN R USDCTSD A.D.R. Rule 2.1. It is anticipated that an agreement may not resolve all of the disputed issues, but the process, nonetheless, can reduce points of contention. Parties and their representatives are required to mediate in good faith, but are not compelled to reach an agreement. IN R USDCTSD A.D.R. Rule 2.1.

        i. *Case selection.* The Court with the agreement of the parties may refer a civil case for mediation. Unless otherwise ordered or as specifically provided in IN R USDCTSD A.D.R. Rule 2.8, referral to mediation does not abate or suspend the action, and no scheduled dates shall be delayed or deferred, including the date of trial. IN R USDCTSD A.D.R. Rule 2.2.

        ii. For more information on mediation, refer to IN R USDCTSD A.D.R. Rule 2.1, et seq.

    c. *Other methods of dispute resolution.* The Local Alternative Dispute Resolution Rules of the United States District Court for the Southern District of Indiana shall not preclude the parties from utilizing any other reasonable method or technique of alternative dispute resolution to resolve disputes to which the parties agree. However, any use of arbitration by the parties will be governed by and comply with the requirements of 28 U.S.C.A. § 654 through 28 U.S.C.A. § 657. IN R USDCTSD A.D.R. Rule 1.5.

    d. For more information on alternative dispute resolution (ADR), refer to IN R USDCTSD A.D.R. Rule 1.1, et seq.

7. *Notice of settlement or resolution.* The parties must immediately notify the court if they reasonably anticipate settling their case or resolving a pending motion. IN R USDCTSD L.R. 7-1(h).

8. *Modification or suspension of rules.* The court may, on its own motion or at the request of a party, suspend or modify any rule in a particular case in the interest of justice. IN R USDCTSD L.R. 1-1(c).

D. Documents

1. *Application for temporary restraining order (with notice)*

    a. *Required documents*

        i. *Notice of motion and motion.* [P]rior to filing any non-dispositive motion (including motions for extension of time), the moving party must contact opposing counsel to determine whether there is an objection to any non-dispositive motion (including motions for extension of time), and state in the motion whether opposing counsel objects to the motion. If an objection cannot be resolved by counsel, the opposing counsel's position shall be stated within the motion. The motion should also indicate whether opposing counsel plans to file a written objection to the motion and the date by which the Court can expect to receive the objection (within the time limits set in IN R USDCTSD L.R. 7-1). If after a reasonable effort, opposing counsel cannot be reached, the moving party shall recite in the motion the dates and times that messages were left for opposing counsel. IN R USDCTSD Case Mgt(General Instructions For All Cases). Refer to the General Requirements section of this document for information on the notice of motion and motion.

   ii.   *Brief.* Refer to the Format section of this document for the format of briefs.

   iii. *Security.* Refer to the General Requirements section of this document for information on the security required.

   iv. *Certificate of service.* FRCP 5(d) requires that the person making service under FRCP 5 certify that service has been effected. FRCP 5(Advisory Committee Notes). Having such information on file may be useful for many purposes, including proof of service if an issue arises concerning the effectiveness of the service. FRCP 5(Advisory Committee Notes).

- *Certificate of service for electronically-filed documents.* A certificate of service must be included with all documents filed electronically. Such certificate shall indicate that service was accomplished pursuant to the Court's electronic filing procedures. IN R USDCTSD ECF Procedures(11). For the suggested format for a certificate of service for electronic filing, refer to IN R USDCTSD ECF Procedures(11).

b. *Supplemental documents*

   i.   *Supporting evidence.* When a motion relies on facts outside the record, the court may hear the matter on affidavits or may hear it wholly or partly on oral testimony or on depositions. FRCP 43(c).

- *Materials necessary for motion.* A party seeking relief under FRCP 26(c) or FRCP 37, or by way of a pretrial motion that could result in a final order on an issue, must file with the motion those parts of the discovery materials relevant to the motion. IN R USDCTSD L.R. 26-2(a).

   ii. *Notice of constitutional question.* A party that files a pleading, written motion, or other paper drawing into question the constitutionality of a federal or state statute must promptly:

- *File notice.* File a notice of constitutional question stating the question and identifying the paper that raises it, if: (1) a federal statute is questioned and the parties do not include the United States, one of its agencies, or one of its officers or employees in an official capacity; or (2) a state statute is questioned and the parties do not include the state, one of its agencies, or one of its officers or employees in an official capacity; and

- *Serve notice.* Serve the notice and paper on the Attorney General of the United States if a federal statute is questioned—or on the state attorney general if a state statute is questioned—either by certified or registered mail or by sending it to an electronic address designated by the attorney general for this purpose. FRCP 5.1(a).

- *Time for filing.* A notice of constitutional challenge to a statute filed in accordance with FRCP 5.1 must be filed at the same time the parties tender their proposed case management plan, if one is required, or within twenty-one (21) days of the filing drawing into question the constitutionality of a federal or state statute, whichever occurs later. IN R USDCTSD L.R. 5.1-1(a).

- *Additional service requirements.* If a federal statute is challenged, in addition to the service requirements of FRCP 5.1(a), the party filing the notice of constitutional challenge must serve the notice and documents on the United States Attorney for the Southern District of Indiana, either by certified or registered mail or by sending it to an electronic address designated for that purpose by that official. IN R USDCTSD L.R. 5.1-1(b).

- *No forfeiture.* A party's failure to file and serve the notice, or the court's failure to certify, does not forfeit a constitutional claim or defense that is otherwise timely asserted. FRCP 5.1(d).

iii. *Nongovernmental corporate disclosure statement*

- *Contents.* A nongovernmental corporate party must file two (2) copies of a disclosure statement that: (1) identifies any parent corporation and any publicly held corporation owning ten percent (10%) or more of its stock; or (2) states that there is no such corporation. FRCP 7.1(a).

- *Time to file; Supplemental filing.* A party must: (1) file the disclosure statement with its first appearance, pleading, petition, motion, response, or other request addressed to the court; and (2) promptly file a supplemental statement if any required information changes. FRCP 7.1(b).

iv. *Index of exhibits.* Any pleading, motion, brief, affidavit, notice, or proposed order filed with the court, whether electronically or with the clerk, must: if it has four (4) or more exhibits, include a separate index that identifies and briefly describes each exhibit. IN R USDCTSD L.R. 5-1(b).

v. *Request for oral argument.* A party may request oral argument by filing a separate motion explaining why oral argument is necessary and estimating how long the court should allow for the argument. The request must be filed and served with the supporting brief, response brief, or reply brief. IN R USDCTSD L.R. 7-5(a).

vi. *Request for evidentiary hearing.* A party may request an evidentiary hearing on a motion or petition by serving and filing a separate motion explaining why the hearing is necessary and estimating how long the court should allow for the hearing. IN R USDCTSD L.R. 7-5(c).

vii. *Copy of authority.* Generally, copies of cited authorities may not be attached to court filings. However, a party must attach to the party's motion or brief a copy of any cited authority if it is not available on Westlaw or Lexis. Upon request, a party must provide copies of any cited authority that is only available through electronic means to the court or the other parties. IN R USDCTSD L.R. 7-1(f).

viii. *Proposed order.* A party must include a suitable form of order with any document that requests the judge or the clerk to enter a routine or uncontested order. IN R USDCTSD L.R. 5-5(b); IN R USDCTSD L.R. 5-10(c); IN R USDCTSD L.R. 7-1(d).

- A service statement and/or list must be included on each proposed order, as required by IN R USDCTSD L.R. 5-5(d). IN R USDCTSD ECF Procedures(11). Any pleading, motion, brief, affidavit, notice, or proposed order filed with the court, whether electronically or with the clerk, must: if it is a form of order, include a statement of service, in the format required by IN R USDCTSD L.R. 5-5(d) in the lower left corner of the document. IN R USDCTSD L.R. 5-1(b).

- A party electronically filing a proposed order—whether voluntarily or because required by IN R USDCTSD L.R. 5-5—must convert the order directly from a word processing program and file it as an attachment to the document it relates to. Proposed orders must include in the lower left-hand corner of the signature page a statement that service will be made electronically on all ECF-registered counsel of record via email generated by the court's ECF system, without listing all such counsel. A service list including the name and postal address of any pro se litigant or non-registered attorney of record must follow, stating that service on the listed individuals will be made in the traditional paper manner, via first-class U.S. Mail. IN R USDCTSD L.R. 5-5(d).

ix. *Copy of document with self-address envelope.* To receive a file-stamped copy of a document filed directly with the clerk, a party must include with the original document an additional copy and a self-addressed envelope. The envelope must be big enough to hold the copy and have enough postage on it to send the copy via regular first-class mail. IN R USDCTSD L.R. 5-10(b).

x. *Notice of manual filing.* When a party who is not exempt from the electronic filing requirement files a document directly with the clerk, the party must: electronically file a notice of manual filing that explains why the document cannot be filed electronically. IN R USDCTSD L.R. 5-2(d)(1). Refer to the Filing and Service Requirements section of this document for more information.

- Where an individual component cannot be included in an electronic filing (e.g. the

component cannot be converted to electronic format), the filer shall electronically file the prescribed Notice of Manual Filing in place of that component. A model form is provided as Appendix C (IN R USDCTSD ECF Procedures(Appendix C)). IN R USDCTSD ECF Procedures(13).

- Before making a manual filing of a component, the filing party shall first electronically file a Notice of Manual Filing (See IN R USDCTSD ECF Procedures(Appendix C)). The filer shall initiate the electronic filing process as if filing the actual component but shall instead attach to the filing the Notice of Manual Filing setting forth the reason(s) why the component cannot be filed electronically. The manual filing should be accompanied by a copy of the previously filed Notice of Manual Filing. A party may seek to have a component excluded from electronic filing pursuant to applicable Federal and Local Rules (e.g., FRCP 26(c)). IN R USDCTSD ECF Procedures(15).

xi. *Courtesy copies.* District Judges and Magistrate Judges regularly receive documents filed by all parties. Therefore, parties shall not bring "courtesy copies" to any chambers unless specifically directed to do so by the Court. IN R USDCTSD Case Mgt(General Instructions For All Cases).

xii. *Copies for three-judge court.* Parties in a case where a three-judge court has been requested must file an original and three copies of any document filed directly with the clerk (instead of electronically) until the court: (1) denies the request; (2) dissolves the three-judge court; or (3) allows the parties to file fewer copies. IN R USDCTSD L.R. 9-2(c).

xiii. *Declaration that party was unable to file in a timely manner due to technical difficulties.* If a party misses a filing deadline due to an inability to file electronically, the party may submit the untimely filed document, accompanied by a declaration stating the reason(s) for missing the deadline. IN R USDCTSD ECF Procedures(16). A model form is provided as Appendix D (IN R USDCTSD ECF Procedures(Appendix D)). IN R USDCTSD ECF Procedures(16).

2. *Application for temporary restraining order (without notice, or "ex parte")*

a. *Required documents*

i. *Motion.* [P]rior to filing any non-dispositive motion (including motions for extension of time), the moving party must contact opposing counsel to determine whether there is an objection to any non-dispositive motion (including motions for extension of time), and state in the motion whether opposing counsel objects to the motion. If an objection cannot be resolved by counsel, the opposing counsel's position shall be stated within the motion. The motion should also indicate whether opposing counsel plans to file a written objection to the motion and the date by which the Court can expect to receive the objection (within the time limits set in IN R USDCTSD L.R. 7-1). If after a reasonable effort, opposing counsel cannot be reached, the moving party shall recite in the motion the dates and times that messages were left for opposing counsel. IN R USDCTSD Case Mgt(General Instructions For All Cases). Refer to the General Requirements section of this document for information on the motion.

ii. *Brief.* Refer to the Format section of this document for the format of briefs.

iii. *Affidavit or verified complaint.* The applicant for an ex parte restraining order must present to the court, in an affidavit or a verified complaint, facts that clearly show irreparable injury. FPP § 2952.

iv. *Certificate of attorney.* The applicant's attorney must certify in writing any efforts made to give notice and the reasons why it should not be required. FEDPROC § 47:81.

v. *Security.* Refer to the General Requirements section of this document for information on the security required.

b. *Supplemental documents*

i. *Supporting evidence.* When a motion relies on facts outside the record, the court may hear the matter on affidavits or may hear it wholly or partly on oral testimony or on depositions. FRCP 43(c).

- *Materials necessary for motion.* A party seeking relief under FRCP 26(c) or FRCP 37, or by way of a pretrial motion that could result in a final order on an issue, must file with the motion those parts of the discovery materials relevant to the motion. IN R USDCTSD L.R. 26-2(a).

ii. *Notice of constitutional question.* A party that files a pleading, written motion, or other paper drawing into question the constitutionality of a federal or state statute must promptly:

- *File notice.* File a notice of constitutional question stating the question and identifying the paper that raises it, if: (1) a federal statute is questioned and the parties do not include the United States, one of its agencies, or one of its officers or employees in an official capacity; or (2) a state statute is questioned and the parties do not include the state, one of its agencies, or one of its officers or employees in an official capacity; and

- *Serve notice.* Serve the notice and paper on the Attorney General of the United States if a federal statute is questioned—or on the state attorney general if a state statute is questioned—either by certified or registered mail or by sending it to an electronic address designated by the attorney general for this purpose. FRCP 5.1(a).

- *Time for filing.* A notice of constitutional challenge to a statute filed in accordance with FRCP 5.1 must be filed at the same time the parties tender their proposed case management plan, if one is required, or within twenty-one (21) days of the filing drawing into question the constitutionality of a federal or state statute, whichever occurs later. IN R USDCTSD L.R. 5.1-1(a).

- *Additional service requirements.* If a federal statute is challenged, in addition to the service requirements of FRCP 5.1(a), the party filing the notice of constitutional challenge must serve the notice and documents on the United States Attorney for the Southern District of Indiana, either by certified or registered mail or by sending it to an electronic address designated for that purpose by that official. IN R USDCTSD L.R. 5.1-1(b).

- *No forfeiture.* A party's failure to file and serve the notice, or the court's failure to certify, does not forfeit a constitutional claim or defense that is otherwise timely asserted. FRCP 5.1(d).

iii. *Nongovernmental corporate disclosure statement*

- *Contents.* A nongovernmental corporate party must file two (2) copies of a disclosure statement that: (1) identifies any parent corporation and any publicly held corporation owning ten percent (10%) or more of its stock; or (2) states that there is no such corporation. FRCP 7.1(a).

- *Time to file; Supplemental filing.* A party must: (1) file the disclosure statement with its first appearance, pleading, petition, motion, response, or other request addressed to the court; and (2) promptly file a supplemental statement if any required information changes. FRCP 7.1(b).

iv. *Index of exhibits.* Any pleading, motion, brief, affidavit, notice, or proposed order filed with the court, whether electronically or with the clerk, must: if it has four (4) or more exhibits, include a separate index that identifies and briefly describes each exhibit. IN R USDCTSD L.R. 5-1(b).

v. *Request for oral argument.* A party may request oral argument by filing a separate motion explaining why oral argument is necessary and estimating how long the court should allow for the argument. The request must be filed and served with the supporting brief, response brief, or reply brief. IN R USDCTSD L.R. 7-5(a).

vi. *Request for evidentiary hearing.* A party may request an evidentiary hearing on a motion or petition by serving and filing a separate motion explaining why the hearing is necessary and estimating how long the court should allow for the hearing. IN R USDCTSD L.R. 7-5(c).

vii. *Copy of authority.* Generally, copies of cited authorities may not be attached to court filings. However, a party must attach to the party's motion or brief a copy of any cited authority if it is not available on Westlaw or Lexis. Upon request, a party must provide copies of any cited authority that is only available through electronic means to the court or the other parties. IN R USDCTSD L.R. 7-1(f).

viii. *Proposed order.* A party must include a suitable form of order with any document that requests the judge or the clerk to enter a routine or uncontested order. IN R USDCTSD L.R. 5-5(b); IN R USDCTSD L.R. 5-10(c); IN R USDCTSD L.R. 7-1(d).

- A service statement and/or list must be included on each proposed order, as required by IN R USDCTSD L.R. 5-5(d). IN R USDCTSD ECF Procedures(11). Any pleading, motion, brief, affidavit, notice, or proposed order filed with the court, whether electronically or with the clerk, must: if it is a form of order, include a statement of service, in the format required by IN R USDCTSD L.R. 5-5(d) in the lower left corner of the document. IN R USDCTSD L.R. 5-1(b).

- A party electronically filing a proposed order—whether voluntarily or because required by IN R USDCTSD L.R. 5-5—must convert the order directly from a word processing program and file it as an attachment to the document it relates to. Proposed orders must include in the lower left-hand corner of the signature page a statement that service will be made electronically on all ECF-registered counsel of record via email generated by the court's ECF system, without listing all such counsel. A service list including the name and postal address of any pro se litigant or non-registered attorney of record must follow, stating that service on the listed individuals will be made in the traditional paper manner, via first-class U.S. Mail. IN R USDCTSD L.R. 5-5(d).

ix. *Copy of document with self-address envelope.* To receive a file-stamped copy of a document filed directly with the clerk, a party must include with the original document an additional copy and a self-addressed envelope. The envelope must be big enough to hold the copy and have enough postage on it to send the copy via regular first-class mail. IN R USDCTSD L.R. 5-10(b).

x. *Notice of manual filing.* When a party who is not exempt from the electronic filing requirement files a document directly with the clerk, the party must: electronically file a notice of manual filing that explains why the document cannot be filed electronically. IN R USDCTSD L.R. 5-2(d)(1). Refer to the Filing and Service Requirements section of this document for more information.

- Where an individual component cannot be included in an electronic filing (e.g. the component cannot be converted to electronic format), the filer shall electronically file the prescribed Notice of Manual Filing in place of that component. A model form is provided as Appendix C (IN R USDCTSD ECF Procedures(Appendix C)). IN R USDCTSD ECF Procedures(13).

- Before making a manual filing of a component, the filing party shall first electronically file a Notice of Manual Filing (See IN R USDCTSD ECF Procedures(Appendix C)). The filer shall initiate the electronic filing process as if filing the actual component but shall instead attach to the filing the Notice of Manual Filing setting forth the reason(s) why the component cannot be filed electronically. The manual filing should be accompanied by a copy of the previously filed Notice of Manual Filing. A party may seek to have a component excluded from electronic filing pursuant to applicable Federal and Local Rules (e.g., FRCP 26(c)). IN R USDCTSD ECF Procedures(15).

xi. *Courtesy copies.* District Judges and Magistrate Judges regularly receive documents filed by all parties. Therefore, parties shall not bring "courtesy copies" to any chambers unless specifically directed to do so by the Court. IN R USDCTSD Case Mgt(General Instructions For All Cases).

xii. *Copies for three-judge court.* Parties in a case where a three-judge court has been requested must file an original and three copies of any document filed directly with the clerk (instead of electronically) until the court: (1) denies the request; (2) dissolves the three-judge court; or (3) allows the parties to file fewer copies. IN R USDCTSD L.R. 9-2(c).

xiii. *Declaration that party was unable to file in a timely manner due to technical difficulties.* If a party misses a filing deadline due to an inability to file electronically, the party may submit the untimely filed document, accompanied by a declaration stating the reason(s) for missing the deadline. IN R USDCTSD ECF Procedures(16). A model form is provided as Appendix D (IN R USDCTSD ECF Procedures(Appendix D)). IN R USDCTSD ECF Procedures(16).

E. Format

1.   *Form of documents.* The rules governing captions and other matters of form in pleadings apply to motions and other papers. FRCP 7(b)(2).

   a.   *Paper (manual filings only).* Any document that is not filed electronically must: be flat, unfolded, and on good-quality, eight and one-half by eleven (8-1/2 x 11) inch white paper. IN R USDCTSD L.R. 5-1(d)(1). Any document that is not filed electronically must: be single-sided. IN R USDCTSD L.R. 5-1(d)(1).

      i.   *Covers or backing.* Any document that is not filed electronically must: not have a cover or a back. IN R USDCTSD L.R. 5-1(d)(1).

      ii. *Fastening.* Any document that is not filed electronically must: be (if consisting of more than one (1) page) fastened by paperclip or binder clip and may not be stapled. IN R USDCTSD L.R. 5-1(d)(1).

         •   *Request for nonconforming fastening.* If a document cannot be fastened or bound as required by IN R USDCTSD L.R. 5-1(d), a party may ask the clerk for permission to fasten it in another manner. The party must make such a request before attempting to file the document with nonconforming fastening. IN R USDCTSD L.R. 5-1(d)(2).

      iii. *Hole punching.* Any document that is not filed electronically must: be two-hole punched at the top with the holes two and three-quarter (2-3/4) inches apart and appropriately centered. IN R USDCTSD L.R. 5-1(d)(1).

   b.   *Margins.* Any pleading, motion, brief, affidavit, notice, or proposed order filed with the court, whether electronically or with the clerk, must: have at least one (1) inch margins. IN R USDCTSD L.R. 5-1(b).

   c.   *Spacing.* Any pleading, motion, brief, affidavit, notice, or proposed order filed with the court, whether electronically or with the clerk, must: be double spaced (except for headings, footnotes, and quoted material). IN R USDCTSD L.R. 5-1(b).

   d.   *Text.* Any pleading, motion, brief, affidavit, notice, or proposed order filed with the court, whether electronically or with the clerk, must: be plainly typewritten, printed, or prepared by a clearly legible copying process. IN R USDCTSD L.R. 5-1(b).

   e.   *Font size.* Any pleading, motion, brief, affidavit, notice, or proposed order filed with the court, whether electronically or with the clerk, must: use at least 12-point type in the body of the document and at least 10-point type in footnotes. IN R USDCTSD L.R. 5-1(b).

   f.   *Page numbering.* Any pleading, motion, brief, affidavit, notice, or proposed order filed with the court, whether electronically or with the clerk, must: have consecutively numbered pages. IN R USDCTSD L.R. 5-1(b).

   g.   *Caption; Names of parties.* Every pleading must have a caption with the court's name, a title, a file number, and a FRCP 7(a) designation. The title of the complaint must name all the parties; the title of other pleadings, after naming the first party on each side, may refer generally to other parties. FRCP 10(a). Any pleading, motion, brief, affidavit, notice, or proposed order filed with the court, whether electronically or with the clerk, must: include a title on the first page. IN R USDCTSD L.R. 5-1(b).

      i.   *Alternative motions.* Motions must be filed separately, but alternative motions may be filed in a single document if each is named in the title. IN R USDCTSD L.R. 7-1(a).

   h.   *Filer's information.* Any pleading, motion, brief, affidavit, notice, or proposed order filed with the court, whether electronically or with the clerk, must: in the case of pleadings, motions, legal briefs, and notices, include the name, complete address, telephone number, facsimile number (where available), and e-mail address (where available) of the pro se litigant or attorney who files it. IN R USDCTSD L.R. 5-1(b).

   i.   *Paragraphs; Separate statements.* A party must state its claims or defenses in numbered paragraphs, each limited as far as practicable to a single set of circumstances. A later pleading may refer by number to a paragraph in an earlier pleading. If doing so would promote clarity, each claim founded on a separate transaction or occurrence—and each defense other than a denial—must be stated in a separate count or defense. FRCP 10(b).

j. *Adoption by reference; Exhibits.* A statement in a pleading may be adopted by reference elsewhere in the same pleading or in any other pleading or motion. A copy of a written instrument that is an exhibit to a pleading is a part of the pleading for all purposes. FRCP 10(c).

k. *Citations*

    i. *Local rules.* The Local Rules of the United States District Court for the Southern District of Indiana may be cited as "S.D. Ind. L.R." IN R USDCTSD L.R. 1-1(a).

    ii. *Local alternative dispute resolution rules.* These Rules shall be known as the Local Alternative Dispute Resolution Rules of the United States District Court for the Southern District of Indiana. They shall be cited as "S.D.Ind. Local A.D.R. Rule _____." IN R USDCTSD A.D.R. Rule 1.1.

l. *Acceptance by the clerk.* The clerk must not refuse to file a paper solely because it is not in the form prescribed by the Federal Rules of Civil Procedure or by a local rule or practice. FRCP 5(d)(4). The clerk will accept a document that violates IN R USDCTSD L.R. 5-1, but the court may exclude the document from the official record. IN R USDCTSD L.R. 5-1(e).

    i. *Sanctions for errors as to form.* The court may strike from the record any document that does not comply with the rules governing the form of documents filed with the court, such as rules that regulate document size or the number of copies to be filed or that require a special designation in the caption. The court may also sanction an attorney or party who files a non-compliant document. IN R USDCTSD L.R. 1-3.

2. *Form of electronic documents.* Any document submitted via the court's electronic case filing (ECF) system must be: otherwise prepared and filed in a manner consistent with the CM/ECF Policies and Procedures Manual (IN R USDCTSD ECF Procedures). IN R USDCTSD L.R. 5-1(c). Electronically filed documents must meet the requirements of FRCP 10 (Form of Pleadings), IN R USDCTSD L.R. 5-1 (Format of Papers Presented for Filing), and FRCP 5.2 (Privacy Protection for Filings Made with the Court), as if they had been submitted on paper. Documents filed electronically are also subject to any page limitations set forth by Court Order, by IN R USDCTSD L.R. 7-1 (Motion Practice), or IN R USDCTSD L.R. 56-1 (Summary Judgment Practice), as applicable. IN R USDCTSD ECF Procedures(13).

a. *PDF format required.* Any document submitted via the court's electronic case filing (ECF) system must be: in .pdf format. IN R USDCTSD L.R. 5-1(c); IN R USDCTSD ECF Procedures(7). Any document submitted via the court's electronic case filing (ECF) system must be: converted to a .pdf file directly from a word processing program, unless it exists only in paper format (in which case it may be scanned to create a .pdf document). IN R USDCTSD L.R. 5-1(c); IN R USDCTSD ECF Procedures(13).

    i. An exhibit may be scanned into PDF format, at a recommended 300 dpi resolution or higher, only if it does not already exist in electronic format. The filing attorney is responsible for reviewing all PDF documents for legibility before submitting them through the Court's Electronic Case Filing system. For technical guidance in creating PDF documents, please contact the Clerk's Office. IN R USDCTSD ECF Procedures(13).

b. *File size limitations.* Any document submitted via the court's electronic case filing (ECF) system must be: submitted as one or more .pdf files that do not exceed ten megabytes (10 MB) each (consistent with the CM/ECF Policies and Procedures Manual (IN R USDCTSD ECF Procedures)). IN R USDCTSD L.R. 5-1(c); IN R USDCTSD ECF Procedures(13).

    i. To electronically file a document or attachment that exceeds ten megabytes (10 MB), the document must first be broken down into two or more smaller files. For example, if Exhibit A is a twelve megabyte (12 MB) PDF file, it should be divided into 2 equal parts prior to electronic filing. Each component part of the exhibit would be filed as an attachment to the main document and described appropriately as "Exhibit A (part 1 of 2)" and "Exhibit A (part 2 of 2)." IN R USDCTSD ECF Procedures(13).

    ii. The supporting items mentioned in IN R USDCTSD ECF Procedures(13) should not be confused with memorandums or briefs in support of motions as outlined in IN R USDCTSD L.R. 7-1 or IN R USDCTSD L.R. 56-1. These memorandums or briefs in support are to be filed as entirely separate documents pursuant to the appropriate rule. Additionally, no motion shall be embodied in the text of a response or reply brief/memorandum unless otherwise ordered by the Court. IN R USDCTSD ECF Procedures(13).

c. *Separate component parts.* A key objective of the electronic filing system is to ensure that as much of the case as possible is managed electronically. To facilitate electronic filing and retrieval, documents to be filed electronically are to be reasonably broken into their separate component parts. By way of example, most filings include a foundation document (e.g., motion) and other supporting items (e.g., exhibits, proposed orders, proposed amended pleadings). The foundation document, as well as the supporting items, are each separate components of the filing; supporting items must be filed as attachments to the foundation document. These exhibits or attachments should include only those excerpts of the referenced documents that are directly germane to the matter under consideration. IN R USDCTSD ECF Procedures(13).

   i. Where an individual component cannot be included in an electronic filing (e.g. the component cannot be converted to electronic format), the filer shall electronically file the prescribed Notice of Manual Filing in place of that component. A model form is provided as Appendix C (IN R USDCTSD ECF Procedures(Appendix C)). IN R USDCTSD ECF Procedures(13).

d. *Exhibits.* Each electronically filed exhibit to a main document must be: (1) created as a separate .pdf file; (2) submitted as an attachment to the main document and given a title which describes its content; and (3) limited to excerpts that are directly germane to the main document's subject matter. IN R USDCTSD L.R. 5-6(a).

   i. When uploading attachments during the electronic filing process, exhibits must be uploaded in a logical sequence and a brief description must be entered for each individual PDF file. The description must include not only the exhibit number or letter, but also a brief description of the document. This information may be entered in CM/ECF using a combination of the Category drop-down menu, the Description text box, or both (see IN R USDCTSD ECF Procedures(13)(Figure 1)). The information that is provided in each box will be combined to create a description of the document as it appears on the case docket (see IN R USDCTSD ECF Procedures(13)(Figure 2)). IN R USDCTSD ECF Procedures(13). For an example, refer to IN R USDCTSD ECF Procedures(13).

e. *Excerpts.* A party filing an exhibit that consists of excerpts from a larger document must clearly and prominently identify the exhibit as containing excerpted material. Either party will have the right to timely file additional excerpts or the complete document to the extent they are or become directly germane to the main document's subject matter. IN R USDCTSD L.R. 5-6(b).

f. For an example illustrating the application of IN R USDCTSD ECF Procedures(13), refer to IN R USDCTSD ECF Procedures(13).

3. *Form of briefs*

a. *Page limits.* Supporting and response briefs (excluding tables of contents, tables of authorities, appendices, and certificates of service) may not exceed thirty-five (35) pages. Reply briefs may not exceed twenty (20) pages. IN R USDCTSD L.R. 7-1(e)(1).

   i. *Permission to exceed limits.* The court may allow a party to file a brief exceeding these page limits for extraordinary and compelling reasons. IN R USDCTSD L.R. 7-1(e)(2).

   ii. *Supporting and response briefs exceeding limits.* If the court allows a party to file a brief or response exceeding thirty-five (35) pages, the document must include:

   - A table of contents with page references;

   - A statement of issues; and

   - A table of authorities including: (1) all cases (alphabetically arranged), statutes, and other authorities cited in the brief; and (2) page numbers where the authorities are cited in the brief. IN R USDCTSD L.R. 7-1(e)(3).

4. *Signing of pleadings, motions and other papers*

   a. *Signature.* Every pleading, written motion, and other paper must be signed by at least one attorney of record in the attorney's name—or by a party personally if the party is unrepresented. The paper must state the signer's address, e-mail address, and telephone number. FRCP 11(a).

      i. *Signatures on manual filings.* Any document that is not filed electronically must: include the original signature of the pro se litigant or attorney who files it. IN R USDCTSD L.R. 5-1(d)(1).

      ii. *Electronic signatures.* Use of the attorney's login and password when filing documents electronically serves in part as the attorney's signature for purposes of FRCP 11, the Local Rules of the United States District Court for the Southern District of Indiana, and any other purpose for which a signature is required in connection with proceedings before the Court. IN R USDCTSD ECF Procedures(14); IN R USDCTSD ECF Procedures(10). A pleading, motion, brief, or notice filed electronically under an attorney's ECF log-in and password must be signed by that attorney. IN R USDCTSD L.R. 5-7(a). A signature on a document other than a document filed as provided under IN R USDCTSD L.R. 5-7(a) must be an original handwritten signature and must be scanned into .pdf format for electronic filing. IN R USDCTSD L.R. 5-7(c); IN R USDCTSD ECF Procedures(14).

         • *Form of electronic signature.* If a document is converted directly from a word processing application to .pdf (as opposed to scanning), the name of the Filing User under whose log-in and password the document is submitted must be preceded by a "s/" and typed on the signature line where the Filing User's handwritten signature would otherwise appear. IN R USDCTSD L.R. 5-7(b). All documents filed electronically shall include a signature block and include the filing attorney's typewritten name, address, telephone number, facsimile number and e-mail address. In addition, the name of the filing attorney under whose ECF login the document will be filed should be preceded by a "s/" and typed in the space where the attorney's handwritten signature would otherwise appear. IN R US-DCTSD ECF Procedures(14). For a sample format, refer to IN R USDCTSD ECF Procedures(14).

         • *Effect of electronic signature.* Filing an electronically signed document under an attorney's ECF log-in and password constitutes the attorney's signature on the document under the Federal Rules of Civil Procedure, under the Local Rules of the United States District Court for the Southern District of Indiana, and for any other reason a signature is required in connection with the court's activities. IN R USDCTSD L.R. 5-7(d).

         • *Documents with multiple attorneys' signatures.* Documents requiring signatures of more than one attorney shall be filed either by: (1) obtaining consent from the other attorney, then typing the "s/ [Name]" signature of the other attorney on the signature line where the other attorney's signature would otherwise appear; (2) identifying in the signature section the name of the other attorney whose signature is required and by the submission of a Notice of Endorsement (see IN R USDCTSD ECF Procedures(Appendix B)) by the other attorney no later than three (3) business days after filing; (3) submitting a scanned document containing all handwritten signatures; or (4) in any other manner approved by the Court. IN R USDCTSD ECF Procedures(14); IN R USDCTSD L.R. 5-7(e).

      iii. *No verification or accompanying affidavit required for pleadings.* Unless a rule or statute specifically states otherwise, a pleading need not be verified or accompanied by an affidavit. FRCP 11(a).

      iv. *Unsigned papers.* The court must strike an unsigned paper unless the omission is promptly corrected after being called to the attorney's or party's attention. FRCP 11(a). The court will strike any document filed directly with the clerk that is not signed by an attorney of record or the pro se litigant filing it, but the court may do so only after giving the attorney or pro se litigant notice of the omission and reasonable time to correct it. Rubber-stamp or facsimile signatures are not original signatures and the court will deem documents containing them to be unsigned for purposes of FRCP 11 and FRCP 26(g) and IN R USDCTSD L.R. 5-10. IN R USDCTSD L.R. 5-10(g).

b. *Representations to the court.* By presenting to the court a pleading, written motion, or other paper—whether by signing, filing, submitting, or later advocating it—an attorney or unrepresented party certifies that to the best of the person's knowledge, information, and belief, formed after an inquiry reasonable under the circumstances:

    i.   It is not being presented for any improper purpose, such as to harass, cause unnecessary delay, or needlessly increase the cost of litigation;

    ii.   The claims, defenses, and other legal contentions are warranted by existing law or by a nonfrivolous argument for extending, modifying, or reversing existing law or for establishing new law;

    iii.   The factual contentions have evidentiary support or, if specifically so identified, will likely have evidentiary support after a reasonable opportunity for further investigation or discovery; and

    iv.   The denials of factual contentions are warranted on the evidence or, if specifically so identified, are reasonably based on belief or a lack of information. FRCP 11(b).

c. *Sanctions.* If, after notice and a reasonable opportunity to respond, the court determines that FRCP 11(b) has been violated, the court may impose an appropriate sanction on any attorney, law firm, or party that violated FRCP 11(b) or is responsible for the violation. FRCP 11(c)(1). Refer to the United States District Court for the Southern District of Indiana KeyRules Motion for Sanctions document for more information.

5. *Privacy protection for filings made with the court.* Electronically filed documents must meet the requirements of. . .FRCP 5.2 (Privacy Protection for Filings Made with the Court), as if they had been submitted on paper. IN R USDCTSD ECF Procedures(13).

a. *Redacted filings.* Unless the court orders otherwise, in an electronic or paper filing with the court that contains an individual's Social Security number, taxpayer-identification number, or birth date, the name of an individual known to be a minor, or a financial-account number, a party or nonparty making the filing may include only:

    i.   The last four (4) digits of the Social Security number and taxpayer-identification number;

    ii.   The year of the individual's birth;

    iii.   The minor's initials; and

    iv.   The last four (4) digits of the financial-account number. FRCP 5.2(a).

b. *Exemptions from the redaction requirement.* The redaction requirement does not apply to the following:

    i.   A financial-account number that identifies the property allegedly subject to forfeiture in a forfeiture proceeding;

    ii.   The record of an administrative or agency proceeding;

    iii.   The official record of a state-court proceeding;

    iv.   The record of a court or tribunal, if that record was not subject to the redaction requirement when originally filed;

    v.   A filing covered by FRCP 5.2(c) or FRCP 5.2(d); and

    vi.   A pro se filing in an action brought under 28 U.S.C.A. § 2241, 28 U.S.C.A. § 2254, or 28 U.S.C.A. § 2255. FRCP 5.2(b).

c. *Limitations on remote access to electronic files; Social Security appeals and immigration cases.* Unless the court orders otherwise, in an action for benefits under the Social Security Act, and in an action or proceeding relating to an order of removal, to relief from removal, or to immigration benefits or detention, access to an electronic file is authorized as follows:

    i.   The parties and their attorneys may have remote electronic access to any part of the case file, including the administrative record;

    ii. Any other person may have electronic access to the full record at the courthouse, but may have remote electronic access only to:

- The docket maintained by the court; and
- An opinion, order, judgment, or other disposition of the court, but not any other part of the case file or the administrative record. FRCP 5.2(c).

  d. *Filings made under seal.* The court may order that a filing be made under seal without redaction. The court may later unseal the filing or order the person who made the filing to file a redacted version for the public record. FRCP 5.2(d). For more information on filing under seal, refer to IN R USDCTSD L.R. 5-11 and IN R USDCTSD ECF Procedures(18).

  e. *Protective orders.* For good cause, the court may by order in a case:

    i. Require redaction of additional information; or

    ii. Limit or prohibit a nonparty's remote electronic access to a document filed with the court. FRCP 5.2(e).

  f. *Option for additional unredacted filing under seal.* A person making a redacted filing may also file an unredacted copy under seal. The court must retain the unredacted copy as part of the record. FRCP 5.2(f).

  g. *Option for filing a reference list.* A filing that contains redacted information may be filed together with a reference list that identifies each item of redacted information and specifies an appropriate identifier that uniquely corresponds to each item listed. The list must be filed under seal and may be amended as of right. Any reference in the case to a listed identifier will be construed to refer to the corresponding item of information. FRCP 5.2(g).

  h. *Waiver of protection of identifiers.* A person waives the protection of FRCP 5.2(a) as to the person's own information by filing it without redaction and not under seal. FRCP 5.2(h).

F. Filing and Service Requirements

1. *Filing requirements.* Any paper after the complaint that is required to be served—together with a certificate of service—must be filed within a reasonable time after service. FRCP 5(d)(1). Motions must be filed separately, but alternative motions may be filed in a single document if each is named in the title. IN R USDCTSD L.R. 7-1(a).

  a. *How filing is made; In general.* A paper is filed by delivering it:

    i. To the clerk; or

    ii. To a judge who agrees to accept it for filing, and who must then note the filing date on the paper and promptly send it to the clerk. FRCP 5(d)(2).

- In certain instances, the court will direct the parties to submit items directly to chambers (e.g., confidential settlement statements). However, absent specific prior authorization, counsel and litigants should not submit letters or documents directly to chambers, and such materials should be filed with the clerk. IN R USDCTSD L.R. 5-1(Local Rules Advisory Committee Comment).

    iii. A document or item submitted in relation to a matter within the court's jurisdiction is deemed filed upon delivery to the office of the clerk in a manner prescribed by the Local Rules of the United States District Court for the Southern District of Indiana or the Federal Rules of Civil Procedure or authorized by the court. Any submission directed to a Judge or Judge's staff, the office of the clerk or any employee thereof, in a manner that is not contemplated by IN R USDCTSD L.R. 5-1 and without prior court authorization is prohibited. IN R USDCTSD L.R. 5-1(a).

  b. *Non-electronic filing.* Any document that is exempt from electronic filing must be filed directly with the clerk and served on other parties in the case as required by those Federal Rules of Civil Procedure and Local Rules of the United States District Court for the Southern District of Indiana that apply to the service of non-electronic documents. IN R USDCTSD L.R. 5-2(c).

i. *When completed.* A document or other item that is not required to be filed electronically is deemed filed:

- Upon delivery in person, by courier, or via U.S. Mail or other mail delivery service to the clerk's office during business hours;

- When the courtroom deputy clerk accepts it, if the document or item is filed in open court; or

- Upon completion of any other manner of filing that the court authorizes. IN R USDCTSD L.R. 5-10(a).

ii. *Document filing by non-exempt party.* When a party who is not exempt from the electronic filing requirement files a document directly with the clerk, the party must:

- Electronically file a notice of manual filing that explains why the document cannot be filed electronically;

- Present the document to the clerk within one (1) business day after filing the notice of manual filing; and

- Present the clerk with a copy of the notice of manual filing when the party files the document with the clerk. IN R USDCTSD L.R. 5-2(d).

c. *Electronic filing*

i. *Authorization of electronic filing program.* A court may, by local rule, allow papers to be filed, signed, or verified by electronic means that are consistent with any technical standards established by the Judicial Conference of the United States. A local rule may require electronic filing only if reasonable exceptions are allowed. A paper filed electronically in compliance with a local rule is a written paper for purposes of the Federal Rules of Civil Procedure. FRCP 5(d)(3).

- IN R USDCTSD L.R. 5-2 requires electronic filing, as allowed by FRCP 5(d)(3). The policies and procedures in IN R USDCTSD ECF Procedures govern electronic filing in this district unless, due to circumstances in a particular case, a judicial officer determines that these policies and procedures (IN R USDCTSD ECF Procedures) should be modified. IN R USDCTSD ECF Procedures(1).

- Unless modified by order of the Court, all Federal Rules of Civil Procedure and Local Rules of the United States District Court for the Southern District of Indiana shall continue to apply to cases maintained in the Court's Case Management/Electronic Case Filing System (CM/ECF). IN R USDCTSD ECF Procedures(3).

ii. *Mandatory electronic filing.* Unless exempted pursuant to IN R USDCTSD L.R. 5-3(e), attorneys admitted to the court's bar (including those admitted pro hac vice) or authorized to represent the United States must use the court's ECF system to file documents. IN R USDCTSD L.R. 5-3(a). Electronic filing by attorneys is required for eligible documents filed in civil and criminal cases pending with the Court, unless specifically exempted by Local Rule or Court Order. IN R USDCTSD ECF Procedures(4).

- *Exceptions.* All civil cases (other than those cases the court specifically exempts) must be maintained in the court's electronic case filing (ECF) system. Accordingly, as allowed by FRCP 5(d)(3), every document filed in this court (including exhibits) must be transmitted to the clerk's office via the ECF system consistent with IN R USDCTSD L.R. 5-2 through IN R USDCTSD L.R. 5-11 except: (1) documents filed by pro se litigants; (2) transcripts in cases filed by claimants under the Social Security Act (and related statutes); (3) exhibits in a format that does not readily permit electronic filing (such as videos and large maps and charts); (4) documents that are illegible when scanned into .pdf format; (5) documents filed in cases not maintained on the ECF system; and (6) any other documents that the court or the Local Rules of the United States District Court for the Southern District of

Indiana specifically allow to be filed directly with the clerk. IN R USDCTSD L.R. 5-2(a). Parties otherwise participating in the electronic filing system may be excused from filing a particular component electronically under certain limited circumstances, such as when the component cannot be reduced to an electronic format. Such components shall not be filed electronically, but instead shall be manually filed with the Clerk of Court and served upon the parties in accordance with the applicable Federal Rules of Civil Procedure and the Local Rules of the United States District Court for the Southern District of Indiana for filing and service of non-electronic documents. IN R USDCTSD ECF Procedures(15).

- *Exemption from participation.* The court may exempt attorneys from using the ECF system in a particular case for good cause. An attorney must file a petition for ECF exemption and a CM/ECF technical requirements exemption questionnaire in each case in which the attorney seeks an exemption. (The CM/ECF technical requirements exemption questionnaire is available on the court's website). IN R USDCTSD L.R. 5-3(e).

iii. *Consequences of electronic filing.* Electronic transmission of a document consistent with the procedures adopted by the Court shall, upon the complete receipt of the same by the Clerk of Court, constitute filing of the document for all purposes of the Federal Rules of Civil and Criminal Procedure and the Local Rules of the United States District Court for the Southern District of Indiana, and shall constitute entry of that document onto the docket maintained by the Clerk pursuant to FRCP 58 and FRCP 79. IN R USDCTSD ECF Procedures(7); IN R USDCTSD L.R. 5-4(c)(1). When a document has been filed electronically: the document, as filed, binds the filing party. IN R USDCTSD L.R. 5-4(c)(3).

- A Notice of Electronic Filing (NEF) acknowledging that the document has been filed will immediately appear on the filer's screen after the document has been submitted. Attorneys are strongly encouraged to print or electronically save a copy of the NEF. Attorneys can also verify the filing of documents by inspecting the Court's electronic docket sheet through the use of a PACER login. IN R USDCTSD ECF Procedures(7). When a document has been filed electronically: the notice of electronic filing for the document serves as the court's date-stamp and proof of filing. IN R USDCTSD L.R. 5-4(c)(4).

- The Court may, upon the motion of a party or upon its own motion, strike any inappropriately filed document. IN R USDCTSD ECF Procedures(7).

iv. For more information on electronic filing, refer to IN R USDCTSD ECF Procedures.

d. *Fax filing.* The clerk may not file a faxed document without court authorization. The court may not authorize the clerk to file faxed documents without finding that compelling circumstances justify it. A party must submit a copy of the document that otherwise complies with IN R USDCTSD L.R. 5-10 to replace the faxed copy within seven (7) days after faxing the document. IN R USDCTSD L.R. 5-10(e).

2. *Service requirements*

a. *Service; When required*

i. *In general.* Unless the Federal Rules of Civil Procedure provide otherwise, each of the following papers must be served on every party:

- An order stating that service is required;

- A pleading filed after the original complaint, unless the court orders otherwise under FRCP 5(c) because there are numerous defendants;

- A discovery paper required to be served on a party, unless the court orders otherwise;

- A written motion, except one that may be heard ex parte; and

- A written notice, appearance, demand, or offer of judgment, or any similar paper. FRCP 5(a)(1).

ii. *If a party fails to appear.* No service is required on a party who is in default for failing to appear. But a pleading that asserts a new claim for relief against such a party must be served on that party under FRCP 4. FRCP 5(a)(2).

iii. *Seizing property.* If an action is begun by seizing property and no person is or need be named as a defendant, any service required before the filing of an appearance, answer, or claim must be made on the person who had custody or possession of the property when it was seized. FRCP 5(a)(3).

b. *Service; How made*

    i. *Serving an attorney.* If a party is represented by an attorney, service under FRCP 5 must be made on the attorney unless the court orders service on the party. FRCP 5(b)(1).

    ii. *Service in general.* A paper is served under FRCP 5 by:

- Handing it to the person;

- Leaving it: (1) at the person's office with a clerk or other person in charge or, if no one is in charge, in a conspicuous place in the office; or (2) if the person has no office or the office is closed, at the person's dwelling or usual place of abode with someone of suitable age and discretion who resides there;

- Mailing it to the person's last known address—in which event service is complete upon mailing;

- Leaving it with the court clerk if the person has no known address;

- Sending it by electronic means if the person consented in writing—in which event service is complete upon transmission, but is not effective if the serving party learns that it did not reach the person to be served; or

- Delivering it by any other means that the person consented to in writing—in which event service is complete when the person making service delivers it to the agency designated to make delivery. FRCP 5(b)(2).

    iii. *Electronic service*

- *Consent.* By registering to use the ECF system, attorneys consent to electronic service of documents filed in cases maintained on the ECF system. IN R USDCTSD L.R. 5-3(d). By participating in the Electronic Case Filing Program, attorneys consent to the electronic service of documents, and shall make available electronic mail addresses for service. IN R USDCTSD ECF Procedures(11).

- *Service on registered parties.* Upon the filing of a document by a party, an e-mail message will be automatically generated by the electronic filing system and sent via electronic mail to the e-mail addresses of all registered attorneys who have appeared in the case. The Notice of Electronic Filing will contain a document hyperlink which will provide recipients with one "free look" at the electronically filed document. Recipients are encouraged to print and/or save a copy of the document during the "free look" to avoid incurring PACER charges for future viewings of the document. IN R USDCTSD ECF Procedures(11). When a document has been filed electronically: transmission of the notice of electronic filing generated by the ECF system to an attorney's e-mail address constitutes service of the document on that attorney. IN R USDCTSD L.R. 5-4(c)(5). The party effectuates service on all registered attorneys by filing electronically. IN R USDCTSD ECF Procedures(11). When a document has been filed electronically: no other attempted service will constitute electronic service of the document. IN R USDCTSD L.R. 5-4(c)(6).

- *Service on exempt parties.* A filer must serve a copy of the document consistent with FRCP 5 on any party or attorney who is exempt from participating in electronic filing. IN R USDCTSD L.R. 5-4(d). It is the responsibility of the filing attorney to conventionally serve all parties who do not receive electronic service (the identity of these parties will be indicated on the filing receipt generated by the ECF system). IN R USDCTSD ECF Procedures(11).

- *Service on parties excused from electronic filing.* Parties otherwise participating in the electronic filing system may be excused from filing a particular component electronically under certain limited circumstances, such as when the component cannot be reduced to an electronic format. Such components shall not be filed electronically, but instead shall be manually filed with the Clerk of Court and served upon the parties in accordance with the applicable Federal Rules of Civil Procedure and the Local Rules of the United States District Court for the Southern District of Indiana for filing and service of non-electronic documents. IN R USDCTSD ECF Procedures(15).

- *Service of exempt documents.* Any document that is exempt from electronic filing must be filed directly with the clerk and served on other parties in the case as required by those Federal Rules of Civil Procedure and Local Rules of the United States District Court for the Southern District of Indiana that apply to the service of non-electronic documents. IN R USDCTSD L.R. 5-2(c).

iv. *Using court facilities.* If a local rule so authorizes, a party may use the court's transmission facilities to make service under FRCP 5(b)(2)(E). FRCP 5(b)(3).

c. *Serving numerous defendants*

i. *In general.* If an action involves an unusually large number of defendants, the court may, on motion or on its own, order that:

- Defendants' pleadings and replies to them need not be served on other defendants;

- Any crossclaim, counterclaim, avoidance, or affirmative defense in those pleadings and replies to them will be treated as denied or avoided by all other parties; and

- Filing any such pleading and serving it on the plaintiff constitutes notice of the pleading to all parties. FRCP 5(c)(1).

ii. *Notifying parties.* A copy of every such order must be served on the parties as the court directs. FRCP 5(c)(2).

G. Hearings

1. *Hearings, generally*

a. *Oral argument.* Due process does not require that oral argument be permitted on a motion and, except as otherwise provided by local rule, the district court has discretion to determine whether it will decide the motion on the papers or hear argument by counsel (and perhaps receive evidence). FPP § 1190; F.D.I.C. v. Deglau, 207 F.3d 153 (3d Cir. 2000).

i. *Request for oral argument.* A party may request oral argument by filing a separate motion explaining why oral argument is necessary and estimating how long the court should allow for the argument. IN R USDCTSD L.R. 7-5(a). Refer to the Documents section of this document for more information.

ii. *No additional evidence at oral argument.* Parties may not present additional evidence at oral argument. IN R USDCTSD L.R. 7-5(b).

b. *Providing a regular schedule for oral hearings.* A court may establish regular times and places for oral hearings on motions. FRCP 78(a).

c. *Providing for submission on briefs.* By rule or order, the court may provide for submitting and determining motions on briefs, without oral hearings. FRCP 78(b).

d. *Request for evidentiary hearing.* A party may request an evidentiary hearing on a motion or petition by serving and filing a separate motion explaining why the hearing is necessary and estimating how long the court should allow for the hearing. IN R USDCTSD L.R. 7-5(c).

e. *Directed by the court.* The court may: (1) grant or deny a request for oral argument or an evidentiary hearing in its sole discretion; (2) set oral argument or an evidentiary hearing without a request from a party; and (3) order any oral argument or evidentiary hearing to be held anywhere within the district regardless of where the case will be tried. IN R USDCTSD L.R. 7-5(d).

2. *Hearing on motion for preliminary injunction after temporary restraining order is issued without notice*

a. *Expediting the preliminary injunction hearing.* If the order is issued without notice, the motion for a preliminary injunction must be set for hearing at the earliest possible time, taking precedence over all other matters except hearings on older matters of the same character. At the hearing, the party who obtained the order must proceed with the motion; if the party does not, the court must dissolve the order. FRCP 65(b)(3). Refer to the United States District Court for the Southern District of Indiana KeyRules Motion for Preliminary Injunction document for more information on the hearing on the motion for preliminary injunction.

3. *Courtroom and courthouse decorum.* For information on courtroom and courthouse decorum, refer to IN R USDCTSD L.R. 83-3.

H. Forms

1. Federal Application for Temporary Restraining Order Forms

a. Ex parte motion; For temporary restraining order and order to show cause; Interference with property rights. AMJUR PP INJUNCTION § 42.

b. Affidavit; In support of ex parte motion for temporary restraining order. AMJUR PP INJUNCTION § 48.

c. Certificate of attorney; In support of ex parte motion for temporary restraining order. AMJUR PP INJUNCTION § 50.

d. Affidavit; In support of ex parte motion for temporary restraining order; Interference with property rights. AMJUR PP INJUNCTION § 51.

e. Motion. 4A FEDFORMS § 5344.

f. Motion; Another form. 4A FEDFORMS § 5345.

g. Motion; Another form. 4A FEDFORMS § 5346.

h. Motion without notice. 4A FEDFORMS § 5347.

i. Motion without notice; Another form. 4A FEDFORMS § 5348.

j. Motion without notice; Another form. 4A FEDFORMS § 5349.

k. Motion without notice; Another form. 4A FEDFORMS § 5350.

l. Motion without notice; Another form. 4A FEDFORMS § 5351.

m. Motion without notice; Another form. 4A FEDFORMS § 5352.

n. Certificate of attorney's efforts to give notice. 4A FEDFORMS § 5353.

o. Certificate of attorney's efforts to give notice; Another form. 4A FEDFORMS § 5354.

p. Certificate of attorney's efforts to give notice; Another form. 4A FEDFORMS § 5355.

q. Certificate of attorney's efforts to give notice; Another form. 4A FEDFORMS § 5356.

r. Motion requesting expedited hearing. 4A FEDFORMS § 5357.

s. Motion seeking temporary restraining order. 4A FEDFORMS § 5359.

t. Motion to dissolve or modify temporary restraining order. 4A FEDFORMS § 5361.

u. Motion for temporary restraining order and preliminary injunction. GOLDLTGFMS § 13A:6.

v. Motion for temporary restraining order; General form. GOLDLTGFMS § 13A:11.

w. Motion for temporary restraining order; Ex parte application. GOLDLTGFMS § 13A:12.

x. Motion for temporary restraining order; Ex parte application; Supporting affidavit by party. GOLDLTGFMS § 13A:13.

y. Motion for temporary restraining order; Ex parte application; Supporting affidavit by party; Copyright infringement. GOLDLTGFMS § 13A:14.

z. Motion for temporary restraining order; Ex parte application; Certificate by counsel. GOLDLTGFMS § 13A:15.

2. Forms for the Southern District of Indiana

a. Notice of endorsement. IN R USDCTSD ECF Procedures(Appendix B).

b. Notice of manual filing. IN R USDCTSD ECF Procedures(Appendix C).

c. Declaration that party was unable to file in a timely manner due to technical difficulties. IN R USDCTSD ECF Procedures(Appendix D).

I. Applicable Rules

1. *Federal rules*

    a. Serving and filing pleadings and other papers. FRCP 5.

    b. Constitutional challenge to a statute; Notice, certification, and intervention. FRCP 5.1.

    c. Privacy protection for filings made with the court. FRCP 5.2.

    d. Computing and extending time; Time for motion papers. FRCP 6.

    e. Pleadings allowed; Form of motions and other papers. FRCP 7.

    f. Disclosure statement. FRCP 7.1.

    g. Form of pleadings. FRCP 10.

    h. Signing pleadings, motions, and other papers; Representations to the court; Sanctions. FRCP 11.

    i. Taking testimony. FRCP 43.

    j. Injunctions and restraining orders. FRCP 65.

    k. Proceedings against a surety. FRCP 65.1.

    l. Hearing motions; Submission on briefs. FRCP 78.

2. *Local rules*

    a. Scope of the rules. IN R USDCTSD L.R. 1-1.

    b. Sanctions for errors as to form. IN R USDCTSD L.R. 1-3.

    c. Format of documents presented for filing. IN R USDCTSD L.R. 5-1.

    d. Constitutional challenge to a statute; Notice. IN R USDCTSD L.R. 5.1-1.

    e. Filing of documents electronically required. IN R USDCTSD L.R. 5-2.

    f. Eligibility, registration, passwords for electronic filing; Exemption from electronic filing. IN R USDCTSD L.R. 5-3.

    g. Timing and consequences of electronic filing. IN R USDCTSD L.R. 5-4.

    h. Attachments and exhibits in cases filed electronically. IN R USDCTSD L.R. 5-6.

    i. Signatures in cases filed electronically. IN R USDCTSD L.R. 5-7.

    j. Non-electronic filings. IN R USDCTSD L.R. 5-10.

    k. Motion practice. [IN R USDCTSD L.R. 7-1, as amended by IN ORDER 16-2319, effective December 1, 2016].

    l. Oral arguments and hearings. IN R USDCTSD L.R. 7-5.

    m. Request for three-judge court. IN R USDCTSD L.R. 9-2.

    n. Filing of discovery materials. IN R USDCTSD L.R. 26-2.

    o. Assignment of cases. IN R USDCTSD L.R. 40-1.

    p. Alternative dispute resolution. IN R USDCTSD A.D.R. Rule 1.1; IN R USDCTSD A.D.R. Rule 1.2; IN R USDCTSD A.D.R. Rule 1.5; IN R USDCTSD A.D.R. Rule 2.1; IN R USDCTSD A.D.R. Rule 2.2.

    q. Instructions for preparing case management plan. IN R USDCTSD Case Mgt.

    r. Electronic case filing policies and procedures manual. IN R USDCTSD ECF Procedures.

Requests, Notices and Applications
Pretrial Conferences, Scheduling, Management

Document Last Updated December 2016

A. Checklist

(I) ❏ Matters to be considered by parties for the pretrial conference

    (a) ❏ Required documents

        (1) ❏ Case management plan

    (b) ❏ Supplemental documents

        (1) ❏ Notice of constitutional question

        (2) ❏ Index of exhibits

        (3) ❏ Copy of document with self-address envelope

        (4) ❏ Notice of manual filing

        (5) ❏ Courtesy copies

        (6) ❏ Copies for three-judge court

        (7) ❏ Declaration that party was unable to file in a timely manner due to technical difficulties

    (c) ❏ Timing

        (1) ❏ The court determines at what stage in the action to hold a pretrial conference

        (2) ❏ Unless otherwise ordered or exempted under IN R USDCTSD L.R. 16-1(g), the parties in a civil case must confer, prepare, and file a joint case management plan: within ninety (90) days after the case was either filed or removed to the court

        (3) ❏ When a party who is not exempt from the electronic filing requirement files a document directly with the clerk, the party must present the document to the clerk within one (1) business day after filing the notice of manual filing

        (4) ❏ Unless the court orders otherwise, the [untimely] document and declaration [that party was unable to file in a timely manner due to technical difficulties] must be filed no later than 12:00 noon of the first day on which the court is open for business following the original filing deadline

(II) ❏ Matters to be considered by parties for the scheduling conference

    (a) ❏ Documents to consider

        (1) ❏ Request for scheduling conference

        (2) ❏ Index of exhibits

        (3) ❏ Copy of document with self-address envelope

        (4) ❏ Notice of manual filing

        (5) ❏ Courtesy copies

        (6) ❏ Copies for three-judge court

        (7) ❏ Declaration that party was unable to file in a timely manner due to technical difficulties

    (b) ❏ Timing

        (1) ❏ If a scheduling conference is called, it is important to recognize that, unlike the ordinary pretrial conference, the scheduling conference occurs before the substantive issues have been defined and is directed toward organizing the processing of the action by setting deadlines for the completion of the various pretrial phases

        (2) ❏ When a party who is not exempt from the electronic filing requirement files a document directly with the clerk, the party must present the document to the clerk within one (1) business day after filing the notice of manual filing

      (3)   ❑   Unless the court orders otherwise, the [untimely] document and declaration [that party was unable to file in a timely manner due to technical difficulties] must be filed no later than 12:00 noon of the first day on which the court is open for business following the original filing deadline

(III)   ❑   Matters to be considered by parties for the discovery planning conference

    (a)   ❑   Required documents

      (1)   ❑   Written report outlining proposed discovery plan

    (b)   ❑   Supplemental documents

      (1)   ❑   Index of exhibits

      (2)   ❑   Copy of document with self-address envelope

      (3)   ❑   Notice of manual filing

      (4)   ❑   Courtesy copies

      (5)   ❑   Copies for three-judge court

      (6)   ❑   Declaration that party was unable to file in a timely manner due to technical difficulties

    (c)   ❑   Timing

      (1)   ❑   Except in a proceeding exempted from initial disclosure under FRCP 26(a)(1)(B) or when the court orders otherwise, the parties must confer as soon as practicable—and in any event at least twenty-one (21) days before a scheduling conference is to be held or a scheduling order is due under FRCP 16(b)

      (2)   ❑   Within fourteen (14) days after the conference, the attorneys of record are responsible for submitting a written report outlining the plan

      (3)   ❑   When a party who is not exempt from the electronic filing requirement files a document directly with the clerk, the party must present the document to the clerk within one (1) business day after filing the notice of manual filing

      (4)   ❑   Unless the court orders otherwise, the [untimely] document and declaration [that party was unable to file in a timely manner due to technical difficulties] must be filed no later than 12:00 noon of the first day on which the court is open for business following the original filing deadline

B. Timing

1. *Pretrial conferences, generally.* The court determines at what stage in the action to hold a pretrial conference. When only one conference is involved, the most favored practice seems to be to wait until after the case has been prepared for trial. FPP § 1524. Although there rarely will be any need to hold a conference in a relatively simple case until after the preliminary motions have been disposed of, the only inherently logical limitation on the court's discretion as to when to hold a conference is that it should not be held before all the necessary and indispensable parties are served. FPP § 1524.

    a. *Case management plan.* Unless otherwise ordered or exempted under IN R USDCTSD L.R. 16-1(f), the parties in a civil case must confer, prepare, and file a joint case management plan: within ninety (90) days after the case was either filed or removed to the court. IN R USDCTSD L.R. 16-1(c)(1); IN R USDCTSD Case Mgt(General Instructions For All Cases). [Editor's note: the reference to IN R USDCTSD L.R. 16-1(f) is likely meant to be a reference to IN R USDCTSD L.R. 16-1(g)].

2. *Scheduling conference.* If a scheduling conference is called, it is important to recognize that, unlike the ordinary pretrial conference, the scheduling conference occurs before the substantive issues have been defined and is directed toward organizing the processing of the action by setting deadlines for the completion of the various pretrial phases. FPP § 1522.1.

3. *Discovery planning conference.* Except in a proceeding exempted from initial disclosure under FRCP 26(a)(1)(B) or when the court orders otherwise, the parties must confer as soon as practicable—and in any event at least twenty-one (21) days before a scheduling conference is to be held or a scheduling order is due under FRCP 16(b). FRCP 26(f)(1).

    a. *Submission of written report outlining proposed discovery plan.* The attorneys of record and all unrepresented parties that have appeared in the case are jointly responsible for arranging the conference, for attempting in good faith to agree on the proposed discovery plan, and for submitting to the court within fourteen (14) days after the conference a written report outlining the plan. FRCP 26(f)(2).

b. *Expedited schedule.* If necessary to comply with its expedited schedule for FRCP 16(b) conferences, a court may by local rule: (1) require the parties' conference to occur less than twenty-one (21) days before the scheduling conference is held or a scheduling order is due under FRCP 16(b); and (2) require the written report outlining the discovery plan to be filed less than fourteen (14) days after the parties' conference, or excuse the parties from submitting a written report and permit them to report orally on their discovery plan at the FRCP 16(b) conference. FRCP 26(f)(4).

4. *Document filing by non-exempt party.* When a party who is not exempt from the electronic filing requirement files a document directly with the clerk, the party must: present the document to the clerk within one (1) business day after filing the notice of manual filing. IN R USDCTSD L.R. 5-2(d)(2).

5. *Declaration that party was unable to file in a timely manner due to technical difficulties.* Unless the Court orders otherwise, the [untimely] document and declaration [that party was unable to file in a timely manner due to technical difficulties] must be filed no later than 12:00 noon of the first day on which the Court is open for business following the original filing deadline. IN R USDCTSD ECF Procedures(16).

6. *Computation of time*

   a. *Computing time.* FRCP 6 applies in computing any time period specified in the Federal Rules of Civil Procedure, in any local rule or court order, or in any statute that does not specify a method of computing time. FRCP 6(a).

      i. *Period stated in days or a longer unit.* When the period is stated in days or a longer unit of time:

         - Exclude the day of the event that triggers the period;
         - Count every day, including intermediate Saturdays, Sundays, and legal holidays; and
         - Include the last day of the period, but if the last day is a Saturday, Sunday, or legal holiday, the period continues to run until the end of the next day that is not a Saturday, Sunday, or legal holiday. FRCP 6(a)(1).

      ii. *Period stated in hours.* When the period is stated in hours:

         - Begin counting immediately on the occurrence of the event that triggers the period;
         - Count every hour, including hours during intermediate Saturdays, Sundays, and legal holidays; and
         - If the period would end on a Saturday, Sunday, or legal holiday, the period continues to run until the same time on the next day that is not a Saturday, Sunday, or legal holiday. FRCP 6(a)(2).

      iii. *Inaccessibility of the clerk's office.* Unless the court orders otherwise, if the clerk's office is inaccessible:

         - On the last day for filing under FRCP 6(a)(1), then the time for filing is extended to the first accessible day that is not a Saturday, Sunday, or legal holiday; or
         - During the last hour for filing under FRCP 6(a)(2), then the time for filing is extended to the same time on the first accessible day that is not a Saturday, Sunday, or legal holiday. FRCP 6(a)(3).

      iv. *"Last day" defined.* Unless a different time is set by a statute, local rule, or court order, the last day ends:

         - For electronic filing, at midnight in the court's time zone; and
         - For filing by other means, when the clerk's office is scheduled to close. FRCP 6(a)(4).

      v. *"Next day" defined.* The "next day" is determined by continuing to count forward when the period is measured after an event and backward when measured before an event. FRCP 6(a)(5).

vi. *"Legal holiday" defined.* "Legal holiday" means:

- The day set aside by statute for observing New Year's Day, Martin Luther King Jr.'s Birthday, Washington's Birthday, Memorial Day, Independence Day, Labor Day, Columbus Day, Veterans' Day, Thanksgiving Day, or Christmas Day;

- Any day declared a holiday by the President or Congress; and

- For periods that are measured after an event, any other day declared a holiday by the state where the district court is located. FRCP 6(a)(6).

b. *Computation of electronic filing deadlines.* Filing documents electronically does not alter filing deadlines. IN R USDCTSD ECF Procedures(7). A document due on a particular day must be filed before midnight local time of the division where the case is pending. IN R USDCTSD L.R. 5-4(a). All electronic transmissions of documents must be completed (i.e. received completely by the Clerk's Office) prior to midnight of the local time of the division in which the case is pending in order to be considered timely filed that day (NOTE: time will be noted in Eastern Time on the Court's docket. If you have filed a document prior to midnight local time of the division in which the case is pending and the document is due that date, but the electronic receipt and docket reflect the following calendar day, please contact the Court). IN R USDCTSD ECF Procedures(7). Although attorneys may file documents electronically twenty-four (24) hours a day, seven (7) days a week, attorneys are encouraged to file all documents during the normal working hours of the Clerk's Office (Monday through Friday, 8:30 a.m. to 4:30 p.m.) when technical support is available. IN R USDCTSD ECF Procedures(7); IN R USDCTSD ECF Procedures(9).

i. *Technical difficulties.* Parties are encouraged to file documents electronically during normal business hours, in case a problem is encountered. In the event a technical failure occurs and a document cannot be filed electronically despite the best efforts of the filing party, the party should print (if possible) a copy of the error message received. In addition, as soon as practically possible, the party should file a "Declaration that Party was Unable to File in a Timely Manner Due to Technical Difficulties." A model form is provided as Appendix D (IN R USDCTSD ECF Procedures(Appendix D)). IN R USDCTSD ECF Procedures(16).

- If a party is unable to file electronically and, as a result, may miss a filing deadline, the party must contact the Clerk's Office at the number listed in IN R USDCTSD ECF Procedures(15) to inform the court's staff of the difficulty. If a party misses a filing deadline due to an inability to file electronically, the party may submit the untimely filed document, accompanied by a declaration stating the reason(s) for missing the deadline. Unless the Court orders otherwise, the document and declaration must be filed no later than 12:00 noon of the first day on which the Court is open for business following the original filing deadline. IN R USDCTSD ECF Procedures(16).

c. *Extending time*

i. *In general.* When an act may or must be done within a specified time, the court may, for good cause, extend the time:

- With or without motion or notice if the court acts, or if a request is made, before the original time or its extension expires; or

- On motion made after the time has expired if the party failed to act because of excusable neglect. FRCP 6(b)(1).

ii. *Exceptions.* A court must not extend the time to act under FRCP 50(b), FRCP 50(d), FRCP 52(b), FRCP 59(b), FRCP 59(d), FRCP 59(e), and FRCP 60(b). FRCP 6(b)(2).

iii. Refer to the United States District Court for the Southern District of Indiana KeyRules Motion for Continuance/Extension of Time document for more information on extending time.

d. *Additional time after certain kinds of service.* When a party may or must act within a specified time after being served and service is made under FRCP 5(b)(2)(C) (mail), FRCP 5(b)(2)(D) (leaving with the clerk), or FRCP 5(b)(2)(F) (other means consented to), three (3) days are added after the period would otherwise expire under FRCP 6(a). FRCP 6(d). Service by electronic mail shall constitute service pursuant to FRCP 5(b)(2)(E) and shall entitle the party being served to the additional three (3) days provided by FRCP 6(d). IN R USDCTSD ECF Procedures(11).

C. General Requirements

1. *Pretrial conferences, generally*

   a. *Purposes of a pretrial conference.* FRCP 16 provides an important mechanism for carrying out one of the basic policies of the Federal Rules of Civil Procedure—the determination of disputes on their merits rather than on the basis of procedural niceties or tactical advantage. FPP § 1522. In any action, the court may order the attorneys and any unrepresented parties to appear for one or more pretrial conferences for such purposes as:

      i. Expediting disposition of the action;

      ii. Establishing early and continuing control so that the case will not be protracted because of lack of management;

      iii. Discouraging wasteful pretrial activities;

      iv. Improving the quality of the trial through more thorough preparation; and

      v. Facilitating settlement. FRCP 16(a).

   b. *When appropriate.* FRCP 16 specifically provides that the court "may order the attorneys and any unrepresented parties to appear for one or more pretrial conferences." This language makes it clear that the utilization of the pretrial conference procedure lies within the discretion of the district court both as a matter of general policy and in terms of whether and when the rule should be invoked in a particular case. FPP § 1523; Mizwicki v. Helwig, 196 F.3d 828 (7th Cir. 1999). There is no requirement that any pretrial conferences be held or not held in certain types of actions. FPP § 1523.

      i. *Initial pretrial conference.* In all cases not exempted under IN R USDCTSD L.R. 16-1(f), the court may order the parties to appear for an initial pretrial conference. IN R USDCTSD L.R. 16-1(a). [Editor's note: the reference to IN R USDCTSD L.R. 16-1(f) is likely meant to be a reference to IN R USDCTSD L.R. 16-1(g)].

   c. *Case management plan, generally.* Unless otherwise ordered or exempted under IN R USDCTSD L.R. 16-1(f), the parties in a civil case must confer, prepare, and file a joint case management plan: (1) within ninety (90) days after the case was either filed or removed to the court; and (2) according to the instructions and form available on the court's website. IN R USDCTSD L.R. 16-1(c); IN R USDCTSD Case Mgt(General Instructions For All Cases). [Editor's note: the reference to IN R USDCTSD L.R. 16-1(f) is likely meant to be a reference to IN R USDCTSD L.R. 16-1(g)].

      i. *Parties' responsibilities for case management plan.* The plaintiff must initiate and coordinate the efforts to confer about, prepare, and file the case management plan. If the plaintiff fails to do so, the defendant must appear at the initial pretrial conference with a proposed case-management plan. IN R USDCTSD L.R. 16-1(d).

         • If the parties cannot agree on all provisions of the case management plan the parties must file a joint plan that contains their respective positions in the disputed portions of the case management plan. The court will enter a case management plan that the court deems most appropriate with or without additional input from the parties. IN R USDCTSD L.R. 16-1(d).

      ii. *Instructions for preparing case management plan.* The provisions in IN R USDCTSD Case Mgt apply to civil cases filed in the United States District Court for the Southern District of Indiana that are not exempt from filing a Case Management Plan ("CMP") under IN R USDCTSD L.R. 16-1. IN R USDCTSD Case Mgt.

         • Unless the plaintiff is pro se, counsel for plaintiff shall be responsible for coordinating timely completion of the CMP. The deadline for filing the CMP is ninety (90) days from the date the case was filed or removed. The deadline for filing the CMP shall not be extended without written motion which establishes good cause to extend the deadline. Regardless of the status of the CMP, the parties are free to engage in discovery in compliance with the Federal Rules of Civil Procedure and the Local Rules of the United

States District Court for the Southern District of Indiana. IN R USDCTSD Case Mgt(General Instructions For All Cases).

- The calculation of all deadlines for the CMP is based on the "Anchor Date," which means the date that the case was filed or removed to the Court. Because all CMP deadlines are linked to the Anchor Date, plaintiffs must promptly effectuate service on all defendants. The Court may entertain requests from defendants to modify/lengthen all CMP deadlines if service is not made promptly. IN R USDCTSD Case Mgt(General Instructions For All Cases).

- Depending on the type of case, the Anchor Date is used to calculate certain deadlines that will govern pretrial management. Please note, however, that the parties are encouraged to shorten these time frames in appropriate cases so that the case may be scheduled for trial more quickly than the outer deadlines otherwise applicable. IN R USDCTSD Case Mgt(General Instructions For All Cases).

- The use of the term "months" for calculating the dates (rather than counting days) is for ease of calculation. Thus, for example, if the Anchor Date is the 20th of the month, most of CMP deadlines will fall on the 20th of the respective months regardless of how many days comprise the intervening months. IN R USDCTSD Case Mgt(General Instructions For All Cases).

- For more information, including special instructions for pro se parties, refer to IN R USDCTSD Case Mgt.

iii. *Cross-motions for summary judgment.* If the parties anticipate cross-motions for summary judgment, the briefing schedule and format should be addressed in the case management plan. IN R USDCTSD L.R. 56-1(Local Rules Advisory Committee Comments).

d. *Attendance at a pretrial conference.* A represented party must authorize at least one of its attorneys to make stipulations and admissions about all matters that can reasonably be anticipated for discussion at a pretrial conference. If appropriate, the court may require that a party or its representative be present or reasonably available by other means to consider possible settlement. FRCP 16(c)(1).

e. *Matters for consideration at a pretrial conference.* At any pretrial conference, the court may consider and take appropriate action on the following matters:

i. Formulating and simplifying the issues, and eliminating frivolous claims or defenses;

ii. Amending the pleadings if necessary or desirable;

iii. Obtaining admissions and stipulations about facts and documents to avoid unnecessary proof, and ruling in advance on the admissibility of evidence;

iv. Avoiding unnecessary proof and cumulative evidence, and limiting the use of testimony under FRE 702;

v. Determining the appropriateness and timing of summary adjudication under FRCP 56;

vi. Controlling and scheduling discovery, including orders affecting disclosures and discovery under FRCP 26 and FRCP 29 through FRCP 37;

vii. Identifying witnesses and documents, scheduling the filing and exchange of any pretrial briefs, and setting dates for further conferences and for trial;

viii. Referring matters to a magistrate judge or a master;

ix. Settling the case and using special procedures to assist in resolving the dispute when authorized by statute or local rule;

x. Determining the form and content of the pretrial order;

xi. Disposing of pending motions;

xii. Adopting special procedures for managing potentially difficult or protracted actions that may involve complex issues, multiple parties, difficult legal questions, or unusual proof problems;

    xiii. Ordering a separate trial under FRCP 42(b) of a claim, counterclaim, crossclaim, third-party claim, or particular issue;

    xiv. Ordering the presentation of evidence early in the trial on a manageable issue that might, on the evidence, be the basis for a judgment as a matter of law under FRCP 50(a) or a judgment on partial findings under FRCP 52(c);

    xv. Establishing a reasonable limit on the time allowed to present evidence; and

    xvi. Facilitating in other ways the just, speedy, and inexpensive disposition of the action. FRCP 16(c)(2).

  f. *Pretrial orders.* After any conference under FRCP 16, the court should issue an order reciting the action taken. This order controls the course of the action unless the court modifies it. FRCP 16(d).

    i. *Deadlines.* Absent court order, deadlines established in any order or pretrial entry under IN R USDCTSD L.R. 16-1 may not be altered unless the parties and the court agree, or for good cause shown. IN R USDCTSD L.R. 16-1(f).

  g. *Additional conferences.* The court may set additional pretrial conferences. The parties must confer before each conference and must be prepared to address case-management plan issues, settlement, trial readiness, and any other matters specifically directed by the court. IN R USDCTSD L.R. 16-1(e).

  h. *Sanctions.* On motion or on its own, the court may issue any just orders, including those authorized by FRCP 37(b)(2)(A)(ii) through FRCP 37(b)(2)(A)(vii), if a party or its attorney: (1) fails to appear at a scheduling or other pretrial conference; (2) is substantially unprepared to participate—or does not participate in good faith—in the conference; or (3) fails to obey a scheduling or other pretrial order. FRCP 16(f)(1).

    i. *Imposing fees and costs.* Instead of or in addition to any other sanction, the court must order the party, its attorney, or both to pay the reasonable expenses—including attorney's fees—incurred because of any noncompliance with FRCP 16, unless the noncompliance was substantially justified or other circumstances make an award of expenses unjust. FRCP 16(f)(2).

2. *Scheduling conference.* A scheduling conference may be requested by the judge or by the parties, but it is not mandatory. FPP § 1522.1.

  a. *Scheduling order.* Except in categories of actions exempted by local rule, the district judge—or a magistrate judge when authorized by local rule—must issue a scheduling order: (1) after receiving the parties' report under FRCP 26(f); or (2) after consulting with the parties' attorneys and any unrepresented parties at a scheduling conference. FRCP 16(b)(1). In actions where a party is unrepresented, the court may issue a scheduling order after consulting with the parties' attorneys and the unrepresented parties at a scheduling conference or by telephone, or other means. IN R USDCTSD L.R. 16-1(b).

    i. *Exempted cases.* Unless otherwise ordered by the court, the following types of cases will be exempted from the scheduling and planning requirements of FRCP 16(b):

      • An action for review of an administrative record;

      • A petition for habeas corpus or other proceeding to challenge a criminal conviction or sentence;

      • An action brought by a person in custody of the United States, a State or a State subdivision;

      • An action to enforce or quash an administrative summons or subpoena;

      • An action by the United States to recover benefit payments;

      • An action by the United States to collect on a student loan guaranteed by the United States;

      • A proceeding ancillary to proceedings in another court;

      • An action to enforce, vacate or modify an arbitration award;

      • Mortgage foreclosures in which the United States is a party; and

- Civil forfeiture cases. IN R USDCTSD L.R. 16-1(g).

ii. *Required contents of the order.* The scheduling order must limit the time to join other parties, amend the pleadings, complete discovery, and file motions. FRCP 16(b)(3)(A).

iii. *Permitted contents of the order.* The scheduling order may:

- Modify the timing of disclosures under FRCP 26(a) and FRCP 26(e)(1);
- Modify the extent of discovery;
- Provide for disclosure, discovery, or preservation of electronically stored information;
- Include any agreements the parties reach for asserting claims of privilege or of protection as trial-preparation material after information is produced, including agreements reached under FRE 502;
- Direct that before moving for an order relating to discovery, the movant must request a conference with the court;
- Set dates for pretrial conferences and for trial; and
- Include other appropriate matters. FRCP 16(b)(3)(B).

b. *Time to issue.* The judge must issue the scheduling order as soon as practicable, but unless the judge finds good cause for delay, the judge must issue it within the earlier of ninety (90) days after any defendant has been served with the complaint or sixty (60) days after any defendant has appeared. FRCP 16(b)(2).

c. *Modifying a schedule.* A schedule may be modified only for good cause and with the judge's consent. FRCP 16(b)(4).

3. *Final pretrial conference.* The court may hold a final pretrial conference to formulate a trial plan, including a plan to facilitate the admission of evidence. FRCP 16(e).

a. *Timing and attendance.* The conference must be held as close to the start of trial as is reasonable, and must be attended by at least one attorney who will conduct the trial for each party and by any unrepresented party. FRCP 16(e).

b. *Modification of final pretrial order.* The court may modify the order issued after a final pretrial conference only to prevent manifest injustice. FRCP 16(e).

4. *Discovery planning conference*

a. *Conference content.* In conferring, the parties must consider the nature and basis of their claims and defenses and the possibilities for promptly settling or resolving the case; make or arrange for the disclosures required by FRCP 26(a)(1); discuss any issues about preserving discoverable information; and develop a proposed discovery plan. FRCP 26(f)(2).

b. *Parties' responsibilities.* The attorneys of record and all unrepresented parties that have appeared in the case are jointly responsible for arranging the conference, for attempting in good faith to agree on the proposed discovery plan, and for submitting to the court within fourteen (14) days after the conference a written report outlining the plan. The court may order the parties or attorneys to attend the conference in person. FRCP 26(f)(2).

c. *Discovery plan.* A discovery plan must state the parties' views and proposals on:

i. What changes should be made in the timing, form, or requirement for disclosures under FRCP 26(a), including a statement of when initial disclosures were made or will be made;

ii. The subjects on which discovery may be needed, when discovery should be completed, and whether discovery should be conducted in phases or be limited to or focused on particular issues;

iii. Any issues about disclosure, discovery, or preservation of electronically stored information, including the form or forms in which it should be produced;

iv. Any issues about claims of privilege or of protection as trial-preparation materials, including—if the parties agree on a procedure to assert these claims after production—whether to ask the court to include their agreement in an order under FRE 502;

    v.   What changes should be made in the limitations on discovery imposed under the Federal Rules of Civil Procedure or by local rule, and what other limitations should be imposed; and

    vi.   Any other orders that the court should issue under FRCP 26(c) or under FRCP 16(b) and FRCP 26(c). FRCP 26(f)(3).

  d.   *Sanctions.* If a party or its attorney fails to participate in good faith in developing and submitting a proposed discovery plan as required by FRCP 26(f), the court may, after giving an opportunity to be heard, require that party or attorney to pay to any other party the reasonable expenses, including attorney's fees, caused by the failure. FRCP 37(f).

5. *Appearances.* Every attorney who represents a party or who files a document on a party's behalf must file an appearance for that party. IN R USDCTSD L.R. 83-7. The filing of a Notice of Appearance shall act to establish the filing attorney as an attorney of record representing a designated party or parties in a particular cause of action. As a result, it is necessary for each attorney to file a separate Notice of Appearance when entering an appearance in a case. A joint appearance on behalf of multiple attorneys may be filed electronically only if it is filed separately for each attorney, using his/her ECF login. IN R USDCTSD ECF Procedures(12). Only those attorneys who have filed an appearance in a pending action are entitled to be served with case documents under FRCP 5(a). IN R USDCTSD L.R. 83-7. For more information, refer to IN R USDCTSD L.R. 83-7 and IN R USDCTSD ECF Procedures(12).

6. *Notice of related action.* A party must file a notice of related action: as soon as it appears that the party's case and another pending case: (1) arise out of the same transaction or occurrence; (2) involve the same property; or (3) involve the validity or infringement or the same patent, trademark, or copyright. IN R USDCTSD L.R. 40-1(d)(2). For more information, refer to IN R USDCTSD L.R. 40-1.

7. *Alternative dispute resolution (ADR)*

  a.   *Application.* Unless limited by specific provisions, or unless there are other applicable specific statutory, common law, or constitutional procedures, the Local Alternative Dispute Resolution Rules of the United States District Court for the Southern District of Indiana shall apply in all civil litigation filed in the U.S. District Court for the Southern District of Indiana, except in the following cases and proceedings:

    i.   Applications for writs of habeas corpus under 28 U.S.C.A. § 2254;

    ii.   Forfeiture cases;

    iii.   Non-adversary proceedings in bankruptcy;

    iv.   Social Security administrative review cases; and

    v.   Such other matters as specified by order of the Court; for example, matters involving important public policy issues, constitutional law, or the establishment of new law. IN R USDCTSD A.D.R. Rule 1.2.

  b.   *Mediation.* Mediation under this section (IN R USDCTSD A.D.R. Rule 2.1, et seq.) involves the confidential process by which a person acting as a Mediator, selected by the parties or appointed by the Court, assists the litigants in reaching a mutually acceptable agreement. It is an informal and nonadversarial process. The role of the Mediator is to assist in identifying the issues, reducing misunderstandings, clarifying priorities, exploring areas of compromise, and finding points of agreement as well as legitimate points of disagreement. Final decision-making authority rests with the parties, not the Mediator. IN R USDCTSD A.D.R. Rule 2.1. It is anticipated that an agreement may not resolve all of the disputed issues, but the process, nonetheless, can reduce points of contention. Parties and their representatives are required to mediate in good faith, but are not compelled to reach an agreement. IN R USDCTSD A.D.R. Rule 2.1.

    i.   *Case selection.* The Court with the agreement of the parties may refer a civil case for mediation. Unless otherwise ordered or as specifically provided in IN R USDCTSD A.D.R. Rule 2.8, referral to mediation does not abate or suspend the action, and no scheduled dates shall be delayed or deferred, including the date of trial. IN R USDCTSD A.D.R. Rule 2.2.

    ii.   For more information on mediation, refer to IN R USDCTSD A.D.R. Rule 2.1, et seq.

  c.   *Other methods of dispute resolution.* The Local Alternative Dispute Resolution Rules of the United

States District Court for the Southern District of Indiana shall not preclude the parties from utilizing any other reasonable method or technique of alternative dispute resolution to resolve disputes to which the parties agree. However, any use of arbitration by the parties will be governed by and comply with the requirements of 28 U.S.C.A. § 654 through 28 U.S.C.A. § 657. IN R USDCTSD A.D.R. Rule 1.5.

    d. For more information on alternative dispute resolution (ADR), refer to IN R USDCTSD A.D.R. Rule 1.1, et seq.

8. *Notice of settlement or resolution.* The parties must immediately notify the court if they reasonably anticipate settling their case or resolving a pending motion. IN R USDCTSD L.R. 7-1(h).

9. *Modification or suspension of rules.* The court may, on its own motion or at the request of a party, suspend or modify any rule in a particular case in the interest of justice. IN R USDCTSD L.R. 1-1(c).

D. Documents

1. *Pretrial conference*

    a. *Required documents*

        i. *Case management plan.* Refer to the General Requirements section of this document for information on the case management plan.

- Even though it is not specifically mentioned in FRCP 16, most courts require the attorney for each side to file a pretrial memorandum or statement prior to the conference, which, if adopted by the court, may be binding at trial. FPP § 1524. The purpose of the memorandum is to reveal the lawyer's theory of the case and the issues counsel believes are in contention in order to aid the court in determining what matters should be considered at the conference itself. FPP § 1524; Manbeck v. Ostrowski, 384 F.2d 970 (D.C. Cir. 1967).

    b. *Supplemental documents*

        i. *Notice of constitutional question.* A party that files a pleading, written motion, or other paper drawing into question the constitutionality of a federal or state statute must promptly:

- *File notice.* File a notice of constitutional question stating the question and identifying the paper that raises it, if: (1) a federal statute is questioned and the parties do not include the United States, one of its agencies, or one of its officers or employees in an official capacity; or (2) a state statute is questioned and the parties do not include the state, one of its agencies, or one of its officers or employees in an official capacity; and

- *Serve notice.* Serve the notice and paper on the Attorney General of the United States if a federal statute is questioned—or on the state attorney general if a state statute is questioned—either by certified or registered mail or by sending it to an electronic address designated by the attorney general for this purpose. FRCP 5.1(a).

- *Time for filing.* A notice of constitutional challenge to a statute filed in accordance with FRCP 5.1 must be filed at the same time the parties tender their proposed case management plan, if one is required, or within twenty-one (21) days of the filing drawing into question the constitutionality of a federal or state statute, whichever occurs later. IN R USDCTSD L.R. 5.1-1(a).

- *Additional service requirements.* If a federal statute is challenged, in addition to the service requirements of FRCP 5.1(a), the party filing the notice of constitutional challenge must serve the notice and documents on the United States Attorney for the Southern District of Indiana, either by certified or registered mail or by sending it to an electronic address designated for that purpose by that official. IN R USDCTSD L.R. 5.1-1(b).

- *No forfeiture.* A party's failure to file and serve the notice, or the court's failure to certify, does not forfeit a constitutional claim or defense that is otherwise timely asserted. FRCP 5.1(d).

        ii. *Index of exhibits.* Any pleading, motion, brief, affidavit, notice, or proposed order filed with the court, whether electronically or with the clerk, must: if it has four (4) or more exhibits, include a separate index that identifies and briefly describes each exhibit. IN R USDCTSD L.R. 5-1(b).

iii. *Copy of document with self-address envelope.* To receive a file-stamped copy of a document filed directly with the clerk, a party must include with the original document an additional copy and a self-addressed envelope. The envelope must be big enough to hold the copy and have enough postage on it to send the copy via regular first-class mail. IN R USDCTSD L.R. 5-10(b).

iv. *Notice of manual filing.* When a party who is not exempt from the electronic filing requirement files a document directly with the clerk, the party must: electronically file a notice of manual filing that explains why the document cannot be filed electronically. IN R USDCTSD L.R. 5-2(d)(1). Refer to the Filing and Service Requirements section of this document for more information.

- Where an individual component cannot be included in an electronic filing (e.g. the component cannot be converted to electronic format), the filer shall electronically file the prescribed Notice of Manual Filing in place of that component. A model form is provided as Appendix C (IN R USDCTSD ECF Procedures(Appendix C)). IN R USDCTSD ECF Procedures(13).

- Before making a manual filing of a component, the filing party shall first electronically file a Notice of Manual Filing (See IN R USDCTSD ECF Procedures(Appendix C)). The filer shall initiate the electronic filing process as if filing the actual component but shall instead attach to the filing the Notice of Manual Filing setting forth the reason(s) why the component cannot be filed electronically. The manual filing should be accompanied by a copy of the previously filed Notice of Manual Filing. A party may seek to have a component excluded from electronic filing pursuant to applicable Federal and Local Rules (e.g., FRCP 26(c)). IN R USDCTSD ECF Procedures(15).

v. *Courtesy copies.* District Judges and Magistrate Judges regularly receive documents filed by all parties. Therefore, parties shall not bring "courtesy copies" to any chambers unless specifically directed to do so by the Court. IN R USDCTSD Case Mgt(General Instructions For All Cases).

vi. *Copies for three-judge court.* Parties in a case where a three-judge court has been requested must file an original and three copies of any document filed directly with the clerk (instead of electronically) until the court: (1) denies the request; (2) dissolves the three-judge court; or (3) allows the parties to file fewer copies. IN R USDCTSD L.R. 9-2(c).

vii. *Declaration that party was unable to file in a timely manner due to technical difficulties.* If a party misses a filing deadline due to an inability to file electronically, the party may submit the untimely filed document, accompanied by a declaration stating the reason(s) for missing the deadline. IN R USDCTSD ECF Procedures(16). A model form is provided as Appendix D (IN R USDCTSD ECF Procedures(Appendix D)). IN R USDCTSD ECF Procedures(16).

2. *Scheduling conference*

a. *Documents to consider*

i. *Request for scheduling conference.* A scheduling conference may be requested by the judge or by the parties, but it is not mandatory. FPP § 1522.1.

ii. *Index of exhibits.* Any pleading, motion, brief, affidavit, notice, or proposed order filed with the court, whether electronically or with the clerk, must: if it has four (4) or more exhibits, include a separate index that identifies and briefly describes each exhibit. IN R USDCTSD L.R. 5-1(b).

iii. *Copy of document with self-address envelope.* To receive a file-stamped copy of a document filed directly with the clerk, a party must include with the original document an additional copy and a self-addressed envelope. The envelope must be big enough to hold the copy and have enough postage on it to send the copy via regular first-class mail. IN R USDCTSD L.R. 5-10(b).

iv. *Notice of manual filing.* When a party who is not exempt from the electronic filing requirement files a document directly with the clerk, the party must: electronically file a notice of manual filing that explains why the document cannot be filed electronically. IN R USDCTSD L.R. 5-2(d)(1). Refer to the Filing and Service Requirements section of this document for more information.

- Where an individual component cannot be included in an electronic filing (e.g. the

component cannot be converted to electronic format), the filer shall electronically file the prescribed Notice of Manual Filing in place of that component. A model form is provided as Appendix C (IN R USDCTSD ECF Procedures(Appendix C)). IN R USDCTSD ECF Procedures(13).

- Before making a manual filing of a component, the filing party shall first electronically file a Notice of Manual Filing (See IN R USDCTSD ECF Procedures(Appendix C)). The filer shall initiate the electronic filing process as if filing the actual component but shall instead attach to the filing the Notice of Manual Filing setting forth the reason(s) why the component cannot be filed electronically. The manual filing should be accompanied by a copy of the previously filed Notice of Manual Filing. A party may seek to have a component excluded from electronic filing pursuant to applicable Federal and Local Rules (e.g., FRCP 26(c)). IN R USDCTSD ECF Procedures(15).

v. *Courtesy copies.* District Judges and Magistrate Judges regularly receive documents filed by all parties. Therefore, parties shall not bring "courtesy copies" to any chambers unless specifically directed to do so by the Court. IN R USDCTSD Case Mgt(General Instructions For All Cases).

vi. *Copies for three-judge court.* Parties in a case where a three-judge court has been requested must file an original and three copies of any document filed directly with the clerk (instead of electronically) until the court: (1) denies the request; (2) dissolves the three-judge court; or (3) allows the parties to file fewer copies. IN R USDCTSD L.R. 9-2(c).

vii. *Declaration that party was unable to file in a timely manner due to technical difficulties.* If a party misses a filing deadline due to an inability to file electronically, the party may submit the untimely filed document, accompanied by a declaration stating the reason(s) for missing the deadline. IN R USDCTSD ECF Procedures(16). A model form is provided as Appendix D (IN R USDCTSD ECF Procedures(Appendix D)). IN R USDCTSD ECF Procedures(16).

3. *Discovery planning conference*

   a. *Required documents*

      i. *Written report outlining proposed discovery plan.* Refer to the General Requirements section of this document for information on the parties' responsibilities for submitting a written report outlining the proposed discovery plan.

   b. *Supplemental documents*

      i. *Index of exhibits.* Any pleading, motion, brief, affidavit, notice, or proposed order filed with the court, whether electronically or with the clerk, must: if it has four (4) or more exhibits, include a separate index that identifies and briefly describes each exhibit. IN R USDCTSD L.R. 5-1(b).

      ii. *Copy of document with self-address envelope.* To receive a file-stamped copy of a document filed directly with the clerk, a party must include with the original document an additional copy and a self-addressed envelope. The envelope must be big enough to hold the copy and have enough postage on it to send the copy via regular first-class mail. IN R USDCTSD L.R. 5-10(b).

      iii. *Notice of manual filing.* When a party who is not exempt from the electronic filing requirement files a document directly with the clerk, the party must: electronically file a notice of manual filing that explains why the document cannot be filed electronically. IN R USDCTSD L.R. 5-2(d)(1). Refer to the Filing and Service Requirements section of this document for more information.

         - Where an individual component cannot be included in an electronic filing (e.g. the component cannot be converted to electronic format), the filer shall electronically file the prescribed Notice of Manual Filing in place of that component. A model form is provided as Appendix C (IN R USDCTSD ECF Procedures(Appendix C)). IN R USDCTSD ECF Procedures(13).

         - Before making a manual filing of a component, the filing party shall first electronically file a Notice of Manual Filing (See IN R USDCTSD ECF Procedures(Appendix C)). The filer shall initiate the electronic filing process as if filing the actual component but shall instead attach to the filing the Notice of Manual Filing setting forth the reason(s) why the component cannot be filed electronically. The manual filing should be accompanied by a copy of the previously filed Notice of Manual Filing. A party may seek to have a component excluded from electronic filing pursuant to applicable Federal and Local Rules (e.g., FRCP 26(c)). IN R USDCTSD ECF Procedures(15).

iv. *Courtesy copies.* District Judges and Magistrate Judges regularly receive documents filed by all parties. Therefore, parties shall not bring "courtesy copies" to any chambers unless specifically directed to do so by the Court. IN R USDCTSD Case Mgt(General Instructions For All Cases).

v. *Copies for three-judge court.* Parties in a case where a three-judge court has been requested must file an original and three copies of any document filed directly with the clerk (instead of electronically) until the court: (1) denies the request; (2) dissolves the three-judge court; or (3) allows the parties to file fewer copies. IN R USDCTSD L.R. 9-2(c).

vi. *Declaration that party was unable to file in a timely manner due to technical difficulties.* If a party misses a filing deadline due to an inability to file electronically, the party may submit the untimely filed document, accompanied by a declaration stating the reason(s) for missing the deadline. IN R USDCTSD ECF Procedures(16). A model form is provided as Appendix D (IN R USDCTSD ECF Procedures(Appendix D)). IN R USDCTSD ECF Procedures(16).

E. Format

1. *Form of documents.* The rules governing captions and other matters of form in pleadings apply to motions and other papers. FRCP 7(b)(2).

   a. *Paper (manual filings only).* Any document that is not filed electronically must: be flat, unfolded, and on good-quality, eight and one-half by eleven (8-1/2 x 11) inch white paper. IN R USDCTSD L.R. 5-1(d)(1). Any document that is not filed electronically must: be single-sided. IN R USDCTSD L.R. 5-1(d)(1).

      i. *Covers or backing.* Any document that is not filed electronically must: not have a cover or a back. IN R USDCTSD L.R. 5-1(d)(1).

      ii. *Fastening.* Any document that is not filed electronically must: be (if consisting of more than one (1) page) fastened by paperclip or binder clip and may not be stapled. IN R USDCTSD L.R. 5-1(d)(1).

      - *Request for nonconforming fastening.* If a document cannot be fastened or bound as required by IN R USDCTSD L.R. 5-1(d), a party may ask the clerk for permission to fasten it in another manner. The party must make such a request before attempting to file the document with nonconforming fastening. IN R USDCTSD L.R. 5-1(d)(2).

      iii. *Hole punching.* Any document that is not filed electronically must: be two-hole punched at the top with the holes two and three-quarter (2-3/4) inches apart and appropriately centered. IN R USDCTSD L.R. 5-1(d)(1).

   b. *Margins.* Any pleading, motion, brief, affidavit, notice, or proposed order filed with the court, whether electronically or with the clerk, must: have at least one (1) inch margins. IN R USDCTSD L.R. 5-1(b).

   c. *Spacing.* Any pleading, motion, brief, affidavit, notice, or proposed order filed with the court, whether electronically or with the clerk, must: be double spaced (except for headings, footnotes, and quoted material). IN R USDCTSD L.R. 5-1(b).

   d. *Text.* Any pleading, motion, brief, affidavit, notice, or proposed order filed with the court, whether electronically or with the clerk, must: be plainly typewritten, printed, or prepared by a clearly legible copying process. IN R USDCTSD L.R. 5-1(b).

   e. *Font size.* Any pleading, motion, brief, affidavit, notice, or proposed order filed with the court, whether electronically or with the clerk, must: use at least 12-point type in the body of the document and at least 10-point type in footnotes. IN R USDCTSD L.R. 5-1(b).

   f. *Page numbering.* Any pleading, motion, brief, affidavit, notice, or proposed order filed with the court, whether electronically or with the clerk, must: have consecutively numbered pages. IN R USDCTSD L.R. 5-1(b).

g. *Caption; Names of parties.* Every pleading must have a caption with the court's name, a title, a file number, and a FRCP 7(a) designation. The title of the complaint must name all the parties; the title of other pleadings, after naming the first party on each side, may refer generally to other parties. FRCP 10(a). Any pleading, motion, brief, affidavit, notice, or proposed order filed with the court, whether electronically or with the clerk, must: include a title on the first page. IN R USDCTSD L.R. 5-1(b).

h. *Filer's information.* Any pleading, motion, brief, affidavit, notice, or proposed order filed with the court, whether electronically or with the clerk, must: in the case of pleadings, motions, legal briefs, and notices, include the name, complete address, telephone number, facsimile number (where available), and e-mail address (where available) of the pro se litigant or attorney who files it. IN R USDCTSD L.R. 5-1(b).

i. *Paragraphs; Separate statements.* A party must state its claims or defenses in numbered paragraphs, each limited as far as practicable to a single set of circumstances. A later pleading may refer by number to a paragraph in an earlier pleading. If doing so would promote clarity, each claim founded on a separate transaction or occurrence—and each defense other than a denial—must be stated in a separate count or defense. FRCP 10(b).

j. *Adoption by reference; Exhibits.* A statement in a pleading may be adopted by reference elsewhere in the same pleading or in any other pleading or motion. A copy of a written instrument that is an exhibit to a pleading is a part of the pleading for all purposes. FRCP 10(c).

k. *Citations*

   i. *Local rules.* The Local Rules of the United States District Court for the Southern District of Indiana may be cited as "S.D. Ind. L.R." IN R USDCTSD L.R. 1-1(a).

   ii. *Local alternative dispute resolution rules.* These Rules shall be known as the Local Alternative Dispute Resolution Rules of the United States District Court for the Southern District of Indiana. They shall be cited as "S.D.Ind. Local A.D.R. Rule _____." IN R USDCTSD A.D.R. Rule 1.1.

l. *Acceptance by the clerk.* The clerk must not refuse to file a paper solely because it is not in the form prescribed by the Federal Rules of Civil Procedure or by a local rule or practice. FRCP 5(d)(4). The clerk will accept a document that violates IN R USDCTSD L.R. 5-1, but the court may exclude the document from the official record. IN R USDCTSD L.R. 5-1(e).

   i. *Sanctions for errors as to form.* The court may strike from the record any document that does not comply with the rules governing the form of documents filed with the court, such as rules that regulate document size or the number of copies to be filed or that require a special designation in the caption. The court may also sanction an attorney or party who files a non-compliant document. IN R USDCTSD L.R. 1-3.

2. *Form of electronic documents.* Any document submitted via the court's electronic case filing (ECF) system must be: otherwise prepared and filed in a manner consistent with the CM/ECF Policies and Procedures Manual (IN R USDCTSD ECF Procedures). IN R USDCTSD L.R. 5-1(c). Electronically filed documents must meet the requirements of FRCP 10 (Form of Pleadings), IN R USDCTSD L.R. 5-1 (Format of Papers Presented for Filing), and FRCP 5.2 (Privacy Protection for Filings Made with the Court), as if they had been submitted on paper. Documents filed electronically are also subject to any page limitations set forth by Court Order, by IN R USDCTSD L.R. 7-1 (Motion Practice), or IN R USDCTSD L.R. 56-1 (Summary Judgment Practice), as applicable. IN R USDCTSD ECF Procedures(13).

   a. *PDF format required.* Any document submitted via the court's electronic case filing (ECF) system must be: in .pdf format. IN R USDCTSD L.R. 5-1(c); IN R USDCTSD ECF Procedures(7). Any document submitted via the court's electronic case filing (ECF) system must be: converted to a .pdf file directly from a word processing program, unless it exists only in paper format (in which case it may be scanned to create a .pdf document). IN R USDCTSD L.R. 5-1(c); IN R USDCTSD ECF Procedures(13).

      i. An exhibit may be scanned into PDF format, at a recommended 300 dpi resolution or higher, only if it does not already exist in electronic format. The filing attorney is responsible for reviewing all PDF documents for legibility before submitting them through the Court's Electronic Case Filing system. For technical guidance in creating PDF documents, please contact the Clerk's Office. IN R USDCTSD ECF Procedures(13).

b.   *File size limitations.* Any document submitted via the court's electronic case filing (ECF) system must be: submitted as one or more .pdf files that do not exceed ten megabytes (10 MB) each (consistent with the CM/ECF Policies and Procedures Manual (IN R USDCTSD ECF Procedures)). IN R USDCTSD L.R. 5-1(c); IN R USDCTSD ECF Procedures(13).

    i.   To electronically file a document or attachment that exceeds ten megabytes (10 MB), the document must first be broken down into two or more smaller files. For example, if Exhibit A is a twelve megabyte (12 MB) PDF file, it should be divided into 2 equal parts prior to electronic filing. Each component part of the exhibit would be filed as an attachment to the main document and described appropriately as "Exhibit A (part 1 of 2)" and "Exhibit A (part 2 of 2)." IN R USDCTSD ECF Procedures(13).

    ii.   The supporting items mentioned in IN R USDCTSD ECF Procedures(13) should not be confused with memorandums or briefs in support of motions as outlined in IN R USDCTSD L.R. 7-1 or IN R USDCTSD L.R. 56-1. These memorandums or briefs in support are to be filed as entirely separate documents pursuant to the appropriate rule. Additionally, no motion shall be embodied in the text of a response or reply brief/memorandum unless otherwise ordered by the Court. IN R USDCTSD ECF Procedures(13).

c.   *Separate component parts.* A key objective of the electronic filing system is to ensure that as much of the case as possible is managed electronically. To facilitate electronic filing and retrieval, documents to be filed electronically are to be reasonably broken into their separate component parts. By way of example, most filings include a foundation document (e.g., motion) and other supporting items (e.g., exhibits, proposed orders, proposed amended pleadings). The foundation document, as well as the supporting items, are each separate components of the filing; supporting items must be filed as attachments to the foundation document. These exhibits or attachments should include only those excerpts of the referenced documents that are directly germane to the matter under consideration. IN R USDCTSD ECF Procedures(13).

    i.   Where an individual component cannot be included in an electronic filing (e.g. the component cannot be converted to electronic format), the filer shall electronically file the prescribed Notice of Manual Filing in place of that component. A model form is provided as Appendix C (IN R USDCTSD ECF Procedures(Appendix C)). IN R USDCTSD ECF Procedures(13).

d.   *Exhibits.* Each electronically filed exhibit to a main document must be: (1) created as a separate .pdf file; (2) submitted as an attachment to the main document and given a title which describes its content; and (3) limited to excerpts that are directly germane to the main document's subject matter. IN R USDCTSD L.R. 5-6(a).

    i.   When uploading attachments during the electronic filing process, exhibits must be uploaded in a logical sequence and a brief description must be entered for each individual PDF file. The description must include not only the exhibit number or letter, but also a brief description of the document. This information may be entered in CM/ECF using a combination of the Category drop-down menu, the Description text box, or both (see IN R USDCTSD ECF Procedures(13)(Figure 1)). The information that is provided in each box will be combined to create a description of the document as it appears on the case docket (see IN R USDCTSD ECF Procedures(13)(Figure 2)). IN R USDCTSD ECF Procedures(13). For an example, refer to IN R USDCTSD ECF Procedures(13).

e.   *Excerpts.* A party filing an exhibit that consists of excerpts from a larger document must clearly and prominently identify the exhibit as containing excerpted material. Either party will have the right to timely file additional excerpts or the complete document to the extent they are or become directly germane to the main document's subject matter. IN R USDCTSD L.R. 5-6(b).

f.   For an example illustrating the application of IN R USDCTSD ECF Procedures(13), refer to IN R USDCTSD ECF Procedures(13).

3.   *Signing of pleadings, motions and other papers*

a.   *Signature.* Every pleading, written motion, and other paper must be signed by at least one attorney of record in the attorney's name—or by a party personally if the party is unrepresented. The paper must state the signer's address, e-mail address, and telephone number. FRCP 11(a).

i. *Signatures on manual filings.* Any document that is not filed electronically must: include the original signature of the pro se litigant or attorney who files it. IN R USDCTSD L.R. 5-1(d)(1).

ii. *Electronic signatures.* Use of the attorney's login and password when filing documents electronically serves in part as the attorney's signature for purposes of FRCP 11, the Local Rules of the United States District Court for the Southern District of Indiana, and any other purpose for which a signature is required in connection with proceedings before the Court. IN R USDCTSD ECF Procedures(14); IN R USDCTSD ECF Procedures(10). A pleading, motion, brief, or notice filed electronically under an attorney's ECF log-in and password must be signed by that attorney. IN R USDCTSD L.R. 5-7(a). A signature on a document other than a document filed as provided under IN R USDCTSD L.R. 5-7(a) must be an original handwritten signature and must be scanned into .pdf format for electronic filing. IN R USDCTSD L.R. 5-7(c); IN R USDCTSD ECF Procedures(14).

- *Form of electronic signature.* If a document is converted directly from a word processing application to .pdf (as opposed to scanning), the name of the Filing User under whose log-in and password the document is submitted must be preceded by a "s/" and typed on the signature line where the Filing User's handwritten signature would otherwise appear. IN R USDCTSD L.R. 5-7(b). All documents filed electronically shall include a signature block and include the filing attorney's typewritten name, address, telephone number, facsimile number and e-mail address. In addition, the name of the filing attorney under whose ECF login the document will be filed should be preceded by a "s/" and typed in the space where the attorney's handwritten signature would otherwise appear. IN R US-DCTSD ECF Procedures(14). For a sample format, refer to IN R USDCTSD ECF Procedures(14).

- *Effect of electronic signature.* Filing an electronically signed document under an attorney's ECF log-in and password constitutes the attorney's signature on the document under the Federal Rules of Civil Procedure, under the Local Rules of the United States District Court for the Southern District of Indiana, and for any other reason a signature is required in connection with the court's activities. IN R USDCTSD L.R. 5-7(d).

- *Documents with multiple attorneys' signatures.* Documents requiring signatures of more than one attorney shall be filed either by: (1) obtaining consent from the other attorney, then typing the "s/ [Name]" signature of the other attorney on the signature line where the other attorney's signature would otherwise appear; (2) identifying in the signature section the name of the other attorney whose signature is required and by the submission of a Notice of Endorsement (see IN R USDCTSD ECF Procedures(Appendix B)) by the other attorney no later than three (3) business days after filing; (3) submitting a scanned document containing all handwritten signatures; or (4) in any other manner approved by the Court. IN R USDCTSD ECF Procedures(14); IN R USDCTSD L.R. 5-7(e).

iii. *No verification or accompanying affidavit required for pleadings.* Unless a rule or statute specifically states otherwise, a pleading need not be verified or accompanied by an affidavit. FRCP 11(a).

iv. *Unsigned papers.* The court must strike an unsigned paper unless the omission is promptly corrected after being called to the attorney's or party's attention. FRCP 11(a). The court will strike any document filed directly with the clerk that is not signed by an attorney of record or the pro se litigant filing it, but the court may do so only after giving the attorney or pro se litigant notice of the omission and reasonable time to correct it. Rubber-stamp or facsimile signatures are not original signatures and the court will deem documents containing them to be unsigned for purposes of FRCP 11 and FRCP 26(g) and IN R USDCTSD L.R. 5-10. IN R USDCTSD L.R. 5-10(g).

b. *Representations to the court.* By presenting to the court a pleading, written motion, or other paper—whether by signing, filing, submitting, or later advocating it—an attorney or unrepresented party certifies that to the best of the person's knowledge, information, and belief, formed after an inquiry reasonable under the circumstances:

    i. It is not being presented for any improper purpose, such as to harass, cause unnecessary delay, or needlessly increase the cost of litigation;

    ii. The claims, defenses, and other legal contentions are warranted by existing law or by a nonfrivolous argument for extending, modifying, or reversing existing law or for establishing new law;

    iii. The factual contentions have evidentiary support or, if specifically so identified, will likely have evidentiary support after a reasonable opportunity for further investigation or discovery; and

    iv. The denials of factual contentions are warranted on the evidence or, if specifically so identified, are reasonably based on belief or a lack of information. FRCP 11(b).

c. *Sanctions.* If, after notice and a reasonable opportunity to respond, the court determines that FRCP 11(b) has been violated, the court may impose an appropriate sanction on any attorney, law firm, or party that violated FRCP 11(b) or is responsible for the violation. FRCP 11(c)(1). Refer to the United States District Court for the Southern District of Indiana KeyRules Motion for Sanctions document for more information.

4. *Privacy protection for filings made with the court.* Electronically filed documents must meet the requirements of. . .FRCP 5.2 (Privacy Protection for Filings Made with the Court), as if they had been submitted on paper. IN R USDCTSD ECF Procedures(13).

a. *Redacted filings.* Unless the court orders otherwise, in an electronic or paper filing with the court that contains an individual's Social Security number, taxpayer-identification number, or birth date, the name of an individual known to be a minor, or a financial-account number, a party or nonparty making the filing may include only:

    i. The last four (4) digits of the Social Security number and taxpayer-identification number;

    ii. The year of the individual's birth;

    iii. The minor's initials; and

    iv. The last four (4) digits of the financial-account number. FRCP 5.2(a).

b. *Exemptions from the redaction requirement.* The redaction requirement does not apply to the following:

    i. A financial-account number that identifies the property allegedly subject to forfeiture in a forfeiture proceeding;

    ii. The record of an administrative or agency proceeding;

    iii. The official record of a state-court proceeding;

    iv. The record of a court or tribunal, if that record was not subject to the redaction requirement when originally filed;

    v. A filing covered by FRCP 5.2(c) or FRCP 5.2(d); and

    vi. A pro se filing in an action brought under 28 U.S.C.A. § 2241, 28 U.S.C.A. § 2254, or 28 U.S.C.A. § 2255. FRCP 5.2(b).

c. *Limitations on remote access to electronic files; Social Security appeals and immigration cases.* Unless the court orders otherwise, in an action for benefits under the Social Security Act, and in an action or proceeding relating to an order of removal, to relief from removal, or to immigration benefits or detention, access to an electronic file is authorized as follows:

    i. The parties and their attorneys may have remote electronic access to any part of the case file, including the administrative record;

    ii. Any other person may have electronic access to the full record at the courthouse, but may have remote electronic access only to:

       • The docket maintained by the court; and

- An opinion, order, judgment, or other disposition of the court, but not any other part of the case file or the administrative record. FRCP 5.2(c).

d. *Filings made under seal.* The court may order that a filing be made under seal without redaction. The court may later unseal the filing or order the person who made the filing to file a redacted version for the public record. FRCP 5.2(d). For more information on filing under seal, refer to IN R USDCTSD L.R. 5-11 and IN R USDCTSD ECF Procedures(18).

e. *Protective orders.* For good cause, the court may by order in a case:

   i. Require redaction of additional information; or

   ii. Limit or prohibit a nonparty's remote electronic access to a document filed with the court. FRCP 5.2(e).

f. *Option for additional unredacted filing under seal.* A person making a redacted filing may also file an unredacted copy under seal. The court must retain the unredacted copy as part of the record. FRCP 5.2(f).

g. *Option for filing a reference list.* A filing that contains redacted information may be filed together with a reference list that identifies each item of redacted information and specifies an appropriate identifier that uniquely corresponds to each item listed. The list must be filed under seal and may be amended as of right. Any reference in the case to a listed identifier will be construed to refer to the corresponding item of information. FRCP 5.2(g).

h. *Waiver of protection of identifiers.* A person waives the protection of FRCP 5.2(a) as to the person's own information by filing it without redaction and not under seal. FRCP 5.2(h).

F. Filing and Service Requirements

1. *Filing requirements.* Any paper after the complaint that is required to be served—together with a certificate of service—must be filed within a reasonable time after service. FRCP 5(d)(1).

   a. *How filing is made; In general.* A paper is filed by delivering it:

      i. To the clerk; or

      ii. To a judge who agrees to accept it for filing, and who must then note the filing date on the paper and promptly send it to the clerk. FRCP 5(d)(2).

         - In certain instances, the court will direct the parties to submit items directly to chambers (e.g., confidential settlement statements). However, absent specific prior authorization, counsel and litigants should not submit letters or documents directly to chambers, and such materials should be filed with the clerk. IN R USDCTSD L.R. 5-1(Local Rules Advisory Committee Comment).

      iii. A document or item submitted in relation to a matter within the court's jurisdiction is deemed filed upon delivery to the office of the clerk in a manner prescribed by the Local Rules of the United States District Court for the Southern District of Indiana or the Federal Rules of Civil Procedure or authorized by the court. Any submission directed to a Judge or Judge's staff, the office of the clerk or any employee thereof, in a manner that is not contemplated by IN R USDCTSD L.R. 5-1 and without prior court authorization is prohibited. IN R USDCTSD L.R. 5-1(a).

   b. *Non-electronic filing.* Any document that is exempt from electronic filing must be filed directly with the clerk and served on other parties in the case as required by those Federal Rules of Civil Procedure and Local Rules of the United States District Court for the Southern District of Indiana that apply to the service of non-electronic documents. IN R USDCTSD L.R. 5-2(c).

      i. *When completed.* A document or other item that is not required to be filed electronically is deemed filed:

         - Upon delivery in person, by courier, or via U.S. Mail or other mail delivery service to the clerk's office during business hours;

         - When the courtroom deputy clerk accepts it, if the document or item is filed in open court; or

- Upon completion of any other manner of filing that the court authorizes. IN R USDCTSD L.R. 5-10(a).

ii. *Document filing by non-exempt party.* When a party who is not exempt from the electronic filing requirement files a document directly with the clerk, the party must:

- Electronically file a notice of manual filing that explains why the document cannot be filed electronically;

- Present the document to the clerk within one (1) business day after filing the notice of manual filing; and

- Present the clerk with a copy of the notice of manual filing when the party files the document with the clerk. IN R USDCTSD L.R. 5-2(d).

c. *Electronic filing*

i. *Authorization of electronic filing program.* A court may, by local rule, allow papers to be filed, signed, or verified by electronic means that are consistent with any technical standards established by the Judicial Conference of the United States. A local rule may require electronic filing only if reasonable exceptions are allowed. A paper filed electronically in compliance with a local rule is a written paper for purposes of the Federal Rules of Civil Procedure. FRCP 5(d)(3).

- IN R USDCTSD L.R. 5-2 requires electronic filing, as allowed by FRCP 5(d)(3). The policies and procedures in IN R USDCTSD ECF Procedures govern electronic filing in this district unless, due to circumstances in a particular case, a judicial officer determines that these policies and procedures (IN R USDCTSD ECF Procedures) should be modified. IN R USDCTSD ECF Procedures(1).

- Unless modified by order of the Court, all Federal Rules of Civil Procedure and Local Rules of the United States District Court for the Southern District of Indiana shall continue to apply to cases maintained in the Court's Case Management/Electronic Case Filing System (CM/ECF). IN R USDCTSD ECF Procedures(3).

ii. *Mandatory electronic filing.* Unless exempted pursuant to IN R USDCTSD L.R. 5-3(e), attorneys admitted to the court's bar (including those admitted pro hac vice) or authorized to represent the United States must use the court's ECF system to file documents. IN R USDCTSD L.R. 5-3(a). Electronic filing by attorneys is required for eligible documents filed in civil and criminal cases pending with the Court, unless specifically exempted by Local Rule or Court Order. IN R USDCTSD ECF Procedures(4).

- *Exceptions.* All civil cases (other than those cases the court specifically exempts) must be maintained in the court's electronic case filing (ECF) system. Accordingly, as allowed by FRCP 5(d)(3), every document filed in this court (including exhibits) must be transmitted to the clerk's office via the ECF system consistent with IN R USDCTSD L.R. 5-2 through IN R USDCTSD L.R. 5-11 except: (1) documents filed by pro se litigants; (2) transcripts in cases filed by claimants under the Social Security Act (and related statutes); (3) exhibits in a format that does not readily permit electronic filing (such as videos and large maps and charts); (4) documents that are illegible when scanned into .pdf format; (5) documents filed in cases not maintained on the ECF system; and (6) any other documents that the court or the Local Rules of the United States District Court for the Southern District of Indiana specifically allow to be filed directly with the clerk. IN R USDCTSD L.R. 5-2(a). Parties otherwise participating in the electronic filing system may be excused from filing a particular component electronically under certain limited circumstances, such as when the component cannot be reduced to an electronic format. Such components shall not be filed electronically, but instead shall be manually filed with the Clerk of Court and served upon the parties in accordance with the applicable Federal Rules of Civil Procedure and the Local Rules of the United States District Court for the Southern District of Indiana for filing and service of non-electronic documents. IN R USDCTSD ECF Procedures(15).

- *Exemption from participation.* The court may exempt attorneys from using the ECF system in a particular case for good cause. An attorney must file a petition for ECF exemption and a CM/ECF technical requirements exemption questionnaire in each case in which the attorney seeks an exemption. (The CM/ECF technical requirements exemption questionnaire is available on the court's website). IN R USDCTSD L.R. 5-3(e).

iii. *Consequences of electronic filing.* Electronic transmission of a document consistent with the procedures adopted by the Court shall, upon the complete receipt of the same by the Clerk of Court, constitute filing of the document for all purposes of the Federal Rules of Civil and Criminal Procedure and the Local Rules of the United States District Court for the Southern District of Indiana, and shall constitute entry of that document onto the docket maintained by the Clerk pursuant to FRCP 58 and FRCP 79. IN R USDCTSD ECF Procedures(7); IN R USDCTSD L.R. 5-4(c)(1). When a document has been filed electronically: the document, as filed, binds the filing party. IN R USDCTSD L.R. 5-4(c)(3).

- A Notice of Electronic Filing (NEF) acknowledging that the document has been filed will immediately appear on the filer's screen after the document has been submitted. Attorneys are strongly encouraged to print or electronically save a copy of the NEF. Attorneys can also verify the filing of documents by inspecting the Court's electronic docket sheet through the use of a PACER login. IN R USDCTSD ECF Procedures(7). When a document has been filed electronically: the notice of electronic filing for the document serves as the court's date-stamp and proof of filing. IN R USDCTSD L.R. 5-4(c)(4).

- The Court may, upon the motion of a party or upon its own motion, strike any inappropriately filed document. IN R USDCTSD ECF Procedures(7).

iv. For more information on electronic filing, refer to IN R USDCTSD ECF Procedures.

d. *Fax filing.* The clerk may not file a faxed document without court authorization. The court may not authorize the clerk to file faxed documents without finding that compelling circumstances justify it. A party must submit a copy of the document that otherwise complies with IN R USDCTSD L.R. 5-10 to replace the faxed copy within seven (7) days after faxing the document. IN R USDCTSD L.R. 5-10(e).

2. *Service requirements*

a. *Service; When required*

i. *In general.* Unless the Federal Rules of Civil Procedure provide otherwise, each of the following papers must be served on every party:

- An order stating that service is required;

- A pleading filed after the original complaint, unless the court orders otherwise under FRCP 5(c) because there are numerous defendants;

- A discovery paper required to be served on a party, unless the court orders otherwise;

- A written motion, except one that may be heard ex parte; and

- A written notice, appearance, demand, or offer of judgment, or any similar paper. FRCP 5(a)(1).

ii. *If a party fails to appear.* No service is required on a party who is in default for failing to appear. But a pleading that asserts a new claim for relief against such a party must be served on that party under FRCP 4. FRCP 5(a)(2).

iii. *Seizing property.* If an action is begun by seizing property and no person is or need be named as a defendant, any service required before the filing of an appearance, answer, or claim must be made on the person who had custody or possession of the property when it was seized. FRCP 5(a)(3).

b. *Service; How made*

i. *Serving an attorney.* If a party is represented by an attorney, service under FRCP 5 must be made on the attorney unless the court orders service on the party. FRCP 5(b)(1).

ii. *Service in general.* A paper is served under FRCP 5 by:

- Handing it to the person;

- Leaving it: (1) at the person's office with a clerk or other person in charge or, if no one is in charge, in a conspicuous place in the office; or (2) if the person has no office or the office is closed, at the person's dwelling or usual place of abode with someone of suitable age and discretion who resides there;

- Mailing it to the person's last known address—in which event service is complete upon mailing;

- Leaving it with the court clerk if the person has no known address;

- Sending it by electronic means if the person consented in writing—in which event service is complete upon transmission, but is not effective if the serving party learns that it did not reach the person to be served; or

- Delivering it by any other means that the person consented to in writing—in which event service is complete when the person making service delivers it to the agency designated to make delivery. FRCP 5(b)(2).

iii. *Electronic service*

- *Consent.* By registering to use the ECF system, attorneys consent to electronic service of documents filed in cases maintained on the ECF system. IN R USDCTSD L.R. 5-3(d). By participating in the Electronic Case Filing Program, attorneys consent to the electronic service of documents, and shall make available electronic mail addresses for service. IN R USDCTSD ECF Procedures(11).

- *Service on registered parties.* Upon the filing of a document by a party, an e-mail message will be automatically generated by the electronic filing system and sent via electronic mail to the e-mail addresses of all registered attorneys who have appeared in the case. The Notice of Electronic Filing will contain a document hyperlink which will provide recipients with one "free look" at the electronically filed document. Recipients are encouraged to print and/or save a copy of the document during the "free look" to avoid incurring PACER charges for future viewings of the document. IN R USDCTSD ECF Procedures(11). When a document has been filed electronically: transmission of the notice of electronic filing generated by the ECF system to an attorney's e-mail address constitutes service of the document on that attorney. IN R USDCTSD L.R. 5-4(c)(5). The party effectuates service on all registered attorneys by filing electronically. IN R USDCTSD ECF Procedures(11). When a document has been filed electronically: no other attempted service will constitute electronic service of the document. IN R USDCTSD L.R. 5-4(c)(6).

- *Service on exempt parties.* A filer must serve a copy of the document consistent with FRCP 5 on any party or attorney who is exempt from participating in electronic filing. IN R USDCTSD L.R. 5-4(d). It is the responsibility of the filing attorney to conventionally serve all parties who do not receive electronic service (the identity of these parties will be indicated on the filing receipt generated by the ECF system). IN R USDCTSD ECF Procedures(11).

- *Service on parties excused from electronic filing.* Parties otherwise participating in the electronic filing system may be excused from filing a particular component electronically under certain limited circumstances, such as when the component cannot be reduced to an electronic format. Such components shall not be filed electronically, but instead shall be manually filed with the Clerk of Court and served upon the parties in accordance with the applicable Federal Rules of Civil Procedure and the Local Rules of the United States District Court for the Southern District of Indiana for filing and service of non-electronic documents. IN R USDCTSD ECF Procedures(15).

- *Service of exempt documents.* Any document that is exempt from electronic filing must be filed directly with the clerk and served on other parties in the case as required by those Federal Rules of Civil Procedure and Local Rules of the United States District Court for the Southern District of Indiana that apply to the service of non-electronic documents. IN R USDCTSD L.R. 5-2(c).

iv. *Using court facilities.* If a local rule so authorizes, a party may use the court's transmission facilities to make service under FRCP 5(b)(2)(E). FRCP 5(b)(3).

c. *Serving numerous defendants*

    i. *In general.* If an action involves an unusually large number of defendants, the court may, on motion or on its own, order that:

- Defendants' pleadings and replies to them need not be served on other defendants;

- Any crossclaim, counterclaim, avoidance, or affirmative defense in those pleadings and replies to them will be treated as denied or avoided by all other parties; and

- Filing any such pleading and serving it on the plaintiff constitutes notice of the pleading to all parties. FRCP 5(c)(1).

    ii. *Notifying parties.* A copy of every such order must be served on the parties as the court directs. FRCP 5(c)(2).

G. Hearings

1. Refer to the General Requirements section of this document for information on pretrial conferences, scheduling conferences, and discovery planning conferences.

H. Forms

1. Federal Pretrial Conferences, Scheduling, Management Forms

a. Plaintiff's informal summary of status of case to judge prior to pretrial conference in complex case. 2C FEDFORMS § 2807.

b. Joint pretrial report. 2C FEDFORMS § 2807.10.

c. Joint statement of undisputed facts. 2C FEDFORMS § 2807.20.

d. Joint statement of disputed facts. 2C FEDFORMS § 2807.30.

e. Joint report of counsel prior to pretrial conference. 2C FEDFORMS § 2807.40.

f. Plaintiff's pretrial conference statement; Insurance case. 2C FEDFORMS § 2807.50.

g. Defendant's pretrial conference statement; Insurance case. 2C FEDFORMS § 2807.60.

h. Plaintiff's list of exhibits to be offered at trial. 2C FEDFORMS § 2811.

i. Defendant's list of prospective witnesses. 2C FEDFORMS § 2811.10.

j. Designation of witnesses whom plaintiff intends to call at trial pursuant to pretrial conference oral stipulation. 2C FEDFORMS § 2811.20.

k. Defendant's list of prospective exhibits. 2C FEDFORMS § 2811.40.

l. Report of parties' planning meeting. 3A FEDFORMS § 3314.

m. Report of parties' discovery conference; Another form. 3A FEDFORMS § 3315.

n. Report of parties' discovery conference; Another form. 3A FEDFORMS § 3316.

o. Joint scheduling report. 3A FEDFORMS § 3316.5.

p. Stipulation and order regarding discovery conference discussions. 3A FEDFORMS § 3316.6.

q. Pretrial statement; By plaintiff; Automobile collision involving corporate defendant. FEDPROF § 1:658.

r. Pretrial statement; By defendant; Automobile collision. FEDPROF § 1:659.

s. Pretrial statement; By parties jointly; Automobile collision. FEDPROF § 1:660.

t. Pretrial statement; Provision; Waiver of abandoned claims or defenses. FEDPROF § 1:661.

u. Status report. GOLDLTGFMS § 34:2.

v. Preliminary pretrial checklist. GOLDLTGFMS § 34:3.

w. Pretrial memorandum. GOLDLTGFMS § 34:4.

    x.   Pretrial memorandum; Short form. GOLDLTGFMS § 34:5.

    y.   Pretrial memorandum; Civil action. GOLDLTGFMS § 34:6.

    z.   Pretrial memorandum; Worker's compensation case. GOLDLTGFMS § 34:7.

2. Forms for the Southern District of Indiana

    a.   Case management plan. IN R USDCTSD Case Mgt(Case Management Plan).

    b.   Notice of endorsement. IN R USDCTSD ECF Procedures(Appendix B).

    c.   Notice of manual filing. IN R USDCTSD ECF Procedures(Appendix C).

    d.   Declaration that party was unable to file in a timely manner due to technical difficulties. IN R USDCTSD ECF Procedures(Appendix D).

I. Applicable Rules

1. *Federal rules*

    a.   Serving and filing pleadings and other papers. FRCP 5.

    b.   Constitutional challenge to a statute; Notice, certification, and intervention. FRCP 5.1.

    c.   Privacy protection for filings made with the court. FRCP 5.2.

    d.   Computing and extending time; Time for motion papers. FRCP 6.

    e.   Pleadings allowed; Form of motions and other papers. FRCP 7.

    f.   Form of pleadings. FRCP 10.

    g.   Signing pleadings, motions, and other papers; Representations to the court; Sanctions. FRCP 11.

    h.   Pretrial conferences; Scheduling; Management. FRCP 16.

    i.   Duty to disclose; General provisions governing discovery. FRCP 26.

    j.   Failure to make disclosures or to cooperate in discovery; Sanctions. FRCP 37.

2. *Local rules*

    a.   Scope of the rules. IN R USDCTSD L.R. 1-1.

    b.   Sanctions for errors as to form. IN R USDCTSD L.R. 1-3.

    c.   Format of documents presented for filing. IN R USDCTSD L.R. 5-1.

    d.   Constitutional challenge to a statute; Notice. IN R USDCTSD L.R. 5.1-1.

    e.   Filing of documents electronically required. IN R USDCTSD L.R. 5-2.

    f.   Eligibility, registration, passwords for electronic filing; Exemption from electronic filing. IN R USDCTSD L.R. 5-3.

    g.   Timing and consequences of electronic filing. IN R USDCTSD L.R. 5-4.

    h.   Attachments and exhibits in cases filed electronically. IN R USDCTSD L.R. 5-6.

    i.   Signatures in cases filed electronically. IN R USDCTSD L.R. 5-7.

    j.   Non-electronic filings. IN R USDCTSD L.R. 5-10.

    k.   Motion practice. [IN R USDCTSD L.R. 7-1, as amended by IN ORDER 16-2319, effective December 1, 2016].

    l.   Request for three-judge court. IN R USDCTSD L.R. 9-2.

    m.   Pretrial procedures. [IN R USDCTSD L.R. 16-1, as amended by IN ORDER 16-2319, effective December 1, 2016].

    n.   Assignment of cases. IN R USDCTSD L.R. 40-1.

    o.   Summary judgment procedure. IN R USDCTSD L.R. 56-1.

    p.   Alternative dispute resolution. IN R USDCTSD A.D.R. Rule 1.1; IN R USDCTSD A.D.R. Rule 1.2; IN R USDCTSD A.D.R. Rule 1.5; IN R USDCTSD A.D.R. Rule 2.1; IN R USDCTSD A.D.R. Rule 2.2.

q. Instructions for preparing case management plan. IN R USDCTSD Case Mgt.

r. Electronic case filing policies and procedures manual. IN R USDCTSD ECF Procedures.

Appendix - Related Court Documents

Complaint

2016 WL 2990802 (N.D.Ind.)

Westlaw Query>>

To find more Complaint filings on Westlaw: access Indiana Trial Court Documents (from the Home page, click Trial Court Documents, then Indiana), click the Advanced Search link, select Complaint, and click Search. Use the Jurisdiction filter on the left to narrow results to Federal.

United States District Court, N.D. Indiana.

BALL CORPORATION, and Indiana corporation and Factory Mutual Insurance Company, a Rhode Island corporation, s subrogee, Plaintiffs,

v.

AIR TECH OF MICHIGAN, INC., a Michigan corporation, Defendant.

No. 16 cv 42.

May 23, 2016.

Complaint

Mark N. Senak, Senak Keegan Gleason Smith & Michaud, Ltd, 621 South Plymouth Court, Suite 100, Chicago, Illinois 60605, T: 312-214-1400 / F: 312-214-1401, Email: msenak@skgsmlaw.com.

JURY DEMAND

Plaintiffs BALL CORPORATION and FACTORY MUTUAL INSURANCE COMPANY, by and through their attorneys, Mark N. Senak and Senak Keegan Gleason Smith & Michaud, Ltd., as their Complaint against Defendant AIR TECH OF MICHIGAN, INC., hereby state as follows:

JURISDICTIONAL STATEMENT

1. The District Court has original jurisdiction over this matter pursuant to 28 U.S.C. § 1332(a)(1).

2. Plaintiff BALL CORPORATION ("BALL") is an Indiana corporation with its principal place of business in Broomfield, Colorado.

3. Plaintiff FACTORY MUTUAL INSURANCE COMPANY ("FACTORY MUTUAL") is a Rhode Island corporation with its principal place of business in Johnston, Rhode Island.

4. Defendant AIR TECH OF MICHIGAN, INC. ("AIR TECH") is a Michigan corporation with its principal place of business in Holland, Michigan.

5. The amount in controversy, exclusive of interest and costs, is in excess of $75,000.

ALLEGATIONS COMMON TO ALL COUNTS

6. Plaintiff FACTORY MUTUAL issued a policy of property insurance to BALL which provided coverage, subject to the applicable terms, conditions, exclusions and exceptions, for damage to the Ball aluminum can manufacturing plant in Monticello, Indiana.

7. On or about May 23, 2014, the Monticello plaint sustained damage as a result of a fire.

8. Pursuant to said policy of insurance, BALL made a claim for reimbursement of the damage caused to the plant, its contents, and related expenses.

9. Pursuant to said policy of insurance, FACTORY MUTUAL paid BALL for the covered expenses less the applicable deductible and uninsured losses.

10. Prior to the commencement of this action and in consideration of the payment by FACTORY MUTUAL under the applicable insurance policy, BALL transferred to FACTORY MUTUAL all of its rights to recover the amount paid by FACTORY MUTUAL to BALL from any party responsible for causing the loss.

11. Pursuant to the applicable insurance policy and related documents, FACTORY MUTUAL is the bona fide subrogee of BALL.

COUNT I: BREACH OF CONTRACT

12. Plaintiffs incorporate by reference the allegations Paragraphs 1 — 11 as the allegation of Paragraph 12.

13. Defendant AIR TECH held itself out to the public and to Plaintiff BALL has having special expertise in the cleaning and servicing of mechanical equipment including, but not limited to, Internal Bake Ovens used by Plaintiff BALL in the production process at the Monticello plant.

14. Plaintiff BALL entered into a contract with Defendant AIR TECH to perform cleaning and maintenance services to Internal Bake Oven No. 2 ("IBO No. 2") and attached ductwork at the Ball plant in Monticello, Indiana.

15. As part of the agreement, Defendant AIR TECH was required to remove residue that accumulates on the internal components of the oven and attached ductwork during the production process.

16. Defendant AIR TECH breached the contract by failing to adequately clean IBO No. 2 to remove the residue that accumulates on the inside of the oven and attached ductwork.

17. As a direct and proximate result of Defendant AIR TECH's breach of the contract, approximately six hours after Defendant AIR TECH completed cleaning IBO No. 2, a fire ignited in IBO No. 2 and the attached ductwork.

18. As a direct and proximate result of Defendant AIR TECH's breach of the contract, Plaintiff BALL sustained fire, smoke, and water damage to IBO No. 2 and the attached ductwork, other parts of the Monticello plant, and to finished product stored at the plant.

19. As a direct and proximate result of the damage to the Monticello plant, the plant was unable to operate resulting in interruption of Plaintiff BALL's production process and related expenses to mitigate interruption of Plaintiff BALL's business operations.

20. The total damages to the Monticello plant, finished product stored at the plant, the resulting business interruption, and efforts to mitigate the business interruption as a direct and proximate result of the fire amount to approximately $12.1 million.

21. Plaintiff BALL performed all of its obligations under the contract.

WHEREFORE, Plaintiffs BALL CORPORATION and FACTORY MUTUAL INSURANCE COMPANY pray judgment be entered in their favor and against Defendant AIR TECH OF MICHIGAN, INC., in an amount in excess of $75,000 plus costs and prejudgment interest, and for such further relief as the Court deems equitable and just.

COUNT II: BREACH OF IMPLIED DUTY OF WORKMANLIKE PERFORMANCE

22. Plaintiffs incorporate by reference the allegations of Paragraphs 1 — 21 as the allegation of Paragraph 22.

23. At all material times, Defendant AIR TECH was under an implied duty to perform the work on IBO No. 2 in a skillful, careful, and workmanlike manner.

24. Defendant AIR TECH breached its duty by one or more of the following acts or omissions:

    a. Failing to adequately remove the residue from inside IBO No. 2 and the attached ductwork to prevent ignition of a fire;

    b. Failing to adequately inspect the work to insure the residue inside IBO No. 2 had been properly removed and prevent ignition of a fire before turning the oven over to Plaintiff BALL;

c. Failing to adequately train its employees on how to properly clean IBO No. 2 and the attached ductwork to remove the accumulated residue to prevent ignition of a fire;

d. Failing to adequately train its employees on the use and operation of an internal bake oven before allowing its employees to perform cleaning and maintenance services on IBO No. 2 at the Monticello plant;

e. Failing to adequately train its employees on the consequences of failing to properly and thoroughly clean IBO No. 2;

f. Failing to provide its employees with proper tools and equipment to adequately clean IBO No. 2 to remove the residue inside the oven and attached ductwork; and

g. Failing to adequately supervise its employees to insure residue inside IBO No. 2 had been properly removed to prevent ignition of a fire.

25. As a direct and proximate result of Defendant AIR TECH's breach of its implied duty, Plaintiff BALL sustained damages as more fully described in paragraphs 17-20, *supra*.

WHEREFORE, Plaintiffs BALL CORPORATION and FACTORY MUTUAL INSURANCE COMPANY pray judgment be entered in their favor and against Defendant AIR TECH OF MICHIGAN, INC., in an amount in excess of $75,000 plus costs and prejudgment interest, and for such further relief as the Court deems equitable and just.

COUNT III: NEGLIGENCE

26. Plaintiffs incorporate by reference the allegations of Paragraphs 1 — 11 as the allegation of Paragraph 26.

27. Defendant AIR TECH owed Plaintiff BALL a duty to use reasonable care both in its work and in course of performing the cleaning and maintenance of IBO No. 2.

28. Defendant AIR TECH breached its duty by one or more of the following acts or omissions:

a. Failing to adequately remove the residue from inside IBO No. 2 and the attached ductwork to prevent ignition of a fire;

b. Failing to adequately inspect the work to insure the residue inside IBO No.2 had been properly removed before turning the oven over to Plaintiff BALL to prevent ignition of a fire;

c. Failing to adequately train its employees on how to properly clean IBO No. 2 and the attached ductwork to remove the accumulated residue to prevent ignition of a fire;

d. Failing to adequately train its employees on the use an operation of an internal bake oven before allowing its employees to perform cleaning and maintenance services on IBO No. 2 at the Monticello plant;

e. Failing to adequately train its employees on the consequences of failing to properly and thoroughly clean IBO No. 2;

f. Failing to provide its employees with proper tools and equipment to adequately clean IBO No.2 to remove the residue inside the oven and attached ductwork; and

g. Failing to adequately supervise its employees to insure residue inside IBO No. 2 had been properly removed to prevent ignition of a fire.

29. As a direct and proximate result of Defendant AIR TECH's breach of its duty, Plaintiff BALL sustained damages as more fully described in paragraphs 17 — 19, *supra*.

WHEREFORE, Plaintiffs BALL CORPORATION and FACTORY MUTUAL INSURANCE COMPANY pray judgment be entered in their favor and against Defendant AIR TECH OF MICHIGAN, INC., in an amount in excess of $75,000 plus costs, and for such further relief as the Court deems equitable and just.

May 23, 2016

Respectfully submitted,

BALL CORPORATION and FACTORY MUTUAL INSURANCE COMPANY

By: s/ *Mark N. Senak*

Mark N. Senak, one of its attorneys

COMPLAINT

Mark N. Senak
SENAK KEEGAN GLEASON SMITH & MICHAUD, LTD
621 South Plymouth Court, Suite 100
Chicago, Illinois 60605
T: 312-214-1400 / F: 312-214-1401
Email: *msenak@skgsmlaw.com*

Answer

2015 WL 12645722 (S.D.Ind.)

United States District Court, S.D. Indiana.

Indianapolis Division

ELI LILLY AND COMPANY and The Trustees of Princeton University, Plaintiffs,

Westlaw Query>>

To find more Answer filings on Westlaw: access Indiana Trial Court Documents (from the Home page, click Trial Court Documents, then Indiana), click the Advanced Search link, select Answer and Counterclaim and click Search. Use the Jurisdiction filter on the left to narrow results to Federal.

v.

NANG KUANG PHARMACEUTICAL CO., LTD. and Canda NX-2, LLC, Defendants.

NANG KUANG PHARMACEUTICAL CO., LTD., and Canda NX-2, LLC, Counter-Plaintiffs,

v.

ELI LILLY AND COMPANY and The Trustees of Princeton University, Counter-Defendants.

No. 1:14-cv-1647-TWP-DKL.

September 11, 2015.

Answer to Complaint, Defenses and Counterclaims

Anthony R. Jost, Riley Bennett & Egloff, LLP, 141 East Washington Street, Fourth Floor, Indianapolis, Indiana 46204, (317) 636-8000, tjost@rbelaw.com, for defendants.

Michael A. Siem (Admitted pro hac vice), Aya Cieslak-Tochigi (Admitted pro hac vice), Farney Daniels PC, 159 20th Street, # 2B-41, Brooklyn, New York 11232, (512) 948-3133, msiem@farneydaniels.com, atochigi@farneydaniels.com; Steven R. Daniels (Admitted pro hac vice), Farney Daniels PC, 800 South Austin Ave., Suite 200, Georgetown, Texas 78626, (512) 582-2828, sdaniels@farneydaniels.com, Of Counsel.

Defendants Nang Kuang Pharmaceutical Co., Ltd. ("Nang Kuang") and CANDA NX-2, LLC (*sic*) ("CANDA") (collectively, "Defendants" or "Counter-Plaintiffs"), by and through the undersigned attorneys, hereby respond to the Complaint for Patent Infringement of Plaintiffs Eli Lilly and Company ("Lilly"), and The Trustees of Princeton University ("Princeton") (collectively, "Plaintiffs" or "Counter-Defendants") as follows:

GENERAL DENIAL

Pursuant to Fed. R. Civ. P. 8(b)(3), Defendants deny all allegations in Plaintiffs' Complaint except those expressly admitted below.

ANSWER

NATURE OF THE ACTION

1. This is an action for patent infringement under the patent laws of the United States, Title 35, United States Code, that arises out of the filing by defendant Nang Kuang Pharmaceutical Co., Ltd. ("Nang Kuang") of an Abbreviated New Drug Application ("ANDA") with the U.S. Food and Drug Administration ("FDA") seeking approval to manufacture and sell generic versions of Lilly's ALIMTA® products prior to the expiration of U.S. Patent Nos. 5,344,932 ("the '932 patent") and 7,772,209 ("the '209 patent"). ALIMTA® is a chemotherapy agent used for the treatment of various types of cancer.

ANSWER: Defendants admit that Plaintiffs have brought an action for infringement of the '932 patent and the '209 patent, and that Nang Kuang has filed an ANDA seeking marketing approval from the FDA for generic versions of Lilly's pharmaceutical products, ALIMTA®. Defendants deny the remaining allegations in paragraph 1.

THE PARTIES

2. Plaintiff Eli Lilly and Company is a corporation organized and existing under the laws of the State of Indiana, having its corporate offices and principal place of business at Lilly Corporate Center, Indianapolis, Indiana 46285.

ANSWER: On information and belief, Defendants admit that Plaintiff Eli Lilly and Company is a corporation operating and existing under the laws of the State of Indiana. Defendants lack knowledge or information sufficient to form a belief as to the truth of the remaining allegations in paragraph 2, and therefore, deny those allegations.

3. Plaintiff The Trustees of Princeton University is a not-for-profit educational institution organized and existing under the laws of the State of New Jersey, having a place of business at One Nassau Hall, Princeton, New Jersey 08540.

ANSWER: On information and belief, Defendants admit that Plaintiff The Trustees of Princeton University is a not-for-profit educational institution organized and existing under the laws of the State of New Jersey. Defendants lack knowledge or information sufficient to form a belief as to the truth of the remaining allegations in paragraph 3, and therefore, deny those allegations.

4. Defendant Nang Kuang Pharmaceutical Co., Ltd. is a Taiwanese company having its offices at No. 1001, Zhongshan Rd, Xinhua Dist., Tainan City, Taiwan. Nang Kuang is in the business of distributing, marketing and/or selling generic pharmaceutical products, directly or indirectly, in the Southern District of Indiana and throughout the United States.

ANSWER: Defendants admit that Nang Kuang is a Taiwanese company having its principal place of business at No. 1001, Zhongshan Rd, Xinhua Dist., Tainan City, Taiwan. Defendants deny the remaining allegations in paragraph 4.

5. Defendant CANDA NK-2, LLC ("CANDA") is a Texas limited liability company having its offices at 1404 S. New Road, Waco, Texas 76711. CANDA holds rights to ANDA No. 207352, which was filed by Nang Kuang. CANDA is in the business of distributing, marketing and/or selling generic pharmaceutical products, directly or indirectly, in the Southern District of Indiana and throughout the United States.

ANSWER: Defendants admit that CANDA is a Texas limited liability company having its principal place of business at 1404 S. New Road, Waco, Texas 76711. Defendants further admit that CANDA holds rights to ANDA No. 207352, which was filed by Nang Kuang. Defendants deny the remaining allegations in paragraph 5.

JURISDICTION AND VENUE

6. This Court has subject matter jurisdiction pursuant to 28 U.S.C. §§ 1331, 1338(a), 2201, and 2202.

ANSWER: Paragraph 6 contains conclusions of law for which no response is required. To the extent a response is required, Defendants deny the allegations in paragraph 6.

7. Venue is proper in this district pursuant to 28 U.S.C. §§ 1391 and 1400(b).

ANSWER: Paragraph 7 contains conclusions of law for which no response is required. To the extent a response is required, Defendants deny the allegations in paragraph 7.

8. This Court has personal jurisdiction over Nang Kuang because, among other things, following any FDA approval of ANDA No. 207352, Nang Kuang intends to distribute (directly and/or through affiliates or subsidiaries) Defendants' ANDA Products throughout the United States and within Indiana and the Southern District of Indiana; if Nang Kuang is permitted to sell Defendants' ANDA Products in the United States prior to the expiration of the '932 and '209 patents, Nang Kuang will cause substantial injury to Lilly, an Indiana corporation headquartered within the Southern District of Indiana, and Nang Kuang knows that Lilly will be injured by such actions in Indiana and the Southern District of Indiana.

ANSWER: Defendants deny the allegations in paragraph 8.

9. In the alternative, this Court has personal jurisdiction over Nang Kuang under Fed. R. Civ. P. 4(k)(2) because this action arises under federal law, Nang Kuang is not subject to jurisdiction in any state's courts of general jurisdiction, and the exercise of jurisdiction over Nang Kuang is consistent with the Constitution and the laws of the United States.

ANSWER: Defendants deny the allegations in paragraph 9.

10. This Court has personal jurisdiction over CANDA because, among other things, following any FDA approval of ANDA No. 207352, CANDA intends to offer to sell and sell (directly and/or through affiliates or subsidiaries) Defendants' ANDA Products throughout the United States and within Indiana and the Southern District of Indiana; if CANDA is permitted to sell Defendants' ANDA Products in the United States prior to the expiration of the '932 and '209 patents, CANDA will cause substantial injury to Lilly, an Indiana corporation headquartered within the Southern District of Indiana, and CANDA knows that Lilly will be injured by such actions in Indiana and the Southern District of Indiana.

ANSWER: Defendants deny the allegations in paragraph 10.

BACKGROUND

11. ALIMTA®, in combination with cisplatin, is indicated (a) for the treatment of patients with malignant pleural mesothelioma, or (b) for the initial treatment of locally advanced or metastatic nonsquamous non-small cell lung cancer. ALIMTA® also is indicated as a single-agent for the treatment of patients with locally advanced or metastatic nonsquamous non-small cell lung cancer after prior chemotherapy. ALIMTA® also is indicated for maintenance treatment of patients with locally advanced or metastatic nonsquamous non-small cell lung cancer whose disease has not progressed after four cycles of platinum-based first-line chemotherapy.

> **ANSWER:** Defendants lack knowledge or information sufficient to form a belief as to the truth of the allegations in paragraph 11, and therefore, deny them.

12. Lilly sells ALIMTA® in the United States pursuant to a New Drug Application that has been approved by the FDA.

> **ANSWER:** Defendants lack knowledge or information sufficient to form a belief as to the truth of the allegations in paragraph 12, and therefore, deny them.

13. The '932 patent, titled "N-(pyrrolo(2,3-d)pyrimidin-3-ylacyl)-Glutamic Acid Derivatives," was duly and legally issued on September 6, 1994. The '932 patent is attached as Exhibit A hereto.

> **ANSWER:** Defendants admit that the '932 patent is entitled "N-(pyrrolo(2,3-d)pyrimidin-3-ylacyl)-Glutamic Acid Derivatives," and the face of the patent indicates that it was issued on or about September 6, 1994. To the extent not expressly admitted, Defendants lack knowledge or information sufficient to form a belief as to the truth of the allegations in paragraph 13, and therefore, deny them.

14. The '209 patent, titled "Antifolate Combination Therapies," was duly and legally issued on August 10, 2010. The '209 patent is attached as Exhibit B hereto.

> **ANSWER:** Defendants admit that the '209 patent is entitled "Antifolate Combination Therapies," and the face of the patent indicates that it was issued on or about August 10, 2010. To the extent not expressly admitted, Defendants lack knowledge or information sufficient to form a belief as to the truth of the allegations in paragraph 14, and therefore, deny them.

15. The '932 and '209 patents have been listed in connection with ALIMTA® in the FDA's publication Approved Drug Products with Therapeutic Equivalence Evaluations.

> **ANSWER:** Defendants admit that the '932 and '209 patents are listed in the FDA's publication Approved

Drug Products with Therapeutic Equivalence Evaluations with respect to ALIMTA®. To the extent not expressly admitted, Defendants deny the allegations in paragraph 15.

16. By letter dated August 25, 2014 ("Defendants' Notice Letter"), Defendants notified Plaintiffs that Nang Kuang had submitted to the FDA ANDA No. 207352 for Defendants' pemetrexed disodium, 100 mg base/vial and 500 mg base/vial for intravenous infusion ("Defendants' ANDA Products"). Defendants' ANDA Products are generic versions of ALIMTA®.

ANSWER: Defendants admit the allegations in paragraph 16.

17. The purpose of the ANDA is to obtain approval under the Federal Food, Drug, and Cosmetic Act ("FDCA") to engage in the commercial manufacture, use, offer for sale, and/or sale of Defendants' ANDA Products prior to the expiration of the '932 and '209 patents.

ANSWER: Defendants deny the allegations in paragraph 17.

COUNT I: INFRINGEMENT OF U.S. PATENT NO. 5,344,932

18. Plaintiffs incorporate each of the preceding paragraphs as if fully set forth herein.

ANSWER: Defendants incorporate each of the preceding paragraphs as if fully set forth herein.

19. As set forth in greater detail in the '932 patent, one or more claims of the '932 patent, incorporated by reference herein, cover ALIMTA®.

ANSWER: Defendants deny the allegations in paragraph 19.

20. Princeton owns the '932 patent. Princeton will be substantially and irreparably damaged by infringement of the '932 patent.

ANSWER: Defendants lack knowledge or information sufficient to form a belief as to the truth of whether Princeton owns the '932 patent, and therefore, deny the allegation. Defendants deny the remaining allegations in paragraph 20.

21. Lilly has been granted an exclusive license under the '932 patent. Lilly will be substantially and irreparably damaged by infringement of the '932 patent.

ANSWER: Defendants lack knowledge or information sufficient to form a belief as to the truth of whether Lilly has been granted an exclusive license under the '932 patent, and therefore, deny the allegation. Defendants deny the remaining allegations in paragraph 21.

22. Defendants' ANDA Products contain pemetrexed disodium.

ANSWER: Defendants admit the allegations in paragraph 22.

23. Defendants' ANDA Products are covered by one or more claims of the '932 patent.

ANSWER: Defendants deny the allegations in paragraph 23.

24. In Defendants' Notice Letter, Defendants notified Plaintiffs that, as part of their ANDA, Defendants filed a certification of the type described in Section 505(j)(2)(A)(vii)(IV) of the FDCA, 21 U.S.C. § 355(j)(2)(A)(vii)(IV), with respect to the '932 patent, asserting that the claims of the '932 patent are invalid, unenforceable, and/or not infringed by the manufacture, use, offer for sale, or sale of Defendants' ANDA Products.

ANSWER: Defendants admit the allegations in paragraph 24.

25. Defendants' submission of ANDA No. 207352 for the purpose of obtaining approval to engage in the commercial manufacture, use, offer for sale, and/or sale of Defendants' ANDA Products prior to the expiration of the '932 patent is an act of infringement of the '932 patent under 35 U.S.C. § 271(e)(2)(A).

ANSWER: Defendants deny the allegations in paragraph 25.

26. Defendants intend to engage in the manufacture, use, offer for sale, sale, marketing, distribution, and/or importation of Defendants' ANDA Products and the proposed labeling therefor immediately and imminently upon approval of ANDA No. 207352, i.e., prior to the expiration of the '932 patent.

ANSWER: Defendants deny the allegations in paragraph 26.

27. Defendants have knowledge of the claims of the '932 patent. Notwithstanding this knowledge, Defendants have

continued to assert their intent to engage in the manufacture, use, offer for sale, sale, marketing, distribution, and/or importation of Defendants' ANDA Products and the proposed labeling therefor immediately and imminently upon approval of ANDA No. 207352.

ANSWER: Defendants deny the allegations in paragraph 27.

28. Defendants plan and intend to, and will, actively induce infringement of the '932 patent when their ANDA is approved, and plan and intend to, and will, do so immediately and imminently upon approval.

ANSWER: Defendants deny the allegations in paragraph 28.

29. The foregoing actions by Defendants constitute and/or will constitute infringement of the '932 patent and active inducement of infringement of the '932 patent.

ANSWER: Defendants deny the allegations in paragraph 29.

30. An actual case or controversy exists between Plaintiffs and Defendants with respect to infringement of the '932 patent.

ANSWER: Defendants admit that there is an actual case or controversy between Plaintiffs and Defendants with respect to the lack of infringement of the '932 patent. To the extent not expressly admitted, Defendants deny the allegations in paragraph 30.

31. Defendants are without a reasonable basis for believing that they will not be liable for infringing the '932 patent and/or actively inducing infringement of the '932 patent.

ANSWER: Defendants deny the allegations in paragraph 31.

32. Unless Defendants are enjoined from infringing the '932 patent and actively inducing infringement of the '932 patent, Plaintiffs will suffer irreparable injury. Plaintiffs have no adequate remedy at law.

ANSWER: Defendants deny the allegations in paragraph 32.

COUNT II: INFRINGEMENT OF U.S. PATENT NO. 7,772,209

33. Plaintiffs incorporate each of the preceding paragraphs as if fully set forth herein.

ANSWER: Defendants incorporate each of the preceding paragraphs as if fully set forth herein.

34. As set forth in greater detail in the '209 patent, one or more claims of the '209 patent, incorporated by reference herein, cover a method of administering pemetrexed disodium to a patient in need thereof that also involves administration of folic acid and vitamin B12.

ANSWER: Defendants lack knowledge or information sufficient to form a belief as to the truth of the allegations in paragraph 34, and therefore, deny them.

35. Lilly owns the '209 patent. Lilly will be substantially and irreparably damaged by infringement of the '209 patent.

ANSWER: Defendants lack knowledge or information sufficient to form a belief as to the truth of whether Lilly owns the '209 patent, and therefore, deny the allegation. Defendants deny the remaining allegations in paragraph 35.

36. Defendants' ANDA Products contain pemetrexed disodium.

ANSWER: Defendants admit the allegations in paragraph 36.

37. Upon information and belief, the use of Defendants' ANDA Products in accordance with Defendants' proposed labeling for Defendants' ANDA Products involves administration of folic acid and vitamins B12.

ANSWER: Defendants deny the allegations in paragraph 37.

38. Upon information and belief, the use of Defendants' ANDA Products in accordance with and as directed by Defendants' proposed labeling for those products will infringe one or more claims of the '209 patent.

ANSWER: Defendants deny the allegations in paragraph 38.

39. In Defendants' Notice Letter, Defendants notified Plaintiffs that, as part of their ANDA, Defendants filed a certification of the type described in Section 505(j)(2)(A)(vii)(IV) of the FDCA, 21 U.S.C. § 355(j)(2)(A)(vii)(IV), with respect to the '209 patent, asserting that the claims of the '209 patent are invalid, unenforceable, and/or not infringed by the manufacture, use, offer for sale, or sale of Defendants' ANDA Products.

ANSWER: Defendants admit the allegations in paragraph 39.

40. Defendants' submission of ANDA No. 207352 for the purpose of obtaining approval to engage in the commercial manufacture, use, offer for sale, and/or sale of Defendants' ANDA Products prior to the expiration of the '209 patent is an act of infringement of the '209 patent under 35 U.S.C. § 271(e)(2)(A).

ANSWER: Defendants deny the allegations in paragraph 40.

41. Defendants intend to engage in the manufacture, use, offer for sale, sale, marketing, distribution, and/or importation of Defendants' ANDA Products and the proposed labeling therefor immediately and imminently upon approval of ANDA No. 207352, i.e., prior to the expiration of the '209 patent.

ANSWER: Defendants deny the allegations in paragraph 41.

42. Defendants have knowledge of the claims of the '209 patent. Notwithstanding this knowledge, Defendants have continued to assert their intent to engage in the manufacture, use, offer for sale, sale, marketing, distribution, and/or importation of Defendants' ANDA Products and the proposed labeling therefor immediately and imminently upon approval of ANDA No. 207352.

ANSWER: Defendants deny the allegations in paragraph 42.

43. Defendants plan and intend to, and will, actively induce infringement of the '209 patent when their ANDA is approved, and plan and intend to, and will, do so immediately and imminently upon approval.

ANSWER: Defendants deny the allegations in paragraph 43.

44. Defendants know that Defendants' ANDA Products are especially made or adapted for use in infringing the '209 patent, and that Defendants' ANDA Products are not suitable for substantial noninfringing use. Defendants plan and intend to, and will, contribute to infringement of the '209 patent immediately and imminently upon approval of ANDA No. 207352.

ANSWER: Defendants deny the allegations in paragraph 44.

45. The foregoing actions by Defendants constitute and/or will constitute infringement of the '209 patent, active inducement of infringement of the '209 patent, and contribution to the infringement by others of the '209 patent.

ANSWER: Defendants deny the allegations in paragraph 45.

46. An actual case or controversy exists between Plaintiffs and Defendants with respect to infringement of the '209 patent.

ANSWER: Defendants admit that there is an actual case or controversy between Plaintiffs and Defendants with respect to the lack of infringement of the '209 patent. To the extent not expressly admitted, Defendants deny the allegations in paragraph 46.

47. Defendants are without a reasonable basis for believing that they will not be liable for infringing the '209 patent, actively inducing infringement of the '209 patent, and/or contributing to the infringement by others of the '209 patent.

ANSWER: Defendants deny the allegations in paragraph 47.

48. Unless Defendants are enjoined from infringing the '209 patent, actively inducing infringement of the '209 patent, and contributing to the infringement by others of the '209 patent, Lilly will suffer irreparable injury. Lilly has no adequate remedy at law.

ANSWER: Defendants deny the allegations in paragraph 48.

PLAINTIFFS' PRAYER FOR RELIEF

Defendants deny that Plaintiffs are entitled to any relief on its claims from the Court.

DEFENSES

Responding further to the Complaint, without any admission as to the burden of proof and without any admission as to any of the averments in the Complaint, Defendants set forth the following defenses:

FIRST DEFENSE

Plaintiffs' Complaint fails to state a claim upon which relief may be granted.

SECOND DEFENSE

The manufacture, use, sale, offer for sale, or importation of Defendants' generic pemetrexed disodium, 100 mg base/vial and 500 mg base/vial for intravenous infusion that is the subject of the Defendants' ANDA has not infringed, does not infringe, and would not, if made, imported, sold, offered for sale, or marketed, infringe any valid and/or enforceable claim of the '932 or the '209 patents.

THIRD DEFENSE

Defendants have not directly, indirectly, by inducement, contributorily, literally or under the doctrine of equivalents, or in any other manner, infringed any valid and enforceable claim of the '932 or the '209 patents.

FOURTH DEFENSE

The claims of the '932 or the '209 patents are invalid for failure to comply with the requirements of the patent laws of the United States, including, without limitation, 35 U.S.C. §§ 101, 102, 103, and/or 112.

FIFTH DEFENSE

Any claim of infringement of the '932 or the '209 patents under the doctrine of equivalents would be limited by prosecution history estoppel.

SIXTH DEFENSE

Defendants' actions in defending this case do not give rise to an exceptional case under 35 U.S.C. § 285.

SEVENTH DEFENSE

Any additional defenses or counterclaims that discovery may reveal.

COUNTERCLAIMS

Defendants Nang Kuang Pharmaceutical Co., Ltd. ("Nang Kuang") and CANDA NK-2, LLC ("CANDA") (collectively, "Counter-Plaintiffs"), by way of counterclaim against Eli Lilly and Company ("Lilly") and The Trustees of Princeton University ("Princeton") (collectively "Counter-Defendants"), state as follows:

PARTIES

1. Nang Kuang is a corporation organized and existing under the laws of Taiwan, with its principal place of business at No. 1001, Zhongshan Rd, Xinhua Dist, Tainan City, Taiwan.

2. CANDA is a limited liability company organized and existing under the laws of Texas, with its principal place of business at 1404 S. New Road, Waco, TX 76711.

3. On information and belief, Counter-Defendant Eli Lilly and Company is a corporation organized and existing under the laws of the State of Indiana, and has a principal place of business at Lilly Corporate Center, Indianapolis, Indiana 46285.

4. On information and belief, Counter-Defendant The Trustees of Princeton University is a not-for-profit educational institution organized and existing under the laws of the State of New Jersey, and has a principal place of business at One Nassau Hall, Princeton, New Jersey 08540.

JURISDICTION AND VENUE

5. These counterclaims arise under the Patent Laws of the United States, 3 U.S.C. § 1 *et seq.* and 35 U.S.C. § 100 *et seq.*; the Declaratory Judgment Act, 28 U.S.C. §§ 2201 and 2202; the Federal Food, Drug and Cosmetic Act, 21 U.S.C. § 301 *et seq.*, as amended by the Drug Price Competition and Patent Term Restriction Act of 1984, Pub. L. No. 98-417, 98 Stat. 1585 (1984 (codified as amended at 21 U.S.C. § 355) (hereinafter, "Hatch-Waxman Amendments"); and the Medicare Prescription Drug, Improvement, and Modernization Act of 2003, Pub. L. No. 108-173, 117 Stat. 2066 (2003) (codified at 21 U.S.C. § 355(j)(5)(C)(i) and 35 U.S.C. § 271(e)(5)) ("the MMA").

6. This Court has subject matter jurisdiction over these counterclaims pursuant to 28 U.S.C. §§ 1331, 1337, 1338, 1367(a), 2201 and 2202, and 35 U.S.C. § 1, *et seq.*

7. This Court does not have personal jurisdiction over Counter-Plaintiffs and the submission of this Counterclaim does not constitute consent by Counter-Plaintiffs to this Court's exercise of personal jurisdiction.

8. This Court has personal jurisdiction over Counter-Defendants because, on information and belief, Counter-Defendants are doing substantial and ongoing business in this judicial district. Further, Counter-Defendants have submitted to the jurisdiction of this Court.

9. This Court has personal jurisdiction over Lilly because its affiliations with the State of Indiana, including by virtue of incorporating and maintaining a principal place of business for Lilly in Indiana, are so continuous and systematic as to render it essentially at home in this forum.

10. This Court also has personal jurisdiction over Lilly because it has consented to jurisdiction in the State of Indiana, including by virtue of the incorporation of Lilly in Indiana.

11. This Court also has personal jurisdiction over Lilly because it has availed itself of the legal protections of the State of Indiana by, among other things, incorporating and maintaining a principal place of business for Lilly in Indiana.

12. Venue is proper in this judicial district under 28 U.S.C. §§ 1391(b) and (c) and 1400(b), 21 U.S.C. § 355 (j)(5)(c)(i)(II), and pursuant to Counter-Defendants' choice of forum.

BACKGROUND

13. On information and belief, on September 6, 1994, the United States Patent and Trademark Office ("USPTO") issued U.S. Patent No. 5,344,932 ("the '932 patent"), entitled "N-(pyrrolo(2,3-d)pyrimidin-3-ylacyl)-Glutamic Acid Derivatives." The face of the patent indicates that the '932 patent was assigned to Princeton.

14. On information and belief, on October 29, 3013, the USPTO issued U.S. Patent No. 7,772,209 ("the '209 patent"), entitled "Antifolate Combination Therapies." The face of the patent indicates that the '209 patent was assigned to Lilly.

15. On information and belief, pursuant to 21 U.S.C. § 355(b)(1)(G), Counter-Defendants caused the FDA to list the '932 and '209 patents in the FDA's Approved Drug Products with Therapeutic Equivalence Evaluations ("the Orange Book") in connection with NDA No. 021462 for ALIMTA® products.

16. By letter dated August 25, 2015 ("the Notice Letter"), Counter-Plaintiffs provided a notice of certification of non-infringement and/or invalidity of the patents to the required parties per 21 C.F.R. § 314.95(a), including Lilly and Princeton. In the Notice Letter, Counter-Plaintiffs notified that it had submitted ANDA No. 207352, seeking approval to engage in the commercial manufacture, use or sale of Counter-Plaintiffs' generic pemetrexed disodium, 100 mg base/vial and 500 mg base/vial for intravenous infusion (the "ANDA products").

17. The Notice Letter states that the ANDA products do not infringe any valid or enforceable claim of the '932 and '209 patents.

18. Despite a clear and unequivocal showing of non-infringement by Counter-Plaintiffs, Counter-Defendants filed a patent infringement Complaint against Nang Kuang and CANDA in this Court on October 8, 2014. As a result of their litigation actions, Counter-Defendants have obtained an automatic 30-month stay of any FDA final approval of the ANDA No. 207352.

19. Counter-Plaintiffs have undertaken substantial efforts in developing and seeking approval for the ANDA products set forth in its ANDA No. 207352.

20. In view of the foregoing, an actual justiciable controversy exists between Counter-Plaintiffs and Counter-Defendants concerning the non-infringement and invalidity of the '932 and '209 patents.

21. Pursuant to 35 U.S.C. § 285, this is an exceptional case, and Counter-Plaintiffs are entitled to an award of attorneys' fees and costs.

FIRST COUNTERCLAIM

(Declaratory Judgment of Non-infringement of the '932 Patent)

22. Counter-Plaintiffs repeat and incorporate the allegations in the foregoing paragraphs 1-21.

23. A case or controversy exists between Counter-Plaintiffs and Counter-Defendants, concerning the non-infringement of the '932 patent, which requires a declaration of rights by this Court.

24. Counter-Plaintiffs' manufacture, use, offer for sale, sale, and/or importation into the United States of its ANDA products pursuant to ANDA No. 207352 will not infringe any valid claim of the '932 patent.

25. Counter-Plaintiffs are entitled to a declaration that the manufacture, use, offer for sale, sale, and/or importation into the United States of its ANDA products pursuant to ANDA No. 206021 will not infringe any valid claim of the '932 patent.

SECOND COUNTERCLAIM

(Declaratory Judgment of Invalidity of the '932 Patent)

26. Counter-Plaintiffs repeat and incorporate the allegations in the foregoing paragraphs 1-25.

27. A case or controversy exists between Counter-Plaintiffs and Counter-Defendants, concerning the invalidity of the '932 patent, which requires a declaration of rights by this Court.

28. The '932 patent claims, including all asserted and unasserted claims, are invalid for failure to comply with the requirements of the patent laws of the Unites States, including, without limitation, 35 U.S.C. §§ 101, 102, 103, and/or 112.

29. Counter-Plaintiffs are entitled to a declaration that the '932 patent claims are invalid.

THIRD COUNTERCLAIM

(Declaratory Judgment of Non-infringement of the '209 Patent)

30. Counter-Plaintiffs repeat and incorporate the allegations in the foregoing paragraphs 1- 29.

31. A case or controversy exists between Counter-Plaintiffs and Counter-Defendants, concerning the non-infringement of the '209 patent, which requires a declaration of rights by this Court.

32. Counter-Plaintiffs' manufacture, use, offer for sale, sale, and/or importation into the United States of its ANDA products pursuant to ANDA No. 207352 will not infringe any valid claim of the '209 patent.

33. Counter-Plaintiffs are entitled to a declaration that the manufacture, use, offer for sale, sale, and/or importation into the United States of its ANDA products pursuant to ANDA No. 207352 will not infringe any valid claim of the '209 patent.

FOURTH COUNTERCLAIM

(Declaratory Judgment of Invalidity of the '209 Patent)

34. Counter-Plaintiffs repeat and incorporate the allegations in the foregoing paragraphs 1- 33.

35. A case or controversy exists between Counter-Plaintiffs and Counter-Defendants, concerning the invalidity of the '209 patent, which requires a declaration of rights by this Court.

36. The '209 patent claims, including all asserted and unasserted claims, are invalid for failure to comply with the requirements of the patent laws of the Unites States, including, without limitation, 35 U.S.C. §§ 101, 102, 103, and/or 112.

37. Counter-Plaintiffs are entitled to a declaration that the '209 patent claims are invalid.

PRAYER FOR RELIEF

WHEREFORE, Counter-Plaintiffs/Defendants Nang Kuang and CANDA, LLC pray that this Court enter judgment in their favor and against Counter-Defendants as follows:

A) Declare that the making manufacture, use, offer for sale, sale, and/or importation into the United States of its ANDA products pursuant to ANDA No. 207352 will not infringe any valid claim of the '932 patent;

B) Declare that the '932 patent and all its claims invalid;

C) Declare that the making manufacture, use, offer for sale, sale, and/or importation into the United States of its ANDA products pursuant to ANDA No. 207352 will not infringe any valid claim of the '209 patent;

D) Declare that the '209 patent and all its claims invalid;

E) Declare that this case is exceptional under 35 U.S.C. § 285;

F) Dismiss Plaintiffs' Complaint with prejudice;

G) Deny Plaintiffs' request for injunctive relief;

H) Order judgment in favor of Counter-Plaintiffs/Defendants;

I) Enjoin Counter-Defendants and their agents, representatives, attorneys, and those persons in active concert or participation with them who receive actual notice hereof from threatening or initiating infringement litigation against Counter-Plaintiffs or their customers, dealers, or suppliers, or any prospective or present sellers, dealers, distributors, or customers of Counter-Plaintiffs, or charging them either orally or in writing with infringement of any patent asserted herein against Counter-Plaintiffs;

J) Award Counter-Plaintiffs costs and reasonable attorneys' fees to the extent permitted by law; and

K) Award Counter-Plaintiffs such other and further relief as the Court deems just and proper.

REQUEST FOR BENCH TRIAL

Defendants Nang Kuang and CANDA request that the Court set this case for a bench trial.

Dated: September 11, 2015

Respectfully submitted,

s/Anthony R. Jost

Anthony R. Jost

RILEY BENNETT & EGLOFF, LLP

141 East Washington Street, Fourth Floor

Indianapolis, Indiana 46204

(317) 636-8000

tjost@rbelaw.com

Attorney for Defendants

OF COUNSEL

Michael A. Siem (*Admitted pro hac vice*)

Aya Cieslak-Tochigi (*Admitted pro hac vice*)

FARNEY DANIELS PC

159 20th Street, # 2B-41

Brooklyn, New York 11232

(512) 948-3133

msiem@farneydaniels.com

atochigi@farneydaniels.com

Steven R. Daniels (*Admitted pro hac vice*)

FARNEY DANIELS PC

800 South Austin Ave., Suite 200

Georgetown, Texas 78626

(512) 582-2828

sdaniels@farneydaniels.com

Amended Pleading

2016 WL 5943060 (N.D.Ind.)

Westlaw Query>>

To find more Amended Pleading filings on Westlaw: access Indiana Trial Court Documents (from the Home page, click Trial Court Documents, then Indiana), enter "DT(amended and complaint answer)" in the search box, and click Search. Use the Jurisdiction filter on the left to narrow results to Federal.

United States District Court, N.D. Indiana.

Lafayette Division

DESIGN BASICS, LLC; and Plan Pros, Inc., Plaintiffs,

v.

MILAKIS HOMES, LLC; Majestic Custom Homes of Lafayette, Inc.; Jim Kiracofe Enterprises, Inc., doing business as Cathedral Homes; Ken Lee L.L.C.; James Kiracofe; Jeff Lee Builders, Inc.; and Jeff Lee, Defendants.

No. 4:16-cv-00053-TLS-SLC.

September 12, 2016.

First Amended Complaint

John D. LaDue (19039-71), Sean J. Quinn (29441-71), LaDue | Curran | Kuehn, 200 First Bank Building, 205 West Jefferson Boulevard, South Bend, Indiana 46601, Telephone: (574) 968-0760, Facsimile: (574) 968-0761, jladue@lck-law.com, squinn@lck-law.com, for plaintiffs Design Basics, LLC, and Plan Pros, Inc.

JURY DEMANDED

Plaintiffs, Design Basics, LLC and Plan Pros, Inc., file this First Amended Complaint as of right under Federal Rule of Civil Procedure 15(a)(1)(B) against Milakis Homes, LLC ("Milakis Homes"); Majestic Custom Homes of Lafayette, Inc. ("Majestic Homes"); Jim Kiracofe Enterprises, Inc., doing business as Cathedral Homes ("Kiracofe Enterprises"); Ken Lee L.L.C. ("Ken Lee LLC"); James Kiracofe ("Mr. Kiracofe"); Jeff Lee Builders, Inc. ("Jeff Lee Builders"); and Jeff Lee ("Mr. Lee") (collectively referred to as "Defendants"), and for their causes of action allege the following:

Parties

1. Design Basics, LLC, is a Nebraska Limited Liability Company with its principal place of business in Omaha, Nebraska. Under Articles of Merger executed on July 1, 2009, Design Basics, LLC, is the successor by merger to Design Basics, Inc., and as such is the owner of all assets (including copyrights, trade and service names, trade and service marks, and all causes of action) that Design Basics, Inc., owned as of that date. Design Basics, LLC, and its predecessor (Design Basics, Inc.) will hereinafter be referred to as "Design Basics."

2. Design Basics is engaged in the business of creating, marketing, publishing and licensing the use of "architectural works" (as that term is defined in the Copyright Act and the Architectural Works Copyright Protection Act of 1990, both codified at 17 U.S.C. § 101 et seq.) and technical drawings depicting such architectural works.

3. Plan Pros, Inc. ("Plan Pros"), is a Nebraska corporation with its principal place of business in Omaha, Nebraska.

4. Plan Pros is engaged in the business of creating, marketing, publishing and licensing the use of "architectural works" (as that term is defined in the Copyright Act and the AWCPA) and technical drawings depicting such architectural works.

5. Defendant Milakis Homes is a limited liability company organized under the laws of the State of Indiana with its principal place of business in Tippecanoe County, Indiana. Milakis Homes may be served through its registered agent, Gregory A. Milakis, 722 E 500 S, Lafayette, Indiana 47909.

6. Defendant Majestic Homes is a corporation organized under the laws of the State of Indiana with its principal place of business in Tippecanoe County, Indiana. Majestic Homes may be served through its registered agent, Gregory Milakis, 722 E 500 S. Lafayette, Indiana 47909.

7. Defendant Kiracofe Enterprises is a corporation organized under the laws of the State of Indiana with its principal place of business in Tippecanoe County, Indiana. Kiracofe Enterprises may be served through its registered agent, James R. Kiracofe, 1202 Stoneripple Court, Lafayette, Indiana 47909.

8. Defendant Jeff Lee Builders is a corporation organized under the laws of the State of Indiana with its principal place of business in Tippecanoe County, Indiana. Jeff Lee Builders may be served through its registered agent, Jeff Lee, 4753 Saintsbury Court, Lafayette, Indiana 47909.

9. Defendant Ken Lee LLC is a limited liability company organized under the laws of the State of Indiana with its principal place of business in Tippecanoe County, Indiana. Ken Lee may be served through its registered agent, Edward L. Kennedy, 338 Main Street, Lafayette, Indiana 47902.

10. Defendant Mr. Kiracofe is a citizen of Indiana residing in Tippecanoe County, Indiana.

11. Mr. Kiracofe is a shareholder of Majestic Homes and Kiracofe Enterprises and controls those companies. Mr. Kiracofe is directly and vicariously liable for the infringing activities of Majestic Homes and Kiracofe Enterprises. He supervised the infringing activities of Majestic Homes and Kiracofe Enterprises as further described below, and has received an obvious and direct financial interest in exploiting Plaintiffs' copyrighted materials.

12. Defendant Mr. Lee is a citizen of Indiana residing in Tippecanoe County, Indiana.

13. Mr. Lee is a shareholder of Jeff Lee Builders and controls the company. Mr. Lee is directly and vicariously liable for the infringing activities of Jeff Lee Builders. He supervised the infringing activities of Jeff Lee Builders as further described below, and has received an obvious and direct financial interest in exploiting Plaintiffs' copyrighted materials.

Jurisdiction and Venue

14. This Court has subject matter jurisdiction of this case under 28 U.S.C. § 1338 because this action arises under federal copyright law, 17 U.S.C. § 101 et seq.

15. Venue is proper in this District under 28 U.S.C. § 1400(a) because Defendants may be found in this District. Furthermore, or in the alternative, venue is proper in this District under 28 U.S.C. § 1391(b) because a substantial part of the events giving rise to the claims at issue occurred in this District; and Defendants reside and do business in this District.

Factual Background

A. *Design Basics' and Plan Pros' Copyrights.*

16. Design Basics and Plan Pros are building design firms which create, market, and license the use of "architectural works" (as that term is defined in the Copyright Act and the Architectural Works Copyright Protection Act of 1990 (the "AWCPA")) and technical drawings depicting architectural works. Design Basics and Plan Pros own copyrights protecting the architectural works and technical drawings they have created.

17. Design Basics is the author and the owner of all copyrights in the following works, each of which has been registered with the United States Copyright Office:

Title / Registration Certificate No.

Plan No. 1330 -- Trenton / VA 314-016, 694-094 & 756-041

Plan No. 1380 -- Paterson / VA 694-094, 314-024 & 726-379

Plan No. 1748 -- Sinclair / VA 371-214, 694-094 & 726-353

Plan No. 2408 -- Crawford / VA 485-123, 756-041 & 1-921-776

Plan No. 3102 -- Aspen / VA 624-138, 624-137 & 726-370

18. Plan Pros is the author and the owner of all copyrights in the following works, each of which has been registered with the United States Copyright Office:

Title / Registration Certificate No.

Plan No. 29333 -- Slater / VA 1-954-612 & 1-954-428

19. The foregoing works described in paragraphs 17-18 above will be referred to collectively as the "Copyrighted Works."

20. The Copyrighted Works have been published in various Design Basics and Plan Pros plan books and publications. The Copyrighted Works have also been published by Design Basics and Plan Pros on the internet at www.designbasics.com.

21. Each of the Copyrighted Works constitutes original material that is copyrightable under federal law.

22. Design Basics is currently, and at all relevant times has been, the sole owner of all right, title and interest in and to the works described in paragraph 17 above.

23. Plan Pros is currently, and at all relevant times has been, the sole owner of all right, title and interest in and to the works described in paragraph 18 above.

B. *Defendants have access to Design Basics's copyrights.*

24. Defendants Milakis Homes, Majestic Homes, Kiracofe Enterprises, Jeff Lee Builders, and Ken Lee LLC have been engaged, at least in part, in the business of creating, publishing, distributing and advertising residential home designs through traditional print media, on the internet on sites such as www.milakis.com and www.majesticcustomhomesoflafayette.com, www.jlbuilders.net, and in marketing, advertising, constructing and selling homes built according to such designs.

25. Milakis Homes, Majestic Homes, Kiracofe Enterprises, and Ken Lee LLC have published, distributed, marketed and advertised certain architectural designs for single family residential homes, each consisting of a floor plan and exterior elevations, that Defendants have identified and marketed under the following model names, and other to be identified through discovery: Lindsey, Nappier, Nappier II, Arlington, Charleston, and Stella III.

26. All Defendants have had access to Design Basics' and Plan Pros' home designs. Milakis Homes, Majestic Homes, Kiracofe Enterprises, Jeff Lee Builders, and Ken Lee LLC received copies of Design Basics's and Plan Pros' plan books and other publications, which included copies of the Copyrighted Works. On information and belief, Mr. Kiracofe and Mr. Lee reviewed the publications containing copies of the Copyrighted Works that Milakis Homes, Majestic Homes, and Jeff Lee Builders received.

27. In addition to the print publications, copies of the Copyrighted Works were also widely disseminated on the internet. Each of the Defendants had access to the internet and the copies of the Copyrighted Works found there.

C. *Defendants violate Design Basics' and Plan Pros' copyrights.*

28. Defendants have violated and continue to violate Design Basics' and Plan Pros' exclusive rights in each of the Copyrighted Works (including the right to reproduce, the right to prepare derivative works and the right to sell), by copying, publishing, distributing, advertising, marketing, selling and/or constructing in the marketplace, plans, drawings and houses which were copied or otherwise derived from the Copyrighted Works.

29. Here are some examples:

a. Kiracofe Enterprises has built at least nine homes that were built using home plans copied or otherwise derived from Design Basics Plan No. 1380: at least three homes in the Landing at Valley Lakes subdivision in Lafayette, Indiana, including homes at 40 Canyon Creek Ct., 1905 Canyon Creek Dr., and 2125 Whisper Valley Drive; at least three homes in the Raineybrook subdivision in Lafayette, including homes at 4803

Osprey Drive East, 4810 Osprey Drive East, and 4812 Admirals Pointe Drive; at least one home in the WakeRobin Estates subdivision of West Lafayette at 2220 Bobolink Drive; and at least two homes at the Commons at Valley Lakes subdivision in Lafayette, including homes at 2006 Kyverdale Drive and 3931 Regal Valley Drive.

b. Milakis Homes has built at least twelve homes that were built using home plans copied or otherwise derived from Design Basics Plan Nos. 1748 or 1752, including 1871 Secretariat Drive and 1867 Secretariat Drive in the Huntington Farms subdivision of West Lafayette and 920 North Commodores Lane and 4641 East Commodores Lane in Lafayette Indiana.

c. Majestic Homes has built at least eight homes that were built using home plans copied or otherwise derived from Design Basics Plan Nos. 1330 or 3102 or Plan Pros Plan No. 29333, including Majestic Homes's "Stella III" model, which infringes the Plan Pros Plan No. 29333, and Majestic Homes's "Charleston" model, which infringes Design Basics Plan No. 3102.

d. Jeff Lee Builders has built at least 24 homes that were built in the Lafayette area using home plans copied or otherwise derived from Design Basics Plan No. 1330.

e. Ken Lee LLC has built at least 7 homes in the Lafayette area using home plans copied or otherwise derived from Design Basics Plan No. 1330 and 1380, including 3740 Westmorland Drive in West Lafayette.

f. Mr. Lee and Mr. Kiracofe personally sold "as joint tenants in common" a home at 6042 Flintrock Drive in West Lafayette that infringes Design Basics Plan No. 3102.

30. Additionally, the following models created by Defendants infringe the Copyrighted Works:

a. Defendants' "Arlington" (and any predecessors, copies or derivatives of that model under the same name or a different name) infringes the Design Basics Plan No. 2408 - Crawford (and any predecessor or derivative thereof).

b. Defendants' "Nappier" (and any predecessors, copies or derivatives of that model under the same name or a different name) infringes the Design Basics Plan No. 1748 - Sinclair (and any predecessor or derivative thereof).

c. Defendants' "Nappier II" (and any predecessors, copies or derivatives of that model under the same name or a different name) infringes the Design Basics Plan No. 1748 - Sinclair (and any predecessor or derivative thereof).

d. Defendants' "Lindsey" (and any predecessors, copies or derivatives of that model under the same name or a different name) infringes the Design Basics Plan No. 1330 - Trenton (and any predecessor or derivative thereof).

e. Defendants' "Charleston" (and any predecessors, copies or derivatives of that model under the same name or a different name) infringes the Design Basics Plan No. 3102 - Aspen (and any predecessor or derivative thereof).

Cause of Action

Copyright Infringement

31. Design Basics and Plan Pros complain of Defendants for copyright infringement and incorporate paragraphs 1 through 30 above by reference.

32. Defendants' construction and sale of houses, and creation of associated design and construction drawings based on Design Basics' and Plan Pros' Copyrighted Works has infringed and continues to infringe Design Basics' and Plan Pros' copyrights in the Copyrighted Works.

33. Defendants' creation and publication of non-pictorial representations based on Design Basics' and Plan Pros' Copyrighted Works has infringed and is infringing Design Basics' and Plan Pros' copyrights in the Copyrighted Works.

34. James Kiracofe controlled Majestic Homes and Kiracofe Enterprises and possessed the right and ability to supervise the infringing activity as well as an obvious and direct financial interest in the exploited copyrighted materials. As such, he is vicariously liable for the infringing acts of Majestic Homes and Kiracofe Enterprises as well his own direct infringement as set forth above.

35. Mr. Lee controlled Jeff Lee Builders and possessed the right and ability to supervise the infringing activity as well as an obvious and direct financial interest in the exploited copyrighted materials. As such, he is vicariously liable for the infringing acts of Jeff Lee Builders as well his own direct infringement as set forth above.

36. Mr. Lee and Mr. Kiracofe are also directly liable to Plaintiffs for copyright infringement for, among other acts, personally selling "as joint tenants in common" a home at 6042 Flintrock Drive in West Lafayette that infringes Design Basics Plan No. 3102.

37. Design Basics and Plan Pros are entitled to recover the actual damages they suffered as a result of the foregoing infringement, and all of Defendants' profits from such infringement, pursuant to 17 U.S.C. § 504(b).

38. In the alternative to the actual damages and infringer profits sought above, Design Basics and Plan Pros are entitled to an award of statutory damages for all infringements of Design Basics' and Plan Pros' Copyrighted Works, as permitted by 17 U.S.C. § 504(c).

39. Pursuant to 17 U.S.C. § 505, Defendants are liable for Design Basics' and Plan Pros' costs and reasonable attorneys' fees incurred in this action.

40. In addition, Design Basics and Plan Pros are entitled to preliminary and permanent injunctions pursuant to 17 U.S.C. § 502 prohibiting Defendants from further infringement of Design Basics' and Plan Pros' copyrights, including but not limited to the further use of infringing plans, creation or use of derivative plans, and construction, sale or rental of infringing structures.

41. Furthermore, this Court should issue an order pursuant to 17. U.S.C. § 503 directing the United States Marshal's Service to (a) impound all copies of the Copyrighted Works, in possession of Defendants or their agents or contractors in violation of Design Basics' and Plan Pros' exclusive rights, and (b) upon final hearing of this case, to destroy or otherwise dispose of those copies.

Conditions Precedent

42. With respect to all counts, Design Basics and Plan Pros generally aver that all conditions precedent to their rights of recovery have occurred or been performed, or have been waived or excused by Defendants.

Jury Demand

43. Pursuant to Federal Rule of Civil Procedure 38, Design Basics and Plan Pros respectfully demand a trial by jury of all issues so triable.

WHEREFORE, Design Basics, LLC, and Plan Pros, Inc., pray that defendants Milakis Homes, LLC; Majestic Custom Homes of Lafayette, Inc.; Jim Kiracofe Enterprises, Inc.; Ken Lee L.L.C.; Jim Kiracofe; Jeff Lee Builders, Inc.; and Jeff Lee be cited to appear and answer; and that upon final trial have and recover from Defendants as set forth above, that they have permanent injunctive relief against Defendants as requested herein, and that they have such and other relief as they may show themselves to be entitled.

Respectfully submitted,

/s/ Sean J. Quinn

John D. LaDue (19039-71)

Sean J. Quinn (29441-71)

LaDue | Curran | Kuehn

200 First Bank Building

205 West Jefferson Boulevard

South Bend, Indiana 46601

Telephone: (574) 968-0760

Facsimile: (574) 968-0761

jladue@lck-law.com

squinn@lck-law.com

Attorneys for Plaintiffs Design Basics, LLC, and Plan Pros, Inc.

Motion to Strike

2015 WL 10371892 (N.D.Ind.)

United States District Court, N.D. Indiana,

South Bend Division.

EQUAL EMPLOYMENT OPPORTUNITY COM-
MISSION, Plaintiff,

v.

SEYMOUR MIDWEST LLC, Defendant.

No. 3:15-cv-00350-TLS-JEM.

October 19, 2015.

Memorandum of Law in Support of Eeoc's Motion to Strike Affirmative Defenses

Laurie A. Young, #11480-49, Regional Attorney, Michelle Eisele, #12070-49, Supervisory Trial Attorney, Jonathan P. Bryant, #24112-49, Trial Attorney, Equal Employment Opportunity Commission, 101 W. Ohio Street, Suite 1900, Indianapolis IN 46204-4203, (317) 226-5588, Fax: (317) 226-5571, E-Mail: jonathan.bryant@eeoc.gov.

When Seymour Midwest learned that Steve Maril was older than its ideal age range, it eliminated Maril from consideration for employment. The Commission has brought this lawsuit under the Age Discrimination in Employment Act as a result. As its third affirmative defense, Seymour Midwest alleges the Commission has an improper motive for bringing this lawsuit because the applicant it ultimately hired was similar in age. But this is not an affirmative defense, and it does not advance the litigation. It should be struck with prejudice. So, too, should Seymour Midwest's first affirmative defense, which is nothing more than a general denial.

Facts and Procedural Background

Seymour Midwest admits that Maril submitted an application for its open position, Senior Vice President of Sales, in July 2014. (Am. Answer, Dkt. No. 11, p.5 at ¶ 11(a).) Seymour Midwest admits that its Executive Vice President - Sales / Strategy asked Maril to confirm that he was in the "ideal age range" of 45 to 52. (*Id.,* ¶11(b).) Seymour Midwest admits that, when Maril responded that he was 58 and asked whether Seymour Midwest wanted to continue the interview process, its Executive Vice President responded, "I was afraid of that . . . I am looking of [sic] a younger candidate . . . If my parameters change, I'll get back to you." (*Id.,* ¶11(c) and (d).)

Legal Standard

Courts are authorized to strike affirmative defenses that are immaterial, impertinent, or scandalous. Fed. R. Civ. Proc. 12(f). Affirmative defenses are "subject to all pleading requirements of the Federal Rules of Civil Procedure," so they " 'must set forth a short and plain statement of the defense,' " and " 'allege the necessary elements of the alleged claims.' " *Puryear v. Indiana Pallet* Co., 2011 WL 5553697 at *1 (N.D. Ind., Nov. 15, 2011), *quoting Heller Fin., Inc. v. Midwhey Powder* Co., 883 F.2d 1286, 1294-95 (7th Cir. 1989) (internal citation omitted). Bare bones or conclusory allegations are insufficient to satisfy the pleading requirements. *See Heller,* 883 F.2d at 1295 (court ordered bare bones, conclusory allegations stricken from the pleadings); *see also, Nat'l Acceptance* Co. *of Am. v.*

Regal Prods., 155 F.R.D. 631, 634 (E.D. Wis. 1994) ("Defenses which amount to nothing more than mere conclusions of law and are not warranted by any asserted facts have no efficacy.").

A court may, despite a general disfavor for doing so, strike an affirmative defense where it would "remove unnecessary clutter from the case" and "serve to expedite, not delay" litigation. *Heller,* 883 F.2d at 1294. Specifically, federal law empowers a court to strike from a pleading an affirmative defense that "is insufficient on the face of the pleading," *Puryear,* 2011 WL 5553697 at *1, *citing Nat'l Accident Ins. Underwriters, Inc. v. Citibank,* 243 F. Supp. 2d 769,770 (N.D. Ill. 2003).

Argument

The third affirmative defense should be struck. It is scandalous and immaterial because it alleges the Commission brings this lawsuit for improper purposes. It is not an affirmative defense because it does not articulate a reason why Seymour Midwest should not be held liable for the damages Seymour Midwest's actions caused Maril. Also, the facts on which the defense is predicated-Seymour Midwest's *favorable* treatment of an individual of approximately the same age as Maril-do not excuse Seymour Midwest's *unfavorable* treatment of Maril. Finally, the first affirmative defense should be struck because it is merely a general denial, not an affirmative defense.

I. The third affirmative defense fails procedurally and substantively.

Seymour Midwest's third affirmative defense alleges, "Plaintiff is aware that Defendant hired an individual of approximately the same age as Maril and brings this lawsuit simply to harass and/or intimidate Defendant." (Am. Answer, Dkt. No. 11, p.6.)

A. The allegation that the Commission brings this lawsuit with an improper motive is unrelated to the suit's claims and defenses.

Affirmative defenses "assume that the allegations of the Complaint are true and then articulate a separate reason why defendant is not liable." *Cottle v. Falcon Holdings Mgmt., LLC,* No. 2:11-cv-95, 2012 U.S. Dist. LEXIS 10478, at *12 (N.D. Ind., Jan. 30, 2012). The Commission's complaint alleges Seymour Midwest violated the ADEA by failing to hire Maril because of his age. Assuming the allegation is true, Maril is entitled to damages and Seymour Midwest should be enjoined from additional discrimination. The Commission's purpose in bringing the lawsuit does not provide a reason why Seymour Midwest should not be liable for its violation of the ADEA. Thus, it is unrelated to the merits of the claims and defenses. *See Va. Lee & Deaf Serv. Ctr. Of Lake & Sumter County, Inc. v. Habashy,* No. 6:09-cv-671, 2009 U.S. Dist. LEXIS 99766, at *12-13 (M.D. Fla., Sept. 30, 2009) (striking improper purpose defense as immaterial and scandalous because it was unrelated to the merits of the claims and defenses at issue).

Seymour Midwest's claim-that the Commission is attempting to harass or intimidate it-suggests the Commission has violated Federal Rule of Civil Procedure 11(b)(1), which requires that a pleading is not "presented for any improper purpose, such as to harass, cause unnecessary delay, or needlessly increase the cost of litigation." If Seymour Midwest believes the Commission violated this obligation, it is not without recourse: it is allowed to move for sanctions "separately from any other motion." Fed. R. Civ. Proc. 11(c)(2). Because Seymour Midwest has failed to properly plead its claim, the third affirmative defense should be struck. *See PepsiCo, Inc. v. J.K. Distribs.,* No 8:07-cv-657, 2007 U.S. Dist. LEXIS 74489, at *6-7 (C.D. Cal., Sept. 14, 2007) (striking affirmative defense alleging complaint was filed for improper purpose); *contra Luellen v. Hodge,* No. 11-cv-6144, 2012 U.S. Dist. LEXIS 38653 (W.D.N.Y., March 21, 2012) (allowing improper purpose affirmative defense where supported by factual allegations of harassing and frivolous litigation in other jurisdictions).

Seymour Midwest's allegation does not advance the litigation. It does not articulate a separate reason why it should not be liable for violating the ADEA, and it is not properly presented. It should be struck with prejudice.

B. Seymour Midwest's "token" evidence does not excuse discrimination.

Seymour Midwest's required short and plain statement of its defense alleges only that the Commission knows Seymour Midwest hired an individual of approximately the same age as Maril. But "there is no token exception to anti-discrimination law." *Diaz v. Kraft Foods Global, Inc.,* 653 F.3d 582, 587-88 (7th Cir. 2011) (noting anti-discrimination laws "would have little force if an employer could defeat a claim of discrimination by treating a single member of the protected class in accordance with the law.")

The Commission is the agency of the United States of America charged with the enforcement of the ADEA, and is expressly authorized to bring this action by the ADEA. 29 U.S.C. 626(b), as amended by Section 2 of Reorganization Plan No. 1 of 1978, 92 Stat. 3781, and by Public Law 98-532 (1984), 98 Stat. 2705. In discharging its duties, the Commission "is not merely a proxy for the victims of discrimination," but it does "act[] at the behest of and for the benefit of specific individuals." *General Telephone Co. of the Northwest v. EEOC,* 446 U.S. 318, 326 (1980).

Here, the Commission acts at the behest of and for the benefit of Steve Maril. To prevail, the Commission "must prove by a preponderance of the evidence . . . that age was the 'but-for' cause of the challenged employment decision." *Gross v. FBL Fin. Servs.,* 557 U.S. 167, 177-78 (2009). The Commission challenges Seymour Midwest's employment decision to reject Maril because of his age. (Compl., Dkt. No. 1, p.3 at ¶ 11.) Seymour Midwest admits that when it learned Maril was older than the identified ideal age range of 45 to 52, it told Maril it was "looking of [sic] a younger candidate" and would "get back to" Maril if the parameters changed. (Answer, Dkt. No. 11, p.5 at ¶ 11(b)-(d).) If Seymour Midwest's point is that the Commission cannot rely on the age of the individual it hired to draw an inference of unlawful discrimination against Maril, the Commission concedes the point. *See O'Connor v. Consol. Coin Caterers Corp.,* 517 U.S. 308, 313 (1996) (no inference of age discrimination arises if comparator is insignificantly younger). But the Commission will not seek to draw such an inference from the age of the individual hired. The age of the individual Seymour Midwest hired does not excuse age discrimination against Maril. Because Seymour Midwest fails to support the third affirmative defense with any other facts, it should be struck with prejudice.

II. Seymour Midwest's allegation that all employment decisions were made for legitimate, non-discriminatory reasons should be struck as a general denial.

Seymour Midwest's first affirmative defense alleges, "All employment decisions made regarding Steve Maril were made for legitimate USDC IN/ND case 3:15-cv-00350-TLS-JEM document 13 filed 10/19/15 page 7 of 8 nondiscriminatory reasons." But this is nothing more than a general denial, not an acceptance as true of the Complaint's allegations, and should therefore be struck with prejudice. *Biglands v. Maysville Regional Water and Sewer Dist.,* No. 1:12-cv-67, 2012 U.S. Dist. LEXIS 81114, at *5-6 (N.D. Ind., June 12, 2012) (striking affirmative defense "amount[ing] to nothing more than a denial of liability or causation, neither of which is an affirmative defense."); *Rizzon v. Ball Horticultural Co.,* 2005 U.S. Dist. LEXIS 9588, at *9-10 (N.D. Ill., April 20, 2005) ("Ball correctly concedes that its first affirmative defense [that it terminated Rizzo for a legitimate, non-discriminatory reason] essentially restates its denial of the allegations in Rizzo's complaint and thus is unnecessary as the reasons for Rizzo's termination will be addressed when the court resolves her wrongful termination claim.").

Conclusion

Seymour Midwest's third affirmative defense misses the mark, twice: it is not appropriate for an affirmative defense and relies on irrelevant evidence. The first affirmative defense is a mere general denial. Neither defense advances the litigation; both defenses add clutter. They should both be struck with prejudice.

Respectfully Submitted,

LAURIE A. YOUNG, #11480-49

Regional Attorney

MICHELLE EISELE, #12070-49

Supervisory Trial Attorney

/s/ Jonathan P. Bryant

Jonathan P. Bryant, #24112-49

Trial Attorney

EQUAL EMPLOYMENT OPPORTUNITY COMMISSION

101 W. Ohio Street, Suite 1900

Indianapolis IN 46204-4203

(317) 226-5588

FAX: (317) 226-5571

E-MAIL: jonathan.bryant@eeoc.gov

Motion for Leave to Amend

2014 WL 7692587 (N.D.Ind.)

Westlaw Query>>

To find more Motion for Leave to Amend filings on Westlaw: access Indiana Trial Court Documents (from the Home page, click Trial Court Documents, then Indiana), enter "DT("leave to amend")" in the search box, and click Search. Use the Jurisdiction filter on the left to narrow results to Federal.

United States District Court, N.D. Indiana,

Fort Wayne Division.

MARION T, LLC, Plaintiff,

v.

FORMALL, INC., Defendant.

Nos. 1:12-CV-456, 1:13-CV-132.

October 23, 2014.

Defendant's Memorandum in Support of Motion for Leave to Amend Pleading and to Submit Counterclaim

Barrett & McNagny LLP, Anthony M. Stites, #14078-71, 215 East Berry Street, P.O. Box 2263, Fort Wayne, IN 46802, Phone: (260) 423-9551, Fax: (260) 423-8920, E-Mail: ams@barrettlaw.com, for defendant, Formall, Inc.

Introduction

The instant case brought by the Plaintiff, Marion T, LLC ("Marion T"), against the Defendant, Formall, Inc. ("Formall") is related to and was consolidated for discovery purposes (Dkt # 14) with a case Marion T brought against Thermoforming Machinery & Equipment, Inc. ("TME"). The underlying facts of these matters are known to this Court since it has since decided and the clerk has entered a final judgment against Marion T and in TME's favor respecting the ownership of certain manufacturing equipment which Marion T claimed. (Dkt# 48).

Following the entry of that judgment, the Court held a hearing on October 9, 2014, consolidated the matters for all purposes, and addressed Formall's filing of a Counterclaim against Marion T. The Court permitted Formall until October 23, 2014 to file a Motion for Leave to file any counterclaim. As moved, Formall seeks to amend its Answer to assert therein its Counterclaim against Marion T and a related affirmative defense for setoff. In so doing, Formall will conform that pleading, originally filed in the Southern District of Indiana, to the local rules of this Court.

Legal Discussion

Leave to amend a pleading is to be "freely given when justice so requires." Fed. R. Civ. P. 15(a). The Supreme Court has stated that leave will generally be given unless factors such as undue prejudice, undue delay, or bad faith are present. *Foman v. Davis,* 371 U.S. 178, 182, 83 S. Ct. 227, 230, 9 L. Ed. 2d 222 (1962). However, since a scheduling order was in place and the deadline to amend the pleadings has passed,[1] Rule 16's standards also apply to a request for leave to permit the filing of an amendment. *See, e.g., Alioto v. Town of Lisbon,* 651 F.3d 715, 719 (7th Cir. 2011).

---

1. In cv-132, the Scheduling Order required amendments to the pleadings to be filed by May 1, 2013 (cv-132 Dkt # 13, 14). This action, cv-456, in which cv-132 has now been consolidated for all purposes, required amendments to the pleadings to be filed by June 28, 2013. (Dkt # 15, 16). Regardless of which deadline is applicable, both have passed.

As discussed below, under either standard the Court should permit the amendment for purposes of asserting a Counterclaim for conversion against Marion T.

As this Court has observed, " 'the good cause standard focuses on the diligence of the party seeking the amendment.' 'In other words, to demonstrate good cause, a party must show that despite its diligence, the time table could not reasonably have been met.' " *Powell v. Furnish,* No. 1:11-CV-88, 2012 WL 2128031, at *2 (N.D. Ind. June 12, 2012) (citations omitted). Here, the proposed counterclaim focuses on property that, until very recently, was held by Marion T. Moreover, the property was claimed by Marion T to be Marion T's property. The threshold issue was not whether the property was Marion T's or Formall's; the dispute over the ownership of the property was between Marion T and another party -- TME. And the dispute over the ownership of the property was not settled until this Court ruled on July 17, 2014, that the property was in fact that of TME, despite a signed, written contract Marion T contended supported its claim that the property was its own.

Formall's rights and claims to the property that is the subject of the proposed Counterclaim were contingent on the determination that TME, the seller from which Formall acquired the property, actually owned the property and could therefore convey to Formall good title. Had the Court concluded the matter in Marion's T's favor, Formall would have had no standing to assert a claim against Marion T for conversion (but would be relegated to pursuing breach of contract and warranty claims against TME). Accordingly, Formall's Counterclaim had not yet ripened by the time the deadline to amend the pleadings passed.

"Ripeness is a doctrine which courts use to enforce prudential limitations upon their jurisdiction." *Peick v. Pension Benefit Guaranty Corp.,* 724 F.2d 1247, 1261 (7th Cir. 1983) (footnote omitted). In *Premcor USA, Inc. v. American Home Assurance Co.,* 400 F.3d 523 (7th Cir. 2005), the Seventh Circuit reversed the district court's grant of summary judgment as unripe for consideration where the issue was whether an insurance company had a duty to indemnify the insured, since the underlying state action against the insured by third parties, which would determine if there was an indemnifiable loss, was still pending. *Id.* at 530 (citing *Outboard Marine Corp. v. Liberty Mut. Ins. Co.,* 607 N.E.2d 1204, 1212 (Ill. 1992) ("[T]he question of whether the insurer has a duty to indemnify the insured for a particular liability is only ripe for consideration if the insured has already incurred liability in the underlying claim against it.") (applying Illinois law). As the Supreme Court has observed, "ripeness is peculiarly a question of timing . . ." *Blanchette v. Connecticut General Ins. Corporations,* 419 U.S. 102, 140, 95 S. Ct. 335, 357, 42 L. Ed. 2d 320 (1974).

Indeed, that the proposed action for conversion (and the resulting, related affirmative defense of setoff) was not ripe is illustrated by the fact that had Formall attempted to litigate its claim for conversion against Marion T, all of the efforts in doing so would have been a complete waste of the Court's (and the parties') resources had Marion T prevailed in enforcing the written agreement it and TME signed, since TME could not, in that case, have conveyed good title to Formall. Other courts have recognized that a case is not ripe where there is still an unresolved dispute as to the ownership of property or a putative plaintiff's standing to sue. *See, e.g., American Premier Underwriters, Inc. v. National R.R. Passenger Corp.,* 704 A.2d 243, 264 (Conn. Ct. App. 1997), (dismissing claims as unripe "because the plaintiff's claim as to [certain real property] had not been adjudicated and, consequently, no determination had been made as to the plaintiff's rights, if any, in the property," thus the trial court was being asked to determine claims that may never come before it since those claims were dependent on a judgment not yet rendered); *Ernst & Young v. Depositors Economic Protection Corp.,* 862 F. Supp. 709, 714-15 (D.R.I. 1994) (finding accounting firm's action to declare statute unconstitutional was unripe since its standing to sue was dependent on the accounting firm's being found liable in a pending underlying action against it brought by third parties) (discussing *Cedars-SinaiMedical Center v. Watkins,* 11 F.3d 1573, 1585 (Fed. Cir. 1993) (dismissing claim challenging the Department of Energy's assertion of rights over a patent as unripe where that assertion depended on outcome of a pending interference action to determine the ownership of the same patent)).

In this case, the Clerk entered a final judgment determining that the property was TMEs (and, thus, TME's to convey to buyers such as Formall) on July 18, 2014. That judgment was subject to Marion T's right to appeal through August 17, 2014. *See* Fed. R. App. P. 4(a)(1)(A). Both of these deadlines were well-past the date to add claims or parties as established by the Court's scheduling order. Formall brought the issue of the Counterclaim to the attention of the Court during the October 8, 2014, hearing, its first appearance before the Court following the entry of judgment and the expiration of Marion T's appeal rights. While there was an earlier telephonic status conference set for September 18, 2014, at which time Formall's former counsel failed to appear, Formall would argue that this delay in bringing the matter to the Court's attention does not amount to a lack of diligence on the part of Formall itself sufficient to defeat its assertion of good cause. Accordingly, Formall believes it has shown good cause under Rule 16 to depart from the deadline for amendment contained in the scheduling order. *See, e.g., Lauer v. Patriot Paint Co.,* No. 1:06-CV-0244, 2007 WL 2068595, at *3 (N.D. Ind. July 17, 2007) (noting that because the Court could not conclude the defendant engaged in dilatory tactics or engaged in undue delay in seeking to amend its pleading good cause had been shown).

Having shown good cause, Formall must also show under Rule 15 that leave to amend should be granted. "Courts must freely give leave to amend under Rule 15(a) where interests of justice so require." *McCauley v. City of Chicago,* 671 F.3d 611, 628 (7th Cir. 2011) (citations omitted) (noting liberal nature of rule). "The Court should freely grant leave to amend a complaint in the absence of undue delay, bad faith, or dilatory motive, a repeated failure to cure deficiencies by previous amendment, undue prejudice to the opposing party, and futility of the amendment." *Barry Aviation, Inc. v. Land O'Lakes Municipal Airport Commission,* 377 F.3d 682, 687 (7th Cir. 2004). Regarding undue delay, as discussed above, there was no undue delay (otherwise Formall would not have satisfied Rule 16). There is also no evidence of a dilatory motive; Formall is ready to proceed to resolve what remains of the claims surrounding the property that had been located at Marion T's facility.

As to undue prejudice, advancing the counterclaim as set forth in the proposed amended pleading will do little (if anything) to expand the issues before the Court and the parties. Marion T has asserted in its Complaint that it was the owner and had the right to possess the property set forth on Exhibit A to the Complaint.[2] (Dkt #1-1). In its Answer, Formall specifically denied those allegations. (Dkt # 3). A defense to a claim of conversion is that the party defending the claim has the right to possess the property. *See, e.g., Newland Resources, LLC v. Branham Corp.,* 918 N.E.2d 763, 775 (Ind. Ct. App. 2009) (conversion requires the exercise of control over the property of another person) (citing Indiana Code Ann. § 35-43-4-3). It cannot be disputed that the ownership of the property and the legality of each party's exercise of control over that property was put into contention as of the filing of the original answer on January 4, 2013 (Dkt. #5). Accordingly, given the common nucleus of facts it is unknown how the assertion of the proposed counterclaim or the affirmative defense of setoff could delay (let alone, unduly delay) the proceedings or force the parties to incur significant additional expenses.

There is no evidence that the proposed amendment would be futile. *See Ray v. Waterfield Mortg.,* No. 1:05-CV-400, 2006 WL 694728, at *1 (N.D. Ind. March 14, 2006) (where the Court can imagine a set of facts that would entitle the party to relief, the amendment should be allowed) (citing *Walker v. Nat'l Recovery, Inc.,* 200 F.3d 500, 503 (7th Cir. 1999)). The issues over ownership and control have existed since the inception of this matter. Moreover, no deadlines respecting discovery have passed in this case. The parties have sufficient time to explore both Marion T's existing claims and the proposed counterclaim and additional affirmative defense, all of which involve the core issues of which entity owned the property and which entity exerted unauthorized control over it. Hence there are no reasons to deny leave under Rule 15.

Conclusion

Because Formall has shown both good cause under Rule 16 and that leave should be given to permit the amendment of its answer to assert a counterclaim for conversion and a related affirmative defense of setoff under Rule 15, the Court should grant Formall's motion and order that the proposed pleading, tendered as Exhibit A to Formall's Motion for Leave to Amend, be filed.

Respectfully submitted,

BARRETT & MCNAGNY LLP

By/s/ Anthony M. Stites

Anthony M. Stites, #14078-71

215 East Berry Street

P.O. Box 2263

Fort Wayne, IN 46802

Phone: (260) 423-9551

---

2. Although the Complaint itself does not set out any distinction, Exhibit A appears to consist of two pages labeled Exhibit A and Exhibit A-1, respectively. (Dkt # 1-1 at 5-6).

Fax: (260) 423-8920

E-Mail: ams@barrettlaw.com

Attorneys for Defendant, Formall, Inc.

Motion for Summary Judgment

2016 WL 5958430 (S.D.Ind.)

Westlaw Query>>

To find more Motion for Summary Judgment filings on Westlaw: access Indiana Trial Court Documents (from the Home page, click Trial Court Documents, then Indiana), click the Advanced Search link, select Motion for Summary Judgment, and click Search. Use the Jurisdiction filter on the left to narrow results to Federal.

United States District Court, S.D. Indiana.

Terre Haute Division

TRUSTGARD INSURANCE COMPANY, Plaintiff,

v.

OLD NATIONAL WEALTH MANAGEMENT, as Personal Representative of the Estate of George Scott Samson, the Estate of Kelly Ann Ecker, By its personal representative, Patricia Ann Leturgez, Patricia Leturgez and Jerrald Anthony Leturgez, As Co-Guardians of L.O.E., and L.O.E. by his Natural parent and Next Best Friend, William Ecker, Defendants.

No. 2:15-cv-0258 JMS DKL.

September 16, 2016.

Memorandum in Support of Motion For Summary Judgment

Thomas R. Schultz, #11670-49, Charles S. Smith, #23148-49, Schultz & Pogue, LLP, for plaintiff.

Plaintiff, Trustgard Insurance Company, by counsel, pursuant to FRCP 56, respectfully moves for summary judgment. In support of its motion, plaintiff states as follows:

STATEMENT OF MATERIAL FACTS NOT IN DISPUTE

This case arises from a shooting in October of 2014. Dr. George Scott Samson married Kelly Ecker on October 4, 2014. [Filing 53-1 at 2]. A judge officiated the wedding. [Filing 53-2 at 2]. Following the wedding, Dr. Samson and Ms. Ecker had a post-reception party at their house located at 4025 North Creal Street in Terre Haute, Indiana. [Filing 53-2 at 3].

Following the party, Dr. Samson and Mrs. Ecker had a terrible fight. [Filing 53-3 at 4]. Ms. Ecker made four calls to 911. [Filing 53-3 at 2-3]. Mrs. Ecker gave the dispatcher the address for her home located at 4025 North Creal Street in Terre Haute. Unfortunately, Mrs. Ecker gave the wrong address, telling the dispatcher that the house was actually located at 4205 North Creal Street until of 4025. [Filing 53-3 at 4-5]. When Ms. Ecker made her fourth call, dispatcher Amanda Leslie took it. [Filing 53-3 at 3-4]. Ms. Leslie heard a female struggling and then saying "He's got a. . ." [Filing 53-3 at 3-4]. Ms. Leslie then heard gunshots. [Filing 53-3 at 3-4]. Dr. Samson's father, George Samson, testified that he heard Dr. Samson and Ms. Ecker arguing. [Filing 53-2 at 5]. Ms. Ecker went into her son, LOE's bedroom. [Filing 53-2 at 5]. Dr. Samson broke open the door to that room and then fired multiple shots at Ms. Ecker. [Filing 53-2 at 5]. Following that, Dr. Samson walked down the hallway, saying "it's too late. It's too late." [Filing 53-2 at 6]. Dr. Samson went to the basement of the house and shot himself in the head. [Filing 53-2 at 6]. *See also* [Filing 53-4 at 4]. LOE lived in Dr. Samson's house. [Filing 53-2 at 7-8].

Upon investigation of the shooting, Sergeant Kristopher Fitzgerald collected casings from nine bullets fired in the room where Dr. Samson shot Ms. Ecker. [Filing 53-4 at 3]. The casings were for a .40 caliber gun. [Filing 53-4 at 2]. Sgt. Fitzgerald recovered a .40 caliber semiautomatic Glock handgun from the basement of Dr. Samson's house. [Filing 53-4 at 5]. The nine-cartridge capacity magazine in the Glock was empty, and the slide was locked to the rear. [Filing 53-4 at 7]. A semiautomatic handgun requires a trigger pull for each bullet. [Filing 53-4 at 6]. In Sgt. Fitzgerald's experience, when he investigates an accidental shooting, there is typically one bullet fired. [Filing 53-4 at 7]. Ms. Ecker was hit by three bullets in LOE's room. [Filing 53-5 at 2].

Prior to getting married, Dr. Samson and Ms. Ecker signed a marriage license. [Filing 7-5 at 6]. The marriage license was not filed due to their deaths. [Filing 7-5 at 6].

Dr. Samson purchased a policy of insurance from Grange Insurance/Trustguard Insurance Company. [Filing 7-1 at 1] The policy number was TH1472837-00. . [Filing 7-1 at 1]. The issue date was 5/21/14, with the effective date 5/21/14. [Filing 7-1 at 1]. The policy provided, in pertinent part, as follows:

DEFINITIONS:

1. "**You**" and "**your**" refer to the Named Insured, which includes the individual named on the Declaration Page or that person's spouse if a **resident** of the same household.

2. "**We**", "**us**" and "**our**" refer to Trustguard Insurance Company.

3. "**Bodily injury**" means bodily harm, sickness or disease, including required care, loss of services, and resulting death. . .

6. "**Insured person**" means:

    a. **you**;

    b. **your** relatives residing in your household; and

    c. any other person under the age of 21 residing in **your** household who is in **your** care or the care of a resident relative. . .

9. "**Occurrence**" means an accident, including continuous or repeated exposure to substantially the same general harmful conditions, which results in **bodily injury** or **property damage** during the policy period. . .

13. "**Resident**" means a person related to **you** by blood, marriage or adoption, includes wards and foster children, and whose principal residence is at the location shown on the Declarations Page. If a court has adjudicated that one parent is the custodial parent, that adjudication shall be conclusive with respect to the minor child's principal residence.

[Filing 7-1 at 36-37].

SECTION II — PERSONAL LIABILITY PROTECTION

COVERAGE E — PERSONAL LIABILITY COVERAGE

We will pay all sums, up to our limit of liability on the Declarations Page for this coverage, arising out of any one loss for which an insured person becomes legally obligated to pay his damages because of bodily injury or property damages, caused by an occurrence covered by this policy. Damages include pre-judgment interest awarded against the insured person.

If a claim is made or suit is brought against the insured person for damages because of bodily injury or property damage caused by an occurrence to which this coverage applies, we will defend the insured person at our expense, using lawyers of our choice. We are not obligated to pay any claim or judgment or to defend after we have paid an amount equal to the limit of our liability shown on the Declarations Page for this coverage. We may investigate or settle any claim or suit as we think appropriate. [Filing 7-1 at 54].

SECTION II — PERSONAL LIABILITY PROTECTION EXCLUSIONS

A. Under Coverage E — Personal Liability Coverage and Coverage F — Medical Payments to Others Coverage, we do not cover: . . .

6. **Bodily injury** or **property damage** caused by the willful, malicious, or intentional act of any person, including any claims alleging negligent supervision, negligent entrustment, or negligent failure to control against any **insured person** arising out of the willful, malicious, or intentional act. . .

8. **Bodily injury** or **property damage** expected or intended by any **insured person**. This includes **bodily injury** or **property damage**:

    a. caused intentionally by or at the direction of an **insured person**; or

    b. which results from any **occurrence** caused by an intentional act of any **insured person** where the results are reasonably foreseeable. . .

18. **Bodily injury** or **property damage** arising from a criminal act or omission which is committed by, or at the direction of an **insured person**. This exclusion applies regardless of whether the **insured person** is actually charged with, or convicted of a crime.

[Filing 7-1 at 57, 59].

B. Under coverage E — personal liability coverage, **we** do not cover: . . .

6. **Bodily injury** to:

    a. **you**;

    b. **your** relatives residing in your household; and

    c. any other person under the age of 21 residing in **your** household who is in **your** care or the care of a **resident** relative.

[Filing 7-1 at p. 59].

COVERAGE F — MEDICAL PAYMENTS TO OTHERS COVERAGE

A. We will pay the **reasonable** expenses incurred, up to our limit of liability shown on the Declarations Page for this coverage, for **necessary** medical, surgical, x-ray and dental services, prosthetic devices, eyeglasses, hearing aids, pharmaceuticals, ambulance, hospital, licensed nursing and funeral services. These expenses must be incurred within three years from the date of an accident causing **bodily injury** covered by this policy.

Each person who sustains **bodily injury** is entitled to this protection when that person is:

1. On an **insured premises** with the permission of an **insured person**; or

2. Elsewhere, if the **bodily injury**:

    a. Arises out of a condition on the **insured premises** or the adjourning way;

    b. Is caused by the activities of an **insured person** or **residence employee** in the course of employment by an **insured person**;

    c. Is caused by an animal owned by or in the care of an **insured person**; or

    d. Is sustained by a **residence employee** arising out of and in the course of employment by an **insured person**.

B. We do not cover injury to:

1. **Insured persons**; or

2. Any other person, except a **residence employee**, who resides regularly on any part of an **insured premises**.

[Filing 7-1 at 54].

SECTION I — PROPERTY PROTECTION AND SECTION II — PERSONAL LIABILITY PROTECTION CONDITIONS

12. Punitive or exemplary damages exclusion.

Regardless of any other provision of this policy, we do not provide coverage for punitive or exemplary damages, or any legal fees or costs associated with them.

[Filing 7-1 at 62, 63].

HOMEOWNERS AMENDATORY ENDORSEMENT- INDIANA (HO 301 IN)

E. SECTION II — PERSONAL LIABILITY PROTECTION

1. The second paragraph under **COVERAGE E — PESONAL LIABILITY COVERAGE** is removed and replaced with:

If a claim is made or suit is brought against the insured person for damages because of **bodily injury** or **property damage** caused by an **occurrence** to which this coverage applies, we will defend the **insured person** at **our** expense, using lawyers of **our** choice. Upon issuance of a reservation of rights letter to any party, **we** reserve the right to recover from any party to whom **we** have provided any defense costs incurred by **us** should a court of competent jurisdiction conclude that we had no duty to provide a defense to that party. The reservation of rights letter will give notice of the coverage issues and **our** right to recover defense costs. Recoverable defense costs include only those attorney fees and costs associated with the defense of the party to whom the reservation of rights letter was issued. **We** are not obligated to pay any claim or judgment or to defend after we have paid an amount equal to the limit of our liability shown on the Declarations Page for this coverage. **We** may investigate or settle any claim or suit as we think appropriate.

[Filing 7-1 at 25].

2. Condition 12. **Punitive or Exemplary Damages Exclusion** is removed and replaced with the following:

12. **Punitive or exemplary damages exclusion**.

Regardless of any other provision of this policy, **we** do not provide coverage for punitive or exemplary damages, or any associated legal fees, interest or costs. Except that if a suit shall have been brought against an **insured person** as defined in this policy with respect to a claim for acts or alleged acts following within the coverage hereof, seeking both compensatory and punitive or exemplary damages, the company will afford a defense to such action. However, the company is not responsible under the policy for the payment of such punitive or exemplary damages.

[Filing 7-1 at 28].

On or about March 11, 2015, the Estate of Kelly Ecker and LOE, by his guardians, filed a complaint against the Estate of George Scott Samson for the death of Mrs. Ecker. [Filing 7-2 at 1]. On or about April 17, 2015, the Estate of Kelly Ann Ecker and LOE filed an amended complaint alleging that Mrs. Ecker's death "was the result of the intentional act and/or negligence of George Scott Samson, now deceased, whose use of a firearm resulted in gunshot wounds which caused the death of Kelly Ann Ecker." [Filing 7-4 at 1]. The amended complaint also alleged claims on behalf of LOE, only with new guardians. Particularly, the complaint alleged that "as a result of the defendant's intentional act and/or negligence, . . .[LOE] has suffered the loss of love, companionship and support, [has] incurred the expenses of healthcare necessitated by the wrongful act, [has] incurred costs associated with funeral and burial, and costs associated with the administration of the estate, including reasonable attorney's fees". [Filing 7-4 at 3]. The amended complaint also alleged:

that George Scott Samson's conduct on October 5, 2014 was so outrageous and reprehensible as to justify the imposition of punitive damages. George Scott Samson's intentional act and/or negligent use of a firearm displayed a wanton and willful disregard of for the law, as well as the rights and safety of Kelly Ann Ecker. As a result, defendant, the Estate of George Scott Samson, should be punished by the assessment of punitive damages in an amount adequate to punish him and to set an example which will deter others in the future. [Filing 7-4 at 3].

On June 9, 2015, LOE, by his next friend, William Ecker, filed an amended complaint for damages. [Filing 7-5 at 1]. LOE alleged that Kelly Ecker died of gunshot wounds which she sustained while in the residence of George Scott Samson, that George Scott Samson intentionally shot and killed Ms. Ecker in front of LOE, and that George Scott Samson negligently, intentionally or recklessly caused LOE to suffer emotional distress, among other things. [Filing 7-5 at 1-3].

DISCUSSION

STANDARD OF REVIEW

A motion for summary judgment asks that the Court find that a trial based on the uncontroverted and admissible evidence is unnecessary because, as a matter of law, it would conclude in the moving party's favor. *See* FRCP 56. To survive a motion for summary judgment, the non-moving party must set forth specific, admissible evidence showing that there is a material issue for trial. FRCP 56(c); *Celotex Corp. v. Catrett*, 477 U.S. 317, 323 (1986). As the current version of Rule 56 makes clear, whether a party asserts that a fact is undisputed or genuinely disputed, the party must support the asserted fact by citing to particular parts of the record, including depositions, documents, or affidavits. FRCP 56(c)(1)(A). A party can also support a fact by showing that the materials cited do not establish the absence or presence of a genuine dispute or that the adverse party cannot produce admissible evidence to support the fact. FRCP 56(c)(1)(B).

The Court need only consider the cited materials, FRCP 56(c)(3), and the Seventh Circuit Court of Appeals has "repeatedly assured the district courts that they are not required to scour every inch of the record for evidence that is potentially relevant to the summary judgment motion before them." *Johnson v. Cambridge Indus.*, 325 F.3d 892, 898 (7th Cir. 2003).

If the non-moving party cannot produce enough evidence to allow a jury to find in their favor, they lose. *See Anderson v. Liberty Lobby, Inc.* 477 U.S. 242 (1986), (holding that a court should grant summary judgment when it is persuaded that, on the same evidence, it would have to reverse a jury verdict in favor of the party opposing summary judgment. The inquiry on a motion for summary judgment "unavoidably asks whether reasonable jurors could find by a preponderance of the evidence that the [non-moving party] is entitled to a verdict—'whether there is [evidence] upon which a jury can properly proceed to find a verdict for the party producing it, upon whom the onus of proof is imposed."' *Id.* at p. 252.) The district court must decide "whether the evidence presents a sufficient disagreement to require submission to a jury or whether it is so one-sided that one party must prevail as a matter of law." *Oest v. Ill. Dep't of Corrections*, 240 F.3d 605, 610 (7th Cir. 2001) (quoting *Liberty Lobby*, 477 U.S. at 248).

"Interpretation of an insurance policy presents a question of law that is particularly suitable for summary judgment." *State Auto Mut. Ins. Co. v. Flexdar, Inc.*, 964 N.E.2d 845, 848 (Ind. 2012). "Clear and unambiguous language in insurance policy contracts, like other contracts, should be given its plain and ordinary meaning." *Cinergy Corp. v. Associated Elec. & Gas Ins. Servs., Ltd.*, 865 N.E.2d 571, 574 (Ind. 2007). "Policy terms are interpreted from the perspective of an ordinary policyholder of average intelligence. If reasonably intelligent persons may honestly differ as to the meaning of the policy language, the policy is ambiguous." *Gasser v. Downing*, 967 N.E.2d 1085, 1087 (Ind. Ct. App. 2012) (citation omitted). "However, an ambiguity does not exist merely because the parties proffer differing interpretations of the policy language." *Buckeye State Mut. Ins. Co. v. Carfield*, 914 N.E.2d 315, 318 (Ind. Ct. App. 2009), *trans. denied* (2010). Also, "a term is not ambiguous simply because it is not defined." *Bastin v. First Ind. Bank*, 694 N.E.2d 740, 746 (Ind. Ct. App. 1998), *trans. denied.*

A split of judicial authority on the meaning of similar contract terms does not necessarily mean that those terms are ambiguous. *Allgood v. Meridian Sec. Ins. Co.*, 836 N.E.2d 243, 248 (Ind. 2005). A disagreement among courts as to the meaning of a particular contractual provision is evidence that an ambiguity may exist. But a division of authority is only evidence of ambiguity. It does not establish conclusively that a particular clause is ambiguous. *Id.* (citation omitted). Where an ambiguity does exist, insurance policies are to be construed strictly against the insurer. *Flexdar*, 964 N.E.2d at 848.

"We construe the policy as a whole and consider all of the provisions of the contract and not just the individual words, phrases or paragraphs." *Nat'l Mut. Ins. Co. v. Curtis*, 867 N.E.2d 631, 634 (Ind. Ct. App. 2007). "We must accept an interpretation of the contract language that harmonizes the provisions, rather than one that supports conflicting versions of the provisions." *Id.* [Courts] "should construe the language of a contract so as not to render any words, phrases, or terms ineffective or meaningless." *Hammerstone v. Ind. Ins. Co.*, 986 N.E.2d 841, 846 (Ind. Ct. App. 2013). "[T]he power to interpret contracts does not extend to changing their terms and we will not give insurance policies an unreasonable construction to provide additional coverage." *Curtis*, 867 N.E.2d at 634.

ARGUMENT

POLICY EXCLUSIONS

The Indiana Court of Appeals has noted that the interpretation of an insurance policy is primarily a question of law for the court, and it is therefore a question which is particularly well-suited for disposition by summary judgment. *See Sans v. Monticello Ins. Co.*, 676 N.E.2d 1099, 1101-02, (Ind.Ct.App.1997). Where there is an ambiguity, policies are to be construed strictly against the insurance company. The insurance company is bound by the plain and ordinary meaning of the words viewed from the standpoint of the insured. However, there is no rule of construction that every term in an insurance contract must be defined, and the mere fact that a term is not defined does not render it ambiguous. Whether a contract is ambiguous is a question of law; and where the court determines there is no ambiguity, the terms of the contract are conclusive and the construction of those terms is also a matter of law to be determined by the court. An insurance contract is ambiguous when it is susceptible to more than one interpretation and reasonably intelligent persons would honestly differ as to its meaning. An ambiguity does not exist simply because a controversy exists between the parties, with each favoring a different interpretation. *Id.*

An unambiguous policy must be enforced according to its terms, even those which limit the insurer's liability. Courts may not extend coverage delineated by the policy, nor may they rewrite the clear and unambiguous language of the policy. However, an exclusionary clause will not be read so broadly as to effectively exclude all coverage. *Id.*

Indiana courts have long upheld standard exclusionary clauses for the insured's intentional acts as in furtherance of the public policy that a person should not be permitted to insure against harms he may intentionally and unlawfully cause others, and thereby acquire a license to engage in such activity. *Id.*

Intentionality and Exclusions 6 and 8

Under the policy at issue in this matter, it appears that there are at least three separate exclusions which could deny coverage to Mrs. Ecker's estate and her son. The first is Exclusion 6, which excludes coverage for bodily injury or property damage caused by the willful, malicious, or intentional act of any person. Additionally, Exclusion 8 bars coverage for bodily injury or property damage expected or intended by any insured person. This exclusion includes bodily injury or property damage caused intentionally by or at the direction of an insured person, or which results from any occurrence caused by any intentional act of any insured person where the results are reasonably foreseeable. Both of these exclusions use comparable analyses to determine coverage.

In *Allstate Insurance Co. v. Herman*, 551 N.E.2d 844 (Ind. 1990), the Indiana Supreme Court found that an individual's act of firing four shots into a fleeing crowd fell within the policy's intentional act exclusion, even if the insured did not actually intend to hit the plaintiff. In that case, the shooter testified that he intentionally shot the gun. The Indiana Supreme Court found that there was no doubt from the evidence that the shooter deliberately fired four shots into a crowd of fleeing people of which the plaintiff was a member. Although there was no evidence that he intended to specifically shoot the plaintiff, he certainly had the intention of shooting into the fleeing crowd with the intent to "hurt somebody". The word intentional "refers . . . to the volitional performance of an act with an intent to cause injury, although not necessarily the precise injury or severity of damage that in fact occurs." *Id.* at 845. The Indiana Supreme Court concluded that when the shooter intentionally fired a gun into the fleeing crowd, of which the plaintiff was part, he was deliberately committing an act which any reasonable person would deem calculated to cause injury. As such, Allstate's exclusionary clause as to intentional acts by the insured entitled it to summary judgment as a matter of law.

Likewise, in *Home Ins. Co. v. Neilsen*, 332 N.E.2d 240 (Ind.Ct.App.1975), the Indiana Court of Appeals analyzed whether a person who intended to punch another person in the face, but did not intend to inflict the injuries he did on the victim, was barred from coverage. The attacker brought a claim for coverage under his homeowner's policy after the insurer refused to defend him. The attacker's insurance policy excluded liability of the company under the comprehensive liability and medical payments provisions "to bodily injury or property damage caused intentionally by or at the direction of the insured." There was no dispute that the underlying suit was strictly for assault and battery, and there was no contention that the attacker did not intend to strike the victim. The Indiana Court of Appeals held that the policy excluded coverage for an action of the insured which was intended to cause injury. The court noted that the intent to injure may be established either by showing actual intent to injure, or by showing the nature and character of the act to be such that intent to cause harm to the other party must be inferred as a matter of law.[1]

Consequently, the "expected or intended" exclusion applied. The Court noted that the Indiana Supreme Court has defined "intentional" as "the volitional performance of an act with an intent to cause injury, although not necessarily the precise injury or severity of damage that in fact occurs." *Id.* at pp. 12-13, quoting *Herman*, 551 N.E.2d 844, 845 (Ind. 1990).

In this matter, the evidence shows that Dr. Samson and Mrs. Ecker were having a fight on the night in question. Within minutes of Mrs. Ecker's call to 911, Dr. Samson shot her three times with a gun. This was not a case of a claimed accidental discharge which unfortunately hit the victim. Rather, this involved a shooter taking aim and pulling a trigger nine separate times in order to shoot Mrs. Ecker. As such, the evidence demonstrates that this is quite like the situation in *Herman*, with the evidence demonstrating that Dr. Samson fired a gun in such a manner that any reasonable person would deem calculated to cause injury. As noted in *Stout v. Underhill*, 734 N.E.2d 717, (Ind. Ct. App. 2000), the nature and character of shooting Ms. Ecker three times with a gun is not one that probably happens without the intent to harm the other party. The nature and character of firing a gun nine times at close range, and shooting Ms. Ecker three times, is such that intent must be inferred as a matter of law.

Likewise, LOE's claim for emotional distress derives from Dr. Samson's intentional shooting of Ms. Ecker. Even if Dr. Samson did not intend to cause LOE harm, like the attacker in *Neilsen*, Dr. Samson intended to engage in an act that was intended to cause injury. Thus, characterizing LOE's claim as one for negligent infliction of emotional distress does not change the underlying intentional nature of Dr. Samson's actions.

Moreover, Exclusion 8 bars coverage for an occurrence (meaning caused by an accident) caused by an intentional act where the results were reasonably foreseeable. Emotional distress for the son of a woman slain in his presence is reasonably foreseeable, and such claim is thereby barred.

Accordingly, under Indiana law, coverage for the incident would be properly excluded under subsections 6 and 8 of Section II of the policy.

Criminal Acts and Exclusion 18

Exclusion 18 provides that the policy does not cover bodily injury or property damage arising from a criminal act or omission which is committed by, or at the direction of an insured person. The exclusion applies regardless of whether the insured person is actually charged with, or convicted of a crime. Had Dr. Samson not killed himself following his shooting of Ms. Ecker, he could have been charged with any number of crimes, from murder to manslaughter to criminal recklessness. Each would be sufficient to bar coverage for Dr. Samson's act.

In *Allstate Ins. Co. v. Carmer*, 794 F.Supp. 871 (S.D. Ind. 1991), Allstate brought a declaratory judgment action to determine that there was no coverage under this exclusion. The underlying facts involved four underage boys drinking beer and driving around Indianapolis. The boys obtained the beer by pooling their money together and finding another person to buy the beer for them. While driving, the boys got into accident. One of the boys, Scott Carmer, and his parents sued the other boys, including Robert Garnett. Both Garnett and Carmer were sitting in the back seat of the car. *Id.* at pp. 871-72. Carmer contended that Garnett was in violation of Ind. Code § 7.1-5-7-8(a) and Ind. Code § 7.1-5-10-15, furnishing alcohol to a minor.

---

1. In *State Farm Fire & Cas. Co. v. Henderson*, the insured, Joyce Henderson, fired a bullet at a man who was fighting with her husband. *See* 2002 U.S. Dist. LEXIS 11062. Ms. Henderson had given a voluntary statement to the police where she said "I pointed the gun at Alan and told him to stop, stop. Alan said he was going to kill me next. I then shot Alan once." At her criminal trial, Ms. Henderson testified that "I got the gun and I pointed it, and they [her husband and Alan, the decedent] was [sic] together and he [Alan] had Bill around the shoulders. I just fired. I don't know how I hit him [Alan] instead of Bill[.]" The United States District Court for the Southern District found that despite Ms. Henderson's claims that she did not intend to kill Alan, it was undisputed that she intended to point the weapon at him, intended to pull the trigger, and did, in fact, pull the trigger of the weapon that discharged the bullet that struck and killed him. As a result, the Court found that Ms. Henderson's volitional acts of pointing the weapon at Alan and pulling the trigger were not accidents and therefore, not covered under the policy. This conclusion applied even if Ms. Henderson did not know how she hit Alan rather than her husband. As such there was no occurrence sufficient to give rise to coverage. *Id.* at pp. 11-12.

The Garnetts had a renters policy which included an exclusion that stated Allstate did "not cover bodily injury. . .resulting from: . . .a) A criminal act or omission. . ." The exclusion also provided that it "applies regardless of whether the insured person is actually charged with, or convicted of, a crime." *Id.* at p. 872.

The Court found that because conviction was not required for the exclusion to be applicable, the question was whether the conduct in question violated a criminal statute, and not whether the actor could be prosecuted criminally. Since Garnett's actions constituted a violation of the Indiana criminal code, the Court held that the exclusion applied.

Likewise, in *Allstate Ins. Co. v. Norris*, 795 F. Supp. 272 (S.D. Ind. 1992), an insured, Norris, was involved in an argument with an individual who fired two shots at the insured and then fled, crouching behind a vehicle parked next to a home. Norris went into his house and returned with a .30 caliber semi-automatic rifle. Norris took the rifle, which was loaded with 20 rounds of ammunition, and began shooting in the direction of the other man. Norris fired a total of nine shots in an effort to "pin down" the man until police could arrive. Unfortunately, the bullets entered a house and struck a young woman and an eighteen month old baby. *Id.* at 273.

Norris eventually pled guilty to felony criminal recklessness, and the teenager and her mother filed a civil suit against Norris. Allstate brought a declaratory judgment action to determine coverage. Like the policy here, Norris's policy expressly did not cover injuries that resulted from any "criminal act or omission" by an insured. Norris's shooting constituted criminal recklessness, so the Court found that under the plain and ordinary meaning of the exclusion, the teenager's injuries, which resulted from that shooting, were not covered by the policy. *Id.* at p. 275.

In this matter, Dr. Samson shot and killed Ms. Ecker at close range. Such conduct constitutes murder under Ind. Code § 35-42-1-1, voluntary manslaughter under Ind. Code § 35-42-1-3, or reckless homicide under Ind. Code 35-42-1-5. The only thing preventing Dr. Samson from being charged with any of those crimes is that he killed himself. Given his commission of these crimes, Exclusion 18 bars any recovery by either the Estate of Ms. Ecker or LOE resulting from those crimes.

The Resident Relative Provision

The other provision which bars coverage for claims arising from Mrs. Ecker's death is the exclusion for bodily injury to the insured or the insured's relatives residing in his household, including any person under the age of 21 residing in the insured's household who is in his care or the care of a resident relative. In this case, Dr. Samson and Ms. Ecker married that night. LOE was residing in the home with his mother at the time of her death. LOE was under the age of 21 at the time of the incident. Indiana's courts have found that a household exclusion is not contrary to public policy. *See Transamerica Insurance Co. v. Henry*, by Henry 563 NE 2d 1265 (Ind 1990).

The policy at issue defines resident as a person related to the insured by blood, marriage or adoption, and whose principal residence is at the location shown on the Declarations Page. Indiana has interpreted these residency requirements on a number of occasions.

In this matter, Ms. Ecker made the 4025 Creal Street home her principal residence. Likewise, Mrs. Ecker had custody over LOE, thereby making him a resident of Dr. Samson's household as well. Ms. Ecker was married to Dr. Samson, making LOE a person under the age of 21 residing in Dr. Samson's household in the care of Dr. Samson's wife, Ms. Ecker. Given these conditions the estate of Mrs. Ecker and LOE would be barred under this exclusion from recovering against Dr. Samson's insurance policy.[2]

PUNITIVE DAMAGES

The policy expressly provides that it does not cover punitive damages. Perhaps as importantly, Indiana law does not permit recovery of punitive damages from the estate of a deceased tortfeasor. *See Crabtree ex rel. Kemp v. Estate of Crabtree*, 837 N.E.2d 135, 139 (Ind. 2005). The central purpose of punitive damages is to punish the wrongdoer and to deter him from future misconduct, not to reward the plaintiff or compensate the plaintiff. *Id.* As Dr. Samson is deceased, he cannot further be punished for his actions, and there is no insurance coverage for such a claim.

---

2. Although LOE is trying to claim that Dr. Samson and Ms. Ecker were not actually married, they did go through the appropriate ceremony and had both signed a license for marriage. See Exhibit 6, p. 6. That they were unable to file the marriage license due to their deaths does not change that, for purposes of interpreting the insurance policy, the two of them were married.

CONCLUSION

For the foregoing reasons, plaintiff Trustgard Insurance Company, pursuant to FRCP 56, respectfully requests that this Court grant summary judgment in its favor and against defendants, and for all other appropriate relief.

Respectfully submitted,

SCHULTZ & POGUE, LLP

By: */s/ Charles S. Smith*

Thomas R. Schultz, #11670-49

Charles S. Smith, #23148-49

Attorneys for Plaintiff

Motion for Sanctions

2015 WL 3856467 (S.D.Ind.)

United States District Court, S.D. Indiana.

Indianapolis Division

CMG WORLDWIDE, INC., Plaintiff,

v.

Jan GLASER, an individual; Tatyana Khomyakova, an Individual; Tatyana Designs, Inc.; and Tatyana, LLC, Defendants.

No. 1:14-cv-00928-RLY-DKL.

March 31, 2015.

Westlaw Query>>

To find more Motion for Sanctions filings on Westlaw: access Indiana Trial Court Documents (from the Home page, click Trial Court Documents, then Indiana), enter "DT("sanctions" 11)" in the search box, and click Search. Use the Jurisdiction filter on the left to narrow results to Federal.

Defendants' Memorandum in Support of Request for Rule 11 Sanctions

Scott E. Shockley, Esq. (#2153-18), Defur Voran, LLP, 400 South Walnut Street, Suite 200, Muncie, Indiana 47305, (760) 288-3651 (t), (765) 288-7068, sshockley@defur.com, Mario L. Herman, Pro Hac Vice Counsel (DC Bar #370706), for defendants counterclaimants/third party plaintiffs, Design Technology Holding, LLC and Design Technology Group, LLC.

On January 9, 2015, this Court dismissed Plaintiff CMG Worldwide, Inc.'s Complaint for failure to state a claim upon which relief can be granted, including Count III: alleging Defendants violated Section 10(b) under the Securities and Exchange Act of 1934 and Rule 10b-5; and Count IV: alleging Defendants violated Section 20(a) of the Act. Defendants requested that the Court determine that Defendants were entitled to an award of sanctions pursuant to the Private Securities Litigation Reform Act ("PSLRA"), and that the Court make specific findings regarding each party . . . with each requirement" of Rule 11." 15 U.S.C. sec 78u-4(c)(1).

On March 13, 2015, this Court held: "The record presents sufficient evidence for the imposition of Rule 11 sanctions against CMG's attorney. Defendants are ORDERED to file a written memorandum in support of an award of attorneys' fees and costs, with designated evidence, in or before April 2, 2015."

Defendants respectfully submit this memorandum, and the Declaration of Mario L. Herman and the Declaration of Mary Klein in support thereof.

Case law has emphasized the punitive rather than compensatory nature of Rule 11 sanctions. In *Pavelic & Le Flore v. Marvel Entertainment Group*, 493 U.S. 120, 110 S.Ct. 456, 107 L.Ed.2d 438 (1989), the Supreme Court stated that the purpose of Rule 11 "is not reimbursement but 'sanction'." *Id.* at 126. In *Cooter & Gell v. Hartmarx Corp.*, 496 U.S. 384, 392, 110 S. Ct. 2447, 2454, 110 L. Ed. 2d 359 (1990), the Court noted that the goal of a Rule 11 sanction is specific and general deterrence. *Id.*, 110 S.Ct. at 2454, 2461. The Court added, however, that proper sanctions could include expenses directly caused by the filing of the lawsuit. *Id.* 110 S.Ct. at 2461. [An appropriate] sanction, may, but need not, include payment of the other parties' expenses. Although the rule must be read in light of concerns that it will spawn satellite litigation and chill vigorous advocacy, any interpretation must give effect to the rule's central goal of deterrence. *Id.* at 2454. Thus deterrence may well include the payment of expenses and attorneys' fees generated as a result of the filing of abusive litigation.

Case law acknowledges compensation as another important objective and purpose for Rule 11. "[O]ne of the goals of Rule 11 is to impose costs on the careless or reckless lawyers. Compensation is one thrust of Rule 11...." *Brown v. Federation of State Medical Boards*, 830 F.2d 1429, 1437 (7th Cir.1987). In our American system which requires each party to bear its own fees and costs, "courts will ensure that each party really *does* bear the costs and does not foist expenses off on its adversaries." *In re TCI, Ltd.*, 769 F.2d 441 (7th Cir.1985). *See also Thornton v. Wahl*, 787 F.2d 1151, 1154 (7th Cir.), *cert. denied*, 479 U.S. 851, 107 S.Ct. 181, 93 L.Ed.2d 116 (1986) ("Counsel who puts the burden of study and illumination on the defendants or the court must expect to pay attorneys' fees under [Rule 11.]").

The sanction should accomplish the twin goals of providing "specific and general deterrence," *Cooter & Gell*, 496 U.S. at 404, 110 S.Ct. at 2460, aimed both to punish the wrongdoer and send a message to the bar that such conduct will not be tolerated. The Seventh Circuit has consistently held that the Rule 11 benchmark is a form of restitution: "Sanctions under Rule 11 frequently are designed to make the adverse party whole--to put the party opposing the motion in as good a position as it would have occupied had the motion never been made." *Mars Steel Corp. v. Cont'l Bank N.A.*, 880 F.2d 928, 939 (7th Cir. 1989); *see also Brandt v. Schal Associates, Inc.*, 960 F.2d 640, 646 (7th Cir.1992) ("Compensation and deterrence ... are sometimes compatible."). In an effort to deter future conduct, the Court may impose a flat sanction or it may direct the offending party to pay the other party's reasonable attorney's fees. *Divane v. Krull Elec. Co.*, 319 F.3d 307, 314 (7th Cir. 2003). Rule 11 authorizes the district court to award reasonable attorneys' fees as a sanction. Fed.R.Civ.P. 11(c)(2).

In setting the amount of an attorneys' fees award, federal courts usually follow the lead of the United States Supreme Court, whose decision on a fee award under 42 U.S.C. § 1988 in *Hensley v. Eckerhart*, 461 U.S. 424, 103 S.Ct. 1933, 76 L.Ed.2d 40 (1983), stated as follows: "The most useful starting point for determining the amount of a reasonable fee is the number of hours reasonably expended on the litigation multiplied by a reasonable hourly rate. This calculation provides an objective basis on which to make an initial estimate of the value of a lawyer's services." 461 U.S. at 434. The product of these two variables is known as the "lodestar," and "the party seeking the fee award bears the burden of proving the reasonableness of the hours worked and the hourly rates claimed." *Spegon v. Catholic Bishop of Chi.*, 175 F.3d 544, 550 (7th Cir.1999) (citing *Hensley*, 461 U.S. at 433). Even where the moving party has provided some documentation for his claims, courts may exercise discretion in setting "reasonable" amounts for hours worked or hourly rate. *Id.* at 550. Once the lodestar amount has been calculated, it is presumptively the correct fee award. *See Pennsylvania v. Del. Valley Citizens' Council for Clean Air*, 478 U.S. 546, 565, 106 S.Ct. 3088, 92 L.Ed.2d 439 (1986).

Courts recognize a presumption that the rates a law firm actually charges its client are reasonable for the geographic market and the type of work performed. *See Cintas Corp. v. Perry*, 517 F.3d 459, 469 (7th Cir.2008) ("[T]he best evidence of whether attorney's fees are reasonable is whether a party has paid them."). Additionally, the reasonableness of an attorney's hourly rate depends upon the prevailing market rate charged by attorneys with similar skill and experience in the legal community. *Blum v. Stenson*, 465 U.S. 886, 895 n. 11 (1984); *Spanish Action Committee v. City of Chicago*, 811 F.2d 1129 (7th Cir.1987); *Tomazzoli v. Sheedy*, 804 F.2d 93 (7th Cir.1986).

Mr. Herman's office charges $520 per hour for his work as an attorney, and Ms. Klein's hours are billed at $85.00 per hour for the work performed by his paralegal ($80.00 for 2014), See Declarations of Mario L. Merman and Mary Klein.[1] Mr. Herman has been a member of the District of Columbia Bar since 1983, and has 32 years of experience practicing law. Mr. Herman's rates for his services and those of his paralegal fall well within the *Laffey Matrix*, which dictates $520 per hour for attorneys with 20+ years of experience, and $150 per hour for paralegal rates.

The *Laffey* Matrix,[2] which has its origins in the case of *Laffey v. Northwest Airlines, Inc.*, 572 F.Supp. 354 (D.D.C.1983), *rev'd in part on other grounds*, 241 U.S.App. D.C. 11, 746 F.2d 4 (1984), is a chart compiled yearly by the Civil Division of the United States Attorney's Office in the District of Columbia. It provides a schedule of hourly rates prevailing in the Washington, D.C. area in each year going back to 1981 for attorneys at various levels of experience. *Piper v. United States Dep't of Justice*, 339 F.Supp.2d 13, 24 n. 8 (D.D.C.2004). It is regularly used

---

1. The Declarations of Mr. Herman and Ms. Klein are attached hereto as Exhibits "A" and "B" respectively.

2. The *Laffey* Matrix for 2014-2015 is attached hereto as Exhibit "C". The *Laffey Matrix* was printed from (*http://www.justice.gov/sites/default/files/usao-dc/legacy/2014/07/14/LaffeyMatrix_2014-2015.pdf.*)

in the federal courts to determine attorneys' fees. *Smith v. District of Columbia*, 466 F.Supp.2d 151, 156 (D.D.C.2006) ("In the District of Columbia, it has been traditional to apply the so-called *Laffey* Matrix ...."); *accord, e.g., Coleman v. District of Columbia*, 2007 WL 1307834 at *2--4, 2007 U.S. Dist. LEXIS 32743 at *13--18 (D.D.C. May 3, 2007); *Piper, supra*, 339 F.Supp.2d at 24 n. 8; *Northwest Coalition for Alternatives to Pesticides v. Browner*, 965 F.Supp. 59, 65 (D.D.C.1997).

As set forth in the Declaration of Mario L. Herman, filed and served herewith, Mr. Herman has spent 35.3 hours ($18,356.00) in connection with the Motion to Dismiss specifically related to the issues related to the securities violations alleged in the Complaint, and this sanctions motion.[3] As set forth in the Declaration of Mary Klein, Mr. Herman's paralegal, Ms. Klein spent a total of 28.25 hours ($2,298.75) in connection with the Motion to Dismiss specifically related to the issues related to the securities violations alleged in the Complaint, and this sanctions motion.

Date: MARCH 31, 2015

Respectfully submitted,

/s/Scott E. Shockley

Scott E. Shockley, Esq. (#2153-18)

DEFUR VORAN, LLP

400 South Walnut Street, Suite 200

Muncie, Indiana 47305

(760) 288-3651 (t)

(765) 288-7068

sshockley@defur.com

/s/Mario L. Herman

Mario L. Herman

Pro Hac Vice Counsel (DC Bar #370706)

Attorney for Defendants

Counterclaimants/Third Party Plaintiffs

DESIGN TECHNOLOGY HOLDING, LLC and DESIGN TECHNOLOGY GROUP, LLC

---

3. Count III: alleging Defendants violated Section 10(b) under the Securities and Exchange Act of 1934 and Rule 10b-5; and Count IV: alleging Defendants violated Section 20(a) of the Act.

Motion to Compel Discovery

2015 WL 10320697 (N.D.Ind.)

United States District Court, N.D. Indiana.

Hammond Division

Gloria JONES, Plaintiff,

v.

GASSER CHAIR COMPANY, Suspa, Inc., and Horseshoe Casino, Defendants.

No. 2:15-cv-00014-PPS.

October 9, 2015.

FRCP Rule 37 Motion to Compel Discovery

Jury Demand

Westlaw Query>>

To find more Motion to Compel Discovery filings on Westlaw: access Indiana Trial Court Documents (from the Home page, click Trial Court Documents, then Indiana), click the Advanced Search link, select Motion to Compel, and click Search. Use the Jurisdiction filter on the left to narrow results to Federal.

NOW COMES Gasser Chair Company, by counsel, pursuant to Federal Rule of Civil Procedure 37 and N.D. Ind. L.R. 37-1, and hereby request(s) this Court to compel discovery responses for certain Interrogatories and Request for Production of Documents propounded by Gasser Chair Company in this cause of action. In support of this Motion, Gasser Chair Company states the following:

1. That on April 31, 2014 Plaintiff mailed to Defendant Answers to Interrogatories. *Exhibits A attached hereto.*

2. That on or about May 20, 2015 Plaintiff mailed to Defendant her response to Defendant's Production Request. *Exhibit B attached hereto.*

3. Plaintiff has refused to sign a HIPPA Release that was provided with the original Discovery Requests from Gasser. *Exhibit C attached hereto.*

4. Federal Rule of Civil Procedure 26(1(a)(2)(B) requires expert opinions to be disclosed by a written report.

5. Federal Rule of Civil Procedure 37(a)(4) states that evasive or incomplete disclosures or answers are to be treated as a failure to disclose or answer.

6. Federal Rule of Civil Procedure 26(e) requires supplementation of disclosures in a timely manner if a disclosure is incomplete.

7. On September 10, 2015 John W. Potter sent to Steven Lang an email outlining 18 issues that Gasser Chair has with Plaintiff's discovery answers. *Exhibit D attached hereto.*

8. On September 14, 2015 Plaintiff attorney Steven Lang and Gasser Chair attorney John W. Potter conducted a conference in good-faith attempting to resolve the discovery issues without Court intervention. *Exhibit D.* Unfortunately, the parties were unable to resolve some of the discovery issues.

9. Interrogatory #3 states: "State the identity and location (full name, last known address and telephone number, both home and business) of each witness who will testify at trial, together with the subject of their testimony." *Exhibit A.* Plaintiff responds with two names and addresses, Debra Williams and Darleen Moore,

but does not provide the subject matter of their testimony. *Exhibit A*. In her initial disclosure, Plaintiff fails to disclose Darleen Moore, and for Dabra [s] Moore advises that she will "testify to the pain and suffering of her friend Gloria Jones (Plaintiff) after the accident and her condition before the accident." Defendant, Gasser, believes that it is entitled to know whether Darleen Moore will be called at trial as a witness, and if yes, what she will testify to. Further, Gasser believes that it is entitled to a more detailed description of the subject matter of Ms. William's testimony.

10. Interrogatory #4 states: "State the full name, address and telephone number of each person who witnessed the occurrence alleged in your Complaint." *Exhibit A*. Plaintiff's answer in part states, "a medical support team arrived on the scene." In discussing the case, Plaintiff disclosed that the medical support team was outside paramedics. Plaintiff refuses to provide any information regarding the paramedics, including: their bill; the run sheet; or the identity of the paramedics. Gasser believes that it is entitled to this information.

11. Interrogatory #5 states: "State the full name, address and telephone number of each person not named in 2 or 3 above who was present or claims to have been present at the scene immediately before, at the time or immediately after the occurrence." *Exhibit A*. Plaintiff responds, "This information is unavailable at this time however investigations are still in progress and we will up-date these interrogatories as information becomes available." Gasser Chair believes that it is entitled to know what investigations are currently ongoing, as there has been no supplementation since the responses were provided in April.

12. Interrogatory #7 states:

With regard to you injuries, did you receive any medical attention, diagnosis, or treatment? If so, for each medical provider, whether hospital, clinic, medical doctor, chiropractor, physical therapist, laboratory, or other, and whether attending or consulting, state:

  a. the name and address of each medical provider;

  b. the date or inclusive dates on which each of them rendered you service;

  c. the amounts to date of their respective bills for services; and

  d. from which of them do you have reports?

Exhibit A. Plaintiff responded: "Northwestern Memorial Hospital, Advocate Trinity Hospital- May 1, 2014; Takashi Nishida, MD-May 6, 2014 (medical bills so far are about $20,000. These interrogatories are on-going and will be updated as more information becomes available." Gasser Chair believes that it is entitled to have the entire interrogatory answered, including subparts.

13. Interrogatory #8 states:

As a result of your personal injuries, were you unable to work? If so, state:

  a. the name and address of your employer, if any, at the time of the occurrence;

  b. the date or inclusive dates on which you were unable to work;

  c. the amount of wage or income loss claimed by you; and

  d. the name and address of your present employer, if any.

Exhibit A. Plaintiff responds, "Career Educational Corporation, 231 Martingale Rd Schamburg Illinois 60173; lost wages from April, 2014 to October 2014; presently unemployed." Gasser Chair believes that it is entitled to the specific dates that Plaintiff was unable to work, as well as the amount of wages or income loss being claimed.

14. Interrogatory #10 states:

During the ten years immediately prior to the date of the occurrence had you been confined in a hospital, treated by a physician or x-rayed for any reason? If so, give the name and address of each such hospital, physician, technician or clinic, the approximate date of the such confinement or service and state, in general, the reason for such confinement or service.

Exhibit A. Plaintiff responds, "At this time there is no information on any hospital confinement or treatment for any reason. However, discovery is ongoing and if any information of such confinement arise these interrogatories will be up-dated immediately." In the discovery conference call, Mr. Lang explained that the answer means that Plaintiff is unaware of any treatment, via a hospital or any other medical provider, during the last ten years. Gasser believes that it is entitled to a more clear answer under oath from Plaintiff, as one could interpret the current answer to mean that Plaintiff is unaware of any hospitalizations only. Further, Gasser Chair believes that it is entitled to an explanation as to what investigation is ongoing. A simple call to Plaintiff's health care provider possibly to answer this question more definitively.

15. Interrogatory #11 states:

Had you suffered any personal injury for which you received medical attention prior to the date of said occurrence? If so, state when, where and in general how you were so injured and describe in general the injuries suffered, and state the name and address of each hospital, physician, technician, or clinic providing treatment, and the approximate dates of treatment.

Exhibit A. Plaintiff answers, "At this time there is no information on any other injuries. However, this discovery is ongoing and if any information of such injury arise these interrogatories will be up-dated immediately." Gasser Chair believes that it is entitled to know the details of the ongoing discovery.

16. Interrogatory #12 states:

Have you suffered either any personal injury or any serious illness, since the date of said occurrence? If so, for any injury, state when, where and in general how you were injured and describe in general the injuries suffered; and, for any illness, state when you were ill and describe in general the illness. For each injury or illness, state the name and address of each hospital, physician, technician, or clinic providing treatment, and the approximate dates of treatment.

Exhibit A. Plaintiff responds, "At this time there is no information on any other injuries. However, this discovery is ongoing and if any information of such injury arise these interrogatories will be up-dated immediately." Gasser Chair believes that it is entitled to know the details of the ongoing discovery.

17. Interrogatory #13 states:

Do you have any continuing complaints, disabilities, or any other problems of any kind resulting from the occurrence? If so, state the nature of the complaint, disability or problem, its frequency, and state what medical attention or treatment you are receiving or taking for it.

Exhibit A. Plaintiff responds, "At this time there is no information on any other injuries. However, this discovery is ongoing and if any information of such injury arise these interrogatories will be up-dated immediately." Gasser Chair believes that it is entitled to an answer that is responsive to the question.

18. Interrogatory #14 states:

Have you ever filed any other lawsuit, application for adjustment of workers' compensation claim, or made any type of claim for your own personal injuries? If so, for each suit or workers' compensation case, state the court or forum which filed, the year filed and the title and docket number of said case, and the status or date of resolution. For each claim, state the type of claim, when the claim was made, state who the claim was made against, and the resolution of the claim.

Exhibit A. Plaintiff answers, "There is no information on any such claim at this time. However, this discovery is ongoing and if any information of such information arise these interrogatories will be up-dated immediately." Gasser Chair believes that it is entitled to know the details of the ongoing discovery.

19. Interrogatory #15 states:

Do you have statements from any witnesses, parties, or employees of parties? If so, for each such statement, identify the name and address of each such person giving the statement, identify by name and address to whom the statement was given, the date of the statement, state whether such statement was written or oral, whether it was recorded or transcribed, and if so, state who has custody of the statement.

Exhibit A. Plaintiff answers, "The Plaintiff was given oral statements from Horseshoe Casino after she reported the incident. Brady Schuler informed the Plaintiff that he believed that "Gasser Chair Company" was liable because of the defect in their design." Gasser Chair believes that it is entitled to know who Brady Schuler is. Is he an employee of the Casino?

20. Interrogatory #16 states: "Were any photographs taken of the scene of the occurrence, or persons, vehicles, products, or instrumentalities involved? If so, state the date or dates on which such photographs were taken, the subjects thereof and who now has custody of them." *Exhibit A.* Plaintiff responds, "The Plaintiff is

still investigating and has no information of photographs as on this time. However, if any become available the plaintiff will up-date these interrogatories immediately." Gasser Chair believes that it is entitled to know the specifics of Plaintiff's ongoing investigation.

21. Interrogatory #17 states: "List the names and addresses of all other persons (other than yourself and persons heretofore listed or specifically excluded) who have knowledge of the facts of the occurrence or of the injuries and damages following therefrom." *Exhibit A*. Plaintiff responds, "At this time the Plaintiff has no other information then that listed in these interrogatories. However, if any become available the plaintiff will up-date these interrogatories immediately." Gasser Chair believes that it is entitled to an answer to this interrogatory. The question specifically excludes people previously listed, so presumably the answer is "none." By globally directing Defendant to all answers provided, Plaintiff renders the answer vague and not susceptible to effective impeachment.

22. Interrogatory #19 states, "State what objects, if any, the Plaintiff was carrying at the time of the occurrence." *Exhibit A*. Plaintiff answers, "Currently it is believed that the Plaintiff was not carrying any object, However, if any become available the plaintiff will up-date these interrogatories immediately." Gasser Chair believes that it is entitled to a straight forward answer to this straight forward question.

23. Interrogatory #24 states:

Have you been insured under a health insurance policy from the time of the accident described in your complaint to present? If your answer is yes, please state: 1) the name of the primary named insured under the policy; 2) the name of the carrier; 3) the address of the carrier; 4) the policy number; and 5) the dates of coverage.

Exhibit A. Plaintiff answers, "Gloria Jones (Plaintiff) is the primary insured, the carrier is Blue Cross, unknown address at this time. However, if any become available the plaintiff will up-date these interrogatories immediately." Gasser Chair believes that it is entitled to the carrier's full name, policy number and address.

24. Interrogatory #26 states:

As to non-retained expert witnesses, please provide: the identity and address of each witness who will testify at trial; state the subjects on which the expert witness will testify at trial; and state the opinions you expect to elicit at trial from each independent expert witness identified in 2(a) above:

Exhibit A. Plaintiff responds:

At this time we are having the chair inspected by two experts (hydraulic Component Services at 8010 New Jersey Ave, Gary Indiana, and Hydraulic Solutions at 5440 West Ridge Road, Gary Indiana. It is expected that both will testify that the hydraulic chair had no safety lock and lacked the appropriate warning tags indicating a date for expiration of its use).

In Plaintiff's Rule 26 Disclose Plaintiff discloses a different expert, Primet Fluidpower located at 7917 New Jersey Ave, Hammond IN 46323. *Exhibit E*. In Plaintiff's supplemental Rule 26 disclosure Plaintiff discloses expert Steven J Roensch, 634 Lake Shore Road, Grafton Wisconsin, as an expert witness. *Exhibit F*. Gasser Chair is left with a muddled and confused picture regarding non-retained and retained experts and believes that it is entitled to clarification and more detailed disclosures from the experts, including C.V.s, reports, and the files from each expert except Mr. Roensch (already provided).

25. Interrogatory #27 states:

As to retained expert witnesses, please provide: the identity and address of each retained expert witness who will testify at trial; state whether such witness is the party, the party's current employee, or the party's retained expert; state the subject matter on which the witness is expected to testify at trial; state the conclusions and opinions of the witness and the bases therefor that will be testified on at trial; state the qualifications of the witness, including a curriculum vitae and/or resume, if any; and provide any reports of the witness regarding this case.

Exhibit A. Plaintiff answers:

C. Samuel martin, PhD, 59 Barque Circle, South Dennis, MA 02660. The witness is not the party nor does he work for the party. The witness is expected to testify on the functions of the hydraulics and the defect of the design. The witness has a PhD in Hydraulics from Georgia Institute of Technology.

Gasser Chair believes that this retained expert disclosure is wholly insufficient and improper. Gasser believes that it is entitled to the entire expert file, a C.V. and a report.

26. Gasser Chair issued a HIPPA Release to Plaintiff to allow it to obtain Plaintiff's medical records and bills for the time period before and after her accident. *Exhibit C*. Plaintiff refuses to sign the HIPPA Release. Gasser Chair believes that Plaintiff has placed both her pre-accident and post accident medical treatment at issue, and therefore Gasser Chair believes that it is entitled to a signed HIPPA Release for all medical treatment before and after her accident.

27. Defendant, Gasser Chair, is also seeking five years of tax returns from before the accident, and two years of W-2 and employment records from before and after the accident. This request was discussed with Steven Lang and is made pursuant to Production Requests 5 and 15. *Exhibit B*.

WHEREFORE, Gasser Chair Company, by counsel, hereby requests this Court to order Plaintiff to comply with the discovery requests by fully answering Interrogatories and responding to Request for Production of Documents within fourteen (14) days of the date of this Order, as well as sign HIPPA Releases for all medical providers and produce tax returns. More specifically, and in accordance with the above outlined issues, Gasser Chair Company asks that Plaintiff be ordered to:

1) Identify all witnesses who she intends to call at trial and the subject matter of their testimony;

2) The identity, medical records and bills from the paramedics that treated Plaintiff at the casino;

3) The specifics of the continuing investigations and discovery regarding interrogatories 5, 10, 11, 12, 14, and 16.

4) A complete answer to interrogatory 7;

5) The amount of lost wages being claimed and the dates on which Plaintiff could not work;

6) A clear and unambiguous answer to interrogatory 10;

7) An answer to interrogatory 13;

8) Information as to who Brady Schuler is;

9) An answer to interrogatory 17;

10) A proper answer to interrogatory 19;

11) A complete answer to interrogatory 24 including the carrier's full name, policy number and address;

12) Complete and accurate answers to interrogatories 26 and 27, stating which experts are going to be called at trial, as well as the entire expert files, their C.V., their prior testimony lists, all correspondence between the experts and Plaintiff attorney and the expert reports;

13) Plaintiff tax returns for five years prior to the accident and two years after the accident including W-2's.

14) Signed HIPPA Releases for all medical providers before and after the accident.

Respectfully submitted,

By: */s/ John W. Potter*

John W. Potter

Motion for Protective Order

2016 WL 3449411 (S.D.Ind.)

Westlaw Query>>

To find more Motion for Protective Order filings on Westlaw: access Indiana Trial Court Documents (from the Home page, click Trial Court Documents, then Indiana), click the Advanced Search link, select Motion for Protective Order, and click Search. Use the Jurisdiction filter on the left to narrow results to Federal.

United States District Court, S.D. Indiana.

Indianapolis Division

In re: COOK MEDICAL, INC. IVC FILTERS MARKETING, SALES PRACTICES AND PRODUCTS LIABILITY LITIGATION.

No. 1:14-ML-02570-RLY-TAB.

April 12, 2016.

MDL No. 2570

Cook's Motion for Protective Order and Brief

Douglas B. King, Esq., James M. Boyers, Esq., Christopher D. Lee, Esq., John C. Babione, Esq., Sandra L. Davis, Esq., Kip S. M. Mcdonald, Esq., doug.king@woodenmclaughlin.com, jim.boyers@woodenmclaughlin.com, chris.lee@woodenmclaughlin.com, kip.mcdonald@woodenmclaughlin.com, sandy.jansen@woodenmclaughlin.com, Wooden McLaughlin LLP, One Indiana Square, Suite 1800, Indianapolis, in 46204-4208, Tel: (317) 639-6151, Fax: (317) 639-6444, Counsel for Cook Defendants.

Pursuant to Fed.R.Civ.Pro. 26(c)(1)(A), Cook respectfully moves for a protective order barring discovery concerning Cook's alleged failure to report adverse events associated with its IVC Filters to the United States Food and Drug Administration ("FDA"), in accordance with 21 CFR Part 803 - Medical Device Reporting.

Whether Cook has complied with the numerous FDA regulations that require manufacturers to submit Medical Device Reports ("MDRs") to FDA is not relevant to the central liability question of whether Cook's IVC Filters were defective when those medical devices left Cook's hands.

Moreover, whether Cook complied with the more than fifty (50) separate FDA regulations in 21 CFR Part 803[1] is an issue for FDA, not for this Court, as "[t]he [Federal Food, Drug and Cosmetics Act ("FDCA")] leaves no doubt that it is the Federal Government rather than private litigants who are authorized to file suit for non-compliance with medical device provisions: 'All such proceedings for the enforcement, or to restrain violations, of this chapter shall be and in the name of the United States.' 21 U.S.C. § 337(a). *Buckman Co. v. Plaintiffs Legal Comm.*, 531 U.S. 341, 349, n.l (2001). Consequently, as noted by the Court in *In re Incretin Mimetics Prods. Liab. Litig*, 2014 U.S. Dist. LEXIS 142227, at *1195 (S.D. Cal.), [t]he judiciary and its litigants are neither the appropriate people nor the appropriate forum for evaluations of compliance with FDA reporting requirements."

On March 11, 2016, Plaintiffs served on Cook a Notice of Taking Rule 30(b)(6) Deposition (the "Notice"), a copy is Exhibit "C." The eight deposition subjects in the Notice show that plaintiffs seek to inquire as to Cook's submissions of MDRs to FDA, as they specifically reference "retroactive[] reporting," "underreport[ing]," and Cook's alleged failure to submit MDRs to FDA. Notice, pp. 7-8. While the Notice prompted this Motion, the Motion goes beyond that Notice to address discovery as to Cook's compliance with 21 CFR Part 803 generally.

---

1. Copies of the FDA regulations in 21 CFR Part 803 are Exhibit "A." A copy of the 47-page Draft FDA Guidance Document on Medical Device Reporting by Manufacturers is Exhibit "B."

On point is In re Incretin Mimetics Prods. Liab. Litig., *supra*; a copy is Exhibit D. There, as here, "Plaintiffs' motion to compel seeks production of the 'underlying documents for each pre- and post-marketing adverse event known to each defendant; and the adverse event databases maintained by each defendant.'" Id., at *186.

Here, as in *In re Incretin Mimetics*, Cook denies any misreporting or underreporting to FDA. But, here, as there, "[p]laintiffs frequently invoke allegations of misreporting and underreporting as a justification for additional discovery. . ." *Id.*, at * 188.

Based upon the Supreme Court's policy in *Buckman* as quoted above, the *Incretin Mimetics* Court denied the plaintiffs' request to discover evidence of the defendant's reporting of postmarketing adverse events, reasoning as follows: "[t]o allow discovery, and by extension judicial consideration, of compliance with federal reporting requirements would erode the FDA's role in pharmaceutical regulation and neglect the policy underlying *Buckman.*" *Id.*, at *197-198. That reasoning plainly applies to these medical device cases no less than to the drug case that is *Incretin Mimetics*.

Further support for Cook's Motion can be found in *In re Trasylol Prods. Liab. Litig.*, 763 F. Supp. 2d 1312 (S.D. Fla. 2010); a copy is Exhibit "E." In *Trasylol*, the Court granted the Bayer defendants' motion *in limine* to preclude the plaintiffs from arguing or proffering evidence that the defendant failed to properly report adverse events to FDA, *id.*, at 1316, reasoning as follows, at 1317:

> [T]he only possible reason for plaintiffs to introduce such evidence would be to argue to the jury that FDA would have reached a different decision regarding warnings or labeling for [the drug] if [the defendant] had provided more timely or "better" information. But what FDA may have done, if anything, with different data and how that information may have ultimately affected [the drug's] regulatory status, if at all, is precisely the type of speculation *Buckman* and Rule 403 prohibit.

The *Trasyolol* Court held that, "evidence or testimony that the defendant failed to adequately or timely provide information to FDA [is] relevant to a fraud-on-the-FDA claim that is preempted by *Buckman.*" *Id.*, at 1329-30, rejecting the plaintiffs' arguments that (1) *Buckman* applies to preclusion of a claim, not evidence; (2) evidence of violations of FDA reporting requirements is evidence of fraudulent concealment and negligence; and (3) that, as plaintiffs argue here, evidence of Bayer's failure to report adverse events to FDA would "'show that Bayer acted negligently in failing to properly disclose information to the FDA, **the medical and scientific communities**, and to the public.'" *Id.*, at 1317 (emphasis added). *See also Bouchard v. Am. Home Prods. Corp.*, 213 F. Supp. 2d 802, 811-12 (N.D. Ohio 2002); *Swank v. Zimmer*, 2004 U.S. Dist. LEXIS 30376, at *5-6 (D. Wyo.); *In re Bextra and Celebrex Mktg., Sales Practices and Prod. Liab. Litig*, No. MDL 05-01699 CRB (N.D. Cal. 2008); *Miller v. DePuy Spine, Inc.*, 638 F. Supp. 2d 1226 (D. Nev. 2009).

The *Trasyolol* court thus rejected the plaintiffs' argument here that what Cook tells FDA is relevant to what it tells doctors. Cook does not seek to prevent discovery by Plaintiffs intended to show that Cook knew of risks associated with its IVC Filters that it failed to disclose to the physicians who implant those filters. Nor does Cook seek to preclude Plaintiffs' discovery of Cook's own post-market surveillance system, i.e., Cook's monitoring and trending of adverse events that are **reported to Cook** for purposes of Cook's assuring the quality of its IVC Filters. Cook seeks only to bar discovery of what it does or does not tell FDA.

Plaintiffs assert that Cook's reporting to FDA is discoverable because it affects FDA's MAUDE database. But, that database is **FDA's**, not Cook's. Per the Honorable Joseph R. Goodwin, District Judge, the defendant's "communication, or alleged lack thereof, with the FDA through the MAUDE database has 'no bearing on whether [the defendant] provided adequate warnings or whether its products were defective . . ..'" *Winebarger v. Boston Sci. Corp.*, 2015 U.S. Dist. LEXIS 53892, at *65-66 (S.D. W. Va.) (citation omitted); a copy is Exhibit "F."

> The MAUDE system is a "passive surveillance system" that does not account for the "potential submission of incomplete, inaccurate, untimely, unverified, or biased data. . . ." FDA warns users that the [MAUDE] data alone "cannot be interpreted or used in isolation to reach conclusions about the existence, severity, or frequency of problems associated with devices."

Id., at *66-67 (citations omitted, but quoting FDA).

Plaintiffs have cited Case Management Order No. 10 in *In Re Bard IVC Products Liability Litigation*, USDC, D. Ariz., No. MDL 15-02641-PHX-DGC; a copy is Exhibit "G." What makes the *Bard* Order different is that Bard had received an "FDA warning letter" *(see* p. 3 of the Order), whereas Cook has not. There is a significant difference between discovery of evidence concerning FDA regulation violations for which FDA has taken action, in Bard's case by issuing a warning letter, and alleged FDA regulation violations for which FDA has not taken action, as here, as the former does not require jury speculation while the latter does. That distinction is important, as the *Trasylol* Court barred Plaintiffs from presenting evidence concerning Bayer's alleged FDA **reporting** violations, but allowed Bayer's evidence that it received FDA's approval to market Trasylol, as "compliance with regulatory requirements provides some evidence that the defendant acted with due care, . . . **requires no speculation** and . . . presents no tension with *Buckman* because the jury is not asked to second-guess the FDA's actual decisions, speculate about its actions or interfere with its judgment." *Trasylol, 163* F. Supp. 2d at 1319 (emphasis added). Moreover, as noted above, Cook does not deny that its "[a]ctual failure rates" are fair game for discovery, as are its "representations made by [it] concerning future rates" **to physicians**, which is what the Arizona District Court found discoverable in its *Bard* Order, p. 3. What is not is what fair game are the representations Cook made to FDA in its MDRs or lack thereof. *See In re Incretin Mimetics;* In re Trasylol, Wineberger v. Boston Scientific.

Based on the foregoing, discovery of Cook's reporting to FDA is not proportional to the needs of the case, considering the importance of the discovery in resolving central liability in this case of whether Cook's IYC filters are somehow defective, and the burden and expense of the proposed discovery outweighs its likely benefit. *See* Fed.R.Civ.Pro. 26(b)(1). Allowing discovery as to whether Cook has complied with 56 arcane FDA regulations explained by FDA in a 47-page Guidance would allow the sideshow to consume the circus. Cook is therefore entitled to a Protective Order under Fed.R.Civ.Pro. 26(c)(1)(A).

s/Douglas B. King

Douglas B. King, Esq.

James M. Boyers, Esq.

Christopher D. Lee, Esq.

John C. Babione, Esq.

Sandra L. Davis, Esq.

Kip S. M. McDonald, Esq.

Doug.King@WoodenMcLaughlin.com

Jim.Boyers@WoodenMcLaughlin.com

Chris.Lee@WoodenMcLaughlin.com

Kip.McDonald@WoodenMcLaughlin.com

Sandy.Jansen@WoodenMcLaughlin.com

Counsel for Cook Defendants

WOODEN MCLAUGHLIN LLP

One Indiana Square, Suite 1800

Indianapolis, IN 46204-4208

Tel: (317) 639-6151

Fax: (317) 639-6444

Motion for Preliminary Injunction

2016 WL 5407549 (S.D.Ind.)

United States District Court, S.D. Indiana.

Indianapolis Division

TRUSTEES OF INDIANA UNIVERSITY, Fred H. Cate, and its research faculty, Dr. Bruce Lamb, and Dr. Debomoy Lahiri, Plaintiffs,

v.

PROSECUTOR OF MARION COUNTY INDIANA, in his Official Capacity, Defendant.

No. 1:16-cv-763-TWP-DML.

May 20, 2016.

Motion for Preliminary Injunction

Faegre Baker Daniels LLP, A. Scott Chinn, #17903-49, Anne K. Ricchiuto, #25760-49, Juliana Yanez, #32201-53, Faegre Baker & Daniels LLP, 300 N. Meridian Street, Suite 2700, Indianapolis, in 46204-1750, Tel: (317) 237-0300, Fax: (317) 237-1000, scott.chinn@faegrebd.com, anne.ricchiuto@faegrebd.com, juliana.yanez@faegrebd.com, for plaintiffs Trustees of Indiana University, Fred H. Cate and its research faculty, Dr. Bruce Lamb, and Dr. Debomoy Lahiri.

The Board of Trustees of Indiana University ("IU"), Fred H. Cate, and research faculty Dr. Bruce Lamb and Dr. Debomoy Lahiri (collectively, "IU Plaintiffs"), by counsel, move this Court pursuant to Rule 65 of the Federal Rules of Civil Procedure for a preliminary injunction in this cause enjoining the defendants from enforcing the portion of House Enrolled Act No. 1337 that is challenged in their complaint in this cause. In support of this motion they state:

1. As noted in their Complaint for Declaratory and Injunctive Relief / Notice of Challenge to Constitutionality of Indiana Statute, IU Plaintiffs are challenging as unconstitutional Indiana Code section 35-46-5-1.5, set to take effect on July 1, 2016.

2. IU Plaintiffs are likely to prevail in their legal challenge.

3. Absent a preliminary injunction, IU Plaintiffs will suffer irreparable injury for which there is no adequate remedy at law.

4. The harm caused to the IU Plaintiffs, as well as to public at large, outweighs any harm that an injunction would cause the defendant.

5. The public interest would be served by the grant of a preliminary injunction.

6. No security is necessary because the preliminary injunction would not impose costs or damages on the defendant. Additionally, as a government entity, IU Plaintiffs are presumed to be excused from security requirements.

7. IU Plaintiffs will simultaneously submit their memorandum of law in support of this motion.

8. This motion and accompanying memorandum are being tendered with the Court's permission while the IU Plaintiffs' motion to intervene is pending. Dkts. 37, 45.

9. If permitted to intervene in this case, IU Plaintiffs will be prepared to participate in the preliminary injunction hearing on June 14, 2016.

WHEREFORE, IU Plaintiffs request that this Court enter a preliminary injunction, without bond, enjoining the defendant and his agents from enforcing Indiana Code § 35-46-5-1.5 (eff. July 1, 2016), until this Court can hold a trial or other proceeding on the merits of IU Plaintiffs' claims. IU Plaintiffs further request that this Court grant such other and further relief as the Court may deem equitable and just.

Respectfully submitted,

FAEGRE BAKER DANIELS LLP

s/ Anne K. Ricchiuto

A. Scott Chinn, #17903-49

Anne K. Ricchiuto, #25760-49

Juliana Yanez, #32201-53

FAEGRE BAKER & DANIELS LLP

300 N. Meridian Street, Suite 2700

Indianapolis, IN 46204-1750

Tel: (317) 237-0300

Fax: (317) 237-1000

scott.chinn@faegrebd.com

anne.ricchiuto@faegrebd.com

juliana.yanez@faegrebd.com

Attorneys for Plaintiffs Trustees of Indiana University, Fred H. Cate and its research faculty, Dr. Bruce Lamb, and Dr. Debomoy Lahiri

Motion to Dismiss for Lack of Subject Matter Jurisdiction

2016 WL 3876820 (N.D.Ind.)

Westlaw Query>>

To find more Motion to Dismiss for Lack of Subject Matter Jurisdiction filings on Westlaw: access Indiana Trial Court Documents (from the Home page, click Trial Court Documents, then Indiana), click the Advanced Search link, select Motion to Dismiss for Lack of Jurisdiction, and click Search. Use the Jurisdiction filter on the left to narrow results to Federal.

United States District Court, N.D. Indiana.

Joseph ULLRICH, Plaintiff,

v.

ARCELORMITTAL USA LLC and National Industrial Maintenance, Inc., Defendants.

No. 2:15-cv-357-TLS-PRC.

February 29, 2016.

National Industrial Maintenance, Inc.'s FRCP 12(B)(6) Motion to Dismiss/Remand for Lack of Subject Matter Jurisdiction

Charles C. Hoppe, Jr., Knight, Hoppe, Kurnik & Knight, Ltd., Attorneys for Click here and enter client's name, 833 West Lincoln Highway, Suite 340E, Schererville, IN 46375-1648, 219/322-0830; Fax: 219/322-0834, Email: Choppe@khkkIaw.com, for defendant National Industrial Maintenance, Inc.

COMES NOW, the Defendant, National Industrial Maintenance, Inc., by one of its attorneys, CHARLES C. HOPPE, JR. (#11869-45), of KNIGHT, HOPPE, KURNIK & KNIGHT, LTD., and pursuant to FRCP12(b)(6) moves this Honorable Court to dismiss or remand this case back to the State Court for lack of subject matter jurisdiction of the Federal Court to proceed with this cause of action. In support hereof, this Defendant states:

1 This cause of action was removed from the Lake County, Indiana Circuit Court, Cause No.: 45C01-1508-CT-000127 to the United States District Court Northern District of Indiana, Hammond, pursuant to Notice of Removal filed by the Defendant, Arcelormittal USA LLC dated September 18, 2015 (docket no. 1) based on diversity of citizenship jurisdiction pursuant to 28 USCA §§ 1332, 1441 and 1446.

2 Pursuant to this Court's Order (docket no. 15) of January 11, 2016, Plaintiff was granted leave to file his Amended Complaint adding National Industrial Maintenance, Inc. as a Party Defendant. National Industrial Maintenance, Inc. was served on February 9, 2016.

3 On February 15, 2016, National Industrial Maintenance, Inc. filed its Appearances (docket no. 18, 19), Jury Demand (docket no. 21), Notice of Automatic Extension of Time to answer up to March 22, 2016 (docket no. 22), and FRCP7.1 Non-Governmental Corporate Disclosure Statement (docket no. 23).

4 Attached hereto and incorporated herein by reference is the sworn Affidavit of William Dennison (Ex. A), President of National Industrial Maintenance, Inc., attesting to the facts that National Industrial Maintenance, Inc. is a corporation incorporated in the State of Indiana and its principal place of business is located at 4530 Baring Avenue, East Chicago, Indiana 46312.

5 Pursuant to 28 USCA § 1332(c)(1), a corporation shall be deemed to be a citizen of every State and foreign states by which it has been incorporated and of the State or foreign states where it has its principal place of business.

6 Pursuant to 28 USCA § 1447(e), if after removal the Plaintiff seeks to join additional defendants where joinder would destroy subject matter jurisdiction, the Court may deny joinder, or permit joinder and remand the action to the State Court.

7 Since the naming of National Industrial Maintenance, Inc., a corporation incorporated in the State of Indiana and

whose principal place of business is in East Chicago, Indiana, and as Plaintiff is a citizen of the State of Indiana, diversity of citizenship jurisdiction has been destroyed and the U.S. District Court no longer has subject matter jurisdiction to hear this cause of action.

WHEREFORE, the Defendant, National Industrial Maintenance, Inc. prays this Honorable Court dismiss this case of action and remand the same back to the Lake County Circuit Court, Lake County, Indiana for further proceedings in the Court from whence this cause of action arose.

Respectfully Submitted,

/s/ Charles C. Hoppe, Jr.

Charles C. Hoppe, Jr. of KNIGHT, HOPPE, KURNIK & KNIGHT, LTD.

Attorney for Defendant National Industrial Maintenance, Inc.

KNIGHT, HOPPE, KURNIK & KNIGHT, LTD.

Attorneys for Click here and enter client's name

833 West Lincoln Highway, Suite 340E

Schererville, IN 46375-1648

219/322-0830; FAX: 219/322-0834

EMAIL: Choppe@khkklaw.com

Motion to Dismiss for Lack of Personal Jurisdiction

2014 WL 8727023 (S.D.Ind.)

Westlaw Query>>

To find more Motion to Dismiss for Lack of Personal Jurisdiction filings on Westlaw: access Indiana Trial Court Documents (from the Home page, click Trial Court Documents, then Indiana), click the Advanced Search link, select Motion to Dismiss for Lack of Jurisdiction, and click Search. Use the Jurisdiction filter on the left to narrow results to Federal.

United States District Court, S.D. Indiana.

Indianapolis Division

Larry G. PHILPOT, Plaintiff,

v.

BAKE ME A WISH, LLC, Defendant.

No. 1:14-cv-1356-SEB-DML.

November 6, 2014.

Defendant's Brief in Support of Motion to Dismiss for Lack of Personal Jurisdiction and for Improper Venue

Matthew Joseph Clark (31263-49), Meitus Gelbert Rose LLP, 47 S. Meridian St., Suite 400, Indianapolis, IN 46204, Phone (317) 464-5307, Fax (317) 464-5111, mclark@mgrfirm.com; Anthony J. Rose, Esq. (15545-53), Meitus Gelbert Rose LLP, 47 S. Meridian St., Suite 400, Indianapolis, IN 46204, Phone (317) 464-5304, Fax (317) 464-5111, arose@mgrfirm.com, for defendant Bake Me A Wish, LLC.

Defendant Bake Me A Wish, LLC ("BMAW") respectfully submits this brief in support of its motion to dismiss Plaintiff Larry G. Philpot's ("Philpot") Complaint for Copyright Infringement and Unfair Competition and Related Claims ("Complaint"), for lack of personal jurisdiction pursuant to Fed. R. Civ. P. 12(b)(2) and for improper venue pursuant to Fed. R. Civ. P. 12(b)(3).

INTRODUCTION AND ALLEGED FACTS

Taking for present purposes the allegations of the Complaint as true, Philpot is a photographer who photographs live musical performances across the United States. (Complaint, ¶ 4). BMAW is an active New York Limited Liability Company, in good standing, with its principal place of business in New York. (Affidavit of Joseph Dornoff, ("Dornoff Affidavit"), ¶ 2). Plaintiff's Complaint alleges a violation of his rights under § 106 of the Copyright Act of 1976, a violation under Section 43 of the Lanham Act (15 U.S.C. § 1125(a)), and a violation of the Digital Millennium Copyright Act as a result of the Defendant's alleged use on its Facebook page of Plaintiff's photograph of popular musician Willie Nelson (Complaint, ¶¶ 1, 28-32, 35, 38-39). Philpot alleges that this Court has personal jurisdiction over BMAW and that venue is proper in this District (Complaint, ¶¶ 2-3). As shown below, however, this Court does not have personal jurisdiction over BMAW, and therefore, venue in this District is improper. Accordingly, the Court should dismiss this case under Fed. R. Civ. P. 12(b)(2)-(3).

STATEMENT OF FACTS

1. BMAW is an active New York Limited Liability Company, in good standing with New York, with its principal place of business at 45 West 45th Street, 7th Floor, New York, NY 10036. (Dornoff Affidavit, ¶ 2).

2. BMAW registered with the New York Secretary of State on August 9, 2005. (Dornoff Affidavit, ¶ 3).

3. BMAW is not registered to do business in Indiana, does not have any offices, employees, shareholders, agents,

or operations in Indiana, has no phone or fax listings in Indiana, has no bank accounts in Indiana, does not own, lease, or control any property or assets in Indiana, and has no authorized dealers or distributors in Indiana. BMAW personnel have never traveled to Indiana in connection with BMAW business. BMAW has never paid any taxes in Indiana. (Dornoff Affidavit, ¶ 4).

4. BMAW operates a website (*www.bakemeawish.com*) and business from New York which ships birthday cakes and gourmet food gifts, including cookies and brownies, upon customers' request. The website generates sales nationally, but primarily in the New York and East Coast region. All sales are derived from the Internet, sent via email, or phoned in via the company's toll free telephone number. (Dornoff Affidavit, ¶ 5).

5. Of these sales, those relating to Indiana have been insubstantial. In the past five years, (a) gifts delivered to Indiana addresses have amounted to no more than 0.86% of total delivered gifts, (b) less than 1.3% of the company's unique system customers list an Indiana residence, and (c) revenue from customers with an Indiana billing address represented no more than 0.66% of total revenue. (Dornoff Affidavit, ¶ 6).

6. BMAW does not advertise in Indiana directly or specifically target Indiana customers in its advertising. Like most e-commerce retailers, BMAW purchases the services of online advertising networks ("Ad Networks"), which integrate BMAW advertisements into third party websites nationwide. The Ad Networks send and store data ("Cookies") onto the computers of visitors to the BMAW website via a script. The Ad Networks then use the Cookies to display BMAW advertisements to prior BMAW website visitors as they visit various other websites. BMAW has no control over the location of BMAW advertisements integrated by the Ad Networks into third party websites. (Dornoff Affidavit, ¶ 7).

ARGUMENT

I. *LEGAL STANDARDS*

Fed. R. Civ. P. 12(b)(2) requires dismissal of suit where personal jurisdiction is lacking. After a defendant moves to dismiss a claim under Rule 12(b)(2), "the plaintiff bears the burden of demonstrating the existence of jurisdiction." *Purdue Research Found. v. Sanofi--Synthelabo, S.A.*, 338 F.3d 773, 782 (7th Cir. 2003). The plaintiff must establish a prima facie case of personal jurisdiction if the court makes its determination solely on the submission of written materials. *GCIU--Employer Ret. Fund v. Goldfarb Corp.*, 565 F.3d 1018, 1023 (7th Cir. 2009). If the defendant submits affidavits or other evidence in opposition to the implementation of jurisdiction, "the plaintiff must go beyond the pleadings and submit affirmative evidence supporting the exercise of jurisdiction." *Purdue*, 338 F.3d at 783.

A federal district court must satisfy a two-step inquiry in order to exercise personal jurisdiction over a non-resident defendant. *Wine and Canvas Dev., LLC v. Weisser*, 886 F. Supp. 2d 930, 938 (S.D. Ind. 2012). The Court's exercise of jurisdiction must comport both with the state's long-arm statute and the requirements of the federal Due Process Clause. *Purdue*, 338 F.3d at 779. Because Indiana's long-arm statute "expand[s] personal jurisdiction to the full extent permitted by the Due Process Clause," due process principles govern the inquiry. *Walters v. Dollar Gen. Corp.*, No. 1:09-cv-1508-SEB-WGH, 2011 WL 759555, at *2 (S.D. Ind. Feb. 24, 2011) (quoting *LinkAmerica Corp. v. Cox*, 857 N.E.2d 961, 966 (Ind. 2006)).

The Due Process Clause of the Fourteenth Amendment requires that a defendant "have certain minimum contacts with [the forum state] such that the maintenance of the suit does not offend traditional notions of fair play and substantial justice." *Int'l Shoe Co. v. Washington*, 326 U.S. 310, 316 (1945). In other words, the defendant's contacts with the forum state must be of a nature that the defendant "should reasonably anticipate being haled into court there." *Burger King Corp. v. Rudzewicz*, 471 U.S. 462, 474 (1985).

Minimum contacts with a forum state may be established by either general jurisdiction or specific jurisdiction. *Int'l Med. Grp., Inc. v. Am. Arbitration Ass'n, Inc.*, 312 F.3d 833, 846 (7th Cir. 2002) (citing *Helicopteros Nacionales de Colombia, S.A. v. Hall*, 466 U.S. 408, 414-15 (1984)). General jurisdiction exists where the contacts with the forum state are unrelated to the subject matter of the suit. *Hyatt Int'l Corp. v. Coco*, 302 F.3d 707, 713 (7th Cir. 2002). Specific jurisdiction, on the other hand, exists "for controversies that arise out of or are related to the defendant's forum contacts." *Id.*

II. *GENERAL JURISDICTION*

If a defendant's contacts with the forum state are "so continuous and systematic that the defendant could reasonably foresee being haled into court in that state for any matter," then the defendant is subject to general jurisdiction. *Int'l Med. Grp.*, 312 F.3d at 846. The defendant's contacts with the state must be so extensive "that it can be treated as present in the state for essentially all purposes." *uBID, Inc. v. GoDaddy Grp., Inc.*, 623 F.3d 421, 426 (7th Cir. 2010). As a result, general jurisdiction over a defendant is "a fairly high standard in practice." *Wilson v. Humphreys (Cayman) Ltd.*, 916 F.2d 1239, 1245 (7th Cir. 1990).

In determining whether a defendant's contacts satisfy the "continuous and systemic" standard, courts consider factors such as whether the defendant "owns any property, pays taxes, conduct[s] any business, or has any offices, agents, employees, or affiliated entities" in the forum state. *Walters*, 2011 WL 759555, at *4. Courts also consider the "volume of a defendant's sales in a forum state" as pertinent to "a court's general jurisdiction analysis." *Draper, Inc. v. Mechoshade Sys., Inc.*, No. 1:10--cv--01443--SEB--TAB, 2011 WL 1258140, at *2 (S.D. Ind. Mar. 31, 2011).

The mere operation of a publicly available website is insufficient, without more, to establish general jurisdiction. *Tamburo v. Dworkin*, 601 F.3d 693, 701 (7th Cir. 2010); *uBID*, 623 F.3d at 426; *Jackson v. The California Newspapers P'ship*, No. 05 C 3459, 2005 WL 2850116, at *2 (N.D.Ill. Oct. 27, 2005). In the Seventh Circuit, "even the operation of a 'highly interactive' website will not, alone, subject a defendant to general jurisdiction." *Collazo v. Enter. Holdings, Inc.*, 823 F. Supp. 2d 865, 869 (N.D. Ind. 2011) (citing *be2 LLC v. Ivanov*, 642 F.3d 555, 559 (7th Cir. 2011). *See also Illinois v. Hemi Grp. LLC*, 622 F.3d 754, 760 (7th Cir. 2010) ("Courts should be careful in resolving questions about personal jurisdiction involving online contacts to ensure that a defendant is not haled into court simply because the defendant owns or operates a website that is accessible in the forum state, even if that site is 'interactive.' "). Rather, the jurisdiction test for Internet-based cases is whether the defendant, through its website, has in some way targeted the forum's market. *Collazo*, 823 F. Supp. 2d at 869 (N.D. Ind. 2011).

BMAW's extremely limited business contacts with Indiana through its New York-based website are neither continuous nor systemic such that it could foresee being haled into an Indiana court for any matter. In fact, other than an insignificant amount of sales into Indiana, BMAW has virtually no contact with this state. BMAW is a New York Limited Liability Company with its principal place of business in New York, and it has never been registered to do business in Indiana. (Facts, ¶¶ 1-3). BMAW does not have any offices, employees, shareholders or agents in Indiana. (Facts, ¶ 3). BMAW does not have any operations in Indiana, has no phone or fax listings in Indiana, and has no bank accounts in Indiana. *Id*. It does not own, lease, or control any property or assets in Indiana, and has no authorized dealers or distributors in Indiana. *Id*. BMAW personnel have never traveled to Indiana in connection with BMAW business, and BMAW has never paid any taxes in Indiana. *Id*.

Moreover, BMAW does not advertise in Indiana directly or specifically target Indiana customers in its advertising. (Facts, ¶ 6). Like most e-commerce retailers, BMAW purchases the services of Ad Networks, which integrate BMAW advertisements into third party websites nationwide via a Cookie. *Id*. The Ad Networks use the Cookies to display BMAW advertisements to prior BMAW website visitors when they visit other websites. *Id*. BMAW has no control over the location of BMAW advertisements integrated by the Ad Networks into third party websites. *Id*. Thus, an Indiana consumer who has browsed BMAW's New York website could later see a BMAW advertisement displayed while browsing a different website (even an Indiana-based one); however, as detailed above, this common type of general advertising over the Internet, by itself, is not sufficient to establish jurisdiction. *See uBID*, 623 F.3d at 431 (stating "the mere fact that the defendant allegedly caused harm by conducting business or advertising over the Internet is not adequate to establish jurisdiction in the plaintiff's chosen forum state").

Although BMAW generates sales nationally from its website, most sales are to the New York and East Coast region. (Facts, ¶ 4). BMAW's sales into Indiana have been insignificant. In the past five years, gifts delivered to Indiana addresses have amounted to no more than .86% of total delivered gifts. (Facts, ¶ 5). During the same time period, less than 1.3% of BMAW's unique system customers list an Indiana residence. *Id*. Total revenue with Indiana customers, i.e., customers with an Indiana billing address, over the last five years equals no more than 0.66% of the company's total. *Id*. This insignificant amount of revenue from Indiana is insufficient to establish general jurisdiction. *See U.S. Sch. of Golf, Inc. v. Biltmore Golf, Inc.*, No. 1:05-CV-0313-DFH-TAB, 2005 WL 3022005, at *3-4 (S.D. Ind. Nov. 10, 2005) (finding no general jurisdiction partly because there was "no evidence that Indiana residents comprise a sizeable percentage of [defendant's] website traffic or purchases"); *L.H. Carbide Corp. v. The Piece Maker Co.*, 852 F. Supp. 1425, 1433 (N.D. Ind. 1994) (limited sales in Indiana ranging from 0.5% to 8% of total annual sales insufficient to establish general jurisdiction); *Commc'ns Depot, Inc. v. Verizon Commc'ns, Inc.*, No. IP01--1587--C--H/K, 2002 WL 1800044, at *5 (S.D. Ind. July 18, 2002) (finding sales from Indiana businesses of less than $10,000 annually to be insufficient to establish substantial, continuous, and systematic contact so as to support general jurisdiction). *See also, e.g., Campbell Pet Co. v. Miale*, 542 F.3d 879, 884 (Fed. Cir. 2008) (no general jurisdiction over defendant where its sales to the forum state amounted to less than 2% of total sales over a period of eight years); *Richter v. INSTAR Enter. Int'l, Inc.*, 594 F. Supp. 2d 1000, 1007 (N.D. Ill. 2009) (sales equaling approximately one tenth of 1% of defendant's overall sales were not enough to confer general jurisdiction); *Lake Assoc., LLC v. DNZ Products LLC*, 886 F. Supp. 2d 1203, 1209 (D. Or. 2012) (annual sales to Oregonians of 2% or less did not establish continuous and systematic contacts with Oregon); *Agape Flights, Inc. v. Covington Aircraft Engines, Inc.*, 771 F. Supp. 2d 1278, 1288 (E.D. Okla. 2011) (Internet sales to Oklahoma customers via its two websites equaling only .04% of defendant's gross revenue over a five-year period were not enough to establish general jurisdiction); *Simplicity, Inc. v. MTS Products, Inc.*, 2006 WL 924993, at *4 (E.D. Pa. Apr. 6, 2006) (sales of less than 1.5% of defendant's total sales over five years were insufficient to confer general jurisdiction).

Finally, as supported above, BMAW's operation of its website and Facebook page, without more, is not enough to subject BMAW to general jurisdiction. *See* U.S. Sch. of Golf, 2005 WL 3022005, at *4 (the fact that Indiana residents could purchase golf equipment and apparel from defendant's website was not enough to subject the defendant to general jurisdiction); *InfoSys Inc. v. Billingnetwork.com, Inc.*, No. 03 C 3047, 2003 WL 22012687, at *4 (N.D. Ill. Aug.27, 2003) ("there is no case where general jurisdiction was conferred on the basis of an interactive website in the absence of non-website factors evidencing intent for a defendant's product or website to reach a particular state"). BMAW's website and Facebook page are not targeted at the Indiana market, (Facts, ¶¶ 4-6), and Plaintiff's Complaint lacks any allegation or evidence suggesting otherwise. Therefore, under these facts and circumstances, the courts of Indiana do not have general jurisdiction over BMAW.

III. *SPECIFIC JURISDICTION*

Specific jurisdiction is satisfied if the defendant purposefully avails itself of the privilege of conducting activities within the forum state and the controversy arises out of or relates to these activities. *Wine and Canvas*, 886 F. Supp. 2d at 939. In other words, where the defendant deliberately engages in activities within the forum state, it is reasonable to subject the defendant to litigation in that forum. *NUCOR Corp. v. Aceros Y Maquilas de Occidente, S.A. de C.V.*, 28 F.3d 572, 580 (7th Cir. 1994). However, a defendant cannot be brought into a jurisdiction "solely as a result of random, fortuitous, or attenuated contacts or of the unilateral activity of another party or a third person." *Burger King*, 471 U.S. at 475. As stated above, in cases involving the Internet, as here, the "defendant must in some way target the forum state's market" to be subject to personal jurisdiction of the Court. *Bell v. Kirchner*, No. 1:13--cv--00012--TWP--DKL, 2014 WL 900923, at *3 (S.D. Ind. Mar. 7, 2014). As stated in *Advanced Tactical Ordnance Sys., LLC v. Real Action Paintball, Inc.*, 751 F.3d 796, 803 (7th Cir. 2014):

> [h]aving an 'interactive website' (which hardly rules out anything in 2014) should not open a defendant up to personal jurisdiction in every spot on the planet where that interactive website is accessible. To hold otherwise would offend 'traditional notions of fair play and substantial justice.'

This case arises from a single post on BMAW's Facebook Page. BMAW's Facebook page does not target Indiana customers, (Facts, ¶¶ 4-6), and Plaintiff's Complaint offers no allegation or evidence suggesting BMAW's Facebook page targets the Indiana market. *See Dillinger, LLC v. Pour House on Lincoln, Inc.*, No. 1:12--cv--714--WTL--TAB, 2012 WL 4527686, at *3 (S.D. Ind. Oct. 1, 2012) ("absent evidence that the Defendants have purposefully targeted Indiana residents with their Facebook page or other advertising, there is simply no basis for this Court to exercise personal jurisdiction over them"). It is questionable whether BMAW's alleged use of the Willie Nelson photograph would even qualify as an advertisement. (See Complaint, ¶ 17 (alleging that BMAW's Facebook page displayed the Willie Nelson photo with the caption, "He may not have always been on our mind, buts his songs sure are. Happy Birthday to country music legend Willie Nelson!")). Again, however, even assuming the alleged use of Plaintiff's Willie Nelson photograph or the use of Facebook itself would qualify as an advertisement, mere advertising over the Internet is not sufficient to establish jurisdiction over the defendant without some evidence that the advertisement was geared towards the Indiana market. *uBID*, 623 F.3d at 431. Here, there is no evidence indicating any significant revenue from the Indiana market due to the alleged use of Plaintiff's photo, and no evidence of any interaction between BMAW and the Indiana market. (Facts, ¶¶ 3-6). *See be2 LLC*, 642 F.3d at 559 (holding defendant's website did not target Illinois residents because there was no indication of advertising, revenue or any interaction between the defendant and Illinois residents as compared against the GoDaddy website in *uBID*, 623 F.3d at 428, in which GoDaddy conducted "a massive and successful exploitation of the Illinois market . . . through an advertising campaign that produced hundreds of thousands of customers in the state and millions of dollars in annual revenues"); *Kirchner*, 2014 WL 900923, at *3 (finding defendant's website did not target Indiana because no indication of advertising, revenue, or any interaction between defendant and Indiana customers). As a result, Plaintiff has failed to show that BMAW has purposefully availed itself of the privilege of conducting activities within Indiana. Accordingly, this Court cannot exercise specific jurisdiction over BMAW.

IV. *IMPROPER VENUE*

Plaintiff's personal jurisdiction and venue allegations are identical. (Complaint, ¶¶ 2-3). Because BMAW is not subject to personal jurisdiction in this District, venue is improper. As such, the case should be dismissed for lack of personal jurisdiction and improper venue.

CONCLUSION

BMAW's contacts and activities with Indiana are insufficient for the exercise of personal jurisdiction by this Court under principles of both general and specific jurisdiction. BMAW respectfully requests that the Court grant its Motion to Dismiss for Lack of Personal Jurisdiction and Improper Venue, and grant BMAW all other just and proper relief.

Respectfully submitted,

s/Matthew J. Clark

Matthew Joseph Clark (31263-49)

Meitus Gelbert Rose LLP

47 S. Meridian St., Suite 400

Indianapolis, IN 46204

Phone (317) 464-5307

Fax (317) 464-5111

mclark@mgrfirm.com

Anthony J. Rose, Esq. (15545-53)

Meitus Gelbert Rose LLP

47 S. Meridian St., Suite 400

Indianapolis, IN 46204

Phone (317) 464-5304

Fax (317) 464-5111

arose@mgrfirm.com

Attorneys for Defendant Bake Me A Wish, LLC

Motion for Judgment on the Pleadings

2016 WL 2772633 (S.D.Ind.)

Westlaw Query>>

To find more Motion for Judgment on the Pleadings filings on Westlaw: access Indiana Trial Court Documents (from the Home page, click Trial Court Documents, then Indiana), click the Advanced Search link, select Motion for Judgment on the Pleadings, and click Search. Use the Jurisdiction filter on the left to narrow results to Federal.

United States District Court, S.D. Indiana.

W.P., a minor, by and through his parents and guardians Kathryn Pierce and Chester Pierce, on behalf of themselves and similarly situated individuals, Plaintiffs,

v.

ANTHEM INSURANCE COMPANIES, INC., an Indiana corporation, Defendant.

No. 1:15-cv-00562-TWP-TAB.

April 11, 2016.

Anthem Insurance Companies, Inc.'s Motion for Partial Judgment on the Pleadings

Anthem Insurance Companies, Inc., One of Its Attorneys, Martin J. Bishop, Rebecca R. Hanson, Reed Smith LLP, 10 S. Wacker Drive, 40th Floor, Chicago, IL 60606, Tel: 312.207.1000, Fax: 312.207.6400, E-Mail: mbishop@reedsmith.com, rhanson@reedsmith.com; Sally Franklin Zweig, No. 11367-49, Kristopher N. Kazmierczak, No. 19430-49, Katz & Korin, PC, 334 North Senate Avenue, Indianapolis, Indiana 46204, Tel: 317.464.1100, Fax: 317.464.1111, E-Mail: szweig@katzkorin.com, kkaz@katzkorin.com.

Defendant Anthem Insurance Companies, Inc. ("Anthem"), by and through its undersigned attorneys and pursuant to Federal Rule of Civil Procedure 12(c), hereby moves this Court for partial judgment on the pleadings with respect to Plaintiffs' putative class action complaint. In support of this motion, Anthem states as follows:

1. Plaintiff W.P., a thirteen-year-old autistic child, and his parents, Kathryn and Chester Pierce (collectively "Plaintiffs"), brought this putative class action against Anthem for allegedly violating Indiana law and federal law, and consequently the Employee Retirement Income Security Act of 1974 ("ERISA"), by partially denying coverage for forty hours per week of a certain modality of therapy known as Applied Behavioral Analysis ("ABA") that Plaintiffs requested to treat W.P.'s autism. (Dkt. 1.) Plaintiffs allege that Anthem's partial denial of W.P.'s request for ABA therapy violated Indiana's so-called "Autism Mandate" and violated the federal Mental Health Parity and Addiction Equity Act of 2008 ("MHPAEA"). *See* Ind. Code 27-8-14.2-4; 29 U.S.C. § 1185a.

2. In Count I, brought pursuant to section 502(a)(1)(B) of ERISA, Plaintiffs seek to recover the benefits allegedly owed to them for Anthem's alleged violations of the Autism Mandate and the MHPAEA. (*Id.* ¶ 8.3.) For Plaintiffs' Count II brought pursuant to 502(a)(3), Plaintiffs seek all "appropriate equitable relief" to redress these alleged wrongful denials. (*Id.* ¶¶ 9.3-9.4.) Plaintiffs also seek to enjoin Anthem from allegedly making offers to ABA therapy providers to temporarily increase coverage for ABA therapy in exchange for members giving up their right to appeal coverage denials. (*Id.* ¶ 9.5.) In Count III, Plaintiffs request "equitable and remedial" relief for Anthem's alleged breach of its fiduciary duties to Plaintiffs pursuant to 502(a)(2) of ERISA. Plaintiffs allege that Anthem breached its fiduciary duty by (i) violating state and federal law in denying coverage for W.P.'s request for forty hours per week of ABA therapy and (ii) making a "take-it-or-leave-it" offer to W.P.'s ABA therapy provider, thus allegedly denying Plaintiffs a reasonable opportunity for a full and fair review of the denial of their requests for coverage. (*Id.* ¶¶ 9.3--9.5, 10.6--10.8.)

3. Partial judgment on the pleadings is proper because Plaintiffs have misinterpreted Indiana law and confused the causes of action and remedies available under ERISA.

4. First, Anthem did not violate Indiana law in applying its benefit plan terms in making coverage determinations for W.P., even if that resulted in coverage for fewer hours of ABA therapy than W.P. or his providers requested. The Autism Mandate regulates the imposition of "dollar limits, deductibles, and coinsurance provisions" in connection with autism coverage in group plans. Ind. Code 27-8-14.2-4(b). It does not, however, mandate that Anthem cover all hours requested by a member or a member's providers, as Plaintiffs allege. Thus, to the extent Plaintiffs claim Anthem has violated Indiana law in approving less than the number of requested hours, Plaintiffs' claim for benefits under the plan in Count I fails as a matter of law.

5. Second, Plaintiffs' claim under 502(a)(3) of ERISA for equitable relief in Count II to redress their denial of benefits is not cognizable; under well-established law, Plaintiffs may not repackage their 502(a)(1)(B) claim for benefits under the plan -- *i.e.*, their claim for *monetary* relief -- as a 502(a)(3) claim for *equitable* relief. *See Varity Corp. v. Howe*, 516 U.S. 489, 512 (1996); *see also Craft v. Health Care Serv. Corp.*, No. 14 C 5853, 2016 U.S. Dist. LEXIS 44810, at *17 (N.D. Ill. Mar. 31, 2016) (granting motion to dismiss for "repackaging" of 502(a)(3) claim); *Karr v. Dow Agrosciences LLC*, No. 1:10-cv-00975-LJM-TAB, 2012 U.S. Dist. LEXIS 55143, at *20-21 (S.D. Ind. Apr. 19, 2012) (sections 502(a)(1)(B) and 502(a)(3) are "mutually exclusive").

6. Third, the Court should grant Anthem judgment on the entirety of Plaintiffs' 502(a)(2) claim in Count III. Because Plaintiffs do not seek relief on behalf of the plan itself, but rather seek relief for alleged injuries to individual members of the plan, their claim in Count III under section 502(a)(2) fails as a matter of law. *See Sharp Elecs. Corp. v. Metro. Life Ins. Co.*, 570 F.3d 505, 512-13 (7th Cir. 2009).

7. Further support for this motion is set forth in Anthem's concurrently filed Memorandum of Law.

WHEREFORE, Defendant Anthem Insurance Companies, Inc. respectfully requests that the Court grant judgment in its favor on the portion of Count I alleging that Anthem's partial denial of coverage for W.P.'s ABA therapy violated the Autism Mandate, on the portions of Count II seeking equitable relief for Anthem's alleged wrongful denial of benefits, and for the entirety of Count III, and for such other relief as is just and proper.

Dated: April 11, 2016

Respectfully submitted,

ANTHEM INSURANCE COMPANIES, INC.

By: */s/ Rebecca R. Hanson*

One of Its Attorneys

Martin J. Bishop

Rebecca R. Hanson

Reed Smith LLP

10 S. Wacker Drive, 40th Floor

Chicago, IL 60606

Tel: 312.207.1000

Fax: 312.207.6400

E-Mail: *mbishop@reedsmith.com*

rhanson@reedsmith.com

Sally Franklin Zweig, No. 11367-49

Kristopher N. Kazmierczak, No. 19430-49

KATZ & KORIN, PC

334 North Senate Avenue

Indianapolis, Indiana 46204

Tel: 317.464.1100

Fax: 317.464.1111

E-Mail: *szweig@katzkorin.com*
kkaz@katzkorin.com

Application for Temporary Restraining Order

2016 WL 4727835 (N.D.Ind.)

United States District Court, N.D. Indiana.

Fort Wayne Division

GLOBAL ARCHERY PRODUCTS, INC., Plaintiff,

v.

Jordan GWYTHER d/b/a Larping.org and Upshot Arrows, Defendant.

No. 1:15-cv-297-JVB-SLC.

February 10, 2016.

Plaintiff Global Archery Products, Inc.'s Brief in Support of Its Motion for Temporary Restraining Order, Preliminary Injunction and Hearing

Dean E. McConnell, Esq. Atty No. 20254-49, Dean McConnell IP Law, 8038 N 600 W, Suite 200, Indianapolis, IN 46055, Phone: (317) 653-2660, Fax: (317) 653-2661, dean@dean-mcconnell.com; Gregg S. Gordon, Attorney No. 19360-49, Of Counsel, Cremer & Cremer, 8038 N 600 W, Ste 400, McCordsville, Indiana 46055, Telephone: (317) 335-3360, Fax: (317) 335-3361, GGordon@Geistlaw.com.

JURY TRIAL DEMANDED

Pursuant to Rule 65 of the Federal Rules of Civil Procedure and N.D. Ind. L.R. 65-1, Plaintiff Global Archery Products, Inc. ("Global"), by counsel and in support of its motion for the entry of a temporary restraining order as well as a preliminary injunction and order against Defendant Jordan Gwyther d/b/a Larping.Org and Upshot Arrows ("Gwyther") shows the Court as follows:

I. ISSUE PRESENTED

Whether a temporary restraining order and preliminary injunction should issue enjoining Gwyther from further committing acts of unfair competition by disseminating press releases, advertisements, and social media postings that falsely, misleadingly, and deceptively misstates the nature and extent of this pending action so that Gwyther can obtain a pecuniary benefit and further damage the goodwill associated with Global and its ARCHERY TAG(r) products?

II. INTRODUCTION

Gwyther has misused and misrepresented to the public Global's complaint in this action to create the false and misleading impression that Global is attempting to assert and protect intellectual property rights far in excess of those at issue in this action. By doing so, Gwyther has deliberately mislead consumers regarding the nature and scope of this action which has resulted in irreparable damage to Global. For this reason, Global seeks a temporary restraining order and preliminary injunction preventing Gwyther from continuing this reckless behavior.

Specifically, on February 8, 2016, Gwyther created a "gofundme" page and posted a YouTube video that creates the false impression in the market place that (a) Global was attempting to interfere with the public's ability to engage in a recreational activity known as Live Action Role Playing ("LARP");[1] (b) Global was attempting to interfere with the public's ability to engage in a recreational activity known as LARP archery; and (c) Global was attempting to assert a patent as to *all* foam tipped arrows. To perpetuate this false and misleading impression, Gwyther used Global's registered trademark ARCHERY TAG(r). Gwyther's conduct has created havoc and confusion in the marketplace for Global, disrupting Global's business and unfairly competing with Global. This was not an "accident" or an "innocent" mistake, but rather, was a calculated maneuver done by Gwyther to unfairly damage Global's reputation, divert sales of Global's products to Gwyther and to dupe the general public into funding Gwyther's defense of this action.

A temporary restraining order and preliminary injunction is the proper remedy to prevent Gwyther from causing further harm to Global and from otherwise unfairly competing with Global. Every day that Gwyther is allowed to continue this course of conduct and without corrective actions, causes the harm done to Global to grow, in the form of lost sales, damaged customer relations, and loss of goodwill.

III. BACKGROUND

Global is the owner of two U.S. Patents (U.S. Patent No. 8,449,413 and U.S. Patent No. 8,932,159) (the "Patents"). *See* Exhibit A, Declaration of John Jackson ("Jackson Declaration"), Paragraph 2. The Patents generally relate to specific forms of a non-lethal arrow that is used in activities marketed and promoted by Global and its authorized licensees under the ARCHERY TAG(r) trademarks. *Id.* Global is the owner of U.S. Trademark Registrations No. 4,208,868 and No. 4,208,868 for the ARCHERY TAG(r) (the "Trademarks"). ARCHERY TAG(r) is a game which is similar to dodgeball but is played using archery bows and non-lethal foam-tipped arrows covered by the Patents. *Id.*

Gwyther is selling and offering for sale in the United States products it refers to as the "Crossbow Bolt", "Flat Tip Larp Arrow", "Glow in the Dark Larp Arrow", and "Round Tip Larp Arrow" (collectively referred to hereinafter as the "Gwyther's Arrows"). *See* Complaint [Doc. 1] at paragraph 10 at p. 4. *See* Defendant's Answer to Complaint and Affirmative Defenses ("Answer") [Doc.11] at paragraph 10. Gwyther has also used the ARCHERY TAG(r) trademark:

- Advertising for Gwyther's Arrows. Complaint at paragraph 11 and Exhibit F;

- As paid key words with one or more search engines such as, by way of example, Google. *Id.* at paragraph 12; and

- On Amazon.com to market and promote competing sets of ARCHERY TAG(r) equipment. *Id.* at paragraph 13;

Gwyther is not authorized or licensed to use the ARCHER TAG(r) trademarks. Jackson Declaration at 5. This action was initiated enforce the Patents as well as the ARCHERY TAG(r) trademarks. The Complaint sets forth nine counts - only two of which involve the Patents. The other seven counts are predicated on Gwyther's misuse and misappropriation of the ARCHERY TAG(r) trademarks, his false advertising, and his tortious interference with Global's business relationships. Thus, only 22.2% of the original action involves the patents, yet Gwyther falsely and misleading omits the other issues in this case in the YouTube video.

On February 8, 2016, Gwyther created a "gofundme" page which solicited funds from the general public purportedly to aid in his legal defense of this action. To induce the general public to donate money to him (and make sales of his products), Gwyther stated, among other things:

- "The End of Larp Archery in North America";

- "I'm reaching out to you today with something *that has the potential to ruin larp in North America as we know it*, specifically in regards to larp archery." (emphasis added)

- "Over the past few months I've become stuck in a legal battle *with someone who claims to own the patent on foam tipped arrows*, the kind we use in larp . . ." (emphasis added)

---

1. LARP is defined as "At it's simplest you could say that larping is a continuation of a table-top roleplaying game that people choose to act out by becoming a character and staging a fantasy world experience in which their character lives." www.larping.org/larp-definition/

- "Very few people in the larp community have a substantial income. I, myself, have a day job and sell these arrows (and other larp equipment) *as a part time hobby which doesn't generate a great deal of income*. However, right now, the state of the entire larp hobby is at risk." (emphasis added)

- "I genuinely believe that this is one of the biggest threats to our hobby in recent times and I cannot defend this threat without your help."

- "In the complaint you will see many claims against me. Some of which are completely untrue, while others are "junk" that is trying to be passed off as breaking the law when in fact *we* have done nothing wrong." (emphasis added).

A true and accurate copy of Gwyther's gofundme page is attached hereton as Exhibit B. (https://www.gofundme.com/savelarparchery). Gwyther also posted a video to YouTube (https://m.youtube.com/watch?v=ey8qr492iY) in which Gwyther repeated the gofundme page representations. Each of the above-referenced statements are false and misleading.

Omitted from these representations, however, are the facts that:

- This action was also initiated to enforce the ARCHER TAG(r) trademarks and stop his false advertising;

- This action was also initiated to prohibit Gwyther from tortious interference with Global's contractual and business relationships; and

- Gwyther has admitted receiving some $47,000.00 from his sale of Gwyther's Arrows. *See* Gwyther's *Motion for Relief from Local Patent Rules, For Limited Discovery, and for a Show-Cause Hearing* at paragraph 2 (Document 16).

As a result of Gwyther's false, deceptive and misleading statements and omission of certain facts (herein "False Advertising"), Global has been inundated with hateful phone calls, emails, and posts on its social media sites. Some of the messages Global has received go so far as stating that they hope that people at Global are "brutally murdered." Jackson Declaration at Group Exhibit 1 thereon. Gwyther, however, has now received over $3,000 from donations from the general public.

See Exhibit B.

IV. ARGUMENT

This is a straightforward case of false advertising under the Lanham Act. *See* 15 U.S.C. 1125(a). Gwyther has falsely, misleading and deceptively issued the smear campaign against Global to unfairly compete with Global. Gwyther's misrepresentations have, and will to continue to, if not enjoined by this Court, irreparably harm Global.

The Seventh Circuit has set forth the legal standard for obtaining for injunctive relief:

To obtain preliminary injunctive relief, the plaintiff must first: (1) show "some likelihood of success on the merits," and (2) show that the plaintiff "has no adequate remedy at law and will suffer irreparable harm if" the requested injunctive relief is denied. *Stuller, Inc. v. Steak N Shake Enterprises, Inc.*, 695 F.3d 676, 678 (7th Cir.2012)(internal quotations omitted)(quoting *Ty, Inc. v. Jones Group, Inc.*, 237 F.3d 891, 895 (7th Cir.2001); *see also Wisconsin Right To Life, Inc. v. Barland*, 751 F.3d 804, 830 (7th Cir.2014) (explaining that "[o]n the merits questions, the burdens at the preliminary injunction stage track the burdens at trial")(internal quotations omitted)(quoting *Gonzales v. O Centro Espirita Beneficente Uniao do Vegetal*, 546 U.S. 418, 429 (2006)).

If the plaintiff satisfies such threshold requirements, in the secondary phase the court must then: (1) "consider the irreparable harm that the nonmoving party will suffer if preliminary relief is granted, balancing such harm against the irreparable harm the moving party will suffer if relief is denied," and (2) "the public interest in granting or denying an injunction." *Stuller*, 695 F.3d at 678. When balancing the harms, the court should use a sliding scale approach, under which "the greater the likelihood of success on the merits, the less heavily the balance of harms must tip in the moving party's favor." *Korte v. Sebelius*, 735 F.3d 654, 665 (7th Cir.2013); *see also Girl Scouts of Manitou Council, Inc. v. Girl Scouts of U.S. of America, Inc.*, 549 F.3d 1079, 1086 (7th Cir.2008)(explaining that the court "must somehow balance the nature and degree of the plaintiff's injury, the likelihood of prevailing at trial, the possible injury to the defendant if the injunction is granted, and the wild card that is the public interest")(internal quotations omitted)(quoting *Lawson Prods., Inc. v. Avnet, Inc.*, 782 F.2d 1429, 1433 (7th Cir.1986)).

In considering irreparable harm, the question is whether the party seeking relief will suffer irreparable harm in the interim period prior to the resolution of its claims. *Girl Scouts of Manitou Counsel*, 549 F.3d at 1086.

A. Global Has a Strong Likelihood of Success on the Merits

The Lanham Act is the statutory basis for a false advertising claim. It states, in relevant part:

(a)(1) Any person who, on or in connection with any goods or services... uses in commerce any word ...or false designation of origin, false or misleading description of fact, or false or misleading representations of fact, which --

...

(B) in commercial advertising or promotion, misrepresents the nature, characteristics, qualities, or geographic origin of his or her or another person's goods, services, or commercial activities,

shall be liable in a civil action by any person who believes that he or she is or is likely to be damaged by such acts.

See 15 U.S.C. § 1125(a)(1)(B).

The Seventh Circuit has established a five element test for plaintiffs seeking to prove liability under the Lanham Act. Specifically, a plaintiff must show that the defendant:

(1) made a false or misleading statement;

(2) that actually deceives or is likely to deceive a substantial segment of the advertisement's audience;

(3) on a subject material to the decision to purchase the goods;

(4) touting goods entering interstate commerce; and

(5) that results in actual or probable injury to the plaintiff.

B. Sanfield, Inc. v. Finlay Fine Jewelry Corp., 168 F.3d 967, 971 (7th Cir. 1999).

"Where the statement in question is actually false, then the plaintiff need not show that the statement either actually deceived consumers or was likely to do so." Id. See *M-3 Associates, Inc. v. Cargo Systems Inc.*, 2004 WL 834690 (N.D. Ind. 2004), (when the statements at issue are literally false, the plaintiff did not need to prove that the statements had a tendency to deceive a substantial segment of the market or that such deception was material "since this is an extension of the second step.")

1. Gwyther Has Made False and Misleading Statements

Gwyther has made false and misleading statements in his False Advertising. *See* Exhibit A and B. The False Advertisement falsely state that this lawsuit is "the end of larp archery in North America" and "has the potential to ruin larp in North America as we know it, specifically in regards to larp archery." Gwyther also falsely states that Global "has made it clear that he wishes for his foam tipped arrow to be used only for the purpose of Archery Tag ..." These statements, amongst other made on the gofundme page and in the YouTube video, are blatantly false and misleading. In fact, Global's products are routinely sold to and used by persons and organizations that LARP. *See* Jackson Declaration at 6. Global has no intent to go after anyone in the LARP community and has no ill will towards anyone in the LARP community. These statements were made purposefully, willfully, and intentionally in order to falsely indicate to the intended audience that Global was attempting to prohibit the general public from engaging in LARP and LARP archery in particular.

Gwyther did this to obfuscate the fact that the instant lawsuit was actually about *his* personal conduct and specifically *his* misuse and misappropriation of Global's ARCHER TAG(r) trademarks, *his* false advertising, and *his* tortious interference with Global's business relationships. In fact, but for these actions, Global might not have even taken action against Gwyther as it was only when Global's licensees started contacting Global and complaining about Gwyther's conduct that Global was forced to take action.

Gwyther then underscored his misrepresentation through the use of a self-serving question and answer:

I dont [sic] use these type of arrows at my game - why should I care? I think *the main point here is that someone is threatening a portion of your hobby, of the nerd community*, is being attacked and will change for the forseeable future. As a community, as a hobby, this is important and we should defend it together so that our hobby can grow and expand instead of being reduced due to greed.

See Exhibit B (emphasis added). No mention is made of the claims against Gwyther for his misuse and misappropriation of Global's ARCHER TAG(r) trademarks at all, and even though Gwyther provides a link to a pdf copy of the Complaint, Gwyther also peremptorily discredits it by stating:

In the complaint you will see many claims against me. Some of which are completely untrue, while others are "junk" that is trying to be passed off as breaking the law when in fact we have done nothing wrong.

Id.

This attempt at discrediting the claims predicated on Gwyther's misuse of Global's ARCHER TAG(r) trademarks, false advertising, and tortious interference with Global's business relationships also ignores Gwyther's own pleadings in this action. In fact, Gwyther has admitted that he has "used the name 'Archery Tag' to describe a particular game that is known by that same name or to refer to the products available by one or more competitors that are used to play a game called Archery Tag, *including the purchase of key words on Google*." *See* Answer at paragraph 12, p. 9 (emphasis added). *See also* paragraph 15 ("Mr. Gwyther Admits that on at least one occasion he has placed a paid advertisement on Google in which he asserts an opinion that his Gwyther's Arrows were 'better than Archery Tag!' ")

Even assuming, for the sake of argument, that Gwyther's False Advertisement is not literally false, it can hardly be argued that Gwyther's False Advertisement does not "convey a false impression or [is] misleading in context, as demonstrated by actual consumer confusion." *Abbott Laboratories v. Mead Johnson & Co.*, 971 F.2d 6, 14 (7th Cir. 1992). As clearly evident by the comments made by the general public both on-line in response to the False Advertising (Exhibit B) and directly to Global (Jackson Declaration at Group Exhibit 1), consumers falsely believe that Global is attempting to interfere with their ability to engage in LARP and LARP archery.

In summary, Gwyther's False Advertisement contains literally false statements that have a tendency to deceive. As such, this factor favors issuance of a temporary restraining order and preliminary injunction enjoining Gwyther from issuing any further false and misleading statements.

2. Gwyther's False Advertisement Actually Deceived and Tend to Deceive a Substantial Portion of the Intended Audience

Gwyther's False Advertisement is directed towards consumers who purchase products sold by both Global and Gwyther. As set forth above, these consumers were deceived by Gwyther's False Advertisement. *See* Exhibits B and C. Gwyther's False Advertisement thus both clearly deceived a substantial portion of the intended audience and obviously tend to deceive a substantial portion of the intended audience. As such, this factor is decisively in Global's favor as well.

3. Gwyther's Statements are Material in that They Influence a Deceived Consumer's Purchasing Decision

A deceived consumer is not going to purchase a hobby product from Global when they have been lead to believe that Global is actively attempting to "ruin" that hobby.

Group Exhibit 1 to Jackson Declaration. Thus, once again, this factor is decisively in favor of the issuance of injunctive relief against Gwyther.

4. Gwyther's False Advertisement Were Introduced Into Interstate Commerce

As set forth above, it is undisputed that Gwyther's False Advertisement was introduced into interstate commerce. This factor also falls decisively in Global's favor.

5. There is a Causal Link Between the False Advertisement and Harm to Global.

Gwyther's False Advertising is causing members of the general public, as well as current customers of Global, to hold Global in complete disdain. A cursory review of Group Exhibit 1 to Jackson's Declaration unequivocally demonstrates this point. As such, Global's business has been unfairly disrupted by having to deal with the public outcry caused by the False Advertisement who falsely believe that Global is attempting to interfere with their hobby. Clearly there is a causal link between the False Advertisements and the harm being done to Global.

B. Global Has and Will Continue to Suffer Irreparable Injury Without an Injunction

"It is well settled that injuries arising from Lanham Act violations are presumed to be irreparable, even if the plaintiff fails to demonstrate a business loss." *Northern Star Industries, Inc. v. Douglas Dynamics LLC*, 848 F.Supp.2d 934, 949 (E.D. Wis. 2012) (citing *Abbott Labs*, 971 F.2d at 16. "This presumption, it appears, is based upon the judgment that it is virtually impossible to ascertain the precise economic consequences of intangible harms, such as damage to reputation and loss of goodwill, caused by such violations." *Id.*

Here, Global's reputation and goodwill in the industry has been and is being irreparably damaged by Gwyther's False Advertisement. Portrayed by Gwyther as the Goliath out to crush all competitors and usurp total and complete control over LARP, Global is now the target of a hate campaign by some of its own customers as well as members of the general public who, but for the False Advertisement, could have become customers of Global. Rather than buy Global's products, the general sentiment now directed to Global is that Global's founders should be brutally murdered. Needless to say, it is doubtful that Global's products would be purchased by these persons or anyone may pass on the False Advertising.

C. Issuance of the Requested Injunctive Relief Will Not Cause Substantial Harm to Others

Global has suffered and will continue to suffer substantial harm if a temporary restraining order and preliminary injunction does not issue. Other than Gwyther's desire to unfairly compete with Global and profit from the False Advertisement, no legitimate purpose is served through allowing Gwyther to continue to make false and misleading statements. No other parties other than Global and Gwyther will be affected by a properly worded temporary restraining order and injunction. Global has invested a substantial amount of time and money in developing its products and getting them to market. Global has also built up a substantial amount of goodwill in the industry that is being harmed by Gwyther's conduct. Any harm that may be caused to Gwyther should be discounted because the harm was brought upon itself by issuing false and misleading statements in the False Advertisement.

D. The Public Interest Is Served by Truthful Advertising

There is a public interest in "preventing confusion and deception in the marketplace and protecting the trademark holder's property interest in the mark." *Lorillard Tobacco Co. v. Amouri's Grand Foods, Inc.*, 453 F.3d 377, 383 (6th Cir. 2006). It should also come as no surprise that courts have found a strong public interest in preventing false and misleading advertising. *See American Home Products Corp. v. Johnson & Johnson*, 654 F. Supp. 568, 590 (S.D.N.Y. 1987). Finally, the public interest favors entry of a preliminary injunction in this case because "the public is equally interested in fair competitive practices and clearly opposed to being deceived in the marketplace." *McNeil Laboratories, Inc. v. American Home Products Corp.*, 416 F.Supp. 804, 809 (D. N.J. 1976). This factor thus also favors entry of a preliminary injunction enjoining Gwyther's unfair trade practice.

V. CONCLUSION

For the foregoing reasons, this Court should grant a temporary restraining order as well as a preliminary injunction enjoining Gwyther from issuing False Advertisements as well as requiring Gwyther to correct the False Advertisement in the market.

Dated: February 10, 2016

s/Dean E. McConnell

Dean E. McConnell, Esq. Atty No. 20254-49

DEAN MCCONNELL IP Law

8038 N 600 W, Suite 200

Indianapolis, IN 46055

Phone: (317) 653-2660

Fax: (317) 653-2661

dean@dean-mcconnell.com

s/Gregg S. Gordon

Gregg S. Gordon, Attorney No. 19360-49

Of Counsel, Cremer & Cremer

8038 N 600 W, Ste 400

McCordsville, Indiana 46055
Telephone: (317) 335-3360
Fax: (317) 335-3361
GGordon@Geistlaw.com

Table of Laws and Rules

UNITED STATES CONSTITUTION

UNITED STATES CODE ANNOTATED

FEDERAL RULES OF CIVIL PROCEDURE

FEDERAL RULES OF CIVIL PROCEDURE—Continued

FEDERAL RULES OF CIVIL PROCEDURE—Continued

FEDERAL RULES OF CIVIL PROCEDURE—Continued

FEDERAL RULES OF CIVIL PROCEDURE—Continued

FEDERAL RULES OF CIVIL PROCEDURE—Continued

FEDERAL RULES OF CIVIL PROCEDURE—Continued

FEDERAL RULES OF CIVIL PROCEDURE—Continued

FEDERAL RULES OF CIVIL PROCEDURE—Continued

FEDERAL RULES OF CIVIL PROCEDURE—Continued

FEDERAL RULES OF CIVIL PROCEDURE—Continued

FEDERAL RULES OF CIVIL PROCEDURE—Continued

FEDERAL RULES OF EVIDENCE

RULES OF THE U.S. DISTRICT COURT FOR THE NORTHERN DISTRICT OF INDIANA

RULES OF THE U.S. DISTRICT COURT FOR THE NORTHERN DISTRICT OF INDIANA—Continued

RULES OF THE U.S. DISTRICT COURT FOR THE NORTHERN DISTRICT OF INDIANA—Continued

RULES OF THE U.S. DISTRICT COURT FOR THE SOUTHERN DISTRICT OF INDIANA

RULES OF THE U.S. DISTRICT COURT FOR THE SOUTHERN DISTRICT OF INDIANA—Continued

RULES OF THE U.S. DISTRICT COURT FOR THE SOUTHERN DISTRICT OF INDIANA—Continued

RULES OF THE U.S. DISTRICT COURT FOR THE SOUTHERN DISTRICT OF INDIANA—Continued

ORDERS OF THE U.S. DISTRICT COURTS FOR THE DISTRICTS OF INDIANA

Table of Cases

TABLE OF CASES